NTA CSIR UGC

NET/SET

JRF & LECTURERSHIP

Life Sciences

Ashish Nagesh
Prashant Kumar
Quisher J. Hossain

ARIHANT PUBLICATIONS (INDIA) LIMITED

Administrative & Production Offices

Regd. Office

'Ramchhaya' 4577/15, Agarwal Road, Darya Ganj, New Delhi -110002
Tele: 011- 47630600, 43518550

Head Office

Kalindi, TP Nagar, Meerut (UP) - 250002
Tel: 0121-7156203, 7156204

Sales & Support Offices

Agra, Ahmedabad, Bengaluru, Bareilly, Chennai, Delhi, Guwahati, Hyderabad, Jaipur, Jhansi, Kolkata, Lucknow, Nagpur & Pune.

PRICE ₹995.00

PO No. : TXT-59-T067593-10-25

Published by Arihant Publications (India) Ltd.

For further information about the books published by Arihant, log on to www.arihantbooks.com or e-mail at info@arihantbooks.com

Follow us on    

NET (National Eligibility Test) determines eligibility for lectureship and for award of Junior Research Fellowship (JRF) for Indian nationals in order to ensure minimum standards for the entrants in the teaching profession and research. The Council of Scientific and Industrial Research (CSIR) conducts the UGC-CSIR NET for other Science subjects, namely, Life Sciences, Physical Sciences, Chemical Sciences, Mathematical Sciences and Earth Sciences jointly with the UGC.

UGC-CSIR NET Tutor for Life Sciences has been designed to help the students get away with their initial qualms & hiccups about the UGC-CSIR NET. In the course of preparation of this book we have followed the pattern & syllabus of the examination for the maximum benefit of the aspirants, difficulty level of the questions has also been kept in mind.

Salient Features of the Book

- Only book in the market which has complete & exhaustive theory exactly on the UGC-CSIR NET pattern & difficulty level.
- For complete understanding all units have been divided into individual chapters with sufficient number of Multiple Choice Questions.
- All types of multiple choice questions covered *viz.*, single option correct, matching type, statement based questions, etc.
- Only book in the market which has Previous Years' Solved Papers & Explanations to all the Sample Questions provided on CSIR website.

We are thankful to Arihant Publications (India) Limited for giving us this opportunity to make such a book which will help the students to get 100% success. We would like to thank Sorabh Chaudhary (Project Coordinator) for giving us their full support during this project.
Any suggestion for the enhancement of the quality of this book is most welcome.

Ashish Nagesh
Prashant Kumar
Quaisher J. Hossain

UNIT V

UNIT VIII

UNIT XI

NET What, Why, When

The National Educational Testing Bureau of University Grants Commission (UGC) conducts National Eligibility Test (NET) to determine eligibility for lecturership and for award of Junior Research Fellowship (JRF) for Indian nationals in order to ensure minimum standards for the entrants in the teaching profession and research. This test is conducted in Humanities (including languages), Social Sciences, Forensic Science, Environmental Sciences, Computer Science and Applications and Electronic Science.

The Council of Scientific and Industrial Research (CSIR) conducts the UGC-CSIR NET for other Science subjects, namely Life Sciences, Physical Sciences, Chemical Sciences, Mathematical Sciences and Earth Atmospheric Ocean & Planetary Sciences jointly with the UGC. The tests are conducted twice in a year generally in the months of June and December. For candidates, who desire to pursue research, the Junior Research Fellowship (JRF) is available for 5 years subject to fulfillment of certain conditions. UGC has allocated a number of fellowships to the universities for the candidates who qualify the test for JRF. The JRFs are awarded to the meritorious candidates from among the candidates qualifying for eligibility for lecturership in the NET. JRFs are available only to the candidates who opt for it in their application forms.

The test for Junior Research Fellowship is being conducted since 1984. The Government of India, through its notification dated 22nd July, 1988 entrusted the task of conducting the eligibility test for lecturership to UGC. Consequently, UGC conducted the first National Eligibility Test, common to both eligibility for Lecturership and Junior Research Fellowship in two parts, that is, in December 1989 and in March 1990.

NET Schedule

UGC conducts NET twice a year, i.e., in the months of June and December. The notifications announcing the June and December examinations are published in the months of March and September respectively in the weekly journal of nation-wide circulation, *viz*, 'Employment News'.

NET Results Declaration Schedule

The result of June, UGC NET is declared generally in the month of October. Similarly December, UGC NET result is usually declared in the month of April. The UGC NET results published in the 'Employment News' are also available on UGC website.

NET FOR SCIENCE SUBJECT

The NET in major Science subjects, viz., Chemical Sciences, Earth Atmospheric Ocean and Planetary Sciences, Life Sciences, Mathematical Sciences and Physical Sciences is conducted jointly with the Council of Scientific and Industrial Research (CSIR), New Delhi. The concerned notifications are issued separately by CSIR.

1

Basic Physical and Chemical Concepts in Biology

Structure of Atoms, Molecules and Chemical Bonds

Syllabus

- Structure of Atoms, Molecules and Chemical Bonds.
- Composition, Structure and Functions of Biomolecules, Carbohydrates, Lipids, Proteins, Nucleic Acids and Vitamins.
- Biomolecular Weak Interactions (van der Waals, Electrostatic force, Hydrogen Bonding, Hydrophobic Interaction, etc.).
- Principles of Biophysical Chemistry (pH, Buffer, Reaction Kinetics, Thermodynamics, Colligative Properties).

A chemical element is a pure chemical substance consisting of one type of atom distinguished by its atomic number, which is the number of protons in its nucleus. The term is also used to refer to a pure chemical substance composed of atoms with the same number of protons.

In total, **118** elements have been observed so far, of which 94 occur naturally on Earth. 80 elements have stable isotopes, namely all elements with atomic numbers 1 to 82, except elements 43 and 61 (technetium and promethium). Elements with atomic numbers 83 or higher (bismuth and above) are inherently unstable, and undergo radioactive decay. The elements from atomic number 83 to 94 have no stable nuclei, but are nevertheless found in nature. Of the total stable elements in nature, fifteen are present in all living things, and a further 8-10 are only found in particular organisms. More than 99% of the atoms in animals' bodies are accounted for by just four elements—hydrogen (H), oxygen (O), carbon (C) and nitrogen (N).

Table 1.1 **Elemental Composition of Earth's Crust**

Element	Per cent by Mass	Element	Per cent by Mass
Oxygen	46.71	Potassium	2.58
Silicon	27.69	Magnesium	2.08
Aluminium	8.07	Titanium	0.62
Iron	5.05	Hydrogen	0.14
Calcium	3.65	Phosphorus	0.13
Sodium	2.75	Carbon	0.094

Table 1.2 **Elemental Composition of Earth's Ocean Water**

Element	Per cent by Mass	Element	Per cent by Mass
Oxygen	85.84	Sulphur	0.091
Hydrogen	10.82	Calcium	0.04
Chlorine	1.94	Potassium	0.04
Sodium	1.08	Bromine	0.0067
Magnesium	0.1292	Carbon	0.0028

Table 1.3 **Composition of Earth's Atmosphere**

Gas	Per cent by Volume	Gas	Per cent by Volume
Nitrogen	78.084	Hydrogen	0.000055
Oxygen	20.946	Nitrous oxide	0.00003
Argon	0.9340	Carbon monoxide	0.00001
Carbon dioxide	0.0390	Xenon	9×10^{-6}
Neon	0.001818	Ozone	$0\text{-}7 \times 10^{-6}$
Helium	0.000524	Nitrogen dioxide	2×10^{-6}
Methane	0.000179	Iodine	1×10^{-6}
Krypton	0.000114	Ammonia	Trace

Table 1.4 **Elemental Composition of the Human Body**

Element	Per cent by Mass	Element	Per cent by Mass
Oxygen	65	Potassium	0.2
Carbon	18	Sulphur	0.2
Hydrogen	10	Chlorine	0.2
Nitrogen	3	Sodium	0.1
Calcium	1.5	Magnesium	0.05
Phosphorus	1.2		
Iron, Cobalt, Copper, Zinc and Iodine	<0.05 each		
Selenium and Fluorine	<0.01 each		

Hydrogen and oxygen are the constituents of water, which alone makes up 60-70% of cell mass. Together with carbon and nitrogen, hydrogen and oxygen are also the major constituents of the **organic compounds** on which most living processes depend. Many biomolecules also contain sulfur (S) or phosphorus (P). The above **macro-elements** are essential for all organisms.

Other biologically important group of elements, which together represent only about 0.5% of the body mass, is present almost exclusively in the form of **inorganic ions**. This group includes the **alkali metals** sodium (Na) and potassium (K), and the **alkaline earth metals** magnesium (Mg) and calcium (Ca). The halogen chlorine (Cl) is also always ionized in the cell. All other elements important for life are present in such small quantities that they are referred to as **trace elements**. These include transition metals such as iron (Fe), zinc (Zn), copper (Cu), cobalt (Co) and manganese (Mn). A few **nonmetals**, such as iodine (I) and selenium (Se), can also be classed as essential trace elements.

H																	He
Li	Be											B	C	N	O	F	Ne
Na	Mg											Al	Si	P	S	Cl	Ar
K	Ca	Sc	Ti	V	Cr	Mn	Fe	Co	Ni	Cu	Zn	Ga	Ge	As	Se	Br	Kr
R	Sr	Y	Zr	Nb	Mo	Tc	Ru	Rh	Pd	Ag	Cd	In	Sn	S	Te	I	Xe
Cs	Ba	La	Hf	Ta	W	Re	Os	Ir	Pt	Au	Hg	Tl	Pb	Bi	Po	At	Rn

Essential to all animals and plants
Essential to several classes of animals and plants
Believed essential to a variety fo species
Possible essential trace elements for some species

Fig. 1.1 Elements known to be essential to living beings. The 11 elements–C, H, O, N, S, P, Na, K, Mg, Ca and Cl–make up 99.9% of the mass of a human being. An additional 13 are known to be essential for higher animals in trace amounts. Boron is essential to higher plants but apparently not to animals, microorganisms or algae.

Electromagnetic Radiation

Electromagnetic radiation is a form of energy transmission in which electric and magnetic fields are propagated as waves through empty space (a vacuum) or through a medium such as glass. According to a theory proposed by **James Clerk Maxwell** (1831-1879) in 1865, electromagnetic radiation—a propagation of electric and magnetic fields, is produced by an accelerating electrically charged particle (particle whose velocity changes).

The SI unit for frequency, s^{-1}, is the **hertz** (Hz), and the basic SI wavelength unit is the meter (m). Because many types of electromagnetic radiation have very short wavelengths, however, smaller units, including those listed below, are also used. The angstrom, named for the **Swedish** physicist **Anders Ångström** (1814-1874), is not an SI unit.

1 centimeter (cm) = 1×10^{-2} m

1 micrometer (mm) = 1×10^{-6} m

1 angstrom (Å) = 1×10^{-10} m = 1×10^{-8} cm = 100 pm

A distinctive feature of electromagnetic radiation is its **constant** speed 2.997925 × 108 ms-1 of in a vacuum, often referred to as the **speed of light**.

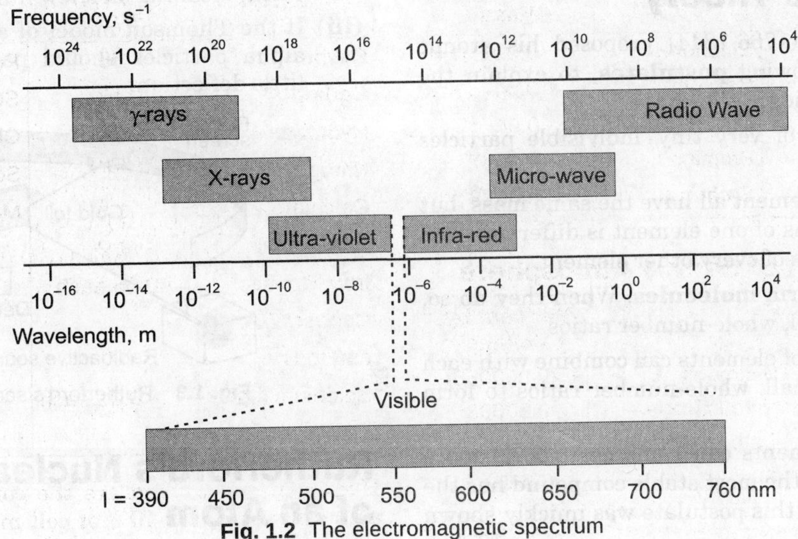

Fig. 1.2 The electromagnetic spectrum

When a beam of white light is passed through a transparent medium, the wavelength components are refracted differently. The light is dispersed into a band of colours, a **spectrum**.

Subatomic Particles

The atom is composed of many types of **subatomic particles**, but only three types will be important in this course. **Protons** and **neutrons** exist in the atom's **nucleus**, and electrons exist outside the nucleus.

An uncombined atom is neither positive nor negative but electrically **neutral**, and thus the number of protons (p) must equal the number of electrons:

Number of protons = Number of electrons (For a neutral atom)

Electron

A negatively charged subatomic particle of an atom or ion that is outside of the nucleus. A neutral atom contains the same number of electrons as there are protons in the nucleus. A negatively charged **Beta Particle** is an electron that is emitted from the nucleus as a result of a nuclear decay process.

Proton

A subatomic particle having a mass of 1.0073 amu and a charge of +1, found in the nuclei of atoms. The nucleus of normal hydrogen is made up of a proton; thus the ionized form of normal hydrogen is often called a proton.

Neutron

An atomic particle found in the nuclei of atoms that is similar to a proton in mass but has no electric charge.

Some Important Terms

- The **atomic number** (Z) is equal to the number of protons (p) in the atom, and determines its identity $Z = p$.
- The number of neutrons in the nuclei of atoms of the same element can differ.
- **Mass number** (A) The sum of the numbers of protons and neutrons in an atom.

$$A = p + n = Z + n$$

- **Atomic mass unit** (amu) One-twelfth of a mass of an atom of the carbon-12 (^{12}C) isotope; a unit used for stating atomic and formula weights; also called a dalton.
- **Isotope** Different forms of a single element that have the same number of protons but have different numbers of neutrons in their nuclei. Radioactive isotopes are unstable and break down until they become stable. Carbon-14 is a radioactive isotope of carbon that is used to date fossilized organic matter.

Structure of Atoms

The word 'atom' has been derived from the Greek word '*a-tomio*' which means 'uncutable' or 'non-divisible'. The atomic theory of matter was first proposed on a firm scientific basis by John Dalton, a British school teacher in 1808. **Dalton's atomic theory**—Atom as the ultimate particle of matter. The experimental observations made by scientists towards the end of nineteenth and beginning of twentieth century have established that atoms can be further divided into subatomic particles, *i.e.*, electrons, protons and neutrons—concept very different from that of Dalton.

Dalton's Atomic Theory

In 1803, **John Dalton** (1766-1844) proposed his atomic theory, including the following **postulates**, to explain the laws of chemical combination:

(i) Matter is made up of very tiny, indivisible particles called **atoms**.

(ii) The atoms of each element all have the same mass, but the mass of the atoms of one element is different from the mass of the atoms of every other element.

(iii) Atoms combine to form **molecules**. When they do so, they combine in small, whole-number ratios.

(iv) Atoms of some pairs of elements can combine with each other in different small, whole-number ratios to form different compounds.

(v) If atoms of two elements can combine to form more than one compound, the most stable compound has the atoms in a 1:1 ratio (this postulate was quickly shown to be incorrect).

The first three postulates have had to be amended, and the fifth was quickly abandoned altogether. But the postulates explained the laws of chemical combination known at the time, and they caused great activity among chemists, which led to more generalizations and further advances in chemistry.

Thomson's Plum Pudding Model of the Atom

In 1904 **Sir JJ Thomson** proposed the first definite theory as to the internal structure of the atom. According to this theory the atom was assumed to consist of a sphere of uniform distribution of about 10^{-10} m positive charge with electrons embedded in it such that the number of electrons equal to the number of positive charges and the atom as a whole is electrically neutral. This model of atom could account the electrical neutrality of atom, but it could not explain the results of gold foil scattering experiment carried out by Rutherford.

Rutherford's Scattering Experiment

Rutherford conducted a scattering experiment in 1911 to find out the arrangement of electrons and protons. He bombarded a thin gold foil with a stream of fast moving positively charged a-particles emanating from radium.

(i) He designs experiment to use alpha particles as atomic bullets The alpha particle was heavy and positively charged, it is a helium nuclei (2 protons and 2 neutrons). The beta particle was light and negatively charged, the electron. Rutherford designed an experiment to use the alpha particles emitted by a radioactive element as probes to the unseen world of atomic structure.

(ii) Rutherford beamed alpha particles through gold foil and detected them as flashes of light or scintillations on a screen. The gold foil was only 0.00004 centimeter thick, meaning on a few hundreds of atoms thick.

(iii) If the Thomson model of atoms was correct, then the alpha particles should pass through with relatively little deflection.

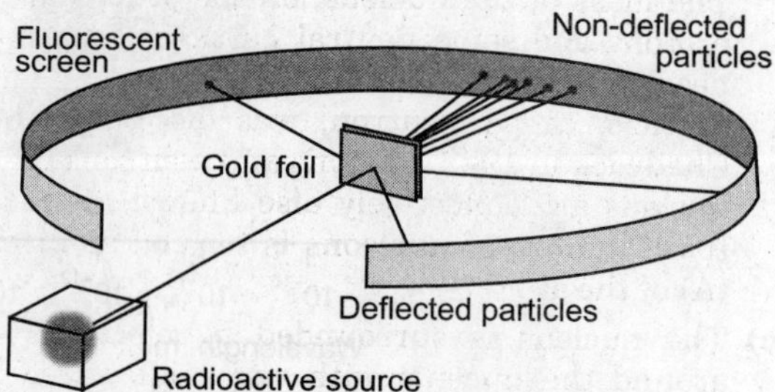

Fig. 1.3 Rutherford's scattering experiment

Rutherford's Nuclear Model of an Atom

This model resulted from conclusion drawn from experiments on the scattering of alpha particles from a radioactive source when the particles were passed through thin sheets of metal foil. According to him

(i) Most of the space in the atom is empty as most of the a-particles passed through the foil.

(ii) A few positively charged α-particles are deflected. The deflection must be due to enormous repulsive force showing that the positive charge of the atom is not spread throughout the atom as Thomson had thought. The positive charge has to be concentrated in a very small volume that repelled and deflected the positively charged α-particles. This very small portion of the atom was called nucleus by Rutherford.

(iii) Calculations by Rutherford showed that the volume occupied by the nucleus is negligibly small as compared to the total volume of the atom. The diameter of the atom is about 10^{-10} m, while that of nucleus is 10^{-15}m.

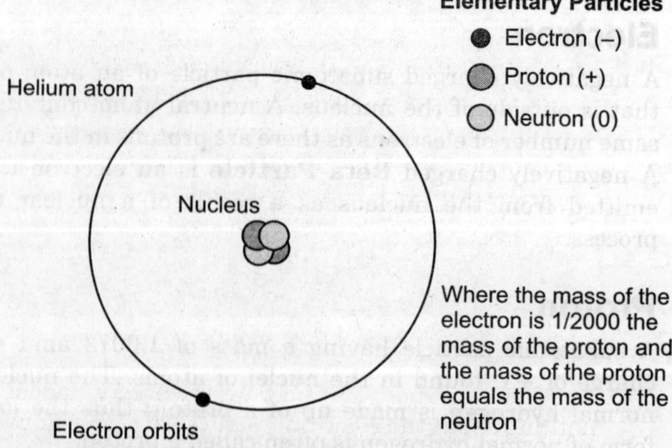

Fig. 1.4 Rutherford's nuclear model of a atom model

On the basis of above observations and conclusions, Rutherford proposed the nuclear model of atom. According to this model:

(a) An atom consists of a tiny positively charged nucleus at its centre.

(b) The positive charge of the nucleus is due to protons. The mass of the nucleus, on the other hand, is due to protons and some neutral particles each having mass nearly equal to the mass of proton. This neutral particle, called neutron, was discovered later on by Chadwick in 1932. Protons and neutrons present in the nucleus are collectively also known as nucleons. The total number of nucleons is termed as mass **number** (A) of the atom.

(c) The nucleus is surrounded by electrons that move around the nucleus with very high speed in circular paths called **orbits**. Thus, Rutherford's model of atom resembles the solar system in which the sun plays the role of the nucleus and the planets that of revolving electrons.

(d) The number of electrons in an atom is equal to the number of protons in it. Thus, the total positive charge of the nucleus exactly balances the total negative charge in the atom making it electrically neutral. The number of protons in an atom is called its atomic number (Z).

(e) Electrons and the nucleus are held together by electrostatic forces of attraction.

Defects of Rutherford's Model

(a) According to Rutherford's model, an atom consists of a positive nucleus with the electrons moving a round it in circular orbits. However JC Maxwell shown that whenever an electron is subjected to acceleration, it emits radiation and loses energy. As a result of this, its orbit should become smaller and smaller and finally it should drop into the nucleus by following a spiral path. This means that atom would collapse and thus Rutherford's model failed to explain stability of atoms.

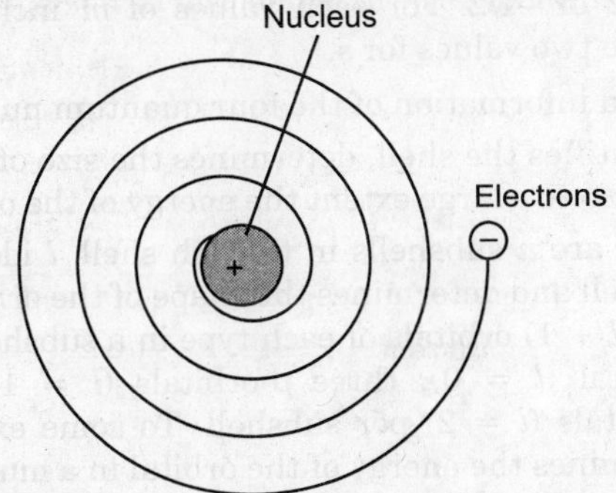

Fig. 1.5 Failure of Rutherford's atom model

(b) Another drawback is that Rutherford's model said nothing about the electronic structure of the atoms, *i.e.*, how the electrons are distributed around the nucleus and what are the energies of these electrons. Therefore, this model failed to explain the existence of certain definite lines in the hydrogen spectrum.

Bohr's Model of an Atom

To overcome the above defects of Rutherford's model, Niels Bohr in 1913 gave a modification based on quantum theory of radiation. The important postulates are:

(i) The electrons revolve round the nucleus only in certain selected circular paths called orbits. These orbits are associated with definite energies and are called energy shells or energy levels or quantum levels. These are numbered as 1, 2, 3, 4 ....., etc. (starting from the nucleus) or designated as *K, L, M, N*, ..., etc.

(ii) As long as an electron remains in a particular orbit, it does not lose or gain energy. This means that energy of an electron in a particular path remains constant. Therefore, these orbits are also called stationary states.

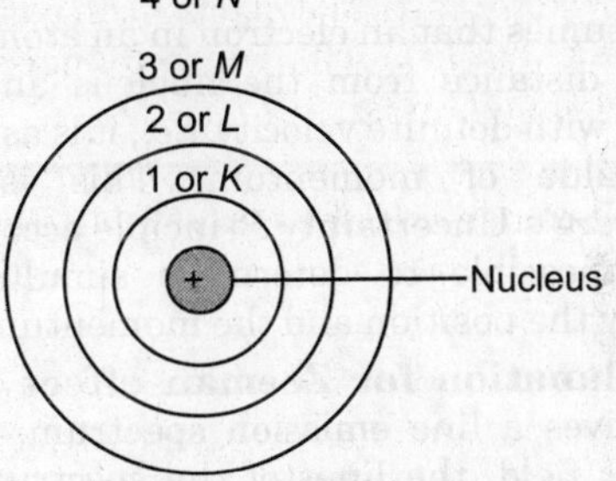

Fig. 1.6 Bohr's orbits

(iii) Only those orbits are permitted in which angular momentum of the electron is a whole number multiple of $h/2\pi$, where 'h' is Planck's constant. An electron moving in a circular orbit has an angular momentum equal to mvr where m is the mass of the electron and v, the angular momentum, the angular momentum, mvr is a whole number multiple of $h/2\pi$, *i.e.*,

$$mvr = nh/2\pi \quad \text{where, } n = 1, 2, 3, \ldots$$

In other words, angular velocity of electrons in an atom is quantised.

(iv) If an electron jumps from one stationary state to another, it will absorb or emit radiation of a definite frequency giving a spectral line of that frequency which depends upon the initial and final levels. When an electron jumps back to the lower energy level, it radiates same amount of energy in the form of radiation.

Limitations of Bohr's Theory

(i) According to Bohr, the radiation results when an electron jumps from one energy orbit to another energy orbit, but how this radiation occurs is not explained by Bohr.

(ii) Bohr' theory had explained the existence of various lines in H spectrum, but it predicted that only a series of lines exist. At that time this was exactly what had been observed. However, as better instruments and techniques were developed, it was realized that the spectral line that had been thought to be a single line was actually a collection of several lines very close together (known as fine spectrum).

(iii) Thus, the appearance of the several lines implies that there are several energy levels, which are close together for each quantum number n. This would require the existence of new quantum numbers.

(iv) Bohr's theory has successfully explained the observed spectra for hydrogen atom and hydrogen like ions (*e.g.*, He^+, Li^{2+}, Be^{3+}, etc.), it can not explain the spectral series for the atoms having a large number of electrons.

(v) There was no satisfactory justification for the assumption that the electron can rotate only in those orbits in which the angular momentum of the electron (mvr) is a whole number multiple of $h/2\pi$, *i.e.*, he could not give any explanation for using the principle of quantisation of angular momentum and it was introduced by him arbitrarily.

(vi) Bohr assumes that an electron in an atom is located at a definite distance from the nucleus and is revolving round it with definite velocity, *i.e.*, it is associated with a fixed value of momentum. This is against the Heisenberg's Uncertainty Principle according to which it is impossible to determine simultaneously with certainty the position and the momentum of a particle.

(vii) No explanation for Zeeman effect If a substance which gives a line emission spectrum, is placed in a magnetic field, the lines of the spectrum get split up into a number of closely spaced lines. This phenomenon is known as Zeeman effect. Bohr's theory has no explanation for this effect.

(viii) No explanation of the Stark effect If a substance which gives a line emission spectrum is placed in an external electric field, its lines get spilt into a number of closely spaced lines. This phenomenon is known as Stark effect. Bohr's theory is not able to explain this observation as well.

Quantum Numbers

The quantum numbers are nothing but the details that are required to locate an electron in an atom. These orbitals are designated by a set of numbers known as quantum numbers. In order to specify energy, size, shape and orientation of the electron orbital, three quantum numbers are required these are discussed below.

The Principal Quantum Number (n)

The electrons inside an atom are arranged in different energy levels called electron shells or orbits. Each shell is characterized by a quantum number called principal quantum number. This is represented by the letter 'n' and have values, 1, 2, 3, 4, etc. The first level is also known as *K*, *L*, *M* and *N* respectively.

The Subsidiary or Azimuthal Quantum Number (l_q)

According to Sommerfeld, the electron in any particular energy level could have circular path or a variety of elliptical paths about the nucleus resulting in slight differences in orbital shapes with slightly differing energies due to the differences in the attraction exerted by the nucleus on the electron. This concept gave rise to the idea of the existence of sub energy levels in each of the principal energy levels of the atom. This is denoted by the letter 'l' and have values from 0 to n –1.

Thus, if

$n = 1$, $l=0$ only one value (one level only) s level.

$n = 2$, $l=0$ and 1 (2 values or 2 sub-levels) s and p level.

$n = 3$, $l=0$, 1 and 2 (3 values or 3 sub-levels) s, p and d level.

$n = 4$, $l=0$, 1, 2 and 3 (4 values or 4 sub-levels) s, p, d and f level.

Magnetic Quantum Number (M_l)

In a strong magnetic field a subshell is resolved into different orientations in space. These orientations called orbitals have slight differences in energy. This explains the appearance of additional lines in atomic spectra produced when atoms emit light in magnetic field. Each orbital is designated by a magnetic quantum number m and its values depend on the value of 'l'. The values are –'l' through zero to +'l' and thus there are ($2l+1$) values. Thus, when

$l = 0$, $m = 0$ (only one value or one orbital)

$l = 1$, $m = -1, 0, +1$ (3 values or 3 orbitals)

$l = 2$, $m = -2, -1, 0, +1, +2$ (5 values or 5 orbitals)

$l = 3$, $m = -3, -2, -1, 0, +1, +2, +3$ (7 values or 7 orbitals).

The three quantum numbers labeling an atomic orbital can be used equally well to label electron in the orbital. However, fourth quanta number, the spin quantum number, (s) is necessary to describe an electron completely.

Spin Quantum Number (M_S)

The electron in the atom rotates not only around the nucleus but also around its own axis and two opposite directions of rotation are possible (clockwise and anti clockwise). Therefore, the spin quantum number can have only two values +1/2 or –1/2. For each values of m including zero, there will be two values for s.

Summarized information of the four quantum numbers:

(a) n identifies the shell, determines the size of the orbital and also to a large extent the energy of the orbit.

(b) There are n subshells in the nth shell. l identifies the subshell and determines the shape of the orbital. There are ($2l + 1$) orbitals of each type in a subshell, *i.e.*, one s-orbital ($l = 0$), three p-orbitals ($l = 1$), and five d-orbitals ($l = 2$) per subshell. To some extent l also determines the energy of the orbital in a multi-electron atom.

(c) m_l designates the orientation of the orbital. For a given value of l, ml has ($2l + 1$) values, the same as the number of orbital's per sub shell. It means that the number of orbitals is equal to the number of ways in which they are oriented.

(d) m_s refer to orientation of the spin of the electron.

Shapes or Boundary Surfaces of Orbitals

s-orbitals

For s-orbital $l = 0$ and hence, m can have only one value, *i.e.*, $m = 0$ This means that the probability of finding the $m = 0$ electron in s-orbital is the same in all directions at a particular distance. In other words s-orbitals are spherically symmetrical.

The electron cloud picture of 1s-orbital is spherical. The s-orbitals are more diffused and have spherical shells within them where probability of finding the electron is zero. These are called nodes. In 2s-orbital there is one spherical node. In the s-orbital, numbers of nodes are $(n - 1)$.

p-orbitals

For p-orbitals $l = 1$ and hence 'm' can have three possible values +1, 0, –1. This means that there are three possible orientations of electron cloud in a p-subshell. The three orbitals of a p-subshell are designated as p_x, p_y and p_z respectively along x-axis, y-axis and z-axis respectively. Each p-orbital is thus dumpbell-shaped.

In the absence of magnetic field these three p-orbitals are equivalent in energy and are, therefore, said to be three-fold degenerate or triply degenerate. In the presence of an external magnetic field, the relative energies of the three p-orbitals vary and depend on their orientation or magnetic quantum number. This probably accounts for the splitting of a single spectral line into a number of closely spaced lines in presence of a magnetic field (fine structure).

d-orbitals

For d-orbitals $l = 2$, $m = 0, \pm1, \pm2$ indicating that d-orbitals have five orientations, *i.e.*, there are five d-orbitals which are named as d_{xy}, d_{yz}, d_{zx} and $d_{x^2} - y^2$. The three orbitals namely d_{xy}, d_{yz} and d_{zx} have their lobes lying symmetrically between the coordinate axes indicated in the subscript to d, *e.g.*, the lobes of d_{xy} orbital are lying between the x-and y-axes. This set of three orbitals is known as T_2g set. $d_{x^2} - y^2$ and d_{z^2} orbitals have their lobes along the axes (*i.e.*, along the axial directions), *e.g.*, the lobes of d-orbital lie along the x and y-axes, while those of d_{z^2} orbital lie along the z-axis. This set is known as E_g set.

Chemical Bonding

The atoms do not remain individually but form bonds among themselves.

In the period from 1916-1919, two Americans, GN Lewis and Irving Langmuir, and a German, Walther Kossel, advanced an important proposal about chemical bonding. Some fundamental ideas associated with Lewis's theory are

(i) Electrons, especially those of the outermost (valence) electronic shell, play a fundamental role in chemical bonding.

(ii) In some cases, electrons are **transferred** from one atom to another. Positive and negative ions are formed and attract each other through electrostatic forces called **ionic bonds.**

(iii) In other cases, one or more pairs of electrons are **shared** between atoms. A bond formed by the sharing of electrons between atoms is called a **covalent bond**.

(iv) Electrons are transferred or shared in such a way that each atom acquires an especially stable electron configuration. Usually this is a noble gas configuration, one with eight outer-shell electrons or an **octet**.

Ionic Bonds

In chemical bonds, atoms can either transfer or share their valence electrons. In the extreme case where one or more atoms lose electrons and other atoms gain them in order to produce a noble gas electron configuration, the bond is called an ionic bond. Typical of ionic bonds are those in the alkali halides such as sodium chloride, NaCl.

Ionization energy, electron affinity and lattice energy influencing the fermation of ionic bonds. Lattice energy is defined as amount of energy released when cations and anions are brought from infinity to their respective equilibrium sites in crystal lattice.

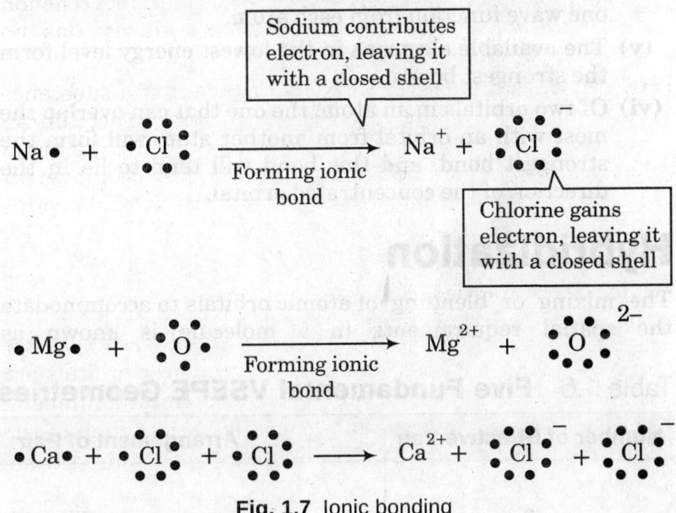

Fig. 1.7 Ionic bonding

Covalent Bonds

Covalent chemical bonds involve the sharing of a pair of valence electrons by two atoms, in contrast to the transfer of electrons in ionic bonds. Such bonds lead to stable molecules if they share electrons in such a way as to create a noble gas configuration for each atom. Hydrogen gas forms the simplest covalent bond in the diatomic hydrogen molecule. The halogens such as chlorine also exist as diatomic gases by forming covalent bonds. The nitrogen and oxygen which makes up the bulk of the atmosphere also exhibits covalent bonding in forming diatomic molecules.

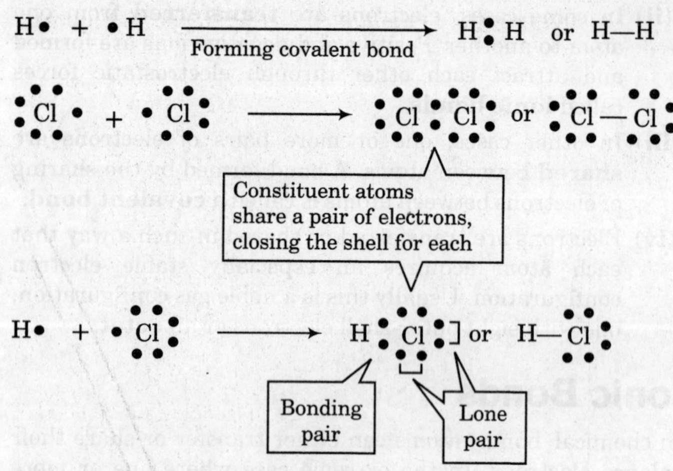

Fig. 1.8 Covalent bonding

Valence Bond Theory

(i) The electron-pair bond forms through the interaction of an unpaired electron on each of two atoms.

(ii) The spins of the electrons have to be opposed.

(iii) Once paired, the two electrons cannot take part in additional bonds.

(iv) The electron-exchange terms for the bond involves only one wave function from each atom.

(v) The available electrons in the lowest energy level form the strongest bonds.

(vi) Of two orbitals in an atom, the one that can overlap the most with an orbital from another atom will form the strongest bond, and this bond will tend to lie in the direction of the concentrated orbital.

Hybridization

The 'mixing' or 'blending' of atomic orbitals to accommodate the spatial requirements in a molecule is known as **hybridization**. Hybridization occurs to minimize electron pair repulsions when atoms are brought together to form molecules. Each of these hybridization schemes corresponds to one of the five fundamental VSEPR geometries.

Sigma (σ) **bonds** arise from the 'end-on' overlap between adjacent orbitals. This leads to a region of high electron density along the inter-nuclear axis (cylindrically symmetrical).

Pi (π) **bonds** arise from the 'side-on' overlap between adjacent orbitals. This leads to two regions of high electron density on opposite sides of the inter-nuclear axis (not cylindrically symmetrical).

Table 1.5 **Shape and Examples of Molecules Predicted from VSEPR Theory**

Number of Electron Pair	Molecular Formula	Molecular Geometry	Example
3	AX_2E	V-shaped molecule	SO_3 and $SnCl_2$
	AX_3	Trigonal planar	BF_3 and SO_3
4	AX_4	Tetrahedral	CH_4 and $SiCl_4$
	AX_3E	Trigonal pyramidal	NH_3 and PF_3
	AX_2E_2	V-shaped molecule	H_2O and H_2S
5	AX_5	Trigonal bipyramidal	PCl_5 and $Fe(CO)_5$
	AX_4E	Irregular tetrahedral	SF_4 and SCl_4
	AX_3E_2	T-shaped	BrF_3 and IBr_3
	AX_2E_3	Linear	XeF_2 and ICl_2^-
6	AX_6	Octahedral	SF_6 and FeF_6^{-3}
	AX_5E	Square pyramidal	BrF_3 and IF_5
	AX_4E_2	Square planar	XeF_4

Table 1.6 **Five Fundamental VSEPE Geometries**

Number of Effective Pair	Arrangement of Pair	Hybridization (symbolic)	Hybridization (figure)
2	⟶ Linear bipyramidal	*sp*	180°
3	⟶ Trigonal planar	sp^2	120°
4	⟶ Tetrahedral	sp^3	109.5°

Number of Effective Pair	Arrangement of Pair	Hybridization (symbolic)	Hybridization (figure)
5	→ Trigonal bipyramidal	dsp^3	90°, 120°
6	→ Octahedral	d^2sp^3	90°, 90°

Water

Water is the **most abundant substance** in living systems, making up 70% or more of the weight of most organisms. The first living organisms doubtless arose in an aqueous environment.

A water molecule is **tetrahedron** with oxygen at its center. The two hydrogens and the unshared electrons of the remaining two sp^3-hybridized orbitals. The 105-degree angle between the hydrogens differs slightly from the ideal tetrahedral angle, 109.5 degrees.

The water molecule and its ionization products, H^+ and OH^-, influence the structure, self-assembly, and properties of all cellular components, including proteins, nucleic acids, and lipids. The noncovalent interactions responsible for the strength and specificity of 'recognition' among biomolecules are decisively influenced by the solvent properties of water, including its ability to form hydrogen bonds with itself and with solutes.

Water has a **higher melting point, boiling point, and heat of vaporization** than most other common solvents. These unusual properties are a consequence of attractions between adjacent water molecules that give liquid water great internal cohesion which is the cause of intermolecular attractions.

Water is a **dipole**, a molecule with electrical charge distributed asymmetrically about its structure. The strongly electronegative oxygen atom and a partial positive charged hydrogen atom. Water, a strong dipole, has a high dielectric **constant**. The dielectric constant for hexane is 1.9; for ethanol is 24.3; and for water is 78.5. Water, therefore greatly decreases the force of attraction between charged and polar species relative to water-free environments with lower **dielectric constants**. Its strong dipole and high dielectric constant enable water to dissolve large quantities of charged compounds such as salts.

Polar biomolecules dissolve readily in water because they can replace water-water interactions with more energetically favorable water-solute interactions. In contrast, non-polar biomolecules interfere with water-water interactions but are unable to form water-solute interactions—consequently, nonpolar molecules are poorly soluble in water. In aqueous solutions, nonpolar molecules tend to cluster together.

Hydrogen bonds are relatively weak. Those in liquid water have a **bond dissociation energy** (the energy required to break a bond) of about 23 kJ/mol, compared with 470 kJ/mol for the covalent OOH bond in water or 348 kJ/mol for a covalent COC bond. The hydrogen bond is about 10% covalent, due to overlaps in the bonding orbitals, and about 90% electrostatic.

Each hydrogen atom of a water molecule shares an electron pair with the central oxygen atom. The oxygen nucleus attracts electrons more strongly than does the hydrogen nucleus (a proton); that is, oxygen is more electronegative. The sharing of electrons between H and O is therefore, unequal; each hydrogen bears a partial positive charge ($2\delta^+$) and the oxygen atom bears a partial negative charge equal to the sum of the two partial positives ($2\delta^-$). As a result, there is an electrostatic attraction between the oxygen atom of one water molecule and the hydrogen of another, called a **hydrogen bond**.

When water is heated, the increase in temperature reflects the faster motion of individual water molecules. At any given time, most of the molecules in liquid water are engaged in hydrogen bonding, but the **lifetime of each hydrogen bond** is just 1 to 20 picoseconds; upon breakage of one hydrogen bond, another hydrogen bond forms, with the same partner or a new one, within 0.1 ps.

Water Influences the Structure of Biomolecules

Water forms about 60-70% of biomass. It directly or indirectly influences the biomolecular structures.

Stabilizes Biological Molecules

The covalent bond is the strongest force that holds molecules together. Non-covalent forces, while of lesser magnitude, make significant contributions to the structure, stability, and functional competence of macromolecules in living cells. These forces, which can be either attractive or repulsive, involve interactions both within the biomolecule and between it and the water that forms the principal component of the surrounding environment.

Folding of Biomolecules

Most biomolecules are **amphipathic** that is, they possess regions rich in charged or polar functional groups as well as regions with hydrophobic character. Proteins tend to fold with the *R*-groups of amino acids with hydrophobic side chains in the interior. Amino acids with charged or polar amino acid side chains (*e.g.,* arginine, glutamate, serine) generally are present on the surface in contact with water. A similar pattern prevails in a phospholipid bilayer, where the charged head groups of phosphatidyl serine or phosphatidyl ethanolamine contact water while their hydrophobic fatty acyl side chains cluster together, excluding water. This pattern maximizes the opportunities for the formation of energetically favorable charge-dipole, dipole-dipole, and hydrogen bonding interactions between polar groups on the biomolecule and water. It also minimizes energetically unfavorable contact between water and hydrophobic groups.

Fig. 1.9 **Left** Association of two dipolar water molecules by a hydrogen bond (dotted line). **Right** Hydrogen-bonded cluster of four water

Note that water can serve simultaneously both as a hydrogen donor and as a hydrogen acceptor.

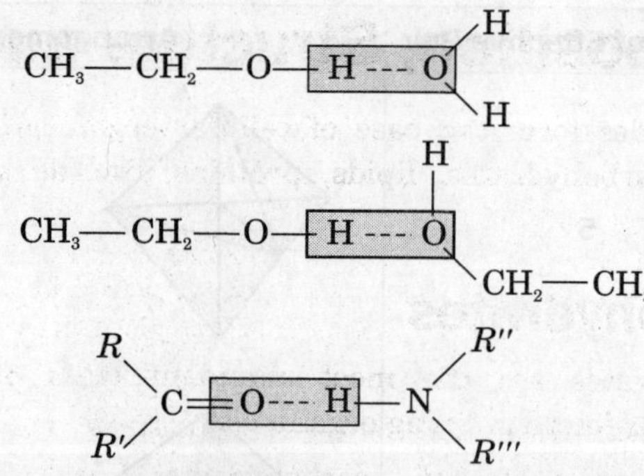

Fig. 1.10 Additional polar groups participate in hydrogen bonding. Shown are hydrogen bonds formed between an alcohol and water, between two molecules of ethanol, and between the peptide carbonyl oxygen and the peptide nitrogen hydrogen of an adjacent amino acid.

Table 1.7 **Bond Energies for Atoms of Biologic Significance**

Bond Type	Energy (kcal/mol)	Bond Type	Energy (kcal/mol)
O—O	34	O=O	96
S—S	51	C—H	99
C—N	70	C=S	108
S—H	81	O—H	110
C—C	82	C=C	147
C—O	84	C=N	147
N—H	94	C=O	164

While the hydrogens of non-polar groups such as the methylene groups of hydrocarbons do not form hydrogen bonds, they do affect the structure of the water that surrounds them. Water molecules adjacent to a hydrophobic group are restricted in the number of orientations (degrees of freedom) that permit them to participate in the maximum number of energetically favorable hydrogen bonds. Maximal formation of multiple hydrogen bonds can be maintained only by increasing the order of the adjacent water molecules, with a corresponding decrease in entropy.

It follows from the second law of thermodynamics that the optimal free energy of a hydrocarbon-water mixture is a function of both maximal enthalpy (from hydrogen bonding) and minimum entropy (maximum degrees of freedom). Thus, nonpolar molecules tend to form droplets with minimal exposed surface area, reducing the number of water molecules affected. For the same reason, in the aqueous environment of the living cell the hydrophobic portions of biopolymers tend to be buried inside the structure of the molecule, or within a lipid bilayer, minimizing contact with water.

Composition, Structure and Functions of Biomolecules

Biomolecules form the base of cellular organization. They include carbohydrates, lipids, proteins, nucleic acids and vitamins.

Carbohydrates

Carbohydrates are the most abundant class of organic compounds found in living organisms.

General formula of carbohydrates is $C_n(H_2O)_n$. Carbohydrates are a major source of metabolic energy, for both plants and animals.

Single units of **sugar**, such as **glucose**, are called monosaccharide. Sugars can be readily linked together to form disaccharides (contains two monosaccharides), **oligosaccharides** (contains several monosaccharides) and **polysaccharides** (contains many monosaccharides).

1. Monosaccharides

The simple sugars, or **monosaccharide** are polyhydroxyaldehydes (aldoses) or polyhydroxyketones (ketoses). All have the composition $(CH_2O)_n$, hence, the family name **carbohydrate**. A typical sugar, and the one with the widest distribution in nature, is glucose.

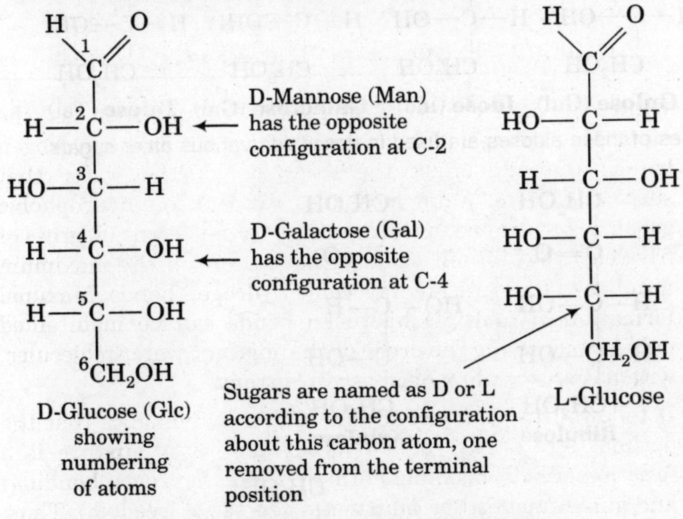

Fig. 1.11 Structures of D and L-glucose

The six-membered ring formed in this way (**pyranose** rings) are especially stable, but five membered **furanose** ring also exist in many carbohydrates.

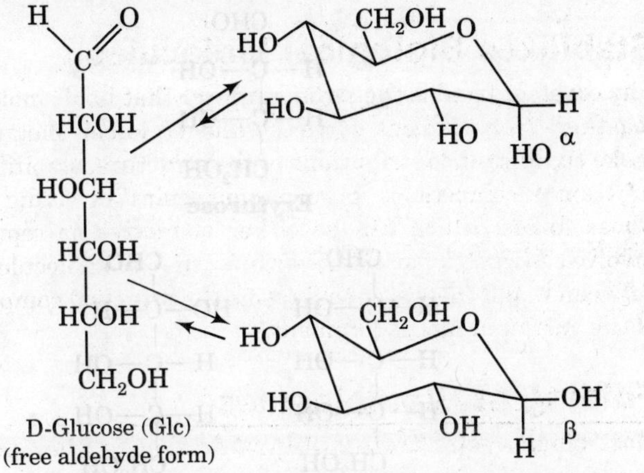

Fig. 1.12 Pyranose ring forms (hemiacetal forms)

The two configurations about this carbon atom are designated a and b as indicated above. In an equilibrium mixture, ring forms of most sugars predominate over open chains. Although polysaccharides are composed almost exclusively of sugar residues in ring forms, the open chain forms are sometimes metabolic intermediates.

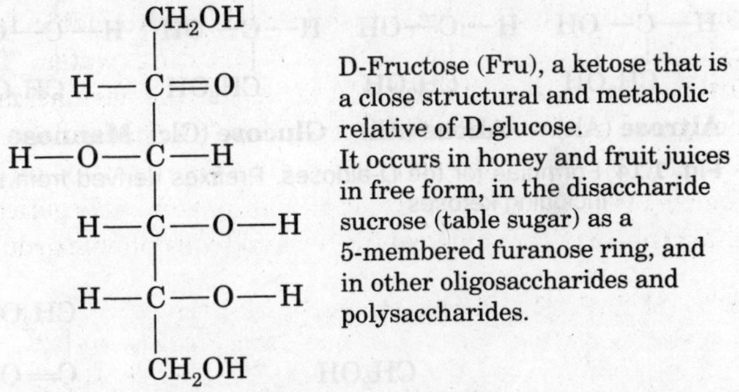

Fig. 1.13 D-fructose

Because of their many polar hydroxyl groups, most sugars are very soluble in water. However, hydrogen bonds between molecules stabilize sugar crystals making them insoluble in non-polar solvents. Intermolecular hydrogen bonds between chains of sugar rings in cellulose account for much of the strength and insolubility of these polysaccharides.

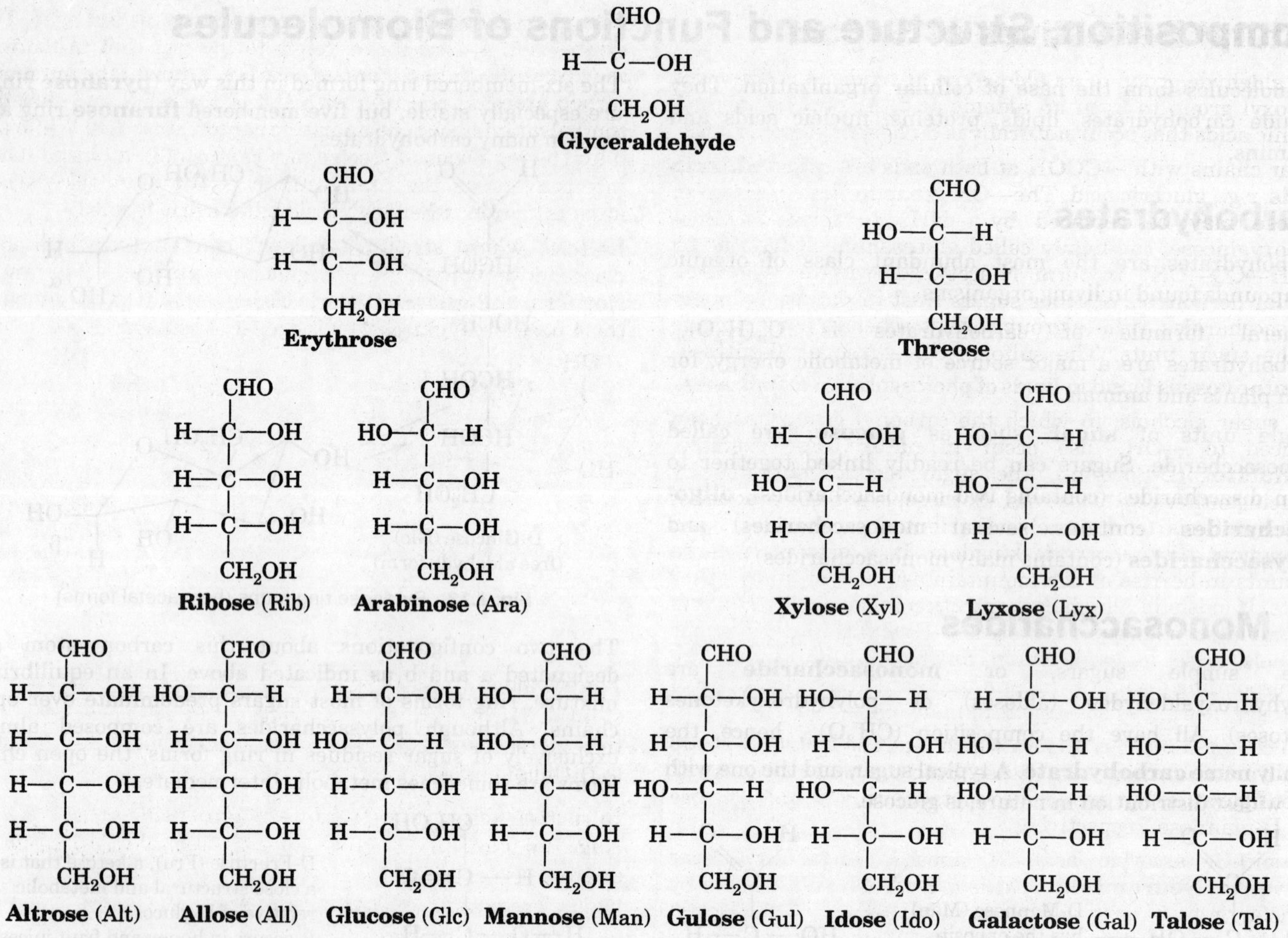

CHO
H—C—OH
CH_2OH
Glyceraldehyde

CHO
H—C—OH
H—C—OH
CH_2OH
Erythrose

CHO
HO—C—H
H—C—OH
CH_2OH
Threose

CHO
H—C—OH
H—C—OH
H—C—OH
CH_2OH
Ribose (Rib)

CHO
HO—C—H
H—C—OH
H—C—OH
CH_2OH
Arabinose (Ara)

CHO
H—C—OH
HO—C—H
H—C—OH
CH_2OH
Xylose (Xyl)

CHO
HO—C—H
HO—C—H
H—C—OH
CH_2OH
Lyxose (Lyx)

CHO
H—C—OH
H—C—OH
H—C—OH
H—C—OH
CH_2OH
Altrose (Alt)

CHO
HO—C—H
H—C—OH
H—C—OH
H—C—OH
CH_2OH
Allose (All)

CHO
H—C—OH
HO—C—H
H—C—OH
H—C—OH
CH_2OH
Glucose (Glc)

CHO
HO—C—H
HO—C—H
H—C—OH
H—C—OH
CH_2OH
Mannose (Man)

CHO
H—C—OH
H—C—OH
HO—C—H
H—C—OH
CH_2OH
Gulose (Gul)

CHO
HO—C—H
H—C—OH
HO—C—H
H—C—OH
CH_2OH
Idose (Ido)

CHO
H—C—OH
HO—C—H
HO—C—H
H—C—OH
CH_2OH
Galactose (Gal)

CHO
HO—C—H
HO—C—H
HO—C—H
H—C—OH
CH_2OH
Talose (Tal)

Fig. 1.14 Formulas for the D-aldoses. Prefixes derived from the names of these aldoses are used in describing various other sugars including ketoses

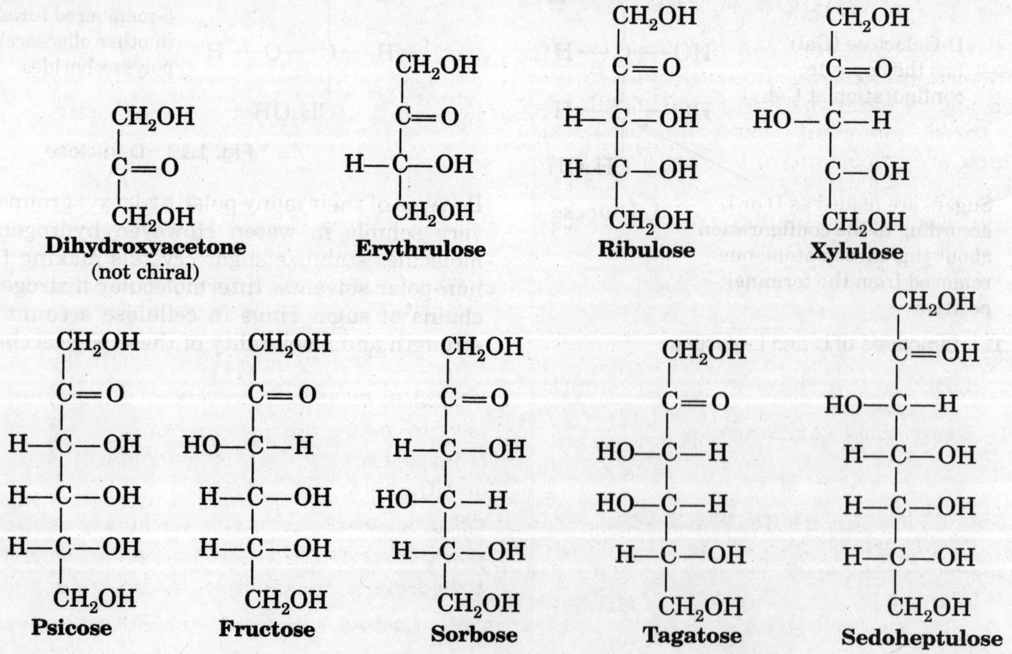

CH_2OH
C=O
CH_2OH
Dihydroxyacetone
(not chiral)

CH_2OH
C=O
H—C—OH
CH_2OH
Erythrulose

CH_2OH
C=O
H—C—OH
H—C—OH
CH_2OH
Ribulose

CH_2OH
C=O
HO—C—H
C—OH
CH_2OH
Xylulose

CH_2OH
C=O
H—C—OH
H—C—OH
H—C—OH
CH_2OH
Psicose

CH_2OH
C=O
HO—C—H
H—C—OH
H—C—OH
CH_2OH
Fructose

CH_2OH
C=O
H—C—OH
HO—C—H
H—C—OH
CH_2OH
Sorbose

CH_2OH
C=O
HO—C—H
HO—C—H
H—C—OH
CH_2OH
Tagatose

CH_2OH
C=OH
HO—C—H
H—C—OH
H—C—OH
H—C—OH
CH_2OH
Sedoheptulose

Fig. 1.15 Formulae for the open forms of the D-ketoses

Natural Derivatives of Sugars

The aldehyde group of an aldose can be oxidized readily to a carboxyl group to form an aldonic acid. Among the several aldonic acids that occur naturally is 6-phosphogluconic acid. Sugar chains with —COOH at both ends are called **aldaric acids**, *e.g.*, glucaric acid. The—OH group in the 2 position of glucose may be replaced by $—NH_2$ to form 2-amino-2-deoxyglucose, commonly called glucosamine (GlcN) or by $—NH—CO—CH_3$ to form N-acetylglucosamine (GlcNAc). Similar derivatives of other sugars exist in nature. In many polysaccharides, sulfate groups are attached in ester linkage to the sugar units. The sulfo ($—SO_3—$) sugar **6-sulfo-a-D-quinovose** is found in lipids of photosynthetic membranes.

The sugar alcohols, in which the carbonyl group has been reduced to —OH, also occur in nature. For example, **D-Glucitol** (D-Sorbitol), the sugar alcohol obtained by reducing either D-Glucose or L-Sorbose, is a major product of photosynthesis and widely distributed in bacteria and throughout the eukaryotic kingdom. It is present in large amounts in berries of the mountain ash and in many other fruits. It exists in a high concentration in human semen and accumulates in lenses of diabetics. D-Glucitol and other sugar alcohols arise in some fungi during metabolism of the corresponding sugars. Mannitol, another product of photosynthesis, is also present in many organisms.

Two common 6-deoxy sugars which lack the hydroxyl group at C-6 are **rhamnose** and fucose. Both are of the 'unnatural' L-configuration but are derived metabolically from D-glucose and D-mannose, respectively.

Vitamin-C (ascorbic acid) is another important sugar derivative. **Neuraminic acid** is a 9-carbon sugar made by transferring a 3-carbon piece onto a hexosamine. Its *N*-acetyl and *N*-glycolyl derivatives are called **sialic acids.**

2. Disaccharides/Oligosaccharides

Two molecules of α-D-glucopyranose can be joined, in an indirect synthesis, to form **maltose**. Maltose is formed by the hydrolysis of starch and is otherwise not found in nature. There are only three abundant naturally occurring **disaccharides** which are important to the metabolism of plants and animals.

Lactose (milk), **Sucrose** (green plants) and **Trehalose** (fungi and insects).

α-D-Glucopyranose (2 molecules)

α-1, 4-Glycosidic linkage

Fig. 1.16 Maltose, a disaccharide

Disaccharides are linked by glycosidic (acetal) linkages. The symbol α-1, 4 used above, refers to the fact that in maltose the glycosidic linkage connects carbon atom 1 (the anomeric carbon atom) of one ring with C-4 of the other and that the configuration about the anomeric carbon atom is a. While the α and β ring forms of free sugars can usually undergo ready interconversion, the configuration at the anomeric carbon atom is 'frozen' when a glycosidic linkage is formed.

Lactose, whose structure follows, can be described as a disaccharide containing one galactose unit in a β-pyranose ring form and whose anomeric carbon atom (C-1) is joined to the 4 position of glucose, giving a β-1, 4 linkage:

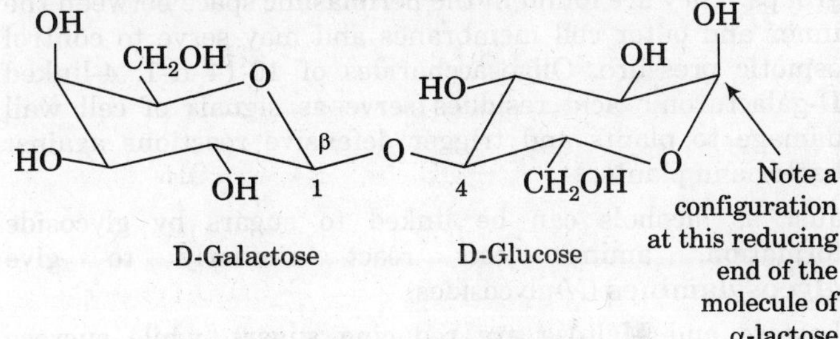

Fig. 1.17 α-Lactose

The systematic name for α-lactose, *O*-β-D-galactopyranosyl (1→4)-α-D-glucopyranose, provides a complete description of the stereochemistry, ring sizes, and mode of linkage (β-D-Gal*p*-(1→4)-α-D-Glc*p*).

In sucrose and in α′, α-trehalose the reducing groups of two rings are joined. Each of these sugars exists in single form. Sucrose serves as the major transport sugar in green plants, while Trehalose plays a similar role in insects, similar to D-glucose in our blood.

Sucrose: Glcpα1→β2Fru*f*

Fig. 1.18 α′, α-Trehalose: Glcapα1→α1Glcf

Trehalose or 'mushroom sugar,' is found not only in fungi but also in many other organisms. It serves as the primary transport sugar in the haemolymph of insects and also acts as 'antifreeze' in many species.

Disaccharides, as well as higher oligosaccharides and polysaccharides, are thermodynamically unstable with respect to hydrolysis, for example, for lactose in aqueous solution:

$$\text{Lactose} + H_2O \longrightarrow \text{D-Glucose} + \text{D-Galactose};$$

$$\Delta G^\circ \approx -8.7 \pm 0.2 \text{ kJ mol}^{-1} \text{ at } 25°\text{C}$$

The joining of additional sugar rings through glycosidic linkages to a disaccharide leads to the formation of **oligosaccharides**, which contain a few residues, and to **polysaccharides**, which contain many residues. Among the well-known oligosaccharides are the substituted sucroses **raffinose**, Gal*p*(1→6) Glc*p*(1→2) Fru*f*, and **stachyose**, Gal*p*(1→6) Gal*p*(1→6) Glc*p*(1→2) Fru*f*. Both sugars are found in many legumes and other green plants in which they are formed by attachment of the galactose rings to sucrose. Oligosaccharides have many functions. For example, Gram negative bacteria often synthesize oligosaccharides of 6-12 glucose units in β-1, 2 linkage joined to *sn*-1-phosphoglyceryl groups. They are found in the periplasmic space between the inner and outer cell membranes and may serve to control osmotic pressure. Oligosaccharides of 10-14 α-1, 4-linked D-galacturonic acid residues serve as signals of cell wall damage to plants and trigger defensive reactions against bacteria in plants.

Just as alcohols can be linked to sugars by glycoside formation, amines can react similarly to give **glycosylamines** (*N*-glycosides).

Lactose and Maltose are reducing sugars, while sucrose non-reducing.

3. **Polysaccharides** (Glycans)

The simple sugars commonly used in the assembly of polysaccharides include D-glucose, D-mannose, D-galactose, D-fructose, D-xylose, L-arabinose, related uronic acids, and amino sugars. These monomer units can be put together in many ways, either as **homopolysaccharides** containing a single kind of monomer or as **heteropolysaccharides** containing two or more different monomers.

Homopolysaccharides

Cell walls of yeasts contain mannans in which the main α-1, 6-linked chain carries short branches of one to three mannose units joined in α-1, 2, α-1, 3 and sometimes α-1, 6 linkages.

The cell walls of some seaweeds contain a β-1, 3-linked **xylan** instead of cellulose.

Fructose, a 6-carbon sugar, is present as five-membered furanose rings in inulin, the storage polysaccharide of the Jerusalem artichoke and other Compositae, and also in sweet potatoes.

The major structural polysaccharide in the exoskeletons of arthropods and of other lower animal forms is **chitin**, a linear β-1, 4-linked polymer of *N*-acetylglucosamine whose structure resembles that of cellulose.

Heteropolysaccharides

Many polysaccharides contain repeating units consisting of more than one different kind of monomer. Some of these are composed of two sugars in a simple alternating sequence. Examples are **hyaluronan** (hyaluronic acid) and the **chondroitin, dermatan, keratan,** and **heparan sulphates**. They are important components of the 'ground substance' or intracellular cement of connective tissue in animals.

Fibres of cellulose, which run like rods through the amorphous matrix of plant cell walls, appear to be coated with a monolayer of **hemicelluloses**. Predominant among the latter is a **xyloglucan**, which has the basic cellulose structure but with α-1, 6-linked xylose units attached to three-fourths of the glucose residues. L-Fucose may also be present in trisaccharide side chains: L-Fucα1 → 2Galα1 → 2Xylα1 →. Pectins of higher plants contain β-1, 4-linked polygalacturonates interrupted by occasional 1, 2-linked L-rhamnose residues. Some of the carboxyl groups of these rhamnogalacturonan chains are methylated. Arabinans and galactans are also present in pectin. A possible arrangement of cellulose fibres, hemicelluloses and pectic materials in a cell wall has been proposed.

Table 1.8 **Some of the Many Polysaccharides Found in Nature**

Name	Source	Monomer	Main Linkage	Branch Linkage
Starch	Green plants			
Amylose		D-Glucose	α-1, 4	
Amylopectin		D-Glucose	α-1, 4	α-1, 6
Glycogen	Animals and bacteria	D-Glucose	α-1, 4	α-1, 6
Cellulose	Green plants and some bacteria	D-Glucose	β-1, 4	
Dextrans	Some bacteria	D-Glucose	α-1, 6	α-1, 3
Pullulan	Yeast	D-Glucose	α-1, 6 + α-1, 4	
Callose	Green plants	D-Glucose	β-1, 3	
Yeast glucan	Yeast	D-Glucose	β-1, 3	
Schizophyllan, curdlan and paramylon		D-Glucose	β-1, 3	β-1, 6 on every third residue
Mannans	Algae	D-Mannose	α-1, 4	
	Yeast	D-Mannose	α-1, 6	

Name	Source	Monomer	Main Linkage	Branch Linkage
Xylans	Green plants Brown seaweed	D-Xylose	β-1, 3	
Inulin	Dahlia plant tubers	D-Fructose	β-2, 6	
Chitin	Fungi and arthropods	*N*-Acetyl-D-Glucosamine	β-1, 4	
Alternating polysaccharides				
Hyaluronan	Animal connective tissue	Glucuronic acid + N-Acetylglucosamine	β-1, 4	
Chondroitin sulphate		D-Glucosamine *N*-Acetyl-D-Galactosamine	β-1, 3 + β-1, 4	
Dermatan sulphate		α-L-Iduronate + *N*-Acetyl-D-Galactosamine	β-1, 3 + β-1, 4	
Pectin	Higher plants	D-galactunonate + others	β-1, 4 + others	
Alginate	Seaweed	D-Mannuronate + L-Guluronate	β-1, 4 + α-1, 4	
Agar-agar	Red seaweed	Galactose	β-1, 4 and α-1, 3	
Carageenan	Red seaweed	Galactose-4-sulphate + 3, 6-anhydro-D-Galactose-2-sulphate	β-1, 4 + α-1, 3	
Murein	Bacterial cell wall	*N*-acetyl D-Glucosamine + *N*-acetyl D-Muramic acid	β-1, 4	

Glucans From glucose alone various organisms synthesize a whole series of polymeric glucans with quite different properties. Of these, **cellulose**, an unbranched β-1, 4-linked polyglucose, is probably the most abundant. It is the primary structural polysaccharide of the cell walls of most green plants. For the whole Earth, plants produce $\sim 10^{14}$ kg of cellulose per year.

Starch, another of the most abundant polymers of glucose, is stored by most green plants in a semicrystalline form in numerous small granules. These granules, which are usually formed within colourless.

Membrane-bounded plastids, have characteristic shapes and appearances that vary from plant to plant. One component of starch, **amylose,** is a linear polymer of many α-D-glucopyranose units in 1, 4 linkage as in maltose. Starch granules always contain a second kind of molecule known as amylopectin. Both amylopectin and **glycogen** (animal starch) consist of highly branched bushlike molecules. Branches are attached to α-1, 4-linked chains through α-1, 6 linkages

Beta-1, 3-linked glucans occur widely in nature. When a new green plant cell is formed the first polysaccharide to be synthesized is not cellulose but the β-1, 3-linked glucose polymer callose. Cellulose appears later. Callose is also produced in some specialized plant tissues, such as pollen tubes, and is formed in massive amounts at the site of wounds or of attack by pathogens. The major structural component of the yeast cell wall is a β-1, 3-linked glucan with some β-1, 6 branches.

Agarose, an alternating carbohydrate polymer consisting of ~120-kDa chains, is the principal component of agar and the compound that accounts for most of the gelling properties of that remarkable substance.

A similar structure has been established for the gelforming **carrageenans** from red seaweed.

Alginates, found in cell walls of some marine algae and also formed by certain bacteria, consist in part of a linear β-1, 4-linked polymer of D-mannuronate with a cellulose-like structure.

Bacteria form and secrete a variety of heteropolysaccharides, several of which are of commercial value because of their useful gelling properties. **Xanthan gum** (formed by Xanthomonas campestris) has the basic cellulose structure but every second glucose residue carries an α-1, 3-linked trisaccharide consisting of 6-*O*-acetylmannose, glucuronic acid, and mannose in the following repeating unit:

$$(4Glc\beta 1\text{-}4Glc\beta n1\text{-})_n$$
$$\uparrow$$
$$6\text{-}O\text{-acetyl-Man-}\alpha\text{-}1$$
$$2$$
$$\uparrow$$
$$\text{Man-}\beta\text{-}1\text{-}4\text{-GlcA}\beta 1$$

Acetan of *Acetobacter xylinum* has pentasaccharide side chains that contain L-rhamnose. A helical structure for the strands has been observed by atomic force microscopy.

Polysaccharides of Bacterial Surfaces

The innermost layer of bacterial cell walls is a porous network of a highly crosslinked material known as **peptidoglycan** or **murein**. The backbone of the peptidoglycan is a β-1, 4-linked alternating polymer of *N*-acetyl-D-glucosamine and *N*-acetyl D-muramic acid. Alternate units of the resulting chitin-like molecule carry unusual peptides that are attached to the lactyl groups of the *N*-acetylmuramic acid units and crosslink the polysaccharide chains. In *E. coli* and other Gram negative bacteria the peptidoglycan forms a thin (2 nm) continuous network around the cell. This 'baglike molecule' protects the organism from osmotic stress. In addition, Gram negative bacteria have an outer membrane and on its outer surface a complex lipopolysaccharide.

Lipids

Lipids are organic compounds, found in living organisms that are soluble in non-polar organic solvents. The solubility of lipids in nonpolar organic solvents results from their significant hydrocarbon component. The hydrocarbon portion of the compound is responsible for its 'oiliness' or 'fattiness'. The word lipid comes from the Greek lipos, which means 'fat'.

Biological Importance of Lipids

(i) Fat under skin serve as thermal insulator against cold.

(ii) Lipids present in myelinated nerves act as insulators for propagation of depolarization wave.

(iii) Fat serves as a source of energy for man like carbohydrates.

(iv) Fat is an ideal form for storing energy in the human body compared to carbohydrates and proteins because: (a) Energy content of fat is higher. (b) Only fat can be stored in a concentrated water free form which is not possible with carbohydrates and proteins.

(v) Lipids are structural components of cell membrane and nervous tissue.

(vi) Some lipids serve as precursors for the synthesis of complex molecules. For example, acetyl Co-A is used for the synthesis of cholesterol.

(vii) Lipoproteins, which are complexes of lipids and proteins are involved in the transport of lipids in the blood and components of cell membrane.

(viii) Some lipids serve as hormones and fat soluble vitamins are lipids.

(ix) Fats are essential for the absorption of fat soluble vitamins.

(x) Fats serve as surfactants by reducing surface tension.

Unlike proteins, polysaccharides, and nucleic acids, most lipids are not polymers. However, they are made by linking together smaller molecules. Among the 'building blocks' of lipids are **fatty acids, glycerol, phosphoric acid** and **sugars**. Many lipids have both polar and non-polar regions. This gives them an **amphipathic** character, *i.e.*, a tendency toward both hydrophobic and hydrophilic behavior, and accounts for their tendency to aggregate into membranous structures.

1. Fatty Acids

Fatty acids are carboxylic acids with long hydrocarbon chains. Fatty acids can be saturated with hydrogen (and therefore have no carbon–carbon double bonds) or unsaturated (have carbon–carbon double bonds). Fatty acids with more than one double bond are called **polyunsaturated fatty acids**. Double bonds in naturally occurring unsaturated fatty acids are never conjugated—they are always separated by one methylene group.

The double bonds in unsaturated fatty acids generally have the cis configuration. This configuration produces a bend in the molecules, which prevents them from packing together as tightly as fully saturated fatty acids. As a result, unsaturated fatty acids have fewer intermolecular interactions and, therefore, lower melting points than saturated fatty acids with comparable molecular weights. The melting points of the unsaturated fatty acids decrease as the number of double bonds increases. For example, an 18-carbon fatty acid melts at 69°C if it is saturated, at 13°C if it has one double bond, at –5°C if it has two double bonds, and at –11°C if it has three double bonds.

Most naturally occurring fatty acids are esterified or combined via amide linkages in complex lipids. For example, ordinary fats are largely the fatty acid esters of glycerol called triacylglycerols (triglycerides).

Most fatty acid chains contain an even number of carbon atoms. In higher plants the C-16 **palmitic acid** and the C-18 unsaturated oleic and linoleic acids predominate. The C-18 saturated stearic acid is almost absent in plants and C-20 to C-24 acids are rarely present except in the outer cuticle of leaves. Certain plants contain unusual fatty acids which may be characteristic of a taxonomic group. For example, the Composite (daisy family) contain acetylene fatty acids and the castor bean contains the hydroxy fatty acid **ricinoleic acid**.

Phospholipids of photoreceptor membranes of the retina contain fatty acid chains as long as C-36. The variety of fatty acids found in animals is greater than in a given plant species.

Bacteria usually lack polyunsaturated fatty acids but often contain branched fatty acids, cyclopropane containing acids, hydroxy fatty acids, and unesterified fatty acids. *Mycobacterium*, including the human pathogen *Mycobacterium tuberculosis*, contains **mycolic acids**.

Table 1.9 **Common and Naturally Occurring Fatty Acids**

Number of Carbon	Common Name	Systematic Name	Structure	Melting Point °C
Saturated				
12	Lauric acid	Dodecanoic acid	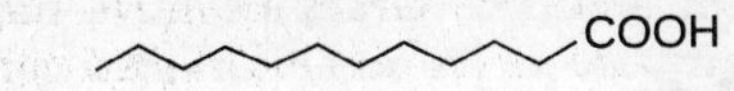 COOH	44
14	Myristic acid	Tetradecanoic acid	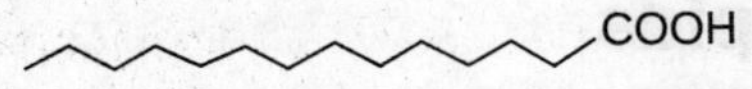 COOH	58
16	Palmitic acid	Hexadecanoic acid	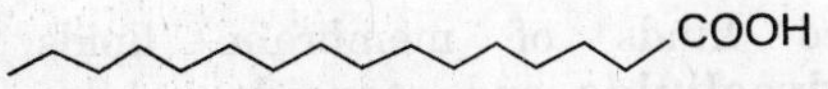 COOH	63
18	Stearic acid	Octadecanoic acid	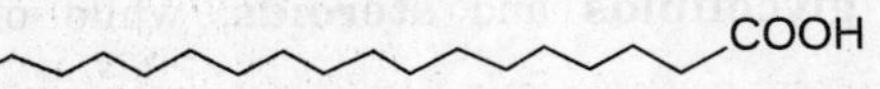 COOH	69
20	Arachidic acid	Eicosanoic acid	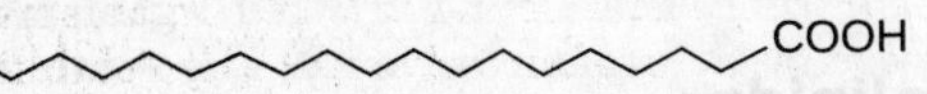 COOH	77
Unsaturated				
16	Palmitoleic acid	(9*Z*)-hexadecenoic acid	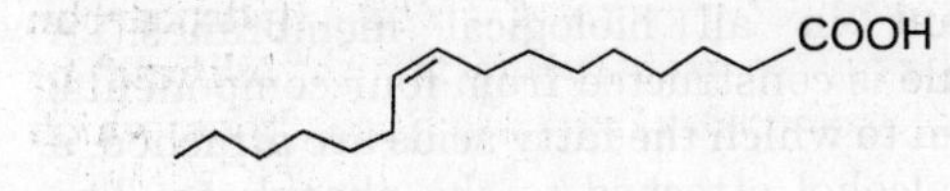 COOH	0
18	Oleic acid	(9*Z*)-octadecenoic acid		13
18	Linoleic acid	(9*Z*, 12*Z*)-octadecadienoic acid	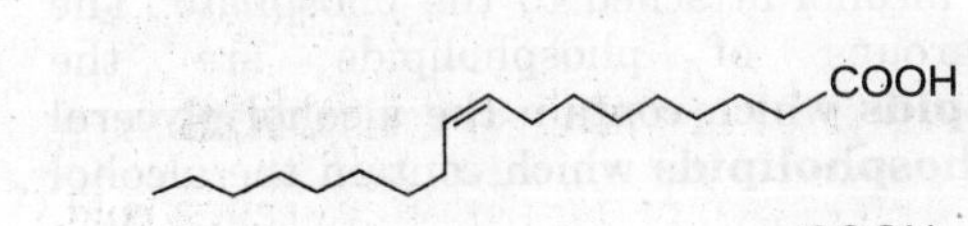 COOH	–5
18	Linolenic acid	(9*Z*, 12*Z*, 15*Z*)-octadecatrienoic acid	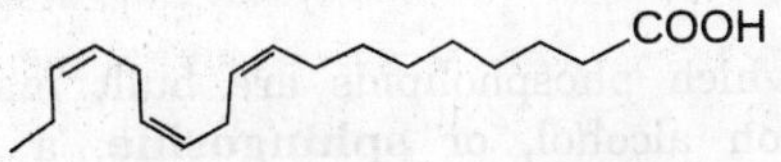 COOH	–11
20	Arachidonic acid	(5*Z*, 8*Z*, 11*Z*, 14*Z*)-eicosatetraenoic acid	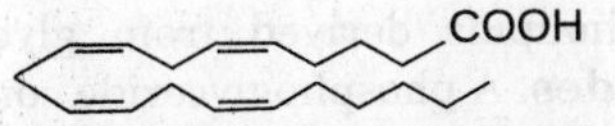 COOH	–50
20	EPA	(5*Z*, 8*Z*, 11*Z*, 14*Z*, 17*Z*)-eicosapentaenoic acid	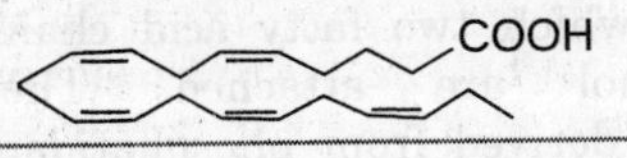 COOH	–50

2. Waxes

Waxes are esters formed from long-chain carboxylic acids and long-chain alcohols. For example, beeswax, the structural material of beehives, has a 16-carbon carboxylic acid component and a 30-carbon alcohol component. Both fatty alcohols and free fatty acids occur in waxes together with esterified forms. These mixtures are found on exterior surfaces of plants and animals.

Carnauba wax is a particularly hard wax because of its relatively high molecular weight, arising from a 32-carbon carboxylic acid component and a 34-carbon alcohol component. Carnauba wax is widely used as a car wax and in floor polishes.

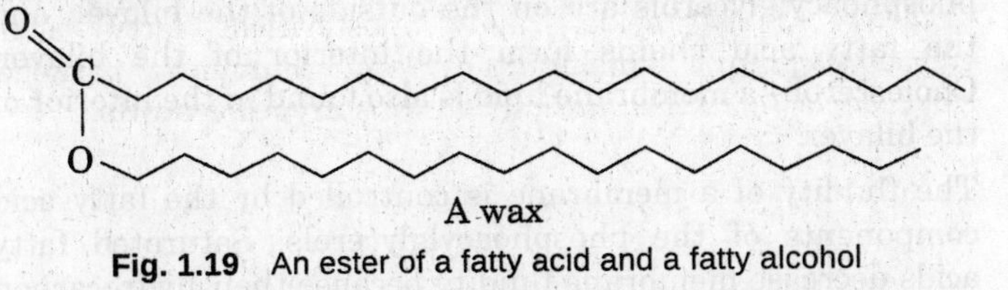

A wax

Fig. 1.19 An ester of a fatty acid and a fatty alcohol

Insects make unsaturated as well as saturated hydrocarbons. The former as well as long-chain alcohols and their esters often form the volatile **pheromones** with which insects communicate.

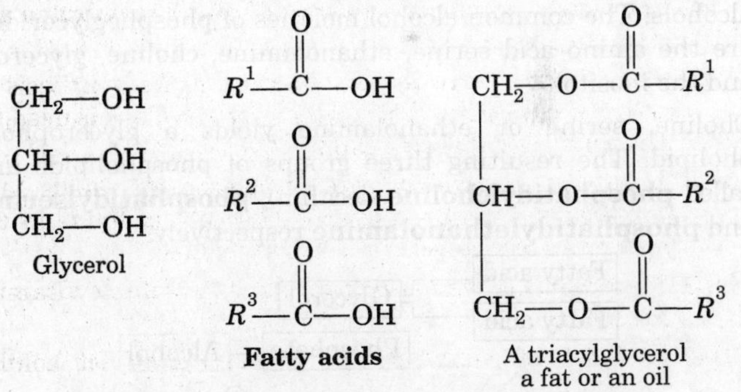

CH_2—OH, CH—OH, CH_2—OH (Glycerol); R^1—C(=O)—OH, R^2—C(=O)—OH, R^3—C(=O)—OH (**Fatty acids**); CH_2—O—C(=O)—R^1, CH—O—C(=O)—R^2, CH_2—O—C(=O)—R^3 (A triacylglycerol a fat or an oil)

Fig. 1.20 Structure of glycerol and fatty acid

Triacylglycerols that are solids or semisolids at room temperature are called **fats**. Fats are usually obtained from animals and are composed largely of triacylglycerols with either saturated fatty acids or fatty acids with only one double bond. The saturated fatty acid tails pack closely together, giving the triacylglycerols relatively high melting points, causing them to be solids at room temperature.

Liquid triacylglycerols are called **oils**. Oils typically come from plant products such as corn, soybeans, olives, and peanuts. They are composed primarily of triacylglycerols with unsaturated fatty acids that cannot pack tightly together. Consequently, they have relatively low melting points, causing them to be liquids at room temperature.

Organisms store energy in the form of triacylglycerols. A fat provides about six times as much metabolic energy as an equal weight of hydrated glycogen because fats are less oxidized than carbohydrates and, since fats are nonpolar, they do not bind water. In contrast, two-thirds of the weight of stored glycogen is water.

Important Lipids

The major three kinds of membrane lipids are **phospholipids**, **glycolipids** and **steroids**, while other present in cells.

1. Phospholipids

These are abundant in all biological membranes. A phospholipid molecule is constructed from four components: fatty acids, a platform to which the fatty acids are attached, a phosphate, and an alcohol attached to the phosphate. The two principal groups of phospholipids are the **glycerophospholipids** which contain the alcohol glycerol and the **sphingophospholipids** which contain the alcohol **sphingosine**.

The platform on which phospholipids are built may be **glycerol**, a 3-carbon alcohol, or **sphingosine**, a more complex alcohol. Phospholipids derived from glycerol are called **phosphoglycerides**. A phosphoglyceride consists of a glycerol backbone to which two fatty acid chains and a phosphorylated alcohol are attached. The major phosphoglycerides are derived from phosphatidate by the formation of an ester bond between the phosphate group of phosphatidate and the hydroxyl group of one of several alcohols. The common alcohol moieties of phosphoglycerides are the amino acid serine, ethanolamine, choline, glycerol, and the inositol.

Choline, serine or ethanolamine yields a glycerophospholipid. The resulting three groups of phospholipids are called **phosphatidylcholine** (lecithin), **phosphatidylserine** and **phosphatidylethanolamine** respectively.

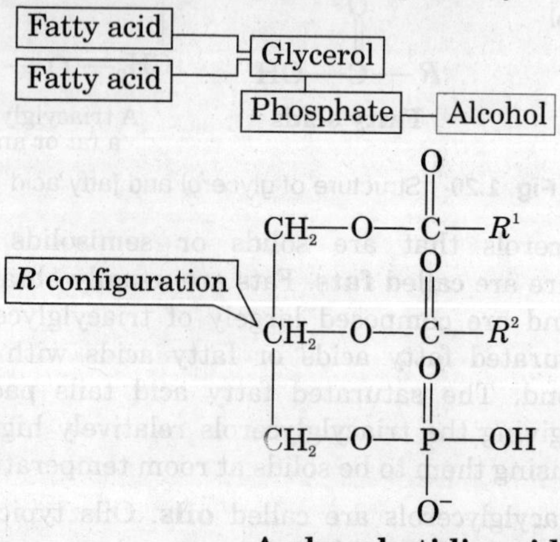

Fatty acid
Fatty acid
Glycerol
Phosphate
Alcohol

R configuration

$$\begin{array}{l} CH_2-O-\overset{O}{\overset{\|}{C}}-R^1 \\ | \\ CH_2-O-\overset{O}{\overset{\|}{C}}-R^2 \\ | \\ CH_2-O-\overset{O}{\overset{\|}{P}}-OH \\ \quad\quad\quad\quad\; | \\ \quad\quad\quad\quad\; O^- \end{array}$$

A phosphatidic acid

Fig. 1.21 Schematic structure of a phospholipid

The alkenyl ether analogs of phosphatidylcholine are called **plasmalogens**. Another group of phosphatides contain the hexahydroxycyclohexane known as **inositol**.

Phosphatidylinositol, as well as smaller amounts of phosphatides derived from phosphate esters of inositol are present in membranes of all eukaryotes. Plays important role in regulating responses of cells to hormones and other external agents.

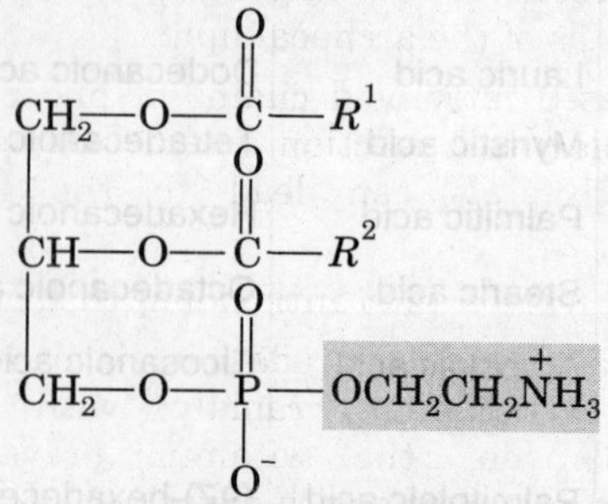

$$\begin{array}{l} CH_2-O-\overset{O}{\overset{\|}{C}}-R^1 \\ | \\ CH-O-\overset{O}{\overset{\|}{C}}-R^2 \\ | \\ CH_2-O-\overset{O}{\overset{\|}{P}}-OCH_2CH_2\overset{+}{N}H_3 \\ \quad\quad\quad\quad\; | \\ \quad\quad\quad\quad\; O^- \end{array}$$

A phosphatidylethanolamine
(a cephalin)

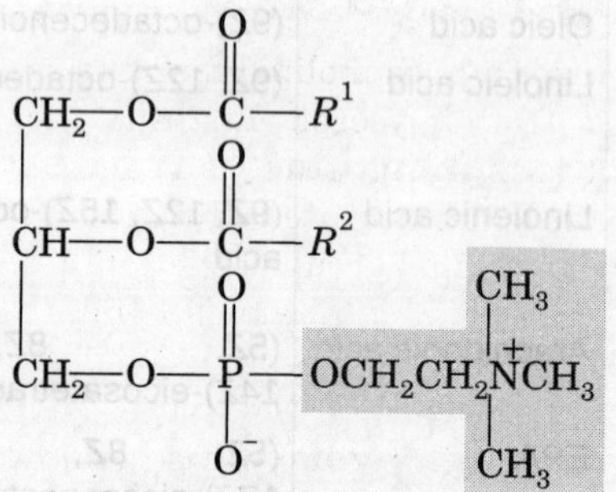

$$\begin{array}{l} CH_2-O-\overset{O}{\overset{\|}{C}}-R^1 \\ | \\ CH-O-\overset{O}{\overset{\|}{C}}-R^2 \\ | \\ CH_2-O-\overset{O}{\overset{\|}{P}}-OCH_2CH_2\overset{+}{N}(CH_3)_2CH_3 \\ \quad\quad\quad\quad\; | \\ \quad\quad\quad\quad\; O^- \end{array}$$

A phosphatidylcholine
(a lecithin)

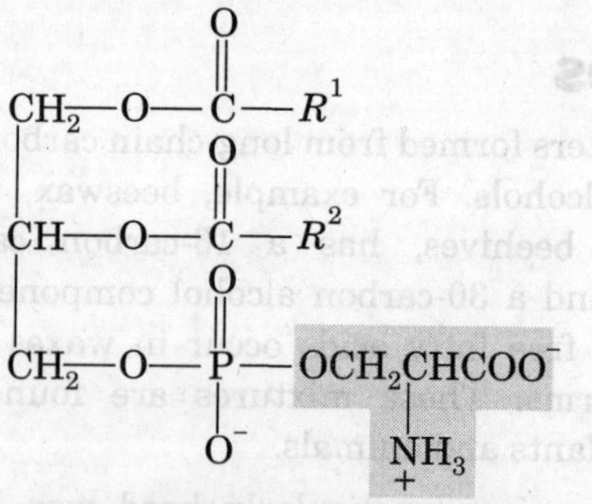

$$\begin{array}{l} CH_2-O-\overset{O}{\overset{\|}{C}}-R^1 \\ | \\ CH-O-\overset{O}{\overset{\|}{C}}-R^2 \\ | \\ CH_2-O-\overset{O}{\overset{\|}{P}}-OCH_2CHCOO^- \\ \quad\quad\quad\quad\; | \quad\quad\quad\quad | \\ \quad\quad\quad\quad\; O^- \quad\quad\quad \overset{+}{N}H_3 \end{array}$$

A phosphatidylserine

Fig. 1.22 Various phospholipids

Phosphoacylglycerols form membranes by arranging themselves in a **lipid bilayer**. The polar heads of the phosphoacylglycerols are on the outside of the bilayer, and the fatty acid chains form the interior of the bilayer. Cholesterol—a membrane lipid is also found in the interior of the bilayer.

The fluidity of a membrane is controlled by the fatty acid components of the phosphoacylglycerols. Saturated fatty acids decrease membrane fluidity because their hydrocarbon chains can pack closely together. Unsaturated fatty acids increase fluidity because they pack less closely together. Cholesterol also decreases fluidity. Only animal membranes contain cholesterol, so they are more rigid than plant membranes.

A Membrane lipid is an amphipathic molecule containing **hydrophilic** and **hydrophobic** moieties. The two hydrophobic fatty acid chains are approximately parallel to each other, whereas the hydrophilic moieties points in the opposite direction. Sphingomyelin has a similar conformation, as of the archaeal lipid.

The unsaturated fatty acid chains of phosphoacylglycerols are susceptible to reaction with O_2. Oxidation of phosphoa-cylglycerols can lead to the degradation of membranes.

Vitamin-E is an important antioxidant that protects fatty acid chains from degradation via oxidation. Because vitamin-E reacts more rapidly with oxygen than triacylglycerols do, the vitamin prevents biological membranes from reacting with oxygen.

2. Sphingolipids

Sphingomyelin is a phospholipid found in membranes that is not derived from glycerol. Instead, the backbone in sphingomyelin is **sphingosine**, an amino alcohol that contains a long, unsaturated hydrocarbon chain. In sphingomyelin, the amino group of the sphingosine backbone is linked to a fatty acid by an amide bond. In addition, the primary hydroxyl group of sphingosine is esterified to phosphoryl choline. Two of the most common kinds of sphingolipids are **sphingomyelins** and **cerebrosides** (Cerebrosides are not phospholipids).

$CH{=}CH(CH_2)_{12}CH_3$

$CH{-}OH$ O

$CH{-}NH{-}C{-}R$

$CH_2{-}O{-}P(=O)(O^-){-}OCH_2CH_2\overset{+}{N}(CH_3)_3$

A sphingomyelin

$CH{=}CH(CH_2)_{12}CH_3$

$CH{-}OH$ O

$CH{-}NH{-}C{-}R$

CH_2

O

H, CH_2OH, HO, O, H, H, HO, OH, H, H

A glucocerebroside

Fig. 1.23 The sphingolipids

The simplest glycolipid, called a **cerebroside**, contains a single sugar residue, either glucose or galactose. More complex glycolipids, such as **gangliosides**, contain a branched chain of as many as seven sugar residues.

3. Glycolipids

The polar heads of the **glycoglycerolipids** lack phospho groups but contain sugars in glycosidic linkage. Chloroplasts also contain the following **sulfolipid**, an anionic sulfonate. Marine algae as well as aquatic higher plants accumulate arsenophospholipids.

4. Prostaglandins

These are found in all body tissues and are responsible for regulating a variety of physiological responses, such as inflammation, blood pressure, blood clotting, fever, pain, the induction of labor, and the sleep–wake cycle. All prostaglandins have a five-membered ring with a seven-carbon carboxylic acid substituent and an eightcarbon hydrocarbon substituent. The two substituents are trans to each other.

H COOH H

Fig. 1.24 Prostaglandin skeleton

5. Terpenes

These are a diverse class of lipids. They can be hydrocarbons, or they can contain oxygen and be alcohols, ketones, or aldehydes. Oxygen-containing terpenes are sometimes called terpenoids. Certain terpenes and **terpenoids** have been used as spices, perfumes, and medicines for many thousands of years.

HO — **Menthol** (peppermint oil)

OH — **Geraniol** (geranium oil)

Zingiberene (oil of ginger)

b-selinene (ril of celery)

Fig. 1.25 Various terpenes

Isoprene is the common name for 2-methyl 1, 3-butadiene, a compound containing five carbon atoms. That isoprene units are linked in a head-to-tail fashion to form terpenes is known as the **isoprene rule**.

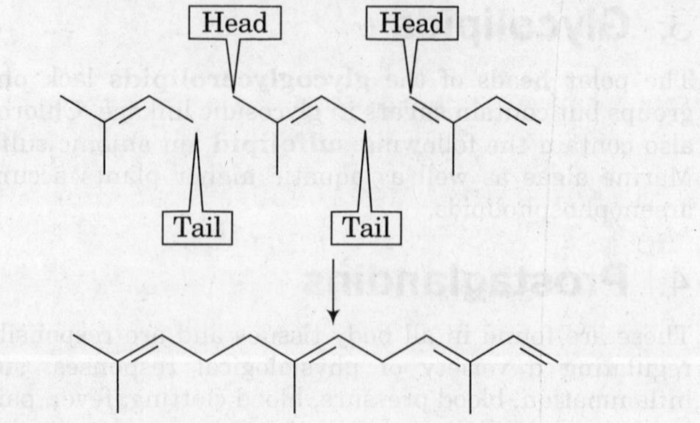

Fig. 1.26 α-farnesene a sesquiterpene found in the waxy coating on apple skins

Terpenes are classified according to the number of carbons they contain. **Monoterpenes** are composed of two isoprene units, so they have 10 carbons. **Sesquiterpenes**, with 15 carbons, are composed of three isoprene units. Many fragrances and flavorings found in plants are monoterpenes and sesquiterpenes. These compounds are known as **essential oils**.

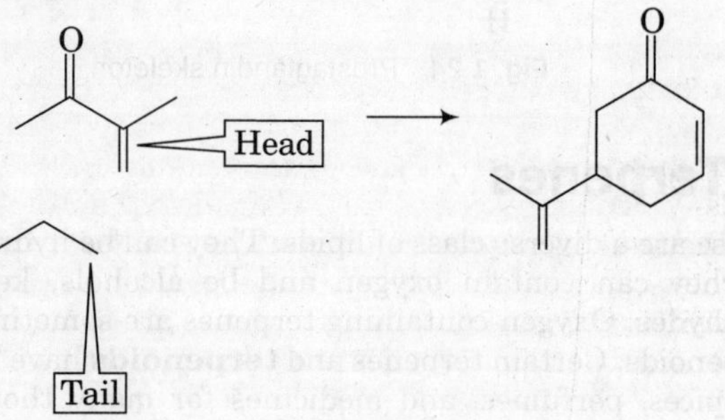

Fig. 1.27 Carvone spearmint oil a monoterpene

Triterpenes (six isoprene units) and **tetraterpenes** (eight isoprene units) have important biological roles. For example, **squalene**, a triterpene, is a precursor of steroid molecules.

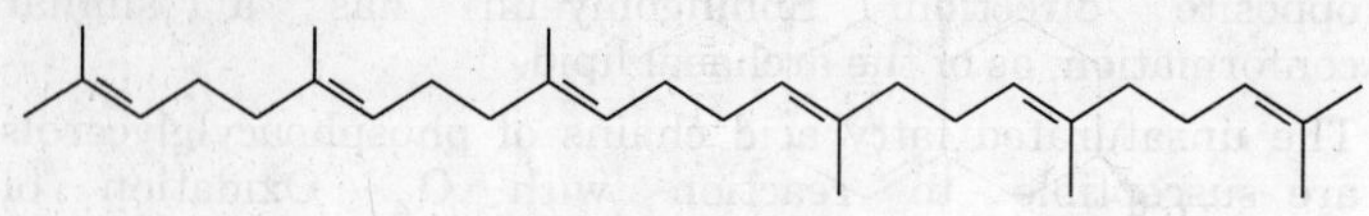

Fig. 1.28 Squalene

Carotenoids are tetraterpenes. Lycopene, the compound responsible for the red colouring of tomatoes and watermelon, and β-carotene, the compound that causes carrots and apricots to be orange, are examples of carotenoids. β-carotene is also the coloring agent used in margarine. The many conjugated double bonds in lycopene and β-carotene cause the compounds to be coloured.

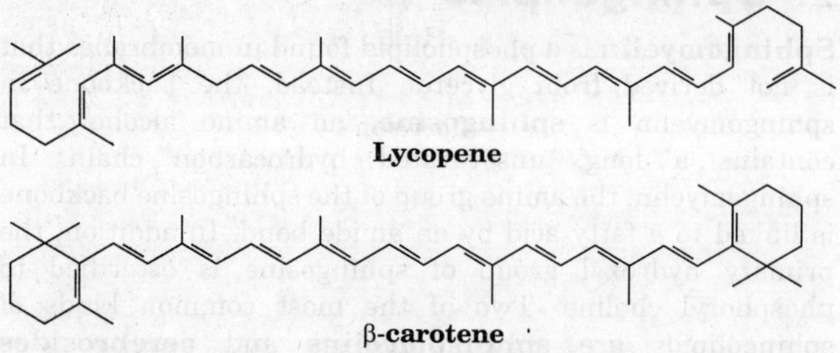

Fig. 1.29 The carotenoid-lycopene and β-carotene

Vitamin-A Vitamin-A, D, E and K are lipid soluble.

Steroids

Many hormones are steroids. Because steroids are non-polar compounds, they are lipids. Their non-polar character allows them to cross cell membranes, so they can leave the cells in which they are synthesized and enter their target cells. All steroids contain a tetracyclic ring system. The four rings are *A*, *B* and *C* are six-membered rings and *D* is a five-membered ring. The rings can be trans fused or cis fused and that *trans* fused rings are more stable. In steroids, the *B*, *C* and *D* rings are all *trans* fused. In most naturally occurring steroids, the *A* and *B* rings are also trans fused.

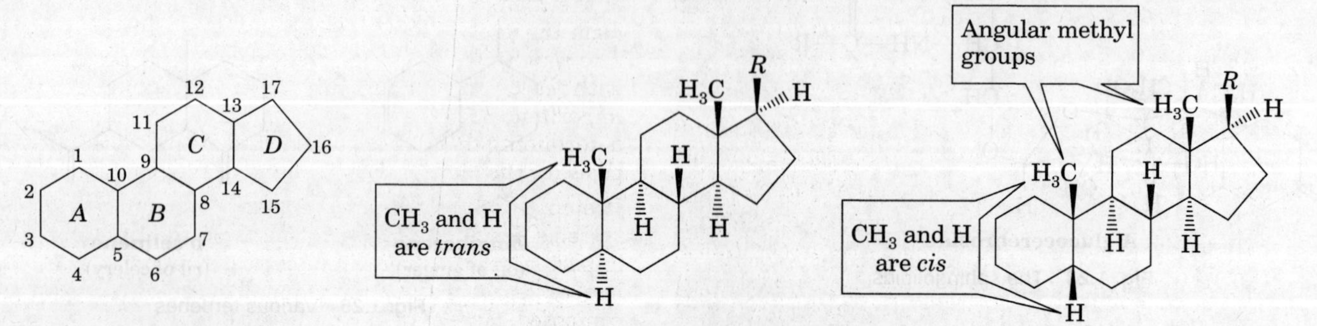

Fig. 1.30 The steroid ring system

The steroid hormones can be divided into five classes: glucocorticoids, mineralocorticoids, androgens, estrogens, and progestins. Glucocorticoids and mineralocorticoids are synthesized in the adrenal cortex and are collectively known as **adrenal cortical steroids**. All adrenal cortical steroids have an oxygen at C-11.

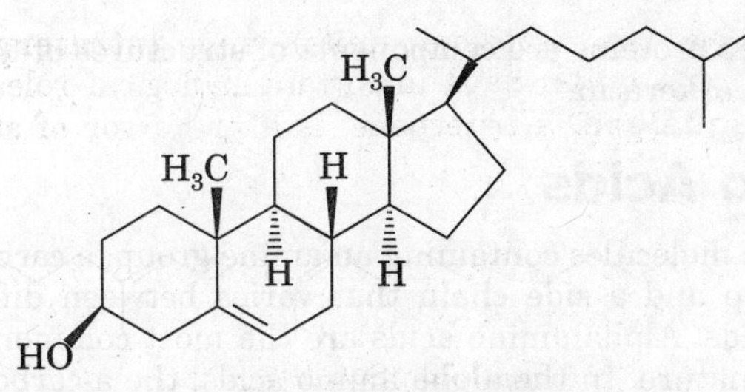

Cholesterol

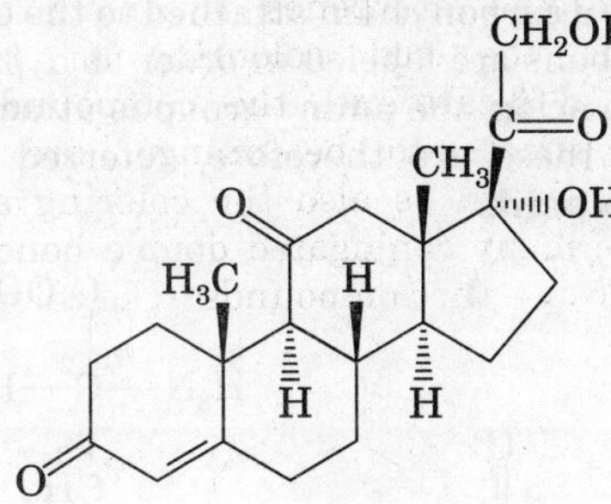

Cortisone

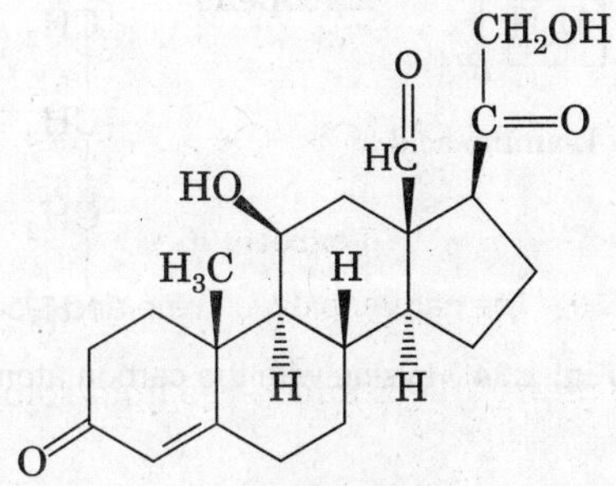

Aldosterone

Fig. 1.31 The cortical steroids

Mineralocorticoids cause increased reabsorption of Na^+, Cl^- and by HCO_3^- the kidneys, leading to an increase in blood pressure. **Aldosterone** is an example of a mineralocorticoid.

The male sex hormones, known as **androgens**, are secreted by the testes. They are responsible for the development of male secondary sex characteristics during puberty. They also promote muscle growth. Testosterone and 5α-dihydrotestosterone are androgens.

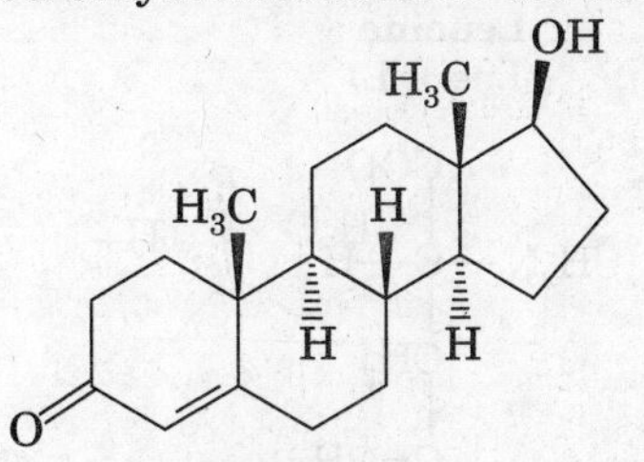

Testosterone

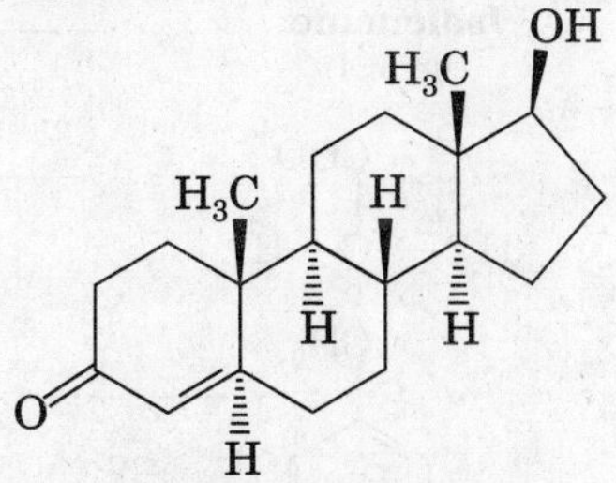

5α-dihydrotestosterone

Fig. 1.32 The androgens

Estradiol and estrone are female sex hormones known as **oestrogens**. They are secreted by the ovaries and are responsible for the development of female secondary sex characteristics. They also regulate the menstrual cycle.

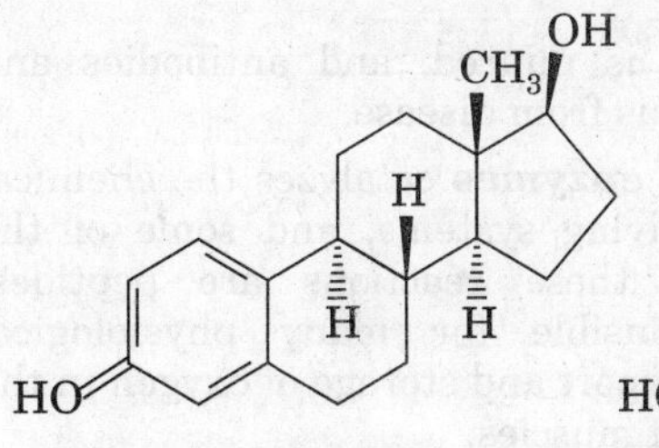

Estradiol 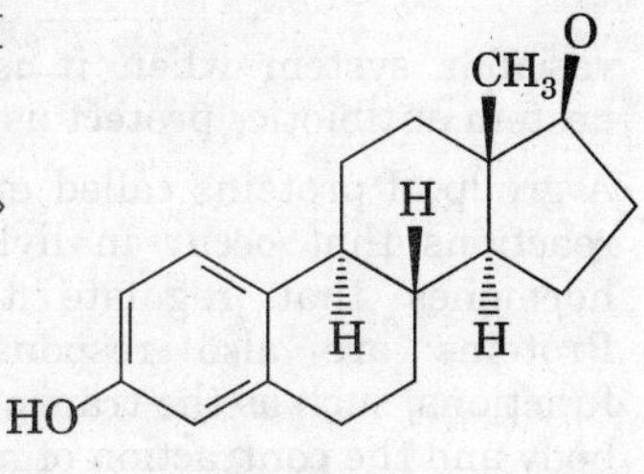 **Estrone**

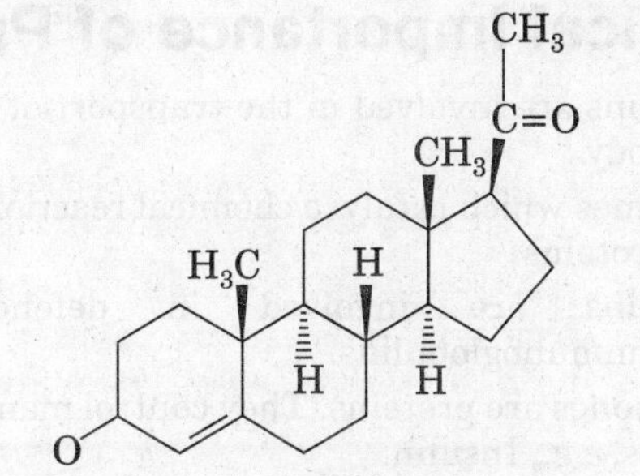

Progesterone

Fig. 1.33 The estrogens

In addition to being the precursor of all the steroid hormones in animals, cholesterol is the precursor of the bile **acids**. In fact, the word cholesterol is derived from the Greek words *chole* meaning 'bile' and *stereos* meaning 'solid'. The bile acids— cholic acid and chenodeoxycholic acid—are synthesized in the liver, stored in the gall bladder and secreted into the small intestine, where they act as emulsifying agents so that fats and oils can be digested by water-soluble digestive enzymes. **Cholesterol** is also the precursor of **vitamin-D**.

Proteins

The amino acid units that make up a protein molecule are joined together in a precise sequence. The chain is then folded, often into a very compact form. Sometimes the chain is then cut in specific places. Pieces may be discarded and parts may be added. A metal ion, a coenzyme derived from a vitamin, or even a single methyl group may be attached to form the biologically active protein. The biological functioning of a protein is determined both by the properties of the chemical groups in the amino acids that are joined to form the protein chain and by the way the chain is folded. The ways in which the different parts of the protein interact with each other and with other molecules are equally important. These interactions play a major role in determining the folding pattern and also provide much of the basis for the biological functioning of proteins.

Proteins and peptides serve many functions in biological systems. Some protect organisms from their environment or impart strength to certain biological structures. Hair, horns, hooves, feathers, fur, and the tough outer layer of skin are all composed largely of a **structural protein**, *e.g.*, keratin, collagen, etc.

Some proteins have other protective functions. Snake venoms and plant toxins, for example, protect their owners from other species, blood-clotting proteins protect the vascular system when it is injured, and antibodies and protein antibiotics protect us from disease.

A group of proteins called **enzymes** catalyzes the chemical reactions that occur in living systems, and some of the hormones that regulate these reactions are peptides. Proteins are also responsible for many physiological functions, such as the transport and storage of oxygen in the body and the contraction of muscles.

Biological Importance of Proteins

(a) Proteins are involved in the transport of substances in the body.

(b) Enzymes which catalyze chemical reactions in the body are proteins.

(c) Proteins are involved in defence function, *e.g.*, Immunoglobulins.

(d) Hormones are proteins. They control many biochemical events, *e.g.*, Insulin.

(e) Some proteins have role in contraction of muscles.

(f) Proteins are involved in the gene expression. They control gene expression and translation, *e.g.*, Histones.

(g) Proteins function as anti-vitamins, *e.g.*, Avidin of egg.

(h) Proteins are infective agents, *e.g.*, Prions which cause mad cow disease are proteins.

(i) Some toxins are proteins, *e.g.*, Enterotoxin of cholera microorganism.

(j) Some proteins provide structural strength and elasticity to the organs and vascular system, *e.g.*, Collagen.

(k) Some proteins are components of structures of tissues, *e.g.*, α-keratin.

Amino Acids

These are molecules containing an amine group, a carboxylic acid group and a side chain that varies between different amino acids. Alpha amino acids are the most common form found in nature. In the alpha amino acids, the a-carbon is a chiral carbon atom, with the exception of glycine. In amino acids that have a carbon chain attached to the carbon (such as lysine) the carbons are labeled in order as α, β, γ, δ and so on. In some amino acids, the amine group is attached to the β or γ-carbon, and these are therefore, referred to as beta or gamma **amino acids**.

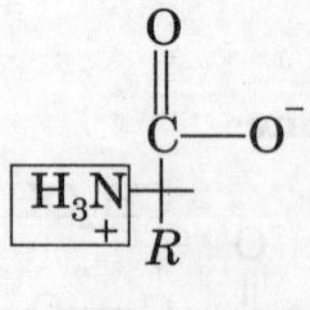

L-amino acid

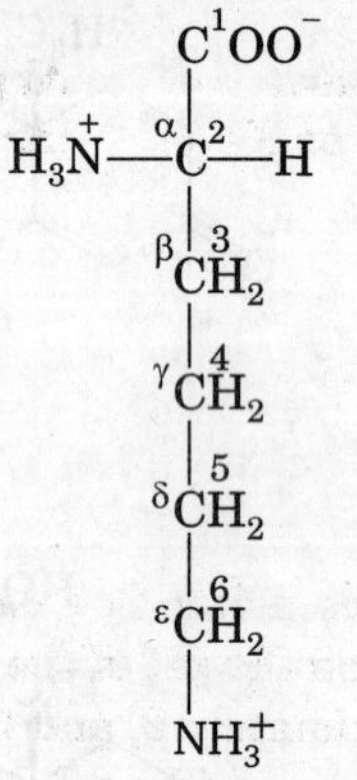

Fig. 1.34 Lysine with the carbon atoms

Amino acids are usually classified by the properties of their side chain into four groups. The side chain can make an amino acid a weak acid or a weak base, and a hydrophile if the side chain is polar or a hydrophobe if it is non-polar.

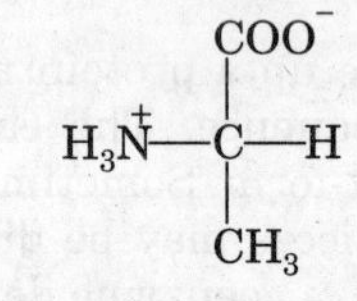

Alanine (Ala or A)

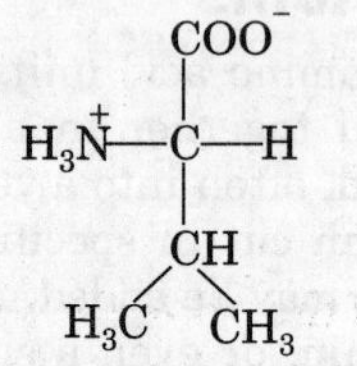

Valine (Val or V)

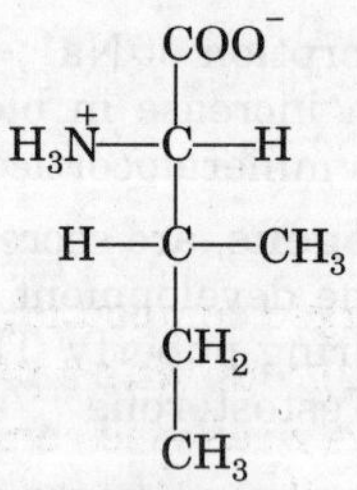

Isoleucine (lie or l)

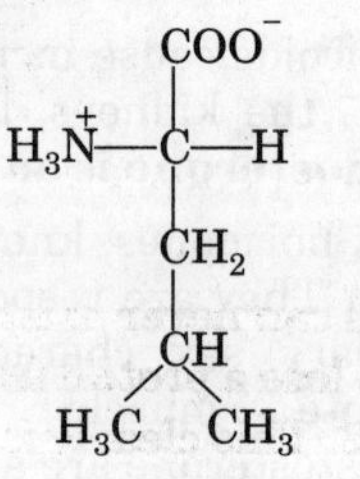

Leucine (Lue or L)

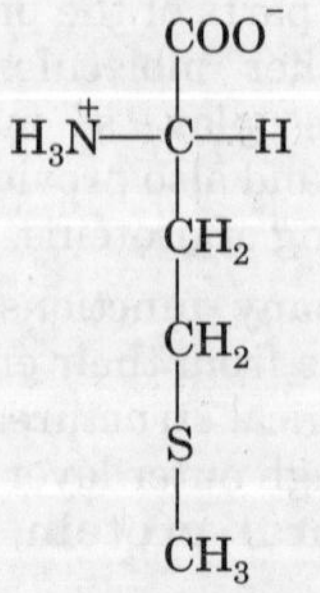

Methionine (Met or M)

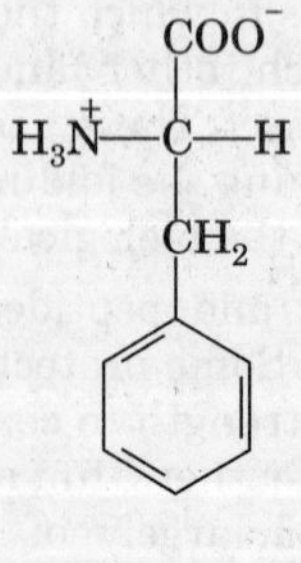

Phenylalanine (Phe or F)

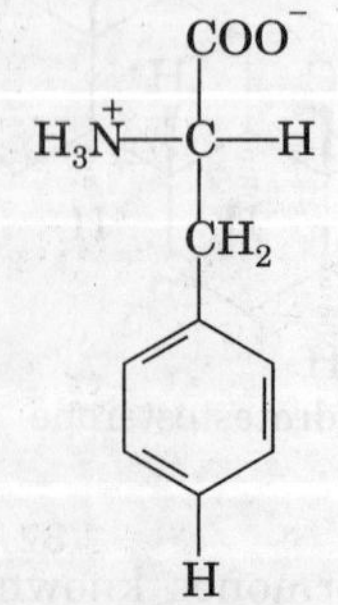

Tyrosine (Tyr or Y)

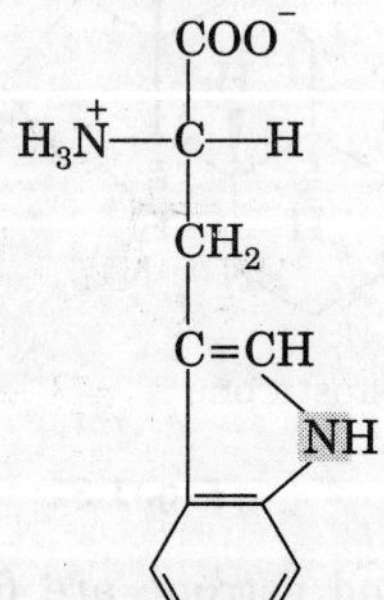

Tryptophan (Trp or W)

Fig. 1.35 Hydrophobic amino acids

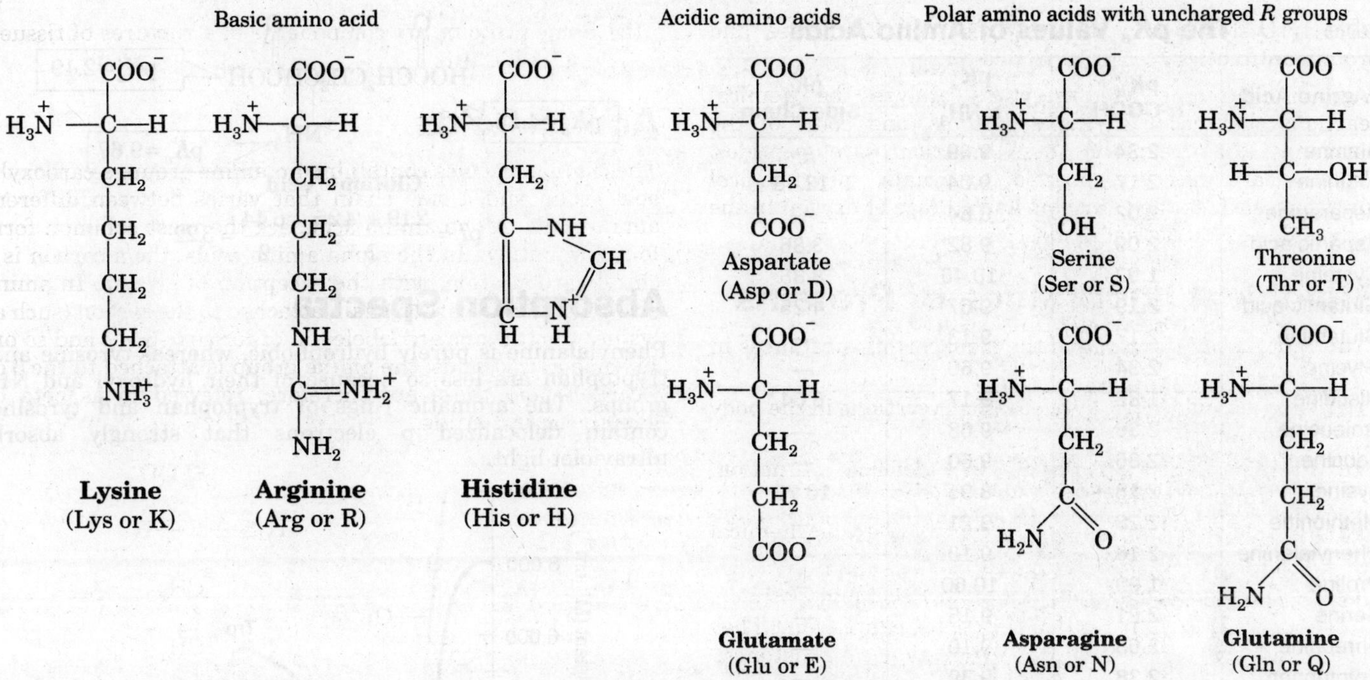

Basic amino acid

$H_3\overset{+}{N}-CH(COO^-)-CH_2-CH_2-CH_2-CH_2-NH_3^+$

Lysine
(Lys or K)

$H_3\overset{+}{N}-CH(COO^-)-CH_2-CH_2-CH_2-NH-C(=NH_2^+)-NH_2$

Arginine
(Arg or R)

$H_3\overset{+}{N}-CH(COO^-)-CH_2-$ (imidazole ring: C—NH, CH, C—N, H H)

Histidine
(His or H)

Acidic amino acids

$H_3\overset{+}{N}-CH(COO^-)-CH_2-COO^-$

Aspartate
(Asp or D)

$H_3\overset{+}{N}-CH(COO^-)-CH_2-CH_2-COO^-$

Glutamate
(Glu or E)

Polar amino acids with uncharged *R* groups

$H_3\overset{+}{N}-CH(COO^-)-CH_2-OH$

Serine
(Ser or S)

$H_3\overset{+}{N}-CH(COO^-)-CH(OH)-CH_3$

Threonine
(Thr or T)

$H_3\overset{+}{N}-CH(COO^-)-CH_2-C(=O)-NH_2$

Asparagine
(Asn or N)

$H_3\overset{+}{N}-CH(COO^-)-CH_2-CH_2-C(=O)-NH_2$

Glutamine
(Gln or Q)

Fig. 1.36 Hydrophilic amino acids

Every amino acid has a carboxyl group and an amino group, and each group can exist in an acidic form or a basic form, depending on the pH of the solution in which the amino acid is dissolved. The carboxyl groups of the amino acids have values of pK_a approximately 2, and the protonated amino groups have pK_a values near 9. Both groups, therefore, will be in their acidic forms in a very acidic solution. At pH = 7, the pH of the solution is greater than the of the carboxyl group, but less than the of the protonated amino group. The carboxyl group, therefore, will be in its basic form and the amino group will be in its acidic form. In a strongly basic solution both groups will be in their basic forms.

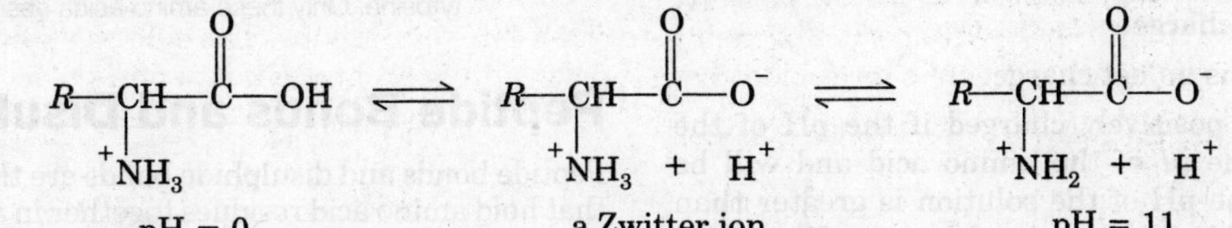

$$\underset{\text{pH = 0}}{R-CH(\overset{+}{N}H_3)-\overset{O}{\overset{\|}{C}}-OH} \rightleftharpoons \underset{\substack{\text{a Zwitter ion} \\ \text{pH = 7}}}{R-CH(\overset{+}{N}H_3)-\overset{O}{\overset{\|}{C}}-O^- + H^+} \rightleftharpoons \underset{\text{pH = 11}}{R-CH(\overset{+}{N}H_2)-\overset{O}{\overset{\|}{C}}-O^- + H^+}$$

An amino acid can never exist as an uncharged compound, regardless of the pH of the solution. To be uncharged, an amino acid would have to lose a proton from an + NH_3 group with a pK_a of about 9 before it would lose a proton from a COOH group with a pK_a of about 2. This clearly is impossible: A weak acid cannot be more acidic than a strong acid. Therefore, at physiological pH (7.3) an amino acid exists as a dipolar ion, called a **Zwitter ion**. A **Zwitter** ion is a compound that has a negative charge on one atom and a positive charge on an adjacent atom.

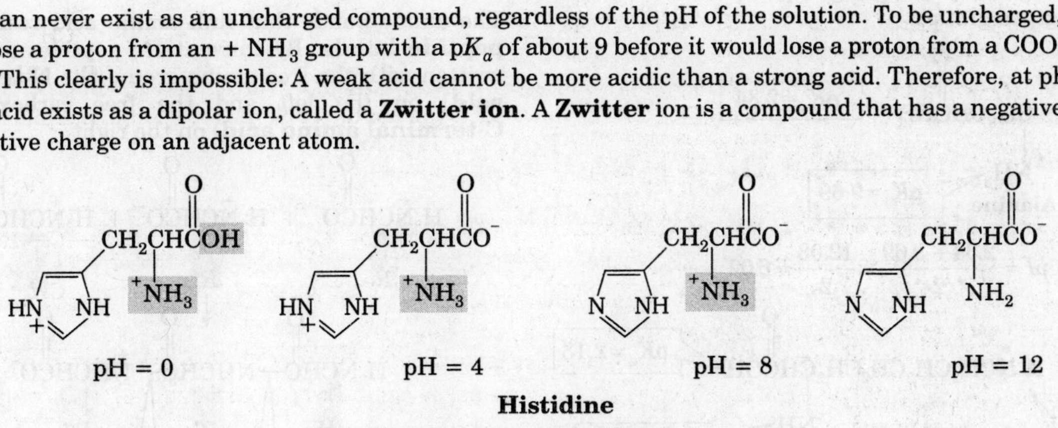

$CH_2CH(\overset{+}{N}H_3)COOH$ (ring: HN, $\overset{+}{N}$H)	$CH_2CH(\overset{+}{N}H_3)COO^-$ (ring: HN, $\overset{+}{N}$H)	$CH_2CH(\overset{+}{N}H_3)COO^-$ (ring: N, NH)	$CH_2CH(NH_2)COO^-$ (ring: N, NH)
pH = 0	pH = 4	pH = 8	pH = 12

Histidine

Fig. 1.37 The Zwitter ion form

Table 1.10 **The pK_a Values of Amino Acids**

Amino Acid	pK_a α-COOH	pK_a α-NH_3^+	pK_a Side Chain
Alanine	2.34	9.69	—
Arginine	2.17	9.04	12.48
Asparagine	2.02	8.84	—
Aspartic acid	2.09	9.82	3.86
Cysteine	1.92	10.46	8.35
Glutamic acid	2.19	9.67	4.25
Glutamine	2.17	9.13	—
Glycine	2.34	9.60	—
Histidine	1.82	9.17	6.04
Isoleucine	2.36	9.68	—
Leucine	2.36	9.60	—
Lysine	2.18	8.95	10.79
Methionine	2.28	9.21	—
Phenylalanine	2.16	9.18	—
Proline	1.99	10.60	—
Serine	2.21	9.15	—
Threonine	2.63	9.10	—
Tryptophan	2.38	9.39	—
Tyrosine	2.20	9.11	10.07
Valine	2.32	9.62	—

The Isoelectric Point

The isoelectric point (pI) of an amino acid is the pH at which it has no net charge. In other words, it is the pH at which the amount of positive charge on an amino acid exactly balances the amount of negative charge:

pI = pH at which there is no net charge.

An amino acid will be positively charged if the pH of the solution is less than the pI of the amino acid and will be negatively charged if the pH of the solution is greater than the pI of the amino acid. At the average of the two pK_a values, the number of negatively charged groups equals the number of positively charged groups.

$CH_3CH(\overset{+}{N}H_3)COOH$ — pK_a=2.34 (COOH), pK_a=9.69 (NH_3^+)

Alanine

$$pI = \frac{2.34 + 9.69}{2} = \frac{12.03}{2} = 6.02$$

$H_3\overset{+}{N}CH_2CH_2CH_2CH_2CH(\overset{+}{N}H_3)COOH$ — pK_a=10.79 (side-chain NH_3^+), pK_a=2.18 (COOH), pK_a=8.95 (α-NH_3^+)

Lysine

$$pI = \frac{8.95 + 10.79}{2} = \frac{19.74}{2} = 9.87$$

$HOOCCH_2CH_2CH(\overset{+}{N}H_3)COOH$ — pK_a=4.25 (side-chain COOH), pK_a=2.19 (α-COOH), pK_a=9.67 (NH_3^+)

Glutamic acid

$$pI = \frac{2.19 + 4.25}{2} = \frac{6.44}{2} = 3.22$$

Absorption Spectra

Phenylalanine is purely hydrophobic, whereas tyrosine and tryptophan are less so because of their hydroxyl and NH groups. The aromatic rings of tryptophan and tyrosine contain delocalized p electrons that strongly absorb ultraviolet light.

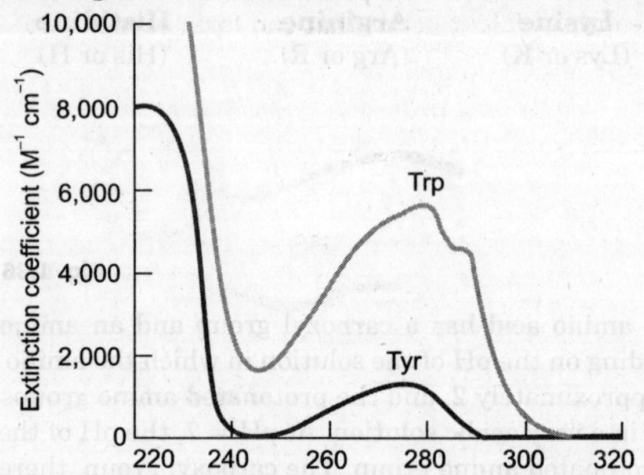

Fig. 1.38 Absorption spectra of the aromatic amino acids tryptophan and tyrosine. Only these amino acids absorb strongly near 280 nm

Peptide Bonds and Disulphide Bonds

Peptide bonds and disulphide bonds are the only covalent bonds that hold amino acid residues together in a peptide or a protein.

Peptide Bonds

The amide bonds that link amino acid residues are called **peptide bonds**. By convention, peptides and proteins are written with the free amino group (the **N-terminal amino acid**) on the left and the free carboxyl group (the **C-terminal amino acid**) on the right.

$H_3\overset{+}{N}CH(R)CO^- + H_3\overset{+}{N}CH(R')CO^- + H_3\overset{+}{N}CH(R'')CO^-$

↓

$H_3\overset{+}{N}CH(R)C(O)-NHCH(R')C(O)-NHCH(R'')CO^- + 2H_2O$

Peptide bonds; The N-terminal amino acid; The C-terminal amino acid

Fig. 1.39 A tripeptide

The Peptide Bond has Partial Double Bond Character

Although peptides are written as if a single bond linked the a-carboxyl and a-nitrogen atoms, this bond in fact exhibits partial double-bond character:

$$\mathrm{O{=}C{-}N(H)} \longleftrightarrow \mathrm{{}^{-}O{-}C{=}\overset{+}{N}(H)}$$

Disulphide bonds When thiols are oxidized under mild conditions, they form disulphides. A disulphide is a compound with an S—S bond.

$$\underset{\text{A thiol}}{2R\text{—SH}} \xrightarrow{\text{Mild oxidation}} \underset{\text{Adisulphide}}{R\text{S—S}R}$$

Two cysteine residues in a protein can be oxidized to a disulphide. This is known as a **disulphide bridge**. Disulphide bridges are the only covalent bonds that can form between non-adjacent amino acids.

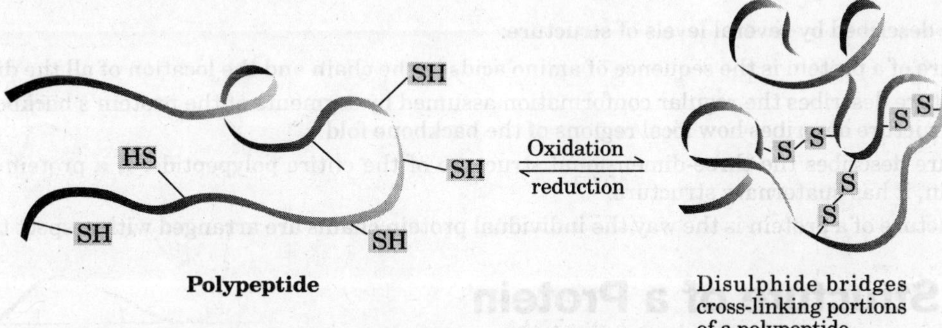

Fig. 1.40 Disulphide bridges cross-linking portions of a peptide

Insulin, a hormone secreted by the pancreas, controls the level of glucose in the blood by regulating glucose metabolism. Insulin is a polypeptide with two peptide chains. The short chain (the *A*-chain) contains 21 amino acids and the long chain (the *B*-chain) contains 30 amino acids. The two chains are held together by two disulphide bridges. These are **interchain disulphide bridges** (between the *A* and *B*-chains). Insulin also has an **intrachain disulphide bridge** (within the *A*-chain).

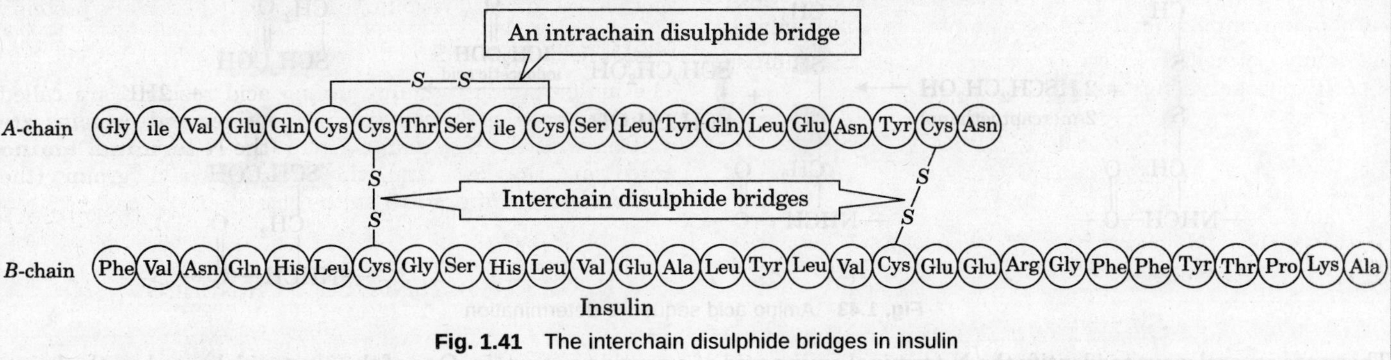

Fig. 1.41 The interchain disulphide bridges in insulin

Some Important Peptides

- **Enkephalins** are pentapeptides that are synthesized by the body to control pain. They decrease the body's sensitivity to pain by binding to receptors in certain brain cells.
- **Bradykinin**, **vasopressin** and **oxytocin** are peptide hormones. They are all nonapeptides. Bradykinin inhibits the inflammation of tissues. Vasopressin controls blood pressure by regulating the contraction of smooth muscle. It is also an antidiuretic. Oxytocin induces labor in pregnant women and stimulates milk production in nursing mothers.
- **Gramicidin** *S* is an antibiotic produced by a strain of bacteria. It is a cyclic decapeptide.

Tyr-Gly-Gly-Phe-Leu leucine enkephalin	Tyr-Gly-Gly-Phe-Leu methionine enkephalin
Bradykinin	Agr-Pro-Pro-Gly-Phe-Ser-Pro-Pho-Arg
Vasoperssin	Cys-Tyr-Phe-Gln-Asn-Cys-Pro-Arg-Gly-NH_2 S — S
Oxytocin	Cys-Tyr-Ile-Gln-Asn-Cys-Pro-Leu-Gly-NH_2 S — S

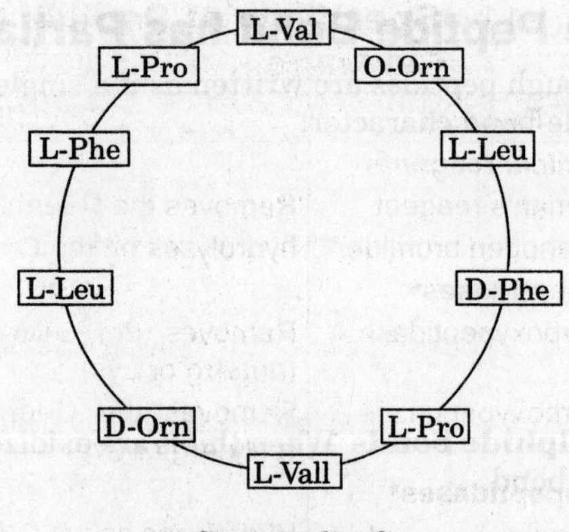

Fig. 1.42 The peptide hormones

Structure of Protein

Protein molecules are described by several levels of structure:

1. Primary structure of a protein is the sequence of amino acids in the chain and the location of all the disulphide bridges.
2. Secondary structure describes the regular conformation assumed by segments of the protein's backbone. In other words, the secondary structure describes how local regions of the backbone fold.
3. Tertiary structure describes the three-dimensional structure of the entire polypeptide. If a protein has more than one polypeptide chain, it has quaternary structure.
4. Quaternary structure of a protein is the way the individual protein chains are arranged with respect to each other.

1. Primary Structure of a Protein

The first step in determining the sequence of amino acids in a peptide or a protein is to reduce any disulphide bridges in the peptide or protein. A commonly used reducing agent is 2-mercaptoethanol, which is oxidized to a disulphide.

Cleaving disulphide bridges

—NHCH—C(=O)— / CH_2 / S—S / CH_2 / —NHCH—C(=O)— + 2 $HSCH_2CH_2OH$ (2-mercaptoethanol) ⟶ —NHCH—C(=O)— / CH_2 / SH SH / CH_2 / —NHCH—C(=O)— + SCH_2CH_2OH / SCH_2CH_2OH —(ICH_2COH (=O), iodoacetic acid)⟶ —NHCH—C(=O)— / CH_2 / SCH_2COH (=O) / SCH_2COH (=O) / CH_2 / —NHCH—C(=O)— + 2HI

Fig. 1.43 Amino acid sequence determination

There are several ways to identify the N-terminal amino acid of a peptide or protein. One of the most widely used methods is to treat the protein with phenyl isothiocyanate (PITC), more commonly known as **Edman's reagent**. This reagent reacts with the N-terminal amino group.

The C-terminal amino acid of the peptide or protein can be identified by treating the protein with carboxypeptidase A. Carboxypeptidase A cleaves off the C-terminal amino acid as long as it is not arginine or lysine. On the other hand, carboxypeptidase B cleaves off the C-terminal amino acid **only** if it is arginine or lysine. Carboxypeptidases are exopeptidases. An **exopeptidase** is an enzyme that catalyzes the hydrolysis of a peptide bond at the end of a peptide chain.

Site where carboxypeptidase cleaves

—NHCHC(=O)—NHCHC(=O)—NHCHC(=O)O⁻ (side chains *R*, *R′*, *R″*)

Table 1.11 **Specificity of Peptide or Protein Cleavage**

Reagent	Specificity
Chemical reagents	
Edman's reagent	Removes the N-terminal amino acid
Cyanogen bromide	hydrolyzes on the C-side of Met
Exopeptidases*	
Carboxypeptidase *A*	Removes the C-terminal amino acid (not Arg or Lys)
Carboxypeptidase *B*	Removes the C-terminal amino acid (only Arg or Lys)
Endopeptidases*	
Trypsin	Hydrolyzes on the C-side of Arg and Lys
Chymotrypsin	hydrolyzes on the C-side of amino acids that contain aromatic six-membered rings (Phe, Tyr and Trp)
Elastase	Hydrolyzes on the C-side of small amino acids (Gly and Ala)

*Cleavage will not occur if Pro is on either side of the bond to be hydrolyzed.

2. Secondary Structure of Proteins

Secondary structure describes the conformation of segments of the backbone chain of a peptide or protein. To minimize energy, a polypeptide chain tends to fold in a repeating geometric structure such as an α-helix or a β-pleated sheet. Three factors determine the choice of secondary structure:

(i) The regional planarity about each peptide bond (as a result of the partial double bond character of the amide bond), which limits the possible conformations of the peptide chain.

(ii) Maximization of the number of peptide groups that engage in hydrogen bonding (*i.e.*, hydrogen bonding between the carbonyl oxygen of one amino acid residue and the amide hydrogen of another).

(iii) Adequate separation between nearby *R* groups to avoid steric hindrance and repulsion of like charges.

In **1951, Linus Pauling** and **Robert Corey** proposed two periodic structures called the α-helix (alpha helix) and the β pleated sheet (beta pleated sheet). Subsequently, other structures such as the α **turn** and **omega** (Ω) **loop** were identified. Although not periodic, these common turn or loop structures are well defined and contribute with α helices and β sheets to form the final protein structure.

Alpha Helix

In the α-helix, the polypeptide backbone is folded in such a way that the —C=O group of each amino acid residue is hydrogen-bonded to the —N—H group of the fourth residue along the chain, *i.e.*, the —C=O group of the first residue binds to the —N—H group of the fifth residue, and so on. The backbone of the helix winds around the long axis, as shown in **Fig. 1.44.** The hydrogen bonds are all aligned approximately parallel to this axis, and side chains protrude outward. Each residue is spaced 0.15 nm from the next one along the axis, and 3.6 residues are required to make a complete turn of the helix.

The α-helix is a right-handed helix; that is, it rotates in a clockwise direction as it spirals down. Each turn of the helix contains 3.6 amino acid residues, and the repeat distance of the helix is 5.4 Å. A proline residue, for example, forces a bend in a helix because the bond between the proline nitrogen and the α-carbon cannot rotate to enable it to fit readily into a helix. Similarly, two adjacent amino acids that have more than one substituent on a β-carbon (valine, isoleucine or threonine) cannot fit into a helix because of steric crowding between the *R* groups. Finally, two adjacent amino acids with like-charged substituents cannot fit into a helix because of electrostatic repulsion between the *R* groups.

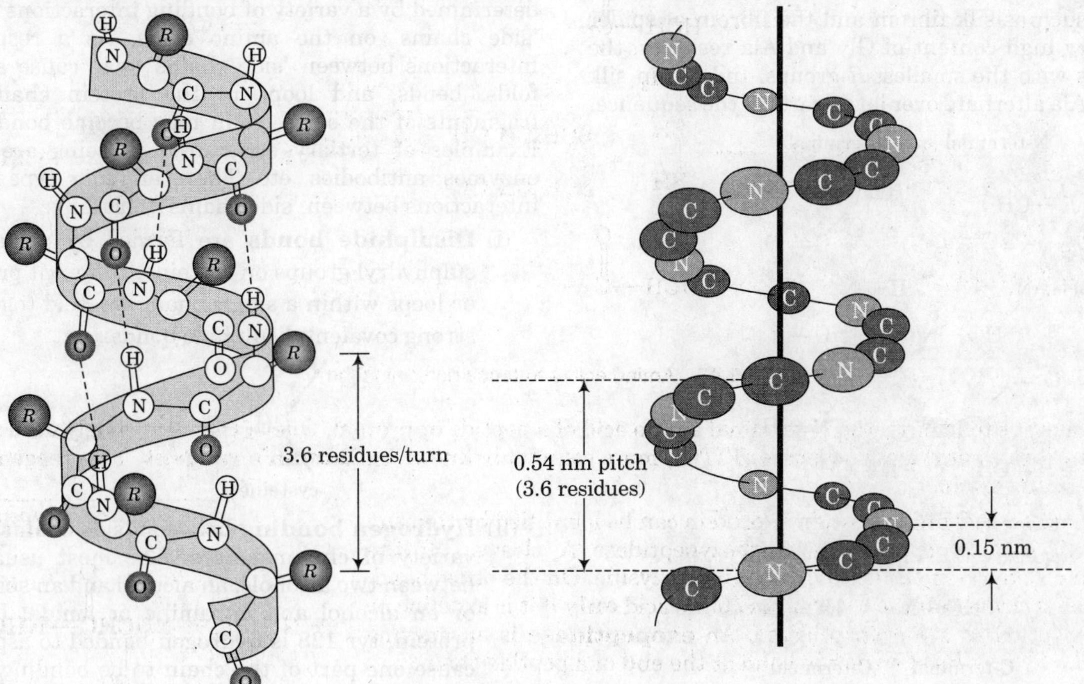

Fig. 1.44 Right-handed α-helix

There are five different kinds of constraints affect the stability of an α-helix: (a) the electrostatic repulsion (or attraction) between successive amino acid residues with charged *R*-groups, (b) The bulkiness of adjacent *R*-groups, (c) The interactions between *R*-groups spaced three (or four) residues apart, (d) the occurrence of Pro and Gly residues, and (e) the interaction between amino acid residues at the ends of the helical segment and the electric dipole inherent to the α-helix.

The mirror image of the α-*R*-helix, the left-handed α-helix (α-L), is rarely found in nature, although it would be energetically 'permissible.'

Beta Sheets

In 1951, the same year Pauling proposed the helix, Pauling and Corey postulated the existence of a different polypeptide secondary structure, the β-sheet. Like the α-helix, the β-sheet uses the full hydrogen-bonding capacity of the polypeptide backbone. In **β-sheets, however, hydrogen bonding occurs between neighboring polypeptide chains rather than within one as in a helix.**

Sheets comprising of two types:

(a) The **antiparallel** **β-sheet**, in which neighboring hydrogen-bonded polypeptide chains run in opposite directions.

(b) The **parallel** **β-sheet**, in which the hydrogen-bonded chains extend in the same direction.

The conformations in which these β-structures are optimally hydrogen bonded vary somewhat from that of the fully extended polypeptide. They therefore, have a rippled or pleated edge-on appearance and for that reason are sometimes called 'pleated sheets.' Successive side chains of a polypeptide chain in a β-Sheet extend to opposite sides of the sheet with a two-residue repeat distance of 7.0 Å.

The β-keratins such as silk fibroin and the fibroin of spider webs have a very high content of Gly and Ala residues, the two amino acids with the smallest *R*-groups. Indeed, in silk fibroin Gly and Ala alternate over large parts of the sequence.

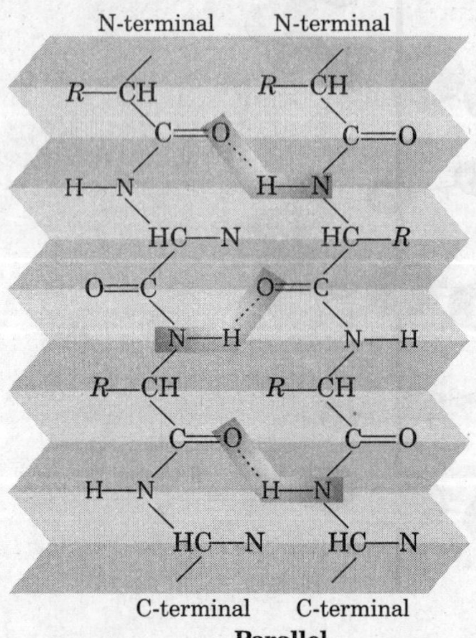

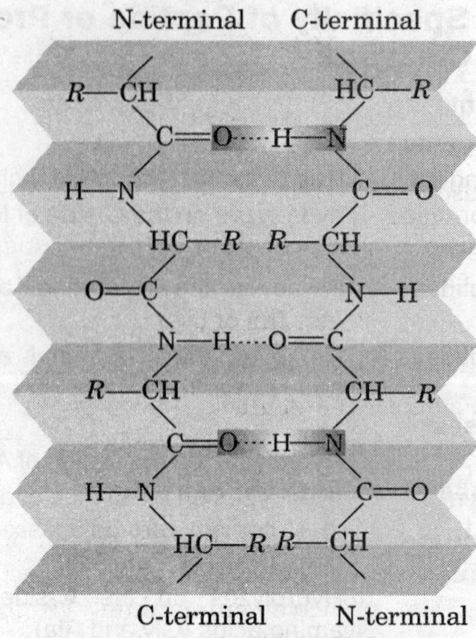

Fig. 1.45 Beta sheets

Coil Conformation

Generally, less than half of a globular protein is in an a-helix or b-pleated sheet. Most of the rest of the protein is still highly ordered but is difficult to describe. These polypeptide fragments are said to be in a coil **conformation** or a **loop conformation**.

3. Tertiary Structure of Proteins

The secondary structure of Polypeptide chain becomes bent and folded extensively to forming a precise, compact, globular shape. This is called tertiary structure. This final shape is determined by a variety of bonding interactions between the 'side chains' on the amino acids. As a result, bonding interactions between 'side chains' may cause a number of folds, bends, and loops in the protein chain. Different fragments of the same chain may become bonded together. Examples of tertiary structured proteins are Myoglobin, enzymes, antibodies, etc. There are four types of bonding interactions between 'side chains' including:

(i) **Disulphide bonds** are formed by oxidation of the sulphydryl groups on cysteine. Different protein chains or loops within a single chain are held together by the strong covalent disulphide bonds.

$$CH_2—S—S—CH_2$$

cysteine   cys

(ii) **Hydrogen bonding** between 'side chains' occurs in a variety of circumstances. The most usual cases are between two alcohols, an alcohol and an acid, two acids, or an alcohol and an amine or amide. In the prion protein, tyr 128 is hydrogen bonded to asp 178, which cause one part of the chain to be bonding with a part some distance away.

$CH_2C(=O)—O^{-}$ (asp) ··· HO— (tyr) —CH_2—

Examples of amino acid side chains that may hydrogen bond to each other:

(a) Two alcohols: ser, thr and tyr.

(b) Alcohol and an acid: asp and tyr

(c) Two acids: asp and glu

(d) Alcohol and amine: ser and lys

(e) Alcohol and amide: ser and asn

(iii) **Salt bridges** result from the neutralization of an acid and amine on side chains. The final interaction is ionic between the positive ammonium group and the negative acid group. Any combination of the various acidic or amine amino acid side chains will have this effect.

$CH_2CH_2—C(=O)—O^{-}$ $H_3\overset{+}{N}—CH_2CH_2CH_2CH_2$

Glutamic acid Lysine

The prion protein with the salt bridge of glutamic acid 200 and lysine 204. In this case a very small loop is made because there are only three other amino acids between them. This salt bridge has the effect of straightening an alpha helix.

(iv) **Non-polar hydrophobic interactions** The hydrophobic interactions of non-polar side chains are believed to contribute significantly to the stabilizing of the tertiary structures in proteins. The non-polar groups mutually repel water and other polar groups and results in a net attraction of the non-polar groups for each other. Hydrocarbon alkyl groups on ala, val, leu, and ile interact in this way. In addition, benzene (aromatic) rings on phe and tyr can 'stack' together.

$CH_2CHCH_3(CH_3)$ CH_3CHCH_2— CH_2—Ph ··· Ph—CH_2—

Leucine Leu **Phenylanine** Phe

(a) In many cases this results in the non-polar side chains of amino acids being on the inside of a globular protein, while the outside of the proteins contains mainly polar groups.

(b) The hydrophobic interactions are quantitatively the most important, being highly significant in maintaining structure in cell membranes.

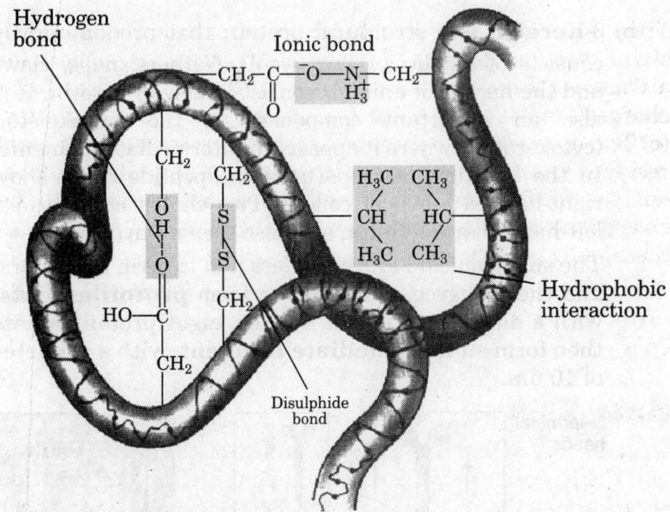

Fig. 1.46 The tertiary structure of proteins showing all type of bonding interaction

Tertiary proteins are broadly classified into two classes:

Fibrous Proteins

It contains long chains of polypeptides that occur in bundles. These proteins are insoluble in water. All the structural proteins described at the beginning of this chapter, such as keratin and collagen, are fibrous proteins.

(a) The **collagen helix is left-handed**, and with a pitch of 0.96 nm and 3.3 residues per turn, it is steeper than the α-helix. In contrast to the α-helix, H bonds are not possible within the collagen helix. However, the conformation is stabilized by the association of three helices to form a right-handed **collagen triple helix**.

Collagen is largely present as a **triple helix** made up of three individual collagen helices.

Denaturation of normal and abnormal collagen fibres Denaturation of collagen containing a normal content of hydroxyproline and of abnormal collagen containing no hydroxyproline. Without hydrogen bonds between hydroxyproline residues, the collagen helix is unstable and loses most of its helical content at temperatures above 20°C. Such collagens are formed by experimental animals (or man) in the absence of ascorbic acid (vitamin-C). Normal collagen is more stable and resists thermal denaturation until a temperature of 40°C is reached.

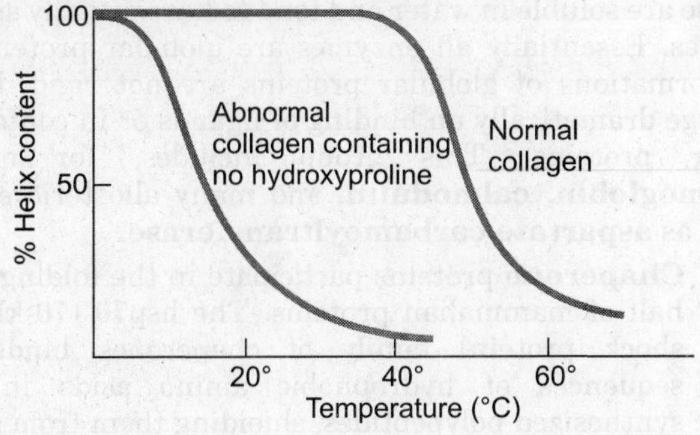

Fig. 1.47 Denaturation of normal and abnormal collagen fibres

(b) β-**Keratin** is a structural protein that predominantly consists of a-helices. Hair (wool), feathers, nails, claws and the hooves of animals consist largely of keratin. It is also an important component of the cytoskeleton (cytokeratin), where it appears in intermediate filaments. In the keratins, large parts of the peptide chain show right-handed a-helical coiling. Two chains each form a left-handed **superhelix**, as is also seen in myosin.

The superhelical keratin dimers join to form tetramers, and these aggregate further to form **protofilaments**, with a diameter of 3 nm. Finally, eight protofilaments then form an **intermediate filament**, with a diameter of 10 nm.

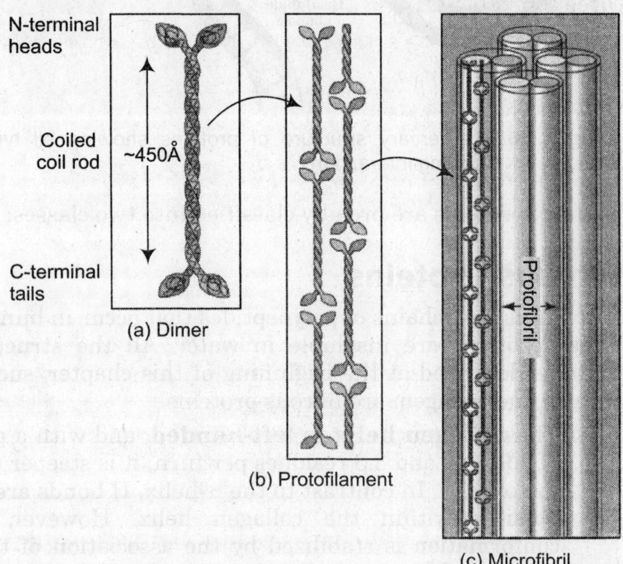

Fig. 1.48 Higher order a keratin structure

(c) **Silk fibroin** Silk is produced from the spun threads from silkworms (the larvae of the moth *Bombyx mori* and related species). The main protein in silk, **fibroin** consists of antiparallel **pleated sheet structures** arranged one on top of the other in numerous layers. In fact, more than 80% of fibroin consists of glycine, alanine and serine, the three amino acids with the shortest side chains. A typical repetitive amino acid sequence is (Gly-Ala-Gly-Ala-Gly-Ser).

Globular Proteins

These are soluble in water and tend to have roughly spherical shapes. Essentially all enzymes are globular proteins. The conformations of globular proteins are not rigid, but can change dramatically on binding of ligands or in contact with other proteins. This group includes, for example, **haemoglobin, calmodulin**, and many allosteric enzymes such as **aspartate carbamoyltransferase.**

(a) **Chaperone** proteins participate in the folding of over half of mammalian proteins. The hsp70 (70-kDa heat shock protein) family of chaperones binds short sequences of hydrophobic amino acids in newly synthesized polypeptides, shielding them from solvent. Chaperones prevent aggregation, thus providing an opportunity for the formation of appropriate secondary structural elements and their subsequent coalescence into a molten globule. The hsp60 family of chaperones, sometimes called **chaperonins**.

(b) **Myoglobin** is rich in α-helix. Oxygen stored in red muscle myoglobin is released during O_2 deprivation (*e.g.*, severe exercise) for use in muscle mitochondria for aerobic synthesis of ATP.

Quaternary Structure of Proteins

Proteins that have more than one peptide chain are called **oligomers**. The individual chains are called **subunits**. A protein with a single subunit is called a **monomer**, one with two subunits is called a *dimer*; one with three subunits is called a **trimer**, and one with four subunits is called a **tetramer**. The subunits are held together by the same kinds of interactions that hold the individual protein chains in a particular three-dimensional conformation: hydrophobic interactions, hydrogen bonding, and electrostatic attractions. The quaternary structure of a protein describes the way the subunits are arranged in space.

Homodimers contain two copies of the same polypeptide chain, while in a heterodimer the polypeptides differ.

Haemoglobins are tetramers comprised of pairs of two different polypeptide subunits. Greek letters are used to designate each subunit type. The subunit composition of the principal haemoglobins are $\alpha_2\beta_2$ (HbA; normal adult haemoglobin), $\alpha_2\gamma_2$ (HbF; fetal haemoglobin), α_2S_2 (HbS; sickle cell haemoglobin), and $\alpha_2\delta_2$ (HbA$_2$; a minor adult haemoglobin). The primary structures of the β, γ and δ chains of human haemoglobin are highly conserved.

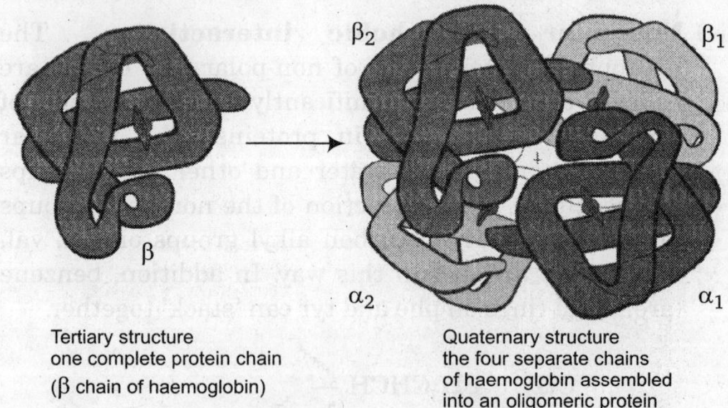

Fig. 1.49 Secondary, tertiary and quaternary structure of haemoglobin

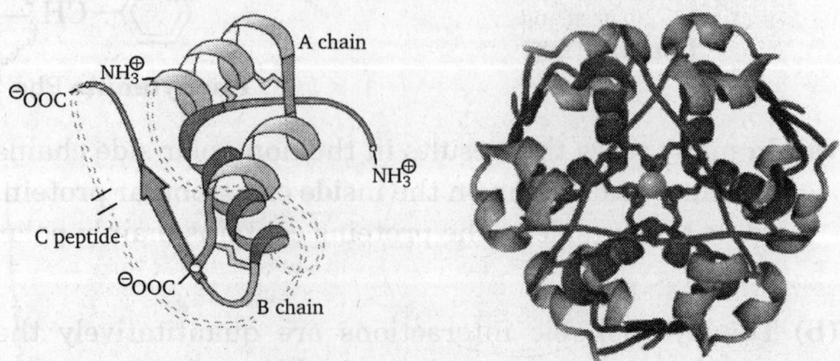

Fig. 1.50 Secondary, tertiary and quaternary structure of insulin

Protein Denaturation

Destroying the highly organized tertiary structure of a protein is called denaturation. The following are some of the ways that proteins can be denatured:

(i) Changing the pH denatures proteins because it changes the charges on many of the side chains. This disrupts electrostatic attractions and hydrogen bonds.

(ii) Certain reagents such as urea and guanidine hydrochloride denature proteins by forming hydrogen bonds to the protein groups that are stronger than the hydrogen bonds formed between the groups.

(iii) Detergents such as sodium dodecyl sulphate denature proteins by associating with the nonpolar groups of the protein, thus interfering with the normal hydrophobic interactions.

(iv) Organic solvents denature proteins by disrupting hydrophobic interactions.

Certain globular proteins denatured by heat, extremes of pH, or denaturing reagents will regain their native structure and their biological activity if returned to conditions in which the native conformation is stable. This process is called **renaturation**.

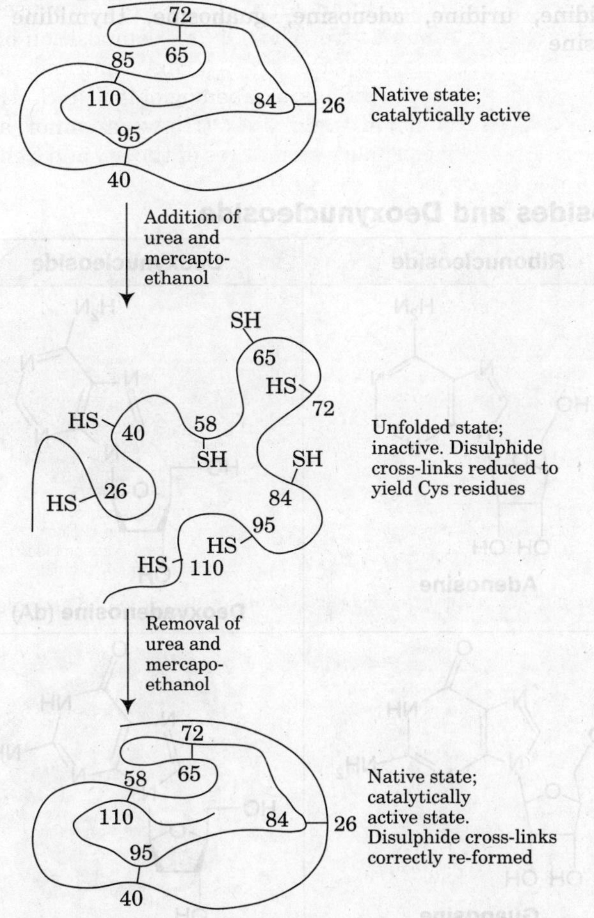

Fig. 1.51 Renaturation of unfolded, denatured ribonuclease

Nucleic Acids

A nucleic acid is a macromolecule. It is composed of chains of monomeric nucleotides. The common nucleic acids are deoxyribonucleic acid (DNA) and ribonucleic acid (RNA). Nucleic acids are universal in living organisms. Nucleic acid was first discovered by **Friedrich Miescher**. He extracted the DNA from pus and called it as *nuclein*.

Chemical Structure

The term 'nucleic acid' is a polynucleotide. It is made up of monomers called **nucleotides**. Each nucleotide consists of three components:

(i) A nitrogenous heterocyclic base (purine or pyrimidine).

(ii) A pentose sugar.

(iii) A phosphate group.

(i) Nitrogenous Heterocyclic Base

Pyrimidines and purines and make up the two groups of nitrogenous bases. These bases make up a part of both deoxyribonucleotides and ribonucleotides, and the basis for the universal genetic code.

Pyrimidine is a heterocyclic aromatic organic compound similar to benzene. It contains two nitrogen atoms at positions 1 and 3 of the six-member ring. There are three pyrimidime bases: cytosine, thymine and uracil.

Pyrimidine ring

Cytosine Thymine Uracil

Purine is a heterocyclic aromatic organic compound, consisting of a pyrimidine ring fused to an imidazole ring. The purine is the most widely distributed nitrogen-containing heterocycle in nature.

The 50% bases in nucleic acids, adenine and guanine, are purines. In DNA, these bases form hydrogen bonds with their complementary pyrimidines (thymine and cytosine). This is called complementary base pairing. In RNA, the complement of adenine is uracil (U) instead of thymine. Other notable purines are hypoxanthine, xanthine, theobromine, caffeine, uric acid and isoguanine.

The name 'purine' (purum uricum) was coined by the German chemist **Emil Fischer** in 1884.

Purine ring

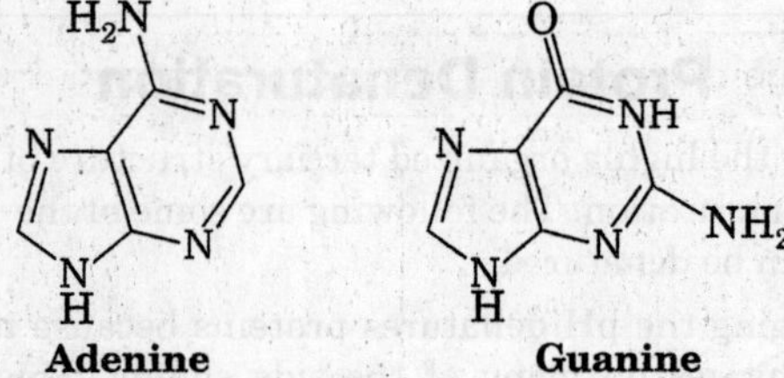

(ii) Pentose Sugar

Ribose primarily D-ribose, is an aldopentose (monosaccharide) containing five carbon atoms, it has aldehyde as functional group in its linear form. The chemical formula of D-ribose is $C_5H_{10}O_5$.

Deoxyribose is also known as D-Deoxyribose and 2-deoxyribose, is also an aldopentose containing five carbon atoms, and an aldehyde as functional group in its linear structure. It is a deoxy sugar derived from the pentose sugar ribose by the replacement of the hydroxyl group at the 2 position with hydrogen, leading to the net loss of an oxygen atom. It has a chemical formula of $C_5H_{10}O_4$; it was discovered in 1929 by **Phoebus Levene**.

D-ribose and Deoxyribose was discovered by **Phoebus Levene** (1905, 1929).

Deoxyribose **D-ribose**

Fig. 1.52 Pentose sugar

(iii) Phosphate Group

Phosphoric acid also known as orthophosphoric acid having the chemical formula H_3PO_4. Orthophosphoric acid molecules combine pentose sugar molecules by phosphodiester bonds.

152 pm, 157 pm

Phosphoric acid

Nucleosides

Nucleosides are glycosylamines made by attaching a nitrogenous base to a ribose or deoxyribose ring. Examples cytidine, uridine, adenosine, guanosine, thymidine and inosine.

Table 1.12 **Nitrogenous Base, Nucleoside, Ribonucleosides and Deoxynucleoside**

Nitrogenous Base	Nucleoside	Ribonucleoside	Deoxynucleoside
Adenine	**Adenosine** (A)	**Adenosine**	**Deoxyadenosine** (dA)
Guanine	**Guanosine** (G)	**Guanosine**	**Deoxyguanosine** (dG)

Nitrogenous Base	Nucleoside	Ribonucleoside	Deoxynucleoside
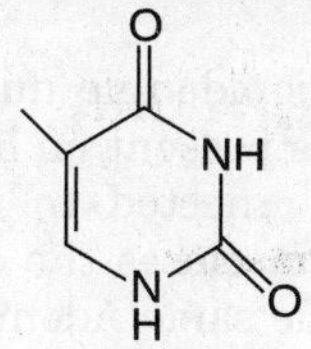 Thymine	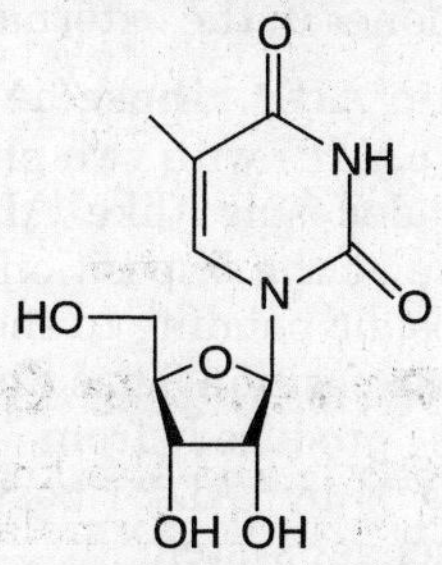 5-methyluridine (m5U)	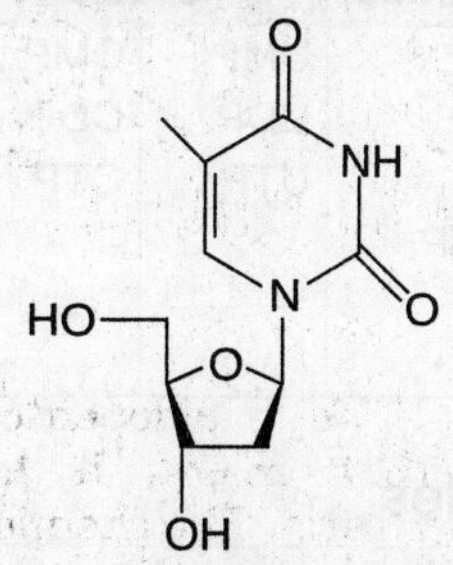 Thymidine	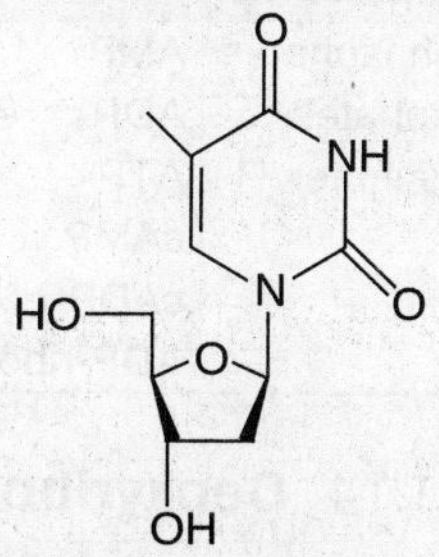 Deoxythymidine (dT)
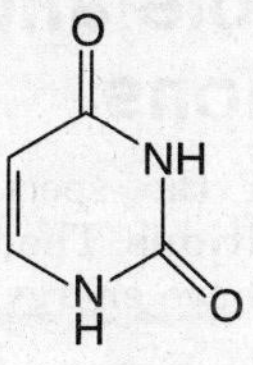 Uracil	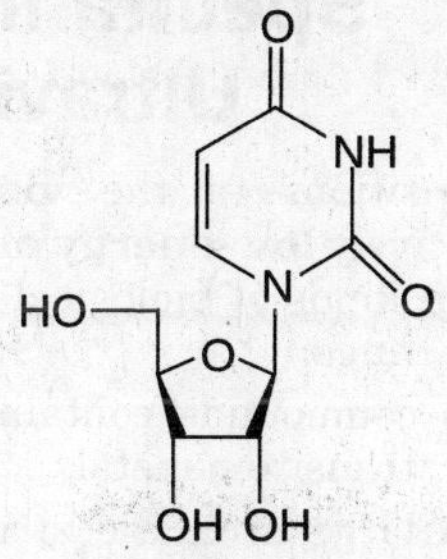 Uridine (U)	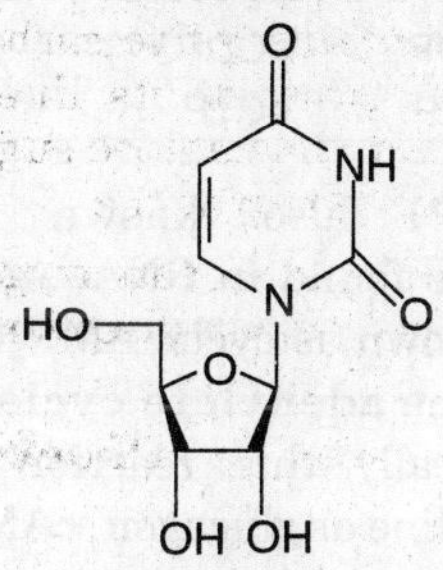 Uridine	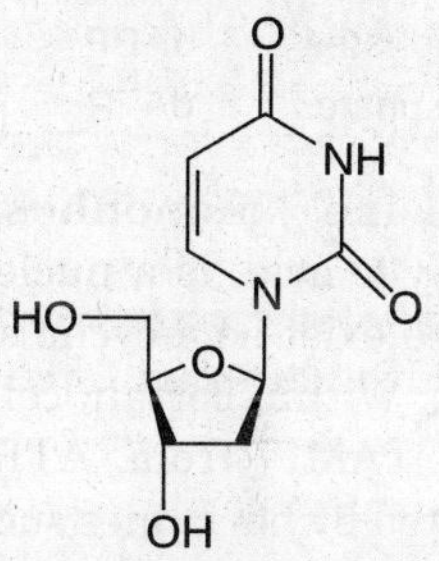 Deoxyuridine (dU)
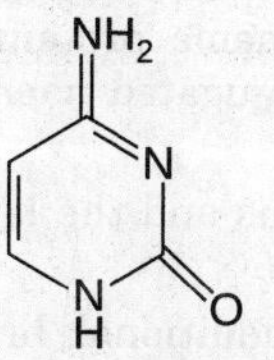 Cytosine	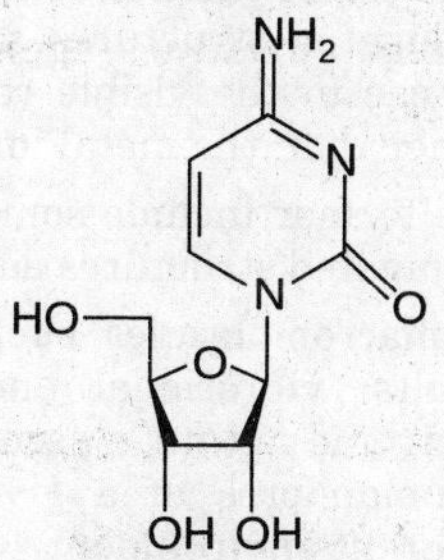 Cytidine (C)	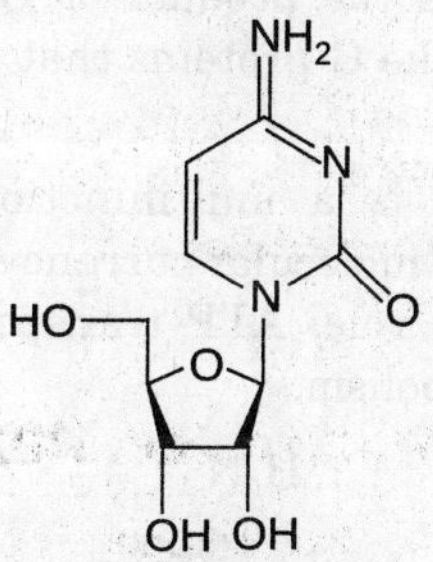 Cytidine	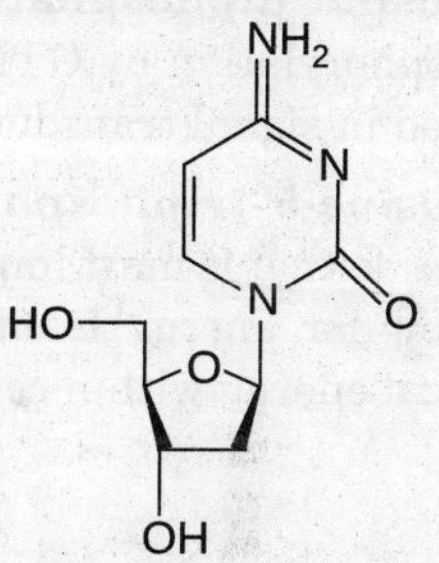 Deoxycytidine (dC)

Nucleotides

Nucleotides are organic the compounds formed by joining three structures: a nitrogenous base (purines or pyrimidines), a sugar (ribose or deoxyribose), and a phosphate group. Nucleotides are the structural units of RNA and DNA.

Nucleotides also serve as important cofactors in cellular signaling and metabolism. These cofactors include Co-A, flavin adenine dinucleotide, flavin mononucleotide, adenosine triphosphate and nicotinamide adenine dinucleotide phosphate.

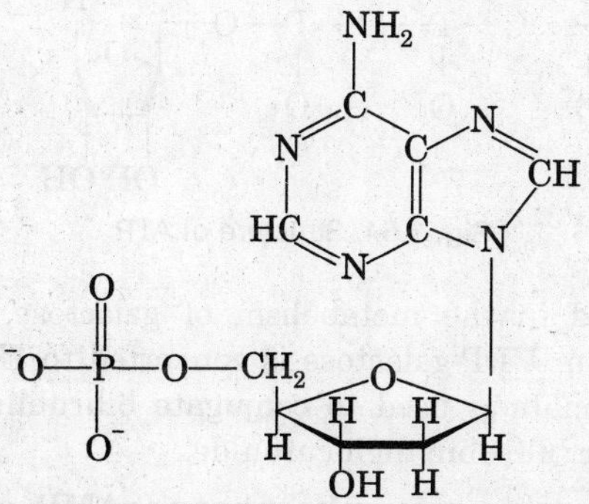

Fig. 1.53 Deoxyadenosine monophosphate (dAMP)

Table 1.13 **Ribonucleotide**

Types Cytosine	Adenine	Guanine	Uracil	
Monophosphates	AMP	GMP	UMP	CMP
Diphosphates	ADP	GDP	UDP	CDP
Triphosphates	ATP	GTP	UTP	CTP
Cyclic	cAMP	cGMP		
	cADPR (Cyclic ADP-ribose)			

Table 1.14 **Deoxyribonucleotides**

Type	Adenine	Guanine	Thymine	Cytosine	Uracil
Monophosphates	dAMP	dGMP	TMP	dCMP	dUMP
Diphosphates	dADP	dGDP	TDP	dCDP	
Triphosphates	dATP	dGTP	TTP	dCTP	

Adenosine monophosphate(AMP) also known as 5′-adenylic acid, is a nucleotide that is found in RNA. AMP can also exist as a cyclic structure known as cyclic AMP (or cAMP). Within certain cells the enzyme **adenylate cyclase** makes cAMP from ATP, and typically this reaction is regulated by hormones such as adrenaline or glucagon. cAMP plays an important role in intracellular signaling.

Guanosine diphosphate (GDP), is the product of GTP dephosphorylation by GTPases, *e.g.*, the G-proteins that are involved in signal transduction.

Adenosine-5′-triphosphate (ATP) is a multifunctional nucleotide that is most important as a 'molecular currency' of intracellular energy transfer. In this role, ATP transports chemical energy within cells for metabolism.

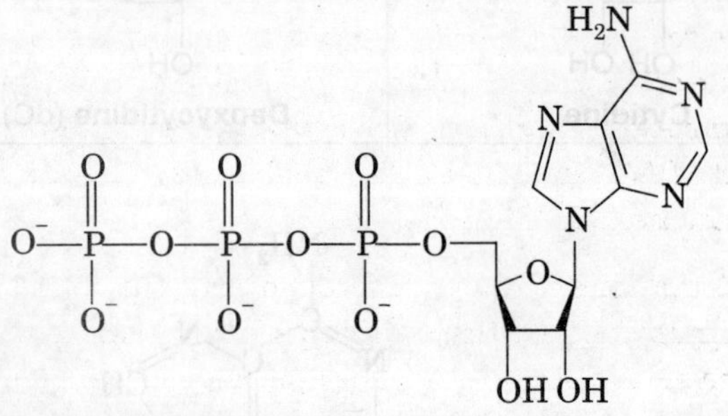

Fig. 1.54 Structure of ATP

UTP is used in the metabolism of galactose, where the activated form UDP-galactose is converted to UDP-glucose. UDP-glucuronate is used to conjugate bilirubin to a more water soluble bilirubin diglucuronide.

Cyclic adenosine monophosphate (cAMP, cyclic AMP or 3′ – 5′ cyclic adenosine monophosphate) is a second messenger that is important in many biological processes. cAMP is derived from adenosine triphosphate (ATP) and used for intracellular signal transduction in many different organisms.

Cyclic guanosine monophosphate (cGMP) is a cyclic nucleotide derived from guanosine triphosphate (GTP). cGMP acts as a second messenger much like cyclic AMP, most notably by activating intracellular protein kinases in response to the binding of membrane-impermeable peptide hormones to the external cell surface.

Cyclic ADP ribose(cADPR) is a cyclic adenine nucleotide (like cAMP) with two phosphate groups present on 5′ OH of the adenosine (like ADP), further connected to another ribose at the 5′ position, which, in turn, closes the cycle by glycosidic bonding to the nitrogen of the same Adenine base (whose position 9 has the glycosidic bond to the other ribose). It is produced from nicotinamide adenine dinucleotide (NAD^+) by ADP-ribosyl cyclases as part of a second messenger system.

Spectra in the Visible and Ultraviolet Regions

Transitions in the **visible region** of the spectrum are relatively **low-energy electronic transitions**. There are two main kinds of biological structures that have energy levels in this range:

(i) compounds containing certain metal ions (particularly transition metals).

(ii) large aromatic structures and conjugated double-bond systems.

The former include some metalloproteins and the latter such conjugated structures as vitamin-A. Haeme proteins absorb intense in the visible region to the conjugated haeme group rather than the metal ion.

The former include some metalloproteins and the latter such conjugated structures as vitamin-A.

In macromolecules such as proteins additional broadening results: vibrational energy accompanying the changes in electronic state ~see from the fact that individual chromophores of a given type may exist in a number of different environment.

In the near-ultraviolet region of the spectrum (200 to 400nm), many biochemicals exhibit strong and useful absorption bands. These biochemicals are often associated with small conjugated ring systems, both aromatic and heterocyclic, whereas the large conjugated systems absorb in the visible region. Thus, among the amino acids, tyrosine, phenylalanine and tryptophan absorb most intensely in this region. Most of the absorption of proteins in the 280 nm region results from the presence of these residues. Similarly, all of the purine and pyrimidines bases absorb strongly in the near ultraviolet.

Macromolecular Structure and Absorption

There is sharp difference between the absorption spectra of macromolecules and those of their monomers. The definite secondary structures of macromolecule have different spectra than its random-coil polymeric structures. These properties can be used for detection of configurational changes.

Consider, for example, the following effect: When a protein is hydrolyzed to its constituent amino acids, the spectrum of the products is somewhat different from that of the intact protein. Similar changes are observed when the protein is

denatured, that is, when its definite secondary and tertiary folding, are disturbed. These observations suggest that the environment of the absorbing residues must be different in the folded protein molecule than when the amino acids are in free contact with the solvent.

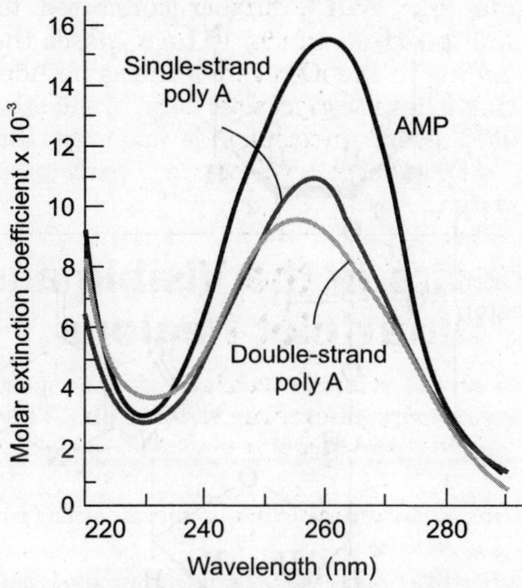

Fig. 1.55 Hypochromism of polyriboadenylic acid. The polymer spectrum differs little from that of the monomer and the intensity of absorption is considerably reduced

The nucleic acids show even more dramatic change in absorption spectra. The above figure polyriboadenylic acid with an equal concentration of its monomer, adenosine monophosphate, while the following figure shows the change produced in the spectrum of *E. coli* DNA by heating to 90°C with accompanying denaturation.

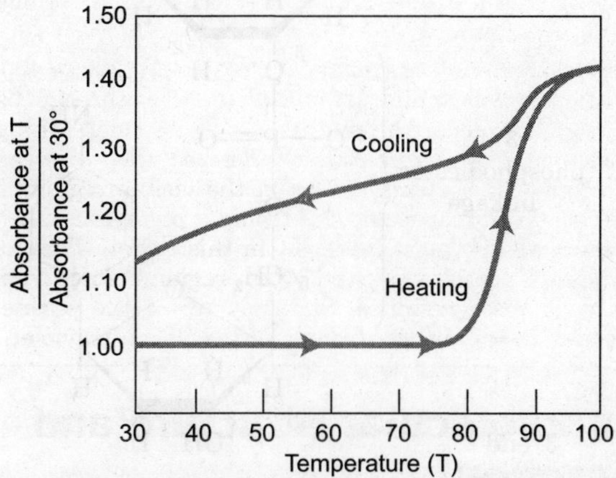

Fig. 1.56 The 'melting' of DNA as followed by absorption at 260 nm. Note that the sharpness of the transition in absorption with change in temperature

The polymer shows lower absorption intensity than the monomer (hypochromism), and in the polymer the maximum is shifted towards the lower wavelength. The hypochromism of polymeric structures arises from intramolecular interactions due to interactions with the solvent and surrounding polymer.

Polynucleotides

Nucleic Acid is a three-dimensional perspective on nucleotide structure, base pairing, and other aspects of DNA and RNA structure. A unit consisting of a base bonded to a sugar is referred to as a **nucleoside.**

In each nucleoside, N-9 of a purine or N-1 of a pyrimidine is attached to C-1 of the sugar. A **nucleotide** is a nucleoside joined to one or more phosphate groups by an ester linkage. The most common site of esterification in naturally occurring nucleotides is the hydroxyl group attached to C-5 of the sugar. A compound formed by the attachment of a phosphate group to the C-5 of a nucleoside sugar is called a **nucleoside 5-phosphate or a 5-nucleotide.**

Nucleotides are the monomers that are linked to form RNA and DNA. The four nucleotide units in DNA are **deoxyadenylate, deoxyguanylate, deoxycytidylate, or deoxythymidylate** and **thymidylate.** Like a polypeptide, a DNA chain has polarity. One end of the chain has a free 5′ —OH group (or a 5′ —OH group attached to a phosphate), and the other end has a 3′ —OH group. By convention, **the base sequence is written in the 5′ to 3′ direction.** The ACG indicates that the unlinked 5 —OH group is on deoxyadenylate, whereas the unlinked 3′—OH group is on deoxyguanylate.

A DNA molecule comprise of many nucleotides to carry the genetic information of an organisms. For example, the DNA a polyoma, virus (cause cancer in certain organisms) is 5100 nucleotides in length. The *E. coli* genome is a single DNA molecule of 4.6 million nucleotides, human genome comprises approximately 3 billion nucleotides, divided among 24 distinct DNA molecules (22 autosomes, X and Y sex chromosomes) of different sizes.

One of the largest known DNA molecules is found in the Indian muntjak (Muntiacus muntjak), $2n = 6$ an Asiatic deer; its genome is nearly as large as the human genome but is distributed on only 3 chromosomes. The largest of these chromosomes has chains of more than 1 billion nucleotides.

Fig. 1.57 Adenosine

Watson-Crick Model

Maurice Wilkins and **Rosalind Franklin** obtained X-ray diffraction photographs of fibers of DNA. The diffraction patterns indicated that DNA was formed of two chains that wound in a regular helical structure. **James Watson** and **Francis Crick** constructed a structural model for DNA that accounted for the diffraction pattern and other functional properties of nucleic acids. The features of the Watson-Crick model of DNA are:

(a) Two helical polynucleotide chains are coiled around a common axis. The chains run in opposite directions.

(b) The sugar-phosphate backbones are on the outside and, therefore, the purine and pyrimidine bases lie on the inside of the helix.

(c) The bases are nearly perpendicular to the helix axis, and adjacent bases are separated by 3.4 Å. The helical structure repeats every 34 Å, so there are 10 bases (= 34 Å per repeat/3.4 Å per base) per turn of helix. There is a rotation of 36 degrees per base (360 degrees per full turn/10 bases per turn).

(d) The diameter of the helix is 20 Å.

In 1950, Erwin Chargaff reported that the ratios of adenine to thymine and of guanine to cytosine were nearly the same in all species studied.

Table 1.15 **Base Compositions Experimentally Determined for a Variety of Organisms**

Species	A : T	G : C	A : G
Human being	1.00	1.00	1.56
Salmon	1.02	1.02	1.43
Wheat	1.00	0.97	1.22
Yeast	1.03	1.02	1.67
Escherichia coli	1.09	0.99	1.05
Serratia marcescens	0.95	0.86	0.70

The adenine:thymine and guanine:cytosine ratios are close to 1, whereas the adenine:guanine ratio varies considerably.

Double-stranded DNA consists of two complementary polynucleotide chains where the bases on one strand form hydrogen-bonded associations with the bases on the other strand. There are two hydrogen bond metween adenine and thymine A=T and three hydrogen bonding between guanine and cytosine G≡C.

The A/T and G/C base pairs each have one purine (A or G) and one pyrimidine (T or C) which means that the size of each of the base pairs from one side to the other is almost the same.

The two strands are said to be complementary because all the bases in one strand are paired with the complementary bases on the other strand (A with T and G with C). The two strands are **antiparallel** one strand runs in the 5′ → 3′ direction from top to bottom while the other strand runs 3′ → 5′.

Fig 1.58 Single strand bonding in DNA

The Reversible Melting of Double Helix

(a) The heating disrupts the hydrogen bonds between base pairs and thereby causes the strands to separate. The dissociation of the double helix is often called **melting** because it occurs relatively abruptly at a certain temperature. The **melting temperature** (T_m) is defined as the temperature at which half the helical structure is lost.

(b) The DNA double helical structure strands may also be separated by adding acid or alkali to ionize the nucleotide bases and disrupt base pairing.

(c) Stacked bases in nucleic acids absorb less ultraviolet light than do unstacked bases, an effect called **hypochromism.** The melting of nucleic acids is followed by increase in the absorption of light at a wavelength of 260 nm.

(d) Separated complementary strands of nucleic acids spontaneously reassociate to form a double helix when the temperature is lowered below T_m. This renaturation process is sometimes called **annealing.**

(e) Proteins called **helicases** use chemical energy (from ATP) to disrupt the structure of double-stranded nucleic acid molecules.

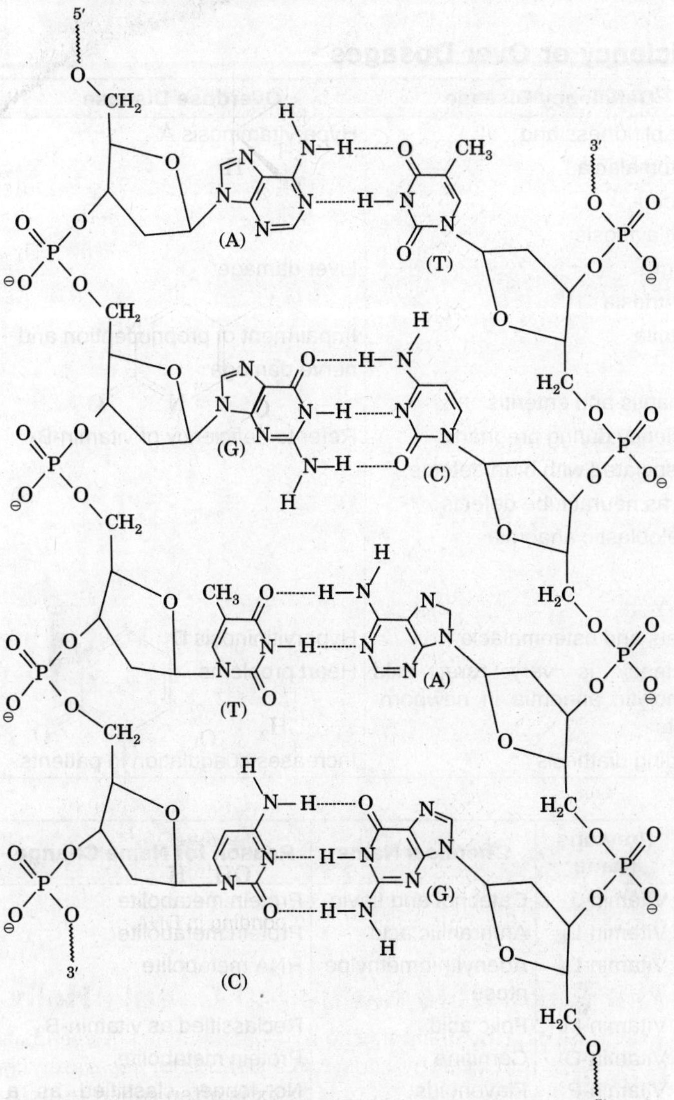

Fig. 1.59 Antiparallel DNA strands

DNA Circular and Supercoiled

The human chromosomes have linear DNA molecules. Some other organisms are circular. The axis of the double helix can itself be twisted into a **superhelix**. A circular DNA molecule without any superhelical turns is known as a **relaxed molecule.** Supercoiling is biologically important for two reasons.

(i) a supercoiled DNA molecule has a more compact shape than does its relaxed counterpart.

(ii) supercoiling may hinder or favour the capacity of the double helix to unwind and thereby affects the interactions between DNA and other molecules.

Ethidium Bromide Binds to DNA

The ethidium bromide is a common salt. Ethidium is a large planer molecule that binds tightly to DNA. It is often used to visualize fragments of DNA that have been separated on gels. The ethidium molecule is fluorescent—when illuminated with ultraviolet light it shines in the visible range.

Ethidium binds to DNA by inserting itself between the stacked bases in double-stranded DNA. The ring structure of ethidium is hydrophobic and resembles the rings of the bases in DNA. Ethidium is capable of forming close van der Waals' contacts with the base pairs and that's why it binds to the hydrophobic interior of the DNA molecule.

Molecules that bind in this manner are called intercalating agents because they intercalate into the compact array of stacked bases. In doing so, they distort the double helix and interfere with DNA replication, transcription, DNA repair, and recombination. This is why intercalating agents are often potent mutagens.

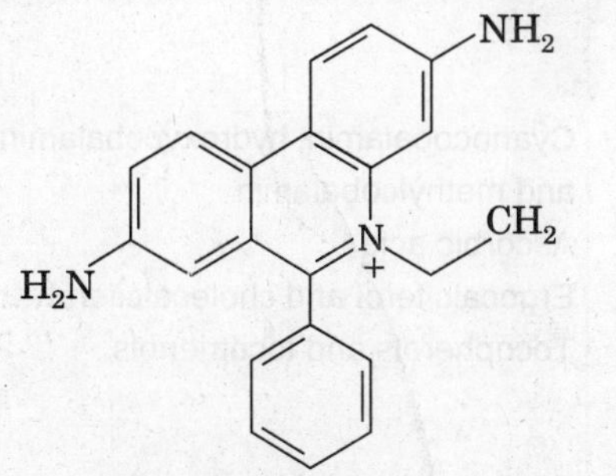

Fig. 1.60 Ethidium bromide

Distortion of the sugar-phosphate backbone takes place when an intercalating agent bind and the DNA is lengthened when intercalating agents bind. This changes the properties of DNA considerably. One of the tricks in separating closed circular molecules of DNA from linear fragments (such as genomic DNA) is to treat the DNA with ethidium bromide. The intercalating agent doesn't bind to closed circular molecules because they can't be lengthened enough to allow insertion of the chemical between the bases. The normal circular plasmid DNA can then be separated from linear DNA with bound ethidium because binding of ethidium changes the overall density of DNA.

Vitamins

The name **vitamin** is derived from the Latin words *vita* (meaning life) and ***amine*** (an organic chemical nitrogen containing molecule). Polish biochemist **Kazimierz Funk** isolated the same complex of micronutrients and proposed the complex be named 'Vitamine' in 1912. Vitamin-C had no amine component, therefore the final 'e' was dropped from the 'amine'.

Biochemical functions of vitamins are:

1. as a hormones (*e.g.*, vitamin-D),
2. antioxidants (*e.g.*, vitamin-E),
3. mediators of cell signaling,
4. regulators of cell and tissue growth and differentiation (*e.g.*, vitamin-A) and
5. largest number of vitamins (*e.g.*, B-complex vitamins) function as precursors for coenzymes.

Vitamins act as catalysts or substrates in metabolism. When it acting as part of a catalyst, vitamins are bound to enzymes and are called **prosthetic groups.** For example, biotin is part of enzymes involved in making fatty acids. Vitamins also act as **coenzymes** to carry chemical groups between enzymes. For example, folic acid carries various forms of carbon group– methyl, formyl and methylene in the cell.

Vitamins are classified as water-soluble vitamins, and fat-soluble vitamins. In general, water-soluble vitamins are readily excreted from the body. Each vitamin is typically used in multiple reactions and, therefore, most have multiple functions. In humans there are 13 vitamins: 4 fat-soluble (A, D, E and K) and 9 water-soluble (8 vitamin-B and vitamin-C).

Table 1.16 **Vitamins and Their Diseases Due to Deficiency or Over Dosages**

Vitamins	Chemical Name(s)	Solubility	Deficiency Disease	Overdose Disease
Vitamin-A	Retinoids (retinol, retinoids and carotenoids)	Fat	Night-blindness and Keratomalacia	Hypervitaminosis A
Vitamin-B_1	Thiamine	Water	Beri-beri	
Vitamin-B_2	Riboflavin	Water	Ariboflavinosis	
Vitamin-B_3	Niacin and niacinamide	Water	Pellagra	Liver damage
Vitamin-B_5	Pantothenic acid	Water	Paresthesia	
Vitamin-B_6	Pyridoxine, pyridoxamine and pyridoxal	Water	Anaemia	Impairment of proprioception and nerve damage
Vitamin-B_7	Biotin	Water	Dermatitis and enteritis	
Vitamin-B_9	Folic acid and folinic acid	Water	Deficiency during pregnancy is associated with birth defects, such as neural tube defects	Refer to deficiency of vitamin-B_6
Vitamin-B_{12}	Cyanocobalamin, hydroxycobalamin and methylcobalamin	Water	Megaloblastic anaemia	
Vitamin-C	Ascorbic acid	Water	Scurvy	
Vitamin-D	Ergocalciferol and cholecalciferol	Fat	Rickets and osteomalacia	Hypervitminosis D
Vitamin-E	Tocopherols and tocotrienols	Fat	Deficiency is very rare; mild haemolytic anaemia in newborn infants	Heart problems
Vitamin-K	Phylloquinone and menaquinones	Fat	Bleeding diathesis	Increases coagulation in patients

The lists of chemicals that had previously been classified as vitamins, and the earlier names of vitamins that later became part of the B-complex:

Table 1.17 **Vitamins and Their Traditional Names**

Previous Name	Chemical Name	Reason for Name Change
Vitamin-B_4	Adenine	DNA metabolite
Vitamin-B_8	Adenylic acid	DNA metabolite
Vitamin-F	Essential fatty acids	Needed in large quantities (does not fit the definition of a vitamin).
Vitamin-G	Riboflavin	Reclassified as vitamin-B_2
Vitamin-H	Biotin	Reclassified as vitamin-B_7
Vitamin-J	Catechol and flavin	Protein metabolite
Vitamin-L_1	Anthranilic acid	Protein metabolite
Vitamin-L_2	Adenylthiomethylpentose	RNA metabolite
Vitamin-M	Folic acid	Reclassified as vitamin-B_9
Vitamin-O	Carnitine	Protein metabolite
Vitamin-P	Flavonoids	No longer classified as a vitamin
Vitamin-PP	Niacin	Reclassified as vitamin-B_3
Vitamin-U	S-Methylmethionine	Protein metabolite

Vitamin-A

(Retinol and Beta-Carotene)

Chemical name Retinol or All-*Trans*-Retinol

Molecular formula $C_{20}H_{30}O$; molecular weight: 286.46 g/mol

Chemical name Beta-carotene

Molecular formula: $C_{40}H_{56}$; Molecular weight: 536.90 g/mol. The pro-vitamin of vitamin-A is β-carotene (orange dye of carrots).

(i) Vitamin-A is a fat-soluble vitamin. Retinol is probably formed by an oxidative splitting of the beta-carotene in the small intestine. That is why beta-carotene is also called **pro-vitamin-A.**

(ii) Beta-carotene is an antioxidant and has in this way cancer preventing properties. Vitamin-A has a protective effect on the epithelia.

(iii) The effect of vitamin-A is essential for the formation of blood capillaries. Therefore, it is important for the nutrition supply to all organs.

(iv) In tissues where most cells are broken down and a continuing replacement of new cells is necessarily (like the skin), a lack of vitamin-A is firstly observed. Insufficient capillary formation and an insufficient capillaries position can cause an accumulation of waste products that serve as food for penetrating bacteria. It can cause serious, often deadly inflammations with pus.

As a result of a retina disturbance of the eye it cause night-blindness.

Properties

(a) Cancer protective properties (beta-carotene for non-smokers).

(b) Prevents and treats skin problems and ageing of the skin.

(c) Improves the eyesight and prevents night-blindness.

(d) Improves the regenerating properties of the body.

(e) Stimulates the growth of strong bones, hair, teeth, skin and gums.

(f) Helps against a too fast working thyroid gland.

Symptoms when Deficiency Occur

(a) Night-blindness

(b) Continuous headaches

(c) Decreased immunity against infections (especially of the airways)

(d) Skin problems

(e) Dry and breakable hair

(f) Kidney stones.

The earliest symptoms of vitamin-A deficiency are night blindness. Other early symptoms include follicular hyperkeratinosis, increased susceptibility to infection and cancer and anaemia equivalent to iron deficient anaemia. Prolonged lack of vitamin-A leads to deterioration of the eye tissue through progressive keratinization of the cornea, a condition known as **xerophthalmia.**

Careful and Toxicity

An overdose of vitamin-A as retinol is poisonous and may not be used by women that are pregnant. Beta-carotene is not poisonous and this vitamin is considered safe for adult and children. High doses of retinol or beta-carotene when you are a smoker because this could increase your change to get lung cancer. Excess accumulation of vitamin-A in the liver can lead to toxicity which manifests as bone pain, hepatosplenomegaly, nausea and diarrhoea.

Natural Sources

Important sources of vitamin-A are only animal products like: liver, fish oil, palm oil, butter, margarine and egg yolk.

Important sources of beta-carotene are green leaf vegetables, carrots and orange vegetables.

Vitamin-B-Complex

When the vitamin-B-complex was discovered people thought it was only one vitamin. This vitamin got the name vitamin-B. Later it was discovered that vitamin-B consisted of more than one vitamin. To distinguish the different vitamins they became numbered from 1 to 13. Later on, some vitamins were removed from the B-complex because they were found not to be real vitamins. Finally, 8 vitamins were left, namely: B_1 (Thiamine), B_2 (Riboflavin), B_3 (Nicotinic acid), B_5 (Pantothenic acid), B_6 (Pyridoxine), Biotin, B_{11} (Folic acid) and B_{12} (Cobalamin).

These vitamins from the B-complex are all active in the metabolism of the body. They are all water-soluble and are all precursors of coenzymes. These vitamins are present especially in meat, bread, potatoes and milk products.

1. Vitamin-B_1 (Thiamine)

Chemical name Thiamine

Molecular formula $C_{12}H_{17}N_4OS$; molecular weight 265.36 g/mol

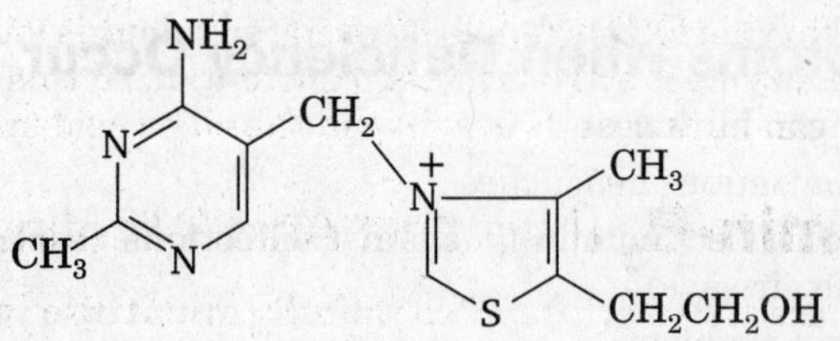

Vitamin-B_1 is a water-soluble and sulphur containing vitamin. It was discovered in 1901 by **Jansen** and **Donath, Windhaus, van Veen** and **Okade.**

Vitamin-B_1 is necessary to regulates the metabolism, especially the carbohydrate break down by which energies are obtained. This vitamin alone can keep someone alive without other vitamins and minerals, also under faulty conditions. Deficiencies can cause numerous organic and functional disturbances. When vitamin-B_1 is lacking and an excess of carbohydrates is present, **beri-beri** arises in the different forms. Also an excess of sugar can arouse a lack of vitamin B_1. Relative deficiencies occur regularly.

Properties

(a) Protects against some negative consequences of alcohol use.

(b) Can help in the treatment of nerve disturbances (especially when these are caused by B_1 deficiency).

(c) Can help in the treatment of anaemia.

(d) Can improve the flexibility of the mind.

(e) Can help to regulate diabetes when a connection exists to a B_1 deficiency.

(f) Helps in the treatment of herpes infections.

(g) Helps to transform sugar into energy in the muscles.

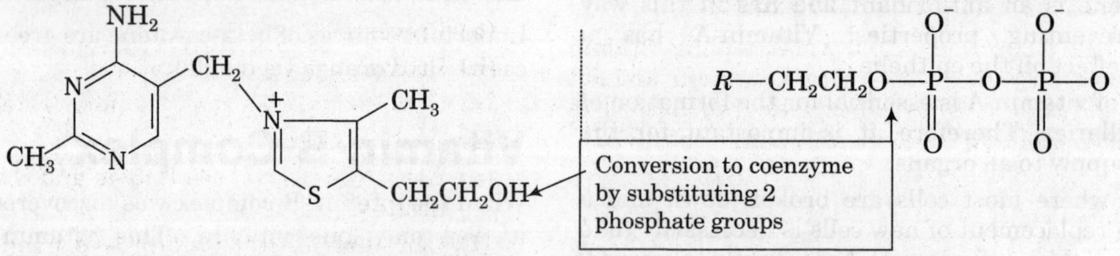

Conversion to coenzyme by substituting 2 phosphate groups

This coenzyme prepares pyruvate for the further breakdown in the citric acid cycle. This coenzyme helps to decarboxylate (= to split off a carbon atom) pyruvate as part of the enzyme **pyruvate dehydrogenase complex.** It is also a part of the enzyme **alpha-ketoglutarate dehydrogenase complex** that is also active in the citric acid cycle. In that way it regulates especially the carbohydrate breakdown in which energies are obtained.

Vitamin-B_2 (Riboflavin)

Chemical name Riboflavin and Lactoflavin

Molecular formula $C_{17}H_{20}O_6N_4$; molecular weight 376.4 g/mol

Symptoms in Case of Deficiencies

The earliest symptoms of thiamin deficiency include constipation, appetite suppression, nausea as well as mental depression, peripheral neuropathy and fatigue. Chronic thiamin deficiency leads to more severe neurological symptoms including ataxia, mental confusion and loss of eye coordination. Other clinical symptoms of prolonged thiamin deficiency are related to cardiovascular and musculature defects.

The severe thiamin deficiency disease known as **Beri-beri**, is the result of a diet that is carbohydrate rich and thiamin deficient. An additional thiamin deficiency related disease is known as **Wernicke-Korsakoff syndrome.** This disease is most commonly found in chronic alcoholics due to their poor dietetic lifestyles.

Careful and Toxicity

Thiamine is not considered poisonous but it is advised not to take more then 400 mg/day.

Dosage and Natural Sources

Vitamin-B_1 is generally present in the diet. Rich in thiamine are yeast, grain germ, meat, peas and beans.

Specific Biochemical Mechanism

Vitamin-B_1 is necessary in the metabolism. It is active in the body as a coenzyme that is called **thiamine di-phosphate or thiamine pyrophosphate.** It is almost the same molecule as thiamine. The only difference is that there are two phosphate groups attached instead of a hydrogen atom.

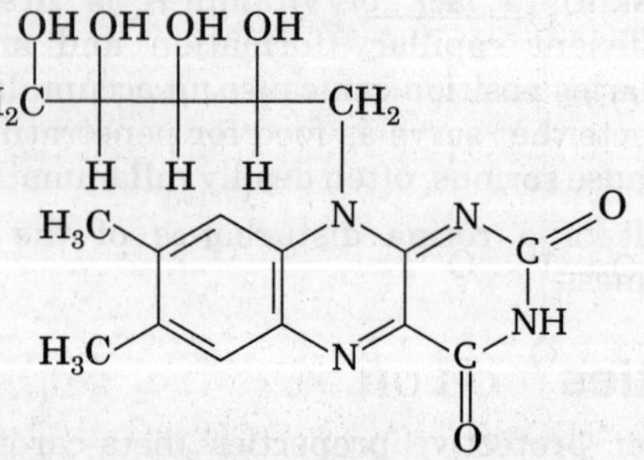

Vitamin-B_2 is a water-soluble vitamin and is also active in the breakdown of carbohydrate, protein and fat.

Properties

(a) Helps the metabolism of fats, proteins and carbohydrates.

(b) Promotes good eyesight.

(c) Promotes the well functioning of the reproductive system.
(d) Promotes athletic performances.
(e) Offers protection against anaemia.

Symptoms in case of Deficiencies

(a) Burst of the skin and mucous membrane.
(b) Redness of the tongue.
(c) Eczema on the skin and the genital organs.
(d) Burning feeling on the skin.
(e) Tiredness.
(f) Sometimes difficulties in the formation of blood.

By absence of vitamin-B_2, a partial damage of the tissue respiration arises. As a consequence of that a standstill of the growth, belly abnormalities, abnormalities of the lips, curved grown finger nail, atrophy of the tongue and stomach and intestine ailment.

Symptoms associated with riboflavin deficiency include, glossitis, seborrhea, angular stomatitis, cheilosis and photophobia. Riboflavin decomposes when exposed to visible light. This characteristic can lead to riboflavin deficiencies in newborns treated for hyperbilirubinemia by phototherapy.

Careful and Toxicity

Riboflavin is poisonous in very high doses. Rarely occurring symptoms are itch and a burning feeling on the skin.

Natural Sources

Rich in vitamins-B_2 are liver, kidney, egg yolk, cheese, yeast, milk, leaf vegetables and meat.

Specific Biochemical Mechanism

Vitamins-B_2 is just as vitamins-B_1 a water-soluble vitamin and it is also active by the carbohydrate, protein and fat breakdown. In the body riboflavin becomes transformed in the coenzyme that is called Flavin Adenine Dinucleotid-FAD.

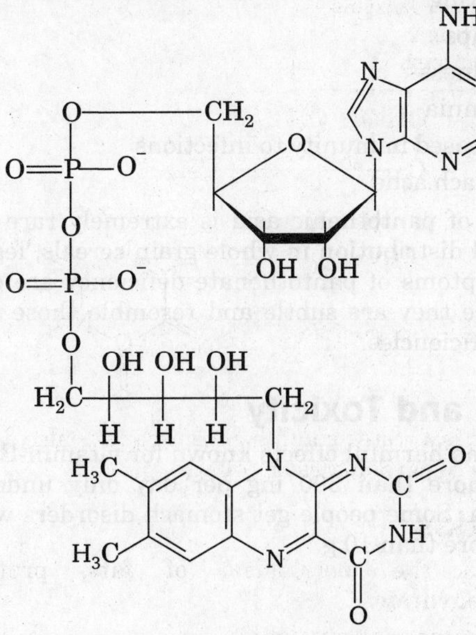

Fig. 1.61 Coenzyme FAD

The coenzyme FAD is represented in red colour is vitamin-B_1. This coenzyme is active as a redox potential. In this molecule energy can be stored. It is active in the citric acid cycle.

Vitamin-B_3 (Nicotinic Acid/Nicotinamide)

There are two forms of vitamin-B_3 **nicotinic acid** and **nicotinamide.**

Chemical name Nicotinic acid

Molecular formula $C_6H_5NO_2$; molecular weight 123.11 g/mol

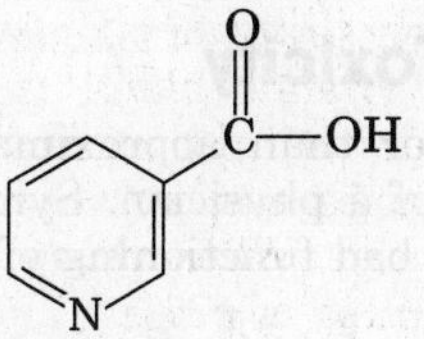

Chemical name Nicotinamide

Molecular formula $C_6H_6N_2O$; molecular weight: 122.13 g/mol

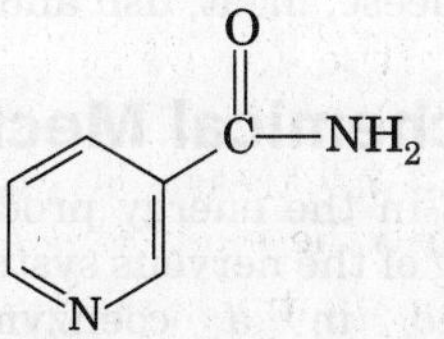

Vitamin-B_3 is a is water-soluble vitamin. This vitamin helps in the energy production and promotes a well working of the nervous system.

Properties

(a) Prevents and treats schizophrenia.
(b) Promotes the cell respiration.
(c) Gets energy from sugar, fat and protein.
(d) Keeps the skin clean.
(e) Keeps the nerves, the tongue and the digestive system healthy.
(f) Can lower the cholesterol levels and offer in this way protection against heart conditions.
(g) Is considered as an antioxidant.
(h) Can prevent migraine.
(i) Lowers the blood pressure.

Symptoms in Case of Deficiencies

(a) Dermatoid (skin illness)
(b) Diarrhoea
(c) Dementia
(d) Pellagra is an ailment with the above-mentioned symptoms that sixty year ago occurred often in South America. This illness was caused by vitamin-B_3 deficiency.

A deficient in niacin (as well as tryptophan) leads to glossitis of the tongue, dermatitis, weight loss, diarrhe, depression and dementia. The severe symptoms, depression, dermatitis and diarrhoea, are associated with the condition known as **pellagra.**

Several physiological conditions (*e.g.*, Hartnup disease and malignant carcinoid syndrome) as well as certain drug therapies (*e.g.*, isoniazid) can lead to niacin deficiency.

In Hartnup disease tryptophan absorption is impaired and in malignant carcinoid syndrome tryptophan metabolism is altered resulting in excess serotonin synthesis. Isoniazid (the hydrazide derivative of isonicotinic acid) is the primary drug for chemotherapy of tuberculosis.

Careful and Toxicity

Avoids doses, higher than approximately 120 mg, unless under supervision of a physician. Symptoms by high doses are depressiveness, bad functioning of the liver, getting red and headache.

Natural Sources

Important sources of vitamin-B_3 are: whole grain products, brown rice, milk, cheese, meat, fish and cashew nut.

Specific Biochemical Mechanism

This vitamin helps in the energy production and promotes the well functioning of the nervous system. In the body niacin becomes converted in a coenzyme that is called **nicotinamine adenine dinucleotide,** NAD.

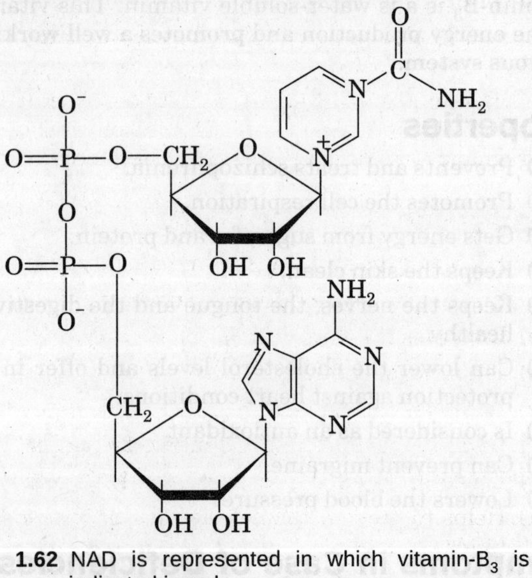

Fig. 1.62 NAD is represented in which vitamin-B_3 is indicated in red

This coenzyme is active as a redox potential, this means that in this molecule energy can be stored and subsequently be taken. The energy is in the form of hydrogen atoms. Because NAD is always recycled by 'recharging' (in the catabolism) and using (in the anabolism), only little (18 mg) of this vitamin is necessary in our daily diet. The coenzyme is active in the citric acid cycle and in the glycolysis.

Vitamin-B_5 (Pantothenic Acid)

Chemical name Pantothenic acid

Molecular formula $C_9H_{16}O_5N$; molecular weight 218.23 g/mol

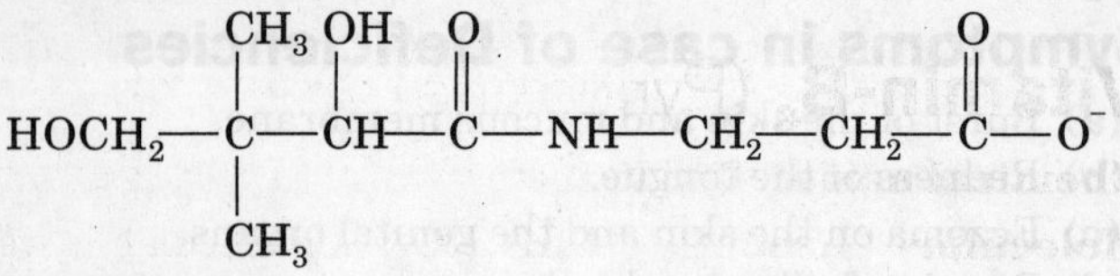

$$HOCH_2-C(CH_3)_2-CH(OH)-C(=O)-NH-CH_2-CH_2-C(=O)-O^-$$

Vitamin-B_5 is just as all vitamin from the vitamin-B complex, water-soluble.

Pantothenic acid can be transformed in the body in coenzyme A (Co-A). This coenzyme breaks down the protein from our food to individual amino acids. This coenzyme also helps to produce human protein from these amino acid building blocks. Coenzyme-A is also active in converting carbohydrates into body energy, for example in the beginning of the citric acid cycle in the decarboxylating reaction.

Properties

(a) Promotes wounds healing.

(b) Helps the body in producing energy.

(c) Decreases stress.

(d) Regulates the immune system.

(e) Prevents tiredness.

(f) Lowers cholesterol levels and offers in this way protection against heart conditions.

(g) Helps to prevent and treat arthritis.

(h) Can prevent baldness and greyness of the hair.

(i) Some hormones can only be formed if sufficient levels of vitamin-B_5 are present in the body.

Symptoms in Case of Deficiencies

(a) Vomiting

(b) Cramps

(c) Tiredness

(d) Insomnia

(e) Decreased immunity to infections

(f) Stomach ache.

Deficiency of pantothenic acid is extremely rare due to its widespread distribution in whole grain cereals, legumes and meat. Symptoms of pantothenate deficiency are difficult to assess since they are subtle and resemble those of other B vitamin deficiencies.

Careful and Toxicity

There are no harmful effects known for vitamin-B_5, but take doses of more than 300 mg per day only under medical supervision. Some people get stomach disorders when using doses of more than 10 g.

Natural Sources

Vitamin-B_5 is present in the following foodstuffs: yeast, whole grain products, green vegetables, mushrooms, meat, organ meat, silver skin rice, eggs and nuts.

Vitamin-B_6 (Pyridoxine)

Chemical name Pyridoxine

Molecular formula $C_8H_{11}NO_3$; molecular weight 169.18 g/mole

Vitamin-B_6 is just like all vitamins from the vitamin-B complex water-soluble.

Pyridoxine together with folic acid and vitamin-B_{12} takes care of the uptake of iron in the body. It is active in the formation of red blood cells. These three vitamins are also important for a good functioning of the nervous system and they are active in the amino acid metabolism.

In the body this vitamin is present as the coenzyme that is called **PLP** (Pyridoxal 5′-phosphate). This coenzyme is active in the glycogen metabolism especially in the glycogen breakdown. PLP together with the enzyme phosphorylase takes care that glycogen can be broken down.

Properties

(a) Raises the immune system.
(b) Helps to regulate diabetes.
(c) Is active in the uptake of proteins and fats.
(d) Helps to fight nauseousness.
(e) Helps to prevent skin and nerve abnormalities.
(f) Treats the symptoms of the premenstrual syndrome (PMS) and the menopause.
(g) Decreases tensions in the muscle.
(h) Works as a natural diuretic.
(i) Helps to protect against cancer.

Symptoms in Case of Deficiencies

(a) Anaemia
(b) Nerve illness
(c) Skin problems

Isoniazid and penicillamine are two drugs that complex with pyridoxal and pyridoxal phosphate resulting in a deficiency in this vitamin.

Careful and Toxicity

Pyridoxine is poisonous in dosages above 200 mg per day. These high doses can leads to serious damages of the nerves. Long periods of high dosages intake of vitamin-B_6 (25-50 mg/day) can lead to excess levels of this vitamin.

Natural Sources

Food stuffs rich in vitamin-B_6 are vegetables, potatoes, bananas, whole grain products, milk, eggs, nuts, fish and meat.

Vitamin-B_{11} (Folic Acid)

Chemical name Folic acid

Molecular formula $C_{19}H_{19}N_7O_6$; molecular weight 441.40 g/mol

Folic acid is just as all vitamin from the vitamin-B family water-soluble.

Folic acid can be transformed in the body in a coenzyme that is called **tetrahydrofolate** (THF).

Folic acid stimulates the formation of gastric juice and is important for a well functioning liver.

This vitamin is active in the metabolism of proteins and fats, it is necessary for the formation of red blood cells (it prevents particular forms of anaemia) and it helps in the metabolism of the brain.

Folic acid is also necessary for the metabolism of DNA and RNA.

This vitamin is indispensable in cell division processes of the body and extra folic acid is for that reason advised to women in pregnancy or women who want to become pregnant.

Properties

(a) Improves the milk production when breast feeding.
(b) Can help to protect against cancer.
(c) Improves the skin.
(d) Is a natural painkiller.
(e) Improves the appetite.
(f) Gives babies and children immunity against infections.
(g) Is necessary for the production of DNA and RNA.
(h) Helps to prevent the developmental birth defect Spina bifida.

Symptoms in Case of Deficiencies

(a) Weak feeling
(b) Apathy
(c) Exceptional tiredness
(d) Insomnia
(e) Irritability
(f) Dementia
(g) Birth defect Spina bifida.

The most pronounced effect of folate deficiency on cellular processes is upon DNA synthesis. This is due to an impairment in dTMP synthesis which leads to cell cycle arrest in S-phase of rapidly proliferating cells, in particular haematopoietic cells.

Careful and Toxicity

Folic acid is poisonous in high dosages. In high dosages it can cause serious neurological problems. Do not take this vitamin if you have a lack of vitamin-B_{12} in the form of anaemia. High doses can cause insomnia and hinder the uptake of zinc in the blood.

Natural Sources

Important food sources of vitamin-B_{11} are: leaf vegetables, eggs, lentils, rice, bread, wheat germ, liver, kidneys, bananas, oranges and peaches.

Vitamin-B_{12} (Cobalamin)

Chemical name Cobalamin

Molecular formula $C_{63}H_{88}CoN_{14}O_{14}P$; molecular weight 1355.4 g/mol.

Vitamin-B_{12} is like all the vitamins from the B family water-soluble.

Cobalamin is together with vitamin-B_6 (pyridoxine) and B_{11} (folic acid) responsible for the uptake of iron in the blood and are necessary for the formation of red blood cells. Deficiencies of these vitamins can lead to anaemia. These three vitamins are also important for a well functioning nervous system and plays a role in the amino acid metabolism.

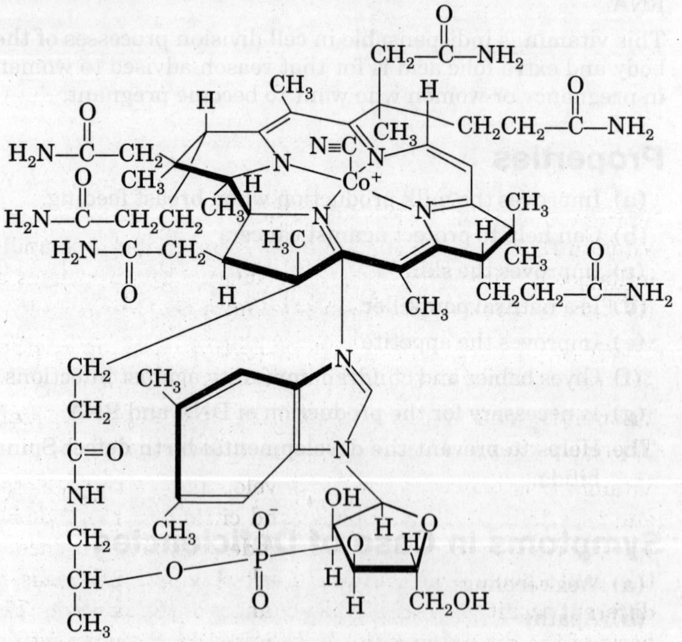

Fig. 1.63 Cobalamin

Properties

(a) Necessarily for the maintenance of the nervous system.

(b) Improves the memory and concentration.

(c) Necessarily for the use of fats, carbohydrates and proteins.

(d) Gives more energy.

(e) Promotes healthy growth for children.

(f) Can give protection against cancer.

(g) Protects against allergens and poisonous elements.

Symptoms in Case of Deficiencies

(a) Anaemia

(b) Menstruation problems

(c) Mental deterioration

(d) Trembling/ shaking

Pernicious anaemia is a megaloblastic anaemia resulting from vitamin-B_{12} deficiency that develops as a result a lack of intrinsic factor in the stomach leading to malabsorption of the vitamin

Neurological complications also are associated with vitamin-B_{12} deficiency and result from a progressive demyelination of nerve cells. The demyelination results due to increase in methylmalonyl Co-A that is due to deficiency of vitamin-B_{12}.

Careful and Toxicity

Vitamin-B_{12} is not considered as poisonous. Yet it is advised not to take more then 200 mg/day.

Natural Sources

Nutrients rich in vitamin-B_{12} are only animal products like: eggs, cheese, pot cheese, milk, fish and meat.

Specific Biochemical Function

In the body vitamin-B_{12} can be converted into a coenzyme (coenzyme-B_{12}) by a addition of a ribose and an adenine molecule as a rest group.

This coenzyme is necessary for the function of two enzymes. **Firstly,** for an enzyme that is functional in the fatty acid metabolism, namely **methylmalonyl Co-A mutase.** This enzyme is one of the enzymes responsible for the breakdown of fatty acids with an odd number of carbon atoms.

Secondly, coenzyme-B_{12} is necessary for the biosynthesis of the amino acid methionin, together with the enzyme **homocystein methyltransferase.** This enzyme puts a methyl group at homocystein by which methionine arises.

Vitamin-C (L-Ascorbic Acid)

Chemical name L-Ascorbic Acid, L-ascorbate

Molecular formula $C_6H_8O_6$; molecular weight 176.12 g/mol

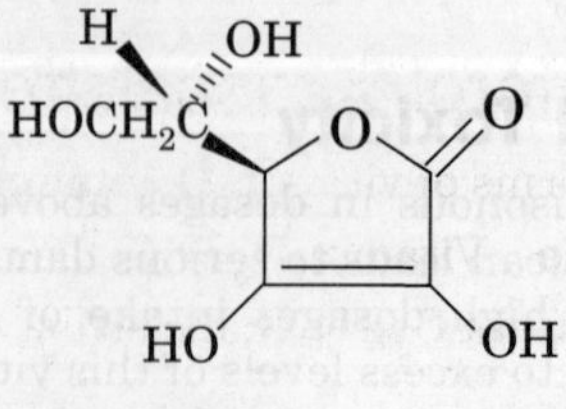

Vitamin-C is a water-soluble vitamin. L-ascorbic acid has as a redox system a task in the oxidative breakdown of the unsaturated fatty acids (linolenic acid).

Vitamins-C also increase the activity of white blood cells and for this reason promotes a better healing of infections. Vitamin-C is easily affected by oxygen (in the presence of heat) and is one of the most sensitive vitamins. Vitamin-C deficiently is also the cause of spring tiredness.

Properties

(a) Antioxidant.
(b) Accelerates the healing of wounds.
(c) Keeps bones, teeth and sexual organs healthy.
(d) Functions as a natural antihistaminic.
(e) Can help to fight infertilities of a man.
(f) Decreases the duration of colds and other virus infections.

Symptoms in Case of Deficiencies

(a) Scurvy
(b) Feeling of weakness
(c) Wounds do not cure well
(d) Tranquillity
(e) Bleeding gums
(f) Easy get bruises
(g) Loose teeth
(h) Pain in the joints
(i) No appetite
(j) Heart problems

Deficiency in vitamin-C leads to the disease **scurvy** due to the role of the vitamin in the post-translational modification of collagens. Scurvy is characterized by easily bruised skin, muscle fatigue, soft swollen gums, decreased wound healing and hemorrhaging, osteoporosis and anaemia.

Careful and Toxicity

Vitamin-C can cause kidney stones and gout. When using high doses some people develop diarrhoea and stomach cramps. Even so this vitamin is considered not harmfully even in very high doses. Very high doses vitamins-C can raise the cholesterol levels in the blood, through which the chance to develop heart diseases increase.

Natural Sources

L-Ascorbic acid is present in many fruits, green plants (leaf vegetables), milk and liver.

Vitamin-D

(Cholecalciferol/Ergocalciferol)

There are two forms of vitamin-D, vitamin-D_3 and D_2.

Chemical name Vitamin-D_3 or Cholecalciferol

Molecular formula $C_{27}H_{44}O$; molecular weight 384.6 g/mol

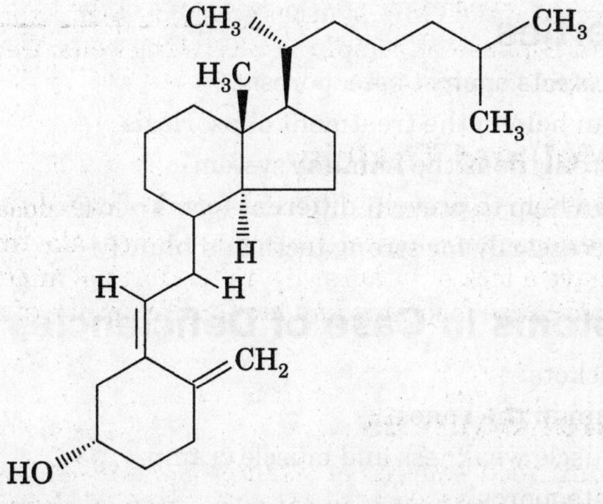

Vitamin-D_2 differs only with one double bond and one methyl group from vitamin-D_3 (indicated with red).

Chemical name Vitamin-D_2, Calciferol or Ergosterol

Molecular formula $C_{28}H_{44}O$; molecular weight: 396.7 g/mol

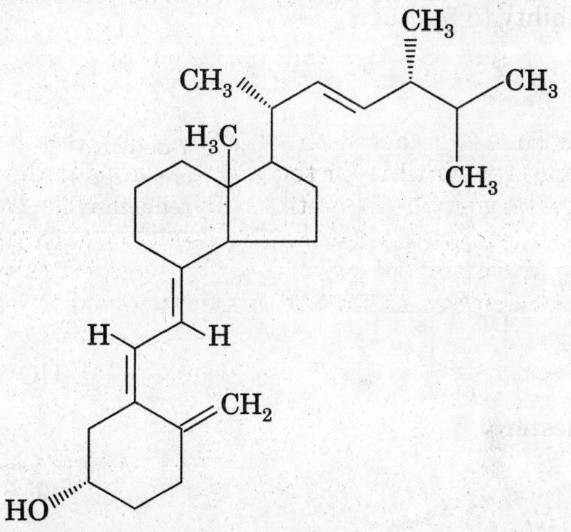

Vitamin-D is an fat-soluble vitamin.

Vitamin-D_3 is formed in our body from cholesterol under influence of ultraviolet light. The antirachitic properties of UV-light rest on the formation of vitamin-D_3.

Vitamin-D_2 is also formed from cholesterol, but *via* another pathway and vitamin-D_2 is vegetable.

Vitamin-D_2 and D_3 have biologically the same function. Therefore vitamin-D_2 is also used as a food supplement.

Vitamin-D is necessary for the development of the skeleton and especially in the phosphate and citric acid metabolism. The function of vitamin-D is dependent on the presence of the pantothenic acid complex. Lack of vitamin-D leads to different rachitic or rachitic like changes of the skeleton. The basis of the disturbance lies in the process of the growth of the cartilage. Therefore a lack of this vitamin is less striking in adults, but still has an effect on the ongoing cell replacement. Determining for damage is the simultaneous drop of break down processes through lacks of other vitamins (C, B etc.), by which the dangerous pre-rachitic state can arise.

Properties

(a) Protects against osteoporosis.
(b) Can help in the treatment of psoriasis.
(c) Strengthens the immune system.
(d) Can help to prevent different forms of cancer.
(e) Necessarily for strong teeth and bluntly.

Symptoms in Case of Deficiencies

(a) Rickets
(b) Pain in the bones.
(c) Muscle weakness and muscle cramp.
(d) Osteoporosis.

The main symptom of vitamin-D deficiency in children is **rickets** and in adults is **osteomalacia.** Rickets is characterized improper mineralization during the development of the bones resulting in soft bones. Osteomalacia is characterized by demineralization of previously formed bone leading to increased softness and susceptibility to fracture.

Careful and Toxicity

Vitamin-D is the most poisonous vitamin of all vitamins and leads to nauseousness, vomiting, headache, depressiveness and other symptoms. It is recommended to take not more then 10 micro grams per day.

Natural Sources

Important foods with vitamin-D are: fish (oil), yeast, leaf vegetables, meat and dairy products.

Specific Biochemical Function

The formation of vitamin-D from cholesterol under influence of ultraviolet-light.

Vitamin-D_3 is formed in the body from cholesterol under influence of ultraviolet light. The antirachitic properties of UV light rests on the formation of vitamin-D_3. From cholesterol, 7-dehydrocholesterol is produced by removing a hydrogen atom from place 7 and 8. This reaction is catalysed by 7-dehydrocholesterol reductase. From this 7-dehydrocholesterol, vitamin-D_3 (cholecalciferol) is produced under the influence of UV light.

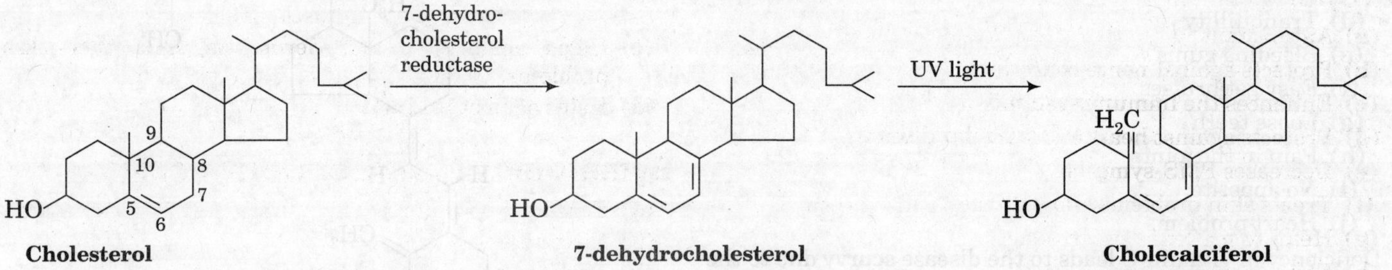

Fig. 1.64 The synthesis of vitamin-D_3

Vitamin-D_2 is also formed from cholesterol, but is vegetable and via another pathway. Vegetable ergosterol is made from cholesterol and this ergosterol is subsequently converted in ergocalciferol (vitamin-D_2) under influence of UV-light Vitamin-D_2 and D_3 have biologically the same function. Therefore, vitamin-D_2 is also used as a food supplement.

Vitamin-D is actually a hormone in the calcium and phosphate metabolism. As vitamin-D it is not active yet. It is made active in subsequent metabolic processes, firstly in the liver and after that in the kidneys. In the liver, an OH group is placed on carbon atom number 25 and in the kidneys also an OH group is placed but now on carbon atom number 1. The synthesized hormone is called 1, 25-dihydroxycholecalciferol or 1, 25(OH)2D.

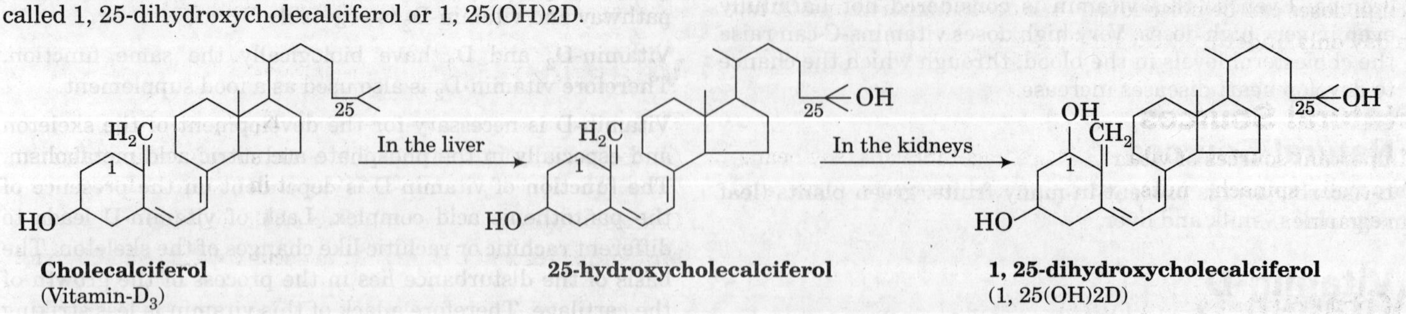

Fig. 1.65 Synthesis of hormone from vitamin-D_3

This hormone stimulates the production of Ca^{2+}-binding protein and is in this way responsible for the increased uptake of calcium (Ca) and phosphate (Pi) in the blood. Ca^{2+} binding protein transports calcium ions and phosphate ions from outside of the cell to the inside of the cell. Hormones in general and also 1, 25-dihydroxycholecalciferol occur in low concentrations in the blood, this also explains why only a little of vitamin-D (5 micrograms) is necessarily in our daily diet.

Vitamin-E (Tocopherol)

Chemical name D-alpha-tocopherol.

Molecular formula $C_{29}H_{50}O_2$; molecular weight 430.7 g/mol

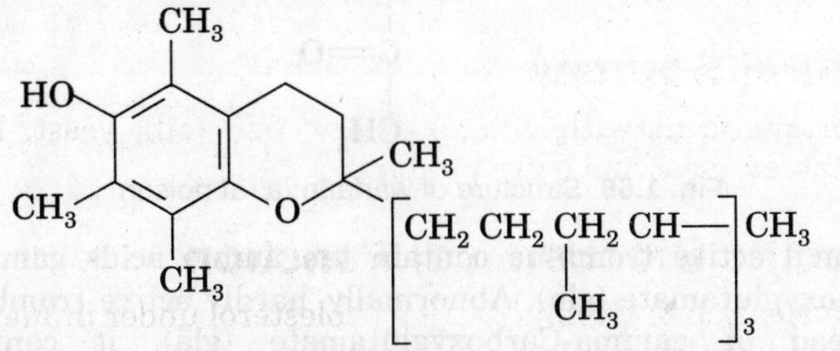

Vitamin-E is a fat-soluble vitamin.

Tocopherol has a preventive effect on ageing conditions. It is like vitamin-C a strong antioxidant (it makes free radicals harmless). Tocopherol is also necessary for the formation of red blood cells and the structure, recovery and maintenance of muscle and other tissue. It also protects plural unsaturated fatty acids that are essential for the body.

Properties

(a) Antioxidant.
(b) Protects against nerve conditions.
(c) Enhances the immune system.
(d) Protects against heart and vascular diseases.
(e) Decreases PMS-symptoms.
(f) Treats skin problems and baldness.
(g) Helps to prevent miscarriages.
(h) Effective as a natural diuretic.
(i) Prevents thickened scar tissue.

Symptoms in Case of Deficiencies

No known symptoms.

Careful and Toxicity

High doses can be poisonous. Take doses higher than 350 mg a day only under medical supervision.

Natural Sources

Important sources of vitamin-E are vegetable oils, soy beans, broccoli, spinach, nuts, whole grain products, eggs and margarine.

Vitamin-H (Biotin)

Chemical name D-Biotin

Molecular formula $C_{10}H_{16}N_2O_3S$; molecular weight 244.3 g/mol

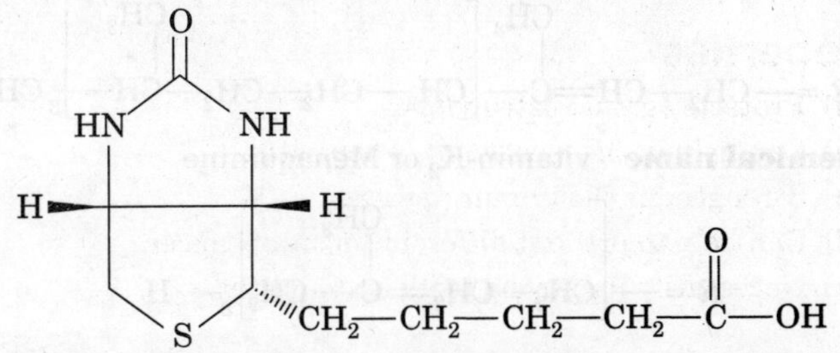

Although biotin is also called vitamin-H, it is part of the B-family and is also called vitamin-B_8. Biotin is a water-soluble vitamin. It can become converted in the body into the coenzyme biocytin (Molecular formula: $C_{16}H_{28}N_4O_4S$; molecular weight: 372.5 g/mol).

Biotin helps to release energy from the diet and in the formation of antibodies.

This vitamin is also responsible for a good condition of the skin and hair.

A deficiency of this vitamin occurs sometimes in babies. This is recognizable from a dry and flaky skin.

Properties

(a) Prevents grey hair.
(b) Lights various forms of muscle pain.
(c) Helps against eczema, dermatitis and other skin problems.
(d) Helps against baldness.

Symptoms in Case of Deficiencies

(a) Eczema
(b) Tiredness
(c) Decline of the metabolism of fat

Careful and Toxicity

Biotin is harmless, but it is advised not to use more then 300 mg per day, unless under medical supervision.

Natural Sources

Important sources of biotin are: eggs, milk, fruit, nuts, soybeans, brewer's yeast, whole rises, meat and fish.

Vitamin-K (Phylloquinone)

There are three forms of vitamin-K: K_1, K_2 and K_3.

All three forms have the same basic structure as indicated below. The rest group (*R*) is different in the three forms.

Chemical name Vitamin-K_1 or Phylloquinone

Molecular formula $C_{31}H_{46}O_2$; molecular weight 450.68 g/mol

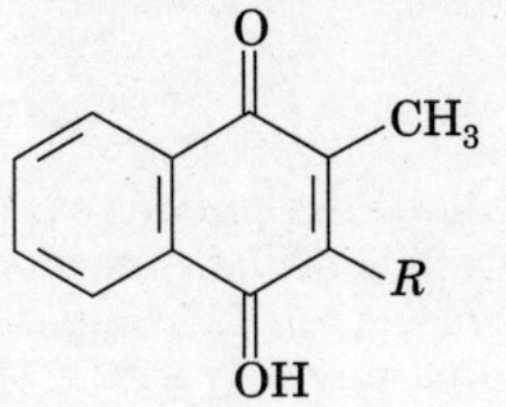

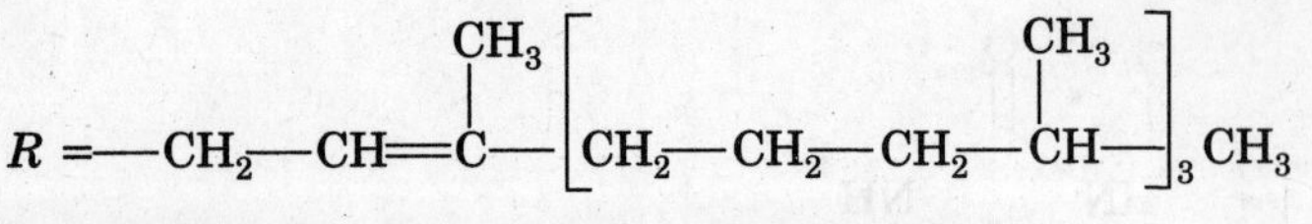

$$R = -CH_2-CH{=}\overset{CH_3}{\overset{|}{C}}-\left[CH_2-CH_2-CH_2-\overset{CH_3}{\overset{|}{CH}}-\right]_3 CH_3$$

Chemical name vitamin-K_2 or Menaquinine

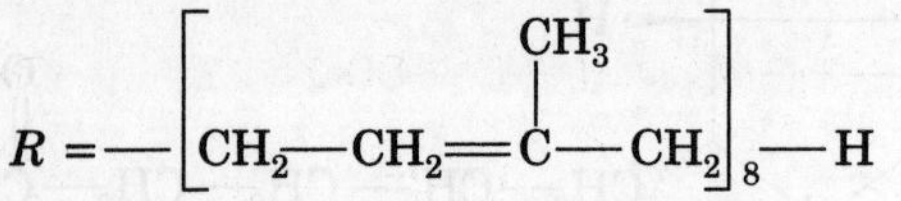

$$R = -\left[CH_2-CH_2{=}\overset{CH_3}{\overset{|}{C}}-CH_2\right]_8-H$$

Chemical name vitamin-K_3 or Menadione

R = -H

Vitamin-K is a fat-soluble vitamin.

This vitamin occurs naturally in vegetable food (green leaves) as a vitamin-K_1 (phylloquinone). In the intestine, it is also produced by our intestinal bacteria as vitamin-K_2 (menaquinone). Synthetic vitamin-K is called vitamin-K_3 (menadione), our body converts this vitamin in active vitamin-K.

Vitamin-K is indispensable in the formation of different coagulation factors, and thus also in the coagulation. Until approximately 3 months after birth it is necessarily that this vitamin is supplied in the diet because till then the intestinal flora is insufficient. Now-a-days this vitamin is added in infants feeding to prevent intracranial haemorrhage.

Properties

Prevents blood clutters.

Careful and Toxicity

There it no information known about toxicity.

Natural Sources

Important sources of phylloquinone are: cauliflower, broccoli, spinach, peas, whole grain products, turnip seed oil and non-fat meat.

Specific Biochemical Function

Vitamin-K is indispensable for the formation of thrombin or prothrombin (thrombinogen) and other coagulation factors in the liver.

When vitamin-K is missing or when a competitive inhibitor is present (like warfarin, a poison for rats), then abnormal trombine is formed, that only show 1% to 2% of the normal activity. **Warfarin has similarities with vitamin-K.**

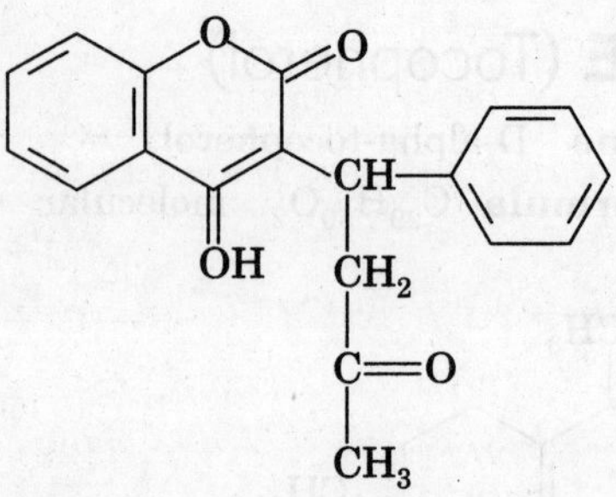

Fig. 1.66 Structure of warfarin, a rat poison

Normal active trombine contain ten amino acids gamma-carboxyglutamate (gla). Abnormally, hardly active trombine instead of gamma-Carboxyglutamate (gla), it contain glutamic acid (glu). Vitamin-K functions as cofactor in the post translational processes in the formation of trombine. Vitamin-K functions in the conversion of glutamic acid (glu) in gamma-carboxyglutamate (gla).

Step 1 Vitamin-K is in its active hydroquinone form and a H^+ ion (a proton) is removed from the 'glu' in an oxygen (O_2) consuming reaction. Because of this reaction a carbon ion arises on the 'glu' molecule.

Step 2 The 'glu' carbon ion reacts with CO_2 so that 'gla' arises.

Step 3 and 4 Active vitamin-K in the hydroquinone form becomes regenerated in two reactions. These reactions are catalysed by the same enzyme that use thiols (like lipoic acid). The rat poison warfarin and also dicoumarol block these regeneration reactions.

In the image above it is shown how vitamin-K becomes re-used. This explains why we only need a little (80 micro grams) of this vitamin in our daily diet.

Antioxidant

An **antioxidant** is a molecule that capable of slowing or preventing the oxidation of other molecules. Oxidation reactions can produce free radicals, which start chain reactions that damage cells. Antioxidants terminate these chain reactions by removing free radical intermediates, and inhibit other oxidation reactions by being oxidized themselves. Antioxidants are often reducing agents such as thiols or polyphenols.

Plants and animals have multiple types of antioxidants, such as **glutathione, vitamin-A, vitamin-C** and **vitamin-E** as well as enzymes such as **catalase, superoxide dismutase** and various **peroxidases.**

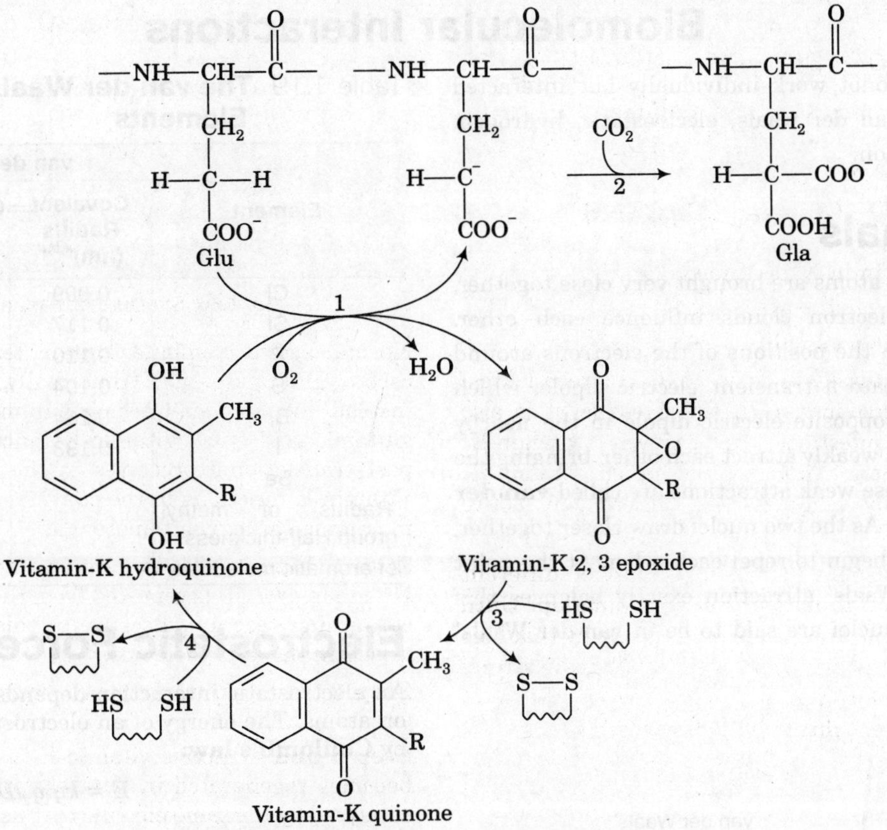

Vitamin-K hydroquinone

Vitamin-K 2, 3 epoxide

Vitamin-K quinone

Fig. 1.67 Conversion of 'glu' into 'gla'

Antioxidant Metabolite	Solubility	Concentration in Human Serum (mM)
Ascorbic acid (vitamin-C)	Water	50-60
Glutathione	Water	325-650
Lipoic acid	Water	0.1-0.7
Uric acid	Water	200-400
Carotenes	Lipid	β-carotene: 0.5-1 retinol (vitamin-A): 1-3
α-tocopherol (vitamin-E)	Lipid	10-40
Ubiquinol (coenzyme Q)	Lipid	5

Ascorbic acid is a reducing agent and can reduce and thereby neutralize reactive oxygen species such as hydrogen peroxide. In addition to its direct antioxidant effects, ascorbic acid is also a substrate for the antioxidant enzyme ascorbate peroxidase, a function that is particularly important in stress resistance in plants.

Glutathione has antioxidant properties since the thiol group in its cysteine moiety is a reducing agent and can be reversibly oxidized and reduced. In cells, glutathione is maintained in the reduced form by the enzyme glutathione reductase and in turn reduces other metabolites and enzyme systems as well as reacting directly with oxidants. Due to its high concentration and its central role in maintaining the cell's redox state, glutathione is one of the most important cellular antioxidants.

Melatonin is a powerful antioxidant that can easily cross cell membranes and the blood-brain barrier. Unlike other antioxidants, melatonin does not undergo redox cycling, which is the ability of a molecule to undergo repeated reduction and oxidation. Redox cycling may allow other antioxidants (such as vitamin-C) to act as pro-oxidants and promote free radical formation. Melatonin, once oxidized, cannot be reduced to its former state because it forms several stable end-products upon reacting with free radicals. Therefore, it has been referred to as a terminal (or suicidal) antioxidant.

Tocopherols and tocotrienols (vitamin-E) has been claimed that the α-tocopherol form is the most important lipid-soluble antioxidant, and that it protects membranes from oxidation by reacting with lipid radicals produced in the lipid peroxidation chain reaction. This reaction produces oxidized α-tocopheroxyl radicals that can be recycled back to the active reduced form through reduction by other antioxidants, such as ascorbate, retinol or ubiquinol.

Antioxidant Compound	Food Containing High Level of These Antioxidant
Vitamin-C (ascorbic acid)	Fruits and vegetables
Vitamin-E (tocopherols and tocotrienols)	Vegetable oils
Polyphenolic antioxidants (resveratrol and flavonoids)	Tea, coffee, soy, fruit, olive oil, chocolate, oregano and red wine.
Carotenoids (lycopene and carotenes)	Fruits and vegetables

Biomolecular Interactions

The biomolecules donot work individually but interacted various forces like van der waals, electrostatic, hydrogen, hydrophobic interaction.

van der Waals

When two uncharged atoms are brought very close together, their surrounding electron clouds influence each other. Random variations in the positions of the electrons around one nucleus may create a transient electric dipole, which induces a transient, opposite electric dipole in the nearby atom. The two dipoles weakly attract each other, bringing the two nuclei closer. These weak attractions are called **van der Waals interactions.** As the two nuclei draw closer together, their electron clouds begin to repel each other. At the point where the van der Waals' attraction exactly balances this repulsive force, the nuclei are said to be in van der Waals' contact.

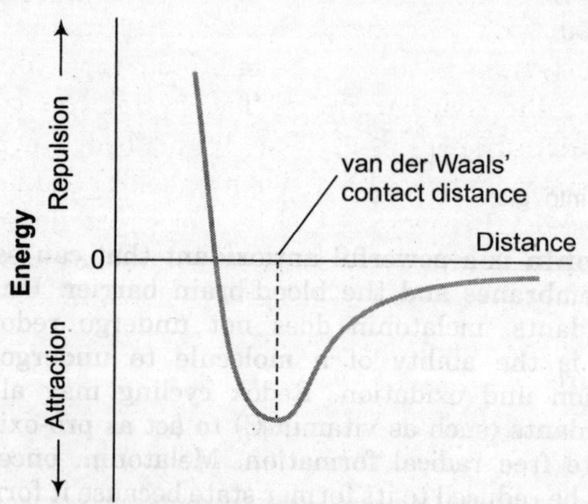

Fig. 1.68 Variation in energy of a van der Waals interaction as two atoms approach. The energy is most favorable at the van der Waals contact distance. The energy rises rapidly as the atoms move closer together than this distance.

Table 1.18 **The Sizes of Some Atoms**[a-c]

Element	Covalent Radius (nm)[a, b, d]	van der Waals' Radii (nm)[d] *a* Sideway Contact[c]	*b* Polar Contact[c]
H	0.030	0.12	
F	0.064	0.138	0.130
C	0.077	0.16	
N	0.070	0.160	0.160

Table 1.19 **The van der Waals' Radii for Some Elements**

Element	Covalent Radius (nm)[a,b,d]	van der Walls radii (nm)[d] a Sideways Contact[c]	b Polar Contact[c]
Cl	0.099	0.178	0.158
Si	0.117		
P	0.110	0.19	
S	0.104	0.203	0.160
Br	0.114	0.184	0.154
I	0.133	0.213	0.176
Se		0.215	0.170
'Radius' of methyl group Half-thickness		0.20	
of aromatic molecules		0.170	

Electrostatic Force

An electrostatic interaction depends on the electric charges on atoms. The energy of an electrostatic interaction is given by **Coulomb's law:**

$$E = kq_1q_2/Dr$$

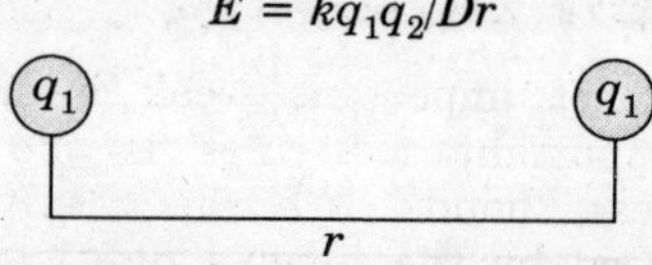

Where, E is the energy, q_1 and q_2 are the charges on the two atoms (in units of the electronic charge), r is the distance between the two atoms (in angstroms), D is the dielectric constant (which accounts for the effects of the intervening medium), and k is a proportionality constant.

Interactions between charged groups shape bimolecular structure. Electrostatic interactions between oppositely charged groups within or between biomolecules are termed **salt bridges.** Salt bridges are comparable in strength to hydrogen bonds but act over larger distances. They thus often facilitate the binding of charged molecules and ions to proteins and nucleic acids.

Fixed positive and negative charges attract each other strongly. Consider a carboxylate ion in contact with $-NH_3^+$ or with an ion of calcium:

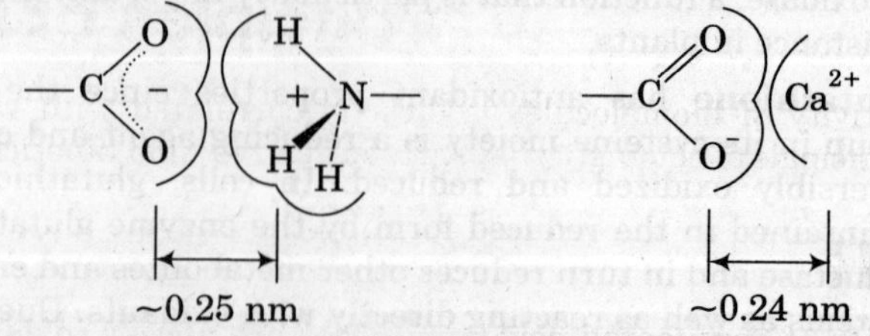

Fig. 1.69 The distance between positive and negative charges

From the van der Waals' radii of above Table and the ionic crystal radius of Ca^{2+} of 0.10 nm, we can estimate an approximate distance between the centers of positive and negative charge of 0.25 nm in both cases. It is of interest to apply Coulomb's law to compute the force F between two charged particles which are almost in contact. Let us choose a distance of 0.40 nm (4.0 Å).

$$F = 8.9875 \times 10^9 \times \frac{qq'}{r^2\varepsilon} \text{ newtons}$$

In this equation r is the distance in meters, q and q' are the charges in coulombs (one electronic charge = 1.6021×10^{-19} coulombs), is the dielectric constant, and F is the force in newtons (N).

Electrostatic forces are of great significance in interactions between molecules and in the induction of changes in conformations of molecules. For example, attraction between $—COO^-$ and $—NH^{3+}$ groups occurs in interactions between proteins. Calcium ions often interact with carboxylate groups, the doubly charged Ca^{2+} bridging between two carboxylate or other polar groups. This occurs in carbohydrates such as agarose, converting solutions of these molecules into rigid gels.

Individual macromolecules as well as cell surfaces usually carry a net negative charge at neutral pH. This causes the surfaces to repel each other. However, at a certain distance of separation the van der Waals attractive forces will balance the electrostatic repulsion.

Hydrogen Bonding

One of the most important weak interactions between biologically important molecules is the hydrogen bond (H-bond). These 'bonds' are the result of electrostatic attraction caused by the uneven distribution of electrons within covalent bonds.

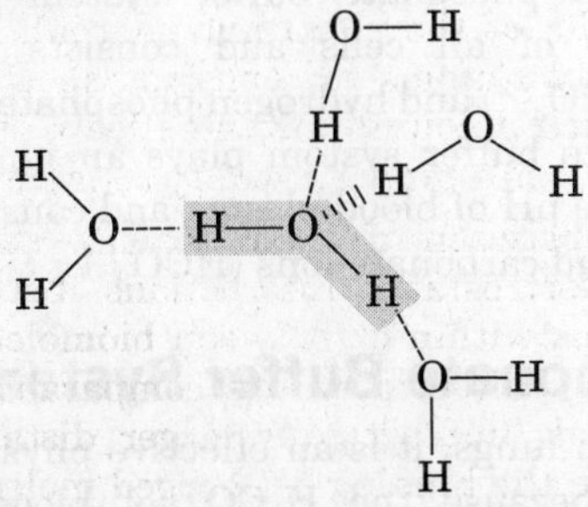

Fig. 1.70 A water molecule hydrogen bonded to four other water molecules; note the tetrahedral arrangement of bonds around the central oxygen

A hydrogen bond is formed when the positively charged end of one of the **dipoles** (polarized bonds) is attracted to the negative end of another dipole. Water molecules tend to hydrogen bond strongly one to another; each oxygen atom can be hydrogen-bonded to two other molecules and each hydrogen to another water molecule. Thus, every water molecule can have up to four hydrogen-bonded neighbours.

The strength of hydrogen bonds, as measured by the bond energy, varies over the range 10-40 kJ/mol. The stronger the hydrogen bond the shorter its length. Hydrogen bonds are strongest when the hydrogen atom and the two heavy atoms to which it is bonded are in a straight line. For this reason hydrogen bonds tend to be linear. However, **the dipoles forming the hydrogen bond do not have to be colinear for strong hydrogen bonding.**

Hydrophobic Interaction

Fats, hydrocarbons, and other materials whose molecules consist largely of nonpolar groups have a low solubility in water and a high solubility in nonpolar solvents. Similarly, the long alkyl groups of fatty acid esters aggregate within membranes and nonpolar side chains of proteins are often packed together in the centers of protein molecules. Because it is as if the nonpolar groups 'fear' water, this is known as the **hydrophobic** effect. The terms hydrophobic forces, hydrophobic interactions, and hydrophobic bonding have also been used. However, the latter term can be misleading because the hydrophobic effect arises not out of any special attraction between non-polar groups but primarily from the strong internal cohesion of the hydrogen-bonded water structure.

When two hydrophobic groups come together to form a 'hydrophobic bond,' water molecules are freed from the structured region around the hydrophobic surfaces and the entropy increases. Various efforts have been made to develop scales of **hydrophobicity** that can be used to predict the probability of finding a given amino acid side chain buried within a protein or in a surface facing water.

Principles of Biophysical Chemistry

Activity of biomolecules is directly correlated with various principals of chemistry like, pH, buffer, reaction kinetics, etc.

pH

Pairs of **conjugated** acids and bases are always involved in proton exchange reactions. The dissociation state of an acid–base pair depends on the H^+ concentration. It is not this concentration itself that is expressed, but its negative decadic logarithm, the **pH value.** The connection between the pH value and the dissociation state is described by the **Henderson–Hasselbalch eqation.**

Standard reaction $HA + H_2O \rightleftharpoons A^{\ominus} + H_3O^{\oplus}$

Law of mass action $K = \dfrac{[A^{\ominus}]\cdot[H_3O^{\oplus}]}{[HA]\cdot[H_2O]}$

Simplified $K_a = \dfrac{[A^{\ominus}]\cdot[H^{\oplus}]}{[HA]}$

Henderson-Hasslbalch equation $pH = pK_a + \log \frac{[A^{\ominus}]}{[HA]}$

Measure of proton transfer potential

As a measure of the **proton transfer potential** of an acid–base pair, its **pK_a value** is used-the negative logarithm of the acid constant K (where *'a'* stands for acid). The *stronger* an acid is, the *lower* its pK_a value. The acid of the pair with the lower pK_a value (the stronger acid-in this case is acetic acid, CH_3COOH) can protonate the base of the pair with the higher pK_a (in this case is NH_3), while ammonium acetate (NH_4^+ and CH_3COO^-) only forms very little CH_3COOH and NH_3.

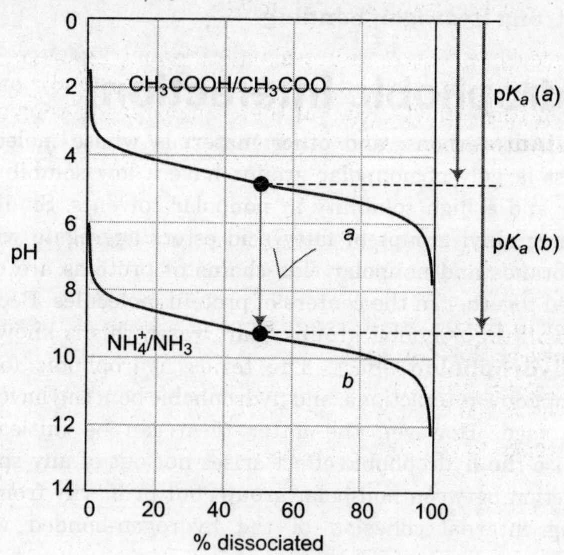

Fig. 1.71 pH correponds to pK_a value

Buffer

A mixture of a weak acid HA and its **conjugate base** A constitutes a buffer which resists changes in pH. This can be seen most readily by taking logarithms of both sides of following equation:

$$HA = A^- + H^+$$

$$K_a = [A^-]\,[H^+]/[HA]$$

where, K_a is acid dissociation constant

By replacing $\log K$ with $-pK_a$ and $\log [H^+]$ with $-pH$ and rearranging we obtain following equation (the Henderson–Hasselbalch equation):

$$pH - pK_a = \log([A]/[HA])$$

It is sometimes useful to rewrite this as,

$$pH - pK_a = \log[\alpha/(1-\alpha)];$$

$$\alpha = [A]/[HA] + [A] = \frac{10^{(pH - pK_a)}}{1 + 10^{(pH - pK_a)}}$$

where, is the fraction of the acid that is dissociated at a given pH.

Buffers are often added to maintain a constant pH in biochemical research and naturally occurring buffer systems within body fluids and cells are very important. Among the most important natural buffers are the proteins themselves, with the imidazole groups of histidine side chains providing much of the buffering capacity of cells around pH 7.

A plot of the dependence of the pH of this solution on the amount of OH— added is called a **titration curve.**

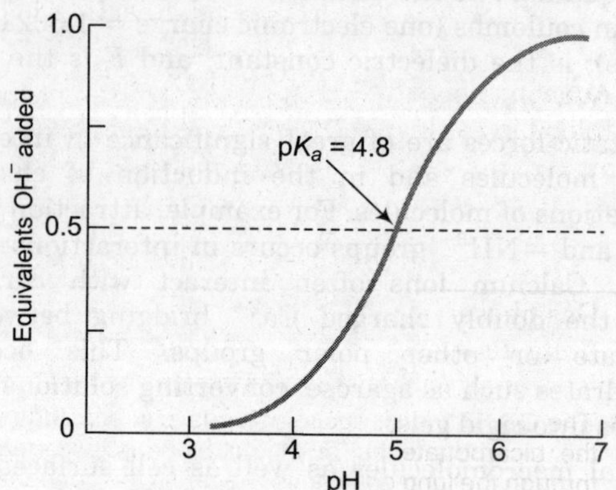

Fig. 1.72 Titration curve of acetic acid

Note that there is an inflection point in the curve at pH 4.8, which is the pK_a of acetic acid. In the vicinity of this pH, a relatively large amount of OH— produces little change in pH. In other words, the buffer maintains the value of pH near a given value, despite the addition of other either protons or hydroxide ions. In general, a weak acid is most effective in buffering against pH changes in the vicinity of its pK_a value.

Two biological buffers (phosphate and bicarbonate) are very important. The phosphate buffer system is effective in internal fluids of all cells and consists of dihydrogan phosphate ($H_2PO_4^{-2}$) and hydrogen phosphate (HPO_4^{-2}) ions. The bicarbonate buffer system plays an important role in maintaining the pH of blood plasma and consists of carbonic acid (H_2CO_3) and carbonate ions (HCO_3^-).

The Bicarbonate Buffer System

In animals with lungs, it is an effective physiological buffer near pH 7.4 because the H_2CO_3 of blood plama is in equilibrium with a large reserve capacity of $CO_2(g)$ in the air space of the lungs. This buffer system involves three reversible equilibria between gaseous CO_2 in the lungs and bicarbonate (HCO_3^-) in the blood plasma (**Fig. 1.72**). When H^+ (from lactic acid produced in muscle tissue for example) is added to blood as it passes through the tissues, reaction 1 proceeds toward a new equilibrium, in which the concentration of H_2CO_3 is increased. This increases the concentration of $CO_2(d)$ in the blood plasma (reaction 2) and thus increases the pressure of $CO_2(g)$ in the air space of the lungs (reaction 3); the extra CO_2 is exhaled.

Conversely, when the pH of blood plasma is raised (by NH_3 production during protein catabolism, for example), the opposite events occur the H^+ concentration of blood plasma is lowered, causing more H_2CO_3 to dissociate into H^+ and HCO^-_3. This in turn causes more $CO_2(g)$ from the lungs to dissolve in the blood plasma. The rate of breathing—that is, the rate of inhaling and exhaling CO_2—can quickly these equilibria to keep the blood pH nearly constant.

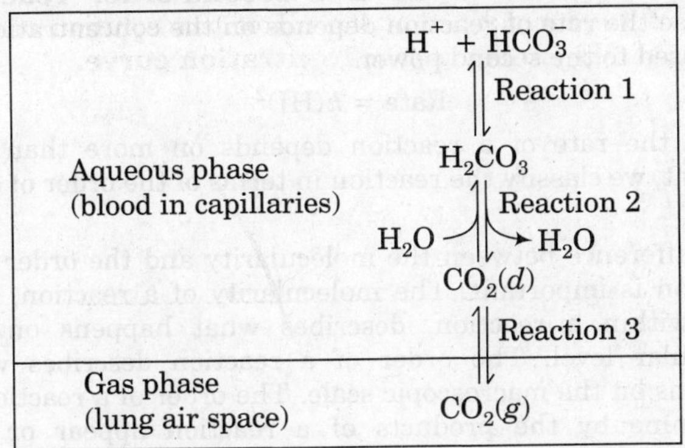

Fig. 1.73 The CO_2 in the air space of lungs is in equilibrium with the bicarbonate buffer in the blood plasma passing through the lung capillaries. Because the concentration of dissolved CO_2 can be adjusted rapidly through changes in the rate of breathing, the bicarbonate buffer system of the blood is in near-equilibrium with a large potential reservoir of CO_2.

Reaction (Chemical) Kinetics

Chemical kinetics (reaction kinetics) is the study of rates of chemical processes. Chemical kinetics investigations how different experimental conditions can influence the speed of a chemical reaction and It provides information about the reaction's mechanism, transition states, and the characteristics of a chemical reaction.

In 1864, **Peter Waage** and **Cato Guldberg** formulating the **law of mass action** which is the start point of development of chemical kinetics. The law of mass action determining the speed of a chemical reaction which is proportional to the quantity of the reacting substances.

The **chemical kinetics** (from a Greek stem meaning 'to move') describes the **rate of reaction**-the rate at which the reactants are transformed into the products of the reaction.

The term rate is often used to describe the change in a quantity that occurs per unit of time. In chemical kinetics, the rate of a reaction is therefore, the change in the concentration of one of the reactants $\Delta(x)$ that occurs during a given period of time Δt.

$$\text{Rate of reaction} = \frac{\Delta x}{\Delta t}$$

Instantaneous Rates of Reaction and the Rate Law for a Reaction

In most reactions, the rate of chemical reaction gradually decreases as the reactants are consumed. This means that the rate of reaction changes while it is being measured.

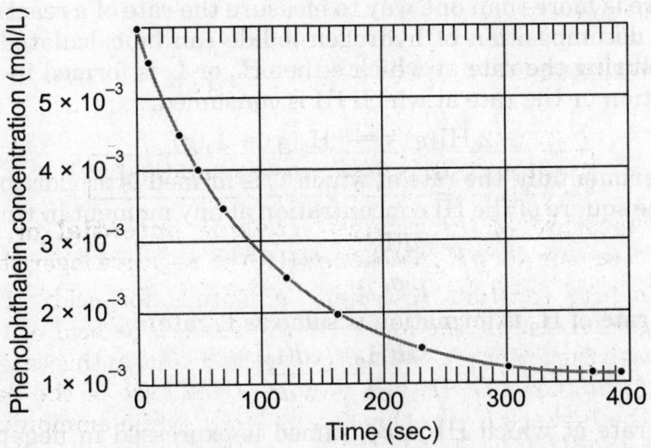

Fig. 1.74 The experiment show the decrease in phenolphthalein concentration in respect to time

The measure the infinitesimally small change in concentration $d(x)$ that occurs over an infinitesimally short period of time dt. The ratio of these quantities is known as the **instantaneous rate of reaction.**

$$\text{Rate} = \frac{d(x)}{dt}$$

The instantaneous rate of reaction at any moment in time can be calculated from a graph of the concentration of the reactant (or product) *versus* time. The rate of reaction at any moment in time is equal to the slope of a tangent drawn to this curve at that moment.

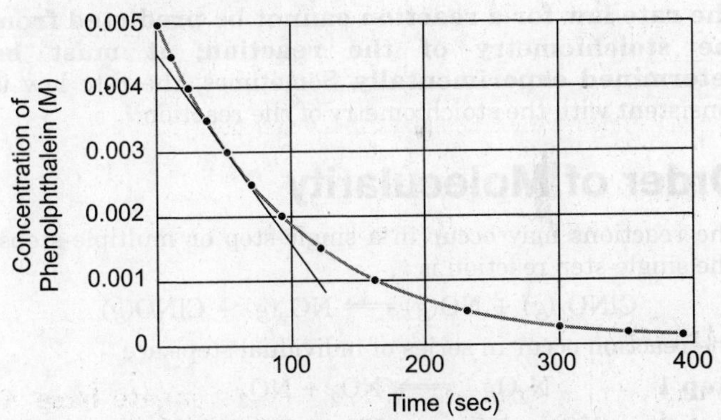

Fig. 1.75 The instantaneous rate of reaction

The instantaneous rate of reaction can be measured at any time between the moment at which the reactants are mixed and the reaction reaches equilibrium.

Rate Laws and Rate Constants

The instantaneous rate of reaction is calculated at various points along the curve in the graph. The rate of reaction at every point on this curve is directly proportional to the concentration of phenolphthalein at that moment in time.

$$\text{Rate} = k\,(\text{phenolphthalein})$$

Because this equation is an experimental law that describes the rate of the reaction, it is called the **rate law** for the reaction. The proportionality constant, k, is known as the **rate constant.**

There is more than one way to measure the rate of a reaction. The decomposition of hydrogen iodide can be calculated by measuring the rate at which either H_2 or I_2 is formed in the reaction or the rate at which HI is consumed.

$$2\,HI(g) \rightleftharpoons H_2(g) + I_2(g)$$

Experimentally, the rate at which I_2 is formed is proportional to the square of the HI concentration at any moment in time.

$$\frac{d(I_2)}{dt} = k(HI)^2$$

The rate of H_2 is formation is same as I_2 rate.

$$\frac{d(H_2)}{dt} = \frac{d(I_2)}{dt}$$

The rate at which HI is consumed is expressed in negative number. By convention, the rate of a reaction is always reported as a positive number.

$$-\frac{d(HI)}{dt} = k'(HI)^2$$

The stoichiometry of the reaction says that two HI molecules are consumed for every molecule of H_2 or I_2 produced. Mathematical it can be xepress as follows.

$$-\frac{d(HI)}{dt} = 2\left\{\frac{d(H_2)}{dt}\right\} = 2\left\{\frac{d(I_2)}{dt}\right\}$$

The rate constant obtained from studying the rate at which H_2 and I_2 are formed in the reaction (k) is not the same as the rate constant obtained by monitoring the rate at which HI is consumed (k')

The rate law for a reaction cannot be predicted from the stoichiometry of the reaction; it must be determined experimentally. Sometimes, the rate law is consistent with the stoichiometry of the reaction.

Order of Molecularity

The reactions may occur in a single-step or multiple-steps. The single-step reaction is

$$ClNO_2(g) + NO(g) \rightleftharpoons NO_2(g) + ClNO(g)$$

The reaction occur in series of individual steps are

Step 1 $N_2O_5 \rightleftharpoons NO_2 + NO_3$

Step 2 $NO_2 + NO_3 \rightleftharpoons NO_2 + NO + O_2$

Step 3 $NO + NO_3 \rightleftharpoons 2\,NO_2$

The steps in a reaction are classified in terms of **Molecularity**, which describes the number of molecules consumed. When a single molecule is consumed, the step is called **unimolecular**. When two molecules are consumed, it is **bimolecular.**

Reactions can also be classified in terms of their **order**. The decomposition of N_2O_5 is a **first-order reaction** because the rate of reaction depends on the concentration of N_2O_5 raised to the first power.

$$\text{Rate} = k(N_2O_5)$$

The decomposition of HI is a **second-order reaction** because the rate of reaction depends on the concentration of HI raised to the second power.

$$\text{Rate} = k(HI)^2$$

When the rate of a reaction depends on more than one reagent, we classify the reaction in terms of the order of each reagent.

The difference between the molecularity and the order of a reaction is important. The molecularity of a reaction, or a step within a reaction, describes what happens on the molecular level. The order of a reaction describes what happens on the macroscopic scale. The order of a reaction is determine by the products of a reaction appear or the reactants disappear.

Elementary Processes or Steps

In the table below, A, B and C represent reactants, intermediates, or products in the elementary process.

Molecularity	Elementary Step	Rate Law
1	$A \rightarrow$ products	rate = $k\,[A]$
2	$A + A \rightarrow$ products	rate = $k\,[A]^2$
	$A + B \rightarrow$ products	rate = $k\,[A]\,[B]$
3	$A + A + A \rightarrow$ products	rate = $k\,[A]^3$
	$A + 2\,B \rightarrow$ products	rate = $k\,[A]\,[B]^2$
	$A + B + C \rightarrow$ products	rate = $k\,[A]\,[B]\,[C]$

Zero-Order Reactions

A **zero-order reaction** has a rate which is independent of the concentration of the reactant(s). Increasing the concentration of the reacting species will not speed up the rate of the reaction. Zero-order reactions are typically found when a material required for the reaction to proceed, such as a surface or a catalyst is saturated by the reactants. The rate law for a zero-order reaction is

$$r = k$$

where, r is the reaction rate and k is the reaction rate coefficient with units of concentration/time. If, and only if, this zero-order reaction. 1) occurs in a closed system, 2) there is no net build-up of intermediates and 3) there are no other reactions occurring.

Table 1.20 **Summary for Reaction Orders 0, 1, 2 and *n***

	Zero-order	First-order	Second-order	nth-order
Rate law	$-\frac{d[A]}{dt} = k$	$-\frac{d[A]}{dt} = k[A]$	$-\frac{d[A]}{dt} = k[A]^2$	$-\frac{d[A]}{dt} = k[A]^n$
Integrated rate law	$[A] = [A]_0 - kt$	$[A] = [A]_0 e^{-kt}$	$\frac{1}{[A]} = \frac{1}{[A]_0} + kt$	$\frac{1}{[A]^{n-1}} = \frac{1}{[A]_0^{n-1}} + (n-1)\,kt$ (Except first order)
Unit of rate constant (*k*)	$\frac{M}{s}$	$\frac{1}{s}$	$\frac{1}{M \cdot s}$	$\frac{1}{M^{n-1}.s}$
Linear plot to determine *k*	$[A]$ vs $\cdot t$	$\ln[A]$ vs $\cdot t$	$\frac{1}{[A]}$ vs $\cdot t$	$\frac{1}{[A]^{n-1}}$ vs $\cdot t$ (Except first order)
Half-life	$t_{1/2} = \frac{[A]_0}{2k}$	$t_{1/2} = \frac{\ln(2)}{k}$	$t_{1/2} = \frac{1}{[A]_0 k}$	$t_{1/2} = \frac{2^{n-1}-1}{(n-1)\,k\,[A_0]^{n-1}}$ (Except first order)

where, *M* stands for concentration (mol · L^{-1}), *t* for time and *k* for the reaction rate constant.

The rate laws for chemical reactions can be explained by the following general rules.

- The rate of any step in a reaction is directly proportional to the concentrations of the reagents consumed in that step.
- The overall rate law for a reaction is determined by the sequence of steps, or the **mechanism**, by which the reactants are converted into the products of the reaction.
- The overall rate law for a reaction is dominated by the rate law for the slowest step in the reaction.

Factors Influence Reaction Rates

Many factors influence rates of chemical reactions, and these are summarized below.

(a) **Nature of reactants** Acid-base reactions, formation of salts, and exchange of ions are fast reactions. Reactions in which large molecules are formed or break apart are usually slow. Reactions breaking strong covalent bonds are also slow.

(b) **Temperature** Usually, the higher the temperature, the faster the reaction. The temperature effect is discussed in terms of activation energy.

(c) **Concentration Effect** The dependences of reaction rates on concentrations are called rate laws. Rate laws are expressions of rates in terms of concentrations of reactants. They are called differential rate laws and integrated rate laws.

(d) Rate laws apply to **homogeneous reactions** in which all reactants and products are in one phase (solution).

(e) Heterogeneous reactions Reactants are present in more than one phase.

For heterogeneous reactions, the rates are affected by surface areas.

(f) **Catalysts** Substances used to facilitate reactions, catalysts play important roles in chemical reactions.

Example 1 Use the data in the above table to calculate the rate at which phenolphthalein reacts with the OH^- ion during each of the following periods:

(a) During the first time interval, when the phenolphthalein concentration falls from 0.0050 M to 0.0045 M.

(b) During the second interval, when the concentration falls from 0.0045 M to 0.0040 M.

(c) During the third interval, when the concentration falls from 0.0040 M to 0.0035 M.

Solution The rate of reaction is equal to the change in the phenolphthalein concentration divided by the length of time over which this change occurs.

(a) During the first time period, the rate of the reaction is 4.8 × 10^{-5} moles per liter per second:

$$\text{Rate} = \frac{\Delta(x)}{\Delta t} = \frac{(0.0050\,M) - (0.0045\,M)}{(10.5s - 0s)}$$

$$= 4.8 \times 10^{-5}\ M/s$$

(b) During the second time period, the rate of reaction is slightly smaller:

$$\text{Rate} = \frac{\Delta(x)}{\Delta t} = \frac{(0.0045\,M) - (0.0040\,M)}{(22.3s - 10.5s)}$$

$$= 4.2 \times 10^{-5}\ M/s$$

(c) During the third time period, the rate of reaction is even smaller:

$$\text{Rate} = \frac{\Delta(x)}{\Delta t} = \frac{(0.0040\,M) - (0.0035\,M)}{(35.7s - 22.3s)}$$

$$= 3.7 \times 10^{-5}\ M/s$$

Example 2 Calculate the rate constant for the reaction between phenolphthalein and the OH^- ion if the instantaneous rate of reaction is 2.5 × 10^{-5} mole per liter per second when the concentration of phenolphthalein is 0.0025 M.

Solution We start with the rate law for this reaction:

$$\text{Rate} = k\,(\text{phenolphthalein})$$

We then substitute the known rate of reaction and the known concentration of phenolphthalein into this equation:

$$\frac{2.5 \times 10^{-5}\ \text{mol/L}}{1\text{s}} = k\,(0.0025\ \text{mol/L})$$

Solving for the rate constant gives the following result:

$$k = 0.010\ \text{s}^{-1}$$

Example 3 Use the rate constant for the reaction between phenolphthalein and the OH^- ion to calculate the initial instantaneous rate of reaction for the experimental data listed in the preceding table.

Solution Substituting the rate constant for the reaction from the preceding problem and the initial concentration of phenolphthalein into the rate law for this reaction gives the following:

$$\begin{aligned}\text{Rate} &= k\,(\text{phenolphthalein})\\ &= (0.010\ \text{s}^{-1})(0.0050\ \text{mol/L})\\ &= 5.0 \times 10^{-5}\ (\text{mol/L})/\text{s}\end{aligned}$$

Because the rate of reaction is the change in the concentration of phenolphthalein divided by the time over which the change occurs, it is reported in units of moles per liter per second. Because the number of moles of phenolphthalein per liter is the molarity of this solution, the rate can also be reported in terms of the change in molarity per second: M/s.

Example 4 Calculate the rate at which HI disappears in the following reaction at the moment when I_2 is being formed at a rate of 1.8×10^{-6} moles per liter per second:

$$2HI(g) \longrightarrow H_2(g) + I_2(g)$$

Solution The balanced equation for the reaction shows that 2 moles of HI disappear for every mole of I_2 formed. Thus, HI is consumed in this reaction twice as fast as I_2 is formed:

$$-\frac{d(HI)}{dt} = \frac{d(I_2)}{dt} = \frac{2(1.8 \times 10^{6})\ \text{mol/L}}{1\text{s}}$$

$$= 3.6 \times 10^{-6}\ \text{M/s}$$

Students sometimes get the wrong answer to this exercise because they become confused about whether the equation for the calculation should be written as:

$$-\frac{d(HI)}{dt} = 2\,\frac{d(I_2)}{dt}$$

or as:

$$\frac{d(I_2)}{dt} = 2\,\frac{d(HI)}{dt}$$

You can avoid mistakes by checking to see whether your answer makes sense. The balanced equation states that 2 moles of HI are consumed for every mole of I_2 produced. HI should therefore, disappear (3.6×10^{-6} M/s) twice as fast as I_2 is formed (1.8×10^{-6} M/s).

Example 5 Determine the molecularity of each step in the reaction by which N_2O_5 decomposes to NO_2 and O_2.

Solution All we have to do is count the number of molecules consumed in each step in this reaction to decide that the first step is unimolecular and the other two steps are bimolecular:

Step 1 $N_2O_5 \rightleftharpoons NO_2 + NO_3$

Step 2 $NO_2 + NO_3 \rightleftharpoons NO_2 + NO + O_2$

Step 3 $NO + NO_3 \rightleftharpoons 2\,NO_2$

Example 6 Classify the order of the reaction between NO and O_2 to form NO_2:

$$2NO(g) + O_2(g) \longrightarrow 2\,NO_2(g)$$

Assume the following rate law for this reaction:

$$\text{Rate} = k(NO)^2(O_2)$$

Solution This reaction is first-order in O_2, second-order in NO, and third-order overall.

Thermodynamics

Thermodynamics is the branch of science that deals with the relationship between heat and other forms of energy, such as work. It can be summarized as three laws that describe restrictions on how different forms of energy can be interconverted. **Chemical thermodynamics** is the portion of thermodynamics that pertains to chemical reactions.

The Laws of Thermodynamics

First law Energy is conserved; it can be neither created nor destroyed.

Second law In an isolated system, natural processes are spontaneous when they lead to an increase in disorder, or entropy.

Third law The entropy of a perfect crystal is zero when the temperature of the crystal is equal to absolute zero (0 K).

The System and Surroundings

One of the basic assumptions of thermodynamics is the idea that we can arbitrarily divide the universe into a **system** and its **surroundings.** The boundary between the system and its surroundings can be as real as the walls of a beaker that separates a solution from the rest of the universe (as shown in the figure below).

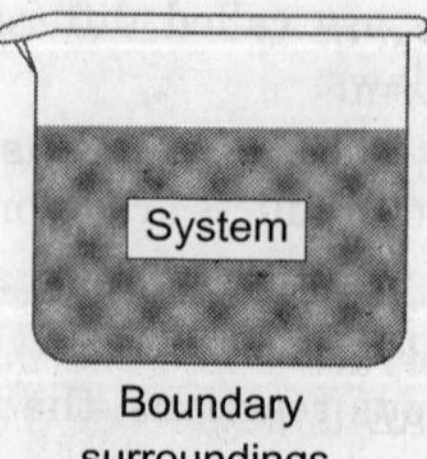

Fig. 1.76 System in universe

Or it can be as imaginary as the set of points that divide the air just above the surface of a metal from the rest of the atmosphere.

If no heat enters or leaves the system during any step of the process it, is called **adiabatic process.**

Internal Energy

One of the thermodynamic properties of a system is its **internal energy,** denoted by U, or sometimes E, which is the sum of the potential and kinetic energies (translational, rotational, vibration motion of molecules) of the particles that form the system. The internal energy of a system can be understood by examining the simplest possible system: an ideal gas. Because the particles in an ideal gas do not interact, this system has no potential energy. The internal energy of an ideal gas is therefore the sum of the kinetic energies of the particles in the gas.

The kinetic molecular theory assumes that the temperature of a gas is directly proportional to the average kinetic energy of its particles. The internal energy of an ideal gas is therefore, directly proportional to the temperature of the gas.

$$E_{sys} = \frac{3}{2}RT$$

In this equation, R is the ideal gas constant in joules per mole Kelvin (J/mol-K) and T is the temperature in Kelvin.

The internal energy of systems is more complex than an ideal gas and can't be measured directly. But the internal energy of the system is still proportional to its temperature. It is not possible to monitor changes in the internal energy of a system by watching the temperature of the system. Whenever the temperature of the system increases it can conclude that the internal energy of the system has also increased.

Any change in the internal energy of the system is equal to the difference between its initial and final values.

$$\Delta E_{sys} = E_f - E_i$$

The First Law of Thermodynamics

The first law of thermodynamics states that the energy of the universe is constant. Energy can be transferred from the system to its surroundings, or *vice versa,* but it can't be created or destroyed.

First Law of Thermodynamics:

$$\Delta E_{univ} = \Delta E_{sys} + \Delta E_{surr} = 0$$

The first law describes how energy is conserved. It says that the change in the internal energy of a system is equal to the sum of the heat gained or lost by the system and the work done by or on the system.

First Law of Thermodynamics:

$$\Delta E_{sys} = q + w$$

When the system gains heat from its surroundings, as a result, both the temperature and the internal energy of the system increase, the ΔE is **positive.** When the system loses heat to its surroundings, as a result, both the temperature and the internal energy of the system decreases, the ΔE is **negative.**

The sign conventions for heat, work, and internal energy are summarized in the figure below. The internal energy and temperature of a system decrease ($\Delta E < 0$) when the system either loses heat or does work on its surroundings. Conversely, the internal energy and temperature increase ($\Delta E > 0$) when the system gains heat from its surroundings or when the surroundings do work on the system.

Fig. 1.77 Working of a system

Enthalpy *vs* Internal Energy

Under a set of conditions where no work is done by the system on its surroundings, or *vice versa*, during a chemical reaction, the heat given off or absorbed by the reaction would be equal to the change in the internal energy of the system.

$$\Delta E_{sys} = q \text{ (if and only if } w = 0)$$

At constant volume, the heat given off or absorbed by the reaction is equal to the change in the internal energy that occurs during the reaction.

$$\Delta E_{sys} = q_v \text{ (at constant volume)}$$

The internal energy of the system is the heat lost or gained by the system and work done by or on system is

$$\Delta E_{sys} = q + w$$

The **enthalpy** (H) is the sum of the internal energy of the system plus the product of the pressure of the gas in the system times the volume of the system.

$$H_{sys} = E_{sys} + pV$$

The relationship can be abbreviated as follows.

$$H = E + pV$$

The change in the enthalpy of the system during a chemical reaction is equal to the change in its internal energy plus the change in the product of the pressure times the volume of the system.

$$\Delta H = \Delta E + \Delta(pV)$$

If the reaction is run at constant pressure, the change in the enthalpy that occurs during the reaction is equal to the change in the internal energy of the system plus the product of the constant pressure times the change in the volume of the system.

$$\Delta H = \Delta E + p\Delta V \text{ (at constant pressure)}$$

Substituting the first law of thermodynamics into this equation gives the following result.

$$\Delta H = (q_p + w) + p\Delta V$$

Assuming that the only work done by the reaction is work of expansion gives an equation in which the $p\Delta V$ terms cancel.

$$\Delta H = (q_p - p\Delta V) + p\Delta V$$

Thus, the heat given off or absorbed during a chemical reaction at constant pressure is equal to the change in the enthalpy of the system.

$$\Delta H = q_p \text{ (at constant pressure)}$$

The relationship between the change in the internal energy of the system during a chemical reaction and the enthalpy of reaction can be summarized as follows.

1. The heat given off or absorbed when a reaction is run at **constant volume** is equal to the change in the internal energy of the system.
$$\Delta E_{sys} = q_v$$
2. The heat given off or absorbed when a reaction is run at **constant pressure** is equal to the change in the enthalpy of the system.
$$\Delta H_{sys} = q_p$$
3. The change in the enthalpy of the system during a chemical reaction is equal to the change in the internal energy plus the change in the product of the pressure of the gas in the system and its volume.
$$\Delta H_{sys} = \Delta E_{sys} + \Delta(pV)$$
4. The difference between ΔE and ΔH for the system is small for reactions that involve only liquids and solids because there is little if any change in the volume of the system during the reaction. The difference can be relatively large, however, for reactions that involve gases, if there is a change in the number of moles of gas in the course of the reaction.

Example 7 Which of the following processes are run at constant volume and which are run at constant pressure?

(a) An acid-base titration

(b) Decomposing $CaCO_3$ by heating limestone in a crucible with a bunsen burner

(c) The reaction bewteen zinc metal and an aqueous solution of Cu^{2+} ions to form copper metal and Zn^{2+} ions

(d) Measuring the calories in a 1-oz. serving of breakfast cereal by burning the cereal in a bomb calorimeter

Solution Processes (a), (b) and (c) are all run under conditions of constant pressure. Only (d) is run at constant volume.

Spontaneous Chemical Reactions

Many chemical and physical processes are reversible and yet tend to proceed in a direction in which they are said to be **spontaneous.** Many spontaneous reactions are exothermic, the driving forces that determines whether a reaction is spontaneous is a tendency to give off energy. The following are all examples of spontaneous chemical reactions that are exothermic.

$$2\,Al(s) + 3\,Br_2(l) \longrightarrow 2AlBr_3(s); \quad \Delta H^o = -511 \text{ kJ/mol } AlBr_3$$

$$2\,H_2(g) + O_2(g) \longrightarrow 2H_2O(g); \quad \Delta H^o = -241.82 \text{ kJ/mol } H_2O$$

$$P_4(s) + 5\,O_2(g) \longrightarrow P_4O_{10}(s); \quad \Delta H^o = -2984 \text{ kJ/mol } P_4O_{10}$$

There are spontaneous reactions that absorb energy from their surroundings. On dissolving Ammonium nitrate spontaneously in water, the energy is absorbed during the reaction.

$$NH_4NO_3(s) \xrightarrow{H_2O} NH_4^+(aq) + NO_3^-(aq); \quad \Delta H^o = 28.05 \text{ kJ/mol}$$

The tendency of a spontaneous reaction to give off energy is one of the driving force behind a chemical reaction. The another factor that determine a spontaneous reaction is known as **entropy,** it is a measure of the disorder of the system.

Entropy as a Measure of Disorder

In 1877 **Ludwig Boltzmann** introduced the concept of the **entropy** of a system as a measure of the amount of disorder in the system. In an ordered system the entropy of the system is zero. The entropy of the system increases with the disorderness of the system.

Boltzmann proposed the following equation to describe the relationship between entropy and the amount of disorder in a system.

$$S = k \ln W$$

In this equation, S is the entropy of the system, k is a proportionality constant equal to the ideal gas constant divided by Avogadro's constant, ln represents a logarithm to the base e, and W is the number of equivalent ways of describing the state of the system. According to this equation, the entropy of a system increases as the number of equivalent ways of describing the state of the system increases.

Entropy and the Second Law of Thermodynamics

The second law of thermodynamics describes the relationship between entropy and the spontaneity of natural processes.

Second Law In an isolated system, natural processes are spontaneous when they lead to an increase in disorder, or entropy.

This statement is restricted to isolated systems; neither heat nor work can be transferred between an isolated system and its surroundings.

The entropy of a system is a state function that is directly proportional to the disorder of the system.

$\Delta S_{sys} > 0$ implies that the system becomes **more disordered** during the reaction.

$\Delta S_{sys} < 0$ implies that the system becomes **less disordered** during the reaction.

For an isolated system, any process that leads to an increase in the disorder of the system will be spontaneous. The following generalizations can help us decide when a chemical reaction leads to an increase in the disorder of the system.

- Solids have a much more regular structure than liquids. Liquids are therefore more disordered than solids.

- The particles in a gas are in a state of constant, random motion. Gases are therefore more disordered than the corresponding liquids.
- Any process that increases the number of particles in the system increases the amount of disorder.

The sign of ΔH for a chemical reaction affects the direction in which the reaction occurs.

Spontaneous reactions often, but not always, give off energy.

The sign of ΔS for a reaction can also determine the direction of the reaction.

In an isolated system, chemical reactions occur in the direction that leads to an increase in the disorder of the system.

In order to decide whether a reaction is spontaneous, it is therefore important to consider the effect of changes in both enthalpy and entropy that occur during the reaction.

Third Law of Thermodynamics

The third law of thermodynamics defines absolute zero on the entropy scale.

The entropy of a perfect crystal is zero when the temperature of the crystal is equal to absolute zero (0 K).

The crystal must be perfect, or else there will be some inherent disorder. It also must be at 0 K; otherwise there will be thermal motion within the crystal, which leads to disorder.

As the crystal warms to temperatures above 0 K, the particles in the crystal start to move, generating some disorder. The entropy of the crystal gradually increases with temperature as the average kinetic energy of the particles increases. The table below provides an example of the difference between the entropy of a substance in the solid, liquid, and gaseous phases.

The entropy of solid, liquid, and gaseous forms of sulphur trioxide.

Compound	So (J/mol-K)
$SO_3(s)$	70.7
$SO_3(l)$	113.8
$SO_3(g)$	256.76

The entropy ΔS of a chemical reaction is equal to the difference between the sum of the entropies of the reactants and the products of the reaction.

$$\Delta S = \sum S(\text{products}) - \sum S(\text{reactants})$$

When this difference is measured under standard-state conditions, the result is the **standard-state entropy of reaction, ΔS^o**.

$$\Delta S^o = \sum S^o(\text{products}) - \sum S^o(\text{reactants})$$

Although standard-state entropies can be measured at any temperature, they are often measured at 25°C.

Example 8 Calculate the standard-state entropy of reaction for the following reactions and explain the sign of ΔS for each reaction.

(a) $Hg(l) \rightleftharpoons Hg(g)$

(b) $2NO_2(g) \rightleftharpoons N_2O_4(g)$

(c) $N_2(g) + O_2(g) \rightleftharpoons 2NO(g)$

Solution

(a) Using a standard-state entropy data table, we find the following information:

Compound	S° (J/mol-K)
Hg(l)	76.02
Hg(s)	174.96

The balanced equation states that 1 mole of mercury vapor is produced for each mole of liquid mercury that boils. The standard-state entropy of reaction is therefore, calculated as follows:

$$\Delta S^o = \sum S^o(\text{products}) - \sum S^o(\text{reactants})$$
$$= [1 \text{ mol Hg(g)} \times 174.96 \text{ J/mol-K}] - [1 \text{ mol Hg}(l) \times 76.02 \text{ J/mol-K}]$$
$$= 98.94 \text{ J/K}$$

The sign of ΔS^o is positive because this process transforms a liquid into a gas, which is inherently more disordered.

(b) Using a standard-state entropy data table, we find the following information:

Compound	S°(J/mol-K)
$NO_2(g)$	240.06
$N_2O_4(g)$	304.29

In this equation, 1 mole of N_2O_4 is formed for every mole of NO_2 consumed, and the value of ΔS^o is calculated as follows:

$$\Delta S^o = \sum S^o(\text{products}) - \sum S^o(\text{reactants})$$
$$= [1 \text{ mol } N_2O_4(g) \times 304.29 \text{ J/mol-K}] - [2 \text{ mol } NO_2(l) \times 240.06 \text{ J/mol-K}]$$
$$= -175.83 \text{ J/K}$$

The sign of ΔS^o is negative because two molecules combine in this reaction to form a larger, more ordered product.

(c) Using a standard-state entropy data table, we find the following information:

Compound	S°(J/mol-K)
NO(g)	210.76
$N_2(g)$	191.61
$O_2(g)$	205.14

The balanced equation for this reaction indicates that 2 mole of NO are produced when 1 mol of N_2 reacts with 1 mole of O_2. Thus, the standard-state entropy of reaction is calculated as follows:

$$\Delta S^o = \sum S^o(\text{products}) - \sum S^o(\text{reactants})$$
$$= [2 \text{ mol NO} \times 210.76 \text{ J/mol-K}] - [1 \text{ mol } N_2 \times 191/61 \text{ J/mol-K} + 1 \text{ mol } O_2 \times 205.14 \text{ J/mol-K}]$$
$$= 24.77 \text{ J/K}$$

ΔS^o for this reaction is small but positive because the product of the reaction (NO) is slightly more disordered that the reactants (N_2 and O_2).

The Difference between Enthalpy of Reaction and Entropy of Reaction

Thermodynamic data for aluminium and its compounds

Substance	DHFo(kJ/mol)	So (J/mol-K)
Al(s)	0	28.33
Al(g)	326.4	164.54
$Al_2O_3(s)$	–1675.7	50.92
$AlCl_3(s)$	–704.2	110.67

The enthalpy of formation of $AlCl_3$, is the heat given off during the reaction.

The absolute entropy of any element or compound can be measured by comparing it with a perfect crystal at absolute zero. The entropy data are therefore, given as absolute numbers, S^o, not entropies of formation, $\Delta S^o{}_f$.

Gibbs Free Energy

Some reactions are spontaneous because they give off energy in the form of heat ($\Delta H < 0$). Others are spontaneous because they lead to an increase in the disorder of the system ($\Delta S > 0$). Calculations of ΔH and ΔS can be used to probe the driving force behind a particular reaction.

The **Gibbs free energy** (G) of a system at any moment in time is defined as the enthalpy of the system minus the product of the temperature times the entropy of the system.

$$G = H - TS$$

The Gibbs free energy of the system is a state function because it is defined in terms of thermodynamic properties that are state functions. The change in the Gibbs free energy of the system that occurs during a reaction is therefore, equal to the change in the enthalpy of the system minus the change in the product of the temperature times the entropy of the system.

$$\Delta G = \Delta H - \Delta(TS)$$

If the reaction is run at constant temperature, this equation can be written as follows.

$$\Delta G = \Delta H - T\Delta S$$

The change in the free energy of a system that occurs during a reaction can be measured under any set of conditions. If the data are collected under standard-state conditions, the result is the **standard-state free energy of reaction** (ΔG^o).

$$\Delta G^o = \Delta H^o - T\Delta S^o$$

The standard-state free energy ΔG^o of the system is negative for any reaction for which ΔH^o is negative and ΔS^o is positive. ΔG^o is therefore negative for any reaction that is favored by both the enthalpy and entropy terms. We can therefore conclude that any reaction for which ΔG^o is negative should be favorable, or spontaneous.

Favourable or spontaneous reactions $\Delta G^o < 0$

Conversely, ΔG^o is positive for any reaction for which ΔH^o is positive and ΔS^o is negative. Any reaction for which ΔG^o is positive is therefore, unfavorable.

Unfavourable or non-spontaneous reactions $\Delta G^o > 0$

Reactions are either **exothermic** ($\Delta H < 0$) or **endothermic** ($\Delta H > 0$) on the basis of whether they give off or absorb heat. Reactions can also be either **exergonic** ($\Delta G < 0$) or **endergonic** ($\Delta G > 0$) on the basis of whether the free energy of the system decreases or increases during the reaction.

When a reaction is favoured by both enthalpy ($\Delta H^o < 0$) and entropy ($\Delta S^o > 0$), there is no need to calculate the value of ΔG^o to decide whether the reaction should proceed. The same can be said for reactions favored by neither enthalpy ($\Delta H^o > 0$) nor entropy ($\Delta S^o < 0$). Free energy calculations become important for reactions favored by only one of these factors.

By definition, the value of ΔG^o for a reaction measures the difference between the free energies of the reactants and products **when all components of the reaction are present at standard-state conditions.** ΔG^o therefore, describes this reaction only when all three components are present at 1 atm pressure.

The sign of ΔG^o tells us the direction in which the reaction has to shift to come to equilibrium. The ΔG^o is negative for this reaction at 25°C means that a system under standard-state conditions at this temperature would have to shift to the right, converting some of the reactants into products, before it can reach equilibrium. The larger the value of ΔG^o, the further the reaction has to go to get to from the standard-state conditions to equilibrium.

Relationship between the free energy of reaction (ΔG) and the standard-state free energy (ΔG^o).

The relationship between the free energy of reaction at any moment in time (ΔG) and the standard-state free energy of reaction (ΔG^o) is described by the following equation.

$$\Delta G = \Delta G^o + RT \ln Q$$

In this equation, R is the ideal gas constant in units of J/mol-K, T is the temperature in kelvin, ln represents a logarithm to the base e, and Q is the reaction quotient at that moment in time.

As we have seen, the driving force behind a chemical reaction is zero ($\Delta G = 0$) when the reaction is at equilibrium ($Q = K$).

$$0 = \Delta G^o + RT \ln K$$

We can therefore, solve this equation for the relationship between ΔG^o and K.

$$\Delta G^o = - RT \ln K$$

This equation allows us to calculate the equilibrium constant for any reaction from the standard-state free energy of reaction or *vice versa*.

Example 9 Calculate ΔH and ΔS for the following reaction and decide in which direction each of these factors will drive the reaction.

$$N_2(g) + 3H_2(g) \longrightarrow 2\,NH_3(g)$$

Solution Using a standard-state enthalpy of formation and absolute entropy data table, we find the following information:

Compound	ΔH_f^o(kJ/mol)	S°(J/mol-K)
$N_2(g)$	0	191.61
$H_2(g)$	0	130.68
$NH_3(g)$	–46.11	192.45

The reaction is exothermic ($\Delta H° < 0$), which means that the enthalpy of reaction favors the products of the reaction:

$$\Delta H^o = \Sigma H_f^o(\text{products}) - \Sigma H_f^o(\text{reactants})$$
$$= [2 \text{ mol } NH_3 \times 46.11 \text{ kJ/mol}] - [1 \text{ mol } N_2 \times 0 \text{ kJ/mol} + 3 \text{ mol } H_2 \times 0 \text{ kJ/mol}]$$
$$= -92.22 \text{ kJ}$$

The entropy of reaction is unfavourable, however, because there is a significant increase in the order of the system, when N_2 and H_2 combine to form NH_3.

$$\Delta S^o = \Sigma S^o(\text{products}) - \Sigma S^o(\text{reactants})$$
$$= [2 \text{ mol } NH_3 \times 192.45 \text{ J/mol-K}] - [1 \text{ mol } N_2 \times 191.61 \text{ J/mol-K} + 3 \text{ mol } H_2 \times 130.68 \text{ J/mol-K}]$$
$$= -198.75 \text{ J/K}$$

Example 10 Calculate ΔH and ΔS for the following reaction:

$$NH_4NO_3(s) + H_2O(l) \longrightarrow NH_4^+(aq) + NO_3^-(aq)$$

Use the results of this calculation to determine the value of ΔG^o for this reaction at 25°C, and explain why NH_4NO_3 spontaneously dissolves is water at room temperature.

Solution Using a standard-state enthalpy of formation and absolute entropy data table, we find the following information:

Compound	ΔH_f^o(kJ/mol)	S°(J/mol-K)
$NH_4NO_3(s)$	–365.56	151.08
$NH_4^+(aq)$	–132.51	113.4
$NO_3^-(aq)$	–205.0	146.4

This reaction is endothermic, and the enthalpy of reaction is therefore, unfavourable:

$$\Delta H^o = \Sigma H_f^o(\text{products}) - \Sigma H_f^o(\text{reactants})$$
$$= [1 \text{ mol } NH_4 \times 132.51 \text{ kJ/mol} + 1 \text{ mol } NO_3^- \times -205.0 \text{ kJ/mol}] - [1 \text{ mol } NH_4NO_3 \times -365.56 \text{ kJ/mol}]$$
$$= 28.05 \text{ kJ}$$

The reaction leads to a significant increase in the disorder of the system, however, and is therefore, favoured by the entropy of reaction:

$$\Delta S^o = \Sigma S^o(\text{products}) - \Sigma S^o(\text{reactants})$$
$$= [1 \text{ mol } NH_4 \times 113.4 \text{ J/mol-K} + 1 \text{ mol } NO_3^- \times 146.4 \text{ J/mol-K}] - [1 \text{ mol } NH_4NO_3 \times 151.08 \text{ J/mol-K}]$$
$$= 108.7 \text{ J/K}$$

To decide whether NH_4NO_3 should dissolve in water at 25°C we have to compare the ΔH^o and $T\Delta S^o$ to see which is larger. Before we can do this, we have to convert the temperature from °C to kelvin:

$$T_K = 25°C + 273.15 = 298.15 \text{ K}$$

We also have to recognize that the units of ΔH^o for this reaction are kilojoules and the units of ΔS^o are joules per Kelvin. At some point in this calculation, we therefore have to convert these quantites to a consistent set of untis. Perhaps the easiest way of doing this is to convert ΔH^o to joules. We then multiply the entropy term by the absolute temperature and subtract this quantity from the enthalpy term:

$$\Delta G^o = \Delta H^o - T\,\Delta S^o$$
$$= 28050 \text{ J} - (298.15 \text{ K} \times 108.7 \text{ J/K})$$
$$= 28050 \text{ J} - 32410 \text{ J}$$
$$= -4360 \text{ J}$$

At 25° C, the standard-state free energy for this reaction is negative because the entropy term at this temperature is larger that the enthalpy term:

$$\Delta G^o = -4.4 \text{ kJ}$$

The reaction is therefore, spontaneous at room temperature.

Colligative Properties

The colligative properties of solutions are those properties that depend upon the number of dissolved molecules or ions, irrespective of their kind. They are the lowering of the vapour pressure, the depression of the freezing point, the elevation of the boiling point, and the osmotic pressure. These properties may be used in determining molecular weights of dissolved substances.

1. Vapour Pressure

When a nonvolatile nonelectrolyte is dissolved in a liquid, the vapor pressure is lowered. **Raoult's law** gives the mathematical relation

$$p = x\, p_o$$

where, p is the vapor pressure of the solution, P_o is the vapour pressure of the pure solvent, and x is the mole fraction of solvent in the solution. The lowering of vapour pressure is not as widely used as some other colligative properties for experimental determinations of molecular weights, because it is difficult to make the measurements precisely.

2. Freezing and Boiling Points of Solutions

The lowering of the vapour pressure by a solute also brings about other changes: the freezing point is lowered, and the boiling point is raised. The amount of the change, ΔT_f or ΔT_B, is determined by the molality *(m)* of the solution. The relationships are

$$\Delta T = K_f m$$
$$\Delta B = K_B m$$

Each solvent has its own characteristic freezing-point constant K_f and boiling point constant K_B, the changes caused by 1 mole, of solute in 1 kilogram of solvent.

The use of boiling-point elevation to determine molecular weights is based upon the same type of calculation, using K_B instead of K_f.

When the substance is soluble in some suitable liquid, we can combine the empirical formula with a molecular-weight determination by freezing-point depression to get the true formula.

3. Osmotic Pressure

When solvent and solution are separated by a semipermeable membrane that permits solvent molecules to pass, an osmotic pressure is developed in the solution. This pressure, π, is defined as the mechanical pressure that must be applied to the solution to prevent solvent molecules from diffusing into it. For water solutions the relationship between Δ and the molal concentration m is given by the equation

$$\pi = (0.0821\ T)\ m$$

where, π is in atmospheres and T is the absolute temperature. The only common practical solvent for osmosis is water, so the only constant we shall consider is 0.0821. A one molal solution at 0.0°C would have an osmotic pressure of

$$\pi = (0.0821)(273)(1.00) = 22.4 \text{ atm}$$

In comparison with the relatively small vapour pressure lowering caused by relatively concentrated solutions, the osmostic effect is gigantic. For example, a 1.00×10^{-4} molal solution at 25.0°C would have an osmotic pressure of

$$\pi = (0.0821)(298)(1.00 \times \text{KT4})$$
$$= 2.45 \times 10{\sim}3 \text{ atm}$$
$$= (2.45 \times 10^{-3} \text{ atm})\ (760 \text{ torr atm})$$
$$= 1.86 \text{ torr}$$

Because of this great sensitivity of osmosis to small changes in concentration, the measurement of osmotic pressure is particularly suitable for the determination of molecular weights of biological materials with extremely high molecular weights. Such solutions will always be of very low molality, partly because of the high molecular weight of the solute and partly because of the generally low solubility of these compounds.

Colligative Properties of Electrolytes

If a mole of NaCl is dissolved in 1 kg of water, the freezing point is not − 1.86°C, as it would be for a mole of sugar on other non electrolyte. Rather, the freezing point is −3.50°C, a depression almost twice as great as we should expect. The theory of ionization provides an explanation for this discrepancy. When NaCl is dissolved, it breaks up into Na^+ and Cl^- ions, so that there are twice as many particles in solution as there would be if the dissociation did not occur. The water does not 'know' whether the particles are molecules or ions, insofar as the colligative properties are concerned. For every mole of NaCl dissolved we have 2 moles in solution: a mole of Na^+ ions, and a mole of Cl^- ions. Thus, we get an abnormal freezing-point depression.

Exercise

1. Which one of the molecules below is a polar molecule?
(a) BF_3 (b) CO_2
(c) CS_2 (d) Ibr
2. The average size of a human gene is
(a) 40000 bp (b) 2×10^6 bp
(c) 1.5×10^8 bp (d) 3×10^9 bp
3. The phenomenon of osmosis is opposite to that of
(a) diffusion (b) effusion
(c) affusion (d) coagulation
4. The ability of the cell membrane to act as a selective barrier depends upon
(a) the lipid composition of the membrane
(b) the pores which allows small molecules
(c) the special mediated transport systems
(d) All of the above
5. The geometry of the ClF_3 molecule is best described as
(a) distorted tetrahedral (b) regular tetrahedral
(c) T-shaped (d) trigonal pyramidal
6. Application of the concepts of the VSEPR theory suggests that the geometric arrangement of the atoms in the carbonate ion, CO_3^{2-} is
(a) octahedral (b) square planar
(c) regular tetrahedral (d) triangular planar
7. Based on conclusions from application of the VSEPR theory, which one of the following species is linear?
(a) BF_3 (b) HCN
(c) H_2CO (d) H_2S
8. The bond angle in Cl_2O is expected to be approximately
(a) 90° (b) 109.5°
(c) 120° (d) 145°
9. The smallest F—S—F bond angle in SF_6 is
(a) 90° (b) 109.5°
(c) 120° (d) 180°
10. Based on observed periodic trends, arrange the following species, HBr, HCl, HF, HI, in order of increasing dipole moment.
(a) HF < HCl < HBr < HI (b) HI < HF < HCl < HBr
(c) HI < HBr < HCl < HF (d) HCl < HBr < HI < HF
11. Which of the following molecules CO_2, CS_2, NO_2, COS is/are polar?
(a) NO_2 only (b) CS_2, NO_2 and COS
(c) CO_2 only (d) COS and NO_2
12. Draw a Lewis structure for the CH_4 molecule. What is the hybrid orbital set used by the carbonatom for bonding?
(a) sp^3d^2 (b) sp^3d
(c) sp^3 (d) sp^2
13. Which one of the following hybrid orbital sets is used by the central atom for σ-bonding in the PCl_3 molecule?
(a) sp (b) sp^2
(c) sp^3 (d) sp^3d
14. Which one of the following hybrid orbital sets is used by the central atom for σ-bonding in the PCl^{4-} ion?
(a) sp^2 (b) sp^3
(c) sp^3d (d) sp^3d^2
15. Which one of the following hybrid orbital sets is used by the central atom for σ-bonding in the SF6 molecule?
(a) sp^2 (b) sp^3
(c) sp^3d (d) sp^3d^2
16. What is the total number of σ-bonds in the benzene molecule?
(a) 0 (b) 1
(c) 2 (d) 3
17. All of the geometries listed below are examples of the five basic geometries for molecules with more than 3 atoms except
(a) planar triangular (b) octahedral
(c) tetrahedral (d) trihedral
18. Three different values can be observed for the bond angles in which of the following basic molecular structures for simple molecules:
(a) planar triangular (b) tetrahedral
(c) trigonal bipyramidal (d) octahedral
19. The basic geometry for molecules in the set below which possesses the smallest bond angles is
(a) planar triangular (b) tetrahedral
(c) trihedral (d) octahedral
20. The basic geometry for molecules in the set below which possesses the largest bond angles is
(a) linear (b) planar triangular
(c) tetrahedral (d) trihedral
21. The concept that electron pairs located in the valence shell of an atom bonded to other atoms tend to stay as far apart as possible so as to minimize repulsions between them is incorporated in the
(a) Pauli principle
(b) Heisenberg uncertainty principle
(c) valence shell electron pair repulsion theory
(d) electronegativity and polar bonds theory
22. Which one of the following arrangements would best accommodate three electron domains in the valence shell of a covalently bonded atom?
(a) Planar triangular (b) Octahedral
(c) Tetrahedral (d) Trihedral
23. Which one of the following arrangements would best accommodate five electron domains in the valence shell of a covalently bonded atom?
(a) Planar triangular (b) Tetrahedral
(c) Trihedral (d) Trigonal bipyramidal
24. Based on the Lewis structure, the number of electron domains in the valence shell of the boronatom in the BF_3 molecule is
(a) 1 (b) 2
(c) 3 (d) 4

25. Based on the Lewis structure, the number of non-bonding domains in the CO_2 molecule is
(a) 1 (b) 2
(c) 3 (d) 4

26. Application of the concepts of VSEPR theory leads us to conclude that the shape of the SO_3 molecule is
(a) trigonal pyramidal (b) square planar
(c) regular tetrahedral (d) triangular planar

27. Application of the concepts of VSEPR theory leads to the prediction that the shape of the PH_3 molecule is
(a) bent (b) trigonal pyramidal
(c) regular tetrahedral (d) triangular planar

28. The geometry of the CS_2 molecule is best described as
(a) bent (b) linear
(c) regular tetrahedral (d) triangular planar

29. In the Lewis structure for the NH_3 molecule, what is the hybrid orbital set used by the nitrogenatom for bonding?
(a) sp^3d^2 (b) sp
(c) sp^3d (d) sp^3

30. Most of water's unique properties result from the fact that water molecules
(a) are very small (b) tend to repel each other
(c) are extremely large (d) tend to stick together

31. In the Lewis structure for the C_2H_4 molecule, what is the hybrid orbital set used by either of the carbon atoms for bonding?
(a) sp^2 (b) sp
(c) sp^3d (d) sp^3

32. The surface tension in intestinal lumen between fat droplets and aqueous medium is decreased by
(a) bile salts (b) bile acids
(c) conc. H_2SO_4 (d) acetic acid

33. The absorption of intact protein from the gut in the foetal and newborn animals takes place by
(a) pinocytosis (b) passive diffusion
(c) simple diffusion (d) active transport

34. The pH of blood is 7.4 when the ratio between H_2CO_3 and $NaHCO_3$ is
(a) 1 : 10 (b) 1 : 20
(c) 1 : 25 (d) 1 : 30

35. Which one is the heaviest particulate component of the cell?
(a) Nucleus (b) Mitochondria
(c) Cytoplasm (d) Golgi apparatus

36. Which one is the largest particulate of the cytoplasm?
(a) Lysosomes (b) Mitochondria
(c) Golgi apparatus (d) Endoplasmic reticulum

37. The average pH of urine is
(a) 7.0 (b) 6.0
(c) 8.0 (d) 0.0

38. The maximum number of hydrogen bonds in which water molecule can participate is?
(a) 1 (b) 2
(c) 3 (d) 4

39. Daily requirement of calcium for normal adult human is
(a) 100 mg (b) 800 mg
(c) 2 g (d) 4 g

40. Normal total serum calcium level varies between
(a) 4-5 mg (b) 9-11 mg
(c) 15-20 mg (d) 50-100 mg

41. The element needed in quantities greater than 100 mg for human beings is
(a) calcium (b) zinc
(c) selenium (d) cobalt

42. The mineral present in the human body in larger amounts than any other cation is
(a) sodium (b) calcium
(c) potassium (d) iron

43. The percentage of the total body calcium present in bones is
(a) 1 (b) 11
(c) 55 (d) 99

44. The percentage of calcium present in extracellular fluid is
(a) 1 (b) 5
(c) 10 (d) 50

45. The physiologically active form of calcium is
(a) protein bond (b) ionized
(c) complexed with citrate (d) complexed with carbonate

46. The normal concentration of calcium in CSF is
(a) 1.5-2.5 mg/100 mL (b) 2.5-4 mg/100 mL
(c) 4.5-5 mg/100 mL (d) 9-10 mg/100 mL

47. Absorption of calcium is increased on a
(a) high protein diet (b) low protein diet
(c) high fat diet (d) low fat diet

48. Calcium absorption is interfered by
(a) protein in diet (b) phytic acid in cereals
(c) alkaline intestinal pH (d) vitamin-D

49. One of the principal cations of soft tissue and body fluids is
(a) Mg (b) S
(c) Mn (d) Co

50. The normal concentration of magnesium in whole blood is
(a) 0-1 mg/100 mL (b) 1-2 mg/100 mL
(c) 2-4 mg/100 mL (d) 4-8 mg/100 mL

51. The normal concentration of magnesium in CSF is about
(a) 1 mg/100 mL (b) 3 mg/100 mL
(c) 5 mg/100 mL (d) 8 mg/100 mL

52. The magnesium content of muscle is about
(a) 5 mg/100 mL (b) 10 mg/100 mL
(c) 21 mg/100 mL (d) 50 mg/100 mL

53. One joule is the energy required to
(a) raise the temperature of 1 gm of water by 1°C
(b) raise the temperature of 1 kg of water by 1°C

(c) move a mass of 1 gm by 1 cm distance by a force of 1 Newton
(d) move a mass of 1 kg by 1 m distance by a force of 1 Newton

54. Organic compound of small molecular size is
(a) urea (b) uric acid
(c) creatinine (d) phosphates

55. Organic substance of large molecular size is
(a) starch (b) insulin
(c) lipids (d) proteins

56. The principal cation in extracellular fluid is
(a) sodium (b) potassium
(c) calcium (d) magnesium

57. The normal concentration of sodium (in mg/100 mL) of human plasma is
(a) 100 (b) 200
(c) 250 (d) 330

58. The principal cation in intracellular fluid is
(a) sodium (b) potassium
(c) calcium (d) magnesium

59. The normal concentration of potassium in whole blood is
(a) 50 mg/100 mL (b) 100 mg/100 mL
(c) 150 mg/100 mL (d) 200 mg/100 mL

60. Chemical score of egg proteins is considered to be
(a) 100 (b) 60
(c) 50 (d) 40

61. Chemical score of milk proteins is
(a) 70 (b) 65
(c) 60 (d) 40

62. Chemical score of proteins of bengal gram is
(a) 70 (b) 60
(c) 44 (d) 42

63. Chemical score of protein gelatin is
(a) 0 (b) 44
(c) 57 (d) 60

64. Which is not correct about saponification number?
I. Smaller the saponification number, higher the MP of fat.
II. It is the number of mg of KOH required to saponify one gram of fat.
III. Measures the extent of unsaturation in fats.
IV. Measures the average molecular weight of fats.
(a) I and II (b) I and III
(c) I, II and III (d) I, II, III and IV

65. Biological value of egg white protein is
(a) 94 (b) 83
(c) 85 (d) 77

66. Net protein utilization of egg protein is
(a) 75% (b) 80%
(c) 91% (d) 72%

67. Net protein utilization of milk protein is
(a) 75% (b) 80%
(c) 86% (d) 91%

68. Fatty acids can be transported into and out of cell membrane by
(a) active transport (b) facilitated transport
(c) diffusion (d) osmosis

69. A lipid bilayer is permeable to
(a) urea (b) fructose
(c) glucose (d) potassium

70. All of the following compounds are capable of forming hydrogen bonds with water except
(a) acetamide (b) methyl acetate
(c) ethanolamine (d) hexane

71. The fatty acids can be transported into and out of mitochondria through
(a) active transport (b) facilitated transfer
(c) non-facilitated transfer (d) None of these

72. All of the following compounds are capable of forming hydrogen bonds with water except
(a) methanol (b) acetamide
(c) methyl acetate (d) hexane

73. The pH of the blood is maintained by
(a) mineral salts (b) globulins
(c) albumins (d) haemoglobin

74. Linkage present in cellulose molecule is
(a) β-(1 $\rightarrow$ 4) (b) α-(1 $\rightarrow$ 4)
(c) α-(1 $\rightarrow$ 6) (d) Both (b) and (c)

75. Active transport
(a) releases energy (b) require energy
(c) produces energy (d) produces toxic material

76. Na^+/K^+-ATPase along with ATP requires
(a) Ca (b) Mn
(c) Mg (d) Cl

77. All the following processes occur rapidly in the membrane lipid bilayer except
(a) flexing of fatty acyl chains
(b) lateral diffusion of phospholipids
(c) transbilayer diffusion of phospholipids
(d) rotation of phospholipids around their long axes

78. Which of the following statement is correct about membrane cholesterol?
(a) The hydroxyl group is located near the centre of the lipid layer
(b) Most of the cholesterol is in the form of a cholesterol ester
(c) The steroid nucleus form forms a rigid, planar structure
(d) The hydrocarbon chain of cholesterol projects into the extracellular fluid

79. The Golgi complex
(a) synthesizes proteins
(b) produces ATP
(c) provides a pathway for transporting chemicals
(d) forms glycoproteins

80. The following points about microfilaments are true except
(a) they form cytoskeleton with microtubules
(b) they provide support and shape
(c) they form intracellular conducting channels
(d) they are involved in muscle cell contraction

81. The following substances are cell inclusions except
(a) melanin (b) glycogen
(c) lipids (d) centrosome

82. The major mechanism of turnover of molecular components of the plasma membrane occurs through
(a) endocytosis of patches of membrane
(b) diffusion of individual molecules into the cytoplasm
(c) recovery of specific components by selective receptors
(d) expulsion of integral molecules into the extracellular medium

83. Cells with abundant apical microvilli are characteristically found in
(a) the reticulo-endothelial system
(b) adipose tissue
(c) neuronal dendrites
(d) absorptive epithelia

84. Cellular proteins destined for secretion are sorted and packaged in the
(a) lysosomes (b) endosomes
(c) endoplasmic reticulum (d) *trans* Golgi

85. Incubation of Gram negative bacteria with lysozyme in an isotonic medium causes rod-shaped bacteria to assume a spherical shape. The cause of this phenomenon is
(a) absorption of water
(b) destruction of the cell wall
(c) destruction of the cytoskeleton
(d) damage to the plasma membrane

86. The pH of the blood is maintained by
(a) mineral salts (b) globulins
(c) albumins (d) haemoglobin

87. Linkage present in cellulose molecule is
(a) $\beta (1 \rightarrow 4)$ (b) $\alpha (1 \rightarrow 4)$
(c) $\alpha (1 \rightarrow 6)$ (d) Both (b) and (c)

88. Active transport
(a) releases energy (b) require energy
(c) produces energy (d) produces toxic material

89. In a substitution nucleophilic first order reaction (S_N1)the stereochemical outcome is
(a) racemisation
(b) inversion of configuration
(c) retention of configuration
(d) difficult to predict

90. In glycoproteins the carbohydrate is in the form of disaccharide units, the number of units are
(a) 50-100 (b) 200-300
(c) 400-500 (d) 600-700

91. The following type of interaction is mainly responsible for aggregation of proteins in dilute solutions
(a) hydrogen bonds (b) hydrophobic interactions
(c) disulphide bonds (d) peptide bonds

92. Disulphides bridge forms between two cystiene residues as a result of
(a) oxidation of sulphydral group
(b) reduction of sulphydral group
(c) amide formation
(d) None of these

93. Which one of the following statements about protein secondary structure is correct?
(a) An α-helix is primarily stabilized by ionic interactions between the side chains of the amino acids
(b) β-sheets exist only in antiparallel form
(c) β turns often contain proline
(d) An α-helix can be composed of more than one polypeptide chain

94. Which of the following statements about natural sterols is incorrect?
(a) Cholestrol is the most abundant sterol in animal tissue
(b) All the carbon atoms of cholestrol are derived from acetyl Co-A
(c) β-sitosterol is the most abundant plant sterol
(d) Dietary β-sterol and cholestrol are absorbed to about the same extent in the intestine of normal human

95. Which statment about nucleotides is correct? Nucleotides
(a) such as ATP are used in the *in vivo* synthesis of nucleic acids
(b) are composed of only a pentose sugar and a nitrogenous purine or pyrimidine base
(c) such as GTP replace ATP in the synthesis of RNA molecules
(d) contain a deoxyribose sugar if they are components of RNA, and a ribose sugar if they are components of DNA

96. The hyperchromic effect refers to
(a) a change in the Optical Rotatory Dispersion (ORD) of a DNA solution upon heating
(b) a maximum rate of denaturation *versus* temperature for duplex DNA
(c) an increase in the absorbance of light at 260 nm upon denaturation of DNA
(d) an increase in the absorbance of light at 260 nm when DNA-RNA hybrids are annealed

97. Which of the following factors favour strand separation in double stranded DNA melting?
(a) Hydrogen bonding between bases
(b) Repulsion between phosphate groups
(c) van der Waals interaction between bases
(d) High content of G + C

98. Cholesterol is essential for normal membrane functions because it
(a) cannot be made by higher organisms, *e.g.*, mammals
(b) spans the thickness of the bilayer
(c) keeps membranes fluid
(d) catalyzes lipid flip-flop in the bilayer

99. Correct statements regarding nucleotide structure include which of the following?
(a) Removal of the 5′-phosphate group from guanylic acid (GMP) yields guanine
(b) Removal of the 5′-phosphate group from adenylic acid (AMP) yields adenosine
(c) Removal of the ribose 5-phosphate from thymidylic acid (TMP) yields uracil
(d) Removal of the ribose 5-phosphate from cytidylic acid (CMP) yields cytidine

100. Disulphide bonds most often stabilize the native structure of
(a) extracellular proteins
(b) dimeric proteins
(c) intracellular proteins
(d) multisubunit proteins

101. The helices in the amino acid supersecondary structure are held together primarily by
(a) charge-charge interactions
(b) covalent cross links
(c) favourable *R* group interactions
(d) main chain hydrogen bonding

102. The quaternary structure of human haemoglobin is best described as a
(a) dimer of two myoglobin dimmers
(b) tetramer of identical subunits
(c) tetramer of four different subunits
(d) tetramer of two different subunits

103. The property of resonance as applied to protein structure is responsible for the
(a) prevention of rotation about the alpha carbon
(b) partial double bond character of the side chain-alpha carbon bond
(c) planar nature of the peptide bond
(d) ability of cochlear cells to detect sound waves by mechanotransduction

104. Which of the following statements is false?
(a) Amino acids tend to be least soluble in water at their isoelectric point
(b) Sickle acids Hb and normal Hb have same value of negative charge
(c) Amino acids are made visible on the chromatogram by treatment with ninhydrin
(d) The net charge on an amino acid is a function of the pH of the solution

105. Glucose and hexanoic acid each contain six carbon atoms, but they have completely different properties. Glucose is necessary in food; hexanoic acid is poisonous. Their differences must be due to different
(a) monomers
(b) macromolecules
(c) quaternary structures
(d) functional groups

106. Which of the following would probably *not* be affected when a protein is denatured?
(a) Primary structure
(b) Secondary structure
(c) Hydrogen bonds
(d) All of the above must be affected for the protein to be denatured

107. Palm oil and coconut oil are more like animal fats than other plant oils. Because they.............than other plant oils, they can contribute to cardiovascular disease.
(a) contain fewer double bonds
(b) are less saturated
(c) contain more sodium
(d) are less soluble in water

108. Certain fatty acids are said to be essential because the body cannot make them itself; they must be obtained in the diet. If your diet were deficient in these essential fatty acids, you would not be able to make certain
(a) fats
(b) glycerol molecules
(c) monosaccharides
(d) you would not be able to make any of the above

109. A solution with a pH of 2, compared to a solutin with pH 4,
(a) is twice as acidic
(b) is 100 times more acidic
(c) is 1000 times more acidic
(d) has two times more $[OH^-]$

110. A buffer
(a) changes pH by a magnitude of 10
(b) absorbs excess OH^-
(c) releases excess H^+
(d) is often a weak acid-base pair

111. Which would be the best method for reducing acid precipitation?
(a) Raise the height of smoke stacks so that exhaust enters the upper atmosphere
(b) Add buffers and bases to bodies of water whose pH has dropped
(c) Use coal burning generators rather than nuclear power to produce electricity
(d) Increase emmission control standards for factories and automobiles

112. Tim added 10 mL of hydrochloric acid and 10 mL of water (pH 7) to a beaker containing 100 mL of water. The pH of the resulting solution was 4. Next he is going to add 10 mL of hydrochloric acid and 10 mL of pH 7 buffer to a different beaker containing 100 mL of water. What do you think will happen?
(a) The resulting pH will be less than 4
(b) The resulting pH will be between 4 and 7
(c) The resulting pH will be 7
(d) The resulting pH will be between 7 and 11

113. A glass of grapefruit juice, at pH 3, contains .... H^+ as a glass of tomato juice, at pH 4.
(a) half as much
(b) twice as much
(c) three times as much
(d) ten times as much

114. Molecules are always moving. Some molecules move faster than other; .... is a measure of their average velocity of movement
(a) polarity
(b) heat
(c) temperature
(d) electronegativity

115. Ice floats because
(a) its moleicules are moving faster than in liquid water
(b) it is more dense than liquid water
(c) its hydrogen molecules bond to the water surface film
(d) its water molecules are farther apart than in liquid water

116. How many different kinds of protein molecules are there in a typical cell?
(a) Four
(b) Twenty
(c) About a hundred
(d) Thousands

117. The smallest particle of water is
(a) an atom (b) a crystal
(c) an element (d) a molecule

118. Which of the following ranks the molecules in the correct order by size?
(a) Water—sucrose—glucose—protein
(b) Protein—water—glucose–sucrose
(c) Water—protein—sucrose—glucose
(d) Protein—sucrose—glucose—water

119. A triple covalent bond would
(a) involve the bonding of three atoms
(b) involve the bonding of six atoms
(c) produce a triangularly shaped molecule
(d) involve the sharing of six electrons

120. Isotopes can be used in studies of metabolic pathways because
(a) their half-life allows a researcher to time an experiment
(b) they are more reactive
(c) the cell does not recognise the extra protons in the nucleus, so isotopes are readily used in metabolism
(d) their location or quantity can be experimentally determined because of their radioactivity

121. Which of the following is not true of cellulose?
(a) It is the most abundant organic compound on Earth
(b) If differs from starch because of the configuration of glucose and the geometry of the glysidic linkage
(c) It may be hydrogen-bonded to neighboring cellulose molecules to form microfibrils
(d) Its monomers are amino sugars

122. Which one of the following statements refers to glycogen, and which one refers to cellulose?
I. Branched molecule containing β-1, 4-glycosidic bond.
II. Straight chain molecule containing β-1, 4-glycosidic bond.
III. Branched molecule containing α-1, 6-glycosidic bond.
IV. Straight chain molecule containing α-1, 6-glycosidic bond.
(a) I – Glycogen IV – Cellulose
(b) II – Glycogen III – Cellulose
(c) III – Glycogen II – Cellulose
(d) IV – Glycogen I – Cellulose

Answers

1. (d)	**2.** (c)	**3.** (a)	**4.** (d)	**5.** (c)	**6.** (d)	**7.** (b)	**8.** (b)	**9.** (a)	**10.** (c)
11. (d)	**12.** (c)	**13.** (c)	**14.** (c)	**15.** (d)	**16.** (d)	**17.** (d)	**18.** (c)	**19.** (d)	**20.** (a)
21. (c)	**22.** (a)	**23.** (d)	**24.** (c)	**25.** (d)	**26.** (d)	**27.** (b)	**28.** (b)	**29.** (d)	**30.** (d)
31. (a)	**32.** (a)	**33.** (a)	**34.** (b)	**35.** (a)	**36.** (b)	**37.** (b)	**38.** (d)	**39.** (b)	**40.** (b)
41. (a)	**42.** (b)	**43.** (d)	**44.** (a)	**45.** (b)	**46.** (c)	**47.** (c)	**48.** (a)	**49.** (a)	**50.** (c)
51. (b)	**52.** (c)	**53.** (d)	**54.** (a)	**55.** (d)	**56.** (a)	**57.** (d)	**58.** (b)	**59.** (d)	**60.** (a)
61. (b)	**62.** (c)	**63.** (a)	**64.** (b)	**65.** (b)	**66.** (c)	**67.** (a)	**68.** (b)	**69.** (a)	**70.** (b)
71. (b)	**72.** (d)	**73.** (a)	**74.** (a)	**75.** (b)	**76.** (c)	**77.** (c)	**78.** (c)	**79.** (d)	**80.** (c)
81. (d)	**82.** (a)	**83.** (d)	**84.** (d)	**85.** (b)	**86.** (a)	**87.** (a)	**88.** (b)	**89.** (c)	**90.** (d)
91. (b)	**92.** (a)	**93.** (c)	**94.** (d)	**95.** (c)	**96.** (c)	**97.** (b)	**98.** (c)	**99.** (b)	**100.** (a)
101. (c)	**102.** (d)	**103.** (c)	**104.** (b)	**105.** (d)	**106.** (a)	**107.** (a)	**108.** (a)	**109.** (b)	**110.** (d)
111. (d)	**112.** (b)	**113.** (d)	**114.** (c)	**115.** (d)	**116.** (d)	**117.** (d)	**118.** (d)	**119.** (d)	**120.** (d)
121. (d)	**122.** (b)								

2 Bioenergetics and Catalysis

Bioenergetics

Bioenergetics or biochemical thermodynamics, is the study of the energy changes accompanying biochemical reactions. Biological systems are essentially **isothermic** and use chemical energy to power living processes. **Gibbs** change in free energy (ΔG) is that portion of the total energy change in a system that is available for doing work, *i.e.,* The useful energy, also known as the **chemical potential.**

Syllabus

- Bioenergetics, Glycolysis, Oxidative Phosphorylation, Coupled Reaction, Group Transfer, Biological Energy Transducer.
- Principles of Catalysis, Enzymes, Mechanism of Enzyme Catalysis, Isozymes, Enzyme Kinetics, Enzyme Regulation.

Metabolism is the sum of all the chemical transformations taking place in a cell or organism, occurs through a series of enzyme-catalyzed reactions that constitute **metabolic pathways.** Each of the consecutive steps in a metabolic pathway brings about a specific, small chemical change, usually the removal, transfer or addition of a particular atom or functional group.

Catabolism is the degradative phase of metabolism in which organic nutrient molecules (carbohydrates, fats and proteins) are converted into smaller, simpler end

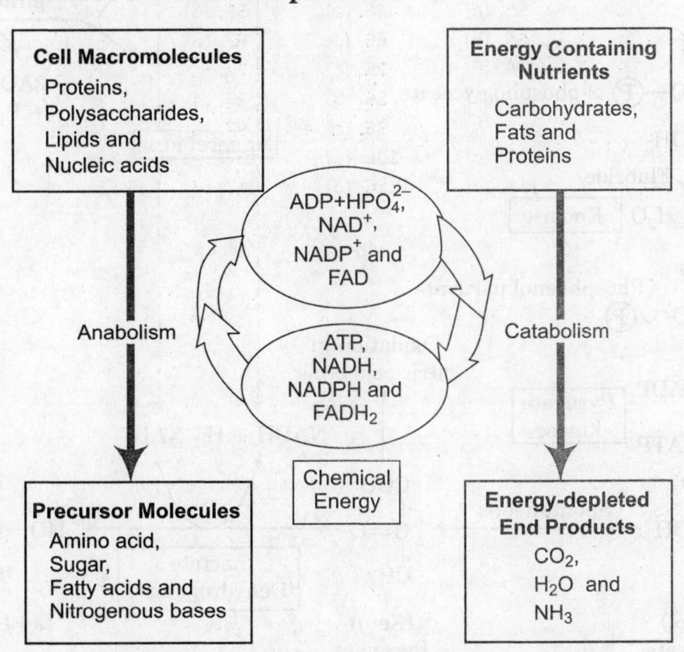

Fig. 2.1 Energy relationship between catabolic and anabolic pathways

products (such as lactic acid, CO_2 and NH_3). Catabolic pathways release energy, some of which is conserved in the formation of ATP and reduced electron carriers (NADH, NADPH and $FADH_2$); the rest is lost as heat.

Anabolism is the synthesis of larger and more complex molecules, including lipids, polysaccharides, proteins and nucleic acids, from small, simple precursors. Anabolic reactions require an input of energy, generally in the form of the phosphoryl group transfer potential of ATP and the reducing power of NADH, NADPH and $FADH_2$.

Glycolysis

Glycolysis is a definite sequence of ten reactions involving ten intermediate compounds. The most common type of glycolysis is the **Embden Meyerhof Parnas** pathway (EMP pathway), which was first discovered by Gustav Embden, Otto Meyerhof and Jakub Karol Parnas. Glycolysis also refers to other pathways, such as the Entner–Doudoroff pathway and homofermentative pathways.

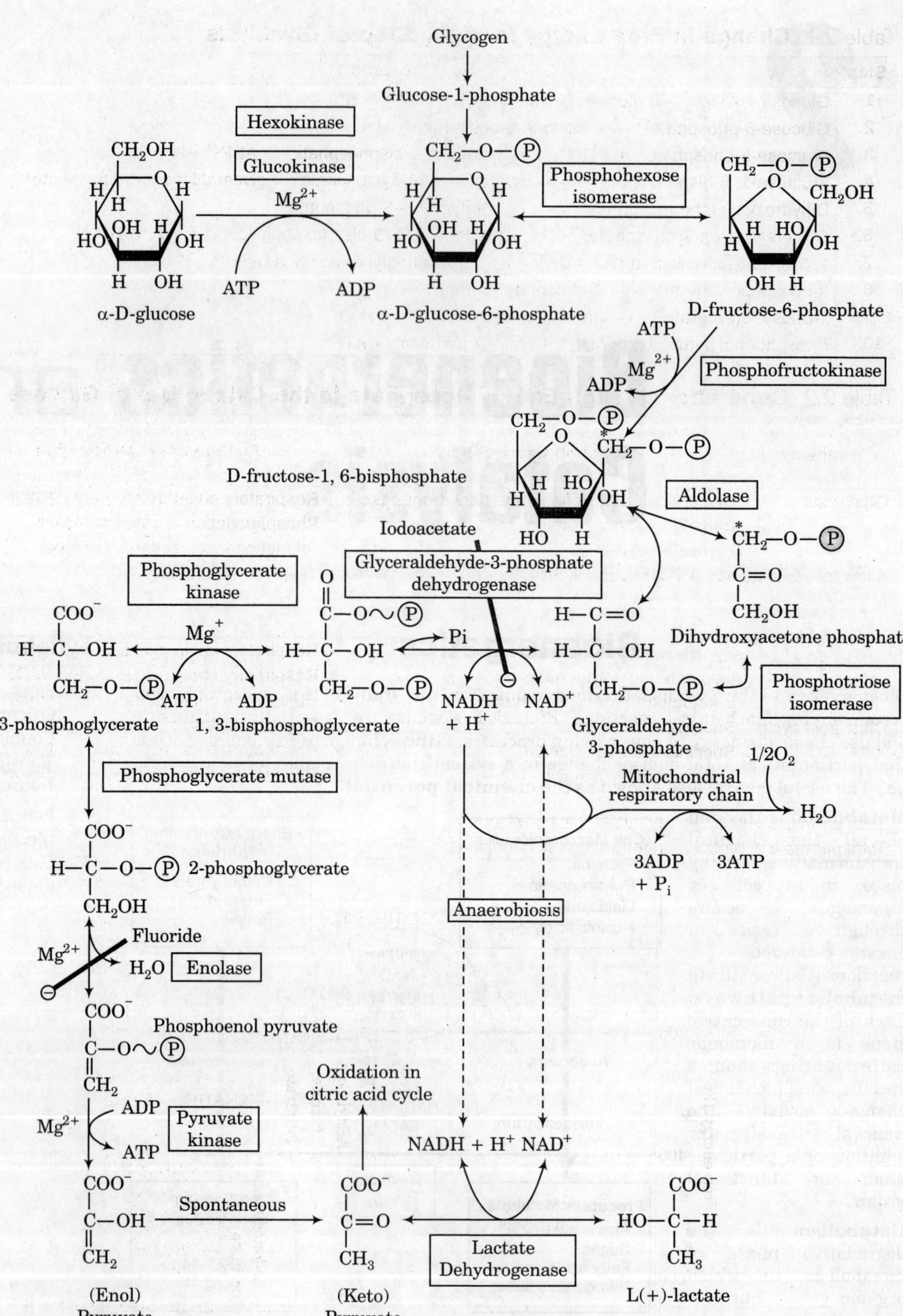

Fig. 2.2 Glycolytic pathway

Table 2.1 **Change in Free Energy for Each Step of Glycolysis**

Step	Reaction	$\Delta G^{o\prime}$/(kJ/mol)
1.	Glucose + ATP^{4-} ⟶ glucose-6-phosphate^{2-} + ADP^{3-} + H^+	–16.7
2.	Glucose-6-phosphate^{2-} ⟶ fructose-6-phosphate^{2-}	1.67
3.	Fructose-6-phosphate^{2-} + ATP^{4-} ⟶ fructose-1, 6-bisphosphate^{4-} + ADP^{3-} + H^+	–14.2
4.	Fructose-1, 6-bisphosphate^{4-} ⟶ dihydroxyacetone phosphate^{2-} + glyceraldehyde-3-phosphate^{2-}	23.9
5.	Dihydroxyacetone phosphate^{2-} ⟶ glyceraldehyde-3-phosphate^{2-}	7.56
6.	Glyceraldehyde-3-phosphate^{2-} + P_i^{2-} + NAD^+ ⟶ 1, 3-bisphosphoglycerate^{4-} + NADH + H^+	6.30
7.	1, 3-bisphosphoglycerate^{4-} + ADP^{3-} ⟶ 3-phosphoglycerate^{3-} + ATP^{4-}	–18.9
8.	3-phosphoglycerate^{3-} ⟶ 2-phosphoglycerate^{3-}	4.4
9.	2-phosphoglycerate^{3-} ⟶ phosphoenol pyruvate^{3-} + H_2O	1.8
10.	Phosphoenol pyruvate^{3-} + ADP^{3-} + H^+ ⟶ pyruvate$^-$ + ATP^{4-}	–31.7

Table 2.2 **Generation of High Energy Phosphate in the Catabolism of Glucose**

Pathway	Reaction Catalyzed by	Method of ~P Production	Number of ~P formed Per Mole of Glucose
Glycolysis	Glyceraldehyde-3-phosphate dehydrogenase	Respiratory chain oxidation of 2 NADH	6*
	Phosphoglycerate kinase	Phosphorylation at substrate level	2
	Pyruvate kinase	Phosphorylation at substrate level	2
Allow for consumption of ATP by reactions catalyzed by hexokinase and phosphofructokinase			10
			–2
			Net 8
	Pyruvate dehydrogenase	Respiratory chain oxidation of 2 NADH	6
	Isocitrate dehydrogenase	Respiratory chain oxidation of 2 NADH	6
	α-ketoglutrate dehydrogenase	Respiratory chain oxidation of 2 NADH	6
Citric acid cycle	Succinate thiokinase	Phosphorylation at substrate level	2
	Succinate dehydrogenase	Respiratory chain oxidation of 2 $FADH_2$	4
	Malate dehydrogenase	Respiratory chain oxidation of 2 NADH	6
			Net 30
Total per mole of glucose under aerobic conditions			38
Total per mole of glucose under anaerobic conditions			2

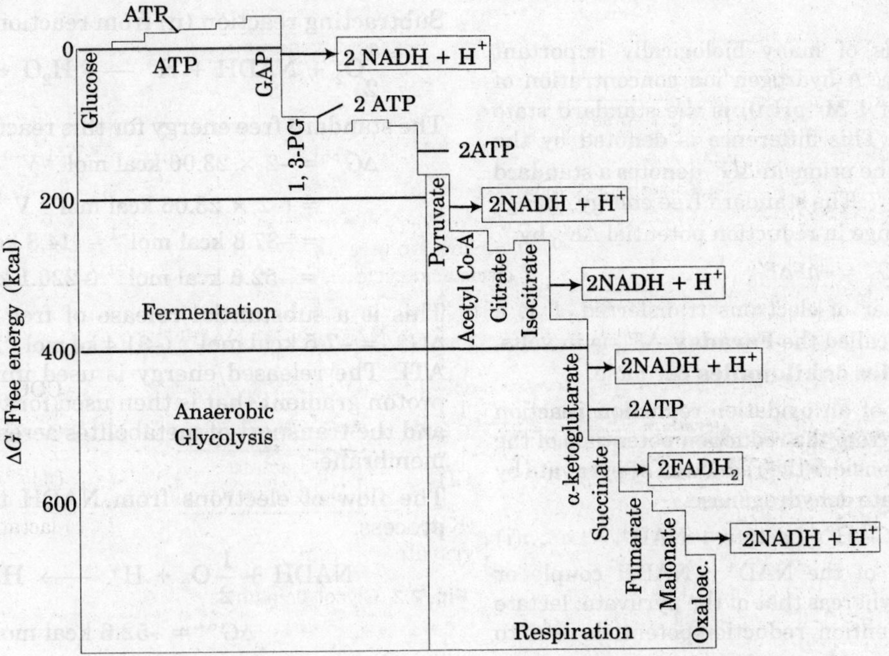

Fig. 2.3 Decrease of free energy (ΔG π) during glycolysis and respiration

Oxidative Phosphorylation

The **phosphate anhydride** (pyrophosphate) linkages of ATP are generated by the joining of ADP and inorganic phosphate by means of special **phosphorylation** reactions. The most important of the latter occur in the photosynthetic membranes of chloroplasts **(photosynthetic phosphorylation)** and in oxygen utilizing membranes of bacteria and of mitochondria **(oxidative phosphorylation).**

The primary function of the citric acid cycle was identified as the generation of NADH and $FADH_2$ by the oxidation of acetyl Co-A. In oxidative phosphorylation, NADH and $FADH_2$ are used to reduce molecular oxygen to water. The highly exergonic reduction of molecular oxygen by NADH and $FADH_2$ occurs in a number of electron transfer reactions, taking place in a set of membrane proteins known as the **electron-transport chain.**

In oxidative phosphorylation, the electron transfer potential of NADH or $FADH_2$ is converted into the phosphoryl transfer potential of ATP. Quantitative expressions for these forms of free energy are required. The measure of phosphoryl transfer potential is given by $\Delta G^{o\prime}$ for the hydrolysis of the activated phosphate compound. The corresponding expression for the electron transfer potential is E'_0, the reduction potential (also called the redox potential or oxidation reduction potential).

A negative reduction potential means that the reduced form of a substance has lower affinity for electrons than does by H_2. A positive reduction potential means that the reduced form of a substance has higher affinity for electrons than does by H_2. A strong reducing agent (such as NADH) is poised to donate electrons and has a negative reduction potential, whereas a strong oxidizing agent (such as O_2) is ready to accept electrons and has a positive reduction potential.

The reduction potentials of many biologically important redox couples are known. A hydrogen ion concentration of 10^{-7} M (pH 7) instead of 1 M (pH 0) is the standard state adopted by biochemists. This difference is denoted by the prime in E'_0. Recall that the prime in $\Delta G^{o\prime}$ denotes a standard free energy change at pH 7. The standard free energy change $\Delta G^{o\prime}$ is related to the change in reduction potential $\Delta E'_0$ by

$$\Delta G^{o\prime} = -nF\Delta E'_0$$

in which n is the number of electrons transferred, F is a proportionality constant called the **Faraday**, $\Delta E'_0$ is in volts, and $\Delta G^{\circ\prime}$ is in **kilocalories** or **kilojoules** per mole.

The free energy change of an oxidation-reduction reaction can be readily calculated from the reduction potentials of the reactants. For example, consider the reduction of pyruvate by NADH, catalyzed by lactate dehydrogenase.

$$\text{Pyruvate + NADH + H}^+ \ \text{Lactate + NAD}^+ \quad \text{...(i)}$$

The reduction potential of the NAD^+ : NADH couple or half-reaction, is –0.32 V, whereas that of the pyruvate: lactate couple is –0.19 V. By convention, reduction potentials refer to partial reactions written as reductions: oxidant + e^{-2} reductant.

Hence,

$$\text{Pyruvate} + 2H^+ + 2e^- \longrightarrow \text{Lactate} \quad E'_0 = -0.19 \text{ V} \quad \text{...(ii)}$$

$$NAD^+ + H^+ + 2e^- \longrightarrow NADH \quad E'_0 = -0.32 \text{ V} \quad \text{...(iii)}$$

To obtain reaction (i) from reactions (ii) and (iii), we need to reverse the direction of reaction (iii) so that NADH appears on the left side of the arrow. In doing so, the sign of E'_0 must be changed.

$$\text{Pyruvate} + 2H^+ + 2e^- \longrightarrow \text{Lactate} \quad E'_0 = -0.19 \text{ V} \quad \text{...(ii)}$$

$$NADH \longrightarrow NAD^+ + H^+ + 2e^- \quad E'_0 = +0.32 \text{ V} \quad \text{...(iv)}$$

For reaction (ii), the free energy can be calculated with $n = 2$.

$$\Delta G^\circ' = -2 \times 23.06 \text{ kcal mol}^{-1}\text{ V}^{-1} \times -0.19 \text{ V}$$
$$= +8.8 \text{ kcal mol}^{-1} \text{ (36.7 kJ mol}^{-1}\text{)}$$

Likewise, for reaction (iv),

$$\Delta G^{\circ\prime} = -2 \times 23.06 \text{ kcal mol}^{-1}\text{ V}^{-1} \times +0.32 \text{ V}$$
$$= -14.8 \text{ kcal mol}^{-1} \text{ (61.7 kJ mol}^{-1}\text{)}$$

Thus, the free energy for reaction (i) is given by

$$\Delta G^{\circ\prime} = \Delta G^{\circ\prime} \text{ (for reaction ii)} + \Delta G^{\circ\prime} \text{ (for reaction iv)}$$
$$= +8.8 + (-14.8)$$
$$= -6.0 \text{ kcal mol}^{-1} \text{ (–25.1 kJ mol}^{-1}\text{)}$$

The driving force of oxidative phosphorylation is the electron transfer potential of NADH or $FADH_2$ relative to that of O_2. How much energy is released by the reduction of O_2 with NADH? Let us calculate $\Delta G^{\circ\prime}$ for this reaction. The pertinent half-reactions are

$$\frac{1}{2} O_2 + 2H^+ + 2e^- \longrightarrow H_2O \quad E_0' = +0.82 \text{ V} \quad \text{...(i)}$$

$$NAD^+ + H^+ + 2e^- \longrightarrow NADH \quad E_0' = -0.32 \text{ V} \quad \text{...(ii)}$$

Subtracting reaction (ii) from reaction (i) yields

$$\frac{1}{2} O_2 + NADH + H^+ \longrightarrow H_2O + NAD^+ \quad \text{...(iii)}$$

The standard free energy for this reaction is then given by

$$\Delta G^{o\prime} = -2 \times 23.06 \text{ kcal mol}^{-1}\text{ V}^{-1} \times +0.82 \text{ V}^-$$
$$= (-2 \times 23.06 \text{ kcal mol}^{-1}\text{ V}^{-1} \times -0.32 \text{ V})$$
$$= -37.8 \text{ kcal mol}^{-1} - (14.8 \text{ kcal mol}^{-1})$$
$$= -52.6 \text{ kcal mol}^{-1} \text{ (–220.1 kJ mol}^{-1}\text{)}$$

This is a substantial release of free energy. Recall that $\Delta G^{\circ\prime} = -7.5$ kcal mol^{-1} (–31.4 kJ mol^{-1}) for the hydrolysis of ATP. The released energy is used initially to generate a proton gradient that is then used for the synthesis of ATP and the transport of metabolites across the mitochondrial membrane.

The flow of electrons from NADH to O_2, an exergonic process.

$$NADH + \frac{1}{2} O_2 + H^+ \longrightarrow H_2O + NAD^+$$

$$\Delta G^{\circ\prime} = -52.6 \text{ kcal mol}^{-1} \text{ (–220.1 kJ mol}^{-1}\text{)}$$

Next, we consider how this process is coupled to the synthesis of ATP, an endergonic process.

$$ADP + P_i + H^+ \longrightarrow ATP + H_2O \qquad \Delta G^{\circ\prime} = +7.3 \text{ kcal mol}^{-1} \ (+30.5 \text{ kJ mol}^{-1})$$

A molecular assembly in the inner mitochondrial membrane carries out the synthesis of ATP. This enzyme complex was originally called the **mitochondrial ATPase** or F_1F_0 **ATPase** because it was discovered through its catalysis of the reverse reaction, the hydrolysis of ATP. ATP synthase, its preferred name, emphas- izes its actual role in the mitochondrion. It is also called as **complex V.**

It was first suggested that electron transfer leads to the formation of a covalent high-energy intermediate that serves as a high phosphoryl transfer potential compound or to the formation of an activated protein conformation, which then drives ATP synthesis. The search for such intermediates for several decades proved fruitless.

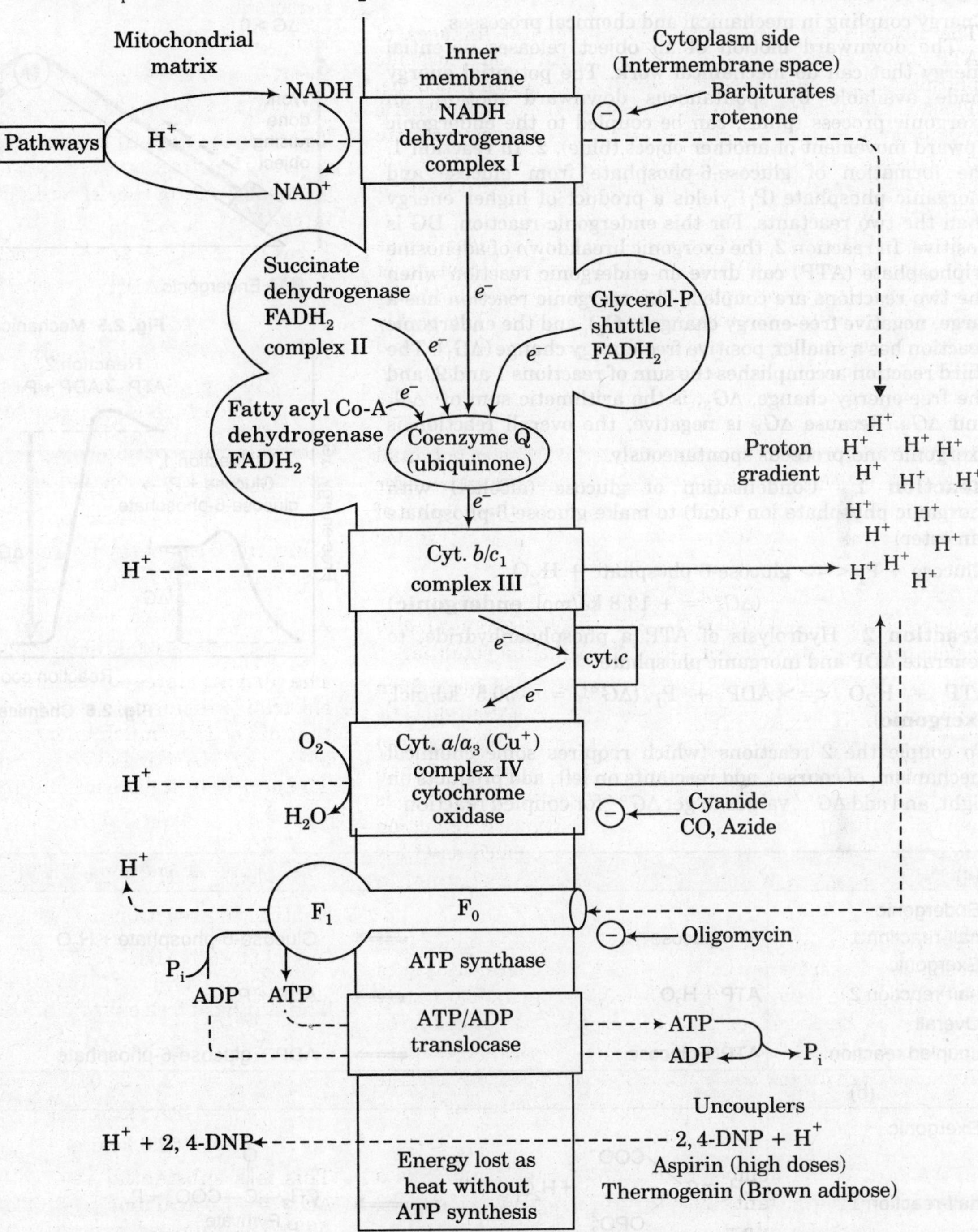

Fig. 2.4 Oxidative phosphorylation

In 1961, **Peter Mitchell** proposed that electron transport and ATP synthesis are coupled by **a proton gradient across the inner mitochondrial membrane** rather than by a covalent high-energy intermediate or an activated protein confor-mation. In his model, the transfer of electrons through the respiratory chain leads to the pumping of protons from the matrix to the cytosolic side of the inner mitochondrial membrane. The H^+ concentration becomes lower in the matrix, and an electrical field with the matrix side negative is generated. Mitchell's idea, called the **chemiosmotic hypothesis,** was that this proton-motive force drives the synthesis of ATP by ATP synthase. Mitchell's highly innovative hypothesis that oxidation and phosphorylation are coupled by a proton gradient is now supported by a wealth of evidence. Indeed, electron transport generates a proton gradient across the inner mitochondrial membrane. The pH outside is 1.4 units lower than inside pH, and the membrane potential is 0.14 V, the outside being positive. The calculated membrane potential corresponds to a free energy of 5.2 kcal (21.8 kJ) per mole of protons.

Coupled Reaction

Energy coupling in mechanical and chemical processes. 1. The downward motion of an object releases potential energy that can do mechanical work. The potential energy made available by spontaneous downward motion, an exergonic process (pink), can be coupled to the endergonic upward movement of another object (blue). 2. In reaction 1, the formation of glucose-6-phosphate from glucose and inorganic phosphate (P_i) yields a product of higher energy than the two reactants. For this endergonic reaction, DG is positive. In reaction 2, the exergonic breakdown of adenosine triphosphate (ATP) can drive an endergonic reaction when the two reactions are coupled. The exergonic reaction has a large, negative free-energy change (ΔG_2), and the endergonic reaction has a smaller, positive free-energy change (ΔG_1). The third reaction accomplishes the sum of reactions 1 and 2, and the free-energy change, ΔG_3, is the arithmetic sum of ΔG_1 and ΔG_2. Because ΔG_3 is negative, the overall reaction is exergonic and proceeds spontaneously.

Reaction 1 Condensation of glucose (alcohol) with inorganic phosphate ion (acid) to make glucose-6-phosphate (an ester)

Glucose + P_i <=> glucose-6-phosphate + H_2O

($\Delta G°'$ = + 13.8 kJ/mol, **endergonic**)

Reaction 2 Hydrolysis of ATP, a phosphoanhydride, to generate ADP and inorganic phosphate

ATP + H_2O <=> ADP + P_i ($\Delta G°'$ = – 30.5 kJ/mol, **exergonic**).

To couple the 2 reactions (which requires some chemical mechanism, of course), add reactants on left, add products on right, and add $\Delta G°'$ values to get $\Delta G°'$ for coupled reaction:

Glucose + ATP <=> glucose-6-phosphate + ADP

($\Delta G°'$ = –16.7 kJ/mol)

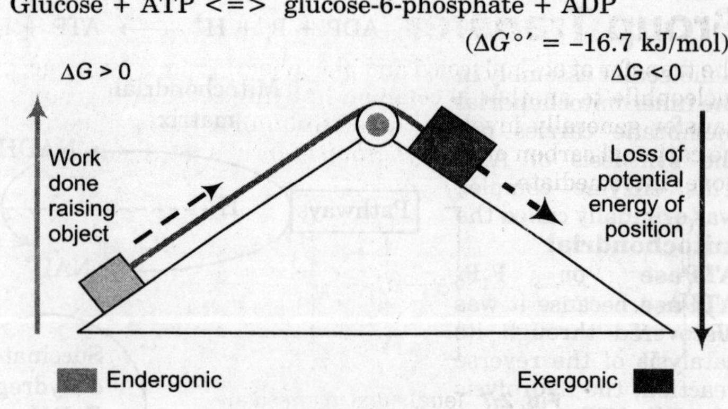

Fig. 2.5 Mechanical process

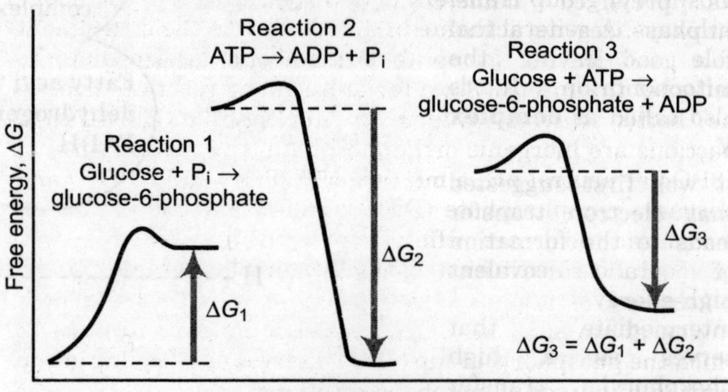

Fig. 2.6 Chemical process

(a)				$\Delta G°'$ (kJ × mol^{-1})
Endergonic half-reaction 1	P_i + glucose	$\rightleftharpoons$	Glucose-6-phosphate + H_2O	+13.8
Exergonic half-reaction 2	ATP + H_2O	$\rightleftharpoons$	ADP + P_i	–30.5
Overall coupled reaction	ATP + glucose	$\rightleftharpoons$	ADP + glucose-6-phosphate	–16.7
(b)				**$\Delta G°'$ (kJ × mol^{-1})**
Exergonic half-reaction 1	$CH_2{=}C(COO^-)(OPO_3^{2-})$ + H_2O Phosphoenol pyruvate	$\rightleftharpoons$	$CH_3{-}C({=}O){-}COO^-$ + P_i Pyruvate	–61.9
Endergonic half-reaction 2	ADP + P_i	$\rightleftharpoons$	ATP + H_2O	+30.5
Overall coupled reaction	$CH_2{=}C(COO^-)(OPO_3^{2-})$ + ADP	$\rightleftharpoons$	$CH_3{-}C({=}O){-}COO^-$ + ATP	–31.4

Group Transfer

The transfer of acyl, glycosyl and phosphoryl groups from one nucleophile to another is common in living cells. Acyl group transfer generally involves the addition of a nucleophile to the carbonyl carbon of an acyl group to form a tetrahedral (to move) intermediate.

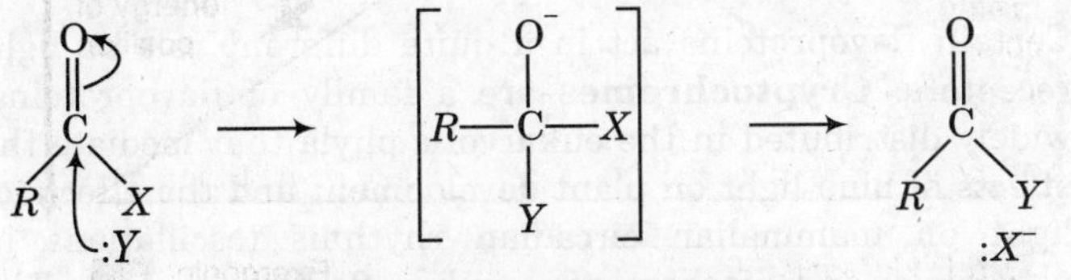

Fig. 2.7 Tetrahedral intermediate

Phosphoryl group transfers play a special role in metabolic pathways. A general theme in metabolism is the attachment of a good leaving group to a metabolic intermediate to 'activate' the intermediate for subsequent reaction. Among the better leaving groups in nucleophilic substitution reactions are inorganic orthophosphate (the ionized form of H3PO4 at neutral pH, a mixture of H_2PO^{4-} and HPO_4^{2-}) and inorganic pyrophosphate ($P_2O_7^{4-}$); esters and anhydrides of phosphoric acid are effectively activated for reaction. Nucleophilic substitution is made more favourable by the attachment of a phosphoryl group to an otherwise poor leaving group such as OOH. Nucleophilic substitutions in which the phosphoryl group ($-PO_3^{2-}$) serves as a leaving group occur in hundreds of metabolic reactions.

The large families of enzymes that catalyze phosphoryl group transfers with ATP as donor are called kinases (Greek *kinein* (to move), hexokinase, 'moves'—a phosphoryl group from ATP to glucose.

Biological Energy Transducers

Cells contain a variety of molecular energy transducers, which convert the energy of electron flow into useful work. Living cells have an analogous biological 'circuit,' with a relatively reduced compound such as glucose as the source of electrons. As glucose is enzymatically oxidized, the released electrons flow spontaneously through a series of electron-carrier intermediates to another chemical species, such as O_2. This electron flow is exergonic, because O_2 has a higher affinity for electrons than do the electron-carrier intermediates. The resulting electromotive force provides energy to a variety of molecular energy transducers (enzymes and other proteins) that do biological work. In the mitochondrion, for example, membrane-bound enzymes couple electron flow to the production of a transmembrane pH difference, accomplishing osmotic and electrical work. The proton gradient thus formed has potential energy, sometimes called the proton-motive force by analogy with electromotive force. Another enzyme, ATP synthase in the inner mitochondrial membrane, uses the proton motive force to do chemical work: synthesis of ATP from ADP and P_i as protons flow spontaneously across the membrane. Similarly, membrane-localized enzymes in *E.coli* convert electromotive force to proton-motive force, which is then used to power flagella motion. The principles of electrochemistry that govern energy changes in the macroscopic circuit with a motor and battery apply with equal validity to the molecular processes accompanying electron flow in living cells.

NADH and NADPH

It act with dehydrogenases as soluble electron carriers. Nicotinamide adenine dinucleotide (NAD^+ in its oxidized form) and its close analog nicotinamide adenine dinucleotide phosphate ($NADP^+$) are composed of two nucleotides joined through their phosphate groups by a phosphoanhydride bond. Because the nicotinamide ring resembles pyridine, these compounds are sometimes called **pyridine nucleotides.** The vitamin niacin is the source of the nicotinamide moiety innicotinamide nucleotides. Both coenzymes undergo reversible reduction of the nicotinamide ring.

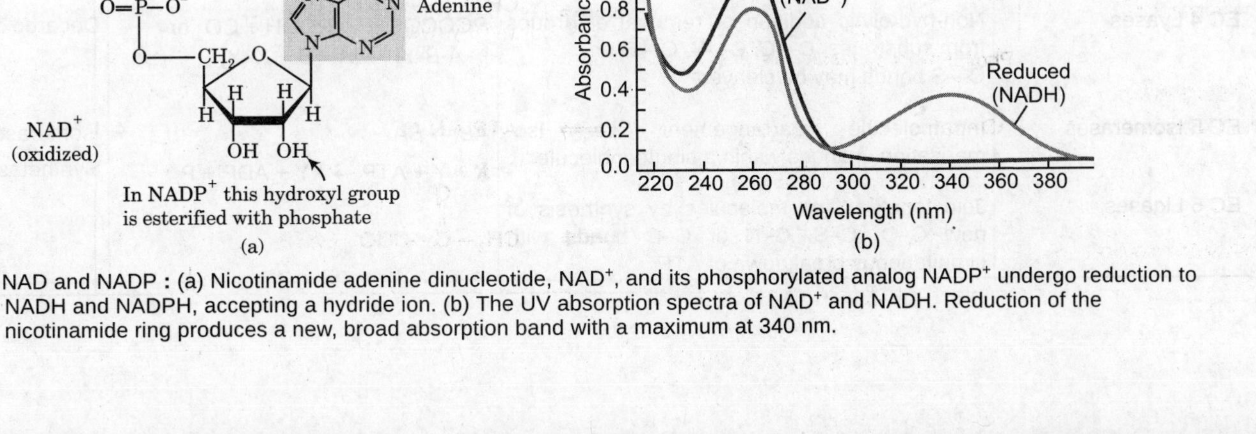

Fig. 2.8 NAD and NADP : (a) Nicotinamide adenine dinucleotide, NAD^+, and its phosphorylated analog $NADP^+$ undergo reduction to NADH and NADPH, accepting a hydride ion. (b) The UV absorption spectra of NAD^+ and NADH. Reduction of the nicotinamide ring produces a new, broad absorption band with a maximum at 340 nm.

More than 200 enzymes are known to catalyze reactions in which NAD^+ (or $NADP^+$) accepts a hydride ion from a reduced substrate NADPH (or NADH) donates a hydride ion to an oxidized substrate.

Flavin Nucleotides Bound in Flavoproteins

Flavoproteins are enzymes that catalyze oxidation-reduction reactions using either flavin mononucleotide (FMN) or flavin adenine dinucleotide (FAD) as coenzyme. These coenzymes, the **flavin nucleotides,** are derived from the vitamin riboflavin. The flavin nucleotide in most flavoproteins is bound rather tightly to the protein and in some enzymes, such as succinate dehydrogenase, it is bound covalently. Such tightly bound coenzymes are properly called prosthetic groups. They do not transfer electrons by diffusing from one enzyme to another; rather, they provide a means by which the flavoproteins can temporarily hold electrons while it catalyzes electron transfer from a reduced substrate to an electron acceptor. One important feature of the flavoproteins is the variability in the standard reduction potential (E^o) of the bound flavin nucleotide.

Certain flavoproteins act in a quite different role as light receptors. **Cryptochromes** are a family of flavoproteins, widely distributed in the eukaryotic phyla that mediate the effects of blue light on plant development and the effects of light on mammalian circadian rhythms (oscillations in physiology and biochemistry, with a 24-hour period). The cryptochromes are homologs of another family of flavoproteins, the photolyases.

Principles of Catalysis

Nearly all biological reactions are catalyzed by catalysts called enzymes. Which function on the basis of vorious principles.

Enzymes

Enzymes are biological catalysts. It catalyzed almost all biological reactions that maintains homeostasis. The macromolecular components of almost all enzymes are composed of protein, except for a class of RNA modifying catalysts known as **ribozymes.** Ribozymes are molecules of ribonucleic acid that catalyze reactions on the phosphodiester bond of other RNAs.

Enzyme Classifications

The **International Union of Biochemists** (IUSs) developed a complex but unambiguous system of enzyme nomenclature. In the IUB system, each enzyme has a unique name and code number that reflect the type of reaction catalyzed and the substrates involved. Enzymes are grouped into six classes, each with several sub-classes. For example, the enzyme commonly called 'hexokinase' is designated 'ATP: D-hexose-6-phosphotransferase EC 2.7.1.1.' This identifies hexokinase as a member of class 2 (transferases), sub-class 7 (transfer of a phosphoryl group), sub-sub-class 1 (alcohol is the phosphoryl acceptor). Finally, the term 'hexose-6' indicates that the alcohol phosphorylated is that of carbon six of a hexose.

For enzymes, the EC numbers; each enzyme is described by a sequence of four numbers preceded by 'EC'. The first number broadly classifies the enzyme based on its mechanism.

Table 2.3 **The Top-level Classification**

Group	Reaction Catalyzed	Typical Reaction	Enzyme Example
EC 1 oxidoreductases	To catalyze oxidation/reduction reactions; transfer of H and O atoms or electrons from one substance to another	$AH + B \rightarrow A + BH$ **(reduced)** $A + O \rightarrow AO$ **(oxidized)**	Dehydrogenase and oxidase
EC 2 Transferases	Transfer of a functional group from one substance to another. The group may be methyl, acyl, amino or phosphate group	$AB + C \rightarrow A + BC$	Transaminase and kinase
EC 3 Hydrolases	Formation of two products from a substrate by hydrolysis	$AB + H_2O \rightarrow AOH + BH$	Lipase, amylase and peptidase
EC 4 Lyases	Non-hydrolytic addition or removal of groups from substrates. C—C, C—N, C—O or C—S bonds may be cleaved	$RCOCOOH \rightarrow RCOH + CO_2$ or $[X\text{-}A\text{-}B\text{-}Y] \rightarrow [A = B + X\text{–}Y]$	Decarboxylase
EC 5 Isomerases	Intramolecule rearrangement, *i.e.*, isomerization changes within a single molecule	$AB \rightarrow BA$ $X + Y + ATP \rightarrow XY + ADP + P_i$	Isomerase and mutase Synthetase
EC 6 Ligases	Join together two molecules by synthesis of new C–O, C–S, C–N or C–C bonds with simultaneous breakdown of ATP		

Prosthetic Groups, Cofactors and Coenzymes

The catalytic activity of many enzymes depends on the presence of small molecules termed **cofactors,** although the precise role varies with the cofactor and the enzyme. Such an enzyme without its cofactor is referred to as an **apoenzyme;** the complete, catalytically active enzyme is called a **holoenzyme.**

Apoenzyme + cofactor = holoenzyme

(i) **Prosthetic groups** are distinguished by their tight, stable incorporation into a protein's structure by covalent or non-covalent forces. Examples include pyridoxal phosphate, flavin mononucleotide (FMN), flavin dinucleotide (FAD), thiamin pyrophosphate, biotin, and the metal ions of Co, Cu, Mg, Mn, Se and Zn. Metals are the most common prosthetic groups. The roughly one-third of all enzymes that contain tightly bound metal ions are termed **metalloenzymes.**

(ii) Some enzymes require no chemical groups for activity other than their amino acid residues. Others require an additional chemical component called a **cofactor**, either one or more inorganic ions, such as Fe^{2-}, Mg^{2-}, Mn^{2-} or Zn^{2-} or a complex organic or metalloorganic molecule called a **coenzyme.** Some enzymes require both a coenzyme.

Fig. 2.9 Enzyme Specificity (a) Trypsin cleaves on the carboxyl side of arginine and lysine residues, whereas (b) Thrombin cleaves Arg-Gly bonds in particular sequences specifically

Table 2.4 **Enzyme Cofactors**

Cofactor	Enzyme
Coenzyme	
Thiamine pyrophosphate	Pyruvate dehydrogenase
Flavin adenine nucleotide	Monoamine oxidase
Pyridoxal phosphate	Glycogen phosphorylase
Nicotinamide adenine dinucleotide	Lactate dehydrogenase
Coenzyme-A (Co-A)	Acetyl Co-A carboxylase
Biotin	Pyruvate carboxylase
5-deoxyadenosyl cobalamin	Methylmalonyl mutase
Tetrahydrofolate	Thymidylate synthase
Metal	
Zn^{2+}	Carbonic anhydrase
Zn^{2+}	Carboxypeptidase
Mg^{2+}	Hexokinase
Mg^{2+}	*Eco* RV
Mo	Xanthine oxidase
Ni^{2+}	Nitrate reductase
Se	Urease
Mn^{2+}	Glutathione peroxidase
	Arginase superoxide dismutase
K^+	Propionyl Co-A carboxylase
Cu^{2+}	Ascorbic acid oxidase

Mechanism of Enzyme Catalysis

The enzyme catalysis is controlled by free energy changes and concentration of substrate and products.

Free Energy of Enzymes

To fully understand how enzymes operate, we need to consider two thermodynamic properties of the reaction. (a) The free-energy difference (ΔG) between the products and reactants. (b) The energy required to initiate the conversion of reactants to products. The former determines whether the reaction will be spontaneous, whereas the later determines the rate of the reaction. Enzymes affect only the latter. First, we will consider the thermodynamics of reactions.

The free-energy change of a reaction (ΔG) tells us if the reaction can occur spontaneously :

- a reaction can occur spontaneously only if ΔG is negative. Such reactions are said to be exergonic.
- a system is at equilibrium and no net change can take place if ΔG is zero.
- a reaction cannot occur spontaneously if ΔG is positive. An input of free energy is required to drive such a reaction. These reactions are termed endergonic.

Two additional points need to be emphasized. The ΔG of a reaction depends only on the free energy of the products (the final state) minus the free energy of the reactants (the initial state). The mechanism of a reaction has no effect on ΔG, *i.e.*,

- The ΔG of a reaction is independent of the path (or molecular mechanism) of the transformation.
- The ΔG provides no information about the rate of a reaction.

The Standard Free-Energy Change of a Reaction

Consider the reaction,

$$A + B \rightleftharpoons C + D$$

The ΔG of this reaction is given by

$$\Delta G = \Delta G^\circ + RT \ln \frac{[C][D]}{[A][B]} \quad \text{...(i)}$$

where,

ΔG° is the standard free-energy change,

R is the gas constant,

T is the absolute temperature and

$[A]$, $[B]$, $[C]$ and $[D]$ are the molar concentrations of the reactants.

ΔG° is the free energy change for this reaction under standard conditions.

The standard free-energy change at pH 7, denoted by the symbol ΔG°. At equilibrium, $\Delta G = 0$. From Eq. (i)

$$0 = \Delta G^{\circ\prime} + RT \ln \frac{[C][D]}{[A][D]} \quad \text{...(ii)}$$

$$\Delta G^{\circ\prime} = - RT \ln \frac{[C][D]}{[A][B]} \quad \text{...(iii)}$$

The equilibrium constant under standard conditions, K'_{eq}, is defined as

$$K'_{eq} = \frac{[C][D]}{[A][B]} \quad \text{...(iv)}$$

$$\Delta G^{\circ\prime} = - RT \ln K'_{eq} \quad \text{...(v)}$$

$$\Delta G^{\circ\prime} = - 2.303RT \log_{10} K'_{eq} \quad \text{...(vi)}$$

(i) Enzymes accelerate the attainment of equilibria but do not shift their positions. The equilibrium position is a function only of the free-energy difference between reactants and products, *i.e.*, equilibrium would be attained rapidly in the presence of a suitable enzyme.

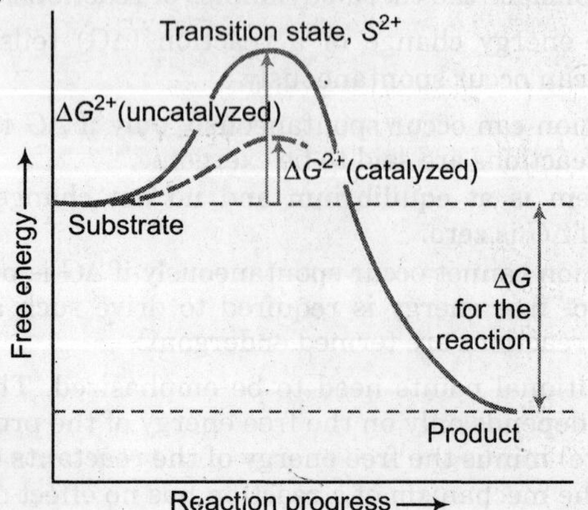

Fig. 2.10 Enzymes decrease the activation energy

Example Calculate ΔG° and ΔG for the isomerization of dihydroxyacetone phosphate (DHAP) to glyceraldehyde-3-phosphate (GAP). This reaction takes place in glycolysis. At equilibrium, the ratio of GAP to DHAP is 0.0475 at 25°C (298 K) and pH 7. Hence, K' eq = 0.0475. Find the standard free-energy change for this reaction.

Solution $\Delta G^{\circ\prime} = -2.303RT \log_{10} K'_{eq}$

$$= -2.303 \times 1.987 \times 10^{-3} \times 298 \times \log_{10}(0.0475)$$

$$= +1.80 \text{ kcal mol}^{-1} \text{ (7.53 kJ mol}^{-1}\text{)}$$

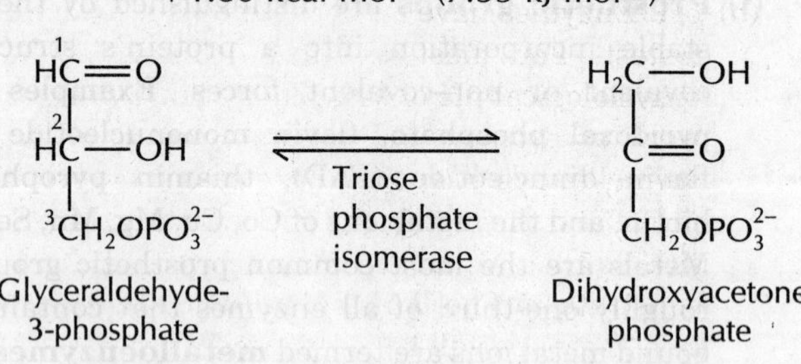

The reaction is endergonic. DHAP will not spontaneously convert to GAP.

Rates of Reactions

The rates of reactions are determined by their activation energy. The **kinetic theory** also called the **collision theory** of chemical kinetics states that for two molecules to react they must

(i) approach within bond-forming distance of one another, or 'collides'; and (ii) Must possess sufficient kinetic energy to overcome the energy barrier for reaching the transition state.

Factors Affecting the Rate of Enzyme Reaction

(a) Temperature Enzymes have an optimum temperature at which they work fastest. For mammalian enzymes this is about 40°C, but there are enzymes that work best at very different temperatures, *e.g.*, enzymes from the Arctic snow flea work at –10°C, and enzymes from thermophilic bacteria work at 90°C.

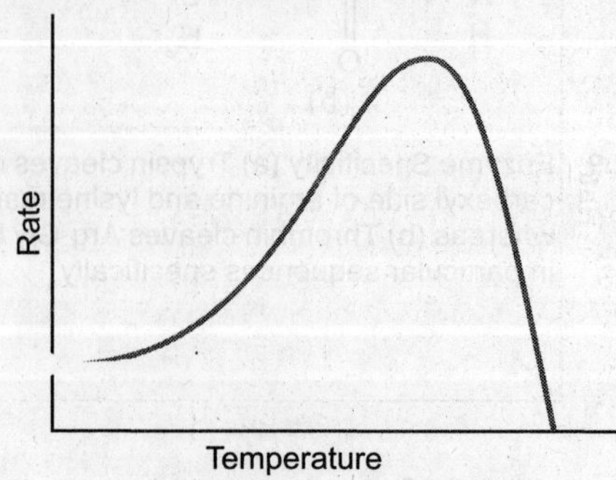

Fig. 2.11 Optimum temperature

Above the optimum temperature, 'the rate decreases as more and more of the enzyme molecules denature. The thermal energy breaks the hydrogen bonds holding the secondary and tertiary structure of the enzyme together, so the enzyme (and especially the active site) loses its shape to become a random coil. The substrate can no longer bind, and the reaction is no longer catalyzed. At very high temperatures this is irreversible. Remember that only the work hydrogen bonds are broken at these mild temperatures to break strong covalent bonds you need to boil in concentrated acid for many hours.

(b) pH Enzymes have an optimum pH at which they work fastest. For most enzymes; this is about pH 7-8 (physiological pH of most cells), but a few enzymes can work at extreme pH, such as protonno enzymes. In animal stomachs, which have an optimum of pH 1. The pH affects the charge of the amino acids at the active site, so the properties of the active site change and the substrate can no longer bind. For example, a carboxyl acid R groups will be uncharged a low pH (COOH), but charged at high pH (COO–).

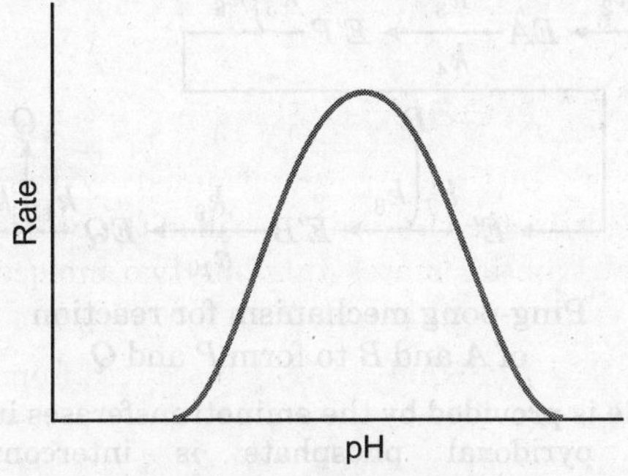

Fig. 2.12 The optimum pH

(c) **Enzyme Concentration** As the enzyme concentration increases, the rate of the reaction increases linearly, because there are more enzyme molecules available to catalyze the reaction. At very high enzyme concentration the substrate concentration may become rate-limiting, so the rate stops increasing. Normally, enzymes are present in cells in rather low concentrations.

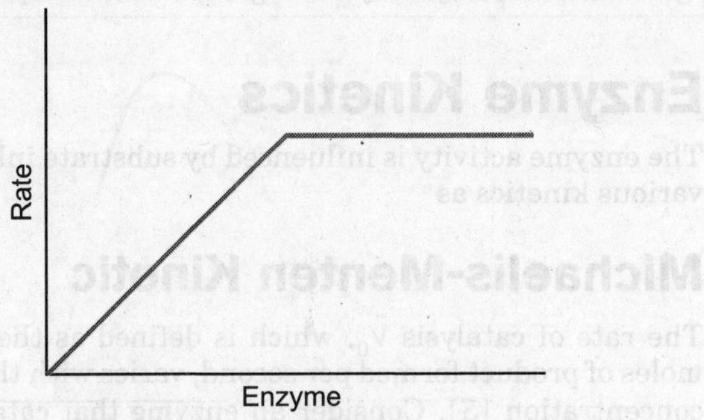

Fig. 2.13 Enzyme concentration

(d) **Substrate Concentration** The rate of an enzyme-catalyzed reaction shows a curved dependence on substrate concentration. As the substrate concentration increases, the rate increases because more substrate molecules can collide with enzyme molecules, so more reactions will take place. At higher concentrations, the enzyme molecules become saturated with substrate, so there are few free enzyme molecules, so adding more substrate doesn't make much difference (though it will increase the rate of E-S collisons).

The maximum rate at infinite substrate concentration is called V_{max} and the substrate concentration that give a rate of half V_{max} is called K_m. These quantities are useful for characterizing an enzyme. A good enzyme has a high V_{max} and a low K_m.

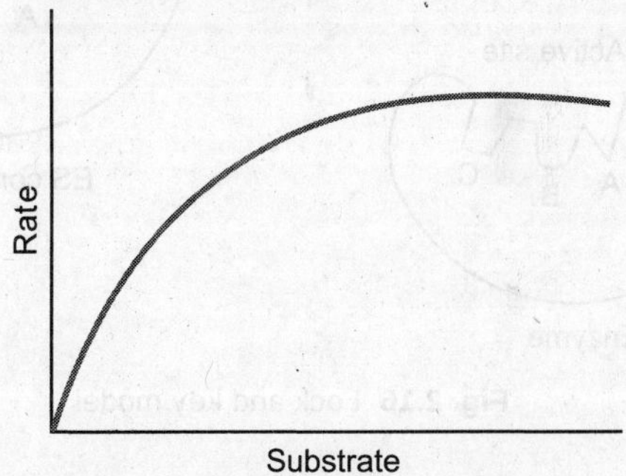

Fig. 2.14 Substrate concentration

Enzyme-Substrate (ES) Complexes

Enzymes promote the formation of the transition states in **enzyme-substrate** (ES) complexes. The substrates are bound to a specific region of the enzyme called the **active site.** Most enzymes are highly selective in the substrates that they bind.

Different models of Enzyme-Substrate (ES) complexes are given below.

Uracil (from substrate)
Threonine side chain
Serine side chain

Fig. 2.15 Hydrogen bonds between an enzyme and substrate

(i) Lock and Key Model of Enzyme-Substrate Binding

In this model, the active site of the unbound enzyme is complementary in shape to the substrate. **Emil Fischer** compared the highly specific fit between enzymes and their substrates to that of a lock and its key. While the 'lock and key model' accounted for the exquisite specificity of enzyme-substrate interactions, the implied rigidity of the enzyme's active site failed to account for the dynamic changes that accompany catalysis.

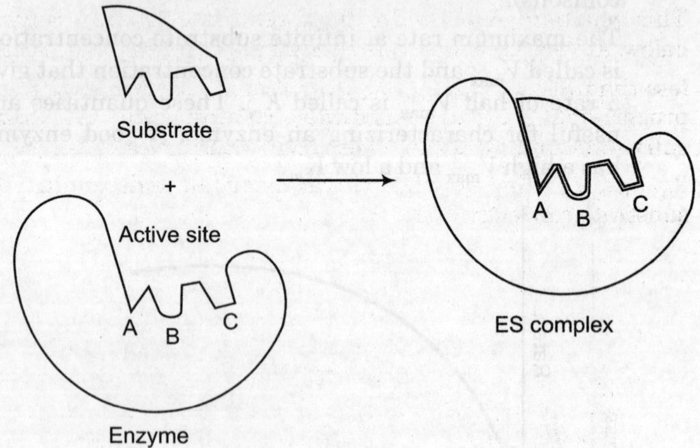

Fig. 2.16 Lock and key model

(ii) Induced-Fit Model of Enzyme-Substrate Binding

In this model, the enzyme changes shape on substrate binding. The active site forms a shape complementary to the substrate only after the substrate has been bound. **Daniel Koshland's induced fit** model, which states that when substrates approach and bind to an enzyme they induce a conformational change, a change analogous to placing a hand (substrate) into a glove (enzyme). A corollary is that the enzyme induces reciprocal changes in its substrates, harnessing the energy of binding to facilitate the transformation of substrates into products.

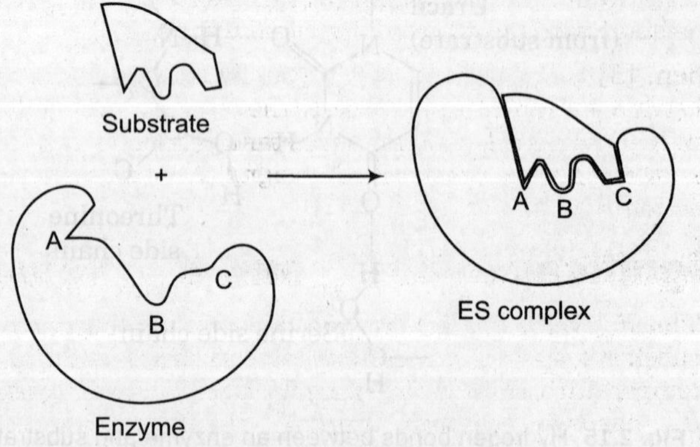

Fig. 2.17 Induced-fit model

Other Models of E-S binding

Covalent Catalysis In covalent catalysis, a transient covalent bond is formed between the enzyme and the substrate.

Metal Ion Catalysis Metals, whether tightly bound to the enzyme or taken up from solution alongwith the substrate, can participate in catalysis in several ways. Ionic interactions between an enzyme-bound metal and a substrate can help orient the substrate for reaction or stabilize charged reaction transition states.

Ping-pong Mechanisms A common type of mechanism that is especially prevalent for enzymes with tightly bound cofactors has been dubbed **ping-pong** because the enzyme alternates between two forms E and E'. Substrate A reacts via complex EA to form E', a modified enzyme that often contains an altered coenzyme. At the same time A is changed to product P still bound to the enzyme. P dissociates leaving E' which is then able to react with the second substrate B and to go through the second half of the cycle during which E' is converted back to E.

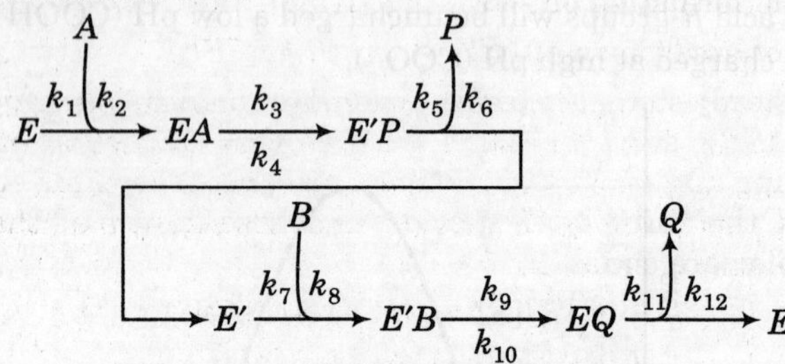

Ping-pong mechanism for reaction of A and B to form P and Q

An example is provided by the aminotransferases in which the coenzyme pyridoxal phosphate is interconvert with pyridoxamine phosphate.

The rate equations of the ping-pong mechanism resemble that for the ordered bimolecular reaction.

Most enzymes employ a combination of several catalytic strategies to bring about a rate enhancement. A good example of the use of both covalent catalysis and general acid-base catalysis is the reaction catalyzed by chymotrypsin. The first step is cleavage of a peptide bond, which is accompanied by formation of a covalent linkage between a Ser residue on the enzyme and part of the substrate the reaction is enhanced by general base catalysis by other groups on the enzyme.

Enzyme Kinetics

The enzyme activity is influenced by substrate inhibitors and various kinetics as

Michaelis-Menten Kinetic

The rate of catalysis V_0, which is defined as the number of moles of product formed per second, varies with the substrate concentration $[S]$. Consider an enzyme that catalyzes the S to P by the following pathway

$$E + E \underset{k_{-1}}{\overset{k_1}{\rightleftharpoons}} ES \underset{k_{-2}}{\overset{k2}{\rightleftharpoons}} E + P$$

At a fixed concentration of enzyme, V_0 is almost linearly proportional to $[S]$ when $[S]$ is small but is nearly independent of $[S]$ when $[S]$ is large. In 1913, **Leonor Michaelis and Maud Menten** proposed a simple model to account for these kinetic characteristics. The critical feature in their treatment is that a specific *ES* complex is a necessary intermediate in catalysis.

An enzyme *E* combines with substrate *S* to form an *ES* complex, with a rate constant k_1. It can also dissociate to *E* and *S*, with a rate constant k_{-1}, or it can proceed to form product *P*, with a rate constant k_2.

The rate of catalysis to the concentrations of substrate and enzyme is equal to the product of the concentration of the *ES* complex and k_2.

$$V_0 = k_2[\text{ES}] \quad \text{...(i)}$$

The rates of formation and breakdown of *ES* are given by

$$\text{Rate of formation of } ES = k_1[E][S] \quad \text{...(ii)}$$

$$\text{Rate of breakdown of } ES = (k_{-1} + k_2)\,[ES] \quad \text{...(iii)}$$

In a steady state, the concentrations of intermediates in this case $[ES]$, stay the same even if the concentrations of starting materials and products are changing. This occurs when the rates of formation and breakdown of the *ES* complex are equal.

$$k_1[E][S] = (k_{-1} + k_2)\,[ES] \quad \text{...(iv)}$$

$$[E][S]/[ES] = (k_{-1} + k_2)/k_1 \quad \text{...(v)}$$

Simplified by defining a new constant, K_m, called the **Michaelis constant**

$$K_\text{m} = \frac{k_{-1} + k_2}{k_1} \quad \text{...(vi)}$$

K_m has the units of concentration. K_m is an important characteristic of enzyme-substrate interactions and is independent of enzyme and substrate concentrations. By solving above equation we get

$$[ES] = \frac{[E][S]}{K_m} \quad \text{...(vii)}$$

The concentration of uncombined substrate $[S]$ is very nearly equal to the total substrate concentration, provided that the concentration of enzyme is much lower than that of substrate. The concentration of uncombined enzyme $[E]$ is equal to the total enzyme concentration $[E]_\text{T}$ minus the concentration of the *ES* complex.

$$[E] = [E]_\text{T} - [ES] \quad \text{...(viii)}$$

Substituting the expression for $[E]$ in the above equation, gives

$$[ES] = \frac{([E]_\text{T} - [ES])\,[S]}{K_m} \quad \text{...(ix)}$$

$$[ES] = d[E]_\text{T}\,\frac{[S]}{[S] + K_m} \quad \text{...(x)}$$

By substituting this expresion for $[ES]$ into Eq (i), we obtain

$$V_0 = K_m[E]_\text{T}\,\frac{[S]}{[S] + K_m} \quad \text{...(xi)}$$

The maximal rate, $V_{\max}$, is attained when the catalytic sites on the enzyme are saturated with substrate that is, when $[ES] = [E]_\text{T}$. Thus,

$$V_{\max} = k_2[E]_\text{T} \quad \text{...(xii)}$$

Substituting Eq. (xii) into Eq. (xi) yields the Michaelis-Menten equation

$$V_0 = \text{V}_{\max}\,\frac{[S]}{[S] + K_m} \quad \text{...(xiii)}$$

This equation accounts for the kinetic data given in Figure below. At very low substrate concentration, when $[S]$ is much less than K_m, $V_0 = (V_{\max}/K_m)[S]$; that is, the rate is directly proportional to the substrate concentration. At high substrate concentration, when $[S]$ is much greater than K_m, $V_0 = V_{\max}$; that is, the rate is maximal, independent of substrate concentration.

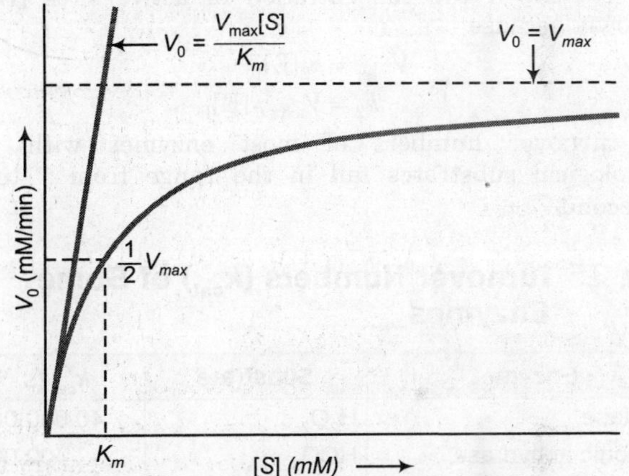

Fig. 2.18 Michaelis-Menten kinetics

This graph shows the kinetic parameters that define the limits of the curve at high and low $[S]$. At low $[S]$, $K_m >> [S]$ and the $[S]$ term in the denominator of the Michaelis-Menten eq (Eq. xiii) becomes in significant. The equation simplifies to $V_0 = V_{\max}[S]/K_m$ and V_0 exhibits a linear dependence on $[S]$, as observed here. At high $[S]$, where $[S] > K_m$, the K_m term in the denominator of the Michaelis Menten equation becomes in significant and the equation simplifies to $V_0 = V_{\max}$; this is consistent with the plateau observed at high $[S]$.

When, $[S] = K_m$, then $V_0 = V_{\max}/2$. Thus K_m is equal to the substrate concentration at which the reaction rate is half its maximal value. K_m is an important characteristic of an enzyme-catalyzed reaction and is significant for its biological function.

Significance of K_m and $V_{\max}$ Values

- The K_m value for an enzyme depends on the particular substrate and on environmental conditions such as pH, temperature, and ionic strength. The Michaelis constant, K_m, has two meanings. First, K_m is the concentration of substrate at which half the active sites are filled. Thus, K_m provides a measure of the substrate concentration required for significant catalysis to occur. Second, K_m is related to the rate constants of the individual steps in the catalytic scheme.

- k_m is defined as $(k_{-1} + k_2)/k_1$. Consider a limiting case in which k_{-1} is much greater than k_2. Under such circumstances, the *ES* complex dissociates to *E* and *S* much more rapidly than product is formed. Under these conditions $(k_{-1} > k_2)$,
- k_m is equal to the dissociation constant of the *ES* complex if k_2 is much smaller than k_{-1}. When this condition is met, K_m is a measure of the strength of the *ES* complex: a high K_m indicates weak binding; a low k_m indicates strong binding. It must be stressed that k_m indicates the affinity of the *ES* complex only when k_{-1} is much greater than k_2.
- The maximal rate, V_{max}, reveals the turnover number of an enzyme, which is the number of substrate molecules converted into product by an enzyme molecule in a unit time when the enzyme is fully saturated with substrate. It is equal to the kinetic constant k_2, which is also called K_{cat}. The maximal rate, V_{max}, reveals the turnover number of an enzyme if the concentration of active sites $[E]_T$ is known, because

$$V_{max} = k_2[E]_T$$
$$k_2 = V_{max} / [E]_T$$

The turnover numbers of most enzymes with their physiological substrates fall in the range from 1 to 10^4 per second.

Table 2.5 **Turnover Numbers (k_{cat}) of Some Enzymes**

Enzyme	Substrate	k_{cat} (s^{-1})
Catalase	H_2O_2	40,000,000
Carbonic anhydrase	HCO_3	400,000
Acetylcholinesterase	Acetylcholine	140,000
β-Lactamase	Benzylpenicillin	2,000
Fumarase	Fumarate	800
RecA protein (an ATPase)	ATP	0

Linear Form of the Michaelis-Menten Equation

A linear form of the Michaelis-Menten equation circumvents this difficulty and permits.

V_{max} and K_m to be extrapolated from initial velocity data obtained at less than saturating concentrations of substrate.

$$\frac{1}{V_0} = \frac{K_m + [S]}{V_{max}[S]} \quad \text{...(xiii)}$$

Where, V_0 is half the maximal velocity ($V_{max}/2$) attainable at a particular concentration of enzyme.

$$\frac{1}{V_0} = \frac{K_m}{V_{max}[S]} + \frac{[S]}{V_{max}[S]}$$

$$\frac{1}{V_0} = \frac{K_m}{V_{max}}\frac{1}{[S]} + \frac{1}{V_{max}}$$

A plot of $1/V_0$ as *y* as a function of $1/[S]$ as *x*, therefore gives a straight line whose *y* intercept is $1/V_{max}$ and whose slope is K_m/V_{max}. Such a plot is called a double reciprocal or Lineweaver-Burk plot. Setting the *y* term of equation equal to zero and solving for *x* reveals that the *x* intercept is $-1/K_m$. K_m is thus most easily calculated from the *x* intercept.

The affinity of an enzyme for its substrate is the inverse of the dissociation constant K_d for dissociation of the enzyme substrate complex *ES*.

$$E + S \underset{k_{-1}}{\overset{k_1}{\rightleftharpoons}} ES$$

$$K_d = \frac{k_{-1}}{k_1}$$

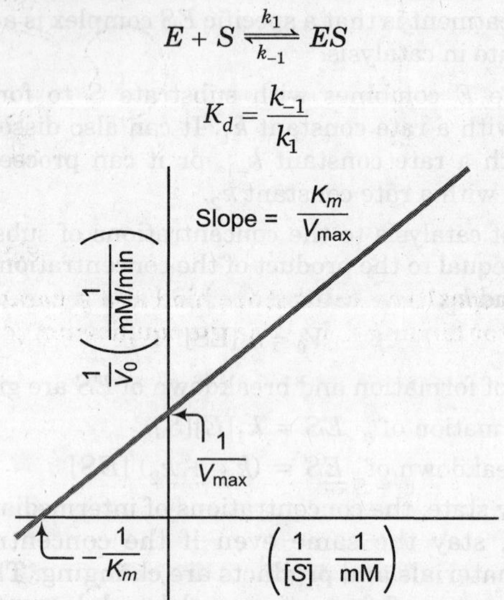

Fig. 2.19 Double reciprocal or Lineweaver-Burk plot of $1/V_0$ *versus* $1/[S]$ used to evaluate K_m and V_{max}

Table 2.6 **K_m for Some Enzymes and Substrates**

Enzyme	Substrate	K_m (mM)
Catalase	H_2O_2	25
Hexokinase (brain)	ATP	0.4
	D-glucose	0.05
	D-fructose	1.5
Carbonic anhydrase	HCO_3^-	26
Chymotrypsin	Glycyltyrosinylglycine	108
	N-Benzoyltyrosinamide	2.5
β-Galactosidase	D-lactose	4.0
Threonine dehydratase	L-threonine	5.0

Enzyme Inhibitors

Enzyme inhibitors are molecular agents that interfere with catalysis, slowing or halting enzymatic reactions. There are two broad classes of enzyme inhibitors reversible and irreversible.

(i) Reversible Inhibition

Three types of reversible inhibition are

(a) **Competitive Inhibitors** bind to the enzyme's active site. V_{max} stays constant and K_m increases, but the inhibitor does not affect the turn over number of the enzyme.

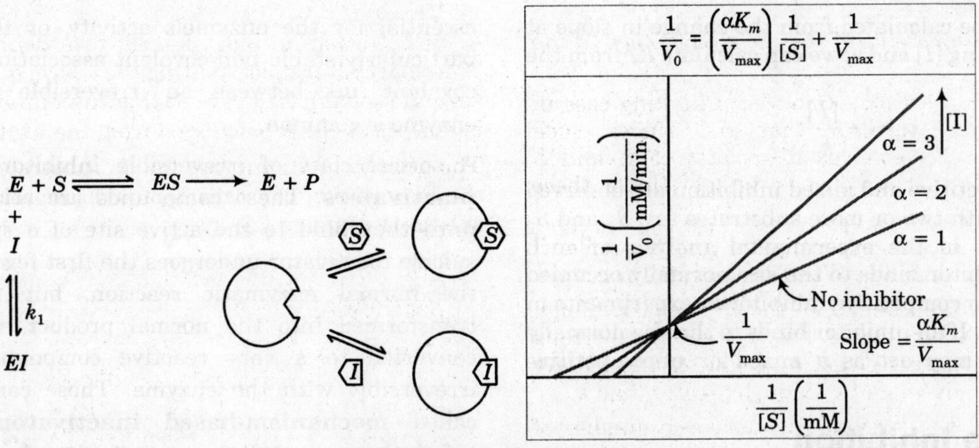

Fig. 2.20 Competitive inhibitors

(b) **Uncompetitive Inhibitors** bind at a separate site, but bind only to the *ES* complex. k_1 is the equilibrium constant for inhibitor binding to E; k_1' is the equilibrium constant for inhibitor binding to ES. V_{max} and K_m both decreases.

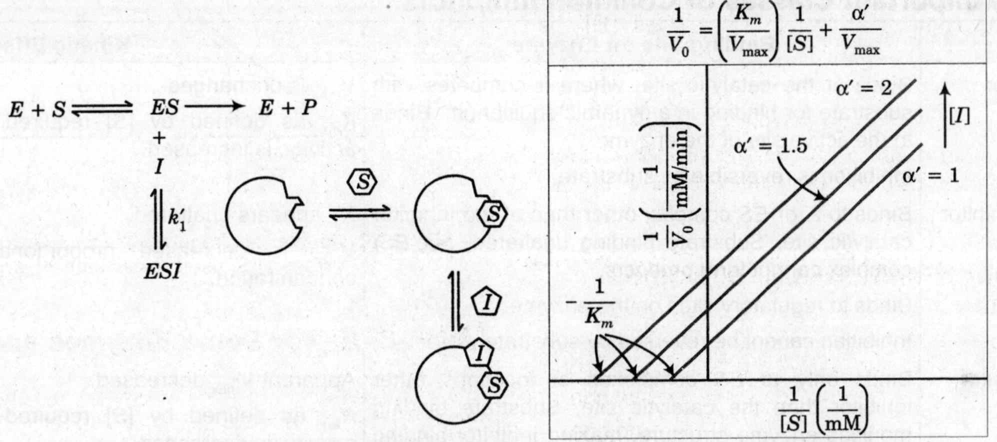

Fig. 2.21 Uncompetitive inhibitors

(c) **Mixed Inhibitors or Non-Competitive Inhibition,** bind at a separate site, but may bind to either *E* or *ES*. Inhibitor binds to the enzyme at a site other than the active site. Inhibitor binding alters the enzyme's three-dimensional configuration and blocks the reaction. V_{max} decreases and K_m stays constant.

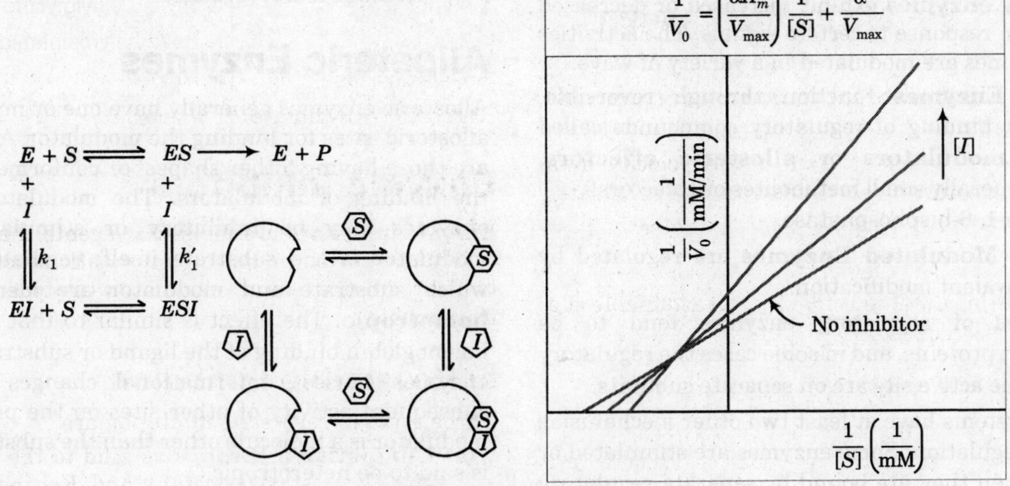

Fig. 2.22 Mixed inhibitors

The value of a can be calculated from the change in slope at any given [*I*]. Knowing [*I*] and a, we can calculate *KI* from the expression

$$\alpha = 1 + \frac{[I]}{k_1}$$

In practice, uncompetitive and mixed inhibition are observed only for enzymes with two or more substrates say, S_1 and S_2 are very important in the experimental analysis of such enzymes. If an inhibitor binds to the site normally occupied by S_1, it may act as a competitive inhibitor in experiments in which $[S_1]$ is varied. If an inhibitor binds to the site normally occupied by S_2, it may act as a mixed or uncompetitive inhibitor of S_1.

(II) Irreversible Inhibition

The **irreversible inhibitors** are those that bind covalently with or destroy a functional group on an enzyme that is essential for the enzyme's activity, or those that form a particularly stable non-covalent association. Formation of a covalent link between an irreversible inhibitor and an enzyme is common.

A special class of irreversible inhibitors is the **suicide inactivators.** These compounds are relatively unreactive until they bind to the active site of a specific enzyme. A suicide inactivator undergoes the first few chemical steps of the normal enzymatic reaction, but instead of being transformed into the normal product, the inactivator is converted to a very reactive compound that combines irreversibly with the enzyme. These compounds are also called **mechanism-based inactivators,** because they hijack the normal enzyme reaction mechanism to inactivate the enzyme.

Table 2.7 **Three Important Classes of Common Inhibitors**

Inhibitor Type	Binding Site on Enzyme	Kinetic Effect
Competitive inhibitor	Binds at the catalytic site, where it competes with substrate for binding in a dynamic equilibrium. Binds to the active site of the enzyme. Inhibition is reversible by substrate.	V_{max} is unchanged. K_m, as defined by [*S*] required for 1/2 maximal activity, is increased.
Non-competitive inhibitor	Binds to *E* or *ES* complex other than at the inhibitor catalytic site. Substrate binding unaltered, but *ESI* complex cannot form products. Binds to regulatory sites on the enzyme. Inhibition cannot be reversed by substrate.	K_m appears unaltered. V_{max} is decreased proportionately to inhibitor concentration.
Uncompetitive inhibitor	Binds only to *ES* complexes at locations other inhibitor than the catalytic site. Substrate binding modifies enzyme structure, making inhibitor-binding site available. Inhibition cannot be reversed by substrate.	Apparent V_{max} decreased. K_m, as defined by [*S*] required for 1/2 maximal activity, is decreased.

Enzyme Regulation

These **regulatory enzymes** exhibit increased or decreased catalytic activity in response to certain signals. The activities of regulatory enzymes are modulated in a variety of ways.

1. **Allosteric Enzymes** function through reversible, non-covalent binding of regulatory compounds called **allosteric modulators** or **allosteric effectors,** which are generally small metabolites or cofactors, *e.g.,* fructose-1, 6-bisphosphatase.
2. **Covalently Modulated Enzymes** are regulated by reversible covalent modification.

   Both classes of regulatory enzymes tend to be multisubunit proteins, and in some cases the regulatory site(s) and the active site are on separate subunits.

   Metabolic systems have at least two other mechanisms of enzyme regulation. Some enzymes are stimulated or inhibited when they are bound by separate regulatory proteins. Others are activated when peptide segments are removed by proteolytic cleavage; unlike effector-mediated regulation, regulation by proteolytic cleavage is irreversible.

Allosteric Enzymes

Allosteric enzymes generally have one or more regulatory, or allosteric, sites for binding the modulator. Allosteric proteins are those having 'other shapes' or conformations induced by the binding of modulators. The modulators for allosteric enzymes may be inhibitory or stimulatory. Often the modulator is the substrate itself; regulatory enzymes for which substrate and modulator are identical are called **homotropic.** The effect is similar to that of O_2 binding to haemoglobin binding of the ligand or substrate, in the case of enzymes causes conformational changes that affect the subsequent activity of other sites on the protein. When the modulator is a molecule other than the substrate, the enzyme is said to be heterotropic.

Uncompetitive and mixed inhibitors, although binds at a second site on the enzyme, but they do not necessarily mediate conformational changes between active and inactive forms, and have distinct kinetic effects.

Allosteric enzymes are generally larger and more complex than non-allosteric enzymes. Most have two or more subunits. Aspartate transcarbamoylase, which catalyzes an early reaction in the biosynthesis of pyrimidine nucleotides, has 12 polypeptide chains organized into catalytic and regulatory subunits.

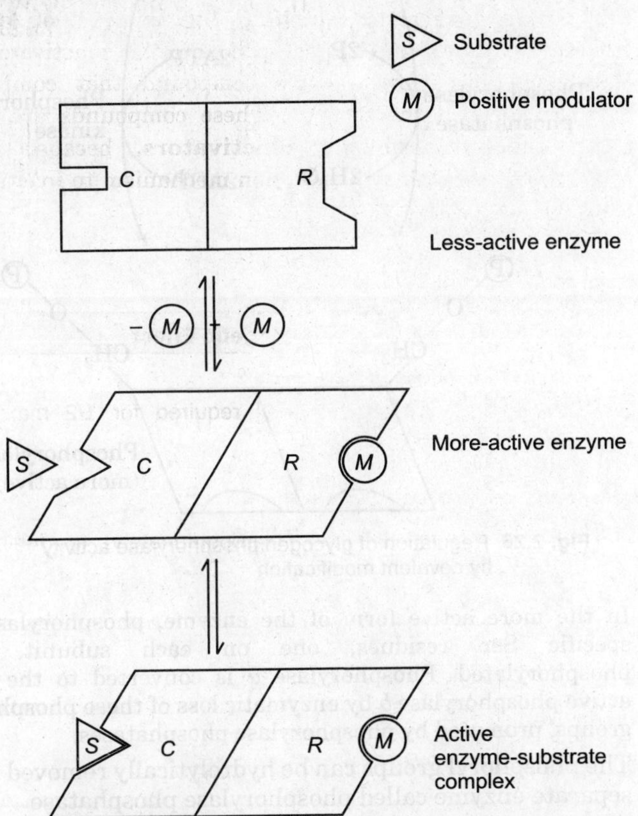

Fig. 2.23 Subunit interactions in an allosteric enzyme

In many allosteric enzymes the catalytic (*C*) and regulatory (*R*) subunits are different. Binding of the positive (stimulatory) modulator (*M*) to its specific site on the regulatory subunit is communicated to the catalytic subunit through a conformational change. This change renders the catalytic subunit active and capable of binding the substrate (*S*) with higher affinity. On dissociation of the modulator from the regulatory subunit, the enzyme reverts to its inactive or less active form.

In some multienzyme systems, the regulatory enzyme is specifically inhibited by the end product of the pathway. This type of regulation is called **feedback inhibition.** One of the first known examples of allosteric feedback inhibition was the bacterial enzyme system that catalyzes the conversion of L-threonine to L-isoleucine **in five steps.**

COO^-

$H_3\overset{+}{N}—C—H$

$H—C—OH$ L-threonine

CH_3

⊗ E_1 Threonine dehydratase

A

E_2

B

E_3

C

E_4

D

E_5

COO^-

$H_3\overset{+}{N}—C—H$

$H—C—CH_3$ L-isoleucine

CH_2

CH_3

Fig. 2.24 Feedback inhibition

The conversion of L-threonine to L-isoleucine is catalyzed by a sequence of five enzymes (E_1 to E_5). Threonine dehydratase (E_1) is specifically inhibited allosterically by L-isoleucine, the end product of the sequence, but not by any of the four intermediates (A to D).

Kinetics of Allosteric Enzymes

(a) **Cooperativity** In relation to multiple subunit enzymes, changes in the conformation of one subunit leads to conformational changes in adjacent subunits. These changes occur at the tertiary and quaternary levels of protein organization and can be caused by an allosteric regulator.

(b) **Homotropic regulation** When binding of one molecule to a multi-subunit enzyme causes a conformational shift that affects the binding of the same molecule to another subunit of the enzyme.

(c) **Heterotropic regulation** When binding of one molecule to a multi-subunit enzyme affects the binding of a different molecule to this enzyme (These terms are similar to those used for oxygen binding to haemoglobin).

Allosteric enzymes do exhibit saturation kinetics at high [S], but they have a characteristic sigmoidal saturation curve rather than hyperbolic curve, when Vo is plotted versus [S]. Addition of an **allosteric activator** (+) tends to shift the curve to a more hyperbolic profile (more like Michaelis-Menten curves), while an **allosteric inhibitor** (–) will result in more pronounced sigmoidal curves.

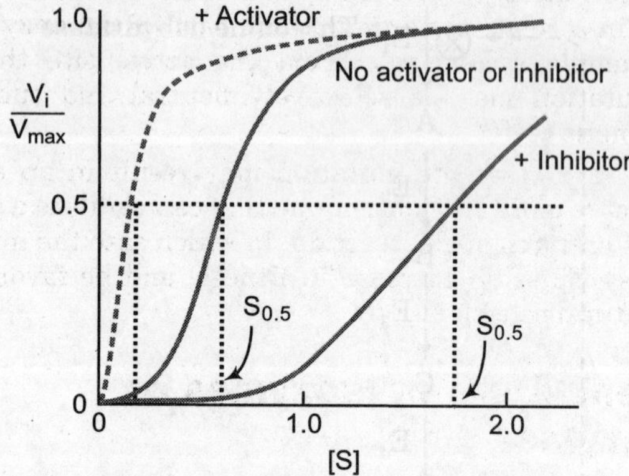

Fig. 2.25 Substrate-activity curves for representative allosteric enzymes

Covalently Modulated Enzymes

A class of regulatory enzymes, whose activity is modulated by covalent modification of the enzyme molecule. Modifying groups include phosphoryl, adenylyl, uridylyl, methyl, and adenosine diphosphate ribosyl groups. These groups are generally linked to and removed from the regulatory enzyme by separate enzymes.

Phosphorylation is the most common type of regulatory modification, one-third to one-half of all proteins in a eukaryotic cell is phosphorylated. Some proteins have only one phosphorylated residue, others have several, and a few have dozens of sites for phosphorylation.

The attachment of phosphoryl groups to specific amino acid residues of a protein is catalyzed by **protein kinases,** removal of phosphoryl groups is catalyzed by **protein phosphatases.**

An important example of regulation by phosphorylation is seen in glycogen phosphorylase of muscle and liver, which catalyzes the reaction.

$$(\text{Glucose})_n + P_i^2 \; (\text{glucose})_{n-1} + \text{glucose-1-phosphate}$$

Glycogen — Shortened glycogen chain

The glucose-1-phosphate so formed can be used for ATP synthesis in muscle or converted to free glucose in the liver. Glycogen phosphorylase occurs in two forms the more active phosphorylase a and the less active phosphorylase *b*. Phosphorylase a has two subunits, each with a specific Ser residue that is phosphorylated at its hydroxyl group. These serine phosphate residues are required for maximal activity of the enzyme.

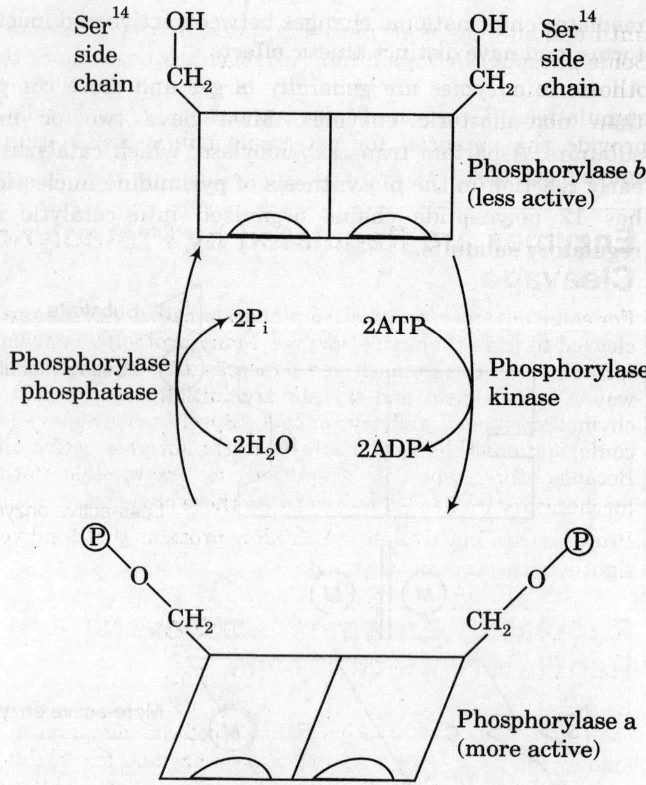

Fig. 2.26 Regulation of glycogen phosphorylase activity by covalent modification

In the more active form of the enzyme, phosphorylase *a*, specific Ser residues, one on each subunit, are phosphorylated. Phosphorylase *a* is converted to the less active phosphorylase *b* by enzymatic loss of these phosphoryl groups, promoted by phosphorylase phosphatases.

The phosphoryl groups can be hydrolytically removed by a separate enzyme called phosphorylase phosphatase

$$\underset{\text{(more active)}}{\text{Phosphorylase } a} + 2H_2O \longrightarrow \underset{\text{(less active)}}{\text{phosphorylase } b} + 2P_i$$

Phosphorylase *b* can in turn be reactivated—covalently transformed back into active phosphorylase *a*—by another enzyme, phosphorylase kinase, which catalyzes the transfer of phosphoryl groups from ATP to the hydroxyl groups of the two specific Ser residues in phosphorylase *b*

$$2\text{ATP} + \underset{\text{(less active)}}{\text{phosphorylase } b} \longrightarrow 2\text{ADP} + \underset{\text{(more active)}}{\text{phosphorylase } a}$$

Phosphorylation of an enzyme can affect catalysis in another way by altering substrate-binding affinity. For example, when isocitrate dehydrogenase (an enzyme of the citric acid cycle) is phosphorylated, electrostatic repulsion by the phosphoryl group inhibits the binding of citrate (a tricarboxylic acid) at the active site.

Glycogen synthase, the enzymes that catalyzes the condensation of glucose monomers to form glycogen, is inactivated by phosphorylation of specific Ser residues and is also modulated by at least four other protein kinases that phosphorylate four other sites in the protein. The protein is not a substrate for glycogen synthase kinase-3, for example, until one site has been phosphorylated by casein kinase II. Some phosphorylations inhibit glycogen synthase more than others, and some combinations of phosphorylations are cumulative. These multiple regulatory phosphorylation provide the potential for extremely subtle modulation of enzyme activity.

Enzymes are Regulated by Proteolytic Cleavage

For some enzymes, an inactive precursor called a **zymogen** is cleaved to form the active enzyme. Many proteolytic enzymes (proteases) of the stomach and pancreas are regulated in this way. Chymotrypsin and trypsin are initially synthesized as chymotrypsinogen and trypsinogen. Specific cleavage causes conformational changes that expose the enzyme active site. Because this type of activation is irreversible, other mechanisms are needed to inactivate these enzymes.

Proteases are inactivated by inhibitor proteins that bind very tightly to the enzyme active site.

Regulatory Enzymes use Several Regulatory Mechanisms

Bacterial glutamine synthetase, which catalyzes a reaction that introduces reduced nitrogen into cellular metabolism, is among the most complex regulatory enzymes known. It is regulated allosterically (with at least eight different modulators) by reversible covalent modification and by the association of other regulatory proteins.

Isozymes or Isoenzymes

Isozymes were first described by **Hunter** and **Markert** (1957) who defined them as different variants of the same enzyme having identical functions and present in the same individual. This definition encompasses :

1. Enzyme variants that are the product of different genes and thus, represent different loci (described as isozymes).
2. Enzymes that are the product of different alleles of the same gene (described as allozymes).

In biochemistry, isozymes or isoenzymes are isoforms (closely related variants) of enzymes. These isoenzymes usually display different enzyme kinetic (*i.e.*, different K_m values), or different regulatory properties. Isozymes are usually the result of gene duplication, but can also arise from polyploidization or hybridization. Over evolutionary time, if the function of the new variant remains identical to the original, then it is likely that one or the other will be lost as mutations accumulate, resulting in a pseudogene. However, if the mutations do not immediately prevent the enzyme from functioning, but instead modify either its function, or its pattern of gene expression, then the two variants may both be favoured by natural selection and become specialized to different functions. For example, they may be expressed at different stages of development or in different tissues.

Allozymes may result from point mutations or from insertion deletion events that affect the DNA coding sequence of the gene. There are following three way formation of a new allozyme :

1. It is most likely that the new allele will be non-functional in which case it will probably result in low fitness and be removed from the population by natural selection.
2. Alternatively, if the amino acid residue that is changed is in a relatively unimportant part of the enzyme, for example a long way from the active site then the mutation may be selectively neutral and subject to genetic drift.
3. In rare cases the mutation may result in an enzyme that is more efficient, or one that can catalyze a slightly different chemical reaction, in which case the mutation may cause an increase in fitness, and be favoured by natural selection.

Nomenclature of Isozymes or Isoenzymes

The 1964 report recommended that individual isoenzymes (isozymes) should be distinguished and numbered on the basis of electrophoretic mobility, with the number 1 being assigned to that form having the highest mobility toward the anode.

Of all the means available to indicate the different properties of isoenzymes (electrophoresis, chromatography, kinetics criteria, chemical structure, etc.), electrophoresis is most widely used for the following reasons.

(i) In the study of enzyme heterogeneity to avoid any artifactual consequences of the handling or 'purification' of enzymes, and zone electrophoresis is one procedure in which the resolution of individual protein species is not unduly influenced by their application in the original state, as tissue homogenates, or the like.

(ii) The degree of resolution is another factor of prime importance in this field, and resolution by electrophoretic procedures is generally more effective than other methods of protein separation.

(iii) Electrophoresis offers the advantages of rapidity and broad applicability.

Isozymes (isoenzymes) or their subunits should not be labelled on the basis of tissue distribution (*e.g.*, brain type, heart type) since confusion may arise on account of species variation, homologous forms may occur in altogether different tissues in other species.

Table 2.8 **Enzyme Isoforms of Lactate Dehydrogenase** (LDH)

Enzymes	Sub-unit	Location
LDH-1	4H	The heart
LDH-2	$3H_1M$	The reticuloendothelial system
LDH-3	$2H_2M$	The lungs
LDH-4	$1H_3M$	The kidneys
LDH-5	4M	The liver and striated muscle

The five isozymes are usually contain four subunits in each isoform. The major isozymes of skeletal muscle and liver is M_4, has four muscle (M) subunits, while the heart isoenzyme is H_4 has four heart (H) subunits. The other variants contain both types of subunits.

The LDH-2 is the predominant form in the serum. The increase in LDH-1 level than the LDH-2 in serum, suggests myocardial infarction (the damaged to heart tissues releases heart LDH, which is rich in LDH-1). The is often use for diagnoses of infarction.

Isoforms of Hexokinase

There are four important mammalian hexokinase isozymes. They vary somewhat in their sub-cellular locations, kinetic characteristics with respect to different substrates and operating conditions and physiological function. They are designated hexokinases I, II, III and IV or hexokinases A, B, C and D.

Hexokinases I, II and III are referred to as 'low-K_m' isozymes because of a high affinity for glucose even at low concentrations. All three are strongly inhibited by their product, glucose-6-phosphate.

(a) Hexokinase I (hexokinase A) is found in all mammalian tissues, it is a 'housekeeping enzyme,'.

(b) Hexokinase III (or C) is inhibited by excessive glucose (substrate inhibition).

(c) Hexokinase IV, also referred to as glucokinase,it is monomeric, displays positive cooperativity with glucose, and is not allosterically inhibited by its product, glucose-6-phosphate. It is located in the liver, pancreas, hypothalamus, small intestine, etc.

Isoforms of Cytochrome P_{450}

(a) Cytochrome P_{450} (CYP, P_{450} or CYP_{450}) is a very large and diverse super-family of haemoproteins found in all domains of life.

(b) Humans have 57 genes and more than 59 pseudogenes divided among 18 families of cytochrome P_{450} genes and 43 sub-families.

(c) The mice have genes for 101 CYPs, and sea urchins have even more (perhaps as many as 120 genes). Most CYP enzymes are presumed to have monooxygenase activity.

Enzyme Isoforms of CPK (Creatine Phosphokinase)

CPK is found primarily in heart and skeletal muscle as well as the brain. Therefore, measurement of serum CPK levels is a good diagnostic for injury to these tissues. The levels of CPK will rise within 6 hours of injury and peak by around 18 hours. If the injury is not persistent the level of CK returns to normal within 2-3 days. Like LDH, there are tissue-specific isozymes of CPK and there designations are described below.

CPK3 (CPK-MM) is the predominant isozyme in muscle and is 100% of the normal serum total.

CPK2 (CPK-MB) accounts for about 35% of the CPK activity in cardiac muscle, but less than 5% in skeletal muscle and is 0% of the normal serum total.

CPK1 (CPK-BB) is the characteristic isozyme in brain and is in significant amounts in smooth muscle and is 0% of the normal serum total.

Since, most of the released CPK after a myocardial infarction is CPK-MB, an increased ratio of CPK-MB to total CPK may help in diagnosis of an acute infarction, but an increase of total CPK in itself may not. CPK-MB levels rise 3-6 hours after a myocardial infarct and peak 12-24 hours later if no further damage occurs and returns to normal 12-48 hours after the infarct.

Abzymes (Catalytic Antibodies)

William Jencks (1969) proposed that antibodies specific for the transition state of a chemical reaction should how catalytic power. When a transition state analog is used as a protein box epitope to stimulate the production of antibodies, the antibodies to bind it are potential catalysis of corresponding reaction. As of monoclonal antibodies catalyse the hydrolysis of esters or carbonates. In these reactions, that attack by water (OH^-) on the carbonyl carbon produces a tetrahedral transition state in which a part negative change has developed on the carbonyl oxygen. Phosphorate compounds mimic the structure.

Exercise

1. Which one is correct about glycolysis?
(a) Breakdown of glucose to two molecules of pyruvate
(b) Occurs in cytoplasm
(c) Two NAD^+ accept, two electrons and become NADH
(d) All of the above

2. A phosphate bond contains an energy
(a) 7.3 kcal (b) 8.3 kcal
(c) 10 kcal (d) 11.7 kcal

3. In anaerobic respiration the process takes place is
(a) Krebs' cycle
(b) glycolysis
(c) oxidative phosphorylation
(d) glycolysis and Krebs' cycle

4. Most of the energy during aerobic respiration is produced by the
(a) electron transport chain
(b) glycolysin
(c) Krebs' cycle
(d) oxidative phosphorylation

5. Which one of the following fixes CO_2 into carbohydrates?
(a) *Rhizobium* (b) *Bacillus*
(c) *Nitrobacter* (d) *Rhodospirillium*

6. The primary acceptor of CO_2 in C_3 plants is
(a) pyruvic acid (b) PEP
(c) RuBP (d) ATP

7. Cytochromes are found in
(a) matrix of mitochondria
(b) cristae of mitochondria
(c) lysosomes
(d) outer wall of mitochondria

8. The power house of the cell is
(a) nucleus (b) cell membrane
(c) mitochondria (d) lysosomes

9. The digestive enzymes of cellular compounds are confined to
(a) lysosomes (b) ribosomes
(c) peroxisomes (d) polysomes

10. Oxidation of which substance in the body yields the most calories
(a) glucose (b) glycogen
(c) protein (d) lipids

11. Differences between the systems involved in the β-oxidation of fatty acids and in their biosynthesis include the
I. intracellular location of the enzymes involved.
II. nature of the thiol acyl carriers.
III. oxidation-reduction state of required pyridine nucleotide cofactors.
IV. participation of high-energy phosphate bonds.
(a) I and II (b) I and III
(c) I, II and III (d) I, II, III and IV

12. The most active site of protein synthesis is the
(a) nucleus (b) ribosome
(c) mitochondrion (d) cell sap

13. The mitochondrial membrane contains a transporter for
(a) NADH (b) acetyl Co-A
(c) GTP (d) ATP

14. If rotenone is added to the mitochondrial electron transport chain
(a) the P/O ratio of NADH is reduced from 3 : 1 to 2 : 1
(b) the rate of NADH oxidation is diminished to two-thirds of its initial value
(c) succinate oxidation remains normal
(d) electron flow is inhibited at site II

15. If cyanide is added to tightly coupled mitochondria that are actively oxidizing succinate
(a) subsequent addition of 2, 4-dinitrophenol will cause ATP hydrolysis
(b) subsequent addition of 2, 4-dinitrophenol will restore succinate oxidation
(c) electron flow will cease, but ATP synthesis will continue
(d) subsequent addition of 2, 4-dinitrophenol and the phosphorylation inhibitor, oligomycin, will cause ATP hydrolysis

16. The chemiosmotic hypothesis involves all of the following except
(a) a membrane impermeable to protons
(b) electron transport by the respiratory chain pumps protons out of the mitochondrion
(c) proton flow into the mitochondria depends on the presence of ADP and P_i
(d) only proton transport is strictly regulated other positively charged ions can diffuse freely across the mitochondrial membrane

17. Suppose the specific defect were a mutant pyruvate dehydrogenase (the first catalytic subunit) with poor binding of its prosthetic group. In this type of defect, sometimes greatly increasing the dietary precursor of the prosthetic group is helpful. In this case increasing which of the following might be helpful?
(a) Thiamine (for TPP)
(b) Niacin (for NAD)
(c) Pantothenic acid (for Co-A)
(d) Riboflavin (for FAD)

18. Dietary triacylglycerols containing long-chain fatty acyl moieties are digested, absorbed from the small intestine, and stored in adipose tissue cells. The following processes occur at different times and sites.
I. Formation of chylomicrons.
II. Hydrolysis by hormone-sensitive triacylglycerol lipase.
III. Micellear formation with bile salts.
IV. Resynthesis from 2-acylglycerols.
V. Hydrolysis by lipoprotein lipase.
VI. Transport in the circulation as free fatty acids bound to serum albumin.

The correct order of these events is given by which of the following sequences?

(a) III, I, V, VI, IV, II (b) III, IV, I, II, VI, V
(c) I, IV, III, V, VI, II (d) III, IV, I, V, II, VI

19. The irreversible reactions of glycolysis include that catalyzed by
(a) phosphoglucose isomerase
(b) 6-phosphofructo-1-kinase
(c) fructose bisphosphate aldolase
(d) glyceraldehyde-3-phosphate dehydrogenase

20. Glucokinase
(a) has a K_m considerably greater than the normal blood glucose concentration
(b) is inhibited by glucose-6-phosphate
(c) is also known as the GLUT-2 protein
(d) has glucose-6-phosphatase activity as well as kinase activity

21. In the Cori cycle
(a) only tissues with aerobic metabolism (*i.e.*, mitochondrial O_2) are involved
(b) a three-carbon compound arising from glycolysis converted to glucose at the expense of energy from fatty acid oxidation
(c) glucose is converted to pyruvate in anaerobic tissues this pyruvate returns to the liver, where it is converted into glucose
(d) the same amount of ATP is used in the liver to synthesis glucose as it is released during glycolysis, leading to no net loss on whole-body energy balance

22. Gluconeogenic enzymes include all of the following except
(a) glucose-6-phosphatase
(b) phosphoenol pyruvate carboxykinase
(c) phosphoglucomutase
(d) pyruvate carboxylase

23. Glycosaminoglycans
(a) are the carbohydrate portion of glycoproteins
(b) contain large segments of a repeating unit typically consisting of a hexosamine and a uronic acid
(c) always contain sulphate
(d) exist in only two forms

24. All of the following statements about acetyl Co-A carboxylase are correct except
(a) it undergoes protomer-polymer interconversion during its physiological regulation
(b) it is inhibited by cAMP-mediated phosphorylation
(c) it is activated by both palmitoyl Co-A and citrate
(d) its content in a cell responds to changes in fat content in the diet

25. The cellular concentration of 5′-phosphoribosyl-1-pyrophosphate (PRPP) is controlled by modulators of PRPP synthetase activity, including

I. inorganic phosphate.
II. nucleoside diphosphates.
III. 2, 3-diphosphoglycerate.
IV. nucleoside triphosphates.

(a) I and II (b) I, II and III
(c) I and III (d) I, II, III and IV

26. Potassium cyanide stops cell activity by
(a) preventing diffusion of O_2
(b) blocking trachea
(c) preventing transfer of electrons from cytochrome - a_3 to O_2
(d) coagulating protein carriers

27. At equilibrium,
(a) no enzymes are functioning
(b) $\Delta G = 0$
(c) the forward and backward reactions have stopped
(d) the products and reactants have equal values of H

28. Which of the following compounds is a member of the electron transport chain?
(a) Octanoyl carnitine
(b) Cytochrome-*c*
(c) Reduced nicotinamide adenine dinucleotide (NADH)
(d) Palmitoyl carnitine

29. Given that the standard free energy change ($\Delta G°$) for the hydrolysis of ATP is –7.3 kcal/mol and that for the hydrolysis of glucose-6-phosphate is –3.3 kcal/mol, what is the $G°$ for the phosphorylation of glucose?

$$\text{glucose} + \text{ATP} \rightarrow \text{glucose-6-phosphate} + \text{ADP}$$

(a) –10.6 kcal/mol (b) –7.3 kcal/mol
(c) –4.0 kcal/mol (d) +4.0 kcal/mol

30. Which of the following reactions generates ATP?
(a) Glucose-6-phosphate to fructose-6-phosphate
(b) Glucose to glucose-6-phosphate
(c) Fructose-6-phosphate to fructose-1, 6-diphosphate
(d) Phosphoenol pyruvate to pyruvate

31. The problem of regenerating NAD^+ from NADH for cytoplasmic processes by using mitochondria is solved in the most energy-efficient manner by which one of the following intercellular shuttle systems?
(a) Citrate pyruvate shuttle
(b) Dihydroxyacetone phosphate-glycerophosphate shuttle
(c) Malate aspartate shuttle
(d) Citrate citrate shuttle

32. Which reaction in the following figure occurs in both muscle and liver but has substantially different qualities in the two?

Glucose

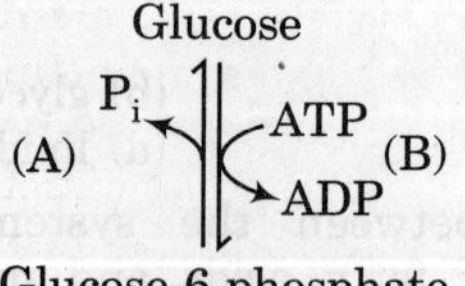

Glucose-6-phosphate

(C) (D)

Fructose-6-phosphate

ATP
(E)
ADP

Fructose-1, 6-bisphosphate

(a) Reaction A (b) Reaction B
(c) Reaction C (d) Reaction E

33. Which of the following is located in the mitochondria?
(a) Cytochrome oxidase
(b) Succinate dehydrogenase
(c) Dihydrolipoyl dehydrogenase
(d) All of the above

34. Diacyiglycerol activates which of the following enzymes?
(a) Protein kinase A (b) Protein kinase C
(c) MAP kinase (d) Tyrosine kinase

35. An enzyme that catalyzes the reaction A $\rightarrow$ B changes the
(a) equilibrium constant
(b) equilibrium concentration of A
(c) entropy of the reaction
(d) rate of both the forward and reverse reactions

36. Hexokinase activity in a desalted cell extract can be measured in a spectrophotometric assay at 340 nanometers. In addition to buffer, Mg2t and lysate, the reaction mixture should contain
(a) glucose, ATP, NADPH and excess glucose-6-phosphate dehydrogenase
(b) glucose, ATP, NADP and excess glucose-6-phosphate dehydrogenase
(c) glucose, ADP, NADP and excess glucose-6-phosphate dehydrogenase
(d) glucose, ATP, NADP and excess 6-phosphogluconate dehydrogenase

37. In all enzymes the active site
(a) contains the substrate-binding site
(b) is contiguous with the substrate-binding site in the primary sequence
(c) contains a metal ion as a prosthetic group
(d) contains the amino acid side chains involved in catalyzing the reaction

38. Enzymes may be specific with respect to all of the except
(a) chemical identity of the substrate
(b) the atomic mass of the elements in the reactive group (*e.g.*, ^{12}C but not ^{14}C)
(c) Optical activity of product formed from a symmetrical substrate
(d) which of a pair of optical isomers will react

39. The transport system that maintains the Na^+ and K^+ gradients across the plasma membrane of cells
(a) involves an enzyme that is an ATPase
(b) moves Na^+ either into or out of the cell
(c) is an electrically neutral system
(d) in the membrane, hydrolyzes ATP independently of the movement of Na^+ and K^+

40. A mediated transport system would be expected to
(a) show a continuously increasing initial rate of transport with in increasing substrate concentration
(b) exhibit structural and/or stereospecificity for the substance transported
(c) be slower than that of a simple diffusion system
(d) establish a concentration gradient across the membrane

41. The group translocation type of transport system
(a) does not require metabolic energy
(b) involves the transport of two different solute molecules simultaneously
(c) has been demonstrated for fatty acids
(d) results in the alteration of the substrate molecule during the transport process

42. ATP-binding cassette (ABC) transporters
(a) all have both a membrane-spanning domain that recombine substrate and an ATP-binding domain
(b) all effect translocation by forming channels
(c) all have two functions-forming a channel and con regulation
(d) are all P-glycoproteins

43. Aminotransferases
(a) usually require α-ketoglutaramate or glutamine as one of the reacting pair
(b) catalyze reactions that result in a net use or production of amino acids
(c) catalyze irreversible reactions
(d) require pyridoxal phosphate as an essential cofactor for the reaction

44. In cooperativity,
(a) a cellular organelle contains all the enzymes needed for a metabolic pathway
(b) a product of a pathway serves as a competitive inhibitor of an early enzyme in the pathway
(c) a molecule bound to the active site of one sub-unit of an enzyme affects the active site of other subunits
(d) the allosteric site is filled with an activator molecule

45. Which is true about enzymes?
(a) They always increase rate of reaction
(b) They always decrease rate of reaction
(c) They do not disturb the equilibrium
(d) Always carry irreversible reactions

46. Blocking action of enzyme through blocking its active site is
(a) allosteric inhibition
(b) feedback inhibition
(c) competitive inhibition
(d) non-competitive inhibition

47. In an enzyme reaction, the reaction velocity becomes more than double when the substrate concentration is doubled. This is possible when the equation governing the kinetics is
(a) Michelis-Menton kinetics
(b) Micheils-Menton kinetics with substrate inhibition
(c) Michelis-Menton kinetics with product inhibition
(d) Hill Equation

48. Sodium Dodecyl Sulphate (SDS) is used while separating proteins by polyacrylanide gel electrophoresis because
(a) it helps in solubilization of proteins thereby making it easier to separate
(b) it binds to proteins and confers uniform negative charge density thereby making them move during electrophoresis
(c) decreases the surface tension of the buffer used for electrophoresis
(d) stabilizes the proteins

49. Which one of the following is without coenzyme activity?
(a) Vitamin-E (b) Thiamine
(c) Biotin (d) Riboflavin

50. Specificity of an enzyme depends upon
(a) active site (b) linear sequence
(c) K_m (d) turn over number

51. Carrier protein can
(a) transport only one substance
(b) transport more than one substance
(c) exchange one substance to another
(d) perform all of these functions

52. Enzymes catalyzing electron transport are present mainly in the
(a) ribosomes
(b) endoplasmic reticulum
(c) lysosomes
(d) inner mitochondrial membrane

53. In a diluted starch solution, a-salivary amylase is added at pH 1.6 and kept at 35°C for half an hour and then Iodine solution is added. What would be the result?
(a) No black colour will appear
(b) Black colour will appear
(c) Solution will be clear and colourless
(d) Solution will be sweet

54. When substrate concentration is much greater than K_m, the velocity is constant and equal to V_{max}. At this point the rate of reaction said to be
(a) 1st order with respect to substrate
(b) 2nd order with respect to substrate
(c) zero order with respect to substrate
(d) None of the above

55. Which of the following regulatory actions involves a reversible covalent modification of an enzyme?
(a) Allosteric modulation
(b) Competitive inhibition
(c) Conversion of zymogen to active enzyme
(d) Phosphorylation of a serine hydroxyl on the enzyme

56. Enzyme action is best measured by noting the
(a) disappearance of the substrate
(b) increase in alkalinity of the solution
(c) sharp rise in temperature of the solution
(d) colour changes that accompany the reaction

57. Which one of the following has isoenzymes?
(a) Lactic dehydrogenase (b) Hexokinase
(c) Citrate synthetase (d) Aldolase

58. A co-enzyme is
(a) organic or inorganic group that is essential for enzyme activity
(b) organic non-proteinaceous group that is essential for enzyme activity
(c) one that shares function of another enzyme
(d) same enzyme found in different organs or tissues

59. Of the following statements about enzymes, which one is true?
I. Enzymes lack in nucleophilic groups.
II. Enzymes are highly specific both in binding chiral substrates and in catalyzing their reactions.
III. Enzymes catalyze chemical reactions by lowering the activation energy.
IV. Pepsin is a proteolytic enzyme.
(a) I and IV (b) I and III
(c) I only (d) II, III and IV

60. Ribozyme is RNA
(a) with extra phosphate (b) without phosphate
(c) without sugar (d) with enzyme activity

61. What is meant by the steady-state assumption that underlies the Michaelis-Menten relationship between substrate concentration and reaction velocity?
(a) The reaction velocity is linearly related to substrate concentration
(b) The reaction velocity is independent of substrate concentration
(c) The rate breakdown of the enzyme substrate complex equals the rate of formation of the complex
(d) The rate of formation of product equals the rate of disappearance of substrate

62. Which of the following vitamins would most likely become deficient in a person who develops a completely carnivorous lifestyle?
(a) Thiamine (b) Niacin
(c) Cobalamin (d) Vitamin-C

63. Abzymes are
(a) enzymes that are highly specific like antibodies
(b) antibodies that have catalytic activities
(c) also referred to as zymogens
(d) enzymes that hydrolyze antiodies

64. In non-competitive type of enzymatic inhibition
(a) the V_{max} decreases and K_m remain unchanged
(b) the V_{max} remain unchanged and K_m increases
(c) V_{max} and K_m both decreases
(d) V_{max} decreases and K_m increases

65. Catalytic antibodies function as enzymes on the principle of
(a) enzymatic conversion of antibodies
(b) stabilizing transition state analogue of substrate
(c) antigen-antibody affinity
(d) monoclonal antibodies with chemical capability

66. Which of the following coenzyme acts as an electron sink to promote catalysis?
(a) Biotin (b) Lipoamide
(c) Co-A (d) Pyridoxal phosphate

67. Which one of the following graphs best represents the effect of substrate concentration on the rate of enzyme reaction?

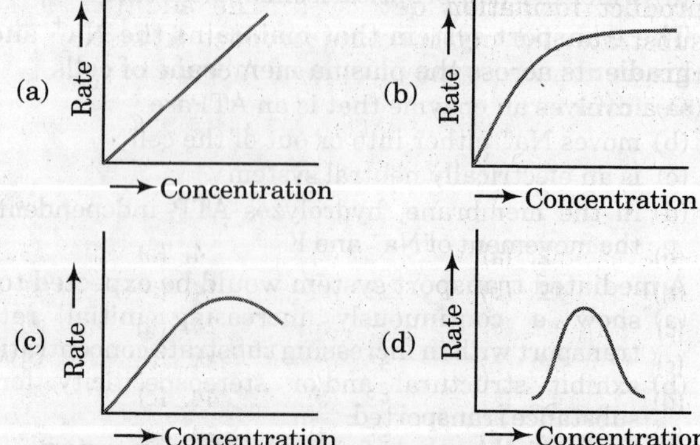

68. Which one of the following is a mitochondrial marker enzyme?
(a) Aldolase (b) Amylase
(c) Succinic dehydrogenase (d) Pyruvate dehydrogenase

69. In an experiment, changing the pH from 7 to 6 resulted in an increase in product formation. From this we could conclude that
(a) the enzyme became saturated at pH 6
(b) the enzyme's optimal pH is 6
(c) the temperature must have increased when the pH was changed to 6
(d) the enzyme was in a more conformation at pH 6

70. According to the induced-fit hypothesis,
(a) the binding of the substrate is an energy requiring process
(b) a competitive inhibitor can out compete the substrate for the active site
(c) the binding of the substrate changes the shape of the enzyme slightly and can stress or bend substrate bonds
(d) the active site creates a microenvironmental ideal for the reaction

71. A negative ΔG means that
(a) the quantity G of energy is available to do work
(b) the reaction is spontaneous
(c) the reactants have mopre free energy than the products
(d) All of the above

72. One way in which a cell maintains metabolic disequilibrium is to
(a) siphon products of a reaction off to the next step in a metabolic pathway
(b) provide a constant supply of enzymes for critical reactions
(c) use feedback inhibition to turn off pathways
(d) use allosteric enzymes that can bind to activators or inhibitors

73. In a reaction in chemical equilibrium,
(a) the forward and reverse reactions are occurring at the same rate
(b) the reactants and products are in equal concentration
(c) the forward reaction has gone further than the reverse reaction
(d) there are equal numbers of atoms on both sides of the equation

74. When substance A was added to an enzyme reaction, product formation decreased. The addition of more substrate did not increase product formation. From this we conclude that substance A could be
(a) a cofactor
(b) an allosteric enzyme
(c) a competitive inhibitor
(d) a non-competitive inhibitor

75. Match list I with list II and select the correct answer using the codes given below the lists.

List I	List II
A. Peripheral reticulum	1. C_3-plants
B. RuBP-carboxylase oxygenase	2. CAM-Plants
C. CO_2-fixation in the dark	3. Photosystem-I
D. Cyclic photophosphorylation	4. C_4-plants
	5. Photosystem-II

Codes

	A	B	C	D
(a)	1	4	2	3
(b)	2	5	4	1
(c)	4	1	2	3
(d)	3	5	1	4

76. The effects of a competitive inhibitor on the kinetics of an enzyme reaction include which of the following?
I. The V_{max} is not changed.
II. Increased concentrations of substrate reverse the inhibition.
III. The K_m is increased.
IV. The inhibitor binds to a site on the enzyme other than the catalytic site.
(a) I and II
(b) I and III
(c) I, II and III
(d) I, II, III and IV

77. Identify the correct parts for the primary functions of the different enzyme classes.

List I	List II
A. Kinases	1. Cleave bonds by elimination
B. Lyases	2. Make large molecules from small molecules
C. Synthase	3. Transfer phosphate group to biomolecules
D. Phosphatases	4. Remove phosphate group from biomolecules

Codes

	A	B	C	D
(a)	4	2	3	1
(b)	3	1	2	4
(c)	4	1	2	3
(d)	3	2	1	4

Answers

1. (d)	2. (a)	3. (c)	4. (a)	5. (d)	6. (c)	7. (b)	8. (c)	9. (a)	10. (d)
11. (d)	12. (b)	13. (d)	14. (a)	15. (a)	16. (d)	17. (a)	18. (d)	19. (b)	20. (a)
21. (c)	22. (c)	23. (b)	24. (b)	25. (b)	26. (c)	27. (b)	28. (c)	29. (c)	30. (d)
31. (c)	32. (b)	33. (d)	34. (b)	35. (d)	36. (b)	37. (b)	38. (b)	39. (a)	40. (b)
41. (d)	42. (a)	43. (d)	44. (c)	45. (c)	46. (c)	47. (d)	48. (b)	49. (a)	50. (a)
51. (d)	52. (d)	53. (a)	54. (c)	55. (d)	56. (a)	57. (a)	58. (c)	59. (b)	60. (a)
61. (c)	62. (d)	63. (b)	64. (a)	65. (d)	66. (d)	67. (b)	68. (c)	69. (d)	70. (c)
71. (d)	72. (a)	73. (a)	74. (d)	75. (c)	76. (c)	77. (c)			

3

Organization and Metabolism of Biomolecules

Conformation of Proteins

Proteins are basic structural molecules of organisms. The structure and conformation of protein is determined by bonding and folding between amino acids in various ways.

Syllabus

- Conformation of Proteins, Ramachandran Plot, Secondary, Tertiary and Quaternary Structure of Proteins.
- Conformation of Nucleic Acids, (A, B and Z-DNA).
- Stability of Proteins and Nucleic Acids.
- Metabolism of Biomolecules, Carbohydrates, Lipids, Amino Acids, Nucleotides and Vitamins.

The Ramachandran Plot

Ramachandran plot also known as Ramachandran map or Ramachandran diagram, developed by **Gopalasamudram Narayana Ramachandran.** He visualized dihedral angles ϕ against ψ of amino acid residues in protein structure. It shows the possible conformations of ϕ and ψ angles for a polypeptide.

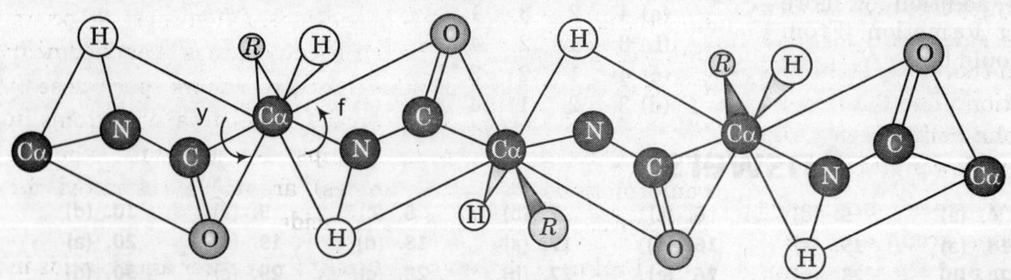

Fig. 3.1 N-C_α and C_α-C bonds in a polypeptide

In a polypeptide, the main chain N-C alpha and C alpha-C bonds relatively are free to rotate. These rotations are represented by the torsion angles phi and psi, respectively. GN Ramachandran used computer models of small polypeptides to systematically vary phi and psi with the objective of finding stable conformations. For each conformation, the structure was examined for close contacts between atoms. Atoms were treated as hard spheres with dimensions corresponding to their van der Waals' radii. Therefore, phi and psi angles which cause spheres to collide correspond to sterically disallowed conformations of the polypeptide backbone.

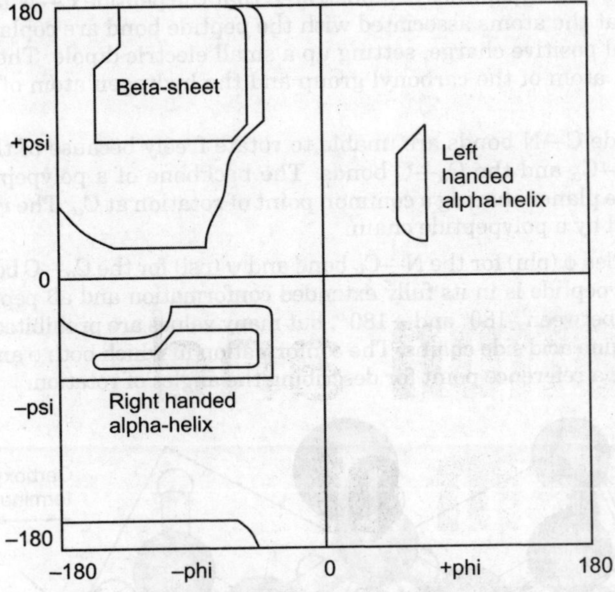

Fig. 3.2 The Ramachandran plot

In the above diagram, the white areas correspond to conformations, where atoms in the polypeptide come closer than the sum of their van der Waals' radii. These regions are sterically disallowed for all amino acids except **glycine which is unique in that it lacks a side chain.** The dark regions correspond to conformations, where there are no steric clashes, *i.e.*, these are the allowed regions namely the alpha-helical and beta-sheet conformations. The light areas show the allowed regions if slightly shorter van der Waals' radii are used in the calculation, *i.e.*, the atoms are allowed to come a little closer together. This brings out an additional region which corresponds to the left-handed alpha-helix.

L-amino acids cannot form extended regions of left-handed helix but occassionally individual residues adopt this conformation. These residues are usually glycine but can also be asparagine or aspartate, where the side chain forms a hydrogen bond with the main chain and therefore, stabilizes this otherwise unfavourable conformation. The 3(10) helix occurs close to the upper right of the alpha-helical region and is on the edge of allowed region indicating lower stability.

Disallowed regions generally involve steric hindrance between the side chain C-beta methylene group and main chain atoms. Glycine has no side chain and therefore, can adopt phi and psi angles in all four quadrants of the Ramachandran plot. Hence, it frequently occurs in turn regions of proteins, where any other residue would be sterically hindered.

1. The larger side chains would result in more restrictions and consequently a smaller allowable region in the Ramachandran plot. In practice this does not appear to be the case; only the methylene group at the β-position has an influence.
2. Glycine has a hydrogen atom, with a smaller van der Waals' radius, instead of a methyl group at the β-position. Hence, it is least restricted and this is apparent in the Ramachandran plot for glycine for which the allowable area is considerably larger.
3. The Ramachandran plot for proline shows only a very limited number of possible combinations of ψ and φ.

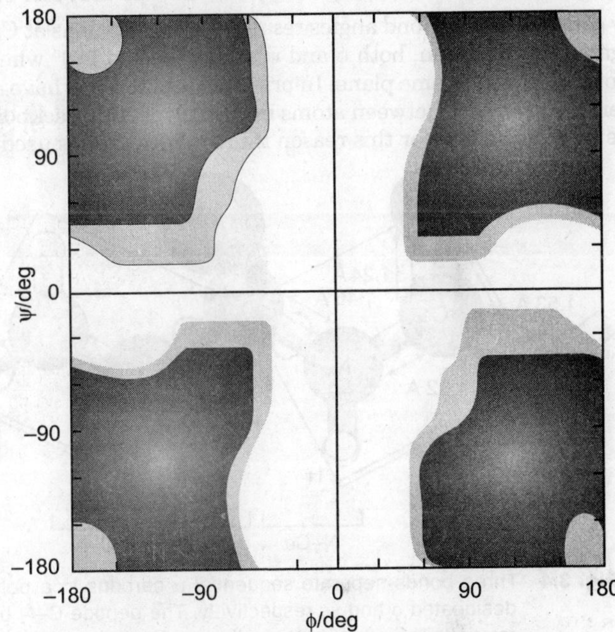

Fig. 3.3 Ramachandran plot for poly-L-glycine. Regions of allowed (dark), outer limit (light) and forbidden (gray) conformations

Ramachandran plots can be constructed for polymers of each of the 20 amino acids. It is significant to note that the Ramachandran plots for many amino acid residues are generally very similar, having only three regions with favourable or tolerated conformations. Differences do occur, however. For instance, where the side-chain is branched near C_α, as in the case of threonine, it occupies more space close to the peptide backbone and restricts the approach of atoms in the neighbouring peptide groups. As a result, allowed conformations (ϕ and ψ angles) are more restricted for polypeptides of branched amino acids.

4. Proline is also quite different from other amino acids in terms of allowed conformations and for polyproline only ϕ values from –85° to –35° are tolerated.
5. The Ramachandran plot for glycine residues in a polypeptide chain differ from the other residues with respect to its conformations.

Secondary, Tertiary and Quaternary Structure of Proteins

The α-carbons of adjacent amino acid residues are separated by three covalent bonds, arranged as C_α—C—N—C_α. X-ray diffraction studies of crystals of amino acids and of simple dipeptides and tripeptides demonstrated that the peptide C—N bond is somewhat shorter than the C—N bond in a simple amine and that the atoms associated with the peptide bond are coplanar. The oxygen has a partial negative charge and the nitrogen a partial positive charge, setting up a small electric dipole. The six atoms of the **peptide group** lie in a single plane, with the oxygen atom of the carbonyl group and the hydrogen atom of the amide nitrogen trans to each other.

From these findings **Pauling** and **Corey** concluded that the peptide C—N bonds are unable to rotate freely because of their partial double-bond character. Rotation is permitted about the N—C_α and the C_α—C bonds. The backbone of a polypeptide chain can thus be pictured as a series of rigid planes with consecutive planes sharing a common point of rotation at C_α. The rigid peptide bonds limit the range of conformations that can be assumed by a polypeptide chain.

By convention, the bond angles resulting from rotations at C_α are labelled ϕ (phi) for the N—C_α bond and ψ (psi) for the C_α—C bond. Again by convention, both ϕ and ψ are defined as 180° when the polypeptide is in its fully extended conformation and all peptide groups are in the same plane. In principle, ϕ and ψ can have any value between –180° and +180°, but many values are prohibited by steric interference between atoms in the polypeptide backbone and amino acid side chains. The conformation in which both ϕ and ψ are 0° is prohibited for this reason this conformation is used merely as a reference point for describing the angles of rotation.

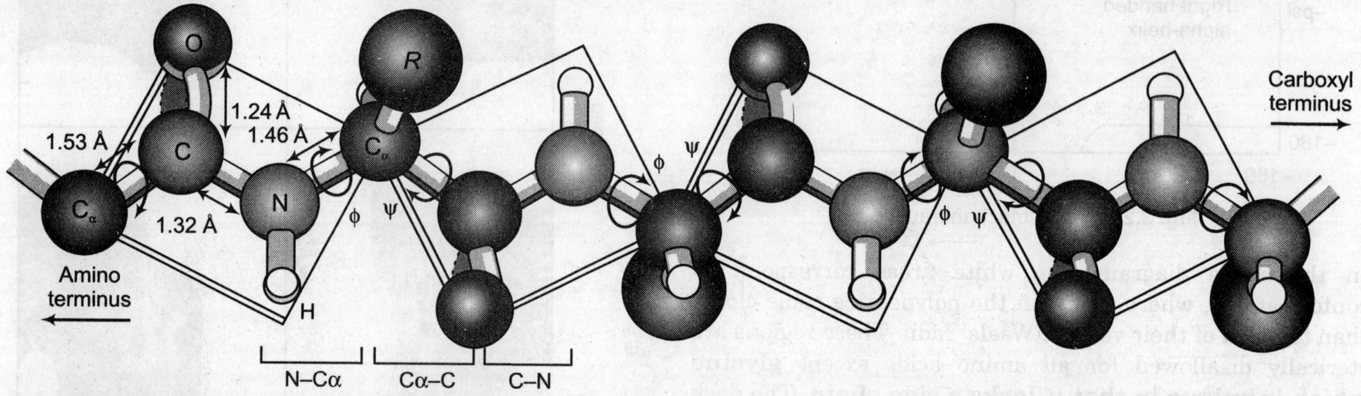

Fig. 3.4 Three bonds separate sequential α carbons in a polypeptide chain. The N–C_α and C_α–C bonds can rotate, with bond angles designated ϕ and ψ, respectively. The peptide C–N bond is not free to rotate. Other single bonds in the backbone may also be rotationally hindered, depending on the size and charge of the *R* groups. In the conformation shown, ϕ and ψ are 180° (or –180°). The α carbon, the ϕ and ψ angles increase as the carbonyl or amide nitrogens (respectively) rotate clockwise.

Secondary Structure

Alpha Helix In the alpha helix, the polypeptide chain is coiled spirally. The 'backbone' of the peptide forms the inner part of the coil while the side chains extend outward from the coil.

Linus Pauling and **Robert Cory,** in 1951, on the basis of X-ray diffraction technique proposed that the secondary structures of protein were either in the form of an alpha (α) helix or the beta (β) sheet (sometime called β-pleated sheet). There is about 60% of a protein's structure alpha helix. The amino acid residues in an α-helix have conformations with ψ = – 45° to –50° and ϕ = –60°, and each helical turn includes 3.6 amino acid residues. The helical twist of the helix found in all proteins is right-handed.

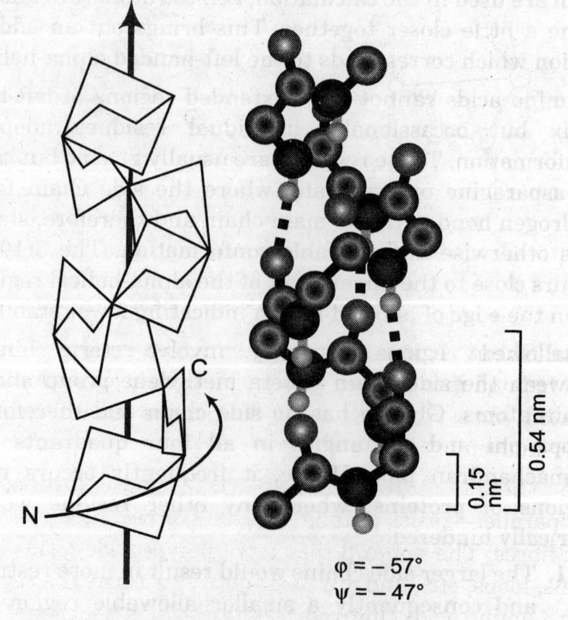

Fig. 3.5 Alpha (α) helix

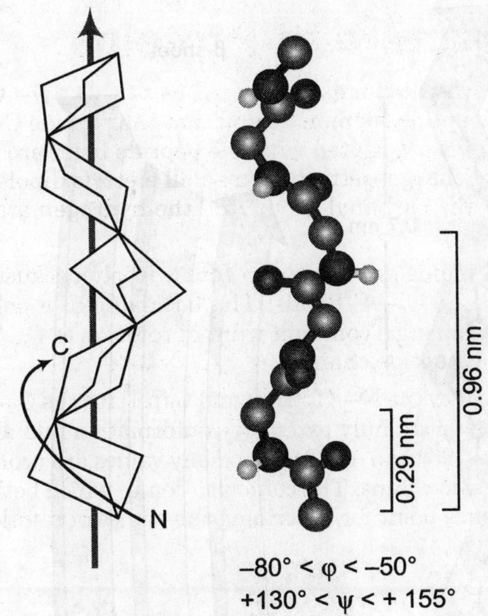

Fig. 3.6 Collagen helix

Helices of smaller and larger diameter than that of the α-helix. The most important is the **3_{10}-helix,** which has exactly three residues per turn. Each NH forms a hydrogen bond to the third C=O on down the chain, thus, the 3_{10}-helix is tighter than the α-helix. Although long 3_{10}-helices are seldom found in proteins, a single turn of this helix occurs as a 'defect' at the end of an α-helix. A polymer of α-aminoisobutyric acid forms long 3_{10} helices because the α-dimethyl side chains constrain φ and ψ to appropriate values. Short helical peptide chains in water may exist as a mixture of α and 3_{10} forms in equilibrium. The **α-helix,** with 4.4 residues per turn is of a larger diameter than the α-helix and has only been found in proteins as a single turn, usually at a C-terminus.

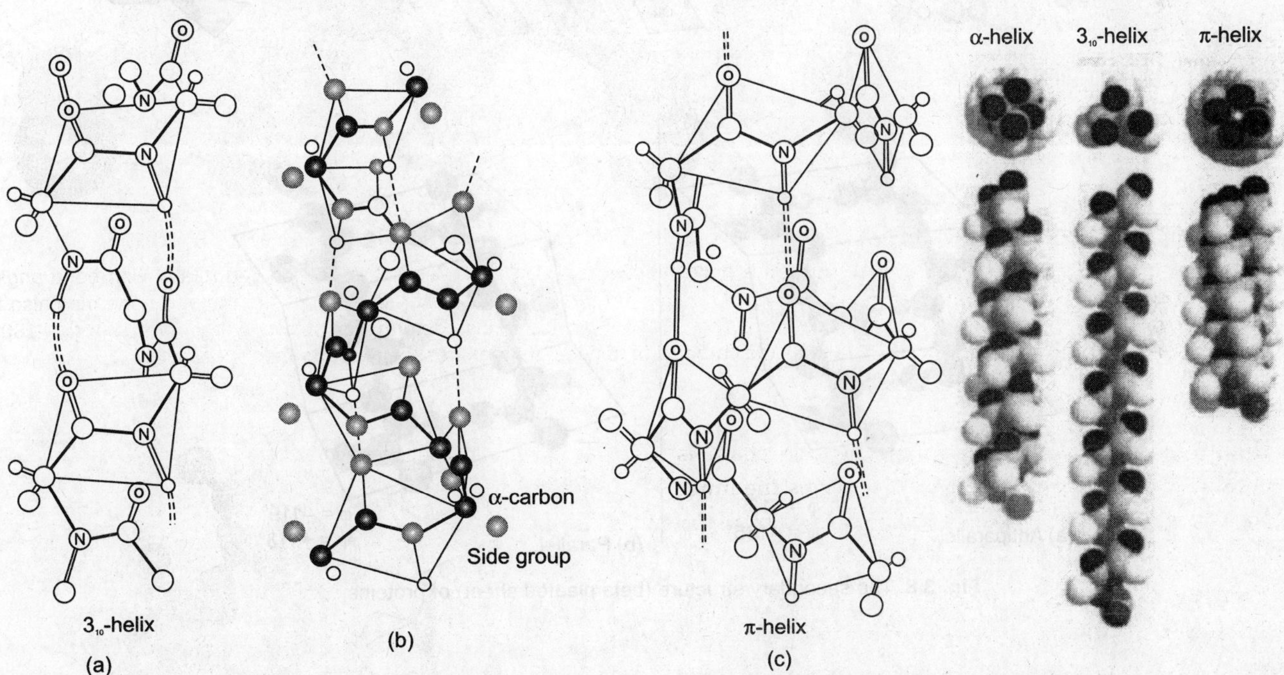

Fig. 3.7 The 3_{10}-helix (a) α-helix (b) π-helix (c) Differ in their patterns of hydrogen bonding

Beta Sheet It is a short segments (5-8 residues) that fold and H-bond into pleated sheets, The linear extended *zig-zag* pleated sheet formed by H-bonds are either intra and inter-molecular chain.

The beta pleated sheet can be parallel and antiparallel—resist pulling (tensile) forces, *e.g.,* strength of silk fibres. The non-α/β regions of polypeptide forms hinges, turns, loops, etc., and are flexibility. The turns is a region of 3 or 4 amino acids that redirect amino acid backbone.

The single β-strands are rarely found in proteins because the structure is not that much more stable than a random coil. However, when two adjacent β-strands line up they can from bridges of hydrogen bonds. This creates a very stable structure known as a β-sheet. In the example shown three parallel β-strands line up edge to edge to form a highly stable sheet with multiple hydrogen bond. The β-sheets can also be formed when antiparallel β-strands align edge to edge. As a matter of fact, the antiparallel conformation is more stable, and more common, than the parallel conformation.

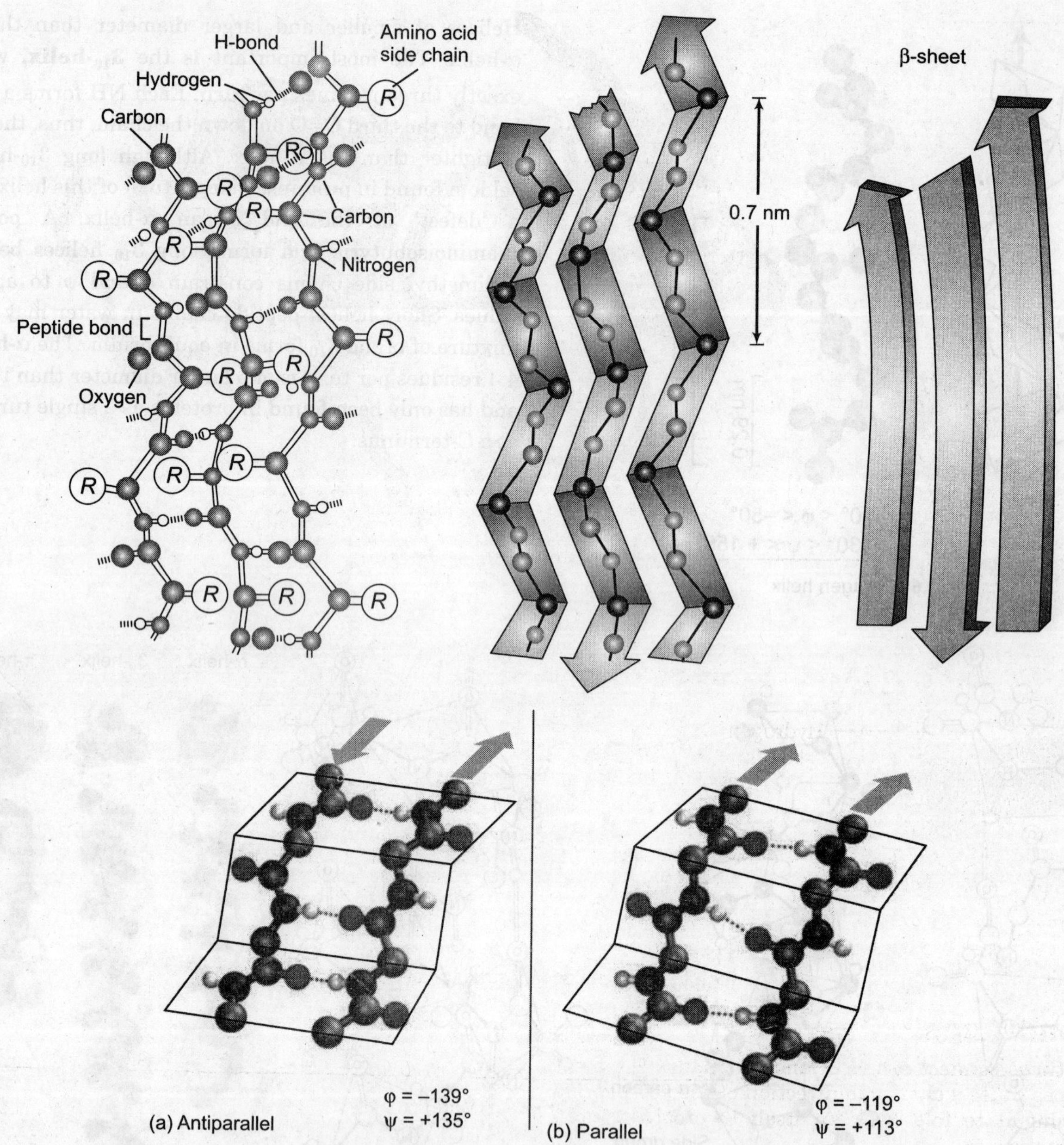

Fig. 3.8 The secondary structure (beta pleated sheet) of proteins

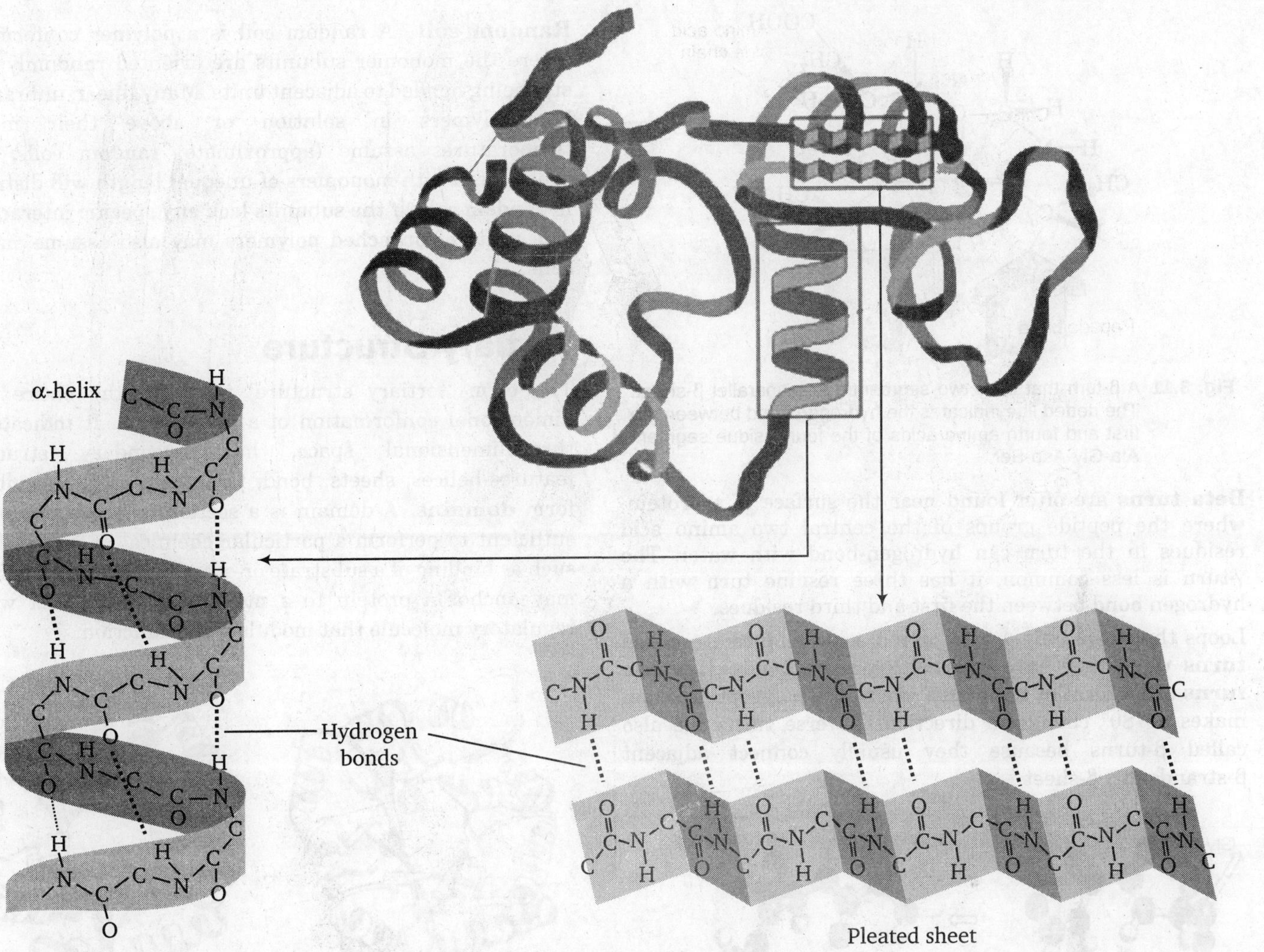

Fig. 3.9 The secondary structure of proteins

Loops and Turns

Loops and turns connect α-helices and β-strands. The most common types cause a change in direction of the polypeptide chain allowing it to fold back on itself to create a more compact structure.

In globular protein half of the residues are in loops, turns, and bends. **Turns** and **Bends** refer to short segments of amino acids that connect the ends of two adjacent segments of an antiparallel β-sheet. The structure is an 180° turn involving four amino acid residues, with the carbonyl oxygen of the first residue forming a hydrogen bond with the amino-group hydrogen of the fourth. The peptides groups of the central two residues do not participate in any inter residue hydrogen bonding.

Proline and glycine often are present in β-**turns**. The former is small and flexible, the latter readily assume the *cis*'-configuration, a form that is particularly amenable to a tight turn.

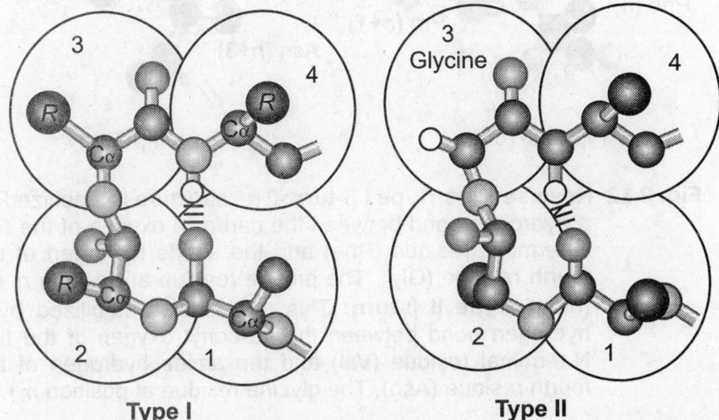

Fig. 3.10 Structures of β-turns. Type I and type II β-turns are most common, type I turns occur more than twice as frequently as type II. Type II β-turns always have Gly, as the third residue. The hydrogen bond between the peptide groups of the first and fourth residues of the bends

Fig. 3.11 A β-turn that links two segments of antiparallel β-sheet. The dotted line indicates the hydrogen bond between the first and fourth amino acids of the four-residue segment Ala-Gly-Asp-Ser.

Beta turns are ofter found near the surface of a protein, where the peptide groups of the central two amino acid residues in the turn can hydrogen-bond with water. The γ-turn is less common, it has three residue turn with a hydrogen bond between the first and third residues.

Loops that have only 4 or 5 amino acid residues are called **turns** when they have internal hydrogen bonds. **Reverse turns** are a form of tight turn where the polypeptide chain makes a 180° change in direction. Reverse turns are also called β-turns because they usually connect adjacent β-strands in a β-sheet.

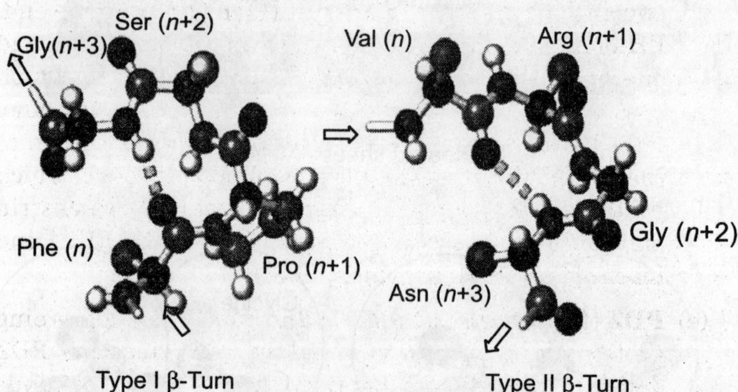

Fig. 3.12 Reverse turns: **Type I β-turn:** The structure is stabilized by a hydrogen bond between the carbonyl oxygen of the first N-terminal residue (Phe) and the amide hydrogen of the fourth residue (Gly). The proline residue at position $n + 1$ (right). **Type II β-turn:** This turn is also stabilized by a hydrogen bond between the carbonyl oxygen of the first N-terminal residue (Val) and the amide hydrogen of the fourth residue (Asn). The glycine residue at position $n + 2$

Loops are regions that contain residues beyond the minimum number necessary to connect adjacent regions of secondary structure. Loops are generally having hydrophilic residues and they are found on the surface of the protein. For many enzymes, the loops that bridge domains responsible for binding substrates often contain aminoacyl residues that participate in catalysis.

Random coil A random coil is a polymer conformation where the monomer subunits are oriented randomly while still being bonded to adjacent units. Many linear, unbranched homopolymers in solution or above their melting temperatures assume (approximate) random coils. Even copolymers with monomers of unequal length will distribute in random coils if the subunits lack any specific interactions. The parts of branched polymers may also assume random coils.

Tertiary Structure

The term 'tertiary structure' refers to the entire three dimensional conformation of a polypeptide. It indicates, in three-dimensional space, how secondary structural features-helices, sheets, bend, turns and loops-assemble to form **domains.** A domain is a section of protein structure sufficient to perform a particular chemical or physical task such as binding of a substrate or other ligand. Other domains may anchor a protein to a membrane or interact with a regulatory molecule that modulates its function.

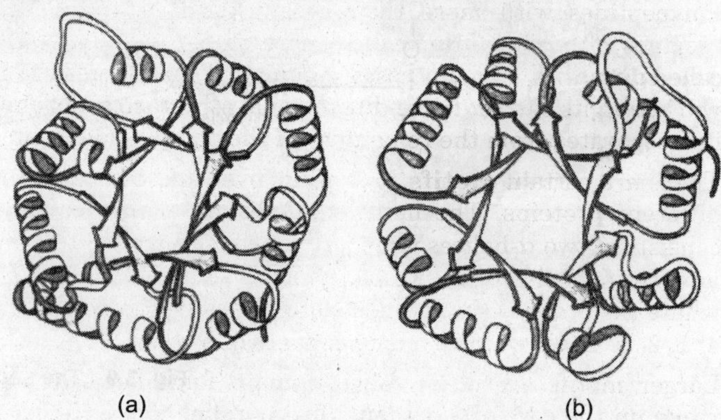

Fig. 3.13 Examples of tertiary structure of proteins. The enzyme triose phosphate isomerase (a) Pyruvate kinase (b) Shows a symmetrical arrangement of alternating β-sheets and α-helices

A small polypeptide such as triose phosphate isomerase or myoglobin may consist of a single domain. Protein kinases catalyze the transfer of a phosphoryl group from ATP to a peptide or protein. The groups that catalyze phosphoryl transfer reside in a loop positioned at the interface of the two domains.

Quaternary Structure

The **quaternary protein structure** involves the clustering of more than one polypeptide or protein chains into a final specific shape. The complex proteins aggregated together with the help of variety of bonding interactions including hydrogen bonding, salt bridges and disulphide bonds hold the various chains into a particular geometry.

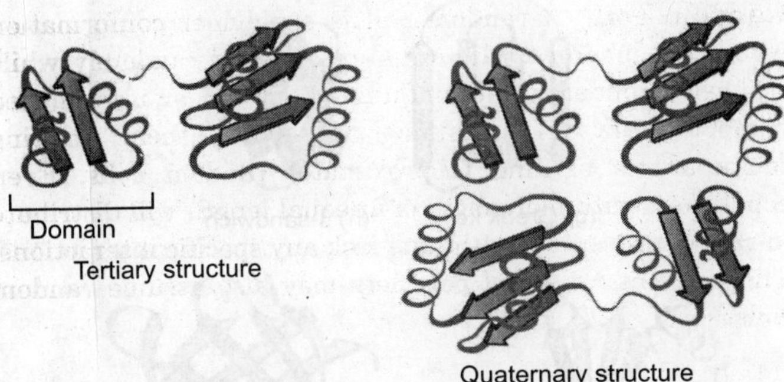

Fig. 3.14 The tertiary and quaternary structure of proteins

Domains, Motif and Folds

The functional unit of a protein is fold that is stable in solution can be defined as protein domain. Actually domain is the fundamental unit of tertiary structure. The terms are also applied to a wide range of structures. Recognized motifs range from simple to complex, sometimes appearing in repeating units or combinations. A single large motif may comprise the entire protein.

Polypeptides with more than a few hundred amino acid residues often fold into two or more stable, globular units called **domains.** In many cases, a domain from a large protein will retain its correct three-dimensional structure even when it is separated from the remainder of the polypeptide chain.

There are certain **motifs** that occur over and over again in different proteins. The helix-loop-helix motif, for example, consists of two α-helices joined by a reverse turn. The Greek key motif consists of four antiparallel β-strands in a β-sheet, where the order of the strands along the polypeptide chain is 4, 1, 2, 3. The β-sandwich is two layers of β-sheet.

Larger motifs are often called domain folds because they make up the core of a domain. The parallel twisted sheet is found in many domains share very stable core structure. The β-barrel structure is found in many membrane proteins. There are dozens of enzymes that have adapted to an α/β-barrel. The β-helix is much less common.

Eukaryotic proteins often contain multiple domains that are attached together by flexible linker peptides. These domains retain both the three-dimensional structure and the function in isolation. Domains are folded, compact and globular. They mostly interact with other proteins and in some cases with other macromolecules such as carbohydrates, lipids and nucleic acids.

Classification of Protein Domains

(i) Intracellular Large Domains

Protein kinase domain, protein phosphatase, other enzymes, leucine-rich repeat domain (LRR), ankyrin repeat domain, armadillo repeat domain, heat repeat domains, etc. These domains consist of repeated motifs. LRRs, 20-22 residues, are repeated multiple times; each repeat is a beta-beta or alpha-beta unit. An armadillo repeat, which roughly contains 40 residues, folds into a three-helix bundle. An ankyrin repeat is formed by 33 amino acids. In each ankyrin repeat two helices define a plane from which a beta hairpin is projected in an orthogonal orientation. These repeated domains are found in many proteins and are primarily involved in the interactions with other macromolecules.

(ii) Intracellular Small Domains (Modules)

(a) **SH2** (Src homology 2) **domain** Many eukaryotic proteins bear this domain. SH2 domain is ~100 residues long. Five-stranded antiparallel beta sheets are flanked by two helices. SH2 domain recognizes phosphotyrosine peptides.

(b) **PTB** (Phosphotyrosine binding) **domain** It was first identified in SHC (Src homology 2, collagen homology) adapter protein. PTB domains are well-defined SH2 domains that bind to phosphotyrosine in non-SH2-dependent manner. Peptide-binding specificity of PTB domain resides in residues at positions amino-terminal to the pY residues. PTB domain binds to NPXpY sequences.

(c) **SH3** (Src homology 3) **domain** These are smaller (60 aa) and bind to proteins containing PXXP sequence (X = at aa). The core of the SH3 is composed of a continuous curved sheet as if two sheets are in perpendicular orientation.

(d) **PH** (Pleckstrin Homology) **domain** It is composed of two antiparallel beta sheets and a long helix at one end. PH domain is approximately 125 amino acids long and one end of the structure is positively charged which presumably interacts with membrane. Phosphatidylinositol 4,5-bisphosphate (PIP2) binds to the N-terminal region of phospholipase Cd-1 which contains a PH domain. The PH domain of pleckstrin and Beta-Adrenergic Receptor Kinase (BARK) bind inositol 1, 4, 5-triphosphate (IP3).

(e) **PDZ** (PSD-90/disc large/201) **domain** PDZ it containing proteins are primarily found in cell junction. PDZ domains interact with peptide found in the C-terminus of K-channels and N-methyl-D-Asp (NMDA) receptor. They are six-stranded beta-sandwich, where one of the strands is shared by both sheets. It binds to peptides of sequence X-T/S-X-Val-COO−.

(f) **WW domain** It is one of the smallest protein domains known. It contains ~40 aa. The domain structure consists of a twisted and bent 3-stranded anti-parallel beta-sheet. Two of the four critical residues Y28 and W39 are located at the bottom of the sheet and the two F29 and W17 located at the top characterize the WW domain. It prefers peptides with PPXY sequence.

(iii) Extracellular Domain

(a) **Immunoglobulin Domain** The cost of the Ig domain is a beta-sandwich between a three-stranded and a four-stranded sheet. CDR (Complementarily-

Determining Region) loops bind to specific antigens. Ig domain is also found in intracellular proteins.

(b) **Cadherins** These molecules have five extracellular domain. Each cadherin has its own specificity of binding. Cadherin dimer of one cell makes homophilic contacts with cadherin of other cell.

(c) **Fibronectin** (Fn) Fn attaches cell to extracellular matrix by binding to integrin family of cell surface proteins. Fn also binds to fibrin and collagen. Type 1 Fn consists of 40 residues. The core of the Fn domain is a beta-sandwich between two small beta sheets (one two-stranded and the other is three-stranded).

(d) **EGF domain** (disulphide bonds) It contain roughly 45 amino acids. It has two stranded beta-sheets. Three disulphide bonds stabilize the folded structure. The domain structure does not show any hydrophobic core. The domain is considerably flexible.

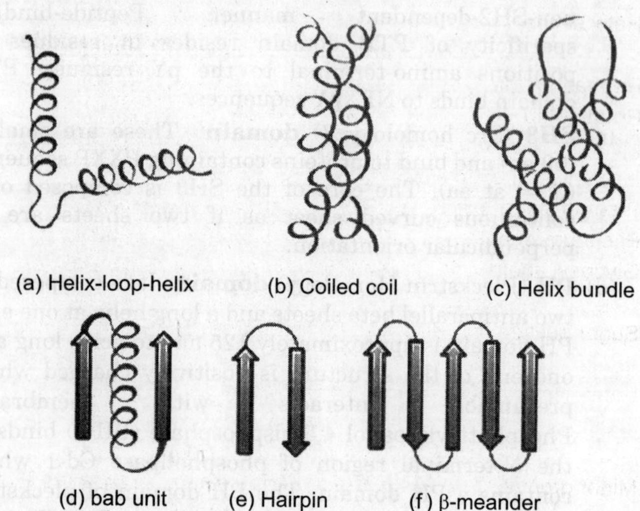

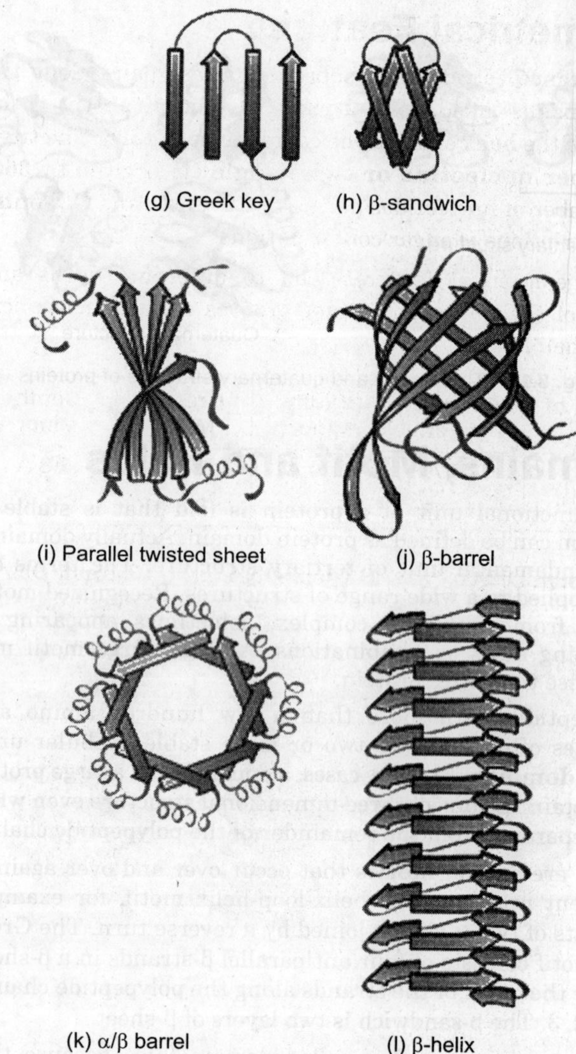

Fig. 3.15 Large motifs

Conformation of Nucleic Acids

The structure and conformation of nucleic acids is determined by various forces and angles their structural components. The DNA is found in various forms based on structure and conformation.

A, B and Z-DNA

In the cell nucleus DNA is complexed with about an equivalent mass of protein to form a structure known as **chromatin.** Chromatin is a periodic structure made up of repeating, regularly spaced subunits, the subunit being the **nucleosome.** Within the nucleosomes the major part of DNA is wrapped around **histones**. The remaning DNA joining each nucleosome is known as **linker DNA.**

The X-ray crystal structure of the nucleosome core particle of chromatin has been determined. It shows in atomic detail how the histone protein octamer is assembled and how 146 base pairs of DNA are organized into a superhelix around it.

1. **A-DNA** is found in solutions with higher salt concentrations or with alcohol added.
2. **Z-DNA** occurs for alternating poly(dG-dC) sequences in solutions with high salt concentrations or alcohol.
3. **B-DNA** is found at low salt concentrations. The native conformation occurring in **chromatin.**
4. There are further nucleic acid conformations like C-DNA, H-DNA, etc.

Geometrical Features

The distance between two subsequent base pairs along the helical axis is called **helical rise (h).** The **pitch (p)** is the length of the helix axis for one complete helix turn. The **turn angle per nucleotide or twist angle (t)** is given by 360° per number of nucleotides per turn. **C2′-endo and C3′-endo** are descriptions of sugar conformations.

These geometrical features lead to different widths and depths of the minor and major grooves of the nucleic acid double helix.

Types of DNA	Groove Major	Width Minor	Groove Major	Depth Minor
A-DNA	2.7 Å	11.0 Å	13.5 Å	2.8 Å
B-DNA	11.7 Å	5.7 Å	8.5 Å	7.5 Å

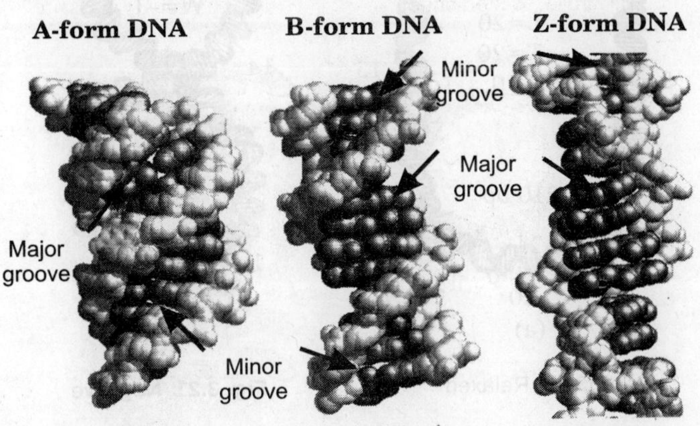

Fig. 3.16 A, B and Z-forms, depending upon salt and water concentrations and sequence

The Sugar Puckering

(i) Conformation of a nucleotide sugar ring characterized by sugar pucker by deviation of the ring from planarity. It is defined by the position of the C2′ and C3′ atoms; relative to the plane (C1′, O4′ and C4′).

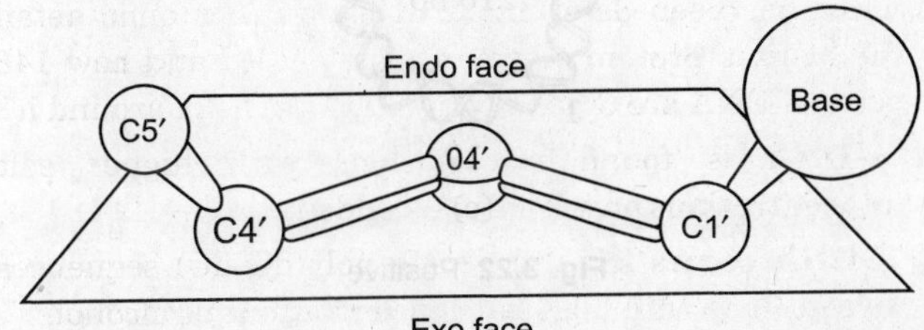

Fig. 3.17 Exo faces and endo faces of sugar

(ii) There are four distinctive types of pucker in which either the C2′ or C3′ atoms deviates from the plane. The devation either above (internal puckering) **(-endo)** or beneath **(-exo)** the plane.

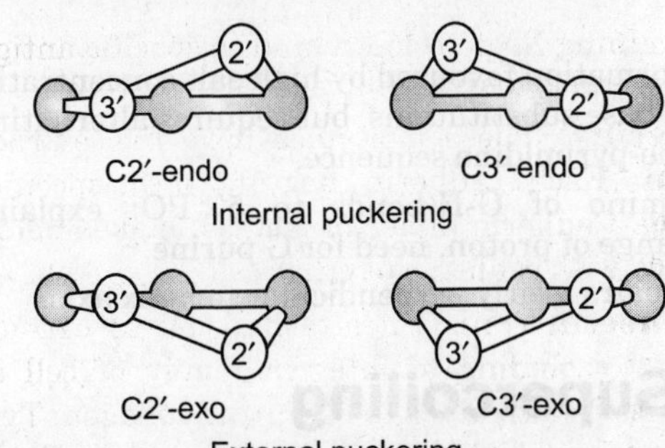

Fig. 3.18 Puckering in sugar

The most frequently occurring nucleic acid model conformations are characterized by the following geometrical parameters:

Table 3.1 **Parameters of Major DNA Helices**

Properties	A	B	Z
Helix sense	Right handed	Right handed	Left handed
Repeating unit	1 bp	1bp	2 bp
Rotation/bp	33.6°	35.9°	30°/
Mean bp/turn	10.7	10.0	12
Inclination of bp to axis	+19°	-1.2°	-9°
Rise/bp along axis	2.3Å	3.32Å	3.8Å
Pitch/turn of helix	24.6Å	33.2Å	45.6Å
Glycosyl angle	Anti	Anti	C: anti, G: syn
Sugar pucker	C3′-endo	C2′-endo	C: C2′-endo, G: C2′-exo
Diameter	26Å	20Å	18Å
Major groove	narrow and deep	wide and deep	Flat
Minor groove	Wide and shallow	Narrow and deep	Narrow and deep

B-form

(i) Most common DNA conformation *in vivo*.

(ii) Wide major groove easily accessible to proteins.

(iii) Favoured conformation at high water concentrations (hydrations of minor groove seems to favour B-form).

(iv) Base pairs nearly perpendicular to helix axis.

A-form

(i) Most RNA and RNA-DNA duplex in this form.

(ii) Shorter, wider helix than B.

(iii) Deep, narrow major groove not easily accessible to proteins.

(iv) Favoured conformation at low water concentrations.

Z-form

(i) It can be formed *in vivo*, given proper sequence and superhelical tension, but function remains obscure.

(ii) Conformation favoured by high salt concentrations, some base substitutions, but requires alternating purine-pyrimidine sequence.

(iii) N2-amino of G-H-bonds to 5′ PO: explains slow exchange of proton, need for G purine.

(iv) Base pairs nearly perpendicular to helix axis.

DNA Supercoiling

Circular B-form DNA, has one helical turn every 10.5 bp, is said to be **relaxed,** as there is no net bending of the DNA axis upon itself. If two points are twisted in opposite directions supercoiling may be created.

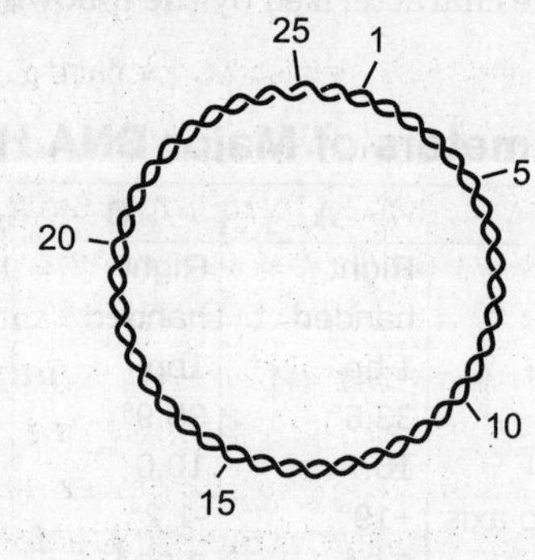

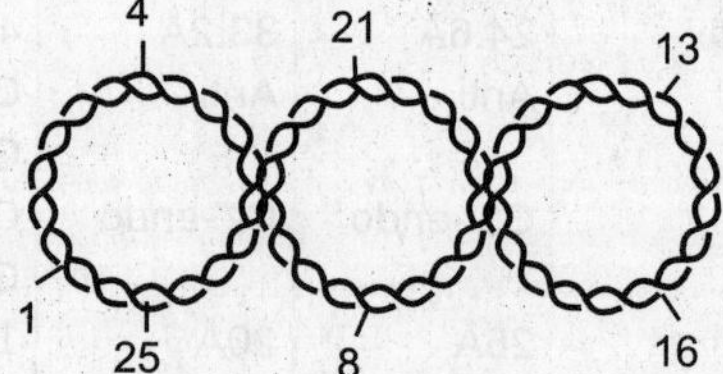

Fig. 3.19 Supercoiling in DNA

Positive and Negative Supercoiling

If the twisting is in the same direction as the double helix (right handed for B-DNA) the supercoiling formed is **positive.** If the twisting is in the opposite direction as the double helix (left handed for B-DNA) the supercoiling formed is **negative.** The level of supercoiling may be quantified in terms of supercoiling density (σ).

$$\sigma = (Lk - Lk^0)/Lk^0$$

Lk^0 is the linking number of the relaxed circular DNA molecule.

DNA isolated from cells is commonly negatively supercoiled by 6 turns per 100 turns of helix. Therefore,

$$\sigma = (94 - 100)/100 = -0.06$$

If the DNA is wound so, that there are fewer bases per turn <9 bp, it is overwound creating positive supercoiling. The angle of twist increases from 34.3° to 37.7°. If there are more bases per turn >11 bp, it is underwound creating negative supercoiling. The angle of twist decreases from 34.3° to 30.9°. The degree of underwinding in cellular DNAs generally falls in the range of 5% to 7% that is,

$$\sigma = -0.05 \text{ to } -0.07$$

Linking number can be broken down into 2 structural components called **writhe** (Wr) and **twist** (Tw). **Writhe** may be thought as a measure of the coiling of the helix axis. **Twist** determine the local twisting or spatial arrangement of neighbouring base pairs.

$$\mathbf{Lk = Tw + Wr}$$

Supercoiled DNA has a higher energy level than relaxed DNA. For negative supercoiling, this energy makes it easier for the DNA helix to be locally unwound or untwisted. Negative supercoiling may therefore, facilitate processes that require DNA unwinding, such as transcription, replication and DNA repair.

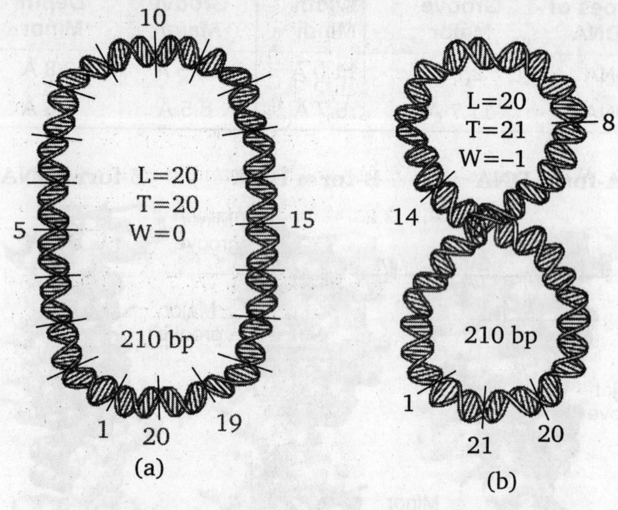

Fig. 3.20 Relaxed **Fig. 3.21** Negative

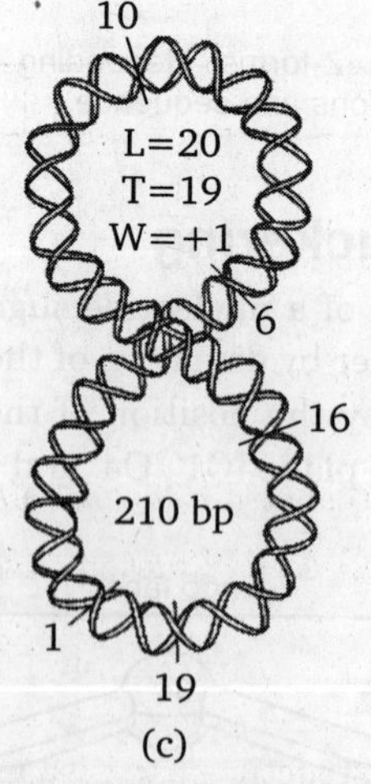

Fig. 3.22 Positive

Hairpin and Cruciform DNA Structures

Palindrome DNA sequences are self-complementary and therefore, have the ability to base-pair with each other. Base pairing of palindrome sequences can result in hairpin or cruciform DNA structures. Palindromes are inverted repeats of DNA.

5′ —T T A G C A C G T G C T A A—3′
3′ —A A T C G T G C A C G A T T —5′

Palindromic sequences are self-complementary within each strand and therefore, have potential to form hairpin or cruciform (cross-shaped) structures.

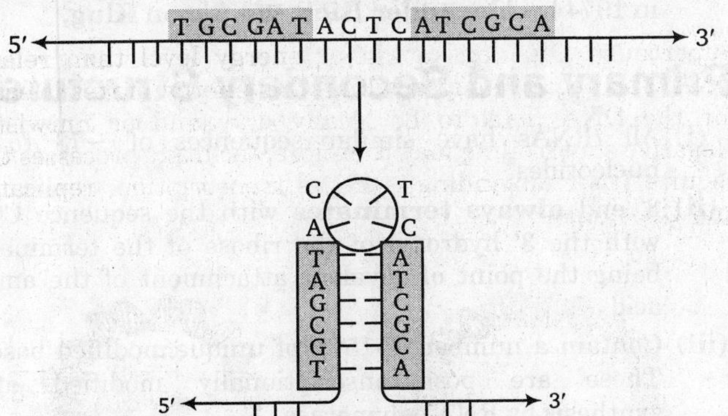

When only a single DNA (or RNA) strand is involved

Fig. 3.23 Hairpin formation

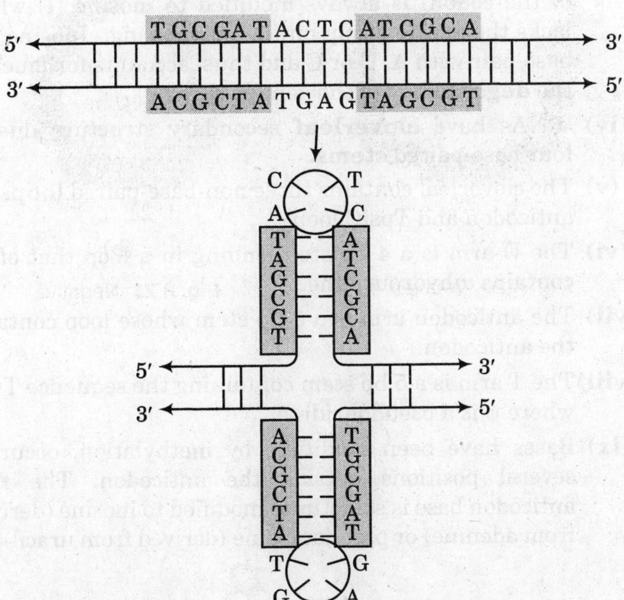

When both strands of a duplex DNA are involved

Fig. 3.24 Cruciform formation

Triple Helix

A triple-stranded structure can also exist at least in the test tube, and possibly during recombination and DNA repair. Triple-helical structures involve, in addition to the normal Watson-Crick base pairing, the **Hoogsteen base pairing.** For example, the first triple helix discovered, poly(U)·poly(A)·poly(U), has an all-purine strand (Pur) paired with two all-pyrimidine strands (Pyr). This type of triple-base bonding is of biological importance. For instance, it helps stabilize structures of *t*RNAs.

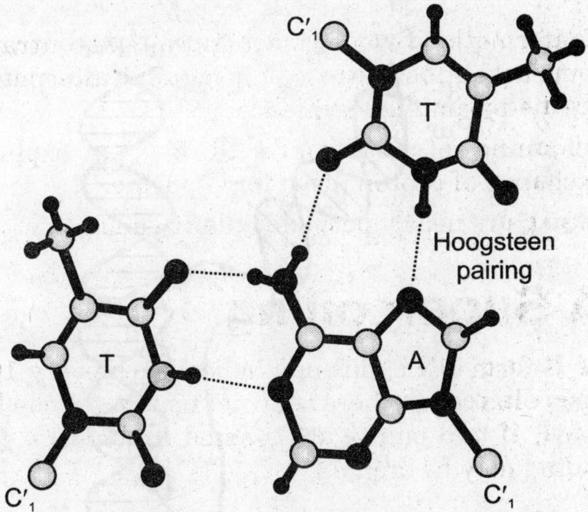

Fig. 3.25 Watson-Crick pairing

In the so, called H-DNA, a portion of the Pyr·Pur duplex denature and loops back to form triple helix, leaving one of the strands from the denatured portion unpaired. The loss of Watson-Crick pairs must have been over compensated by the formation of **Hoogsteen base pairs.** In fact, cocrystallization of monomeric adenine and thymine derivatives invariably leads to Hoogsteen pairs, suggesting that Hoogsteen base pairing is more stable for A·T pairs than is Watson-Crick base pairing.

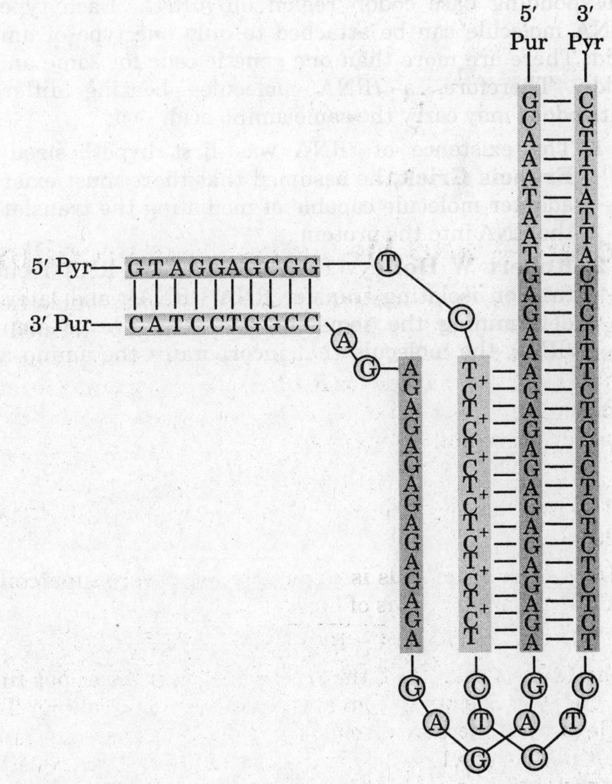

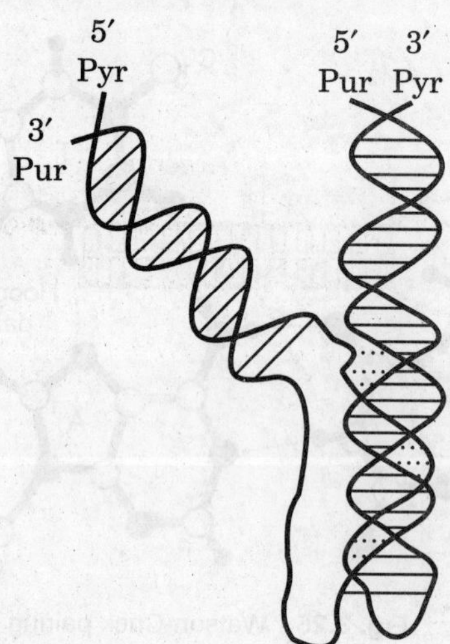

Fig. 3.26 The triple helix bonding

Transfer RNA

Transfer RNA (*t*RNA) is a small RNA (~73-93 nucleotides) that transfers a specific amino acid to a growing polypeptide chain at the ribosomal site during translation. The *t*RNA has a 3′ terminal site for amino acid attachment. The amino acid is covalently linked to *t*RNA. This linkage is catalyzed by an aminoacyl *t*RNA synthetase. The *t*RNA has three base region called the anticodon that base pair with the three crossponding base codon region on *m*RNA. Each type of *t*RNA molecule can be attached to only one type of amino acid. There are more than one genetic code for some amino acids. Therefore, a *t*RNA molecules bearing different anticodons may carry the same amino acid.

1. The existence of *t*RNA was first hypothesized by **Francis Crick,** he assumed that there must exist an adapter molecule capable of mediating the translating the RNA into the protein.
2. **Robert W Holley** (1965) research on RNA focused first on isolating transfer RNA (*t*RNA), and later on determining the sequence and structure of alanine *t*RNA, the molecule that incorporates the amino acid alanine into proteins. Holley's team determined the *t*RNAs structure by using two ribonucleases to split the tRNA molecule into pieces, the team eventually determined the entire structure of the molecule.
3. The secondary and tertiary structures were derived from X-ray crystallography studies reported independently in 1974 by **Alexander Rich** and **Aaron Klug.**

Primary and Secondary Structure

(i) All *t*RNAs have similar sequences of ~73 to 93 nucleotides.

(ii) 3′ end **always terminates** with the sequence CCA, with the 3′ hydroxyl of the ribose of the terminal A being the point of covalent attachment of the amino acid.

(iii) Contain a number (7-15%) of unique/modified bases. These are post-transcriptionally modified after synthesis by RNA polymerase.

– In particular, adenosine (A) in first or 5′ position of the anticodon (corresponding to the third or 3′ position of the codon) is always modified to inosine (I) which lacks the amino group on the purine ring. Inosine can base-pair with A, U or C and thus, accounts for much of the **degeneracy** of the genetic code.

(iv) *t*RNAs have **cloverleaf** secondary structure due to four base-paired **stems.**

(v) The cloverleaf contains three non-base-paired **loops**, D, anticodon and TpsiC loop.

(vi) The D-arm is a 4 bp stem ending in a loop that often contains dihydrouridine.

(vii) The anticodon arm is a 5-bp stem whose loop contains the anticodon.

(viii) The T-arm is a 5 bp stem containing the sequence TψC, where ψ is a pseudouridine.

(ix) Bases have been modified, by methylation, occur in several positions outside the anticodon. The first anticodon base is sometimes modified to inosine (derived from adenine) or pseudouridine (derived from uracil).

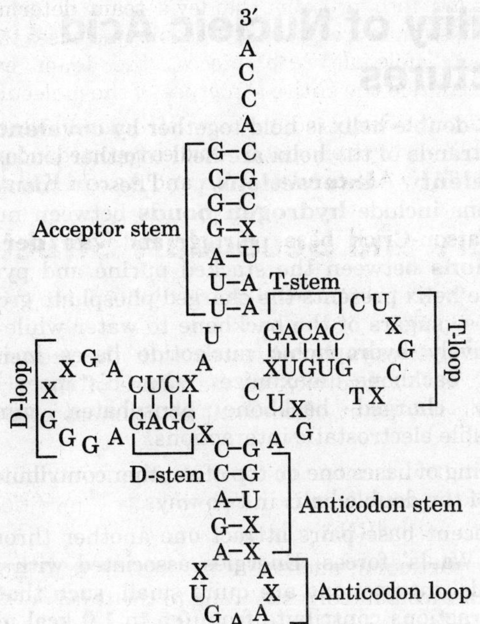

Fig. 3.27 Standard *t*RNA representation

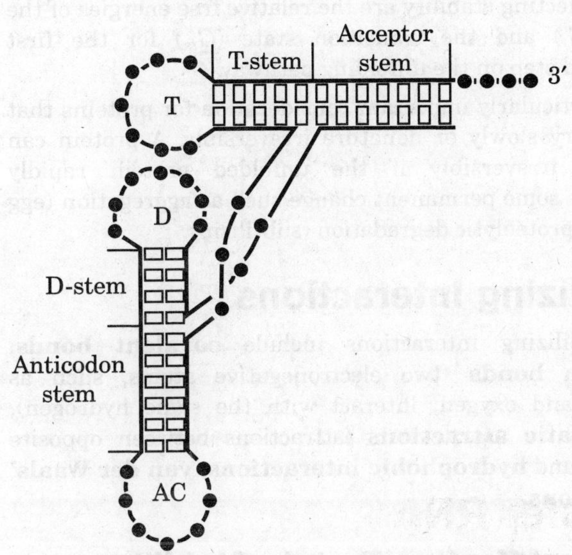

Fig. 3.28 Two distinct domains: First domain (vertical) : D-stem and anticodon stem. Second domain (horizontal) : T-stem and acceptor stem

Stability of Proteins and Nucleic Acids

The stability of various macromolecules including proteins and nucleic acids is determined by various weak interactions and thermodynamics.

Stability of Protein

Proteins fold spontaneously in solution in order to maximize their stability. Every time there is a stabilizing interaction between two atoms, free energy is released. The more free energy released (the more negative the $\Delta G°$), the more stable the protein. So, a protein tends to fold in a way that maximizes the number of stabilizing interactions.

Thermodynamic Stability

The conformational entropy change ΔS_{conf} works against folding, but the enthalpy of internal interactions and the hydrophobic entropy change favour folding. Therefore, the overall $\Delta G_{folding}$ is negative, and the folded structure is stable.

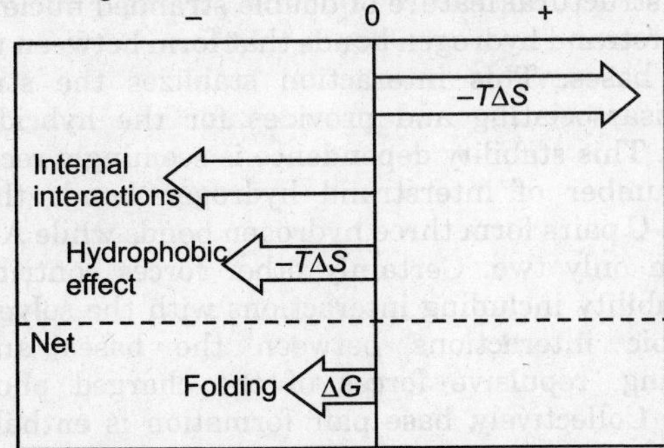

Fig. 3.29 The thermodynamic stability

The physical biochemist, on the one hand, would probably discuss protein stability primarily in terms of the **thermodynamic stability** of a protein that unfolds and refolds rapidly, reversibly, cooperatively and with a simple, two-state mechanism:

$$\text{Folded} \xrightleftharpoons{K_u} \text{Unfolded}$$

where, K_u is the equilibrium constant for unfolding.

In these cases, the stability of the protein is simply the difference in Gibbs free energy, ΔG, between the folded and the unfolded states. The only factors affecting stability are the relative free energies of the folded (G_f) and the unfolded (G_u) states. The larger and more positive ΔG_u, the more stable is the protein to denaturation.

$$\Delta G_u = G_u - G_f$$

The Gibbs free energy G, is made up the two terms enthalpy (H) and entropy (S), related by the equation:

$$G = H - TS$$

where, T is the temperature in Kelvin.

The folding free energy difference, ΔG_u, is typically small, of the order of 5-15 kcal/mol for a globular protein (compared to, *e.g.*, ~30-100 kcal/mol for a covalent bond).

In case of irreversible or slowly unfolding proteins, it is kinetic stability or the rate of unfolding that is important. A protein that is kinetically stable will unfold more slowly than a kinetically unstable protein. In a kinetically stable protein, a large free energy barrier to unfolding is required and the factors affecting stability are the relative free energies of the folded (G_f) and the transition state (G_{ts}) for the first committed step on the unfolding pathway.

It is a particularly important consideration for proteins that unfold very slowly or denature irreversibly. A protein can denature irreversibly if the unfolded protein rapidly undergoes some permanent change such as aggregation (egg white) or proteolytic degradation (subtilisin).

Stabilizing Interactions

The stabilizing interactions include **covalent bonds, hydrogen bonds** (two electronegative atoms, such as nitrogen and oxygen, interact with the same hydrogen), **electrostatic attractions** (attractions between opposite charges), and **hydrophobic interactions, van der Waals' interactions.**

Factors Affecting Protein Stability

(a) Hydrophobic interactions
(b) Hydrogen bonds
(c) Conformational entropy
(d) Salt bridges
(e) Aromatic-aromatic interactions
(f) Metal binding and
(g) Disulphide bonds

The **conformational entropy** of unfolding makes the greatest contribution to stabilization of the unfolded state is its conformational entropy. It has been proposed that decreasing the conformational flexibility of the unfolded chain (by substitution with proline or by replacement of glycine) should lead to an increase in the stability of the folded relative to the unfolded protein.

The **aromatic-aromatic interactions** about 60% of the aromatic side chains (Phe, Tyr and Trp), found in proteins are involved in aromatic pairings.

Its geometry is perpendicular, such that the partially positively charged hydrogens on the edge of one ring can interact favourably with the pi electrons and partially negatively charged carbons of the other. Such interactions make a contribution to protein stability.

Another method by which the folded state of proteins can be stabilized is **metal binding,** in which metal ions are coordinated, usually by lone pair donation from oxygen or nitrogen atoms.

The stabilizing interactions can occur between peptide groups (atoms in the backbone of the protein), between side-chain groups and between peptide and side-chain groups. Disulphide bonds are the only covalent bonds that can form when a protein folds. The other bonding interactions that occur in folding are much weaker.

Stability of Nucleic Acid Structures

The DNA double helix is held together by **covalent bonds,** the two strands of the helix are held together exclusively by **non-covalent interactions.** These non-covalent interactions include **hydrogen bonds** between nucleotide bases (Watson-Crick base pairing) and **van der Waals' interactions** between the stacked purine and pyrimidine bases. The helix presents the charged phosphate groups and polar ribose sugars of the backbone to water while burying the relatively hydrophobic nucleotide bases inside. The extended backbone maximizes the distance between negatively charged backbone phosphates, minimizing unfavourable electrostatic interactions.

The stacking of bases one on top of another contributes to the stability of the double helix in two ways.

1. Adjacent base pairs attract one another through van der Waals' forces. Energies associated with van der Waals' interactions are quite small, such that typical interactions contribute from 0.5 to 1.0 kcal mol^{-1} per atom pair. In the double helix, however, a large number of atoms are in van der Waals' contact and the net effect, summed over these atom pairs, is substantial.
2. The double helix is stabilized by the hydrophobic effect, base stacking or hydrophobic interactions between the bases, results in the exposure of the more polar surfaces to the surrounding water. This arrangement is reminiscent of protein folding, where hydrophobic amino acids are interior in the protein and hydrophilic are exterior. Base stacking in DNA is also favoured by the conformations of the relatively rigid five-membered rings of the backbone sugars. The sugar rigidity affects both the single-stranded and the double-helical forms.

A nucleic acid in aqueous solution is in equilibrium between the native conformation and its uncoiled conformation. The stability of the native state is based on the magnitude of the Gibbs free energy (ΔG) of the system and the thermodynamic relationships between enthalpy (ΔH) and entropy (ΔS) changes. A positive ΔG indicates the native state is more stable than the denatured state the more positive the ΔG, the greater the stability. For a DNA molecule to melt, stabilizing forces need to be broken.

A central structural feature of double stranded nucleic acids is the interstrand hydrogen bonds that form between the A-T and G-C bases. This interaction stablizes the structure against disassociating and provides for the hybridization specificity. This stability dependence is seemingly reconciled by the number of interstrand hydrogen bonds that are formed. G-C pairs form three hydrogen bonds while A-T base pairs form only two. Certainly other forces contribute to duplex stability including interactions with the solvent, the hydrophobic interactions between the bases and the destabilizing, repulsive forces of the charged phosphate backbone. Collectively, base pair formation is enthalpically favourable, summing up to ~–8.5 kcals mol A-T base pair-1 and ~–9.4 kcals mol G-C base pair-1.

Metabolism of Biomolecules

The enzyme-catalyzed chemical reactions are functionally organized into sequences of consecutive reactions, called **pathways.** Some pathways degrade organic nutrients into simple end products in order to convert it into a form useful to the cell such a reactions are designated **catabolism.** Other pathways start with small precursor molecules and convert them to progressively larger and more complex molecules, such as proteins and nucleic acids. Such synthetic pathways, designated **anabolism**. The overall network of enzyme-catalyzed pathways constitutes cellular **metabolism**.

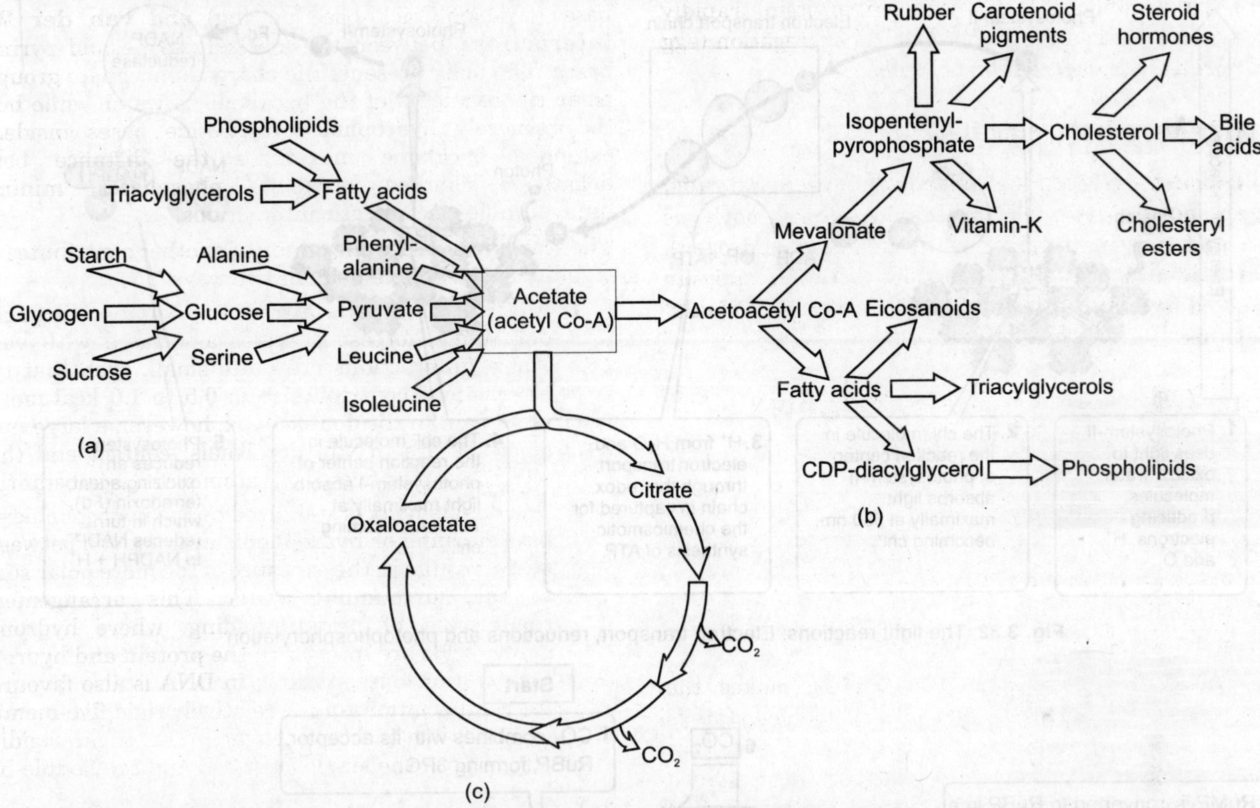

Fig. 3.30 Three types of metabolic pathways. (a) Converging catabolic (b) Diverging anabolic and (c) Cyclic, in which one of the starting materials is regenerated and reenters the pathway.

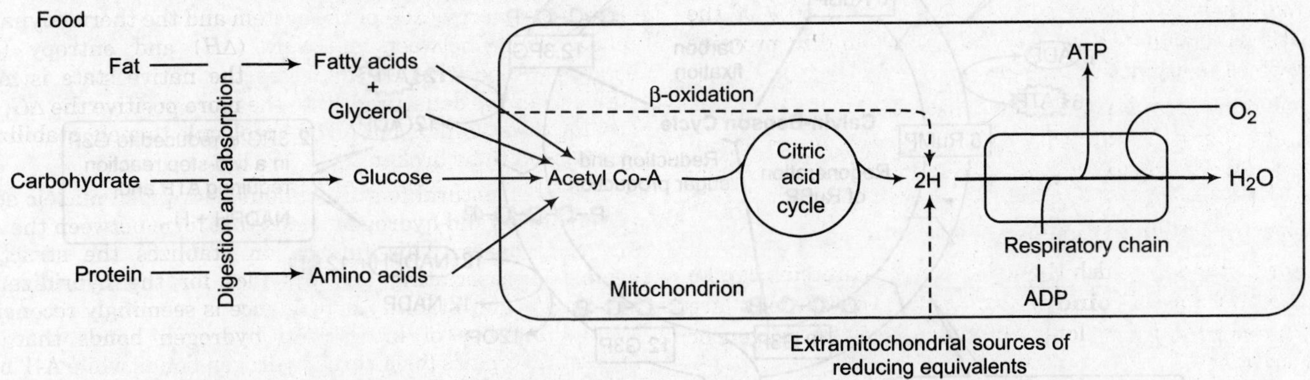

Fig. 3.31 Role of the respiratory chain of mitochondria in the conversion of food energy to ATP

Carbohydrates

Carbohydrates is primary energy providing biomolecule composed of C, H and O. It is synthesized by plants but catalysed by all organisms.

Carbohydrate Biosynthesis

Carbohydrate is synthesized through photosynthesis. There are two pathways in photosynthesis.

(i) The **light reactions** are driven by light energy. This pathway produces ATP and a reduced electron carrier (NADPH + H^+).

(ii) The second pathway, called the **dark reaction** (Calvin–Benson cycle, C_4, CAM) does not use light directly. It uses ATP, NADPH + H^+ (made by the light reactions) and CO_2 to produce sugars.

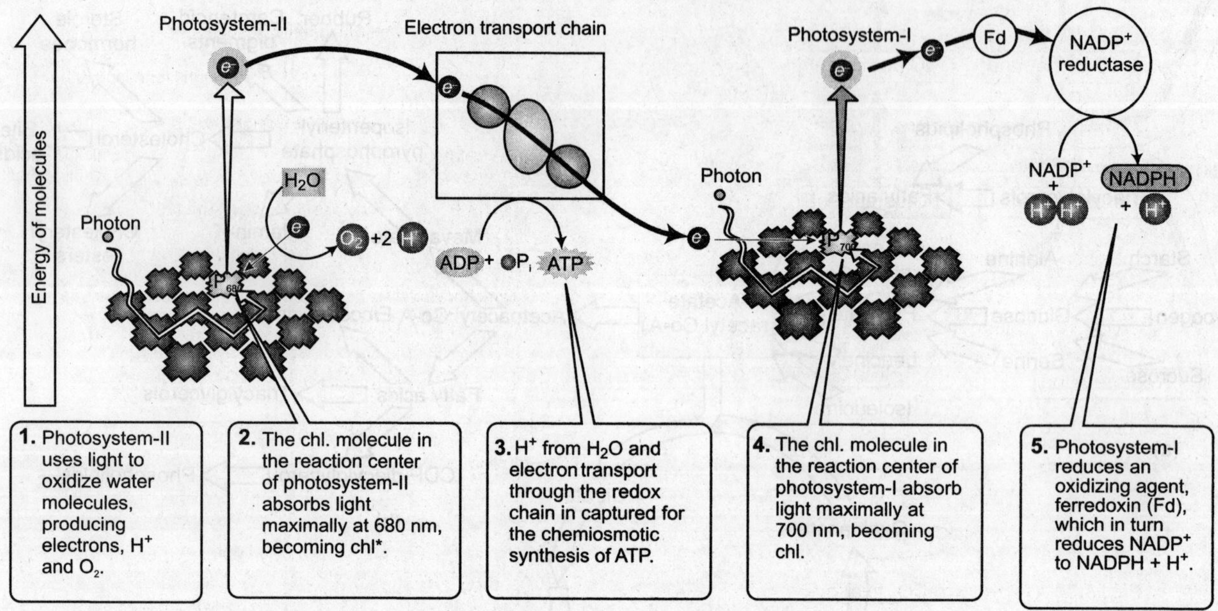

Fig. 3.32 The light reactions: Electron transport, reductions and photophosphorylation

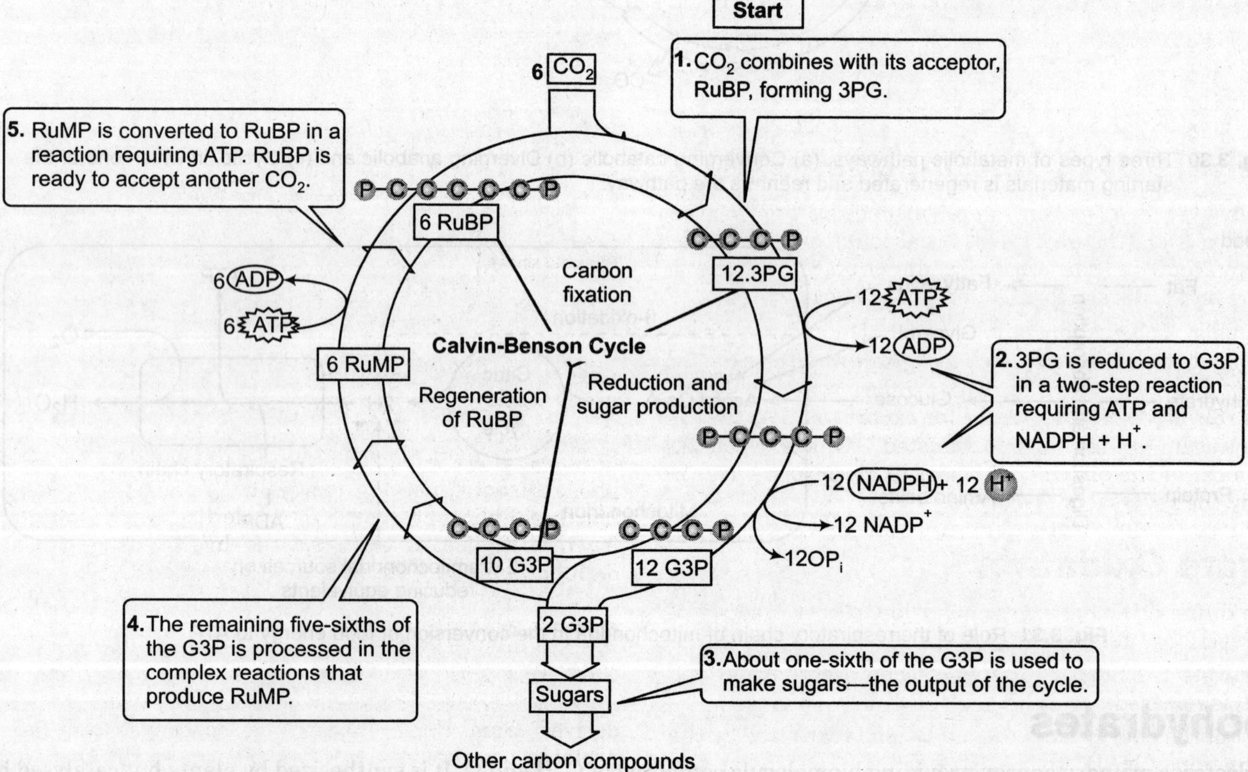

Fig. 3.33 The Calvin-Benson cycle. The Calvin-Benson cycle uses CO_2 and the ATP and NADPH + H^+ generated in the light reactions to produce glucose

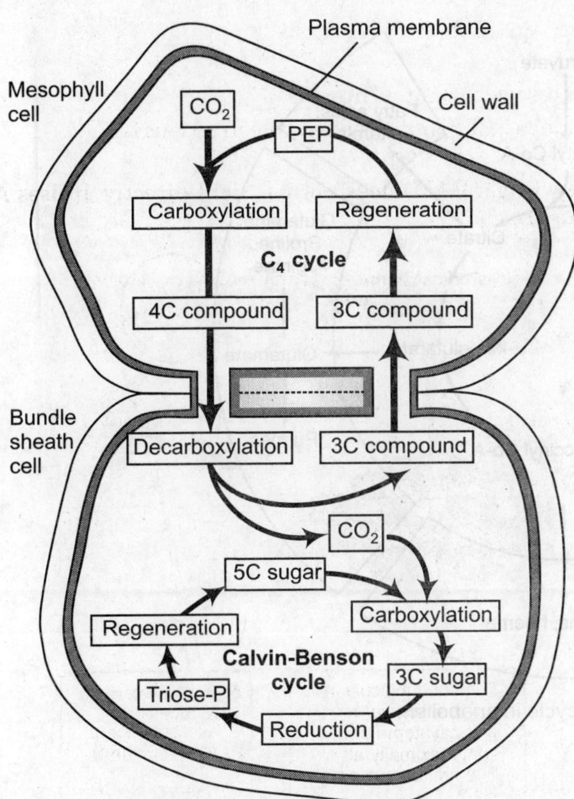

Fig. 3.34 C_4 cycle of CO_2 fixation

Carbohydrates Catabolism

Oxidation of carbohydrate mainly glucose is necessary for energy. In presence of O_2 it is oxidized to CO_2 water and energy through glycolysis and Krebs' cycle.

Glycolysis and Gluconeogenesis

The pathways of glycogen metabolism provide, in the catabolic direction, the energy essential to oppose the forces of entropy and in the anabolic direction, biosynthetic precursors and a storage form of metabolic energy.

In animals the formation of D-glucose from non-carbohydrate precursor is called **gluconeogenesis.** In mammals, gluconeogenesis occurs primarily in the **liver**, where its role is to provide glucose for export to other tissues when glycogen stores are exhausted. Gluconeogenesis employs most of the enzymes that act in glycolysis, but it is not simply the reversal of glycolysis.

Pyruvate Oxidation

Pyruvate diffuses into the mitochondrion, where a series of coupled reactions takes place:

(a) Pyruvate is oxidized to a two-carbon acetyl group and CO_2 is released.

(b) Part of the energy from the oxidation is captured by the reduction of NAD^+ to NADH + H^+.

(c) Some of the remaining energy is stored temporarily by the combining of the acetyl group with Co-A, forming acetyl Co-A:

$$\text{Pyruvate} + NAD^+ + \text{Co-A} \rightarrow \text{Acetyl Co-A} + NADH + H^+ + CO_2$$

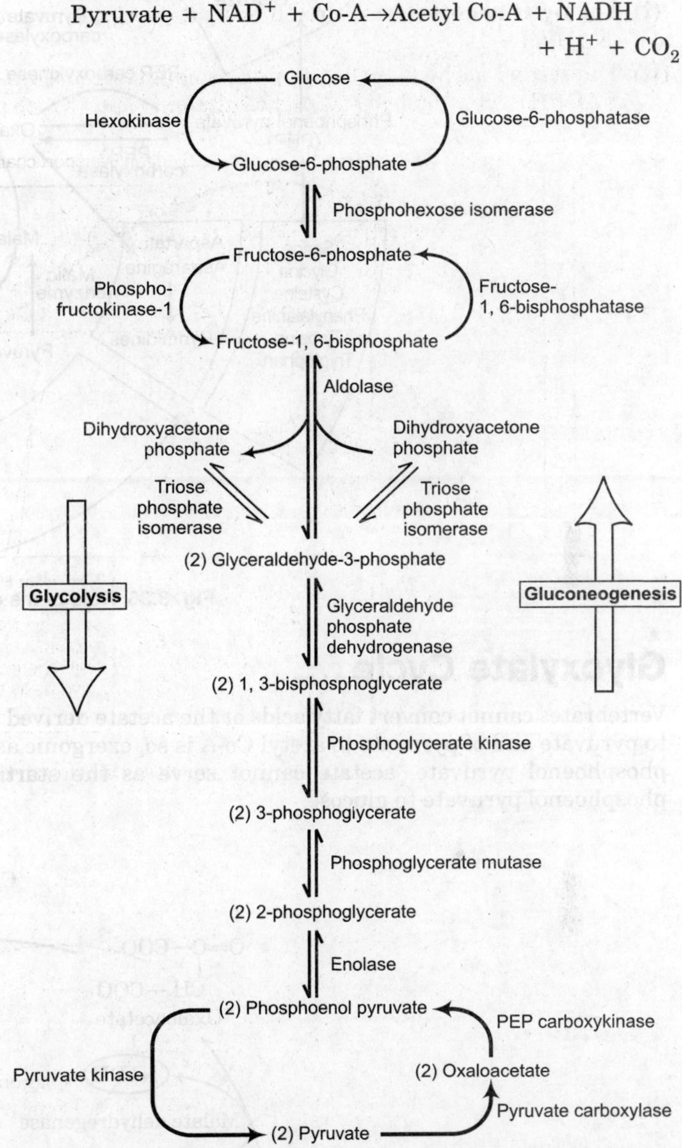

Fig. 3.35 Glycolysis and gluconeogenesis

When two reactions occur simultaneously at a high rate in the same cell they can cause loss of large amount of energy as heat. Such ATP degrading cycle is called futile cycle. As phosphofructokinase catalyses phosphorylation of fructose-6-phosphate by ATP while its by pass counterpart fructose diphosphatase catalyses hydrolysis of fructose-1, 6-diphosphate to yield fructose-6-phosphate.

Citric Acid Cycle

The citric acid cycle (Krebs' cycle, TCA cycle) is a nearly universal central catabolic pathway in which compounds derived from the breakdown of carbohydrates, fats and proteins are oxidized to CO_2, with most of the energy of oxidation temporarily held in the electron carriers $FADH_2$ and NADH.

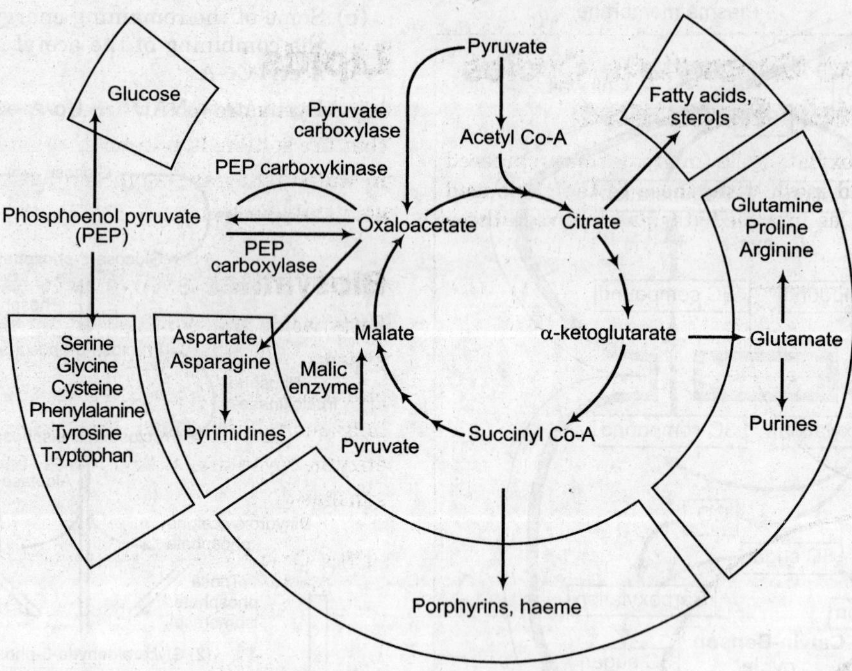

Fig. 3.36 Role of the citric acid cycle in anabolism

Glyoxylate Cycle

Vertebrates cannot convert fatty acids or the acetate derived from them, to carbohydrates. Conversion of phosphoenol pyruvate to pyruvate and of pyruvate to acetyl Co-A is so, exergonic as to be essentially irreversible. If a cell cannot convert acetate into phosphoenol pyruvate, acetate cannot serve as the starting material for the gluconeogenic pathway, which leads from phosphoenol pyruvate to glucose.

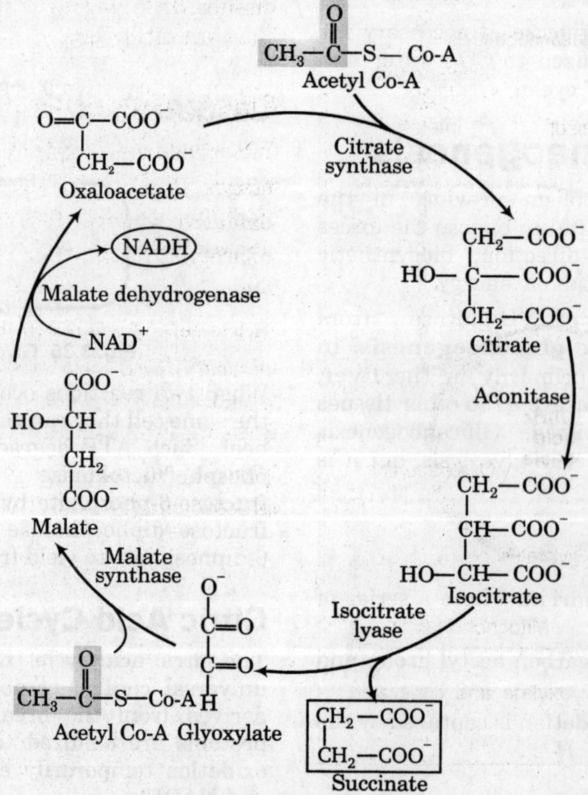

Fig. 3.37 Glyoxylate cycle

Citric Acid and Glyoxylate Cycles are Coordinately Regulated

The reactions of the glyoxylate cycle (in glyoxysomes) proceed simultaneously with and mesh with, those of the citric acid cycle (in mitochondria), as intermediates pass between these compartments.

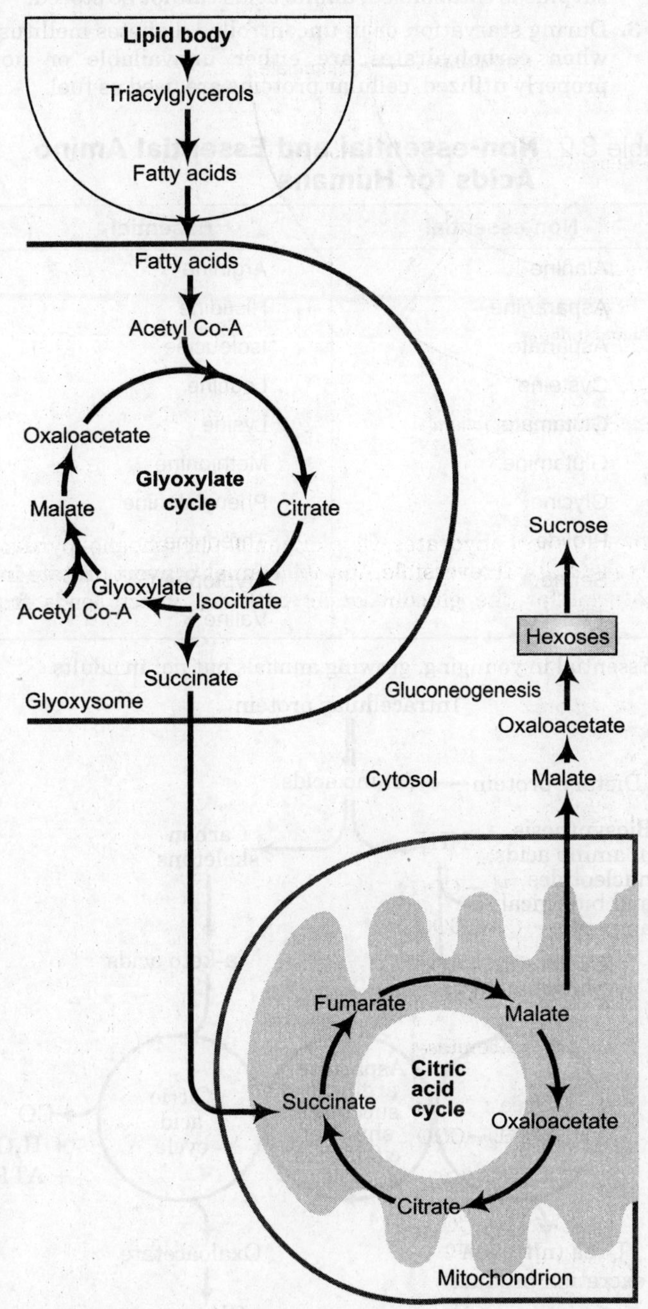

Fig. 3.38 Relationship between the glyoxylate and citric acid cycles

Lipids

Lipids are a group of naturally occurring organic compounds that are soluble in non-polar organism solvents but insoluble in water. They are composed of C, H and O in form of fatty acid and glycerol.

Biosynthesis of Fatty Acids

Fatty acids are synthesized by an **extra mitochondrial system**, which is responsible for the complete synthesis of palmitate from acetyl Co-A in the cytosol. The synthesis of long-chain fatty acids (lipogenesis) is carried out by two enzyme systems, acetyl Co-A carboxylase and fatty acid synthase.

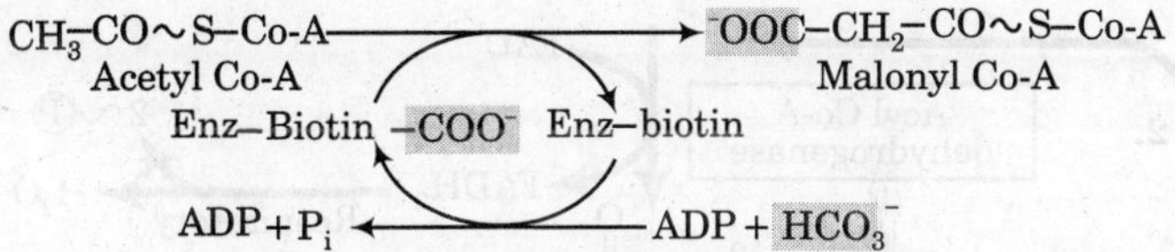

Fig. 3.39 Biosynthesis of malonyl Co-A

Fatty Acid Catabolism

The oxidation of long-chain fatty acids to acetyl Co-A is a central energy-yielding pathway in many organisms and tissues. In higher plants, acetyl Co-A serves primarily as a biosynthetic precursor, only secondarily as fuel.

Oxidation of Fatty Acids

Mitochondrial oxidation of fatty acids takes place in three stages. In the first stage is β-oxidation of fatty acids undergo oxidative removal of successive two-carbon units in the form of acetyl Co-A, starting from the carboxyl end of the fatty acyl chain.

In the second stage of fatty acid oxidation, the acetyl groups of acetyl Co-A are oxidized to CO_2 in the citric acid cycle, which also takes place in the mitochondrial matrix. Acetyl Co-A derived from fatty acids thus enters a final common pathway of oxidation with the acetyl Co-A derived from glucose *via* glycolysis and pyruvate oxidation.

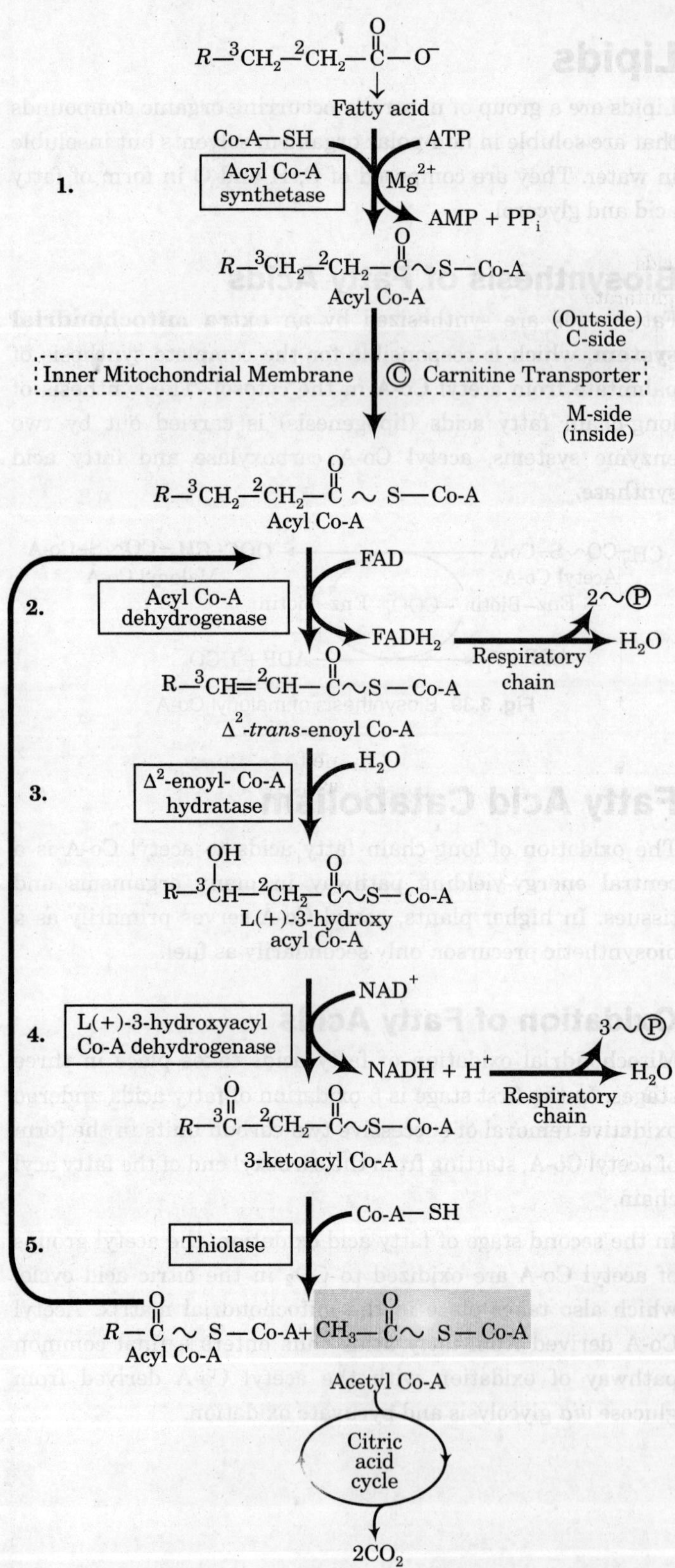

Fig. 3.40 β-Oxidation of fatty acids. Long-chain acyl Co-A is cycled through reactions 2-5, acetyl Co-A being split off, each cycle, by thiolase (reaction 5)

Amino Acids

In animals, amino acids undergo oxidative degradation in three different metabolic circumstances:

1. During the normal synthesis and degradation of cellular proteins (oxidative degradation).
2. When a diet is rich in protein and the ingested amino acids exceed the body's needs for protein synthesis, the surplus is catabolized; amino acids cannot be stored.
3. During starvation or in uncontrolled diabetes mellitus, when carbohydrates are either unavailable or not properly utilized, cellular proteins are used as fuel.

Table 3.2 **Non-essential and Essential Amino Acids for Humans**

Non-essential	Essential
Alanine	Arginine*
Asparagine	Histidine
Aspartate	Isoleucine
Cysteine	Leucine
Glutamate	Lysine
Glutamine	Methionine
Glycine	Phenylalanine
Proline	Threonine
Serine	Tryptophan
Tyrosine	Valine

* Essential in younging, growing animals but not in adults.

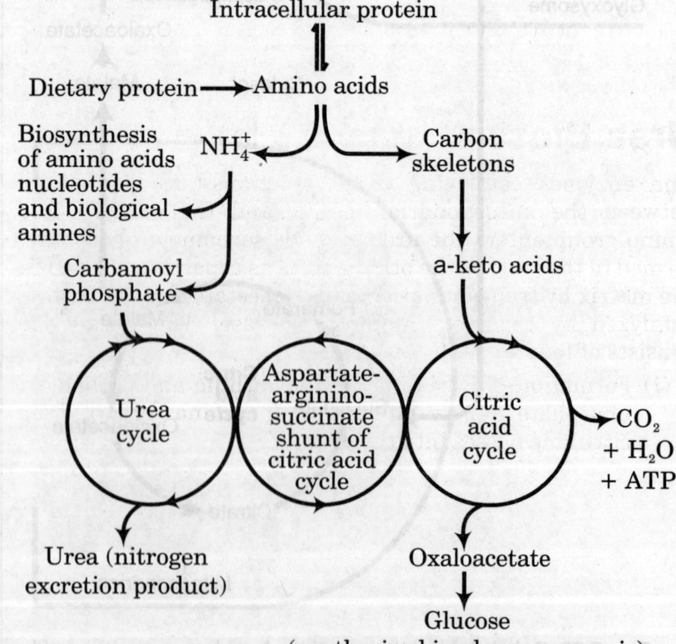

Fig. 3.41 Overview of amino acid catabolism in mammals

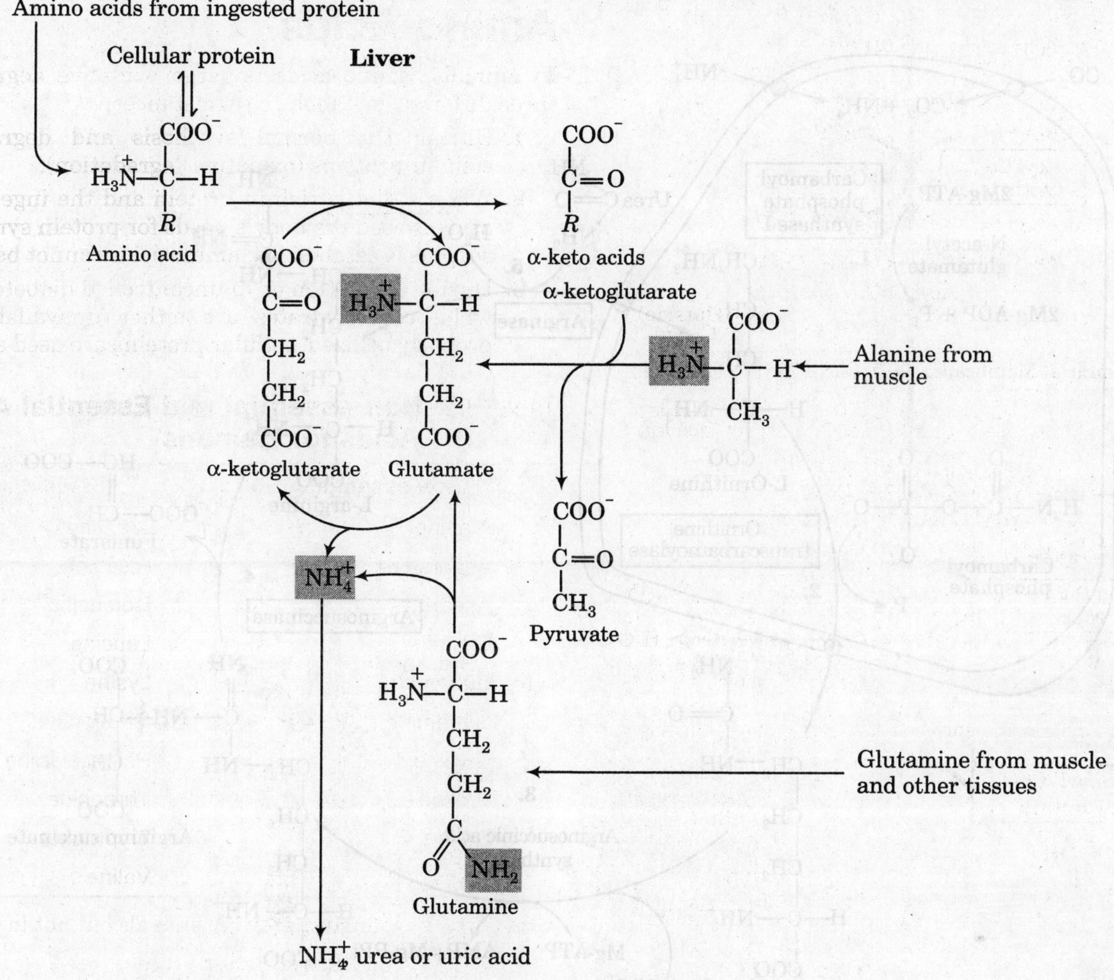

Fig. 3.42 Amino group catabolism

Urea Biosynthesis (Cycle)

The enzymes catalyzing these reactions are distributed between the mitochondrial matrix and the cytosol. One amino group enters the urea cycle as carbamoyl phosphate, formed in the matrix; the other enters as aspartate, formed in the matrix by transamination of oxaloacetate and glutamate, catalyzed by aspartate aminotransferase. The urea cycle consists of four steps.

(i) Formation of citrulline from ornithine and carbamoyl phosphate (entry of the first amino group); the citrulline passes into the cytosol.

(ii) Formation of argininosuccinate through a citrullyl-AMP intermediate (entry of the second amino group).

(iii) Formation of arginine from argininosuccinate; this reaction releases fumarate, which enters the citric acid cycle.

(iv) Formation of urea; this reaction also regenerates, ornithine.

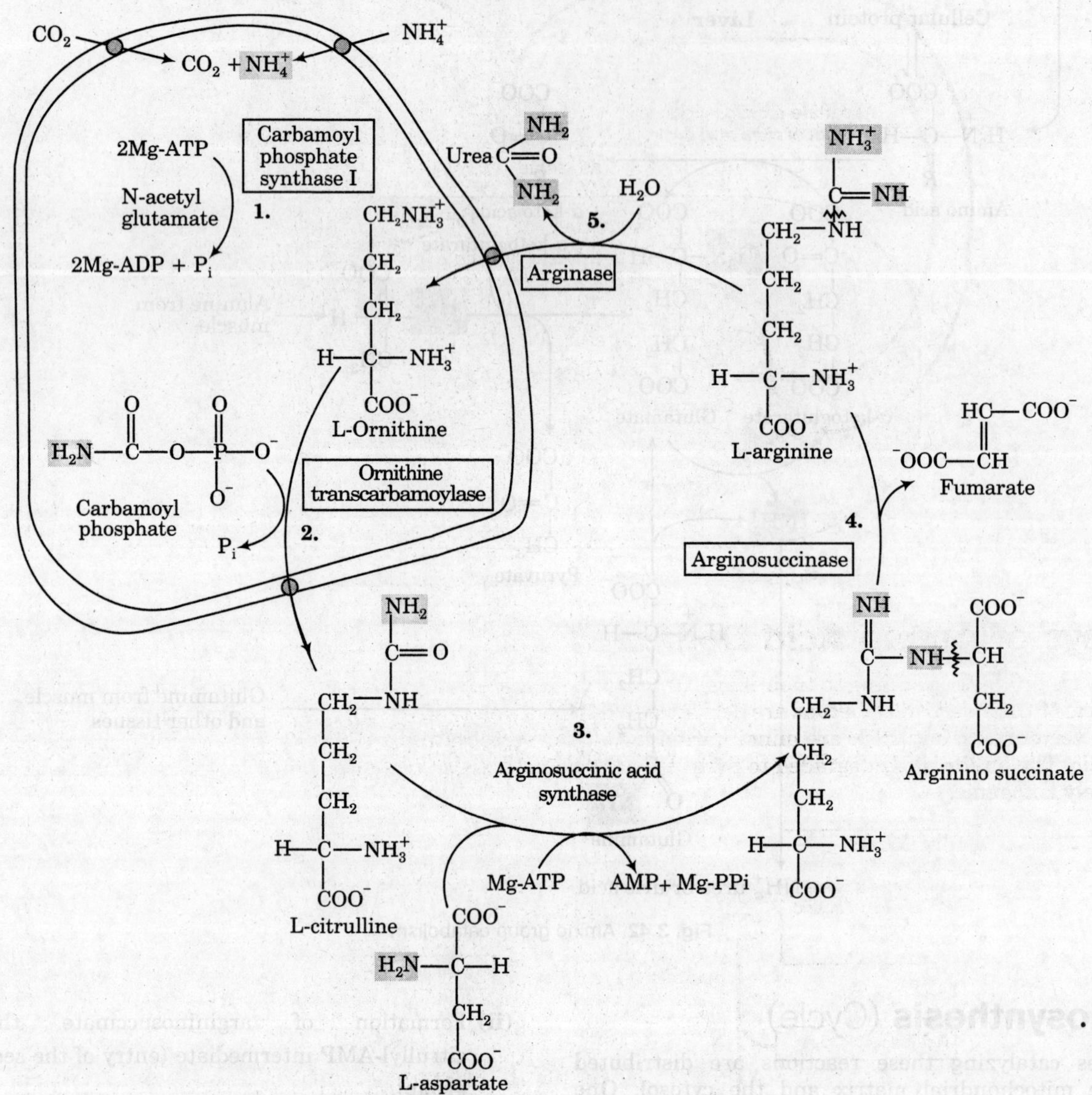

Fig. 3.43 Reactions and intermediates of urea biosynthesis. The nitrogen-containing groups that contribute to the formation of urea are shaded

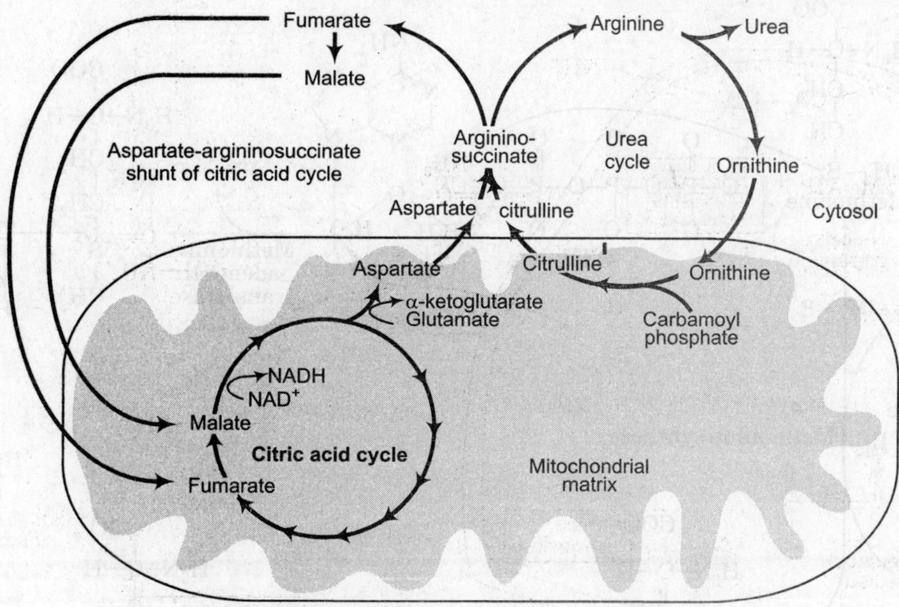

Fig. 3.44 Links between the urea cycle and citric acid cycle

Pathways of Amino Acid Degradation

Amino acids are grouped according to their major degradative end product. Some amino acids are listed more than once because different parts of their carbon skeletons are degraded to different end products. The figure shows the most important catabolic pathways in vertebrates, but there are minor variations among vertebrate species. Five of the amino acids are both glucogenic and ketogenic. The amino acids degraded to pyruvate are also potentially ketogenic. Only two amino acids, leucine and lysine, are exclusively ketogenic.

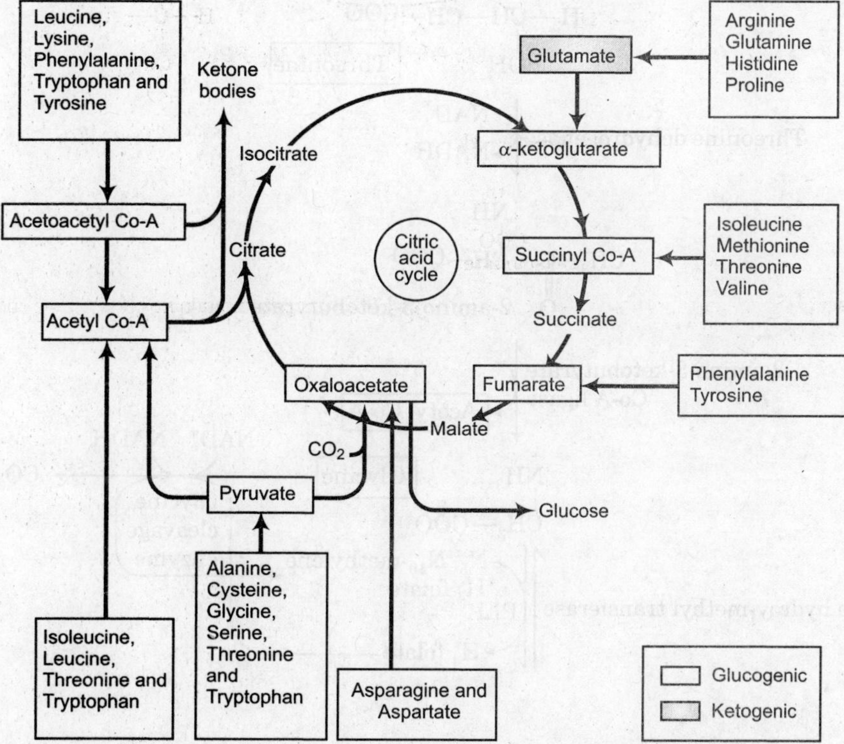

Fig. 3.45 Summary of points of entry of standard amino acids into citric acid cycle

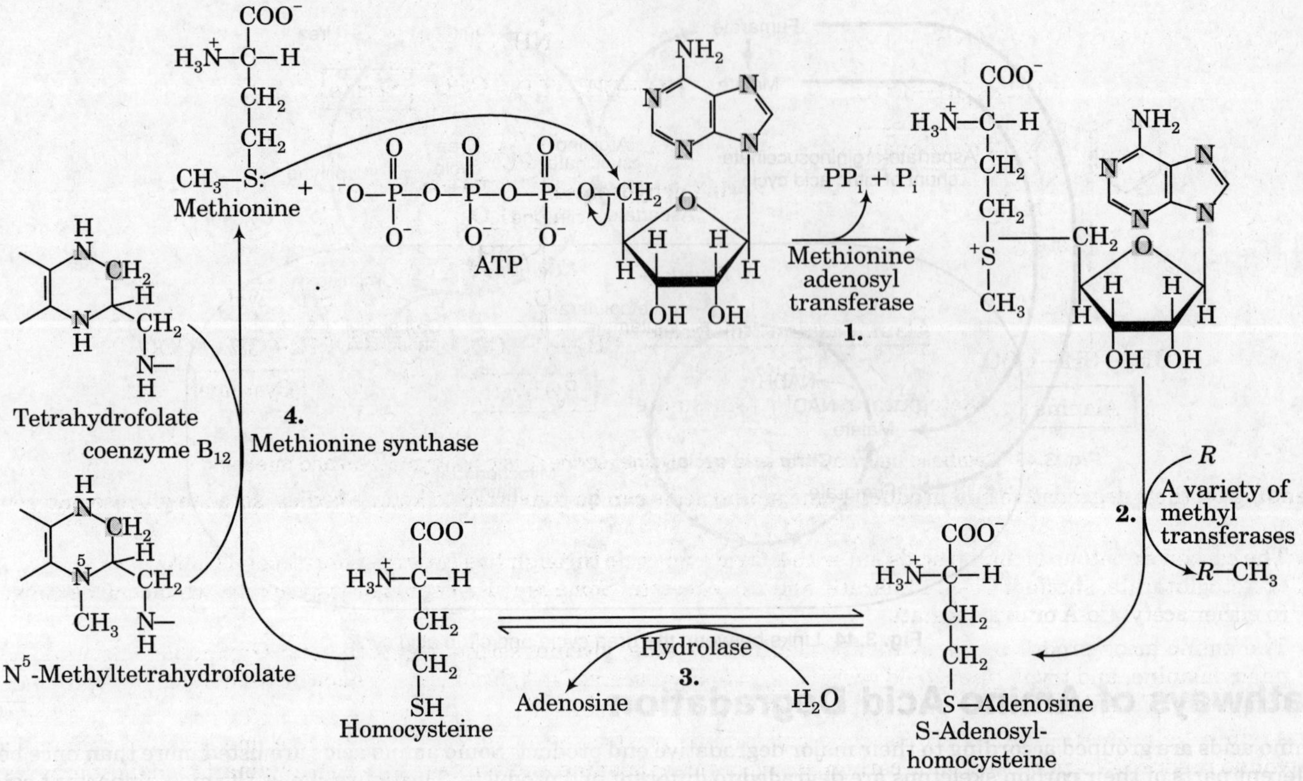

Fig. 3.46 Synthesis of methionine and *S*-adenosylmethionine in an activated-methyl cycle

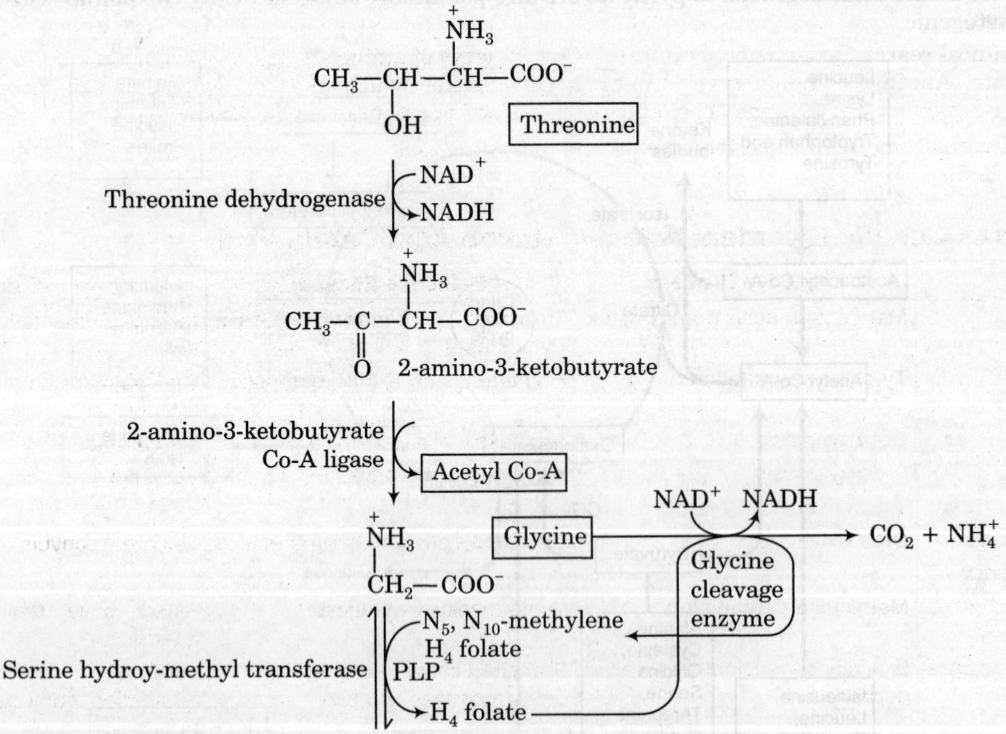

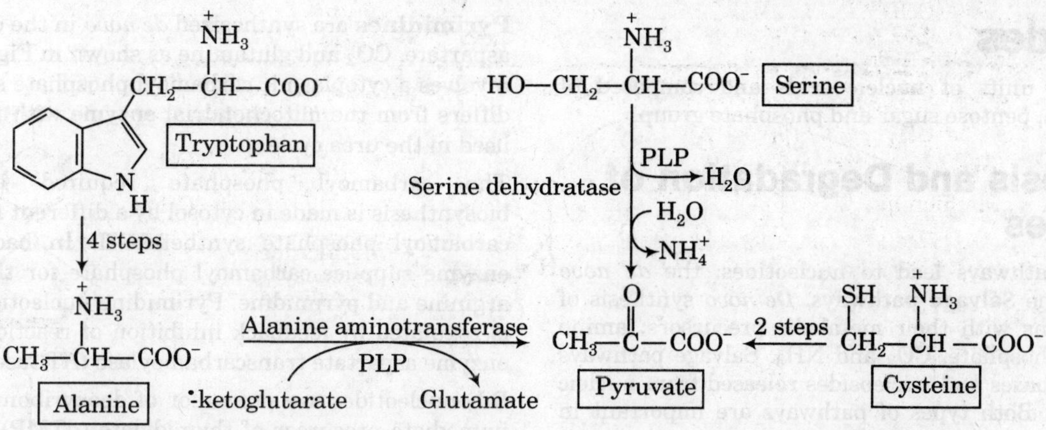

Fig. 3.47 Catabolic pathways for alanine, glycine, serine, cysteine, tryptophan and threonine

Depending on their degradative end product, some amino acids can be converted to ketone bodies, some to glucose and some to both.

(i) **The carbon skeletons of amino acids enter the citric acid cycle through five intermediates: acetyl Co-A, α-ketoglutarate, succinyl Co-A, fumarate, and oxaloacetate. Some are also degraded to pyruvate, which can be converted to either acetyl Co-A or oxaloacetate.**

(ii) **The amino acids producing pyruvate are alanine, cysteine, glycine, serine, threonine and tryptophan. Leucine, lysine, phenylalanine, and tryptophan yield acetyl Co-A *via* acetoacetyl Co-A. Isoleucine, leucine, threonine and tryptophan also form acetyl Co-A directly.**

(iii) **Arginine, glutamate, glutamine, histidine and proline produce α-ketoglutarate; isoleucine, methionine, threonine and valine produce succinyl Co-A; four carbon atoms of phenylalanine and tyrosine give rise to fumarate and asparagine and aspartate produce oxaloacetate.**

(iv) **The branched-chain amino acids (isoleucine, leucine and valine), unlike the other amino acids, are degraded only in extra hepatic tissues.**

There are two chemical rearrangements occur in catabolic pathways of amino acids. One is transamination reaction requiring pyridoxal phosphate. Another common type is one carbon transfer which usually involves one of three cofactors-biotin, tetrahydrofolate or S-adenosylmethionine. The later two are also important in nucleotide metabolism.

These one carbon transfer reactions are required in the biosynthesis of serine, methionine, glycine, choline and the purine nucleotides and dTMP.

Table 3.3 **Human Genetic Disorders Affecing Amino Acid Catabolism**

Disorder	Defective Process	Defective Enzyme	Effects
Albinism	Melanin synthesis from tyrosine	Tyrosine 3-mono-oxygenase (tyrosinase)	Lack of pigmentation; white hair, pink skin
Alkaptonuria	Tyrosine degradation	Homogentisate 1, 2-dioxygenase	Dark pigment in urine; late-developing arthritis
Argininemia	Urea synthesis	Arginase	Mental retardation
Argininosuccinic acidemia	Urea synthesis	Argininosuccinate lyase	Vomiting, convulsions
Carbamoyl phosphate synthetase I deficiency	Urea synthesis	Carbamoyl phosphate synthetase I	Lethargy, convulsions, early death
Homocystinuria	Methionine degradation	Cystathionine β-synthase	Faulty bone development, mental retardation
Maple syrup urine disease (branched-chain ketoaciduria)	Isoleucine, leucine and valine degradation	Branched-chain α-keto acid dehydrogenase complex	Vomiting, convulsions, metal retardation, early death
Methylmalonic acidemia	Conversion of propionyl Co-A to succinyl Co-A	Methylmalonyl Co-A mutase	Vomiting, convulsions, mental retardation, early death
Phenylketonuria	Conversion of phenylalanine to tyrosine	Phenylalanine hydroxylase	Neonatal vomiting; mental retardation

Nucleotides

Nucleotides are units of nucleic acids and composed of nitrogenous base, pentose sugar and phosphate group.

Biosynthesis and Degradation of Nucleotides

Two types of pathways lead to nucleotides: the *de novo* pathways and the **Salvage pathways.** *De novo* synthesis of nucleotides begins with their metabolic precursors: amino acids, ribose-5-phosphate, CO_2 and NH_3. Salvage pathways recycle the free bases and nucleosides released from nucleic acid breakdown. Both types of pathways are important in cellular metabolism.

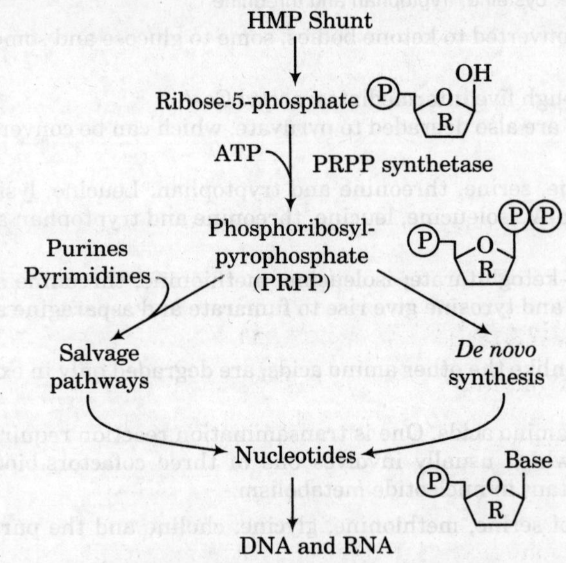

Fig. 3.48 Nucleotide synthesis by Salvage and *de novo* pathways

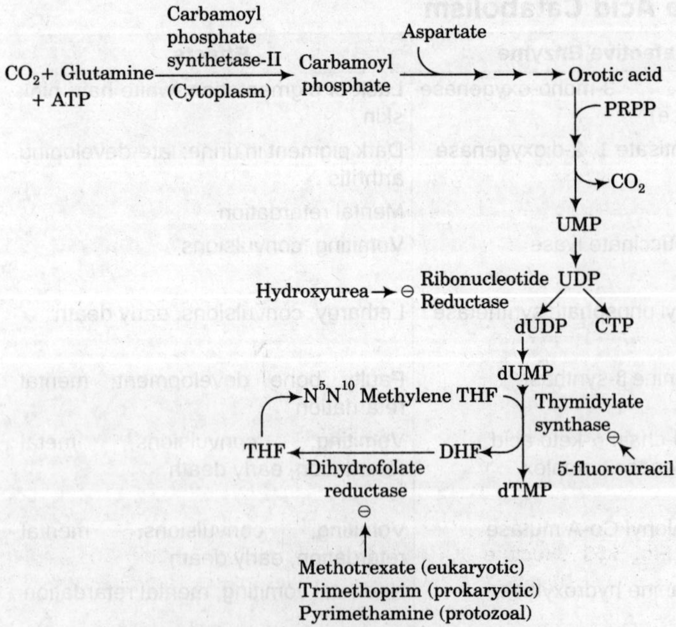

Fig. 3.49 *De novo* pyrimidine synthesis

Pyrimidines are synthesized *de novo* in the cytoplasm from aspartate, CO_2 and glutamine as shown in Figure . Synthesis involves a cytoplasmic carbamoyl phosphate synthetase that differs from the mitochondrial enzyme with the same name used in the urea cycle.

The carbamoyl phosphate required in pyrimidine biosynthesis is made in cytosol by a different form of enzyme carbamoyl phosphate synthetase-II. In bacteria a single enzyme supplies carbamoyl phosphate for the synthesis of arginine and pyrimidine. Pyrimidine nucleotide biosynthesis is regulated by feedback inhibition of reaction catalyzed by enzyme aspartate transcarbamoylase (ATCase).

Ribonucleotides are precursor of deoxyribonucleotides. The immediate precursor of thymidylate (dTMP) is dUMP. This reaction is catalyzed by thymidylate synthase.

Pyrimidines may be completely catabolized (NH_4^+ is produced) or recycled by pyrimidine Salvage enzymes.

Purines are synthesized *de novo* beginning with PRPP as shown in figure. The most important enzyme is PRPP amidotransferase, which catalyzes the first and rate-limiting reaction of the pathway. It is inhibited by the three purine nucleotide end products AMP, GMP and IMP.

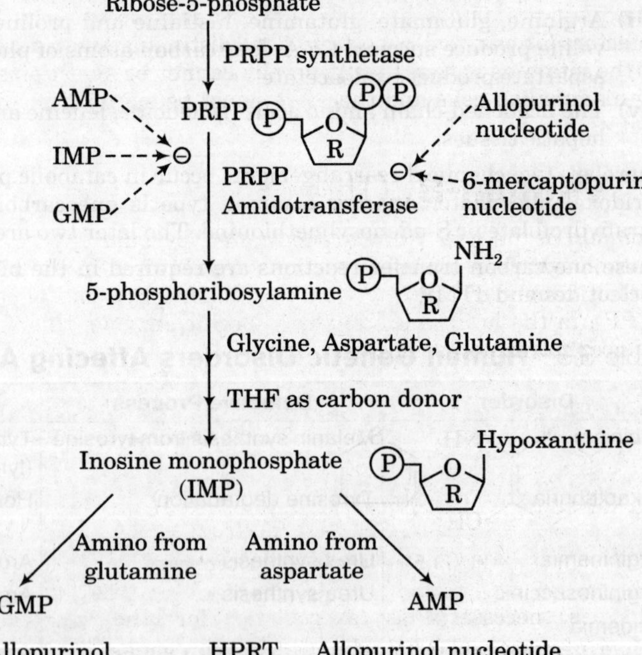

Fig. 3.50 *De novo* synthesis of purine nucleotides

Excess purine nucleotides or those released from DNA and RNA by nucleases are catabolized first to nucleosides (loss of P) and then to free purine bases (release of ribose or deoxyribose). Salvage enzymes recycle normally about 90% of these purines and 10% are converted to uric acid and excreted in urine. When purine catabolism is increased significantly, a person is at risk for developing hyperuricemia and potentially gout.

Purine nucleotide adenylate yields adenosine which is deaminated to inosine by adenosine deaminase and inosine is hydrolyzed to hypoxanthine and D-ribose. Hypoxanthine is oxidized successively to xanthine and then uric acid by xanthine oxidase (a-flavoenzyme with an atom of Mo and four Fe-S centres). GMP first hydrolyzed to guanosine which cleaved to free guanine and ultimately to uric acid. In primates, birds and some other animals uric acid is excreted but in many other vertebrates further degraded to allantoin by action of urate oxidase.

(i) Pyrimidine degradation leads to NH_4^+ production and thus to urea, synthesis.

(ii) A genetic lack of hypoxanthin-guanine phosphoribosyltransferase activity results in a bizarre set of symptoms called Lilsch-Nyhan syndrome exclusively in male children.

(iii) Many chemotherapeutic agents like azaserine and acivicin (inhibit) glutamine amidotransferases) fluorouracil (inhibit thymidylate synthase), methotrexate and amino petrin (inhibitor of dihydrofolate reductase).

Vitamins

The most prominent function of the vitamin is to serve as cofactors for enzymatic reactions. The distinguishing feature of the vitamins is that they generally cannot be synthesized by mammalian cells and therefore, must be supplied in the diet.

1. Vitamin-B$_1$ (Thiamin)

Thiamin is derived from a substituted pyrimidine and a thiazole which are coupled by a methylene bridge. Thiamin is rapidly converted to its active form, thiamin pyrophosphate (TPP), in the brain and liver by a specific enzyme, thiamin diphosphotransferase.

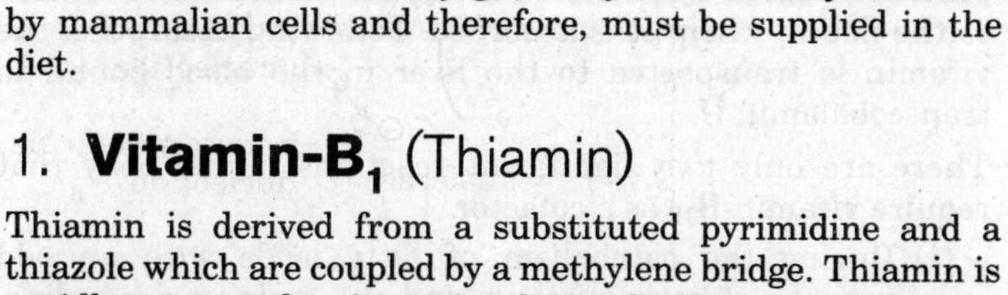

Fig. 3.51 Thiamin pyrophosphate

TPP is necessary as a cofactor for the pyruvate dehydrogenase and α-ketoglutarate dehydrogenase catalyzed reactions as well as the transketolase catalyzed reactions of the pentose phosphate pathway. A deficiency in thiamin intake leads to a severely reduced capacity of cells to generate energy as a result of its role in these reactions.

2. Vitamin-B$_2$ (Riboflavin)

Riboflavin is the precursor for the coenzymes, flavin mononucleotide (FMN) and Flavin Adenine Dinucleotide (FAD). The enzymes that require FMN or FAD as cofactors are termed flavoproteins. Several flavoproteins also contain metal ions and are termed metalloflavoproteins. Both classes of enzymes are involved in a wide range of redox reactions, *e.g.,* succinate dehydrogenase and xanthine oxidase. During the course of the enzymatic reactions involving the flavoproteins the reduced forms of FMN and FAD are formed, $FMNH_2$ and $FADH_2$, respectively.

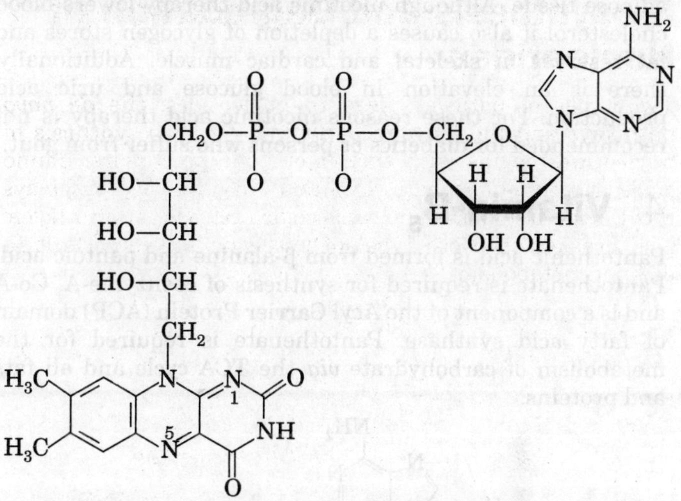

Fig. 3.52 Structure of FAD (Hydrogens of $FADH_2$ are on nitrogens 1 and 5)

3. Vitamin-B$_3$ (Niacin)

Niacin (nicotinic acid and nicotinamide) can serve as the dietary source of vitamin-B$_3$. Niacin is required for the synthesis of the active forms of vitamin-B$_3$, nicotinamide adenine dinucleotide (NAD^+) and nicotinamide adenine dinucleotide phosphate ($NADP^+$). Both NAD^+ and $NADP^+$ function as cofactors for numerous dehydrogenases, *e.g.,* lactate dehydrogenase and malate dehydrogenase.

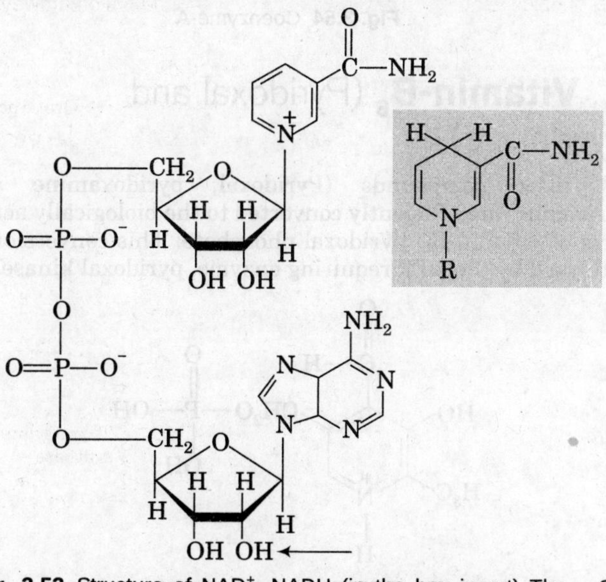

Fig. 3.53 Structure of NAD^+. NADH (in the box insert) The —OH phosphorylated in $NADP^+$ is indicated by the red arrow

Niacin is not a true vitamin in the strictest definition since it can be derived from the amino acid tryptophan.

Nicotinic acid (but not nicotinamide) when administered in pharmacological doses of 2-4 g/day lowers plasma cholesterol levels and has been shown to be a useful therapeutic for hypercholesterolemia. The major action of nicotinic acid in this capacity is a reduction in fatty acid mobilization from adipose tissue. Although nicotinic acid therapy lowers blood cholesterol it also causes a depletion of glycogen stores and fat reserves in skeletal and cardiac muscle. Additionally, there is an elevation in blood glucose and uric acid production. For these reasons nicotinic acid therapy is not recommended for diabetics or persons who suffer from gout.

4. Vitamin-B$_5$

Pantothenic acid is formed from β-alanine and pantoic acid. Pantothenate is required for synthesis of coenzyme-A, Co-A and is a component of the Acyl Carrier Protein (ACP) domain of fatty acid synthase. Pantothenate is required for the metabolism of carbohydrate *via* the TCA cycle and all fats and proteins.

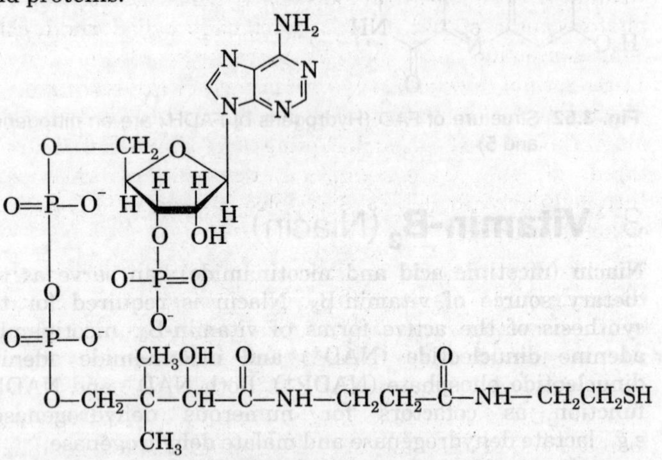

Fig. 3.54 Coenzyme-A

5. Vitamin-B$_6$ (Pyridoxal and Pyridoxine)

All three compounds (Pyridoxal, pyridoxamine and pyridoxine) are efficiently converted to the biologically active form of vitamin-B$_6$, pyridoxal phosphate. This conversion is catalyzed by the ATP requiring enzyme, pyridoxal kinase.

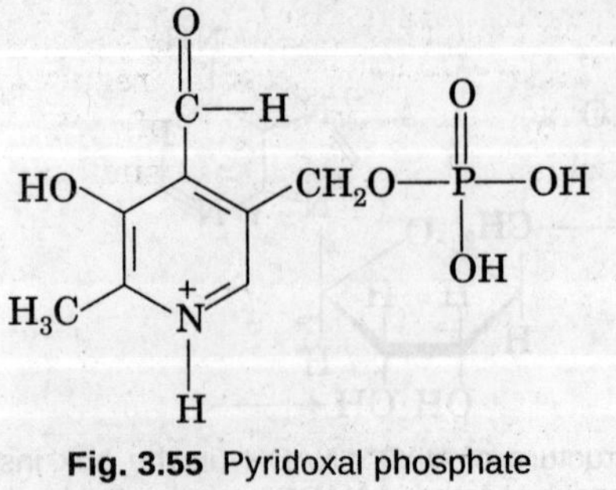

Fig. 3.55 Pyridoxal phosphate

Pyridoxal phosphate functions as a cofactor in enzymes involved in transamination reactions required for the synthesis and catabolism of the amino acids as well as in glycogenolysis as a cofactor for glycogen phosphorylase.

Biotin (Vitamin H or B$_8$)

Biotin is the cofactor required of enzymes that are involved in carboxylation reactions, *e.g.*, acetyl Co-A carboxylase and pyruvate carboxylase.

Biotin is found in numerous foods and also is synthesized by intestinal bacteria and as such deficiencies of the vitamin are rare. Deficiencies are generally due to long antibiotic therapies which deplete the intestinal fauna or following excessive consumption of raw eggs. The latter is due to the affinity of the avidin (egg white protein) for biotin preventing intestinal absorption of the biotin.

6. Vitamin-B$_{12}$ (Cobalamin)

Vitamin-B$_{12}$ is composed of a complex tetrapyrrol ring structure (corrin ring) and a cobalt ion in the center. Vitamin-B$_{12}$ is synthesized exclusively by microorganisms and is found in the liver of animals bound to protein as methycobalamin or 5′-deoxyadenosylcobalamin. The vitamin must be hydrolyzed from protein in order to be active. Hydrolysis occurs in the stomach by gastric acids or the intestines by trypsin digestion following consumption of animal meat. The vitamin is then bound by intrinsic factor, a protein secreted by parietal cells of the stomach and carried to the ileum, where it is absorbed. Following absorption the vitamin is transported to the liver in the blood bound to transcobalamin II.

There are only two significant reactions in the body that require vitamin-B$_{12}$ as a cofactor.

(i) During the catabolism of fatty acids with an odd number of carbon atoms and the amino acids valine, isoleucine and threonine the resultant propionyl Co-A is converted to succinyl Co-A for oxidation in the TCA cycle. One of the enzymes in this pathway, methylmalonyl Co-A mutase, requires vitamin-B$_{12}$ as a cofactor in the conversion of methylmalonyl Co-A to succinyl Co-A. The 5′-deoxyadenosine derivative of cobalamin is required for this reaction.

(ii) The second reaction requiring vitamin-B$_{12}$ catalyzes the conversion of homocysteine to methionine and is catalyzed by methionine synthase. This reaction results in the transfer of the methyl group from N^5-methyltetrahydrofolate to hydroxycobalamin generating tetrahydrofolate (THF) and methylcobalamin during the process of the conversion.

7. Vitamin-B$_{10}$ (Folic Acid)

Folic acid is a conjugated molecule consisting of a pteridine ring structure linked to para-aminobenzoic acid (PABA) that forms pteroic acid. Folic acid itself is then generated through the conjugation of glutamic acid residues to pteroic acid.

In the liver or ingested folic acid exists in a polyglutamate form. Intestinal mucosal cells remove some of the glutamate residues through the action of the lysosomal enzyme, conjugase. The removal of glutamate residues makes folate less negatively charged (from the polyglutamic acids) and therefore, more capable of passing through the basal lamenal membrane of the epithelial cells of the intestine and into the bloodstream. Folic acid is reduced within cells (principally the liver where it is stored) to tetrahydrofolate (THF also H_4 folate) through the action of dihydrofolate reductase (DHFR), an NADPH-requiring enzyme.

The function of THF derivatives is to carry and transfer various forms of one carbon units during biosynthetic reactions. The one carbon units are either methyl, methylene, methenyl, formyl or formimino groups.

Role of Vitamin-B_{12}

(a) It has ability to acquire choline and amino acids from the diet and to salvage the purine nucleotides.

(b) The vitamin-B_{12} and N^5-methyl THF can convert homocysteine to methionine.

8. **Vitamin-C** (Ascorbic Acid)

Ascorbic acid is derived from glucose *via* the uronic acid pathway. The enzyme L-gulonolactone oxidase responsible for the conversion of gulonolactone to ascorbic acid is absent in primates making ascorbic acid required in the diet.

Function of Ascorbate

(a) The active form of vitamin-C is ascorbate acid. The main function of ascorbate is as a reducing agent in a number of different reactions.

(b) Vitamin-C has the potential to reduce cytochromes-*a* and *c* of the respiratory chain as well as molecular oxygen.

(c) Ascorbate is required as a cofactor in the hydroxylation of proline residues in collagen.

(d) The catabolism of tyrosine and the synthesis of epinephrine from tyrosine and the synthesis of the bile acids.

9. **Vitamin-A** (Retinol)

Vitamin-A consists of three biologically active molecules, retinol, retinal (retinaldehyde) and retinoic acid.

Physiology of Vitamin-A

Ingested β-carotene is cleaved in the lumen of the intestine by β-carotene dioxygenase to yield retinal. Retinal is reduced to retinol by retinaldehyde reductase, an NADPH requiring enzyme. Retinol is esterified to palmitic acid and delivered to the blood *via* chylomicrons. The uptake of chylomicron remnants by the liver results in delivery of retinol to this organ for storage as a lipid ester within lipocytes. Transport of retinol from the liver to extrahepatic tissues occurs by binding of hydrolyzed retinol to aporetinol binding protein (RBP). The retinol-RBP complex is then transported to the cell surface within the Golgi and secreted. Within extrahepatic tissues retinol is bound to cellular retinol binding protein (CRBP). Plasma transport of retinoic acid is accomplished by binding to albumin.

Vision and the Role of Vitamin-A

Photoreception in the eye is the function of two specialized cell present in the retina; the rod and cone cells. Both rod and cone cells contain a photoreceptor pigment in their membranes.

The photosensitive compound of most mammalian eyes is a protein called **opsin** is covalently coupled with aldehyde of vitamin-A. The opsin of rod cells is called **scotopsin.** The photoreceptor of rod cells is specifically called **rhodopsin.** This compound is a complex between scotopsin and the 11-*cis*-retinal (also called 11-*cis*-retinene) form of vitamin-A. Rhodopsin is a serpentine receptor imbedded in the membrane of the rod cell. Coupling of 11-*cis*-retinal occurs at three of the transmembrane domains of rhodopsin. Intracellularly, rhodopsin is coupled to a specific G-protein called transducin.

When the rhodopsin is exposed to light it is bleached releasing the 11-*cis*-retinal from opsin. Absorption of photons by 11-*cis*-retinal initiate a conformational change to all-*trans*-retinal. The release of opsin results in a conformational change in the photoreceptor. This conformational change activates transducin, leading to an increased GTP-binding by the a-subunit of transducin. Binding of GTP releases the α-subunit from the inhibitory β and γ-subunits. The GTP-activated α-subunit in turn activates an associated phosphodiesterase; an enzyme that hydrolyzes cyclic-GMP (cGMP) to GMP. Cyclic GMP is required to maintain the Na^+ channels of the rod cell in the open conformation. The drop in cGMP concentration results in complete closure of the Na^+ channels. The closing of the channels leads to hyperpolarization of the rod cell with concomitant propagation of nerve impulses to the brain.

Retinol also functions in the synthesis of certain glycoproteins and mucopolysaccharides necessary for mucous production and normal growth regulation. This is accomplished by phosphorylation of retinol to retinyl phosphate which then functions similarly to dolichol phosphate.

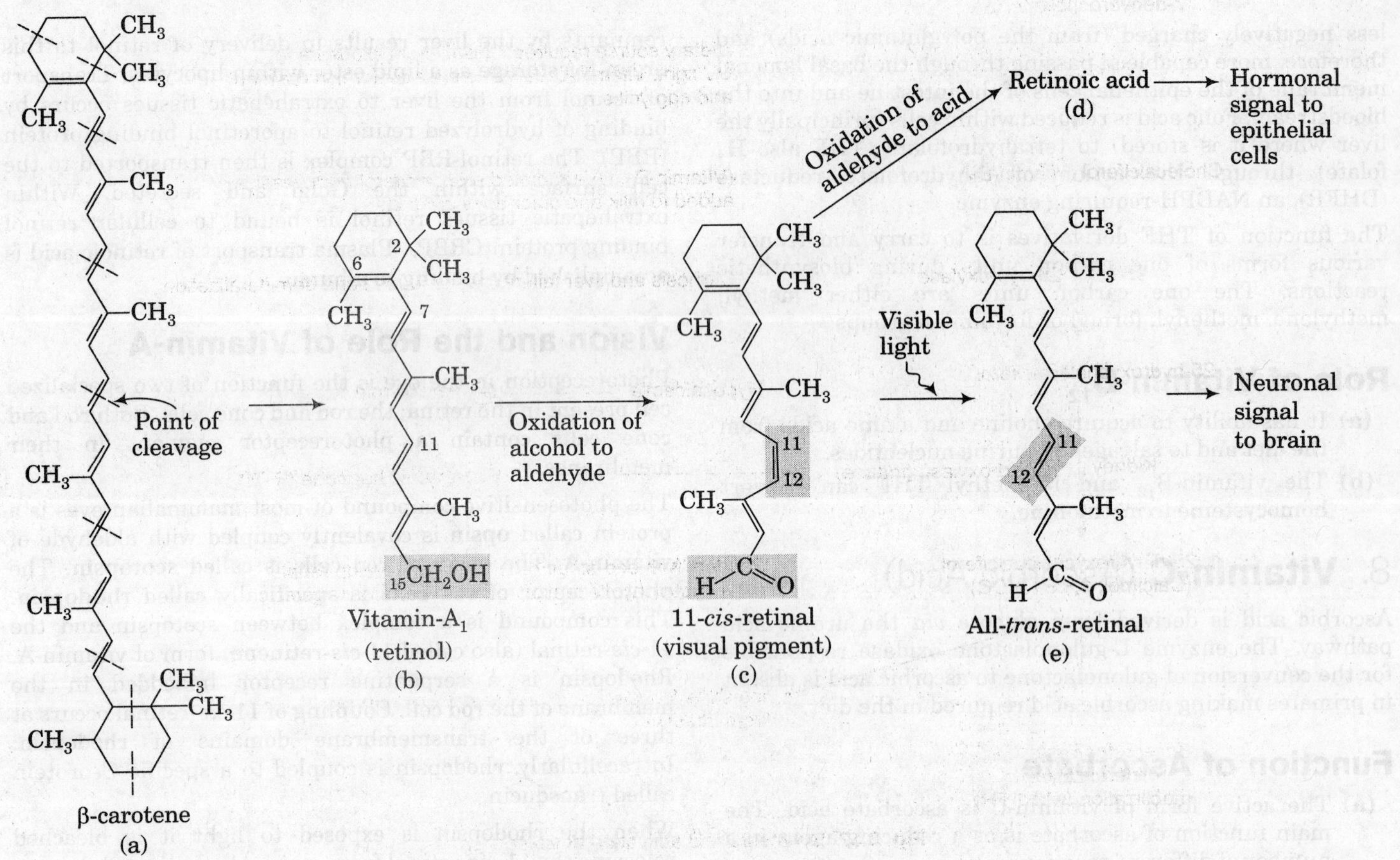

Fig. 3.56 Vitamin-A_1 and its precursor and derivatives

10. Vitamin-D

Humans can synthesize calcitriol from 7-dehydrocholesterol derived from cholesterol in the liver. Three steps are involved, each occurring in a different tissue. The relation of vitamin-D to calcium homeostasis and its *in vivo* activation are shown in figure.

Vitamin-D is a steroid hormone that functions to regulate specific gene expression following interaction with its intracellular receptor. The biologically active form of the hormone is 1, 25-dihydroxy vitamin-D_3 (1, 25-$(OH)_2D_3$, also termed calcitriol). Calcitriol functions primarily to regulate calcium and phosphorus homeostasis.

Active calcitriol is derived from ergosterol (produced in plants) and from 7-dehydrocholesterol (produced in the skin). Ergocalciferol (vitamin-D_2) is formed by UV irradiation of ergosterol. In the skin 7-dehydrocholesterol is converted to cholecalciferol (vitamin-D_3) following UV irradiation.

Vitamin-D_2 and D_3 are processed to D_2-calcitriol and D_3-calcitriol, respectively, by the same enzymatic pathways in the body. Cholecalciferol (or ergocalciferol) are absorbed from the intestine and transported to the liver bound to a specific vitamin-D-binding protein. In the liver cholecalciferol is hydroxylated at the 25 position by a specific D_3-25-hydroxylase generating 25-hydroxy-D_3 [25-$(OH)D_3$] which is the major circulating form of vitamin-D. Conversion of 25-$(OH)D_3$ to its biologically active form, calcitriol, occurs through the activity of a specific D_3-1-hydroxylase present in the proximal convoluted tubules of the kidneys and in bone and placenta. 25-$(OH)D_3$ can also be hydroxylated at the 24 position by a specific D_3-24-hydroxylase in the kidneys, intestine, placenta and cartilage.

Calcitriol functions in concert with parathyroid hormone (PTH) and calcitonin to regulate serum calcium and phosphorus levels. PTH is released in response to low serum calcium and induces the production of calcitriol. In contrast, reduced levels of PTH stimulate synthesis of the inactive 24, 25-$(OH)_2D_3$. In the intestinal epithelium, calcitriol functions as a steroid hormone in inducing the expression of calbindin D_{28K}, a protein involved in intestinal calcium absorption. The increased absorption of calcium ions requires concomitant absorption of a negatively charged counter ion to maintain electrical neutrality. The predominant counter ion is Pi. When plasma calcium levels fall the major sites of action of calcitriol and PTH are bone, where they stimulate bone resorption and the kidneys where they inhibit calcium excretion by stimulating reabsorption by the distal tubules. The role of calcitonin in calcium homeostasis is to decrease elevated serum calcium levels by inhibiting bone resorption.

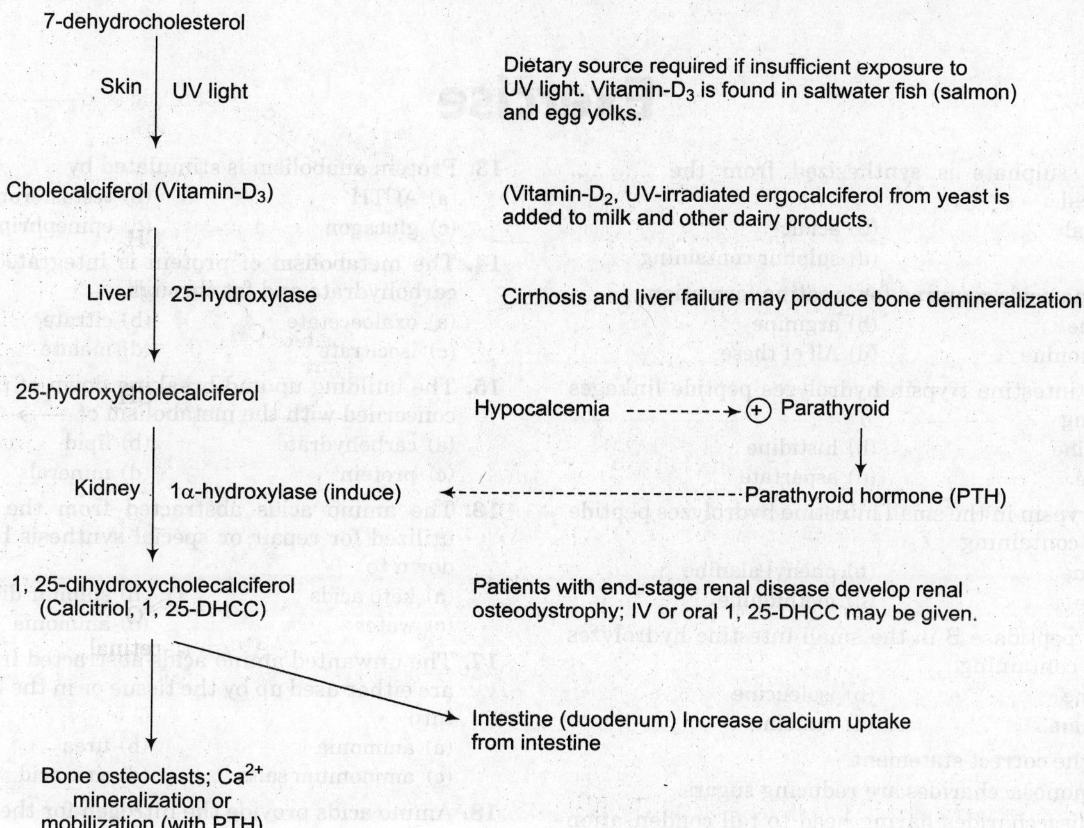

Fig. 3.57 Synthesis and activation of vitamin-D

Vitamin-E (Tocopherol)

Vitamin-E is a mixture of several related compounds known as tocopherols. The α-tocopherol molecule is the most potent of the tocopherols.

The major function of vitamin-E is to act as a natural antioxidant by scavenging free radicals and molecular oxygen. In particular vitamin-E is important for preventing peroxidation of polyunsaturated membrane fatty acids. Active α-tocopherol can be regenerated by interaction with vitamin-C following scavenge of a peroxy free radical. Alternatively, α-tocopherol can scavenge two peroxy free radicals and then be conjugated to glucuronate for excretion in the bile.

Vitamin-K (Phylloquinone)

The vitamins-K exist naturally as K_1 (phylloquinone) in green vegetables and K_2 (menaquinone) produced by intestinal bacteria and K_3 is synthetic menadione. When administered, vitamin-K_3 is alkylated to one of the vitamin-K_2 forms of menaquinone.

The major function of the vitamins-K is in the maintenance of normal levels of the blood clotting proteins, factors II, VII, IX, X and protein C and protein S, which are synthesized in the liver as inactive precursor proteins. Conversion from inactive to active clotting factor requires a post-translational modification of specific glutamate (E) residues. This modification is a carboxylation and the enzyme responsible requires vitamin-K as a cofactor. The resultant modified E residues are γ-carboxyglutamate (gla). This process is most clearly understood for factor II, also called preprothrombin. Prothrombin is modified preprothrombin. The gla residues are effective calcium ion chelators. Upon chelation of calcium, prothrombin interacts with phospholipids in membranes and is proteolysed to thrombin through the action of activated factor X (Xa).

During the carboxylation reaction reduced hydroquinone form of vitamin-K is converted to a 2, 3-epoxide form. The regeneration of the hydroquinone form requires an uncharacterized reductase. This latter reaction is the site of action of the coumarin based anticoagulants such as warfarin.

Exercise

1. Ethereal sulphate is synthesized from the .... amino acid.
(a) neutral (b) acidic
(c) basic (d) sulphur containing

2. The amino acids required for creatine formation
(a) glycine (b) arginine
(c) methionine (d) All of these

3. In small intestine trypsin hydrolyzes peptide linkages containing
(a) arginine (b) histidine
(c) serine (d) aspartate

4. Chymotrypsin in the small intestine hydrolyzes peptide linkages containing
(a) alanine (b) phenyl alanine
(c) valine (d) methionine

5. Carboxy peptidase B in the small intestine hydrolyzes peptides containing
(a) leucine (b) isoleucine
(c) arginine (d) cysteine

6. Choose the correct statement.
I. All monosaccharides are reducing sugars.
II. All disaccharides having head to tail condensation are reducing sugar.
III. Ascorbic acid is an aldonic acid.
IV. Sucrose is dextrorotatory.
(a) I and II (b) II and III
(c) I, II and III (d) I, II, III and IV

7. The third active process for amino acids transport involves
(a) acidic amino acids
(b) basic amino acids
(c) neutral amino acids
(d) sulphur containing amino acids

8. If one amino acid is fed excess, the absorption of another is
(a) slightly accelerated (b) moderately accelerated
(c) highly accelerated (d) retarded

9. Under normal conditions, food proteins are generally readily digested up to the present
(a) 67 to 73 (b) 74 to 81
(c) 82 to 89 (d) 90 to 97

10. By overheating the nutritional value of cereal proteins is
(a) increased (b) decreased
(c) unchanged (d) None of these

11. More than half of the protein of the liver and intestinal mucosa are broken down and resynthesized in
(a) 10 days (b) 12 days
(c) 15 days (d) 18 days

12. The half-life of antibody protein is about
(a) 4 weeks (b) 3 weeks
(c) 2 weeks (d) 1 week

13. Protein anabolism is stimulated by
(a) ACTH (b) testosterone
(c) glucagon (d) epinephrine

14. The metabolism of protein is integrated with that of carbohydrate and fat through
(a) oxaloacetate (b) citrate
(c) isocitrate (d) malate

15. The building up and breaking down of protoplasm are concerned with the metabolism of
(a) carbohydrate (b) lipid
(c) protein (d) minerals

16. The amino acids abstracted from the liver are not utilized for repair or special synthesis but are broken down to
(a) keto acids (b) sulphur dioxide
(c) water (d) ammonia

17. The unwanted amino acids abstracted from the tissues are either used up by the tissue or in the liver converted into
(a) ammonia (b) urea
(c) ammonium salts (d) uric acid

18. Amino acids provide the nitrogen for the synthesis of
(a) the bases of the phospholipids
(b) uric acid
(c) glycolipids
(d) chondroitin sulphates

19. The metabolism of all proteins ingested over and above the essential requirements is called
(a) exogenous metabolism (b) endogenous metabolism
(c) Both (a) and (b) (d) None of these

20. Sulphur containing amino acids after catabolism produces a substance which is excreted
(a) SO_2 (b) HNO_3
(c) H_2SO_4 (d) H_3PO_4

21. When egg albumin is heated till it is coagulated, the secondary and tertiary structures of the proteins are completely lost resulting in a mixture of randomly arranged
(a) dipeptide chains (b) tripeptide chains
(c) polypeptide chains (d) All of these

22. Proteins that are embedded in or reach across a membrane are characterized by
I. A stretch of at least 16 to 21 hydrophobic.
II. A high lysine, arginine and histidine content.
III. A high glutamate and aspartate content.
IV. At least one α-helical or β-sheet domain.
(a) I and II (b) I and III
(c) I and IV (d) I, II, III and IV

23. Achylia gastrica is said to be when absence of
(a) pepsin (b) Both (a) and (b)
(c) HCl (d) All of these

24. A limiting amino acid is an essential amino acid
(a) that is most deficient in proteins
(b) that is most excess in proteins
(c) that which increases the growth
(d) that which increases the weight gain

25. The limiting amino acid of rice is
(a) lysine (b) tryptophan
(c) phenylalanine (d) tyrosine

26. The limiting amino acid of fish proteins is
(a) tryptophan (b) cysteine
(c) lysine (d) threonine

27. Pulses are deficient in
(a) lysine (b) threonine
(c) methionine (d) tryptophan

28. A trace element deficient in the milk is
(a) magnesium (b) copper
(c) zinc (d) chloride

29. A conjugated protein present in the egg yolk is
(a) vitellin (b) livetin
(c) albuminoids (d) ovo-mucoid

30. The chief protein of cow's milk is
(a) albumin (b) vitellin
(c) livetin (d) casein

31. The hydrogen bonds between peptide linkages are interfered by
(a) guanidine (b) uric acid
(c) salicylic acid (d) oxalic acid

32. The digestability of certain denatured proteins by proteolytic enzymes
(a) decreases (b) increases
(c) normal (d) None of these

33. The antigenic antibody functions of proteins by denaturation are frequently
(a) not changed (b) changed
(c) Both (a) and (b) (d) None of these

34. In case of severe denaturation of protein, there is
(a) reversible denaturation
(b) moderate reversible denaturation
(c) irreversible denaturation
(d) None of the above

35. Which of the following porphyrins gives stools their characteristic brown colour?
(a) Biliverdin (b) Urobilinogen
(c) Haeme (d) Stercobilin

36. Which of the following is most characteristic of a sphingolipidosis?
(a) Variable activities of abnormal enzyme in different patient tissues
(b) Deficiency of a hydrolytic enzyme
(c) Abnormalities of sphingolipid synthesis
(d) Accumulation of ceramide-containing lipids

37. Which one of the following contributes nitrogen atoms to both purine and pyrimidine rings?
(a) Aspartate (b) Carbamoyl phosphate
(c) Carbon dioxide (d) Glutamine

38. Which of the following amino acids is a precursor to cysteine?
(a) Threonine (b) Methionine
(c) Glutamine (d) Lysine

39. A short length of double stranded DNA molecule contains 120 adenine and 120 cytosine bases. The total number of nucleotides in this DNA fragment is
(a) 60 (b) 120
(c) 240 (d) 480

40. A newborn baby has a sibling with sickle cell anaemia and is at risk for the disease. The appropriate diagnostic test for sickle cell anaemia in this baby will include
(a) DNA amplification (b) haemoglobin antibodies
(c) DNA restriction (d) red cell counting

41. A polymorphism is best defined as
(a) one phenotype, multiple genotypes
(b) non-random allele association
(c) one locus, multiple abnormal alleles
(d) one locus, multiple normal alleles

42. Single stranded DNA is found in
(a) coliphage $\phi \times 174$ virus (b) reovirus
(c) wound tumour virus (d) TMV

43. DNA replication is
(a) continuous and conservative
(b) discontinuous and semiconservative
(c) semidiscontinuous and semiconservative
(d) conservative and semidiscontinuous

44. Which of the following is called amber?
(a) AUG (b) UAA
(c) UAG (d) UGA

45. Initiation of polypeptide chain in protein synthesis is induced by
(a) methionine (b) glycine
(c) leucine (d) lysine

46. Exchange of segments between non-homologous chromosomes is called
(a) inversion (b) duplication
(c) translocation (d) deletion

47. Following ultraviolet damage of DNA in skin
(a) a specific excinuclease detects damaged areas
(b) purine dimers are formed
(c) both strands are cleaved
(d) endonuclease removes the strand

48. Which of the following statements correctly describes eukaryotic nuclear chromosomal DNA?
(a) Each discontinuous piece making up the chromosomes of eukaryotes is about the same size as each prokaryotic chromosome
(b) Unlike bacterial DNA, no histones are associated with it
(c) It is not replicated semiconservatively
(d) It is a linear and unbranched molecule

49. Xeroderma pigmentosum is an inherited human skin disease that causes a variety of phenotypic changes in skin cells exposed to sunlight. The molecular basis of the disease appears to be

(a) the inactivation of temperature-sensitive transport enzymes in sunlight
(b) the induction of a virulent provirus on ultraviolet exposure
(c) the inability of the cells to synthesize carotenoid-type compounds
(d) a defect in an excision-repair system that removes thymine dimers from DNA

50. Which of the following statements describes both the spiral structure of double-stranded DNA and the spiral structure found in certain segments of protein?
(a) They are repeating spiral structures with intervals of pleated sheets
(b) They have four alternative units arranged in polymeric chains
(c) They are held together by hydrogen bonding
(d) They have covalently linked backbones

51. Which of the following descriptions of DNA replication is not common to the synthesis of both leading and lagging strands?
(a) RNA primer is synthesized
(b) DNA polymerase III synthesizes DNA
(c) Helicase (rep protein) continuously unwinds duplex DNA at the replication fork during synthesis
(d) DNA ligase repeatedly joins the ends of DNA along the growing strand

52. Which of the following statements describing restriction endonucleases is true?
(a) They always yield overhanging single-stranded ends
(b) They recognize methylated DNA sequences
(c) They recognize triplet repeats
(d) They cleave both strands in duplex DNA

53. DNA fingerprinting is used for paternity testing and forensic identification of suspects. Which of the following is the most accurate description of DNA fingerprinting?
(a) DNA can be isolated from blood, skin or sperm and analyzed for variable patterns of restriction fragments arising from tandemly repeated sequences (microsatellites)
(b) DNA is copied from blood, skin or sperm RNA using reverse transcriptase and analyzed for the pattern of complementary DNAs
(c) DNA is isolated from blood, skin or sperm and its fragment size distribution is analyzed by gel electrophoresis
(d) DNA is isolated from blood, skin or sperm and hybridized with probes from the HLA locus to visualize HLA gene patterns

54. The first drug to be effective against AIDS, including the reduction of maternal-to-child AIDS transmission by 30%, was AIDS drug azidothymidine (AZT). Which of the following describes its mechanism of action?
(a) It inhibits viral protein synthesis
(b) It inhibits RNA synthesis
(c) It inhibits viral DNA polymerase
(d) It inhibits viral reverse transcriptase

55. Which of the following statement is correct?
I. Change in the optical rotation of sucrose upon hydrolysis is known as inversion.
II. Fructose is a ketose sugar having furan ring.
III. A monosaccharide with 'n' chiral center will form 2nd number of steroisomer.
IV. The most abundant organic molecule synthesized by living system is cellulose.
(a) I and II (b) I, II and III
(c) II, III and IV (d) I, II, III and IV

56. Which of the following statements correctly describes the recombinant DNA tool known as plasmids?
(a) They are found more commonly in viruses than in bacteria
(b) They are single-stranded circles
(c) They sometimes enhance bacterial susceptibility to antibiotics
(d) They sometimes enhance bacterial resistance to antibiotics

57. Which of the following molecules is found in a nucleoside?
(a) A pyrophosphate group
(b) A 1′-base linked to a pentose sugar
(c) A 5′-phosphate group linked to a pentose sugar
(d) A 3′-phosphate group linked to a pentose sugar

58. Which is the most correct sequence of events in gene repair mechanisms in patients without a mutated repair process?
(a) Nicking, excision, replacement, sealing, recognition
(b) Sealing, recognition, nicking, excision, replacement
(c) Recognition, nicking, excision, replacement, sealing
(d) Nicking, sealing, recognition, excision, replacement

59. Which of the following enzymes can be described as a DNA-dependent RNA polymerase?
(a) DNA ligase (b) Primase
(c) DNA polymerase III (d) DNA polymerase I

60. In mammalian cells *r*RNA is produced mainly in the
(a) Endoplasmic reticulum (b) Ribosome
(c) Nucleolus (d) Nucleus

61. Genetic information of nuclear DNA is transmitted to the site of protein synthesis by
(a) *r*RNA (b) *m*RNA
(c) *t*RNA (d) Polysomes

62. Intestinal absorption of magnesium is increased in
(a) calcium deficient diet (b) high calcium diet
(c) high oxalate diet (d) high phytate diet

63. Small amount of urinary oxalates is contributed by the amino acid
(a) glycine (b) tyrosine
(c) alanine (d) serine

64. Choose the correct statement.
I. Singal sequence present near N-terminus on nascent polypeptide consists of a segment of hydrophobic amino acids.
II. Chaperone, BiP helps in folding of polypeptide.
III. COPI coated vesicles transport proteins in the retrograde directions.

IV. Mannose-6-phosphate receptors in the membrane of the *trans*-Golgi bind proteins bearing mannose 6-phosphate and direct their transfer of lysosome.
(a) I and II (b) I and III
(c) I and IV (d) I, II, III and IV

65. The amino acids involved in the synthesis of creatine are
(a) arginine, glycine and active methionine
(b) arginine, alanine and glycine
(c) glycine, lysine and methionine
(d) arginine, lysine and methionine

66. Tay-Sachs disease results due to lack of enzyme
(a) glucokinase (b) hexosaminidase A
(c) pyruvate kinase (d) Na^+–K^+ ATPase

67. Cystic fibrosis is a disease in which
(a) Na^+ ions fail to pass through plasma membrane
(b) Cl^- ions fail to pass through plasma membrane
(c) K^+ ions fail to pass through plasma membrane
(d) Both (a) and (b)

68. A promoter gene defines the
(a) site for initial binding of RNA polymerase
(b) direction of transcription
(c) copying the strand
(d) All of the above

69. Radiation therapy is employed for many cancers, including irradiation of the central nervous system to destroy lymphoblasts in leukemia. Which of the following accounts for the destruction of rapidly growing cells?
(a) Cross-linking of DNA
(b) Cleavage of DNA double strands
(c) Disruption of DNA-RNA transcription complexes
(d) Disruption of purine rings in DNA

70. Mammalian chromosomes have specialized structures with highly repetitive DNA at their ends (telomeres). Which aspect of telomeric DNA replication is different from that of other chromosomal regions?
(a) The DNA polymerase uses an RNA primer but does not degrade it
(b) The DNA polymerase contains an RNA molecule that serves as template for DNA synthesis
(c) The DNA polymerase must cross-link the 5′ and 3′-termini
(d) The DNA polymerase has a σ-subunit that facilitates binding to repetitive DNA

71. Mature erythrocytes do not contain
(a) glycolytic enzymes
(b) HMP shunt enzymes
(c) pyridine nucleotide
(d) ATP

72. Restriction Fragment Length Polymorphism (RFLP) analysis can only be used to follow the inheritance of a genetic disease if
(a) the disease causing mutation is at or closely linked to an altered restriction site
(b) proteins of mutated and normal genes migrate differently upon gel electrophoresis
(c) mutations are outside of restriction sites so that cleaving still occurs
(d) restriction fragments remain the same size but their charge changes

73. It is well known that DNA polymerases synthesize DNA only in the 5′-3′ direction. Yet, at the replication fork, both strands of parental DNA are being replicated with the synthesis of new DNA. How is it possible that while one strand is being synthesized in the 5′-3′ direction, the other strand appears to be synthesized in the 3′-5′ direction? This apparent paradox is explained by
(a) 3′-5′ DNA repair enzymes
(b) 3′-5′ DNA polymerase
(c) Okazaki fragments
(d) lack of RNA primer on one of the strands

74. Given that the chromosomes of mammalian cells may be 20 times as large as those of *Escherichia coli*, how can replication of mammalian chromosomes be carried out in just a few minutes?
(a) Eukaryotic DNA polymerases are extraordinarily fast compared with prokaryotic polymerases
(b) The higher temperature of mammalian cells allows for an exponentially higher replication rate
(c) Hundreds of replication forks work simultaneously on each piece of chromosomal DNA
(d) A great many different RNA polymerases carry out replication simultaneously on chromosomal DNA

75. The process that occurs at the 5 position of cytidine and often correlates with gene inactivation is
(a) gene conversion (b) pseudogene
(c) gene rearrangement (d) DNA methylation

76. A child presents with severe growth failure, accelerated ageing that causes adult complications such as diabetes and coronary artery disease and microcephaly (small head) due to increased nerve cell death. *In vitro* assay of labelled thymidine incorporation reveals decreased levels of DNA synthesis compared to controls, but normal-sized labelled DNA fragments. The addition of protein extract from normal cells, gently heated to inactivate DNA polymerase, restores DNA synthesis in the child's cell extracts to normal. Which of the enzymes used in DNA replication is likely to be defective in this child?
(a) DNA-directed DNA polymerase
(b) Unwinding proteins
(c) DNA polymerase I
(d) DNA-directed RNA polymerase

77. Patients with hereditary non-polyposis colon cancer have genes with microsatellite instability, that is, many regions containing abnormal, small loops of unpaired DNA. This is a result of a mutation affecting
(a) mismatch repair (b) chain break repair
(c) base excision repair (d) depurination repair

78. If a completely radioactive double-stranded DNA molecule undergoes two rounds of replication in a solution free of radioactive label, what is the radioactivity status of the resulting four double-stranded DNA molecules?

(a) Half should contain no radioactivity
(b) All should contain radioactivity
(c) Half should contain radioactivity in both strands
(d) One should contain radioactivity in both strands

79. Sickle cell anaemia is the clinical manifestation of homozygous genes for an abnormal haemoglobin molecule. The mutation in the β-chain is known to produce a single amino acid change. The most likely mechanism for this mutation is
(a) two-base insertion
(b) three-base deletion
(c) non-disjunction
(d) single-base substitution (point mutation)

80. Parents bring their newborn daughter to you for consultation about diagnosis and management. Their first two children, a boy and a girl, have a complete form of albinism with pink irides, blond hair and pale skin. Which of the following represents your correct advice concerning the newborn child?
(a) A 1/8 risk for albinism and skin cancer from DNA cross-linkage
(b) A 1/4 risk for albinism and skin cancer from DNA point mutations
(c) A 1/4 risk for albinism and skin cancer from DNA deletions
(d) A 1/4 risk for albinism and skin cancer from DNA cross-linkage

81. A culture of bacteria not resistant to tetracycline develops an infection from a virus that is derived from the lysis of tetracycline-resistant bacteria. Most of the bacterial progeny of the original culture is found to have become resistant to tetracycline. What phenomenon has occurred?
(a) Conjugation (b) Recombination
(c) Transformation (d) Transduction

82. Retinitis pigmentosa (RP) is a genetically heterogeneous disease characterized by progressive photoreceptor degeneration and ultimately blindness. Mutations in more than 20 different genes have been identified in clinically affected patients. Recent studies have mapped an RP locus to the chromosomal location of a new candidate gene at 5q31. One might expect this gene to encode a polypeptide required for the activity of a
(a) receptor tyrosine kinase
(b) cGMP phosphodiesterase
(c) phospholipase C
(d) adenyl cyclase

83. A 27 year old woman with epilepsy has been taking phenytoin to control her seizures. She is now pregnant, and her physician is considering changing her medication to prevent potential bleeding episodes in the infant. What biochemical activity might be deficient in the infant if her medication is continued?
(a) Glucuronidation of bilirubin
(b) Reduction of glutathione
(c) γ-carboxylation of glutamate
(d) Oxidation of lysine

84. A 75 year old woman is seen in the emergency room with a fractured arm. Physical examination revealed multiple bruises and perifollicular haemorrhages, periodontitis and painful gums. Her diet consists predominately of weak coffee, bouillon, rolls and plain pasta. Lab results indicated mild microcytic anaemia. Which of the following enzymes should be less active than normal in this patient?
(a) Homocysteine methyltransferase
(b) γ-glutamyl carboxylase
(c) Dihydrofolate reductase
(d) Prolyl hydroxylase

85. A drug which prevents uric acid synthesis by inhibiting the enzyme xanthine oxidase is
(a) aspirin (b) allopurinol
(c) colchicine (d) probenecid

86. Which of the following phospholipids is localized to a greater extent in the outer leaflet of the membrane lipid bilayer?
(a) Choline phosphoglycerides
(b) Ethanolamine phosphoglycerides
(c) Inositol phosphoglycerides
(d) Serine phosphoglycerides

87. Primary bile acids
(a) are any bile acids that are found in the intestinal tract
(b) are any bile acids reabsorbed from the intestinal tract
(c) are synthesized in hepatocytes directly from cholesterol
(d) are converted to secondary bile acids by conjugation with glycine or taurine

88. Structural features that are common to all prostaglandins include
(a) 20-carbon atoms
(b) an oxygen-containing internal heterocyclic ring
(c) a peroxide group at C-15
(d) two double bonds

89. Amino acids considered non-essential for humans are
(a) those not incorporated into protein
(b) not necessary in the diet if sufficient amounts of precursors are present
(c) the same for adults as for children
(d) generally not provided by the ordinary diet

90. The amide nitrogen of glutamine
(a) represents a non-toxic transport form of ammonia
(b) is a major source of ammonia for urinary excretion
(c) is used in the synthesis of asparagine., purines and pyrimidines
(d) can be recovered as ammonia by the action of glutaminase

91. S-adenosylmethionine
(a) contains a positively charged sulphur (sulphonium) that facilitates the transfer of substituents to suitable acceptors
(b) yields α-ketobutyrate in the reaction in which the methyl is transferred
(c) donates a methyl group in a freely reversible reaction
(d) generates H_2S by transsulphuration

92. In humans, sulphur of cysteine may participate in all of the following except
(a) the conversion of cyanide to less toxic thiocyanate
(b) the formation of thiosulphate
(c) the formation of taurine
(d) the donation of the sulphur for methionine formation

93. Deletion 1: Genes bde are lost.
Deletion 2: Genes ac are lost.
Deletion 3: Genes abd are lost.
The genes abcde are determined to be closely linked on the *E. coli* chromosome. Three random short deletions are created in the region, resulting in the removal of various genes as shown above. Which of the following gene orders is possible based on the deletion analysis?
(a) abcde (b) acbed
(c) bdeac (d) cadbe

94. Temperate bacteriophages differ from other bacteriophages in that temperate bacteriophages
(a) reproduce at moderate temperatures
(b) inhibit synthesis of host-cell proteins
(c) fragment the host-cell chromosome
(d) can lysogenize the host cell

95. Which of the following is the most likely mechanism for the origin of multigene families?
(a) Endosymbiosis
(b) Gene duplication
(c) Convergent evolution of dissimilar genes
(d) Horizontal gene transfer

96. Which of the following are found only in organisms containing polycistronic *m*RNA?
(a) Missense mutations
(b) Polar mutations
(c) Temperature-sensitive mutations
(d) Alternative splicing sites

97. Which of the following is not required for RecA-dependent recombination between two DNA molecules?
(a) Strand migration (b) Ligation
(c) Mismatch repair (d) Nuclease digestion

98. Which of the following occurs as a result of epinephrine binding to its receptor?
(a) Glycogen accumulates
(b) Phosphorylase kinase is phosphorylated and glycogen synthase is dephosphorylated
(c) Phosphodiesterase is activated to prolong the effect of cAMP
(d) A phosphatase inhibitor is activated by phosphorylation

99. All of the following compounds are capable of forming hydrogen bonds with water except
(a) methanol (b) acetamide
(c) methyl acetate (d) hexane

100. A water-soluble globular protein is most likely to have the highest proportion of which of the following amino acid residues buried within its core?
(a) Serine (b) Histidine
(c) Isoleucine (d) Glutamate

101. A protein having both structural and enzymatic traits is
(a) actin (b) haemoglobin
(c) myosin (d) myoglobin

102. The most striking example of an unique point mutation is found in a disease called
(a) night blindness (b) thalassemia
(c) down syndrome (d) sickle cell anaemia

103. Successful replication of chromosomes does not require the presence of
(a) ribosomes (b) DNA template
(c) nuclear enzymes (d) ATP

104. The factor required only for accurate initiations of transcription in prokaryotes is
(a) alpha (α) (b) beta (β)
(c) rho (ρ) (d) sigma (σ)

105. A mixture separated on HPLC gives clearly defined peaks, whereas in a manually run column the peaks tend to blend into each other. This is primarily because
(a) the small size of the packing material used in the HPLC column
(b) the better control of flow in HPLC
(c) the use of high pressure in HPLC
(d) the use of better detection systems in HPLC

106. A 4 Kb covalently closed circular (ccc) plasmid has 2 (two) sites for a restriction enzyme 1 kb apart. It is partially digested by the enzyme. The maximum number of bands that could be seen on a gel will be
(a) 1 (b) 2
(c) 3 (d) 4

107. A post-transcriptional processing event that occurs in the formation of both messenger RNA (*m*RNA) and transfer RNA (*t*RNA) in eukaryotes is
(a) the addition of the sequence CCA to 3-ends
(b) the removal of introns by splicing
(c) the modification of some of their bases
(d) cleavage event before polyadenylation

108. Eukaryotic *m*RNAs differ from prokaryotic *m*RNAs in that
(a) they do not have a 5′-untranslated region
(b) their coding regions are separated by spacers
(c) they do not have 3′-UTR
(d) they have a free 3′-hydroxy group on each of their ends

109. Degeneracy of the genetic code means that
(a) a given base triplet can code for more than one amino acid
(b) there is no punctuation in the code sequence
(c) the third base in a codon is net important for coding
(d) a given amino acid can be coded for by more than one base triplet

110. Which one of the following sequences is most likely to be a restriction enzyme recognition site?
(a) CGGC (b) CGC
(c) GTAATG (d) GTCGAC

111. Which step is the first in the formation of a double stranded complementary DNA (*c*DNA) target for cloning?
(a) Blunt end ligation
(b) DNA dependent DNA synthesis
(c) Restriction enzyme cleavage
(d) Primer annealing

112. Cyclic AMP regulates the lactose (*lac*) operon by
(a) binding to the operator to turn on transcription
(b) binding to the *lac* repressor to prevent transcription
(c) combining with the catabolitic activator protein (CAP) to form a complex that enhances transcriptions upon binding to the promoter
(d) combining with the CAP to remove CAP's inhibition of transcription

113. Which of the following chemotherapeutic agents works by impairing *de novo* purine synthesis?
(a) Acyclovir (acycloguanosine)
(b) 5-fluorouracil (antimetabolite)
(c) Methotrexate (anti folate)
(d) Hydroxyurea

114. Which of the following element plays an important role in nitrogen fixation?
(a) Manganese (b) Molybdenum
(c) Zinc (d) Copper

115. An important cause of water intoxication is
(a) nephrogenic diabetes insipidus
(b) renal failure
(c) gastroenteritis
(d) fanconi syndrome

116. Minimum excretory urinary volume for waste products elimination during 24 h is
(a) 200-300 mL (b) 200-400 mL
(c) 500-600 mL (d) 800 mL

117. In primary dehydration
(a) intracellular fluid volume is reduced
(b) intracellular fluid volume remains normal
(c) extracellular fluid volume is much reduced
(d) extracellular fluid volume is much increased

118. An important cause of secondary dehydration is
(a) dysphagia (b) oesophageal varices
(c) oesophageal varices (d) gastroenteritis

119. Important finding of secondary dehydration is
(a) intracellular oedema (b) cellular dehydration
(c) thirst (d) muscle cramps

120. Urine examination in secondary dehydration shows
(a) ketonuria (b) low specific gravity
(c) high specific gravity (d) albuminuria

121. The total calcium of the human body is about
(a) 100-150 g (b) 200-300 g
(c) 1-1.5 kg (d) 2-3 kg

122. The pH of gastric juice become low in
(a) Haemolytic anaemia
(b) pernicious anaemia
(c) Both (a) and (b)
(d) None of the above

123. A water-soluble globular protein is most likely to have the highest proportion of which of the following amino acid residues buried within its core?
(a) Serine (b) Histidine
(c) Isoleucine (d) Glutamate

124. Virus-mediated transfer of cellular genetic material from one bacterial cell to another by means of virus particles is called
(a) induction (b) transfection
(c) transformation (d) transduction

125. Which of the following is required for crystallization and storage of the hormone insulin?
(a) Mn^{2+} (b) Mg^{2+}
(c) Ca^{2+} (d) Zn^{2+}

126. Milk is deficient in which vitamins?
(a) Vitamin-C (b) Vitamin-A
(c) Vitamin-B_2 (d) Vitamin-K

127. Milk is deficient of which mineral?
(a) Phosphorus (b) Sodium
(c) Iron (d) Potassium

128. Synthesis of prostaglandins is inhibited by
(a) aspirin (b) arsenic
(c) fluoride (d) cyanide

129. HDL is synthesized and secreted from
(a) pancreas (b) liver
(c) kidney (d) muscle

130. Which are the cholesterol esters that enter cells through the receptor-mediated endocytosis of lipoproteins hydrolyzed?
(a) Endoplasmin reticulum
(b) Lysosomes
(c) Plasma membrane receptor
(d) Mitochondria

131. Calcium absorption is increased by
(a) vitamin-D (b) vitamin-C
(c) vitamin-K (d) vitamin-E

132. In serum product of Ca × p (in mg/100mL) in children is normally
(a) 20 (b) 30
(c) 50 (d) 60

133. In rickets, the product of Ca × p (in mg/ 100 mL) in serum is below
(a) 30 (b) 50
(c) 70 (d) 100

134. In man, the amount of calcium in gms filtered in 24 h period by the renal glomeruli is
(a) 5 (b) 10
(c) 15 (d) 20

135. The percentage of the calcium eliminated in faeces is
(a) 10-20 (b) 30-40
(c) 50-60 (d) 70-90

136. Renal ricket is caused by renal tubular defect (usually inherited) which interferes with reabsorption of
(a) calcium (b) phosphorus
(c) sodium (d) chloride

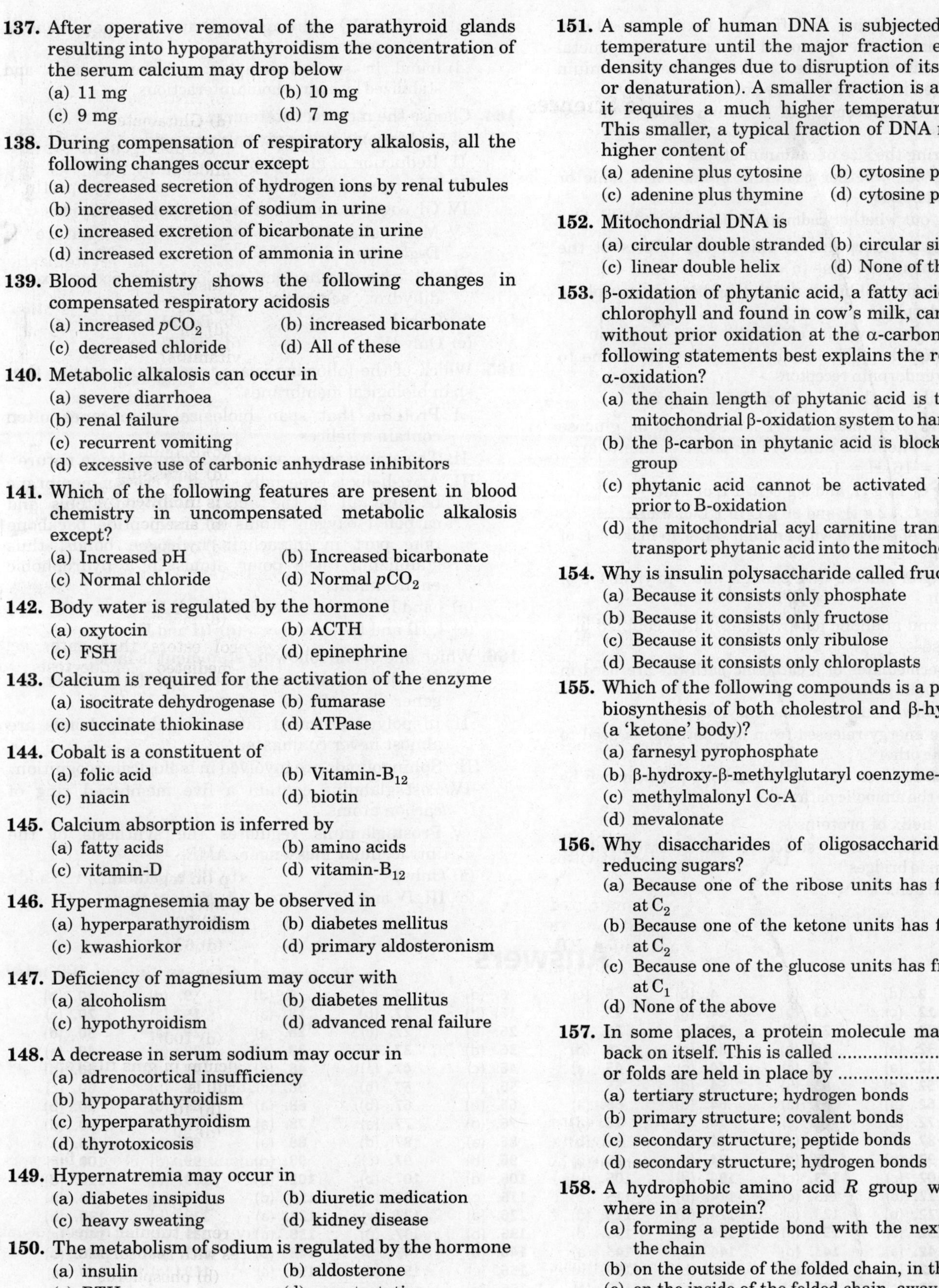

137. After operative removal of the parathyroid glands resulting into hypoparathyroidism the concentration of the serum calcium may drop below
(a) 11 mg (b) 10 mg
(c) 9 mg (d) 7 mg

138. During compensation of respiratory alkalosis, all the following changes occur except
(a) decreased secretion of hydrogen ions by renal tubules
(b) increased excretion of sodium in urine
(c) increased excretion of bicarbonate in urine
(d) increased excretion of ammonia in urine

139. Blood chemistry shows the following changes in compensated respiratory acidosis
(a) increased pCO_2 (b) increased bicarbonate
(c) decreased chloride (d) All of these

140. Metabolic alkalosis can occur in
(a) severe diarrhoea
(b) renal failure
(c) recurrent vomiting
(d) excessive use of carbonic anhydrase inhibitors

141. Which of the following features are present in blood chemistry in uncompensated metabolic alkalosis except?
(a) Increased pH (b) Increased bicarbonate
(c) Normal chloride (d) Normal pCO_2

142. Body water is regulated by the hormone
(a) oxytocin (b) ACTH
(c) FSH (d) epinephrine

143. Calcium is required for the activation of the enzyme
(a) isocitrate dehydrogenase (b) fumarase
(c) succinate thiokinase (d) ATPase

144. Cobalt is a constituent of
(a) folic acid (b) Vitamin-B_{12}
(c) niacin (d) biotin

145. Calcium absorption is inferred by
(a) fatty acids (b) amino acids
(c) vitamin-D (d) vitamin-B_{12}

146. Hypermagnesemia may be observed in
(a) hyperparathyroidism (b) diabetes mellitus
(c) kwashiorkor (d) primary aldosteronism

147. Deficiency of magnesium may occur with
(a) alcoholism (b) diabetes mellitus
(c) hypothyroidism (d) advanced renal failure

148. A decrease in serum sodium may occur in
(a) adrenocortical insufficiency
(b) hypoparathyroidism
(c) hyperparathyroidism
(d) thyrotoxicosis

149. Hypernatremia may occur in
(a) diabetes insipidus (b) diuretic medication
(c) heavy sweating (d) kidney disease

150. The metabolism of sodium is regulated by the hormone
(a) insulin (b) aldosterone
(c) PTH (d) somatostatin

151. A sample of human DNA is subjected to increasing temperature until the major fraction exhibits optical density changes due to disruption of its helix (melting or denaturation). A smaller fraction is a typical in that it requires a much higher temperature for melting. This smaller, a typical fraction of DNA must contain a higher content of
(a) adenine plus cytosine (b) cytosine plus guanine
(c) adenine plus thymine (d) cytosine plus thymine

152. Mitochondrial DNA is
(a) circular double stranded (b) circular single stranded
(c) linear double helix (d) None of these

153. β-oxidation of phytanic acid, a fatty acid derived from chlorophyll and found in cow's milk, cannot take place without prior oxidation at the α-carbon. Which of the following statements best explains the requirement for α-oxidation?
(a) the chain length of phytanic acid is too long for the mitochondrial β-oxidation system to handle
(b) the β-carbon in phytanic acid is blocked by a methyl group
(c) phytanic acid cannot be activated by coenzyme-A prior to B-oxidation
(d) the mitochondrial acyl carnitine transferase will not transport phytanic acid into the mitochondrial matrix

154. Why is insulin polysaccharide called fructosane?
(a) Because it consists only phosphate
(b) Because it consists only fructose
(c) Because it consists only ribulose
(d) Because it consists only chloroplasts

155. Which of the following compounds is a precursor in the biosynthesis of both cholestrol and β-hydroxybutyrate (a 'ketone' body)?
(a) farnesyl pyrophosphate
(b) β-hydroxy-β-methylglutaryl coenzyme-A (HMG Co-A)
(c) methylmalonyl Co-A
(d) mevalonate

156. Why disaccharides of oligosaccharides are called reducing sugars?
(a) Because one of the ribose units has free—OH group at C_2
(b) Because one of the ketone units has free—OH group at C_2
(c) Because one of the glucose units has free —OH group at C_1
(d) None of the above

157. In some places, a protein molecule may twist or fold back on itself. This is called .... and the coils or folds are held in place by ....
(a) tertiary structure; hydrogen bonds
(b) primary structure; covalent bonds
(c) secondary structure; peptide bonds
(d) secondary structure; hydrogen bonds

158. A hydrophobic amino acid R group would be found where in a protein?
(a) forming a peptide bond with the next amino acid in the chain
(b) on the outside of the folded chain, in the water
(c) on the inside of the folded chain, away from water
(d) forming hydrogen bonds with other R groups

159. Researchers studying the effects of toxic wastes knew that animals were poisoned by the heavy metal cadmium, but they wanted to know where cadmium accumulated in the body. They could find out by
(a) tracing the movement of cadmium isotopes in test animals
(b) measuring the size of cadmium atoms
(c) finding out whether cadmium atoms form ionic or covalent bonds
(d) finding out whether cadmium is acidic in water

160. The ability of morphine to mimic the effects of the body's endorphins is due to
(a) a chemical equilibrium developing between morphine and endorphins
(b) the one-way conversion of morphine into endorphin
(c) molecular shape similarities that allow morphine to bind to endorphin receptors
(d) the similarities between morphine and heroin

161. How would you make a 0.1 M solution of glucose ($C_6H_{12}O_6$)? The mass numbers for these elements are C = 12, O = 16, H = 1.
(a) Mix 6 g C, 12 g H, and 6 g O in 1 L of water
(b) Mix 72 g C, 12 g H, and 96 g O in 1 L of water
(c) Mix 18 g of glucose with enough water to make 1 L of solution
(d) Mix 29 g of glucose with enough water to yield 1 L of solution

162. Catabolic and anabolic pathways are often coupled in a cell because
(a) the intermediates of a catabolic pathway are used in the anabolic pathway
(b) both pathways use the same enzymes
(c) the free energy released from one pathway is used to drive the other
(d) the activation energy of the catabolic pathway can be used in the anabolic pathway

163. The alpha helix of proteins is
(a) part of the tertiary structure and is stabilized by disulphide bridges
(b) a double helix
(c) stabilized by hydrogen bonds and commonly found in fibrous proteins
(d) found in some regions of globular proteins and stabilized by hydrophobic interactions

164. Choose the incorrect statement.
I. Aldose oxidizes to give aldonic acids.
II. Reduction of glucose gives sorbitol.
III. Glycogen is highly branched form of amylopectin.
IV. Glycogen is a major structural polysaccharides.
V. Most abundant monosaccharide in nature is D-glucose.
VI. All monosaccharides are optically active except dihydroxy acetone.
(a) Only I (b) Both I and II
(c) Only IV (d) III, IV and V

165. Which of the following is/are true about proteins that span biological membranes?
I. Proteins that span biological membranes often contain a helices.
II. The amino acides would be hydrophobic in nature.
III. An α-helix is especially suited to cross a membrane because all of the amide hydrogen atoms and carbonyl oxygen atoms of the peptide backbone take part in intrachain hydrogen bonds, thus stabilizing these polar atoms in a hydrophobic environment.
(a) I and II (b) I and III
(c) I, III and II (d) III and II

166. Which one of the following statement is false?
I. Double bounds in unsaturated fatty acids are generally in the *cis* configuration.
II. In polyunsaturated fatty acid, double bonds are almost never conjugated.
III. Sphingolipids are involved in biological recognition.
IV. Postaglandins contain a five membered ring of carbon atoms.
V. Prostaglandins regulates the synthesis of the intracellular messenger cAMP.
(a) Only I (b) Both I and II
(c) III, IV and V (d) None of these

Answers

1. (d)	**2.** (d)	**3.** (a)	**4.** (b)	**5.** (c)	**6.** (d)	**7.** (c)	**8.** (d)	**9.** (d)	**10.** (b)
11. (a)	**12.** (c)	**13.** (b)	**14.** (a)	**15.** (c)	**16.** (d)	**17.** (b)	**18.** (a)	**19.** (a)	**20.** (c)
21. (c)	**22.** (c)	**23.** (c)	**24.** (a)	**25.** (a)	**26.** (a)	**27.** (c)	**28.** (a)	**29.** (a)	**30.** (d)
31. (a)	**32.** (a)	**33.** (b)	**34.** (c)	**35.** (d)	**36.** (d)	**37.** (a)	**38.** (b)	**39.** (d)	**40.** (a)
41. (d)	**42.** (a)	**43.** (c)	**44.** (c)	**45.** (a)	**46.** (c)	**47.** (a)	**48.** (d)	**49.** (d)	**50.** (d)
51. (d)	**52.** (d)	**53.** (a)	**54.** (d)	**55.** (d)	**56.** (d)	**57.** (b)	**58.** (c)	**59.** (b)	**60.** (c)
61. (d)	**62.** (a)	**63.** (a)	**64.** (d)	**65.** (a)	**66.** (b)	**67.** (b)	**68.** (a)	**69.** (d)	**70.** (b)
71. (c)	**72.** (a)	**73.** (c)	**74.** (c)	**75.** (d)	**76.** (b)	**77.** (a)	**78.** (a)	**79.** (d)	**80.** (d)
81. (d)	**82.** (b)	**83.** (c)	**84.** (d)	**85.** (b)	**86.** (a)	**87.** (d)	**88.** (a)	**89.** (b)	**90.** (a)
91. (a)	**92.** (b)	**93.** (d)	**94.** (d)	**95.** (b)	**96.** (b)	**97.** (c)	**98.** (d)	**99.** (d)	**100.** (c)
101. (d)	**102.** (c)	**103.** (c)	**104.** (d)	**105.** (b)	**106.** (d)	**107.** (b)	**108.** (b)	**109.** (d)	**110.** (d)
111. (d)	**112.** (c)	**113.** (c)	**114.** (b)	**115.** (b)	**116.** (c)	**117.** (a)	**118.** (d)	**119.** (a)	**120.** (b)
121. (c)	**122.** (b)	**123.** (c)	**124.** (d)	**125.** (d)	**126.** (a)	**127.** (c)	**128.** (a)	**129.** (b)	**130.** (b)
131. (a)	**132.** (c)	**133.** (a)	**134.** (b)	**135.** (d)	**136.** (b)	**137.** (d)	**138.** (d)	**139.** (d)	**140.** (c)
141. (d)	**142.** (a)	**143.** (d)	**144.** (b)	**145.** (a)	**146.** (b)	**147.** (a)	**148.** (b)	**149.** (a)	**150.** (b)
151. (d)	**152.** (a)	**153.** (b)	**154.** (b)	**155.** (b)	**156.** (c)	**157.** (d)	**158.** (c)	**159.** (a)	**160.** (c)
161. (c)	**162.** (c)	**163.** (c)	**164.** (c)	**165.** (c)	**166.** (d)				

4 The Cell : Structure and Function

Syllabus

- Membrane : Structure and Function, Structure of Model Membrane, Lipid Bilayer and Membrane Protein Diffusion, Osmosis, Ion Channels, Active Transport, Ion Pumps, Mechanism of Sorting and Regulation of Intracellular Transport, Electrical Properties of Membranes.
- Structure and Function of Intracellular Organelles: Cell Wall, Nucleus, Mitochondria, Golgi Bodies, Lysosomes, Endoplasmic Reticulum, Peroxisomes, Plastids, Chloroplast, Vacuoles, Cytoskeleton and its Role in Motility.

Membrane : Structure and Function

Cell is a structural and functional unit of all organisms. The cell was discovered by **Robert Hooke** in 1665. Hooke's description were actually non-living cell wall was published in *Micrographia*. The first man to witness a live cell under a microscope was **Antony von Leeuwenhoek** (but the first man to make a compound microscope was Zacharias Janssen), who in 1674, described the algae (*Spirogyra*) and named organisms animalcules, meaning 'little animals'.

MJ Schleiden a German botanist and **T Schwann,** a German zoologist (1838-1839), stated that cell is the basic structural and functional unit of all organisms. It was later known as 'cell theory'. Most of the biologist accepted the cell theory given by Schleiden and Schwann except **Rudolf Virchow** an embryologist had powerful dictum that 'all cells arise from pre-existing cell' (*omnis cellula e cellula*).

The Cell Theory

Schleiden and Schwann proposed the cell theory in 1838-39 cell biology research was forever changed. The cell theory states that:

1. All life forms are made from one or more cells.
2. Cells only arise from pre-existing cells.
3. The cell is the smallest form of life.

The cell theory also provides us with an operational definition of 'life.'

Around 1833 **Robert Brown,** reported the discovery of the **nucleus.**

Structure of Model Membrane

Plant cell protoplasts were permeable to water but not to larger macromolecules like sucrose (de Vries; 1871). Pfeffer (1877), was the first to study the osmotic pressure within cells and formulated the idea that the protoplasm of cells is surrounded by a thin layer, which he called the **plasma membrane.**

Charles Ernest Overton (1895), Overton's findings led to the hypothesis that the thin membranes surrounding cells have the properties of oil. He called the layers surrounding cells as 'lipoids' made from lipids and cholesterol.

Langmuir (1917), developed an apparatus in which molecular layers of lipids were spread at the air-water interface. Langmuir proposed that in the molecular film the polar head groups were directed toward the water, whereas the hydrophobic hydrocarbons are pointed toward the air phase.

Gorter and **Grendel** (1925), experimentally concluded that cell membranes are made of two opposing thin molecular layers and they proposed that this double layer is constructed such that two lipid layers form a **bilayer** with the polar head groups pointing toward the aqueous environment.

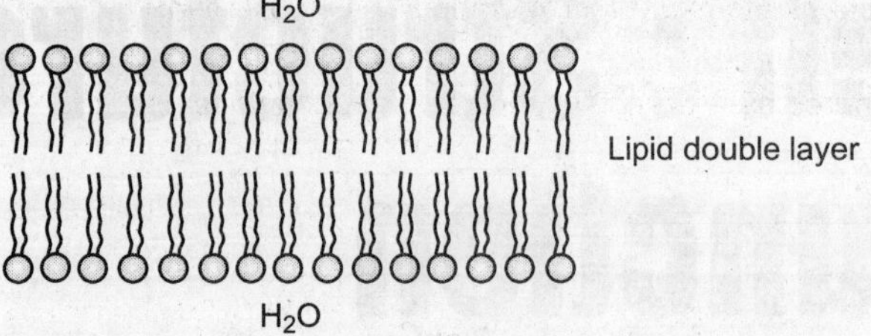

Fig. 4.1 The lipid bilayer cell membrane proposed by Gorter and Grendel

JR Danielli and **H Davson** (1935), proposed the molecular model for the biomembrane structure including known as the **Sandwich Model.**

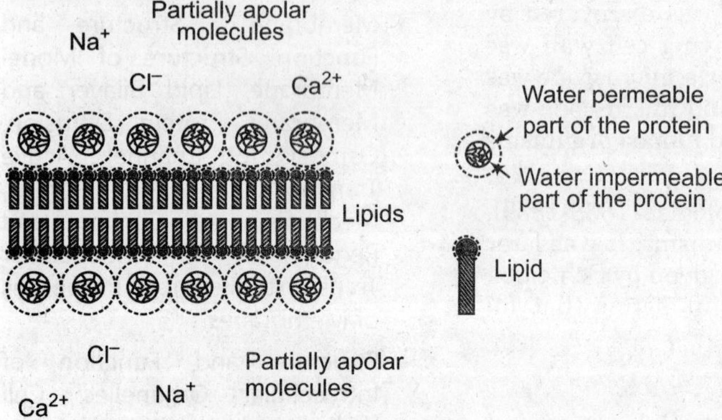

Fig. 4.2 Danielli and Davson proposed a membrane model including proteins

In particular, they assumed that the membrane has both a lipophilic and a hydrophilic character. Water containing regions in the membrane give rise to ion transport depending on water content of the membrane and its charge; lipophilic parts are responsible for the transport of water-insoluble molecules.

JD Robertson (1959), proposed the unit membrane model (Trilamellar concept). The electron microscopic studies of plasma membrane reveals that it is three layered. The two outer layers are dense and approximately 20Å thick and the middle layer is about 35Å thick. This three layered structure is called the **unit membrane.** This trilamellar concept was proposed by **Robertson** (1959). According to **Robertson,** even all bio-membranes present inside the cell and around the cell organelles have a trilamellar (protein-lipid-protein) arrangement.

Fig. 4.3 Robertson collected electron microscopy images of a biological membrane which resembles that of Danielli and Davson

SJ Singer and **GL Nicolson** (1972), proposed **fluid mosaic model**—a widely accepted and best suited model to explain the structure and physiological nature of the cell membrane. **Singer** and **Nicolson** concluded that proteins may also span through membranes. The model can be summarized as follows: (a) Membranes are constructed from lipids and proteins. (b) The proteins form mainly two classes: **peripheral proteins** are those proteins that are only loosely attached to the membrane surface and can easily be separated from the membrane by mild treatment (*e.g.*, cytochrome-*c* in mitochondria or spectrin in erythrocytes) and **integral proteins** cannot easily be separated from the lipids. They form the major fraction of membrane proteins. The structure forming unit (matrix) is the lipid double layer (bilayer). Proteins may be either adsorbed to the membrane surface or span through the membrane.

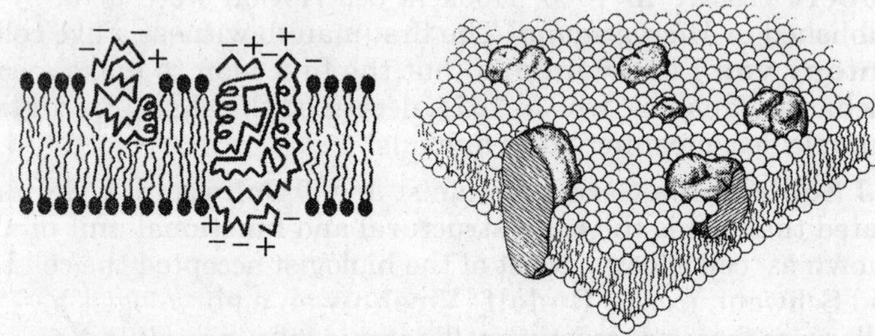

Fig. 4.4 The 'fluid mosaic model' of Singer and Nicolson. The left side shows the lipid bilayer including globular proteins intercalated with the membrane and transmembrane proteins

Hilleir and **Hoffman** proposed micellar theory which states that plasma membrane consists of mosaic of globular subunits or micells of lipid molecules.

Lipid Bilayer and Membrane Protein Diffusion

The physical organization and functioning of all biological membranes depend on their constituents: lipids, proteins and carbohydrates. **Proteins** embedded in the phospholipid bilayer have a number of functions, including moving materials through the membrane and receiving chemical signals from the cell's external environment. The **carbohydrates** associated with membranes are attached either to the lipids or to protein molecules. They are located on the outside of the plasma membrane. Carbohydrates are crucial in recognizing specific molecules. Membrane associated carbohydrates may be covalently bound to lipids or to proteins; these are: 1. **Glycolipids** consist of a carbohydrate covalently bound to a lipid; they serve as recognition signals for interactions between cells. 2. **Glycoproteins** consist of a carbohydrate covalently bound to a protein. The bound carbohydrates are oligosaccharide chains. Glycoproteins enable a cell to be recognized by other cells and proteins. Both glycoproteins and glycolipids are especially abundant in the plasma membranes of eukaryotic cells; they are absent from the inner mitochondrial membrane, chloroplast lamellae and several other intracellular membranes.

The molecule responsible for cell recognition and adhesion in sponges is a huge membrane glycoprotein (80% sugar) that is partly embedded in the plasma membrane, with the recognition part sticking out and exposed to the environment. One important consequence of such interactions is illustrated by the A, B and O blood-group antigens. These three structurally related oligosaccharide components of certain glycoproteins and glycolipids are expressed on the surfaces of human erythrocytes and many other cell types.

Table 4.1 **Modes of Membrane Protein Binding to the Membrane**

Mode of Membrane Protein	Example
Bound to other 'anchor' proteins	Succinate dehydrogenase
Electrostatic binding to bilayer	Myelin basic protein
Hydrophobic interaction with bilayer without substantial penetration	*E. coli* pyruvate oxidase
Anchored by a short terminal segment	Cytochrome-b_5
Single transmembrane segment	Glycophorin
Multiple transmembrane segments	Lactose premease, ion channels
Anchored by a covalently bound lipid	Eukaryotic alkaline phosphatase

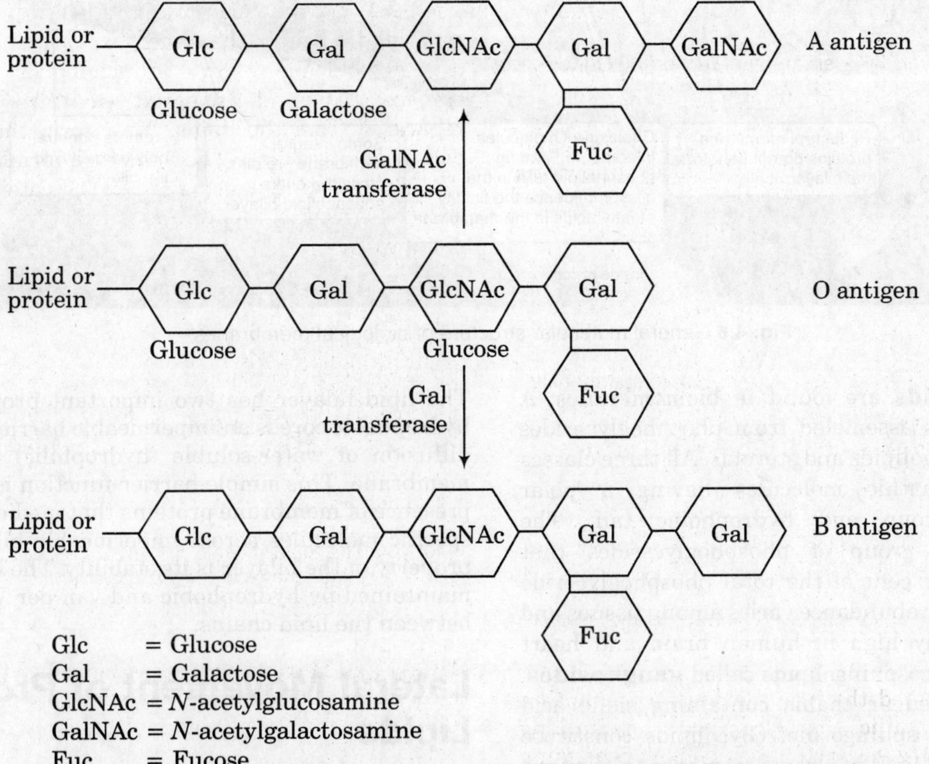

Fig. 4.5 Human ABO blood-group antigens. These antigens are oligosaccharide chains covalently attached to glycolipids or glycoproteins in the plasma membrane. The terminal oligosaccharide sugars distinguish the three antigens. The presence or absence of the glycosyltransferases that add galactose (Gal) or *N*-acetylgalactosamine (GalNAc) to O antigen determine a person's blood type.

Lipids constitute the bulk of a membrane. Most of the lipids in biological membranes are phospholipids. Some compounds are hydrophilic (water-loving) and others are hydrophobic (water-hating). Phospholipids have both hydrophilic regions and hydrophobic regions and thus, are amphipathic.

1. **Hydrophilic regions** The phosphorus-containing 'head' of the phospholipid is electrically charged and hence, associates with polar water molecules.
2. **Hydrophobic regions** The long, non-polar fatty acid 'tails' of the phospholipid associate with other non-polar materials, but they do not dissolve in water or associate with hydrophilic substances.

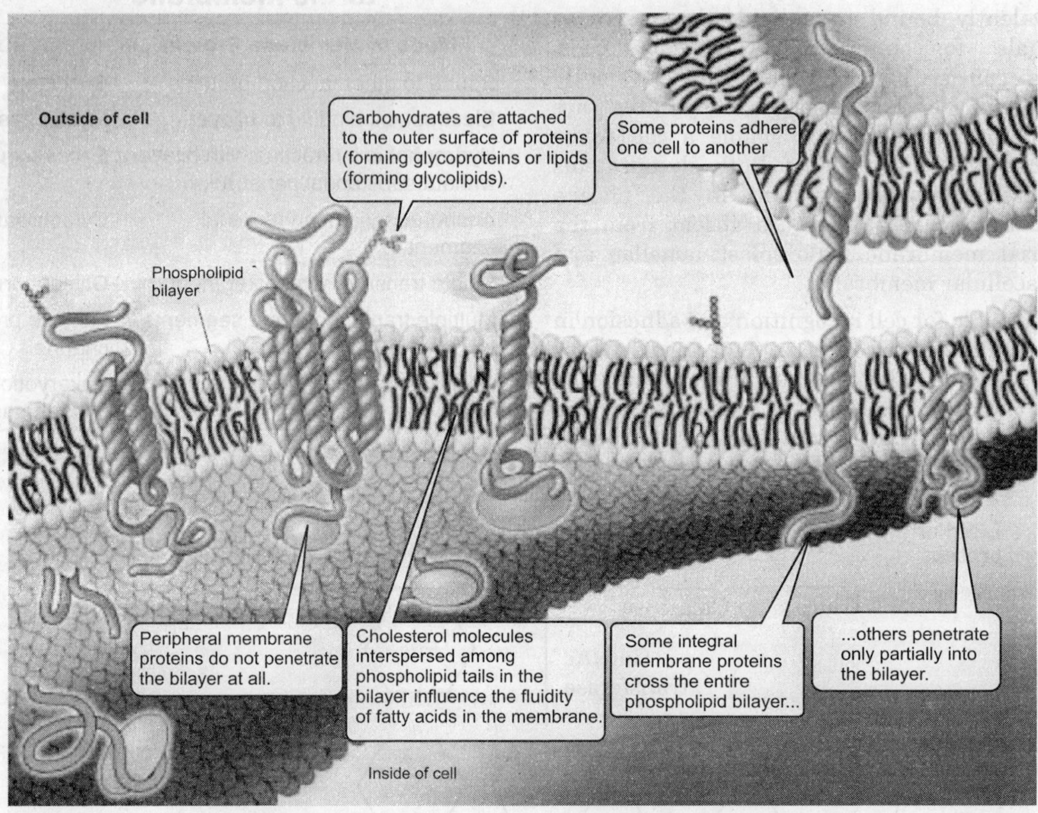

Fig. 4.6 General molecular structure of biological membranes

Three classes of lipids are found in biomembranes. A typical biomembrane is assembled from phosphoglycerides (most abundant), sphingolipids and steroids. All three classes of lipids are amphipathic molecules having a polar (hydrophilic) head group and hydrophobic tail. The **plasmalogens** are a group of phosphoglycerides that constitute about 20 per cent of the total phosphoglyceride content in human. Their abundance varies among tissues and species but is especially high in human brain and heart tissue. The complex glycosphingolipids called **gangliosides**, one or two branched sugar chains containing sialic acid groups are attached to sphingosine. Glycolipids constitute 2-10 per cent of the total lipid in plasma membranes; they are most abundant in nervous tissue. **Cholesterol** is especially abundant in the plasma membranes of mammalian cells but is absent from most prokaryotic cells. As much as 30-50 per cent of the lipids in plant plasma membranes consist of certain steroids unique to plants.

The lipid bilayer has two important properties. **First,** the hydrophobic core is an impermeable barrier that prevents the diffusion of water-soluble (hydrophilic) solutes across the membrane. This simple barrier function is modulated by the presence of membrane proteins that mediate the transport of specific molecules across impermeable bilayer. The **second** property of the bilayer is its stability. The bilayer structure is maintained by hydrophobic and van der Waals' interactions between the lipid chains.

Lateral Movement of Proteins and Lipids

The amount of cholesterol present in membranes, alongwith the degree of saturation of the fatty acids present, can increase or decrease membrane fluidity. Shorter fatty acid chains make for a more fluid membrane, as do unsaturated fatty acids.

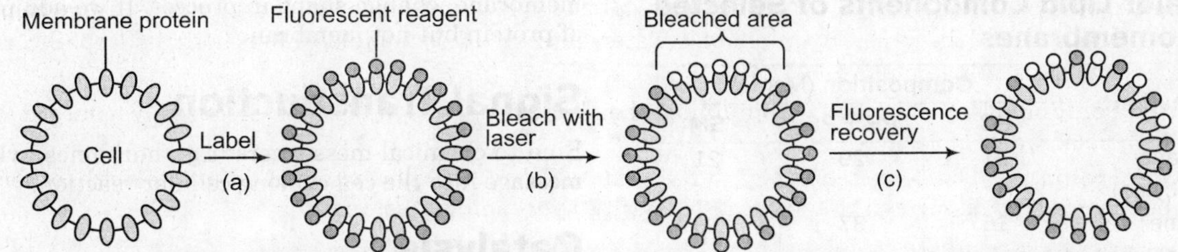

Fig. 4.7 Fluorescence recovery after photobleaching experiments can quantify the lateral movement of proteins and lipids within the plasma membrane

Phospholipids form bilayer in an aqueous solution. Lipid molecules readily exchange places laterally with their neighbours on one side of the bilayers but occasionally move from one monolayer to other. This movement is called flip-flop movement (migration or process). Lateral movement occurs much frequently than flip-flop migration.

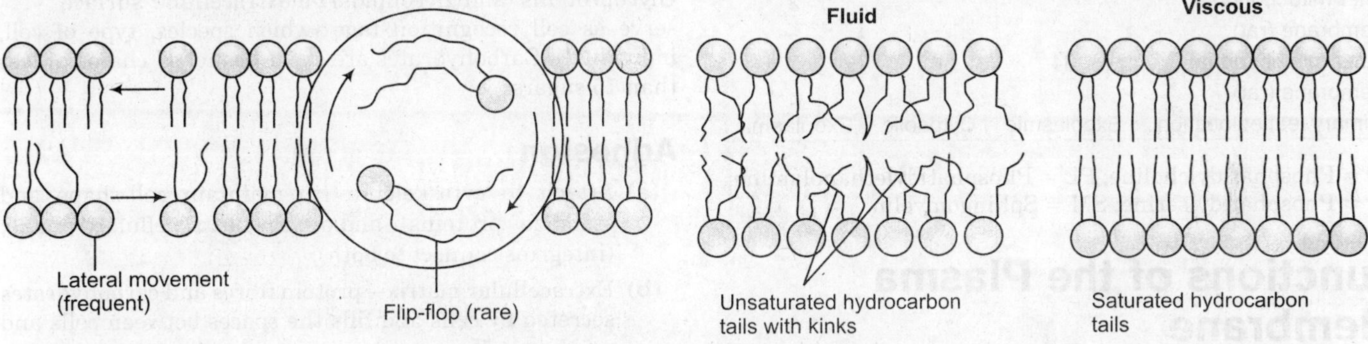

Fig. 4.8 Various types of movement of phospholipids molecules in lipid bilayer

Membrane Protein Asymmetry

Proteins are asymmetrically distributed on the inner and outer surfaces of a membrane. Integral membrane proteins that protrude on both sides of the membrane, known as transmembrane proteins, show different 'faces' on the two membrane surfaces.

Plasma membranes have one protein molecule for every 25 phospholipid molecules. This ratio varies depending on membrane function. In the inner membrane of the mitochondrion, which is specialized for energy processing, there is one protein for every 15 lipids. On the other hand, myelin, a membrane that encloses some nerve cells and uses the properties of lipids to act as an electrical insulator, has only one protein per 70 lipids. Like phospholipids, these proteins are also amphipatic.

(i) **Hydrophilic regions** Stretches of amino acids with hydrophilic R groups (side chains) give certain regions of the protein a polar character. Those regions interact with water, sticking out into the aqueous extracellular environment or cytoplasm.

(ii) **Hydrophobic regions** Stretches of amino acids with hydrophobic R groups give other regions of the protein a non-polar character. Those domains interact with the fatty acid chains in the interior of the lipid bilayer, away from water.

Many proteins are free to migrate in the membrane, others are not, but rather appear to be 'anchored' to a specific region of the membrane. For example, the protein in the membrane of a muscle cell that recognizes a molecular signal from nerve cells is normally found only at the site, where a nerve cell meets the muscle cell. None of this protein is found elsewhere on the surface of the muscle cell. There are two ways to restrict the movement of proteins within a membrane:

(a) The cytoskeleton have components just below the inner face of the membrane that are attached to membrane proteins protruding into the cytoplasm.

(b) Lipid rafts, groups of lipids in a puasifluid state, may trap proteins within a region.

These lipids have a different composition from the surrounding phospholipids; for example, they may have very long fatty acid chains.

Table 4.2 **Major Lipid Components of Selected Biomembranes**

Source/Location	Composition (Mol %)		
	PC	PE + PS	SM
Plasma membrane (human erythrocytes)	21	29	21
Myelin membrane (human neurons)	16	37	13
Plasma membrane (*E. coli*)	0	85	0
Endoplasmic reticulum membrane (rat)	54 45	26 20	5 13
Golgi membrane (rat)	45	45	2
Inner mitochondrial membrane (rat)			2
Outer mitochondrial membrane (rat)	34	46	2
Primary leaflet location	Exoplasmic	Cytosolic	Exoplasmic

PC = Phosphatidylcholine; PE = Phosphatidylethanolamine; PS = Phosphatidylserine; SM = Sphingomyelin

Functions of the Plasma Membrane

Transport

Channel proteins forms channel for lipid insoluble molecules and ions to pass freely through membrane. **Carrier proteins** bind to a substance and carry it across membrane, change shape in process. If we add protein fix in of protein but not membrane.

Signal Transduction

Bind to chemical messengers (*e.g.*, hormones) which sends a message into the cell causing cellular reaction.

Catalysis

Carry out enzymatic reactions right at the membrane when a substrate binds to the active site.

Cell Recognition Proteins

Glycoproteins (and glycolipids) on extracellular surface serve as cell recognition tags (which species, type of cell, individual). Carbohydrates are short branched chains of less than 15 sugars.

Adhesion

(a) Attach to cytoskeleton (to maintain cell-shape and stabilize proteins) and/or the extracellular matrix (integrins connect to both).

(b) Extracellular matrix—protein fibres and carbohydrates secreted by cells and fills the spaces between cells and supports cells in a tissue.

(c) Extracellular matrix can influence activity inside the cell and coordinate the behaviour of all the cells in a tissue.

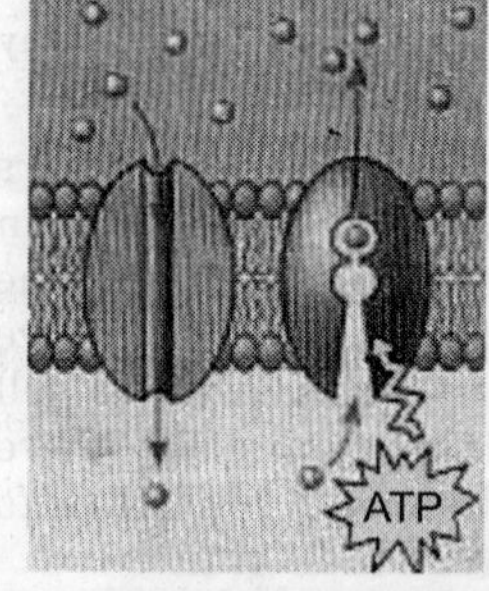

Fig. 4.9 Channel and carrier proteins

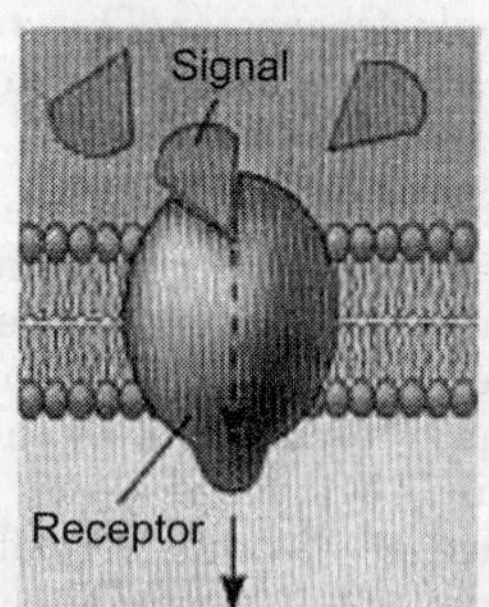

Fig. 4.10 Receptor proteins

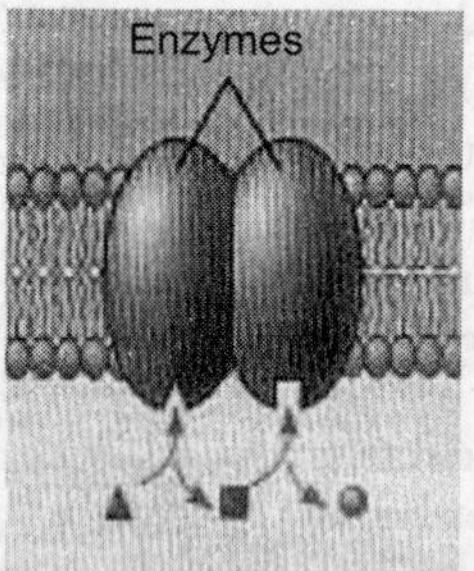

Fig. 4.11 Enzymatic proteins

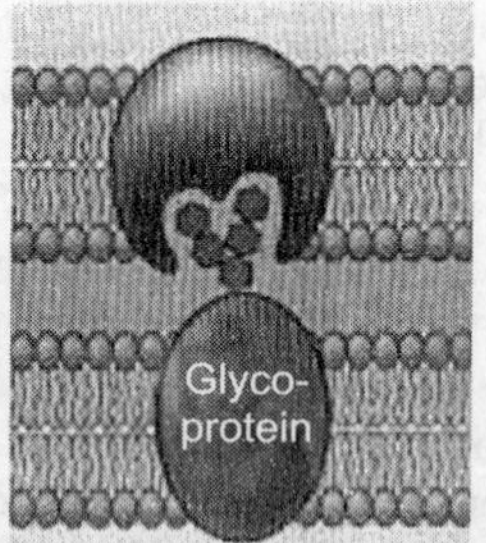

Fig. 4.12 Cell recognition proteins

Fig. 4.13 Attachment proteins

Intercellular Junction Proteins

These proteins bind cells together:

(a) **Tight Junctions** Transmembrane proteins of opposite cells attach in a tight zipper-like fashion, no leakage is found. For example–intestine, kidneys, epithelium of skin.

(b) **Desmosomes** Cytoplasmic plaques of two cells bind with the aid of intermediate filaments of keratin, it allows stretching. For example–stomach, bladder, heart.

(c) **Gap Junctions** Channel proteins of opposite cells join together providing channels for ions, sugars, amino acids and other small molecules to pass, it allows communication between cells. For example–heart muscle, animal embryos.

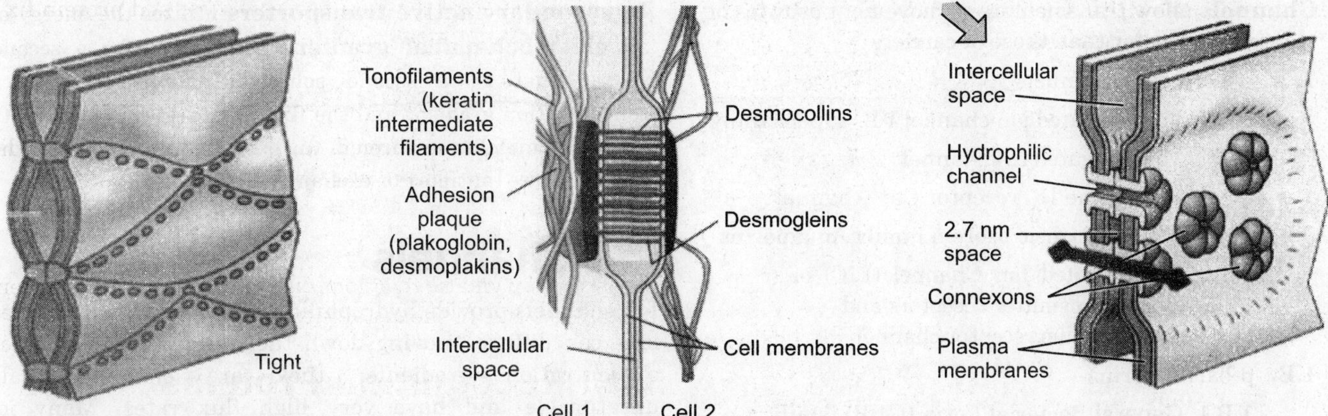

Fig. 4.14 Tight junction proteins **Fig. 4.15** Desmosome proteins **Fig. 4.16** Gap junction proteins

Gap junctions are a means of communication. Whereas tight junctions and desmosomes have mechanical roles, gap junctions facilitate communication between cells. Each gap junction is made up of specialized protein channels, called **connexins,** that span the plasma membranes of two adjacent cells and the intercellular space between them. Dissolved molecules and electric signals can pass from cell to cell through these junctions.

Osmosis

Osmosis is the diffusion of water molecules (solvent) across a selectively permeable membrane. Water will diffuse from a region of its higher concentration (lower concentration of solutes) to a region of its lower concentration (higher concentration of solutes). When water moves into a body by osmosis, hydrostatic pressure or osmotic pressure may build up inside the body.

Terms are used to compare the solute concentrations of two solutions separated by a membrane:

1. **Isotonic** solutions have equal solute concentrations.
2. **Hypertonic** solution has a higher solute concentration than the other solution with which it is being compared.
3. **Hypotonic** solution has a lower solute concentration than the other solution with which it is being compared.

In bacteria and plants, the plasma membrane is surrounded by a non-expandable cell wall of sufficient rigidity and strength to resist osmotic pressure and prevent osmotic lysis.

Certain freshwater protists that live in a highly hypotonic medium have contractile vacuole that pumps water out of the cell.

In multicellular animals, blood plasma and interstitial fluid are maintained at an osmolarity close to that of the cytosol.

The high concentration of albumin and other proteins in blood plasma contributes to its osmolarity. Cells also actively pump out ions such as Na^+ into the interstitial fluid to stay in osmotic balance with their surroundings.

Passive transport is always down an electrochemical gradient, toward equilibrium. Active transport is against an electrochemical gradient and requires an input of energy.

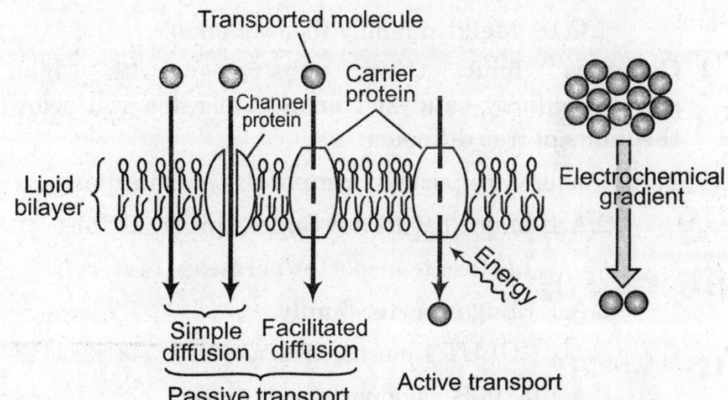

Fig. 4.17 Transportation of molecules of ions membrane

Uniport system moves one type of molecule bidirectionally.

In **cotransport** systems, the transfer of one solute depends upon the stoichiometric simultaneous or sequential transfer of another solute.

Uniport system moves one type of molecule bidirectionally.

A **symport** moves these solutes in the same direction. For example, proton-sugar transporter in bacteria and the Na^+–sugar transporters (for glucose and certain other sugars) and Na^+–amino acid transporters in mammalian cells.

Antiport systems move two molecules in opposite directions (*e.g.*, Na^+ in and Ca^{2+} out).

Classification of Transporters

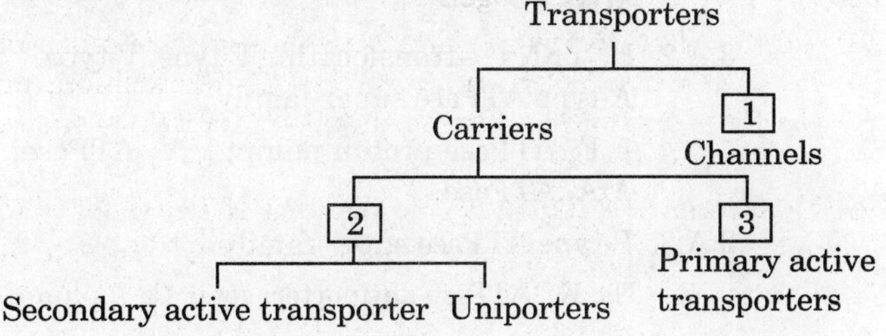

1. **Channels** allow transmembrane movement at rates of magnitude greater than those of carriers

1. A. α-helix type channels

1.A.1. Voltage-gated ion channel VIC super-family Voltage-gated K^+ channel

1.A.3. Ryanodine/IP_3 receptor Ca^{2+} channel

1.A.8. Major intrinsic protein family Aquaporins

1.A.9. Ligand-gated Ion Channel (LIC) of neurotransmitter receptors and acetylcholine receptor/channel

1.B. β-barrel porins

1.B.1. General Bacterial Porin (GBP) family

1.C. Pore-forming toxins

1.C.7. Diphtheria toxin family

1.C.18. Mellitin family (bee venoms)

2. **Carriers** bind their substrates with high stereospecificity, catalyze transport at rates well below the limits of free diffusion

2. A. Porters: uniporters, symporters and antiporters

2.A.1. Major Facilitator Super-family (MFS) Lactose transporter/permease of *E. coli*

2.A.1.1 Sugar porter family GLUT 1 glucose transporter of erythrocyte

2.A.1.9. P_i-H^+ symporter

2.A.12. ATP-ADP antiporter (AAA) family

2.A.13. C_4-dicarboxylate uptake (Dcu) family

2.A.21. Solute-Na^+ symporter (SSS) family Na^+-glucose symporter in epithelial cells

2.A.73. HCO_3^- transporters $HCO_3^- - Cl^-$ antiporter

2.B. Non-ribosomally synthesized porters

2.B.1. Valinomycin carrier family Valinomycin

3. **Primary active transporters** there is a direct coupling to a reaction such as the hydrolysis of ATP to 'pump' the solute across the membrane.

3. A. Diphosphate bond hydrolysis-driven transporters (use PP_i, not ATP)

3.A.1. ATP-binding cassette (ABC) super-family CFTR Cl^- channel; multidrug transporter MDR1

3.A.2. H^+ or Na^+ –translocating F-type, V-type, A-type ATPase super-family

F_0F_1 ATPase proton pump; V_0V_1 ATPase; A_0A_1 ATPase

3.A.3. P-type ATPase super-family Na^+K^+ ATPase antiporter; serca Ca^{2+} pump.

In secondary active transporters utilizes the energy of an **electrochemical gradient** established for a second solute; that is, a second solute is pumped against a concentration gradient and the first solute is then allowed to cross the membrane through an exchange process with the second solute (antiport or exchange diffusion).

Ion Channels

Ion channels provide hydrophilic pores through which select ions can diffuse, moving down their electrical or chemical concentration gradients; they are characteristically unsaturable and have very high flux rates. Many ion channels are highly specific for one ion and most are gated by either voltage or a ligand.

In bacterial K^+ channels, a selectivity filter provides ligands are voltage gated. The acetylcholine receptor/channel is gated by acetylcholine, which triggers subtle conformational changes that open and close the transmembrane path.

Ion channels, together with in pumps such as the Na^+ K^+ ATPase, determine a plasma membrane's permeability to specific ions and regulate the cytosolic concentration of ions and the membane potential.

Properties Characterize Ion Channels

(i) Ion channels can be highly selective for particular ions.

(ii) Ion channels exist in open and closed states.

(iii) Most cells have a variety of Na^+, K^+, Ca^{2+} and Cl^- channels.

(iv) Open states of channels often spontaneously convert into inactivated conformation.

(v) Transitions between the open and the closed states are regulated. Ion channels are divided into two classes: Ligand-gated channels and voltage-gated channels. Ligand-gated channels open and close in response to the binding of specific chemicals, whereas voltage-gated channels open and close in response to the electrical potential across the membrane.

Most organisms contain a large number of ion channels. One of these, which plays a key role in nerve conduction, is the **voltage-gated K^+ channel.** It is closed most of the time but opens when a nerve impulse arrives, dropping the membrane potential from its resting –50 to –70 mV (negative inside) value to below zero. This voltage change opens the channel, allowing a very rapid outflow of K^+ ions. The channels then close spontaneously. The conduction channel is lined largely with hydrophobic groups.

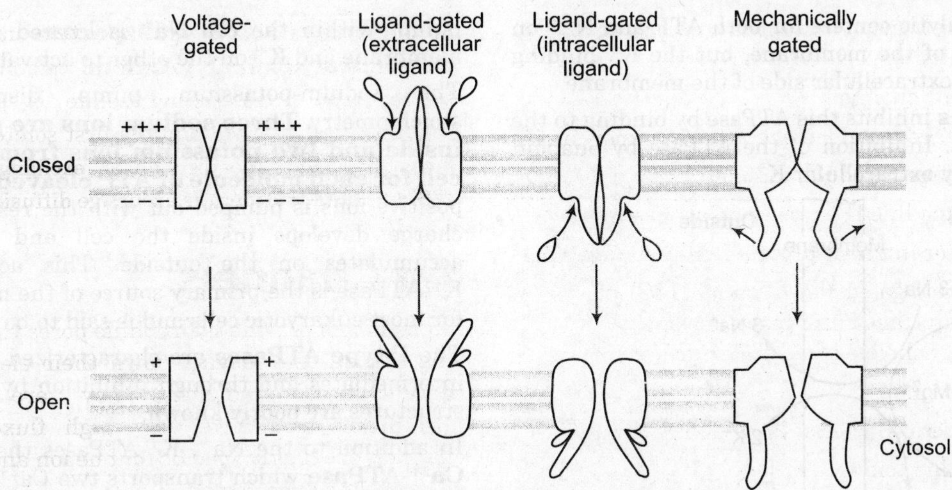

Fig. 4.18 Ion channels open in response to special stimulus

- **Ionophores** Certain microbes synthesize small organic molecules, ionophores, that function as shuttles for the movement of ions across membranes. These ionophores contain hydrophilic centers that bind specific ions and are surrounded by peripheral hydrophobic regions; this arrangement allows the molecules to dissolve effectively in the membrane and diffuse transversely therein. Example polypeptide gramicidin, form channels.
- **Aquaporins** In certain cells (*e.g.*, red cells, cells of the collecting ductuless of the kidney), the movement of water by simple diffusion is augmented by movement through water channels. These channels are composed of tetrameric transmembrane proteins named aquaporins. A family of integral proteins discovered by **Peter Agre**, the **aquaporins** (AQPs), provide channels for rapid movement of water molecules across all plasma membranes.

These are distinguished from ion transporters in atleast three ways :

First, the rate of flux through channels can be several orders of magnitude greater than the turnover number for a transporter.

Second, ion channels are not saturable: rates do not approach a maximum at high substrate concentration.

Third, they are 'gated'—opened or closed in response to some cellular event.

1. **Ligand-Gated Channel** (generally oligomeric), binding of an extracellular or intracellular small molecule forces an allosteric transition in the protein, which opens or closes the channel.
2. **Voltage-Gated Ion Channels,** a change in transmembrane electrical potential (V_m) causes a charged protein domain to move relative to the membrane, opening or closing the ion channel.

Both types of gating can be very fast. A channel typically opens in a fraction of a millisecond and may remain open for only milliseconds, making these molecular devices effective for very fast signal transmission in the nervous system.

Table 4.3 **Some Diseases Resulting from Ion Channel Defects**

Ion Channel	Disease
Na^+ (voltage-gated and skeletal muscle)	Hyperkalemic periodic paralysis or paramyotonia congenita
Na^+ (voltage-gated and neuronal)	Generalized epilepsy with febrile seizures
Na^+ (voltage-gated and cardiac muscle)	Long QT syndrome 3
Ca^{2+} (neuronal)	Familial hemiplegic migraine
Ca^{2+} (voltage-gated and retina)	Congenital stationary night blindness
Ca^{2+} (polycystin-1)	Polycystic kidney disease
K^+ (neuronal)	Dominant deafness
K^+ (voltage-gated and neuronal)	Benign familian neonatal convulsions
Non-specification (cGMP-gated and retinal)	Retinitis pigmentosa
Acetylcholine receptor (skeletal muscle)	Congenital myasthenic syndrome
Cl^-	Cystic fibrosis

Active Transport

In active transport molecules are transported away from thermodynamic equilibrium; hence, **energy is required.** This energy come from the hydrolysis of ATP, from **electron movement** or from **light.** The maintenance of electrochemical gradients in biological systems is so important that it consumes almost 30-40% of the total energy expenditure in a cell.

In general, cells maintain a low intracellular Na^+ concentration and a high intracellular K^+ concentration, along with a net negative electrical potential inside. The pump that maintains these gradients is an **ATPase** that is activated by Na^+ and K^+. The ATPase is an integral membrane protein and requires phospholipids for activity.

The ATPase has catalytic centers for both ATP and Na^+ on the cytoplasmic side of the membrane, but the K^+ binding site is located on the extracellular side of the membrane.

Ouabain or **digitalis** inhibits this ATPase by binding to the extracellular domain. Inhibition of the ATPase by ouabain can be antagonized by extracellular K^+.

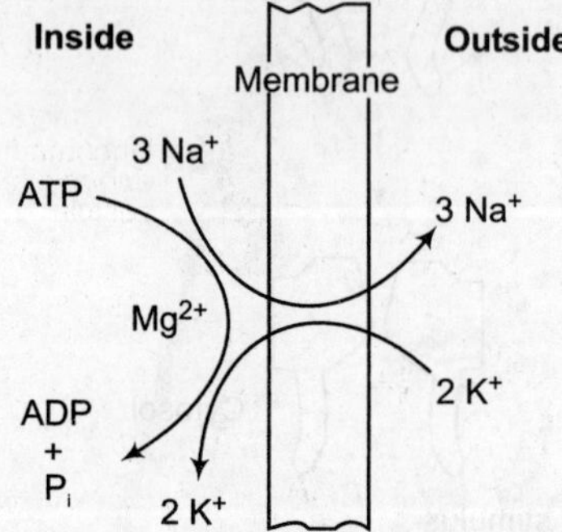

Fig. 4.19 The Na^+-K^+ ATPase pump. This pump moves three Na^+ ions from inside the cell to the outside and brings two K^+ ions from the outside to the inside for every molecule of ATP hydrolyzed to ADP by the membrane associated ATPase

Table 4.4 **Comparison of Various Molecules Outside and Inside a Mammalian Cell**

Substance	Extracellular Fluid	Intracellular Fluid
Na^+	140 mmol/L	10 mmol/L
K^+	4 mmol/L	140 mmol/L
Ca^{2+} (free)	2.5 mmol/L	0.1 mmol/L
Mg^{2+}	1.5 mmol/L	30 mmol/L
Cl^-	100 mmol/L	4 mmol/L
HCO_3^-	27 mmol/L	10 mmol/L
PO_4^{3-}	2 mmol/L	60 mmol/L
Glucose	5.5 mmol/L	0-1 mmol/L
Protein	2 g/dL	16 g/dL

Ion Pumps

Cells have an active **ion pump** that removes Na^+ from cells and introduces K^+. For example, the cytoplasm of the giant axons of nerves of squid can be squeezed out and replaced by ionic solutions.

An ($Na^+ + K^+$) activated ATPase (often abbreviated Na^+, K^+-ATPase) as synonymous with the membrane-bound ion pump. Within the cell Na^+ is located on one side of the membrane and K^+ on the other to activate this enzyme.

The sodium-potassium pump displays a curious stoichiometry. **Three sodium ions are pumped from the inside and two potassium ions from the outside of a cell for each molecule of ATP cleaved.** Thus, an excess of positive ions is pumped out with the result that a negative charge develops inside the cell and a positive charge accumulates on the outside. This action of the Na^+, K^+-ATPase is the primary source of the membrane potential for most eukaryotic cells and is said to be **electrogenic.**

The **P-type ATPases** are characterized by phosphoenzyme intermediates and through inhibition by vanadate ion. The structures are poorly known.

In addition to the Na^+, K^+-ATPases there is a very active **Ca^{2+}-ATPase** which transports two Ca^{2+} from the inside of cells to the outside while returning two H^+ from outside per ATP.

Mechanism of Sorting and Regulation of Intracellular Transport

There is considerable intracellular traffic of proteins. The Golgi apparatus plays a major role in the sorting of proteins for their correct destinations. The protein biosynthetic pathways in cells can be considered to be **one large sorting system.** Many proteins carry **signals** (sequences of amino acids) that direct them to their destination.

The entire pathway of ER, Golgi apparatus, plasma membrane is often called the **secretory** or **exocytotic pathway.** Golgi apparatus or the plasma membrane are carried in **transport vesicles;** a brief description of the formation of these important particles will be given subsequently. Other proteins destined for secretion are carried in **secretory vesicles** proteins that are transported by vesicles are called the **cargo.** These are prominent in the pancreas and certain other glands. Their mobilization and discharge are regulated and often referred to as **regulated secretion,** whereas the secretory pathway involving transport vesicles is called **constitutive light.**

Translocation is occur **post-translationally,** after the matrix proteins are released from the cytosolic polyribosomes. Interactions with a number of cytosolic proteins that act as **chaperones** (Protein foling machineries) RER and as targeting factors occur prior to translocation.

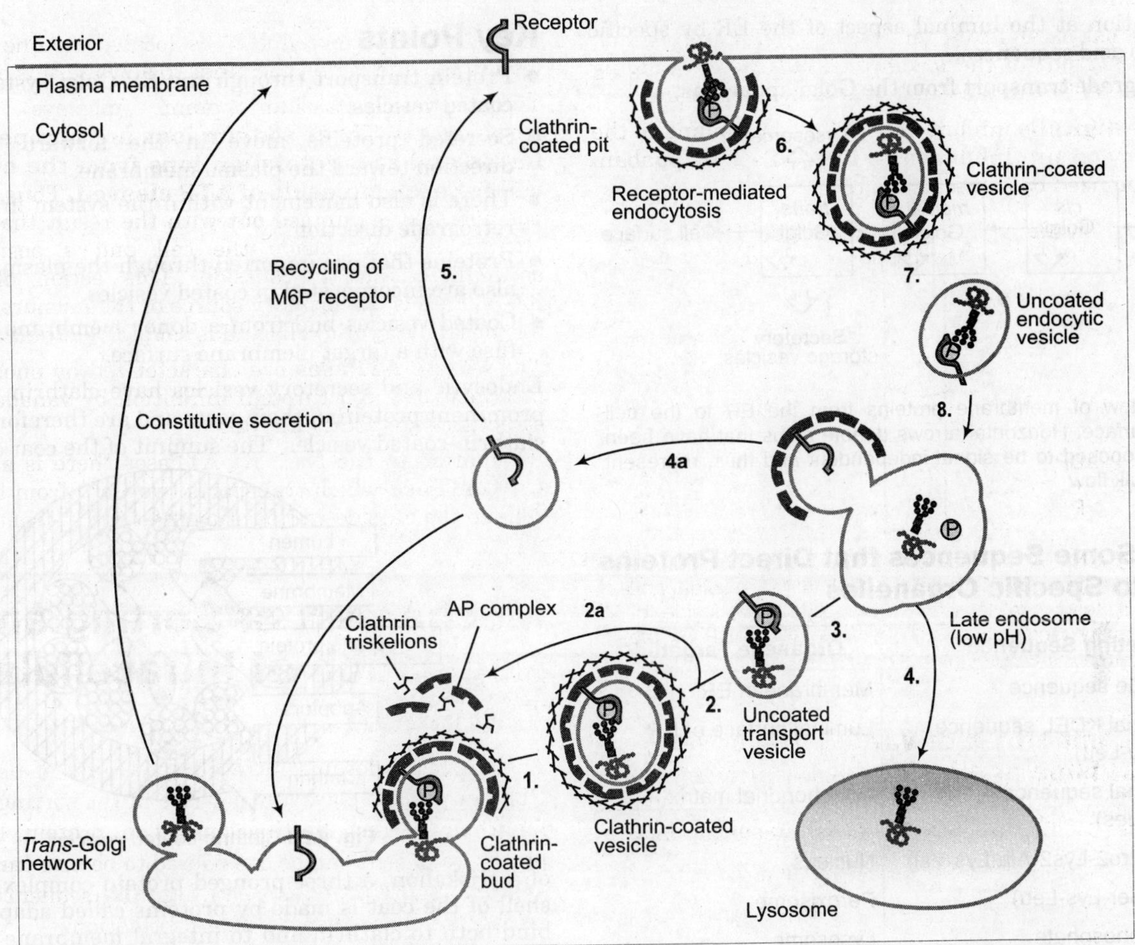

Fig. 4.20 Diagrammatic representation of the rough endoplasmic reticulum branch of protein sorting

The **signal hypothesis** was proposed by **Blobel** and **Sabatini** to explain the distinction between free and membrane-bound polyribosomes. They found that proteins synthesized on membrane-bound polyribosomes contained a peptide extension (signal peptide) at their amino terminals which mediated their attachment to the membranes of the ER. The *m*RNA for secreted protein encodes an amino terminal **signal peptide** (leader sequence). The protein is inserted into the ER membrane at the same time as its *m*RNA is being translated on polyribosomes, so-called **co-translational insertion.** As the signal peptide emerges from the large subunit of the ribosome, it is recognized by a **signal recognition particle** (SRP). The SRP contains six proteins and has a 7 S RNA associaosely related to the Alu family of highly repeated DNA sequences. The SRP-impose block until the SRP-signal peptide-polyribosome complex has bound to the so-called **docking protein** (SRP-R, a receptor for the SRP) on the ER membrane; the SRP thus, guides the signal peptide to the SRP-R and prevents premature folding and expulsion of the protein being synthesized into the cytosol.

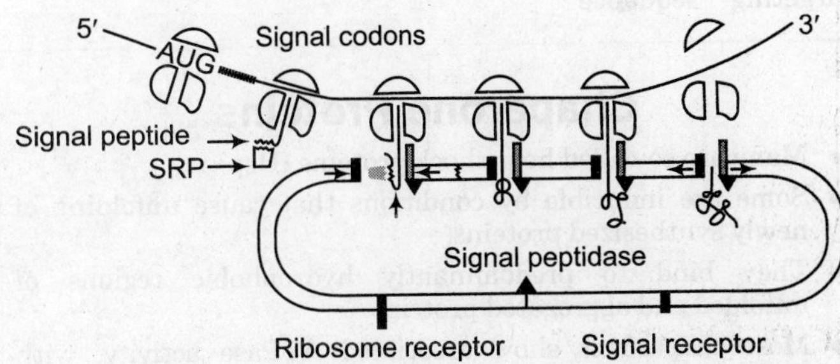

Fig. 4.21 Diagram of the signal hypothesis for the transport of secreted proteins across the ER membrane

The insertion of the signal peptide into the conducting channel, while the other end of the parent protein is still attached to ribosomes, is termed **co-translational insertion.**

Routes of Proteins Assembly

Proteins follow several routes to be inserted into or attached to the membranes of the endoplasmic reticulum:

(i) Co-translational insertion.

(ii) Synthesis on free polyribosomes and subsequent attachment to the ER membrane.

(iii) Retention at the luminal aspect of the ER by specific amino acid sequences.

(iv) Retrograde transport from the Golgi apparatus.

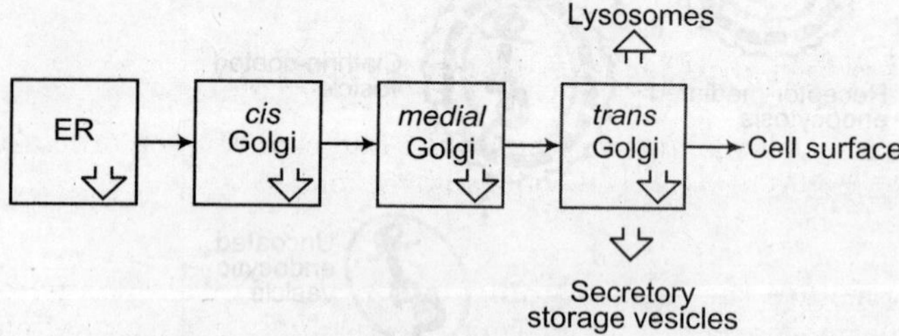

Fig. 4.22 Flow of membrane proteins from the ER to the cell surface. Horizontal arrows denote steps that have been proposed to be signal independent and thus, represent bulk flow

Table 4.5 **Some Sequences that Direct Proteins to Specific Organelles**

Targeting Sequence	Organelle Targeted
Signal peptide sequence	Membrane of ER
Amino terminal KDEL sequence (Lys-Asp-Glu-Leu)	Luminal surface of ER
Amino terminal sequence (20-80 residues)	Mitochondrial matrix
NLS* (*e.g.*, Pro2-Lys2-Ala-Lys-Val)	Nucleus
PTS* (*e.g.*, Ser-Lys-Leu)	Peroxisome
Mannose-6-phosphate	Lysosome

* NLS, nuclear localization signal; PTS, peroxisomal-matrix targeting sequence

Chaperone Proteins

- Many are so-called heat shock proteins (Hsp).
- Some are inducible by conditions that cause unfolding of newly synthesized proteins.
- They bind to predominantly hydrophobic regions of unfolded and aggregated proteins.
- Most chaperones show associated ATPase activity, with ATP or ADP being involved in the protein-chaperone interaction.
- Found in various cellular compartments such as cytosol, mitochondria and the lumen of the endoplasmic reticulum.

Coated Vesicles

Vesicles are used to transport proteins both out of the cell and into the cell. The secretion of proteins is called **exocytosis;** internalization of proteins is called **endocytosis.** Proteins are transported in coated vesicles. Constitutive (bulk flow) transport from ER through the Golgi takes place by COP-coated vesicles. Clathrin coated vesicles are used for both regulated exocytosis and endocytosis.

Key Points

- Protein transport through the ER-Golgi system occurs in coated vesicles.
- Secreted proteins move in the forward, anterograde direction toward the plasma membrane.
- There is also movement within the system in the reverse, retrograde direction.
- Proteins that are imported through the plasma membrane also are incorporated in coated vesicles.
- Coated vesicles bud from a donor membrane surface and fuse with a target membrane surface.

Endocytic and secretory vesicles have clathrin as the most prominent protein in their coats and are therefore, known as clathrin-coated vesicles. The subunit of the coat consists

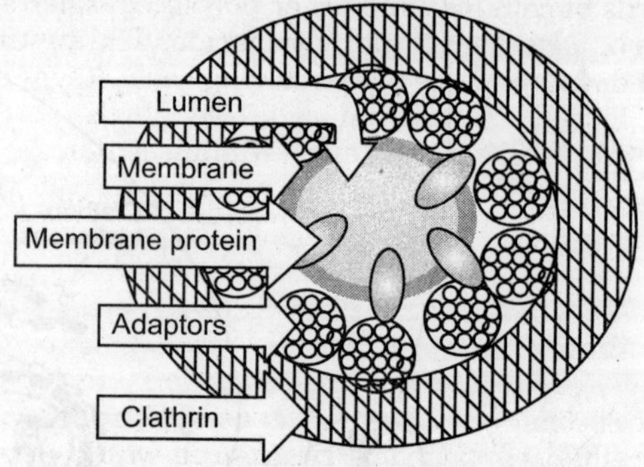

Fig. 4.23 Clathrin-coated vesicles

of a triskelion, a three-pronged protein complex. The inner shell of the coat is made by proteins called adaptors, which bind both to clathrin and to integral membrane proteins of the vesicle.

The inner shell of the coat is made by proteins called adaptors, which bind both to clathrin and to integral membrane proteins of the vesicle. COP-I-coated vesicles are responsible for retrograde transport from the Golgi to the ER. COP-II vesicles undertake forward movement from the ER to Golgi.

In the pathway for regulated secretion of proteins, proteins are sorted into clathrin-coated vesicles at the Golgi *trans* face. Some vesicles may fuse into (larger) secretory granules. Vesicles also move to endosomes, which control trafficking to the cell surface. Secretory vesicles are stimulated to unload their cargos at the plasma membrane by extracellular signals. Similar vesicles are used for endocytosis, the pathway by which proteins are internalized from the cell surface.

Electrical Properties of Membranes

All animal cells are surrounded by a plasma membrane. The fluid on both sides of the membrane contains high concentrations of mobile ions, of which sodium (Na^+), potassium (K^+), chloride (Cl^-) and calcium (Ca^{2+}) are the most important. The membrane potential arises from the interaction of ion channels and ion pumps embedded in the membrane, which maintain different ion concentrations on the intracellular and extracellular sides of the membrane.

The membrane potential has two basic functions: first, it provides power to operate a variety of 'molecular devices' embedded in the membrane; second, in electrically excitable cells such as neurons, it is used for transmitting signals between different parts of a cell. Opening or closing of ion channels in the membrane produces a local change in the membrane potential, which causes electric current to flow rapidly to other points in the membrane.

Structure and Function of Intracellular Organelles

The eukaryotic cell is composed of a number of organells some of which are membrane bound (like mitochondria) chloroplast, nucleus, ER, Golgi body) while other are non-membranous. The plant cells also has cell walls and vacuoles.

Cell Wall

The thick wall of higher plant cell provide strength and rigidity to plants and, at the same time, allow rapid elongation during periods of growth. The cell wall contains microfibrils of cellulose and other polysaccharides embedded in a matrix, also largely polysaccharide. The **primary cell wall** laid down in green plants during early stages of growth contains loosely interwoven cellulose fibrils ~ 10 nm in diameter and with an ~ 4 nm crystalline center.

The **microfibrils** in green plants are most often cellulose but may contain other polysaccharides as well. Some algae are rich in fibrils of xylan and mannan. The materials present in the matrix phase vary with the growth period of the plant. During initial phases **pectin** (polygalacturonic acid derivatives) predominate but later xylans and a variety of other polysaccharides known as **crosslinking glycans** (or hemicelluloses) appear. Primary cell wall constituents of dicotyledons include **xyloglucans** (linear glucan chains with xylose, galactose and fucose units in branches). The xyloglycans, which comprise 20% of the cell wall in some plants, have a backbone of α-1,4-linked glucose units with numerous α-1, 6-linked xylose rings.

Pectins form a porous gel on the inside surface of plant cell walls. A major component is a **homogalacturonan,** which consists of α-1, 4-linked galacturonic acid (GalA). A second is rhamnogalacturonan I, an alternating polymer of (2-L-Rhaα1 4GalAα) units. The most interesting pectin component is **rhamnogalacturonan II,** one of the less abundant constituents of pectin. Calcium and magnesium pectate form middle lamella of plant cell wall.

The principal cell wall components of plants are carbohydrates, proteins account for 5-10% of the mass. Predominant among these are glycoprotein **extensins.** Like collagen, they are rich in 4-hydroxyproline which is glycosylated with arabinose oligosaccharides and galactose. During advanced stages as the walls harden into wood, large amounts of **lignins** are laid down in some plant cells.

The effect of the **gibberellins** cause very rapid elongation of plant cell wall may depend to some extent upon chemical cleavage and reforming of crosslinking polysaccharides. It is mediated by proteins called **expansins**, is the ability of plant tissues to extend rapidly when incubated in a mildly acidic buffer of pH < 5.5. Expansins are also involved in ripening of fruit. They may disrupt non-covalent bonding between cellulose fibrils and the hemicelluloses. The β-expansins of grasses are allergens found in grass pollens.

Plasmodesmata are cytoplasmic channels through relatively large pores in the cell wall allowing fusion of plasma membranes from two adjacent cells. A single tubular structure the **desmotubule** lies in the central channel of plasmodesmata. Endoplasmic recticulum cisterna often approach the plasmodesmata on either side and make connection between cells. The ring of cytoplasm between desmotubule and membrane that lines the plasmodesmata is called **annulus.** Calcium appears to regulate movement through plasmodesmata.

Nucleus

The nucleus was described in more detail in 1831 by Scottish botanist **Robert Brown.** The nucleus is the largest cellular organelle in animals. The presence of a nucleus is the principal feature that distinguishes eukaryotic from prokaryotic cells. Prokaryotes have nuclear region in the cytoplasm which is called **nucleoid.** While the eukaryotes have double membrane envelops nucleus.

Bacterial Genome

The bacterial nucleoid is ~80% DNA by mass and can be unfolded by agents that act on RNA or protein. The proteins that are responsible for condensing the DNA have not been identified. Several DNA-binding proteins with a superficial resemblance to eukaryotic chromosomal proteins have been isolated in *E. coli*. **Protein HU** is a dimer that condenses DNA, possibly wrapping it into a bead-like structure. **Protein HI** (also known as H-NS) binds DNA, interacting preferentially with sequences that are bent.

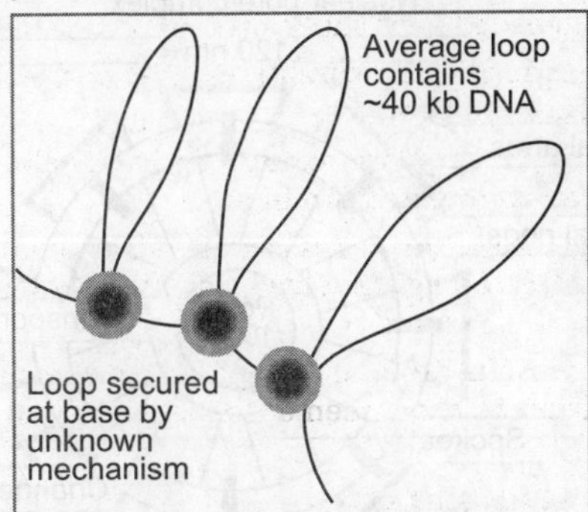

Fig. 4.24 Bacterial nucleoid

The bacterial genome is supercoiled. The nucleoid has ~100 independently negatively supercoiled domains. The supercoiling in each domain is not affected by events in the other domains. The average density of supercoiling is — 1 turn/100 bp.The supercoiling in each domain is not affected by events in the other domains. Supercoiling is an important feature of transcription.

The first evidence for the presence of genes outside the nucleus was provided by non-Mendelian inheritance in plants. It is the failure of the progeny of a mating to display Mendelian segregation for parental characters. Non-Mendelian inheritance results from the presence in mitochondria and chloroplasts of DNA genomes that are inherited independently of nuclear genes.

The nuclear fluid present in nucleus is called **nucleoplasm.** The nuclear envelope which cover the nucleus contains **nuclear pores.** The pore is enclosed by circular structure called **annuli.** The pore and annuli together constitute **nuclear pore complex** that control the passage of molecules in and out of the nucleus.

Nuclear Pore Complex

The nuclear pore is an annular structure with 8-folds symmetry. There are matching annuli at the outer and inner membranes, comprising the surfaces that project into the cytosol and into the nucleus and each is connected to the spokes, which form a central ring. Proteins are transported through the central pore. The **Nuclear Localization Signal** (NLS) and **NES** (nuclear export signal) consist of short sequences that are necessary and sufficient for proteins to be transported through the pores into or out of the nucleus. A protein may have both an NLS and an NES, the former used for its import into the nucleus and the latter for its export. Exportins transport substrates from nucleus to cytoplasm; importins transport substrates from cytoplasm to nucleus. Exportins and importins interact with nucleoporins in the pore. Transport can be divided into two stages: **docking,** which consists of binding to the pore; and **translocation,** which consists of movement through it. Translocation through the pore is inhibited by wheat germ agglutinin, a lectin (glycoprotein). The component proteins of the pore that bind to lectins were originally called **nucleoporins.**

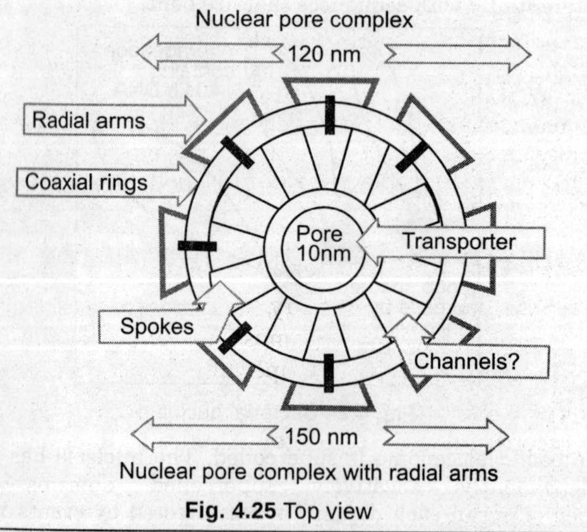

Fig. 4.25 Top view

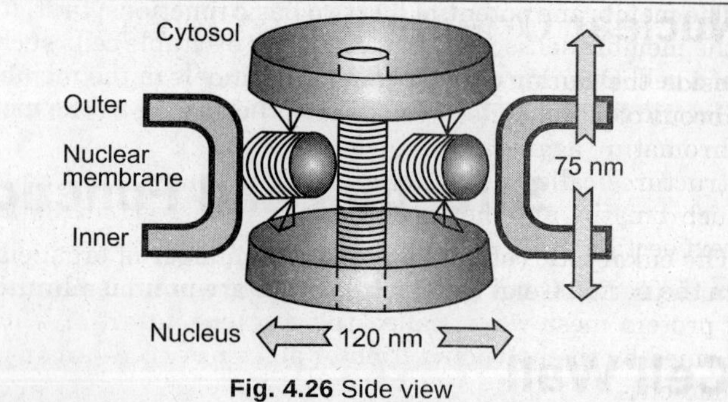

Fig. 4.26 Side view

RNA is exported by several systems. There are (at least) three export systems for RNA. Each consists of an exportin that binds particular types of RNA. Nuclear pore complex providing a channel for bidirectional transport of molecules and macromolecules between the nucleus and the cytosol. The nuclear pores are used for both import and export of material.

Import	Histones
	Non-histone proteins
	Ribosomal proteins
Export	Ribosomal subunits
	*m*RNA

Ribosomal proteins assemble with the *r*RNA in nucleolus, they first imported protein into the nucleus. So ribosomal proteins shuttle into the nucleus as free proteins and out into cytoplasm again as assembled ribosomal subunits. The central channel is large enough to allow proteins of 5-5O kD to pass.

The condensed state of DNA due to binding with basic proteins. The positive charges of proteins neutralize the negative charges of the DNA. Thus, structure of the nucleoprotein complex is determined by the interactions of the proteins with the DNA (or RNA).

Nucleolus

The **nucleolus** is a dense, spherical-shaped structure present inside the nucleus. Some eukaryotic organisms contains up to four nucleoli. The nucleolus plays an indirect role in protein synthesis by producing ribosomes. Ribosomes are cell organelles made up of RNA and proteins; they are transported to the cytoplasm. Ribosomes are the protein-producing structures of a cell. Nucleolus disappears when a cell undergoes division and is reformed after the completion of cell division. It was discovered by **Fontana** in 1781 and nucleolus was termed by **Bowman** (1840). Nucleoli are formed around specific genetic loci called **Nucleolar Organizing Regions** (NORs), first described by **Barbara** McClintock. A NOR is composed of tandem repeats of *r*RNA genes, which can be found in several different chromosomes. The human genome contains more than 200 clustered copies of the *r*RNA genes on five different chromosomes (13, 14, 15, 21, 22).

Nuclear Orientation of DNA

Inside the nucleus, DNA combines with proteins to form a fibrous complex called **chromatin**. Prior to cell division, the chromatin aggregates to form discrete, readily visible structures called **chromosomes**. Chromatin is divided into euchromatin and heterochromatin (discussed in detail in next section).

At the periphery of the nucleus, the chromatin is attached to a protein mesh-work, called the **nuclear lamina,** which is formed by the polymerization of proteins called **lamins** into filaments.

Eukaryotic DNA

Eukaryotic DNA has loops and domains attached to a scaffold. DNA of interphase chromatin is negatively supercoiled into independent domains of ~85 kb. Metaphase chromosomes have a protein scaffold to which the loops of supercoiled DNA are attached. The overall compression of the DNA can be described by the packing ratio, the length of the DNA divided by the length of the unit that contains it. Ethidium bromide intercalates between base pairs to generate positive superhelical turns in 'closed' circular DNA molecules. Supercoiling measured by the response to ethidium bromide corresponds to about one negative supercoil/200 bp. These supercoils can be removed by nicking with DNAase, although the DNA remains in the form of the 10 nm fibre. The protein-depleted chromosomes take the form of a central **scaffold** surrounded by a halo of DNA. DNA sites attached to proteinaceous structures in interphase nuclei are called **MAR** (Matrix Attachment Regions); they are sometimes also called **SAR** (Scaffold Attachment Regions). The MARs are A-T rich but do not have any specific consensus sequence.

A eukaryotic chromosome is held on the mitotic spindle by the attachment of microtubules to the kinetochore (centromeric region). Centromeres often have heterochromatin that is rich in satellite DNA sequences. The sites in the two regions, where, microtubule ends are organized—in the vicinity of the centrioles at the poles and at the chromosomes—are called MTOCs (Microtubule Organizing Centers). Chromosomes are pulled to the poles *via* microtubules that attach at the centromeres. The sister chromatids are held together until anaphase by glue proteins (cohesins).

Centromeres have short DNA sequences in *S. cerevisiae.* A CEN fragment is identified as the minimal sequence that have the ability to allow a plasmid to segregate accurately at mitosis. CEN elements consists of short conserved sequences CDE-I and CDE-III that flank the A-T-rich region CDE-II. They are used only to attach the chromosome to the spindle and play no role in distinguishing one chromosome from another.

Telomeres have simple repeating sequences. It is required for the stability of the chromosome end and consists of a simple repeat, where a C+A rich strand has the sequence $C_{>7}(A/T)_{1-4}$.

Chromosomes Banding Patterns

Centromeric heterochromatin is can be visualized by a technique in which all the centromeres show as darkly staining regions. It is called **C-bands**. Certain staining techniques cause the chromosomes to have the appearance of a series bands. The bands are lower in G-C content than the interbands. Genes are concentrated in the G-Crich interbands.

When chromosomes subjected to certain treatments and then stained with the chemical dye Giemsa, chromosomes generate a series of transverse bands **G-bands.** (shown in figure)

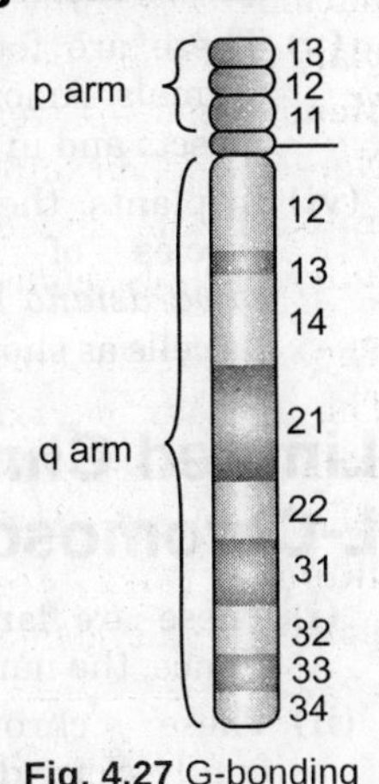

Fig. 4.27 G-bonding

Special Type of Chromosomes

Lampbrush Chromosomes The Lampbrush chromosomes are present in primary oocyte nuclei of vertebrate, invertebrate and spermatocyte nuclei of fruitfly. It has a length of 800-1000 μ. Lampbrush chromosome is made up of two homologous chromosomes held at several places by chiasmata. Each chromosome has an axis with alternate chromomeres and interchromatic area. From each chromomeres there arise 1-9 loops in pairs. This loop is made up of DNA. Due to pairs of loops these chromosome appears like Lampbrush. Sites of gene expression on Lampbrush chromosomes show loops that are extended from the chromosomal axis. These chromosomes form a large number of nucleoli but their significance is unknown.

Polytene Chromosomes (Salivary Gland Chromosomes) It was discovered by **Balbiani** (1881) in the salivary gland of *Chironomus tantans*. It is present in salivary glands (and Malpighian tubules) of many insect larvae. In plant it is found in the antipodal cell, suspensor cells and endosperm. Salivary gland chromosome is up to 2000μ (2 mm) in size. These chromosome show distinct dark and light bands. These chromosome form **puffs or loops** which are called **Balbiani puffs or Balbiani rings** where synthesis of *m*RNA occurs. The name polytene was given by **Kollar.** The polytene chromosome is formed by somatic pairing of homologous chromosomes followed by repeated replication or endomitosis.

Accessory or B-Chromosomes

(i) These are unnecessary, unwanted chromosomes genetically or the chromosomes which simply inner chromosome number (supernumerary) in a genome.

(ii) Their effect on phenotype of an individual is not recorded hence, called **genetically unnecessary.**

(iii) These chromosomes are smaler than normal chromosomes and their number varies from individual, *i.e.,* not constant in all the individuals of a species.

(iv) Supernumerary chromosomes are non-homologous to any of the normal chromosome and do not form synapse with them. These, however can form synapse among themselves.

(v) These are found more commonly in plants than in animals. Among animals, these are mostly reported in insects and in two species of flatworms.

(vi) In plants, these chromosomes are reported in several species of an angiosperms, *e.g.*, *Tradescantia edwardsiana* has five supernumerary chromosomes in its cells as shown below:

Limited Chromosomes of L-Chromosomes

(i) These are large and limited to germ line cell only. Hence, the name limited chromosome.

(ii) These chromosomes are reported in the family–Sciaridae of order–Diptera of insects.

(iii) These chromosomes differ from supernumerary chromosomes in that, these are constant to all individuals of a species having them, while supernumerary chromosomes are found only in some individuals.

M-Chromosomes or Minute Chromosomes

(i) These are so called because of their extremely small size, *i.e.*, 0.5 μ or less.

(ii) These are normally seen during meiosis but occassionally during mitosis.

(iii) These chromosomes are present in all the individuals of a species and as these can undergo pairing that's why not considered to be supernumerary chromosomes.

(iv) These are seen in bryophytes and bugs of family–Coreidae (order–Heteroptera, *i.e.*, with different wings) called rice bug.

S and E or Somatic and Eliminative Chromosomes

(i) These are present in both germ line as well as in somatic cells.

(ii) S-chromosomes are elimated from somatic cells and present in germ line cells only are called E-chromosomes.

(iii) The elimination takes place during the cleavage stages of embryo.

(iv) Such chromosomes are reported in insects of family–Coecidomyiidae (gall insects) and family–Chironomidae (order–Diptera).

Megachromosomes

(i) These are the chromosomes, which have their length up to 15 times the length of normal chromosomes.

(ii) These are normally described in the few species of *Nicotiana* hybrids.

(iii) The number of megachromosomes vary from 1 to 7 per cell in different individuals.

(iv) Megachromosomes are heterochromatic in nature, *i.e.*, these contain heterochromatin in them. These may have a single centromere or may be dicentric or acentric.

Mitochondria

Mitochondria is constituted of the following parts:

Outer membrane This is constituted of a semipermeable phospholipid bilayer, made of porins (protein structures). This layer is permeable to ions, ATP (adenosine triphosphate), ADP (adenosine diphosphate) and nutrient molecules.

Inner membrane This is a complex but permeable membrane made of complex molecules of electron transport system, ATP synthetase complex and transport proteins. This layer allows oxygen, water and carbon dioxide.

Cristae Cristae are in folds in inner membrane. This helps in increasing surface area of inner mitochondrial membrane.

Intermembrane space This is the space between outer membrane and inner membrane. Intermembrane space is primarily responsible for oxidative phosphorylation.

Cytoplasmic matrix Cytoplasmic matrix contains the DNA molecules of mitochondria (responsible for cellular respiration), enzymes (responsible for citric acid cycle reactions), dissolved gases (like oxygen, carbon dioxide), recyclable intermediates (serve as energy shuttles) and water.

Different parts of mitochondria have distinct marker enzymes for histochemical markings, such as **cytochrome oxidase** for inner membrane, **monoamine oxidase** for outer membrane, **malate dehydrogenase** for matrix and **adenylate kinase** for outer chamber.

Mitochondrial Genome

This genetic material of mitochondria is known as mitochondrial DNA or *mt*DNA. In humans, mitochondrial DNA spans about 16500 DNA building blocks (base pairs), representing a small fraction of the total DNA in cells. Mitochondrial DNA contains 37 genes, all of which are essential for normal mitochondrial function. Thirteen of these genes provide instructions for making enzymes involved in oxidative phosphorylation. The remaining genes provide instructions for making molecules called transfer RNA (*t*RNA) and ribosomal RNA (*r*RNA). These types of RNA help assemble protein building blocks (amino acids) into functioning proteins. Animal cell mitochondrial DNA is extremely compact and typically codes for 13 proteins, 2 *r*RNAs and 22 *t*RNAs. Yeast mitochondrial DNA is 5x longer than animal cell *mt*DNA because of the presence of long introns. Replication is by D-loop mechanism.

Table 4.6 **Comparison of Prokaryotes, Chloroplasts and Mitochondria with Eukaryotes**

Organelle	Prokaryote, Chloroplast and Mitochondria	Eukaryote
DNA	• Circular • Not contained in • chromosomes • Not contained in nucleus	• Linear • Contained in chromosomes • Contained in a nucleus
Ribosomes	Smaller (70 S)	Larger (80 S)
Sensitivity to antibiotics	Protein synthesis inhibited by chloramphenicol, not cycloheximide	Protein synthesis inhibited by cycloheximide
Average diameter	Prokaryotic cell: 0.5-3 μm Chloroplast: 3-5 μm Mitochondrion: 1μm	Eukaryote cell: 20 μm

Table 4.7 **Transport Systems of Inner Mitochondrial Membrane**

System	Exchange
Decarboxylate carrier	Exchange for mole-for-mole basis of malate, succinate, fumarate and phosphate between matrix and cytosol.
Tricarboxylate carrier	Exchange on mole-for-mole basis citrate and isocitrate between matrix and cytosol.

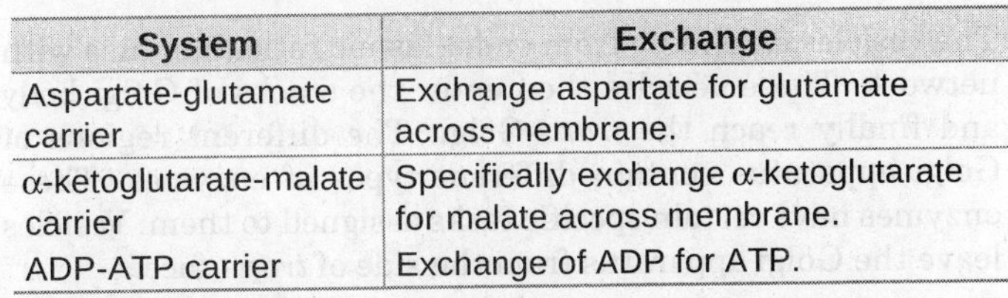

System	Exchange
Aspartate-glutamate carrier	Exchange aspartate for glutamate across membrane.
α-ketoglutarate-malate carrier	Specifically exchange α-ketoglutarate for malate across membrane.
ADP-ATP carrier	Exchange of ADP for ATP.

Functions

(a) **Glycolysis** The term 'glycolysis' itself means **Splitting sugar**. This is the first stage of cellular respiration. Products of glycolysis are two molecules of ATP, two molecules of pyruvic acid and two NADH (Nicotinamide adenine dinucleotide) molecules (which are electron carrying molecules).

(b) **Citric Acid Cycle** This is the second phase of cellular respiration. The intermediary reactions of this process yields ATP molecules of energy and NAD and FAD (flavin adenine dinucleotide) molecules. NAD and FAD molecules are further reduced in the Krebs' cycle to high energy electrons.

(c) **Electron Transport** The electron transport chain is constitute of a series of electron carriers generated in the membrane of the mitochondria, from Krebs' cycle. A eukaryotic cell produces about 36 ATP molecules after cellular respiration.

(d) Cell signaling for neurons.

(e) Role of mitochondria in apoptosis.

(f) Controlling cell cycle.

(g) Monitoring cell differentiation, growth and development.

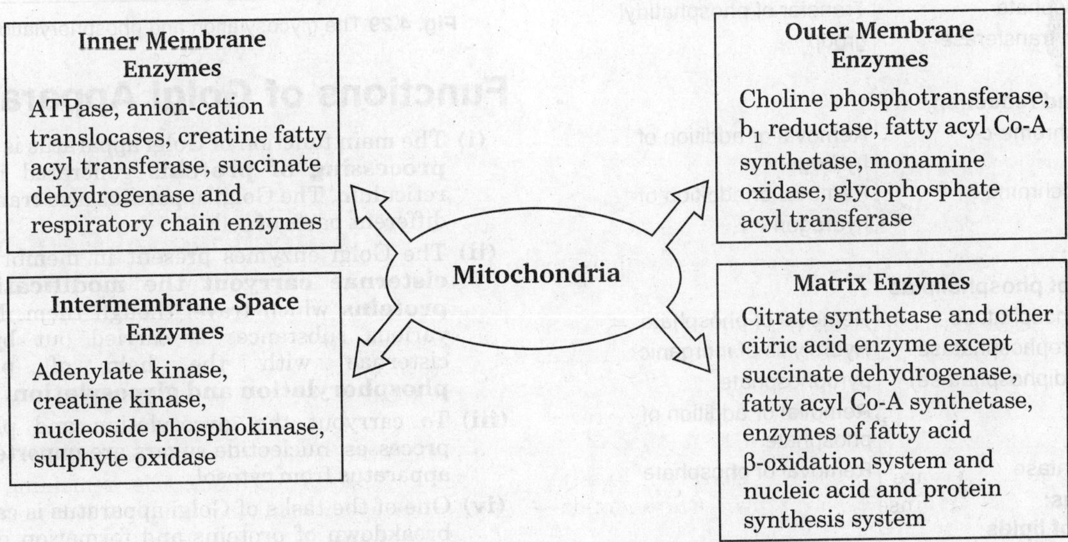

Fig. 4.28 Various enzymes found in mitochondria

Golgi Bodies

The Golgi apparatus which is also known as **Golgi body** is a eukaryotic cell organelle identified by **Camillo Golgi**, an Italian physicist in the year 1898. Golgi body is actually a pile/stack of membranous structures called cisternae. The number of cisternae in a single stack vary between 6-8. In some protists, however, the number could extend upto 60.

The Golgi bodies are found in both plant and animal cells. The cisternae of Golgi body have four structural components, *i.e.*, *cis*-**Golgi**, *endo*-**Golgi**, *medial*-**Golgi** and *trans*-**Golgi**.

The vesicles extending from endoplasmic reticulum fuse with network. These vesicles then enter the stacks of Golgi body and finally reach the *trans*-Golgi. The different regions of Golgi apparatus contain different types of enzymes. These enzymes have certain specific tasks assigned to them. Vesicles leave the Golgi apparatus from the side of *trans*-face.

The Golgi apparatus is an important organelle of eukaryotic cells. Directing the carbohydrates and proteins required by the body to their correct destination is the primary job of Golgi body. In this process of directing molecules to appropriate destinations, they (molecules such as proteins and carbohydrates) are tagged with destination information and structural modifications (see mechanism of sorting and regulation of intracellular transport).

Table 4.8 **Some Enzymes of the Golgi Apparatus and their Function in Animal Cells**

Enzyme : Class and Type	Function
Glycosyl transferases:	
Glycoprotein biosynthesis	
Sialyl transferases	Transfers sialic acid from CMP-sialic acid
Galactosyl transferases	Transfer galactose to lipids or proteins
Sulpho and glycotransferases:	
Glycolipid biosynthesis	
Sulphotransferase	Transfer of sulphate from activated donor
Lysolecithin acetyl transferase	Transfer of acyl groups to phospholipid
Glycero-phosphate phosphatidyl transferase	Transfer of phosphatidyl group
Oxireductases:	
Oxidation and reduction	
NADH-cytochrome-c-reductase	Removal or addition of hydrogen
NADPH-cytochrome-c-reductase	Removal or addition of hydrogen
Phosphatases:	
Hydrolysis of phospholipids	
Glucose-6-phosphatase	Removal of phosphate
Thiamine pyrophosphatase (Nucleoside diphosphatase)	Hydrolysis of inorganic pyrophosphate
ATPase	Removal or addition of phosphate
Acid phosphatase	Removal of phosphate
Phospholipases:	
Hydrolysis of lipids	
Phospholipase A_1	Removal of non-specific fatty acid chains from phospholipids
Phospholipase A_2	Removal of fatty acid chains
Kinases:	
Phosphorylation	
Casein phosphokinases	Phosphorylation of casein
Mannosidases :	
Removal of mannose	
Mannosidase I and II	Removal of mannose residue from oligosaccharide

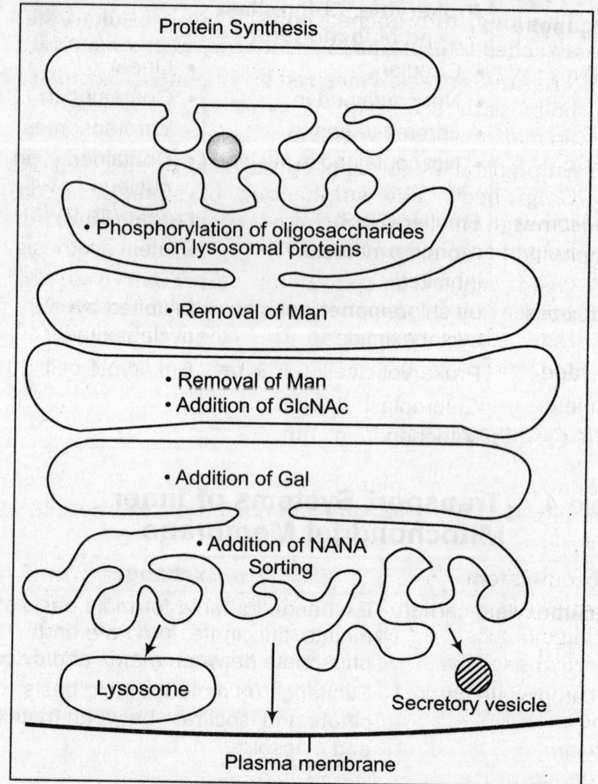

Fig. 4.29 The glycosylation and phosphorylation processes

Functions of Golgi Apparatus

(i) The main function of Golgi apparatus is to carryout the **processing of proteins** generated in endoplasmic reticulum. The Golgi apparatus also transports it to the different parts of cell.

(ii) The Golgi enzymes present in membranous disks of **cisternae carryout the modification of cargo proteins** which travel though them. Modification of various substances is carried out by enzymes in cisternae with the help of processes like **phosphorylation and glycosylation.**

(iii) To carryout the glycosylation and phosphorylation processes, nucleotide sugars are imported by the Golgi apparatus from cytosol.

(iv) One of the tasks of Golgi apparatus is carrying out the breakdown of proteins and formation of small, active fragments.

(v) Incorporation of phosphate molecules onto molecules of proteins is also an important task carried out in the Golgi apparatus.

(vi) Transportation of lipids around cells and creation of lysosomes are the important functions carried out by Golgi apparatus.

(vii) Synthesis of proteoglycans is carried out by the Golgi body. The proteoglycans are found in extracellular matrix of animal cells.

(viii) Carbohydrates are synthesized in the Golgi body. The process of carbohydrate synthesis involves production of polysaccharides and glucosaminoglycans (GAGs).

(ix) The long, unbranched polysaccharides and GAGs are attached to proteins in order to form proteoglycans.

(x) The GAGs are polymerized by enzymes present in Golgi body with the help of xylose link; it leads to the formation of core proteins.

(xi) Sulphation is an important task carried out by the Golgi body. The sulphaction of substances passing through the lumen of Golgi body is carried out with the help of sulphotransferases.

(xii) Golgi apparatus plays an important role in the prevention of destruction of cells (or apoptosis). The Bcl-2 genes present in the Golgi are used for this purpose.

Lysosomes

Christain de Duve isolated a class of particles, which had a high content of acid phosphatase and other hydrolytic enzymes now called **lysosome.**

Lysosomes are actually membranous sacs filled with enzymes. They are found in all eukaryotic cells and act as 'garbage disposal' or the 'digester' of the cell. Lysosomes are spherical bag-like structures that are bound by a single layer membrane, however, the lysosome shape and size may vary to some extent in different organisms. The lysosome size ranges between 0.1 to 1.2μm. The membane that surrounds the lysosome, protects the rest of the cell from the hydrolytic or digestive enzymes that are contained in the lysosomes.

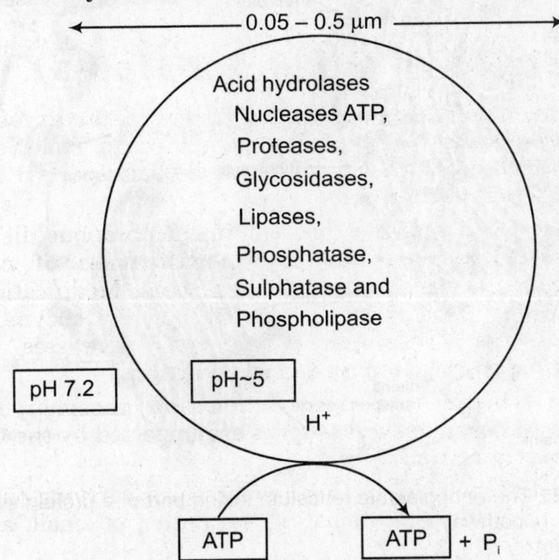

Fig. 4.30 Lysosomes and its characteristics

Lysosome contains more than 50 hydrolytic enzymes involved in intracellular digestion that breakdown proteins, carbohydrates, nucleic acids. Lysosomes are ruptured in the injured or dead cells and releases the hydrolytic enzymes to digest its own cellular contents. Because of this property lysosome is called suicidal bag. The lysosome maintains a slightly acidic pH 5 in its interior, a pH at which lysosomal enzymes are maximally active. The contents of the lysosomes are isolated from the cytoplasm by the lysosomal membrane, keeping the pH distinct from the neutral pH of the cytoplasm.

Types of Lysosomes

There are four types of lysosomes, of which the first is the **primary lysosomes** and other three are grouped together as **secondary lysosomes.**

(i) The Primary Lysosomes (Storage Granules)

It is a small body, whose enzymatic content is synthesized by the ribosomes and accumulated in the endoplasmic reticulum. From ER it penetrates into the Golgi region. The primary lysosome may be charged preferentially with one type of enzyme or another. It is only in the secondary lysosomes, where the full complement of acid hydrolases is present.

(ii) The Secondary Lysosome or Heterophagosome (Digestive Vacuole)

It is formed by the fusion of primary lysosome with the phagosome or engulfed vesicle. The engulfed material is progressively digested by the hydrolytic enzymes of lysosome. This digestion produces products of low molecular weight, which pass through the lysosomal membrane and are incorporated into the cell for many metabolic pathway.

Residual Bodies

If the digestion is incomplete then residual bodies are formed. By the process of **defecation** these residual bodies are eliminated in some cells (like *Amoeba* and other Protozoa), while in other cells they may remain for a long time and may be responsible for ageing process. In some metabolic disease the absence of some of the lysosomal enzymes may lead to enormous accumulation of products in the cell.

The Autophagic Vacuole, Cytolysosome or Autophagosome

In this case, the lysosome contains part of the cell in a process of digestion (*e.g.*, a mitochondrion or portions of the endoplasmic reticulum). A large number of these vacuoles are formed in certain physiologic and pathologic process. This is a mechanism by which the cell can achieve the degradation of its own constituents which is irreparable.

Functions of Lysosome

Three important functions of lysosomes are :

(a) **Digestion of external particles** that enter the cell by endocytosis (b) **Digestion of intra-cellular** substances (Autophagy) (c) **Extracellular Digestion** Lysosomal enzymes may be discharged outside the cell to produce lytic effects. The lysosomal enzymes function in: the breakdown of foreign particles by leucocytes. The dissolution of the structure, surrounding the egg cell by sperms during the course of fertilization and bone digesting activities of osteoclast cells are carried out by lysosome.

Any malfunctioning of the lysosomes or any of the digestive proteins, results in lysosomal storage diseases, such as **Tay-Sachs disease** and **Pompe's disease.** These diseases are caused by defective function of the lysosomes or in absence of any of the digestive proteins or lysosomal hydrolytic enzymes.

Endoplasmic Reticulum

The first of the two words 'endoplasmic' (*endo* = inside) means that this organelle is contained within the cytoplasm of a eukaryotic cell. The second word '*reticulum*' means that this is a type of network that is spread within the cell cytoplasm. The name 'endoplasmic reticulum' was coined in 1953 by **Porter** who in 1945 had observed it in electron micrographs of liver cells.

The endoplasmic reticulum is a continuously connected network of **tubules**, **cisterns** and **vesicles** that is spread throughout the cytoplasm and is covered with a special membrane. The **cisternae** are long, flattened, sac-like, unbranched tubules having the diameter of 40 to 50 μm which have synthetic roles as the cells of pancreas, notochord and brain. The **vesicles** are oval, membrane-bound vacuolar structures having the diameter of 25 to 500 μm. They especially abundant in the SER. The **tubules** are branched structures forming the reticular system along with the cisternae and vesicles. They usually have the diameter from 50 to 190 μm.

There are two types of endoplasmic reticulum. One is **Smooth Endoplasmic Reticulum** (SER) and the other is **Rough Endoplasmic Reticulum** (RER) and both of these types are interconvertible. The rough endoplasmic reticulum has ribosomes attached to the surface, which are sites for protein synthesis, while the smooth endoplasmic reticulum is purely a transport system for the ions and steroids in particular.

SER synthesize lipids and steroids, metabolize carbohydrates and steroids and regulate calcium concentration, drug detoxification and attachment of receptors on cell membrane proteins. **Sarcoplasmic reticulum** solely regulate calcium levels. The smooth ER also contains the enzyme glucose-6-phosphatase which converts glucose-6-phosphate to glucose, a step in gluconeogenesis. The SER consists of tubules and vesicles that branch forming a network.

Ribosomes are membranous particles of *r*RNA and proteins, they may be 70 S type in prokaryotes and 80 S type is eukaryotes. They attach to ER by ribophosis I and II. There are site of protein synthesis.

The membrane of the **RER** is continuous with the outer layer of the nuclear envelope. Although there is no continuous membrane between the RER and the Golgi apparatus, membrane-bound vesicles shuttle proteins between these two compartments.

Functions of RER

The RER is key in multiple functions:

(i) Lysosomal enzymes with a **mannose-6-phosphate marker added in the *cis*-Golgi network.**

(ii) **Secreted proteins,** either secreted constitutively or regulated secretion involving clathrin and paired basic amino acids in the signal peptide.

(iii) **Integral membrane proteins** are imbedded in the membrane as vesicles exit and bind to new membranes.

(iv) **Initial glycosylation** as assembly continues. This is either N-linked (O-linking occur in the Golgi). N-linked glycosylation: if the protein is properly folded.

The smooth ER is the site at which **some drugs are modified** by microsomal enzymes which include the cytochrome P_{450} enzymes.

Table 4.9 **Distribution of Enzymes in the Membranes of Endoplasmic Reticulum**

Enzyme	Surface Localization
Cytochrome-b_5 (involved in synthesis of unsaturated fatty acids)	Cytoplasmic face
NADH-Cytochrome-b_5 reductase	Cytoplasmic face
NADP-Cytochrome-*c* reductase	Cytoplasmic face
Cytochrome P_{450} (most abundant)	Both on cytoplasmic and luminal face
ATPase	Cytoplasmic face
5′-nucleotidase	Cytoplasmic face
Nucleoside pyrophosphatase	Cytoplasmic face
GDP-mannosyl transferase	Cytoplasmic face
Nucleoside diphosphatase	Luminal face
Glucose-6-phosphatase (histochemical marker enzyme)	Luminal face
Acetanilide-hydrolysing esterase	Luminal face
β-glucuronidase	Luminal face

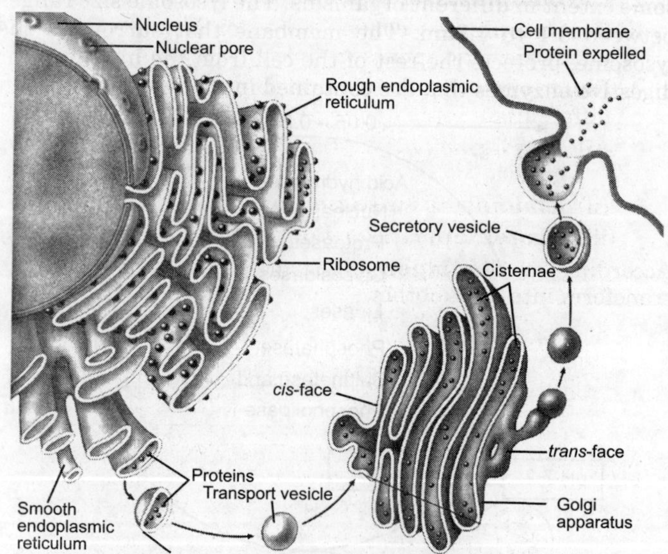

Fig. 4.31 The endoplasmic reticulum taking part of a protein sorting pathway

The endoplasmic reticulum is also part of a protein sorting pathway. The majority of endoplasmic reticulum resident proteins are retained in the endoplasmic reticulum through a retention motif. This motif is composed of four amino acids at the end of the protein sequence. The most common retention sequence is **KDEL** (lys-asp-glu-leu). However, variation on KDEL does occur. There are three KDEL receptors in mammalian cells and they have a very high degree of sequence identity. The functional differences between these receptors remain to be established.

Peroxisomes

This organelle is responsible for protecting the cell from its own production of toxic hydrogen peroxide. As an example, white blood cells produce hydrogen peroxide to kill bacteria. The oxidative enzymes in peroxisomes breakdown the hydrogen peroxide into water and oxygen. **Peroxisomes** are found in animal cells and in the leaves of higher plants. They contain catalases and oxidases (*e.g.*, D-amino oxidase and urate oxidase). In plant cells, peroxisomes remain associated with ER, chloroplasts and mitochondria and are involved in photorespiration. **Glyoxysomes** occur only in fat rich plant cells and involved in glyoxylate cycle.

A major function of the peroxisome is the breakdown of very long chain fatty acids through beta-oxidation, hydrogen peroxide metabolism, glycolate pathway, photorespiration, etc.

Plastids

Plastids are responsible for photosynthesis, storage of products like starch and for the synthesis have the ability to differentiate or redifferentiate, between these and other forms. Proplastids and young chloroplasts commonly divide, but more mature chloroplasts also have this capacity. Undifferentiated plastids (proplastids) may develop into any of the following plastids:

1. **Chloroplasts** for photosynthesis;
2. **Chromoplasts** for pigment synthesis and storage.
3. **Gerontoplasts** control the dismantling of the photosynthetic apparatus during senescence.
4. **Leucoplasts** for monoterpene synthesis; it is further differentiate into:
   (i) **Amyloplasts** for starch storage and detecting gravity.
   (ii) **Elaioplasts** for storing fat.
   (iii) **Proteinoplasts** for storing and modifying protein.

According to **Schimper,** different kinds of plastids can transform into one another.

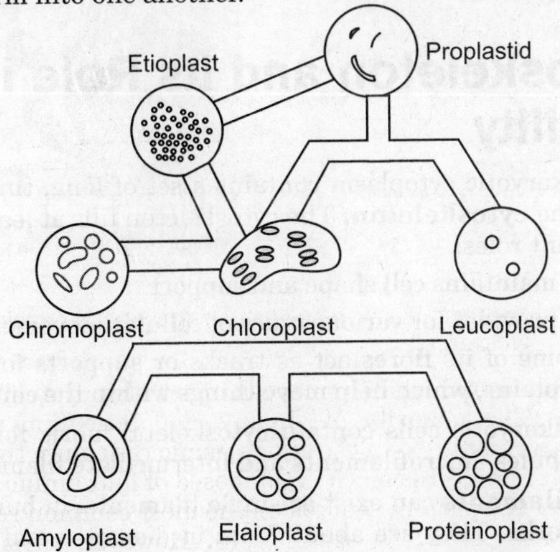

Fig. 4.32 Differentiation of plastids (proplastids)

Plastids are thought to have originated from endosymbiotic cyanobacteria. They developed around 1500 million years ago and allowed eukaryotes to carry out oxygenic photosynthesis. Complex plastids start by secondary endosymbiosis, when a eukaryote engulfs a red or green alga and retains the algal plastid, which is typically surrounded by more than two membranes.

Chromoplasts synthesize and store pigments such as orange carotene, yellow xanthophylls and various other red pigments; as such, their colour varies depending on what pigment they contain.

Leucoplasts have been observed in epidermal cells of roots, hypocotyls and petals and in callus and suspension culture cells of tobacco. In some cell types at certain stages of development, leucoplasts are clustered around the nucleus with stromules extending to the cell periphery, as observed for proplastids in the root meristem.

Etioplasts are pre-granal, immature chloroplasts but can also be chloroplasts which have been deprived of light, lack active pigment.

Chloroplasts

Chloroplasts have a double-membrane envelope, called the **chloroplast envelope**. Each membrane is a phospholipid bilayer, between 6 and 8 nm thick and the two are separated by a gap of 10-20 nm, called the **intermembrane space.** The **outer membrane** is permeable to most ions and metabolites, but the **inner membrane** is highly specialized with transport proteins. Carbohydrates are transported across the outer membrane by a triose phosphate translocator.

Within the inner membrane, in the region called the stroma, there is a system of interconnecting flattened membrane compartments, called the **thylakoids.** The membranes of the thylakoid contain **photosystems I and II** which harvest solar energy to excite electrons which travel down **the electron transport chain.**

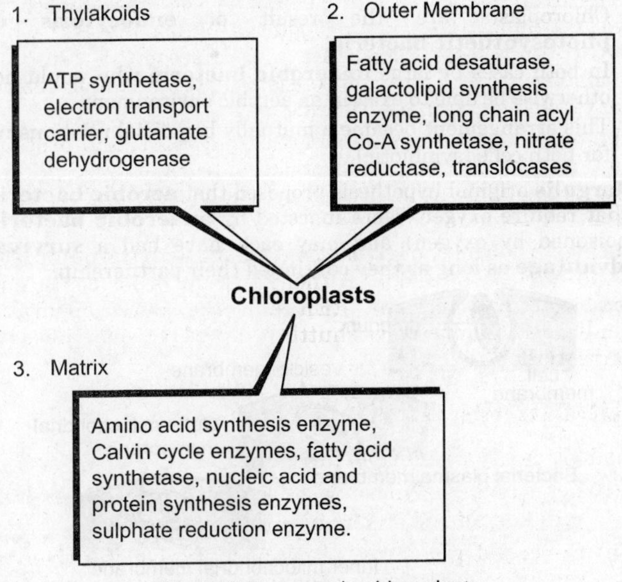

Fig. 4.33 Enzymes in chloroplasts

The **chloroplast genome** codes for many proteins and RNAs. Chloroplast genomes vary in size, but are large enough to code for 50-100 proteins as well as the *r*RNAs and *t*RNAs. The chloroplast genome in land plants codes for 4 *r*RNAs, 30 *t*RNAs and ~ 60 proteins.

Chloroplast Genome

Chloroplast DNAs vary in length from 120-190 kb. The sequenced chloroplast genomes (>10 in total) have from 87-183 genes.

Gene	Type
RNA-coding	
16 S *r*RNA	1
23 S *r*RNA	1
4.5 S *r*RNA	1
5 S *r*RNA	1
*t*RNA	30-32
Gene Expression	
r-proteins	20-21
RNA polymerase	3
Others	2
Chloroplast functions	
Rubisco and thylakoids	31-32
NADH dehydrogenase	11
Total	**105-113**

Organelle genomes (mitochondria and chloroplast) are usually circular molecules of DNA. Organelle genomes code for some but not all of the proteins found in the organelle.

The Endosymbioic Theory

First postulated by Lynn Margulis in the 1967. She proposed that the similarities between prokaryotes and organelles, together with their appearance in the fossil record, could best be explained by 'endosymbiosis'. **Hypothesis** originally proposed that:

- Mitochondria are the result of **endocytosis of aerobic bacteria.**
- Chloroplasts are the result of **endocytosis of photosynthetic bacteria.**
- In both cases by large **anaerobic bacteria** who would not otherwise be able to exist in an aerobic environment.
- This arrangement became a mutually beneficial relationship for both cells (symbiotic).

Margulis original hypothesis proposed that **aerobic bacteria** (that require oxygen) were ingested by **anaerobic bacteria** (poisoned by oxygen) and may each have had a **survival advantage** as long as they continued their partnership.

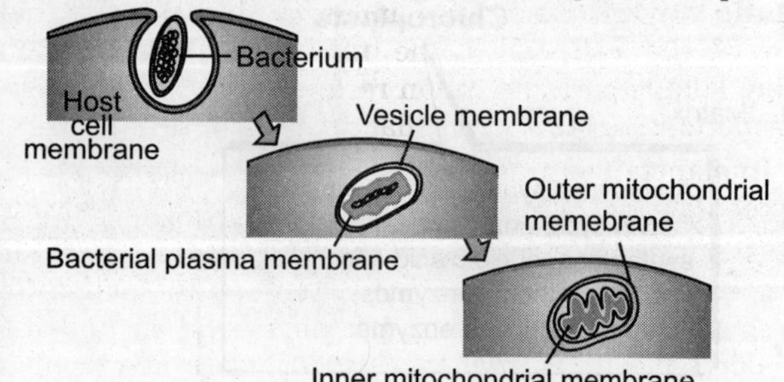

Fig. 4.34 Endosymbiosis process

Vacuoles

A **vacuole** is a membrane-bound organelle which is present in all plant and animal and bacterial cells. Vacuoles are enclosed compartments which are filled with water, inorganic and organic molecules including enzymes in solution. Vacuoles are formed by the fusion of multiple membrane vesicles. In general, the functions of the vacuole include:

1. Isolating harmful or a threat to the cell materials.
2. Containing waste products.
3. Maintaining internal hydrostatic pressure or turgor within the cell.
4. Maintaining an acidic internal pH.
5. Allows plants to support structures such as leaves and flowers due to the pressure of the central vacuole.
6. In seeds, stored proteins needed for germination are kept in 'protein bodies', which are modified vacuoles.

In plant cell, a vacuole is surrounded by a membrane called the **tonoplast** (word origin: Gk *ton*(os), meaning 'stretching', 'tension', 'tone'. Gk *plastos* formed, molded). In young cell vacuoles are extremely small in size or may be absent. The vacuole may be of four type: Sap vacuoles, contractile vacuoles, food vacuoles and gas or air vacuoles.

Vacuoles play a major role in autophagy, maintaining a balance between biogenesis (production) and degradation (or turnover) of many substances and cell structures in certain organisms.

Contractile vacuoles are found in many freshwater protists. Their function is to get rid of the excess water that rushes into the cell because of the imbalance in salt concentration between the relatively salty interior of the cell and its freshwater environment.

Food vacuoles are found in some simple and evolutionarily ancient groups of organisms—single-celled protists and simple multicellular organisms such as sponges. In these organisms, the cells engulf food particles by phagocytosis, generating a food vacuole. Fusion of this vacuole with a lysosome results in digestion and small molecules leave the vacuole and enter the cytoplasm for use or distribution to other organelles.

Cytoskeleton and its Role in Motility

The eukaryotic cytoplasm contains a set of long, thin fibres called the **cytoskeleton.** The cytoskeleton fills at least three important roles:

1. It maintains cell shape and support.
2. It provides for various types of cellular movement.
3. Some of its fibres act as tracks or supports for motor proteins, which help move things within the cell.

Most eukaryotic cells contain cytoskeletal fabric formed of microtubules, microfilaments and intermediate filaments.

Microfilaments can exist as single filaments, in bundles or in networks. They are about 7 nm in diameter and several micrometers long. They are assembled from **actin,** a protein that exists in several forms and has many functions among members of the animal phyla. The polymerization of actin into microfilaments is reversible and they can disappear from cells, breaking down into units of free actin. Microfilaments have two major roles:

4. They help the entire cell or parts of the cell to move.
5. They stabilize cell shape.

In muscle cells, actin fibres are associated with another protein, **myosin** and the interactions of these two proteins account for the contraction of muscles. In non-muscle cells, actin fibres are associated with localized changes of shape in the cell.

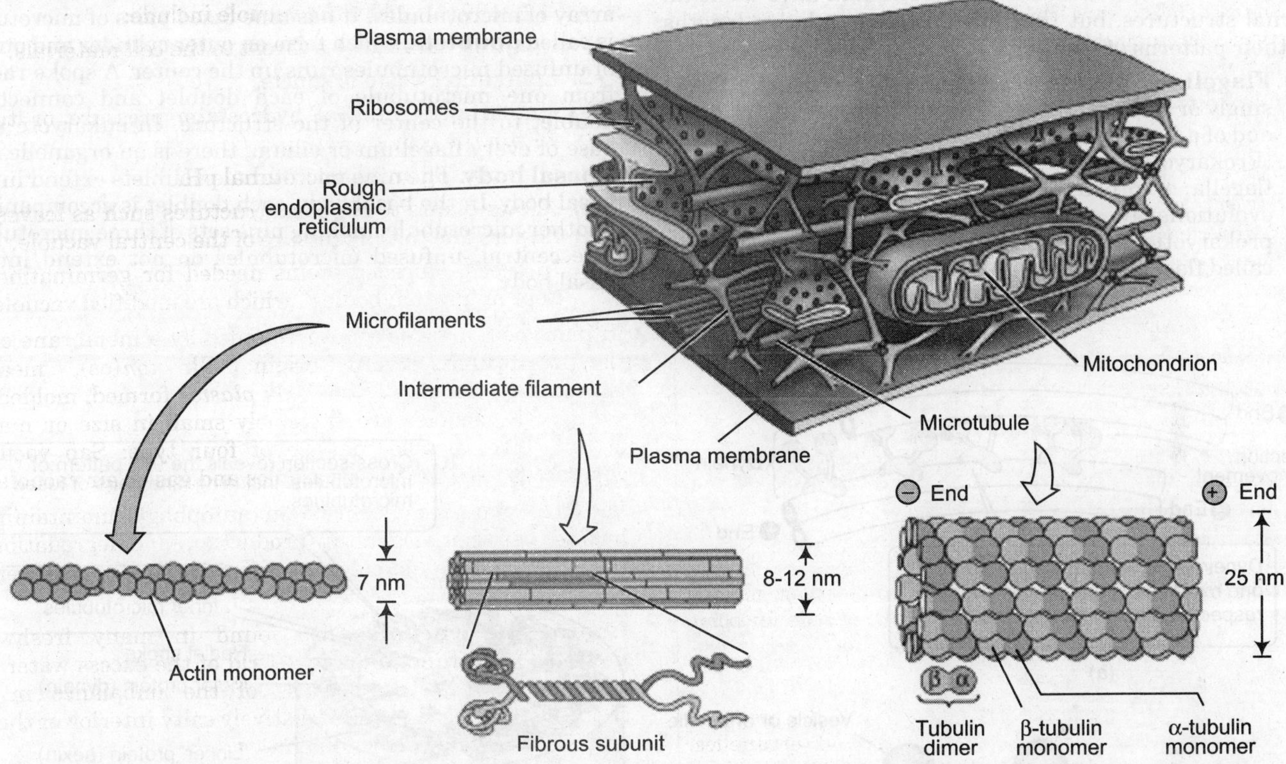

Fig. 4.35 The cytoskeleton Three important structural components of the cytoskeleton. These structures maintain and reinforce cell shape and contribute to cell movement

Microfilaments are involved in a flowing movement of the cytoplasm called **cytoplasmic streaming,** division of an animal cell into two daughter cells and formation of cellular extensions called **pseudopodia** (*pseudo* = false; *podia* = feet) that enable some cells to move.

Intermediate filaments are found only in multicellular organisms. In contrast to the other components of the cytoskeleton, there are at least 50 different kinds of intermediate filaments. They generally fall into six molecular classes, based on amino acid sequence and share the same general structure, being composed of fibrous proteins of the keratin family. In cells, these proteins are organized into tough, rope-like assemblages 8-12 nm in diameter. Intermediate filaments have two major structural functions:

1. They stabilize cell structure.
2. They resist tension.

Intermediate filaments radiate from the nuclear envelope and maintain the positions of the nucleus and other organelles in the cell. The lamins of the nuclear lamina are intermediate filaments. Intermediate filaments stabilize and help maintain rigidity in surface tissues by connecting desmosomes between adjacent cells.

Microtubules are long, hollow, unbranched cylinders about 25 nm in diameter and up to several micrometers long. Microtubules have two roles in the cell:

1. They form a rigid internal skeleton for some cells.
2. They act as a framework along which motor proteins can move structures in the cell.

Microtubules are assembled from molecules of the protein **tubulin**. Tubulin is a **dimer,** made up of two monomers. known as **α-tubulin and β-tubulin.** Tubulin dimers can be added or subtracted, mainly lengthening or shortening the microtubule. This change length rapidly makes microtubules **dynamic structures.** Many microtubules radiate from a region of the cell called the **microtubule organizing center.** Tubule polymerization results in rigidity and tubule depolymerization leads to a collapse of this rigid structure.

1. In plants, microtubules control the arrangement of the cellulose fibres of the cell wall.
2. Microtubules serve as tracks for **motor proteins,** specialized molecules that use energy to change their shape and move. Motor proteins bond to and move along the microtubules, carrying materials from one part of the cell to another.

3. Microtubules are essential in distributing chromosomes to daughter cells during cell division.
4. Microtubules are associated with movable cell appendages: the flagella and cilia.

Many eukaryotic cells have **flagella** or **cilia** or both. Cilia and eukaryotic (but not prokaryotic) flagella are both assembled from specialized microtubules and have identical internal structures, but they differ in their relative lengths and their patterns of beating:

(i) Flagella are longer than cilia and are usually found singly or in pairs. Waves of bending propagate from one end of a flagellum to the other in snake-like undulation. (Prokaryotic flagella lack microtubules and dynein. The flagella of prokaryotes are neither structurally nor evolutionarily related to those of eukaryotes. The prokaryotic flagellum is assembled from a protein called flagellin).

(ii) Cilia are shorter than flagella and are usually present in great numbers. They beat stiffly in one direction and recover flexibly in the other direction, so that the recovery stroke does not undo the work of the power stroke.

In cross section, a typical cilium or eukaryotic flagellum is surrounded by the plasma membrane and contains a '9 + 2' array of microtubules. It has nine fused pairs of microtubules is called **doublets,** which form an outer cylinder and one pair of unfused microtubules runs up the center. A spoke radiates from one microtubule of each doublet and connects the doublet to the center of the structure. In eukaryote at the base of every flagellum or cilium, there is an organelle called a **basal body.** The nine microtubule doublets extend into the basal body. In the basal body, each doublet is accompanied by another microtubule, making nine sets of three microtubules. The central, unfused microtubules do not extend into the basal body.

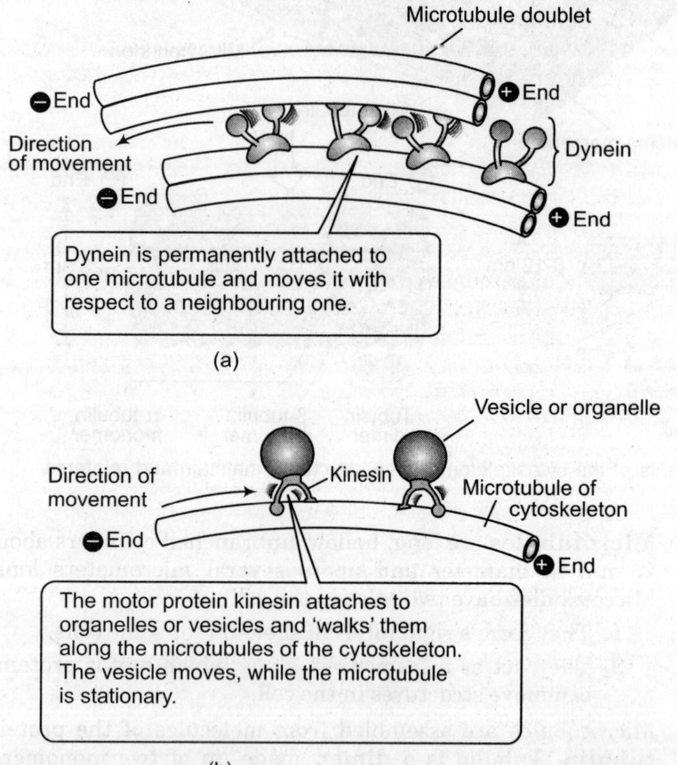

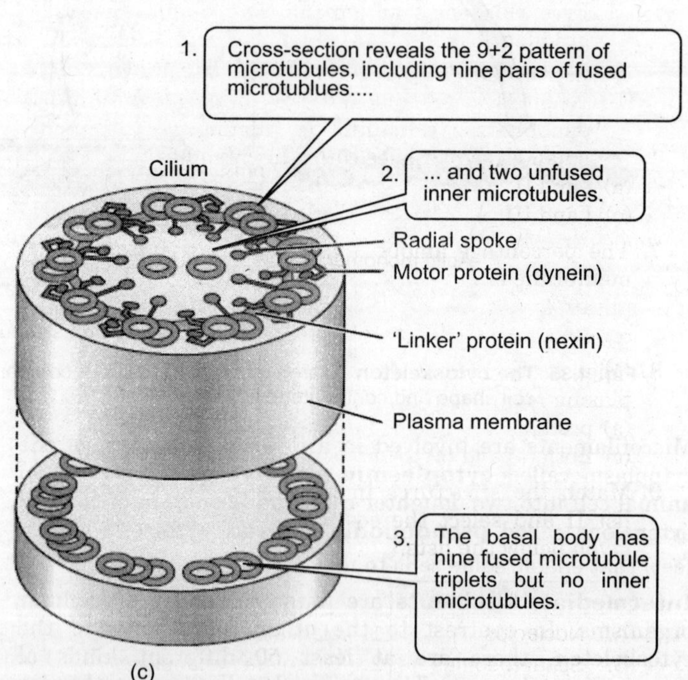

Fig. 4.36 Motor proteins use energy from ATP to move (a) Dynein is responsible for flagellar movement. (b) Kinesin delivers vesicles to various parts of the cell (c) Cross section of a single cilium

The nine microtubule doublets of cilia and flagella are linked by proteins. The motion of cilia and flagella results from the sliding of the microtubules past each other. This sliding is driven by a motor protein called **dynein** by changing its shape.

All motor proteins undergo reversible shape changes powered by energy from ATP. Dynein molecules attached to one microtubule doublet bind to a neighbouring doublet. As the dynein molecules change shape, they move the microtubule past its neighbour.

Dynein and another motor protein, **kinesin,** are responsible for carrying protein-laden vesicles from one part of the cell to another. Dynein moves attached organelles toward the minus end, while kinesin moves them toward the plus end.

Centrioles are almost identical to the basal bodies of cilia and flagella. Centrioles are found in all eukaryotes except the flowering plants, pine trees and their relatives and some protists. It is made up of a precise bundle of microtubules arranged as nine sets of three fused microtubules each. Centrioles lie in the microtubule organizing center in cells that are about to divide. They are involved in the formation of the mitotic spindle, to which the chromosomes attach.

Exercise

1. Lysosomes are the
(a) digestive centres (b) respiratory centres
(c) excretory centres (d) energy centres

2. Electron transport system is located in
(a) mitochondrial matrix (b) cytosol
(c) cristae (d) All of these

3. The acrosome of the sperm is formed from the
(a) mitochondria (b) centrosome
(c) lysosome (d) Golgi bodies

4. Plant cell wall is generally made up of
(a) cellulose and pectin (b) cellulose
(c) chitin (d) murin

5. Nucleus is absent in
(a) sieve tube (b) cambium
(c) phloem parenchyma (d) None of these

6. Which of the following is the correct statement?
I. Free ribosomes and membrane bound ribosomes are identical.
II. 5-5 bond formation occurs in the ER-lumen.
III. When cells are disrupted by homogenization, the endoplasmic reticulum is fragmented into many small closed vesicles called microsomes.
(a) I and II (b) II and III
(c) I and III (d) I, II and III

7. The percentage amount of integral protein of plasma membrane is
(a) 40 % (b) 50 %
(c) 60 % (d) 70 %

8. Oligosaccharide are usely attached to extrinsic phase of plasma membrane by
(a) proteins (b) lipids
(c) Both (a) and (b) (d) not specific

9. Match the structures in list I with the functions in list II and select the correct answer using the codes given below the lists.

List I	List II
A. Nucleolus	1. Lipid storage
B. Sphaerosomes	2. Glycolate metabolism
C. Peroxisomes	3. Transport of macromolecules
D. Plasmodesmata	4. RNA-synthesis

	A	B	C	D
(a)	4	1	3	2
(b)	1	2	4	3
(c)	4	1	2	3
(d)	1	3	2	4

10. Of the following organelles, which group is involved in manufacturing substances needed by the cell?
(a) Lysosome, vacuole and ribosome
(b) Ribosome, rough ER and smooth ER
(c) Vacuole, rough ER and smooth ER
(d) Smooth ER, ribosome and vacuole

11. The internal skeleton of a cell is composed of
(a) microtubules, intermediate filaments and microfilaments
(b) cellulose and intermediate filaments
(c) cellulose, microtubules and centrioles
(d) microfilaments

12. Select the correct statement concerning membrane
(a) Carbohydrates are only found associated with the membranes of prokaryotic cells
(b) Glucose is the most abundant membrane carbohydrate
(c) Cell membranes consist of protein and phospholipid; carbohydrate is not a membrane component
(d) Membrane carbohydrates function primarily in cell-cell recognition

13. Collagens
(a) are high in glycine, hydroxylysine and hydroxyproline
(b) are the most abundant proteins in vertebrates
(c) are the most abundant component of the extracellular matrix in animals
(d) All of the above

14. The ECM of animals, cells consists of what three classes of molecules?
(a) Protein-polysaccharides, structural proteins and microtubules
(b) Structural proteins, lipid bilayers, adhesive glycoproteins
(c) Lipoproteins, polysaccharides and adhesive glycoproteins
(d) Structural proteins, protein-polysaccharides, adhesive glycoproteins

15. The fluid mosaic model of plasma membrane given by Singer and Nicolson is applicable to
(a) only prokaryotic membrane
(b) only eukaryotic membrane
(c) Both (a) and (b)
(d) only to organelle membranes

16. Hemidesmosomes are structure found between
(a) two adjacent plant cells
(b) two adjacent animal cells
(c) between cell and extracellular matrix
(d) within a bacteria

17. Thylakoid membrane has lateral asymmetrical positioning of photosystem in chloroplast. Which statement is correct?
(a) PS-I in non-appressed portion and PS-II in appressed portion
(b) PS-II in non-appressed portion and PS-I in appressed portion
(c) Both PS-I and PS-II in appressed portion
(d) Both PS-I and PS-II in non-appressed portion of thylakoid

18. In the Krebs' cycle, the electrons are moved from NADH to
(a) $FADH_2$ (b) pyruvate
(c) ethanol (d) oxygen

19. Which of the following constitutes the secondary level of protein structure?
(a) Disulphide bonds cystine molecules between of polypeptide chain
(b) Linear sequence of amino acids joined by peptide bonds
(c) Beta pleated sheet
(d) Alpha cells

20. Which cellular organelle functions in ribosome synthesis?
(a) The endoplasmic reticulum
(b) The nucleolus
(c) The nucleus
(d) The Golgi bodies

21. Which of the following statements is true regarding cellular respiration?
(a) The end product of glycolysis is acetyl coenzyme-A, which enters the Krebs' cycle
(b) The majority of ATP production results from glycolysis
(c) Pyruvate is converted to lactate
(d) NADH and $FADH_2$ function as electron carriers

22. The centriole/centrosome takes part in
(a) nucleus formation
(b) start of cell division
(c) cell plate formation
(d) spindle formation

23. Which of the following sequences represents a possible pathway in the production of a secretory protein?
(a) Rough ER → Secretory vesicle → Ribosomes → Golgi apparatus
(b) Ribosomes → Rough ER → Golgi apparatus → Secretory vesicle
(c) Secretory vesicle → Golgi apparatus → Ribosomes → Rough ER
(d) Rough ER → Ribosomes → Secretory vesicles → Golgi apparatus

24. Cytoplasmic streaming results into mobility of substances and organalles involves interaction of
(a) tubulin and kinesin (b) tubulin and myosin
(c) actin and kinesin (d) actin and myosin

25. Which organelle require intact membrane system for ATP synthesis?
(a) Chloroplast (b) Mitochondria
(c) Both (a) and (b) (d) Endoplasmic reticulum

26. Post-translational modification take place in
(a) nucleus (b) mitochondria
(c) ribosome (d) endoplasmic reticulum

27. Which of the following in not true of the nuclear envelope?
(a) The nuclear envelope is exactly like other cellular membranes
(b) The nuclear envelope separates the genetic material from the cytoplasm
(c) The nuclear envelope is a pair of concentric membranes
(d) The nuclear envelope is studded with pores

28. Which cytoplasmic fibrils are most like the nuclear lamins?
(a) Microtubules (b) Microfilaments
(c) Intermediate filaments (d) Actomyosin

29. RER is found abundantly in goblet cells, pancreatic cells and liver cells is mainly engaged in
(a) glycosylation of protein
(b) folding and secondary structure formation
(c) production of secretory and cytosolic protein
(d) production and excretion of protein

30. Microsomes are not found in cell in natural condition. They are
(a) present only in certain bacteria
(b) broken pieces of ER during centrifugation
(c) broken pieces of Golgi during centrifugation
(d) present in certain fungi

31. Which of the following statement is correct?
I. Flagella having 9 + 2 arrangement of microtubules.
II. Centriole having 9 + 0 arrangement of microtubules.
III. Structure of kinetosome and centriole is same.
(a) I and II (b) I and III
(c) II and III (d) I, II and III

32. *r*RNA originates from
(a) nucleus (b) nucleolus
(c) cytoplasm (d) ER

33. Which organelle is presenting zone of exclusion and have definite polarity?
(a) Golgi body (b) ER
(c) Nucleus (d) Ribosome

34. Lysosomes are abundant in
(a) WBCs and osteoblasts (b) RBCs and spleen
(c) Liver and spleen (d) WBCs and spleen

35. Lysosome membrane is strengthened by cortisol, cortisone, antihistamine, heparin, chloroquinone and cholesterol but becomes fragile
(a) low bile salts and energy radiations
(b) in absence of oxygen
(c) low vitamin-A and E
(d) low progesterone and oestrogen

36. Fruit rotting can be checked by slowing down the action of enzyme polygalactouronose of the organelle
(a) Golgi (b) lysosomes
(c) glyoxysome (d) peroxisome

37. In prokaryotes where the mitochondria is absent, the site of oxidative phosphorylation and electron transport chain including dehydrogenases is
(a) mesosomes (b) endosomes
(c) plasma membrane (d) microsomes

38. Which statement, best characterizes the nuclear localization signal?
(a) The NLS is typically a small molecular weight metabolic intermediate
(b) The NLS is a stretch of hydrophobic amino acids on a protein's N-terminus
(c) The NLS is one or two stretches of basic amino acids on a protein's C-terminus
(d) The NLS is a steroid that binds to DNA

39. RNA molecules that exhibit catalytic activity are called
(a) *m*RNAs
(b) ribonucleases
(c) ribozymes
(d) ribonucleotides

40. Which part of translational modification of proteins does not occur in lumen of ER?
(a) Glycosylation
(b) Ubiquination
(c) Conformation folding and formation of quaternary structure
(d) Formation of disulphide bonds

41. In muscle cells the .... is specialized for the storage and release of calcium.
(a) smooth ER (b) the Golgi apparatus
(c) contractile vacuoles (d) rough ER

42. The characteristic property of metabolically active cell is
(a) low nucleo-cytoplasmic ratio
(b) high nucleo-cytoplasmic ratio
(c) high volume to surface area ratio
(d) small nucleus

43. The chromatin is made up of repetitive units known as
(a) chromosomes (b) chromonemata
(c) nucleosomes (d) nucleotides

44. Proteins are transported around the cell in membranous vesicles. These vesicles
I. form when a section of membrane protrudes and buds off
II. gave a layer of coat protein around the inside of the vesicle.
III. use their protein coat to find their target membrane.
IV. are uncoated after they reach their target.
(a) I, II (b) I, III
(c) I, III, IV (d) I, II, III and IV

45. Cytochrome oxidase and cytochrome-*c* deficiency in mitochondria causes
(a) Menke's disease
(b) Kearns-Says syndrome and Menke's disease
(c) Kearns-Says syndrome
(d) Leber's optic neuropathy

46. Photophosphorylation occurs in
(a) plastids (b) mitochondria
(c) cytoplasm (d) cell membrane

47. In the plasma membrane the functional as well as structural role is played by
(a) proteins (b) lipids
(c) cholesterol (d) oligosaccharides

48. Lipid nature of plasma membrane can be destroyed by
(a) hexane (b) benzene
(c) chloroform (d) NaOH

49. The plasma membrane of intestine is highly folded into microvilli. The main function of microvilli is
(a) to secrete digestive enzymes
(b) to help in blood circulation
(c) to increase its absorptive surface
(d) for ageing of worn out cells

50. The structure formed where two adjacent membrane are thickened with disc-shaped adhesive material in between and tonofibrils radiating out from adhesive region is
(a) gap junction (b) tight junctions
(c) desmosomes (d) plasmodesmata

51. The outer part of cytoplasm is usually termed as
(a) plasmasol (b) plasmagel
(c) nucleoplasm (d) protoplasm

52. Endoplasmic reticulum originates from
(a) nuclues (b) nucleolus
(c) Golgi complex (d) plasma membrane

53. The endoplasmic reticulum which constitute 50% of cell is absent in
(a) ova (b) embryonic cells
(c) mature erythrocytes (d) All of these

54. Lysosomes are polymorphous organelles enclosed by a single membrane. They contain vast array of hydrolytic enzymes which can digest any foreign material except
(a) cellulose (b) starch
(c) glycogen (d) lipids

55. Spectrin of erythrocytes and cytochrome-*c* of mitochondria, which can be easily dissociated by high ionic strength and metal ion chelating agent are example of
(a) extrinsic protein (b) intrinsic protein
(c) tunnel protein (d) cytoplasmic protein

56. Microtubules are 25 nm thick, 15nm core formed of 13 helically arranged protofilaments made up of
(a) α-tubulin (b) β-tubulin
(c) myosin (d) Both (a) and (b)

57. Intermediate filaments are made up of
(a) non-contractile proteins (b) β-tubulin
(c) myosin (d) actin

58. In hexose monophosphate shunt, the CO_2 molecules evolved is
(a) same as in glycolysis
(b) less then glycolysis
(c) more then glycolysis
(d) much lesser then glycolysis

59. Human mitochondria
(a) are inherited as an X-linked trait
(b) are all inherited from the father
(c) have linear DNA
(d) are all inherited from the mother

60. Both chloroplasts and mitochondria
(a) are found within the nucleus
(b) have linear DNA
(c) carry extranuclear genes
(d) are inherited from both parents

61. Among the following which is longest cell?
(a) Hemp (b) Ramie
(c) Jute (d) Nerve fibre

62. The middle lamella of plant cells is made up of calcium magnesium pectate. Pectic acid is polymer of
(a) α-1, 4 D-glucose
(b) α-1, 6-D-glucose
(c) α-1, 4-D-galactouronic acid
(d) α-1, 4-D-galactouronic acid

63. Which of the following would not be considered part of a cell's cytoplasm?
(a) A ribosome (b) The nucleus
(c) A mitochondrion (d) A microtubule

64. The maximum size of a cell is limited by
(a) its need for enough surface area for exchange with its environment
(b) the number of organelles that can be packed inside
(c) the materials needed to build it
(d) the amount of flexibility it needs to be able to move

65. You would expect a cell with an extensive Golgi apparatus to
(a) make a lot of ATP (b) secrete a lot of material
(c) move actively (d) perform photosynthesis

66. Which of the following correctly matches an organelle with its function?
(a) Mitochondrion — Photosynthesis
(b) Nucleus — Cellular respiration
(c) Ribosome — Manufacture of lipids
(d) Central vacuole — Storage

67. Mitochondria and cholorplasts share several common features, for example,
(a) both are capable of semiautonomous growth and reproduction
(b) neither are components of the endomembrane system
(c) each contains a small amount of DNA
(d) All of the above

68. The characteristic strength of woody tissues is due to
(a) the secondary cell wall (b) hemicellulose
(c) the middle lamina (d) the primary cell wall

69. The rule is derived from the ER and is continuous with the ER of two adjacent plant cells.
(a) Middle lamina (b) Annulus
(c) Plasmodesma (d) Desmotubule

70. Dye injected into a plant cell might be able to enter an adjacent cell through a
(a) tight junction (b) microtubule
(c) desmosome (d) plasmodesma

71. The protein in the membrane was actually slightly different from the protein made in the ER. The protein was probably changed in the
(a) Golgi apparatus (b) smooth ER
(c) mitochondrion (d) nucleus

72. When elongated, tube-shaped cells from the lining of the intestine are treated with a certain chemical, the cells sag and become round blobs. The internal structures disrupted by this chemical are probably
(a) cell junctions (b) microtubules
(c) rough ER (d) dynein

73. Cell fractionation is the most appropriate procedure for preparing .... for study.
(a) isolated cells which are normally found tightly attached to neighbouring cells
(b) cells without a functional cytoskeleton
(c) isolated organelle
(d) the basic macromolecules

74. Which of the following clues would tell you whether a cell is prokaryotic or eukaryotic?
(a) The presence or absence of a rigid cell wall
(b) Whether or not the cell is partitioned by internal membranes
(c) The presence or absence of ribosomes
(d) Whether or not the cell carries out cellular metabolism

75. A plant cell was grown in a test tube containing radioactive nucleotides, the parts from which DNA is built. Later examination of the cell showed the radioactivity to be concentrated in the
(a) rough ER (b) peroxisome
(c) nucleus (d) central vacuole

76. When isolated liver cells are combined with non-polar toxins initial processing in the .... increases the solubility of these compounds as an initial step in their excretion.
(a) smooth ER (b) Golgi apparatus
(c) mitochondrion (d) rough ER

77. Discontinuous segments of DNA are joined by
(a) telomerase (b) DNA ligase
(c) exonuclease (d) DNA polymerase

78. Phospholipid molecules in a membrane are arranged with their .... on the exterior and their .... on the interior.
(a) hydrophobic heads; hydrophilic tails
(b) hydrophilic heads; hydrophobic tails
(c) non-polar heads; polar tails
(d) hydrophobic tails; hydrophilic heads

79. The concentration of calcium in a cell is 0.3%. The concentration of calcium in the surrounding fluid is 0.1%. How could the cell obtain more calcium?
(a) Passive transport (b) Diffusion
(c) Active transport (d) Osmosis

80. A plant cell is placed in a solution whose solute concentration is twice as great as the concentration of the cell cytoplasm. The cell membrane is selectively permeable, allowing water but not the solutes to pass through. What will happen to the cell?
(a) No change will occur because it is a plant cell
(b) The cell will shrivel because of osmosis
(c) The cell will swell because of osmosis
(d) The cell will shrivel because of active transport of water

81. One consequence of the sidedness of the plasma membrane is that
(a) molecules that begin on the inside face of the ER end up on the inside face of the plasma membrane
(b) the asymmetrical distribution for membrane proteins, lipids and carbohydrate must be determined when the membrane is first constructed
(c) some proteins on the cytoplasmic side of the membrane are attached to the cytoskeleton
(d) the inside of an ER vesicle is topographical equivalent to the extracellular surface of the plasma membrane

82. The reason urine does not seep out of the bladder is due to the role of
(a) adherens junctions (b) hemidesmosomes
(c) gap junctions (d) tight junctions

83. Desmosomes and hemidesmosomes are anchored in the cytoplasm by
(a) desmocollins (b) actin fibres
(c) collagen (d) tonofilaments

84. Gap junctions consist of channels formed by
(a) hydrophilic and connexons
(b) hydrophobic and cadherins
(c) hydrophobic and connexons
(d) hydrophilic and cadherins

85. The iron containing protein, transferrin, is taken up by fibroblast cells in culture. In what order will the iron atoms of this molecule follow the heterophagy pathway?

I. Coated vesicle at cell surface

II. Endosome vesicle

III. Primary lysosome

IV. Residual body

V. Secondary lysosome

(a) I, II, V and IV (b) I, III, IV and V
(c) I, III, V and IV (d) I, II, V and III

86. Procollagen consists of .... and is formed in the lumen of the ....

(a) 2 β-sheets; lysosomes (b) 3 β-sheets; ER
(c) 3 α-chains; Golgi (d) 3 α-chains; ER

87. The flexibility of the lungs is due mainly to

(a) laminins (c) elastins
(b) collagens (d) fibronectins

88. A difference between collagen and elastin is that

(a) elastin has hydroxylysines and collagen does not
(b) collagen does not have hydroxylated proline residues
(c) there are over 15 types of elastins and less than 5 types of collagens
(d) elastin molecules are crosslinked by covalent bonds between lysine residues and collagen is not

89. Which is the correct order from least to most complex?

(a) Glucuronate, hyaluronate, proteoglycans, GAG
(b) Hyaluronate, glucuronate, GAG chains, proteoglycans
(c) GAG chains, hyaluronate, glucuronate, proteoglycans
(d) Glucuronate, hyaluronate, GAG chains, proteoglycans

90. Two of the most common adhesive glycoproteins in the ECM are

(a) laminins and elastins
(b) collagens and elastins
(c) fibronectins and laminins
(d) collagens and fibronectins

91. Roles of the glycocalyx include

(a) cell adhesion
(b) cell recognition
(c) creation of permeability barriers
(d) All of the above

92. The three most common cell junctions in animals are

(a) adhesive junctions, tight junctions and gap junctions
(b) adhesive junctions, tight junctions and plasmodesmata
(c) tight junctions, plasmodesmata and adhesive junctions
(d) gap junctions, tight junctions and plasmodesmata

93. Which of the following stores calcium, important in muscle contraction?

(a) Mitochondria (b) Smooth ER
(c) The Golgi apparatus (d) Contractile vacuoles

94. Of the following organelles, which group is involved in manufacturing substances needed by the cell?

(a) Lysosome, vacuole and ribosome
(b) Ribosome, rough ER and smooth ER
(c) Vacuole, rough ER and smooth ER
(d) Smooth ER, ribosome and vacuole

95. The internal skeleton of a cell is composed of

(a) microtubules, intermediate filaments and microfilaments
(b) cellulose and intermediate filaments
(c) cellulose, microtubules and centrioles
(d) microfilaments

96. The proton pump in plant cells is the functional equivalent of an animal cells

(a) cotransport mechanism
(b) sodium-potassium pump
(c) contractile vacuole for osmoregulation
(d) receptor-mediated endocytosis of cholesterol

97. Pinocytosis involves

(a) the fusion of a newly formed food vacuole with a lysosome
(b) receptor-mediated endocytosis and the formation of vesicles
(c) the pinching in of the plasma membrane around droplets of external fluid
(d) pseudopod extension as vesicles move along the cytoskeleton and fuse with the plasma membrane

98. Support for the fluid mosaic model of membrane structure comes from the

(a) freeze-fracture technique of electron microscopy
(b) movement of proteins in hybrid cells
(c) amphipathic nature of membrane proteins
(d) All of the above

99. Glycoproteins and glycolipids are important for

(a) facilitated diffusion
(b) active transport
(c) cell-cell recognition
(d) signal-transduction pathways

100. A single layer of phospholipid molecules coats the water in a beaker. Which part of the molecules will face the air?

(a) The phosphate groups
(b) The hydrocarbon tails
(c) Both head and tail because the molecules are amphipathic and will lie sideways
(d) The phospholipids would dissolve in the water and not form a membrane coat

101. The innermost portion of a mature plant cell wall is the

(a) primary cell wall (b) secondary cell wall
(c) plasma membrane (d) plasmodesmata

102. Contractile elements of muscle cells are

(a) intermediate filaments (b) centrioles
(c) microtubules (d) actin filaments

103. Microtubules are components of all of the following except

(a) centrioles
(b) the spindle apparatus for separating chromosomes in cell division
(c) tracks along which organelles can move using motor molecules
(d) the pinching apart of the cytoplasm in animal cell division

104. Desmosomes are

(a) formed during bacterial conjugation
(b) small vesicles found in pancreatic cells

(c) synthesized during cell wall formation in plant cells
(d) specialized regions of cell membrane for adhesion to other cells in animal tissues

105. Plasmodesmata in plant cells are similar in function to
(a) desmosomes (b) tight junctions
(c) gap junctions (d) the extracellular matrix

106. Which of the following would be least likely to diffuse through a cell membrane without the help of a transport protein?
(a) A large polar molecule
(b) A large non-polar molecule
(c) A small polar molecule
(d) Any of the above would easily diffuse through the membrane

107. A cell has mitochondria, ribosomes, smooth ER and other parts. Based on this information, it could not be a
(a) cell from a pine tree (b) grasshopper cell
(c) yeast (fungus) cell (d) bacterium

108. Dye injected into a cell might be able to enter an adjacent cell through a
(a) tight junction (b) microtubule
(c) vacuole (d) plasmodesma

109. A plant cell is placed in a solution whose solute concentration is twice as great as the concentration of the cell cytoplasm. The cell membrane is selectively permeable, allowing water but not the solutes to pass through. What will happen to the cell?
(a) No change will occur because it is a plant cell
(b) The cell will shrivel because of osmosis
(c) The cell will swell because of osmosis
(d) The cell will shrivel because of active transport of water

110. Choose the statement that is not correct for cytoskeletal protein actin.
(a) α-actins are found in various types of muscles.
(b) Polymerization of pure actin *in vitro* requires GTP.
(c) Actin filaments have a slow growing minus end and a fast growing plus end.
(d) Cytochalasins are the inhibitors for actin polymerization.

111. Mitochondrial morphology is maintained by balancing the active absorption of water and active secretion by the mitochondrion. Hence mitochondria are likely to swell in the presence of
(a) ATP
(b) hypertonic solution
(c) uncoupling agent
(d) uncoupling catalysing oxidative phosphorylation

112. Which of the following is not a similarity among the nucleus, chloroplasts and mitochondria?
(a) They contain DNA
(b) They are bounded by a double phospholipid bilayer membrane
(c) They can divide to reproduce themselves
(d) They are derived from the endoplasmic reticulum system

113. Zone of exclusion is zone of cytoplasm surrounding Golgi complex where
(a) ribosomes and glycogen are absent
(b) ribosomes glycogen and cell organelles are absent
(c) cell organelles like mitochondria and chloroplasts are scarce or absent
(d) Golgi complex synthesizes new material

114. Cotransport may involve
(a) active transport of two solutes through a transport protein
(b) ion diffusion against the electrochemical gradient created by an electrogenic pump
(c) first and second messengers in a single-transduction pathway
(d) transport of one solute against its concentration gradient in tandem with another that is diffusing down its concentration gradient

115. The following statement about biological membrane is correct.
(a) They are symmetric bileaflet structure.
(b) Their constituent lipid and protein moieties are held together by covalent interaction.
(c) They are rigid assemblies of protein, lipid and carbohydrates.
(d) Their lipid moieties are amphipathic in nature.

116. Osmosis is a form of diffusion in which
(a) the solute moves freely from a region of higher concentration to lower concentration through semipermeable membrane
(b) the solvent move through a semipermeable membrane from region, where a solute is in higher concentration to region of lower concentration
(c) the solvent moves through a semipermeable membrane from a region, where a solute is in lower concentration to a region of higher concentration
(d) None of the above

117. Purple cabbage leaves do not loose their colour in cold water but do so in the boiling water because
(a) boiling water can enter the cell cavity
(b) plasmalemma get killed in boiling water
(c) the pigment is not soluble in cold water
(d) cell wall is killed in boiling water

118. The fluidity of membranes in a plant in cold weather may be maintained by
(a) increasing the number of phospholipids with saturated hydrocarbon tails
(b) activating a H^+ pump
(c) increasing the concentration of cholesterol in the membrane
(d) increasing the number of phospholipids with unsaturated hydrocarbon tails

119. Which one of the following is not a function of the Golgi apparatus?
(a) Protein synthesized by the ribosomes on the RER are transferred to Golgi, where it is accumulated in the sacs. These sacs may migrate to the surface of cell and discharge their content outside
(b) Protein filled sac may be retained within the cell as lysosome
(c) It is the site, where glycosylation of lipid takes place
(d) It is the site, where synthesis of phospholipid takes place

120. Which of the following enables a cell to pick up and concentrate a specific kind of molecule?
(a) Passive transport
(b) Diffusion
(c) Osmosis
(d) Receptor-mediated endocytosis

121. A researcher made an interesting observation about a protein made by the rough ER and eventually used to build a cell's plasma membrane. The protein in the membrane was actually slightly different from the protein made in the ER. The protein was probably changed in the
(a) Golgi apparatus (b) smooth ER
(c) mitochondrion (d) nucleus

122. If the nucleus is a cell's 'control center' and chloroplasts its 'solar collectors,' which of the following might be called the cell's combination 'food processor' and 'garbage disposer'?
(a) Lysosome (b) Golgi apparatus
(c) Flagellum (d) Ribosome

123. Which of the following is not true of the carrier molecules involved in facilitated diffusion?
(a) They increase the speed of transport across a membrane
(b) They can concentrate solute molecules on one side of the membrane
(c) They have specific binding sites for the molecules they transport
(d) They may undergo a conformational change upon binding of solute

124. Suppose you were to treat a normal mammalian cell with a substance that inhibits the Na-K ATPase. Would be the most immediate effect upon the cell?
(a) There would be no change at all
(b) The cell's osmotic balance were be disrupted and the cell would begin to swell
(c) The cell membrane potential would immediately drop to zero
(d) The cell would very quickly run out of ATP

125. The glyoxysomes in a plant cell
(a) detoxify the hydrogen peroxide produced in the cell
(b) store the waste products released in the carbohydrate metabolism
(c) breakdown the fatty acids during the respiration of lipid
(d) convert glycolate into glycine

126. The mitochondrial DNA (*mt*DNA) is
(a) capable of producing only one kind of RNA, the *mt*RNA also known as mitochondrion specific RNA
(b) unique in producing both mitochondrial *t*RNA and mitochondrial *m*RNA
(c) able to produce three classes of mitochondrial RNA, namely *m*RNA, *t*RNA and *r*RNA
(d) characterized by the fact that it produces its own *r*RNA and *r*RNA which interact directly with *mt*DNA codons for protein synthesis

127. Organelles involved in energy conversion are the
(a) rough ER and Golgi apparatus
(b) nucleus and smooth ER
(c) nucleus and chloroplast
(d) mitochondrion and chloroplast

128. The maximum size of a cell is limited by
(a) its need for enough surface area for exchange with its environment
(b) the number of organelles that can be packed inside
(c) the materials needed to build it
(d) the amount of flexibility it needs to be able to move

129. You would expect a cell with an extensive Golgi apparatus to
(a) make a lot of ATP (b) secrete a lot of material
(c) move actively (d) perform photosynthesis

130. Consider the following statements.
I. In plant cells, cytokinesis starts with the formation of the phragmoplast.
II. Phragmoplast comprises interozonal microtubules and Golgi vesicles.
III. Primary cell wall is produced by microtubules.
Which of the above statements are correct?
(a) I and III (b) I and II
(c) II and III (d) I, II and III

131. Which statements about the glycosylation of secreted proteins are true?
I. Almost all secreted proteins are glycosylated.
II. Glycosylation occurs exclusively on the NH_2 group of asparagine.
III. An oligosaccharide is formed on the lipid dolichol and then transferred to the protein.
IV. The oligosaccharide is trimmed by the removal of mannose residues.
(a) I and II (b) I and III
(c) I, III and IV (d) I, II, III and IV

132. Match list I with list II and select the correct answer using the codes given below the lists.

List I	List II
A. Conduction of secretions to the different organelles in a cell	1. Nuclear pores
B. Intracellular osmosis	2. Endoplasmic reticulum
C. Exchange of granular material between the nucleus and the cytoplasm	3. Cell membrane

Codes

	A	B	C
(a)	2	3	1
(b)	1	3	2
(c)	3	1	2
(d)	2	1	3

133. Match list I (mitochondrial enzymes) with list II (location of enzymes) and select the correct answer using the codes given below the lists.

List I (Mitochondrial Enzyme)	List II (Location of Enzyme)
A. Cytochrome oxidase	1. Outer chamber of mitochondria
B. Fatty acid Co-A ligase	2. Inner membrane of mitochondria
C. Adenylate kinase	3. Mitochondrial matrix
D. Malate dehydrogenase	4. Outer membrane of mitochondria
	5. Polyribosomes attached to mitochondria

Codes

	A	B	C	D
(a)	3	5	4	
(b) 2	4	1	3	
(c) 1	4	5	3	
(d) 2	3	1	4	

134. Match list I (sub-structures) with list II (functions) and select the correct answer using the codes given below the lists.

List I (Sub-Structures)	List II (Functions)
A. Nucleosome	1. Cell adhering junctions
B. Tubulin	2. Battery of degradative enzymes
C. Desmosomes	3. Structural units of chromatin
D. Lysosomes	4. Protein units on microtubules
	5. Oxidative phosphorylation

Codes

	A	B	C	D
(a)	3	4	1	2
(b)	2	5	4	3
(c)	3	5	4	2
(d)	2	4	1	3

135. Match list I with list II and select the correct answer using the codes given below the lists.

List I	List II
A. Nuclear membrane	1. Single layered membrane
B. Lysosome	2. *Cis* and *trans* faces
C. Golgi apparatus	3. Double layered membrane
D. Cell membrane	4. Endocytosis and exocytosis
	5. Polysome

Codes

	A	B	C	D
(a)	3	1	2	4
(b)	3	1	4	5
(c)	1	3	2	4
(d)	1	3	4	5

Answers

1. (a)	**2.** (c)	**3.** (d)	**4.** (a)	**5.** (a)	**6.** (d)	**7.** (d)	**8.** (c)	**9.** (c)	**10.** (b)
11. (a)	**12.** (d)	**13.** (d)	**14.** (d)	**15.** (c)	**16.** (c)	**17.** (a)	**18.** (a)	**19.** (c)	**20.** (b)
21. (d)	**22.** (d)	**23.** (b)	**24.** (d)	**25.** (c)	**26.** (d)	**27.** (a)	**28.** (c)	**29.** (d)	**30.** (b)
31. (d)	**32.** (b)	**33.** (a)	**34.** (d)	**35.** (b)	**36.** (c)	**37.** (c)	**38.** (c)	**39.** (c)	**40.** (b)
41. (a)	**42.** (b)	**43.** (c)	**44.** (c)	**45.** (b)	**46.** (a)	**47.** (a)	**48.** (b)	**49.** (c)	**50.** (c)
51. (b)	**52.** (a)	**53.** (d)	**54.** (a)	**55.** (a)	**56.** (b)	**57.** (a)	**58.** (c)	**59.** (d)	**60.** (c)
61. (d)	**62.** (d)	**63.** (b)	**64.** (a)	**65.** (b)	**66.** (d)	**67.** (d)	**68.** (a)	**69.** (d)	**70.** (d)
71. (a)	**72.** (b)	**73.** (c)	**74.** (b)	**75.** (b)	**76.** (a)	**77.** (b)	**78.** (b)	**79.** (c)	**80.** (b)
81. (d)	**82.** (d)	**83.** (d)	**84.** (a)	**85.** (a)	**86.** (d)	**87.** (c)	**88.** (d)	**89.** (d)	**90.** (c)
91. (d)	**92.** (a)	**93.** (b)	**94.** (b)	**95.** (a)	**96.** (b)	**97.** (b)	**98.** (d)	**99.** (c)	**100.** (b)
101. (b)	**102.** (d)	**103.** (d)	**104.** (d)	**105.** (c)	**106.** (a)	**107.** (d)	**108.** (d)	**109.** (b)	**110.** (b)
111. (c)	**112.** (d)	**113.** (b)	**114.** (d)	**115.** (d)	**116.** (c)	**117.** (b)	**118.** (d)	**119.** (d)	**120.** (d)
121. (a)	**122.** (a)	**123.** (b)	**124.** (c)	**125.** (c)	**126.** (d)	**127.** (d)	**128.** (a)	**129.** (b)	**130.** (d)
131. (c)	**132.** (a)	**133.** (b)	**134.** (a)	**135.** (c)					

5 Structure of Chromosome and Cell Cycle

Organization of Gene and Chromosome

DNA is the genetic material in most of the organisms. This DNA with histone and non-histone protein constitutes the chromatin. The chromatin organized into chromosome during cell division and is composed of two chromatids.

Structure of Chromatin and Chromosomes

The nucleosome is a bead-like structure of chromatin fibres. The **nucleosome** contains ~200 bp of DNA, organized by an octamer of small, basic proteins called **histones.** The nucleosome provides the first level of organization, giving a packing ratio of ~6. The second level of organization is the coiling of the series of nucleosomes into a helical array to constitute the fibre of diameter ~30 nm (interphase chromatin). In chromatin this brings the packing ratio of DNA to ~40. The final packing ratio is determined by the third level of organization, the packaging of the 30 nm fibre. This gives an overall packing ratio of ~ 1000 in euchromatin.

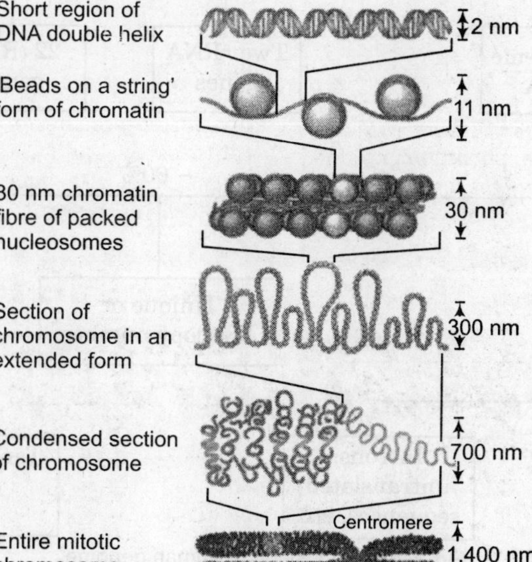

Fig. 5.1 Organization of chromosome

Syllabus

- Organization of Gene and Chromosome: Structure of Chromatin and Chromosomes, Unique and Repetitive DNA, Heterochromatin *vs* Euchromatin, Operon Concept, Interrupted Genes, Gene Families, Transposons.
- Cell Cycle and Cell Division: Mitosis, Meiosis, Steps in Cell Cycle, Control of Cell Cycle.
- Microbial Physiology: Growth, Yield and Characteristic, Strategies of Cell Division, Stress Response.

The **nucleosome** contains ~200 bp of DNA associated with a histone octamer that consists of two copies each of H2A, H2B, H3, and H4. These are known as the **core histones.** Histones H3 and H4 are among the most conserved proteins. The H2A and H2B show appreciable species-specific variation in sequence. Histone H1 proteins show appreciable variation between tissues and between species (and are absent from yeast). The length of DNA per nucleosome varies for individual tissues in a range from 154-260 bp.

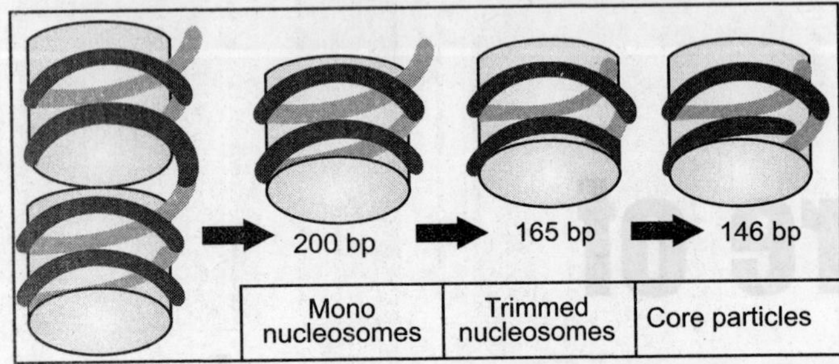

Fig. 5.2 Cleaves by micrococcal nuclease

The histone octamer has a kernel of a $H3_2$-$H4_2$ tetramer associated with two H2A-H2B dimers. Each histone is extensively interdigitated with its partner. All core histories have the structural motif of the histone fold. N-terminal tails extend out of the nucleosome. Histone octamers are not conserved during replication, but H2A-H2B dimers and $H3_2$-$H4_2$ tetramers are conserved.

RNA polymerase displaces histone octamers during transcription. Nucleosomes reform on DNA after the polymerase has passed, unless transcription is very intensive (such as in *r*DNA) when they may be displaced completely.

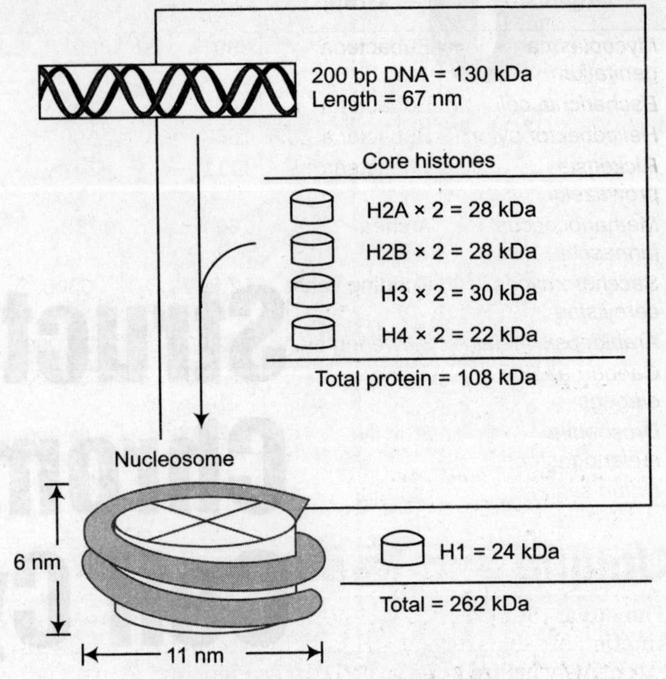

Fig. 5.3 Nucleosome and histone

- **Human Genome**
  - Nuclear genome 3300 Mb ~ 80000 genes
    - ~ 25% Genes and gene-related sequences
      - Unique or moderately repetitive
        - ~ 10% Coding DNA
        - ~ 90% Non-coding DNA
          - Pseudogenes
          - Gene fragments
          - Introns, untranslated sequences, etc.
    - ~ 75% Extragenic DNA
      - ~ 60% Unique or low copy number
      - ~ 40% Moderate to highly repetitive
        - Tandemly repeated or clustered repeats
        - Interspersed repeats
  - Mitochondrial genome 16.6 kb 37 genes
    - Two *r*RNA genes
    - 22 *t*RNA genes
    - 13 polypeptide-encoding genes

Fig. 5.4 Composition of human genome

Table 5.1 **Genome Size and Number of Genes Present in Some Organisms**

Organisms	Group	Genome Size (kb)	Number of Genes
Mycoplasma genitalium	Eubacteria	580	468
Escherichia coli	Eubacteria	4639	4289
Helicobactor pylori	Eubacteria	1667	1590
Rickettsia prowazekii	Eubacteria	1111	834
Methanococcus jannaschii	Archea	1664	1750
Saccharomyces cerevisiae	Budding yeast	12,069	~ 6300
Arabidopsis thaliana	Flowering plant	142,000	~ 26,000
Caenorhabditis elegans	Worm	97,000	~ 19,000
Drosophila melanogaster	Fruit fly	137,000	~ 14,000
Homo sapiens	Human	32,000,000	~ 30,000

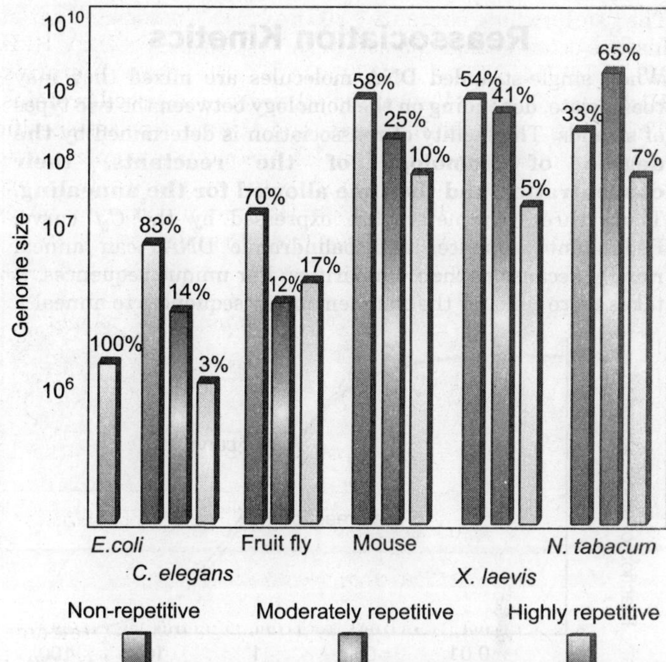

Fig. 5.5 The absolute content of non-repetitive DNA increases with genome size, but reaches a plateau at~2 × 10^9 bp [Non-repetitive/Unique (red); Moderately repetitive (blue); Highly repetitive (green)]

Unique and Repetitive DNA

The eukaryotic genome can be assessed by the reassociation kinetis of denatured DNA. This technique was used extensively before large scale DNA sequencing. Reassociation kinetics identify two general types of genomic sequences:

1. **Non-repetitive/Unique DNA** It consists of sequences that are unique; that is only one copy in a haploid genome.
2. **Repetitive DNA** It consists of sequences that are present in more than one copy in each genome. Repetitive DNA is often divided into two general types:

(i) **Moderately repetitive DNA** consists of relatively short sequences (10-100bp) in the genome. The sequences are dispersed throughout the genome. It is also responsible for the high degree of secondary structure formation in pre-*m*RNA (inverted repeats in the introns pair to form duplex regions).

(ii) **Highly repetitive DNA** consists of very short sequences (typically <100 bp) in the genome. The sequences are present many thousands of times in the genome, as a long tandem.

Neither **moderately repetitive nor Highly repetitive** DNA represents any protein.

> **Key Points**
>
> - A comparison of the human and puffer fish (*Fugu rubripes* has 365 million base pairs and about 30,000 genes; the human genome has one third fewer genes in eight times the amount of DNA.) genomes showed that many genes in the two organisms are similar. A major difference between the two genomes is in repetitive DNA sequences, which make up 40 percent of the human genome but a much smaller proportion in the puffer fish.
> - Prokaryotes contain only non-repetitive DNA.
> - Most of the DNA of lower eukaryotes is non-repetitive (<20% are moderately repetitive components).
> - In animal cells, up to half of the DNA is occupied by moderately and highly repetitive components.
> - In plants and amphibians, the moderately and highly repetitive components may account for up to 80% of the genome.
> - The moderately repetitive DNA consists of transposons, short sequences of DNA (~1 kb) that have the ability to move to new locations in the genome.

The length of the non-repetitive DNA component tends to increase with overall-genome size. The non-repetitive DNA content of genomes is synonym with the relative complexity of the organism. *E. coli* has 4.2 and 10^6 bp, *C. elegans* increases to 6.6 and 10^7 bp, *D. melanogaster* increases further to ~10^8 bp and mammals increase another order of magnitude to ~2 × 10^9 bp.

Reassociation kinetics show that *m*RNA is derived from non-repetitive DNA. The amount of non-repetitive DNA indicate total DNA of the coding potential. Many exons have related sequences. **Exon sequences are conserved but introns vary.** Such exons evolve by a duplication to give copies that initially are identical, but which then diverge in sequence during evolution.

Reassociation Kinetics

When single-stranded DNA molecules are mixed they may reassociate, depending on the homology between the two types of strands. The facility of reassociation is determined by **the degree of homology of the reactants, their concentration and the time allowed for the annealing.** These three parameters are expressed by the C_0t curve. Redundant sequences and palindromic DNAs can anneal rapidly because of their similarities. For unique sequences, it takes more time for the complementary sequences to anneal

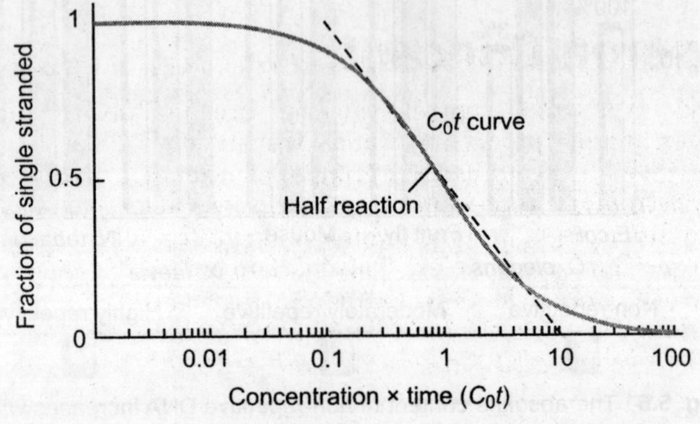

Fig. 5.6 C_0t curve of nucleic acid reassociation is an ideal second-order reaction

The reassociation of *E. coli* DNA generally takes place between C_0t values of about 0.1 and 10 (ca. 4.7×10^6 bp, mainly unique DNA), whereas for a large and complex genome of rye containing about 80% redundancy in the 7.9×10^9 bp.

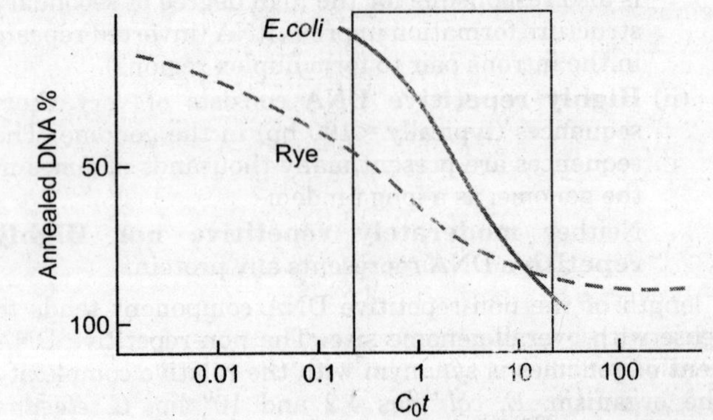

Fig. 5.7 The reassociation kinetics of two genomes (7.9×10^9 bp of rye and 4.7×10^6 *E. coli*) of different complexities

Repetitive sequences account for >50% of the human genome. The repetitive sequences fall into five classes:

- Transposons (either active or inactive) account for 45% of the genome.
- Processed pseudogenes(~0.1% of total DNA). Pseudogenes are dead ends of evolution.
- Simple sequence repeats account for ~3%.
- Segmental duplications account for ~5%.
- Tandem repeats sequence (at centromeres and telomeres).

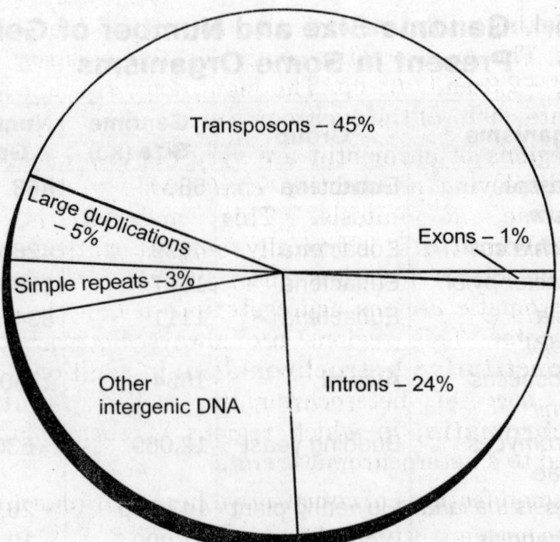

Fig. 5.8 Component repetitive sequences of the human genome

Heterochromatin Vs. Euchromatin

Chromatin is divided into euchromatin and heterochromatin. The euchromatin comprises the majority of the genome. The identified genome sequence represents ~90% of the euchromatin. In addition to providing information on the genetic content of the genome, the sequence also identifies features that may be of structural importance.

Euchromatin does not absorb the common nuclear stains during interphase and is normally transcribed into *m*RNA. In the human genome, the euchromatic fraction varies a great deal among the chromosomes. In chromosome 2 an almost 160 Mb sequence is less than 60% euchromatic, whereas a more than 30 Mb sequence in chromosome 21 is almost entirely euchromatic.

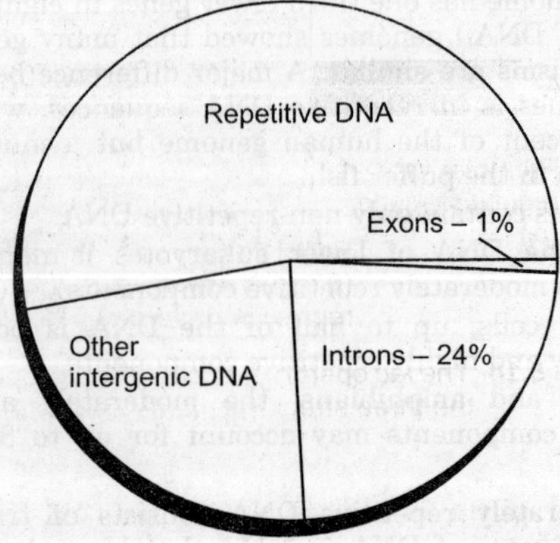

Fig. 5.9 Genes occupy 25% of the human genome, but only 1% of the human genome consists of coding regions (protein coding sequences)

The human (haploid) genome contains 22 autosomes plus the X or Y. The chromosomes range in size from 45-279 Mb of

DNA, making a total genome content of 3,286 Mb (~3.3 and 10^9 bp). The euchromatin comprises the majority of the genome, ~2.9 and 10^9 bp. The identified genome sequence represents ~90% of the euchromatin.

Some regions of chromatin are very densely packed with fibres, displaying a condition comparable to that of the chromosome at mitosis. This material is called **heterochromatin.** It is typically found at centromeres, but occurs at other locations also. It often the various heterochromatic regions aggregate into a densely staining chromocenter. This regions are always heterochromatic, called **constitutive hetrochromatin;** in addition, there is another sort of heterochromatin, called **facultative heterochromatin,** in which regions of euchromatin are converted to a heterochromatic state.

The common features of **constitutive heterochromatin** are

1. It is permanently condensed.
2. It often consists of multiple repeats of a few sequences of DNA that are not transcribed.
3. The density of genes in this region, is very much reduced compared with heterochromatin; and genes that are translocated into or near it are often inactivated.
4. It replicates late in S-phase and has a reduced frequency of genetic recombination.

Facultative heterochromatin behaves as a heterochromatin only under certain conditions, like in the mammalian X-chromosome when present in more than a single copy.

The reduced acetylation of histone proteins, increased methylation of one histone protein and hypermethylation of cytidine bases in DNA. These molecular changes cause the condensation of the material, which is responsible for inactivity. Although active genes are contained within euchromatin, only a small minority of the sequences in euchromatin are transcribed at any time. So, location in **euchromatin is necessary for gene expression, but is not sufficient for it.**

Satellite DNAs are found in regions of heterochromatin. Heterochromatin is the regions of chromosomes that are permanently tightly coiled up and inert, in contrast with the euchromatin that represents most of the genome. Heterochromatin is commonly found at centromeres (kinetochores, the regions controlling chromosome movement). The centromeric location of satellite DNA suggests some structural function in the chromosome which is connected with the process of chromosome segregation.

Operon Concept

Gene expression control can be broadly divide into transcription, processing, and translation. This is a functionally coordinated group of genes producing polycistronic transcripts (co-transcription). Operons have been discovered in prokaryotes, eukaryotes also contain operons but are complex. The mechanism is the operon, elegantly worked out by **Francois Jacob and Jacques Monod.** They distinguished between two types of sequences in DNA sequences that code for *trans*-**acting** products, and *cis*-**acting** sequences that function exclusively within the DNA. Gene activity is regulated by the specific interactions of the *trans*-acting products (usually proteins) with the *cis*-acting sequences (usually sites in DNA).

Operons are functional units of transcription. A short stretch of DNA called the **operator** lies in this position. It can bind very tightly to a special type of protein molecule, called a **repressor**, to create such an obstacle. When the repressor protein is bound to the operator, it blocks the transcription of *m*RNA. When the repressor is not attached to the operator, *m*RNA synthesis proceeds rapidly. The whole unit, consisting of the closely linked structural genes and the DNA sequences that control their transcription, is called an **operon.**

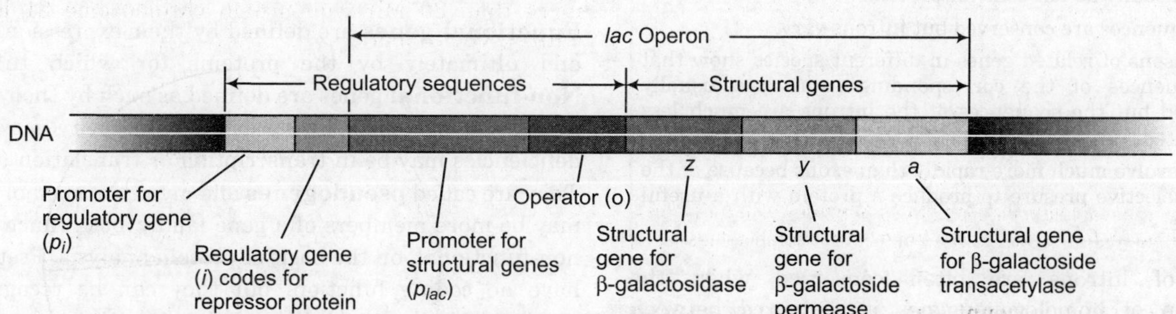

Fig. 5.10 The *lac* operon of *E. coli.* The *lac* operon of *E. coli* is a segment of DNA that includes a promoter, an operator and the three structural genes that code for lactose-metabolizing enzymes

A **structural gene** is simply any gene that codes for a protein (or RNA) product. A **regulator gene** simply describes a gene that codes for a protein (or an RNA) involved in regulating the expression of other genes. A promoter serves to initiate transcription only of the gene or genes physically connected to it on the same stretch of DNA.

Interrupted Genes

Eukaryotic genomes contain interrupted genes that consist of an alternation of **exons** (represented in the final RNA product) and **introns** (removed from the initial transcript). An interrupted gene is longer than its final RNA product because of the presence of the introns.

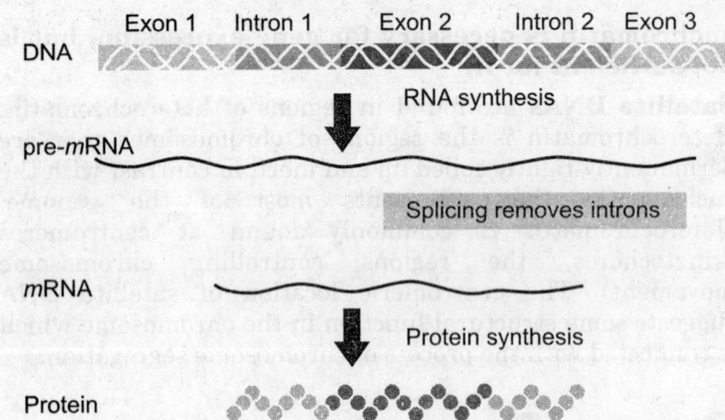

Fig. 5.11 An interrupted gene. The introns are the intervening sequences that are removed

Introns can be detected by the presence of additional regions when genes are compared with their RNA products by restriction mapping or electron microscopy, but the ultimate definition is based on comparison of sequences.

The positions of introns are usually conserved when homologous genes are compared between different organisms, but the lengths of the corresponding introns may vary greatly.

Introns usually do not code for proteins.

Key Concepts

- Introns can be detected by the presence of additional regions when genes are compared with their RNA products by restriction mapping or electron microscopy, but the ultimate definition is based on comparison of sequence.
- The positions of introns are usually conserved when homologous genes are compared between different organisms, but the lengths of the corresponding introns may vary greatly.
- Introns usually do not code for proteins.
- Exon sequences are conserved but introns vary.
- Comparisons of related genes in different species show that the sequences of the corresponding exons are usually conserved but the sequences of the introns are much less well related.
- Introns evolve much more rapidly than exons because of the lack of selective presure to produce a protein with a useful sequence.

Positions of introns are often conserved when the organization of homologous genes is compared between species. Intron sequences vary, and may even be unrelated, although exon sequences remain well related. The conservation of exons can be used to isolate related genes in different species. Introns become larger early in the higher eukaryotes, when gene sizes therefore increase significatly. The range of gene sizes in mammals is generally from 1-100 kb, but it is possible to have even larger genes, the longest known case is dystrophin at 2000 kb.

Gene Families

A set of genes descended by duplication and variation from some ancestral gene is called a gene family. Its members may be clustered together or dispersed on different chromosomes (or a combination of both). Genome analysis shows that many genes belong to families, the 40,000 genes identified in the human genome fall into ~ 15,000 families so, the average gene has a couple of relatives in the genome. Thus, a gene family is a set of several similar genes, formed by duplication of a single original gene and generally with similar biochemical functions. One such family are the genes for human haemoglobin subunits, the ten genes are in two clusters on different chromosomes, called the α-globin and β-globin loci. If the genes of a gene family encode proteins, the term protein family is often used in an analogous manner to gene family.

Duplicated genes may diverge to generate different genes or one copy may become inactive. All globin genes are descended by duplication and mutation from an ancestral gene that had three exons. The ancestral gene gave rise to myoglobin, leghaemoglobin and α and β-globins. The α and β-globin genes separated in the period of early vertebrate evolution, after which duplications generated the individual clusters of separate α-like and β-like genes. Once a gene has been inactivated by mutation, it may accumulate further mutations and become a pseudogene, which is homologous to the active gene(s) but has no functional role.

Functional genes are defined by their expression in RNA, and ultimately by the proteins for which they code. **Non-functional** genes are defined as such by their inability to code for proteins, the reasons for inactivity vary and the deficiencies may be in transcription or translation (or both). They are called **pseudogenes** and given the symbol ψ. There may be more members of a gene family, both functional and non-functional, on the basis of protein analysis. Pseudogenes have no coding function, but they can be recognized by sequence similarities with existing functional genes. They arise by the accumulation of mutations in (formerly) functional genes.

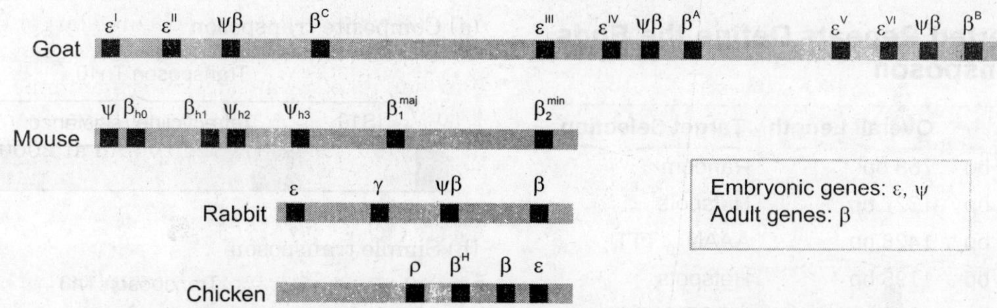

Fig. 5.12 Clusters of β-globin genes and pseudogenes are found in vertebrates

Mutations accumulate more rapidly in silent sites than in replacement sites (which affect the amino acid sequence). The rate of divergence at replacement sites can be used to establish a clock, calibrated in percent divergence per million years.

A tandem cluster consists of many copies of a repeating unit that includes the transcribed sequence(s) and a non-transcribed spacer(s). *r*RNA gene clusters code only for a single *r*RNA precursor. Maintenance of active genes in clusters depends on mechanisms such as gene conversion or unequal crossing-over that cause mutations to spread through the cluster, so, that they become exposed to evolutonary pressure.

Transposons

It discovered by **Barbara McClintock.**

Genomes evolve by rearranging the existing sequences. Rearrangements are sponsored by processes internal to the genome. There two of the major causes of rearrangements:

1. Unequal recombination results from mispairing by the cellular systems for homologous recombination.
2. Another major cause of variation is provided by **transposable elements** or **transposons.** These are discrete sequences in the genome that are mobile—they are able to transport themselves to other locations within the genome.

Transposons that **mobilize** *via* DNA are found in both prokaryotes and eukaryotes. Each **bacterial transposon** carries gene(s) that code for the enzyme activities required for its own transposition. **In eukaryotes,** their enzymatic functions are not so, well characterized. A genome may contain both functional and non-functional (defective) elements. Often the majority of elements in a eukaryotic genome are defective, and have lost the ability to transpose independently, although they may still be recognized as substrates for transposition by the enzymes produced by functional transposons. A eukaryotic genome contains a large number and variety of transposons.

Insertion Sequences—Simplest Transposons

The simplest and shortest transposons, known as insertion sequences, were first found in bacteria. They are designated IS1, IS2, etc. Typical insertion sequences are 750 to 1,500 base pairs (bp) long with terminal inverted repeats of 10 to 40 bp. Insertion sequences only encode a single enzyme, the **transposase,** the enzyme needed for movement. Between the inverted repeats is a region that actually contains two open reading frames. This gene product is a transcriptional regulator that controls the production of transposase and of itself.

An insertion sequence is a transposon that codes for the enzyme(s) needed for transposition flanked by short inverted terminal repeats. The target site at which a transposon is inserted is duplicated during the insertion process to form two repeats in direct orientation at the ends of the transposon. The length of the direct repeat is 5-9 bp and is characteristic for any particular transposon.

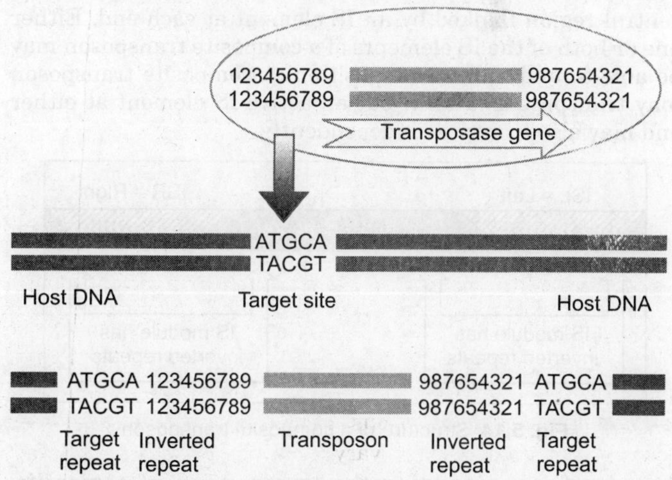

Fig. 5.13 Transposons have inverted terminal repeats and generate direct repeats of flanking DNA at the target site

The IS DNA is always flanked by very short direct repeats. The sequence of the direct repeat varies among individual transposition events undertaken by a transposon, but the length is constant for any particular IS element. The most common length for the direct repeats is 9 bp.

Table 5.2 **The Inverted Repeats Define the Ends of a Transposon**

			Overall Length	Target Selection
IS1	9 bp	23 bp	768 bp	Random
IS2	5 bp	41 bp	1327 bp	Hotspots
IS4	11-13 bp	18 bp	1428 bp	$AAAN_{20}$ TTT
IS5	4 bp	16 bp	1195 bp	Hotspots
IS10R	9 bp	22 bp	1329 bp	NGCTNAGCN
IS50R	9 bp	9 bp	1531 bp	Hotspots
IS903	9 bp	18 bp	1057 bp	Random

Composite Transposons

These transposons are named Tn followed by a number. One class of larger transposons are called composite elements, because a central region carrying the drug marker(s) is flanked on either side by 'arms' that consist of IS elements.

Table 5.3 **Some Common Composite Transposons**

Example	Left End	Markers	Right End
Tn903	IS903	*kan*^{R}	Both IS ends functional
Tn10	IS10L non-functional	*tet*^{R}	IS10R functional
Tn5	IS50L non-functional	*kan*^{R}	IS50R functional

Transposons can carry other genes in addition to those coding for transposition. Composite transposons have a central region flanked by an IS element at each end. Either one or both of the IS elements of a composite transposon may be able to undertake transposition. A composite transposon may transpose as a unit, but an active IS element at either end may also transpose independently.

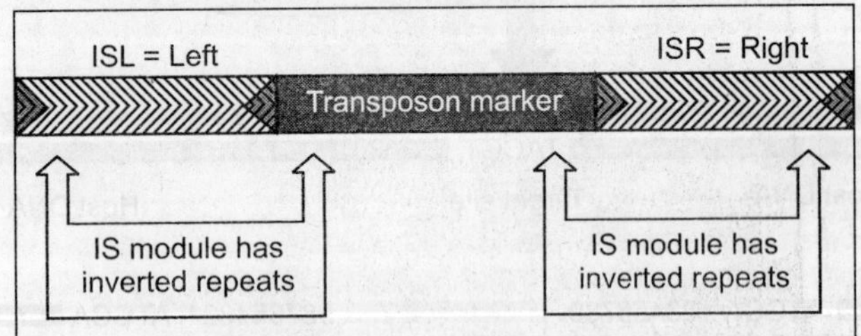

Fig. 5.14 Structure of a composite transposon

A major force supporting the transposition of composite. Transposons is selection for the marker(s) carried in the central region. An IS10 module is free to move around on its own and mobilizes an order of magnitude more frequently than Tn10. But Tn10 is held together by selection for *tet*$^{R-}$; so that under selective conditions, the relative frequency of intact Tn10 transposition is much increased.

(a) Composite transposon

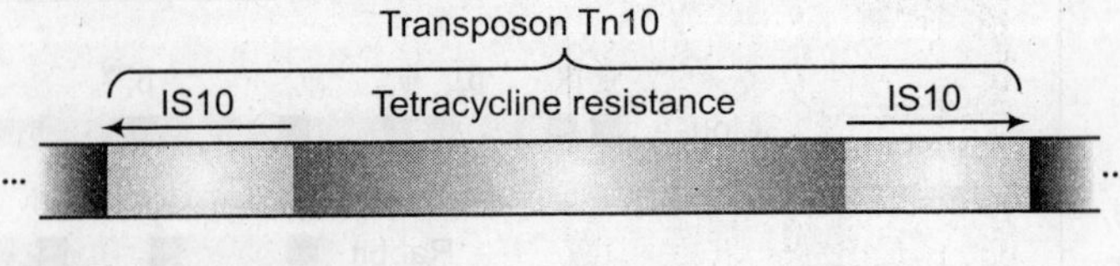

(b) Simple transposon

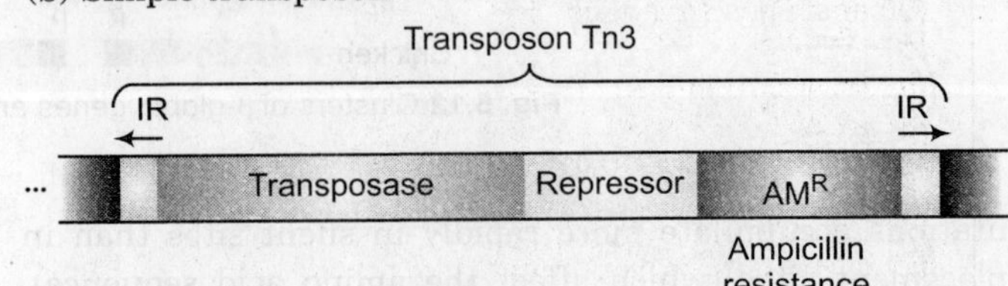

Fig. 5.15 Structural features of composite and simple transposons

Transposition—Replicative and Non-replicative Mechanisms

In replicative transposition, the element is duplicated during the reaction, so that the transposing entity is a copy of the original element. Replicative transposition involves two types of enzymatic activity, a transposase that acts on the ends of the original transposon and a resolvase that acts on the duplicated copies. A group of transposons related to TnA move only by replicative transposition. Replicative transposition proceeds through a cointegrate.

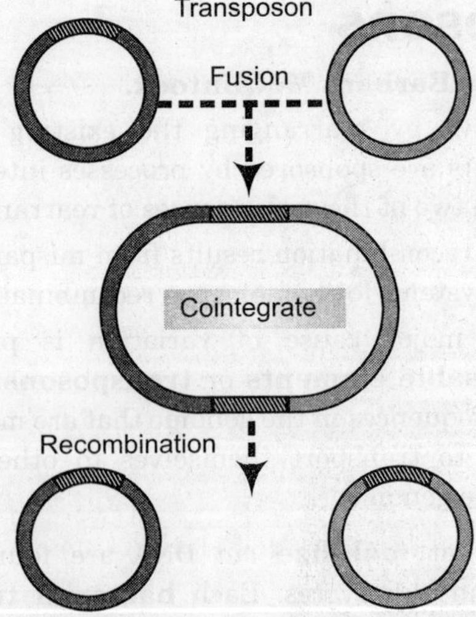

Fig. 5.16 Basic structures involved in replicative transposition are illustrated

In **non-replicative transposition**, the transposing element moves as a physical entity directly from one site to another, and is conserved. The insertion sequences and composite transposons Tn10 and Tn5 use the mechanism. Non-replicative transposition proceeds by breakage and reunion.

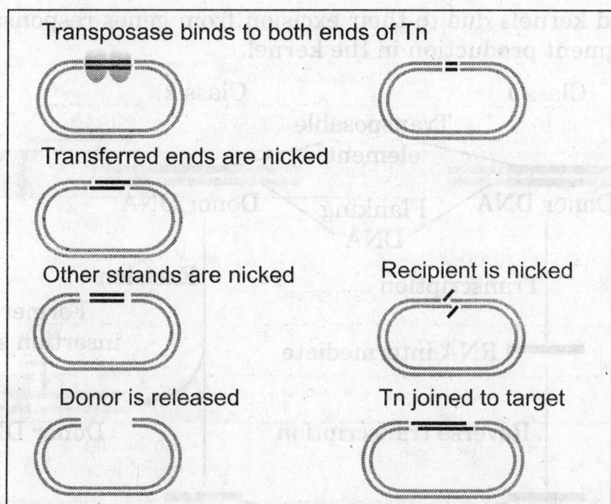

Fig. 5.17 The cut and paste pathway is used by Tn10, is illustrated

Conservative transposition describes another sort of non-replicative event, in which the element is excised from the donor site and inserted into a target site by a series of events in which every nucleotide bond is conserved.

Transposons Cause Rearrangement

Transposons cause rearrangement of DNA. Homologous recombination between multiple copies of a transposon causes rearrangement of host DNA. Homologous recombination between the repeats of a transposon may lead to precise or imprecise excision.

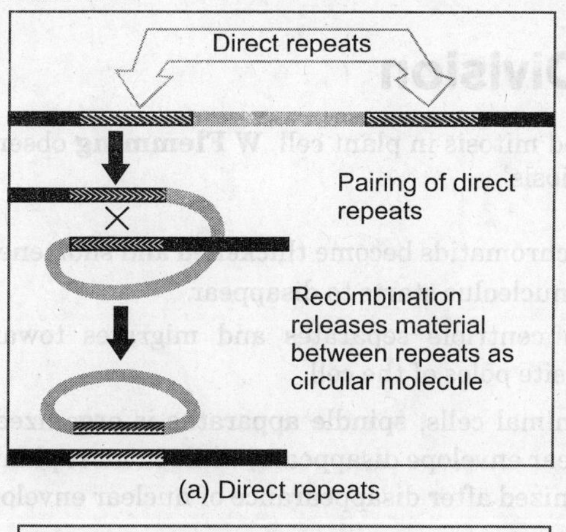

(a) Direct repeats

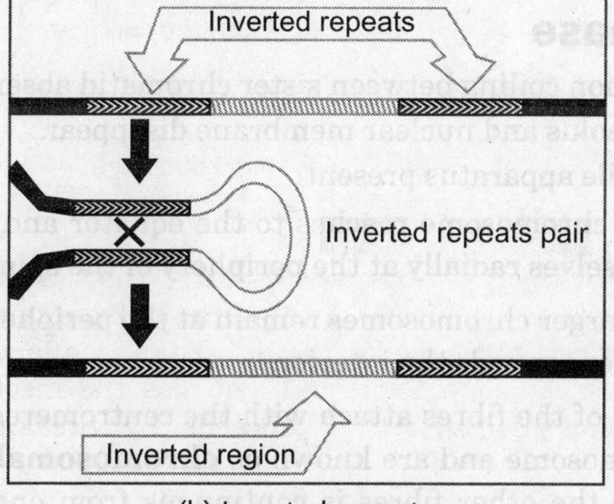

(b) Inverted repeats

Fig. 5.18 Rearrangement of DNA by transposons

TnA Transposition Organization

Transposition of Tn10 has multiple controls.

Multicopy inhibition (phenomenon of 'multicopy inhibition' reveals that expression of the IS 10R transposase gene is regulated) reduces the rate of transposition of any one copy of a transposon when other copies of the same transposon are introduced into the genome. Multiple mechanisms affect the rate of transposition.

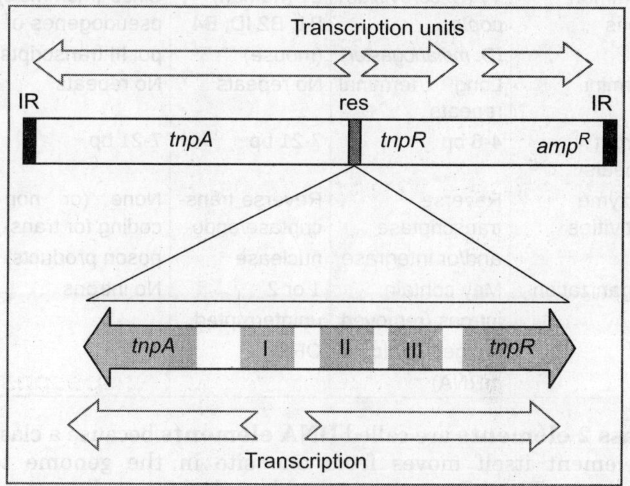

Fig. 5.19 TnA transposition organization is conserved

Replicative transposition of TnA requires a transposase to form the cointegrate structure and a resolvase to release the two replicons.

The best characterized transposons in plants are the controlling elements of maize, which fall into several families. Each family contains a single type of autonomous element, analogous to bacterial transposons in its ability to mobilize. The first transposon was discovered in the plant maize (*Zea mays*, corn species) and is named dissociator (Ds). Transposition of maize elements (in particular Ac) is non-replicative, probably requiring only a single transposase enzyme coded by the element. P elements in *D. melanogaster* are responsible for hybrid dysgenesis, which could be a forerunner of speciation.

Eukaryotic Transposable Elements Eukaryotic transposable elements fall into one of two classes, called class 1 and class 2 elements.

Class 1 elements are also called **RNA elements** because the DNA element in the genome is transcribed into an RNA copy. The RNA copy is converted back into a DNA copy that can then insert into another (target) site in the host genome. The elements are also called **retro-elements** because their movement (called **retrotransposition**) is characterized by the reverse flow of genetic information, from RNA to DNA.

There are three main sub-classes of retrotransposons:

- **Viral** encode reverse transcriptase (to reverse transcribe RNA into DNA), have long terminal repeats (LTRs), similar to retroviruses.
- **LINEs** encode reverse transcriptase, lack LTRs, transcribed by RNA polymerase II.

- **Non-viral super-family** do not code for reverse transcriptase, transcribed by RNA polymerase III.

Table 5.4 **Mammalian Genome has Three Type of Retro-Elements**

	Viral Super-family	Lines	Normal Super-family
Common types	Ty (*S. cerevisiae*) *copia* (*D. melanogaster*)	L1 (human) B1, B2 ID, B4 (mouse)	Sines (mammals) pseudogenes of pol III transcripts
Termini	Long terminal repeats	No repeats	No repeats
Target repeats	4-6 bp	7-21 bp	7-21 bp
Enzyme activities	Reverse transcriptase and/or integrase	Reverse trans-criptase/endo-nuclease	None (or non-coding for trans-poson products)
Organization	May contain introns (removed subgeonomic *m*RNA)	1 or 2 uninterrupted ORFs	No introns

Class 2 elements are called **DNA elements** because a class 2 element itself moves from one site in the genome to another. The first transposable elements discovered genetically in maize were class 2 elements that led to unusual spotted kernels due to their excision from genes responsible for pigment production in the kernel.

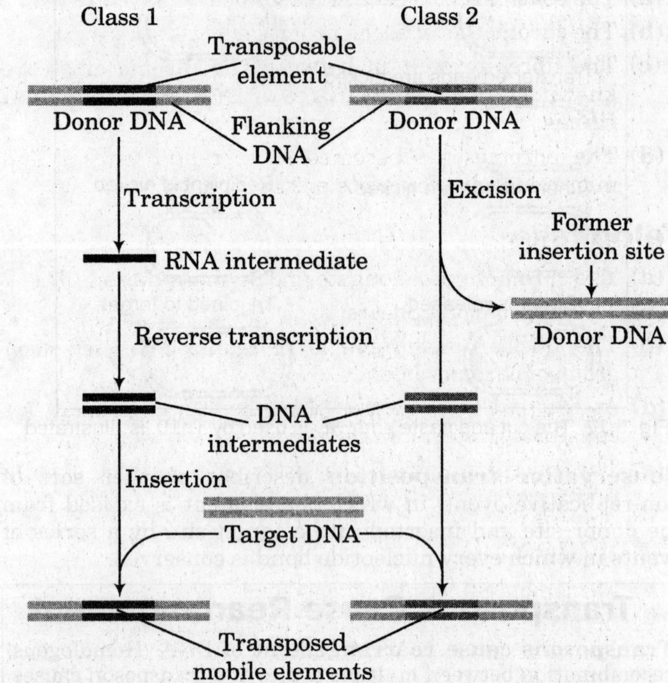

Fig. 5.20 Two classes of transposable elements in eukaryotes

Cell Cycle and Cell Division

W Flemming (1882) gave the term mitosis. **E Strasburger** (1875) observed mitosis in plant cell. **W Flemming** observed the mitosis in animal cell. **JB Farmer** and **Moore** in 1905 coined the term 'meiosis'.

Mitosis

The process of mitosis occurs in somatic cell so, it is known as **somatic cell division.** In mitotic cell division two daughter cells are formed, which resembles the parent cells morphologically and genetically. The mitosis can be divided into following steps.

Interphase

The resting phase between the two mitotic division is called **intermitotic phase** or **interphase.** The chromosomes do not divide during interphase. The interphase is the longest phase of the mitotic cycle.

Mitotic Phase

Following are the main phases of mitotic division.

Prophase

(a) The cell becomes spheroid, refractive and viscous.

(b) The nuclear envelope starts disintegrating.

(c) DNA duplicated during the interphase, each chromosome now possesses two chromatids.

(d) The chromatids become thickened and shortened.

(e) The nucleolus starts to disappear.

(f) Each centriole separates and migrates towards the opposite poles of the cell.

(g) In animal cells, spindle apparatus is organized before nuclear envelope disappears; while in most plant cells it organized after disappearance of nuclear envelope.

Metaphase

(a) Relation coiling between sister chromatid absent.

(b) Nucleolus and nuclear membrane disappear.

(c) Spindle apparatus present.

(d) Each chromosome reaches to the equator and arrange themselves radially at the periphery of the spindle.

(e) The larger chromosomes remain at the periphery, while smaller towards the interior.

(f) Some of the fibres attach with the centromeres of each chromosome and are known as **chromosomal fibres,** while the other fibres is continuous from one pole to another and is known as **continuous fibres.**

Anaphase

(a) The centromere of each chromosome divides into two.

(b) The chromatids of each chromosome get separated.

(c) The fibres present in between the chromosomes are known as **inter-zonal fibres** or **inter-chromosomal fibres.**

(d) The chromosome becomes shorter and thicker and migrate towards opposite poles of the cell.

Telophase

(a) The chromosomes elongate and becomes thread-like.

(b) The nucleolus reappears.

(c) The nuclear membrane is reorganized around each group of chromosome.

(d) At the end of telophase phragmoplast appear at the equatorial plate of the cell.

(e) The microtubules of the aster and mitotic spindle rearrange and disappear.

Cytokinesis

(a) Phragmoplast formed at the equatorial plate.

(b) In plant cell separation of cytoplasm begins at the centre of the cell and gradually extend outward each side of the cell. In animal cell separation of cytoplasm begins simultaneously with furrowing or invagination from all side of plasmalemma.

Meiosis

Meiosis is sometimes called **reductive cell division.** In meiosis DNA replication is completed in two rounds of cell division. The first round of division is called **meiosis-I,** which produces two intermediate daughter cells. The second round of division is called **meiosis-II,** which results in four genetically distinct haploid gametes.

Meiotic Division-I or Reductional Division

The meiotic division-I also known as reductional division because the homologous chromosome separate during this phase. The chromosomal number is reduced to half. It can be divided into following stages:

Prophase-I

During this stage, chromatin condenses, the spindle fibres are formed and the nucleoli and nuclear membrane disappear. The homologous chromosomes came together and interwined in a process called **synapsis.** At this stage each chromosome consists of two sister chromatids, each synaptic pair of homologous chromosomes contains four copies of the genome and are called **tetrad.** The prophase-I is the longest phase. It can be divided into following sub-stages:

Leptotene or Leptonema

(Gk. *Leptonema* = thin thread) The chromosome becomes uncoiled and appears in a thread-like shape. The centriole duplicates and each daughter centriole migrates towards the opposite poles of the cell. The **Bouquet formation** is observed during this stage.

Zygotene or Zygonema

(Gk. *Zygonema* = paired threads) The pairing of homologous chromosomes takes place in this stage. The pairing of homologous chromosomes is known as **synapsis.** The synapsis begins at one or more points along the length of the homologous chromosomes.

- The synapsis or pairing leads to formation of **bivalents.**
- The development of **synaptonemal complex** occurs.

Pachytene or Pachynema

(Gk. *Pachynema* = thick thread) The pair of chromosomes become twisted and cannot be distinguished separately.

- As a consequence of synapsis the number of observable chromosome is only half of somatic chromosome number.
- The pachynema chromosome consists of four chromatids closely joined together in one complex unit called a bivalent.
- The crossing over takes place in pachytene stage.

It involves mutual exchange of hereditary material of two parents between two homologous chromosomes. The crossing-over is accompanied by the **chiasmata formation.** The nucleolus associated with the nucleolar-organizer region of the chromosome.

Diplotene or Diplonema

(Gk. *Diplonema* = two thread) The force of attraction between the two homologous chromosomes decreases. The homologous chromosomes starts moving away from each other. During the separation of homologous chromosome of each bivalent; it found that the chromosomes are attached with each other at one or more point. This attachment is known as **chiasma.**

Diakinesis

The bivalent chromosomes become more condensed. The nucleolus separates from the nucleolar organizer and finally disappear. The chiasma moves towards the ends of the chromosomes and the intermediate chiasmata diminished. Such types of movement of chiasmata is known as **chiasma terminalization.**

Metaphase-I

The homologous chromosomal pairs (tetrads) align at the equatorial plane of the dividing cells and each homologous pair attaches to spindle fibres produced by kinetochore.

Anaphase-I

The homologous pairs of chromosomes (not sister chromatids) are pulled to opposite poles of the cell by spindle fibres. Each daughter cell at this point has one chromosome, each contains two sister chromatids. The sister chromatids remain together during meiotic anaphase-I and separate during the second round of meiotic cell division. In meiotic anaphase-I, each chromosome of paternal origin separates from its homologous chromosome of maternal origin. The separation of homologous chromosomes during meiosis is called **disjunction.**

Telophase-I

The nuclear membrane is formed around each new nucleus of the daughter cells I. At this point, each chromosome still consists of sister chromatids joined at the centromere. The cell divides through cytokinesis into two daughter cells, each of daughter cell receives a nucleus containing the haploid number of chromosomes.

Meiotic Division-II on Equatorial Division

In general the meiotic division-II or equatorial division is similar to mitosis, except that it is not proceeded by a round of DNA replication. The division of haploid cells occurs during meiotic division-II rather than diploid cell as in case of mitosis. There are following phases in the meiotic division-II.

Prophase-II The centrioles migrate to opposite poles and spindle apparatus is formed.

Metaphase-II The chromosomes line up along the equatorial plane.

Anaphase-II It is the shortest phase of meiosis. The sister chromatids are separated and pulled to opposite poles by the spindle fibres.

Telophase-II The nuclear membrane is formed around each new haploid nucleus. The cytokinesis results in formation of two daughter cells. Thus in the process of meiosis four haploid daughter cells are produced from single diploid cell.

Steps in Cell Cycle

The period between two mitotic divisions defines the somatic cell cycle.The cycle is divided into four different phases (G_1, S, G_2 and M, in that sequence). The time from the end of one mitosis to the start of the next is called **interphase** (comprising **gap 1, synthesis** and **gap 2**).

1. The period of actual division, corresponding to the visible mitosis, is called **M-phase.**
2. **G_1-phase,** when RNAs and proteins are synthesized, but there is no DNA replication.
3. The transition from G_1-phase to the period of **S-phase** is defined as lasting until all of the DNA has been replicated, the total content of DNA increases from the diploid value of $2n$ to the fully replicated value of $4n$.
4. The period from the end of S-phase until mitosis is called **G_2-phase;** during this period, the cell has two complete diploid sets of chromosomes.

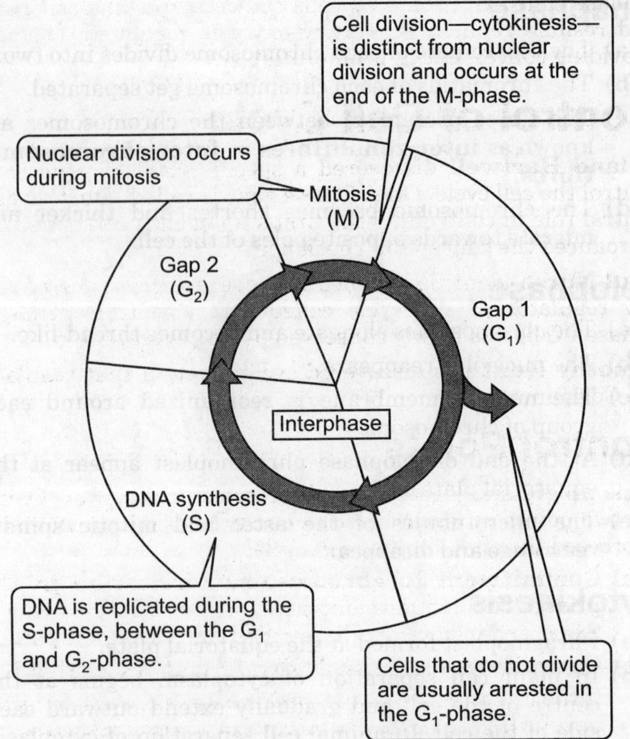

Fig. 5.21 The eukaryotic cell cycle : The cell cycle consists of a mitotic (M) phase and interphase. Interphase has three sub-phases (G_1, S and G_2) in cells that divide

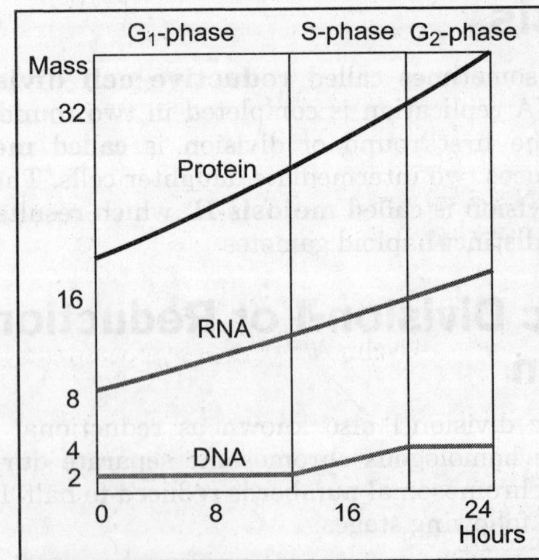

Fig. 5.22 The changes in cellular components

In yeasts and other fungi, the nuclear envelope does not breakdown during mitosis. In these organisms, the mitotic spindle forms within the nuclear envelope, which then pinches off, forming two nuclei at the time of cytokinesis.

Rapidly replicating human cells progress through the full cell cycle in about 24 hours: mitosis takes ≈30 minutes; G_1, 9 hours; the S-phase, 10 hours and G_2, 4.5 hours. In contrast, the full cycle takes only ≈90 minutes in rapidly growing yeast cells.

Some cells (*e.g.,* nerve cells and cells of the eye lens) of the organism remains without dividing again. Such **post-mitotic** cells generally exit the cell cycle in G_1, entering a phase called G_0. Some G_0 cells can return to the cell cycle and resume replicating, this re-entry is regulated, thereby providing control of cell proliferation.

Control of Cell Cycle

Leland Hartwell discovered a specific class of gene that control the cell cycle. One of these gene is called 'Start' It has central role in controlling the first step in each cell cycle. He introduced the concept of 'check point'.

Paul Nurse identified, cloned and characterized one of the key regulator of cell cycle called Cdk (Cyclic Dependent Kinase). Cdk was highly conserved during evolution.

Timothy Hunt has discovered cyclin protein that regulate the Cdk function.

Control Points

Cycle progression depends on discrete control points. There are two points at which a decision may be taken on whether to proceed through another cell cycle.

(a) **Commitment to chromosome replication in G_1 phase** The commitment point in yeast cells is called **Start** and in animal cells is called the **restriction point.**

(b) **Commitment to mitotic division at the end of G_2** If the cell does not divide at this point then the cell will have twice the normal complement of chromosomes.

In animal cells, G_1 control is the major point of decision and G_2/M control is subsidiary. Cells spend the longest part of their cycle in G_1, and it is the length of G_1 that is adjusted in response to growth conditions.

Cell halt in G_2 In the diploid organisms these cells usually likely to be called upon to divide again, *e.g.*, nuclei at some stages of insect embryogenesis divide and rest in the tetraploid state. In the haploid organisms, it is more common for cells to rest in G_2, this provide some protection against damage to DNA, since there are two copies of the genome instead of the single copy present in G_1. Some yeasts can use either G_1 or G_2 as the primary control point, depending on the nutritional conditions. Some (haploid) mosses usually use G_2 as the control point.

Checkpoints

Checkpoints occur throughout the cell cycle. It control the orderly progress of cell through the cell cycle, which prevent one stage from proceeding unless necessary earlier stages have been completed.

Checkpoints assess the readiness of the cell to proceed on the pathway. **Each checkpoint represents a control loop that makes the initiation of one event in the cell cycle dependent on the successful completion of an earlier event.** A checkpoint works by acting directly on the factors that control progression through the cell cycle.

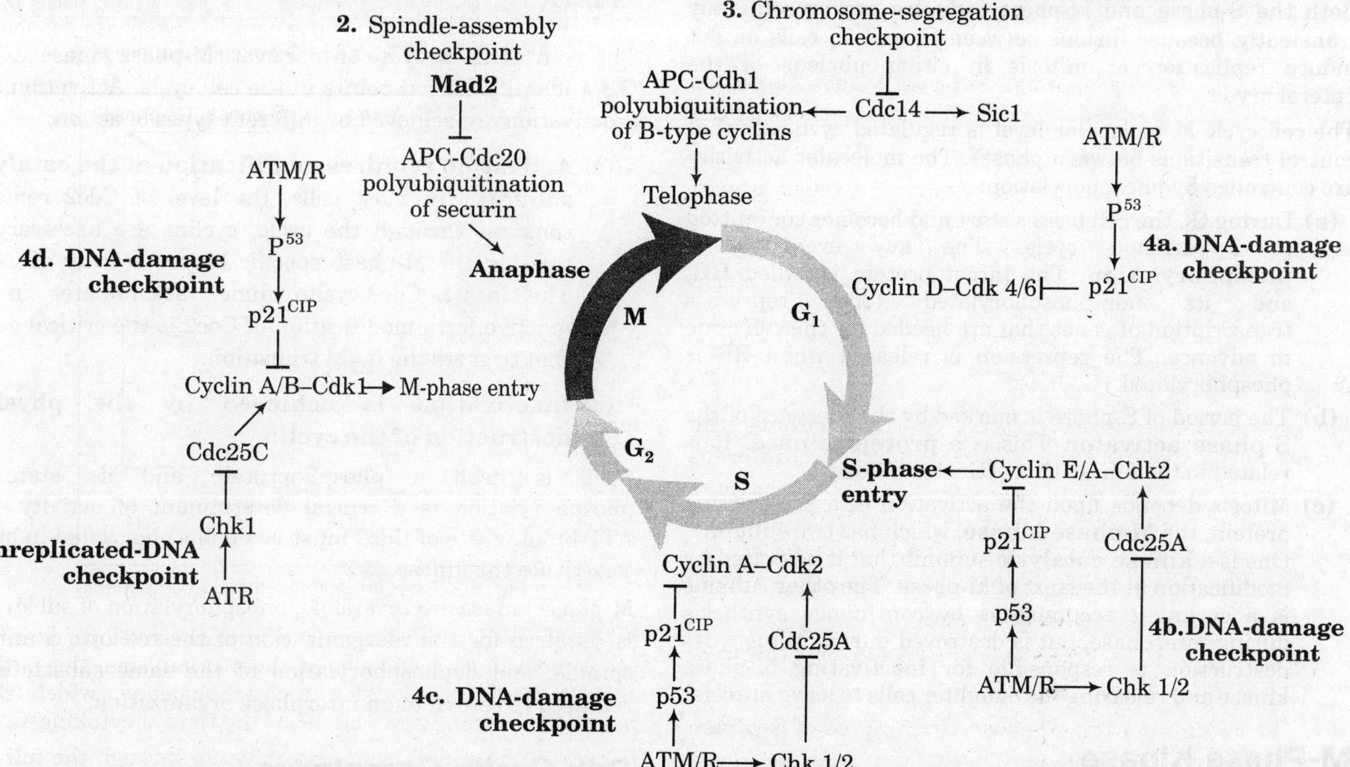

Fig. 5.23 Overview of checkpoint controls in the cell cycle. The unreplicated-DNA checkpoint 1. Prevents activation of cyclin A-Cdk1 and cyclin B-Cdk1, Spindle-assembly checkpoint 2. Inhibit activation of the APC specificity factor (Cdc20), thereby preventing entry into anaphase. The chromosome-segregation checkpoint 3. Prevents release of the Cdc14 phosphatase from nucleoli, thereby blocking activation of the APC specificity factor (Cdh1) as a result, the decrease in MPF activity required for the events of telophase does not occur; DNA-damage checkpoint 4a, the ATM or ATR protein kinase (ATM/R) is activated. The active kinases then trigger two pathways, the Chk-Cdc25A pathway 4b and 4c, blocking entry into or through the S-phase, and the P53-P21^{CIP} pathway, leading to arrest in G_1, S, and G_2 4a-4b.

Checkpoints within S-phase prevent continuing of replication and other checkpoint establishes that all the DNA has been replicated. Completion of DNA replication is a prerequisite for cell division.

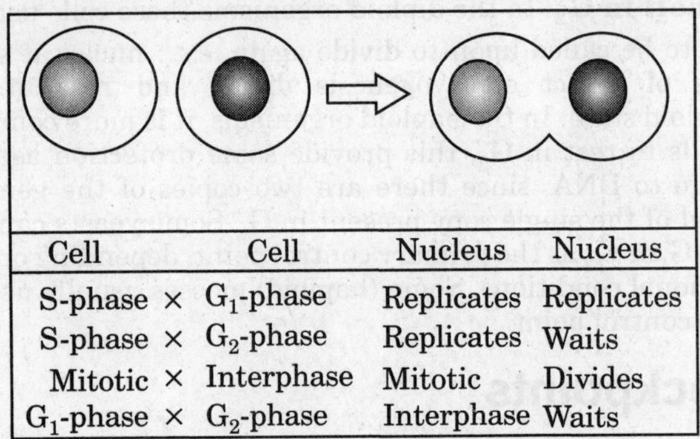

Cell	Cell	Nucleus	Nucleus
S-phase ×	G_1-phase	Replicates	Replicates
S-phase ×	G_2-phase	Replicates	Waits
Mitotic ×	Interphase	Mitotic	Divides
G_1-phase ×	G_2-phase	Interphase	Waits

Fig. 5.24 Cell fusion experiments

Cell fusion is performed by mixing the cells in the presence of either a chemical or viral agent that causes their plasma membranes to fuse, generating a hybrid cell called a heterokaryon, that contains two (or more) nuclei in a common cytoplasm.

Cell Cycle Induces

Both the S-phase and M-phase inducers are present only transiently, because fusions between G_1 and G_2 cells do not induce replication or mitosis in either nucleus of the heterokaryon.

The cell cycle at molecular level is regulated cyclically that control transitions between phases. The molecular activities are controlled by phosphorylation:

(a) During G_1, the cell passes start and becomes committed to a division cycle. The key event is a **phosphorylation.** The target protein is called **RB,** and its non-phosphorylated form represses transcription of genes that are needed for the cell cycle to advance. The repression is released when RB is phosphorylated.

(b) The period of S-phase is marked by the presence of the **S-phase activator.** This is a **protein kinase.** It is related to the kinase that activates mitosis.

(c) Mitosis depends upon the activation of a pre-existing protein, the **M-phase kinase,** which has two subunits. One is a **kinase catalytic** subunit that is activated by modification at the start of M-phase. The other subunit is a cyclin, it accumulates by continuous synthesis during interphase, but is destroyed during mitosis. Its destruction is responsible for inactivating M-phase kinase and releasing the daughter cells to leave mitosis.

M-Phase Kinase

M-phase kinase regulates entry into mitosis. **Maturation Promoting Factor** (MPF) has a general responsibility for causing somatic cells to enter M-phase, MPF is now understood to stand for **M-phase promoting factor.** As the mitosis are completed and S-phase occurs, the MPF activity disappears.

MPF causes germinal vesicle (nuclear envelope) breakdown when injected into *Xenopus* oocytes and induces several mitotic events in a cell-free system, including nuclear envelope disaggregation, chromosome condensation and spindle formation. MPF is a kinase that can phosphorylate a variety of protein substrates. This immediately suggests a mode for its action by **phosphorylating target proteins at a specific point in the cell cycle, MPF controls their ability to function.** In fact, the activity of the enzyme is most often assayed by its ability to phosphorylate target proteins and so, the name **M-phase kinase** provides a better description.

M-Phase Kinase: A Catalytic Subunit and a Regulatory Cyclin

M-phase kinase consists of two types of subunit with different functions

- Cdc2 is the **catalytic subunit** which phosphorylates serine and threonine residues in target proteins. It is named for the homologous protein in *Saccharomyces pombe.*
- Its partner is a cyclin, this is a regulatory subunit which is necessary for the kinase to function with appropriate substrates.

An M-phase kinase typically has a single type of catalytic subunit (Cdc2), but may have any one of several alternative cyclin partners. There are two general types of mitotic cyclins, A and B.

The events that activate or inactivate M-phase kinase at G_2/M identify crucial points in the cell cycle. Activation and inactivation are achieved by different types of action:

(a) **Activation requires modification of the catalytic subunit** In most cells, the level of Cdc2 remains constant through the cycle, cyclins are necessary to turn on the M-phase specific kinase activity of Cdc2. The intact Cdc2-cyclin dimer accumulates in an inactive form modification of Cdc2 is the critical event that triggers the G_2/M transition.

(b) **Inactivation is achieved by the physical destruction of the cyclin.**

Cdc2 is itself a phosphoprotein and its state of phosphorylation is a crucial determinant of activity. The ATP-binding site of Cdc2 must be dephosphorylated in order to activate the kinase.

M-phase kinase are reversible, phosphorylation of substrates is required for the reorganization of the cell into a mitotic spindle, and dephosphorylation of the same substrates is required to return to an interphase organization.

Cdk-Cyclin Complexes

The animal cell cycle is controlled by many Cdk-cyclin complexes. Catalytic subunits that associate with cyclins are called cyclin-dependent kinases (Cdks). Many dimeric kinases with a Cdc2-like catalytic subunit (Cdk) are found in animal cells. Cdk2 and Cdk4 are the catalytic subunits that are usually bound to G_1 cyclins. The dimers are controlled by phosphorylation of cdk subunits and by availability of cyclin subunits.

In each phase of cell cycle, a special **Ser/Thr-specific protein kinases** are formed, which are known as cyclin-dependent kinases (Cdks), bind an activator protein (cyclin) in order to become active. The Cdk–cyclin complex is activated by phosphorylation and/or dephosphorylation. The activated complex in turn phosphorylates **transcription factors,** which finally lead to the formation of the proteins that are required in the cell cycle phase (enzymes, cytoskeleton components, other Cdks and cyclins). The activity of the Cdk–cyclin complex is then terminated again by proteolytic **cyclin degradation.**

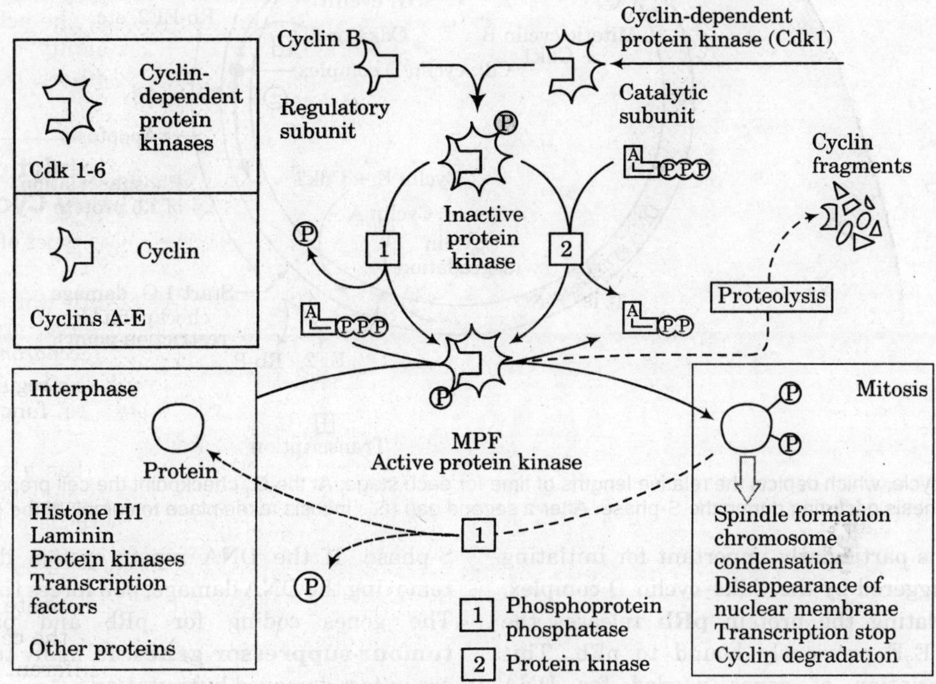

Fig. 5.25 Control of the cell cycle

Key Concepts

- **RB is a major substrate for Cdk-cyclin complexes** It is an important target for Cdk-G_1 cyclin complexes, its phosphorylation is required for initiation of S-phase.
- **G_0/G_1 and G_1/S transitions involve Cdk inhibitors** CKI proteins are inhibitors of Cdk-cyclin dimers. Different CKI proteins have specificities for different Cdk-cyclin complexes.
- **Cyclins are degraded at two points** during mitosis, cyclin A during metaphase and B cyclins to terminate mitosis. The APC (anaphase promoting complex) is an E_3 ubiquitin ligase that targets a substrate for degradation.
- **Cohesins hold sister chromatids together** Cohesins associate with chromatin at S-phase and hold sister chromatids together. A securin is a protein that sequesters a separin and keeps it in an inactive state. Anaphase in yeast is triggered when CDC20 causes the APC to degrade the securin Pds lp. Degradation of the securin releases the separin (Esp1 in yeast) which is a protease that cleaves the cohesin Scc1p. Cleavage of Scc1p releases the sister chromatids.

Entry of animal cells into mitosis is based on the **MPF. MPF** consists of **Cdk1** (cdc2) and **cyclin B.** The intracellular concentration of cyclin B increases constantly until mitosis starts and then declines again rapidly. MPF is initially inactive, because Cdk1 is phosphorylated and cyclin B is dephosphorylated.

The M-phase is triggered when a **protein phosphatase** dephosphorylates the Cdk while cyclin B is phosphorylated by a **kinase.** In its active form, MPF phosphorylates various proteins that have functions in mitosis, *e.g.*, **histone H1,** components of the cytoskeleton such as the **laminins** in the nuclear membrane, **transcription factors, mitotic spindle** proteins and various enzymes.

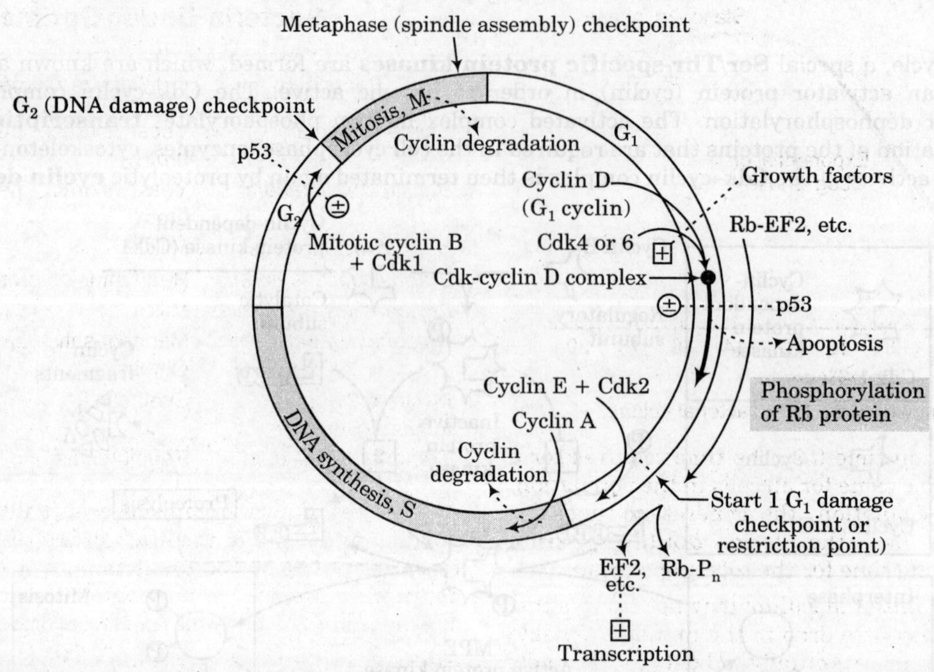

Fig. 5.26 The cell cycle, which depicts the relative lengths of time for each stage. At the G_1 checkpoint the cell prepares to divide, with DNA synthesis occurring during the S-phase. After a second gap (G_2) mitosis takes place to complete the cycle

The G_1–S transition is particularly important for initiating the cell cycle. It is triggered by the Cdk4–cyclin D complex, which by phosphorylating the protein **pRb** releases the transcription factor E_2F previously bound to pRb. This activates the transcription of genes needed for DNA replication. If the DNA is damaged by mutagens or ionizing radiation, the protein **p53** initially delays entry into the S-phase. If the DNA repair system does not succeed in removing the DNA damage, p53 forces the cell into apoptosis. The genes coding for pRb and p53 belong to the **tumour-suppressor genes.** In many tumours, these genes are in fact damaged by mutation.

Microbial Physiology

Like that of other organisms the microorganism including bacteria fungi, viruses, some algae and protozoans also have a characteristic pattern of growth, division and stress response and is studied under physiology.

Growth, Yield and Characteristic

Growth cycle is the cell division commences immediately and proceeds continuously for a protracted period of time, prokaryotic cell division follows a geometric progression:

$$2^0 \rightarrow 2^1 \rightarrow 2^2 \rightarrow 2^3 \rightarrow 2^4 \rightarrow 2^5 \rightarrow 2^6 \rightarrow 2^7 \rightarrow 2^8 \rightarrow 2^9 \rightarrow \text{, etc.}$$

This progression may be expressed as a function of 2 as shown in the line above. The number of cells (b) present at a given time may be expressed as

$$b = 1 \times 2^n$$

The total number of cells (b) is dependent on the number of generations (n = number of divisions) occurring during a given time period. Starting with an inoculum containing more than one cell, the number of cells in the population can be expressed as

$$b = a \times 2^n$$

where a is the number of organisms present in the original inoculum. Since the number of organisms present in the population (b) is a function of the number 2. Plotting the logarithm of the number, a linear function is obtained as shown in figure 5.27. For convenience, logarithms to the base 10 are used. This is possible because the logarithm to the base 10 of a number is equal to 0.3010 times the logarithm to the base 2 of a number.

Solving the equation for n, the number of generations that occurred between the time of inoculation and the time of sampling is

$$n = \frac{\log_{10} b - \log_{10} a}{0.3010}$$

The generation time (tg) or doubling time may be determined by dividing the time elapsed (t) by the number of generations (n):

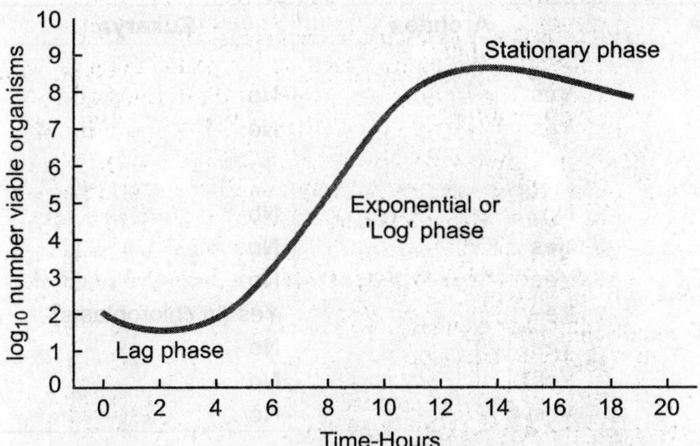

Fig. 5.27 A typical growth curve for a bacterial culture

The individual generation time (*i.e.,* the time required for a single cell to divide) is the same for all cells in the population. However, in a given population, the generation times for individual cells vary so, the term **doubling time** encompasses the doubling time for the total population.

Some of the cells in the initial inoculum may not survive this **lag phase** and there may be a drop in the number of viable cells. The surviving cells eventually adjust to the new environment and begin to divide at a more rapid rate, until conditions in the medium begin to deteriorate (*e.g.,* nutrients are exhausted). Since plotting the cell number logarithm during this period results in a linear function, this phase of growth is referred to as the **logarithmic** (log) **phase** or more correctly, the **exponential phase.**

Table 5.5 **Generation Times of Some Common Bacteria Under Optimal Conditions**

Bacterium	Culture Medium	Generation Time (min)
Escherichia coli	Yeast extract, peptone broth	20
Bacillus megaterium	Yeast extract, peptone broth	25
Streptococcus lactis	Milk	26
Staphylococcus aureus	Heart infusion broth	27-30
Lactobacillus acidophilus	Milk	66-87
Rhizobium japonicum	Mannitol-salts-yeast extract	344-461
Mycobacterium tuberculosis	Synthetic	792-932
Treponema pallidum	Rabbit testes	1980

All cultures of microorganisms eventually reach a maximum population density in the **stationary phase.** Exhaustion of essential nutrients, accumulation of toxic waste products, depletion of oxygen, or development of an unfavourable pH are the factors responsible for the decline in the growth rate.

Although cell division continues during the stationary phase, the number of cells that are able to divide (viable cells) are approximately equal to the number that are unable to divide (non-viable cells). Thus, the stationary phase represents an equilibrium between the number of cells able to divide and the number that are unable to divide.

The death of organisms in the population results in a decline in the viable population and the **death phase** ensues.

Table 5.6 **Summary of Major Differential Features Among Bacteria, Archaea and Eukarya**

Characteristic	Bacteria	Archaea	Eukarya
Morphological and Genetic Features			
Prokaryotic cell structure	Yes	Yes	No
DNA present in covalently closed and circular form	Yes	Yes	No
Histone proteins present	No	Yes	Yes
Membrane enclosed nucleus	Absent	Absent	Present
Cell wall	Muramic acid present	Muramic acid absent	Muramic acid absent
Ribosomes (mass)	70 S	70 S	80 S
Initiator *t*RNA	Formylmethionine	Methionine	Methionine
Introns in most genes	No	No	Yes
Operons	Yes	Yes	No
Capping and poly-A tailing of *m*RNA	No	No	Yes
Plasmids	Yes	Yes	Rare
Ribosome sensitivity to diphtheria toxin	No	Yes	Yes
RNA polymerases	One (4 subunits)	Several (8-12 subunits each)	Three (12-14 subunits each)
Transcription factors required	No	Yes	Yes
Promoter structure	–10 and –35 sequences (Pribnow box)	TATA box	TATA box
Sensitivity to chloramphenicol, streptomycin and kanamycin	Yes	No	No

Characteristic	Bacteria	Archaea	Eukarya
Physiological/Special Structures			
Methanogenesis	No	Yes	No
Dissimilative reduction of S^o or SO_4^{2-} or to H_2S or Fe^{3+} to Fe^{2+}	Yes	Yes	No
Nitrification	Yes	No	No
Denitrification	Yes	Yes	No
Nitrogen fixation	Yes	Yes	No
Chlorophyll-based photosynthesis	Yes	Yes	Yes (in chloroplasts)
Rhodopsin based energy metabolism	Yes	Yes	No
Chemolithotrophy (Fe, S and H_2)	Yes	Yes	No
Gas vesicles	Yes	Yes	No

Strategies of Cell Division

The flow of metabolites and timing of the individual activities be intricately coordinated so, that it lead to the orderly process of cell duplication. The processes that take place during the cell cycle are the coordination of chromosome replication with formation of a division septum, the production and activity of various proteins essential to the cell division process and the regulation of these events.

The cell wall peptidoglycan of *E. coli* and other Gram negative bacteria is extended by a process of intercalation of new wall material by numbers of enzymes. At a point, a series of events results in the assembly of a large group of proteins into a ring, where a constriction occurs between two daughter cells. This ring structure and its component parts are called a **divisome**.

The cell division can be inhibited without disrupting the continued linear elongation of the cell. The action of certain β-lactam antibiotics directly affect the process of cell division can result in the formation of filaments lacking septation.

The proposed steps in the cell division in *E. coli* involved three main groups of enzymes.

1. The first group contains enzymes that form the peptidoglycan sacculus around the growing cell. In the absence of modifying activities, this set of enzymes produces the minimum amount of peptidoglycan needed to completely surround the cell—that is, it produces spherical cells that enlarge without division.
2. The second groups modifying reactions—contains for example, the RodA-PBP2 system—that results in the development of a cylindrical shape to the peptidoglycan sacculus. These functions must be active over the entire surface (except at the poles) because pre-existing cylindrical surfaces are converted to spherical surfaces after inactivation of either of these two gene products. Also, a spherical surface formed in the absence of these products is replaced by or converted to a cylindrical surface after reactivation of this system.
3. The third group, responsible for cell division through the formation of new septation sites, acts periodically and is confined to the site of septation at the cell surface. A switch to formation of the type of peptidoglycan (murein) required for septation occurs late in the *E. coli* cell cycle.

   Inhibition by β-lactam agents gives rise to long, multinucleate non-septate filaments. Switching from cell elongation to septum formation may result from the change in the relative availability of the different peptide chains required by the two competing systems.

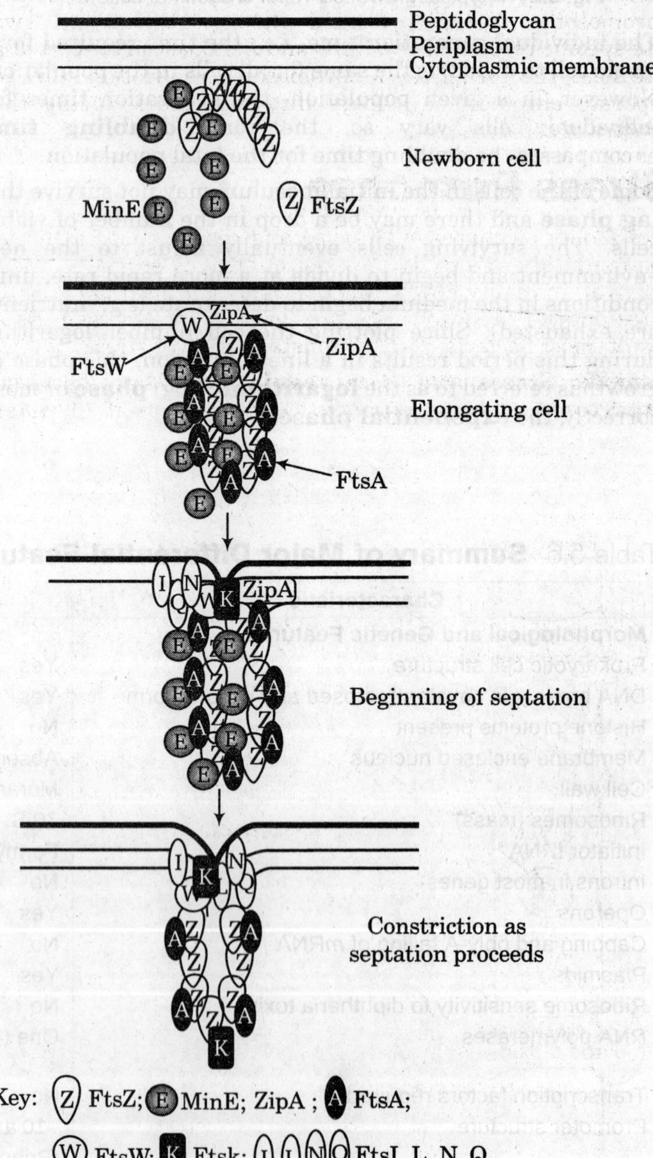

Fig. 5.28 The role of cell division components in *E. coli* (conceptual). The process begins with the assembly of FtsZ at the midpoint of the cell and targets MinE to the same location.

This penicillin-binding protein (FtsI) is a late recruit to the division site and its septal location is dependent on interaction with FtsZ, FtsA, FtsQ and FtsL as well as an intact membrane anchor. The FtsZ protein acts at an early stage of the septation process. FtsZ is a Mg-dependent GTPase dispersed throughout the cell. Just prior to the onset of septal invagination, FtsZ is recruited from the cytoplasm to the division site.

The cell division does not take place until a round of replication has been completed. The cell division is triggered by events that occur at or near the termination of replication. The most important of these is decatenation of the replicated chromosomes. The separated chromosomes are then partitioned into the two daughter cells. Division occurs subsequent to or simultaneously with partitioning. In *E. coli* several enzymes appear to participate in resolving chromosome dimmers formed during replication. Two site-specific recombinases, XerC and XerD, act in concert at a site near the terminus of chromosome replication (*dif*) to separate chromosome dimers into monomers during the process of cell division.

Stress Response

The ability of microbes to sense and respond (correctly) to imprompt alterations in the environment is crucial to their survival. In reality, conditions that allow for maximal growth rates outside the laboratory are few and far between. As a result, most bacteria live in a constant state of stress.

Osmotic Stress and Osmoregulation Many bacteria, **hypertonic** or **hyperosmotic** conditions result in water loss from the cytoplasm, causing the cell to shrink **(plasmolysis). Hypotonic** or **hypoosmotic** conditions result in an influx of water into the cytoplasm, which causes the cell to swell **(plasmoptysis)** and perhaps burst in a process referred to as **osmotic lysis.** Microbial membranes are freely permeable to water and therefore, water inside the cell is essentially at equilibrium with the outside of the cell. Microbes with cell walls can and do maintain a high cytoplasmic solute concentration relative to the outside.

The most rapid response to this osmotic upshock is an **increase in K^+ ion influx** through, at least, three uptake systems in *E. coli*, *Salmonella enterica* and other bacteria.

Many microbes also accumulate the **disaccharide trehalose** (composed of two glucose residues) as a **compatible solute** in response to osmotic stress as well as starvation, thermal stress and desiccation stress.

Complex sugars, known as **membrane-derived oligosaccharides** found in the periplasm of Gram negative bacteria can induced by growth in conditions of low osmolality.

Aerobic to Anaerobic Transitions Facultative microorganisms such as *E. coli* and *S. enterica* are capable of modifying their metabolism to accommodate growth under either aerobic or anaerobic conditions. The transition between aerobic and anaerobic metabolism is accompanied by alterations in the rate, route and efficiency of pathways of electron flow.

Under anaerobic conditions without alternate electron acceptors, pyruvate is converted to formate, acetate or ethanol, CO_2 and H_2 gas.

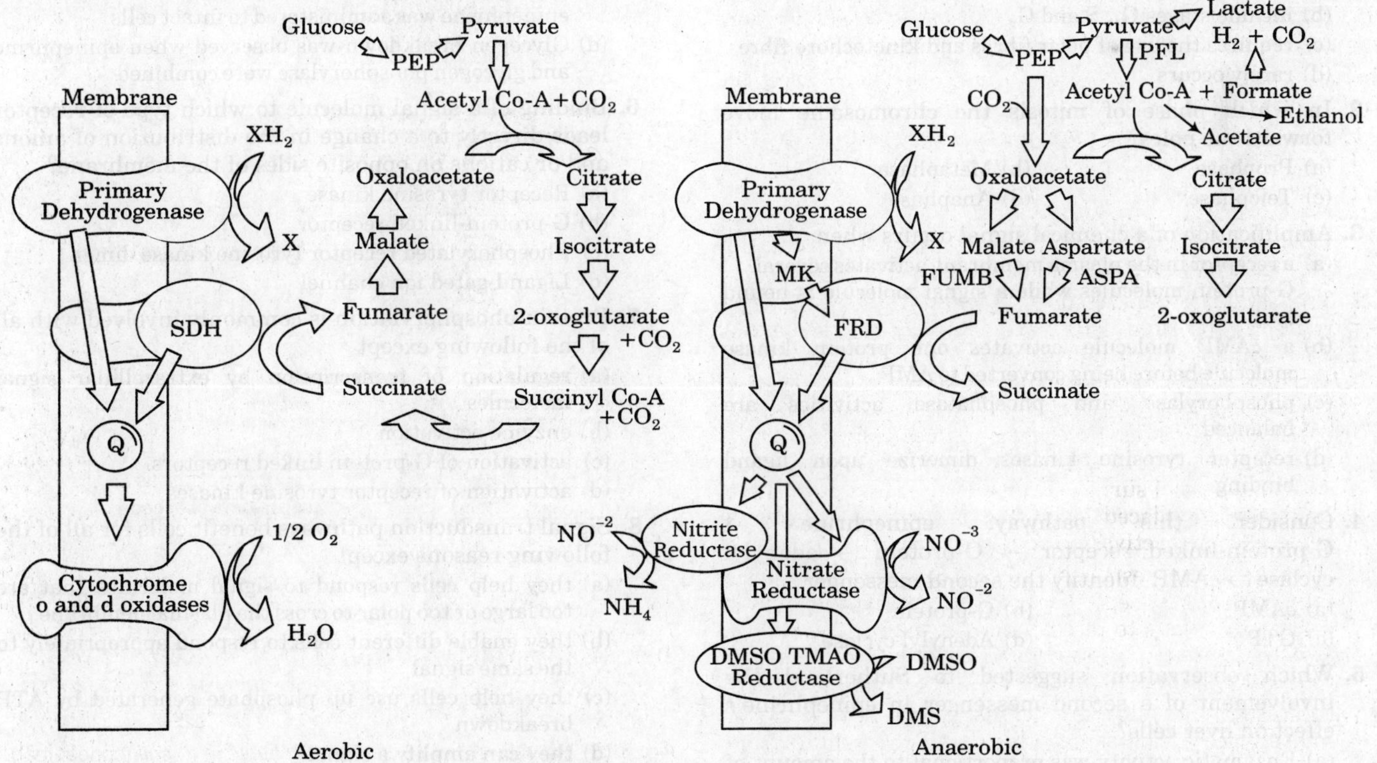

Fig. 5.29 Basic aerobic and anaerobic metabolic pathways of *E. coli*

Obligate anaerobic lack both superoxide dismutase and catalase that deal with reactive oxygen species, thus oxygen is toxic to them, *e.g., Clostridium.* **Microaerophiles** (capnophiles) only grow is low concentration of O_2 (< 21%) likes *Campylobacter jejuni, Neisseria gonorrhoea, Streptococcus.*

Most bacteria grow in ranges between 0.85% sodium chloride (physiological saline) and 3.5% sodium chloride (seawater). Most microorganisms are non-halophile like *E. coli* is salt intolerent. *Halophiles* grow in extreme high salt environment (15-30% salt). *Halobacterium* grow best in environment having 18% salt concentration.

Acidophiles (*Lactobacillus, Thiobacillus thioxidans*) maintain an internal pH of 6.5 over an external range 1-5.0. **Neutrophiles** (*E. coli*) cannot withstand pH condition greater than 8 or below 4.5 **Alkalophiles** (*Bacillus, Alcaligens faecalis* and *Vibrio cholerae*) mantain internal pH of 9.5 over on extreme pH range 9-11.

Thermal stress and the heat shock response upon a shift from 30 to 42°C, *E. coli* and other bacteria transiently increase the rate of synthesis of a set of proteins called Heat Shock Proteins (HSPs). Many of these HSPs are required for cell growth or survival at more elevated temperatures (thermotolerance). There are nearly 50 heat shock-inducible proteins identified in *E. coli*. They can be sub-divided into those regulated by alternative factors and two component regulatory systems.

B. subtilis has four classes of heat shock genes. All of them are not described here, but one is particularly interesting because of the mechanism used to control the genes. Class I heat shock genes include the major chaperones DnaK-DnaJ-GrpE and GroEL-GroES.

Psychrophilic Organisms The psychrophilic yeast *Leucosporidium* grows well at 1°C. In this organism, there is a positive correlation between the growth temperature and the unsaturated fatty acid composition of the cell lipids. The psychrophilic bacterium *Micrococcus cryophilus* also undergoes alteration in its lipid composition with changes in growth temperature.

Exercise

1. Interphase
(a) is the same as prophase, metaphase anaphase and telophase
(b) include stages G_1, S and G_2
(c) requires the use of polar fibres and kinetochore fibres
(d) rarely occurs

2. In which phase of mitosis the chromosome move forward the poles?
(a) Prophase (b) Metaphase
(c) Telophase (d) Anaphase

3. Amplification of a chemical signal occurs when
(a) a receptor in the plasma membrane activates several G-protein molecules while a signal molecule is bound to it
(b) a *c*AMP molecule activates one protein kinase molecule before being converted to AMP
(c) phosphorylase and phosphatase activities are balanced
(d) receptor tyrosine kinases dimerize upon ligand binding

4. Consider this pathway: epinephrine → G-protein-linked receptor → G-protein → adenylyl cyclase → *c*AMP. Identify the second messenger.
(a) *c*AMP (b) G-protein
(c) GTP (d) Adenylyl cyclase

5. Which observation suggested to Sutherland the involvement of a second messenger in epinephrine's effect on liver cells?
(a) Enzymatic activity was proportional to the amount of calcium added to a cell-free extract
(b) Receptor studies indicated that epinephrine was a ligand
(c) Glycogen breakdown was observed only when epinephrine was administered to intact cells
(d) Glycogen breakdown was observed when epinephrine and glycogen phosphorylase were combined

6. Binding of a signal molecule to which type of receptor leads directly to a change in the distribution of anions and/or cations on opposite sides of the membrane?
(a) Receptor tyrosine kinase
(b) G-protein-linked receptor
(c) Phosphorylated receptor tyrosine kinase dimer
(d) Ligand-gated ion channel

7. Protein phosphorylation is commonly involved with all of the following except
(a) regulation of transcription by extracellular signal molecules
(b) enzyme activation
(c) activation of G-protein linked receptors
(d) activation of receptor tyrosine kinases

8. Signal transduction pathways benefit cells for all of the following reasons except
(a) they help cells respond to signal molecules that are too large or too polar to cross the plasma membrane
(b) they enable different cells to respond appropriately to the same signal
(c) they help cells use up phosphate generated by ATP breakdown
(d) they can amplify a signal

9. Phosphorylation cascades involving a series of protein kinases are useful for cellular signal transduction because
(a) they are species specific
(b) they always lead to the same cellular response
(c) they amplify the original signal many fold
(d) they counter the harmful effects of phosphatases

10. The activation of receptor tyrosine kinases is always characterized by
(a) dimerization and phosphorylation
(b) IP_3 binding
(c) a phosphorylation cascade
(d) GTP hydrolysis

11. Lipid-soluble signal molecules, such as testosterone, cross the membranes of all cells but affect only target cells because
(a) only target cells retain the appropriate DNA segments
(b) intracellular receptors are present only in target cells
(c) most cells lack the Y-chromosome required
(d) only target cells possess the cytosolic enzymes that transduce the testosterone

12. Which of the following provides the best evidence that cell signalling pathways evolved early in the history of life?
(a) They are seen in 'primitive' cells such as yeast
(b) Yeast cells signal each other for mating
(c) Signal transduction molecules found in distantly related organisms are similar
(d) Signals can be sent long distances by cells

13. Which if these cells produce and secrete antibodies?
(a) Plasma cells (b) Cytotoxic T-cells
(c) Helper T-cells (d) Macrophages

14. What kind of white blood cells defend against parasitic invaders?
(a) Basophils (b) Monocytes
(c) Eosinophils (d) Neutrophils

15. .... proliferate in the bone marrow and .... mature in the thymus.
(a) B-cells; T-cells (b) NK-cells; T-cells
(c) T-cells; B-cells (d) B-cells; NK-cells

16. Correct statements concerning heterochromatin include which of the following?
I. It is not easily transcribed.
II. It occurs in the centromeres of chromosomes.
III. It is associated with histone H1.
IV. It is relatively dispersed and stains poorly.
(a) I and II (b) I, II and III
(c) I and III (d) I, II, III and IV

17. What kind of molecules must pass between the nucleus and the cytoplasm?
(a) DNA (b) Protein
(c) Lipids (d) Carbohydrates

18. In a cell if acidity of lysome is lost, then loss of
(a) phagocytosis of invading bacteria
(b) elevated phosphatase level
(c) glycogen degradation
(d) no major effect

19. Bacterial genomes is prevented by its own endonucleases by
(a) methylation at restriction sites
(b) immune mechanism
(c) muclease resistant genome
(d) are not much effective on bacterial genome

20. The difference which distinguish prokaryotic cell from eukaryotic is
(a) ER (b) mesosome
(c) nuclear membrane (d) plasma membrane

21. Extra nuclear genetic material is found in
(a) ribosome (b) ER
(c) chloroplast (d) centriole

22. Holiday junction is observed during
(a) mitosis (b) interphase
(c) recombination (d) DNA repair

23. Which one of the following is correct for structure of cell wall of fungi and bacteria?
(a) Both have glycopeptide
(b) Both are made up of N-acetylglucasamine
(c) Both are made up of murin
(d) Both are made up of chitin

24. Post-translation modification of secretary proteins occurs in
(a) RER (b) SER
(c) mitochondria (d) nucleus

25. The cell wall of microorganisms is coated with certain plasma protein promoting the attachment of microbe to phagocytes, only then they can be phagocytosized. The coat protein are called as
(a) globins (b) opsonins
(c) ovulbumins (d) phagosonins

26. Which of the following is not a function of mitotic cell division in?
(a) Repair of damaged organs
(b) Production of gametes
(c) Asexual reproduction
(d) Growth

27. During cytokinesis in plants
(a) a bundle of actin microfilaments called the contractile ring, pinch the cell in half
(b) small vesicles, directed by the phragmoplast, move to the spindle
(c) a cleavage furrow encircles the cell
(d) cytoplasmic division is called cleavage

28. Which of the following occurs during meiosis but not during mitosis?
(a) Chromosomes align at the metaphase plate
(b) Chromosomes condense
(c) Chromosomes migrate to opposite poles
(d) Synapsis

29. At the end of telophase-I and cytokinesis there are
(a) 4 haploid cells
(b) 2 diploid cells
(c) 1 haploid ovum and 3 polar bodies
(d) 2 haploid cells

30. Synapsis occurs during
(a) anaphase-I (b) prophase-I
(c) cytokinesis (d) prophase-II

31. During anaphase-II
(a) homologues separate and migrate towards opposite poles
(b) sister chromatids separate and migrate towards opposite poles
(c) nuclei reform
(d) chromosomes line up in a single file

32. During anaphase-I
(a) homologues separate and migrate towards opposite poles
(b) sister chromatids separate and migrate towards opposite poles
(c) nuclei reform
(d) chromosomes line up in a single file

33. Cytokinesis is the
(a) exchange of homologous regions of non-sister chromatids
(b) formation of tetrads
(c) independent assortment of chromosomes
(d) division of one cell into two

34. Centrioles separate during
(a) cytokinesis
(b) prophase-I and prophase-II
(c) metaphase-I and metaphase-II
(d) anaphase-I and anaphase-II

35. Crossing over occurs during
(a) cytokinesis (b) metaphase-I
(c) prophase-II (d) prophase-I

36. Regions where non-sister chromatids cross are called
(a) inversions (b) homologues
(c) tetrads (d) chiasmata

37. An bacterial operon contains three structural genes A, B and C in the same order. If polar mutation occurs in gene B, then the effect in protein would be observed in
(a) in all proteins A, B and C
(b) only in B and C
(c) only in B
(d) complete loss of all proteins

38. Exponential growth in bacteria would be expected during
(a) lag phase (b) log phase
(c) stationary phase (d) deceleration phase

39. The movement of chloroplast is mediated by
(a) dynein (b) kinesin
(c) actin (d) myosin

40. The flagellin protein is associated with
(a) bacteria (b) protist
(c) virus (d) eukaryotic cell

41. Starch filled plastids are responsible for geotropism in columella cell beneath the root cap. They are termed as
(a) amyloplast (b) elioplast
(c) chloroplast (d) proplastid

42. ABC transporter in plants which are responsible for detoxification of xenobiotics and prevent oxidative damage are located at
(a) tonoplast (b) peroxisome
(c) ER (d) plasma membrane

43. Which of the following is true regarding the phage lambda, a virus which infects bacteria?
(a) In the lytic cycle, the bacterial host replicates viral DNA, passing it on to daughter cells during binary fission.
(b) In the lysogenic cycle, the bacterial host replicates viral DNA, passing it on to daughter cells during binary fission.
(c) In the lytic cycle, viral DNA is integrated into the host genome.
(d) In the lysogenic cycle, the host bacterial cell bursts, releasing phases.

44. Which of the following cells have cilia?
(a) Cells lining the human respiratory tract
(b) *Euglena*
(c) Cells lining the human urinary tract
(d) Human sperms cells

45. Which of the following contains thymine?
(a) DNA (b) *r*RNA
(c) *r*RNA (d) *m*RNA

46. Which of the following statements is false regarding SDS-polyacrylamide gel electrophoresis?
(a) Proteins are separated by molecular weight
(b) SDS is a detergent which gives charge to protein
(c) Large proteins move more slowly through the gel
(d) SDS is used to maintain the three dimensional structure of protein

47. Regulation of *trp* operon by binding of trytophan to *trp* repressor is termed as
(a) repression (b) induction
(c) anti termination (d) atteneution

48. The Mendelian law of independent assortment is due to arrangement of chromosome during
(a) anaphase-I (b) anaphase-II
(c) S-phase (d) cytokinesis

49. Minisatellite repeats
I. Contain fewer individual repeats per cluster than satellite repeats.
II. Have a core repeat of 10-15 nucleotides.
III. Frequently vary in sluster size between individuals in a population.
IV. Are not active in DNA recombination.
(a) I and II (b) I and IV
(c) II and IV (d) I, II and III

50. Among the following which organelle is involved in apoptosis?
(a) Lysosome (b) ER
(c) Golgi (d) Mitochondria

51. Taxol, an anti-cancerous drug effects
(a) inhibiting polymerization of tubulin
(b) inhibiting depolymerization of tubulin
(c) polymerization of actin
(d) favouring depolymerizaton of tubulin

52. Polytene chromosome is generated due to
(a) failure of DNA replication
(b) repeated DNA replication without segregation chromosomes
(c) pairing of homologous chromosomes
(d) due to extensive transcription process

53. Which sequence represents increasing levels of chromosomal organization, from most dispersed to most condensed?
(a) Nucleosomes–30 nm filaments–supercoiled loops–mitotic chromosomes
(b) Nucleosomes–supercoiled loops–30 nm filaments–mitotic chromosomes
(c) Nucleosomes–30 nm filaments–mitotic chromosomes–supercoiled loops
(d) Mitotic chromosomes–30 nm filaments–supercoiled loops–nucleosomes

54. When chromatin is treated with non-specific nucleases, what is the length of the resulting pieces of DNA?
(a) Random numbers of base pairs
(b) About 60 base pairs
(c) About 8 base pairs
(d) About 200 base pairs

55. Which of the following statements about histones is not true?
(a) Histones are very similar between species
(b) Histones have many basic amino acids
(c) Histones are rich in lysine and arginine
(d) Each histone has one single gene that codes for it

56. In mammalian cells, the DNA of the centromere is characteristic of
(a) facultative heterochromatin
(b) constitutive heterochromatin
(c) euchromatin
(d) dispersed chromatin

57. Why are adult women genetic mosaics?
(a) Inactivated X-chromosomes are all derived from the male parent
(b) Inactivated X-chromosomes are all derived from the female parent
(c) Inactivated X-chromosomes can be from either the male or the female parent
(d) None of the above

58. What do telomeres do?
(a) They protect the chromosomes from degradation by nucleases
(b) They prevent the ends of chromosomes from fusing with one another
(c) They are required for complete chromosomal replication
(d) All of the above

59. When all or a piece of a chromosome becomes attached to another chromosome, the aberration is called a(n)
(a) inversion
(b) translocation
(c) deletion
(d) duplication

60. If there were a mutation in the regulatory gene of an inducible promoter rendering the protein incapable of binding to the repressor, then
(a) the structural genes would always be expressed
(b) the structural genes would never be expressed
(c) the structural genes would only be expressed in the presence of the inducer
(d) the structural genes would only be expressed in the absence of the inducer

61. Which of the following is a difference between inducible *versus* repressible operons?
(a) In an inducible operon, the inducer binds to the regulator protein
(b) In a repressible operon, the corepressor-regulator complex binds to the operator
(c) In a repressible operon, all the structural gene products have related functions
(d) In an inducible operon, RNA polymerase binds to the promoter

62. Eukaryotes regulate gene expression at all of the following levels except
(a) transcription
(b) translation
(c) RNA processing
(d) All of these

63. To stimulate transcription, enhancer sequences
(a) must be within a few base pairs of the gene they enhance
(b) must be within a few hundred base pairs of the gene they enhance
(c) can be tens of thousands of base pairs away from the genes they enhance
(d) will not function if they are moved experimentally

64. Coactivators assist in transcriptional activity by
(a) interacting with general transcription factors
(b) modifying the activity of RNA polymerase II directly
(c) changing chromatin structure to make transcription of certain genes more accessible
(d) All of the above

65. Alternate splicing means that
(a) the same gene can code for several different proteins
(b) several different genes can code for the same protein
(c) gene expression can be regulated at the level of transcription
(d) pieces of DNA can move around within the genome

66. Which of the following statements is true?
(a) A cell can potentially make fewer different proteins than the number of different genes it contains
(b) A cell can potentially make only the same number of different proteins as the number of different genes it contains
(c) A cell can potentially make more different proteins than the number of different genes it contains
(d) None of the above

67. The longevity of *m*RNA is related to
(a) the length of the poly (A) tail
(b) the 5′ cap on the *m*RNA
(c) Both (a) and (b)
(d) None of the above

68. Freshly broken chromosome ends are sticky and tend to fuse, however ends of intact chromosomes are stable. Their stability is due to presence of
(a) centromeres
(b) telomeres
(c) special membrane around chromosomes
(d) kinetochores

69. Simple sequence DNA
I. Reassociates with the intermediate component of a $C_0t_{½}$ curve.
II. Consists of individual short repeated sequences that are dispersed throughout the genomes.
III. Accounts for approximately 10% of mammalian genomes.
IV. Has a characteristic buoyant density based on its nucleotide composition.
(a) I and II (b) I and IV
(c) III and IV (d) I, II and III

70. It is difficult to observe individual chromosomes with a light microscope during interphase because
(a) they have uncoiled to form long, thin strands
(b) they leave the nucleus and are dispersed to other parts of the cell
(c) the DNA has not been replicated yet
(d) the spindle must move them to the metaphase plate before they become

71. One can estimate the length of M-phase by knowing the
(a) S-phase (b) mitotic index
(c) age of the cell (d) generation time

72. Cells will usually divide if they receive the proper signal at
(a) M (b) S
(c) G_2 (d) G_1

73. The electron microscope has been particularly useful in studying bacteria, because
(a) electrons can penetrate tough bacterial cell walls
(b) bacteria are so small
(c) bacteria move so quickly they are hard to photograph
(d) with few organelles present, bacteria are distinguished by differences in individual macromolecules

74. Sister chromatids
(a) are created when DNA is replicated
(b) are separated during mitosis
(c) are attached at the centromere prior to division
(d) All of the above

75. Which of the following correctly matches a phase of the cell cycle?
(a) S, immediately precedes cell division
(b) M, duplication of DNA
(c) G_1, immediately follows cell division
(d) G_2, cell division

76. The kinetochores
(a) are the primary centromere structures that maintain the attachment
(b) attach to the ring of actin along the cytoplasmic surface of the plasma membrane
(c) move along spindle microtubules during anaphase, dragging
(d) are located at the center of the centromere their function is to provide attachment site to spindle fibre

77. A biochemist measured the amount of DNA to be doubled during the cells in growing stages
(a) between prophase and anaphase
(b) between anaphase and telophase
(c) during the M-phase of the cell cycle
(d) between the G_1 and G_2-phases

78. DNA damaged by sunlight
(a) has undergone depurination
(b) has lost its phosphate groups
(c) has formed pyrimidine dimers
(d) has lost its hydrogen bonds

79. Which of the following functional processes results from the presence of protein within the plasma membrane?
(a) Enzymatic activity
(b) Signal transduction
(c) Intercellular joining
(d) All of the above

80. Progression through the eukaryotic cell cycle is regulated by
(a) microtubules (b) the p53 gene
(c) cyclin-dependent kinases(d) DNA ligase

81. The result of the operation of an electrogenic pump would be
(a) an electrochemical gradient on the cell membrane
(b) a resting potential across the membrane
(c) plasmolysis
(d) a cell with a positively charged interior

82. The p53 gene
(a) is the most frequently mutated gene in human cancer
(b) can lead to cell cycle arrest at the G_1 checkpoint
(c) can trigger apoptosis
(d) All of the above

83. When a dividing cell is treated with hydrogen peroxide, the spindle fibres precipitate due to formation of disulphide bridges. This reaction indicates that the spindle fibres and the microtubules are
(a) glycosyl structures
(b) proteinaceous structures
(c) non-polar organic structures
(d) None of the above

84. Brachymeiosis is
(a) failure of meiosis-I or meiosis-II
(b) failure of metaphase
(c) failure of prophase
(d) doubling of chromosome

85. In zygotene, homologous chromosomes undergo pairing to form bivalent having two homologous chromosomes. These two chromosomes are attached laterally due to
(a) U protein
(b) swielase
(c) ribonucleoprotein
(d) endonuclease

86. Isochromosome refers to the
(a) chromosome which has been isolated from the rest of the complement
(b) chromosome which has reached the equatorial plane earlier than the other chromosomes
(c) translocated chromosome having identical arms
(d) lagging chromosome which has not moved to either of the poles

87. During cell division, mitochondria
(a) accumulate near the spindle and form rings around the myofibrillar bands in the muscle cell
(b) split into two equal halves in readiness to migrate to each daughter cell
(c) arrange themselves at the equator and twist to form coils
(d) migrate to terminal poles on long threads and split vertically

88. Colchicine arrests any mitotically dividing cell at metaphase by
(a) preventing the polymerization of tubulin into microtubules of the spindle
(b) preventing the movement of spindle fibres as a result of which chromosomes fail to go the opposite poles
(c) destroying the contractile property of the spindle protein which eventually coagulate
(d) dislodging chromosomes from the fibrous elements of the spindle and consequently the chromosomes remain confined to the equatorial plane

89. Mitotic chromosomes are transcriptionally inactive because
(a) ribonucleoside triphosphates are sparingly available as they walk over to cytoplasm in the absence of a nuclear membrane
(b) energy needed for transcription is diverted towards spindle-apparatus formation
(c) RNA polymerase, specially its s-factor, gets denatured after getting combined with spindle forming molecules
(d) condensed form of chromatin prevents RNA polymerase from gaining access to DNA

90. A cell that passes the restriction point will most likely
(a) undergo chromosome duplication
(b) have just completed cytokinesis
(c) continue to divide only if it is a cancer cell
(d) show a drop in MPF concentration

91. The rhythmic changes in cyclin concentration in a cell cycle are due to
(a) its increased production once the restriction point is passed
(b) the cascade of increased production once its enzyme in phosphorylated by MPF
(c) its degradation by an enzyme phosphorylated by MPF
(d) the changing ratio of cytoplasm to genome

92. Which of the following does not lead to genetic variability?
(a) Random fertilization
(b) Crossing over during meiosis
(c) Division of chromosomes during anaphase of mitosis
(d) Orientation of chromosomes during metaphase-I of meiosis

93. Most cells will divide if they receive the proper signal at a checkpoint in the .... phase of the cell cycle.
(a) M (b) G_1
(c) S (d) G_2

94. Geneticists suspect that the extrachromosome seen in Down syndrome usually comes from the egg, rather than the sperm, because
(a) eggs are produced so rapidly that there is more chance for error
(b) Down syndrome is due to dominant gene in women, a recessive gene in men
(c) most women inherit Down syndrome from their mothers
(d) meiosis takes longer in the ovary, increasing the likelihood of error

95. There are a number of differences between fission of a bacterium and human cell division.
Which of the following is not one of them?
(a) A bacterium has only one chromosome
(b) Duplicated bacterial chromosomes attach to the plasma membrane
(c) Bacteria are smaller and simpler than human cells
(d) Bacteria have to duplicate their DNA before dividing

96. You would be unlikely to see which of the following human cells dividing?
(a) Nerve cell (b) Skin cell
(c) Cancer cell (d) Cell from an embryo

97. Sister chromatids
(a) cross over during prophase-I of meiosis
(b) separate during the first meiotic division
(c) are produced during S-phase between cell divisions
(d) cross over during prophase-II of meiosis

98. A picture of a dividing pigeon cell taken through a microscope shows that the cell contains 7 chromosomes, each consisting of 2 chromatids. The picture must have been taken during
(a) metaphase of mitosis
(b) prophase-I of meiosis
(c) telophase-II of meiosis
(d) prophase-II of meiosis

99. One chromosome of a homologous pair carries the genes *J* and *K*. The other chromosome of the pair carries the genes *j* and *k* at corresponding loci. Crossing over results in exchange of chromosome segments and production of gametes with new combinations of genes. A 'recombinant'- type gamete resulting from this crossover might contain
(a) genes *J* and *K* (b) genes *j* and *K*
(c) genes *J* and *j* (d) genes *j* and *k*

100. In certain fungi and algae, cells undergo mitosis repeatedly without subsequently undergoing cytokinesis. What would result from this?
(a) A decrease in chromosome number
(b) Inability to duplicate DNA
(c) Division of the organism into many cells, most lacking nuclei
(d) Large cells containing many nuclei

101. Which of the following is not a function of mitotic cell division in animals?
(a) Asexual reproduction
(b) Growth
(c) Repair of damaged organs
(d) Production of gametes

102. Which of the following is not true of a cell plate?
(a) It forms at the site of the metaphase plate
(b) It results from the fusion of microtubules
(c) It fuses with the plasma membrane
(d) A cell wall is laid down between its membranes

103. A cell biologist carefully measured the quantity of DNA in grasshopper cells growing in cell culture. Cells examined during the G_2-phase of the cell cycle contained 200 units of DNA. What would be the amount of DNA in one of the grasshopper daughter cells seen in telophase of mitosis?
(a) 50 units
(b) 100 units
(c) between 50 and 100 units
(d) 200 units

104. Match list I (distinguishing feature based on chromosomal appearance) with list II (stage of meiosis) and select the correct answer using the codes given below the lists.

List I	List II
A. Terminalized chiasmata	1. Pachytene
B. Exchange of segments of chromatids	2. Zygotene
C. Synapsis of homologous chromosomes	3. Diakinesis
D. Appearance of chiasmata	4. Leptotene
	5. Diplotene

	A	B	C	D
(a)	4	2	3	1
(b)	3	1	2	5
(c)	2	5	1	3
(d)	2	4	3	1

105. All histones undergo post-translational modification of specific amino acids. These modifications
I. Alter the charge of the histone molecule.
II. Are permanent.
III. Occur (in part) on the N-terminal arms of the histones, which are thought to extend out from the core.
IV. Occur at specific times during the cell cycle.
(a) I and II
(b) I and IV
(c) I, III and IV
(d) I, II and III

106. Match the following lists.

List I	List II
A. DNA found at the ends of linear euksaryotic chromosomes	1. Centromere
B. Protein structure on eukaryotic chromosomes, where spindle fibres attach	2. Telomere
C. DNA site, where kinetochores are found	3. Nucleolar oganizer
D. DNA sequence that serves as the template for the synthesis and amplification of ribosomal DNA	4. Kinetochore

	A	B	C	D
(a)	1	4	2	3
(b)	2	4	1	3
(c)	4	3	1	2
(d)	3	4	3	2

Answers

1. (b)	2. (d)	3. (a)	4. (a)	5. (c)	6. (d)	7. (c)	8. (c)	9. (c)	10. (a)
11. (b)	12. (c)	13. (a)	14. (c)	15. (a)	16. (b)	17. (b)	18. (c)	19. (a)	20. (c)
21. (c)	22. (c)	23. (b)	24. (a)	25. (b)	26. (b)	27. (b)	28. (d)	29. (d)	30. (b)
31. (b)	32. (a)	33. (d)	34. (b)	35. (d)	36. (d)	37. (c)	38. (b)	39. (d)	40. (a)
41. (a)	42. (a)	43. (b)	44. (a)	45. (a)	46. (d)	47. (a)	48. (a)	49. (d)	50. (d)
51. (b)	52. (b)	53. (c)	54. (a)	55. (d)	56. (b)	57. (b)	58. (d)	59. (b)	60. (a)
61. (b)	62. (d)	63. (c)	64. (d)	65. (a)	66. (c)	67. (c)	68. (b)	69. (c)	70. (a)
71. (b)	72. (d)	73. (b)	74. (d)	75. (c)	76. (c)	77. (d)	78. (c)	79. (d)	80. (c)
81. (b)	82. (d)	83. (b)	84. (a)	85. (c)	86. (c)	87. (a)	88. (a)	89. (c)	90. (a)
91. (c)	92. (c)	93. (b)	94. (d)	95. (d)	96. (a)	97. (c)	98. (d)	99. (b)	100. (d)
101. (d)	102. (b)	103. (b)	104. (b)	105. (c)	106. (b)				

6

DNA Replication, Repair and Recombination

Fundamental Processes

There are a number of processes necessary for the continuation of generation, growth and development of organisms called fundamental process. These includes replication of genetic material, damage and repair and recombination in genetic material.

Syllabus

- DNA Replication, Unit of Replication
- Enzymes Involved
- Replication Origin and Replication Fork
- Fidelity of Replication
- Extrachromosomal Replicon
- DNA Damage, DNA Repair
- Homologous and Site-Specific Recombination

DNA Replication

DNA replication is a process of cloning of DNA molecule, in which each strand of DNA molecule acts as a template to guide the synthesis of its complementary strand.

Basic Features of DNA Replication

Synthesis of DNA involves three steps

(a) Chain initiation, (b) Chain extension or elongation, (c) Chain termination

Modes of DNA Replication

Semiconservative Conservative Dispersive

Parental DNA

First-generation progeny DNA

Second-generation progeny DNA

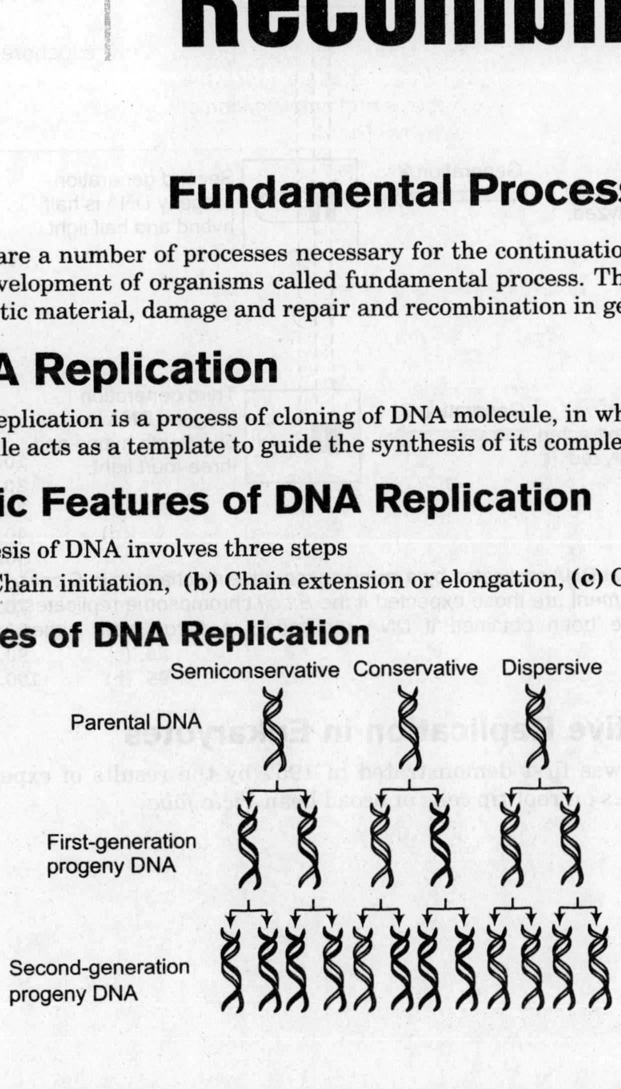

Fig. 6.1 Three possible modes of DNA replication:

(a) Semiconservative, in which each strand of the parental double helix is conserved and directs the synthesis of a new complementary progeny strand.

(b) Conservative, in which the parental double helix is conserved and directs the synthesis of a new progeny double helix.

(c) Dispersive, in which segments of each parental strand are conserved and direct the synthesis of new complementary strand segments that are subsequently joined to produce new progeny strands.

Semiconservative Replication

(a) Each parental strand is conserved and serves as template for the synthesis of a new complementary strand.
(b) It is based on complementary base pairing as proposed by Watson and Crick.

Experimental Evidence of Semi-conservative Replication in Prokaryotes

- Elucidated by Meselson and Stahl in 1958 in *E. coli*.

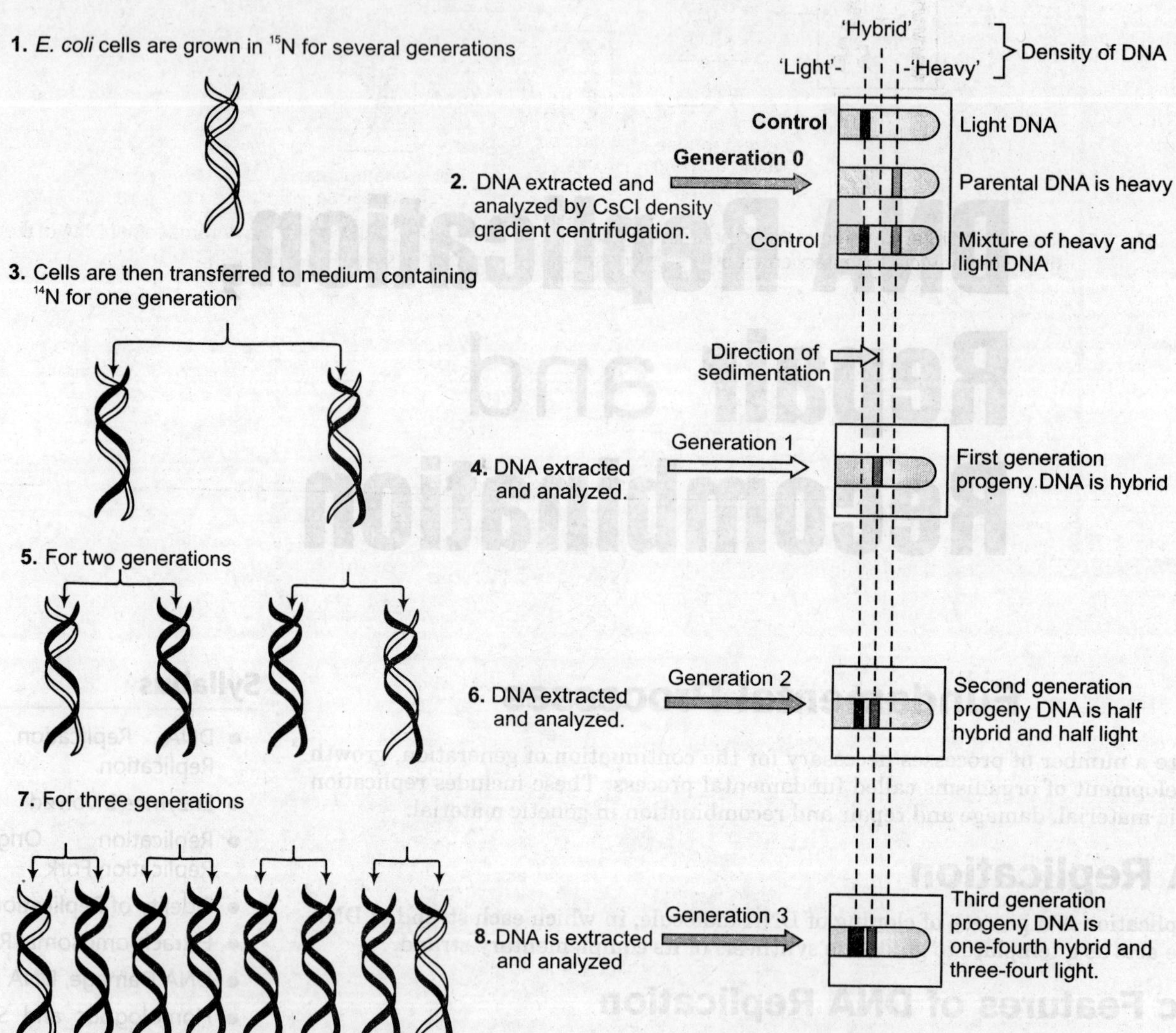

Fig. 6.2 Meselson and Stahl's experiment demonstrating that DNA replicates by a semiconservative mechanism in *E.coli*. The diagram shows that the results of their experiment are those expected if the *E.coli* chromosome replicates semiconservatively. Different results would have been obtained if DNA replication in *E.coli* were either conservative or dispersive.

Experimental Evidence of Semi-conservative Replication in Eukaryotes

The semiconservative replication of eukaryotic chromosome was first demonstrated in 1957 by the results of experiments carried out by **J Herbert Taylor, Philip Wood** and **Walter Hughes** on root tip cells of broad bean *Vicia faba*.

3. Duplication without labelled thymidine

4. Autoradiography

2. Autoradiography

1. Duplication with labelled thymidine

1st c-metaphase after labelling

2nd c-metaphase after labelling

Fig. 6.3 Results and interpretation of the experiment by **Taylor** and colleagues showing that the chromosomal DNA of the broad bean. *Vicia faba*, replicates by a semiconservative mechanism

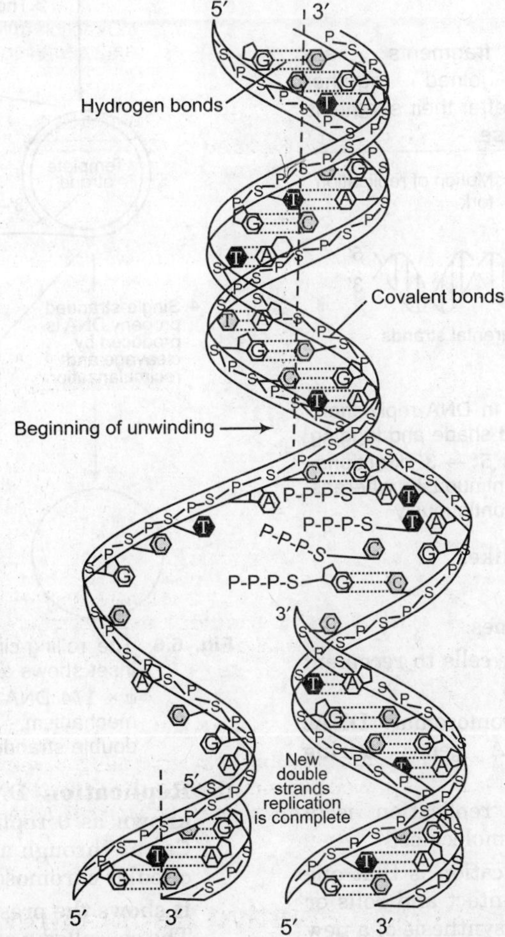

Fig. 6.4 Semiconservative model of DNA replication based on complementary base-pairing as proposed by Watson and Crick. Note that each of the parental strands is conserved and serves as a template for the synthesis of a new complementary strand, that is, the base sequence of each progeny strand is determined by the hydrogen-bonding potentials of the bases in the parental strand

Unique Origin of Replication

In bacterial and viral chromosomes, there is usually one unique origin of replication per chromosome and the single origin controls the replication of entire chromosome.

In large chromosomes of eukaryotes, multiple origins collectively controls the replication of giant DNA molecule present in each chromosome.

Each origin controls the replication of a unit of DNA called Replicon, thus most prokaryotic chromosomes contains a single replicon, whereas eukaryotic chromosomes usually contains many replicons.

Semidiscontinuous Replication Model

(a) It was proposed by **Reiji Okazaki** in 1968.

(b) The two parental strands are replicated in different ways.

Leading Strand	Lagging Strand
The newly synthesized DNA that extends 5′→3′ in the direction of replication fork movement is called leading strand.	It is also synthesized in 5′→3′ direction but discontinuously as Okazaki fragment.
It is continuously synthesized in 5′→3′ direction.	Okazaki fragments are covalently joined together sometimes after their synthesis by DNA ligase.

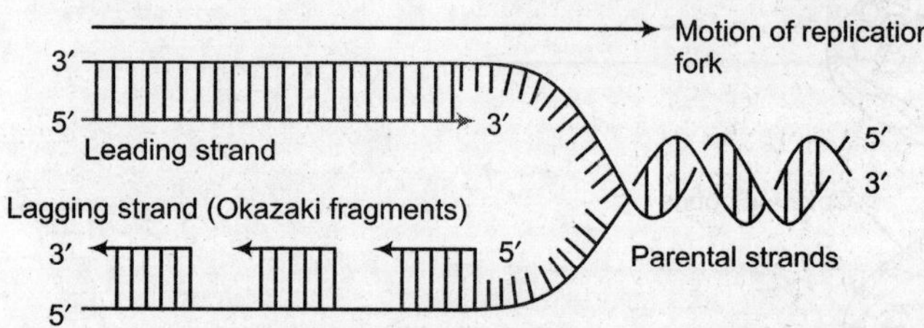

Fig. 6.5 Semidiscontinuous DNA replication. In DNA replication, both daughter strands (leading strand shade and lagging strand black) are synthesized in their 5′ → 3′ directions. The leading strand is synthesized continuously, whereas the lagging strand is synthesized discontinuously

There are a number of replication models like.

(a) **Rolling Circle Replication**

- By many viruses to duplicate their genomes.
- In bacteria to transfer DNA from donor cells to recepient cells during one type of genetic exchange
- In amphibians to amplify extrachromosomal DNAs carrying clusters of ribosomal RNA genes during oogenesis.
- As the name implies, rolling circle replication is a mechanism for replicating circular DNA molecules.
- The unique aspect of rolling circle replication is that one parental circular DNA strand remains intact and rolls or spins while serving as a template for the synthesis of a new complementary strand.
- Replication is initiated when a sequence specific endonuclease cleaves one strand at the origin producing 3′–OH and 5′–phosphate termini.

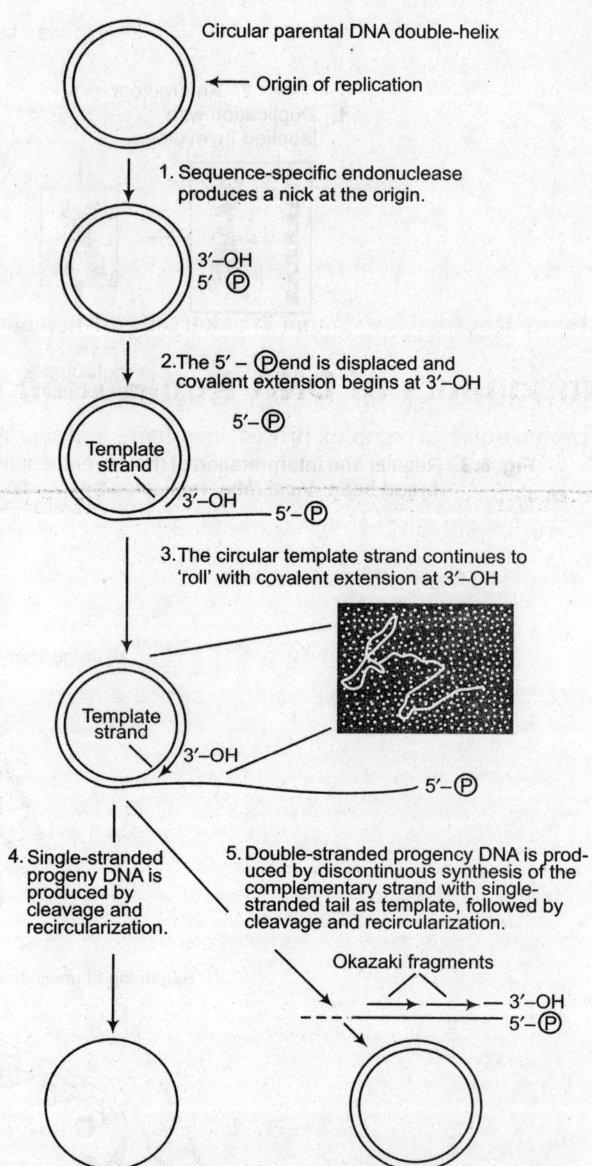

Fig. 6.6 The rolling-circle mechanism of DNA replication. The inset shows an electron micrograph of a bacteriophase ϕ × 174 DNA molecule replicating by the rolling-circle mechanism. A single-stranded tail extends from a double-stranded, circular, replicative DNA

(b) **Replication** DNA relication involving θ structures is known as θ replication. This was elucidated by **John Cairns** through autoradiography of replicating DNA of circular chromosomes.

It shows the presence of replication 'eyes' or 'bubbles'. The so, called q structure indicate that double stranded DNA (ds DNA) replicates by the progressive seperation of its two parental strands accompanied by the synthesis of their complementary strand to yield two semi-conservatively replicated duplex daughter strands.

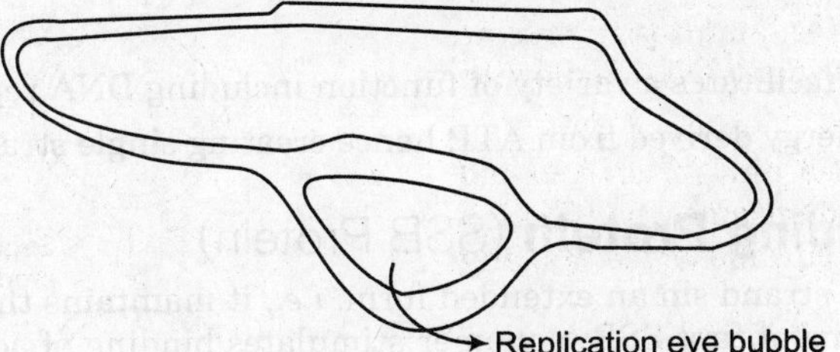

Fig. 6.7 Replicating *E. coli* chromosome

(c) **Linear Replication** Found in eukaryotic DNA replication.

Components of DNA Replication in Prokaryotes

DNA replication is a complex process involving a great variety of enzymes and proteins.

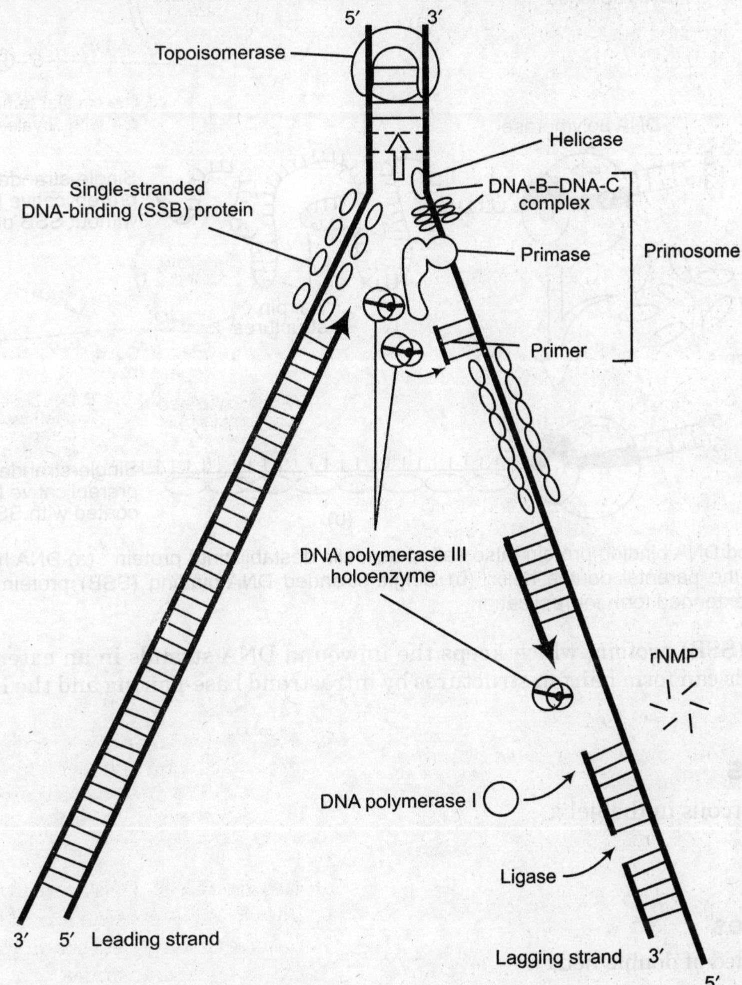

Fig. 6.8 Diagram of a replication fork in *E. coli* showing the major components of the replication apparatus

DNA-A Protein

Responsible for the localized strand separation at *Ori*C (Origin of replication). It is an ATP requiring process, causes double stranded DNA to melt forming single stranded DNA.

DNA-C Protein

Joins the initiation complex and contributes to formation of two bidirectional replication fork.

DNA Helicases

Form a diverse group of enzymes that facilitates a variety of function including DNA replication, recombination, repair, etc. It unwounds the double helix using energy derived from ATP, hence creating single stranded DNA.

Single-Stranded DNA Binding Protein (SSB Protein)

SSB protein keeps the unwound DNA strand sin an extended form, *i.e.,* it maintains the single stranded form for replication. SSB binding is cooperative, *i.e.,* Binding of first SSB monomer stimulates binding of additional monomers to single stranded DNA. It also protects the DNA from nuclease that cleaves single stranded DNA.

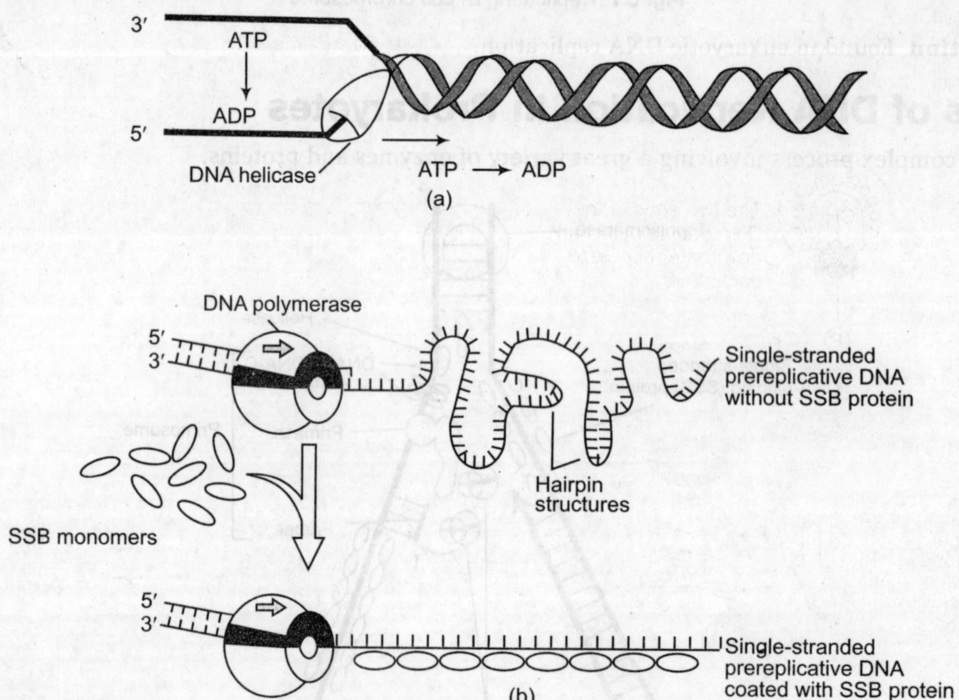

Fig. 6.9 Single-stranded DNA binding protein [also called as Helix destabilizing] protein : (a) DNA helicase catalyzes the unwinding of the parental double helix, (b) Single-stranded DNA-binding (SSB) protein keeps the unwound strands in an extended form for replication

Single-stranded DNA-binding (SSB) protein, which keeps the unwound DNA strands in an extended form. In the absence of SSB protein, DNA single strands can form hairpin structures by intrastrand base-pairing and the hairpin structures will retard or arrest DNA synthesis.

DNA Topoisomerases

Responsible for removing supercoils in the helix.

Types

Type I DNA topoisomerases

- Reversibly cut a single stranded of double helix
- They have both nuclease (strand cutting) and ligase (strand sealing) activity.
- They do not require ATP.

1. One end of the DNA, double helix connot roate relative the other end.

2. DNA topoisomerase I covalently attaches to a DNA phosphate, thereby breaking a phosphodiester linkage in one DNA strand.

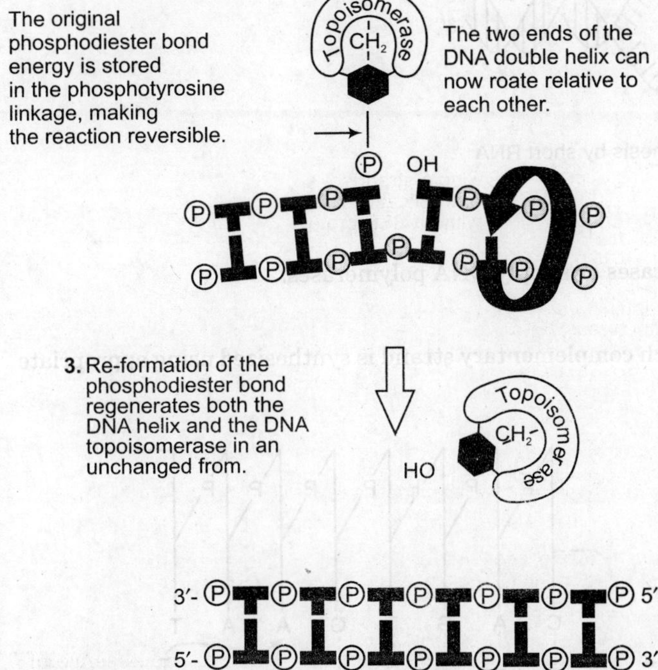

Fig. 6.10 DNA topoisomerase I produces transient single strand breaks in DNA that act space of rotation or swivels during DNA replication

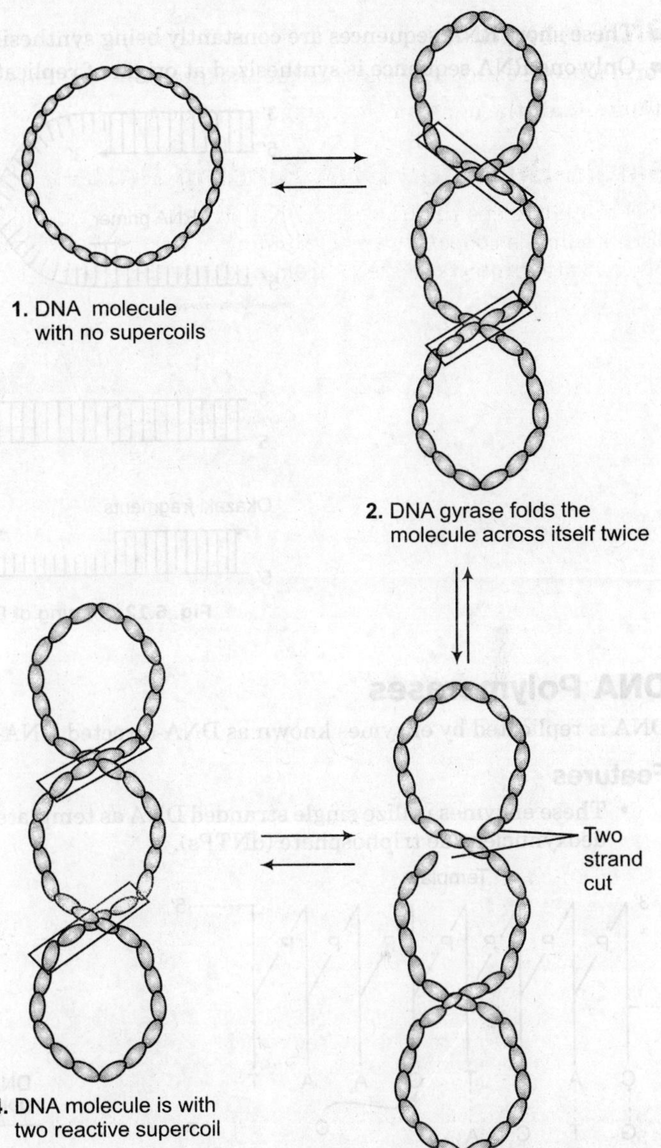

Fig. 6.11 Mechanism of action of DNA gyrase

Type II DNA Topoisomerases

- Binds tightly to DNA double helix and makes transient breaks in both strands.
- The enzyme then causes a second stretch of the DNA double helix to pass through the break and finally, reseals the breaks.
- DNA gyrase, a type II topoisomerase found in *E.coli* has the unusual property of being able to introduce negative supercoils into relaxed circular DNA using energy from the hydrolysis of ATP.

RNA Primers

RNA primer is a short double stranded region consisting of RNA base-paired to the DNA template with a free hydroxyl group on the 3′ end of RNA strand. This hydroxyl group serves as the first acceptor of nucleotide by action of DNA polymerase. *E. coli* has two enzymes that catalyze the formation of these RNA primers.

(a) RNA polymerase, which mediates transcription.

(b) Primase synthesizes the short stretches of RNA approximately ten nucleotide long that are complementary and antiparallel to DNA template.

- These short RNA sequences are constantly being synthesized at replication fork on Lagging strand.
- Only one RNA sequence is synthesized at origin of replication on the leading strand.

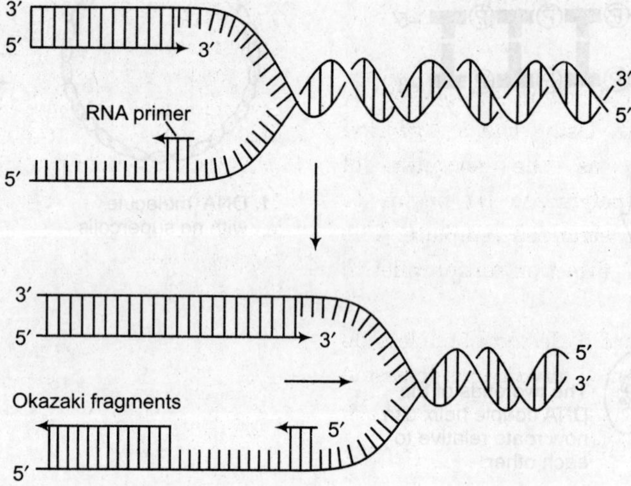

Fig. 6.12 Priming of DNA synthesis by short RNA

DNA Polymerases

DNA is replicated by enzymes known as DNA-directed DNA-polymerases or simply DNA polymerases.

Features

- These enzymes utilize single stranded DNA as template on which complementary strand is synthesized using appropriate deoxynucleoside triphosphate (dNTPs).

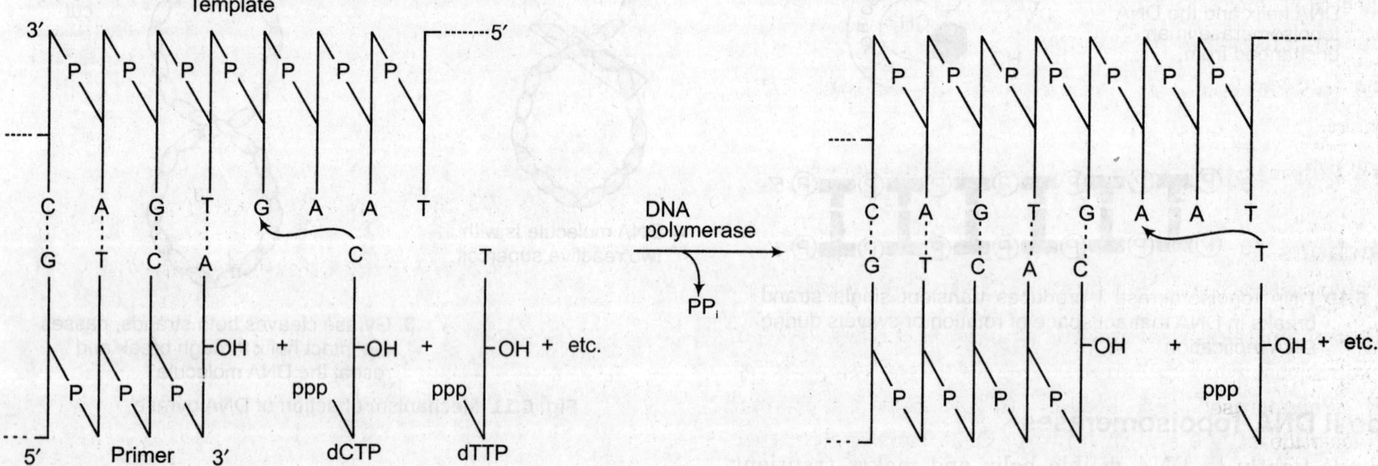

Fig. 6.13 Action of DNA polymerase. DNA polymerases assemble incoming deoxynucleoside triphosphates on single-stranded DNA templates such that the growing strand is elongated in its 5′→ 3′ direction

- All DNA polymerases have an absolute requirement of a free 3′OH on the primer strandand all DNA synthesis occurs in 5′→3′ direction. They are able to read parental nucleotide sequence in 3′→5′ direction.
- All DNA polymerases requires a primer strand which extended and a template strand which is copied.
- Prokaryotic DNA polymerases elongates a new DNA strand by adding deoxyribonucleotides, one at a time, to the 3′ end of growing chain.

Types

1. **DNA polymerase III** It is a multisubunit enzyme which consists of atleast ten types of subunits.

Function

- **DNA chain elongation** DNA chain elongation is catalyzed by DNA plymerase III. Using the 3′ hydroxyl group of the RNA primer as the acceptor of first-deoxyribonucleotide, DNA polymease III begins to add nucleotides along the single stranded template. The new DNA strand grows in 5′→3′ direction antiparallel to the parental strand.
  The nucleotide building blocks are 5′-deoxyribonucleoside triphosphate. All the four deoxyribonucleoside triphosphates (dATP, dCTP, dTTP and dGTP must be present for DNA replication to occur.
- Proofreading of newly synthesized DNA
  To ensure the replicated DNA sequence to be with as few errors as possible because misreading of template sequence could result in lethal mutations.
  DNA polymerase III has a "proofreading activity". If DNA polymerase mispairs a nucleotide with the template. It uses its 3′→5′ exonuclease activity to excise the mismatched nucleotides. Exonuclease moves in 3′→5′ direction, because excision must be done in reverse direction from that of synthesis.

DNA polymerase II Participates in repairing DNA damages.

DNA Polymerase I Discovered by Arthur Kornberg

Functions

- Polymerase activity Synthesizes DNA in 5′→3′ direction.
- Editing mistakes/Proofreading activity It can act as 3′→5′ exonuclease which proofreads the newly synthesized DNA. If Polymerase/I erroneously incorporates a wrong nucleotide at the end of growing DNA chain polymerase activity is inhibited and 3′→5′ exonuclease excise the offending nucleotide.
- Excision of RNAprimers and their replacement by DNA: It can act as 5′→3′ exonuclease that is able to hydrolytically remove the RNA primes. DNA polymerase I's 5′→3′ exonuclease remove the RNA primers at the 5′ ends of the newly synthesized DNA while its 5′-3′ polymerase activity fills the resulting gaps.

Table 6.1 **Comparison of Various Prokaryotic DNA Polymerases**

DNA Polymerase Particular ↓	Polymerase I	Polymerase II	Polymerase III
Structural gene	Polymerase A	Polymerase B	Polymerase C
Polymerization 5′ → 3′	+	+	+
Exonuclease 3′ → 5′	+	+	+
Exonuclease 5′ → 3′	+	–	–
	1. DNA synthesis 2. Proofreading 3. Excision of RNA primers and their replacement by DNA	DNA repair	1. DNA chain elongation 2. Proofreading of newly synthesized DNA.

DNA Ligase

The final phosphodiester linkage between the 5′ phosphate group of DNA chain synthesized by DNA Polymerase III and 3′ hydroxyl group on the chain made by DNA polymerase I is catalyzed by DNA Ligase. This process is energy requiring.

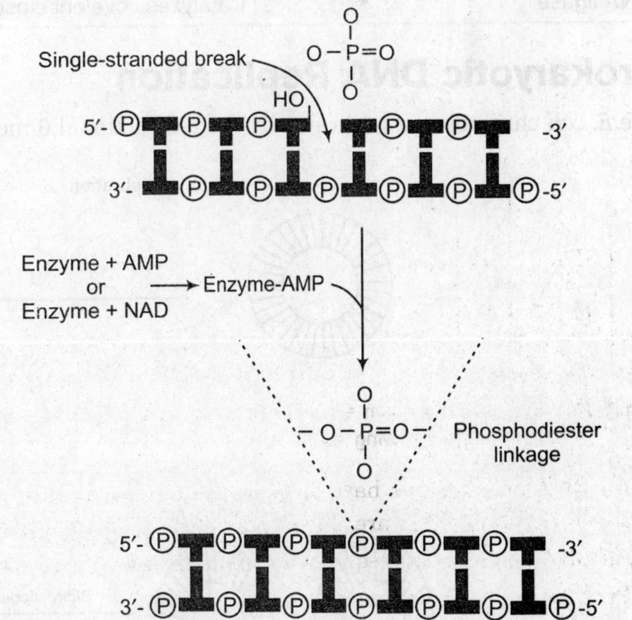

Fig. 6.14 DNA ligase catalyzes the covalent closure of nicks in DNA. The energy required to form the ester linkage is provided by either adenosine triphosphate (ATP) or nicotinamide-adenine dinucleotide (NAD), depending on the series

Table 6.2 **Components of DNA Replication**

Components		Main Functions
DNA-A Protein		Responsible for localized strand separation at *OriC* forming single stranded DNA
DNA-C Protein		Contributes to formation of two bidirectional replication fork
DNA helicases		Catalyzes unwinding of parental double helix
Single stranded		Keeps the unwound DNA strand in an extended
DNA binding protein		Form for replication
Topoisomerases		Responsible for removing supercoils in the helix
Primase		Synthesizes short stretches of RNA once on the leading strand and continuously on lagging strand which is elongated by DNA polymerases.
DNA polymerase I		(a) DNA synthesis in 5′→ 3′ direction (b) Proofreading activity (3′ → 5′ exonuclease) (c) Excision of RNA primers (5′→ 3′ exonuclease activity).
DNA Polymerase III (holoenzyme)		
α	DNAE	Polymerization
ε	DNAQ	3′→ 5′ editing
RNAse-H	rnh A	Removes RNA primers
q	holE	Present in core (∝ εQ)s
β	DNAN	Sliding clamp
τ*	DNAX	Organizes complex, joins leading and lagging DNA pol III
τ*	DNAX	Binds clamp loaders and SSB proteins
δ	holA	Clamp loading
δ′	holB	Clamp loading
χ	holC	Binds SSB
ψ	holD	Binds SSB
DNA ligase		Catalyzes covalent closure of micks in DNA

Prokaryotic DNA Replication

The *E. coli* chromosome replicates by the bidirectional θ mode from a single replication origin

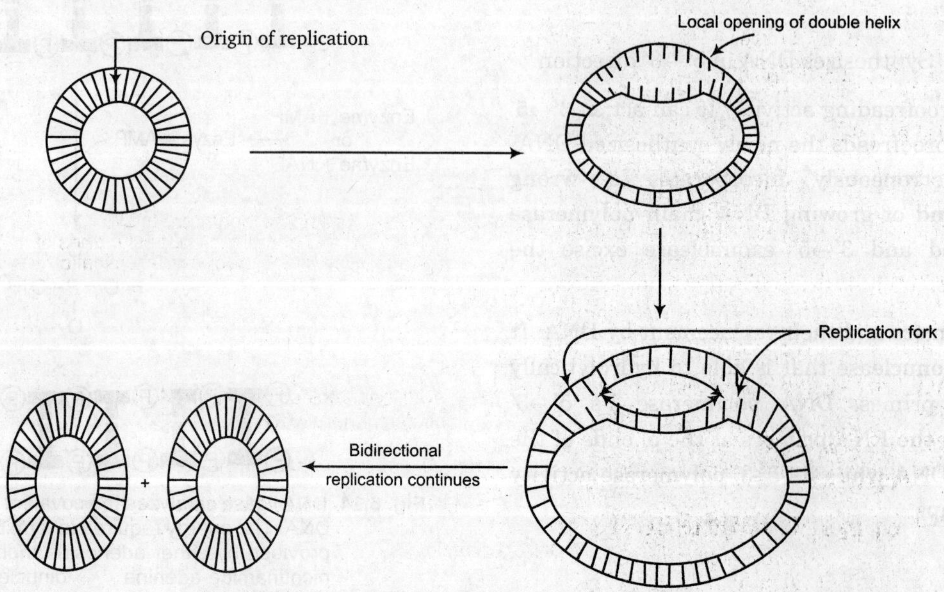

Fig. 6.15 Replication of DNA: Small prokaryotic circular DNA

Process

DNA replication involves three steps

(a) Initiation **(b)** Extension or Elongation **(c)** Termination

DNA Replication Initiation

In prokaryotic organisms, DNA replication begins at a single, unique nucleotide sequence-a site called origin of replication. The replication origin of *E. coli* Ichromosome consists of a unique 245 bp segment known as *oriC* locus.

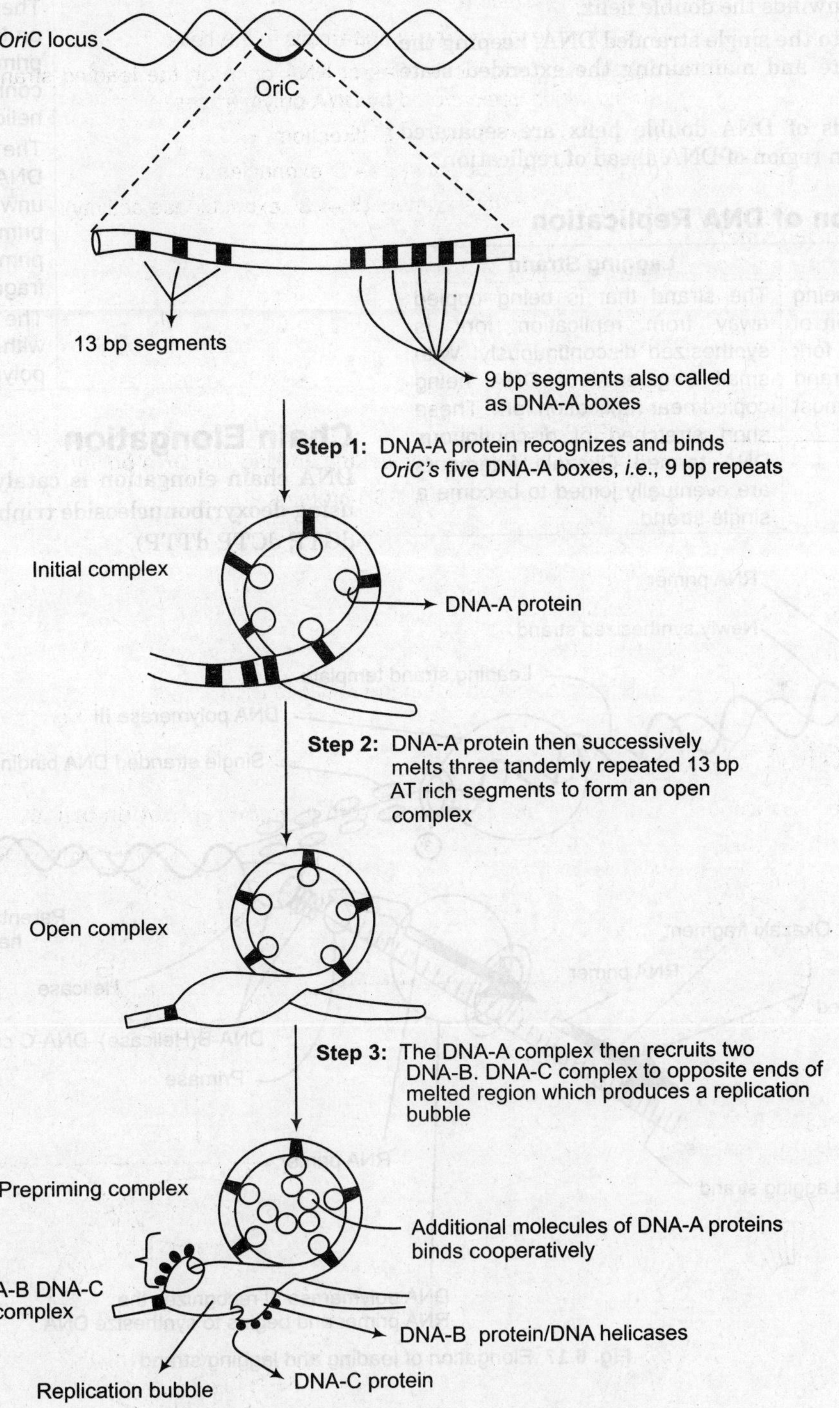

Fig. 6.16 DNA replication initiation in prokaryotes

Formation of Replication Fork

As the two strands unwind and separate they form a 'V' where active synthesis occurs. This region is called replication fork. It moves along the DNA molecules as synthesis occurs.

Events

- After strand separation catalyzed by DNA-A protein, DNA helicases further unwinds the double helix.
- SSB protein binds to the single stranded DNA, keeping the two strand separate and maintaining the extended state for replication.
- As the two strands of DNA double helix are separated supercoils appear in region of DNA ahead of replication.

Table 6.3 **Direction of DNA Replication**

Leading Strand	Lagging Strand
The strand that is being copied in the direction of advancing replication fork is called the leading strand and is synthesized almost continuously.	The strand that is being copied away from replication fork is synthesized discontinuously. With small fragments of DNA being copied near replication fork. These short stretched of discontinuous DNA termed Okazaki fragments are eventually joined to become a single strand.

Leading Strand	Lagging Strand
Synthesis of new DNA strand is initiated by RNA primers synthesized by DNA primase.	The new strand of DNA produced by this mechanism is termed lagging strand.
A single RNA primer is required for continuous replication	RNA primers are required for starting the synthesis of Okazaki fragment.
	The initiation of Okazaki fragments on lagging strand is carried out by primasome, a protein complex containing DNA primase + DNA helicase.
	The primasome moves along the DNA molecule, DNA helicase unwinds the double helix and DNA primase synthesizes the RNA primers for succesive Okazaki fragments.
	The RNA primers are extended with deoxyribonucleotides by DNA polymerase III.

Chain Elongation

DNA chain elongation is catalyzed by DNA polymerase III using deoxyribonucleoside triphosphates (dNTPs, *e.g.*, dATP, dGTP, dCTP, dTTP).

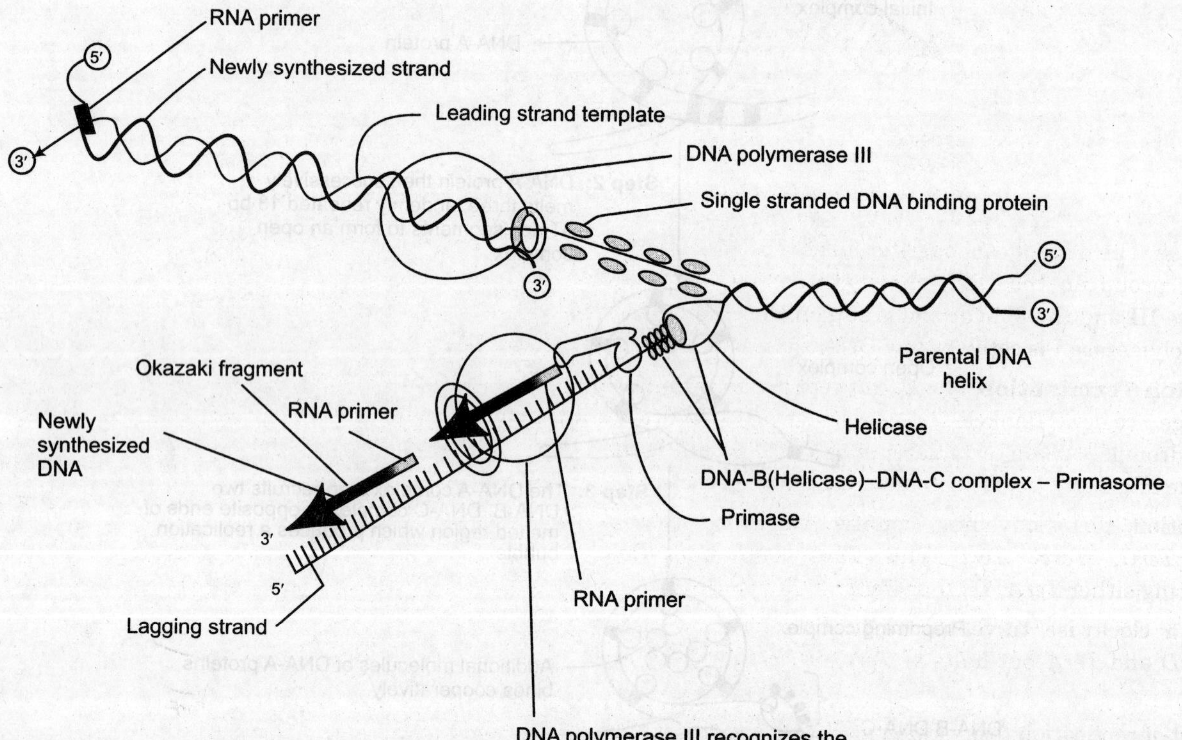

Fig. 6.17 Elongation of leading and lagging strand

Excision of RNA primers and their replacement by DNA RNA primers are excised by DNA polymerase I by its 5′ → 3′ Exonuclease activity and replaces DNA by its 5′→3′ polymerase activity

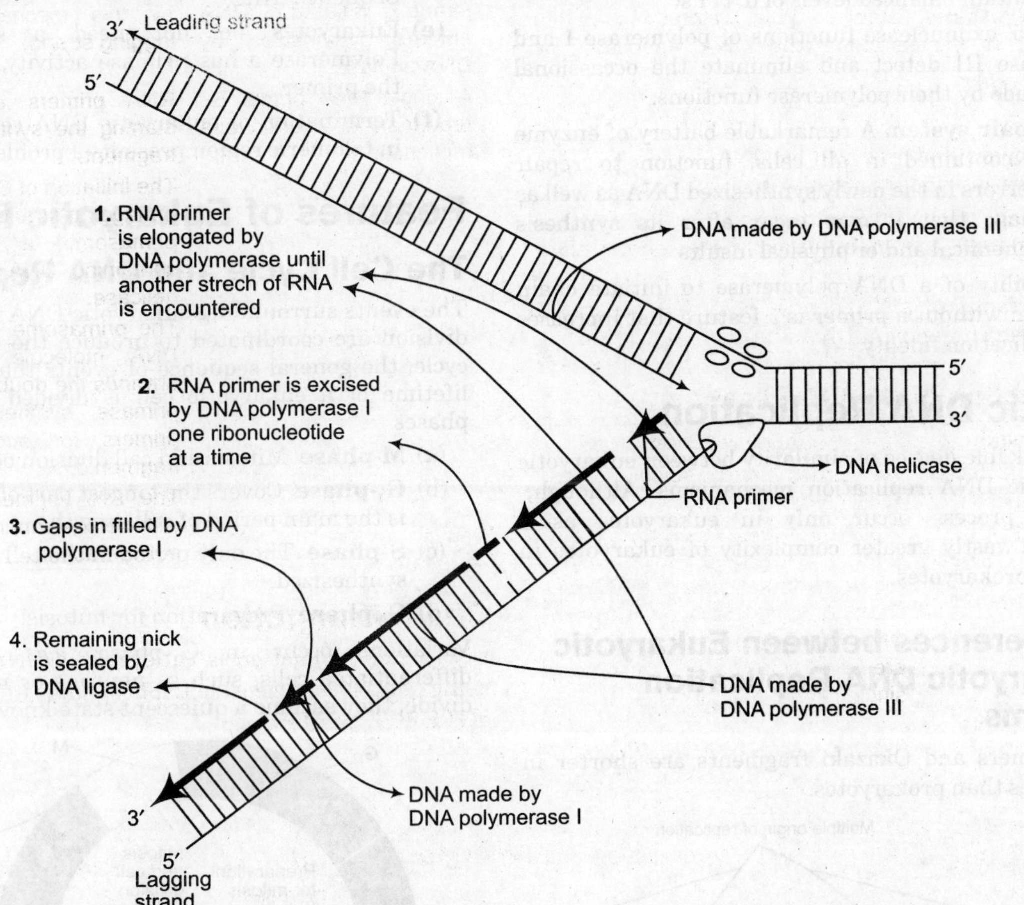

Fig. 6.18 Removal of RNA primer and filling of the resulting gaps by DNA polymerase-I

DNA ligase The final phosphodiester linkage between the 5′ phosphate group on the DNA chain synthesized by DNA polymerase III and the 3′ hydroxyl group on the chain made by DNA polymerase I is catalyzed by DNA ligase.

Replication Termination The *E. coli* replication terminus is a large region flanked by seven nearly identical non-palindromic ~ 23 bp terminator sites *TerE*, *D* and *TerA* on one side and *TerG*, *TerF*, *TerB* and *TerC* on the other.

A replication fork travelling counter clockwise passes through *TerG*, *TerF*, *TerB* and *TerC* but stops on encountering either *TerA*, *TerD* or *TerE*.

Similary a clockwise travelling replication fork transists *TerE*, *TerD* and *TerA* but halts at *TerC* or *TerB* or *TerF* or *TerG*.

The arrest of replication fork motion at *Ter* sites requires the action of *Tus* protein a product of tus gene *Tus* binds specifically to *Ter* site and prevents strand displacement by DNA-B (helicase), thereby arresting the replication fork motion.

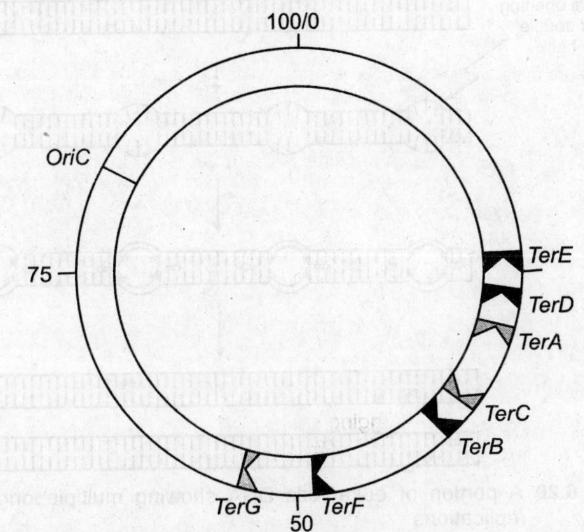

Fig. 6.19 Map of *E.coli* chromosome showing the positions of the *Ter* sites and the *OriC* site

Fidelity of Replication The process of DNA replication is highly accurate so as to preserve the integrity of the genome from generation to generation.

Achieved High replication accuracy arises from following sources

(a) Cells maintain balanced levels of dNTPs

(b) The 3′→5′ exonuclease functions of polymerase I and polymerase III detect and eliminate the occassional errors made by their polymerase functions.

(c) **DNA repair system** A remarkable battery of enzyme systems, contained in all cells, function to repair residual errors in the newly synthesized DNA as well as any damage that it may incur after its synthesis through chemical and/or physical insults.

(d) The inability of a DNA polymerase to initiate chain elongation without a primer is a feature that increases DNA replication fidelity.

Eukaryotic DNA Replication

There is remarkable degree of similarity between eukaryotic and prokaryotic DNA replication mechanisms. Although, some of the process occur only in eukaryotes as a consequence of vastly greater complexity of eukaryotes in comparison to prokaryotes.

Major Differences between Eukaryotic and Prokaryotic DNA Replication Mechanisms

(a) RNA primers and Okazaki fragments are shorter in eukaryotes than prokaryotes.

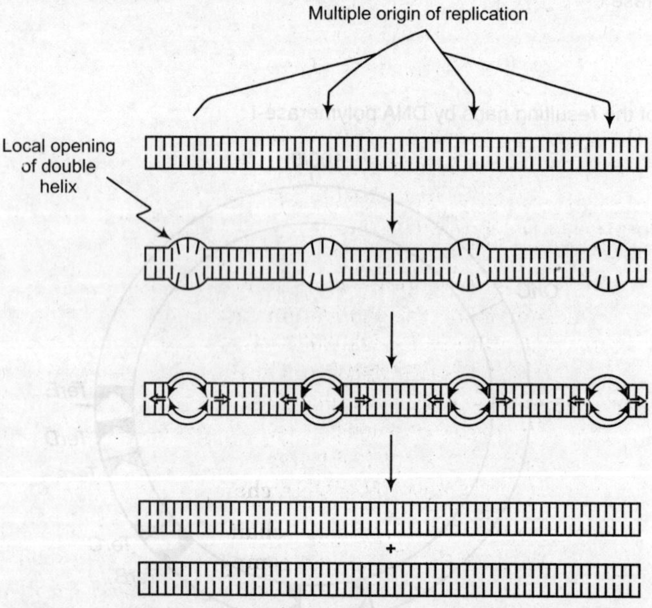

Fig. 6.20 A portion of eukaryotic DNA showing multiple origin of replications

(b) DNA synthesis takes place within a small portion of cell cycle in eukaryotes not continuously as in prokaryotes.

(c) Eukaryotic chromosomes contain multiple origin of replication.

(d) Eukaryotic DNA replication starts at origin of replication designated as Autonomous Replicative Sequence (ARS)

(e) Eukaryotes do not need a separate Primase. Polymerase a has primase activity, *i.e.*, it synthesizes the primer.

(f) Termination of eukaryotic DNA replication especially in telomeric region presents a problem in replication.

Features of Eukaryotic Replication

The Cell Cycle and DNA Replication

The events surrounding eukaryotic DNA replication and cell division are coordinated to produce the cell cycle. The cell cycle, the general sequence of events that occur during the lifetime of a eukaryotic cell is divided into four distinct phases

(a) **M-phase** Mitosis and cell division occurs.

(b) **G_1-phase** Covers the longest part of the cell cycle. This is the main period of cell growth.

(c) **S-phase** The only period in the cell cycle when DNA is synthesized.

(d) **G_2 phase** Preparation for mitosis.

Variations occur in G_1-phase, *e.g.*, many terminally differentiated cells, such as neurons or muscle cells, never divide, they assume a quiescent state known as G_0-phase.

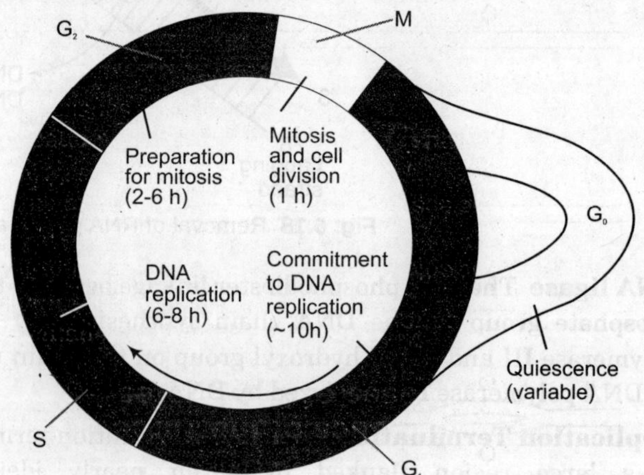

Fig. 6.21 The eukaryotic cell cycle. Cells in G_1 may enter a quiescent phase (G_0) rather than continuing about the cycle

- In rapidly dividing embryonic cells, G_1 and G_2 are very short or non-existent.
- In all cells, decisions to continue on through the cell cycle occurs at two points.

  1. Entry into S-phase 2. Entry into mitosis

These checkpoints helps to ensure that DNA replicates once and only once during each cell division.

Multiple Replicons Per Chromosome

A segment of DNA whose replication is under the control of one origin and two termini is called a Replicon. In prokaryotes the entire chromosome has usually one replicon.

The existence of multiple replicons per eukaryotic chromosome has been verified directly by electron microscopy.

Reason for multiple replicons per chromosomes

(a) Multiple origin of replication are required to allow the very large DNA molecule in eukaryotic chromosome to replicate within observed cell division time.

(b) Replication is initiated at more sites during very rapid cell division of embryogenesis than during later stages of development.

Experimental Evidence

The first evidence of multiple origins in eukaryotic chromosomes resulted from pulse labelling experiments with Chinese hamster cells growing in culture, in 1968 when Joel Huberm Caum and Arthur Riggs pulse-labelled cells with ^{3}H-thymidine for a few minutes, extracted the DNA and performed autoradiographic analysis of labelled DNA.

Interpretations

- Individual macromolecule of DNA contains multiple origin of replication.
- Replication in eukaryotes is bi-directional as it is most prokaryotes.

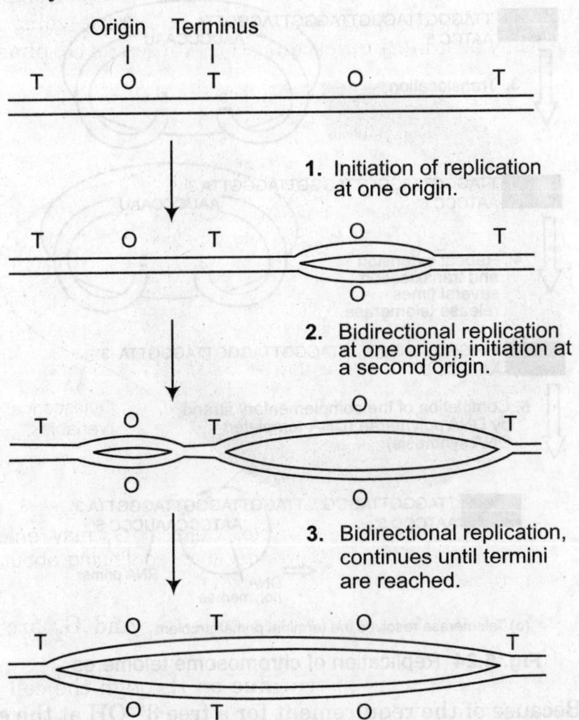

Fig. 6.22 Diagrammatic interpretation of the replication of the DNA

Replication Apparatus in Eukaryotes

(a) It is more complex than prokaryotes.

(b) Although, knowledge of the structure of the replicative machinery in eukaryotes is still limited many features of DNA replication are similar in eukaryotes and prokaryotes.

(c) Most of the knowledge about eukayotic DNA Replication mechanism is learned from studies on budding yeast. (*Saccharomyces cerevisiae*) and fission yeast (*Schizosacharomyces pombe*).

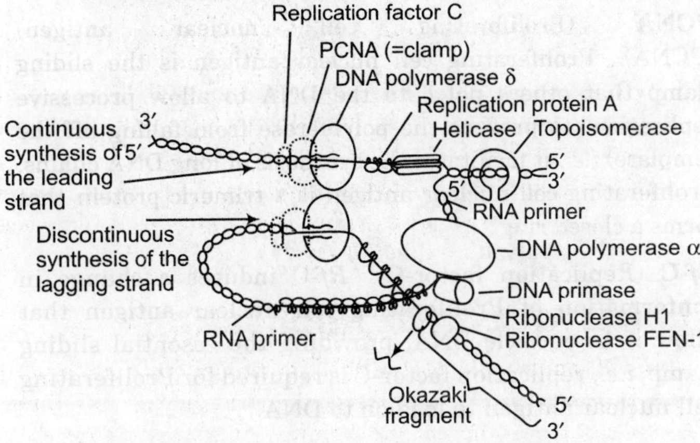

Fig. 6.23 Replication apparatus in eukaryotes showing important components

Brief description of components of eukaryotic replication apparatus along with their functions.

Eukaryotic DNA Polymerases

At least five classes of eukaryotic DNA polymerase has been identified and characterized.

Polymerase	Function	Proofreading
Pol α	• Contains primase • Initiates DNA synthesis	–
Pol β	• Repair	–
Pol γ	• Replicates mitochondrial DNA	+
Pol δ	• Elongates leading strand and Okazaki fragments	+
Pol ε	• Repair	+

Pol α is a multisubunit enzyme which is required for the initiation of replication at origin and for the priming of Okazaki fragments during the discontinuous synthesis of the lagging strand.

Pol a exists in a stable complex with DNA primase. Primase synthesizes RNA primess which are extended with deoxyribonucleotides by polymerase α to produce RNA–DNA chains.

Pol δ RNA–DNA primer chains are extended by polymerase δ, *i.e.*, it completes the synthesis of Okazaki fragment in lagging strand and catalyzes continuous synthesis of leading strand.

Polymerase α interacts with protein pCNA and *Rf*-C (Replication factor C) to be active. It also fills the gap iniated by excision of RNA primers by ribonuclease H! and ribonuclease FEN! Polymerase δ also contains the 3′→5′ exonuclease activity required for proofreading.

DNA Topoisomerase and DNA Helicases Unwinds the parental DNA strand as in prokaryotes.

Replication Protein A (Rp-A) are the single strand DNA-binding protein which keeps the unwound strand in extended state.

PCNA (Proliferating cell nuclear antigen) (PCNA) Proliferating cell nuclear antigen is the sliding clamp that others pol δ to the DNA to allow processive replication (to prevent the polymerase from falling off the template) *i.e.*, it facilitates the synthesis of long DNA chains. Proliferating cell nuclear antigen is a trimeric protein that forms a closed ring.

***Rf*-C** (Replication factor-C) *Rf*-C induces a change in conformation of Proliferating cell nuclear antigen that allow it to encircle DNA, providing the essential sliding clamp, *i.e.*, replication factor-C is required for Proliferating cell nuclear antigen to load on to DNA.

Ribonuclear H1 and Ribonuclease FEN-1 RNA Primers are excised by ribonuclease H1 which degrades RNA present in RNA-DNA duplexes and ribonuclease FEN-1.

DNA Ligase Seals the nicks, producing covalently closed progeny strands.

Replication of Telomeres

Eukaryotic cells face a special problem in replicating the ends of their linear DNA molecules. Following removal of the RNA primer from the extreme 5′ end of the lagging strand, there is no way to fill in the remaining gap with DNA.

To solve this problem and to protect the ends of chromosomes from attack by nucleases, the special structure of telomere provides a mechanism for the addition of telomeres by an RNA containing enzyme called telomerase. The telomerase of humans, contain the tandemly repeated sequence TTAGGG.

(a) Telomerese recognise the G-rich telomere sequence on the 3′ overhang and extend it 5′→3′ one repeat unit at a time.

(b) Telomerase does not fill in the gap opposite the 3′ end of the template strand it simply extends the 3′ end of the template strand. The unique feature of telomerase is that it contains a built in RNA template. After several telomere repeat units are added by telomerase, DNA polymerase catalyzes the synthesis of complementary strand. Without telomerase activity linear chromosomes would become progressively shorter.

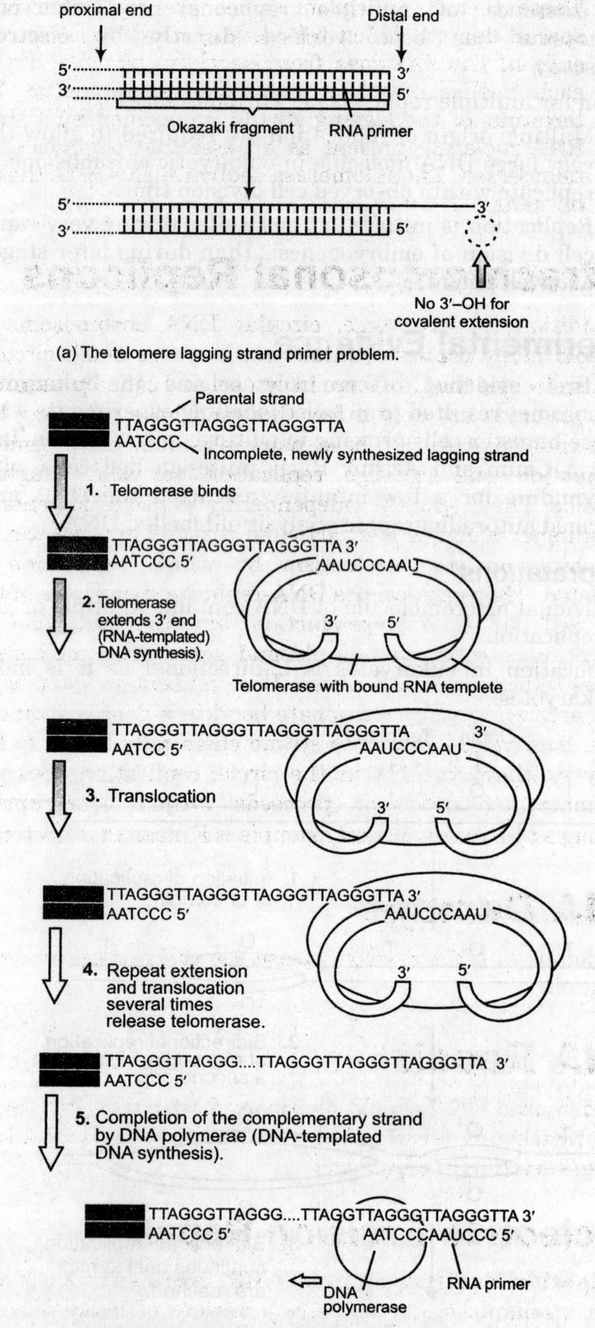

Fig. 6.24 Replication of chromosome telomeres

(a) Because of the requirement for a free 3′–OH at the end of the primer strand. DNA polymerases cannot replace an RNA primer that initiates DNA synthesis close to or at the terminus of the lagging strand.

(b) These termini of chromosomes are replicated by a special enzyme called telomerase, which prevents the ends of chromosomes from becoming shorter during each replication. The nucleotide sequence at the terminus of the lagging strand is specified by a short RNA molecule present as an essential component of telomerase. The telomerase sequence shown is that of humans.

Extrachromosonal Replicons

In addition to very large, circular DNA chromosome in nucleoid many bacteria contain one or more small circular DNA molecules that are force in cytosol and called **plasmids**. Most plasmids are only a few thousand base pair long but some contain over 10^5 base pairs plasmids carry genetic information and undergo replication to yield daughter plasmids. They replicate independently to bacterial genome. The number of copies of a particular plasmid in a cell varries depending on the mechanism by which replication is regulated. They relay on the DNA-replication enzymes of the host cell for their reproduction but the initiation of replication is controlled by plasmid genes. The replication follows rolling circle replication. Here replication starts with a cut at specific sugar phosphate bond in a double stranded circle. Because the displaced strand chemically linked to the newly synthesized DNA in the circle, replication does not terminate and extension proceeds without interruption forming a tail. An important example is F plasmid is bacteria.

DNA Damage

For details of DNA damage please see the chapter on gene mutation.

DNA Repair

The damaged DNA should be repaired otherwise it leads to malformation or termination of polypeptide and ultimately lead to variation in organisms.

Nucleotide Excision Repair

Nucleotide Excision Repair (NER) operates by a cut and patch mechanism that removes a variety of bulky lesions, including pyrimidine dimers and nucleotides to which various chemical groups have become attached. Two distinct NER pathways can be distinguished.

(i) **A transcription-coupled pathway** in which the template strands of genes that are being actively transcribed are preferentially repaired. Repair of a template strand is thought to occur as the DNA is being transcribed, and the presence of the lesion may be signaled by a stalled RNA polymerase. This preferential repair pathway ensures that those genes of greatest importance to the cell, which are the genes the cell is actively transcribing, receive the highest priority on the 'repair list.'

(ii) A slower, less efficient **global genomic pathway** that corrects DNA strands in the remainder of the genome. Although recognition of the lesion is probably accomplished by different proteins in the two nucleotide excision repair pathways. One of the key components of the nucleotide excision repair machinery is TFIIH, a huge protein that also participates in the initiation of transcription. The discovery of the involvement of TFIIH established a crucial link between transcription and DNA repair, two processes that were previously assumed to be independent of one another. Included among the various subunits of TFIIH are two subunits (XPB and XPD) that possess helicase activity, these enzymes separate the two strands of the duplex in preparation for removal of the lesion. The damaged strand is then cut on both sides of the lesion by a pair of endonucleases, and the segment of DNA between the incisions is released. Once excised, the gap is filled by a DNA polymerase and the strand is sealed by DNA ligase.

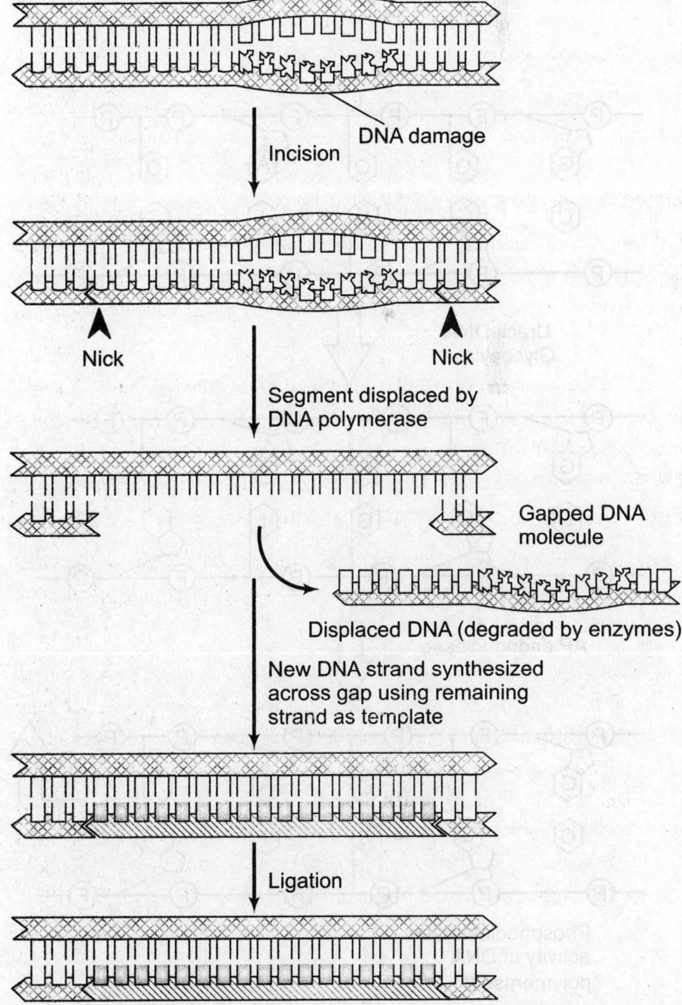

Fig. 6.25 Mechanism of excision repair After a multienzyme complex recognizes a bulky legion such as pyrimidine dimer, one cut is made on each side of lesion, DNA helicase remove the entire portion of damaged DNA shared.

Mechanism of other Excision Repairs

(i) A separate excision repair system operates to remove altered nucleotides generated by reactive chemicals present in the dietor produced by metabolism.

(ii) The steps in this repair pathway in eukaryotes, which is called **base excision repair** (BER), are shown in Fig. 6.26.

(iii) Base Excision Repair is initiated by a **DNA glycosylase** that recognizes the alteration (step 1) and removes the base by cleavage of the glycosidic bond holding the base to the deoxyribose sugar (step 2). A number of different DNA glycosylases have been identified, each more or less specific for a particular type of altered base, including uracil (formed by the hydrolytic removal of the amino group of cytosine), 8-oxoguanine (caused by damage from oxygen free radicals,), and 3-methyladenine (produced by transfer of a methyl group from a methyl donor).

(iv) Structural studies of the DNA glycosylase that removes the highly mutagenic 8-oxoguanine (oxoG) indicate that this enzyme diffuses rapidly along the DNA 'inspecting' each of the G-C base pairs within the DNA duplex. Figure 6.27(step 1). In step 2, the enzyme has come across an oxoG-C base pair.

(v) When this occurs, the enzyme inserts a specific amino acid side chain into the DNA helix, causing the nucleotide to rotate ('flip') 180 degrees out of the DNA helix and into the body of the enzyme (step 2).

(vi) If the nucleotide does, in fact, contain an oxoG, the base fits into the active site of the enzyme (step 3) and is cleaved from its associated sugar.

(vii) In contrast, if the extruded nucleotide contains a normal guanine, which only differs in structure by two atoms from oxoG, it is unable to fit into the enzyme's active site (step 4) and it is returned to its appropriate position within the stack of bases.

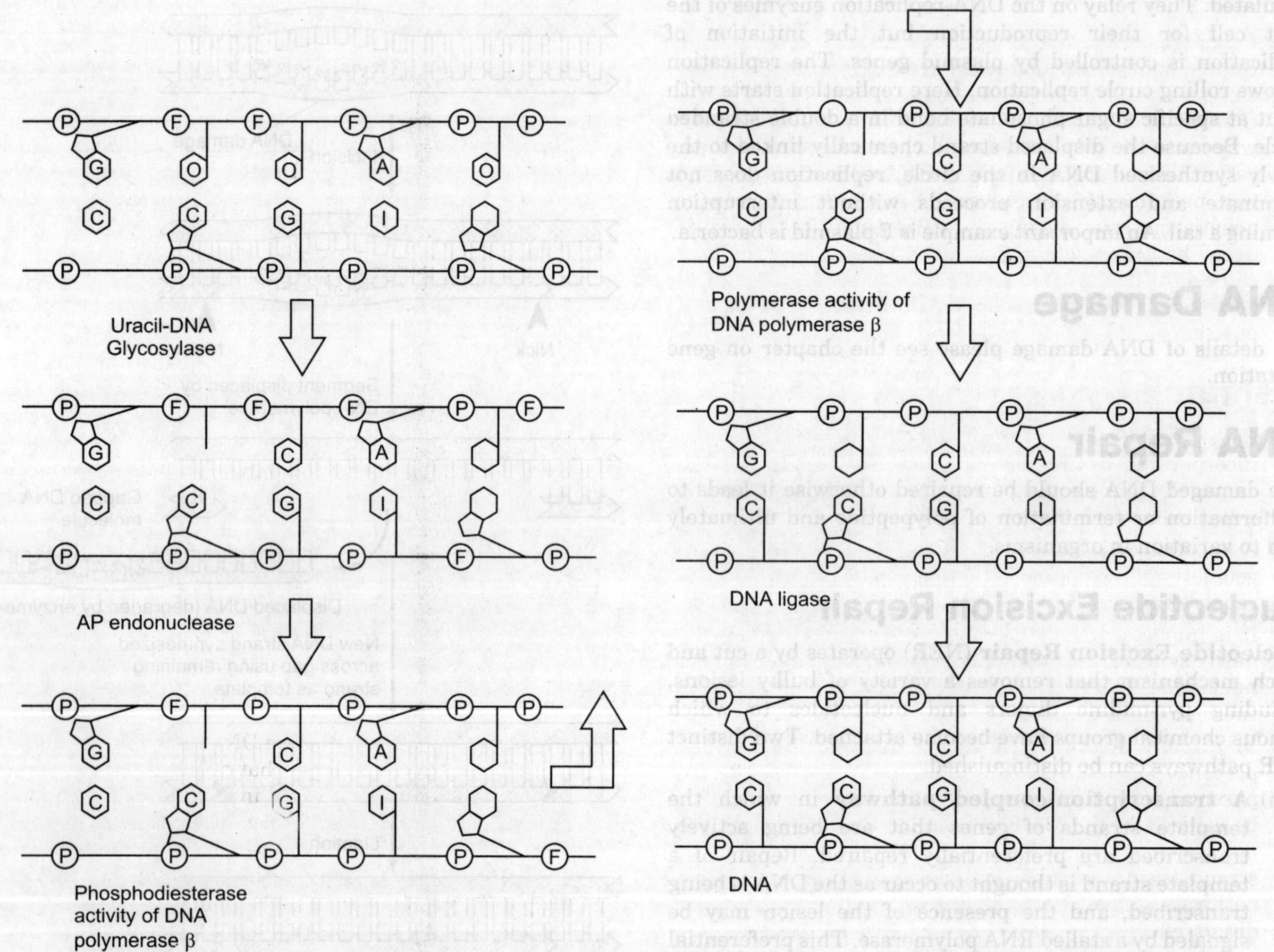

Fig. 6.26 Base excision repair. BER also has been shown to have distinct transcription coupled and global repair pathways

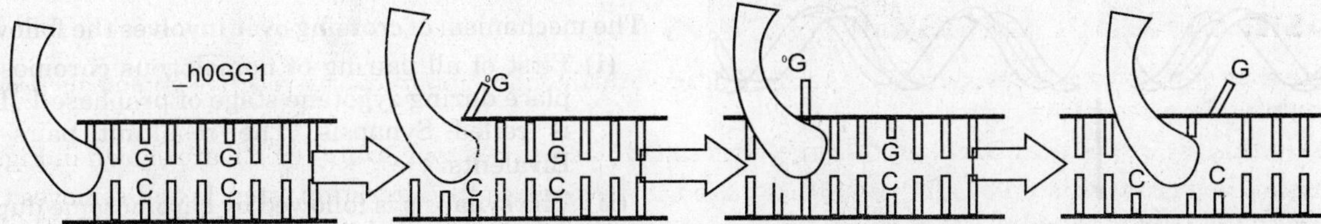

Fig. 6.27 Deteching damaged bases during BER. In step 1, a DNA glycosylase (named hOGG1) is inspecting a nucleotide that is paired to a cytosine. In step 2, the nucleotide is flipped out of the DNA duples. In this case, the base is an oxidized varsion of guanine, 8-oxoguanine, and it is able to fit into the active site of the enzyme (step 3) where it is cleaved from its attached sugar. The subsequent steps in BER were shown in fig. In step 4, the extruded base is a normal guanine, which is unable to fit into the active site pf the glycosylase and is rturned to the base stack. Failure to remove oxoG would have resulted in a G to T mutation.

(viii) Once an altered purine or pyrimidine is removed by a glycosylase, the 'beheaded' deoxyribose phosphate remaining in the site is excised by the combined action of a specialized (AP) endonuclease and a DNA polymerase. AP endonuclease cleaves the DNA backbone (Figure 26 step 3) and a phosphodiesterase activity of polymerase removes the sugar–phosphate remnant that had been attached to the excised base (step 4).

(ix) Polymerase then fills the gap by inserting a nucleotide complementary to the undamaged strand (step 5), and the strand is sealed by DNA ligase III (step 6). The fact that cytosine can be converted to uracil may explain why natural selection favored the use of thymine, rather than uracil, as a base in DNA, even though uracil was presumably present in RNA when it served as genetic material during the early evolution of life. If uracil had been retained as a DNA base, it would have caused difficulty for repair systems to distinguish between a uracil that belonged at a particular site and one that resulted from an alteration of cytosine.

Mismatch Repair

(i) Cells can remove mismatched bases that are incorporated by the DNA polymerase and escape the enzyme's proofreading exonuclease. This process is called **mismatch repair** (MMR).

(ii) A mismatched base pair causes a distortion in the geometry of the double helix that can be recognized by a repair enzyme.

(iii) It is important that the repair system distinguish the newly synthesized strand, which contains the incorrect nucleotide, from the parental strand, which contains the correct nucleotide.

(iv) In *E. coli*, the two strands are distinguished by the presence of methylated adenosine residues on the parental strand. DNA methylation does not appear to be utilized by the MMR system in eukaryotes, and the mechanism of identification of the newly synthesized strand remains unclear. Several different MMR pathways have been identified and will not be discussed.

Double-Strand Breakage Repair

(i) When these forms of radiation (X-rays, gamma rays, and particles released by radioactive atoms) collide with a fragile DNA molecule, they often break both strands of the double helix.

(ii) **Double-strand breaks** (DSBs) can also be caused by certain chemicals, including several (*e.g.,* bleomycin) used in cancer chemotherapy, and free radicals produced by normal cellular metabolism.

(iii) Double strand breaks are also introduced during replication of damaged DNA.

(iv) A single double-strand break can cause serious chromosome abnormalities, which can have grave consequences for the cell. Double Strand Breaks can be repaired by several alternate pathways. The predominant pathway in mammalian cells is called **Non-Homologous End Joining** (NHEJ), in which a complex of proteins bind to the broken ends of the DNA duplex and catalyze a series of reactions that rejoin the broken strands.

(v) The major steps that occur during NHEJ are shown in Fig. 6.28 and described in the accompanying legend. This NHEJ repair protein is seen to localize at the site of the DSBs immediately following their appearance. Another DSB repair pathway known as **homologous recombination** requires a homologous chromosome to serve as a template for repair of the broken strand. The steps that occur during homologous recombination are similar to those of genetic recombination depicted. Defects in both repair pathways have been linked to increased cancer susceptibility.

Recombination

An important property of the DNA in cells is its ability to undergo rearrangements that can vary the particular combination of genes present in any individual genome as well as the timing and level of expression of these genes. This DNA rearrangement is caused by **genetic recombination.** Two main classes of genetic recombination are general or homologous recombination and site specific recombination.

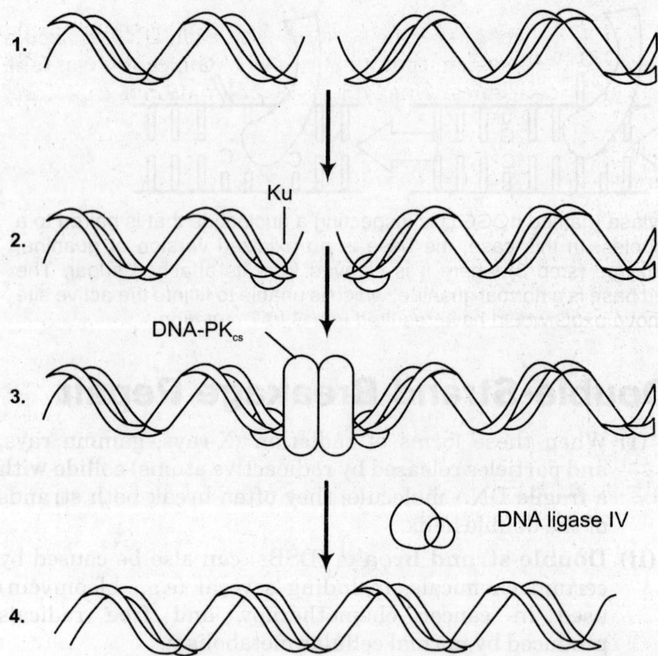

Fig. 6.28 Repairing double-strand breaks (DSBs) by non-homologous end joining. (a) In this simplified model of double-strand break repair, the lesion (step 1) is detected by a heterodimeric, ring-shaped protein called Ku, that binds to the broken ends of the DNA (step 2). The DNA-bound Ku recruits another protein, called DNA-PK$_{cs}$, which is the catalytic subunit of a DNA-dependent protein kinase (step 3). Most of the substrates phosphorylated by this protein kinase have not been identified. These proteins bring the ends of the broken DNA together in such a way that they can be joined by DNA ligase IV to regenerate an intact DNA duplex (step 4).

Homologous Recombination

If chromosomes remain intact during inheritance than only parental combinations must appear in F_2-generations. But in most of the cases, though parental combinations are more numerous, the non-parental combinations also appear. Presence of these non-parental combinations indicate that in the linked genes, their occur a process of interchange of alleles (homologous segments) between non-sister chromatids of homologous chromosomes. **Morgan** termed this phenomenon as **crossing over**. Thus, the phenomenon of crossing over can be defined as the phenomenon of recombinations of linked genes which is the result of interchange of homologous segments between the non-sister chromatids of homologous chromosome pair. For example, a cross between grey bodied vestigial wings (BB vv) and black bodied-long wings (bb VV) of *Drosophila* produces four types of offsprings in F_2-generation on test cross as:

- Grey-Vestigial–41.5%
- Black-Long–41.5%
- Black-Vestigial–8.5%
- Grey-Long–8.5%

The mechanism of crossing over involves the following steps:

(i) First of all pairing of homologous chromosomes takes place during zygotene stage of prophase-I. This pairing is called Synapsis. The resultant pairs are called Bivalents.

(ii) The synapsis is followed by chromosome duplication, in which each homologous chromosome of bivalent splits longitudinally to form two identical sister chromatids, which remain held together by an unsplitted centromere. At this stage, each bivalent contains four arms or two chromatids hence, are called Bivalent (tetrad).

(iii) After tetrad formation, crossing over occur, during which two non-sister chromatids exchange their segments. After exchange, the chromosomal parts start repelling each other except at the point of contact. The result will be seen in the form of cross-shaped or X-shaped structures called Chiasmata. The crossing over that takes place at this point thus, resulting to several chiasmata. The number of chiasmata depends upon the length of chromosome and the type of cross over. It is interesting to note:

- **Stern** and **Hotta** (1969) have described that the breakage of chromatids is brought about by a nuclear enzyme **endonuclease.** The fusion of broken segments takes place due to action of another enzyme ligase. Thus, these two enzymes help in exchange of segments during crossing over.
- The formation of chiasmata between any two gene loci has a characteristic probability, *i.e.,* the more apart two genes are located, the greater probability of chiasmata formation they have.

(iv) After chiasmata formation, the chromosomes start separating progressively from each other beginning at centromere and moving towards the chiasma. Similarly, the chiasma itself move in a zipper fashion towards the ends of tetrads. This zipper movement of chiasma is called **terminalization** and results to complete separation of homologous pairs.

Site Specific Recombination

This type of recombination is guided by a recombination enzyme that recognizes specific nucleotide sequences present on one or both of recombining DNA molecules. This type of recombination enables various types of mobile DNA sequence to move about within and between chromosomes by separating and joining double stranded DNA molecules at specific sites. Site specific recombination was first discovered when bacteriophage lambda moves its genome unto and out of the *E. coli* genome. When this virus enters a cell a virus encoded enzyme called **lambda integrase** (resamble DNA topoisomerase) is synthesized. This enzyme catalyses the recombination process which begins after tight binding of integrase protein to a specific DNA sequence. The integrase than catalyse the cutting and resealing of DNA using a short region of chromosome to form heteroduplex.

Site-specific recombination enzymes that break and rejoin two DNA double helices at specific sequences on each DNA molecule often do this in a reversible way: as for lambda bacteriophage. The same enzyme system that joins two DNA molecules can take them apart again, precisely restoring the sequences of the two original DNA molecules. This type of recombination is therefore, called **conservative site-specific recombination.**

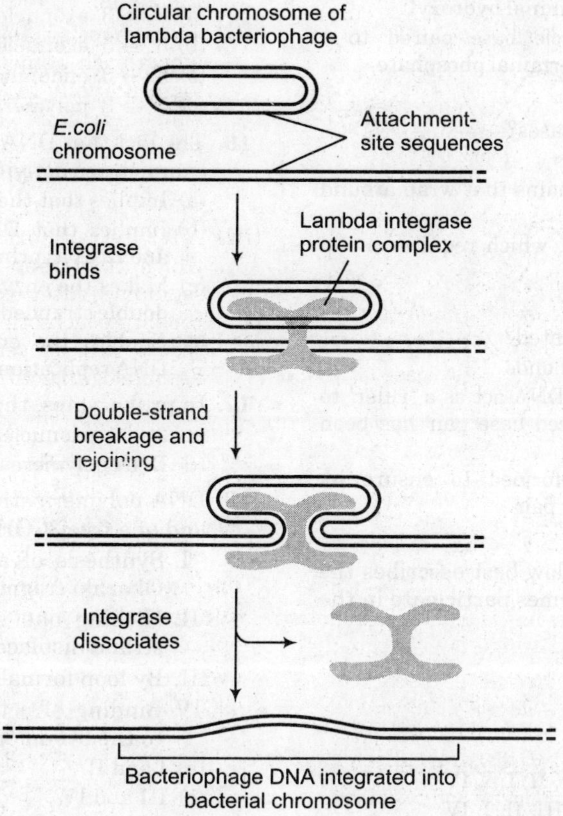

Fig. 6.29 The insertion of bacteriophage lambda DNA into the *E.coli* chromosome

Exercise

1. The observed error rate in DNA replication is
(a) 1 per 106 nucleotides
(b) 1 per 104 nucleotides
(c) 1 per 1010 nucleotides
(d) 1 per 1015 nucleotides

2. Which of the following is (are) true?
(a) Naturally occurring DNA usually has negative supercoiling
(b) Forms with same linking number can be interconverted without cleavage
(c) The twist value rarely changes in naturally occurring DNA
(d) Both (a) and (b)

3. The mechanism by which type II topoisomerase relaxes DNA includes which of the following?
(a) The OH of *Tyr* 723 attacks a phosphate group on one DNA strand
(b) When the backbone of one strand is cleaved, the DNA rotates
(c) ATP binds, leading to a conformation change
(d) Both (a) and (b)

4. Replication moves from
(a) 5′ → 3′ direction (b) 3′ → 5′ direction
(c) 5′ → 5′ direction (d) 3′ → 3′ direction

5. In the Meselson and Stahl experiment, *E. coli* cells grown on heavy nitrogen were transferred to light nitrogen. What percentage of DNA can be expected of light nitrogen after three generation of multiplication?
(a) 25 (b) 50
(c) 75 (d) 100

6. Isotope used for proving semi-conservative replication of DNA are
(a) N^{14} and P^{31} (b) N^{14} and N^{15}
(c) N^{14} and C^{14} (d) C^{14} and P^{31}

7. A solution contains DNA polymerase I, Mg^{2+}, salts of dATP, dGTP, dCTP and dTTP, and an appropriate buffer. Which of the following DNA molecule would

serve as a template for DNA synthesis when added to this solution?
(a) A single stranded closed circle
(b) A single stranded closed circle base paired top a shorter linear strand with 3′ terminal hydroxyl
(c) A single stranded closed circle base paired to a shorter linear strand with a 3′ terminal phosphate
(d) A double stranded closed circle

8. What is true about DNA polymerases?
(a) There are five structural classes
(b) All have finger and thumb domains that wrap around the DNA
(c) All catalyze the same reaction, which requires metal cofactors
(d) All of the above

9. How is replication specificity dictated?
(a) Formation of proper hydrogen bonds
(b) Enzyme interactions with the DNA act as a 'ruler' to determine if the properly spaced base pair has been formed
(c) The bond is broken and reformed to ensure its accurate placement at each base pair
(d) Both (a) and (b)

10. Which of the sequences listed below best describes the order in which the following enzymes participate in the replication of DNA in bacteria?
I. DNA polymerase I
II. 5′ → 3′ Exonuclease
III. DNA polymerase III
IV. DNA ligase
(a) V, III, I, II, IV (b) III, II, I, V, IV
(c) V, III, IV, II, I (d) V, III, II, I, IV

11. In genetics, an origin is
(a) a protein that binds to DNA at the point where replication begins
(b) a protein that binds to RNA at the point where translation begins
(c) the point in DNA where transcription starts
(d) the point in DNA where replication starts

12. Replication of DNA in eukaryotes commences from
(a) one end of chromatid extending to the other end
(b) both ends of the chromatid simultaneously
(c) the centromere to either of the ends of chromatids
(d) several sites of the DNA of the chromatid simultaneously

13. The synthesis of DNA was shown to be template dependent and semiconservative. This would predict that
(a) no organism can have a single stranded genome
(b) RNA cannot serve as the genome of any organism
(c) all single stranded genomes would be synthesized *via* a double stranded intermediate
(d) template independent DNA polymerases do not exist in nature

14. One function of the two metal cations that are required by DNA polymerases is
(a) to stabilize the negative charge of the transition state
(b) to bind ATP
(c) to complex with a *Tyr* residue in the active site
(d) Both (b) and (c)

15. Which of the following property is not associated with DNA polymerase I?
(a) 5′ → 3′ exonuclease activity
(b) 3′ → 5′ exonuclease activity
(c) 5′ → 3′ endonuclease activity
(d) 5′ → 3′ polymerase activity

16. The fact that DNA polymerase I from *E. coli* has 5′ → 3′ exonuclease activity
(a) Implies that the enzyme has multiple subunits
(b) Implies that DNA polymerase I can use both DNA and RNA as primers
(c) Makes the enzyme able to detect thymine dimmers in double stranded DNA
(d) Enables the enzyme to play an important role in DNA replication

17. In prokaryotes, the lagging primers are removed by
(a) 3′→ 5′ exonuclease (b) DNA ligase
(c) DNA polymerase I (d) DNA polymerase III

18. DNA polymerization requires the presence of template and of a free 3′-OH end. This end may be generated by
I. Synthesis of an RNA primer at the origin or at Okazaki fragments start points
II. Nicking one strand of duplex DNA followed by strand displacement
III. By loop formation at the 3′ end (self-priming)
IV. Binding of a terminal nucleotide-carrying protein to the 3′ end of template
(a) I and II (b) I and III
(c) III and IV (d) I, II, III and IV

19. The function of *E. coli* DNA polymerase II in the cell is to
(a) initiate replication at the origins
(b) carry out 'fill in' reaction at the Okazaki fragments after RNA primer removal
(c) synthesis of leading strand only
(d) replication restart at the stalled replication fork

20. Huntington disease is caused by
(a) pyrimidine dimers (b) trinucleotide expansion
(c) suppressor mutants (d) All of these

21. Okazaki fragments
(a) require the activity of only a DNA polymerase for synthesis
(b) require only RNA polymerase activity for synthesis
(c) are made when DNA is exposed to UV radiation
(d) are composed of both DNA and RNA

22. Okazaki fragments are used to elongate
(a) the leading strand towards the replication fork
(b) the lagging strand towards the replication fork
(c) the leading strand away from the replication fork
(d) the lagging strand away from the replication fork

23. Approximately how many Okazaki fragments are synthesized during one round of replication of the *E. coli* genome?
(a) 5000-10000 (b) 4×10^6
(c) 2500-5000 (d) 2

24. During replication of DNA, which one of the following enzyme polymerizes the Okazaki fragments
(a) DNA polymerase I (b) DNA polymerase II
(c) DNA polymerase III (d) RNA polymerase I

25. Which enzyme removes the RNA primer and fills in deoxyribonucleotides in prokaryotic replicons?
(a) DNA polymerase III (b) DNA polymerase II
(c) DNA polymerase I (d) Exonuclease MFI

26. Which of the following reactions is required for proofreading (*i.e.*, correcting replication errors) during DNA replication by DNA polymerase III?
(a) $3' \rightarrow 5'$ exonuclease activity
(b) $5' \rightarrow 3'$ exonuclease activity
(c) $3' \rightarrow 5'$ endonuclease activity
(d) $5' \rightarrow 3'$ endonuclease activity

27. The bacterial enzyme that changes positively super coiled DNA into negatively super coiled DNA is
(a) DNA helicase
(b) DNA gyrase
(c) single strand binding protein
(d) polymerase

28. The exonuclease activity of the DNA polymerases functions to
(a) remove the RNA primer sequences
(b) proofread the new DNA strand and remove inappropriate nucleotides
(c) maximize the fidelity of DNA replication
(d) All of the above

29. In prokaryotes, the lagging strand primers are removed by
(a) $3' \rightarrow 5'$ exonuclease (b) DNA ligase
(c) DNA polymerase I (d) DNA polymerase III

30. T_4 DNA ligase
(a) requires ATP
(b) joins double stranded DNA fragments with an adjacent 3′ phosphate and 5′-OH
(c) requires NADH
(d) joins single stranded DNA

31. DNA ligase of *E. coli* requires which of the following cofactors?
(a) FAD as an electron acceptor
(b) $NADP^+$ as a phosphate donor
(c) NAD^+ to form an active adenyl enzyme
(d) NAD^+ as an electron acceptor

32. In eukaryotes, RNA primers are removed after replication by
(a) DNA polymerase δ (b) helicase
(c) FEN I (d) DNA polymerase

33. Which of the following DNA polymerase has proofreading property in animal cells?
(a) DNA polymerase α (b) DNA polymerase δ
(c) DNA polymerase β (d) All of these

34. How does the mismatch repair system distinguish between the parental (*i.e.*, correct) DNA strand and the newly synthesized strand containing the mismatched base?
(a) Thymine in the parental strand of the helix is methylated at GATC
(b) Thymine in the new strand of the helix is methylated at GATC
(c) Guanine in the parental strand of the helix is methylated at GATC
(d) Guanine in the new strand of the helix is methylated at GATC

35. What is the name of the DNA repair system in *E. coli* in which dual incisions are made in the damaged part of the double helix, and a 12-13 base segment is removed and replaced with new DNA?
(a) Mismatch repair
(b) Base excision repair
(c) Nucleotide excision repair
(d) AP site repair

36. Which of the following DNA polymerase in eukaryote has $5' \rightarrow 3'$ exonuclease activity?
(a) DNA polymerase α (b) DNA polymerase β
(c) DNA polymerase δ (d) None of these

37. Eukaryotic DNA synthesis is inhibited by
(a) aphidicoline (b) cyclohexamide
(c) chloramphenicol (d) ampicillin

38. Action of topoisomerase leads to change in
(a) linking number of single-stranded linear DNA
(b) linking number of double-stranded linear DNA
(c) linking number of closed circular single stranded DNA
(d) linking number of closed circular double stranded DNA

39. All of the following cell types contain the enzyme telomerase which protects the length of telomeres at the end of chromosomes, except
(a) germinal (b) somatic
(c) haemopoetic (d) tumour

40. Mitochondrial DNA is replicated from
(a) a single *ori* site bidirectionally
(b) two different *ori* sites in the same direction
(c) two different *ori* sites at different times in opposite directions
(d) many sites bidirectionally, like nuclear chromosomes

41. Chloroplast DNA is replicated from
(a) a single *ori* site bidirectionally
(b) two different *ori* sites in the same direction
(c) two different *ori* sites simultaneously and in opposite directions
(d) many sites bidirectionally, like nuclear chromosomes

42. A triple stranded intermediate is postulated to occur during
(a) eukaryotic DNA replication
(b) *Rec* A-mediated DNA recombination
(c) excision repair
(d) thymidine dimer photo reactivation

43. In bacteria, which enzyme unwinds double stranded DNA until it meets a chi site and then cuts one strand of the DNA
(a) *Rec* A (b) *Rec* BCD
(c) *Uvr* ABC (d) *Uvr* D

44. The *Rec* A protein of *E. coli* has several functions. Which of the following statements is false?
(a) *Rec* A acts as a co-protease
(b) *Rec* A protein has an affinity for single-stranded DNA
(c) *Rec* A binds pyrimidine dimers and initiates their repair
(d) *Rec* A is required for homologous recombination

45. In a mating between two strains of yeast that differ at a single locus (wild type x mutant), 15% of the tetrads contain wild type and mutant spores in the ratio of 3:1 or 1:3. The most likely explanation for this observation is
(a) gene conversion
(b) deletion of the mutant allele
(c) allelic exclusion
(d) reversion

46. Gene conversion is observed when
(a) During meiosis, one allele is replaced by another allele
(b) During meiosis, the expected 2:2 ratio of alleles is replaced with a 4:0 ratio
(c) During meiosis, the expected 2:2 ratio of alleles is replace with a 3:1 ratio
(d) All of the above

47. Any DNA polymerase that is involved in cellular DNA replication, when used to synthesize DNA in a test tube reaction, cannot synthesize DNA that is as long as the DNA that it makes in cells because in the test tube it
(a) lacks a sliding clamp
(b) has proofreading activity
(c) lacks RNAase H activity
(d) cannot synthesize DNA without a primer

48. During replication in all cells, the DNA in one of the two strands of DNA is replicated before the other strand because
(a) one strand is unwound before the other one
(b) only one strand is replicated in the same direction that the DNA is being unwound
(c) the two strands are replicated by different replication forks that start at different times
(d) one strand is more highly methylated than the other

49. DNA ligase uses the energy of ATP to close nicks in DNA and this involves a mechanism which includes
(a) an AMP in a phospho-ester linkage to the 5′-hydroxyl at one side of the nick
(b) an AMP in a phospho-ester linkage to the 5′-hydroxyl at one side of the nick
(c) an AMP in a phospho-anhydride linkage to the side-chain of a tyrosine in DNA ligase
(d) a linkage of the side-chain of a tyrosine in DNA ligase to the 5′-phosphate at one side of the nick

50. Mutations that do not kill a cell
(a) are almost always repaired after homologous recombination
(b) almost always change the amino acid sequence of a protein
(c) are irreversible, so, they accumulate in progeny cells
(d) always contribute to causing cancer

51. Unwinding dsDNA, whether for transcription or for replication,
(a) consumes negative supercoils to the dsDNA
(b) requires that the unwound strands pass through each other *via* a topoisomerase I-like reaction
(c) adds negative supercoils to the dsDNA
(d) has no impact on the supercoiling of the dsDNA

52. Photoreactivation
(a) repairs dimmers in DNBA using an endonuclease
(b) uses light to activate an endonuclease
(c) removes alkylating agents from bases
(d) deaminate bases

53. Enzyme DNA photolyase which is involved in direct repair of damaged DNA like thymine dimer
(a) can work only in the presence of light
(b) can work in dark
(c) is independent of light
(d) None of the above

54. Nucleotide excision repair of DNA in *E. coli*
(a) replaces strands of the DNA in the damaged region
(b) uses high energy phosphate bonds
(c) utilizes RNA polymerase to make primer
(d) requires *Uvr* ABC exonuclease

55. The most common modification of DNA is methylation. In prokaryotes, this serves to
I. identify damaged DNA for repair.
II. distinguish the strands after replication and allow/disallow continued replication.
III. identify methylated foreign DNA for recombinational incorporation into the genome.
IV. protect its own DNA but not foreign DNA from restriction by endonuclease.
(a) I and II
(b) II and III
(c) III and IV
(d) I, II and IV

56. When two replication forks meet,
(a) the DNA polymerases on the leading strands meet and the DNA polymerases on the lagging strand meet
(b) the Okazaki fragment from one fork is extended onto the lagging strand of the other fork
(c) the primer for the Okazaki fragment on each lagging strand is extended until it meets the DNA polymerase on the leading strand from the other fork
(d) each leading strand stops when it hits the primer for the last Okazaki fragment on the lagging strand from the other fork

57. In all cells (both prokaryotes and eukaryotes), DNA replication is initiated
(a) at each end of each chromosome
(b) at multiple sites on each chromosome, with each site generating one replication fork
(c) at multiple sites on each chromosome, with each site generating two replication fork
(d) in a tightly regulated manner so, that replication is initiated once per cell cycle at each initiation site

58. The unique feature of semi-conservative mode of replication of DNA is
(a) both half of each new molecule of DNA are old ones
(b) both half of each new molecule of DNA are new ones

(c) one half of each new molecule of DNA is an old one and other half is newly synthesized
(d) one half of each new molecule of DNA will be transcribed, while the other half is silent

59. In *E. coli*, which of the following repair systems is most error-prone?
(a) Photoactivation (b) Excision repair
(c) Recombinational repair (d) SOS repair

60. The SOS repair mechanism is activated by which of the following?
(a) 5-bromouracil (b) Acridine orange
(c) Hydroxylamine (d) Thymidine dimers

61. Semi-conservative mode of replication DNA was proved by
(a) Watson and Crick (b) H Khorana
(c) Lederberg (d) Meselson and Stahl

62. The mechanism of DNA replication was originally characterized in
(a) bacteria (b) algae
(c) fungi (d) virus

63. Which of the type of DNA polymerase is not involved in the replication process of *E. coli*?
(a) DNA polymerase I (b) DNA polymerase II
(c) DNA polymerase III (d) DNA polymerase IV

64. Which type of DNA polymerase posseses most abundant replicating activity in *E. coli* and also ensures the fidelity of replication?
(a) DNA polymerase I (b) DNA polymerase II
(c) DNA polymerase III (d) DNA polymerase IV

65. Replication of the *E. coli* genome is mainly carried out by
(a) DNA polymerase I (b) DNA polymerase II
(c) DNA polymerase III (d) DNA polymerase IV

66. The newly synthesized discontinuous segments of polynucleotides in replication process, is called as
(a) Kimura fragments (b) Suzuki fragments
(c) Okazaki fragments (d) Pinaki fragments

67. The ability of a particular polymerase to remain associated with the template strand is termed as its
(a) associate ship (b) linking
(c) attachment (d) processivity

68. Torsional stress created during replication of DNA is relieved by
(a) helicase (b) primase
(c) topoisomerase (d) DNA ligase

69. The gaps that exist between the 3′—OH of one leading strand and the 5′-phosphate of another is repaired by the
(a) helicase (b) primase
(c) topoisomerase (d) DNA ligase

70. Which of the statement is correct regarding recombination of DNA?
(a) It results in the process which leads to new molecules of DNA that contain a mix of genetic information from each parental strand
(b) It refers to the phenomenon whereby two parental strands of DNA are tied together resulting in an exchange of portions of their respective strands
(c) Both (a) and (b)
(d) None of the above

71. Which of the following is a type of DNA recombination
(a) Homologous recombination
(b) Site-specific recombination
(c) Transposition
(d) All of the above

72. Which of the following is a way of DNA repair in mammalian cells?
(a) Mismatch repair of single base mispairs
(b) Single and multi-step base excision mechanism
(c) Multi-step reactions involving multiple protein components
(d) All of the above

73. Transposons are
(a) short DNAs that bind to RISC and direct the specificity of degradation of *m*RNA by RISC
(b) are important for DNA repair because they facilitate sister-chromatid exchanges of DNA
(c) an uncommon form of DNA recombination that causes rearrangement of the immunoglobulin locus to contribute to the high amount of antibody diversity in the immune system
(d) short DNAs that can move around in the genome *via* transpositional recombination

74. Homologous DNA recombination mainly benefits cells by its role in
(a) post-replication repair of DNA
(b) genetic recombination
(c) unnatural recombination used by biotechnology
(d) retroviral integration into the genome

75. Cells normally delay replication until DNA damage and replication errors have been repaired because
(a) DNA polymerase cannot function when the DNA is damaged or there are replication errors present
(b) replication of damaged or mismatched DNA results in mutations
(c) repair is more resource intensive if done after replication because it requires homologous recombination
(d) it is not possible to do repair and replication at the same time

76. If a guanine is lost from DNA due to hydrolysis of the glycosidic bond, this is repaired by
(a) base excision repair
(b) DNA polymerase adding the guanine back by forming a new glycosidic bond
(c) purine salvage pathway
(d) nucleotide excision repair

77. Position-specific scoring matrices, consensus sequences, and sequence logo are needed because a transcription factor
(a) always binds to the same DNA sequence found in many locations in the genome
(b) always binds to a specific DNA sequence but its affinity varies with the genomic location of that sequence
(c) often binds to DNA with any one of several very similar sequences
(d) often binds to other transcription factors

78. Though the molecular details have not yet been revealed by experiments, DNA recombination is known to be essential in the repair of
(a) large amounts of DNA damage
(b) small DNA damage limited to a single nucleotide
(c) double-stranded DNA breaks
(d) erroneous DNA methylation

79. One of the biggest functional differences between DNA polymerases and RNA polymerases is that, unlike DNA polymerases, RNA polymerases
(a) supply their own template
(b) do not require a primer
(c) synthesize nucleic acid with the same polarity as the template, rather than anti-parallel
(d) function only in the nucleus of eukaryotic cells

80. The information carried by a DNA molecule is in
(a) its amino acid sequence
(b) the sugars and phosphates forming its backbone
(c) the order of the bases in the molecule
(d) the total number of nucleotides it contains

81. In an important experiment, bacteriophages were allowed to infect bacteria. In the first trial, the phages used contained radioactive DNA, and radioactivity was detected in the bacteria. Next, other phages containing radioactive protein were allowed to infect bacteria, and no radioactivity was detected in the bacteria. When the experimenters compared the results of these two trials, they concluded that
(a) genes are made of DNA
(b) bacteriophages can infect bacteria
(c) DNA is made of nucleotides
(d) genes carry information for making proteins

82. DNA replication occurs
(a) whenever a cell makes protein
(b) to repair gene damage caused by mutation
(c) before a cell divides
(d) whenever a cell needs RNA

83. A geneticist raised a crop of T_2 bacteriophages in a medium containing radioactive phosphorus, so that the DNA of the bacteriophages was labelled with radioactivity. The labelled phages were then allowed to infect non-radioactive bacteria. In a few hours, these bacteria burst open, releasing many bacteriophages. Some of these phages contained labelled.
(a) DNA (b) RNA
(c) protein (d) All of these

84. Meselson and Stahl
(a) provided evidence for the semiconservative model of DNA replication
(b) were able to separate phage protein coats from *E. coli* by using a blender
(c) found that DNA labelled with ^{15}N was of intermediate density
(d) grew *E. coli* on labelled phosphorus and sulphur

85. Researchers have found homeotic genes in humans, but they are not yet certain how these genes shape the human phenotype. Considering the functions of homeotic genes in other animals, which of the following is most likely to be their function in humans?
(a) determining skin and hair colour
(b) regulating cellular metabolic rate
(c) determining head and tail, back and front
(d) determining whether an individual is male or female

86. One of the reasons most scientists believed proteins were the carriers of genetic information was that
(a) Proteins were more heat stable than nucleic acids
(b) The protein content of duplicating cells always doubled prior to division
(c) Proteins were much more complex molecules than nucleic acids
(d) Early experimental evidence pointed to proteins as the hereditary material

87. Which of the following statements about DNA polymerase in incorrect?
(a) It joins complementary base pairs to each other
(b) It is able to proofread and correct for errors in its base-pairing in bacteria
(c) It is unable to join free nucleotides unless an RNA primer is present
(d) It only works in the $5' \rightarrow 3'$ direction

88. Thymine dimers, covalent links between adjacent thymine bases in DNA, may be induced by UV light. When they occur, they are repaired by
(a) excision enzymes (b) DNA polymerase
(c) ligase (d) All of these

89. Watson and Crick concluded that each base could not pair with itself because
(a) There would not be room for the helix to make a full turn every 3.4 nm
(b) The width of 2 nm would not permit two purines to pair together
(c) The bases could not be stacked 0.34 nm apart
(d) Identical bases could not hydrogen-bond together

90. The joining of nucleotides in the polymerization of DNA requires energy from
(a) DNA polymerase
(b) the hydrolysis of the terminal phosphate group of ATP
(c) the hydrolysis of GTP
(d) the hydrolysis of phosphates from nucleoside triphosphates

91. Eukaryotes differ from prokaryotes in mechanism of DNA replication due to
(a) discontinuous rather than semi-discontinuous
(b) DNA primers instead of RNA primers
(c) different enzymes for lagging and leading strands
(d) unidirectional rather than bidirectional

92. In the carbon skeleton of the pentose sugar in DNA, what is the attachment point of a base to form a nucleoside?
(a) C_1
(b) C_2
(c) C_3
(d) C_4

93. Heterochromatin
(a) has a higher degree of packing than does euchromatin
(b) is visible with the light microscope during interphase
(c) is not actively involved in transcription
(d) All of the above

94. DNA methylation of cytosine residues
(a) can be induced by drugs that reactive genes
(b) may contribute to long-term gene inactivation
(c) produces the promoter region that specifically bind RNA polymerase
(d) makes satellite DNA a different density so it can be separated by ultracentrifugation

95. Chromosome puffs along the polytene chromosomes of *Drosophila*
(a) appear at specific sites during developmental stages and give visual evidence of selected gene activation
(b) are associated with the presence of nonsteroid hormones that act *via* a second messenger
(c) are regions of DNA methylation causing highly compacted and inactive areas on the chromosome
(d) contain collections of multigene families

96. Which of the following statements about DNA polymerase I is correct?
(a) It functions as a DNA repair enzyme but is not involved in the DNA replication process
(b) It requires a template and a primer to polymerize deoxyribonucleoside triphosphates
(c) It joins together Okazaki fragments to complete the lagging strand during DNA replication
(d) It produces Okazaki fragments linked to RNA primer chains

97. DNA ligase of *E. coli* requires which of the following cofactors?
(a) Flavin-adenine dinucleotide as an electron acceptor
(b) Nicotinamide-adenine dinucleotide phosphate as a phosphate donor
(c) Nicotinamide-adenine dinucleotide (NAD^+) to form an active adenyl enzyme
(d) NAD^+ as an electron acceptor

98. How does the DNA of the circular *E. coli* chromosome replicate?
(a) Unidirectionally—it starts at one point on the chromosome and replicates in one direction
(b) Bidirectionally—it starts at one point on the chromosome and replicates in both directions.
(c) Multidirectionally—it starts at several points on the chromosome proceeding in both directions
(d) All the above statement is true

99. How are the eight human globin genes organized?
(a) They are randomly distributed on the human chromosomes
(b) They are in two clusters, one on chromosome 11 and the other on 16
(c) They are in a single cluster on the X-chromosome
(d) They are in four clusters, alpha, beta, gamma and delta

100. Which of the following statements about topoisomerases is incorrect?
(a) They alter the linking number of topoisomers
(b) They break and reseal phosphodiester bonds
(c) They require NAD^+ is a cofactor to supply the energy to drive the conversion of a supercoiled molecule to its relaxed form
(d) They form covalent intermediates with their DNA substrates

101. Which of the following statement is incorrect?
(a) Unequal crossing over changes gene organization but not total gene number
(b) Histone genes and *r*RNA genes are typically organized in tandem units in eukaryotic genomes
(c) Organelles genomes are mostly circular and dsDNA
(d) $Cot_{1/2}$ values are affected by genome size but not by the complexity of genome

102. In the widely accepted nucleosome model of chromosome the following are found
(a) histone core with DNA molecule wrapped around it
(b) four types of basic histone, one acidic histone and DNA molecule loosely linked
(c) one acidic histone forming the core with 4 histone and DNA molecule present in separate whorls
(d) DNA core surrounded by five histone protein

103. 'Zinc fingers' are important in cellular function because they are
(a) the catalytic site of many metabolic enzymes
(b) structural motifs in many DNA-binding proteins
(c) structures with high redox potential
(d) characteristic of palindromic stretches of unique DNA sequence

104. The difference in DNA and RNA structure is the presence of uracil in RNA instead of thymine in DNA. At molecular level there is only a difference of
(a) methyl group (b) aldehyde group
(c) carboxylic group (d) ketone group

105. Cot ½ of DNA is defined as
(a) the time taken by a denatures molecule to reanneal
(b) the Initial concentration (Co) in moles/L multiplied by time (*t*) in second taken for 50% of DNA to reanneal
(c) the concentration of DNA in a cell at any particular time
(d) amount of cytosine bases in a single strand by DNA

106. DNA is made up of two antiparallel polynucleotide chains, the word antiparallel means
(a) the distance between the two strands is not constant throughout
(b) the strands have opposite polarity, *i.e.*, One is from 3′-5′ and the other is 5′-3′ directed
(c) that they are not complementary
(d) that one grows faster than the other strand

107. When a growing structurally unsynchronized culture of a strain of *E. coli* is exposed to a three-minute pulse of [^{3}H] thymidine, a great majority of individual bacteria become radioactivity, this indicates that
(a) DNA synthesis occupies only fraction of the time required for cell division
(b) transcription of DNA to form *m*RNA is continuously taking place
(c) bacterial DNA replication is taking place in a semi-conservative manner
(d) DNA synthesis is taking place for almost the entire duration on of the division cycle

108. Consider the following events in DNA replication
I. Formation of RNA primers by RNA polymerase.
II. Removal of RNA primers and formation of Okazaki fragments.
III. Formation of DNA strands on RNA primers by poly III-copoly III complex.
IV. Recognition of initiation point by initiator protein
V. Dissociation of hydrogen bonds and opening of a bubble in the duplex by unwinding proteins.
VI. Filling up the gaps between Okazaki fragments and formation of DNA strand.

The correct sequence of these events is
(a) IV, V, I, III, II, VI (b) IV, I, V, II, III, VI
(c) IV, V, II, I, III, VI (d) IV, V, I, II, III, VI

109. Radioactive thymidine when added to the medium surrounding living mammalian cells gets incorporated into the newly synthesized DNA. Which of the following types of chromatin is expected to become radioactive if cells are exposed to radioactive thymidine as soon as they enter the S-phase?
(a) Neither heterochromatin nor euchromatin but only the nucleus
(b) Heterochromatin
(c) Euchromatin
(d) Both (b) and (c)

110. During DNA replication, the synthesis of the leading strand occurs in the $5' \rightarrow 3'$; direction alongwith the movement of the replication fork. Which one of the following statements is true about the synthesis of the lagging strand?
(a) DNA polymerase II, which has an additional activity of polymerization in $3' \rightarrow 5'$ direction, is utilized
(b) DNA polymerase I is utilized, which can carry out DNA synthesis in the absence of any primer
(c) synthesis of the lagging strand occurs in the small fragments by DNA polymerase in $5' \rightarrow 3'$ direction using a *de novo* synthesized DNA primer
(d) synthesis of the lagging strand occurs in the small fragments in $5' \rightarrow 3'$ direction utilizing RNA primer

111. What is the role of gyrase in DNA replication?
(a) To relax or prevent supercoiling of the double helix
(b) To separate the two template strands of DNA at each replication fork
(c) To synthesize a short RNA primer for each new DNA strand
(d) To protect single-stranded regions of DNA from damage

112. The large (Klenow) fragment of *E. coli* DNA polymerase I contains which of the following activities?
(a) Reverse transcriptase activity and nick-translation activity
(b) Polymerase activity and $3' \rightarrow 5'$ exonuclease activity
(c) Polymerase activity and nick-translation activity
(d) $5' \rightarrow 3'$ exonuclease activity

113. In a reaction containing dNTPs and DNA polymerase in buffer, on which of the following molecules DNA synthesis would occur
(a) a single-stranded closed circular DNA
(b) a double stranded closed circular DNA
(c) a single-stranded closed circular DNA paired with a short oligonucleotide with a 3′ terminal phosphate
(d) a single-stranded closed circular DNA paired with a short oligonucleotide with a 3′ hydroxyl group

114. Match the following lists.

List I	List II
A. DNA ligase	1. Catalyses the covalent anion of segments of an interrupted sugar phosphate strand in double-stranded DNA
B. DNA polymerase	2. Endonuclease that digest either single-stranded or double stranded DNA
C. DNAase I	3. Produces single or double-stranded breaks in DNA during replication to release tension brought about by the separation of double-strands
D. DNA topoisomerase	4. Catalyses the formation of DNA form deoxyribonucleotides using one strand of DNA as template

Codes

	A	B	C	D
(a)	1	4	3	D
(b)	4	1	2	3
(c)	1	4	2	3
(d)	4	1	3	2

Answers

1. (c)	**2.** (d)	**3.** (d)	**4.** (a)	**5.** (c)	**6.** (b)	**7.** (b)	**8.** (d)	**9.** (d)	**10.** (d)
11. (d)	**12.** (d)	**13.** (c)	**14.** (a)	**15.** (c)	**16.** (d)	**17.** (c)	**18.** (d)	**19.** (d)	**20.** (b)
21. (d)	**22** (d)	**23.** (c)	**24.** (c)	**25.** (c)	**26.** (a)	**27.** (b)	**28.** (d)	**29.** (c)	**30.** (a)
31. (c)	**32.** (c)	**33.** (b)	**34.** (d)	**35.** (c)	**36.** (d)	**37.** (a)	**38.** (d)	**39.** (b)	**40.** (c)
41. (c)	**42.** (b)	**43.** (b)	**44.** (c)	**45.** (a)	**46.** (c)	**47.** (a)	**48.** (b)	**49.** (b)	**50.** (c)
51. (a)	**52.** (b)	**53.** (a)	**54.** (d)	**55.** (d)	**56.** (d)	**57.** (d)	**58.** (c)	**59.** (d)	**60.** (d)
61. (d)	**62.** (a)	**63.** (d)	**64.** (a)	**65.** (c)	**66.** (c)	**67.** (d)	**68.** (c)	**69.** (d)	**70.** (c)
71. (d)	**72.** (d)	**73.** (d)	**74.** (a)	**75.** (b)	**76.** (a)	**77.** (c)	**78.** (c)	**79.** (b)	**80.** (c)
81. (a)	**82.** (c)	**83.** (a)	**84.** (a)	**85.** (c)	**86.** (c)	**87.** (a)	**88.** (d)	**89.** (d)	**90.** (d)
91. (a)	**92.** (a)	**93.** (d)	**94.** (b)	**95.** (a)	**96.** (b)	**97.** (c)	**98.** (b)	**99.** (b)	**100.** (c)
101. (d)	**102.** (a)	**103.** (b)	**104.** (a)	**105.** (b)	**106.** (b)	**107.** (c)	**108.** (c)	**109.** (a)	**110.** (d)
111. (a)	**112.** (b)	**113.** (d)	**114.** (c)						

7 RNA Synthesis and Processing

Syllabus

- Transcription Factors and Machinery, Formation of Initiation Complex, Transcription Activator and Repressor RNA Polymerases Capping, Elongation and Termination (RNA Processing RNA Editing, Splicing and Polyadenylation)
- RNA Transport

Transcription

Transcription is the first step in gene expression which transfers the genetic information stored in DNA/genes into RNA molecules.

All RNA except the genomes of many RNA viruses are produced through transcription. During transcription only one strand of a DNA Molecule is transcribed and called antisense or template strand, while other strand is called coding or sense stand. The general features of transcription are

(a) Precursors for RNA synthesis are ribonucleoside triphosphates.

(b) Only one strand of DNA is used as a template for the synthesis of a complementary RNA chain in any given region.

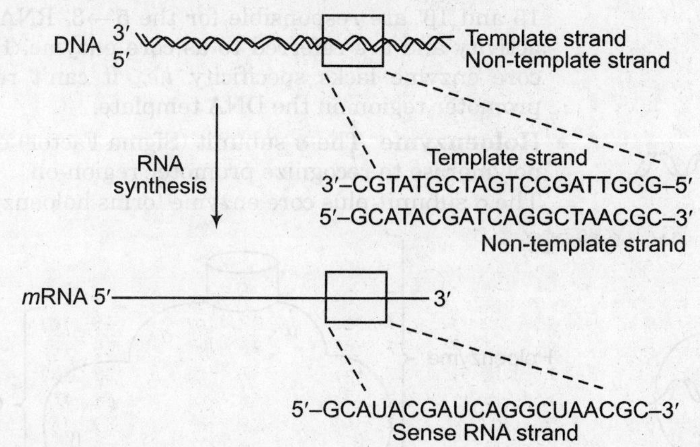

Fig. 7.1 RNA synthesis utilizes only one DNA strand of a gene as template

(c) RNA chains can be initiated *de novo*, without any requirement for a pre-existing primer strand.

(d) The synthesis of RNA chains occurs in the 5′→3′ direction with the addition of ribonucleotides to the 3′-hydroxyl group at the end of the chain.

(e) RNA synthesis takes place within a locally unwound segment of DNA, sometimes called a **replication bubble,** which is produced by RNA polymerase.

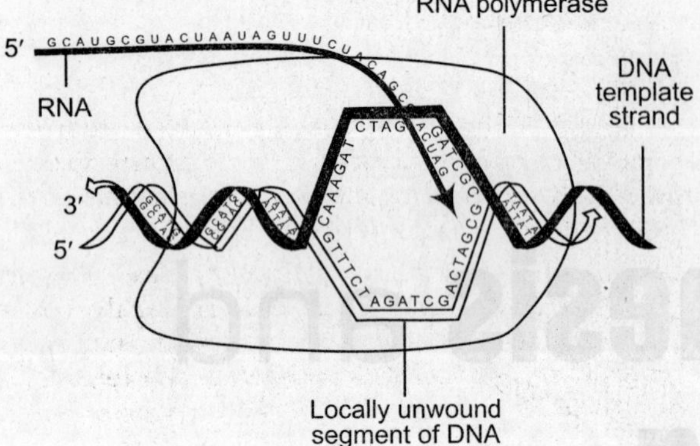

Fig. 7.2 RNA synthesis occurs within a locally unwound segment of DNA. This transcription bubble allows a few nucleotides in the template strand to base-pair with the growing end of the RNA chain. The unwinding and rewinding of the DNA molecule are catalyzed by RNA polymerase.

(f) The process of transcription involves three steps :
- Initiation
- Elongation
- Termination

1. **RNA chain initiation**

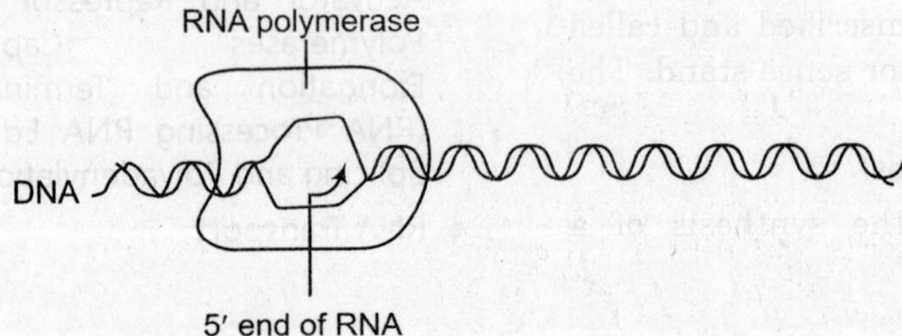

2. **RNA chain elongation**

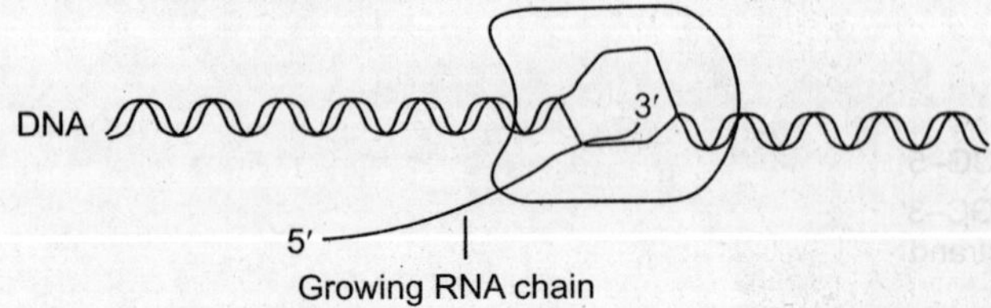

3. **RNA chain termination**

Fig. 7.3 The three stages of transcription: initiation elongation and termination

Prokaryotic Transcription: Components

Transcriptions and translation in prokaryotes takes place in cytoplasm. The transcription unit is composed of RNA polymerase, promoters transcription factors, etc.

RNA Polymerase

RNA polymerase, the enzyme responsible for the DNA-directed synthesis of RNA was discovered independently in 1960 by **Samuel Weiss** and **Jerard Hurwitz.**

(a) The enzyme couples together the ribonucleoside triphosphate ATP, CTP, GTP and UTP on DNA template in a reaction that is driven by release and subsequent hydrolysis of PP_i.

$$(RNA)_n \text{ residues} + NTP \rightleftharpoons (RNA)_{n+1 \text{ residues}} + PP_i$$

(b) RNA polymerase initiates transcription at specific nucleotide sequences called **promoters** which are different in prokaryotes and eukaryotes.

(c) A single RNA polymerase carries out all transcription in most prokaryotes, whereas three different RNA polymerases are present in eukaryotes with each polymerase responsible for synthesis of a distinct class of RNAs.

(d) It makes a complementary RNA copy of the template DNA strand and then recognizes the termination region of the DNA sequence to be transcribed.

(e) The product of process of transcription by RNA polymerase is termed as **primary transcript.**

(f) RNA polymerase does not require a primer and has no ability to repair mistakes in the RNA.

Components of Prokaryotic RNA Polymerase

- **Core Enzyme** Four of the enzyme's peptide subunits 2α, 1β and 1β′ are responsible for the 5′→3′ RNA polymerase activity and are referred to as core enzyme. However, the core enzyme lacks specificity, *i.e.,* it can't recognize the promoter region on the DNA template.
- **Holoenzyme** The σ subunit (Sigma Factor) enables RNA polymerase to recognize promoter region on the DNA. The σ subunit plus core enzyme forms holoenzyme.

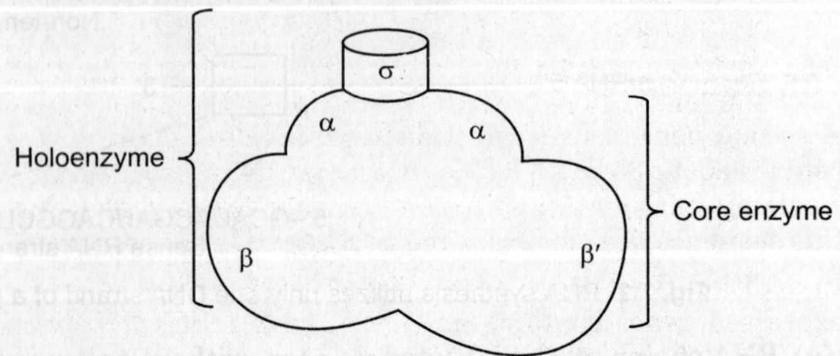

Fig. 7.4 Diagram of RNA polymerase holoenzyme

Functions of RNA Polymerase Subunits

RNA polymerase is a multi-subunit enzyme of 480 KD molecular weight. It comprises of following subunits 2α, $1\beta'$, 1β and 1σ:

Table 7.1 **RNA Polymerase Subunits and their Function**

RNA Polymerase Subunit	Function
α-subunit	• Involved in assembly of the tetrameric core ($\alpha_2\ \beta\ \beta'$) of RNA polymerase.
β-subunit	• Contains ribonucleoside triphos-phate binding site.
β'-subunit	• Contains DNA template binding region.
σ-factor	• Involved only in the initiation of transcription. • It plays no role in chain elongation. • Main function is to recognize and bind RNA polymerase to the transcription initiation or promoter sites in DNA. • After chain initiation has occurred it is released which is catalyzed by core enzyme ($\alpha_2\ \beta\beta'$).

Transcription Unit

A transcription unit is a strech of DNA that codes for an RNA molecule and the sequences necessary for its transcription. Within a transcription unit there are three critical regions.

(a) A promoter
(b) An RNA coding sequence
(c) A terminator

Promoter

The promoter is a DNA sequence that transcription apparatus recognizes and bind. In most transcription units promoter is located next to transcription start site but is not itself transcribed.

Two short sequences within the promoter are –10 sequence and –35 sequence. These sequences are highly conserved. The nucleotide sequences that are present in such conserved genetic elements are called **consensus sequences.** These are recognized by prokaryotic RNA polymerase σ factor.

Pribnow box/ -10 sequence

It is named after David Pribnow, who pointed its existence in 1975. This is a strech of six nucleotides whose consensus sequence is : 5′ –TATAAT –3′. The AT rich -10 sequence facilitates the localized unwinding of DNA which is an essential pre-requisite to synthesis of a new RNA chain.

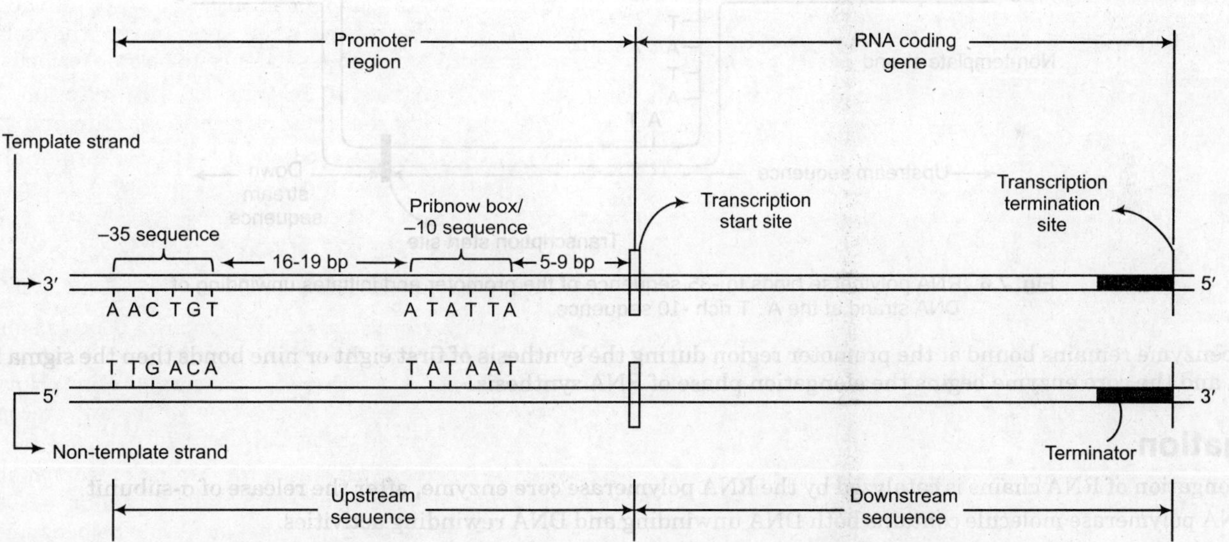

Fig. 7.5 A prokaryotic transcription unit showing position of various sequences

–35 Sequence

A second consensus nucleotide sequence 5′–TTGACA -3′ is centred about 35 bases left to the transcription start site. The s-subunit initially recognizes and binds to –35 sequence thus, this sequence, is sometimes called recognition sequence.

In addition **Richard Gourse** discovered that certain highly expressed genes contains an A + T rich segment between position –40 and –60, the Upstream Promoter (UP) element which binds to the C-terminal Domain of RNA polymerase's α-subunit. The UP element containing genes include those encoding the ribosomal RNAs.

RNA Coding Gene

A sequence of DNA nucleotides that is copied into an RNA molecule.

Terminator

A sequence of nucleotides that signals, where transcription is to end. Terminators are usually part of the coding sequence; that is, transcription stops only after the terminator has been copied into RNA.

Steps/Phases of Transcription

There are three phases of transcription

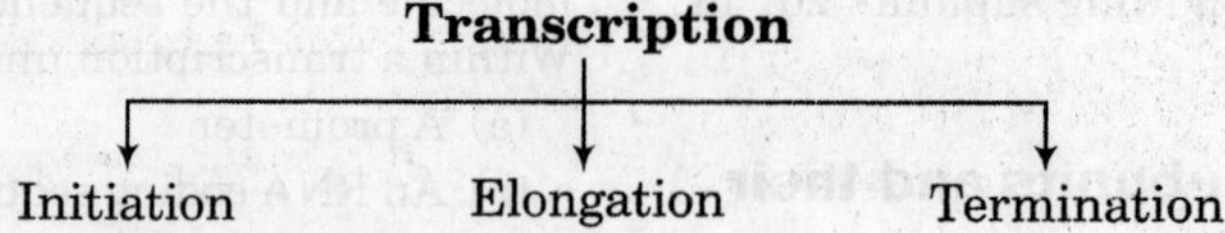

Initiation

Initiation of RNA chains involves three steps :

(a) **Promoter Recognition** Binding of RNA polymerase holoenzyme to a promoter region in DNA, that are recognized by σ-factor. The σ-subunit initially recognizes and binds to –35 sequence.

(b) **Formation of Trasnscription Bubble** RNA polymerase catalyzes localized unwinding of the two strands of DNA, providing a template strand free to base pair with ribonucleotides.

(c) The formation of phosphodiester bonds between the first few ribonucleotides in the nascent RNA chain.

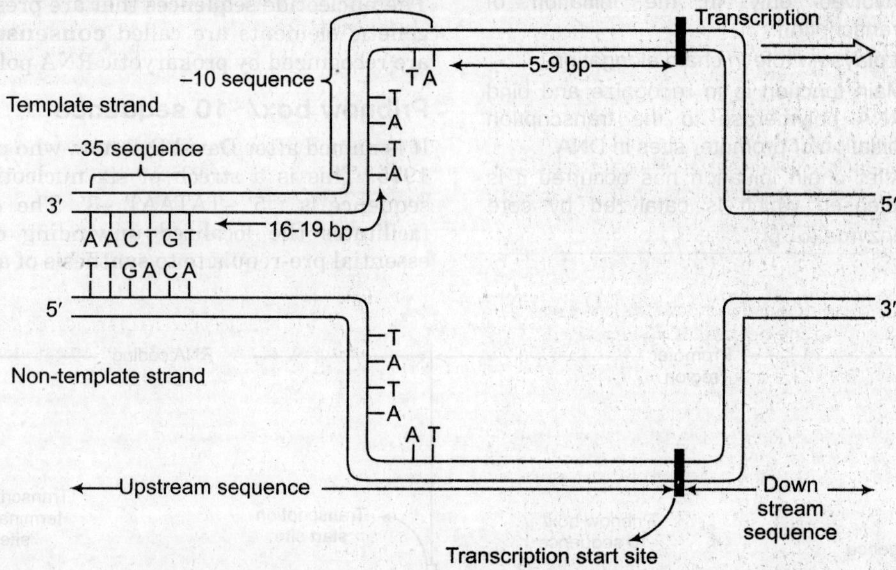

Fig. 7.6 RNA polymerse binds to -35 sequence of the promoter and initiates unwinding of DNA strand at the A : T rich -10 sequence

The holoenzyme remains bound at the promoter region during the synthesis of first eight or nine bonds then the sigma factor is released and the core enzyme begins the elongation phase of RNA synthesis.

Elongation

(a) Elongation of RNA chains is catalyzed by the RNA polymerase core enzyme, after the release of σ-subunit.

(b) RNA polymerase molecule contains both DNA unwinding and DNA rewinding activities.

(c) RNA polymerase continuously unwinds the DNA double helix ahead of the polymerization site and rewinds the complementary DNA strand behind the polymerization site as it moves along the double helix.

(d) RNA polymerases uses ribonucleoside triphosphates and releases pyrophosphate each time a nucleotide is added to the growing chain.

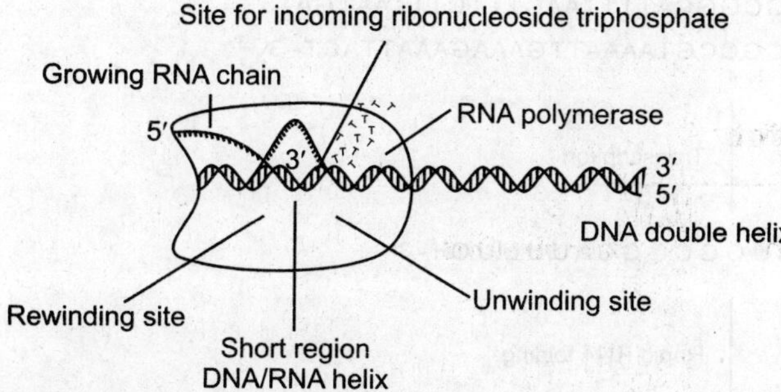

(a) RNA polymerase is bound to DNA and is covalently extending the RNA chain

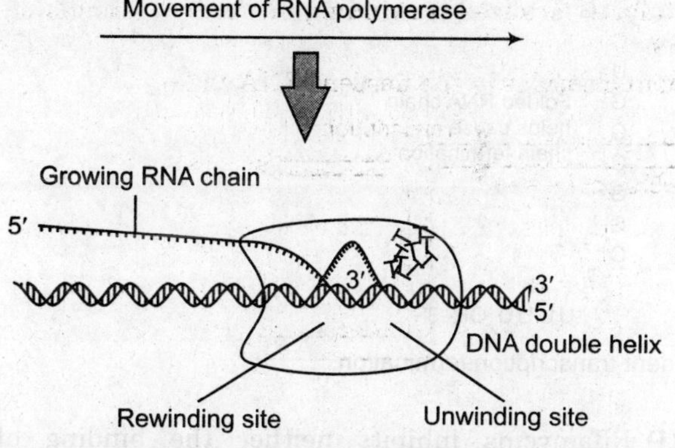

(b) RNA polymerase has moved downstream from its position in (a), processively extending the nascent RNA chain.

Fig. 7.7 Elongation of an RNA chain catalyzed by RNA polymerases in *E. coli*

Termination

Termination of RNA chains occurs when RNA polymerase encounters a termination signal. When it does the transcription complex dissociates releasing nascent RNA molecule.

Two Types of Transcription Termination

rho (ρ) Dependent Termination

Requires the participation of an additional protein ρ (rho) factor therefore, such termination sequences are called **rho-dependent termination.**

rho (ρ) Independent Termination

RNA polymerase in some instances, recognizes termination region of the DNA template therefore, termination of transcription occurs without the involvement of rho. Such sequences are called rho independent termination.

rho-Independent Termination The transcription termination sequence of many *E.coli* genes share two common features.

(a) A series of 4-10 consequtive AT's with A's on template strand. The transcribed RNA is terminated in or just past this sequence.

(b) A G + C rich region with a palindromic sequence that is immediately upstream of the series of AT's.

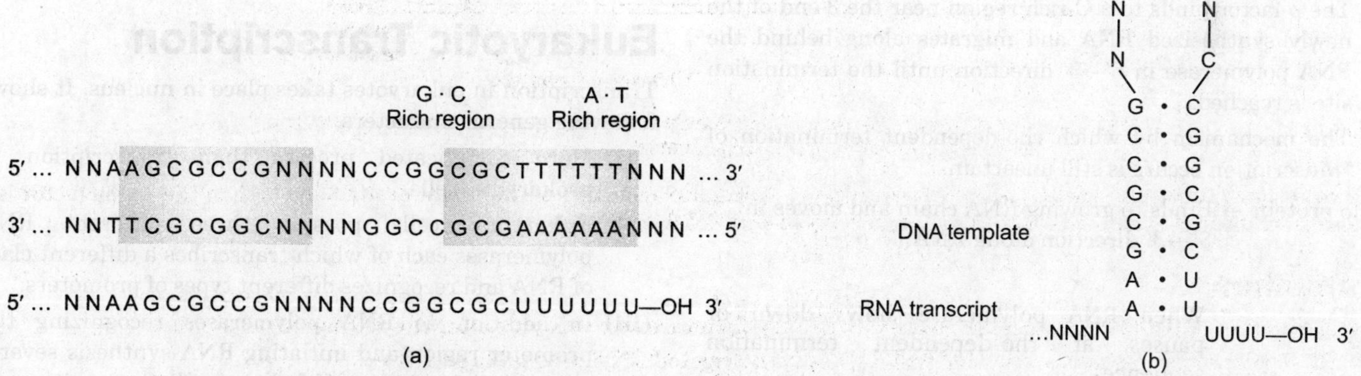

Fig. 7.8 (a) Transcript RNA (b) RNA hairpin structure and poly U tail that triggers transcription termination

The RNA transcript of this region can therefore, form a self complementary 'hairpin' structure that is terminated by several U residues. The formation of G + C rich hairpin causes RNA polymerase to pause for several second at termination site. This structure retards the movement of RNA polymerase along the DNA molecule, which results in the termination of transcription and the release of the nascent RNA chain.

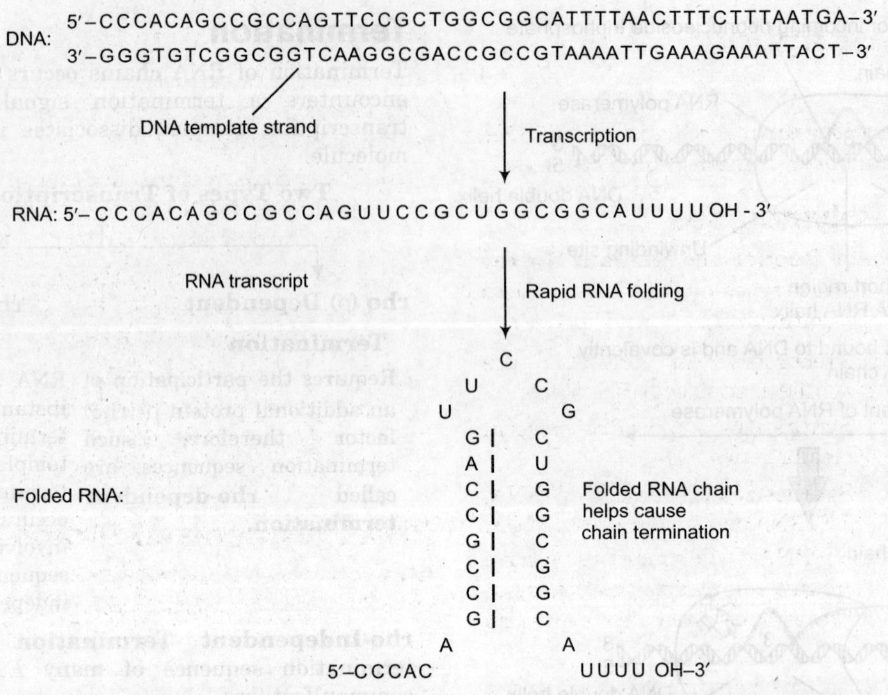

Fig. 7.9 Overall process of rho-independent transcription termination

rho-Dependent Termination

- rho-factor has ATP dependent RNA-DNA helicase activity that hydrolyzes ATP and uses the energy to unwind the 3′ end of the transcript from the template.
- rho-dependent termination sequences are 50-90 bp long and specify RNA transcripts that are rich in C residues.
- The ρ-factor binds to a C-rich region near the 3′end of the newly synthesized RNA and migrates along behind the RNA polymerase in 5′→3′ direction until the termination site is reached.
- The mechanism by which rho-dependent termination of transcription occurs is still uncertain.

rho protein → Binds to growing RNA chain and moves in 5′→3′ direction along RNA.

↓

When RNA polymerase slows down or pauses at rho-dependent termination sequence.

↓

rho protein pulls the nascent RNA chain from transcription bubble.

Inhibitor of Prokaryotic Transcription Initiation

Two related antibiotics rifamycin B which is produced by *Streptomyces mediterranei* and its semi synthetic derivative **rifampicin** specifically inhibits transcription by prokaryotic, but not eukaryotic RNA polymerases.

(i) Rifamycins inhibits neither the binding of RNA polymerase to promoter nor the formation of the first phosphodiester bond, but they prevent further chain elongation.

(ii) Once RNA chain initiation have occurred they have no effect on the subsequent chain elongation process.

Eukaryotic Transcription

Transcription in eukaryotes takes place in nucleus. It shows following general characters.

(i) More complicated process than transcription in prokaryotic cells.

(ii) Eukaryotic cells possess three different RNA polymerases each of which transcribes a different class of RNA and recognizes different types of promoters.

(iii) In addition to RNA polymerases recognizing the promoter region and initiating RNA synthesis several transcription factors binds to distinct sites on DNA-either within the promoter region or some distance from it. The binding of different factors determines which genes are to be transcribed.

(iv) Most actively transcribed genes are found in a relatively relaxed form of chromatin called **euchromatin,** whereas most inactive segments of DNA are found in highly condensed **heterochromatin.**

(v) In eukaryotes RNA is synthesized in the nucleus and most RNAs that encode proteins must be transported to cytoplasm for translation on ribosomes.

Eukaryotic Transcription: Components

The eukaryotic transcription unit is composed of RNA polymerase, promoters, enhancer, transcription factors, etc.

Eukaryotic RNA Polymerases

Eukaryotic nuclei as **Robert Roeder** and **William Rutter** discovered contain three distinct types of RNA polymerases that differs in the RNA they synthesize.

RNA Polymerase I : Precursors of *r*RNAs are synthesized except 5 S *r*RNA.

RNA Polymerase II : Synthesizes hnRNA/protein coding genes.

RNA Polymerase III : Synthesizes precursors of *t*RNA, 5 S *r*RNA and small nuclear RNAs.

(a) Eukaryotic nuclear RNA Polymerases have considerably greater subunit complexity than those of prokaryotes. These enzymes have molecular masses up to 600 KD.

(b) All the three eukaryotic RNA polymerases require the assistance of other proteins called transcription factors in order to initiate the synthesis of RNA chains.

(c) The three RNA polymerases exhibit very different sensitivity to inhibition by α-amanitin, a metabolic poison produced by the mushroom *(Amanita phalloides)*. Thus, α-aminitin can be used to determine which RNA polymerase catalyze the transcription of a particular gene.

Table 7.2 **Characteristics of the Three RNA Polymerases of Eukaryotes**

Enzyme	Location	Products	Sensitivity to α-Amanitin
RNA polymerase I	Nucleolus	Ribosomal RNAs, excluding 5 S *r*RBA	No sensitivity
RNA polymerase II	Nucleus	Nuclear pre-*m*RNAs	Complete sensitivity
RNA polymerase III	Nucleus	*t*RNAs, 5 S *r*RNA, and other small nuclear RNAs	Intermediate sensitivity

Promoters

The promoter is defined as the region containing binding sites that can support transcription at normal efficiency and with proper control.

(a) The major feature defining the promoter for an eukaryotic *m*RNA is the location of binding site for transcription factors.

(b) Each promoter contains characteristics set of short conserved sequences that are recognized by the appropriate class of factors.

(c) The promoters for RNA polymerase I and RNA polymerase II are mostly upstream of the start point but some promoters of RNA polymerase III lies downstream of the start point.

RNA Polymerase I Promoter

RNA polymerase transcribes from a single type of promoter only the genes for ribosomal RNA. The transcript includes the sequences of both large and small *r*RNAs which are later released by cleavage and processing.

(a) RNA polymerase I has a bipartite promoter.

(b) The promoter consists of two separate region.

Core Promoter Element	Upstream Promoter Element
• It surrounds the start point extending from −45 to +20 and is sufficient for transcription to initiate.	• It is also a GC rich sequence related to core promoter element and extends from −180 to 107.
• It is generally GC rich except a short AT rich sequence around the start point.	• It increases the core promoter's efficiency.

(c) This type of organization is common to RNA polymerase I promoter but the actual sequences vary widely.

Start point →

−180 −170 −160 −150 −140 −130 −120 −110 | −40 −30 −20 −10 | +10 +20

Upstream promoter element | Core promoter

Fig. 7.10 RNA polymerase I promoter

RNA Polymerase III Promoters

The promoters of genes transcribed by RNA polymerase III can be located entirely within the gene's transcribed regions.

RNA polymerase III has two types of promoters

(a) **Internal promoters** have short consensus sequences located within the transcription unit and cause initiation to occur a fixed distance upstream.

Example The promoters for 5 S *r*RNA and *t*RNA genes are internal; they lie downstream of the start point.

(b) **Upstream promoters** can contain three short consensus sequences upstream of the start point and that are bound by transcription factors.

Example The promoters for snRNA genes lies upstream of the start point.

RNA Polymerase II Promoters

The promoters recognized by RNA Polymerase II are considerably longer and more diverse.

(a) **GC Box** The structural genes, which are expressed in all tissues, *i.e.*, the **house keeping genes** have one or more copies of the sequence GGGCGG located upstream from their transcription start sites structural genes that are **selectively expressed** in one or few type of cells often a lack these GC rich sequences.

(b) **Tata Box** Many structural genes that are selectively expressed contains a conserved at rich sequence located 25 to 30 bp upstream from their transcription start site. It is the conserved element closest to the transcription start site (position + 1) and has **consensus sequence** TATAAT.

- TATA box plays an important role in positioning the transcription start point.
- TATA box deletions and mutations generates heterogeneties in the transcriptional start site thereby indicates that TATA box participates in selecting this site.

(c) **CAAT Box** It has consensus sequence CCAAT. Many eukaryotic structural genes including those encoding the various globins have a conserved consensus CCAAT located between about –70 and –90, whose alternation greatly reduces genes transcription rate.

(d) **Octamer Box** It is oftenly present in the RNA polymerase II promoter and has the consensus sequence ATTTGCAT. It influences the efficiency of a promoter in initiating transcription.

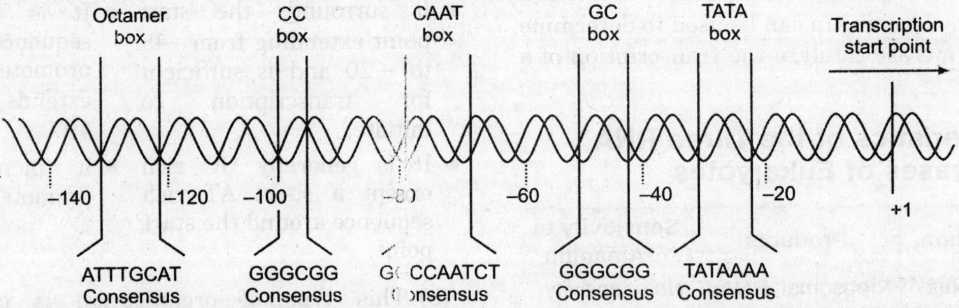

Fig. 7.11 Structure of a promoter recognized by RNA polymerase II

- The TATA and CAAT boxes are located at about same position in promoters of most nuclear genes encoding proteins.
- The GC and octamer boxes may be present or absent when present, they occur at many different locations either singly or in multiple copies.

Enhancers

The enhancer is another type of site involved in initiation. It is identified by sequences that stimulate initiation, but that are located a considerable distance from the start point.

(a) The components of an enhancer resemble those of the promoter in that they consist of a variety of modular elements. The elements of an enhancer however are organized in a closely packed array and function like those in the promoter.

(b) The enhancer does not need to be near the start point.

(c) Proteins bound at enhancer elements interacts with proteins bound at promoter element.

(d) The position of enhancer relative to the promoter need not to be fixed, but they can vary substantially. It can be either upstream or downstream.

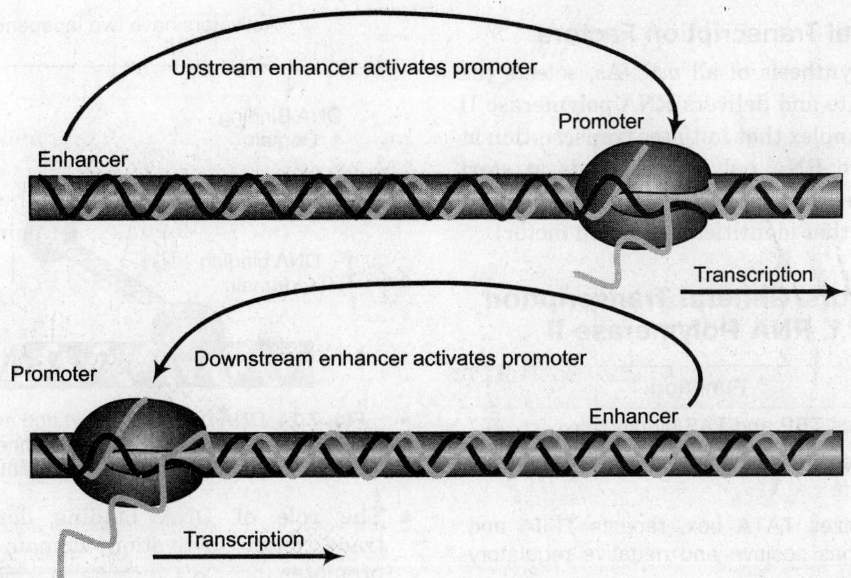

Fig. 7.12 An enhancer can activate a promoter from upstream or downstream locations, and its sequence can be inverted relative to the promoter

Transcription Factors

Initiation of transcription requires the enzyme RNA polymerase and transcription factors. Any factor that is needed for the initiation of transcription but which is not itself part of RNA polymerase is defined as a transcription factor.

(a) Transcription factors are needed for initiation but are not required subsequently.

(b) Transcription factors are principally responsible for recognizing the promoter for the three eukaryotic RNA polymerases.

- They act by recognizing the binding sites on DNA.
- For all eukaryotic RNA polymerases the factors create a structure at the promoter to povide the target that is recognized by the enzyme.
- A factor may recognize another factor, or may recognize RNA polymerase, or may be incorporated into an initiation complex.

(c) Initiation of transcription involves many protein-protein interaction among transcription factors bound at the promoter or at an enhancer as well as with RNA polymerase.

Types of Transcription Factors

We can divide the factors required for transcription into several classes.

(a) **Basal factors**

(b) **Activators** binds directly to DNA at promoter or at enhancer.

(c) **Coactivators** binds to both activators and basal apparatus.

(d) **Regulators** acts on chromatin structure.

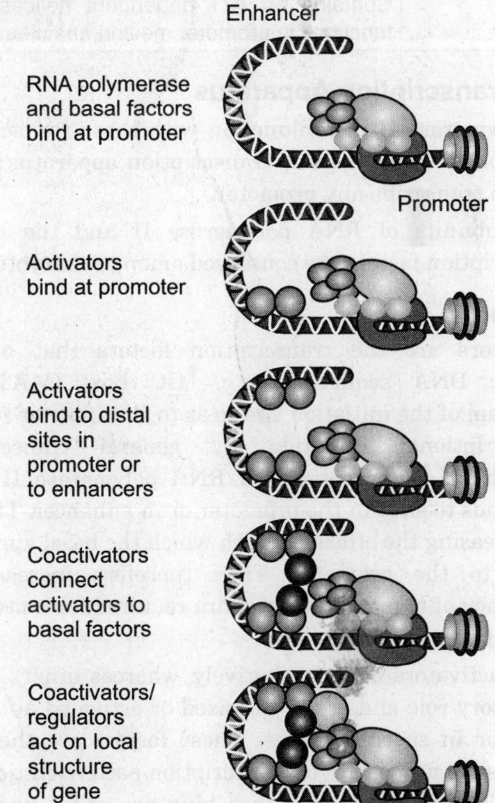

Fig. 7.13 Diagram showing different types of transcription factors and their actions

Basal Factors/General Transcription Factors

These are required for synthesis of all *m*RNAs, selects the transcription initiation site and delivers RNA polymerase II to it thereby forming a complex that initiates transcription at basal rate. Together with RNA polymerase binds at start point and TATA box. The general factors are described as TFIIX (where, X is letter that identities individual factor).

Table 7.3 **Basal Factors/General Transcription Factors w.r.t. RNA Polymerase II**

Factor	Function
TFIIA	Stabilizes TBP and TAF binding
TFIIB	Stabilizes TBP binding, influences start site selection.
TFIID TBP TAFs	Recognizes TATA box, recruits TFIIA and TFIIB, has positive and negative regulatory functions.
TFIIE	An $\alpha_2\beta_2$ heterotetramer recruits TFIIH and stimulates its helicase activity; enhances promoter melting.
TFIIF	Facilitates promoter targetting stimulates elongation, recruits RNA polymerase II.
TFIIH	Contains an ATP-dependent helicase that functions in promoter melting and clearance.

Basal Transcription Apparatus

RNA polymerase II in conjunction with these transcription factors constitutes the basal transcription apparatus that is needed to transcribe any promoter.

- The subunits of RNA polymerase II and the general transcription factors are conserved among eukaryotes.

Activators

- Activators are the transcription factors that bind to specific DNA sequences (*e.g.*, GC box, CAAT box) upstream of the initiation site so as to stimulate or repress. Transcriptional initiation by general transcription factor/basal factor complexed RNA polymerase II. They also binds to sites in the promoter or in enhancer. They act by increasing the efficiency with which the basal apparatus binds to the promoter. They therefore increase the frequency of transcription and are required for a promoter to function at adequate level.
- Some activators act constitutively, whereas others have a regulatory role and are synthesized or activated at specific times or in specific tissues. These factors are therefore, responsible for control of transcription pattern in time and space. The sequence that they bind are called **response elements.**

How does activators recognize their target DNA sequences?

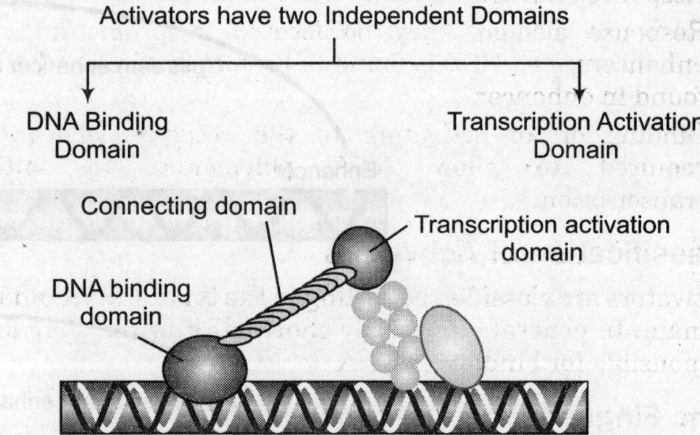

Fig. 7.14 DNA binding domain and activating domain are independent and are connected in a way that allows the activating domain to interact with basal apparatus

- The role of DNA binding domain is to bring the transcription activation domain into the vicinity of promoter.
- A transcription activating domain works by making protein-protein contacts with general transcription factors that provide assembly of the basal apparatus contact with basal apparatus may be made with any of the several basal factors but typically occurs with TFIID, TFIIB or TFIIA. All of these factors participates in early stages of assembly of the basal apparatus.

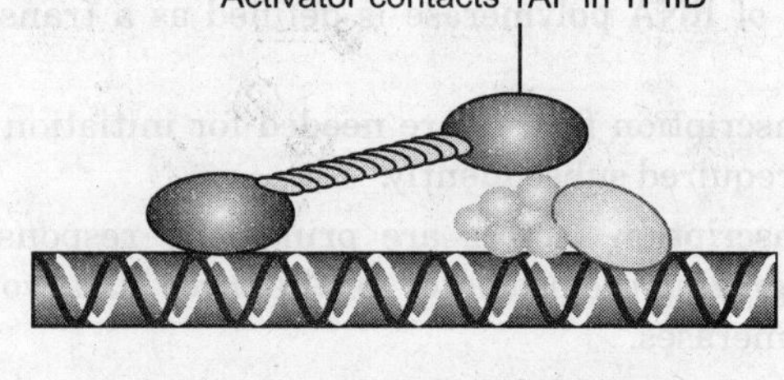

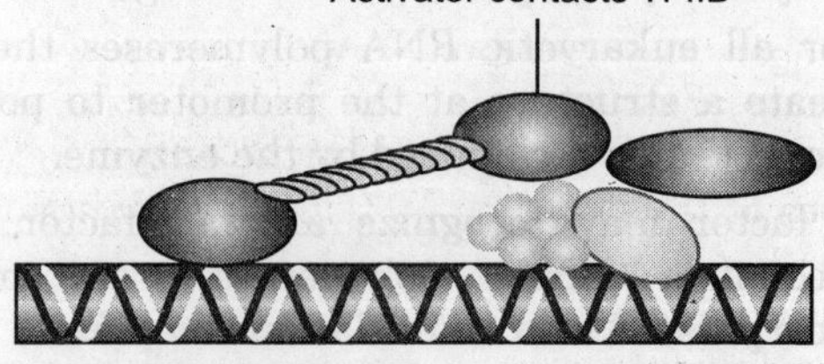

Fig. 7.15 Activators may work at different stages of initiation by contacting the TAFs of TFIID or by contacting

- Hence, the upstream elements are recognized by activators that interact with the basal apparatus to determine the efficiency with which the promoter is used.

Response Elements are Recognized by Activators An element that causes a gene to repond to such a factor (activator) is called response element.

Example HSE (Heat Shock Response Element)
GRE (Glucocorticoid Response Element)
SRE (Serum Response Element)

- Response elements contains short consensus sequences.
- Response element may be located in promoter or in enhancers, *e.g.,* HSE is found in promoter, whereas GRE is found in enhancer.
- Binding of an activators to the response element is required to allow RNA polymerase to initiate transcription.

Classification of Activators

Activators are classified according to the type of DNA binding domain. In general a relatively short motif in this domain is responsible for binding to DNA.

Zinc Finger Motif

The xinc finger motif comprises a DNA binding domain. It was originally recognized in factor TFIIIA which is required for RNA polymerase III to transcribe 5 S *r*RNA gene. It has since been identified in several other transcription factors. A distinct form of this motif is also found in steroid receptors.

- A zinc finger is a loop of ~23 amino acids that protrudes from a zinc binding site formed by it His and Cys amino acids. The zinc is held in a tetrahedral structure formed by conserved Cys and His residues.

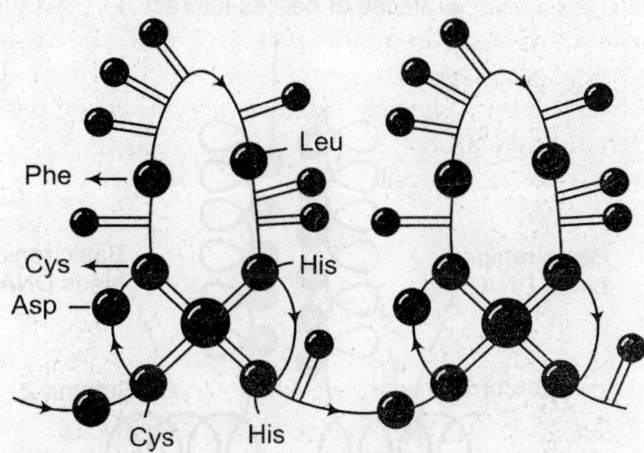

Fig. 7.16 Zinc finger motif

- A zinc finger takes its name from the structure in which a small group of conserved amino acids binds a zinc ion to form an independent domain in the protein.
- Two types of DNA binding proteins have structure of this type :
- The classic zinc finger proteins.
- The steroid receptors.

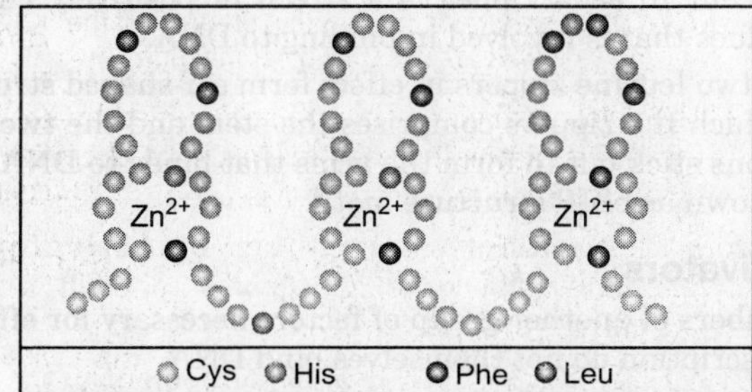

Fig. 7.17 Transcription factor SP1 has a series of three zinc fingers, each with a characteristic pattern of cysteine and histidine residues that constitute the zinc-binding site

- The crystal structure of DNA bound by a protein with three fingers suggests the C-terminal part of each finger forms α-helices that binds DNA; the N-terminal part form a β-sheet.

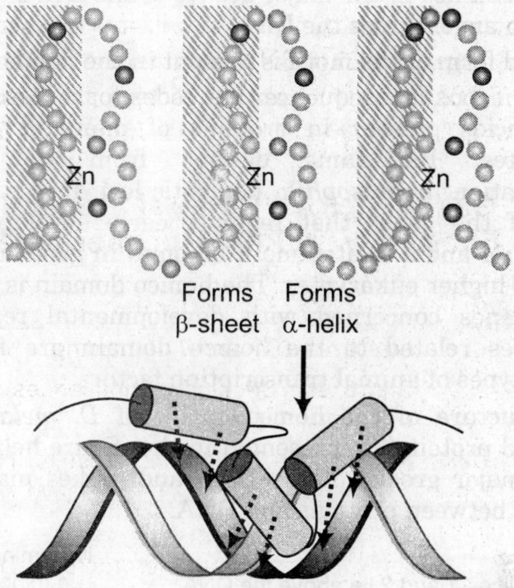

Fig. 7.18 Zinc fingers may form α helices that insert into the major groove, which is associated with β-sheets on the other side

Steroid Receptors

Steroid receptors are defined as the group by functional relationship, *i.e.,* each receptor is activated by binding a particular steroid.

- Steroid receptors are examples of ligand responsive activators that are activated by binding a steroid.
- There are separate DNA-binding and ligand binding domains (hormone binding) that are in same relative locations.
- These diverse compounds share a common mode of action. Each is a small molecule that binds to a specific receptor that activates gene transcription.
- The DNA binding domain of a steroid receptor is a type of zinc finger that has Cys but not His residues.

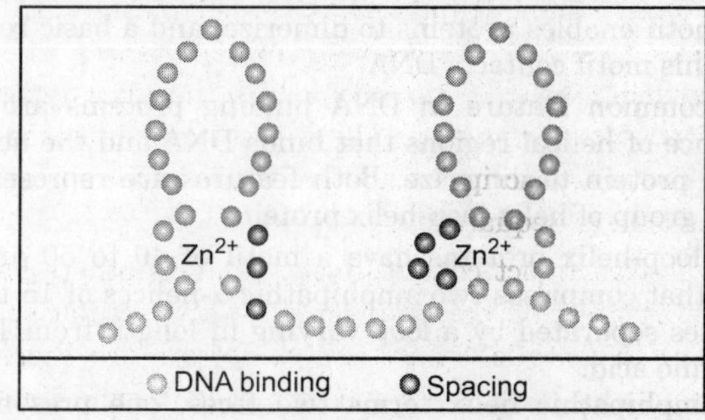

Fig. 7.19 The first finger of a steroid receptor controls which DNA sequence is bound (positions shown in light shade); the second finger controls spacing between the sequences (positions shown in dark shade)

Helix Turn Helix Motif

- It was originally identified as DNA-binding domain of phage repressors.
- One α-helix lies in the major groove of the DNA; the other lies at an angle across the DNA.
- A related form of the motif is present in the homeodomain.
- The homeobox is a sequence that codes for a domain of 60 amino acids present in proteins of many or even all eukaryotes. Its name derives from its original identification in *Drosophila* homeotic loci. It is present in many of the genes that regulate early development in *Drosophila* and a related motif is found in genes in a wide range of higher eukaryotes. The homeo domain is found in many genes concerned with developmental regulation. Sequences related to the homeo domain are found in several types of animal transcription factors.
- The structure of the homeodomain of *D. melanogaster* engrailed protein is represented in the figure helix 3 bind in the major groove of the DNA and makes majority of contacts between proteins and DNA.

Helices 1 and 2 lie above the DNA

N-terminal arm lies in minor groove

Helix 3 lies in the major groove

Fig. 7.20 Helix 3 of the homeodomain binds in the major groove of DNA, with helices 1 and 2 lying outside the double helix. Helix 3 contacts both the phosphate backbone and specific bases. The N-terminal arm lies in the minor groove, and makes additional contacts

Helix-Loop Helix Motif

It has been identified in some developmental regulators and in genes encoding for eukaryotic DNA-binding proteins.

- The motif enables proteins to dimerize, and a basic region near this motif contacts DNA.
- Two common feature in DNA binding proteins are the presence of helical regions that binds DNA and the ability of the protein to dimerize. Both features are represented in the group of helix-loop-helix proteins.
- Helix-loop-helix proteins have a motif of 40 to 50 amino acids that comprises two amphipathic α-helices of 15 to 16 residues separated by a loop varying in length from 12 to 28 amino acid.
  (An amphipathic helix forms two faces, one presenting hydrophobic amino acids and other presenting charged amino acids).
- The helices are responsible for dimer formation. The proteins from both homodimers and heterodimers by means of interaction between the hydrophobic residues on the corresponding faces of the two helices.
- Most HLH proteins contains a region adjacent to the HLH motif that is itself highly basic, and which is needed for binding to DNA. Members of the group with such a region are called bHLH proteins.
- bHLH proteins falls into two general groups :
  - Class A consists of proteins that are ubiquitously expressed.
  - Class B consists of proteins that are expressed in a tissue specific manner, including mammalian myo-D, myogenin, Myf-S (a group of activators that are involved in myogenesis).

Leucine Zipper

- Consists of a stretch of amino acids with leucine residues in every seventh position, leucine residues provides dimerization motif.
- A leucine zipper in one polypeptide interacts with zipper in another polypeptide to form a dimer.

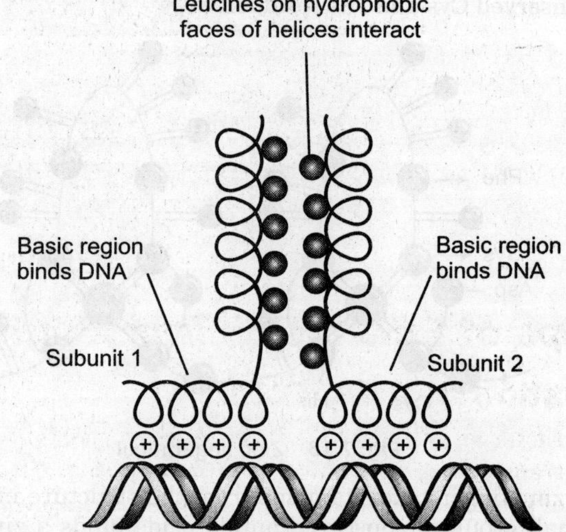

Fig. 7.21 The basic regions of the bZIP motif are held together by the dimerization at the adjacent zipper region when the hydrophobic faces of two leucine zippers interact in parallel orientation

- Adjacent to each zipper is a strech of positively charged residues that is involved in binding to DNA.
- The two leucine zippers in effect form a Y-shaped structure in which the zippers comprises the stem and the two basic regions stick out to form the arms that binds to DNA. This is known as bZIP structure motif.

Coactivators

- Members of another group of factors necessary for efficient transcription do not themselves bind DNA.
- Coactivators provide a connection between activators and basal apparatus. They work by protein-protein interaction forming bridges between activators and basal transcription apparatus.

- In some cases the activators does not itself have a transcription activation domain, but binds another protein a coactivator that has a transcription activation domain.
- Hence, coactivators are transcription factors whose specificity is conferred by the ability to bind to DNA, binding transcription factor instead of directly to DNA.

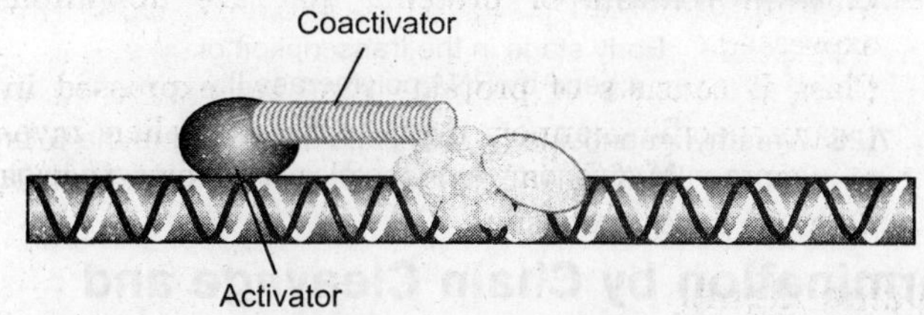

Fig. 7.22 An activator may bind a coactivator that contacts the basal apparatus

Eukaryotic Transcription Unit

Contents in a typical gene transcribed by RNA polymerase II

(a) **Gene** Generally contains a single gene.

(b) **Promoter** Promoter extends upstream from the site, where transcription is initiated promoter contains several short sequence elements that bind transcription factors dispersed over > 200 bp.

(c) **Enhancer** An enhancer contain- ing a more closely packed array of elements that also bind transcription factors may be located several kb distant.

(d) **Termination** Termination occurs beyond the end of coding region. Termination lacks the regulatory importance that applies in prokaryotic systems.

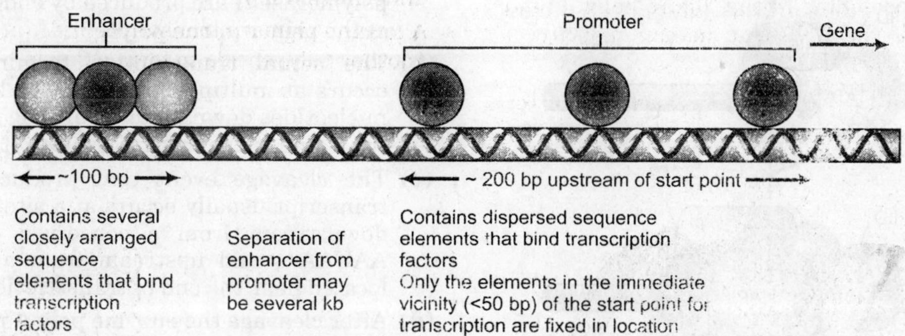

Fig. 7.23 A typical gene transcribed RNA polymerase II

Steps of Eukaryotic Transcription

Initiation of RNA Chains

(a) Eukaryotic RNA polymerases can't initiate transcription by themselves, the require the assistance of protein transcription factors to start the synthesis of an RNA chain.

(b) Transcription factors must bind to a promoter region in DNA and form an appropriate initiation complex before RNA polymerase will bind and initiate transcription.

(c) Different promoters and transcription factors are utilized by RNA polymerase I, II and III.

Transcription Initiation by RNA Polymerase II

- Initiation of transcription involves the formation of a locally unwound segment of DNA providing a DNA strand that is free to function as a template for the synthesis of a complementary strand of RNA.
- The accurate transcriptional initiation of most structural genes requires the presence of six general transcription factors most of which are multiprotein complexes named TFIIA, TFIIB, TFIID, TFIIE, TFIIF and TFIIH.
(TF: for transcription factor and II for class II gene, *i.e.,* those that are tanscribed by RNA polymerase II).
- These GFTs combine in an ordered pathway with RNA polymerase II and promoter containing DNA near the transcriptional start site to form a so called **pre-initiation complex** that supports a basal level of transcription.
- The so called **core promoter** in structural genes are largely upstream of the transcriptional start site and often contain a TATA Box that is centered at around position –27 and whose consensus sequence is TATA A/T A A/T.
- The remaining position of promoter to which various transcription factors are targetted are known as upstream activation sequences. An entire eukaryotic promoter extends over ~ 100 bp.

Process

- Binding of TATA Box **binding protein** (TBP) to the tata box, thereby identifying the transcriptional start site.
- TBP is then joined by a series of~10 TBP **associated factors** (TAFs) to form the ~700 KD multi-subunit complex TFIID.
- TFIIA then binds to TFIID-DNA complex so as to stabilize it followed by TFIIB.
- At this point TFIIF recruits RNA polymerase II to the promoter.

- Finally TFIIE and TFIIH join in that order to form the **pre-initiation complex.**
- Once this complex has been assembled an ATP dependent activation step mediated by TFIIH's helicase function to melt the promoter, is required to initiate transcription at a basal rate.

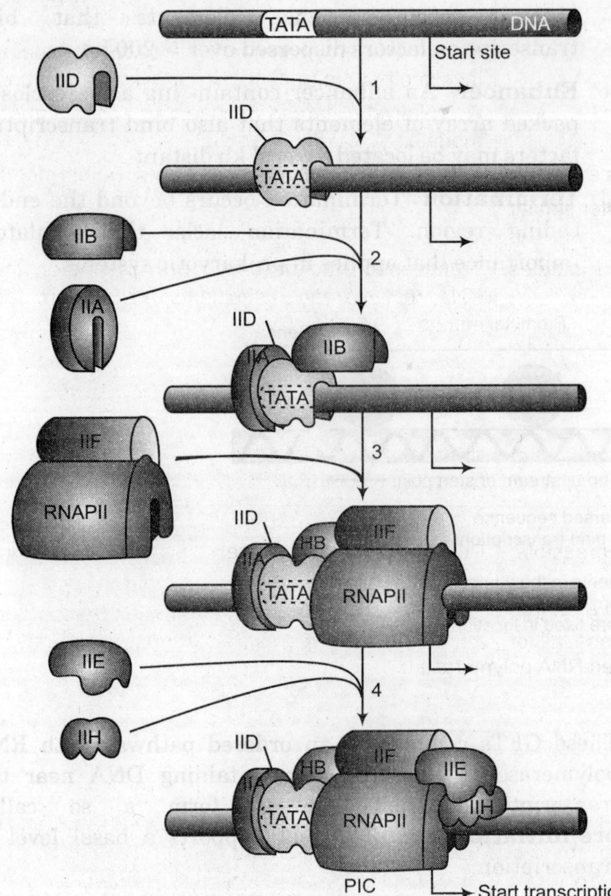

Fig. 7.24 Assembly of the pre-initiation complex (PIC) on a TATA Box-containing promoter. 1. TFIID assembles on the TATA Box beginning with the binding of TATA Box-binding protein (TBP) to the TATA Box. 2. TFIIA and TFIIB then bind to the growing complex. 3. TFIIF then binds to RNA polymerase II and escorts it to the complex. 4. Finally, TFIIE and TFIIH are sequentially recruited to the complex, thereby completing the PIC. [After Zawel L and Reinberg D., *Curr. Opin.* Cell Biol.

RNA Chain Elongation and Addition of 5-Methyl Guanosine Caps

(a) After release from initiation complex, RNA polymerase catalyze RNA chain elongation.

(b) Early in the elongation process, the 5′ ends of the eukaryotic pre-*m*RNA's are modified by the addition of 7-methyl guanosine (7-MG) caps. The 7-MG caps are added when the growing RNA chains are only about 30 nucleotide lo:.g.

(c) 7-MG caps are recognized by protein factors involved in the initiation of translation and also help protect the growing RNA chains from degradation by nucleases.

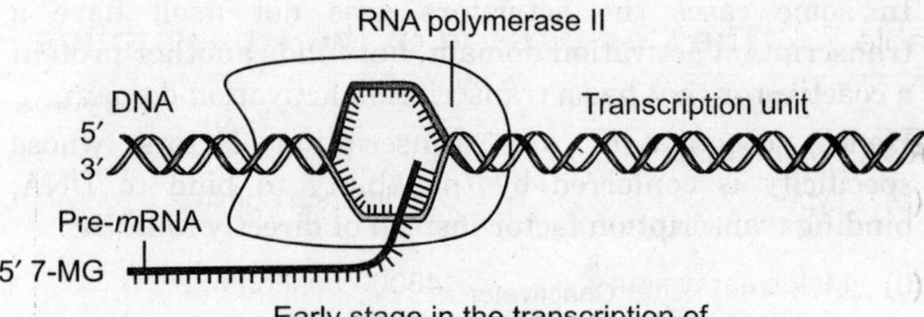

Fig. 7.25 7-methyl guanosine (7-MG) caps are added to the 5′ ends of pre-*m*RNAs shortly after the elongation process begins

Termination by Chain Cleavage and Addition of 3 is Poly A Tails

(a) The 3′ ends of RNA transcripts synthesized by RNA polymerase II are produced by endonucleolytic cleavage of the primary transcript.

(b) The actual transcription termination events often occurs at multiple sites that are located 1000 to 2000 nucleotides downstream from the site that will become the 3′ end of the mature transcript.

(c) The cleavage event that produces the 3′ end of a transcript usually occurs at a site 11 to 30 nucleotides downstream from a conserved consensus sequence AAUAAA, and upstream from a G U-rich sequence located near the end of transcription unit.

(d) After cleavage the enzyme poly A polymerase adds poly A tails, to the 3′ end of transcripts. The addition of poly A tails to the eukaryotic *m*RNAs is called **polyadenylation.** The poly A tails of eukaryotic *m*RNAs enhance their stability and plays an important role in their transport from the nucleus to the cytoplasm.

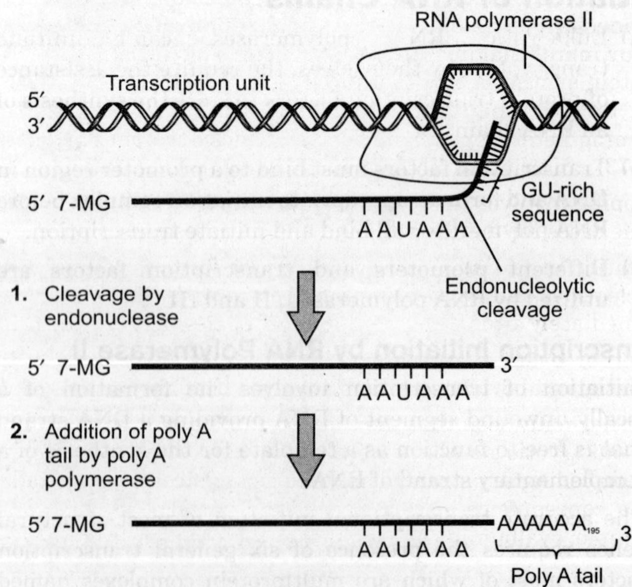

Fig. 7.26 Poly A tails are added to the 3′ ends of transcripts by the enzyme poly A polymerase. The 3′ end substrates for poly A polymerase are reduced by endonucleolytic cleavage of the transcript downstream from a polyadenylation signal, which has the consensus sequence AAUAAA.

Table 7.4 **The Comparison of the Transcription Process in Prokaryotes and Eukaryotes**

Characteristics	Prokaryotes	Eukaryotes
RNA Polymerase		
(a) Types	One in each species	Three; RNA polymerase I, II and III 500000 daltons
(b) Molecular weight	~480000 daltons	Two large subunits + <10 smaller subunits.
(c) Subunits	$\alpha_2 \beta\beta'\sigma$	Many different types of transcription factors; involved both in transcription and its regulation.
Transcription factors	Not known	A relatively larger sequence; has variable modules.
Promoter	A simpler and relatively smaller sequence.	Present at variable distances from the promoter.
Enhancer	A part of the promoter may act in a manner similar to enhancer.	
Transcription initiation	The holoenzyme binds to promoter and initiates transcription.	Transcription factors first bind to promoter, then RNA polymerase associates with them and initiates.
Transcription Complex		
(a) Composition	Core RNA polymerase + σ factor	RNA polymerase and transcription factors.
(b) Separation of components	σ factor dissociates from the core enzyme after initiation.	Transcription factors dissociate when transcription is initiated
End Product Regulation	Polycistronic RNA transcripts	Monocistronic RNA transcripts
(a) Type	Mainly negative control: inducible or repressible; positive control is less common.	Primarily positive, rarely negative; inducible control
(b) Genes under the same regulation	Located in a single Operon forming a single transcription unit; regulation results since all of them are controlled by a single promoter.	Located at divergent sites; regulation results since all of them have the same response elements.

RNA Processing

Maturation of eukaryotic *m*RNA from primary *m*RNA transcripts involves many complex steps, which generally referred to as **processing.** The initial processing step involves addition of a cap at 5′ end and a tail at 3′ end. Other extensive modification occur in internal nucleotide sequences. The initially formed RNAs are most often much larger than those that are required for protein synthesis, sometimes, called pre *m*RNAs. They are part of a group of molecules than those found only in the nucleus, *i.e.,* **heterogeneous nuclear RNA** (hnRNA). These RNA molecules are of variable size and are complexed with proteins, forming heterogeneous nuclear ribonucleoprotein particles (hnRNAs). Heterogeneous nuclear RNA as defined by **Weinberg** (1973) are all those RNAs, which have a sedimentation coefficient greater than 8 S.

Capping involves the formation of a cap at the 5′ end by the condensation of guanylate residues. This capping is necessary in some cases for the formation of *m*RNA ribosome complete.

Addition of tail at 3′ end occurs in the form of adding poly A or polyadenylate sequence. This sequence consists of 180-200 nucleotides and its addition takes place with the help of enzyme **poly A synthetase.** This polyadenylation takes place either immediately after transcription or after cleavage of transcripts. This poly A sequence suppose to play role in stabilizing *m*RNA.

Another event of processing is **methylation,** *i.e.,* the addition of methyl group to a few adenylate residues. There is experimental evidence, which suggests that the capping and methylation takes place before polyadenylation.

It is normally seen that the codon for one amino acid is immediately adjacent to the codon for the next amino acid. But some of the eukaryotic genes are mosaics, *i.e.,* consisting of coding nucleotide sequences which are separated from each other by blocks of non coding sequences. The coding sequences here are called **exons** and intervening non-coding sequences are called **introns**. As a consequence of this alternating pattern of exons and introns, genes bearing them are often called **split genes.** For example, ovalbumin gene is chicken, β-globin genes of mice and rabbit, *t*RNA genes of rabbit, ribosomal genes of *Drosophila,* etc.

RNA Splicing

Just like the uninterrupted genes, the split genes are transcribed into a single RNA copy of entire gene. Thus, the primary transcript from a typical eukaryotic gene contains introns as well as exons. Introns are removed from this primary transcript or pre-*m*RNA by a process called **RNA splicing**. The complete process right from transcription looks like:

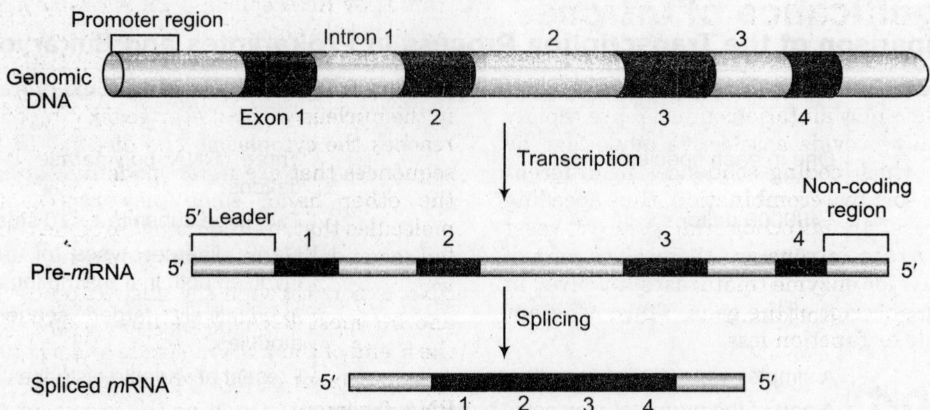

Fig. 7.27 Split gene with transcription and splicing

The process of splicing involves two successive transesterification reactions in which phosphodiester linkages within the pre-*m*RNA are broken and then new linkage is formed. The complete process is carried out with the help of a large complex called **spliceosome.** The complex comprises about 150 proteins and five RNAs and is similar in size to a ribosome. The five RNAs present here are called **small nuclear RNAs** (*m*RNAs), each of these is 100-300 nucleotides long and is complexed with many proteins. These RNA protein complexes are small nuclear ribonucleor proteins (sn RNPs or pronounced as snurps).

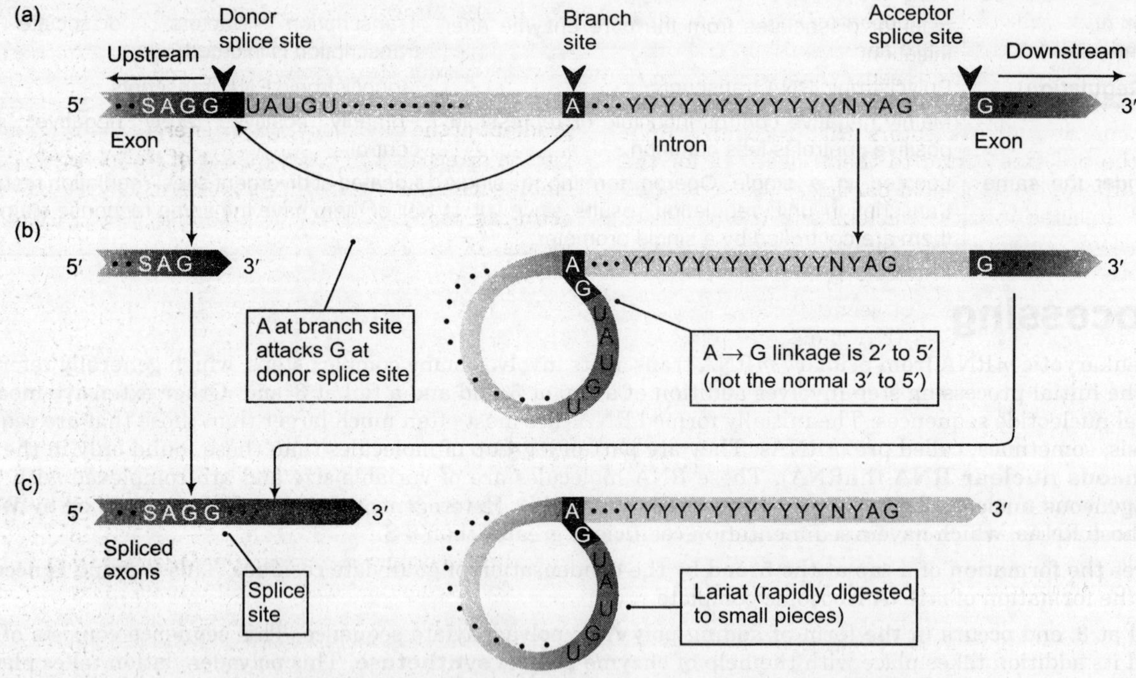

Fig. 7.28 Splicing with removal of one intron (molecular level)

A remarkable event is noticed in the splicing of a ribosomal RNA precursor in a ciliate Tetrahymena. Here, the intron is found to work as an enzyme in catalysing the splicing reaction. This self-splicing Tetrahymena RNA molecule was the first example of a RNA molecule that could function as an enzyme in catalysing a chemical reaction. Such enzymatic RNA molecules are usually called as **ribozymes** (Thomas Cech; 1981). For the discovery of ribozymes, **Thomas Cech** got the **Nobel Prize in 1986**.

Facts About Splicing

(a) ESE and ISE ESE are Exonic Splicing Enhancers and ISE are Intronic Splicing Enhancers. These are specialized proteins, which have the tendency to enhance splicing at nearby splice sites when bind to specific sites.

(b) Alternative Splicing Isoforms When two or more functional *m*RNA are developed from a single primary transcripts due to difference in splicing pattern, their splicing is called alternative splicing. Thus, through alternative splicing multiple protein products can be produced from a single gene. These different proteins are called isoforms.

Biological Significance of Introns

Introns are highly variable in size ranging from flow few to thousands base pair long. In several genes the introns have been shown to accumulate new mutations much more rapidly than exons. Introns may provide a selective advantage by increasing the rate at which coding sequences in different exons of a gene can reassort by recombination, thus speeding up the evolution process. In mitochondrial gene of yeast coding for cytochrome-*b*, the introns are themselves part of the exons for gene coding for enzyme (maturases) involved in processing of primary transcript of the gene. Thus, different intron play different role or function less.

RNA Transport

The RNA synthesized in nucleus of eukaryotic cell must transported to cytoplasm for protein and ribosome synthesis. The export of new ribosomal subunits and messenger RNA molecules through the nuclear pores depends on a selective transport system. If 20 nm-diameter gold spheres, are coated with small RNA molecules (*t*RNA or 5 S RNA) and then injected into the nucleus of a frog oocyte, they are rapidly transported through the nuclear pores into the cytosol. If they are injected into the cytosol of the oocyte, on the other hand, they remain there. Thus it seems that, in addition to receptors that recognize nuclear protein import signals, the pore contains one or more receptors that recognize RNA molecules (or the proteins bound to them) destined for the cytosol. Using differently sized gold particles, one set coated with RNA and injected into the nucleus and the other set coated with nuclear protein import signals, it can be shown that a single pore complex allows traffic in both directions.

An average primary RNA transcript seems to be at most 10 times longer than the mature *m*RNA molecule generated from it by RNA splicing. Yet it has been estimated that only about one-twentieth of the total mass of RNA made ever leaves the nucleus. Therefore, a substantial fraction of the primary transcripts (about half) may be completely degraded in the nucleus without ever generating an RNA molecule that reaches the cytoplasm. The discarded RNAs may consist of sequences that are never made into an *m*RNA molecule; on the other hand, some may represent potential *m*RNA molecules that are functional in some cell types but in others fail to get delivered to the cytoplasm.

RNA export through the nuclear pores is an active process, and for most RNAs it requires a specific nucleotide cap at the 5′ end of the RNA molecule and a poly-A tail at the 3′ end. A requirement of this type makes sense, since it keeps junk RNA fragments (such as the intron sequences removed by RNA splicing) out of the cytosol. But having the proper types of ends is not enough for transport: *m*RNAs are directed to specific intracellular locations by signals in the *m*RNA sequence itself, before the sequence has been translated into an amino acid sequence. The signal is typically located in the 3′ untranslated region (UTR) of the *m*RNA molecule–a region that extends from the stop codon, to the start of the poly A tail in the *Drosophila* egg, the *m*RNA encoding the bicoid gene regulatory protein is attached to the cortical cytoskeleton at the anterior tip of the developing egg. When the translation of this *m*RNA is triggered by fertilization, a gradient of the bicoid protein is generated that plays a crucial part in directing the development of the anterior part of the embryo. Similarly the *m*RNA that encodes is localized to the actin-filament-rich cell cortex in mammalian fibroblasts by means of a 3′ UTR signal, presumably because it is advantageous for the cell to position its *m*RNAs close to the sites, where the protein produced from the *m*RNA is required.

Exercise

1. What is the 'central dogma'?
(a) Genetic information flows from RNA to DNA to protein
(b) Genetic information flows from RNA to protein to DNA
(c) Genetic information flows from DNA to RNA to protein
(d) Genetic information flows from DNA to protein to RNA

2. Mark all true statements.
I. Exons are found in the same order in the genome.
II. All cells in the human body have the same set of genes.
III. All cells in the human body express the same set of genes.
IV. All cells in the human body splice *m*RNAs for each gene in the same way.
(a) I and IV (b) I and II
(c) III and IV (d) II and III

3. Which of the following features of transcription is similar to that of replication?
(a) No primer is required for polymerization
(b) Polymerization does not have proof reading activity
(c) Newly synthesized strand starts failing off the template before complete RNA is synthesized
(d) RNA synthesis requires DNA topoisomerase action

4. Synthesis of *m*RNA on DNA template is
(a) unidirectional
(b) bidirectional
(c) bidirectional with the help of primer
(d) unidirectional with the help of primer

5. Which of the following does not have a mechanism that checks to make sure that the right monomer is incorporated into the polymer?
(a) Protein synthesis
(b) Double stranded rolling circle DNA synthesis
(c) RNA synthesis
(d) Excision repair DNA synthesis

6. Which of the following enzyme does not require a primer?
(a) RNA dependent DNA polymerase
(b) DNA dependent DNA polymerase
(c) DNA dependent RNA polymerase
(d) *Taq* DNA polymerase

7. Which one of the following statement about *E. coli* RNA polymerase is false?
(a) The holoenzyme includes the sigma factor
(b) The core enzyme includes the sigma factor
(c) It requires Mg^{2+} for its activity
(d) It requires Zn^{2+} for its activity

8. RNA polymerases join nucleotides through what kind of bond?
(a) Phosphodiester (b) Hydrogen
(c) Peptide (d) Glycosidic

9. The DNA binding protein that initiates the transcription of bacterial genes is called a/an
(a) operator (b) promoter
(c) repressor (d) sigma factor

10. Sigma subunit of RNA polymerase
(a) specifies the site for transcription
(b) initiates replication
(c) provides contact between ribonuclease and DNA template
(d) terminates transcription

11. Binding of a given sigma factor depends on the
(a) recognition of the length and spacing of promoter consensus sequences
(b) interaction with core enzyme
(c) length of the transcription unity
(d) distance of the transcriptional start codon

12. What is the role of the promoter region of a gene?
(a) It is the site where the ribosome binds to the *m*RNA
(b) It is the site where RNA polymerase binds to the DNA
(c) It is the site where DNA polymerase binds to the DNA
(d) It is the site where Shine-Dalgarno sequence present

13. Pribnow box is centered at
(a) +10 position (b) –10 position
(c) –35 position (d) +35 position

14. The prokaryotic RNA polymerase holoenzyme has the subunit structure
(a) ααββ′σ (b) αβσ
(c) αβ (d) αββ

15. To begin transcription, RNA polymerase recognizes nucleotide sequences in what region of the DNA?
(a) Promoter region (b) Template region
(c) G C-rich region (d) Terminator region

16. Rho dependent termination
(a) require the RNA involved to take one a specific secondary structure before termination can occur
(b) require that a specific protein bind to the RNA and cause termination
(c) require that the RNA be cut before transcription terminates further downstream
(d) only occurs on *t*RNA genes in eukaryotes

17. Which one of the following is a common feature found in the 3′ terminal segment of prokaryotic *m*RNAs?
(a) Poly A-stretch
(b) Cap
(c) Shine-Dalgarno sequence
(d) Stem loop structure

18. Mode of activation of rifampicin in *E. coli* is through
(a) cell division
(b) initiation of transcription
(c) RNA polymerase binding to DNA template
(d) inhibition of the oxidation potential

19. In eukaryotes the ribosomal RNA genes are transcribed by
(a) reverse transcriptase
(b) RNA dependent RNA polymerase
(c) RNA polymerase I
(d) RNA polymerase III

20. A promoter of a typical eukaryotic gene is composed of a binding site for
(a) the sigma factor (b) TATA binding protein
(c) transcription factor IID (d) transcription factor IIB

21. About 25-35 bp upstream of the transcriptional start site in most plant genes is a short sequence, which serves as site of assembly of the transcriptional initiation complex called
(a) CAAT box (b) GC box
(c) TATA box (d) Repressor

22. The TATA Box plays a key role in assembling active transcription complexes by
(a) binding with TATA-box binding protein
(b) binding with DNA protein
(c) binding with RNA protein
(d) it does not bind with any protein

23. Which one of the following transcription factors binds to TATA Box?
(a) TFIID (b) TFIIB
(c) TFIIIA (d) TFIIE

24. At which site on the DNA of a gene does RNA polymerase release its newly made RNA?
(a) Promoter (b) Template
(c) Stop codon (d) Terminator

25. Which of the following is not true about RNA processing?
(a) Exons are excised and hydrolyzed before *m*RNA moves out of the nucleus
(b) The presence of introns may facilitate crossing over between regions of a gene that code for polypeptide domains
(c) RNA splicing may be catalyzed spliceosomes
(d) A primary transcript is often much longer than the final RNA molecule that leaves the nucleus

26. Most eukaryotic pre *m*RNAs are matured by which of the following modifications to their ends?
(a) Capping at the 3′ end, cleavage and polyadenylation at the 5′ end
(b) Addition of a GMP to the 5′ end, cleavage and polyadenylation to create the 3′ end

(c) Addition of a guanine residue to the 5′ end, cleavage and polyadenylation to create the 3′ end
(d) Addition of a GMP to the 5′ end, polyadenylation, then cleavage to create the 3′ end

27. Mature eukaryotic *m*RNAs have 5′ cap that is residue of
(a) 2-methylguanosine (b) 3-methylguanosine
(c) 5-methylguanosine (d) 7-methylguanosine

28. Which one of the following regions in the mature *m*RNA is not found in the gene for the *m*RNA?
(a) Start codon (b) Leader sequence
(c) Poly A tail (d) Exon

29. In eukaryotes, what must assemble at a promoter before RNA polymerase can transcribe a gene?
(a) Nucleotides required in transcription
(b) General transcription factors
(c) Sigma factor
(d) An RNA primer

30. What is the purpose of storing information in exons separated by introns?
(a) It keep the exons safe from infecting viral DNA
(b) Eukaryotes are able to then use the information in one DNA sequence in alternative ways
(c) It allows for multiple copies of instructions to be hidden within several chromosomes
(d) There appears to be no significance to this arrangement

31. Which one of the following statements is not correct about eukaryotic *m*RNAs?
(a) It contains a poly A tail of up to 250 residues
(b) The poly A tail is coded by the DNA template
(c) The primary nuclear transcripts are much larger than the cytoplasmic *m*RNAs and contain introns
(d) A guanosine residue is attached to the 5′ terminus in an unusual 5′-5′ linkage

32. The co-linearity of gene and product clearly seen in prokaryote system is obscured in eukaryotes because
(a) DNA sequences coding for proteins are interrupted by non-coding sequences that are not transcribed
(b) the sequences of bases in the *m*RNA is modified in the cytoplasm prior to interaction with the ribosomes
(c) ribosomes in eukaryotes only translate exon regions of the *m*RNA
(d) the coding sequences in DNA is interrupted by DNA sequences that are transcribed and the spliced out of the *m*RNA

33. Spliceosomes, complex of snRNA, protein and pre-*m*RNA is found in
(a) eukaryotic cell (b) prokaryotic cell
(c) Both (a) and (b) (d) only in plant cell

34. Spliceosomes mediated splicing of GU-AG intron
(a) requires ATP
(b) involves transesterification reaction
(c) involves the nucleophilic attack of an OH group on the sugar phosphate backbone
(d) All of the above

35. Mark the true statement about snRNAs
(a) snRNAs are strictly localized to the nucleus
(b) most snRNAs are very abundant
(c) some snRNAs can base pair with intron consensus sequences
(d) All of the above

36. Introns are released as lariats during splicing of
(a) pre-*m*RNA transcripts and group II intron containing transcripts
(b) pre-*m*RNA transcripts only
(c) group I intron containing transcripts
(d) *t*RNA precursors

37. Alternate splicing means that
(a) the same gene can code for several different proteins
(b) several different genes can code for the same protein
(c) gene expression can be regulated at the level of transcription
(d) places of DNA can move around within the genome

38. In which of the following splicing events, the intermediates do not form the lariat or the branched structure?
(a) Trans splicing (b) Group I intron splicing
(c) Group II intron splicing (d) hnRNA splicing

39. Which ribonuclease is involved in producing mature *t*RNA in *E. coli*?
(a) RNAse A, D, E and F (b) RNAse D, E, F and H
(c) RNAse D, E, F and P (d) RNAse A, D, H and P

40. The footprinting assay can be used to
(a) map the position of nucleosome in chromatin
(b) determine the level of expression of a specific transcript
(c) determine the DNA-binding site for a transcription factor
(d) map the ends of a transcripts

41. Which of the following is not post-transcriptional modification?
(a) Splicing (b) 5′ capping
(c) 3′ adenylation (d) Glycosylation

42. All promoters are stimulated by negative supercoiling.
(a) The above statement is true in all cases
(b) The above statement is not true in all cases
(c) The above statement is not true only for the promoters of gyrase
(d) The above statement is not true only for the promoters of topoisomerase

43. The core enzyme binds to the DNA template
(a) less strongly than holoenzyme
(b) more strongly than holoenzyme
(c) as strongly as that of holoenzyme
(d) its binding depends on the type of DNA it binds

44. The significance of the absence of poly A tail from histone *m*RNA is
(a) absence of poly A tail hinders is the transfer of *m*RNA from nucleus to cytoplasm which is a favourable condition for histone protein
(b) absence of poly A tail facilitates the quick transfer of histone *m*RNA from nucleus to cytoplasm
(c) poly A tail inhibits with the transcription of histone *m*RNA
(d) poly A tail formation is not possible with the histone *m*RNA

45. A genetic defect in humans results in the absence of sweat glands in the skin. Some men have this defect all over their bodies, but in women it is usually expressed in a peculiar way. A woman with the defect typically has small patches of skin with sweat glands and other patches where sweat glands are lacking. This pattern suggests the phenotypic effect of

(a) a mutation (b) chromosome inactivation
(c) RNA splicing (d) an operon

46. A bacterium makes the amino acid glycine or absorbs it form its surroundings. A biochemist found that glycine binds to a repressor protein and causes the repressor to bind to the bacterial chromosome, 'turning off' an operon. If this is like other operons, the genes of this operon probably code for enzymes that

(a) control bacterial cell division
(b) breakdown glycine
(c) produce glycine
(d) cause the bacterium to differentiate

47. In humans, the hormone testosterone enters cells and binds to specific proteins, which in turn bind to specific sites on the cells' DNA.

These proteins probably act to

(a) help RNA polymerase transcribe certain genes
(b) alter the pattern of DNA splicing
(c) stimulate protein synthesis
(d) unwind the DNA so that its genes can be transcribed

48. Which of the following is the first thing that happens when a signal molecule acts on a target cell?

(a) A transcription factor acts on the DNA
(b) The signal molecule binds to the DNA
(c) A new protein is made in the target cell
(d) The signal molecule binds to a receptor

49. How does RNA polymerase 'know' where to start transcribing a gene into *m*RNA?

(a) It starts at one end of the chromosome.
(b) Transfer RNA acts to translate the message to RNA polymerase
(c) It starts at a certain nucleotide sequence called a promoter
(d) The ribosome directs it to the correct portion of the DNA molecule

50. After an *m*RNA molecule is transcribed form a eukaryotic gene, portions called .... are removed and the remaining .... are spliced together to produce an *m*RNA molecule with a continuous coding sequence.

(a) operators; promoters (b) exons; introns
(c) silencers; enhancers (d) introns; exons

51. Which of the following mechanisms of gene regulation operates after *m*RNA transcription but before translation of *m*RNA into protein?

(a) *m*RNA splicing
(b) DNA packing
(c) Repressors and activators
(d) Protein degradation

52. Homeobox polypeptide segments

(a) serve as histones, facilitating DNA packing
(b) bind to DNA and activate or repress gene transcription
(c) are vastly different in different organisms
(d) acts as enzymes, carrying out important chemical reactions

53. Which one of the following statements correctly describes the splicing process undergone by most eukaryotic pre-*m*RNAs?

(a) In a two-step reaction, the spliceosome removes the exon as lariat and joins the two atoms introns together
(b) Splicing requires conserved sequences, which are the 5′-splice site, the 3′-splice site, the branch point and the polypurine tract
(c) The UI snRNP initially binds to the 5′-splice site, U2 to the branch point sequence and then the three snRNP, U4, U5 and U6 can bind
(d) In the first step of splicing the G at the 3′-end of the intron is joined to the 2′ hydroxyl group of the A residue of the branch point sequence to create a lariat

54. How do retroviruses, such as HIV, differ from other viruses?

(a) They are much simpler than other viruses
(b) They contain DNA that is used as a template to make RNA
(c) They can reproduce only inside of living cells
(d) They contain RNA that is used as a template to make DNA

55. A ribozyme is

(a) an exception to the one gene-one RNA molecule axiom
(b) an enzyme that adds the 5′ cap and poly A tail to *m*RNA
(c) an example of rearrangement of protein domains caused by RNA splicing
(d) an RNA molecule that functions as an enzyme

56. Retroviruses have a gene for reverse transcriptase that

(a) uses viral RNA as a template for making complementary RNA strands
(b) protects viral DNA from degradation by restriction enzymes
(c) destroys the host cell DNA
(d) uses viral RNA as a template for DNA synthesis

57. Which of the following is not true of enhancers?

(a) They may be located thousands of nucleotides upstream from the genes they effect
(b) When bound with transcription factors, they interact with the promoter region and other transcription factors to increase the activity of a gene
(c) They may complex with steroid-activated receptor proteins and thus, selectively activate specific genes at appropriate stages in development
(d) They are located within the promoter, and, when complexed with a steroid or other small molecule, they release an inhibitory protein and thus make DNA more accessible to RNA polymerase

58. The colinearity of gene and product clearly seen in prokaryotic system is obscured in eukaryotes because

(a) the DNA sequences coding for proteins is interrupted by non-coding sequences that are not transcribed

(b) the sequence of bases in the *m*RNA is modified in the cytoplasm prior to interaction with the ribosomes
(c) ribosomes in eukaryotes only translate exon regions of the *m*RNA
(d) the coding sequence in DNA is interrupted by DNA sequences that are transcribed and then spliced out of the *m*RNA

59. Which of the following statements regarding the supercoiling of duplex DNA is correct?
(a) DNA replication promotes positive supercoiling downstream from the replication fork
(b) DNA polymerase II can replicate positively supercoiled duplex DNA
(c) DNA topoisomerases unwind duplex DNA into single-stranded DNA chains
(d) DNA topoisomerases unwind positively supercoiled duplex DNA without cutting the phosphosugar backbone

60. Which of the following statement regarding the termination of transcription of DNA is correct?
(a) The rho protein binds tightly to RNA polymerase and inactivities the polymerization activity
(b) Termination sites of DNA contain an inverted-repeat base sequence that results in the RNA formed adopting a 'stem and loop' configuration
(c) Each termination site contains a unique base where transcription stops
(d) All prokaryote termination sites contain the 'stem and loop' promoting sequence and also require the participation of the rho protein to halt RNA synthesis

61. Which one of the following statements about general transcription factors is false?
(a) TFII D binds to the TATA Box
(b) TFII D is a multiprotein complex consisting of TBP and TAF
(c) TBP is a common factor in transcription by RNA Pol I, RNA Pol II and RNA Pol III
(d) TFII H dephosphyorylates the carboxylterminal domain (CTD)

62. Which of the following is not an example of the control of gene expression that occurs after transcription?
(a) *m*RNA stored in the cytoplasm needing a control signal to initiate translation
(b) The length of time *m*RNA lasts before it is degraded
(c) *r*RNA genes amplified in tandem arrays
(d) RNA processing before *m*RNA exits from the nucleus

63. During the processing of introns, a single snRNP complex catalyzes both the cleavage of the RNA and the joining of the cut ends. What would be the consequence if these two processes were catalyzed by separate enzymes not associated in a single complex?
(a) the rate of RNA processing would be much faster
(b) the cell would be unable to identify the correct cleavage sites
(c) the atoms might not be joined in the correct sequence
(d) exons instead of introns would be cleaved from the RNA molecule

64. Binding of a given sigma factor depends on the
(a) recognition of the length and spacing of promoter consensus sequences
(b) interaction with core enzyme
(c) length of the transcription unit
(d) distance of the translational start codon

65. A cell biologist found that two different proteins with largely different structures were translated from two different *m*RNAs. These *m*RNAs, however, were transcribed from the same gene in the cell nucleus. What mechanism below could best account for this?
(a) Different systems of DNA unpacking could result in two different *m*RNAs
(b) A mutation might have altered the gene
(c) Exons from the same gene could be spliced in different ways to make different *m*RNAs
(d) The two *m*RNAs could be transcribed from different chromosome puffs

66. Which of the following statement is false?
(a) DNAse I hypersensitive sites are regions where the DNA is free of nucleosomes
(b) when gene is active, the promoter is generally free of nucleosome
(c) Hl phosphorylation occurs mainly before mitosis and phosphates are removed when cell division is complete
(d) DNA sequences called matric or scaffold associated regions are generally CG-rich

67. Scientists estimate that greater numbers of proteins produced in humans than the number of predicted genes. This is because
(a) the relationship between genes and proteins is not known
(b) primary RNA transcripts can be alternatively spliced to make different *m*RNA
(c) DNA replication occurs throughout life, so that genes are produced as a person gets older
(d) both the coding and the template strand of a single gene is transcribed

68. Which one of the following statements about retrotransposons is not correct?
(a) They are mobile genetic elements residing in the genomes of all classes of organisms
(b) They are transposons that behave much like retroviruses and have a retroviruses like structure
(c) The reverse transcriptase makes a cDNA copy of the retrotransposon
(d) The retrotransposan RNA is packed into virus particles

69. Rho-dependent terminators
(a) require the RNA involved to take on a specific secondary structure before termination can occur
(b) require that a specific protein bind to the RNA and cause termination
(c) require that the RNA be cut before transcription terminates further downstream
(d) only occurs on *t*RNA genes in eukaryotes

70. Alternative splicing means that
(a) the same gene can code for several different proteins
(b) several different genes can code for the same protein
(c) gene expression can be regulated at the level of transcription
(d) pieces of DNA can move around within the genome

71. Most eukaryotic pre-*m*RNAs are matured by which of the following modifications to their ends?

(a) capping at the 3′-end, cleavage and polyadenylation at the 5′-end
(b) addition of a GMP to the 5′-end, cleavage and polyadenylation to create the 3′-end
(c) addition of a guanine residue to the 5′-end, cleavage and polyadenylation to create the 3′-end
(d) addition of a GMP to the 5′-end, polyadenylation, then cleavage to create the 3′-end

72. What is the role of the rho protein in termination of transcription?

(a) It is a subunit of RNA polymerase that binds to RNA hairpins and stalls transcription
(b) It is a DNA-binding protein that blocks the movement of RNA polymerase down the template
(c) It is a helicase the actively breaks base pairs between the template and transcript
(d) It is a nuclease that degrades the 3′ ends to RNA transcripts

73. Transcription termination of *m*RNA genes in eukaryotes occurs

(a) at polyadenylation sites by the action of a termination factor
(b) by the formation of a strong hairpin structure in the vicinity of polyadenylation site
(c) termination factor bound to the termination site in the vicinity of polyadenylation site
(d) at pause sites following the polyadenylation sites

74. Cyclic adenosine monophosphate regulates the lactose (*lac*) operon by

(a) binding to the operator to turn on transcription
(b) binding to the *lac* repressor to prevent transcription
(c) combining with the catabolite activator protein (CAP) to form a complex that turns on transcription by binding to the promoter
(d) None of the above

75. Dioxin, produced as a byproduct of various industrial chemical processes, is suspected of causing cancer and birth defects in animals and humans. It apparently acts by entering cells and binding to proteins, altering the pattern of gene expression. The proteins affected by dioxin are probably

(a) enzymes (b) DNA polymerases
(c) transcription factors (d) enhancers

76. Which one of the following statements about eukaryotic RNA polymerases I, II and III is false?

(a) RNA pol II is very sensitive to a-amanitin
(b) RNA pol II is located in the nucleoplasm
(c) RNA pol III transcribes the genes for *t*RNA
(d) The carboxyl end of RNA pol II contains a short sequence of only seven amino acids which is called the CTD and which may be phosphorylated

77. Transfer RNA specifies amino acid, during proteins synthesis. *t*RNA is charged with amino acid at 3′ end and its anticodon pairs with codon of *m*RNA. Select the incorrect statement out of the following.

(a) Information is transmitted between 3′ end of *t*RNA and anticodon
(b) Codon-anticodon interaction occurs in A-site of ribosome
(c) Each *t*RNA has specific anticodon
(d) Each codon is triplet

78. Which of the following is not true of RNA processing?

(a) Exons are excised and hydrolyzed before *m*RNA moves out of the nucleus
(b) The presence of introns may facilitate crossing over between regions of a gene that code for polypeptide domains
(c) RNA splicing may be catalyzed by spliceosomes
(d) A primary transcript is often much longer than the final RNA molecule that leaves the nucleus

79. Which one of the following statements is not correct about eukaryotic *m*RNAs?

(a) It contains a poly-A tail of upto 250 residues
(b) The poly-A-tail is coded by the DNA template
(c) The primary nuclear transcripts are much larger than the cytoplasmic *m*RNAs and contain introns
(d) A guanosine residue is attached to the 5′ terminus in an unusual 5′-5′ linkage

80. 'Enhancer' elements are known to increase the rate of transcription when present at the upstream side of the promoter sequences, if the same enhancer element is placed in reverse orientation

(a) the rate of transcription increases
(b) the rate of transcription decreases
(c) the rate transcription remains same
(d) no transcription is observed

81. Genes that have been artificially synthesized without non-coding sequences often fail to yield proteins when placed inside a cell, because

(a) they are not transcribed
(b) they curl up
(c) they bond to the DNA
(d) their *m*RNA molecules fail to move through the pores in the nuclear envelope

82. Changes in RNA polymerase III promoters result in changes in the sequence of the gene product. This is because

(a) RNA polymerase III initiates transcription at various positions
(b) the promoter elements are located within the coding region of the gene
(c) promoters are located far upstream of the gene transcribed
(d) polymerase is unable to bind to the promoter

83. Which one of the following statements about the primary transcripts in eukaryotes is incorrect?

(a) They are usually longer than the fundamental RNA
(b) They contain no modified bases
(c) They contain nucleotide sequences which are complementary to the DNA template
(d) They contain the TATA Box sequence

84. What is the purpose in storing information in exons separated by introns?

(a) It keeps the exons safe from infecting viral DNA
(b) Eukaryotes are able to then use the information in one DNA sequence in alternative ways

(c) It allows for multiple copies of instructions to be hidden within several chromosomes
(d) There appears to be no significance to this arrangement

85. The poly A end of eukaryotic *m*RNAs originates from
(a) transcription of corresponding poly T region of the respective gene
(b) addition of a pre-synthesized poly—A tail to the 3′ end of the primary transcript
(c) sequential addition of A residues at the 3′ end of the primary transcript
(d) by as set an unknown mechanism

86. Histone acetylation increase transcription of gene because
(a) it increases the DNA histone interaction
(b) the acetyl groups on histones are recognized by the RNA polymerase
(c) histone acetylation loosens the DNA histone complex, thereby making it more accessible to RNA polymerase
(d) histone acetylation induces DNA bending which is recognized by RNA polymerase

87. Similarities between RNA polymerase and DNA polymerase activities in prokaryotes include
I. The requirement for a template
II. The requirement for a primer
III. Synthesis of the nascent chain in the 5′ to 3′ direction
IV. The 3′ to 5′ exonuclease editing function
(a) I and II (b) I and III
(c) I and IV (d) I, II and III

88. The introns in *t*RNA
I. Are removed by a two-step transesterification mechanism.
II. Have a sequence complementary to the anticodon.
III. All form a similar secondary structure.
IV. Are removed by protein enzymes (endonuclease and ligase).
(a) I and II
(b) I and III
(c) I and IV
(d) II, III and IV

89. Addition of the poly-(A)-tail to a pre-*m*RNA
I. Involves a two-step transesterification mechanism.
II. Requires a conserved AAUAAA sequence.
III. Proceed by the stepwise assembly of a multi component complex.
IV. Is carried out by a template-dependent RNA polymerase.
(a) I and II (b) I and III
(c) I and IV (d) II, III and IV

90. In mammalian cells, RNA editing
I. Can change the coding capacity of a gene after transcription.
II. Creates a stop codon in the middle of the apo-B *m*RNA in intestinal cells but not in liver cells.
III. Usually makes many changes in each *m*RNA.
IV. Can change specific nucleotides by deamination.
(a) I and II (b) I and III
(c) I, II and IV (d) II, III and IV

91. Alternative splicing
I. Uses a completely different mechanism than 'constitutive' splicing.
II. Allows generation of protein isoforms (variants that differ by addition or deletion of a small number of amino acids) from a single gene.
III. Involves the use of different 5′ and 3′ splice sites.
IV. Is used to make different proteins in different tissues and at different developmental stages.
(a) I and II (b) I and III
(c) I and IV (d) II, III and IV

92. Consider the following statement.
A factor called 'sigma factor' is involved in the transcription process during protein synthesis. This factor.
I. Interacts with the core enzyme RNA-polymerase and Forms the complete active enzyme.
II. Recognizes the start signal on DNA and directs the binding of the enzyme to the promoter region.
III. Along with the rho factor helps RNA to dissociate from RNA-polymerase and thus, helps to terminate transcription.
Which of these statements are correct?
(a) I and II (b) I and III
(c) II and III (d) I, II and III

Answers

1. (c)	**2.** (b)	**3.** (d)	**4.** (a)	**5.** (c)	**6.** (c)	**7.** (b)	**8.** (a)	**9.** (d)	**10.** (a)
11. (a)	**12.** (b)	**13.** (b)	**14.** (a)	**15.** (a)	**16.** (b)	**17.** (d)	**18.** (b)	**19.** (c)	**20.** (b)
21. (c)	**22.** (a)	**23.** (a)	**24.** (d)	**25.** (a)	**26.** (b)	**27.** (d)	**28.** (c)	**29.** (b)	**30.** (b)
31. (b)	**32.** (d)	**33.** (a)	**34.** (d)	**35.** (d)	**36.** (a)	**37.** (a)	**38.** (b)	**39.** (c)	**40.** (c)
41. (d)	**42.** (b)	**43.** (b)	**44.** (b)	**45.** (b)	**46.** (c)	**47.** (a)	**48.** (d)	**49.** (c)	**50.** (d)
51. (a)	**52.** (b)	**53.** (c)	**54.** (d)	**55.** (d)	**56.** (d)	**57.** (d)	**58.** (d)	**59.** (a)	**60.** (b)
61. (d)	**62.** (c)	**63.** (c)	**64.** (a)	**65.** (c)	**66.** (d)	**67.** (b)	**68.** (d)	**69.** (b)	**70.** (a)
71. (b)	**72.** (c)	**73.** (d)	**74.** (c)	**75.** (c)	**76.** (d)	**77.** (a)	**78.** (a)	**79.** (b)	**80.** (c)
81. (d)	**82.** (b)	**83.** (d)	**84.** (b)	**85.** (c)	**86.** (c)	**87.** (d)	**88.** (d)	**89.** (c)	**90.** (c)
91. (a)	**92.** (b)								

8 Protein Synthesis and Processing

Translation

Translation involves the transfer of information in *m*RNA molecules into the amino acid sequences of polypeptides according to the specifications of the genetic code.

The translation takes place on ribosome in cytoplasm of cell. It is simultaneous in prokaryotic transcription, while required processing *m*RNA in eukaryotes. Its general features are

(i) It is a complex process requiring the function of a large number of macro-molecules, *e.g.*,

(a) Over 50 polypeptides and three to five RNA molecules present in each ribosome.

(b) At least 20 amino acid activating enzymes.

(c) 40-60 different *t*RNA molecules.

(d) Numerous soluble proteins involved in polypeptide chain initiation, elongation and termination.

(ii) The nucleotide sequence of an *m*RNA molecule is translated into appropriate amino acid sequence according to the dictations of the genetic code.

(iii) Of the 64 possible nucleotide triplets, 61 specify amino acids two of which also function as polypeptide chain initiation signal, and three specify polypeptide chain termination.

(iv) *m*RNA is translated from its 5′ end to its 3′ end, *i.e.*, Ribosomes read *m*RNA in 5′→3′ direction.

(v) Polypeptide synthesis proceeds from N-terminus to C-terminus.

(vi) Active translation occurs on polyribosomes. Electron micrographs revealed that ribosomes engaged in protein synthesis are tandemly arranged on *m*RNAs like beads on a string. The individual ribosomes in these polyribosomes are separated by a gap of 50 to 150 Å so, they have a maximum density on *m*RNA of ~1 ribosomes per 80 nucleotides.

Syllabus

- Translation
- Genetic code
- Ribosome
- Formation of Initiation Complex
- Initiation Factors and their Regulation,
- Elongation and Elongation Factors,
- Termination,
- Aminocylation of *t*RNA,
- *t*RNA-identity,
- Aminoacyl *t*RNA Synthetase and Translational Proofreading
- Translational Inhibitors: Antibiotics
- Post-translational Modification of Proteins

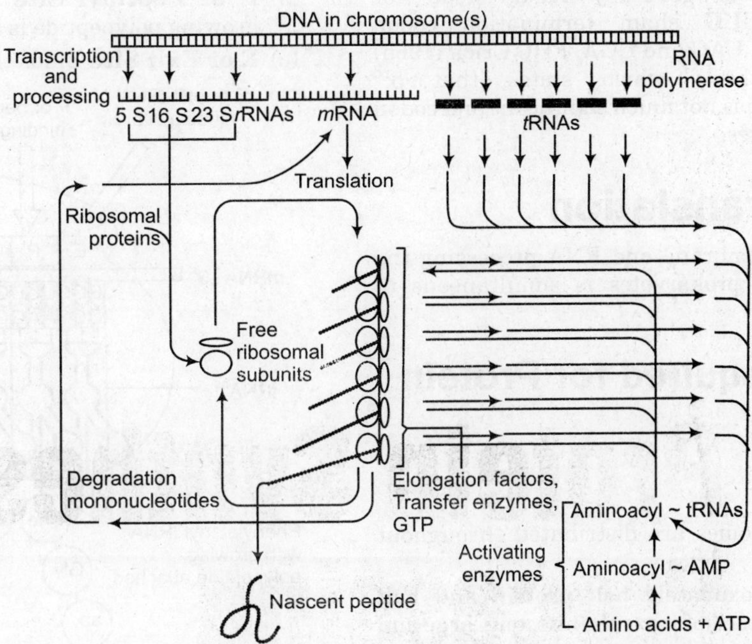

Fig. 8.1 Overview of protein synthesis. The sizes of the *r*RNA molecules shown are correct for bacteria, larger *r*RNAs are present in eukaryotes. For simplicity, all RNA species have been transcribed from contiguous segments of a single DNA molecule. In reality, the various RNAs are transcripts of genes located at different positions on form one to many chromosomes.

Genetic Code

Genetic code was discovered by Nirenberg and Matthaei 1961 may be defined as the sequence of nucleotides in polynucleotide chain (DNA molecule) which determine sequence of amino acids in a polypeptide chain. The genetic code is triplet (*i.e.*, 3-letter codon), degenerate (*i.e.*, more than one codon are available for single amino acid). Commaless, non-overlapping, non-ambiguous (one codon always and code for same amino acid) and universal.

First Position (5′ end)	**Second Position**				**Third Position (3′ end)**
	U	C	A	G	
U	U U U Phe } F	U C U Ser } S	U A U Tyr } Y	U G U Cys } F	U
	U U C Phe	U C C Ser	U A C Tyr	U G C Cys	C
	U U A Leu } L	U C A Ser	**U A A Stop**	**U G A Stop**	A
	U U G Leu	U C G Ser	**U A G Stop**	U G G Trp W	G
C	C U U Leu } L	C C U Pro } P	C A U His } H	C G U Arg } R	U
	C U C Leu	C C C Pro	C A C His	C G C Arg	C
	C U A Leu	C C A Pro	C A A Gln } Q	C G A Arg	A
	C U G Leu	C C G Pro	C A G Gln	C G G Arg	G
A	A U U Ile } I	A C U Thr } T	A A U Asn } N	A G U Ser } S	U
	A U C Ile	A C C Thr	A A C Asn	A G C Ser	C
	A U A Ile	A C A Thr	A A A Lys } K	A G A Arg } R	A
	A U G Met M	A C G Thr	A A G Lys	A G G Arg	G
G	G U U Val } V	G C U Ala } A	G A U Asp } D	G G U Gly } G	U
	G U C Val	G C C Ala	G A C Asp	G G C Gly	C
	G U A Val	G C A Ala	G A A Glu } E	G G A Gly	A
	G U G Val	G C G Ala	G A G Glu	G G G Gly	G

Fig. 8.2 The standard genetic code

Chain initiation codon is generally AUG (code for methionine) or rarly GUG chain termination codon (non-sence codon are UAA, UAG and UGA, FHC Crick (1965) proposed wobble hypothesis which states that 3rd nitrogenous base of a codon is not much significant and codon is specified by first two bases.

Prokaryotic Translation

Due to lack of nuclear membrane and RNA processing the process of translation in prokaryotes is simultaneous to transcription is cytoplasm.

Components Required for Protein Synthesis

Ribosomes

(a) In prokaryotes ribosomes are distributed throughout cells.

(b) Ribosomes are approximately half protein and half RNA. They are composed of two subunits, one large and one small, which dissociate when translation of an *m*RNA molecule is completed and reassociate during initiation of translation.

(c) Ribosome sizes are most frequently expressed in terms of their rates of sedimentation during centrifugation, in Svedberg unit.

(d) The prokaryotic ribosome has a size of 70 S.

(e) Although the size and macromolecular composition of ribosomes vary, the overall three dimensional structure of ribosome is basically the same in all organisms.

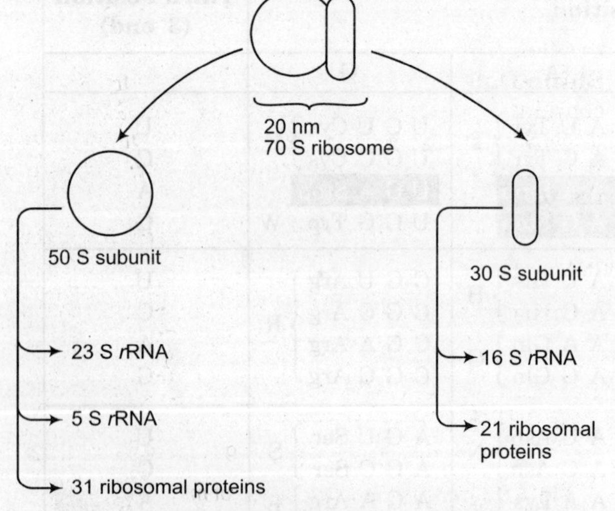

Fig. 8.3 Prokaryotic ribosomes: Macromolecular composition

*t*RNA Binding Sites on Ribosomes

(a) **A or Aminoacyl site** Binds the incoming aminoacyl *t*RNA, the *t*RNA carrying the next amino acid to be added to the growing polypeptide chain.

(b) **P or Peptidyl Site** Binds the *t*RNA to which the growing polypeptide is attached.

(c) **E or Exit Site** Binds the departing uncharged *t*RNA.

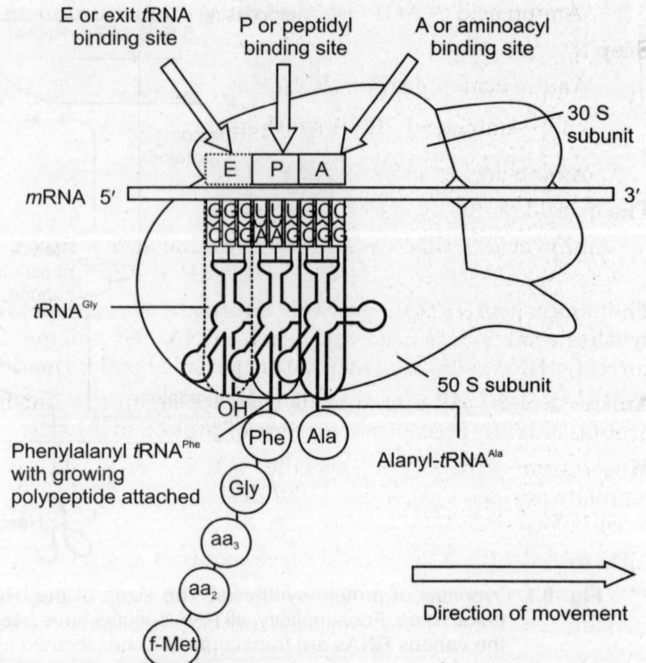

Fig. 8.4 Binding sites for *t*RNA on 70 S ribosome

Transfer RNAs

The translation of a coded *m*RNA message into a sequence of amino acids in a polypeptide requires *t*RNA molecule. Atleast one specific type of *t*RNA is required per amino acid. Also a single *t*RNA may recognize two or three codons all specifying one single amino acid.

Anticodon *t*RNA molecule, contain a triplet nucleotide sequence the anticodon (5′ nucleotide), which is complementary to and base pairs with the codon (3′ nucleotide) sequence in *m*RNA during translation. Because of *t*RNAs ability to both carry a specific amino acid and to recognize the codon for that amino aciod *t*RNAs are also known as adaptor molecule.

Amino Acid Attachment Site The amino acids are attached to the *t*RNAs by high energy bond (symbolized ~) between the carboxyl group of the amino acids and the 3′-hydroxyl termini of the *t*RNAs.

Aminoacyl *t*RNA Synthetases The *t*RNAs are activated or charged with amino acids in two step process, with both reactions catalyzed by the same enzyme aminoacyl *t*RNA synthetase. There is at least one aminoacyl *t*RNA synthetases for each of the twenty amino acids.

Step 1 Aminoacyl *t*RNA synthesis involves activation of the amino acid using energy from adenosine triphosphate (ATP).

$$\text{Amino acid} + \text{ATP} \xrightarrow{\text{Aminoacyl } t\text{RNA synthetase}} \text{Amino acid} \sim \text{AMP} + (P) \sim (P)$$

Step 2

$$\text{Amino acid} \sim \text{AMP} + t\text{RNA} \xrightarrow{\text{Aminoacyl } t\text{RNA synthetase}} \text{Amino acyl} \sim t\text{RNA} + \text{AMP}$$

The overall amino acylation reaction is

$$\text{Amino acid} + t\text{RNA} + \text{ATP} \rightleftharpoons \text{Amino acyl} \sim t\text{RNA} + \text{AMP} + \text{PP}_i$$

The aminoacyl *t*RNAs are the substrate for polypeptide synthesis on ribosomes, with each *t*RNA recognizing the correct *m*RNA codon and facilitating peptide bond formation.

Amino Acids All amino acids that appear in the finished protein must be present at the time of protein synthesis.

Messenger RNA The specific *m*RNA required as a template for the synthesis of the desired polypeptide chain must be present.

ATP and GTP ATP and GTP are required as the source of energy.

Protein Factors Initiation, elongation, termination/release factors are required for peptide synthesis.

Table 8.1 **The Soluble Protein Factors of *E. coli* Protein Synthesis**

Factor	Number of Residue[a]	Function
Initiation Factors		
IF-1	71	Assists IF3 binding
IF-2	890	Binds initiator *t*RNA and GTP
IF-3	180	Release *m*RNA and *t*RNA from recycled 30 S subunit and aids new *m*RNA binding
Elongation Factors		
EF-Tu	393	Binds amino acyl *t*RNA and GTP
EF-Ts	282	Displaces GDP from EF-Tu
EF-G	703	Promotes translocation through GTP binding and hyrolysis
Release Factors		
RF-1	360	Recognizes UAA and UAG stop codons
RF-2	365	Recognizes UAA and UGA stop codons
RF-3	528	Stimulates RF-1/RF-2 release *via* GTP hydrolysis
RRF	185	Together with EF-G, induces ribosomal dissociation to small and large subunits

[a] All *E.coli* translational factors are monomeric proteins.

Steps in Prokaryotic Translation

The translation of the sequence of nucleotides in an *m*RNA molecule into the sequence of amino acids in its polypeptide product can be divided into three stages

(i) Polypeptide chain initiation
(ii) Chain elongation
(iii) Chain termination

Initiation

The initiation of translation includes all events that precedes the formation of a peptide bond between the first two amino acids of the new polypeptide chain. Initiation is a complex process in which two ribosomal subunits and f^{met} $t\text{RNA}_f^{met}$ assemble on a properly aligned *m*RNA to form a complex that is competent to commense chain elongation. This assembly process also requires the participation of protein initiation factors that are not permanently associated with ribosome. Initiation involves three initiation factors designated IF–1, IF–2 and IF-3.

$t\text{RNA}_f^{met}$

$t\text{RNA}_f^{met}$ initiates synthesis of polypeptides, in response to the translation initiation codon (usually AUG). Therefore, all polypeptide begins with methionine during synthesis. The amino terminal methionine is subsequently cleaved from many polypeptides. Thus, functional proteins need not have an amino terminal methionine.

- The methionyl-$t\text{RNA}_f^{met}$ interacts with protein initiation factor IF-2 to begin the process.
- The methionyl-$t\text{RNA}_f^{met}$ is the only amino-acyl *t*RNA that can enter the P-site directly.
- The methionyl-$t\text{RNA}_f^{met}$ also binds to ribosome in response to alternate initiator codon GUG, that occurs in some *m*RNA molecules.
- **Shine-Dalgarno Sequence** Prokaryotic *m*RNA contains a conserved consensus AGGAGG located seven nucleotide upstream from the AUG initiation codon. It is complementary to a sequence near 3′-terminus of the 16 S ribosomal RNA.

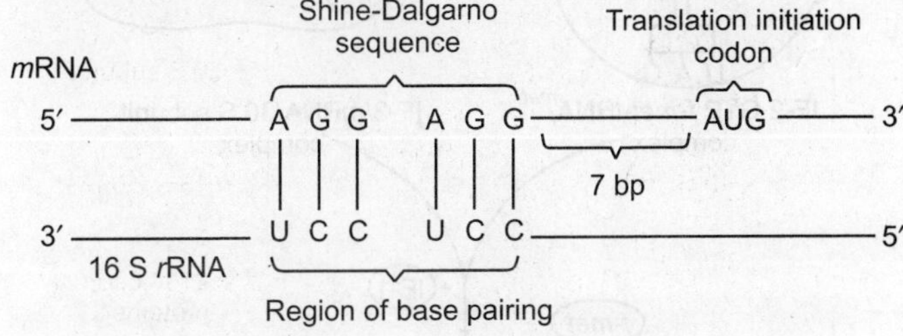

Fig. 8.5 Shine-Dalgarno sequence of *m*RNA and 16*r*RNA

- This base pairing plays an important role in the translation and leads to the formation of *m*RNA/30 S ribosomal subunit initiation complex.

Stages in Prokaryotic Initiation

The initiation sequence in the *E.coli* ribosomes has three stages.

Stage 1 On completing a cycle of polypeptide synthesis the 30 S and 50 S subunits remain associated as an inactive 70 S ribosome. IF-3 binds to the 30 S subunit of this complex so as to promote dissociation.

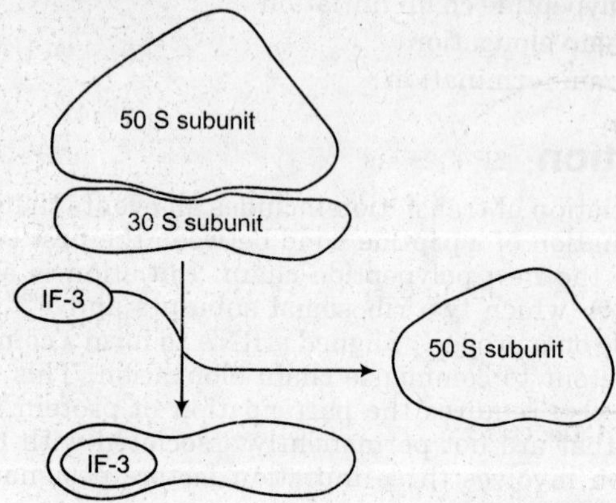

Fig. 8.6 Binding of IF-3 to ribosomes subunit

Stage 2 Formation of IF-2·GTP·^{fmet}-*t*RNA$_f^{met}$ and IF-3/*m*RNA/30 S subunit complexes. Subsequently these two complexes combine with each other along with IF-1 to form the complete 30 S initiation complex.

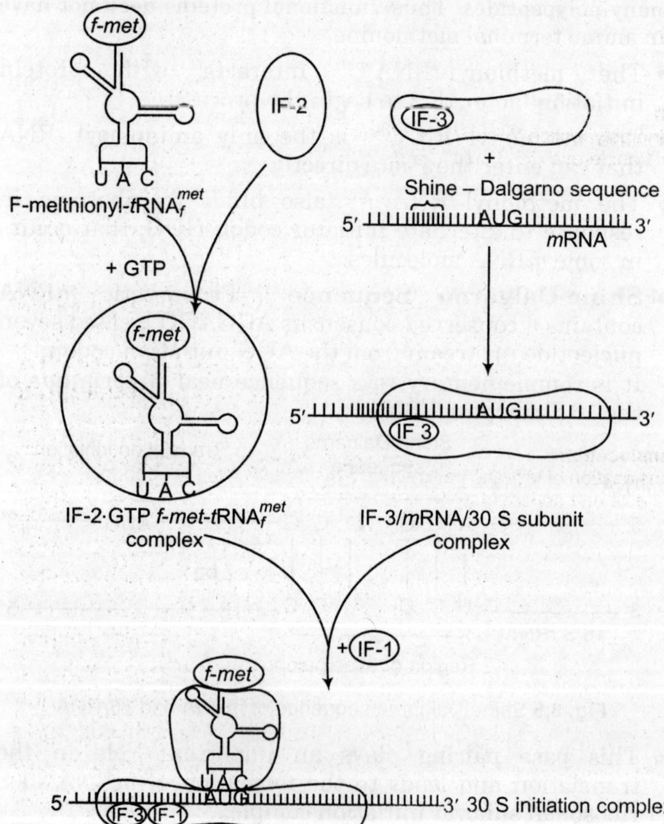

Fig. 8.7 Formation of IF, *t*RNA and 30 S subunit complex

Stage 3 Release of IF-1 and IF-3. The 50 S subunit joins the 30 S initiation complex in a manner that stimulates IF-2 to hydrolyze its bound GTP to GDP + P$_i$. This irreversible reaction conformationally rearranges the 30 S subunit and release IF-2 for participation in further initiation reaction.

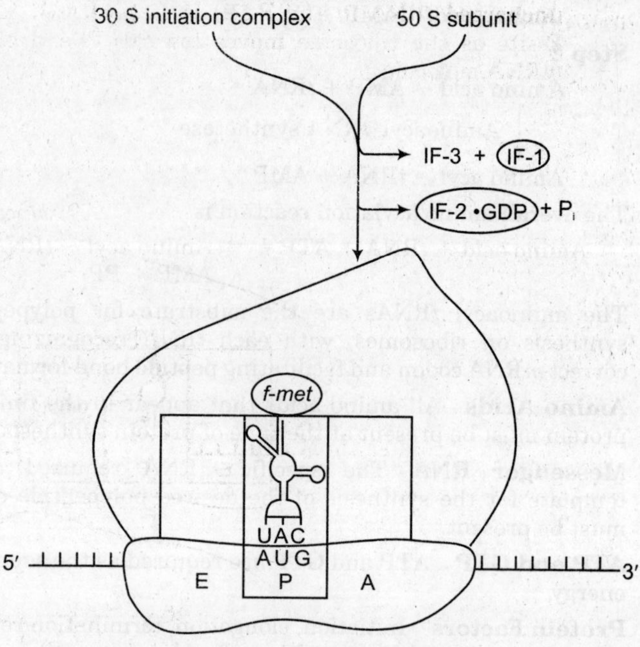

Fig. 8.8 70 S initiation complex

- Initiation results in the formation of an *f-met-t*RNA$_f^{met}$ *m*RNA • Ribosome complex in which the *f-met-t*RNA$_f^{met}$ occupies the ribosomes P-site while its A-site is poised to accept an incoming aminoacyl *t*RNA.

Chain Elongation

Ribosomes elongate polypeptide chains in a three stage, reaction cycle that adds amino acid residue to a growing polypeptide C-terminus.

(a) **Decoding** in which ribosome selects and binds an amino acyl *t*RNA, whose anticodon is complementary to the *m*RNA codon in the A-site.

This step rquires elongation factor T$_u$ carrying a molecule of GTP (EF–T$_u$ · GTP) which combines with aminoacyl *t*RNA. The complex aminoacyl *t*RNA. EF-T$_u$· GTP binds to ribosome in a reaction that hydrolyze GTP to GDP + P$_i$. Aminoacyl *t*RNA binds to ribosomal A-site and EF – T$_u$ · GDP + P$_i$ is released.

- EF–T$_u$ · GDP is inactive and is activated by elongation factor Ts (EF – Ts).
- EF–T$_u$ interacts with all aminoacyl *t*RNAs except methionyl-*t*RNA.

(b) **Transpeptidation** in which the peptidyl group on the P-site *t*RNA is transferred to the aminoacyl group in the A-site through the formation of peptide bond.

- This uncouples the growing chain from *t*RNA in the P-site and covalently joins the chain to the *t*RNA in the A-site.
- This reaction is catalyzed by peptidyl transferase an enzymatic activity built into the 50 S subunit of the ribosome.

(c) **Translocation** peptidyl *t*RNA present in A-site of the ribosome is translocated to the P-site and the uncharged *t*RNA in the P-site is translocated to the E-site as the ribosome moves towards 3′-end of the *m*RNA molecule.

- This translocation step requires GTP and elongation factor G (EF – G).

These three steps are repeated in a cyclic manner throughout the elongation process.

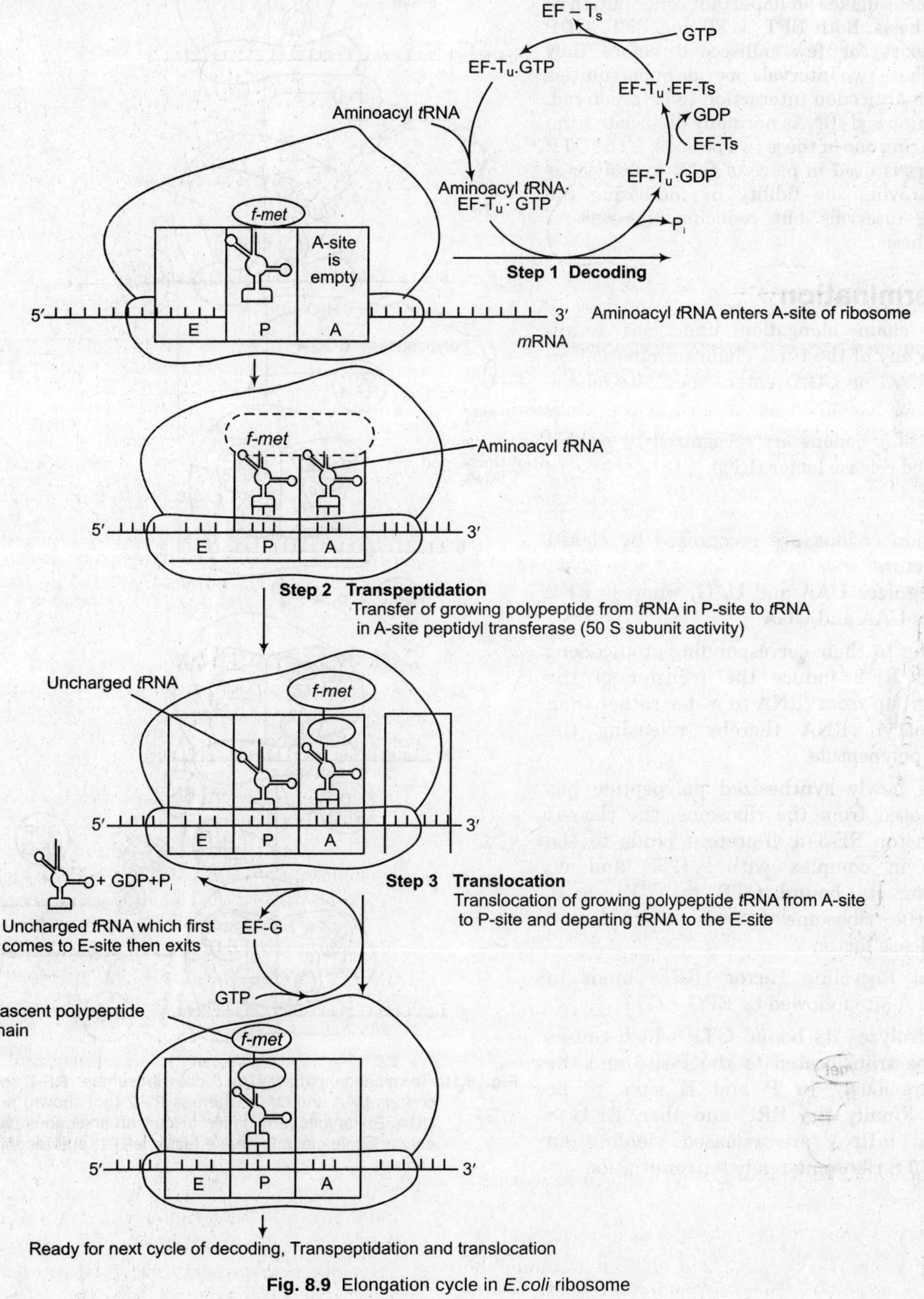

Fig. 8.9 Elongation cycle in *E.coli* ribosome

Translational Proofreading

Proofreading mechanism on ribosome establish only that proper codon-anticodon pairing has taken place. The GTPas activity of EET_u during the first step in prokaryotic cells makes an important contribution to protein synthesis. Both EFT_u GTP and EFT_u GDP complexes exist for few milisecond before they dissociate. These two intervals provide opportunities for the codon anticodon interaction to be proofread. Incorrect aminoacyl *t*RNAs normally dissociate from the A-site during one of these two periods. If the GTP analog GTPrs is used in place of GTP, hydrolysis is slowed, improving the fidility by increasing the proofreading intervals but reducing the rate of protein synthesis.

Chain Termination

Polypeptide chain elongation undergoes termination when any of the three chain termination codon (UAA, UAG or UGA) enters the Asite on the ribosome.

These three stop codons are recognized by soluble proteins called release factor (RFs).

Steps

- Termination codons are recognized by class-I release factors.
  RF-1 recognizes UAA and UAG, whereas RF-2 recognizes UAA and UGA.
- On binding to their corresponding stop codons RF-1 and RF-2 induce the transfer of the peptidyl group from *t*RNA to water rather than to aminoacyl *t*RNA thereby releasing the complete polypeptide.
- Once the newly synthesized polypeptide has been released from the ribosome, the class-II release factor RF-3 a G-protein binds to the ribosome in complex with GTP and on hydrolyzing its bound GTP to GDP + P_i induces the ribosome to release its bound class-I release factor.
- Ribosomal Recycling Factor (RRF) binds in ribosomal A-site followed by EFG • GTP.
- EF-G hydrolyzes its bound GTP which causes RRF to be translocated to the P-site and the *t*RNAs previously in P and E sites to be released. Finally the RRF and then EF-G • GDP and *m*RNA are released yielding an inactive 70 S ribosome ready for reinitiation.

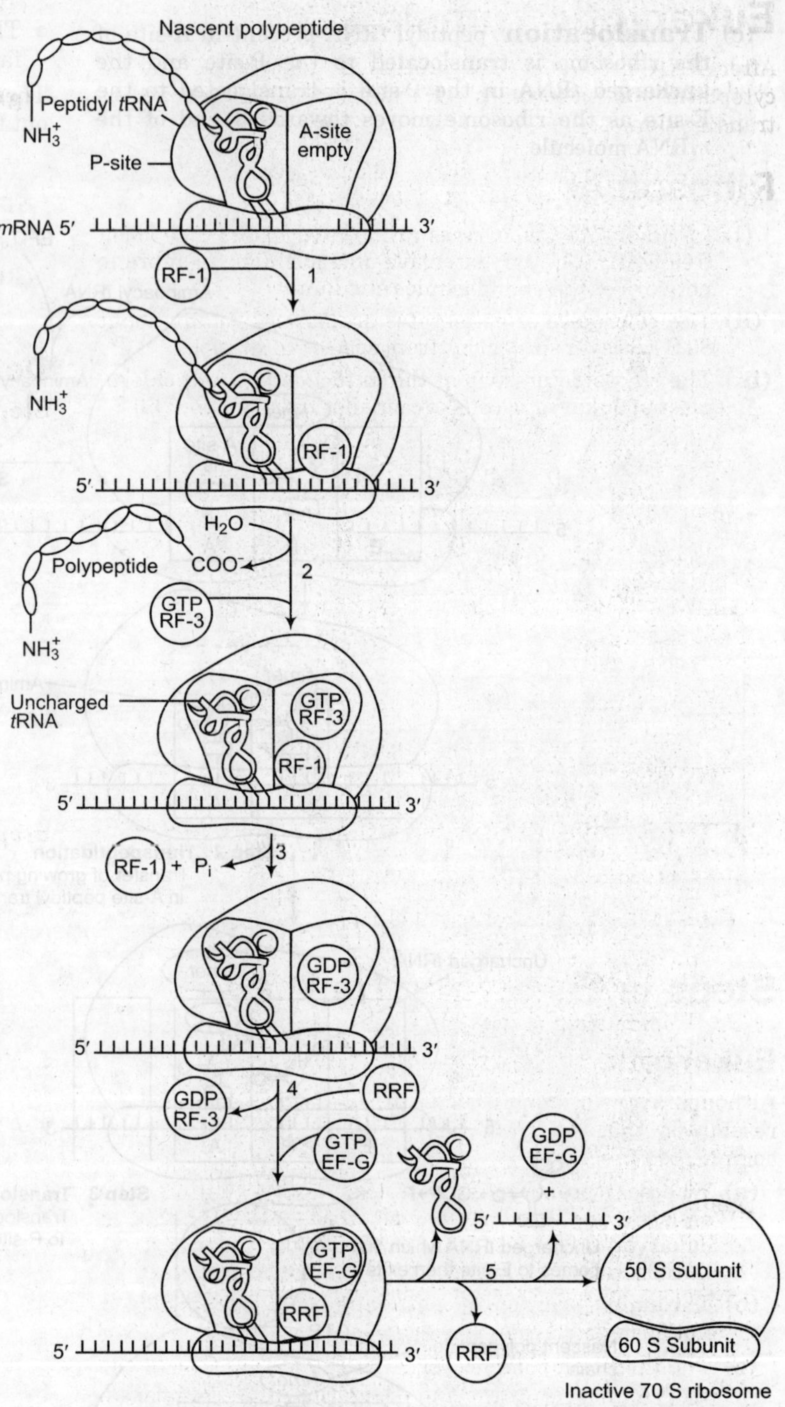

Fig. 8.10 Termination pathway in *E.coli* ribosomes. RF-1 recognizes the stop codons UAA and UAG, whereas RF-2 (not shown) recognizes UAA and UGA. Eukaryotic termination follows an analogous pathway but requires only a single class I release factor, eRF1, that recognizes all three stop codons

Eukaryotic Translation

After RNA processing the process of translation star in cytoplasm on ribosomes. It is not simultaneous to transcription.

Ribosomes

(i) In eukaryotes, ribosomes are located in the cytoplasm frequently on the extensive intracellular membrane network of the endoplasmic reticulum.

(ii) The ribosomes of eukaryotes are larger, usually about 80 S however size varies from species to species.

(iii) The ribosome present in the mitochondria and chloroplast of eukaryotic cells are smaller usually about 60 S.

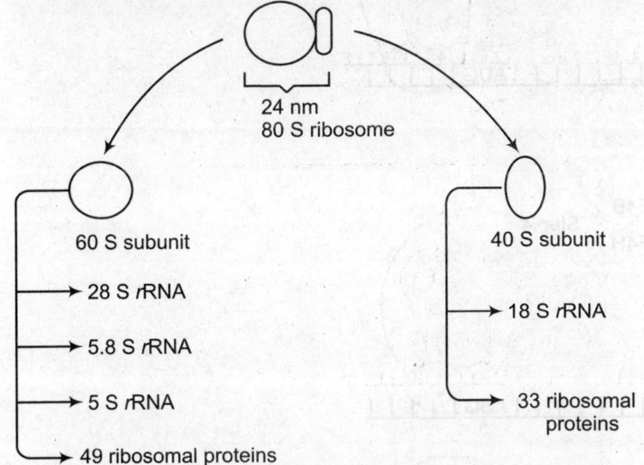

Fig. 8.11 Eukaryotic ribosome : Macromolecular composition

Steps in Eukaryotic Translation

Eukaryotic Initiation

Although translation initiation in eukaryotes superficially resembles that in prokaryotes, it is infact far more complicated process.

(a) Whereas prokaryotic initiation only requires the assistance of three monomeric initiation factor, that in eukaryotes involves the participation of atleast 11 initiation factor designated eIF_n ('e' for eukaryotes).

(b) The amino group of the methionine on initiator *t*RNA is not formylated as in prokaryotes.

(c) The initiation complex forms at the 5′-terminus of the *m*RNA, not at the Shine-Dalgarno/AUG translation start site as in *E. coli*.

(d) In eukaryotes, translation frequently begins at the AUG closest to the 5′-terminus of the *m*RNA molecule, although the efficiency with which a given AUG is used to initiate translation depends on the contigous nucleotide sequence 5′—GCC (A or G) CC AUG G–3′. This sequence requirement for optimal translation initiation in eukaryotes are called Kozak's rule.

(e) Eukaryotes contains a special initiator *t*RNA, *t*RNA$_i^{met}$ ('*i*' for initiator), but the amino group of the methionyl-*t*RNA$_i^{met}$ is not formylated.

(f) The initiator methionyl-*t*RNA$_i^{met}$ interacts with a soluble initiation factor and enters the P-site directly during the initiation process.

(g) The entire initiation complex means 5′→3′ along the *m*RNA molecule, searching for an AUG codon. When an AUG triplet is found, the initiation factor dissociate from the complex and the large (60 S) subunit binds to the methionyl *t*RNA/*m*RNA/40 S subunit complex forming the complete 80 S ribosome.

(h) The 80 S ribosome/*m*RNA/*t*RNA complex is ready to begin the second phase of translation, chain elongation.

Detailed Process

Step 1 Binding of eIF3 and eIF1A (homolog of bacterial IF-1) to the 40 S subunit in inactive 80 S ribosome so, that, *i.e.*, releases the 50 S subunit.

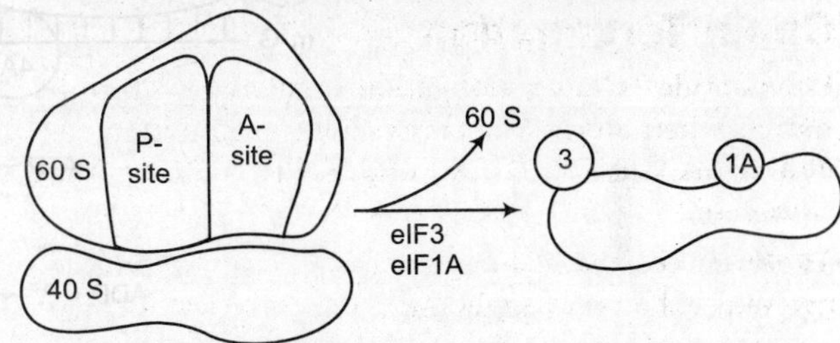

Fig. 8.12 Binding of eIF3 and eIF1A to 40 S subunit

Step 2 The complex of eIF2, GTP and *met-t*RNA$_i^{met}$ binds to the 40 S ribosomal subunit accompanied by eIF1 to form 43 S pre-initiation complex.

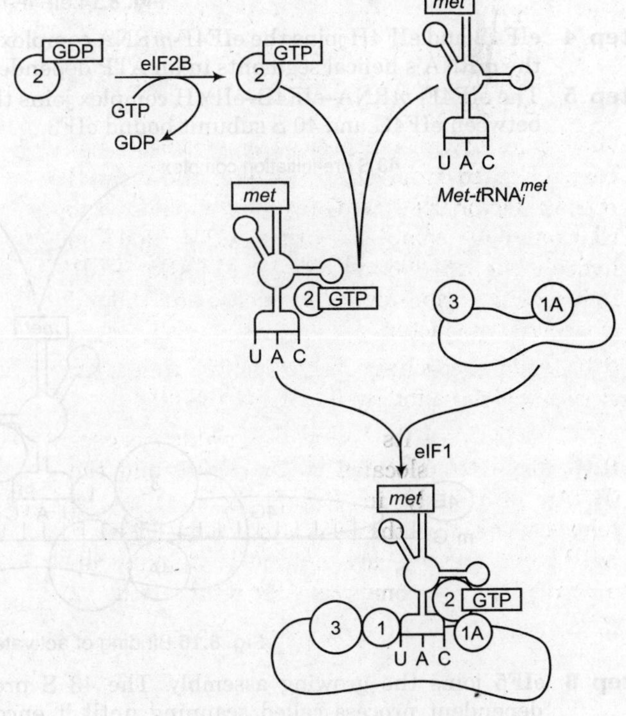

Fig. 8.13 43 S pre-initiation complex

Step 3 Eukaryotic *m*RNAs nearly all of which have an m^{7}G cap and poly (A) tail are invariably monocistronic and almost always initiate translation at their leading AUG. This AUG which occurs at the end of a 5′ untranslated region of 50 to 70 nucleotides is embedded in consensus sequence CCAUGG.

- The recognition of the initiation site begins by binding of eIF4F to the m^{7}G cap. eIF4F is a heterotrimeric complex of eIF4E, eIF4G and eIF4A in which eIF4E (cap binding protein) recognizes the *m*RNAs m^{7}G cap.

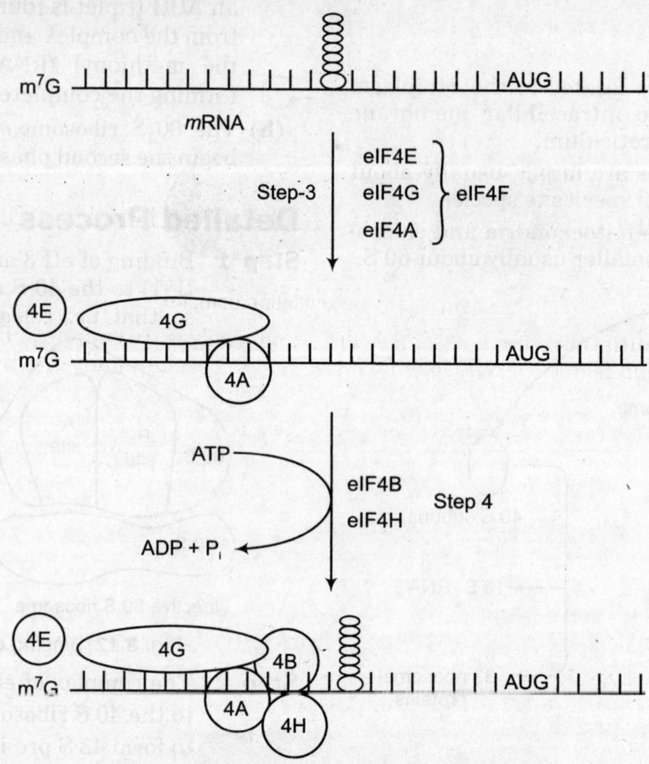

Fig. 8.14 eIF4F-*m*RNA-eIF$_4$B-e-IF4 complex

Step 4 eIF4B and eIF4H joins the eIF4F-*m*RNA complex, where they stimulate the RNA helicase activity of eIF4A to unwind the *m*RNA's helical segments in an ATP dependent process.

Step 5 The eIF4F–*m*RNA–eIF4B–eIF4H complex joins the 43 S pre-initiation complex through a protein-protein interaction between eIF4G and 40 S subunit bound eIF3.

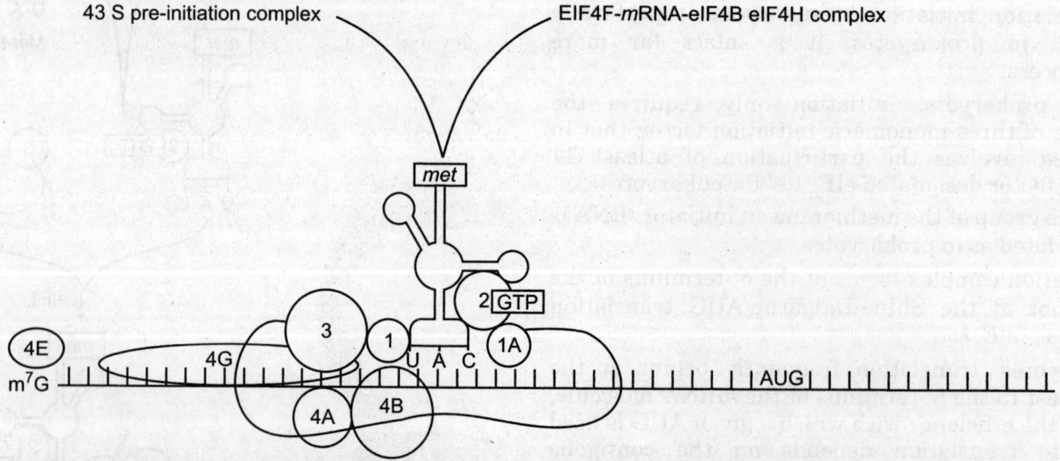

Fig. 8.15 Binding of activated *t* RNA to ribosome *m*RNA complex

Step 6 eIF5 joins the growing assembly. The 43 S pre-initiation complex then translocates along the *m*RNA, an ATP dependent process called scanning until it encounters the *m*RNAs AUG initiation codon thereby yielding 48 S initiation complex.

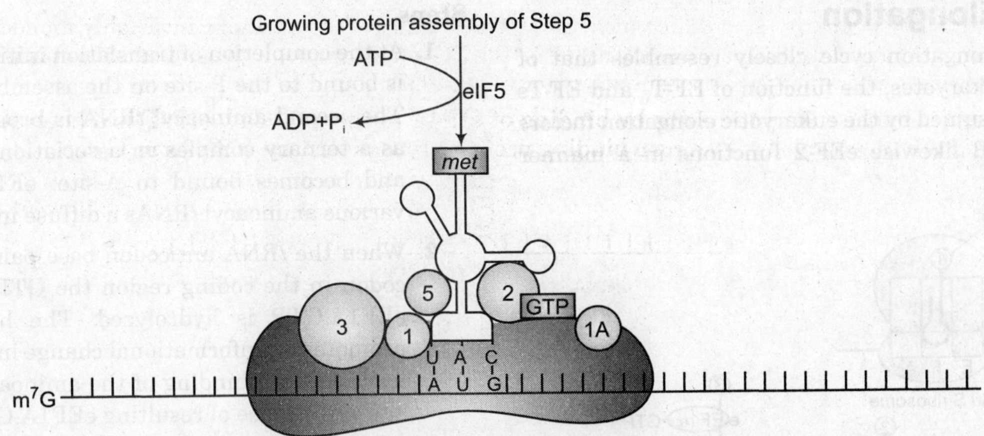

Fig. 8.16 48 S initiation complex

Step 7 The formation of 48 S initiation complex induces eIF2 to hydrolyze its bound GTP to GDP + P_i, which results in the release of all the initiation factor thereby leaving *met-t*RNA$_i^{met}$ in the small subunits P-site. The hydrolysis reaction is stimulated by eIF5.

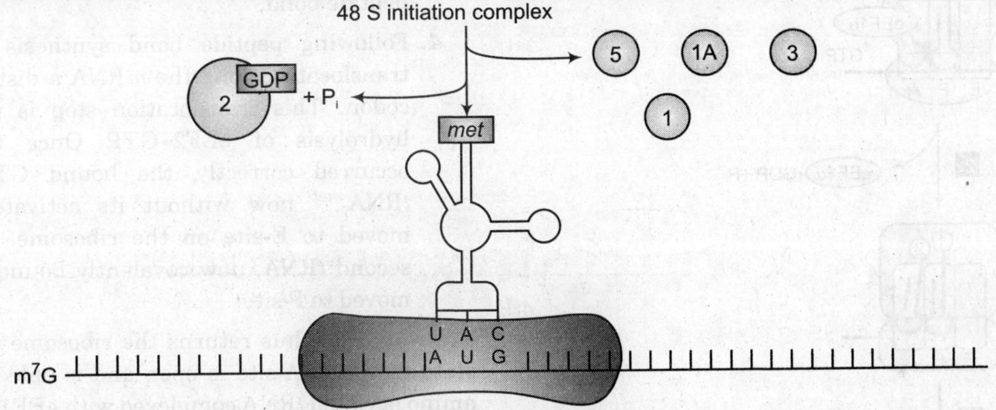

Fig. 8.17 Release of initiation factors

Step 8 The 60 S subunit then joins the *m*RNA bound *met-t*RNA$_i^{met}$ - 40 S subunit complex in a GTPase reaction mediated by eIF5B thereby yielding the 80 S ribosomal initiation complex. Thus, eukaryotic translation initiation consumes 2GTPs *versus* one for prokaryotic initiation.

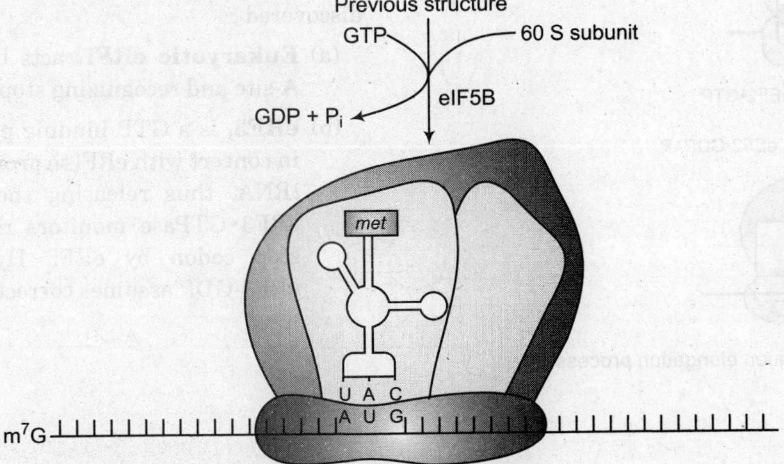

Fig. 8.18 80 S initiation complex

Eukaryotic Elongation

The eukaryotic elongation cycle closely resembles that of prokaryotes. In eukaryotes, the function of EF-T_u and EF-Ts are respectively assumed by the eukaryotic elongation factors eEF1A and eEF1B likewise eEF-2 functions in a manner analogous to EF-G.

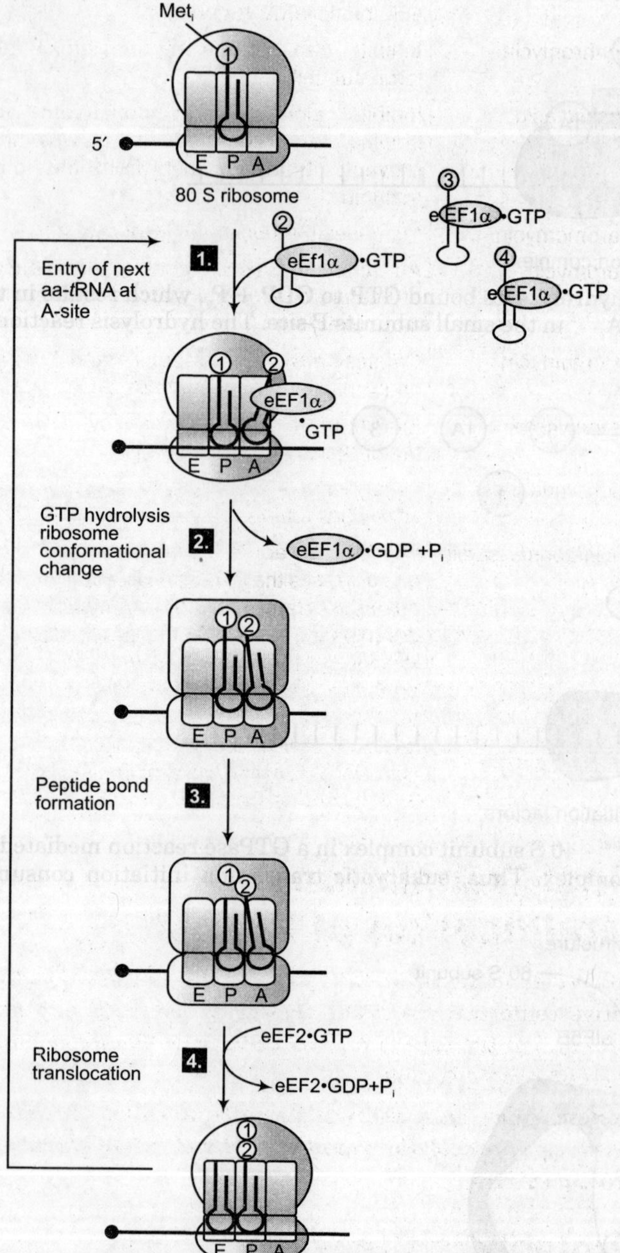

Fig. 8.19 Translation elongation process

Steps

1. At the completion of translation initiation *met-t*RNA_i^{met} is bound to the P-site on the assembled 80 S ribosome. The second aminoacyl *t*RNA is brought into ribosome as a ternary complex in association with eEF1A-GTP and becomes bound to A-site. eF1A•GTP bound to various aminoacyl *t*RNAs a diffuse into the A-site.
2. When the *t*RNA anticodon base pairs with the second codon in the coding region the GTP in the associated eEF1A.GTP is hydrolyzed. The hydrolysis of GTP promotes a conformational change in the ribosome that leads to tight binding of the aminoacyl *t*RNA in the A site and release of resulting eEF1A.GDP complex.
3. With the initiating *met-t*RNA_i^{met} at the P-site and second aminoacyl *t*RNA tightly bound at the A-site, the α-amino group of the second amino acid reacts with the 'activated' methionine on the initiator *t*RNA forming peptide bond.
4. Following peptide bond synthesis the ribosome is translocated along the *m*RNA a distance equal to one codon. This translocation step is monitored by the hydrolysis of eEF2•GTP. Once translocation has occurred correctly, the bound GTP is hydrolyzed *t*RNA_i^{met} now without its activated methionine is moved to E-site on the ribosome. Concurrently the second *t*RNA, now covalently bound to a dipeptide is moved to P-site.

Translocation thus returns the ribosome conformation to a state in which A-site is open and is able to accept another amino acylated *t*RNA complexed with eEF1A•GTP beginning another cycle of chain elongation.

Chain Termination

Two types of specific protein release factors (RFs) have been discovered :

(a) **Eukaryotic eRFl** acts by binding to the ribosomal A-site and recognizing stop codons directly.

(b) **eRF3,** is a GTP binding protein. The eRF3•GTP acts in concert with eRFl to promote cleavage of the peptidyl *t*RNA, thus releasing the completed protein chain. eRF3•GTPase monitors the correct recognition of a stop codon by eRFl. Hydrolysis of eRF3-GTP to eRF3-GDP assumes correct termination of translation.

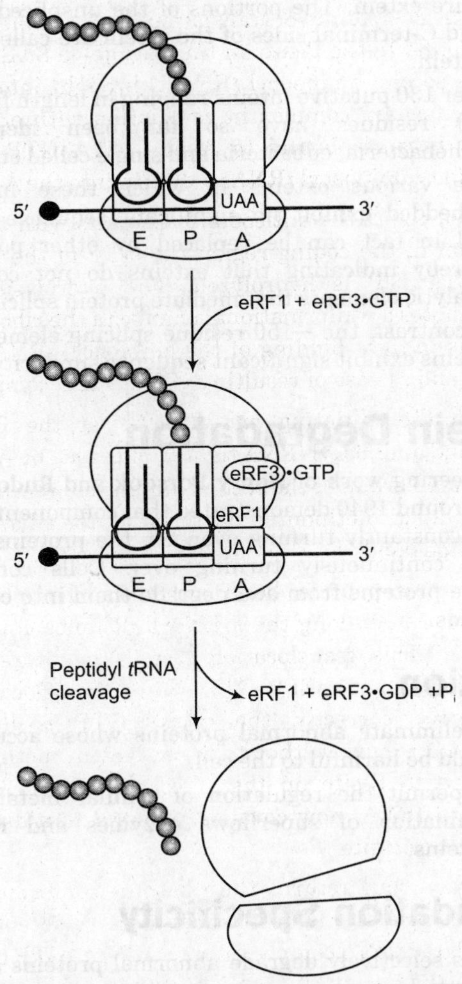

Fig. 8.20 Termination of translation in eukaryotes

- Bacteria have two release factors (RF1 and RF2 that are functionally analogous to eRF1 and a GTP binding factor (RF3) that is analogous to eRF3.

Translational Inhibitors: Antibiotics

Antibiotics are bacterially or fungally produced substances that inhibit the growth of other organism. Antibiotics are known to inhibit a variety of essential biological processes, including DNA replication (*e.g.,* ciprofloxin) transcription (*e.g.,* rifamycin B) and bacterial cell wall synthesis (*e.g.,* penicillin). However the majority of known antibiotics, including a great variety of medically useful substances, blocks translation. This situation is presumably a consequence of the translation machinery's enormous complexity which makes it vulnerable to disruption in many ways. Antibiotics have also been useful in analyzing ribosomal mechanisms.

Table 8.2 **Some Translation Inhibitors**

Inhibitor	Action
Chloramphenicol	Inhibits peptidyl transferase on the prokaryotic large subunit.
Cycloheximide	Inhibits peptidyl transferase in the eukaryotic large subunit.
Erythromycin	Inhibits translocation by the prokaryotic large subunit.
Fusidic acid	Inhibits elongation in prokaryotes by binding to EF-G • GDP in a way that prevents its dissociation from the large subunit.
Paromomycin	Increases the ribosomal error rate.
Puromycin	An aminoacyl *t*RNA analog that causes premature chain termination in prokaryotes and eukaryotes.
Streptomycin	Causes *m*RNA misreading and inhibits chain initiation in prokaryotes.
Tetracycline	Inhibits the binding of aminoacyl *t*RNAs to the prokaryotic small subunit.
Diphtheria toxin	Catalytically inactivates eEF2 by ADP-ribosylation.
Ricin/abrin/α-sarcin	Ricin and abrin are poisonous plant glycosidases that catalytically inactivate the eukaryotic large subunit by hydrolytically depurinating a specific highly conserved A residue of the 28 SRNA, which is located on the so, called sarcin-ricin loop that forms a critical part of the ribosomal factor binding center; α-sarcin is a fungal protein that cleaves a specific phosphodiester bond in the sarcin-ricin loop.

Post-Translational Modification of Protein

To become mature proteins, polypeptides must fold to their native conformations, their disulphide bonds, if any must form and in the case of multi-subunit proteins the subunits must properly combine.

Proteins may be post-translationally modified in various ways, *e.g.,* proteolytic cleavage, covalent modification and protein splicing.

Proteolytic Cleavage

Proteolytic cleavage is the most common type of post translational modification. Probably all mature proteins have been so modified if by nothing less than proteolytic removal of their leading Met (or *f-met*) residue shortly after it emerges from the ribosome.

(i) Proteolytic cleavage usually by specific peptidases activates proproteins. The signal peptides of preproteins are removed by signal peptidases.

(ii) Inactivative proteins that are activated by the removal of polypeptides are called proproteins, whereas the excised polypeptides are called propeptides.

Example

(a) Conversion of trypsinogen and chymotripsinogen to their active forms by cleavage of specific peptide bonds.

(b) Formation of active insulin from the 84 residue proinsulin by the excision of its internal 33 residue C-chain.

Covalent Modification

Covalent modification alters many types of side chains in a variety of ways that modulate the catalytic activities of enzymes, provide recognition markers and stabilize protein structures.

Proteins are subject to specific chemical derivatizations both at the functional groups of their side chains and at their terminal amino or carboxyl groups.

These includes

(a) Acetylation
(b) Glycosylation
(c) Hydroxylation
(d) Methylation
(e) Nucleotidylations
(f) Phosphorylation
(g) ADP ribosylation as well as numerous miscellaneous modifications.

Phosphorylation

Phosphorylation occurs on the hydroxyl groups of serine, threonine or less frequently, tyrosine residues in a proteins. Phosphorylation is catalyzed by one of a family of protein kinases and may be reversed by action of cellular protein phosphatases. Phosphorylation may increase or decrease the functional activity of a protein.

Glycosylation

Many of the proteins that are destined to become part of plasma membrane or lysosome or to be secreted from cell have a carbohydrate chain attached to serine or threonine hydroxyl group (O-linked or amine nitrogen of asparagine (N-linked).

Hydroxylation

Proline and lysine residues of the α-chains of collagen are extensively hydroxylated in endoplasmic reticulum.

Protein Splicing

Protein splicing is a post-transcriptional modification process in which an internal protein segment (an intein) excises itself from the surrounding external protein, which ligates to form the mature extein. The portions of the unspliced extein on the N-and C-terminal sides of the intein are called N-extein and C-extein.

(i) Over 130 putative inteins ranging in length from 134 to 600 residues have so far been identified in archebacteria, eubacteria and single celled eukaryotes.

(ii) The various exteins in which these inteins are embedded exhibit no significant sequence similarity and in fact can be replaced by other polypeptides thereby indicating that exteins do not contain the catalytic elements that mediate protein splicing.

(iii) In contrast, the ~150 residue splicing elements of the Inteins exhibit significant sequence similarity.

Protein Degradation

The pioneering work of **Henry Borsook** and **Rudolf Schoen Heimer** around 1940 demonstrated that components of living cells are constantly turning over. So, the proteins in living cells are continuously turning over. Cells continuously synthesize proteins from and degrade them into component amino acids.

Function

(i) To eliminate abnormal proteins whose accumulation would be harmful to the cell.

(ii) To permit the regulation of cellular metabolism by elimination of superflows enzymes and regulatory proteins.

Degradation Specificity

(i) Cells selectively degrade abnormal proteins and is an essential recycling mechanism that prevents the build up of substances that would otherwise interfere with cellular processes.

(ii) The most rapidly degraded enzymes all occupy importat metabolic control points, whereas the relatively stable enzymes have nearly constant catalytic activities under all physiological conditions.

(iii) The rate of protein degradation in a cell also varies with its nutritional and hormonal state. Under conditions of nutritional deprivation cell increase their rate of protein degradation so, as to provide the necessary nutrients for indespensible metabolic processes.

Degradation Mechanisms

Eukaryotic cells have dual systems for protein degradation.

(i) Lysosomal mechanism.
(ii) ATP-dependent cytosolically based mechanisms.

Lysosomal Mechanism

Lysosomes mostly degrade proteins non-selectively lysosomes are membrane encapsulated organelles that contain ~50 hydrolytic enzymes including a variety of proteases known as **cathepsins.** The lysosomes maintain an internal pH of ~5 and its enzyme have acidic pH optima. This situation presumably protects the cells against accidental lysosomal leakages since lysosomal enzymes are largely inactive at cytosolic pH's.

(a) Lysosomes recycle intracellular constituents by fusing with membrane enclosed bits of cytoplasm known as autophagic vacuoles and subsequently breaking down their contents. They similarily degrade substances that the cells takes up *via* endocytosis.

(b) Lysosomal protein degradation in well nourished cells appears to be non-selective. Lysosomes also have a selective pathway which is activated only after a prolonged fast, that takes up and degrade proteins containing the pentapeptide Lys-Phe-Glu-Arg-Gn (KFERQ) or a closely related sequence.

ATP Dependent Cytosolically Based Mechanism

Proteins that are selected for degradation are so marked by covalently linking them to ubiquitin. A cytosolically based ATP dependent system degrades normal as well as abnormal proteins in process that flags these proteins by the covalent attachment of polyubiquitin chains to their Lys-residues. This process is mediated by three consecutively activating enzymes

(a) Ubiquitin activating enzyme (E1).

(b) Ubiquitin conjugating enzyme (E2).

(c) Ubiquitin protein ligase (E3).

Most cells have one species of E1, several species of E2 and many species of E3, each of which is served by one or a few E2s. These polyubiquitinated proteins is proteolytically degraded in the 26 S proteasome.

Ubiquitin It is required for ATP dependent protein degradation. This 76 residue monomeric protein is so named because it is ubiquitous as well as abundant in eukaryotes, and is the most highly conserved protein known.

26 S Proteasome A ubiquitinated protein is proteolytically degraded to short peptide in an ATP dependent process mediated by a large multisubunit protein complex named 26 S proteasome.

Exercise

1. The formation of the peptide bond is catalyzed by
(a) aminoacyl *t*RNA synthetase
(b) GTP
(c) tryptophan
(d) peptidyl transferase

2. The charged initiator *t*RNA binds initially to the .... in protein synthesis.
(a) 3′ end of *m*RNA (b) P-site
(c) A-site (d) E-site

3. The shift of *m*RNA by three nucleotides in order to bring another codon into position in the ribosome is called
(a) transport (b) translation
(c) translocation (d) transcription

4. The final location in the ribosome that the uncharged *t*RNA is thought to move to before exiting the ribosome is called the
(a) termination codon (b) A-site
(c) P-site (d) E-site

5. If a genetic code is degenerate, it means that
(a) a given base triplet can code for more than one amino acid
(b) there is no punctuation in the code sequences
(c) the third base in a codon is not important in coding
(d) a given amino acid can be coded for by more than one base triplet

6. Which of the following amino acids has the greatest number of codons?
(a) Proline (b) Leucine
(c) Tryptophan (d) Aspartic acid

7. 'Isoaccepting *t*RNAs' are
I. Multiple *t*RNAs that recognize synonym *m*RNA codons (third base degeneracy).
II. Multiple *t*RNAs that react with the same codon.
III. Multiple *t*RNAs representing the same amino acid.
IV. Multiple *t*RNAs recognized by the same aminoacyl *t*RNA synthetase.
(a) I and II (b) II and III
(c) III and IV (d) I, II, III and IV

8. The Wobble hypothesis refers to the less stringent base pairing specificity of the
(a) 5′ end base of the codon
(b) 3′ end base of the anticodon
(c) Middle base of the anticodon
(d) 5′ end base of the anticodon

9. Which base(s) in the anticodon contribute to the degeneracy in codon reading?
(a) First (b) Second
(c) Third (d) Both (a) and (b)

10. Transfer RNA specifies amino acids, during proteins synthesis. *t*RNA is charged with amino acid at 3′ end and its anticodon pairs with codon of *m*RNA. Select the incorrect statement out of the following?
(a) Information is transmitted between 3′ end of *t*RNA and anticodon
(b) Codon-anticodon interaction occurs in A-site of ribosome
(c) Each *t*RNA has specific anticodon
(d) Each codon is triplet

11. IF2 and GTP are examples of
(a) elongation factors (b) translation factors
(c) *t*RNA factors (d) initiation factors

12. The growing polypeptide chain in the ribosome during translation is attached to the
(a) 3′ end of a *t*RNA (b) 3′ end of the *m*RNA
(c) 5′ end of the *m*RNA (d) small subunit

13. EF-T_u is an example of
(a) an elongation factor
(b) an enzyme catalyzing peptide bond formation
(c) a termination factor
(d) an anticodon

14. How many polypeptides chains can be formed simultaneously by a given ribosome?
(a) One
(b) Up to 30
(c) Variable, deadening on the length of the *m*RNA
(d) Variable, depending both on length of *m*RNA and temperature

15. Three of the four eukaryotic *r*RNAs are synthesized from a single transcription unit consisting of the *r*DNA. Which one of the following does not belong to this group?
(a) 5.8 S (b) 5 S
(c) 18 S (d) 28 S

16. Wobble base pairs function during protein synthesis by allowing a non Watson-Crick base pair to be formed between?
(a) G at 5′ end of the anticodon and U at the 3′ end of the codon
(b) G at the 3′ end of the anticodon and U at the 5′ end of the codon
(c) A at the 5′ end of the anticodon and G at the 3′ end of the codon
(d) A at the 3′ end of the anticodon and G at the 5′ end of the codon

17. A genetic unit that codes amino acid sequence of a complete functional polypeptide could be termed as
(a) recon (b) intron
(c) exon (d) cistron

18. An amioacyl *t*RNA synthetase is responsible for
(a) formation of a peptide bond
(b) binding of *m*RNA to ribosomes
(c) attaching an amino group to an organic acid
(d) joining an amino acid to *t*RNA

19. The number of amnioacyl *t*RNA synthetase is determined by the
(a) number of existing *t*RNAs
(b) number of transferable *m*RNA codons
(c) number of utilized amino acids
(d) individual organism species

20. GTP is required by which of the following steps in protein synthesis?
(a) Aminoacyl *t*RNA synthetase activation of amino acids
(b) Attachment of ribosomes to ER
(c) Translocation of *t*RNA-nascent protein complex from A to P-sites
(d) Attachment of *m*RNA to ribosomes

21. Translation of *m*RNA in a ribosome proceeds ....
(a) from the 3′ end to the 5′ end
(b) from the middle to the 3′ end and then from the middle to the 5′ end
(c) from either the 5′ or 3′ end, depending on the enzymes present
(d) from the 5′ end to the 3′ end

22. Multiple sites translating simultaneously the code sequence on different parts of a single *m*RNA molecule constitute a
(a) polymorphism (b) polynucleotide
(c) polypeptide (d) polyribosome

23. In a polysome, which ribosomes will have synthesized the longest peptide chains at any one time?
(a) The ones nearest the 5′ end of the *m*RNA molecule
(b) The ones nearest the AUG codon in the *m*RNA
(c) The ones nearest the 3′ end of the *m*RNA molecule
(d) The ones nearest the middle of the *m*RNA molecule

24. Formylmethionine *t*RNA is present in
(a) yeast (b) bacteria
(c) insects (d) mammals

25. All of the following factors are required to initiate translation of *m*RNA in prokaryotes except
(a) formylmethionine *t*RNA
(b) 30 S ribosomal subunits
(c) guanosine triphosphate
(d) EF-T_u

26. GUG codes for valine in both prokaryotes and eukaryotes but when GUG is initiation codon, this codes
(a) methionine (b) valine
(c) tryptophane (d) None of these

27. At initiation the two ribosomal subunits combine with *m*RNA and
(a) therionine charged *t*RNA
(b) methionine charged *t*RNA
(c) serine charged *t*RNA
(d) proline charged *t*RNA

28. Shine-Dalgarno sequence of *m*RNA is helpful in
(a) recognition of 50 S ribosomal subunit
(b) recognition of 60 S ribosomal subunit
(c) recognition of 5 S *r*RNA
(d) recognition of 30 S subunit of ribosome

29. 'Kozak' is associated with
(a) transcription (b) DNA replication
(c) DNA repair (d) translation

30. Based on the schematic animation that you have just seen, which of the following would you say is true?
(a) The large subunit acts primarily to decode *m*RNA
(b) The large subunit acts primarily to form peptide bonds
(c) The small subunit acts primarily to form peptide bonds
(d) The small subunit acts primarily to decode *t*RNA

31. Initiation of protein synthesis from most eukaryotic *m*RNA requires
(a) a 3′ poly A tail (b) a 5′ cap
(c) a 3′ cap (d) Both (a) and (b)

32. In the protein synthesis, *t*RNA carrying the initiating amino acid enters in which site of ribosome?
(a) A-site (b) P-site
(c) Anticodon site (d) Recognition site

33. Which of following protein factors are required for the addition of an amino acid residue to a growing polypeptide chain during protein biosynthesis in *E. coli*?
(a) IF1, IF2 and IF3 (b) Factor G
(c) Factor R (d) Factors T_u and T_s

34. Synthesis of peptide bond is catalyzed by
(a) A-site of ribosome (b) P-site of ribosome
(c) 23 S *r*RNA (d) *t*RNA

35. *E. coli* release factor 1 (RF1) recognizes which codon?
(a) UAA only (b) UGA only
(c) Both (a) and (b) (d) UAG and UAA

36. What is the E-site of the ribosome?
(a) The site, where eukaryotic *m*RNA is processed
(b) An exciting term made up by your instructor
(c) The site, where *t*RNA exists the prokaryotic ribosome
(d) The site, where the endonuclease *Eco* RI restricts the ribosome

37. How many energy bonds are expended in the formation of a peptide bond?
(a) 2 (b) 4
(c) 3 (d) 6

38. Ribosomes are located
(a) in the cytoplasm
(b) on the endoplasmic reticulum
(c) in the nucleus
(d) in the cytoplasm and on the endoplasmic reticulum

39. Which of the following is not an antibacterial antibiotic?
(a) Tetracycline (b) Streptomycin
(c) Nystatin (d) Nalidixic acid

40. Chloramphenicol inhibits
(a) cell wall synthesis in bacteria
(b) protein synthesis on 70 S ribosome
(c) protein synthesis on 80 S ribosome
(d) DNA replication

41. An antibiotic that resembles the 3′ end of a charged *t*RNA molecule is
(a) streptomycin (b) penicillin
(c) tetracycline (d) puromycin

42. Chaperone protein help in
(a) protein folding and assembly
(b) protein stability
(c) Both (a) and (b)
(d) None of the above

43. Which of the following post-translational modifications of proteins does not occur in the lumen of the ER?
(a) Glycosylation
(b) Formation of disulphide bonds
(c) Folding and formation of quaternary structure
(d) Ubiquitination

44. The term 'protein splicing' refers to
(a) removal of intervening sequences between the genes
(b) splicing out of introns from RNA
(c) removal of intervening protein sequences from the translated protein
(d) joining (splicing) of two different gene products to generate a novel protein

45. Which one of the following statements is true about *t*RNA?
(a) It binds to DNA initiating translation
(b) It has a greater molecular weight than *m*RNA
(c) Transfers the code from the nucleus to cytoplasm
(d) There is at least one form for each kind of amino acid

46. The second event in translation after *m*RNA binding is
(a) synthesis of amino acids from glucose and ammonia
(b) translocation of the nuclear envelope
(c) joining together of the two ribosomal subunits
(d) rotation of the polysomal unit

47. The enzyme aminocyl synthetase facilitates
(a) joining two neighbouring amino acids on ribosomes
(b) transfer of aminoacyl *t*RNA from the ribosomal A-site to P-site
(c) insertion of aminoacyl *t*RNA into the ribosome sites
(d) adoption of amino acid by a *t*RNA molecule of its type

48. Non-sense codon takes part in
(a) formation of unspecified amino acids
(b) releasing *t*RNA from polypeptide chain
(c) conversion of sense DNA into non-sense one
(d) terminating message of gene controlled protein synthesis

49. Which one of the following statements about protein synthesis in an eukaryotic cell is true?
(a) Formylated *t*RNA is important for initiation of translation
(b) Cycloheximide blocks elongation during translation
(c) Single *m*RNAs specify for more than one gene product
(d) Erythromycin inhibits elongation during translation

50. Protein synthesis in bacteria stops when an antibiotic, puromycin, is added because
(a) puromycin resembles tyrosyl *t*RNA
(b) it binds at 'A' binding site and terminates the polypeptide chain
(c) it binds to peptide with the C-terminus of growing polypeptide resulting in termination of polypeptide chain
(d) its peptidyl end resembles the tyrosyl *t*RNA and helps binding of the amino acid tyrosine

51. The polypeptide chain initiation in a prokaryotic cell always begins with the amino acid F-methionine because
(a) no peptide bond formation can take place at the amino end of F-methionine as it is formylated
(b) F-methionine is available in abundance is formylated
(c) F-methionine can help chain elongation
(d) only one *t*RNA can attach with F-methionine

52. Eukaryotic proteins are isoprenylated,
(a) isoprenyl group is attached at the 3′ end of the polypeptide chain
(b) isoprenyl group is deleted from the protein
(c) a thioester bond is formed between the isoprenyl group and cys residue of the protein
(d) an ester bond is formed between isoprenyl group and ser residue of the protein

53. The bonds between the anticodon of a *t*RNA molecule and the complementary codon of *m*RNA are
(a) formed by the input of energy from GTP
(b) formed by the input of energy from ATP
(c) hydrogen bonds
(d) catalyzed by aminoacyl *t*RNA synthetase

54. It is possible for a cell to make proteins that last for months; haemoglobin in red blood cells is a good example. However, many proteins are not this long-lasting. They may be degraded in days or even hours. Why do cells make proteins with such short lifetimes if it is possible to make them last longer?
(a) Most proteins are used only once
(b) Most cells in the body live only a few days
(c) Only cancer cells, which can keep dividing contain long-lasting proteins
(d) This enables cells to control the amount of protein present

55. A sequence of pictures of polypeptide synthesis shows a ribosome holding two transfer RNAs. One *t*RNA has a polypeptide chain attached to it; the other *t*RNA has a single amino acid attached to it. What does the next picture show?
(a) The polypeptide chain moves over and bonds to the single amino acid
(b) The *t*RNA with the amino acid leaves the ribosome
(c) The amino acid moves over and bonds to the polypeptide chain
(d) The *t*RNA with the polypeptide chain leaves the ribosome

56. Which of the following processes occurs in the cytoplasm of a eukaryotic cell?
(a) DNA replication
(b) Translation
(c) DNA replication and translation
(d) Translation and transcription

57. Beadle and Tatum showed that each kind of mutant bread mold lacked a specific enzyme. This experiment demonstrated that
(a) genes carry information for making proteins
(b) mutations are changes in genetic information
(c) genes are made of DNA
(d) enzymes are required to repair damaged DNA information

58. Which of the following statements is not true for Ubiquitin mediated proteolysis?
(a) Ubiquitinylated proteins are degraded in the lysosome
(b) Ubiquitin is polypeptide of 76 amino acids
(c) Ubiquitination occurs at a specific amino acid of the target proteins
(d) Following ubiquitination, proteins are degraded by proteasomes

59. Imagine an error occurring during DNA replication in a cell, so that where there is supposed to be a T in one of the genes there is instead a G. What effect will this probably have on the cell?
(a) Each of its kinds of proteins will contain an incorrect amino acid
(b) An amino acid will be missing from each of its kinds of proteins
(c) One of its kinds of proteins might contain an incorrect amino acid
(d) An amino acid will be missing from one of its kinds of proteins

60. In Beadle and Tatum's study of *Neurospora,* they were able to identify three classes of arginine auxotrophs, mutants that needed arginine added to minimal media in order to grow. The pathway in the production of arginine includes the following steps: precursor → ornithine → citrulline → arginine. What nutrient (s) had to be added to the minimal medium in order for the class of mutant with a defective enzyme for the precursor → ornithine step to grow?
(a) Precursor only
(b) Ornithine only
(c) Citrulline only
(d) Ornithine or citrulline

61. Which of the following is not true of an anticodon?
(a) It consists of three nucleotides
(b) It is the basic unit of the genetic code
(c) It extends from one end of a *t*RNA molecule
(d) It may pair with more than one codon, especially if it has the base inosine in its third position

62. RNA polymerase
(a) is the protein responsible for the production of ribonucleotides
(b) is the enzyme that creates hydrogen bonds between nucleotides on the DNA template strand and their complementary RNA nucleotides
(c) is a ribozyme composed of snRNPs
(d) begins transcription at a promoter sequence and moves along the template strand of DNA in 5′ → 3′ direction

63. What is the function of initiation factor IF3?
(a) If bound to the 40 S subunit, it facilitates the association of the 40 S and 60 S subunits
(b) If bound to the 30 S subunit, it prevents the association of the 30 S and 50 S subunits
(c) If bound to the 30 S subunit, it allows the 16 S *r*RNA of the 30 S subunit to interact with the Shine-Dalgarno sequence of the *m*RNA
(d) It directs the initiator *t*RNA to enter the partial P-site on the 30 S subunit bound to *m*RNA

64. A loss of function mutation in the gene that encodes the catabolite activator protein of *E. coli* would have what effect on expression of the *lac* operon?
(a) Expression would be very high in the presence of lactose and off in its absence regardless of the presence or absence of glucose
(b) Expression would be low in the presence of lactose and off in its absence, regardless of the presence or absence of glucose
(c) Expression would be low in the presence of glucose and very high in its absence, regardless of the presence or absence of lactose
(d) Expression would be off in the presence of glucose and low in its absence, regardless of the presence or absence of lactose

65. Translocation involves,
(a) the hydrolysis of a GTP molecule
(b) the movement of the *t*RNA in the A-site to the P-site
(c) the movement of the *m*RNA strand one triplet length in the A-site
(d) All of the above

66. Changes in a polypeptide following translation may involve,
(a) the addition of sugars or lipids to certain amino acids
(b) the action of enzymes to add amino acids at the beginning of the chain
(c) the removal of poly-A from the end of the chain
(d) the addition of a 5′ cap of a modified guanosine residue
(e) All of the above

67. Several proteins may be produced at the same time from a single *m*RNA by
(a) the action of several ribosomes in a cluster called a polyribosome
(b) several RNA polymerase molecules working sequentially
(c) signal sequences that associate ribosomes with rough ER
(d) containing several promoter regions

68. Which enzyme is responsible for the synthesis of *t*RNA?
(a) RNA replicase
(b) RNA polymerase
(c) Aminoacyl *t*RNA synthetase
(d) Ribosomal enzymes

69. During peptide bond synthesis, which of the following step does not require an input of energy?
(a) An amino acid activation
(b) The formation of the 70 S initiation complex of prokaryotes
(c) The binding of the aminoacyl *t*RNA to the A-site on the ribosome
(d) The movement of peptidyl *t*RNA to the P-site

70. All of the following statements about amino acid activation are correct except
(a) aminoacyl *t*RNA synthetases transfer the amino acids to the A on the 3′ end of *t*RNA *via* an aminoacyl adenosine monophosphate intermediate
(b) the aminoacyl *t*RNA synthetase is specific for a given amino acid
(c) there may be more than one kind of *t*RNA for a given amino acid
(d) the activation step requires the hydrolysis of the terminal phosphate group of guanosine triphosphate

71. Which one of the following statements correctly describes initiation of protein synthesis in *E. coli?*
(a) The initiator *t*RNA binds to the Shine-Dalgarno sequence
(b) Three initiation factors are involved and IF2 binds to GTP
(c) The intermediate containing IF1, IF2, IF3 initiator *t*RNA and *m*RNA is called the 30 S initiation complex
(d) Binding of the 50 S subunit releases IF1, IF2, GMP and PP_i

72. Which of the following staements about the diphtheria toxin are correct?
(a) It is cleaved on the surface of susceptible eukaryotic cells into two fragments, one of which enters the cytosol
(b) It binds to peptidyl transferase and inhibits protein synthesis
(c) It reacts with ATP to phosphorylate eIF2 and prevent the insertion of the *met-t*RNA_i into the P-site
(d) It reacts with NAD^+ to add ADP-ribose to eEF2 and prevent movement of the peptidyl *t*RNA from the A to the P-site

73. The Wobble hypothesis explains
(a) how multiple different types of *t*RNA are charged with a single type of amino acid?
(b) how multiple stop codons can associate with the same release factor?
(c) how multiple stop codons can associate with the same codon?
(d) how one *t*RNA can associate with multiple codons?

74. Which of the following occurs when the eukaryotic translational machinery encounters the UAG codon?
(a) The ribosome can recognize the UAG codon as a translational stop codon and does not allow any *t*RNA to bind the *m*RNA
(b) The termination factors recognize this codon and translation ends
(c) This codon is recognized by the corresponding anticodon of an empty *t*RNA molecule that is not linked to an amino acid
(d) The non-recognition of this codon by any *t*RNA ultimately causes the translational machinery to stop

75. Characteristics of prokaryotic ribosomes include which of the following?
I. They are composed of two subunit particles with sedimentation coefficients of 30 I and 50 S.
II. They are composed of about 65% RNA and about 35% protein.
III. They can be split into their component subunits by treatment with a Mg^{2+} chelator.
IV. They have all of their protein in the 50 S subunit.
(a) I and II (b) II and III
(c) I, II and III (d) I, II, III and IV

76. Which of the following statements about the ribosomal peptidyl transferase activity is correct?
I. The peptidyl transferase activity resides in the large (50 S or 60 S) ribosomal subunit.
II. It facilitates transfer of the C-terminus of the peptide chain from the peptidyl *t*RNA to the N-terminus of the aminoacyl *t*RNA in the A-site.
III. If facilitates transfer of the N-terminus of the aminoacyl *t*RNA from the A-site to the C-terminus of the peptidyl *t*RNA in the P-site by deacylation of aminoacyl *t*RNA.
IV. It hydrolyses GTP in order to allow for translocation of the ribosome.
(a) I and II (b) II and III
(c) I, II and III (d) I, II, III and IV

77. Peptide bond synthesis requires an input of energy during

I. An amino acid activation.
II. The formation of the 70 S initiation complex of prokaryotes.
III. The binding of the aminoacyl *t*RNA to the A-site on the ribosome.
IV. The movement of the peptidyl *t*RNA to the P-site and the associated movement of the *m*RNA.

(a) I and II (b) I and II
(c) I, II and III (d) I, II, III and IV

78. During the synthesis of secretory proteins the following events happen.

I. The signal recognition particle (SRP) binds to the signal sequence.
II. The two parts of a cytosolic ribosome binds to the *m*RNA.
III. Protein synthesis stops.
IV. The signal sequence is translated.
V. The ribosome and protein are transferred to a translocation.
VI. The secretory protein folds.
VII. The signal sequence is cleaved by a signal peptidase.
VIII. The SRP binds to its receptor in the ER membrane.

The correct order for these events is

(a) IV, I, II, III, VI, VIII, VII, V
(b) II, IV, I, III, VIII, V, VII, VI
(c) I, IV, II, III, VI, V, VIII, VII
(d) II, IV, I, III, V, VIII, VII, VI

79. Which of the following statements about antibiotic inhibitors of protein synthesis is correct?

I. Chloramphenicol inhibits the peptidyl transferase activity of the large ribosomal subunit in eukaryotes.
II. Cycloheximide inhibits the peptidyl transferase activity of the large ribosomal subunit in eukaryotes.
III. Puromycin blocks protein synthesis in prokaryotes only.
IV. Streptomycin inhibits protein synthesis by binding to 30 S ribosomal subunits

(a) I and II
(b) II and III
(c) II and IV
(d) I, II, III and IV

80. Which two of the following statements about initiation of eukaryotic protein synthesis are true?

I. Eukaryotes use a *m*RNA scanning method to locate the correct start codon.
II. There are at least nine eukaryotic initiation factors (eIFs).
III. Eukaryotic initiation uses N-formylmethionine.
IV. The 80 S initiation complex completes the initiation process and contains the initiator *t*RNA base paired to the start codon in the A-site.

(a) I and III (b) II and IV
(c) I, II and III (d) I, II, III and IV

Answers

1. (d)	**2.** (b)	**3.** (c)	**4.** (d)	**5.** (d)	**6.** (b)	**7.** (c)	**8.** (d)	**9.** (a)	**10.** (a)
11. (d)	**12.** (a)	**13.** (a)	**14.** (a)	**15.** (b)	**16.** (a)	**17.** (d)	**18.** (d)	**19.** (c)	**20.** (c)
21. (d)	**22.** (d)	**23.** (c)	**24.** (b)	**25.** (d)	**26.** (a)	**27.** (b)	**28.** (d)	**29.** (d)	**30.** (b)
31. (d)	**32.** (b)	**33.** (d)	**34.** (c)	**35.** (d)	**36.** (c)	**37.** (b)	**38.** (d)	**39.** (c)	**40.** (b)
41. (d)	**42.** (c)	**43.** (d)	**44.** (c)	**45.** (d)	**46.** (c)	**47.** (d)	**48.** (d)	**49.** (d)	**50.** (c)
51. (a)	**52.** (c)	**53.** (c)	**54.** (d)	**55.** (a)	**56.** (b)	**57.** (a)	**58.** (a)	**59.** (c)	**60.** (d)
61. (b)	**62.** (d)	**63.** (b)	**64.** (b)	**65.** (d)	**66.** (a)	**67.** (a)	**68.** (b)	**69.** (d)	**70.** (d)
71. (b)	**72.** (d)	**73.** (d)	**74.** (b)	**75.** (c)	**76.** (a)	**77.** (c)	**78.** (b)	**79.** (c)	**80.** (a)

9

Control of Gene Expression

By switching genes off when they are not needed, cells can prevent resources from being wasted. There should be natural selection favouring the ability to switch genes on and off. Complex multicellular organisms are produced by cells that switch genes on and off during development. A typical human cell normally expresses about 3% to 5% of its genes at any given time. Cancer results from genes that do not turn off properly. Cancer cells have lost their ability to regulate mitosis, resulting in uncontrolled cell division. Regulation of gene expression (or gene regulation) includes the processes that cells and viruses use to regulate the way that the information in genes is turned into gene products. Although a functional gene product can be RNA, the majority of known mechanisms regulate protein coding genes. Any step of the gene's expression may be modulated, from DNA-RNA transcription to the post-translational modification of a protein.

Gene regulation is essential for viruses, prokaryotes and eukaryotes as it increases the versatility and adaptability of an organism by allowing the cell to express protein when needed. Although in 1951, **Barbara McClintock** showed interaction between two genetic loci, Activator (Ac) and Dissociator (Ds), the first discovery of a gene regulation system is widely considered to be the identification in 1961, of the *lac* operon, discovered by **Jacob** and **Monod,** in which protein involved in lactose metabolism are expressed by *E. coli* only in the presence of lactose and absence of glucose.

Furthermore, gene regulation drives the processes of cellular differentiation and morphogenesis, leading to the creation of different cell types in multicellular organisms where, the different types of cells may possess different gene expression profiles though they all possess the same genome sequence. Gene expressions are strictly controlled at many levels to ensure the organism having the appropriate response to its environment or internal changes. In bacteria many functional-related genes are clustered and transcribed under the same types of regulation (operons). An operon usually contains regulatory genes and structure genes. The most studied operons in bacteria are *lac* operons and *trp* operons, in both of which cases the activation or inactivation of repressors plays key roles in gene regulation. This is also true in I phage in terms of regulating its lytic and lysogenic cycles: When cI proteins predominate, phage remains in the lysogenic state; when *cro* proteins predominate, phage enters the lytic state.

Syllabus

- Regulated Stages of Gene Expression, Prokaryotic and Eukaryotic Genes.
- Regulating the Expression of
- Regulation of Expression of Viral and Phage Genes.
- Role of Chromatin in Gene Expression.
- Gene Silencing

Regulated Stages of Gene Expression

Any step of gene expression may be modulated, from the DNA-RNA transcription step to post-translational modification of a protein. The following is a list of stages, where gene expression is regulated the most extensively utilized point is transcription initiation:

1. Chromatin domains
2. Transcription
3. Post-transcriptional modification
4. RNA transport
5. Translation
6. *m*RNA degradation.

Regulation of Transcription

Regulation of transcription controls when transcription occurs and how much RNA is created. Transcription of a gene by RNA polymerase can be regulated by at least five mechanisms:

(i) Specificity factors alter the specificity of RNA polymerase for a given promoter or set of promoters, making it more or less likely to bind to them (*i.e.*, sigma factors used in prokaryotic transcription).

(ii) Repressors bind to non-coding sequences on the DNA strand that are close to or overlapping the promoter region, impeding RNA polymerase's progress along the strand, thus impeding the expression of the gene.

(iii) General transcription factors position RNA polymerase at the start of a protein-coding sequence and then release the polymerase to transcribe the *m*RNA.

(iv) Activators enhance the interaction between RNA polymerase and a particular promoter, encouraging the expression of the gene. Activators do this by increasing the attraction of RNA polymerase for the promoter, through interactions with subunits of the RNA polymerase or indirectly by changing the structure of the DNA.

(v) Enhancers are sites on the DNA helix that are bound to by activators in order to loop the DNA bringing a specific promoter to the initiation complex. Enhancers are much more common in eukaryote than prokaryotes, where only a few examples exist (to date).

Post-transcriptional Regulation

After the DNA is transcribed and *m*RNA is formed, there must be some sort of regulation on how much the *m*RNA is translated into proteins. Cells do this by modulating the capping, splicing, addition of a poly A tail, the sequence-specific nuclear export rates, and, in several contexts, sequestration of the RNA transcript. These processes occur in eukaryotes but not in prokaryotes. This modulation is a result of a protein or transcript that, in turn, is regulated and may have an affinity for certain sequences.

Translational Regulation

The translation of *m*RNA can also be controlled by a number of mechanisms, mostly at the level of initiation. Recruitment of the small ribosomal subunit can indeed be modulated by *m*RNA secondary structure, antisense RNA binding, or protein binding. In both prokaryotes and eukaryotes, a large number of RNA binding proteins exist, which often are directed to their target sequence by the secondary structure of the transcript, which may change depending on certain conditions, such as temperature or presence of a ligand (aptamer). Some transcripts act as ribozymes and self-regulate their expression.

Examples of Gene Regulation

(a) Enzyme induction is a process in which a molecule (*e.g.*, a drug) induces (*i.e.*, initiates or enhances) the expression of an enzyme.

(b) The induction of heat shock proteins in the fruit fly *Drosophila melanogaster.*

(c) The *lac* operon is an interesting example of how gene expression can be regulated.

(d) Viruses, despite having only a few genes, possess mechanisms to regulate their gene expression, typically into an early and late phase, using collinear systems regulated by anti-terminators (lambda phage) or splicing modulators (HIV).

(e) A large number of studied regulatory systems come from developmental biology.

Examples

- The colinearity of the *Hox* gene cluster with their nested antero-posterior patterning.
- It has been speculated that pattern generation of the hand (digits-inter digits). The gradient of Sonic hedgehog (secreted inducing factor) from the zone of polarizing activity in the limb, which creates a gradient of active Gli3, which activates gremlin, which inhibits BMPs also secreted in the limb, resulting in the formation of an alternating pattern of activity as a result of this reaction-diffusion system.
- Somitogenesis is the creation of segments (somites) from a uniform tissue (Pre-Somitic Mesoderm, PSM). They are formed sequentially from anterior to posterior. This is achieved in amniotes possibly by means of two opposing gradients, retinoic acid in the anterior (wave front) and Wnt and Fgf in the posterior, coupled to an oscillating pattern (segmentation clock) composed of FGF + Notch and Wnt in anti-phase.
- Sex determination in the soma of a *Drosophila* requires the sensing of the ratio of autosomal genes to sex chromosome encoded genes, which results in the production of sexless splicing factor in females, resulting in the female isoform of double sex.

Gene Regulatory Network

Various types of gene regulatory networks are given here.

Up-regulation and Down-regulation

Up-regulation is a process that occurs within a cell triggered by a signal (originating internal or external to the cell), which results in increased expression of one or more genes and as a result the protein(s) encoded by those genes. On the converse, down-regulation is a process resulting in decreased gene and corresponding protein expression.

(a) Up-regulation occurs, for example, when a cell is deficient in some kind of receptor. In this case, more receptor protein is synthesized and transported to the membrane of the cell and thus, the sensitivity of the cell is brought back to normal, reestablishing homeostasis.

(b) Down-regulation occurs, for example, when a cell is over stimulated by a neurotransmitter, hormone, or drug for a prolonged period of time, and the expression of the receptor protein is decreased in order to protect the cell (see also tachyphylaxis).

Inducible *Versus* Repressible Systems

Gene regulation can be summarized by the response of the respective system:

(a) **Inducible systems** An inducible system is off unless there is the presence of some molecule (called an inducer) that allows for gene expression. The molecule is said to 'induce expression'. The manner by which this happens is dependent on the control mechanisms as well as differences between prokaryotic and eukaryotic cells.

(b) **Repressible systems** A repressible system is on except in the presence of some molecule (called a corepressor) that suppresses gene expression. The molecule is said to 'repress expression'. The manner by which this happens is dependent on the control mechanisms as well as differences between prokaryotic and eukaryotic cells.

Theoretical Circuits

(a) Repressor/Inducer: an activation of a sensor results in the change of expression of a gene.

(b) Negative feedback: the gene product down regulates its own production directly or indirectly, which can result in.

(c) Keeping transcript levels constant/proportional to a factor.

(d) Inhibition of run-away reactions when coupled with a positive feedback loop.

(e) Creating an oscillator by taking advantage in the time delay of transcription and translation, given that the *m*RNA and protein half-life is shorter.

(f) Positive feedback: the gene product upregulates its own production directly or indirectly, which can result in.

(g) Signal amplification.

(h) Bistable switches when two genes inhibit each other and both have positive feedback.

(i) Pattern generation.

Gene Regulatory Mechanisms in Prokaryotes

Much of our understanding of gene control comes from studies of prokaryotes. They are usually mechanisms that involve the rapid turn-on and turn-off of gene expression in response to environmental changes. They are comprised of pre programmed circuits or cascades of gene expression. They involve sequential expression of genes.

Prokaryotes have two levels of gene control. Transcriptional mechanisms control the synthesis of *m*RNA and translational mechanisms control the synthesis of protein after *m*RNA has been produced.

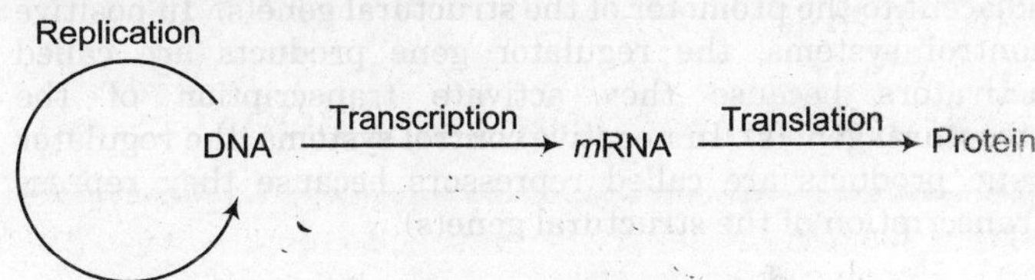

Fig. 9.1 The central dogma

Constitutive, Inducible and Repressible Gene Expression

Genes that specify cellular components that perform housekeeping function, for example, the ribosomal RNAs and proteins involved in protein synthesis—are expressed constitutively. Other genes often are expressed only when their products are required for growth.

Constitutive Genes

Certain gene products (*e.g.*, *t*RNAs, *r*RNAs, ribosomal proteins, RNA polymerase subunits, enzymes catalyzing housekeeping functions) are essential components of almost all living cells. Genes that specify products of this type are continuously expressed in most cells.

Inducible and Repressible Genes

Other gene products are needed for cell growth only under certain environmental conditions. Regulatory mechanisms allow the synthesis of these gene products only, when they are needed.

In prokaryotes, genes that specify housekeeping functions such as *r*RNAs, *t*RNAs and ribosomal proteins are expressed constitutively. Other genes usually are expressed only when their products are needed. Genes that encode enzymes involved in catabolic pathways often are expressed only in the presence of the substrates of the enzymes; their expression is inducible. Genes that encode enzymes involved in anabolic pathways usually are turned off in the presence of the end product of the pathway; their expression is repressible. Although gene expression can be regulated at many levels, transcriptional regulation is the most common.

Positive and Negative Control of Gene Expression

In some cases, the product of a regulatory gene is required to initiate the expression of one or more genes. In other cases, the product of a regulatory gene is required to turn off the expression of one or more genes. Regulator genes encode products that regulate the expression of other genes. In positive control mechanisms, the product of the regulator gene is required to turn on the expression of structural genes. In negative control mechanisms, the product of the regulator gene is necessary to shut off the expression of structural genes. The product of the regulator gene acts by binding to a site called the Regulator Protein Binding Site (RPBS) adjacent to the promoter of the structural gene(s). In positive control systems, the regulator gene products are called activators because they activate transcription of the structural gene(s). In negative control systems, the regulator gene products are called repressors because they repress transcription of the structural gene(s).

Effector Molecules

Whether or not a regulator protein can bind to the RPBS depends on the presence or absence of effector molecules in the cell. Inducers are effector molecules involved in induction of gene expression. Co-repressors are effector molecules involved in repression of gene expression. Small molecules such as amino acids, sugars and similar metabolites.

Allosteric Transitions

Effector molecules bind to regulator gene products and cause conformational changes in protein structure called allosteric transitions. Allosteric transitions caused by the binding of effector molecules to activators and repressors alter their ability to bind to the RPBS. Conformational changes in proteins.

Regulatory Mechanisms

In a positive control mechanism, the activator is involved in turning on gene expression. In a negative control mechanism, the repressor is involved in turning off gene expression. With both positive and negative control mechanisms, whether gene expression is inducible or repressible depends on whether the free regulator protein or the regulator protein/effector molecule complex binds to the RPBS.

Gene expression is controlled by both positive and negative regulatory mechanism. In positive control mechanisms, the product of a regulator gene, an activator, is required to turn on the expression of the structural gene(s). In negative control mechanisms, the product of a regulator gene, a repressor, is required to turn off the expression of the structural gene(s). The examples are presented later. Activators and repressors regulate gene expression by binding to sites adjacent to the promoters of structural genes. Whether or not the regulator proteins can bind to their binding sites depends on the presence or absence of small effector molecules that form complexes with the regulator proteins. The effector molecules are called **inducers in inducible systems** and **co-repressors** in **repressible systems.**

Operons

Operons are groups of genes that function to produce proteins needed by the cell. There are two different kinds of genes in operons:

Structural genes code for proteins needed for the normal operation of the cell. For example, they may be proteins needed for the breakdown of sugars. The structural genes are grouped together and a single *m*RNA molecule is produced during their transcription.

Regulator genes code for proteins that regulate other genes.

A single *m*RNA transcript carries the coding information of an entire operon. Operons containing more than one structural gene are multigenic. All structural genes in an operon are co-transcribed and, therefore are coordinately expressed. In bacterial, genes with related functions frequently occur in coordinately regulated units called operons. Each operon contains a set of contiguous structural genes, a promoter (the binding site for RNA polymerase), and an operator (the binding site for a regulatory protein called a repressor). When a repressor is bound to the operator, RNA polymerase cannot transcribe the structural genes in the operon. When the operator is free of repressor, RNA polymerase can transcribe the operon. Operons have not been found in eukaryotes.

The *lac* Operon

Lactose is a sugar found in milk. If lactose is present, *E. coli* (the common intestinal bacterium) needs to produce the necessary enzymes to digest it. Three different enzymes are needed.

In the diagrams below, genes A, B and C represent the genes whose products are necessary to digest lactose. In the normal condition, the genes do not function because a repressor protein is active and bound to the DNA preventing transcription. When the repressor protein is bound to the DNA, RNA polymerase cannot bind to the DNA. The protein must be removed before the genes can be transcribed.

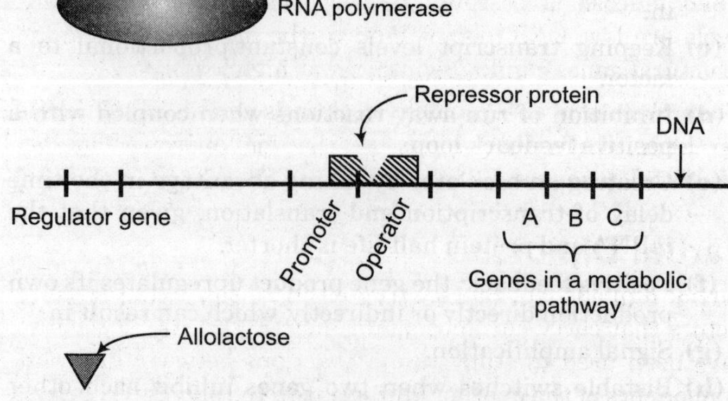

Fig. 9.2 Structure of *lac* operon

Below: Allolactose, an isomer of lactose, binds with the repressor protein inactivating it.

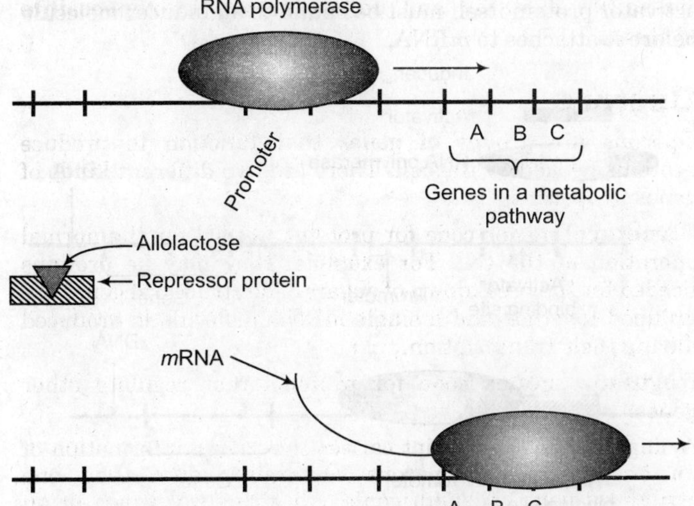

Fig. 9.3 Allolactose binding and activation of structural genes

The repressor protein is produced by a **regulator gene.** The region of DNA, where the repressor protein binds is the operator site. The promoter site is a region of DNA, where RNA polymerase can bind. The entire unit (promoter, operator and genes) is an operon. The operator acts like a switch that can turn several genes on or off at the same time. The *lac* operon is an example of an inducible operon because the structural genes are normally inactive. They are activated when lactose is present.

The *lac* promoter has two components:

1. The RNA polymerase binding site
2. A binding site for Catabolite Activator Protein (CAP). Binding of CAP to the promoter activates transcription of the *lac* operon from being induced when glucose is absent. CAP binds to the promoter only when cyclic AMP (cAMP) is present at sufficient concentrations.

CAP Exerts Positive Control of the *lac* Operon; cAMP is the Effector

When glucose is present adenylcyclase is inactive. cAMP levels are low. CAP cannot bind to the *lac* operon. The *lac* structural genes cannot be induced at high levels.

When glucose is absent adenylcyclase is active. cAMP levels are high. CAP/cAMP binds to the *lac* operon. The *lac* structural genes can be induced.

Partial Diploids

Partial diploids can be constructed in *E. coli* using fertility factors that carry chromosomal genes (F Factors). F Factors have been used to study the interactions between different components of the operon. Mutations in the structural genes, the operator and the repressor can be studied in this way.

The *E. coli lac* operon is a negative inducible and catabolite repressible system; the three structural genes in the *lac* operon are transcribed at high levels only in the presence of lactose and the absence of glucose. In the absence of lactose, the *lac* repressor binds to the *lac* operator and prevents RNA polymerase from initiating transcription of the operon.

Catabolite repression keeps operons such as *lac* encoding enzymes involved in carbohydrate catabolism from being induced in the presence of glucose, the preferred energy source.

The *trp* Operon

Repressible operons are the opposite of inducible operons. Transcription occurs continuously and the repressor protein must be activated to stop transcription. The structural genes in the tryptophan operon are transcribed only when tryptophan is absent or present in low concentrations. The expression of the genes in the *trp* operon is regulated by repression of transcriptional initiation and by attenuation (premature termination) of transcription when tryptophan is prevalent in the environment.

Tryptophan is an amino acid needed by *E. coli* and the genes that code for proteins that produce tryptophan are continuously transcribed as shown below.

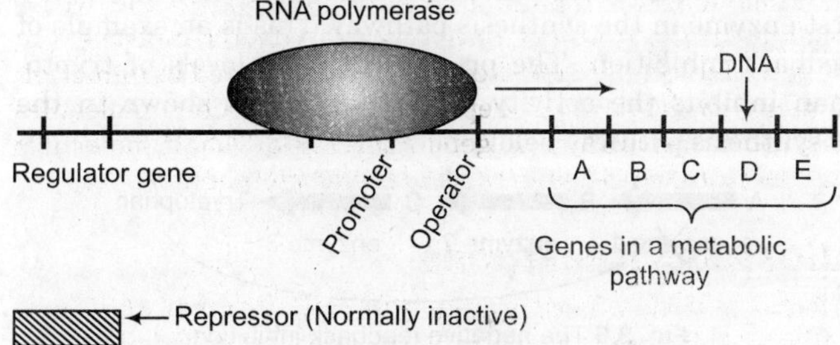

Fig. 9.4 Tryptophan operon

If tryptophan is present in the environment, however, *E. coli* does not need to synthesize it and the tryptophan-synthesizing genes should be turned off. This occurs when tryptophan binds with the repressor protein, activating it. Unlike the repressor discussed with the *lac* operon, this repressor will not bind to the DNA unless it is activated by binding with tryptophan. Tryptophan is therefore, a core-pressor.

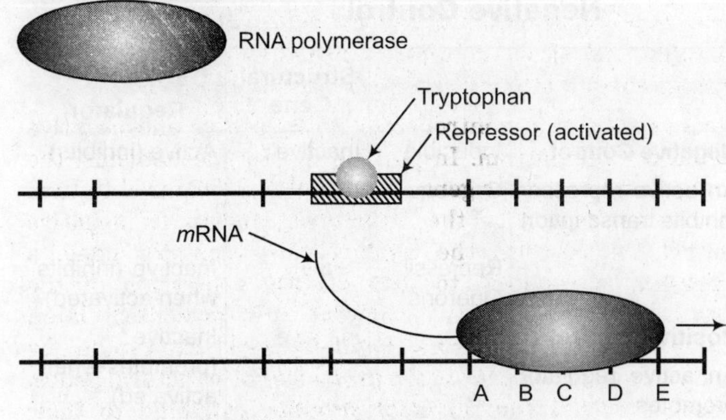

Fig. 9.5 Tryptophan as corepressor

The *trp* operon is an example of a repressible operon because the structural genes are active and are inactivated when tryptophan is present.

The *E. coli trp* operon is a negative repressible system; transcription of the five structural genes in the *trp* operon is repressed in the presence of significant concentrations of tryptophan. Operons such as *trp* that encode enzymes involved in amino acid biosynthetic pathways often are controlled by a second regulatory mechanism called attenuation. Attenuation occurs by the premature termination of transcription at a site in the *m*RNA leader sequence (the sequence 5′ to the coding region) when tryptophan is prevalent in the environment in which the bacteria are growing.

	Structural Gene	Repressor
Inducible Operons	Inactive	Active (inhibits)
Repressible Operons	Active	Inactive (inhibits when activated)

Negative Feedback Inhibition

In addition to genetic regulation, tryptophan can inhibit the first enzyme in the synthesis pathway. This is an example of feedback inhibition. The presence of high levels of tryptophan inhibits the activity of the enzyme as shown in the biosynthesis pathway below.

Fig. 9.6 The negative feedback inhibition

Negative and Positive Control

The *trp* and *lac* operons discussed above are examples of negative control because a repressor blocks transcription. In one case (*lac* operon) the repressor is active and prevents transcription. In the other case (*trp*) the repressor is inactive and must be activated to prevent transcription.

Table 9.1 **Comparison between Positive and Negative Control**

		Structural Gene	Repressor or Regulator
Negative Control An active repressor inhibits transcription	Inducible Operons	Inactive	Active (inhibits)
	Repressible Operons	Active	Inactive (inhibits when activated)
Positive Control An active regulator promotes transcription		Inactive	Inactive (promotes when activated)

Positive control mechanisms require the presence of an activator protein before RNA polymerase will attach. The activator protein itself must be bound to an inducer molecule before it attaches to *m*RNA.

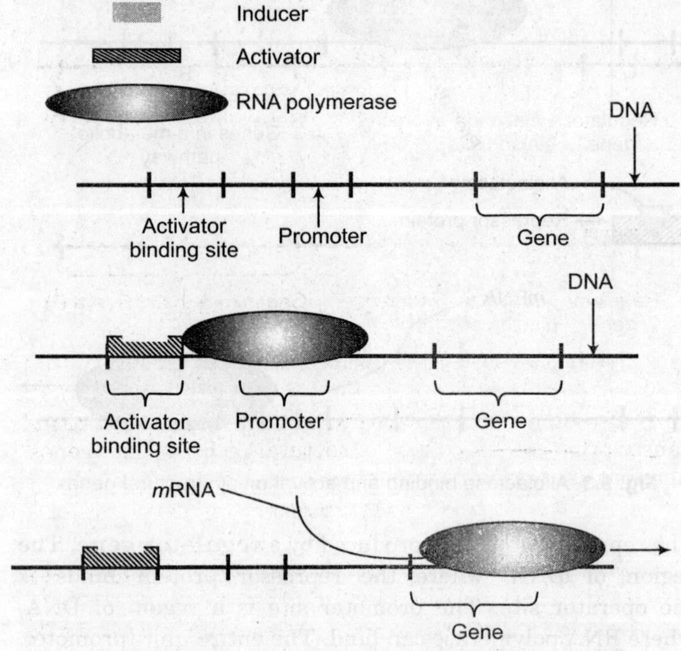

Fig. 9.7 The positive control mechanism

Genes which code for enzymes necessary for the digestion of maltose are regulated by this mechanism. Maltose acts as the inducer, binding to an activator and then to *m*RNA. The activator bound to *m*RNA stimulates the binding of RNA polymerase.

The *Arabinose* Operon

The *arabinose* operon uses both positive and negative control.

The operon contains three different genes (*ara* A, *ara* B and *ara* D) that code for three enzymes needed to convert arabinose to a usable form. A fourth gene codes for a protein (*ara* C) that acts to regulate the structural genes.

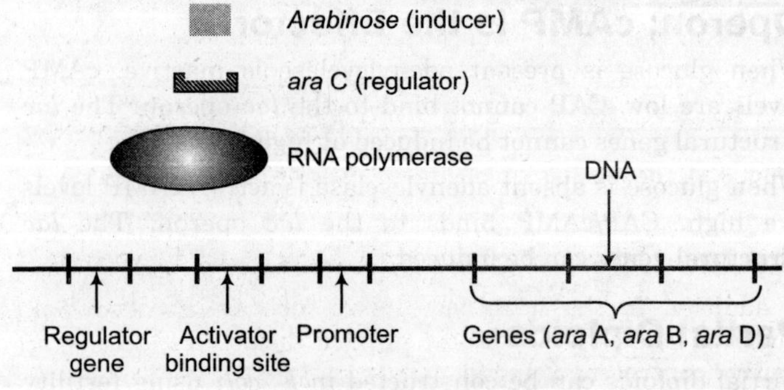

Fig. 9.8 The *arabinose* operon

The regulator protein (*ara* C) is needed for transcription of the three structural genes (*ara* A, *ara* B and *ara* D). It binds to its own structural gene preventing its own transcription, thus autoregulating its own level. When the level of *ara* C is low, transcription occurs and more *ara* C is synthesized.

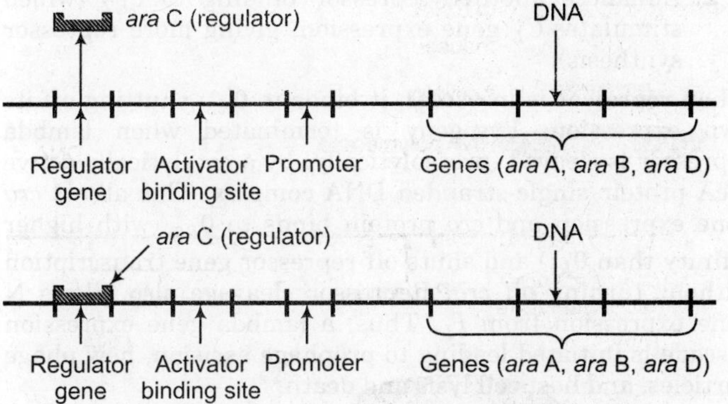

Fig. 9.9 The negative control of *arabinose* operon

ara C also binds to other sites within the operon, inhibiting transcription of the three structural genes. The genes, therefore are normally not active.

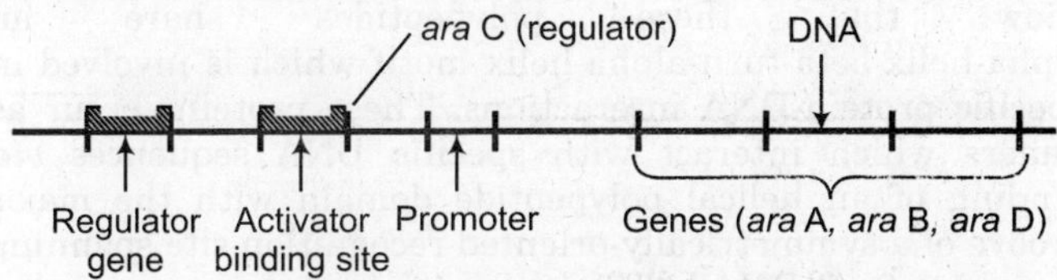

Fig. 9.10 The *arabinase* gene

When *arabinose* is present, it binds to *ara* C causing it to change shape. The new shape promotes the attachment of RNA polymerase to the DNA, thus allowing transcription to occur.

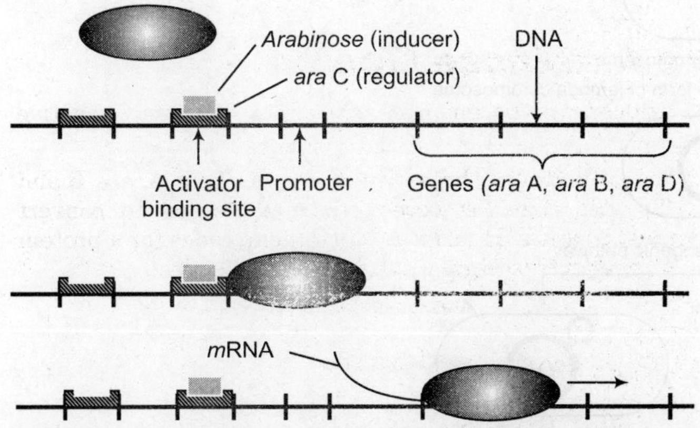

Fig. 9.11 The mechanism of positive control of *arabinose* operon

The *lac* Operon also has Positive Control

In addition to the negative control mechanism described earlier in this chapter, the *lac* operon is also regulated by a positive control mechanism.

E. coli prefer glucose when both glucose and lactose are present. When allolactose binds to and inhibits the repressor, the genes that code for enzymes needed to digest lactose are transcribed but only at a low level. Much of the cell's energy comes from glucose instead of lactose.

When the level of glucose is low, the level of cAMP increases. Cyclic AMP activates a molecule (CAP), which then binds to the *lac* promoter and enhances the rate of transcription.

Promoters and Sigma Factors

The nucleotide sequence of promoters is similar but not identical. The more similar the sequence is to a consensus sequence, the more likely that RNA polymerase will attach and produce *m*RNA from the associated genes.

Part of the RNA polymerase enzyme that recognizes the promoter is called the sigma factor. After transcription begins, this unit dissociates from the enzyme.

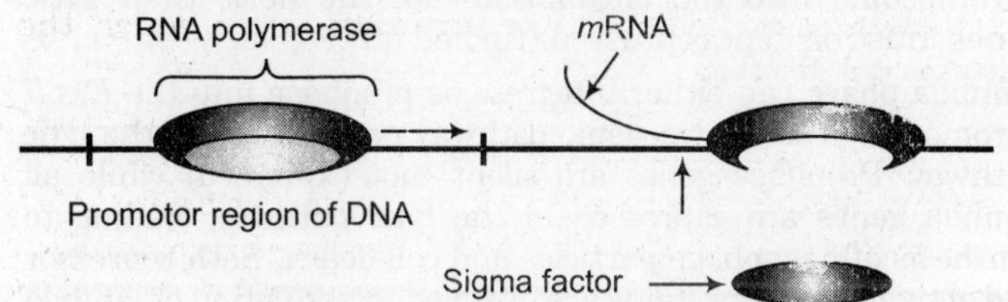

Fig. 9.12 The promoter region of DNA

Different sigma factors recognize different promoters and thus, the availability of sigma factors can regulate the transcription of genes associated with these promoters.

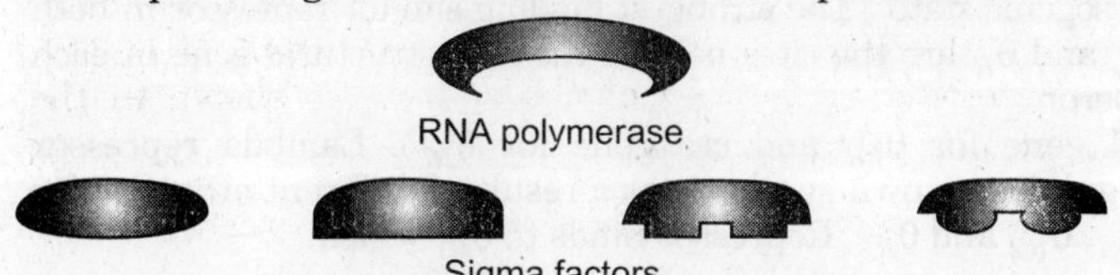

Fig. 9.13 The structure of sigma factor

The availability of sigma factors can be used to regulate sets of genes. For example, a group of genes whose product is rarely needed might have a different promoter sequence than other genes and thus, require different sigma factors. These genes would only be transcribed when the correct sigma factor became available.

Example of Translational Control in Prokaryotes

Antisense RNA

Normally, *m*RNA is synthesized off of the template (antisense) strand of DNA. Antisense RNA is synthesized from the non-coding (sense) strand of DNA. The two *m*RNA mole- cules bond together, inactivating the *m*RNA.

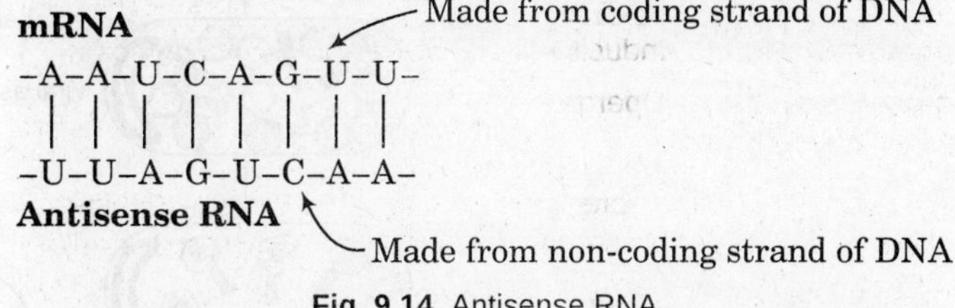

Fig. 9.14 Antisense RNA

This mechanism appears to be universal among bacteria. It has not been shown to be a normal means in eukaryotes.

Antisense RNA can be injected into eukaryotic cells as a control mechanism.

Regulation of Viral Gene Expression

Bacteriophage Lambda: Repression of Lambda Lytic Pathway Genes During Lysogeny

When temperate bacteriophages, such as phage, enter the lysogenic pathway, during which they covalently insert their chromosome into the chromosome of the host, their lytic genes must be kept repressed (turned off).

Lambda phage can either integrate as prophage into the *E.coli* chromosome *via* the lysogenic pathway or it can enter the lytic pathway. Prophage genes are silent (not expressed) while all lambda genes are expressed in the lytic pathway, leading to synthesis of new phage particles and cell death. Both repressor and activator (*cro*) proteins are involved in regulation of lambda gene expression. Repressor (C_L gene product) binds to two pairs (0_L and 0_R) of operator regions, each of which has three binding sites for the repressor (these sites have dyad symmetry). This repressor binding keeps lambda genes turned off in the prophage (lysogenic state). The strongest binding site for repressor in both 0_L and 0_R are the sites nearest the first structural gene in each operon

(N gene for 0_{LR} and cro gene for 0_{RL}). Lambda repressor regulates its own synthesis as a result of different affinities for 0_{R1}, 0_{R2} and 0_{R3}. Repressor binds to 0_{R1} which.

1. Shuts off *cro* expression.
2. Enhances another repressor binding to 0_{R2} (which stimulates C_L gene expression, giving more repressor synthesis).

When repressor is in excess, it binds to 0_{R3}, shutting off its own expression. Lysogeny is terminated when lambda repressor is cleaved (proteolytically) by a catalytically active recA protein/single-stranded DNA complex. This allows *cro* gene expression and *cro* protein binds to 0_{R3} (with higher affinity than 0_{R1}) and shuts off repressor gene transcription without turning off *cro*. Repressor cleavage also allows N gene expression from P_L. Thus, a lambda gene expression cascade is initiated leading to prophage excision, new phage particles, and host cell lysis and death.

Regulatory Proteins have a Helix-Turn-Helix Motif

Three-dimensional models of cro, lambda repressor and CAP show that these polypeptides share an alpha-helix-beta-turn-alpha-helix motif which is involved in specific protein-DNA interactions. These proteins occur as dimers which interact with specific DNA sequences *via* binding of an helical polypeptide domain with the major groove of a symmetrically-oriented recognition site spanning one turn of a B-DNA helix.

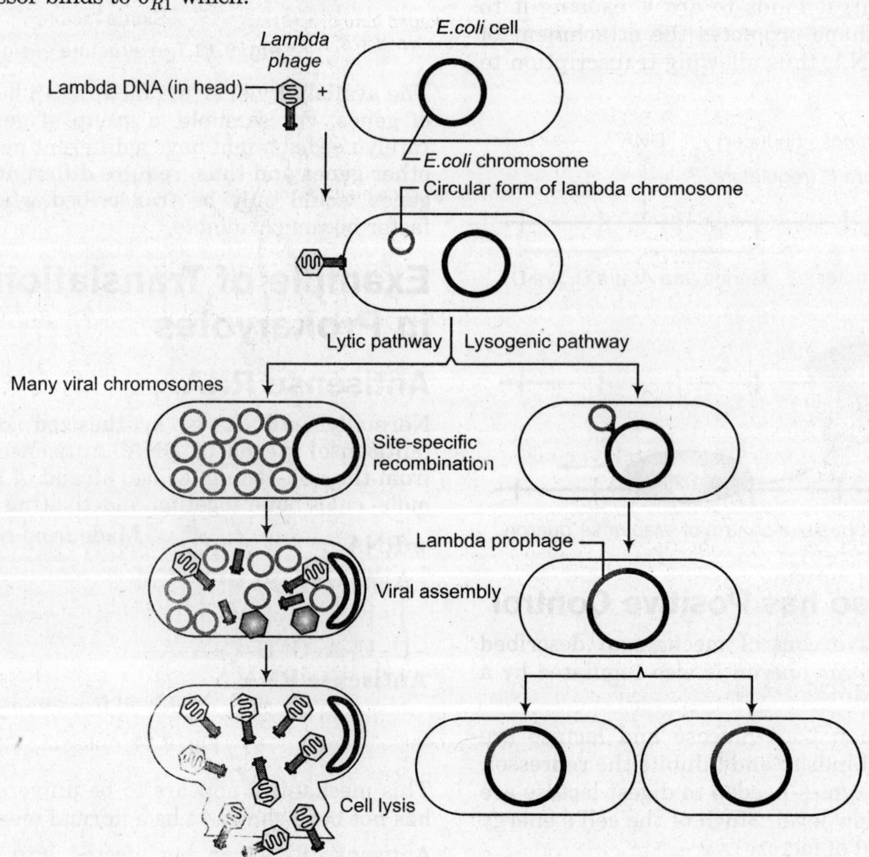

Fig. 9.15 Infection with phage: Lysis or lysogeny

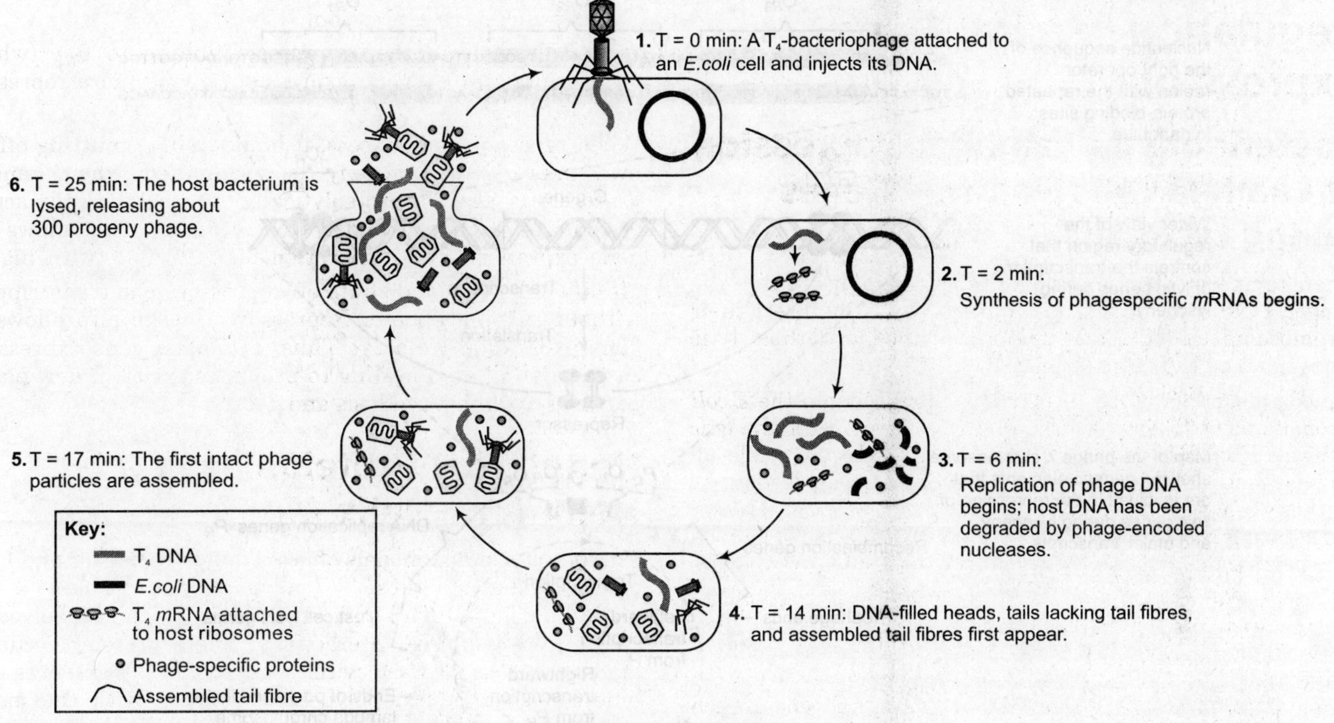

Fig. 9.16 The lytic pathway

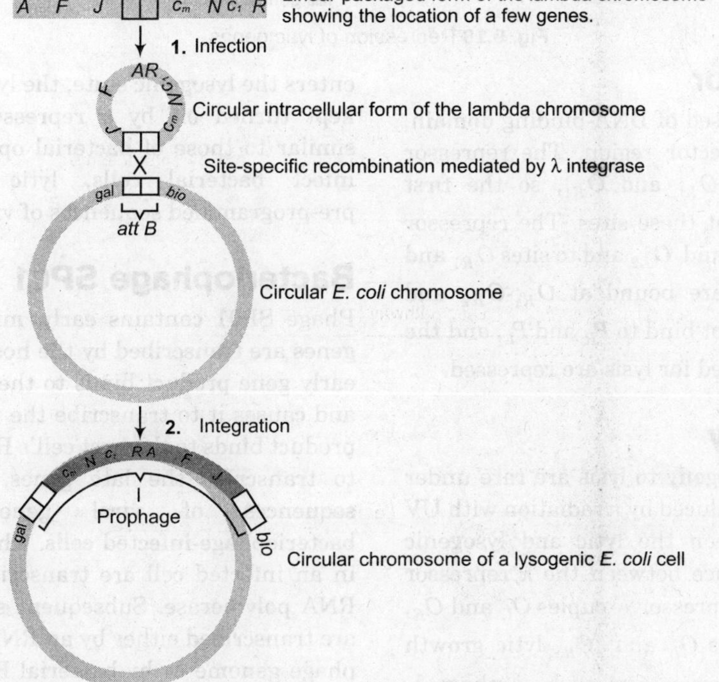

Fig. 9.17 The lysogenic pathway

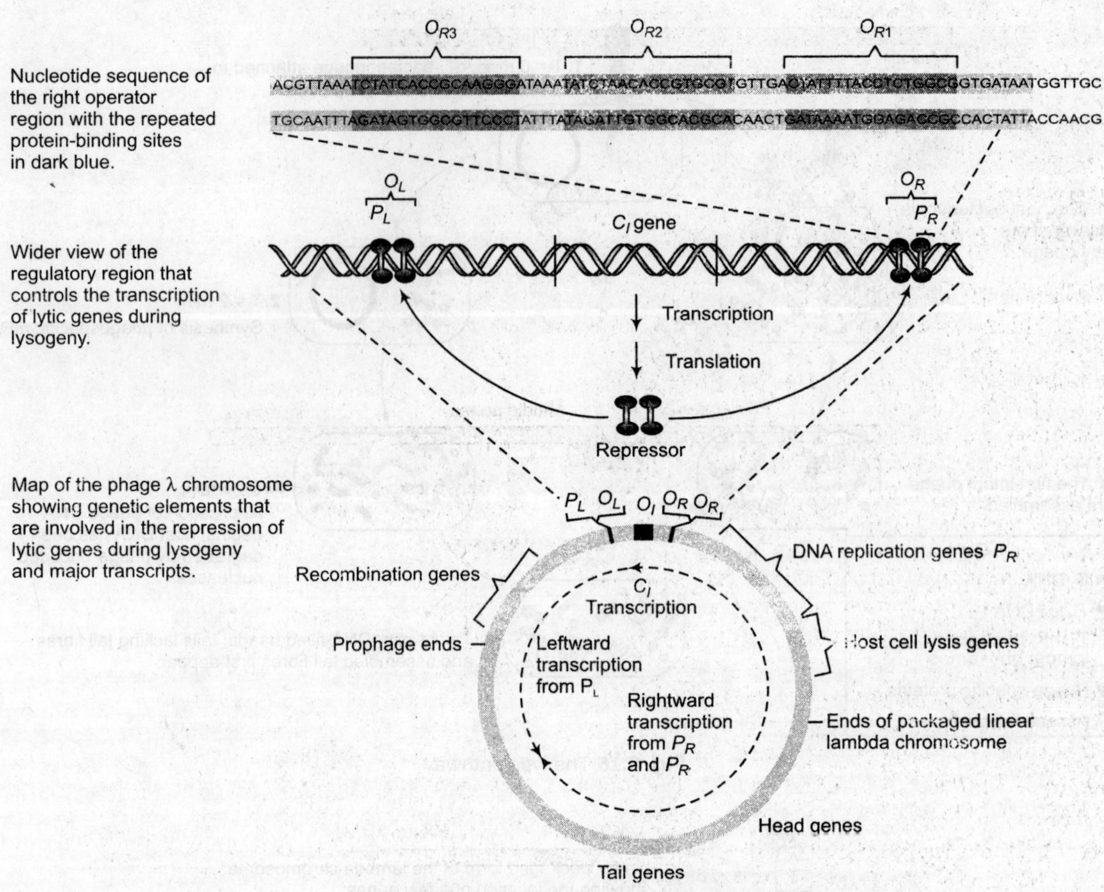

Fig. 9.18 Repression of lytic genes

The Lambda Repressor

The lambda repressor is comprised of DNA-binding domain, dimerization domain and connector region. The repressor has highest affinity for sites O_{L1} and O_{R1}, so the first repressor dimers usually bind at these sites. The repressor binds cooperatively to sites O_{L1} and O_{L2} and to sites O_{R1} and O_{R2}. When repressor dimers are bound at O_{R1}-O_{R2} and O_{L1}-O_{L2}, RNA polymerase cannot bind to P_R and P_L, and the genes encoding functions required for lysis are repressed.

Lysis *versus* Lysogeny

Spontaneous switches from lysogeny to lysis are rare under normal conditions but may be induced by irradiation with UV light. The initial choice between the lytic and lysogenic pathways depends on the balance between the λ repressor and the *Cro* protein. If the λ repressor occupies O_L and O_R, lysogeny occurs; if *Cro* occupies O_L and O_R, lytic growth occurs. When a temperate bacteriophage, such as phage λ, enters the lysogenic state, the lytic genes of the prophage are kept turned off by a repressor-operator-promoter circuit similar to those of bacterial operons. When bacteriophages infect bacterial cells, lytic growth is governed by pre-programmed sequences of viral gene expression.

Bacteriophage SP01

Phage SP01 contains early, middle, and late genes. Early genes are transcribed by the host cell's RNA polymerase. An early gene product binds to the host cell's RNA polymerase and causes it to transcribe the middle genes. A middle gene product binds to the host cell's RNA polymerase and causes it to transcribe the late genes. Pre-programmed temporal sequences of viral gene expression occur in bacteriophage-infected cells. The first viral genes expressed in an infected cell are transcribed by unmodified bacterial RNA polymerase. Subsequent sets of expressed viral genes are transcribed either by an RNA polymerase encoded by the phage genome or by bacterial RNA polymerase modified by the addition of viral protein(s).

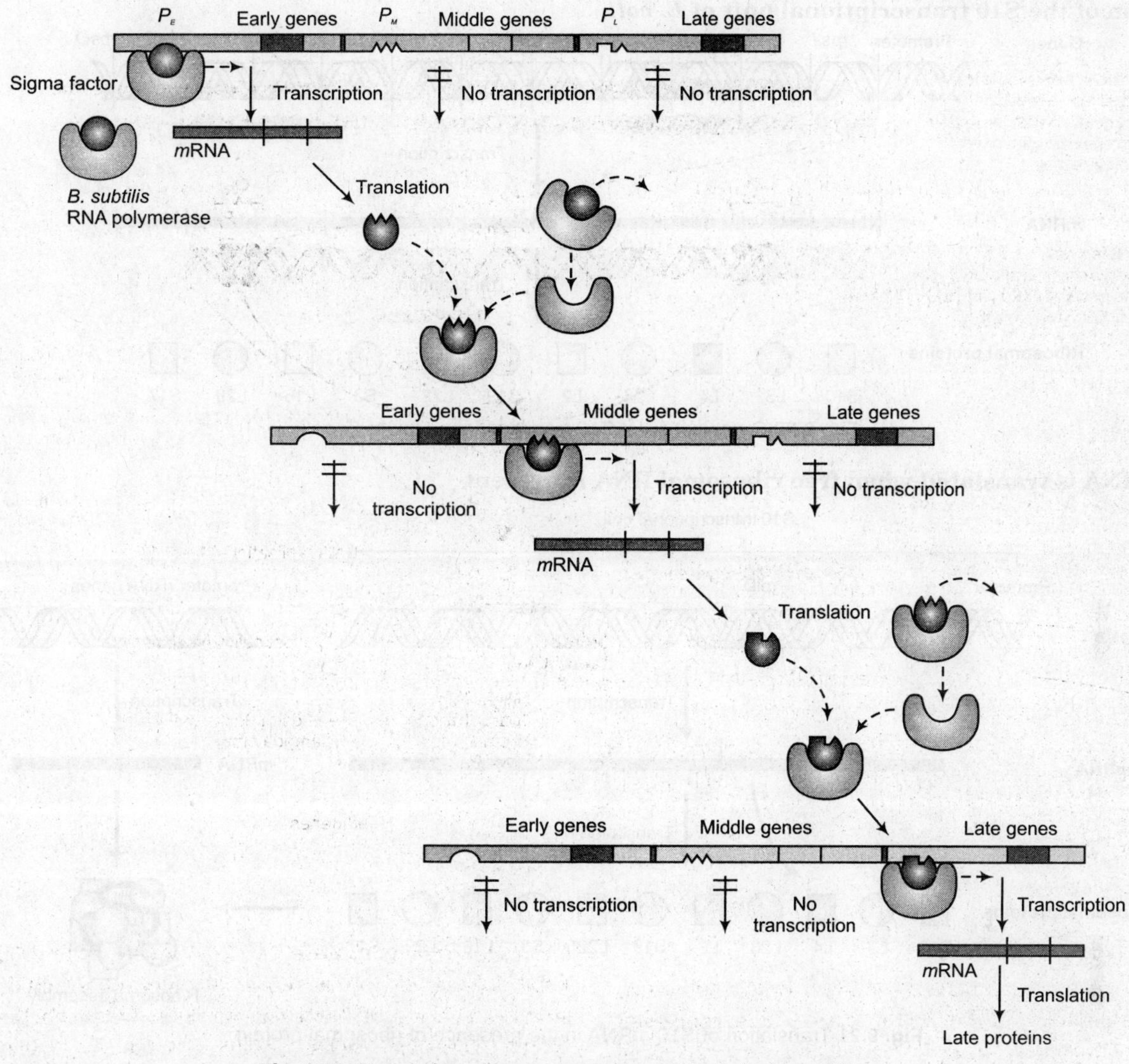

Fig. 9.19 Regulation of gene expression in bacteriophase SPo1

Translational Control of Gene Expression

The regulation of gene expression is often fine-tuned by modulating either the frequency of initiation of translation or the rate of polypeptide chain elongation. There is unequal efficiencies of translational initiation as well as altered efficiencies of ribosome movement through intergenic regions. There is differential rate of degradation of specific regions of *m*RNA molecules.

The Ribosomal Protein S10 Gene Cluster

The S_{10} transcriptional unit contains 11 coordinately regulated genes, all encoding ribosomal proteins. The product of one of the genes (*rplD*) inhibits translation of the multigenic transcript through a mechanism called **negative self-regulation** or negative autogenous regulation.

Regulation of the S10 Transcriptional Unit

When free *r*RNAs are present, nascent L4 protein binds to the RNA and is assembled into ribosomes. In the absence of *r*RNA, the L_4 protein binds to the 5′ end of the S_{10} transcriptional unit and inhibits its translation; this mechanism prevents synthesis of unneeded ribosomal proteins. Regulatory fine-tuning frequently occurs at the level of translation by modulation of the rate of polypeptide chain initiation or chain elongation. Sometimes gene expression is regulated by the differential degradation of specific regions of polygenic *m*RNAs.

Organization of the S10 transcriptional unit of *E. coli*

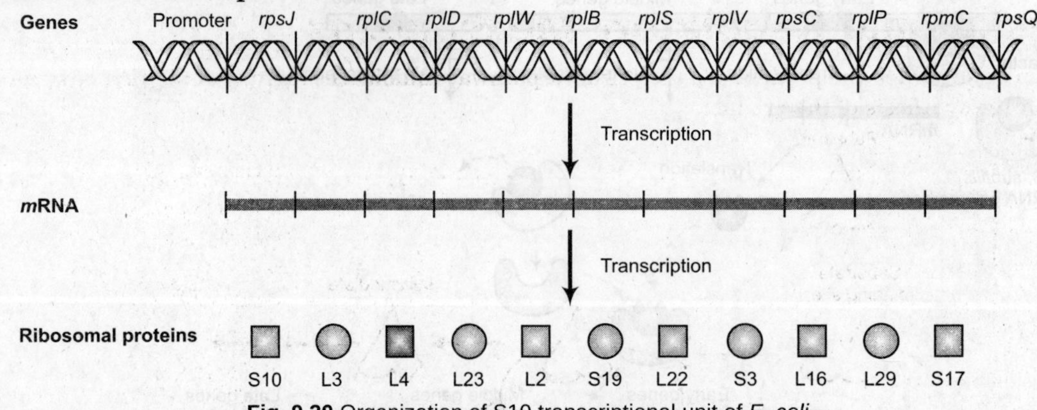

Fig. 9.20 Organization of S10 transcriptional unit of *E. coli*

The S10 *m*RNA is translated when free ribosomal RNA is present

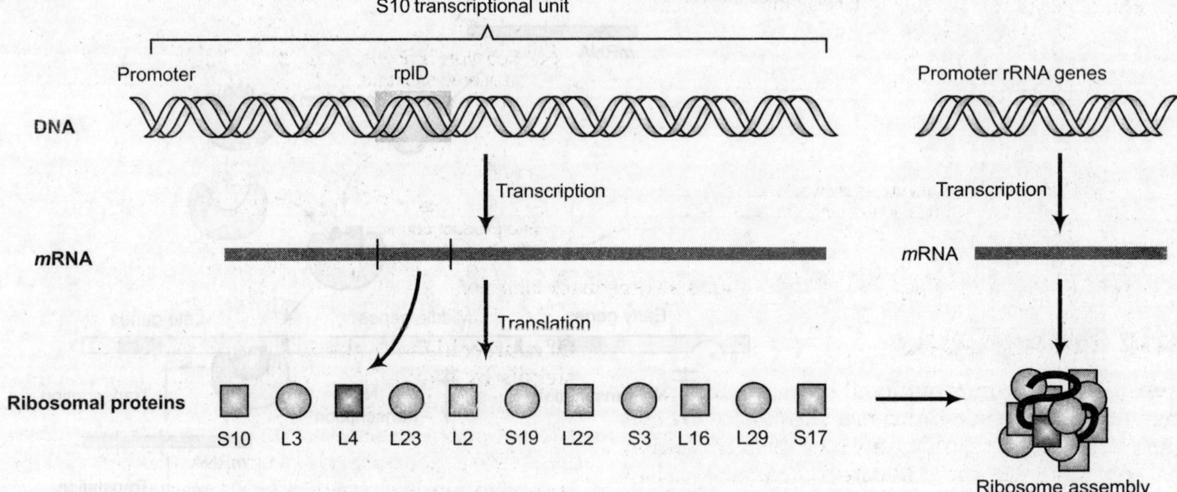

Fig. 9.21 Translation of S10 *m*RNA in the presence of ribosomal protein

Protein L4 blocks translation of the S10 *m*RNA when no free ribosomal RNA is present

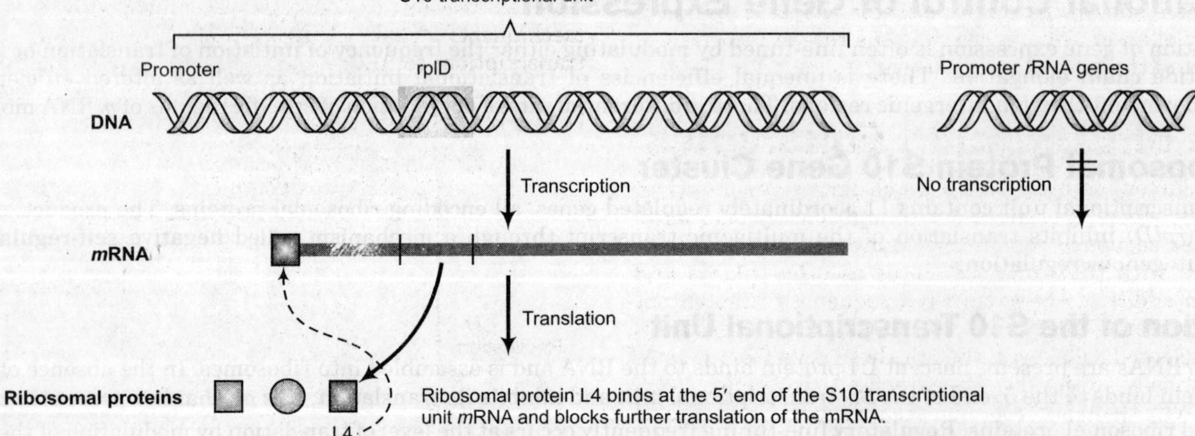

Fig. 9.22 Blocking of S10 *m*RNA by L4 protein in the absence of ribosomal protein

Post-Translational Regulatory Mechanisms

Feedback inhibition occurs when the product of a biosynthetic pathway inhibits the activity of the first enzyme in the pathway, rapidly shutting off the synthesis of the product.

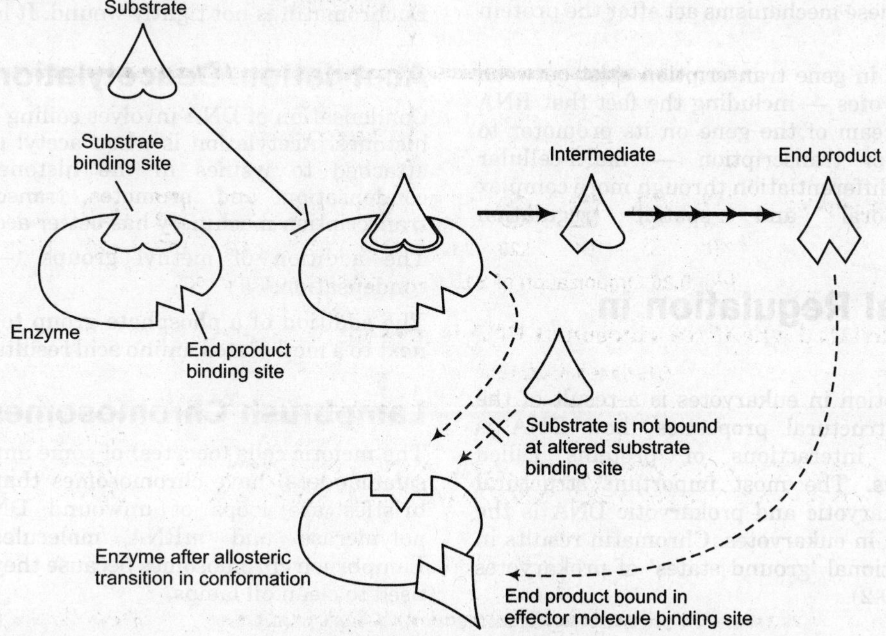

Fig. 9.23 Feedback Inhibition

Allosteric Transitions

Allosteric transitions are conformational changes that occur upon binding of a cofactor to an enzyme. Binding of an end product to an enzyme can result in an allosteric transition that reduces enzymatic activity. Allosteric transitions can also result in enzyme activation when binding of a substrate or cofactor increases enzymatic activity. Feedback inhibition occurs when the product of a biosynthetic pathway inhibits the activity of the first enzyme in the pathway, rapidly arresting the biosynthesis of the product. Enzyme activation occurs when a substrate or other effector molecule enhances the activity of an enzyme, increasing the rate of synthesis of the product of the biosynthetic pathway.

Types of Control in Eukaryotes

Multi-cellular eukaryotes have a much larger genome than prokaryotes, which is organized into multiple chromosomes with greater sequence complexity. Many eukaryotic species carry genes with the same sequences as other plants and animals. In addition, the same DNA sequences (though not the same proteins) are found within all of an organism's diploid, nucleated cells, even though these cells form tissues with drastically different appearances, properties, and functions. Why then, is there such great variation among and within such organisms? Quite simply, the mechanism by which different genes are switched on and off in specific cells generate the variety we observe in nature. In other words, specific functions of different cell types are generated through differential gene regulation.

Of course, higher eukaryotes still respond to environ- mental signals by regulating their genes. But there is an additional layer of regulation that results from cell-to-cell interactions within the organism that orchestrate development. Specifically, gene expression is controlled on two levels. First, transcription is controlled by limiting the amount of *m*RNA that is produced from a particular gene. The second level of control is through post-transcriptional events that regulate the translation of *m*RNA into proteins. Even after a protein is made, post-translational modifications can affect its activity.

Gene expression in eukaryotes is controlled by a variety of mechanisms that range from those that prevent transcription to those that prevent expression after the protein has been produced. The diagram below shows five kinds of general mechanisms that can be used.

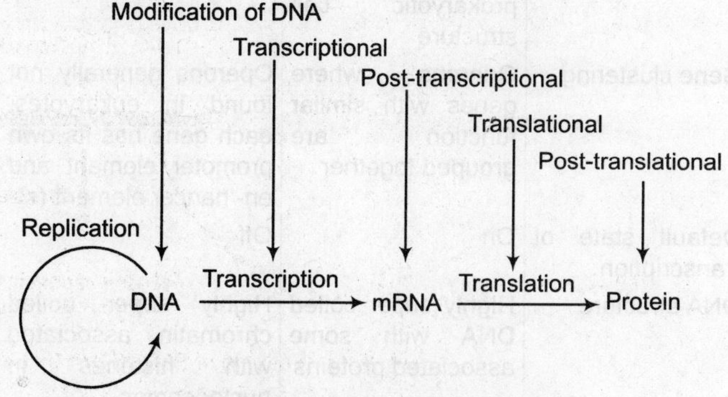

Fig. 9.24 The regulation mechanism

Transcriptional These mechanisms prevent transcription.

Post-transcriptional These mechanisms control or regulate mRNA after it has been produced.

Translational These mechanisms prevent translation. They often involve protein factors needed for translation.

Post-translational These mechanisms act after the protein has been produced.

While basic similarities in gene transcription exist between prokaryotes and eukaryotes — including the fact that RNA polymerase binds upstream of the gene on its promoter to initiate the process of transcription — multi-cellular eukaryotes control cell differentiation through more complex and precise temporal and spatial regulation of gene expression.

Transcriptional Regulation in Eukaryotes

Regulation of transcription in eukaryotes is a result of the combined effects of structural properties (how DNA is 'packaged') and the interactions of proteins called **transcription factors.** The most important structural difference between eukaryotic and prokaryotic DNA is the formation of chromatin in eukaryotes. Chromatin results in the different transcriptional 'ground states' of prokaryotes and eukaryotes (Table 9.2).

Table 9.2 **Overview of Differences between Prokaryotic and Eukaryotic Gene Expression and Regulation**

Character	Prokaryotes	Eukaryotes
Structure of genome	Single, generally circular genome some-times accompanied by smaller pieces of accessory DNA, like plasmids	Genone found in chromosomes; nucleosome structure limits DNA accessibility
Size of genome	Relatively small	Relatively large
Location of gene transcription and	Coupled; no nucleoid envelope barrier	Nuclear transcription and cytoplasmic
Translation	Because of prokaryotic cell structure	Translation
Gene clustering	Operons where genes with similar function are grouped together	Operons generally not found in eukaryotes; each gene has its own promoter element and en- hancer element (s)
Default state of transcription	On	Off
DNA structure	Highly super coiled DNA with some associated proteins	Highly super coiled chromatin associated with histones in nucleosomes

These mechanisms prevent mRNA from being synthesized.

Heterochromatin and Euchromatin

Heterochromatin is tightly wound DNA and visible during interphase. It is inactive because DNA cannot be transcribed while it is tightly wound.

Euchromatin is not tightly wound. It is active.

Acetylation/Deacetylation of DNA

Condensation of DNA involves coiling around proteins called histones. Acetylation is when acetyl groups (—$COCH_3$) are attached to lysines in the histone tails. This reduces condensation and promotes transcription because the transcription machinery has better access to the DNA.

The addition of methyl groups (—CH_3) also promotes condensation.

The addition of a phosphate group to an amino acid that is next to a methylated amino acid results in less condensation.

Lampbrush Chromosomes

The meiotic cells (oocytes) of some amphibians (frogs, toads, salamanders) have chromosomes that appear bristled. The bristles are loops of unwound DNA with many RNA polymerase and mRNA molecules. They are called Lampbrush chromosomes because they resemble the brushes used to clean oil lamps.

Puffs on Polytene Chromosomes

Polytene chromosomes are seen in the salivary glands of fruit fly larvae and the larvae of some other insects.

They have about 1000 chromatids; produced by DNA replication without mitosis. When viewed under a microscope, the many chromatids look like a giant chromosome. The large number of chromatids allows the cell to produce more mRNA and therefore, more gene product (protein).

Developmental stages in the larva are associated with the appearance of chromosomal puffs. These are where DNA is unwound and actively being transcribed. As development proceeds, some puffs disappear and others appear indicating that some genes become inactive while others become active.

DNA Methylation and Epigenic Inheritance

The DNA can also be methylated (usually cytosine). Inactive DNA such as the Barr body (inactive X-chromosome in females) is usually more methylated.

Methylated DNA usually remains methylated after cell division. This allows clusters of cells to develop into tissues that have the same genes inactivated.

Epigenic inheritance is the inheritance of traits that are not due to change in the DNA sequence.

Transcription Factors

RNA polymerase requires the presence of general transcription factors before transcription can begin. Interactions between the transcription factors, RNA polymerase, and the promotor allow the polymerase to move along the gene and begin transcription.

Higher levels of transcription occur with the presence of specific transcription factors as described below.

The activators shown below are specific transcription factors. They function by binding to a region of the DNA called the **enhancer.** The enhancer may be located at a distance from the gene. Bending proteins assist in bending the DNA so that the enhancer is near the promoter. Activators, general transcription factors, and other proteins attach, forming an initiation complex. Transcription begins when the initiation complex is formed.

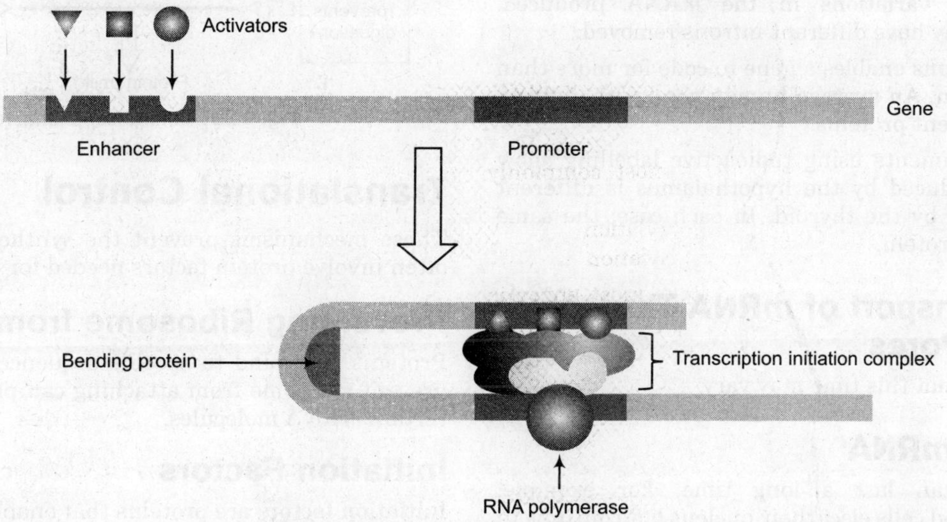

Fig. 9.25 The transcriptional regulation

Hundreds of different transcription factors have been discovered; each recognizes and binds with a specific nucleotide sequence in the DNA. A specific combination of transcription factors is necessary to activate a gene.

Transcription factors are regulated by signals produced from other molecules. For example, hormones activate transcription factors and thus, enable transcription. Hormones, therefore activate certain genes.

Transcription Factors and Combinatorial Control

Transcription factors (TFs) are regulatory proteins whose function is to activate (or more rarely, to inhibit) transcription of DNA by binding to specific DNA sequences. TFs have defined DNA-binding domains with up to 10^6-fold higher affinity for their target sequences than for the remainder of the DNA strand. These highly conserved sequences have been used to categorize the known TFs into various 'families', such as the MADS box-containing proteins, SOX proteins, and POU factors. Transcription factors can also be classified by their three-dimensional protein structure, including basic helix-turn-helix, helix-loop-helix, and zinc finger proteins. These different structural motifs result in transcription factor specificity for the consensus sequences to which they bind.

Sequence-specific transcription factors are considered the most important and diverse mechanisms of gene regulation in both prokaryotic and eukaryotic cells. In eukaryotes, regulation of gene expression by transcription factors is said to be combinatorial, in that it requires the coordinated interactions of multiple proteins (in contrast to prokaryotes, in which a single protein is usually all that is required).

Many genes, known as housekeeping genes, are needed by almost every type of cell and appear to be unregulated or constitutive. But at the core of cellular differentiation, manifested in the variety of cell types observed in different organisms, is the regulation of gene expression in a tissue-specific manner. The same genome is responsible for making the entire cadre of cell types, each of which has its own function—for example, red blood cells exchange oxygen, muscle cells expand and contract, and cells in the immune system recognize pathogens. Genes that regulate cell identity are turned on under very specific temporal, spatial, and environmental conditions to ensure that a cell is able to perform its designated function.

Take the example of the gene for beta-globin, a protein used in red blood cells for oxygen exchange. Every cell in the human body contains the beta-globin gene and the corresponding upstream regulatory sequences that regulate expression, but no cell type other than red blood cells expresses beta-globin. Scientists can use a technique called DNA foot printing to map, where transcription factors bind to specific regulatory sequences. When the beta-globin promoter in different cell types were examined, it was found that the transcription factors that could bind to the promoter sequences required for beta-globin expression were expressed only in erythroblasts (immature adult red blood cells). The two consensus sequences in the beta globin promoter known for binding transcription factors, CCAAT and CACC, were protected in the erythroid cells (E), but not the other cell types.

Post-transcriptional Control

These mechanisms control or regulate *m*RNA after it has been produced.

Alternative RNA Splicing

This can produce variations in the *m*RNA produced. Different *m*RNA may have different introns removed.

The removal of introns enables a gene to code for more than one different protein. An average human gene is thought to code for three different proteins.

For example, experiments using radioactive labelling show that calcitonin produced by the hypothalamus is different from that produced by the thyroid. In each case, the same gene produces the protein.

Speed of Transport of *m*RNA Through the Nuclear Pores

Evidence suggests that this time may vary.

Longevity of *m*RNA

Messenger RNA can last a long time. For example, mammalian red blood cells eject their nucleus but continue to synthesize haemoglobin for several months. This indicates that *m*RNA is available to produce the protein even though the DNA is gone.

Ribonucleases

Ribonucleases are enzymes that destroy *m*RNA.

Messenger RNA has non-coding nucleotides at either end of the molecule. These segments contain information about the number of times *m*RNA is transcribed before being destroyed by ribonucleases.

Hormones stabilize certain *m*RNA transcripts.

Example

Prolactin is a hormone that promotes milk production because it affects the length of time the *m*RNA for casein (a major milk protein) is available.

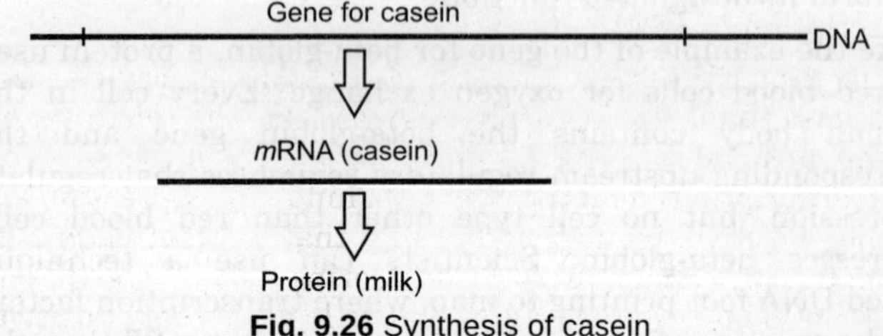

Fig. 9.26 Synthesis of casein

Ribonucleases destroy the *m*RNA.

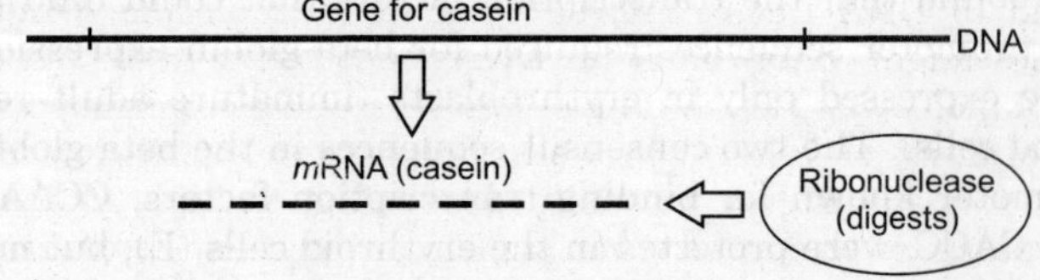

Fig. 9.27 Role of ribonuclease

Prolactin is a hormone that prevents destruction of the *m*RNA.

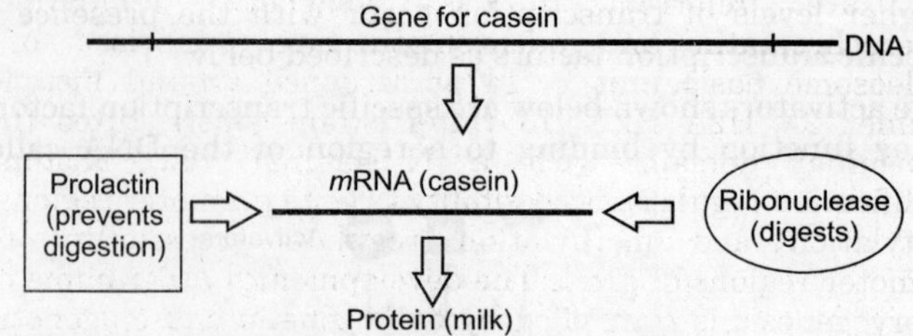

Fig. 9.28 Post transcriptional regulation

Translational Control

These mechanisms prevent the synthesis of protein. They often involve protein factors needed for translation.

Preventing Ribosome from Attaching

Proteins that bind to specific sequences in the *m*RNA and prevent ribosome from attaching can prevent translation of certain *m*RNA molecules.

Initiation Factors

Initiation factors are proteins that enable ribosome to attach to *m*RNA. These factors can be produced when certain proteins are needed. For example, the eggs of many organisms contain *m*RNA that is not needed until after fertilization. At this time, an initiation factor is activated.

Post-translational Control

These mechanisms act after the protein has been produced.

Protein Activation

Some proteins are not active when they are first formed. They must undergo modification such as folding, enzymatic cleavage, or bond formation.

Example Pro-insulin is a precursor to the hormone insulin. It must be cleaved into two polypeptide chains and then some amino acids must be removed to form insulin.

Many proteins are activated by adding phosphate groups. They can be inactivated by removing phosphate groups. For example, kinases activate by adding phosphate groups and phosphodiesterase inactivates by removing the phosphate groups.

Feedback Control

Some enzymes in a metabolic pathway may be negatively inhibited by products of the pathway.

Modification of DNA

A different layer of transcriptional regulation is there which influence gene expression. It includes histone modifications and DNA methylation in **chromatin.** In eukaryotes, the accessibility of large regions of DNA can depend on its chromatin structure, which can be altered as a result of histone modifications directed by DNA methylation, ncRNA, or DNA-binding protein. Hence, these modifications may up or down regulate the expression of gene. Certain of these modifications that regulate gene expression are inheritable and are referred to as epigenetic regulation. Heterochromatin and euchromatin are comprised of nucleosome basic unit = 147pb wrapped around histone octamer 2X H2A H2B H3 H4. Histone consti- tutes the C-terminal domain with a N-terminal tail. Histone modification regulates accessibility to gene promoter regions. Acetylation and methylation regulate accessibility to promoter regions of genes.The developmental programme of embryogenesis is controlled by both genetic and epigenetic mechanisms. Regulation of chromatin structures is crucial for genome reprogramming during early embryogenesis and for tissue-specific gene expression and global gene silencing.

(i) Chemical Modification

Methylation of DNA is a common method of gene silencing. DNA is typically methylated by methyltransferase enzymes on cytosine nucleotides in a CpG dinucleotide sequence (also called 'CpG islands' when densely clustered). Analysis of the pattern of methylation in a given region of DNA (which can be a promoter) can be achieved through a method called bisulphite mapping. Methylated cytosine residues are unchanged by the treatment, whereas unmethylated ones are changed to uracil. The differences are analyzed by DNA sequencing or by methods developed to quantify SNPs, such as pyrosequencing (Biotage) or massArray (Sequenom), measuring the relative amounts of C/T at the CG dinucleotide. Abnormal methylation patterns are thought to be involved in oncogenesis.

(ii) Structural Modification

Transcription of DNA is dictated by its structure. In general, the density of its packing is indicative of the frequency of transcription. Octameric protein complexes called **nucleosomes** are responsible for the amount of supercoiling of DNA, and these complexes can be temporarily modified by processes such as phosphorylation or more permanently modified by processes such as methylation. Such modifications are considered to be responsible for more or less permanent changes in gene expression levels.

Histone acetylation is also an important process in transcription. Histone acetyltransferase enzymes (HATs) such as CREB-binding protein also dissociate the DNA from the histone complex, allowing transcription to proceed. Often, DNA methylation and histone deacetylation work together in gene silencing. The combination of the two seems to be a signal for DNA to be packed more densely, lowering gene expression.

Gene Amplification

In *Drosophila* (fruit flies), the chorion (egg shell) gene is copied many times in certain cells of the oviduct. These cells make large quantities of the protein needed to surround the egg. In other cells of the body, there is only one copy of this gene.

The Immunoglobin Genes

Immunoglobins (antibodies) are proteins that are used to defend the body against foreign invaders. They are able to do this because they have a shape that matches a shape found on the invader, allowing it to become attached. Particles that have antibodies attached are quickly destroyed by other cells in the immune system. Our bodies contain millions of different antibodies, each produced by a type of white blood cell called a lymphocyte. A single lymphocyte can produce only one specific kind of antibody; thus, there are millions of different kinds of lymphocytes. The genes that code for these antibodies differ from one lymphocyte to the next because when the lymphocytes are produced, different regions of the DNA are deleted so that each lymphocyte has a somewhat different version of the genes involved.

Transposons

Transposons are segments of DNA that are capable of moving to another location, either on the same chromosome or on a different one. If a transposon inserts itself within another gene, it can prevent the gene from expressing itself. Sometimes the transposon carries a gene which can become activated if it becomes inserted downstream from an active promoter.

The Ground State of DNA Expression

RNA polymerase in prokaryotes can access almost any promoter in a DNA strand without the presence of activators or repressors. Thus, the 'ground state' of DNA expression in prokaryotes is said to be non-restrictive, or 'on'. In eukaryotes, however, the ground state of expression is restrictive in that, although strong promoters might be present, they are inactive in the absence of some sort of recruitment to the promoter by transcription factors. For instance, RNA polymerase II, which transcribes *m*RNA, cannot bind to promoters in eukaryotic DNA without the help of transcription factors. In many eukaryotic organisms, the promoter contains a conserved gene sequence called the TATA Box. Various other consensus sequences also exist and are recognized by the different TF families. Transcription is initiated when one TF binds to one of these promoter sequences, initiating a series of interactions between multiple proteins (activators, regulators and repressors) at the same site, or other promoter, regulator, and enhancer sequences. Ultimately, a transcription complex is formed at the promoter that facilitates binding and transcription by RNA polymerase.

As in prokaryotes, eukaryotic repressor molecules can sometimes bind to silencer elements in the vicinity of a gene and inhibit the binding, assembly, or activity of the transcription complex, thus turning off expression of a gene. Positive regulation by TFs that are activators is common in eukaryotes. Considering the restrictive transcriptional ground state, it is logical that positive regulation is the predominant form of control in all systems characterized to date. Many activating TFs are generally bound to DNA until removed by a signal molecule, while others might only bind to DNA once influenced by a signal molecule. The binding of one type of TF can influence the binding of others, as well. Thus, gene expression in eukaryotes is highly variable, depending on the type of activators involved and what signals are present to control binding.

The Role of Chromatin in Gene Expression

Even when transcription factors are present in a cell, transcription does not always occur, because often the TFs cannot reach their target sequences. The association of the DNA molecule with proteins is the first step in its silencing. The associated DNA and histone proteins are collectively called chromatin; the complex is tightly bonded by attraction of the negatively charged DNA to the positively charged histones. The state of chromatin can limit access of transcription factors and RNA polymerase to DNA promoters, contributing to the restrictive ground state of gene expression. In order for gene transcription to occur, the chromatin structure must be unwound.

Chromatin structure contributes to the varying levels of complexity in gene regulation. It allows simultaneous regulation of functionally or structurally related genes that tend to be present in widely spaced clusters or domains on eukaryotic DNA. Interactions of chromatin with activators and repressors can result in domains of chromatin that are open, closed, or poised for activation. Chromatin domains have various sizes and different extents of stability. These variations allow for phenomena found solely in eukaryotes, such as transcription at various stages of develop- ment and epigenetic memory throughout cell division cycles. They also allow for the maintenance of differentiated cellular states, which is crucial to the survival of multicellular organisms.

Multiple Interactions Provide Synchronous Control

The state of chromatin structure at a specific region in eukaryotic DNA, along with the presence of specific transcription factors, works to regulate gene expression in eukaryotes. However, this complex interplay between proteins that serve as transcriptional activators or repressors and accessibility to the regulatory sequence is still just part of the story. Epigenetic mechanisms, including DNA methylation and imprinting, non-coding RNA, post-translational modifications, and other mechanisms, further enrich the cellular portfolio of gene expression control activities.

RNA Interference

RNA interference is gene silencing mediated by short RNA molecules produced from double stranded RNA (dsRNA). Short RNAs are produced by cleavage of dsRNA by the nuclease called dicer. Dicer produces short dsRNA called siRNA duplexes. Then, a complex of proteins called RISC unwinds the duplex and produces siRNA. siRNA hybridize to the target *m*RNA which is degraded. Non-coding RNAs play a significant role in the control of epigenetic regulation, chromosomal dynamics, and long-range interactions, as well as phenomena that have an impact on normal cellular differentiation and organismal development. Small RNA molecules that are products of the RNAi machinery can achieve transcriptional gene silencing (TGS) through chromatin changes, particularly characterized by histone methylation, and/or, in particular systems, DNA methylation. It has been recognized for some time that the 'canonical' RNAi pathway uses small interfering RNAs (siRNAs) to induce degradation of cognate messenger RNAs in a sequence-specific manner. This involves the processing of dsRNA by dicer, the RNA substrate of which may be exogenously introduced by experimental manipulation, viruses, endogenous parasitic elements or repetitive sequences. The enzyme dicer belongs to the RNAs III family of ribonucleases, which creates, through its action, small interfering RNAs (siRNAs) that are central to RNAi and related phenomena. These small RNAs are then loaded into dedicated machinery, known as the RISC complex (RNA-induced silencing complex), whose nuclease activity is encoded by the Argonaute-two protein. RNAi is also involved in the regulation of translation, in which endogenous micro RNA precursors (pre-miRNAs) are sequentially processed by the Drosha and Dicer RNAs III enzymes, yielding microRNAs (miRNAs). miRNAs bind the 3′-UTR of their target genes and inhibit translation by a currently unknown mechanism. miRNAs are responsible for key processes of development such as patterning, cell symmetry, and proliferation, and are implicated in disease.

RNAi Acts on Chromatin

Centromeres produce dsRNA and Dicer as well as the RISC are required for centromere silencing. Transposons induce gene silencing in a similar manner. Heterochromatin stabilizes repetitive DNA sequences or multiple copies of transposable elements at centromeres, telomeres, and other regions of the genome by preventing recombination between homologous sequences.

Gene Silencing

In many differentiated cells depending on the cellular requirements certain genes are permanently silenced and other are turned on or off. Initially it was beleived that gene silencing is a passive process and non-transcribing gene automatically inactivated, but later found that gene silencing is actively controlled. Certain genes which are turned on and off depending on the cellular requirement are sometimes kept inactive by a mechanism (called repression). Repression is mediated by a group of proteins called repressor which target specific sequences in gene promoter and inhibit their expression. Like enhances modular DNA sequences (called silences) involved in silencing of a particular gene. Silences are targeted by a number of sequence specific DNA binding proteins. In multicellular organisms long term gene silencing is mediated by methylation of cytosine base (5 methyl cytosine) on DNA without affecting the base pairing. Following methylation a group of proteins binds to methylated DNA and *via* interaction with chromatin remodeling complexes condense the chromatins leading to its long term silencing. Such methylation play an important role in gene regulation of vertebrates.

Exercise

1. The products of constitutive genes may be
I. Involved in catabolic pathways.
II. Involved in anabolic pathways.
III. Continuously synthesized.
IV. Involved in the synthesis of structural elements in the cell.
(a) I and II (b) I and III
(c) I and IV (d) I, II, III and IV

2. It is generally thought that the 'default' condition of chromatin is a(n) .... state.
(a) repressed (b) activated
(c) enhanced (d) Both (b) and (c)

3. The addition of methyl groups to the histones generally leads to .... of transcription.
(a) activation (b) baseline stability
(c) repression (d) enhancement

4. Genes whose products are constantly needed for cellular activity are called
(a) regulator genes (b) structural genes
(c) housekeeping genes (d) smart genes

5. Which of the following processes is not an example of allosteric regulation?
(a) Regulation of phosphofructokinase activity by fructose 2, 6-biphosphate
(b) Inactivation of nitrogenase by ADP ribosylation
(c) Regulation of the *lac* operon by allolactose in *E. coli*
(d) Catabolic repression by CAP in *E. coli*

6. In bacteria, the genes that codes for the enzymes of a metabolic pathway are usually arranged consecutively to form a functional unit called
(a) an induction system
(b) an end product repression system
(c) an operon
(d) a constitutive enzyme system

7. A series of genes that transitionally regulated in *trans* by DNA-binding proteins are called a/an
(a) transcriptor (b) repressor
(c) promoter (d) operon

8. Operons
(a) are of approximately uniform in size
(b) do not bind proteins
(c) are found in some eukaryotic genes
(d) are shorter and smaller in lower eukaryotes than higher eukaryotes

9. Which of the following genes is not transcribed from the promoter for β-galactosidase?
(a) *lac Z* (b) *lac I*
(c) *lac Y* (d) *lac A*

10. Which of the following compounds is a gratuitous inducer of β-galactosidase in *E. coli*?
(a) Glucose
(b) Allolactose
(c) Isopropylthiogalactoside
(d) Lactose

11. Induction of β-galactosidase activity by IPTG is the result of
(a) stimulation of *lac* repressor function
(b) IPTG binding to *lac* operon and inducing transcription
(c) IPTG binding to *lac*-I gene product and inhibiting its activity
(d) inhibition of β-galactosidase degradation

12. If there is a deletion mutation in the operator for the *lac* operon, the expression of *lac* structural gene will be
(a) permanently stop
(b) constitutively expressed
(c) not expressed
(d) resistant to catabolic expression

13. Bacteria utilized glucose first, even if other sugars are present, through a mechanism called
(a) operon repression
(b) enzyme repression
(c) catabolic repression
(d) glucose utilization

14. Catabolic Activator Protein (CAP) acts as
(a) apo repressor (b) co-repressor
(c) apo inducer (d) inducer

15. cAMP regulates the *lac* operon by
(a) binding the operator to turn on transcription
(b) binding to the *lac* repressor to prevent transcription
(c) combining with the catabolic activator protein to form a complex that turns on transcription after binding near promoter
(d) None of the above

16. Full expression of the *lac* operon requires
(a) lactose and cAMP
(b) allolactose and cAMP
(c) lactose
(d) allolactose

17. A positively controlled operon can be identified by mutation in the regulatory gene
(a) leading to constitutive expression
(b) very high levels of expression
(c) inducibility of the operon
(d) repression of the operon

18. In case of inducible *lac* operon, the transcription is inhibited by
(a) the binding of repressor top operator
(b) the presence of lactose
(c) the interaction of repressor with lactose
(d) the interaction of lactose with the operator

19. Enzymes that place acetyl groups on histones are called
(a) histone acetylases
(b) histone deacetylases
(c) histone acetyltransferases
(d) histone deacetyltransferases

20. Which of the following is not true for histones?
(a) They are associated with the nucleosome
(b) H1, H2, H3 and H4 form the nucleosome core
(c) They are found in the nucleus
(d) None of the above

21. What is the current area of study regarding enhancers?
(a) Enhancers (b) Enhanciomeres
(c) Enhancesomes (d) Enhansases

22. What is the chemical basis of gene imprinting?
(a) Phosphorylation of DNA (b) Methylation of DNA
(c) Oxidation of DNA (d) Glycosylation of DNA

23. Which of the following is an epigenetic factor for gene expression in eukaryotes?
(a) Recombination
(b) DNA methylation
(c) Protein phosphorylation
(d) DNA protein interaction

24. The yeast two hybrid system is designed to identify which of the following?
(a) All of the components of multi-protein complex
(b) Human proteins that are required for binding RNA poly- merase
(c) Two proteins that directly interact with one another
(d) Two proteins that are involved in the same metabolic pathway

25. siRNA
(a) forms a complex in the spliceosomes
(b) recruits histone acetyl transferase to the nucleus
(c) forms a complex with RISC proteins tro inhibits translation or cause degradation of complementary *m*RNA
(d) is not transmitted to daughter cells after cell division

26. The enhancer must/may be on a/the .... chromosome.
(a) different (b) same
(c) lateral (d) All of these

27. What gene, as discussed in class, has different enhancers, based on location of gene expression?
(a) *Pax6* (b) *GSP*
(c) *ZP1* (d) *CCmP*

28. Which of the following regulators are said to act in *cis*?
(a) The *lac* repressor and *lac* operator
(b) The operator and mammalian transcriptional factors
(c) The *lac* operator and mammalian enhancers
(d) Mammalian transcription factors and enhancers

29. Tryptophan operon in *E. coli* is an example of
(a) inducible operon
(b) positively regulated operon
(c) repressible operon
(d) All of the above

30. The expression of the *trp* operon in *E. coli* is regulated in part by the availability of the amino acid tryptophan; this regulatory process is referred to as?
(a) Attenuation
(b) Translational read-through
(c) Anti-termination
(d) Non-sense suppression

31. The leader region (*trpL)* of the tryptophan biosynthetic operon codes for RNA that may function as the operon's?
(a) Co-repressor (b) Holo-repressor
(c) Apo-repressor (d) Attenuator

32. Which of the following statements about enhancers is incorrect?
(a) They function as promoters
(b) They function in any orientation
(c) They function even when located many base pairs away from the promoter
(d) They function in tissue specific manner

33. In the RNAi regulatory pathway, the dicer enzyme cleaves
(a) RNA polymerase into non-functional pieces
(b) single-stranded DNA into repetitive sequences
(c) double-stranded RNA into short strands
(d) *m*RNA of genes to be repressed

34. Function of an enhancer during transcription of an eukaryotic gene is to
(a) initiate transcription
(b) stimulate the rate of transcription
(c) elongate transcriptions
(d) enhance *m*RNA stability

35. DNA sequences to which hormone receptors bind are called
(a) response element (b) carboxyl terminal domain
(c) operator (d) promoter

36. Which one of the following factors is involved in the epigenetic control of gene expression in eukaryotes?
(a) RNA polymerase II (b) DNA methyl transferase
(c) TFIID (d) TFIIH

37. Enhancers, despite possible conditions, are often .... the target gene.
(a) far away from (b) in the middle of
(c) immediately preceding (d) near to

38. Which is not an example of control of gene expression at the level of translation?
(a) Differential *m*RNA longevity
(b) Lack of 5′ CAP
(c) Formation of a circular *m*RNA
(d) Presence of enhancers and activators

39. Which one of the following statements about the trypto-phan (*trp*) operon is true?
(a) The RNA product of the *trp* operon is very stable
(b) The *trp* repressor is a product of the *trp* operon
(c) The *trp* repressor, like the *lac* repressor, is a tetramer of identical subunit
(d) The *trp* repressor binds to tryptophan

40. In case of *lac* operon when disaccharide enters the cell
(a) it binds to the bound-repressor to the operator and the structural gene are transcribed because the RNA polymerase can recognize and bind the transcription initiation site
(b) it binds to the repressor and structural genes are transcribed because the repressor has an altered conformation, is inactivated and does not bind to the operator

(c) the membrane protein interacts with the operator and the RNA polymerase can recognize the transcription initiation
(d) the membrane protein has an altered conformation and does not interact with the operator, thus leading to the transcri- ption of the structural gene

41. The control of gene expression is more complex in eukaryotic cells because
(a) chromosomes are contained in a nucleus
(b) gene expression differentiates specialized cells
(c) the chromosomes are linear and more numerous
(d) operons are controlled by more than one promoter region

42. In a eukaryotic, a repressor protein may block gene expression by binding to a DNA site called
(a) an operon (b) a histone
(c) an enhancer (d) a silencer

43. Gene expression in animal development seems to be regulated largely by
(a) controlling gene packing and unpacking
(b) controlling the transcription of genes into *m*RNAs
(c) controlling the translation of *m*RNAs into protein
(d) selectively eliminating certain genes from the genome

44. Operons enable bacteria to
(a) function in frequently changing environment
(b) resist attack by predators
(c) correct mutations that might interfere with their genetic instructions
(d) differentiate

45. If the nucleus of a frog egg is destroyed and replaced with the nucleus of an intestine cell from a tadpole, the egg can develop into a normal tadpole. This demonstrates that
(a) intestine cells are fully differentiated
(b) there is little difference between an egg celi and an intestine cell
(c) an intestine cell possesses a full set of genes
(d) intestine cells are not differentiated

46. DNA packing–the way DNA is folded into chromosomes–affects gene expression by
(a) controlling access to DNA
(b) positioning related genes near each other
(c) protecting DNA from mutations
(d) enhancing recombination of genes

47. Regulation of polygenic transcription in prokaryotes can be at the level of
(a) RNA polymerase holoenzyme recruitment to DNA (sigma factor specificity for promoters)
(b) enhancer binding protein-induced isomerization of the binary complex (DNA:Es)
(c) repressor and anti-termination of transcription
(d) All of the above

48. In cells that have not been previously exposed to lactose, how does lactose enter the cells to induce *lac* operon?
(a) IPTG would induce the expression instead of lactose
(b) lactose would enter by diffusion across the membrane without the need for permease
(c) some other transport protein facilitates the entry of lactose
(d) basal level of expression of *lac*, operon, leading to the low level synthesis of permease

49. A mutant of *Escherichia coli* was isolated that synthesized greater than normal levels of tryptophan synthesizing enzymes in the absence of tryptophan. It was found to make normal *trp* repressor and also had normal *trp* operator. Which of the following mutations might result in the observed phenotype?
(a) Deletion in the *trp* promoter
(b) Deletion just after the promoter-operator region
(c) Deletion just before the coding sequences for the *trp* enzymes
(d) Deletion in the rho-independent transcription termination signal

50. When a certain bacterium encounters the antibiotic tetracycline, the antibiotic molecule enters the cell and attaches to a repressor protein. This keeps the repressor from binding to the bacterial chromosome, allowing a set of genes to be transcribed. These genes code for enzymes that breakdown the antibiotic. This set of genes is best described as
(a) an exon (b) regulatory genes
(c) an operon (d) a homeobox

51. Regulatory genes are genes that
(a) code for repressor proteins
(b) are transcribed continuously
(c) are not contained in the operon they control
(d) All of the above

52. Inducible enzymes
(a) are usually involved in anabolic pathways
(b) are produced when a catabolite inactivates the repressor protein
(c) are produced when an activator molecule enhances the attachment of RNA polymerase with the operator
(d) are regulated by inherently inactive repressor molecules

53. Enhancer elements are segments of DNA that
I. are required for the transcription of certain genes.
II. activate transcription of a gene irrespective of their relative position in the DNA chain.
III. have no polarity (*i.e.,* they can be inverted).
IV. are non-specific for tissue or species.
(a) I and II (b) II and IV
(c) I, II and III (d) I, II, III and IV

54. Which of the following statement is correct?
I. Promoter-proximal elements present both upstream or down stream of the start point.
II. Upstream Activating Sequences (UASs), present in yeast function similarly to enhancer.
III. True major sigma factor in *E.coli* is S^{70}.
IV. *lac* operon has a strong promoter.
(a) I and II (b) II and III
(c) I, II and III (d) I, II, III and IV

55. Homeodomain proteins
I. Form a structure with three α-helices
II. Contact DNA primarily through α-helix 3 and an N-terminal arm

III. Are similar in structure to prokaryotic helix-turn-helix proteins like the λ-repressor
IV. The always present in the cell nucleus
(a) I and II (b) I and III
(c) I, II and III (d) I, II, III and IV

56. Choose the incorrect pair.
(a) The DNA sequence — Promoter site to which RNA polymerase binds
(b) The DNA sequence — Enhancer sequence to which sigma factors bind
(c) The DNA sequence — Structural gene that codes for a protein'
(d) The DNA sequence — Operator site to which repressors bind

57. Match the following lists.

List-I	List-II
A. Operator gene	1. Provides a site for binding activator proteins and RNA polymerase
B. Promoter gene	2. Makes enzymes that control metabolism such as lactose in the cell
C. Regulator gene	3. Switches on cistern activity
D. Structural gene	4. Synthesises a molecule that blocks a gene adjacent to structural genes

Codes

	A	B	C	D
(a)	2	1	3	4
(b)	3	1	4	2
(c)	2	3	4	1
(d)	3	4	1	2

58. Which of the following statements about the repressor of the lactose operon of *E.coli* are true?
I. It is the gene product of the regulatory gene.
II. It binds to the operator region of the DNA of the *lac* operon.
III. It blocks the transcription of structural genes.
IV. It combines with allolactose and the combination will not bind to the operator.
(a) I and II
(b) I and II
(c) I and IV
(d) I, II, III and IV

59. The following are basic properties of a prokaryotic operon. The operon
I. Usually consists of multiple genes that are organized between a promoter and a terminator.
II. The operon is usually under autogenous transcriptional control.
III. Member genes are coordinately regulated.
IV. The operon contains exclusively genes that encode proteins involved in stress tolerance.
(a) I and II
(b) I and III
(c) I and III
(d) I, III and IV

Answers

1. (d)	**2.** (a)	**3.** (c)	**4.** (c)	**5.** (b)	**6.** (c)	**7.** (d)	**8.** (c)	**9.** (b)	**10.** (c)
11. (c)	**12.** (b)	**13.** (c)	**14.** (c)	**15.** (c)	**16.** (b)	**17.** (d)	**18.** (a)	**19.** (c)	**20.** (b)
21. (c)	**22.** (b)	**23.** (b)	**24.** (c)	**25.** (c)	**26.** (b)	**27.** (a)	**28.** (c)	**29.** (c)	**30.** (a)
31. (d)	**32.** (a)	**33.** (c)	**34.** (b)	**35.** (a)	**36.** (b)	**37.** (d)	**38.** (d)	**39.** (d)	**40.** (b)
41. (b)	**42.** (d)	**43.** (b)	**44.** (a)	**45.** (c)	**46.** (a)	**47.** (d)	**48.** (d)	**49.** (c)	**50.** (c)
51. (d)	**52.** (b)	**53.** (c)	**54.** (b)	**55.** (c)	**56.** (b)	**57.** (b)	**58.** (d)	**59.** (b)	

10

Host Parasite Interactions

Microbes are consistently associated with the body surfaces of animals and plants. There are many more microbial cells on the surface of a human (including the gastrointestinal tract) than there are human cells that make up the animal. The bacteria and other microbes that are consistently associated with an animal/plant are called the **normal flora** or more properly the **indigenous microbiota,** of the animal/plant. Many bacteria have such a full range of **symbiotic interactions** with their animal hosts.

In biology, **symbiosis** is defined as 'life together', *i.e.,* two organisms live in an association with one another. Thus, there are at least three types of relationships based on the quality of the relationship for each member of the symbiotic association.

Syllabus

- Recognition and Entry of Different Pathogens Like Bacteria, Viruses into Animal and Plant Host Cells.
- Alteration of Host Cell Behaviour by Pathogens.
- Virus Induced Cell Transformation.
- Pathogen Induced Diseases in Animals and Plants.

Mutualism

Both members of the association benefit. For human, one classic mutualistic association is that of the lactic acid bacteria that live on the vaginal epithelium of a woman. The bacteria are provided habitat with a constant temperature and supply of nutrients (glycogen) in exchange for the production of lactic acid, which protects the vagina from colonization and disease caused by yeast and other potentially harmful microbes.

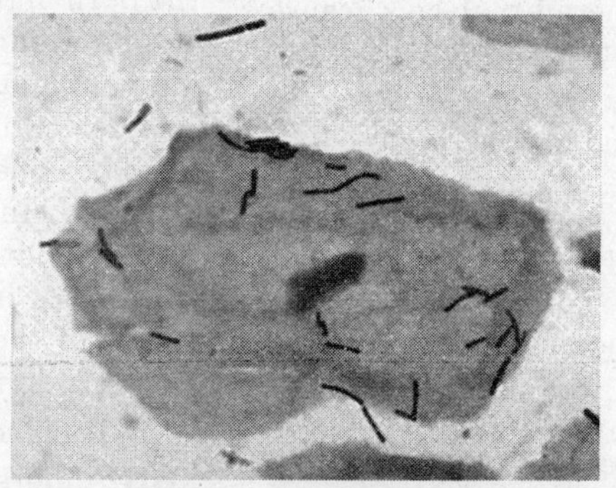

Fig. 10.1 Loctobacilli in association with a vaginal epithelical cell

Commensalism

There is no apparent benefit or harm to either member of the association. A problem with commensal relationships is that if you look at one long enough and hard enough, you often discover that at least one member is being helped or harmed during the association. Consider our relationship with *Staphylococcus epidermidis*, a consistent inhabitant of the skin of human. Probably, the bacterium produces lactic acid that protects the skin from colonization by harmful microbes that are less acid tolerant. But it has been suggested that other metabolites that are produced by the bacteria are an important cause of body odours (good or bad, depending on your personal point of view) and possibly associated with certain skin cancers. 'Commensalisms' best works when the relationship between two organisms is unknown and not obvious.

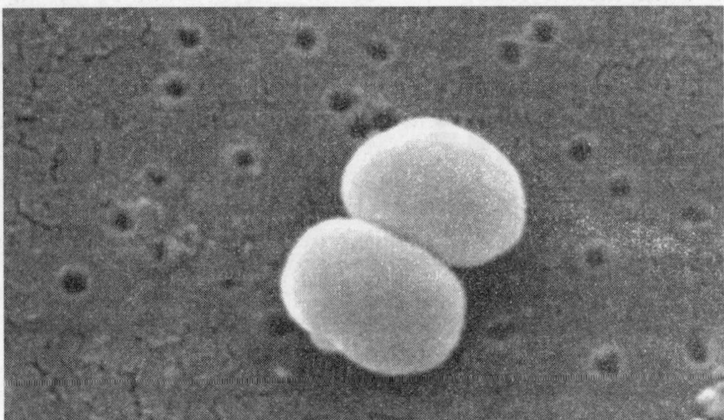

Fig. 10.2 Electron micrograph of *Staphylococcus epidermidis*

Parasitism

In biology, the term **parasite** refers to an organism that grows, feeds and is sheltered on or in a different organism while contributing nothing to the survival of its host. In microbiology, the mode of existence of a parasite implies that the parasite is capable of causing damage to the host. This type of a symbiotic association draws our attention because a parasite may become pathogenic if the damage to the host results in disease. Some parasitic bacteria live as normal flora of human while waiting for an opportunity to cause disease. Other non-indigenous parasites generally always cause disease if they associate with a non-immune host.

Parasitology is actually a branch of microbiology, refers to the scientific study of parasitism and a **pathogen** is a microorganism or virus that is able to produce disease. **Pathogenicity** is the ability of a microorganism to cause disease in another organism, namely the **host** for the pathogen. As implied above, pathogenicity may be a manifestation of a host-parasite interaction, *e.g.*, in human, some of the normal bacterial flora (*e.g.*, *Staphylococcus aureus*, *Streptococcus pneumoniae* and *Haemophilus influenzae*) are **potential pathogens** that live in a commensal or parasitic relationship without producing disease. They do not cause disease in their host unless they have an opportunity brought on by some compromise or weakness in the host's anatomical barriers, tissue resistance or immunity. Furthermore, the bacteria are in a position to be transmitted from one host to another, giving them additional opportunities to colonize or infect.

There are some pathogens that do not associate with their host except in the case of disease. These microbes may be thought of as **obligate pathogens,** even though some may rarely occur as normal flora, in asymptomatic or recovered carriers, or in some form, where they cannot be eliminated by the host.

Recognition and Entry of Different Pathogens

Microbes which cause a disease in a compromised host which typically would not occur in a healthy (non-compromised) host are acting as **opportunistic pathogens.**

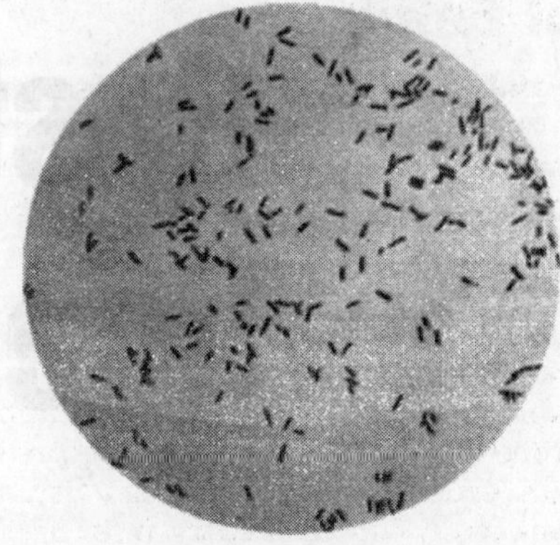

Fig. 10.3 Photomicrograph of *Pseudomonas aeruginosa*

Pseudomonas aeruginosa, bacterium causes urinary tract infections, respiratory system infections, dermatitis, soft tissue infections, bacteremia and a variety of systemic infections, particularly in cancer and AIDS patients who are immuno-suppressed.

Infection

It is necessary that pathogens must first gain access to the host, *i.e.*, it must adhere and penetrate before infection is established and then it must continually evade host defenses the normal flora, as well as any 'contaminating' microbe from the environment, is all found on the body surfaces of the animal/plant; the blood and internal tissues are sterile. If a microbe, whether or not a component of the normal flora, breaches one of these surfaces, an **infection** is said to have occurred. Infection does not necessarily lead to infectious disease. But other factors, such as the route of entry, the number of infectious microbes, and (most importantly) the status of the host defenses, play a role in determining the outcome of infection. To cause disease a pathogen must.

(i) Gain access to the host.

(ii) Adhere to host tissues.

(iii) Penetrate or evade host defenses.

(iv) Damage the host, either directly or through accumulation of microbial wastes.

Properties of the Host

The **host** in a **host-parasite interaction** is the animal or a plant that maintains the parasite. The host and parasite are in a dynamic interaction, the outcome of which depends upon the properties of the parasite and of the host. The **microbial parasite has its determinants of virulence** that allow it to invade and damage the host and to resist the defenses of the host. The **host has various degrees of resistance** to the parasite in the form of the **host defenses.**

Entry of Pathogen into Host

Most pathogens must gain access to the host, adhere to host tissue, penetrate or evade host defenses and damage the host tissue. Pathogens can enter to human body or other host through several avenues called portals of entry.

Portals of Entry

(i) **Mucous membranes** (moist mucosa) is the most common route for most pathogens/entry through mucus membranes is achieved in respiratory tract (most common), gastrointestinal tract, urinary/genital tracts and conjunctiva.

(ii) **Skin** (keratinized cutaneous membrane), while some pathogens infect hair follicles and sweat glands, few can colonize surface. Unless broken, skin is usually an impermeable barrier to microbes. It is important that most microbes must enter through their preferred portal of entry in order to cause disease. Some can cause disease from many routes of entry, most usually also exit the host from the same original portal to spread disease.

(iii) **Parenteral route** Some pathogens penetrate skin through punctures, injections, bites, cuts, surgery, etc., and deposit organisms directly into deeper tissues.

Numbers of Invading Microbes

The likelihood of disease increases as the number of invading pathogens increases. $\mathbf{ID_{50}}$ (Infectious Dose) is the number of microbes required to produce infection in 50% of the population. Usually there is different ID^{50} for different pathogens. Also there is different ID^{50} for different portals of entry for the same pathogen. $\mathbf{LD_{50}}$ (Lethal Dose) is defined as the amount of toxin or pathogen necessary to kill 50% of the population in a particular time frame.

Adherence

It is the attachment to the host by the microbe at portal of entry and is usually necessary for virulence. In fact , blocking adhesion can prevent disease. Usually pathogen has surface molecules called **adhesions** or **ligands** that bind specifically to the host surface receptors. Most microbial adhesions are glycoproteins or lipoproteins located on the glycocalyx, capsule, capsid, pili, fimbriae or flagella. Most host receptors are typically proteins (for virus) or carbohydrates (for bacteria) in the wall or membrane of host cell. Adhesions/ligands bind to receptors on host cells.

(a) **Glycocalyx** *Streptococcus mutans*

(b) **Fimbriae** *Escherichia coli*

(c) **M protein** *Streptococcus pyogenes*

(d) **Opa protein** *Neisseria gonorrhoeae*

(e) **Tapered end** *Treponema pallidum*.

Table 10.1 **Specific Attachments of Bacteria to Cell or Tissue Surfaces**

Bacterium	Adhesion	Host Receptor	Attachment Site	Disease
Streptococcus pyogenes	Protein F	Amino terminus of fibronectin	Pharyngeal epithelium	Sore throat
Streptococcus mutans	Glucan	Salivary glycoprotein	Pellicle of tooth	Dental caries
Streptococcus salivarius	Lipoteichoic acid	Unknown	Buccal epithelium of tongue	None
Streptococcus pneumoniae	Cell-bound protein	N-acetyloxamine galactose disaccharide	Mucosal epithelium	Pneumonia
Staphylococcus aureus	Cell-bound protein	Amino terminus of fibronectin	Mucosal epithelium	Various
Neisseria gonorrhoeae	N-methylpheny-ealanine pili	Glucosamine galactose carbohydrate	Urethral/cervical epithelium	Gonorrhoea
Enteroxigenic *E.coli*	Type I fimbriae (pili)	Species-specific carbohydrate(s)	Intestinal epithelium	Diarrhoea
Uropathogenic *E.coli*	Type I fimbriae (pili)	Complex carbohydrate	Urethral epithelium	Urethritis
Uropathogenic *E.coli*	P pill (pylonephritis-associated (pili)	P-blood group	Upper urinary tract	Pyelonephritis
Bordetella pertussis	Pili (filamentous haemagglutinin) glycolipids	Galactose on sulphated Glycolipids	Respiratory epithelium	Whooping cough
Vibrio cholerae	N-methylpherry-nylalanine pili	Fructose and mannose carbohydrate	Intestinal epithelium	Cholera
Treponema pallidum	Peptide in outer membrane	Surface protein (fibronectin)	Mucosal epithelium	Syphilis
Mycoplasma	Membrane protein	Sialic acid	Respiratory epithelium	Pneumonia
Chlamydia	Unknown	Sialic acid	Conjunctiva or urethral epithelium	Conjunctivitis or urethritis

Biofilms

They are formed when microbes adhere to a surface that is usually moist and contains organic matter. Each microbe secretes glycocalyx thus, allowing other microbes to adhere hence, a large mass is formed. The biofilm formed is resistant to disinfectants and antibiotics (outer layer protects inner layers). This poses a problem for catheters and surgical implants and infact serves as chronic reservoir.

Enzymes

(a) **Coagulase** Coagulate blood.
(b) **Kinases** Digest fibrin clots.
(c) **Hyaluronidase** Hydrolyzes hyaluronic acid.
(d) **Collagenase** Hydrolyzes collagen.
(e) **IgA proteases** Destroy IgA antibodies.
(f) **Siderophores** Take iron from host iron-binding proteins.
(g) **Antigenic variation** Alter surface proteins.

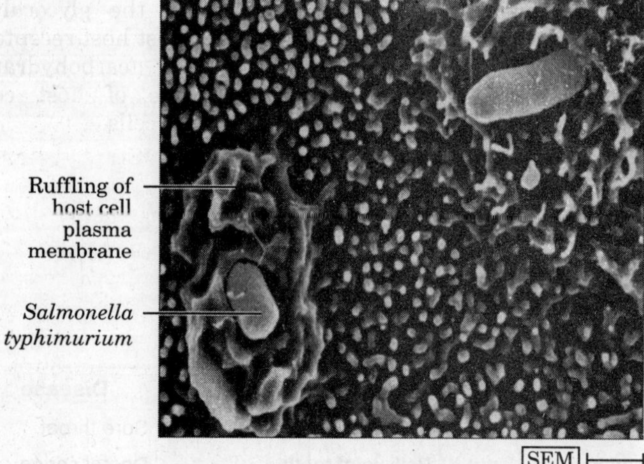

Fig. 10.4 Electron micrograph of *Salmonella* effect on target cell

Toxins

(a) **Toxin** Substances that contribute to pathogenicity.
(b) **Toxigenicity** Ability to produce a toxin.
(c) **Toxemia** Presence of toxin in the host's blood.
(d) **Toxoid** Inactivated toxin used in a vaccine.
(e) **Antitoxin** Antibodies against a specific toxin.

Determinants of Virulence

Pathogenic microbes are able to produce disease because they possess certain **structural** or **biochemical** or **genetic** traits that render them pathogenic or **virulent** (the term **virulence** is best interpreted as referring to the **degree of pathogenicity**). The sums of the characteristics that allow a given microbe to produce disease are the pathogen's **determinants of virulence.** Some pathogens may rely on a single determinant of virulence, such as toxin production, to cause damage to their host, while others maintain a large repertoire of virulence determinants and consequently are able to produce a more complete range of diseases that affect different tissues in their host.

Host Defenses

A healthy animal can defend itself against pathogens at different stages in the infectious disease process. The host defenses may be of such a degree that infection can be prevented entirely. Or, if infection does occur, the defenses may stop the process before disease is apparent. At other times, the defenses that are necessary to defeat a pathogen may not be effective until infectious disease is well into progress.

Typically the host defense mechanisms are divided into two groups :

Innate Defenses

Defenses common to all healthy animals. These defenses provide general protection against invasion by normal flora, or colonization, infection and infectious disease caused by pathogens. Innate defenses include anatomical and structural barriers, inflammation, phagocytosis and the presence of a normal bacterial flora. The innate defenses have also been referred to as 'natural' or 'constitutive' resistance, since **they are inherent to the host.**

Inducible Defenses

Defense mechanisms that **must be induced or turned on by host exposure to a pathogen** (as during an infection). Unlike the innate defenses, they are not immediately ready to come into play until after the host is appropriately exposed to the parasite. The inducible defenses are synonymous with **acquired** or **adaptive immunity** and involve the immunological responses to a pathogen causing an infection.

Adaptive immunity is generally quite specifically directed against an invading pathogen. The innate defenses are not so specific and are directed toward general strategic defense. Innate defenses, by themselves, may not be sufficient to protect a host against pathogens. Such pathogens that evade or overcome the relatively **non-specific innate defenses** are usually susceptible to the more **specific inducible defenses,** once they have developed the immune system.

The inducible defenses are so called because they are induced upon primary exposure to a pathogen or one of its products. The inducible defenses are a function of the **immunological system** and the **immune responses.** The innate defenses are immediately available for host defense. The inducible defenses must be triggered in a host and initially take time to develop. The type of resistance thus, developed in the host is called **acquired immunity.** The term **immune** usually means the ability to resist infectious disease. **Immunity** refers to the relative state of resistance of the host to a specific pathogen brought on by the activities of the immunological system.

Acquired or **Adaptive Immunity,** itself, is sometimes divided into two types, based on how it is acquired by the host.

In **active immunity, the host undergoes an immunological response** and produces the cells and factors responsible for the immunity, *i.e.,* the host produces its own antibodies and/or immuno-reactive lymphocytes. Active immunity can persist a long time in the host, up to many years in human.

In passive immunity there is acquisition by a host of immune factors which were produced in another animal, *i.e.,* the host receives antibodies and/or immuno-reactive lymphocytes originally produced in another animal. Passive immunity is typically short-lived and usually persists only a few weeks or months.

Antigens

Antigens are chemical substances of relatively high molecular weight, that stimulate the immune response in animals. Bacteria are composed of various macromolecular components that are antigens or **antigenic** in their host and bacterial antigens interact with the host immunological system in a variety of ways.

Natural Antibodies

Studies on germ-free animals have confirmed that a normal bacterial flora in the gastrointestinal tract is necessary for full development of immunological (lymphatic) tissues in the intestine. Furthermore, the interaction between these immune tissues and intestinal bacteria results in the production of **serum** and **secretory antibodies** that are directed against bacterial antigens. These antibodies probably help protect the host from invasion by its own normal flora and they can cross react with antgenically-related pathogens. For example, antibodies against normal *E.coli* could react with closely-related pathogenic *Shigella dysenteriae*. These types of antibodies are sometimes called **natural** or **cross-reactive antibodies.**

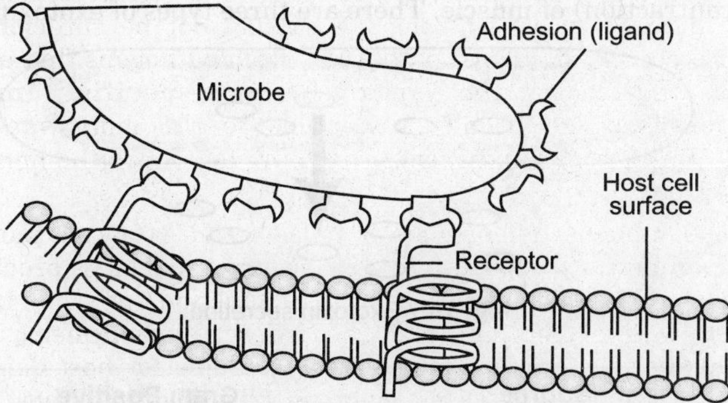

Fig. 10.5 The mechanism of microbial attachment to host cell

Penetration of Host Defenses

There are various levels of host defenses to overcome by pathogen for disease development. The various penetration processes are

Capsules

The organized glycocalyx layer (carbohydrates) outside cell wall is known to impair phagocytosis. It prevents engulfment and destruction by leukocytes. If present, it is usually required for virulence even though some of them are non-antigenic.

Cell Wall Components

(a) M protein of *Streptococcus pyogenes* is a heat and acid resistant molecule which mediates attachment of bacterium to epithelial cells and resists phagocytosis by leukocytes.

(b) Fimbriae + Opa (membrane protein) is used by *Neisseria gonorrhoeae* and promotes attachment and uptake by host epithelial cells and leukocytes. *Neisseria* then grows inside these cells.

(c) Mycolic acid (waxy) of *Mycobacterium tuberculosis* resists digestion by phagocytes. *Mycobacterium* then grows inside phagocyte.

Enzymes (Exo-enzymes)

(a) Coagulases are a clot fibrin in blood to create protective barrier against host defenses.

(b) Kinases is used to dissolve clots (fibrinolysis) to allow escape from isolated wounds, *e.g.,* Streptokinase (*Streptococcus pyogenes*), Staphylokinase (*Staphylococcus aureus*).

(c) Hyaluronidases used to hydrolyzes hyaluronic acid (glue that holds together connective tissues and epithelium barriers) thereby allowing deeper invasion, *e.g., Clostridium* species. It allows them to cause gangrene (tissue necrosis).

(d) Collagenase usually breaks down collagen (fibrous part of connective tissue) for invasion into muscles and organs, *e.g., Clostridium* species.

(e) IgA proteases destroys host IgA antibodies found in mucous secretions to allow adherence and passage at mucus membranes, *e.g., Neisseria* species that infect CNS.

Antigenic Variation

Here the pathogen alters its surface antigens to escape attack by antibodies and immune cells, *e.g., Neisseria gonorrhoeae* has many versions of the Opa gene. It can alter which one is being expressed, *e.g.,* influenza virus, where there is constant genetic recombination between flu viruses leading to always new spike proteins.

Penetration into Host Cytoskeleton

This involves the use of actin of host cell to penetrate and move within the cell. It involves several proteins like :

(a) **Invasins** They are the surface proteins produced by bacteria to control actin, *e.g., Salmonella* which rearranges actin thereby causing the cell membrane to wrap around the microbe and take it into the cell (endocytosis). It also allows *Salmonella* to penetrate intestinal epithelium. Further in *Shigella* and *Listeria* it triggers endocytosis which polymerizes actin behind bacterium to propel through host cell.

(b) **Cadherin** It allows penetration between cells at intercellular junctions, *e.g.*, *Shigella* and *Listeria* which move between cells at cell junctions.

Using Hosts Nutrients

Iron is required for all cells (electron transport chain cytochromes) by both the host and the pathogen. However host usually does not have free iron available (free iron leads to easy colonization by pathogens). In the case of human bind unused iron to transport proteins like transferrin. The pathogens can produce siderophores which are secreted by bacteria to compete iron from host proteins and siderophore iron complex then absorbed by bacteria.

Alteration of Cell Behaviour by Pathogens

Host tissues show different types of responses to activities of the pathogen after it has established infection and when it starts parasitic and pathogen activities. In the initial stages of penetration these may be a striking increase in protoplasmic strands and the nucleus of the cell may move to the site of penetration. Normal physiological activities of the host cell are disturbed and anatomical and morphological changes appear as visible changes. The main harmful effects are due to pathogen enzymes, hormonal inbalance and metabolic disturbance.

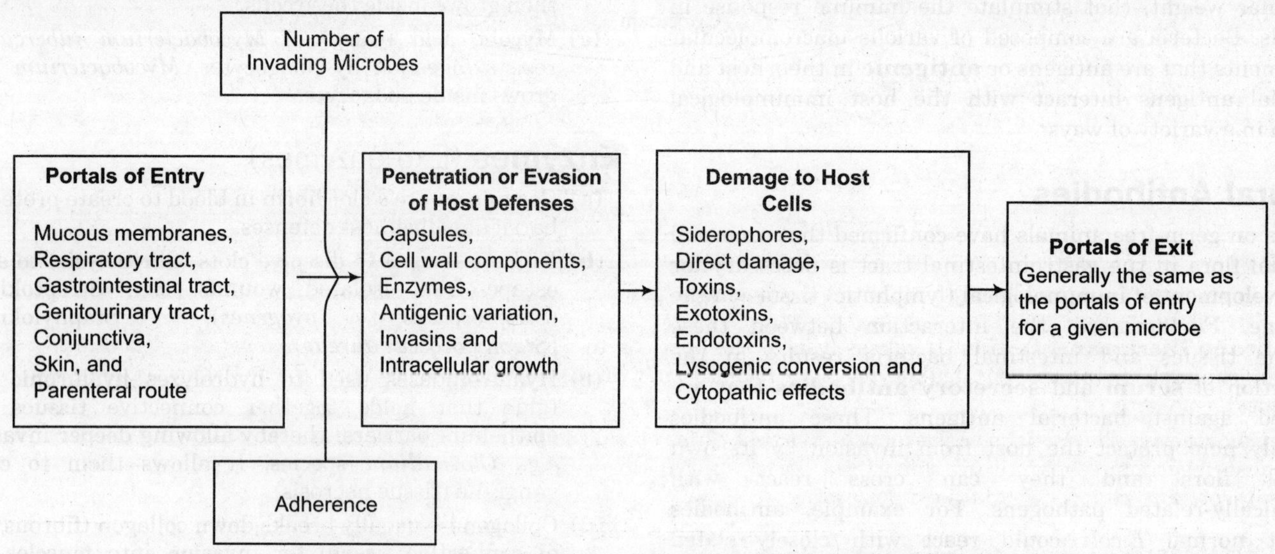

Fig. 10.6 Microbial mechanism of pathogenicity and damage to host cell

Direct Damage to Colonized Area

The growth and replication in host cells resulting in host cell lysis are during penetration through host cells (mucosa, organs) hence, causing damage and finally lysis of host cells to obtain nutrients.

Production of Toxins

Toxins are usually poisonous substance produced by microbes which tend to cause widespread damage/disease in host. They may be necessary for virulence. The various types are:

Exotoxins

They are produced inside the bacteria and either secreted or released following microbe lysis. The toxin genes are often found on plasmids or *via* lysogenic phages. Most of them are enzymes and function to destroy certain host cell parts or inhibit particular metabolic functions. The damage from toxin results in the particular signs or symptoms of a disease and can be named for the disease, type of cell attacked or organism that produces it, *e.g.*, tetanus toxin: causes tetanus (contraction) of muscle. There are three types of exotoxins:

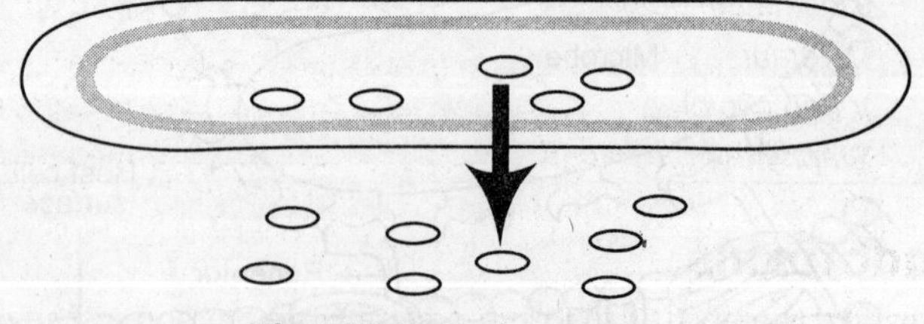

Fig. 10.7 Exotoxin secretion

Source	Gram Positive
Relation to microbe	By-products of growing cell
Chemistry	Protein
Fever	No
Neutralized by antitoxin	Yes
LD^{50}	Small

B-toxins

It is composed of two parts, where A is the enzyme that disrupts some cell activity, while B-binds surface receptors to bring A into the host cell, *e.g.*, botulinum and tetanus toxin.

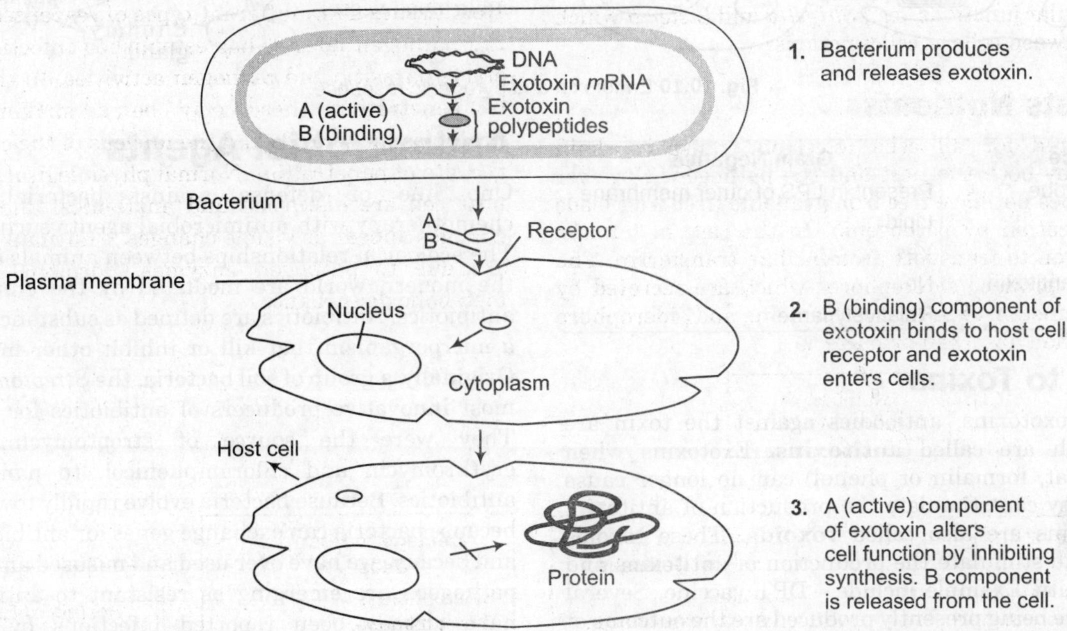

Fig. 10.8 Action of exotoxin

Membrane Disrupting Toxins It causes lysis of the host cell by disrupting the plasma membrane, *e.g.*, leukocidins: make protein channels in phagocytic leukocytes *e.g.*, haemolysins: make protein channels in RBCs (haemolysis: *Streptococcus pyogenes*).

Super Antigens They are the bacterial proteins that cause proliferation of T-cells and release of cytokines excessive cytokines can cause fever, nausea, vomiting, diarrhoea, shock and death (septic shock), *e.g.*, toxic shock syndrome (*Staphylococcus*), *e.g.*, enterotoxins: Staphylococcal food poisoning.

Table 10.2 **Microorganism and their Exotoxin**

Microorganism	Exotoxin	Lysogenic Conversion
Corynebacterium diphtheriae	A-B-toxin inhibits protein synthesis	+
Streptococcus pyogenes	Membrane-disrupting erythrogenic	+
Clostridium botulinum	A-B-toxin, neurotoxin	+
C. tetani	A-B-toxin, neurotoxin	
Vibrio cholerae	A-B-toxin, enterotoxin	+
Staphylococcus aureus	Superantigen	+

Endotoxins

They are the part of the outer membrane portion of the cell wall of Gram negative bacteria, *e.g.*, Lipopolysaccharide (LPS) which is released when dead cells lyse in blood, causes macrophages to release high levels of cytokines resulting in chills, fever, weakness, aches, small blood clots, tissue necrosis, shock and death. Also endotoxic shock which is basically the critical loss of blood pressure is caused due to bacterial endotoxins (LPS). Sterile solutions can contain LPS because bacteria dies in sterilization but LPS is unaltered Due to serious consequences at very low levels of LPS, it is essential to test medical devices and solutions for endotoxin presence.

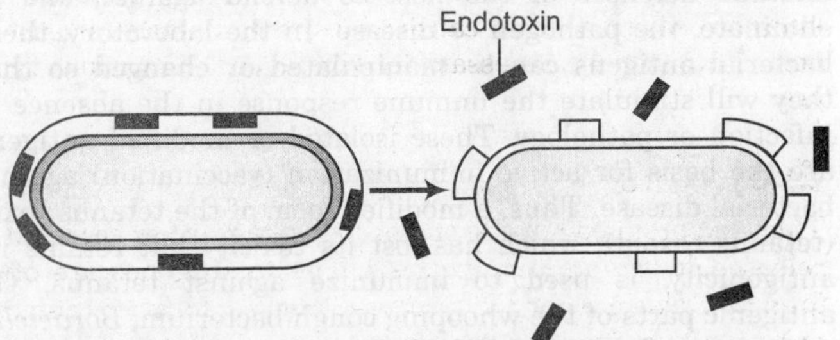

Fig. 10.9 Endotoxins are part of the outer portion of the cell wall of Gram negative bacteria. They are liberated when the bacteria die and the cell wall breaks apart.

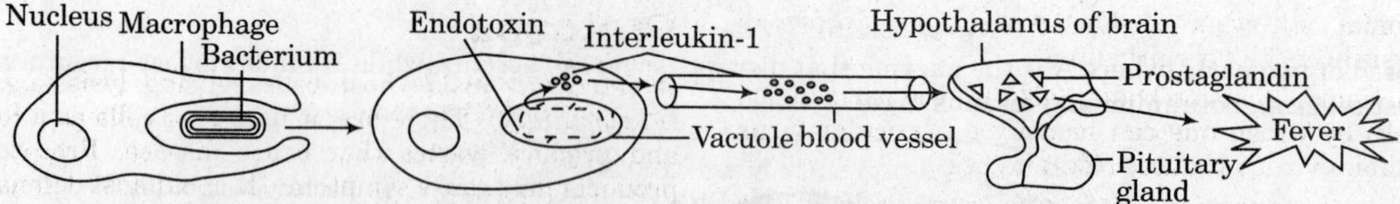

Fig. 10.10 Endotoxin and pyrogenic response

Source	Gram Negative
Relation to microbe	Present in LPS of outer membrane
Chemistry	Lipid
Fever	Yes
Neutralized by antitoxin	No
LD^{50}	Relatively large

Response to Toxins

If exposed to exotoxins, antibodies against the toxin are produced which are called **antitoxins.** Exotoxins when inactivated (heat, formalin or phenol) can no longer cause disease, but they can stimulate the production of antitoxin. Altered exotoxins are also called **toxoids.** These toxoids when injected to stimulate the production of antitoxins and provide immunity. Example include – DPT vaccine. Several vaccines that are being presently produced are the outcome of such attenuated toxoids.

Plasmids, Lysogeny and Pathogenicity

Usually plasmids carry genes for resistance to anti-biotics and/or virulence factors (*e.g.,* exotoxins, fimbriae) between bacteria allowing new bacteria to become pathogenic, *e.g.,* haemorrhagic *E. coli* (fimbriae + shiga toxin). Also prophages can result in lysogenic conversion that results in pathogenic ability of the bacteria carrying them (new production of endotoxin), *e.g.,* Diphtheria toxin (*Corynebacterium*), Cholera toxin (*Vibrio*) phage can be transmitted to non-pathogenic strains making them virulent.

Bacterial Antigens Made into Vaccines

In another way, bacterial antigens that are the components or products of pathogens are the substances that induce the immune defenses of the host to defend against, and to eliminate, the pathogen or disease. In the laboratory, these bacterial antigens can be manipulated or changed so that they will stimulate the immune response in the absence of infection or pathology. These isolated or modified antigens are the basis for active immunization (vaccination) against bacterial disease. Thus, a modified form of the tetanus toxin (tetanus toxoid), which has lost its toxicity but retains its antigenicity, is used to immunize against tetanus. Or, antigenic parts of the whooping cough bacterium, *Bordetella pertusis,* can be used to induce active formation of antibodies that will react with the living organism and thereby prevent infection.

Antimicrobial Agents

One line of defense against bacterial infection is chemotherapy with antimicrobial agents such as antibiotics. The ecological relationships between animals and bacteria in the modern world are mediated by the omni presence of antibiotics. Antibiotics are defined as substances produced by a microorganism that kill or inhibit other microorganisms. Originally, a group of soil bacteria, the *Streptomyces*, were the most innovative producers of antibiotics for clinical usage. They were the source of streptomycin, tetracycline, erythromycin and chloramphenicol, to name just a few antibiotics. Because bacteria evolve rapidly toward resistance because bacteria can exchange genes for antibiotic resistance, and because we have over used and misused antibiotics, many pathogens are emerging as resistant to antibiotics. There have already been reported infections by *Enterococcus*, *Staphylococcus aureus* and *Pseudomonas aeruginosa* that are refractory to all known antibiotics. Bacterial resistance to antimicrobial agents has become part of a pathogen's determinants of virulence. These are examples of genetic means by which bacteria exert their virulence.

The usage of antibiotics to control the growth of parasites is an artificial way to intervene in the natural process of the host-parasite interaction. But, of course, it is done for the obvious purpose of curing the disease. The body heals itself: most antibiotics just stop bacterial growth and the host must rely entirely on its native defenses to accomplish the neutralization of bacterial toxins or the elimination of bacterial cells. The judicious use of antibiotics in the past five decades has saved millions of lives from infections caused by bacteria.

Pathogenic Properties of Virus

Viruses are a group of sub-microscopic entities showing obligate relationship with living cells of the host and ability to cause specific disease. The viruses

(i) Grow inside host cells to hide from immune defense.

(ii) Kill immune cells, *e.g.,* HIV kills T_H cells thereby evading immunity.

Cytopathic Effects

They are the visible effects of viral infection on host cell: some effects will kill the cell; some will just change the cell

(i) These virus stop DNA, RNA and/or protein synthesis, *e.g.,* Herpes virus blocks mitosis.

(ii) Lysosomal autolysis of host cells, *e.g.*, Influenza autolysis bronchiolar epithelium.

(iii) Production of inclusion bodies (visible viral parts inside the cell) by which one can identify a particular virus *e.g.*, Rabies virus produces Negri bodies.

(iv) Syncytium formation (neighbouring cells fuse together), *e.g.*, Varicella zoster virus.

(v) Change in cell function, *e.g.*, Measles.

(vi) Production of interferons by host cell (triggers host immune response).

(vii) Induce antigenic changes on host cell surface (triggers destruction of infected cell by host immune response).

(viii) Induce chromosomal changes.

(ix) Cell transformation may activate or deliver oncogenes resulting in loss of contact inhibition (cancer), *e.g.*, Papilloma virus.

Table 10.3 **Cytopathic Effects of Selected Viruses**

Virus	Cytopathic Effect
Poliovirus (Enterovirus)	Cytocidal (cell death)
Papovavirus (family–Papovaviridae)	Acidophilic inclusion bodies in nucleus
Adenovirus (Mastadenovirus)	Basophilic inclusion bodies in nucleus
Rhabdovirus (family–Rhabdoviridae)	Acidophilic inclusion bodies in cytoplasm
Cytomegalovirus	Acidophilic inclusion bodies in nucleus and cytoplasm
Measles virus (Morbillivirus)	Cell fusion
Polyomavirus	Transformation
HIV (Lentivirus)	Destruction of T-cells

Eukaryotic Pathogens

A number of eukaryotic also causes diseases in plants and animals. The eukaryotic pathogens are fungi, Protozoa and algae.

Fungi

It produces toxins causing allergies or disease, *e.g.*, chronic sinusitis is caused by black molds, while *Stachybotrys* leads to headaches, vomiting, mental, disturbance and invasive systemic mycosis in immune compromised patients is caused by *Candida*. In mushrooms, the mycotoxins produced may be hallucinogenic or deadly.

(i) Fungal waste products may cause symptoms.

(ii) Chronic infections provoke an allergic response.

(iii) Tichothecene toxins inhibit protein synthesis, *e.g.*, *Fusarium*

(iv) Proteases, *e.g.*, *Candida*, *Trichophyton*

(v) Capsule prevents phagocytosis, *e.g.*, *Cryptococcus*

(vi) Ergot toxin, *e.g.*, *Claviceps*

(vii) Aflatoxin, *e.g.*, *Aspergillus*

(viii) Mycotoxins

(ix) Nurotoxins: Phalloidin, amanitin, *e.g.*, *Amanita*

Protozoa

It can grow inside host cells causing lysis, *e.g.*, malaria (*Plasmodium*). Therefore, it uses host cells as a food source and produce wastes that cause disease. Protozoan waste products may cause symptoms. It avoid host defenses by

(i) Growing in phagocytes.

(ii) Antigenic variation.

Algae

It produces neurotoxic substances, *e.g.*, shellfish causes poisoning due to dinoflagellates.

Virus Induced Cell Transformation

Viral transformation can impose characteristically determinable features upon a cell. Typical phenotypic changes include high saturation density, anchorage-independent growth, loss of contact inhibition, loss of orientated growth, immortalization and disruption of the cell's cytoskeleton.

Epidemiological studies suggest that malignant transformation of cells by viruses occurs *via* multiple steps. This involves initiation, promotion and progression events. Viruses act alongwith other factors to transform cells. The persistence of at least part of the viral genome within the cell is required for cell transformation. This is accompanied by the continual expression from a number of viral genes. These genes interfere with a cell's signaling pathway causing the observed phenotypic changes of the cell. The end result is a transformed cell showing increased cell division, which is favourable to the virus.

Host Parasite Interaction in Plants

Even though the vast majority of plant pathogens are fungi, however, plant diseases are also caused by insects, bacteria, nematodes, viruses and phytoplasmas. Disease-like symptoms can also be caused by abiotic factors such as temperature, light, chemical agents and water or nutrient deficiencies.

Symptoms

Symptoms of disease include death and destruction of host tissue, wilting, abnormal growth and differentiation and discolouration of host tissue.

Necrotic Lesions

Some parasites, called **necrotrophs,** secrete enzymes that kill host tissue, extract nutrients from the cells and then live in the dead tissue thereby causing localized or extensive lesions finally leading to plant's death.

Wilting

It occurs when water loss is greater than water intake due to either interference with water and nutrient absorption at the roots, interference with water conduction within the plant (*i.e.*, infection of the vascular tissue), or loss of control of transpiration.

Abnormal Growth and Differentiation

It results from deviation from the complex balance of interrelated reactions that take place in plants, *e.g.*, altered hormonal balance in plants causing an abnormal increase in the size or number of cells, resulting in abnormal growth and differentiation, for example, the formation of galls.

Discolouration of tissue is most commonly by chlorosis or mosaics of leaves (abnormal production of chlorophyll), both of which can have a number of causes. **Mosaicism** is a symptom of many virus infections and is characterized by alternating light and dark green areas on the leaves.

Survival of Pathogen

Most pathogens possess mechanisms to survive intercrop periods or periods of unfavourable environmental conditions.

Continuous Infection Chains

The survival of most plant pathogens requires the repeated infection of host plants, *i.e.*, the infection chain. The infection chain can be continuous or discontinuous (incorporating a resting phase). Continuous infection chains can involve the same or alternative hosts. It is a necessary step in the infection cycle.

Discontinuous Infection Chains

Discontinuous infection chains usually involve an epiphytic, saprophytic or resting phase. Nematode eggs can survive for long periods in egg cysts or gelatinous egg masses, which reduce the rate of egg desiccation.

Dispersal of Inoculum

Inoculum can be classified as primary or secondary inoculum.

Primary inoculum consists of propagules of a pathogen that start the disease cycle in a new growing season.

Secondary inoculum distributes the pathogen within the main growing season of the crop. It is usually secondary inoculum that leads to the development of epidemics.

Inoculum can be carried from plant to plant by a variety of methods like air currents, through the soil, by water splash or *via* a vector species such as an insect, other animal, fungus or plant.

Insect vectors often have piercing and sucking mouthparts, penetrating the plant surface and providing an infection pathway for viruses, phytoplasmas and plant parasitic Protozoa that they are carrying inside their bodies. Some bacteria and fungi are spread by sticking to the outside of insect vectors. Disease can also be dispersed in planting material, such as clones and seeds. About one fifth of known plant viruses are dispersed *via* seed.

The Infection Process

The 'infection process' can be divided into three phases–**pre-entry, entry** and **colonization.** The process of infection is influenced by properties of the pathogen, the host and the external environment.

Pre-Entry

Parasites colonize the outside of the plant (ectoparasites) or enter the host plant by **penetration** or *via* a wound. Pathogens may negotiate its surface before entering the host through specialized penetration structures, such as appressoria, through wounds or stomata pores or *via* vectors such as fungi or insects. After inoculation pathogen development is differentially influenced by temperature, moisture, light, aeration, nutrient availability and pH. The conditions necessary for survival and successful infection differ between pathogens.

Entry

Fungal pathogens often use **direct penetration** of the plant surface to enter the host. This requires adhesion to the plant surface (attachment of the appressorium), followed by the application of pressure and then enzymatic degradation (cutinase, cellulase, pectinase and protease) of the cuticle and cell wall, in order to overcome the physical barriers presented by the plant's surface.

The alternative pathway for pathogen entry is *via* a **pre-existing opening** (natural openings like stomatal pores, hydathode, lenticels, unusual openings like nectaries, styles and **ectodesmata** or a wound) in the plant surface.

Colonization

A successful infection requires the establishment of a parasitic relationship between the pathogen and the host, once the host has gained entry to the plant.

Types of Pathogens in Plants

Two broad categories of pathogens are **biotrophs** (those that establish an infection in living tissue) and **necrotrophs** (those that kill cells before colonizing them, by secreting toxins that diffuse ahead of the advancing pathogen). The toxins produced by necrotrophs can be specific to the host or non-specific. Necrotrophs often enter the plant through wounds and cause immediate and severe symptoms. An intermediate category of parasite is the **hemibiotrophs,** which start off as biotrophs and eventually become necrotrophic, employing tactics from both classes of pathogen.

Pathogens that colonize the surface of plants, extracting nutrients through haustoria in epidermal or mesophyll cells are termed **ectoparasites.**

Some parasites colonize the area between the cuticle and the outer wall of the epidermal cells, penetrating host epidermal and mesophyll cells with haustoria. These are called **sub-cuticular infections.**

Pathogens can also form colonies deeper in the plant, tissues. These are **mesophyll** and **parenchyma infections** and can be necrotrophic, hemibiotrophicor biotrophic relation- ships.

Vascular infections usually cause wilting and discolouration as a result of the physical blockage of infected xylem vessels. True vascular wilt pathogens colonize the vascular tissue exclusively, although other pathogens can cause the same symptoms if they infect the vascular system as well as other tissues.

There are a few pathogens that manage to achieve **systemic infection** of their host. For example, many viruses can spread to most parts of the plant, although not necessarily all tissues. Some downy mildews can also systemically infect their host by invading the vascular tissue and growing throughout the host, causing deformation, rather than necrosis.

Finally, there are some pathogens that complete their entire life cycle within the cells of their host, and may spread from cell to cell during cytokinesis. These are **endobiotic infections.**

Disease Physiology

While necrotrophs have little effect on plant physiology, since they kill host cells before colonizing them, biotrophic pathogens become incorporated into and subtly modify various aspects of host physiology, such as respiration, photosynthesis, translocation, transpiration and growth and development.

Host Resistance

Resistant hosts prevent or slow the development and reproduction of the majority of pathogen propagules that they come into contact with. Resistance can be expressed at many stages in the infection process, from inhibition of propagule germination and penetration, to the restriction of colony development after the pathogen has become established. The defence barriers erected by plants are a coordinated system of molecular, cellular and tissue-based responses to pathogen attack.

Protection from a pathogen's initial invasion is achieved *via* passive defenses, such as physical and/or chemical barriers.

Physical barriers largely involve properties of the plant surface, that is, the cuticle, stomata and cell walls (presence of enzymes, thickness and size).

Chemical barriers include compounds, such as **phyto-anticipins,** that have antimicrobial activity and compounds that affect the vectors of plant viruses. Phenols and quinones are two classes of antimicrobial compounds produced by some plants. Lactones, cyanogenic glucosides, saponins, terpenoids, stilbenes and tannins are also plant-produced compounds associated with pathogen resistance.

Another group of defensive compounds are the plant **defensins,** which interfere with pathogen nutrition and retard their development.

Pathogen Recognition

Plants use a vast array of signals originating from micro-organisms and the environment to recognize pathogens and elicit plant defence responses.

Non-specific elicitors of biotic and abiotic origin induce host defenses in a broad range of host species. **Abiotic elicitors** such as heavy metal ions or UV light can induce stress responses in exposed tissues, which may provide an additional barrier to invading pathogens or alternatively, increase the plant's susceptibility to infection. **Biotic elicitors** include cell wall fragments released from fungi and bacteria, hydrolytic enzymes of plant or pathogen origin, some peptides, glycoproteins and polyunsaturated fatty acids.

Specific elicitors enable defence against a very specific pathogen, and are conditioned by avirulence genes in that pathogen. Avirulence genes determine the pathogen's host range, but are only able to function in the presence of another set of genes, the 'hypersensitive response and pathogenicity' (Hrp) gene cluster. Some Hrp gene products are involved in disguising the pathogen from host recognition, thus playing a role in both virulence and avirulence.

For a biotroph to form a successful infection, it must establish a basic **compatibility** with its host. **Incompatibility** between a host and a pathogen results in the recognition of the pathogen and activation of defence mechanisms, while compatibility results in infection.

Specific elicitors are encoded by **avirulence** genes, and these peptides are believed to bind to receptor peptides, encoded by host resistance genes.

Host-parasite specific resistance is determined by the interaction of between products of pathogen avirulence genes. Specific elicitors and products of host resistance genes.

Rapid Active Defenses

Almost every host-parasite interaction is unique in the details of the activation, localization, timing and magnitude of the defence responses.

The Membrane

The host membrane appears to be involved in the earliest stages of pathogen recognition and signal transduction. A **change in membrane permeability** after exposure to a pathogen causes fluxes in ions, such as K^+, H^+, Ca^{2+} and **oxidative burst** results in changes to gene activation and the triggering of the defence responses.

The Cell Wall

Reinforcement of the cell wall, *i.e.,* intensification of cytoplasmic streaming and the accumulation of host cytoplasm around the site of attempted penetration which can improve host resistance, begin very quickly after a pathogen attempts to penetrate a host cell.

The Hypersensitive Response

Hypersensitive cell death is another widespread mechanism used by hosts to prevent the spread of a pathogen. Infected cells and those which surround them 'suicide', using lignifications and synthesizing anti-microbial compounds thereby preventing further spread and in some cases, killing the pathogen.

Antibiotic Compounds

Phytoalexins are low molecular weight antibiotics produced by many (but not all) plants in response to infection. Phytoalexins inhibit the growth of bacteria and fungi *in vivo* and *in vitro*, and production of these antibiotics during an infection can induce resistance to subsequent infections by that pathogen. Over 350 phytoalexins are known in over 100 plant species. They include pterocarpans, sesquiterpenes, cryptophenols, isocoumarins, isoflavenoids, and others.

Delayed Active Defenses

Delayed active defenses include containment of the pathogen, wound repair, expression of pathogenesis-related proteins and the acquisition of systemic resistance. These mechanisms restrict the spread of the pathogen after infection is established and contain the damage to host tissues.

Systemic Acquired Resistance

Systemic acquired resistance, or induced resistance, is characterized by the increased resistance of a plant to a wide range of pathogens following infection by one pathogen and rather than providing immunity *per se*, systemic acquired resistance reduces the severity of later diseases and role of salicylic acid has been observed.

Coordination of Defence Responsess

The success of defence responses is increased if activated in combination. Passive mechanisms, coupled with rapid active responses and slower follow up defenses provide a broad defence front to the plant. The specific interaction between host and pathogen is of course crucial to the success of the plant's resistance or the pathogen's invasion and is mediated by the many pathways involved in producing or detecting elicitors, enhancers, suppressors and secondary signals.

Non-Specific Plant Disease Resistance

Non-specific plant disease resistance is multi-component, relying upon a foundation of passive plant defenses and usually also involving the activation of active defenses by non-specific elicitors of biotic origin . The combination of defenses involved in this type of resistance is highly coordinated and similar for all plant-pathogen interactions. However, substantial variation in both the timing and degree of the active component of plant defense and in environmental factors has been shown to be critical to its success. Whilst stronger, more timely non-specific defense responses are responsible for many incompatible plant-pathogen interactions, weaker non-specific defence responses are often overcome by the pathogen in compatible interactions, and have also been observed in symbiotic relationships with endophytic fungi.

The genetic basis underlying non-specific plant disease resistance is complex and involves multiple genes that encode proteins with a diversity of functions in both partners of the plant-pathogen interaction. These can be divided into **pathogenicity genes** that determine the ability of the pathogen to cause disease and **defence-related genes** that enable the plant host to execute defense responses. Both classes of genes contain members that are expressed in a constitutive manner, in addition to genes that are only expressed in response to the interaction of plant and pathogen. Pathogen genes that govern pathogenicity usually encode proteins that have a negative impact on disease resistance. The majority of pathogenicity genes in plant pathogens condition the ability to establish infection, and these include genes that encode proteins with specific roles in adhesion to the plant surface, the formation of penetration structures, cell wall degradation and the synthesis of toxic compounds. However, a number of pathogenicity genes instead govern the ability of the pathogen to defeat plant defences, such as those encoding proteins involved in the detoxification of phytoalexins. Plant defense-related genes encode proteins that enable the detection of non-specific elicitors and the activation of an intracellular signaling pathway leading to plant defences, as well as those themselves involved in passive and active plant defences.

Specific Plant Disease Resistance

In contrast to non-specific resistance, specific plant disease resistance appears to be governed by a single gene or a small number of related genes, which encode proteins capable of altering the outcome of an otherwise compatible plant-pathogen interaction. Genes conditioning host-pathogen specificity are found in particular sub-populations of the pathogen, plant host, or both interacting organisms and specific plant disease resistance can be sub-divided into three major categories on this basis.

Race-Specific Resistance

Race-specific resistance is induced in response to only a particular race of pathogen, but occurs in all cultivars of the host plant. This type of specific disease resistance is dependent upon **genetic variation** within the pathogen species and the production of proteins capable of altering the outcome of an otherwise compatible plant-pathogen interaction in only certain pathogen races.

Cultivar-Specific Resistance

Cultivar-specific resistance is activated only in a specific host plant cultivar, but in reaction to all races of a pathogen species. In a few plant-pathogen systems where, non-specific resistance limits the host range of the pathogen to a plant genus, this type of resistance occurs at the level of the host plant species and is termed **species-specific resistance.**

Race-Cultivar-Specific (Gene-for-Gene) Resistance

If both pathogen and host specificity are involved, plant disease resistance is termed **race-cultivar-specific resistance,** since it results only from the interaction of a particular pathogen race with a particular cultivar of the host plant. This type of resistance is usually referred to as **gene-for-gene resistance,** because in most cases it requires the presence of both a race-specific **avirulence (*avr*) gene** in the pathogen and one or more corresponding cultivar-specific **resistance (*R*) genes** in the host plant.

Mechanisms Underlying Specific Plant Disease Resistance

The biochemical mechanisms responsible for the induction of specific resistance in plant-pathogen interactions are poorly understood, but are likely to vary with both the type of specific resistance and the plant-pathogen system involved. The three most common mechanisms underlying specific resistance appear to be race-specific elicitors, host-selective toxins and race-specific suppressors, but others, as yet unknown, may also exist.

Race-Specific Elicitors

The majority of cases of race-specific resistance appear to result from the generation by a pathogen of race-specific elicitors of active plant defences and the recognition of these by the plant host. Resistance with this biochemical basis is often also cultivar-specific (and thus gene-for-gene), since the elicitor interacts with a corresponding plant receptor that is usually unique to a particular cultivar of the host plant. The recognition of the elicitor by its receptor is proposed to occur at the plant plasma membrane for most fungal pathogens, and within the plant cell for bacterial and viral pathogens. In bacterial biotrophs such as *Xanthomonas* and *Pseudomonas*, which are extracellular plant pathogens, this event is dependent upon a bacterial membrane transport protein that delivers the elicitor into the plant cell, and is encoded by the *hrp* gene complex. Interaction of the elicitor and receptor activates a complex signal transduction pathway resulting in the induction of plant defences against pathogen races harbouring the elicitor. The elicitor is generally the protein that is encoded by the avirulence gene, however in some plant-pathogen interactions the elicitor has been found to be the product of a reaction catalyzed by this protein. Resistance genes in some cases directly encode cultivar-specific receptors of race-specific elicitors, and in these cases a direct physical interaction between avirulence and resistance gene products may occur. However, resistance proteins are more likely to function by registering interactions between the elicitor and an unknown target protein, or act as unique links in the signalling pathway leading to active plant defences.

Host-Selective Toxins

Race-cultivar-specific pathogen resistance can also occur due to the production of compounds that are toxic to plants. These Host-Selective Toxins (HSTs) are generated in a race-specific manner, mainly by necrotrophic species of the fungal genera *Alternaria* and *Cochliobolus*. A few of the approximately twenty known host-selective toxins are proteins or peptides that are directly encoded by race-specific pathogen genes. However, most are non-protein compounds of low molecular weight that are synthesized in reactions catalyzed by proteinaceous race-specific gene products. Following transport into the host plant cell *via* a highly coordinated delivery system, host-selective toxins cause cellular damage, but only in toxin-sensitive cultivars that harbour a single gene conditioning toxin sensitivity. The mode of action of host-selective toxins is highly variable, but appears to always involve either activation or inhibition of a cultivar-specific protein. For example, T-toxin, produced by *C. heterostrophus*, serves to activate a cultivar-specific protein capable of forming destructive membrane pores, whereas HC-toxin from *C. carbonum* inhibits a cultivar-specific version of an enzyme that modifies DNA-bound proteins to cause disturbances in gene expression.

Race-Specific Suppressors

Race-specific resistance can also result from pathogen production of race-specific suppressors that inhibit a non-specific resistance response. To date, race-specific suppressors have been described for only a few species of biotrophic plant-pathogenic fungi, including *Phytophthora infestans*. In contrast to race-specific elicitors, they are proposed to interfere with elicitor binding, signal transduction, gene expression or plant defences to suppress the non-specific resistance response towards races that harbour them. Race-specific suppressors may be proteins directly encoded by pathogen genes governing race-specificity, or may be non-protein compounds produced by reactions catalyzed by these proteins. Plant disease resistance in cases involving race-specific suppressors may or may not also be cultivar-specific (and thus gene-for-gene), depending on whether or not the actual mechanism of suppression involves a cultivar-specific plant molecule.

Table 10.4 **Factors that Affect Disease Development**

Pathogen	Host	Environment
Presence of pathogen Pathogenicity Adaptability Dispersal efficiency Survival efficiency Reproductive fitness	Susceptibility Growth stage and form Population density and structure General health	Temperature Rainfall/Dew Leaf wetness period Soil properties Wind Fire history Air pollution Herbicide damage

Table 10.5 **Some of the Most Common Terms Used to Describe Symptoms of Plant Diseases**

Disease	Character
Blight	A disease characterized by widespread death of plant tissue.
Canker	A sunken necrotic lesion often of a main stem, branch or root.
Damping-off	Collapse and rot of seedlings near soil level before emergence or soon after emergence caused by *Pythium* sp., *Phytophthora* sp., *Fusarium* sp. and *Rhizoctonia* sp.
Dieback	Partial defoliation, twig and branch death and even complete death of plants.
Downy mildew	White or grey 'bloom' on leaves and stems caused by production of sporangiophores and sporangia by members of the peronosporales (downy mildew fungi).
Gall	An abnormal growth or swelling produced as a result of pathogenic invasion.
Mosaic	Patchy variation of normal green colour in leaves, usually light and dark green mosaic, symptomatic of many viral diseases.
Powdery mildew	White powdery 'bloom' on the plant surface caused by the production of fungal mycelium, conidiophores and conidia by members of the Erysiphales (powdery mildew fungi).
Pustule	A blister-like spore mass breaking through a plant epidermis.
Rot	Disintegration of tissue, often caused by enzymes or toxins produced by pathogens.
Rust	Rust-coloured pustules formed by members of the Uredinales (rust fungi).
Scab	A discrete, superficial roughened lesion.
Smut	A disease characterized by black spore masses on leaves, stems or inflorescences, caused by members of the Ustilaginales (smut fungi).
Vascular wilt	A disease in which the pathogen is confined to the vascular system of the host and in which wilting is a characteristic symptom; plants lose their turgidity and become flaccid, leaves collapse.

Pathogen Induced Diseases in Plants

Table 10.6 **Viral Diseases of Plants**

Disease	Causal Virus
Tobacco mosaic	Tobacco mosaic virus
Papaya mosaic	Papaya mosaic virus
Abutilon mosaic	Abutilon mosaic virus
Cucumber mosaic	Cucumber mosaic virus
Tomato leaf curl	Tomato leaf curl virus
Potato mild mosaic	Potato virus-X
Potato rugose mosaic	Potato virus-Y
Potato leaf roll	Potato leaf roll virus
Ratoon stunt of sugarcane	Ratoon stunt virus
Rosette of groundnut	Groundnut mosaic virus
Tristeza of citrus	*Citrus tristeza* virus
Sugarcane mosaic	Sugarcane virus-I
Bunchy top of banana	Banana bunchy top virus

Table 10.7 **Some Important Plant Diseases Caused by Bacteria**

Disease	Causal Bacteria	Disease	Causal Bacteria
Angular leaf spot of cotton	*Xanthomonas malvacearum*	Fire blight of pear and apple	*Erwinia amylovora*
Angular leaf spot of tobacco	*Pseudomonas angulata*	Gummosis of sugarcane	*Xanthomonas vasculorum*
Black leg or soft rot of potato	*Erwinia carotovora*	Leaf spot of cucumber	*Xanthomonas cucurbitae*
Black rot of cabbage	*Xanthomonas campestris*	Leaf spot of peach	*Xanthomonas pruni*
Blight of beans	*Pseudomonas phaseolicola*	Red stripe of sugarcane	*Pseudomonas rubrilineans*
Blight of paddy	*Xanthom onas oryzae*	Scab of potato	*Streptomyces scabies*
Brown rot/wilt of potato	*Pseudomonas solanacearum*	Stalk rot of maize	*Erwinia carotovora*
Canker of citrus	*Xanthomonas citri*	Tundu of wheat	*Corynebacteri-um tritici*
Canker of stone fruits	*Pseudomonas syringae*	Wilt of maize	*Xanthomonas stewartii*
Crown gall of apple	*Agrobacterium tumefaciens*	Soft rot of mango	*Erwinia cartovora*
Ear rot of wheat	*Corynebacteri um tritici*	Wild fire of tobacco	*Pseudomonas tobaci*

Pathogen Induced Diseases in Animals

Table 10.8 **Viral Diseases of Human Beings**

Disease	Pathogen	Reservoir	Vector/Epidemiology
AIDS	HIV	STD	Destroys immune defence, resulting in death by infection or cancer. Over 39.5 million people were living with HIV in 2006 and 3.6 million were infected in India by 2007.
Chickenpox	Human herpes virus (*Varicella zoster*)	Humans	Spread through contact with infected individuals. Rarely fatal. Vaccine approved in US in early 1995.
Ebola	Filoviruses	Unknown	Acute haemorrhagic fever; virus attacks connective tissue leading to massive haemorrhage and death. Peak mortality is 50-90%, if the disease is untreated. Outbreaks confined to local regions of central Africa.
Hepatitis-B (viral)	Hepatitis-B Virus (HBV)	Humans	Highly infectious through contact with infected body fluids. Vaccine available, can be fatal.
Herpes	Herpes Simplex Virus (HSV)	Humans	Fever, blisters; spread primarily through contact with infected saliva. Very prevalent, worldwide. Exhibits latency–the disease can be dormant for several years.
Influenza	Influenza viruses	Humans and ducks	Historically, a major killer (22 million died in 18 months in 1918-1919); wild Asian ducks, chicken and pigs are major reservoirs. The ducks are not affected by the flu. virus, which shuffles its antigen gene while, multiplying within them, leading to new flu strains.
Measles	Paramyxoviruses	Humans	Extremely contagious through contact with infected individuals. Vaccine available. Usually contracted in childhood, when it is not serious; more dangerous to adults.
Mononucleosis	Epstein-Barr Virus (EBV)	Humans	Spreads through contact with infected saliva. May last for several weeks; common in young adults. Rarely fatal.
Mumps	Paramyxovirus	Humans	Spreads through contact with infected saliva. Vaccine available; rarely fatal.
Pneumonia	Influenza virus	Humans	Acute infection of the lungs, often fatal without treatment.
Polio	Poliovirus	Humans	Acute viral infection of the CNS that can lead to paralysis and is often fatal. Salk's vaccine.
Rabies	Rhabdovirus	Wild and domestic Canidae (dogs, foxes, wolves, coyotes), bats and raccoons	An acute viral encephalomyelitis transmitted by the bite of an infected animal. Fatal if untreated.
Smallpox	Variola virus	Formerly humans, now only exists into research labs–may be eliminated	Historically, a major killer; the last recorded case of smallpox was in 1977. Last case of smallpox was found in 1984, but not confirmed, in Bangladesh. A worldwide vaccination compaign wiped out the disease completely.
Yellow fever	Flavivirus	Humans and mosquitoes	Spread from individual to individual by mosquito bites; a notable cause of death during the construction of the Panama canal. If untreated, this disease has a peak mortality rate of 60%.

Table 10.9 **Important Human Diseases Caused by Bacteria**

Disease	Pathogen	Vector/Reservoir	Epidemiology
Anthrax	*Bacillus anthracis*	Animals, including processed skins	Bacterial infection that can be transmitted through contact or ingestion. Rare, except in sporadic outbreaks. May be fatal.
Botulism	*Clostridium botulinum*	Improperly prepared food	Contracted through ingestion or contract with wound. Produces acute toxic poison; can be fatal.
Chlamydia	*Chlamydia trachomatis*	Humans and STD	Urogenital infections with possible spread to eyes and respiratory tract.
Cholera	*Vibrio cholerae*	Human faeces and plankton	Causes severe diarrhoea that can lead to death by dehydration; 50% peak mortality if the disease goes untreated.
Dental caries	*Streptococcus*	Humans	A dense collection of this bacteria on the surface of teeth leads to the secretion of acids that destroy minerals in tooth enamel; sugar alone can not cause caries.
Diphtheria	*Corynebacterium diphtheriae*	Humans	Acute inflammation and lesions of mucous membrane. Spread through contact with infected individual. Vaccine available.
Gonorrhoea	*Neisseria gonorrhoeae*	Humans only	STD, on the increase worldwide. Usually not fatal.
Hansen's disease (leprosy)	*Mycobacterium leprae*	Humans and feral armadilos	Chronic infection of the skin; worldwide incidence about 10-12 million, especially in South-East Asia. Spread through contact with infected individuals.
Lyme disease	*Borrelia bergdorferi*	Ticks, deer and small rodents	Spread through the bite of infected tick. Lesion followed by malaise, fever, fatigue, pain, stiff neck and headache.
Peptic ulcers	*Helicobacter pylori*	Humans	Originally thought to be caused by stress or diet, most peptic ulcers now appear to be caused by this bacterium; good news for ulcer sufferers as it can be treated with antibiotics.
Plague	*Yersinia pestis*	Fleas of wild rodents rats	Killed 1/4 of the population of Europe in the 14th and squirrels century; endemic in wild rodent populations of the Western US today.
Pneumonia	*Streptococcus, Mycoplasma* and *Chlamydia*	Humans	Acute infection of the lungs, often fatal without treatment.
Tuberculosis	*Mycobacterium tuberculosis*	Humans	An acute bacterial infection of the lungs, lymph and meninges. Its incidence is on the rise, complicated by the development of new strains of the bacteria that are resistant to antibiotics.
Typhoid fever	*Salmonella typhi*	Humans	A systemic bacterial disease of worldwide incidence. The disease is spread through contaminated water or foods (such as improperly washes fruits and vegetables). Vaccines are available for travellers.
Typhus	*Rickettsia typhi*	Lice, rat fleas and humans	Historically, a major killer in times of crowding and poor sanitation; transmitted from human to human through the bite of infected lice and fleas. Typhus has a peak untreated mortality rate of 70%.

Exercise

1. Pathogenicity is
(a) ability to cause disease (b) degree of disease
(c) virulence (d) All of these

2. Entry of pathogen *via* parenteral route includes entry though
(a) mucous membranes (b) skin
(c) punctures and injections (d) All of these

3. M protein of *Streptococcus pyogenes* is
(a) heat and acid resistant
(b) mediates attachment of bacterium to epithelial cells
(c) resists phagocytosis by leukocytes
(d) All of the above

4. Invasins are surface proteins produced by bacteria
(a) to control actin
(b) to allow penetration between cells at intercellular junctions
(c) Both (a) and (b)
(d) None of the above

5. .... produce neurotoxic substances in shellfish poisoning.
(a) Dinoflagellates (b) Protozoa
(c) Virus (d) Bacteria

6. Soft rot caused by *Erwinia carotovara* effects
(a) fleshy tissue fruits (b) herbaceous plants
(c) ornamental plants (d) weeds

7. Late blight of potato is caused by
(a) *Phytophthora infestans* (b) *Endothia parsitica*
(c) *Puccinia graminis* (d) *Ustilago maydis*

8. Diseases contracted *via* the gastrointestinal tract are
(a) salmonellosis (b) shigellosis
(c) cholera (d) All of these

9. *Mycobacterium tuberculosis*, *Neisseria gonorrhoeae* and *Plasmodium* sp., are
(a) Strict pathogens (b) Opportunistic pathogens
(c) Both (a) and (b) (d) None of these

10. *Staphylococcus, S. aureus, Corynebacteria* and *Propionibacteria* are found
(a) skin surface (b) mouth
(c) oral cavity (d) pharynx

11. Bacterial triggering of actin rearrangement in host cells is responsible for
(a) forced phagocytosis of bacteria by normally non phagocytic host cells
(b) movement within host cells
(c) movement from one host cell to another
(d) All of the above

12. Pathogens adhere through
(a) fimbriae (b) capsules
(c) spikes (d) All of these

13. Adhesions/ligands bind to receptors on host cells in *Treponema pallidum*
(a) glycocalyx (b) fimbriae
(c) opa (d) tapered ends

14. What low molecular weight proteins are produced by a host cell in response to viral infection which protects a pre-infected cell from a viral infection?
(a) Antibodies (b) Phytotoxins
(c) Interferons (d) Phytoalexins

15. The plant viruses that multiply within their insect vector are called,
(a) persistant (b) non-presistant
(c) propagative (d) circulative

16. Chronic infection has
(a) long duration
(b) short duration
(c) restriction to limited area
(d) All of the above

17. The basic principle involved in the working of anti-AIDS drug is that
(a) they block protein synthesis
(b) they inhibits of reduce the replication potentials by disturbing reverse transcriptase
(c) they dissolve the protein coat of virus
(d) they block the enzymatic reactions necessary for metabolism of virus

18. F_e receptors are commonly seen on the surface
(a) of erythrocytes
(b) thrombocytes
(c) beutrophils and macrophages
(d) All of the above

19. All the following represent nonspecific mechanisms of body defence except
(a) IgM
(b) stomach acids
(c) phagocytosis
(d) mucus that traps particles in respiratory tract

20. TCR are transmembrane structure consisting of
(a) four polypeptide chains (2a + 2b)
(b) two polypeptide chains (1a + 1b)
(c) four polypeptide chains (2a + 2)
(d) lipid bilayer

21. HIV the human immunodeficiency virus belongs to which of the following viral groups?
(a) Reoviruses (b) Retroviruses
(c) Rhabdoviruses (d) None of these

22. Match List I with List II.

List I	List II
A. Pathogen	1. A localized response with in infected tissue
B. Mast cells	2. Protein produced by virus infected cells
C. Inflammation	3. Release histamine to initiate an inflammatory response
D. Interferons	4. A disease causing organism

	A	B	C	D
(a)	3	4	2	1
(b)	4	3	1	2
(c)	2	1	4	3
(d)	1	2	3	4

23. The vehicle borne transmission of disease is occurring through
I. Certain vectors like arthropods.
II. Agencies like water, ice, food or blood.
III. Through infectious clothes.
IV. Through air.
(a) I, II, III are correct
(b) II, III, IV are correct
(c) II and III ae correct
(d) I and IV are correct

Answers

1. (a)	**2.** (c)	**3.** (d)	**4.** (a)	**5.** (a)	**6.** (a)	**7.** (a)	**8.** (d)	**9.** (a)	**10.** (a)
11. (d)	**12.** (d)	**13.** (d)	**14.** (c)	**15.** (c)	**16.** (a)	**17.** (b)	**18.** (c)	**19.** (a)	**20.** (b)
21. (b)	**22.** (b)	**23.** (d)							

11

Cell Signaling and Cellular Communication

Cell Signaling

A cell needs to communicate with its environment, so that it can make appropriate responses in terms of basic cellular activities (development, tissue repair and immunity as well as normal tissue homeostasis) and coordinates cell actions.

Traditional work in biology has focused on studying individual parts of cell signaling pathways. Cells adjacent to one another frequently communicate through cell to cell contact. While there are other forms of communication cover larger distances with the help of extracellular signaling molecules.

Cell signaling has been most extensively studied in the context of human diseases and signaling between cells of a single organism. However, cell signaling may also occur between the cells of two different organisms. In many mammals, early embryo cells exchange signals with cells of the uterus. In the human gastrointestinal tract, bacteria exchange signals with each other and with human epithelial and immune system cells. For the yeast *Saccharomyces cerevisiae* during mating, some cells send a peptide signal (mating factor pheromones) into their environment. The mating factor peptide may bind to a cell surface receptor on other yeast cells and induce them to prepare for mating.

Receptors for Cell Moves

Cells receive information from their neighbours through a class of proteins known as receptors. Notch is a cell surface protein that are expressed on adjacent cells and functions as a receptor. Animals have a small set of genes that code for signaling proteins that interact specifically with notch receptors and stimulate a response in cells

Syllabus

- Hormones and their Receptors
- Cell Surface Receptor, G-protein Coupled Receptors
- Second Messengers
- Signal Transduction Pathways
- Regulation of Signaling Transduction
- Bacterial and Plant Two Component Systems
- Bacterial Chemotaxis and Quorum Sensing
- Cell Adhesion and Adhesion Molecules
- Extracellular Matrix
- Integrins
- Principles of Cell Communication
- Haematopoiesis and its Regulation
- Gap Junctions
- Neurotransmission and its Regulation

that express notch on their surface. Molecules that activate (or, in some cases, inhibit) receptors can be classified as hormones, neurotransmitters, cytokines and growth factors, but all of these are called receptor ligands, while many receptors are cell surface proteins, some are found inside cells.

A number of transmembrane receptors for molecules that include peptide hormones and of intracellular receptors for steroid hormones exist, giving to a cell the ability to respond to a great number of hormonal and pharmacological stimuli.

For several types of intercellular signaling molecules that are unable to permeate the hydrophobic cell membrane due to their hydrophilic nature, the target receptor is expressed on the membrane. When such signaling molecule activates its receptor, the signal is carried into the cell usually by means of a second messenger such as *c*AMP.

The external signal may enter a cell *via* four major pathways:

(i) Hydrophobic molecules.

(ii) Ion channels.

(iii) G-protein coupled receptors.

(iv) Extra cellular signaling.

Signaling molecules are released by signaling cells and the signal is called the ligand. The ligand binds to its specific receptor on a target cell. This ligand receptor interaction induces a conformational or shape change in the receptor and produces a specific response. This is called the cellular response which can include a vast array of compounds, *e.g.*, small amino acid derivatives, small peptides, proteins, etc.

Cell to cell communication by extracellular signaling usually involves six steps

(i) Synthesis of the signaling molecule by the signaling cell.

(ii) Release of the signaling molecule by the signaling cell.

(iii) Transport of the signal to the target cell.

(iv) Detection of the signal by a specific receptor protein receptor ligand specificity.

(v) A change in cellular metabolism, function, or development leading to a cellular response triggered by the receptor → ligand complex → specific to the ligand → receptor complex.

(vi) Removal of the signal, which usually terminates the cellular response → degradation of ligand.

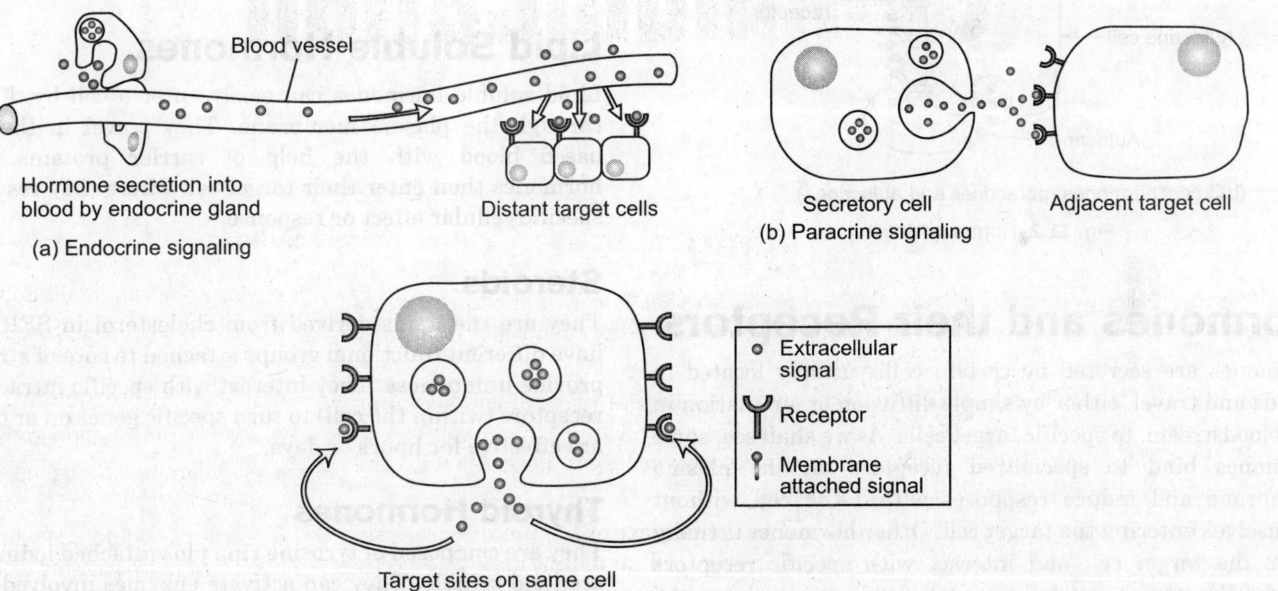

Fig. 11.1 Various distance mode signaling

Extracellular signaling can occur over

(i) Large distances or endocrine signaling, signaling molecules are called hormones which act on target cells distant from their site of synthesis and are usually carried through the bloodstream.

(ii) Short distances or paracrine signaling, affects target cells within proximity to the cell that synthesized the molecule and are usually mediated by neurotransmitters and some growth factors.

(iii) No distance or autocrine signaling, the signal feedback and affects itself. This is observed as the action of many growth factors. These compounds generally act on themselves to regulate proliferation and is seen frequently in tumour cells.

Many compounds can act through two or even three types of cell signaling, *e.g.*, growth factors (*e.g.*, EGF), which is paracrine and autocrine and endocrine, epinephrine–endocrine and paracrine.

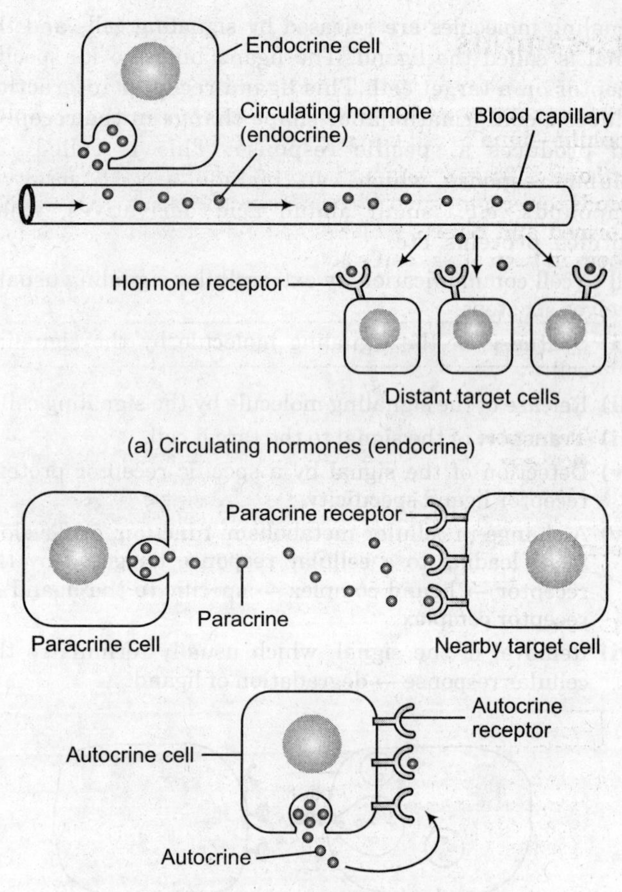

Fig. 11.2 Hormonal action

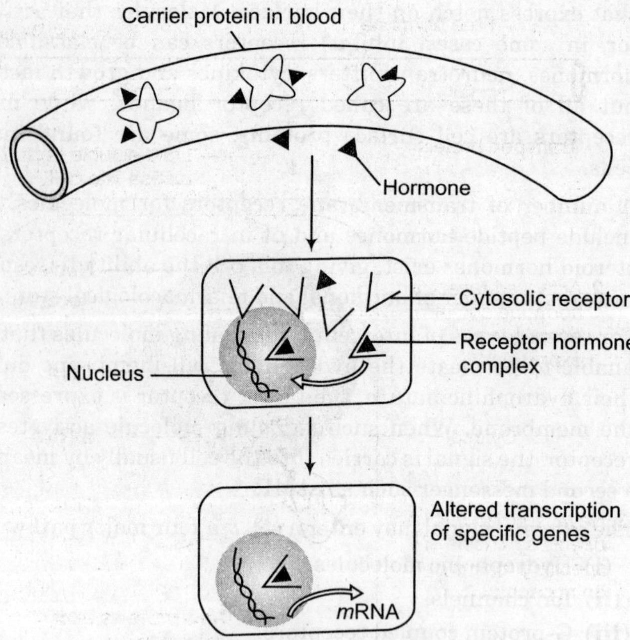

Fig. 11.3 Intracellular receptors

Hormones and their Receptors

Hormones are secreted by certain cells, usually located in glands and travel, either by simple diffusion or circulation in the bloodstream, to specific target cells. As we shall see, some hormones bind to specialized receptors on the plasma membrane and induce responses within the cell without themselves entering the target cell. Other hormones actually enter the target cell and interact with specific receptors there. By these mechanisms, hormones regulate the metabolic processes of various organs and tissues, facilitate and control growth, differentiation, reproductive activities, learning and memory, and help the organism cope with changing conditions and stresses in its environment.

Hormones are of two types, *i.e.,* lipid soluble and water soluble.

Lipid Soluble Hormones

Lipid soluble hormones can easily enter a cell by diffusing through the plasma membrane. They travel in the water based blood with the help of carrier proteins. These hormones then enter their target cell where they result in a specific cellular effect or response.

Steroids

They are the lipids derived from cholesterol in SER which have different functional groups attached to core of structure provide uniqueness. They interact with specific intracellular receptors (within the cell) to turn specific genes on or off and are effective for hours or days.

Thyroid Hormones

They are composed of tyrosine ring plus attached iodines and are lipid soluble. They can activate enzymes involved in the catabolism of fats and glucose and help set our basal metabolic rate.

Retinoids

They are the vitamin-A derivatives. They have dramatic effects on proliferation and differentiation plus cellular death (*i.e.,* apoptosis).

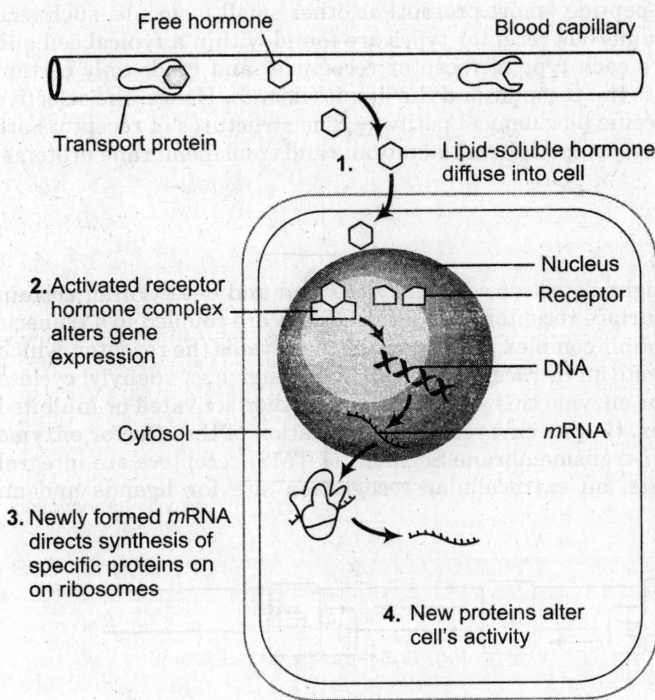

Fig. 11.4 Action of lipid soluble hormones

Water Soluble Hormones

Water soluble hormones can easily travel within the blood. They enter a cell and result in a cellular response by binding to specific cell surface receptors. This binding activates the receptor and results in a series of cellular events called the second messenger system.

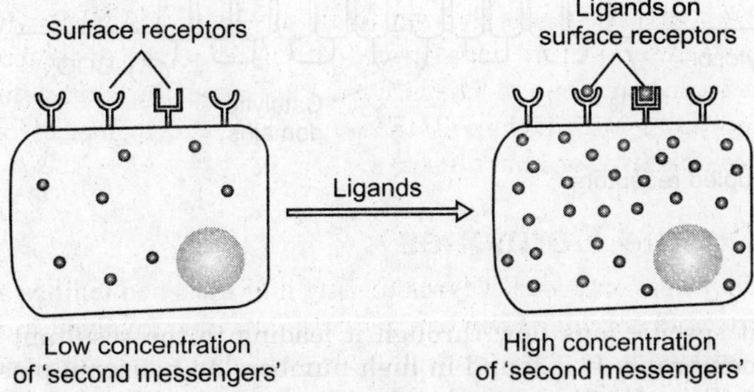

Fig. 11.5 Cell surface receptors

Amino Acid Derivatives, Small Peptides and Protein Hormones

They are the modified amino acids or amino acids put together, *e.g.*, serotonin, melatonin, histamine and epinephrine.

Larger Peptide Hormones

This mainly includes insulin and glucagon.

Eicosanoids

They are derived from arachidonic acid (fatty acid), prostaglandins or leukotriene. Prostaglandins despite being lipophilic—bind to cell surface receptors.

Hormone diffuses through phospholipid bilayer and into cell. It binds to receptor turning on/off specific genes. New *m*RNA is formed and directs synthesis of new proteins. This new protein in turn alters cell's activity.

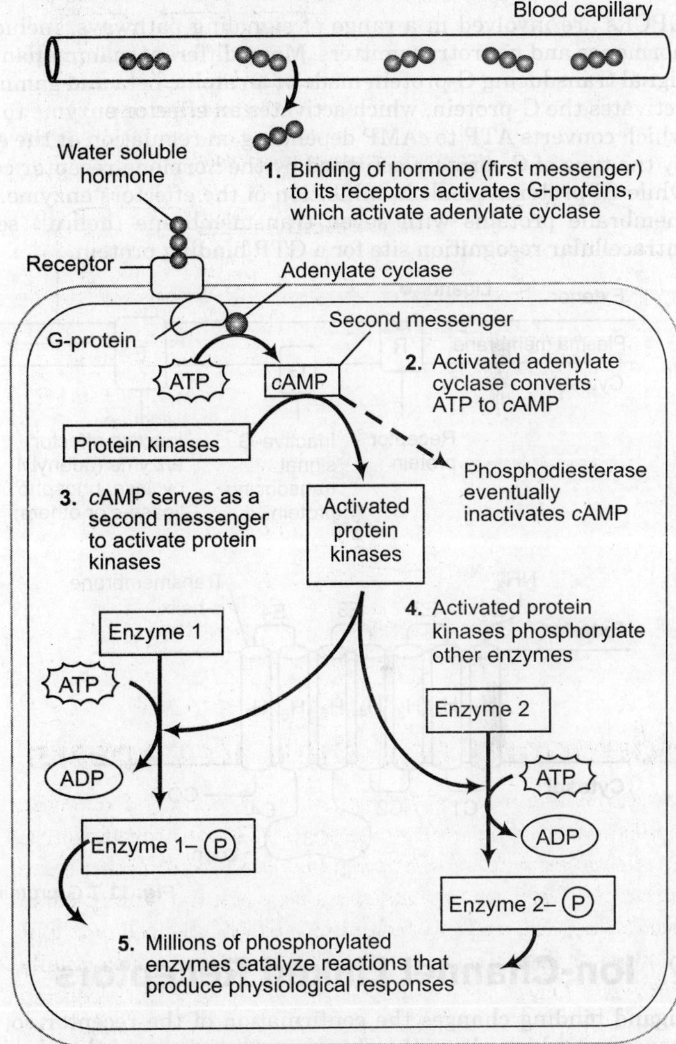

Fig. 11.6 Action of water soluble hormones

These hormones cannot diffuse through plasma membrane. Hormone receptors are integral membrane proteins which act as first messenger. Receptor protein activates G-protein in the membrane. This G-protein activates adenylate cyclase to convert ATP to *c*AMP in the cytosol.

Cell Surface Receptors

Receptors are protein molecules, embedded in either the plasma membrane (cell surface receptors) or the cytoplasm or nucleus (nuclear receptors) of a cell, to which one or more specific kinds of signaling molecules may attach. A molecule which binds (attaches) to a receptor is called a ligand and may be peptide (short protein) or other small molecule, such as a neurotransmitter, a hormone, a pharmaceutical drug or a toxin. Numerous receptor types are found within a typical cell and each type is linked to a specific biochemical pathway. Furthermore each type of receptor recognizes and binds only certain ligand shapes (in analogy to a lock and key where the lock represents the receptor and the key, its ligand). Hence, the selective binding of specific a ligand to its receptor activates or inhibits a specific biochemical pathway. The structures of receptors are very diverse and can broadly be classified into the following categories, *i.e.*, peripheral membrane and transmembrane proteins. The various type of transmembrane protein receptors are

1. G-Protein Coupled Receptors

GPCRs are involved in a range of signaling pathways, including light detection, odorant detection and detection of certain hormones and neurotransmitters. Many different mammalian cell surface receptors including GPCRs are coupled to a trimeric signal transducing G-protein made of an alpha, beta and gamma subunit complex. Ligand binding activates the receptor, which activates the G-protein, which activates an effector enzyme to generate an intracellular second messengr, *e.g.*, adenylyl cyclase which converts ATP to *c*AMP depending on regulation at the effector enzyme this pathway can be either activated or inhibited by the type of G- protein activated by the hormone-receptor complex. Gs-proteins result in stimulation of the effector enzyme while Gi-proteins result in inhibition of the effectors enzyme. The 7-transmembrane Segment (7-TMS) receptors are integral membrane proteins with seven transmembrane (helical) segments, an extracellular recognition site for ligands and an intracellular recognition site for a GTP binding protein.

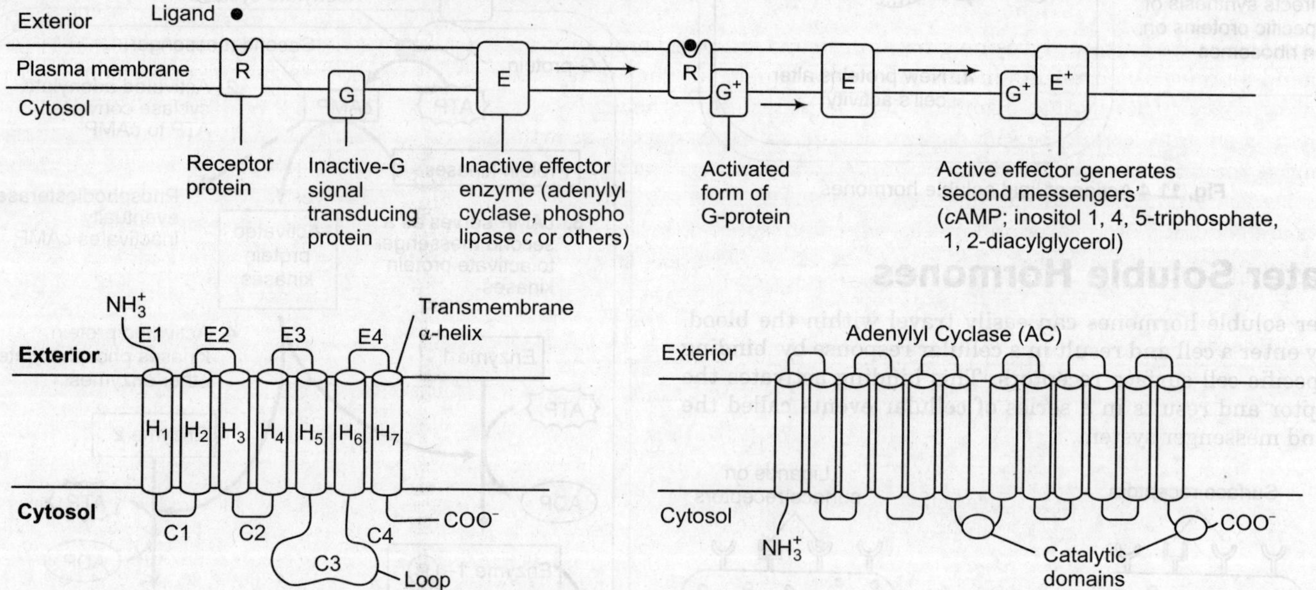

Fig. 11.7 G-protein-coupled receptors

2. Ion-Channel Linked Receptors

Ligand binding changes the confirmation of the receptor so, that specific ions flow through it leading to the resultant ion movement which alters the electric potential across the plasma membrane. It is found in high numbers on neuronal plasma membranes, *e.g.*, ligand gated channels for sodium and potassium. It is also found on the plasma membrane of muscle cells, binding of acetylcholine results in ion movement and eventual contraction of muscle.

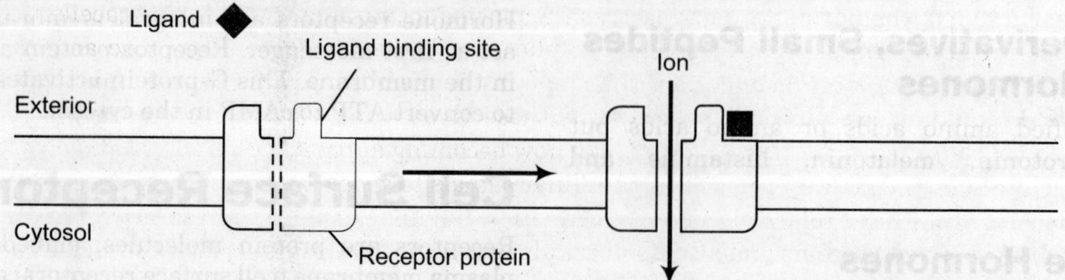

Fig. 11.8 Ion-channel receptors

3. Tyrosine Kinase Linked Receptors

They lack intrinsic catalytic activity and binding of the ligand results in the formation of a receptor dimer (two receptors). This dimer than activates a class of protein called tyrosine kinases. This activation results in the phosphorylation of downstream targets by these tyrosine kinases (stick phosphate groups onto tyrosine within the target protein).

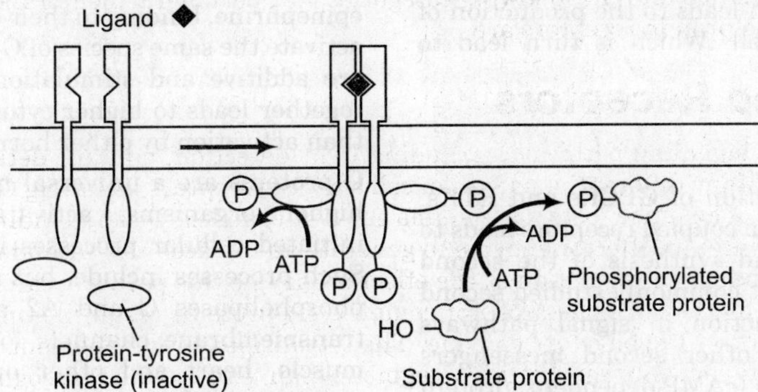

Fig. 11.9 Tyrosine kinase linked receptors

They are also called receptor tyrosine kinases or ligand triggered protein kinases and are similar to tyrosine linked receptors in the ligand binding which results in formation of a dimer but: they differ from tyrosine linked receptors in terms of intrinsic catalytic activity. It means that ligand binding activates it and the activated receptor acts as a kinase which in turn recognize soluble or membrane bound peptide or protein hormones that act as growth factors, *e.g.,* NGF, PDGF, insulin. In all of them binding of the ligand stimulates the receptor's tyrosine kinase activity resulting in phosphorylation of multiple amino acid residues within its target such as serine and threonine residues. This phosphorylation activates downstream targets and its targets are generally other protein kinases which phosphorylate their own downstream targets.

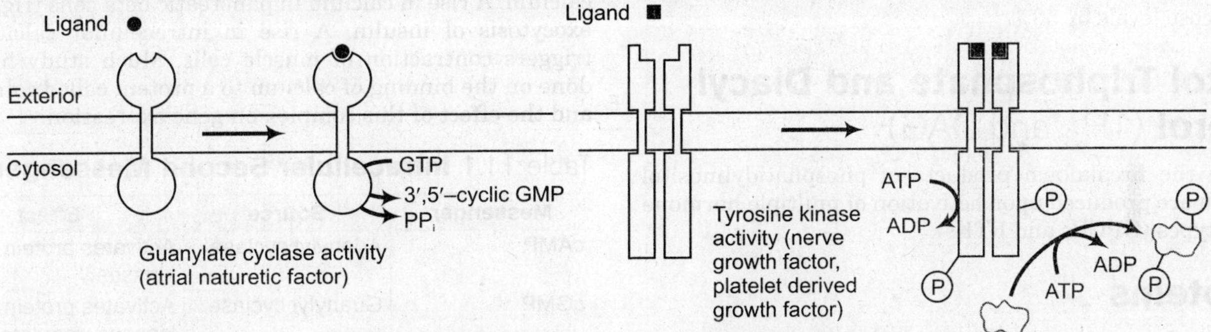

Fig. 11.10 Receptors with intrinsic enzymatic activity

Signal Transduction Cascades

The successive phosphorylation or activation of multiple kinases results in a cascade of phosphorylation or activation and this cascade is frequently called a signal transduction cascade. This cascade eventually leads to a specific cellular response, *e.g.,* changes in cell physiology and or patterns of gene expression. These pathways are involved in regulation of cell proliferation and differentiation, promotion of cell survival and modulation of cellular metabolism. Hormonal regulation depends upon the transduction of the hormonal signal across the plasma membrane to specific intracellular sites, particularly the nucleus. Many steps in these signaling pathways involve phosphorylation of serine, threonine and tyrosine residues on target proteins. The complexity of signal transduction is thus manifested in the estimates that the human genome may contain between 1000 and 3000 protein kinases. Although only a few of these kinases and other signaling proteins and molecules have been identified, the principles that govern these pathways are now becoming apparent. Signaling pathways must operate with speed and precision, facilitating the accurate relay of intracellular signals to specific targets. But how does this happen? Many protein kinases and phosphatases have relatively broad specificities, but they depend upon interactions between specialized recognition domains on the involved proteins and also upon cellular strategies for localization of the signaling molecules. As we shall see later, modular proteins having one or more protein protein or protein–lipid recognition domains mediate these events.

Second Messengers

Cells respond to their environment by taking cues from hormones or other external chemical signal. The interaction of these extracellular chemical signals (first messenger) with receptors on the cell surface often leads to the production of second messengers inside the cell. Which is turn lead to adaptive changes in cell interior.

Cyclic AMP (cAMP)

They are produced by the activation of GPCRs and RTKs. Hormone stimulation of Gs protein coupled receptors leads to activation of adenylyl cyclase and synthesis of the second messenger *c*AMP. This is the most commonly studied second messenger. *c*AMP does not function in signal pathways initiated by RTKs. *c*AMP and other second messengers activate specific protein kinases (*c*AMP-dependent protein kinases or PKAs). *c*AMP has a wide variety of effects depending on the cell type and the downstream PKAs and other kinases. In adipocytes, increased *c*AMP activates a PKA that stimulates production of fatty acids in ovarian cells another PKA will respond to *c*AMP by increase estrogen synthesis. Second messenger systems allow for amplification of an extracellular signal. One epinephrine molecule can bind one GPCR – this can result in the synthesis of multiple *c*AMP molecules which can go on to activate and amplified number of PKAs. A blood level as low as 10^{-10} M epinephrine can raise blood glucose levels by 50%.

Inositol Triphosphate and Diacyl Glycerol ($1P_3$ and DAG)

They are the breakdown products of phosphatidylinositol (PI) which are produced upon activation of multiple hormone receptor types (GPCRs and RTKs).

G-Proteins

Typically, G-proteins are heterotrimers consisting of α–(45 to 47 kD), β-(35 kD) and γ-(7 to 9 kD) subunits. The a subunit binds GDP or GTP and has an intrinsic, slow GTPase activity. The G $\alpha\beta\gamma$ complex in the inactivated state has GDP at the nucleotide site. Binding of hormone to receptor stimulates a rapid exchange of GTP for GDP on G α. The binding of GTP causes G α to dissociate from G $\beta\gamma$ and to associate with an effector protein such as adenylyl cyclase. Binding of G α (GTP) activates adenylyl cyclase. The adenylyl cyclase actively synthesizes *c*AMP as long as G α (GTP) remains bound to it. However, the intrinsic GTPase activity of G α eventually hydrolyzes GTP to GDP, leading to dissociation of G α (GDP) from adenylyl cyclase and reassociation with the G $\beta\gamma$ dimer, regenerating the inactive heterotrimeric G $\alpha\beta\gamma$ complex.

Two stages of amplification occur in the G-protein mediated hormone response. First, a single hormone-receptor complex can activate many G-proteins before the hormone dissociates from the receptor. Second and more obvious, the G α activated adenylyl cyclase synthesizes many *c*AMP molecules. Thus, binding of hormone to a very small number of membrane receptors stimulates a large increase in concentration of *c*AMP within the cell. The hormone receptor, G-protein and cyclase constitute a complete hormone signal transduction unit.

A given G-protein can be activated by several different hormone-receptor complexes. For example, either glucagon or epinephrine, binding to their distinctive receptor proteins, can activate the same species of G-protein in liver cells. The effects are additive and stimulation by glucagon and epinephrine together leads to higher cytoplasmic concentrations of *c*AMP than activation by either hormone alone.

G-proteins are a universal means of signal transduction in higher organisms, activating many hormone receptor initiated cellular processes in addition to adenylyl cyclase. Such processes include, but are not limited to, activation of phospholipases C and A2 and the opening or closing of transmembrane channels for K^+ Na^+ and Ca^{2+} in brain, muscle, heart and other organs. G-proteins are integral components of sensory pathways such as vision and olfaction. More than 100 different G-protein-coupled receptors and at least 21 distinct G-proteins are known. At least a dozen different G-protein effectors have been identified, including a variety of enzymes and ion channels.

Calcium

IP3 production results in the opening of calcium channels on the plasma membrane of the ER leading to the release of calcium. A rise in calcium in pancreatic beta cells triggers the exocytosis of insulin. A rise in intracellular calcium also triggers contraction of muscle cells. Much study has been done on the binding of calcium to a protein called calmodulin and the effect of this complex on gene expression.

Table 11.1 **Intracellular Second Messengers**

Messenger	Source	Effect
cAMP	Adenylyl cyclase	Activates protein kinases
cGMP	Guanylyl cyclase	Activates protein kinases, regulates ion channels, regulates phosphodiestereases
Ca^{2+}	Ion channels in ER and plasma membrane	Activates protein kinases, activates Ca^{2+} modulated proteins
IP_3	PLC action on PI	Activates Ca^{2+} channels
DAG	PLC action on PI	Activates protein kinase C
Phosphatidic acid	Membrane component and product of PLD	Activates Ca^{2+} channels, inhibits adenylyl cyclase
Ceramide	PLC action on sphingomyelin	Activates protein kinases
Nitric oxide (NO)	NO synthase	Activates guanylyl cyclase, relaxes smooth muscle
Cyclic ADP ribose	cADP-ribose synthase	Activates Ca^{2+} channels

- IP_3 is inositol-1, 4, 5-triphosphate, PLC is phospholipase C, PLD is phospholipase D, PI is phosphatidylinositol, DAG is diacylglycerol.

Signal Transduction Pathways

In some cases, receptor activation caused by ligand binding to a receptor is directly coupled to the cell's response to the ligand. For example, the neurotransmitter GABA can activate a cell surface receptor that is part of an ion channel. GABA binding to a GABA a receptor on a neuron opens a chloride selective ion channel that is part of the receptor. GABA a receptor activation allows negatively charged chloride ions to move into the neuron, which inhibits the ability of the neuron to produce action potentials. However, for many cell surface receptors, ligand receptor interactions are not directly linked to the cell's response. The activated receptor must first interact with other proteins inside the cell before the ultimate physiological effect of the ligand on the cell's behaviour is produced. Often, the behaviour of a chain of several interacting cell proteins is altered following receptor activation. The entire set of cell changes induced by receptor activation is called a signal transduction mechanism or pathway. In the case of notch-mediated signaling, the signal transduction mechanism can be relatively simple. Activation of notch can cause the notch protein to be altered by a protease. Part of the notch protein is released from the cell surface membrane and can act to change the pattern of gene transcription in the cell nucleus. This causes the responding cell to make different proteins, resulting in an altered pattern of cell behaviour. Cell signaling research involves studying the spatial and temporal dynamics of both receptors and the components of signaling pathways that are activated by receptors in various cell types.

Another pathway involves changes of protein-protein interactions inside the cell, induced by an external signal. Many growth factors bind to receptors at the cell surface and stimulate cells to progress through the cell cycle and divide. Several of these receptors are kinases that start to phosphorylate themselves and other proteins when binding to a ligand. This phosphorylation can generate a binding site for a different protein and thus, induce protein-protein interaction. The ligand [called epidermal growth factor (EGF)] binds to the receptor (called EGFR). This activates the receptor to phosphorylate itself. The phosphorylated receptor binds to an adaptor protein (GRB2), which couples the signal to further downstream signaling processes. For example, one of the signal transduction pathways that are activated is called the Mitogen Activated Protein Kinase (MAPK) pathway. The signal transduction component labelled as 'MAPK' in the pathway was originally called 'ERK', so the pathway is called the MAPK or ERK pathway. The MAPK protein is an enzyme, a protein kinase that can attach phosphate to target proteins such as the transcription factor MYC and, thus, alter gene transcription and, ultimately, cell cycle progression. Many cellular proteins are activated downstream of the growth factor receptors (such as EGFR) that initiate this signal transduction pathway.

Some signaling transduction pathways respond differently, depending on the amount of signaling received by the cell. For instance, the Hedgehog protein activates different genes, depending on the amount of Hedgehog protein present.

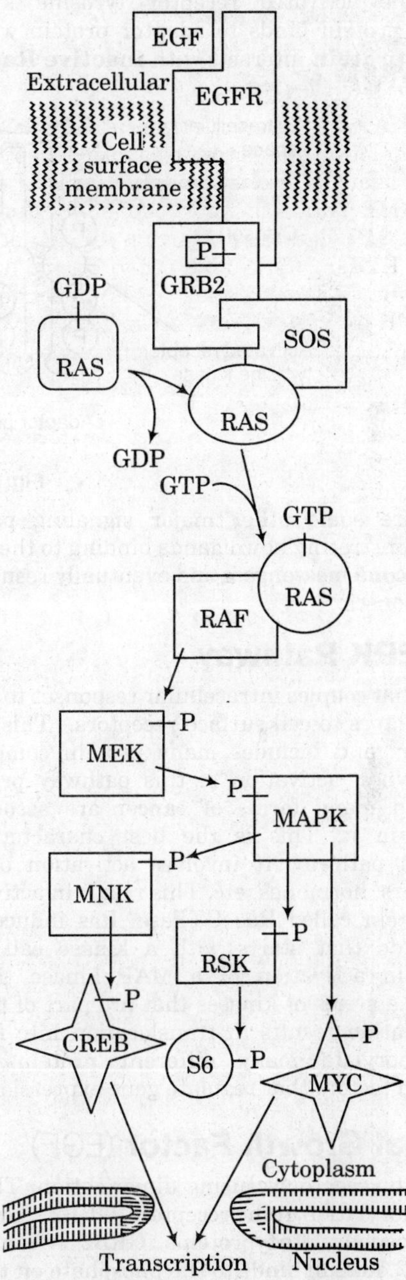

Fig. 11.11 Diagram showing key components of a signal transduction pathway

Complex multicomponent signal transduction pathways provide opportunities for feedback, signal amplification and interactions inside one cell between multiple signals and signaling pathways.

Major Pathways of Signal Transduction

Signaling/adaptor proteins bind to phosphorylated receptors wherein signalers pass signal on to the **adaptors** which link/bind to other proteins like **adaptor protein** binds to the activated receptor tyrosine kinase, **Ras activating** protein binds to adaptor protein wherein **Ras activating protein** interacts with **inactive Ras protein.**

Ras Protein

It is a G-protein and an integral membrane protein. The lipid tail is responsible for localization in the plasma membrane. Ras is synthesized in the cytoplasm on cytoplasmic ribosome while the addition of the lipid tail occurs in the cytoplasm (monomeric G-proteins bind to the cytoplasmic face of the outer cell membrane and these proteins can also bind to the face of the ER). Ras protein releases GDP and binds GTP and active Ras transmits signals to other molecules.

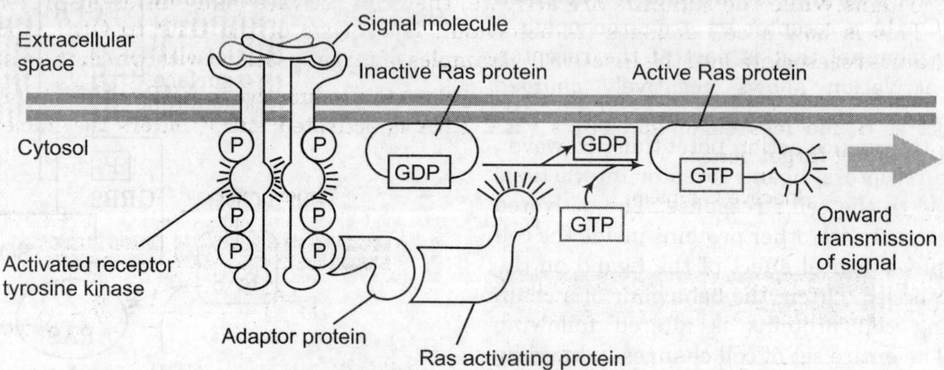

Fig. 11.12 Pathway of Ras protein action

Following are some other major signaling pathways in details, demonstrating how ligands binding to their receptors can affect second messengers and eventually result in altered cellular responses.

MAPK/ERK Pathway

A pathway that couples intracellular responses to the binding of growth factors to cell surface receptors. This pathway is very complex and includes many protein components. In many cell types, activation of this pathway promotes cell division, and many forms of cancer are associated with aberrations in it. This is the best characterized signal transduction pathway. It involves activation of RTKs by growth factors, hormones, etc. This result in activation of an adaptor protein called Ras GTPase. Ras induces a kinase signal cascade that starts with a kinase called rac and culminates in activation of a MAP kinase (MAPK). In between are a series of kinases that are part of the cascade. MAPK activation results in translocation into the nucleus and phosphorylate many different proteins, including transcription factors that regulate gene expression.

Epidermal Growth Factor (EGF)

EGF binds to receptors causing dimerization. This leads to cross phosphorylation of the receptors. GRB2 adaptor protein binds to phosphorylated proteins. GRB2 is composed of 2 domains SH2 domain binds to the phosphate on the receptor protein and SH3 domain binds to the Sos protein. Sos activator protein (a GNRP) links GRB2 (SH3 domain) to inactive Ras. Sos is a Ras activator protein also called the Son of seven less. Sos activates Ras protein and causes release of GDP. This GTP binds to the Ras protein and Ras becomes activated by binding GTP. Ras sends out signals and Sos disassociates from Ras. Raf protein binds to activated Ras. A specific protein which floats in the cytoplasm, *i.e.,* Raf becomes activated after binding to activate Ras (GTP bound). Raf protein is activated. This activated Raf protein binds to and phosphorylates MEK. Phosphorylated MEK activates MAP-KKK (MAP-kinase-kinase-kinase). Activation of MAP-KKK is achieved by phosphorylation by MEK. Phosphorylation occurs through converting ATP to ADP (not known). MAP-KKK activates MAP-KK while MAP-KK activates MAP-K. Phosphatases clip off the phosphates from the receptor and stop the procedure.

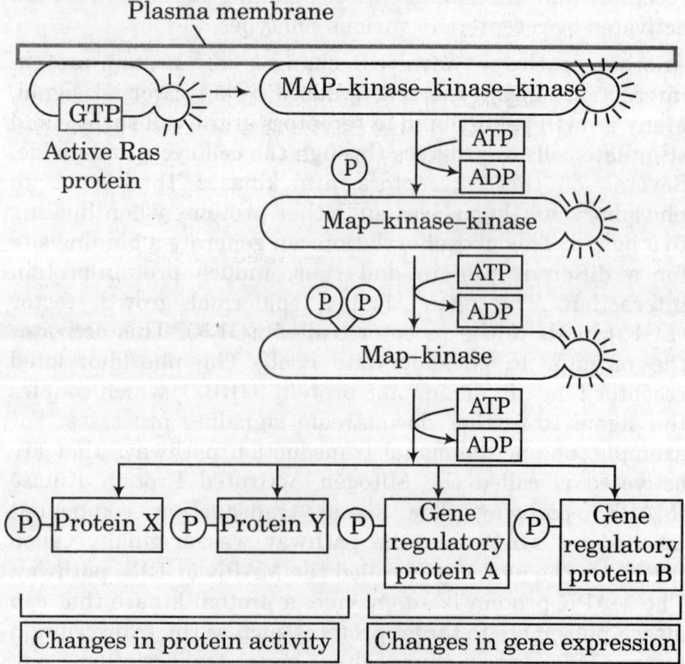

Fig. 11.13 Serine-threonine phosphorylation cascade activated by Ras and C-kinase and involving a series of kinases

cAMP Dependent Pathway

In humans, *c*AMP works by activating protein kinase A (PKA, cAMP dependent protein kinase) and thus, further effects mainly depend on *c*AMP dependent protein kinase, which vary based on the type of cell. G-protein linked receptors are 7 pass transmembrane protein while G-protein (trimeric) with 3 subunits. α-subunit has GDP or GTP bound to it. It has a lipid tail while β-subunit binds to subunit. Signal molecule binds to receptor protein and the receptor undergoes a conformational change. The G-protein releases the receptor protein because α-subunit is altered by losing GDP and binding GTP. α-subunit separates from β subunit and in this way, the 7PTM receptor serves as a GNRP. α-subunit separates from βγ subunit. β-subunit remains bound to subunit (β-complex), separated a subunit can diffuse through the plasma membrane. β-subunit becomes activated when it separates from α. Each subunit (β or α) can activate other membrane proteins. Activated subunits bind to and activate target proteins.While the subunits are activate, they can activate many different proteins or in some cases, deactivate proteins. This is how a cell changes its behaviour. Hydrolysis of the GTP to GDP inactivates the subunit. α-subunits and β-subunits reassociate into the inactive β. Examples of target proteins with which the a subunit can interact:

Adenylyl cyclase α-subunit reacts with the enzyme adenylyl cyclase to produce cyclic AMP (*c*AMP)/ *c*AMP dependent kinase (PKA). *c*AMP can act as α 2nd messenger and binds PKA. PKA is activated and it enters the nucleus. It stimulates the transcription of a whole set of target genes.

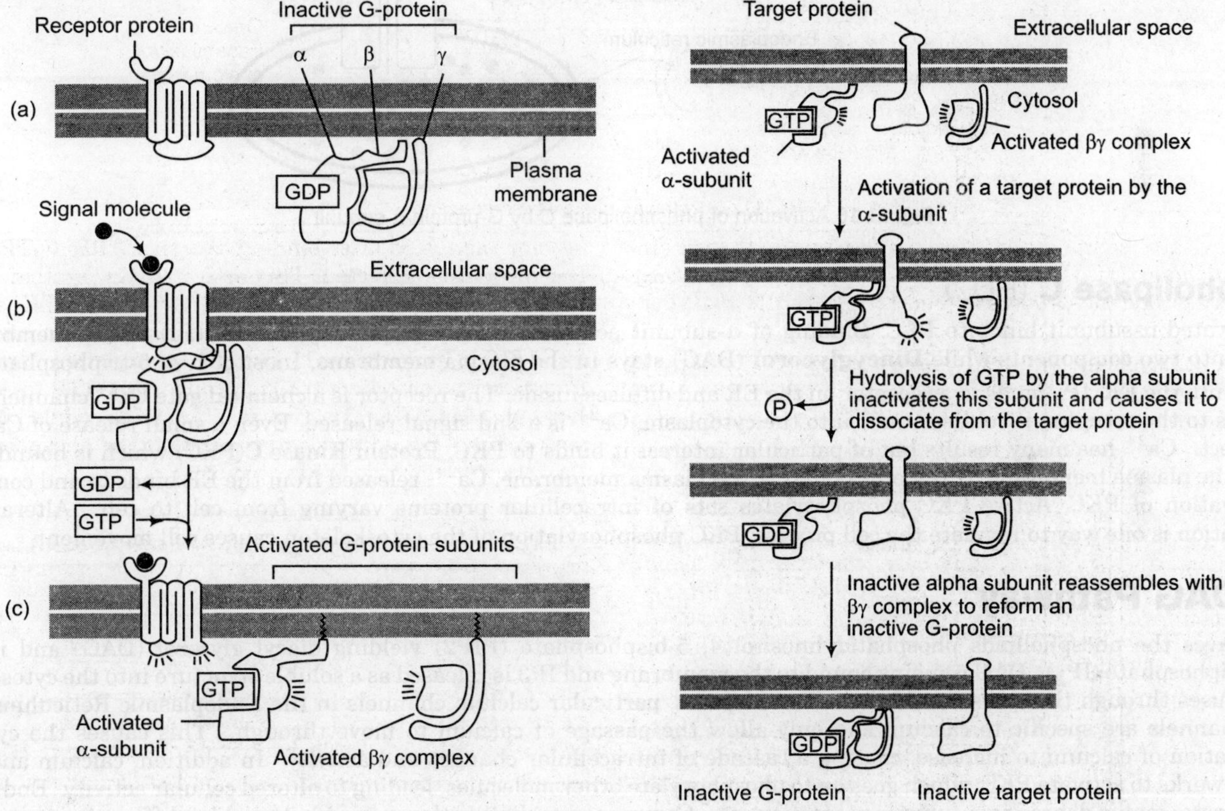

Fig. 11.14 Cyclic AMP dependent signal transduction pathway

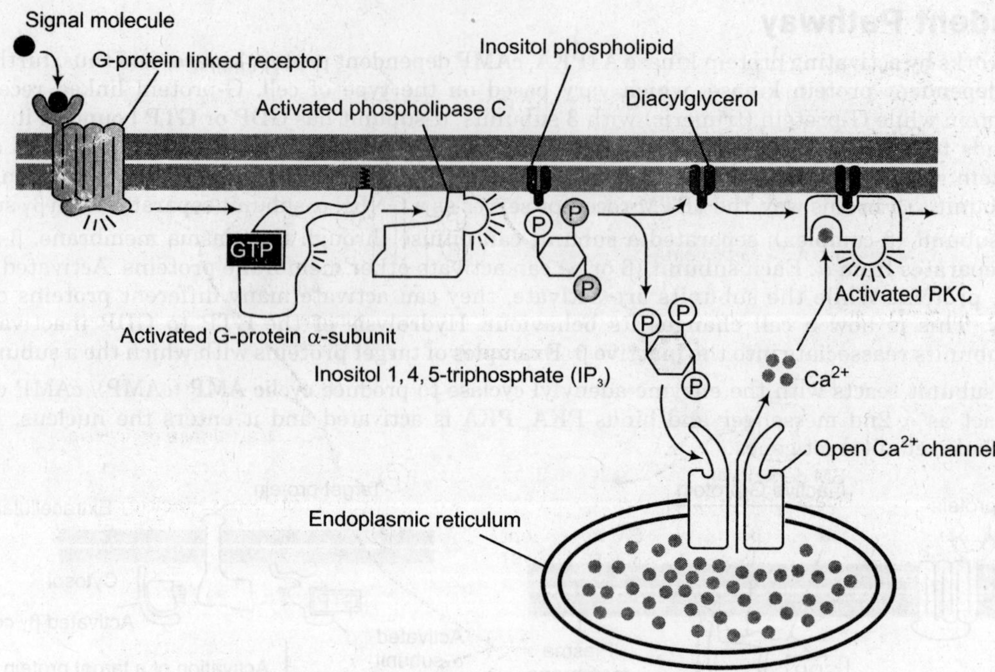

Fig. 11.15 Activation of phospholipase C by G-protein α-subunit

Phospholipase C (PLC)

The activated α-subunit binds to PLC. Binding of α-subunit activates PLC. Phosphatidylinositol (PI) in the membrane is cleaved into two components while **Diacyglycerol** (DAG) stays in the plasma membrane, Inositol 1, 4, 5-triphosphate (IP_3) diffuses into the ER. IP_3 binds to a receptor on the ER and diffuses inside. The receptor is a chemical gate Ca^{2+} channel. When IP_3 binds to the receptor, it releases Ca^{2+} into the cytoplasm. Ca^{2+} is a 2nd signal released. Even a small release of Ca^{2+} is a huge effect. Ca^{2+} has many results but of particular interest it binds to PKC. Protein Kinase C(PKC) which is bound to the DAG in the plasma membrane. It remains bound at the plasma membrane. Ca^{2+}, released from the ER binds to and completes the activation of PKC. Active PKC phosphorylates sets of intracellular proteins varying from cell to cell. Alteration of transcription is one way to regulate the cell process. PKC phosphorylation of the cytoskeleton causes cell movement.

IP3/DAG Pathway

PLC cleaves the phospholipids phosphatidylinositol 4, 5-bisphosphate (PIP2) yielding diacyl glycerol (DAG) and inositol 1, 4, 5-triphosphate (IP_3). DAG remains bound to the membrane and IP3 is released as a soluble structure into the cytosol. IP_3 then diffuses through the cytosol to bind to IP_3 receptors, particular calcium channels in the Endoplasmic Reticulum (ER). These channels are specific to calcium and only allow the passage of calcium to move through. This causes the cytosolic concentration of calcium to increase, causing a cascade of intracellular changes and activity. In addition, calcium and DAG together works to activate PKC, which goes on to phosphorylate other molecules, leading to altered cellular activity. End effects include taste, manic depression, tumour promotion, etc. Common signaling pathways are initiated by different receptors in a class.

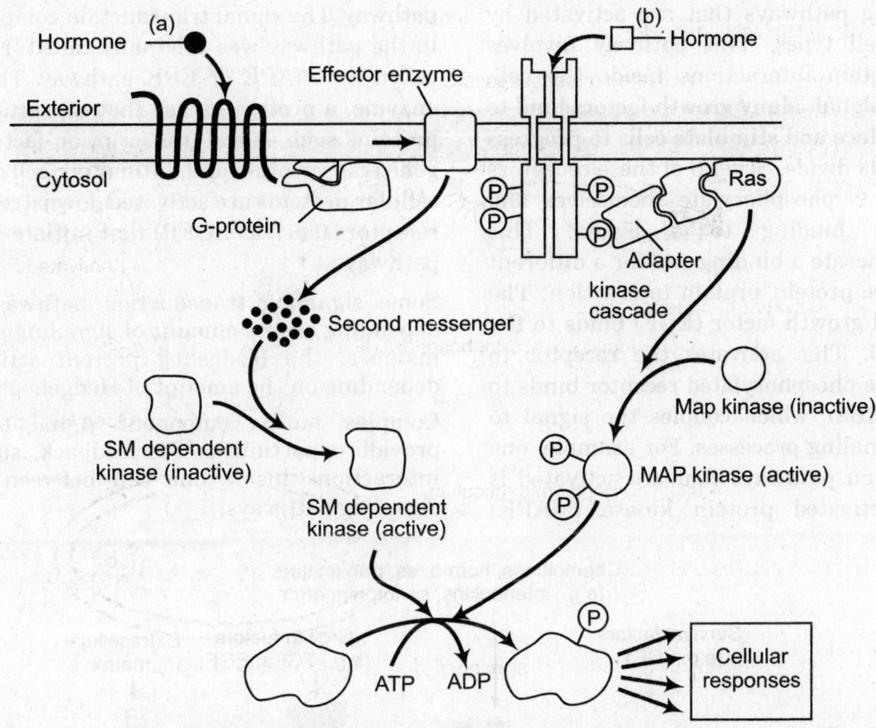

Fig. 11.16 (a) GPCR Pathway and (b) RTK Pathway

The effects of activation of GPCRs and RTKs are more complicated than a simple step by step cascade. Stimulation of either GPCRs or RTKs often leads to production of multiple second messengers and both types of receptors promote or inhibit production of many of the same second messengers.

In addition, RTKs can promote a signal transduction cascade that eventually acts on the same target as the GPCR. Therefore, the same cellular response may be induced by multiple signaling pathways by distinct mechanisms. Interaction of different signaling pathways permits fine tuning of cellular activities.

MAPK/ERK Pathway

In some cases, receptor activation caused by ligand binding to a receptor is directly coupled to the cell's response to the ligand. For example, the neurotransmitter GABA can activate a cell surface receptor that is part of an ion channel. GABA binding to a GABA. A receptor on a neuron opens a chloride-selective ion channel that is part of the receptor. GABA A receptor activation allows negatively charged chloride ions to move into the neuron, which inhibits the ability of the neuron to produce action potentials. However, for many cell surface receptors, ligand receptor interactions are not directly linked to the cell's response. The activated receptor must first interact with other proteins inside the cell before the ultimate physiological effect of the ligand on the cell's behaviour is produced. Often, the behaviour of a chain of several interacting cell proteins is altered following receptor activation. The entire set of cell changes induced by receptor activation is called a signal transduction mechanism or pathway.

In the case of notch mediated signaling, the signal transduction mechanism can be relatively simple. Activation of notch can cause the notch protein to be altered by a protease. Part of the notch protein is released from the cell surface membrane and can act to change the pattern of gene transcription in the cell nucleus. This causes the responding cell to make different proteins, resulting in an altered pattern of cell behaviour. Cell signaling research involves studying the spatial and temporal dynamics of both receptors and the

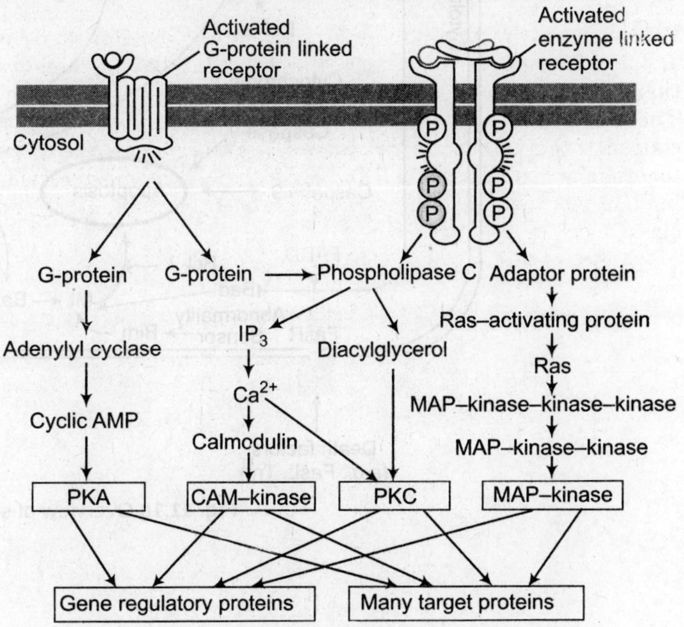

Fig. 11.17 Multicomponent signal transduction pathway

components of signaling pathways that are activated by receptors in various cell types. This pathway involves changes of protein–protein interactions inside the cell, induced by an external signal. Many growth factors bind to receptors at the cell surface and stimulate cells to progress through the cell cycle and divide. Several of these receptors are kinases that start to phosphorylate themselves and other proteins when binding to a ligand. This phosphorylation can generate a binding site for a different protein and thus, induce protein–protein interaction. The ligand (called epidermal growth factor (EGF) binds to the receptor (called EGFR). This activates the receptor to phosphorylate itself. The phosphorylated receptor binds to an adaptor protein (GRB2), which couples the signal to further downstream signaling processes. For example, one of the signal transduction pathways that are activated is called the mitogen activated protein kinase (MAPK) pathway. The signal transduction component labeled as MAPK in the pathway was originally called 'ERK, so, the pathway is called the MAPK or ERK pathway. The MAPK protein is an enzyme, a protein kinase that can attach phosphate to target proteins such as the transcription factor MYC and thus, alter gene transcription and, ultimately, cell cycle progression. Many cellular proteins are activated downstream of the growth factor receptors (such as EGFR) that initiate this signal transduction pathway.

Some signaling transduction pathways respond differently, depending on the amount of signaling received by the cell. For instance, the Hedgehog protein activates different genes, depending on the amount of Hedgehog protein present.

Complex multi component signal transduction pathways provide opportunities for feedback, signal amplification and interactions inside one cell between multiple signals and signaling pathways.

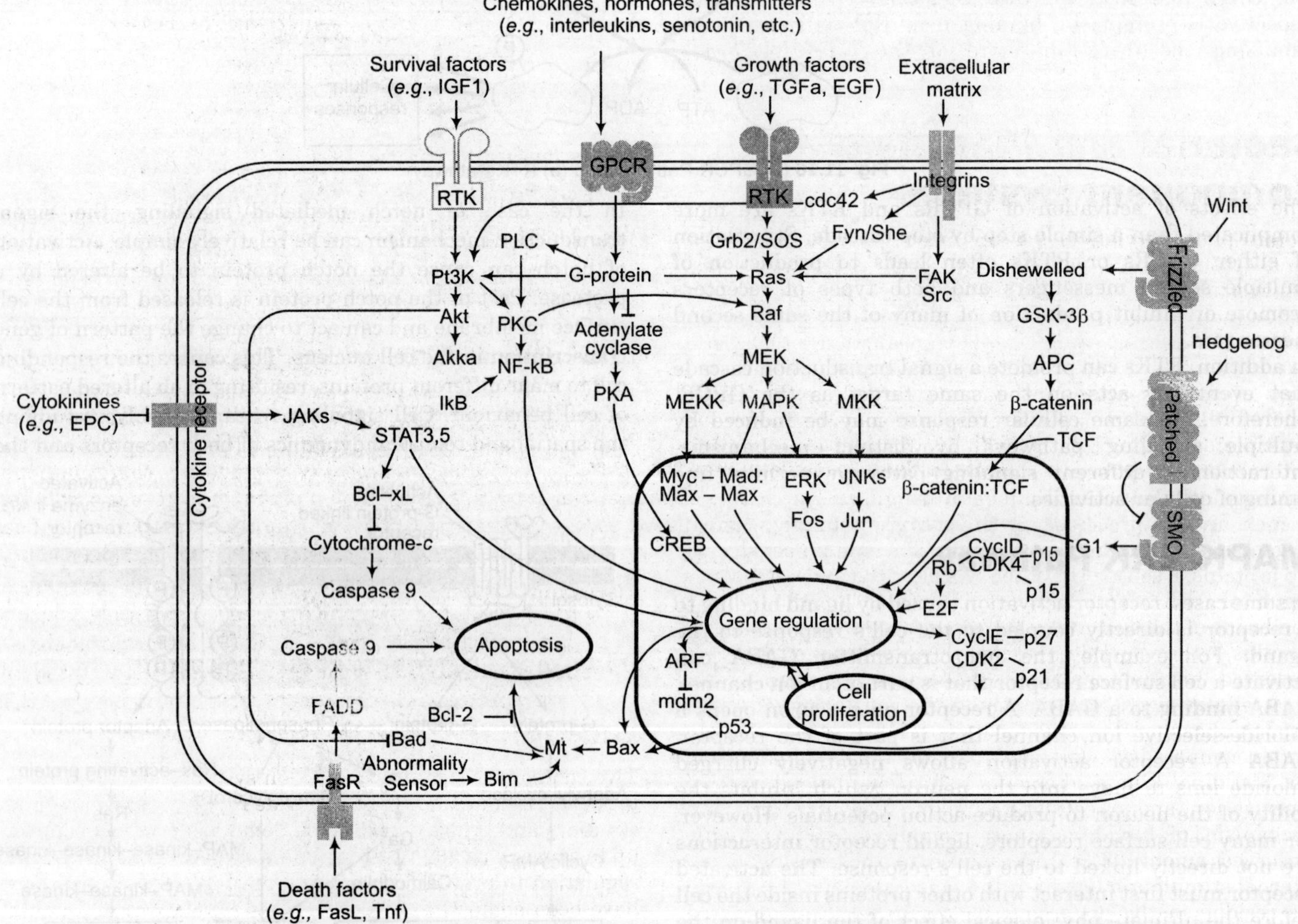

Fig. 11.18 Overview of signal transduction pathways

Regulation of Signal Transduction

RGSs and GAPs—Switches that turn off G-proteins. Nature has made ras p21 and Gsa very poor enzymes by design. These G-proteins are active only in the GTP bound state and downstream targets will dissociate upon GTP hydrolysis. If ras p21 and Gsa were efficient enzymes, the GTP bound state would be short lived, and G-protein mediated signaling would be ineffective. But how can G-proteins be switched off if they are inherently poor GTPases? The answer is provided by GTPase activating proteins (GAPs) and regulators of G-protein signaling (RGS), which cause dramatic increases in GTPase activity when bound to G-proteins. RGS proteins accelerate Gsa catalyzed GTP hydrolysis by nearly 100-fold. In both ras p21 and Gsa, GTPase activity and the conversion from GTP bound to GDP bound forms of the protein involve conformation changes in the switch regions, portions of the G-protein structure that surround the GTP/GDP binding site. GAPs and RGS increase GTPase activities of their respective G-proteins by binding near the active site and stabilizing the transition state of the GTP hydrolysis reaction.

Bacterial and Plant Two Component Systems

Protein phosphorylation is a key mechanism for regulating signal transduction pathways in both prokaryotes and eukaryotes. In eukaryotes, regulatory phosphorylation predominantly occurs at serine, threonine and tyrosine residues. In contrast, many signal transduction pathways in bacteria employ a so, called 'two component system' that relies upon phosphorylation of histidine and aspartic acid residues. Plants also make use of two component systems and these perform important roles in growth and development. Two component systems confer upon bacteria the ability to sense and respond to environmental stimuli and are involved in such diverse processes as chemotaxis, osmotic sensing, oxygen sensing and host recognition. The system consists of two proteins, a sensor Histidine Kinase (HK) and a Response Regulator (RR). The receptor is located in the plasma membrane of the bacterium. In response to an environmental stimulus, the histidine kinase autophosphorylates a conserved histidine residue. HK senses an extra or an intra-cellular signal and transmits the sensed signal to RR through phosphoryl transfer reactions. HK is a multidomain protein composed of sensor and histidine kinase domains and the histidine kinase domain is further divided into a dimerization and a catalytic domain. The structure and mechanism of histidine kinase domain of HK is highly conserved among TCS. In response to the sensing of an external stimuli or a ligand in the sensor domain, the special His residue in the dimerization domain is phosphorylated using ATP, which is catalyzed by the catalytic domain (autophosphorylation). HKs function in the dimeric form and the autophosphorylation reaction occur in transmanner, *i.e.*, the catalytic domain of one subunit phosphorylates His in other subunit. The phosphoryl group on the His residue is transferred to the special Asp residue in RR (RR-kinase). Phosphorylation of the response regulator modulates its ability to mediate downstream signaling.

In bacteria, many of the response regulators are transcription factors. Thus, two proteins create a signaling circuit, capable of converting an external stimulus into a change in transcription. There are permutations on the two component system. Of particular relevance to the plant two component systems are multi-step phospho relays. These make use of a 'hybrid' kinase that contains histidine kinase and receiver domains in one protein, a histidine containing phosphotransfer (HPt) protein and a separate response regulator. In these multi step phosphorelays, the phosphate is transferred from amino acid to amino acid in sequence His to Asp to His to Asp. Interestingly, the canonical histidyl-aspartyl-phosphorelay is apparently not found in animals.

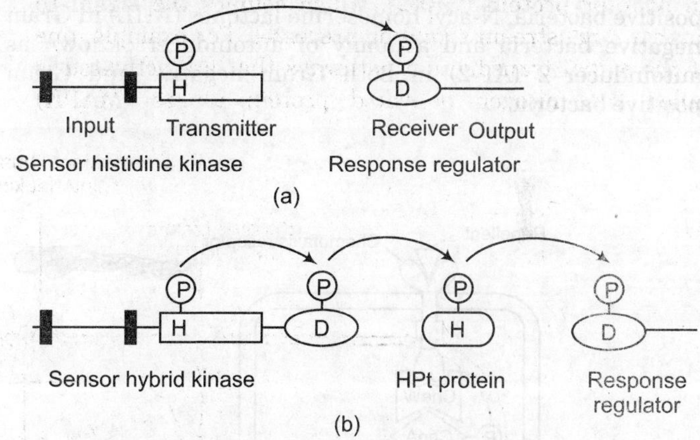

Fig. 11.19 Two component system

Histidyl-Aspartyl Phosphorelay

Histidine kinase domains are indicated by rectangles, receiver domains by ovals, HPt proteins by rounded rectangles and transmembrane domains by black bars. Sites of phosphorylation upon histidine (H) and aspartic acid (D) residues are indicated.

(i) Simple two component system that employs a histidine kinase and a response regulator.

(ii) Multi step phosphorelay that employs a hybrid histidine kinase with both histidine kinase and receiver domains, a histidine containing phosphotransfer protein (HPt) and a response regulator.

Biological Significance

Two component signal transduction systems enable bacteria to sense, respond and adapt to a wide range of environments, stressors and growth conditions. Some bacteria can contain up to as many as 200 two component systems that need tight regulation to prevent unwanted cross talk. These pathways have been adapted to response to a wide variety of stimuli, including nutrients, cellular redox state, changes in osmolarity, quorum signals, antibiotics, temperature, osmolarity, chemoattractants, pH and more. In *E. coli* the EnvZ/OmpR osmoregulation system controls the differential expression of the outer membrane porin proteins OmpF and OmpC.

Bacterial Chemotaxis and Quorum Sensing

Quorum sensing is a system of stimulus and response correlated to population density. Many species of bacteria use quorum sensing to coordinate gene expression according to the density of their local population. Bacteria use quorum sensing to coordinate certain behaviours based on the local density of the bacterial population. Quorum sensing can occur within a single bacterial species as well as between diverse species and can regulate a host of different processes, in essence, serving as a simple communication network. A variety of different molecules can be used as signals. Common classes of signaling molecules are oligopeptides in Gram positive bacteria, N-acyl homoserine lactones (AHL) in Gram negative bacteria and a family of autoinducers known as autoinducer–2 (AI–2) in both Gram negative and Gram positive bacteria.

Mechanism of Action

Bacteria that use quorum sensing constantly produce and secrete certain signaling molecules (called autoinducers or pheromones). These bacteria also have a receptor that can specifically detect the signaling molecule (inducer). When the inducer binds the receptor, it activates transcription of certain genes, including those for inducer synthesis. There is a low likelihood of a bacterium detecting its own secreted inducer. Thus, in order for gene transcription to be activated, the cell must encounter signaling molecules secreted by other cells in its environment. When only a few other bacteria of the same kind are in the vicinity, diffusion reduces the concentration of the inducer in the surrounding medium to almost zero, so, the bacteria produce little inducer. However, as the population grows, the concentration of the inducer passes a threshold, causing more inducer to be synthesized. This forms a positive feedback loop, and the receptor becomes fully activated. Activation of the receptor induces the up regulation of other specific genes, causing all of the cells to begin transcription at approximately the same time. This coordinated behaviour of bacterial cells can be useful in a variety of situations especially chemotaxis.

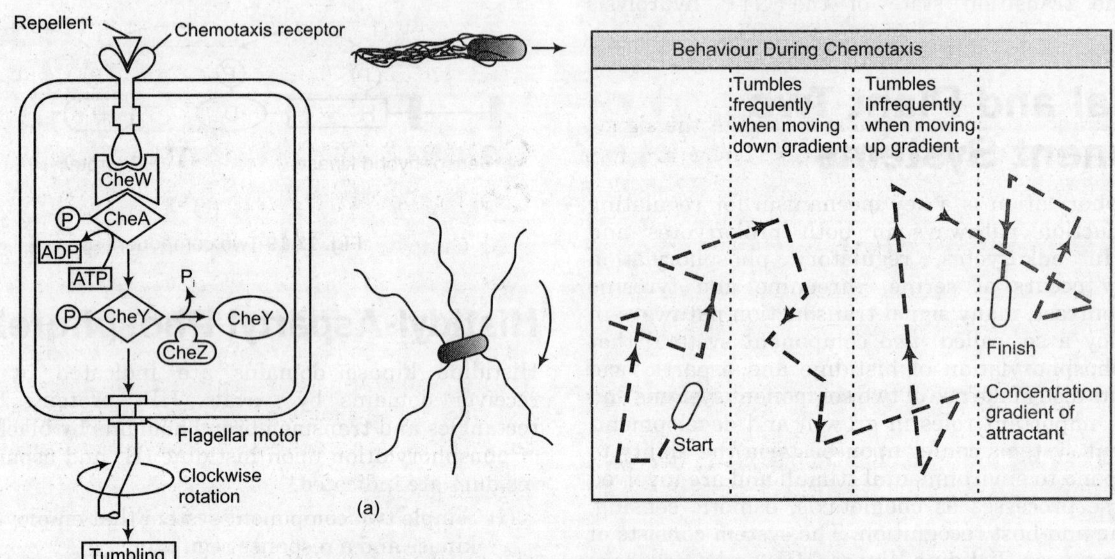

Fig. 11.20 Mechanism of chemotaxis and quorum sensing

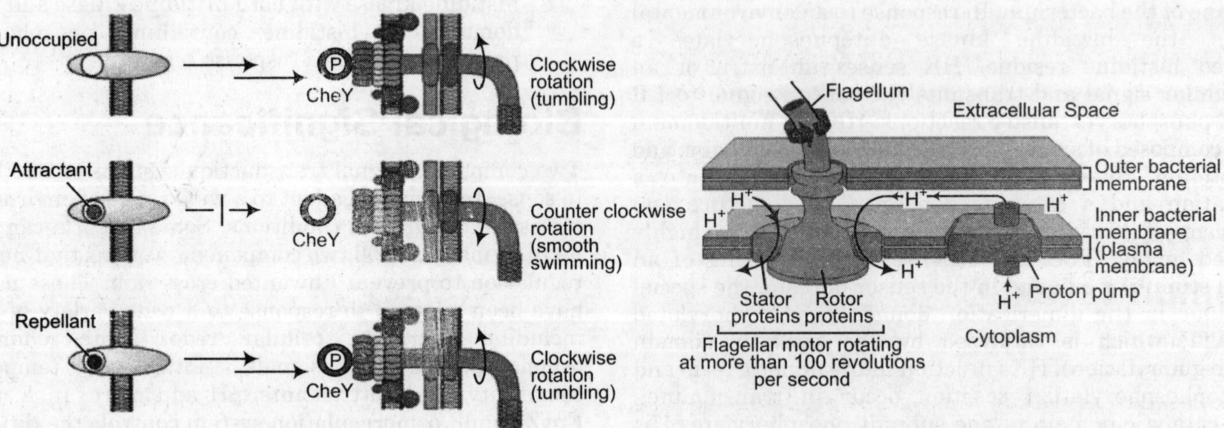

Fig. 11.21 Flagellar movement during chemotaxis

The two component pathway that enables flagellar motor during bacterial chemotaxis. Thus, in the presence of repellant the flagellar motion is clockwise while in the presence of attactant, the flagellar motion is counter clockwise.

(i) When the flagella rotate counter clockwise, they are drawn together into a single bundle, which acts as a propeller to produce smooth swimming.

(ii) When the flagella rotate clockwise, they fly apart and produce tumbling. The rotation of the bacterial flagellum is driven by H^+ flow.

Cellular Communication

An important aspect of cell communication is cell signaling. The topic has been discussed in details in the last topic.

An important concept of cell signaling is signal transduction. The basic constituents of the process are:

1. **Signaling cell** sends a signal to a target cell *via* a signal molecule.
   (a) **Signal molecule** carries a message to the target cell.
2. **Target cell** detects the signal molecule (receives the message).
   (i) **Receptor proteins**
   (a) Found on the target cell/receiver.
   (b) Recognize and respond specifically to the signal molecule.

The mechanism of the process entails sending of the signals which act over long and short distances. There are four categories of signaling:

Neuronal Communication (Will be Discussed in Details Later)

(i) Neurons delivering messages across long distances.

(ii) Acts quickly.

(iii) Conversion of electrical impulses to chemical and *vice versa*.

Example — Poke big toe, stimulus travels along nerves to the brain and converts a stimulus that travels back to the toe indicating pain.

Endocrine Communication

(i) Long distance signaling.

(ii) Very often it occurs through the systemic circulation.

(iii) Hormones released into the blood stream and bind to receptors to the sites.

Example—Pancreas producing insulin and which regulates glucose uptake in cells all over the body.

Paracrine and Autocrine Communication

(i) Signaling in the neighbourhood or communication to neighbouring cells.

(ii) Act as local mediators to influence neighbouring cells, released to the local extracellular space.

(iii) Depend upon diffusion and regulated by factors that influence diffusion distance/rate.

(iv) Paracrine *versus* autocrine

(a) Autocrine signaling

A certain type of cell will release the signal and the same type of cell will respond to the signal.

Example—Epithelial cell communicates with an epithelial cell.

(b) Paracrine signaling

A certain type of cell will release the signal and a different type of cell will respond to the signal.

Example—Epithelial communicates with a smooth muscle cell.

Contact Dependent Communication (Juxtacrine)

(i) Occurs between two cells that are next to each other.

(ii) Difference between juxtacrine and paracrine is that:

(a) A cell is never released into the extracellular space.

(b) The two cells in a sense hold hands. They must be adjacent and in direct contact with one another.

(c) Example—Occurs when WBC are trying to leave the circulation and enter the site of injury.

Signaling molecules expressed on the surface of the epithelial cells are not released into the blood stream but stick to their cell surfaces. The WBCs notice the signal and bind so, that the cell can be extravasated into the infection site.

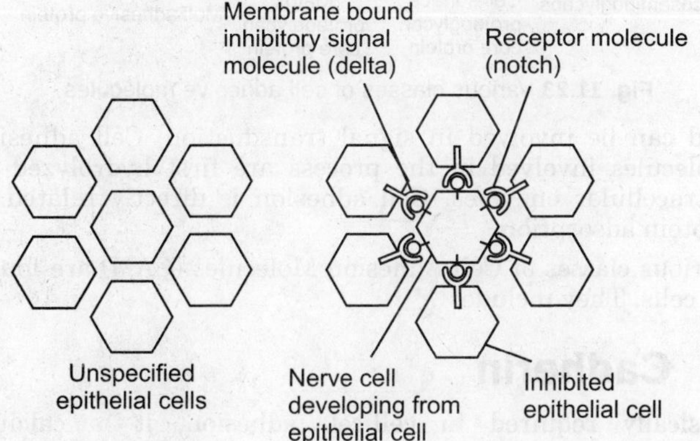

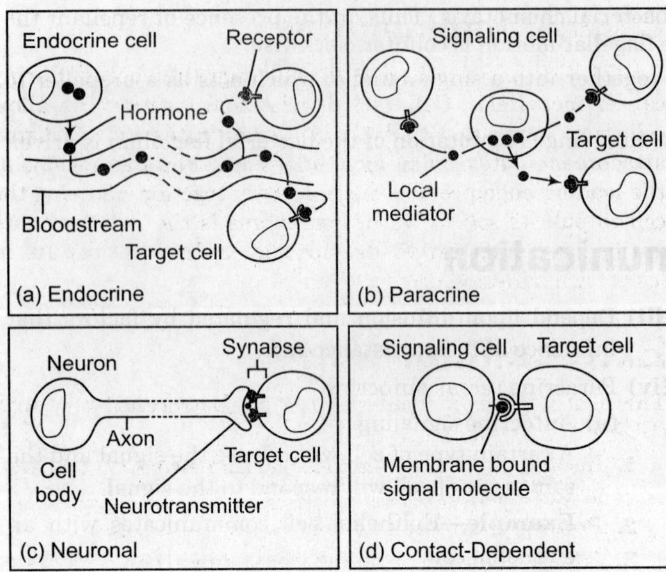

Fig. 11.22 Four signalling pathways

Cell Adhesion and Adhesion Molecules

Cellular adhesion is the binding of a cell to a surface, extra cellular matrix or another cell using cell adhesion molecules such as selectins, integrins and cadherins. Correct cellular adhesion is essential in maintaining multicellular structure. Cellular adhesion can link the cytoplasm of cells.

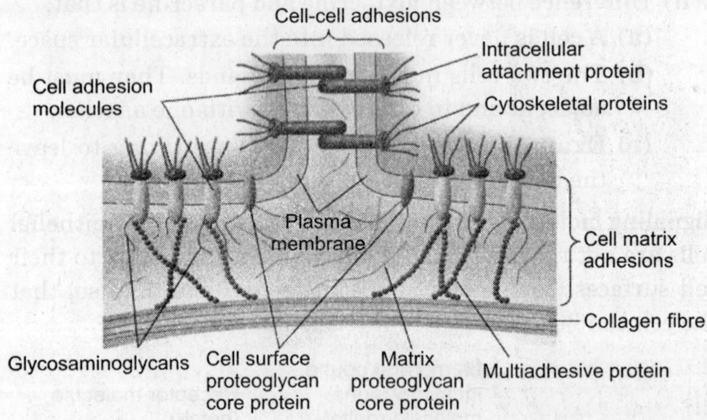

Fig. 11.23 Various classes of cell adhesive molecules

and can be involved in signal transduction. Cell adhesion molecules involved in the process are first hydrolyzed by extracellular enzymes. Cell adhesion is directly related to protein adsorption.

Various classes of Cell Adhesion Molecules (CAM) are found on cells. They include:

1. Cadherin

Basically required in cell-cell adhesion, it is calcium dependent in nature. Over 40 different cadherins are known, *e.g.,* include E cadherin, P cadherin. CAMs are major molecules of cell-cell adhesion (homophilic). Tissues have specialized junctions made of cadherins.

Cadherin Containing Junctions

There are two major types :

Adherens junction A continuous band of cadherins is found in epithelial cells. It connects cells tightly and interact with the actin portion of the cytoskeleton.

Desmosomes It is also found in high densities in epithelial tissues wherein cells attach *via* cadherins and connect to protein 'plaques' that attach to the plasma membrane and to intermediate filaments within the cytoskeleton.

2. Ig Super Family of CAMs

Again required in cell-cell adhesion, it is however calcium independent, *e.g.,* include N-CAM, V-CAM. Some are found enriched on specific cell types N-CAM.

3. Integrin

It is a major cell matrix adhesion molecule, *e.g.,* a1 integrin, b1 integrin.

Cellular Adhesions in Eukaryotes

Eukaryotic protozoans express multiple adhesion molecules. An example of a pathogenic protozoan is the malarial parasite (*Plasmodium falciparum*), which uses one adhesion molecule called the circum sporozoite protein to bind to liver cells and another adhesion molecule called the merozoite surface protein to bind red blood cells. In human cells, which have many different types of adhesion molecules, the major classes are named integrins, Ig super-family members, cadherins and selectins. Each of these adhesion molecules has a different function and recognizes different ligands. Defects in cell adhesion are usually attributable to defects in expression of adhesion molecules.

Cell junctions allow cells to adhere. There are four types of cell junctions:

(i) Anchoring junctions, which transmit stress through tothering to cytoskeleton are cell-cell or cell matrix.

(ii) Occluding junctions, which seal gaps between cells, making an impermeable barrier.

(iii) Channel forming junctions aka gap junctions, which links cytoplasm of adjacent cells.

(iv) Signal relaying junction, synapses in nervous systems.

Cell-cell adhesions in anchoring junctions are mediated by cadherins. Cell matrix adhesions however, are usually mediated by intergrins. Selective cell-cell adhesion enables vertebrate cells to assemble into organized tissues. Homophilic attachment allows selective recognition resulting. Cells of a similar type stick together where as cells of a different type stay segregated.

Prokaryotes

Prokaryotes have adhesion molecules usually termed 'adhesins'. Adhesins may occur on pili (fimbriae), flagellae or the cell surface. Adhesion of bacteria is the first step in colonization and regulates tropism (tissue or cell specific interactions).

Viruses

Viruses also have adhesion molecules required for viral binding to host cells. For example, influenza virus has a hemagglutinin on its surface that is required for recognition of the sugar sialic acid on host cell surface molecules. HIV has an adhesion molecule termedgp 120 that binds to its ligand CD^4, which is expressed on lymphocytes.

Differential Adhesion Hypothesis

The **differential adhesion hypothesis** (sometimes called the 'thermodynamic hypothesis') is a theory of cell adhesion advanced by **Malcolm Steinberg** in 1964 to explain the mechanism by which heterotypic cells in mixed aggregates sort out into isotypic territories. The DAH postulates that tissues are visco-elastic liquids and as such possess measurable tissue surface tensions. These surface tensions have been determined for a variety of tissues, including embryonic tissues and cell lines. The surface tensions correspond to the mutual sorting behaviour, the tissue type with the higher surface tension will occupy an internal position relative to a tissue with a lower surface tension (if these tissues can interact with each other through their adhesion machinery). Quantitative differences in homo and heterotypic adhesion are supposed to be sufficient to account for the phenomenon without the need to postulate cell type specific adhesion systems, fairly generally accepted, although some tissue specific cell adhesion molecules are now known to exist.

Clinical Implications

Dysfunction of cell adhesion and cell migration occurs during cancer metastasis. Cellular adhesion and traction can allow cells to migrate. Cells can form integrin mediated attachments sites called focal adhesions. Focal adhesions at the leading edge provide the necessary traction allowing the cell to pull its self forward. Pemphigus is the result of auto antibodies which target desmosomal cadherins, results in loss of cell adhesion.

Extracellular Matrix

There are three components to the Extracellular Matrix (ECM)

1. Insoluble collagens—structural framework of the ECM, provides strength and resiliency.
2. Proteoglycans—cushions cells.
3. Adhesive matrix proteins—bind these components to receptors on the cell surface.

Different combinations result in unique ECM compositions which can directly affect the activity of the cells. The interaction of ECM components with specific CAMs (*i.e.,* ECM receptors) can turn certain signaling paths ON or OFF. Also the ECM is capable of sequestering growth factors and hormones by binding them and making them unavailable to turn cellular signaling on or off.

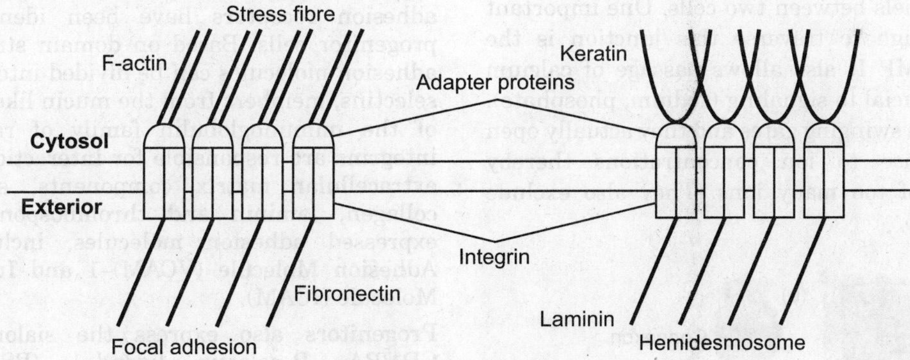

Fig. 11.24 Cell matrix interactions

Integrins

Integrins allow connection between the extracellular matrix with the cytoskeleton of the cell. They also can mediate cell-cell interactions (weak). Basically made of an alpha and a beta subunit, 17 types of a chains, 8 types of β-chains. These αβ complexes act as receptors to specific matrix components, *e.g.,* α1β1 – collagen and laminin α5 β1 fibronectin. Cells will express multiple integrin types and attachment can be regulated by up or down regulated expression of these integrins. Activation of these integrins can promote cell signaling, *e.g.,* formation and activation of focal adhesions triggers a cascade initaited by a Focal Adhesion Kinase (FAK) which modulates cell growth and motility.

Integrins can also form very specific adhesive junctions:

Focal Adhesions (FN to actin) It is a complex of more than twenty proteins and can increase and decrease based on physical stress.

Hemidesmosomes (intermediate filaments to collagens and laminins), *e.g.,* include epithelial cells.

Principles of Cell Communication

Mechanisms enabling one cell to influence the behaviour of another almost certainly existed in the world of unicellular organisms long before multicellular organisms appeared on Earth.

1. Extracellular signal molecules bind to specific receptors.

2. Extracellular signal molecules can act over either short or long distances.
3. Autocrine signaling can coordinate decisions by groups of identical cells.
4. Gap junction allow signaling information to be shared by neighbouring cells.
5. Each cell is programmed to respond to specific combinations of extracellular signal molecules.
6. Different cells can respond differently to the same extracellular signal molecule.
7. The concentration of a molecule can be adjusted quickly only if the lifetime of the molecule is short.
8. Some intracellular signaling proteins act as molecular switches.
9. Intracellular signaling complexes enhance the speed, efficiency and specificity of the respnse.
10. Interactions between intracellular signaling proteins are mediated by modular binding domains.
11. Cells can respond abruptly to a gradually increasing concentration of an extracellular signal.
12. A cell can remember the effect of some signals.
13. Cells can adjust their sensitivity to a signal.

Gap Junctions

Almost all cells have specialized junctions that allow the free passage of materials (*e.g.*, signaling molecules) back and forth. These junctions are called **gap junctions.** They are made of a channel protein called **connexon.** Connexons interact to form channels between two cells. One important compound small enough to traverse this junction is the second messenger *c*AMP. It also allows passage of calcium ions and other ions crucial to signaling (sodium, phosphate). These gaps are not free swinging gates and they actually open and close in response to ion concentrations thereby restricting the flow of too many ions. They also exclude materials based on size.

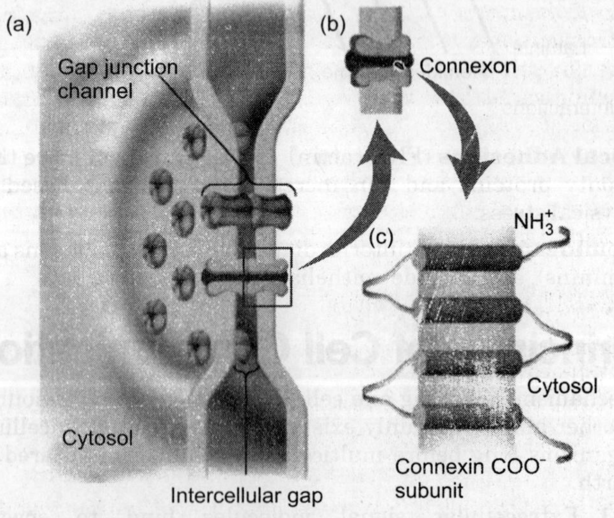

Fig. 11.25 Communication through gap junctions

Haematopoiesis and its Regulation

Haematopoiesis is a complex process in which haematopoietic stem cells self replicate and differentiate to generate all the different mature blood cells. Under steady state conditions, stem cells and haematopoietic progenitor cells reside in the Bone Marrow (BM) medullary cavity in contact with the bone marrow microenvironment. Most, if not all, the factors required for the orderly development of stem cells are present in the BM microenvironment. These include mesenchymal cells as well as other haematopoietic cells that secrete haematopoietic cytokines and extracellular matrix components. More than 40 different growth factors, cytokines and chemokines interact with stem and progenitor cells through specific receptors and regulate proliferation, differentiation and cell fate. Haematopoietic growth factors are produced by mesenchymal cells and haematopoietic cells and are present in cell bound forms, bound to the Extra Cellular Matrix (ECM) or in solution. Stem and progenitor cells express adhesion receptors that provide specific cell-cell and cell–ECM interactions. Aside from retaining stem and progenitor cells in the BM, engagement of adhesion receptors on stem and progenitor cells by BM stromal ligands also plays an important role in the regulation of the haematopoietic process. Adhesive interactions serve as growth or survival signals but also may modulate growth factor dependent signals. In addition, cytokines and growth factors affect adhesive interactions between stem and progenitor cells and their adhesive ligands in the BM, providing a further level of regulation of haematopoiesis. More than twenty different adhesion receptors have been identified on stem and progenitor cells. Based on domain structure and function, adhesion molecules can be divided into integrins, cadherins, selectins, members from the mucin like family and members of the immunoglobulin family of receptors. β1 and β2 integrins are responsible for interactions between cells and extracellular matrix components, such as fibronectin, collagen, laminin and thrombospondin or cell surface expressed adhesion molecules, including Vascular Cell Adhesion Molecule (VCAM)–1 and Intercellular Adhesion Molecule (ICAM).

Progenitors also express the sialomucins CD^{34}, CD^{43}, CD^{45}RA, P–selectin ligand–1 (PSGL–1), CD^{164} and podocalyxin like protein–1 (PCLP–1).

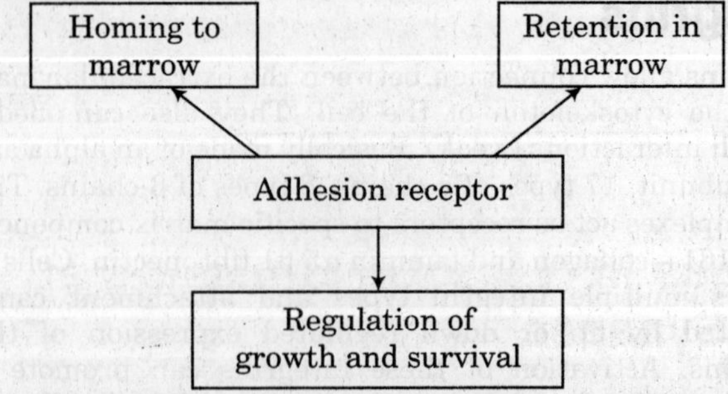

Fig. 11.26 Role of adhesion molecule in haematopoiesis

It is believed that adhesion molecules contribute to retention of stem and progenitor cells in the BM and are essential for homing of stem and progenitor cells to the BM. Besides their role in trafficking and location, adhesion receptors transmit signals from the extracellular milieu into the cell. Aside from anchoring cells in a given microenvironment, adhesion receptors also play an important role in regulation of cell behaviour, either through direct activation of signal pathways important for cell survival, cell growth and cell fate decision making processes or by modulating responses to growth factors.

Neurotransmission and its Regulation

The presynaptic neuron releases neurotransmitter, which activates receptors on the postsynaptic cell dark.

Neurotransmission, also called **synaptic transmission,** is the process by which signaling molecules called neurotrans mitters are released by a neuron (the presynaptic neuron), and bind to and activate the receptors of another neuron (the postsynaptic neuron). Neurotransmission usually takes place at a synapse and occurs when an action potential is initiated in the pre-synaptic neuron. The binding of neurotransmitters to receptors in the postsynaptic neuron can trigger either short term changes, like changes in the membrane potential called postsynaptic potentials or longer term changes by the activation of signaling cascades. Nerve impulses are essential for the propagation of signals. These signals are sent to and from the central nervous system *via* efferent and afferent neurons in order to coordinate smooth, skeletal and cardiac muscles, bodily secretions and organ functions critical for the long term survival of multicellular vertebrate organisms such as mammals.

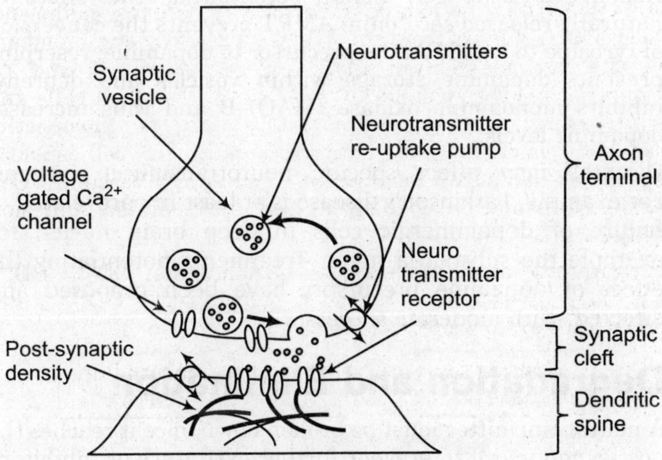

Fig. 11.27 Neurotransmission

Stages in Neurotransmission at the Synapse

(i) Synthesis of the neurotransmitter. This can take place in the cell body, in the axon or in the axon terminal.

(ii) Storage of the neurotransmitter in storage granules or vesicles in the axon terminal.

(iii) Calcium enters the axon terminal during an action potential, causing release of the neurotransmitter into the synaptic cleft.

(iv) After its release, the transmitter binds to and activates a receptor in the post-synaptic membrane.

(v) Deactivation of the neurotransmitter. The neurotrans-mitter is either destroyed enzymatically or taken back into the terminal from which it came, where it can be reused or degraded and removed.

Summation

Each neuron is connected with numerous other neurons, receiving numerous impulses from them. **Summation** is the adding together of these impulses at the axon hillock. If the neuron only gets excitatory impulses, it will also generate an action potential but if the neuron gets as many inhibitory as excitatory impulses, the inhibition cancels out the excitation and the nerve impulse will stop there. Summation takes place at the axon hillock. **Spatial summation** means several firings on different places of the neuron, that in themselves are not strong enough to cause a neuron to fire. However, if they fire simultaneously, their combined effects will cause an action potential. **Temporal summation** means several firings at the same place, that won't cause an action potential if they have a pause in between, but when there are several firings in rapid succession, they will cause the neuron to reach the threshold for excitation.

Convergence and Divergence

Neurotransmission implies both a convergence and a divergence of information. First one neuron is influenced by many others, resulting in a convergence of input. When the neuron fires, the signal is sent to many other neurons, resulting in a divergence of output. Many other neurons are influenced by this neuron.

Cotransmission

Cotransmission is the release of several types of neurotransmitters from a single nerve terminal. Cotransmission allows for more complex effects at post-synaptic receptors and thus, allows for more complex communication to occur between neurons. Some neurons can release at least two neurotransmitters at the same time, the other being a cotransmitter, in order to provide, the stabilizing negative feedback required for meaningful encoding, in the absence of inhibitory interneurons. Examples include GABA–glycine corelease.

Neurotransmitter

A chemical can be classified as a neurotransmitter if it meets the following conditions:

(i) There are precursors and or synthesis enzymes located in the pre-synaptic side of the synapse.

(ii) The chemical is present in the pre-synaptic element.

(iii) It is available in sufficient quantity in the pre-synaptic neuron to affect the post-synaptic neuron.

(iv) There are post-synaptic receptors and the chemical is able to bind to them.

(v) A biochemical mechanism for inactivation is present.

Types of Neurotransmitters

There are many different ways to classify neurotransmitters. Dividing them into amino acids, peptides and monoamines is sufficient for some classification purposes.

Major Neurotransmitters

(a) Amino acids: Glutamate, aspartate, D-serine, γ-aminobutyric acid (GABA), glycine

(b) Monoamines and other biogenic amines: Dopamine (DA), norepinephrine (noradrenaline, NE, NA), epinephrine (adrenaline), histamine, serotonin, (SE, 5–HT)

(c) Others: Acetylcholine (ACh), adenosine, anandamide, nitric oxide, etc.

Actions

As explained above, the only direct action of a neurotransmitter is to activate a receptor. Therefore, the effects of a neurotransmitter system depend on the connections of the neurons that use the transmitter and the chemical properties of the receptors that the transmitter binds to.

Here are a few examples of important neurotransmitter actions:

(a) Glutamate is used at the great majority of fast excitatory synapses in the brain and spinal cord. It is also used at most synapses that are 'modifiable', *i.e.*, capable of increasing or decreasing in strength. Modifiable synapses are thought to be the main memory storage elements in the brain. Excessive glutamate release can lead to excitotoxicity causing cell death.

(b) GABA is used at the great majority of fast inhibitory synapses in virtually every part of the brain.
Many sedative/tranquilizing drugs act by enhancing the effects of GABA. Correspondingly glycine is the inhibitory transmitter in the spinal cord.

(c) Acetylcholine is distinguished as the transmitter at the neuromuscular junction connecting motor nerves to muscles. The paralytic arrow poison curare acts by blocking transmission at these synapses. Acetylcholine also operates in many regions of the brain, but using different types of receptors.

(d) Dopamine has a number of important functions in the brain. It plays a critical role in the reward system, but dysfunction of the dopamine system is also implicated in Parkinson's disease and schizophrenia.

(e) Serotonin is a monoamine neurotransmitter. Most of it is produced by and found in the intestine (approximately 90%), and the remainder in central nervous system neurons. It functions to regulate appetite, sleep, memory and learning, temperature, mood, behaviour, muscle contraction, and function of the cardiovascular system and endocrine system. It is speculated to have a role in depression, as some depressed patients are seen to have lower concentrations of metabolites of serotonin in their cerebrospinal fluid and brain tissue. Substance P is an undecapeptide responsible for transmission of pain from certain sensory neurons to the central nervous system.

Neurons expressing certain types of neurotransmitters sometimes form distinct systems, where activation of the system affects large volumes of the brain, called volume transmission. Major neurotransmitter systems include the noradrenaline (norepinephrine) system, the dopamine system, the serotonin system and the cholinergic system.

Drugs as the Regulators

Drugs targeting the neurotransmitter of such systems affect the whole system, this fact explains the complexity of action of some drugs. Cocaine, for example, blocks the reuptake of dopamine back into the presynaptic neuron, leaving the neurotransmitter molecules in the synaptic gap longer. Since the dopamine remains in the synapse longer, the neurotransmitter continues to bind to the receptors on the postsynaptic neuron, eliciting a pleasurable emotional response. Physical addiction to cocaine may result from prolonged exposure to excess dopamine in the synapses, which leads to the downregulation of some postsynaptic receptors. After the effects of the drug wear off, one might feel depressed because of the decreased probability of the neurotransmitter binding to a receptor. Prozac is a Selective Serotonin Reuptake Inhibitor (SSRI), which blocks reuptake of serotonin by the presynaptic cell. This increases the amount of serotonin present at the synapse and allows it to remain there longer, hence potentiating the effect of naturally released serotonin. AMPT prevents the conversion of tyrosine to L–DOPA, the precursor to dopamine; reserpine prevents dopamine storage within vesicles and deprenyl inhibits monoamine oxidase (MAO)–B and thus increases dopamine levels.

Diseases may affect specific neurotransmitter systems. For example, Parkinson's disease is at least in part related to failure of dopaminergic cells in deep brain nuclei, for example the substantia nigra. Treatments potentiating the effect of dopamine precursors have been proposed and effected, with moderate success.

Degradation and Elimination

A neurotransmitter must be broken down once it reaches the post-synaptic cell to prevent further excitatory or inhibitory signal transduction. For example, acetylcholine (ACh), an excitatory neurotransmitter, is broken down by acetylcholinesterase (AChE). Choline is taken up and recycled by the pre-synaptic neuron to synthesize more ACh. Other neurotransmitters such as dopamine are able to diffuse away from their targeted synaptic junctions and are eliminated from the body *via* the kidneys or destroyed in the liver. Each neurotransmitter has very specific degradation pathways at regulatory points, which may be the target of the body's own regulatory system or recreational drugs.

Exercise

1. Neuron response after an immediate shock is an example of
(a) paracrine signaling (b) endocrine signaling
(c) synaptic signaling (d) direct touch signaling

2. Which of the enzyme is responsible for adding a phosphate to a protein in order to generate a signal?
(a) Phosphatase
(b) Protein kinase
(c) Phosphate transferase
(d) Phosphate group transfer protein

3. Which of the following is a sub-class of membrane receptors?
(a) Channel linked receptors
(b) Enzymatic receptors
(c) G-protein coupled receptor
(d) All of the above

4. Synaptic signaling involves
(a) endocrine signals (b) paracrine signals
(c) autocrine signals (d) neurotransmitters

5. Characteristics of intracellular receptors that regulate gene transcription include all of the following except
(a) a DNA binding site
(b) an extracellular binding sitre
(c) a transcription activating domain
(d) may be signaled by lipid soluble molecules

6. In eukaryotes, which of the following is not a second messenger?
(a) 1, 2-diacyl glycerol
(b) Cyclic AMP
(c) Inositol 1, 4, 5-triphosphate
(d) Cyclins

7. Which of the following compounds does not act second messenger during signaling process?
(a) *c*AMP
(b) Calcium ions
(c) Inositol 3, 4, 5-triphosphate
(d) Triacylglycerol

8. Cell surface receptors may be any of the following except?
(a) G-protein linked
(b) Enzymatic receptors
(c) Transcription factors
(d) Ligand gated ion channels

9. The .... surrounds the cell like a belt, preventing the passage of substances between the cells.
(a) gap junction (b) desmosome
(c) hemidesmosome (d) tight junction

10. All of the following statements apply to G-proteins except
(a) G-proteins transmit a signal from the cell surface to the interior of the cell
(b) G-proteins do not use second messengers but transmit the signal directly into the nucleus
(c) All G-proteins have a similar structure
(d) G-proteins act to amplify the signal creating a cascade response in the cell

11. Which subunit of trimetric G-protein acts as GTPase switch protein subunit?
(a) Alpha (b) Beta
(c) Gamma (d) Beta-gamma

12. G-proteins are involved in recycling signals through G-protein linked receptors. Which of the following forms of G-protein is considered to be in active state?
(a) G-protein–ADP (b) G-protein–ATP
(c) G-protein–GDP (d) G-protein–GTP

13. In most cases protein kinases
(a) hydrolyze proteins
(b) polymerize amino acids
(c) stimulate adenylyl cyclase
(d) add phosphate groups to proteins

14. Receptor tyrosine kinases
I. Have a cytoplasmic kinase domain.
II. Dimerize upon ligand binding.
III. Change conformation of their cytoplasmic domains upon ligand binding.
IV. Become catalytically active after the conformational change.
(a) I and II (b) I and III
(c) II, III and IV (d) I, II, III and IV

15. Narrow gaps between nerve cells through which paracrine signals travel are called
(a) desmosomes (b) calmodulins
(c) synapses (d) integrins

16. .... is a common second messenger.
(a) *c*AMP (b) cGTP
(c) cMHC (d) cATP

17. Paracrine signals
(a) are long-lived with widespread effects
(b) are short-lived, but with widespread effects due to cascades
(c) are long-lived, but are acting locally
(d) are short-lived with local effects

18. All of the following statemnents about monomeric G-proteins are true except
(a) they are regulated by GTP–GDP exchange proteins
(b) they are regulated by GTPase activating proteins
(c) they regulate vesicle fusion
(d) they helps in uncoating of proteins from vesicle

19. The signaling system that operates over the shortest range is
(a) contact dependent cell signaling, as in the inhibition of neighbours by diffrebriating nerve cells
(b) paracrine secretion, as in the secretion of histamine by mast cells
(c) neural signaling, as in the transmission of a nerve impulse
(d) None of the above

20. Which of the following reactions is most commonly utilized by living cells to propogate?
(a) Acylation (b) Phosphorylation
(c) Methylation (d) Decarboxylation

21. With respect to the plasma membrane, most enzymic receptors are
(a) entirely internal (b) seven pass
(c) multipass (d) single pass

22. A single pass protein that acts as a 'self' marker is
(a) GTP (b) MHC
(c) GMP (d) MCA

23. In the *c*AMP pathway, the G-protein stimulates
(a) phospholipase *C* (b) adenylate
(c) the ER (d) calmodulin

24. Dacylglycerol activates
(a) protein kinase A (b) protein kinase *C*
(c) MAP kinase (d) tyrosine kinase

25. Which of the following is involved in cell signaling process?
(a) Cytochrome-P_{450} (b) Protein kinase *C*
(c) Zinc fingers (d) All of these

26. Calmodulin activates protein kinases in response to a transient incrase in
(a) *c*AMP (b) calcium ions
(c) DAG (d) NO

27. With respect to the plasma membrane, most enzymic receptors are
(a) single pass (b) seven pass
(c) entirely on the surface (d) multipass

28. Plasmodesmata
(a) encircle cells of a tight junction like a belt
(b) connect to intermediate fibers of the cytoskeleton
(c) connect the cytoplasm of one plant cell to that of another
(d) connect actin fibres of one cell to the extracellular matrix of another

29. The signaling molecules that travel the farthest are
(a) endocrine (b) paracrine
(c) neurotransmitter (d) intracel

30. When a signal molecule arrives at a G-protein-linked receptor, the G-protein
(a) becomes deactivated
(b) binds to the signal molecule
(c) becomes activated
(d) binds with a Ca^{2+}

31. Which of the following is a component in the signaling pathway stimulated by receptor tyrosine kinase?
(a) Adenylate cyclase
(b) Adaptor proteins
(c) Autophosphorylating receptor
(d) Ras activatoing protein

32. Cells interact through the actions of chemical signals which either bind to receptors on the membrane or
(a) pass through the plasma membrane
(b) bind to intracellular receptors
(c) activate receptors that bind to DNA
(d) All of the above

33. In some tissues subject to mechanical stress, special junctions called .... connect the cytoskeletons of adjacent cells.
(a) cadherin junctions (b) tight junctions
(c) stress junctions (d) anchoring junctions

34. Gap junctions are formed by
(a) the fusion of plasma membranes to form a single membrane
(b) the insertion of protein complexes that form tunnels between cells
(c) protein hooks that extend into the membrane of adjacent cells
(d) gaps in the cell wall of plants

35. The receptor for NO is
(a) intercellular (b) intracellular
(c) extracellular (d) transcellular

36. Which of the following statements is false for the NO gas?
(a) An intracellular signaling molecule
(b) Deamination of histidine results into NO production
(c) Stimuilates guanylyl cyclase to produce *c*GMP
(d) Can be activated neutrophils

37. Which of the following passes through the cell membrane, binds to its intracellular receptors and activates it?
(a) Estrogens (b) Non-epinephrine
(c) Aceylcholine (d) Glucagons

38. Hormones are relatively long lived signals that travel throughout the body. This type of signaling is called
(a) paracrine signaling (b) synaptic signaling
(c) autocrine signaling (d) endocrine signaling

39. All of the following statements apply to G-proteins except
(a) G-proteins transmit a signal from the cell surface to the interior of the cell
(b) all G-proteins have a similar structure
(c) G-proteins do not use second messengers but transmit the signal directly into the nucleus
(d) G-proteins act to amplify the signal creating a cascade response in the cell

40. The receptors for which of the following hormone is a transcription factor?
(a) Insulin (b) Glucagon
(c) Estradiol (d) Adrenaline

41. Receptors that are recognized by the immune system are
(a) immunoglobulins (b) MHC proteins
(c) T-receptor (d) All of these

42. Hormones
(a) are secreted by exocrine glands
(b) act only on neighbouring cells
(c) are always peptides
(d) are secreted into the blood

43. G-protein activation
(a) leads to changes in gene expression
(b) always causes an increase in cyclic AMP
(c) leads to the generation of second messengers
(d) always results in a decrease in cyclic AMP

44. Steroid hormones such as aldosterone
(a) bind to nuclear receptors to regulate gene expression
(b) activate G-protein cascades
(c) activate receptors on the cell membrane
(d) directly regulate protein synthesis

45. Which of the following signal molecules binds to a receptor situated in the cytoplasm, not the outer membrane of the cell?
(a) Progesterone
(b) Adrenaline (Epinephrine)
(c) Epidermal growth factor
(d) Interferon

46. Which of the following signals does not activate a serpentine receptor which in turn activates a heterotrimeric G-protein?
(a) Glucagon
(b) Insulin
(c) Light in retinal rod and cones cells
(d) Vasopressin

47. Which of the following molecule is water soluble?
(a) Adrenaline
(b) Epidermal growth factor
(c) Interferon
(d) All of the above

48. Protein kinase G
(a) AKA *c*AMP-dependent kinase that is active in the presence of *c*AMP
(b) Concentration of ligand at which half the receptors are bound
(c) Bind to four *c*AMP and release the catalytic subunits which are activated
(d) AKA *c*GMP dependent kinase is active in the presence of *c*GMP

49. Ras protein
(a) breaks down phosphatidyl inositol phosphate (PIP2) into inositol triphosphate (IP_3) and diacylglycerol
(b) receptors for growth factors and usually associated with transmembrane tyrosine specific protein kinases
(c) serve as high affinity binding sites for intracellular signaling proteins in the target cell
(d) monomeric GTPase that functions as a switch, cycling between GTP active and inactive state

50. Which of the following cell junction link cell together (intercellular junctions)?
(a) Focal contacts (b) Adhesion plaques
(c) Hemidesmosomes (d) Adherens

51. Which of the following cell junction can be seen through light microscope?
(a) Tight junction (b) Hemidesmosomes
(c) Desmosomal junctions (d) Adhesion plaques

52. Which of the following cell junction is also known as zonula occludens?
(a) Tight junctions
(b) Adherens junctions
(c) Desmosomes
(d) Hemidesmosomes

53. Which of the following statement is incorrect regarding tight junction?
(a) It is a site where the membranes of two cells come very close together, in fact, the outer leaflets of the membranes of the contacting cells appear to be fused
(b) They does not act as a barrier so, that materials can pass between two interacting cells
(c) The protein components of the tight junction are arranged like beads on a string that span the adjacent membranes of each tight junction
(d) Tight junctions often occur in a belt completely encircling the cell

54. Which of the following feature specifically distinguish desmosomes from hemidesmosomes?
(a) Association with the keratin based cytoskeleton
(b) Adhesion properties
(c) Type of adhesion molecules
(d) Both (a) and (c)

55. .... are specialized protein complexes that create an aqueous pore between the cytoplasms of two adjacent cells.
(a) Hormones (b) Receptors
(c) Gap junctions (d) Ion channels

56. How do most hydrophobic chemical messengers get transported to a target cell?
(a) They dissolve easily in the circulatory fluids
(b) They bind to hormones in the blood
(c) They move from cell to cell through gap junctions
(d) They bind to carrier proteins in the blood

57. When a chemical messenger (or ligand) reaches a target cell, it binds to a receptor. A hydrophobic ligand binds to a(n)...................., whereas a hydrophilic ligand binds to a(n) ....
(a) intracellular receptor; transmembrane receptor
(b) transmembrane receptor; intracellular receptor
(c) aganist receptor; antagonist receptor
(d) autocrine receptor; paracrine receptor

58. The strength of binding between a ligand and a receptor is usually expressed as the
(a) K_m
(b) endocrine constant
(c) affinity constant (*Ka*)
(d) paracrine constant

59. Which of the following statements about receptor enzymes is false?
(a) A receptor-enzyme has an extracellular ligand-binding domain, a transmembrane domain, and an intracellular catalytic (enzyme) domain.
(b) Three types of receptor–enzymes found in animals are 1) receptor guanylate cyclases 2) receptor tyrosine kinases and 3) receptor serine/threonine kinases.
(c) The signal transduction pathways of receptor-enzymes involve phosphorylation cascades.
(d) Receptor-enzymes interact with an intracellular protein called a 'G-protein'.

60. Which of the following is not a chemical class of hormones?
(a) Amines (b) Peptides
(c) MAP kinases (d) Steroids

61. Norepinephrine, acetylcholine and serotonin are what kind of hormones?
(a) Peptide hormones (b) Steroids
(c) Prohormones (d) Amines

62. What is ecdysone?
(a) A G-protein coupled receptor found only in invertebrates
(b) A neurotransmitter found only in invertebrates
(c) A steroid hormone found only in vertebrates
(d) A steroid hormone found only in invertebrates

63. Which of the following is a property of peptide hormones?
(a) They bind to intracellular receptors
(b) They alter transcription rates of target cells
(c) They are shuttled around the plasma by binding to carrier proteins
(d) They are often synthesized as large inactive polypeptides and stored before their release

64. Which of the following statements related to the evolution of cell signaling is false?
(a) All vertebrates use a series of related steroid hormones as chemical messengers, including estrogens, androgens and glucocorticoids.
(b) The endocrine and nervous systems evolved at about the same time.
(c) Invertebrates have very few endocrine glands and most of their endocrine signaling utilizes neurohormones.
(d) The similarities of endocrine systems likely stem from the evolution of endocrine systems from a shared set of basic signal transduction mechanisms involved in paracrine communication.

65. Paracrine are
(a) growth factors (b) G-protein pathways
(c) epinephrine (d) detects target cell

66. Protein activity regulation adds phosphate from ATP to
(a) interfere with G-protein function
(b) in tissues with high mechanical stress
(c) local signaling (short distance signaling)
(d) a protein which activates more proteins

67. Carrier mediated transport may be divided into .... diffusion and active transport.
(a) active (b) passive
(c) facilitated (d) None of these

68. Simple diffusion, osmosis, and facilitated diffusion are all considered .... transport.
(a) active (b) passive
(c) facilitated (d) None of these

69. Metastasis of some cancer cells results when the cancer cells produce active forms of .... (two words), the enzymes that are normally inactive and act to breakdown the collagen of the basal lamina.
(a) DNAase (b) matrix metalloproteinase
(c) simple proteinase (d) urease

70. When describing body fluids such as plasma, the total molality of that fluid is usually expressed as its
(a) molarity (b) formality
(c) normality (d) osmolarity

71. Neurons located in the hypothalamus that are responsible for sensing blood plasma osmolality and osmotic pressure are called
(a) thermoreceptors (b) osmoreceptors
(c) chemoreceptors (d) baroreceptors

72. .... hormone is released from the posterior pituitary whenever plasma osmolality increases.
(a) LH (b) FSH
(c) ADH (d) TSH

73. Primary active transport pumps require recognition of a carrier protein and the hydrolysis of cellular energy in the form of
(a) GTP (b) ATP
(c) CTP (d) TTP

74. The equilibrium potential for potassium is measured at .... mV.
(a) –10 (b) +10
(c) –90 (d) +90

75. The concentration of sodium ion is .... outside the cell.
(a) lower (b) similar
(c) higher (d) static

76. The plasma ion that must be monitored carefully to prevent alterations in the resting membrane potential and the generation of aberrant electrical activity in the heart is
(a) K^+ (b) Ca^{2+}
(c) Na^+ (d) PO^{4-}

77. The Na^+/K^+ pump transports (spell out number) Na^+ ions out of the cell for every two K^+ ions that it moves into the cell, helping to generate a potential difference across the membrane.
(a) 1 (b) 2
(c) 3 (d) 4

78. The interstitial fluid comprises of the extracellular fluid.
(a) 80% (b) 67%
(c) 33% (d) 20%

79. Urea will move freely through a non-living dialysis membrane by
(a) simple diffusion (b) facilitated diffusion
(c) active transport (d) osmosis

80. Which of the following substances is least able to diffuse through a living cellular membrane?
(a) Glucose (b) Carbon dioxide
(c) Cholesterol (d) Water

81. The sodium equilibrium potential, E_{Na}, is about .... mV.
(a) +60 (b) 0
(c) –65 (d) –90

82. The E_K of a cell is about –90 mV and the E_{Na} is +60 mV. Both potassium and sodium ions contribute to actual resting membrane potential of a cell that is typically about .... mV.
(a) +60 (b) +75
(c) –15 (d) –65

83. Which of the following is statement not correct?
(a) Sodium and potassium ions, being very small, can easily pass through the phospholipid layer of a cell membrane.
(b) A living cell normally has a relatively high concentration of K^+ inside the cell and a low concentration of K^+ in the extracelluar fluid.
(c) The living cell membrane is much more permeable to sodium than any other cation.
(d) The term, potential difference, means the amount of electrical charge (voltage) that exists across a cell membrane at any moment.
(e) The potassium equilibrium potential (E_K) is also the normal resting potential of a cell.

84. Which of the following statement is incorrect?
(a) Osmosis is the net diffusion of water through a semipermeable membrane, so, pure water has a lower osmotic pressure than any solution
(b) Osmosis is the movement of water through a semipermeable membrane from the side with a more concentrated solution to the side with a more dilute solution
(c) A given osmolality will lower the freezing point of a solution the same amount no matter what solutes are in the solution
(d) Oxygen and carbon dioxide gas molecules can move in and out of cells by simple diffusion

85. Calmodulin activates protein kinases in response to a transient increase in
(a) *t*AMP (b) calcium ions
(c) DAG (d) NO

86. The signaling system that operates over the shortest range is
(a) contact-dependent cell signaling, as in the inhibition of neighbours by differentiating nerve cells
(b) paracrine secretion, as in the secretion of histamines by mast cells
(c) neural signaling, as in the transmission of a nerve impulse
(d) None of the above

87. Cyclin-dependent kinase (Cdk) activity increases steadily during G_2 as a result of
(a) phosphorylation of mitotic cyclins by Cdks
(b) activation of mitotic Cdk-cyclins through the activity of a phosphatase
(c) phosphorylation of Cdks at a point not located inside the catalytic site of the cdk-cyclin complex
(d) transient increase in the cytosolic GTP concentration

88. Which one of the following is involved in cell?
(a) Cytochrome-P_{450} (b) Protein kinase C
(c) Zinc fingers (d) All of these

89. In the *c*AMP pathway, the G-protein stimulates
(a) phospholipase C
(b) adenylyl cyclase
(c) the endoplasmic reticulum
(d) calmodulin

90. Identify the correct order in which the extracellular signals are transmitted
(a) adenylate cyclase-*c*AMP protein kinase A
(b) protein kinase A-adenylate cyclase-*c*AMP
(c) protein kinase A-*c*AMP-adenylate cyclase
(d) *c*AMP-adenylate cyclase-protein kinase A

91. Which of the following hormone passes through the cell membrane, binds to its intracellular receptors and activates it?
(a) Estrogen (b) Non-epinephrine
(c) Acetylcholine (d) Glucagons

92. The mechanism of signal transduction by steroid hormones differs from amine and peptide hormones because
(a) steroids use small, water soluble second messengers
(b) they bind with specific receptor proteins on target-cell plasma membranes
(c) they bind to cytoplasmic or nuclear receptors and affect gene expression
(d) they are secreted from exocrine glands

93. Synaptic signaling involves
(a) endocrine signals (b) paracrine signals
(c) autocrine signals (d) neurotransmitters

94. Characteristics of intracellular receptors that regulate gene transcription include all of the following except
(a) a DNA binding site
(b) an extracellular binding site
(c) a transcription activating domain
(d) may be signaled by lipid soluble molecules

95. Cell surface receptors may be any of the following except
(a) G-protein linked
(b) enzymatic receptors
(c) signal-pass transmembrane proteins for neurotransmitters
(d) ligand-gated ion channels

96. Which of the following is incorrect?
(a) Endocrine signaling molecules acts on target cell distant from site of synthesis
(b) Paracrine signaling molecules affect target cells only in close proximity
(c) Autocrine signaling molecules affect the same cells that release
(d) None of the abvoe

97. Which one of the following compounds does not acts second messenger during signaling process?
(a) cAMP
(b) Calcium ions
(c) Inositol 3, 4, 5-triphosphate
(d) Triacylglycerol

98. MAP kinases
I. Are activated by the Ras pathway.
II. Phosphorylate their targets on tyrosine residues.
III. Act to stimulate or repress the transcription of target genes through the phosphorylation of transcription factors.
IV. Become active when phosphorylated by MEK kinases.
(a) I and II (b) I and III
(c) I, II and III (d) I, II, III and IV

99. Match list I (Enzyme) with list II (Product) that it produces.

List I	List II
A. Guanylcyclase	1. cAMP
B. Adenylcyclase	2. DAG and IP_3
C. Phospholipase-C	3. cGMP
D. Phosphatidylinositol	4. Phosphatidylinositol 4-phosphate 4, 5-bisphosphate (PIP) kinase (PIP2)

Codes

	A	B	C	D
(a)	3	1	2	4
(b)	2	3	1	4
(c)	4	3	2	1
(d)	4	1	4	3

100. Signal transduction describes the ways in which external molecules cause internal changes in cells. These processes

I. Always involve the movement of ligands across the membrane.

II. Amplify the strenght of the external stimulus.

III. Rely on cell surface receptors that can interact with intracellular proteins.

IV. Can trigger the production of a second messenger inside the cell.

(a) I and II

(b) I and III

(c) II, III and IV

(d) I, II, III and IV

Answers

1. (c)	**2.** (b)	**3.** (d)	**4.** (d)	**5.** (b)	**6.** (d)	**7.** (d)	**8.** (c)	**9.** (d)	**10.** (b)
11. (a)	**12.** (d)	**13.** (d)	**14.** (b)	**15.** (c)	**16.** (a)	**17.** (d)	**18.** (d)	**19.** (a)	**20.** (b)
21. (d)	**22.** (b)	**23.** (b)	**24.** (b)	**25.** (b)	**26.** (b)	**27.** (a)	**28.** (c)	**29.** (a)	**30.** (c)
31. (d)	**32.** (d)	**33.** (d)	**34.** (b)	**35.** (b)	**36.** (b)	**37.** (a)	**38.** (d)	**39.** (c)	**40.** (c)
41. (d)	**42.** (d)	**43.** (c)	**44.** (a)	**45.** (a)	**46.** (b)	**47.** (d)	**48.** (d)	**49.** (d)	**50.** (d)
51. (d)	**52.** (a)	**53.** (b)	**54.** (d)	**55.** (c)	**56.** (d)	**57.** (a)	**58.** (c)	**59.** (d)	**60.** (c)
61. (d)	**62.** (d)	**63.** (d)	**64.** (b)	**65.** (a)	**66.** (a)	**67.** (c)	**68.** (d)	**69.** (b)	**70.** (d)
71. (b)	**72.** (c)	**73.** (b)	**74.** (c)	**75.** (c)	**76.** (a)	**77.** (c)	**78.** (a)	**79.** (a)	**80.** (a)
81. (a)	**82.** (d)	**83.** (d)	**84.** (b)	**85.** (b)	**86.** (a)	**87.** (a)	**88.** (b)	**89.** (b)	**90.** (a)
91. (a)	**92.** (c)	**93.** (d)	**94.** (b)	**95.** (c)	**96.** (d)	**97.** (d)	**98.** (c)	**99.** (a)	**100.** (c)

12 Cancer

Introduction

Cancer is one of the most common diseases in the developed world and 1 in 4 deaths are due to cancer in which 1 in 17 deaths are due to lung cancer, lung cancer is the most common cancer in men while breast cancer is the most common cancer in women. There are over 100 different forms of cancer. Normal body cells grow, divide and die in an orderly fashion. The division of normal cells is normally precisely controlled. During the early years of a person's life, normal cells divide more rapidly until the person becomes an adult. After that, cells in most parts of the body divide only to replace worn out or dying cells and to repair injuries. Cancerous cells divide repeatedly out of control even though they are not needed, they crowd out other normal cells and function abnormally. They can also destroy the correct functioning of major organs. Although there are many kinds of cancer, they all start because of out of control growth of abnormal cells.

Cancer cells develop because of damage to DNA. This substance is in every cell and directs all its activities. Most of the time when DNA becomes damaged the body is able to repair it. In cancer cells, the damaged DNA is not repaired. People can inherit damaged DNA, which accounts for inherited cancers. Many times though, a person's DNA becomes damaged by exposure to something in the environment, like smoking. Cancer arises from the mutation of a normal gene. Mutated genes that cause cancer are called **oncogenes.** Any agent that causes cancer is called a carcinogen and is described as carcinogenic. Carcinogens include ionizing radiation like X-rays, UV light, chemicals like tar from cigarettes and virus infection like papilloma virus can be responsible for cancer. Some families are **more susceptible** to getting certain cancers. There are two types of tumours benign and malignant. Benign tumours do not spread from their site of origin, but can crowd out (squash) surrounding cells, *e.g.,* brain tumour, warts. Malignant tumours can spread from the original site and cause **secondary tumours.** This is called **metastasis.** They interfere with neighbouring cells and can block blood

Syllabus

- Genetic Rearrangements in Progenitor Cells
- Cancer Genes (Oncogenes)
- Tumour Suppressor Genes
- Apoptosis
- Virus Induced Cancer
- Cancer and the Cell Cycle
- Therapeutic Interventions of Uncontrolled Cell Growth (Cancer Treatment)

vessels, the gut, glands, lungs, etc. Both types of tumour can tire the body out as they both need a huge amount of nutrients to sustain the rapid growth and division of the cells. Most tumours induce the formation of new blood vessels for nourishment which is known as angiogenesis. Many tumours produce growth factor that stimulate angiogenesis like Basic Fibroblast Growth Factor (bFGF), transforming growth factors.

Table 12.1 **Comparison of Benign and Malignant Tumour**

Characteristic	Benign	Malignant
Growth pattern	Expansive	Infiltrative
Rate of growth	Slow	Fast
Differentiation	Good	Atypical and poor
Metastasis	Absent	Typical

Types of Cancers

(i) **Adenoma** A cancer of hormone secreting cells. Many cancers of reproductive tracts.
(ii) **Carcinoma** Cancer of epithelioid tissue.
(iii) **Fibroblast** Tissue derived from connective tissue.
(iv) **Fibropapilloma** Solid tumour of cells derived from connective tissue.
(v) **Hepatocellular carcinoma** A cancer of liver epithelial cells.
(vi) **Endothelioma** Overproduction of erythrocytes.
(vii) **Leukaemia** A cancer of white blood cells.
(viii) **Lymphoma** A cancer of lymphoid tissue.
(ix) **Retinoblastoma** Cancer of retinal cells.
(x) **Sarcoma** A cancer of fibroblasts.

Hallmarks of Cancer

They reflect six changes for cancer found in most, if not all, cancers:

(i) Self-sufficiency in growth signals.
(ii) Insensitivity to growth-inhibitory signals.
(iii) Evasion of apoptosis.
(iv) Limitless replicative capacity.
(v) Sustained angiogenesis.
(vi) Tissue invasion and metastasis.

Prognosis or Prediction of Outcome

(i) Criteria are different for each cancer type.
(ii) Grade, stage, histology routine criteria.
(iii) Patient characteristics are important.
(iv) Treatment considerations critical.

Prognostic factors include grade, stage, tumour type and biomarkers (slide based and molecular techniques).

Transformed Cells

Much of what we know about cancer is derived from studies of transformed cells. These cells have abnormal growth parameters and behaviours like:

(i) Immortality can grow indefinitely.
(ii) Reduced requirement for serum growth factors.
(iii) Loss of capacity for growth arrest upon nutrient deprivation.
(iv) High saturation densities.
(v) Loss of contact inhibition.
(vi) Anchorage independent (can grown in soft agar).
(vii) Altered morphology (rounded and refractile).
(viii) Tumorogenic can cause tumours when transplanted into animals.

Causes of Cancer

(i) Mutations are

(a) DNA mutations due to

- Radiation and other environmental factors (tobacco, alcohol, radon, asbestos, etc).
- Random somatic mutations.
- Inherited germ-line mutations.

(b) Genetic predisposition

- Rb, p53, APC, CDKN2A, BRCA1, BRCA2.

(ii) Infectious agents are

(a) Viral

- HPV – Cervical cancer
- Hepatitis – Liver cancer

(b) Bacterial like *H. pylori* – Stomach cancer.

Genetic Rearrangements in Progenitor Cells

Within every nucleus of every one of the human body's 30 trillion cells exists DNA, the substance that contains the information needed to make and control every cell within the body. Usually DNA is an exact copy of the DNA from which it came. When the parent cell divided to create two cells, the cell's DNA is also divided, creating two identical copies of the original DNA.

Mutation of DNA

However sometimes the DNA suffers a mutation, either through mis-copying (when its parent cell divided) or through the damaging effects of exposure to radiation or a chemical carcinogen.

Genetically Altered Cell

Body cells replicate through mitosis, they respond to their surrounding cells and replicate only to replace other cells. Sometimes a genetic mutation causes a cell and its descendants to reproduce even though replacement cells are not needed. The DNA of such cells has a mutation that causes the cell to replicate even though this tissue doesn't need replacement cells at this time or at this place.

Spread and Second Mutation

The genetically altered cells, over time, reproduce unchecked, crowding out the surrounding normal cells. The growth may contain one million cells and be the size of a pinhead. At this point the cells continue to look the same as the surrounding healthy cells. After about a million divisions, there's a good chance that one of the new cells have mutated further. This cell, now carrying two mutant genes, would have an altered appearance and be even more prone to reproduce unchecked.

Third Mutation

Not all mutations that lead to cancerous cells result in the cells reproducing at a faster, more uncontrolled rate. For example, a mutation may simply cause a cell to keep from self destructing. All normal cells have surveillance mechanisms that look for damage or for problems with their own control systems. If such problems are found, the cell destroys itself.

Over time and after many cell divisions, a third mutation may arise. If the mutation gives the cell some further advantage, that cell will grow more vigorously than its predecessors and thus, speed up the growth of the tumour.

Fourth Mutation

The new type of cells grows rapidly, allowing for more opportunities for mutations. The next mutation paves the way for the development of an even more aggressive cancer. At this point the tumour is still contained. Cells have a finite life and ability to replicate due to chromosome shortening. The ends of chromosome are called telomeres (hexamer repeats - TTAGGG). There is a Hay flick limit ~ 50-80 doublings and they reach replicative senescence by inactivating pRb/p53 which extends lifespan by 30 doublings. Subsequently cells reach crisis due to continued chromosome shortening, Chromosomal fusions, genetic loss and cell death. Rare mutations usually lead to immortalization thereby activation of telomerase occurs.

Breaking through the Membrane

The newer, wilder cells created by another mutation push their way through the epithelial tissue's basement membrane, which is a meshwork of protein that normally creates a barrier. The invasive cells in this tumour are no longer contained. At this point the cancer is still too small to be detected.

Angiogenesis

Often during the development of earlier stages of the tumour, or perhaps by the time the tumour has broken through the basement membrane, angiogenesis takes place. Angiogenesis is the recruitment of blood vessels from the network of neighbouring vessels. Without blood and the nutrients it carries, a tumour would be unable to continue growing. With the new blood supply, however, the growth of the tumour accelerates, it soon contains **thousand million cells** and now the size of a small grape, is large enough to be detected as a lump. VEGF and FGF1 and FGF2 are activated in tumours and signal endothelial cell proliferation and growth of blood vessels occurs.

Invasion and Dispersal

The tumour now invades the tissue beyond the basement membrane. Individual cells from the tumour enter into the network of newly formed blood vessels, using these vessels as highways by which they can move to other parts of the body. A tumour as small as a gram can send out a million tumour cells into blood vessels a day. It is usually associated with activated motility and local tissue independence *in vitro* and is a balance between tissue destruction and synthesis. Cell surface and extracellular matrix play important roles.

Tumour Cells Travel–Metastasis

What makes most tumours so, lethal is their ability to metastasis that is, establish new tumour sites at other locations throughout the body. Metastasis is then underway, as tumour cells from the original cancer growth travel throughout the body. Most of these cells die soon after entering the blood or lymph circulation. It basically requires acquisition of additional tumour characteristics beyond those necessary for invasion, *i.e.,* multiple lesions and organ specificity. To form a secondary tumour, a tumour cell needs to leave the vessel system and invade tissue. The cell must attach itself to a vessel's wall. Once this is done, it can work its way through the vessel and enter the tissue. Although perhaps less than one in 10000 tumour cells will survive long enough to establish a new tumour site, a few survivors can escape and initiate new colonies of the cancer. The mechanisms of spread is mainly haematogenous or through lymphatics. Other mechanisms of spread include direct extension, seeding and surgical or procedural transplantation (iatrogenic).

Pathogenesis of Cancer

(i) **Initiators** carcinogens **attack** the genetic material of the cells and **alter** their constituents.

(ii) **Promoters** carcinogens **stimulate** the growth of abnormal (altered) cells.

(iii) Initiators have **long** latent period while promoters have **short** latent period.

Theories of Cancer Genesis

(i) Standard dogma
  (a) Proto-oncogenes (Ras-melanoma).
  (b) Tumour suppressor genes (p53-various cancers).

(ii) Modified dogma
  (a) Mutation in a DNA repair gene leads to the accumulation of unrepaired mutations (xeroderma pigmentosum).

(iii) Early instability theory.

Cancer Genes

Proliferation and growth are two different things and both of them are required for the spread of cancer. As 80-90% of the dry mass of a cell is protein hence the rate of protein accumulation dictates the growth rate of cancer. In most cell types the number of *m*RNA molecules is greater than the number of ribosomes therefore, growth rates and increase in cancer cells is observed if they produce more ribosomes. Further master genes required for adequate cell reproduction are disabled, resulting in aneuploidy (*Philadelphia* chromosome). The below described factors play a crucial role in the growth of cancer.

1. **Proliferation** Oncogenes and tumour suppressor genes.
2. **Cell survival** Apoptosis *vs* DNA repair.
3. **Epithelial-stromal interactions** Angiogenesis, invasion and metastasis.
4. **Cell surface markers** Immune evasion.
5. **Membrane pumps** Drug resistance and response to therapy.
6. **Metabolism** Allow more rapid growth (*e.g.*, ribogenesis).

Virtually any gene product may be a target for therapy as long as :

1. It's expression level/structure/activity is sufficiently different between normal and tumour cells.
2. It is required for continued growth/survival of the tumour cells.
3. Many are involved in cellular signaling pathways.

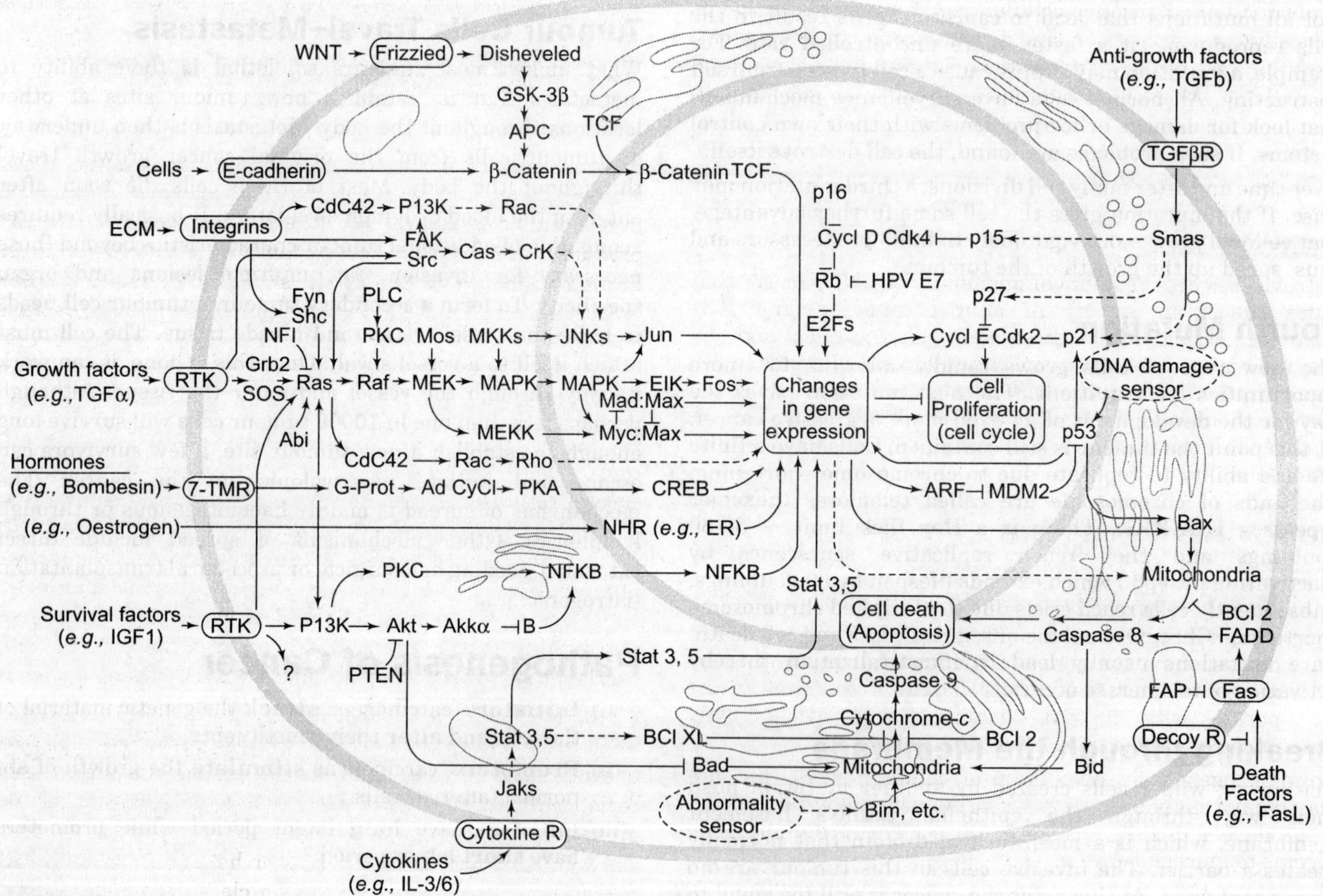

Fig. 12.1 A systematic representation of the various follows responsible for alteration/regulation of gene expression at different check points in cell growth

Oncogenes

Originally coined as a genetic term to describe any gene capable of causing cancer. But, later found to be tumour suppressor in nature and it is the loss of these function genes which leads to cancer. Oncogenes refers to genes that contribute to cancer in a gain of function manner and are dominate at the cellular level. Proto-oncogenes are the normal genes. Over 100 oncogenes have been identified. These genes code for proteins that are capable of stimulating cell growth and division. In normal tissues and organisms, such growth stimulating proteins are regulated, so, that growth is appropriately limited. However, mutations in these genes may result in loss of growth regulation, leading to uncontrolled cell proliferation and tumour development.

These mutant genes are known as oncogenes, because they induce the oncogenic state cancer. The normal precursors of these genes are termed proto-oncogenes and are essential for normal cell growth and differentiation. Oncogenes are dominant, because a mutation of only one of the cell's two copies of that gene can lead to tumour formation. Oncogene causes cancer by affecting:

(i) Cell proliferation examples are, Ras, Raf, EGF.

(ii) Cell differentiation example, PML/RAR that inhibits the differentiation of promyelocyte to granulocyte which will maintain the cell in its active proliferate state.

(iii) Cell survival (example, Pl-3/AKT which will activate BCL-2 inhibit apoptosis and maintain cell survival.

Retroviral Transduction

Transduction of normal cellular genes by transduction is basically over expression and formation of mutant genes. Mutations are usually Ras activating mutations in codons 12, 13 and 61. Over-expression usually involves gene amplification. In the case of tyrosine kinase receptors and translocations and re-arrangements in the case of autocrine signaling, transcription factors.

Retroviruses

Retroviruses are members of one family of RNA viruses that cause cancer in variety of animals and humans. The retrovirus is made up of three main genes gag, pol and env that are required for virus replication but not play role in cell transformation. A retrovirus can transform cells from normal to cancer, if they include a specific gene that is capable of inducing cell transformation this gene is known as 'Oncogene'.

Retrovirus Oncogene

There are two main types of oncogenes:

(a) **Viral Oncogene** Gene from the retrovirus itself.

(b) **Non–viral Oncogene** (Cellular oncogene) Genes derived from the genes of the host cell that are in an inactive form usually. Occasionally if the gene incorporates with the viral genome it will form a highly oncogenic virus.

Proto-oncogenes, are the form of cellular genes that are inactive normally but can incorporate with the viral genome to produce a highly oncogenic virus. The proto-oncogene become an oncogene by:

Mutation

Example Mutation in Ras gene → Continuous activation of Ras by (constitutively in the GTP-bound conformation) → Unregulated cell proliferation → Cell transformation.

Abnormal Activity

Removal of the regulatory domain in the Raf gene and replaced by gag gene → Raf kinase domain consciously active → Cell transformation.

Gene Translocation

c-myc gene is translocated from chromosome 8 to the IgH on the chromosome 14 resulting in abnormal *c-myc* expression → Cell transformation.

Amplification

Amplification of N-myc → neuroblastoma. Amplification of erbB-2 → breast and ovarian carcinomas.

Functions of Oncogene

(i) Growth factor example, Epithelium growth factor EGF, and platelet derived growth factor PDGF.

(ii) Growth factor receptor example, PDGFR.

(iii) Signal translation example, Ras, Raf and MEK.

(iv) Transcription factor example, *Jun*, *Fos*, *Elk*–1 and *myc*.

Tumour Suppressor Genes (TSG)

Tumour suppressor genes: These genes code for proteins whose normal function is to turn off cell growth. A mutation in one of these growth limiting genes may result in a protein product that has lost its growth limiting ability. The normal forms of such genes have been shown to suppress tumour growth and are known as tumour suppressor genes. Because both cellular copies of a tumour suppressor gene must be mutated to foil its growth limiting action, these genes are recessive in nature.

Careful molecular analysis of cancerous tissue has shown that tumour development may result from mutations in several proto–oncogenes or tumour suppressor genes. The implication is that there is redundancy in cellular growth regulation. Many (if not all) tumours are either the result of interactions of two or more oncogene products or arise from simultaneous mutations in a proto-oncogene and both copies of a tumour suppressor gene. Cells have thus evolved with overlapping growth-control mechanisms. When one is compromised by mutation, others take over.

TSGs are altered by inactivating mutations and this can lead to cancer. The mutations invoved are point mutations, delete regions of chromosomes, LOH, altered methylation of the promotor, epigenetics or Knudson's 'two hit' model, *i.e.*, dominant negative as in p53 or haploinsufficiency. The two major TSG are RB and p53. In classic RB gene usually germline mutations in RB and one acquired somatic mutation is observed. It leads to retinoblastoma wherein the development of retinoblastoma can be either hereditary, *i.e.*, a defective copy of Rb gene is inherited from the affected parents or non-hereditary in which two normal Rb genes are inherited and develop mutation during life. Retinoblastoma is developed if two somatic mutations inactivate both copies of Rb in the same cell. 80% of small cell lung cancers have an RB mutation.

In p^{53}, 50-75% of all cancers have a p53 mutation and usually there is a loss of both or dominant negative gene.

Tumour suppressor genes, are genes that act to inhibit cell proliferation and tumour development and if TSG was mutated or inactivated, it will lead to cell transformation. **Example**, deletion of Rb gene will cause retinoblastoma.

Function of TSG

(i) Antagonize the action of oncogene (Example, PTEN which converts PIPIII to PIPII because PIPIII will activate Pl-3/AKT which will activate BCL-2 that will inhibit apoptosis and induce cell transformation.)

(ii) Transcription factors

(a) **Repressor transcription factors, example,** WT1 is a repressor that appears to suppress transcription factor (insulin like growth factor) which will contribute in the development of tumour.

(b) **Activator transcription factors, example,** SMAD family that are activated by TGF-β, leading to inhibition of cell proliferation.

(iii) Regulate cell cycle

(a) **Rb gene** that inhibits the cell cycle in the G_1-phase decrease cell proliferation.

(b) **INK-4** gene that produces P^{16} that inhibits Cdk4/cyclin D action (to phosphorylate Rb gene to inactivate it's action).

(c) $\mathbf{P^{53}}$, that produces P^{21} that has the same action of P^{16} in inhibiting the action of Cdk4/cyclin D.

(iv) Induce apoptosis.

$\mathbf{P^{53}}$, release will $\longrightarrow$ increase Bax $\longrightarrow$ form holes in the mitochondria $\longrightarrow$ release cytochrome-*c* $\longrightarrow$ activate apoptosis.

Apoptosis

According to a Japanese saying, 'Once we are in the land of the living, we will eventually die.' True as this may be for human beings, it is also true of the cells of our bodies. In the ongoing cycle of cell division and differentiation, many surplus and/or harmful cells are produced. These cells must be removed or killed to maintain the integrity and homeostasis of the organism. The magnitude of such cell death is often surprising, more than 95% of thymocytes die during maturation of the thymus. The cell death that occurs during embryogenesis, metamorphosis, and normal cell turnover is termed 'programmed cell death' or apoptosis (where the second 'p' is silent).

Apoptosis can be initiated in a variety of ways. One of these involves 'death factors', proteins such as Fas ligand and tumour necrosis factor, or TNF, that are members of the cytokine family of proteins. These factors bind to specific plasma membrane receptors Fas and TNF-receptor, respectively, prompting trimeric associations of the receptor proteins in the membrane. These receptor proteins possess intracellular death domains, polypeptide motifs that adopt an unusual structure consisting of six antiparallel, amphipathic α-helices. These receptor death domains form oligomeric associations with other, similar death domains on adaptor proteins (known as FADD or MORT1). This prompts special death effector domains on FADD/MORT1 to bind to cysteine proteases known as caspases (so, named with a 'c' for cysteine and 'asp' indicating that these proteases cleave after an Asp residue in their protein substrates). Sequential activation in a cascade of caspases, together with other events, triggers apoptosis (cell death).

In appropriate apoptosis underlies the cause of certain human diseases, including neuro degenerative disorders and cancer. An unusual caspase cleavage appears to play a role in Huntington's Disease (HD), the cause of the death of folk singer Woody Guthrie. The mutation responsible for HD is an expansion of a CAG trinucleotide repeat at the 59th end of the gene Hdh, which encodes an essential protein (huntingtin) of unknown function. The CAG extension results in an extended polyglutamine domain on the N-terminus of the protein. Huntington's disease is manifested if this Gln repeat region exceeds 35 residues. Downstream of the poly-Gln region is a cluster of five DXXD motifs that are cleaved specifically by caspase 3. The longer the poly-Gln region, the greater is the activity of caspase 3 in cleaving the DXXD motifs. The released poly-Gln domains are cytotoxic, provoking death of affected neurons, progressive loss of control of voluntary movements, general loss of neural function and eventual death.

Apoptosis is a critical defense against cancer. Evasion of apoptosis is done when receptors transmit death signals either through FAS and FAS receptor, TNF α and TNF αR1 or decoy receptor that don't signal can promote survival. Alternatively evasion is done through intracellular proteins that monitor DNA damage like p53. Biochemical events lead to characteristic cell changes (morphology) and death. These changes include blebbing, cell shrinkage, nuclear fragmentation, chromatin condensation and chromosomal DNA fragmentation. Unlike necrosis, apoptosis produces cell fragments called apoptotic bodies that phagocytic cells are able to engulf and quickly remove before the contents of the cell can spill out onto surrounding cells and cause damage. In contrast to necrosis, which is a form of traumatic cell death that results from acute cellular injury, apoptosis, in general, confers advantages during an organism's life cycle. For example, the differentiation of fingers and toes in a developing human embryo occurs because cells between the fingers apoptose. Between 50 and 70 billion cells die each day due to apoptosis in the average human adult. In addition to its importance as a biological phenomenon, defective apoptotic processes have been implicated in an extensive variety of diseases. Excessive apoptosis causes atrophy, whereas an insufficient amount results in uncontrolled cell proliferation, such as cancer.

Apoptosis is evolutionarily conserved and occurs in all multicellular animals studies (plants too). The stages and genes are conserved from nematodes (worms) and flies to mice and humans.

Table 12.2 **Forms of Cell Death**

Necrosis	Apoptosis	Mitotic Catastrophe
Passive	Active	Passive
Pathological	Physiological or pathological	Pathological
Swelling and lysis	Condensation and crosslinking	Swelling and lysis
Dissipates	Phagocytosed	Dissipates
Inflammation	No inflammation	Inflammation
Externally induced	Internally or externally induced	Internally

General Feature of Apoptosis

(i) A number of activities take place, *i.e.*,

(a) Occupation of death receptors.

(b) Dimerization of Bcl-2 family members.

(c) Release of cytochrome-*c*.

(d) Activation of caspases.

(e) Activation of DNAase.

(ii) Translocation of phosphatidylserine.

(iii) ATP-dependency.

(iv) Internucleosomal DNA fragmentation (ladder pattern).

(v) No apoptosis at +4°C.

(vi) No inflammation.

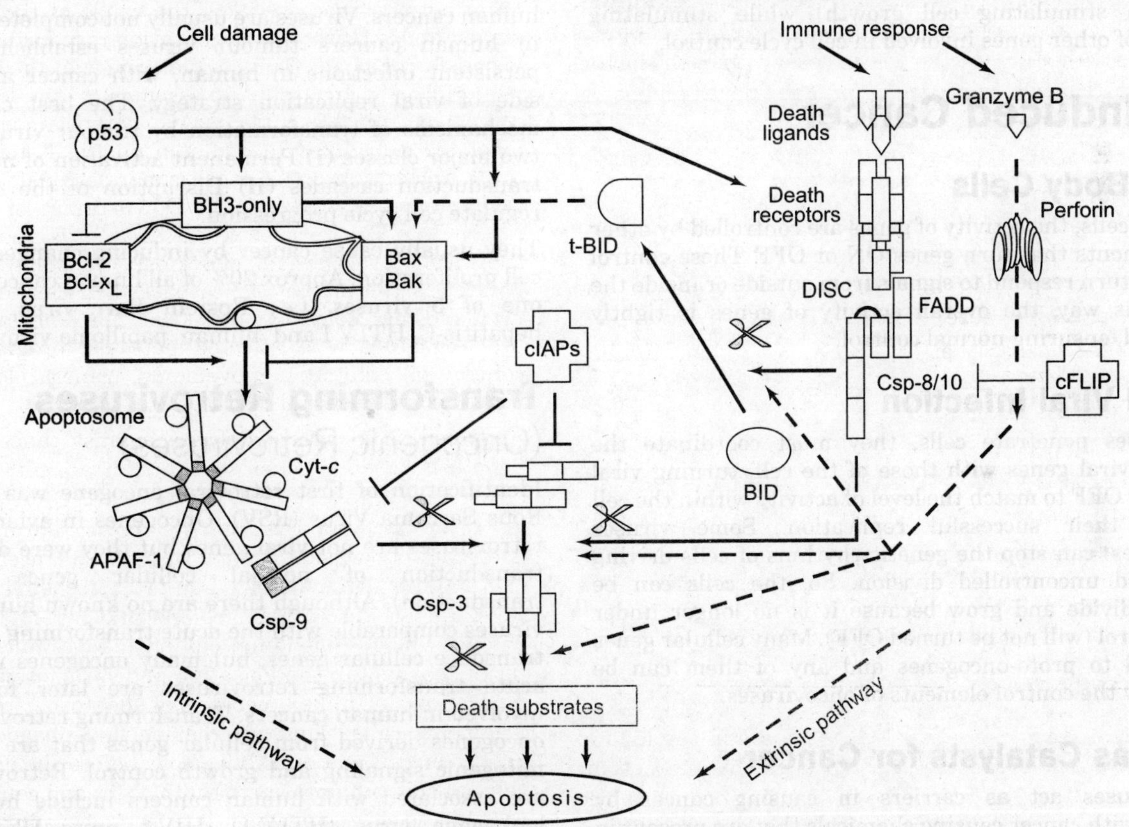

Fig. 12.2 The various regulatory pathways of apoptosis

Methodology

The process of apoptosis is controlled by a diverse range of cell signals, which may originate either extracellularly (extrinsic inducers) or intracellularly (intrinsic inducers). Extracellular signals may include toxins, hormones, growth factors, nitric oxide or cytokines, that must either cross the plasma membrane or transduce to effect a response. These signals may positively (*i.e.*, trigger) or negatively (*i.e.*, repress, inhibit or dampen) affect apoptosis. Before the actual process of cell death is precipitated by enzymes, apoptotic signals must cause regulatory proteins to initiate the apoptosis pathway. This step allows apoptotic signals to cause cell death, or the process to be stopped, should the cell no longer need to die. Several proteins are involved, but two main methods of regulation have been identified, targeting mitochondria functionality, or directly transducing the signal via adaptor proteins to the apoptotic mechanisms (TNF path and Fas path). Another extrinsic pathway for initiation identified in several toxin studies is an increase in calcium concentration within a cell caused by drug activity, which also can cause apoptosis *via* a calcium binding protease calpain.

Caspases

Caspases are proteins that are highly conserved, cysteine-dependent aspartate specific proteases. There are two types of caspases, initiator caspases, caspase 8, 10, 9, 2 and effector caspases, caspase 3, 7, 6. The activation of initiator caspases requires binding to specific oligomeric adaptor protein. Effector caspases are then activated by these active initiator caspases through proteolytic cleavage. The active effector caspases then proteolytically degrade a host of intracellular proteins to carry out the cell death program. There also exists a caspase-independent apoptotic pathway that is mediated by AIF (apoptosis-inducing factor).

p53

It suppresses progression through the cell cycle in response to DNA damage. It initiates apoptosis if the damage to the cell is severe. It also acts as a tumour suppressor. It is a transcription factor and once activated, it represses transcription of one set of genes (several of which are involved in stimulating cell growth) while stimulating expression of other genes involved in cell cycle control.

Virus Induced Cancer

Normal Body Cells

In all living cells, the activity of genes are controlled by other genetic elements that turn genes ON or OFF. These control elements in turn respond to signals from outside or inside the cells. In this way, the overall activity of genes is tightly orchestrated, ensuring normal control.

Cell and Viral Infection

When viruses penetrate cells, they must coordinate the function of viral genes with those of the cell, turning viral genes ON or OFF to match the level of activity within the cell to ensure their successful replication. Some viruses (Onco-viruses) can stop the genetic rhythms of cells driving them toward uncontrolled division. So, the cells can be ordered to divide and grow because it is no longer under cellular control (will not be turned OFF). Many cellular genes are changed to proto-oncogenes and any of them can be turned on by the control elements of oncoviruses.

Viruses as Catalysts for Cancer

Human viruses act as carriers in causing cancer by interacting with cancer causing chemicals that are present in too small quantity.

Relation between microorganisms and malignancy.

It is difficult to prove **causal relationship** (due to length of time). A general criteria for deciding if cancer is caused by a microorganism includes:

(a) Strong statistical association.

(b) Consistency in different populations.

(c) Specific association between factor and disease.

(d) Dose response relation.

Some articles and researches documented that cancer is an infectious disease caused by pleomorphic cell wall deficient bacteria. In the absence of a protective immune response, these bacteria may become pathogenic and lead to cancer. Examples include all patients with prostate cancer have been found to be heavily infested with intestinal parasites. Therefore, it has been suggested that parasites are probably a cause of cancer prostate. Skin cancers are forms of fungus growth and a simple application of oil of cloves is recommended for treatment.

Tumour Viruses

Viruses that directly cause cancer in either experimental animals or humans include RNA viruses and DNA viruses. Viruses as etiological factors of human cancer is reflected as ~15% of all human tumours worldwide are caused by viruses. Tumour viruses contributes to the formation of current concepts of cancer biology and molecular mechanisms of cancer formation and the recognition of the etiology of some human cancers. Viruses are usually not complete carcinogens in human cancers tumour viruses establish long term persistent infections in human, with cancer an accidental side of viral replication strategy. The best characterized mechanisms of transformation by tumour viruses fall into two major classes **(i)** Permanent activation of mitotic signal transduction cascades **(ii)** Disruption of the circuits that regulate cell cycle progression.

They usually cause cancer by inducing changes that affect cell proliferation. Approx 20% of all human cancers causes by one of 5 viruses, *i.e.,* Epstein Barr virus, hepatitis-B, hepatitis-C, HTLV I and human papilloma viruses.

Transforming Retroviruses (Oncogenic Retroviruses)

Identification of first retroviral oncogene was from avian Rous Sarcoma Virus (RSV). Oncogenes in avian or murine retroviruses are not viral genes but they were derived from transduction of normal cellular genes (retroviral transduction). Although there are no known human tumour viruses comparable with the acute transforming viruses that transduce cellular genes, but many oncogenes identified in acute transforming retroviruses are later found to be involved in human cancers. Transforming retroviruses carry oncogenes derived from cellular genes that are involved in mitogenic signaling and growth control. Retroviruses that are associated with human cancers include human T-cell leukaemia virus (HTLV-1), HIV-1 proto DNA. Tumour viruses encode oncogenes of viral origin that is essential for both viral replication and cellular transformation study of DNA tumour viruses lead to the discovery of cellular tumour suppressor genes.

Viral Transforming Genes V-oncogenes

It is characteristic of transforming viruses and of cellular origin. Picked up by retroviruses, it is a typical fusions of viral plus cellular genes where viral sequences alter expression, regulation and localization of gene products, *e.g.,* over expression of myc is sufficient to induce transformation and *v–erb*B is a truncated form of the epithelial growth factor receptor whose expression stimulates growth of cells by mimicking the 'ON' state of the receptor.

Viral Proteins that Alter Cellular Signaling Pathways

They are constitutively active viral receptors of viral origin which do not resemble cellular proteins. Proteins specifically recruit and activate signal transduction pathways, *e.g.*, LMP-1 in Epstein Barr virus.

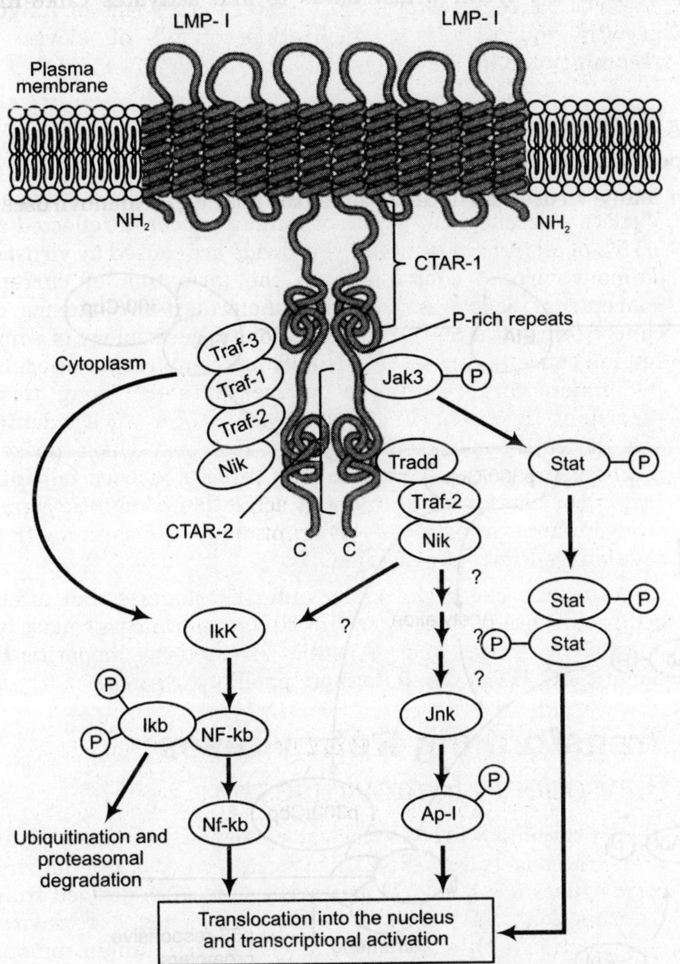

Fig. 12.3 Various active viral receptors

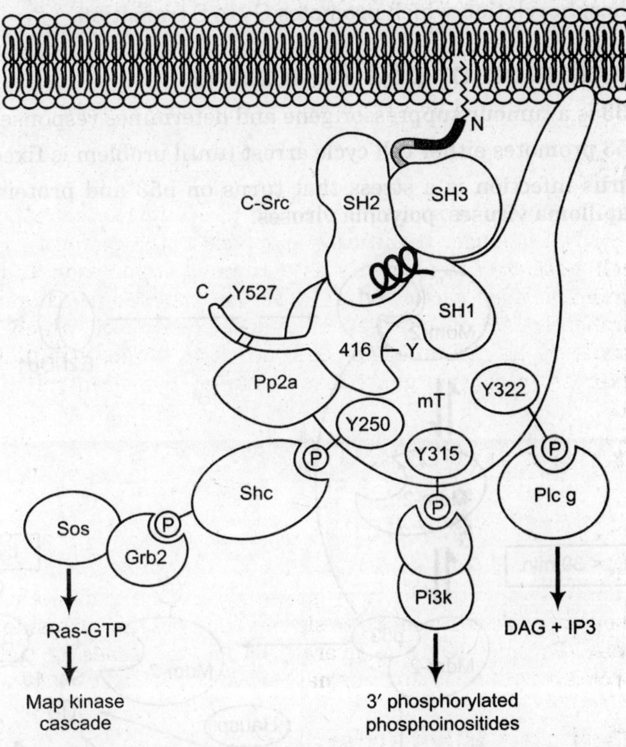

Fig. 12.4 Viral adapter proteins that alter cellular signaling pathways

These adapter proteins bind to cellular tyrosine kinases and permanently activate them. It also turns on cellular signal transduction pathways, *e.g.*, mT protein of polyomavirus activates *c–src* tyrosine kinase

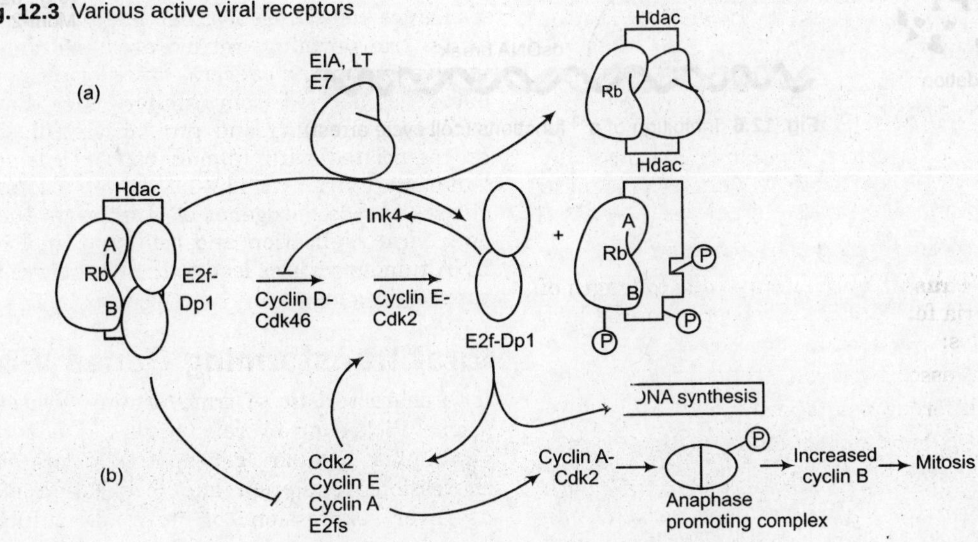

Fig. 12.5 Cell cycle regulation by the Rb protein

Transformation *via* Cell Cycle Control Pathways

Predominantly there is inhibition of Rb function by viral proteins. Many viruses actively inhibit Rb function therefore, there is bypass of restriction point control, *i.e.*, the passage from G_1 to S-phase, *e.g.*, $_5$V40 LT, adenovirus E1A, HPV E7 proteins. Also there is production of virus specific cyclins, *e.g.*, human herpes virus 8 v-cyclin which binds to and activates Cdk6-Rb phosphorylation which promotes G_1 to S transition.

Inhibition of p53 Functions

p53 is a tumour suppressor gene and determines response of cells to DNA damage and hypoxia.

p53 promotes either cell cycle arrest (until problem is fixed) or apoptosis (unfixable problem).

Virus infection is a stress that turns on p53 and proteins from many viruses mislocalize or block p53, *e.g.*, Adenoviruses, papilloma viruses, polyoma viruses.

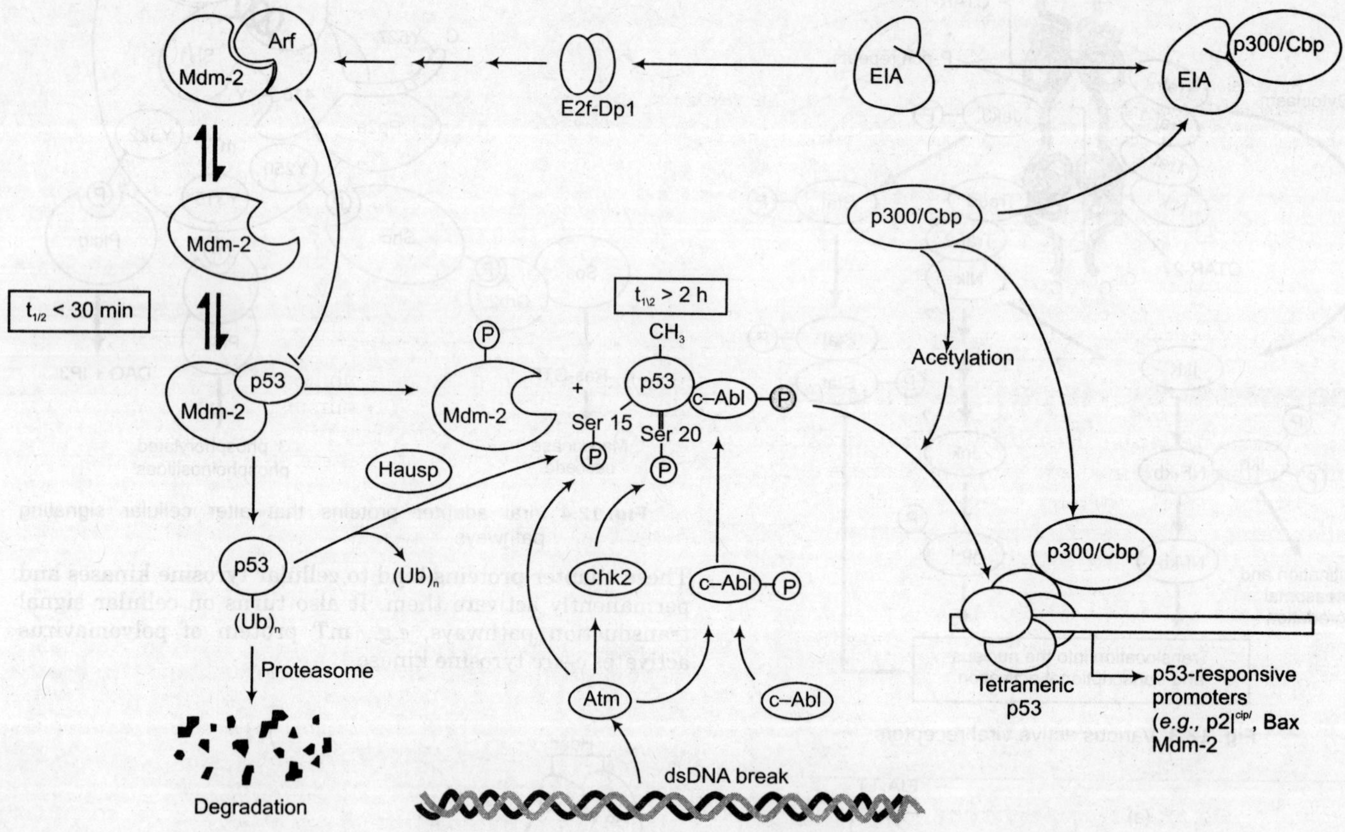

Fig. 12.6 Inhibition of p^{53} functions (cell cycle arrest)

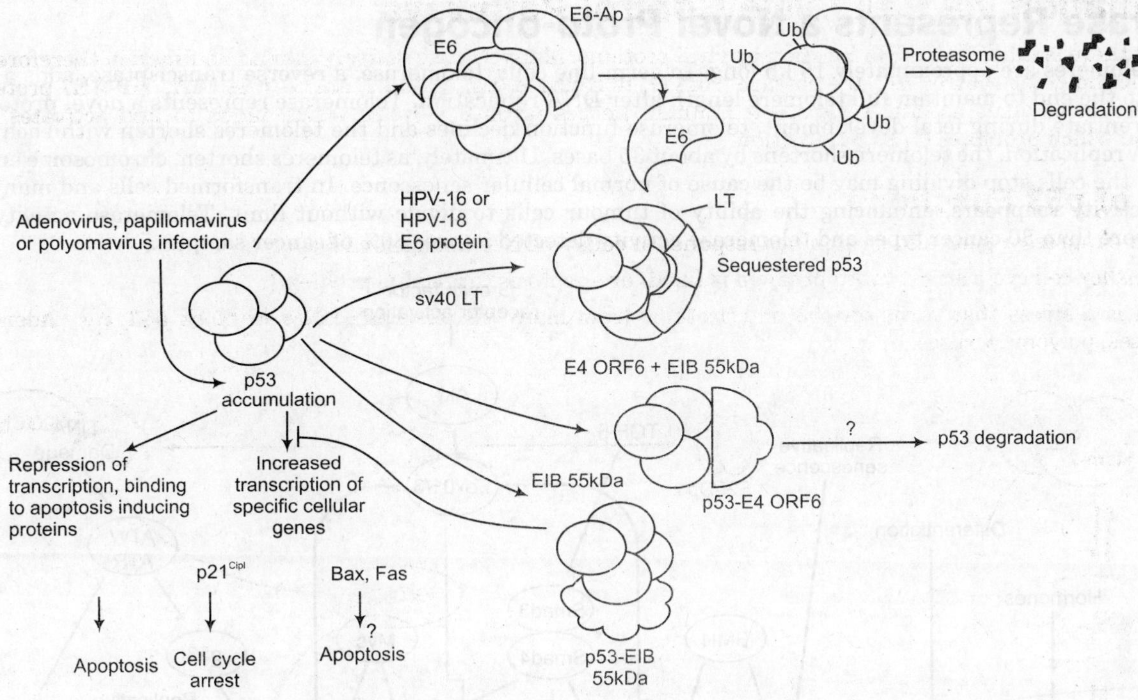

Fig. 12.7 Inhibition of p53 functions (Apoptosis)

Oncogenesis by Hepatitis Viruses

Hepatitis-B (Hepadna virus), Hepatitis-C (Flavi virus) are persistent infections. Sustained low level lever damage due to immune system attack thereby there is lots of cell proliferation/regeneration and lots of cellular DNA replication plus lots of oxidative stress leads to increased chance of mutation.

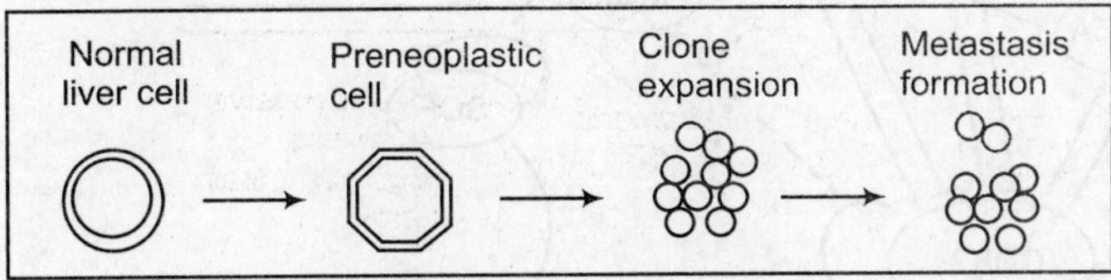

Fig. 12.8 Oncogenesis in liver

Immune defenses	Hyperplasia to replace cleared HBV-infected liver cells; DNA damage by free radicals		
Viral proteins	X protein: inhibition of DNA repair and increased susceptibility to chemical carcinogens	Stimulation of proliferation by X and truncated MHBs proteins, inhibition of apoptosis by X protein	X protein: increased migration *via* modulation of cell adhesion matrix X

Oncogene is defined by their ability to transform cells in culture or induce cancer in animals. There is a gain of function by mutations of proto-oncogenes (cellular counterpart of oncogenes). Dominant effect, *i.e.*, mutations in only one of the two alleles is sufficient for inducing oncogenesis. Originally identified from transforming retroviruses (viral oncogenes), identification of cellular oncogenes in human cancers is done by gene transfer assays. Proto-oncogenes can be activated by genetic changes affecting either protein expression or structure. Actions of oncogenes include uncontrolled growth promoting signals and production of hyperactive products (qualitative changes) example: constitutive Ras activity in cancer cells. Over expression of protein products (quantitative change) example includes over-expression of Myc8.

Mechanisms to activate proto-oncogenes include:

(i) Retroviral transduction—*v-src*

(ii) Promoter/enhancer insertion (insertional mutagenesis)—*myc*

(iii) Point mutation—rasoncogene

(iv) Amplification—*erb*B, *myc*

(v) Chromosomal translocation—*myc*

c-*myc* proto-oncogene can be activated by retroviral transduction, provirus insertion, gene amplification and chromosomal translocation. All of these mechanisms lead to over expression of *myc* gene. Proto-oncogenes can be activated by genetic changes affecting protein expression. Structural changes in proto-oncogenes can also lead to oncogenic activation. *H-ras* carries by Harvey sarcoma virus contains a point mutation and is over expressed. c-*ras* proto-oncogene can be activated by retroviral insertion and somatic mutations. Both mechanisms result in oncogenic *ras* with point mutations. Both activation mechanisms (regulatory and structural alterations) might collaborate to create an active oncogene.

Telomerase Represents a Novel Proto-oncogen

Full length telomeres are approximately 15 kb long. In germ-line cells, telomerase, a reverse transcriptase, adds a hexameric DNA repeat to the end to maintain full telomere length after DNA replication. Telomerase represents a novel proto-oncogene. As cells differentiate during fetal development, telomerase function declines and the telomeres shorten with each successive round of DNA replication, the telomere shortens by about 35 bases. Ultimately, as telomeres shorten, chromosome ends become damaged and the cells stop dividing may be the cause of normal cellular senescence. In transformed cells and many tumours, telomerase activity reappears, enhancing the ability of tumour cells to divide without limit. Telomerase activity has been detected in more than 30 cancer types and telomerase activity detected in over 80% of cancer samples.

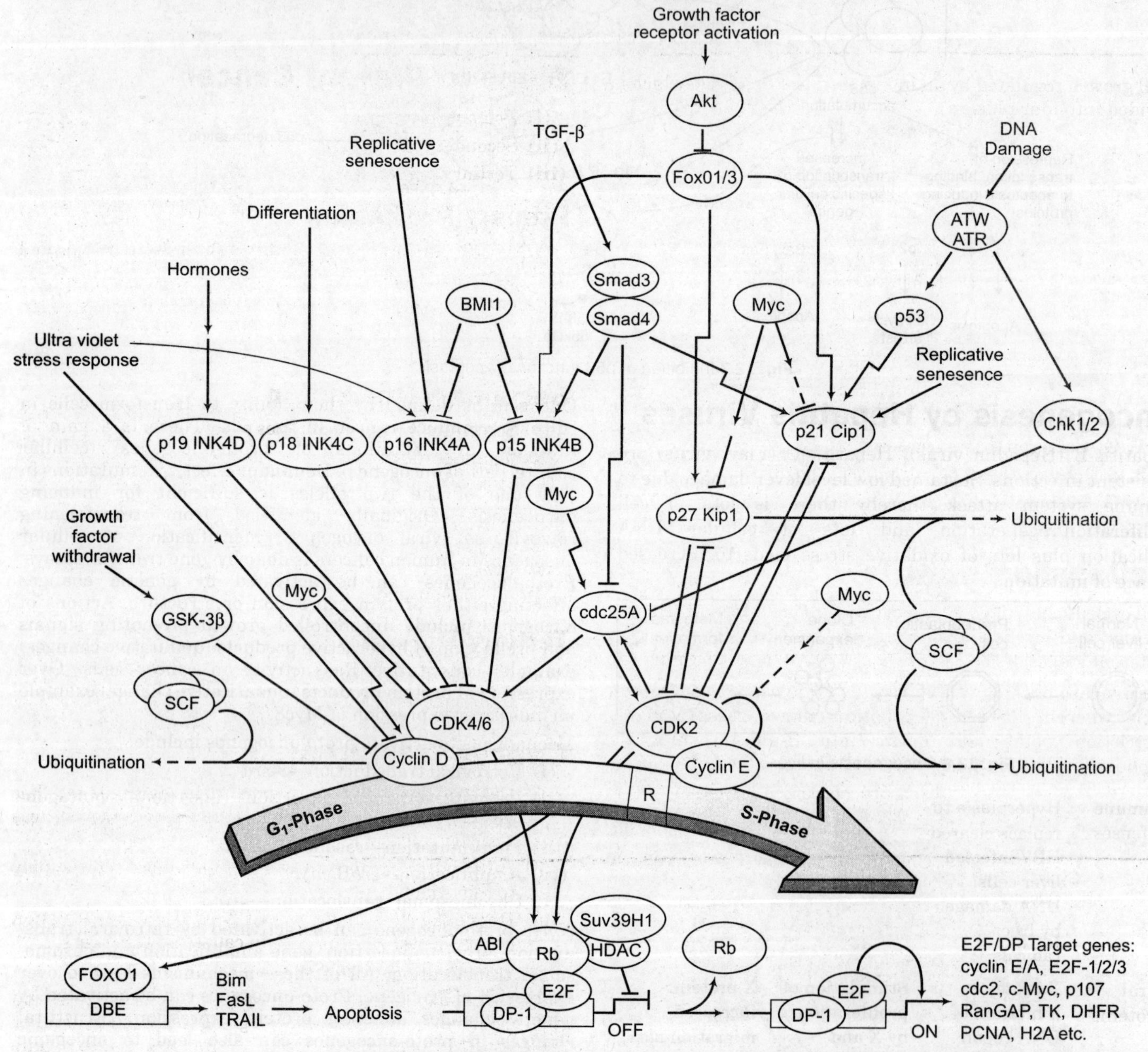

Fig. 12.9 Regulation of cell cycle and cell functioning

Cancer and the Cell Cycle

1. Cells must sense what is going on around them.
2. Cell surface receptors interact with ligands.
3. Signal transduction cascades.
4. Second messengers.
5. Activation and repression of genes.

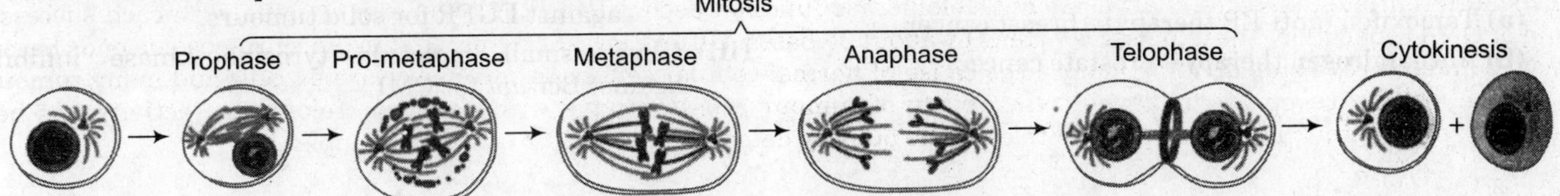

Fig. 12.10 Various phases of mitosis

Cell growth regulated by an internal timer: cell cycle which is divided into four phases:

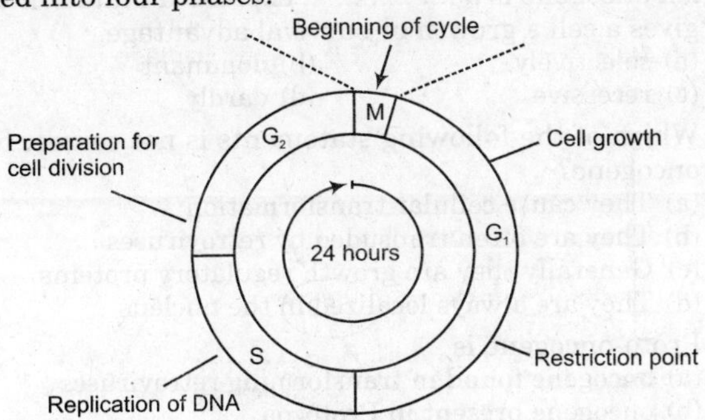

Fig. 12.11 Cell cycle

1. G_1-Cell growth, restriction point.
2. S-DNA synthesis.
3. G_2-Preparation for cell division.
4. M-Mitosis.

Cell Cycle Control

Cell cycle is controlled by the cyclin-Cdk machinery. Different cyclins and cyclin dependent kinases are expressed at different stages of the cell cycle.

Rb protein phosphorylation status of Rb used to control cell cycle wherein Rb phosphorylation allows passage of G_1 restriction point and entry into S-phase while Rb dephosphorylation signals end of M-phase.

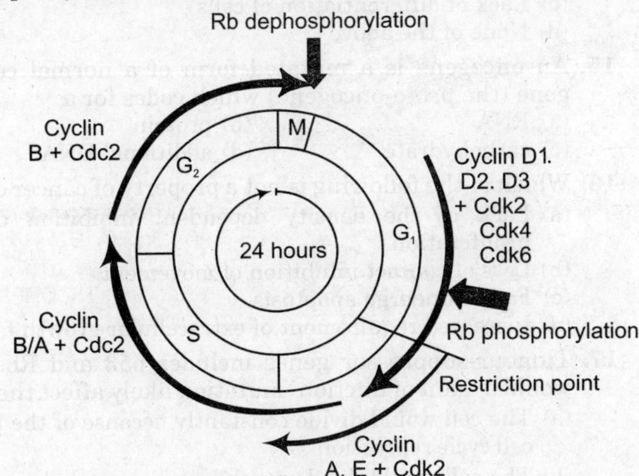

Fig. 12.12 Cell cycle control

Steps to Prevent Cancer

(i) Primary prevention.
(ii) Secondary prevention.
(iii) Tertiary prevention.

Primary Prevention

(a) Health education: to modify life style, diet, alcohol, smoking, etc.
(b) Avoid or reduce exposure to known risk factors, *e.g.*, drugs, hormones, radiation.
(c) Occupational preventive measures.

Secondary Prevention

Screening for different types of cancer

(a) Mammography
(b) Cervical smear
(c) PSA
(d) Blood film
(e) CEA
(f) Alpha fetoprotein

Tertiary Prevention

(a) Physical rehabilitation.
(b) Psychological rehabilitation.

Cancer Treatment

(i) **Chemotherapy** Deals with DNA damage and has affinity to all proliferating cells not specifying if it was a cancer cell or not.
(ii) **Inhibiting Angiogenesis** Inhibit blood flow/supply to the tumour cells.
(iii) **Decrease Franesylation of Ras** Decrease activation of Ras, because Ras mutation causes most cancers.
(iv) Monoclonal antibody.

Primary tumour usually can be excised by the surgeon and then chemo and/or radiotherapy is given to kill of any local or disseminated metastatic cells. Tumours have gene alterations/lost tumour suppressor genes; gained mutations (oncogenes), *i.e.,* Cancer genes and result frequently defective in their apoptotic pathways so, are resistant to chemo and/or radiotherapy. Hence cells that escaped from the primary tumour lead to metastatic tumours colon to liver breast to lymph glands and bone.

Examples of Targeted Therapies in Clinical Use

(i) Anti-endocrine therapies

(a) Tamoxifen (anti-ER therapy) – breast cancer.

(b) Anti-androgen therapy – prostate cancer.

(ii) Anti-receptor tyrosine kinase therapies:

(a) Herceptin—immunotherapy against HER2/ ERBB2 in breast cancer.

(b) Iressa—small molecule tyrosine kinase inhibitor against EGFR for solid tumours.

(iii) Glivec—small molecule tyrosine kinase inhibitor against Bcr-*abl* for CML.

Exercise

1. Which of the following statements is not true about cancer?
(a) A cancer is a genetic disease which is often inherited
(b) Cancer is primarily a disease of old age
(c) A cancer is caused by accumulation of a small number of mutations, each of which gives the cell a growth advantage
(d) A tumour is not regarded as malignant until it spreads to other parts of the body forming secondary tumours

2. Which of the following best defines an oncogene?
(a) An oncogene is a dominantly expressed mutation which gives a cell a growth or survival advantage
(b) An oncogene codes for a mutated form of a protein which forms part of a signal transduction pathway
(c) An oncogene codes for a protein which prevents the cell from undergoing apoptosis
(d) An oncogene codes for a cell cycle control protein

3. How does p53 prevent the development of cancer?
(a) p53 is a transcription factor
(b) p53 prevents the replication of cells with damaged DNA
(c) p53 prevents cells from triggering apoptosis
(d) p53 stimulates synthesis of DNA repair enzymes which replace telomeres

4. To form a malignant cancer a cell must acquire a small number of mutations (probably about ....) each of which gives the cell a growth or survival advantage.
(a) 2 (b) 3
(c) 6 (d) 13

5. Because cells have to accumulate mutations before they become malignant cancers, most cancers arise in
(a) infants (b) teen
(c) elders (d) young

6. Incidence rates for most forms of cancers rise .... with increasing age.
(a) arithmetically (b) logarithmically
(c) exponentially (d) steadily

7. Cells which have accumulated some growth .... mutations give rise to tumours located at a single site.
(a) promoting (b) retarding
(c) independent (d) dependent

8. Initial tumours are regarded as benign until cells start to leave the tumour and establish secondary tumours at other sites. This process is called
(a) statis (b) metastasis
(c) signaling (d) translocation

9. An oncogene is a .... expressed mutation which gives a cell a growth or survival advantage.
(a) selectively (b) dominant
(c) recessive (d) dardly

10. Which of the following statements is not correct for an oncogene?
(a) They cause cellular transformation
(b) They are often transuded by retroviruses
(c) Generally they are growth regulatory proteins
(d) They are always localized in the nucleus

11. Proto-oncogene is
(a) oncogene found in transforming retroviruses
(b) oncogene present in Protozoa
(c) genes encoding oncogene related proteins in extinct organisms
(d) cellular genes encoding proteins related to viral oncogene

12. Choose the mismatch.
(a) Rho — GTP-binding proteins
(b) Raf — serine/therionine kinase
(c) p53 — tumour suppressor gene
(d) *myc* — proto-oncogene

13. The oncoprotein Ras is a
(a) kinase (b) ATPase
(c) GTPase (d) phosphatase

14. Which of the following is not a characteristic feature malignant tumour?
(a) Invasiveness
(b) Metastatsis
(c) Lack of differentiation of cells
(d) None of the above

15. An oncogene is a mutated form of a normal cellular gene (the proto-oncogene) which codes for a
(a) RNA (b) protein
(c) carbohydrate (d) additional DNA

16. Which of the following is not a property of cancer cells?
(a) Lack of the density dependent inhibition of cell proliferation
(b) Loss of contact inhibition of movement
(c) Fail to undergo apoptosis
(d) Increased requirement of extracellular growth factors

17. Tumour-suppressor genes includes p53 and Rb. How would a 'gain of unction' mutation likely affect the cell?
(a) The cell would divide constantly because of the loss of cell cycle repression
(b) The cell would divide much less frequently because of the extra cell cycle repression

(c) The cell would divide normally because these genes have no effect on cell cycle control
(d) The cell would commit suicide by apoptosis

18. How would the cell cycle be affected if you removed the phosphorylation sites in the Rb protein?
(a) The cell cycle would not be affected because pRb is not phosphorylated normally
(b) The cell cycle would be blocked in G_1
(c) The cell cycle would be blocked in G_2
(d) The cell cycle would be shorter

19. One difference between a cancer cell and a normal cell is that
(a) the cancer cell is unable to synthesize DNA
(b) the cell cycle of the cancer cell is arrested at the S-phase
(c) cancer cells continue to divide even when they are tightly packed
(d) cancer cells cannot function properly because they suffer from density-dependent inhibition

20. Choose the incorrect statement.
(a) *c-abl*, a proto-oncogene encode a tyrosine kinase
(b) translocation of *c-abl* from chromosome 9 to chromosome 22 results in chromic mylogenous leukaemia
(c) all retrovirus are oncovirus
(d) p53 gene located on chromosome 17 of human

21. Which of the following statements about tumour suppressor genes is false?
(a) The retinoblastoma gene is a tumour suppressor gene
(b) Tumour suppressor gene act in a genetically dominant manner
(c) Tumour suppressor, p53 can trigger apoptosis
(d) None of the above

22. The normal cellular counterparts of oncogenes are important for the following functions except?
(a) Promotion of cell cycle progression
(b) Inhibition of apoptosis
(c) Promotion of DNA repair
(d) Promotion of nuclear transcription

23. During the early years of cancer research, there were two schools of thought regarding the causes of cancer: I. That cancer was caused entirely by environmental factors, II. That cancer was caused by genetic factors. Which was correct?
(a) I because we have identified many potential carcinogens
(b) II because we know of many proto-oncogenes
(c) II because we know of many tumour-suppressor genes
(d) Both were correct; most chemical carcinogens function by altering genes

24. Too much time in a tanning booth probably causes DNA damage to epithelial cells. The most likely effect would be
(a) depurination
(b) pyrimidine dimers
(c) deamination
(d) single-stranded nicks in the phosphodiester backbone

25. The term 'cancer' means
(a) cell division (b) out of control
(c) crab (d) lobster

26. Cancer is often the result of activation of .... to .... and the inactivation of .... genes.
(a) oncogenes; tumour-suppressor genes; proto-oncogenes
(b) proto-oncogenes; oncogenes; tumour-suppressor genes
(c) oncogenes; proto-oncogenes; tumour-suppressor genes
(d) proto-suppressor genes; suppressors; oncogenes

27. It was found that normal stem cells isolated from a tissue have a doubling time of 24 hours, wheras tumour derived cells have a doubling time of 12 hours. Both these cell types were grown in the presence of radioactive thymidine for 24 hours, following which they were grown in normal media. At the end of a week, radioactivity per cell will be
(a) double in stem cells as compared to cancer cells
(b) half in stem cells as compared to cancer cells
(c) same in both stem and cancer cells
(d) none in stem cells and high levels in cancer cells

28. About 50% of all human cancers may involve an abnormal or missing
(a) oncogene (b) proto-oncogene
(c) p53 gene (d) BRCA-1 gene

29. Inherited retinoblastoma requires .... mutation(s) or deletion(s).
(a) one (b) two
(c) three (d) four

30. In which of the human cells listed below is telomerase active?
(a) Blood (b) Bone
(c) Muscle (d) Sperm

31. Which of the following statements correctly describes p53?
(a) It is a membrane receptor that binds to a cell growth hormone
(b) Cell division stops until p53 binds to DNA and repairs the damage
(c) p53 is an example of an oncogene and its expression causes uncontrolled cell division
(d) Activation of p53 leads to inhibition of the S-phase cyclin-Cdk complex

32. Retroviruses are capable of causing cancer because they
(a) produce a very high number of progeny viruses per infected cell
(b) often contain point mutations in their pol gene
(c) transducer mutant versions of cellular genes that normally regulate cell growth
(d) infect cells more efficiently than other viruses

33. Which of the following is not a characteristic of cancer cells?
(a) Loss of cell cycle control (b) Transplantability
(c) Loss of contact inhibition (d) All are characteristic

34. The philadelphia chromosome is associated with which type of cancer?
(a) Breast (b) Thyroid
(c) Nerve (d) Leukaemia

35. Some oncogene retroviruses can transform normal mammalian cells to cancer cells *in vitro*. This transformation of a best cell is generally associated with
(a) conversion of the host DNA into viral RNA
(b) presence of viral particles in the host's cell membrane
(c) integration of the viral genome into host's nuclear DNA
(d) release of numerous viral particles and concomitant death of host cells

36. Apoptosis refers to
(a) limb regeneration in vertebrates
(b) metamorphosis in *C. elegens*
(c) genetically cell death
(d) formation of imaginal disc in *Drosophila*

37. An increasing number of women in the rural south die from .... cancer.
(a) breast (b) colon
(c) lung (d) mouth

38. The p53 protein normally promotes
(a) DNA repair (b) tumour formation
(c) cell division (d) apoptosis

39. Which of the following is least likely to cause a protooncogene to become an oncogene?
(a) A gene is incorporated into a retroviral genome
(b) A gene is moved into centrometric heterochromatin, silencing its transcription
(c) A gene is moved close to an enhancer, causing excess product to be made
(d) A gene is truncated, yielding a protein with modified activity

40. A mutation in which gene makes nearby DNA more susceptible to replication errors?
(a) APC (b) BRCA1
(c) P^{53} (d) RB

41. p53 protein is associated with all of the following except
(a) tumour suppression
(b) programmed cell death
(c) transcription
(d) post-transcription modifications

42. Movement of cancer cells to a new site where a secondary tumour begins is called
(a) anaplasia (b) metastasis
(c) promotion (d) vascularization

43. Increased blood flow to a cancerous tumour is called
(a) anaplasia (b) metastasis
(c) malignancy (d) vascularization

44. A cancer-causing gene is called a(n)
(a) initiator (b) promoter
(c) oncogene (d) proto-oncogene

45. The versions of genes that most often occur naturally are called
(a) natural genes
(b) wild-type genes
(c) HF (high-frequency) genes
(d) LM (low-mutation) genes

46. Cancer cells have the ability to divide indefinitely. They have become
(a) immortalized (b) desensitized
(c) transduced (d) indestructible

47. Which of the following only appears during plant cell mitosis?
(a) Cell plate (b) Spindle fibres
(c) Chromatids (d) Centrioles

48. Apoptosis is programmed cell death. Which one of the following brings out apoptosis in humans?
(a) Great reduction in the size of appendix
(b) Degeneration of neurons resulting in loss of memory
(c) Leaching out of osteocytes in menopausal women
(d) Webbing erosion between fingers in the second month of embryo development

49. Which of these are properties typically displayed by cancer cells?
(a) Dependence on growth factors for continued cell division
(b) Secretion of proteases that degrade the extracellular matrix
(c) Growth inhibition upon contact with neighbouring cells
(d) High nucleo-cytoplasmic ratio

50. Which of the following statements is not correct for an oncogene?
(a) They cause cellular transformation
(b) They are often transduced by retroviruses
(c) Generally they are growth regulatory proteins
(d) They are always localized in the nucleus

51. Apoptosis is a phenomenon, which leads to
(a) Limb regeneration in vertebrates
(b) Formation of cardiac tissues
(c) Programmed cell death
(d) Frame-shift mutations in *Drosophila*

52. Which statement about cyclins are true?
I. There are several families of cyclins that differ in amino acid sequence and in their properties.
II. Cyclins are present at a constant steady state level throughout the cell cycle.
III. Cyclins are degraded rapidly when the cell enters mitosis.
IV. Cyclins regulate the activity of the M-phase kinase.
(a) I and II (b) I and III
(c) I, III and IV (d) I, II, III and IV

53. M-phase kinase
I. Can cause G_2-blocked *Xenopus laevis* oocytes to enter M-phase.
II. Contains a kinase subunit called p34.
III. Contains a regulatory subunit that is a cyclin.
IV. Phosphorylates target proteins at specific times in the cell cycle.
(a) I and II (b) I and III
(c) III and IV (d) I, II, III and IV

Answers

1. (a)	**2.** (a)	**3.** (b)	**4.** (c)	**5.** (c)	**6.** (c)	**7.** (a)	**8.** (b)	**9.** (b)	**10.** (d)
11. (d)	**12.** (a)	**13.** (c)	**14.** (d)	**15.** (b)	**16.** (d)	**17.** (b)	**18.** (b)	**19.** (c)	**20.** (c)
21. (b)	**22.** (c)	**23.** (d)	**24.** (b)	**25.** (c)	**26.** (b)	**27.** (c)	**28.** (c)	**29.** (b)	**30.** (d)
31. (d)	**32.** (c)	**33.** (d)	**34.** (d)	**35.** (c)	**36.** (c)	**37.** (d)	**38.** (d)	**39.** (b)	**40.** (a)
41. (d)	**42.** (b)	**43.** (d)	**44.** (c)	**45.** (b)	**46.** (a)	**47.** (d)	**48.** (d)	**49.** (b)	**50.** (c)
51. (c)	**52.** (c)	**53.** (d)							

13 Immune System

Immunology is a broad field encompassing both basic and clinical applications and deals with antigens, antibodies and cell mediated host defense functions, especially as they relate to immunity to disease, hypersensitivity biological reactions, allergies and rejection of foreign tissues.

Immunity is the body defense against exogenous (microbes) and endogenous (tumour cells) agents. It is comprised of

1. Innate (natural and non-adaptive or non-specific) immunity.
2. Adaptive (acquired or specific) immunity. It occurs after exposure to antigen. It is mediated by either antibodies (humoral immunity) or lymphoid cells (cellular immunity). It can be:
   - (i) Passive immunity
   - (ii) Active immunity.

Syllabus

- Innate and Adaptive Immunity
- Primary and Secondary Immune Defences.
- Antigens, Antigen Processing and Presentation
- B and T-Cell Epitopes
- Structure and Function of Antibody Molecules, Generation of Antibody Diversity
- Monoclonal Antibodies and Antibody Engineering
- Antigen-Antibody Interactions
- MHC Molecules
- B and T-cell Receptors, Activation and Differentiation of B and T-Cells
- Humoral and Cell-Mediated Immune Responses (Cellular Basis)
- The Complement System
- Toll-Like Receptors
- Cell-Mediated Effector Functions
- Inflammation Cytokines, Interferons Hypersensitivity and Autoimmunity
- Parasitic (malaria) and Viral (HIV) Infections
- Vaccines, Immunodeficiencies

Non-Specific Host Defenses/Innate Immunity

1. Physiological barriers at the portal of entry
   - (i) The skin
   - (ii) Mucous membranes.
2. Non-adaptive immunologic mechanisms.
   - (i) **Reticuloendothelial System** Mononuclear phagocytic cells in blood, lymphoid tissue, liver, spleen, bone marrow, lung and other tissues that are efficient in uptake and removal of particulate matter from lymph channels and the blood stream.
   - (ii) Alternative pathway of complement C3 parasites, endotoxins, microbial surface C5, C6, C7, C8, C9 (Opsonization, lysis of bacteria).
   - (iii) **Phagocytosis** Engulfment and killing of microbes by phagocytic cells which include microphage (granulocytes, polymorphs) and macrophage.
     The process of killing includes both non-oxidative and oxidative mechanisms.

(iv) Inflammatory response.
(v) Fever Endotoxins and interleukin 1.
(vi) Interferon Virus induced proteins that have antiviral activity after 48 hours of viral infection. IFN a, IFN b, INF g.
(vii) NK cells Lyse tumour cells and virus infected cells.

Acquired Immunity (Adaptive Immunity/Specific Immunity)

This type of immunity occurs in response to infection called **Adaptive** as the immune system must adapt itself to previously unseen molecules. It forms 3rd line of defence Following recovery from certain infections with a particular microorganism, individuals will never again develop infection with the same organism, but can become infected with other microorganisms, *i.e.,* he/she is protected against one microorganism. This form of protection is called **Immunity** and an individual is said to be **Immunised** against that organism. The induction of immunity by infection or with a vaccine is called **Active Immunity.**

Historically it has been shown that a non immune individual can be made immune by transferring serum or lymphocytes from an immune individual. **Passive Immunity,** serum constituents **(Antibodies)** and **Lymphocytes** are involved in immunity.

It has been observed that the immune system responds to microorganisms but not to its own cells and that the system knows that the body has been infected previously with a particular organism. This implies:

Immunological recognition.
Self/Non-self discrimination.
Immunological specifity.
Immunological memory.

Immunity is mediated by the **Immune System,** which responds to infection by mounting an **Immune Response.** An immune response must:

recognize a microorganism as foreign (non-self) as distinct from self (Afferent limb).

respond to a microorganism by production of specific antibodies and specific lymphocytes.

mediate the elimination of microorganisms (Efferent limb).

An agent which evokes an immune response is called an **Immunogen.** The term **antigen** is applied to a substance which reacts with antibody.

Prevention of Entry of Organisms

Mechanical barriers at body surfaces, skin, mucous membranes disruption leads to infection.

Antibacterial substances in secretions, lysozyme, lactoferrin, low pH of stomach contents.

Prevention of stasis.

Peristalsis/flow of urine/upward movement of secretions in bronchial tree.

Clinical relevance, urinary infection with urinary obstruction, decreased bronchial.

Ciliary activity, bronchiectasis (Kartagener's syndrome).

Coughing, Vomiting.

Non-specific elimination of microorganisms.

(i) Phagocytosis Ingestion and killing of microorganisms by specialized cells (phagocytes). Phagocytes-polymorphonuclear leukocytes (neutrophils)-mononuclear phagocytes (monocytes, macrophages).

(ii) Opsonization The process of coating microorganisms with some of the proteins found in plasma, to make them more easily phagocytosable. An **Opsonin** is a plasma protein binding to bacteria. This promotes adhesion between the opsonized bacteria and macrophages because the opsonin binds to receptors on phagocyte membrane, *e.g.,* complement with complement receptors and phagocytes. Opsonization and phagocytosis are more efficient in immune individuals.

Inflammation complement and phagocytes exist mainly in blood so, a mechanism is required to recruit these elements to the site of tissue invasion **Inflammatory Response** (inflammation).

Antigens

Antigens are some chemicals that creates immune response. Most of them are proteins or large polysaccharides from a foreign organism, *e.g.,* In microbes include, capsules, cell walls, toxins, viral capsids, flagella, etc., while in Non-microbes it includes. Pollen, egg white, red blood cell surface molecules, serum proteins, and surface molecules from transplanted tissue. Antigens are comprized of epitopes which are a small part of an antigen that interacts with an antibody, they are usually 10-12 amino acids. Any given antigen may have several epitopes and each epitope is recognized by a different antibody. Epitopes are basically antigen regions that interact with antibodies. An antigen may or may not be able to elicit an immune response while an immunogen always elicits an immune response. Usually post-translational modification especially glycosylation assist an antigen to become a good immunogen. Addition of adjuvant helps an antigen to generate a good immune response. The features that determine immunogenicity substances that stimulate the immune response are, foreignness, molecular size, chemical and structural complexity, molecular weight, > 10000, dosage, route and timing of Ag administration. Incomplete Ag which can be conjugated with a carrier protein to form a complete Ag.

Epitopes (Antigenic Determinants)

Antibody molecule do not kind to the whole of an infections agent. These may be several different antibodies for a given pathogen, each binding to a different antigen an that pathogen's surface. Each antibody kinds to a restricted part of antigen called **epitope.** A single antigen can have several different epitopes. T-cell and B-cell epitopes are distinct. In two peptides of antigen glucagon antibody is primarily directed to epitope at N-terminus while the C-terminal peptide stimulates T-cell response.

Antigen Processing and Presentation

The antigen is first degraded into short peptides of 8-18 amino acids long by antigen presenting cells, and the process is called **antigen processing.** These short peptides then bind within cleft of MHC I or MHC II molecules within the APCs and the peptide-MHC complexes are transformed to and displayed at the cell surface of APCs. This process is known as **antigen presentation.** Those cells that process and present antigenic peptides in association with class II MHC molecules, and deliver a costimulatory signal required for T_H cells activation are called antigen presenting cells. There are two pathway of antigen processing.

(a) **Cytosolic pathway** Intracellular antigens are eliminated by cytotoxic T-lymphocytes.

(b) **Endocytic pathway** Extracellular antigens are eliminated by secreted antibodies.

Primary and Secondary Immune Defences

Non-specific Immunity (Innate) offers general protection from all pathogens. It includes first line of defense (*i.e.,* skin) and second line of defense (*i.e.,* phagocytosis inflammation).

Skin—The Largest Organ of the Body in Terms of Surface Area

(i) Epidermis Outer thin layer contains stratified squamous epithelium. It forms a barrier against most pathogens. Keratinocytes secrete keratin, a type of wax. Most microbiota is located here.

(ii) Dermis Skin's inner thicker part composed of connective tissue made of collagen.

(a) Dendritic cells are a type of phagocyte found in the skin derived from monocytes. These cells migrate to the lymph nodes after phagocytosis.

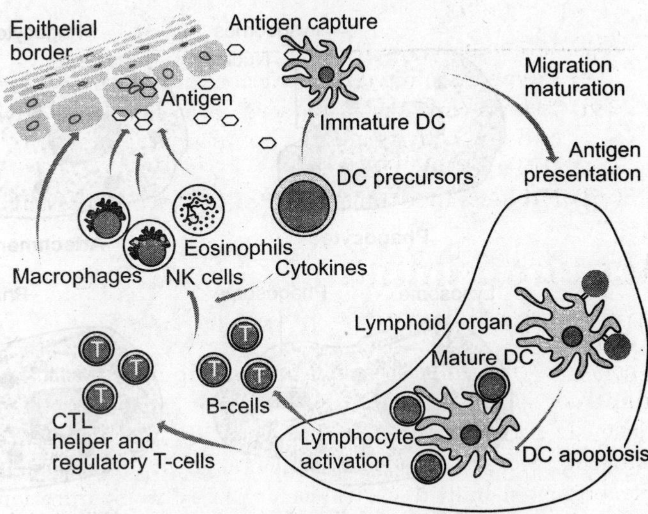

Fig. 13.1 Dandritic cells in immune functioning

(b) Mast cells release histamine during inflammation. Not normally in circulation but in the skin.

(c) Suderiferous glands produce sweat. Sweat contains lysozyme and NaCl which inhibits most bacteria except *Staphylococcus epidermidis*.

(d) Sebacous glands produce sebum, an unsaturated fatty acid, lowers skin pH to 4.0.

(iii) Subcutaneous Tissue – mostly the membranes that line the G.I.T., G.U.T. and R.T.

(a) Goblet cells secrete mucus. It prevent cells from drying out and cracking. It keeps bacteria flowing over the surface of cells lining tracts of the body.

(b) Ciliated columnar cells wave dirt, dust and bacteria out of the body. In the R.T., cilia wave particles up toward the epiglottis where they are swallowed. Also called the 'muco ciliary escalator'.

(c) Hydrochloric Acid (HCl) pH 1.8 stomach.

(d) Salivary glands one liter of saliva per day. Bathes teeth with lysozyme (it destroys peptidoglycan layer).

(e) Lacrimal glands produce tears, contain lysozyme.

Phagocytic System—Phagocytosis (To Eat)

(i) Mechanism

(a) **Chemotaxis** Chemical attraction of phagocytes to a microbe.

(b) **Adherence** Attachment

(c) **Ingestion** Pseudopods extend around microbe.

(d) **Digestion** The plasma membrane of a phagocytic cell pinches off into the cell and forms a vacuole (phagosome). Lysosomes fuse with phagosome. It contain nitric oxide and lysozyme which kills microbes, and digestive enzymes that degrade microbes.

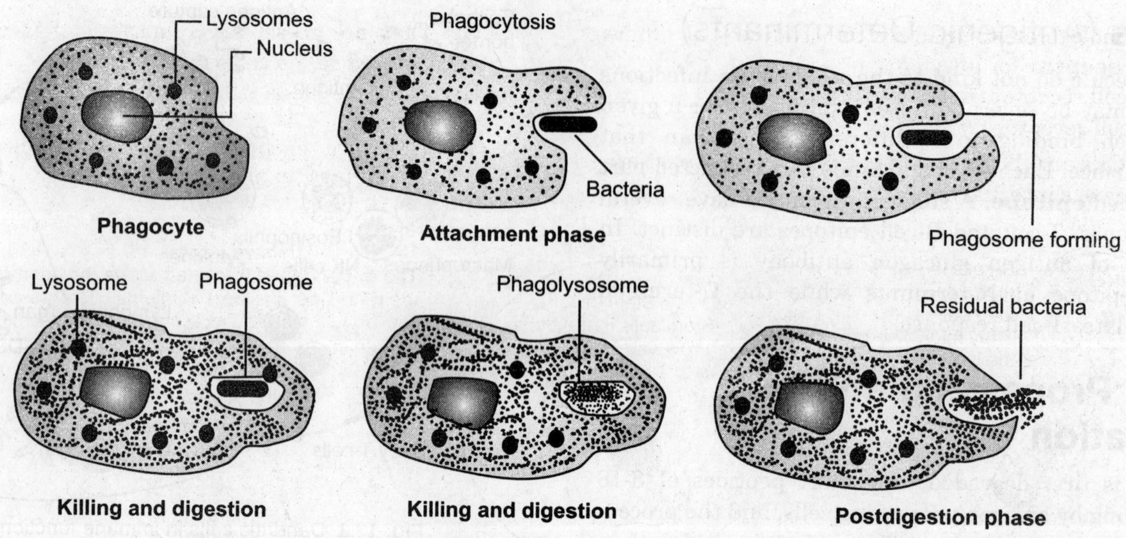

Fig. 13.2 Phagocytosis process

(ii) Five types of leukocytes (WBCs) are made in the bone marrow. They are comprised of three granulocytes with granules in cytoplasm.

(a) Neutrophils stain poorly and have 2-7 nuclei. It is the first phagocytes to arrive at site of inflammation. They are 60% of blood leukocytes.

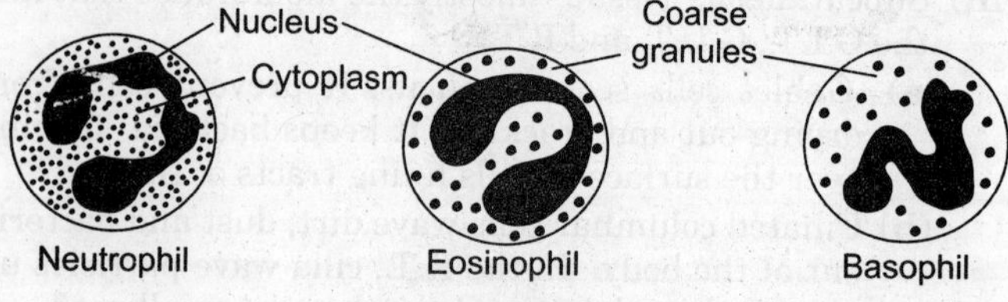

Fig. 13.3 Neutrophils

(b) Eosinophils stain red have two nuclei and phagocytize large parasites (protozoans, worms and fungi). 2-4% of the total population.

(c) Basophils stain blue and release histamine during inflammation. Non-phagocytic in nature. They are comprised of < 1% of the total leukocytes.

Two agranulocytes no granules in cytoplasm.

(d) **Monocytes** It is comprised of horseshoe-shaped nucleus. It is the largest leukocyte. They migrate out of the circulatory system and wander into any tissue of the body scavenging for foreign substances.

If they are out of the circulation, they are called macrophage (MP). Ingest 100 bacteria at once 3-8% of WBCs all in blood.

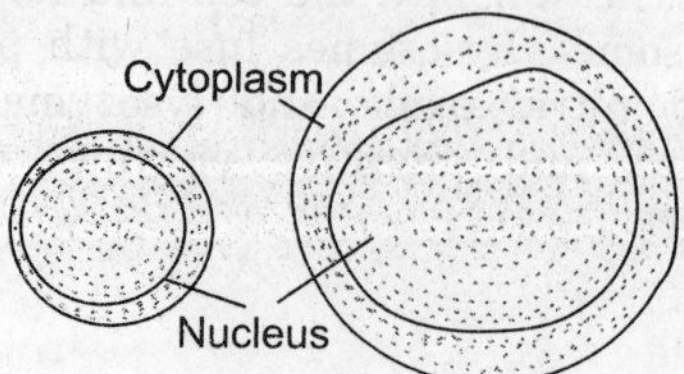

Fig. 13.4 Agranulocytes

(e) **Lymphocytes** make up 20% of all leukocytes. Function in specific immunity. There are basically two types, T-cells and B-cells.

(ii) Platelets or thrombocytes, basically are small cells that form blood clots.

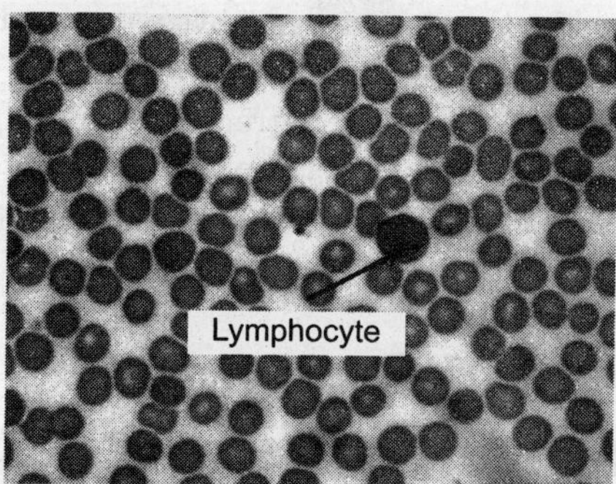

Fig. 13.5 Platelets

B-cells and T-cells with their Receptors

Lymphocytes are one of the five kinds of (**white blood cells** or **leukocytes**), circulating in the blood. Although mature lymphocytes all look pretty much alike, they are extraordinarily diverse in their functions. The most abundant lymphocytes are:

1. B-lymphocytes (often simply called **B-cells**) and
2. T-lymphocytes (likewise called **T-cells**).

B-cells are not only produced in the **bone marrow** but also mature there. However, the precursors of T cells leave the bone marrow and mature in the **thymus** (which accounts for their designation).

Each B-cell and T-cell is **specific** for a particular **antigen.** What this means is that each is able to recognize and **bind to** a particular molecular structure. The specificity of binding resides in a **receptor** for antigen:

1. The B-cell receptor (**BCR**) for antigen
2. The T-cell receptor (**TCR**) respectively.

Both BCRs and TCRs **share** the following properties:

(i) They are internal membrane proteins.

(ii) They are present in thousands of identical copies exposed at the cell surface.

(iii) They are made before the cell ever encounters an antigen.

(iv) They are encoded by genes assembled by the recombination of segments of DNA.

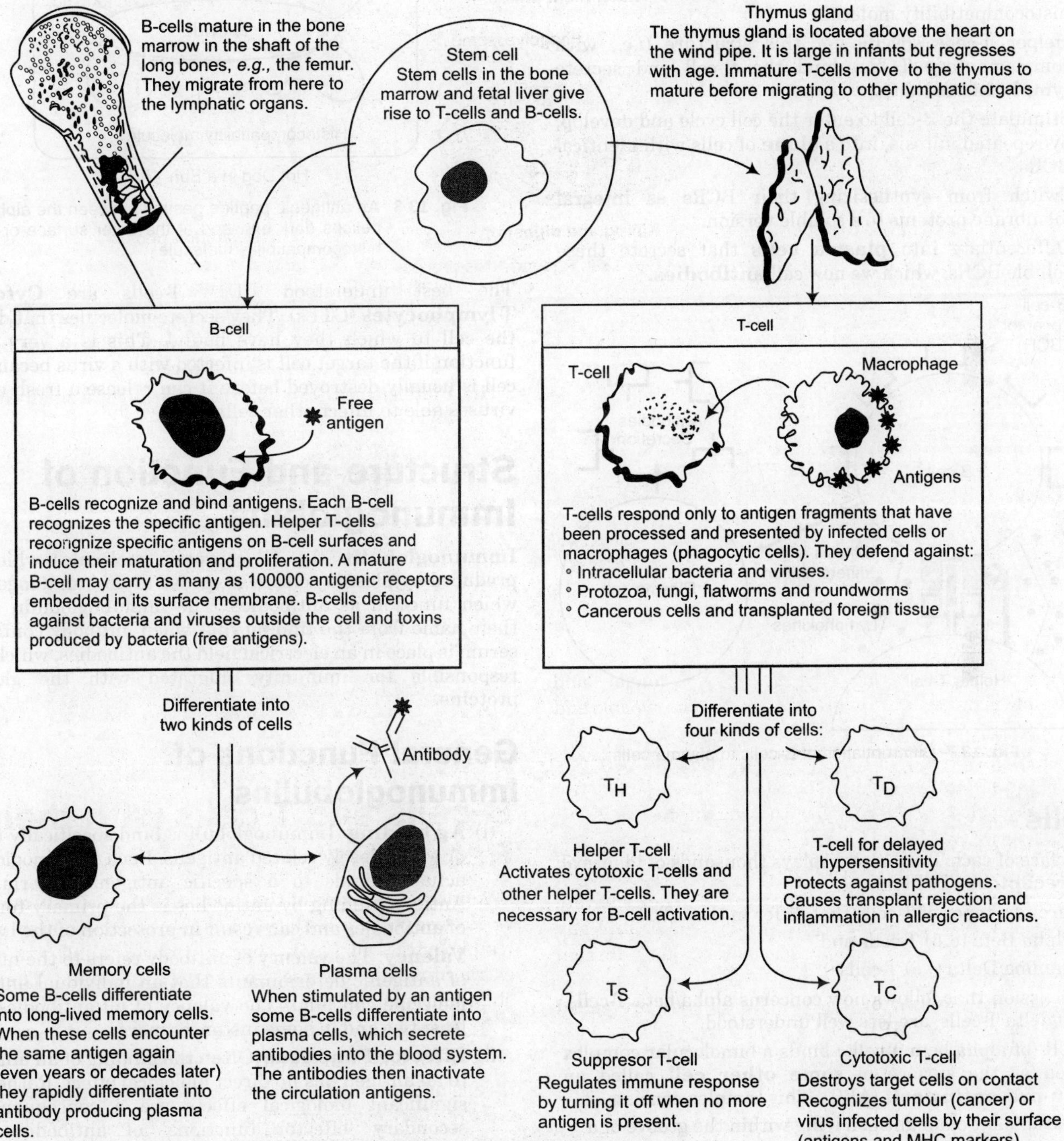

Fig. 13.6 Lymphocytes and their functions

B-Cells

(i) BCRs bind soluble antigens (like diphtheria toxoid, the protein introduced into your body in the DTP vaccine).

(ii) The bound antigen molecules are engulfed into the B-cell by receptor mediated endocytosis.

(iii) The antigen is digested into fragments which are then displayed at the cell surface nestled inside a class II histocompatibility molecule.

(iv) Helper T-cells specific for this structure (*i.e.,* with complementary TCRs) bind the B-cell and secrete **lymphokines** that:

(a) Stimulate the B-cell to enter the cell cycle and develop, by repeated mitosis, into a **clone** of cells with identical BCRs.

(b) Switch from synthesizing their BCRs as integral membrane proteins to a soluble version.

(c) Differentiate into **plasma cells** that secrete these soluble BCRs, which we now call **antibodies.**

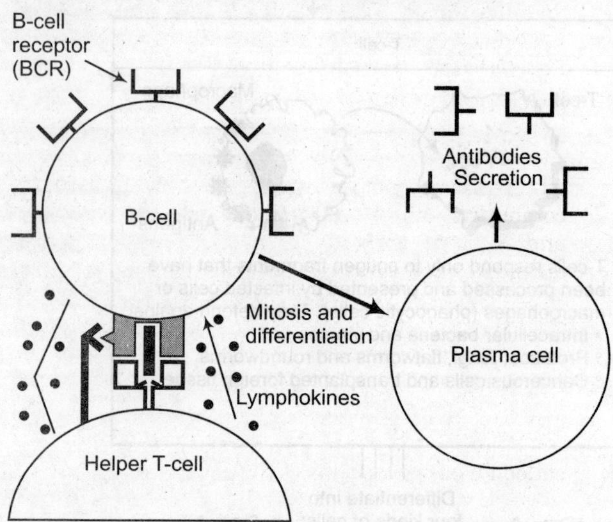

Fig. 13.7 Differentiation of B-cells to plasma cells

T-cells

The surface of each T-cell also displays thousands of identical **T-cell receptors** (TCRs).

There are two types of T-cells that differ in their TCR:

(i) Alpha/Beta (α β) T-cells and

(ii) Gamma/Delta (γ δ) T-cells.

The discussion that follows now concerns alpha/beta T-cells. Gamma/delta T-cells, are less well understood.

The TCR (of alpha/beta T-cells) binds a bimolecular complex displayed at the surface of **some other cell** called an **antigen-presenting cell** (APC). This complex consists of

(iii) A fragment of an antigen lying within the groove of a

(iv) Histocompatibility molecule.

The complex has been compared to a 'hot dog in a bun'. Most of the T-cells in the body belong to one of two subsets. These are distinguished by the presence on their surface of **one or the other** of two glycoproteins designated:

CD^4 binds epitopes of class II, histocompatibility molecules present on dendritic cells, B-cells and macrophages.

CD^8 bind epitopes of class I, histocompatibility molecules. Almost all the cells of the body express class I molecules.

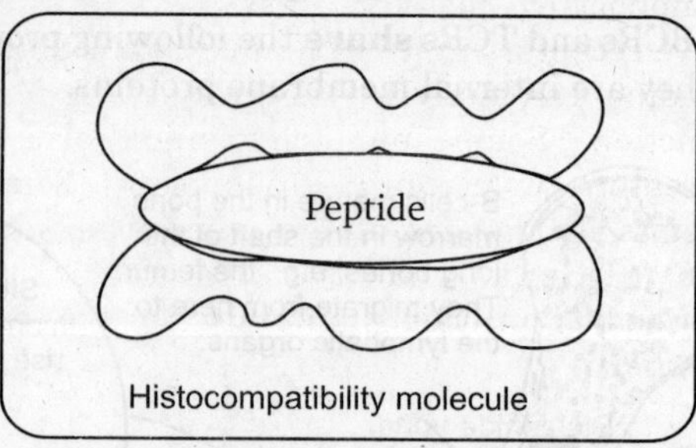

Fig. 13.8 An antigenic peptide nestled between the alpha helices dark exposed at the outer surface or a histocompatibility molecule

The best understood CD^{8+} T-cells are **Cytotoxic T-lymphocytes** (CTLs). They secrete molecules that destroy the cell to which they have bound. This is a very useful function if the target cell is infected with a virus because the cell is usually destroyed before it can release a fresh crop of viruses able to infect other cells.

Structure and Function of Immunoglobins

Immunoglobulin (Ig) Glycoprotein molecules which are produced by plasma cells in response to an immunogen and which function as antibodies. The immunoglobulin derive their name from the finding that when antibody containing serum is place in an electrical field the antibodies, which were responsible for immunity, migrated with the globular proteins.

General Functions of Immunoglobulins

(i) **Ag binding** Immunoglobulins bind specifically to one or a few closely related antigens. Each immunoglobulin actually binds to a specific antigenic determinant. Antigen binding by antibodies is the primary function of antibodies and can result in protection of the host.

Valency The valency of antibody refers to the number of antigenic determinants that an individual antibody molecule can bind. The valency of all antibodies is at least two and in some instances more.

(ii) **Effector Functions** Often the binding of an antibody to an antigen has no direct biological effect. Rather, the significant biological effects are a consequence of secondary 'effector functions' of antibodies. The immunoglobulins mediate a variety of these effector functions. Usually the ability to carry out a particular effector function requires that the antibody bind to its antigen. Not every immunoglobulin will mediate all effector functions.

(a) Fixation of complement—lysis of cells, release of biologically active molecules.

(b) Binding to various cell types—phagocytic cells, lymphocytes, platelets, mast cells, and basophils have receptors that bind immunoglobulins and the binding can activate the cells to perform some function. Some immunoglobulins also bind to receptors on placental trophoblasts. The binding results in transfer of the immunoglobulin across the placenta and the transferred maternal antibodies provide immunity to the fetus and newborn.

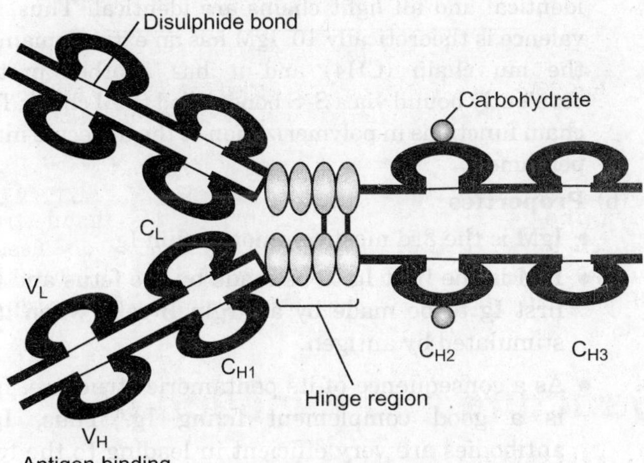

Fig. 13.9 Structure of immunoglobulin

HVR or CDRs

Comparisons of the amino acid sequences of the variable regions of Ig's show that most of the variability resides in three regions called the hypervariable (HVR) regions or the complementarity determining regions (CDRs) as illustrated in figure 3. Antibodies with different specificities (*i.e.,* different combining sites) have different CDRs, while antibodies of the exact same specificity have identical CDRs (*i.e.,* CDR —> Ab Combing site). CDRs are found in both the H and the L chains.

Framework Regions

The regions between the CDRs in the variable region are called the framework regions (FR). Based on similarities and differences in the framework regions the immunoglobulin heavy and light chain variable regions can be divided into groups and subgroups. These represent the products of different variable region genes.

The effector functions of immunoglobulins are mediated by this part of the molecule. Different functions are mediated by the different domains in this fragment. Normally the ability of an antibody to carry out an effector function requires the prior binding of an antigen. However, there are exceptions to this rule.

F(ab')2

Treatment of immunoglobulins with pepsin results in cleavage of the heavy chain after the H–H inter chain disulphide bonds resulting in a fragment that contains both antigen binding sites. This fragment was called F(ab')2 because it was divalent. The Fc region of the molecule is digested into small peptides by pepsin. The F(ab')2 binds antigen but it does not mediate the effector functions of antibodies.

Immunoglobulin Fragments Structure/Function Relationships

Immunoglobulin fragments produced by proteolytic digestion have proven very useful in elucidating structure/function relationships in immunoglobulins.

(i) **Fab** Digestion with papain breaks the immunoglobulin molecule in the hinge region before the H–H inter chain disulfide bond. This results in the formation of two identical fragments that contain the light chain and the V_H and C_{H1} domains of the heavy chain.

(ii) **Antigen binding** These fragments were called the Fab fragments because they contained the antigen binding sites of the antibody. Each Fab fragment is monovalent, whereas the original molecule was divalent. The combining site of the antibody is created by both V_H and V_L. An antibody is able to bind a particular antigenic determinant because it has a particular combination of V_H and V_L. Different combinations of a V_H and V_L result in antibodies that can bind a different antigenic determinants.

(iii) **Fc** Digestion with papain also produces a fragment that contains the remainder of the two heavy chains each containing a CH_2 and CH_3 domain. This fragment was called Fc because it was easily crystallized.

Types of Immunoglobulins

Immunoglobulins can also be classified by the type of light chain that they have. Light chain types are based on differences in the amino acid sequence in the constant region of the light chain. These differences are detected by serological means.

(i) Kappa light chains
(ii) Lambda light chains

Immunoglobulin Sub-types

The light chains can also be divided into subtypes based on differences in the amino acid sequences in the constant region of the light chain.

(a) Lambda sub-types

- Lambda 1
- Lambda 2
- Lambda 3
- Lambda 4

- **Nomenclature** Immunoglobulins are named based on the class, or subclass of the heavy chain and type or subtype of light chain. Unless it is stated precisely you are to assume that all subclass, types and subtypes are present. IgG means that all subclasses and types are present.

- **Heterogeneity** Immunoglobulins considered as a population of molecules are normally very heterogeneous because they are composed of different classes and subclasses each of which has different types and subtypes of light chains. In addition, different immunoglobulin molecules can have different antigen binding properties because of different V_H and V_L regions.

IG Classes and Sub-classes

The immunoglobulins can be divided into five different classes based on differences in the amino acid sequences in the constant region of the heavy chains. All immunoglobulins within a given class will have very similar heavy chain constant regions. These differences can be detected by sequence studies or more commonly by serological means (*i.e.*, by the use of antibodies directed to these differences).

(i) **IgG** Gamma heavy chains
(ii) **IgM** Mu heavy chains
(iii) **IgA** Alpha heavy chains
(iv) **IgD** Delta heavy chains
(v) **IgE** Epsilon heavy chains.

IgG

(a) Structure All IgGs are monomers (7S immunoglobulin). The subclasses differ in the number of disulphide bonds and length of the hinge region.

IgG sub-classes

(a) **IgG1** Gamma 1 heavy chains
(b) **IgG2** Gamma 2 heavy chains
(c) **IgG3** Gamma 3 heavy chains
(d) **IgG4** Gamma 4 heavy chains

(b) Properties Most versatile immunoglobulin because it is capable of carrying out all of the functions of immunoglobulin molecules.

- IgG is the major Ig in serum 75% of serum Ig is IgG.
- IgG is the major Ig in extra vascular spaces.
- Placental transfer IgG is the only class of Ig that crosses the placenta. Transfer is mediated by receptor on placental cells for the Fc region of IgG. Not all sub-classes cross equally, IgG2 does not cross well.
- **Fixes complement** Not all subclasses fix equally well, IgG4 does not fix complement.
- **Binding to cells** Macrophages, monocytes, PMN's and some lymphocytes have Fc receptors for the Fc region of IgG. Not all subclasses bind equally well. IgG2 and IgG4 do not bind to Fc receptors. A consequence of binding to the Fc receptors on PMN's, monocytes and macrophages is that the cell can now internalize the antigen better. The antibody has prepared the antigen for eating by the phagocytic cells. The term opsonin is used to describe substances that enhance phagocytosis. IgG is a good opsonin. Binding of IgG to Fc receptors on other types of cells results in the activation of other functions.

IgM

(a) **Structure** IgM normally exists as a pentamer (19S immunoglobulin) but it can also exist as a monomer. In the pentameric form all heavy chains are identical and all light chains are identical. Thus, the valence is theoretically 10. IgM has an extra domain on the mu chain (CH4) and it has another protein covalently bound via a S–S bond called the J chain. This chain functions in polymerization of the molecule into a pentamer.

(b) **Properties**

- IgM is the 3rd most common serum Ig.
- IgM is the first Ig to be made by the fetus and the first Ig to be made by a virgin B cells when it is stimulated by antigen.
- As a consequence of its pentameric structure, IgM is a good complement fixing Ig. Thus, IgM antibodies are very efficient in leading to the lysis of microorganisms.
- As a consequence of its structure, IgM is also a good agglutinating Ig. Thus, IgM antibodies are very good in clumping microorganisms for eventual elimination from the body.
- IgM binds to some cells via Fc receptors.
- B-cell surface Ig surface IgM exists as a monomer and lacks J-chain but it has an extra 20 amino acids at the C-terminal end to anchor it into the membrane. Cell surface IgM functions as a receptor for antigen on B-cells. Surface IgM is non-covalently associated with two additional proteins in the membrane of the B-cell called Ig-alpha and Ig–beta. These additional proteins act as signal transducing molecules since the cytoplasmic tail of the Ig molecule itself is too short to transduce a signal. Contact between surface immunoglobulin and an antigen is required before a signal can be transduced by the Ig-alpha and Ig-beta chains. In the case of T independent antigens, contact between the antigen and surface immunoglobulin is sufficient to activate B-cells to differentiate into antibody secreting plasma cells. However, for T dependent antigens, a second signal provided by helper T-cells is required before B-cells are activated.

IgA

(a) **Structure** Serum IgA is a monomer but IgA found in secretions is a dimer. When IgA exits as a dimer, a J chain is associated with it.

When IgA is found in secretions is also has another protein associated with it called the secretory piece or T piece, sIgA is sometimes referred to as 11S immunoglobulin. Unlike the remainder of the IgA which is made in the plasma cell, the secretory piece is made in epithelial cells and is added to the IgA as it passes into the secretions. The secretory piece helps IgA to be transported across mucosa and also protects it from degradation in the secretions.

These are two sub-classes

(a) IgA1 – Alpha 1 heavy chain

(b) IgA2 – Alpha 2 heavy chain.

(b) **Properties**

- IgA is the 2nd most common serum Ig.
- IgA is the major class of Ig in secretions tears, saliva, colostrum, mucus. Since it is found in secretions secretory IgA is important in local (mucosal) immunity.
- Normally IgA does not fix complement, unless aggregated.
- IgA can binding to some cells - PMN's and some lymphocytes.

IgD

(a) **Structure** IgD exists only as a monomer.

(b) **Properties**

- IgD is found in low levels in serum; its role in serum uncertain.
- IgD is primarily found on B-cell surfaces where it functions as a receptor for antigen. IgD on the surface of B-cells has extra amino acids at C terminal end for anchoring to the membrane. It also associates with the Ig alpha and Ig beta chains.

(c) IgD does not bind complement.

IgE

(a) **Structure** IgE exists as a monomer and has an extra domain in the constant region.

(b) **Properties**

- IgE is the least common serum Ig since it binds very tightly to Fc receptors on basophils and mast cells even before interacting with antigen.
- Involved in allergic reactions - As a consequence of its binding to basophils an mast cells, IgE is involved in allergic reactions. Binding of the allergen to the IgE on the cells results in the release of various pharmacological mediators that result in allergic symptoms.
- IgE also plays a role in parasitic helminth diseases. Since serum IgE levels rise in parasitic diseases, measuring IgE levels is helpful in diagnosing parasitic infections. Eosinophils have Fc receptors for IgE and binding of eosinophils to IgE coated helminths results in killing of the parasite.
- IgE does not fix complement.

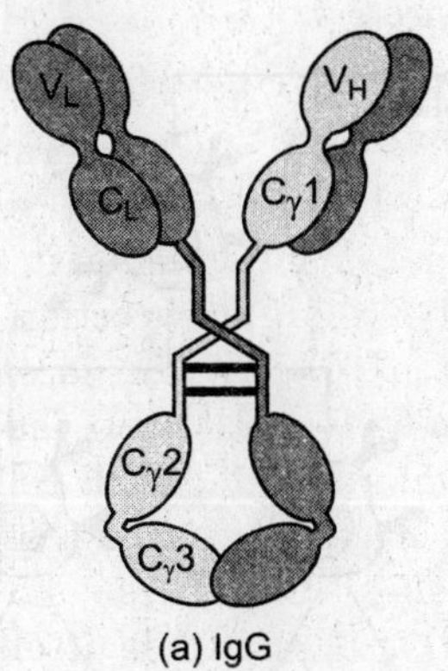

(a) IgG

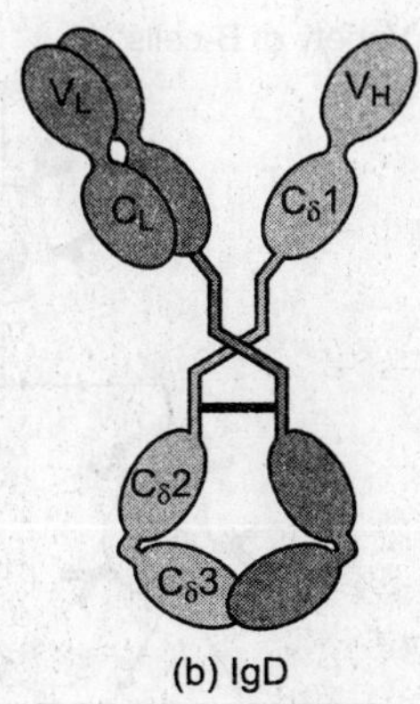

(b) IgD

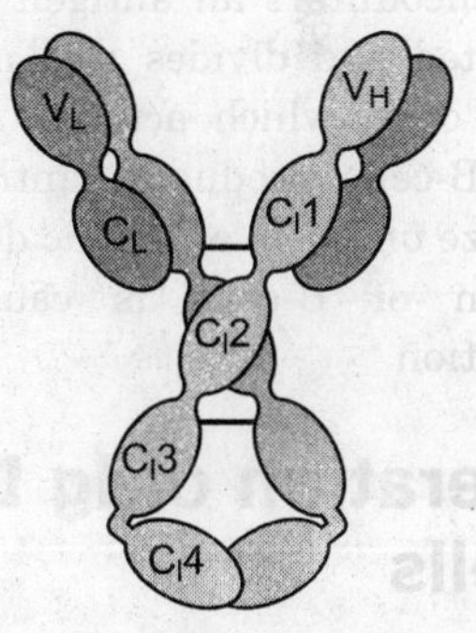

(c) IgE

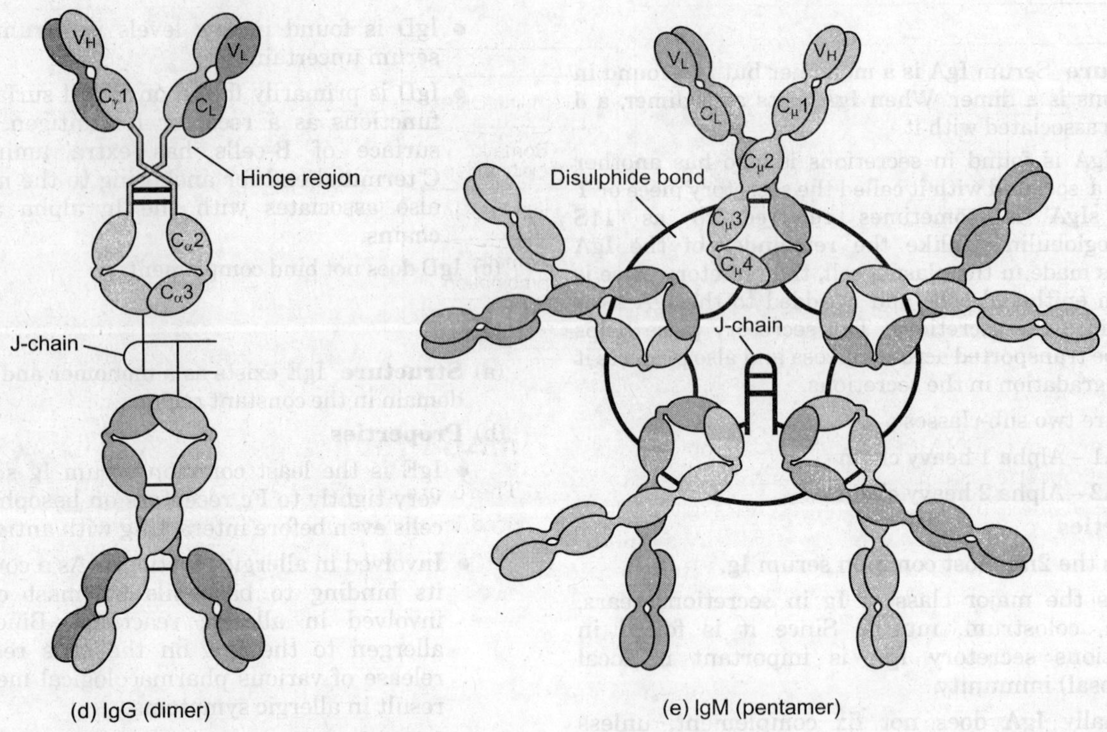

Fig. 13.10 Classes of immunoglobulins

B-Cells Produce Antibodies

B-cells develop from stem cells in the bone marrow of adults (liver of fetuses). After maturation B-cells migrate to lymphoid organs (lymph node or spleen). Clonal selection: When a B-cell encounters an antigen it recognizes, it is stimulated and divides into many clones called plasma cells, which actively secrete antibodies. Each B-cell produces antibodies that will recognize only one antigenic determinant. Clonal selection of B-cells is caused by antigenic stimulation.

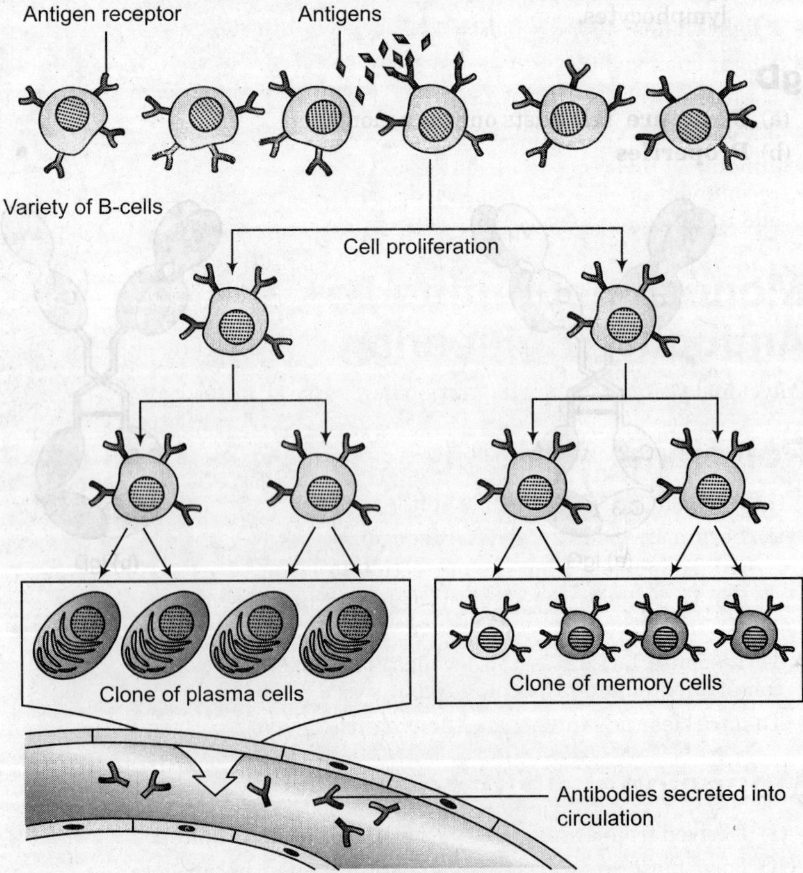

Fig. 13.11 Production of antibody by B-cells

Generation of Ig Diversity in B-cells

Before encounter with antigen (primary repertoire) the body can produce billions of different antibodies (although a single B-cell produces one specificity only) part of this diversity is produced by th various combinations of H and L-chain polypeptides no ready made genes in the germ line. Ig heavy and light chain loci consist of families of gene segments. Some of these segments are rearranged to somatically generate the immunoglobulin genes in B-lymphocytes (only) the rearrangement process generates the enormous diversity.

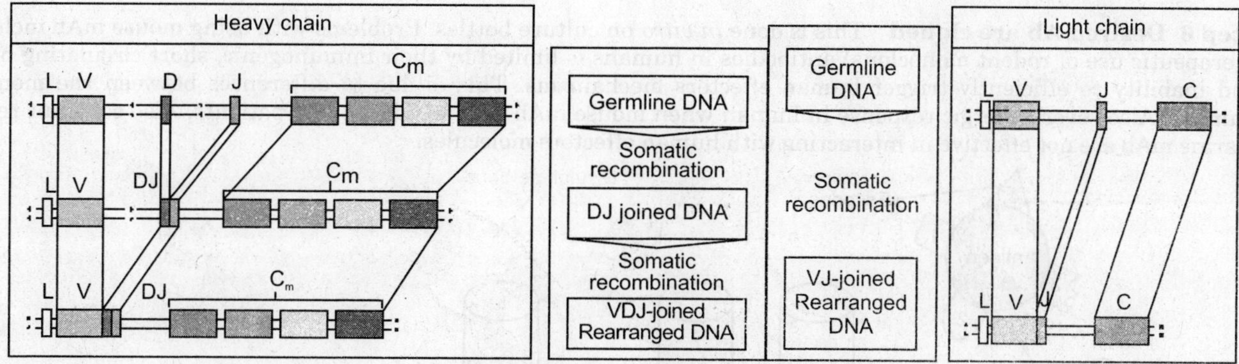

Fig. 13.12 Ig diversity by recombination

This unique process of DNA rearrangement happens (daily) when a hemopoetic stem cell differentiates into a B-lymphocyte. Unfortunately, the one gene segment that needs to be joined to the D or J segments is called V, similar to the V region of the H or L chain polypeptide. However, it encodes only part of the V polypeptide sequence. There are several copies of the V, D and J segments, respectively. Different B-cells choose different copies. This creates diversity in the antigen binding sites of antibodies generated by all B-cells, even though an individual B-cell produces only one kind of antibody.

Generation of antibody diversity:

- κ light chains: 40 Vκ × 5 Jκ = 200
- λ light chains: 30 Vλ × 4 Jλ = 120
- H-chains: 40 VH × 27 DH × 6JH = 6,480
- 320 L-chains × 6,480 H-chains = 2.1 × 106
- Junctional diversity (addition or deletion of nucleotides at recombination sites, especially of H-chain), estimated to add 3×107 fold to overall diversity.

Monoclonal Antibodies and Antibody Engineering

Polyclonal *versus* monoclonal antibodies

Polyclonal Antibody

(i) Antigens possess multiple epitopes.

(ii) Serum antibodies are heterogeneous.

- **(a)** To increase immune protection *in vivo*
- **(b)** To reduces the efficacy of antiserum for various *in vitro* uses

- To response facilitates the localization, phagocytosis, and complementediated lysis of antigen.
- To have clear advantages for the organism *in vivo*.

Monoclonal Antibody (mAb)

(i) Derived from a single clone, specific for a single epitope.

(ii) For most research, diagnostic, and therapeutic purposes.

mAb Production

There are currently two widely adopted methods used to produce monoclonal Ab. *In vivo* and *in vitro*, there are advantages and disadvantages for both methods.

The generation of mAb producing cells are typically done in mice. This method involves fusing a B-cell with a myeloma cell (tumour cell).

(a) **Step 1 Immunization of mice** Mice are immunized with an antigen (attached to adjuvant). The antigen can be whole cells, membrane fragment, or complex molecules. Mice serum's are screened using various techniques such as ELISA. When sufficient titer is reached the mice are euthanize and spleen is removed as a source of cells for cell fusion.

(b) **Step 2 Preparation of myeloma cells** Myeloma cells are immortalized cells that are capable of dividing indefinitely. These cells are treated with 8-azaguanine to ensure sensitivity to HAT.

(c) **Step 3 Fusion of myeloma cells with spleen cells** Spleen cells harvested from mice are fused with myeloma cells. Fission is done through co centrifuging in polyethylene glycol. Cells are plated in selection medium. Hypoxanthine–Aminopterin–Thymidine (HAT) selection medium inhibitor of aminopterin which blocks nucleotide synthesis. Only fused cells with grow on HAT. Cells are distributed on feeder cells (murine bone marrow) to promote growth of the hybridomal cells.

(d) **Step 4 Cloning of hybridoma cells** A mouse is inoculated with the cell and thereby becomes a factory for producing the mAb. Ascites are collected from the mouse.

(e) **Step 5 Ab are screened and purified** Ab are screened using specific Ag binding. Advantage of *in vivo* process include it being relatively inexpensive and easy while the disadvantage includes ethical concerns with using animals.

(f) **Step 6 Desired Ab are cloned** This is done *in vitro* on culture bottles. Problems with using mouse mAb include the therapeutic use of rodent monoclonal antibodies in humans is limited by their immunogenic, short circulating half life, and inability to efficiently trigger human effectors mechanisms. This is due to differences between the mouse and humans. Also severe allergic response in human when mouse mAb are introduced to a patients. Also constant region of marine mAb are not effective in interacting with human effectors molecules.

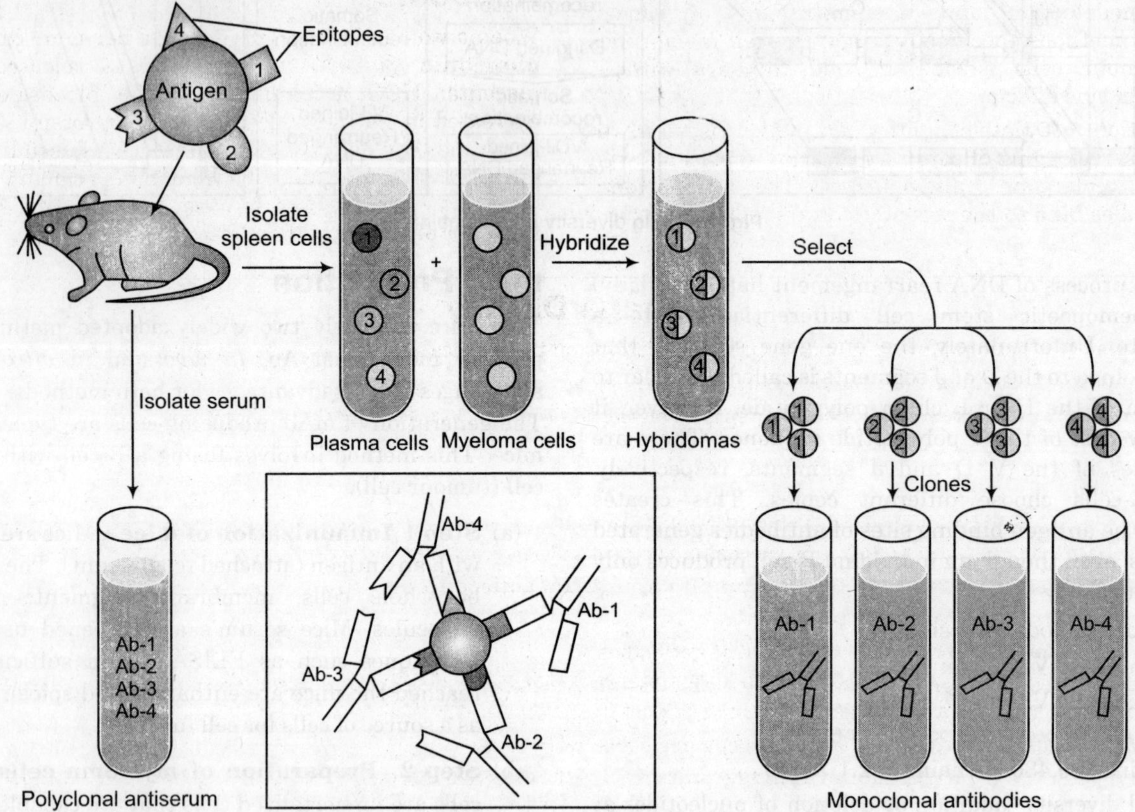

Fig. 13.13 The process of monoclonal antibody production

Chimeric mAb

mAb are genetically engineered using a molecular approach. Chimeric Ab are obtained by genetically fusing the mouse variable domains to human constant domains. Variable regions are isolated using Polymerase Chain Reaction (PCR). Issues with Chimeric mAb are that there are problems that can arise from using mouse human Ab. Sometimes the body may elicit an anti-chimeric Ab in the present of these genetically engineered Ab.

Human Monoclonal Antibodies

(i) There are numbers of technical difficulties; The lack of human myeloma cells to exhibit immortal growth, be susceptible to HAT selection, to not secrete antibody, and support antibody production in the hybridoma made with them, human B-cell sometimes have immortality. That is the difficulty of readily obtaining antigen activated B-cells.

(ii) To culture human B-cells *in vitro* to produce human monoclonal antibody Transplant human cells with immune response into SCID mice (lack a functional immune system).

(iii) To address this problem, the complementary regions (CDRs), which are the responsible for antigen binding within the variable regions, have been transferred to human frameworks creating 'CDR–grafted' or 'humanized' antibodies. This is, in essence a human Ab with small segments containing mouse Ab genes.

Application of Monoclonal Antibodies

Diagnostic Uses

(a) Detecting the presence of pathogens such as *Chlamydia* and *Streptococcus* bacteria, distinguishing between Herpesvirus I and II and diagnosing AIDS.

(b) Measuring protein, toxin or drug levels in serum.

(c) Blood and tissue typing.

(d) Detection of antibiotic residues in milk.

Therapeutic Uses

(a) Neutralizing endotoxins produced by bacteria in blood infections.

(b) Used to prevent organ rejection, *e.g.,* in kidney transplants, by interfering with the T-cells involves with the rejection of transplanted tissue.

(c) Used in the treatment of some auto-immune disorders such as rheumatoid arthritis and allergic asthma. The monoclonal antibodies bind to and inactivate factors involved in the cascade leading to the inflammatory response.

(d) Immunodetection and immunotherapy of cancer. Newer methods specifically target the cell membranes of tumour cells, shrinking solid tumours without harmful side effects.

(e) Inhibition of platelet clumping, which is used to prevent reclogging of coronary arteries in patients who have undergone angioplasty. The monoclonal antibodies bind to the receptors on the platelet surface that are normally linked by fibrinogen during the clotting process.

Detecting Pregnancy Using Monoclonal Antibodies

When a women becomes pregnant, a hormone called **human chorionic gonadotropin** (HCG) is released from the placenta. HCG accumulates in the bloodstream and is excreated in the urine. HCG is a glycoprotein, which means antibodies can be produced against it and used in simple test kits (below) to determine if a woman in pregnant. Monoclonal antibodies are also used in other home testing kits, such as those for detecting ovulation time (far left).

Phage Display

(i) The display of functional foreign peptides or small proteins on the surface of bacteriophage particles.
(ii) As an important tool in protein engineering.
(iii) As a powerful way to screen and select for peptides on the basis of binding or molecular recognition.

Advantages

(a) More efficiently than through conventional hybridoma system.
(b) Cheaper to produce recombinant antibodies using bacteria, rather than mammalian cell line.
(c) Easier to maintain and grow bacterial cultures for recombinant antibody production.
(d) Bypass immunization in antibody selection.
(e) Bypass the use of animal cells for production of antibodies.
(f) Producing the combinatorial library (ideally with 108 to 109 members) of functional antibodies to generate a larger repertoire of antibodies than those available through conventional hybridoma technology.
(g) Easy isolation and expression of the cloned gene in a bacterial host.
(h) Excellent potential to further improve binding properties of the selected antibody by protein engineering techniques.

Filamentous Phage

(a) Long, thin, and flexible particles that contain a closed circular single strained DNA molecule, such as fd, f1, and M13.
(b) The major coat protein is pVIII. The minor coat proteins pIII and pVI are located at one end of the phage, pVII and pIX are located at the other end of the phage.
(c) To infect Gram negative bacteria.
(d) To adsorb specifically to the tip of F pili on male cells.
(e) Be able to accommodate foreign DNA fragments.
(f) Its non-lysogenic characteristic to permits the extrusion of recombinant phage into the culture supernatant.

Filamentous Bacteriophage Vector

(a) To construct filamentous bacteriophage vectors enabled the 'biological' generation of the hundreds of millions of unique peptides.
(b) Be the double-stranded replicative form from a culture of inserted host cell.
(c) Be inserted an antibiotic resistance gene.
(d) Be introduced a pair of specifically situated endonuclease restriction sites to allow cloning of DNA insert into a position to express a foreign fusion protein with capsid protein.

Recombinant Monoclonal Antibodies

Recombinant antibody engineering involves the use of viruses or yeast to create antibodies, rather than mice. Phage display library construction of V_H and V_L gene libraries and expression of them on a filamentous bacteriophage. The phage expressing an antigen bonding domain specific for a particular antigen to screen the mAbs.

Transgenic Animals

Transgenic (genetically engineered) mouse to produce more human like antibodies (Abgenix,CA) Such mice have human antibody gene loci inserted into their bodies (using the embryonic stem cell method). Their own genes for making antibodies are 'knocked out'.

Clinical Uses of Monoclonal Antibodies

(i) Very useful as diagnostic, imaging and therapeutic reagents in clinical medicine

(a) Monoclonal antibodies were used primarily as *in vitro* diagnostic reagents.

(b) Radiolabelled monoclonal antibodies can also be used *in vivo* detecting or locating.

(ii) Immunotoxins

(a) To compose of tumour specific monoclonal antibodies coupled to lethal toxin.

(b) Valuable therapeutic reagent.

Antigen-Antibody Interactions

The antigen antibody interactions are characterized as non-covalent interaction (similar to 'lock and key' fit of enzyme substrate). It does not lead to irreversible alteration of Ag or Ab and this this exact and specific interaction has led to many immunological assays used to detect **Ag** or **Ab,** diagnose **disease,** measure magnitude of **humoral IR and** identify molecules of biological and medical interest.

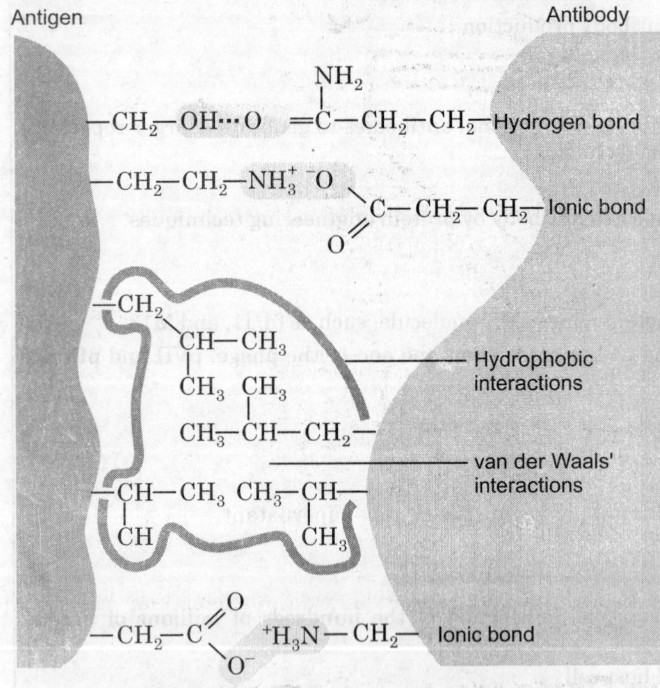

Fig. 13.14 Antigen-Antibody interaction

Ag-Ab interactions are major comprized of hydrogen bond, ionic bond, hydrophobic interactions and van der Waals' forces. Each bond is weak however when together they provide a strong linkage. To 'hold' they must be close thereby requiring high amts of complementarity.

Measuring affinity of Ab to Ag

Association between CDR and monovalent Ag can be expressed as :

$$Ag + Ab \underset{k_{-1}}{\overset{k1}{\rightleftharpoons}} Ag\text{–}Ab;$$

K1 = forward (association) rate constant
Whereby $K1/K-1 = K_a$

K − 1 = reverse (dissociation) rate constant
the association/equilibrium constant

K_a = [Ag-Ab] value of K_a depends on K1,
[Ag] [Ab] for small haptens, K1 is high
for large protein Ag's, K1 is lower

K_a is determined by equilibrium dialysis

Affinity The strength of binding between a single binding site and a single ligand [A][B] / [AB].

Avidity The strength of binding between a molecule and a complex ligand, *e.g.,* if there are multiple binding sites then the avidity may be increased by increasing the number of binding sites or by increasing the affinity of those binding sites.

IgM is produced early in an immune response when the affinity for antigen often is low, as an immune response continues, antibody affinity is improved, this is combined by 'class switching' to the use of smaller molecules (IgG, IgE and IgA). The increased affinity compensates for the decrease in number of binding sites in maintaining the overall avidity for antigen.

Major Histocompatibility Complex (MHC)

MHC complex is group of genes on a single chromosome that codes the MHC antigens. Major as well as minor histocompatibility antigens (also called transplantation antigens) mediate rejection of grafts between two genetically different individuals. However, the role played by the major histocompatibility antigens supersedes the minor histocompatibility antigens. HLA (human leukocyte antigens) are the MHC antigens of humans, and called so, because they were first detected on leukocytes. H-2 antigens are their equivalent MHC antigens of mouse. A set of MHC alleles present on each chromosome is called an MHC haplotype. Monozygotic human twins have the same histocompatibility molecules on their cells, and they can accept transplants of tissue from each other. Histocompatibility molecules of one individual act as antigens when introduced into a different individual. George Snell, Jean Dausset and Baruj Benacerraf received the Nobel Prize in 1980 for their contributions to the discovery and understanding of the MHC in mice and humans MHC gene products were identified as responsible for graft rejection. MHC gene products that control immune responses are called the immune response (Ir) genes. Immune response genes influence responses to infections. The essential role of the HLA antigens lies in the induction and regulation of the immune response and defense against microorganisms. The physiologic function of MHC molecules is the presentation of peptide antigen to T-lymphocytes. These antigens and their genes can be divided into three major classes, class I, class II and class III.

Class I MHC Molecule

Class I MHC molecules contain two separate polypeptide chains, the heavier (44-47 KDa) alpha chain and the lighter (12 KDa) beta chain. The polymorphism among class I MHC gene products creates variation in the chemical surface of the peptide–binding groove so, that various peptide molecules can be accommodated. The specific binding of a peptide molecule in the peptide binding groove of MHC requires the peptide to have one or more specific amino acid at a fixed position. Such sites are termed anchor sites. The other amino acids can be variable so, that each MHC molecule can bind many different peptides.The $\alpha1$ and $\alpha2$ domains also bind T-cell receptor (TCR) of CD^8 T-lymphocytes. CD^8 molecules present on CD^8 T-lymphocytes binds to this region.

Class II MHC Molecule

Class II MHC molecules comprise two non identical and non-covalently associated polypeptide chains (α and β). These two chains have amino ends on the surface, a short transmembrane stretch and intracytoplasmic carboxyl ends. Both α chain (34 kDa) and β chain (28 kDa) are MHC encoded and polymorphic. During antigen presentation, CD^4 molecule of helper T lymphocyte binds to $\beta2$ domain of the class II MHC molecules.Exogenous antigens (fragments of bacterial cells or viruses that are engulfed and processed by antigen presenting cell) are presented to helper T-cells along with MHC II molecules.

HLA Typing

Because some HLA antigens are recognized on almost all of the tissues of the body (with few exceptions), the identification of HLA antigens is also described as 'Tissue Typing'. HLA matching between donor and recipient is desirable for allogenic transplantation. Class I typing methods include test such as microcytoxicity (for typing A, B, C loci) and cellular techniques such as CML (for HLA-DPw typing). Class II typing involves cellular techniques such as MLR/MLC (for DR typing) and molecular techniques such as PCR and direct sequencing (for DR, DQ typing).

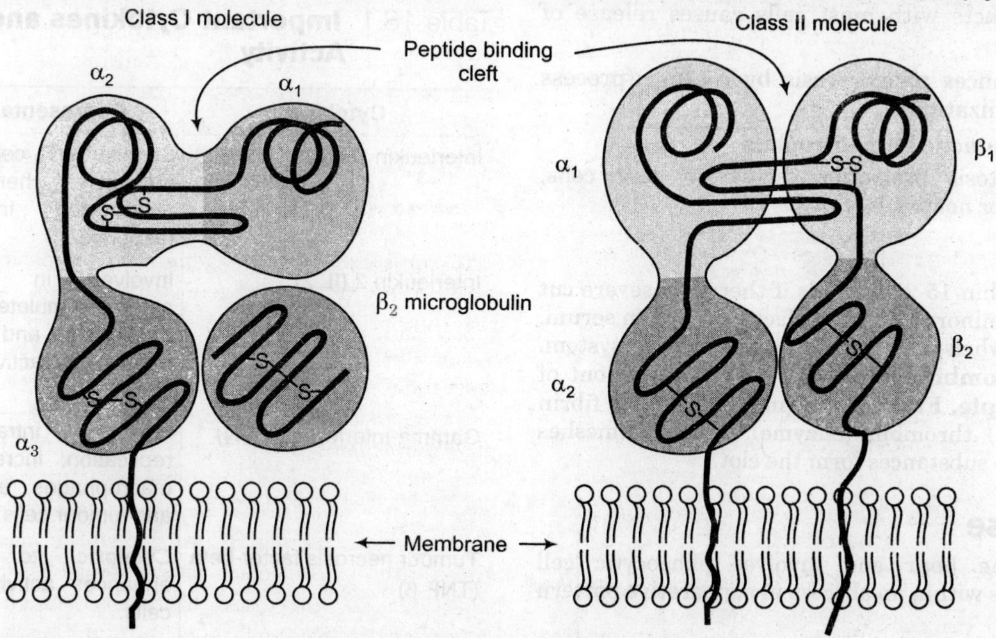

Fig. 13.15 Major histocompatibility molecule I and II

Inflammation

Inflammation is a non-specific host defense mechanism designed to mobilize components to the site of injury, destroy microbes, and set repair processes into motion.

Four Cardinal Signs of Inflammation

(i) **Rubor** Redness or erythema
(ii) **Dolar** Pain
(iii) **Calor** Heat
(iv) **Halor** swelling, can be fluid (oedema) or cellular (tumour).

Five Patterns of Inflammation

(i) **Serous** Water blister and mild burns
(ii) **Fibrinous** Scar tissue formation
(iii) **Pseudomembrane** New membrane formed over the old.
(iv) **Suppurative** Pus formation, dead neutrophils and target bacteria within an abscess.
(v) **Ulcer** Crater from inflammed tissue.

Three Phases of Inflammatory Response

Fluid Phase (Chemical Mediators)

(a) **Bradykinin** produced in kidney, causes pain and vasodilation (found in bee venom).

(b) **Histamine** releazed by mast cells causes vasodilation and smooth muscle contraction (problem–asthma).

(c) **Prostaglandin**-lipid releazed by somatic (body) and mast cells, causes vasodilation.

(d) **Heparin** by mast cells, anticoagulant.

(e) **Leukotrienes** by leukocytes, squeezing effect on capillaries + (bronchial constriction).

(f) **Seratonin** releazed by platelets causes vasodilation.

(g) **Histamine** releazed by basophils (vasodilation).

(h) **Complement** consists of 20 serum proteins that bind to antibody in an ordered sequence or cascade.

- **C3a** Interacts with mast cells causes release of histamine.
- **C3b** Enhances phagocytosis by coating (process called opsonization).
- **C5a** Chemotactic for neutrophils.

(i) LPF leukocytosis promotion factor by mast cells, chemotactic for neutrophils.

Haemostasis

Clotting begins within 15-20 seconds if there is a severe cut and 1-2 minutes if minor. 12 clotting factors found in serum. It gets activated when they leave the circulatory system. **Example, Prothrombin** (in blood) $\longrightarrow$ thrombin (out of circulation). **Example, Fibrinogen** (in blood) $\longrightarrow$ fibrin (out of circulation) thrombin (enzyme). Fibrin enmeshes platelets.These two substances form the clot.

Cellular Phase

Occurs within one hour and involves phagocytic cell infiltration. Occurs within an abscess in supparative pattern of inflammation.

(a) Low pH kills microbes.

(b) Macrophages attack escaping microbes.

(c) Body temperature increases due to macrophage signaling the hypothalamus with lymphokine (a chemical secreted by white blood cells that regulates the immune response) called IL-1 (interleukin I). **Note: Specific immunity begins here.**

Healing Phase

Fibroblast cells produce beta interferon.

(a) Lymphokine secreted by cells of the body that regulates the immune response). This chemical signals the immune system to stop.

(b) Fibroblasts proliferate and produce collagen fibres.

(c) Macrophage also produce collagen.

(d) Intact connective tissue reforms.

Cytokines

Cytokines are chemicals secreted by cells of the body that regulate the immune response. 'Chemical messengers' cytokines produced by leukocytes are lymphokines.

Table 13.1 **Important Cytokines and their Activity**

Cytokine	Representative Activity
Interleukin 1 (IL 1)	Stimulates T_H cells in presence of antigens; chemically attracts phagocytes in inflammatory response.
Interleukin 2 (IL 2)	Involved in proliferation of antigen-stimulated T_H cells, proliferation and differentiation of B-cells and activation of T_C cells and N_K cells.
Gamma-interferon (γ-IFN)	Inhibits intracellular viral replication; increases activity of macrophages against microbes and tumour cells.
Tumour necrosis factor-beta (TNF-β)	Cytotoxic to tumour cells; enhances activity of phagocytic cells.
Granulocyte-macrophage colony-stimulating factor(GM-CSF)	Stimulates the formation of red and white blood cells from stem cells.

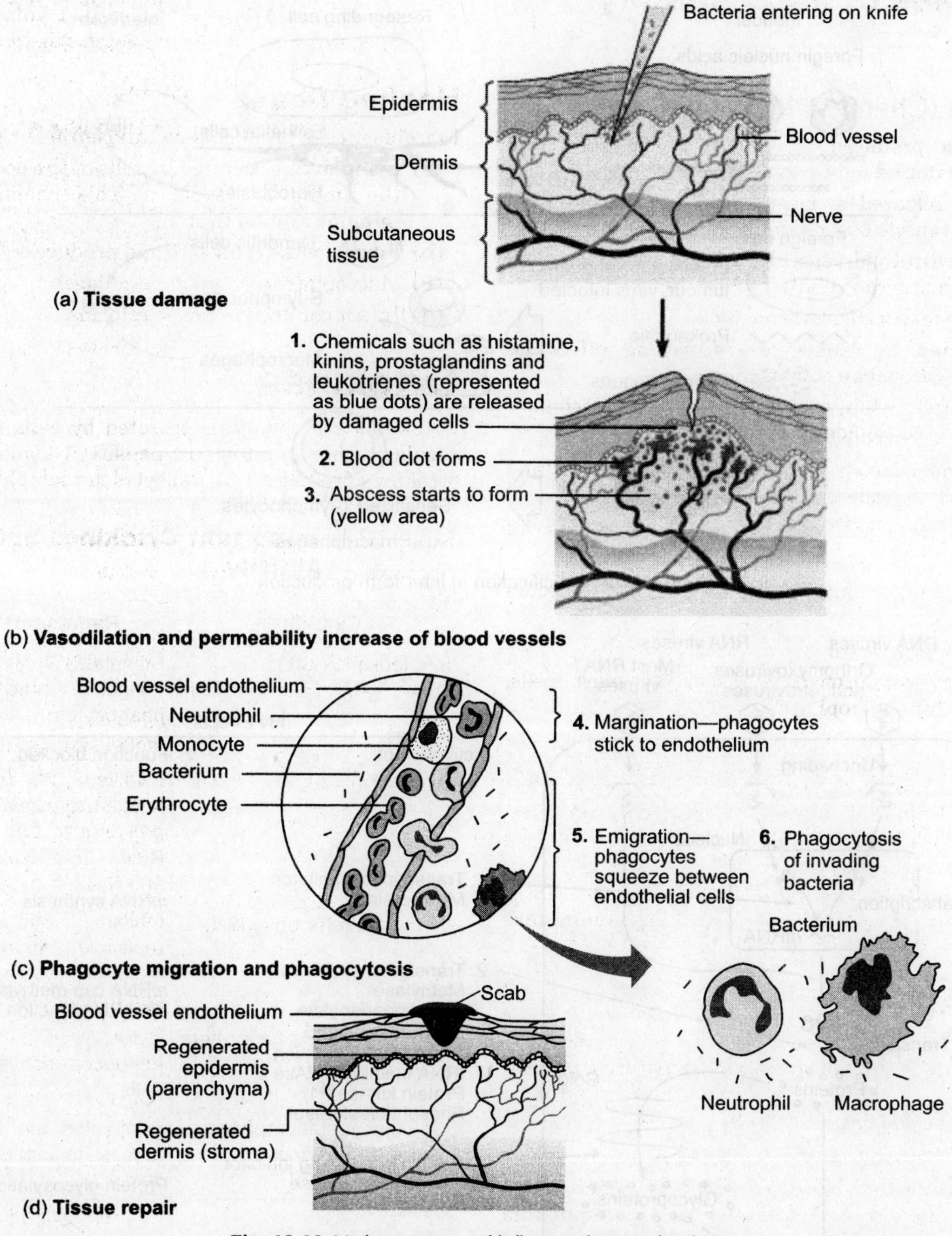

Bacteria entering on knife
Epidermis
Dermis
Subcutaneous tissue
Blood vessel
Nerve
(a) Tissue damage
1. Chemicals such as histamine, kinins, prostaglandins and leukotrienes (represented as blue dots) are released by damaged cells
2. Blood clot forms
3. Abscess starts to form (yellow area)
(b) Vasodilation and permeability increase of blood vessels
Blood vessel endothelium
Neutrophil
Monocyte
Bacterium
Erythrocyte
4. Margination—phagocytes stick to endothelium
5. Emigration—phagocytes squeeze between endothelial cells
6. Phagocytosis of invading bacteria
Bacterium
Neutrophil
Macrophage
(c) Phagocyte migration and phagocytosis
Scab
Blood vessel endothelium
Regenerated epidermis (parenchyma)
Regenerated dermis (stroma)
(d) Tissue repair

Fig. 13.16 Various stages of inflammation mechanism

Interferon (IFN)

(i) **Beta interferon** Produced by fibroblasts. Activates T-suppressor (TS) cells to end the inflammatory response.

(ii) **Alpha interferon** Viruses trigger neighbouring cells to produce antiviral proteins. Used to treat symptoms of varian cancer, multiple sclerosis, Kaposi's Sarcoma and HCV.

(iii) **Gamma interferon** Produced by T-helper cells (TH1) in response to viruses. Gamma-IFN activates macrophages (MP) and Natural Killer (NK) cells for specific immunity.

Interferon
Signal
Transduction
Activation of gene
mRNA
Translation Inhibitory Protein (TIP)
Translation of gene
Ribosome
Viral RNA

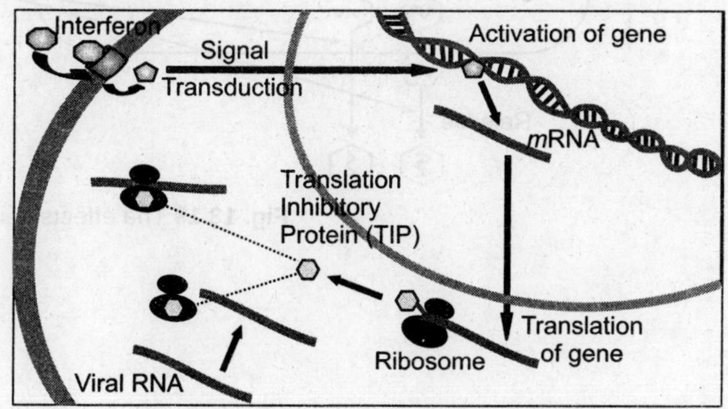

Fig. 13.17 Antiviral action of interferon

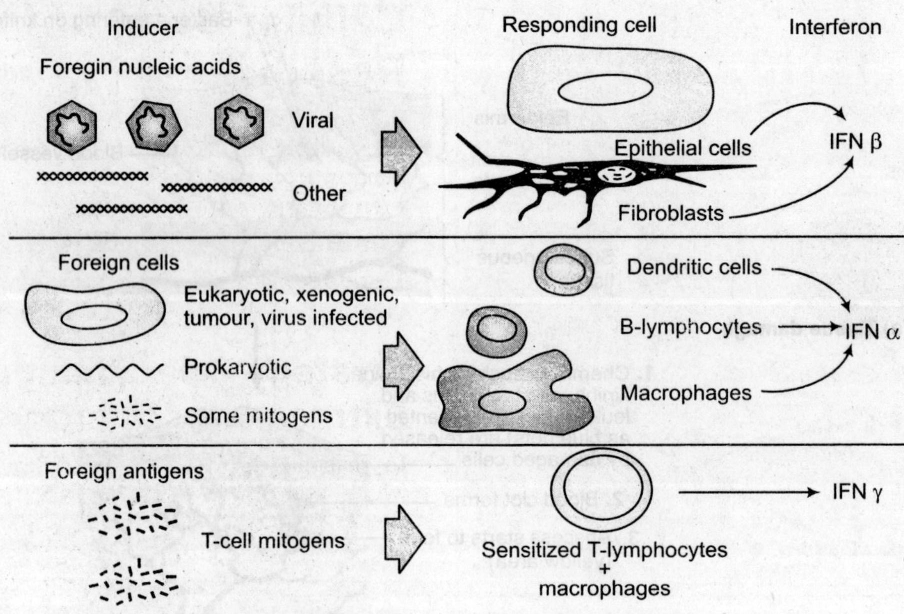

Fig. 13.18 Specification in inter form production

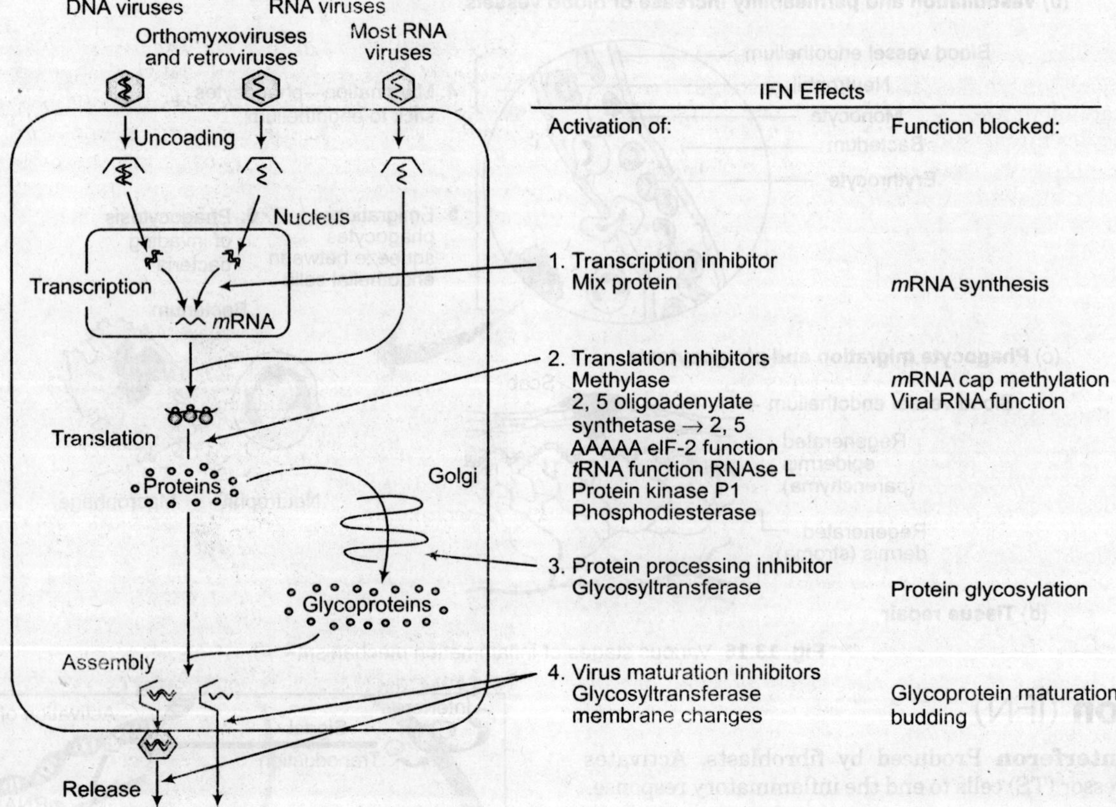

Fig. 13.19 The effects of interferon during viral multiplication

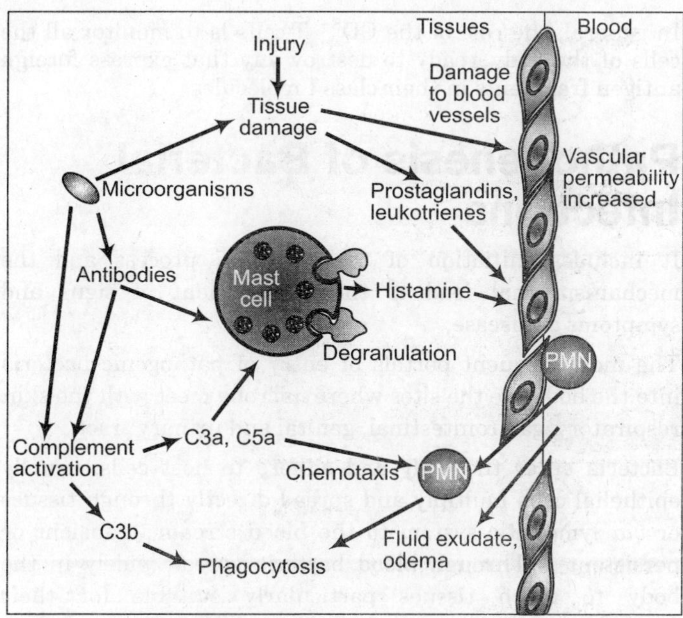

Fig. 13.20 Stimulation of inflammation

Inflammation involves

(a) Opening up of junctions between endothelial cells in post capillary venule to allow plasma proteins to escape.

(b) Adhesion of leukocytes to endothelial cells of post-capillary venule, followed by emigration of phagocytes into tissues.

Inflammation is localized to area of infection/tissue injury by release of substances from microorganisms or chemicals (chemical mediators) releazed from cells in tissues, *e.g.,* histamine from **Mast cells.** Once organisms destroyed inflammation settles down (resolves).

Cell-Cell Interaction

Antigen Processing

When the macrophage eats bacteria, proteins (antigens) from the bacteria are broken down into short peptide chains and those peptides are then 'displayed' on the macrophage surface attached to special molecules called MHC II (for major histocompatibility complex class II). Bacterial peptides are similarly processed and displayed on MHC II molecules on the surface of B lymphocytes.

Helper T-Cell Stimulating B-Cell

When a T-lymphocyte 'sees' the same peptide on the macrophage and on the B-cell, the T-cell stimulates the B-cell to turn on antibody production.

Antibody Production

The stimulated B-cell undergoes repeated cell divisions, enlargement and differentiation to form a clone of antibody secreting plasma cells. Hence, through specific antigen recognition of the invader, clonal expansion and B-c ll differentiation you acquire an effective number of plasma cells all secreting the same needed antibody. That antibody then binds to the bacteria making them easier to ingest by white cells. Antibody combined with a plasma component called 'complement' may also kill the bacteria directly.

Cellular Basis of Immune Response

Key cells are lymphocytes, which have capacity to recognise microorganisms. There are two types which develop in bone marrow from a common precursor.

(i) **T-cells** mature in thymus.

(ii) **B-cells** mature in bone marrow.

These two types of lymphocyte are used in three ways to fight infection.

Strategy One: Elimination of Extracellular Microorganisms

In response to infection B-cells mature into plasma cells which secrete soluble recognition molecules (antibodies). B-cells recognise microbes because they express membrane bound antibody which acts as an antigen receptor.

At time of first infection there is no antibody in blood and level does not begin to increase until between 7-10 days afterwards. The level of antibody rises slowly to a low peak and then gradually declines towards baseline **primary response.**

On subsequent exposure to same microorganisms the level of antibody begins to increase within 24 hours and reaches a high level which is sustained **secondary response.**

Antibody recognises structures on surface of bacteria (proteins/ carbohydrates/lipids). When we have an infection we produce antibodies which recognise many different types of structure on bacterial surface. Thus, serum from an immune individual contains many different types of antibodies each of which recognise different structures on surface of membrane. Each of these structures is called an **epitope** (or antigenic determinant).

Antibody is soluble and diffuses through tissues to target extracellular microorganisms. Binding of antibody to microorganisms activate two **effector** mechanisms to eliminate microorganisms.

- Activation of complement system – bacterial lysis/ opsonization.
- Phagocytosis by neutrophils and macrophages with intracellular killing.

Strategy Two : Elimination of Intracellular Microorganisms

(i) Even when antibody and complement opsonise certain bacteria and phagocytosis occurs, they are not killed but survive and multiply in macrophages, *e.g., Mycobacterium tuberculosis*. Elimination occurs by use of a sub-population of cells called **Helper T-cells.** These cells recognise macrophages containing intracellular bacteria by means of T-cells antigen receptor, which is not an antibody. They help macrophages to kill bacteria by synthesising soluble molecules (cytokins) which stimulate bacterial killing mechanisms of macrophages.

Strategy Three : Elimination of Microorganisms Infecting non-immune Cells

Viruses are obligate intracellular pathogens, can infect any type of cells and most cells do not possess antimicrobial mechanisms. During intracellular replication virus proteins appear on the surface of the infected cell. A second subset of T-cells cytotoxic T-cells recognises these viruses (foreign) antigens and secretes cytotoxic molecules which kill the infected cells.

An example will show the beauty and biological efficiency of this mechanism.

Every time you get a virus infection, say influenza (flu), the virus invades certain cells of your body (in this case cells of the respiratory passages). Once inside, the virus subverts the metabolism of the cell to make more virus. This involves synthesizing a number of different macromolecules encoded by the viral genome.

In due course, these are assembled into a fresh crop of virus particles that leave the cell (often killing it in the process) and spread to new target cells.

Except while in transit from their old homes to their new, the viruses work inside of your cells safe from any antibodies that might be present in blood, lymph, and secretions.

But early in the process, infected cells display fragments of the viral proteins in their surface class I molecules. CTLs specific for that antigen will be able to bind to the infected cell and often will be able to destroy it before it can release a fresh crop of viruses.

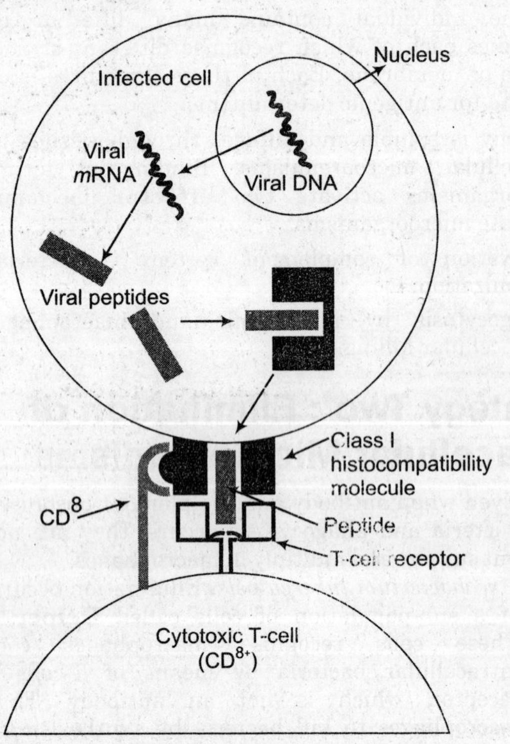

Fig. 13.21 Role of cytotoxic T-cell

In general, the role of the CD^{8+} T-cells is to monitor all the cells of the body, ready to destroy any that express foreign antigen fragments in their class I molecules.

Pathogenesis of Bacterial Infections

It includes initiation of the infection process and the mechanism that lead to the development of signs and symptoms of disease.

The most frequent portals of entry of pathogenic bacteria into the body are the sites where microbe meet with the skin respiratory, gastrointestinal, genital and urinary tract.

Bacteria enter the body and adhere to host cells, usually epithelial cells multiply and spread directly through tissues or *via* lymphatic system to the blood stream (transient or persistent). Through blood bacteria spread widely in the body to reach tissues particularly suitable for their multiplication.

Bacterial Virulance Factors

(a) Adherence factors

(b) Invasion of host cells and tissues – Enzyme production, capsule.

(c) Toxin production – Exotoxins, endotoxins, enteroxins.

(d) Intracellular pathogenicity.

The Complement System

The complement system plays an essential role in host defence against infectious agents and in the inflammatory process. It consists of about twenty plasma proteins that function either as enzymes or as binding proteins. In addition to these plasma proteins, the complement system includes multiple distinct cell surface receptors that exhibit specificity for the physiological fragments of complement proteins and that occur on inflammatory cells and cells of the immune system. There are also several regulatory membrane proteins that function to prevent autologous complement activation and protect host cells from accidental complement attack (1).

The role of complement in host defence has been established through genetic deficiencies of certain complement components, which may result in life threatening recurrent bacterial infections or immune complex diseases.

The role of complement in inflammation and tissue injury has become apparent through clinical investigations and discoveries that the pathogenesis of certain experimental inflammatory diseases is complement dependent.

The complement system can be activated by two different pathways, the **classical** complement pathway and the **alternative** complement pathway.

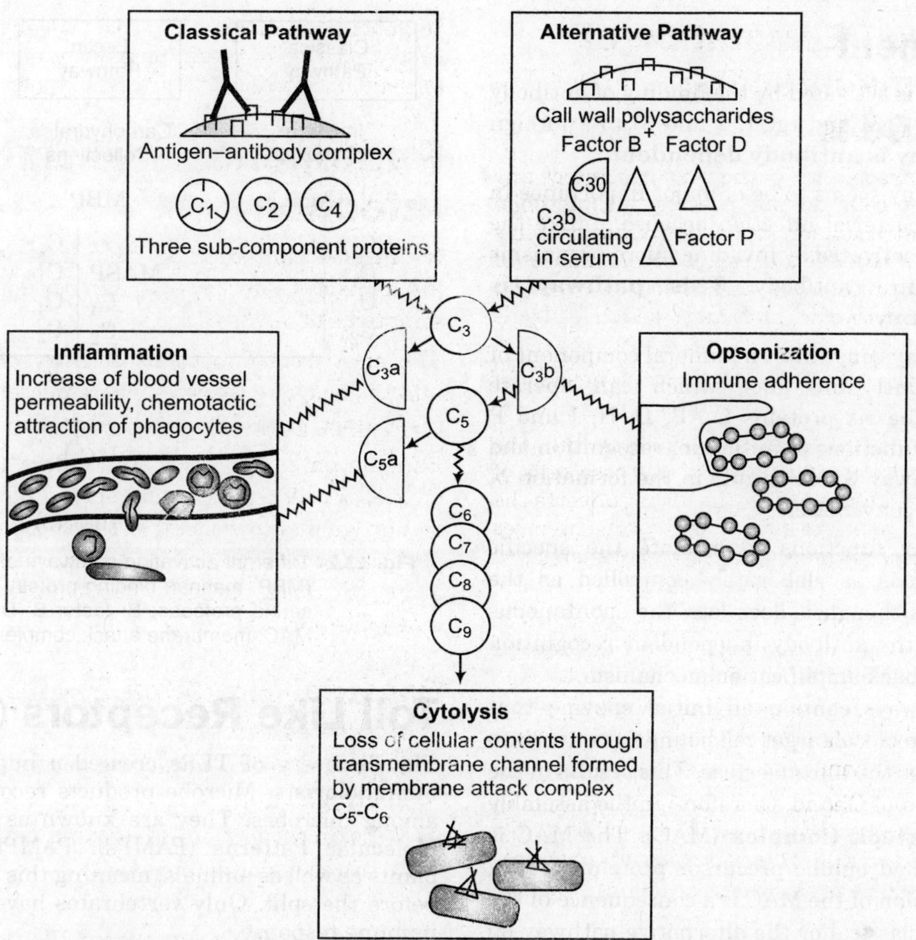

Fig. 13.22 Complement activation via classical and alternative pathway. Cleavage of C_3 into C_3a and C_3b fragments induce three kinds of consequences distructive to microbes

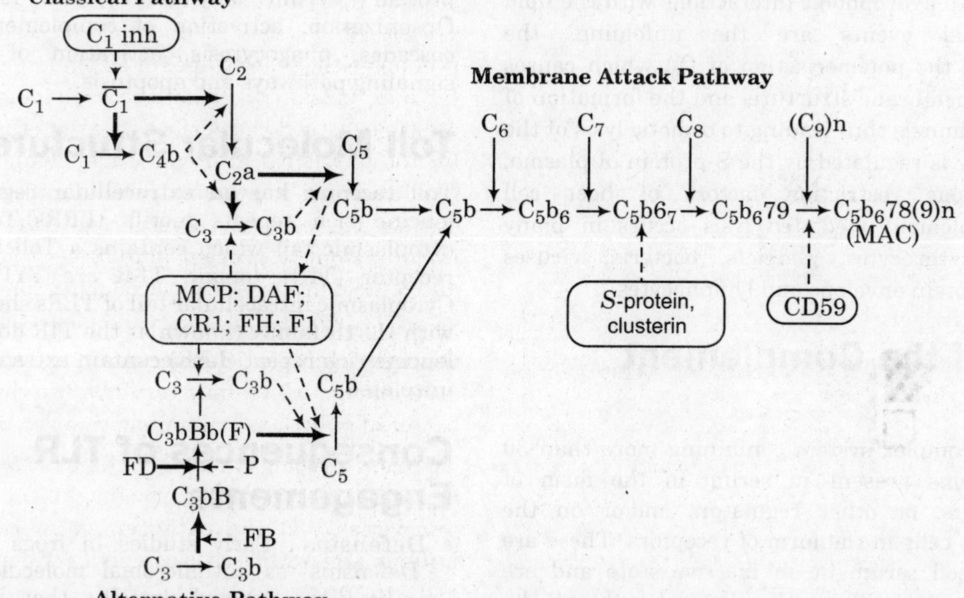

Fig. 13.23 The complement pathway and its regulation. Enzymatic steps are represented by heavy arrows. Regulatory proteins are boxed membrane regulators in plain text, fluid phase regulators in italics. Abbreviations: C1 inh, C1 esteraser inhibitor, MCP, membrane cofactor protein, DAF, decay accelerating factor, CR1, complement receptor 1, FH, factor H, FB, factor B, FD, factor D, P, properdin, MAC, membrane attack complex.

The Complement

The classical pathway is activated by the binding of antibody molecules (specifically IgM and IgG1, 2 and 3) to a foreign particle. **This pathway is antibody dependent.**

The alternative pathway seems to be of major importance in host defence against bacterial infection because, unlike the classical pathway, it is activated by invading micro-organisms and does not require antibody. **This pathway is antibody-independent.**

The alternative pathway constitutes a humoral component of natural defence against infections, which can operate without antibodies. The six proteins C_3, B, D, H, I and P together perform the functions of initiation, recognition and activation of this pathway which results in the formation of activator bound C_3/C_5 convertase.

The classical pathway functions to mediate the specific antibody response. It is as elaborately controlled as the alternative pathway, although it does lack the spontaneous initiation ability, *i.e.*, the antibody independent recognition function, and the feedback amplification mechanism.

Both activation pathways contain an initial enzyme that catalyses the formation of the target cell bound C_3 convertase which in turn generates the C_5 convertase. This results in the cleavage and activation of C_5 and, therefore, in the assembly of the **Membrane Attack Complex** (MAC). The MAC is assembled from five hydrophilic precursor proteins C_5, C_6, C_7, C_8, and C_9. Activation of the MAC is a consequence of the activity of either the classical or the alternative pathway on the surface of a cell. Through its metastable membrane binding site, the forming MAC binds firmly to target membranes owing to hydrophobic interactions with the lipid bilayer. The final events are the unfolding, the oligomerisation, or the polymerisation of C_9, which causes the weakening of membrane structure, and the formation of transmembrane channels thus leading to osmotic lysis of the cell. MAC assembly is regulated by the S-protein of plasma, and by homologous restriction factors of host cell membranes. Complement mediated lysis occurs in many kinds of cells erythrocytes, platelets, bacteria, viruses possessing a lipoprotein envelope and lymphocytes.

Products of the Complement System

Complement is a complex system containing more than 30 various glycoproteins present in serum in the form of components, factors, or other regulators and/or on the surface of different cells in the form of receptors. These are present in the blood serum in an inactive state and are activated by immune complexes (the classical pathway), by carbohydrates (the lectin pathway), or by other substances, mainly of bacterial origin (the alternative pathway).

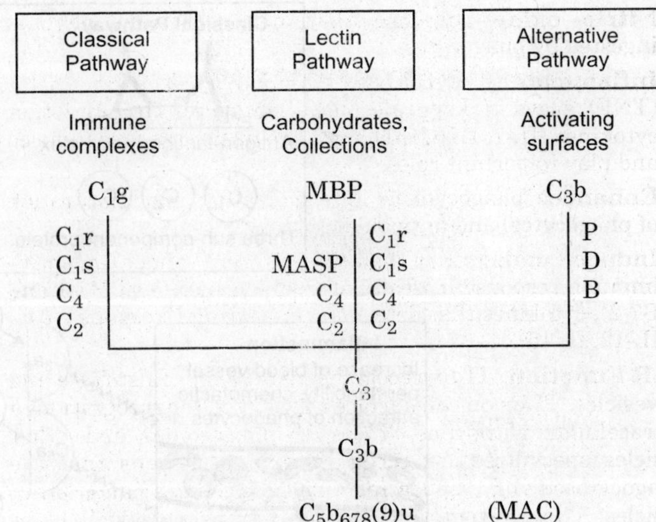

Fig. 13.24 Different activation pathways of the complement system (MBP: mannan binding protein, MASP: MBP associated serine protease; B: factor B; D: factor D; P: properdin; MAC: membrane attack complex)

Toll Like Receptors (TLRs)

The discovery of TLRs created a huge excitement among immunologists. Microbe products recognized are conserved among microbes. They are known as Pathogen Associated Molecular Patterns (PAMPs). PAMPs are recognized by plants as well as animals, meaning this innate response arose before the split. Only vertebrates have evolved an adaptive immune response.

Pattern Recognition Receptors (PRRs) They include Toll like receptors, mannose binding lectin (MBL), C reactive protein, Serum amyloid P. The functions of PRRs. Opsonization, activation of complement and coagulation cascades, phagocytosis, activation of pro inflammatory signaling pathways and apoptosis.

Toll Molecular Structure

Toll receptor has an extracellular region which contains leucine rich repeats motifs (LRRs).Toll receptor has a cytoplasmic tail which contains a Toll interleukin–1 (IL-1) receptor (TIR) domain TLR are TYPE 1 glycoproteins. Cytoplasmic intracellular tail of TLRs shows a high homology with IL–1R family (known as the TIR domain), although the leucine rich repeat (LRR) contain extra cellular domains are unrelated.

Consequences of TLR Engagements

- **Defensins** Early studies in frogs and flies identified 'Defensins' as antimicrobial molecules. They are small (<10 kDa) secreted proteins that insert into microbe membranes and lyse the microbes. Toll in *Drosophila* triggers defensin production.

Immune Regulation

A defect in any arm of the immune system can trigger autoimmunity. Autoimmunity is hard to classify as strictly a B-cell or T-cell mediated disease as multiple arms of the immune system are involved. The key to treating autoimmunity is immuno modulation.

Treatment Options

Anti-inflammatory drugs like NSAIDS, corticosteroids, immunosuppressant drugs like methotrexate, radiation, plamapheresis; cell blocking reagents like aCD^{20} (rituxan), aCD^{3} (teplizumab) and cytokine blocking reagents, TNF (humira and enbrel).

Vaccine

A vaccine is a non-pathogenic antigen that mimics a particular pathogen in order to elicit an immune response as if that actual pathogen were in the body. The overall goal of a vaccine is to establish immunity against that particular pathogen.

Mechanism of Vaccine Action

In an ideal scenario, whenever a vaccine is first administered, it is phagocytized by an Antigen Presenting Cell (APC). Recent research suggest that it is particularly important that the vaccine be taken up by a dendritic cell. This is because dendritic cells play a key role in activating T-cells, which become helper T-cells (Th cells). From there, the activated Th cells goes on to activate mature B-cells. These activated B-cells divides into two cell types, antibody-producing plasma cells and, most importantly, memory B-cells. Memory T-cells are also established, however, they usually have a shorter half-life than memory B-cells, thus, they play only a minor role in long-term immunity. Usually, there are no cytotoxic T-cells formed whenever the body responds to a vaccine.

Potential Shortcomings of Vaccines

In some rare cases, a vaccine may directly activate a B-cell, without stimulation from Th cells. Such antigens are known as T-independent (TI) antigens. The problem with such a response is that only Ig-M antibodies are produced and there are no memory cells established.Thus, such a vaccine will be useless against establishing immunity. Sometimes, the vaccine may be cleared from the body before it has the chance to properly stimulate the immune system.Some pathogens, particularly viruses, has a tendency to mutate and change there surface antigens, making a vaccine against them ineffective. This is especially true of malaria, which is constantly changing its surface antigens. Several different types of pathogens may cause similar infections, thus, several different vaccines may be required for them.For example, *Haemophilus influenzae*, a bacterium, and influenza virus, a virus, causes diseases with similar symptoms.

The Importance of the Secondary Immune Response (Vaccines)

During the secondary immune response, the body mounts a quicker, more robust attack on the pathogen. Thus, the pathogen is cleared from the body before it has the chance to cause an infection. But in some cases, a pathogen may be so, virulent that it causes illness, even during the secondary immune response.In this situation, a vaccine may be ineffective

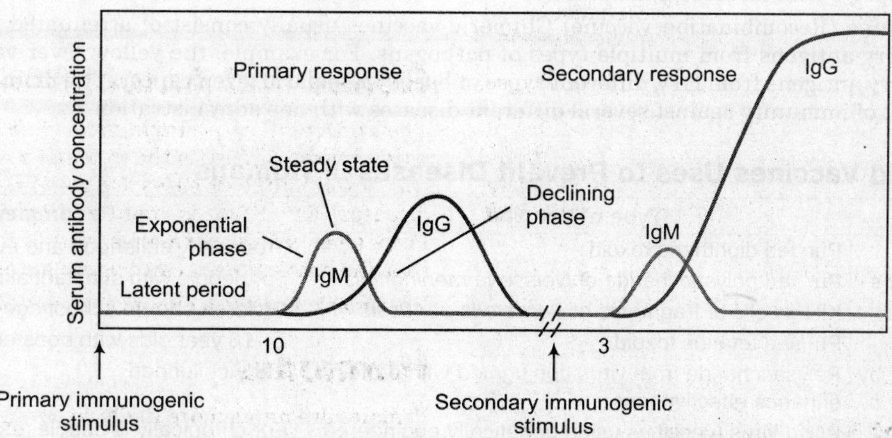

Fig. 13.25 Primary and secondary immune response to an antigen

Adjuvents

An adjuvant is a chemical substance that can be added to a vaccine in order to enhance the immune response to the vaccine.

Routes of Administration

There are three different routs of administration, intradermal administration, three types are intravenous, intramuscular, and subcutaneous, oral administration vaccine is usually given in liquid form. Foods, such as tomatoes, have been engineered to produce a vaccine, intranasal administration.

Boosters

For most vaccines, the immunity against a particular pathogen has a tendency to wear off over time. In this case, a periodic 'booster' administration must be given in order to strengthen and lengthen the duration of immunity. Boosters can also be given during the primary response in order to prolong and strengthen the immune response against the vaccine.

Types of Vaccines

There are numerous types of vaccines. Each different type of has its own unique properties.There function, however, is the same, to establish immunity against a particular pathogen.

(i) **Attenuated Virus/Bacteria** (Weakend) These vaccines consist of live, but weakened, viruses or bacteria. These organisms have been altered, either genetically or chemically, in a way that they are not pathogenic. An example is the attenuated virus vaccine for yellow fever, which utilizes the YF17D strain, a weakened form of the wild virus other examples are measles vaccine mumps and rubella (MMR).

(ii) **Killed Whole Organism** (Inactivated) This vaccine consist of the actual pathogen, however, it has been killed, either by a heat treatment or chemically.
An example is the Salk vaccine for polio, which utilizes whole polioviruses that have been inactivated by formaldehyde rabies vaccine.

(iii) **Toxoids** Some species of bacterial produce what is known as exotoxens. Toxoids are vaccines which consist of exotoxins that have been inactivated, either by heat or chemicals. These vaccines are intended to build an immunity against the toxins, but not necessarily the bacteria that produce the toxins. Some examples are tilanusbotulinum antitoxin and diphtheria antitoxin.

(iv) **Surface Molecule** (Conjugated vaccines) Proteins, carbohydrates, and lipids, that are found on the surface of pathogens, are isolated and used as a vaccine. Proteins are usually large and complex enough to be used on there own. Carbohydrates and lipids requires conjugated with a large protein in order to be immunogenic. An example of surface molecules used as a vaccine are hepatitis B surface antigens.

(v) **Anti–Idiotype Vaccines** In this unique type of vaccine, antibodies from a sick individual are isolated. These antibodies are then injected into a lab animal, which may then produce an antibody whose antigen binding site mimics the epitope that the original antibody binds to. These antibodies are then isolated and injected into a healthy individual, who may produce antibodies with an antigen binding site that binds to the antigen binding site of the animals antibodies. Because the animals binding site resembles the epitope of an antigen on a particular pathogen, the individual will have an immunity against that pathogen.

(vi) **DNA Vaccines** DNA vaccines consist of plasmids that contains genes for certain types of antigens.
Once administered, the plasmid is taken up by the target cell and the genes are expressed. The cell then either excretes the antigen or displays it on an MHC-I molecule.

(vii) **Chimeric Vaccines** (Recombination vaccine) Chimeric vaccines usually consist of attenuated viruses that have been engineered to carry antigens from multiple types of pathogens. For example, the yellow fever vaccine YF17D has been engineered to carry antigens from HIV, different types of bacteria, malaria, even cancer. The main of a chimeric vaccine is the establishment of immunity against several different diseases with one administration.

Table 13.5 **Selected Vaccines Uses to Prevent Diseases in Humans**

Disease	Type of Vaccine	Recommendation
Diphtheria	Purified diphtheria toxoid	From early childhood and every 10 years for adults
Meningococcal meningitis	Purified polysaccharide of *Neisseria meningitidis*	For people with substantial risk of infection
Whooping cough	Killed cells or fragments of *Bordetella pertussis*	Children prior to school age
Tetanus	Purified tetanus toxoid	14-16 year olds with booster every 10 years
Meningitis caused by *Haemophilus influenzae b*	Polysaccharide from virus conjugated with protein to enhance effectiveness	Early childhood
Influenza	Killed virus (vaccines using genetically engineered antigenic fragments are also being developed)	For chronically ill people, especially with respiratory diseases, or for healthy people over 65 years of age
Measles	Attenuated virus	Early childhood
Mumps	Attenuated virus	Early childhood
Rubella	Attenuated virus	Early childhood; for females of child-bearing age who are not pregnant
Polio	Attenuated or killed virus (enhanced potency type)	Early childhood
Hepatitis-B	Antigenic fragments of virus	Early childhood

Vaccine Production Methods

There are three main vaccine manufacturing strategies: *in vivo*, *in vitro* and chemical synthesis. Some vaccines can be produced using any one of the three methods, while for other vaccines, only one method will work.

***In vivo* Method** In *in vivo* manufacturing, the vaccine is produced inside a living organism. Embryonated chicken eggs are are commonly used, particularly in producing flu vaccines. Vaccines, such as anti-idiotype, can also be produced in lab animals, such as mice. There are even some species of plant, such as bananas, that have been genetically engineered to produce a vaccine.

***In vitro* method** Here, using recombinant DNA technology, vaccines can be produced in yeast cultures, bacterial cultures, or cell cultures. Recombinant vaccines, such as chimeric vaccines, are produced in this manor. Attenuated virus/bacteria vaccines can also be produced this way.

Chemical synthesis Here, instead of using biological systems to produce a vaccine, a vaccine can be produced in a lab. Vaccines that utilize synthetic peptides as well as conjugated lipids and polysaccharides are manufactured this way. Usually, this method is used in combination with either *in vivo* or *in vitro* production.

Risks Associated With Vaccines

The primary risk associated with vaccines, especially vaccines that utilize live organisms, is that the vaccine itself causes illness. This happened with the orally administered Sabin vaccine for polio, where some individuals became ill and, in rare cases, even spread the illness to other individuals who were not exposed to the vaccine. Another risk is that the vaccine may behave as a super antigen and over stimulate the immune system. Yet a third risk is that some individuals may have an allergic reaction to the vaccine, especially vaccines produced in embrionated chicken eggs and in transgenic plants.

Immunoeficiency Disease

Immunodeficiency disease (IDD), results from a genetic or developmental defect or acquired factors in the immune system, and is a syndrome mostly characterized by infection in clinic. Immunodeficiency (or immune deficiency) is a state in which the immune system's ability to fight infectious disease is compromised or entirely absent. Immunodeficiency may also decrease cancer immunosurveillance. Most cases of immunodeficiency are acquired (secondary) but some people are born with defects in their immune system, or primary immunodeficiency. Transplant patients take medications to suppress their immune system as an anti-rejection measure, as do some patients suffering from an overactive immune system. A person who has an immunodeficiency of any kind is said to be immuno compromised. An immuno compromised person may be particularly vulnerable to opportunistic, in addition to normal infections that could affect everyone.

An individual is immune deficient if defective in any of the following components of the immune system, *i.e.*, signaling molecules in TCR activation, key transcriptional factors of immune cells, molecules and organs for lymphocyte development, antigen presentation, phagocyte function, cytokines and co-stimulation molecules, immune cell migration and adhesion, complement and DNA recombination and metabolism.

Types

By Affected Component

(a) Humoral immune deficiency, with signs or symptoms depending on the cause, but generally include signs of hypogammaglobulinemia (decrease of one or more types of antibodies) with presentations including repeated mild respiratory infections, and/or a gammaglobulinemia (lack of all or most antibody production) which results in frequent severe infections and is often fatal.

(b) T-cell deficiency, often caused secondary disorders such as acquired immune deficiency syndrome.

(c) **Granulocyte deficiency,** including decreased numbers of granulocytes (called granulocytopenia or if absent, agranulocytosis) such as of neutrophil granulocytes (termed neutropenia).

Granulocyte deficiencies also include decreased function of individual granulocytes, such as in chronic granulomatous disease.

(d) Asplenia, where there is no function of the spleen

(e) Complement deficiency is where the function of the complement system is deficient

In reality, immunodeficiency often affects multiple components, with notable examples including severe combined immunodeficiency (which is primary) and acquired immune deficiency syndrome (which is secondary).

Primary *vs* Secondary

Distinction between primary versus secondary immunodeficiencies are based on, respectively, whether the cause originates in the immune system itself or is, in turn, due to insufficiency of a supporting component of it or an external decreasing factor of it.

Primary Immunodeficiency (PID)

A number of rare diseases feature a heightened susceptibility to infections from childhood onward. Primary Immunodeficiency is also known as congenital immunodeficiencies. Many of these disorders are hereditary and are autosomal recessive or X-linked. There are over 80 recognised primary immunodeficiency syndromes, they are generally grouped by the part of the immune system that is malfunctioning, such as lymphocytes or granulocytes.

Secondary Immunodeficiency

Secondary immunodeficiencies, also known as acquired immunodeficiencies, can result from various immuno suppressive agents, for example, malnutrition, aging and particular medications (*e.g.*, chemotherapy, disease modifying antirheumatic drugs, immunosuppressive drugs after organ transplants, glucocorticoids).

Many specific diseases directly or indirectly cause immunosuppression. This includes many types of cancer, particularly those of the bone marrow and blood cells (leukemia, lymphoma, multiple myeloma), and certain chronic infections. Immuno deficiency is also the hallmark of acquired immuno deficiency syndrome (AIDS), caused by the human immunodeficiency virus (HIV). HIV directly infects a small number of T-helper cells, and also impairs other immune system responses indirectly.

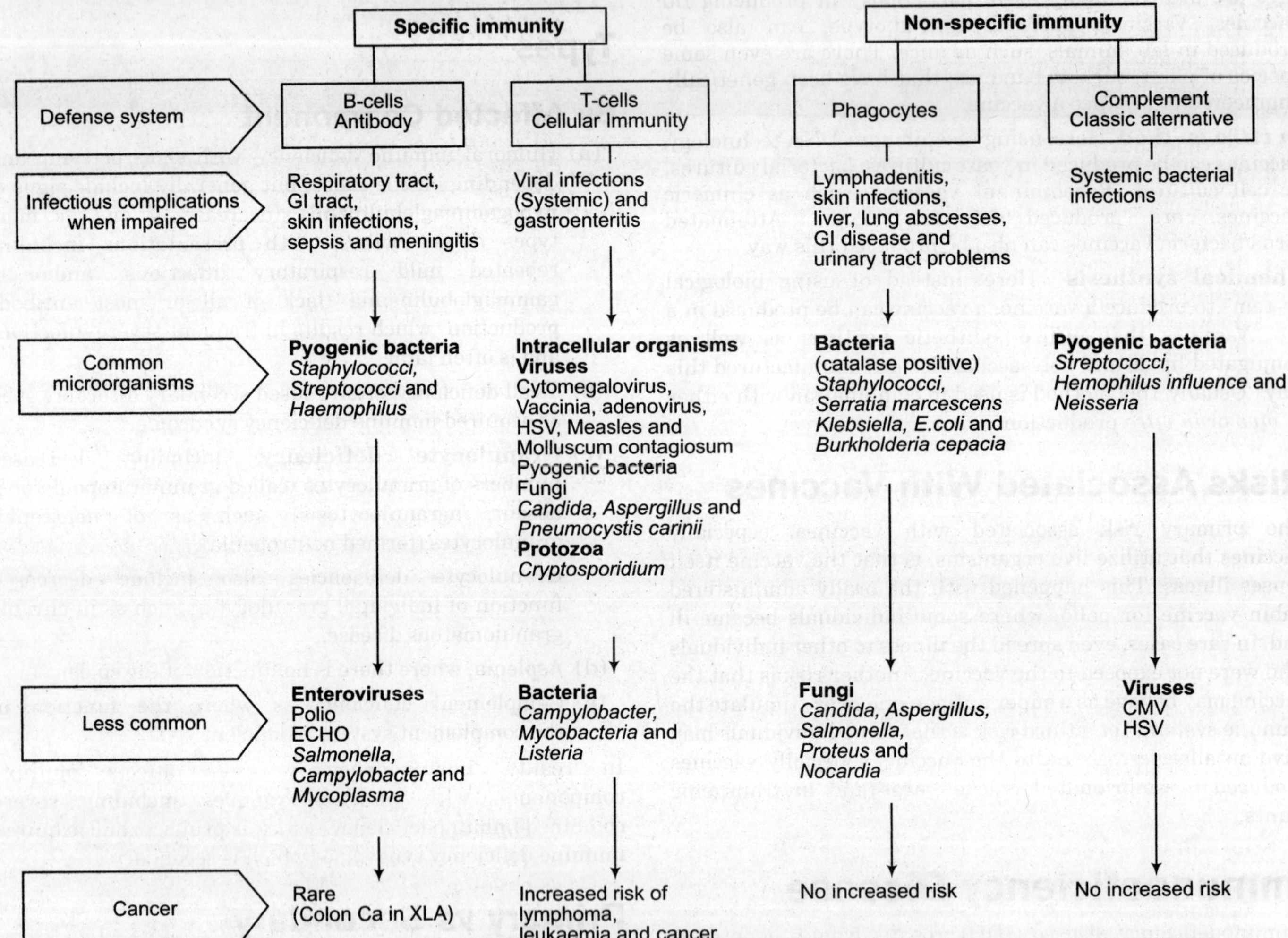

Fig. 13.26 Types of infections and risk of malignancies in immunodeficiency diseases affecting different defenses systems

Exercise

1. Short lived immunity acquired by foetus/ infant from mother through placenta/milk is
(a) active immunity
(b) passive immunity
(c) cellular immunity
(d) innate non-specific immunity

2. The antigen binding site of antibody is found in
(a) variable region of light chain
(b) variable region of heavy chain
(c) variable region of both heavy and light chains
(d) constant region of light chain

3. The cells active in production of antibodies are
(a) Kupffer cells (b) plasma cells
(c) mast cells (d) Langerhans cells

4. The disease erythroblastosis foetalis of human baby is due to
(a) incompatibility of blood groups of the couple
(b) incompatibility of blood groups of embryo and mother
(c) maladjustment of Rh factor
(d) All of the above

5. Gall bodies are characteristic cytoplasmic structure of
I. T_H cells II. T_C cells
III. B-cells IV. Plasma cells
Choose the correct options :
(a) I and II (b) I and III
(c) II and III (d) I, II and III

6. What is the function of lymphocytes?
(a) Destruction of poisonous substances
(b) Destruction of bacteria
(c) Destruction of RBC
(d) None of the above

7. A blood group has both 'A' and 'B' antigens but no antibodies. It is
(a) A (b) O
(c) AB (d) B

8. A molecule that produces an immune response is
(a) antigen (b) antibody
(c) carcinogen (d) mutagen

9. A person is injected with gammaglobulin against hepatitis-B. It is
(a) artificially acquires passive immunity
(b) artificially acquires active immunity
(c) naturally acquires active immunity
(d) naturally acquires passive immunity

10. Active immunity means
(a) resistance developed before disease
(b) resistance developed after disease
(c) increased heart beat
(d) increased flow of blood

11. AIDS is caused by
(a) RNA virus (b) DNA virus
(c) herpes virus (d) hepatitis virus

12. Which is most abundant immunoglobulin?
(a) IgA (b) IgD
(c) IgG (d) IgM

13. An insect bite may result in inflammation of that spot. It is triggered by alarm chemicals such as
(a) histamine and dopamine
(b) histamine and kinins
(c) interferon and opsonin
(d) interferons and histones

14. Monoclonal antibodies can be used to detect
I. Protozoan infections II. Diabetes
III. Drug abuse IV. Viral pathogenesis
Codes
(a) I, II, and III (b) I, II, III and IV
(c) II, III and IV (d) III and IV

15. Antibody formation and immunity production by globulin protein is found in
(a) haemoglobin of RBCs (b) blood platelets
(c) plasma (d) cytoplasm of RBCs

16. Antigens are found
(a) inside cytoplasm (b) inside nucleus
(c) on nuclear envelope (d) on cell surface

17. Blood group is due to
(a) specific antigens on the surface of WBC
(b) specific antibodies on the surface of RBC
(c) specific antigens on the surface of RBC
(d) types of haemoglobin

18. Cells of immune system that cause pore formation in the antigen are
(a) helper T-cells (b) killer T-cells
(c) suppressor T-cells (d) B-cells

19. Chemically an antibody is
(a) protein (b) lipoprotein
(c) lipid (d) nucleoprotein

20. During inflammation which of the following is secreted by connective tissue
(a) heparin (b) serotonin
(c) glucagon (d) histamine

21. Hay fever is due to
(a) hepatitis (b) allergy
(c) dengue (d) helper T-cells

22. Hypersensitivity to an allergen is due to
(a) increase in temperature
(b) food habits
(c) age
(d) aberrent functioning of immune system

23. If a man is Rh^+ and woman Rh^-
(a) their first child will die
(b) no child will be born
(c) the first child will survive
(d) All the children will survive

24. Inflammation reaction is brought about by
(a) plasma cells (b) mast cells
(c) macrophages (d) adipose cells

25. Which one engulfs foreign materials?
(a) Macrophages (b) Plasma cells
(c) Mast cells (d) Lymphocytes

26. Macrophages are derived from
(a) neutrophils (b) lymphocytes
(c) monocytes (d) basophils

27. The inflammatory response includes all of the following except
(a) vessel constriction (b) temperature increase
(c) increased blood flow (d) phagocyte attack

28. The immunoglobulin found in a mother's milk is
(a) IgM (b) IgA
(c) IgE (d) IgG

29. A person with anti-A and anti-B antibodies in their blood has what blood type?
(a) A (b) B
(c) AB (d) O

30. Your body has millions of different antibodies for detecting millions of different antigens because
(a) you have millions of different antibody genes
(b) antibody genes undergo somatic rearrangement and somatic mutation
(c) antibody genes undergo antigen shifting
(d) All of the above

31. Which type of surface marker is present on every nucleated cell in your body?
(a) B receptor (b) T receptor
(c) MHC-I (d) MHC-II

32. Of the five classes of antibody heavy chains, which one's function is still partially unclear?
(a) IgE (b) IgM
(c) IgG (d) IgD

33. Diseases in which a person's immune system attacks the person's own normal tissue are called
(a) secondary immune diseases
(b) autoimmune diseases
(c) primary immune diseases
(d) clonal selection diseases

34. Hypersensitivity reactions
(a) are sometimes mediated by IgE
(b) may involve immune complexes
(c) may involve complement, histamine, neutrophils or IgG
(d) All of the above

35. The pharyngeal tonsils are found in the
(a) oropharynx (b) laryngopharynx
(c) nasopharynx (d) None of these

36. Vaccinations are an example of
(a) naturally acquired active immunity
(b) artificially acquired active immunity
(c) naturally acquired passive immunity
(d) artificially acquired passive immunity

37. A single IgA dimer can bind .... antigens.
(a) 1 (b) 2
(c) 3 (d) 4

38. Macrophages are examples of
(a) antibody-secreting T-lymphocytes
(b) antigen presenting cells
(c) activated plasma cells
(d) All of the above

39. Which of the following are involved in B-cell activation?
(a) Antigen (b) T-helper cell
(c) Cytokine (d) All of these

40. Which of the following is true of the spleen?
(a) It's located on the right side of the stomach
(b) Its primary function is lymphocyte production
(c) A histological section of the spleen would typically contain more white pulp than red pulp
(d) It contains smooth muscle within its capsule

41. Acute epiglottis is caused by
(a) *H. influenzae*
(b) *Pneumoccocus*
(c) beta haemolytic *Streptococci*
(d) *Staphylococcus*

42. Chancroid is caused by
(a) *H. ducreyi* (b) *Staphylococci*
(c) *Streptococci* (d) None of these

43. Allergy and anaphylaxis are due to
(a) IgE (b) IgA
(c) IgG (d) IgM

44. Innate immune responses are most effective against
(a) antigens resembling self antigens
(b) common antigens on bacteria
(c) genetically engineered antigens
(d) viruses that have previously caused infection

45. Inflammation does not involve
(a) cytokine production by macrophage
(b) migration of leukocyte out of the circulation
(c) pain and swelling at the site of infection
(d) secretion of antibodies

46. The primary purpose of the adaptive immune system is to
(a) block all pathogens from entering the body
(b) cure allergic reactions
(c) kill tumor cells
(d) protect from disease upon re-infection with a specific pathogen

47. Viral replication within cells in inhibited by
(a) IL-4 (b) IL-1
(c) IFN alpha (d) TNF alpha

48. Active immunity means
(a) resistance developed after disease
(b) resistance developed before disease
(c) increasing rate of heart beat
(d) increasing quantity of blood

49. Which of the following is not a characteristic of a secondary immune response?
(a) IgG isotype (b) Low affinity antibodies
(c) High affinity antibodies (d) No lag phase

50. Which one group of the following cells is not phagocytic in nature?
(a) Neutrophil polymorphonuclear leukocytes
(b) B-lymphocytes
(c) Microglial cells
(d) Macrophages

51. The macrophage rich mass found at the site of injection of an adjuvant is called
(a) myeloma
(b) granuloma
(c) adjuvant activated lymphoma
(d) None of the above

52. Mature dendritic cells are capable of which of the following?
(a) Activation antigen specific T-cells
(b) Removing red blood cells
(c) Producing bradykinin
(d) Extracellular killing of target cells

53. Most antibodies are synthesized by the
(a) central lymphoid organs
(b) peripheral lymphoid organs
(c) primary lymphoid organs
(d) macrophages

54. The common myeloid progenitor cell gives rise to
(a) Neutrophils alone
(b) Neutrophil, basophils and mast cells
(c) PMNs and mononuclear leukocytes
(d) Neutrophils, basophils and monocytes

55. Haptens
(a) require carrier molecules to be immunogenic
(b) react with specific antibodies when homologous carriers are
(c) interact with specific antibody, even if the haptens are monovalent
(d) All of the above

56. Agretope is the region of antigen that is interacting with
(a) TCR (b) MHC
(c) Both (a) and (b) (d) antibody

57. Which of the following cell/cells expresses MHC-II on the surface?
(a) Lymphocytes (b) Macrophages
(c) Dendritic cells (d) All of these

58. Antigenic peptides are presented to T-cells by
(a) TCR/CD^3 (b) CD^{28}
(c) CTL A4 (d) MHC

59. Generation of antigenic peptide for MHC class I occurs in
(a) endoplasmic reticulum (b) cytosol
(c) Golgi apparatus (d) endosome

60. How many disulphide bonds are there in a typical immunoglobulin molecule?
(a) 2-5 (b) 6-9
(c) 10-20 (d) 28

61. The class of immunoglobulin that can get transported across epithelial cells is
(a) IgG (b) IgE (c) IgA (d) IgM

62. Number of antigen binding sites in IgM
(a) 5 (b) 8 (c) 4 (d) 10

63. Joining chain is found in
(a) IgM (b) IgA
(c) IgM and IgA (d) IgE

64. The immunoglobulin that results in histamine release is
(a) IgG (b) IgA
(c) IgE (d) IgD

65. The predominant antibody in saliva is
(a) IgG (b) IgA
(c) IgM (d) IgD

66. Immunoglobulin in the serum of a newborn will be mostly
(a) IgM of maternal origin (b) IgG of maternal origin
(c) IgG of endogenous origin (d) IgM of endogenous origin

67. A polyclonal antibody response
(a) is not antigen-specific
(b) is produced only in response to polymeric antigens
(c) is produced by several B-cells recognizing different epitopes on the same antigen
(d) occurs during the lag phase of the immune response

68. Antibody diversity is generated by
(a) protein splicing
(b) somatic mutation
(c) allelic exclusion
(d) inter chromosomal recombination

69. Which of the following chemical bonds is not involved in antigen binding by antibody?
(a) Hydrogen bonds (b) Hydrophobic forces
(c) Covalent bonds (d) van der Waal' forces

70. Cells that release histamine and other vasoactive substances in response to allergens are
(a) neutrophils (b) macrophages
(c) NK cells (d) mast cells

71. Live vaccine is
(a) low dose of the infectious bacteria administered as prophylactic
(b) a dose of bacterial strain in a modified form which retains immunogenicity but is not pathogenic
(c) a low dose of toxin that is produced by the bacterium
(d) a sample of cells from a patient who recently recovered from the disease

72. For the first six months of its life, a child depends on antibodies
(a) received in food
(b) obtained forms its mother
(c) produced from its immune system cells
(d) acquired from the environment

73. Antibody formation and immunity production by globulin protein is found in
(a) cytoplasm of RBCs (b) haemoglobin of RBCs
(c) plasma (d) blood platelets

74. Artificial immunity can be acquired from a
(a) serious illness
(b) vaccination
(c) repeated exposure to the same microbes
(d) treatment with penicillin

75. In idiopathic thrombocytopenia a person produces antibodies against self
(a) RBC membrane protein
(b) platelet membrane proteins
(c) leucocyte membrane protein
(d) all membrane protein

76. Surface bound receptor proteins are characteristic feature of
(a) B-cells (b) Plasma cells
(c) T-cells (d) None of these

77. Match the terms given in List I with their description in List II and select the correct codes.

List I	List II
A. Helper T-cells	1. Cells that are active in production of antibodies
B. Plasma cells	2. Activated T or B-lymphocytes to become plasma cells
C. Killer T-cells	3. Protein produced by virus infected cell
D. Interferon	4. Combine with antigen causing lysis and release of cytokinese

Codes

	A	B	C	D
(a)	4	1	2	3
(b)	3	2	1	4
(c)	1	3	4	2
(d)	2	1	4	3

78. Match List I with List II.

List I	List II
A. Suppressor T-cells	1. Bind to and destroy target cells
B. Cytotoxic T-cells	2. Activate cytotoxic T-cells
C. Interleukin-I	3. Inhibit production of cytotoxic T-cells
D. Helper T-cells	4. Produced by APCs to activate helper T-cells

Codes

	A	B	C	D
(a)	3	1	4	2
(b)	4	3	1	2
(c)	1	3	2	4
(d)	4	2	1	3

Answers

1. (b) **2.** (b) **3.** (b) **4.** (c) **5.** (a) **6.** (b) **7.** (c) **8.** (a) **9.** (a) **10.** (b)
11. (a) **12.** (c) **13.** (b) **14.** (b) **15.** (c) **16.** (d) **17.** (c) **18.** (b) **19.** (a) **20.** (d)
21. (b) **22.** (d) **23.** (c) **24.** (b) **25.** (a) **26.** (c) **27.** (a) **28.** (b) **29.** (d) **30.** (b)
31. (c) **32.** (b) **33.** (b) **34.** (d) **35.** (c) **36.** (b) **37.** (d) **38.** (b) **39.** (d) **40.** (d)
41. (a) **42.** (a) **43.** (a) **44.** (b) **45.** (d) **46.** (b) **47.** (b) **48.** (c) **49.** (b) **50.** (b)
51. (b) **52.** (b) **53.** (a) **54.** (d) **55.** (d) **56.** (b) **57.** (d) **58.** (d) **59.** (b) **60.** (c)
61. (c) **62.** (d) **63.** (c) **64.** (c) **65.** (b) **66.** (b) **67.** (c) **68.** (b) **69.** (c) **70.** (d)
71. (b) **72.** (b) **73.** (c) **74.** (b) **75.** (b) **76.** (c) **77.** (d) **78.** (a)

14 Concepts and Early Development in Plants and Animals

Basic Concepts of Development

Potency, Commitment and Specification

Potency is the capacity to differentiate into specialized cell types. In the strictest sense, this requires stem cells to be either **totipotent** or **pluripotent** — to be able to give rise to any mature cell type, although **multipotent** or **unipotent** progenitor cells are sometimes referred to as stem cells.

1. **Totipotent** Stem cells are produced from the fusion of an egg and sperm cell. Cells produced by the first few divisions of the fertilized egg are also totipotent. These cells can differentiate into embryonic and extraembryonic cell types.
2. **Pluripotent** Stem cells are the descendants of totipotent cells and can differentiate into cells derived from any of the three germ layers.

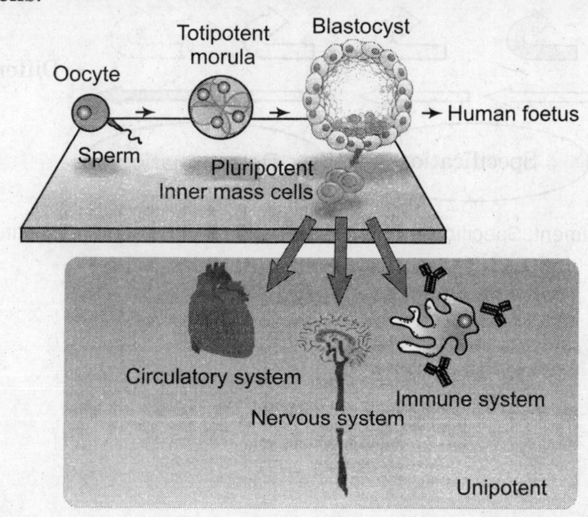

Fig. 14.1 The capacity to differentiate into specialized cell types

Syllabus

- Basic Concepts of Development; Potency, Commitment, Specification, Induction and Competence, Determination and Differentiation, Morphogenetic Gradients; Cell Fate and Cell Lineages, Stem Cells, Genomic Equivalence and the Cytoplasmic Determinants, Imprinting; Mutants and Transgenics in Analysis of Development.
- Gametogenesis, Fertilization and Early Development : Production of Gametes in Animals, Production of Gametes in Plants, Cell Surface Molecules in Sperm Egg Recognition in Animals, Double Fertilizatior in Plants; Zygote Formation, Cleavage and Blastula Formation, Embryonic Fields or Morphogenetic Field Gastrulation and Formation of Germ Layers in Animals; Embryogenesis and Establishment of Symmetry in Plants; Seed Formation and Germination.

3. **Multipotent** Stem cells can produce only cells of a closely related family of cells (*e.g.*, haematopoietic stem cells differentiate into red blood cells, white blood cells, platelets, etc.).
4. **Unipotent** Cells can produce only one cell type, but have the property of self-renewal which distinguishes them from non-stem cells (*e.g.*, muscle stem cells).

Differentiation is an overt change in cellular biochemistry, structure, physiology and function. It is preceded by the covert **commitment** of cells to particular pre-destined fates. Commitment is also a staged process divided into two stages, specification and determination. Specification implies early, reversible steps, whereas determination is irreversibility.

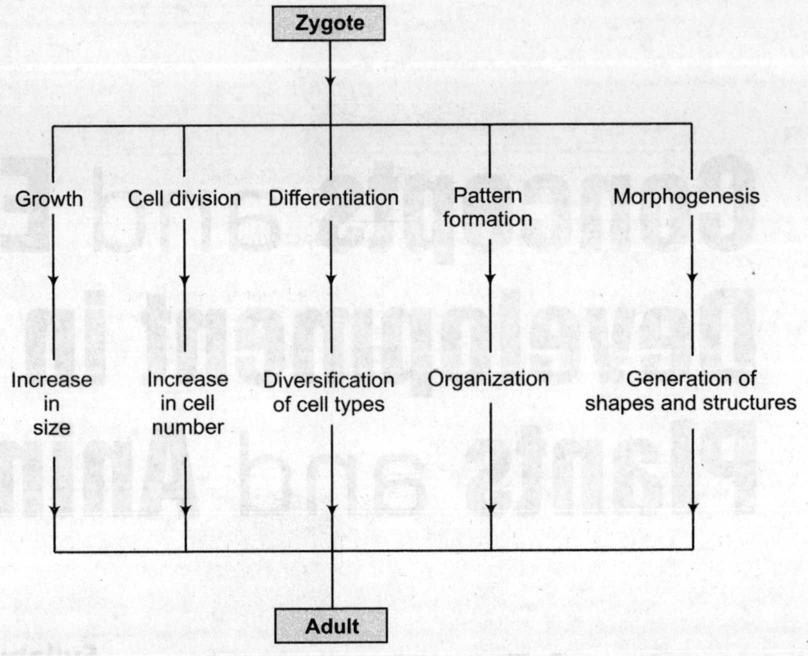

Fig. 14.2 An overview of developmental processes

Stages of Cell Commitment

(a) **Specification** Capable of autonomous differentiation when placed in a neutral environment; not when placed in non-neutral environment.

(b) **Determination** Capable of autonomous differentiation even when placed into another embryonic region.

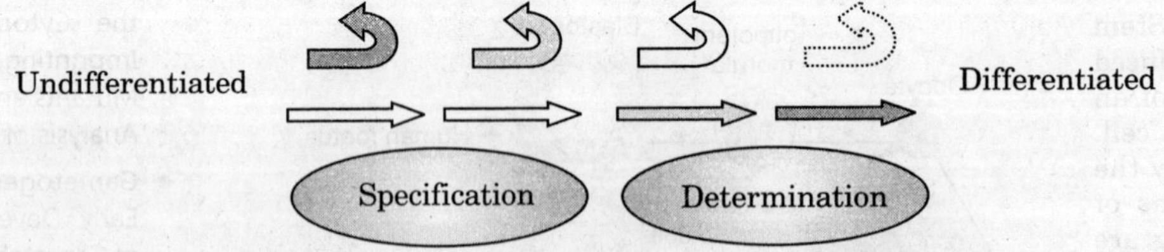

Fig. 14.3 Stages of cell commitment: Specification (reversible) and determination (essentially irreversible)

Specification Types

(a) Autonomous specification
(b) Syncytial specification
(c) Conditional specification

Autonomous Specification

Cells are specified by differential distribution of cytoplasmic components during cleavage of the egg and early embryo.

Modes of Cell Type Specification and their Characteristics

- Characteristic of most invertebrates.
- Specification by differential acquisition of certain cytoplasmic molecules present in the egg.
- Invariant cleavages produce the same lineages in each embryo of the species. Blastomere fates are generally invariant.
- Cell type specification precedes any large-scale embryonic cell migration.
- Produces 'mosaic' development cells cannot change fate if a blastomere is lost.

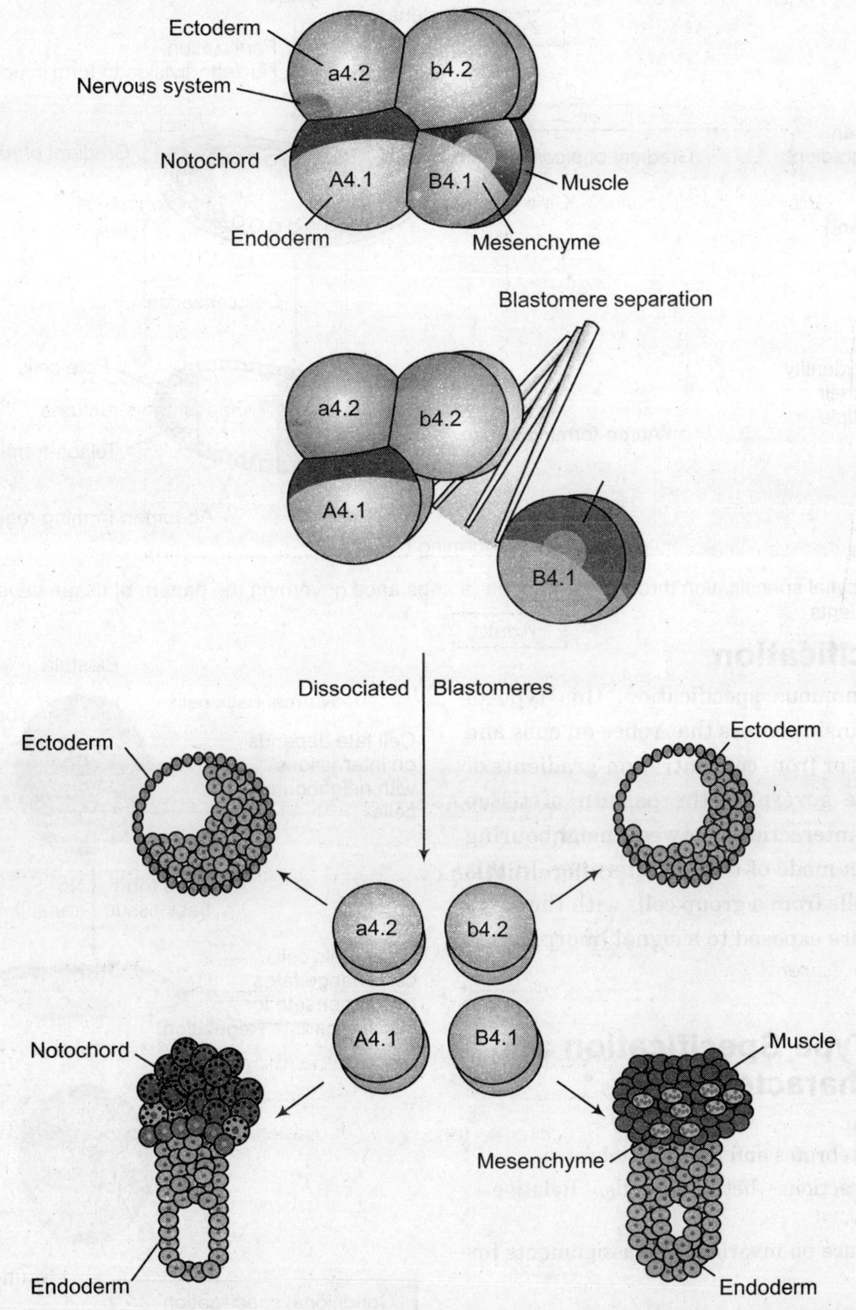

Fig. 14.4 Autonomous specification in Tunicate (sea squirt). Blastomeres are committed at a very early stage in mosaic development. If split, each dissociated blastomere pair forms original structures. Each blastomere contains positional information in the form of specific proteins and genes

Syncytial Specification

Nuclear division without cell division, results in cytoplasm with many nuclei.

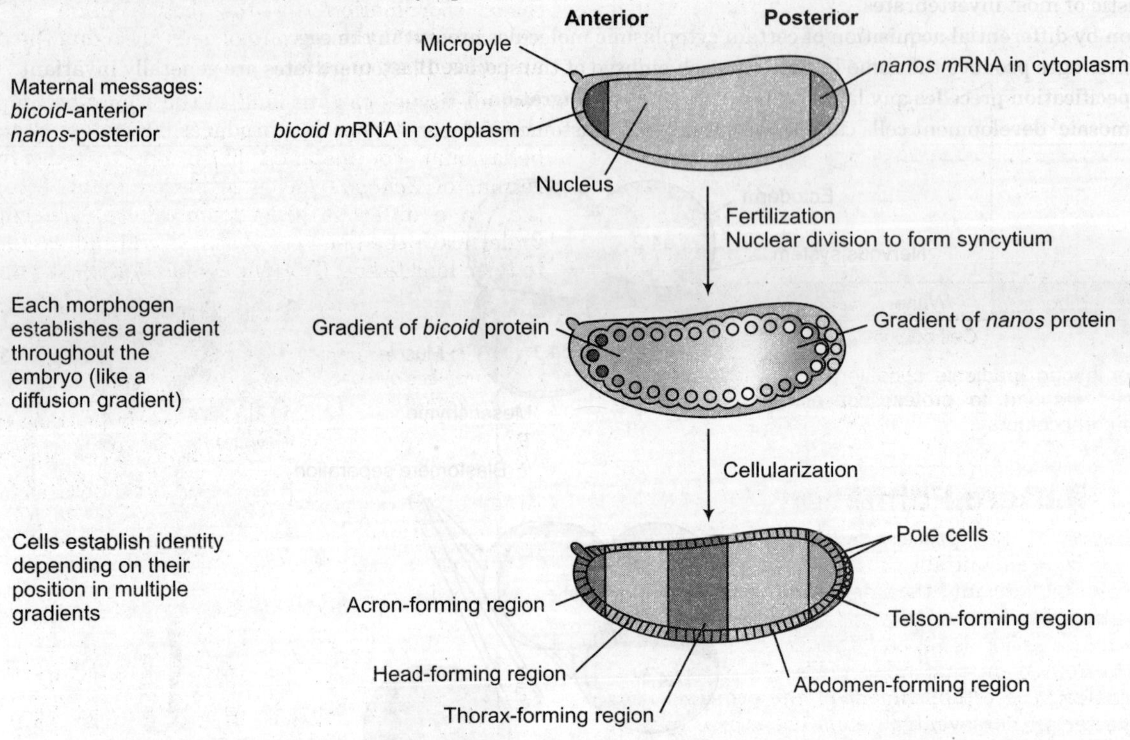

Fig. 14.5 Syncytial specification through morphogen (a substance governing the pattern of tissue development) gradients

Conditional Specification

In contrast to the autonomous specification, this type of specification is a cell-extrinsic process that relies on cues and interactions between cells or from concentration-gradients of morphogens (a substance governing the pattern of tissue development). Inductive interactions between neighbouring cells are the most common mode of tissue patterning. In this mechanism, one or two cells from a group cells with the same developmental potential are exposed to a signal (morphogen) from outside the group.

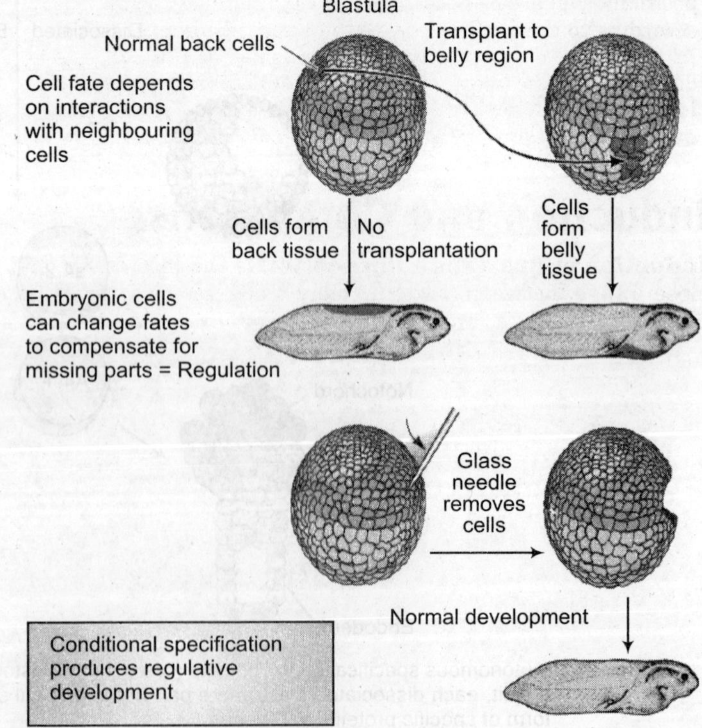

Fig. 14.6 Conditional specification

Modes of Cell Type Specification and their Characteristics

- Conditional specification.
- Characteristic of all vertebrates and few invertebrates.
- Specification by interactions between cells. Relative positions are important.
- Variable cleavages produce no invariant fate assignments to cells.
- Massive cell rearrangements and migrations precede or accompany specification.
- Capacity for 'regulative' development: allows cells to acquire different functions.

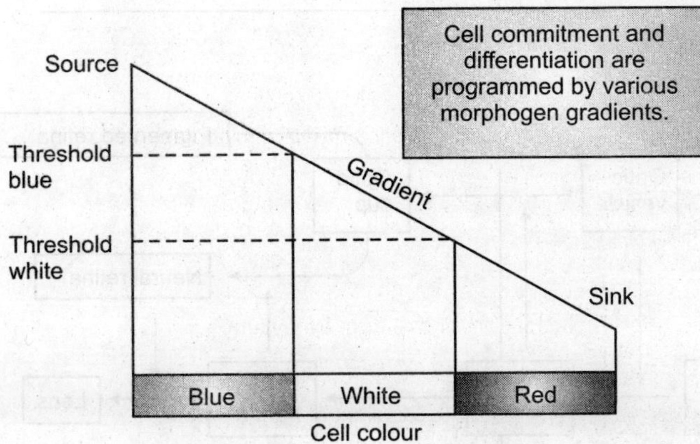

Fig. 14.7 Morphogen gradients conditional specification. Here, cells respond to protein concentration by turning different colours

Pattern Formation

Pattern formation is the process by which cells become organized in the embryo, initially to form the basic rudiments of the body plan and later into the fine structure of individual organs. The process by which cells become specialized according to their position is called **regional specification.** The first patterning event that takes place in the embryo is axis **specification,** the establishment of the principal body axes (anteroposterior, dorsoventral, etc). These axes may be pre-determined by the distribution of maternal gene products in the egg. Once the principal axes are established, the position of cells along each axis is specified and allocating each a positional value. The positional values to cells may be assigned according to the position of a cell in a **morphogen gradient**. A diversity of patterning mechanisms occurs later in development, including **asymmetric cell division, specific localized interactions between cells** and the **generation of regular spacing patterns by lateral inhibition**.

Induction and Competence

Induction or **proximate interaction** is the interaction at close range between two or more cells or tissues with different histories and properties. For example, in the vertebrate eye, the diameter of lens tissue is controlled by muscle tissue, which meets the tissue of the neural retina. Such coordination in the construction of organs is accomplished by one group of cells changing the behaviour of an adjacent set of cells.

Not all tissues can respond to the signal being produced by the inducer (tissue that produces a signal to changes cellular behaviour). For instance, if the optic vesicle (presumptive retina) of *Xenopus laevis* is placed in an ectopic location (*i.e.,* in a different place from where it normally forms) underneath the head ectoderm, it will induce that ectoderm to form lens tissue. Therefore, optic vesicle is an inducer.

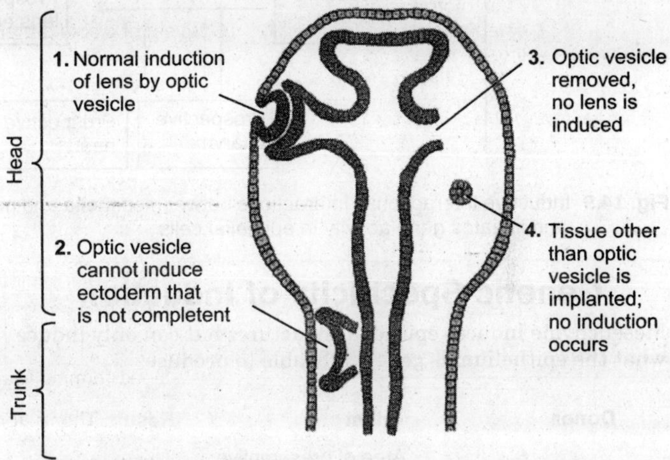

Fig. 14.8 Ectodermal ability to respond to the optic vesicle inducer in *Xenopus laevis*

1. The optic vesicle is able to induce lenses in the anterior portion of the ectoderm, but not in the presumptive trunk and abdomen.
2. If the optic vesicle is removed.
3. The surface ectoderm forms either an abnormal lens or no lens at all.
4. Most other tissues are not able to substitute for the optic vesicle.

Competence is ability to respond to a specific inductive signal. Competence is an actively acquired condition.

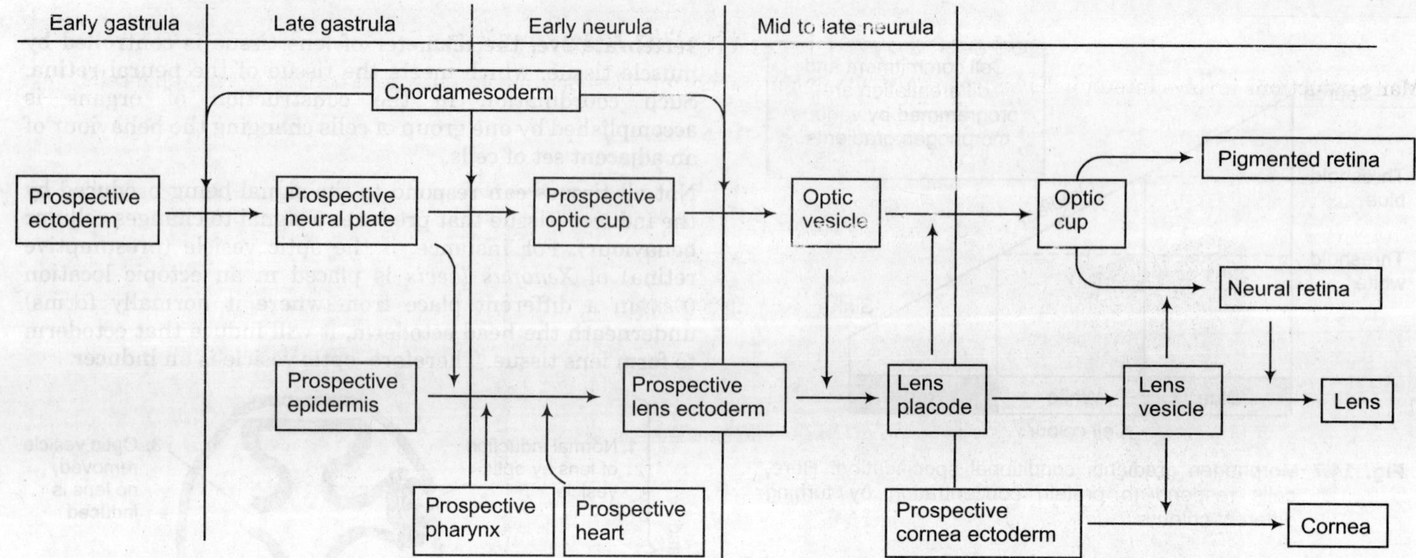

Fig. 14.9 Inductive Interactions : Interactions between epithelia and mesenchyme: mesenchyme plays an instructive role (as the inducing tissue); and initiates gene activity in epithelial cells

Genetic Specificity of Induction

Mesenchyme induces epithelial structures but can only induce what the epithelium is genetically able to produce.

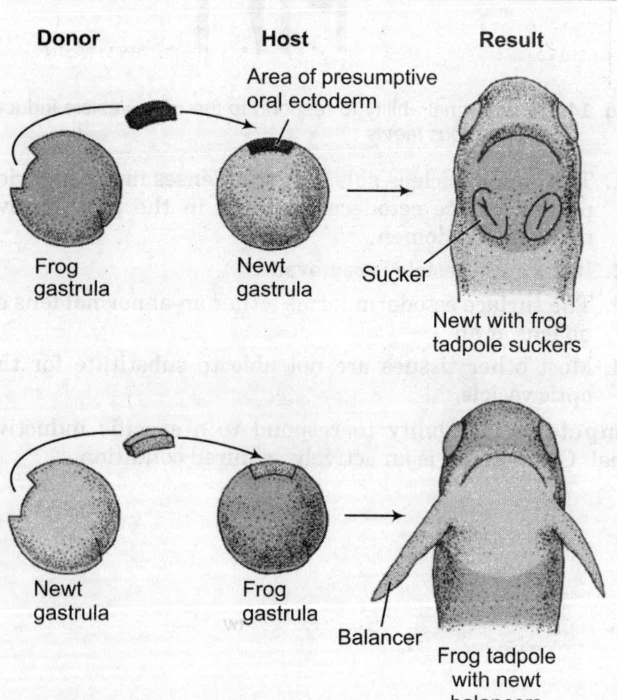

Fig. 14.10 Genetic specificity showing epithelial response is limited to genomic capability

For example, in the developing chick and mammalian eye, the *Pax6* protein appears to be important in making the ectoderm competent to respond to the inductive signal from the optic vesicle. *Pax6* expression is seen in the head ectoderm, which can respond to the optic vesicle by forming lenses and it is not seen in other regions of the surface ectoderm.

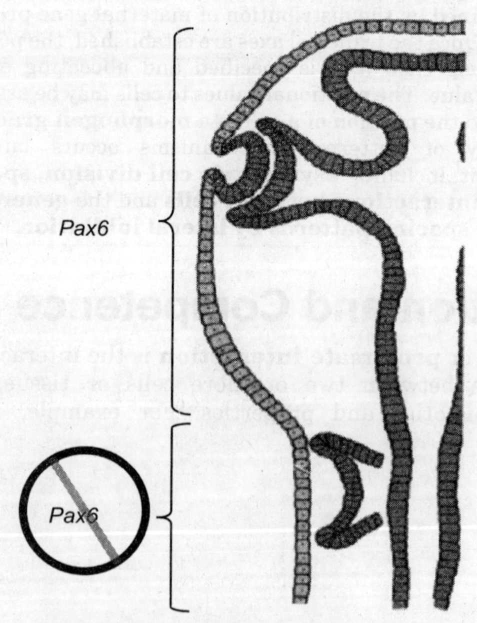

Fig. 14.11 *Pax6* is a competence factor for lens induction. During lens induction *Pax6* is expressed in the head ectoderm, but not in other regions of surface ectoderm

Mesenchymal-Epithelial Interactions

Many inductions involve interactions between epithelia and mesenchyme. Mesenchyme initiates gene activity in epithelial cells.

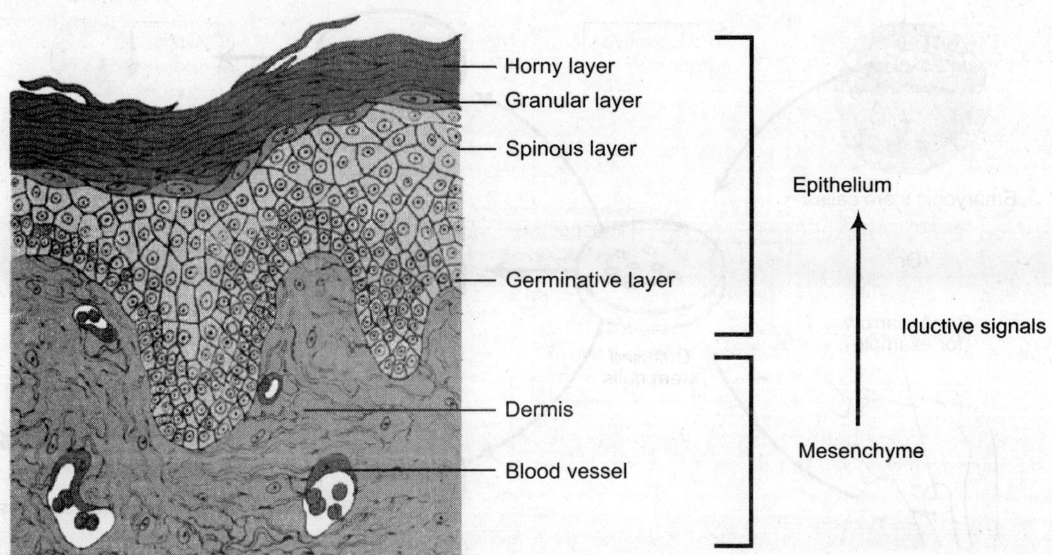

Fig 14.12 Epithelial derivatives (hair, scales, feathers, mammary glands, sweat glands) type depends on restrictions by region and genetics

In **regional specificity,** source of the mesenchyme (inducing tissue) determines the structure of the epithelial derivative.

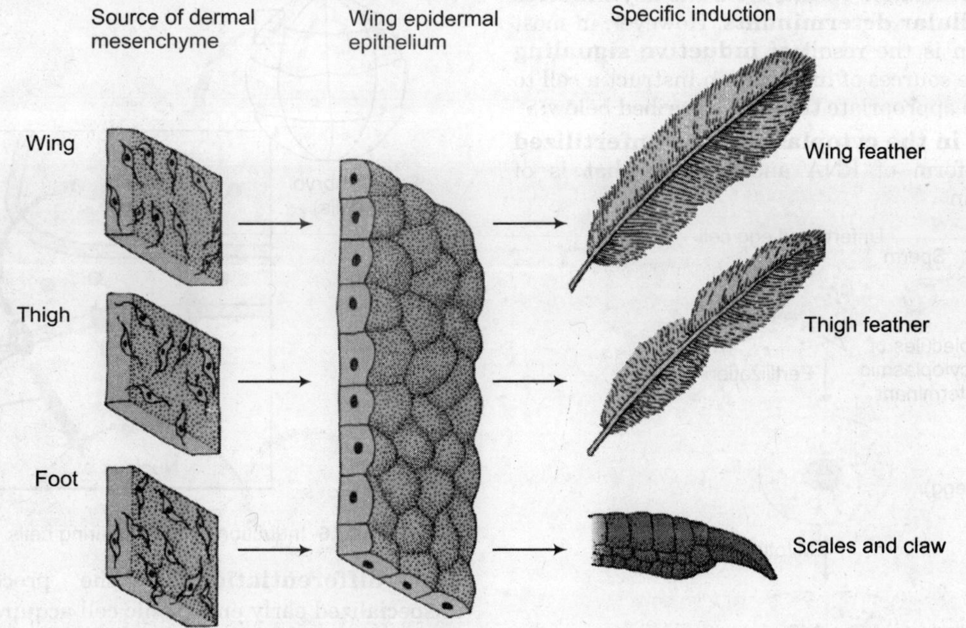

Fig. 14.13 Regional specificity of induction

Determination and Differentiation

Cell determination is the process by which portions of the genome are selected for expression in different embryonic cells. This involves developmental decisions that gradually restrict cell fate. Cells can progress from totipotent to pluripotent to determined.

Molecular Basis of Determination

The result of determination is the presence of tissue-specific proteins characteristic of a cell's structure and function.

Early human embryo at blastocyst stage (mammalian equivalent of blastula)
Embryonic stem cells
Or
Bone marrow (for example)
Adult stem cell
Cultured stem cells
Different culture conditions
Liver cells
Nerve cells
Heart muscle cells
Different types of differentiated cells

Fig. 14.14 Molecular basis of determination of cells in the presence of tissue-specific proteins

In some cases, determination results from the **asymmetric segregation of cellular determinants**. However, in most cases, determination is the result of **inductive signaling between cells**. The sources of information instruct a cell to express genes at the appropriate time are described below:

(i) **Information in the cytoplasm of the unfertilized egg,** in the form of RNA and protein, that is of maternal origin

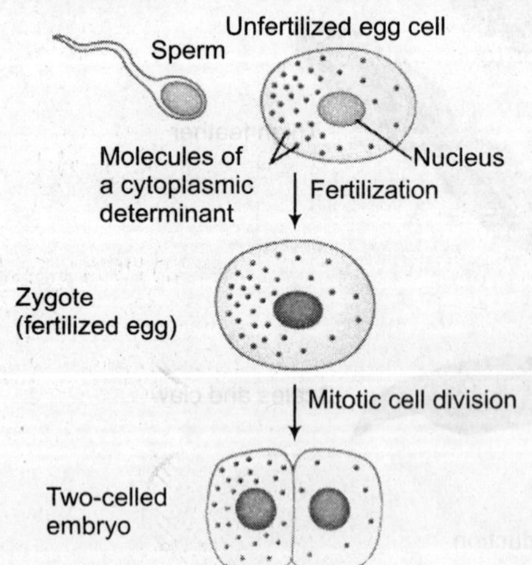

Fig. 14.15 Cytoplasmic determinants in egg

(ii) **Chemical signals produced by neighbouring embryonic cells,** such signals, through a process called 'induction' influence the growth and differentiation of adjacent cells.

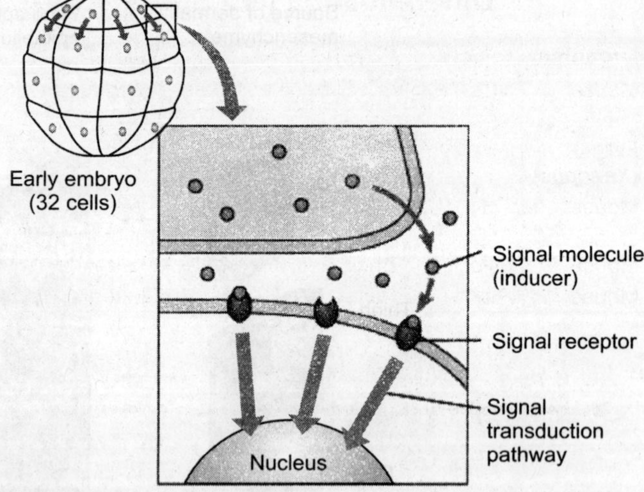

Fig. 14.16 Induction of neighbouring cells

Cell differentiation is the process whereby an unspecialized early embryonic cell acquires the features of a specialized cell such as a heart, liver or muscle cell.

Differentiation follows determination, as the cell elaborates a cell-specific developmental program. Differentiation results in the presence of cell types that have clear-cut identities, such as muscle cells, nerve cells, and skin cells.

Differentiated cell remain totipotent as differentiated cells are used in most of the cloning of animal by nuclear transfer (See table ahead).

Table 14.1 **Cloning Animals from Differentiated Cells by Nuclear Transfer**

Year	Animal	Nucleus Source
1962	Frog	Tadpole intestine
1997	Sheep	Mammary gland
1998	Cow	Adult cumulus cell
1998	Mouse	Adult fibroblast
1999	Goat	Foetal fibroblast
2000	Pig	Granulosa cell

Principle of Cell Differentiation

(i) Each differentiated cell contains a complete genome.

(ii) The differences between the cell types are only due to expression of different kinds of proteins, that is, a set of genes are expressed in a certain type of cell, but not in another type of cell.

Cell Differentiation is Controlled by Transcription

Tissue specific transcription factors are the proteins that cause the expression of a group of proteins that together give cell its identity.

Table 14.2 **Tissue Specific Transcription Factors That Cause Cell Differentiation into Specific Tissue**

Organism	Factor	Type of Factor	Tissue Specified
Mouse	SCL/*Tal*1	Basic helix-loop-helix	Haematopoetic cells
Frog (*Xenopus*)	*neuroD*	Basic helix-loop-helix	Neurons
Mouse	*Tcf4*	HMG box	Intestinal epithelium
Mouse	*MyoD*	Basic helix-loop-helix	Skeletal muscle
Mouse	*Pax7*	Paired-box	Skeletal muscle

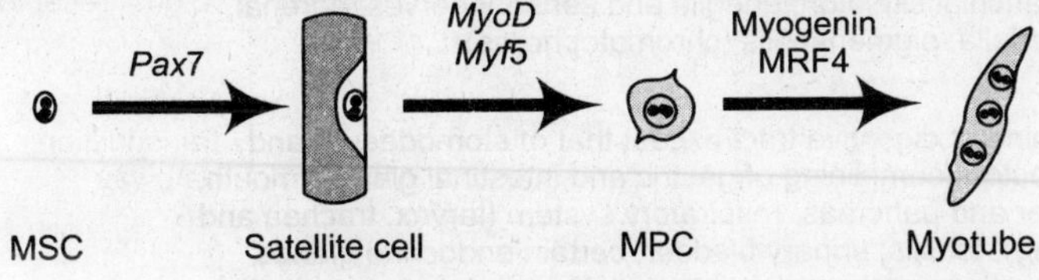

Fig. 14.17 Muscle differentiation, transcription factors in muscle differentiation

Cell differentiation is reversible

(a) Embryonic Stem (ES) cell can complete the whole process of differentiation in proper environment.

(b) Differentiated cell can undergo dedifferentiation or *trans*-differentiation.

(c) Cancer cell can be induce to differentiate.

Morphogenetic Gradients

Morphogenesis is the process of cellular differentiation, distribution and growth that takes place during the embryonic development of an organism. The **morphogenes** (proteins that control morphogenesis) that determine the fate of cells and elicits different responses at different concentration thresholds. A morphogen synthesized at one end of an axis would establish a concentration gradient along the axis. The gradient of morphogen is translated into a gradient of intracellular signal transduction and ultimately differential gene expression. Morphogens can establish gradients by free diffusion but alternative mechanisms are required for extracellular secreted proteins such as Hedgehog, Wingless/Wnt and Decapentaplegic/BMP.

The **morphogenetic determinants** (certain proteins or *m*RNAs) are placed in different regions of the egg cytoplasm and are apportioned to the different cells as the embryo divides. These morphogenetic determinants specify the cell type.

Morphogenetic Gradients in *Drosophila melanogaster*

The morphogenes (or transcription factors) displayed are the proteins *bicoid* (*bicoid* is a maternally transcribed gene that organizes the anterior development in *Drosophila*) and *hunchback* (*hunchback* is the 'partner' of *bicoid* in anterior/posterior development in *Drosophila*). These proteins play an important role in determining the anterior part of the body (head and thorax) from the posterior part (abdomen).

In *Drosophila*, antennae and legs are created by the same process, the only differ is a single transcription factor. If this transcription factor is damaged, the fly grows legs instead of antennae. This is due to 'antennapedia' mutant.

In the early stages of morphogenesis in an insect embryo, four types of differentiation can be distinguished:

- Anterior (head and thorax)
- Posterior (abdomen)

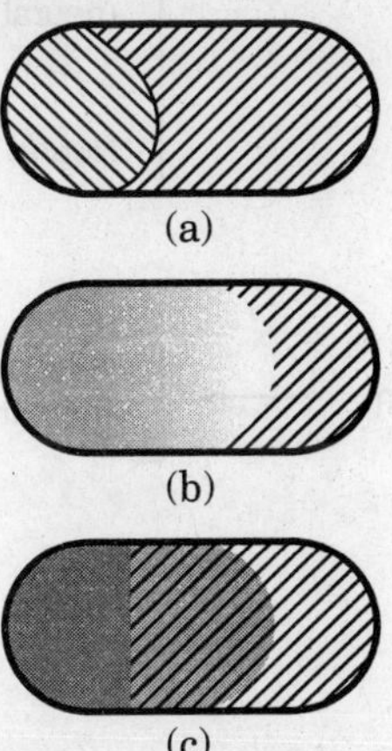

Fig. 14.18 Schematic drawing of morphogene gradients in *Drosophila*

(a) The *bicoid* *m*RNA (messenger RNA) is an intermediate copy of a piece of the DNA. It is transported to the ribosomes, where protein biosynthesis takes place) is located on the left side of the embryo. All cells of the embryo have inactive *hunchback* DNA.

(b) The *bicoid* *m*RNA is expressed as *bicoid* protein, resulting in a protein gradient with the highest concentration of protein on the left side of the embryo.

(c) The *hunchback* DNA is activated once the amount of *bicoid* protein passes a certain threshold. This results in a sharp borderline, which divides the part, where *hunchback* is expressed from the part where *hunchback* is not expressed.

- Dorso-ventral (front-and backside)
- Terminal (special structures at the unsegmented ends of the embryo)

In the later stages of development, these basic compartments become more and more divided. The same transcription factor can be used several times, having diffrent meanings in the different body parts.

The term 'morphogenesis' can be used to describe the development of unicellular life forms that do not have an embryonic stage in their life cycle. Morphogenetic responses may be induced in organisms by hormones or by environmental chemicals.

Cell Fate and Cell Lineages

Fate is the sum of all structures that the cell or its descendants will form at a later stage of normal development. It is the ultimate differentiated state to which a cell has become committed. Fate maps are the bases for experimental embryology.

The **cell lineage** of an organism is the pattern of cell divisions during its development. Cell lineages are described by following cell divisions in living individuals or by marking cells and examining their progeny.

Cell Lineage Patterns

(i) Some organisms or precursor cells display **cell lineage patterns are invariant** patterns of cell division, in which specification of cell fates is correlated with cell division patterns.

(ii) In other organisms, **cell lineage patterns are variable** and not correlated with cell fates. Invariant cell lineages reflect both cell-autonomous mechanisms of fate determination and highly reproducible cell-cell interactions. Genetic analysis of cell lineages has focused on systems, where cell lineage and cell fates are correlated.

Fate Mapping Methods

Fate maps have been generated in several ways:

(i) **Observing living embryos** In certain invertebrates, it is actually possible to look through the microscope and trace the descendants of a particular cell into the organs they generate. This type of study was performed about a century ago by **Edwin G Conklin.**

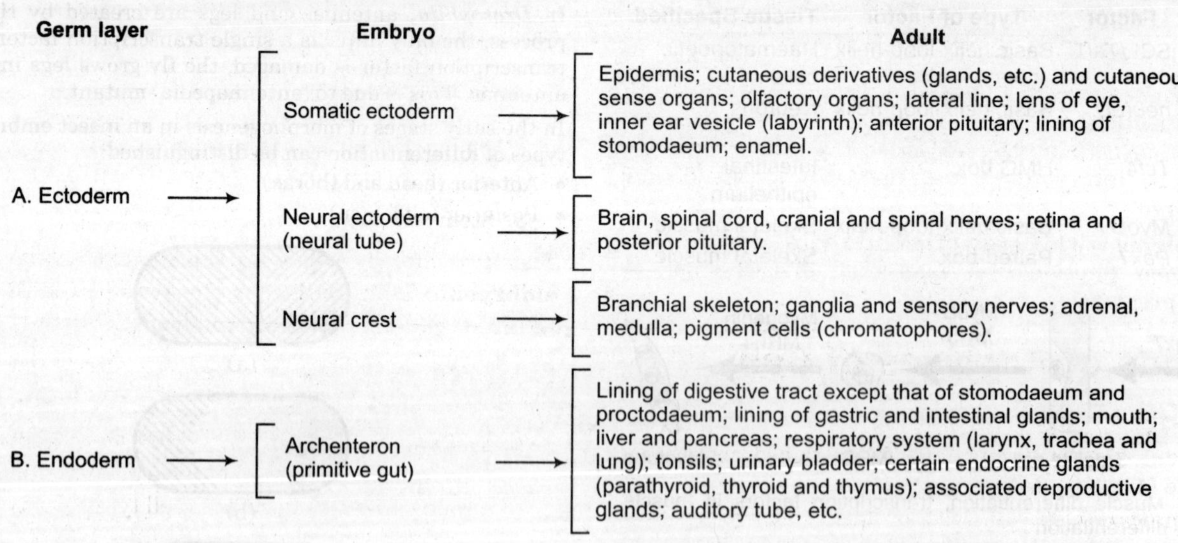

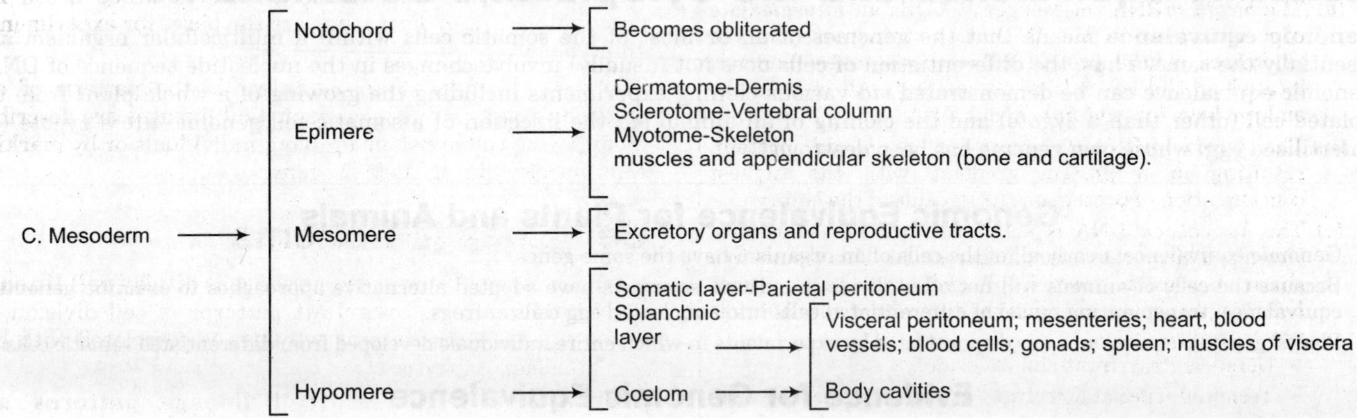

Fig. 14.19 Fate of three germ layers

(ii) Vital dye marking In the early years of the twentieth century, **Vogt** (1929) traced the fates of different areas of amphibian eggs by applying vital dyes to the region of interest. Vital dyes will stain cells but not kill them.

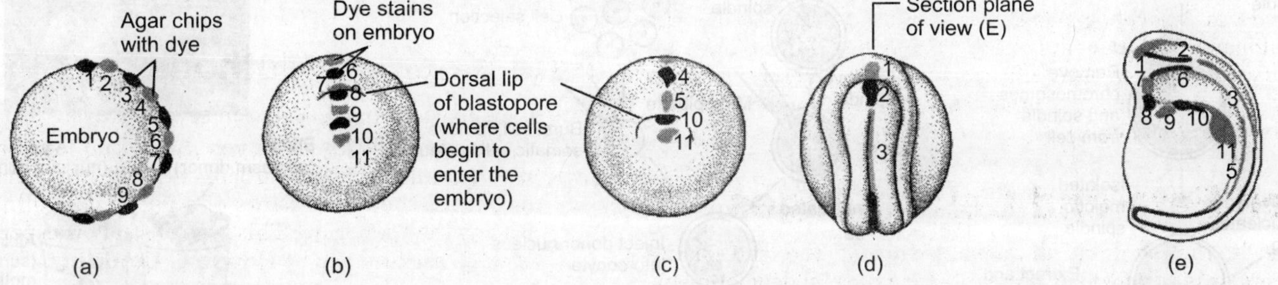

Fig. 14.20 Vital dye staining of amphibian embryos. (a) Specific cells of the embryonic surface with vital dyes. (b-d) Dorsal surface views of stain on successively later embryos. (e) Medial sagittal section to show the stained cells

(iii) Radioactive labelling and fluorescent dyes In this method, a donor embryo is usually grown in a solution containing radioactive thymidine. This base will be incorporated into the DNA of the dividing embryo.

The **problems with radioactive and vital dye marking** include their dilution over many cell divisions and the laborious preparation of the slides.

Methods of Analyses of Cell Lineage

(i) **Direct observation** Same as described above under 'Fate Mapping Methods'.

(ii) **Clonal analysis** In large, opaque or slowly developing embryos, direct observation of cell divisions is not feasible. To analyze cell lineages in such cases, it is necessary to mark individual cells by physical or genetic means and later to identify their progeny by expression of the marker. Here, the progeny of a single cell forms a clone.

Stem Cells

Stem cells are a class of undifferentiated cells (*i.e.*, lacking certain tissue specific differentiation markers) that are able to differentiate into specialized cell types.

All stem cells have three general properties.

1. Stem cells are capable of dividing and renewing themselves for long periods.
2. Stem cells are unspecialized.
3. Stem cells can give rise to specialized cells.

The two broad types of mammalian stem cells are **embryonic stem cells** that are found in blastocysts and **adult stem cells** that are found in adult tissues.

In a developing embryo, stem cells can differentiate into all of the specialized embryonic tissues.

4. Embryonic stem cells are primitive (undifferentiated) cells from the embryo that have the potential to become a wide variety of specialized cell types.
5. Human embryonic stem cells are derived from blastocyst.

Embryonic stem cells develop from eggs that have been fertilized *in vitro* or *in vivo*. Another potential source of embryonic stem cells is Somatic Cell Nuclear Transfer (SCNT). **Adult stem cell** is an undifferentiated cell found among differentiated cells in a tissue or organ. One population is haematopoietic stem cells and the second population is bone marrow stromal cells.

Genomic Equivalence and the Cytoplasmic Determinants

Genomic equivalence means that the genomes of all or most of the somatic cells within a multicellular organism are essentially the same. Thus, the differentiation of cells does not (usually) involve changes in the nucleotide sequence of DNA. Genomic equivalence can be demonstrated *via* various cloning experiments including the growing of a whole plant from an isolated cell (other than a zygote) and the cloning of an animal *via* the injection of a somatic-cell genome into a zygote (or unfertilized egg) whose own genome has been destroyed.

Genomic Equivalence for Plants and Animals

- Genomic equivalence; nearly all of the cells of an organism have the same genes.
- Because the cells of animals will not often divide in culture, scientists have adopted alternative approaches to examine genomic equivalence: transplanting nuclei of differentiated cells into enucleated egg cells of frogs.
- Plants' genomic equivalence was demonstrated by experiments in which entire individuals developed from differentiated somatic cells.

Evidence for Genomic Equivalence

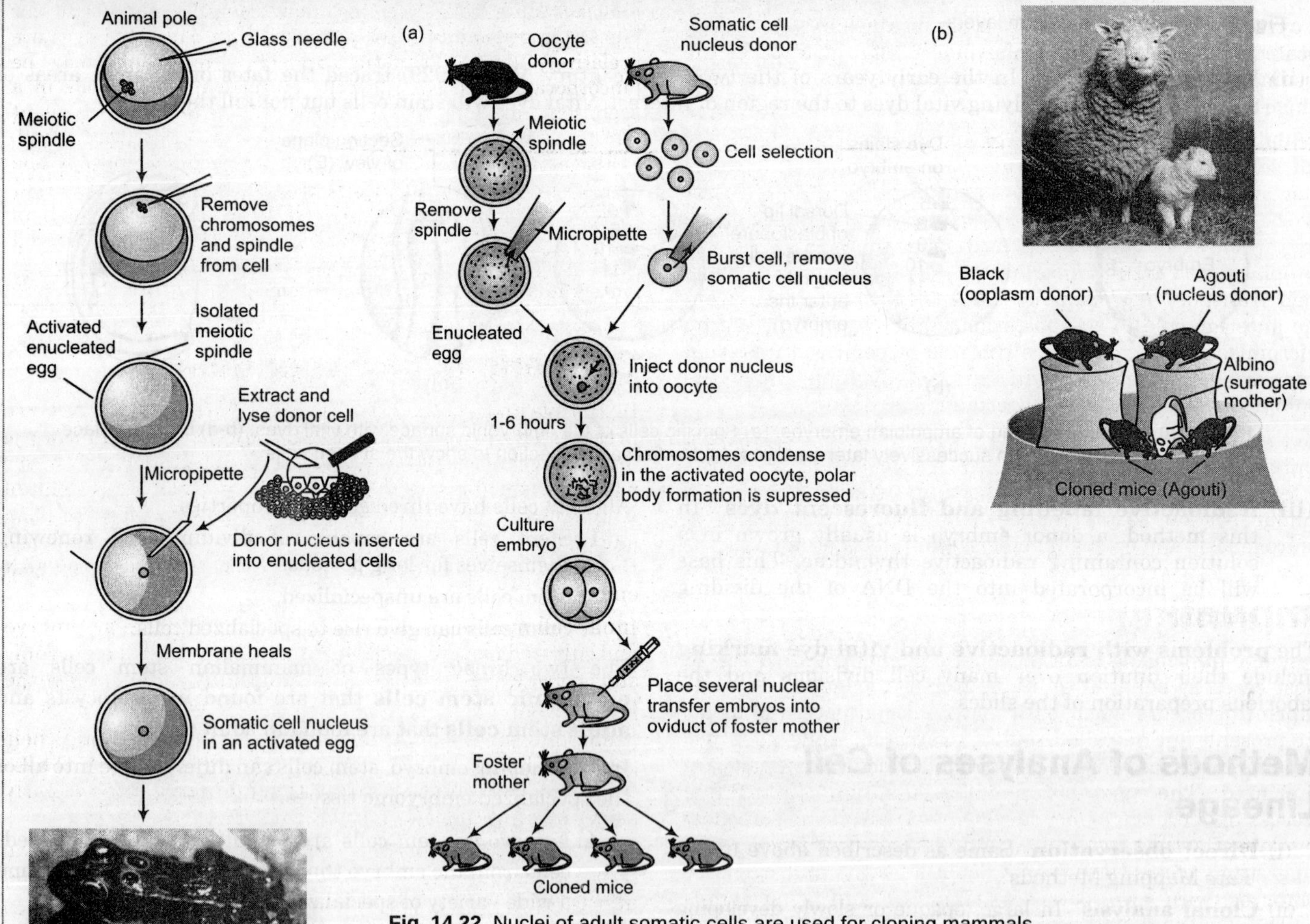

Fig. 41.21 Procedure for transplanting blastula nuclei into activated enclеated *Rana pipiens* eggs. The relative dimensions of the meiotic spindle have been exaggerted to show the technique

Fig. 14.22 Nuclei of adult somatic cells are used for cloning mammals

(a) The upper left dark mouse is the occyte donor, while the upper right light (agouti) mouse is the nucleus donor. The white mouse in the lower row is the mouse into whose uterus the resulting embryos were implanted. The two agouti mice beside her are cloned mice, derived from the injection of the agouti nucleus into the occyte of the black-furred parent.

(b) Similarly, Dolly, the adult sheep, was derived by fusing a mammary gland cell nucleus with an enucleated occyte, which was then implanted in a surrogate mother (of a different breed of sheep who gave birth to dolly.)

Table 14.3 **Examples of Genomic Non-equivalence During Development**

Mechanism	Examples
DNA amplification	Selective amplification of *r*RNA genes in *Xenopus* oocytes. Amplification of the chorion genes during oogenesis in *Drosophila.*
DNA loss	In mammals, loss of nuclei in differentiated erythrocytes and keratinocytes.
DNA rearrangement	In vertebrates, VDJ recombination and class switching during B-cell and T-cell development.

A **cytoplasmic determinant** is a substance or substances, located in part of an egg or blastomere, that guarantees the assumption of a particular state of commitment by the cells which inherit it during cleavage.

Cytoplasmic determinants are of considerable importance for the very earliest stages of embryonic development because they are often responsible for the establishment of the first two or three distinctly specified regions in the embryo. There are established experimental techniques that reorganize the cytoplasm and thus redistribute the determinants or block their transport. For example, the transfer of cytoplasm from the anterior pole to the posterior of the *Drosophila* egg by microinjection demonstrates the role of polarized maternal cytoplasmic determinants in axis specification, since the embryo develops with two heads and no abdomen.

In the early stages of *C. elegans* development a complex containing PAR3, PAR6 and aPKC becomes localized in the anterior and controls the fate of the first two blastomeres. A similar system seems to be involved in later events of neurogenesis and epithelial polarization in other animals.

Imprinting

Genomic imprinting is an epigenetic phenomenon which, in most cases, is believed to occur in gametogenesis. Genomic imprinting occurs when both maternal and paternal alleles are present, but one allele will be expressed, while the other remains inactive. It is not completely evident why genes are imprinted. The most prominent assumption is that this process is necessary for development and may somehow regulate growth in the embryo and neonate. Evidence for this suggestion came from experiments with androgenotes (embryos with two paternal genomes) and gynogenotes (embryos with two maternal genomes), which were produced by nuclear transplantation. These zygotes were formed, but neither type was able to undergo further development. From this situation, it is possible to suggest that the maternal and paternal effects are complementary.

The optimal method for gene imprinting is DNA methylation. This process is carried out with the enzyme DNA methyltransferase (DNA MTase) in mammals. DNA MTase acts on the DNA sequence 5-CpG-3. Some organisms (primarily higher eukaryotes) have aggregates of CpG (known as CpG islands) in their genomes. These islands are rarely methylated in animal cells. This may be due to the bound transcription factors that block DNA MTase.

Mutants and Transgenics in Analysis of Development

Recently developed techniques have enabled us to study gene function by moving certain genes into and out of embryonic cells.

Technique of Inserting DNA into a Cell

Cloned pieces of DNA can be isolated, modified (if so desired) and inserted into cells by several means. **Microinjection,** in which a solution containing the cloned gene is injected into the nucleus of a cell. This technique is especially useful for inserting genes into newly fertilized eggs, since the eggs are relatively large. **Transfection,** DNA fragments may be incorporated directly into cells by incubating the cells in a solution containing new DNA. The chances of a DNA fragment incorporation into the chromosomes are relatively small. **Electroporation,** in which a high-voltage pulse 'pushes' the DNA into the cells. **Transposable element** or **retroviral vector,** a more 'natural' way of getting genes into cells is to insert the cloned gene into a transposable element or retroviral vector. These naturally occurring mobile regions of DNA can integrate themselves into the genome of an organism.

Chimeric Mice Experiments

In the blastocyst, there is a stage when two cell types are present: **The outer trophoblast cells,** which will form the fetal portion of the placenta and the **Inner Cell Mass** (ICM), whose cells will give rise to the embryo itself. Separation of ICM cells can lead to twins and if an ICM blastomere from one mouse is transferred into the embryo of a second mouse, the donor ICM cell can contribute to every organ of the host embryo.

Inner cell mass blastomeres can be isolated from an embryo and cultured *in vitro*, such cultured cells are called embryonic stem cells (ES cells). ES cells are almost totipotent, except the trophoblast.

Embryonic stem cells from a mouse are cultured and their genome altered by the addition of a cloned gene. These transgenic cells are selected and then injected into the early stages of a host mouse embryo.

The transgenic embryonic stem cells integrate with the host's embryonic stem cells. The embryo is placed into the uterus of a pregnant mouse, where it develops into a **chimeric mouse**. The treated cells can become part of the germ line of the mouse. If such a chimeric mouse is mated with a wild-type mouse, some of its progeny will carry one copy of the inserted gene. When these heterozygous progeny are mated to one another, about 25 percent of the resulting offspring will be homozygous for the inserted gene in every cell of their bodies. Thus, a gene cloned from some other organism will be present in both copies of the chromosomes within these mouse genomes. Strains of such transgenic mice have been particularly useful in determining how genes are regulated during development.

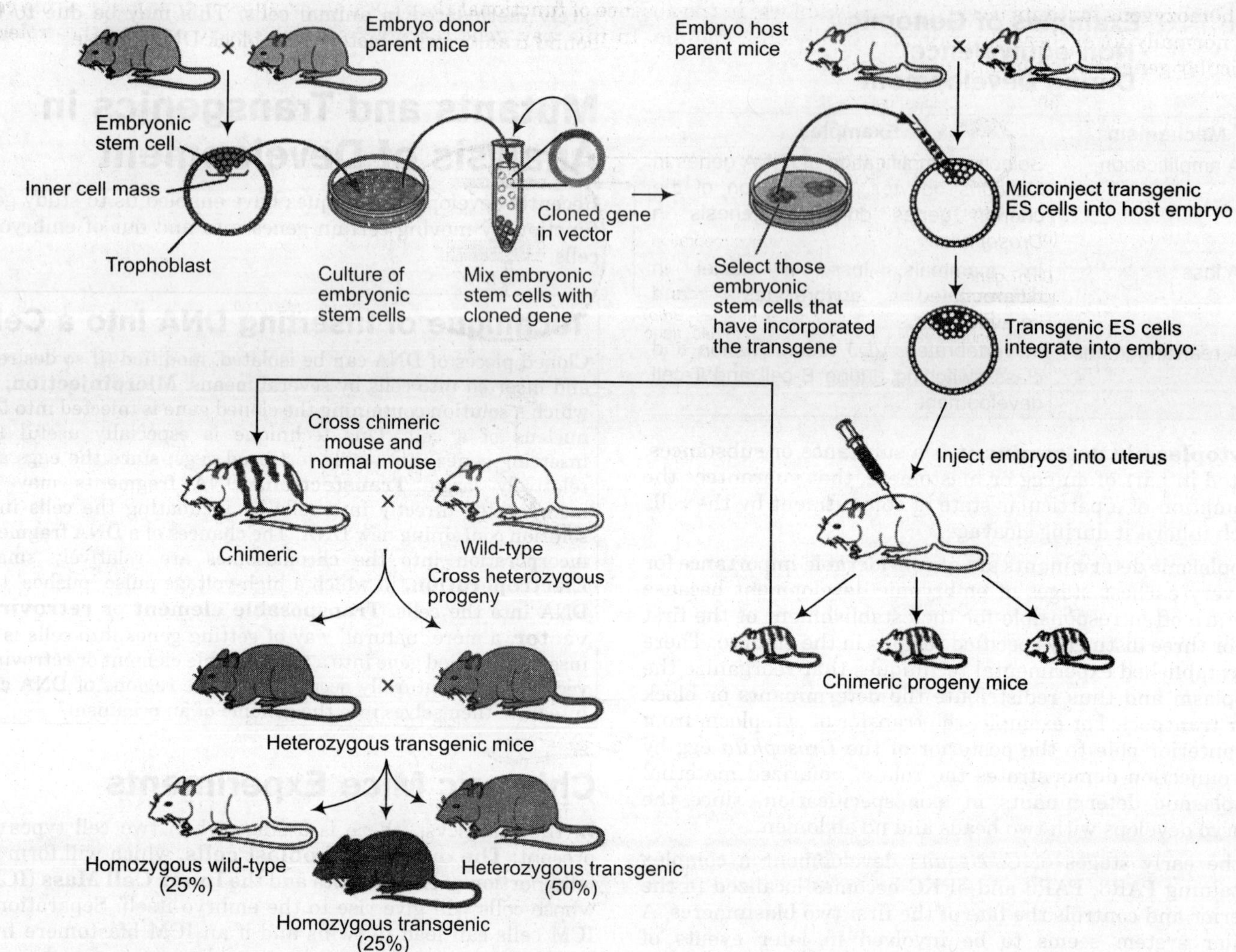

Fig. 14.23 Production of transgenic mice

Gene Targeting (Gene Knockout) Experiments

The analysis of early mammalian embryos has been done by the techniques of **gene targeting** (gene knockout). This technique involves adding genes, gene targeting replaces wild-type alleles with mutant ones. As an example, a knockout of the gene for bone morphogenetic protein 7 (*Bmp*7) is considered in the following discussion.

Bone morphogenetic proteins are involved in numerous developmental interactions. *Bmp*7 has been implicated as a protein that prevents cell death and promotes cell division in several developing organs.

To find the function of *Bmp*7 in the development of the mouse. First, isolate the (*Bmp*7) gene, cut it at one site with a restriction enzyme and inserted a bacterial gene for neomycin resistance into that site. This mutated the *Bmp*7 gene has destroyed the ability of the gene's product (*Bmp*7 protein) to function. These mutant (*Bmp*7) genes were electroporated into embryonic stem cells that were naturally sensitive to neomycin. Once inside the nucleus of an ES cell, the mutated *Bmp*7 gene may replace a normal allele of *Bmp*7 by a process called homologous recombination. Thus, the enzymes involved in DNA repair and replication incorporate the mutant gene in the place of the normal copy. It's a rare event, but such cells can be selected by growing the ES cells in neomycin. The resulting cells have one normal *Bmp*7 gene and one mutated *Bmp*7 gene. These heterozygous ES cells were then microinjected into mouse blastocysts, where they were integrated into the cells of the embryo. The resulting chimeric mice had wild-type cells from the host embryo and heterozygous *Bmp*7-containing cells from the donor ES cells. The chimeras were mated to wild-type mice, producing progeny that were heterozygous for *Bmp*7. These heterozygous mice were then bred with each other and about 25 percent of their progeny carried two copies of the mutated *Bmp*7 gene.

The homozygous mutants lacked eyes and kidneys. In the absence of functional *Bmp*7 protein, it appears that many of the cells that normally form these two organs stop dividing and die. In this way, gene targeting can be used to analyze the roles of particular genes during mammalian development.

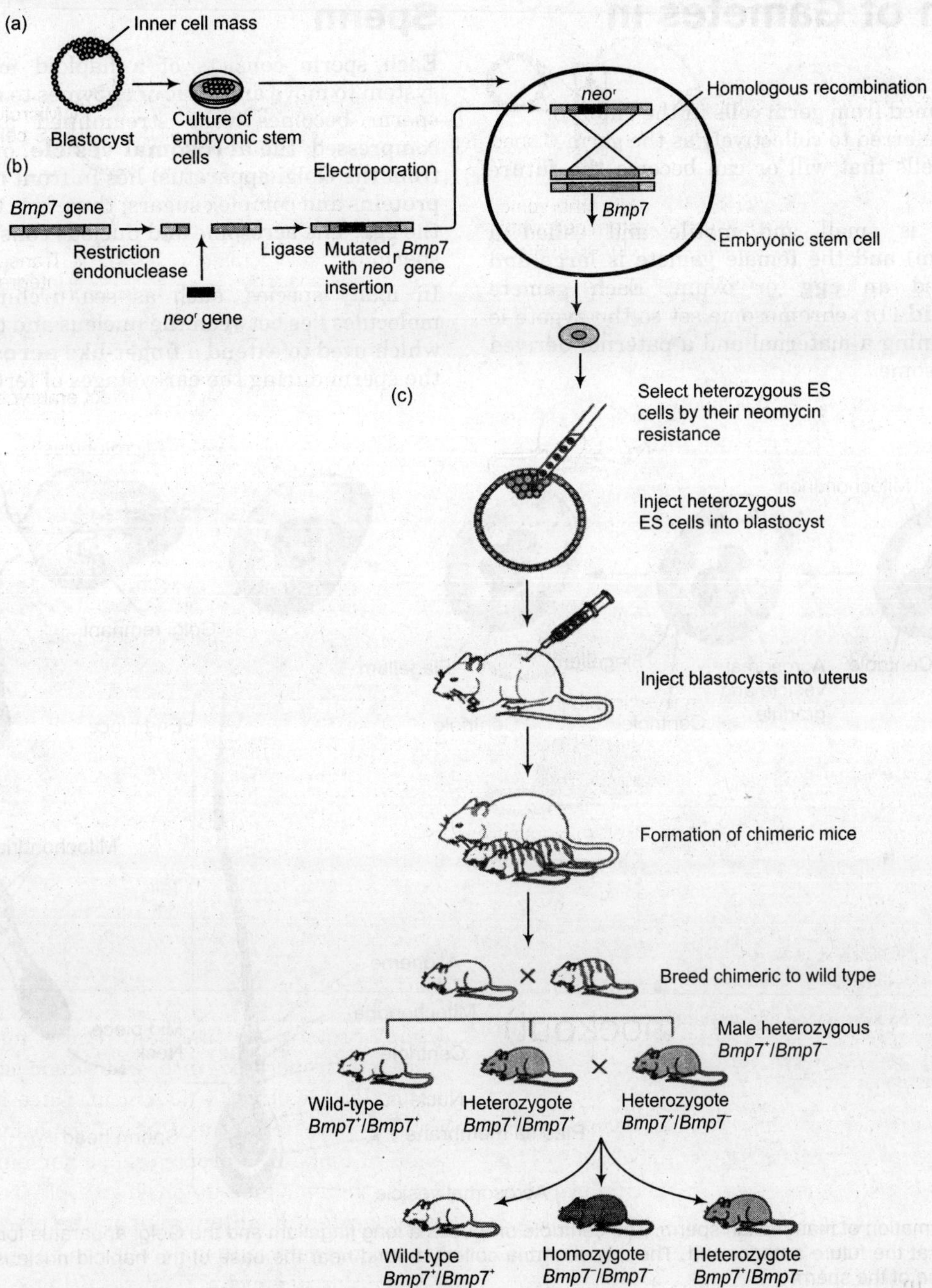

Fig. 14.24 Technique for gene targeting. In this case, the targeted gene is *Bmp*7

(a) Embryonic stem cells from a mouse blastocyst are cultured.

(b) Cloned *Bmp*7 genes are cut with a restriction enzyme and a neomycin resistance gene is inserted into the region that encodes the DNA-binding site of the protein. These mutant *Bmp*7 genes are electroporated into ES cells. In some of the cells, homologous recombination exchanges a wild-type gene for the mutant copy. These cells are selected by their neomycin resistance

Gametogenesis, Fertilization and Early Development

Production of Gametes in Animals

The gametes are formed from germ cells in the embryo. The germ cells are referred to collectively as the germ line, consisting of cells that will or can become the future gametes.

The male gamete is small and motile and called a spermatozoon (sperm) and the female gamete is large and immotile and called an **egg** or ovum. Each gamete contributes a **haploid** ($1n$) chromosome set so the zygote is **diploid** ($2n$), containing a maternal and a paternal-derived copy of each chromosome.

Sperm

Each sperm consists of a haploid nucleus, a propulsion system to move and a sac of enzymes to enter the egg. Mature sperm becomes very streamlined and DNA is tightly compressed; the **acrosomal vesicle**, or **acrosome** (derived from the Golgi apparatus) lies in front of nucleus that digest proteins and complex sugars; thus, lyse the outer coverings of the egg. The acrosome and nucleus constitute the head of the sperm.

In many species, such as sea urchins, a globular actin molecules lies between the nucleus and the acrosomal vesicle, which used to extend a finger-like **acrosomal process** from the sperm during the early stages of fertilization.

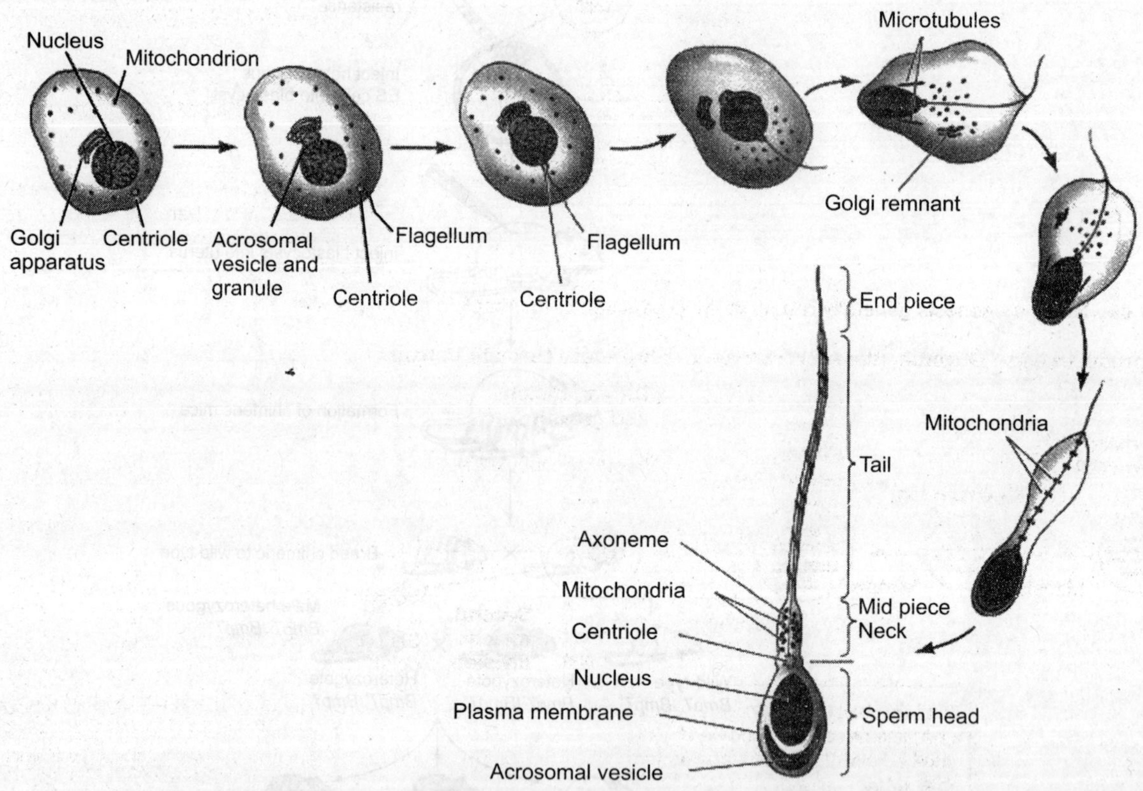

Fig. 14.25 The formation of mammalian sperm. The centriole produces a long flagellum and the Golgi apparatus forms the acrosomal vesicle at the future anterior end. The mitochondria collect around near the base of the haploid nucleus and become the midpiece of the sperm

In most species, sperm travel by whipping its **flagellum.** Flagella are complex structures. The major motor portion of the flagellum is called the **axoneme**. It is formed by microtubules emanating from the centriole at the base of the sperm nucleus.

The force for sperm propulsion is provided by **dynein**, a protein that is attached to the microtubules. Dynein hydrolyzes molecules of ATP and can convert the released chemical energy into the mechanical energy that propels the sperm.

The differentiation of mammalian sperm is not completed in the testes. The pre-mature sperm moves through the lumen of the seminiferous tubules into the epididymis, where they acquire the ability to move. The sperm released during ejaculation are able to move, but they do until the sperm has been inside the female reproductive tract for a certain period of time. The final stages of sperm maturation are called capacitation.

Gamete Formation or Gametogenesis

Spermatogenesis produces sperm. Primary spermatocytes undergo the first meiotic division to form **secondary spermatocytes**, which are haploid. The second meiotic division produces four haploid **spermatids** for each primary spermatocyte that entered meiosis.

Spermatogenesis
Male germ cell (2*n*)
Mitosis
Spermatogonium (2*n*)
Mitosis
Primary spermatocyte (2*n*)
First meiotic division
Secondary spermatocytes (*n*)
Cytoplasmic bridge
Second meiotic division
Differentiation and maturation into gametes
Spermatids (*n*)
Sperm cells (*n*)
The first meiotic division produces haploid cells.
Spermatids, each of which is different genetically, will differentiate into individual sperm.

Fig. 14.26. Spermatogenesis generally results in the production of four haploid sperm per meiosis

Oogenesis produces eggs. Oogonia, like spermatogonia, proliferate through mitosis.

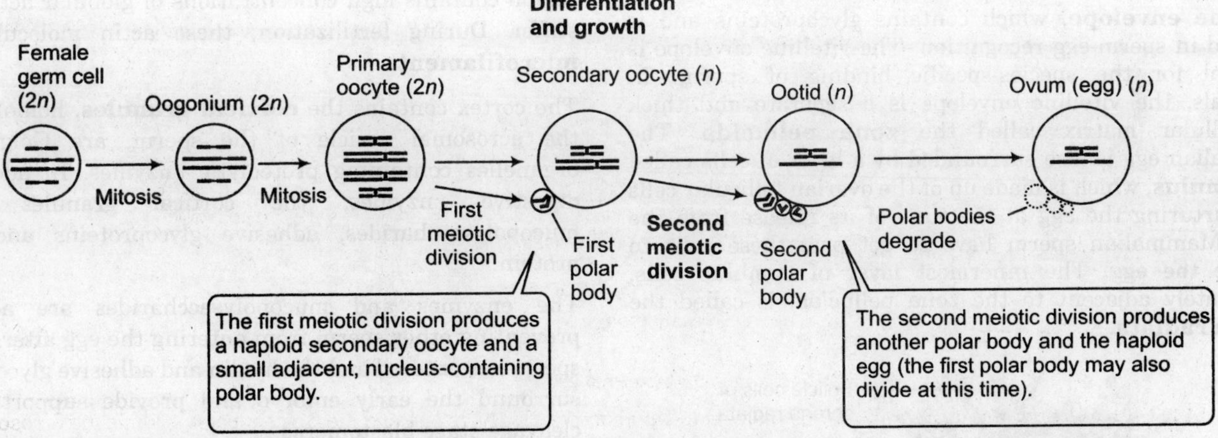

Fig. 14.27 Oogenesis generally results in the formation of one egg and two polar bodies (first polar body has the same chromosome number but twice the DNA content as second polar body)

The Egg

The germ cell, following the last mitotic division is known as an **oocyte**. It is a **primary oocyte** until completion of the first meiotic division and a **secondary oocyte** until completion of the second meiotic division. The developing egg (called the **oocytes** before it reaches the stage of meiosis at which it is fertilized).

All the material necessary for the beginning of growth and development must be stored in the mature egg (the ovum).

In some species (*e.g.*, sea urchins), the nucleus is already haploid at the time of fertilization. In other species (including many worms and most mammals), the egg nucleus is still diploid and the sperm enters before the meiotic divisions are completed. The stage of the egg nucleus at the time of sperm entry in different species is different.

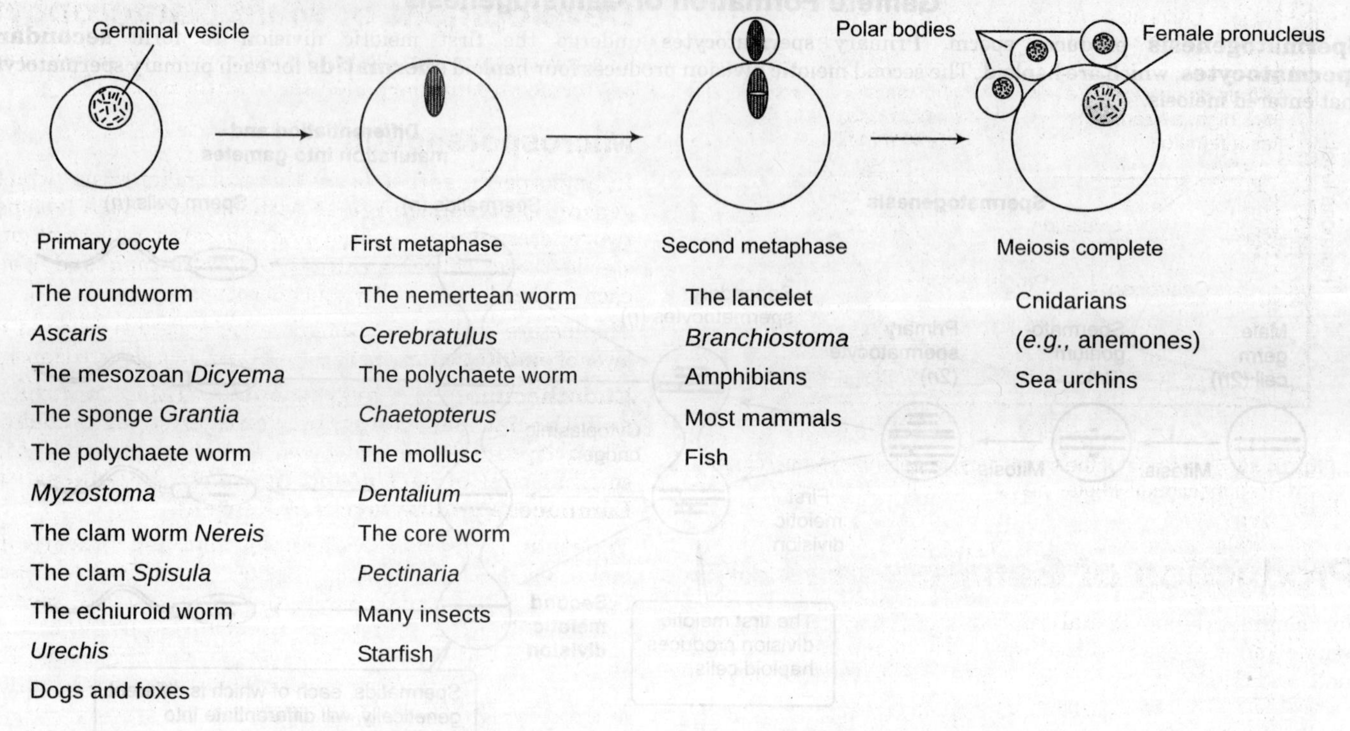

Fig. 14.28 Stages of egg maturation at the time of sperm entry in different animal species

The egg **plasma membrane** regulate the flow of certain ions during fertilization and capable of fusing with the sperm plasma membrane. Outside the plasma membrane is the **vitelline envelope**, which contains glycoproteins and is involved in sperm-egg recognition. The vitelline envelope is essential for the species-specific binding of sperm. In mammals, the vitelline envelope is a separate and thick extracellular matrix called the **zona pellucida**. The mammalian egg is also surrounded by a layer of cells called the **cumulus**, which is made up of the ovarian follicular cells that nurturing the egg at the time of its release from the ovary. Mammalian sperm have to get past these cells to fertilize the egg. The innermost layer of cumulus cells, immediately adjacent to the zona pellucida, is called the **corona radiata.**

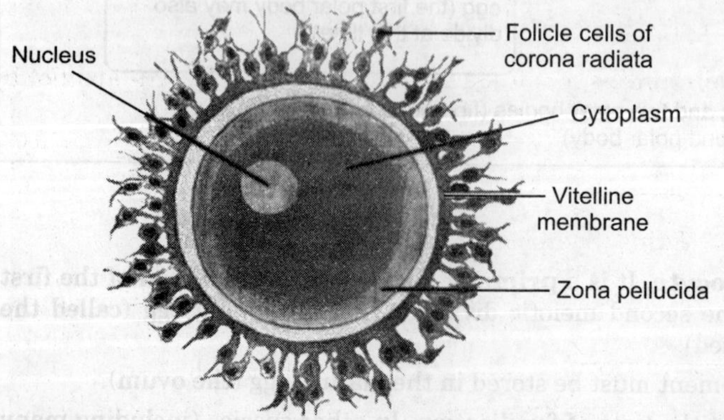

Fig. 14.29 Structure of egg

Immediately beneath the plasma membrane is a thin shell of gel-like cytoplasm called the **cortex**. The cytoplasm in this region contains high concentrations of globular actin and is stiffer. During fertilization, these actin molecules form **microfilaments**.

The cortex contains the **cortical granules,** homologous to the acrosomal vesicle of the sperm, are Golgi-derived organelles containing proteolytic enzymes. In addition to digestive enzymes, the cortical granules contain mucopolysaccharides, adhesive glycoproteins and hyalin protein.

The enzymes and mucopolysaccharides are active in preventing other sperm from entering the egg after the first sperm has entered and the hyalin and adhesive glycoproteins surround the early embryo and provide support for the cleavage-stage blastomeres.

Parthenogenetic Reproduction in a Species of Whiptail Lizard

In whiptail lizard (*Cnemidophorus uniparens*), there are no males in this species, but females act as males, engaging in all aspects of courtship display and mating, even though no sperm are produced or transferred. Whether a specific female acts as a female or as a male depends on her hormonal state at the time, but sexual activity is required to stimulate release of eggs from the ovary.

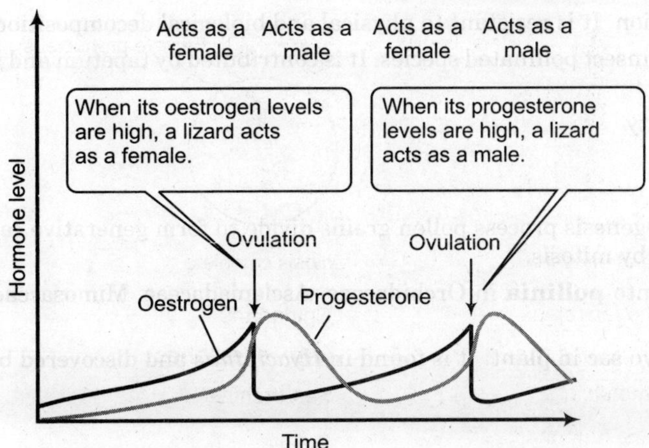

Fig. 14.30 The stage of the ovarian cycle determines the role an individual whiptail plays

Production of Gametes in Plants

For completion of sexual reproduction male gamete and female gametes are required which are formed by meiosis in male and female reproductive organs respectively.

Development of Male Gametophyte

The male gamete producing structures called pollen grains, are formed within the pollen sac of anthers.

Microsporangium

In angiosperm, anther bears the sporangial tissue which is generally **tetrasporangiate** with two lobe. Each lobe bears two microsporangia, which are separated by a column of sterile tissue called **connective.** In *Moringa* and *Wolffia* each anther lobe has only one microsporangium.

The mature anther wall comprises an epidermis followed by a layer of **endothecium,** middle layers and single layered tapetum.

Endothecium is **hygroscopic. This nature of endothecial cell helps in dehiscence of anther at maturity.** In *Pisum* and *Lens*, endothecium wall contains small amount of **pectin and lignin. In Najadaceae and Lamnaceae middle layers are absent.**

Tapetum is physiologically important and provides food materials for sporogenous tissue. In *Alectra thomsonii* tapetal cell is dimorphic, larger towards interior (C-tapetum) and smaller on the outer side (P-tapetum). DNA content is enormously increased in taptal cells due to endomitosis, polyteny and restitution nuclei. Tapetum secrete **callose enzyme** which dissolves **callose.**

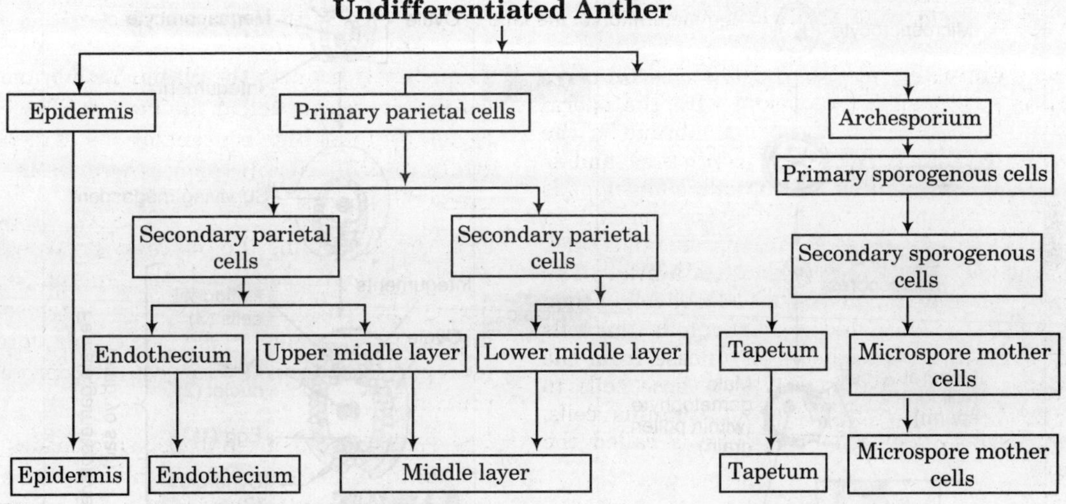

Fig. 14.31 Typical development pathway of microsporangium *(Alectra thomsonii)*

Tapetal cells contain numbers of spherical bodies called **pro-ubisch bodies,** produced only by glandular tapetum and not by amoeboid tapetum. They rapidly become coated with **sporopollenin** called **ubisch bodies.**

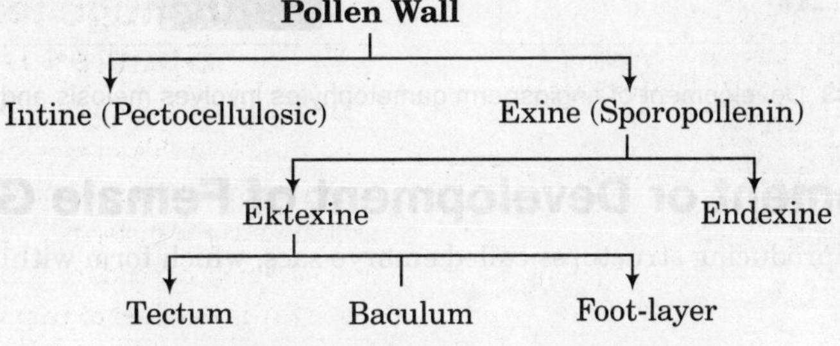

Fig. 14.32 Different sections of pollen wall

Sporopollenin is derived from carotenoids by oxidative polymerization. It is resistant to physical and biological decomposition.

Pollenkit is an oily layer found outside the mature pollen grains of insect pollinated species. It is contributed by tapetum and is made up of lipid and carotenoids.

Auxin, maleic hydrazide and dalapon selectively induce male sterility.

Development of Male Gamete

Microspore is the male gametophyte in higher plant. In the gametogenesis process pollen grains divide to form generative cell and vegetative cell. The generative cell produces two male gametes by mitosis.

Microspore is in **tetrad** during mitosis, the microspore is united into **pollinia** in Orchidaceae, Asclepiadaceae, Mimosaceae, etc., or as **massulae** in *Neottia*.

Nemec phenomenon is the appearance of pollen grain like embryo sac in plant. It is found in *Hyacinthus* and discovered by **Nemec (1898).**

(a) Pollen of *Ambrosia* (Compositae) cause hay fever.

(b) Pollens of *Seryania* lethalis are poisonous.

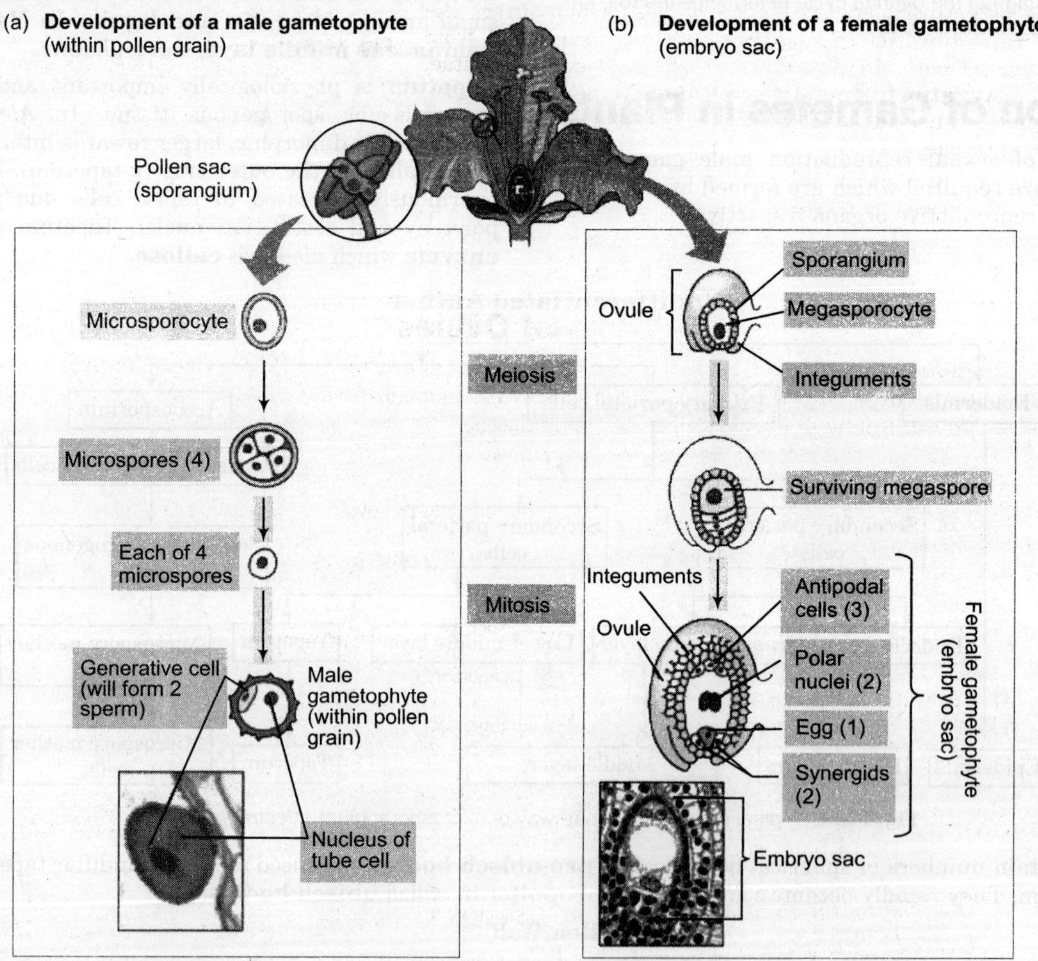

Fig. 14.33 Development of angiosperm gametophytes involves meiosis and mitosis

Embyo Sac Development or Development of Female Gametophyte

The female gametophytes are egg-producing structures called embryo sacs, which form within the ovules in ovaries.

Megasporangium

Megasporangium is the female gametophytic structure with a protective coating and called **ovule**. The ovules attached to the wall of ovary by a **placenta.** The ovule is attached to placenta by a stalk called **funicle** or **funiculus.** The point of attachment of funicle to the ovules is called **hilum.**

The ovules may be as **unitegmic ovule** (single integument) or **bitegmic ovules** (two integuments). The **unitegmic ovule** is the characteristics of gamopetalae and **bitegmic ovules** are the characteristics of polypetalae and monocotyledons. The ovules without any integument are called **ategmic ovules,** *e.g., Solanum, Loranthus, Liriosma* and *Oxalix.*

Endothecium is the innermost layer of embryo sac function as nutritive tissue. These tissues found in sympetalae with unitegmic, tenuinucellate ovule. In some bitegmic ovules **endothetium is generally single layered.** In **compositae** it is multilayered, *e.g.,* in sunflower it is twelve-layered.

Obturator is the structure associated with ovules, which direct the growth of pollen tube towards the microphyle. It is originated from placenta or funiculus or both. In Acanthaceae, Anacardiaceae, Labiatae, Magnoliaceae, etc., **obturator formed by swelling** of funicle. In *Crinum,* the funicle becomes knee-shaped. Placental obturator occurs in Euphorbiaceae, Cuscutaceae, etc.

Tenuinucellate condition of ovule is found in advanced families. Most of the families show the crassinucellate condition.

Perisperm is the remnant of nucellus, *e.g., Mirabilis jalapa, Nymphaea, Zingiber, Portulaca,* etc.

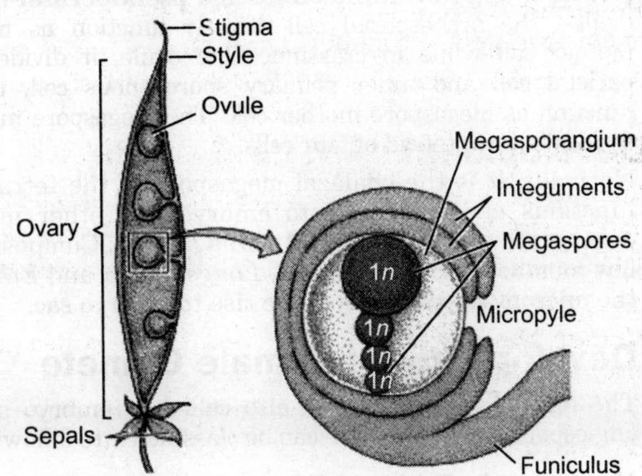

Fig. 14.34 The carpel contains one or more ovules, these contain megasporangia protected by two layers of integument cells. The megasporangia divide meiotically to produce haploid megaspores, all of the carpel is diploid except for the megaspores, which divide mitotically to produce the embryo sac (the female gametophyte)

Types of Ovules

Orthotropous or Atropous ovules This is primitive and simplest type of ovules, *e.g.,* Polygonaceae, Piperaceae.

Anatropous or Inverted ovules This is most common type of ovules in angiosperms, *e.g.,* Sympetalae.

Hemianatropous or Hemitropous, *e.g.,* Malpighiaceae, Primulaceae.

Campylotropous, *e.g.,* Chapparidaceae, Chenopodiaceae, Cruciferae.

Amphitropous, *e.g.,* Papaveraceae, Alismaceae, Butomaceae.

Circinotropous Ovules are straight but later, due to more growth on one side the ovule, inverted and completely rounded.

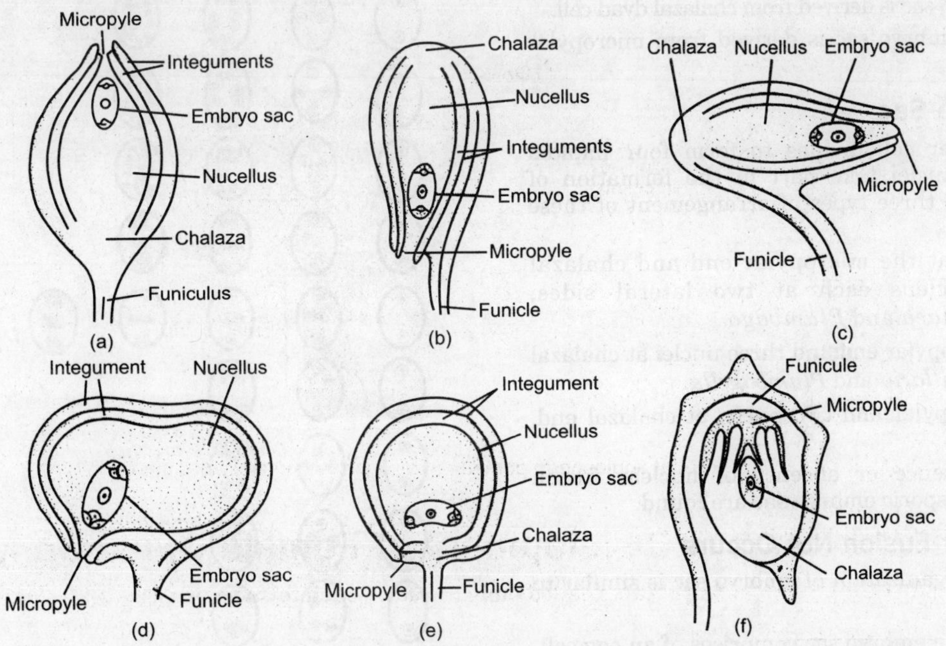

Fig. 14.35 Types of ovule in longitudinal section. (a) Orthotropous (b) Anatropous (c) Hemianatropous (d) Campylotropous (e) Amphitropous (f) Circinotropous

The single hypodermal cell of nucellus functions as archesporium. In **tenuincellate** and **pseudocrassi-nucellate** ovules, the archesporial cell directly function as megaspore mother cell while in crassinucellate ovule, it divide to form parietal cell and inner primary sporogenous cell, the latter function as megaspore mother cell. The megaspore mother cell divides to form tetrad of four cells.

Normally, it is the chalazal megaspore of the tetrad, which functions and gives rise to embryo sac, other megaspore degenerate and disappears. In Onagraceae, Compositae (in a few members), *Balanosphora, Longsdorffia* and *Ethytranthe* the micropylar megaspore give rise to embryo sac.

Development of Female Gamete

The female gametophyte is also called as embryo sac. The angiospermic gametophyte can be classified into following types

Monosporic Embryo Sacs

It is develop from single megaspore. It has following types of embryo sac.

- ***Polygonum* type** The embryo sacs formed by chalazal megaspore of the tetrads, embryo sac comprises of an egg apparatus, three antipodal cells, and a binucleate central cell.
- ***Oenothera* type** The embryo sac is derived from micropylar megaspore of the tetrad. It comprises of an egg apparatus and a uninucleate central cell.
- *Schisandra chinesis* have similar type of embryo sac, in this species chalazal megaspore is functional.

Bisporic Embryo Sacs

The megaspore mother cell divides to form dyad. Only one dyad cell undergoes meiotic division and other degenerates. The embryo sac is organized similar to *Polygonum* type. It has following types of embryo sacs.

- **Allium** type Embryo sac is derived from chalazal dyad cell.
- **Endymion** type Embryo sac is derived from micropylar dyad cell.

Tetrasporic Embryo Sac

The megaspore mother cell divides to form four haploid nuclei. All the four nuclei take part in the formation of embryo sac. There are three types of arrangement of these four nuclei

- One nucleus each at the micropylar end and chalazal end, and one nucleus each at two lateral sides, *e.g., Peperomia, Penaea* and *Plumbago*.
- One nucleus at micropylar end and three nuclei at chalazal end, *e.g., Drusa, Fritillaria* and *Plumbagella*.
- Two nuclei at micropylar and two nuclei at chalazal end, *e.g., Adoxa*.

On the basis of presence or absence of nuclear fusion following types of tetrasporic embryo sac are found.

Megaspore Nuclear Fusion Not Occurs

- ***Adoxa* type** The organization of embryo sac is similar to *Polygonum* type.
- ***Plumbago* type** The embryo sac comprises of an egg cell, a four nucleate central cell and three nuclei at the periphery.
- ***Penaea* type** The embryo sac comprises of group of three nuclei each at micropylar, chalazal and two groups present laterally. Four nuclei behave as polar nuclei. Triad at micropylar function as egg apparatus.
- ***Peperomia* type** The embryo sac comprises of an egg, a synergid, six peripheral cells and a central cell with eight polar nuclei.
- ***Drusa* type** The embryo sac comprises of three celled egg apparatus, two polar nuclei and eleven antipodal cells.

Megaspore Nuclei Fuse to form Triploid

- ***Fritillaria* type** The embryo sac comprises of an egg apparatus of three haploid cells, three triploid antipodal cells and a central cell with two polar nuclei, one is haploid and one is triploid.
- ***Plumbagella* type** The embryo sac comprises of an egg apparatus of haploid nuclei at the micropylar end, one triploid antipodal cell and two polar cells, one is haploid and other is triploid.
- The three haploid nuclei at chalazal end fuse to form triploid in *Fritillaria* and *Plumbagella* type of embryo sac. This phenomenon was first reported by **Bambacioni** (1928). This phenomenon is often called Bambacioni effect.

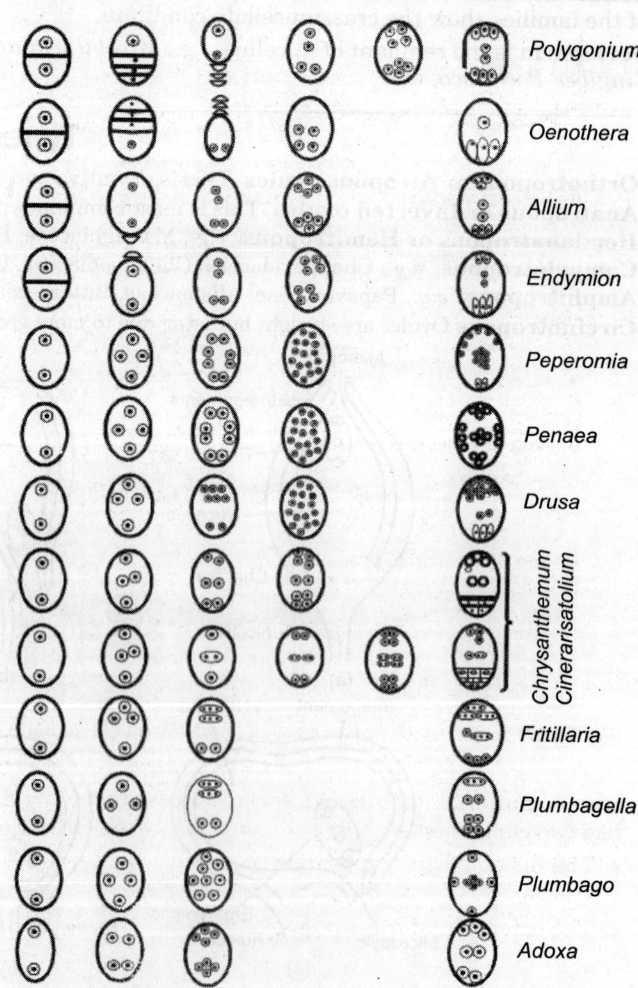

Fig. 14.36 Female gametophyte development of different types of embryo sacs in angiosperms

Cell Surface Molecules in Sperm-Egg Recognition in Animals

The interaction of sperm and egg generally proceeds according to five basic steps :

Step 1 The chemoattraction of the sperm to the egg by soluble molecules secreted by the egg.
Step 2 The exocytosis of the acrosomal vesicle to release its enzymes.
Step 3 The binding of the sperm to the extracellular envelope (vitelline layer or zona pellucida) of the egg.
Step 4 The passing of the sperm through this extracellular envelope.
Step 5 Fusion of egg and sperm cell plasma membranes.

In mammalian fertilization steps 2 and 3 are reversed and the sperm binds to the egg before releasing the contents of the acrosome.

Many marine organisms release their gametes into the environment and use species-specific attraction of sperm and species-specific sperm activation. For example, Mollusca, Cnidaria, Echinodermata and Orochordata. The mechanisms involve **chemotaxis,** by following a gradient of a chemical secreted by the egg.

The mechanisms of chemotaxis differ among species. One chemotactic molecule, a 14 amino acid peptide called **resact,** has been isolated from the egg jelly of the sea urchin *Arbacia punctulata*. *A. punctulata* sperm have receptors in their plasma membranes that bind resact and can swim up a concentration gradient of this compound until they reach the egg. Resact also acts as a **sperm-activating peptide.**

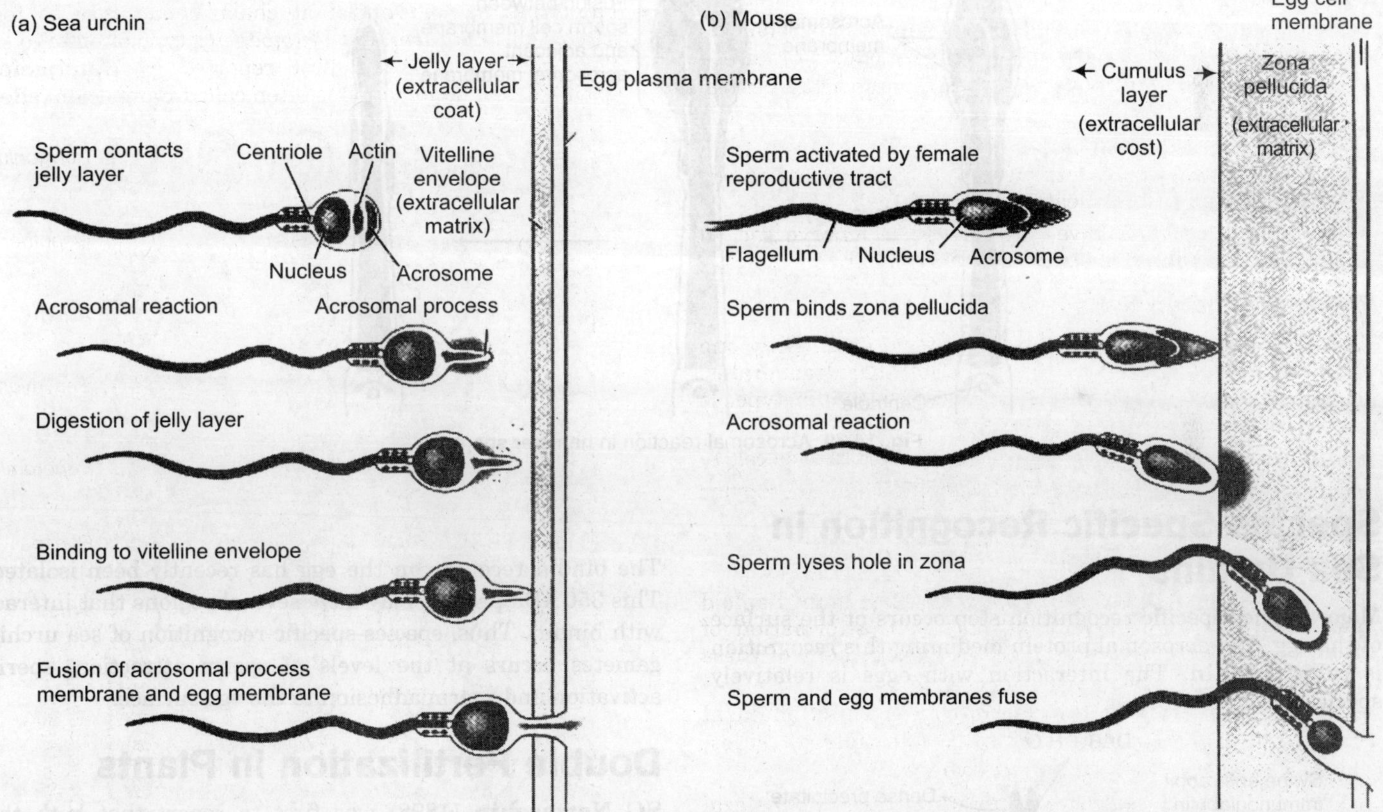

Fig. 14.37 Summary of events leading to the fusion of egg and sperm plasma membranes in the sea urchin and the mouse. Sea urchin fertilization is external

A second interaction between sperm and egg is the **acrosomal reaction.** In most marine invertebrates, the acrosomal reaction has two components :

- The fusion of the acrosomal vesicle with the sperm plasma membrane (results in the release of the contents of the acrosomal vesicle).
- The extension of the acrosomal process.

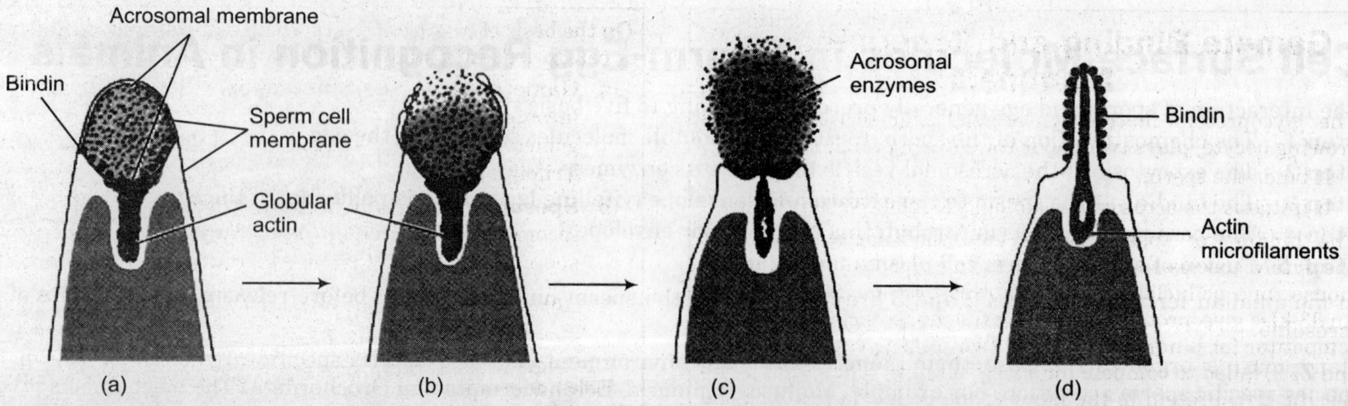

Fig. 14.38 Acrosomal reaction in sea urchin sperm. The acrosomal reaction is initiated by a fucose-containing polysaccharide in the egg jelly that binds to the sperm and allows calcium to enter into the sperm head. The exocytosis of the acrosomal vesicle is caused by the calcium-mediated fusion of the acrosomal membrane with the adjacent sperm plasma membrane

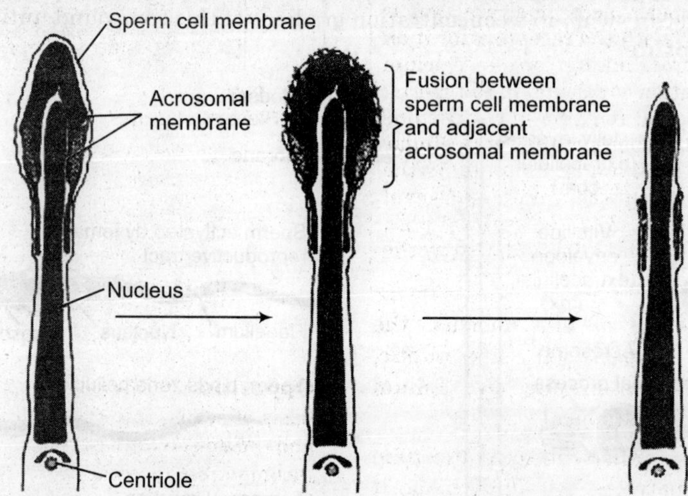

Fig. 14.39 Acrosomal reaction in hamster sperm

Species-Specific Recognition in Sea Urchins

Major species-specific recognition step occurs at the surface of the egg. The acrosomal protein mediating this recognition is called **bindin.** The interaction with eggs is relatively species-specific.

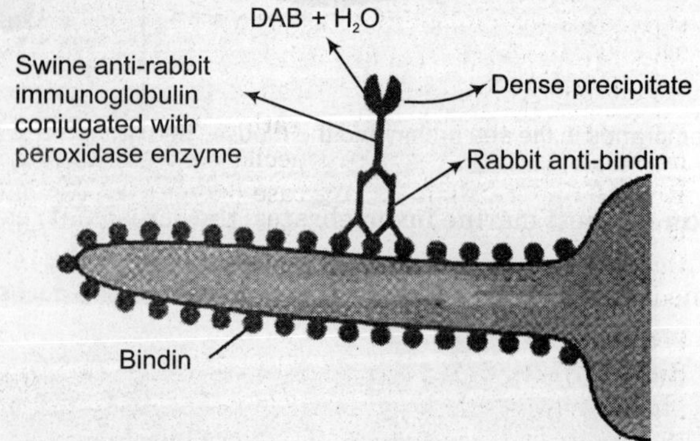

Fig. 14.40 Localization of bindin on the acrosomal process

The bindin receptor on the egg has recently been isolated. This 350 kDa protein may have several regions that interact with bindin. Thus, species-specific recognition of sea urchin gametes occurs at the levels of sperm attraction, sperm activation and sperm adhesion to the egg surface.

Double Fertilization in Plants

SG Nawaschin (1898) was first to report that both the sperms are involved in fertilization. One sperm is fused with egg and other fuse with secondary nuclei. This process is called **double fertilization** which is unique to angiosperms. Most of the plants have two polar nuclei and therefore, second fusion involves the fusion of three nuclei. This process is called **triple fusion.** Fusion of male nuclei and polar nuclei takes place earlier than the fusion of male nuclei and egg. Fusion of egg nucleus with sperm nucleus is called **syngamy.**

Gamete Binding and Recognition in Mammals

The glycoprotein matrix synthesized and secreted by the growing oocyte, plays two major roles during fertilization

- It binds the sperm.
- It initiates the acrosomal reaction after the sperm is bound.

The binding of sperm to the zona is relatively, but not absolutely, species-specific. The binding of mouse sperm to the mouse zona pellucida can be inhibited by zona glycoproteins. An 83-kDa glycoprotein, **ZP3,** from the mouse zona is the active competitor for binding. The other two zona glycoproteins, ZP1 and ZP2, failed to compete for sperm binding. Thus, ZP3 is the specific glycoprotein in the mouse zona pellucida to which the sperm bind. ZP3 also initiates the acrosomal reaction after sperm have bound to it. Unlike the sea urchin, the acrosomal reaction in mammals occurs only after the sperm has bound to the zona pellucida. The mouse sperm acrosomal reaction is induced by the crosslinking of ZP3 with the receptors for it on the sperm membrane. This crosslinking opens calcium channels to increase the concentration of calcium in the sperm. The difference between the acrosomal reaction in sea urchins and mammals may be due to the thickness of the extracellular envelopes surrounding the egg. The secondary binding to the zona is accomplished by proteins in the inner acrosomal membrane that bind specifically to ZP2. In guinea pigs, secondary binding to the zona is thought to be mediated by the protein PH-20.

Depending upon the mitotic state of egg nucleus, the syngamy can be of three types: **(i)** Pre-mitotic, *e.g.*, Gramineae, Compositae **(ii)** Post-mitotic, *e.g.*, Lilium fritillaria **(iii)** Intermediate e.g., Impatiens.

Polyspermy When more than one pollen tube or pollen tube with more than two sperms penetrates the embryo sac it releases more than two sperms in embryo sac. This situation is referred to as **polyspermy.** It results in fertilization of egg by more than one male sperm nucleus or sperms. May fertilize other component of embryo sac such as synergids or antipodals nuclei.

The zygote of the angiosperm produces only a single embryo, the zygote of the gymnosperm, on the other hand, produces two or more embryos after cell division begins, by a process known as cleavage embryogenesis. Double fertilization, first identified a century ago, is generally restricted to the angiosperms, but it has also been found in the gymnosperms *Ephedra* and *Gnetum,* although no endosperm forms.

Pollen Incompatibility

Interspecific incompatibility refers to the failure of pollen from one species to germinate and/or grow on the stigma of another species. **Intraspecific incompatibility** is incompatibility that occurs within a species.

Self-incompatibility is incompatibility between the pollen and the stigmas of the same individual. It is an example of intraspecific incompatibility. Self-incompatibility blocks fertilization between two genetically similar gametes, increasing the probability of new gene combinations by promoting outcrossing.

On the basis of origin of factors which determining mating type is categorized into following types

(a) **Gametophytic self-incompatibility** (GSI) The incompatibility is determined by genotype of male gametophyte, *e.g.*, Gramineae, Liliaceae, Solanaceae, Trifolium.

(b) **Sporophytic self-incompatibility** (SSI) The incompatibility process is controlled by genotype of sporophytic tissue of plant, *e.g.*, compositae, cruciferae.

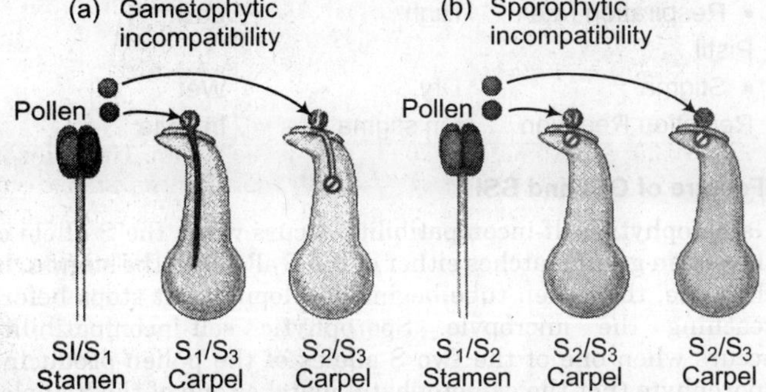

Fig. 14.41 Self-incompatibility. S1, S2 and S3 are different alleles of the self-incompatibility (S) locus
(a) Plants with gametophytic self-incompatibility reject pollen only when the genotype of the pollen matches one of the carpel's two alleles.
(b) In sporophytic self-incompatibility, the genotype of the pollen parent, not just of the haploid pollen grain itself, can trigger an incompatibility response.

Opposition S-alleles hypothesis has described the Genetic basis of sexual incompatibility. It was first proposed by **East** and **Mangelsdorf** (1925). This hypothesis describe the incompatibility reaction is controlled by single gene called **S-gene** with its several alleles. The pollen component of gametophytic self-incompatibility in the petunia, SLF (S-locus, F-box), is an F-box gene within the S locus

In *Brassica*, one of the genes of the S locus encodes a transmembrane serine-threonine kinase (SRK) that functions in the epidermis of the stigma and binds a cysteine-rich peptide (SCR) from the pollen. Self-incompatibility results from the binding of SRK and SRC proteins of self (from allelic S loci) rather than nonself.

1. **Gametophytic self-incompatibility** (GSI) Recognition and rejection reaction, irrespective of S-alleles, occurs in style after the pollen tube has grown to a certain length. The recognition factor is contributed by male gametophyte. In grasses (Gramineae and *Oenothera*) rejection occurs on stigma rather than in style. At molecular level there are two mechanism of rejection. The **RNAse mechanism.** In this case pollen tube elongation is halted when pollen tube reached a one-third the way through style. The **S-glycoprotein mechanism.** In this case, pollen growth is inhibited within a minute of its placement on stigma.
2. **Sporophytic Self-incompatibility** (SSI) In this case plants behave similarly to GSI irrespective of S-allele they carry. A plant with S_1 S_2 alleles produce pollen S_1 and S_2 would behave in similar way, *i.e.*, both pollens is non-functional with respect to particular style. Here

pollen fails to germinate or malformed tube unable to penetrate stigma. This clearly suggests that barrier is restricted to stigma. SSI is determined by diploid genotype.

Characters	Incompatibility	
	SSI	GSI
Pollen		
• Cytology	3-celled	2-celled
• *In vitro* germination	Difficult	Easy
• Respiration rate	High	Low
Pistil		
• Stigma	Dry	Wet
Rejection Reaction	On stigma	In style

Feature of GSI and SSI

Gametophytic self-incompatibility occurs when the S allele of the pollen grain matches either of the S alleles of the stigma. In this case, the pollen tube begins developing, but stops before reaching the micropyle. Sporophytic self-incompatibility occurs when one of the two S alleles of the pollen-producing sporophyte (not the gametophyte) matches one of the S alleles of the stigma. Most likely, sporophyte contributions to the exine are responsible. A ligand on the pollen is thought to bind to a membrane-bound kinase receptor in the stigma that starts a signaling process leading to pollen rejection.

Exception Three-celled pollen with high respiratory rate is an example of GSI in Gramineae, *Oenothera organesis* and *Theobroma cacao.*

Zygote Formation

Recognition of sperm by the vitelline envelope or zona pellucida is followed by the lysis of that portion of the envelope or zona in the region of the sperm head by the acrosomal enzymes. This lysis is followed by the fusion of the sperm plasma membrane with the plasma membrane of the egg.

In the sea urchin, all regions of the egg plasma membrane are capable of fusing with sperm. In several other species, certain regions of the membrane are specialized for sperm recognition and fusion. Fusion is an active process, often mediated by specific 'fusogenic' proteins. In mammals, the **fertilin** proteins in the sperm plasma membrane are essential for sperm membrane-egg membrane fusion.

Prevention of Polyspermy

In normal **monospermy,** where only one sperm enters the egg, a haploid sperm nucleus and a haploid egg nucleus combine to form the diploid nucleus of the fertilized egg (zygote). The entrance of multiple sperm leads to **polyspermy**.

The **fast block to polyspermy** is achieved by changing the electric potential of the egg plasma membrane. This membrane provides a selective barrier between the egg cytoplasm and the outside environment.

If the sperm bound to the vitelline envelope are not somehow removed. The removal is accomplished by the cortical granule reaction, a **slower, mechanical block to polyspermy** that becomes active about a minute after the first successful sperm-egg attachment.

The slow block to polyspermy in the sea urchin is mediated by the phosphatidyl inositol-bisphosphate (PIP_2) second messenger system. Activation of the bindin receptors activates phospholipase C, which cleaves PIP_2 in the egg plasma membrane, releasing inositol triphosphate (IP_3) into the egg cell cytoplasm. IP_3 diffuses to the endoplasmic reticulum, where it opens calcium channels.

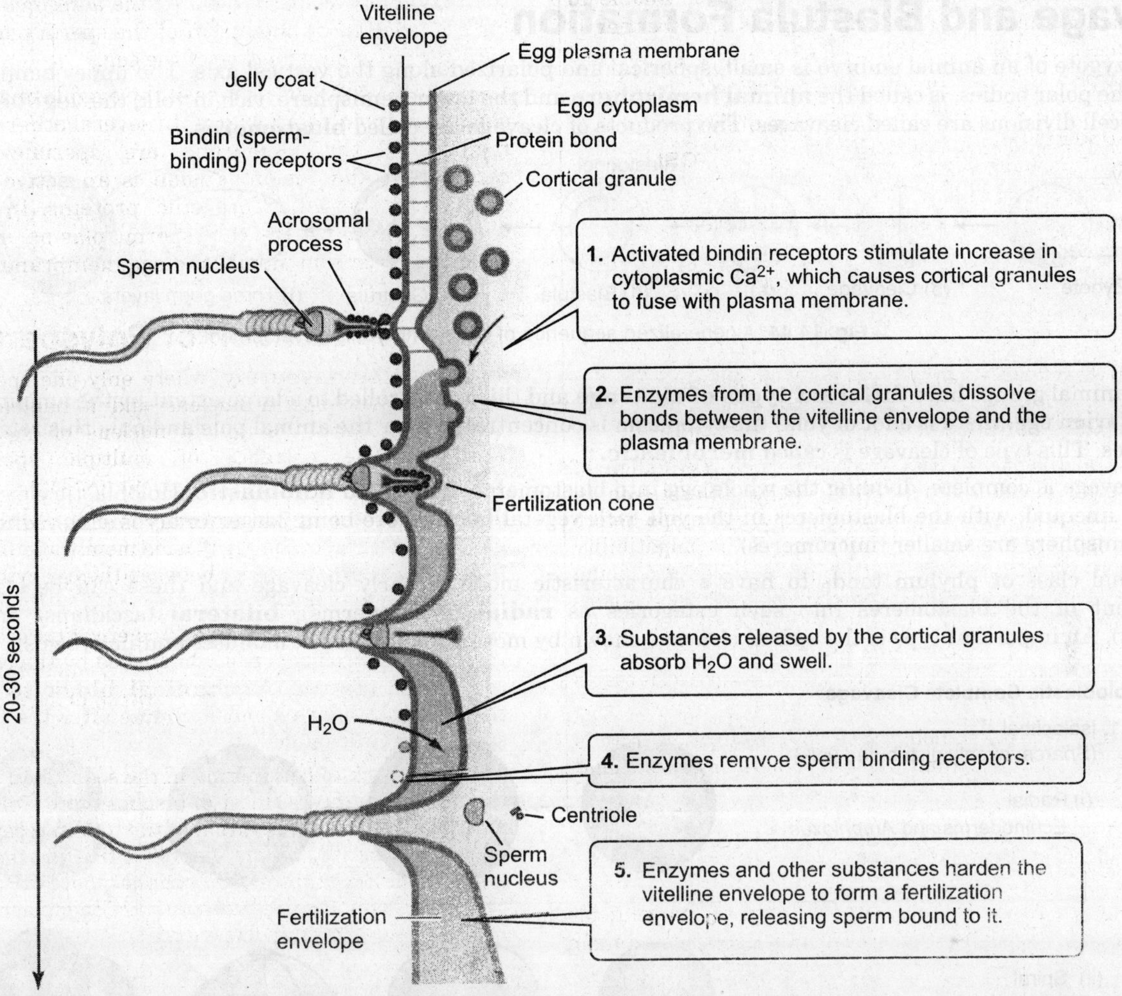

Vitelline envelope
Egg plasma membrane
Jelly coat
Egg cytoplasm
Bindin (sperm-binding) receptors
Protein bond
Cortical granule
Acrosomal process
Sperm nucleus
1. Activated bindin receptors stimulate increase in cytoplasmic Ca^{2+}, which causes cortical granules to fuse with plasma membrane.
2. Enzymes from the cortical granules dissolve bonds between the vitelline envelope and the plasma membrane.
Fertilization cone
20-30 seconds
3. Substances released by the cortical granules absorb H_2O and swell.
H_2O
4. Enzymes remvoe sperm binding receptors.
Centriole
Sperm nucleus
5. Enzymes and other substances harden the vitelline envelope to form a fertilization envelope, releasing sperm bound to it.
Fertilization envelope

Fig. 14.42 The slow block to polyspermy Enzymes from the sea urchin egg's cortical granules trigger the slow block to polyspermy

Na^+ influx
Membrane potential change
Fast block to polyspermy
Activation of NAD^+ kinase
Conversion of NAD^+ to $NADP^+$
Sperm binding and/or fusion to egg cell membrane
Slow block to polyspermy
IP_3 production
Ca^{2+} release
Cortical granule exocytosis
Formation of hyaline layer
Tyrosine kinase stimulation?
Phospholipase C activation
Stimulation of protein synthesis, DNA replication, and cytoplasmic movements of morphogenetic material
Diacylglycerol production
Protein kinase C activation
Na^+/H^+ exchange
Increase in intracellular pH

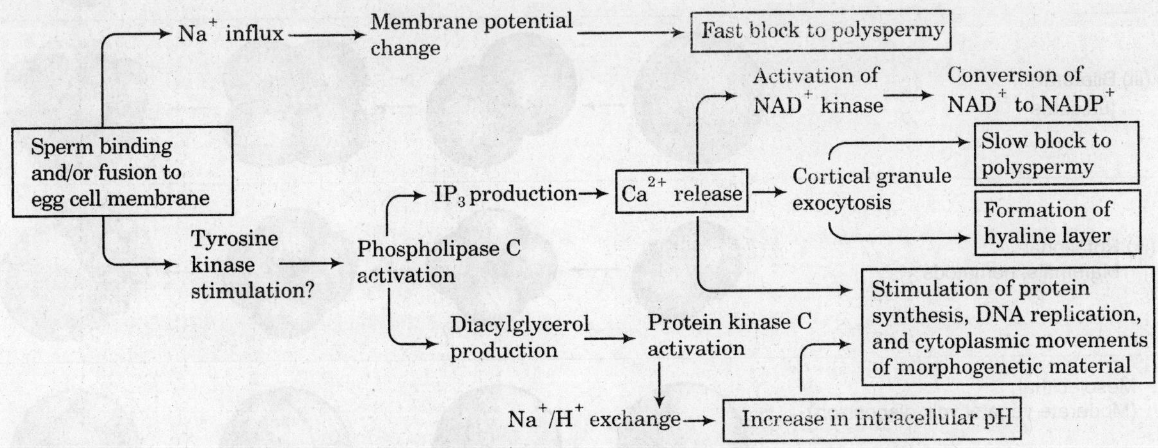

Fig. 14.43 Model of possible pathway of egg activation in the sea urchin

The male pronucleus and the female pronucleus migrate toward each other, replicating DNA as they move. In sea urchins, the two pronuclei merge and a **diploid zygote nucleus** is formed. In mammals, the pronuclei disintegrate as they approach each other, and their chromosomes gather around a common metaphase plate.

Cleavage and Blastula Formation

A typical zygote of an animal embryo is small, spherical and polarized along the vertical axis. The upper hemisphere, usually carrying the polar bodies, is called the **animal hemisphere** and the lower hemisphere, rich in yolk, the **vegetal hemisphere.** The early cell divisions are called cleavages. The products of cleavage are called **blastomeres.**

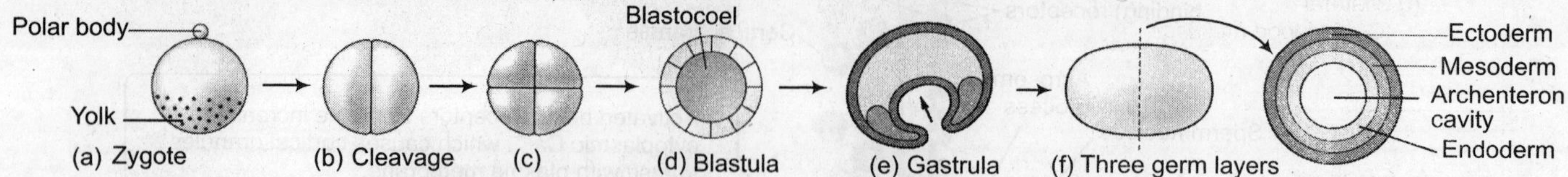

Fig. 14.44 A generalized sequence of early embryonic development

Different animal groups have **different types of cleavage** and this is controlled to a large extent by the amount of yolk in the egg. In an avian egg, there is a lot of yolk, the cytoplasm is concentrated near the animal pole and only this region cleaves into blastomeres. This type of cleavage is called **meroblastic.**

Where cleavage is complete, dividing the whole egg into blastomeres, it is called **holoblastic**. Holoblastic cleavages are often somewhat unequal, with the blastomeres in the yolk-rich vegetal hemisphere being larger (macromeres), while those in the animal hemisphere are smaller (micromeres).

Each animal class or phylum tends to have a characteristic mode of early cleavage and these can be classified by the arrangement of the blastomeres into such categories as **radial** (echinoderms), **bilateral** (ascidians) and **rotational** (mammals). An important type is the **spiral** cleavage shown by most annelid worms, molluscs and flatworms.

Holoblastic Complete Cleavage

1. Isolecithal
(Sparce, evenly distributed yolk)

(i) Radial
Echinoderms and *Amphioxus*

(ii) Spiral
Annelids, molluscs and flatworms

(iii) Bilateral
tunicates

(iv) Rotational
Mammals, nematods

2. Mesolecithal
(Moderate vegetal yolk disposition)

Radial
Amphibians

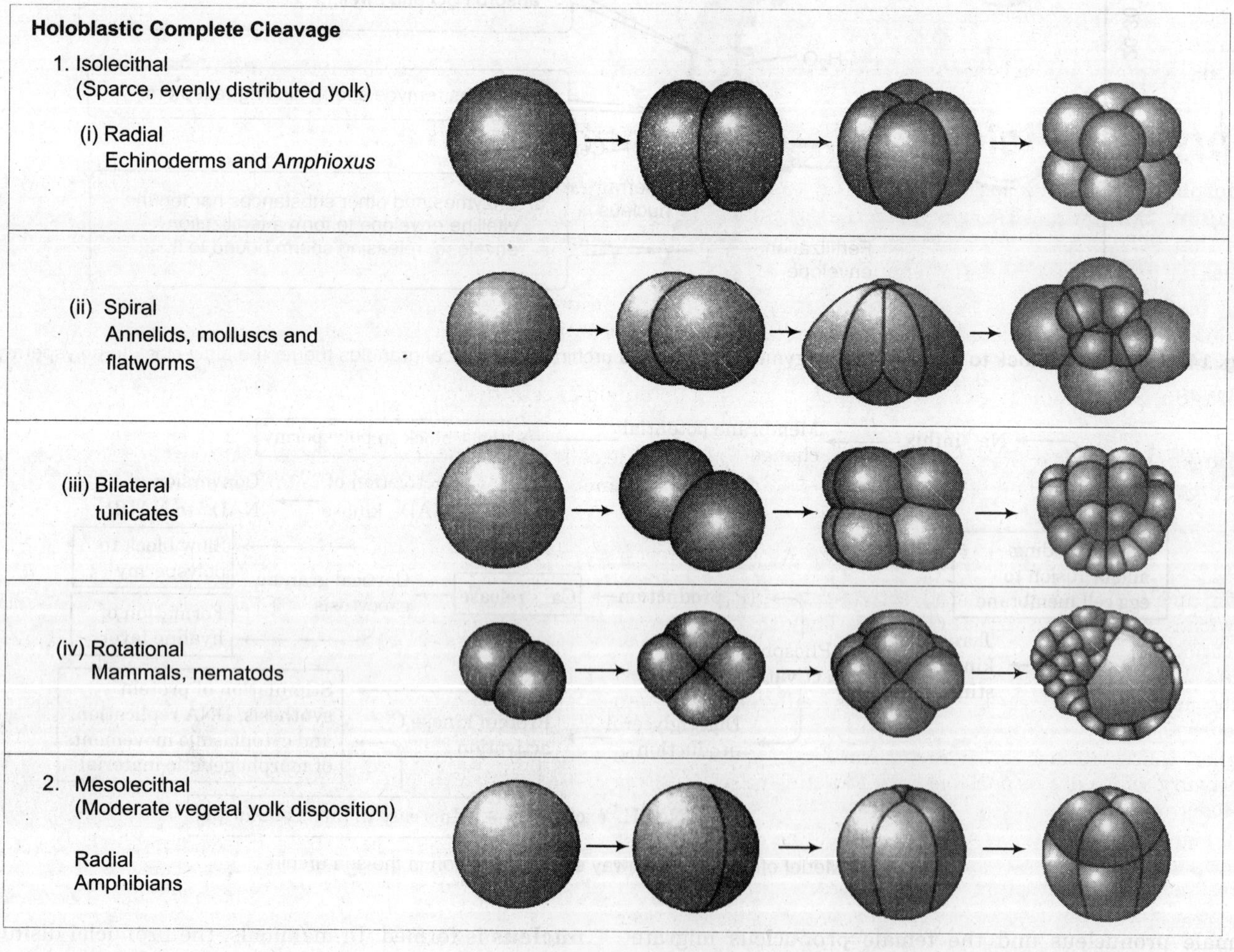

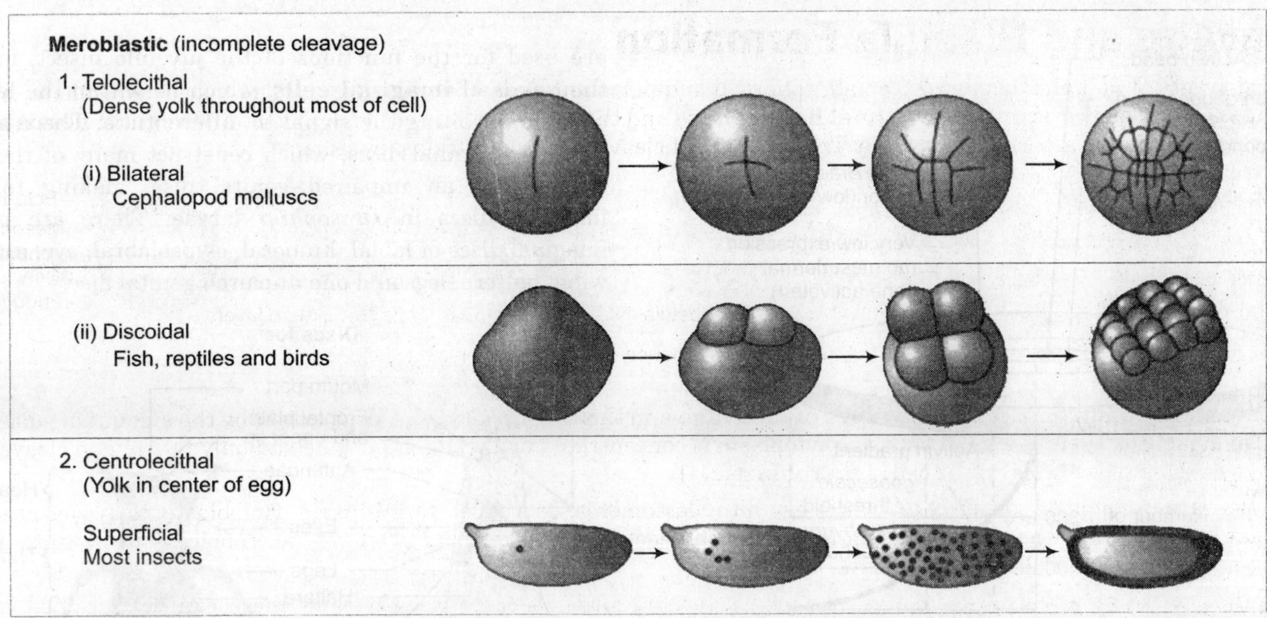

Fig. 14.45 Summary of the main patterns of cleavage

Most insects and some crustaceans show a special type of cleavage called **superficial cleavage.** Here only the nuclei divide and there is no cytoplasmic cleavage at the early stages. During the cleavage phase a cavity usually forms in the center of the ball of cells. This is known as the **blastocoel.** At this stage of development the embryo is called a **blastula.**

Embryonic Fields or Morphogenetic Field

The morphogenetic field has been referred to as a 'field of organization' (Spemann; 1921) and as a 'cellular ecosystem' (1923, 1939). Spemann (1938) reviewed the concepts and definitions of **embryonic field,** according to him it is an inductive system that will give rise to some structure. The classical embryonic field has no boundaries, but rather displays a graded potential for developmental morphogenesis.

The key feature of the field is the presence of **morphogen gradients** within it. This feature explains the ability of the classical embryonic field to recreate complete structures when the field is sectioned, as well as its apparent properties of orientation and self-organization.

Morphogen Signal molecule that can impose a pattern on a field of cells by causing cells in different places to adopt different fates.

Morphogen gradients Morphogen may specify more than one cell type by forming a **concentration gradient.** The concept of morphogen gradients had been used to model another phenomenon of regulative development **regeneration.**

A Gradient of Activin in *Xenopus* Animal Cap Cells

Gurdon and his colleagues placed activin-releasing beads into 'sandwiches' of *Xenopus* animal cap cells. They found following observation

- Little or no activin failed to express any of the genes associated with mesodermal tissues. These cells differentiated into ectoderm.
- Higher concentrations of activin turned on genes such as brachyury, which are responsible for instructing cells to become mesoderm.
- Still higher concentrations of activin caused the cells to express genes such as goosecoid, which are associated with the most dorsal mesodermal structure, the notochord.

The expression of the brachyury and *goosecoid* genes has been correlated with the number of activin receptors on each cell.

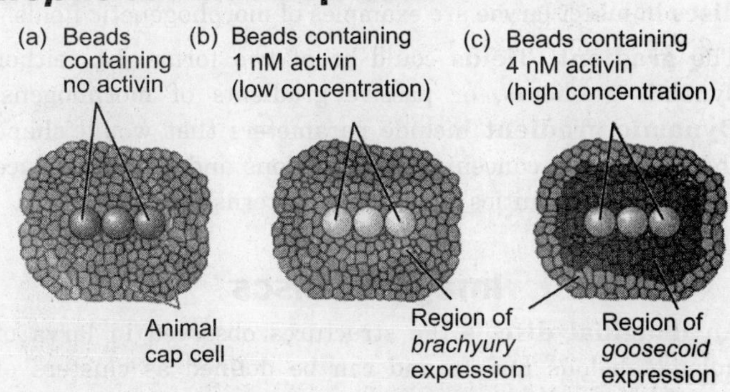

Fig. 14.46 A gradient of activin causes different gene expression in *Xenopus* animal cap cells

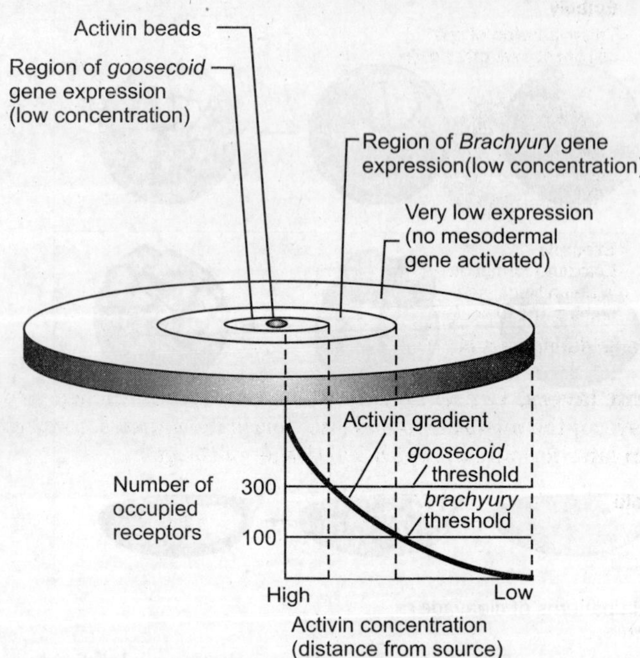

Fig. 14.47 Interpretation of activin gradient by *Xenopus* animal cap cells. High concentrations of activin activate the *goosecoid* gene, while lower concentrations activate the *brachyury* gene. This pattern correlates with the number of activin receptors occupied on the individual cells. A threshold value determines whether a cell will express *goosecoid, brachyury* or neither gene

The original control of differentiation is exerted in what may be called a **morphogenetic field.** Within these fields various processes concerned with morphogenesis is quantitatively graded. These fields are the fundamental unit of development.

A **morphogenetic field** can be described as a group of cells whose position and fate are specified with respect to the same set of boundaries. The general fate of a morphogenetic field is determined, thus, a particular field of cells will give rise to its particular organ (forelimb, eye, heart, etc.) even when transplanted to a different part of the embryo. **Imaginal discs** in insect larvae are examples of morphogenetic fields.

The **gradient fields** could be of two forms, *i.e.*, either dynamic gradients, or passive gradients of morphogens. **Dynamic gradient** include parameters that would shape the morphogen concentration functions and might produce spatial discontinuities and shaped patterns.

Imaginal Discs

An **imaginal disc** is the structures observed in larva of holometabolous insects and can be defined as clusters of undifferentiated embryonic cells in holometabolous insects that proliferate during larval stages and then differentiate during the pupal stage upon induction by ecdysone but in the absence of juvenile hormone.Thus, within any larva, there are two distinct populations of cells **the larval cells**, which are used for the functions of the juvenile insect, and the thousands of **imaginal cells,** which lie within the larva in clusters, awaiting the signal to differentiate. There are ten pairs of imaginal discs, which construct many of the adult organs and an unpaired genital disc, making total 21 imaginal discs in *Drosophila* larvae. There are pair of imaginal discs of labial, humeral, clypeolabral, eye, antenna, wing, haltere, legs and one unpaired genital disc.

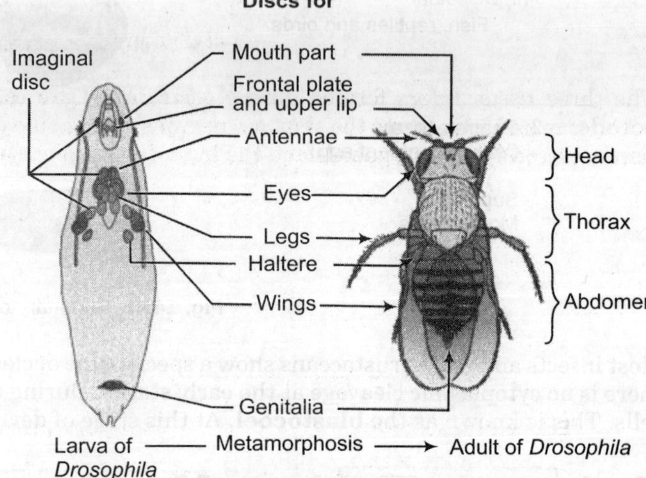

Fig. 14.48 The locations and developmental fates of the imaginal discs in *Drosophila melanogaster*

Gastrulation and Formation of Germ Layers in Animals

Following the formation of the blastula, all animal embryos show a phase of cell and tissue movements called **gastrulation** that converts the simple ball or sheet of cells into a three-layered structure known as the **gastrula.**

The movements of gastrulation involve the entire embryo, and cell migrations in one part of the gastrulating embryo must be intimately coordinated with other movements occurring simultaneously. Gastrulation usually involves some combination of the following types of movements.

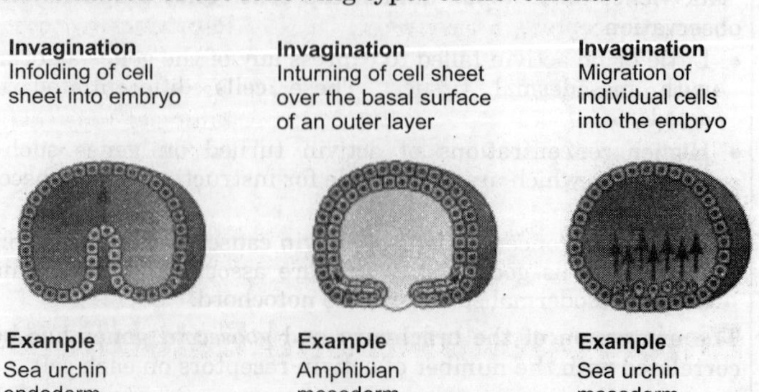

Delamination
Splitting or migration of one sheet into two sheets

Example
Mammalian and bird hypoblast formation

Epiboly
The expansion of one cell sheet over other cells

Example
Ectoderm formation in amphibians, sea urchins and tunicates

Fig. 14.49 Types of cell movements during gastrulation

The three tissue layers formed during gastrulation are called **germ layers.** Conventionally the outer layer is known as the **ectoderm** and later forms the skin and nervous system; the middle layer is the **mesoderm** and later forms the muscles, connective tissue, excretory organs, gonads and the inner layer is the **endoderm** later forming the epithelial tissues of the gut.

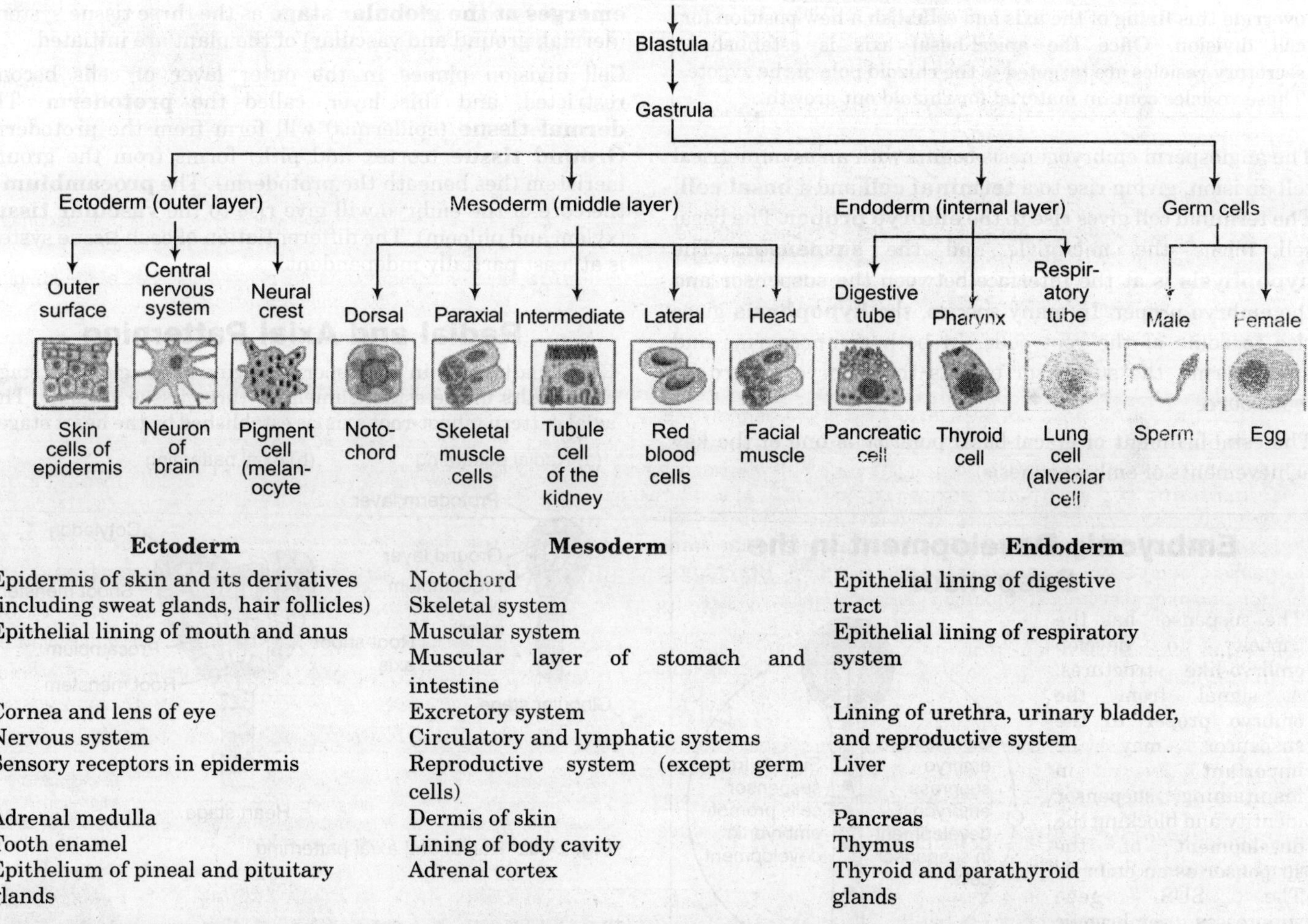

Ectoderm	**Mesoderm**	**Endoderm**
Epidermis of skin and its derivatives (including sweat glands, hair follicles)	Notochord	Epithelial lining of digestive tract
Epithelial lining of mouth and anus	Skeletal system	Epithelial lining of respiratory system
	Muscular system	
	Muscular layer of stomach and intestine	
Cornea and lens of eye	Excretory system	Lining of urethra, urinary bladder, and reproductive system
Nervous system	Circulatory and lymphatic systems	
Sensory receptors in epidermis	Reproductive system (except germ cells)	Liver
Adrenal medulla	Dermis of skin	Pancreas
Tooth enamel	Lining of body cavity	Thymus
Epithelium of pineal and pituitary glands	Adrenal cortex	Thyroid and parathyroid glands

Fig. 14.50 The three germ layers. The cell types are organized according to the germ layers from which they arise. The germ cells (precursors of the sperm and egg) are shown as not arising from any of the germ layers

Embryogenesis and Establishment of Symmetry in Plants

In plants, the term **embryogenesis** covers development from the time of fertilization until dormancy occurs. The basic body plan of the sporophyte is established during embryogenesis, the major events of embryogenesis are

1. To establish the basic body plan. **Radial patterning** produces three tissue systems, and **axial patterning** establishes the apical-basal (shoot-root) axis.
2. To set aside meristematic tissue for postembryonic elaboration of the body structure (leaves, roots, flowers, etc.).
3. To establish an accessible food reserve for the germinating embryo.

Establishment of Polarity in Brown Algae

In brown algae, the initial cell division results in one smaller cell, which will form the rhizoid and one larger cell, which gives rise to the thallus. The point of sperm entry fixes the position of the rhizoid end of the apical-basal axis, which is perpendicular to the plane of the first cell division. F-actin accumulates at the rhizoid pole. However, light or gravity can override this fixing of the axis and establish a new position for cell division. Once the apical-basal axis is established, secretory vesicles are targeted to the rhizoid pole of the zygote. These vesicles contain material for rhizoid out growth.

The angiosperm embryogenesis begins with an asymmetrical cell division, giving rise to a **terminal cell** and a **basal cell.** The terminal cell gives rise to the **embryo proper.** The basal cell forms the micropyle and the **suspensor.** The **hypophysis** is at the interface between the suspensor and the embryo proper. In many species, the **hypophysis** gives rise to some of the root cells. In both gymnosperms and angiosperms, the suspensor orients the embryo toward its food source.

The establishment of apical-basal polarity is one of the key achievements of embryogenesis.

Embryonic Development in the Suspensor

The suspensor has the capacity to develop embryo-like structures. A signal from the embryo proper to the suspensor may be important in maintaining suspensor identity and blocking the development of the suspensor as an embryo. The SUS gene suppresses embryonic development in the suspensor.

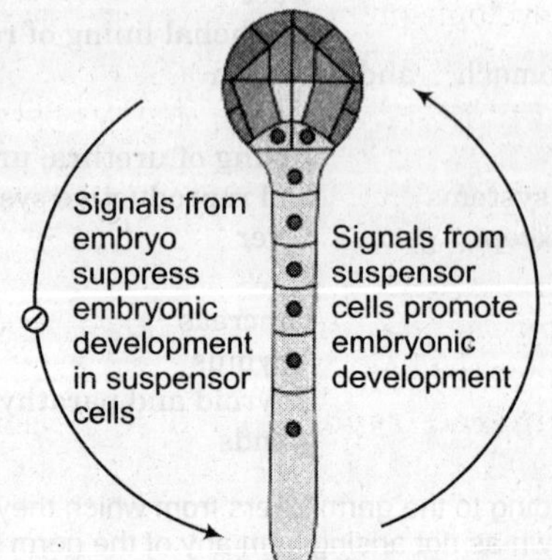

Fig. 14.51 Model showing the embryo proper suppresses embryonic development in the suspensor and the suspensor provides feedback information to the embryo

Maternal effect is key to establishing embryonic pattern. The three potential sources of influence in plant embryogenesis sporophytic tissue, gametophytic tissue, and the polyploid endosperm. All of these tissues are in close association with the egg/zygote.

Maternal genes could also affect endosperm development. **Sporophytic maternal effect genes** and **gametophytic maternal effect genes** have been identified in Arabidopsis. The first identified maternal effect gene is Short Integuments 1 (SIN1). Transcription factors FBP7 and FBP11 are needed in the petunia sporophyte for normal endosperm development. A female gametophytic maternal effect gene, MEDEA, has protein domains that is expressed by the female gametophyte and by maternally inherited alleles in the zygote, but not by paternally inherited alleles.

Radial and axial patterns develop as cell division and differentiation continue. The cells of the embryo proper divide to form a globular stage. **Radial patterning emerges at the globular stage** as the three tissue systems (dermal, ground and vascular) of the plant are initiated.

Cell division planes in the outer layer of cells become restricted, and this layer, called the **protoderm**. The **dermal tissue** (epidermis) will form from the protoderm, **Ground tissue** (cortex and pith) forms from the ground meristem (lies beneath the protoderm). The **procambium** is the core of the embryo will give rise to the **vascular tissue** (xylem and phloem). The differentiation of each tissue system is at least partially independent.

Radial and Axial Patterning

Radial patterning in angiosperms begins in the globular stage and results in the establishment of three tissue systems. The axial pattern (shoot-root axis) is established by the heart stage.

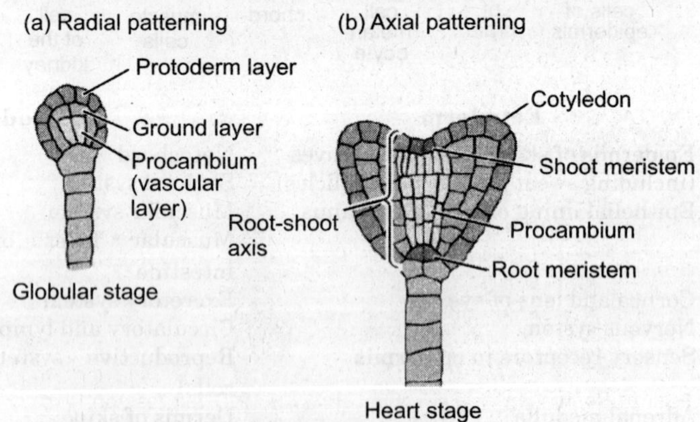

Fig. 14.52 Radial and axial patterning

The globular shape of the embryo is lost as **cotyledons** (first leaves) begin to form. Dicots have two cotyledons, which plan is evident by this **heart stage** of development.

The **shoot apical meristem** and **root apical meristem** persist in the postembryonic plant and give rise to most of the sporophyte body. In some species the root meristem is partially derived from the hypophysis. Rest of the parts sporophyte body are derived from the embryo proper.

Shoot-root Axis

The hormone auxin plays a key role in establishing the apical-basal axis of the embryo. Very early in embryogenesis, the family of pinformed (PIN) auxin efflux carriers is asymmetrically distributed. The pinoid (PID) protein kinase aids in the asymmetric localization of PIN proteins. At the 4-cell stage, auxin moves apically, but by the globular stage, the efflux carriers direct the flow of auxin to the hypophysis, which organizes as the root meristem.

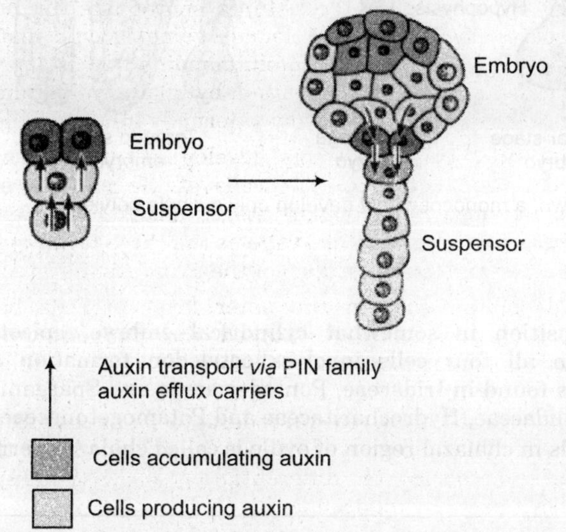

Fig. 14.53 A family of PIN auxin efflux carriers is responsible for the early apical flow of auxin in the embryo and the shift to basal auxin flow as the apical end of the globular stage embryo begins to produce auxin

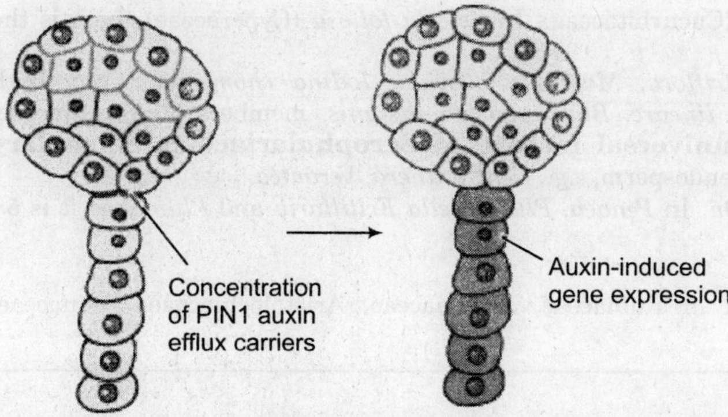

Fig. 14.54 In wild-type globular embryos, PID expression leads to the accumulation of PIN1 at the basal end of the embryo. When an auxin-response gene is fused with GFP and expressed, basal accumulation and normal embryonic development occur

Disruption of the auxin morphogenetic gradient, either through mutation or over expression of PID allows auxin to accumulate more apically and root development is abnormal or inhibited.

Genetics of the Shoot and Root Meristems

- STM gene in *Arabidopsis* affect the development of the root axis during embryogenesis.
- HOBBIT gene in *Arabidopsis* affect the hypophysis derivatives and eliminate root meristem function.
- *dek*23 gene in maize form a root meristem.

Although most embryonic cells are pluripotent and can generate organs such as cotyledons and leaves, only meristems retain this capacity in the postembryonic plant body.

In **most of angiosperms zygote divide transversely** into small **apical cell** and large **basal cell** towards micropyle.

Embryogeny in Dicotyledons

Schnarf (1929) and **Johansen** (1945) identified the five principal type of embryos in dicotyledons. These may be classified as follows :

The Apical Cell of 2-celled Proembryo Divide Longitudinally

Crucifer type or Onagrad type The basal cell play minor role in subsequent development of embryo, *e.g.*, Ranunculaceae, Annonaceae, Onagraceae, Cruciferae, Pedaliaceae and Scrophulariaceae.

Asterad type The basal cell and apical cell both contribute to development of embryo, *e.g.*, Balsaminaceae, Vitaceae, Violaceae and Compositae.

The Apical Cell of Two Cell Proembryo Divide Transversely

Solanad type The basal based cell play minor role in development of embryo. The basal cell form suspensor, *e.g.*, Campanulaceae, Theaceae, Linaceae and Solanaceae.

Caryophyllad type The basal based cell play minor role in development of embryo. The basal cell undergo no further division, and suspensor if present is derived from terminal cell, *e.g.*, Crassulaceae, Haloragaceae and Caryophyllaceae.

Chenopodial type The basal cell and apical cell both contribute to development of embryo, *e.g.*, Boraginaceae and Chenopodiaceae.

Piperad type The first division of zygote is vertical, *e.g.*, Loranthaceae and Piperaceae.

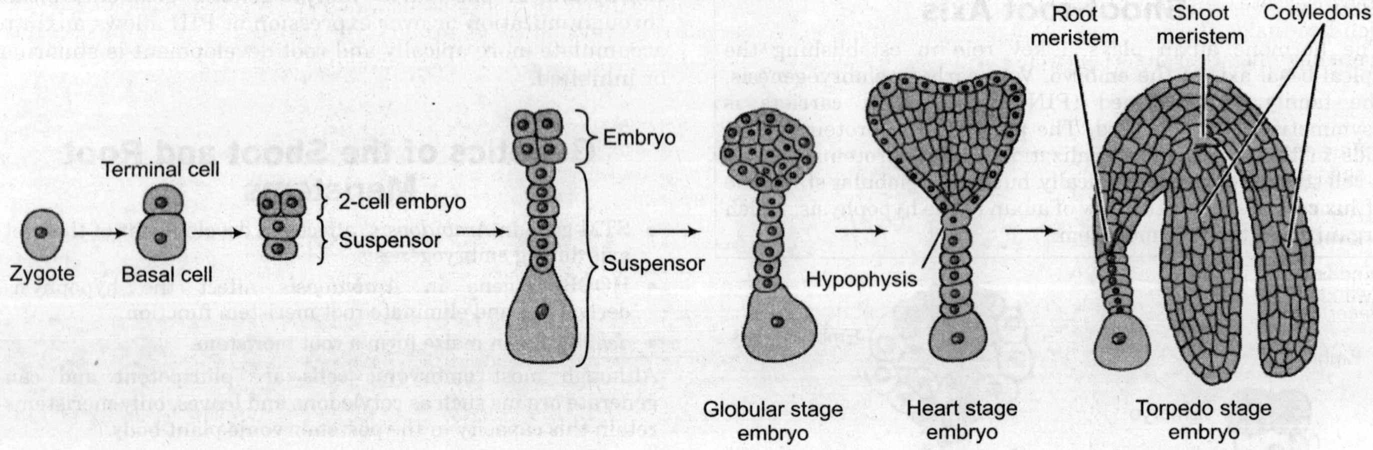

Fig. 14.55 Angiosperm embryogenesis. A representative dicot is shown; a monocot would develop only a single cotyledon

Embryogeny in Monocotyledons

In the monocotyledon embryo, shoot apex occupies a lateral position in somewhat cylindrical embryo, epicotyl in monocotyledon embryo is terminal in position. In monocotyledon all four cells involves cotyledon formation as in **Philydraceae**, three cells of quadrant involve in embryo formation is found in Iridaceae, Pontederiaceae and Sparganiaceae and two adjacent cells involve in embryo formation is found in Amaryllidaceae, Hydrocharitaceae and Potamogetonaceae. Grass embryo has single cotyledon called **scutellum**. The nucellar cells in chalazal region of ovule is called chalaza sperm and provide nutrition to embryo.

Endosperm

- In angiosperm, endosperm is not formed in the member of families **Orchidaceae, Podostemaceae** and **Trapaceae**
- Cellular endosperm is mostly found in dicotyledonous families. Aracaceae and Lemnaceae (monocotyledon) show cellular type of endosperms.
- Helobial endosperm mostly found in monocotyledons.
- Longest endosperm haustorium is reported in *Echinocystis lobata* (Cucurbitaceae). In *Scleria foliosa* (Cyperaceae) there is the occurrence of both chalazal and micropylar endosperm haustoria.
- Chalazal haustorium is occurs in *Impatiens roylei, Hydrocera triflora, Magnolia obovata, Iodina rhombifolia,* etc. Both **Micropylar** and **Chalazal haustorium** found in *Melampyrum lineare, Blumenbachia insignis,* members of Acanthaceae, Hydrophyllaceae, Lobeliaceae, etc. **This type of haustoria is universal feature of Scrophulariaceae. Secondary haustorium** develop from other than micropylar or chalazal cell of endosperm, *e.g., Centranthera, Veronica.*
- Endosperm tissue is generally triploid ($3n$), but in peperomia it is $9n$. In *Penaea, Plumbigella Fritillaria* and *Plumbago* it is $5n$ while in *Oenothera* it is $2n$.
- Endosperm in gymnosperms is **haploid**.
- Ruminate endosperm (surface with ridge and furrow) is found in Rubiaceae, Annonaceae, Aristolochiaceae, Palmaceae, Myristicaceae, etc.

Seed Formation and Germination

The seeds of some plant species are capable of germinating as soon as they have matured. But many other species have seeds that are dormant at maturity. There are three principal strategies dominate

1. Exclusion of water or oxygen from the embryo by means of an impermeable seed coat.
2. Mechanical restraint of the embryo by means of a tough seed coat.
3. Chemical inhibition of embryonic development.

Advantages of Seed Dormancy

Seed dormancy helps annual plants encounter the effects of year-to-year variation in the environment. The seeds of other plants germinate at specific times during the year, increasing the likelihood that at least some of the seedlings will encounter conditions favourable for their growth. Dormancy may also increase the likelihood of a seed's germinating in the right place. Some cypress trees, for example, grow in standing water and their seeds germinate only if inhibitors are leached by water.

The first step in germination is the uptake of water, called **imbibitions.** In germinating barley and other cereal seeds, the embryo secretes **gibberellins.** Gibberellins diffuse through the endosperm to a surrounding tissue called the aleurone layer, which lies inside the seed coat. The gibberellins trigger a cascade of events in the aleurone layer, causing it to synthesize and secrete enzymes that digest proteins and starch stored in the endosperm.

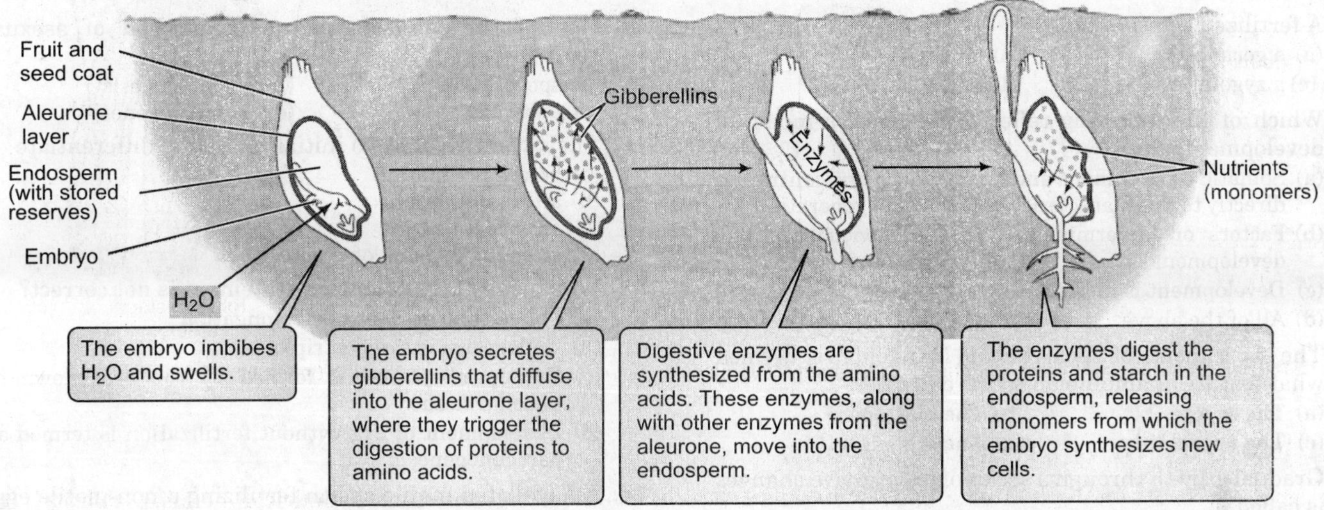

Fig. 14.56 Embryos mobilize their reserves during seed germination

The process of germination is irreversible, *i.e.*, once germination begins it cannot be revert back to dormant state. There are two types of seed germination.

Epigeal Germination

When hypocotyl grows it first pushes the cotyledonary and other part of seed out of soil. This is called epigeal germination. This type of germination is shown by dicotyledons and few monocotyledons. Examples,

(i) **Dicotyledonous exalbuminous seeds** Cucurbits, mustards, tamarind, french bean, sunflower.

(ii) **Dicotyledonous albuminous seeds** Castor.

(iii) **Monocotyledonous exalbuminous seeds** *Alisme plantego.*

(iv) **Monocotyledonous albuminous seeds** Rare, occur in onion.

Hypogeal Germination

When epicotyl grows, it first pushes the plumule out of soil. The cotyledonary nodes and cotyledons remains under the soil. This type of germination is called hypogeal germination this type of germination is shown by most of the monocotyledons. Examples,

(i) **Dicotyledonous exalbuminous seeds** Gram, broad beans, mango and jackfruit.

(ii) **Monocotyledonous albuminous seeds** Rice, maize, wheat, coconut, date, areca nut and palmyra.

Vivipary

It is the germination of seed within fruit, while it is still attached to parent plant. Common example is *Rhizophora mucronata, Ceriops roxburghiana, Burguiera gymnorhiza*, etc., of Rhizophoraceae and *Sechium edule* of Cucurbitaceae.

Exercise

1. A fertilized egg is called
(a) a germ cell (b) an embryo
(c) a zygote (d) a blastula

2. Which of the following reflects Weismann's model of development?
(a) Somatic development and change does not contribute directly to the characteristics of the next generation
(b) Factors or 'determinants', in the nucleus regulate development
(c) Development is mosaic
(d) All of the above

3. The experiments of Spemann and Mangold first defined what feature of amphibian embryos?
(a) The zygote (b) The blastopore
(c) The neural tube (d) The organizer

4. Gradual growth through a series of progressive changes is called
(a) growth (b) development
(c) cleavage (d) transduction

5. Epigeal germination occurs in
(a) castor (b) gram
(c) pea (d) maize

6. As a fertilized egg develops into an embryo, it undergoes
(a) one meiotic cell division
(b) many meiotic cell divisions
(c) one mitotic cell division
(d) many mitotic cell divisions

7. In which of the following types of ovules do the micropyle and the funiculus come to lie in one straight line?
(a) Orthotropous (b) Anatropous
(c) Hemianatropous (d) Campylotropous

8. With reference to sexual incompatibility in angiosperms, consider the following statements.
I. Gametophytic self-incompatibility is found in all species of Brassicaceae.
II. Sporophytic self-incompatibility is found in all species of Solanaceae.
Which of the statements given above is/are correct?
(a) I only (b) II only
(c) Both I and II (d) Neither I nor II

9. The tapetum in anther originates from
(a) sporogeneous tissue and epidermis
(b) parietal layer and sporogenous tissue
(c) cells of the connective tissue and epidermis
(d) parietal layer and cells of the connective tissue

10. In angiosperms, germinable adventive embryos develop from
(a) endosperm
(b) nucellus
(c) antipodal cells and/or synergids
(d) synergids

11. One of the following is not a method of asexual reproduction
(a) sporulation (b) gametogenesis
(c) apomixis (d) parthenogenesis

12. The adventive embryo initials of *Citrus* differentiate
(a) before pollination
(b) after pollination
(c) after fertilization
(d) after the division of zygote

13. Which one of the following statement is not correct?
(a) Pollen tube grows by cell elongation
(b) Endosperm is always triploid
(c) Pseudoembryo sac is formed by the breakdown of nucellar tissue
(d) Development of egg without fertilization is termed as parthenogenesis

14. A flagellated motile sperm fertilizing a non-motile egg, this syngamy is called
(a) isogamy (b) anisogamy
(c) oogamy (d) All of these

15. A type of syngamy in which both fusing gametes are flagellated but different in size are known as
(a) isogamy (b) anisogamy
(c) oogamy (d) All of these

16. A type of syngamy in which both fusing gametes are flagellated and same in size are known as
(a) isogamy (b) anisogamy
(c) oogamy (d) All of these

17. In angiosperms, the entry of pollen tube into the embryo sac at the micropylar end is
(a) between synergid and central cell
(b) through filiform apparatus
(c) between synergid and egg
(d) directly into the egg

18. Reproduction of egg without fertilization by sperm is termed as
(a) parthenogenesis (b) parthenocarpy
(c) regeneration (d) budding

19. Match list I (name of the plant) with list II (type of seeds to which the given plants belong) and select the correct answer using the codes given below the lists.

List I	List II
A. Mango	1. Dicotyledonous and albuminous
B. Castor	2. Monocotyledonous and albuminous
C. Orchid	3. Monocotyledonous and exalbumious
D. Barley	4. Dicotyledonous and exalbumious

Codes

	A	B	C	D
(a)	4	1	3	2
(b)	1	2	4	3
(c)	2	4	1	3
(d)	4	1	2	3

20. Fraternal twins
(a) can be only two boys
(b) can be only two girls
(c) can not be one boy and one girl
(d) can be one boy and one girl

21. Sexual reproduction is important to avoid
(a) variation (b) chances of survival
(c) genetic monotomy (d) All of these

22. Which of the following cell type is haploid?
(a) Primary spermatocyte (b) Spermatogonium
(c) Sertoli cell (d) Secondary spermatocyte

23. Spermatogenesis and oogenesis both involve
(a) mitosis (b) meiosis
(c) Both (a) and (b) (d) None of these

24. After meiosis, the .... differentiates into the mature sperm.
(a) primary spermatocyte (b) spermatid
(c) secondary spermatocyte (d) spermatogonium

25. The animals which lay eggs are called
(a) oviparous (b) viviparous
(c) dioecious (d) neuter

26. In terrestrial conditions, which type fertilization is more common
(a) external (b) internal
(c) self (d) None of these

27. In mammalian males, the reproductive and excretory system share the same
(a) ureter (b) vas deferens
(c) urinary bladder (d) urethra

28. External male genitalia are
(a) vasa efferentia and penis
(b) seminiferous tubules and penis
(c) scrotum and penis
(d) None of the above

29. Human testes are packed with about .... seminiferous tubules which produce about .... million sperms every day.
(a) 200; 20 (b) 300; 40
(c) 500; 30 (d) 500;10

30. Three sets of glands secrete fluids which combine with the sperm to form
(a) interstitial fluid (b) semen
(c) amniotic fluid (d) Both (a) and (b)

31. A human female has around .... oocytes in each of her ovary.
(a) 30000 (b) 200000
(c) 300000 (d) 20000

32. Fertilization of human eggs most often takes place in the
(a) ovary (b) uterus
(c) oviduct (Fallopian tube) (d) cervix

33. In human female only one ovum is usually discharged from the ovary at one time it is called
(a) parturition (b) menstruation
(c) ovulation (d) implantation

34. The uterus opens into the .... through cervix.
(a) Fallopian tube (b) urethra
(c) vagina (d) All of these

35. The follicle cells, after release of the egg, are modified to form a special structure called
(a) endometrium (b) perimetrium
(c) Graafian follicle (d) corpus luteum

36. In mammals that are seasonal breeders, females are receptive only once a year. This is called
(a) a follicular cycle (b) an oestrous cycle
(c) a menstrual cycle (d) a luteal cycle

37. Consider the following statements
The function of fertilization is to
I. facilitate the contents of the nuclei of the gametes to unite.
II. mix the paternal and maternal characters in the offspring.
III. restore the normal diploid number.
Which of the following statements given above is/are correct?
(a) I, II and III are correct (b) I and II are correct
(c) II and III are correct (d) I and III are correct

38. What event occurs in the menstrual cycle when the level of progesterone decline?
(a) Ovulation
(b) Beginning of menses
(c) Formation of corpus luteum
(d) Maturation of ovarian follicle

39. .... is produced mainly by the corpus luteum in the ovary following ovulation.
(a) Progesterone
(b) Follicle stimulating hormone
(c) Luteinizing hormone
(d) Chorionic gonadotrophic hormone

40. From which of the following structures is the secondary oocyte ovulated?
(a) Corpus luteum (b) Graafian follicle
(c) Primary follicle (d) Germinal epithelium

41. The process by which .... becomes embedded in endometrium is called ....
(a) morula; parturition (b) blastocyst; parturition
(c) blastocyst; implantation (d) morula; implantation

42. .... controls the release of milk form the mammary glands.
(a) Oxytocin
(b) Follicle stimulating hormone
(c) Luteinizing hormone
(d) None of the above

43. An egg fertilized in the laboratory and then implanted in the uterus for development is called
(a) cloning (b) test tube baby
(c) Both (a) and (b) (d) *in vivo* fertilization

44. The period starting from conception up to the birth of baby is called
(a) implantation period (b) gestation period
(c) extra uterine period (d) imprinting period

45. Menopause in female comes at the age of
(a) 30 to 40 years (b) 45 to 50 years
(c) 60 to 65 years (d) 70 years

46. This hormone from the hypothalamus stimulates release of FSH from the anterior pituitary
(a) gonadotropin (b) oxytocin
(c) luteinizing hormone (d) progesterone

47. Sexually Transmitted Disease (STD) caused by *Treponema pallidum* is
(a) syphilis (b) genital herpes
(c) gonorrhoea (d) AIDS

48. The rapid growth of pollen tube is restricted to the
(a) basal region
(b) middle region
(c) apical region
(d) zone behind the apical region

49. If the egg is not fertilized, ... occurs.
(a) menstruation (b) pregnancy
(c) implantation (d) All of these

50. It is a tube that connects a developing embryo or foetus to the placenta
(a) amnion (b) chorionic villum
(c) umbilical cord (d) allantois

51. The protein in the pollen wall that causes allergy is contributed by
(a) exine (b) pollen cytoplasm
(c) tapetum (d) intine

52. Infertility is overcome by a technique known as
(a) *in vitro* fertilization (b) *in vivo* fertilization
(c) Both (a) and (b) (d) None of these

53. The pattern of cleavage in which only part of the ovum is divided into cells. It is also called incomplete cleavage and is usually observed in embryos with large amounts of yolk
(a) meroblastic cleavage (b) discoidal cleavage
(c) holoblastic cleavage (d) Both (a) and (b)

54. The divided germinal disc of a megalecithal egg forms a layer of cells termed as
(a) blastoderm (b) blastocoel
(c) blastocyst (d) Both (a) and (c)

55. The peripheral region of the chick blastodisc surrounding the area pellucida and in direct contact with the yolk is
(a) area ascarosida (b) area vitellina
(c) area opaca (d) area vasculosa

56. One of a pair of twisted, cords of albumen found at each of an egg, joining the shell membrane to the yolk and supporting the yolk centrally within the shell is
(a) nucellus (b) chalaza
(c) choenoderm (d) latebra

57. The central region of blastodisc is known as
(a) area pellucida (b) area vitellina
(c) area opaca (d) area vasculosa

58. Animals begin their lives as a single, diploid cell called
(a) zygote (b) embryo
(c) gastrula (d) All of these

59. Increase in size of organs to attain maturity is called
(a) differentiation (b) localization
(c) growth (d) Both (b) and (c)

60. Cells of the blastoderm surface migrate posteriorly and medially and involute (turn in) along a line called the
(a) hypoblast (b) germinal disc
(c) primitive streak (d) latebra

61. Due to the migration of mesodermal cells from the epiblast, a groove is formed known as
(a) neural groove (b) primitive groove
(c) somatopleure (d) splanchnopleure

62. The hypoblast is mainly presumptive
(a) ectoderm (b) endoderm
(c) mesoderm (d) blastoderm

63. The membrane composed of ectoderm and somatic mesoderm is known as
(a) somatopleure (b) splanchnopleure
(c) visceralopleure (d) All of these

64. The cellular layer consisting of splanchnic mesoderm and endoderm is known as
(a) somatopleure (b) splanchnopleure
(c) visceralopleure (d) parietopleure

65. The lateral plate mesoderm is differentiated into two sheet like layers, *i.e.*, somatic mesoderm and
(a) chorda mesoderm (b) proper mesoderm
(c) splanchnic mesoderm (d) dermatogenic mesoderm

66. In chick gastrula .... and .... formation do not occur.
(a) somatopleure; splanchnopleure
(b) primitive streak; dorsal lip
(c) invagination; archentron
(d) primitive streak; ventral lip

67. Mesomere somite gives rise
(a) digestive system (b) muscles
(c) skeleton (d) excretory system

68. Muscles, axial skeleton and connective tissues are differentiated from
(a) epimeres (b) mesomere
(c) hypomere (d) endoderm

69. Coelom is formed from
(a) epimere (b) hypomere
(c) mesomere (d) None of these

70. In 24 hours chick embryo the foldings of neural plate are clearly visible. At this stage embryo is called
(a) morula (b) blastula
(c) neurula (d) blastocyst

71. A tube of tissue formed by a thickening and rolling up of the neural plate during embryonic neurulation. It will later form the brain and spinal cord of the animal. This is called
(a) neurocoel (b) neural groove
(c) neurospore (d) neural tube

72. .... is the process of selection of activation of some genes by a cell, which are not activated by other cells of the embryo.
(a) cell induction (b) cell transformation
(c) cell differentiation (d) cell mediation

73. When the primitive streak reaches its maximum length, the cells of the most anterior region of the streak appear morphologically distinct. This region is known as
(a) node of Ranvier (b) Schwann's node
(c) Henson's node (d) None of these

74. Mechanism of differentiation depends upon .... organization of unfertilized egg.
(a) homogenous (b) heterogeneous
(c) exogenous (d) All of these

75. The situation where one embryonic tissue influences an other so that the responding tissue differentiates is known as
(a) instruction (b) evocation
(c) induction (d) None of these

76. The control development of cap in *Acetabularia* is through production of developmentally active substance in
(a) nucleus (b) cytoplasm
(c) gray crescent (d) Both (a) and (b)

77. The technique of producing a genetically identical copy of an organism by replacing the nucleus of an unfertilized ovum with the nucleus of a body cell from the organism is
(a) test tube baby (b) cloning
(c) *in vitro* fertilization (d) All of these

78. The study of degenerative changes in ageing is called
(a) Developmental biology (b) Paedology
(c) Gerontology (d) Chronology

79. The science of studying and treating malformations and monstrosities of organisms is called
(a) Gerontology (b) Teratology
(c) Dermatology (d) Etiology

80. The normal process of development is disturbed by abnormalities. These abnormalities are due to
(a) abnormal functioning of glands
(b) abnormal chromosomal number
(c) UV radiations
(d) All of the above

81. In birds and mammals regeneration is mostly limited to the small wounds by the formation of a new tissue
(a) callus (b) scar
(c) serous (d) None of these

82. Notochord is formed from
(a) epimeres (b) mesomeres
(c) hypomeres (d) Henson's node

83. A condition in which heart is present towards right side of the chest is called
(a) sinistrocardia (b) dextrocardia
(c) laterocardia (d) Both (a) and (b)

84. Decreased ability or inability of blood to clot is
(a) thalassemia (b) sickle cell anaemia
(c) haemophilia (d) haemolysis

85. Regarding 3-celled pollen, which one of the following statements is not correct?
(a) It exhibits short viability
(b) It is difficult to germinate *in vitro*
(c) It occurs in cereals
(d) It is characterized by low respiratory rate

86. A condition characterized by split in the upper lip and gap in the roof of mouth is
(a) microcephaly (b) polydactyly
(c) Klinefelter's syndrome (d) cleft palate

87. Which one of the following is correct about thalassemia?
(a) Decreased clotting ability
(b) Increased clotting ability
(c) Abnormal sickle shaped RBC
(d) Fragile RBC cause haemolytic anaemia

88. Which one of the following is correct about microcephaly?
(a) Small skull
(b) Five fingers
(c) Gap in the roof of the mouth
(d) Upper lip folded

89. Gray crescent is present in
(a) eye of frog (b) retina of cockroach
(c) brain of frog (d) zygote of frog

90. The flowering process is a .... response.
(a) phototropic (b) photoperiodic
(c) gravitropic (d) thigmotropic

91. Match list I (embryological features) with list II (plants) and select the correct answer using the codes given below.

List I	List II
A. Longitudinal division of zygote	1. *Cyperus*
B. Only one of the four microspores in a tetrad is functional	2. *Dendropthoe*
C. Plant regeneration from *in vitro* fertilized egg	3. *Zea*

Codes

	A	B	C
(a)	1	2	3
(b)	3	1	2
(c)	1	3	2
(d)	2	1	3

92. Consider the following statement.
Self-incompatibility is defined as
I. A pre-zygotic barrier to self-fertilization in plants that otherwise produce fully functional gametes.
II. An intraspecific reproductive barrier regulated by genetically determined self-recognition, self-rejection mechanism.
III. An intraspecific reproductive barrier, where cell-to-cell recognition allows the pistil to recognize and reject pollen from genetically related individual.
IV. A pre-zygotic barrier to self-fertilization in plants that produce non-functional male gametes.

Which of the statements given above is/are correct?
(a) I, II, III and IV (b) I, II and III
(c) III and IV (d) I only

93. Which one of the following features is not associated with grasses?
(a) Aleurone tissue (b) Scutellum
(c) Cellular endosperm (d) 3-celled pollen

94. Russell *et. al,* demonstrated the occurrence of dimorphic sperms in the pollen of
(a) *Amaryllis* (b) *Clivia*
(c) *Plumbago* (d) *Orchis*

95. In sporophytic self-incompatibility, rejection of the male gametophyte occurs at the level of
(a) ovary
(b) stigma surface
(c) transmitting tract of the stigma
(d) stylar canal

96. What is advantage of sexual reproduction?
(a) Genetically varied individuals are born
(b) Chances of survival increases
(c) Chances of evolution increases
(d) All of the above

97. In angiosperms, normally after fertilization
(a) the zygote divides before the division of the primary endosperm
(b) the primary endosperm nucleus divides before the division of the zygote
(c) both the zygote and the primary endosperm nucleus divide simultaneously
(d) both the zygote and the primary endosperm nucleus undergo a resting period and then divide simultaneously

98. Artificial method(s) of asexual reproduction in plants is (are)
(a) cuttings
(b) tissue culture
(c) Both (a) and (b)
(d) alternation of generation

99. A single mushroom may produce .... spores a minute at the peak of its reproduction.
(a) 500000 (b) 50000
(c) 80000 (d) 200000

100. Perennating organs are associated with which type of asexual reproduction?
(a) Sporulation (b) Apomixis
(c) Vegetative propagation (d) Cutting

101. In apomixis, an embryo is created from a diploid cell in the
(a) pollen tube (b) leaf
(c) ovule (d) All of these

102. Asexual reproduction differs from sexual reproduction in that it does not require
(a) one parent (b) two parents
(c) spores (d) vegetative parts

103. In the embryonic development of *Drosophila melanogaster.* How long does embryonic development take in this organism?
(a) One hour (b) Three hours
(c) One day (d) Ten days

104. The portion of the blastoderm-stage embryo which will give rise to most ectodermal, mesodermal and endodermal tissues is called the
(a) ventral (b) germ band
(c) imaginal discs (d) amnioserosa

105. The grafting of a second polarizing region into the anterior of a limb bud results in
(a) degeneration of the bud
(b) formation of a second bud at the site of the graft
(c) formation of extra copies of the anterior-most digit, digit 2, is the only possible result.
(d) a new axis can be formed if the second polarizing region is large and a second full set of digits can form with mirror-image orientation to the normal set of digits

106. Match list I (type of placenta) with list II (example) and select the correct answer using the codes given below.

List I	List II
A. Epitheliochorial	1. Dog
B. Syndesmochorial	2. Platypus
C. Endotheliochorial	3. Rabbit
D. Homochorial	4. Pig
	5. Deer

Codes

	A	B	C	D
(a)	2	4	1	3
(b)	4	5	3	1
(c)	2	4	3	1
(d)	4	5	1	3

107. The muscle-forming cells of the vertebrate limb come from
(a) the ectodermal epithelium of the limb bud
(b) the mesodermal mesenchyme of the limb bud, derived from lateral plate ectoderm
(c) mesodermal cells that migrate into the limb bud from the somites
(d) the progress zone

108. Ontogeny is
(a) development of the ear
(b) the evolutionary history of a species or group
(c) the study of cancer
(d) the development of an individual organism

109. In humans, the branchial arches have evolved to give rise to
(a) bones in the human ear
(b) gills that form during embryonic stages
(c) vertebrae of the neck
(d) the skull

110. Which of the following statement is a true statement?
(a) Limbs evolved from fins
(b) Kidneys evolved from jaws
(c) Bat wings evolved from horse's hooves
(d) Insects evolved from crustaceans

111. The absence of limbs in snakes may be attributable to the evolution changes in
(a) collagen proteins
(b) apical ectodermal ridge formation
(c) BMP signaling
(d) HOX gene expression

112. Hedgehog family genes specify the .... position in both vertebrate and insect wings.
(a) dorsal (b) ventral
(c) anterior (d) posterior

113. The HOX gene complexes of mice and other mammals have evolved by
(a) the splitting of one cluster into two
(b) the duplication of a single ancestral HOX gene such as the one found in insects
(c) the duplication of the ancestral cluster
(d) the loss of three clusters from the ancestral condition of four clusters

114. Consider the following plants
I. *Avicennia*
II. *Aegiceras*
III. *Sonneratia*
Which of the above plant/plants exhibit vivipary?
(a) I only (b) I and II
(c) II and III (d) I, II and III

115. Changes in the timing of developmental events is called
(a) neoteny (b) ontogeny
(c) heterochrony (d) phylogeny

116. A key evolutionary event that allowed the evolution of the bilaterally symmetric triploblasts from the common ancestor of the triploblasts and the diploblasts would have been the evolution of
(a) limbs (b) a nervous system
(c) a gut (d) the mesoderm

117. Consider the following families.
I. Orchidaceae
II. Podostemaceae
III. Trapaceae
In which of the above does the embryo possess extensively developed suspensor haustoria?
(a) I only (b) I and II
(c) II and III (d) I, II and III

118. Consider the following statements.
I. Aleurone tissue forms the outermost layer of endosperm in maize.
II. Aleurone tissue helps in the nutrition of embryo during germination.
Which of the statements given above is/are correct?
(a) I only (b) II only
(c) Both I and II (d) Neither I nor II

119. Regarding pollination in angiosperms, consider the following statements.
I. Anemophily is associated with the reduction in the number of ovules per ovary.
II. All hydrophytes are pollinated through water.
Which of the statements given above is/are correct?
(a) I only (b) I only
(c) Both I and II (d) Neither I nor II

120. With reference is sperms and ova of vertebrates, consider the following statements.
I. In the spermatozoon, the middle piece containing nucleus and the tail contains mitochondrion.
II. The mature ovum contains a centriole which later helps the zygote in its division.
Which of the statements given above is/are correct?
(a) I only (b) II only
(c) Both I and II (d) Neither I nor II

121. The exine proteins responsible for the pollen 'rejection reaction' on the incompatible stigma are derived from
(a) anther locule (b) tapetum
(c) connective tissue (d) microspore cytoplasm

122. The term 'chalazosperm' refers to the
(a) absence of endosperm
(b) persistent nucellus
(c) prominent tissue formed by the nucellar cells above the vascular bundle and arising from chalazal region of ovule
(d) cleavage and proliferation of embryo

123. In all, a minimum of how many meiotic divisions are required to form 100 sexual seeds?
(a) 25 (b) 50
(c) 100 (d) 125

124. Xenogamy refers to
(a) pollination between flowers borne by two different plants of the same species
(b) pollination between two flowers borne by the same plant
(c) pollination between two flowers borne by two different plants of allied species or genera
(d) pollination within the same bisexual flowers

125. Seed germination in grasses and sedges is
(a) hypogeal (b) epigeal
(c) cryptogeal (d) mesogeal

126. What does it tell us about aging that cells from different organisms are capable of a fixed number of divisions in culture and that number of divisions reflects the relative lifespan of the organism?
(a) The cells from these different organisms are not all equally adapted to growth in culture
(b) In each organism, the cells seems to be capable of a genetically determined number of divisions, after which the organism undergoes senescence and dies
(c) Cells growing in culture live for the same number of years that the organism from which they are derived would be expected to live, indicating a genetically determined lifespan
(d) The conditions cells encounter in culture lead to oxidative damage which reflects the kind of damage that normally leads to ageing in the organism

127. Why is meiosis required for germ cell formation, yet is never used by somatic cells?
(a) Meiosis is the cell division process that produces haploid products

(b) Meiosis is a process that produces one sperm and one egg from each dividing germ cell
(c) Meiosis is a specialized, highly efficient process of cell division, which is used because of the large numbers of germ cells required by an organism
(d) Meiosis is a specialized form of cell division that produces four diploid cells instead of just two, facilitating the production of large numbers of germ cells

128. Two human disorders, Prader-Willi syndrome and Angelman syndrome, occur when the mother contributes a copy of chromosome 15 that contains a small deletion in a specific region. Why does this small deletion not behave as a recessive allele, that is, why is its loss not made up for by the good copy of the region on the paternally contributed chromosome 15?
(a) This portion of chromosome 15 is invariably mutated in males, so the father, too, contributes recessive alleles that are thus homozygous and perturb development
(b) The father's copy of chromosome 15 has genes in the region of the deletion that are imprinted and thus inactive, in the absence of any active copies of these genes, development cannot proceed normally.
(c) The genes in this portion of chromosome 15 are special in that they are required in two copies for normal development, and so the loss of one set does not allow normal development
(d) Two copies of every gene in the genome are required for development, so loss of one of the copies from this region perturbs development

129. What is the 'acrosomal reaction'?
(a) The acrosomal reaction is a repulsive interaction between the sperm and the egg
(b) The acrosomal reaction is the digestion of the acrosome by the sperm when it encounters an egg
(c) The acrosomal reaction is the digestion of the zona pellucida, permitting the sperm to contact the egg
(d) The acrosomal reaction is the fusion of the sperm and egg plasma membranes

130. What is the cortical reaction and why is it important?
(a) The cortical reaction is the fusion of the egg cortex with the egg plasma membrane, which allows the sperm to enter
(b) The cortical reaction is the entry of Ca^{2+} ions into the egg, which initiates development
(c) The cortical reaction is the exocytosis of the cortical granules during egg maturation, which contain the components of the zona pellucida
(d) The cortical reaction is the release of the cortical granules after sperm entry, which converts the vitelline membrane into the fertilization membrane which blocks polyspermy

131. In humans, an individual with an XXY chromosomal complement will develop as
(a) a male (b) a female
(c) an hermaphrodite (d) a super-female

132. Adherens junctions play an important role in development they are composed of
(a) cadherins linked to other cadherins extracellularly, and to actin filaments intracellularly
(b) cadherins linked to other cadherins extracellularly, and to intermediate filaments intracellularly
(c) immunoglobulin super-family (IgSF) molecules linked to other IgSF molecules extracellularly, and to the cytoskeleton intracellularly
(d) integrins linked to extracellular matrix molecules extracellularly, and to the cytoskeleton intracellularly

133. If embryos are disaggregated with chemicals or proteases and the individual cells are mixed together in culture, what will happen?
(a) The cells will regulate to form one or more normal embryos
(b) The cells will often sort themselves so that like cells are together
(c) The cells will reaggregate to form a normal embryo capable of continuing development
(d) The cells will associate with one another randomly

134. What type of cleavage is used in frog embryos?
(a) Radial (b) Unequal
(c) Spiral (d) Superficial

135. The process in which the three germ layers form is called
(a) fertilization (b) cleavage
(c) gastrulation (d) organogenesis

136. During gastrulation in *Xenopus*, the future mesoderm and endoderm move inside the embryo through the 'blastopore' in contrast, in chickens, gastrulation involves cells moving inward through the
(a) blastoderm (b) yolk
(c) cleavage furrow (d) primitive streak

137. In mammalian development, the embryo will form from which population of cells?
(a) The blastocyst (b) The inner cell mass
(c) The trophectoderm (d) The blastocoel

138. Genes control development by
(a) controlling where and when proteins are synthesized
(b) containing small preformed body parts and organs that become 'expressed' during development
(c) directly controlling phenotypes, without intermediates or influence from the environment
(d) acting as enzymes to build proteins

139. A mature pollen grain contains
(a) 2 tube cells and 2 generative cells
(b) 2 tube cells and 1 generative cell
(c) 1 tube cell and 1 generative cell
(d) 1 tube cell and 2 generative cells

140. Which one of the following structures arises from the funiculus during post fertilization development of the ovule?
(a) Caruncle (b) Aril
(c) Operculum (d) Perisperm

141. In which one of the following families does the seed contain endosperm?
(a) Poaceae (b) Trapaceae
(c) Podostemaceae (d) Orchidaceae

142. Maternal factors are
(a) energy rich proteins and lipids packaged into the vegetal pole

(b) hormonal influences encountered in the uterus in mammals
(c) *m*RNAs and proteins packaged into the egg by the mother, which act to control early development in the embryo
(d) genes contributed to the embryo by the maternal haploid genome

143. The role of maternal factors (such as Vg-1, Xwnt-1 and VegT) packaged into the vegetal region of the *Xenopus* oocyte is
(a) in establishing the future dorso-ventral body axis.
(b) to allow the vegetal region to divide during cleavage
(c) to specify the future animal-vegetal body axis
(d) to provide energy and nutrients for the developing embryo

144. Between fertilization and the first cleavage division, actin filaments pull the cytoplasm of the frog egg toward the point of sperm entry in a process called
(a) cortical rotation (b) dorsalization
(c) blastulation (d) gastrulation

145. Consider the following statements.
I. Orchid seed are albuminous.
II. *Pinus* seed are exalbuminous
Which of the statements given above is/are correct?
(a) I only (b) II only
(c) Both I and II (d) Neither I nor II

146. In mammals, dosage compensation is carried out by
(a) decreasing the transcription of the X in males
(b) increasing the transcription of the X in males
(c) inactivating one X-chromosome in females by condensation as heterochromatin
(d) inactivating one X-chromosome in males by condensation as heterochromatin

147. Many cells in the body divide only rarely, if at all; neurons, red blood cells and keratinocytes are extreme examples. In which portion of the cell cycle would such cells be considered to be?
(a) M-phase (b) G_1-phase
(c) G_0-phase (d) S-phase

148. The size of a cell is generally controlled by the amount of DNA in the nucleus. The more DNA, the larger the cell. What do experiments in which the amount of DNA is doubled (tetraploidy in salamanders) tell us about growth control?
(a) The animals grow to a normal size, and contain only half as many cells, indicating that growth is regulated at the level of absolute size, rather than cell number
(b) The animals grow to twice the normal size, indicating that growth is regulated at the level of the number of cells present
(c) The animals end up with cells that are twice as big, but only half as many, resulting in an animal that is half its normal size, indicating that the number of cells is the critical determinant of growth
(d) The animals grow to a normal size, and contain only half as many cells, indicating that growth is regulated by the total amount of DNA present in an organism

149. Disease, injuries and birth defects that compromise the function of the pituitary may lead to decreased stature (height). What treatment might be prescribed and what would be its rationale?
(a) Since the pituitary is damaged or missing, the only possible treatment would be the transplantation of a donor pituitary
(b) Loss of pituitary function could lead to decreased growth hormone production and hence short stature, recombinant human growth hormone might be prescribed
(c) Since growth hormone controls growth hormone releasing hormone and somatostatin production in the hypothalamus, its absence would be compensated for by administration of those hormones
(d) Since the pituitary is located under the brain, above the roof of the mouth, no intervention is possible since this location is hard to reach

150. Adult human bone.
(a) grows only at the extreme ends (epiphysis)
(b) grows only in the center (diaphysis)
(c) grows only at the growth plates between the epiphysis and the diaphysis
(d) grows throughout its length

151. What is especially exciting about research into regeneration in zebrafish?
(a) Amputation of a fin leads to regeneration of a limb, implying an evolutionary homology between the two structures
(b) Removal of the eye results in regeneration of the eye, and since zebrafish and humans have very similar eyes, this research may lead to new therapies for eye damage in humans
(c) Limited regeneration of heart muscle can occur in zebrafish and the ability to study zebrafish genetically will enhance our ability to understand the genetic basis of regeneration
(d) Mutations have been found that enhance the regenerative powers of zebrafish and it is hoped that the genes found can be exploited in enhancing human regeneration

152. The middle piece of mammalian sperm includes which one of the following sets of structures?
(a) Golgi apparatus, mitochondria and centriole
(b) Golgi apparatus, mitochondria and axial filament
(c) Golgi apparatus, centriole and axial filament
(d) Mitochondria, centriole and axial filament

153. In the endospermous seeds the growth of the embryo starts
(a) concurrently with the endosperm
(b) before the endosperm starts growing
(c) after the endosperm has started growing
(d) after the endosperm is fully developed

154. The type of enzymes released by sperm acrosome at the time of acrosome reaction during fertilization is
(a) ligase
(b) peptidase
(c) hydrolase
(d) dehydrogenase

155. Which one of the following is the correct statement?

Cortical reaction of egg during fertilization is necessary to

(a) inhibit polyspermy and solubilize the egg membranes
(b) inhibit polyspermy and harden the egg membranes
(c) solubilize the egg membranes
(d) allow polyspermy and harden the egg membranes

156. What are osteoblasts?

(a) Osteoblasts are the stem cells that give rise to chondrocytes
(b) Osteoblasts are the proliferating precursors of the chondrocytes
(c) Osteoblasts are enlarged chondrocytes present in the hypertrophic zone of the growth plate
(d) Osteoblasts are bone-forming cells that derive from stem cells in the bone marrow and therefore have no lineage relationship to chondrocytes

157. Cancer is believed to often arise from stem cells, rather than fully differentiated cells. Which of the following are consistent with this view?

(a) Stem cells are actively dividing and express few differentiated functions, so they may have fewer changes to undergo than do fully differentiated cells in becoming cancer cells
(b) DNA replication is necessary for mutations to occur, and stem cells are replicating their DNA, whereas differentiated cells are for the most part not replicating their DNA
(c) Stem cells require genes like Wnt for the maintenance of their stem cell function, and many such genes can also function as oncogenes
(d) All of the above are reasons that cancer cells may more readily arise from stem cells than from fully differentiated cells

158. In developmental biology, what is meant by the concept of 'growth'?

(a) Growth occurs through increases in cell size
(b) Growth occurs through increases in cell number
(c) Cell death is an important determinant of overall growth
(d) All of the above

159. The process that sperm undergoes in female genital tract of mammals before fertilization is called

(a) decapacitation (b) capacitation
(c) activation (d) deactivation

160. Which of the following statements regarding endosperm is are false?

I. Primary endosperm nucleus divides along with zygotic division
II. All types of endosperm produce haustorial appendages
III. Usually the endosperm is a triploid tissue
IV. Ruminate endosperm is of common occurrence in Compositae and Gramineae

(a) I and II (b) only IV
(c) I and IV (d) None of these

161. Match list I with list II and select the correct answer using the codes given below the lists.

List I (Development Processes)	List II (Animal)
A. Parthenogenesis	1. Urochordates
B. Retrogressive metamorphosis	2. Honeybee
C. Paedogenesis	3. Lepidopteran insect
D. Blastokinesis	4. Amphibia

Codes

	A	B	C	D
(a)	1	2	3	4
(b)	2	1	3	4
(c)	1	2	4	3
(d)	2	1	4	3

162. Match list I with list II.

List I (Foetal Membranes)	List II (Functions of Foetal Membranes)
A. Yolk sac	1. Elimination of metabolic wastes
B. Chorion	2. Shock absorption
C. Allantois	3. Food storage and digestion
D. Amnion	4. Exchange of substances between mother and embryo

Codes

	A	B	C	D
(a)	4	3	1	2
(b)	4	3	2	1
(c)	3	4	2	1
(d)	3	4	1	2

163. Match list I with list II and select the correct answer using the codes given below the lists.

List I	List II
A. Pollinia	1. Litchi
B. Aril	2. Pollen tube
C. Virus elimination	3. Orchids
D. Tip growth	4. Meristem culture
	5. Palynology

Codes :

	A	B	C	D
(a)	3	2	4	5
(b)	2	1	3	4
(c)	4	3	5	2
(d)	3	1	4	2

164. Match list I with list II.

List I (Cell Type)	List II (Characteristic)
A. Spermatogonium	1. Does not divide
B. Spermatocyte	2. Divides meiotically
C. Spermatic	3. Divides mitotically
D. Sertoli cell	4. Divides both mitotically and meiotically
	5. Nourishes other cell types

Codes

	A	B	C	D
(a)	5	3	1	4
(b)	1	3	4	5
(c)	3	2	4	1
(d)	3	2	1	5

165. Match list I with list II and select the correct answer using the codes given below the lists.

List I (Structures)	List II (Originated from)
A. Retina	1. Endodermal cells
B. Nephric tubules	2. Ectodermal cells
C. Pigment pattern of skin	3. Neural crest cells
D. Allantois	4. Mesodermal cells

Codes

	A	B	C	D
(a)	1	2	3	4
(b)	4	3	2	1
(c)	2	4	3	1
(d)	3	4	1	2

166. Match list I with list II and select the correct answer using the codes given below the lists.

List I	List II
A. Triple fusion	1. Transference of pollen grains on the stigma
B. Pollination	2. Fussion of male and female gametes
C. Parthenocarpy	3. Seedless development of fruit
D. Syngamy	4. Fusion of polars and male gametes

Codes

	A	B	C	D
(a)	1	2	3	4
(b)	4	1	3	2
(c)	2	1	3	4
(d)	4	1	2	3

Answers

1. (c)	**2.** (d)	**3.** (d)	**4.** (b)	**5.** (a)	**6.** (d)	**7.** (a)	**8.** (c)	**9.** (d)	**10.** (b)
11. (b)	**12.** (b)	**13.** (b)	**14.** (c)	**15.** (b)	**16.** (a)	**17.** (c)	**18.** (a)	**19.** (a)	**20.** (d)
21. (c)	**22.** (d)	**23.** (c)	**24.** (b)	**25.** (a)	**26.** (b)	**27.** (d)	**28.** (c)	**29.** (c)	**30.** (b)
31. (b)	**32.** (c)	**33.** (c)	**34.** (c)	**35.** (d)	**36.** (b)	**37.** (a)	**38.** (b)	**39.** (a)	**40.** (b)
41. (c)	**42.** (a)	**43.** (b)	**44.** (b)	**45.** (b)	**46.** (a)	**47.** (a)	**48.** (c)	**49.** (a)	**50.** (c)
51. (b)	**52.** (a)	**53.** (d)	**54.** (a)	**55.** (c)	**56.** (b)	**57.** (a)	**58.** (a)	**59.** (c)	**60.** (c)
61. (b)	**62.** (b)	**63.** (a)	**64.** (b)	**65.** (c)	**66.** (c)	**67.** (d)	**68.** (a)	**69.** (b)	**70.** (c)
71. (d)	**72.** (c)	**73.** (c)	**74.** (b)	**75.** (c)	**76.** (a)	**77.** (b)	**78.** (c)	**79.** (b)	**80.** (d)
81. (b)	**82.** (d)	**83.** (b)	**84.** (c)	**85.** (d)	**86.** (d)	**87.** (d)	**88.** (a)	**89.** (d)	**90.** (b)
91. (a)	**92.** (c)	**93.** (c)	**94.** (c)	**95.** (b)	**96.** (d)	**97.** (b)	**98.** (c)	**99.** (a)	**100.** (c)
101. (c)	**102.** (b)	**103.** (c)	**104.** (b)	**105.** (d)	**106.** (d)	**107.** (c)	**108.** (d)	**109.** (a)	**110.** (a)
111. (d)	**112.** (d)	**113.** (c)	**114.** (d)	**115.** (c)	**116.** (d)	**117.** (d)	**118.** (c)	**119.** (c)	**120.** (b)
121. (b)	**122.** (c)	**123.** (d)	**124.** (a)	**125.** (d)	**126.** (b)	**127.** (a)	**128.** (b)	**129.** (c)	**130.** (d)
131. (a)	**132.** (a)	**133.** (b)	**134.** (a)	**135.** (c)	**136.** (d)	**137.** (b)	**138.** (a)	**139.** (c)	**140.** (b)
141. (a)	**142.** (c)	**143.** (a)	**144.** (a)	**145.** (d)	**146.** (c)	**147.** (c)	**148.** (a)	**149.** (b)	**150.** (c)
151. (c)	**152.** (d)	**153.** (c)	**154.** (c)	**155.** (b)	**156.** (d)	**157.** (d)	**158.** (d)	**159.** (d)	**160.** (c)
161. (a)	**162.** (a)	**163.** (d)	**164.** (d)	**165.** (c)	**166.** (b)				

15

Morphogenesis and Organogenesis in Plants and Animals

Morphogenesis and Organogenesis in Animals

The life of an individual begins when two genetically different mature gametes (egg and sperm) undergo fertilization to form zygote. It is followed by growth and differentiation to form complete individual like its parent.

Cell Aggregation and Differentiation in *Dictyostelium*

Dictyostelium discoideum shows a type of multicellular organization derived from unicellular organisms. Haploid spores give rise to myxamoebae, which can reproduce asexually to form more haploid myxamoebae.

In asexual cycle, solitary haploid amoebae (called myxamoebae) live on decaying logs, eating bacteria and reproducing by binary fission. When they have exhausted their food supply, tens of thousands of these **myxamoebae** join together to form moving streams of cells called a tight aggregate. Subsequently, a tip arises at the top of this mound and the tight aggregate bends over to produce the migrating **slug** (pseudoplasmodium or grex) with the tip at the front. The grex begins to migrate (in dark and moist environment) with its anterior tip slightly raised, migration ceases in an illuminated area and the grex differentiates into a fruiting body composed of spore cells and a **stalk.** The stalk cells die and the **spore cells,** elevated above the stalk, become spore cells. These spore cells disperse, each one forms a new myxamoeba.

Syllabus

- Morphogenesis and Organogenesis in Animals : Cell Aggregation and Differentiation in *Dictyostelium;* Axes and Pattern Formation in *Drosophila,* Amphibia and Chick; Organogenesis, Vulva Formation in *Caenorhabditis elegans*; Eye Lens Induction, Limb Development and Regeneration in Vertebrates; Differentiation of Neurons, Post Embryonic Development-Larval Formation, Metamorphosis; Environmental Regulation of Normal Development; Sex Determination.
- Morphogenesis and Organogenesis in Plants : Organization of Shoot and Root Apical
- Meristem; Shoot and Root Development; Leaf Development and Phyllotaxy; Transition to Flowering, Floral Meristems and Floral Development in *Arabidopsis* and *Antirrhinum.*
- E. Programmed Cell Death, Ageing and Senescence.

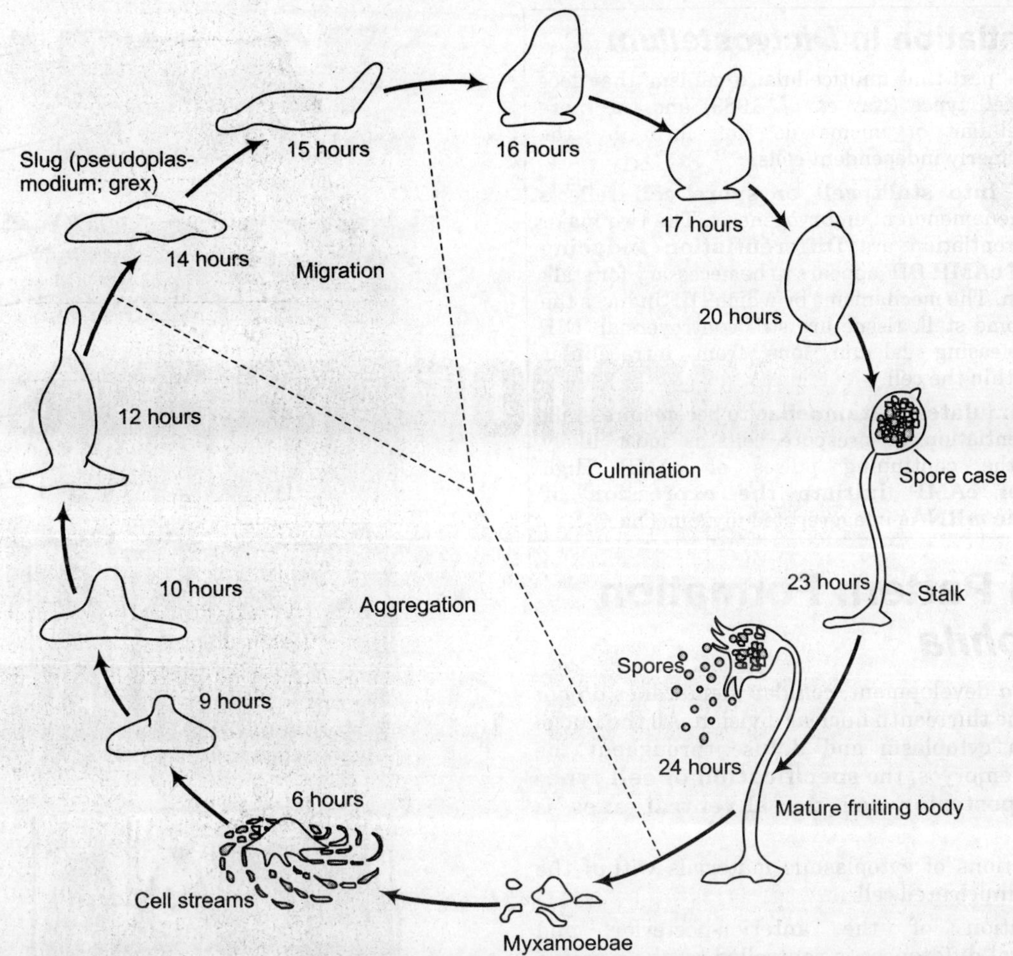

Fig. 15.1 Life history of *Dictyostelium discoideum*

In addition to this asexual cycle, two myxamoebae of the *Dictyostelium* can fuse to create a giant cell, which digests all the other cells of the aggregate.

The aggregation of thousands of myxamoebae into a single organism is an incredible feat of organization.

Bonner (1947) and **Shaffer** (1953) showed that this movement is due to chemotaxis the cells are guided to aggregation centres by a soluble substance. This substance was later identified as cyclic adenosine 3′, 5′ -monophosphate (cAMP).

Aggregation is initiated as each of the cells begins to synthesize cAMP. Neighbouring cells respond to cAMP in two ways they initiate a movement toward the cAMP pulse and they release cAMP of their own. After this the cell is unresponsive to further cAMP pulses for several minutes. The result is a rotating spiral wave of cAMP that is propagated throughout the population of cells. As each wave arrives, the cells take another step toward the centre.

Raper (1940) and **Bonner** (1957) demonstrated that the anterior cells normally become stalk, while the remaining, posterior cells are usually destined to form spores but the cells have ability to change their developmental fates according to their location within the whole organism and thereby compensate by **regulation.**

Individual cells stick together to form a cohesive organism by developmentally regulated cell adhesion molecules.

Cell Adhesion Molecules in *Dictyostelium*

Dictyostelium cells do not adhere to one another, while growing on bacteria. However, once cell division stops, the cells become increasingly adhesive around eight hours after starvation.

The **initial cell-cell adhesion is mediated** by a glycoprotein that is absent in myxamoebae but appears shortly after division ceases. Once this initial aggregation has occurred, it is stabilized by a second cell adhesion molecule. The second cell adhesion system seems to be needed for retaining a large enough number of cells to form large fruiting bodies. A third cell adhesion system is activated late in development.

The **glycoprotein** (80 kDa) is synthesized during the aggregation phase. If it is defective or absent, the fruiting bodies will be only about one third the normal size. This protein also important in the movement of the pre-stalk cells to the apex of the mound.

Differentiation in *Dictyostelium*

Dictyostelium is a 'part time multicellular organism' that does not form many cell types (Kay *et. al,* 1989) and the more complex multicellular organisms do not form by the aggregation of formerly independent cells.

Differentiation into stalk cell or spore cell reflects another major phenomenon of embryogenesis. The two major factors for differentiation are **Differentiation Inducing Factor** (DIF) and **cAMP.** DIF appears to be necessary for stalk cell differentiation. The mechanisms by which DIF induces the grex cells to become stalk tissue are still controversial. DIF may act by releasing calcium ions from intracellular compartments within the cell.

Although **DIF stimulates myxamoebae** to become pre-stalk cells, the differentiation of prespore cells is most likely controlled by the continuing pulses of *c*AMP. High concentrations of **cAMP initiate the expression of prespore specific *m*RNAs** in aggregated myxamoebae.

Axes and Pattern Formation in *Drosophila*

During *Drosophila* development, cellular membranes do not form until after the thirteenth nuclear division. All the nuclei share a common cytoplasm and diffuse throughout the embryo. In these embryos, the **specification of cell types** along **anterior-posterior** and **dorsal-ventral axes** is accomplished by:

1. The interactions of cytoplasmic materials within the single, multinucleated cell.
2. The initiation of the anterior-posterior and dorsal-ventral differences is controlled by the position of the egg within the mother's ovary.
3. The sperm entry site may fix the axes in ascidians and nematodes, but in the fly's anterior-posterior and dorsal-ventral axes are specified by interactions between the egg and its surrounding follicle cells.

Formation of the Cellular Blastoderm in *Drosophila*

The zygote nucleus undergoes several mitotic divisions within the central portion of the egg. The nuclei then migrate to the periphery of the egg, where the mitosis continue, albeit at a progressively slower rate. Most of the other nuclei arrive at the periphery of the embryo at tenth cycle and then undergo four more divisions at progressively slower rates. During these stages of nuclear division, the embryo is called a **syncytial blastoderm** (nuclei are contained within a common cytoplasm without cell membranes except egg itself). The nuclei and their associated cytoplasmic islands are called **energids.** Following thirteenth cycle, the oocyte plasma membrane folds inward between the nuclei and partitioning each somatic nucleus into a single cell. This process creates the **cellular blastoderm**, in which all the cells are arranged in a single layered jacket around the yolky core of the egg. This process can be inhibited by drugs that block microtubules as formation of the cellular blastoderm involves a delicate interplay of microtubules and microfilaments.

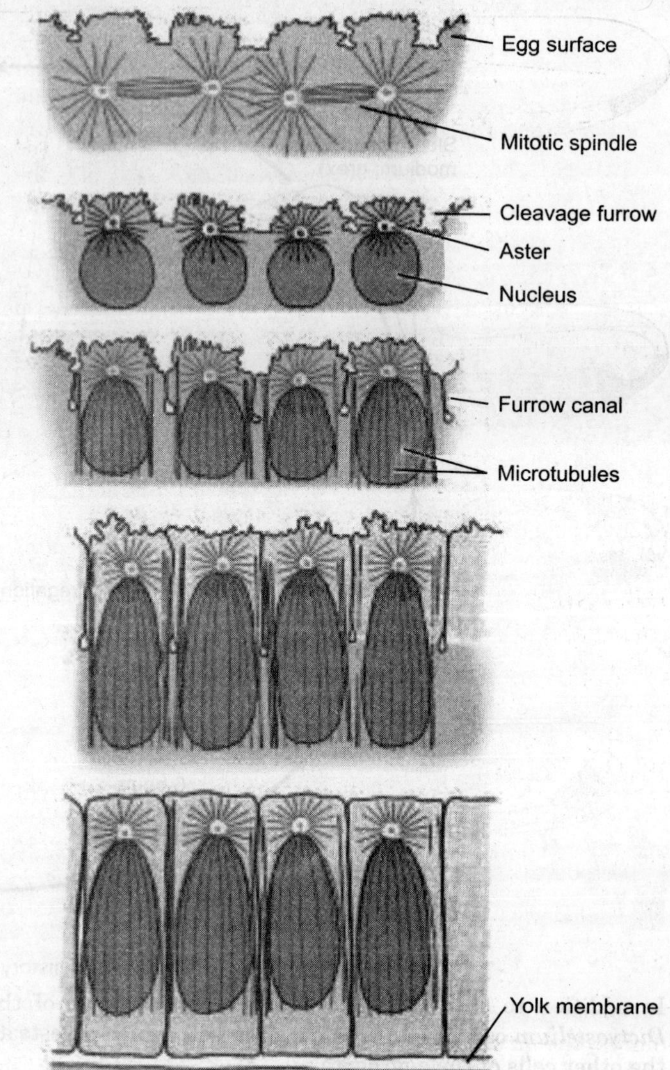

Fig. 15.2 Developmental series showing the progressive cellularization

The first movements of *Drosophila* gastrulation segregate the presumptive mesoderm, endoderm and ectoderm. The mesoderm (about 1000 cells) folds inward to produce the **ventral furrow.** This furrow eventually becomes a ventral tube within the embryo. The **pole cells are internalized** alongwith the endoderm. At this time, the embryo bends to form the cephalic furrow.

The ectodermal cells on the surface and the mesoderm undergo convergence and extension, migrating toward the ventral midline to form the **germ band.**

While the germ band is in its extended position, several key morphogenetic processes occur organogenesis, segmentation and the segregation of the imaginal discs (imaginal discs are those cells set aside to produce the adult structures). In addition, the nervous system forms from two regions of ventral ectoderm. In *Drosophila*, the nervous system is located ventrally, rather than being derived from a dorsal neural tube as in vertebrates.

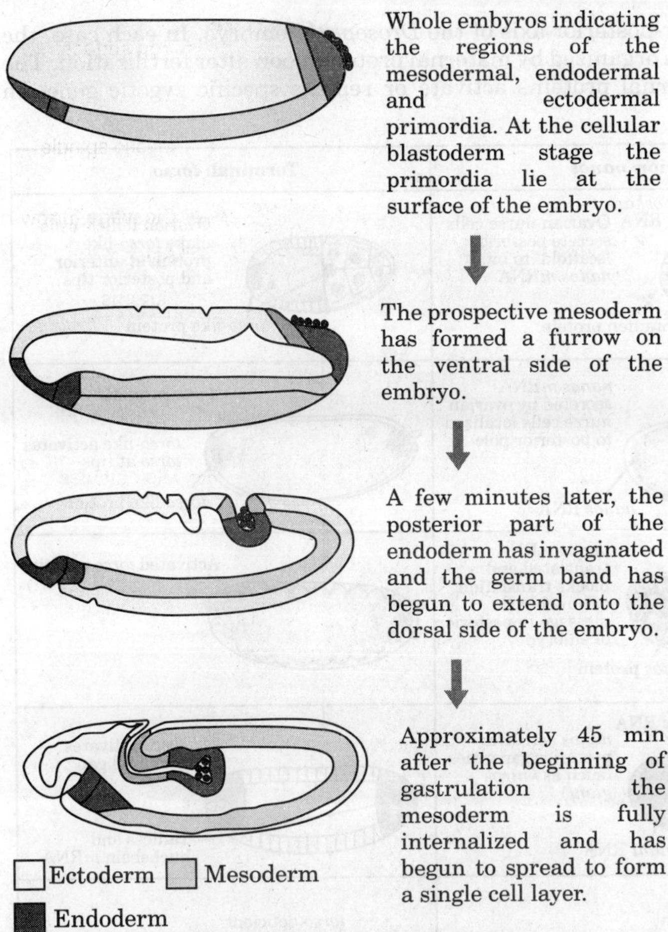

Fig. 15.3 Four stages of gastrulation

The general body plan of *Drosophila* is the same in the embryo, the larva and the adult, each of which has a distinct head end and a distinct tail end, between which are repeating segmental units. Each segment of the adult fly has its own identity.

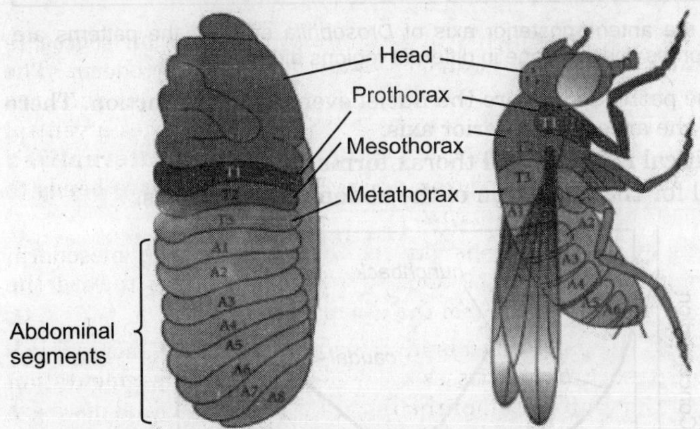

Fig. 15.4 Comparison of larval and adult segmentation in *Drosophila*

The **anterior-posterior** and **dorsal-ventral axes** of *Drosophila* form at right angles to one another and they are both determined by the position of the oocyte within the follicle cells of the ovary.

Origins of Anterior-Posterior Polarity
(Patterning)

The anterior-posterior polarity of the embryo, larva and adult has its origin in the anterior-posterior polarity of the egg. The **maternal effect genes** encode transcriptional and translational regulatory proteins that diffuse through the syncytial blastoderm and activate or repress the expression of certain zygotic genes. Two of these proteins, ***bicoid*** and ***hunchback***, regulate the production of anterior structures, while another pair of maternally specified proteins, ***nanos*** and ***caudal***, regulates the formation of the posterior parts of the embryo. The **gap genes** is the zygotic genes and are among the first genes transcribed in the embryo, it regulated the expression of maternal factors. The gap gene proteins cause the transcription of **pair rule genes**, each of which divides the embryo into regions about two segments wide results in a striped pattern of seven vertical bands perpendicular to the anterior-posterior axis. The pair rule gene proteins activate the transcription of the **segment polarity genes**, whose products divide the embryo into 14 segment wide units. The protein products of the **gap genes**, **pair rule genes** and **segment polarity genes** interact to regulate another class of genes, the **homeotic selector genes**, whose transcription determines the developmental fate of each segment.

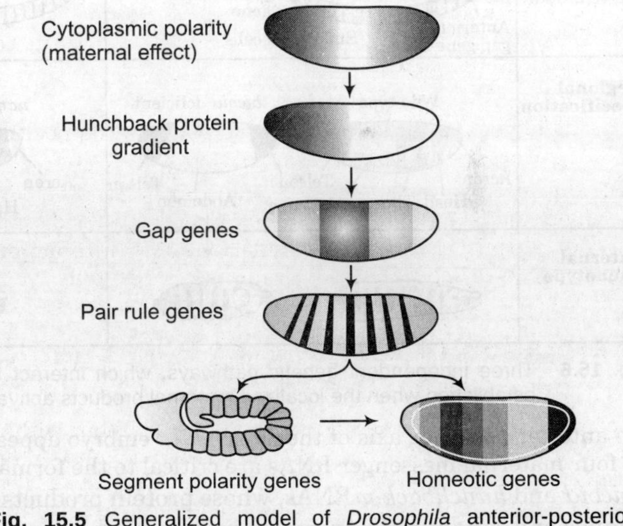

Fig. 15.5 Generalized model of *Drosophila* anterior-posterior pattern formation

The egg sequesters an RNA that generates a gradient of anterior forming material.

The gradient hypothesis was united with a genetic approach to the study of *Drosophila* embryogenesis and found that **one set of genes encoded gradient morphogens** for the anterior part of the embryo, **another set of genes encoded morphogens** responsible for organizing the posterior region of the embryo and a **third set of genes encoded proteins** that produced the terminal regions at both ends of the embryo.

Three independent genetic pathways interact to form the anterior-posterior axis of the *Drosophila* embryo. In each case, the initial asymmetry is established during oogenesis and the pattern is organized by maternal proteins soon after fertilization. The realization of the pattern comes about when the localized maternal proteins activate or repress specific zygotic genes in different regions of the embryo.

Stage	Anterior: *bicoid*	Posterior: *nanos*	Terminal: *torso*
Mid oogenesis	Nurse cells; *bicoid* *m*RNA; Ovarian nurse cells secrete *bicoid* *m*RNA into oocyte; oocyte nucleus interacts with posterior follicle cells; Oocyte	*nanos* RNA; *oskar* RNA; Ovarian nurse cells secrete posterior 'scaffold' to bind *nanos* *m*RNA; Staufen protein	Ovarian follicle cells make *torso*-like protein at anterior and posterior tips; *torso*-like protein
Completion of oogenesis	*bicoid* *m*RNA; *bicoid* *m*RNA localized in anterior by products of exuparantia and swallow, nucleus migrates to the dorsal anterior region	Maternal *hunchback* RNA; *nanos* *m*RNA secreted by ovarian nurse cells localized to posterior pole; *nanos* RNA	*torso* protein; *torso*-like activates *torso* at tips; *torso* like protein
Syncytial blastoderm	Bicoid protein; *bicoid* *m*RNA translated and forms protein gradient; it represses caudal *m*RNA translation; *Caudal* protein	*Hunchback* protein; *nanos* *m*RNA translated and blocks translation of hunchback message in posterior of embryo; *nanos* protein	Activated *torso* protein
Cellular blastoderm	*hunchback* protein gradient; Pole cells; *bicoid* protein activates anterior gap genes such as **orthodentical, buttonhead** and the *hunchback* gene; Anterior gap gene RNA; Embryonic cells	*knirps* RNA; *nanos* activates posterior gap genes (such as *knirps giant*); *giant* RNA	*torso* activates terminal gap genes; Tailless and huckebein *m*RNA
Regional specification	Wild type: Acron, Head, Thorax, Abdomen, Telson; *bicoid* deficient: Abdomen, Telson	*nanos* deficient: Acron, Head, Thorax, Telson	*torso* deficient: Head, Thorax, Abdomen
External phenotype			

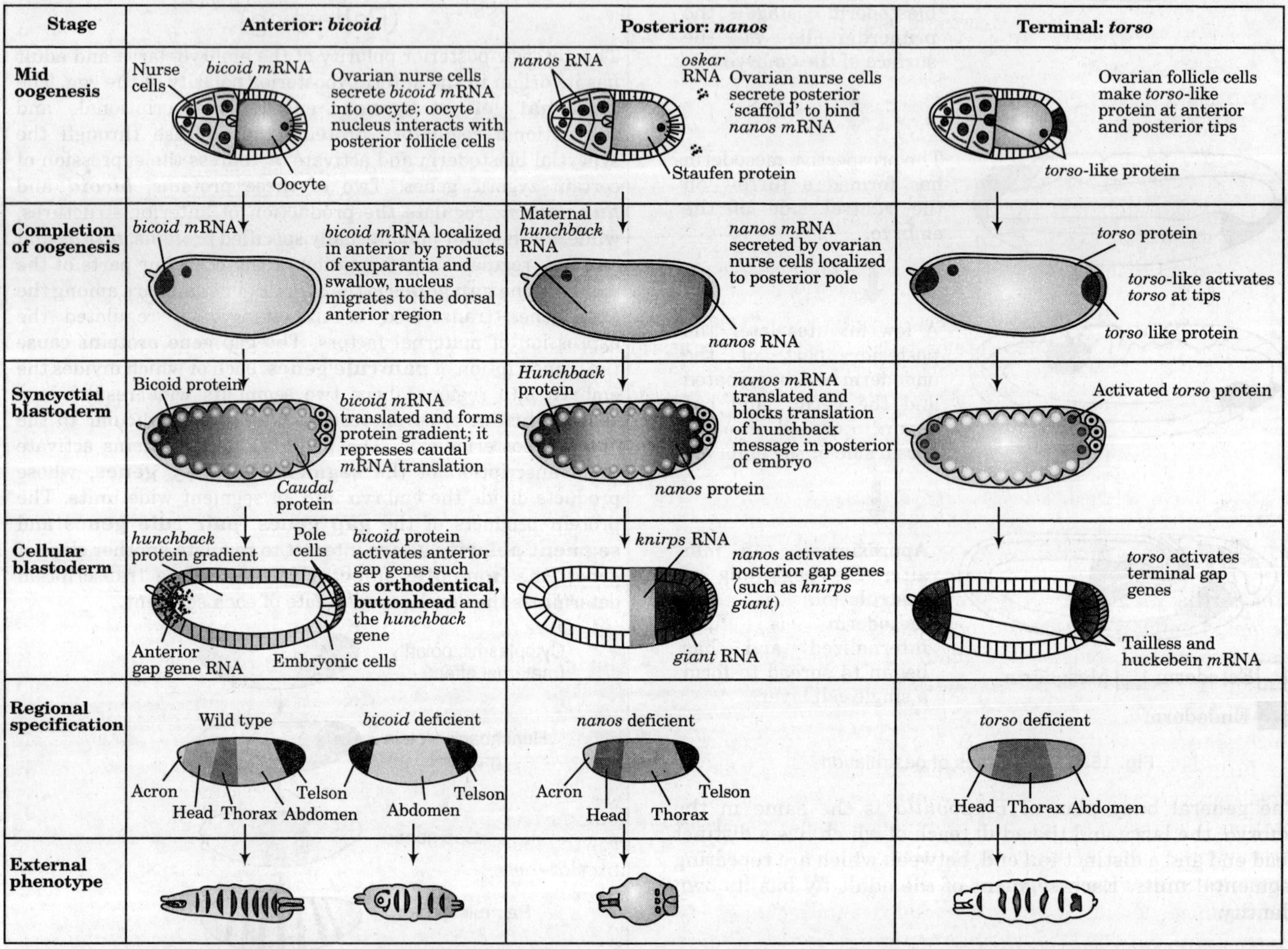

Fig. 15.6 Three independent genetic pathways, which interact to form the anterio-posterior axis of *Drosophila* embryo; the patterns are established when the localized maternal products activate or repress specific gene in different regions of the embryo

The anterior-posterior axis of the *Drosophila* embryo appears to be patterned before the nuclei even begin to function. There are four maternal messenger RNAs are critical to the formation of the anterior-posterior axis:

- *bicoid* and *hunchback* *m*RNAs, whose protein products are critical for head and thorax formation.
- *nanos* and *caudal* *m*RNAs, whose protein products are critical for the formation of the abdominal segments.

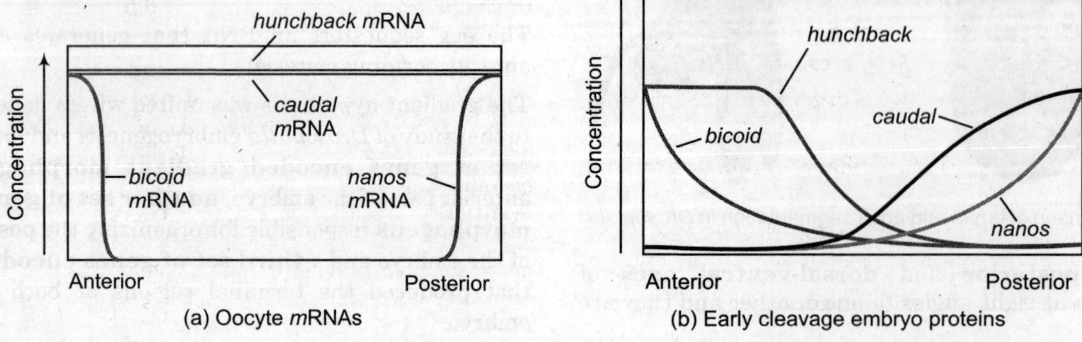

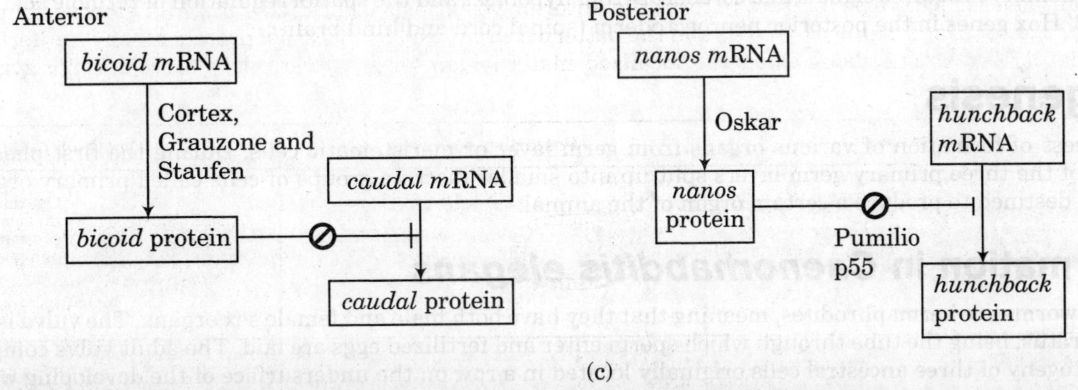

Fig. 15.7 A model of anterior-posterior pattern generation by the *Drosophila* maternal effect genes

(a) The *hunchback* and *caudal* mRNAs are distributed throughout the oocytes. At the anterior pole, the *bicoid* is translated and at the anterior pole, the *nanos* message is translated.

(b) *bicoid* also elevates the level of *hunchback* protein in the anterior of the embryo by binding to the enhancers of the *hunchback* gene and stimulating its transcription.

(c) *bicoid* protein inhibits the translation of the *caudal* RNA, allowing *caudal* protein to be synthesized only in the posterior of the cell. Conversely, *nanos* protein, in conjunction with pumilio protein, binds to *hunchback* RNA, preventing its translation in the posterior portion of the embryo.

Axes and Pattern Formation in Amphibia

After fertilization and before first cleavage in amphibian (*Xenopus*) embryo, the cortical cytoplasm of zygote rotates relative to central cytoplasm by about 30 degree. The cortical rotation is powered by microtubules motors moving along parallel arrays of cartical microtubules. The gray crescent which is uncovered by rotation of cortical cytoplasm marks the future dorsal side of the embryo, *i.e.*, formation of dorsal/ventral axis can be prevented by blocking this rotation. The tissue which is able to induce the formation of dorsal/ventral axis is called **organizer** and the chemical substance emitted to enfluence this effect is called **evocator.** The organizer is induced from a dorsal vegetal region called **Nieuwkoop center.** The vegetal cap can give rise to only endodermal cells, while the animal cap can give rise to only epidermal cell types. The marginal zone can give rise to most structure in embryo including mesoderm.

The entire development of an organism is due to a series of induction. The structure which induces the formation of another structure is called the organizer or inductor. In animals three types of organizers are found.

1. **Primary Organizer** Dorsal lip of blastopore. This organizer originates from grey crescent.
2. **Secondary Organizer** The organizer which induce formation of various organs.
3. **Tertiary Organizer** Secondary organizers induce formation tertiary organizer.

Organizer has the ability of self-differentiation and organization. It has following roles:

1. Induce nearby cells to form certain organs and part of organ.
2. Induces the surrounding cells to transform into secondary inductor centre.
3. Determine the main features of axiation and organization of the embryo.
4. Does not interfere with work of another organizer.

The anterior/posterior patterning of the embryo occurs sometime before or during gastrulation. The anterior inducing ability comes from the X_{wnt} – 8 (which expressed throughout the ventral and lateral mesoderm) antagonising signals. Cereberus Dickkopf and FrZb (These signals bind to X_{wnt} – 8 to prevent it from binding to its receptor). Anterior head development also requires the function of insulin like growth factors (IGFs) expressed in dorsal middle and anterior neural tube. In the posterior a fibroblast growth factor homologue (eFGF) and retinoic acid.

Axes and Pattern Formation in Chick

The orientation of cells with respect to the yolk defined the dorsal/ventral axis in chick. The animal is up, while ventral is down with respect to yolk. This axis is defined by the creation of a pH difference inside and outside of blastoderm between the sub-germinal space (pH = 6.5) and albumin on the outside (pH = 9.5).

The anterior/posterior axis is defined during the initial tilting of the embryo when the egg shell is being deposited. There is a partial stratification of the yolk by constant rotation of egg in a consistent direction. The lighter yolk components will become the future posterior. The accumulation of cells eventually results in posterior marginal zone which expresses both Vg1 and nuclear localized β-catenin. The posterior marginal zone induce Hensen's node (equivalent to organizer) which is the site, where gastrulation begins and it becomes the dorsal mesoderm. The anterior/posterior

patterning of the embryo requires signals like coreberus from hypoblast and the spatiol regulation of retinoic acid accumulation to activate the 3′ Hox genes in the posterior neuroectoderm (spinal cord and hind brain).

Organogenesis

This is the process of formation of various organs from germ layer or meristematic cells. During the first phase continuous masses of cells of the three primary germ layers split up into smaller discrete groups of cells called primary organ rudiment, each of which is destined to produce a certain organ of the animal.

Vulva Formation in *Caenorhabditis elegans*

Most *C. elegans* worms are hermaphrodites, meaning that they have both male and female sex organs. The vulva is part of the female sex apparatus, being the tube through which sperm enter and fertilized eggs are laid. The adult vulva comprises 22 cells which are the progeny of three ancestral cells originally located in a row on the undersurface of the developing worm.

Each of these ancestral cells becomes committed to the differentiation pathway that leads to production of vulva cells. The central cell, called P6.p, adopts the primary vulva cell fate and divides to produce eight new cells. The other two cells, P5.p and P7.p, take on the secondary vulva cell fate and divide into seven cells each. These 22 cells then reorganize their positions to construct the vulva.

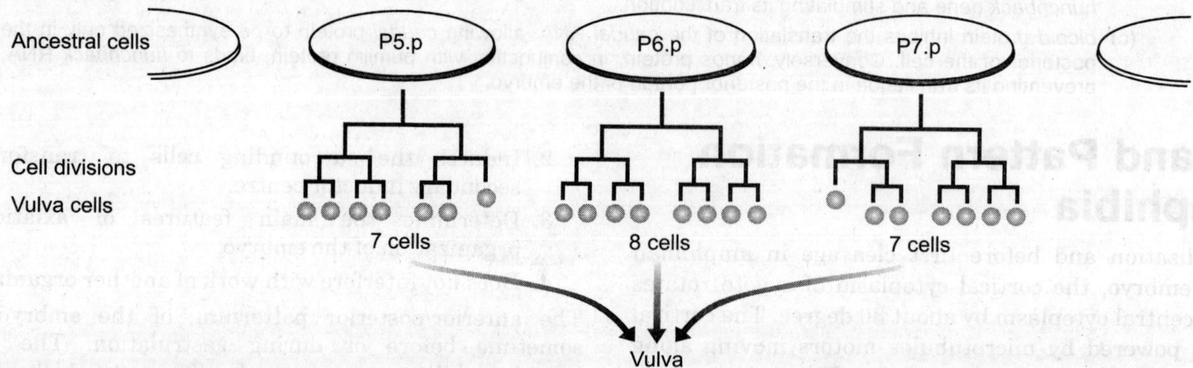

Fig. 15.8 Cell divisions resulting in production of the vulva cells of *Caenorhabditis elegans*

A critical aspect of vulva development is that it must occur in the correct position relative to the gonad, the structure containing the egg cells. If the vulva develops in the wrong place then the gonad will not receive sperm and the egg cells will never be fertilized. The positional information needed by the vulva progenitor cells is provided by a cell within the gonad called the anchor cell. In the absence of the anchor cell, a vulva does not develop.

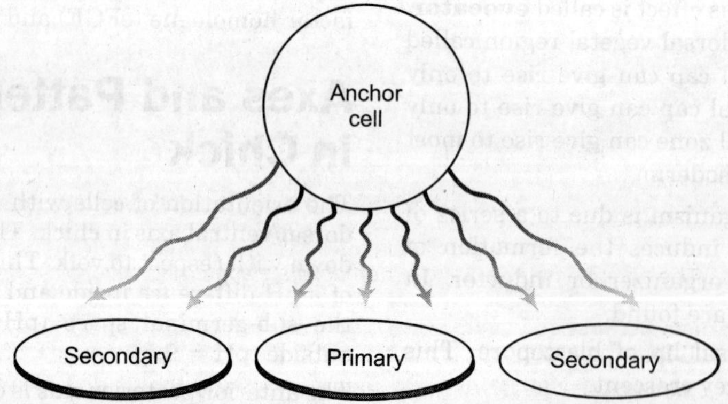

Fig. 15.9 The anchor cell in determining cell fate during vulva development in *Caenorhabditis elegans*

The signal that commits P5.p and P7.p to their secondary fates might not come directly from the anchor cell but *via* P6.p in the form of a different extracellular signalling compound whose synthesis by P6.p is switched on by LIN-3 activation.

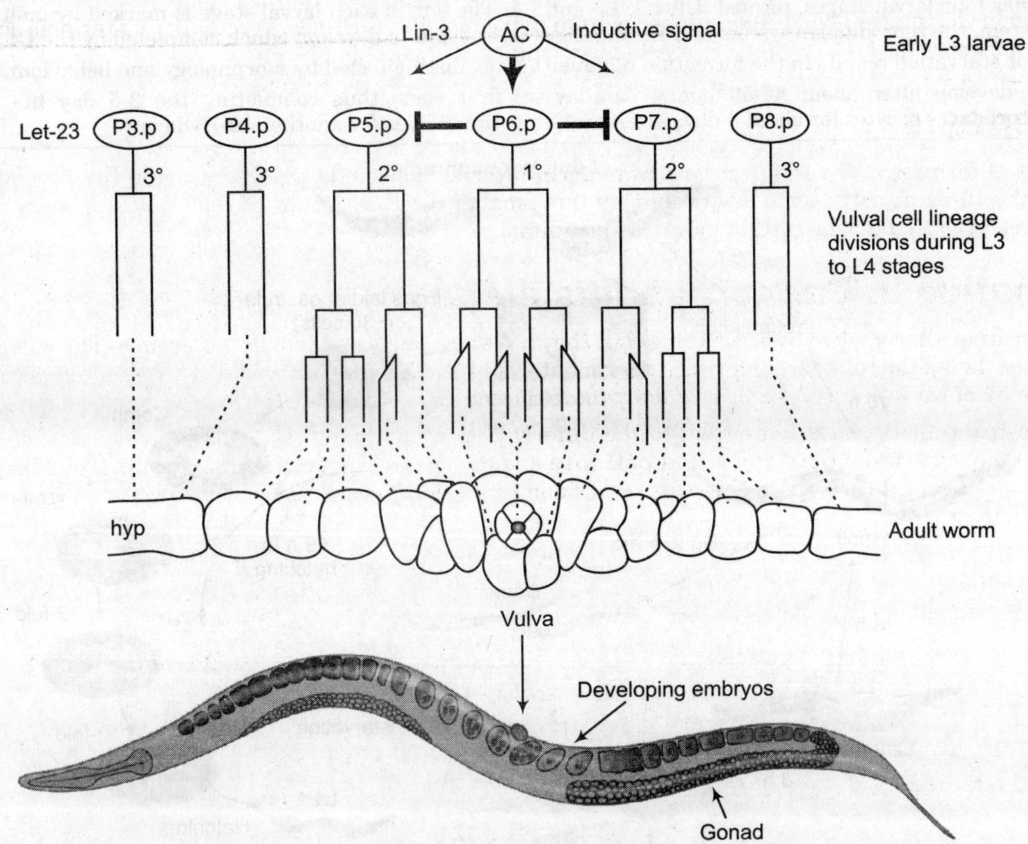

Fig. 15.10 The formation of the *Caenorhabditis elegans* vulva involves a series of signalling events

Caenorhabditis elegans as a Model Organism

The organisms are protostomes, unlike deuterostomes, by the order of formation of the mouth and anus.

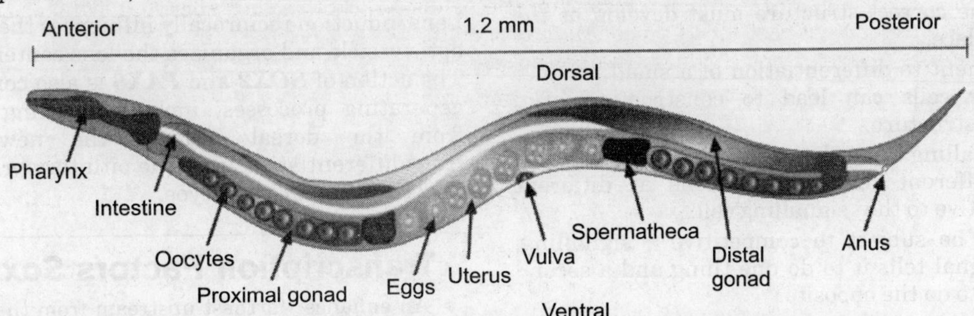

Fig. 15.11 The adult hermaphrodite *Caenorhabditis elegans* with labelled body parts

- *C. elegans* is an ideal model organism because the adult hermaphrodite contains exactly 959 cells and the position of each cell in the adult is derived from a strict cell lineage, which was precisely defined in by John Sulston *et. al.*
- It was the first organism in which small interfering RNAs were used successfully for gene silencing by Craig Mello and Andrew Fire.
- It was the first animal to be studied with a reporter protein namely, Green Fluorescent Protein (GFP) from the jellyfish *Aequorea victoria*.
- It was the organism in which apoptosis was discovered by H Robert Horvitz.
- It was the first metazoan to have its genome sequenced.

C. elegans is transparent and individual cells can be easily visualized through all stages of development. The worm exists as two sexes, hermaphrodite or male (no female organisms exist). In the hermaphrodite, the gonad is bilobed, with each lobe connecting *via* an oviduct and spermatheca to a shared midventral vulva and uterus (see figure above). Eggs pass through the spermatheca, where fertilization takes place by stored sperm (male sperm is stored in the spermatheca) and the eggs begin to develop inside the mother.

Stage of developmental of *C. elegans*

- Gastrulation begins prior to egg laying, its proliferation results in an undifferentiated embryo.

- The organism has four larval stages, termed L1, L2, L3 and L4. The end of each larval stage is marked by molting. In L1 larvae, the nervous system, the reproductive system and the digestive tract begin to develop, which completed by the L4 stage.
- Overcrowding or starvation results in the formation of dauer larvae, distinguished by morphology and behaviour.
- Mature adults develop after about 45-50 hours, can lay its first eggs, thus completing the 3-5 day life cycle. The adult hermaphrodite produces oocytes for about 4 days afterward, the animal lives for another 10-15 days.

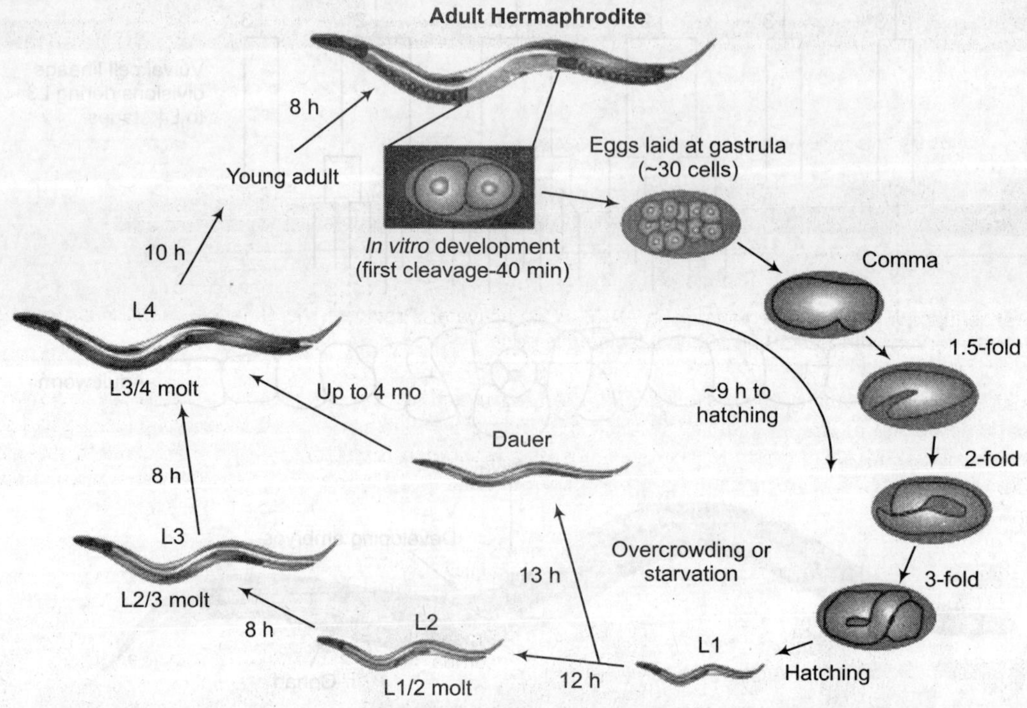

Fig. 15.12 Life cycle of *C. elegans*

In summary, the general concepts to emerge from vulva development in *C. elegans* are as follows:

(i) In a multicellular organism, positional information is important, the correct structure must develop at the appropriate place.

(ii) The commitment to differentiation of a small number of progenitor cells can lead to construction of a multicellular structure.

(iii) Cell-cell signalling can utilize a concentration gradient to induce different responses in cells at different positions relative to the signalling cell.

(iv) A cell might be subject to competitive signalling, where one signal tells it to do one thing and a second signal tells it to do the opposite.

Eye Lens Induction

Lens tissue develops from the embryonic head ectoderm through its interaction with the retinal primordium, the optic vesicle. This developmental mechanism has served as a paradigm of embryonic tissues induction.

The application of modern techniques for gene manipulation and monitoring gene activities in developing embryonic tissues have revealed the two optic vesicle dependent mechanisms that underlie the lens induction process:

(i) Local activation of the cooperative transcription factors ***SOX2*** (SRY-related-HMG-box 2) and ***PAX6*** (paired box 6) in the head ectoderm;

(ii) Elimination of the influence of the cephalic neural crest, which is otherwise inhibitory to lens development.

Lens induction reciprocally influences the development of the optic vesicle and organizes the lens centered optic cup.

The action of ***SOX2*** and ***PAX6*** is also common to other lens generating processes, including during lens regeneration from the dorsal iris in the newt eye and lens transdifferentiation from the pituitary primordium as occurs in certain mutant embryos.

Transcription Factors *Sox2* and *Pax6*

- An enhancer farthest upstream from the promoter contains the regions necessary for ***PAX6*** expression in the pancreas.
- A second enhancer activates ***PAX6*** expression in surface ectoderm (lens, cornea and conjunctiva).
- A third enhancer resides in the leader sequence and it contained the sequences that direct ***Pax6*** expression in the neural tube.
- A fourth enhancer sequence, located in an intron shortly after the translation initiation sequence, determines the expression of ***PAX6*** in the retina.
- ***SOX2*** is not usually found in the outer ectoderm, but it appears in those outer ectodermal cells that will become lens by virtue of their being induced by the optic vesicle evaginating from the brain. Thus, only those cells that contain both ***SOX2*** and ***PAX6*** can express the lens crystallin gene.

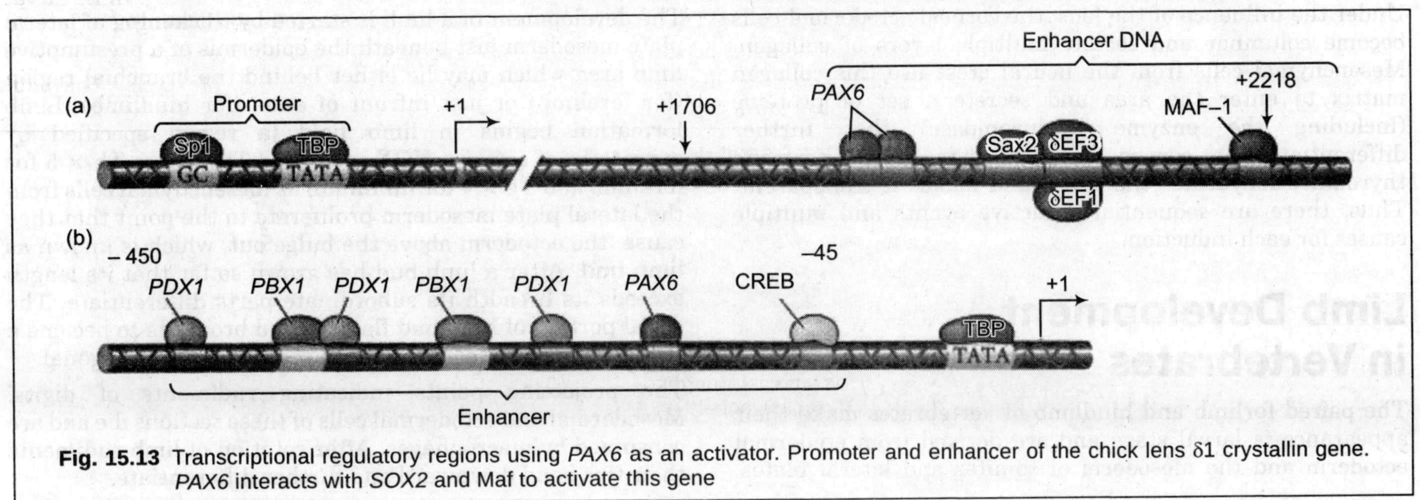

Fig. 15.13 Transcriptional regulatory regions using *PAX6* as an activator. Promoter and enhancer of the chick lens δ1 crystallin gene. *PAX6* interacts with *SOX2* and Maf to activate this gene

The mouse lens at 9th day of embryo, the optic vesicle extends toward the surface ectoderm from the forebrain. The lens placode appears as a local thickening of the surface ectoderm near the optic vesicle the lens placode then enlarged and the optic vesicle formed an optic cup. The central portion of the lens forming ectoderm invaginates, while the two layers of the retina become distinguished. The lens consists of anterior cuboidal epithelial cells and elongating posterior fibre cells. The cornea develops in front of the lens.

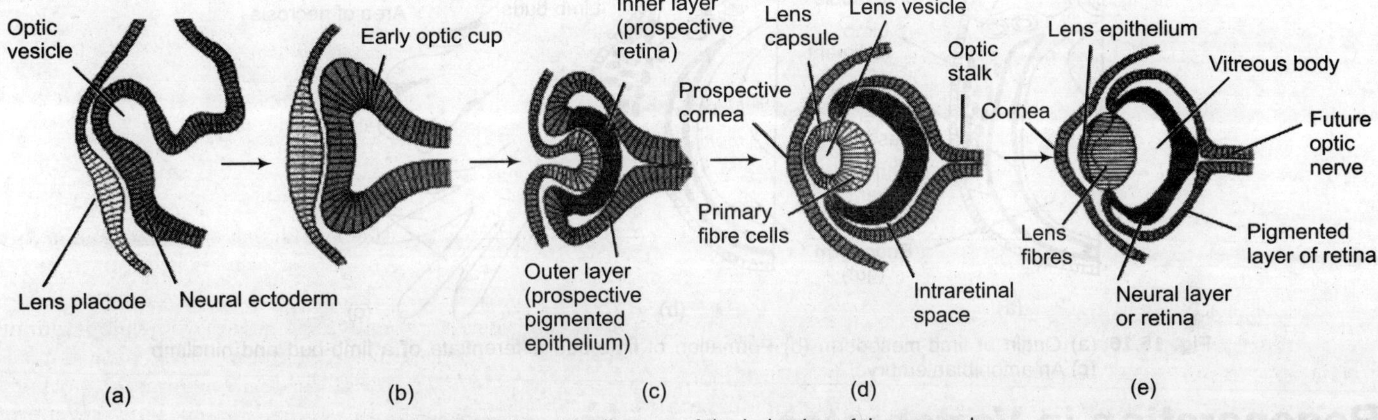

Fig. 15.14 Schematic diagram of the induction of the mouse lens

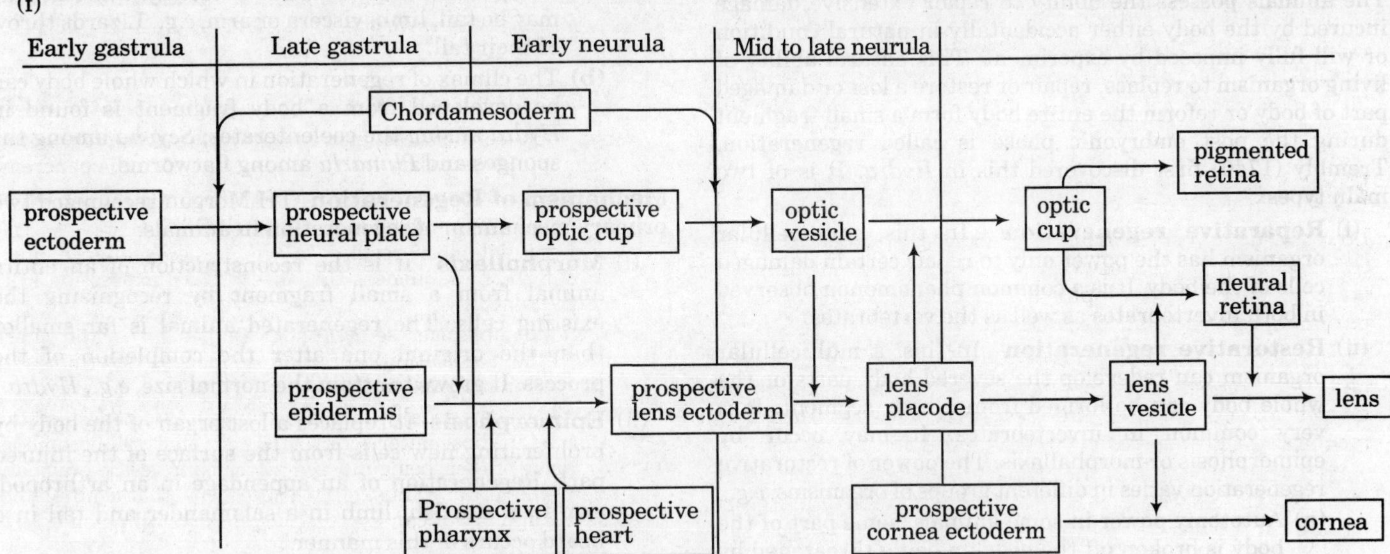

Fig. 15.15 Summary of some of the inductive interactions during eye development

Under the influence of the lens, the corneal ectodermal cells become columnar and secrete multiple layers of collagen. Mesenchymal cells from the neural crest use this collagen matrix to enter the area and secrete a set of proteins (including the enzyme hyaluronidase) that further differentiate the cornea. A third signal, the hormone thyroxine, dehydrates the tissue and makes it transparent. Thus, there are sequential inductive events and multiple causes for each induction.

Limb Development in Vertebrates

The paired forlimb and hindlimb of vertebrates make their appearance is larval stage and are derived from epidermal ectoderm and the mesoderm of somites and lateral plates.

The development of a limb is started by thickening of lateral plate mesoderm just beneath the epidermis of a presumptive limb area which may lie either behind the branchial region (for forelimb) or just infront of anus (for hindlimb). Limb formation begins in limb field (a region specified by expression of certain *HOX* genes and TbX genes Tb × 5 for forelimb and Tb × 4 for hindlimb) as mesenchymal cells from the lateral plate mesoderm proliferate to the point that they cause, the ectoderm above the bulge out, which is known as **limb bud.** After a limb bud has grown so far that its length exceeds its breadth its subordinate parts differentiate. The distal portion of limb bud flattens and broadens to become a circular hand or foot plate which soon become pentagonal.

The projecting points indicating rudiments of digits. Mesodermal and ectodermal cells of these sections die and are consumed by macrophages. After rotation of limb rudiments their tips bend downward and further differentiate.

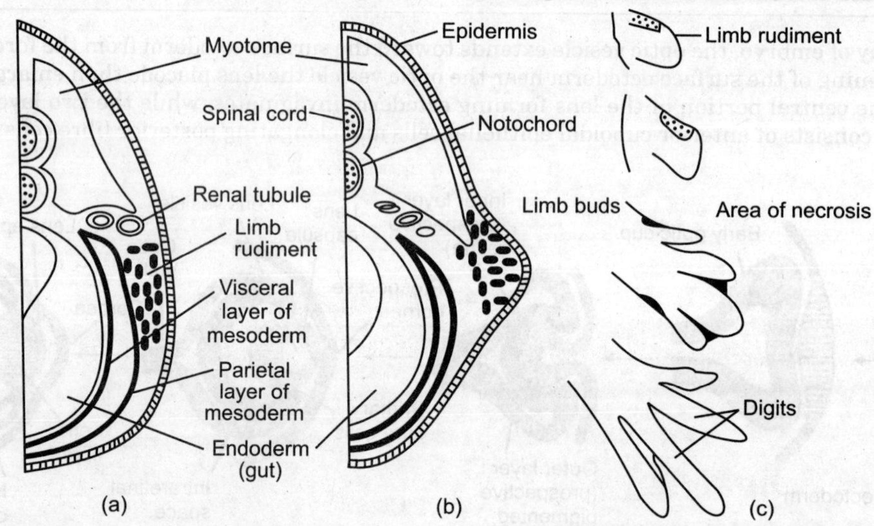

Fig. 15.16 (a) Origin of limb-mesoderm (b) Formation of limb-bud differentiate of a limb-bud and hindlimb (c) An amphibian embryo

Regeneration in Vertebrates

The animals possess the ability to repair extensive damage incured by the body either accidentally in natural condition or will fully imposed by experiment. This natural ability of living organism to replace, repair or restore a lost or damaged part of body or reform the entire body form a small fragment during the post embryonic phase is called regeneration. Trembly (1740) first discovered this in *Hydra.* It is of two main types:

(i) **Reparative regeneration** In this, multicellular organism has the power only to repair certain damaged cells of the body. It is a common phenomenon observed in both invertebrates as well as the vertebrates.

(ii) **Restorative regeneration** In this, a multicellular organism can redevelop the severed body parts or the whole body can be formed from a body segment. It is very common in invertebrates. It may occur by epimorphosis or morphallaxis. The power of restorative regeneration varies in different groups of organisms, *e.g.,*

(a) Autotomy power in some animals, some part of the body is broken off the body on being threatened by the enemy or predator. This phenomenon of self mutilation of body is called autotomy. The lost part may be tail, limb, viscera or arm, *e.g.,* Lizards throw of their tail.

(b) The climax of regeneration in which whole body can be developed from a body fragment is found in *Hydra* among the coelenterates; *Scypha* among the sponges and *Planaria* among flatworms.

Mechanism of Regeneration TH Morgan recognized two primary mechanism of regeneration in animals.

(i) **Morphallaxis** It is the reconstruction of an entire animal from a small fragment by recognizing the existing cells. The regenerated animal is far smaller than the original one after the completion of the process. It grows to attain the normal size, *e.g., Hydra.*

(ii) **Epimorphosis** It replaces a lost organ of the body by proliferating new cells from the surface of the injured part. Regeneration of an appendage in an arthropod, arm in a starfish, limb in a salamander and tail in a lizard occurs in this manner.

Differentiation of Neurons

The central nervous system, peripheral nervous system and the eyes develop from the neural ectoderm. The dorsal thickening of ectoderm forms neural or medullary plate which form the primary rudiment (*i.e.,* neural tube) of the central nervous system. The newly formed neural tube is of unequal diameter throughout. Its anterior end is expanded with a brooder cavity and thicker walls than posterior part of the tube. Which develops into brain. The spinal cord develops from posterior thin walled narrow part.

Development of Brain

The neural tube expands anteriorly into bulb-like future brain. The most anterior is prosencephalon (forebrain), the mid region is mesencephalon (midbrain) and posterior most region, which is continuous with spinal cord is the rhombencephalon (hindbrain). The three vesicles soon become five by paired out pocketing of anterior end of forebrain called **telencephalon** and a median outpocketing of the hindbrain forming metancephalon. The telencephalon will form the cerebral hemisphere end the remaining part of forebrain to become the **diencephalon** or **thalamencephalon.** Antero-ventral part of the telencephalon grows forward to differentiate into olfactory lobes constituting the rhincephalon. From the midbrain grows out paired dorsal outgrowths called optic lobes. The metencephalon gives rise to cerebellum the remaining hindbrain called myelencephalon develops into medulla oblongata.

Development of Spinal Cord

The posterior portion of the original neural tube which does not develop into brain becomes the spinal cord. The ependymal cells (lining neurocoel) do not contribute to formation of any nervous element. The outside of the spinal cord is derived from original nervous ectoderm lying beneath the original epidermis. Some of the neuroepithelial cells slip outward and become neuroblasts (embryonic nerve cells) which differentiate into **neurons.** Some neuroblast cells differentiate into neuroglial cells (embryonic supporting cells) which form the connective tissue of CNS. Numerous neurons and neuroglia accumulate between neurocoel and mantle forming **gray matter.** Outside the mantle the developing neuroblasts send out processes (axons) which ascend or descend in the spinal cord. When axons get ensheathed by fatty myelin sheath, this layer is called **white matter.** Both the matter differentiated further.

Postembryonic Development

After formation of embryo from an egg the embryo undergoes a number of process of development. These include larval formation and metamorphosis.

Larval Formation

The newly formed individual partially developing within the egg membranes or in maternal body, which later born or hatched from the egg. The condition and characteristics of new organism at the time of birth or hatching differs in various groups of animals. Like in frog embryos emerge from egg membrane when the main organs have already begin to develop but differentiate of the tissue is not completed. Similarly certain precocial birds emerge from the egg covered with downy feathers and can run about, soon after hatching while altricial birds hatch naked with only rudimentary feather and are unable to move. Among mammals there is great variation in degree of development at birth, as in marsupials (*e.g.,* opossums and kangaroo) the young born under developed and very small and then kept in pouch of mother for long time. Many small mammals are helpless at birth. In birds, the hard egg shell is broken by hatching's break. A similar egg tooth appears on the tip of snout of hatching reptiles.

There are various advantages of development of embryo into larva rather than complete organism the young are called larvae which transform into adult form by a process of metamorphosis.

Table 15.1 **Different Groups with their Characteristic Larva**

Group	Larva
Porifera	Amphiblastula and Parenchymula
Coelenterata	Planula
Platyhelminthes	Turbellaria
Trematodes	Muller's larva, Miracidium, Sporocyst, Redia, Cercaria and Metacercaria
Cestodes	Cysticercus
Nemertinea	Pillidium
Annelida	Trochophore
Mollusca	Trochophore, Veliger and Glochidium
Arthropoda	Nauplius, Zoea, Metazoea, Cypris
Bryozoa, Ectoprocta	Megalopa, Phyllosoma, Caterpillar Cyphonantes
Echinodermata	Pluteus, Bipinaria, Auricularia, etc.
Protochordata	Tornaria, Tadpole and Gastrula Larva
Cyclostomata	Ammocoetus
Amphibia	Tadpole of Frog, Axolotl, etc.

Metamorphosis

It is the postembryonic activation of morphogenetic processes associated with adramatic change in habitat, structure funct n and consequent way of life during a brief discrete period. This process is observed in those animals in which the embryo develops into a larva and the larva is transformed into adult. Based upon presence or absence of metamorphosis the development may be **direct** or **indirect.** These are two types of metamorphosis met among vertebrates.

Table 15.2 **Metamorphic Changes with Functional Activities in Frog**

Characteristic	Change	Functions
Morphological		
Skin	Pigmentation changes	Protection colouration.
	Hardening	Protection against water loss on land.
Mouth	Loss of horny beaks to mouth.	Adaptation to new diet.
	Widening of mouth. Teeth develop in upper jaw.	
Head	Development of tympanum, repositioning of eyes.	Accommodation to aerial sensory input.
Limbs	Complete growth of fore and hindlimbs.	Locomotion on land.
Tail	Complete resorption.	Loss of swimming as major mode of locomotion.
Anatomical		
Digestive system	Development of long muscular and bifid tongue from the floor of buccal cavity.	
	Major shortening of gut. Repositioning of anus.	
	Resorption of gills.	Change from herbivorous to carnivorous diet.
	Development of lungs.	
Respiratory system	Development of hyoid cartilages and muscles for respiration.	Change from water-to-air-based respiratory system.
Eye	Development of nictitating membrane and eyelids.	To protect eyes in the water.
Nervous system	Growth of new neurones and nerves.	Innervation of new structures.
Lateral line organ	Degeneration of lateral line organs.	Not required for terrestrial life.
Reproductive system	Development of gonads.	Sexual maturity only in adult form.
Biochemical		
Skin	Melanin synthesis.	Protective colouration.
	Induction of Na-K-ATPase.	Maintenance of electrolyte balance.
	Serotonin synthesis.	
	Changes in collagen deposition and breakdown.	
Eye	Change in visual pigment from porphyropsin to rhodopsin.	
Liver	Synthesis of urea cycle enzymes.	Change in excretory product from ammonia to urea.
	Synthesis of serum albumin.	Maintenance of homeostasis.
	Synthesis of ceruloplasmin.	Connected with changed iron utilization.
Erythropoietic tissue	Change from synthesis of larval haemoglobin to adult haemoglobin.	Lower affinity oxygen carrier for air-based respiration.
Gut	Synthesis of hydrolytic enzymes.	Resorption of tissue.
	Appearance of peptic activity in foregut.	Change to digestion of animal tissue.
Tail	Synthesis of hydrolytic enzymes.	Resorption of tissue.

Progressive Metamorphosis

The larva undergoes many rapid changes in which larval organs are lost while other undergoes extensive modification and organs of the adult are completed. This is found in amphibians.

Retrogressive Metamorphosis

During this type of metamorphosis certain advanced characters of larval stage start degenerating and adult appears as a degenerated form. This is common in ascidians.

Hormonal Control of Metamorphosis

Etkin (1968) has suggested that changes in amphibians during metamorphosis are brought about by concentration of thyroid hormone. It is presumed that some genetic mechanism render the hypothalamus sensitive to the low level of thyroid hormone in the blood.

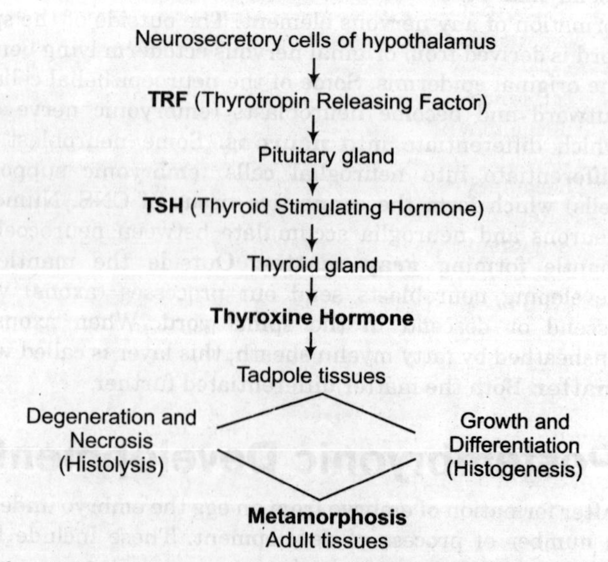

Fig. 15.17 Mechanism of hormonal secretion in metamorphosis

Environmental Regulation of Normal Development

In initial the embryo is simply a group of similar cells but gradually the size and position of cells begin to different. The interplay among the cell's activities, its environment and the properties of neighbouring cells provide information that cells use to select which role they will assume in the embryo.

The development of organism is controlled genetically as well as environmentally. A number of environmental factors affect the development. Some of which are:

1. **Source of food** In many mosquitoes (especially blood sucking) egg production is triggered by digested product of blood meal which stimulate the brain to secrete egg development neurosecretory hormone also known as ovarian ecdysteroidogenic hormone. This hormone stimulates the ovary to make ecdysteroids (which instruct the fat body cells to make vitellogenin for the oocytes) in *Aedes aegypti*.
2. **Larval settlement** A free swimming marine larva often needs to settle near a source of food or on stable substrate on which it can metamorphose. In some cases, the prey supply the matter while in other cases, the substrate gives off molecules used by the larvae to achieve settlement.
3. **Symbiosis** In some organisms symbiotic association also positively influence the development. In some cases, the symbionts become so, tightly integrated into the host organism that the host can not develop without them. Symbiosis between egg mass and photosynthetic algae is critical for the development of several species. In tight packing oxygen supply limits the rate of development.
4. **Gravity and pressure** Some predictable components such as gravity and pressure affect the

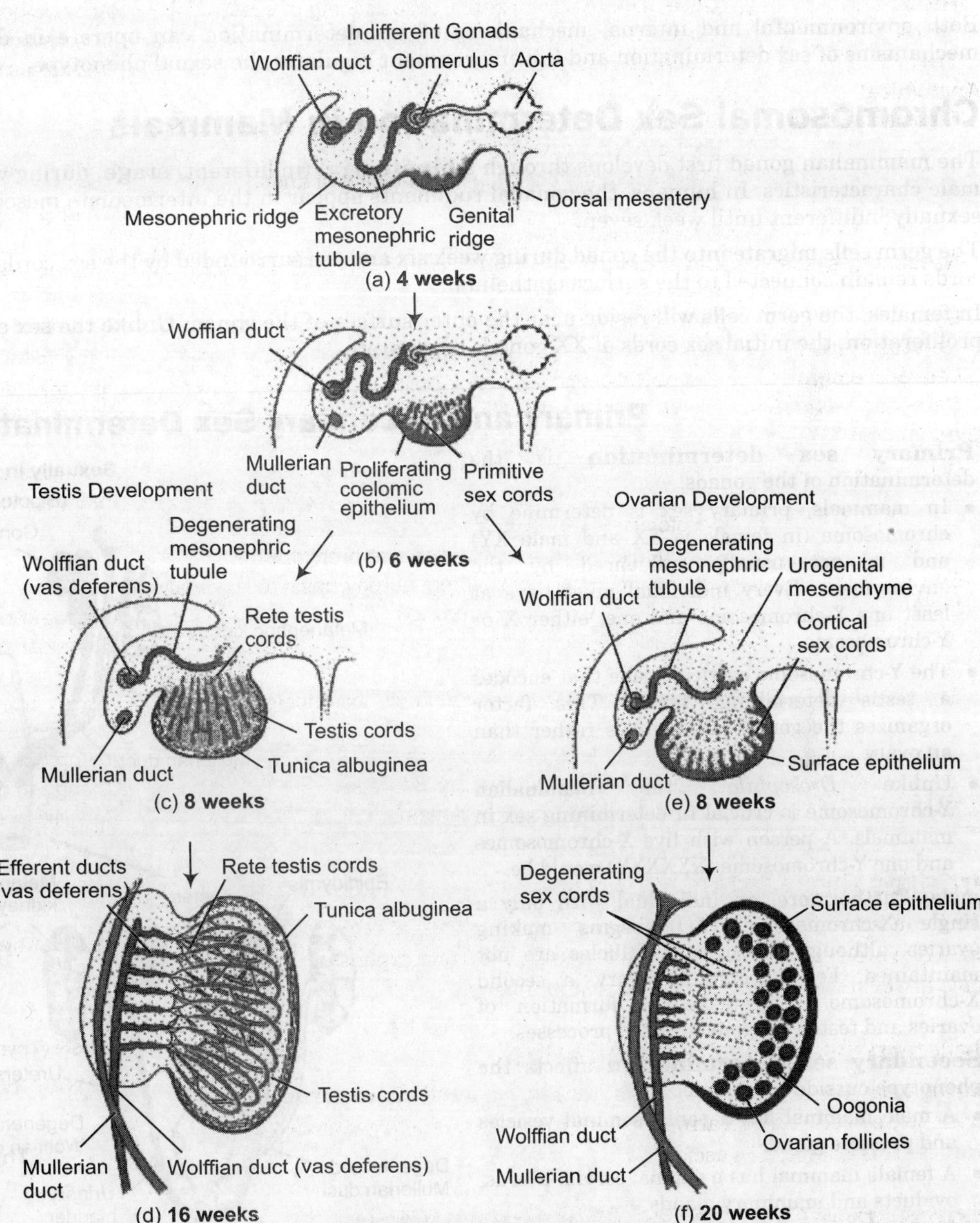

Fig. 15.18 Differentiation of human gonads, (a) Genital ridge of 4-week embryo. (b) Genital ridge of a 6-week indifferent gonad showing primitive sex cords. (c) Testis development in the eighth week. The sex cords lose contact with the cortical epithelium and develop the rete testis. (d) In sixteenth week, the development of testis cords is continuous with the rete testis and connects with the Wolffian duct. (e) Ovary development in an 8-week human embryo, as primitive sex cords degenerate. (f) The 20-week human ovary does not connect to the Wolffian duct and new cortical sex cords surround the germ cells that have migrated into the gential ridge

development process. These are several bones whose formation is dependent on stresses occasioned by the movement of embryo. Such, stresses are responsible for formation of human patella (knee cap).

5. **Temperature** The temperature, daylight length and season are used by many species to adjust their development to a changing environment. The season also affected sex in aphids. The temperature dependence of sex determination in fishes and reptiles is known.

Sex Determination

Both environmental and internal mechanisms of sex determination can operate in different species. The chromosomal mechanisms of sex determination and the environment regulates the sexual phenotype.

Chromosomal Sex Determination in Mammals

The mammalian gonad first develops through a **bipotential** (indifferent) **stage,** during which time it has neither female nor male characteristics. In humans, the gonadal rudiments appear in the intermediate mesoderm during week four and remains sexually indifferent until week seven.

The germ cells migrate into the gonad during week six and are surrounded by the sex cords. In both XY and XX gonads, the sex cords remain connected to the surface epithelium.

In females, the germ cells will reside near the outer surface of the gonad. Unlike the sex cords in males, which continue their proliferation, the initial sex cords of XX gonads degenerate.

Primary and Secondary Sex Determination

Primary sex determination is the determination of the gonads.

- In mammals, primary sex is determine by chromosome (in female is XX and male XY) and is not usually influenced by the environment. Every individual must have at least one X-chromosome and one, either X or Y-chromosome.
- The Y-chromosome carries a gene that encodes a testis determining factor. This factor organizes the gonad into a testis rather than an ovary.
- Unlike *Drosophila*, the mammalian Y-chromosome is crucial in determining sex in mammals. A person with five X-chromosomes and one Y-chromosome (XXXXXY) would be male. Furthermore, an individual with only a single X-chromosome (XO) begins making ovaries, although the ovarian follicles are not maintained. For a complete ovary, a second X-chromosome is needed. The formation of ovaries and testes are gene directed processes.

Secondary sex determination affects the phenotype outside the gonads.

- A male mammal has a penis, seminal vesicles and prostate gland.
- A female mammal has a vagina, cervix, uterus, oviducts and mammary glands.
- These secondary sex characteristics are determined by hormones secreted from the gonads. However, in the absence of gonads, the female phenotype is generated regardless of whether they were XX or XY.

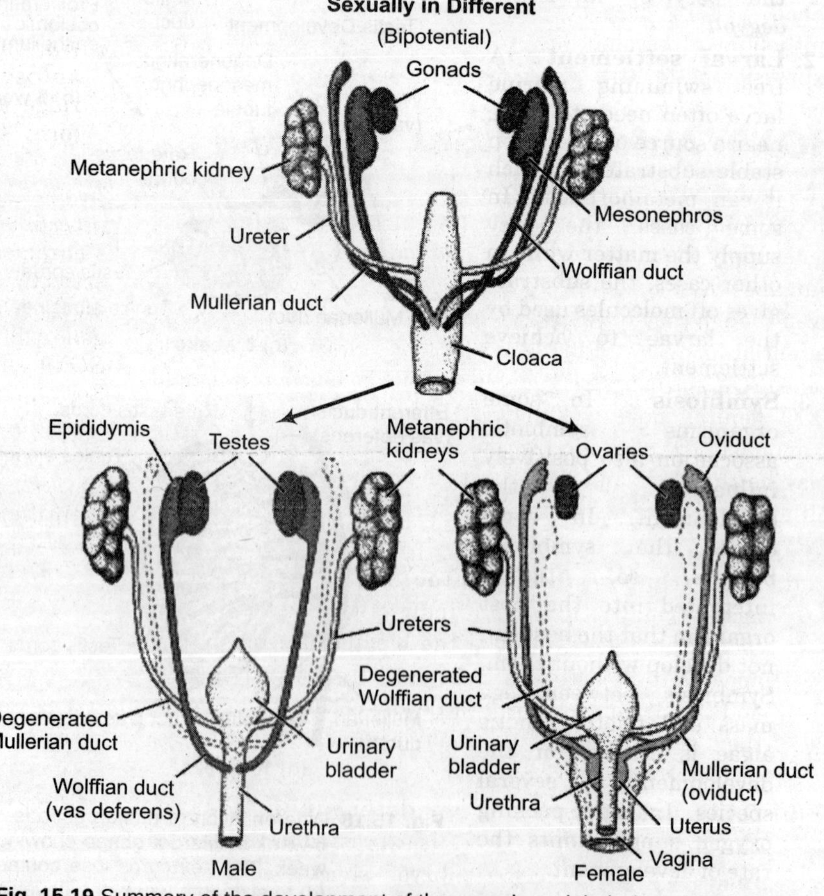

Fig. 15.19 Summary of the development of the gonads and their ducts in mammals

Gonads—Gonadal type, Testis, Ovary, Sex cords, Medullary (internal), Cortical (external)

Ducts—Remaining duct for germ cells, Wolffian, Mullerian, Duct differentiation, Vas deferens, epididymis and seminal vessicle, Oviduct, uterus, cervix, upper portion of vagina.

SRY: The Y-Chromosome Sex Determinant

In humans, the major gene for the testis determining factor resides on the short arm of the Y-chromosome. Individuals who are born with the short arm but not the long arm of the Y-chromosome are male, while individuals born with the long arm of the Y-chromosome but not the short arm are female.

The testis determining gene located near the tip of the short arm of the Y-chromosome called *SRY* (sex determining region of the Y-chromosome). *SRY* is found in normal XY males and in the rare XX males and it is absent from normal XX females and from many XY females.

The homologous gene found in mice. The mouse gene (*Sry*) also correlates with the presence of testes; it is present in XX males and absent in XY females. *Sry*/*SRY* is necessary, but not sufficient, for the development of the mammalian testis. SRY may have more than one mode of action in converting the bipotential gonads into testes. *SRY* in the genital ridge cells induces the cells to secrete a chemotactic factor that permits the migration of mesonephric cells into the XY gonad. These mesonephric cells induce the gonadal epithelium to become Sertoli cells with male specific gene expression patterns.

*SOX*9: Autosomal Sex Reversal

The autosomal genes involved in sex determination are *SOX9*. Individuals having only one functional copy of this gene have a syndrome called campomelic dysplasia. XX humans who have an extra copy of *SOX*9 develop as males, even though they have no *SRY* gene. It appears that *SOX*9 is essential for testis formation. The mouse homologue of this gene, *SOX*9, is expressed only in male (XY) but not in female (XX) genital ridges. While *SRY* is found specifically in mammals, *SOX*9 is found throughout the vertebrates. *SOX*9 may be the older and more central sex determination gene although in mammals it became activated by its relative, *SRY*.

(i) The **transcription factor SF1** (steroidogenic factor 1) may be directly or indirectly activated by SRY. *SF1* is necessary to make the bipotential gonad. *SF1* appears to be active in masculinizing both the Leydig and the Sertoli cells. In the Leydig cells, *SF1* activates the genes encoding the enzymes that make testosterone.

(ii) ***DAX1* is a potential ovary determining gene on the X-chromosome.** *DAX*1 is expressed in the genital ridges of the mouse embryo, shortly after *SRY* expression. *DAX*1 antagonize the function of *SRY* and it down regulates *SF1* expression thus, involve in ovary determination.

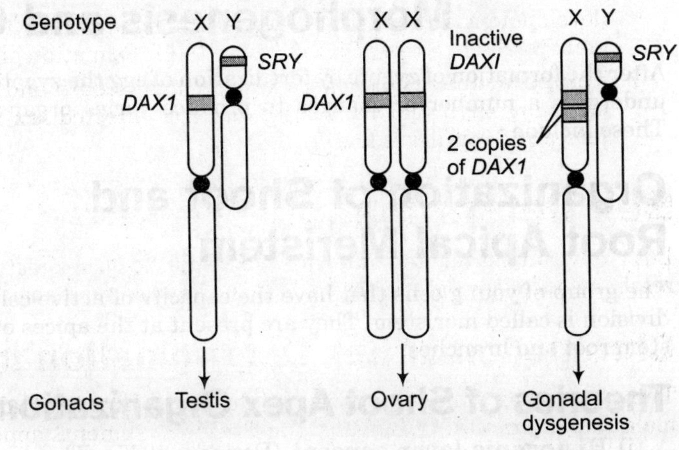

Fig. 15.20 Phenotypic sex reversal in humans having two copies of the *DAX*1 locus. *DAX*1 (on the X-chromosome) plus *SRY* (on the Y-chromosome) produces testes. *DAX*1 without *SRY* (since the other *DAX*1 locus is on the inactive X-chromosome) produces ovaries. Two active copies of *DAX*1 (on the active X-chromosome) plus *SRY* (on the Y-chromosome) lead to a poorly formed gonad. Since, the gonad makes neither AMH nor testosterone, the phenotype is female.

- ***Wnt*4 is a potential ovary determining gene on an autosome.** This gene is expressed in the mouse genital ridge while it is still in its bipotential stage. *SRY* may form testes by repressing *Wnt*4 expression in the genital ridge, as well as by Promoting *SF*1.

In this model (shown below), *SRY* competes with the *DAX*1 protein to activate or repress the *SF*1 gene. If a single X and Y-chromosome are present, the *SRY* will be favoured and the activation of *SF*1 will occur. If two copies of *DAX*1 are present on the X-chromosome (or no on the Y-chromosome), the *SF*1 gene will not be activated. The *SF1* protein is activate the *SOX*9 gene, which instructs the sex cords to develop into the Sertoli cells of the testes and may also repress *Wnt*4, which would otherwise cause the differentiation of the gonad into an ovary.

Most of the genes activated by *Wnt*4 and *SOX*9 have not been identified and the mechanisms by which *SRY* and *DAX*1 function are not yet known.

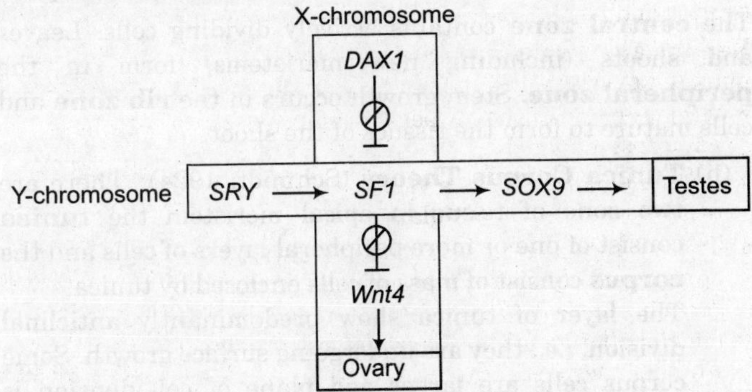

Fig. 15.21 Possible mechanism for primary sex determination in mammals. This model attempts to organize the data into a coherent sequence

Morphogenesis and Organogenesis in Plants

After the formation of zygote by fertilization of egg the zygote undergoes a number of changes to produce varies organs. These include :

Organization of Shoot and Root Apical Meristem

The group of young cells that have the capacity of active cell division is called meristem. They are present at the apices of stem root and branches.

Theories of Shoot Apex Organization

(i) **Histogenic layer concept** (Dermen; 1947) There is no distinct layer of apical meristem. On the basis of origin apical meristem are L1, L2, L3, etc. **Layer 1** produces the epidermis that surrounds the shoot. Here cells divide to generate only a single layer. Beneath it, **layer 2** divides to generate the layers of cells beneath the epidermis. Layer 1 and layer 2 together are known as the **tunica.**

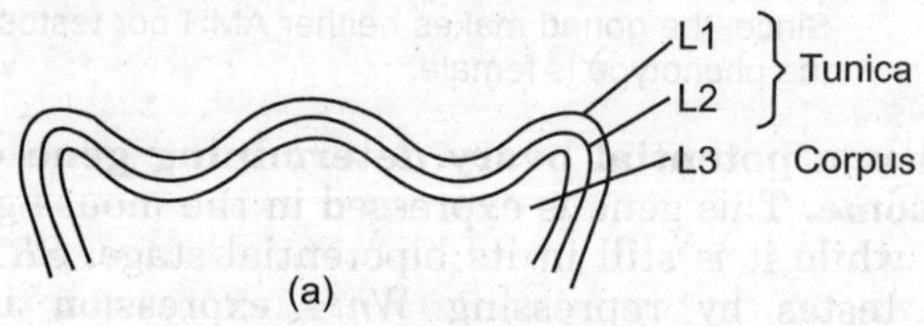

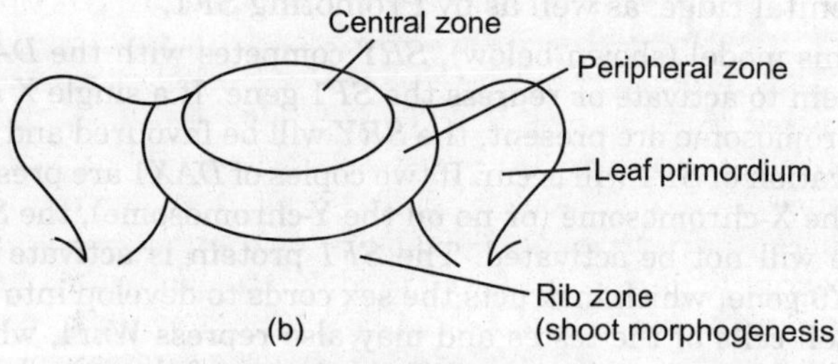

Fig. 15.22 A schematic representation of a longitudinal section through a shoot apical meristem (a) Tunica corpus (b) Histogenic layers

Layer 3 produces all the other tissues of the shoot, the cortex, pith and vascular tissues and is known as the **corpus.**

The **central zone** contains actively dividing cells. Leaves and shoots (including new meristems) form in the **peripheral zone.** Stem growth occurs in the **rib zone** and cells mature to form the tissues of the shoot.

(ii) **Tunica Corpus Theory** (Schmidt; 1924) There are two zone of tissue in apical meristem the **tunica** consist of one or more peripheral layers of cells and the **corpus** consist of mass of cells enclosed by tunica.
The layer of tunica show predominantly anticlinal division, *i.e.,* they are undergoing surface growth. Some corpus cells are larger and plane of cell division is irregular. In tunica the number of layers of tunica is equal to number of initial. The corpus arises from single tier of initials which divide periclinally.

(iii) **Mantle Core Concept** (Popham and Chan; 1950) The concept is comparable to tunica-corpus organization. He used term mantle instead of tunica and core instead of corpus.

(iv) **Histogen concept** (Hanstein; 1870) According to this theory there are three groups of initials in shoot apex namely **dermatogen** (outermost), which gives rise to epidermis, **periblem** (middle), which gives rise to cortex including endodermis and **plerome** (inner most) which gives rise to vascular tissue.

The vegetative shoot apices vary in shape, size and cytohistological structure. The shoot apex may be narrow and conical (*Pinus* and conifers) broad and flat (in *Cycas* and *Ginkgo*). The apical meristem may elevate young leaf primordia (in grasses and monocotyledons) or shunken beneath young leaf primordia (in dicotyledons).

Pteridophytes

The growth at the apex proceeds either from one or few initials.

(a) **Tetrahedral** (Pyramid like) New cells are formed on three side except at base, *e.g.,* Psilotales, Equisetaceae.

(b) **Sided apical cell** Two side form new cells, *e.g., Salvinia, Azolla.*

(c) **Apical growth by one, three or four sided apical cell** or from group of initials, *e.g., Selaginella.*

(d) **Eusporangiate** Two or four initials.

(e) **Leptosprorangiate** one initial.

Ontogenically, in ferns an apex with several initials is more primitive than the one with single apical cells (Bower; 1935, Wardlaw; 1945).

Gymnosperms

It has several inter related growth zone derived from the group of surface initials. The apical initials divide periclinally, peripheral zone is seat of origin of leaf primordia. The pith cell derived at base of mother cell.

In cycads, mother cell zone is ill defined, *Pinus* and conifers have less diversified than cycads and less well defined than *Ginkgo*. Gnetales have definite separation between surface layer and inner core derived from its own initials. *Ephedra* and *Gnetum* have been described as having tunica corpus pattern of growth.

Angiosperms

The stem apex of angiosperms have tunica corpus organization.

(a) Dicotyledons have one to five layer tunica and monocotyledons have one to three layer tunica.

(b) *Saccharum officinarum* tunica corpus organization is not found.

Theories of Root Apex Organization

(i) **Apical Cell Theory** (Nageli; 1858) The apical cell was interpreted as constant structure. It is a functional unit of apical meristem which governs the whole process of growth. The vascular cryptogams (pteridophytes) have solitary apical cell, *e.g.*, horsetail, fern, *Selaginella*, *Dryopteris*. Gymnosperms have two group of initials and angiosperms have three, rarely four group of initials.

(ii) **Korper-kappe Theory** (Schuepp; 1917) Roots changes its diameter during growth there are various points at which single longitudinal file of cell has become a double file as a result of cell division. At this point a cell first divides transversely and thereafter one of its daughter cell divides longitudinally. This is known as T-division.

(iii) **Histogen concept** (Henstein; 1868) According to this concept root apex has three group of initials namely **dermatogen** which gives rise to epiblema or piliferous layer, **periblem** which gives rise to cortex including endodermis and **plerome** which gives rise to vascular tissue.

(iv) **Quiescent Centre Concept** (Clowes; 1956) According to this concept there is an inactive region in the root apex having low DNA, RNA and protein content and acts as a reservoir of active initials.

Leaf Development and Phyllotaxy

Leaf developed from the leaf primordium which differentiates little below the shoot apical meristem. The leaf primordium form a cone-shaped structure around the apex. The midrib starts to differentiate at the top and smaller veins on both sides of its base. After acheiving 8 mm size a cavity develops at the base of primordium and the ligule, auricles and collar differentiated. This collar separated the blade and sheath. The blade start to elongate due to meristem activity. During this time other tissues and structures are also formed. The internal structure of blade have fully developed when it emerges and enrolls from its tip down to the base. At the same time leaf sheath starts to elongate and the internal structure also start to differentiate in sheath.

Phyllotaxy is the arrangement of leaves on both mains stem and branches. The following types of phyllotaxy is found in plants.

1. **Alternate** For example, *Mangifera indica*, *Brassica*, *Nicotiana*.
2. **Opposite** Each node two leaves.
   (i) **Superposed** *Eugenia*, *Ixora*, *Quisqualis*.
   (ii) **Decussate** *Calotropis*, *Ocimum*.
3. **Whorled** For example, *Alstonia*, *Nerium*, *Vangueria*.

Floral Meristems and Floral Development in *Arabidopsis* and *Antirrhinum*

An active area of plant developmental genetics research utilizes a small flowering plant called *Arabidopsis thaliana* as a model genetic system. The most intensively studied developmental process in *Arabidopsis* is flower pattern formation. Just as the homeotic gene cluster controls segmental identity in animal development, a series of transcriptional regulators determine the fate of the four layers (whorls) of the flower. The outermost whorl of the flower normally develops into the sepals, the next whorl, the petals, the next, the stamens and the innermost develops into the carpels. Several genes have been identified that, when knocked out or ectopically expressed, transform one or more of these whorls into another. For example, the gene *AP*1 (*Apetala*-1) causes the homeotic transformation of the outer two whorls into the inner two. Analogously to the homeotic mutants in animals, the number of whorls remains the same (four), but their identities are transformed. The study of the spatial expression patterns and mutant phenotypes of the various flower identity genes has produced a model in which whorl fate is established through the combinatorial action of multiple transcription factors. Thus, sepal (outermost whorl fate) is established through the action of transcription factors expressed by genes of the class A type only. Petal fate is established through the action of transcription factors produced by simultaneous expression of the class A and class B genes. Stamen fate is established through the action of transcription factors produced by simultaneous expression of class B and class C genes. Finally, carpel fate is established through the action of transcription factors expressed by class C genes. Just as the homeotic segment identity genes in animals encode a series of structurally related (homeodomain containing) transcription factors, the flower identity genes encode a series of structurally related transcription factors called MADS transcription factors, found in all eukaryotic kingdoms.

The word MADS is composed of the first letters of the names of four prototypic member genes of this family. Thus, although different in detail, the overall strategy of differentially expressed transcription factors is one of the approaches by which plant cell fate is established. With its combination of sophisticated genetics and genomics, findings from studies of *Arabidopsis* pattern formation should reveal much about the ways in which plants develop.

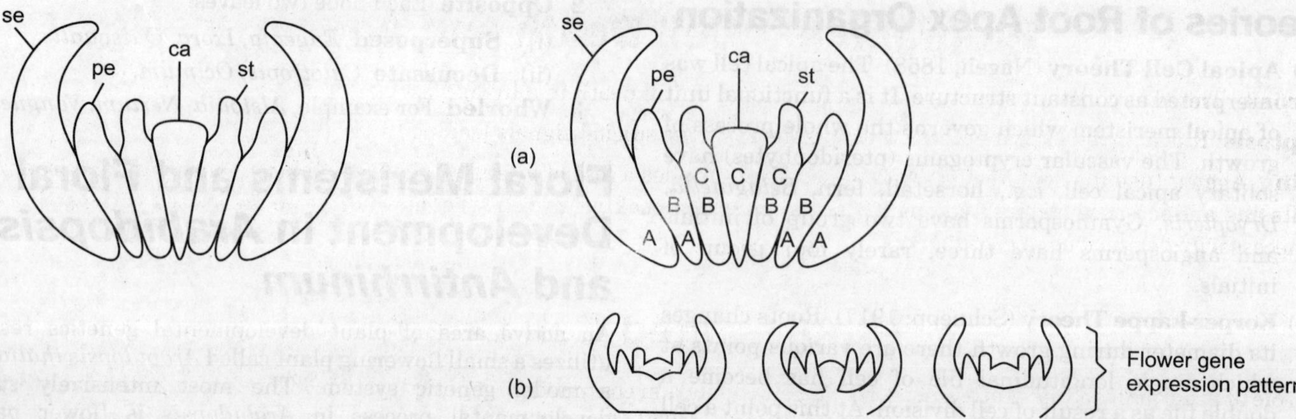

Fig. 15.23 Flower development in *Arabidopsis thaliana.* Flower identity gene expression and the establishment of whorl fate. A cross-sectional diagram of the developing flower, with the normal fates of the four whorls indicated. From outermost to innermost, they are sepal (se), petal (pe), stamen (st) and carpel (ca).
(a) The patterns of gene expression corresponding to the different whorl fates.
(b) The shaded regions of the cross-sectional diagrams of the developing flower indicate the gene expression patterns for genes of the A, B and C classes.

Flower development takes place in two phases, floral induction and pattern formation. In floral induction, the **shoot apical meristem** sets aside a **floral meristem.** The organ primordia are then generated. There are four primordia, in the form of four whorls that make up a flower. Outermost is the sepal whorl, then the petal whorl, then the stamen whorl, responsible for the male parts of the flower and finally the innermost carpel whorl, responsible for the female parts of the flower. The genetics of development in plants is studied by mutational analysis, selective ablation (removal or killing) of cells during development and other techniques used in animal studies. Many genes have been isolated that affect the sequence of steps of floral induction and pattern formation.

The first stage to be controlled in floral induction is its timing. That is, flower formation usually occurs at a specific time in the life cycle of a plant, affected by environmental cues (day length, temperature). In *Arabidopsis*, at least three dozen genes have been isolated that affect the timing of flower formation. These genes include **Constans,** a late flowering gene, **Early Flowering 1,** an early flowering gene and **Gibberellin Insensitive,** a gene for late flowering only in short days (autumn). The next stage in floral induction is generating floral meristem at the point, where a flower will form. Atleast five genes are known that impart identity on floral meristem (floral meristem identity genes), when mutated, these genes result in either shoots instead of flowers or in highly abnormal flowers.

These genes include **leafy, unusual floral organs,** ***Apetala1*** and ***Apetala2.***

Floral development continues by the creation of organ primordia. Although far removed from animals in both taxonomy and DNA sequences, plants have homeotic genes, some producing proteins homologous to those produced by animal genes. Currently, floral homeotic genes are classified into three categories-A, B and C. Genes from category A affect sepals and petals, genes from category B affect petals and stamens and genes from category C affect stamens and carpels. This is not unlike the model of action in *Drosophila's* homeotic gene clusters, which acts sequentially, controlling development along the head to tail axis of the fly. It appears that genetic control of floral development is highly conserved across angiosperms, the dominant plant group.

An example of a homeotic gene is **agamous,** a gene in the C group required for the development of stamens and carpels. Expression of this gene takes place in the third and fourth whorls of the flower, the stamen and carpel whorls. After its expression in the appropriate whorls, **agamous** is repressed. Its repressor is another gene, **curly leaf.** When the protein product of **curly leaf** was compared with protein sequences from *Drosophila,* it proved to have similarities in amino acid sequence with a gene in *Drosophila* called **enhancer of zeste.** This gene is also a repressor of a homeotic gene, but in fruit flies. Thus, several valuable conclusions come from this study of *Arabidopsis*. Most important is the fact that plants and animals seem to use similar mechanisms in development. Both groups have repeated units (segments) in development, both have homeotic genes that control developmental pathways in these units, both have repressors of homeotic genes that maintain the proper developmental fate in their segments and, despite large taxonomic distances, there is some homology between the proteins in plants and animals.

Programmed Cell Death and Ageing

Necrosis The sum of the morphologic changes that follow cell death in a living tissue or organ.

Apoptosis It is a physiological process that includes specific suicide signals leading to cell death.

Ageing Ageing (usually synonymous with senescence) implies a loss of vitality, a reduced ability to withstand environmental insults and an increased chance of dying with time. Strictly speaking, **ageing** means any change associated with getting older, not necessarily deleterious (*e.g.*, puberty).

Programmed Cell Death

The role of programmed cell death (apoptosis) in cell population control during growth and development suggests that these are inherent cellular mechanisms that lead the cell to destruct. This form of cell death differ from any other form a cell death.

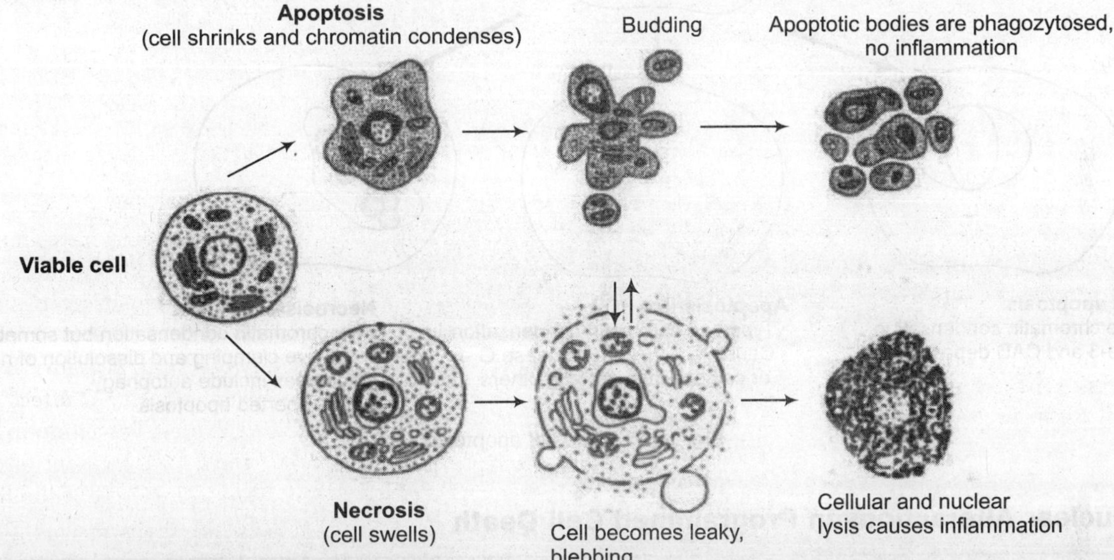

Fig. 15.24 The apoptotic and necrotic cell death process. Apoptosis includes cellular shrinking, chromatin condensation and margination at the nuclear periphery with the eventual formation of membrane bound apoptotic bodies that contain organelles, cytosol and nuclear fragments and are phagocytosed without triggering inflammatory processes. The necrotic cell swells, becomes leaky and finally is disrupted and releases its contents into the surrounding tissue resulting in inflammation

Necrosis *Versus* Apoptosis

Necrosis	Apoptosis
A pathological response to cellular injury	A physiological response to specific suicide signals, or lack of survival signals.
Chromatin clumps	Chromatin condenses and migrates to nuclear membrane. Internucleosomal cleavage leads to laddering of DNA at the nucleosomal repeat length, ca. 200 bp.
Mitochondria swell and rupture	Cytoplasm shrinks without membrane rupture.
Plasma membrane lyses	Blebbing of plasma and nuclear membranes.
Cell conents spill out	Cell contents are packaged in membrane bounded bodies, internal organelles still functioning, to be engulfed by neighbours.
General inflammatory response is triggered	Epitopes appear on plasma membrane marking cell as a phagocytic target.
	No spillage, no inflammation

Types of Apoptosis

Autophagic Cell Death (type II programmed cell death) The cytoplasm is actively destroyed long before nuclear changes become apparent.

Classical Apoptotic Cell Death The chromatin marginates and the cell and nucleus fragment before morphological changes are seen in intracellular organelles.

Nuclear Alterations in Programmed Cell Death

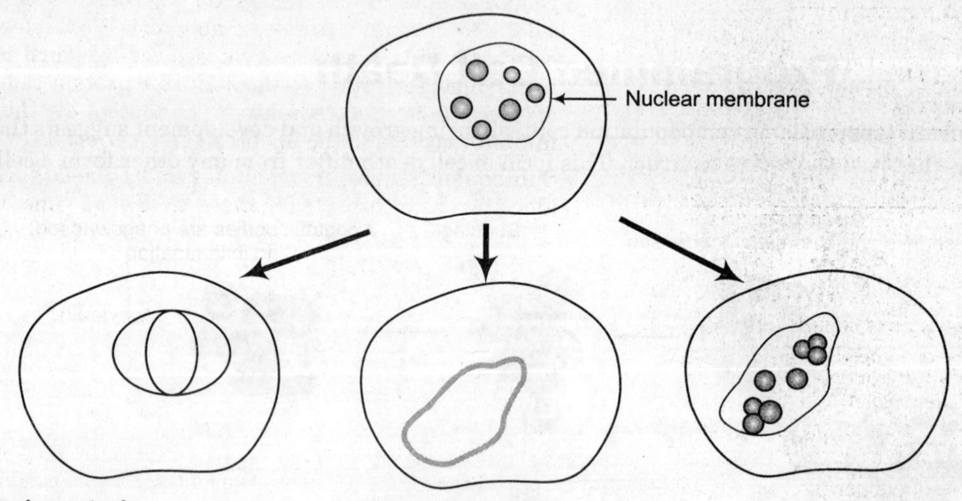

Fig. 15.25 Types of apoptosis

Table 15.3 **Nuclear Alteractions in Programmed Cell Death**

Classical Apoptosis	Apoptosis like PCD
Caspase dependent strong chromatin compaction Capase dependent chromatin compaction at the nuclear periphery fragmented into two compact spheres.	Caspase independent, AIF- driven lumpy chromatin condensation. Caspase independent lumpy chromatin condensation without nuclear fragmentation.

Apoptosis in *Caenorhabditis Elegans*

The life cycle of *C. elegans* from egg to sexual maturity is about 3 days· ced-1, 3, 4 and 9 (cell death determining) proteins in *C.elegans* are closely related to mammalian apoptosis regulating genes. The adult hermaphrodite consists of exactly 959 somatic cells of precisely determined lineage and function. Individual cells are named and their relationships to their neighbours are known. Overall, the 959 somatic cells of adult *C.elegans* arise from 1090 original cells, exactly 131 somatic cells undergo programmed cell death in the wild type worm.

Of the 1090 cells, 302 are neurons and many of the programmed deaths also lie in the neuronal lineage.

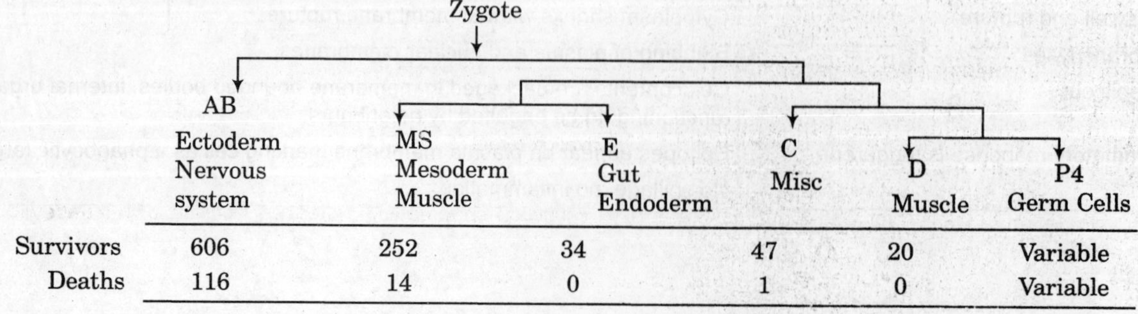

Molecular Mechanisms of Apoptosis Signaling Pathways

This general overview of basic apoptotic signalling pathways and of the molecular machinery responsible for the induction and execution of apoptosis is discussed in context of their function and of the mechanisms involving the initiation, mediation, execution and regulation of apoptosis. It is complex interplay between factors that promote or suppress apoptosis, resulting in a regulatory network which determines the fate of an individual cell.

Various Death Signals Activate Common Signaling Pathways

Apoptosis is a tightly regulated and genetically encoded. Apoptosis can be triggered by various stimuli from outside or inside the cell, such as.

(a) by ligation of cell surface receptors.
(b) by DNA damage as a cause of defects in DNA repair mechanisms.
(c) treatment with cytotoxic drugs or irradiation.
(d) by a lack of survival signals.
(e) contradictory cell cycle signaling.
(f) by developmental death signals.

Much of the understanding of cell death has come from genetic studies in the nematode *C. elegans* (See box in left side). The proximal cause of apoptosis in *C. elegans* is the activation of the cysteine protease ced-3, which is mediated by its oligomerization at the activator protein ced-4. Activity of the ced-3/ced-4 complex is regulated by the apoptosis inhibitor ced-9 and the apoptosis inducer egl-1.

Subsequent studies in mammals and *D. melanogaster*, have identified counterparts for these *C. elegans* genes.

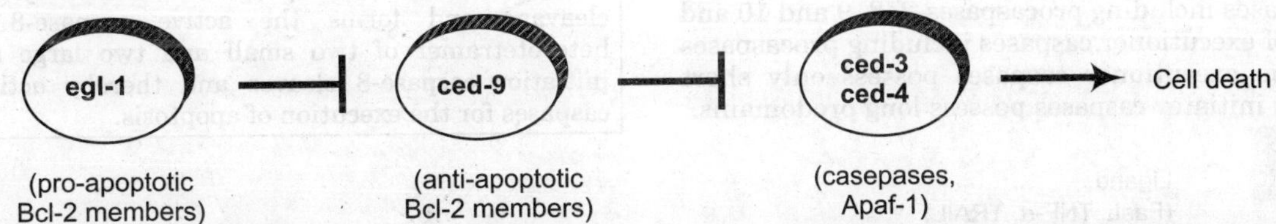

Fig. 15.26 *C. elegans* as a model system contains basic components of the cell death machinery. Apoptosis factors of *C. elegans* is analogous to the components found in higher organisms such as **egl-1** is the representative for mammalian proapoptotic BH3 only proteins, **ced-9** belongs to the antiapoptotic Bcl-2 family, **ced-3** is the only caspase and **ced-4** is homologous to mammalian Apaf-1

Caspases Central Initiators and Executioners of Apoptosis

The caspases, cysteine proteases homologous to *C. elegans* ced-3, are activated in most cases of apoptotic cell death. The cell death can be classified to follow a classical apoptotic mode if execution of cell death is dependent on caspase activity.

The term 'caspases' is derived from **cysteine dependent aspartate specific proteases:** Their catalytical activity depends on a critical cysteine residue within a highly conserved active site pentapeptide QACRG and the caspases specifically cleave their substrates after Asp residues.

So, far, 7 different caspases have been identified in *Drosophila and* 14 different members of the caspase family have been described in mammals, with caspase-11 and caspase-12 only identified in the mouse.

Caspases

- Caspases were implicated in apoptosis with the discovery that CED-3 is related to caspase 1 (interleukin-1 -β-converting enzyme).
- They are expressed as proenzymes (30-50 kD) that contain three domains, N-terminal, large domain (L) and small domain (S). Proteolytical activation remove N-terminal, then the association of L and S to form a heterodimer active enzyme.
- Caspases recognize four amino acid N-terminal to the cleavage site aspartic acid with high substrate specificity.

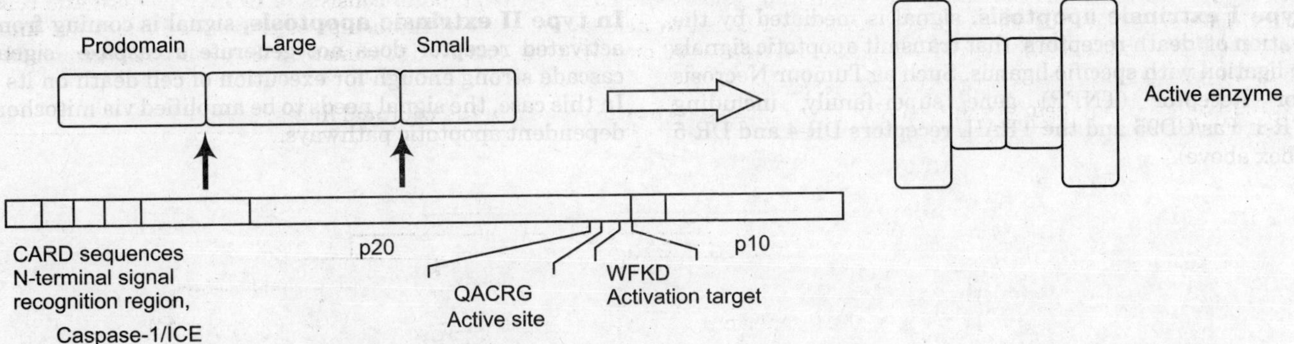

Fig. 15.27 The target sequence for Ced-3 and caspases (Cys catalytic Asp targetting proteases) consists of a tetrapeptide with C-terminal Asp (D)

Caspase-1 is ICE (Interleukin-1β-converting enzyme), the first mammalian caspase homologue to ced-3. Caspase-1, 4, 5, 11 and 12 appear to be mainly involved in the proteolytic maturation of pro-inflammatory cytokines.

Mice deficient for **caspase-1** or **caspase-11** develop normally and cells from those knockout mice remain sensitive to various death stimuli. **Caspase-2, 3, 6, 7, 8, 9** and **10** have been recognized to play an important role in the apoptotic signaling machinery.

In the cell, **caspases are synthesized** as inactive zymogens, the so, called **procaspases,** which at their N-terminus carry a prodomain followed by a large and a small subunit **(See box above).** Upon maturation, the procaspases are proteolytically processed between the **large and small subunit.** The prodomain is generally removed during the activation process. A heterotetramer consisting of each two small and two large subunits then forms an active caspase.

The **proapoptotic caspases** can be divided into the group of initiator caspases including procaspases-2, 8, 9 and 10 and into the group of executioner caspases including procaspases 3, 6 and 7. The executioner caspases possess only short prodomains, the initiator caspases possess long prodomains.

The **executioner caspases** possess only short prodomains, the **initiator caspases** possess long prodomains, containing Death Effector Domains (DED) in the case of procaspases-8 and 10 or caspase recruitment domains (CARD) as in the case of procaspase-9 and procaspase-2.

The initiator caspases, *via* prodomains, activated at death inducing signaling complexes either in response to the ligation of cell surface death receptors (extrinsic apoptosis pathways) or in response to signals originating from inside the cell (intrinsic apoptosis pathways).

Extrinsic Apoptosis Pathways

Upon ligation by its cognate ligand, the trimeric death receptor recruits adaptor molecules *via* its cytoplasmic Death Domains (DD), the adaptors additionally contain Death Effector Domains (DED) which recruit procaspase-8 to the receptor complex which now is called the Death Inducing signalling Complex (DISC). Procaspase-8 is activated by autoproteolytic cleavage and forms the active caspase-8 which is a heterotetramer of two small and two large subunits. The initiatior caspase-8 cleaves and thereby activates effector caspases for the execution of apoptosis.

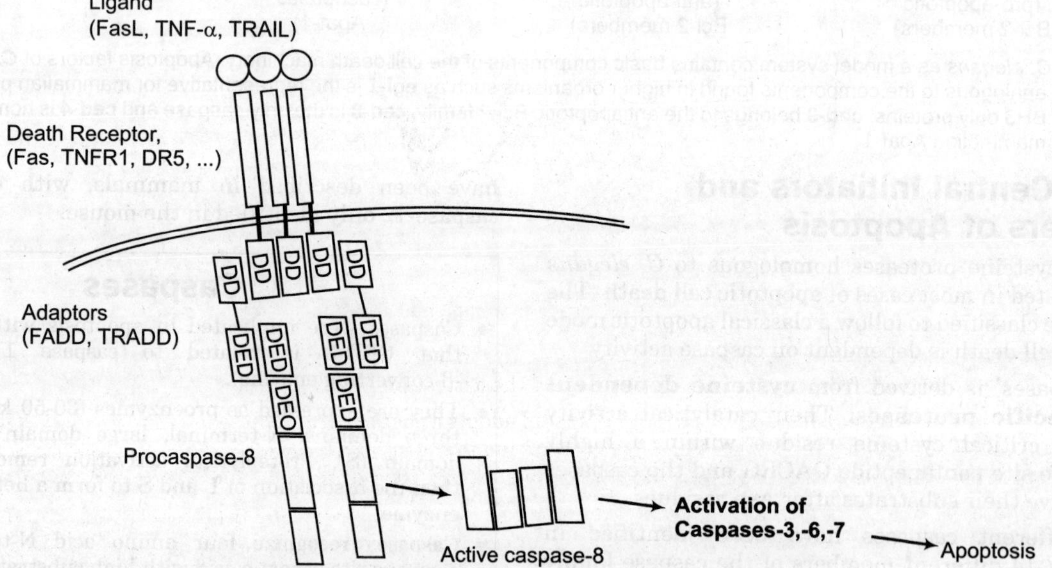

Fig. 15.28 Receptor-mediated caspase activation at the DISC

In type I extrinsic apoptosis, signal is mediated by the activation of 'death receptors' that transmit apoptotic signals after ligation with specific ligands. Such as Tumour Necrosis Factor Receptor (TNFR) gene super-family, including TNFR-1, Fas/CD95 and the TRAIL receptors DR-4 and DR-5 (see box above).

In type II extrinsic apoptosis, signal is coming from the activated receptor does not generate a caspase signalling cascade strong enough for execution of cell death on its own. In this case, the signal needs to be amplified via mitochondria dependent apoptotic pathways.

Intrinsic Apoptosis Pathways

Intrinsic apoptosis pathways involve procaspase-9 which is activated downstream of mitochondrial proapoptotic events at the so, called apoptosome, a cytosolic death signalling protein complex that is formed upon release of cytochrome *c* from the mitochondria. In this case it is the dimerization of procaspase-9 molecules at the Apaf-1 scaffold that is responsible for caspase-9 activation.

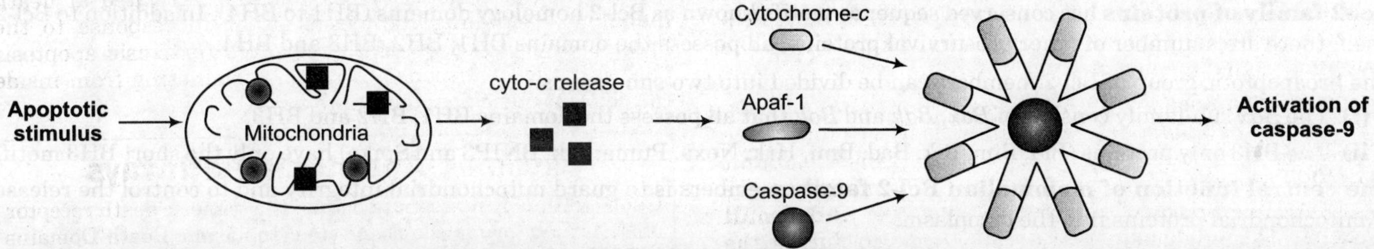

Fig. 15.29 Mitochondrial pathway of caspase activation

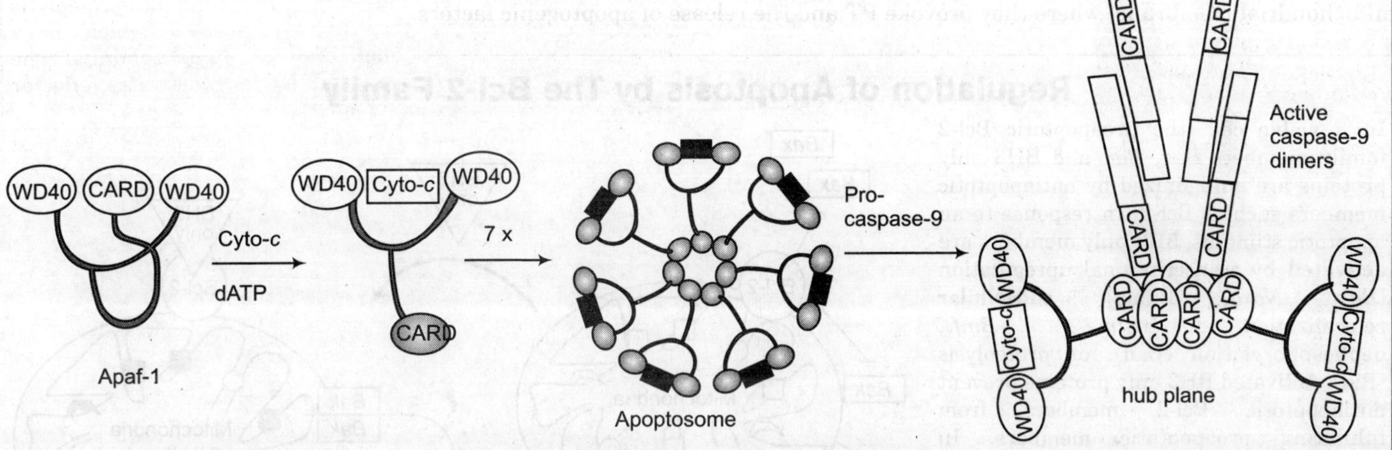

Fig. 15.30 Apoptosome formation and activation

Apoptotic stimuli trigger the release of apoptogenic factors from the mitochondrial intermembrane space to the cytosol, such as cytochrome-c which induces the formation of the apoptosome and the activation of procaspase-9.

By the action of cytochrome-c (Cyto-*c*) and dATP the Apaf-1 protein adopts a conformation that allows the formation of a heptameric, wheel-like structure, the apoptosome. Procaspase-9 molecules can bind to the inner 'hub' region of the apoptosome and are activated by dimer formation. Active caspase-9 dimers further mediate activation of effector caspases.

The effector procaspases-3, 6 and 7 which subsequently cleave a specific set of protein substrates resulting in the mediation and amplification of the death signal and eventually in the execution of cell death is observed.

In type II extrinsic apoptosis, the mitochondria is provided by the Bcl-2 family member Bid. Bid is cleaved by caspase-8 and translocates to the mitochondria, where it acts together with the proapoptotic Bcl-2 family members Bax and Bak to induce the release of cytochrome *c* and other mitochondrial proapoptotic factors into the cytosol.

Cytosolic cytochrome-*c* is binding to monomeric Apaf-1 which then oligomerizes to assemble the apoptosome, that triggers the activation of the initiator procaspase-9. Activated caspase-9 subsequently initiates a caspase cascade, ultimately resulting in cell death.

Mitochondria as central regulators of intrinsic apoptosis pathways. They contain many pro-apoptotic proteins such as Apoptosis Inducing Factor (AIF), Smac/DIABLO and cytochrome-c. These factors are released from the mitochondria following the formation of a pore in the mitochondrial membrane called the permeability transition pore or PT pore. These pores are thought to form through the action of the pro-apoptotic members of the Bcl-2 family of proteins. Besides the mitochondria, the Endoplasmic Reticulum (ER) is a second compartment participating in intrinsic apoptosis.

Regulatory Mechanism in Apoptosis Signaling

The Bcl-2 Family

Bcl-2, an oncogene, which in follicular lymphoma is linked to an immunoglobulin locus by the chromosome translocations (14, 18)(q32, q21), was the first example of an oncogene that inhibits cell death rather than promoting proliferation.

Bcl-2 family of proteins has conserved sequence motifs known as Bcl-2 homology domains (BH1 to BH4). In addition to Bcl-2 itself, there are a number of other prosurvival proteins, all possess the domains BH1, BH2, BH3 and BH4.

The proapoptotic group of Bcl-2 members can be divided into two sub-groups:

(i) The *Bax* sub-family consists of *Bax*, *Bak* and *Bok* that all possess the domains BH1, BH2 and BH3,

(ii) The BH3 only proteins (Bid, Bim, Bik, Bad, Bmf, Hrk, Noxa, Puma, Blk, BNIP3 and Spike) have only the short BH3 motif.

The central function of mammalian Bcl-2 family members is to guard mitochondrial integrity and to control the release of mitochondrial proteins into the cytoplasm.

A specific apoptotic stress signals trigger the activation of particular BH3 only proteins, which then interact with antiapoptotic members on the outer mitochondrial (but also nuclear/ER) membrane, resulting in the release of *Bax* like proapoptotic factors. *Bax*-like factors undergo a conformational change (possibly assisted by some BH3 only proteins), insert into the outer mitochondrial membrane, where they provoke PT and the release of apoptogenic factors.

Regulation of Apoptosis by The Bcl-2 Family

In a viable cell, the proapoptotic Bcl-2 family members *Bax*, *Bak* and BH3 only proteins are antagonized by antiapoptotic members such as Bcl-2. In response to an apoptotic stimulus, **BH3 only members are activated** by transcriptional upregulation (*Bax*, *Noxa*, Puma), subcellular relocalization (*Bim*, *Bmf*), dephosphorylation (Bad), or proteolysis (Bid). Activated BH3 only proteins prevent antiapoptotic Bcl-2 members from inhibiting proapoptotic members. In addition, they might directly induce a conformational change of *Bax* and *Bak* which subsequently oligomerize and insert into the mitochondrial membrane where they form pores either by themselves or by associating with the permeability transition pore complex.

In consequence, proapoptotic factors are released from the inner mitochondrial membrane into the cytosol, such as cytochrome-*c* which contributes to the formation of the apoptosome and the subsequent activation of the caspase cascade.

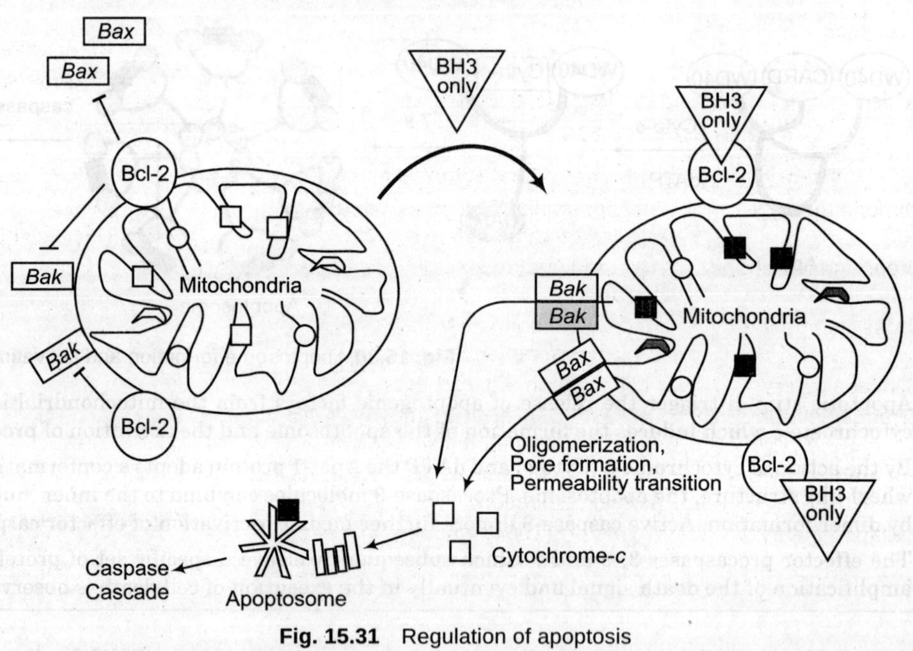

Fig. 15.31 Regulation of apoptosis

Inhibitors of apoptosis proteins (IAPs), whose prototype originally was described in baculovirus with many homologues found to be conserved across several species. So, far, eight human IAP homologues have been identified. All IAPs contain Baculovirus IAP Repeat (BIR) domains, 70 amino acid motifs, which are essential for the antiapoptotic properties of IAPs because it is the interaction between the BIR domains and caspases that is believed to confer most of the antiapoptotic activity of IAPs.

Apoptosis and p53 Tumour Suppressor Gene

p53, a major mediator of the intrinsic pathway, is very frequently mutated gene in cancer. Stabilized and activated p53 can translocate into the nucleus, where it activates the transcription of proapoptotic genes and suppresses the transcription of antiapoptotic genes what under certain conditions can result in the induction of apoptosis.

Ageing

In all metazoans the life cycle includes two developmental period—the **embryonic period** which extends from zygote to offspring and **post embryonic period** which includes growth, adulthood, reproduction and ageing. The field of developmental biology that deals with process and problems of ageing is known as **Gerontology.** There are three types of changes observed in ageing.

1. **Changes at organ level** Decrease in heart efficiency, blood volume, capacity of lungs, nerve impulse propagation, volume of urine, oxygen uptake and accomodation power of eyes.
2. **Cellular changes** These includes decline in cell volume, accumulation of exhaustion pigments and appearance of lipid vacuoles.
3. **Physiological changes** Chromosomal aberrations and gene mutations, decrease in permeability of cell membrane (due to Ca^{+2} deposition), protein synthesis, rate of metabolism and increase activity of aldolase in liver.

Table 15.3 **Theories of Ageing with Characteristics**

Theory	Characteristic
Immune theory	Disappearance of thymus gland which weakens natural defense.
Urear and tear theory	Regenerative capacity progressively declines.
Cross linkage theory	Increase of bonds between protein and nucleic acid molecules.
Clinker's theory	Accumulation of metabolic waste.
Error catastrophy	Orgal (1963), error in reading genetic code, results in defective proteins.
Fre eradical theory	Oxygen free radicals as byproduct of normal respiration.
Collagen theory	F Verzer (1964) change in collagen protein in interstitial fluid.

Senescence

Senescence is a functional decline near the end of a life span. Death is sudden, but senescence involves a progressive increase in the probability of dying. Senescence is a fundamental, intrinsic property of all animals.

Hayflick first described cellular senescence in the 1960s as a cell cycle arrest that accompanies the exhaustion of the replicative potential of human diploid fibroblasts in culture. Senescence cells continue to be metabolically active. Senescence is a highly irreversible form of growth arrest.

At the molecular level, replicative senescence of human cells is triggered by telomere attrition, which is registered by the cell as DNA damage and results eventually in the activation of p53. During replicative senescence the cdk inhibitor $p16^{ink4a}$ accumulates in the cell, inhibiting the cdk–mediated phosphorylation of Rb, therefore contributing to a G_1 cell cycle arrest. These two pathways (the p53 and the $p16^{ink4a}$/Rb pathways) are central to senescence control.

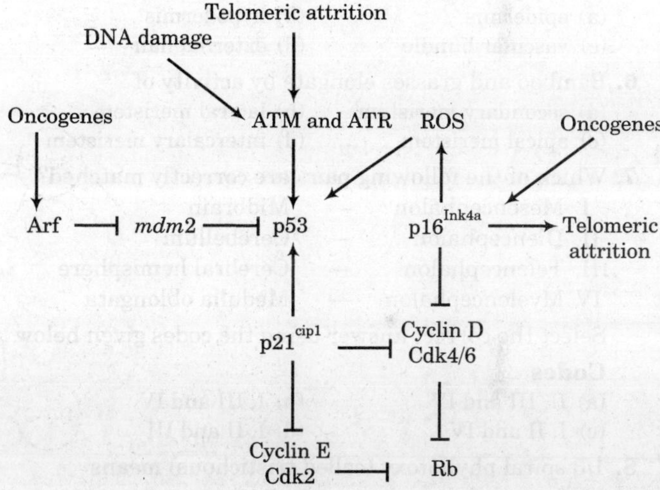

Fig. 13.32 Cellular senescence, Schema of the pathways involved in senescence and the entry points where various stimuli engage them

Exercise

1. At high temperature the rate of growth stops due to
(a) excessive transpiration (b) enzyme loss
(c) Both (a) and (b) (d) All of these

2. In plants red light favours
(a) elongation of cells
(b) maturation of cells
(c) formation of cells
(d) division of cells

3. Tunica corpus theory was proposed by
(a) Schmidt (b) Strasburger
(c) Nageli (d) Hofmeister

4. There is no distinction between tunica and corpus layers in the stem apices of
(a) some pteridophytes (b) some gymnosperms
(c) all pteridophytes (d) all angiosperms

5. According to histogen theory the plerome gives rise to
(a) epidermis (b) hypodermis
(c) vascular bundle (d) external hair

6. Bamboo and grasses elongate by activity of
(a) secondary meristem (b) lateral meristem
(c) apical meristem (d) intercalary meristem

7. Which of the following pairs are correctly matched?

I. Mesencephalon	—	Midbrain
II. Diencephalon	—	Cerebellum
III. Telencephalon	—	Cerebral hemisphere
IV. Myelencephalon	—	Medulla oblongata

Select the correct answer using the codes given below.

Codes
(a) II, III and IV (b) I, III and IV
(c) I, II and IV (d) I, II and III

8. 1/3 spiral phyllotoxy (called tristichous) means
(a) 3 rows of alternate rows
(b) in one circle there are three leaves
(c) angular divergence between two leaves is 120°
(d) All of the above

9. If there is more than one tunica layer in a stem apex, which among the following is most likely to happen
(a) all the layers will develop into epidermal cells
(b) only the outer layer will develop into epidermal cells
(c) all the layers will develop into cortex
(d) inner layer develops into cortex

10. Trees may be damaged by animals which rub against them, wearing away a strip of bark right around the tree trunk and exposing the xylem. The tree will then
(a) die quickly, because the leaves are deprived of food and water
(b) die quickly, because fungi enter the trunk through the wounds
(c) continue to grow, because bark always regrows to cover a wound
(d) die slowly, because the roots cannot replenish their food reserves

11. Considering the root apex of monocotyledons, there are three groups of initials
(a) the terminal ones form the dermatogen and the cap, the median forms the periblem and the innermost ones form the plerome
(b) the terminal ones form the cap, the median ones form the dermatogen and the innermost ones form the periblem and plerome
(c) the terminal ones form the cap, the median ones form the dermatogen and periblem and the innermost ones form the plerome
(d) the terminal ones form the cap and the dermatogen, the median ones are non-functional and the innermost ones form the periblem and plerome

12. As a person becomes old, a degenerative process sets in the body which causes
(a) a gradual alteration in the connective tissue components only
(b) increase in the collagen content of the connective tissues only
(c) increase in the mucopolysaccharides content of the most of the connective tissues only
(d) Both (a) and (b)

13. Which of these possesses good regenerating power?
(a) Brain (b) Kidney
(c) Lung (d) Liver

14. Which one of the following is gradually reduced and degenerated in ageing according to immunity theory?
(a) Thyroid (b) Parathyroids
(c) Thymus (d) Pituitary

15. The quiescent centre in root meristem serves as a
(a) site for storage of food, which is utilized during maturation
(b) reservior of growth hormones
(c) reserve for replenishment of damaged cells of the meristem
(d) region for absorption of water

16. Root cap is a specialized protective structure found on the tips of the terrestrial vascular plants only. The cells of this root cap are
(a) simple and usually forms a homogenous parenchymatous tissue of short-lived cells
(b) Simple and usually forms a homogenous collenchymatous tissue
(c) complex and consists of outer collenchyma and inner sclerenchyma
(d) complex and consists of outer suberised cells and inner parenchyma

17. This hormone would be at an increased level in a mother who is breast feeding
(a) thyroxine (b) prolactin
(c) aldosterone (d) insulin

18. The contractions of the muscles of uterus during parturition are stimulated by
(a) prolactin (b) GnRH
(c) FSH (d) oxytocin

19. During females fertile years only about .... oocytes develop into mature eggs.
(a) 20,000 (b) 250,000
(c) 300,000 (d) 450

20. Which hormone stimulates process of ovulation?
(a) Prolactin (b) LH
(c) FSH (d) Oxytocin

21. Undifferentiated tissue from which new cells are formed, as at the tip of a stem or root.
(a) Meristele (b) Merithallus
(c) Meristem (d) All of these

22. Primary growth depends upon activity of
(a) apical meristem (b) secondary meristem
(c) lateral meristem (d) vascular cambium

23. Secondary growth is made possible by the .... which increases the girth of plant.
(a) primary meristem (b) apical meristem
(c) lateral meristem (d) None of these

24. In .... plants whole body is capable of growth.
(a) angiosperms (b) gymnosperms
(c) Bryophyta (d) All of these

25. The correct sequence of growth phases in plants is
(a) elongation–formative –maturation
(b) maturation– elongation–formative
(c) formative –maturation– elongation
(d) formative – elongation–maturation

26. During elongation phase the cells become enlarged due to
(a) transpiration pressure (b) plasmolytic pressure
(c) turgor pressure (d) Both (b) and (c)

27. During which phase the elongated cells are modified into permanent cells.
(a) Formative phase (b) Elongation phase
(c) Both (a) and (b) (d) Maturation phase

28. The growth in diameter is called
(a) primary growth (b) secondary growth
(c) apical growth (d) intercalary growth

29. During secondary growth xylem rings are produced on the .... side of dividing cambium.
(a) inner side (b) outer side
(c) Both (a) and (b) (d) None of these

30. In a cross section of a tree or log, one of the ribbons of tissue extending radially from the pith form
(a) cortical rays (b) necrotic rays
(c) medullary rays (d) All of these

31. The internal factors that influence the growth of plants are
(a) hormones (b) genes
(c) Both (a) and (b) (d) None of these

32. .... are parts of apical meristem which have become separated from the apex by permanent tissues.
(a) Primary meristem (b) Intercalary meristem
(c) Lateral meristem (d) None of these

33. One of the most important correlative effects in plants is
(a) morphogenesis (b) apical dominance
(c) de-differentiation (d) re-differentiation

34. The removal of apex releases the lateral buds from apical dominance, it is known as
(a) inhibitory effect (b) reciprocal effect
(c) compensatory effect (d) apical effect

35. During the process of .... the miniature seedling comes and enter the second phase ....
(a) fertilization; development
(b) fertilization; cleavage
(c) germination; growth
(d) cleavage; differentiation

36. The correct sequence of process of development after fertilization and cleavage is
(a) gastrulation–organogenesis – growth
(b) organogenesis – gastrulation – growth
(c) gastrulation –blastulation–growth
(d) organogenesis – morulation – blastulation

37. It is series of mitotic cell division that changes zygote into multicellular embryo
(a) gastrulation (b) gametogenesis
(c) blastulation (d) cleavage

38. Cell divisions, migrations and rearrangements produce three germ layers in
(a) morulation (b) blastulation
(c) gastrulation (d) All of these

39. The egg of hen is
(a) alecithal (b) meolecithal
(c) mesolecithal (d) polylecithal

40. In hen, the egg is released from the ovary as
(a) primary oocyte (b) secondary oocyte
(c) ootid (d) None of these

41. In hen, the egg is fertilized at the stage of
(a) primary oocyte (b) secondary oocyte
(c) ootid (d) Both (a) and (b)

42. During development of chick the fertilized egg is laid .... hours after the fertilization.
(a) 24 (b) 36
(c) 40 (d) 45

43. After .... days of incubation, the chick finally begins its escape from the shell.
(a) 16 (b) 19
(c) 20 (d) 21

44. Which of the following is consistent with a model for aging in which stresses leading to DNA damage cause senescence and ageing?
(a) The DAF-16 protein of *C. elegans* is involved in the activation of stress responses
(b) Dietary restriction in mammals reduces the production of DNA-damaging free radicals in the mitochondria
(c) Werner's syndrome is a premature aging illness, possibly caused by a defect in DNA repair
(d) All of the above are consistent with a model for aging based on DNA damage

45. What generalization can be applied to the pole plasm of *Drosophila*, the P granules of *C. elegans*, the yolk free vegetal cytoplasm of *Xenopus* and the localized *m*RNA for vasa in zebra fish?
(a) All mark the posterior end of the antero-posterior axis
(b) All are present at fertilization in the vegetal pole of the egg
(c) All are determinants that specify the dorso-ventral axis of the fertilized egg
(d) All mark the special region of cytoplasm, the germplasm, that is involved in specification of germ cells

46. What is the role of semaphorins and Eph ligands in development of the nervous system?
(a) The semaphorins and Eph ligands are growth factors that stimulate cell division of neurons
(b) The semaphorins and Eph ligands act as signals for the outgrowth of neuronal growth cones, in general, both lead growth cones to turn away
(c) The semaphorins and Eph ligands act as signals for the outgrowth of neuronal growth cones, in general, both lead growth cones to come toward them
(d) The semaphorins and Eph ligands are cell-cell adhesion molecules that bind adjacent neurons together

47. What is the consequence for the ability of motor neurons to find their correct targets, if a section of the spinal cord is rotated, so, that the antero-posterior axis is reversed?
(a) Anterior motor neurons enter the limb in a bundle in the posterior instead of the anterior, but then take novel pathways to find the correct anterior muscles to innervate
(b) Anterior motor neurons enter the limb in a bundle in the posterior instead of the anterior and follow pathways intended for posterior neurons to make contacts with posterior muscles
(c) Anterior motor neurons change their course to enter the limb in the anterior, but take their usual pathways to find the correct anterior muscles
(d) The motor neurons grow over to the other side of the spinal cord and resume their normal pathways into muscles on their normal side of the body

48. What does the experiment in which a frog's eye is rotated tell us about the spatial relationships between the retina and the tectum?
(a) When the right retina makes connections to the right tectum, nasal (anterior) neurons go to the anterior tectum and temporal (posterior) neurons go to the posterior tectum
(b) When the right retina makes connections to the right tectum, nasal (anterior) neurons go to the posterior tectum and temporal (posterior) neurons go to the anterior tectum
(c) When the right retina makes connections to the left tectum, nasal (anterior) neurons go to the posterior tectum and temporal (posterior) neurons go to the anterior tectum
(d) When the right retina makes connections to the left tectum, nasal (anterior) neurons go to the anterior tectum and temporal (posterior) neurons go to the posterior tectum

49. The 'synaptic cleft' of a neuromuscular junction is
(a) a groove in the muscle cell plasma membrane through which neurons grow
(b) that portion of the cell surface receptor molecule on the surface of a muscle cell, into which the ligand binds
(c) a depression at the end of an axon from which neurotransmitters are secreted
(d) the space between the plasma membrane of a neuron on the pre-synaptic side of the synapse and the plasma membrane of the muscle cell on the post-synaptic side of the synapse

50. Do neurons make synapses with other neurons?
(a) No, the only role of neurons is to cause muscles to contract
(b) No, neurons can enervate tissues other than muscle, but there is no need for them to enervate other neurons
(c) Yes, neurons make contacts with other neurons that are identical to those they make with muscle cells
(d) Yes, however, the connections neurons make with each other differ from those they make with muscle cells in that cell-cell adhesion molecules link the pre-synaptic and post-synaptic membranes together

51. Why can't babies see well when they are first born?
(a) The multiple connections between the retina and the visual cortex present at birth become refined in response to visual stimuli, through changes in connectivity and cell death
(b) At birth, the eyes are not yet connected to the visual cortex and processing of visual stimuli occurs only at the level of the geniculate nucleus
(c) Synapses have formed at birth, but are not functional until visual stimuli begin to occur
(d) The lens of the eye is not fully formed at birth

52. In the development of the nervous system, which is the correct order of events?
(a) First, cells must be specified to be neurons, second, these neurons must make connections with their targets, third, the neurons must migrate to their final position and fourth, the neurons refine their synaptic connections
(b) First, cells must be specified to be neurons, second, the neurons must migrate to their final position, third, these neurons must make connections with their targets and fourth, the neurons refine their synaptic connections
(c) First, cells must migrate to their final position, second, these cells must be specified to be neurons, third, the neurons must make connections with their targets and fourth, the neurons refine their synaptic connections
(d) First, the prospective neurons must make connections with their targets, second, the neurons refine their synaptic connections, third, the neurons must migrate to their final position and fourth, the cells are specified to become neurons

53. In *Drosophila*, the neurectoderm is located ventrally during gastrulation, while in mice or frogs, the neurectoderm is located dorsally. Which statement best describes how the two systems are similar or different?

(a) There are no similarities between flies and vertebrates in development of the nervous system
(b) Although gastrulation is completely different in invertebrates and vertebrates, the formation of a neural tube is identical in the two types of animals
(c) There is little similarity, since the neurectoderm of invertebrates forms their nervous system with no further morphological changes, while in vertebrates, the neural tube forms a bundle of neurons running along the antero-posterior axis called the spinal cord
(d) Although the invertebrate nervous system is a ventrally located nerve cord and the vertebrate spinal cord is located dorsally, homologous genes play a role and neurons are ultimately specified through a process of lateral inhibition in both cases

54. How does lateral inhibition work to specify individual neurons in the neural epithelium of invertebrates and vertebrates?
(a) Prospective neurons first arise in a cluster, but then, by chance, one cell will come to signal more strongly through Delta and Notch than its neighbours and become the only neuron in the cluster, by inhibiting its neighbours' specification as neurons
(b) Stripes of prospective neurons will inhibit formation of neurons in stripes lateral to themselves
(c) A gradient of inhibition spreads from the cells lateral to the neural epithelium, inhibiting their specification of neurons until a threshold is reached, at which point a single neuron is permitted to develop
(d) Only one cell in each cluster of prospective neurons is fated to become a neuron and it does so, by inhibiting neural development in its lateral neighbours

55. The ventricular proliferative zone is a region of cell division in
(a) the neural plate
(b) Henson's node
(c) the neurectoderm of *Drosophila*
(d) the neural tube

56. In thinking about the development of the wing imaginal disc of *Drosophila*, what is the significance of 'compartments'?
(a) A compartment is a signaling center that controls antero-posterior patterning
(b) Compartments are developmental units, in that the wing forms from the 'wing compartment'
(c) Compartments are epithelial sacs, set aside during embryogenesis, that will give rise to adult structures such as wings after metamorphosis
(d) Since cells in adjacent compartments have different lineage histories, adjacent compartments can adopt different fates and differentiation patterns, as in the formation of the anterior and posterior portions of the wing blade

57. Engrailed comes to be expressed in posterior compartments during *Drosophila* embryogenesis, what is the consequence of engrailed activation of hedgehog (Hh) signaling from the posterior compartment of the wing disc?
(a) Hh activates decapentaplegic (Dpp) signaling at the compartment boundary, Dpp then acts as a morphogen to pattern the development of veins in the wing blade
(b) Hh signaling from the posterior compartment specifies the adjacent compartment as an anterior compartment
(c) Hh signaling in the posterior compartment acts as a morphogen to pattern the posterior portion of the wing
(d) Hh signaling controls the identity of the imaginal discs, in this case, specifying the disc as the wing disc

58. Keeping in mind the fact that genes are often named for the phenotype of a mutation in that gene, what might be the phenotype of a mutation of the Distalless gene of *Drosophila*?
(a) Mutations of distalless would fail to pattern the wing veins along their antero-posterior axis
(b) Distalless mutants would form only distal structures, like the tarsus (distal end) of the legs without a coxa (proximal end)
(c) Distalless mutants would form only proximal structures, like the coxa (proximal end) of the legs without a tarsus (distal end)
(d) Distalless mutants would fail to form the signaling center that controls dorso-ventral patterning

59. The development of drugs to block the activity of vascular endothelial growth factor (VEGF) has been applied to the control of the growth of cancers. What is the rationale for such a strategy?
(a) VEGF acts as a growth factor to stimulate the growth of many solid tumours
(b) Tumour cells produce VEGF to stimulate angiogenesis in their vicinity and tumours cannot continue to grow without this supply of blood
(c) Blocking VEGF prevents vasculogenesis in the embryo and if done properly prevents cancer later in life
(d) VEGF causes blood vessels to grow toward cancers, which kills the cancer due to too much blood

60. Heart development begins as
(a) a folding process in the mesoderm below the notochord that is exactly like neural tube formation
(b) an outgrowth of the endoderm above the gut that forms a tube that will become the heart
(c) a pair of tubes in the lateral plate mesoderm that move together and fuse to form a single tube that will become the heart
(d) cells from the somitic myotome, which migrate ventrally and form the heart

61. Teeth form from
(a) mesoderm, since they are clearly akin to bone
(b) ectodermal epidermis, since they are clearly related to fingernails and toenails
(c) endoderm, since they reside in the mouth, an extension of the gut
(d) a combination of oral epithelium and neural crest derived mesenchyme in the jaw

62. *Hedgehog* signaling at the compartment boundary in the *Drosophila* wing disc leads to the expression of what signaling molecule in the adjacent anterior cells?
(a) Engrailed (b) Wingless
(c) Decapentaplegic (d) Sonic hedgehog

63. The segmental identity of imaginal discs is determined by
(a) Hox genes (b) gap genes
(c) segment polarity genes (d) maternal genes

64. The heart forms from
(a) dorsal ectoderm
(b) lateral plate mesoderm
(c) endoderm
(d) mesenchyme

65. The kidney forms from
(a) endoderm (b) somites
(c) mesoderm (d) ectoderm

66. Where are the stem cells that renew the epithelium of the gut found?
(a) In the bone marrow
(b) In the inner cell mass
(c) In the villi, underlying the dead outer layer of keratinocytes
(d) Near the bottom of the crypt

67. What happens if you introduced the gene *myo D* into fibroblast cells growing in culture?
(a) The fibroblasts will express muscle specific proteins, fuse and form functional muscle in culture
(b) Nothing will happen because fibroblasts are derived from a different cell population in the embryo than are the muscle precursors that respond to *myo D*
(c) The fibroblasts will undergo apoptosis, due to the abnormal effects of *myo D* on their normal differentiation
(d) *myo D* will activate expression of myogenin, but the muscle specific genes will not be able to activate

68. In what way are *mrf* 4, *myo D* and the other muscle inducing genes similar to the homeotic genes of *Drosophila*?
(a) *mrf 4, myo D* and the others encode homeobox containing proteins
(b) *mrf 4, myo D* and the others encode 'master switch' transcription factors, which initiate a cascade of gene expression that leads to the differentiation of cells
(c) *mrf 4, myo D* and the others act as homeotic genes in *Drosophila*
(d) *mrf 4, myo D* and the others are expressed exclusively in muscle, as are the homeotic genes of *Drosophila*

69. Neural crest cells that follow a dorso-lateral route of migration under the skin will become melanocytes, how is their differentiation into melanocytes triggered during their migration?
(a) The neural crest cells are already determined to become melanocytes before they leave the neural tube
(b) N-cadherin and E-cadherin are lost from the neural crest cells when they initiate their migration and this signals the cells to become melanocytes
(c) BMP and noggin control the fate of neural crest cells
(d) The cells in the skin express a ligand (stem cell factor, SCF, also known as steel) on their surface, which interacts with a receptor (Kit, also known as white spotting) on the surface of the neural crest derived cells, this interaction triggers their differentiation as melanocytes

70. Which of the following cells would be considered differentiated?
(a) Blastomere (b) Spemann organizer
(c) Myotome of the somite (d) Muscle cell

71. Differentiated cells express the genes and proteins characteristic of their final identity in the adult and that identity can be altered only under special circumstances. How does the concept of differentiation, as described here, differ from the concept of determination?
(a) Determined cells have begun to differentiate, but are not fully differentiated
(b) Determined cells are embryonic cells that will give rise to all the cell types of the adult organism, but have not yet begun to express the genes and proteins characteristic of their final fates
(c) Determined cells will continue to follow their fate if grafted into a different place in a host embryo, even though they do not yet express the genes and proteins characteristic of their final fate
(d) Determination describes fully differentiated cells whose identity can no longer be altered

72. What is the role of stem cells with regard to the function of adult tissues and organs?
(a) Stem cells are undifferentiated cells that divide asymmetrically, giving rise to one daughter that remains a stem cell and one daughter that will differentiate to replace damaged and worn out cells in the adult tissue or organ
(b) Stem cells are embryonic cells that persist in the adult and can give rise to all of the cell types in the body
(c) Stem cells are determined cells that reside in fully differentiated tissues and can, when needed, differentiate to supply new cells for growth of the tissue
(d) Stem cells are differentiated cells that have yet to express the genes and proteins characteristic of their differentiated state and do so, when needed for repair of tissues and organs

73. The immunoglobulin genes are expressed in B-cells and the β-globin gene is expressed in red blood cells. What manipulations might be carried out to get the β-globin gene to be expressed in B-cells?
(a) The coding region of an immunoglobulin gene could be combined with the *cis*-regulatory region of the β-globin genes and this artificial gene would then express β-globin in B-cells
(b) The *cis*-regulatory region of the β-globin gene could be inserted into B-cells, which would then express their own version of the β-globin gene
(c) The *cis*-regulatory region of an immunoglobulin gene could be combined with the coding region of the β-globin genes and this artificial gene would then express β-globin in B-cells
(d) The transcription factors GATA-1 and GATA-2 (which activate the β-globin gene in erythrocytes) could be introduced into B-cells, which would then express their own copy of the β-globin gene

74. Imagine that in an attempt to get the β-globin gene to be expressed in B-cells, the transcription factors (GATA-1 and GATA-2) known to control the β-globin gene in erythrocytes were introduced into B-cells, yet the β-globin gene was not expressed. What is a likely explanation for this result?

(a) The erythrocyte transcription factors are degraded rapidly in the B-cell and so, cannot act on the β-globin gene
(b) The β-globin gene in the B-cells is packaged into heterochromatin and the erythrocyte transcription factors are insufficient to remodel that chromatin into an active state
(c) Erythrocyte transcription factors cannot interact with their target DNA sequences in B-cells, even though those sequences are present and accessible
(d) Even though the necessary erythrocyte specific transcription factors are now present in the B-cells, the general transcription factors required for β-globin gene expression would not be present

75. What type of cell-cell signaling protein exerts its effect in gene expression through a receptor that is a transcription factor?

(a) The Wnt protein
(b) The Hedgehog protein, whose receptor is patched
(c) Peptides like EGF and FGF, whose receptors are tyrosine kinases
(d) Hydrophobic molecules like steroid hormones and retinoic acid

76. What is the developmental pathway by which the haematopoietic stem cell gives rise to a macrophage?

(a) The haematopoietic stem cell divides, giving rise to a daughter cell that remains a stem cell and a daughter cell that differentiates directly into a macrophage
(b) The haematopoietic stem cell can give rise to either a lymphoid progenitor or a myeloid progenitor, the myeloid progenitor differentiates directly into a macrophage
(c) The haematopoietic stem cell gives rise to a variety of cells referred to as granulocytes, any one of which can differentiate further into a macrophage
(d) The haematopoietic stem cell must first generate a cell of the myeloid lineage (as opposed to the lymphoid lineage), then a granulocyte/macrophage progenitor, then a monocyte and finally a macrophage

77. How do the endodermal cells of the sea urchin embryo carry out gut formation during gastrulation?

(a) They move inside the blastocoel and form the skeletal structures that will support the adult animal
(b) They move into the blastocoel as mesenchyme and crawl ventrally, to mark the location of the future mouth
(c) Changes in cell shape initiate the invagination, convergent extension extends the sheet of cells into the blastocoel and finally, filopodia make contact with the future mouth region and pull the tip of the gut to that point
(d) The crawl inside the blastocoel and form a solid rod, which is then hollowed out to form the tube of the gut

78. Contrast involution, epiboly and convergent extension.

(a) Involution is the movement of cells toward an axis to extend that axis, epiboly is a flattening and spreading of epithelial cells to increase the amount of surface they cover and convergent extension is the movement of cells inside the embryo as a coherent sheet
(b) Involution is the movement of cells inside the embryo as a coherent sheet, epiboly is a flattening and spreading of epithelial cells to increase the amount of surface they cover and convergent extension is movement of cells toward an axis to extend that axis
(c) Involution is a flattening of epithelial cells to increase the amount of surface they cover, epiboly is the movement of cells inside the embryo as a coherent sheet and convergent extension is movement of cells toward an axis to extend that axis
(d) Involution is the movement of cells inside the embryo as a coherent sheet, epiboly is movement of cells toward an axis to extend that axis and convergent extension is a flattening and spreading of epithelial cells to increase the amount of surface they cover

79. During gastrulation in the frog, the very first cells to move into the interior of the embryo through the blastopore come from the surface layer of cells in the marginal zone, they will become

(a) ectoderm (b) mesoderm
(c) endoderm (d) yolk

80. Gastrulation in sea urchins, *Drosophila* and *Xenopus* all begin with a change in cell shape, in which the apical surface of an epithelial sheet contracts. This process is called

(a) involution (b) convergent extension
(c) epiboly (d) invagination

81. In *Xenopus*, the mesoderm moves in through the blastopore by rolling around the dorsal lip in a process called

(a) involution (b) convergent extension
(c) epiboly (d) invagination

82. In *Xenopus*, the elongation of the mesoderm toward the anterior results from the intercalation of cells during a process called

(a) involution (b) convergent extension
(c) epiboly (d) invagination

83. In chicks, the formation of the neural tube relies on what cell biological processes?

(a) Changes in cell shape in the neural plate are the only process required for neural tube formation
(b) Changes in adhesiveness between the prospective neural tube cells and the prospective epidermis in the ectoderm are the only changes required for neural tube formation
(c) Both changes in cell shape in the neural plate and changes in adhesion molecule expression in the neural tube are required during formation of the neural tube
(d) Prospective neural tube cells in the ectoderm undergo medio-lateral intercalation, then involute and form the neural tube

84. Neural crest cells will become
(a) medullary cells of the adrenal gland
(b) neurons in the sympathetic ganglia of the autonomic nervous system
(c) neurons in the dorsal root ganglia of the peripheral nervous system
(d) All of the above are derived from neural crest cells

85. Neural crest cells taking the dorso-lateral route will become
(a) dorso-lateral route ganglia
(b) adrenal medulla
(c) sympathetic ganglia
(d) melanocytes

86. At the molecular and cellular level, how does morphogenesis differ from the establishment of embryonic axes and the specification of cellular identity?
(a) Previously, we have studied only gene expression patterns, whereas now we are concerned with cell-cell signaling as well
(b) Previously, cell-cell signaling has been the major focus, whereas in morphogenesis we will be concerned with gene expression primarily
(c) The specification of pattern and fate has been presented as being completely under maternal control, whereas now we are concerned with zygotic control over development
(d) The formation of embryonic axes and the specification of cell fates rely heavily on cell-cell signaling events and their influence over gene expression patterns, whereas morphogenesis relies primarily on cell-cell adhesion and cell motility

87. Which of the following is the only true statement regarding compaction in the mouse embryo?
(a) Compaction involves the activation of cadherins, resulting in an increase in cell-cell adhesion among the eight cells of the embryo
(b) Compaction involves a polarization of the cells of the embryo, such that ions can be pumped from the outer surface of the embryo into the central cavity, resulting in an influx of water into the central cavity and formation of the blastocoel
(c) Compaction gives subsequent cell divisions an orientation, such that cell divisions that occur tangential (parallel) to the cell surface will result in one cell being inside the embryo, where it can contribute to the inner cell mass
(d) All of the above are true of compaction in the mouse embryo

88. Where would leaf primordium number seven appear?
(a) Directly on the proximal (toward the center) side of leaf primordium number six
(b) Directly opposite leaf primordium number six, at the proximal junction of leaf primordia number four and number five
(c) Directly opposite leaf primordium number six, on the distal (toward the outside) side of the junction of leaf primordia number one and number two
(d) Adjacent to leaf primordium number six, on the proximal side of primordium number four

89. Which of the following describes the pathway in *Arabidopsis* by which day length is translated into a signal that coverts a vegetative shoot meristem into a floral meristem?
(a) The constans protein is degraded in the dark, but accumulates in the leaves as the days get longer
(b) The *FT m*RNA travels to the shoot meristem, where it is translated, the protein then participates in activation of leafy and *AP1*
(c) Leafy and *AP1* re-specify the shoot meristem into a floral meristem, capable of producing flowers
(d) A through the above describe, in order, the pathway by which shoot meristems are turned into floral meristems

90. What is meant by the word 'whorl' in discussing floral meristems?
(a) When leaf primordia first arise, they arise in a pattern described as a 'whorl'
(b) Flowers consist of four different types of organs, which occur in concentric rings called 'whorls'
(c) The floral meristem as to spin around during flower formation, giving the process the name 'whorl'
(d) The six stamens in a dicot flower like that of *Arabidopsis* form a ring that is called the flower's 'whorl'

91. In what way are the homeotic genes of flowering plants similar to those of *Drosophila* and other animals?
(a) All homeotic genes are transcription factors of the homeobox class
(b) The homeotic genes of flowers are derived during evolution from the same primordial genes used in animals
(c) Mutations in the homeotic genes of flowers cause transformation of one organ into another
(d) The homeotic genes of plants are arranged in a cluster on the chromosome and are expressed from one end to the other in an anterior-posterior order

92. What is the phenotype of a mutation in the agamous homeotic gene of *Arabidopsis* (Recall, genes are often named for the mutant phenotype.)?
(a) Agamous mutants fail to restrict the expression of class A genes, resulting in four whorls composed of sepals and petals, with no stamens or carpels
(b) Agamous mutants fail to make the central most whorl, which gives rise to carpels and are thus left with only three whorls
(c) Agamous mutants make only the outer two whorls, resulting in two whorls composed of sepals and petals, with no stamens or carpels
(d) Agamous mutants make only the gamete forming structures, stamens and carpels, with no petals or sepals

93. How is the ABC model for floral identity in *Arabidopsis* reminiscent of the models for homeotic gene function derived from studies in *Drosophila*?
(a) In both organisms, homeobox genes specify the identity of regions of the mature organism
(b) The key responsibility of the homeotic genes in both organisms is patterning of dorso-ventral asymmetry

(c) In both organisms, one homeotic gene is expressed at the two ends, a second expressed in to domains more central to that of the first and a third expressed most centrally, thus contributing unambiguous identities to all regions of the organism

(d) In both organisms, the homeotic genes interact, so, that it is often the combination of genes present that is critical in unambiguously specifying structures in the adult

94. In a comparison of plant and animal development, it is found that

(a) animals evolved from plants and animal developmental strategies are derived from those of plants

(b) fully differentiated cells of plants are still totipotent and will readily form a complete fertile plant, whereas, the differentiated state of animal cells is difficult to reverse

(c) gene regulation evolved later than the split between plants and animals and is executed differently in the two kingdoms

(d) basic metabolic pathways and intracellular structures evolved separately in plants and animals and are fundamentally different

95. Why has the diploid genome been an advantage in studying the development of *Arabidopsis*?

(a) It is assumed that polyploidy plants use developmental mechanisms that are unlike those of animals, whereas the developmental mechanisms used by *Arabidopsis* are identical to those of animals, since both are diploid

(b) The diploid genome of *Arabidopsis* provides a marker for the *Arabidopsis* cells in chimeras made with other plants

(c) The diploid genome allows genetic analysis of development, in a manner analogous to the genetic analysis that has been done with *Drosophila*

(d) The development of polyploid plants is too variable to be of any use in studies of development

96. The fate map of the *Arabidopsis* embryo at the heart stage indicates that

(a) the primordia of the leaves, stems and roots have already formed

(b) the three germ layers that will give rise to roots, stems and leaves have formed

(c) although none of the adult structures have formed, the regions that will give rise to the meristems, which will in turn give rise to adult structures, can be identified

(d) development in plants is so, indeterminate that a true fate map cannot be drawn

97. One of the earliest events in *Arabidopsis* development is formation of the .... axis, in response to a gradient of ....

(a) apical-basal; auxin

(b) dorsal-ventral; miRNA

(c) apical-basal; Pin-1 and Pin-7

(d) animal-vegetal; nodal

98. Do Hox genes play a role in the development of *C. elegans*?

(a) No, *C. elegans* does not have Hox genes

(b) No, *C. elegans* has Hox genes but none of them are used during development

(c) Yes, *C. elegans* has 4 clust rs of Hox genes, just like mammals, that are required for specification of the identity of structures during embryogenesis

(d) Yes, but only one Hox gene is required in the embryo, the others provide positional identity in the larva

99. What are the *lin*-4 and *lin*-14 genes of *C. elegans*?

(a) *Lin*-4 encodes a *mi*RNA that represses *lin*-14 translation, which in turn regulates the timing of larval development

(b) *Lin*-4 and *lin*-14 are genes that are named for their control of the first division and hence the lineage of the AB and P1 cells

(c) *Lin*-4 and *lin*-14 are *C. elegans* versions of the Hox genes

(d) *Lin*-4 and *lin*-14 both encode *m*RNAs that serve as cell-cell signaling molecules in *C. elegans*

100. The ability of the sea urchin embryo to regulate its development illustrates the fact that there are maternally determined differences along the animal vegetal axis that are necessary for normal development. Which of the following statements about regulation in sea urchin embryos is consistent with that fact?

(a) Up until the hatching of the embryo as a pluteus larva, any blastomere can be separated from the others and will regulate to go on and develop into a fully formed and full sized larva

(b) Up until the hatching of the embryo as a pluteus larva, any blastomere can be separated from the others and will regulate to go on and develop into a fully formed, yet smaller, larva

(c) Blastomeres from the animal or vegetal poles of the embryo can be isolated and will go on to form an embryo, as long as either an animal or vegetal pole is included

(d) Blastomeres at the 4-cell stage each still possesses a portion of the original animal vegetal axis and if isolated will go on to form a fully formed, yet smaller, larva

101. In which way is the organizer region of the sea urchin similar to that in frogs?

(a) The organizer induces the dorso-ventral axis

(b) The organizer forms near the dorsal lip of the blastopore

(c) The organizer accumulates β-catenin, which in turn activates the expression of cell-cell signaling molecules

(d) The organizer will become the mesoderm

102. Which statement(s) best describes gastrulation in sea urchins?

(a) Gastrulation is initiated by invagination of the micromeres at the vegetal pole

(b) The mouth of the pluteus larva will form from mesomeres on the oral side of the 60-cell embryo

(c) The gut will form from the macromeres at the 16-cell stage

(d) All of the above

103. In the ascidian, *Styela*, the yellow pigmented myoplasm marks cells fated to become muscle cells in the tail, however, at the molecular level, the key determinant of tail muscle seems to be
(a) localization of β-catenin to the nuclei in the vegetal portion of the embryo
(b) the sperm centrosome
(c) the gene product of *macho*-1 gene
(d) expression of the *Brachyury* gene

104. In flies, frogs and chicks, gradients of morphogens determine the future antero-posterior and dorso-ventral axes of the developing embryo. How is the antero-posterior axis determined in *C. elegans*?
(a) *bicoid* protein is translated in the anterior of the fertilized egg, leading to a gradient that determines the antero-posterior axis
(b) Opposing gradients of chordin and BMP-4 establish the antero-posterior axis
(c) β-catenin becomes localized to the nucleus in the future anterior cells after fertilization
(d) Sperm entry leads to a reorganization of the cytoskeleton and redistribution of maternally packaged PAR proteins, which in turn determine the antero-posterior axis

105. The role of the *Brachyury* gene in ascidians is similar to that in *Xenopus* in that
(a) *Brachyury* sets up the animal vegetal axis
(b) *Brachyury* is characteristic of the organizer region
(c) The *Brachyury* gene is expressed specifically in those cells that will form somites and hence muscle
(d) Signaling that leads to induction of the mesoderm results in expression of the *Brachyury* gene in the mesoderm

106. Which statement describes *Dictyostelium*?
(a) *Dictyostelium* cells can live as single, free living cells, until they are stimulated by starvation to aggregate and sporulate
(b) *Dictyostelium* is a fungus that forms a cap with spores, like a mushroom
(c) *Dictyostelium* is a plant that forms a fruiting body instead of a flower
(d) *Dictyostelium* is related to snails and other slugs that have evolved from snails through loss of their shells

107. What is the role of cAMP in *Dictyostelium* development?
(a) cAMP induces differentiation of cells as prestalk cells
(b) cAMP is secreted by individual cells in response to starvation and serves to attract nearby cells resulting in formation of aggregate
(c) cAMP signals lead cells to express DIF-1, which in turn stimulates aggregation
(d) cAMP is used as an energy source for migrating *Dictyostelium* cells

108. Hox genes
(a) encode transcription factors which specify a position along the anterior-posterior axis in vertebrates
(b) make signaling molecules used during somite formation
(c) control the formation of vertebrae in mice, but are not found in other animals
(d) are expressed only in the mesoderm

109. The effect of grafting an extra piece of notochord into a dorsal position adjacent to pre-somitic mesoderm is
(a) the pre-somitic mesoderm will degenerate
(b) somites will form but fail to differentiate
(c) the somite will be converted almost entirely to muscle forming cells
(d) the somite is incorporated into the neural tube

110. The grafting of the dorsal lip of the blastopore from an early *Xenopus* gastrula onto the ventral side of an early embryo will result in
(a) the formation of two separate and independent embryos
(b) the formation of two complete embryos joined along the ventral axis
(c) the formation of two sets of posterior structures joined along the ventral axis, a two tailed embryo
(d) no effect, only dorsal lips from early embryos have organizer activity

111. The 'default model' for neural tissue formation states that
(a) no mechanism is required to form nervous tissue in the embryo, it forms unless signals direct development of epidermal tissue
(b) neural tissue formation is the default state, such that special induction is required to form mesoderm, endoderm and epidermis, but not neurectoderm
(c) neurectoderm formation is inhibited by the BMP proteins present throughout the early embryo and this inhibition is relieved by BMP antagonists from the organizer, such as chordin
(d) the induction of neural tissue is the default state in embryos and all other inductions are special

112. The use of segments as a developmental strategy in vertebrates is evident in the
(a) endoderm (b) axial skeleton
(c) hindbrain (d) Both (b) and (c)

113. A fate map of a *Xenopus* blastula, just before gastrulation begins, shows that the top portion of the embryo will become ectoderm (skin and nerve), the central portion will become mesoderm (bone, muscle and blood) and the lowest portion will become endoderm (gut). How is it that the endoderm and mesoderm, shown on the outside in the fate map, end up on the inside in the embryo after gastrulation?
(a) The endodermal cells begin first to move into the embryo through the blastopore, displacing the blastocoel and forming a gut, as gastrulation proceeds, the blastopore spreads sideways and the mesoderm follows the endoderm in, ending up between the endoderm and the ectoderm
(b) The ectodermal cells divide and spread down over the rest of the embryo, so, that the endoderm ends up on the bottom, ventral, surface of the embryo and the mesoderm ends up around the middle, just as is shown in the fate map
(c) The three germ layers adopt their final positions through, first, the growth of the mesodermal marginal zone down over the endoderm, followed by, secondly, the growth of ectoderm down and over the mesoderm
(d) The cells, having already been fated to form endoderm and mesoderm, migrate directly into the interior of the embryo and take up residence in appropriate places

114. What property of the mammalian embryo permits the production of chimeric mice?
(a) The inner cell mass is highly regulative, so, that extra cells derived from the inner cell mass of a different embryo are incorporated without causing defects
(b) If half of the cells of the inner cell mass are removed and replaced with cells from half of a different embryo's inner cell mass, the embryo will heal and develop normally
(c) The embryo can develop outside the womb, making surgical manipulations possible
(d) Blastomeres separated at the two-cell stage will regulate and each forms a normal embryo

115. If cells from the animal pole of a frog blastula (animal cap cells) are placed into contact with cells from the vegetal hemisphere, after removing the cells fated to form mesoderm, what is the result?
(a) The cells regulate to form a normal embryo
(b) Animal cap cells are induced to form mesodermal derivatives
(c) Vegetal hemisphere cells are induced by the animal cap cells to form mesodermal derivatives
(d) An embryo forms with only ectodermal and endodermal derivatives

116. The 'mid blastula transition' is the point in development when
(a) translation of maternal *m*RNA is initiated
(b) cell determination becomes fixed
(c) cell division in the embryo ends
(d) transcription of zygotic genes begins

117. What is the mechanism by which cells fated to be mesoderm form in the marginal zone of the *Xenopus* embryo?
(a) Vegetal region cells migrate toward the animal pole and become mesoderm
(b) Cells in the marginal zone are fated to be mesoderm, but they do not become specified or determined as mesoderm until after they move internally during gastrulation
(c) Maternal factors packaged into the marginal zone act on these cells to instruct them to become mesoderm
(d) Secreted signals of the TGF-β family are released by the cells of the vegetal region and act on the adjacent cells of the marginal zone to instruct them to adopt a mesodermal fate

118. How is the Spemann organizer distinguished from the other mesodermal cells during induction by the cells of the vegetal region?
(a) The cells of the Spemann organizer become different as they pass over the dorsal lip of the blastopore during gastrulation
(b) β-catenin, which has become localized to the nucleus in the Nieuwkoop center as a result of cortical rotation, turns on high levels of the TGF-β signaling molecule, nodal and this relatively high level distinguishes the adjacent cells of the Spemann organizer from the rest of the mesoderm
(c) The Spemann organizer is formed from cells of the Nieuwkoop center, which have migrated upward in the embryo
(d) BMP-4 signaling from ventral mesodermal cells toward the dorsal region specify the dorsal-most cells as organizer

119. Patterning of the *Xenopus* mesoderm along the dorso-ventral axis involves an antagonistic relationship between chordin and BMP-4. Is there an analogy here to dorso-ventral patterning in the *Drosophila* embryo?
(a) Yes, the *Drosophila* homolog of BMP-4, Decapentaplegic (Dpp), is antagonized by the *Drosophila* homolog of chordin, short gastrulation (Sog), in patterning of the dorso-ventral axis
(b) Yes, *Drosophila* also uses BMP-4 to specify ventral fates and chordin to specify dorsal fates
(c) Yes, the *Drosophila* dorsal protein is identical to the vertebrate BMP-4 protein and specifies the ventral region of the embryo
(d) No, insect development is totally different than that of real animals like frogs and chickens

120. In which portion of the frog's life cycle would a frog appear most similar to a mammal?
(a) The fertilized eggs of frogs and mammals are similar in size and look nearly identical
(b) A frog blastula is very similar to a mammalian blastocyst
(c) The events of gastrulation in frogs are highly similar to gastrulation and extraembryonic membrane formation in mammals
(d) Late in organogenesis, at the phylotypic stage, the body plans of frogs and mammals are remarkably similar

121. The notochord is a .... structure in vertebrate embryos that lies under the .... and is flanked by ....
(a) mesodermal; neural tube; somites
(b) endodermal; mesoderm; the gut
(c) ectodermal; neural tube; mesoderm
(d) mesodermal; ectoderm; endoderm

122. During gastrulation in *Xenopus*, the blastocoel
(a) becomes the gut
(b) is filled with endodermal cells and disappears
(c) is filled with mesoderm and disappears
(d) is displaced and its original location becomes an endoderm lined cavity, the archenteron, which is a precursor to the gut

123. The development of the antero-posterior axis of *Drosophila* is initiated when
(a) the mother packages *bicoid* and *nanos* *m*RNA into the developing oocyte
(b) the toll receptor is activated after fertilization, leading to nuclear localization of dorsal protein
(c) the terminal group protein *torso* sets up the anterior and posterior poles of the embryo
(d) the homeotic genes specify the fate of individual segments

124. Which would lead to a dorsalized embryo? (Recall that genes in *Drosophila* are named for their mutant phenotype).

(a) Dorsal mutant (b) Cactus mutant
(c) Toll mutant (d) Spätzle mutant

125. A gap gene mutation might cause which of the following defects in the embryonic body plan?

(a) Every other segment would be missing, resulting in T1, T3, A2, A4, etc., but no T2, A1, A3 and so, on
(b) Segments A2 through A6 would be missing, but the rest of the pattern is essentially normal
(c) No segmentation would be evident
(d) Patterning within each segment would be abnormal, causing for example denticle belts to form across the entire segment

126. The activation of zygotic *hunchback* expression by *bicoid* protein illustrates what principle in the establishment of positional information in embryos?

(a) The mother can influence development through the packaging of materials into the egg
(b) A gradient of a protein can activate a gene in a discrete region of an embryo through a threshold effect
(c) The identity of segments in the embryo is a reflection of their position in the embryo
(d) A cascade of gene activations occurs in the syncitial blastoderm

127. The portion of the *Drosophila* body plan which will produce the wing is called

(a) telson (b) dorsal
(c) abdomen (d) thorax

128. The adult body plan of the fly is based on reiterating structures called segments, segment precursors (parasegments) are first positioned at the cell by cell level by which group of genes?

(a) Maternal genes such as *bicoid*
(b) Gap genes such as *Kruppel*
(c) Pair rule genes such as even skipped
(d) Segmentation genes such as engrailed

129. Mutations in homeotic genes can lead to what type of developmental defect?

(a) The anterior portion of the embryo does not develop
(b) Several adjacent segments will be missing from an otherwise intact embryo
(c) The embryo will develop with every other segment failing to form
(d) The development of segments will be changed wholesale from their normal identity to that of a different segment

130. Which of the following, first discovered through mutagenesis studies in *Drosophila*, also function in the development of mammals like ourselves?

(a) Hedgehog (b) Homeobox genes
(c) The Wnt family (d) All of these

131. What would be the effect on the timing of somite formation, if a piece of the pre-somitic mesoderm of a chick embryo is rotated by 180° and reinserted in its original position?

(a) There would be no effect because the embryo would regulate and development would proceed normally
(b) Antero-posterior development would be blocked at that point and more posterior structures would fail to form
(c) The rotated mesoderm would degenerate and a gap would form in the antero-posterior pattern
(d) The timing of somite formation will be reversed in the rotated block only, proceeding from posterior to anterior, but the rest of the somites will form in a normal fashion, proceeding from anterior to posterior

132. Relative to the primitive streak and Henson's node, somite formation in the chick embryo occurs

(a) anterior to Henson's node, after the primitive steak has retracted past that point
(b) posterior to Henson's node, as cells from the lateral portions of the epiblast move in through the primitive streak to become mesoderm
(c) adjacent to Henson's node, as the primitive streak migrates toward the anterior of the embryo
(d) somite formation occurs simultaneously along the axis, after Henson's node has fully retracted

133. The genetic analysis of *Arabidopsis* development was strongly influenced by genetic analysis of *Drosophila* development and as is the case in *Drosophila*, genes that influence development are often named for

(a) extinct royal families of Europe
(b) mythical creatures from Greek *mythology*
(c) their location on a chromosome, as determined by karyotype analysis
(d) the phenotype observed when the gene is mutated

134. Maintenance of the shoot meristems in adult *Arabidopsis* plants relies on which of the following mechanisms?

(a) A transcription factor encoded by the shoot meristemless gene is expressed in shoot meristem cells and maintains them in their undifferentiated state
(b) A homeobox transcription factor encoded by the Wuschel gene is expressed in the organizing center and initiates a signal to the overlying cells to behave as stem cells
(c) Shoot meristems cells secrete proteins encoded by the clavata family that antagonize Wuschel expression, thereby restricting the size of the shoot meristems
(d) All of the above are involved in specification and maintenance of shoot meristems

135. Haematopoietic stem cells can be isolated and grown in culture, if one wished to control their differentiation into either neutrophils or macrophages, what colony stimulating factors could be used?

(a) First, GM-CSF and IL-3 would be added to trigger formation of the granulocyte/macrophage lineage, then, the addition of either G-CSF or M-CSF would select between further differentiation as neutrophils or macrophages, respectively
(b) Since Stem Cell Factor (SCF) would maintain the cells as stem cells, the elimination of SCF would trigger differentiation into granulocyte/macrophage precursors, no further manipulation would be necessary

(c) The stem cells could be simultaneously stimulated with G–CSF, M–CSF, GM–CSF and IL–3, half would become neutrophils and the other half would become macrophages, no further control is possible
(d) Since haematopoietic stem cells can become only erythrocytes, neutrophils, or macrophages and no other cell types, the elimination of erythropoietin (EPO) would be sufficient to trigger formation of neutrophils and macrophages

136. What is globin gene switching?
(a) Globin gene switching refers to the switching on of the globin genes during erythrocyte differentiation
(b) Globin gene switching refers to the switching from α-globin to β-globin, so, that $\alpha_2\beta_2$ haemoglobin can be made
(c) Globin gene switching refers to the molecular basis for the genetic disease, sickle cell anaemia
(d) Globin gene switching refers to the transition, during fetal development, from the production of haemoglobin containing ε-globin, to γ-globin, to β-globin

137. What do 'V', 'J' and 'C' mean in the context of the genes for immunoglobulins?
(a) V, J and C are the three exons of an immunoglobulin gene, which are spliced together to produce a mature immunoglobulin *m*RNA
(b) There are several V and J exons in an immunoglobulin gene, one of each is joined to a C exon during splicing, through a process of alternative splicing
(c) There are several V and J exons in an immunoglobulin gene, one of each is selected during a rearrangement in the DNA to produce an immunoglobulin gene capable of being expressed, the V and J segments that are not selected are lost from the genome
(d) The V and J genes exist in many copies, the choice of one of these many genes contributes to antibody diversity

138. Cartilage (bone forming tissue) and connective tissue of the vertebrate limb form from
(a) the ectodermal epithelium of the limb bud
(b) the mesodermal mesenchyme of the limb bud, derived from lateral plate ectoderm
(c) mesodermal cells that migrate into the limb bud from the somites
(d) the polarizing region

139. Which of the following correctly describes the sequence of events by which the position of limbs along the antero-posterior axis of vertebrates is specified?
(a) Hox gene expression in the mesoderm activates Wnt signaling, which turns on FGF expression and formation of the limb bud
(b) Wnt signaling activates Hox gene expression, which turns on FGF expression and formation of the limb bud
(c) FGF expression in the mesoderm activates Wnt signaling, which turns on Hox gene expression and formation of the limb bud
(d) Hox gene expression in the mesoderm activates FGF signaling, which turns on Wnt expression and formation of the limb bud

140. Removal of the apical ridge leads to
(a) regeneration of the entire limb bud from underlying mesoderm
(b) formation of structures proximal to the apical ridge, but no formation of new distal structures
(c) degeneration of the limb bud
(d) regeneration of a new apical ridge from adjacent epidermal tissue

141. Cells of the muscle forming region of the somite, the myotome, express *Pax3*, *Pax3* activates expression of *myo D* and *myf 5*, but muscle differentiation does not occur until the cells stop dividing. When they enter the limb bud, *Pax 3* is down regulated, division ceases and differentiation begins. At this point, what gene is the next to be activated as the cells differentiate into muscle?
(a) Hoxd13 (b) Myogenin
(c) *mrf4* (d) *Wnt*

142. What is the relationship between dorso-ventral patterning of the neural tube and patterning of the somites?
(a) The somites pattern the neural tube after they form
(b) The neural tube plays the role of organizer in being the sole influence on patterning in the somites
(c) Sonic Hedgehog from the notochord and floorplate of the neural tube confers ventral fates on both the neural tube and the somite, while BMPs confer more dorsal fates
(d) Both the neural tube and the somites acquire their dorso-ventral patterning during gastrulation

143. What role, if any, do Hox genes play in specification of neuronal fate?
(a) Different Hox genes are activated along the dorso-ventral axis by the gradient of Shh
(b) Different combinations of Hox genes specify the identities of neurons along the antero-posterior axis
(c) Hox genes determine the identity of the segments along the axis of the vertebrate spinal cord
(d) Hox genes determine the different subtypes of neurons that form along the dorso-ventral axis

144. Secretion of Mullerian inhibiting substance by Sertoli cells
(a) causes the Mullerian ducts to develop into the oviducts
(b) causes the Mullerian ducts to develop into Wolffian ducts
(c) causes the Wolffian duct to develop into the vas deferenes
(d) causes the testis to produce testosterone

145. In what way, if any, does the chromosomal determination of sex differ in *Drosophila* and humans?
(a) In humans, the Y-chromosome determines maleness, with female development being a default state, but in *Drosophila*, the presence of two X-chromosomes determines femaleness and male development is the default state
(b) In humans, the Y-chromosome determines maleness, but in *Drosophila*, the ratio of X-chromosomes to autosomes determines maleness or femaleness

(c) In humans, it is the presence of only one X-chromosome that triggers male development and two X-chromosomes trigger female development, just as occurs in *Drosophila*
(d) In human males, a single Y-chromosome is present in the absence of an X-chromosome, while in *Drosophila*, a single X-chromosome is present in the absence of a Y-chromosome

146. What is the molecular activity of the sex lethal protein of *Drosophila*?
(a) Sex lethal is a transcription factor that activates female-specific genes
(b) Sex lethal is a repressor of the transcription of male specific genes
(c) Sex lethal controls the splicing of specific *m*RNAs such that certain proteins required for female development are produced only in females
(d) Sex lethal protein is equivalent to testosterone in mammals, in determining male development

147. The treatment of *Xenopus* embryos with lithium dorsalizes the embryos by interfering with cell-cell signaling pathways. What, if anything, is the effect of lithium on *Hydra* and what might we infer about its mechanism of action?
(a) Lithium has no effect in *Hydra*
(b) Lithium dorsalizes *Hydra* just as it does *Xenopus*, so, we would assume its mechanism of action is identical in the two organisms
(c) Lithium causes the formation of extra basal discs, which we might infer arise through interference with cell-cell signaling pathways
(d) Lithium causes the formation of extra head regions, since the head of *Hydra* is mechanistically analogous to the dorsal side of *Xenopus* embryos

148. In frogs, maternally packaged Xwnt-1 leads to nuclear localization of .... in the ...., which in response signals to adjacent cells to become the ....
(a) β-catenin; Nieuwkoop center; Spemann organizer
(b) nodal; signaling center; shield
(c) Vg-1; vegetal region; Nieuwkoop center
(d) Sonic Hedgehog; limb bud; posterior

149. Remarkably, Vg-1 and Wnt are used in both frogs and chicks to establish a body axis, although in chicks this is the antero-posterior axis instead of the dorso-ventral axis. What is the region of the chick embryo that is thus, analogous to the Nieuwkoop center?
(a) Area pellucida (b) Blastoderm
(c) Primitive streak (d) Posterior marginal zone

150. Although the vertebrate body plan outwardly displays a mirror image symmetry with regard to left and right, the internal organs are not symmetrical. How does this left-right asymmetry develop?
(a) The two cells of the Nieuwkoop center (at the 32-cell stage) signal each other and become either left or right
(b) Maternal factors that determine left and right are packaged into the egg, just as dorsalizing factors are
(c) Differential release of Ca^{2+} ions on the left side leads to expression of Nodal and Pitx2 on the left
(d) Gravity determines the left-right axis, that side which is down becomes right and that side which is up becomes left

151. The process of gastrulation in amphibian embryos starts from the dorsal lip of blastopore by
(a) epiboly (b) involution
(c) evagination (d) delamination

152. What may be the molecular trigger that causes cells in the presomitic mesoderm to finally condense into somites?
(a) A gradient of retinoic acid exists that emanates both anteriorly and posteriorly from the somites
(b) The FGF gradient drops off in the region that is forming somites
(c) Signaling from the receptor notch is required for somite formation
(d) Different Hox gene combinations are expressed along the antero-posterior axis of the embryo

153. What important lesson for the mechanisms of development can we derive from the ability to clone frogs by nuclear transfer?
(a) That the selective gene expression seen in differentiated cells does not result from an irreversible loss of genes, or their potential for expression
(b) That a piece of a frog can be 'planted' to obtain a new, cloned individual, just like in plants
(c) That the pattern of gene expression in a differentiated cell can only be reversed if the nucleus is removed from the cell
(d) That the mechanisms of development are irreversible in all organisms except frogs

154. What is the difference between apoptosis and necrosis?
(a) Apoptosis is a controlled program of cellular destruction, necrosis is cell death due to damage
(b) Apoptosis is a property of all differentiated cells, necrosis only occurs to undifferentiated cells
(c) Apoptosis is cell death due to damage that occurs during embryogenesis, necrosis is cell death due to damage that occurs during adulthood
(d) Apoptosis is the death of a differentiated cell, necrosis is the death of an undifferentiated cell

155. What is the role of the caspases in apoptosis?
(a) Caspase is a term used to refer to the initial signal that causes apoptosis
(b) Caspases are enzymes that are inactivated during apoptosis and in their absence the cell dies
(c) Caspases are inhibitors of apoptosis, the destruction of the caspases causes apoptosis to begin
(d) Caspases are proteases that carry out the controlled destruction of the cell's components during apoptosis

156. If apoptosis in the developing limb were blocked, what feature of a normal limb would not form?
(a) The bones and muscles would not form
(b) The overlying epidermis would not form
(c) The proximo distal patterning would not occur normally
(d) The digits would be connected by webbing and would not be separated

157. If the nerve supply to a newt limb is severed before amputation, how will this affect regeneration?
(a) It will have no effect, since regeneration involves growth of new muscle, bone and connective tissue
(b) Regeneration of most tissues will occur normally, but regeneration of the nerves will not occur
(c) Outgrowth will occur, but the identity of the limb will be lost and normal proximo-distal patterning will not occur
(d) A blastema will form but will not grow and regeneration will fail

158. 'Intercalary growth' in a regenerating amphibian limb means that if a distal blastema is grafted to a proximal stump
(a) the distal blastema grows back, to regenerate proximal elements, then out, to regenerate distal structures
(b) the stump grows out to regenerate proximal structures, until the positional values of the blastema are produced, at which time the distal blastema takes over and completes outgrowth of distal structures
(c) the distal blastema grows out, regenerating distal structures, resulting in a limb lacking intermediate structures
(d) the distal blastema grows proximally, intercalating intermediate structures between it and the stump, then growth stops, resulting in a regenerate lacking distal structures

159. How does the dose-dependence of retinoic acid treatment support the notion that a gradient of retinoic acid can act as a morphogen along the proximo-distal axis in the limb?
(a) Treatment with high levels of retinoic acid causes a proximal blastema to be respecified as a distal blastema and only distal structures are regenerated
(b) Treatment with high levels of retinoic acid causes any blastema to form only distal structures
(c) Treatment with high levels of retinoic acid causes any blastema to be respecified as a proximal blastema, but it will form only proximal structures
(d) Treatment with high levels of retinoic acid causes a distal blastema to be respecified as a proximal blastema and regeneration of a full limb may be initiated from proximal values

160. Is there a difference between oncogenes and tumour suppressor genes?
(a) Yes, oncogenes are genes that can cause cancer when they become mutated to become proto-oncogenes, whereas tumour suppressor genes play no role in cancer
(b) Yes, oncogenes prevent cancer from forming unless they are mutated to become proto-oncogenes, whereas tumour suppressor genes stimulate the formation of cancer even in the absence of mutation
(c) No, oncogenes and tumour suppressor genes both stimulate the development of cancer, even in the absence of their becoming mutated
(d) Yes, oncogenes are mutated versions of genes that promote abnormal cell division (such as ras and myc), whereas tumour suppressor genes are genes that normally hold cell division in check when it is not appropriate (such as Rb and p53)

161. Insects such as *Drosophila* undergo three molts before becoming a pupa and undergoing metamorphosis. Molting, which is also called 'ecdysis', is controlled by what hormone?
(a) Ecdysone
(b) Juvenile hormone
(c) Auxin
(d) Cytokinin

162. Metamorphosis of amphibians is triggered by environmental cues that act on the
(a) thyroid (b) pituitary
(c) hypothalamus (d) eye

163. Which one of the following acts as a precocious urinary bladder in which nitrogenous waste accumulates during the development of chick?
(a) Amnion (b) Allantois
(c) Somatopleure (d) Yolk sac

164. Which one of the following statement is not correct about metamorphosis in frog?
(a) The forelimbs, which develop under cover of the opercular membrane, break through to the exterior
(b) The middle ear develops in connection with the third pharyngeal pouch
(c) The eyes protrude on the dorsal surface of the head and develop eyelids
(d) The tongue is developed from the floor of the mouth

165. Consider the following developmental stages of frog
I. Neurula
II. Blastula
III. Morula
IV. Gastrula
Which of the above lack a blastopore?
(a) I and IV (b) II and III
(c) I, II and III (d) II, III and IV

166. With reference to gastrulation in chick, consider the following statements.
I. In the gastrulation of chick, there is neither invagination nor archenteron.
II. The place of origin of endoderm is anterior part of the blastoderm.
Which of the statements given above is/are correct?
(a) I only (b) II only
(c) Both I and II (d) Neither I nor II

167. Consider the following statements on extra-embryonic membranes in chick.
I. Allantois has inner layer of endoderm and outer layer of splanchnic mesoderm.
II. Yolk sac has an inner layer of endoderm and outer layer of splanchnic mesoderm.
III. Allantois has inner layer of splanchnic mesoderm and outer layer of endoderm.
IV. Yolk sac has inner layer of splanchnic mesoderm and outer layer of endoderm.
Which of the statements given above are correct?
(a) I and II (b) II and III
(c) III and IV (d) I and IV

168. Which statement correctly characterizes regeneration in the mammalian nervous system?

(a) In some instances, peripheral nerves can regenerate an axon if cut, such as when motor neurons regenerate axons to make correct connections with muscles
(b) Killed cells of the peripheral nervous system can be regenerated and will extend axons to restore connectivity with targets
(c) Cells of the brain can regenerate if damaged, but the peripheral nervous system is incapable of regeneration
(d) Fully functional regeneration in the mammalian nervous system has been shown to be possible when adult stem cell transplants are used

169. Is regeneration in *Hydra* similar to regeneration in vertebrates or is it fundamentally different in some way?

(a) Regeneration in *Hydra* occurs through a repatterning of existing cells by morphallaxis, unlike regeneration in vertebrates, which occurs through epimorphosis
(b) Regeneration in *Hydra* occurs through the reinitiation of cell division in existing cells, followed by repatterning of those cells, very much like regeneration in vertebrates
(c) Regeneration in *Hydra* occurs through the reinitiation of cell division in existing cells, followed by repatterning of those cells, which is totally different from regeneration in vertebrates
(d) Regeneration in *Hydra* occurs through the reinitiation of cell division in existing cells, followed by repatterning of those cells, whereas regeneration in vertebrates occurs through a process of repatterning of existing cells

170. What is the difference between 'fate' and 'specification'?

(a) If cells are transplanted from their normal region in an embryo to a different region in a recipient embryo, such cells will alter their fate, but not their specification
(b) Cell fate describes the allocation of cells to the germ layers, ectoderm, mesoderm or endoderm, whereas specification describes the exact tissues that each cell will ultimately become
(c) The fate map of an embryo does not change during development — the fate map of an egg is the same as the fate map of a late blastula — whereas the specification map of an embryo changes continually as the embryo's development proceeds
(d) The specification state of a cell is determined by transplantation of cells to recipient embryos, whereas the fate of a cell is determined by the culture of those cells in an artificial medium

171. The folding of sheets of cells, the migration of cells and cell death are all mechanisms of

(a) cleavage division (b) pattern formation
(c) morphogenesis (d) differentiation

172. The process by which developing cells achieve their functional, mature identity as liver or muscle or nerve is called

(a) cleavage division (b) pattern formation
(c) morphogenesis (d) differentiation

173. The establishment of the anterior-posterior or dorsal-ventral body axes is called

(a) division (b) pattern formation
(c) morphogenesis (d) differentiation

174. What observation might explain how somites originally become specified to form structures appropriate to their position along the antero-posterior axis?

(a) If pre-somitic mesoderm is rotated, the somites form in a reversed order
(b) Somites in the anterior of the embryo form before somites in the more posterior regions
(c) A gradient of retinoic acid exists that emanates both anteriorly and posteriorly from the somites
(d) Periodic waves of c-hairy1 are expressed in the presomitic mesoderm, such that cells in the more anterior somites will have been exposed to fewer waves of c-hairy1 than the cells in more posterior somites

175. With reference to the embryonic development of vertebrates, consider the following statements.

I. In the chick, the aminon and chorion have no blood vessels.
II. There is almost no yolk in mammalian eggs and therefore, their embryos have no yolk sac.

Which of the statements given above is/are correct?

(a) I only (b) II only
(c) Both I and II (d) Neither I nor II

176. The central zone overlying the sub-germinal cavity of developing egg of a chick is called

(a) area pellucida (b) area opaca
(c) epiblast (d) hypoblast

177. Consider the following statements.

I. By examining embryos and foetal stages of a vertebrate group, it is impossible to identify the group to which they belong.
II. Structural similarities exist in embryonic and larval stages, which are not apparent in adults.
III. During the development, chick first resembles a fish, then an amphibian and later a reptile.

Which of the statements given above is/are correct?

(a) I and II (b) I only
(c) II and III (d) I, II and III

178. Which one of the following is formed by mesoderm of gastrula?

(a) Central nervous system (b) Epidermis
(c) Circulatory system (d) Liver and pancreas

179. Which of the following changes are involved in retrogressive metamorphosis in ascidians?

I. Increase in the number of pharyngeal stigmata.
II. Complete disappearance of tail.
III. Disappearance of the endostyle and other parts of feeding mechanism.
IV. Disappearance of the eye and the otocyst.

Select the correct answer using the codes given below:

(a) II and IV (b) I and III
(c) I, II and IV (d) II, III and IV

180. In Eutherian mammals, the extraembryonic membrane (s) taking part in the formation of placenta is/are

(a) yolk sac

(b) allantois

(c) yolk sac and chorion

(d) chorion and allantois

181. Match the following lists.

List I (Extraembryonic Layers in Rabbit)	List II (Characteristic function of the Extraembryonic Layers)
A. Amnion	1. Somatopleure protects the embryo from mechanical shocks
B. Chorion	2. Splanchnopleure supplies O_2 and nutrients to the foetus
C. Allantois	3. Splanchnopleure develops villi
	4. Somatopleure develops villi

Codes

	A	B	C
(a)	2	4	1
(b)	2	1	3
(c)	1	3	2
(d)	1	4	2

182. Match the list I with litst II.

List I (Structure)	List II (Availability)
A. Amnion	1. Mammalian ovum
B. Primitive streak	2. Amphibian gastrula
C. Dorsal lip of blastopore	3. Chick's gastrula
D. Zona radiata	4. Reptilian embryo

Codes

	A	B	C	D
(a)	4	3	2	1
(b)	4	3	2	1
(c)	3	4	2	1
(d)	3	4	1	2

183. Match the list I with litst II.

List I (Pattern of Cleavage)	List II (Group of Animals)
A. Radial	1. Echinodermata
B. Spiral	2. Mollusca
C. Bilateral	3. Ascidia
D. Irregular	4. Coelenterata

Codes

	A	B	C	D
(a)	1	2	3	4
(b)	1	3	2	4
(c)	4	3	2	1
(d)	3	2	3	1

Answers

1. (c)	**2.** (a)	**3.** (a)	**4.** (d)	**5.** (c)	**6.** (d)	**7.** (b)	**8.** (d)	**9.** (b)	**10.** (a)
11. (c)	**12.** (d)	**13.** (d)	**14.** (c)	**15.** (c)	**16.** (a)	**17.** (b)	**18.** (d)	**19.** (d)	**20.** (b)
21. (c)	**22.** (a)	**23.** (c)	**24.** (c)	**25.** (d)	**26.** (c)	**27.** (d)	**28.** (b)	**29.** (a)	**30.** (c)
31. (c)	**32.** (b)	**33.** (b)	**34.** (c)	**35.** (c)	**36.** (a)	**37.** (d)	**38.** (c)	**39.** (d)	**40.** (a)
41. (b)	**42.** (a)	**43.** (d)	**44.** (d)	**45.** (d)	**46.** (b)	**47.** (a)	**48.** (c)	**49.** (d)	**50.** (d)
51. (a)	**52.** (b)	**53.** (d)	**54.** (a)	**55.** (d)	**56.** (d)	**57.** (a)	**58.** (c)	**59.** (b)	**60.** (c)
61. (d)	**62.** (c)	**63.** (a)	**64.** (b)	**65.** (c)	**66.** (d)	**67.** (a)	**68.** (b)	**69.** (d)	**70.** (d)
71. (c)	**72.** (a)	**73.** (c)	**74.** (b)	**75.** (d)	**76.** (d)	**77.** (c)	**78.** (b)	**79.** (c)	**80.** (d)
81. (a)	**82.** (b)	**83.** (c)	**84.** (d)	**85.** (d)	**86.** (d)	**87.** (d)	**88.** (d)	**89.** (d)	**90.** (b)
91. (c)	**92.** (a)	**93.** (d)	**94.** (b)	**95.** (c)	**96.** (d)	**97.** (a)	**98.** (d)	**99.** (a)	**100.** (d)
101. (c)	**102.** (d)	**103.** (c)	**104.** (d)	**105.** (d)	**106.** (a)	**107.** (b)	**108.** (a)	**109.** (d)	**110.** (d)
111. (c)	**112.** (d)	**113.** (a)	**114.** (a)	**115.** (b)	**116.** (d)	**117.** (d)	**118.** (b)	**119.** (a)	**120.** (d)
121. (a)	**122.** (d)	**123.** (a)	**124.** (a)	**125.** (b)	**126.** (b)	**127.** (d)	**128.** (c)	**129.** (d)	**130.** (d)
131. (d)	**132.** (a)	**133.** (d)	**134.** (d)	**135.** (a)	**136.** (d)	**137.** (c)	**138.** (b)	**139.** (a)	**140.** (b)
141. (b)	**142.** (c)	**143.** (b)	**144.** (a)	**145.** (b)	**146.** (c)	**147.** (c)	**148.** (a)	**149.** (d)	**150.** (c)
151. (b)	**152.** (b)	**153.** (a)	**154.** (a)	**155.** (d)	**156.** (d)	**157.** (d)	**158.** (b)	**159.** (d)	**160.** (d)
161. (a)	**162.** (c)	**163.** (b)	**164.** (b)	**165.** (b)	**166.** (d)	**167.** (a)	**168.** (a)	**169.** (a)	**170.** (b)
171. (c)	**172.** (d)	**173.** (b)	**174.** (d)	**175.** (d)	**176.** (a)	**177.** (c)	**178.** (c)	**179.** (d)	**180.** (d)
181. (c)	**182.** (b)	**183.** (a)							

16

Physiological Metabolism in Plants

Photosynthesis

The term **photosynthesis** means literally **synthesis using light.** Photosynthetic organisms use solar energy to synthesize carbon compounds. More specifically, light energy drives the synthesis of carbohydrates from carbon dioxide and water with the generation of oxygen:

$$6CO_2 + 12H_2O \longrightarrow C_6H_{12}O_6 + 6O_2 + 6H_2O$$

Energy stored in these molecules can be used later to power cellular processes in the plant and can serve as the energy source for all forms of life. The most active photosynthetic tissue in higher plants is the mesophyll of leaf. Mesophyll cells have many chloroplast, which contain the specialized light absorbing green pigment, the **chlorophyll.**

The light dependent reactions of photosynthesis take place in the specialized internal membranes of the chloroplast called thylakoids. The end products of these thylakoid reactions are the high energy compounds ATP and NADPH, which are used for the synthesis of sugars in the **carbon fixation reactions.**

In the chloroplast, light energy is converted into chemical energy by two different functional units called **photosystems.** The absorbed light energy is used to power the transfer of electrons through a series of compounds that act as electron donors and electron acceptors. The majority of electrons ultimately reduce $NADP^+$ to NADPH and oxidize water to oxygen. Light energy generate a proton motive force across the thylakoid membrane, which is used to synthesize ATP.

Chloroplast pigment belongs to two main groups:

1. Chlorophylls (green pigment) with two principle types
   Chlorophyll-*a* ($C_{55}H_{72}O_5N_4Mg$) bluish green
   Chlorophyll-*b* ($C_{55}H_{70}O_6N_4Mg$) olive green
2. Carotenoids (orange or yellow pigment) with two principle types
   Carotene (orange) β-carotene ($C_{40}H_{56}$)
   Xanthophylls (yellow) lutein ($C_{40}H_{56}O_2$)

Syllabus

- Photosynthesis: Light Harvesting Complexes, Mechanisms of Electron Transport; Photoprotective Mechanisms; CO_2 Fixation, C_3, C_4 and CAM Pathways.
- Respiration and Photorespiration: Glycolysis: A Cytosolic Process, Citric Acid Cycle; Plant Mitochondrial Electron Transport, ATP Synthesis, Alternate Oxidase; Photorespiratory Pathway.
- Nitrogen Metabolism: Nitrate and Ammonium Assimilation; Amino Acid Biosynthesis.

Chlorophyll appears green to our eyes because it absorbs light mainly in the red and blue parts of the spectrum, and some of the light enriched in green wavelengths (about 550 nm) is reflected into our eye.

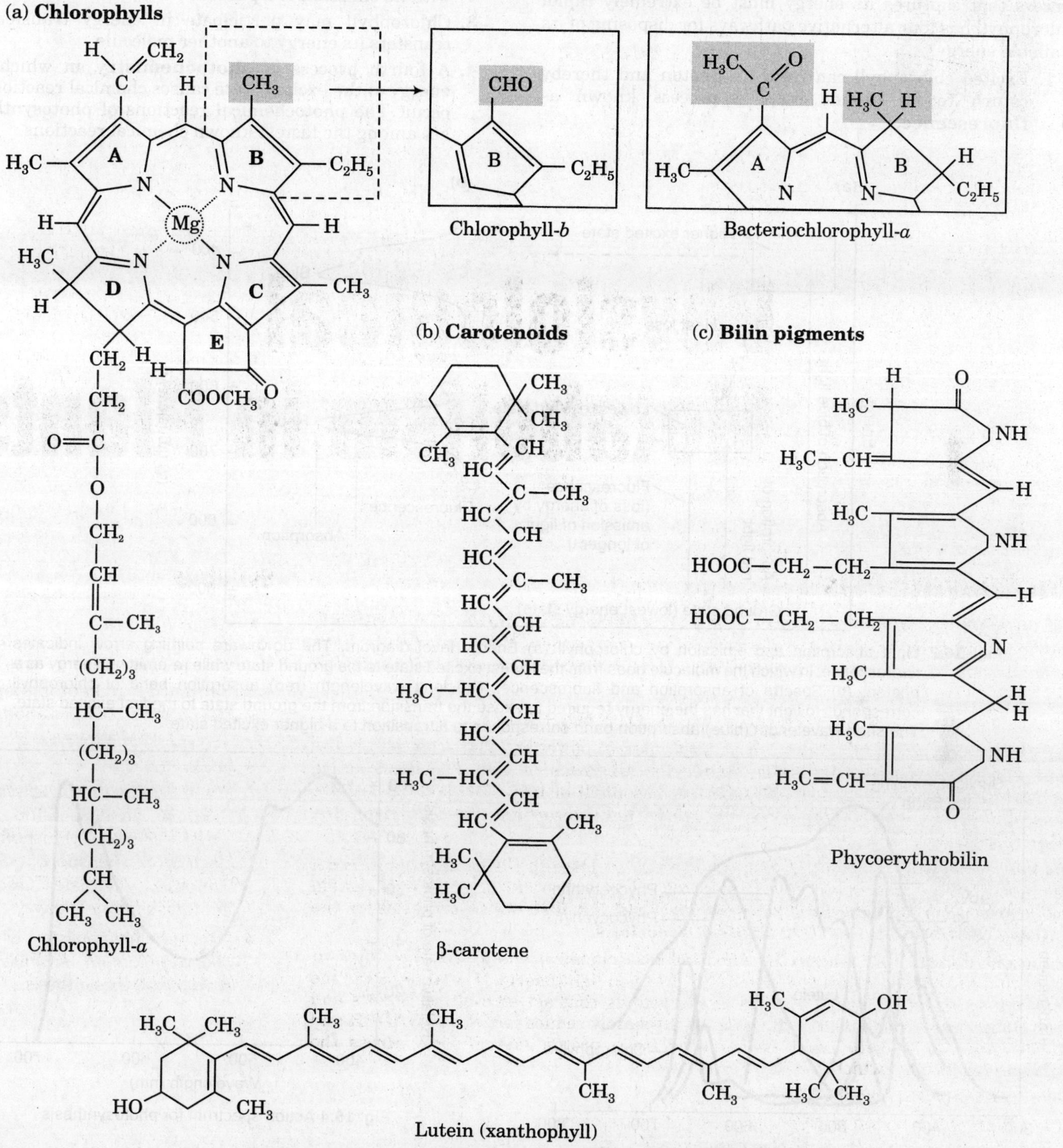

Fig. 16.1 Plant pigments chlorophyll, carotenoids and bilin pigments

The absorption of light by chlorophyll (Chl) in its lowest energy, or ground state makes a transition to a higher energy or excited state (Chl*).

$$\text{Chl} + h\nu \longrightarrow \text{Chl}^*$$

The distribution of electrons in the excited molecule is different from the distribution in the ground state molecule.

Absorption of **blue light** excites the chlorophyll to a higher energy state than absorption of **red light** because the energy of photons is higher when their wavelength is shorter. In the higher excited state, chlorophyll is extremely unstable, very rapidly gives up some of its energy to the surroundings as heat, and enters the lowest excited state, where it can be stable for a maximum of several nanoseconds (10^{-9} s). Because of this inherent instability of the excited state, any process that captures its energy must be extremely rapid. Chlorophyll has four alternative pathways for disposing of its available energy.

1. Excited chlorophyll can reemit a photon and thereby return to its ground state a process known as **fluorescence**.
2. The excited chlorophyll can return to its ground state by directly converting its excitation energy into heat, with no emission of a photon.
3. Chlorophyll may participate in energy transfer, by transfers its energy to another molecule.
4. A fourth process is **photochemistry**, in which the energy of the excited state causes chemical reactions to occur. The photochemical reactions of photosynthesis are among the fastest known chemical reactions.

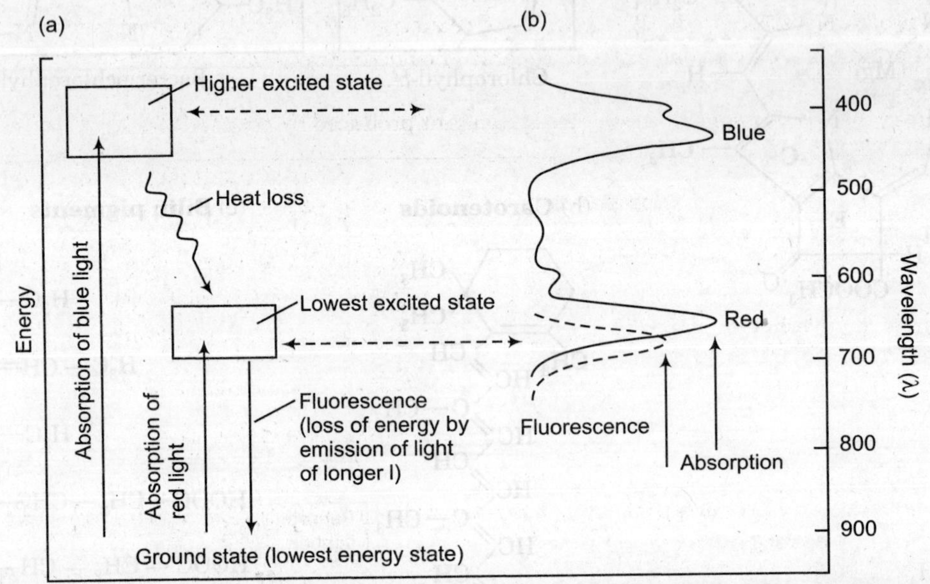

Fig. 16.2 Light absorption and emission by chlorophyll (a) Energy level diagram. The downward pointing arrow indicates fluorescence, in which the molecule goes from the lowest excited state to the ground state while re-emitting energy as a photon. (b) Spectra of absorption and fluorescence. The long wavelength (red) absorption band of chlorophyll corresponds to light that has the energy required to cause the transition from the ground state to the first excited state. The short wavelength (blue) absorption band corresponds to a transition to a higher excited state.

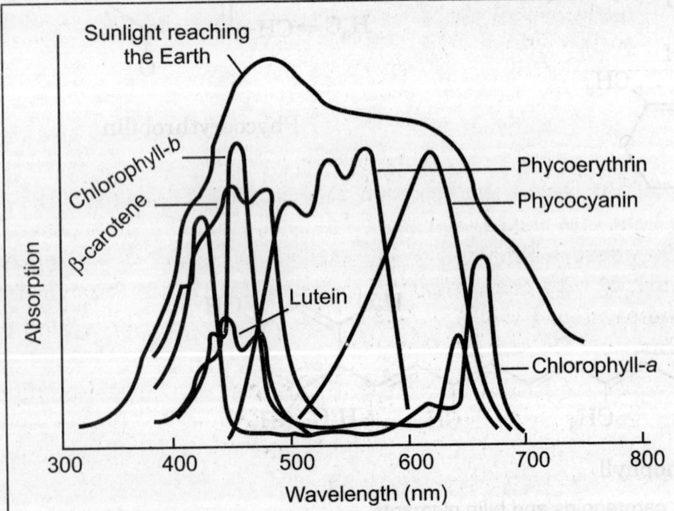

Fig. 16.3 Absorption of visible light by photopigments

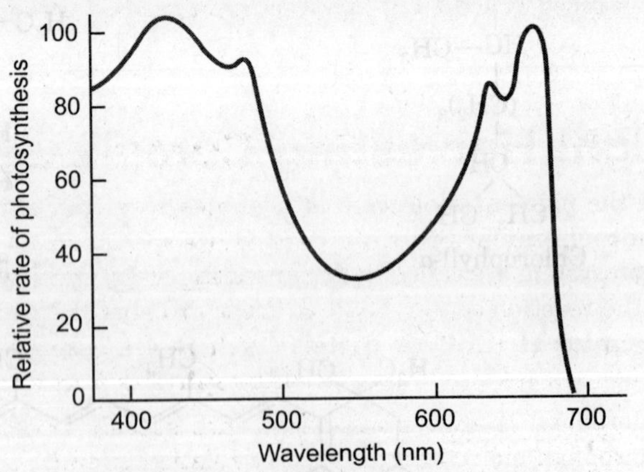

Fig. 16.4 Action spectrum for photosynthesis

Plants are green because their pigments absorb light from the red and blue regions of the spectrum, leaving primarily green light to be reflected or transmitted.

An action spectrum (as shown here) describes the relative rate of photosynthesis for illumination with a constant number of photons of different wavelengths. An action spectrum is useful because, by comparison with absorption spectra, it suggests which pigments can channel energy into photosynthesis.

Photosynthesis in plants encompasses two processes the **light dependent reactions** or **light reactions,** which occur only when plants are illuminated, and the **carbon-assimilation reactions** (or **carbon fixation reactions**). In the light reactions, chlorophyll and other pigments of photosynthetic cells absorb light energy and conserve it as ATP and NADPH, simultaneously, O_2 is evolved. In the carbon assimilation reactions, ATP and NADPH are used to reduce CO_2 to form triose phosphates, starch sucrose and other products derived from them.

Oxygen evolving organisms have two photosystems that operate in series. These two photosystems came into a light due to phenomenon of **red drop** and **enhancement effect**. These observations were eventually explained by experiments performed in the 1960s that led to the discovery that two photochemical complexes, now known as **photosystems-I** and **II** (**PS-I** and **PS-II**), operate in series to carry out the early energy storage reactions of photosynthesis.

1. Photosystem-I produces a strong reductant, capable of reducing $NADP^+$ and a weak oxidant.
2. Photosystem-II produces a very strong oxidant, capable of oxidizing water and a weaker reductant than the one produced by photosystem-I.

The reductant produced by photosystem-II rereduces the oxidant produced by photosystem-I.

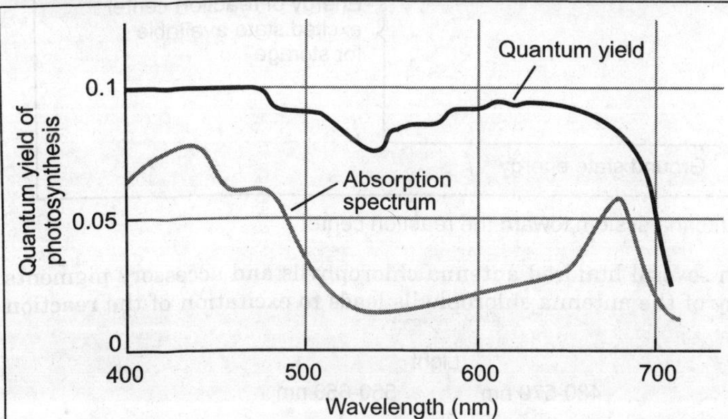

Fig. 16.5 Red drop effect

The quantum yield of photosynthesis falls off drastically for far red light of wavelength greater than 680 nm, indicating that far-red light alone is inefficient in driving photosynthesis. The slight dip near 500 nm reflects the somewhat lower efficiency of photosynthesis using light absorbed by accessory pigments, carotenoids.

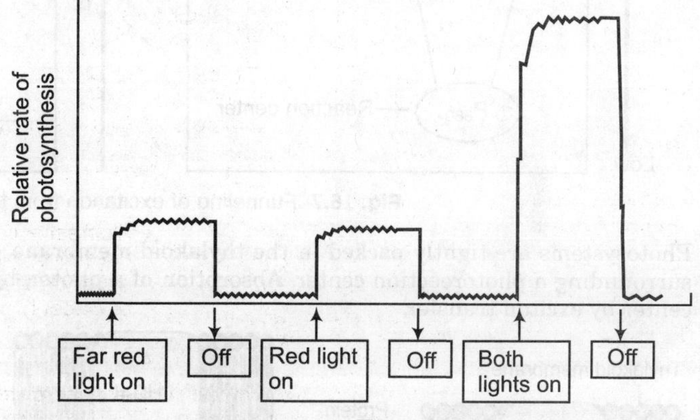

Fig. 16.6 Enhancement effect

The rate of photosynthesis when red and far-red light are given together is greater than the sum of the rates when they are given apart. The enhancement effect provided essential evidence in favour of the concept that photosynthesis is carried out by two photochemical systems working in tandem but with slightly different wavelength optima.

Light Harvesting Complexes

All the pigment molecules in a photosystem can absorb photons, but only a few chlorophyll molecules associated with the **photochemical reaction center** are specialized to transduce light into chemical energy. The other pigment molecules in a photosystem are called light harvesting or antenna molecules. They absorb light energy and transmit it rapidly and efficiently to the reaction center. Some of these proteins are associated primarily with photosystem-II and are called **Light Harvesting Complex-II** (LHC-II) proteins, others are associated with photosystem-I and are called **LHCI** proteins. These antenna complexes are also known as **chlorophyll-*a*/*b* antenna proteins.**

Chlorophyll is always associated with specific binding proteins, forming **Light Harvesting Complexes** (LHCs) in which chlorophyll molecules are fixed in relation to each other, to other protein complexes, and to the membrane. It contains seven molecules of chlorophyll-*a*, five of chlorophyll-*b*, and two of the accessory pigment lutein. Cyanobacteria and red algae employ **phycobilins** such as phycoerythrobilin and phycocyanobilin as their light harvesting pigments.

The association of **LHC-II** with **PS-II** is regulated by light intensity and wavelength. In bright sunlight (with a large component of blue light), PS-II absorbs more light than PS-I and produces reduced plastoquinone (plastoquinol, PQH_2) faster than PS-I can oxidize it. The resulting accumulation of PQH_2 activates a protein kinase that phosphorylates a Thr residue on LHC-II. Phosphorylation weakens the interaction of LHC-II with PS-II, and some LHC-II dissociates and moves to the stromal lamellae, here it captures photons for PS-I, speeding the oxidation of PQH_2 and reversing the imbalance between electron flow in PS-I and PS-II. In less intense light (in the shade, with more red light), PS-I oxidizes PQH2 faster than PS-II can make it, and the resulting increase in PQ concentration triggers dephosphorylation of LHC-II, reversing the effect of phosphorylation.

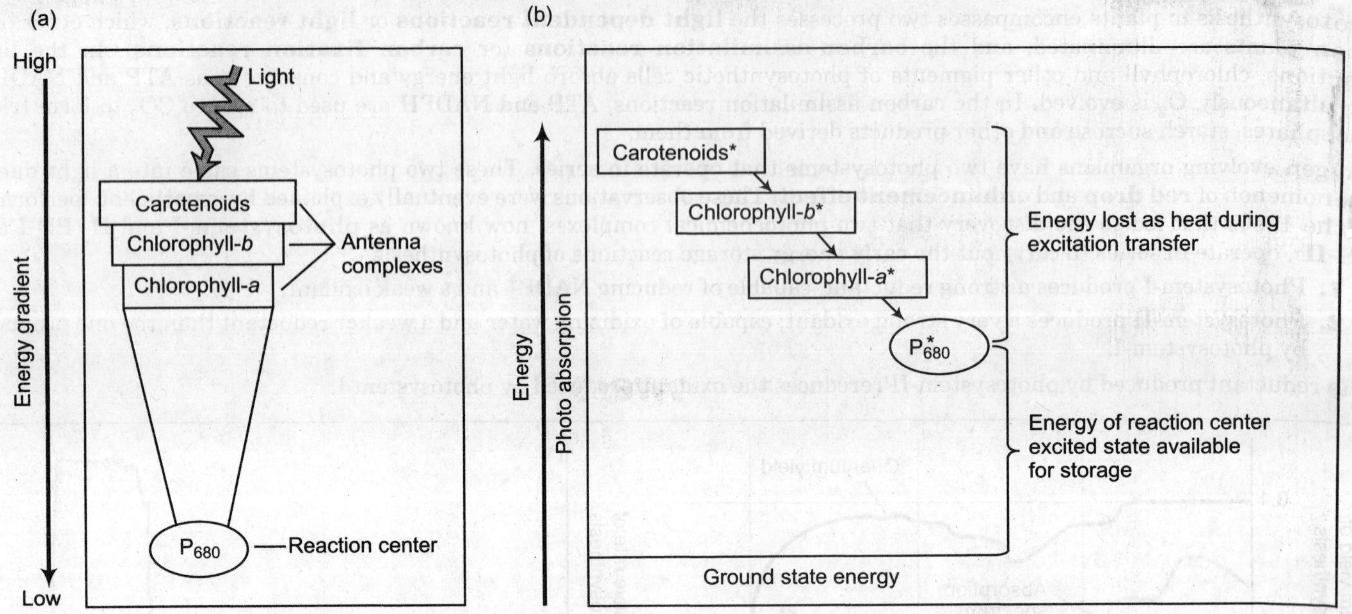

Fig. 16.7 Funneling of excitation from the antenna system toward the reaction center

Photosystems are tightly packed in the thylakoid membrane, with several hundred antenna chlorophylls and accessory pigments surrounding a photoreaction center. Absorption of a photon by any of the antenna chlorophylls leads to excitation of the reaction center by exciton transfer.

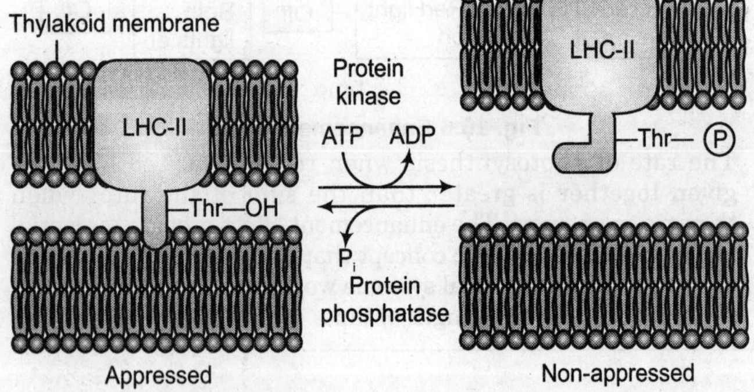

Fig. 16.8 Equalization of electron flow in PS-I and PS-II by modulation of granal stacking. A hydrophobic domain of LHCII in one thylakoid lamella inserts into the neighbouring lamella and closely appresses the two membranes

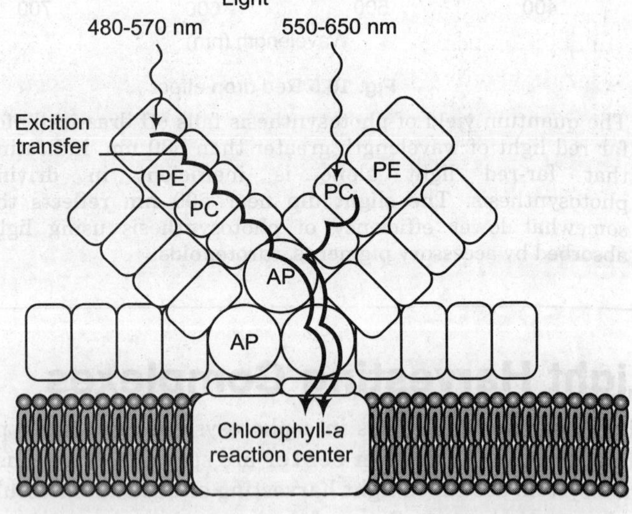

Fig. 16.9 Transfer of light energy by phycobilisome

In these highly structured assemblies found in cyanobacteria and red algae, phycobilin pigments bound to specific proteins forming complexes called phycoerythrin (PE), phycocyanin (PC) and allophycocyanin (AP). The energy of photons absorbed by PE or PC is conveyed through AP (a phycocyanobilin binding protein) to chlorophyll-*a* of the reaction center by exciton transfer.

Cyanobacteria and red algae employ **phycobilins** such as phycoerythrobilin and phycocyanobilin as their light harvesting pigments. These open chain tetrapyrroles have the extended polyene system found in chlorophylls, but not their cyclic structure or central Mg^{2+}. Phycobilins are covalently linked to specific binding proteins, forming **phycobiliproteins,** which associate in highly ordered complexes called phycobilisomes that constitute the primary light harvesting structures in these microorganisms.

Photosystem-I and **II** are spatially separated in the thylakoid membrane. Photosystem-II is located predominantly in the stacked regions of the thylakoid membrane photosystem I and ATP synthase are found in the unstacked regions protruding into the stroma. Cytochrome-b_6f complexes are evenly distributed. This lateral separation of the two photosystems requires that electrons and protons produced by photosystem-II be transported a considerable distance before they can be acted on by photosystem-I and the ATP coupling enzyme.

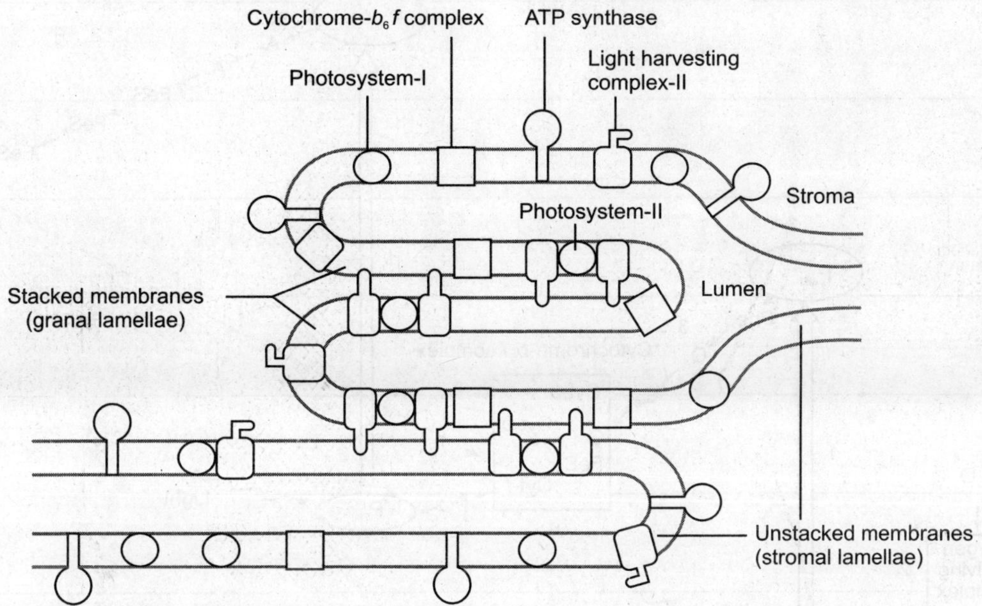

Fig. 16.10 Organization of the protein complexes of the thylakoid membrane

Most measurements of the relative quantities of photosystems I and II have shown that there is an excess of photosystem-II in chloroplasts. Most commonly, the ratio of PS-II to PS-I is about 1.5:1, but it can change when plants are grown in different light conditions.

Anoxygenic photosynthetic bacteria have a reaction center similar to that of photosystem-II. Non-oxygen evolving (anoxygenic) organisms, such as the purple photosynthetic bacteria of the genera *Rhodobacter* and *Rhodopseudomonas*, contain only a single photosystem.

Mechanisms of Electron Transport

The scheme of photosynthesis depicted in figure below called the ***Z*** (*zig-zag*) **scheme**, has become the basis for understanding O_2 evolving (oxygenic) photosynthetic organisms. It accounts for the operation of two physically and chemically distinct photosystems (I and II), each with its own antenna pigments and photochemical reaction center. The two photosystems are linked by an electron transport chain.

In *Z* scheme of O_2 evolving photosynthetic organisms.

The redox carriers are placed at their midpoint redox potentials.

1. The vertical arrows represent photon absorption by the reaction center chlorophylls P_{680} for photosystem-II (PS-II) and P_{700} for photosystem-I (PS-I). The excited PS-II reaction center chlorophyll, $P_{680}{}^*$, transfers an electron to pheophytin (Pheo).
2. On the oxidizing side of PS-II (to the left of the arrow joining P_{680} with $P_{680}{}^*$), P_{680} oxidized by light is re-reduced by Y_z , that has received electrons from oxidation of water.
3. On the reducing side of PS-II, **pheophytin** transfers electrons to the acceptors Q_A and Q_B, which are plastoquinones.
4. The cytochrome-b_6f complex transfers electrons to plastocyanin (PC), a soluble protein, which in turn reduces $P_{700}{}^*$ (oxidized P_{700}).
5. The acceptor of electrons from $P_{700}{}^*$ (A_0) is thought to (A_1) be a chlorophyll, and the next acceptor is a quinone. A series of membrane bound iron-sulphur proteins (F_eS_X, F_eS_A and F_eS_B) transfers electrons to soluble ferredoxin (Fd).
6. The soluble flavoprotein ferredoxin–NADP reductase (FNR) reduces $NADP^+$ to NADPH, which is used in the Calvin cycle to reduce CO_2.

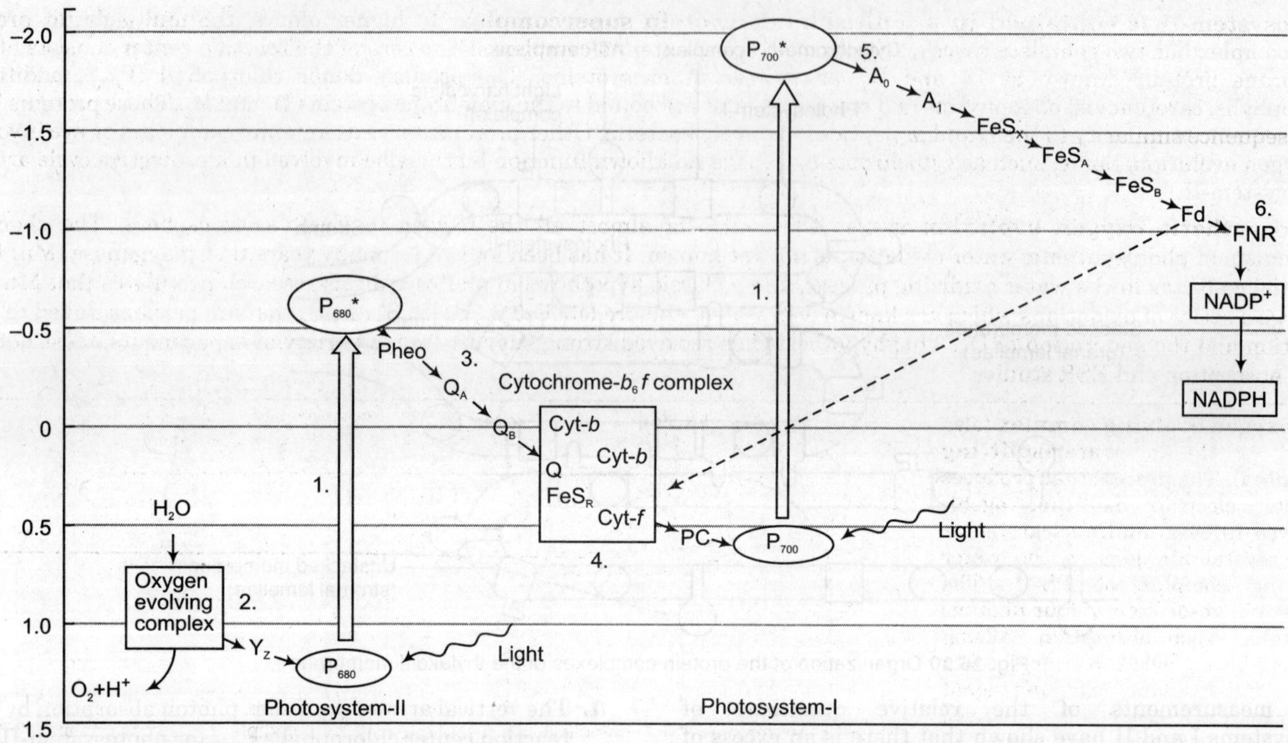

Fig. 16.11 *Z* scheme of photosynthesis. Red light absorbed by photosystem-II (PS-II) produces a strong oxidant and a weak reductant. Far-red light absorbed by photosystem-I (PS-I) produces a weak oxidant and a strong reductant. The strong oxidant generated by PS-II oxidizes water, while the strong reductant produced by PS-I reduces $NADP^+$. This scheme is basic to an understanding of photosynthetic electron transport. P_{680} and P_{700} refer to the wavelengths of maximum absorption of the reaction center chlorophylls in PS-II and PS-I, respectively.

The transfer of electrons and protons in the thylakoid membrane is carried out by four protein complexes. Water is oxidized and protons are released in the lumen by PS-II.

PS-I reduces $NADP^+$ to NADPH in the stroma, *via* the action of ferredoxin (Fd) and the flavoprotein ferredoxin–NADP reductase (FNR). Protons are also transported into the lumen by the action of the cytochrome-b_6 *f* complex and contribute to the electrochemical proton gradient. These protons must then diffuse to the ATP synthase enzyme, where their diffusion down the electrochemical potential gradient is used to synthesize ATP in the stroma. Reduced plastoquinone (PQH_2) and plastocyanin transfer electrons to cytochrome-b_6 *f* and to PS-I, respectively.

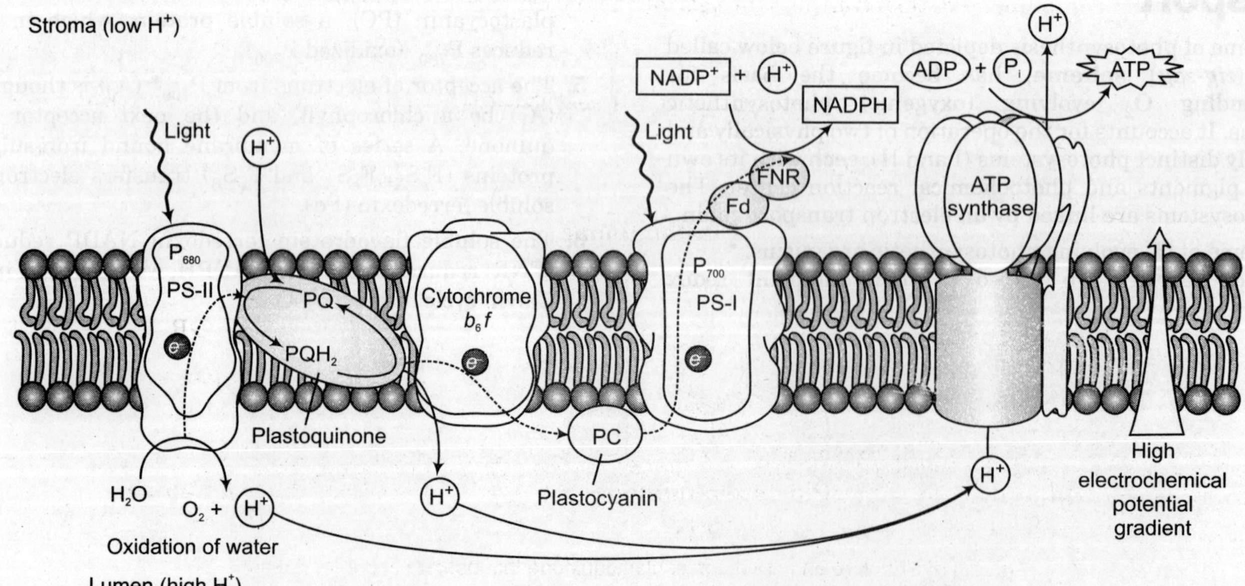

Fig. 16.12 The transfer of electrons and protons in the thylakoid membrane

Photosystem-II is contained in a multisubunit protein supercomplex. In higher plants, the multisubunit protein supercomplex has two complete reaction centers and some antenna complexes. The core of the reaction center consists of two membrane proteins known as D_1 and D_2, as well as other proteins. The primary donor chlorophyll (P_{680}), additional chlorophylls, carotenoids, pheophytins and plastoquinones are bound to the membrane proteins D_1 and D_2. These proteins have some sequence similarity to the L and M peptides of purple bacteria. Other proteins serve as antenna complexes or are involved in oxygen evolution. Some, such as cytochrome-b_{559}, have no known function but may be involved in a protective cycle around photosystem-II.

Photosynthetic oxygen evolution is also the source of almost all the oxygen in Earth's atmosphere. The chemical mechanism of photosynthetic water oxidation is not yet known. It has been known for many years that manganese (Mn) is an essential co-factor in the water oxidizing process, and a classic hypothesis in photosynthesis research postulates that Mn ions undergo a series of oxidations which are known as S states, and are labelled S_0, S_1, S_2,S_3 and S_4 that are perhaps linked to H_2O oxidation and the generation of O_2. This hypothesis has received strong support from a variety of experiments, most notably X-ray absorption and ESR studies.

The **oxygen evolving complex** (also called the **water-splitting complex**). The process that produces a four electron oxidizing agent, believed to be a multinuclear center with several Mn ions in the water splitting complex of PS-II. The sequential absorption of four photons (excitons), each absorption causing the loss of one electron from the Mn center, produces an oxidizing agent that can remove four electrons from two molecules of water, producing O_2. The electrons lost from the Mn center pass one at a time to an oxidized Tyr residue in a PS-II protein, then to P_{680}^*.

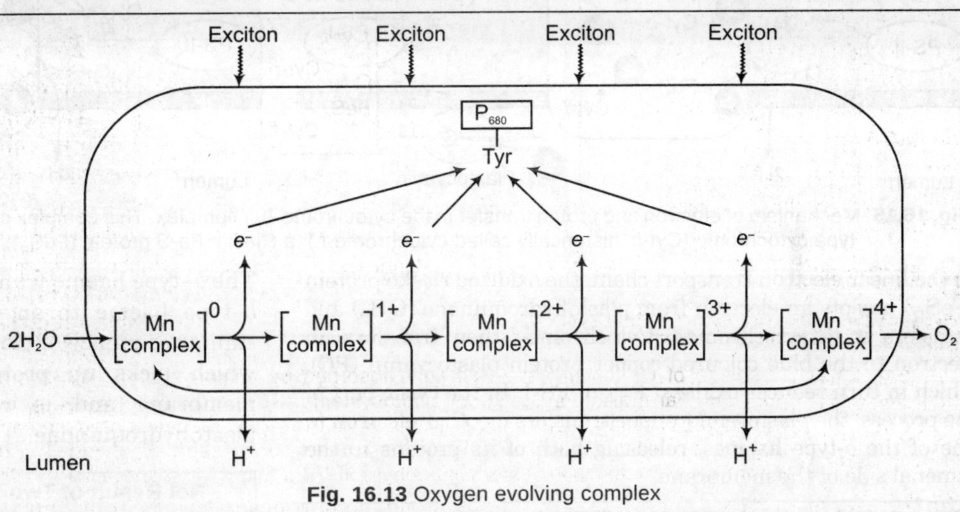

Fig. 16.13 Oxygen evolving complex

One electron carrier, Y_z, functions between the oxygen evolving complex and P_{680}. This species has been identified as a radical formed from a tyrosine residue in the D_1 protein of the PS-II reaction center.

Pheophytin is a chlorophyll in which the central magnesium atom has been replaced by two hydrogen atoms. This chemical change gives pheophytin chemical and spectral properties that are slightly different from those of chlorophyll.

Two plastoquinones (Q_A and Q_B) are bound to the reaction center and receive electrons from pheophytin in a sequential fashion. The plastohydroquinone in turn transfers its electrons to the cytochrome-b_6 *f* complex.

H_3C, H_3C, O, O, $-(CH_2-C(CH_3)=CH-CH_2)_9-H$

Plastoquinone

Quinone (Q) $+ e^- \longrightarrow$ **Plastosemiquinone** ($Q^{\cdot-}$) $+ 1e^- \longrightarrow + 2H^+ \longrightarrow$ **Plastohydroquinone** (QH_2)

Fig. 16.14 Structure and reactions of plastoquinone that operate in photosystem II

The cytochrome-b_6 *f* complex is a large multisubunit protein with several prosthetic groups . It contains two *b* type haemae and one *c* type haeme (**cytochrome-*f***). In *c* type cytochromes the haeme is covalently attached to the peptide; in *b* type cytochromes the chemically similar protoheme group is not covalently attached.

In **Q cycle mechanism**, plastohydroquinone (QH_2) is oxidized, and one of the two electrons is passed along a linear electron transport chain toward photosystem-I, while the other electron goes through a cyclic process that increases the number of protons pumped across the membrane.

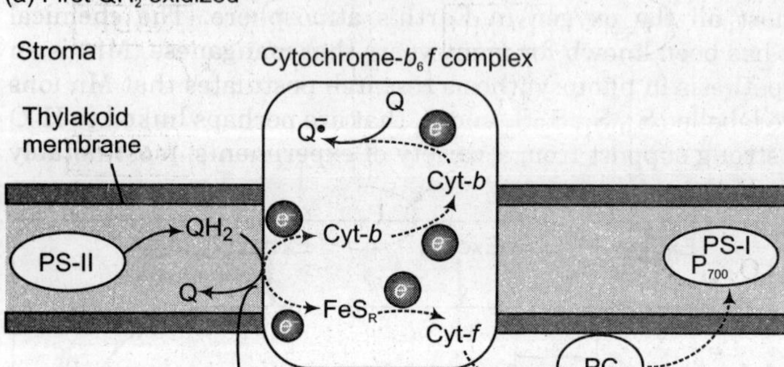

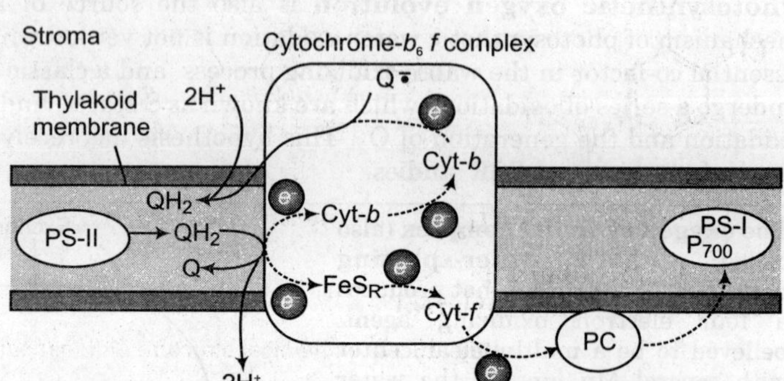

Fig. 16.15 Mechanism of electron and proton transfer in the cytochrome-b_6 *f* complex. This complex contains two *b*-type cytochromes (Cyt-*b*), a *c* type cytochrome (Cyt-*c*, historically called cytochrome-*f*), a Rieske Fe-S protein (FeS_R), and two quinone oxidation-reduction sites

In the linear electron transport chain, the oxidized rieske protein (**FeS_R**) accepts an electron from plastohydroquinone (QH_2) and transfers it to cytochrome-*f*. Cytochrome-*f* then transfers an electron to the blue coloured copper protein plastocyanin (PC), which in turn reduces oxidized P_{700} of PS-I. In the cyclic part of the process, the plastosemiquinone transfers its other electron to one of the *b*-type haemes, releasing both of its protons to the lumenal side of the membrane.

Structural model of the PS-I reaction center. Components of the PS-I reaction center are organized around two major proteins, PsaA and PsaB. Minor proteins PsaC to PsaN are labelled C to N.

Electrons are transferred from plastocyanin (PC) to P_{700} and then to a chlorophyll molecule, A_0, to phylloquinone, A_1, to the FeS_X, FeS_A and FeS_B and finally to the soluble iron–sulphur protein, ferredoxin (Fd)

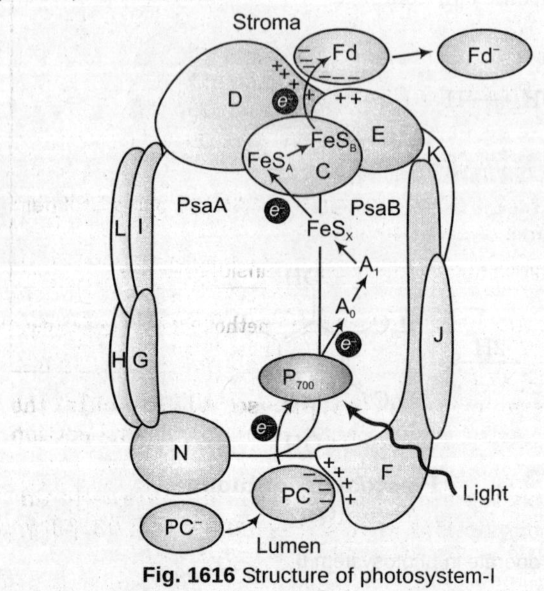

Fig. 1616 Structure of photosystem-I

The *b*–type haeme transfers its electron through the second *b*–type haeme to an oxidized quinone molecule. Another similar sequence of electron flow reduces the plastoquinone, which picks up protons from the stromal side of the membrane and is released from the b_6f complex as plastohydroquinone.

Net Result of Two Turnovers of the Cytochrome-b_6 *f* complex	
Electrons are transferred to P_{600}	Two
Plastohydroquinones are oxidized to the quinone	Two
Oxidized plastoquinone is reduced to the hydroquinone	One
Protons transferred from the stromal to the lumenal side of the membrane	Four

The cytochrome-b_6 *f* complex, electron flow connecting the acceptor side of the PS-II reaction center to the donor side of the PS-I reaction center also gives rise to an electrochemical potential across the membrane. This electrochemical potential is used to **power the synthesis of ATP**.

Plastoquinone and **plastocyanin** carry electrons between photosystems-II and I. The cytochrome-b_6 *f* complex is distributed equally between the grana and the stroma regions of the membranes, but its large size makes, plastoquinone or plastocyanin to serve as mobile carriers to connect the two photosystems.

Plastocyanin is a small (10.5 kDa), water soluble, copper-containing protein that transfers electrons between the cytochrome-b_6 *f* complex and P_{700}. This protein is found in the lumenal space.

In certain green algae and cyanobacteria, a-***c*-type cytochrome** is sometimes found instead of plastocyanin, which of these two proteins is synthesized depends on the amount of copper available to the organism.

Chemical structure of dichlorophenyl-dimethylurea (DCMU) and methyl viologen (paraquat), two herbicides that block photosynthetic electron flow. DCMU is also known as diuron.

Sites of action of the two herbicides. DCMU blocks electron flow at the quinone acceptors of photosystem II, by competing for the binding site of plastoquinone. Paraquat acts by accepting electrons from the early acceptors of photosystem-I.

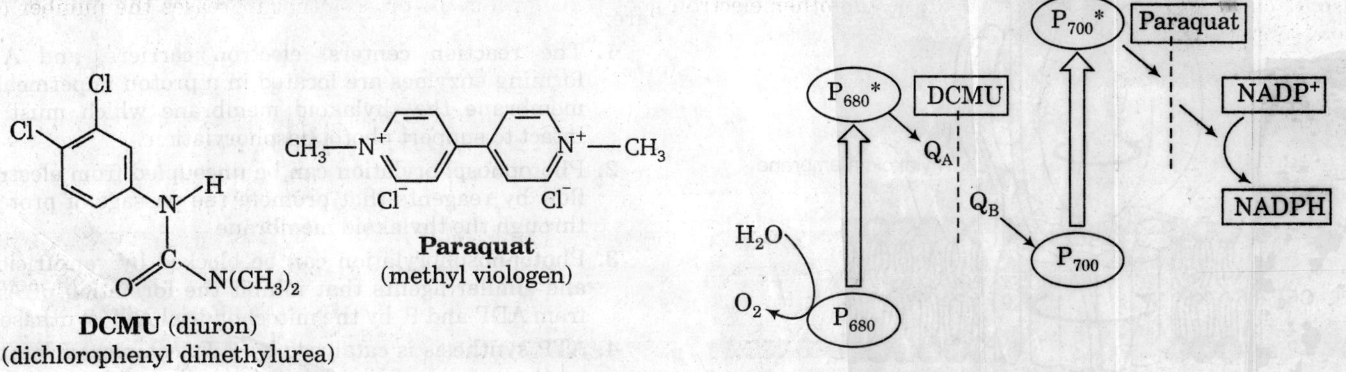

Fig. 16.17 Chemical structure and mechanism of action of two important herbicides

Agents that Interfere with Oxidative Phosphorylation or Photophosphorylation

Type of Interference	Compound*	Target/Mode of Action
Inhibition of electron transfer	Cyanide Carbon monoxide	Inhibit cytochrome oxidase
	Antimycin A	Blocks electron transfer from cytochrome-*b* to cytochrome-c_1
	Myxothiazol Rotenone Amytal Piericidin A	Prevent electron transfer from Fe-S center to ubiquinone
	DCMU	Competes with Q_B for binding site in PS-II
Inhibition of ATP synthase	Aurovertin	Inhibits F_1
	Oligomycin Venturicidin	Inhibit F_0 and CF_0
	DCCD	Blocks proton flow through F_0 and CF_0
Uncoupling of phosphorylation from electron transfer	FCCP DNP	Hydrophobic proton carriers
	Valinomycin	K^+ ionophore
	Thermogenin	In brown fat, forms proton conducting pores in inner mitochondrial membrane
Inhibition of ATP-ADP exchange	Atractyloside	Inhibits adenine nucleotide translocase

*DCMU is 3-(3, 4-dichlorophenyl)-1, 1-dimethylurea, DCCD, dicylohexylcarbodimide, FCCP, cyanide-*p*-trifluoromethoxphenyl-hydrazone, DNP, 2, 4-dinitrophenol.

The ATP is synthesized by a large (400 kDa) enzyme complex known by several names, **ATP synthase**, **ATPase** (after the reverse reaction of ATP hydrolysis), and **CF_0-CF_1**. This enzyme consists of two parts, a hydrophobic membrane bound portion called CF_0 and a portion that sticks out into the stroma called CF_1.

This enzyme consists of a large multisubunit complex, CF_1, attached on the stromal side of the membrane to an integral membrane portion, known as CF_0. CF_1 consists of five different polypeptides, with a stoichiometry of α3, β3, γ, δ, ε. CF_0 contains probably four different polypeptides, with a stoichiometry of α, β, β′, γ_{12}.

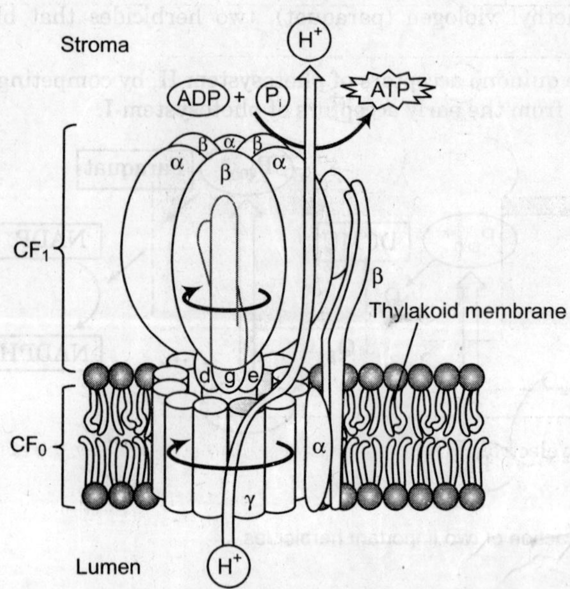

Fig. 16.18 Structure of ATP synthase

The light energy captured by the photosynthetic systems of these organisms is transformed into the phosphate bond energy of ATP. This process is called **photophosphorylation.** Properties of photosynthetic electron transfer and photophosphorylation in chloroplasts are:

1. The reaction centers, electron carriers, and ATP forming enzymes are located in a proton impermeable membrane the thylakoid membrane which must be intact to support photophosphorylation.
2. Photophosphorylation can be uncoupled from electron flow by reagents that promote the passage of protons through the thylakoid membrane.
3. Photophosphorylation can be blocked by venturicidin and similar agents that inhibit the formation of ATP from ADP and P_i by the mitochondrial ATP synthase.
4. ATP synthesis is catalyzed by F_0F_1 complexes, located on the outer surface of the thylakoid membranes, that are very similar in structure and function to the F_0F_1 complexes of mitochondria.

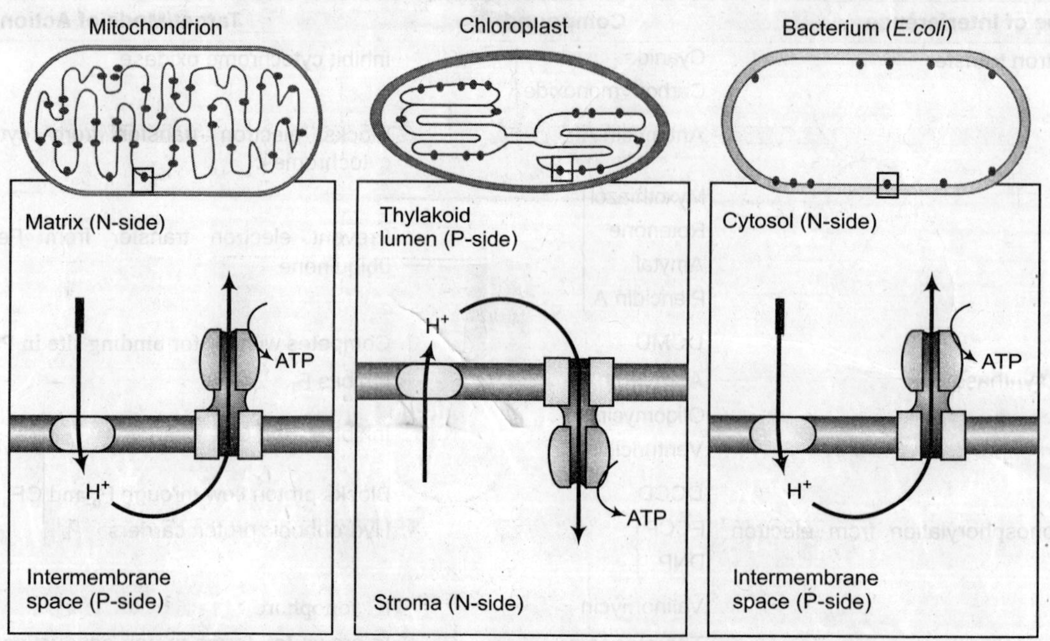

Fig. 16.19 Topology of proton movement and ATP synthase orientation

Similarities of photosynthetic and respiratory electron flow in bacteria, chloroplasts and mitochondria. In all three, electron flow is coupled to proton translocation, creating a transmembrane proton motive force. The energy in the proton motive force is then used for the synthesis of ATP by ATP synthase.

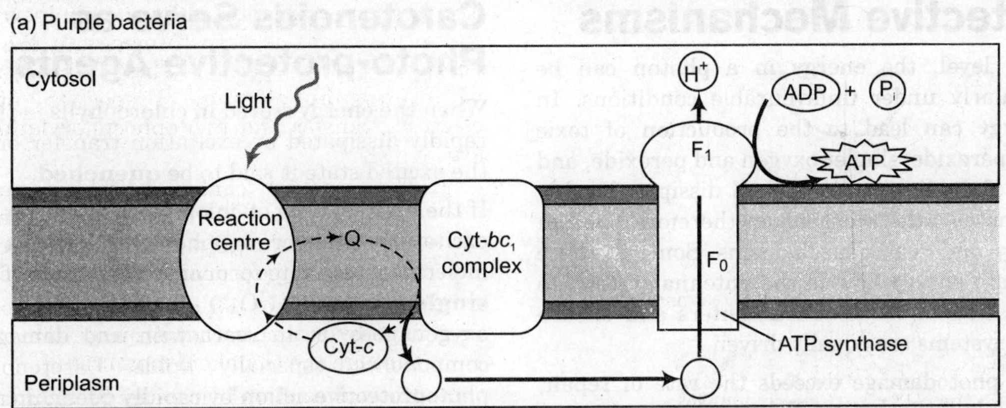

A reaction center (RC) in purple photosynthetic bacteria carries out cyclic electron flow, generating a proton potential by the action of the cytochrome-bc_1 complex.

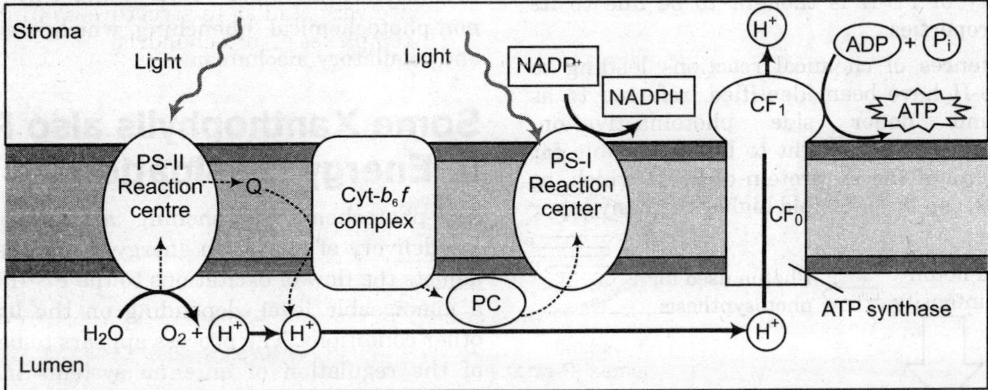

Chloroplasts carry out non-cyclic electron flow, oxidizing water and reducing $NADP^+$. Protons are produced by the oxidation of water and by the oxidation of PQH2 (Q) by the cytochrome-b_6f complex.

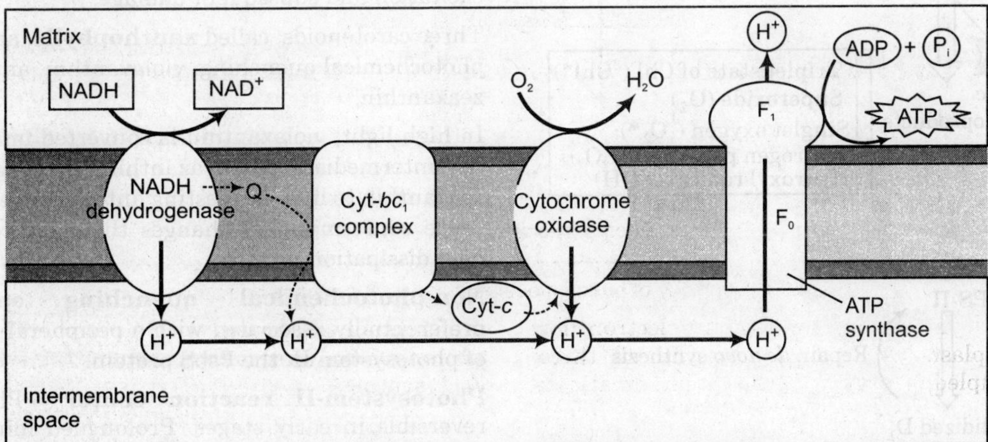

Fig. 16.20 Photosynthetic and respiratory electron flow

Mitochondria oxidize NADH to NAD^+ and reduce oxygen to water. Protons are pumped by the enzyme NADH dehydrogenase, the cytochrome-bc_1 complex and cytochrome oxidase. The ATP synthases in the three systems are very similar in structure.

Photoprotective Mechanisms

At the molecular level, the energy in a photon can be damaging, particularly under unfavourable conditions. In excess, light energy can lead to the production of toxic species, such as superoxide, singlet oxygen and peroxide, and damage can occur if the light energy is not dissipated safely (Photodamage). Photosynthetic organisms therefore, contain complex regulatory and repair mechanisms. Some of these mechanisms regulate energy flow in the antenna system, to avoid excess excitation of the reaction centers and ensure that the two photosystems are equally driven.

When the rate of photodamage exceeds the rate of repair, there is a drop in photosynthetic efficiency, a phenomenon known as **photoinhibition.**

The main site of photodamage is the PS-II reaction center. PS-I is relatively immune from photodamage, and the particular sensitivity of PS-II is thought to be due to its unusual chemical properties.

Two different sequences of chemical reactions leading to photodamage of PS-II have been identified, referred to as acceptor side and donor side photoinactivation. Photoinactivation of PS-II is thought to be responsible for the high turnover rate of the D_1 protein of PS-II which, at high light intensities, can be 50-80 fold higher than any other thylakoid protein.

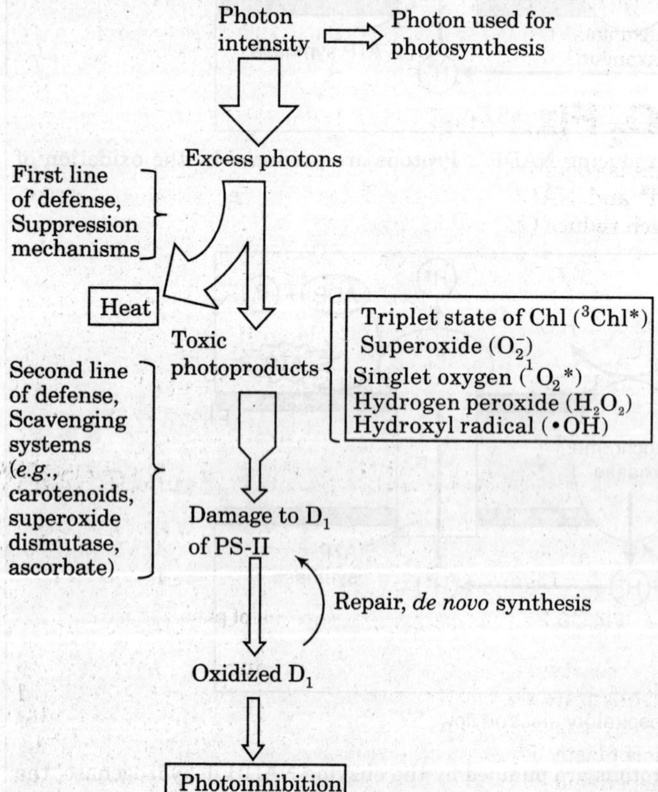

Fig. 16.21 Overall picture of the regulation of photon capture and the protection and repair of photodamage. Protection against photodamage is a multilevel process

Carotenoids Serve as Photo-protective Agents

When the energy stored in chlorophylls in the excited state is rapidly dissipated by excitation transfer or photochemistry, the excited state is said to be **quenched**.

If the excited state of chlorophyll is not rapidly quenched by excitation transfer or photochemistry, it can react with molecular oxygen to form an excited state of oxygen known as **singlet oxygen** ($^1O_2$*). The extremely reactive singlet oxygen goes on to react with and damage many cellular components, especially lipids. Carotenoids exert their photoprotective action by rapidly quenching the excited state of chlorophyll. The excited state of carotenoids does not have sufficient energy to form singlet oxygen, so, it decays back to its ground state while losing its energy as heat.

Recently carotenoids were found to play a role in non-photochemical quenching, which is a second protective and regulatory mechanism.

Some Xanthophylls also Participate in Energy Dissipation

Non-photochemical quenching, a major process regulating the delivery of excitation energy to the reaction center that adjusts the flow of excitations to the PS-II reaction center to a manageable level, depending on the light intensity and other conditions. The process appears to be an essential part of the regulation of antenna systems in most algae and plants.

Non-photochemical quenching is thought to be involved in protecting the photosynthetic machinery against over excitation and subsequent damage.

Three carotenoids, called **xanthophylls**, are involved in non photochemical quenching, violaxanthin, antheraxanthin and zeaxanthin.

In high light, violaxanthin is converted into zeaxanthin, *via* the intermediate antheraxanthin. Binding of protons and zeaxanthin to light harvesting antenna proteins is thought to cause conformational changes that lead to quenching and heat dissipation.

Non-photochemical quenching appears to be preferentially associated with a peripheral antenna complex of photosystem II, the PsbS protein.

Photosystem-II reaction center Photoinhibition is reversible in early stages. Prolongued inhibition, however, results in damage to the system such that the PS-II reaction center. The main target of this damage is the D_1 protein that makes up part of the PS-II reaction center complex. When D_1 is damaged by excess light, it must be replaced with a newly synthesized molecule. The other components of the PS-II reaction center are not damaged by excess excitation and are thought to be recycled, so, the D_1 protein is the only component that needs to be synthesized.

Low light

Violaxanthin

H_2O NADPH $2H + O_2$ | 2H Ascorbate H_2O

Antheraxanthin

H_2O NADPH $2H + O_2$ | 2H Ascorbate H_2O

Zeaxanthin

High light

Fig. 16.22 Chemical structure of violaxanthin, antheraxanthin and zeaxanthin. The highly quenched state of photosystem-II is associated with zeaxanthin, the unquenched state with violaxanthin

Photosystem I reaction center Photosystem I is protected from active oxygen species. The ferredoxin acceptor of PS-I is a very strong reductant that can easily reduce molecular oxygen to form superoxide (O_2^-). This reduction competes with the normal channeling of electrons to the reduction of $NADP^+$ and other processes. Superoxide can be eliminated by the action of a series of enzymes, including superoxide dismutase and ascorbate peroxidase.

Thylakoid membranes contain a protein kinase that can phosphorylate a specific threonine residue on the surface of LHC-II. When LHC-II is not phosphorylated, it delivers more energy to photosystem-II, and when it is phosphorylated, it delivers more energy to photosystem-I.

The kinase is activated when plastoquinone, one of the electron carriers between PS-I and PS-II, accumulates in the reduced state. The phosphorylated LHC-II then migrates out of the stacked regions of the membrane into the unstacked regions.

If plastoquinone becomes more oxidized because of excess excitation of photosystem-I, the kinase is deactivated and the level of phosphorylation of LHC-II is decreased by the action of a membrane bound phosphatase. LHC-II then moves back to the grana.

CO_2 Fixation

Light is required for the generation of ATP and NADPH. The ATP and NADPH are consumed by the carbon reactions, which reduce CO_2 to carbohydrate.

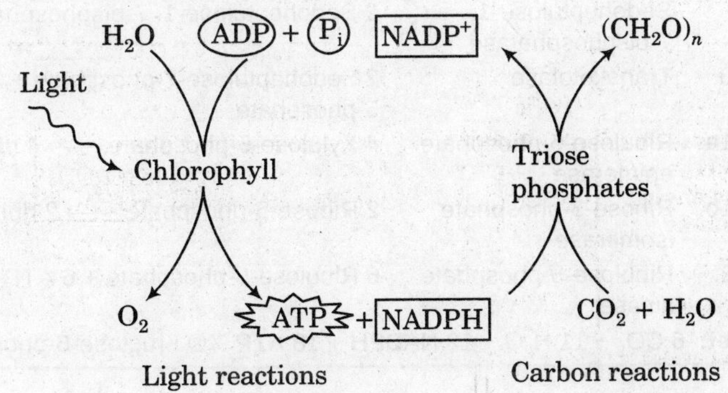

Fig. 16.23 Light and carbon reactions of photosynthesis

The reactions catalyzing the reduction of CO_2 to carbohydrate are coupled to the consumption of NADPH and ATP by enzymes found in the stroma, the soluble phase of chloroplasts. These stroma reactions were long thought to be independent of light and, as a consequence, were referred to as the dark reactions. The three pathway of CO_2 fixation are C_3, C_4 and CAM pathway.

C_3 Pathways

The photosynthetic carbon reduction cycle originally described for C_3 species [the **Calvin cycle** or **Reductive Pentose Phosphate** (RPP) **cycle**. The most primitive alga to the most advanced angiosperm, reduce CO_2 to carbohydrate *via* Calvin cycle.

The Calvin cycle was elucidated as a result of a series of elegant experiments by **Melvin Calvin** and his colleagues in the 1950s, for which a Nobel Prize was awarded in 1961.

In the Calvin cycle, CO_2 and water from the environment are enzymatically combined with a five carbon acceptor molecule to generate two molecules of a three carbon intermediate (3-phosphoglycerate).

The Calvin cycle proceeds in three stages:

(i) Carboxylation of the CO_2 acceptor ribulose 1,5-bisphosphate, forming two molecules of 3-phosphoglycerate, the first stable intermediate of the Calvin cycle.

(ii) Reduction of 3-phosphoglycerate, forming gyceraldehyde-3-phosphate, a carbohydrate.

(iii) Regeneration of the CO_2 acceptor ribulose-1, 5-bisphosphate from glyceraldehyde-3-phosphate.

Various Reactions of the Calvin Cycle

	Enzyme	Reaction
1.	Ribulose-1, 5-bisphosphate carboxylase/oxygenase	6 Ribulose 1, 5-bisphosphate + $6CO_2$ + $6H_2O$ ⟶ 12 (3-phosphoglycerate) + $12H^+$
2.	3-phosphoglycerate kinase	12 (3-phosphoglycerate) + 12 ATP ⟶ 12 (1, 3-bisphosphoglycerate) + 12 ADP
3.	NADP, glyceraldehyde 3-phosphate dehydrogenase	12 (1, 3-bisphosphoglycerate) + 12 NADPH + 12 H+ ⟶ 12 glyceraldehyde-3-phosphate + 12 $NADP^+$ + $12P_i$
4.	Triose phosphate isomerase	5 Glyceraldehyde-3-phosphate ⟶ 5 dihydroxyacetone-3-phosphate
5.	Aldolase	3 Glyceraldehyde 3-phosphate + 3 dihydroxyacetone-3-phosphate ⟶ 3 fructose-1, 6-bisphosphate
6.	Fructose-1, 6-bisphosphatase	3 Fructose-1, 6-bisphosphate $3H_2O$ ⟶ 3 fructose-6-phosphate + $3P_i$
7.	Transketolase	2 Fructose-6-phosphate + 2 glyceraldehyde-3-phosphate ⟶ 2 erythrose 4-phosphate + 2 xylulose 5-phosphate
8.	Aldolase	2 Erythrose-4-phosphate + 2 dihydroxyacetone-3-phosphate ⟶ 2 sedoheptulose-1, 7-bisphosphate
9.	Sedoheptulose-1, 7-bisphosphatase	2 Sedoheptulose-1, 7-bisphosphate + $2H_2O$ ⟶ 2 sedoheptulose 7-phosphate + $2P_i$
10.	Transketolase	2 Sedoheptulose-7-phosphate + 2 glyceraldehyde-3-phosphate ⟶ 2 ribose-5-phosphate + 2 xylulose 5-phosphate
11a.	Ribulose-5-phosphate epimerase	4 Xylulose-5-phosphate ⟶ 4 ribulose-5-phosphate
11b.	Ribose-5-phosphate isomerase	2 Ribose-5-phosphate ⟶ 2 ribulose-5-phosphate
12.	Ribulose-5-phosphate kinase	6 Ribulose-5-phosphate + 6 ATP ⟶ 6 ribulose-1, 5-bisphosphate +6 ADP + 6H+
Net:		6 CO_2 + 11 H_2O + 12 NADPH + 18 ATP ¾® Fructose-6-phosphate + 12 $NADP^+$ + $6H^+$ + 18 ADP + 17 P_i

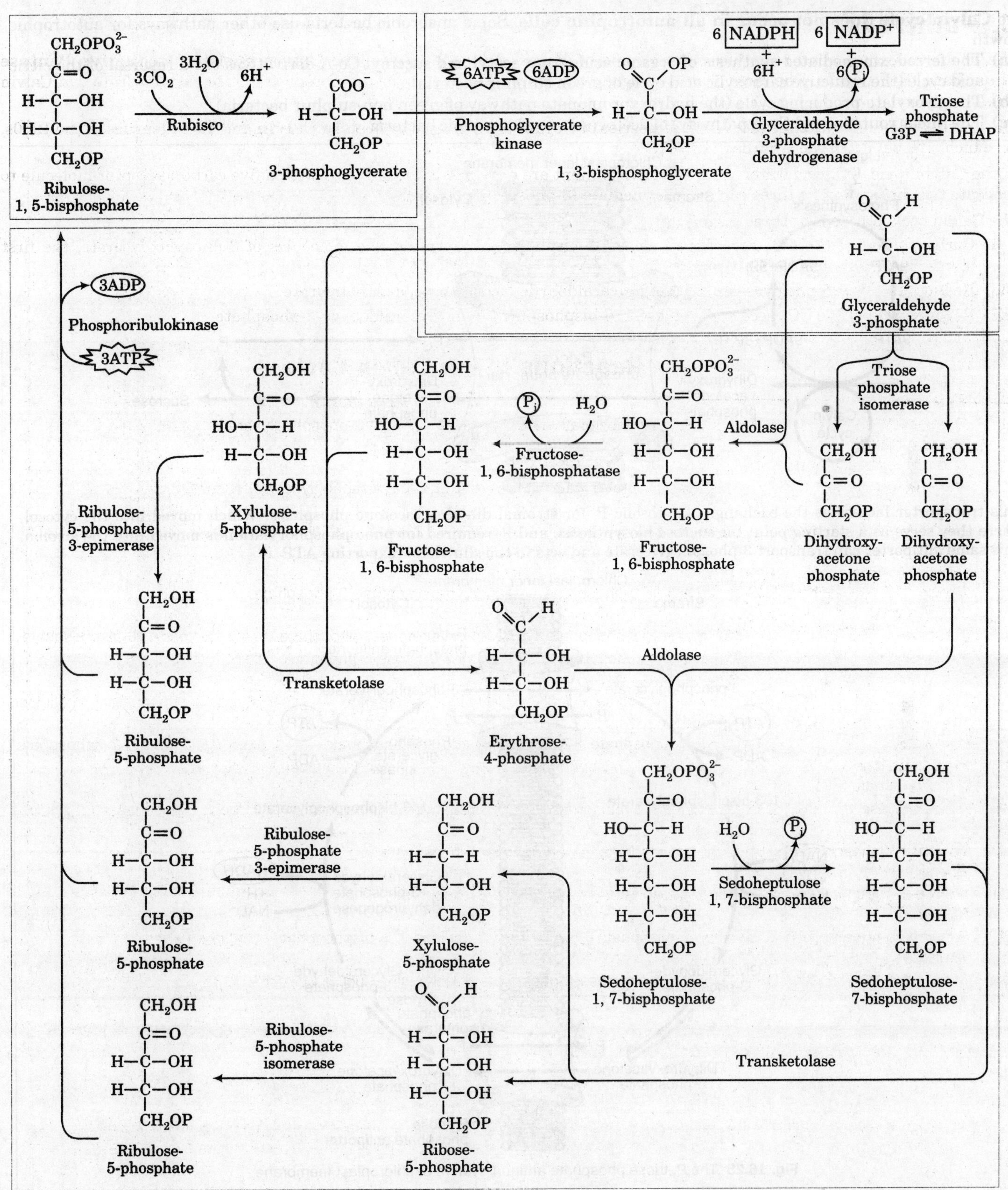

Fig. 16.24 The Calvin cycle

The **Calvin cycle does not occur in all autotrophic cells**. Some anaerobic bacteria use other pathways for autotrophic growth

(a) The ferredoxin mediated synthesis of organic acids from acetyl and succinyl Co-A derivatives *via* a reversal of the citric acid cycle (the reductive carboxylic acid cycle of green sulphur bacteria).

(b) The glyoxylate-producing cycle (the hydroxypropionate pathway of green non-sulphur bacteria).

(c) The linear route (acetyl Co-A pathway) of acetogenic, methanogenic bacteria.

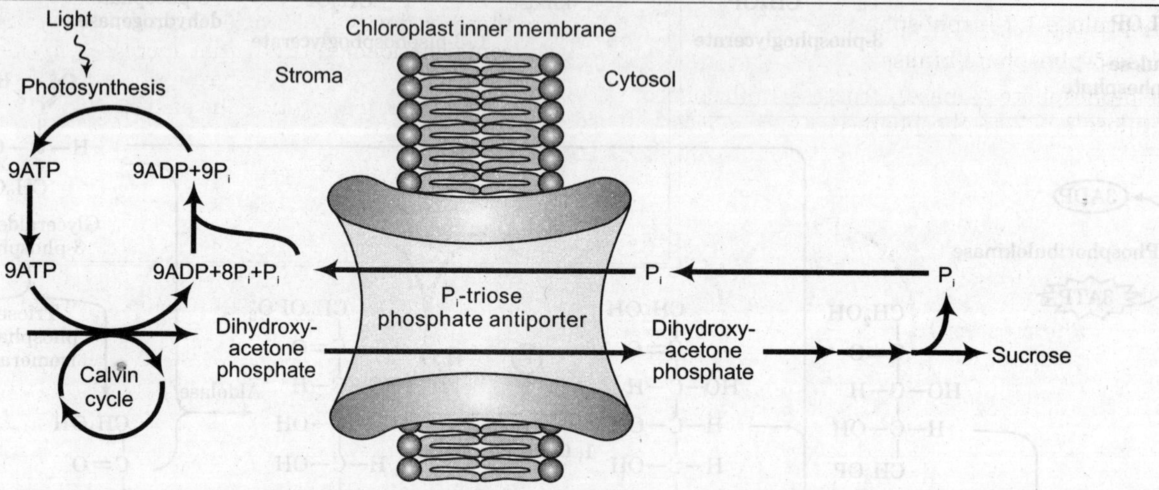

This transporter facilitates the exchange of cytosolic P_i for stromal dihydroxyacetone phosphate. Which moved into the cytosol, where they serve as a starting point for sucrose biosynthesis, and P_i required for photophosphorylation is moved into the stroma. This same antiporter can transport 3-phosphoglycerate and acts in the shuttle for exporting ATP.

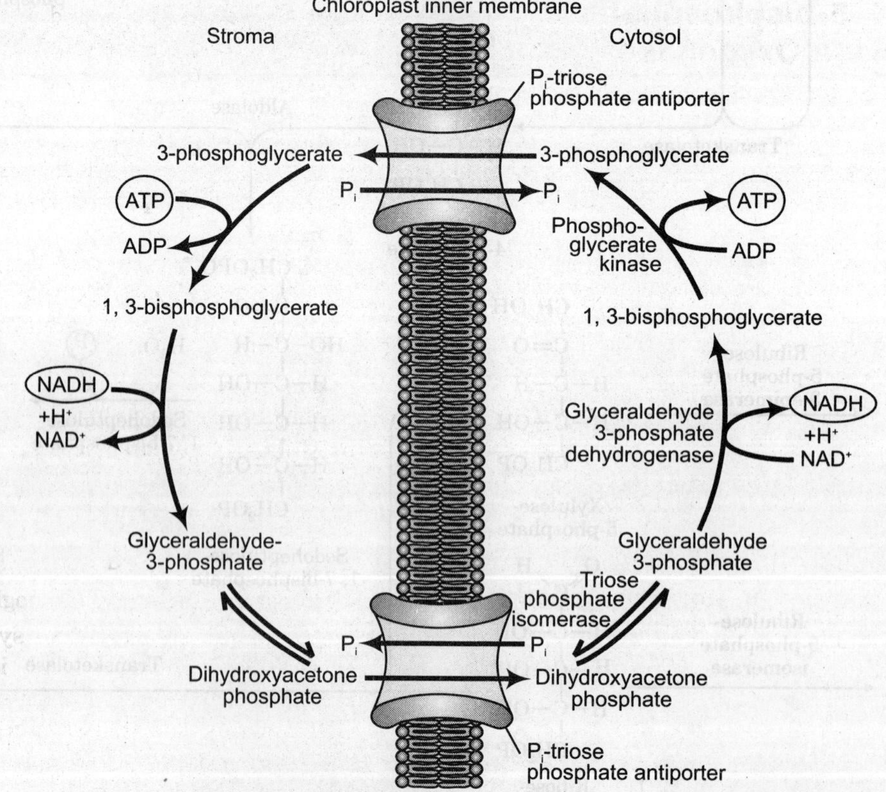

Fig. 16.25 The P_i-triose phosphate antiport system of chloroplast membrane

Dihydroxyacetone phosphate leaves the chloroplast and is converted to glyceraldehyde-3-phosphate in the cytosol. The cytosolic glyceraldehyde 3-phosphate dehydrogenase and phosphoglycerate kinase reactions then produce NADH, ATP and 3-phosphoglycerate. The latter re-enters the chloroplast and is reduced to dihydroxyacetone phosphate.

Light Dependent Enzyme Regulates the Calvin Cycle Five light-regulated enzymes operate in the Calvin cycle:

- Rubisco
- NADP, glyceraldehyde-3-phosphate dehydrogenase
- Fructose-1, 6-bisphosphatase
- Sedoheptulose-1,7-bisphosphatase
- Ribulose-5-phosphate kinase

Ribulose-5-phosphate kinase, fructose-1,6-bisphosphatase, sedoheptulose-1, 7-bisphosphatase, and glyceraldehyde 3-phosphate dehydrogenase are activated by light driven reduction of disulphide bonds between two Cys residues critical to their catalytic activities. When these Cys residues are disulphide bonded (oxidized), the enzymes are inactive, this is the normal situation in the dark.

Reduced thioredoxin donates electrons for the reduction of the disulphide bonds of the light activated enzymes, and these reductive cleavage reactions are accompanied by conformational changes that increase enzyme activities. In the dark, the —SH groups undergo reoxidation to disulphides, inactivating the enzymes.

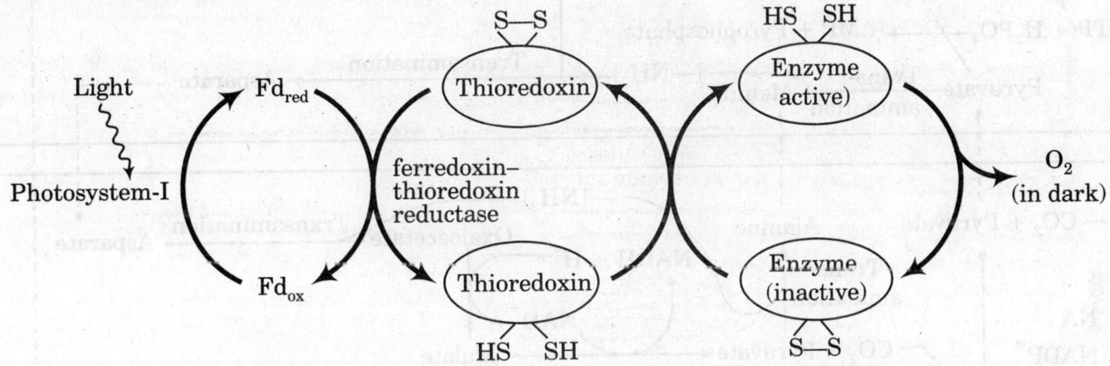

Fig. 16.26 Light activation of several enzymes of the Calvin cycle

Ribulose-1, 5-bisphosphate Carboxylase Oxygenase

Rubisco is very abundant, representing upto 40% of the total soluble protein of most leaves. The activity of rubisco is also regulated by light, but the enzyme itself does not respond to thioredoxin. The three-dimensional structure of the photosynthetic enzyme, rubisco, appears to have been established early in evolution, since its form in the plant chloroplast is very close to that found in photosynthetic bacteria.Thus, the quaternary structure of both these rubiscos has the same standard eight small and eight large subunits (L_8S_8). That rubisco has evolved from simpler forms of the enzyme is apparent from the fact that there are in bacteria forms with fewer components (L_6S_6 in *Pseudomonas oxalates*) and one which completely lacks the small subunits (L_2 in *Rhodospirillum rubrum*). Plant rubisco has a complex structure with **eight identical large subunits** (encoded in the chloroplast genome, or plastome), each containing a catalytic site, and **eight identical small subunits** (encoded in the nuclear genome) of uncertain function. The rubisco of photosynthetic bacteria is simpler in structure, having two subunits that in many respects resemble the large subunits of the plant enzyme.

C_4-Pathways

Inseveral plants like sugarcane, maize, *Euphorbia*, *Amaranthus*, *Sorghum*, first stable product in dark reaction is oxaloacetic acid (the 4-carbon compound, hence named). First CO_2 fixation occur in mesophyll chloroplast, while second in bundle sheath.

Two aspect of C_4 model are:

(i) **First Aspect** Asparate and malate decarboxylate are formed in bundle sheath cells. There are three such mechanisms depending on species.

(a) **Asparate formers** (Species form more asparate than malate), **asparate** moves into bundle sheath cell is changed back to **oxaloacetate** by transmination. Next, oxaloacetal reduced to **malate** by NADH dependent malate dehydrogenase. Malate is oxidatively decarboxylated by malic enzyme to **pyruvate.** It is then converted to **alanine** by another transamination. As alanine moves back to mesophyll cells, it lose NH_2 and converted to asparate and is transported to bundle sheath cells.

(b) **Malate formers** (species mostly form malate) transfer **malate** into bundle sheath, where it is oxidatively decarboxylated to CO_2 and **pyruvate.** This process uses malic enzyme in presence of NADP. The NADPH formed by this enzyme is help to reduce 3-PGA 3-phosphoglyceraldehyde.

(iii) The **third decarboxylation system** operate mainly in **asparate formers** and involves oxaloacetate formed in bundle sheath. This system is catalyzed by **EP carboxykinase, oxaloacetate** which react with ATP to release CO_2, **PEP** and ADP. The CO_2 fixed by **rubisco** is converted into carbohydrate by Calvin cycle.

(ii) **Second aspect** is how 3-carbon acid that transport back to mesophyll cells can regenerate PEP, which is needed for continued fixation of CO_2. Alanine is converted back to pyruvic by other transaminase. The chloroplast enzyme pyruvate phosphate dikinase uses ATP to convert **pyruvate** to **PEP** and **P_i**

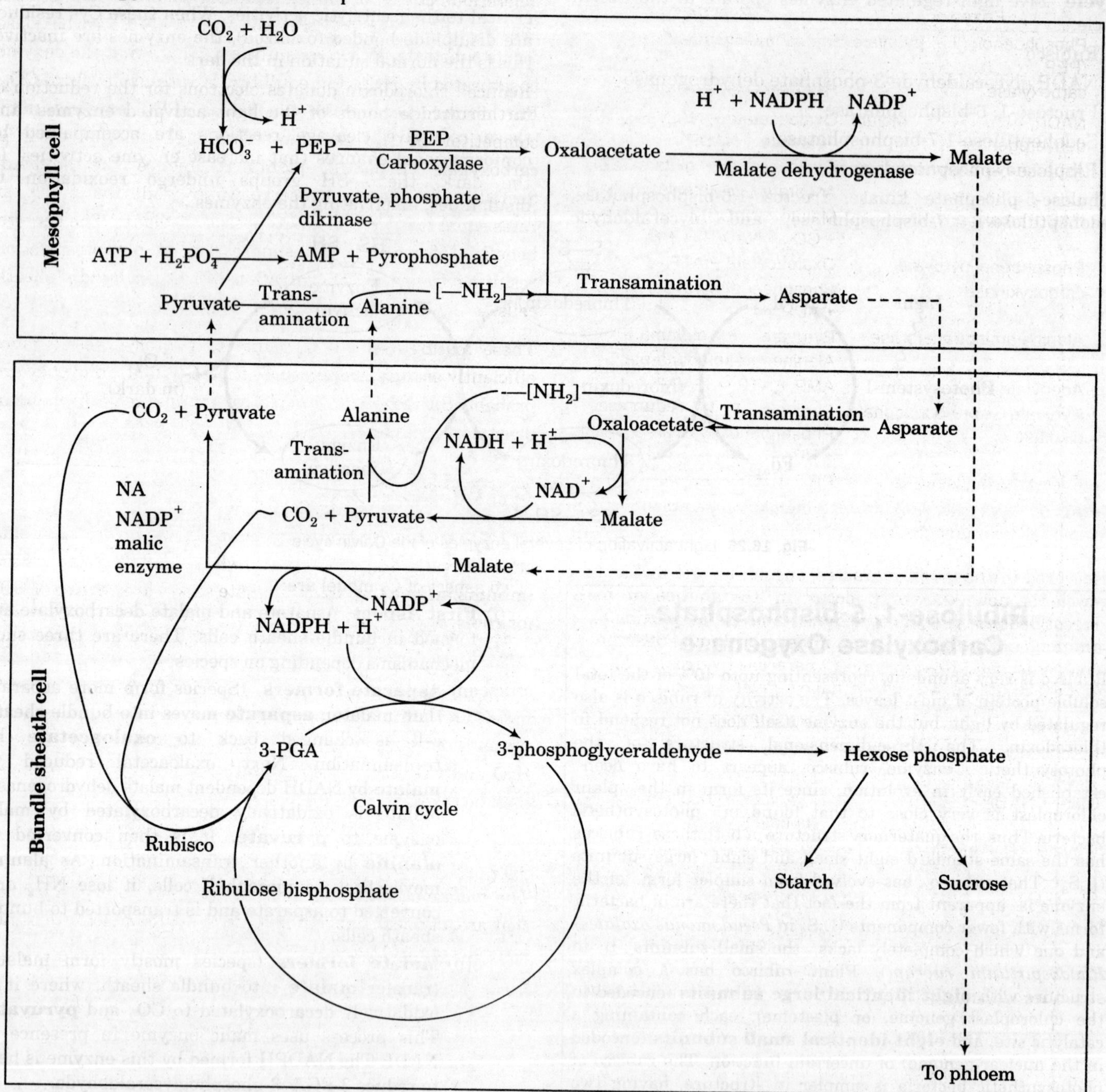

Fig. 16.27 The C_4 photosynthetic pathway. The hydrolysis of two ATP drives the cycle in the direction of the arrows, thus pumping CO_2 from the atmosphere to the Calvin cycle of the chloroplasts from bundle sheath cells.

The basic C_4 cycle consists of four stages:

(a) Fixation of CO_2 by the carboxylation of phosphoenol pyruvate in the mesophyll cells to form a C_4 acid (malate and/or asparate).

(b) Transport of the C_4 acids to the bundle sheath cells.

(c) Decarboxylation of the C_4 acids within the bundle sheath cells and generation of CO_2, which is then reduced to carbohydrate *via* the Calvin cycle.

Reactions of the C_4 Photosynthetic Carbon Cycle	
Enzyme	**Reaction**
1. Phosphoenol pyruvate (PEP) carboxylase	Phosphoenolpyruvate + $HCO_3^- \rightarrow$ Oxaloacetate + P_i
2. NADP, malate dehydrogenase	Oxaloacetate + NADPH + H^+ $\rightarrow$ Malate + $NADP^+$
3. Aspartate aminotransferase	Oxaloacetate + glutamate $\rightarrow$ Asparate + α–ketoglutarate
4. NAD(P) malic enzyme	Malate + $NAD(P)^+ \rightarrow$ Pyruvate + CO_2 + NAD(P)H + H^+
5. Phosphoenol pyruvate carboxykinase	Oxaloacetate + ATP $\rightarrow$ Phosphoenol pyruvate + CO_2 + ADP
6. Alanine aminotransferase	Pyruvate + glutamate $\leftrightarrow$ Alanine + α-ketoglutarate
7. Adenylate kinase	AMP + ATP $\rightarrow$ 2 ADP
8. Pyruvate orthophosphate dikinase	Pyruvate + P_i + ATP $\rightarrow$ Phosphoenol pyruvate + AMP + PP_i
9. Pyrophosphatase	$PP_i + H_2O \rightarrow 2P_i$

Note: P_i and PP_i stand for inorganic phosphate and pyrophosphate, respectively.

Discovered in the tropical grasses, sugarcane and maize, the C_4-cycle is now known to occur in 16 families of both monocotyledons and dicotyledons, and it is particularly prominent in Gramineae (corn, millet, sorghum, sugarcane), Chenopodiaceae (*Atriplex*) and Cyperaceae (sedges).
About 1% of all known species have C_4 metabolism.

Energetics of the C_4 Photosynthetic Carbon Cycle		
Phosphoenol pyruvate + H_2O + NADPH + CO_2 (mesophyll)	$\rightarrow$	Malate + NADP+ + P_i (mesophyll)
Malate + NADP+	$\rightarrow$	Pyruvate + NADPH + CO_2 (bundle sheath)
Pyruvate + P_i + ATP	$\rightarrow$	Phosphoenolpyruvate + AMP + PP_i (mesophyll)
$PP_i + H_2O$	$\rightarrow$	2Pi (mesophyll)
AMP + ATP	$\rightarrow$	2ADP
Net: CO_2 (mesophyll) + ATP + $2H_2O$	$\rightarrow$	CO2 (bundle sheath) + 2ADP + $2P_i$
Cost of concentrating CO_2 within the bundle sheath cell = 2ATP per CO_2		

Two features of the C_4-cycle in C_4-plants overcome the deleterious effects of higher temperature on photosynthesis that were noted earlier. **First**, the affinity of PEP carboxylase for its substrate, HCO_3^-, is sufficiently high that the enzyme is saturated by HCO_3^- in equilibrium with air levels of CO_2. Furthermore, because the substrate is HCO_3^-, oxygen is not a competitor in the reaction. This high activity of PEP carboxylase enables C_4-plants to reduce the stomatal aperture and thereby conserve water while fixing CO_2 at rates equal to or greater than those of C_3-plants. The **second** beneficial feature is the suppression of photorespiration resulting from the concentration of CO_2 in bundle sheath cells.

These features enable C_4-plants to photosynthesize more efficiently at high temperatures than C_3-plants, and they are probably the reason for the relative abundance of C_4-plants in drier, hotter climates.

CAM Pathway

In CAM plants, CO_2 is fixed into malate in the dark and stored in vacuoles until daylight, when the stomata are closed (minimizing water loss) and malate serves as a source of CO_2 for rubisco.

CAM plants such as cacti achieve their high water use efficiency by opening their stomata during the cool, desert, nights and closing them during the hot, dry days. Closing the stomata during the day minimizes water loss, but because H_2O and CO_2 share the same diffusion pathway, CO_2 must then be taken up at night.

CO_2 is incorporated *via* carboxylation of phosphoenol pyruvate to oxaloacetate, which is then reduced to malate. The malate accumulates and is stored in the large vacuoles that are a typical, but not obligatory, anatomic feature of the leaf cells of CAM plants.

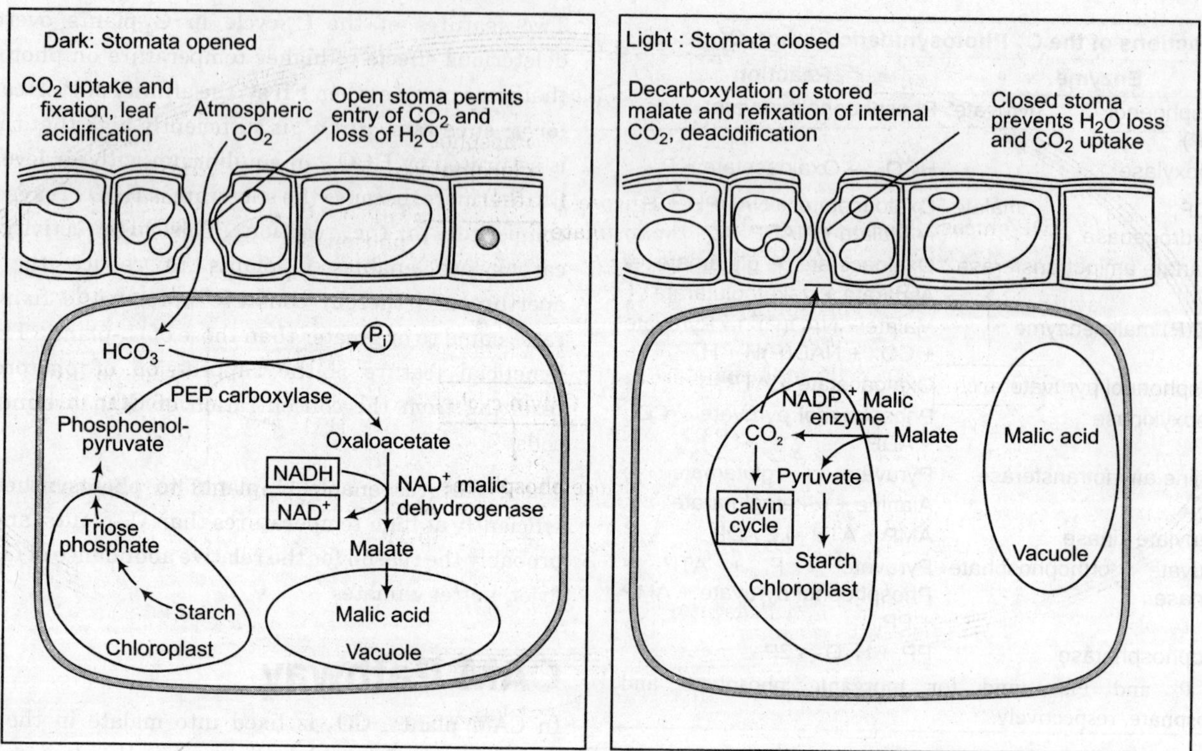

Fig. 16.28 Crassulacean acid metabolism (CAM). Temporal separation of CO_2 uptake from photosynthetic reactions, CO_2 uptake and fixation take place at night, and decarboxylation and refixation of the internally released CO_2 occur during the day.

Diurnal regulation of CAM phosphoenolpyruvate (PEP) carboxylase. Phosphorylation of the serine residue (Ser–OP) yields a form of the enzyme which is active during the night and relatively insensitive to malate. During the day, dephosphorylation of the serine (Ser–OH) gives a form of the enzyme which is inhibited by malate.

In both C_4 and CAM plants, PEP carboxylase is inhibited by malate and activated by glucose-6-phosphate. C_4 and CAM plants utilize PEP carboxylase to fix CO_2, and they separate that enzyme from rubisco either spatially (C_4 plants) or temporally (CAM plants).

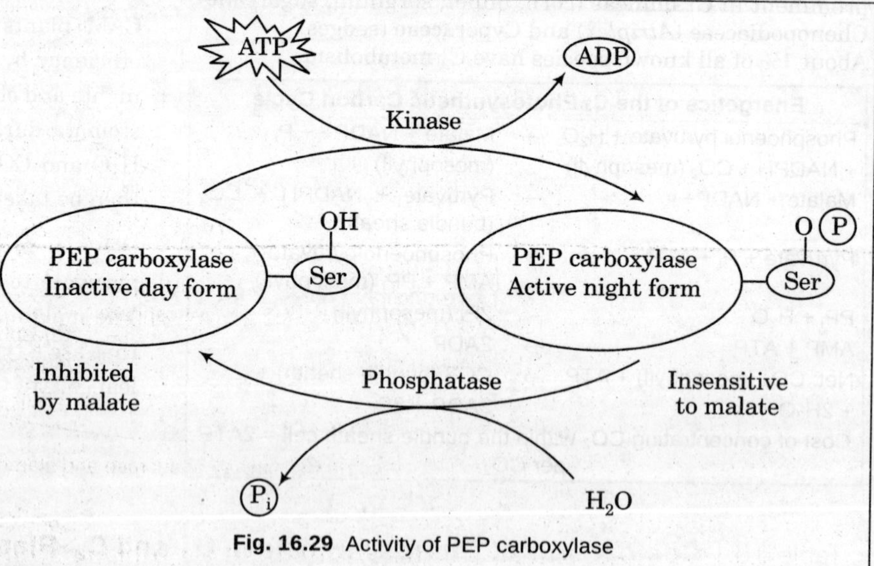

Fig. 16.29 Activity of PEP carboxylase

Synthesis of Starch and Sucrose

The synthesis of starch and sucrose are competing processes that occur in the chloroplast and the cytosol, respectively. When the cytosolic P_i concentration is high, chloroplast triose phosphate is exported to the cytosol *via* the P_i in exchange for P_i, and sucrose is synthesized. When the cytosolic P_i concentration is low, triose phosphate is retained within the chloroplast, and starch is synthesized.

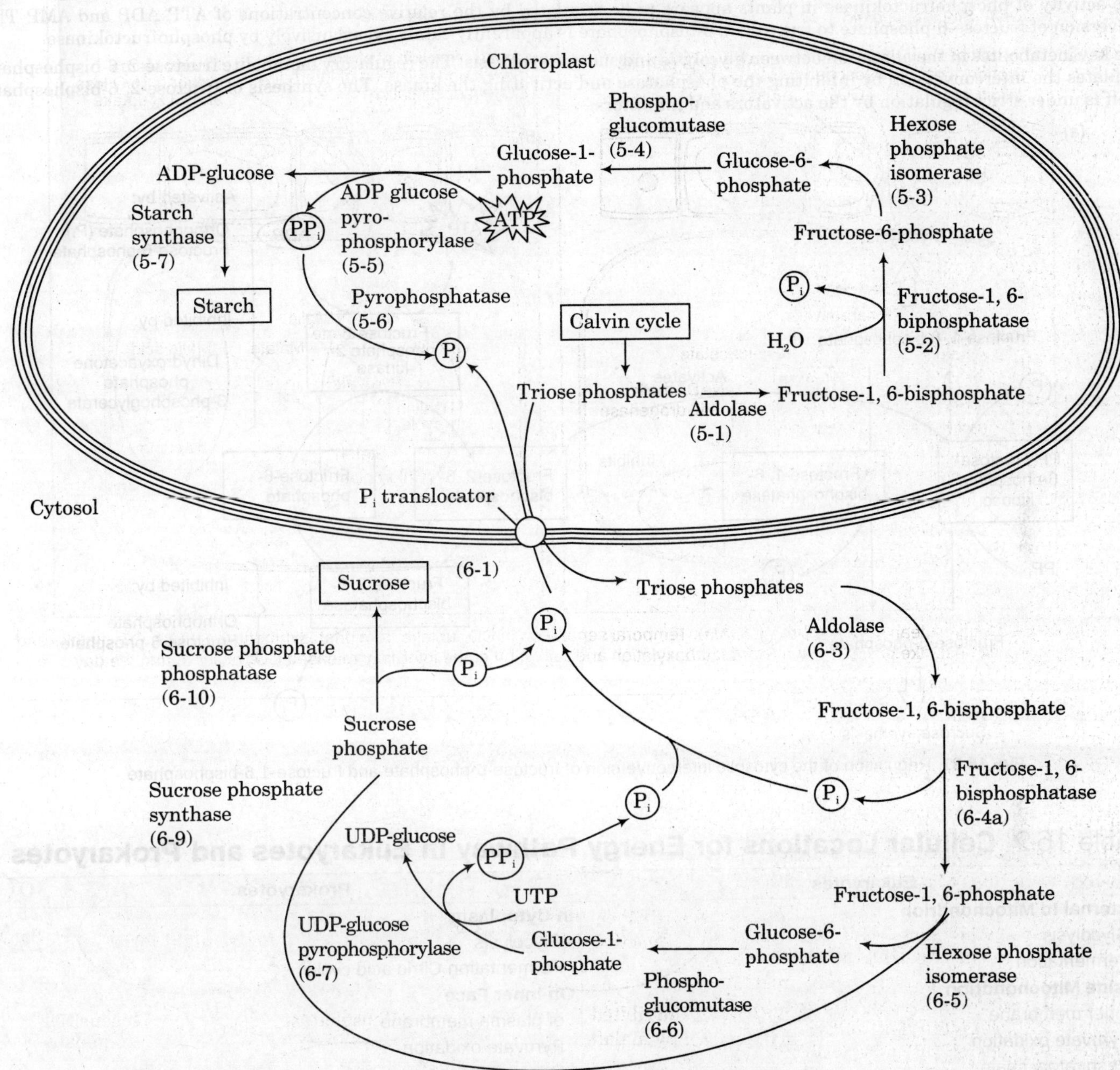

Fig. 16.30 Pathway of sucrose and starch synthesis

Table 16.1 **Comparison of Photosynthesis in C_3 and C_4-Plants**

Variable	C_3-Plants	C_4-Plants
Photorespiration	Extensive	Minimal
Perform Calvin-Benson cycle?	Yes	Yes
Primary CO_2 acceptor	RuBP	PEP
CO_2-fixing enzyme	Rubisco (RuBP carboxylase/oxygenase)	PEP carboxylase and rubisco
First product of CO_2 fixation	3PG (3-carbon compound)	Oxaloacetate(4-carbon compound)
Affinity of carboxylase for CO_2	Moderate	High
Photosynthetic cells of leaf	Mesophyll	Mesophyll + bundle sheath
Classes of chloroplasts	One	Two

The activity of phosphofructokinase in plants appears to be regulated by the relative concentrations of ATP, ADP and AMP. The conversion of fructose-6-phosphate to fructose-1, 6-bisphosphate is apparently catalyzed exclusively by phosphofructokinase.

The key metabolites in the allocation between glycolysis and sucrose synthesis. The regulatory metabolite fructose-2, 6-bisphosphate regulates the interconversion by inhibiting the phosphatase and activating the kinase. The synthesis of fructose-2, 6-bisphosphate itself is under strict regulation by the activators and inhibitors.

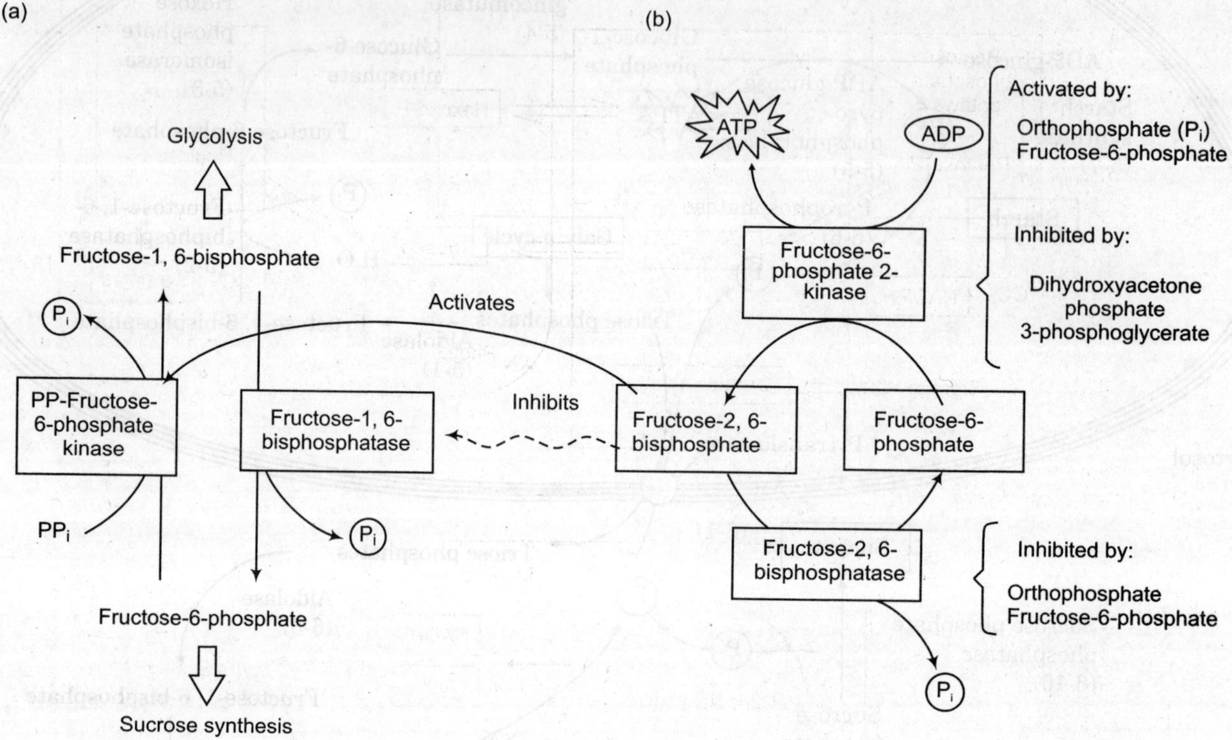

Fig. 16.31 Regulation of the cytosolic interconversion of fructose-6-phosphate and fructose-1,6-bisphosphate

Table 16.2 **Cellular Locations for Energy Pathway in Eukaryotes and Prokaryotes**

Eukaryotes	Prokaryotes
External to Mitochondrion	**In Cytoplasm**
Glycolysis	Glycolysis
Fermentation	Fermentation Citric acid cycle
Inside Mitochondrion	**On Inner Face**
Inner membrane	of plasma membrane
Pyruvate oxidation	Pyruvate oxidation
Respiratory chain	Respiratory chain
Matrix	
Citric acid cycle	

Respiration and Photorespiration

Aerobic (oxygen-requiring) respiration is common to nearly all eukaryotic organisms, the respiratory process in plants is similar to that found in animals and lower eukaryotes. However, some specific aspects of plant respiration distinguish it from its animal counterpart. During respiration, free energy is released and transiently stored in a compound, ATP, which can be readily utilized for the maintenance and development of the plant. **Aerobic respiration** is the biological process by which reduced organic compounds are mobilized and subsequently oxidized in a controlled manner.

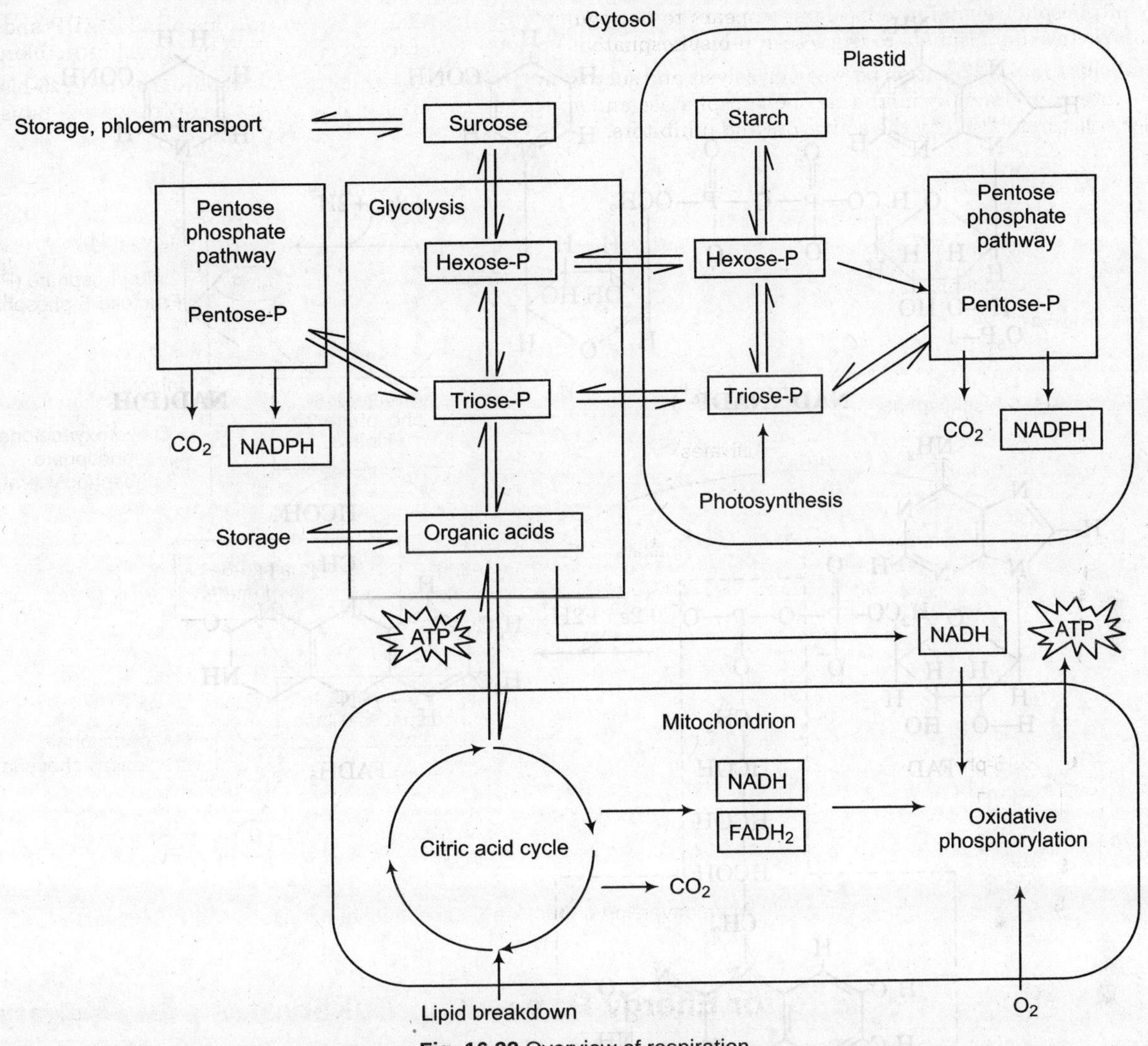

Fig. 16.32 Overview of respiration

Some Coenzymes of Oxidation and Reduction Processes

Coenzymes are organic molecules which acts as carriers of atoms or electroms. These are NAD, NADP, FMN, FAD, cytochromes, Co-A etc.

(i) NAD

(Nicotinamide Adenine dinucleotide/NADP)

Coenzyme for most degradative dehydrogenations. Also called coenzyme I and it was previously designed as diphosphopyridine nucleotide (DPN). NADH or NADPH is the reduced form of NAD or NADP. Nicotinamide is a vitamin constituent. NADP is commonly called coenzyme II. Earlier it was referred as TPN (Triphospho Pyridine Nucleotide). This coenzyme is most frequently associated with synthetic reactions (photosynthesis). It also functions in hexose monophosphate shunt. The oxidation reduction potential of NADP is low (– 0.32 V).

(ii) FMN and FAD

Riboflavin is key constituent of FMN (Flavin mononucleotide) and FAD (Flavin adenine dinucleotide) FMN is coenzyme of lactic acid dehydrogenase, while FAD is that of aldehyde oxidase, D-amino oxidase and fatty acyl Co-A dehydrogenase.

(iii) Cytochromes

Transfer electrons from flavoprotein or other carrier enzyme to cytochrome oxidase.

(iv) Coenzyme-A

Needed for acetylation reactions. It contains thioethanolamine-vitamin-B pantothenic acid, pyrophosphate and nucleotide adenylic acid.

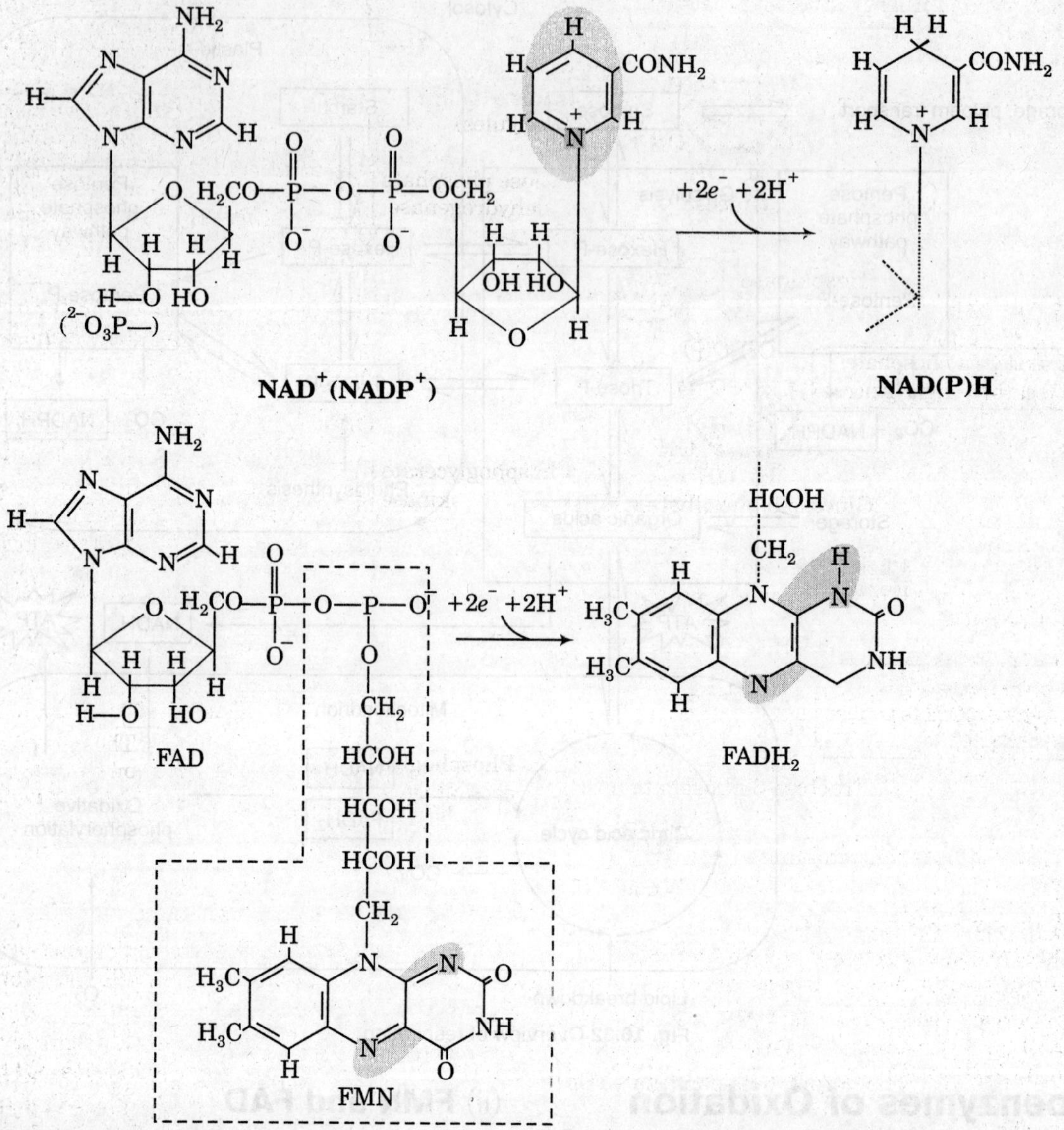

$NAD^+(NADP^+)$

NAD(P)H

FAD

$FADH_2$

FMN

Fig. 16.33 Structures and reactions of the major electron carrying coenzymes involved in respiratory bioenergetics

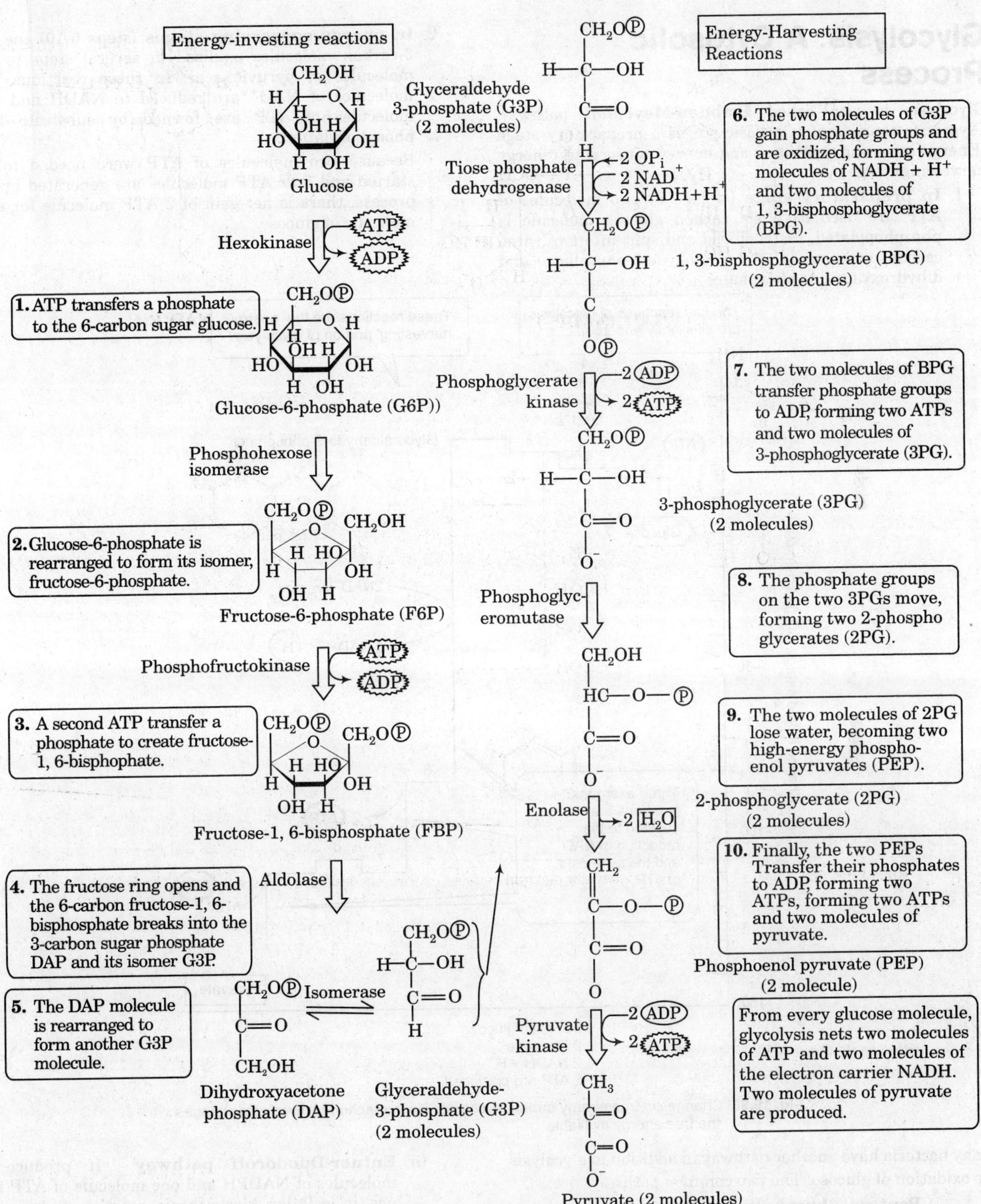

Fig. 16.34 Glycolysis converts glucose to pyruvate ten enzymes, starting with hexokinase, catalyze ten reactions in turn. Along the way, ATP is produced (reactions 7 and 10), and two NAD^+ are reduced to two NADH + H^+ (reaction 6)

Glycolysis: A Cytosolic Process

Glycolysis is also called **Embden-Meyerhof** pathway. Glycolysis consists of two basic stages a preparatory stage (Energy investing reactions) and energy conserving (energy harvesting) stage.

1. **In preparatory stage** (steps 1-5) two molecules of ATP are used as a six carbon glucose molecule is phosphopylated, restructured and split into two three carbon compounds glyceraldehyde-3-phosphate and dihydroxyacetone phosphate.
2. **In energy conserving stages** (steps 6-10) the two 3-carbon molecules oxidized in several steps to two molecules of pyruvic acid. In these reactions, two molecules of NAD^+ are reduced to NADH and four molecules of ATP are formed by substrate level phosphorylation.

Because two molecules of ATP were needed to get started and four ATP molecules are generated by the process, there is net gain of 2 ATP molecule for each molecule of glucose.

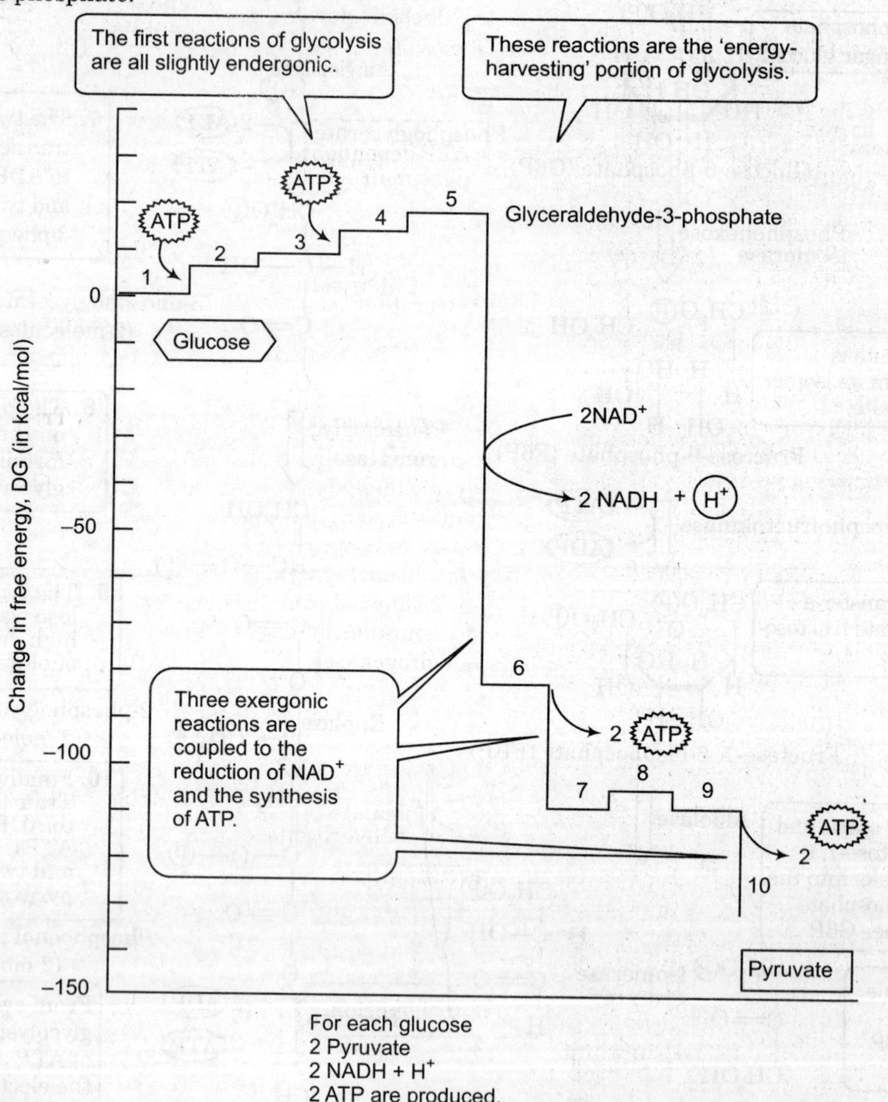

Fig. 16.35 Changes in free energy during glycolysis. Each reaction of glycolysis changes the free energy available

Many bacteria have another pathway in addition to glycolysis for oxidation of glucose. The two common pathways are:

(i) **Pentose phosphate pathway** Cyclic pathway operates simultaneously with glycolysis for breakdown of 5-carbon sugar.

(ii) **Entner-Duodoroff pathway** It produce 2 molecules of NADPH and one molecule of ATP for use in cellular biosynthesis reaction from each glucose molecule. It is found in *Rhizobium*, *Pseudomonas* and *Agrobacterium* (All Gram negative).

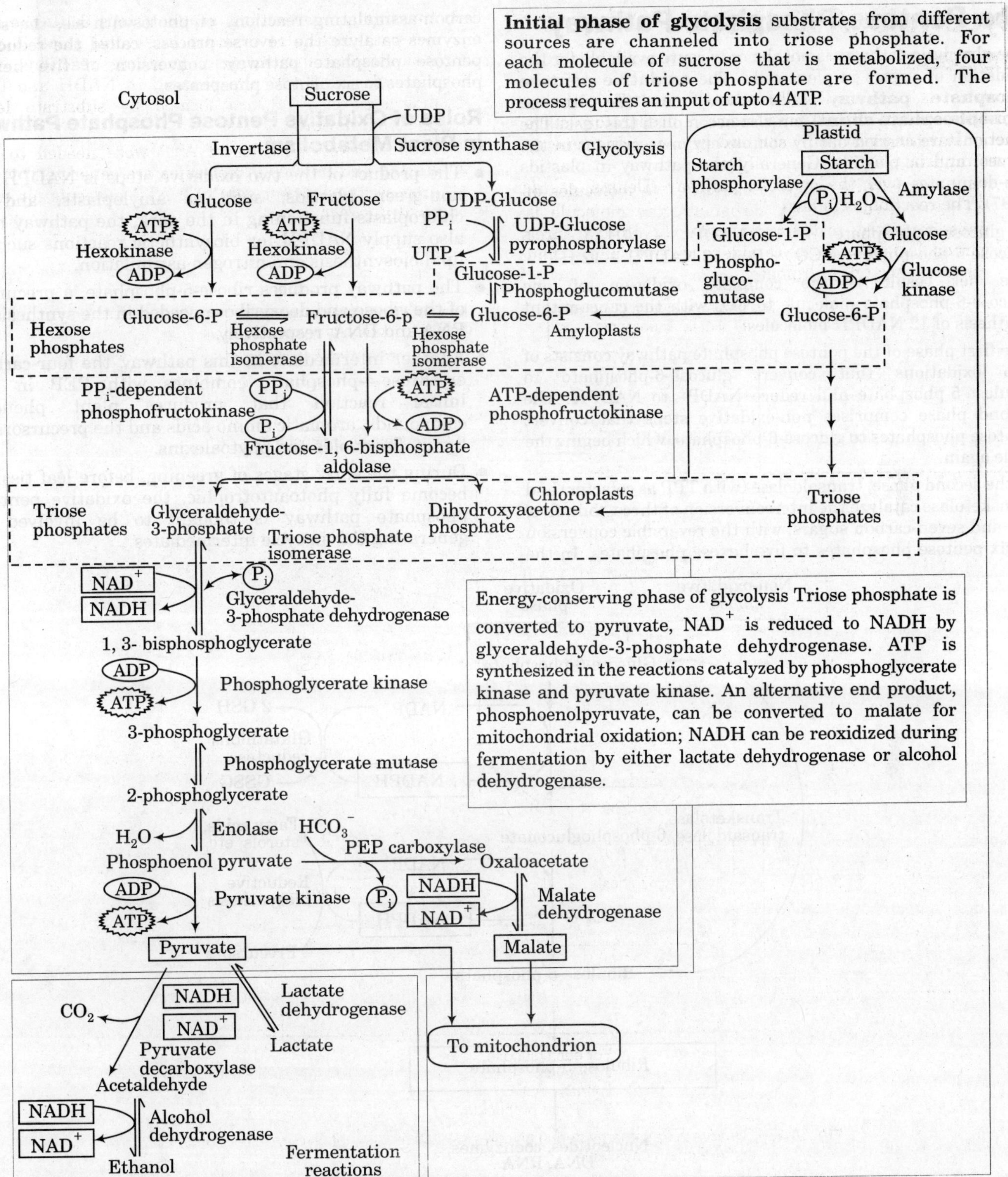

Fig. 16.36 Reactions of plant glycolysis and fermentation. In the main pathway, sucrose is oxidized to the organic acid pyruvate. The double arrows denote reversible reactions; the single arrows, essentially irreversible reactions

The Pentose Phosphate Pathway

The glycolytic pathway is not the only route available for the oxidation of sugars in plant cells. The **oxidative pentose phosphate pathway** (also known as the **hexose monophosphate shunt**) can also accomplish this task. The reactions are carried out by soluble enzymes present in the cytosol and in plastids. Generally, the pathway in plastids pre-dominates over the cytosolic pathway (Dennis, *et. al.*, 1997). The reaction as follows:

6 glucose-6-phosphate + 12 $NADP^+$ + 7H_2O $\rightarrow$ 5 glucose-6-phosphate + 6 CO_2 + P_i + 12 NADPH + 12 H^+

The net result is the complete oxidation of one glucose-6-phosphate molecule to CO_2 with the concomitant synthesis of 12 NADPH molecules.

The first phase of the pentose phosphate pathway consists of two oxidations that convert glucose-6-phosphate to ribulose-5-phosphate and reduce $NADP^+$ to NADPH. The second phase comprises non-oxidative steps that convert pentose phosphates to glucose-6-phosphate, which begins the cycle again.

In the second phase, transaldolase (with TPP as cofactor) and transketolase catalyze the interconversion of three, four, five, six, and seven-carbon sugars, with the reversible conversion of six pentose phosphates to five hexose phosphates. In the carbon-assimilating reactions of photosynthesis, the same enzymes catalyze the reverse process, called the reductive pentose phosphate pathway: conversion of five hexose phosphates to six pentose phosphates.

Roles of Oxidative Pentose Phosphate Pathway in Plant Metabolism

- The product of the two oxidative steps is NADPH. In non-green plastids, such as amyloplasts, and in chloroplasts functioning in the dark, the pathway may also supply NADPH for biosynthetic reactions such as lipid biosynthesis and nitrogen assimilation.
- The pathway produces ribose-5-phosphate, a precursor of the ribose and deoxyribose needed in the synthesis of RNA and DNA, respectively.
- Another intermediate in this pathway, the four-carbon erythrose-4-phosphate, combines with PEP in the initial reaction that produces plant phenolic compounds, aromatic amino acids and the precursors of lignin, flavonoids and phytoalexins.
- During the early stages of greening, before leaf tissues become fully photoautotrophic, the oxidative pentose phosphate pathway is thought to be involved in generating Calvin cycle intermediates.

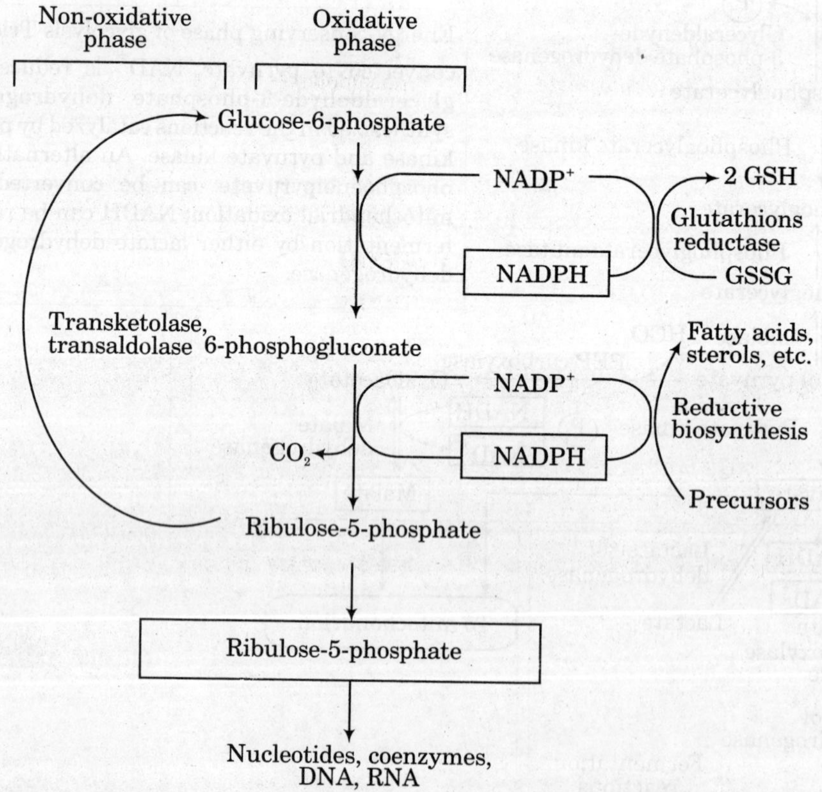

Fig. 16.37 General scheme of the pentose phosphate pathway

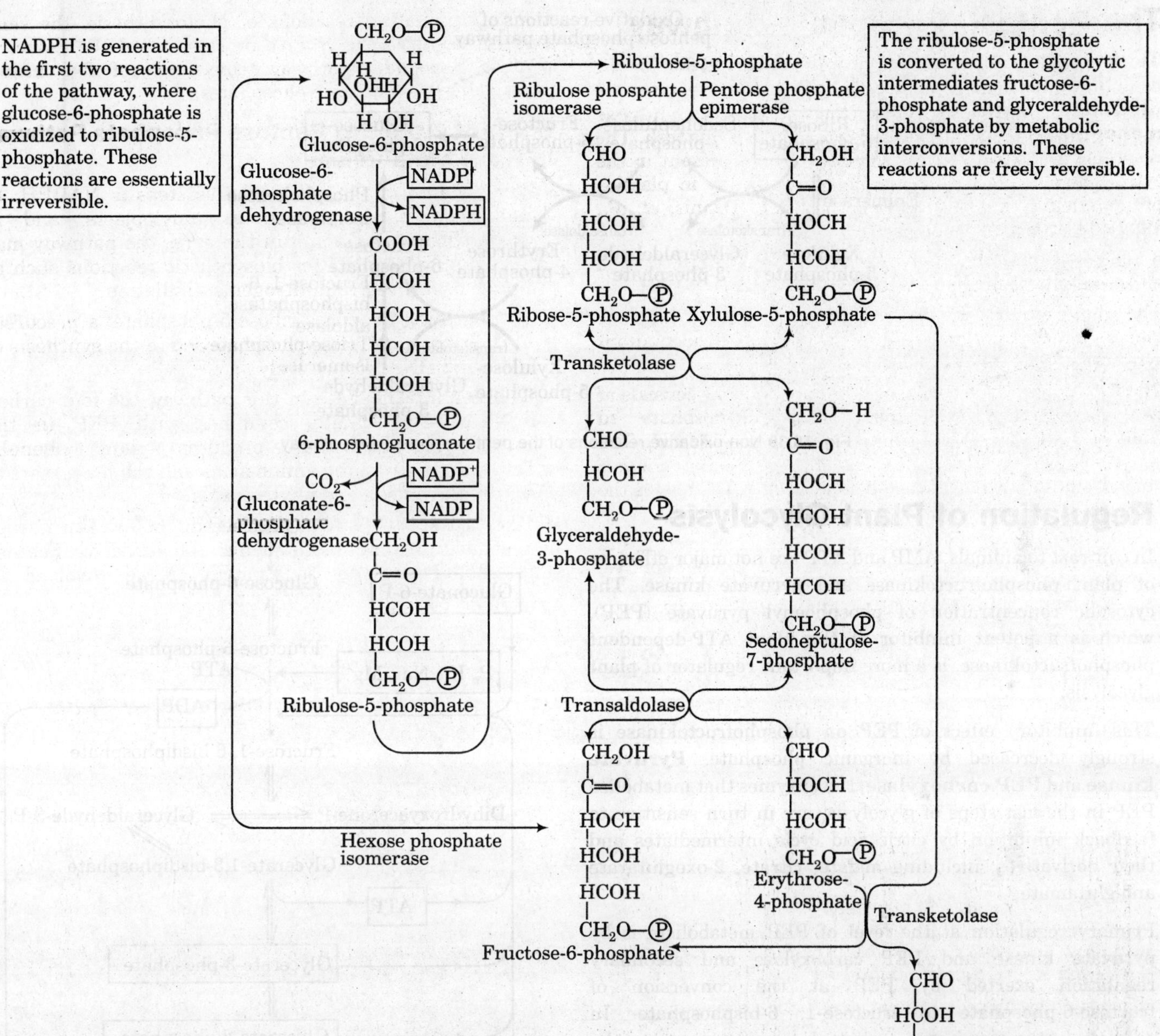

Fig. 16.38 Reactions of the oxidative pentose phosphate pathway in higher plants

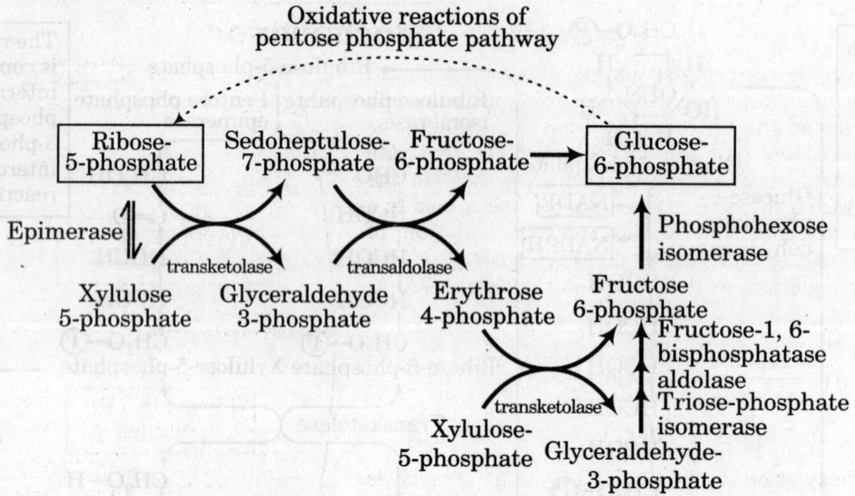

Fig. 16.39 Non-oxidative reactions of the pentose phosphate pathway

Regulation of Plant Glycolysis

In contrast to animals, AMP and ATP are not major effectors of plant phosphofructokinase and pyruvate kinase. The cytosolic concentration of phosphoenyl pyruvate (PEP), which is a potent inhibitor of the plant ATP-dependent phosphofructokinase, is a more important regulator of plant glycolysis.

This inhibitory effect of PEP on phosphofructokinase is strongly decreased by inorganic phosphate. **Pyruvate kinase** and **PEP carboxylase**, the enzymes that metabolize PEP in the last steps of glycolysis, are in turn sensitive to feedback inhibition by citric acid cycle intermediates and their derivatives, including malate, citrate, 2-oxoglutarate and glutamate.

Primary regulation at the level of PEP metabolism is by pyruvate kinase and PEP carboxylase and secondary regulation exerted by PEP at the conversion of fructose-6-phosphate to fructose-1, 6-bisphosphate. In animals, the primary control operates at the phosphofructokinase and secondary control at the pyruvate kinase.

The regulation of the conversion of fructose-6-phosphate to fructose-1, 6-bisphosphate is also complex. Fructose-2, 6-bisphosphate, another hexose bisphosphate, is present at varying levels in the cytosol. It markedly inhibits the activity of cytosolic fructose-1, 6-bisphosphatase but stimulates the activity of PP_i-dependent phosphofructokinase.

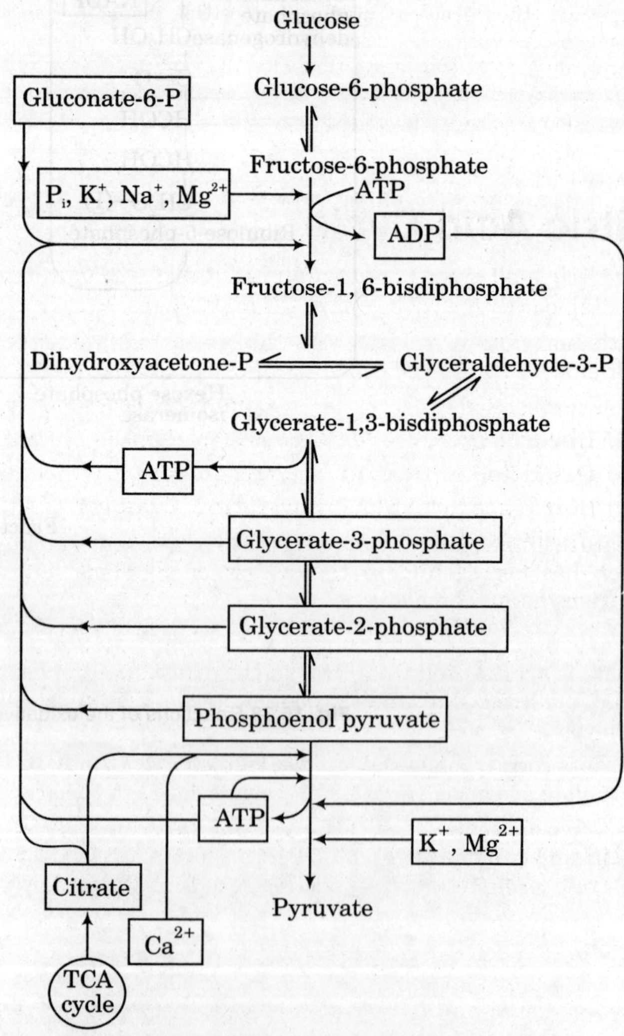

Fig. 16.40 A scheme for the regulation of glycolysis

Pyruvate in Mitochondrion

The pyruvate generated in the cytosol during glycolysis transported through the impermeable inner mitochondrial membrane *via* a specific transport protein. Once inside the mitochondrial matrix, pyruvate is decarboxylated in an oxidation reaction by the enzyme pyruvate dehydrogenase. The products are NADH, CO_2 and acetic acid in the form of acetyl-Co-A, in which a thioester bond links the acetic acid to a sulphur-containing cofactor, coenzyme-A (Co-A). The oxidation of pyruvate to acetyl coenzyme-A is catalyzed by an enzyme complex, in a three-step process: decarboxylation, oxidation and conjugation to Co-A.

- Pyruvate (CH_3–CO–CO_2^-) + TPP → CO_2 + CH_3–HC(–OH)–TPP
- CH_3–HC(–OH)–TPP + Lipoate → TPP + CH_3–C(=O)–DHL
- CH_3–C(=O)–DHL + HSCo-A → CH_3–C(=O)–SCo-A

In the first step, decarboxylation occurs and the acetyl moiety is transferred to thiamine pyrophosphate (TPP) with reduction of the carboxyl group, then this intermediate, a-hydroxyethyl TPP, undergoes another transfer to lipoate, during which the two hydrogen atoms of a-hydroxyethyl TPP reduce lipoate to dihydrolipoate (DHL). The final stage in the process involves another transfer reaction with coenzyme-A, with the release of DHL and the formation of the coenzyme-A ester of acetate. The enzyme complex has a tightly bound FAD coenzyme which is linked as an electron acceptor to NAD^+ and energy is released from the reaction as NADH.

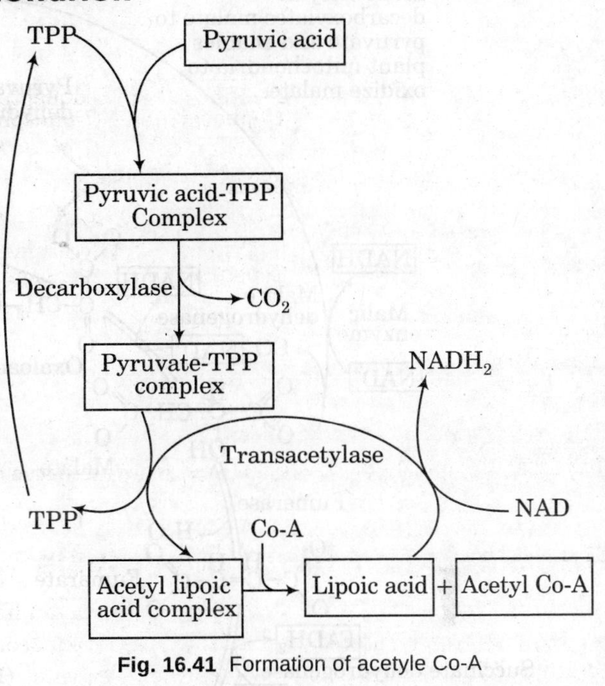

Fig. 16.41 Formation of acetyle Co-A

Citric Acid Cycle

The citric acid cycle reactions in plant are not identical with those carried out by animal mitochondria. For example, the step catalyzed by succinyl Co-A synthetase produces ATP in plants and GTP in animals.

All the enzymes associated with the citric acid cycle are found in plant mitochondria. Some of them may be associated in multienzyme complexes, which would facilitate movement of metabolites between the enzymes.

Chemical reactions of Krebs' cycle fall into three main categories:

(i) **Decarboxylation** All three carbon atoms in pyruvic acid are eventually released as CO_2 in Krebs' cycle.

(ii) **Oxidation reduction** Oxidation of carbon compounds while reduction of NAD^+ and FAD^+.

(iii) **Substrate level phosphorylation** Synthesis of ATP (GTP) by accepting phosphate from the substrate.

A feature of the plant citric acid cycle that is absent in many other organisms is the significant activity of NAD^+ malic enzyme, which has been found in the matrix of all plant mitochondria analyzed to date. This enzyme catalyzes the oxidative decarboxylation of malate:

$$\text{Malate} + NAD^+ \rightarrow \text{Pyruvate} + CO_2 + NADH$$

Malate is synthesized from PEP in the cytosol *via* the enzymes PEP carboxylase and malate dehydrogenase. The presence of NAD^+ malic enzyme enables plant mitochondria to operate alternative pathways for the metabolism of PEP derived from glycolysis.

Malate is then transported into the mitochondrial matrix, where NAD^+ malic enzyme can oxidize it to pyruvate. Alternatively, the malate produced *via* the PEP carboxylase can replace citric acid cycle intermediates used in biosynthesis.

Every two molecules of acetyl Co-A that enters the cycle four molecules of CO_2 are liberated by decarboxylation, six molecules of NADH and two molecules of $FADH_2$ are produced by oxidation reduction reactions and two molecules of ATP are produced by substrate level phosphorylation. Many of the intermediates play a role in other pathway especially amino acid biosynthesis.

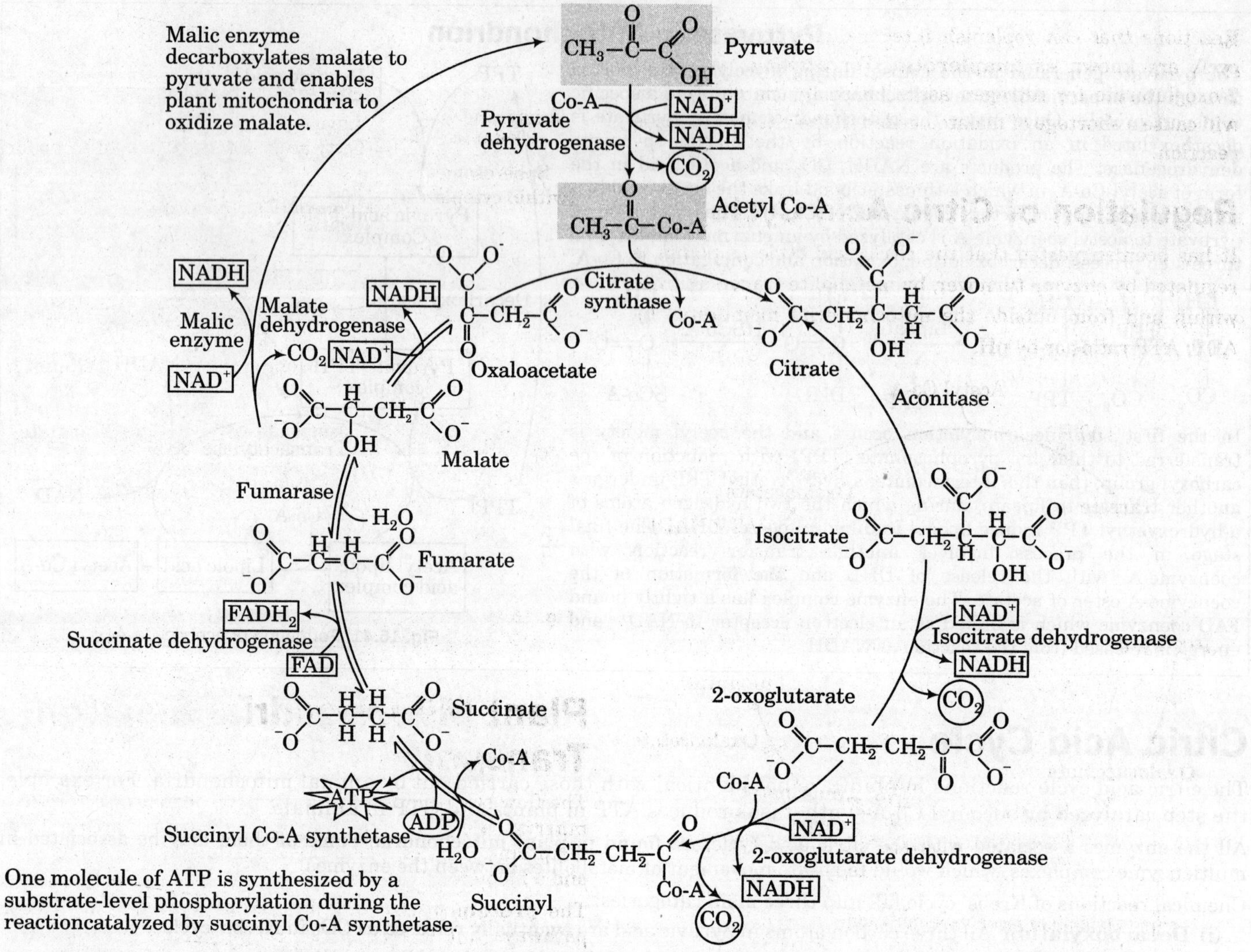

Malic enzyme decarboxylates malate to pyruvate and enables plant mitochondria to oxidize malate.

One molecule of ATP is synthesized by a substrate-level phosphorylation during the reactioncatalyzed by succinyl Co-A synthetase.

Fig. 16.42 Plant citric acid cycle. Pyruvate is oxidized to three molecules of CO_2. The electrons released during these oxidations are used to reduce four molecules of NAD^+ to NADH and one molecule of FAD to $FADH_2$

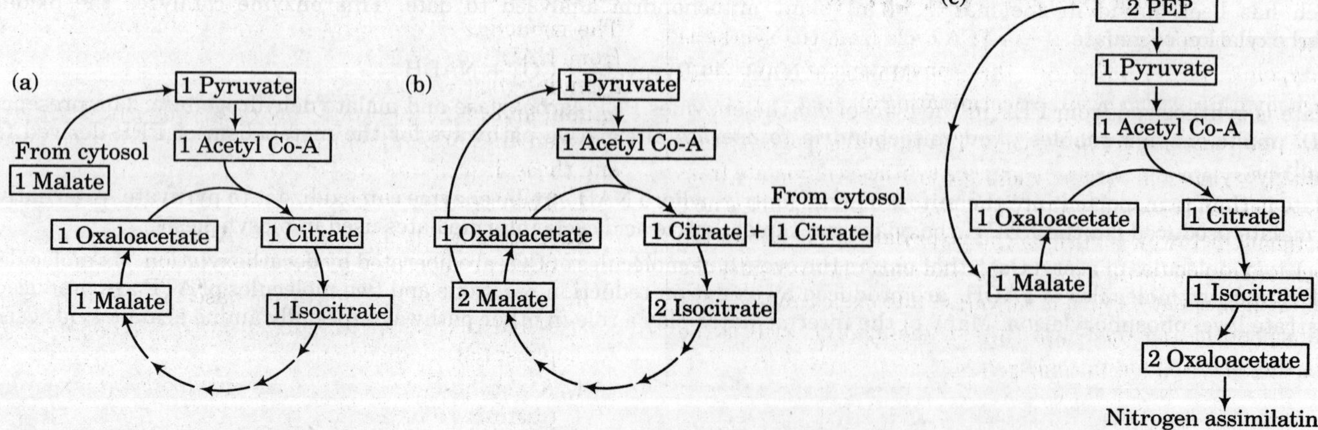

Fig. 16.43 Malic enzyme and PEP carboxylase provide plants with metabolic flexibility for the metabolism of phosphoenolpyruvate. Malic enzyme makes it possible for plant mitochondria to oxidize both malate (a) and citrate (b) to CO_2 without involving pyruvate delivered by glycolysis. The joint action of PEP carboxylase and pyruvate kinase can convert glycolytic PEP to 2-oxoglutarate, which is used for nitrogen assimilation (c).

Reactions that can replenish intermediates in a metabolic cycle are known as **anaplerotic**. For example, export of 2-oxoglutarate for nitrogen assimilation in the chloroplast will cause a shortage of malate needed in the citrate synthase reaction.

Regulation of Citric Acid Cycle

It has been suggested that the citric acid cycle in plants is regulated by enzyme turnover, by metabolite transport from within and from outside the mitochondrial membrane, by ADP: ATP ratios or by pH.

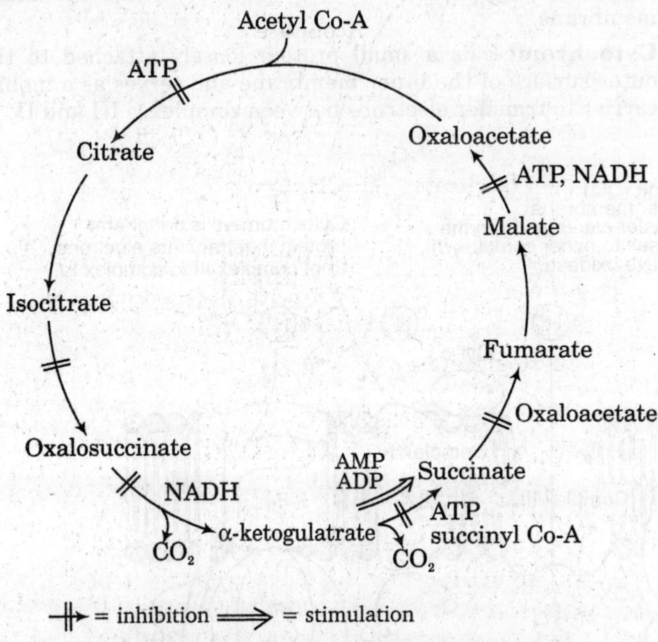

Fig. 16.44 Regulation of steps in citric acid cycle

Role of the TCA cycle

The most important role of the TCA cycle from the synthetic viewpoint, is its place in the conversion of lipid into carbohydrate, which occurs in germinating oil seed.

Two new reactions are introduced: The conversion of isocitrate into glyoxylate and succinate and the synthesis of malate from glyoxylate and external acetyl coenzyme-A. This ingenious new metabolic pathway, known as the glyoxylate cycle, allows the cycle to keep on turning over and at the same time provides the cell with succinate, which is converted into oxaloacetate in the mitochondria and then into PEP in the cytosol. PEP is the starting material for gluconeogenesis.

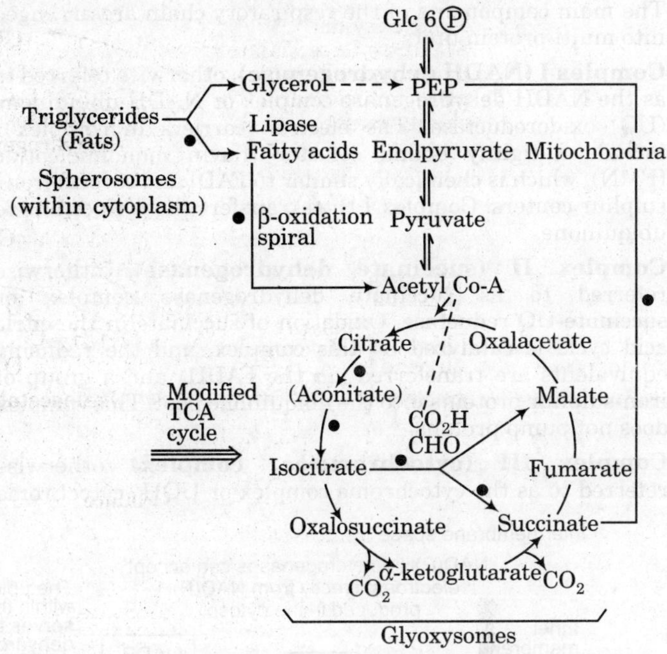

Fig. 16.45 The glyoxylate cycle. Solid dots indicate the pathway of carbon in the cycle

Plant Mitochondrial Electron Transport

The flow of electrons causes pumping of **protons from the matrix side to the intermembrane space**. This maintains a proton motive force composed of a pH gradient and a membrane potential.

The **protons flow back into the matrix** along various pathways but particularly through the ATP synthesizing complex embedded in the membrane during ATP synthesis. The central feature of this process of oxidative phosphorylation is the generation of proton gradient and its accompanying membrane potential.

The sequence of events that mediate the flow of electrons from NADH or $FADH_2$ to O_2 *via* cytochrome oxidase (the cyanide-sensitive pathway) appears to be similar in both animal and plant mitochondria. Some important differences between animal and plant mitochondria have been observed and these differences in plants are

1. The respiratory-linked oxidation of external NADH.
2. A cyanide and antimycin-A-insensitive alternative electron transport pathway.
3. A second NADPH dehydrogenase that oxidizes external NADPH produced mainly from the oxidative pentose phosphate pathway.
4. A rotenone-insensitive oxidation of internal NADH (distinct from complex I).

The main components of the respiratory chain are arranged into multi-protein units.

Complex I (NADH dehydrogenase), otherwise referred to as the NADH dehydrogenase complex or NADH-ubiquinone (UQ) oxidoreductase. The electron carriers in complex I include a tightly bound cofactor [flavin mononucleotide (FMN), which is chemically similar to FAD] and several iron–sulphur centers. Complex I then transfers these electrons to ubiquinone.

Complex II (succinate dehydrogenase), otherwise referred to as succinate dehydrogenase complex or succinate-UQ reductase. Oxidation of succinate in the citric acid cycle is catalyzed by this complex, and the reducing equivalents are transferred *via* the $FADH_2$ and a group of iron-sulphur proteins into the ubiquinone pool. This complex does not pump protons.

Complex III (cytochrome-bc_1 complex) otherwise referred to as the cytochrome complex or UQH_2-cytochrome reductase. This complex oxidizes reduced ubiquinone (ubiquinol) and transfers the electrons *via* an iron-sulphur center, two *b*-type cytochromes (b_{565} and b_{560}), and a membrane-bound cytochrome-c_1 to cytochrome-*c*.

Complex IV (cytochrome-*c* oxidase), otherwise referred to as the cytochrome oxidase complex. This complex contains two copper centers (Cu_A and Cu_B) and cytochromes-*a* and a_3. Complex IV is the terminal oxidase and brings about the four-electron reduction of O_2 to two molecules of H_2O.

The complexes are hydrophobic in nature. However, the cytochrome component between complex III and IV is a water-soluble peripheral protein on the outside of the mitochondrial membrane. **Ubiquinone**, a small lipid-soluble electron and proton carrier, is located within the inner membrane.

Cytochrome-*c* is a small protein loosely attached to the outer surface of the inner membrane and serves as a mobile carrier to transfer electrons between complexes III and IV.

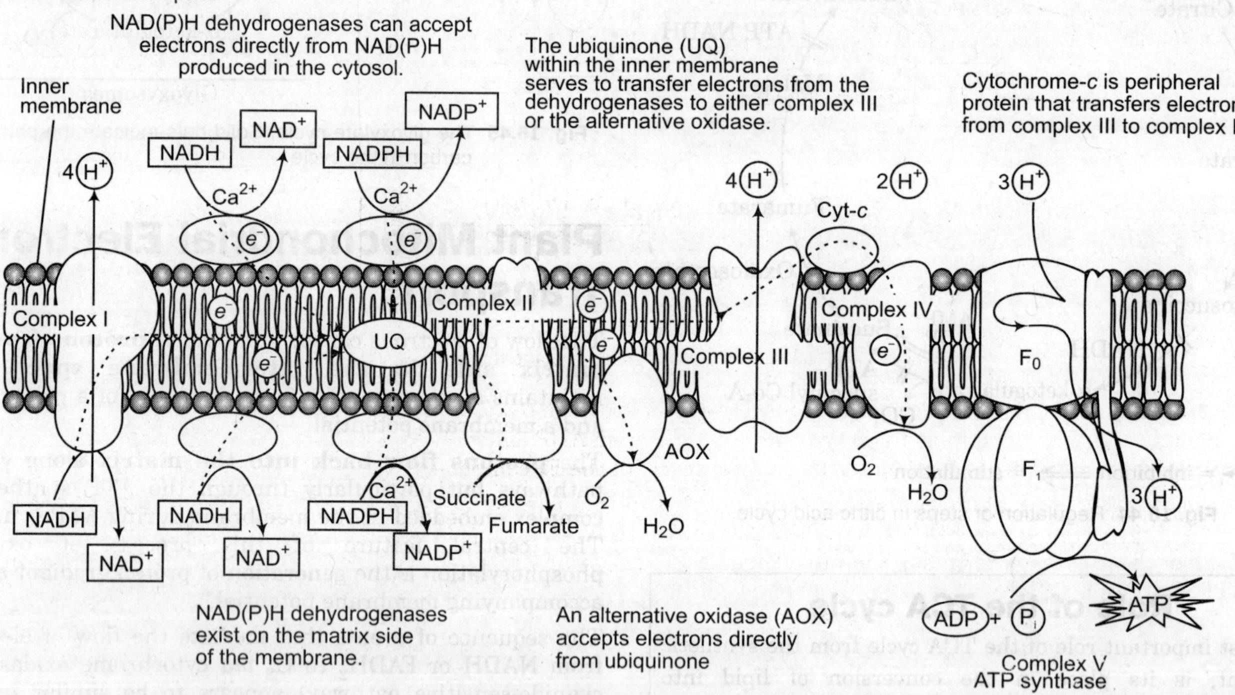

Fig. 16.46 A schematic representation of the distribution of redox components within the inner mitochondrial membrane. None of these additional enzymes pumps protons

Specific Inhibitors Tools to Investigate the Electron Transport Chain of Plant Mitochondria

Inhibitors	Acts On
Rotenone*	Complex I
Antimycin	Complex III
Cyanide	Complex IV
Salicylhydroxamic Acid (SHAM)	Alternative oxidase

*Rotenone is insensitive to **NAD(P)H dehydrogenases (highlighted in green in above diagram)** exist on the matrix and the cytosol side of the membrane.

The **F_0 F_1-ATP synthase** (also called **complex V**) consists of two major components, F_1 and F_0. **F_1** is a peripheral membrane protein complex that is composed of five different subunits and the catalytic site for converting ADP to ATP. This complex is attached to the matrix side of the inner membrane. **F_0** is an integral membrane protein complex that consists of at least three different polypeptides that form the channel through which protons cross the inner membrane.

ATP Synthesis

The mechanism of mitochondrial ATP synthesis is based on the chemiosmotic hypothesis, which was first proposed in 1961 by Nobel laureate **Peter Mitchell** across biological membranes. According to the chemiosmotic theory, the electrochemical energy inherent in the difference in proton concentration and separation of charge across the inner mitochondrial membrane—the proton-motive force—drives the synthesis of ATP as protons flow passively back into the matrix through a proton pore associated with **ATP synthase.**

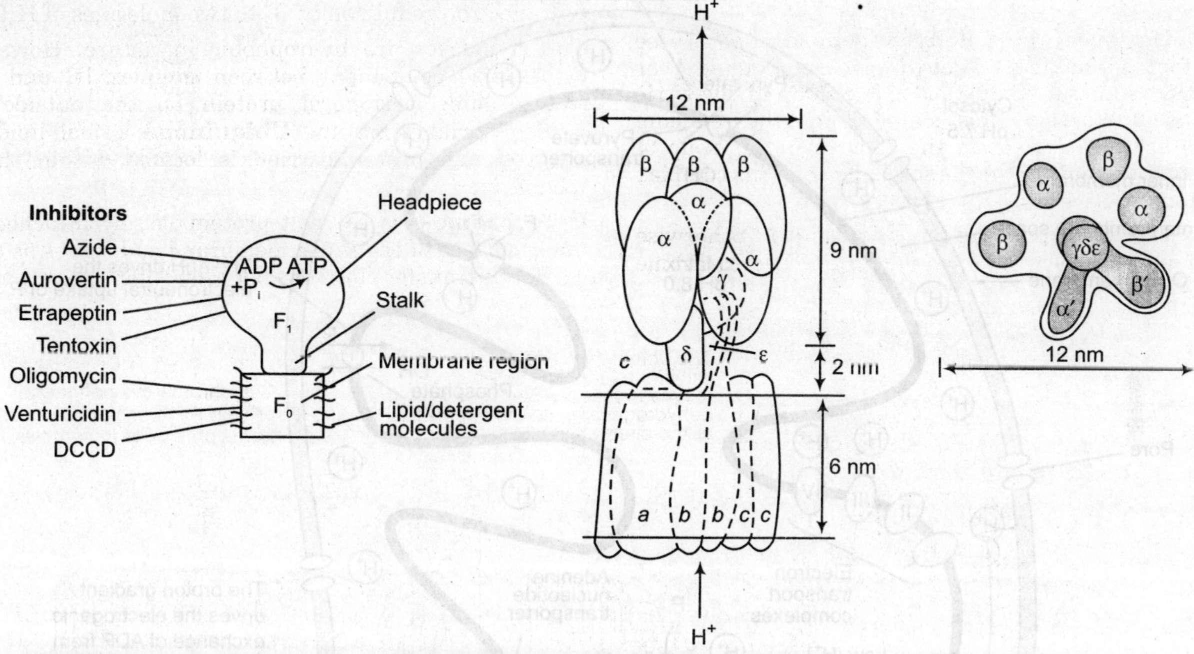

Fig. 16.47 ATP synthase in mitochondria

ATP synthesis in the mitochondrion is coupled to electron transport. In oxidative phosphorylation, the transfer of electrons to oxygen via complexes I to IV is coupled to the synthesis of ATP from ADP and P_i via the ATP synthase (complex V). The passage of protons through the channel is coupled to the catalytic cycle of the F_1 component of the ATP synthase.

The chemiosmotic theory explains the action mechanism of uncouplers, a wide range of chemically unrelated compounds (including 2, 4-dinitrophenol and FCCP) that decreases mitochondrial ATP synthesis but often stimulates the rate of electron transport. All of these compounds make the inner membrane leaky to protons, which prevents the buildup of a sufficiently H^+ to drive ATP synthesis.

Transmembrane Transport in Plant Mitochondria

An electrochemical proton gradient consisting of a membrane potential. Alkaline is established inside across the inner mitochondrial membrane during electron transport. Specific metabolites are moved across the inner membrane by specialized proteins, called transporters or carriers.

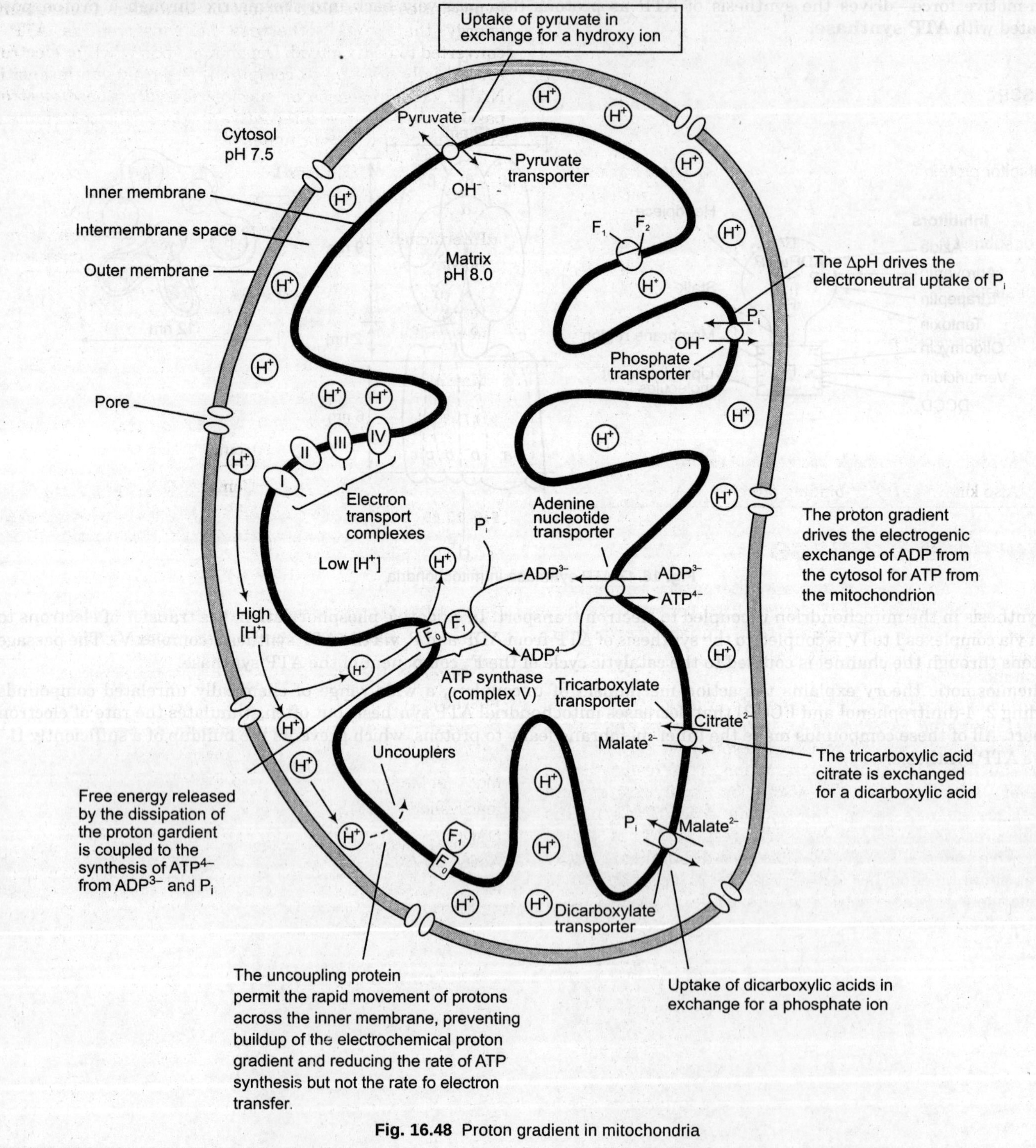

Fig. 16.48 Proton gradient in mitochondria

A Comparison of the Nomenclature of ATP Synthase Subunits

Mitochondria	Chloroplast	E. coli
F_1		
α	α	α
β	β	β
γ	γ	γ
OSCP	δ	δ
δ	ε	ε
ε	–	–
Inhibitor protein	–	some homology with ε
F_0		
a or subunit 6	IV	a
b	I, II[a]	b
c or subunit 9[b]	III[b]	c[b]
d	–	–
F_6 (coupling factor 6)	–	–
A6L		
e	–	–
f	–	–
g	–	–

[a]In some photosynthetic bacteria and chloroplasts.

[b]Also known as DCCD-binding protein.

Alternate Oxidase

Most, if not all, plants have an 'alternative' respiratory pathway for the reduction of oxygen. This pathway involves the so-called alternative oxidase that, unlike cytochrome-*c* oxidase, is insensitive to inhibition by cyanide, azide or carbon monoxide.

In animals cyanide, carbon monoxide and azide inhibitors completely inhibit respiratory O_2 uptake. In root and leaves of spinach or pea cyanide resistant respiration may account for as much as 40% of total respiration. This respiration is however sensitive to inhibition by hydroxamic acid derivatives such as Salicyl Hydroxamic Acid (SHAM). This cyanide resistant SHAM-sensitive respiration is called alternative oxidase. The enzyme has been difficult to study by conventional biochemical techniques, the proteins appear to be relatively unstable and loses its activity rapidly upon isolation from membrane.

This alternative oxidase is composed of two identical subunits (a homodimer) that span the inner mitochondrial membrane, with the active site facing the matrix side of the membrane. It functions as a ubiquinone, O_2 oxidoreductase that is it accepts electrons from the ubiquinone pool and transfers them to oxygen. In alternative oxidase the electrons bypass atleast two sites for proton extrusion. Consequently energy that would otherwise be conserved as ATP is converted to heat instead. Depending upon whether electrons are initially donated to complex I, the rotenone insensitive NADH dehydrogenase or succinic dehydrogenase electrons passing through the alternative oxidase will contribute to synthesis of one ATP or none.

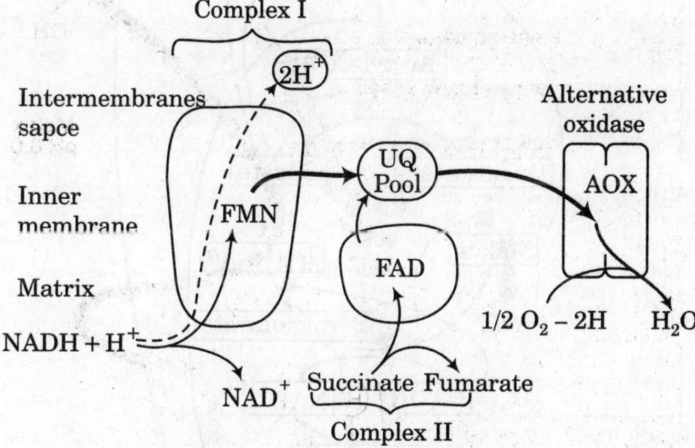

Fig. 16.49 The alternative respiratory pathway. Electrons intercepted by the alternative oxidase (AOX) pass through one or no phosphorylating sites

Table 16.3 **Regulation of Pyruvate Dehydrogenase** (PDH) **Activity**

Effect of PDH Activity	Mechanism
Activating	
Pyruvate	Inhibits kinase
ADP	Inhibits kinase
Mg^{2+} (or Mn^{2+})	Stimulates phosphatase
Inactivating	
NADH	Inhibits PDH stimulates kinase
Acetyl Co-A	Inhibits PDH stimulates kinase
NH_4^+	Inhibits PDH stimulates kinase

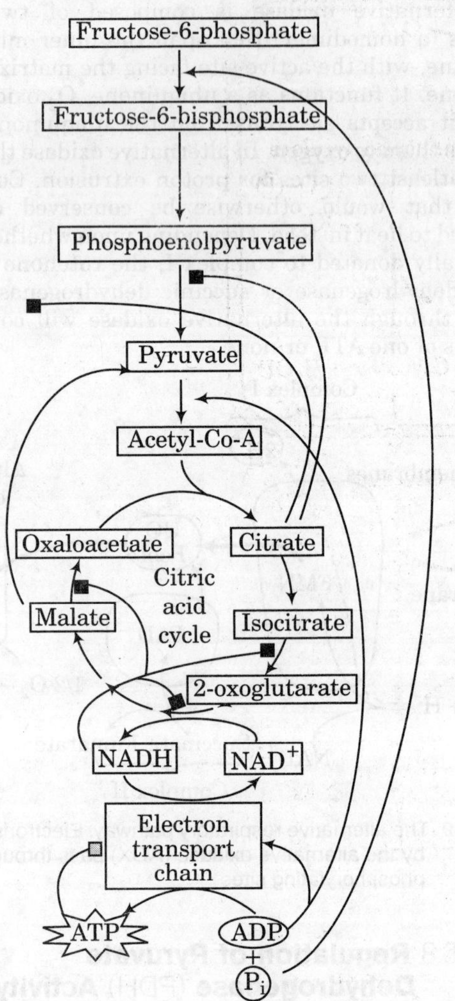

Fig. 16.50 Concept of bottom-up regulation of plant respiration

Stimulate enzymes in early steps of the pathways (green arrows). Accumulation of products (*e.g.,* ATP) inhibits (squares).

Photorespiratory Pathway

This process involves the reoxidation of products just previously assimilated in photosynthesis. This pathway involves different cell organelles (chloroplast, mitochondria and peroxisome) and result in net loss of carbon from cell (as CO_2 is evolved). It is light dependent evolution of CO_2.

An important property of rubisco is its ability to catalyze both the carboxylation and the oxygenation of RuBP. Oxygenation is the primary reaction in a process known as **photorespiration**. Because photosynthesis and photorespiration work in diametrically opposite directions, photorespiration results in loss of CO_2 from cells that are simultaneously fixing CO_2 by the Calvin cycle.

Oxygenation of RuBP leads to the production of one molecule of glycerate-3-phosphate and one of glycolate-2-phosphate.

The K_m (CO_2) of Rubisco is about 10μM, which is about the same as the concentration of CO_2 dissolved in water at 20°C, but the CO_2 concentration would be rather less in the mesophyll cells of a leaf in air. The K_m (O_2) is about 535μM, which is about double the O_2 concentration in a leaf at 20°C. Under these conditions, Rubisco catalyzes both carboxylation and oxygenation of RuBP. The two substrates are competitive, so that raising the CO_2 concentration will inhibit oxygenation and *vice versa*.

Reactions of the C_2 Oxidative Photosynthetic Carbon Cycle

Enzyme	Reaction
1. Ribulose-1, 5-bisphosphate carboxylase/oxygenase (chloroplast)	2 Ribulose-1, 5-bisphosphate + $2O_2 \rightarrow$ 2 phosphoglycolate + 2, 3-phosphoglycerate + $4H^+$
2. Phosphoglycolate phosphatase (chloroplast)	2 Phosphoglycolate + $2H_2O \rightarrow$ 2 glycolate + $2P_i$
3. Glycolate oxidase (peroxisome)	2 Glycolate + $2O_2 \rightarrow$ 2 glyoxylate + $2H_2O \rightarrow 2$
4. Catalase (peroxisome)	$2H_2O_2 \rightarrow 2H_2O + O_2$
5. Glyoxylate: glutamate aminotransferase (peroxisome)	2 Glyoxylate + 2 glutamate $\rightarrow$ 2 glycine + 2 α-ketoglutarate
6. Glycine decarboxylase (mitochondrion)	Glycine + NAD^+ + H^+ H_4-folate $\rightarrow$ NADH + CO_2 + NH_4^+ + methylene-H_4-folate
7. Serine hydroxymethyl transferase (mitochondrion)	Methylene-H_4-folate + H_2O + glycine $\rightarrow$ serine + H_4-folate
8. Serine aminotransferase (peroxisome)	Serine + α-ketoglutarate $\rightarrow$ Hydroxypyruvate + glutamate
9. Hydroxypyruvate reductase peroxisome)	Hydroxypyruvate - NADH + $H^+ \rightarrow$ Glycerate + NAD^+
10. Glycerate kinase (chloroplast)	Glycerate + ATP $\rightarrow$ 3-phosphoglycerate + ADP + H^+

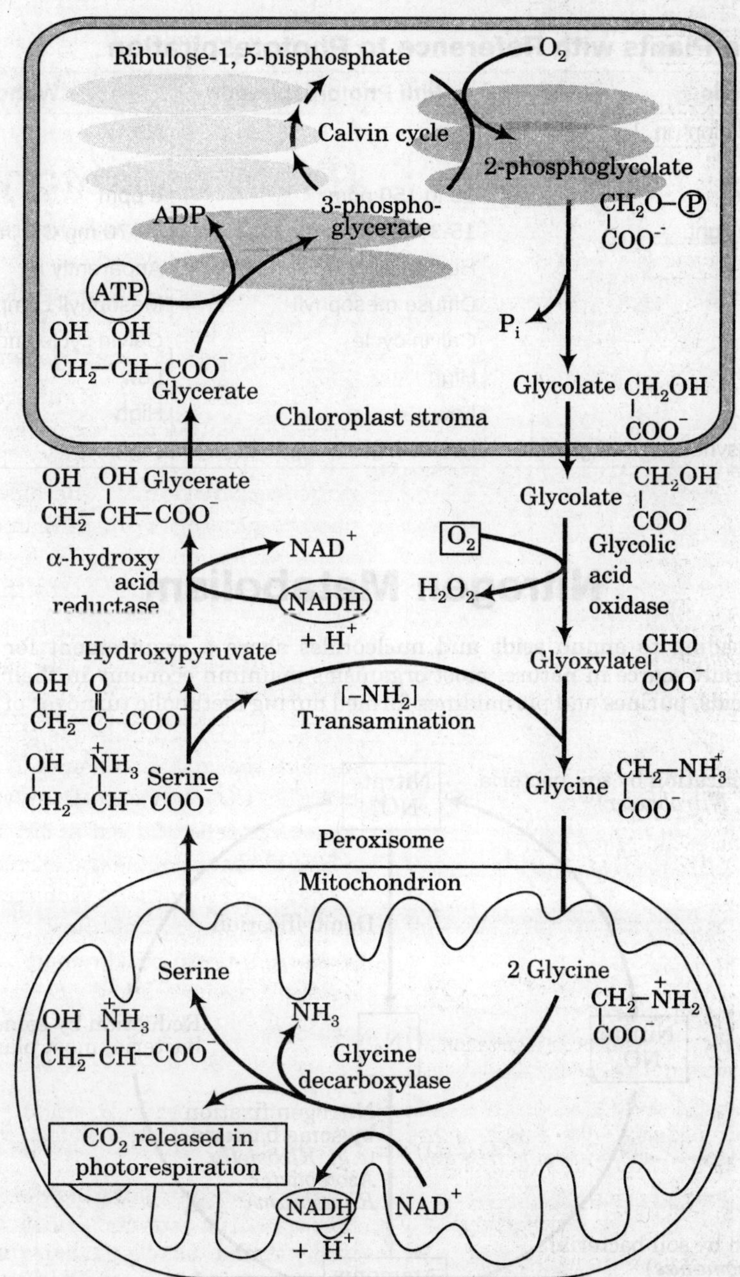

Fig. 16.51 The photorespiratory pathway. OAA-oxaloacetic acid

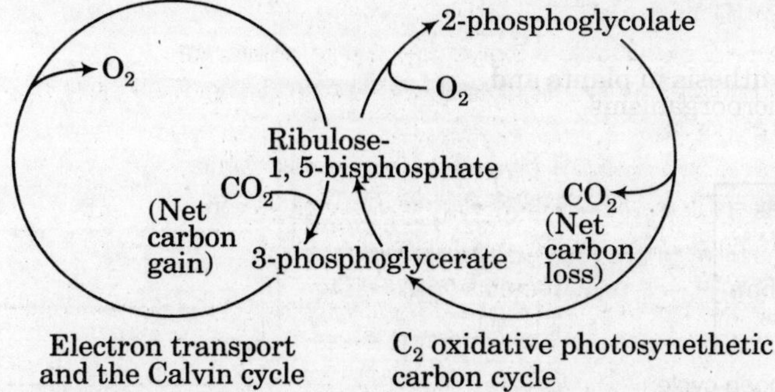

Fig. 16.52 The flow of carbon in the leaf between the Calvin cycle and C_2 oxidative photosynthetic carbon cycle

The flow of carbon in the leaf is determined by the balance between two mutually opposing cycles. Whereas the Calvin cycle is capable of independent operation in the presence of adequate substrates generated by photosynthetic electron transport, the C_2 oxidative photosynthetic carbon cycle requires continued operation of the Calvin cycle to regenerate its starting material, ribulose-1, 5-bisphosphate.

Photorespiration depends upon concentration of O_2 and goes on increasing with higher concentration of oxygen even upto 100%.

Table 16.4 **Differences in Plants with Reference to Photorespiration**

Characteristic	With Photorespiration	Without Photorespiration
Enhancement of CO_2 assimilation in light and low oxygen.	Yes	No
CO_2 compensation point in light.	15 to 150 ppm	0 ppm
CO_2 assimilation rate in intense light.	15-35 mg CO_2/dm2/h	50-70 mg CO_2/dm2/h
CO2 evolution in light.	High rate	Apparently nil
Internal structure of leaf.	Diffuse mesophyll	Mesophyll compact about vascular bundles
Carbon pathway.	Calvin cycle	Calvin cycle and Hatch and Slack pathway both
Carbonic anhydrase activity.	High	Low
Translocation rate from leaf.	Low	High
Temperature optimum for photosynthesis and growth.	Low to high	High

Nitrogen Metabolism

The biosynthetic pathways leading to amino acids and nucleotides share a requirement for nitrogen. Biologically useful nitrogen compounds are generally scarce in nature, most organisms maintain economy in their use of ammonia, amino acids and nucleotides. Free amino acids, purines and pyrimidines formed during metabolic turnover of proteins and nucleic acids are often reused.

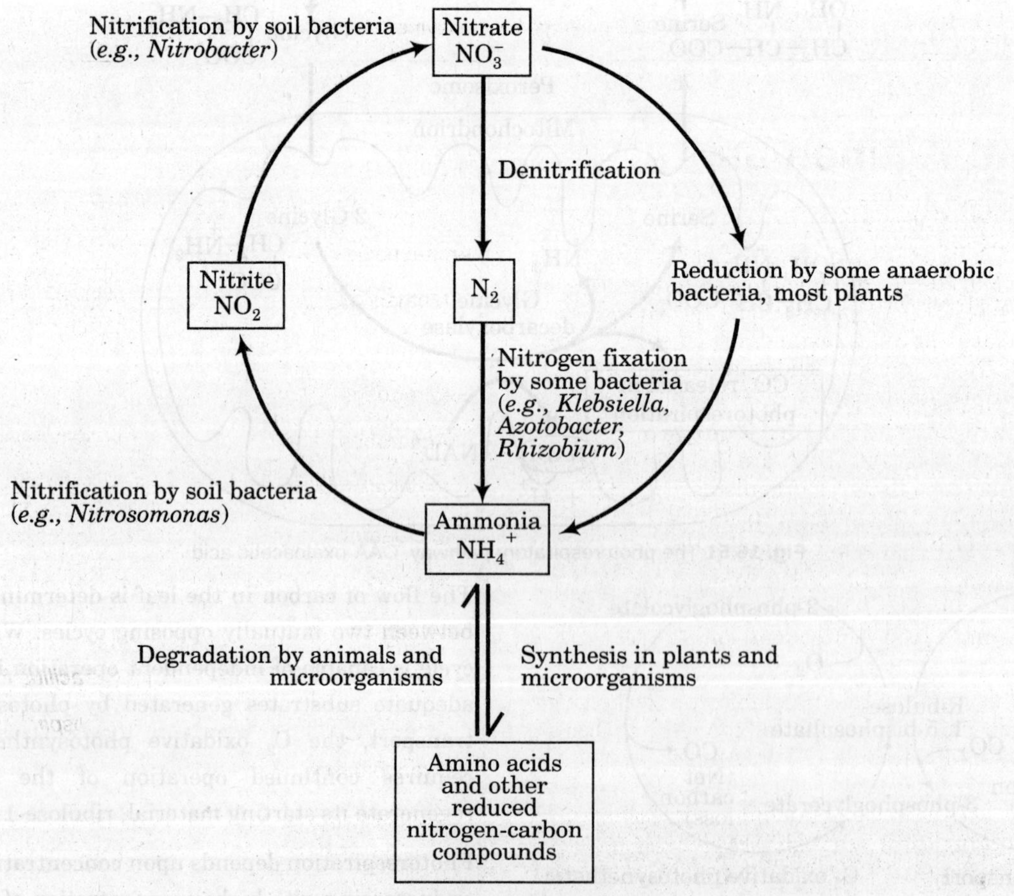

Fig. 16.53 The nitrogen cycle

Nitrogenase Enzyme Complex Fixes N_2

The reaction catalyzed by nitrogenase. Ferredoxin reduces the Fe protein. Binding and hydrolysis of ATP to the Fe protein is thought to cause a conformational change of the Fe protein that facilitates the redox reactions. The Fe protein reduces the MoFe protein, and the MoFe protein reduces the N_2.

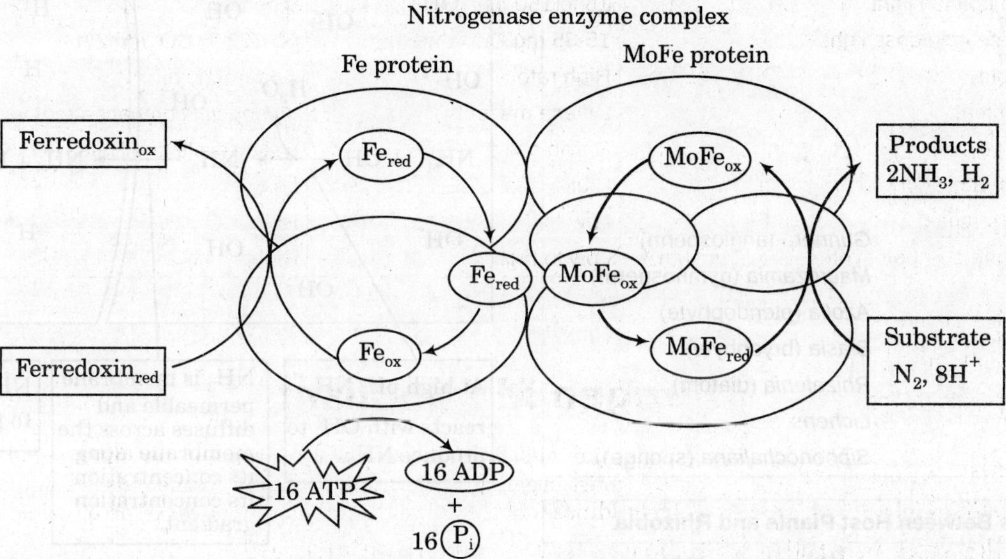

Fig. 16.54 Nitrogenase enzyme complex

Nitrate and Ammonium Assimilation

Many mineral nutrients absorbed from the soil by the roots and incorporation into the organic compounds that are essential for growth and development. This incorporation of mineral nutrients into organic substances such as pigments, enzyme cofactors, lipids, nucleic acids and amino acids is termed **nutrient assimilation**.

Assimilation of nitrogen and sulphur requires a complex series of biochemical reactions that are among the most energy-requiring reactions in living organisms:

1. In **nitrate (NO_3^-) assimilation**, the nitrogen in NO_3^- is converted to a higher-energy form in nitrite (NO_2^-), then to a yet higher-energy form in ammonium (NH_4^+), and finally into the amide nitrogen of glutamine. This process consumes the equivalent of 12 ATPs per nitrogen.
2. Plants such as legumes form symbiotic relationships with nitrogen-fixing bacteria to convert molecular nitrogen (N_2) into ammonia (NH_3). Ammonia (NH_3) is the first stable product of natural fixation; at physiological pH, however, ammonia is protonated to form the **ammonium ion (NH^{4+})**. The process of **biological nitrogen fixation**, together with the subsequent assimilation of NH_3 into an **amino acid**, consumes about 16 ATPs per nitrogen.

Free Living Nitrogen Fixing Organisms	
Archaebacteria	
Methanogens	*Methanococcus volate*
Eubacteria	
Heterotrophs	
Anaerobes	*Clostridium pasteurianum*
Facultative anaerobes/	*Klebsiella pneumoniae*
Microaerobes	*Azotobacter vinelandii*
Aerobes	*Azospirillum lipoferum*
Autotrophs	
Chemotrophic bacteria	*Thiobacillus ferriooxidans*
Photosynthetic bacteria	*Rhodospirillum rubrum*
Cyanobacteria	
Unicellular	*Gloeothece* sp.
Filamentous	*Oscillatoria* sp.
Heterocystous	*Anabaena, Nostoc* sp.

Symbiotic Nitrogen Fixing Organisms	
Name	**Host**
Rhizobiaceae	Legumes and Parasponia
Azorhizobium	
Bradyrhizobium	
Photorhizobium	
Rhizobium	
Sinorhizobium	
Actinomycetales	
Frankia	
Cyanobacteria	*Gunnera* (angiosperm)
	Macrozamia (gymnosperm)
	Azolla (pteridophyte)
	Blasia (bryophyte)
	Rhizalenia (diatom)
	Lichens
	Siphonochaliana (sponge)

Associations Between Host Plants and Rhizobia	
Plant host	**Rhizobial symbiont**
Parasponia (a non-legume, formerly called Trema)	*Bradyrhizobium* sp.
Soyabean (*Glycine max*)	*Bradyrhizobium japonicum* (slow-growing type); *Sinorhizobium fredii* (fast-growing type)
Alfalfa (*Medicago sativa*)	*Sinorhizobium meliloti*
Sesbania (aquatic)	*Azorhizobium* (forms both root and stem nodules; the stems have adventitious roots)
Bean (*Phaseolus*)	*Rhizobium leguminosarum* var. *phaseoli*; *Rhizobium tropicii*; *Rhizobium etli*
Clover (*Trifolium*)	*Rhizobium leguminosarum* var. *trifolii*
Pea (*Pisum sativum*)	*Rhizobium leguminosarum* var. *viciae*
Aeschenomene (aquatic)	*Photorhizobium* (photosynthetically active rhizobia that form stem nodules, probably associated with adventitious roots)

In contrast to nitrate, high levels of ammonium are toxic to both plants and animals. Ammonium dissipates transmembrane proton gradients that are required for both photosynthetic and respiratory electron transport.

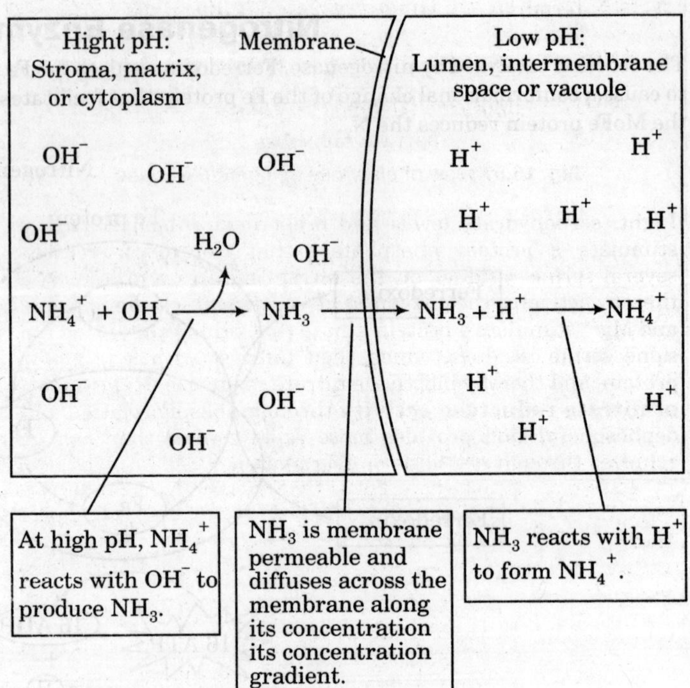

Fig. 16.55 NH_4^+ toxicity can dissipate pH gradients

Nitrate Reductase

Plants assimilate most of the nitrate absorbed by their roots into organic nitrogen compounds. The first step of this process is the reduction of nitrate to nitrite in the cytosol (Oaks; 1994). The enzyme **nitrate reductase** catalyzes this reaction.

$$NO_3^- + NAD(P)H + H^+ + 2e^- \rightarrow NO_2^- + NAD(P)^+ + H_2O$$

Nitrate Reductases

The nitrate reductases of higher plants are composed of two identical subunits, each containing three prosthetic groups: **FAD (Flavin Adenine Dinucleotide)**, **haeme**, and **a molybdenum complexed** to an organic molecule called a **pterin.**

Fig. 16.56 A pterin (fully oxidized)

Nitrate reductase is the main molybdenum-containing protein in vegetative tissues and one symptom of molybdenum deficiency is the accumulation of nitrate.The three-domain model for nitrate reductase function coordinately. The FAD-binding domain accepts two electrons from NADH or NADPH. The electrons then pass through the haeme domain to the molybdenum complex, where they are transferred to nitrate.

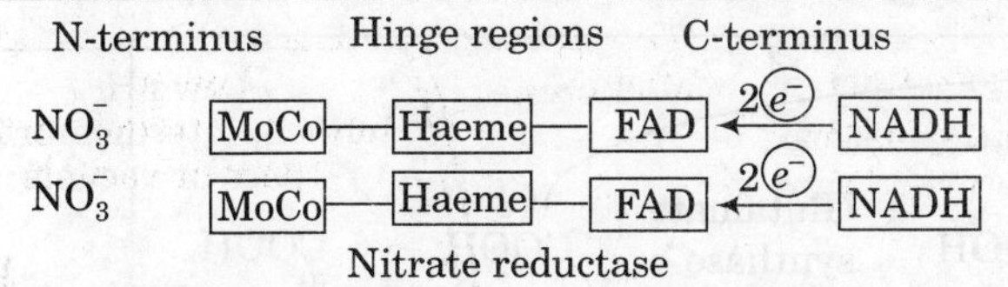

Fig. 16.57 Flow of electrons in nitrate reductase

Light, carbohydrate levels and other environmental factors stimulate a protein phosphatase that **dephosphorylates** several serine residues on the nitrate reductase protein and thereby activates the enzyme. The reverse direction, darkness and Mg^{2+} stimulate a protein kinase that **phosphorylates** the same serine residues, which then interact with a inhibitor protein, and thereby inactivate nitrate reductase. **Regulation of nitrate reductase activity** through phosphorylation and dephosphorylation provides more rapid control than can be achieved through synthesis or degradation.

Nitrite Reductase Converts Nitrite to Ammonium

Plant cells immediately transport the nitrite generated by nitrate reduction from the cytosol into chloroplasts in leaves and plastids in roots. In these organelles, the enzyme nitrite reductase reduces nitrite to ammonium.

$$NO_2^- + 6\,Fd_{red} + 8\,H^+ + 6\,e^- \rightarrow NH_4^+ + 6\,Fd_{ox} + 2\,H_2O$$

Chloroplasts and root plastids contain different forms of the enzyme, but both forms consist of a single polypeptide containing two prosthetic groups: an iron–sulphur cluster (Fe_4S_4) and a specialized heme. These groups acting together bind nitrite and reduce it directly to ammonium.

Nitrite reductase is encoded in the nucleus and synthesized in the cytoplasm with an N-terminal transit peptide that targets it to the plastids.

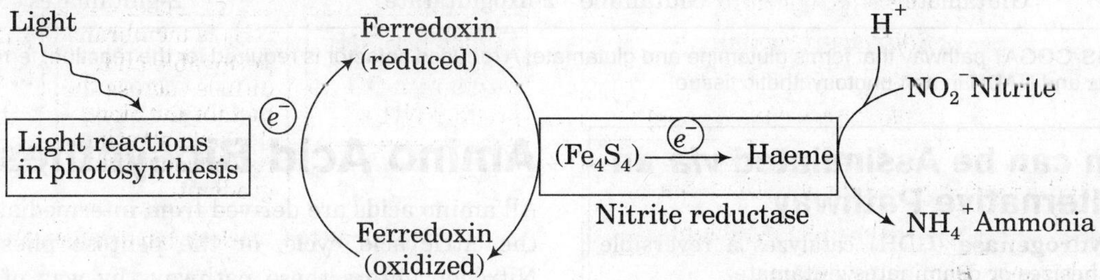

Fig. 16.58 Model for coupling of photosynthetic electron flow, *via* ferredoxin, to the reduction of nitrite by nitrite reductase

Plants Assimilate Nitrate in both Roots and Shoots

In many plants, when the roots receive small amounts of nitrate, nitrate is reduced primarily in the roots. In plants such as the cocklebur (*Xanthium strumarium*), nitrate metabolism is restricted to the shoot; in other plants, such as white lupine (*Lupinus albus*), most nitrate is metabolized in the roots. Generally, species native to temperate regions rely more heavily on nitrate assimilation by the roots than do species of tropical or subtropical origins.

Ammonium Assimilation

Plant cells avoid ammonium toxicity by rapidly converting the ammonium generated from nitrate assimilation or photorespiration into amino acids.

The primary pathway for conversion of ammonium to amino acids involves the sequential actions of **glutamine synthetase** and **glutamate synthase**.

- **Glutamine synthetase** (GS) combines ammonium with glutamate to form glutamine.

$$\text{Glutamate} + NH_4^+ + \text{ATP} \rightarrow \text{Glutamine} + \text{ADP} + P_i$$

Elevated plastid levels of glutamine stimulate the activity of **glutamate synthase** (also known as glutamine-2-oxoglutarate aminotransferase or **GOGAT**). This enzyme transfers the amide group of glutamine to 2-oxoglutarate, yielding two molecules of glutamate. Plants contain two types of GOGAT: One accepts electrons from **NADH**; the other accepts electrons from **ferredoxin (Fd)**.

$$\text{Glutamine} + \text{2-oxoglutarate} + \text{NADH} + H^+ \rightarrow 2\ \text{glutamate} + NAD^+$$

$$\text{Glutamine} + \text{2-oxoglutarate} + Fd_{red} \rightarrow 2\ \text{glutamate} + Fd_{ox}$$

The **NADH type of the enzyme** (NADH-GOGAT) is located in plastids of non-photosynthetic tissues such as roots or vascular bundles of developing leaves.

The **ferredoxin-dependent type** of glutamate synthase (Fd- GOGAT) is found in chloroplasts and serves in photorespiratory nitrogen metabolism.

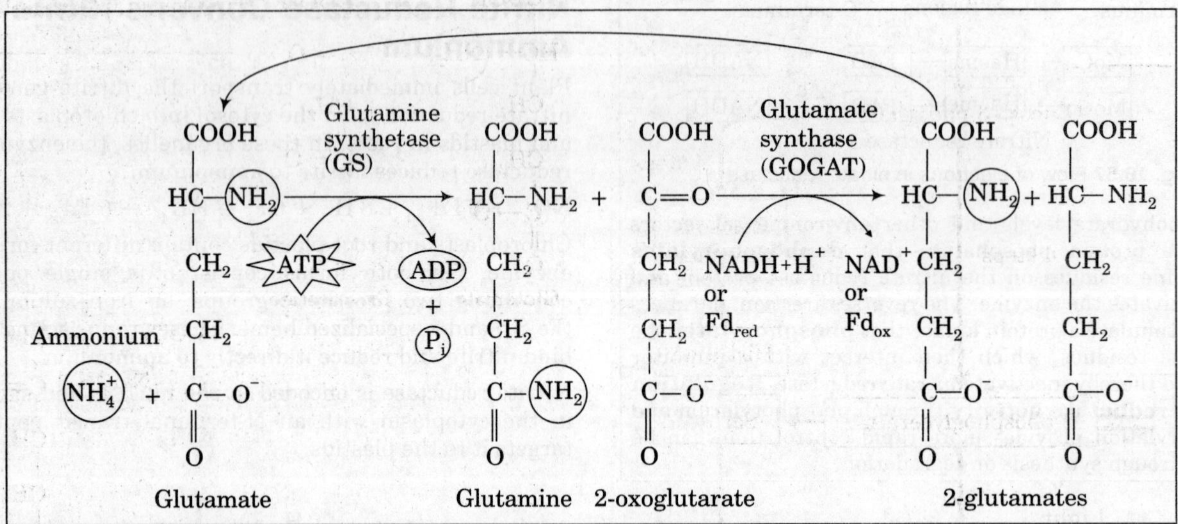

Fig. 16.59 The GS-GOGAT pathway that forms glutamine and glutamate. A reduced cofactor is required for the reaction: ferredoxin in green leaves and NADH in non-photosynthetic tissue.

Ammonium can be Assimilated *via* an Alternative Pathway

Glutamate dehydrogenase (GDH) catalyzes a reversible reaction that synthesizes or deaminates glutamate.

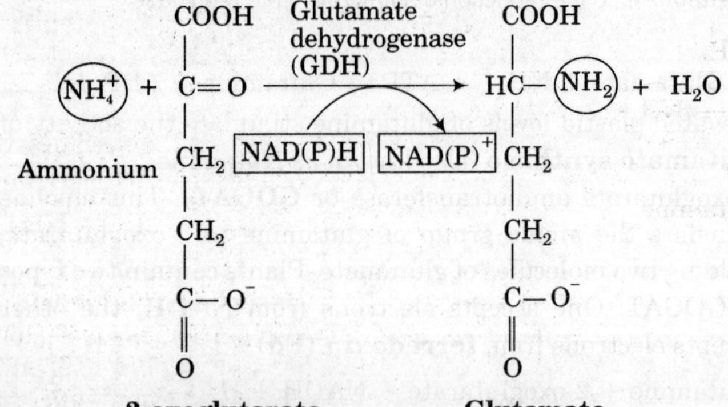

Fig. 16.60 The GDH pathway that forms glutamate using NADH or NADPH as a reductant

An NADH-dependent form of GDH is found in mitochondria and an NADPH-dependent form is localized in the chloroplasts of photosynthetic organs.

Amino Acid Biosynthesis

All amino acids are derived from intermediates in glycolysis, the citric acid cycle, or the pentose phosphate pathway. Nitrogen enters these pathways by way of glutamate and glutamine.

Once assimilated into glutamine and glutamate, nitrogen is incorporated into other amino acids *via* transamination reactions. The enzymes that catalyze these reactions are known as **aminotransferases**, *e.g.,* **Asparate aminotransferase (Asp-AT).** All transamination reactions require pyridoxal phosphate (vitamin-B_6) as a cofactor.

Aminotransferases are found in the cytoplasm, chloroplasts, mitochondria, glyoxysomes and peroxisomes.

Asparagine, isolated from asparagus as early as 1806, was the first amide to be identified. It serves not only as a protein precursor, but as a key compound for nitrogen transport and storage.

Asparagine synthetase (AS), the enzyme that catalyzes this reaction, is found in the cytosol of leaves and roots and in nitrogen-fixing nodules.

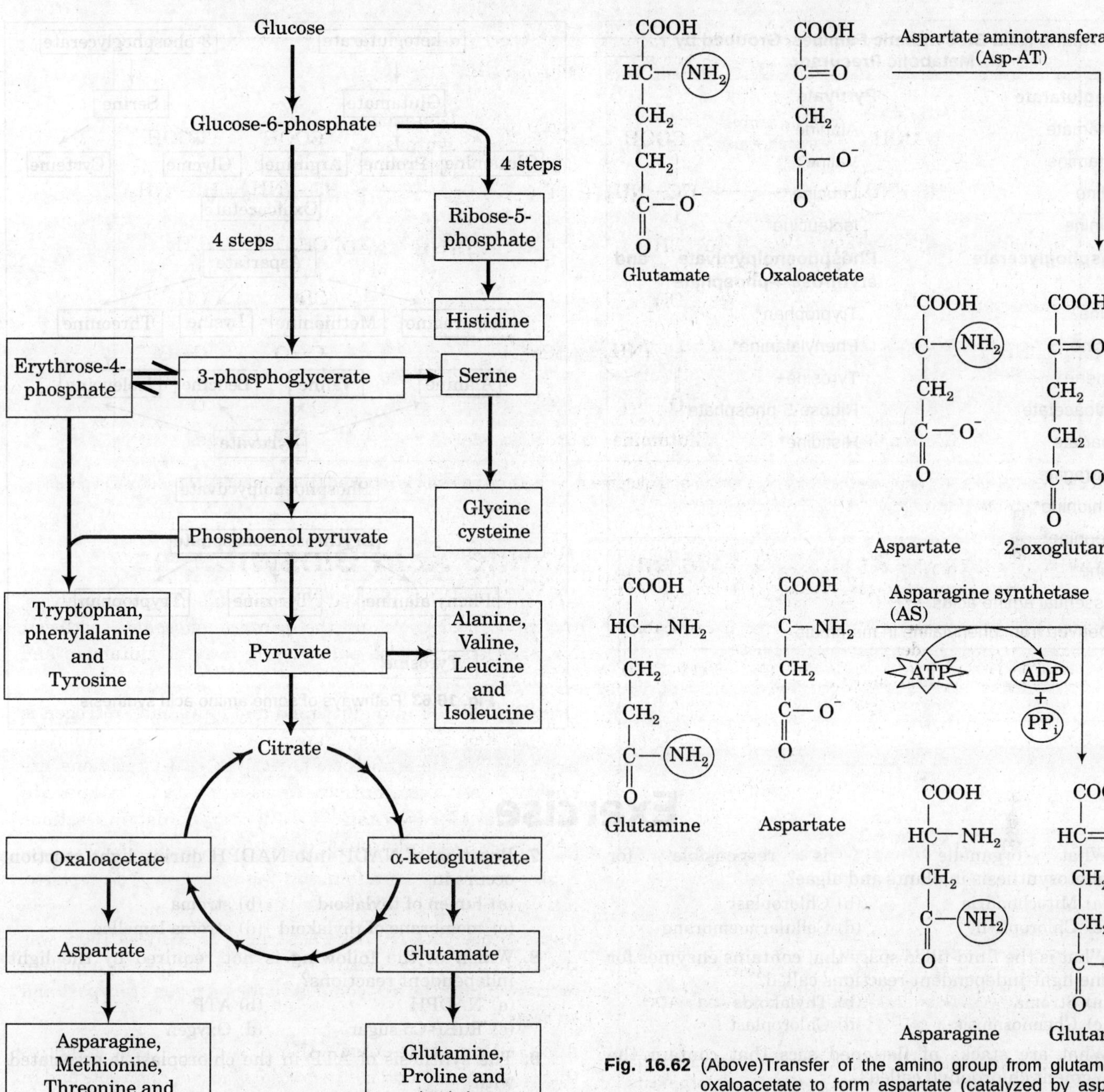

Fig. 16.61 Overview of amino acid biosynthesis

Fig. 16.62 (Above)Transfer of the amino group from glutamate to oxaloacetate to form aspartate (catalyzed by aspartate aminotransferase). (Below) Synthesis of asparagine by transfer of an amino acid group from glutamine to aspartate (catalyzed by asparagine synthesis)

Amino Acid Biosynthetic Families, Grouped by Metabolic Precursor	
α-ketoglutarate	**Pyruvate**
Glutamate	Alanine
Glutamine	Valine*
Ptoline	Leucine*
Arginine	Isoleucine*
3-phosphoglycerate	**Phosphoenolpyruvate and erythrose 4-phosphate**
Serine	Tryptophan*
Glycine	Phenylalanine*
Cystene	Tyrosine+
Oxaloacetate	Ribose-5-phosphate
Aspartate	Histidine*
Asparagine	
Methionine*	
Threonine*	
Lysine*	

* Essential amino acids.

\+ Derived from phenylaline in mammals.

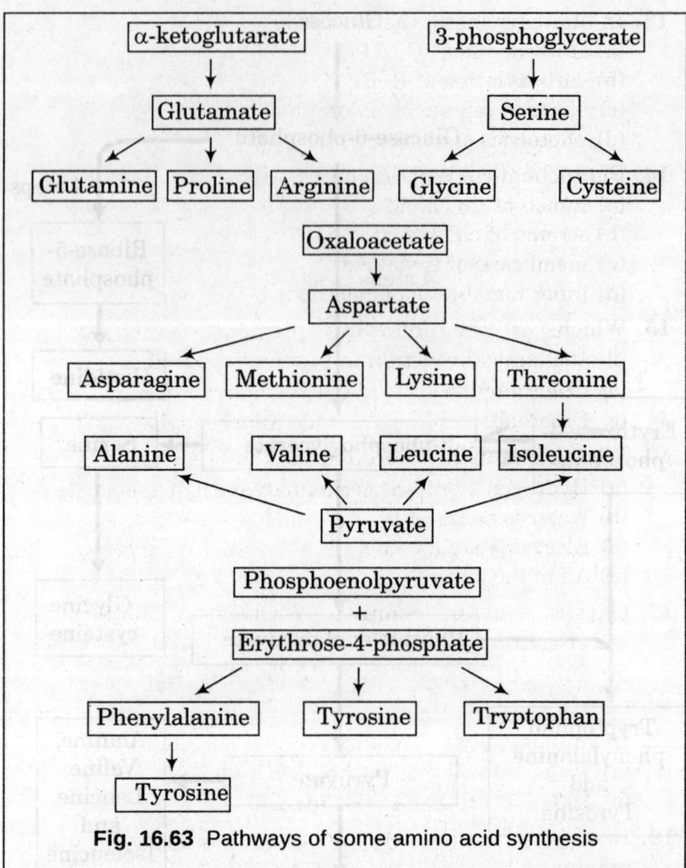

Fig. 16.63 Pathways of some amino acid synthesis

Exercise

1. What organelle is responsible for photosynthesis in plants and algae?
(a) Mitochondria (b) Chloroplast
(c) Chlorophyll (d) Cellular membrane

2. What is the fluid-filled space that contains enzymes for the light-independent reactions called?
(a) Stroma (b) Thylakoids
(c) Chemiosmosis (d) Chloroplast

3. What are stacks of flattened sacs that contain the pigment chlorophyll called?
(a) Stroma (b) Thylakoids
(c) Chemiosmosis (d) Chloroplast

4. Which is a light-independent reaction?
(a) Chemiosmosis (b) Electron pathway
(c) PS I (d) Calvin cycle

5. When electrons in the reaction-center chlorophyll become so excited; they escape to a nearby
(a) primary electron acceptor molecule
(b) secondary electron acceptor molecule
(c) chloroplast
(d) cellular membrane

6. What relationship are respiration and photosynthesis?
(a) Recipical (b) Reverse
(c) Same (d) No relationship

7. Reaction of NADP into NADPH during light reaction occurs in
(a) lumen of thylakoid (b) stroma
(c) membrane of thylakoid (d) stroma lamellae

8. Which of the following is not required by the light independent reactions?
(a) NADPH (b) ATP
(c) RuBP-C5 sugar (d) Oxygen

9. The synthesis of ATP in the chloroplast is associated with
(a) non-cyclic electron flow
(b) an accumulation of H^+ in the thylakoid lumen
(c) electron flow between PS-II to PS-I
(d) All of the above

10. What is the site of the light-dependent reactions?
(a) Stroma (b) Thylakoids
(c) Chemiosmosis (d) Chloroplast

11. Sugar moves in phloem vessels as
(a) cellulose (b) glucose
(c) starch (d) sucrose

12. .... ions help in photolysis of water
(a) Mn^{2+} (b) Mg^{2+}
(c) Cl^- (d) Both (a) and (c)

13. In photosynthesis the first step is
(a) conversion of PG to PGA
(b) carboxylation of RuBP
(c) electron release by chlorophyll-*a*
(d) photolysis of water

14. Photochemical reaction occurs in
(a) lumen of thylakoid
(b) stroma of chloroplast
(c) membrane of thylakoid
(d) inner membrane of chloroplast

15. Which of the following pigment is involved in photochemical reaction in pigment system?
(a) Chlorophyll-*b* (b) Chlorophyll-*a*
(c) Carotene (d) Xanthophylls

16. What happens in chloroplast in the presence of light?
(a) Hydrogen's protons accumulate in thylakoid spaces
(b) Water is being spilit
(c) Electrons are moving
(d) All of the above

17. Oxygen evolving complex, involved in photolysis of water contain
(a) Mn^{2+}, Cl^- and K^+ (b) Mg^{2+}, Cl^- and Ca^{2+}
(c) Mn^{2+}, Cl^- and CO (d) Mn^{2+}, Cl^- and Ca^{2+}

18. In young leaves ratio of carotene to xanthophyll is
(a) 2 : 1 (b) 3: 1
(c) 1: 3 (d) 1: 2

19. In which of the following light, rate of photosynthesis is maximum?
(a) White (b) Discontinuous white
(c) Red (d) Blue

20. During light phase of photosynthesis...................... is oxidized and .... is reduced.
(a) CO_2 and water
(b) water and CO_2
(c) water and NADP
(d) $NADPH_2$ and CO_2

21. The visible product of photosynthesis is
(a) glucose (b) cellulose
(c) starch (d) fructose

22. Glycolytic reversal is a part of
(a) aerobic respiration
(b) anaerobic respiration
(c) light phase of photosynthesis
(d) dark phase of photosynthesis

23. During non-cyclic photophosphorylation, plants and cyanobacteria produce
(a) ATP (b) NADPH
(c) NADPH and ATP (d) NADH and ATP

24. Electron carriers in non-cyclic flow of electrons
(a) pass electrons from a more negative to a more positive reduction potential
(b) pass electrons from higher free energy to lower energy
(c) pass electrons from a more positive to more negative reduction potential
(d) Both (a) and (b)

25. Cooperation of the two photosystems of the chloroplast is required
(a) for ATP synthesis
(b) reduction of $NADP^+$
(c) oxidation of the reaction centre of PS-I
(d) generation of proton motive force

26. In the presence of light, pH of the lumen of thylakoid
(a) increases (b) decreases
(c) remain same (d) None of these

27. The proton motive force develops across the thylakoid membrane in the presence of light is results of
(a) only pH gradient
(b) only voltage gradient
(c) sum of both pH and voltage gradient
(d) None of the above

28. Which one of the following compound in non-cyclic photophosphorylation in light reaction contains copper?
(a) Cytochrome (b) Ferredoxin
(c) Plastoquinone (d) Plastocyanin

29. The source of CO_2 during Calvin cycle in C_4 plant is
(a) malic acid (b) OAA
(c) PEP (d) RuDP

30. Dimorphic chloroplast are present in
(a) *Zea mays* (b) *Saccharum officinale*
(c) *Sorghum bicolor* (d) All of these

31. The pigment molecules responsible for photosynthesis are located in the
(a) cytoplasm of the cell
(b) stroma of the chloroplast
(c) thylakoid membrane of the chloroplast
(d) All of the above

32. Photooxidation of chlorophyll is prevented by
(a) carotenoid (b) anthocyanin
(c) phycobilin (d) fucoxanthin

33. Which pigment will have higher absorbance in red region?
(a) Chlorophyll-*a*
(b) Chlorophyll-*b*
(c) Both have same absorbance
(d) Carotene

34. Colours of light most useful in photosynthesis are
(a) green, yellow and orange (b) red, violet and blue
(c) infrared, red and yellow (d) red, white and blue

35. Name a plant which do not perform photosynthesis is
(a) algae (b) *Bryophyllum*
(c) *Cuscutta* (d) pitcher plant

36. In Calvin cycle,
(a) fructose-1, 6-diphosphate undergoes dephosphorylation.
(b) ATP is formed during dephosphorylation of fructose
(c) 1, 3 di PGA undergo phosphorylation
(d) None of the above

37. What will happen to the rate of photosynthesis if sodium bicarbonate is added in the water having *Hydrilla* plant in a beaker?
(a) It will remain normal (b) It will be decreased
(c) It will be stopped (d) It will be accelerated

38. Photooxidation of chlorophyll and cell contents as a result of high light intensity is known as
(a) solarization (b) photolysis
(c) photoperiodism (d) photorespiration

39. Photosynthesis yield will be more in
(a) continuous red light (b) continuous blue light
(c) intermittent white light (d) green light

40. For the process of photosynthesis all except one of the following items are essential. Point out the exception
(a) CO_2, optimum temperature
(b) glucose and oxygen
(c) water and minerals
(d) light and chlorophyll

41. The prerequisities of Calvin cycle are
(a) H_2O, CO_2 and ATP (b) ATP, H_2O and $NADPH_2$
(c) CO_2, ATP and $NADPH_2$ (d) $NADPH_2$ and H_2O, CO_2

42. The function of water in photosynthesis is to
(a) absorb light energy
(b) supply electrons in the light dependent reactions
(c) transport H^+ ions in the light independent reactions
(d) provide O_2 for the light independent reactions

43. Which organism does not evolve oxygen in photosynthesis?
(a) *Anabaena* (b) *Funaria*
(c) Higher plants (d) *Rhodospirillum*

44. In the Calvin cycle, the assimilatory power is used during
(a) formation of-3PGA
(b) conversion of-3PGA to-3PGAL
(c) formation of fructose-1, 6-diphsophate from PGAL
(d) formation of glucose, from fructose-1, 6-diphosphate

45. Which is sensitive to longer wavelength of light?
(a) Photolysis (b) PS-I
(c) PS-II (d) Photophosphorylation

46. Reduction of co-enzyme NADP depends on
(a) reduction of CO_2 (b) evolution of O_2
(c) photolysis of water (d) formation of ATP

47. Ribbon-shaped chloroplast is present in
(a) *Zygnema* (b) *Spirogyra*
(c) *Chlorobium* (d) *Chromatinum*

48. In anoxygenic photosynthesis, the green and purple bacteria do not use the following one as electron source
(a) H_2O (b) H_2
(c) H_2S (d) elemental sulphur

49. In chloroplast, PS-I present on the
(a) appeared membrane of the thylakoid
(b) non-appeared membrane of the thylakoid
(c) lumen of the thylakoid
(d) inner membrane of chloroplast

50. The two photosystem-I and II during non-cyclic photophosphorylation acts in
(a) parallel (b) series
(c) Both (a) and (b) (d) None of these

51. Assimilatory powers produced during photosynthesis are
(a) RuBP and Rubisco (b) H_2O and O_2
(c) ATP and NADPH (d) $C_6H_{12}O_6$ and PGAL

52. Which of the following protist is a photoautotroph?
(a) *Thiobacillus* (b) *Ferrobacillus*
(c) Diatoms (d) *Chlorobium*

53. During photosynthesis the reaction when PGA is converted into PGAL, is called
(a) isomerization (b) reduction
(c) oxidation (d) phosphorylation

54. In C_3-pathway, the first stable compound is
(a) PGAL (b) OAA
(c) PGA (d) RuDP

55. The photochemical process in photosynthesis which needs both PS-I and PS-II also involves
(a) photolysis of water
(b) Z-scheme of electron transfer
(c) synthesis of assimilatory power
(d) All of the above

56. Which of the following is false statement?
(a) All NH_4^+ seems to be converted first into the amide group of glutamine
(b) Conversion of organic nitrogen to NH_4^+ by soil microbes is called ammonification
(c) Cl^- is required for photochemical reaction involved in photolysis of water
(d) Plant roots absorb ions as well as the salts

57. When DCPIP (Hill reagent) accepts electron from H_2O its colour changes to
(a) blue (b) red
(c) colourless (d) None of these

58. The experiment model used by Van Neil, to prove that O_2 comes out from the water was
(a) *Chlorella pyrenoidosa* (b) *Scendesmus*
(c) Blue green algae (d) *Chromatium vinosum*

59. Non-cyclic photophosphorylation in photosynthesis activates
(a) PS-II only
(b) PS-I then PS-II
(c) PS-II then PS-I
(d) PS-I and PS-II simultaneously

60. ATP synthesis during light reaction is
(a) Photophosphorylation
(b) Photolysis
(c) Oxidative phosphorylation
(d) Phosphorylation

61. Bundle sheath chloroplast of C_4-plants are
(a) large and agranal (b) large and granal
(c) small and granal (d) small and agranal

62. Carbon dioxide is fixed in
(a) llight reaction (b) dark reaction
(c) aerobic respiration (d) anaerobic respiration

63. Carbon dioxide joins the photosynthetic pathway in
(a) PS-I (b) PS-II
(c) light reaction (d) dark reaction

64. Cyclic photophosphorylation produces
(a) NADPH (b) ATP and NADPH
(c) ATP, NADPH and O_2 (d) ATP

65. Ferredoxin is a constituent of
(a) PS-I (b) PS-II
(c) Hill reaction (d) P_{680}

66. Which of the following lists these compounds from lowest redox potential to highest?
(a) Glucose-NAD-electron transport chain-oxygen
(b) Oxygen-glucose-NAD-electron transport chain
(c) Electron transport chain-NAD-oxygen-glucose
(d) Glucose-electron transport chain-NAD-oxygen

67. Which of the following is false about glyoxylate cycle?
(a) It is a variant of citric acid cycle
(b) It occurs in glyoxisome
(c) It results in the formation of succinate from acetyl Co-A
(d) It occurs in all eukaryotic cells

68. All of the following occur in mitochondria except
(a) citric acid cycle (Krebs' cycle)
(b) glycogenolysis
(c) fatty acid oxidation
(d) electron transport chain

69. Glucose is metabolized through glycolysis and Kreb's cycle. How do amino acids and fat get metabolized?
(a) There are separate cycle and pathways for such metabolism
(b) They are broken down, modified, and fed into various points in the same pathway as is used by glucose
(c) They are first converted to glucose molecules
(d) Only the amino group on the amino acids can be used for energy, the rest is just degraded, while fats are only stored

70. The function of the TCA cycle is catalyzed by all of the following statements except
(a) it generates reduced NAD^+ and reduced FAD
(b) it generates guanosine triphosphate
(c) it catalyses the complete oxidation of acetate to carbon dioxide and water
(d) it causes the net synthesis of oxaloacetate from acetyl Co-A

71. Which of the reactions of the tricarboxylic acid cycle listed below results in the formation of a high energy phosphate compounds?
(a) Isocitrate dehydrogenase
(b) Succinyl coenzyme-A synthase
(c) Succintate dehydrogenase
(d) Citrate synthetase

72. Most carbon dioxide from catabolism of glucose is released during
(a) glycolysis
(b) the Krebs' cycle
(c) lactate fermentation
(d) oxidative phosphorylation

73. All of the following enzymes of the TCA cycle are located in the mitochondrial matrix except
(a) citrate synthetase
(b) α-ketoglutarate dehydrogenase
(c) succinate dehydrogenase
(d) fumarase

74. Which of the following citric acid cycle products is disposed of by our respiratory system when we exhale?
(a) CO_2 (b) ATP
(c) NADH (d) $FADH_2$

75. The release of carbon dioxide results from which of the following reactions in the TCA cycle?
I. Isocitrate to α-ketoglutarate
II. Malate to oxaloacetate
III. α-ketoglutarate to succinyl Co-A
IV. Succinate to fumarate
(a) I and II (b) I and III
(c) I, II and III (d) I, II, III and IV

76. Substrate level phosphorylation in the citric acid cycle depends directly on the energy of the
(a) thioester bond of succinyl Co-A
(b) oxidative decarboxylation of isocitrate to α-ketoglutarate
(c) formation of citrate from oxaloacetate and acetyl Co-A
(d) FAD-dependent oxidation of succinate to fumarate

77. In a radiolabelling metabolic experiment radiolabelled ($4\text{-}^{14}C$) oxaloacetate is fed to mitochondria. After one turn of the CAC, which carbon(s) of succinate would be labelled?
(a) C-4
(b) Equally distributed between C-1 and C-4
(c) Equally distributed between C-2 and C-3
(d) None of the above

78. If 1 mol of acetyl coenzyme-A labelled with ^{14}C in both carbon position of the acetate moiety goes through one turn of the TCA cycle, how many moles of the $^{14}CO_2$ would be produced?
(a) 0 (b) 1
(c) 2 (d) 4

79. Which C-atom of glucose was tagged with ^{14}C so that after one cycle of glycolysis and Krebs' cycle none of the radioactive C-atom is found in intermediates?
(a) C-6 (b) C-1
(c) C-3 (d) C-2

80. The electrons that enter the electron transport system are carried there by
(a) NADH (b) $FADH_2$
(c) Both (a) and (b) (d) None of these

81. The electron transport system is located in the
(a) stroma (b) matrix
(c) cytosol (D) cristae

82. Which of the following statement correctly describes the relationship between the Krebs' cycle and electron transport pathways?
(a) The Krebs' cycle releases H^+ used by the electron transport
(b) The electron transport pathway obtains electrons from the CO_2 produced by the Krebs' cycle
(c) ATP produced by the Krebs' cycle derives electron transport and formation of a H^+ gradient
(d) NADH produced by the Krebs' cycle is used to make ATP by electron transport

83. All of the following electron carriers are components of the mitochondrial electron transport chain except
(a) nicotinamide-adenine dinucleotide
(b) nicotinamide-adenine dinucleotide phosphate
(c) flavin mononucleotide
(d) flavin-adenine dinucleotide

84. All of the following statement about NAD^+ are true except
(a) NAD^+ is reduced to NADH during both glycolysis and the Krebs' cycle
(b) NAD^+ has more chemical energy than NADH
(c) NAD^+ is reduced by the action of enzymes called dehydrogenases
(d) NAD^+ can receive electrons for use in oxidative phosphorylation

85. Electrons from NADH enter the mitochondrial electron transport chain at the level of
(a) coenzyme Q
(b) NADH-Q reductase (complex I)
(c) CoH_2-cytochrome-*c* reductase (complex III)
(d) cytochrome-*c* oxidase (complex IV)

86. ATP synthetase is multifunctional enzyme with a subunit constitution of $\alpha_3\beta_3\gamma$. The pair constituent subunits taking part in nucleotide binding and catalysis is
(a) $\alpha_1\beta_1$ (b) $\alpha_2\beta_2$
(c) $\alpha_3\beta_3$ (d) $\alpha_4\beta_4$

87. Some of the free energy released in the mitochondrial electron transport chain can be harnessed to the formation of ATP. How many moles of ATP can be formed per mole-pair of electrons transferred from NADH to oxygen?
(a) 0 (b) 1
(c) 2 (d) 2.5

88. In aerobic cellular respiration, which generates more ATP substrate level phosphorylation or chemiosmosis?
(a) Substrate level phosphorylation
(b) Chemiosmosis
(c) Both genarte the same amount of ATP
(d) Neither generates any ATP

89. The uncoupling of oxidative phosphorylation in a mitochondrial system describes which of the following actions?
(a) The phosphorylation of ADP continues but oxygen uptake stops
(b) The phosphorylation of ADP stops but oxygen uptake continues
(c) Oxygen uptake stops
(d) The phosphorylation of ADP to ATP accelerates

90. Uncoupling of oxidative phosphorylation implies that
(a) the ATPase activity of mitochondria is abolished
(b) the mitochondria cease to oxidize succinate
(c) ATP formation ceases but respiration continues
(d) ATP formation continue but respiration ceases

91. DCCD is a reagent that reacts with Asp residue. The addition of DCCD blocks the ATP synthesizing activity F_0F_1-ATPase by inhibiting the
(a) flow of protons by F_0
(b) binding of ADP with beta subunits
(c) release of ATP from beta subunit
(d) protonation and deprotonation of alpha subunit

92. It is possible for variety of substrates to use a common pathway for the transfer of electrons to oxygen because
(a) the substrates are oxidized in the mitochondria
(b) many of the substrates are oxidized by enzymes linked to oxidized NAD^+ or FAD
(c) the substrates are all oxidized by the same enzymes
(d) None of the above

93. The electrons from all substrates are transferred to the common acceptor, ATP. The place in the mitochondrion where pH is lower during aerobic respiration in the
(a) matrix (b) cytosol
(c) intermembrane space (d) mitochondrial ribosome

94. Pumping of H^+ across the inner membrane, from the matrix space to inter membrane space in mitochondria cause
(a) lower pH in matrix than in cytosol
(b) higher pH in matrix than in cytosol
(c) Both (a) and (b)
(d) None of the above

95. In the chemosomatic hypothesis for energy generation in mitochondria
(a) electron transport carriers set up a proton gradient
(b) a pH gradient drives the hydrolysis of ATP to ADP
(c) ATP must be continually translocated into the mitochondria
(d) electron transport carriers, use energy of moving electron in up hill direction to form ATP

96. In ATP synthase, F_0 acts as
(a) H^+ channel (b) Cl^- carrier
(c) electron carrier (d) ATPase

97. F_1 ATPase, part of ATP synthase synthesize ATP when proton passes through it
(a) against their electrochemical proton gradient
(b) down their K^+ gradient
(c) down their electrochemical proton gradient
(d) All of the above

98. Which statement about ATP synthesis is false?
(a) ATP is synthesized only in chloroplast and mitochondria
(b) ATP synthesis in the chloroplast occurs in the thylakoid region of this organelle
(c) Proton motive force (proton gradient) drives the formation of ATP in mitochondria
(d) ATP synthesis are protein complexes that allow protons to cross membrane

99. Essential elements are
(a) not required for normal reproduction
(b) not replaceable by other elements
(c) not directly involved with metabolism
(d) required only in those processes leading to increased growth

100. Which of the following is an incorrect match of the essential element and function?
(a) Mn-structural component of chlorophyll
(b) Ca-component of the middle lamella
(c) Zn-enzyme activator
(d) Fe-component of ferredoxin

101. Legume root nodules contain leghaemoglobin. Its function is to regulate
(a) expression of *nif* genes (b) dinitrogenase activity
(c) oxygen supply (d) nodule growth

102. How many ATP are required for the conversion of one N_2 to $2NH_4^+$ during biological nitrogen fixation?
(a) 8 ATP (b) 10 ATP
(c) 12 ATP (d) 16 ATP

103. Carnivorous adaptation of plants mainly compensate for soil that has a relatively low content of
(a) K (b) N_2
(c) PO_4 (d) Ca

104. Which of the following is not correct about nitrogen fixation?
(a) It requires metabolic energy
(b) Carried out only by few prokaryotic organism termed Diazatrophs
(c) Enzyme that catalyses the reduction of nitrogen is taked nitrogenase complex
(d) None of the above

105. Nitrogen fertilizers disrupt ecosystem structure and function by
(a) promoting heterotrophic growth causing an imbalance in CO_2 levels
(b) decreasing filamentous fungal development which causes loss of soil crumb structure and subsequent soil fertility
(c) causing more antibiotic producing bacteria to grow and produce antibiotics which stunt the growth of plants
(d) reducing the number of nitrogen fixing bacteria in soils

106. Addition of nitrogen-containing fertilizers affects gas exchange processes in the soil
(a) resulting in release of NO and N_2O which are greenhouse gasses
(b) causing methane gas to be consumed
(c) causing methane gas to be produced
(d) causing antibiotic production in bacteria which leads to antibiotic resistance

107. The reservoir for nitrogen is
(a) the atmosphere (b) rocks
(c) ammonia (d) nitrates

108. Biological Nitrogen Fixation (BNF) occurs when atmospheric nitrogen is converted into ammonia by an enzyme called
(a) ammonia synthase (b) nitrogenase
(c) ATPase (d) glutamate synthase

109. Choose the mismatch

Mineral nutrient		**Function**
(a) B	—	Cell elongation
(b) Mo	—	N_2 fixation
(c) Na	—	C_3 pathway
(d) Cl	—	Photosynthesis of water

110. Conversion of NO_3^- to NO_2^- occurs in plant cells
I. Occur in the cytosol.
II. Catalyzed by nitrate reductase.
III. Requires Mo and FAD as cofactor.
IV. Reduced ferredoxin acts as electron donor.
Which of the following is correct?
(a) I and IV (b) I, II and III
(c) I, II, III, and IV (d) II Only

111. Which of the following statement is correct about nitrate reductase?
(a) FAD, Mo and haeme act as prosthetic groups
(b) Catalyses conversion of NO_3^- to NH_4^+
(c) $FADH_2$ acts as electron donor
(d) Very sensitive to O_2

112. Match list I with list II and select the correct answer using the codes given below the lists.

List I	List II
A. The amount of energy accumulation in green plants through the process of photosynthesis	1. Gross Primary Productivity
B. The total organic matter synthesized by the producers in the process of photosyn- thesis per unit time and area	2. Primary productivity
C. Rate of storage of organic matter in plant tissues in excess of the respiratory utilization during the measurement period	3. Secondary productivity
D. Rate of energy storage at consumer level	4. Net primary productivity

Codes

	A	B	C	D
(a)	1	2	3	4
(b)	2	1	3	4
(c)	1	3	4	2
(d)	2	1	4	3

113. Consider the following statements.
I. Copper is present in cytochrome oxidase.
II. Pantothenic acid is the precursor of Co-enzyme A.
III. Thiamine pyrophosphate is the prosthetic group in decarboxylases.
IV. Zinc is present in RNA and DNA polymerases.
Which of these statements are correct?
(a) I and II (b) II, III and IV
(c) I, II, III and IV (d) I, III and IV

114. Match list I with list II and select the correct answer using the codes given below the lists.

List I	List II
A. Nitrogen fixation	1. Conversion of NH_4^+ into nitrite and nitrate
B. Denitrification	2. Conversion of nitrite or nitrate into atmospheric nitrogen
C. Nitrification	3. Conversion of atmospheric nitrogen into ammonia
D. Ammonification	4. Conversion of organic nitrogen into ammonia

Codes

	A	B	C	D
(a)	3	2	1	4
(b)	2	1	3	4
(c)	3	2	4	1
(d)	2	4	1	3

115. Match list I with list II and select the correct answer using the codes given below the lists.

List I	List II
A. Conversion of glucose to pyruvate	1. Krebs' cycle
B. Conversion of pyruvate to acetyl Co-A system	2. Electron Transport
C. Breakdown of acetyl-Co-A	3. Glycolysis to yield reduced Co-enzymes
D. Synthesis of ATP	4. Oxidative decarboxylation

Codes

	A	B	C	D
(a)	3	4	1	2
(b)	3	4	2	1
(c)	4	3	2	1
(d)	3	1	4	2

116. Match list I and list II and select the correct answer using the codes given below the lists.

List I	List II
A. Biotin	1. Carboxylation
B. Coenzyme-A	2. Active aldehyde transfer
C. Thymine pyrophosphate	3. Sugar transfer
D. Uridine diphosphate	4. Acyl group transfer

Codes

	A	B	C	D
(a)	1	4	2	3
(b)	1	4	3	2
(c)	4	1	2	3
(d)	4	1	3	2

117. Which of the following statement is correct?

I. Electron transport generates the proton motive force.

II. Peroxisomal oxidation of fatty acids generates no ATP.

III. Proton motive force in mitochondria is largely due to voltage gradient across the membrane.

IV. Total of $10H^+$ are translocated from the matrix across the inner membrane per electron pair moving from NADH to O_2.

(a) I and II (b) I and III
(c) I, II and III (d) I, II, III and IV

118. Consider the following

I. cytochrome-b_6 II. cytochrome-f
III. plastocyanin IV. plastoquinone

What is the sequence of these in the photoinduced electron carriers between PS-II and PS-I in photosynthesis?

(a) IV, I, II and III (b) III, IV, I and II
(c) I, II, III and IV (d) II, III, IV and I

119. Match list I and list II and select the correct answer using the codes given below the lists.

List I	List II
A. Peripheral reticulum	1. C_3-plants
B. RuBP-carboxylase-oxygenase	2. CAM-plants
C. CO_2-fixation in the dark	3. Photosystem-I
D. Cyclic photophosphorylation	4. C_4-plants
	5. Photosystem-II

Codes

	A	B	C	D
(a)	1	4	2	3
(b)	2	5	4	1
(c)	4	1	2	3
(d)	3	5	1	4

120. Which of the following are true?

I. NADH yields less ATP than $FADH_2$.

II. More NADH is produced in the Krebs' cycle than in glycolysis.

III. The final acceptor of electrons is ATP synthase.

IV. ETS pumps H^+ into the intermembrane space.

(a) I only (b) II and III
(c) II and IV (d) I, II and IV

Answers

1. (b)	**2.** (a)	**3.** (b)	**4.** (d)	**5.** (a)	**6.** (b)	**7.** (b)	**8.** (d)	**9.** (d)	**10.** (b)
11. (b)	**12.** (d)	**13.** (c)	**14.** (c)	**15.** (b)	**16.** (d)	**17.** (d)	**18.** (d)	**19.** (b)	**20.** (c)
21. (a)	**22.** (d)	**23.** (c)	**24.** (d)	**25.** (b)	**26.** (b)	**27.** (c)	**28.** (d)	**29.** (a)	**30.** (d)
31. (c)	**32.** (a)	**33.** (a)	**34.** (d)	**35.** (d)	**36.** (a)	**37.** (d)	**38.** (a)	**39.** (c)	**40.** (b)
41. (c)	**42.** (b)	**43.** (d)	**44.** (b)	**45.** (b)	**46.** (c)	**47.** (b)	**48.** (a)	**49.** (b)	**50.** (b)
51. (c)	**52.** (c)	**53.** (b)	**54.** (c)	**55.** (d)	**56.** (d)	**57.** (c)	**58.** (d)	**59.** (d)	**60.** (a)
61. (a)	**62.** (b)	**63.** (d)	**64.** (d)	**65.** (a)	**66.** (a)	**67.** (d)	**68.** (b)	**69.** (b)	**70.** (d)
71. (b)	**72.** (b)	**73.** (c)	**74.** (a)	**75.** (b)	**76.** (a)	**77.** (d)	**78.** (a)	**79.** (c)	**80.** (c)
81. (d)	**82.** (d)	**83.** ()	**84.** ()	**85.** (b)	**86.** (c)	**87.** (d)	**88.** (b)	**89.** (b)	**90.** (c)
91. (a)	**92.** (b)	**93.** (c)	**94.** (b)	**95.** (a)	**96.** (a)	**97.** (c)	**98.** (a)	**99.** (b)	**100.** (a)
101. (c)	**102.** (d)	**103.** (b)	**104.** (d)	**105.** (b)	**106.** (a)	**107.** (a)	**108.** (b)	**109.** (c)	**110.** (b)
111. (a)	**112.** (d)	**113.** (a)	**114.** (a)	**115.** (a)	**116.** (b)	**117.** (c)	**118.** (a)	**119.** (c)	**120.** (c)

17

Growth Hormone and Photobiology

Plant Hormones

Plants produce signaling molecules, called **hormones**, that have profound effects on development at vanishingly low concentrations. Plant development was thought to be regulated by only five types of hormones—auxins, gibberellins, cytokinins, ethylene and abscisic acid. However, there is evidence for the existence of plant steroid hormones, the brassinosteroids, that have a wide range of morphological effects on plant development. Following are the some growth regulating substances:

1. **Auxins** (cell elongation)
2. **Gibberellins** (cell elongation + cell division — translated into growth)
3. **Cytokinins** (cell division + inhibits senescence)
4. **Abscisic acid** (abscission of leaves and fruits + dormancy induction of buds and seeds)
5. **Ethylene** (promotes senescence, epinasty and fruit ripening)
6. Flowering hormones.
7. Miscellaneous natural substance; cyclitols, phytochromes.
8. Synthetic growth retardants; CCC, morphactins, maleic dehydrogenase (MH).
9. Miscellaneous jasmonic acid, salicylic acid and the polypeptide systemin.

Both **auxin** and **cytokinin** differ from the other plant hormones and signaling agents in one important respect: They are **required for viability.** Thus far, no mutants lacking either auxin or cytokinin have been found, suggesting that mutations that eliminate them are lethal.

Syllabus

- Plant Hormones
- Biosynthesis, Storage, Breakdown and Transport, Physiological Effects and Mechanisms of Action
- Sensory Photobiology
- Structure, Functions and Mechanisms of Action of Phytochromes
- Cryptochromes and Phototropins
- Stomatal Movement
- Photoperiodism and Biological Clocks

Plant Hormones Differ from Animal Hormones

Unlike animal hormones, plant hormones are not made in tissues specialized for hormone production (*e.g.*, sex hormones made in the gonads, human growth hormone in pituitary gland).

Unlike animal hormones, plant hormones do not have definite target areas (*e.g.*, auxins can stimulate adventitious root development in a cut shoot or shoot elongation or apical dominance or differentiation of vascular tissue, etc.).

Plant growth regulators are necessary for, but do not control, many aspects of plant growth and development.

Their effect on plant physiology is dependent on the amount of hormone present and tissue sensitivity to the plant growth regulator.

Auxins

Auxin is a Greek *auxein*, meaning 'to increase' or 'to grow. Auxin were the first to be identified as growth hormones. The auxins free (easily extracted) or bound (require organic solvent for extraction.

Chemical Nature of Auxins

Indole-3-acetaldehyde, indole-3-acetonitrile, indole-3-ethanol, 4-chloro-IAA are found in plants. Certain other substances identical to properties of auxins are: indole butyric acid (IBA) α and β-nephthalene acetic acids, 2, 4-dichloro-phenoxyacetic acid (2, 4-D) 2, 4, 5-trichlorophenoxy acetic acid (2, 4, 5-T), indole propionic acid (IPA), etc.

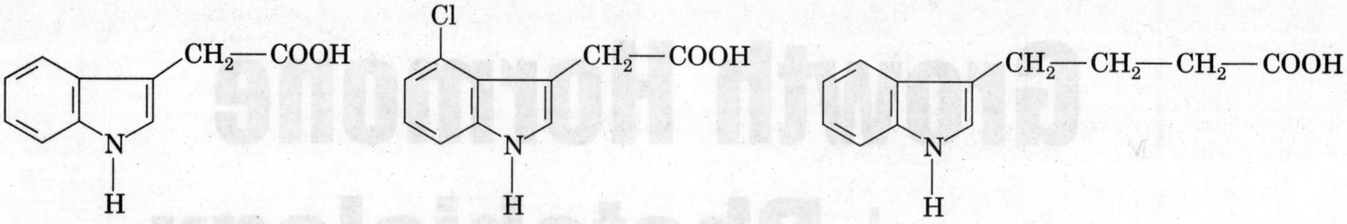

Indole-3-acetic acid (IAA) **4-chloroindole-3-acetic acid (4-Cl-IAA)** **Indole-3-butyric acid (IBA)**

Fig. 17.1 Structure of three natural auxins. Indole-3-acetic acid (IAA) occurs in all plants, peas contain 4-chloroindole-3-acetic acid. Mustards and corn contain indole-3-butyric acid (IBA)

2, 4-dichlorophenoxyacetic acid (2, 4-D) **2-methoxy-3, 6-dichlorobenzoic acid (dicamba)**

Fig. 17.2 Structures of two synthetic auxins. Most synthetic auxins are used as herbicides in horticulture and agriculture

A **bioassay** is a measurement of the effect of a known or suspected biologically active substance on living material.

Avena coleoptile curvature test The coleoptile curved because the increase in auxin on one side stimulated cell elongation, and the decrease in auxin on the other side (due to the absence of the coleoptile tip) caused a decrease in the growth rate—a phenomenon called **differential growth.**

Biosynthetic

During early stages of hydathode differentiation a center of high auxin synthesis is evident. Multiple pathways exist for the biosynthesis of IAA, such as **indole-3-pyruvic acid (IPA) pathway, tryptamine (TAM) pathway (tomato) and indole-3-acetonitrile (IAN) pathway** (Brassicaceae, Poaceae and Musaceae).

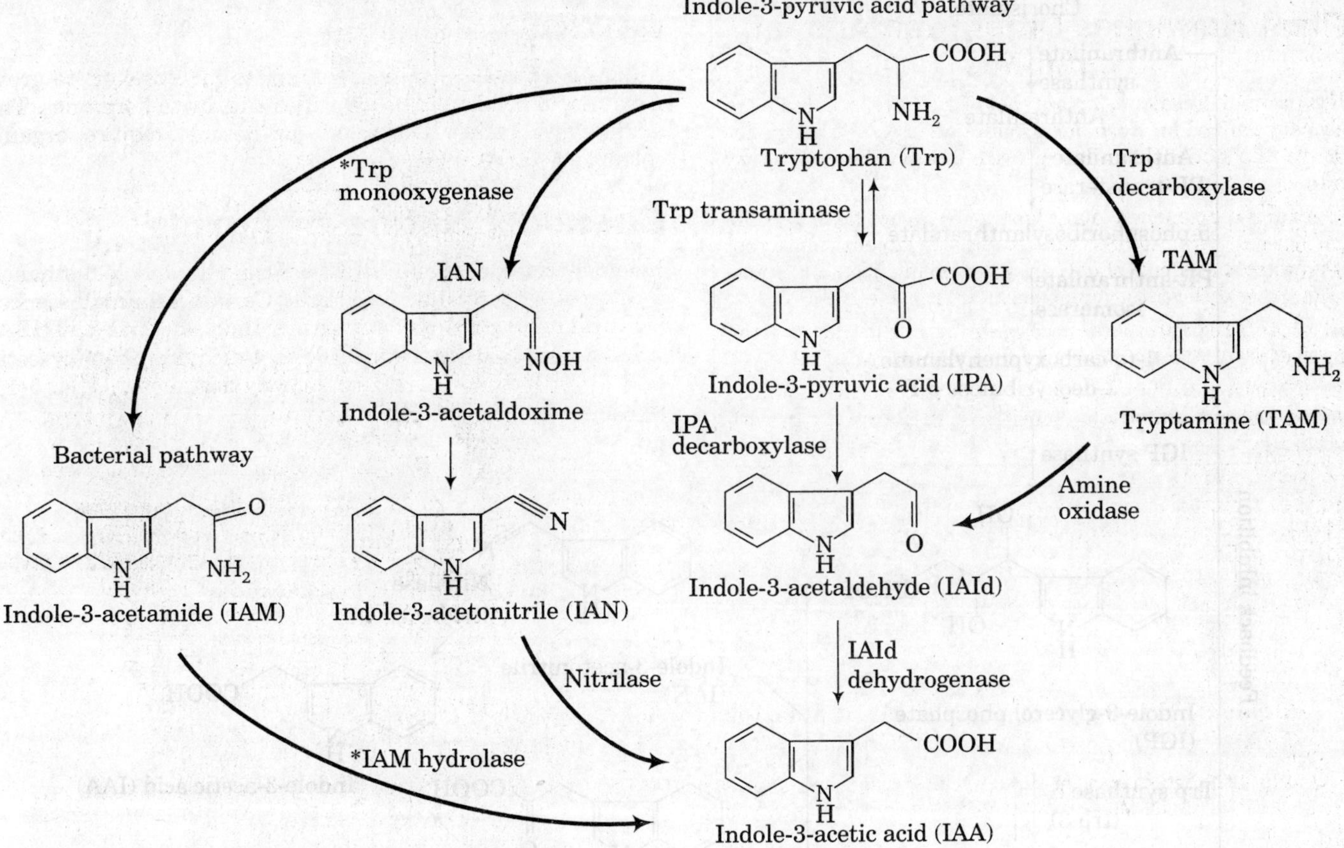

Fig. 17.3 Tryptophan-dependent pathways of IAA biosynthesis in plants and bacteria. The enzymes that are present only in bacteria are marked with an asterisk

Four genes (NIT_1 through NIT_4) that encode nitrilase enzymes have now been cloned from *Arabidopsis*. When NIT_2 was expressed in transgenic tobacco, the resultant plants acquired the ability to respond to IAN as an auxin by hydrolyzing it to IAA.

Another tryptophan-dependent biosynthetic pathway—one that uses **indole-3-acetamide** (IAM) as an intermediate, is used by various pathogenic bacteria, such as *Pseudomonas savastanoi* and *Agrobacterium tumefaciens*.

IAA is also synthesized from indole or from indole-3-glycerol phosphate. IAN and IPA are possible intermediates, but the immediate precursor of IAA in the tryptophan-independent pathway has not yet been identified. The discovery of the tryptophan-independent pathway has drastically altered our view of IAA biosynthesis, but the relative importance of the two pathways (tryptophan dependent *versus* tryptophan-independent) is poorly understood.

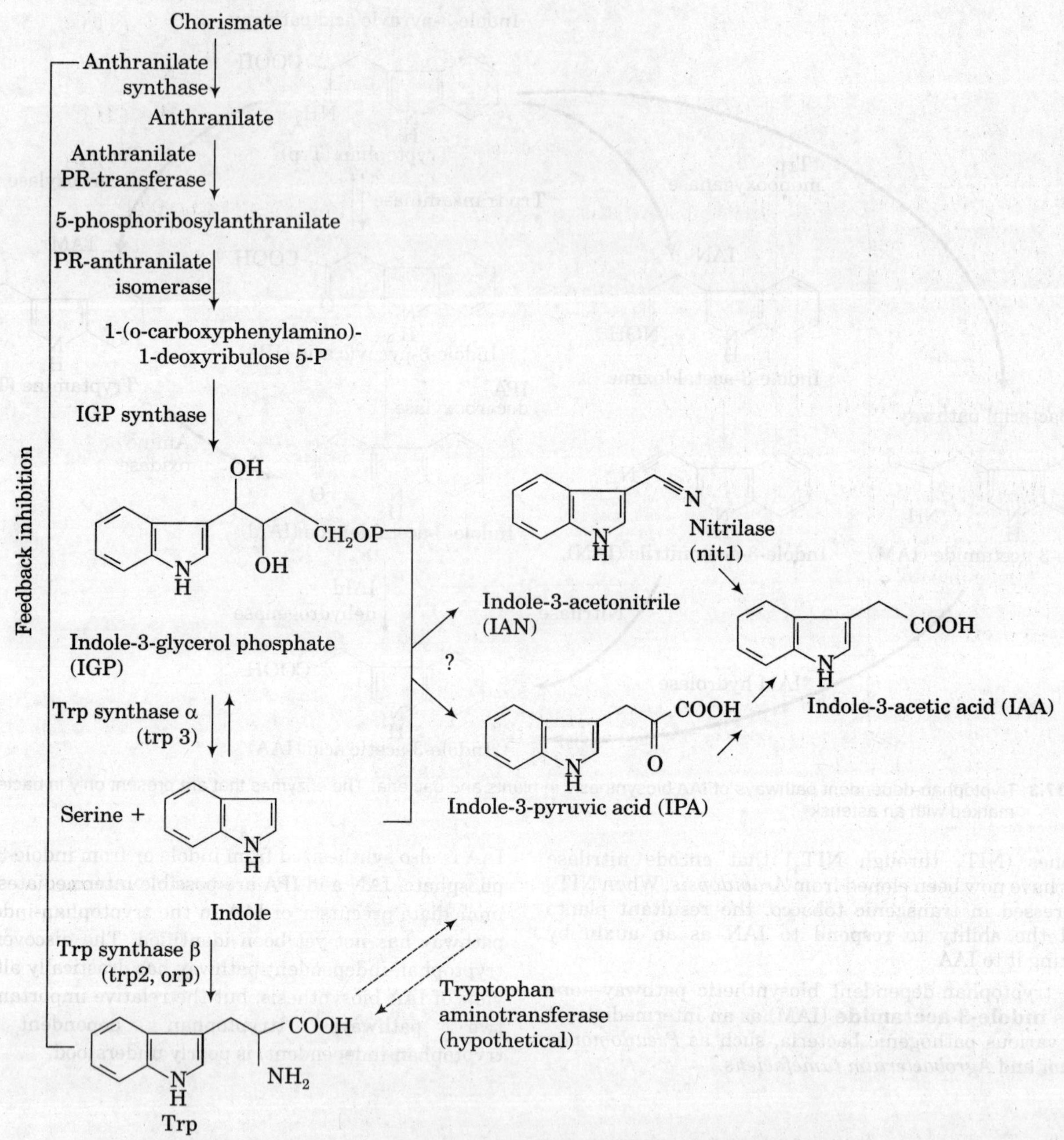

Fig. 17.4 Tryptophan-independent pathways of IAA biosynthesis in plants

Two Sub-cellular Pools of IAA Exist: The Cytosol and the Chloroplasts

The distribution of IAA in the cell appears to be regulated largely by pH. Because IAA does not cross membranes unaided, whereas IAAH readily diffuses across membranes, auxin tends to accumulate in the more alkaline compartments of the cell.

IAA is Degraded by Multiple Pathways

Like IAA biosynthesis, the enzymatic breakdown (oxidation) of IAA may involve more than one pathway. The distribution of IAA and its metabolites has been studied in tobacco cells. About one-third of the IAA is found in the chloroplast and the remainder is located in the cytosol.

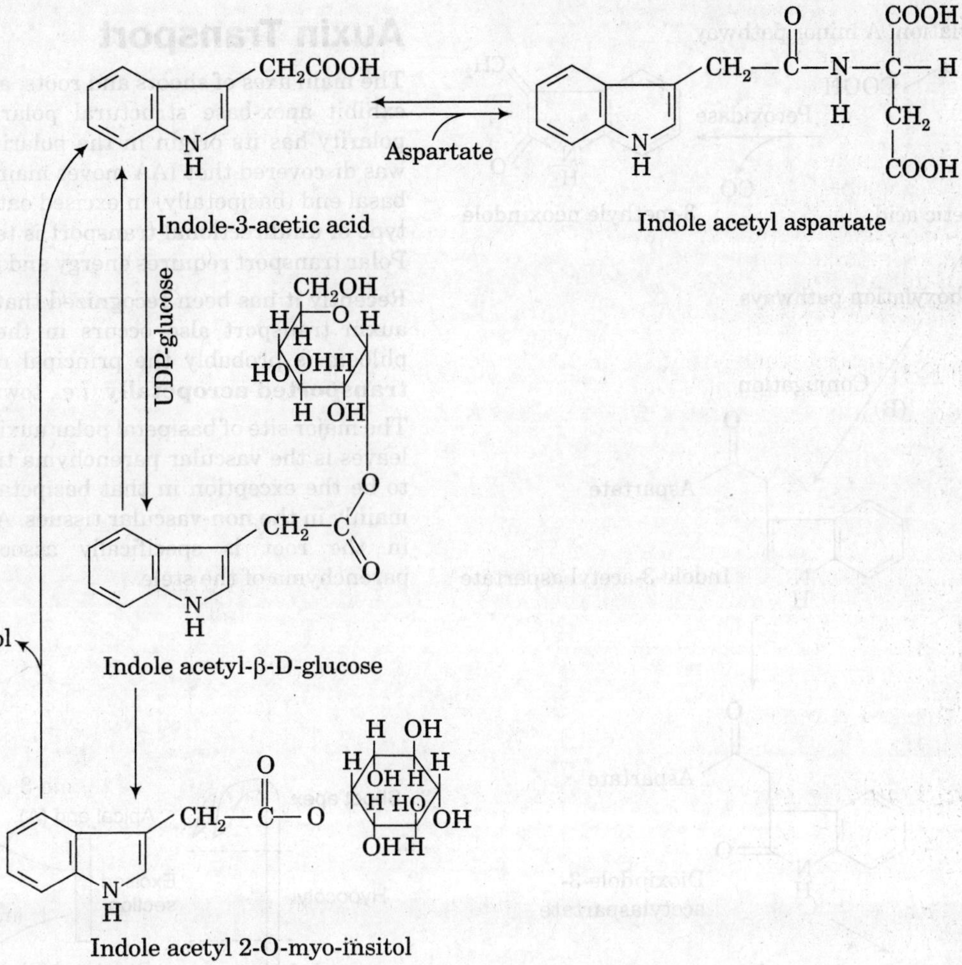

Indole-3-acetic acid

Aspartate

Indole acetyl aspartate

UDP-glucose

Indole acetyl-β-D-glucose

myo-inositol

Indole acetyl 2-O-myo-insitol

Fig. 17.5 Structures and proposed metabolic pathways of bound auxins. The diagram shows structures of various IAA conjugates and proposed metabolic pathways involved in their synthesis and breakdown

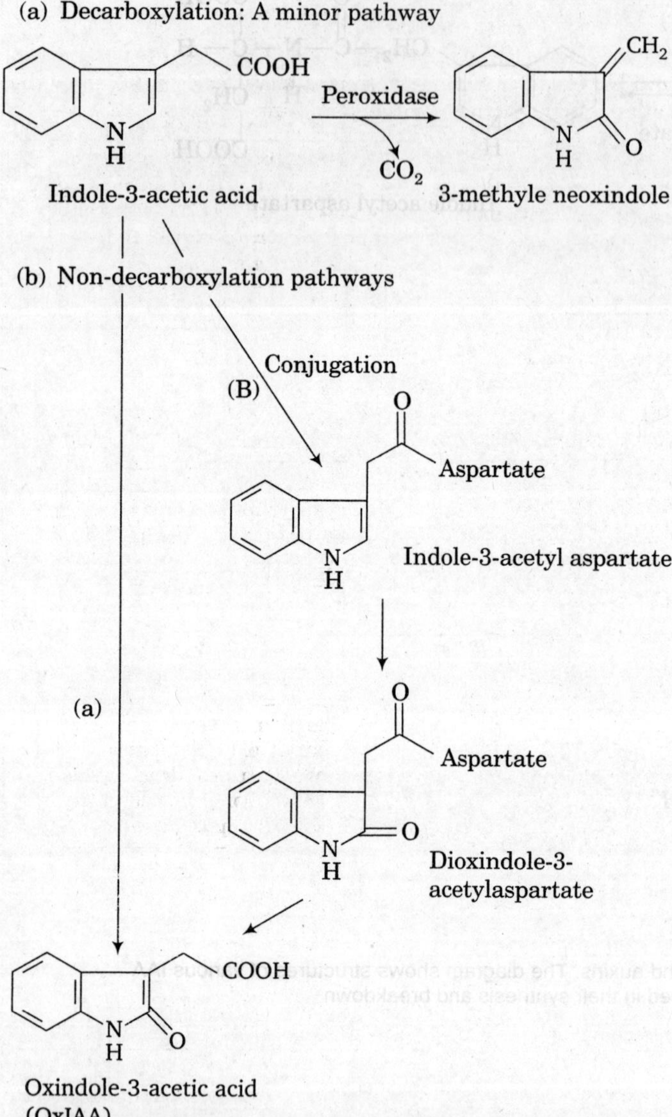

Fig. 17.6 Biodegradation of IAA (a) The peroxidase route (decarboxylation pathway) plays a relatively minor role. (b) The two non-decarboxylation routes of IAA oxidative

Auxin Transport

The main axes of shoots and roots, alongwith their branches, exhibit apex-base structural polarity, and this structural polarity has its origin in the polarity of auxin transport. It was discovered that IAA moves mainly from the apical to the basal end (basipetally) in excised oat coleoptile sections. This type of unidirectional transport is termed **polar transport.** Polar transport requires energy and is gravity **independent**.

Recently it has been recognized that a significant amount of auxin transport also occurs in the phloem, and that the phloem is probably the principal route by which auxin is **transported acropetally** (*i.e.*, toward the tip) in the root.

The major site of basipetal polar auxin transport in stems and leaves is the vascular parenchyma tissue. Coleoptiles appear to be the exception in that basipetal polar transport occurs mainly in the non-vascular tissues. Acropetal polar transport in the root is specifically associated with the xylem parenchyma of the stele.

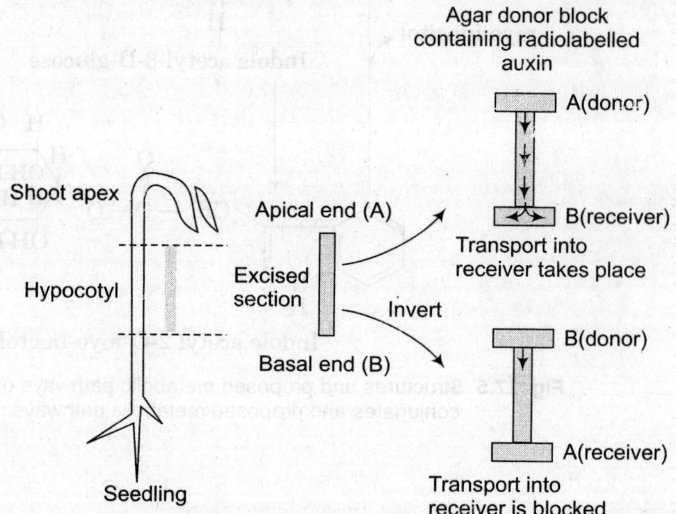

Fig. 17.7 The standard method for measuring polar auxin transport. The polarity of transport is independent of orientation with respect to gravity

Chemiosmotic Model for Polar Auxin Transport

The discovery of the chemiosmotic mechanism of solute transport in the late 1960s led to the application of this model to polar auxin transport. According to the now generally accepted **chemiosmotic model** for polar auxin transport, auxin uptake is driven by the proton motive force ($\Delta E + \Delta pH$) across the plasma membrane, while auxin efflux is driven by the membrane potential, ΔE.

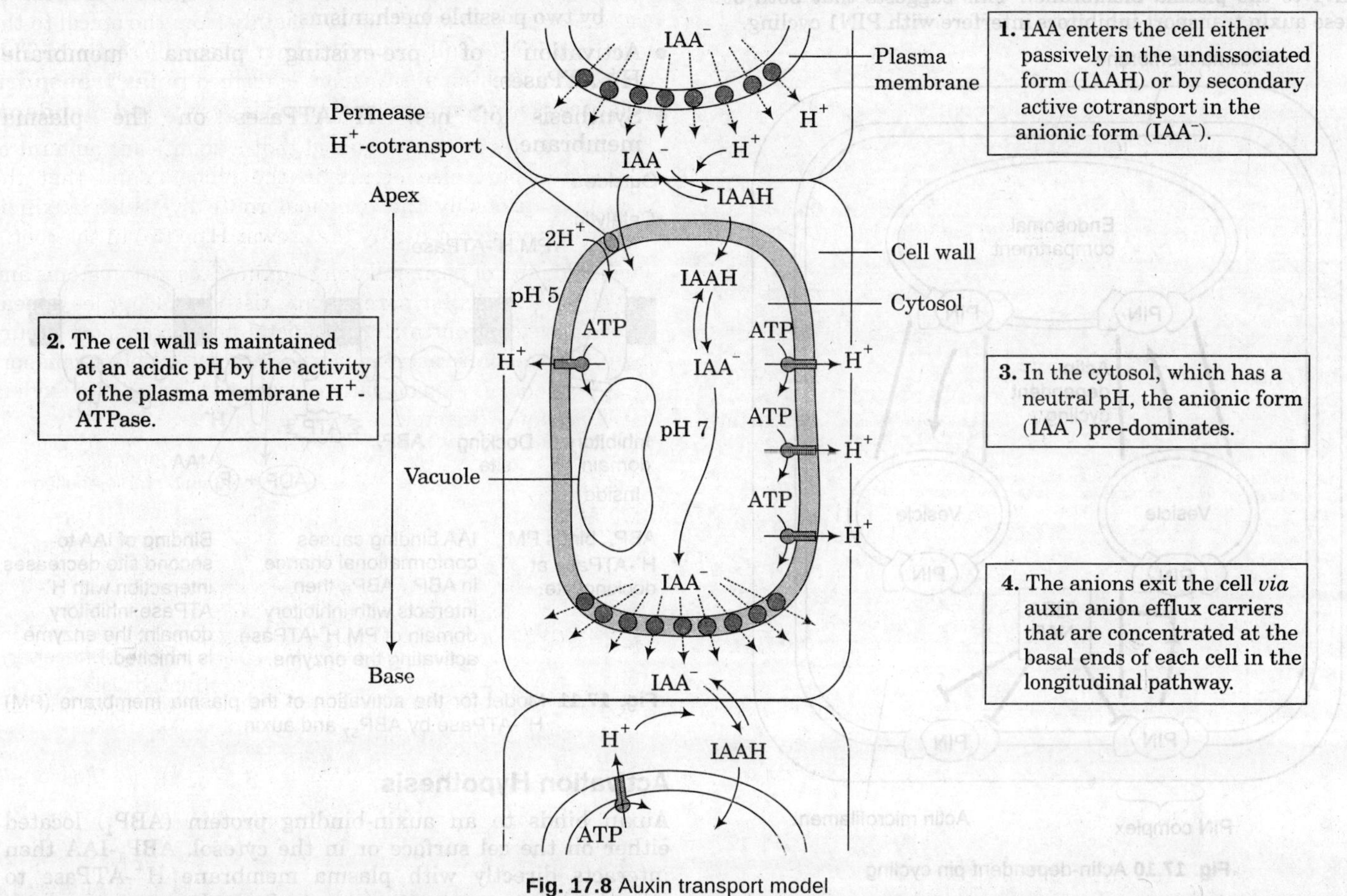

Fig. 17.8 Auxin transport model

Several compounds have been synthesized that can act as **Auxin Transport Inhibitors** (ATIs), including NPA (1-N-naphthylphthalamic acid) and TIBA (2, 3, 5-triiodobenzoic acid)

Auxin transport inhibitors not found in plants

NPA (1-N-naphthylphthalmic acid)

TIBA (2, 3, 5-triiodobenzoic acid)

1-NOA (1-naphthoxyacetic acid)

Naturally occurring auxin transport inhibitors

Quercetin (flavonol)

Genistein

Fig. 17.9 Structures of auxin transport inhibitors

Actin-dependent PIN cycling between the plasma membrane and an endosomal compartment. Auxin transport inhibitors TIBA and NPA both interfere with relocalization of PIN1 proteins to basal plasma membranes after BFA washout (auxin transport inhibitors block secretion of the auxin efflux carrier PIN1 to the plasma membrane). This suggests that both of these auxin transport inhibitors interfere with PIN1 cycling.

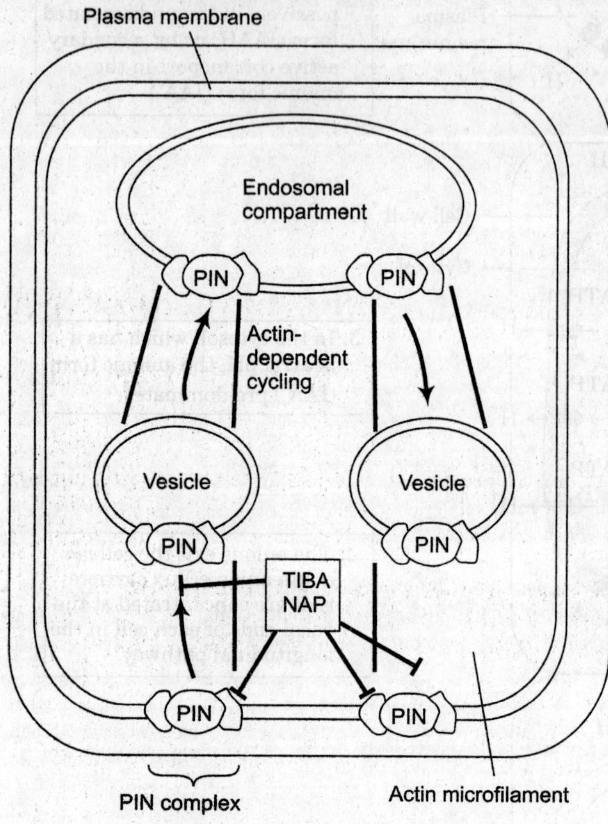

Fig. 17.10 Actin-dependent pin cycling

Physiological Effects of Auxin

Cell Elongation

(a) Auxins promote growth in stems and coleoptiles, while inhibiting growth in roots.

(b) The outer tissues of dicot stems are the targets of auxin action.

(c) Auxin rapidly increases the extensibility of the cell wall.

(d) Auxin-induced proton extrusion acidifies the cell wall and increases cell extension.

(e) Auxin-induced proton extrusion, may involve both activation and synthesis.

In theory, auxin could increase the rate of proton extrusion by two possible mechanisms:

- Activation of pre-existing plasma membrane H^+-ATPases.
- Synthesis of new H^+-ATPases on the plasma membrane.

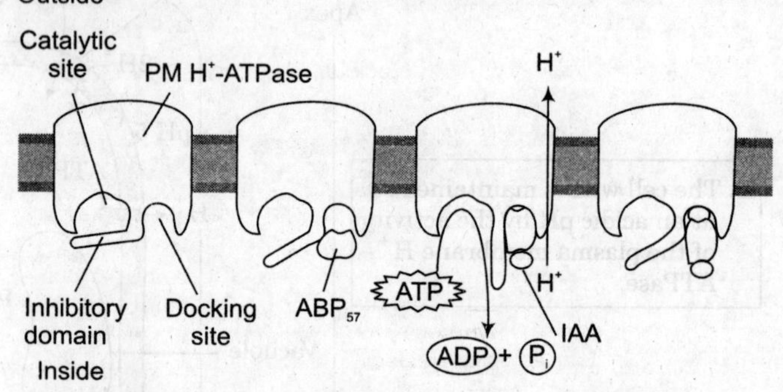

Fig. 17.11 Model for the activation of the plasma membrane (PM) H^+-ATPase by ABP_{57} and auxin

Activation Hypothesis

Auxin binds to an auxin-binding protein (ABP_1) located either on the cel surface or in the cytosol. ABP_1-IAA then interacts directly with plasma membrane H^+-ATPase to stimulate proton pumping (step 1). Second messengers, such as calcium or intracellular pH, could also be involved.

Synthesis Hypothesis

IAA-induced second messengers activate the expression of genes (step 2) that encode the plasma membrane H^+-ATPase (step 3). The protein is synthesized on the rough endoplasmic reticulum (step 4) and targeted *via* the secretory pathway to the plasma membrane (steps 5 and 6). The increase in proton extrusion results from an increase in the number of proton pumps on the membrane.

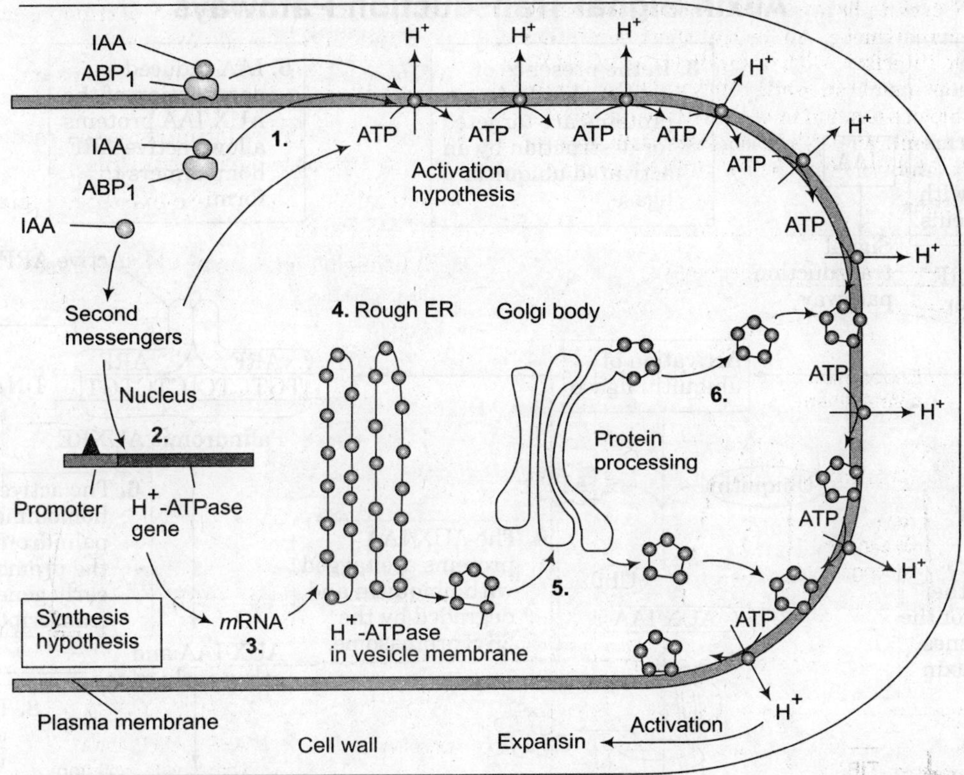

Fig. 17.12 Current models for IAA-induced H^+ extrusion. In many plants, both of these mechanisms may operate. Regardless of how H^+ pumping is increased, acid-induced wall loosening is thought to be mediated by expansins

Phototropism and Gravitropism

Three main guidance systems control the orientation of plant growth **phototropism, gravitropism and thigmotropism.**

Phototropism and gravitropism is mediated by the lateral redistribution of auxin.

Two flavoproteins, phototropins 1 and 2 are the photoreceptors for the blue-light signaling pathway that induces phototropic bending in *Arabidopsis* hypocotyls and oat coleoptiles under both high- and low-fluence conditions.

The **Cholodny-Went hypothesis** and the **acid growth hypothesis,** the apoplastic pH on the shaded side of a phototropically bending stem or coleoptile is more acidic than the side facing the light.

Statoliths serve as gravity sensors in shoots and roots. All parts of the plant experience the gravitational stimulus equally. Amyloplasts that function as gravity sensors are called **statoliths,** and the specialized gravity-sensing cells in which they occur are called **statocytes.** In shoots and coleoptiles, gravity is perceived in the **starch sheath,** a layer of cells that surrounds the vascular tissues of the shoot.

The **starch-statolith hypothesis** of gravity perception in roots is supported by several lines of evidence. Amyloplasts are the only organelles that consistently sediment in the columella cells of different plant species and the rate of sedimentation correlates closely with the time required to perceive the gravitational stimulus.

Auxin Regulates Apical Dominance

In most higher plants, the growing apical bud inhibits the growth of lateral (axillary) buds—a phenomenon called **apical dominance.** Removal of the shoot apex (decapitation) usually results in the growth of one or more of the lateral buds.

Other Physiological Effects of Auxin

(a) Auxin promotes the formation of lateral and adventitious roots.

(b) Auxin delays the onset of leaf abscission.

(c) Auxin transport regulates floral bud development.

(d) Auxin promotes fruit development.

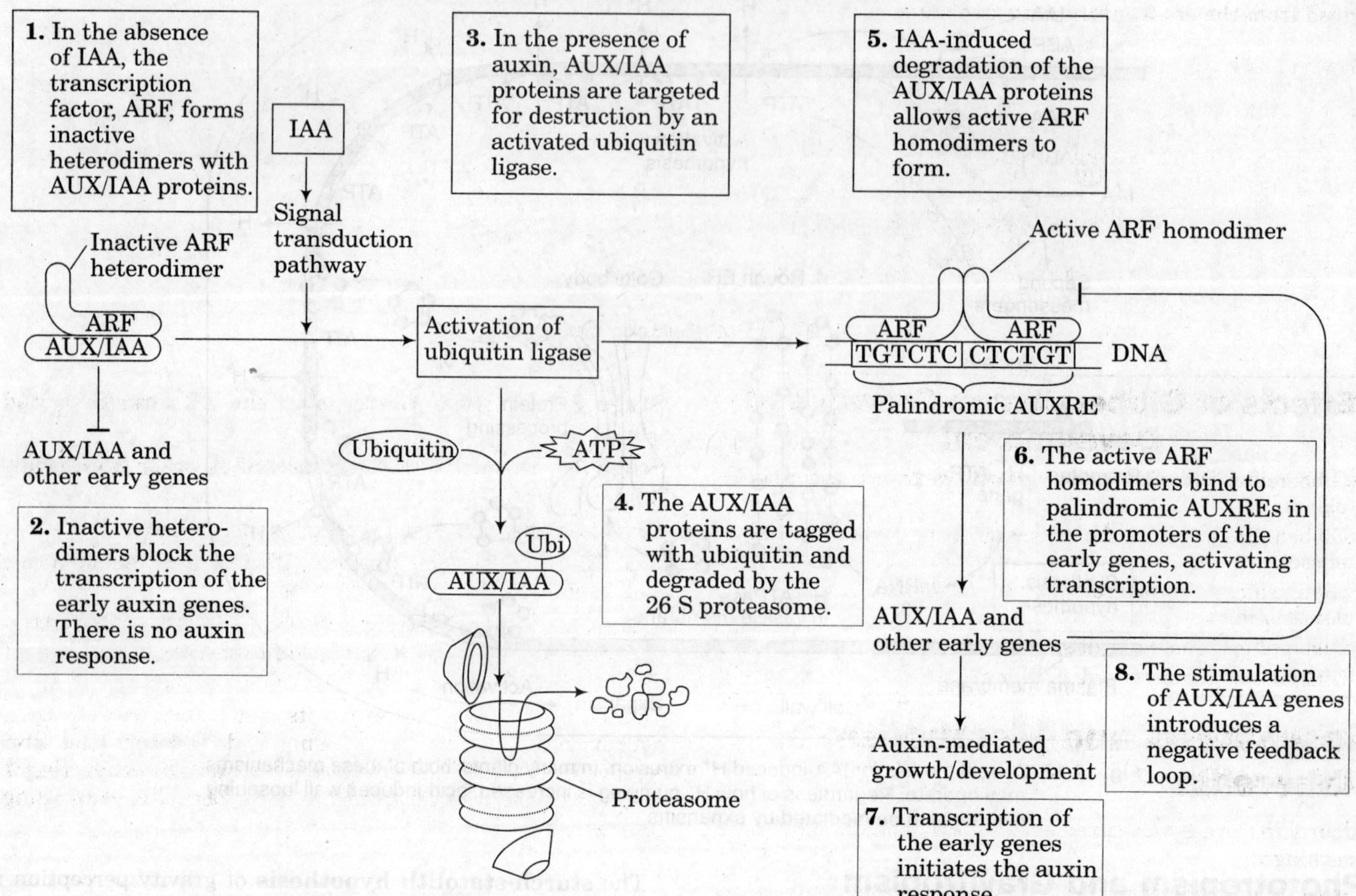

Fig. 17.13 A model for auxin regulation of transcriptional activation of early response genes by auxin

Gibberellins

In the 1930s, Japanese scientists succeeded in obtaining impure crystals of two fungal growth-active compounds, which they termed gibberellin A and B. Until the mid-1950s, scientists at Tokyo University isolated three gibberellins from the original gibberellin A and named them gibberellin A_1, gibberellin A_2, and gibberellin A_3. Gibberellin A_3 and gibberellic acid proved to be identical. In 1958, a gibberellin (gibberellin A_1) was conclusively identified from a higher plant (runner bean seeds, *Phaseolus coccineus*).

Gibberellic acid (GA_3)

Gibberellic acid A_1 (GA_1)

Fig. 17.14 Structure of gibberellic acid (GA_3 and GA_1)

The structural feature that all gibberellins have in common, and that defines them as a family of molecules, is that they are derived from the ent-kaurene ring structure:

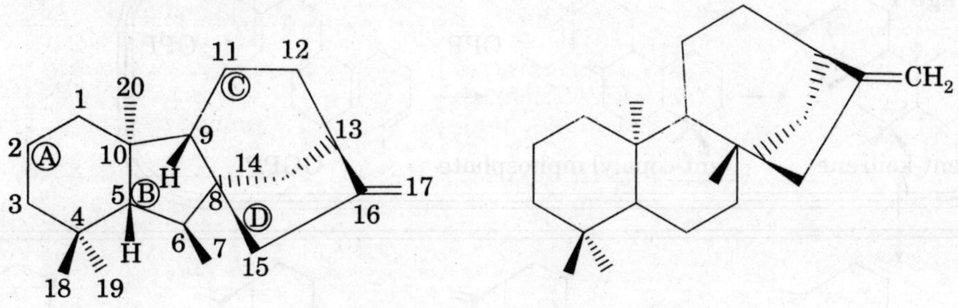

Fig. 17.15 Ent-gibberellic structure

Effects of Gibberellin on Growth and Development

- Gibberellins stimulate stem growth in dwarf and rosette plants.
- Gibberellins regulate the transition from juvenile to adult phases.
- Gibberellins influence floral initiation and sex determination.
- Gibberellins promote fruit set.
- Gibberellins promote seed germination.

Biosynthesis and Metabolism of Gibberellin

Gibberellins are synthesized *via* the terpenoid pathway in three stages:

Stage 1 Production of terpenoid precursors and entkaurene in plastids.

Stage 2 Oxidation reactions on the ER form GA_{12} and GA_{53}.

Stage 3 Formation in the cytosol of all other gibberellins from GA_{12} or GA_{53}.

Two basic chemical changes occur in most plants:

1. Hydroxylation at carbon 13 (on the endoplasmic reticulum) or carbon 3 or both.
2. A successive oxidation at carbon 20 ($CH_2 \rightarrow CH_2OH \rightarrow$ CHO). The final step of this oxidation is the loss of carbon 20 as CO_2.

Finally, GA_1 is inactivated by its conversion to GA_8 by a hydroxylation on carbon 2. This hydroxylation can also remove GA_{20} from the biosynthetic pathway by converting it to GA_{29}. GA_1 is the biologically active gibberellin controlling stem growth.

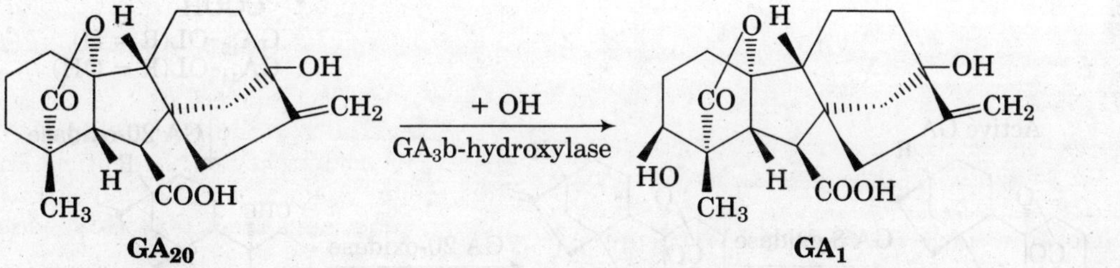

Fig. 17.16 Conversion of GA_{20} to GA_1 by GA 3β-hydroxylase, which adds a hydroxyl group (OH) to carbon 3 of GA_{20}

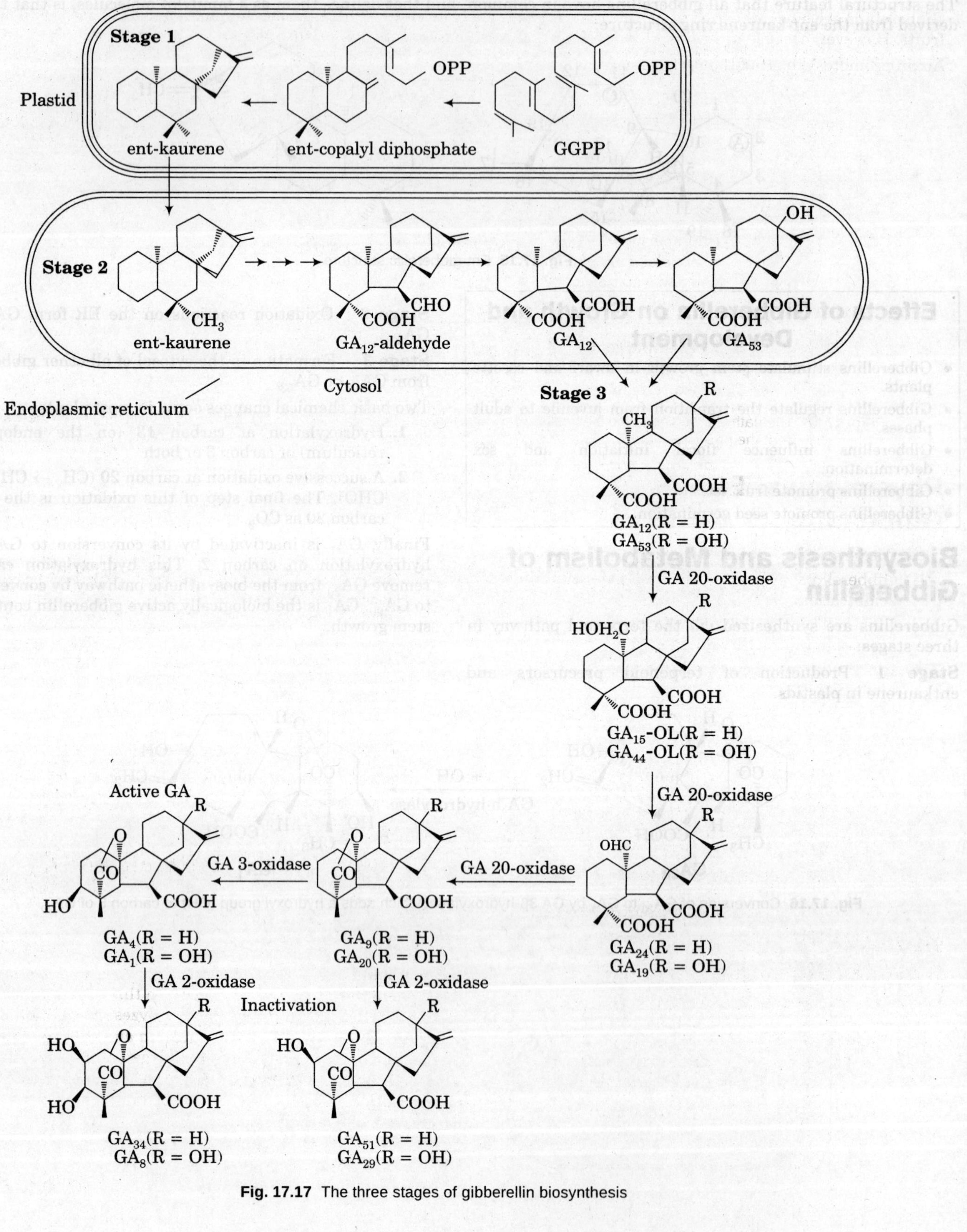

Stage 1

Plastid

ent-kaurene ← ent-copalyl diphosphate ← GGPP

OPP OPP

Stage 2

ent-kaurene (CH_3) → → → GA$_{12}$-aldehyde (CHO, COOH) → GA$_{12}$ (COOH, COOH) → GA$_{53}$ (OH, COOH, COOH)

Cytosol

Endoplasmic reticulum

Stage 3

GA$_{12}$(R = H)
GA$_{53}$(R = OH)

GA 20-oxidase

HOH_2C

GA$_{15}$-OL(R = H)
GA$_{44}$-OL(R = OH)

GA 20-oxidase

OHC

GA$_{24}$(R = H)
GA$_{19}$(R = OH)

GA 20-oxidase

GA$_9$(R = H)
GA$_{20}$(R = OH)

GA 3-oxidase

Active GA

GA$_4$(R = H)
GA$_1$(R = OH)

GA 2-oxidase

Inactivation

GA 2-oxidase

GA$_{34}$(R = H)
GA$_8$(R = OH)

GA$_{51}$(R = H)
GA$_{29}$(R = OH)

Fig. 17.17 The three stages of gibberellin biosynthesis

Gibberellins are biosynthesized in apical tissues. The highest levels of gibberellins are found in immature seeds and developing fruits. However, because the gibberellin level normally decreases to zero in mature seeds.

Auxin promotes gibberellin biosynthesis

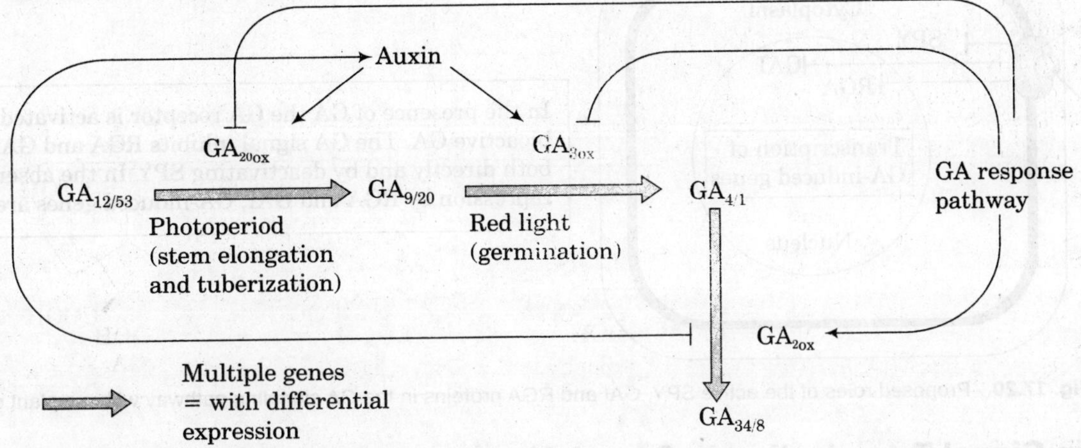

Fig. 17.18 The pathway of gibberellin biosynthesis showing the identities of the genes for the metabolic enzymes and the way that their transcription is regulated by feedback, environment and other endogenous hormones

Physiological Effects of Gibberellin

(i) Gibberellins stimulate cell elongation and cell division.

(ii) Gibberellins enhance cell wall extensibility without acidification.

(iii) Gibberellins regulate the transcription of cell cycle kinases in intercalary meristems.

(iv) Gibberellin response mutants have defects in signal transduction.

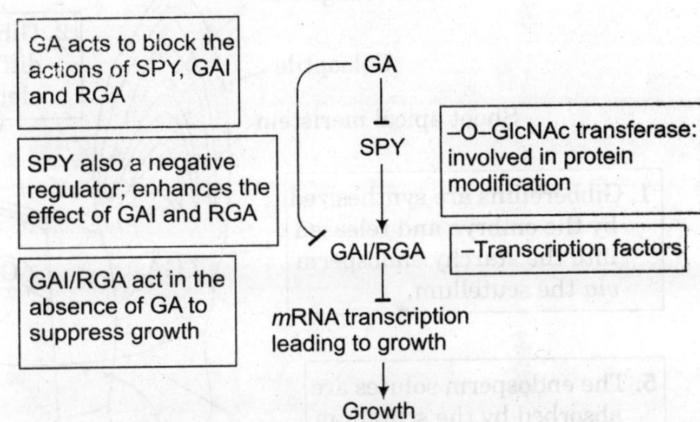

Fig. 17.19 Interactions between gibberellin and the genes SPY, GAI and RGA in the regulation of stem elongation

GA-deficient plant cell: No growth

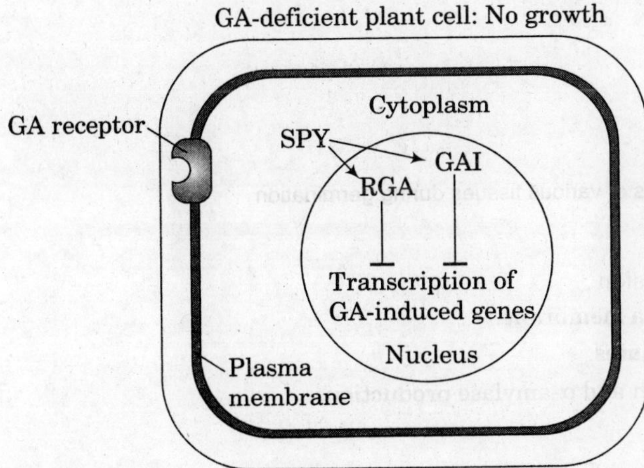

In a GA-deficient cell in a GA biosynthesis mutant or a wild-type cell without the GA signal, the transmembrane GA receptor is inactive in the absence of GA signal. In this situation, SPY is an active O-GlcNAc transferase that catalyzes the addition of a ginal GlcNAc residue (from UDP-GlcNAc) *via* an O linkage to specific serine and/or threonine residues of target proteins, possibly RGA and GAI. Active RGA and GAI function as repressors of transcripti · and they indirectly or directly inhibit the expression of GA-induced genes.

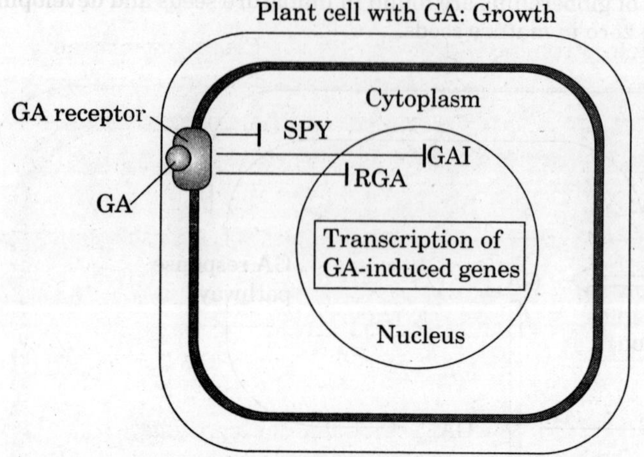

Fig. 17.20 Proposed roles of the active SPY, GAI and RGA proteins in the GA signaling pathway within a plant cell

Gibberellin Signal Transduction in Cereal Aleurone Layers

(a) Gibberellin from the embryo induces α-amylase production by aleurone layers.

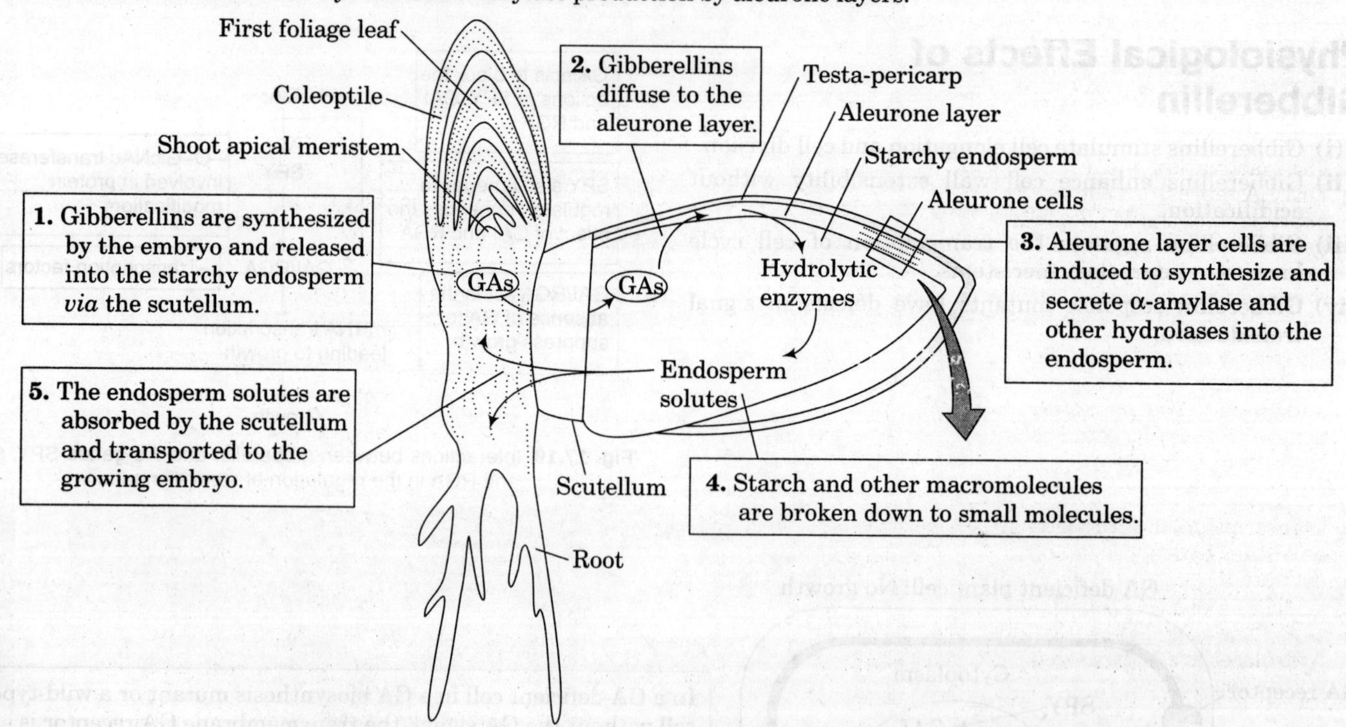

Fig. 17.21 Structure of a barley grain and the functions of various tissues during germination

(b) Gibberellic acid enhances the transcription of α-amylase *m*RNA.

(c) A GA-MYB transcription factor regulates α-amylase gene expression.

(d) Gibberellin receptors may interact with G-proteins on the plasma membrane.

Cyclic GMP, Ca^{2+} and protein kinases are possible signaling intermediates.

The gibberellin signal transduction pathway is similar for stem growth and α-amylase production.

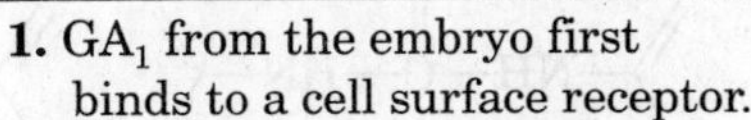

1. GA$_1$ from the embryo first binds to a cell surface receptor.

2. The cell surface GA receptor complex interacts with a heterotrimeric G-protein, initiating two separate signal transduction chains.

3. A calcium-independent pathway, involving *c*GMP, results in the activation of a signaling intermediate.

4. The activated signaling intermediate binds to DELLA repressor proteins in the nucleus.

5. The DELLA repressors are degraded when bound to the GA signal.

6. The inactivation of the DELLA repressors allows the expression of the MYB gene, as well as other genes, to proceed through transcription, processing and translation.

7. The newly synthesized MYB protein then enters the nucleus and binds to the promoter genes for α-amylase and other hydrolytic enzymes.

8. Transcription of α-amylase and other hydrolytic genes is activated.

9. α-amylase and other hydrolases are synthesized on the rough ER.

10. Proteins are secreted *via* the Golgi.

11. The secretory pathway requires GA stimulation *via* a calcium-calmodulin-dependent signal transduction pathway.

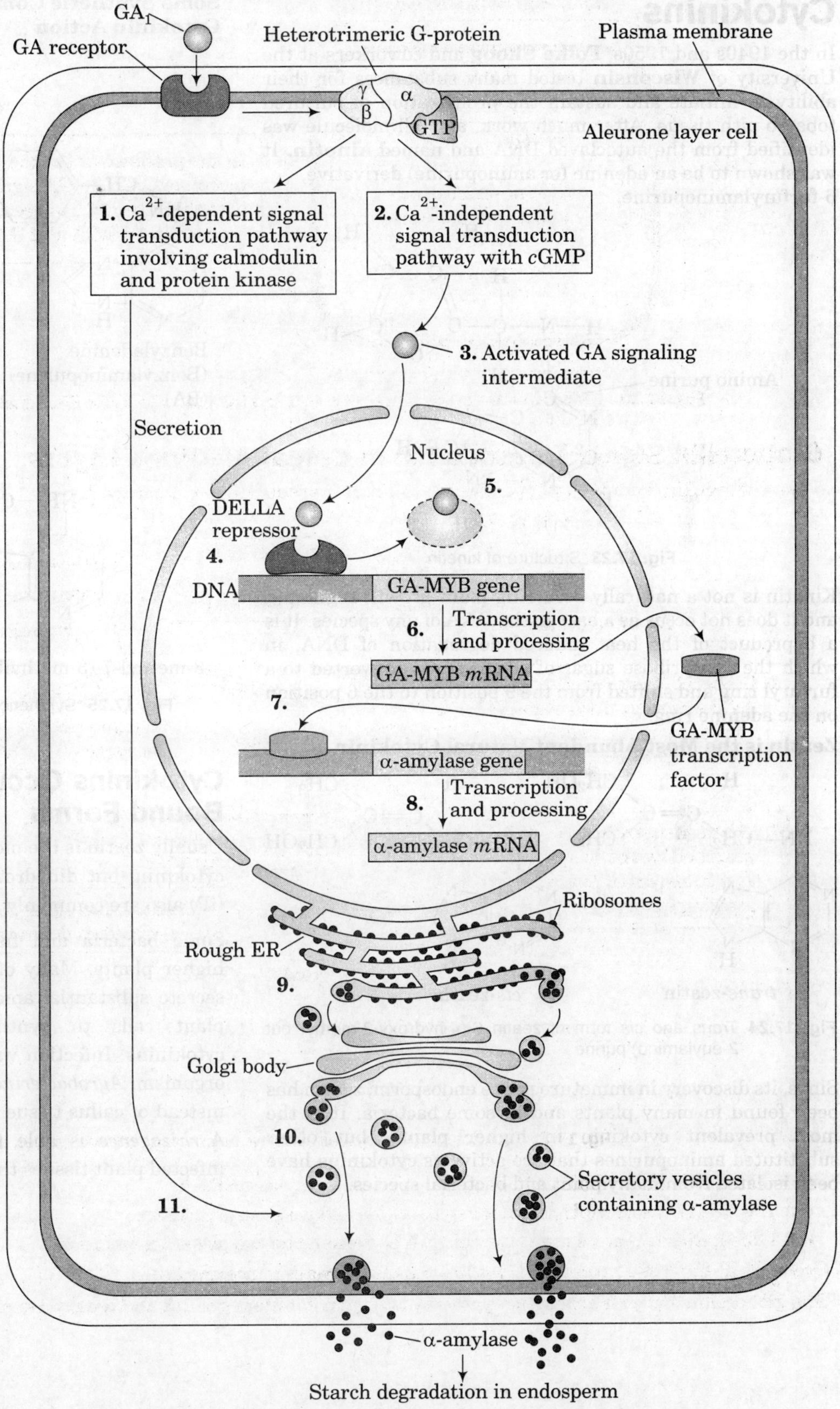

Fig. 17.22 Composite model for the induction of α-amylase synthesis in barley aleurone layers by gibberellin. A calcium-independent pathway induces α-amylase gene transcription; a calcium-dependent pathway is involved in α-amylase secretion

Cytokinins

In the 1940s and 1950s, **Folke Skoog** and coworkers at the University of **Wisconsin** tested many substances for their ability to initiate and sustain the proliferation of cultured tobacco pith tissue. After much work, a small molecule was identified from the autoclaved DNA and named **kinetin.** It was shown to be an adenine (or aminopurine) derivative, 6-furfurylaminopurine.

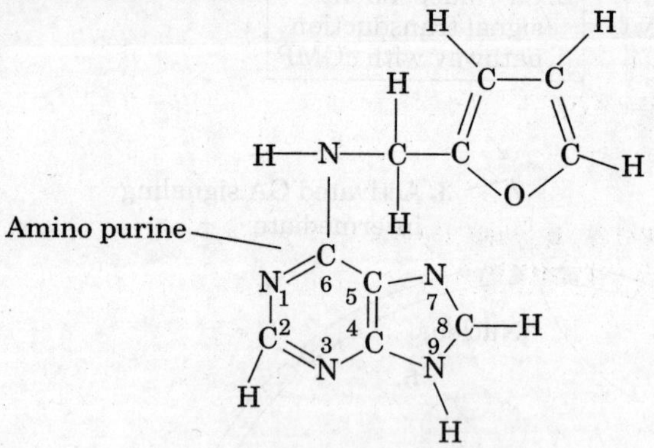

Amino purine

Fig. 17.23 Structure of kinetin

Kinetin is not a naturally occurring plant growth regulator, and it does not occur as a base in the DNA of any species. It is a byproduct of the heat induced degradation of DNA, in which the deoxyribose sugar of adenosine is converted to a furfuryl ring and shifted from the 9 position to the 6 position on the adenine ring.

Zeatin is the Most Abundant Natural Cytokinin

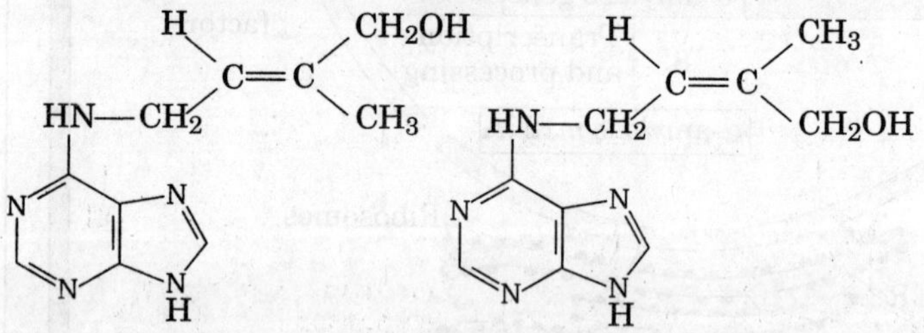

trans-zeatin *cis*-zeatin

Fig. 17.24 *Trans* and *cis* form of zeatin 6-(4-hydroxy-3-methyl but 2-enylamino) purine

Since, its discovery in immature maize endosperm, zeatin has been found in many plants and in some bacteria. It is the most prevalent cytokinin in higher plants, but other substituted aminopurines that are active as cytokinins have been isolated from many plant and bacterial species.

Some Synthetic Compounds can Mimic or Antagonize Cytokinin Action

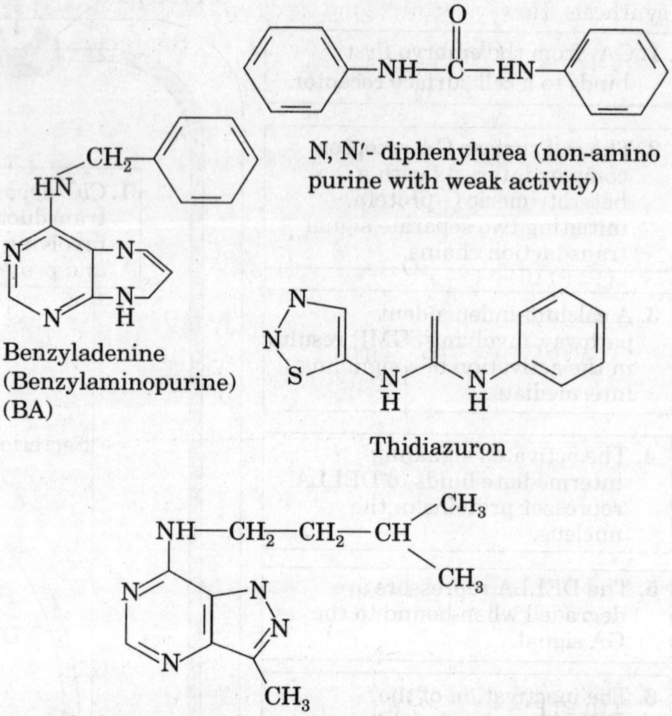

N, N'- diphenylurea (non-amino purine with weak activity)

Benzyladenine (Benzylaminopurine) (BA)

Thidiazuron

3-methyl-7-(3-methylbutylamino)pyrazolo(4,3-D)pyrimidin

Fig. 17.25 Synthetic compounds mimicing cytokinin action

Cytokinins Occur in Both Free and Bound Forms

Usually zeatin is the most abundant naturally occurring free cytokinin, but dihydrozeatin (DZ) and isopentenyl adenine (iP) also are commonly found in higher plants and bacteria.

Some bacteria and fungi are intimately associated with higher plants. Many of these microorganisms produce and secrete substantial amounts of cytokinins and/or cause the plant cells to synthesize plant hormones, including cytokinins. Infection with a close relative of the crown gall organism, *Agrobacterium rhizogenes*, causes masses of roots instead of callus tissue to develop from the site of infection. *A. rhizogenes* is able to modify cytokinin metabolism in infected plant tissues through a mechanism.

Biosynthesis of Cytokinins

It is visualized that earlier stages of cytokinin biosynthesis are similar to those of all purines. Root tip is an important site for its synthesis. However developing seeds and cambial tissue are also the site for synthesis.

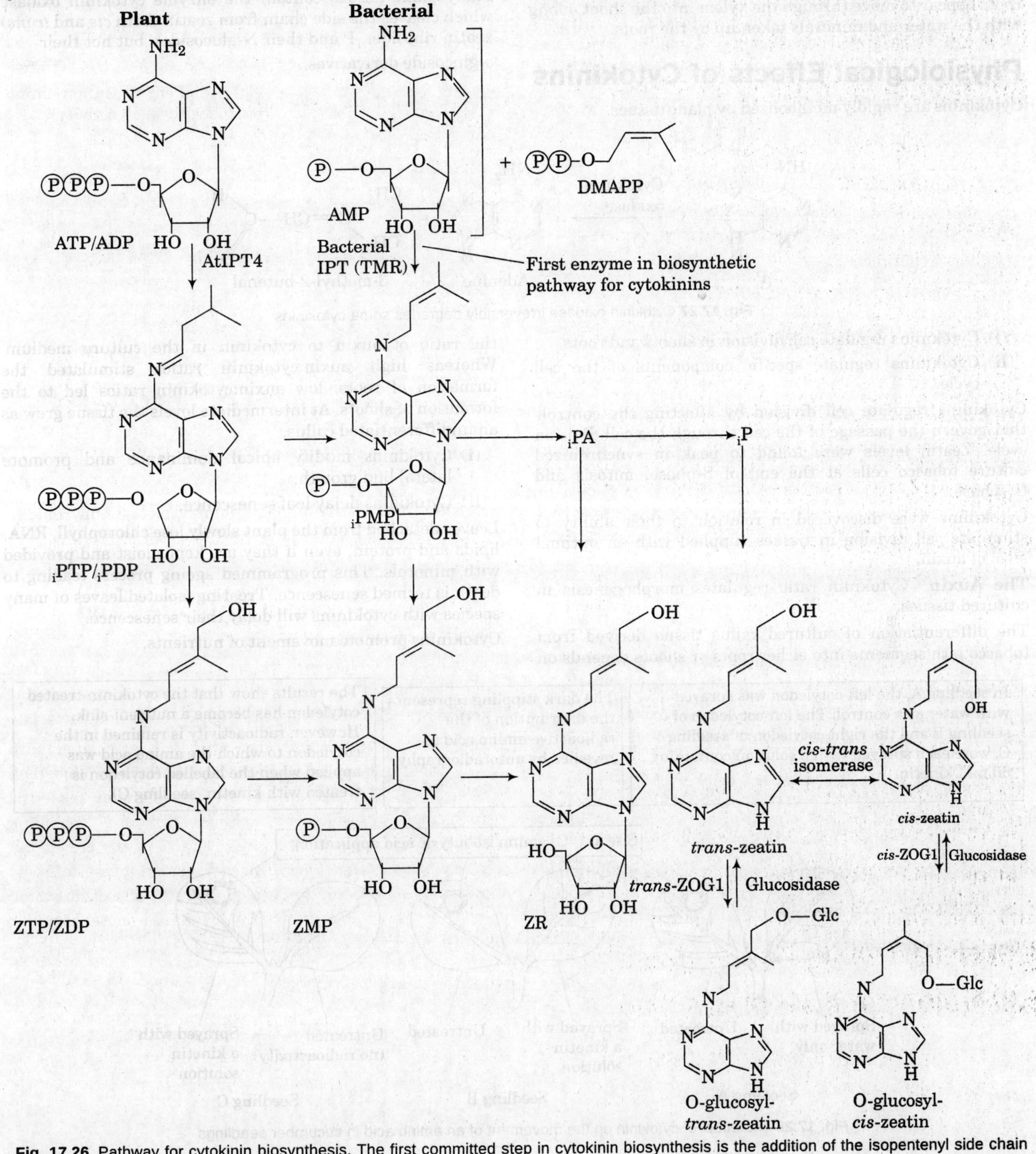

Plant

Bacterial

ATP/ADP

AMP

DMAPP

AtIPT4

Bacterial IPT (TMR)

First enzyme in biosynthetic pathway for cytokinins

PTP/PDP

iPMP

iPA

iP

ZTP/ZDP

ZMP

ZR

trans-zeatin

cis-trans isomerase

cis-zeatin

trans-ZOG1 Glucosidase

cis-ZOG1 Glucosidase

O-glucosyl-*trans*-zeatin

O-glucosyl-*cis*-zeatin

Fig. 17.26 Pathway for cytokinin biosynthesis. The first committed step in cytokinin biosynthesis is the addition of the isopentenyl side chain from DMAPP to an adenosine moiety

Transport of Cytokinins

Root apical meristems are major sites of synthesis of the free cytokinins in whole plants. The cytokinins synthesized in roots appear to move through the xylem into the shoot, along with the water and minerals taken up by the roots.

Physiological Effects of Cytokinins

Cytokinins are rapidly metabolized by plant tissues.

Free cytokinins are readily converted to their respective nucleoside and nucleotide forms. Such interconversions likely involve enzymes common to purine metabolism. Many plant tissues contain the enzyme cytokinin oxidase, which cleaves the side chain from zeatin (both *cis* and *trans*), zeatin riboside, $_i$P and their N-glucosides, but not their *o*-glucoside derivatives.

$_i$P $\xrightarrow[O_2]{\text{Cytokinin oxidase}}$ Adenine + 3-methyl-2-butenal

Fig. 17.27 Cytokinin oxidase irreversibly degrades some cytokinins

(i) Cytokinins regulate cell division in shoots and roots.

(ii) Cytokinins regulate specific components of the cell cycle.

Cytokinins regulate cell division by affecting the controls that govern the passage of the cell through the cell division cycle. Zeatin levels were found to peak in synchronized culture tobacco cells at the end of S-phase, mitosis and G_1-phase.

Cytokinins were discovered in relation to their ability to stimulate cell division in tissues supplied with an optimal level of auxin.

The Auxin Cytokinin ratio regulates morphogenesis in cultured tissues.

The differentiation of cultured callus tissue derived from tobacco pith segments into either roots or shoots depends on the ratio of auxin to cytokinin in the culture medium. Whereas high auxin:cytokinin ratios stimulated the formation of roots, low auxin:cytokinin ratios led to the formation of shoots. At intermediate levels the tissue grew as an undifferentiated callus.

(i) Cytokinins modify apical dominance and promote lateral bud growth.

(ii) Cytokinins delay leaf senescence.

Leaves detached from the plant slowly lose chlorophyll, RNA, lipids and protein, even if they are kept moist and provided with minerals. This programmed ageing process leading to death is termed senescence. Treating isolated leaves of many species with cytokinins will delay their senescence.

Cytokinins promote movement of nutrients.

In seedling A, the left cotyledon was sprayed with water as a control. The left cotyledon of seedling B and the right cotyledon of seedling C, were each sprayed with a solution containing 50 mM kinetin.

The dark stippling represents the distribution of the radioactive amino acid as revealed by autoradiography.

The results show that the cytokinin-treated cotyledon has become a nutrient sink. However, radioactivity is retained in the cotyledon to which the amino acid was applied when the labelled cotyledon is treated with kinetin (seedling C).

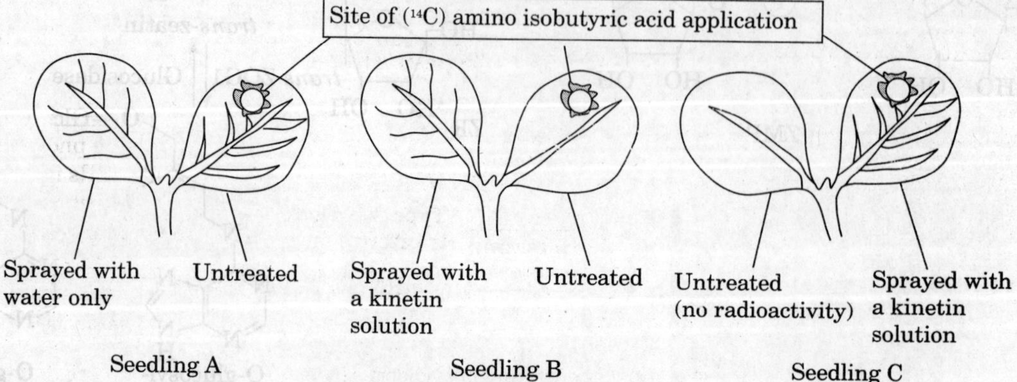

Fig. 17.28 The effect of cytokinin on the movement of an amino acid in cucumber seedlings

(i) Cytokinins promote chloroplast development.

(ii) Cytokinins promote cell expansion in leaves and cotyledons.

(iii) Cytokinins regulate growth of stems and roots.

Cellular and Molecular Modes of Cytokinin Action

Model of cytokinin signaling. The near future should see significant refinement of this model, the tools are now in hand to analyze the interactions among these elements.

The first clue to the nature of the cytokinin receptor came from the discovery of the CKI1 gene. Plant cells generally require cytokinin in order to divide in culture. However, a cell line that overexpresses CKI1 is capable of growing in culture in the absence of added cytokinin. Cytokinins cause a rapid increase in the expression of response regulator genes. Histidine phosphotransferases may mediate the cytokinin signaling cascade. Cytokinin-induced phosphorylation activates transcription factors.

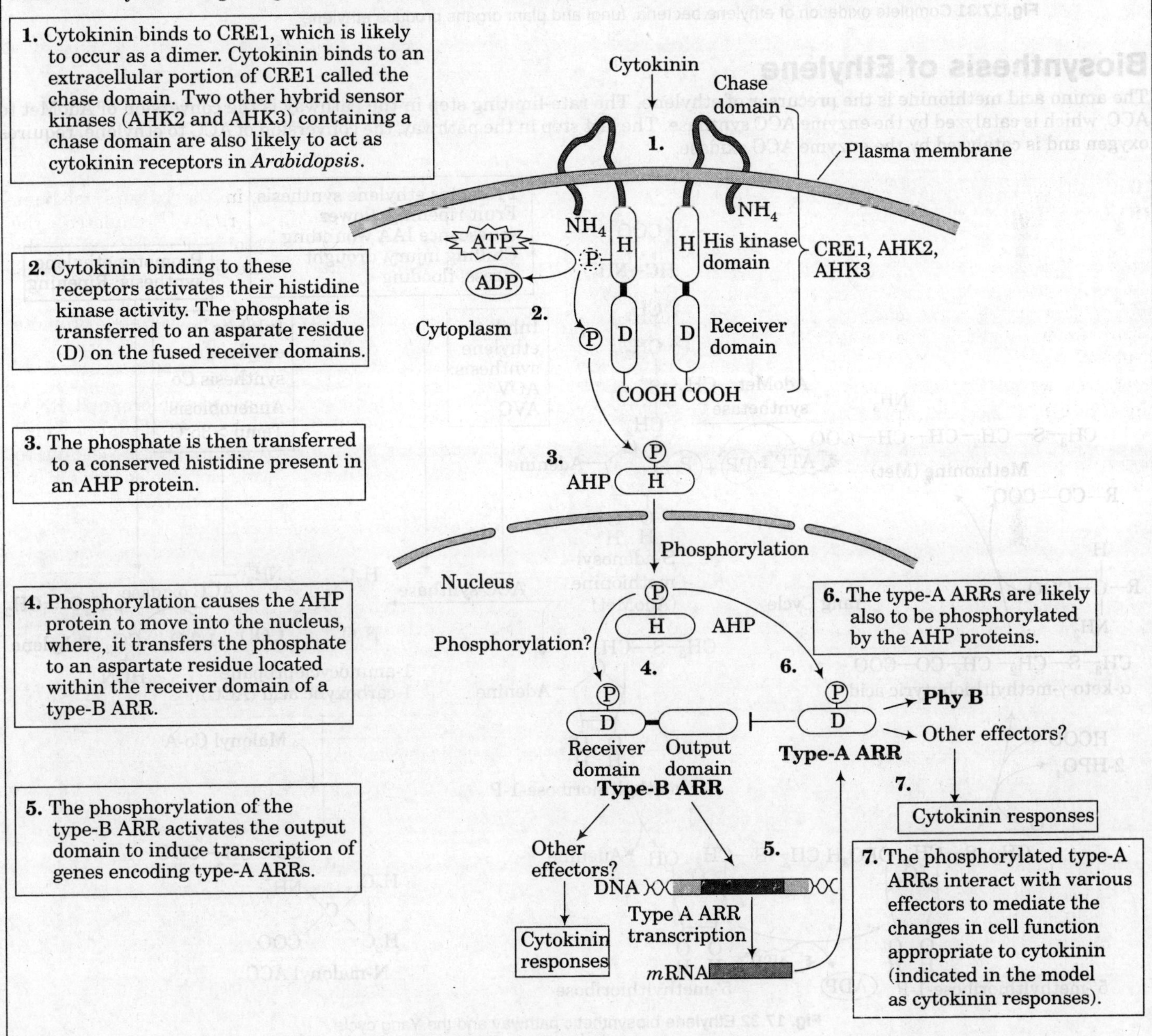

Fig. 17.29 Mechanism of cytokinin action

Ethylene

Ethylene is the simplest known olefin (its molecular weight is 28), and it is lighter than air under physiological conditions:

It is flammable and readily undergoes oxidation. Ethylene can be oxidized to ethylene oxide.

In most plant tissues, ethylene can be completely oxidized to CO_2, in the following reaction:

$$H_2C{=}CH_2 \xrightarrow{[O]} H_2C{-}O{-}CH_2 \xrightarrow{O_2} HOOC{-}COOH \rightarrow CO_2$$

Ethylene — Ethylene oxide — Oxalic acid — Carbon dioxide

Fig. 17.31 Complete oxidation of ethylene bacteria, fungi and plant organs produce ethylene

$$H_2C{=}CH_2$$

Fig. 17.30 Structure of ethylene

Biosynthesis of Ethylene

The amino acid methionine is the precursor of ethylene. The rate-limiting step in the pathway is the conversion of AdoMet to ACC, which is catalyzed by the enzyme ACC synthase. The last step in the pathway, the conversion of ACC to ethylene, requires oxygen and is catalyzed by the enzyme ACC oxidase.

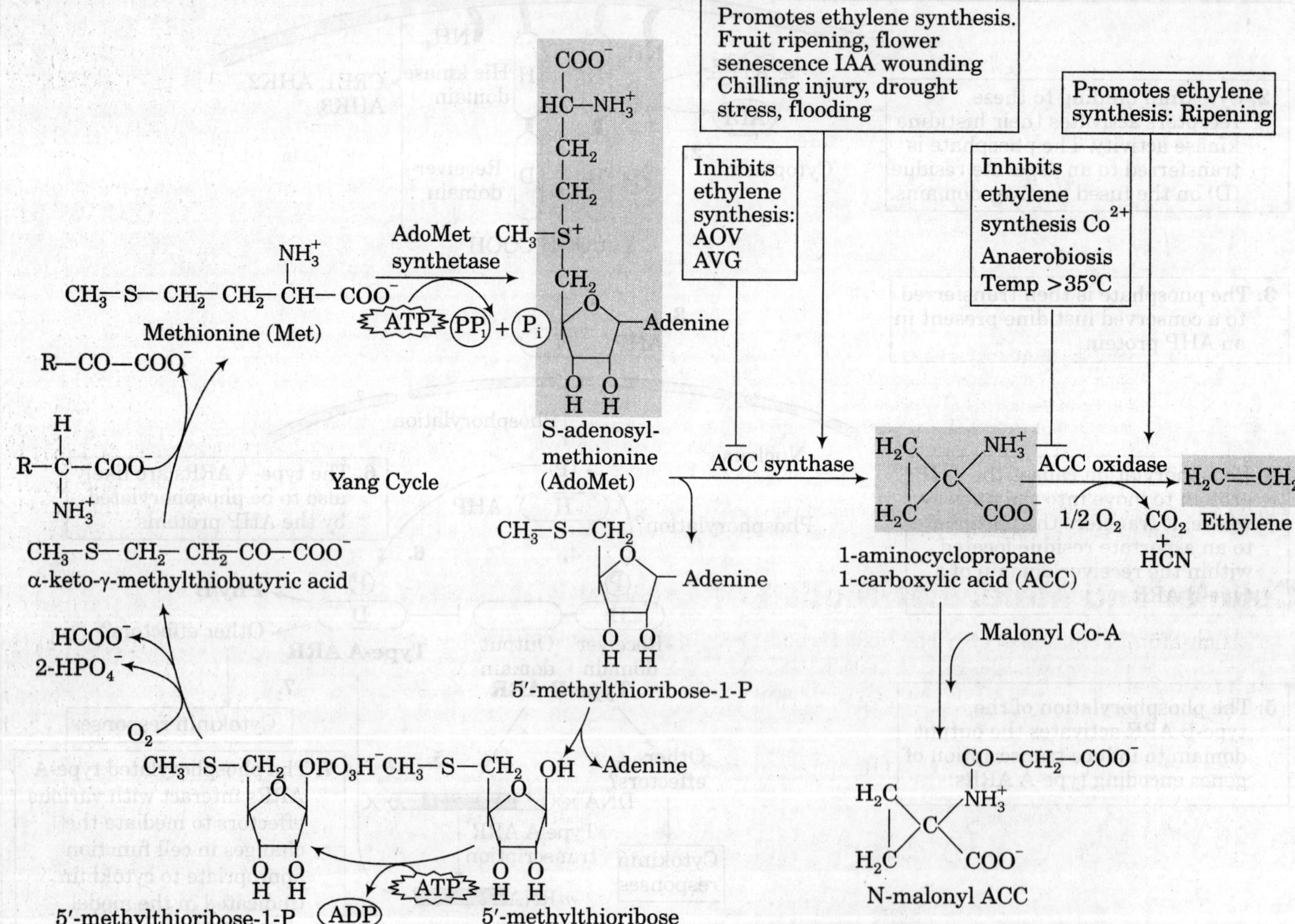

Fig. 17.32 Ethylene biosynthetic pathway and the Yang cycle

Ethylene biosynthesis is increased by stress conditions such as drought, flooding, chilling, exposure to ozone or mechanical wounding.

As fruits mature, the rate of ACC and ethylene biosynthesis increases, due to increased enzymatic activities of both ACC oxidase and ACC synthase.

In some instances, auxins and ethylene can cause similar plant responses, such as induction of flowering in pineapple and inhibition of stem elongation. These responses might be due to the ability of auxins to promote ethylene synthesis by enhancing ACC synthase activity.

Physiological Effects of Ethylene

(i) Ethylene promotes the ripening of some fruits.

> **Plants Genetically Engineered and Ethylene**
>
> Analysis of *m*RNA from tomato fruits from wild-type and transgenic tomato plants genetically engineered to lack ethylene has revealed that gene expression during ripening is regulated by at least two independent pathways:
> 1. **An ethylene-dependent pathway** includes genes involved in lycopene and aroma biosynthesis, respiratory metabolism and ACC synthase. 2. **A developmental, ethylene-independent pathway** includes genes encoding ACC oxidase and chlorophyllase.

(ii) Leaf epinasty results when ACC from the root is transported to the shoot.

(iii) Ethylene induces lateral cell expansion.

(iv) The hooks of dark-grown seedlings are maintained by ethylene production.

(v) Ethylene breaks seed and bud dormancy in some species.

(vi) Ethylene induces the formation of roots and root hairs.

(vii) Ethylene promotes the elongation growth of submerged aquatic species.

(viii) Ethylene induces flowering in the pineapple family.

(ix) Ethylene enhances the rate of leaf senescence.

(x) The role of ethylene in defense responses is complex.

Ethylene production generally increases in response to pathogen attack in both compatible (*i.e.*, pathogenic) and non-compatible (non-pathogenic) interactions.

Ethylene biosynthesis in the abscission zone is regulated by auxin

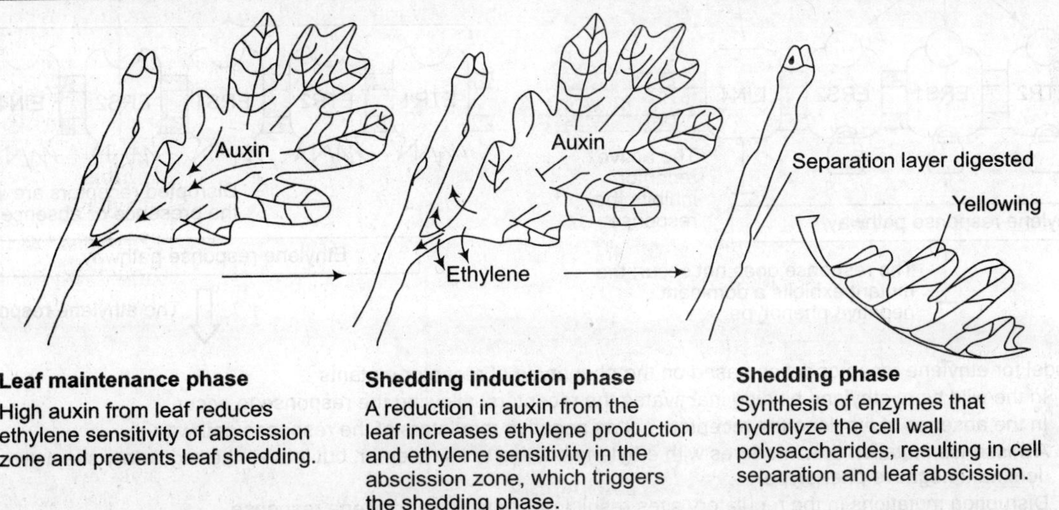

Fig. 17.33 Schematic view of the roles of auxin and ethylene during leaf abscission. In the shedding induction phase, the level of auxin decreases, and the level of ethylene increases. These changes in the hormonal balance increase the sensitivity of the target cells to ethylene

Cellular and Molecular Modes of Ethylene Action

High-affinity binding of ethylene to its receptor requires a copper cofactor.

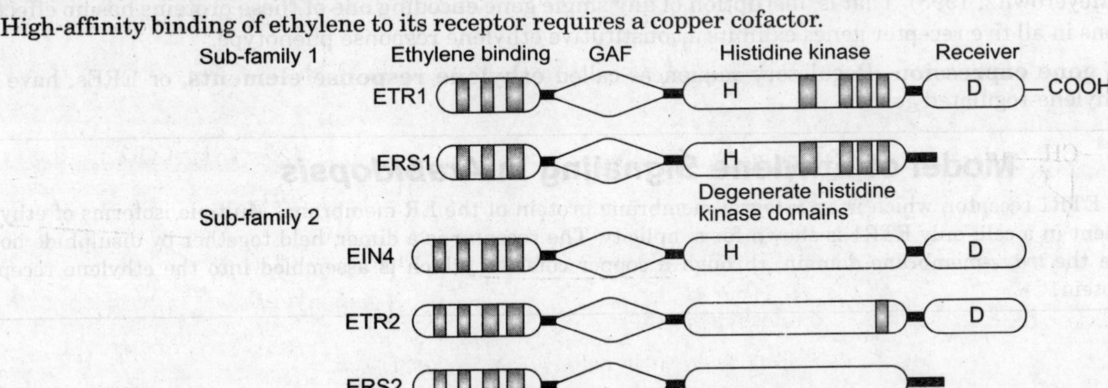

Fig. 17.34 Schematic diagram of five ethylene receptor proteins and their functional domains. The GAF domain is a conserved cGMP-binding domain found in a diverse group of proteins. Note that EIN4, ETR2 and ERS2 have degenerate histidine kinase domains

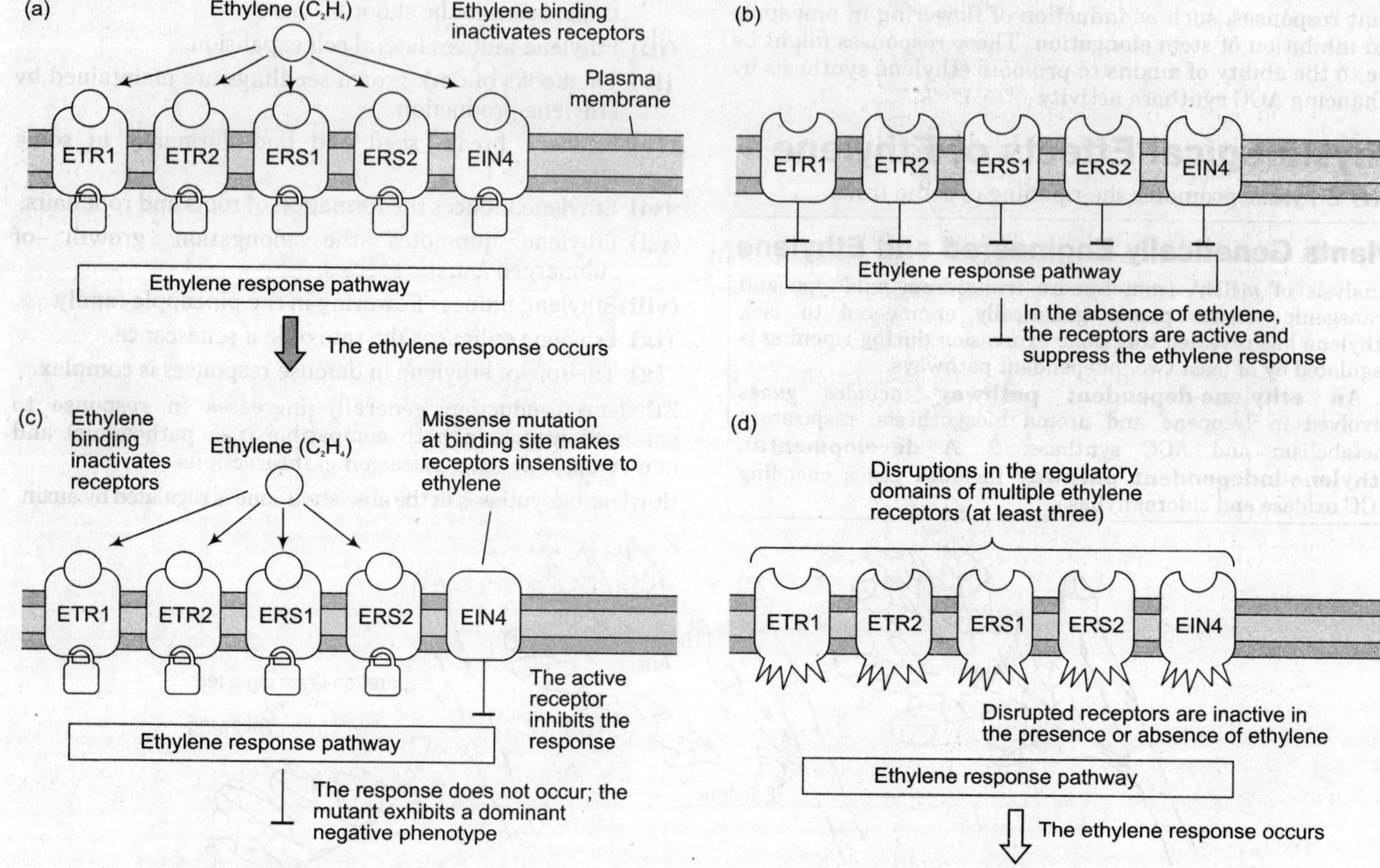

Fig. 17.35 Model for ethylene receptor action based on the phenotype of receptor mutants
(a) In the wild type, ethylene binding inactivates the receptors, allowing the response to occur.
(b) In the absence of ethylene the receptors act as negative regulators of the response pathway.
(c) A missense mutation that interferes with ethylene binding to its receptor, but leaves the regulatory site active, results in a dominant negative phenotype.
(d) Disruption mutations in the regulatory sites result in a constitutive ethylene response.

Unbound ethylene receptors are negative regulators of the response pathway In *Arabidopsis*, tomato and probably most other plant species, the ethylene receptors are encoded by multigene families. Targeted disruption (complete inactivation) of the five *Arabidopsis* ethylene receptors (ETR1, ETR2, ERS1, ERS2 and EIN4) has revealed that they are functionally redundant (Hua and Meyerowitz; 1998). That is, disruption of any single gene encoding one of these proteins has no effect, but a plant with disruptions in all five receptor genes exhibits a constitutive ethylene response phenotype.

Ethylene regulates gene expression Regulatory sequences called **ethylene response elements,** or EREs, have been identified from the ethylene-regulated genes.

Model of Ethylene Signaling in *Arabidopsis*

Ethylene binds to the ETR1 receptor, which is an integral membrane protein of the ER membrane. Multiple isoforms of ethylene receptors may be present in a cell; only ETR1 is shown for simplicity. The receptor is a dimer, held together by disulphide bonds. Ethylene binds within the *trans*-membrane domain, through a copper cofactor, which is assembled into the ethylene receptors through the RAN1 protein.

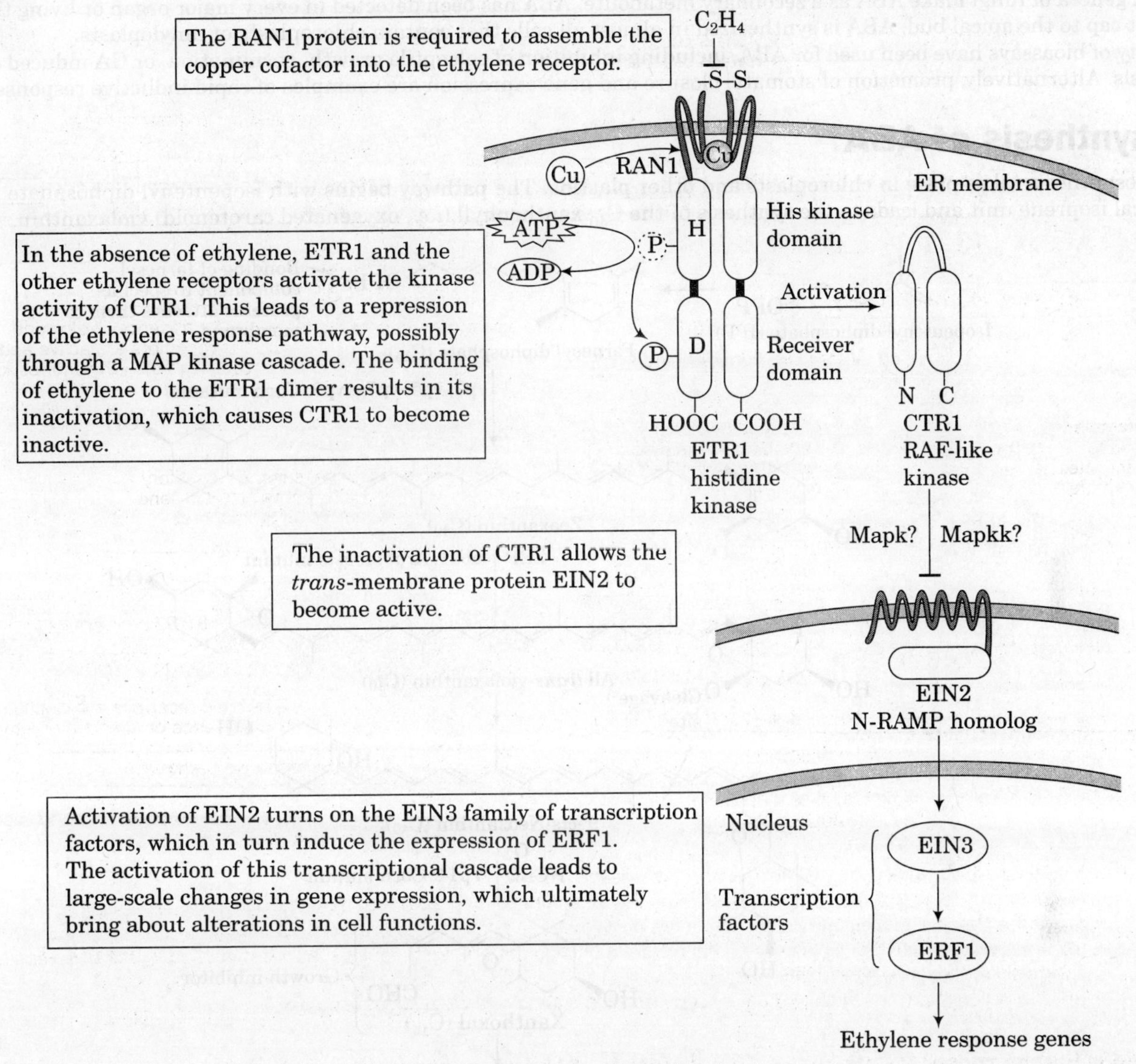

Fig. 17.36 Ethylene signaling

Abscisic Acid (ABA)

Early experiments led to the identification of a group of growth-inhibiting compounds, including a substance known as **dormin** purified from sycamore leaves collected in early autumn, when the trees were entering dormancy. Upon discovery that dormin was chemically identical to a substance that promotes the abscission of cotton fruits, **abscisin II,** the compound was renamed **abscisic acid** (ABA).

Another important function is its regulation of seed maturation and dormancy.

H_3C CH_3 5 CH_3 3 4 5′ 6′ 1′ 2 OH 2′ 3′ 1 O 4′ CH_3 COOH

(*S*)-*cis*-ABA
(naturally occurring active form)

H_3C CH_3 CH_3 OH O CH_3 COOH

(*R*)-*cis*-ABA
(inactive in stomatal closure)

H_3C CH_3 CH_3 COOH OH O

(*S*)-2-*trans*-ABA (inactive, but interconvertible with active [*cis*] form)

Fig. 17.37 The chemical structures of the S (counterclockwise array) and R (clockwise array) forms of *cis*-ABA, and the (S)-2-*trans* form of ABA

Several genera of fungi make ABA as a secondary metabolite. ABA has been detected in every major organ or living tissue from the root cap to the apical bud. ABA is synthesized in almost all cells that contain chloroplasts or amyloplasts.
A variety of bioassays have been used for ABA, including inhibition of coleoptile growth, germination, or GA induced α-amylase synthesis. Alternatively, promotion of stomatal closure and gene expression are examples of rapid inductive responses.

Biosynthesis of ABA

ABA biosynthesis takes place in chloroplasts and other plastids. The pathway begins with isopentenyl diphosphate (IPP), the biological isoprene unit and leads to the synthesis of the C_{40} xanthophyll (*i.e.*, oxygenated carotenoid) violaxanthin.

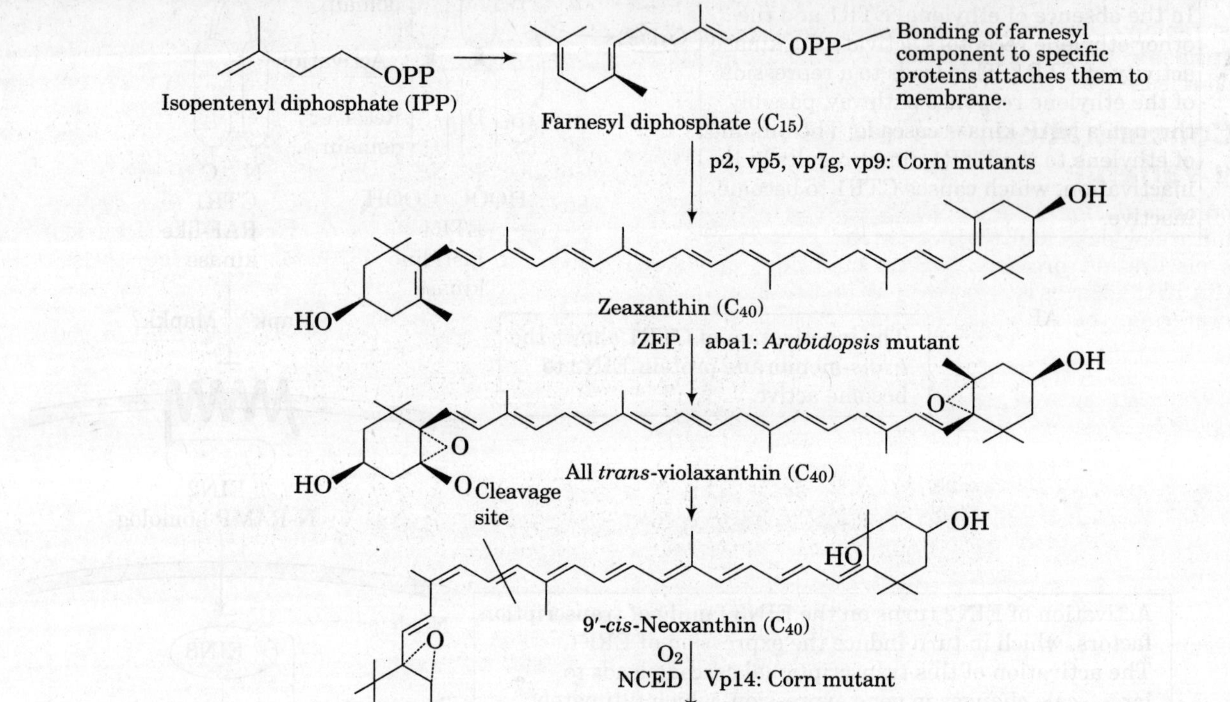

OPP
Isopentenyl diphosphate (IPP)
OPP
Bonding of farnesyl component to specific proteins attaches them to membrane.
Farnesyl diphosphate (C_{15})
p2, vp5, vp7g, vp9: Corn mutants
OH
HO
Zeaxanthin (C_{40})
ZEP | aba1: *Arabidopsis* mutant
OH
O
O
HO
O Cleavage site
All *trans*-violaxanthin (C_{40})
OH
HO
O
HO
9′-*cis*-Neoxanthin (C_{40})
O_2
NCED | Vp14: Corn mutant
O
HO
CHO
Xanthoxal (C_{15})
Growth inhibitor
OH
O
CHO
ABA-aldehyde (C_{15})
Flacca, Sitiens, Tomato mutants
droopy: Potato mutants
aba3: *Arabidopsis* mutant
nar2a: Barley mutant
ABA inactivation by oxidation
ABA inactivation by conjugation with monosaccharides
H
O
OH
OH
COOH
4′-dihydrophaseic acid (DPA)
O
O
OH
COOH
Phaseic acid (PA)
Oxidation
O
OH
COOH
Abscisic acid (C_{15}) (ABA)
Conjugation
O
OH
C–O
O
CH_2OH
O
OH
OH
OH
ABA-β-D-glucose ester

Fig. 17.38 ABA biosynthesis and metabolism. In higher plants, ABA is synthesized *via* the terpenoid pathway. The pathways for ABA catabolism include conjugation to form ABA-β-D-glucosyl ester or oxidation to form phaseic acid and then dihydrophaseic acid. ZEP – zeaxanthin epoxidase; NCED – nine-*cis*-epoxycarotenoids dioxygenase.

Violaxanthin is converted to the C_{40} compound **9′-*cis*-neoxanthin,** which is then cleaved to form the C_{15} comstress as a result of synthesis in the leaf, redistribution within the mesophyll cell, import from the roots, and recirculation from other leaves. The concentration of ABA declines after rewatering because of degradation and export from the leaf, as well as a decrease in the rate of synthesis.

ABA can be inactivated by oxidation or conjugation A major cause of the inactivation of free ABA is oxidation, yielding the unstable intermediate 6-hydroxymethyl ABA, which is rapidly converted to **Phaseic Acid** (PA) and **dihydrophaseic acid** (DPA). Esterase enzymes in plant cells could release free ABA from the conjugated form.

ABA Concentrations in Tissues are Highly Variable

In developing seeds, for example, ABA levels can increase 100 fold within a few days and then decline to vanishingly low levels as maturation proceeds. Under conditions of water stress, ABA in the leaves can increase 50 fold within 4 to 8h. Upon rewatering, the ABA level declines to normal in the same amount of time.

As with other plant hormones, the concentration of free ABA, in the cytosol is also regulated by degradation, compartmentation, conjugation and transport. For example, cytosolic ABA increases during water stress as a result of synthesis in the leaf, redistribution within the mesophyll cell, import from the roots and recirculation from other leaves.

ABA is Translocated in Vascular Tissue

ABA is transported by both the xylem and the phloem, but it is normally much more abundant in the phloem sap. Destruction of the phloem by a stem girdle prevents ABA accumulation in the roots, indicating that the hormone is transported in the phloem sap. ABA synthesized in the roots can also be transported to the shoot *via* the xylem. Whereas, the concentration of ABA in the xylem sap.

Stress-induced alkalinization of the apoplast favours formation of the dissociated form of abscisic acid, ABA, which does not readily cross membranes. Hence, less ABA enters the mesophyll cells, and more reaches the guard cells *via* the transpiration stream.

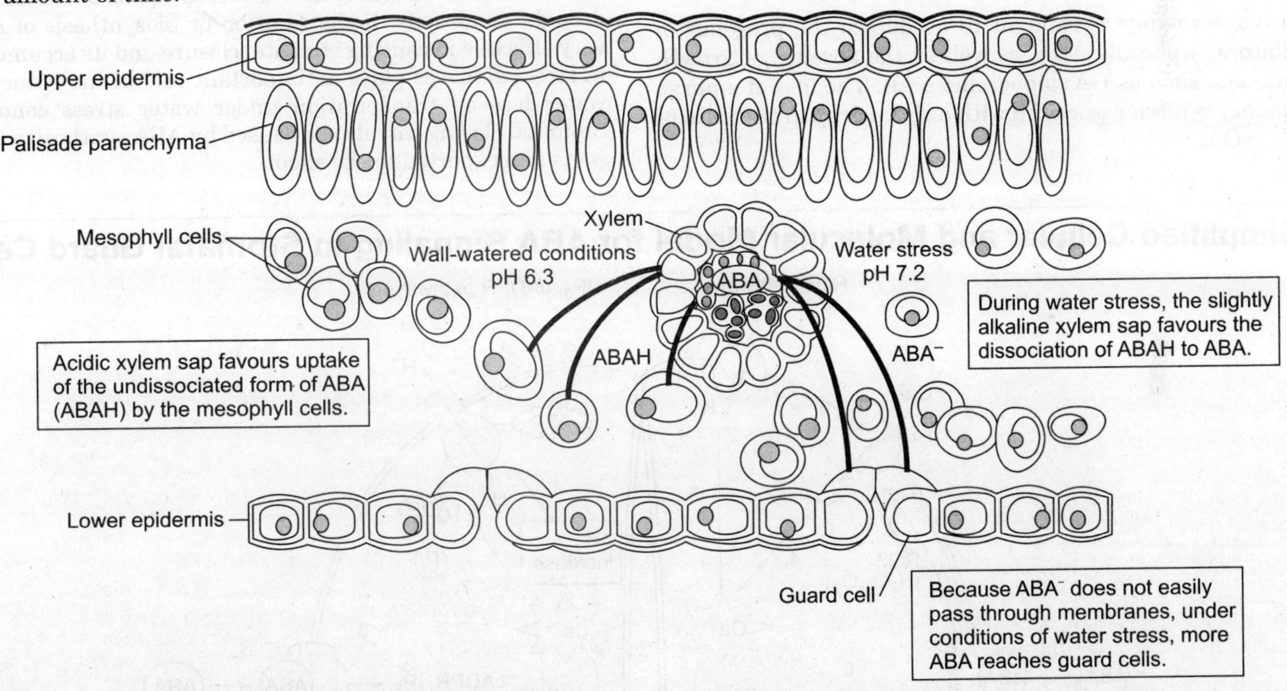

Fig. 17.39 Redistribution of ABA in the leaf resulting from alkalinization of the xylem sap during water stress

Physiological Effects of ABA

Abscisic acid plays primary regulatory roles in the initiation and maintenance of seed and bud dormancy and in the plant's response to stress, particularly water stress.

ABA influences many other aspects of plant development by interacting, usually as an antagonist, with auxin, cytokinin, gibberellin, ethylene and brassinosteroids.

ABA Levels in Seeds Peak during Embryogenesis

Seed development can be divided into three phases:

(i) During the first phase, which is characterized by cell divisions and tissue differentiation.

(ii) During the second phase, cell divisions cease and storage compounds accumulate.

(iii) In the final phase, the embryo becomes tolerant to desiccation, and the seed dehydrates, losing upto 90% of its water.

Typically, the ABA content of seeds is very low early in embryogenesis, reaches a maximum at about the halfway point, and then gradually falls to low levels as the seed reaches maturity.

ABA synthesis in the embryo and endosperm and is essential to dormancy induction, whereas the maternal genotype controls the major, early peak of ABA accumulation and helps suppress vivipary in mid embryogenesis.

ABA Promotes Desiccation Tolerance in the Embryo Synthesis of many **Late-Embryogenesis-Abundant** (LEA proteins thought to be involved in desiccation tolerance) proteins, or related family members, can be induced by ABA treatment of either young embryos or vegetative tissues. Thus, the synthesis of most LEA proteins is under ABA control.

ABA Promotes the Accumulation of Seed Storage Protein during Embryogenesis Exogenous ABA promotes accumulation of storage proteins in cultured embryos of many species, and some ABA-deficient or insensitive mutants have reduced storage protein accumulation.

ABA not only regulates the accumulation of storage proteins during embryogenesis; it can also maintain the mature embryo in a dormant state until the environmental conditions are optimal for growth.

Seed Dormancy may be Imposed by the Coat or the Embryo Seed coats and pericarps may contain relatively high concentrations of growth inhibitors, including ABA, that can suppress germination of the embryo.

Embryo dormancy is thought to be due to the presence of inhibitors, especially ABA, as well as the absence of growth promoters, such as GA (gibberellic acid). The loss of embryo dormancy is often associated with a sharp drop in the ratio of ABA to GA.

Seed Dormancy is Controlled by the Ratio of ABA to GA Although the role of ABA in initiating and maintaining seed dormancy is well established, other hormones contribute to the overall effect. For example, in most plants the peak of ABA production in the seed coincides with a decline in the levels of IAA and GA.

ABA inhibits precocious germination and vivipary

- ABA accumulates in dormant buds.
- ABA promotes root growth and inhibits shoot growth at low water potentials.

ABA promotes leaf senescence independently of ethylene.

ABA Inhibits GA-Induced Enzyme Production ABA exerts this inhibitory effect *via* atleast two mechanisms:

(i) An activator of ABA-induced gene expression, acts as a transcriptional repressor of some GA-regulated genes.

(ii) ABA represses the GA-induced expression of GAMYB, a transcription factor that mediates the GA induction of α-amylase expression.

ABA Closes Stomata in Response to Water Stress ABA concentrations in leaves can increase up to 50 times under drought conditions. Redistribution or biosynthesis of ABA is very effective in causing stomatal closure and its accumulation in stressed leaves plays an important role in the reduction of water loss by transpiration under water stress conditions. Stomatal closing can also be caused by ABA synthesized in the roots and exported to the shoot.

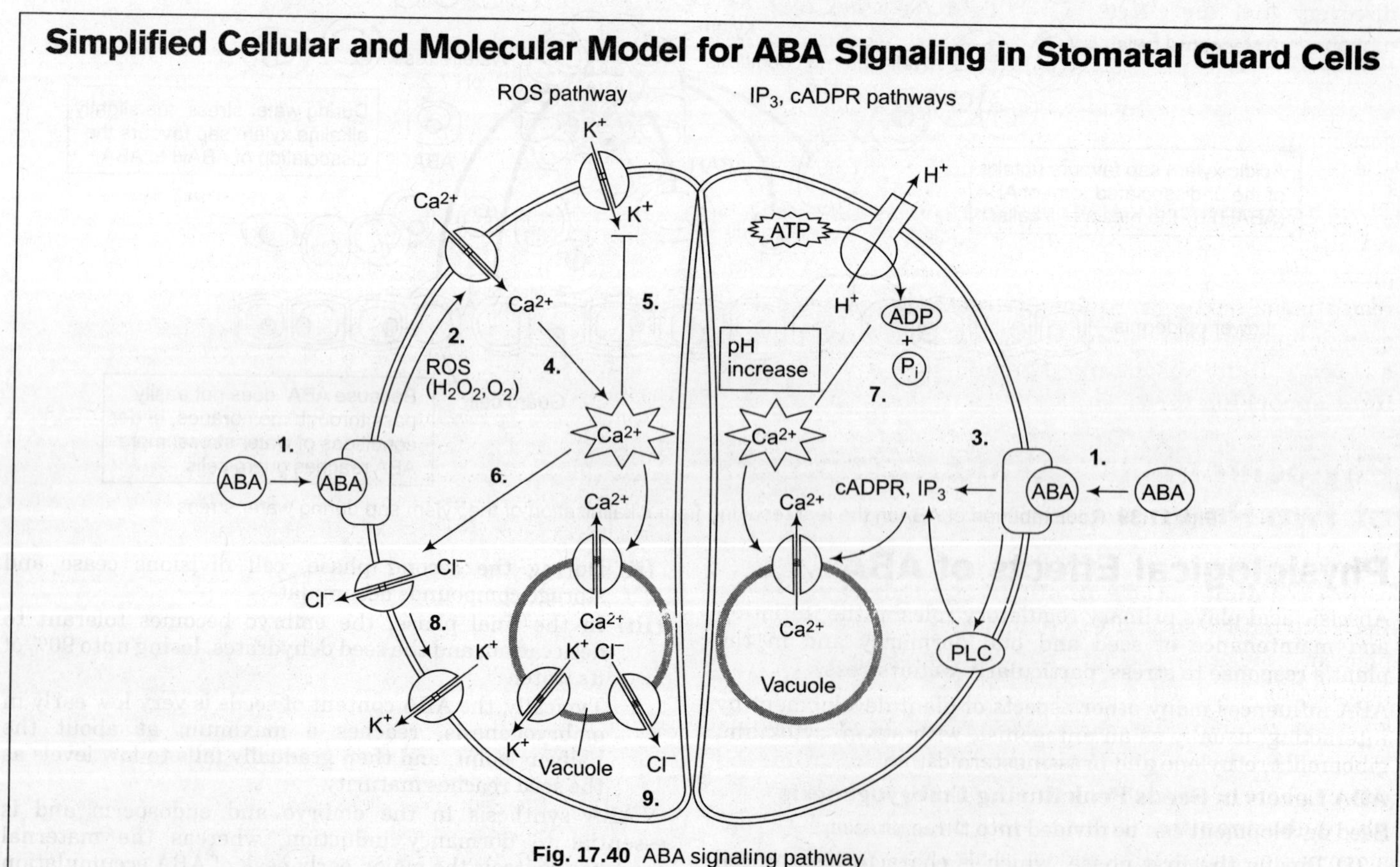

Fig. 17.40 ABA signaling pathway

1. ABA binds to its receptors.
2. ABA binding induces the formation of reactive oxygen species, which activate plasma membrane Ca^{2+} channels.
3. ABA increases the levels of cyclic ADP-ribose and IP_3, which activate additional calcium channels on the tonoplast.
4. The influx of calcium initiates intracellular calcium oscillations and promotes the further release of calcium from vacuoles.
5. The rise in intracellular calcium blocks K^+ in channels.
6. The rise in intracellular calcium promotes the opening if Cl^- out (anion) channels on the plasma membrane, causing membrane depolarization.
7. The plasma membrane proton pump is inhibited by the ABA-induced increase in cytostolic calcium and a rise in intracellular pH, further depolarizing the membrane.
8. Membrane depolarization activates K^+ out channels.
9. K^+ and anions to be releazed across the plasma membrane are first releazed from vacuoles into the cytosol.

The net effect is the loss of potassium and its anion (Cl^- or malate^{2-}) from the cell. (R–receptor; ROS–reactive oxygen species; cADPR–cyclic ADP-ribose; G-protein–GTP-binding protein; PLC–phospholipase C.)

Sensory Photobiology

Phytochromes

Phytochrome, a blue protein pigment with a molecular mass of about 125 kDa (kilodaltons). However, many of the biological properties of phytochrome had been established earlier in studies of whole plants.

A key break through in the history of phytochrome was the discovery that the effects of red light **(650-680 nm)** on morphogenesis could be reversed by a subsequent irradiation with light of **longer wavelengths (710-740 nm),** called far-red light. This phenomenon was first demonstrated in germinating seeds, but was also observed in relation to stem and leaf growth, as well as floral induction.

These interpretations suggest that there are two pigments, a red light-absorbing pigment and a far-red light-absorbing pigment and the two pigments act antagonistically in the regulation of seed germination. Alternatively, there might be a single pigment that can exist in two interconvertible forms: a **red light-absorbing form** and a **far-red light-absorbing form.**

Phytochrome is a Dimer Composed of Two Polypeptides

Native phytochrome is a soluble protein (MW 250 kDa). It occurs as a **dimer made up of two equivalent subunits.** Each subunit consists of two components: a light-absorbing pigment molecule called the **chromophore** and a polypeptide chain called the **apoprotein.**

The apoprotein monomer (MW 125 kDa) and its chromophore make up the **holoprotein.** In higher plants the chromophore of phytochrome is a linear tetrapyrrole termed **phyto-chromobilin.** There is only one chromophore per monomer of apoprotein, and it is attached to the protein through a thioether linkage to a cysteine residue.

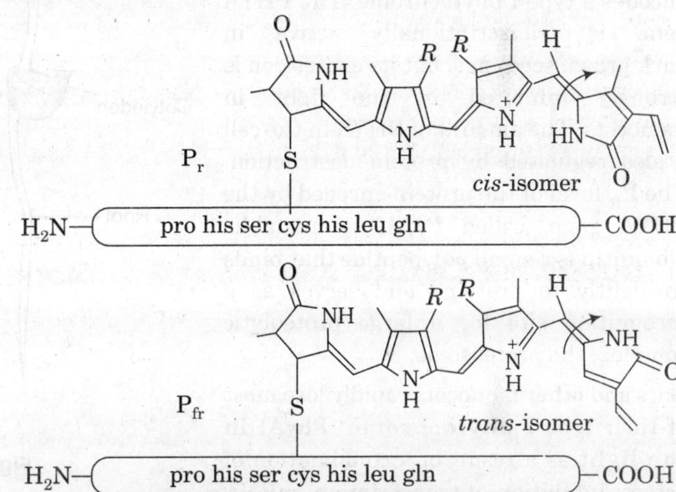

Fig. 17.41 Structure of the P_r and P_{fr} forms of the chromophore (phytochromobilin) and the peptide region bound to the chromophore through a thioether linkage. Red light converts *cis* form to *trans* form

The polypeptide folds into two major domains separated by a 'hinge' region. The **larger N-terminal domain** (MW 70 kDa) bears the chromophore; the **smaller C-terminal domain** (MW 55 kDa) contains the site, where the two monomers associate with each other to form the dimer.

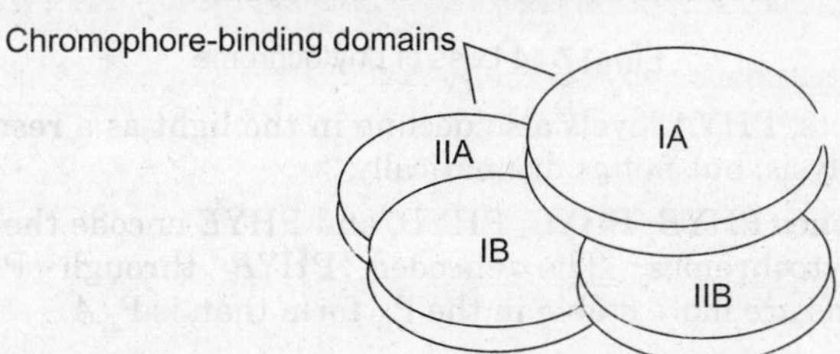

Fig. 17.42 Structure of the phytochrome dimer. The monomers are labelled I and II. Each monomer consists of a chromophore-binding domain (A) and a smaller non-chromophore domain (B)

Phytochromobilin is synthesized inside plastids and is derived from 5-aminolevulinic acid *via* a pathway that branches from the chlorophyll biosynthetic pathway. It is thought to leak out of the plastid into the cytosol by a passive process.

Both chromophore and protein undergo conformational changes upon absorption of light, the P_r chromophore undergoes a *cis-trans* isomerization of the double bond between carbons 15 and 16 and rotation of the C14 –C15 single bond. During the conversion of P_r to P_{fr}, the protein moiety of the phytochrome holoprotein also undergoes a subtle conformational change.

Phytochrome is most abundant in etiolated seedlings. Very little phytochrome is extractable from green tissues. There are two different classes of phytochrome with distinct properties. These have been termed **type I** and **type II phytochromes.** Type I is about nine times more abundant than type II in dark-grown pea seedlings; in light-grown pea seedlings the amounts of the two types are about equal.

This phytochrome gene family is named PHY, and its five individual members are PHY*A*, PHY*B*, PHY*C*, PHY*D* and PHY*E*. PHY genes encode two types of phytochrome, PHY*A* is the only gene that encodes a type I phytochrome. The PHY*A* gene is transcriptionally active in dark-grown seedlings, but its expression is strongly inhibited in the light in monocots. The amount of PHY*A* in the cell s also regulated by protein destruction. The P_{fr} form of the protein encoded by the PHY*A* gene, called $\mathbf{P_{fr}A}$, is unstable. Ubiquitin is a small polypeptide that binds covalently to proteins and serves as a recognition site for a large proteolytic complex, the proteasome.

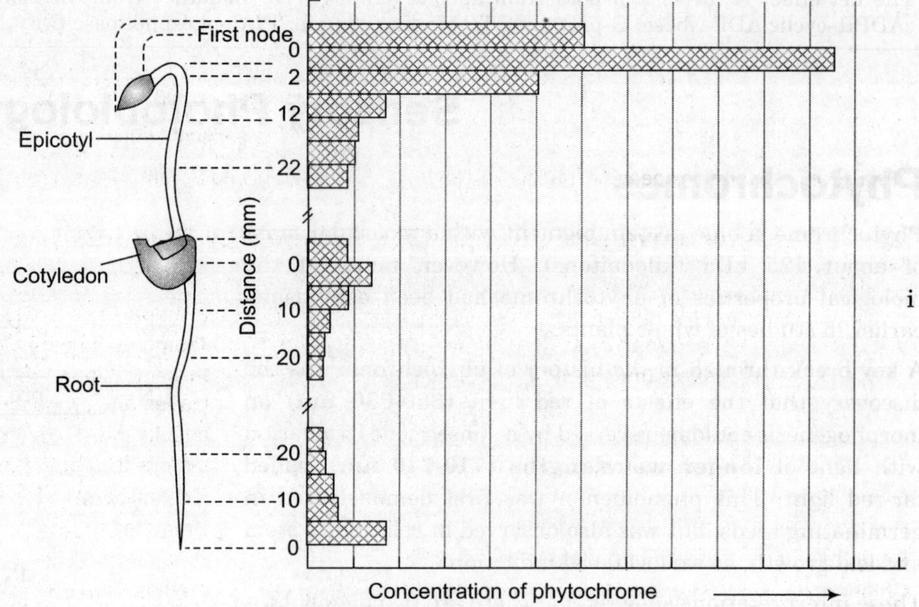

Fig. 17.43 Localization of phytochrome in tissues and cells

Oats and other monocots rapidly lose most of their type **I phytochrome** (PhyA) **in the light** as a result of a combination of actors: inhibition of transcription, *m*RNA degradation, and proteolysis:

PHYA → *m*RNA → P_r ⇄ (Red / Far red) P_{fr} → Response

*m*RNA → Degradation; P_{fr} + Ubiquitin + ATP → Ubiquitin → Degradation

Fig. 17.44 Loss of phytochrome

In dicots, PHY*A* levels also decline in the light as a result of proteolysis, but not as dramatically.

The genes PHY*B*, PHY*C*, PHY*D*, and PHY*E* encode the type II phytochromes. The encoded PHY*B* through PHY*E* proteins are more stable in the P_{fr} form than is $P_{fr}A$.

Function of Phytochromes

In dark-grown or etiolated plants, phytochrome is present in a red light-absorbing form, referred to as P_r because it is synthesized in this form. P_r, which to the human eye is blue, is converted by red light to a far-red light-absorbing form called $\mathbf{P_{fr}}$, which is blue-green. P_{fr}, in turn, can be converted back to P_r by far-red light. This is known as **photo-reversibility.**

When P_r molecules are exposed to red light, most of them absorb it and are converted to P_{fr}, but some of the P_{fr} also absorbs the red light and is converted back to P_r because both P_r and P_{fr} absorb red light. Thus, the proportion of phytochrome in the P_{fr} form after saturating irradiation by red light is only about 85%. Similarly, the very small amount of far-red light absorbed by P_r makes it impossible to convert P_{fr} entirely to P_r by broad spectrum far-red light. Instead, an equilibrium of 97% P_r and 3% P_{fr} is achieved. This equilibrium is termed the **photostationary state.**

In addition to absorbing red light, both forms of phytochrome absorb light in the blue region of the spectrum. Which can convert P_r to P_{fr} and *vice versa*. Blue-light responses can also result from the action of one or more specific blue-light photoreceptors.

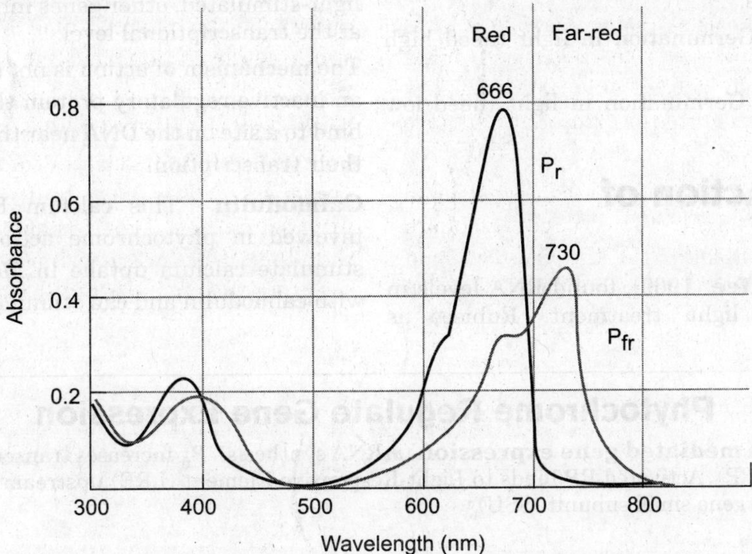

Fig. 17.45 Absorption spectra of purified oat phytochrome in the P_r and P_{fr} forms overlap. P_{fr} is the physiologically active form of phytochrome

Table 17.1 **Photoreversible Responses Induced by Phytochrome**

Group	Genus	Stage of Development	Effect of Light
Angiosperms	*Lactuca* (lettuce)	Seed	Promotes germination.
	Avena (oat)	Seedling (etiolated)	Promotes de-etiolation (*e.g.*, leaf unrolling).
	Sinapis (mustard)	Seedling	Promotes formation of leaf primordia, development of primary leaves and production of anthocyanin.
	Pisum (pea)	Adult	Inhibits internode elongation.
	Xanthium (cocklebur)	Adult	Inhibits flowering (photoperiodic response).
Gymnosperms	*Pinus* (pine)	Seedling	Enhances rate of chlorophyll accumulation.
Pteridophytes	*Onoclea* (sensitive fern)	Young gametophyte	Promotes growth.
Bryophytes	*Polytrichum* (moss)	Germling	Promotes replication of plastids.
Chlorophyta	*Mougeotia* (alga)	Mature gametophyte	Promotes orientation of chloroplasts to directional dim light.

The R:FR ratio and shading An important function of phytochrome is that it enables plants to sense shading by other plants. Plants that increase stem extension in response to shading are said to exhibit a **shade avoidance response.** As shading increases, the R:FR ratio decreases.

The R:FR ratio and seed germination. Light quality also plays a role in regulating the germination of some seeds. In general, large-seeded species, with ample food reserves to sustain prolonged seedling growth in darkness (*e.g.*, underground), do not require light for germination. However, a light requirement is often observed in the small seeds of herbaceous and grassland species, many of which remain dormant, even while hydrated, if they are buried below the depth to which light penetrates.

Phytochrome-Mediated Responses

A. **Low Fluence** (LF) **Responses** These are the 'classic' responses that are induced by red light and reversed by far red. Examples include:

- Light-sensitive seed germination
- Reversal of etiolation
- Change surface charge

Chloroplast rotation in *Mougeotia*

B. **Very Low Fluence** (VLF) **Responses** These are extremely sensitive to low levels of light. These are not photoreversible and saturate at 50 n mol m^{-2}. Examples include

- Mesocotyl elongation in cereals
- *Arabidopsis* seed germination

C. **High Fluence** (HF) **or High Irradiance Response** (HIR) Prolonged or continuous light; fluence rate is important; and not fully photoreversible. Apparently what is important is maintaining a low level of P_{fr} over time. Another pigment is likely involved - a blue-UVA receptor. Examples of phenomena involved in this reaction include:

- Anthocyanin synthesis in seedlings and apple skins.
- Inhibition of hypocotyl elongation in mustard, lettuce and petunia.
- Plume hook opening in lettuce.
- Cotyledon enlargement in lettuce.
- Ethylene production in sorghum.

Seeds can be one of two types.

Positively photoblastic Germination in light (need high P_{fr}/P_r).

Negatively photoblastic Germination in light (need low P_{fr}/P_r).

Mechanisms of Action of Phytochromes

Stimulates transcription **Jaffee** (1969), found RNA levels in pea increased after red light treatment. Rubisco is light-stimulated, other genes inhibited. Phytochrome involved at the transcriptional level.

The mechanism of action is not clear, but the P_{fr} may activate an inactive regulatory protein that moves into the nucleus to bind to a site on the DNA near the genes of interest to promote their transcription.

Calmodulin This calcium P_{fr} binding protein may be involved in phytochrome action. P_{fr} has been shown to stimulate calcium uptake in *Mougeotia*. Calcium complexes with calmodulin and can stimulate enzymes.

Phytochrome Regulate Gene Expression

P_{fr} is directly involved in mediated gene expression (*m*RNA synthesis). P_{fr} increases transcription rates of these genes· P_{fr} activates regulatory protein (RP)· Activated RP binds to Light-Responsive Element (LRE) upstream of light-responsive gene· This activates transcription of that gene small subunit (SSU)

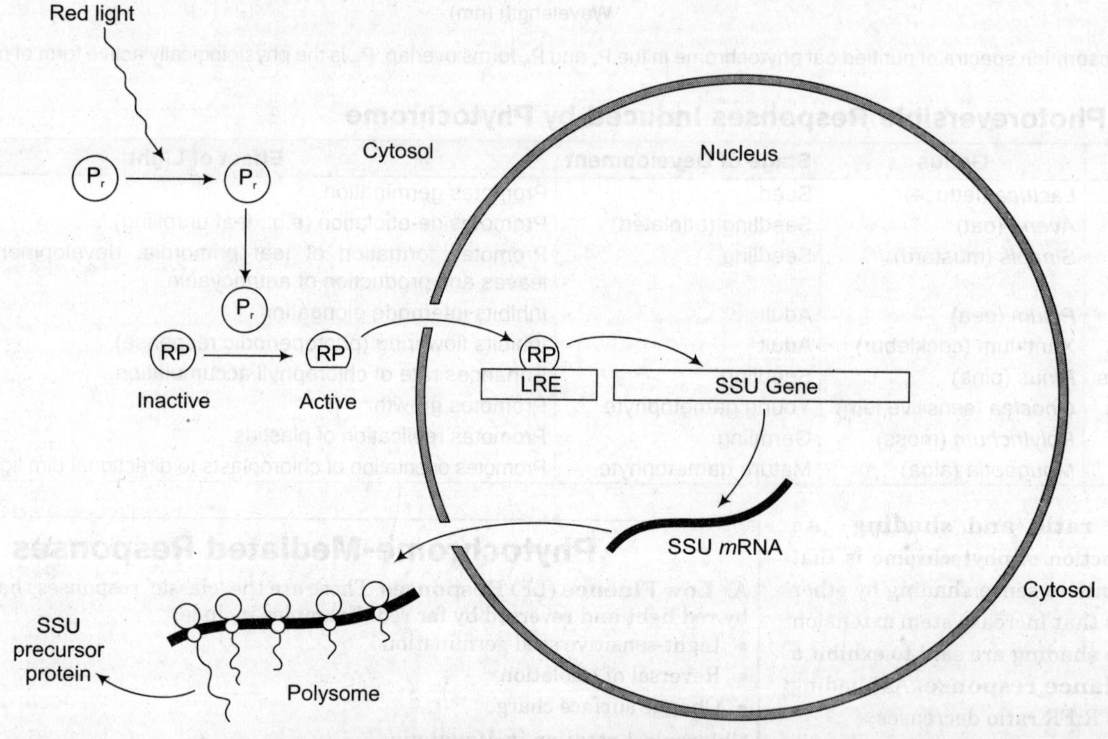

Fig. 17.46 Mediation of P_{fr} in gene expression

- Gene regulatory proteins alter gene expression in association with P_{fr}.
- Regulatory proteins can enter nucleus to affect gene expression. The subcellular location of P_{fr} is affected by light.
- A regulatory protein (PIF3) binds to the promoter of a light-sensitive gene.
- PIF3 alone does not activate transcription of this gene.
- P_{fr} enters the nucleus and binds to PIF3.
- This binding changes the shape of PIF3, letting it turn on transcription.
- Amount of R/FR regulates binding to PIF3 and thus, transcription of gene.

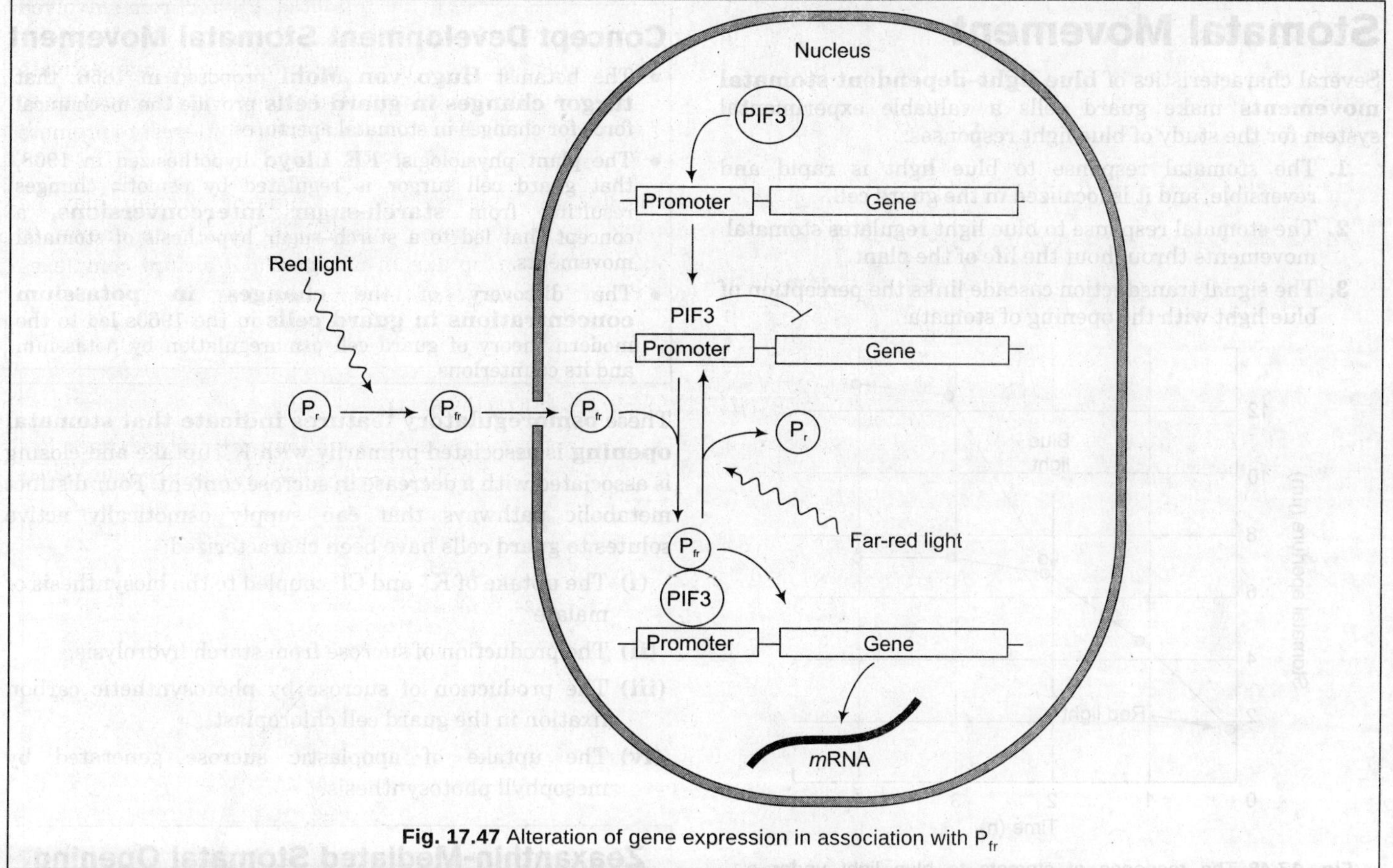

Fig. 17.47 Alteration of gene expression in association with P_{fr}

Cryptochromes and Phototropins

Plants also respond to **higher energy** light (blue, UV-A) using other photosensor molecules. The three photoreceptors associated with blue-light responses are—**cryptochromes, phototropins** and **zeaxanthin.**

Cryptochromes are a family of flavoproteins, widely distributed in the eukaryotic phyla, that mediate the effects of blue light on plant development. Cryptochromes are involved in the inhibition of stem elongation.

The hy4 mutant of *Arabidopsis* lacks the blue light–stimulated inhibition of hypocotyl elongation. Isolation of the hy4 gene showed that it encodes a 75 kDa protein with significant sequence homology to microbial DNA **photolyase,** a blue light–activated enzyme that repairs pyrimidine dimers in DNA formed as a result of exposure to ultraviolet radiation. The hy4 protein, later renamed **cryptochrome** 1 (cry1), was proposed to be a blue-light photoreceptor mediating the inhibition of stem elongation.

Photolyases are pigment proteins that contain a flavin adenine dinucleotide and a pterin. **Pterins** are light-absorbing, pteridine derivatives that often function as pigments in insects, fishes and birds.

In addition, cry1 has been shown to be involved in the setting of the circadian clock in *Arabidopsis* and both **cry1 and cry2 have been shown to play a role in the induction of flowering.** Cryptochrome homologs have been found to regulate the circadian clock in *Drosophila*, mouse and humans.

Phototropins are involved in phototropism and chloroplast movements. The nph1 mutant lacks a phototropic response in the hypocotyl but has normal blue light stimulated inhibition of hypocotyl elongation, while hy4 has the converse phenotype. Recently the nph1 gene was renamed phot1 and the protein it encodes was named **phototropin.**

The **C-terminal half of phototropin is a serine/threonine kinase.** The N-terminal half contains two repeated domains, of about 100 amino acids. Proteins with sequence similarity to the N-terminus of phototropin bind flavin cofactors. These proteins are oxygen sensors in *Escherichia coli* and *Azotobacter* and voltage sensors in potassium channels of *Drosophila* and vertebrates. When expressed in insect cells, the N-terminal half of phototropin binds flavin mononucleotide (FMN).

Under strong light, the **chloroplasts move to the cell surfaces** that are parallel to the incident light (the 'avoidance' response), thus minimizing light absorption. Cells from the phot2 mutant show a normal accumulation response but lack the avoidance response. Thus, phot2 plays a key role in the avoidance response, and that both phot1 and phot2 contribute to the accumulation response.

Stomatal Movement

Several characteristics of **blue light–dependent stomatal movements** make guard cells a valuable experimental system for the study of blue light responses:

1. The stomatal response to blue light is rapid and reversible, and it is localized in the guard cell.
2. The stomatal response to blue light regulates stomatal movements throughout the life of the plant.
3. The signal transduction cascade links the perception of blue light with the opening of stomata.

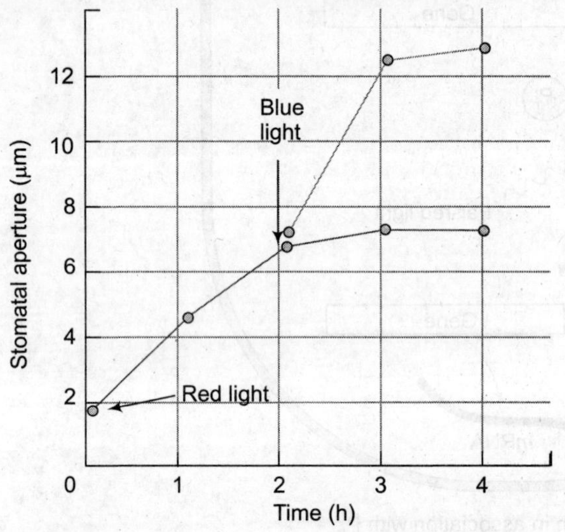

Fig. 17.48 The response of stomata to blue light under a red-light background. In a parallel treatment, stomata illuminated with red light were also illuminated with blue light. The increase in stomatal opening above the level reached in the presence of saturating red light indicates that a different photoreceptor system, stimulated by blue light, is mediating the additional increases in opening.

Blue Light Activates a Proton Pump at the Guard Cell Plasma Membrane.

Irradiated with blue light under background red-light illumination, the pH of the suspension medium becomes more acidic. Acidification of a suspension medium of guard cell protoplasts of *Vicia faba* stimulated by a 30 s pulse of blue light. The acidification results from the stimulation of an **H^+-ATPase at the plasma membrane and it is associated with protoplast swelling.** This blue light induced acidification is blocked by inhibitors that dissipate pH gradients, such as CCCP (carbonyl cyanide *m*-chlorophenylhydrazone), and by inhibitors of the proton-pumping H^+-ATPase, such as vanadate.

Concept Development Stomatal Movement

- The botanist **Hugo von Mohl** proposed in 1856, that **turgor changes in guard cells** provide the mechanical force for changes in stomatal apertures.
- The plant physiologist **FE Lloyd** hypothesized in 1908, that guard cell turgor is regulated by osmotic changes resulting from **starch-sugar interconversions,** a concept that led to a starch–sugar hypothesis of stomatal movements.
- The discovery of the **changes in potassium concentrations in guard cells** in the 1960s led to the modern theory of guard cell osmoregulation by potassium and its counterions.

These **osmoregulatory features indicate that stomatal opening** is associated primarily with K^+ uptake and closing is associated with a decrease in sucrose content. Four distinct metabolic pathways that can supply osmotically active solutes to guard cells have been characterized:

(i) The uptake of K^+ and Cl^- coupled to the biosynthesis of malate^{2-}.

(ii) The production of sucrose from starch hydrolysis.

(iii) The production of sucrose by photosynthetic carbon fixation in the guard cell chloroplast.

(iv) The uptake of apoplastic sucrose generated by mesophyll photosynthesis.

Zeaxanthin-Mediated Stomatal Opening

The **carotenoid zeaxanthin has been implicated as a photoreceptor in blue light** stimulated stomatal opening. zeaxanthin is one of the three components of the xanthophyll cycle of chloroplasts, which protects photosynthetic pigments from excess excitation energy. The **absorption spectrum of zeaxanthin closely matches the action spectrum for blue light stimulated stomatal opening.** The blue-light sensitivity of guard cells increases as a function of their zeaxanthin concentration. **Blue light stimulated stomatal opening** is completely inhibited by 3 mM dithiothreitol (DTT), and the inhibition is concentration dependent. Zeaxanthin formation is blocked by DTT. The specificity of the inhibition of blue light–stimulated stomatal opening by DTT, and its concentration dependence, indicate that guard cell zeaxanthin is required for the stomatal response to blue light. In the facultative CAM species *Mesembryanthemum crystallinum,* **salt accumulation shifts its carbon metabolism from C_3 to CAM mode.** In the C_3 mode, stomata accumulate zeaxanthin and show a blue-light response. CAM induction inhibits the ability of guard cells to accumulate zeaxanthin, and to respond to blue light.

Blue Light-Stimulated Stomatal Opening

A sensory transduction cascade of blue light–stimulated stomatal opening.

Zeaxanthin formation is blocked by DTT, a reducing agent that reduces S—S bonds to –SH groups and effectively inhibits the enzyme that converts violaxanthin into zeaxanthin. The specificity of the inhibition of blue light–stimulated stomatal opening by DTT, and its concentration dependence, indicate that guard cell zeaxanthin is required for the stomatal response to blue light.

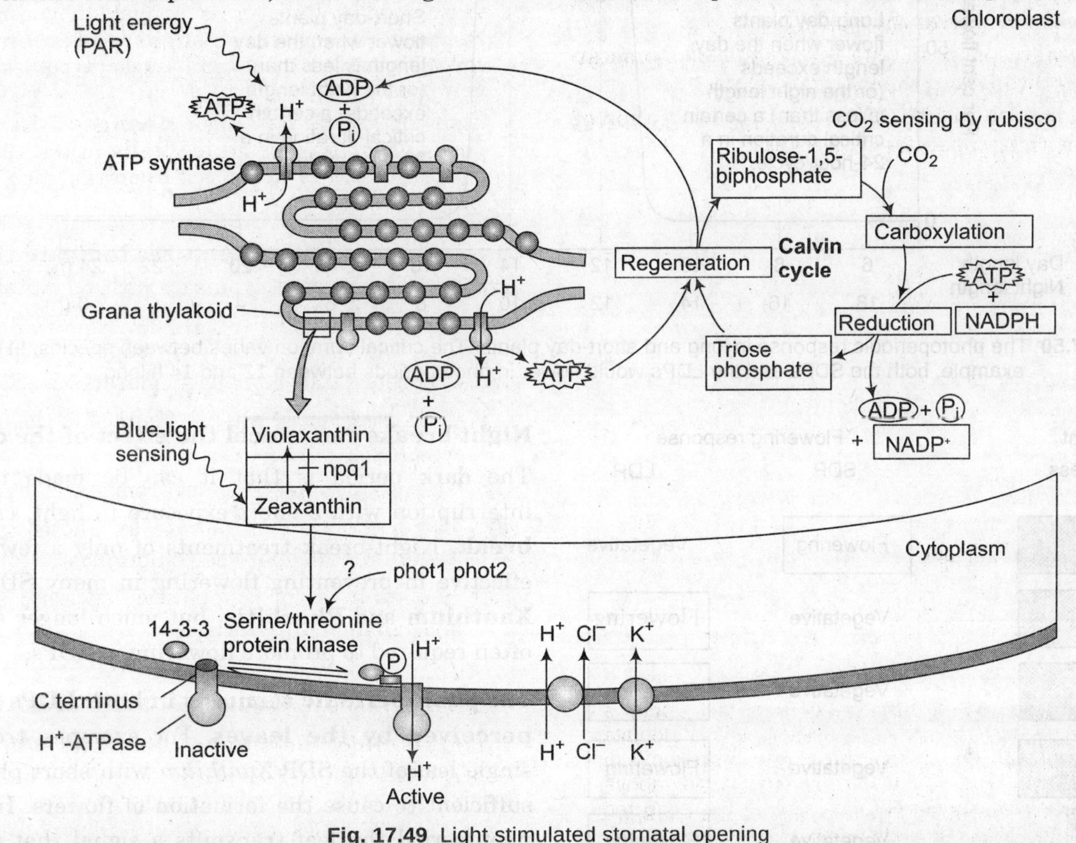

Fig. 17.49 Light stimulated stomatal opening

Daily Movement of Stomata

Loftfield classified stomata on the basis of other daily movement into four main categories:

(i) **Alfa alfa type** Stomata, remain open throughout the day and closed all night, *e.g.*, radish mustard, turnip, pea, apple.

(ii) **Potato type** Stomata remain open throughout the day and night except for few hours following sunset, *e.g.*, cabbage, pumpkin, onion.

(iii) **Barley type** Stomata remain closed throughout night and open, only for few hours during day, *e.g.*, barley, maize, wheat, oat.

(iv) **Equisetum type** Stomata never close, *e.g.*, *Equisetum*.

Photoperiodism

Photoperiodism and vernalization are two of the most important mechanisms underlying seasonal responses. **Photoperiodism** is a response to the length of day; **vernalization** is the promotion of flowering—at subsequent higher temperatures—brought about by exposure to cold.

Effects of the duration of the dark period on flowering can classified plant into:

Short-Day Plants *Chrysanthemum*, Rice, *Kalanchoe*, *Poinsettias*, Morning glory (*Pharbitis*), Cocklebur (*Xanthium*), Soyabean.

Long-Day Plants *Hibiscus*, *Fuchsia*, Spinach, *Arabidopsis*, Sugarbeet, Radish.

Day-Neutral Plants Kidney bean, desert plants, cucumber, tomato.

Different photoperiods shows that the length of the dark period is critical.

Short-day (long-night) **plants flower** When night length exceeds a critical dark period. Interruption of the dark period by a brief light treatment (a night break) prevents flowering.

Long-day (short-night) **plants flower** If the night length is shorter than a critical period. In some long-day plants, shortening the night with a night break induces flowering.

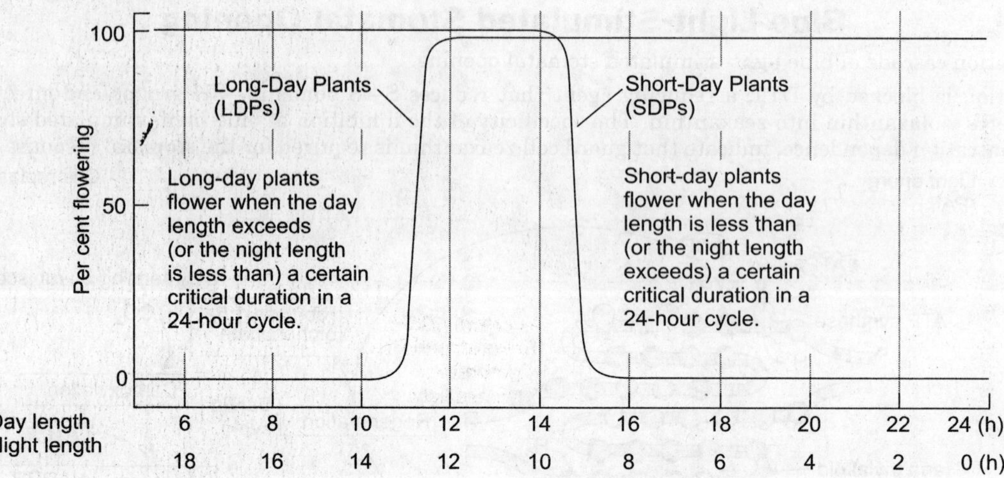

Fig. 17.50 The photoperiodic response in long and short-day plants. The critical duration varies between species: In this example, both the SDPs and the LDPs would flower in photoperiods between 12 and 14 h long

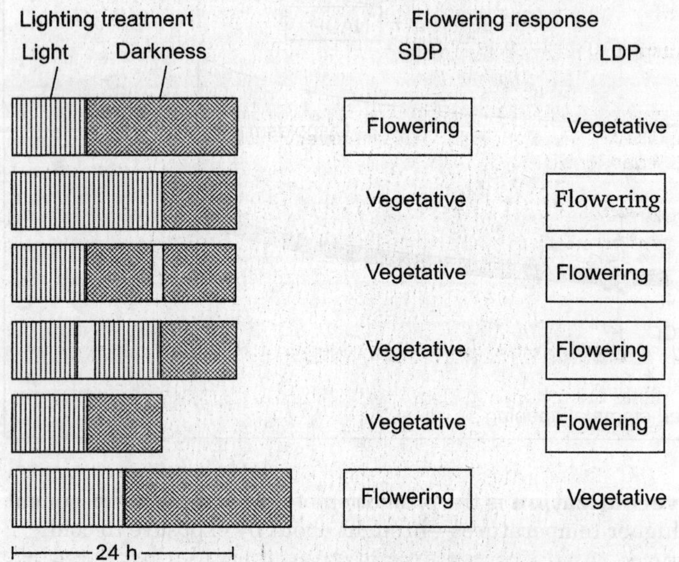

Fig. 17.51 Effects of the duration of the light or dark period on SDP and LDP. Treating short and long-day plants with different photoperiods clearly shows that the critical variable is the length of the dark period

Night breaks can cancel the effect of the dark period

The dark period is that it can be made ineffective by interruption with a short exposure to light, called a **night break.** Night-break treatments of only a few minutes are effective in preventing flowering in many SDPs, including **Xanthium** and **Pharbitis,** but much longer exposures are often required to promote flowering in LDPs.

The **photoperiodic stimulus in both LDPs and SDPs is perceived by the leaves.** For example, treatment of a single leaf of the SDP *Xanthium* with short photoperiods is sufficient to cause the formation of flowers. In response to photoperiod the leaf transmits a signal that regulates the transition to flowering at the shoot apex. The photoperiod-regulated processes that occur in the leaves resulting in the transmission of a floral stimulus to the shoot apex are referred to collectively as **photoperiodic induction.** Once produced, the flowering stimulus appears to be **transported to the meristem** ***via*** **the phloem.**

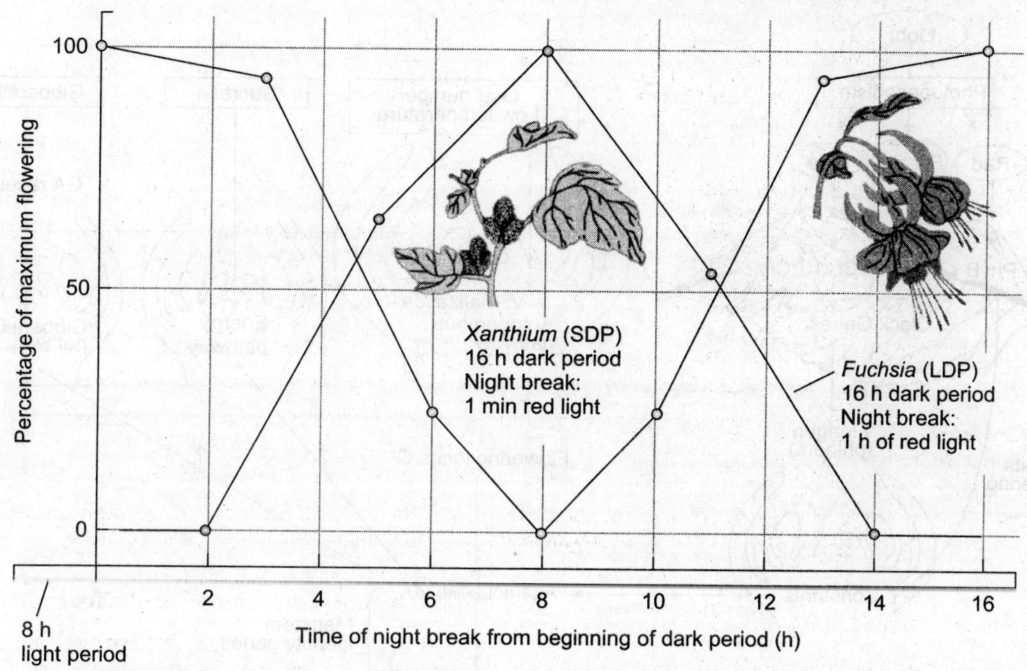

Fig. 17.52 The time when a night break is given determines the flowering response. When given during a long dark period, a night break promotes flowering in LDPs and inhibits flowering in SDPs. In both cases, the greatest effect on flowering occurs when the night break is given near the middle of the 16 h dark period

Phytochrome is the primary photoreceptor in photoperiodism

In many SDPs, a night break becomes effective only when the supplied dose of light is sufficient to saturate the photoconversion of P_r (phytochrome that absorbs red light) to P_{fr} (phytochrome that absorbs far-red light). A subsequent exposure to far-red light, which photoconverts the pigment back to the physiologically inactive P_r form, restores the flowering response.

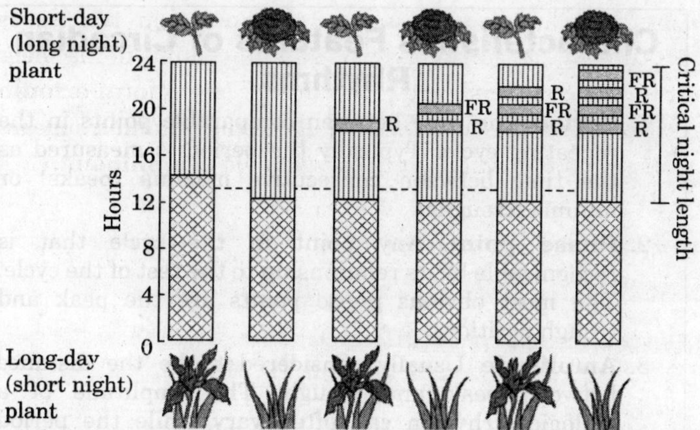

Fig. 17.53 A flash of red light during the dark period induces flowering in a **long-day plant,** and effect is reversed by far-red light. It involves phytochromes. In a **short-day plant,** red light prevents flowering, and effect is reversed by flash of far-red light

In some LDPs, a night break of red light promoted flowering, and a subsequent exposure to far-red light prevented this response.

Biochemical Signaling in Flowering

The transition to flowering involves multiple factors and pathways.

1. The photoperiodic pathway involves phytochromes and cryptochromes.
2. In the dual autonomous/vernalization pathway, flowering occurs either in response to internal signals—the production of a fixed number of leaves—or to low temperatures.
3. The carbohydrate or sucrose, pathway reflects the metabolic state of the plant. Sucrose stimulates flowering in *Arabidopsis* by increasing LFY expression, although the genetic pathway is unknown.
4. The gibberellin pathway is required for early flowering and for flowering under non-inductive short days. All four pathways converge by increasing the expression of the key floral meristem identity gene agamous like 20 (AGL20).

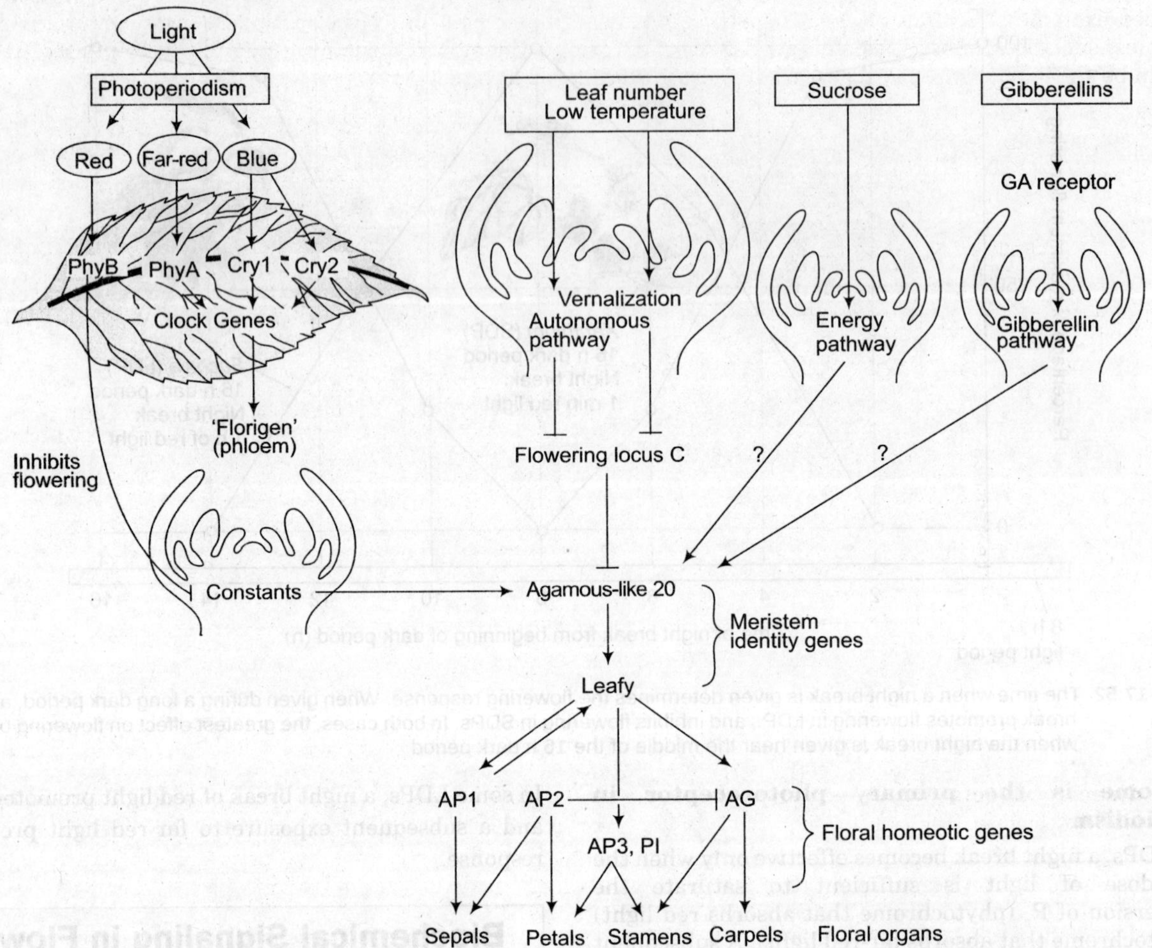

Fig. 17.54 Four developmental pathways for flowering in *Arabidopsis* the photoperiodism, autonomous/vernalization, sucrose and gibberellin pathways. A transmissible floral stimulus (florigen) from leaves is only involved in the photoperiodic pathway

Biological Clocks

Organisms are normally exhibit rhythmic behaviour in association with daily cycles of light and darkness, in both plants and animals such changes often alternate through high-activity and low-activity phases with a regular periodicity of about 24 h. These rhythmic changes are referred to as **circadian rhythms.**

Examples of such rhythms include **leaf and petal movements** (day and night positions), **stomatal opening and closing, growth and sporulation patterns in fungi** (*e.g., Pilobolus* and *Neurospora*), as well as metabolic processes such as photosynthetic capacity and respiration rate. The stimulus for biological clock may be in form of sudden change in the light intensity, temperature or environment. It require a supply of energy to operate and this energy is provided by metabolism.

Characteristics Features of Circadian Rhythms

1. **Period** The time between comparable points in the repeating cycle. Typically the period is measured as the time between consecutive maxima (peaks) or minima (troughs).
2. **Phase point** Any point in the cycle that is recognizable by its relationship to the rest of the cycle. The most obvious phase points are the peak and trough positions.
3. **Amplitude** Usually considered to be the distance between peak and trough. The amplitude of a biological rhythm can often vary while the period remains unchanged.

The rhythm persists in the absence of external controlling factors, it is considered to be **endogenous.** Light is a strong modulator of rhythms in both plants and animals.

Phytochrome regulates the sleep movements of leaves. The sleep movements of leaves, referred to as **nyctinasty,** are a well-described example of a plant circadian rhythm that is regulated by light. Nyctinastic leaf movements are exhibited by many legumes, such as *Mimosa*, *Albizia* and *Samanea*, as well as members of the *Oxalis* family. The phase of the rhythm, however, can be shifted by various exogenous signals, including red or blue light.

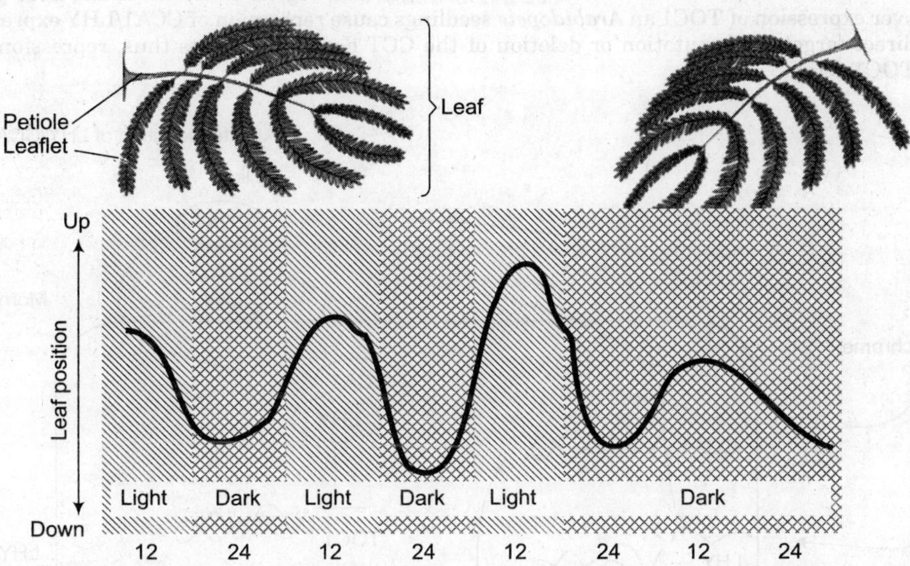

Fig. 17.55 Circadian rhythm in the diurnal movements of *Albizia* leaves. The leaves are elevated in the morning and lowered in the evening

Light also directly affects movement Blue light stimulates closed leaflets to open, and red light followed by darkness causes open leaflets to close.

Physiological Mechanism of Leaf Movement

Ion fluxes between the dorsal and ventral motor cells of *Albizia pulvini* regulate leaflet opening and closing.

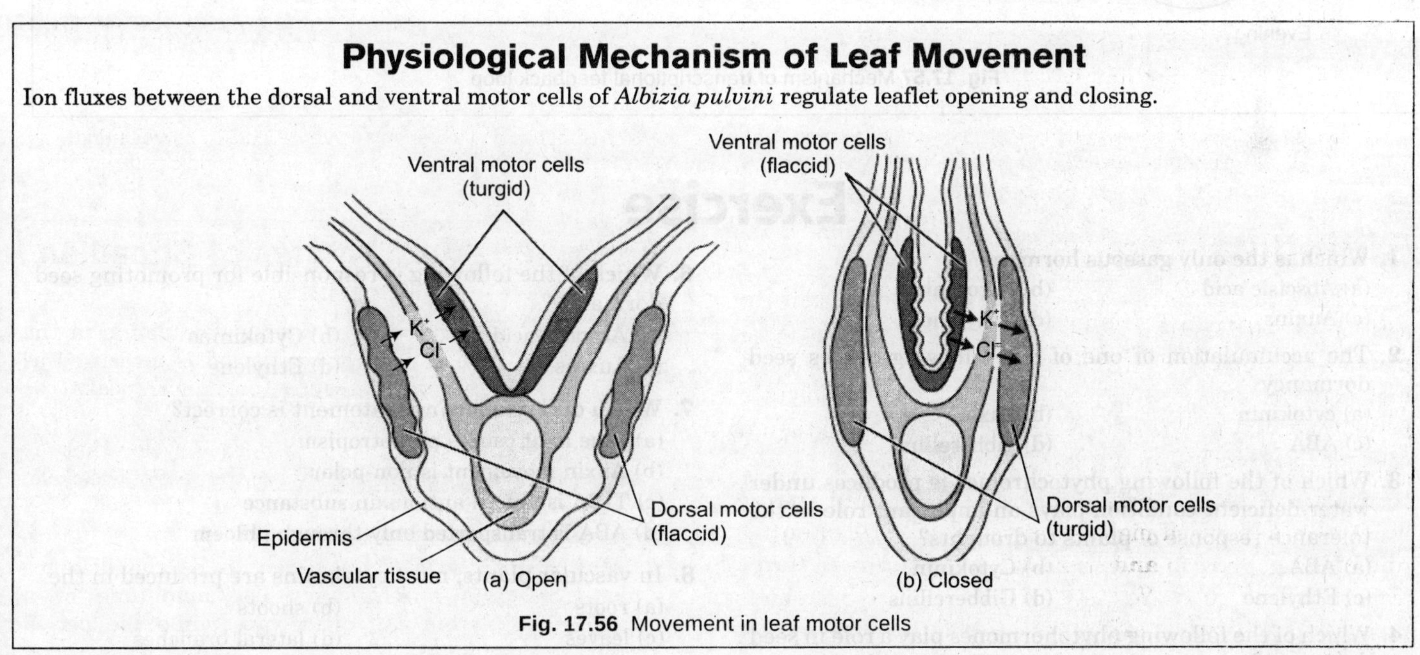

Fig. 17.56 Movement in leaf motor cells

Phytochrome can also interact with circadian rhythms at the level of gene expression. The expression of genes in the LHCB family, encoding the light harvesting chlorophyll-*a*/*b*–binding proteins of photosystem II, is regulated at the transcriptional level by both circadian rhythms and phytochrome.

Transcriptional Feedback Loop in *Arabidopsis*

Transcriptional feedback loops are a feature of circadian clocks in both plants and animals. Late Elongated Hypocotyl (LHY) and Circadian clock Associated (CCA1) are considered negative elements due to its repression against Timing of Cab Expression1 (TOC1) in the morning while TOC1 is considered a positive element because it results in increased transcription of LHY and CCA1 during the evening because of its accumulation. TOC1 occupies specific genomic region in the CCA1 and LHY promotors. Chemical induction and transient over expression of TOC1 an *Arabidopsis* seedlings cause repression of CCA1/LHY expression demonstrating that TOC1 can repress direct targets and mutation or deletion of the CCT domain prevents thus, repression showing that DNA binding is necessary for TOC1 action.

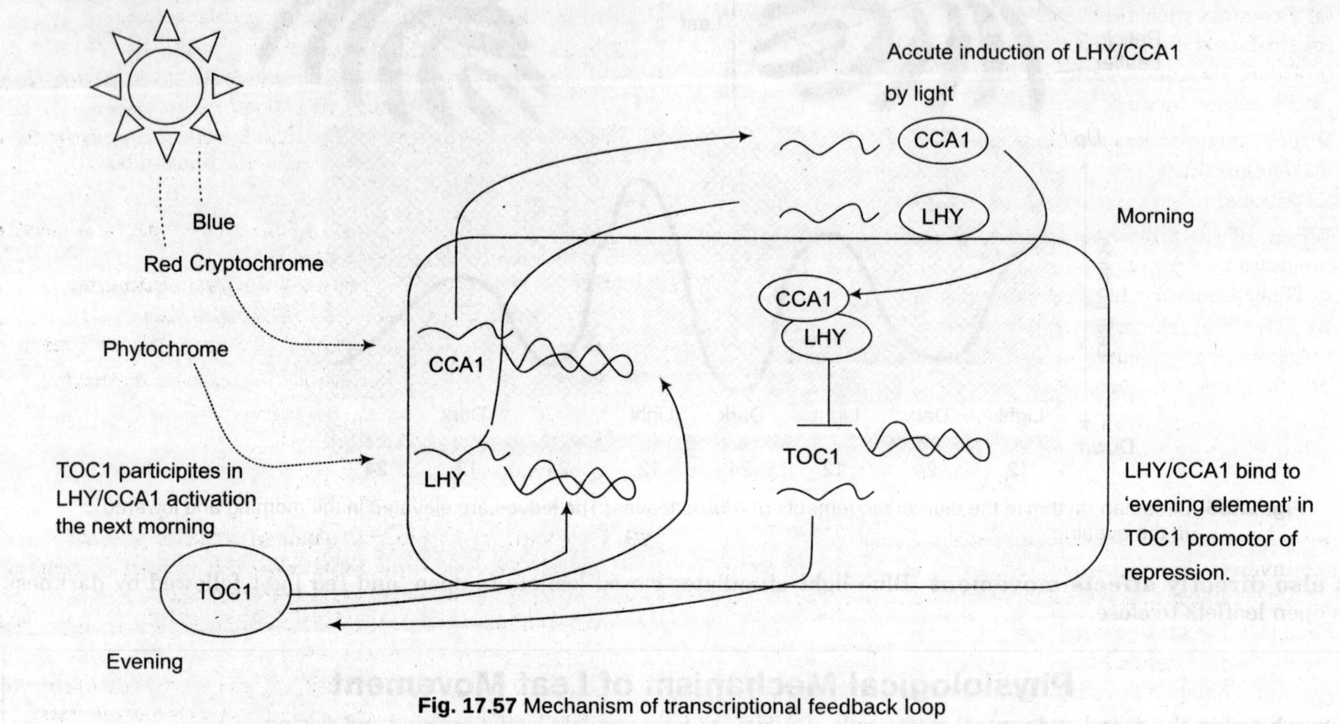

Fig. 17.57 Mechanism of transcriptional feedback loop

Exercise

1. Which is the only gaseous hormone?
(a) Abscisic acid (b) Cytokinins
(c) Auxins (d) Ethylene

2. The accumulation of one of the following causes seed dormancy
(a) cytokinin (b) auxin
(c) ABA (d) gibberellins

3. Which of the following phytochromes is produces under water-deficient condition plays an important role in the tolerance response of plants to droughts?
(a) ABA (b) Cytokinin
(c) Ethylene (d) Gibberellins

4. Which of the following phytohormones play a role in seed dormancy?
(a) Gibberellins (b) ABA
(c) Cytokinin (d) Auxins

5. ABA controls which of the following?
(a) Abscission (b) Fruit climacteric
(c) Stomatal closure (d) Cell elongation

6. Which of the following is responsible for promoting seed dormancy?
(a) Abscisic acid (b) Cytokinins
(c) Auxins (d) Ethylene

7. Which of the following statement is correct?
(a) Blue light causes phototropism
(b) Auxin movement is non-polar
(c) TIBA is not an anti auxin substance
(d) ABA is transported only through phloem

8. In vascular plants, most cytokinins are produced in the
(a) roots (b) shoots
(c) leaves (d) lateral branches

9. Which of the following is not part of the triple response of etiolated pea seedlings to ethylene?
(a) Stunted growth
(b) Increased radial expansion of cells of the stem
(c) Loss of gravity perception
(d) Unfolding of the apical hook of the seedling

10. Which of the hormones regulates cell division and differentiation?
(a) Gibberellins (b) Cytokinins
(c) Auxins (d) Ethylene

11. Which hormone instigates 'the triple response'?
(a) Abscisic acid (b) Cytokinins
(c) Auxins (d) Ethylene

12. Which of the following is not related to cytokinin?
(a) Promotes apical dominance
(b) Promotes chloroplast maturation
(c) Cause Richmond-Lang effect
(d) Promotes nutrient mobilization

13. Which hormone has anti-ageing effects?
(a) Gibberellins (b) Cytokinins
(c) Auxins (d) Ethylene

14. Which of the following is not a characteristic of plant hormone?
(a) They are active in small concentration
(b) They are pleiotropic in their effects
(c) They are synthesized in specific glands and tissues
(d) Plant hormones are tissue and time specific

15. The geotropic response in roots
(a) involves the redistribution of calcium ions
(b) primarily involves the basipetal transport of ABA in the root cortex
(c) can be abolished by the removal of root cap
(d) involves the increased transport of auxin into the lower side of the root elongation zone

16. Bioassay for gibberellins is
(a) *Avena* coleoptiles test
(b) alpha amylase induction iun cereal endosperms
(c) callus formation in tobacco from pith tissue
(d) ormation of abscission layer in cotton

17. Which hormone is responsible to stem elongation?
(a) Gibberellins (b) Cytokinins
(c) Auxins (d) Ethylene

18. Lateral stem development is controlled by the relative levels of
(a) cytokinins and auxins (b) ABA and auxins
(c) auxins and gibberellins (d) auxins and ethylene

19. Which of the following hormone, in combination with auxin, stimulates cell division in plants and determines the course of differentiation?
(a) Ethylene (b) Indol eacetic acid
(c) Gibberellins (d) Cytokinin

20. Ethylene receptor
(a) is a membrane bound receptor dimer of two component system
(b) is a soluble protein in the cytoplasm
(c) has a chromophore similar to phytochrome
(d) it has pterin and flavin as prosthetic groups

21. Which hormone allows seeds to ignore environmental conditions and germinate?
(a) Abscisic acid (b) Cytokinins
(c) Auxins (d) Gibberellins

22. Leaf abscission
(a) is followed by leaf senescence
(b) is regulated by the hormone ABA
(c) is a passive process, involving nothing more than death of petiole cells
(d) is associated with an increase in ethylene production by petiole cells

23. Stomatal pores open when
(a) H^+ ions are pumped into the guard cells
(b) K^+ ions are pumped out of the guard cells
(c) water moves into the guard cells in response to a decrease in water potential in the guard cells
(d) water moves out of the guard cells in response to a decrease in water potential in the guard cells

24. What is a tropism?
(a) An internal chemical signal that controls a plant's growth and development
(b) A movement in response to an external stimulus
(c) A movement in response to light stimulus
(d) A pigment that absorbs light and affects seed germination

25. What is the term for growth in response to gravity?
(a) Tropism
(b) Phototropism
(c) Growth regulator
(d) Gravitropism

26. How would phototropism be beneficial to plants?
(a) By keeping the leaves oriented perpendicularly to light, the plant can increase water loss
(b) By keeping the leaves oriented parallel to light, the plant can increase water loss
(c) By keeping the leaves oriented perpendicularly to light, the plant can increase the photosynthesis rate
(d) By keeping the leaves oriented parallel to light, the plant can decrease the photosynthesis rate

27. Which part of a plant cell is thought to aid plants in sensing gravity in their roots?
(a) Amyloplasts
(b) Chloroplasts
(c) Nucleus
(d) Mitochondria

28. What is phytochrome?
(a) A pigment that absorbs light and affects photosynthesis
(b) A pigment that absorbs light and affects seed germination
(c) A pigmentthat senses gravity and affects seed germination
(d) A macronutrient

29. Which of the following wavelengths of light would stimulate germination?
(a) 450 nm (b) 540 nm
(c) 660 nm (d) 730 nm

30. A plant that appears pale and spindly with small leaves is referred to as
(a) gravitropic (b) wilted
(c) etiolated (d) an albino

31. Light stimulates seed germination, promotes chlorophyll synthesis and the development of chloroplasts and promotion of leaf expansion. These responses induced by the light are examples of
(a) photoperiodism (b) photomorphogenesis
(c) phototropism (d) photosynthesis

32. In lettuce, red light is most effective in breaking seed dormancy because it
(a) stimulates water absorption
(b) reverses the inhibitory effect of far-red light
(c) induces active transport
(d) induces GA_3 production

33. The pigment that plays a key role in photomorphogenesis is
(a) chlorophyll (b) phytochrome
(c) cytochrome (d) anthocyanin

34. Photoreversebility defines involvement of which plant pigment/photoreceptor in plant growth and development
(a) chlorophyll (b) cryptochrome
(c) phototropin (d) phytochrome

35. Type I phytochrome
(a) is destroyed in the light
(b) is synthesized in the far-red absorbing form (P_{fr})
(c) reverts to type II phytochrome in the dark
(d) senses red light, white type II senses far-red light

36. Which of the following function is not associated with phytochrome?
(a) Nyctinastic movement in *Mimosa*
(b) Seed germination in lettuce
(c) Stomatal opening
(d) Circadian rhythms

37. Which statement about photomorphogenesis is false?
(a) Involves the protein pigment phytochrome
(b) Is only important at the seedling stage of plant development
(c) Is affected by red, far-red and blue light
(d) Can be defined as light dependent changes in plant growth, development and metabolism

38. The light which stimulates flowering in an inducible plant
(a) is perceived by the apical meristem
(b) is perceived throughout the plant
(c) is perceived by the leaves
(d) None of the above

39. Phototropism refers to how plants respond to sunlight by bending towards the light. This is due to
(a) cell division on the side of the stem closer to the light source
(b) cell division on the side of the stem away from the light source
(c) cell differentiation on the side of the stem away from the light source
(d) cell elongation on the side of the stem away from the light source

40. Unlike tropisms, nastic movements are in response to
(a) paratonic stimuli (b) gravity
(c) non-directional stimuli (d) directional stimuli

41. Which of the following movements of plants are reversible and allow the plant to advantageously orient leaves?
(a) Thigmotropisms (b) Turgor movements
(c) Phototropisms (d) Gravitropisms

42. Choose the correct statement.
(a) Tropic movement is autonomic movement
(b) Nastic movement depends on direction of stimulus
(c) Growth of pollen tube is chemotactic movement
(d) None of the above

43. Nyctinasty occurs due to
(a) differential growth rate
(b) change in pressure potential
(c) movement of bulliform cell
(d) None of the above

44. In 1925, the Japanese biologist Kurosawa showed that the bakanae (foolish seedling) disease of rice was caused by a substance produced by the fungus *Gibberella fujikuroi*. The substance was named gibberellin and was shown to cause elongation of stem tissues. Which of the following statements about gibberellin is false?
(a) Pea plants carrying the dwarf mutation would be expected to have higher levels of gibberellin in their stems than normal plants
(b) If gibberellin is applied to the stems of dwarf pea plants, the stems elongate so that plant reach normal height
(c) Dwarf pea plants have a mutation in the gibberellin biosynthetic pathway
(d) The gibberellin produced by the fungus caused normal healthy rice plants to become unusually tall

45. Which statement concerning stomatal function is false?
(a) To close stoma, potassium ions diffuse passively out of the guard cells
(b) When stomata are about to open, potassium ions are actively transported into the guard cells from the surrounding cells of the epidermis
(c) Stomata are open when the turgor pressure of the guard cells decreases
(d) Low levels of carbon dioxide stimulate the opening of stomata

46. Charles Darwin and his son Francis experimented with phototropism of grass seedlings by placing a metal for blindfold over different parts of the seedlings coleoptiles. A simplified version of their results is shown below. Which of the following statements best explains their results?
(a) The light signal is perceived below the tip, and these cells cause the coleoptiles to grow toward the light
(b) Both ehe seedling root and coleoptiles perceive and respond to light in the same manner
(c) A chemical messenger must travel from the base of the coleoptile to the tip
(d) The light signal is perceived at the tip of the coleoptile, but the growth response occurs a few millimeters below the tip

47. Match list I with list II and select the correct answer using the codes given below the lists.

List I	List II
A. *Glycine max*	1. Long day plant
B. *Lycopersicon esculentum*	2. Short day plant
C. *Hyoscyamus niger*	3. Day neutral plant
D. *Cestrum nocturnum*	4. Short day-long day plant
	5. Long day-short day plant

Codes

	A	B	C	D
(a)	1	3	4	5
(b)	2	3	4	5
(c)	2	5	1	4
(d)	3	4	5	1

48. Match list I (plant hormone) with list II (typical physiological effect) and select the correct answer using the codes given below the lists.

List I	List II
A. Auxin	1. Apical dominance
B. Gibberellin	2. Cell division
C. Cytokinin	3. Fruit ripening
D. Ethylene	4. Internodal elongation

Codes

	A	B	C	D
(a)	1	4	2	3
(b)	1	4	3	2
(c)	4	1	2	3
(d)	4	1	3	2

49. Match list I (phenomena) with list II (growth regulators) and select the correct answer using the codes given below the lists.

List I	List II
A. Root differentiation	1. Kinins followed by auxins
B. Vegetative bud differentiation	2. Auxins followed by kinins
C. Flower bud differentiation	3. Auxins plus gibberellins
D. Fruit development	4. Auxins plus carbohydrates

Codes

	A	B	C	D
(a)	4	3	1	2
(b)	4	1	2	3
(c)	3	2	1	4
(d)	1	4	3	2

50. Match list I with list II and select the correct answer using the codes given below the lists.

List I	List II
A. Increase in wall elongation	1. Gibberellins
B. Bolting and flowering	2. Auxins
C. Cell division	3. Abscisic acid
D. Dormancy	4. Cytokinins

Codes

	A	B	C	D
(a)	2	1	3	4
(b)	2	1	4	3
(c)	1	2	4	3
(d)	1	2	3	4

51. Match list I with list II and select the correct answer using the codes given below the lists.

List I	List II
A. Antigibberellin	1. Scopoletin
B. Growth inhibitor	2. Caffeic acid
C. Germination inhibitor	3. Abscisic acid
D. IAA-oxidase inhibitor	4. Cycocel

Codes

	A	B	C	D
(a)	2	3	1	4
(b)	4	2	3	1
(c)	3	1	4	2
(d)	4	3	1	2

Answers

1. (d)	**2.** (c)	**3.** (a)	**4.** (b)	**5.** (c)	**6.** (a)	**7.** (a)	**8.** (a)	**9.** (c)	**10.** (b)
11. (d)	**12.** (a)	**13.** (b)	**14.** (c)	**15.** (c)	**16.** (b)	**17.** (a)	**18.** (a)	**19.** (d)	**20.** (a)
21. (d)	**22.** (d)	**23.** (c)	**24.** (b)	**25.** (d)	**26.** (c)	**27.** (a)	**28.** (b)	**29.** (c)	**30.** (c)
31. (b)	**32.** (b)	**33.** (b)	**34.** (d)	**35.** (a)	**36.** (c)	**37.** (b)	**38.** (c)	**39.** (d)	**40.** (c)
41. (b)	**42.** (d)	**43.** (b)	**44.** (a)	**45.** (c)	**46.** (d)	**47.** (b)	**48.** (a)	**49.** (c)	**50.** (b)
51. (d)									

18

Solute Transport and Stress Physiology

Syllabus

- Solute Transport and Photoassimilate Translocation: Uptake, Transport and Translocation of Water, Ions, Solutes and Macromolecules (from Soil, through Cells, Across Membranes, through Xylem and Phloem) Transpiration; Mechanisms of Loading and Unloading of Photoassimilates.
- Secondary Metabolites – Biosynthesis of Terpenes, Phenols and Nitrogenous Compounds and their Roles.
- Stress Physiology: Responses of Plants to Biotic (Pathogen and Insects) and Abiotic (Water, Temperature and Salt) Stresses: Mechanisms of Resistance to Biotic Stress and Tolerance to Abiotic Stress.

Solute Transport and Photoassimilate Translocation

Molecular and ionic movement from one location to another is known as **transport**. Local transport of solutes into or within cells is regulated mainly by membranes. Larger-scale transport between plant and environment or between leaves and roots, is also controlled by membrane transport at the cellular level. For example, the transport of sucrose from leaf to root through the phloem, referred to as **translocation**, is driven and regulated by membrane transport into the phloem cells of the leaf, and from the phloem to the storage cells of the root.

According to **Fick's first law**, the movement of molecules by diffusion always proceeds spontaneously, down a gradient of concentration or chemical potential, until equilibrium is reached. The spontaneous 'downhill' movement of molecules is termed **passive transport.**

The movement of substances against or up a gradient of chemical potential (*e.g.*, to a higher concentration) is termed **active transport**.

The **chemical potential** for any solute is defined as the sum of the concentration, electric, and hydrostatic potentials.

$$\tilde{\mu}_j = \mu_j^* + RT \ln C_j + z_jFE + \bar{V}_jP$$

$\tilde{\mu}_j$	=	μ_j^*	+	$RT \ln C_j$	+	z_jFE	+	$\bar{V}_jP$
Chemical potential for a given solute, *j*		Chemical potential of *j* under standard conditions		Concentration (activity) component		Electric potential component		Hydrostatic pressure

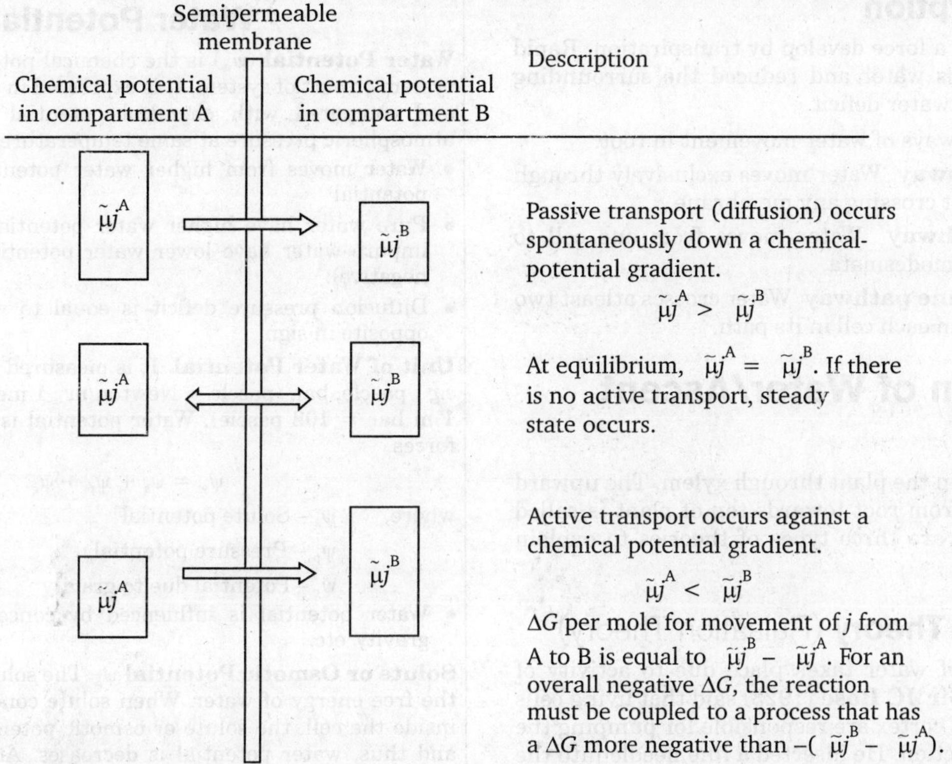

Fig. 18.1 Relationship between the chemical potential, and the transport of molecules across a permeability barrier. The net movement of molecular species j between compartments A and B depends on the relative magnitude of the chemical potential of j in each compartment.

Uptake, Transport and Translocation of Water

Large amount of water is continuously absorbed from the soil and moved through the plant during its life cycle. Water acts as good solvent and is essential for all physiological activities. Without constant supply of water the plant could not carry on any of its physiological activities such as photosynthesis respiration and growth.

Means of Transport/Uptake

Diffusion The movement of molecules of gases, liquids and solutes from the region of higher concentration or high diffusion pressure to the region of lower concentration or lower diffusion pressure is known as **diffusion**. The diffusion pressure of pure solvent is maximum as compared to same solvent in solution.

Facilitated diffusion A type of passive transport in which substances move across the membrane along their concentration gradient in the presence of certain carrier protein molecules called permeases present in the membrane. It helps in transportation of glucose in liver cells and RBCs through their cell membrane. Also helps in absorption of fructose and nucleotides in small intestine.

Osmosis The diffusion of solvent from a hypotonic solution (having lower concentration) to hypotonic solution (having higher concentration) through a semipermeable membrane to keep the concentration in equilibrium. Osmotic pressure is that equivalent of maximum hydrostatic pressure which is produced in the solution when this solution is separated from its pure solvent by a semipermeable membrane.

Imbibition The phenomenon of absorption of water or any other liquid without forming a solution. The liquid which is imbibed is called imbibate while the material is called imbibants.

The plant cell when placed in pure water swells but not burst. The hydrostatic pressure developed inside this cell against the cell wall due to endosmosis is called **turgor pressure**. There are two methods of water uptake/absorption.

Active Absorption

This type of absorption need energy. These are two theories of active absorption.

(a) **Osmotic theory** The water is absorbed due to osmotic differences between soil water and cell sap. Absorption directly requires no expenditure of metabolic energy and higher DPD of cell sap causes endosmosis of soil water across the semipermeable plasma membrane. Absorption continues till DPD become zero.

(b) **Non-osmotic theory** Water absorbed with the help of energy provided by respiration in form of ATP.

Passive Absorption

This is caused due to a force develop by transpiration. Rapid transpiration removes water and reduced the surrounding root cells to make up water deficit.

There are three pathways of water movement in root.

(a) **Apoplast pathway** Water moves exclusively through cell wall without crossing any membrane.

(b) **Symplast pathway** Water moves from one cell to another by plasmodesmata.

(c) **Transmembrane pathway** Water crosses atleast two membranes from each cell in its path.

Translocation of Water/Ascent of Sap

Water rises upwards in the plant through xylem. The upward movement of water from root towards top of plant is called ascent of sap. These are three types of theories to explain ascent of sap.

(a) **Vital Force Theory** (Pulsation Theory)

Upward movement of water takes place due to activity of living cells of plant. **Sir JC Bose** (1923) said that living cells of inner most layer of cortex are responsible for pumping the water in upward direction. He inserted a fine needle into the stem of *Desmodium* and connected to a galvanometer which showed slow oscillations.

(b) **Root Pressure Theory**

When a well watered plant is cut near the base the xylem sap is seen to flow out through the cut end with a pressure called root pressure (developed as a result of metabolic activities of root). The value of root pressure is 2-5 atm. Which is not sufficient for taller plants like *Eucalyptus* to raise the water up.

(c) **Physical Force Theory** (Transpiration Pull Theory)

Originally proposed by **Dixon** and **Jolly** (1894). Cohesive and adhesive properties of water developed an unbroken continuous water column in xylem. The mutual attraction between water molecules is called **cohesion** (upto 350 atm). The walls of tracheids and vessels of xylem are made up of lignin and cellulose and have strong affinity for water called **adhesion.** Transpiration develops a negative pressure or tension in xylem sap, which is transmitted down to the root. Due to transpiration of water DPD in mesophyll cells increases. Water is therefore absorbed by the cell walls from protoplasm which in turn takes water from vacuole of cell. DPD of xylem elements increases. Due to these cohesive and adhesive forces water column does not break and pulled upward by a force called **transpiration pull.** It does not require metabolic energy.

Water Potential

Water Potential (ψ_w) is the chemical potential of water in a system or part of system. It is expressed in the unit of pressure and compared with chemical potential of pure water in atmospheric pressure at same temperature and pressure.

- Water moves from higher water potential to lower water potential
- Pure water have higher water potential (zero pascal) and impure water have lower water potential (value always in negative).
- Diffusion pressure deficit is equal to water potential but opposite in sign.

Unit of Water Potential It is measured in unit of pressure. *e.g.*, pascle, bar. (pascle = Newton/m^2; 1 mega pascle = 10 bar; 1 m bar = 102 pascle). Water potential is sum total of three forces

$$\psi_w = \psi_s + \psi_p + \psi_g$$

where, ψ_s – Solute potential

ψ_p – Pressure potential

ψ_g – Potential due to gravity

- Water potential is influenced by concentration, pressure, gravity, etc.

Solute or Osmotic Potential ψ_s The solute potential reduce the free energy of water. When solute concentration increase inside the cell, the solute or osmotic potential (ψ_s) is lowered and thus, water potential is decreases. At high temperature osmotic potential increases. Its value is always in negative.

Pressure Potential or Hydrostatic Pressure ψ_p The positive hydrostatic pressure is called turgor pressure. The wall pressure will increase if turgor pressure keep on increasing. The pressure potential have always positive value.

Gravity Potential ψ_g It depends on height of water above reference point of water. ψ_g is negative if vertical distance is less than 5 m.

- ψ_m is the matric potential used for the surface such as soil particles or cell wall to which water molecules are adsorbed. It has negative value.
- In a fully turgid cell, osmotic potential and pressure potential are equal but opposite in sign, so that water potential is zero.

Transport of Ions Across a Membrane Barrier

Diffusion potentials develop when oppositely charged ions move across a membrane at different rates.

The cytosol and the vacuole are the most important intracellular compartments that determine the ionic relations of plant cells. In mature plant cells, the central vacuole often occupies 90% or more of the cell's volume, and the cytosol is restricted to a thin layer around the periphery of the cell.

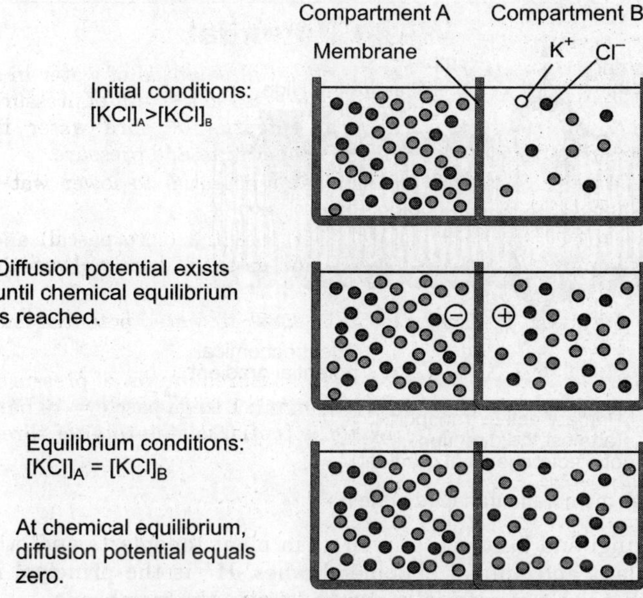

Fig. 18.2 Development of a diffusion potential and a charge separation between two compartments separated by a membrane that is preferentially permeable to potassium. If the concentration of potassium chloride is higher in compartment A ($[KCl]_A > [KCl]_B$), potassium and chloride ions will diffuse at a higher rate into compartment B, and a diffusion potential will be established. When membranes are more permeable to potassium than to chloride, potassium ions will diffuse faster than chloride ions, and charge separation (+ and –) will develop

Plants absorb the mineral from soil and translocated them to other part. The movement of mineral ions take place by mass flow (along water due to transpiration), ion exchange Donnan equilibrium (fixed or non-diffusible anions) or active process.

Ion Concentrations in the Cytosol and the Vacuole

- Potassium is accumulated passively by both the cytosol and the vacuole, except when extracellular K^+ concentrations are very low, in which case it is taken up actively.
- Sodium is pumped actively out of the cytosol into the extracellular spaces and vacuole.
- Excess protons, generated by intermediary metabolism, are also actively extruded from the cytosol. This process helps maintain the cytosolic pH near neutrality, while the vacuole and the extracellular medium are generally more acidic by one or two pH units.
- All the anions are taken up actively into the cytosol.
- Calcium is actively transported out of the cytosol at both the cell membrane and the vacuolar membrane, which is called the tonoplast.

Many different ions permeate the membranes of living cells simultaneously, but K^+, Na^+ and Cl^- have the highest concentrations and largest permeabilities in plant cells.

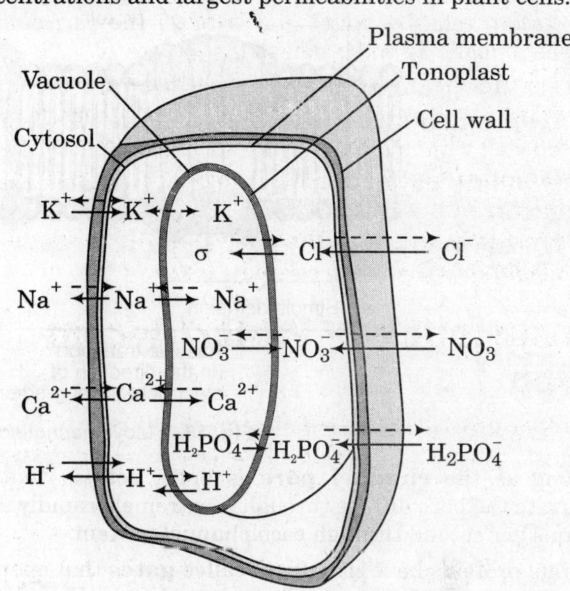

Fig. 18.3 Ion concentrations in the cytosol and the vacuole are controlled by passive (dashed arrows) and active (solid arrows) transport processes. In most plant cells the vacuole occupies up to 90% of the cell's volume and contains the bulk of the cell solutes. Control of the ion concentrations in the cytosol is important for the regulation of metabolic enzymes. The cell wall surrounding the plasma membrane does not represent a permeability barrier and hence, is not a factor in solute transport

Three Classes of Membrane Transport Proteins

Three types of membrane transporters enhance the movement of solutes across membranes: channel, carriers and pumps. Channels are transmembrane proteins that function as selective pores, through which molecules or ions can diffuse across the membrane. Channels and **carriers** can mediate the passive transport of solutes across membranes (by simple diffusion or facilitated diffusion), down the solute's gradient of electrochemical potential. **Channel proteins** act as membrane pores, and their specificity is determined primarily by the biophysical properties of the channel. **Carrier proteins** bind the transported molecule on one side of the membrane and release it on the other side. Primary active transport is carried out by **pumps** and uses energy directly, usually from ATP hydrolysis, to pump solutes against their gradient of electrochemical potential.

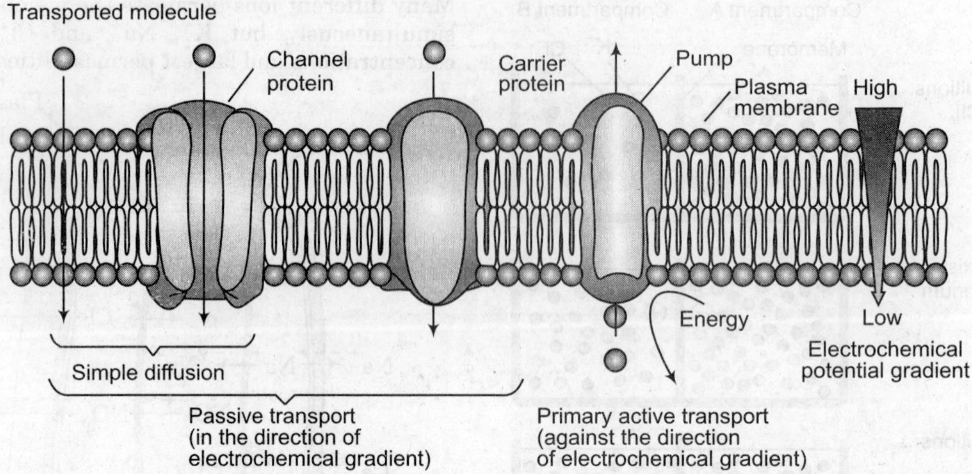

Fig. 18.4 Movement of solutes through membrane transport protein

As long as the **channel pore** is open, solutes that can penetrate the pore diffuse through it extremely rapidly about 10^8 ions per second through each channel protein.

Channel proteins have structures called **gates** that open and close the pore in response to external signals. Signals that can open or close gates include voltage changes, hormone binding, or light.

Carriers Bind and Transport Specific Substances

The substance being transported is initially bound to a specific site on the carrier protein. Carriers therefore specialize in the transport of specific organic metabolites. Binding causes a conformational change in the protein. Transport is complete when the substance dissociates from the carrier's binding site. Typically, carriers may transport 100 to 1000 ions or molecules per second, which is about 10^6 times slower than transport through a channel.

Carrier-mediated transport (unlike transport through channels) can be either passive or active. **Passive transport** on a carrier is sometimes called **facilitated diffusion**, although it resembles diffusion only in that it transports substances down their gradient of electrochemical potential, without an additional input of energy.

Primary active transport is coupled directly to a source of energy other than ATP hydrolysis, an oxidation-reduction reaction. The membrane proteins that carry out primary active transport are called **pumps**. Most pumps transport ions, such as H^+ or Ca^{2+}.

Ion pumps can be further characterized as either electrogenic or electroneutral. In general, **electrogenic transport** refers to ion transport involving the net movement of charge across the membrane. In contrast, **electroneutral transport**, as the name implies, involves no net movement of charge. The Na^+/K^+ ATPase is therefore an electrogenic ion pump, *e.g.,* plasma membranes of plants, fungi and bacteria, as well as in plant tonoplasts and other plant and animal endomembranes, H^+ is the principal ion that is electrogenically pumped across the membrane.

Solutes can be actively transported across a membrane against their gradient of electrochemical potential is by coupling of the uphill transport of one solute to the downhill transport of another. This type of carrier mediated cotransport is termed **secondary active transport**. The proton motive force generated by electrogenic H^+ transport is used in secondary active transport to drive the transport of many other substances against their gradient of electrochemical potentials.

There are two types of secondary transport—symport and antiport. **Symport** (and the protein involved is called a symporter) because the two substances are moving in the same direction through the membrane. **Antiport** (facilitated by a protein called an antiporter) refers to coupled transport in which the downhill movement of protons drives the active (uphill) transport of a solute in the opposite direction.

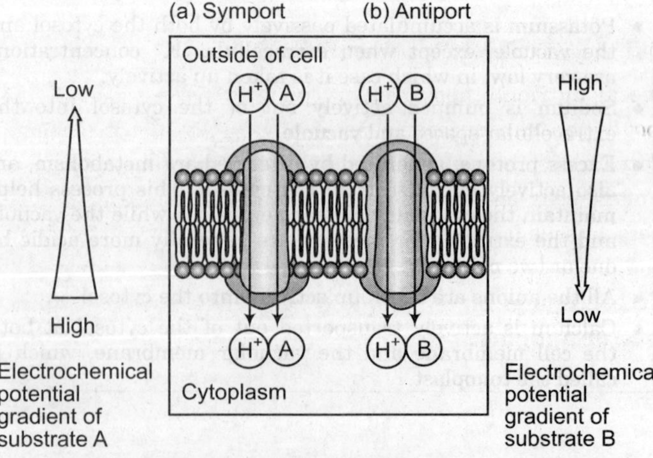

Fig. 18.5 Two examples of secondary active transport coupled to a primary proton gradient

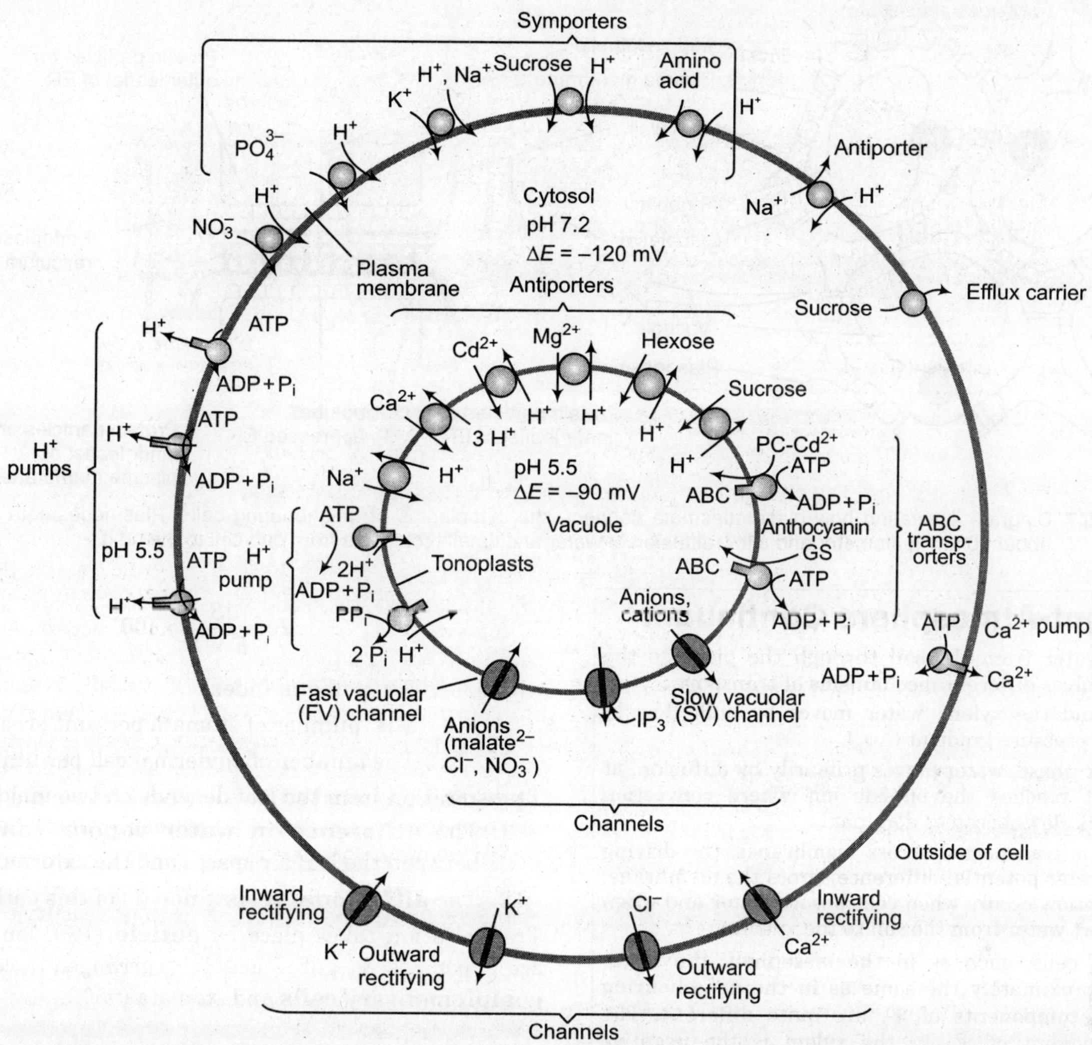

Fig. 18.6 Overview of the various transport processes on the plasma membrane and tonoplast of plant cells

Ion Transport in Roots

Mineral nutrients absorbed by the root are carried to the shoot by the transpiration stream moving through the xylem. Solutes move through both apoplast and symplast. Because all plant cells are separated by cell walls, ions can diffuse across a tissue (or be carried passively by water flow) entirely through the cell wall space without ever entering a living cell. This continuum of cell walls is called the **extracellular space or apoplast.**

The cytoplasms of neighbouring cells form a continuous phase, collectively referred to as the **symplast**. Plant cells are interconnected by cytoplasmic bridges called **plasmodesmata**, cylindrical pores 20 to 60 nm in diameter. Each plasmodesma is lined with a plasma membrane and contains a narrow tubule, the desmotubule, that is a continuation of the endoplasmic reticulum.

Ions moving through the root cross both symplastic and apoplastic spaces. Ion absorption by the roots is more pronounced in the root hair zone than in the meristem and elongation zones.

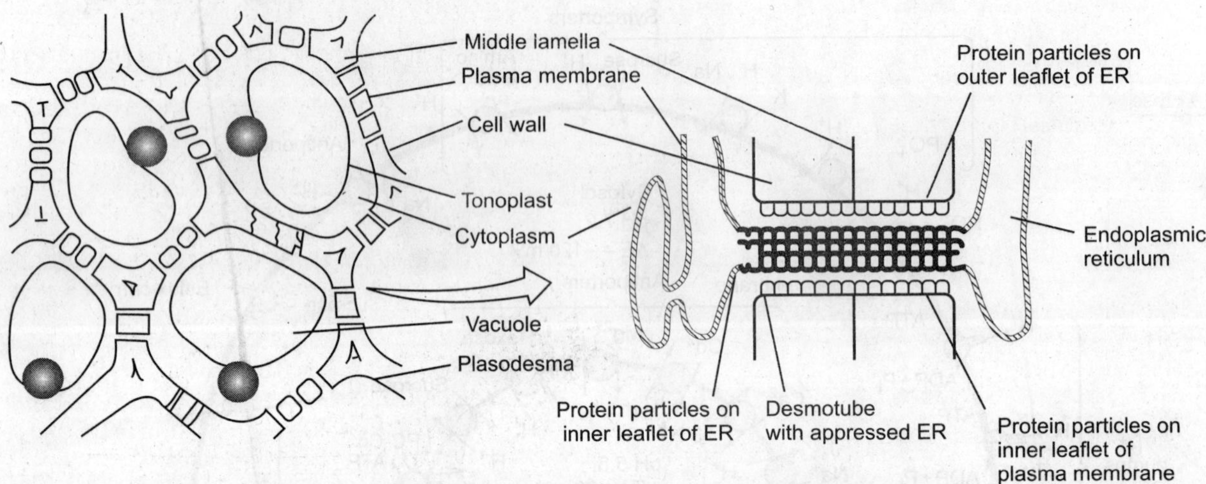

Fig. 18.7 Diagram illustrating how plasmodesmata connect the cytoplasms of neighbouring cells. Plasmodesmata are about 40 nm in diameter and allow diffusion of water and small molecules from one cell to the next

Soil-Plant-Atmosphere Continuum

Movement of water from the soil through the plant to the atmosphere involves different mechanisms of transport:

- In the soil and the xylem, water moves by bulk flow in response to a pressure gradient ($\Delta\psi_p$).
- In the vapour phase, water moves primarily by diffusion, at least until it reaches the outside air, where convection (a form of bulk flow) becomes dominant.
- When water is transported across membranes, the driving force is the water potential difference across the membrane. Such osmotic flow occurs when cells absorb water and when roots transport water from the soil to the xylem.

Inside the leaf cells, such as in the mesophyll, the water potential is approximately the same as in the neighbouring xylem, yet the components of Ψ_w are quite different. The dominant component of Ψ_w in the xylem is the negative pressure (Ψ_p), whereas in the leaf cell Ψ_p is generally positive. This large difference in Ψ_p occurs across the plasma membrane of the leaf cells. Within the leaf cells, water potential is reduced by a high concentration of dissolved solutes (low Ψ_s).

Transpiration

Transpiration is an important means of dissipating the heat input from sunlight. Heat dissipates because the water molecules that escape into the atmosphere have higher than-average energy, which breaks the bonds holding them in the liquid.

During the plant's lifetime, water equivalent to 100 times the fresh weight of the plant may be lost through the leaf surfaces.

Transpiration ratio It is the amount of water loss through transpiration per unit of dry matter produced during growing season.

Stomatal index It is the number of stomata per unit area of leaf surface.

$$I = \frac{S}{E + S} \times 100$$

where, I is stomatal index.
S is number of stomata per unit area.
E is number of epidermal cell per unit area.

Transpiration from the leaf depends on two major factors:

1. The **difference in water vapour concentration** between the leaf air spaces and the external air
2. The **diffusional resistance** (r) of this pathway.

Transpiration takes place by **cuticle** (1%), lenticels which are composed of lossely arranged cells called **complementary cells** and stomata (95%).

Mechanism of Opening and Closing of Stomata

Stomata are minute pores found in epidermis of leaves, stem, etc. There are two kidney-shaped guard cells surrounded by subsidiary or accessory cells. Opening and closing of stomata takes place due to turgor change in guard cells. There are two main theories replaining opening and closing of stomata.

(i) Starch Sugar Inter Conversion Hypothesis

According to **Steward** (1964) CO_2 accumulates in guard cells in dark thus reducing the pH (acidity increases) which favour sugar to starch conversion. This results in exosmosis causing stomata to close.

During day time CO_2 is consumed in photosynthesis. This increasing the pH (reducing acidity) which favoured hydrolysis of starch to sugar. Due to increase in osmotic concentration endosmosis occur in guard cells and stomata open.

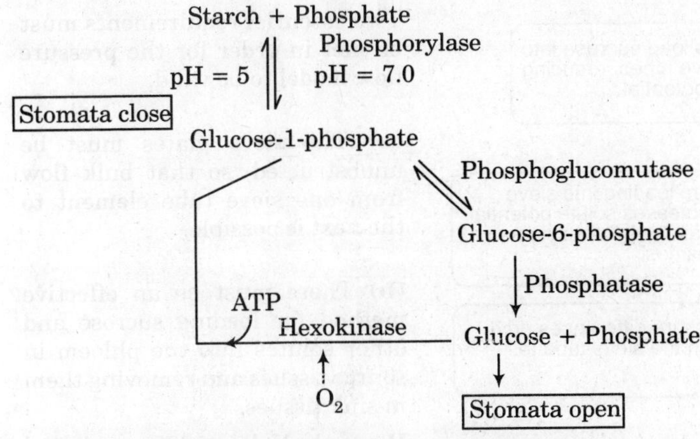

Fig. 18.8 Steward starch sugar hypothesis

(ii) Active K⁺ Theory

Levitt (1974) proposed the proton transport concept to explain the mechanism of opening and closing of stomata. According to this theory the opening and closing of stomata is the result of active transport of K^+ into guard cells and out from them. He observed that proton (H^+) uptake by guard cells, chloroplasts takes place with the help of ATP. This leads to increase in pH of guard cells, which favour conversion of starch to organic acid like malic acid.

$$\text{Starch} \longrightarrow \text{Phosphoglyceric acid} \xrightarrow{\text{Carboxylase}} \text{Phosphoenol pyruvic acid} + CO_2$$

$$\text{Malic acid} \longleftarrow \text{Oxaloacetic acid} \longleftarrow$$

Malic acid further dissociate to H^+ and malate. The uptake of K^+ is balanced by uptake of Cl^- or transport of H^+ from organic acid such as malic acid or by negative charge of organic acid when they loss H^+. The potassium malate transport to vacuole, which caused endosmosis and increase in turgor pressure. This leads to stomatal opening. The stomatal closure is considered to be brought about by passive excretion of K^+ and Cl^- from the guard cells to epidermal cells. Closure mechanism also involves participation of an inhibitor hormone abscissic acid (ABA). In dark ABA inhibits K^+ uptake by changing the diffusion and permeability of guard cells. Mesophyll cells with intercellular spaces and stomata are essential for gaseous exchange required for photosynthesis and respiration. Transpiration is therefore called as **necessary evil** (Curtis; 1926).

Antitranspirants PMA (phenyl mercuric acetate), aspirin, salicyclic acid, ABA (abscisic acid) and CO_2 (0.05%).

Guttation It is the loss of water from plant in form of liquid. Plants show guttation through **hydathodes.** The hydothodes has loosely arranged mass of parenchyma which is termed as **epithem**.

Mechanisms of Loading and Unloading of Photoassimilates

Photosynthesis takes place in the mesophyll cells and, in C_4 plants, in the bundle sheath cells of the leaf. The products of photosynthesis (primarily carbohydrates) diffuse to the nearest small vein, where they are actively transported into sieve tube elements.

Sieve element contain active cytoplasm. Companion cells are believed to provide metabolic support for sieve tube member and are involved in translocation of sucrose into sieve tube. Phloem parenchyma cells in minor leaf veins of some plants develop extensive outgrowths of cell walls. Such cells are called **transfer cells.** They are responsible for collecting and passing on organic solutes.

Substances in the phloem move from sources to sinks. A **source** is an organ (such as a mature leaf or a storage root) that produces (by photosynthesis or by digestion of stored reserves) more sugars than it requires. A **sink** is an organ (such as a root, a flower, a developing fruit or tuber, or an immature leaf) that consumes sugars for its own growth and storage needs.

Phloem sap contains sucrose (50-90%) organic acids (malate etc.) amino acids, some cations (K^+), anions (like NO_3^-) and hormones. Sucrose may be loaded into sieve elements of veinlet endings *via* symplast (through plasmodesmata)or apoplast (through cell wall) pathway. Unloading can also occur *via* symplastic or apoplastic pathway.

Pressure Flow Model (Munch)

The sap flows under pressure through the sieve tubes, moving from one sieve tube element to the next by bulk flow through the sieve plates, without crossing a membrane. Two steps in translocation require metabolic energy:

(i) Transport of sucrose and other solutes into the sieve tubes at sources, called **loading**.

(ii) Removal of the solutes, called **unloading,** where the sieve tubes enter sinks.

According to the **pressure flow model** of translocation in the phloem, sucrose is actively transported into sieve tube elements at a source, giving those cells a greater sucrose concentration than the surrounding cells. Water therefore, enters the sieve tube elements by osmosis. The entry of this water causes a greater pressure potential in the sieve tube, so that the entire fluid content of the sieve tube is pushed toward the sink end of the tube, the sap moves by bulk flow in response to a pressure gradient. In the sink, the sucrose is unloaded by active transport, maintaining the gradients of solute potential and water potential needed for movement.

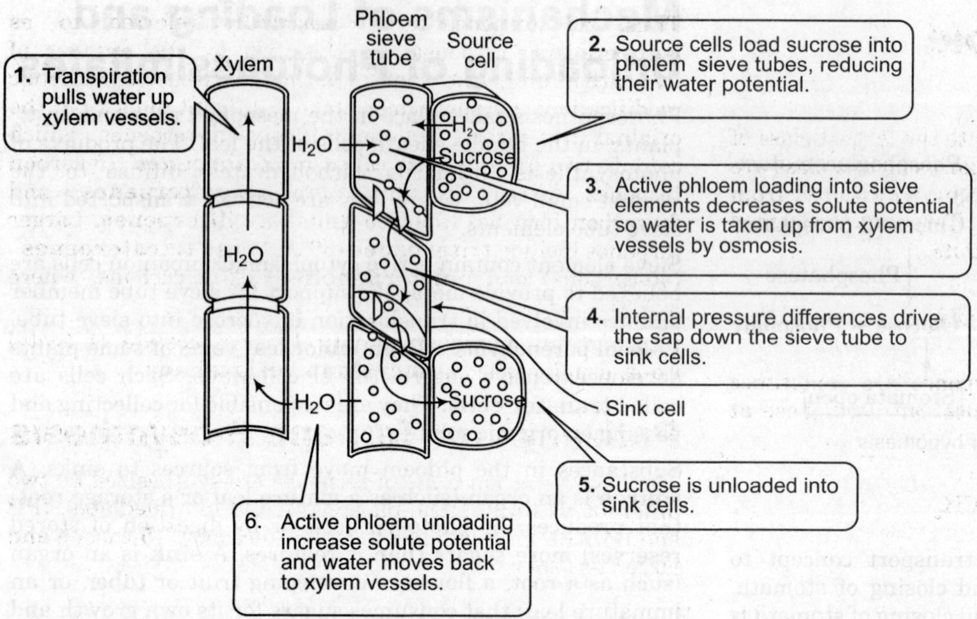

Fig. 18.9 The pressure flow model combined pressure potential and water potential differences drive the bulk flow of sieve tube sap from a source to a sink

Two essential requirements must be met in order for the pressure flow model to be valid:

(a) The sieve plates must be unobstructed, so that bulk flow from one sieve tube element to the next is possible.

(b) There must be an effective method for loading sucrose and other solutes into the phloem in source tissues and removing them in sink tissues.

Hugo de Vries (1885) suggested that cyclosis or cytoplasmic streaming is a type of active translocation and movement is caused by combination of diffusion and cytoplasmic streaming. **Curtis** (1935) supported this theory.

Secondary Metabolites

The compound which are not required for normal growth and development by general metabolic pathway, which common to all plant, are sometime referred to as **secondary compound, secondary product** or **secondary metabolite.**

Secondary metabolite can be of following categories:

1. Alkaloids
2. Isoprenoids/terpenes
3. Rubber like polymers/ polyisoprenes
4. Phenolic compounds
5. Rare amino acids
6. Plant amines
7. Glycosides

Secondary metabolite occurs usually only in special differentiated cells.

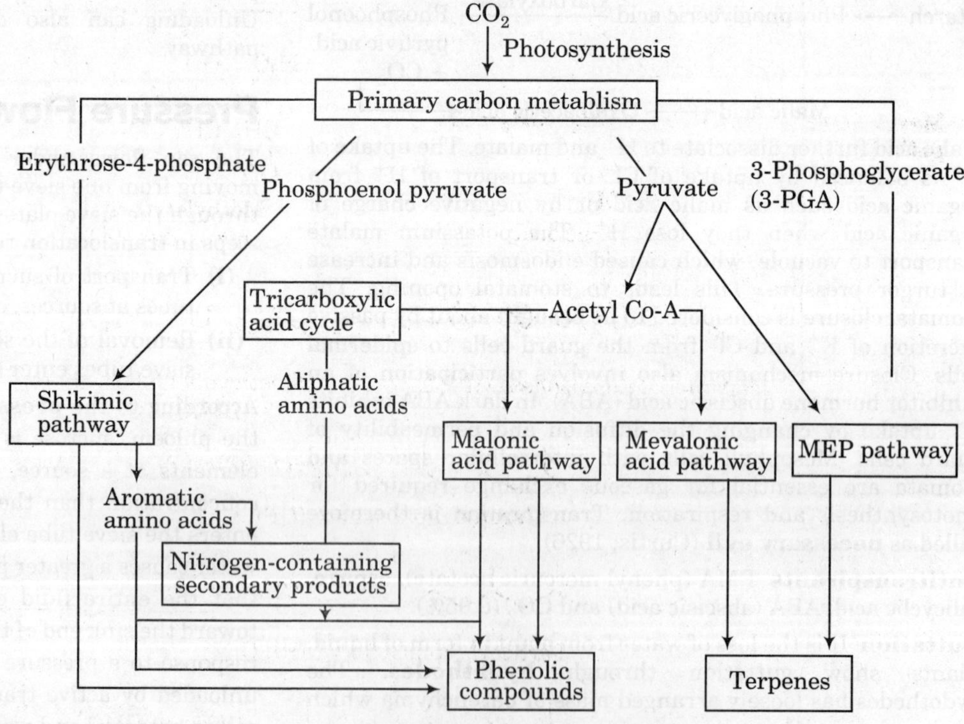

Fig. 18.10 A simplified view of the major pathways of secondary-metabolite. Biosynthesis and their interrelationships with primary metabolism

Biosynthesis and Role of Terpenes

The **terpenes** or **terpenoids,** constitute the largest class of secondary products. The diverse substances of this class are generally insoluble in water. They are biosynthesized from acetyl Co-A or glycolytic intermediates. Terpenes are formed by the fusion of five- carbon isoprene units.

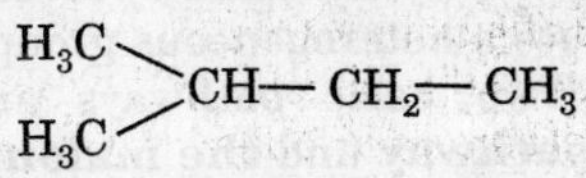

$$(H_3C)_2CH{-}CH_2{-}CH_3$$

The basic structural elements of terpenes are sometimes called **isoprene units** because terpenes can decompose at high temperatures to give isoprene:

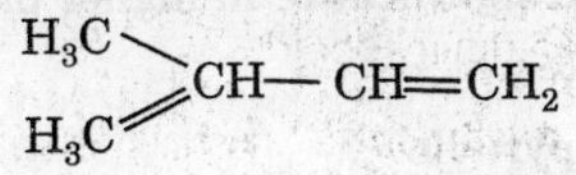

$$H_3C(H_2C{=})C{-}CH{=}CH_2$$

Thus, all terpenes are occasionally referred to as **isoprenoids.** Terpenes are classified by the number of five-carbon units they contain, although extensive metabolic modifications can sometimes make it difficult to pick out the original five-carbon residues. 10-carbon terpenes, which contain two C5 units, are called **monoterpenes**; 15-carbon terpenes (three C5 units) are **sesquiterpenes**; and 20-carbon terpenes (four C5 units) are **diterpenes**. Larger terpenes include **triterpenes** (30 carbons), **tetraterpenes** (40-carbons) and **polyterpenoids** [(C5)n carbons, where $n > 8$].

Isoprene unit synthesized entirely from acetate of acetyl Co-A, usually called as **mevalonic** acid pathway.

Pathways for Terpene Biosynthesis

The basic 5-carbon units of terpenes are synthesized by two different pathways. The phosphorylated intermediates, IPP and DMAPP are combined to make 10-carbon, 15-carbon and larger terpenes.

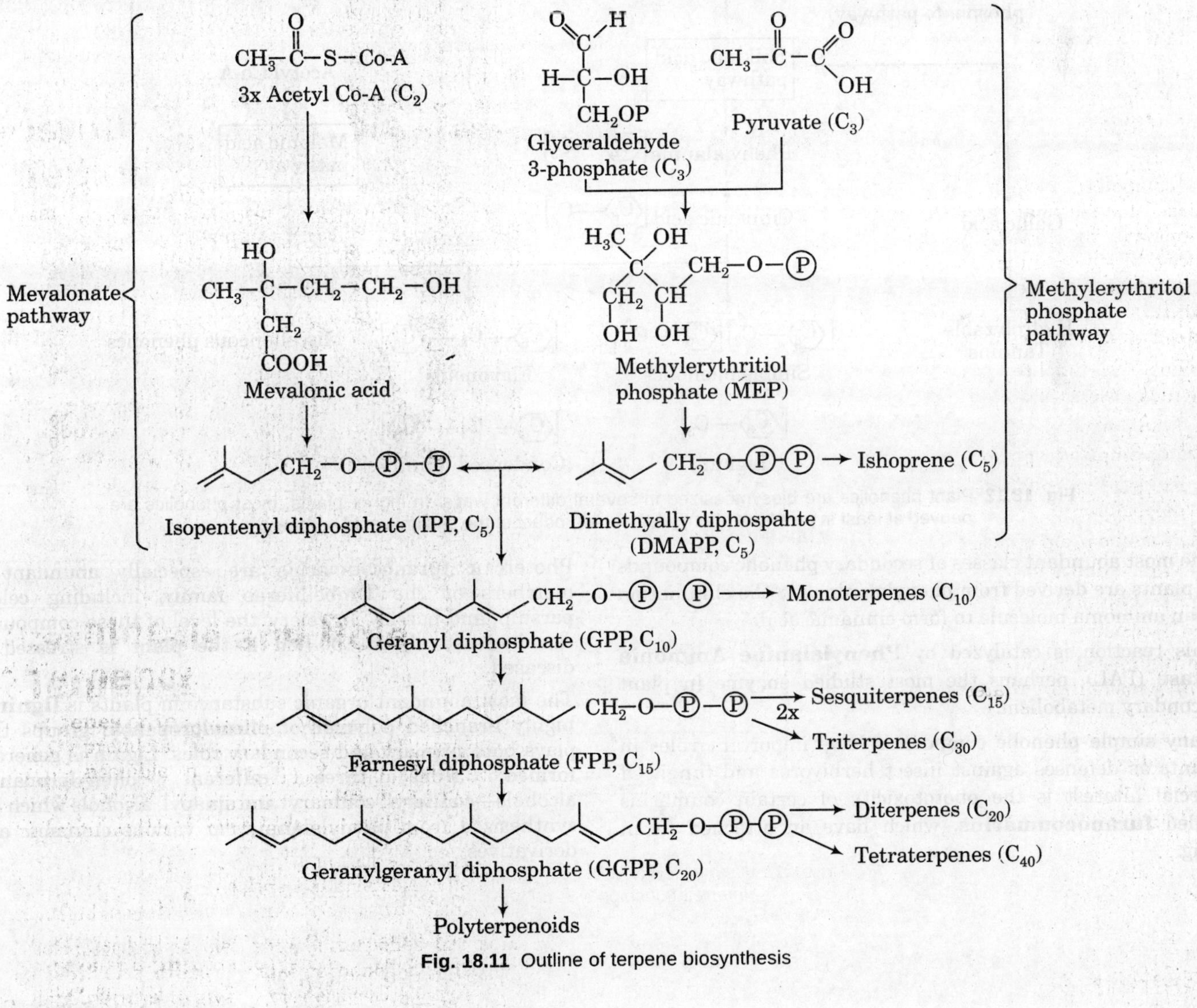

Mevalonate pathway:

$CH_3{-}CO{-}S{-}Co\text{-}A$ — 3x Acetyl Co-A (C_2)

↓

$CH_3{-}C(OH)(CH_2COOH){-}CH_2{-}CH_2{-}OH$ — Mevalonic acid

↓

$CH_2{-}O{-}Ⓟ{-}Ⓟ$ — Isopentenyl diphosphate (IPP, C_5)

Methylerythritol phosphate pathway:

$H{-}C(=O)$, $H{-}C{-}OH$, CH_2OP — Glyceraldehyde 3-phosphate (C_3)

$CH_3{-}CO{-}COOH$ — Pyruvate (C_3)

↓

H_3C, OH, C, $CH_2{-}O{-}Ⓟ$, CH_2, CH, OH OH — Methylerythritiol phosphate (MEP)

↓

$CH_2{-}O{-}Ⓟ{-}Ⓟ$ → Ishoprene (C_5) — Dimethyally diphospahte (DMAPP, C_5)

IPP ⟷ DMAPP

↓

$CH_2{-}O{-}Ⓟ{-}Ⓟ$ → Monoterpenes (C_{10}) — Geranyl diphosphate (GPP, C_{10})

↓

$CH_2{-}O{-}Ⓟ{-}Ⓟ$ → Sesquiterpenes (C_{15}); 2x → Triterpenes (C_{30}) — Farnesyl diphosphate (FPP, C_{15})

↓

$CH_2{-}O{-}Ⓟ{-}Ⓟ$ → Diterpenes (C_{20}); → Tetraterpenes (C_{40}) — Geranylgeranyl diphosphate (GGPP, C_{20})

↓

Polyterpenoids

Fig. 18.11 Outline of terpene biosynthesis

Many plants contain mixtures of volatile monoterpenes and sesquiterpenes, called **essential oils**, that lend a characteristic odour to their foliage. Many conifers respond to bark beetle infestation by producing additional quantities of monoterpenes.

The non-volatile terpene antiherbivore compounds are the **limonoids**, a group of triterpenes (C_{30}) well known as bitter substances in citrus fruit. Perhaps the most powerful detergent to insect feeding known is azadirachtin, a complex limonoid from the neem tree (*Azadirachta indica*) of Africa and Asia.

Triterpenes that are active against vertebrate herbivores include cardenolides and saponins. **Cardenolides** are glycosides (compounds containing an attached sugar or sugars) that taste bitter and are extremely toxic to higher animals.

Biosynthesis of Phenols and their Roles

All phenolic compounds have an aromatic ring that contains various attached substituent groups such as hydroxyl, carboxyl and methoxyl (—O—CH_3) group and often other non-aromatic ring structures.

Plant phenolics are biosynthesized by several different routes and thus constitute a heterogeneous group from a metabolic point of view. Two basic pathways are involved: **The shikimic acid pathway** and **the malonic acid pathway**. The shikimic acid pathway participates in the biosynthesis of most plant phenolics. The malonic acid pathway, although an important source of phenolic secondary products in fungi and bacteria, is of less significance in higher plants.

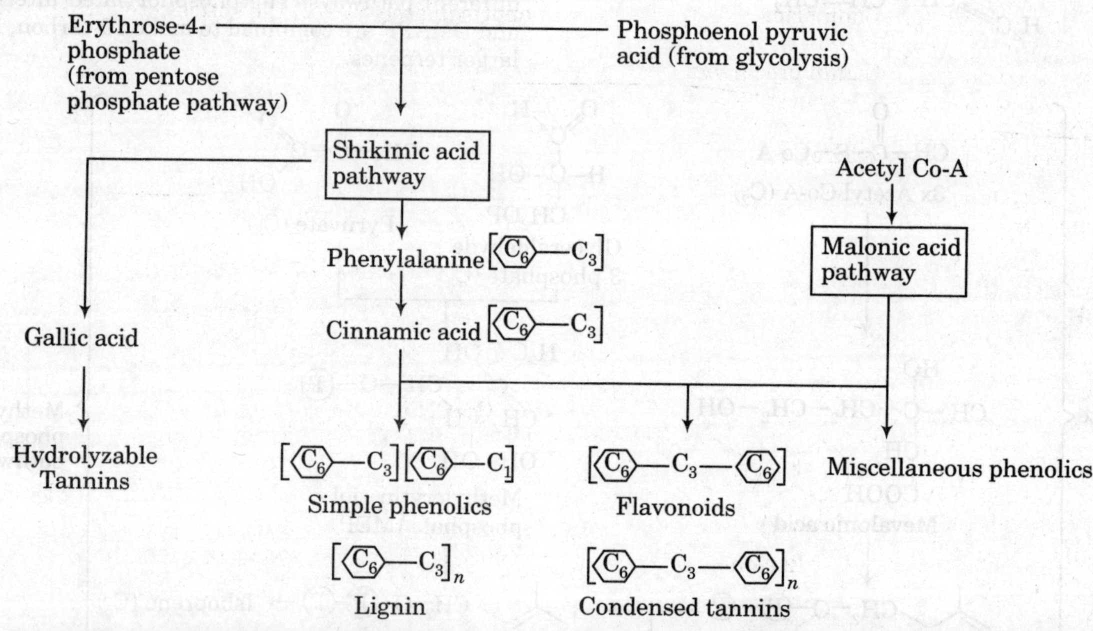

Fig. 18.12 Plant phenolics are biosynthesized in several different ways. In higher plants, most phenolics are derived at least in part from phenylalanine, a product of the shikimic acid pathway

The most abundant classes of secondary phenolic compounds in plants are derived from phenylalanine *via* the elimination of an ammonia molecule to form cinnamic acid.

This reaction is catalyzed by **Phenylalanine Ammonia Lyase** (PAL), perhaps the most studied enzyme in plant secondary metabolism.

Many simple phenolic compounds have important roles in plants as defenses against insect herbivores and fungi. Of special interest is the phototoxicity of certain coumarins called **furanocoumarins**, which have an attached furan ring.

Phototoxic furanocoumarins are especially abundant in members of the Umbelliferae family, including celery, parsnip, and parsley. In celery, the level of these compounds can increase about 100-fold if the plant is stressed or diseased.

The most abundant organic substance in plants is **lignin**, a highly branched polymer of phenylpropanoid groups that plays both primary and secondary roles. Lignin is generally formed from three different phenylpropanoid alcohols—coniferyl, coumaryl and sinapyl, alcohols which are synthesized from phenylalanine *via* various cinnamic acid derivatives.

COOH
NH_2
Phenylalanine
NH_3 Phenylalanine Ammonia Lyase (PAL)
COOH
Benzoic acid derivatives
trans-cinnamic acid
COOH
Caffeic acid and other simple phenylpropanoids
HO
p-coumaric acid
Co-A-SH
Coumarins
COS Co-A
Lignin precursors
HO
p-coumaryl Co-A
3-malonyl Co-A molecules
Chalocone synthase
OH
HO OH
OH O
Chalcones
OH
HO O
OH O
Flavones
OH
HO O
OH O
Flavanones
HO O
OH O
OH
Isoflavones (isoflavonoids)
OH
HO O
OH
OH O
Dihydroflavonols
OH
HO O
OH
OH O
Flavonols
Anthocyanins
Condensed tannins

Fig. 18.13 Outline of phenolic biosynthesis from phenylalanine. The formation of many plant phenolics, including simple phenylpropanoids, coumarins, benzoic acid derivatives, lignin, anthocyanins, isoflavones, condensed tannins and other flavonoids, begins with phenylalanine.

Biosynthesis of Nitrogenous Compounds and their Roles

A large variety of plant secondary metabolites have nitrogen in their structure. Included in this category are such well-known antiherbivore defenses as **alkaloids** and **cyanogenic glycosides**, which are of considerable interest because of their toxicity to humans and their medicinal properties.

Various nitrogen-containing secondary metabolites, are alkaloids, cyanogenic glycosides, glucosinolates, and non-protein amino acids.

The **alkaloids** are a large family of more than 15000 nitrogen-containing secondary metabolites found in approximately 20% of the species of vascular plants.

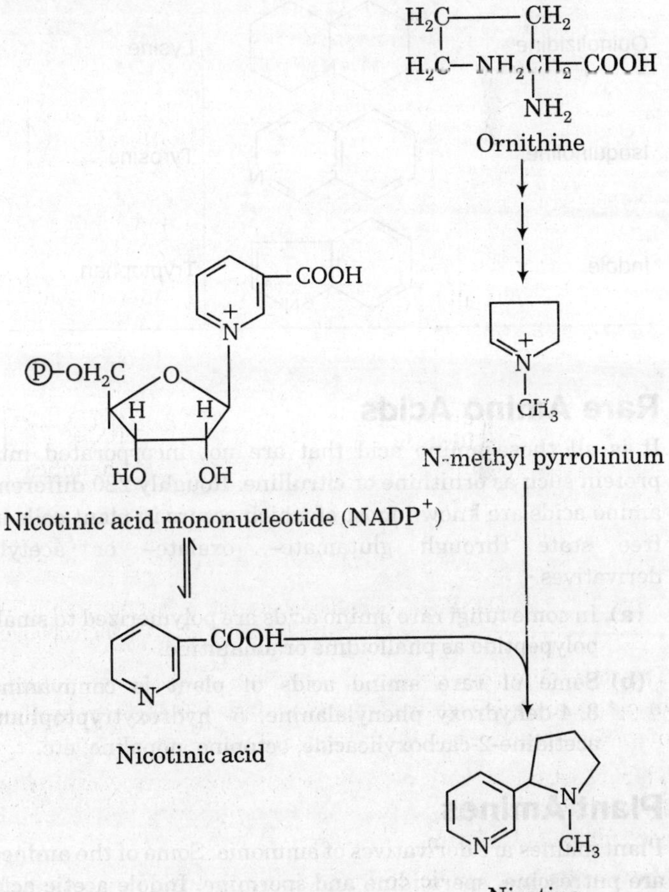

Fig. 18.14 Nicotine biosynthesis begins with the biosynthesis of the nicotinic acid (niacin) from aspartate and glyceraldehyde-3-phosphate. Nicotinic acid is also a component of NAD^+ and $NADP^+$, important participants in biological oxidation-reduction reactions. The five-membered ring of nicotine is derived from ornithine, an intermediate in arginine biosynthesis

Table 18.1 **Major Types of Alkaloids, their Amino Acid Precursors and Well-Known Examples**

Alkaloid Class	Structure	Biosynthetic Precursor	Example	Human Use
Pyrrolidine		Ornithine (asparate)	Nicotine	Stimulant, depressant and transquilizer
Tropane		Ornithine	Atropine	Prevention of intestinal spasms, antidote to other poisons, dilation of pupils for examination
			Cocaine	Stimulant of the central nervous system and local anesthetic
Piperidine		Lysine (or acetate)	Conline	Poison (paralyzes motor neurons)
Pyrrolizidine		Ornithine	Retrorshine	None
Quinolizidine		Lysine	Lupinine	Restoration of heart rhythm
Isoquinoline		Tyrosine	Codeine Morphine	Analgesic (pain relief), treatment of coughs analgesic
Indole		Tryptophan	Psilocybin	Haluconogen

Rare Amino Acids

It is all those amino acid that are not incorporated into protein such as ornithine or citrulline. Roughly 220 different amino acids are known most of which occurs in plant cells in free state through glutamate–, oxalate– or acetyl– derivatives.

(a) In some fungi rare amino acids are polymerized to small polypeptide as phalloidine or amanitine.

(b) Some of rare amino acids of plant is canavanine 3, 4-dehydroxy phenylalanine, 5- hydroxytryptophan, acetidine-2-carboxylicacide, octopine, nopaline, etc.

Plant Amines

Plant amines are derivatives of ammonia. Some of the amines are putrescine, spermidine and spermine. Indole acetic acid (IAA) and serotonin are tryptamines.

Alkaloid

Plant containing aromatic nitrogenous compounds are called alkaloids. Relatively few monocots and gymnosperms possess alkaloid. The first alkaloids to be isolated and crystallized was the drug **morphine** isolated from *Papaver somniferum*.

Table 18.2 **Plant Species Producing Alkaloids**

Alkaloid	Plant Species
Nicotine	Tabaccum (leaf)
Cocaines	*Erythroxylon coca* (leaf)
Quinine	Cuprea (bark)
Caffeine	Coffee (bean), tea (leaf)
Strychnine	*Strychnos nuxvomica* (seed)
Theobromine	Cocoa (bean)
Atropine	*Atropa belladonna*
Colchicine	*Colchicum byzantium*
Mescaline	*Lophophora williamsii*
Lycoctonine	*Delphinium barbeyi*

Stress Physiology

Deviations from the physiological normal type to suboptimal or damaging quantities or intensities of environmental factors are termed as **stress**. Thus stress and reactions caused by it (stress reactions) can be used as a measure of the strength of the stress on a scale of intensity, ranging from deficiency to excessive supply.

Environmental factors deviating from the optimal intensity or quantity for the plant are called **stress factors**.

Stress is caused of the following factors: **light** (weak light, strong light), **temperature** (cold, heat), water (drought, flooding), **nutrients** (lack of ions, over-fertilization, salt stress), **carbon dioxide** and **oxygen** (photosynthesis, respiration/photorespiration, oxidative stress, anaerobiosis).

Biotic environmental factors resulting from interactions with other organisms.

Environmental noxae are stress factors which trigger stress reactions when applied in any concentration or intensity.

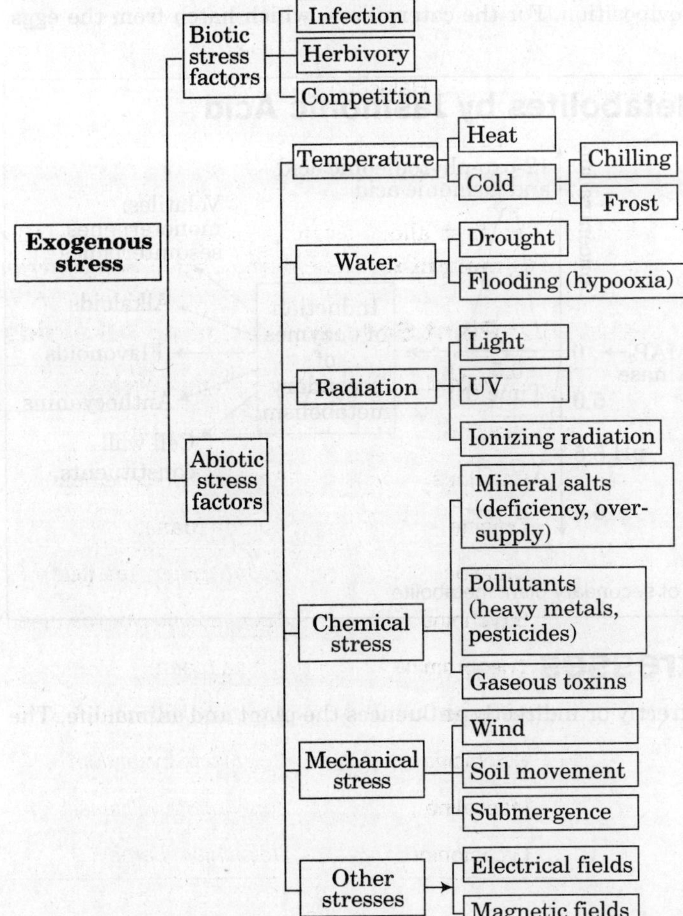

Fig. 18.15 Biotic and abiotic environmental factors creating stress for plants

Quantification of Damage of Stress to Plant Tissue

1. Counting necrotic areas after stress application.
2. Absorption and accumulation of neutral red in the vacuole of undamaged cells.
3. Plasmolysis of undamaged cells.
4. Measurement of electrical conductivity: loss of ions from damaged cells into distilled water.
5. Measurement of chlorophyll fluorescence in photosynthesis.

Responses of Plants to Biotic (Pathogen and Insects) Stress

There are many plants that are practically never touched or only attacked by pathogen and insects, so-called **poisonous plants**. These plants are protected by secondary plant metabolites, which are constitutively formed (so called anticipators) and accumulated in the vacuoles or cell walls during the life of the plant. Examples are **alkaloids, terpenoids, steroids** (*e.g.*, saponin, bittering agents, heart active glycosides), phenolic **compounds** (*e.g.*, **tannins), cyanogenic compounds** and **mustard oil glycosides** (which are hydrolyzed upon damage of the cells releasing HCN or mustard oils) and many more.

These defence compounds do not provide complete protection, particularly regarding phytophagous insects. Some phytophagous insects detoxify the cyanide ion by binding it with fJ-cyanoalanine synthase to serine or cysteine. Other phytophages take up such toxins with their food, for example, the butterflies of the genus *Zygaena* accumulate the cyanogenic glycosides linamarin and lotaustralin from the birds-foot trefoil (*Lotus corniculatus*) and protect themselves against their enemies by releasing hydrogen cyanide. Hymenopteran and dipteran insects, on the other hand, when parasitising these phytophages, are able to detoxify HCN with rhodanese.

Compatible and Incompatible Interactions

(i) In **compatible interactions** host and pathogen 'get alongwith each other', *i.e.* **infestation is strong, the pathogen is virulent** and the plant is susceptible.

(ii) In **incompatible interactions**, the infested plant can cope with the attack of pathogens by establishing defence reactions, *i.e.*, **it is resistant and the pathogens are called avirulent**. In compatible interactions, pathogens are able to circumvent, inactivate or tolerate the plant defences.

Secondary plant metabolites as potential toxins Release of hydrogen cyanide from seeds of many Rosaceae. Amygdalin occurs in many seeds (embryos) of stone and pome-fruit plants. On imbibition of the seeds or after wounding, the glucosidases amygdalin hydrolase and prunasin hydrolase become active, followed by the hydroxynitrilases, which finally lead to the release of hydrogen cyanide.

Table 18.3 **Reactions which are Induced by Stress and/or During Developmental Phases**

Process	Signal(s)	Protein(s)/Reaction	Gene Sequence Known
Wounding	S, JA, ABA and Et	Proteinase inhibitors	Yes
Pathogen attack	JA and SA	Thionins, 'pathogenesis-related proteins'	Yes
Elicitor (fungal) application	JA and Et	Phytoalexin-producing enzymes	Yes
Contact	JA	Tendril movement	No
Drought stress	ABA and JA	Dehydrins and JIPS	Yes
Osmotic stress	ABA and JA	JIPs	Yes
Salt stress	ABA, JA and Et	Osmotin	Yes
Nitrogen storage	JA	N-storage proteins in vegetative tissues	Yes
Fruit ripening	JA and Et	ACC oxidase	No
Senscene	JA and Et	Lipoxygenase and JIPS	Yes
Stabilization of the cell	JA	Hydroxyproline and glycine-rich proteins	Yes

ABA-Abscisic acid; ACC-aminocyclo propane carboxylate oxidase; Et-ethylene; JA-jasmonic acid; j {Psjasmonate-induced proteins; S-systemin; SA-salicylic acid.

Defence compounds as attractants. When cabbage leaves are damaged, **sinigrin**, a mustard oil **glucoside**, is released from the vacuole and simultaneously a **thioglucosidase** (**myrosinase**) is released from the lytic compartment (Golgi vesicles, etc.) Removal of glucose by myrosinase results in a reactive intermediate, which, on hydrolysis of the sulphate residue, is converted into volatile **allyl isothiocyanate** (**allyl mustard oil**). This compound, which has a pungent flavour to humans, is extremely toxic to many insects. For the large cabbage white butterfly (*Fieris brassicae*), the allyl mustard oil is, however, an attractant which stimulates the female butterfly to oviposition. For the caterpillars, which hatch from the eggs, sinigrin and its derivatives are feeding stimulants.

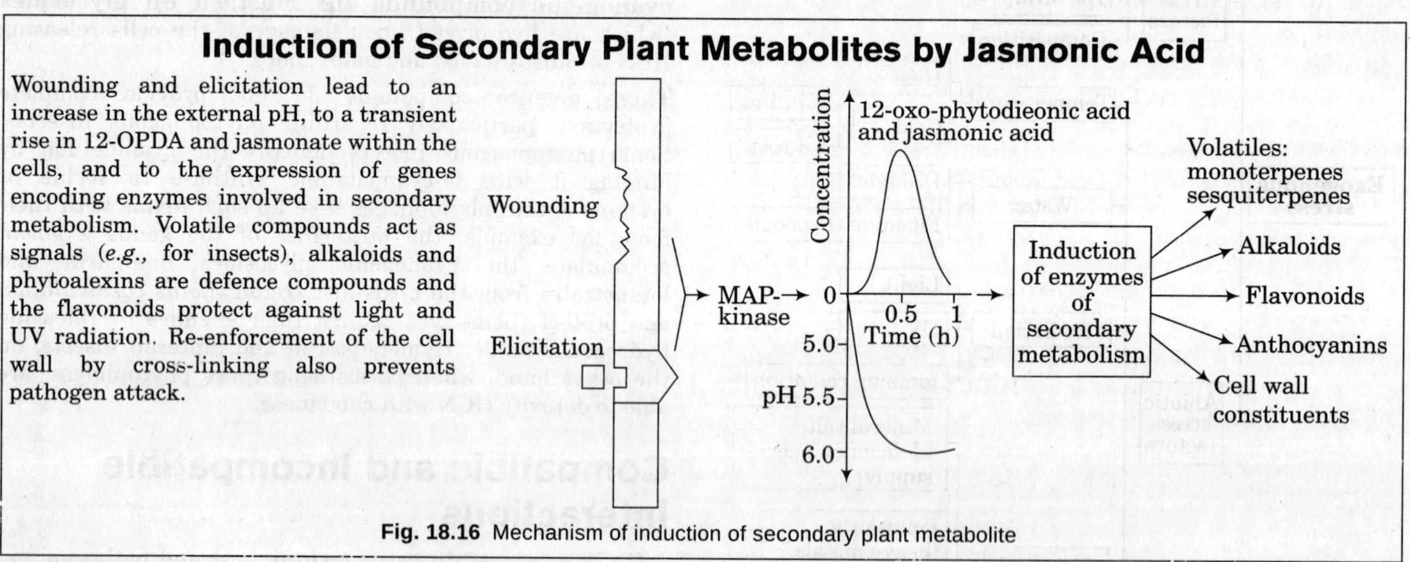

Fig. 18.16 Mechanism of induction of secondary plant metabolite

Responses of Plants to Abiotic Stresses

The abiotic factors include water, salts, temperature etc., which directly or indirectly enfluences the plant and animal life. The various plant activities due to abiotic stress are described here.

Water Stress

Water stress may cause the following changes

(i) Shrinkage of the protoplast.
(ii) Concentration of cellular solutions.
(iii) Decrease or loss of turgor pressure.
(iv) Changes in the water potential gradient across membranes.
(v) In the worst cases, disintegration of biomembranes and denaturing of proteins.

Table 18.4 **Accumulation of Metabolic Products in Terrestrial Plants Under Drought Stress and their Physiological Effects**

Types of Compound	Compound	Function Upon Drought	Cross-Protection
Ions	Potassium	Osmotic balance, acquisition of macronutrients, sodium exclusion and export.	Salt
Proteins	LEA/dehydrins, osmotin and SOD/catalyses	Membrane and protein protection, pathogen-related proteins, detoxification of radicals.	Frost and defense against pathogens
Amino acids	Proline and ecotin	Osmotic balance, membrane and protein protection.	Frost
Sugars	Sucrose and fructans	Osmotic balance, membrane and protein protection, storage of carbohydrates.	Frost
Polyols	Acylic (*e.g.,* mannitol) and cyclic (*e.g.,* pinitol)	Osmotic balance, membrane protection, storage of carbohydrates and radical scavengers.	Frost and salt
Polyamines	Spermine and spermidine	Ion balance and protection of chromatin.	Anaerobiosis
Quaternary amines	Glycinebetaine and β-alaninebetaine	Membrane protection	Frost and salt
Tertiary sulfonium compounds	Dimethyl sulfoniopropionate	Membrane protection	Frost and salt
Pigments and carotenoids	Carotenoids, anthocyanins and betalains	Protection against excess light and photoinhibition.	

Abscisic acid is synthesized continuously at a low rate in mesophyll cells and tends to accumulate in the chloroplasts. When the mesophyll becomes mildly dehydrated, two things happen:

(a) Some of the ABA stored in the chloroplasts is released to the apoplast (the cell wall space) of the mesophyll cell.

(b) ABA is synthesized at a higher rate and more ABA accumulates in the leaf apoplast. The higher ABA concentrations resulting from the higher rates of ABA synthesis appear to enhance or prolong the initial closing effect of the stored ABA. The mechanism of ABA-induced stomatal closure.

Table 18.5 **Water use Efficiency, Photosynthesis and Biomass Production of C_3, C_4 and CAM Plants**

Type of Photosynthesis	C_3	C_4	CAM
Water use efficiency (g water/g C)	450-950	250-350	18-100 (night-time); 150-600 (day-time)
Maximum rate of net photosynthesis (μmol CO_2 m^2 s^1)	9-25	25-50	0.6-8
Growth (g biomass m^2 day^1)	50-200	400-500	1.5-1.8

Water deficit limits photosynthesis within the chloroplast. Osmotic adjustment of cells helps maintain plant water balance. Osmotic stress induces crassulacean acid metabolism in some plants. Water deficit increases wax deposition on the leaf surface, and alters energy dissipation from leaves.

Stress-Responsive Genes are Regulated by ABA Dependent and ABA-Independent Processes

Gene transcription is controlled through the interaction of regulatory proteins (transcription factors) with specific regulatory sequences in the promoters of the genes they regulate.

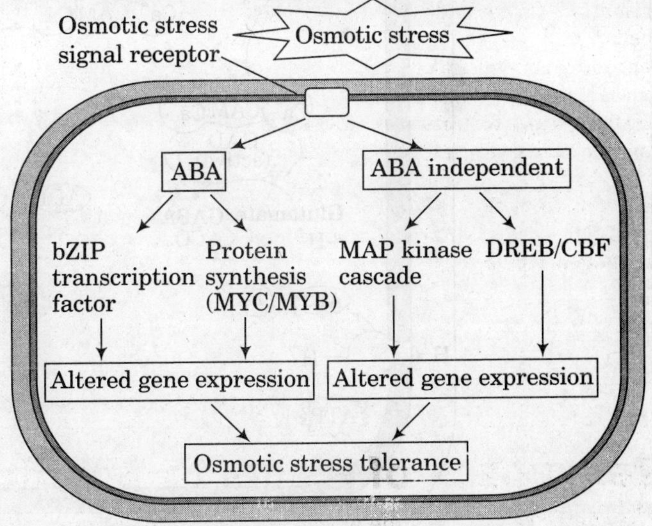

Fig. 18.17 Signal transduction pathways for osmotic stress in plant cells

Osmotic stress is perceived by an as yet unknown receptor in the plasma membrane activating ABA-independent and an ABA-dependent signal transduction pathways. Protein synthesis participates in one of the ABA-dependent pathways involving MYC/MYB. The bZIP ABA-dependent pathway involves recognition of ABA-responsive elements in gene promoters. Two ABA independent pathways, one involving the MAP kinase signaling cascade and the other involving DREBP/CBF related transcription factors have also been demonstrated.

The promoters of ABA-regulated genes contain a six nucleotide sequence element referred to as the **ABA Response Element** (ABRE). The promoters of these genes, which are regulated by osmotic stress in an ABA-dependent manner, contain an alternative nine-nucleotide regulatory sequence element, the **Dehydration Response Element** (DRE). The genes that are regulated by osmotic stresses appear to be regulated either by signal transduction pathways mediated by the action of ABA (ABA-dependent genes) or by an **ABA-independent**, osmotic stress-responsive signal transduction pathway.

Temperature Stress

Types of organisms constitutively adapted to cold are called **psychrophiles** and those requiring high temperatures are called **thermophiles** (extreme thermophiles), but most organisms are **mesophiles**.

Seed germination behaviour can be modified by inhibitory mechanisms (*e.g.*, the requirement for a prolonged exposure of imbibed seeds to cold-**stratification** or the fire-dependent opening of seeds in **pyrophytes**), which prevent premature germination at unfavourable times.

Frost represents a long-term stress situation in contrast to, for example, fire and can last for hours, days and even months. Frost acts not only as a temperature stress, but primarily as a drought stress due to the freezing of tissue water.

The **melting point** and **viscosity of the lipids** of their biomembranes depend on the length of the component fatty acids and the degree of their unsaturation. The longer the chain length of the fatty acids and the lower the number of double bonds, the higher the melting point. Organisms are able to adapt the viscosity of their biomembranes to temperature to a certain extent by incorporating more saturated fatty acids into the membranes.

Adaptation to Heat Stress is Mediated by Cytosolic Calcium

Heat stress causes a reduction in cytosolic pH from the normal slightly alkaline value, probably by inhibiting proton-pumping ATPases and pyrophosphatases that pump protons across the plasma membrane or into the vacuole.

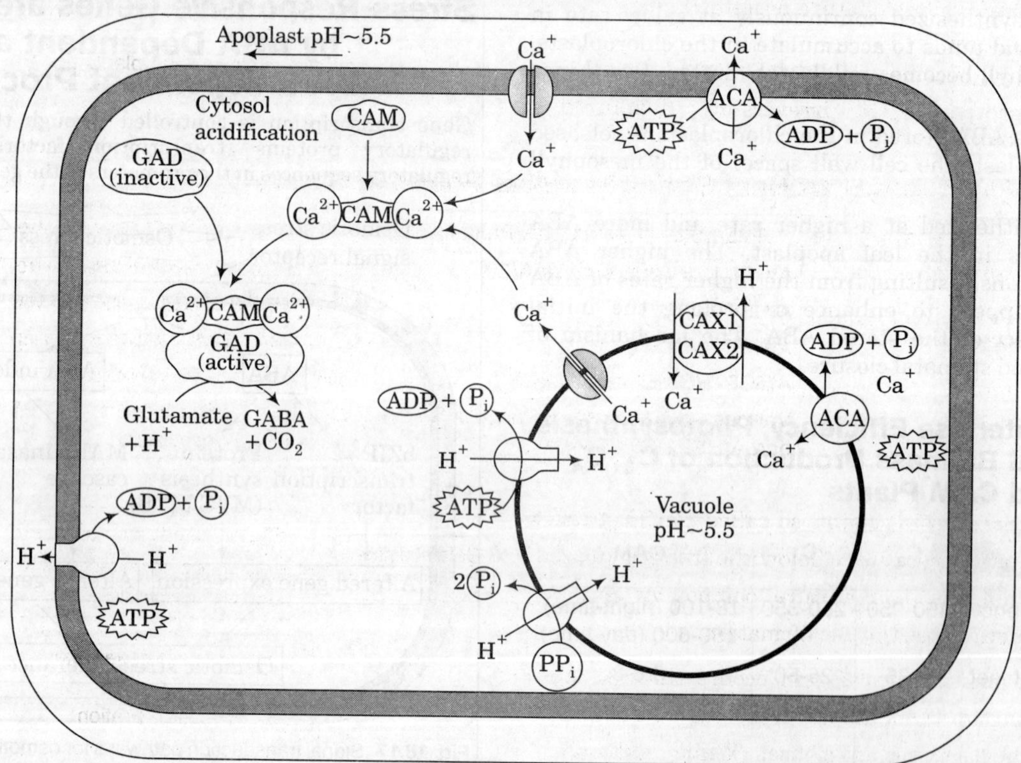

Fig. 18.18 Adaptation to heat stress

Heat stress effects a change in calcium homeostasis inside the cell by affecting the influx of calcium into the cytosol through either plasma membrane or vacuolar calcium channels, or by action on efflux ATPases or proton cotransporters. This increase in cytosolic calcium leads to the activation of calmodulin (CAM), which binds to glutamate decarboxylase (GAD) converting it from the inactive to the active form. Glutamate conversion to γ-aminobutyric acid (GABA) is then accomplished consuming protons in the process and mediating an increase in cytosolic pH. CAX1 and CAX2 are transport proteins, ACA: Ca^{2+} ATPase.

Heat shock is a short- or longer-term increase of temperature within the range of temperature which can still be tolerated.

The so-called **heat shock reaction** of the cell is quite a different matter. For plants with a temperature optimum between 15°C and 25°C, this reaction takes place at temperatures above +35 PC and consists of:

(i) The slowing down of housekeeping reactions particularly of the expression of the housekeeping genes.

(ii) An almost exclusive synthesis of so-called **heat shock proteins** (HSPs).

(iii) Cessation of the production of the HSPs after 6-8 h.

(iv) A gradual resumption of the expression of the housekeeping genes.

Most HSPs are constitutively expressed proteins, so called **molecular chaperones** (governesses), and are present under 'normal' conditions only in very small amounts. During stress, the housekeeping genes are 'switched off' and subsequently only HSPs are produced.

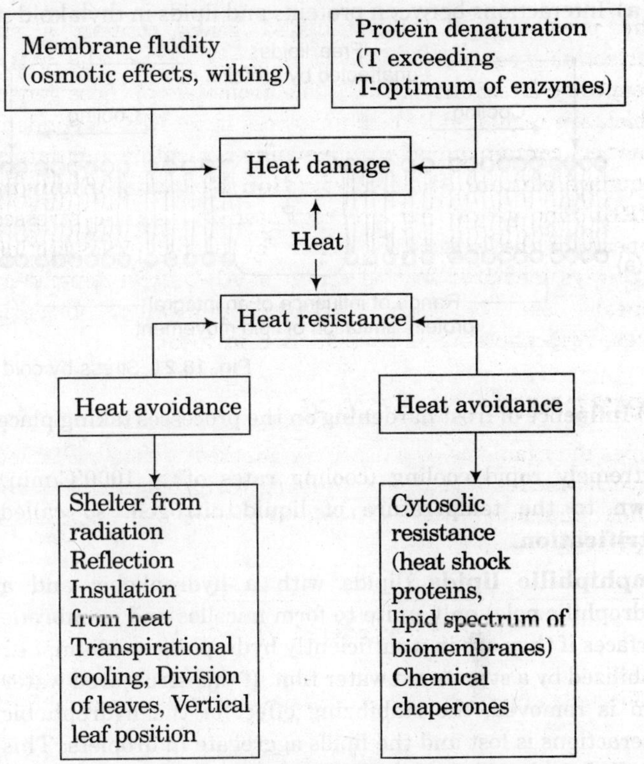

Fig. 18.19 The effects of heat on plants and the ways in which they react to the heat stress

Function of Heat Shock Proteins

Heat shock proteins have atleast three different functions in relation to the stresses which denature proteins:

(a) Chaperone function.

(b) Conservation of housekeeping *m*RNA in HS granules.

(c) Catalyzing proteolysis of irreversibly denatured, aggregated proteins.

Table 18.6 **The Five Classes of Heat Shock Proteins Found in Plants**

HSP Class	Size (kDa)	Examples (*Arabidopsis*/Prokaryotic)	Cellular Location
HSP 100	100-114	AtHSP101/ ClpB and ClpA/C	Cytosol, mitochondria and chloroplasts
HSP 90	80-94	AtHSP90/HtpG	Cytosol and endoplasmic reticulum
HSP 70	69-71	AtHSP70/Dnak	Cytosol/nucleus, mitochondria and chloroplasts
HSP 60	57-60	AtTCP-1/GroEL and GroES	Mitochondria and chloroplasts
smHSP	15-30	Various AtHSP22, AtHSP20, AtHSP 18.2 and AtHSP17.6/IBPA/B	Cytosol, mitochondria, chloroplasts and endoplasmic reticulum

Cold stress above the freezing point, so called **chilling** and stress by frost, *i.e.*, at temperatures below the freezing point, which always includes a temperature component and a desiccation component caused by ice formation.

In heat stress the physiological strain occurs through the (dissimilar) speeding up of metabolic processes culminating in the specific heat stress response. While metabolic processes also get out of equilibrium during cold stress due to the different activation energies of individual reactions.

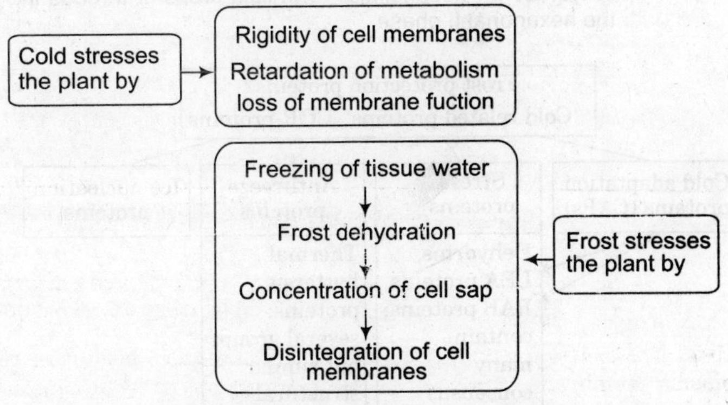

Fig. 18.20 Stress from cold and frost

(a) Interactions between proteins and lipids in thylakoid membranes during cooling.

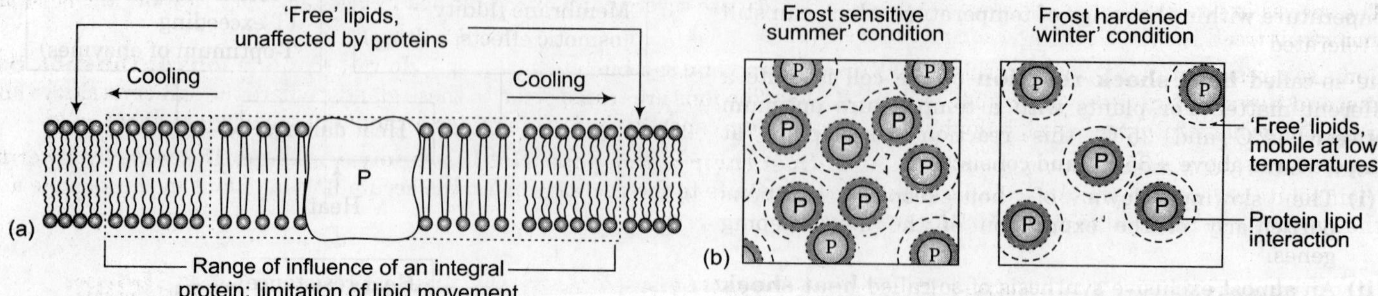

Fig. 18.21 Stress by cold above the freezing point (chilling)

(b) Influence of frost hardening on the processes taking place during cooling of the thylakoid membranes of *Pinus sylvestris.*

Extremely rapid cooling (cooling rates of > 1000'C/min) down to the temperature of liquid nitrogen, so called **vitrification.**

Amphiphilic lipids (lipids with a hydrophobic and a hydrophilic pole) only unite to form micelles and membrane surfaces if they are in a sufficiently hydrophilic medium, *i.e.,* stabilized by a structured water film. If this structured water film is removed, the stabilizing effect of the hydrophobic interactions is lost and the lipids aggregate in droplets: This is called the lipid hexagonal II phase.

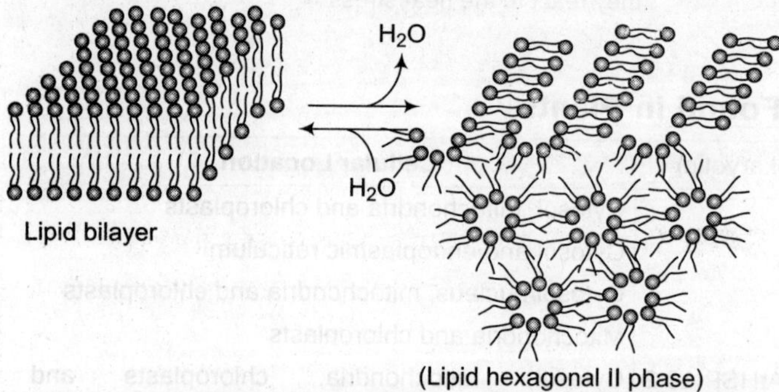

Fig. 18.22 Disintegration and reconstruction of a phospholipid bilayer by water removal (*e.g.,* freeze dehydration) and rehydration. Phospholipids form lipid drops or threads in the hexagonal II phase

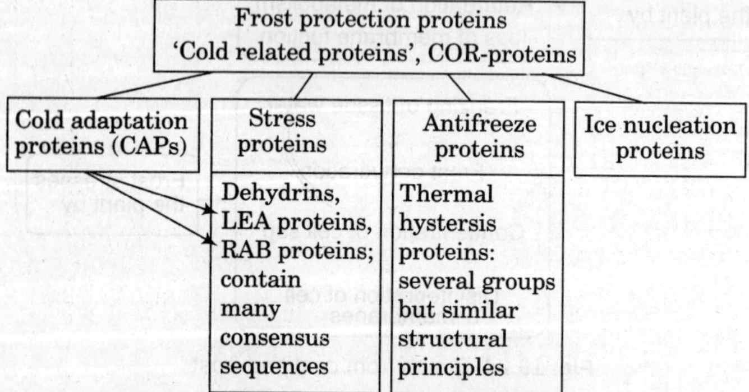

Fig. 18.23 The different types of frost protection proteins

Salt Stress

Salts found in nature (mainly NaCl and $CaSO_4$) may occur at concentrations which are either toxic, tolerated or even required as an osmoticum and plants are accordingly referred to as glycophytes (non-salt plants) or halophytes (salt plants).

Species Relative to Salinity

The growth of different species subjected to salinity relative to that of unsalinized controls. The curves dividing the regions are based on data for different species. Plants were grown for 1 to 6 months.

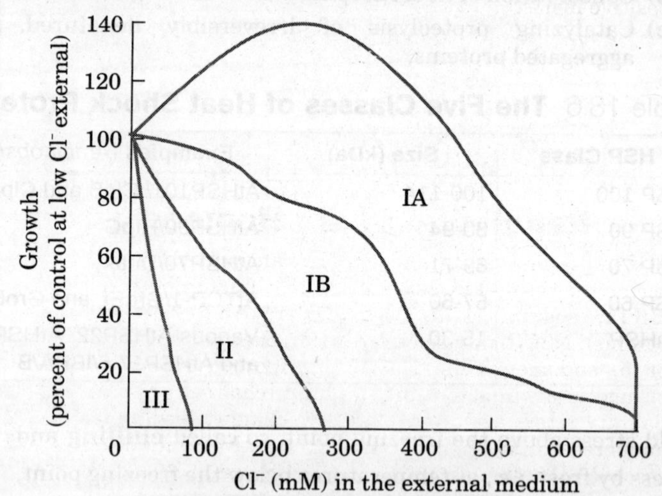

Fig. 18.24 Species relative to salinity

Group IA (halophytes) includes sea blite (*Suaeda maritima*) and salt bush (*Atriplex nummularai*). These species show growth stimulation with Cl^- levels below 400 nM.

Group IB (halophytes) includes Townsend's cordgrass (*Spartinari townsendii*) and sugarbeet (*Beta vulgaris*). These plants tolerate salt, but their growth is retarded.

Group II (halophytes and non-halophytes) includes salt-tolerant halophytic grasses that lack salt glans, such as *Festuca rubra* subsp. red descue (*Littoralis*) and *Puccinellia peisonis* and non-halophytes, such as cotton (*Gossypium* sp.) and barely (*Hordeum vulgare*). All are inhibited by high salt concentatios. Within this group, tomato (*Lycopersicon esculentum*) is intermediate, and common bean (*Phaseolus vulgaris*) and soyabean (*Glycine max*) are sensitive.

The species in Group III(very salt-sensitive non-halophytes) are severely inhibited or killed by low salt concentration. Included are many fruit trees, such as citrus, avocado and stome fruit.

Some salt-resistant plants, such as salt cedar (*Tamarix* sp.) and salt bush (*Atriplex* sp.), **do not exclude ions at the root, but instead have salt glands** at the surface of the leaves. The ions are transported to these glands, where the salt crystallizes and is no longer harmful. In general, halophytes have a greater capacity than glycophytes for ion accumulation in shoot cells.

Some plants, such as mangroves, plant cells can **adjust their water potential in response to osmotic stress** by lowering their solute potential. Two intracellular processes contribute to the decrease in *Ys*: the accumulation of ions in the vacuole and the synthesis of compatible solutes in the cytosol.

Membrane Transport Proteins Mediating Sodium, Potassium and Calcium Transport during Salinity Stress

SOS1, plasma membrane Na^+/H^+ antiporter; ACA, plasma/tonoplast membrane Ca^{2+}-ATPase; KUP1/TRH1, high-affinity K^+-H^+ co-transporter; atHKT1, sodium influx transporter; AKT1, K^+ in channel; NSCC, non-selective cation channel; CAX1 or 2, Ca^{2+}/H^+ antiporter; atNHX1, 2 or 5, endomembrane Na^+/H^+ antiporter. Also indicated in the figure are proteins that have been implicated in ion homeostasis, but whose molecular identity is either not presently known or cofirmed in plants. These include plasma membrane and tonoplast calcium channel proteins and vacuolar proton-pumping ATPases and pyrophosphatases. The membrane potential difference across the plasma membrane is typically 120 to 200 mV, negative inside; across the tonoplast 0 to 20 mV; positive inside.

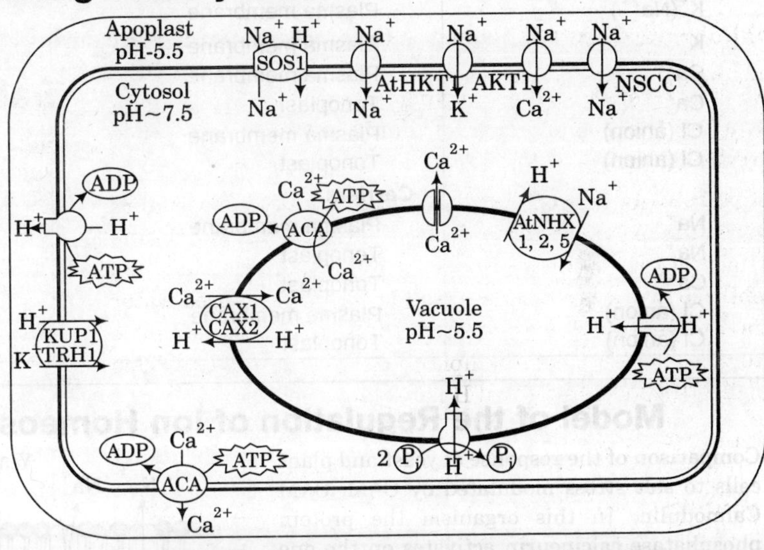

Fig. 18.25 Transport of cations during salinity stress

Regulation of Ion Homeostasis by the SOS Signal Transduction Pathway

SOS1, plasma membrane Na^+/H^+ antiporter; SOS2, serine/threonine kinase; SOS3, Ca^{2+} binding protein; HKT1, sodium influx transporter; AKT1, K^+ in channel; NSCC, non-selective cation channel; NHX1, 2 or 5, endomembrane Na^+/H^+ antiporter; shown in orange is an undetermined calcium channel protein. Salinity stress activates a calcium channel leading to an increase in cytosolic calcium that activates the SOS cascade through SOS3. The SOS cascade must negatively regulate HKT1 which in turn secondarily regulates AKT1. At the same time, the SOS cascade increases the activity of SOS1 and AKT1. Working through an as yet undefined transcription factor the SOS cascade increases transcription of SOS1, while decreasing transcription of NHX gene(s). At low calcium NSCC can also function as an alternative sodium influx system, but this transporter is inhibited at high calcium levels. The membrane potential difference across the plasma membrane is typically 120 to 200 mV, negative inside, that of the tonoplast is 0 to 20 mV, positive inside.

Red arrows indicate positive regulation of the effected transport protein while blue arrows indicate negative regulation. Proteins shown in yellow are activated by salinity stress.

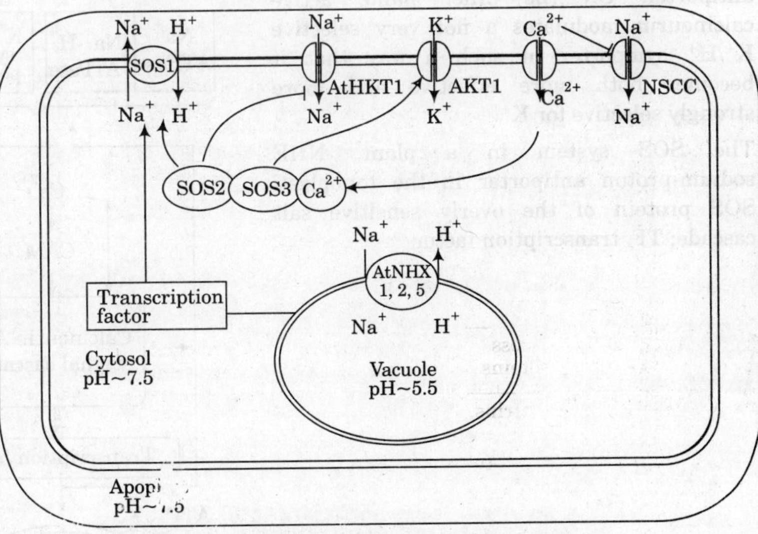

Fig. 18.26 SOS singal transduction pathway

Table 18.7 **Transport Systems Potentially Involved in Ion Homeostasis in the Plasma Membrane and the Tonoplast**

Substrate	Sub-cellular Localization	Direction	Source of Energy or Counter Ion
	Pumps		
H^+	Plasma membrane	Apoplast	ATP
H^+	Tonoplast	Vacuole	ATP
H^+	Tonoplast	Vacuole	PP
Ca^{2+}	Plasma membrane	Apoplast	ATP
Ca^{2+}	Tonoplast	Vacuole	ATP
	Channels		
$K^+(Na^{2+})$	Plasma membrane	Cytosol	Membrane potential
$K^+(Na^{2+})$	Plasma membrane	Cytosol	H^+ (symport)
K^+	Plasma membrane	Cytosol	H^+ Na^+ (symport)
Ca^{2+}	Plasma membrane	Cytosol	Membrane potential
Ca^{2+}	Tonoplast	Cytosol	Membrane potential
Cl (anion)	Plasma membrane	Apoplast	Membrane potential
Cl (anion)	Tonoplast	Vacuole	Membrane potential
	Carriers		
Na^+	Plasma membrane	Apoplast	H^+ (antiport)
Na^+	Tonoplast	Vacuole	H^+ (antiport)
Ca^{2+}	Tonoplast	Vacuole	H^+ (antiport)
Cl (anion)	Plasma membrane	Cytosol	H^+ (symport)
Cl (anion)	Tonoplast	Vacuole	H^+ (antiport)

Model of the Regulation of Ion Homeostasis by Ca^{2+} Under Salt Stress

Comparison of the response of yeast and plant cells to salt stress modulated by CAM. CAM Calmodulin. In this organism the protein phosphatase calcineurin activates on the one hand transcription factors, which lead to increased expression of a plasma membrane Na^+-ATPase and a tonoplastic Na^+/H^+ antiporter. On the other hand, active calcineurin modulates a not very selective K^+/H^+ symporter in such a way that it becomes both more effective and more strongly selective for K^+.

The SOS system in a plant. NHE sodium-proton antiporter in the tonoplast; SOS protein of the overly sensitive salt cascade; TF, transcription factor.

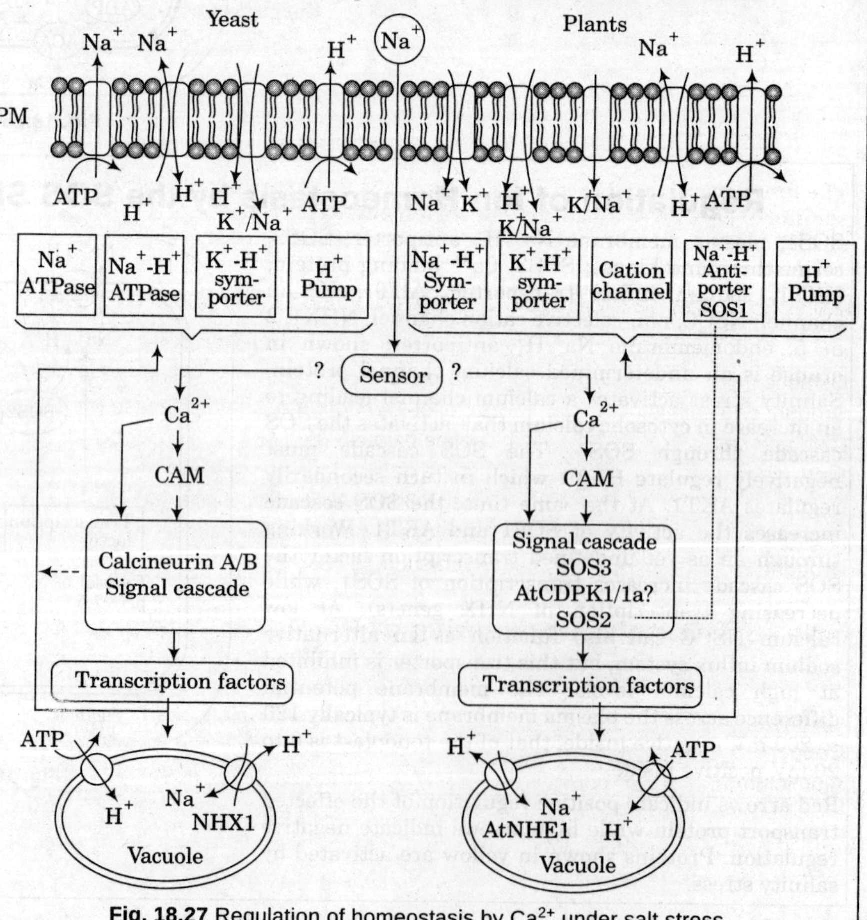

Fig. 18.27 Regulation of homeostasis by Ca^{2+} under salt stress

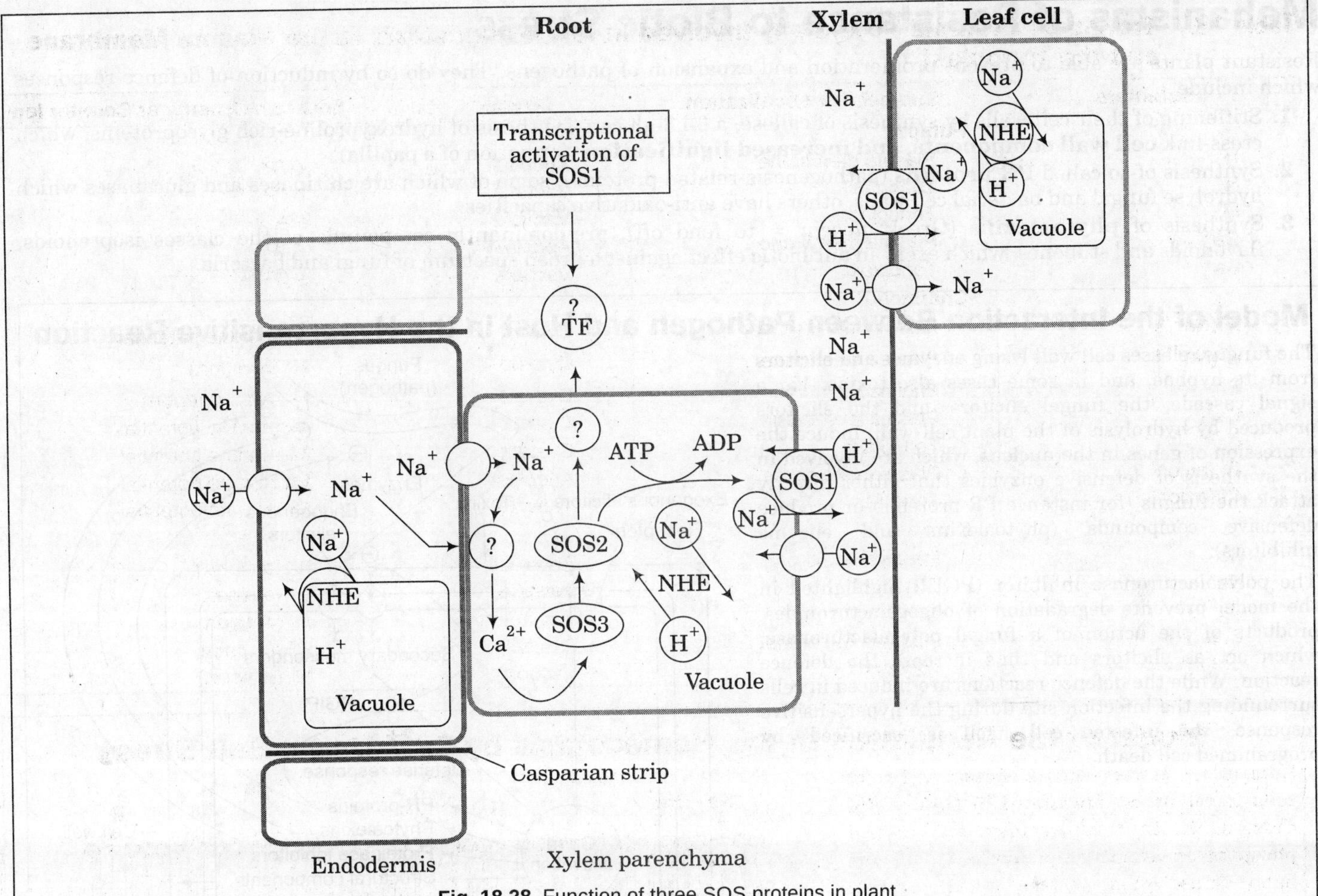

Fig. 18.28 Function of three SOS proteins in plant

The functions of three SOS proteins have now been elucidated: SOS1 is a Na^+-H^+ antiporter in the plasma membrane, **SOS2 is a serinethreonine protein kinase which activates SOS1,** and SOS3 is a calcium-binding protein with an EF-hand domain typical of such proteins, which - after being activated - itself activates SOS2.

Table 18.8 **Genetic Engineering of Plants for Tolerance to Abiotic Stresses**

Stress	Gene/Enzyme	Source
Osmotic	Delta-pyrrolling-5-carboxylate synthetase (P5CS)	Mothbean (*V. aconitifolia*)
Drought and salinity	Mannitol-1-phosphate dehydrogenase (mt 1D)	*E. coli*
Cold and salt	Choline oxidase (cod A)	*Arthrobactor gobiformis*
Salt	Choline dehydrogenase (bet A)	*E. coli*
Cold	Omega-3-fatty acid desaturase (fad 7)	*Arabidopsis*
Drought	Trehalose-6-phosphate synthase	Yeast
Drought	Levan sucrase (Sac B)	*Bacillus subtilis*

Table 18.9 **Genetic Engineering of Plants for Tolerance to Heavy Metal**

Stress	Gene/Enzyme	Source
Cadmium	Metallothionein-I (MT-I)	Mouse
Copper	Metallothionein-like (PsMTA)	Pea
Aluminium	Citrate synthase (CSb)	*P. aeruginosa*

Mehanisms of Resistance to Biotic Stress

Resistant plants are able to prevent proliferation and expansion of pathogens. They do so by induction of defence responses which include

1. Stiffening of their cell walls by synthesis of callose, a β-1,3-glucan, synthesis of hydroxyproline-rich glycoproteins, which cross-link **cell wall components, and increased lignification** (formation of a papilla).
2. Synthesis of so called **PR proteins** (pathogenesis-related proteins), some of which are chitinases and glucanases which hydrolyse fungal and bacterial cell walls, others have anti-oxidative capacities.
3. Synthesis of **phytoalexins** (Greek *alekein* = to fend off), pre-dominantly compounds of the classes isoprenoids, flavonoids and stilbenes, which exert an antibiotic effect against a broad spectrum of fungi and bacteria.

Model of the Interaction Between Pathogen and Host in the Hypersensitive Reaction

The fungus releases cell wall lysing enzymes and elicitors from its hyphae, and in some cases also toxins. *Via* a signal cascade, the fungal elicitors, and the elicitors produced by hydrolysis of the plant cell wall, induce the expression of genes in the nucleus, which are involved in the synthesis of defensive enzymes that either directly attack the fungus (for instance PR proteins) or produce defensive compounds (phytoalexins and enzyme inhibitors).

The polygalacturonase inhibitor (PGIP) highlighted in the model prevents degradation of oligogalacturonides, products of the action of a fungal polygalacturonase, which act as elicitors and thus increase the defence reaction. While the defence reactions are induced in cells surrounding the infection site during the hypersensitive response, the infected cell itself is 'sacrificed' by programmed cell death.

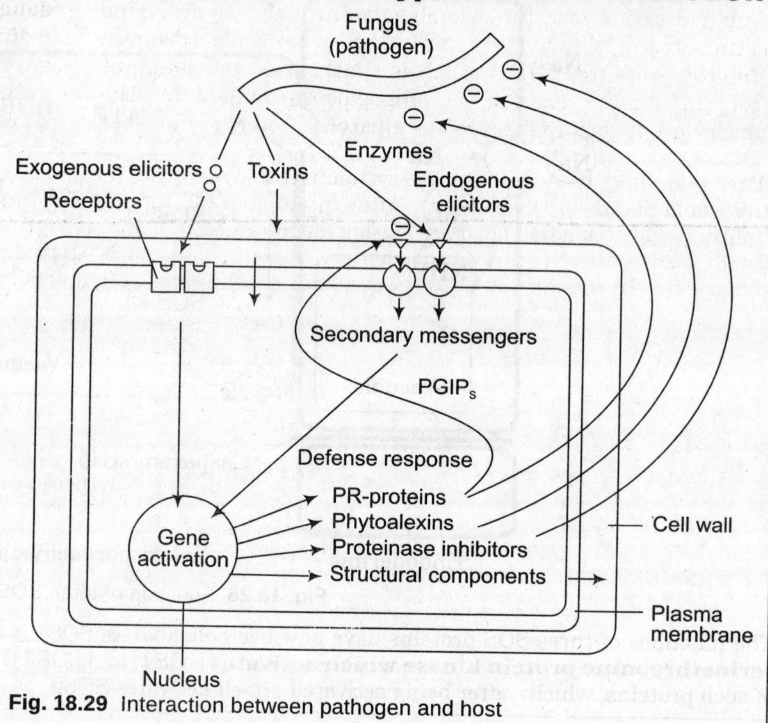

Fig. 18.29 Interaction between pathogen and host

The defence responses are induced in cells surrounding the infested cell. One mediator of the induction of **PR proteins is salicylic acid**. Salicylic acid can be produced *via* several biosynthetic pathways, either *via* cinnamic acid coenzyme-A thioester or *via* cinnamic acid glucose ester.

L-phenylalanine
PAL
Co-A-ligase
Cinnamoyl Co-A
Benzoyl Co-A
Salicyloyl-Co-A
trans-cinnamic acid
Free benzoic acid
Salicylic acid
C4H
GTase
p-coumaric acid
Lignin
Phytoalexins
Cinnamoyl-glucose
Benzoyl-glucose
Salicyloyl-glucose ester
Salicin

Fig. 18.30 Biosynthetic pathways of salicylic acid

In resistant plants, the infested cell itself often dies by programmed cell death, the final result of the so called **hypersensitive response (HR)**

Plants contain **R genes** (resistance genes), while pathogens contain **avr genes** (avirulence genes) or **vir genes** (virulence genes). The products of R genes are often integral plasma membrane proteins which function as receptors. Binding of a proper elicitor to the receptor then induces *via* a signal transduction chain–the defence responses.

The products of avr genes may be the elicitors in most cases, avr genes encode proteins which are involved in the **synthesis of elicitors**. This elicitor is produced by the combined action of a fungal polygalacturonase (hydrolysing pectin of the plant cell wall) and a polygalacturonase inhibitor protein (PGIP), which is synthesized by the plant after infection, leading to oligogalacturonides of the appropriate length to function as elicitor.

Many interactions between plants and herbivores and plants and pathogens are known. Less well known is that plants affect the growth of other plants. Such a phenomenon, allelopathy (Greek *allelos,* 'another'; *pathos*, 'suffering').

The classical **example for allelopathy** is the inhibitory effect on germination by leaves of the walnut trees *(Juglans regia* and *J. nigra)*. The inhibition is caused by juglone (1-hydroxynaphthalene), which is formed from 5-glucosyl-1, 4, 5-trihydroxynaphthalene under the influence of bacteria.

A good **example of intraspecific allelopathy** is shown by several representatives of the genus *Kalanchoe,* where root exudates from the mother plant inhibit growth of the daughter plants which are formed at the edge of the leaf. The main components of the root exudate (in decreasing amounts) are gallic acid, caffeic acid, *p*-hydroxybenzoic acid, protocatechuic acid and *p*-coumaric acid, again all phenolic substances.

After wounding, the signal peptide systemin is released from the precursor protein prosystemin. Systemin is distributed throughout the whole plant *via* the phloem. After interaction of systemin with its receptor and/or by influence of other exogenous factors, linolenic acid is released from the plasma membrane. Linolenic acid is the starting point of the so called octadecanoid pathway, which finally leads to the synthesis of jasmonate. The phytohormone ABA may modulate the activity of this pathway. Jasmonate in turn induces the expression of defence genes, often in combined action with ethylene.

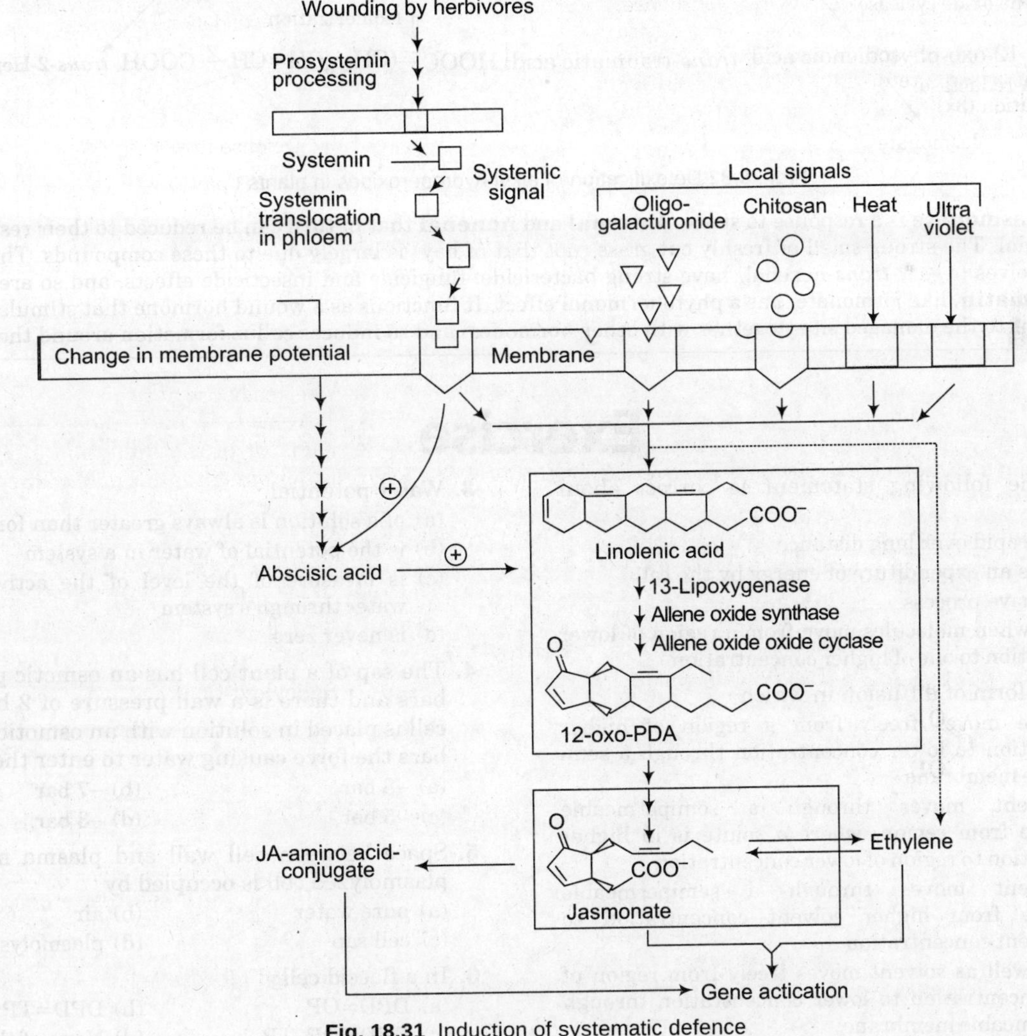

Fig. 18.31 Induction of systematic defence

Metabolism (Detoxification) of Alkyl Hydroperoxides in Plants

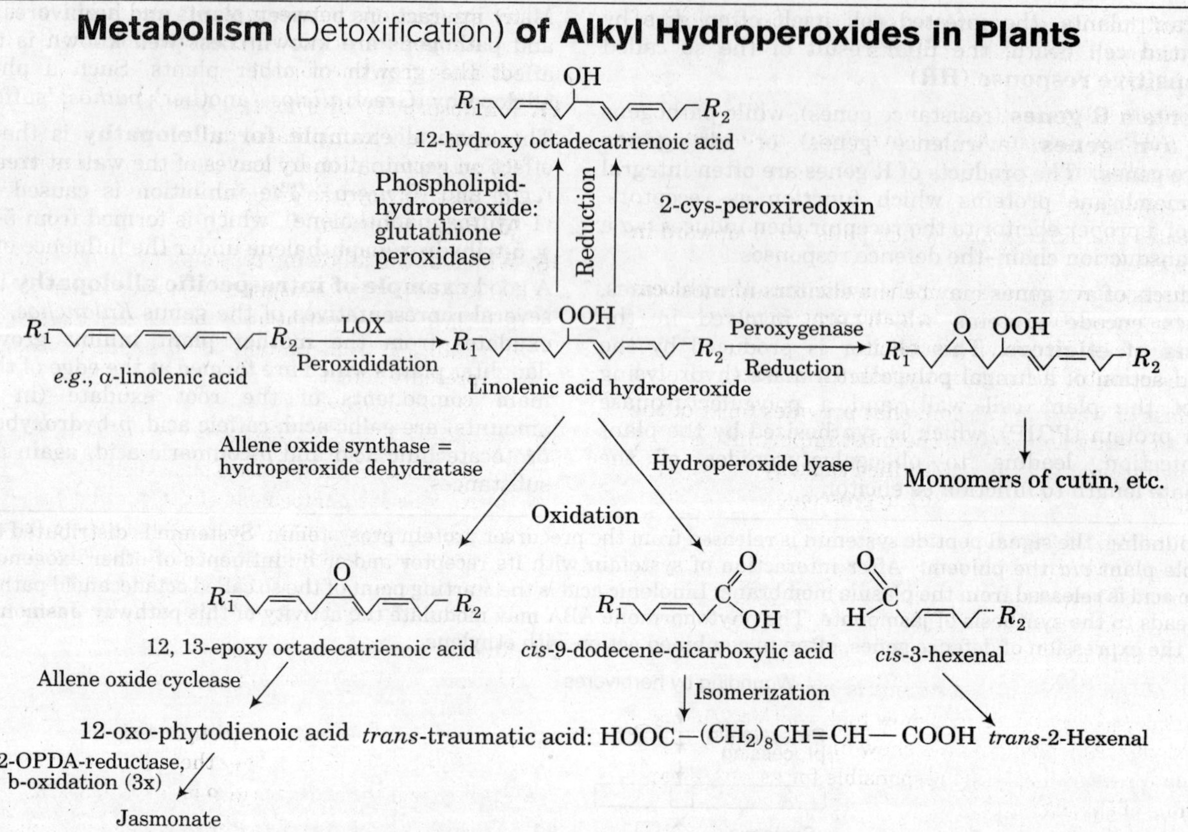

Fig. 18.32 Detoxification of alkyl hydroperoxides in plants

The formation of **jasmonate** is a response to stress. **Hexenal** and **nonenal** that in turn can be reduced to their respective alcohols hexanol and nonenol. The strong smell of freshly cut grass (not that of hay) is largely due to these compounds. The **unsaturated aldehydes** themselves (*e.g.*, 2-*trans*-hexenal) have strong bactericide, fungicide and insecticide effects, and so are potent defence compounds. **Traumatin**, like jasmonate, has a phytohormonal effect. It functions as a wound hormone that stimulates cell division in the cells adjacent to the damaged site (together with other hormones) and so induces callus formation around the wound.

Exercise

1. Which of the following statement is correct about diffusion?
(a) It is very rapid over long distance
(b) It requires an expenditure of energy by the cell
(c) It is a passive process
(d) It occurs when molecules move from a region of lower concentration to one of higher concentration

2. Osmosis is a form of diffusion in which
(a) the solute moves freely from a region of higher concentration to lower concentration through a semi permeable membrane
(b) the solvent moves through a semipermeable membrane from region, where a solute is in higher concentration to region of lower concentration
(c) the solvent moves through a semipermeable membrane from higher solvent concentration to lower solvent concentration
(d) solute as well as solvent moves freely from region of higher concentration to lower concentration through a semipermeable membrane

3. Water potential
(a) of a solution is always greater than for pure water
(b) is the potential of water in a system
(c) is measure of the level of the active movement of water through a system
(d) is never zero

4. The sap of a plant cell has an osmotic potential of –10 bars and there is a wall pressure of 2 bars. When this cell is placed in solution with an osmotic potential of –3 bars the force causing water to enter the cell is
(a) –8 bar (b) –7 bar
(c) –5 bar (d) –3 bar

5. Space between cell wall and plasma membrane in a plasmolyzed cell is occupied by
(a) pure water (b) air
(c) cell sap (d) plasmolysing solution

6. In a flaccid cell
(a) DPD=OP (b) DPD=TP
(c) DPD=OP–TP (d) None of these

7. Which of the following plays no role in the movement of water through the xylem of plants?
(a) Capillarity
(b) Root pressure
(c) H^+/ATPase pump at the xylem element membrane
(d) Transpirational pull

8. Water cohesion
(a) creates the pulling force which pulls water upward in the xylem
(b) causes water to move from the xylem into the phloem in response to differences in water concentration
(c) is an energy requiring process
(d) is responsible for making the column of water

9. The class of water in the soil, that provides most of the water to plants and is thus the most important, is
(a) gravitational (b) flied capacity
(c) capillary (d) hygroscopic

10. Root pressure is a/an
(a) non-osmotic phenomenon
(b) osmotic phenomenon
(c) positive hydrostatic pressure
(d) more than one correct

11. Which of the following statement is correct?
(a) Members of gymnosperm show high root pressure
(b) Activity transpiring plants show high root pressure
(c) Root pressure is mainly responsible for ascent of sap
(d) None of the above

12. Transpiration pull depends on
(a) adhesion of water molecules to the walls of phloem cells
(b) capillarity
(c) the very negative water potential of the atmosphere
(d) cohesion of water molecules to each other

13. The source of energy driving the transport of water through the xylem is
(a) ATP produced by photosynthesis
(b) ATP generated by respiration
(c) the sun
(d) transpiration

14. Which of the following properties of water is most directly related to its ability to rise in the capillary spaces of plants?
(a) Neutral pH
(b) High density
(c) Low compressibility
(d) High surface tension

15. Which of the following observations shows that ion uptake in plants is energy dependent?
(a) Ion uptake shows saturation kinetics
(b) Ion uptake rates are different for different ions
(c) Some ions accumulate against a concentration gradient
(d) Some ions enter the symplast before reaching the endodermis

16. Ion absorption by plant roots
(a) can be explained by the nutrient-carrier hypothesis
(b) is basically ions passively soaking in root cells alongwith soil water
(c) explains the movement of ions from a dilute soil solution into a more concentrated solution
(d) more than one correct

17. Ion absorption by symplast occurs
(a) passively by facilitated diffusion
(b) actively by primary and secondary active transport
(c) passively by free diffusion
(d) Both (a) and (b)

18. Which of the following statement(s) is/are correct?
(a) Water lost by transpiration is pure water
(b) The cause of guttation is mainly root pressure
(c) Rate of transpiration is dependent upon vapour pressure deficit
(d) All of the above

19. Stomatal pores open when
(a) H^+ ions are pumped into guard cells
(b) K^+ ions are pumped out of the guard cells
(c) water moves into the guard cells in response to decrease in water potential in the guard cells
(d) water moves out of the guard cells in response to a decrease in water potential of the guard cells

20. Most of the water taken up by the plant is
(a) spilt during photosynthesis as a source of electrons and hydrogen
(b) lost by transpiration through stomata
(c) absorbed by cells during their elongation
(d) incorporated directly into organic material

21. The part of root involved in water absorption is zone of
(a) cell division (b) root hairs
(c) elongation (d) root cap

22. In plants, water rises upwards through
(a) cambium (b) stomata
(c) xylem (d) phloem

23. When water enters the cell, one of the pressures is exerted on cell wall
(a) osmotic pressure (b) suction pressure
(c) turgor pressure (d) root pressure

24. Diffusion of water through semipermeable membrane from dilute solution to concentrated solution is
(a) imbibition (b) osmosis
(c) plasmolysis (d) necrosis

25. Osmosis is the diffusion of
(a) water (b) solute particles
(c) gases (d) energy

26. The membrane which allows the movement of only water molecules to pass through it and not the solute particles
(a) permeable membrane
(b) semipermeable membrane
(c) impermeable membrane
(d) not permeable

27. The membrane which allows passage of solvent as well as some selective solutes and prevents others is called
(a) permeable membrane
(b) semipermeable membrane
(c) selectively permeable membrane
(d) impermeable membrane

28. Cell wall of root hair has two layers outer and inner which are made up of
(a) pectin and lignin respectively
(b) pectin and cellulose respectively
(c) cellulose and pectin respectively
(d) lignin and cellulose respectively

29. The outer solution having equal concentration as that of the cell sap is called
(a) hypotonic solution (b) isotonic solution
(c) hypertonic solution (d) neutral solution

30. The process of imbibition involves
(a) diffusion (b) capillary action
(c) absorption (d) Both (a) and (b)

31. A cell increase in volume when it is placed in
(a) hypertonic solution (b) hypotonic solution
(c) isotonic solution (d) None of these

32. Which of the following will be zero in a fully turgid cell?
(a) Wall pressure (b) Suction pressure (DPD)
(c) Turgor pressure (d) Imbibitional pressure

33. Endosmosis occurs when the plant cell is placed in
(a) strong solution (b) isotonic solution
(c) hypotonic solution (d) hypertonic solution

34. Cell becomes turgid because of
(a) plasmolysis (b) exosmosis
(c) endosmosis (d) diffusion

35. Pressure developed on cell wall of plant cell caused by osmotic movement of water is called as
(a) turgor pressure (b) osmotic pressure
(c) suction pressure (d) DPD

36. Isoprenoids, alkaloids and flavonoids are the example of
(a) secondary metabolites (b) essential nutrients
(c) plant hormones (d) plant scents

37. Which of the following is derived as a product of Shikimate pathway?
(a) Aromatic amino acids (b) Hydroxyl benzoic acid
(c) Aliphatic amino acid (d) Both (a) and (b)

38. Alkaloids and flavonoids are derived from
(a) hydroxyl benzoic acid (b) aromatic amino acids
(c) aliphatic amino acids (d) 6-deoxyxylulose

39. Which of the following is an example of secondary metabolite?
(a) Abietic acid (b) Kaurenoic acid
(c) Pipecolic acid (d) Both (a) and (c)

40. 29000 terpenes derived from the isopentenyl diphosphate (IPP) precursor which is .... in nature?
(a) C3 (b) C4
(c) C5 (d) C6

41. Find out the mismatch.

	Metabolite		Compartment
(a)	Chloroplast		Alkaloid and terpenoids
(b)	Mitochondria	—	Some amine and alkaloids
(c)	Vesicles	—	Protoberberines
(d)	ER	—	Hydrophilic compounds

42. Water soluble secondary metabolites are generally stored in
(a) vacuole (b) resin ducts
(c) glandular hairs (d) trichomes

43. Rubber is an example of
(a) secondary metabolite
(b) an essential compound to plant
(c) non useful for humans
(d) protective component for plant

44. Which of the following statement proves the hypothesis that secondary metabolites are not a waste product to plants?
(a) Production of SMs in young tissues
(b) Plants are autotrophs and waste products are typical and needed for heterotrophic animals that cannot degrade their food completely for energy production
(c) Tight spatial and temporal regulation of SMs biosynthesis
(d) All of the above

45. Find out the unmatch one.

	Metabolite		Compartment
(a)	Rutin	—	Visual pollinator attractant
(b)	Rotenone	—	Insect feeding deterrent
(c)	DIMBOA	—	Olfactory pollinator attractant
(d)	Brassilexin	—	Antifungal toxin

46. Which of the following is potential targets for different plant secondary metabolites?
(a) Nervous system (b) Muscles and motility
(c) Digestion (d) All of these

47. Which of the following statement is false regarding secondary metabolite?
(a) These are exclusively produced by plants
(b) They serve various functions like protection against pests, as colouring, scent or attractants and as the plant's own hormones
(c) Secondary metabolite is of no use in human physiology
(d) Secondary metabolites do not have nutrient characteristics for human beings

48. Plant phenolics are biosynthesized by
(a) shikimic acid pathway (b) malonic acid pathway
(c) Both (a) and (b) (d) None of these

49. Halophytes such as mangroves meet high osmotic pressure in the soil. They overcome the problem of water uptake by
(a) increase in the root to shoot ratio
(b) reduction in the number of stomata to reduce transpiration
(c) accumulation of electrolytes in the vacuoles
(d) growth at relatively high humidity to reduce transpiration

50. If both leaf water potential and leaf osmotic potential in mid afternoon on a hot summer day equal-15 bars
(a) the leaf is probably wilted
(b) the whole plant is at the permanent wilting point
(c) leaf cells have highest wall pressure
(d) the soil is at the plant's permanent wilting point

51. Various physiological responses of *Arabidopsis* upon exposure to salinity is an example of
(a) hormonal control (b) plant movement
(c) response toward stress (d) None of these

52. The non-living variable must influence the
(a) cell constituent (b) tissue formation
(c) Both (a) and (b) (d) environment

53. Biotic stress includes living disturbances as
(a) fungi (b) insects
(c) Both (a) and (b) (d) green plants

54. World wide abiotic stress is the most harmful factor concerning
(a) the growth of crops (b) the productivity of crops
(c) Both (a) and (b) (d) None of these

55. Abiotic stressors include
(a) high winds (b) extreme temperature
(c) drought (d) All of these

56. A plant's is first line of defense against abiotic stress lies in its
(a) leaf (b) root
(c) stem (d) leaf apex

57. If a plant cell is placed in deionized water the water potential of that cell becomes
(a) more positive because the pressure potential become more positive
(b) more positive because the osmotic potential becomes more negative
(c) more negative because the pressure potential becomes more negative
(d) less negative because the pressure potential becomes more positive

58. Which of the following observations provides direct support for Munch's hypothesis?
(a) Transpiration occurs from open stomata on leaves and stems during the day
(b) Turgor pressure in the sieve tubes of a fully expanded tomato leaf is higher than the turgor in the sieve tubes of a developing tomato fruit
(c) Carbohydrates move within the plant from sink to source
(d) The osmotic potential of the sieve tubes in a root tip is more negative than that of the sieve tubes in the leaf

59. Transport of the products of photosynthesis is thought to occur by pressure flow through the sieve tubes of the phloem from a source to a sink which of the following statements about phloem transport is false?
(a) Water enters the sieve tubes by osmosis
(b) Sieve tubes in a source have a low hydrostatic pressure
(c) Water and solutes move through the sieve tubes along a pressure gradient
(d) Solutes are swept along by the bulk flow of water in the sieve tube

60. The negative impact of non-living factors on the living organisms in a specific environment, is called
(a) abiotic stress (b) biotic stress
(c) fecundity (d) stratification

61. Which of the following is not a difference between sugar translocation in phloem (sieve tubes) and water movement in the xylem (vessels or tracheids)?
(a) Sugar translocation is a metabolically active process, while water movement is entirely passive
(b) Pressure in positive in sieve tubes, while xylem is usually under tension
(c) Sieve tubes are living cells, while mature xylem is dead
(d) All of the above

62. Match list I and list II and select the correct answer using the codes given below the lists.

List I	List II
A. Chloride	1. Essential for the biosynthesis of indole-3-acetic acid
B. Zinc	2. Enzyme activator for photolysis
C. Boron	3. Necessary for translocation of sugars

Codes

	A	B	C
(a)	1	2	3
(b)	2	1	3
(c)	2	3	1
(d)	3	1	2

63. Match the following list I (essential elements) with list II (their respective roles) and select the correct answer using the codes given below the lists.

List I	List II
A. Chlorine	1. Constituent of plastocyanin
B. Copper	2. Constituent of nitrate reductase
C. Molybdenum	3. Constituent of alcohol dehydrogenase
D. Zinc	4. Required for O_2 evolution in photosynthesis
	5. Required for phosphate transfer

Codes

	A	B	C	D
(a)	4	1	3	2
(b)	1	2	5	3
(c)	1	4	5	2
(d)	4	1	2	3

64. Match list I with list II and select the correct answer using the codes given below the lists.

List I	List II
A. Field capacity	1. Forces which hold water to the soil
B. Permanent wilting	2. Combined effect of accelerated water loss and retarded water absorption
C. Water deficit	3. Water content of a soil
D. Soil misture	4. Loss of water from plant with little chance of regaining turgidity

Codes

	A	B	C	D
(a)	3	4	2	1
(b)	1	2	3	4
(c)	2	4	3	1
(d)	3	1	2	4

65. Consider the following statements

Osmosis is a process of transport of water across a semipermeable membrane

I. down the water potential gradient.

II. up the water potential gradient.

III. up the water potential gradient.

IV. actively.

V. passively.

Of these statements

(a) I and III are correct (b) II and III are correct

(c) II and IV are correct (d) I and IV are correct

66. Match list I with list II.

List I (Essential Element)	List II (Deficiency Symptom)
A. Boron	1. Die-back disease
B. Copper	2. Interveinal chlorosis
C. Iron	3. Little leaf disease
D. Zinc	4. Terminal leaf necrosis

Codes

	A	B	C	D
(a)	1	4	3	2
(b)	1	4	2	3
(c)	4	1	3	2
(d)	4	1	2	3

67. Match list I with list II and select the correct answer using the codes given below the lists.

List I (Significance of the Phenomenon in Cell Water Relation)	List II (Quantity)
A. Degree of hydration of protoplasm	1. Wall pressure
B. Stretches cell walls and may lead to their enlargement if the walls are sufficiently plastic	2. Water potential
C. Increases the free energy of water molecule	3. Turgor pressure
D. Indicates the direction of diffusion of water	4. Osmotic potential

Codes

	A	B	C	D
(a)	1	3	2	4
(b)	4	3	1	2
(c)	4	1	2	3
(d)	3	4	2	1

Answers

1. (c)	**2.** (c)	**3.** (b)	**4.** (c)	**5.** (d)	**6.** (a)	**7.** (c)	**8.** (d)	**9.** (d)	**10.** (d)
11. (d)	**12.** (c)	**13.** (c)	**14.** (d)	**15.** (c)	**16.** (d)	**17.** (d)	**18.** (d)	**19.** (c)	**20.** (b)
21. (b)	**22.** (c)	**23.** (c)	**24.** (b)	**25.** (a)	**26.** (b)	**27.** (c)	**28.** (b)	**29.** (b)	**30.** (d)
31. (b)	**32.** (b)	**33.** (c)	**34.** (c)	**35.** (a)	**36.** (a)	**37.** (d)	**38.** (b)	**39.** (d)	**40.** (c)
41. (d)	**42.** (a)	**43.** (a)	**44.** (d)	**45.** (c)	**46.** (d)	**47.** (c)	**48.** (c)	**49.** (c)	**50.** (a)
51. (c)	**52.** (d)	**53.** (c)	**54.** (c)	**55.** (d)	**56.** (b)	**57.** (d)	**58.** (b)	**59.** (b)	**60.** (a)
61. (a)	**62.** (b)	**63.** (d)	**64.** (a)	**65.** (d)	**66.** (d)	**67.** (a)			

19 Digestion and Respiratory System

Digestive System

Syllabus

- Digestion
- Absorption
- Energy Balance
- BMR
- Transport of Gases
- Exchange of Gases
- Neural and Chemical Regulation of Respiration
- Comparison of Respiration in Different Species

The digestive tract organs in the body are amongst the most important ones. The 30+ foot long tube that goes from the mouth to the anus is responsible for the many different body functions. The gastrointestinal tract is imperative for our well being and our life-long health. A non-functioning or poorly functioning gastrointestinal tract can be the source of many chronic health problems that can interfere with your quality of life. In many instances the death of a person begins in the intestines.

The old saying 'you are what you eat' perhaps would be more accurate if worded 'you are what you absorb and digest'. Here we will be looking at the importance of these two functions of the digestive system—absorption and digestion.

Gastrointestinal Tract

The gastrointestinal system is responsible for the breakdown and absorption of various foods and liquids needed to sustain life. Many different organs have essential roles in the digestion of food, from the mechanical disrupting of the teeth to the creation of bile (an emulsifier) by the liver. Bile production of the liver plays an important role in digestion: from being stored and concentrated in the gall bladder during fasting stages to being discharged to the small intestine. In order to understand the interactions of the different components we shall follow the food on its journey through the human body. During digestion two main processes occur at the same time.

The GI tract starts with the mouth and proceeds to the oesophagus, stomach, small intestine (duodenum, jejunum, ileum), and then to the large intestine (colon), rectum, and terminates at the anus.

Layers of the GI Tract

The GI tract is composed of four layers, or tunics. Each layer has different tissues and functions. From the inside out they are called mucosa, submucosa, muscularis and serosa.

Mucosa

The mucosa is the absorptive and secretory layer. It is composed of simple epithelium cells and a thin connective tissue. There are specialized goblet cells that secrete mucus throughout the GI tract located within the mucosa. On the mucosa layer there are villi and microvilli.

Submucosa

The submucosa is relatively thick, is highly vascular and serves the mucosa. The absorbed elements that pass through the mucosa are picked up from the blood vessels of the submucosa. The submucosa also has glands and nerve plexuses.

Muscularis

The muscularis is responsible for segmental contractions and peristaltic movement in the GI tract. The muscularis is composed of two layers of muscle—an inner circular and outer longitudinal layer of smooth muscle. These muscles cause food to move and churn with digestive enzymes down the GI tract.

Serosa

The last layer is a protective layer. It is composed of a vascular connective tissue and simple squamous epithelium. It secretes lubricating serous fluid. This is the visible layer on the outside of the organs.

Accessory Organs

(i) Salivary glands
- **(a)** Parotid gland
- **(b)** Submandibular gland
- **(c)** Sublingual gland

(ii) Tongue
(iii) Teeth
(iv) Liver
(v) Gall bladder
Bile storage
(vi) Pancreas
(vii) Vermiform appendix

Digestion

The first step in the digestive system can actually begin before the food is even in your mouth. When you smell or see something that you just have to eat, you start to salivate in anticipation of eating, thus beginning the digestive process.

Food is the body's source of fuel. Nutrients in food give the body's cells the energy they need to operate. Before food can be used it has to be broken down into tiny little pieces so it can be absorbed and used by the body. In human, proteins need to be broken down into amino acids, starches into sugars, and fats into fatty acids and glycerol.

During digestion two main processes occur at the same time.

Mechanical Digestion

Larger pieces of food get broken down into smaller pieces while being prepared for chemical digestion. Mechanical digestion starts in the mouth and continues into the stomach.

Chemical Digestion

Several different enzymes breakdown macromolecules into smaller molecules that can be more efficiently absorbed. Chemical digestion starts with saliva and continues into the intestines.

The digestive system is made up by the alimentary canal, or the digestive tract, and other abdominal organs that play a part in digestion such as the liver and the pancreas. The alimentary canal is the long tube of organs that runs from the mouth (where the food enters) to the anus (where indigestible waste leaves). The organs in the alimentary canal include the esophagus, stomach and the intestines. The average adult digestive tract is about thirty feet (30′) long. While in the digestive tract the food is really passing through the body rather than being in the body. The smooth muscles of the tubular digestive organs move the food efficiently along as it is broken down into absorbable atoms and molecules. During absorption, the nutrients that come from food (such as proteins, fats, carbohydrates, vitamins and minerals) pass through the wall of the small intestine and into the blood stream and lymph. In this way nutrients can be distributed throughout the rest of the body. In the large intestine there is reabsorption of water and absorption of some minerals as faces are formed. The parts of the food that the body passes out through the anus is known as faeces.

Mastication

Digestion begins in the mouth. A brain reflex triggers the flow of saliva when we see or even think about food. Saliva moistens the food while the teeth chew it up and make it easier to swallow. Amylase, which is the digestive enzyme found in saliva, starts to breakdown starch into simpler sugars before the food even leaves the mouth. The nervous pathway involved in salivary excretion requires stimulation of receptors in the mouth, sensory impulses to the brain stem and parasympathetic impulses to salivary glands.

Swallowing your food happens when the muscles in your tongue and mouth move the food into your pharynx. The pharynx, which is the passage way for food and air, is about five inches (5") long. A small flap of skin called the epiglottis closes over the pharynx to prevent food from entering the trachea and thus choking. For swallowing to happen correctly a combination of 25 muscles must all work together at the same time. Salivary glands also produce an estimated three liters of saliva per day.

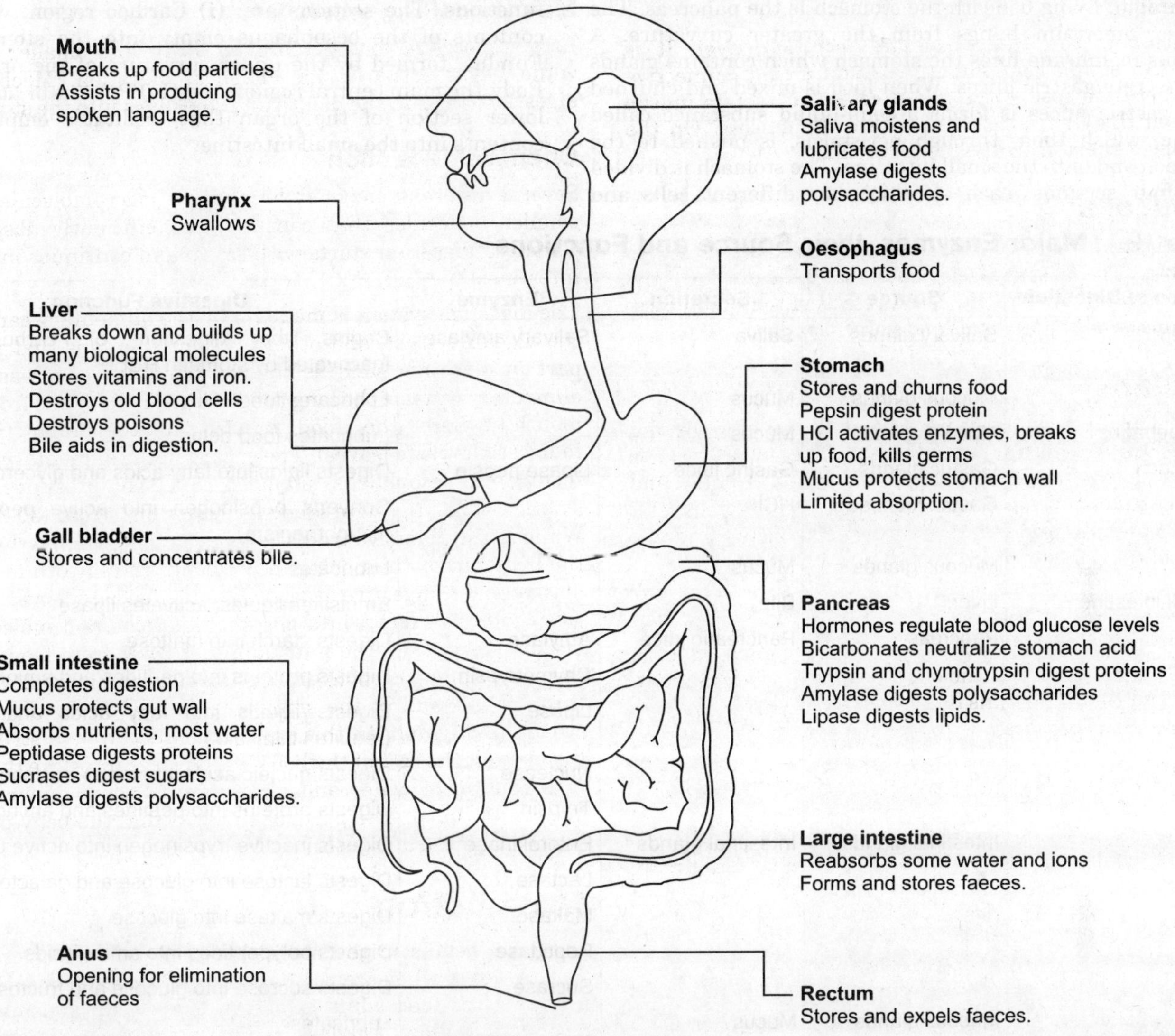

Fig. 19.1 Digestive system of man

Oesophagus

The oesophagus (also spelled esophagus) or gullet is the muscular tube in vertebrates through which ingested food passes from the mouth area to the stomach. The oesophagus is continuous with the laryngeal part of the pharynx at the level of the C6 vertebra. Food is passed through the oesophagus by using the process of peristalsis. It connects the pharynx, which is the body cavity that is common to both the digestive and respiratory systems behind the mouth, with the stomach, where the second stage of digestion is initiated (the first stage is in the mouth with teeth and tongue masticating food and mixing it with saliva).

Histology

The oesophagus is lined with mucus membranes, and uses peristaltic action to move swallowed food down to the stomach. The oesophagus is lined by a stratified squamous epithelium, which is rapidly turned over, and serves a protective effect due to the high volume transit of food, saliva, and mucus into the stomach. The lamina propria of the oesophagus is sparse. The mucus secreting glands are located in the submucosa, and are connective structures called papillae. The muscularis propria of the oesophagus consists of straited muscle in the upper third (superior) part of the oesophagus. The middle third consists of a combination of smooth muscle and straited muscle, and the bottom (inferior) third is only smooth muscle. The distal end of the oesophagus is slightly narrowed because of the thickened circular muscles. This part of the oesophagus is called the lower oesophageal sphincter. This aids in keeping food down and not being regurgitated. The oesophagus has a rich lymphatic drainage as well.

Stomach

The stomach lies between the esophagus and the first part of the small intestine (the duodenum). It is on the left side of the abdominal cavity; the fundus of the stomach lying against the diaphragm. Lying beneath the stomach is the pancreas. The greater omentum hangs from the greater curvature. A mucous membrane lines the stomach which contains glands that secrete gastric juices. When food is mixed and churned with gastric juices it forms a semi-liquid substance called chyme, which then, through peristalsis, is pushed to the stomach and onto the small intestine. The stomach is divided into four sections, each of which has different cells and functions. The sections are: **(i)** Cardiac region, where the contents of the oesophagus empty into the stomach, **(ii)** Fundus, formed by the upper curvature of the organ, **(iii)** Body, the main central region, and **(iv)** Pylorus or atrium, the lower section of the organ that facilitates emptying the contents into the small intestine.

Table 19.1 **Major Enzymes, their Source and Functions**

Place of Digestion	Source	Secretion	Enzyme	Digestive Function
Mouth	Salivary glands	Saliva	Salivary amylase	Begins the digestion of carbohydrates; inactivated by stomach HCl
	Mucous glands	Mucus	–	Lubricates food bolus
Oesophagus	Mucous glands	Mucus	–	Lubricates food bolus
Stomach	Gastric glands	Gastric juice	Lipase pepsin	Digests liqids into fatty acids and glycerol
	Gastric mucosa	HCl	–	Converts pepsinogen into active pepsin; kills microorganism
	Mucous glands	Mucus	–	Lubricates
Small intestine	Liver	Bile	–	Emulsifies liquids; activates lipase
	Pancreas	Pancreatic juice	Amylase	Digests starch into maltose
			Chymotrypsin	Digests proteins into peptides and amino acids
			Lipase	Digests liquids into fatty acids and glycerol (requires bile salts)
			Nuclease	Digests nucleic acids into mono-nucleotides
			Trypsin	Digests proteins into peptides and amino acids
	Intestinal glands	Intestinal glands	Enterokinase	Digests inactive trypsinogen into active trypsin
			Lactase	Digests lactose into glucose and galactose
			Maltase	Digests maltose into glucose
			Peptidase	Digests polypeptides into amino acids
			Sucrase	Digests sucrose into glucose and fructose
	Mucous glands	Mucus	–	Lubricates
Large intestine	Mucous glands	Mucus	–	Lubricates

Two smooth muscle valves, or sphincters, keep the contents of the stomach contained. They are the: **(i)** Cardiac or esophageal sphincter, dividing the tract above, and **(ii)** Pyloric sphincter, dividing the stomach from the small intestine. The gastric juice, which is in the stomach, is highly acidic with a pH of 1-3. Gastric acid may cause or compound damage to the stomach wall or its layer of mucus, causing a peptic ulcer. On the inside of the stomach there are folds of skin call the gastric rugae. Gastric rugae make the stomach very extendable, especially after a very big meal.

Gastric Glands

There are many different gastric glands and they secret many different chemicals. Parietal cells secrete hydrochloric acid; chief cells secrete pepsinogen; goblet cells secrete mucus; argentaffin cells secrete serotonin and histamine; and G-cells secrete the hormone gastrin.

Vessels and Nerves Arteries

The arteries supplying the stomach are the left gastric, the right gastric and right gastroepiploic branches of the hepatic, and the left gastroepiploic and short gastric branches of the lineal. They supply the muscular coat, ramify in the submucous coat, and are finally distributed to the mucous membrane.

Capillaries

The arteries break up at the base of the gastric tubules into a plexus of fine capillaries, which run upward between the tubules, anatomizing with each other, and ending in a plexus of larger capillaries, which surround the mouths of the tubes, and also form hexagonal meshes around the ducts.

Veins

From these the veins arise, and pursue a straight course downward, between the tubules, to the submucous tissue; they end either in the lineal and superior mesenteric veins, or directly in the portal vein.

Lymphatics

The lymphatics are numerous: They consist of a superficial and a deep set and pass to the lymph glands found along the two curvatures of the organ.

Nerves

The nerves are the terminal branches of the right and left urethra and other parts, the former being distributed upon the back, and the latter upon the front part of the organ. A great number of branches from the celiac plexus of the sympathetic are also distributed to it. Nerve plexuses are found in the submucous coat and between the layers of the muscular coat as in the intestine. From these plexuses fibrils are distributed to the muscular tissue and the mucous membrane.

Small Intestine

The small intestine is the site, where most of the chemical and mechanical digestion is carried out. Tiny projections called villi line the small intestine which absorbs digested food into the capillaries. Most of the food absorption takes place in the jejunum and the ileum.The functions of a small intestine is, the digestion of proteins into peptides and amino acids principally occurs in the stomach but some also occurs in the small intestine. Peptides are degraded into amino acids lipids (fats) are degraded into fatty acids and glycerol; and carbohydrates are degraded into simple sugars. The three main sections of the small intestine is duodenum, jejunum, ileum.

Duodenum

In anatomy of the digestive system, the duodenum is a hollow jointed tube connecting the stomach to the jejunum. It is the first and shortest part of the small intestine. It begins with the duodenal bulb and ends at the ligament of treitz. The duodenum is almost entirely retroperitoneal. The duodenum is also where the bile and pancreatic juices enter the intestine.

Jejunum

The jejunum is a part of the small bowel, located between the distal end of duodenum and the proximal part of ileum. The jejunum and the ileum are suspended by an extensive mesentery giving the bowel great mobility within the abdomen. The inner surface of the jejunum, its mucous membrane, is covered in projections called villi, which increase the surface area of tissue available to absorb nutrients from the gut contents. It is different from the ileum due to fewer goblet cells and generally lacks Peyer's patches.

Ileum

Its function is to absorb vitamin-B_{12} and bile salts. The wall itself is made up of folds, each of which has many tiny finger-like projections known as villi, on its surface. In turn, the epithelial cells which line these villi possess even larger numbers of microvilli. The cells that line the ileum contain the protease and carbohydrate enzymes responsible for the final stages of protein and carbohydrate digestion. These enzymes are present in the cytoplasm of the epithelial cells. The villi contain large numbers of capillaries which take the amino acids and glucose produced by digestion to the hepatic portal vein and the liver.

Large Intestine

The large intestine (colon) extends from the end of the ileum to the anus. It is about 5 feet long, being one-fifth of the whole extent of the intestinal canal. It's caliber is largest at the commencement at the caecum, and gradually diminishes as far as the rectum, where there is a dilatation of considerable size just above the anal canal. It differs from the small intestine in by the greater caliber, more fixed position, sacculated form, and in possessing certain appendages to its external coat, the appendices epiploicae. Further, its longitudinal muscular fibres do not form a continuous layer around the gut, but are arranged in three longitudinal bands or taeniae. The large intestine is divided into the caecum, colon, rectum, and anal canal. In its course, describes an arch which surrounds the convolutions of the small intestine. It commences in the right iliac region, in a dilated part, the caecum. It ascends through the right lumbar and hypochondriac regions to the under surface of the liver; here it takes a bend, the right colic flexure, to the left and passes transversely across the abdomen on the confines of the epigastric and umbilical regions, to the left hypochondriac region; it then bends again, the left colic flexure, and descends through the left lumbar and iliac regions to the pelvis, where it forms a bend called the sigmoid flexure; from this it is continued along the posterior wall of the pelvis to the anus.

There are trillions of bacteria, yeasts, and parasites living in our intestines, mostly in the colon. Over 400 species of organisms live in the colon. Most of these are very helpful to our health, while the minority are harmful. Helpful organisms synthesize vitamins, like B_{12}, biotin, and vitamin-K. They breakdown toxins and stop proliferation of harmful organisms. They stimulate the immune system and produce short chain fatty acids (SCFAs) that are required for the health of colon cells and help prevent colon cancer. There are many beneficial bacteria but some of the most common and important are lactobacillus acidophilus and various species of bifidobacterium. These are available as 'probiotics' from many sources.

Anus

The human anus is situated between the buttocks, posterioo the peritomeum. It has two anal sphincters, one internal, the other external. These hold the anus closed until defection occurs. One sphincter consists of smooth muscle and its action is involuntary; the other consists of striated muscle and its action is voluntary. In many animals, the anus is surrounded by anal sacs. Role of the anus is when the rectum is full, the increase in intra-rectal pressure forces the walls of the anal canal apart allowing the faecal matter to enter the anal canal. The rectum shortens as material is formed into the anal canal and peristaltic waves propel the faeces out of the rectum. The internal and external sphincters of the anus allow the faeces to be passed by muscles pulling the anus up over the exiting faeces.

Role of Accessory Organs in Digestion

The pancreas, liver and gall bladder are essential for digestion. The pancreas produces enzymes that help digest proteins, fats, and carbohydrates, the liver produces bile that helps the body absorb fat, and the gall bladder stores the bile until it is needed. The enzymes and bile travel through special channels called ducts and into the small intestine, where they help breakdown the food.

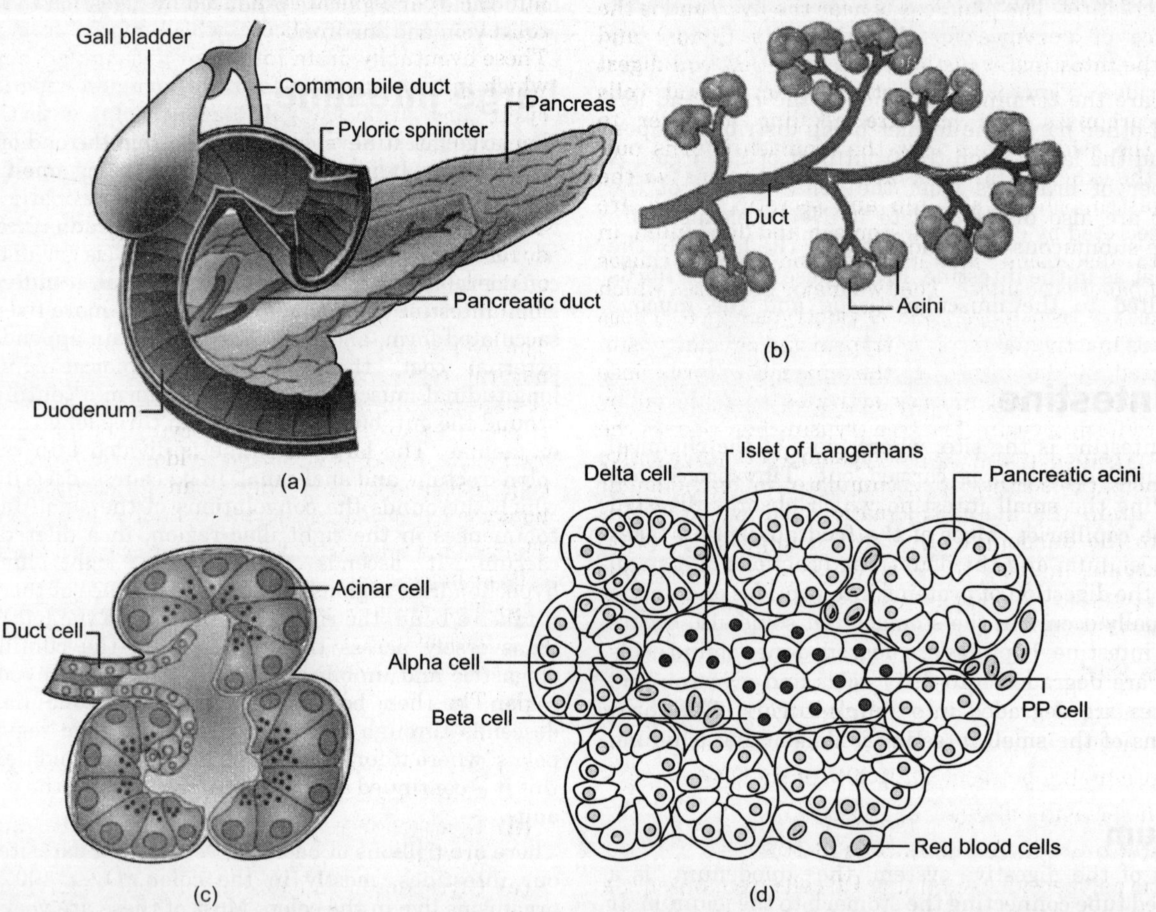

Fig. 19.2 Pancreas Exocrine and endocrine pancreas are made of specific cell types specialized in their functions

Pancreas

The pancreas is located posterior to the stomach and in close association with the duodenum. In human, the pancreas is a 6″-10″ inch elongated organ in the abdomen located retro peritoneal. It is often described as having three regions: a head, body and tail. The pancreatic head abuts the second part of the duodenum while the tail extends towards the spleen. The pancreatic duct runs the length of the pancreas and empties into the second part of the duodenum at the ampulla of Vater. The common bile duct commonly joins the pancreatic duct at or near this point. The pancreas is supplied arterially by the pancreaticoduodenal arteries, themselves branches of the superior mesenteric artery of the hepatic artery (branch of celiac trunk from the abdominal aorta). The superior mesenteric artery provides the inferior pancreaticoduodenal arteries while the gastroduodenal artery (one of the terminal branches of the hepatic artery) provides the superior pancreaticoduodenal artery. Venous drainage is *via* the pancreatic duodenal veins which end up in the portal vein. The splenic vein passed posterior to the pancreas but is said to not drain the pancreas itself. The portal vein is formed by the union of the superior mesenteric vein and splenic vein posterior to the body of the pancreas. In some people (as many as 40%) the inferior mesenteric vein also joins with the splenic vein behind the pancreas, in others it simply joins with the superior mesenteric vein instead.

The function of the pancreas is to produce enzymes that break down all categories of digestible foods (exocrine pancreas) and secrete hormones that affect carbohydrates metabolism (endocrine pancreas).

Exocrine Part

The pancreas is composed of pancreatic exocrine cells, whose ducts are arranged in clusters called acini (singular acinus). The cells are filled with secretory granules containing the precursor digestive enzymes (mainly trypsinogen, chymotrypsinogen, pancreatic lipase, and amylase) that are secreted into the lumen of the acinus. These granules are termed zymogen granules (zymogen referring to the inactive precursor enzymes.) It is important to synthesize inactive enzymes in the pancreas to avoid autodegradation, which can lead to pancreatitis. The pancreas is near the liver, and is the main source of enzymes for digesting fats (lipids) and proteins—the intestinal walls have enzymes that will digest polysaccharides. Pancreatic secretions from ductal cells contain bicarbonate ions and are alkaline in order to neutralize the acidic chyme that the stomach churns out. Control of the exocrine function of the pancreas are *via* the hormone gastrin, cholecystokinin and secretin, which are hormones secreted by cells in the stomach and duodenum, in response to distension and/or food and which causes secretion of pancreatic juices. The two major proteases which the pancreas are trypsinogen and chymotrypsinogen. These zymogens are inactivated forms of trypsin and chymotrypsin. Once released in the intestine, the enzyme enterokinase present in the intestinal mucosa activates trypsinogen by cleaving it to form trypsin. The free trypsin then cleaves the rest of the trypsinogen and chymotrypsinogen to their active forms. Pancreatic secretions accumulate in intralobular ducts that drain the main pancreatic duct, which drains directly into the duodenum. Due to the importance of its enzyme contents, injuring the pancreas is a very dangerous situation. A puncture of the pancreas tends to require careful medical intervention.

Endocrine Part

Scattered among the acini are the endocrine cells of the pancreas, in groups called the islets of Langerhans. They are:

- Insulin producing beta-cells (50-80% of the islet cells),
- Glucagon-releasing alpha-cells (15-20%),
- Somatostatin-producing delta-cells (3-10%),
- Pancreatic polypeptide-containing PP-cells (remaining %).

The islets are a compact collection of endocrine cells arranged in clusters and cords and are criss crossed by a dense network of capillaries. The capillaries of the islets are lined by layers of endocrine cells in direct contact with vessels, and most endocrine cells are in direct contact with blood vessels, by either cytoplasmic processes or by direct apposition.

Liver

The liver is an organ in vertebrates, including human. It plays a major role in metabolism and has a number of functions in the body including glycogen storage, plasma protein synthesis, and drug detoxification. It also produces bile, which is important in digestion. It performs and regulates a wide variety of high-volume biochemical reaction requiring specialized tissues. The liver normally weighs between 1.3-3.0 kg and is a soft, pinkish-brown 'boomerang-shaped' organ. It is the second largest organ (the largest being the skin) and the largest gland within the human body. Its anatomical position in the body is immediately under the diaphragm on the right side of the upper abdomen. The liver lies on the right side of the stomach and makes a kind of bed for the **gall bladder.**

The liver is supplied by two main blood vessels on its right lobe—the hepatic artery and the portal vein. The hepatic artery normally comes off the celiac trunk. The portal vein brings venous blood from the spleen, pancreas, and small intestine, so that the liver can process the nutrients and byproducts of food digestion. The hepatic veins drain directly into the inferior vena cava. The bile produced in the liver is collected in bile canaliculi, which merge from bile ducts. These eventually drain into the right and left hepatic ducts, which in turn merge to form the common hepatic duct. The cystic duct (from the gall bladder) joins with the common hepatic duct to form the common bile duct. Bile can either drain directly into the duodenum *via* the common bile duct or be temporarily stored in the gall bladder *via* the cystic duct. The common bile duct and the pancreatic duct enter the duodenum together at the ampulla of Vater. The branching's of the bile ducts resemble those of a tree, and indeed term 'biliary tree' is commonly used in this setting.

The liver is among the few internal human organs capable of natural regeneration of lost tissue: as little as 25% of remaining liver can regenerate into a whole liver again. This is predominantly due to hepatocytes acting as unipotential stem cells. There is also some evidence of bio potential stem cells, called oval cell, which can differentiate into either hepatocytes or cholangiocytes (cells that line bile ducts).

The various functions of the liver are carried out by the liver cells or hepatocytes.

(a) The liver produces and excretes bile requires for dissolving fats. Some of the bile drains directly into the duodenum, and some is stored in the gall bladder.

(b) The liver performs several roles in carbohydrate metabolism.

(c) Gluconeogenesis (the formation of glucose from certain amino acids, lactate or glycerol).

(d) Glycogenolysis (the formation of glucose from glycogen).

(e) Glycogenesis (the formation of glycogen from glucose)

(f) The breakdown of insulin and other hormones.

(g) The liver is responsible for the mainstay of protein metabolism.

(h) The liver also performs several roles in lipid metabolism.

(i) Cholesterol synthesis.

(j) The production of triglycerides (fats).

(k) The liver produces coagulation factors I (fibrinogen), II (prothrombin), V, VII, IX, X and XI, as well as protein C, protein S and antithrombin.

(l) The liver breaks down haemoglobin, creating metabolites that are added to bile as pigment.

(m) The liver breaks down toxic substances and most medicinal products in a process called drug metabolism. This sometimes results in toxication, when the metabolite is more toxic than its precursor.

(n) The liver converts ammonia to urea.

(o) The liver stores a multitude of substances, including glucose in the form of glycogen, vitamin-B_{12}, iron and copper.

(p) In the first trimester fetus, the liver is the main site of red blood cell production. By the 32nd weeks of gestation, the bone marrow has almost completely taken over that task.

(q) The liver is responsible for immunological effects the reticuloendothelial system if the liver contains many immunologically active cells, acting as a 'sieve' for antigens carried to it *via* the portal system.

Gall Bladder

The gall bladder is a pear-shaped organ that stores about 50 mL of bile (or gall) until the body needs it for digestion. The gall bladder is about 7-10 cm long in humans and is dark green in appearance due to its contents (bile), not its tissue. It is connected to the liver and the duodenum by biliary tract. The gall bladder is connected to the main bile duct through the gall bladder duct (cystic duct). The main biliary tract runs from the liver to the duodenum, and the cystic duct is effectively a 'cul de sac', serving as entrance and exit to the gall bladder. The surface marking of the gall bladder is the intersection of the midclavicular line (MCL) and the trans pyloric plane, at the tip of the ninth rib. The blood supply is by the cystic artery and vein, which runs parallel to the cystic duct. The cystic artery is highly variable, and this is of clinical relevance since, it must be clipped and cut during a cholecystectomy. The gall bladder has a epithelial lining characterized by recesses called Aschoff's recesses, which are pouches inside the lining. Under epithelium there is a layer of connective tissue, followed by a muscular wall that contracts in response to cholecystokinin, a peptide hormone by the duodenum. The gall bladder stores bile, which is released when food containing fat enters the digestive tract, stimulating the secretion of cholecystokinin (CCK). The bile emulsifies fats and neutralizes acids in partly digested food. After being stored in the gall bladder, the bile becomes more concentrated than when it left the liver, increasing its potency and intensifying its effect in fats.

Absorption

The total quantity of fluid that must be absorbed each day by the intestines is equal to the ingested fluid (about 1.5 liters) plus that secreted in the various gastrointestinal secretions (about 7 liters). This comes to a total of 8 to 9 liters. All but about 1.5 liters of this is absorbed in the small intestine, leaving only 1.5 liters to pass through the ileocecal value into the colon each day.

The stomach is poor absorptive area of the gastrointestinal tract because it lacks the typical villus type of absorptive membrane, and also because the junctions between the epithelial cells are tight junctions. Only a few highly lipid-soluble substances, such as alcohol and some drugs like aspirin, can be absorbed in small quantities.

The absorptive surface of small intestinal mucosa showing many folds called folds of kerckring which increase the surface area about three fold. 8 millions of villi are also located on the epithelial surface of small intestine which increase the absorptive area 10 fold more. Each intestinal epithelial cell on each villus is characterized by brush border. Consisting of as many as 1000 microvilli (1 × 0.1 μm) protruding into intestinal chyme. The combination of folds of kerckring, the villi and microvilli increases the total absorptive area of mucosa perhaps 1000 folds.

Absorption in Small Intestine

Absorption from the small intestine each day consists of several hundred grams of carbohydrates, 100 or more grams of fat, 50 to 100 grams of amino acids, 50 to 10 grams of ions, and 7 to 8 liters of water. The absorptive capacity of the normal small intestine is far greater than this: as much as several kilograms of carbohydrates per day, 500 grams of fat per day, 500 to 700 grams of proteins per day, and 20 or more liters of water per day. The large intestine can absorp still additional water and ions, although very few nutrients.

Water is transported through the intestinal membrane entirely by diffusion. Further more, this diffusion obeys the usual laws of osmosis. Therefore, when the chyme is dilute enough, water is absorbed through the intestional mucosa into the blood of the villi almost entirely by osmosis. Sufficient water may be transferred by osmosis into chyme to make the chyme isoosmotic with plasma 20-30 gm of Na is secreted in the intestinal secretion each day.

The motive power for sodium absorption is provided by active transport of sodium from inside the epithelial cells through the basal and side walls for these cells into paracellular spaces.

In the upper part of small intestine, chloride ions absorbed rapidly by diffusion along the electrical gradient to follow sodium ions.

Often large quantities of bicarbonate ions must be reabsorbed from the upper small intestine because large amounts of bicarbonate ions have been secreted into the duodenum in both pancreatic secretion and bile. There is active absorption of bicarbonate ions. The epithelial cells on the surface of villi in the ileum as well on the surface of large intestine have a special capability of secreting bicarbonate ions in exchange for absorption of chloride ions. It provides alkaline bicarbonate ions that neutralize acid products formed by bacteria in large intestine.

Extreme diarrhoeal secretion is initiated by entry of a subunit of cholera toxin into the epithelial cells. This stimulates formation of excess cyclic adenosine monophosphate, which opens tremendous numbers of chloride channels, allowing chloride ions to flow rapidly from inside the cell into the intestinal crypts. In turn, this is believed to activate a sodium pump that pumps sodium ions into the crypts to go alongwith the chloride ions. Finally, all this extra sodium chloride causes extreme osmosis of water from the blood, thus providing rapid flow of fluid along with the salt. All this excess fluid washes away most of the bacteria and is of value in combating the disease, but too much of a good thing can be lethal because of serious dehydration of the whole body that might ensue.

Calcium ions absorption is controlled by parathyroid hormone and vitamin-D. Fe ions are actively absorbed from small intestine. K, Mg, phosphate and probably still other ions can also be actively absorbed through the intestinal mucosa.

Absorption of Carbohydrates

Essentially all the carbohydrates in the food are absorbed in the form of monosaccharides; only a small fraction are absorbed as disaccharides and almost none as larger carbohydrate compounds. By far the most abundant of the absorbed monosaccharides is glucose, usually accounting for more than 80 percent of carbohydrate calories absorbed. The reason for that is that giucose is the final digestion product of our most abundant carbohydrate food, the starches. The remaining 20 percent of absorbed monosaccharides are composed almost entirely of galactose and fructose, the galactose derived from milk and the fructose as one of the monosaccharides digested from cane sugar. Glucose and galactose are transported by sodium co-transport mechanism while, fructose is transported by facilitated diffusion.

Absorption of Proteins

Most proteins, after digestion, are absorbed through the luminal membranes of the intestinal epithelial cells in the form of dipeptides, tripeptides, and a few free amino acids. The energy for most of this transport is supplied by a sodium co-transport mechanism in the same way that sodium co-transport of glucose occurs. That is, most peptide or amino acid molecules bind in the cell's microvillus membrane with a specific transport protein that requires sodium binding before transport can occur. After binding, the sodium ion then moves down its electrochemical gradient to the interior of the cell and pulls the amino acid or peptide alongwith it. This is called cotransport (secondary active transport) of the amino acids and peptides. A few amino acids do not require this sodium cotransport mechanism but instead are transported by special membrane transport proteins in the same way that fructose is transported, by facilitated diffusion.

Atleast five types of transport proteins for transporting amino acids and peptides have been found in the luminal membranes of intestinal epithelial cells.

Absorption of Fats

When fats are digested to form monoglycerides and free fatty acids, both of these digestive and products first become dissolved in the central lipid portions of bile micelles. As the molecular dimensions of these micelles are only 3 to 6 nanometers in diameter, and because of their highly charged exterior, they are soluble in chyme. In this form, the monoglycerides and free fatty acids are carried to the surfaces of the microvilli of the intestinal cell brush border and then penetrate into the recesses among the moving, agitating microvilli. Here, both the monoglycerides and fatty acids diffuse immediately out of the micelles and into the interior of the epithelial cells, which is possible because the lipids are also soluble in the epithelial cell membrane. This leaves the bile micelles still in the chyme, where they function again and again to help absorb still more monoglycerides and fatty acids.

In this way the micelles perform a 'ferrying' function that is highly important for fat absorption. In the presence of an abundance of bile micelles, about 97 per cent of the fat is absorbed; in the absence of the bile micelles, only 40 to 50 percent can be absorbed. After entering the epithelial cell, the fatty acids and monoglycerides are taken up by the cell's smooth endoplasmic reticulum; here they are mainly used to form new triglycerides that are subsequently released in the form of chylomicrons through the base of the epithelial cell, to flow upward through the thoracic lymph duct and empty into the circulating blood. Small quantity of short and median chain fatty acids are absorbed directly by way of lymphatics without converted into glycerides.

Absorption in Large Intestine

Most of the absorption in the large intestine occurs in the proximal one half of the colon, giving this portion the name absorbing colon, whereas the distal colon functions principally for faeces storage, until a propitious time for faeces excretion and is, therefore called the storage colon.

The mucosa of the large intestine, has a high capability for active absorption of sodium, and the electrical potential gradient created by absorption of the sodium causes chloride absorption as well. The tight junctions between the epithelial cells of the large intestinal epithelium are much tighter than those of the small intestine. This prevents significant amounts of back-diffusion of ions through these junctions, thus allowing the large intestinal mucosa to absorb sodium ions far more completely–that is, against a much higher concentration gradient–than can occur in the small intestine.

The mucosa of the large intestine secreted bicarbonate ions while it simultaneously absorbs an equal number of chloride ions in an exchange transport process that has already been described. The bicarbonate helps neutralize the acidic end products of bacterial action in the large intestine.

Absorption of sodium and chloride ions creates an osmotic gradient across the large intestinal mucosa which in turn causes absorption of water.

Bacteria are present absorping colon, which are capable of digesting cellulose. In herbivores animals. This source of energy (from cellulose) is significant.

Other substances formed as a result of bacterial activity are vitamin-K, vitamin-B_{12}, thiamine, riboflavin and various gases that contribute to flatus in the colon, especially carbon dioxide, hydrogen gas and methane. The bacteria formed vitamin-K is especially important because this vitamin in the daily ingested foods is normally, insufficient to maintain adequate blood coagulation.

Composition of the Faeces

The faeces normally contains three-fourths water and one-fourth solid matter that itself is composed of about 30 per cent dead bacteria, 10 to 20 per cent fat, 10 to 20 per cent inorganic matter, 2 to 3 per cent protein, and 30 per cent undigested roughage from the food and dried constituents of digestive juices, such as bile pigment and sloughed epithelial cells. The brown colour of faeces is caused by stercobilin and urobilin derivatives of bilirubin. The odour is caused principally by products of bacterial action. Including indole, skatole, mercaptans and hydrogen sulphide.

Energy Balance and Body Weight

Energy is measured in units called calories. A calorie is the amount of energy that is needed to raise the temperature of 1 gram of water by one degree celsius. Because a calorie is such a small amount, scientists use a larger unit to measure intake, called a kilocalorie. A kilocalorie is also referred to often as a capital 'C' calorie, and is equal to 1000 cal. When we 'count' calories, we are actually counting the big calories.

The old saying, 'you are what you eat' is very much true. According to scientists, the average adult consumes 900000 calories per year. Most people tend to take in more calories than their body needs. An intake of 12 extra calories a day or around 5% excess in calories, yields an annual increase of 12 extra pounds of body weight. The more developed countries tend to consume more calories than others because of the increasing availability and dieting habits of eating refined foods with little nutrition in them and lots of saturated fat. In our society, there is a huge emphasis put on a person's image and how thin they are, and less emphasis put on what's most imporant—the nutrition our body receives. While our body do need calories every day to keep us going, we need to watch the amount of calories we consume in order to maintain good health and proper body weight. Our caloric intake is linked directly to our health status. Being overweight is generally defined as being 15-20% above ideal body weight, while obesity is defined as being more than 20% above it. People who weigh 10% less than ideal are considered underweight. This is less common in the more developed countries. In less developed countries such as South Africa, being underweight is quite common because they lack the nutrition to maintain good health. How do we gain weight? When we consume more calories than our body can burn in a day, the excess energy is stored in specialized cells as fat. It is also important to know that the three classes of nutrients have different caloric contents. Carbohydrates and proteins contain only four calories per gram, while fat contains about nine. Because of this, it is essential that we watch our amount of fat intake. If we continuously feed our body more calories than is needed, our body will reduce more fat cells, to store the excess energy. This contributes to gaining weight. It is more difficult for chronically overweight persons to lose weight than normal-weight persons. This is because they are constantly fighting the body's own weight-control system, which responds as if the excess weight were normal. Our body is capable of measuring how much we intake, and maintaining our weight. When an overweight person goes on a diet, and consumes less calories, their body will respond as if they are starving, and try to save energy where, it can to make up for the decrease in received calories. Maintaining a healthy body weight. To maintain a stable body weight, our consumption of calories needs to be equal to the amount of calories we use in a day. You can determine your daily energy needs by determining your basal metabolic rate (BMR). Your BMR is the energy your body needs to perform essential activities. Some examples of essential activities are breathing, and maintaining organ function. Your metabolic rate can be influenced by your age, gender, muscular activity, body surface area and environmental temperature.

Physical Activity to Use Calories

Although the BMR stays about the same, we can dramatically change the amount of calories we burn in a day by participating in physical activity. It is important to note that heavier people do more work per hour than normal-weight people, for the same level of activity. We must spend about 3500 calories to lose one pound of fat. The best approach to weight loss, recommended by nutritionists, is to reduce the caloric intake by a small amount each day while gradually increasing your amount of physical activity.

BMR

There are several factors that influence the BMR. Each person's body has different needs. BMR needs vary with gender and body composition. Muscle tissue consumes more energy than fat tissue. Typically, males need more calories than females, because they generally have more muscle tissue. Males use up calories faster than women. BMR also varies with your age as well. As we age, our body needs less and less calories. In addition, some health conditions can contribute to our needed calories. Health conditions such as fever, infections and hyperthyroidism are examples of health conditions that lower your BMR. Our stress level effects our needed calorie intake as well. So does our increase or decrease in consumption, and our rate of metabolism, which varies with individual genetics.

Calculating Your BMR

Here are the steps to determining your BMR, or the amount of energy your body needs to perform essential activities:

(i) First calculate your weight into kilograms. This is obtained by dividing the number of pounds by 2.2.

(ii) For males multiply your weight in kilograms by 1.0. For females multiply your weight in kilograms by 0.9.

(iii) This number approximates the number of calories you consumer per hour. Now multiply this number by 24 to estimate how many calories you need per day to support basic metabolic functions.

(iv) The end result is basal metabolic rate.

Respiratory System

The respiratory system is crucial to every human being. Without it, we would cease to live outside of the womb. During inhalation or exhalation air is pulled towards or away from the lungs, by several cavities, tubes and openings. The organs of the respiratory system make sure that oxygen enters our bodies and carbon dioxide leaves our bodies.

The Pathway of Air

When one breathes air in at sea level, the inhalation is composed of different gases. These gases and their quantities are oxygen which makes up 21%, nitrogen which is 78%, carbon dioxide with 0.04% and others with significantly smaller portions. In the process of breathing, air enters into the nasal cavity through the nostrils and is filtered by coarse hairs (vibrissae) and mucous that is found there. The vibrissae filter macroparticles, which are particles of large size. Dust, pollen, smoke, and fine particles are trapped in the mucous that lines the nasal cavities (hollow spaces within the bones of the skull that warm, moisten, and filter the air). There are three bony projections inside the nasal cavity. The superior, middle and inferior nasal conchae. Air passes between these chonchae *via* the nasal meatuses. Air then travels past the nasopharynx, oropharynx and laryngopharynx, which are the three portions that make up the pharynx. The pharynx is a funnel-shaped tube that connects our nasal and oral cavities to the larynx. The tonsils which are part of the lymphatic system form a ring at the connection of the oral cavity and the pharynx. Here, they protect against foreign invasion of antigens.

Therefore, the respiratory tract aids the immune system through this protection. Then the air travels through the larynx. The larynx closes at the epiglottis to prevent the passage of food or drink as a protection to our trachea and lungs. The larynx is also our voicebox; it contains vocal cords, in which it produces sound. Sound is produced from the vibration of the vocal cords when air passes through them.

The trachea, which is also known as our windpipe, has ciliated cells and mucous secreting cells lining it, and is held open by C-shaped cartilage rings. One of its functions is similar to the larynx and nasal cavity, by way of protection from dust and other particles. The dust will adhere to the sticky mucous and the cilia helps propel it back up the trachea, to where it is either swallowed or coughed up.

The mucociliary escalator extends from the top of the trachea all the way down to the bronchioles. Through the trachea, the air is now able to pass into the bronchi.

Inspiration

Inspiration is initiated by contraction of the diaphragm and in some cases the intercostals muscles when they receive nervous impulses. During normal quiet breathing, the phrenic nerves stimulate the diaphragm to contract and move downward into the abdomen. This downward movement of the diaphragm enlarges the thorax. When necessary, the intercostal muscles also increase the thorax by contacting and drawing the ribs upward and outward.

The active increase of the thorax changes the stability set up in a resting lung. As the thoracic wall moves away from lung which increases the space between the thoracic wall and lung and decreases the pressure in the intrapleural cavity. This decrease in pressure causes the pressure in the alveoli to become greater than the elastic recoil that is inherent in lung tissue. Thus, when contraction of the diaphragm and the intercostal muscles actively increase the size of the thorax, the lungs are passively forced to expand. This expansion increases the size of the alveoli which decreases pressure in the alveoli. Pressure within the alveoli is now lower than atmospheric pressure which allows air to move into the lungs through the structures discussed above.

Expiration

During quiet breathing, expiration is normally a passive process and does not require muscles to work. When the lungs are stretched and expanded, stretchy receptors within the alveoli send inhibitory nerve impulses to the medulla oblongata, causing it to stop sending signals to the rib cage and diaphragm to relax and rise. This elastic recoil causes the lungs and chest cavity to shrink and increase the air pressure within the lungs. This increased positive air pressure pushes the air out of the lungs. Expiration happens as the diaphragm relaxes. Although the respiratory system is primarily under involuntary control, and regulated by the medulla oblongata, we have some voluntary control over it also. This is due to the higher brain function of the cerebral cortex. When under physical or emotional stress, more frequent and deep breathing is needed, and both inspiration and expiration will work as active processes. Additional muscles in the rib cage forcefully contract and push more air out of the lungs (this cannot occur during rest) In addition to deeper breathing, when coughing or sneezing we exhale forcibly. Our abdominal muscles will contract suddenly (when there is an urge to cough or sneeze), raising the abdominal pressure. The rapid increase in pressure pushes the relaxed diaphragm up against the pleural cavity. This causes air to be forced out of the lungs.

Another function of the respiratory system is to sing and to speak. Our exertion of conscious control over our breathing is what allows us to speak and sing.

Lung Compliance

Lung compliance is the magnitude of the change in lung volume produced by a change in pulmonary pressure. Compliance can be considered the opposite of stiffness. A low lung compliance would mean that the lungs would need a greater than average change in intrapleural pressure to change the volume of the lungs. A high lung compliance would indicate that little pressure difference in intrapleural pressure is needed to change the volume of the lungs. More energy is required to breathe normally in a person with low lung compliance. Persons with low lung compliance due to disease therefore tend to take shallow breaths and breathe more frequently. Determination of lung compliance two major things determine lung compliance. The first is the elasticity of the lung tissue. Any thickening of lung tissues due to disease will decrease lung compliance. The second is surface tensions at air water interfaces in the alveoli. The surface of the alveoli cells is moist. The attractive force, between the water cells on the alveoli, is called surface tension. Thus, energy is required not only to expand the tissues of the lung but also to overcome the surface tension of the water that lines the alveoli. To overcome the forces of surface tension, certain alveoli cells secret a protein and lipid complex called 'surfactant'.

The Respiratory Tracts

For the sake of convenience, we will divide the respiratory system into the upper and lower respiratory tracts:

Upper Respiratory Tract

The upper respiratory tract consists of the nose and the pharynx. Its primary function is to receive the air from the external environment and filter, warm and humidify it before it reaches the delicate lungs where gas exchange will occur. Air enters through the nostrils of the nose and is partially filtered by the nose hairs, then flows into the nasal cavity. The nasal cavity is lined with epithelial tissue, containing blood vessels, which help warm the air and secrete mucous, which further filters the air. The endothelial lining of the nasal cavity also contains tiny hair-like projections, called cilia. The cilia serve to transport dust and other foreign particles, trapped in mucous, to the back of the nasal cavity and to the pharynx. There the mucus is either coughed out, or swallowed and digested by powerful stomach acids. After passing through the nasal cavity, the air flows down the pharynx to the larynx.

Lower Respiratory Tract

The lower respiratory tract starts with the larynx, and includes the trachea, the two bronchi that branch from the trachea, and the lungs themselves. This is where gas exchange actually takes place.

Larynx

The larynx (pl. larynges), colloquially known as the voice box, is an organ in our neck involved in protection of the trachea and sound production. The larynx houses the vocal cords, and is situated just below, where the tract of the pharynx splits into the trachea and the esophagus. The larynx contains two important structures—the epiglottis and the vocal cords. The epiglottis is a flap of cartilage located at the opening to the larynx. During swallowing, the larynx (at the epiglottis and at the glottis) closes to prevent swallowed material from entering the lungs; the larynx is also pulled upwards to assist this process. Stimulation of the larynx by ingested matter produces a strong cough reflex to protect the lungs. Note: choking occurs when the oesophagus fails to cover the trachea, and food becomes lodged in our windpipe. The vocal cords consist of two folds of connective tissue that stretch and vibrate when air passes through them, causing vocalization. The length the vocal cords are stretched determines what pitch the sound will have. The strength of expiration from the lungs also contributes to the loudness of the sound. Our ability to have some voluntary control over the respiratory system enables us to sing and to speak. In order for the larynx to function and produce sound, we need air. That is why we can't talk when we're swallowing.

Right and Left Lungs

The right primary bronchus is the first portion we come to, it then branches off into the lobar (secondary) bronchi, segmental (tertiary) bronchi, then to the bronchioles which have little cartilage and are lined by simple cuboidal epithelium. The bronchi are lined by pseudostratified columnar epithelium. Objects will likely lodge here at the junction of the carina and the right primary bronchus because of the vertical structure. Items have a tendency to fall in it, where as the left primary bronchus has more of a curve to it which would make it hard to have things lodge there.

The left primary bronchus has the same set up as the right with the lobar, semental bronchi and the bronchioles. The lungs are attached to the heart and trachea through structures that are called the roots of the lungs. The roots of the lungs are the bronchi, pulmonary vessels, bronchial vessels, lymphatic vessels and nerves. These structures enter and leave at the hilus of the lung which is 'the depression in the medial surface of a lung that forms the opening through which the bronchus, blood vessels, and nerves pass'. There are a number of terminal bronchioles connected to respiratory bronchioles which then advance into the alveolar ducts that then become alveolar sacs. Each bronchiole terminates in an elongated space enclosed by many air sacs called alveoli which are surrounded by blood capillaries. Present there as well, are alveolar macrophages, they ingest any microbes that reach the alveoli. The pulmonary alveoli are microscopic, which means they can only be seen through a microscope, membranous air sacs within the lungs. They are units of respiration and the site of gas exchange between the respiratory and circulatory systems.

Transport of Gases

The oxygen which is diffused from the alveoli into the pulmonary blood is transported to peripheral tissue capillaries in combination with haemoglobin. In the body cells the O_2 reacts with food stuffs to form CO_2. This CO_2 enters the tissue capillaries and transported back to the lungs.

1. **Transport of oxygen from lungs to body tissue** Oxygen is transported (about 97%) throughout the body chemically bound to respiratory pigment haemoglobin inside the red blood cells. In the mucles oxygen from haemoglobin is transferred to and retained by myoglobin (a molecule chemically similar to haemoglobin except that is consist of one haeme-globin unit). Myoglobin releasing the oxygen during period of prolonged muscular activity. If the myoglobin store is exhausted the muscle respire anaerobically releasing lactic acid. This lactic acid transported to liver, where it is metabolized. The most important factor determining

how much oxygen is carried by haemoglobin is the level of oxygen in blood. Oxygen diffuses from the alveoli into the pulmonary capillary blood because the oxygen partial pressure (pO_2) in the alveoli is greater than pO_2 is the pulmonary capillary blood.

As oxygen level increases, more oxygen combines with haemoglobin (Hb). Hb saturation remains high, even at low oxygen tensions. Fetal Hb has a high affinity for oxygen and carries 20-30% more than maternal Hb. Myoglobin in skeletal muscle has a very high affinity for oxygen and will take up oxygen from haemoglobin in the blood.

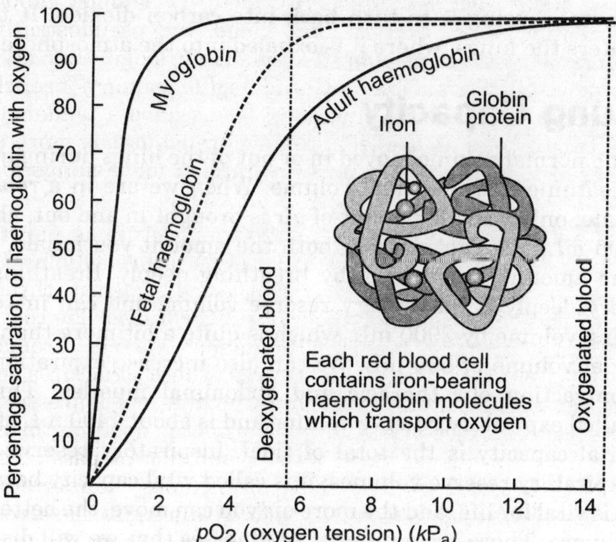

Fig. 19.3 Dissociation curves for haemoglobin and myoglobin at normal body temperature for fetal and adult human blood.

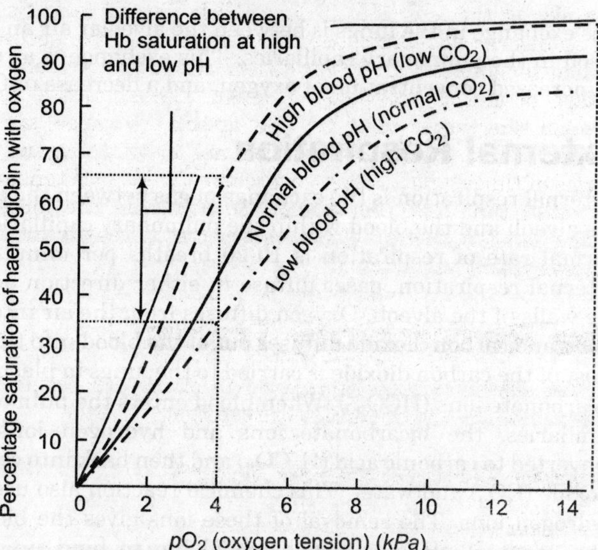

Fig. 19.4 Oxygen-haemoglobin dissociation curves for human blood at normal body temperature at different blood pH

As pH increases (lower CO_2), more oxygen combines with Hb. As the blood pH decreases (higher CO_2), Hb binds less oxygen and releases more to the tissues (the Bohr effect). The difference between Hb saturation at high and low pH represents the amount of oxygen released to the tissues.

About 1.3% of O_2 is transported by blood is dissolved form in plasm.

2. **Transport of carbon dioxide** When oxygen is metabolized in the cells the carbon dioxide produced rises the pressure (pCO_2) which causes carbon dioxide to diffuse into the tissue capillaries. About 7% of CO_2 is transported by blood as carbonic acid while about 70% as sodium and potassium bicarbonates and the remaining 23% as carbaminohaemoglobin which is formed by combination of CO_2 and haemoglobin.

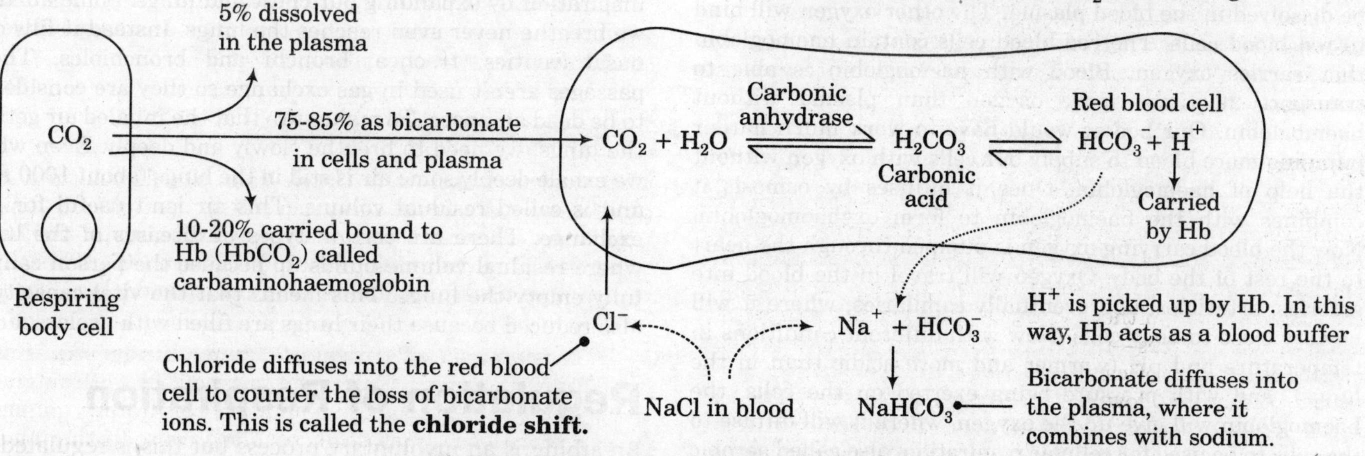

Fig. 19.5 Transport of carbon dioxide in the blood

Homeostasis and Gas Exchange

Homeostasis is maintained by the respiratory system in two ways—gas exchange and regulation of blood pH. Gas exchange is performed by the lungs by eliminating carbon dioxide, a waste product given off by cellular respiration. As carbon dioxide exits the body, oxygen needed for cellular respiration enters the body through the lungs. ATP, produced by cellular respiration, provides the energy for the body to perform many functions, including nerve conduction and muscle contraction. Lack of oxygen affects brain function, sense of judgment, and a host of other problems.

Gas exchange in the lungs is between the alveolar air and the blood in the pulmonary capillaries. This exchange is a result of increased concentration of oxygen, and a decrease of CO_2.

External Respiration

External respiration is the exchange of gas between the air in the alveoli and the blood within the pulmonary capillaries. A normal rate of respiration is 10-20 breaths per minute. In external respiration, gases diffuse in either direction across the walls of the alveoli. Oxygen diffuses from the air into the blood and carbon dioxide diffuses out of the blood into the air. Most of the carbon dioxide is carried to the lungs in plasma as bicarbonate ions (HCO_3^-). When blood enters the pulmonary capillaries, the bicarbonate ions and hydrogen ions are converted to carbonic acid (H_2CO_3) and then back into carbon dioxide (CO_2) and water. This chemical reaction also uses up hydrogen ions. The removal of these ions gives the blood a more neutral pH, allowing haemoglobin to bind up more oxygen.

Internal Respiration

Internal respiration is the exchanging of gases at the cellular level. The passage way from the trachea to the bronchioles. There is a point at the inferior portion of the trachea, where it branches into two directions that form the right and left primary bronchus. This point is called the carina, which is the keel-like cartilage plate at the division point. We are now at the bronchial tree. It is named so because it has a series of respiratory tubes that branch off into smaller and smaller tubes as they run throughout the lungs.

First the oxygen must diffuse from the alveolus into the capillaries. It is able to do this because the capillaries are permeable to oxygen. After it is in the capillary, about 5% will be dissolved in the blood plasma. The other oxygen will bind to red blood cells. The red blood cells contain haemoglobin that carries oxygen. Blood with haemoglobin is able to transport 26 times more oxygen than plasma without haemoglobin. Our bodies would have to work much harder pumping more blood to supply our cells with oxygen without the help of haemoglobin. Once it diffuses by osmosis it combines with the haemoglobin to form oxyhaemoglobin. Now the blood carrying oxygen is pumped through the heart to the rest of the body. Oxygen will travel in the blood into arteries, arterioles, and eventually capillaries, where it will be very close to body cells. Now with different conditions in temperature and pH (warmer and more acidic than in the lungs), and with pressure being exerted on the cells, the haemoglobin will give up the oxygen, where it will diffuse to the cells to be used for cellular respiration, also called aerobic respiration.

Cellular Respiration

Cellular respiration is the process of moving energy from one chemical form (glucose) into another (ATP), since all cells use ATP for all metabolic reactions. It is in the mitochondria of the cells, where oxygen is actually consumed and carbon dioxide produced. Oxygen is produced as it combines with hydrogen ions to form water at the end of the electron transport chain (see chapter on cells). As cells take apart the carbon molecules from glucose, these get released as carbon dioxide. Each body cell releases carbon dioxide into nearby capillaries by diffusion, because the level of carbon dioxide is higher in the body cells than in the blood. In the capillaries, some of the carbon dioxide is dissolved in plasma and some is taken by the haemoglobin, but most enters the red blood cells where it binds with water to form carbonic acid. It travels to the capillaries surrounding the lung, where a water molecule leaves, causing it to turn back into carbon dioxide. It then enters the lungs, where it is exhaled into the atmosphere.

Lung Capacity

The normal volume moved in or out of the lungs during quiet breathing is called tidal volume. When we are in a relaxed state, only a small amount of air is brought in and out, about 500 mL. You can increase both the amount you inhale, and the amount you exhale, by breathing deeply. Breathing in very deeply is inspiratory reserve volume and can increase lung volume by 2900 mL, which is quite a bit more than the tidal volume of 500 mL. We can also increase expiration by contracting our thoracic and abdominal muscles. This is called expiratory reserve volume and is about 1400 mL of air. Vital capacity is the total of tidal, inspiratory reserve and expiratory reserve volumes; it is called vital capacity because it is vital for life, and the more air you can move, the better off you are. There are a number of illnesses that we will discuss later in the chapter that decrease vital capacity.

Vital Capacity

It can vary a little depending on how much we can increase inspiration by expanding our chest and lungs. Some air that we breathe never even reaches the lungs. Instead it fills our nasal cavities, trachea, bronchi and bronchioles. These passages aren't used in gas exchange so they are considered to be dead air space. To make sure that the inhaled air gets to the lungs, we need to breathe slowly and deeply. Even when we exhale deeply some air is still in the lungs (about 1000 mL) and is called residual volume. This air isn't useful for gas exchange. There are certain types of diseases of the lung, where residual volume builds up because the person cannot fully empty the lungs. This means that the vital capacity is also reduced because their lungs are filled with useless air.

Regulation of Respiration

Breathing is an involuntary process but this is regulated by nervous and chemical way.

1. **Nervous control** The basic rhythm of breathing is controlled by the respiratory centre (a cluster of neurons located in the medulla oblongata). These centres are for inspiration, expiration and pneumotaxic (lies in pons varolii) pneumotaxic centre increases the rate of respiration but decreas the depth of respiration so causing evaporation from the respiratory membrane.

2. **Chemical control** There are chemoreceptors in the aorta, the carotid arteries, and in the medulla oblongata of the brainstem that are sensitive to pH. As carbon dioxide levels increase there is a buildup of carbonic acid, which releases hydrogen ions and lowers pH. Thus, the chemoreceptors do not respond to changes in oxygen levels (which actually change much more slowly), but to pH, which is an indirect measure of carbon dioxide levels. In other words, CO_2 is the driving force for breathing. The receptors in the aorta and the carotid arteries stimulate an immediate increase in breathing rate and the receptors in the medulla stimulate a sustained increase in breathing until blood pH returns to normal. This response can be experienced by running a 100 m dash. During this exertion (or any other sustained exercise) your muscle cells must metabolize ATP at a much faster rate than usual, and thus will produce much higher quantities of CO_2. The blood pH drops as CO_2 levels increase, and you will involuntarily increase breathing rate very soon after beginning the sprint. You will continue to breathe heavily after the race, thus expelling more carbon dioxide, until pH has returned to normal.

Role of Respiratory System

Regulation of Blood pH

Many of us are not aware of the importance of maintaining the acid/base balance of our blood. It is vital to our survival. Normal blood pH is set at 7.4, which is slightly alkaline or 'basic'. If the pH of our blood drops below 7.2 or rises above 7.6 then very soon our brains would cease functioning normally and we would be in big trouble. Blood pH levels below 6.9 or above 7.9 are usually fatal if they last for more than a short time. Another wonder of our amazing bodies is the ability to cope with every pH change – large or small. There are three factors in this process—the lungs, the kidneys and buffers.

When blood pH is too low and the blood becomes too acidic (acidosis), the presence of too many H^+ ions is to blame. Buffers help to soak up those extra H^+ ions. On the other hand, the lack of H^+ ions causes the blood to be too basic (alkalosis). In this situation, buffers release H^+ ions. Buffers function to maintain the pH of our blood by either donating or grabbing H^+ ions as necessary to keep the number of H^+ ions floating around the blood at just the right amount. The most important buffer we have in our bodies is a mixture of carbon dioxide (CO_2) and bicarbonate ion (HCO_3^-). CO_2 forms carbonic acid (H_2CO_3) when it dissolves in water and acts as an acid giving up hydrogen ions (H^+) when needed. HCO_3 is a base and soaks up hydrogen ions (H^+) when there are too many of them. In a nutshell, blood pH is determined by a balance between bicarbonate and carbon dioxide.

Bicarbonate Buffer System

With this important system our bodies maintain homeostasis. (Note that H_2CO_3 is carbonic acid and HCO_3 is bicarbonate)

$$CO_2 + H_2O \longleftrightarrow H_2CO_3 \longleftrightarrow (H^+) + HCO_3$$

(i) If pH is too high, carbonic acid will donate hydrogen ions (H^+) and pH will drop.

(ii) If pH is too low, bicarbonate will bond with hydrogen ions (H^+) and pH will rise.

Too much CO_2 or too little HCO_3^- in the blood will cause acidosis. The CO_2 level is increased when hypoventilation or slow breathing occurs, such as if you have emphysema or pneumonia. Bicarbonate will be lowered by ketoacidosis, a condition caused by excess fat metabolism (diabetes mellitus). Too much HCO_3 or too little CO_2 in the blood will cause alkalosis. This condition is less common than acidosis. CO_2 can be lowered by hyperventilation. So, in summary, if you are going into respiratory acidosis the above equation will move to the right. The body's H^+ and CO_2 levels will rise and the pH will drop. To counteract this body will breathe more and release H^+. In contrast, if you are going into respiratory alkalosis the equation will move to the left. The body's H^+ and CO_2 levels will fall and the pH will rise. So the body will try to breathe less to release HCO_3^-. One can think of it like a leak in a pipe: where ever there is a leak, the body will "fill the hole".

Comparative Account of Respiration in Animals

Adaptations for External Respiration

(i) Primary organs in adult vertebrates are external and internal gills, swim bladders or lungs, skin and the buccopharyngeal mucosa.

(ii) Less common respiratory devices include filamentous outgrowths of the posterior trunk and thigh (African hairy frog), lining of the cloaca, and lining of oesophagus.

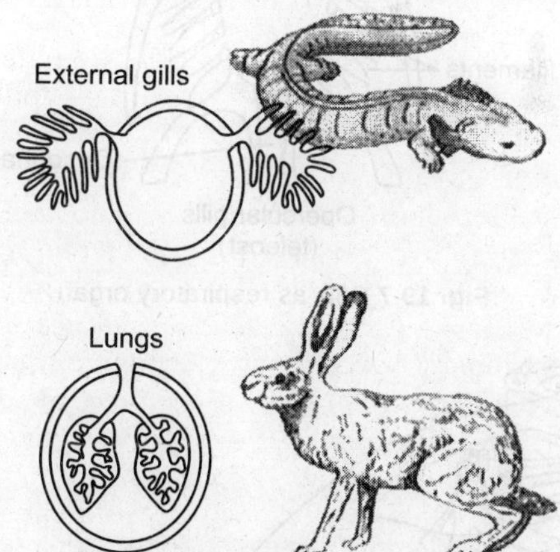

Fig. 19.6 Gas exchange organs

Respiratory Organs

1. Cutaneous respiration
   (i) Respiration through the skin can take place in air, water or both.
   (ii) Most important among amphibians (especially the family N-Plethodontidae).
2. Gills (see Respiration in Fishes)
   Cartilaginous fishes:
   (a) 5 'naked' gill slits

(b) Anterior and posterior walls of the 1st 4 gill chambers have a gill surface (demibranch). Posterior wall of last (5th) chamber has no demibranch.
(c) Interbranchial septum lies between 2 demibranchs of a gill arch.
(d) Gill rakers protrude from gill cartilage and 'guard' entrance into gill chamber.
(e) 2 demibranchs + septum and associated cartilage, blood vessels, muscles and nerves = holobranch

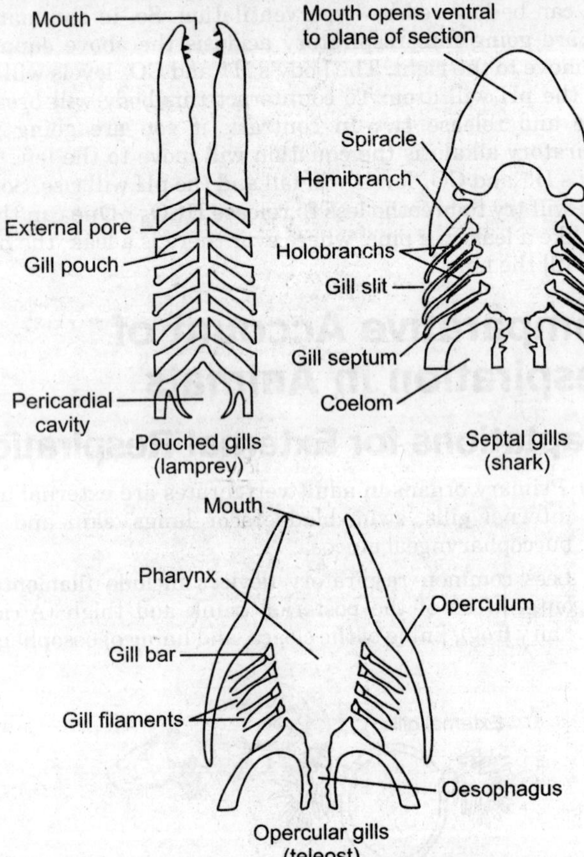

Fig. 19.7 Gills as respiratory organ

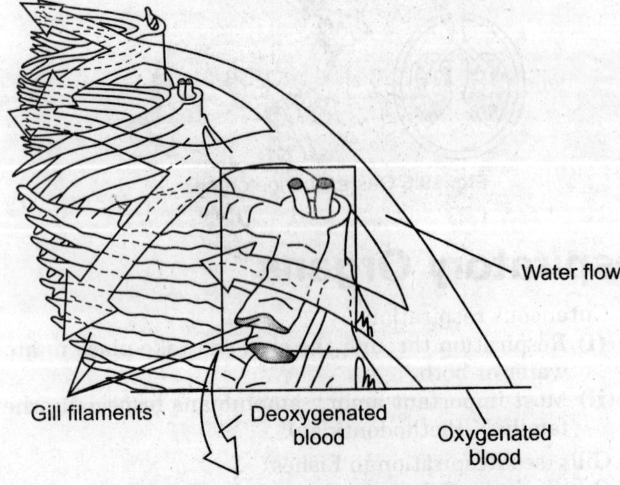

Fig. 19.8 Mechanism of transport in gills

3. Bony fishes (teleosts) (See 'ventilation in teleost fishes')
(i) Usually have 5 gill slits.
(ii) Operculum projects backward over gill chambers.
(iii) Interbranchial septa are very short or absent.

4. Agnathans:
(i) 6-15 pairs of gill pouches.
(ii) Pouches connected to pharynx by afferent branchial (or gill) ducts and to exterior by efferent branchial (or gill) ducts.

5. Larval gills
(i) External gills
(a) Outgrowths from the external surface of one or more gill arches.
(b) Found in lungfish and amphibians.
(ii) Filamentous extensions of internal gills
(a) Project through gill slits.
(b) Occur in early stages of development of elasmobranchs.
(iii) Internal gills-hidden behind larval operculum of late anuran tadpoles.

Swim Bladder and Origin of Lungs

Most vertebrates develop an outpocketing of pharynx or oesophagus that becomes one or a pair of sacs (swim bladders or lungs) filled with gases derived directly or indirectly from the atmosphere. Similarities between swim bladders and lungs indicate they are the same organs.

Vertebrates without swim bladders or lungs include cyclostomes, cartilaginous fish, and a few teleosts (*e.g.*, flounders and other bottom-dwellers).

Swim Bladders

(i) May be paired or unpaired.
(ii) Have, during development, a pneumatic duct that usually connects to the oesophagus. The duct remains open (physostomous) in bowfins and lungfish, but closes off (physoclistous) in most teleosts.
(iii) Serve primarily as a hydrostatic organ (regulating a fish's specific gravity).
(iv) Gain gas by way of a 'red body' (or red gland); gas is resorbed *via* the oval body on posterior part of bladder.

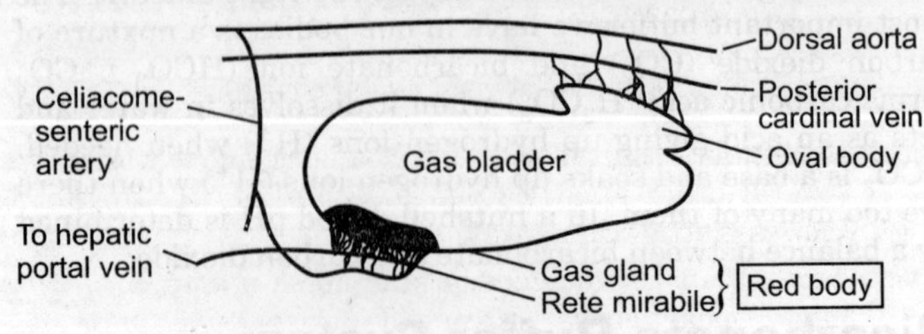

Fig. 19.9 Physoclistous gas bladder

(v) May also play important roles in:
(a) **Hearing** some freshwater teleosts (*e.g.*, catfish, goldfish and carp) 'hear' by way of pressure waves transmitted *via* the swim bladder and small bones called Weberian ossicles.

(b) **Sound production** muscles attached to the swim bladder contract to move air between 'sub-chambers' of the bladder. The resulting vibration creates sound in fish such as **croakers**, **grunters** and **midshipman** fish.

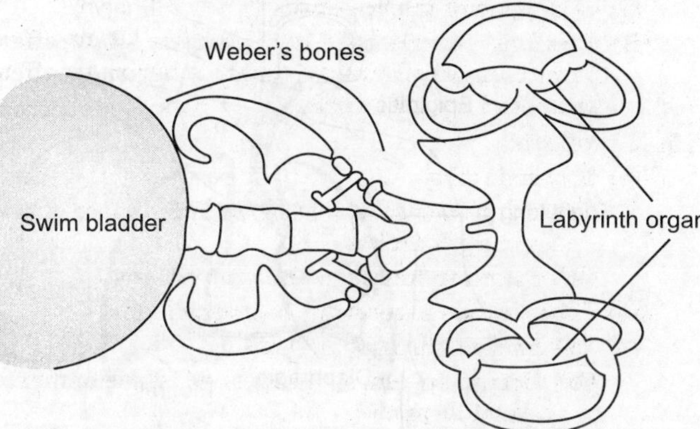

Fig. 19.10 Swim bladder of lung fishes

(c) **Respiration** the swim bladder of **lungfish** has number sub-divisions or septa (to increase surface area) and oxygen and carbon dioxide is exchanged between the bladder and the blood.

Lungs and Associated Structures

Larynx

(a) Tetrapods besides mammals – two pair of cartilages—artytenoid and cricoid.

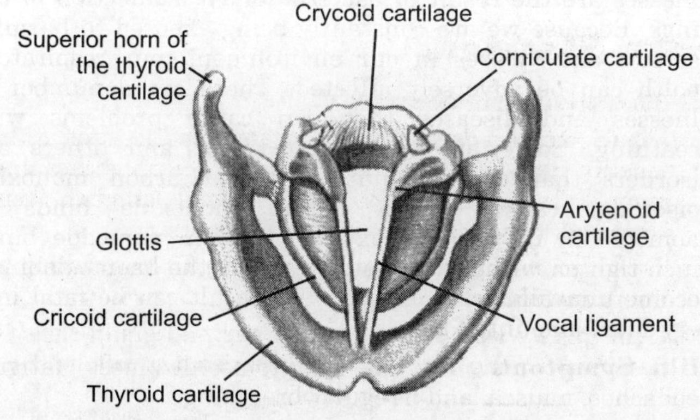

Fig. 19.11 The larynx viewed from above

(b) Mammals – paired arytenoids + cricoid + thyroid + several other small cartilages including the epiglottis (closes glottis when swallowing).

(c) Amphibians, some lizards and most mammals - also have vocal cords stretched across the laryngeal chamber.

Trachea and syrinx

Trachea

(a) Usually about as long as a vertebrates neck (except in a few birds such as cranes).

(b) Reinforced by cartilaginous rings (or c-rings).

(c) Splits into two primary bronchi and in birds only, forms the syrinx at that point.

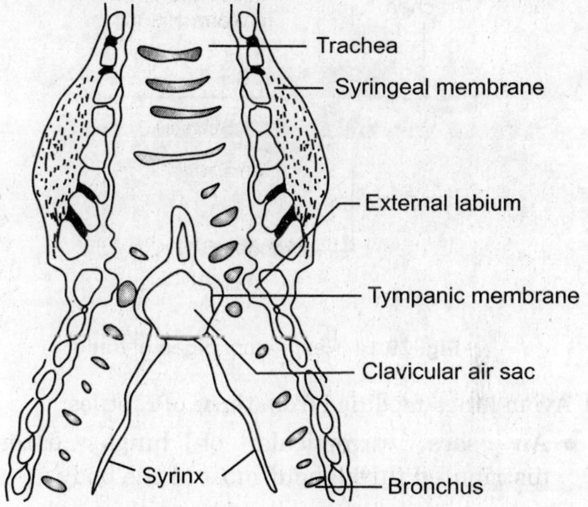

Fig. 19.12 Structure of trachea and syrinx

Lungs

(a) Amphibian lungs :

- Two simple sacs.
- Internal lining may be smooth or have simple sacculations or pockets.
- Air exchanged *via* positive-pressure ventilation.

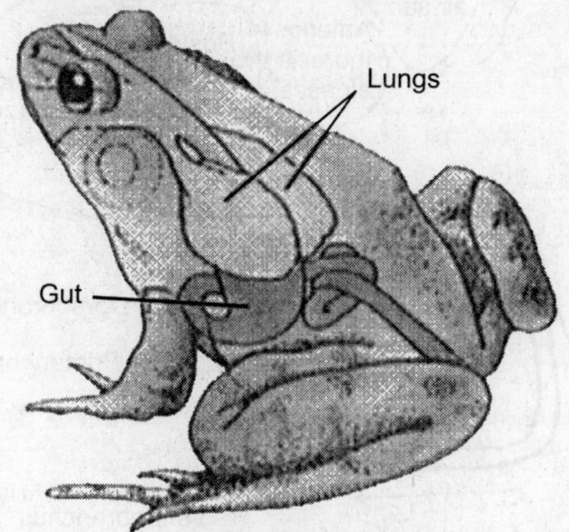

Fig. 19.13 Lung in Amphibia

(b) Reptilian lungs

- Simple sacs in sphenodon and snakes.
- Lizards, crocodilians and turtles-lining is septate, with lots of chambers and sub-chambers.
- Air exchanged *via* positive-pressure ventilation.

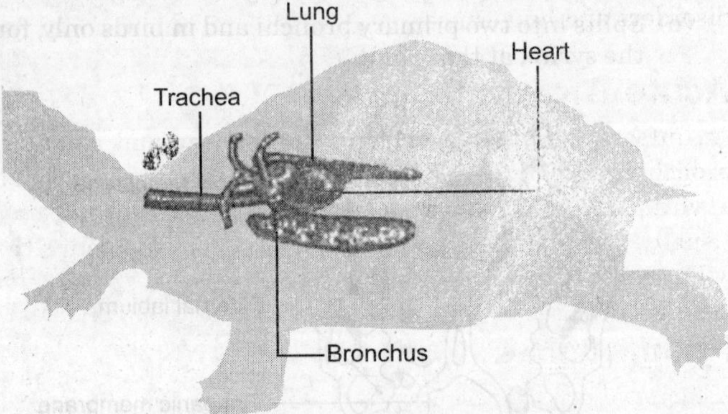

Fig. 19.14 Respiratory organ of turtle

(c) Avian lungs-modified from those of reptiles:

- Air sacs (diverticula of lungs) extensively distributed throughout most of the body.
- Arrangement of air ducts in lungs → no passageway is a dead-end.
- Air flow through lungs (parabronchi) is unidirectional.

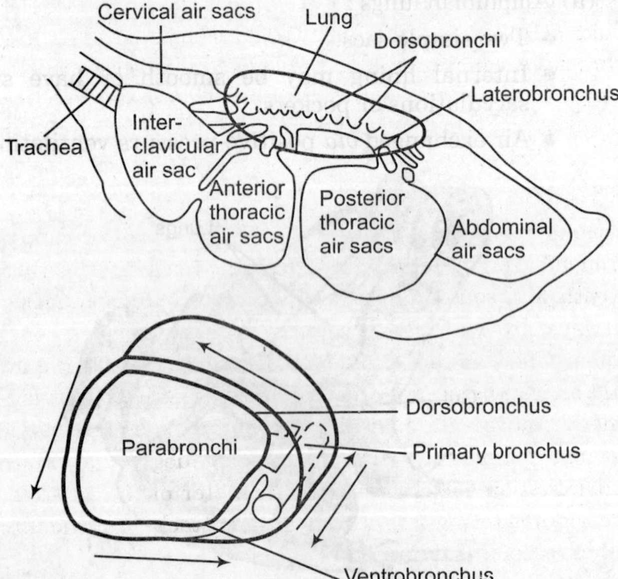

Fig. 19.15 Bird lung in cross section

(d) Mammalian lungs:

- Multi-chambered and usually divided into lobes
- Air flow is bidirectional:
  Trachea ↔ primary bronchi ↔ secondary bronchi ↔ tertiary bronchi ↔ bronchioles ↔ alveoli

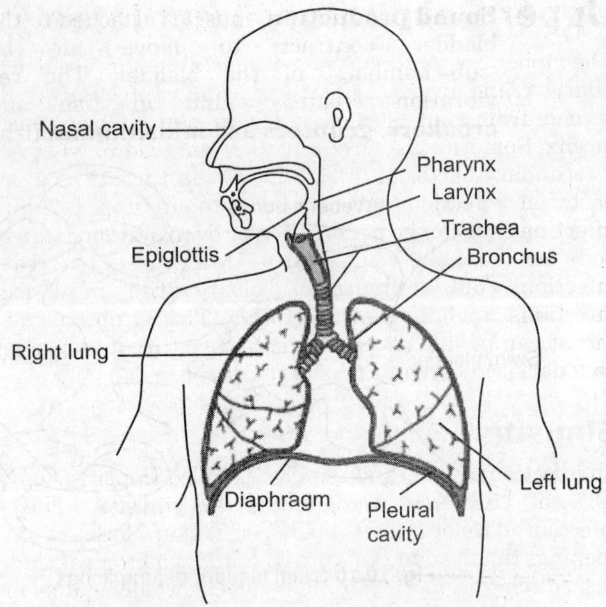

Fig. 19.16 Human respiratory system

- Air exchanged *via* negative pressure ventilation, with pressures changing due to contraction and relaxation of diaphragm and intercostal muscles

Respiratory Diseases

The environment of the lung is very moist, which makes it a hospitable environment for bacteria. Many respiratory illnesses are the result of bacterial or viral infection of the lungs. Because we are constantly being exposed to harmful bacteria and viruses in our environment, our respiratory health can be adversely affected. There are a number of illnesses and diseases that can cause problems with breathing. Some are simple infections, and others are disorders that can be quite serious. Carbon monoxide poisoning: caused when carbon monoxide binds to haemoglobin in place of oxygen. Carbon monoxide binds much tighter, without releasing, causing the haemoglobin to become unavailable to oxygen. The result can be fatal in a very short amount of time.

Mild Symptoms flu like symptoms, dizziness, fatigue, headaches, nausea, and irregular breathing.

Moderate Symptoms chest pain, rapid heart beat, difficulty thinking, blurred vision, shortness of breath and unsteadiness.

Severe Symptoms seizures, palpitations, disorientation, irregular heart beat, low blood pressure, coma and death.

Pulmonary Embolism blockage of the pulmonary artery (or one of its branches) by a blood clot, fat, air or clumped tumour cells. By far the most common form of pulmonary embolism is a thromboembolism, which occurs when a blood clot, generally a venous thrombus, becomes dislodged from its site of formation and embolizes to the arterial blood supply of one of the lungs. Symptoms may include difficulty breathing, pain during breathing, and more rarely circulatory instability and death. Treatment, usually, is with anticoagulant medication.

Upper Respiratory Tract Infections

The upper respiratory tract consists of our nasal cavities, pharynx, and larynx. Upper Respiratory Infections (URI) can spread from our nasal cavities to our sinuses, ears, and larynx. Sometimes a viral infection can lead to what is called a secondary bacterial infection. 'Strep throat' is a primary bacterial infection and can lead to an upper respiratory infection that can be generalized or even systemic (affects the body as a whole). Antibiotics aren't used to treat viral infections, but are successful in treating most bacterial infections, including strep throat. The symptoms of strep throat can be a high fever, severe sore throat, white patches on a dark red throat, and stomach ache.

Sinusitis

An infection of the cranial sinuses is called sinusitis. Only about 1-3% of URI's are accompanied by sinusitis. This 'sinus infection' develops when nasal congestion blocks off the tiny openings that lead to the sinuses. Some symptoms include: post nasal discharge, facial pain that worsens when bending forward and sometimes even tooth pain can be a symptom. Successful treatment depends on restoring the proper drainage of the sinuses. Taking a hot shower or sleeping upright can be very helpful. Otherwise, using a spray decongestant or sometimes a prescribed antibiotic will be necessary.

Otitis Media

Otitis media in an infection of the middle ear. Even though the middle ear is not part of the respiratory tract, it is discussed here because it is often a complication seen in children who has a nasal infection. The infection can be spread by way of the 'auditory (Eustachian) tube that leads form the nasopharynx to the middle ear. The main symptom is usually pain. Sometimes though, vertigo, hearing loss, and dizziness may be present. Antibiotics can be prescribed and tubes are placed in the eardrum to prevent the buildup of pressure in the middle ear and the possibility of hearing loss.

Tonsillitis

Tonsillitis occurs when the tonsils become sollen and inflamed. The tonsils located in the posterior wall of the nasopharynx are often referred to as adenoids. If you suffer from tonsillitis frequently and breathing becomes difficult, they can be removed surgically in a procedure called a tonsillectomy.

Laryngitis

An infection of the larynx is called laryngitis. It is accompanied by hoarseness and being unable to speak in an audible voice. Usually, laryngitis disappears with treatment of the URI. Persistent hoarseness without a URI is a warning sign of cancer, and should be checked into by your physician.

Lower Respiratory Tract Disorders

Lower respiratory tract disorders include infections, restrictive pulmonary disorders, obstructive pulmonary disorders and lung cancer.

Acute Bronchitis

An infection that is located in the primary and secondary bronchi is called bronchitis. Most of the time, it is preceded by a viral URI that led to a secondary bacterial infection. Usually, a non-productive cough turns into a deep cough that will expectorate mucus and sometimes pus.

Pneumonia

A bacterial or viral infection in the lungs, where the bronchi and the alveoli fill with a thick fluid. Usually it is preceded by influenza. Symptoms of pneumonia include high fever and chills, with headache and chest pain. Pneumonia can be located in several lobules of the lung and obviously, the more lobules involved, the more serious the infection. It can be caused by bacteria that are usually held in check, but due to stress or reduced immunity has gained the upper hand.

Pulmonary Fibrosis

Vital capacity is reduced in these types of disorders because the lungs have lost their elasticity. Inhaling particles such as sand, asbestos, coal dust or fiberglass can lead to pulmonary fibrosis, a condition where fibrous tissue builds up in the lungs. This makes it so our lungs cannot inflate properly and are always tending toward deflation.

Asthma

Asthma is a respiratory disease of the bronchi and bronchioles. The symptoms include wheezing, shortness of breath and sometimes a cough that will expel mucus. The airways are very sensitive to irritants which can include pollen, dust, animal dander and tobacco. Even being out in cold air can be an irritant. When exposed to an irritant, the smooth muscle in the bronchioles undergoes spasms. Most asthma patients have at least some degree of bronchial inflammation that reduces the diameter of the airways and contributes to the seriousness of the attack. While asthma is not curable, it is treatable.

Exercise

1. Organ that produces bile is
(a) pancreas (b) oesophagus
(c) liver (d) stomach

2. The component in bile which helps to emulsify fat in the duodenum is
(a) bile salts (b) biliverdin
(c) bilirubin (d) cholesterol

3. The HCl in gastric juice converts
(a) disaccharide to monosaccharide
(b) pepsinogen to pepsin
(c) prorennin to rennin
(d) polypeptide to peptide

4. Enzymes that is found on the mucosa of the intestinal villi is
(a) peptidase (b) trypsin
(c) amylase (d) lipase

5. The respiratory control centers are located in the
(a) heart
(b) lungs
(c) diaphragm and rib muscles
(d) brain

6. The glucose is converted into glycogen in liver and stored in
(a) liver and spleen (b) liver and muscle
(c) liver (d) spleen and muscles

7. The movements in the gut wall are known as
(a) metachronal (b) diastole
(c) systole (d) peristalsis

8. Which one of the following statements is true regarding digestion and absorption of food in human?
(a) About 60% of starch is hydrolyzed by salivary amylase in our mouth
(b) Oxyntic cells in our stomach secrete the proenzyme pepsinogen
(c) Fructose and amino acids are absorbed through intestinal mucosa with the help of carrier ions like Na^+
(d) Chylomicrons are small lipoprotein particles that are transported from intestine into blood capillaries

9. The energy needed to fuel essential body processes is called
(a) essential nutrient level
(b) recommended daily allowance
(c) optimum energy intake
(d) basal metabolic rate

10. Why are bird lungs more efficient than human lungs?
(a) They use countercurrent exchange
(b) They have more surface area than human lungs
(c) They are able to concentrate the oxygen to much higher levels
(d) They use a one-way rather than an in-out air flow system

11. Peyer's patches found in the small intestine are
(a) epithelial tissue (b) glandular tissue
(c) lymphatic tissue (d) haemopoietic tissue

12. A fish opens and closes its mouth and gill covers. A dog plants. A marine worm waves long, filmy gills in the water. All of these movements
(a) are examples of ventilation
(b) show how circulation aids respiration
(c) are examples of breathing
(d) slow diffusion of CO_2

13. In respiration energy not converted in ATP is
(a) liberated alongwith CO_2
(b) converted into heat
(c) transferred to organic compounds
(d) transferred to water

14. One gram mole of glucose on complete oxidation to CO_2 and H_2O produces about
(a) 686000 cal (b) 6860 cal
(c) 6860000 cal (d) 68600 cal

15. In respiration, pyruvic acid is
(a) formed only when the cell is with mitochondria
(b) formed only when oxygen is available
(c) formed only when cell is performing aerobic respiration
(d) commonly formed as intermediate product of aerobic and anaerobic respiration

16. A disease called emphysema decrease the springiness of the lungs. This decreases .... and makes it harder to breathe
(a) the volume of each breath (b) respiratory rate
(c) countercurrent exchange (d) vital capacity

17. The .... is a structure specialized for diffusion of gases and nutrients between the blood of the mother and the fetus.
(a) uterus (b) placenta
(c) lamella (d) alveolus

18. Patients with chronic lung disease and difficulty breathing often adapt to the high concentration of CO_2 in their blood. The breathing centers stop responding to CO_2 level. If such a patient has difficulty breathing, medical personnel are reluctant to give the patient pure oxygen. Based on what you know about control of breathing, why do you think this the case?
(a) The petient's body would use the oxygen to make even more CO_2
(b) The oxygen would increase concentration of bicarbonate, altering pH
(c) Increased oxygen in the blood might slow or stop breathing
(d) The body is not used to the oxygen and the patient would overdose

19. Removal of hydrogen and CO_2 from substrate is called
(a) oxidation (b) decarboxylation
(c) reductive carboxylation (d) oxidative decarboxylation

20. Aerobic respiration of one glucose produces
(a) 12 NADH + $2FADH_2$ + 38 ATP
(b) 12 NADH + 30 ATP + H_2O
(c) 8 NADH + $2FADH_2$ + 2ATP
(d) 10 $NADH_2$ + 2 $FADH_2$ + 2 ATP + 2 GTP

21. End products of aerobic respiration are
(a) sugar and oxygen
(b) water and energy
(c) carbon dioxide and energy
(d) carbon dioxide, water and energy

22. Deposit-feeders
(a) feed mostly on mineral substrates
(b) filter small organisms from water
(c) feed on detritus
(d) live in or on their food, eating their way through

23. The energy content of fats
(a) is released by bile salts
(b) may be lost unless an herbivore eats some of its faeces
(c) is approximately two times that of carbohydrate or protein
(d) can reverse the effects of malnutrition

24. Which of the following would have the same O_2 content?
(a) Blood entering the lungs-blood leaving the lungs
(b) Blood entering the right side of the heart-blood entering the left side of the heart
(c) Blood entering the tissue capillaries-blood leaving the tissue capillaries
(d) Blood entering the right side of the heart-blood leaving the right side of the heart

25. Which of the following is more likely to be found in animals with gastrovascular cavities than in those with alimentary canals?
(a) A large surface area for absorption of predigested nutrients
(b) Extracellular digestion
(c) Intracellular digestion
(d) Suspension feeding

26. Ruminants
(a) have teeth adapted for an omnivorous duct
(b) use microorganisms to digest cellulose
(c) eat their faeces to obtain nutrients digested from cellulose by microorganisms
(d) house symbiotic bacteria and microorganisms in a caecum

27. Zymogens are
(a) hormones that stimulate release of pancreatic enzymes
(b) enzymes attached to the brush border that hydrolyze nucleosides
(c) hydrolytic enzymes manufactured in inactive forms to protect the cells that produce them
(d) protein digesting enzymes that are activated by hydrochloric acid

28. The tracheae of insects
(a) are stiffened with chitinous rings and lead into the lungs
(b) are filled by positive pressure breathing
(c) ramify along capillaries of the circulatory system for gas exchange
(d) are highly branched, coming into contact with almost every cell for gas exchange

29. Which of the following is not involved in speeding up breathing?
(a) A drop in the pH of the blood
(b) Stretch receptors in the lungs
(c) Impulses from the breathing centers in the medulla
(d) Severe deficiencies of oxygen

30. The binding of an O_2 atom to the first iron atom of a haemoglobin molecule
(a) occurs at a very low partial pressure of oxygen
(b) produces a conformational change that lowers the other subunits affinity for oxygen
(c) is an example of cooperatively as O_2 readily binds to the other subunits
(d) is the signal for haemoglobin to release H^+ so that bicarbonate converts to CO_2.

31. Fluid is moved back into the capillaries at the downstream end of a capillary bed by
(a) active transport
(b) hydrostatic pressure
(c) osmosis
(d) bulk transport

32. Which of the following is not a factor in the exchange of substances in capillary beds?
(a) Endocytosis and exocytosis
(b) Passive diffusion through clefts between endothelial cells
(c) Hydrostatic pressure
(d) Bulk flow through the apoplast

33. Which of the following is an organic molecule needed by the body in small amounts?
(a) Protein (b) Zinc
(c) Vitamin-C (d) Monosaccharide

34. Breathing rate will increase when .... CO_2 in your blood causes a .... in pH.
(a) increased / rise
(b) increased / drop
(c) decreased / rise
(d) it is the level of O_2 in the blood that normally signals changes in breathing rate

35. The acid pH of the stomach
(a) hydrolyzes proteins
(b) is regulated by the release of gastrin
(c) is neutralized by gastric juice
(d) triggers the release of enterogastrone

36. After a meal of greasy french fries, which hormones and enzymes would you expect to be most active?
(a) salivary, pancreatic amylase and disaccharidases
(b) bile salts, lipase and enterogastrone
(c) pepsin, trypsin, chymotrypsin, amino carboxypeptidases, dipeptidases and CCK
(d) Both (a) and (b)

37. Chylomicrons are
(a) lipoproteins transported by the circulatory system
(b) small branches of the lymphatic system
(c) protein-coated fat globules excreted out of epithelial cells into a lacteal
(d) small peptides acted upon by chymotrypsin

38. Which of the following is not a common component of faeces?
(a) Intestinal bacteria (b) Cellulose
(c) Saturated fats (d) Bile pigments

39. The hepatic portal vessel
(a) suppiies the capillaries of the intestines
(b) carries absorbed nutrients to the liver for processing
(c) carries blood from the liver to the heart
(d) drains the lacteals of the villi

40. In countercurrent exchange,
(a) the flow of fluids in opposite directions maintains a favourable diffusion gradient along the length of an exchange surface
(b) oxygen is exchanged for carbon dioxide
(c) double circulation keeps oxygenated and deoxygenated blood separate
(d) oxygen moves from a region of high partial pressure to one of low partial pressure, but carbon dioxide moves in the opposite direction

41. Smoking destroys the chilia in the respiratory passage ways. This
(a) makes it harder to move air in and out of the lungs
(b) decreases the surface area for respiration
(c) slows blood flow through lung blood vesels
(d) makes it harder to keep the lungs clean

42. The lungs are folded into many small air sacs and blood vessels, which divide to form many small capillaries that increase the transfer of substances through their walls. The structures in the digestive system similar in function to these air sacs and capillaries are the
(a) villi (b) colon and rectum
(c) gastric glands (d) high-density lipoproteins

43. Imagine that you have eaten a meal containing the following nutrients. Which would not have to be digested before being absorbed?
(a) Protein (b) Polysaccharide
(c) Nucleic acid (d) Amino acid

44. Aunt rose had her gall bladder removed and afterward
(a) could not eat foods containing large amounts of fat
(b) had trouble digesting proteins
(c) could eat monosaccharides and disaccharides but not polysaccharides
(d) needed to take an amino acid supplement

45. Laxatives work in the large intestine to relieve constipation. Which of the following would probably not be an effective laxative? A substance that
(a) contains lots of fibre
(b) promotes water absorption in the large intestine
(c) speeds up movement of material through the large intestine
(d) decreases water absorption in the large intestine

46. Which of the answers below would not work in the following sentence? 'In order for the body to absorb and use ...., they must be broken down by hydrolysis into ....
(a) polysaccharides; monosaccharides
(b) amino acids; proteins
(c) fats; glycerol and fatty acids
(d) disaccharides; monosaccharides

47. How does a gastrovascular cavity differ from an alimentary canal? The gastrovascular cavity
(a) stores food but does not digest it
(b) is usually much larger
(c) has only one opening
(d) functions in digestion but not absorption

48. Joe is trying to decide whether to buy a candy bar or some gumdrops to reward himself for losing 10 pounds. Both are 300 calories. Most of the calories in the gumdrops come from carbohydrate. If Joe wants to keep his weight under control, it would be best to buy the
(a) gumdrops, because the body tends to hoard carbohydrates
(b) gumdrops, because the body tends to hoard fat
(c) candy bar, because the body tends to hoard carbohydrates
(d) candy bar, because the body tends to hoard fat

49. In humans, most nutrient molecules are absorbed by the
(a) stomach (b) liver
(c) small intestine (d) large intestine

50. After nutrients are absorbed, the blood carries them first to the
(a) brain (b) pancreas
(c) kidneys (d) liver

51. An advantage of gas exchange in water, compared with gas exchange in air, is that
(a) water usually contains a higher concentration of O_2 than air
(b) water is easier to move over the respiratory surface
(c) the respiratory surface does not dry out in water
(d) the respiratory surface does not have to be as extensive in water

52. Transport epithelia are responsible for
(a) pumping water across a membrane
(b) forming an impermeable boundary at an interface with the environment
(c) the exchange of solutes for osmoregulation or excretion
(d) filtering blood to form the filtrate in Bowman's capsule

53. Match list I with list II and select the correct answer using codes given below the lists.

List I	List II
A. Xerophthalmia	1. ACTH
B. Tetany	2. Vitamin-A
C. Beri-beri	3. Vitamin-B_1
D. Cushings disease	4. Parathyroid
	5. Vitamin-B_2

Codes

	A	B	C	D
(a)	2	3	1	4
(b)	2	4	3	1
(c)	2	5	3	1
(d)	4	5	2	3

54. Which of the following pairs is/are correctly matched?

Enzyme		Action of the enzyme
I. Pepsin	—	Converts proteins into proteoses and peptones
II. Trypsin	—	Converts proteins into proteoses, peptones and polypeptides
III. Dipeptidases	—	Convert polypeptides into dipeptides

Select the correct answer using the codes given below

Codes

(a) I, II and III (b) I and II
(c) I and III (d) II only

55. Match list I with list II and select the correct answer using the codes given below the lists.

List I (Digestive enzyme)	List II (Substrate)
A. Cathepsin	1. Triglyceride
B. Pancreatic amylase	2. Oligosaccharide
C. Lipase	3. Protein
D. Glucosidase	4. Lipoprotein
	5. Polysaccharide

Codes

	A	B	C	D
(a)	3	5	1	2
(b)	4	3	1	2
(c)	4	3	2	1
(d)	3	5	2	1

56. Consider the following statements regarding the chambers of the stomach namely rumen, reticulum, omasum and abomasum of ruminants.

I. All these chambers are present in all the ruminants.
II. One of these chambers may not be present in some ruminants.
III. Water cells are present in rumen and reticulum.
IV. Water cells are present in both rumen and reticulum.

Which of the statements given above is/are correct?

(a) I and III are correct (b) II and III are correct
(c) III and IV are correct (d) I and IV are correct

57. Match list I with list II and select the correct answer using the codes given below the lists.

List I	List II
A. Liver	1. Amylase
B. Beta cells	2. Chymotrypsin
C. Duodenum	3. Insulin
D. Parotid gland	4. Stercobilin

Codes

	A	B	C	D
(a)	3	5	1	2
(b)	4	3	1	2
(c)	4	3	2	1
(d)	3	5	2	1

Answers

1. (c)	**2.** (a)	**3.** (b)	**4.** (a)	**5.** (d)	**6.** (c)	**7.** (d)	**8.** (c)	**9.** (d)	**10.** (d)
11. (c)	**12.** (a)	**13.** (b)	**14.** (a)	**15.** (d)	**16.** (d)	**17.** (b)	**18.** (c)	**19.** (d)	**20.** (d)
21. (d)	**22.** (c)	**23.** (c)	**24.** (d)	**25.** (c)	**26.** (b)	**27.** (c)	**28.** (d)	**29.** (b)	**30.** (c)
31. (c)	**32.** (d)	**33.** (c)	**34.** (b)	**35.** (b)	**36.** (d)	**37.** (c)	**38.** (c)	**39.** (b)	**40.** (a)
41. (d)	**42.** (a)	**43.** (d)	**44.** (a)	**45.** (b)	**46.** (b)	**47.** (c)	**48.** (b)	**49.** (c)	**50.** (d)
51. (c)	**52.** (c)	**53.** (b)	**54.** (d)	**55.** (a)	**56.** (b)	**57.** (b)			

20 Blood Vascular System

Blood and Circulation

Blood is the fluid connective tissue present in vertebrates. The primary function of blood is to supply nutrients and constitutional elements to tissues and to remove waste products. Blood also enables cells and different substances to be transported between tissues and organs. Problems with blood composition or circulation can lead to downstream tissue malfunction. Blood is also involved in maintaining homeostasis by acting as a medium for transferring heat to the skin and by acting as a buffer system for bodily pH. The blood is circulated around the lungs and body by the pumping action of the heart. Additional return pressure may be generated by gravity and the actions of skeletal muscles.

Oxygen (O_2) is carried throughout the body by the blood circulation. Pulmonary circulation happens when blood leaves the heart, enters the lungs and becomes saturated with oxygen. Once this saturated blood exits the heart, it delivers the oxygen to all organs throughout the body. This oxygen depleted blood is then delivered back to the lungs to be renewed with fresh oxygen.

Blood is a circulating tissue composed of fluid plasma and cells (red blood cells, white blood cells and platelets). Anatomically, blood is considered a connective tissue, due to its origin in the bones and its function. Blood is the means and transport system of the body used in carrying elements (*e.g.*, nutrition, waste and heat) from one location in the body to another, by way of blood vessels. Blood is made of two parts:

1. Plasma which makes up 45-55% of blood volume.
2. Formed cellular elements (red, white blood cells and platelets) which combine to make the remaining blood volume.

Syllabus

- Blood Plasma
- Blood Corpuscles
- Haemoglobin
- Haemostasis
- Haemopoiesis
- Blood Group system
- Myogenic Heart
- Heart as a Pump
- Comparative Anatomy of Heart Structure
- Cardiac Cycle
- Neural and Chemical Regulation of Heart Beat
- ECG—Its Principle and Significance
- Blood Pressure

Blood Plasma

Plasma is made up of 90% water, 7-8% soluble proteins (albumin maintains bloods osmotic integrity, others clot, etc.), 1% electrolytes and 1% elements in transit. One percent of the plasma is salt, which helps with the pH of the blood. The largest group of solutes in plasma contains three important proteins to be discussed. There are albumins, globulins and clotting proteins. Albumins are the most common group of proteins in plasma and consist of nearly two-thirds of them (60-80%). They are produced in the liver. The main function of albumins is to maintain the osmotic balance between the blood and tissue fluids and is called colloid osmotic pressure. In addition, albumins assist in transport of different materials, such as vitamins and certain molecules and drugs (*e.g.,* bilirubin, fatty acids and penicillin). Globulins are a diverse group of proteins, designated into three groups– gamma, alpha and beta. Their main function is to transport various substances in the blood. Gamma globulins assist the body's immune system in defense against infections and illness. Clotting proteins are mainly produced in the liver as well. There are atleast 12 substances, known as 'clotting factors' that participate in the clotting process. One important clotting protein that is part of this group is fibrinogen, one of the main components in the formation of blood clots. In response to tissue damage, fibrinogen makes fibrin threads, which serve as adhesive in binding platelets, red blood cells and other molecules together, to stop the blood flow.

Blood Corpuscles

The blood corpuscles are the cells which float freely in plasma. These form about 40-45% of blood. These are generally three types of blood corpuscles.

1. Red Blood Cells (RBCs)

Red blood cell (erythrocyte) also known as **RBCs**. RBCs are formed in the myeloid tissue or most commonly known as red bone marrow, although when the body is under severe conditions the yellow bone marrow, which is also in the fatty places of the marrow in the body will also make RBCs. The formation of RBCs is called erythropoiesis (erythro/red; poiesis/formation). Red blood cells lose nuclei upon maturation and take on a biconcave, dimpled-shape. They are about 7-8 micrometers in diameter. There are about 1000 × more red blood cells than white blood cells. RBCs live about 120 days and do not self repair. RBCs contain haemoglobin which transports oxygen from the lungs to the rest of the body, such as to the muscles, where it releases the oxygen load. The haemoglobin gets it's red colour from their respiratory pigments.

Shape

RBCs have a shape of a disk that appears to be 'caved in' or almost flattened in the middle; this is called biconcave. This biconcave shape allows the RBC to carry oxygen and pass through even the smallest capillaries in the lungs. This shape also allows RBCs to stack like dinner plates and bend as they flow smoothly through the narrow blood vessels in the body. RBCs lack a nucleus (no DNA) and no organelles, meaning that these cells cannot divide or replicate themselves like the cells in our skin and muscles. RBCs have a short life span of about 120 days, however, as long as our myeloid tissue is working correctly, we will produce about 2-3 million RBCs per second. That is about 200 billion a day. This allows us to have more to replace the ones we lose.

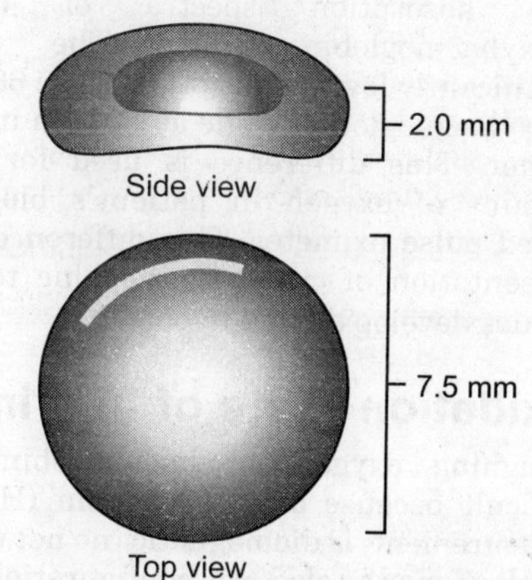

Fig. 20.1 RBCs are biconcave in shape

Haemoglobin

Haemoglobin was discovered by **Hunefeld** in 1840. The role of haemoglobin in the blood was elucidated by physiologist **Claude Bernard.** The name haemoglobin is derived from the words haeme and globin, reflecting the fact that each subunit of haemoglobin is a globular protein with an embedded haeme group. Each haeme group contains one iron atom, that can bind one oxygen molecule through ion-induced dipole forces. The most common type of haemoglobin in mammals contains four such subunits. Haemoglobin is involved in the transport of other gases: it carries some of the body's respiratory carbon dioxide (about 10% of the total) as carbaminohaemoglobin, in which CO_2 is bound to the globin protein. The molecule also carries the important regulatory molecule nitric oxide bound to a globin protein thiol group, releasing it at the same time as oxygen.

Structure

Haemoglobin has a quaternary structure characteristic of many multi-subunit globular proteins. Most of the amino acids in haemoglobin form alpha helices, connected by short non-helical segments. Hydrogen bonds stabilize the helical sections inside this protein, causing attractions within the molecule, folding each polypeptide chain into a specific shape. Haemoglobin's quaternary structure comes from its four subunits in roughly a tetrahedral arrangement.

In most vertebrates, the haemoglobin molecule is an assembly of four globular protein subunits. Each subunit is composed of a protein chain tightly associated with a non-protein haeme group. Each protein chain arranges into a set of alpha-helix structural segments connected together in a globin fold arrangement, so called because this arrangement is the same folding motif used in other haeme/globin proteins such **asmyoglobin.** This folding pattern contains a pocket that strongly binds the haeme group.

A haeme group consists of an iron (Fe) ion (charged atom) held in a heterocyclic ring, known as a **porphyrin.** This porphyrin ring consists of four pyrrole molecules cyclically linked together (by methene bridges) with the iron ion bound in the center. The iron ion, which is the site of oxygen binding, coordinates with the four nitrogens in the center of the ring, which all lie in one plane. The iron is bound strongly (covalently) to the globular protein *via* the imidazole ring of the F8 **histidine** residue (also known as the proximal histidine) below the porphyrin ring. A sixth position can reversibly bind oxygen by a coordinate covalent bond, completing the octahedral group of six ligands. Oxygen binds in an 'end-on bent' geometry, where one oxygen atom binds Fe and the other protrudes at an angle. When oxygen is not bound, a very weakly bonded water molecule fills the site, forming a distorted octahedron.

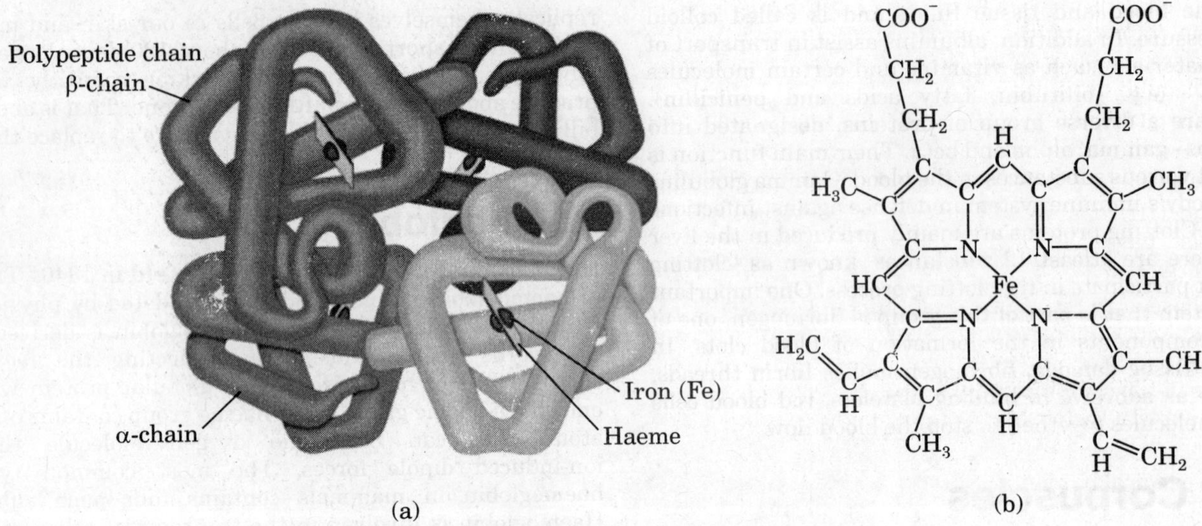

Fig. 20.2 Structure of (a) Haemoglobin (b) Haeme

Even though carbon dioxide is carried by haemoglobin, it does not compete with oxygen for the iron-binding positions, but is actually bound to the protein chains of the structure.

The iron ion may be either in the Fe^{2+} or in the Fe^{3+} state, but ferrihaemoglobin (methaemoglobin) (Fe^{3+}) cannot bind oxygen. In binding, oxygen temporarily and reversibly oxidizes (Fe^{2+}) to (Fe^{3+}), while oxygen temporally turns into superoxide, thus iron must exist in the +2 oxidation state to bind oxygen. If superoxide ion associated to Fe^{3+} is protonated the haemoglobin iron will remain oxidized and incapable to bind oxygen. In such cases, the enzyme **methaemoglobin** reductase will be able to eventually reactivate methaemoglobin by reducing the iron center.

In adult humans, the most common haemoglobin type is a tetramer (which contains 4 subunit proteins) called **haemoglobin A,** consisting of two α and two β sub-units non-covalently bound, each made of 141 and 146 amino acid residues, respectively. This is denoted as $\alpha_2\beta_2$. The subunits are structurally similar and about the same size. Each subunit has a molecular weight of about 17000 daltons, for a total molecular weight of the tetramer of about 64000 daltons (64458 g/mol). Thus, 1 g/dL = 0.1551 mmol/L. Haemoglobin A is the most intensively studied of the haemoglobin molecules.

In human infants, the haemoglobin molecule is made up of 2 α-chains and 2 γ-chains. The γ-chains are gradually replaced by β-chains as the infant grows.

The four polypeptide chains are bound to each other by salt bridges, hydrogen bonds, and the hydrophobic effect. There are two kinds of contacts between the α and β-chains: $\alpha_1\beta_1$ and $\alpha_1\beta_2$.

Oxygen Saturation

In general, haemoglobin can be saturated with oxygen molecules (oxyhaemoglobin) or desaturated with oxygen molecules (deoxyhaemoglobin).

Oxyhaemoglobin

It is formed during physiological respiration when oxygen binds to the haeme component of the protein haemoglobin in red blood cells. This process occurs in the pulmonary capillaries adjacent to the alveoli of the lungs. The oxygen then travels through the blood stream to be dropped off at cells where, it is utilized in glycolysis and in the production of ATP by the process of oxidative phosphorylation. It does not, however, help to counteract a decrease in blood pH. Ventilation, or breathing, may reverse this condition by removal of carbon dioxide thus, causing a shift up in pH.

Haemoglobin exists in two forms, a **taut form** (T) and a **relaxed form** (R). Various factors such as low pH, high CO_2 and high 2,3 BPG at the level of the tissues favour the taut form, which has low oxygen affinity and releases oxygen in the tissues. Conversely, a high pH, low CO_2 or low 2, 3 BPG favours the relaxed form which can better bind oxygen.

Deoxygenated Haemoglobin

It is the form of haemoglobin without the bound oxygen. The absorption spectra of oxyhaemoglobin and deoxyhaemoglobin differ. The oxyhaemoglobin has significantly lower absorption of the 660 nm wavelength than deoxyhaemoglobin, while at 940 nm its absorption is slightly higher. This difference is used for measurement of the amount of oxygen in patient's blood by an instrument called pulse oximeter. This difference also accounts for the presentation of cyanosis, the blue to purplish colour that tissues develop during hypoxia.

Oxidation State of Iron in Haemoglobin

Assigning oxygenated haemoglobin's oxidation state is difficult because oxyhaemoglobin (HbO_2), by experimental measurement, is diamagnetic (no net unpaired electrons), yet the low-energy electron configurations in both oxygen and iron are paramagnetic (suggesting atleast one unpaired electron in the complex). The lowest energy form of oxygen, and the lowest energy forms of the relevant oxidation states of iron, are these:

(a) Triplet oxygen, the lowest energy molecular oxygen species, has two unpaired electrons in antibonding π^* molecular orbitals.

(b) Iron (II) tends to exist in a high-spin configuration, where unpaired electrons exist in Eg antibonding orbitals.

(c) Iron (III) has an odd number of electrons, and thus must have one or more unpaired electrons, in any energy state.

All of these structures are paramagnetic (have unpaired electrons), not diamagnetic. Thus, a non-intuitive (*e.g.*, a higher energy for at least one species) distribution of electrons in the combination of iron and oxygen must exist, in order to explain the observed diamagnetism and no unpaired electrons.

The three logical possibilities to produce diamagnetic (no net spin) HbO_2 are:

(a) Low-spin Fe^{2+} binds to singlet oxygen. Both low-spin iron and singlet oxygen are diamagnetic. However, the singlet form of oxygen is the higher-energy form of the molecule.

(b) Low-spin Fe^{3+} binds to O_2^- (the superoxide ion) and the two unpaired electrons couple antiferromagnetically, giving diamagnetic properties.

(c) Low-spin Fe^{4+} binds to peroxide, O_2^{2-}. Both are diamagnetic.

Besides the oxygen ligand, which binds to haemoglobin in a cooperative manner, haemoglobin ligands also include competitive inhibitors such as carbon monoxide (CO) and allosteric ligands such as carbon dioxide (CO_2) and nitric oxide (NO). The carbon dioxide is bound to amino groups of the globin proteins as carbaminohaemoglobin, and is thought to account for about 10% of carbon dioxide transport in mammals. Nitric oxide is bound to specific thiol groups in the globin protein to form an S-nitrosothiol which dissociates into free nitric oxide and thiol again, as the haemoglobin releases oxygen from its haeme site. This nitric oxide transport to peripheral tissues is hypothesized to assist oxygen transport in tissues, by releasing vasodilatory nitric oxide to tissues in which oxygen levels are low.

Cooperative

When oxygen binds to the iron complex, it causes the iron atom to move back toward the center of the plane of the porphyrin ring. At the same time, the imidazole side-chain of the histidine residue interacting at the other pole of the iron is pulled toward the porphyrin ring. This interaction forces the plane of the ring sideways toward the outside of the tetramer, and also induces a strain in the protein helix containing the histidine as it moves nearer to the iron atom. This strain is transmitted to the remaining three monomers in the tetramer, where it induces a similar conformational change in the other haeme sites such that binding of oxygen to these sites becomes easier.

In the tetrameric form of normal adult haemoglobin, the binding of oxygen is, thus, a cooperative process. The binding affinity of haemoglobin for oxygen is increased by the oxygen saturation of the molecule, with the first oxygen bound influencing the shape of the binding sites for the next oxygen, in a way favourable for binding. This positive cooperative binding is achieved through steric conformational changes of the haemoglobin protein complex as discussed above, *i.e.*, when one subunit protein in haemoglobin becomes oxygenated, a conformational or structural change in the whole complex is initiated, causing the other subunits to gain an increased affinity for oxygen. As a consequence, the oxygen binding curve of haemoglobin is sigmoidal or S-shaped, as opposed to the normal hyperbolic curve associated with non-cooperative binding.

Competitive

Haemoglobin's oxygen-binding capacity is decreased in the presence of carbon monoxide because both gases compete for the same binding sites on haemoglobin, carbon monoxide binding preferentially in place of oxygen.

The binding of oxygen is affected by molecules such as carbon monoxide (CO) (for example, from tobacco smoking, car exhaust, and incomplete combustion in furnaces). CO competes with oxygen at the heme binding site. Haemoglobin binding affinity for CO is 250 times greater than its affinity for oxygen, meaning that small amounts of CO dramatically reduce haemoglobin's ability to transport oxygen. Since carbon monoxide is a colourless, odourless and tasteless gas, and poses a potentially fatal threat detectors have become commercially available to warn of dangerous levels in residences. When haemoglobin combines with CO, it forms a very bright red compound called **carboxyhaemoglobin,** which may cause the skin of CO poisoning victims to appear pink in death, instead of white or blue. When inspired air contains CO levels as low as 0.02%, headache and nausea occur; if the CO concentration is increased to 0.1%, unconsciousness will follow. In heavy smokers, up to 20% of the oxygen-active sites can be blocked by CO.

In similar fashion, haemoglobin also has competitive binding affinity for cyanide (CN^-), sulphur monoxide (SO), nitric oxide (NO) and sulphide (S^{2-}), including hydrogen sulphide (H_2S). All of these bind to iron in haeme without changing its oxidation state, but they never the less inhibit oxygen-binding, causing grave toxicity.

The iron atom in the haeme group must initially be in the ferrous (Fe^{2+}) oxidation state to support oxygen and other gases binding and transport (it temporarily switches to ferric during the time oxygen is bound, as explained above). Initial oxidation to the ferric (Fe^{3+}) state without oxygen converts haemoglobin into 'haemiglobin' or methaemoglobin (pronounced 'met-haemoglobin'), which cannot bind oxygen. Haemoglobin in normal red blood cells is protected by a reduction system to keep this from happening. Nitric oxide is capable of converting a small fraction of haemoglobin to methaemoglobin in red blood cells. The latter reaction is a remnant activity of the more ancient nitric oxide dioxygenase function of globins.

Allosteric

Carbon dioxide occupies a different binding site on the haemoglobin. Carbon dioxide is more readily dissolved in deoxygenated blood, facilitating its removal from the body after the oxygen has been released to tissues undergoing metabolism. This increased affinity for carbon dioxide by the venous blood is known as the **Haldane effect.** Through the enzyme carbonic anhydrase, carbon dioxide reacts with water to give carbonic acid, which decomposes into bicarbonate and protons:

$$CO_2 + H_2O \longrightarrow H_2CO_3 \longrightarrow HCO_3^- + H^+$$

Hence, blood with high carbon dioxide levels is also lower in pH (more acidic). Haemoglobin can bind protons and carbon dioxide, which causes a conformational change in the protein and facilitates the release of oxygen. Protons bind at various places on the protein, while carbon dioxide binds at the α-amino group. Carbon dioxide binds to haemoglobin and forms carbaminohaemoglobin. This decrease in haemoglobin's affinity for oxygen by the binding of carbon dioxide and acid is known as the **Bohr effect** (shifts the O_2 saturation curve to the right). Conversely, when the carbon dioxide levels in the blood decrease (*i.e.,* in the lung capillaries), carbon dioxide and protons are released from haemoglobin, increasing the oxygen affinity of the protein. A reduction in the total binding capacity of haemoglobin to oxygen (*i.e.,* shifting the curve down, not just to the right) due to reduced pH is called the **root effect.** This is seen in bony fish.

It is necessary for haemoglobin to release the oxygen that it binds; if not, there is no point in binding it. The sigmoidal curve of haemoglobin makes it efficient in binding (taking up O_2 in lungs), and efficient in unloading (unloading O_2 in tissues).

In people acclimated to high altitudes, the concentration of 2, 3-biphosphoglycerate (2, 3-BPG) in the blood is increased, which allows these individuals to deliver a larger amount of oxygen to tissues under conditions of lower oxygen tension. This phenomenon, where molecule Y affects the binding of molecule X to a transport molecule Z, is called a **heterotropic allosteric effect.**

A variant haemoglobin, called **fetal haemoglobin** (HbF, $\alpha_2\gamma_2$), is found in the developing fetus, and binds oxygen with greater affinity than adult haemoglobin. This means that the oxygen binding curve for fetal haemoglobin is left-shifted (*i.e.,* a higher percentage of haemoglobin has oxygen bound to it at lower oxygen tension), in comparison to that of adult haemoglobin. As a result, fetal blood in the placenta is able to take oxygen from maternal blood.

Haemoglobin also carries nitric oxide in the globin part of the molecule. This improves oxygen delivery in the periphery and contributes to the control of respiration. NO binds reversibly to a specific cysteine residue in globin; the binding depends on the state (R or T) of the haemoglobin. The resulting S-nitrosylated haemoglobin influences various NO-related activities such as the control of vascular resistance, blood pressure and respiration. NO is not released in the cytoplasm of erythrocytes but transported by an anion exchanger called AE1 out of them.

A study was performed to examine the influence of the form of haemoglobin (Hb) on the partitioning of inhaled Volatile Organic Compounds (VOCs) into (human and animal) blood. Benzene was the prototypic VOC used in the investigations for this research due to the similar properties it shares with many other VOCs. To be specific, this study analyses the influence of the water solubility of Hb on the partitioning coefficient (PC) of a VOC as compared to the influence of the 'species' or form of Hb. The different forms of blood used include: human haemoglobin (HbA), rat Hb and sickle-cell haemoglobin (HbS). Rat Hb contains little water and is in a quasi-crystalline form, found inside the Red Blood Cells (RBCs), meaning they are more hydrophobic than human Hb, which are water-soluble. Sickle-cell haemoglobin (HbS) is water-soluble; however it can become water-insoluble, forming hydrophobic polymers, when deoxygenated. The findings state that the benzene PC for rat Hb was much higher than human that for Hb; however, the tests that measured the PCs of the oxygenated and deoxygenated forms of HbA and HbS did not differ, indicating that the affinity of benzene was not affected by the water solubility of Hb.

Other Oxygen Binding Proteins

There are a number of oxygen binding proteins present in other organisms and also in other organs/tissue in human body. They include

Myoglobin

It is found in the muscle tissue of many vertebrates, including humans, it gives muscle tissue a distinct red or dark gray colour. It is very similar to haemoglobin in structure and sequence, but is not a tetramer; instead, it is a monomer that lacks cooperative binding. It is used to store oxygen rather than transport it.

Haemocyanin

The second most common oxygen-transporting protein found in nature, it is found in the blood of many **arthropods** and molluscs. Uses copper prosthetic groups instead of iron haeme groups and is blue in colour when oxygenated.

Haemoerythrin

Some marine invertebrates and a few species of annelid use this iron containing non-haeme protein to carry oxygen in their blood. Appears pink/violet when oxygenated, clear otherwise.

Chlorocruorin

It is found in many annelids, it is very similar to erythrocruorin, but the haeme group is significantly different in structure. Appears green when deoxygenated and red when oxygenated.

Vanabins

Also known as **vanadium chromagens,** they are found in the blood of sea **squirts.** There were once hypothesized to use the rare metal vanadium as an oxygen binding prosthetic group. However, although they do contain vanadium by preference, they apparently bind little oxygen and thus, have some other function, which has not been elucidated (sea squirts also contain some haemoglobin). They may act as toxins.

Erythrocruorin

It is found in many annelids, including earthworms, it is a giant free-floating blood protein containing many dozens—possibly hundreds—of iron and haeme-bearing protein subunits bound together into a single protein complex with a molecular mass greater than 3.5 million daltons.

Pinnaglobin

Only seen in the mollusc *Pinna squamosa*. Brown manganese based porphyrin protein.

Leghaemoglobin

In leguminous plants, such as alfa-alfa or soyabeans, the nitrogen fixing bacteria in the roots are protected from oxygen by this iron haeme containing oxygen-binding protein. The specific enzyme protected is nitrogenase, which is unable to reduce nitrogen gas in the presence of free oxygen.

Coboglobin

A synthetic cobalt-based porphyrin. Coboprotein would appear colourless when oxygenated, but yellow when in veins.

The balance can be measured by the acid and base levels in the blood. This is called pH. Normal pH of blood ranges between 7.35-7.45; this normal blood is called alkaline (less acidic then water). A drop in pH is called acidic. This condition is also called acidosis. A jump in pH higher the 7.45 is called 'alkalis'. To maintain the homeostasis (or balance) the blood has tiny molecules within the RBC that help prevent drops or increases from happening.

Destruction

Red blood cells are broken down and haemoglobin is released. The globin part of the haemoglobin is broken down into amino acid components, which in turn is recycled by the body. The iron is recovered and returned to the bone marrow to be reused. The haeme portion of the molecule experiences a chemical change and then gets excreted as bile pigment (bilirubin) by the liver. Haeme portion after being broken down contributes to the colour of faeces and your skin colour changing after being bruised.

2. White Blood Cells (WBCs)

White blood cells are different from red cells in the fact that they are usually larger in size 10-14 micrometers in diameter. White blood cells do not contain haemoglobin which in turn makes them translucent. Many times in diagrams or pictures white blood cells are represented in a blue colour, mainly because blue is the colour of the stain used to see the cells. White blood cells also have nuclei; that are some what segmented and are surrounded by electrons inside the membrane.

Functions

White blood cells (leukocytes) are also known as 'WBCs'. White blood cells are made in the bone marrow but they also divide in the blood and lymphatic systems. They are commonly amoeboid (cells that move or feed by means of temporary projections, called **pseudopods** (false feet) and escape the circulatory system through the capillary beds. The different types of WBCs are basophils, eosinophils, eutrophils, monocytes, B and T-cell lymphocytes. Neutrophils, eosinophils and basophils are all granular leukocytes. Lymphocytes and monocytes are agranular leukocytes.

Table 20.1 **Characteristics of Different Types of White Blood Cells**

Characters	Neutrophils	Basophils	Acidophils	Monocytes	Lymphocytes
Percentage of leucocytes	60-65%	0.5-1%	2-3%	6-8%	20-25%
Diameter	10-12 μm	8-10 μm	10-15 μm	12-15 μm	8-12 μm
Nucleus	Multilobed	S-shaped	Bilobed	Kidney-shaped	Rounded
Cytoplasm	Neutrophilic	Basophilic	Eosinophilic	Basophilic	Basophilic
Granules	Fine granular	Coarse granular	Coarse granular	Absent	Absent
Lifespan	10-12 hours	8-12 hours	14 hours	10-20 hours	Months to years
Formation	Red bone marrow	Red bone marrow	Red bone marrow	Spleen and lymph nodes	Lymph nodes and Thymus
Functions	Soliders acting as phagocytes	Heparin and histamine secretion	Antiallergic and healing of wounds	Scavenger	Antibodies formation

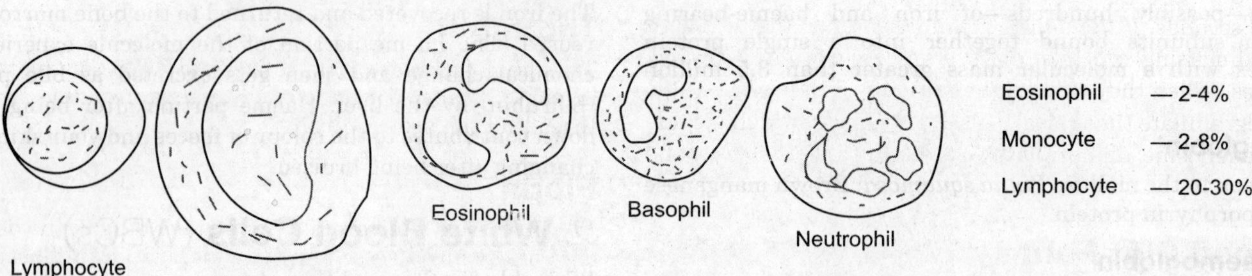

Fig. 20.3 The differential type of leucocytes in human blood

These special cells help our bodies defend themselves against pathogens. Not only do they help our immune system but they remove toxins, wastes, and abnormal or damaged cells. WBCs main function is being phagocytic which means to engulf or swallow cells.

3. Platelets

Platelets, also called thrombocytes, are membrane-bound cell fragments. Platelets have no nucleus, are between one to two micrometers in diameter, and are about $1/10^{th}$ to $1/20^{th}$ as abundant as white blood cells. Less than 1% of whole blood consists of platelets.

They result from fragmentation of large cells called megakaryocytes which are cells derived from stem cells in the bone marrow. Platelets are produced at a rate of 200 billion per day. Their production is regulated by the hormone called **thrombopoietin.** The circulating life of a platelet is 8-10 days. The sticky surface of the platelets allows them to accumulate at the site of broken blood vessels to form a clot. This aids in the process of hqemostasis (blood stopping). Platelets secrete factors that increase local platelet aggregation (*e.g.,* thromboxane A), enhance vasoconstriction (*e.g.,* serotonin), and promote blood coagulation (*e.g.,* thromboplastin).

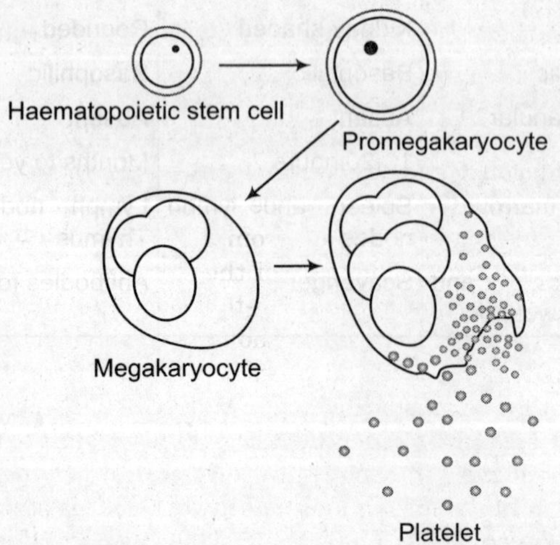

Fig. 20.4 Blood platelets: Cellular derivatives of megakaryocytes

Haemostasis

Haemostasis is the natural process of stopping blood flow or loss of blood following an injury (*haemo* = blood; *stasis* = standing). It has three stages:

(i) Vascular spasm, vasoconstriction, or intense contraction of blood vessels.

(ii) Formation of a platelet plug.

(iii) Blood clotting or coagulation. Once the flow of blood has been stopped, tissue repair can begin.

1. Vascular Spasm or Vasoconstriction

In a normal individual, immediately after a blood vessel has been cut and endothelial cells are damaged, vasoconstriction occurs, thus slowing blood flow to the area. Smooth muscle in the vessel wall goes through spasms or intense contractions that constrict the vessel. If the vessels are small, spasms compress the inner walls together and may be able to stop the bleeding completely. If the vessels are medium to large-sized, the spasms slow down immediate outflow of blood, lessening the damage but still preparing the vessel for the later steps of haemostasis. These vascular spasms usually last for about 30 min, long enough for the next two stages of haemostasis to take place.

2. Formation of a Platelet Plug

Within 20 of an injury, coagulation is initiated. Contrary to popular belief, clotting of a cut on the skin is not initiated by air or drying out, but by platelets adhering to and activated by collagen in the blood vessels endothelium. The activated platelets then release the contents of their granules, which contain a variety of substances that stimulate further platelet activation and enhance the haemostatic process. When the lining of a blood vessel breaks and endothelial cells are damaged, revealing collagen proteins in the vessel wall, platelets swell, grow spikey extensions and start clumping together. They start to stick to each other and the walls of the vessel. This continues as more platelets congregate and undergo these same transformations. This process results in a platelet plug that seals the injured area. If the injury is small, a platelet plug may be able to form and close it within several seconds. If the damage is more serious, the next step of blood clotting will take place. Platelets contain secretory granules. When they stick to the proteins in the vessel walls, they degranulate thus releasing their products, which include ADP (adenosine diphosphate), serotonin and thromboxane A2.

A Blood Clot Forms

If the platelet plug is not enough to stop the bleeding, the third stage of haemostasis begins: the formation of a blood clot. First, blood changes from a liquid to a gel. Atleast 12 substances called clotting factors take part in a series of chemical reactions that eventually create a mesh of protein fibres within the blood. Each of the clotting factors has a very specific function. Three of the substances discussed here prothrombin, thrombin and fibrinogen.

Prothrombin

When blood vessels are damaged, vessels and nearby platelets are stimulated to release a substance called prothrombin activator, which in turn activates the conversion of prothrombin, a plasma protein, into an enzyme called thrombin. This reaction requires calcium ions.

Thrombin

Thrombin facilitates the conversion of a soluble plasma protein called fibrinogen into long insoluble fibres or threads of the protein fibrin.

Fibrin

Fibrin threads wind around the platelet plug at the damaged area of the blood vessel, forming an interlocking network of fibres and a framework for the clot. This net of fibres traps and helps hold platelets, blood cells and other molecules tight to the site of injury, functioning as the initial clot. This temporary fibrin clot can form in less than a minute and usually does a good job of reducing the blood flow. Next, platelets in the clot begin to shrink, tightening the clot and drawing together the vessel walls. Usually, this whole process of clot formation and tightening takes less than a half hour. The use of adsorbent chemicals, such as zeolites and other haemostatic agents, are also being explored for use in sealing severe injuries quickly.

It is essential that platelets become activated only at the site of a broken vessel. Otherwise activated platelets would form plugs and induce clots in inapropriate places. Healthy vessels secrete an enzyme called prostacyclin that functions to inhibit platelet activation and aggregation.

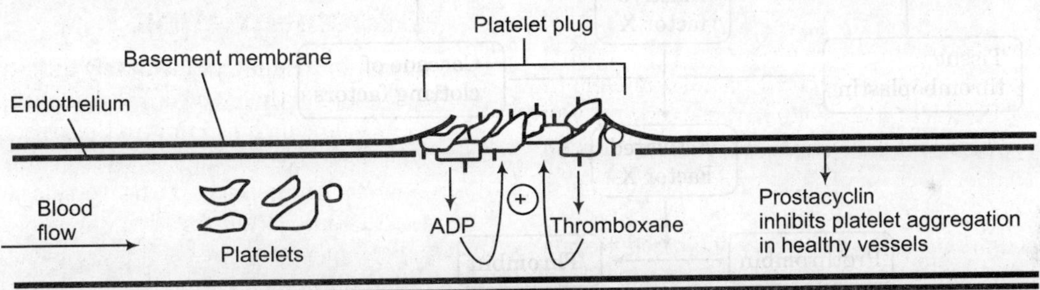

Fig. 20.5 Platelet plug in a damaged blood vessel

Aspirin inhibits platelet activation by inhibiting the action of thromboxane. By inhibiting platelet activation, aspirin limits blood clotting in general. Aspirin is used clinically as a 'blood thinner' in individuals that are at risk for developing life-threatning clots. Patients with advanced atherosclerosis take one baby aspirin per day to reduce the probability of heart attack and stroke.

Thrombocytopenia Small tears of the capillaries and arterioles are happening all the time. Platelets are responsible for quickly sealing these tears before the slower process of clotting completes the job. In the absence of adequate numbers of platelets these micro-tears allow blood to seep into the tissues. This is evidenced by purple blotches (thrombocytopenia purpura) visible on the skin. Thrombocytopenia can be acute or chronic and has many causes. Severe, untreated cases result in death.

3. Clotting of Blood

The blood contains about a dozen clotting factors. These factors are proteins that exist in the blood in an inactive state, but can be called into action when tissues or blood vessels are damaged. The activation of clotting factors occurs in a sequential manner. The first factor in the sequence activates the second factor, which activates the third factor and so on. This series of reactions is called the clotting cascade.

Blood clotting is the transformation of liquid blood into a semisolid gel. Clots are made from fibres (polymers) of a protein called fibrin (see the diagram below). **Fibrin** monomers come from an inactive precursor called **fibrinogen.** The body of the fibrinogen molecule has caps on its ends that mask fibrin-to-fibrin binding sites. If the caps are removed then fibrin monomers polymerize to form fibrin polymers. This process requires **thrombin,** the enzyme that converts fibrinogen to fibrin. This process also requires **calcium,** which acts as a kind of glue to hold the fibrin monomers to each other to form the polymeric fibre. The fibrin fibres form a loose meshwork that is stabilized by clotting **factor XIII.** The stabilized meshwork of fibrin fibres traps erythrocytes, thus forming a clot that stops the flow of blood.

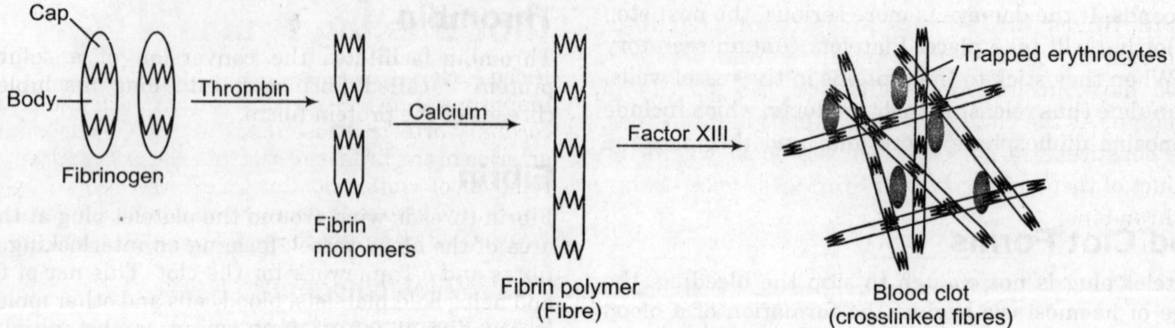

Fig. 20.6 Formation of blood clot

Control of the Clotting Cascade

From the diagram above we can see that thrombin is the key to the clotting mechanism. If thrombin is present then clotting will procede, but if thrombin is absent then clotting will not occur. How then is thrombin controlled? Thrombin is derived from an inactive precursor called **prothrombin.** There are two pathways that lead to the conversion of prothrombin to thrombin;

(i) The intrinsic pathway

(ii) The extrinsic pathway

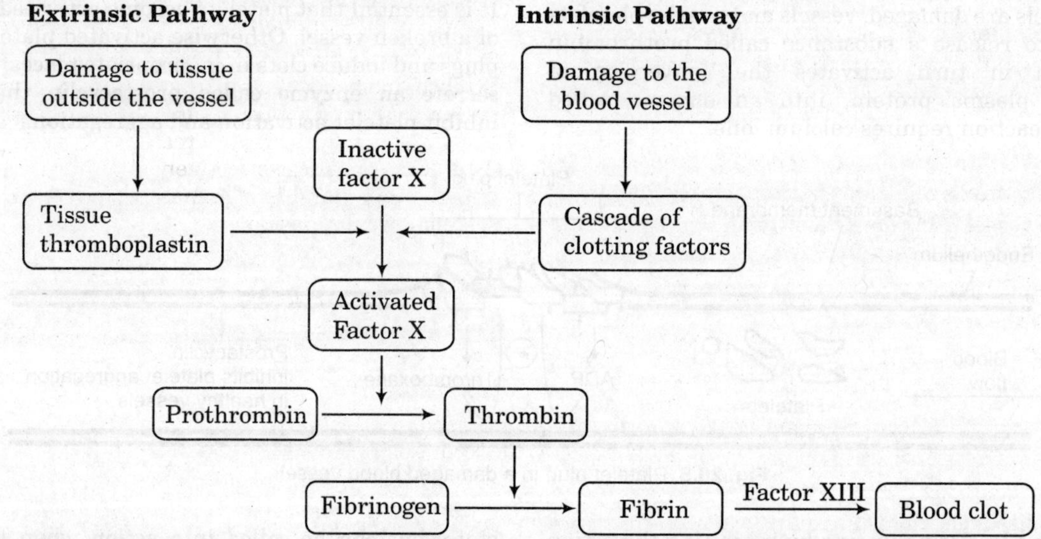

Fig. 20.7 Blood clotting cascade

Intrinsic Pathway

The intrinsic pathway, which is triggered by elements that lie within the blood inself (intrinsic to the blood), occurs in the following way. Damage to the vessel wall stimulates the activation of a cascade of clotting factors (for the sake of simplicity we will not consider the individual factors). This cascade results in the activation of factor X. Activated factor X is an enzyme that converts prothrombin to thrombin. Thrombin converts fibrinogen to fibrin monomers, which then polymerize in fibrin fibres. Fibrin fibres form a loose meshwork that is stabilized by crosslinks created by factor XIII. The stabilzed meshwork of fibrin fibres is now a clot that traps red blood cells and platelets and thus stops the flow of blood.

Extrinsic Pathway

The extrinsic pathway is triggered by tissue damage outside of the blood vessel. This pathway acts to clot blood that has escaped from the vessel into the tissues. Damage to tissue stimulates the activation of **tissue thromboplastin,** an enzyme that catalyzes the activation of factor X. At this point the intrinsic and extrinsic pathways converge and the subsequent steps are the same as those described above.

Inhibition of Excessive Clotting

It would be dangerous if blood clotting were to continue to expand beyond the boundaries of the injury. Excessive clotting is inhibited because:

(a) Clotting factors are rapidly inactivated

There are enzymes in the blood that function to inactivate clotting factors. As clotting factors are taken away from the site of injury by the blood stream, they become inactivated by these enzymes. This ensures that clotting will only occur at the site of injury and not progress steadily down the vessel.

(b) Fibrin fibres inhibit the activity of thrombin Thrombin acts to convert fibrinogen to fibrin, yet fibrin fibres have an inhibitory effect on the activity of thrombin. As the clot grows this inhibition intensifies. This constitutes a negative feedback loop, where the product of thrombin activity (fibrin) feeds back to shut off thrombin.

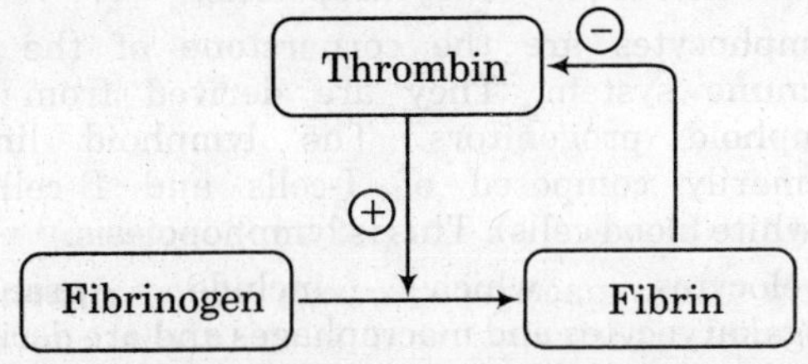

Fig. 20.8 Inhibition of blood clotting

Clot Removal

Blood clots are designed to be temporary. After the clot has formed, the process of vessel repair begins. Epithelial cells at the margin on the injury undergo cell division. These new cells eventually fill the gap in the vessel created by the injury. Also, cells called fibroblasts are recruited to the area. Fibroblasts form connective tissue that repairs the basement membrane of the vessel (fibroblasts also form scar tissue that may or may not be removed over time). At this point the vessel is healed and the blood clot is no longer needed. The clot is removed in the following way:

The clot itself stimulates the secretion of **Tissue Plasminogen Activator** (TPA) from the surrounding vascular epithelium. TPA is an enzyme that catalyzes the conversion of **plasminogen** to **plasmin.** Plasminogen is an inactive precursor molecule found in the blood, but plasmin is an enzyme that dissolves clots. Plasmin levels are not very high so clot removal is a slow process. By the time the clot has been completely dissolved by plasmin, the vessel has had a chance to heal itself. In summary, the clot, which forms rapidly, calls for its own destruction by initiating the activation of plasmin.

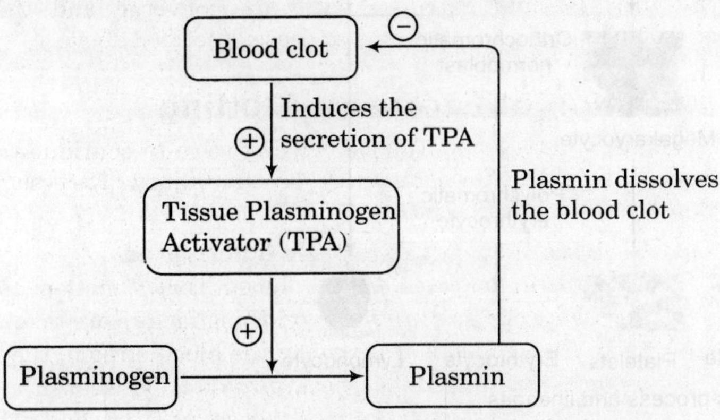

Fig. 20.9 Removal of blood clot

Clot Busting Drugs

Blood clots can be life-threatening if they form inappropriately in critical locations. Clots that block coronary arteries cause heart attacks, while clots that block arteries in the brain cause stroke. Drugs that can mediate the removal of clots, 'clot busters', are used in cases of heart attack and stroke to decrease the damage caused by the clot. Drugs used clinically to remove clots include:

Tissue Plasminogen Activator (TPA)

Tissue Plasminogen Activator (TPA) was recently cloned and is now produced in mass quantities by the biotech firm, Amgen. It is used clinically to dissolve clots in coronary arteries following a heart attack. It is also used to dissolve clots in the brain following stroke.

Streptokinase

Streptokinase is an enzyme that directly dissolves blood clots. It is produced by *Streptococcus* bacteria. The bacteria use streptokinase to dissolve clots that negatively effects their growth in the human host. This clot dissolving enzyme is apparently as effective as recombinant TPA.

Streptokinase is not a human enzyme, therefore the immune system sees it as a foreign molecule that should be destroyed. The immune response increases with repeated use of the drug. This limits the effectiveness of the drug over time. TPA, on-the other hand is a human molecule which the immune system does not destroy.

Anticoagulants Substances that Inhibit the Process of Clotting

(a) Heparin

- Produced primarily in the liver and lung (usually obtained from pigs or cows).
- Acts as an anticoagulant by inhibiting the activity of thrombin.
- Used clinically for acute problems, also used to prevent clotting in IVs (heplock).
- Fast acting, but short-lived drug. It must be injected to be effective.

(b) Coumadin (Dicoumarol and Warfarin)

- Taken orally in small doses for long-term control of blood clotting.
  Acts as an anticoagulant by inhibiting the processing of vitamin-K, which is required for the synthesis of several clotting factors including prothrombin.
- It is slow acting, requiring days to have an effect.

(c) Citrates

- Calcium is required for polymerization of fibrin.
- Citrates bind up (chelate) calcium and thus inhibit the formation of clots.
- Citrates are used in long term blood storage.
- Transfusion of large amounts of citrate-containing blood can be dangerous. The citrates chelate calcium in the body and thus disrupt processes such as nerve transmission and muscle contraction.

Haematopoiesis

Haematopoiesis is the formation of blood cellular components. All cellular blood components are derived from haematopoietic stem cells. In a healthy adult person, approximately 10^{11}-10^{12} new blood cells are produced daily in order to maintain steady state levels in the peripheral circulation.

Haematopoietic Stem Cells (HSCs) reside in the medulla of the bone (bone marrow) and have the unique ability to give rise to all of the different mature blood cell types. HSCs are self-renewing when they proliferate, atleast some of their daughter cells remain as HSCs, so the pool of stem cells does not become depleted. The other daughters of HSCs (myeloid and lymphoid progenitor cells), however can each commit to any of the alternative differentiation pathways that lead to the production of one or more specific types of blood cells, but cannot self-renew. This is one of the vital processes in the body.

In developing embryos, blood formation occurs in aggregates of blood cells in the yolk sac, called blood islands. As development progresses, blood formation occurs in the spleen, liver and lymph nodes. When bone marrow develops, it eventually assumes the task of forming most of the blood cells for the entire organism. However, maturation, activation, and some proliferation of lymphoid cells occurs in secondary lymphoid organs (spleen, thymus and lymph nodes). In children, haematopoiesis occurs in the marrow of the long bones such as the femur and tibia. In adults, it occurs mainly in the pelvis, cranium, vertebrae and sternum. All blood cells are divided into three lineages.

1. Erythroid cells are the oxygen carrying red blood cells. Both reticulocytes and erythrocytes are functional and are released into the blood. In fact, a reticulocyte count estimates the rate of erythropoiesis.
2. Lymphocytes are the cornerstone of the adaptive immune system. They are derived from common lymphoid progenitors. The lymphoid lineage is primarily composed of T-cells and B-cells (types of white blood cells). This is lymphopoiesis.
3. Myelocytes, which include granulocytes, megakaryocytes and macrophages and are derived from common myeloid progenitors, are involved in such diverse roles as innate immunity, adaptive immunity, and blood clotting. This is myelopoiesis.

Granulopoiesis (or granulocytopoiesis) is haematopoiesis of **granulocytes.**

Megakaryocytopoiesis is haematopoiesis of **megakaryocytes.**

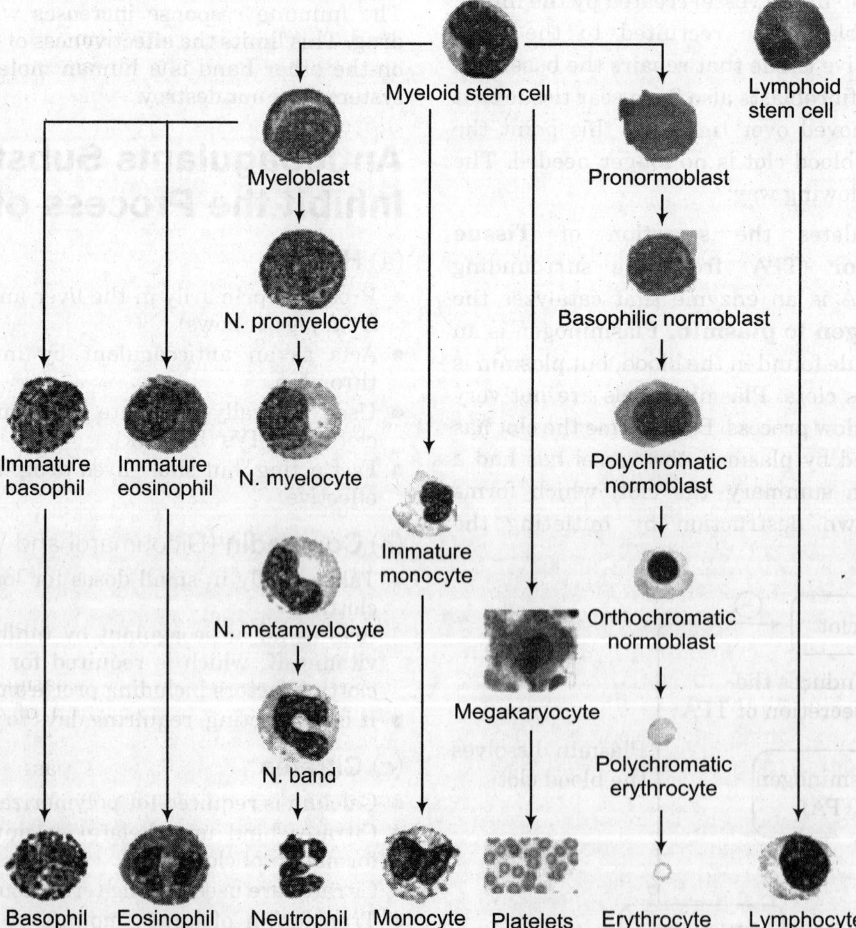

Fig. 20.10 Haematopoiesis process and lineages

Blood Group System

The ABO blood group is represented by substances on the surface of Red Blood Cells (RBCs). These substances are important because they contain specific sequences of amino acid and carbohydrates which are antigenic. As well as being on the surface of RBCs, some of these antigens are also present on the cells of other tissues. A complete blood type describes the set of 29 substances on the surface of RBCs, and an individual's blood type is one of the many possible combinations of blood group antigens. Usually only the ABO blood group system and the presence or absence of the Rhesus D antigen (also known as the rhesus factor or Rh factor) are determined and used to describe the blood type. Over 400 different blood group antigens have been found, many of these being very rare. If an individual is exposed to a blood group antigen that is not recognized as self, the individual can become sensitized to that antigen; the immune system makes specific antibodies which binds specifically to a particular blood group antigen and an immunological memory against that particular antigen is formed. These antibodies can bind to antigens on the surface of transfused red blood cells (or other tissue cells) often leading to destruction of the cells by recruitment of other components of the immune system. Knowledge of a individual's blood type is important to identify appropriate blood for transfusion or tissue for organ transplantation.

Surface Antigens

Several different RBC surface antigens stemming from one allele (or very closely linked genes) are collectively labelled as a blood group system or blood group. The two most important blood group systems were discovered during early experiments with blood transfusion, the ABO group in **1901** and the rhesus group in 1937. These two blood groups are reflected in the common nomenclature A positive, O negative, etc. With letters referring to the ABO group and positive/negative to the presence/absence of the Rh D antigen of the rhesus group. Development of the Coombs test in 1945, and the advent of transfusion medicine led to discovery of more blood groups. Blood Group AB individuals have both A and B antigens on the surface of their RBCs, and their blood serum do not contain any antibodies against either A or B antigen. Therefore, an individual with type AB blood can receive blood from any group (with AB being preferable), but can only donate blood to another group AB individual. Blood Group A individuals have the A antigen on the surface of their RBCs, and blood serum containing IgM antibodies against the B antigen. Therefore, a group A individual can only receive blood from individuals of groups A or O (with A being preferable), and can donate blood to individuals of groups A or AB. Blood group B individuals have the B antigen on their surface of their RBCs, and blood serum containing IgM antibodies against the A antigen. Therefore, a group B individual can only receive blood from individuals of groups B or O (with B being preferable), and can donate blood to individuals of groups B or AB. Blood group O individuals do not have either A or B antigens on the surface of their RBCs, but their blood serum contains IgM antibodies against both A and B antigens. Therefore, a group O individual can only receive blood from a group O individual, but they can donate blood to individuals of any ABO blood group (*i.e.*, A, B, O or AB). Inheritance blood types are inherited and represent contributions from both parents.

The ABO blood type is controlled by a single gene with three alleles: i, IA, and IB. The gene encodes an enzyme that modifies the carbohydrate content of the red blood cell antigens. IA gives type A, IB gives type B, i give types O

IA and IB are dominant over i, so ii people have type O, IAIA or IAi have A and IBIB or IBi have type B. IAIB people have both phenotypes because A and B are codominant, which means that type A and B parents can have an AB child. Thus, it is extremely unlikely for a type AB parent to have a type O child (it is not, however, direct proof of illegitimacy): the *cis*-AB phenotype has a single enzyme that creates both A and B antigens. The resulting red blood cells do not usually express A or B antigen at the same level that would be expected on common group A or B red blood cells, which can help solve the problem of an apparently genetically impossible blood group.

Rh Factor

Many people have the Rh factor on the red blood cell. Rh carriers do not have the antibodies for the Rh factor, but can make them if exposed to Rh. Most commonly Rh is seen when anti-Rh antibodies cross from the mother's placenta into the child before birth. The Rh factor enters the child destroying the child's red blood cells. This is called **haemolytic disease.**

Haemolytic Disease of the Newborn

Often a pregnant woman carries a foetus with a different blood type to herself, and sometimes the mother forms antibodies against the red blood cells of the foetus, leading to low foetal blood counts, a condition known as haemolytic disease of the newborn. Haemolytic disease of the newborn (also known as HDN) is an alloimmune condition that develops in a foetus when the IgG antibodies produced by the mother and passing through the placenta include ones which attack the red blood cells in the foetal circulation. The red cells are broken down and the foetus can develop reticulocytosis and anaemia. The foetal disease ranges from mild to very severe and foetal death from heart failure hydrops fetalis can occur. When the disease is moderate or severe many erythroblasts are present in the foetal blood and so these forms of the disease can be called **erythroblastosis fetalis.**

Before birth, options for treatment include intrauterine transfusion or early induction of labour when pulmonary maturity has been attained, foetal distress is present or 35 to 37 weeks of gestation have passed. The mother may also undergo plasma exchange to reduce the circulating levels of antibody by as much as 75%. After birth, treatment depends on the severity of the condition, but could include temperature stabilization and monitoring, phototherapy, transfusion with compatible packed red blood, exchange transfusion with a blood type compatible with both the infant and the mother, sodium bicarbonate for correction of acidosis and/or assisted ventilation. Rh negative mothers who have had a pregnancy with or are pregnant with a Rh positive infant, are given Rh immune globulin (RhIG) also known as Rhogam, during pregnancy and after delivery to prevent sensitization to the D antigen. It works by binding any fetal red cells with the D antigen before the mother is able to produce an immune response and form anti-D IgG. A drawback to pre-partum administration of RhIG is that it causes a positive antibody screen when the mother is tested which is indistinguishable from immune reasons for antibody production.

Rh Antigens (Rh^+ and Rh^- People)

About 85 per cent of all white people are Rh^+ and 15 per cent, Rh^-. In American blacks, the percentage of Rh^+ is about 95, whereas in African blacks, it is virtually 100 per cent.

There are six common types of Rh antigens, each of which is called an **Rh factor.** These types are designated C, D, E, c, d and e. A person who has a C antigen does not have the c antigen, but the person missing the C antigen always has the c antigen. The same is true for the D-d and E-e antigens. Also, because of the manner of inheritance of these factors, each person has one of each of the three pairs of antigens.

The type D antigen is widely prevalent in the population and considerably more antigenic than the other Rh antigens. Anyone who has this type of antigen is said to the Rh^+, whereas a person who does not have type D antigen is said to be Rh^-. However, it must be noted that even in Rh-negative people, some of the other Rh antigens can still cause transfusion reactions although the reactions are usually much milder.

Compatibility in Blood Transfusions

Blood transfusions between donor and recipient of incompatible blood types can cause severe acute immunological reactions, haemolysis (RBC destruction), renal failure, shock and sometimes death. Antibodies can be highly active and can attack RBCs and bind components of the complement system to cause massive haemolysis of the transfused blood. A patient should ideally receive their own blood or type-specific blood products to minimize the chance of a transfusion reaction. If time allows, the risk will further be reduced by cross-matching blood, in addition to blood typing both recipient and donor. Cross-matching involves mixing a sample of the recipient's blood with a sample of the donor's blood and checking to see if the mixture agglutinates or forms clumps. Blood bank technicians usually check for agglutination with a microscope and if it occurs, that particular donor's blood cannot be transfused to that particular recipient. Blood transfusion is a potentially risky medical procedure and it is vital that all blood specimens are correctly identified, so in cross-matching labeling is standardized using a barcode system known as ISBT 128.

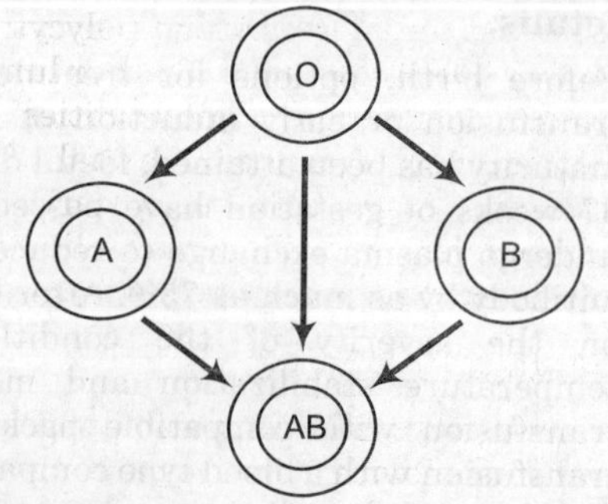

Fig. 20.11 Compatibility of blood types

Diseases of the Blood

Disseminated Intravascular Coagulation

Disseminated Intravascular Coagulation (DIC), also called **consumptive coagulopathy,** is a pathological process in the body, where the blood starts to coagulate throughout the whole body. This depletes the body of its platelets and coagulation factors and there is a paradoxically increased risk of haemorrhage. It occurs in critically ill patients, especially those with Gram negative sepsis (particularly meningococcal sepsis) and acute promyelocytic leukaemia.

Haemophilia

Haemophilia is a disease where, there is low or no blood protein, causing an inability to produce blood clots. There are two types of haemophilia: type A, which is a deficiency in factor VIII and type B (Christmas disease) a deficiency on factor IX. Because people with haemophilia do not have the ability to make blood clots, even a little cut may kill them or the smallest bump or jar to the body could cause severe bruising that doesn't get better for months. Haemophilia is passed down from mothers to their sons. Haemophilia is sometimes known as the 'Royal Disease'. This is because Queen Victoria, Queen of England (1837-1901), was a carrier of haemophilia. The haemophilia disease was passed down to her son Leopold who ended up dying at age 31. Queen Victoria also had two daughters who were carriers. These daughters passed haemophilia into the Spanish, German and Russian royal families. One of the most famous stories is that of the Russian royal family. Alexandra, grand daughter to Queen Victoria, married Nicholas (Tsar of Russia in the 1900s). Alexandra was a carrier of the disease and passed the disease to their first son, Tsarevich Alexi, who was heir to the throne of Russia. The family tried to keep their son's secret from the people, but Alexi suffered with serious bruises and extreme pain. The family found help from a monk named Rasputin. He kept their secret and gained a great deal of power over the family, making them think he was their only hope. During this time of great turmoil in Russia, Nicholas and Alexandra spent most of their attentions on their son, and not on the people. It wasn't long before the Bolshevik revolution of 1917 began.

Factor V Leiden

The opposite of haemophilia, factor V Leiden is the name given to a variant of human factor V that causes a hypercoagulability disorder. In this disorder the Leiden variant of factor V, cannot be inactivated by activated protein C. Factor V Leiden is the most common hereditary hypercoagulability disorder amongst Eurasians. It is named after the city Leiden (The Netherlands), where it was first identified in 1994 by **Prof R Bertina** *et.al.* Those that have it are at a slightly higher risk of developing blood clotts than those without. Those that test positive for factor V should avoid (oral contreseptives, obesity, smoking, and high blood pressure).

Anaemia

Anaemia (AmE) or anaemia (BrE), from the Greek (νατμια) meaning 'without blood', refers to a deficiency of red blood cells (RBCs) and/or haemoglobin. This results in a reduced ability of blood to transfer oxygen to the tissues, causing hypoxia. Since all human cells depend on oxygen for survival, varying degrees of anaemia can have a wide range of clinical consequences. Haemoglobin (the oxygen-carrying protein in the red blood cells) has to be present to ensure adequate oxygenation of all body tissues and organs.

The three main classes of anaemia include excessive blood loss (acutely such as a haemorrhage or chronically through low-volume loss), excessive blood cell destruction (haemolysis) or deficient red blood cell production (ineffective haematopoiesis). In menstruating women, dietary iron deficiency is a common cause of deficient red blood cell production.

Sickle Cell

Sickle cell disease is a general term for a group of genetic disorders caused by sickle haemoglobin (Hgb S or Hb S). In many forms of the disease, the red blood cells change shape upon deoxygenation because of polymerization of the abnormal sickle haemoglobin. This process damages the red blood cell membrane, and can cause the cells to become stuck in blood vessels. This deprives the downstream tissues of oxygen and causes ischemia and infarction. The disease is chronic and lifelong. Individuals are most often well, but their lives are punctuated by periodic painful attacks.

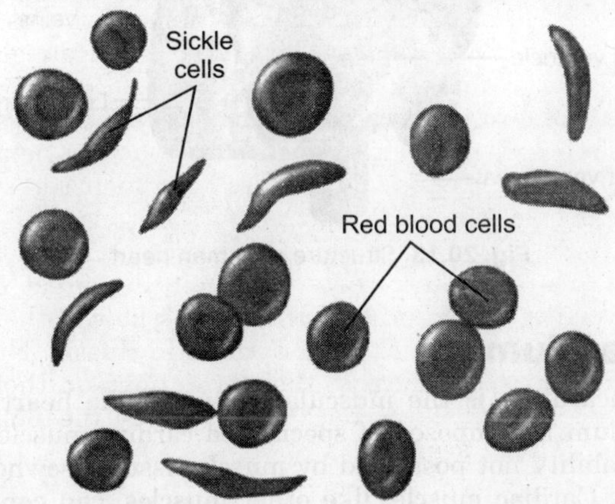

Fig. 20.12 Sickle-shaped RBCs responsible for sickle cell anaemia

In addition to periodic pain, there may be damage of internal organs and/or stroke. Life span is often shortened with sufferers living to an average of 40 years. It is common in people from parts of the world, where malaria is or was common, especially in sub-Saharan Africa or in descendants of those peoples. Sickle cell disease is inherited in the autosomal recessive pattern, depicted above. The allele responsible for sickle cell anaemia is autosomal recessive. A person who receives the defective gene from both father and mother develops the disease; a person, who receives one defective and one healthy allele remains healthy, but can pass on the disease and is known as a carrier. If two parents who are carriers have a child, there is a 1-in-4 chance of their child developing the illness and a 1-in-2 chance of their child just being a carrier.

Polycythemia

Polycythemia is a condition in which there is a net increase in the total circulating erythrocyte (red blood cell) mass of the body. There are several types of polycythemia.

Primary Polycythemia

In primary polycythemia, there may be 8 to 9 million and occasionally 11 million erythrocytes per cubic millimeter of blood (a normal range for adults is 4-5 million), and the hematocrit may be as high as 70 to 80%. In addition, the total blood volume can increase to as much as twice as normal. The entire vascular system can become markedly engorged with blood, and circulation times for blood throughout the body can increase up to twice the normal value. The increased numbers of erythrocytes can increase the viscosity of the blood to as much as five times normal. Capillaries can become plugged by the very viscous blood, and the flow of blood through the vessels tends to be extremely sluggish. As a consequence of the above, people with untreated. Polycythemia are at a risk of various thrombotic events (deep venous thrombosis, pulmonary embolism), heart attack and stroke, and have a substantial risk of Budd-Chiari syndrome (hepatic vein thrombosis). The condition is considered chronic; no cure exists. Symptomatic treatment (see below) can normalize the blood count and most patients can live a normal life for years.

Secondary Polycythemia

Secondary polycythemia is caused by either appropriate or inappropriate increases in the production of erythropoietin that result in an increased production of erythrocytes. In secondary polycythemia, there may be 6 to 8 million and occasionally 9 million erythrocytes per cubic millimeter of blood. A type of secondary polycythemia in which the production of erythropoietin increases appropriately is called **physiologic polycythemia.** Physiologic polycythemia occurs in individuals living at high altitudes (4275 to 5200 m), where oxygen availability is less than at sea level. Many athletes train at higher altitudes to take advantage of this effect — a legal form of blood doping. Actual polycythemia sufferers have been known to use their condition as an athletic advantage for greater stamina.

Other causes of secondary polycythemia include smoking, renal or liver tumours or heart or lung diseases that result in hypoxia. Endocrine abnormalities, prominently including pheochromocytoma and adrenal adenoma with Cushing's syndrome, are also secondary causes. Athletes and body-builders who abuse anabolic steroids or erythropoietin may develop secondary polycythemia.

Relative Polycythemia

Relative polycythemia is an apparent rise of the erythrocyte level in the blood; however, the underlying cause is reduced blood plasma. Relative polycythemia is often caused by fluid loss, *i.e.,* burns, dehydration and stress polycythemia.

Leukaemia

Leukaemia is a cancer of the blood or bone marrow characterized by an abnormal proliferation of blood cells, usually white blood cells (leukocytes). It is part of the broad group of diseases called **haematological neoplasms.** Damage to the bone marrow, by way of displacing the normal marrow cells with increasing numbers of malignant cells, results in a lack of blood platelets, which are important in the blood clotting process. This means people with leukaemia may become bruised, bleed excessively, or develop pin-prick bleeds (petechiae). White blood cells, which are involved in fighting pathogens, may be suppressed or dysfunctional, putting the patient at the risk of developing infections. The red blood cell deficiency leads to anaemia, which may cause dyspnea. All symptoms may also be attributable to other diseases for diagnosis, blood tests and a bone marrow biopsy are required.

Cardiovascular System

The cardiovascular system, in addition to needing to maintain itself within certain levels, plays a role in maintenance of other body systems by transporting hormones (heart secretes ANP and BNP) and nutrients (oxygen, EPO to bones, etc.), taking away waste products, and providing all living body cells with a fresh supply of oxygen and removing carbon dioxide. Homeostasis is disturbed if the cardiovascular or lymphatic systems are not functioning correctly. Our skin, bones, muscles, nervous system, endocrine, lymphatic system, lungs, digestive tract, urinary system and reproductive use the cardiovascular system as its 'road' or 'highway' as far as distribution of things that go on in our body. There are many risk factors for an unhealthy cardiovascular system. Some diseases associated are typically labelled 'uncontrollable' or 'controllable.' The main uncontrollable risk factors are age, gender and a family history of heart disease, especially at an early age.

The heart is the life-beating, always-thumping muscle in your chest. From inside the womb until death, the thump goes on. The heart for the average human will contract about 3 billion times; never resting, never stopping to take a break except for a fraction of a second between beats. If a person lives to be 80 years old, his or her heart will continue to beat an average of 100000 times a day. Many believe that the heart is the first organ to become functional. Within weeks of conception the heart starts its mission of supplying the body with nutrients even though the embryo is no bigger than a capital letter on this page. The primary function of the heart is to pump blood throgh the arteries, capillaries, and veins. There is an estimated 60000 miles of vessels throughout an adult body.

Myogenic Heart

The heart may be **neurogenic** (regulated by nerves, found in annelids, crustaceans and insects) or **myogenic** (regulated by muscles found in molluscs and vertebrates). Mammalian heart is a hollow, muscular organ about the size of a fist. It is responsible for pumping blood through the blood vessels by repeated, rhythmic contractions. The heart is composed of cardiac muscle, an involuntary muscle tissue that is found only within this organ. The term 'cardiac' (as in cardiology) means 'related to the heart' and comes from the Greek word *kardia*, for 'heart.' It has a four chambered, double pump and is located in the thoracic cavity between the lungs.

The cardiac muscle is self-exciting, meaning it has its own conduction system. This is in contrast with skeletal muscle, which requires either conscious or reflex nervous stimuli. The heart's rhythmic contractions occur spontaneously, although the frequency or heart rate can be changed by nervous or hormonal influence such as exercise or the perception of danger.

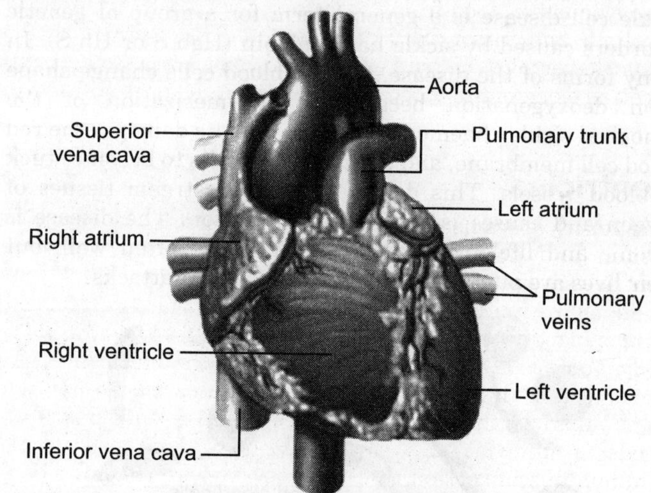

Fig. 20.13 Structure of human heart

Myocardium

The myocardium is the muscular tissue of the heart. The myocardium is composed of specialized cardiac muscle cells with an ability not possessed by muscle tissue elsewhere in the body. Cardiac muscle, like other muscles, can contract, but it can also conduct electricity, like nerves. The blood to the myocardium is supplied by the coronary arteries. If these arteries are occluded by atherosclerosis and/or thrombosis, this can lead to angina pectoris or myocardial infarction due to ischemia (lack of oxygen). Failure of the heart to contract properly (for various reasons) is termed heart failure, generally leading to fluid retention, edema, pulmonary edema, renal insufficiency, hepatomegaly, a shortened life expectancy and decreased quality of life.

Pericardium

The pericardium is the thick, membranous sac that surrounds the heart. It protects and lubricates the heart.

There are two layers to the pericardium — the fibrous pericardium and the serous pericardium. The serous pericardium is divided into two layers; in between these two layers there is a space called the pericardial cavity.

Epicardium

The layer next to the heart is the visceral layer, also known as the **epicardium.** This is the inner most layer and consists of connective tissue.

Heart Chambers

The heart has four-chambers, two atrium and two ventricles. The atriums are smaller with thin walls, while the ventricles are larger and much stronger.

Atrium

There are two atria on either side of the heart. On the right side is the atrium which holds blood that needs oxygen. The left atrium holds that blood which has been oxygenated and is ready to be sent to the body. The right atrium receives de-oxygenated blood from the superior vena cava (from head, forelimb and upper part of chest) and inferior vena cava (from lower part of trunk and hindlimbs). The left atrium receives oxygenated blood from the left and right pulmonary veins.

Ventricles

The ventricle is a heart chamber which collects blood from an atrium and pumps it out of the heart. There are two ventricles: the right ventricle pumps blood into the pulmonary circulation for the lungs, and the left ventricle pumps blood into the systemic circulation for the rest of the body. Ventricles have thicker walls than the atria and thus, can create the higher blood pressure. Comparing the left and right ventricle, the left ventricle have thicker walls because it needs to pump blood to the whole body. This leads to the common misconception that the heart lies on the left side of the body.

Septum

The interventricular septum (ventricular septum or during development septum inferious) is the stout wall separating the lower chambers (the ventricles) of the heart from one another. The ventricular septum is directed backward and to the right and is curved toward the right ventricle. The greater portion of it is thick and muscular and constitutes the muscular ventricular septum. Its upper and posterior part, which separates the aortic vestibule from the lower part of the right atrium and upper part of the right ventricle, is thin and fibrous, and is termed the membranous ventricular septum.

Valves

The two atrioventricular (AV) valves are a one-way valve that ensures blood flows from the atria to the ventricles, and not the other way. The two semilunar (SL) valves are present in the arteries leaving the heart; they prevent blood from flowing back into the ventricles. The sound heard in a heart beat is the heart valves shutting. The right AV valve is also called the **tricuspid valve** because it has three flaps. It is located between the right atrium and the right ventricle. The tricuspid valve allows blood to flow from the right atrium into the right ventricle when the heart is relaxed during diastole. When the heart begins to contract, the heart enters a phase called **systole,** and the atrium pushes blood into the ventricle. Then, the ventricle begins to contract and blood pressure inside the heart rises. When the ventricular pressure exceeds the pressure in the atrium, the tricuspid valve snaps shut. The left AV valve is also called the bicuspid valve because it has two flaps. It is also known as **the mitral valve** due to the resemblance to a bishop's mitre (a type of hat). This valve prevents blood in the left ventricle from flowing into the left atrium. As it is on the left side of the heart, it must cope with a lot of strain and pressure; this is why it is made of only two cusps, as there is less to go wrong. There are two remaining valves called the **semilunar valves.** They have flaps that resemble half moons. The pulmonary semilunar valve sits between the right ventricle and the pulmonary trunk. The aortic semilunar valve sits between the ventricle and the aorta.

Subvalvular Apparatus

The chordae tendinae are attached to papillary muscles that cause tension to better hold the valve. Together, the papillary muscles and the chordae tendinae are known as the **subvalvular** apparatus. The function of the subvalvular apparatus is to keep the valves from prolapsing into the atria when they close. The subvalvular apparatus have no effect on the opening and closing of the valves. This is caused entirely by the pressure gradient across the valve.

Complications with the Heart

The most common congenital abnormality of the heart is the bicuspid aortic valve. In this condition, instead of three cusps, the aortic valve has two cusps. This condition is often undiagnosed until the person develops calcific aortic stenosis. Aortic stenosis occurs in this condition usually in patients in their 40s or 50s, an average of 10 yr earlier than in people with normal aortic valves.

Another common complication of rheumatic fever is thickening and stenosis (partial blocking) of the mitral valve. For patients who have had rheumatic fever dentist are advised to prophylactally administer antibiotics prior to dental work to prevent bacterial endocarditis that occurs when bacteria from the teeth enter the circulation and attach to damaged heart valves.

The Circulation of Blood Through

The circulatory system is extremely important in sustaining life. It's proper functioning is responsible for the delivery of oxygen and nutrients to all cells, as well as the removal of carbon dioxide, waste products, maintenance of optimum pH, and the mobility of the elements, proteins and cells, of the immune system. In developed countries, the two leading causes of death, myocardial infarction and stroke are each direct results of an arterial system that has been slowly and progressively compromized by years of deterioration.

While it is convenient to describe the flow of the blood through the right side of the heart and then through the left side, it is important to realize that both atria contract at the same time and that both ventricles contract at the same time. The heart works as two pumps, one on the right and one on the left that works simultaneously. The right pump pumps the blood to the lungs or the pulmonary circulation at the same time that the left pump pumps blood to the rest of the body or the systemic circulation. Venous blood from systemic circulation (deoxygenated) enters the right atrium through the superior and inferior vena cava. The right atrium contracts and forces the blood through the tricuspid valve (right atrioventricular valve) and into the right ventricles. The right ventricles contract and force the blood through the pulmonary semilunar valve into the pulmonary trunk and out the pulmonary artery. This takes the blood to the lungs, where the blood releases carbon dioxide and receives a new supply of oxygen. The new blood is carried in the pulmonary veins that take it to the left atrium. The left atrium then contracts and forces blood through the left atrioventricular, bicuspid or mitral, valve into the left ventricle. The left ventricle contracts forcing blood through the aortic semilunar valve into the ascending aorta. It then branches to Arteries carrying oxygen rich blood to all parts of the body.

Blood flow after the heart is — Aorta → Arteries → Arterioles → Capillaries → Venules → Veins → Vena cava.

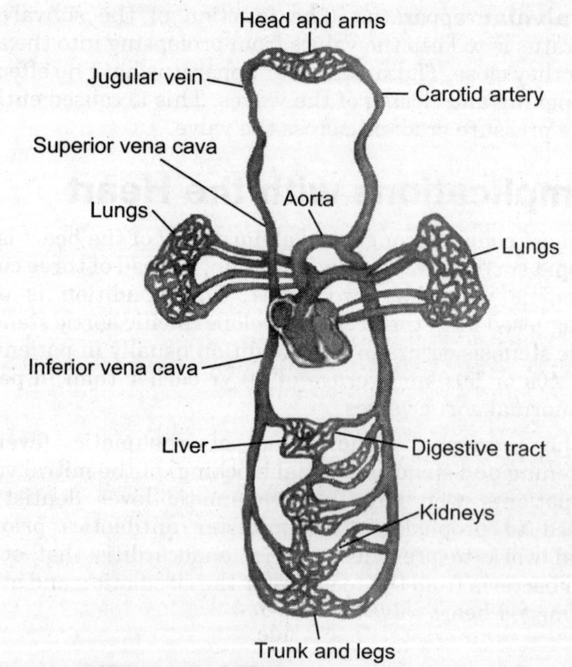

Fig. 20.14 Blood circulation: Light colour represents oxygenated blood and dark indicates deoxygenated blood

Arteries

Arteries are muscular blood vessels that carry oxygenated blood away from the heart to the body. The only exception being the pulmonary artery that carries deoxygenated blood to the lungs. Arteries have a thick wall that consists of three layers. The inside layer is called the endothelium, the middle layer is mostly smooth muscle and the outside layer is connective tissue. The artery walls are thick so that when blood enters under pressure the walls can expand.

Arterioles

An arteriole is a small artery that extends and leads to capillaries. Arterioles have thick smooth muscular walls. These smooth muscles are able to contract (causing vessel constriction) and relax (causing vessel dilation). This contracting and relaxing affects blood pressure, the higher number of vessels dilated, the lower blood pressure will be. Arterioles are just visible to the naked eye.

Capillaries

Capillaries are the smallest of a body's vessels, they connect arteries and veins, and most closely interact with tissues. They are very prevalent in the body; total surface area is about 6300 square meters. Because of this, no cell is ever very far from a capillary. The walls of capillaries are composed of a single layer of cells, the endothelium. This layer is so thin that molecules such as oxygen, water and lipids can pass through them by diffusion and enter the tissues. Waste products such as carbon dioxide and urea can diffuse back into the blood to be carried away for removal from the body. The 'capillary bed' is the network of capillaries present throughout the body. These beds are able to be 'opened' and 'closed' at any given time, according to need. This process is called **autoregulation** and capillary beds usually carry no more than 25% of the amount of blood it could hold at any time. The more metabolically active the cells, the more capillaries it will require to supply nutrients.

Capillaries Come in Three Categories

- **Continuous** Continuous capillaries have a sealed epithelium and only allow small molecules, water and ions to diffuse.
- **Fenestrated** Fenestrated capillaries (as their name implies 'fenster') have openings that allow larger molecules to diffuse.
- **Sinusoidal** Sinusoidal capillaries are special forms of fenestrated capillaries that have larger opening allowing RBCs and serum proteins to enter.

Veins

Veins carry deoxygenated blood to the heart. The only exception to this is in the pulmonary vein that carries oxygenated blood to the heart. Most of the blood volume is found in the venous system; about 70% at any given time. The veins outer walls have the same three layers as the artery, differing only because there is a lack of smooth muscle in the inner layer and less connective tissue on the outer layer. Veins have low blood pressure compared to arteries and need the help of skeletal muscles to bring blood back to the heart. Most veins have one-way valves called venous valves to prevent back flow caused by gravity. They also have a thick collagen outer layer, which helps maintain blood pressure and stop blood pooling. If a person is standing still for long periods or is bedridden, blood can accumulates in veins and can cause varicose veins. The hollow internal cavity in which the blood flows is called the lumen. A muscular layer allows veins to contract, which puts more blood into circulation. Veins are used medically as points of access to the blood stream, permitting the withdrawal of blood specimens (venipuncture) for testing purposes, and enabling the infusion of fluid, electrolytes, nutrition and medications (intravenous delivery).

Venules

A venule is a small vein that allows deoxygenated blood to return from the capillary beds to the larger blood veins. Venules have three layers; they have the same make up as arteries with less smooth muscle, making them thinner.

Cardiovascular Pathways

The double circulatory system of blood flow refers to the separate systems of pulmonary circulation and the systemic circulation in amphibians, birds and mammals (including humans). In contrast, fishes have a single circulation system. For instance, the adult human heart consists of two separated pumps, the right side with the right atrium and ventricle (which pumps deoxygenated blood into the pulmonary circulation), and the left side with the left atrium and ventricle (which pumps oxygenated blood into the systemic circulation). Blood in one circuit has to go through the heart to enter the other circuit. Blood circulates through the body two to three times every minute. In one day, the blood travels a total of 19000 km (12000 miles).

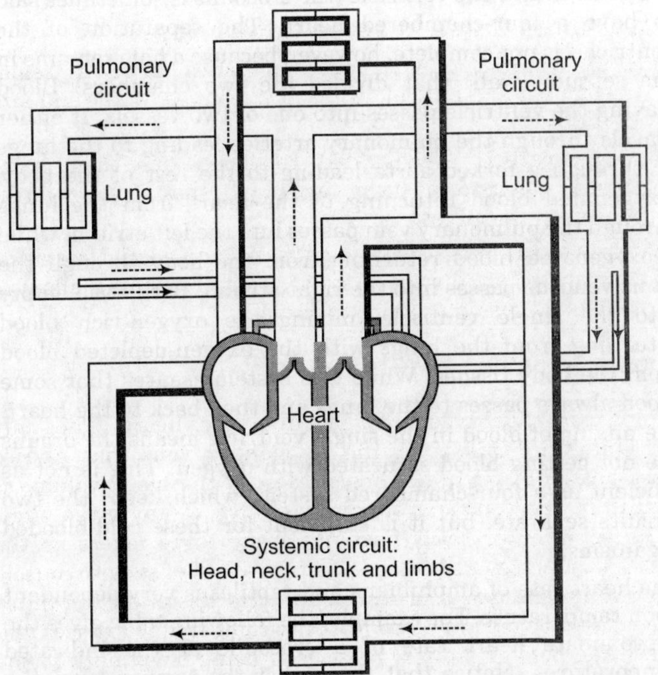

Fig. 20.15 Representation of pulmonary and systemic circulation

Pulmonary Circuit

In the pulmonary circuit, blood is pumped to the lungs from the right ventricle of the heart. It is carried to the lungs *via* pulmonary arteries. At lungs, oxygen in the alveolae diffuses to the capillaries surrounding the alveolae and carbon dioxide inside the blood diffuses to the alveolae. As a result, blood is oxygenated which is then carried to the heart's left half to the left atrium *via* pulmonary veins. Oxygen rich blood is prepared for the whole organs and tissues of the body. This is important because mitochondria inside the cells should use oxygen to produce energy from the organic compounds.

Systemic Circuit

The systemic circuit supplies oxygenated blood to the organ system. Oxygenated blood from the lungs is returned to the left atrium, then the ventricle contracts and pumps blood into the aorta. Systemic arteries split from the aorta and direct blood into the capillaries. Cells consume the oxygen and nutrients and add carbon dioxide, wastes, enzymes and hormones. The veins drain the deoxygenated blood from the capillaries and return the blood to the right atrium.

Aorta

The aorta is the largest of the arteries in the systemic circuit. The blood is pumped from the left ventricle into the aorta and from there it branches to all parts of the body. The aorta is an elastic artery and as such is able to distend. When the left ventricle contracts to force blood into the aorta, the aorta expands. This stretching gives the potential energy that will help maintain blood pressure during diastole, as during this time the aorta contracts passively.

Superior Vena Cava

The Superior Vena Cava (SVC) is a large but short vein that carries deoxygenated blood from the upper half of the body to the heart's right atrium. It is formed by the left and right brachiocephalic veins (also referred to as the innominate veins) which receive blood from the upper limbs and the head and neck. The azygous vein (which receives blood from the ribcage) joins it just before it enters the right atrium.

Inferior Vena Cava

The Inferior Vena Cava (or IVC) is a large vein that carries de-oxygenated blood from the lower half of the body into the heart. It is formed by the left and right common iliac veins and transports blood to the right atrium of the heart. It is posterior to the abdominal cavity, and runs along side of the vertebral column on its right side.

Coronary Arteries

The coronary circulation consists of the blood vessels that supply blood to, and remove blood from, the heart muscle itself. Although blood fills the chambers of the heart, the muscle tissue of the heart or myocardium, is so thick that it requires coronary blood vessels to deliver blood deep into the myocardium. The vessels that supply blood high in oxygen to the myocardium are known as **coronary arteries.** The vessels that remove the deoxygenated blood from the heart muscle are known as cardiac veins. The coronary arteries that run on the surface of the heart are called **epicardial coronary arteries.** These arteries, when healthy, are capable of autoregulation to maintain coronary blood flow at levels appropriate to the needs of the heart muscle. These relatively narrow vessels are commonly affected by atherosclerosis and can become blocked, causing angina or a heart attack. The coronary arteries are classified as 'end circulation', since they represent the only source of blood supply to the myocardium: there is very little redundant blood supply, which is why blockage of these vessels can be so critical. In general, there are two main coronary arteries, the left and right.

(a) Right coronary artery

(b) Left coronary artery

Both of these arteries originate from the beginning (root) of the aorta, immediately above the aortic valve. As discussed below, the left coronary artery originates from the left aortic sinus, while the right coronary artery originates from the right aortic sinus. Four percent of people have a third, the posterior coronary artery. In rare cases, a patient will have one coronary artery that runs around the root of the aorta.

Hepatic Veins

In human anatomy, the hepatic veins are the blood vessels that drain deoxygenated blood from the liver and blood cleaned by the liver (from the stomach, pancreas, small intestine and colon) into the inferior vena cava.

They arise from the substance of the liver, more specifically the central vein of the liver lobule. They can be differentiated into two groups, the upper group and lower group. The upper group of three typically arises from the posterior aspect of the liver and drain the quadrate lobe and left lobe. The lower group rise from the right lobe and caudate lobe, are variable in number and are typically smaller than those in the upper group. None of the hepatic veins have valves.

Comparative Anatomy of Heart Structure

The heart and blood vessels changed greatly as vertebrates moved from water to land and an endothermy evolved. In amphibians and reptiles, the evolution of a double circulatory circuits in which blood passes through the heart twice during its circuits through the body has over come the problem of two chamber heart.

Fish

Fish possess the simplest type of true heart — a two-chambered organ composed of one atrium and one ventricle. A rudimentary valve is located between the two-chambers. Blood is pumped from the ventricle through the conus arteriosus to the gills. The conus arteriosus is like the aorta in other species. At the gills, the blood receives oxygen and gets rid of carbon dioxide. Blood then moves on to the organs of the body, where nutrients, gases and wastes are exchanged. There is no division of the circulation between the gills and the body. That is, the blood travels from the heart to the gills, and then directly to the body before returning to the atrium through the sinus venosus to be circulated again. The heart rates of fish fall within the wide range of 60-240 beats per minute, depending upon species and water temperature. The fish's heart rate will be slower at lower temperatures.

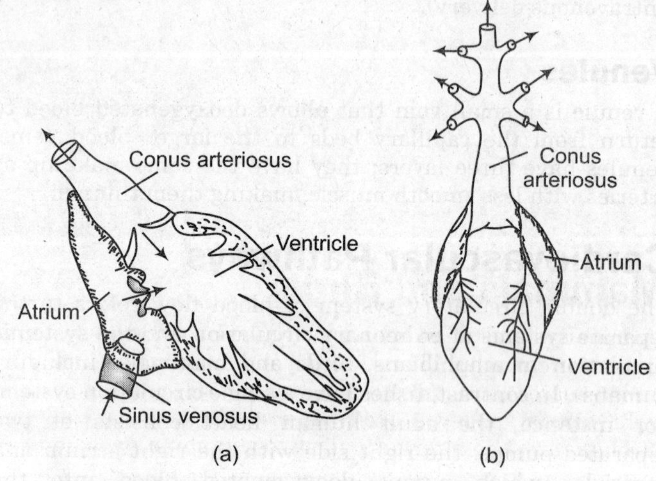

Fig. 20.16 Fish heart (a) Internal view (b) External view

Amphibians and Reptiles

Amphibians and Reptiles, by contrast, have a three-chambered heart. The three-chambered heart consists of two atria and one ventricle (the crocodile is sometimes said to have a four-chambered heart. The separation of the ventricles is not complete, however, because a hole remains in the septum (wall) that divides the two chambers) Blood leaving the ventricle passes into one of two vessels. It either travels through the pulmonary arteries leading to the lungs or through a forked aorta leading to the rest of the body. Oxygenated blood returning to the heart from the lungs through the pulmonary vein passes into the left atrium, while deoxygenated blood returning from the body through the sinus venosus passes into the right atrium. Both atria empty into the single ventricle, mixing the oxygen-rich blood returning from the lungs with the oxygen-depleted blood from the body tissues. While this system assures that some blood always passes to the lungs and then back to the heart, the mixing of blood in the single ventricle means the organs are not getting blood saturated with oxygen. This is not as efficient as a four-chambered system, which keeps the two circuits separate, but it is sufficient for these cold-blooded organisms.

The heart rate of amphibians and reptiles is very dependent upon temperature. For example, the following table gives the approximate heart rate of a crocodile at the indicated temperatures. Notice that the higher the temperature, the faster the heart beat.

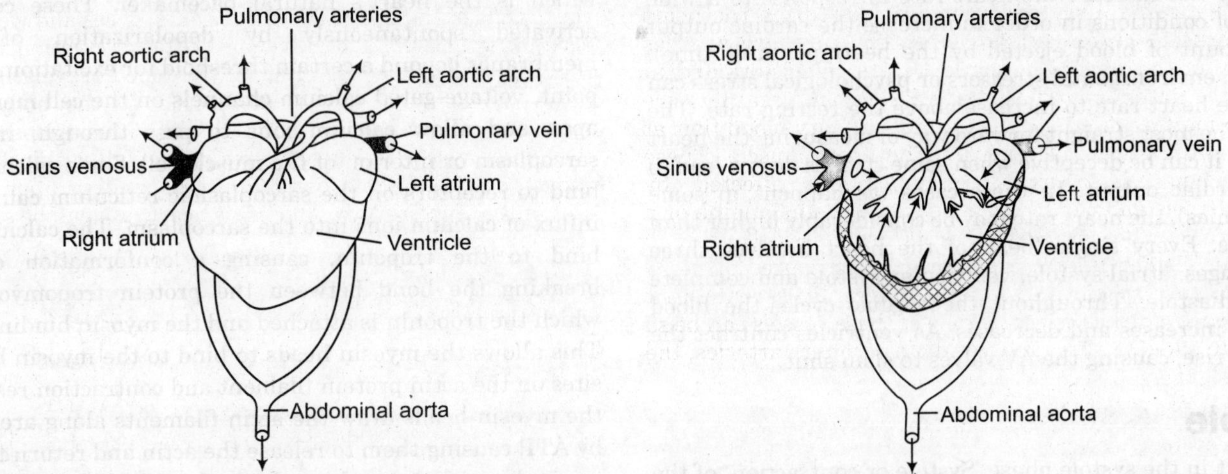

Fig. 20.17 Structure of amphibian heart: (a) External view (b) Internal view

Mammals and Birds

Mammalian and avian hearts have four chambers—two atria and two-ventricles. This is the most efficient system, as deoxygenated and oxygenated bloods are not mixed. The right atrium receives deoxygenated blood from the body through both the inferior and superior vena cava. The blood then passes to the right ventricle to be pumped through the pulmonary arteries to the lungs, where it becomes oxygenated. It returns to the left atrium *via* the pulmonary veins, this oxygen-rich blood is then passed to the left ventricle and pumped through the aorta to the rest of the body. The aorta is the largest artery and has an enormous amount of stretch and elasticity to withstand the pressure created by the pumping ventricle. The four-chambered heart ensures that the tissues of the body are supplied with oxygen-saturated blood to facilitate sustained muscle movement. Also, the larger oxygen supply allows these warm-blooded organisms to achieve thermoregulation (body temperature maintenance).

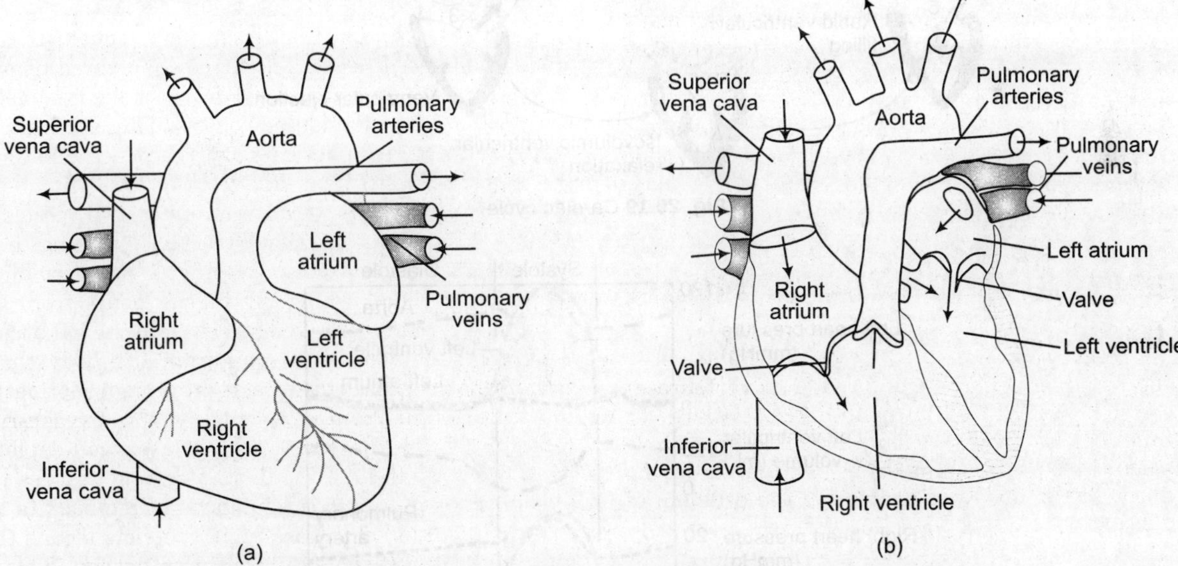

Fig. 20.18 Structure of mammalian heart (a) External view (b) Internal view

Cardiac Cycle

Cardiac cycle is the term used to describe the relaxation and contraction that occur, as a heart works to pump blood through the body. Heart rate is a term used to describe the frequency of the cardiac cycle. It is considered one of the four vital signs. Usually it is calculated as the number of contractions (heart beats) of the heart in one minute and expressed as 'beats per minute' (bpm). When resting, the adult human heart beats at about 70 bpm (males) and 75 bpm (females), but this rate varies between people. However, the reference range is nominally between 60 bpm (if less termed **bradycardia**) and 100 bpm (if greater, termed **tachycardia**). Resting heart rates can be significantly lower in athletes and significantly higher in the obese.

The body can increase the heart rate in response to a wide variety of conditions in order to increase the cardiac output (the amount of blood ejected by the heart per unit time). Exercise, environmental stressors or psychological stress can cause the heart rate to increase above the resting rate. The pulse is the most straight forward way of measuring the heart rate, but it can be deceptive when some strokes do not lead to much cardiac output. In these cases (as happens in some arrhythmias), the heart rate may be considerably higher than the pulse. Every single 'beat' of the heart involves three major stages: atrial systole, ventricular systole and complete cardiac diastole. Throughout the cardiac cycle, the blood pressure increases and decreases. As ventricles contract the pressure rise, causing the AV valves to slam shut.

Systole

The heart in the systole phase. Systole or contraction, of the heart is initiated by the electrical cells of the sinoatrial node, which is the heart's natural pacemaker. These cells are activated spontaneously by depolarization of their membranes beyond a certain threshold for excitation. At this point, voltage-gated calcium channels on the cell membrane open and allow calcium ions to pass through, into the sarcoplasm or interior, of the muscle cell. Some calcium ions bind to receptors on the sarcoplasmic reticulum causing an influx of calcium ions into the sarcoplasm. The calcium ions bind to the troponin, causing a conformation change, breaking the bond between the protein tropomyosin, to which the troponin is attached and the myosin binding sites. This allows the myosin heads to bind to the myosin binding sites on the actin protein filament and contraction results as the myosin heads draw the actin filaments along are bound by ATP, causing them to release the actin and return to their original position, breaking down the ATP into ADP and a phosphate group.

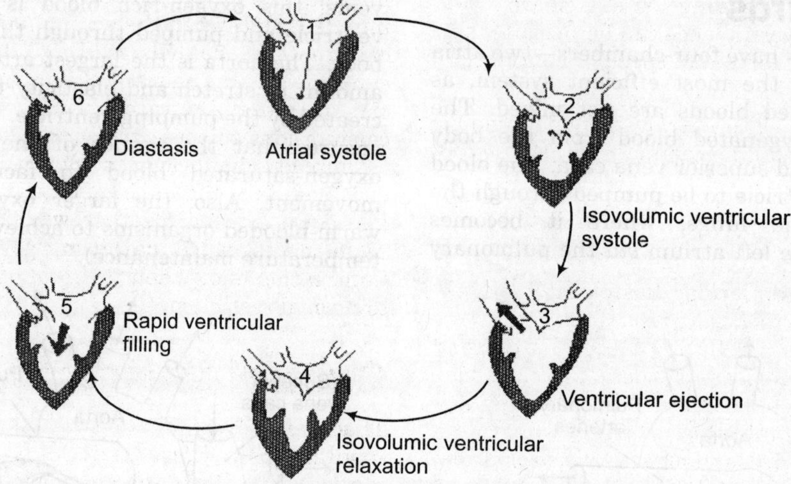

Fig. 20.19 Cardiac cycle

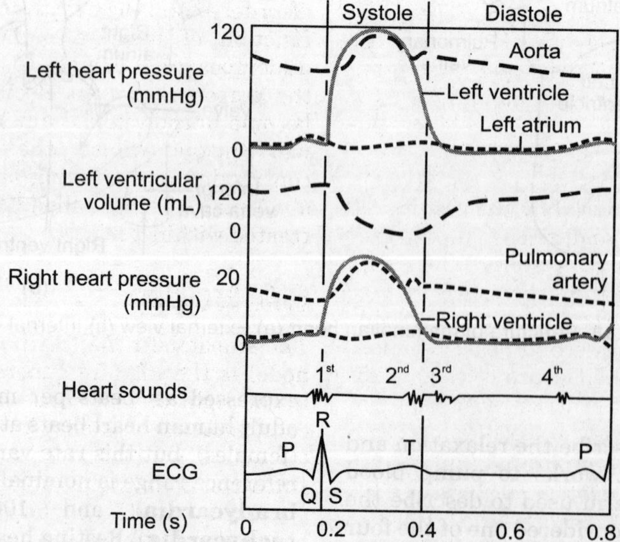

Fig. 20.20 Diagrammatic representation of the cardiac cycle

The action potential spreads *via* the passage of sodium ions through the gap junctions that connect the sarcoplasm of adjacent myocardial cells. Norepinephrine (noradrenaline) is released by the terminal boutons of depolarized sympathetic fibres, at the sinoatrial and atrioventricular nodes. Norepinephrine diffuses across the synaptic cleft binds to the β1-adrenoreceptors – G-protein linked receptors, consisting of seven transmembrane domains – shifting their equilibrium towards the active state. The receptor changes its conformation and mechanically activates the G-protein which is released. The G-protein is involved in the production of cyclic adenyl monophosphate (camp) from adenosine triphosphate (ATP) and this in turn activates the protein kinase (β-adrenoreceptor kinase). β-adrenoreceptor kinase phosphorylates the calcium ion channels in the sarcolema, so that calcium ion influx is increased when they are activated by the appropriate transmembrane voltage. This will of course, cause more of the calcium receptors in the sarcoplasmic reticulum to be activated, creating a larger flow of calcium ions into the sarcoplasm. More troponin will be bound and more myosin binding sites cleared (of tropomyosin) so that more myosin heads can be recruited for the contraction and a greater force and speed of contraction results.

Noradrenaline also affects the atrioventricular node, reducing the delay before continuing conduction of the action potential *via* the bundle of His.

Diastole

The heart in the diastole phase. Cardiac diastole is the period of time when the heart relaxes after contraction in preparation for refilling with circulating blood. Ventricular diastole is when the ventricles are relaxing, while atrial diastole is when the atria are relaxing. Together they are known as complete cardiac diastole. During ventricular diastole, the pressure in the (left and right) ventricles drops from the peak that it reaches in systole. When the pressure in the left ventricle drops to below the pressure in the left atrium, the mitral valve opens, and the left ventricle fills with blood that was accumulating in the left atrium. Likewise, when the pressure in the right ventricle drops below that in the right atrium, the tricuspid valve opens and the right ventricle fills with blood that was in the right atrium.

Heart Sounds

The first heart tone, or S1, 'Lub' is caused by the closure of the atrioventricular valves, mitral and tricuspid, at the beginning of ventricular contraction or systole. When the pressure in the ventricles rises above the pressure in the atria, these valves close to prevent regurgitation of blood from the ventricles into the atria. The second heart tone, or S2 (A2 and P2), 'Dub' is caused by the closure of the aortic valve and pulmonic valve at the end of ventricular systole. As the left ventricle empties, its pressure falls below the pressure in the aorta, and the aortic valve closes. Similarly, as the pressure in the right ventricle falls below the pressure in the pulmonary artery, the pulmonic valve closes. During inspiration, negative intrathoracic pressure causes increased blood return into the right side of the heart. The increased blood volume in the right ventricle causes the pulmonic valve to stay open longer during ventricular systole. This causes an increased delay in the P2 component of S2. During expiration, the positive intrathoracic pressure causes decreased blood return to the right side of the heart. The reduced volume in the right ventricle allows the pulmonic valve to close earlier at the end of ventricular systole, causing P2 to occur earlier, and 'closer' to A2. It is physiological to hear the splitting of the second heart tone by younger people and during inspiration. During expiration normally the interval between the two components shortens and the tone becomes merged.

Cardiac Muscle Contraction

After an action potential excites the plasma membrane of the cardiac muscle cell the contraction is due to an increase in the cytoplasmic concentration of calcium ions. Similar to skeletal muscle, the release of Ca^{+} ions from the sarcoplasmic reticulum binds to troponin which allows actin to bind with myosin. The difference between skeletal muscle and cardiac muscle is that when the action potential opens voltage gated calcium ion channels in the T-tubules. The increase in cytosolic calcium causes calcium ions to bind to receptors on the surface of the sarcoplasmic reticulum. The binding of calcium ions to these receptors causes the opening of more calcium ion channels in the SR membrane. Calcium ions then rush out of the SR and bind to troponin and allow the myosin and actin to bind together which causes contraction. This sequence is called **calcium induced calcium release.** Contraction ends when the level of cytosolic calcium returns to normal resting levels.

Control of Heart Beat

The heart contains two cardiac pacemakers that spontaneously cause the heart to beat. These can be controlled by the autonomic nervous system and circulating adrenaline. If the cardiac muscles just contracted and relaxed randomly at a natural rhythm the cycle would become disordered and the heart would become unable to carry on its function of being a pump. Sometimes when the heart undergoes great damage to one part of the cardiac muscle or the person incurs an electric shock, the cardiac cycle can become uncoordinated and chaotic. Some parts of the heart will contract whilst others will relax so that instead of contracting and relaxing as a whole, the heart will flutter abnormally. This is called **fibrillation** and can be fatal if not treated within 1 min.

SA Node

The sinoatrial node (SA node or SAN, also called the sinus node) is the impulse generating (pacemaker) tissue located in the right atrium of the heart. Although all of the heart's cells possess the ability to generate the electrical impulses (or action potentials) that trigger cardiac contraction, the sinoatrial node is what normally initiates it, simply because it generates impulses slightly faster than the other areas with pacemaker potential. Because cardiac myocytes, like all nerve cells, have refractory periods following contraction during which additional contractions cannot be triggered, their pacemaker potential is over ridden by the sinoatrial node. The SA node emits a new impulse before either the AV or Purkinje fibres reach threshold. The sinoatrial node (SA node) is a group of cells positioned on the wall of the right atrium, near the entrance of the superior vena cava. These cells are modified cardiac myocytes. They possess some contractile filaments, though they do not contract. Cells in the SA node will naturally discharge (create action potentials) at about 70-80 times/minute. Because the sinoatrial node is responsible for the rest of the heart's electrical activity, it is sometimes called the primary pacemaker. If the SA node doesn't function, or the impulse generated in the SA node is blocked before it travels down the electrical conduction system, a group of cells further down the heart will become the heart's pacemaker. These cells form the atrioventricular node (AV node), which is an area between the right atrium and ventricle, within the atrial septum. The impulses from the AV node will maintain a slower heart rate (about 40-60 beats per a minute). When there is pathology in the AV node or Purkinje fibres, an ectopic pacemaker can occur in different parts of the heart. The ectopic pacemaker typically discharges faster than the SA node and causes an abnormal sequence of contraction. The SA node is richly innervated by vagal and sympathetic fibres. This makes the SA node susceptible to autonomic influences. Stimulation of the vagus nerve causes decrease in the SA node rate (thereby causing decrease in the heart rate). Stimulation *via* sympathetic fibres causes increase in the SA node rate (thereby increasing the heart rate). The sympathetic nerves are distributed to all parts of the heart, especially in ventricular muscles. The parasympathetic nerves mainly control SA and AV nodes, some atrial muscle and ventricular muscle. Parasympathetic stimulation from the vagal nerves decreases the rate of the AV node by causing the release of acetylcholine at vagal endings which in turn increases the K^+ permeability of the cardiac muscle fibre. Vagal stimulation can block transmission through AV junction or stop SA node contraction which is called 'ventricular escape.' When this happens, the Purkinje fibres in the AV bundle develops a rhythm of their own. In the majority of patients, the SA node receives blood from the right coronary artery, meaning that a myocardial infarction occluding it will cause ischemia in the SA node unless there is a sufficiently good anastomosis from the left coronary artery. If not, death of the affected cells will stop the SA node from triggering the heart beat.

AV Node

The atrioventricular node (AV node) is the tissue between the atria and the ventricles of the heart, which conducts the normal electrical impulse from the atria to the ventricles. The AV node receives two inputs from the atria: posteriorly *via* the crista terminalis, and anteriorly *via* the interatrial septum. An important property that is unique to the AV node is decremental conduction. This is the property of the AV node that prevents rapid conduction to the ventricle in cases of rapid atrial rhythms, such as atrial fibrillation or atrial flutter. The atrioventricular node delays impulses for 0.1 s before spreading to the ventricle walls. The reason it is so important to delay the cardiac impulse is to ensure that the atria are empty completely before the ventricles contract. The blood supply of the AV node is from a branch of the right coronary artery in 85% to 90% of individuals, and from a branch of the left circumflex artery in 10% to 15% of individuals. In certain types of supraventricular tachycardia, a person could have two AV nodes; this will cause a loop in electrical current and uncontrollably rapid heart beat. When this electricity catches up with itself, it will dissipate and return to normal heart beat speed.

AV Bundle

The bundle of His is a collection of heart muscle cells specialized for electrical conduction that transmits the electrical impulses from the AV node (located between the atria and the ventricles) to the point of the apex of the fascicular branches. The fascicular branches then lead to the Purkinje fibres which innervate the ventricles, causing the cardiac muscle of the ventricles to contract at a paced interval. These specialized muscle fibres in the heart were named after the **Swiss** cardiologist **Wilhelm His, Jr.,** who discovered them in 1893. Cardiac muscle is very specialized, as it is the only type of muscle that has an internal rhythm; *i.e.,* it is myogenic which means that it can naturally contract and relax without receiving electrical impulses from nerves. When a cell of cardiac muscle is placed next to another, they will beat in unison. The fibres of the bundle of His allow electrical conduction to occur more easily and quickly than typical cardiac muscle. They are an important part of the electrical conduction system of the heart as they transmit the impulse from the AV node (the ventricular pacemaker) to the rest of the heart. The bundle of His branches into the three bundle branches: the right left anterior and left posterior bundle branches that run along the intraventricular septum. The bundles give rise to thin filaments known as Purkinje fibres. These fibres distribute the impulse to the ventricular muscle. Together, the bundle branches and Purkinje network comprise the ventricular conduction system. It takes about 0.03-0.04s for the impulse to travel from the bundle of His to the ventricular muscle. It is extremely important for these nodes to exist as they ensure the correct control and co-ordination of the heart and cardiac cycle and make sure all the contractions remain within the correct sequence and in sync.

Purkinje Fibres

Purkinje fibres or Purkinje tissue are located in the inner ventricular walls of the heart, just beneath the endocardium. These fibres are specialized myocardial fibres that conduct an electrical stimulus or impulse that enables the heart to contract in a coordinated fashion. Purkinje fibres work with the sinoatrial node (SA node) and the atrioventricular node (AV node) to control the heart rate. During the ventricular contraction portion of the cardiac cycle, the Purkinje fibres carry the contraction impulse from the left and right bundle branches to the myocardium of the ventricles. This causes the muscle tissue of the ventricles to contract and force blood out of the heart — either to the pulmonary circulation (from the right ventricle) or to the systemic circulation (from the left ventricle). They were discovered in 1839 by **Jan Evangelista** Purkinje, who gave them his name.

Intrinsic Control of Heart Beat

(a) SA node (located in the right atrium near the entrance of the superior vena cava).

(b) AV node (located at the base of right atrium).

(c) AV bundle (located in the intraventricular septum between the two ventricles that go in two directions right and left bundle branches that leave the septum to enter the walls of both ventricle).

(d) Bundle branches (the branching off the septum to the walls of the ventricles that run into the Purkinje fibres that then make contact with ventricular myocardial cells to spread the impulse to the rest of the ventricles).

Extrinsic Control of Heart Beat

Autonomic system with two sub-divisions — the sympathetic division and the parasympathetic division. Hormonal control of blood pressure

(a) Epinephrine

(b) Norepinephrine

(c) ANP (Atrial Natriuretic Peptide)

(d) ADH (Antidiuretic Hormone)

(e) Renin angiotension system

Fibrillation

Fibrillation is when the heart flutters abnormally. This can be detected by an electrocardiogram which measures the waves of excitation passing through the heart and plotting a graph of potential difference (voltage) against time. If the heart and cardiac cycle is functioning properly the electrocardiogram shows a regular, repeating pattern. However, if there is fibrillation there will be no apparent pattern. In a hospital the monitor would make a sound and alert the doctors to treat the fibrillation by passing a huge current through the chest wall and shocking the heart out of its fibrillation. This causes the cardiac muscle to stop completely for 5 s and when it begins to beat again the cardiac cycle would have resumed to normal and the heart will be beating in a controlled manner again. Fibrillation is an example of 'circus movement' of impulses through the heart muscle. Circus movement occurs when an impulse begins in one part of the heart muscle and spreads in a circuitous pathway through the heart then returns to the originally excited muscle and 're-enters' it to stimulate it once more. The signal never stops. A cause of circus movement is long length pathway in which the muscle is no longer in a refractory state when the stimulus returns to it. A 'flutter' is a circus movement in coordinated, low frequency waves that cause rapid heart rate. If the bundle of His is blocked, it will result in dissociation between the activity of the atria and that of the ventricles, otherwise called **a third degree heart block.** The other cause of a third degree block would be a block of the right, left anterior, and left posterior bundle branches. A third degree block is very serious medical condition that will most likely require an artificial pacemaker.

ECG

Also known as the electrocardiogram. Cardiac electrophysiology is the science of the mechanisms, functions and performance of the electrical activities of specific regions of the heart. The ECG is the recording of the heart's electrical activity as a graph. The graph can show the heart's rate and rhythm, it can detect enlargement of the heart, decreased blood flow, or the presence of current or past heart attacks. ECG's are inexpensive, Non-invasive, quick and painless. Depending of the results, the patient's medical history and a physical exam; further tests or a combination of medications and lifestyle changes may be ordered.

Read an ECG

ECG Wave form

P-wave (0.08-0.10 s) QRS (0.06-0.10 s)

P-R interval (0.12-0.20 s) $Q\text{-}T_C$ interval (≤ 0.44 s)*

$^*QT_C = OT/\sqrt{RR}$

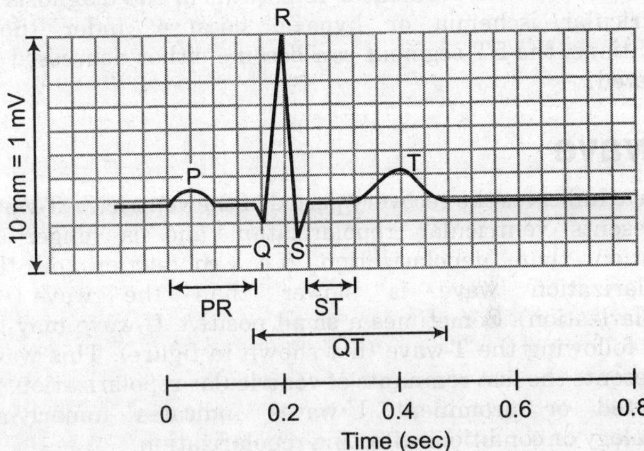

Fig. 20.21 Electrocardiogram representing normal wave output

P-Wave

The P-wave represents the wave of depolarization that spreads from the SA node throughout the atria, and is usually 0.08 to 0.1 s (80-100 ms) in duration. The brief isoelectric (zero voltage) period after the P-wave represents the time in which the impulse is traveling within the AV node (where the conduction velocity is greatly retarded) and the bundle of His. Atrial rate can be calculated by determining the time interval between P-waves. The period of time from the onset of the P-wave to the beginning of the QRS complex is termed the P-R interval, which normally ranges from 0.12 to 0.20 s in duration. This interval represents the time between the onset of atrial depolarization and the onset of ventricular depolarization. If the P-R interval is >0.2 s, there is an **AV conduction block,** which is also termed a **first-degree heart block** if the impulse is still able to be conducted into the ventricles.

QRS Complex

QRS complex-indicates that the ventricles are electrically stimulated to pump blood out, *i.e.,* ventricular depolarization. The duration of the QRS complex is normally 0.06 to 0.1 s. This relatively short duration indicates that ventricular depolarization normally occurs very rapidly. If the QRS complex is prolonged (> 0.1 s), conduction is impaired within the ventricles. This can occur with bundle branch blocks or whenever a ventricular foci (abnormal pacemaker site) becomes the pacemaker driving the ventricle. Such an ectopic foci nearly always results in impulses being conducted over slower pathways within the heart, thereby increasing the time for depolarization and the duration of the QRS complex. The shape of the QRS complex in the previous page is idealized. In fact, the shape changes depending on which recording electrodes are being used. The shape will also change when there is abnormal conduction of electrical impulses within the ventricles.

ST Segment

The isoelectric period (ST segment) following the QRS is the time at which the entire ventricle is depolarized and roughly corresponds to the plateau phase of the ventricular action potential. The ST segment is important in the diagnosis of ventricular ischemia or hypoxia because under those conditions, the ST segment can become either depressed or elevated.

T-wave

T-wave indicates the recovery period of the ventricles. T-wave represents ventricular repolarization and is longer in duration than depolarization (*i.e.,* conduction of the repolarization wave is slower than the wave of depolarization). Sometimes a small positive U-wave may be seen following the T-wave (not shown in figure). This wave represents the last remnants of ventricular repolarization. Inverted or prominent U-waves indicates underlying pathology or conditions affecting repolarization.

Q-T interval

The Q-T interval represents the time for both ventricular depolarization and repolarization to occur, and therefore, roughly estimates the duration of an average ventricular action potential. This interval can range from 0.2 to 0.4 s depending upon heart rate. At high heart rates, ventricular action potentials shorten in duration, which decreases the Q-T interval. Because prolonged Q-T intervals can be diagnostic for susceptibility to certain types of tachyarrhythmias, it is important to determine if a given Q-T interval is excessively long. In practice, the Q-T interval is expressed as a 'corrected Q-T (QTc)' by taking the Q-T interval and dividing it by the square root of the R-R interval (interval between ventricular depolarizations). This allows an assessment of the Q-T interval that is independent of heart rate. Normal corrected Q-Tc intervals are less than 0.44 s.

There is no distinctly visible wave representing atrial repolarization in the ECG because it occurs during ventricular depolarization. Because the wave of atrial repolarization is relatively small in amplitude (*i.e.,* has low voltage), it is masked by the much larger ventricular generated QRS complex.

Blood Pressure

Blood pressure is the pressure exerted by the blood on the walls of the blood vessels. Unless indicated otherwise, blood pressure refers to systemic arterial blood pressure, *i.e.,* the pressure in the large arteries delivering blood to body parts other than the lungs, such as the brachial artery (in the arm). The pressure of the blood in other vessels is lower than the arterial pressure. Blood pressure values are universally stated in millimeters of mercury (mm Hg). The systolic pressure is defined as the peak pressure in the arteries during the cardiac cycle; the diastolic pressure is the lowest pressure (at the resting phase of the cardiac cycle). The mean arterial pressure and pulse pressure are other important quantities. Typical values for a resting, healthy adult are approximately 120 mm Hg systolic and 80 mm Hg diastolic (written as 120/80 mm Hg), with large individual variations. These measures of blood pressure are not static, but undergo natural variations from one heart beat to another or throughout the day (in a circadian rhythm); they also change in response to stress, nutritional factors, drugs, or disease.

Systolic Pressure

Systolic pressure is the highest when the blood is being pumped out of the left ventricle into the aorta during ventricular systole. The average high during systole is 120 mm Hg.

Diastolic Pressure

Diastolic blood pressure lowers steadily lowers to a low of 80 mm Hg during ventricular diastole.

Cardiovascular Disease

Cardiovascular disease refers to the class of diseases that involve the heart and/or blood vessels (arteries and veins). While the term technically refers to any disease that affects the cardiovascular system, it is usually used to refer to those related to atherosclerosis (arterial disease). These conditions have similar causes, mechanisms and treatments. Over 50 million Americans have cardiovascular problems and most other Western countries face high and increasing rates of cardiovascular disease. It is the number 1 cause of death and disability in the **United States** and most **European** countries. By the time that heart problems are detected, the underlying cause (atherosclerosis) is usually quite advanced, having progressed for decades. There is therefore, increased emphasis on preventing atherosclerosis by modifying risk factors, such as healthy eating, exercise and avoidance of smoking.

Hypertension

Hypertension or high blood pressure is a medical condition where in the blood pressure is chronically elevated. Persistent hypertension is one of the risk factors for strokes, heart attacks, heart failure and arterial aneurysm and is a leading cause of chronic renal failure.

Atherosclerosis

Atherosclerosis is a disease affecting the arterial blood vessel. It is commonly referred to as a 'hardening' or 'furring' of the arteries. It is caused by the formation of multiple plaques within the arteries. Arteriosclerosis (hardening of the artery) results from a deposition of tough, rigid collagen inside the vessel wall and around the atheroma. This increases the stiffness, decreases the elasticity of the artery wall. Atherosclerosis typically begins in early adolescence, is usually found in most major arteries and yet is asymptomatic and not detected by most diagnostic methods during life. It most commonly becomes seriously symptomatic when interfering with the coronary circulation supplying the heart or cerebral circulation supplying the brain, and is considered the most important underlying cause of strokes, heart attacks, various heart diseases including congestive heart failure and most cardiovascular diseases in general.

Plaque

Plaque atheroma or commonly known as plaque is an abnormal inflammatory accumulation of macrophage white blood cells within the walls of arteries.

Circulatory Shock

Circulatory shock is a severe condition that results from reduced blood circulation.

Thrombus

A thrombus or blood clot, is the final product of the blood coagulation step in haemostasis. It is achieved *via* the aggregation of platelets that form a platelet plug, and the activation of the humoral coagulation system (*i.e.*, clotting factors). A thrombus is physiologic in cases of injury, but pathologic in case of thrombosis. Preventing blood clots reduces the risk of stroke, heart attack and pulmonary embolism. Heparin and warfarin are often used to inhibit the formation and growth of existing blood clots, thereby allowing the body to shrink and dissolve the blood clots through normal methods.

Embolism

An embolism occurs when an object (the embolus) migrates from one part of the body (through circulation) and causes a blockage (occlusion) of a blood vessel in another part of the body. Blood clots form the most common embolic material by far: other possible embolic materials include fat globules (a fat embolism), air bubbles (an air embolism), septic emboli (containing pus and bacteria), or amniotic fluid.

Stroke

A stroke, also known as **cerebrovascular accident** (CVA), is an acute neurological injury whereby the blood supply to a part of the brain is interrupted. Strokes can be classified into two major categories: ischemic and haemorrhagic. ~80% of strokes are due to ischemia.

(a) **Ischemic Stroke** In ischemic stroke, which occurs in approximately 85-90% of strokes, a blood vessel becomes occluded and the blood supply to part of the brain is totally or partially blocked. Ischemic stroke is commonly divided into thrombotic stroke, embolic stroke, systemic hypoperfusion (watershed or border zone stroke) or venous thrombosis.

(b) **Haemorrhagic Stroke** A haemorrhagic stroke, or cerebral haemorrhage, is a form of stroke that occurs when a blood vessel in the brain ruptures or bleeds. Like ischemic strokes, haemorrhagic strokes interrupt the brain's blood supply because the bleeding vessel can no longer carry the blood to its target tissue. In addition, blood irritates brain tissue, disrupting the delicate chemical balance and, if the bleeding continues, it can cause increased intracranial pressure which physically impinges on brain tissue and restricts blood flow into the brain. In this respect, haemorrhagic strokes are more dangerous than their more common counterpart, ischemic strokes.

There are two types of haemorrhagic stroke: intracerebral haemorrhage and subarachnoid haemorrhage.

The term 'brain attack' is starting to come into use in the United States for stroke, just as the term 'heart attack' is used for myocardial infarction, where a cutoff of blood causes necrosis to the tissue of the heart. Many hospitals have 'brain attack' teams within their neurology departments specifically for swift treatment of stroke.

Heart Attack

Acute Myocardial Infarction (AMI or MI), commonly known as a **heart attack.** A heart attack occurs when the supply of blood and oxygen to an area of heart muscle is blocked, usually by a clot in a coronary artery. Often, this blockage leads to arrhythmias (irregular heart beat or rhythm) that cause a severe decrease in the pumping function of the heart and may bring about sudden death. If the blockage is not treated within a few hours, the affected heart muscle will die and be replaced by scar tissue. It is the leading cause of death for both men and women all over the world.

Angina Pectoris

Angina pectoris is chest pain due to ischemia (a lack of blood and hence oxygen supply) of the heart muscle, generally due to obstruction or spasm of the coronary arteries (the heart's blood vessels).

Coronary Bypass

Coronary artery bypass surgery, coronary artery bypass graft surgery and heart bypass are surgical procedures performed on patients with coronary artery disease for the relief of angina and possible improved heart muscle function. Veins or arteries from elsewhere in the patient's body are grafted from the aorta to the coronary arteries, bypassing coronary artery narrowing caused by atherosclerosis and improves the blood supply to the myocardium (heart muscle).

Congestive Heart Failure

Congestive Heart Failure (CHF), also called **Congestive Cardiac Failure** (CCF) or just heart failure is a condition that can result from any structural or functional cardiac disorder that impairs the ability of the heart to fill with or pump a sufficient amount of blood throughout the body. It is not to be confused with 'cessation of heartbeat', which is known as asystole, or with cardiac arrest, which is the cessation of normal cardiac function in the face of heart disease. Because not all patients have volume overload at the time of initial or subsequent evaluation, the term 'heart failure' is preferred over the older term 'congestive heart failure'. Congestive heart failure is often undiagnosed due to a lack of a universally agreed definition and difficulties in diagnosis, particularly when the condition is considered 'mild'.

Aneurysm

An aneurysm (or aneurism) is a localized dilation or ballooning of a blood vessel by more than 50% of the diameter of the vessel and can lead to instant death at anytime. Aneurysms most commonly occur in arteries at the base of the brain (the circle of Willis) and in the aorta (the main artery coming out of the heart) — this is an aortic aneurysm. This bulge in a blood vessel, much like a bulge on an over-inflated inner tube, can lead to death at anytime. The larger an aneurysm becomes, the more likely it is to burst. Aneurysms are also described according to their shape: Saccular or fusiform. A saccular aneurysm resembles a small sack; a fusiform aneurysm is shaped like a spindle.

Exercise

1. The term that refers to the percentage of packed erythrocytes per unit volume of blood is the
   (a) differential count (b) haemoglobin
   (c) haematocrit (d) haemopoiesis
2. Which of the following is a circulating blood cell that is capable of differentiating into a plasma cell?
   (a) Neutrophil (b) Basophil
   (c) B-lymphocyte (d) T-lymphocyte
3. The component of plasma responsible for maintaining the osmotic pressure of blood is
   (a) plasmin (b) albumin
   (c) fibrinogen (d) gamma globulin
4. Plasma is
   (a) blood that has no red blood cells
   (b) the liquid portion of blood including the clotting factors
   (c) the liquid portion of blood minus the clotting factors
   (d) the proteins of blood
5. The Fe^{3+} portion of the haemoglobin is eventually
   (a) converted into transferrin in the large intestine
   (b) converted into ferritin in the kidney
   (c) excreted from the body
   (d) None of the above
6. .... eventually become macrophages.
   (a) Neutrophils (b) Basophils
   (c) Monocytes (d) Macrocytes
7. Which of the following activates platelets during haemostasis?
   (a) Eosinophil degranulation
   (b) Exposed collagen or endothelial basement membrane
   (c) Fibrin thread formation
   (d) Thromboplastin
8. An individual with type B^+ blood has which of the following antibodies in their blood?
   (a) Anti-A and anti-O (b) Anti-B and anti-Rh
   (c) Anti-A (d) Anti-B
9. Which of the following blood cells have some properties similar to connective tissue mast cells?
   (a) Basophils
   (b) Neutrophils
   (c) Eosinophils
   (d) Monocytes
10. Examples of erythrocytes can be found in almost all histological sections. Therefore, knowledge of the approximate diameter of a red blood cell is useful because it can serve as a built in ruler on the tissue section. Which of the following best describes the diameter of red cells?
    (a) 5-6 μm (b) 6-7 μm
    (c) 7-8 μm (d) 8-9 μm
11. Select from the following terms. Matching with some may be used more than once or not at all
    1. Lymphocytes 2. Monocytes
    3. Eosinophils 4. Basophils
    5. Neutrophils 6. All of these
    A. Leukocytes
    B. Least numerous of the circulating leukocytes
    C. First line of cellular defense against a bacterial invasion
    D. Found in the buffy coat in a haematocrit tube
    E. Most numerous of the circulating leukocytes
    F. Specific granules contain heparin and histamine
    G. Capable of diapedesis
    H. May be found in loose connective tissue
    (a) EFDDFFEF (b) EDFFDEF
    (c) FDDFFEFE (d) FDEFEDFF
12. Together, leukocytes and platelets comprise approximately .... percent of total blood volume.
    (a) 1 (b) 15
    (c) 23 (d) 10

13. Which of the following is characteristic of all leukocytes?
(a) They are nucleated
(b) They have lobed mitochondria
(c) They have cytoplasmic granules
(d) They are phagocytic

14. The thickest layer of the wall of veins is the
(a) tunica media (b) tunica externa
(c) tunica interna (d) internal elastic lamina

15. The basic tissue types found in large blood vessels include
(a) muscle (b) nerve
(c) epithelium (d) All of these

16. When compared to arteries, veins generally
(a) are thinner walled
(b) gave more muscle in the tunica media
(c) carry faster moving blood
(d) have thicker endothelium

17. The blood vessels that play the most important role in the regulation of blood flow to a tissue and blood pressure are the
(a) arterioles (b) veins
(c) capillaries (d) venules

18. A patient with a hypothalamic tumour has hypersecretion of ADH. Which of the following BP readings would be most likely for this patient?
(a) 95/65 (b) 115/80
(c) 120/60 (d) 165/100

19. The difference between the systolic and the diastolic pressures is known as the
(a) blood pressure (b) pulse pressure
(c) mean arterial pressure (d) end-ventricular pressure

20. The tunica interna
(a) includes a layer of dense connective tissue
(b) contains some small capillaries
(c) contains some striated smooth muscle fibres
(d) includes a layer of simple squamous epithelium

21. Which of the following represents the primary kind of tissue found in the tunica media of blood vessels?
(a) Skeletal muscle
(b) Longitudinally arranged striated muscle
(c) Concentric layers of smooth muscle
(d) Reticular connective tissue

22. Large diameter capillaries found primarily in the liver, spleen and bone marrow are called
(a) continuous capillaries (b) fenestrated capillaries
(c) sinusoidal capillaries (d) megacapillaries

23. As a subject's age increases, his/her arterial compliance
(a) increase (b) decrease
(c) not change (d) not related

24. As depth of respiration increases, venous return
(a) increase (b) decrease
(c) not change (d) not related

25. As plasma ANP increases, blood volume
(a) increase (b) decrease
(c) not change (d) not related

26. As blood flows from the arteries into capillaries, BP
(a) increase (b) decrease
(c) not change (d) not related

27. As venous BP increases, tissue edema
(a) increase (b) decrease
(c) not change (d) not related

28. Which statement is true of arteries?
(a) All arteries carry oxygenated blood away from the heart
(b) All arteries carry blood low in carbon dioxide away from the heart
(c) Some elastic arteries release significant amounts of renin
(d) All arteries lack valves

29. Peripheral resistance
(a) decreases with increasing blood vessel length
(b) decreases if blood vessel diameter is reduced by 50%
(c) decreases in cases of polycythemia
(d) None of the above

30. The arteries that directly feed into the capillary beds are called
(a) veins (b) arterioles
(c) capillaries (d) venules

31. A deficiency of albumin would result in
(a) increased blood volume
(b) increased blood oncotic pressure
(c) loss of water by osmosis from the blood stream
(d) All of the above

32. As blood flows from the aorta to the capillaries of the gastrocnemius, its velocity of flow will
(a) increase (b) decrease
(c) stay the same (d) not related

33. Which of the following is true?
(a) Arteries typically have thinner walls than veins
(b) Veins typically have a much wider tunica media than arteries
(c) Veins typically have much more elastin than conducting arteries
(d) You typically would find fewer valves in arteries than in veins

34. Increasing blood vessel length will cause peripheral resistance to
(a) increase (b) decrease
(c) not change (d) not related

35. As you go from arteries to capillaries, the fluid pressure exerted by blood on the vessel walls
(a) increase (b) decrease
(c) stays the same (d) not related

36. If MAP increased by 10 mmHg, how much must the diastolic pressure have changed?
(a) –10 mmHg (b) +10 mmHg
(c) 0 mmHg (d) Cannot be determined

37. As heart rate decreases, diastolic pressure will
(a) increase (b) decrease
(c) not change (d) not related

38. If MAP = 100mmHg, and SBP = 120, then what must DBP be?
(a) 80 mmHg (b) 90 mmHg
(c) 100 mmHg (d) 120 mmHg

39. Histologically, the tunica .... is squamous epithelium underlain by a sparse connective tissue layer.
(a) interna (b) externa
(c) media (d) None of these

40. Arrange the following in the proper order for blood flow.
I. Muscular arteries II. Arterioles
III. Elastic arteries
(a) I, II, III (b) II, I, III
(c) III, I, II (d) III, II, I

41. The femoral artery is an example of a(n) artery.
(a) muscular (b) elastic
(c) venus (d) capillary

42. 65% of the blood volume is contained within the
(a) artery (b) veins
(c) arterioles (d) venule

43. Atherosclerosis refers to ailment of
(a) kidney (b) heart
(c) lungs (d) liver

44. Which one of the following statements is correct regarding blood pressure?
(a) 190/110 mmHg may harm vital organs like brain and kidney
(b) 130/90 mmHg is considered high and requires treatment
(c) 100/55 mmHg is considered an ideal blood pressure
(d) 105/50 mmHg makes one very active

45. A muscular wall is absent in
(a) capillary (b) vein
(c) venule (d) arteriole

46. The space in the middle of the thoracic cavity, where the heart resides is the
(a) pericardial cavity (b) pericardium
(c) pleural cavity (d) mediastinum

47. The foramen ovale in the fetal heart is located in the
(a) right atrium (b) left atrium
(c) interventricular septum (d) interatrial septum

48. Which blood vessel does not bring deoxygenated blood directly to the heart?
(a) Pulmonary vein (b) Coronary sinus
(c) Inferior vena cava (d) Superior vena cava

49. If communication between the SA node and the AV node became blocked, which will most likely occur?
(a) The rate of ventricular contraction will decrease
(b) After load will increase
(c) The rate of atrial contraction will decrease
(d) Stroke volume will increase to 5L/beat

50. A valve damaged by rheumatic fever fails to open completely. This is known as
(a) stenosis (b) heart block
(c) ischemia (d) MI

51. Cardiac output is equal to
(a) HR × SV (b) HR/SV
(c) EDV – ESV (d) HR × BP

52. Increased sympathetic stimulation will cause HR to
(a) increases (b) decreases
(c) not change (d) not related

53. Moderate increase in preload will cause SV to
(a) increase (b) decrease
(c) not change (d) not related

54. Decreased cardiac contractility will cause SV to .... and will cause CO to ....
(a) increase; increase (b) increase; decrease
(c) decrease; increase (d) decrease; decrease

55. Decreased SV as with congestive heart failure will cause ESV to
(a) increase (b) decrease
(c) not change (d) not related

56. Excessively high HR will cause PR interval to ...., ventricular fill time to ...., EDV to ...., preload to ...., and SV to ....
(a) increase; increase; increase; increase; increase
(b) increase; decrease; increase; decrease; decrease
(c) decrease; increase; increase; decrease; decrease
(d) decrease; decrease; decrease; decrease; decrease

57. Moderate to intense (but not maximal) exercise will cause HR to ...., SV to ...., and CO to ....
(a) increase; increase; increase
(b) increase; decrease; increase
(c) decrease; increase; increase
(d) decrease; decrease; decrease

58. As atrial EDV increases, plasma ANP levels
(a) increase (b) decrease
(c) not change (d) not related

59. Name the pacemaker of the heart.
(a) Sinoatrial node (b) AV node
(c) Pulmonary artery (d) Endocardium

60. Which portion of the heart's intrinsic conduction system has the lowest conduction velocity?
(a) SA node cells (b) AV node cells
(c) Pulmonary artery (d) Aorta

61. During ventricular systole the AV valves are
(a) closed (b) opened
(c) partially closed (d) partially opened

62. Which heart structure has the greatest rate of spontaneous depolarization?
(a) SA node (b) AV node
(c) VA node (d) AS node

63. Which great vessel delivers blood to the lungs?
(a) Aorta (b) Pulmonary trunk
(c) SA node (d) AV node

64. Shortly after (100ms to be precise) the QRS complex of the ECG. The mitral valve is .... and the aortic valve is ....
(a) closed; closed (b) closed; open
(c) open; closed (d) open; open

65. Which of the following neurotransmitters could have caused this response?

(a) Norepinephrine (b) Acetylcholine
(c) Epinephrine (d) Dopamine

66. A patient with which of the following conditions would probably not be helped by injections of purified stem cells?

(a) Impaired resistance to infection
(b) Leukaemia
(c) AIDS
(d) Hypertension

67. Which of the following is not a similarity between open and closed circulatory systems?

(a) Some sort of pumping device helps to move blood through the body
(b) Some of the circulation of blood is a result of movements of the body
(c) The blood and interstitial fluid are distinguishable from each other
(d) All tissues come into close contact with the circulating body fluid so that the exchange of nutrients and wastes can take place

68. In a system with double circulation,

(a) blood is pumped at two separate locations as it circulates through the body
(b) there is no countercurrent exchange within the gills
(c) Haemolymph circulates both through a pumping blood vessel and through body sinuses
(d) Blood is pumped to the gas-exchange organ and returning blood is then pumped through systemic vessels

69. During diastole,

(a) blood flows passively into the ventricles
(b) the elastic recoil of the arteries maintains hydrostatic pressure on the blood
(c) the semilunar valves are closed but the atrioventricular valves are open
(d) All of the above

70. An atrioventricular valve prevents the backflow or leakage of blood from

(a) the right ventricle into the right atrium
(b) the left atrium into the left ventricle
(c) the aorta into the left ventricle
(d) the pulmonary vein into the right atrium

71. Blood flows more slowly in the arterioles than in the artries because the arterioles

(a) have thoroughfare channels to venules that are often closed off
(b) collectively have a larger cross-sectional area than do the arteries
(c) must provide opportunity for exchange with the interstitial fluid
(d) have sphincters that restrict flow to capillary beds

72. Which of the following cannot move freely in and out of a capillary?

(a) Sugar (b) Oxygen
(c) Carbon dioxide (d) Plasma protein

73. Heart valves function to

(a) keep blood moving forward through the heart
(b) mix blood thoroughly as it passes through the heart
(c) control the amount of blood pumped by the heart
(d) slow blood down as it passes through the heart

74. If all the body's capillaries were open at the same time,

(a) Blood pressure would fall dramatically
(b) Blood would move too rapidly through the capillary beds
(c) The amount of blood returning to the heart would increase
(d) The increased gas exchange would allow for strenunous exercise

75. Rhythmic stretching of the arteries caused by heart contractions is called

(a) hypertension (b) heart murmur
(c) haemophilia (d) pulse

76. The heart specialist listened to Paul's heart through a stethoscope. Instead of the normal 'lub-dupp, lub-dupp' heart sounds, he heard 'siss-dupp, siss-dupp'. The doctor said,

Hmm ... I'm not sure it is anything to worry about, but I think there is something wrong with

(a) one of your coronary arteries
(b) the pacemaker
(c) an atrioventricular valve
(d) your aorta

77. If cells are not receiving enough oxygen, a hormone signals the bone marrow to produce more

(a) leukocytes (b) plasma
(c) platelets (d) erythrocytes

78. The primary sealants that plug leaks in blood vessels are

(a) platelets and fibrin
(b) red blood cells and albumin
(c) fibrin and white blood cells
(d) white blood cells and platelets

79. A recording of the electrical activity of a patient's heart shows that the atria are contracting regularly and normally, but every few beats the ventricles fail to contract. Which of the following is probably not functioning properly?

(a) AV node (b) Semilunar valve
(c) Coronary artery (d) Pacemaker

80. The amount of blood flowing to skeletal muscles is greatly increased during exercise. This redirection of blood into muscles is accomplished by

(a) contraction of muscle in the wall of arteries
(b) relaxation of muscle in wall of arterioles
(c) opening of valves in veins
(d) opening of valves in arteries

81. What is the sequence of blood flow to and fro from the heart of a mammal?

(Where, SV = Sinus Venosus, LA and RA = Left and Right Auricles LV and RV = Left and Right Ventricles)

(a) SV → LA → LV → pulmonary arteries → lungs → pulmonary veins → RA → RV → truncus arteriosus → organs
(b) SV → LA → conus arteriosus → L V → pulmonary arteries → lungs → pulmonary veins → RA → RV → aorta → organs
(c) Superior and inferior vena cava → RA → RV → pulmonary arteries → lungs → pulmonary veins → LA → LV → truncus arteriosus → organs
(d) Superior and inferior vena cava → RA → RV → pulmonary arteries → lungs → pulmonary veins → LA → LV → aorta → organs

82. Consider the following features.

I. Generation of enormous pressure for the ejection of nucleus to the exterior.
II. Increase in the surface area for an effective exchange of O_2 and CO_2.
III. It keeps the cell small and pliable enough for percolation through capillaries.
IV. Enlargement of pores in cell membrane for the release of waste products.

The advantages arising out of the biconcave nature of mammalian red blood cell would include

(a) I and II (b) II and IV
(c) II, III and IV (d) I, II and IV

83. Consider the following processes.

I. Generation of cytotoxic T-cells.
II. Stimulation of interferon release.
III. Formation of bursin.
IV. Release of opsin.

Which of the above are the functions in mammalian tissues performed by interleukin (T-cell growth factor) which is secreted by certain activated T-lymphocytes?

(a) I and II (b) I and III
(c) II and III (d) III and IV

84. Consider the following statements. Constriction of the renal artery would result in an increase in mean arterial pressure due to

I. Increased renin secretion.
II. Increased angiotensin-II formation.
III. Decreased plasma bradykinin levels.
IV. Increased aldosterone secretion.

Which of these statements are correct?

(a) I, II and III (b) II, III and IV
(c) I and IV (d) I, II, III and IV

Answers

1. (c)	**2.** (c)	**3.** (b)	**4.** (b)	**5.** (d)	**6.** (c)	**7.** (b)	**8.** (c)	**9.** (a)	**10.** (c)
11. (d)	**12.** (a)	**13.** (a)	**14.** (b)	**15.** (d)	**16.** (a)	**17.** (a)	**18.** (d)	**19.** (b)	**20.** (d)
21. (c)	**22.** (c)	**23.** (b)	**24.** (a)	**25.** (b)	**26.** (b)	**27.** (a)	**28.** (d)	**29.** (d)	**30.** (b)
31. (c)	**32.** (b)	**33.** (d)	**34.** (a)	**35.** (b)	**36.** (d)	**37.** (b)	**38.** (b)	**39.** (a)	**40.** (c)
41. (a)	**42.** (b)	**43.** (b)	**44.** (a)	**45.** (a)	**46.** (d)	**47.** (d)	**48.** (a)	**49.** (a)	**50.** (a)
51. (a)	**52.** (a)	**53.** (a)	**54.** (d)	**55.** (a)	**56.** (d)	**57.** (a)	**58.** (a)	**59.** (a)	**60.** (b)
61. (a)	**62.** (a)	**63.** (b)	**64.** (b)	**65.** (b)	**66.** (d)	**67.** (c)	**68.** (d)	**69.** (d)	**70.** (a)
71. (b)	**72.** (d)	**73.** (a)	**74.** (a)	**75.** (d)	**76.** (c)	**77.** (d)	**78.** (a)	**79.** (a)	**80.** (b)
81. (b)	**82.** (b)	**83.** (a)	**84.** (d)						

21

Excretory System and Thermoregulation

Excretory System

Animals perform their metabolic processes, protein and nucleic acids, both of which contain nitrogen are degraded. This nitrogen is partially used for the synthesis of new nitrogen containing molecules while majority of it cannot be used and must be disposed of from body as waste. Typically, the first nitrogen containing molecule that is formed in all organisms is ammonia; which is highly soluble in water.

Depending upon the mode of excretion of nitrogen organisms have been divided into:

1. **Ammonotelic** Excretes ammonia (highly soluble in water), reside in aquatic habitats, *e.g.*, fishes.
2. **Uricotelic** Excretes uric acid (poorly soluble in water), water scarce habitats, *e.g.*, lizards, birds.
3. **Ureotelic** Excretes urea (highly soluble in water), sufficient water is available, *e.g.*, humans.

In addition, certain organisms excrete nitrogenous waste in form of **allantoin** which is a cell proliferator as well, *e.g.*, blow fly larvae.

Syllabus

- Excretory System: Comparative Physiology of Excretion, Kidneys, Formation of Urine Waste Elimination, Micturition, Regulation of Acid-Base Balance.
- Thermoregulation: Comfort Zone, Body Temperature Regulation (Acclimatization) Thermoregulation in Humans.
- Stress and Adaptation.

Table 21.1 **Various Excretory Compounds with their Toxicity and Presence**

Compound	Chemical Formula	Toxicity	Water Solubility	Animals
Ammonia	NH_3	High	High	Aquatic animals
Urea	$(NH_2)_2CO$	Moderate	Moderate	Terrestrial animals
Uric acid	$C_5H_4N_4O_3$	Low	Low	Reptiles and birds

The **excretory system** constitutes a passive organ system that removes excess, unnecessary or dangerous materials. It is responsible for the elimination of the **waste products** of **metabolism** as well as other liquid and gaseous wastes. As most healthy functioning organs produce metabolic and other wastes, the entire **organism** depends on the function of the system; however, only the organs specifically for the excretion process are considered a part of the excretory system. The substances are filtered out from the body in the form of urine. Urine is a liquid produced by the kidneys, collected in the bladder and excreted through the urethra. Urine is used to extract excess minerals or vitamins as well as blood corpuscles from the body. The urinary organs include the kidneys, ureters, bladder and urethra. The urinary system works with the other systems of the body to help maintain homeostasis. The kidneys are the main organs of homeostasis because they maintain the acid base balance and the water salt balance of the blood.

Comparative Account of Excretion in Animals

Diverse mechanisms have evolved that enable the various animal species to inhabit a wide range of environment. In animals whose bodies consist of a single layer of cells, waste disposal is accomplished principally by diffusion from the site of waste production to the outside environment. This method is efficient when the distances over which wastes diffuse are relatively short, when there is a high surface area to volume relationship and when the rate of waste production is relatively low. In more complex animals, however, waste elimination by diffusion through the body wall to the exterior is less efficient because individual cells are further removed from the exterior surface of the organism. The presence of specialized mechanisms of elimination in higher animals enables wastes to be rapidly transported to the exterior surface of the body.

Protista

No specialized elimination mechanisms are present in algae, fungi, protozoans and **slime moulds,** the main groups of protists. Metabolic wastes (carbon dioxide, water, oxygen and nitrogenous compounds) diffuse through the cell membranes of these **unicellular organisms** into the outside environment. Particulate wastes pass from the bodies of certain protozoans to the exterior by way of small openings in the body surface—anal pores and other cell openings. Elimination in protists is carried out passively and therefore, requires little or no expenditure of metabolic energy on the part of the organism.

Sponges

Phylogenetically, the sponges (phylum–Porifera) are the simplest of animals. They are multicellular and composed of specialized cells, arranged in a single layer, for the maintenance of life processes. Elimination in these aquatic animals proceeds by diffusion of gaseous wastes into the surrounding water and by the ejection of solid wastes and indigestible material from the digestive cells into the streams of water that constantly flow through the animal.

Cnidarians

The jellyfishes, coral animals, ctenophores and comb jellies have a rudimentary canal-like cavity in their two-layered bodies for the ingestion, digestion and egestion of food and wastes. Gaseous wastes are eliminated by diffusion and solid wastes in dissolved or undissolved form pass out through an opening in the body wall that serves the dual purposes of food intake and waste elimination.

Flatworms

Flatworm bodies consist of three layers of cells and in this aquatic group elimination is similar to that of the less complex animals. Food and solid wastes enter and leave through a common opening in the well-developed digestive tract, which consists of a mouth, pharynx and gastrovascular cavity.

Nemertine Worms

The digestive and **excretory system** of the aquatic proboscis worms is more efficient than that of lower animals in that a well-defined mouth, intestine and excretory opening (anus) permit the one-way flow of food and waste through the animal. Egested food and nitrogenous wastes, which are secreted into the intestine, are passed along it to the anus by peristaltic waves of the **smooth muscle** lining the intestinal walls.

Nematodes

An additional excretory structure has evolved in the roundworms. Excretory canals located on both sides of the intestine facilitate waste disposal by carriage of material to an excretory pore in the body wall.

Other Invertebrates

In invertebrates, increasing structural complexity is accompanied by more efficient waste-disposal mechanisms. In the phylum–Mollusca (clams, snails, oysters, molluscs, octopuses and squids), gills add another more efficient channel for waste disposal. A heart increases the rate of flow in the circulatory system and speeds the transport of wastes to the gills. An excretory, kidney-like organ removes metabolic wastes from the circulation and body fluid prior to excretion. All basic mechanisms of excretion are thus present in relatively simple animals. As invertebrates become more specialized and complex, as in the arthropods (insects, crabs and other joint-legged animals) and annelids (segmented worms), adaptations in excretion methods allow survival in non-aquatic environments.

Vertebrates

Though the wastes produced by vertebrates differ little qualitatively from those of higher invertebrates, increased structural complexity and body size, in combination with environmental adaptations, require more specific waste-disposal mechanisms in order to maintain a constant internal environment. The presence of highly efficient, water-retaining kidneys, for example, permits vertebrates to inhabit arid, hot regions of the earth. It seems proper, within the vertebrate group, to consider elimination schemes as variations of mechanisms common to all higher animals but which enable animals to inhabit widely diversified environments.

Excretory Mechanisms

The meaning of excretion is most easily understood in the context of vertebrate physiology. The animal swallows food (ingestion). In the stomach and intestine some of the food is broken down into soluble products (digestion) that are absorbed into the body (assimilation). In the body these soluble products undergo further **chemical change (metabolism);** some are used by the body for growth, but most provide energy for the various activities of the body. Metabolism involves the uptake of oxygen and the elimination of **carbon dioxide** in the lungs (respiration). Besides carbon dioxide, compounds of nitrogen arise from metabolism and are eliminated, chiefly by the kidney, in the urine (excretion). Food not digested is eliminated through the anus (defecation).

Osmotic Pressure

In order to understand the advantages of the excretion of uric acid over urea it is necessary to know something about the behaviour of **molecules** in **solution.** Molecules of a solute (*e.g.,* salt and sugar) in water tend to move by diffusion from a region, where they are in high concentration to one where they are in low concentration and molecules of **water** tend to move in the opposite direction. If a porous membrane is placed between these regions, the movements of molecules may be variously restricted depending upon their size in relation to the size of the submicroscopic pores in the membrane. The passage of water molecules from pure water through such a membrane into a solution containing molecules that are too large to pass is called **osmosis,** a process that takes place spontaneously and does not require energy. This process can be reversed by applying hydrostatic pressure to the solution, a process that does require energy. The level of **hydrostatic pressure** at which there is no net movement of water in either direction across the membrane is called the **osmotic pressure** of that particular solution; the greater the concentration of dissolved molecules in the solution the greater is its osmotic pressure and the greater the force needed to remove water from it.

These principles explain why more energy is required to remove water from urine containing urea than from urine containing the same weight of uric acid. The molecule of urea is smaller than that of uric acid, so that with the same weight, there are more molecules of urea to exert osmotic pressure. But an even more important difference is that whereas urea is highly soluble in water, uric acid is not. As water is progressively removed from a solution of urea, the osmotic pressure opposing further removal progressively increases. For the uric acid solution, however, as water is removed, the uric acid comes out of solution or precipitates, when the solution is at a lower concentration and therefore, at a lower osmotic pressure, which does not increase further.

Regulation of Water and Salt Balance

The mechanisms of detoxication that animals use are related to their modes of life. This is true, with greater force of the mechanisms of **homeostasis,** the ability of organisms to maintain internal stability. A desert-living mammal constantly faces the problem of water conservation; but a freshwater fish faces the problem of getting rid of the water that enters its body by osmosis through the skin. At the level of the individual cell, whether it is the cell that constitutes **a unicellular organism** or a cell in the body of a **multicellular organism,** the problems of homeostasis present themselves in similar ways.

To continue its intracellular processes a cell must maintain an intracellular chemical environment in which the concentrations of various **ions** (see below) are kept constant in the face of changing concentrations in the medium surrounding the cell. This is the task of the **cell membrane.** In the higher animals, the task is easier since cells in the interior of their bodies are bathed in an internal medium—**the blood** whose composition is regulated so as to minimize the effects of changes in the external medium. This regulatory function is undertaken by specialized cells or organs such as the kidney, thereby lessening the regulatory burden of the other cells of the body.

The biological necessity for homeostatic mechanisms is particularly urgent for controlling the inorganic components of cells and body fluids. Inorganic salts can exert even greater osmotic pressure against membranes impermeable to them than urea. This is so because, under the conditions in the body, they are almost completely dissociated into their component ions. For example, a molecule of **common salt** (sodium chloride) is dissociated into two inorganic ions—a positively charged **sodium ion** and a negatively charged chloride ion—both of which can exert osmotic pressure.

Aside from their osmotic effects, inorganic ions have profound effects upon metabolic processes, which in general will take place only in the presence of appropriate concentrations of these ions. The most important inorganic ions in organisms are the positively charged hydrogen, sodium, potassium, calcium and magnesium ions and the negatively charged chloride, phosphate and bicarbonate ions. The membranes of cells are not completely impermeable to these ions and are in fact endowed with the ability to transport ions between the inside and outside of the cell, whereby they control the concentrations of ions within the cells; when such transport is in the direction that requires a supply of energy, it is called active transport (see cell: The plasma membrane).

Osmotic regulation is the maintenance of the normal concentration of the body fluids *i.e.,* the total concentration of all dissolved substances (solutes) that would exert osmotic pressure against a membrane impermeable to them. Osmotic regulation controls the amount of water in the body fluids relative to the amount of osmotically active solutes. Ionic regulation is the maintenance of the concentrations of the various ions in the body fluids relative to one another. There is no consistent distinction between the two processes; organs that participate in one process at the same time participate in the other.

Principal Excretory Structures

Whereas, the kidney is the principal organ subserving both nitrogenous excretion and osmotic and **ionic regulation** in the mammalian body, these functions are not always performed by a single organ in other animals. As indicated earlier, primitive aquatic animals do not require any special provision for nitrogenous excretion. But by reason of their permeable skins they may have serious problems of osmotic and ionic regulation, especially in **freshwater,** where cells covering the surface of the body have the ability to actively transport salts into or out of the animal. In some cases, these non-kidney regulatory activities are performed by certain specialized cells, *e.g.,* in the gills of fishes (see below **vertebrate excretory systems: fishes).** In other cases, specialized cells are assembled into organs of salt uptake or salt elimination *e.g.,* the salt glands of birds (see below **vertebrate excretory systems: birds and reptiles).**

This dispersal of the regulatory function may be the primitive condition, for it is only in the more highly evolved terrestrial animals that the regulatory function is restricted to an excretory system proper. This is readily understandable in view of the need of terrestrial animals to conserve water. This evolutionary development toward one system reaches its climax in the birds, reptiles and terrestrial insects, in which all the processes of elimination that might involve loss of water—defecation, nitrogenous excretion and ionic regulation—converge upon the same final channel.

For the excretory organs of a wide variety of vertebrate and invertebrate animals, there is evidence that the primary process of urine production is non-selective, in that in those animals all substances dissolved in their body fluids, with the possible exception of proteins, are found in the primary urine. In many animals, the primary urine is produced by filtration from the blood. At a later stage, substances in the primary urine that are useful to the body are selectively reabsorbed. In addition, a few substances are known to be actively transported (secreted) into the urine.

The non-selective formation of primary urine serves another aspect of excretion: the elimination of foreign substances. Mechanisms of active transport are highly specific to the substances transported. All dissolved constituents of the body fluids pass freely into the primary urine and then specific reabsorptive mechanisms gather up the 'wanted' substances. In this way, a natural economy automatically eliminates 'unwanted' substances simply by not providing mechanisms for their reabsorption.

Invertebrate-Excretory Systems

In their detoxication mechanisms, so far as they have been investigated, the invertebrates in general conform to the principles applying to all animals, namely, that aquatic forms get rid of ammonia by diffusion through the surface of the body; terrestrial forms convert ammonia to uric acid. This implies that in aquatic forms the excretory organ is principally of importance for the composition of their body fluids. Normally, the body fluids of marine invertebrates have the same concentration as sea water; they usually differ, however, in the proportions of ions, with relatively more potassium and less magnesium than sea water. Furthermore, their urine normally has the same concentration as sea water, but correspondingly it contains less potassium and more magnesium. In freshwater invertebrates, the urine is commonly, though not invariably, more dilute than the body fluids. By producing dilute urine a freshwater invertebrate conserves the salt content of its body while eliminating the water that enters its body by osmosis through its water-permeable surface.

Some invertebrates, notably echinoderms, cnidarians and sponges, have no organs to which an excretory function can be confidently ascribed. Since all of these animals are aquatic, it is reasonable to suppose that they excrete nitrogen (as ammonia) by simple diffusion. Their body fluids (where present) are closely similar to sea water in composition and it may be presumed that regulation operates only at the cellular level.

The excretory organs of other invertebrates are of diverse evolutionary origin. This is not to say, however, that each invertebrate phylum has evolved its own particular type of excretory organ; rather, there appear to be five main types of invertebrate excretory organ: **contractile vacuole, nephridium, renal gland, coxal gland and Malpighian tubule.**

Contractile Vacuoles of Protozoans

Some protozoan animals possess an organelle having the form of an internal sac or vacuole, which enlarges by the accumulation of a clear fluid and then discharges its contents to the exterior. The cycle of filling and emptying may be repeated as frequently as every half minute. The chief role of the contractile vacuole appears to be in osmotic regulation, not in nitrogen excretion.

Contractile vacuoles occur more frequently and are more active in freshwater species than in closely related marine species. In fresh water, the concentration of dissolved substances in the cell is greater than in the external medium and the cell takes in water by osmosis. If the contractile vacuole is put out of action, the cell increases in volume. If the concentration of salts in the medium increases—which would have the effect of decreasing the rate of osmosis—the rate of output by the contractile vacuole diminishes. The fluid eliminated by the vacuole is more dilute than the cytoplasm.

Nephridia of Annelids, Nemertines, Flatworms and Rotifers

The word **nephridium** applies in its strict sense only to the excretory organs of **annelids,** but it may usefully be extended to include the excretory organs of other phyla having similar characteristics. Annelids are segmented animals that typically contain a pair of nephridia on each segment. Each nephridium has the form of a very fine tubule, often of considerable length; one end usually opens into the

body cavity and the other to the exterior. In some annelids, however, the tubule does not open into the body cavity but ends internally in a cluster of cells of a special type known as solenocytes or flame cells. The possession of **solenocytes** by some annelids is one of the characteristics that allies them with other non-segmented phyla that have no true body cavity. They also have a system of tubules opening at the surface and ending internally in flame cells embedded among the other cells of the body. In most cases, there is no regular arrangement of the various parts of the system. Animals belonging to all of these phyla are primarily aquatic and in the few cases known, the main excretory product is ammonia. How much of it leaves the body by the nephridia and how much through the body surface is not known.

Few physiological studies have been made on nephridia other than those of the earthworm. Although the earthworm is considered a terrestrial animal, its relationships with its environment are characteristically those of a freshwater animal. The nephridium of the earthworm is longer and more complex than that of marine annelids, four regions being distinguishable. Body fluid enters the nephridium *via* an internal opening called the **nephridiostome.** As the fluid passes along the tubule, probably driven by cilia, its composition is modified. In the two lower regions of the tubule the fluid becomes progressively more dilute, presumably as a result of the reabsorption of salts. Finally, a very dilute urine passes into the bladder (an enlarged portion of the tubule) and then to the exterior through the external opening or **nephridiopore.** The rate of urine flow for an earthworm may be as much as 60 per cent of its body weight in a period of 24 h.

Renal Glands of Molluscs

The anatomical form of the renal gland varies from one class of molluscs to another, but a common plan is clearly evident. The renal gland is a relatively wide tube opening from a sac (the pericardium) surrounding the heart, at one end and to the **mantle cavity** (effectively to the exterior) at the other. There is a single pair of renal glands; in some forms one member of the pair may be reduced or absent. **Clams** have the simplest arrangement; the region nearest to the pericardium has glandular walls and gives way to a non-glandular, wider tube that extends to the urinary opening.

The vast majority of molluscs are aquatic and excrete nitrogen in the form of ammonia. In **octopuses,** however, nitrogen is excreted as **ammonium chloride,** which is quite strongly concentrated in the urine. Terrestrial **snails** and **slugs** excrete uric acid but may also excrete ammonia when living in moist surroundings.

In all molluscs so far investigated the primary process in urine production appears to be **filtration** of the blood. This may take place through the wall of the heart into the pericardium or from **blood vessels** that supply the glandular part of the renal gland. The composition of the primary urine may be altered by reabsorption or secretion or both. In freshwater molluscs salts are reabsorbed in the glandular tube and in the wide tubule and the **final urine** is more dilute than the blood. The rate of urine flow is high, upto 45 per cent of the body weight per day in the **freshwater mussel.** In marine molluscs the urine has the same concentration as the blood, but (in the few cases examined) its ionic composition is different.

Coxal Glands of Aquatic Arthropods

Coxal glands are tubular organs, each opening on the basal region (coxa) of a limb. Since, arthropods are segmented animals, it is reasonable to suppose that the ancestral arthropod had a pair of such glands in every segment of the body. In modern **crustaceans** there is, as a rule, only a single pair of glands and in higher crustaceans these open at the bases of the antennae. Each **antennal gland** is a compact organ formed of a single tubule folded upon itself. When unraveled the tubule is seen to comprise three or four easily recognizable regions. The tubule arises internally as a small sac, the coelomic sac, which opens into a wider region, the labyrinth, having complex infoldings of its walls. The labyrinth opens either directly into the bladder, as in marine lobsters and crabs or into a narrow part of the **tubule,** the canal, which in turn opens into the bladder, as in freshwater crayfishes.

The coelomic sac, well supplied with blood vessels, gives evidence that the primary process in urine production is filtration of the blood through the wall of the coelomic sac in a manner analogous to filtration in the glomerulus and Bowman's capsule of the vertebrate kidney (see below). In lobsters and marine crabs the urine in all parts of the organ has the same ion concentration as the blood. In fresh water **crayfishes** the urine has the same concentration as far as the end of the labyrinth; from that point on reabsorption takes place in the canal and the urine leaves the body as a very dilute solution. The addition of the canal to the system demonstrates one way crustaceans have adapted to life in freshwater. But this is not the only way in which the regulatory problem is solved in freshwater crustaceans. In freshwater crabs, for example, there is a great decrease in the water permeability of the surface (principally the gills) so that water enters by osmosis quite slowly. In contrast to the rate of urine flow in a freshwater crayfish (about 5 per cent of the body weight per day), that of the freshwater **crab** is 100 times less (about 0.05 per cent). In the crab the urine has the same concentration as the blood, but because the flow is so small the salt loss *via* the urine is negligible. A few semiterrestrial crabs are known to produce urine more concentrated than the blood.

In all crustaceans for which analyses are available the concentrations of ions in blood and urine differ. At a urine flow of 5 per cent of the body weight per day the activities of the **antennal glands** are certainly capable of effecting changes in the composition of the blood. These activities are somehow coordinated with salt uptake by the cells of the body surface so as to subserve homeostasis. The role of the antennal glands in nitrogenous excretion seems to be unimportant.

Malpighian Tubules of Insects

Although some terrestrial arthropods (*e.g.,* land crabs and ticks) retain the coxal glands of their aquatic ancestors, others, the insects, have evolved an entirely different type of excretory system. The Malpighian tubules, which vary in number from two in some species to more than 100 in others, end blindly in the body cavity (which is a blood space) and open not directly to the exterior but to the **alimentary canal** at the junction between midgut and hindgut. The primary urine issuing from the Malpighian tubules has to pass through the rectum before it leaves the **insect's** body and in the **rectum** its composition is markedly changed. The insect excretory system therefore, comprises the Malpighian tubules and the rectum acting together.

The Malpighian tubules are bathed in the insect's blood, but since, they are not rigid it is impossible for any hydrostatic pressure to be developed across their walls, such as could bring about filtration. The primary urine is formed by a process of secretion in the following way potassium ions are actively transported from the blood into the cavity of the tubule and are necessarily followed by negatively charged ions so as to maintain electroneutrality. In turn, water follows the ions, probably by osmosis and various other substances—sugars, amino acids and urate ions—also enter the primary urine by diffusion from the blood.

The primary urine, together with soluble products of digestion and insoluble indigestible matter from the midgut, then passes to the rectum. There (or in some insects at an earlier stage) the urine is acidified and the soluble urate is thereby converted to insoluble uric acid, which comes out of solution. Water is then reabsorbed together with the soluble products of digestion and other useful substances, including the bulk of the ions that entered the primary urine. In insects that live in dry surroundings the rectum has remarkable powers of reabsorption, its contents finally being voided as hard, dry pellets containing solid uric acid.

The activity of the excretory system in insects is under hormonal control. This has been most clearly demonstrated in the case of *Rhodnius*, a bloodsucking bug. Immediately after the ingestion of blood meal there is a rapid flow of urine whereby most of the water taken in with the blood meal is eliminated. The distension of the body after ingestion is the stimulus that causes certain cells in the **central nervous system** to release a hormone that acts upon the Malpighian tubules to promote a brisk flow of primary urine.

Vertebrate Excretory System

Studies of the embryonic development of primitive vertebrates, such as the dogfish shark, clearly show that the excretory system arises from a series of tubules, one pair in every segment of the body between the heart and the tail. This continuous series of tubules constitutes the **archinephros,** the name implying that the **kidney** of the ancestral vertebrate had some such form as this. Each tubule opens internally to the body cavity and may, in the remote past, have opened separately to the exterior; but in all living vertebrates the tubules open on each side into a longitudinal duct, the **archinephric duct.** At the posterior end of the body cavity the two archinephric ducts unite before opening to the exterior. Later in development, Bowman's capsule arises as a diverticulum of each tubule, subsequently becoming indented by the glomerulus. Eventually, the tubules usually lose their internal openings to the body cavity. The most anterior tubules of the archinephros (pronephros) usually degenerate in the adult.

These ducts and tubules also subserve the reproductive function and for this reason they are also called the **urogenital system.** The extent to which the ducts and tubules are shared is greater in the male than in the female. In the male the spermatic tubules of the testis connect with the kidney tubules in the middle region of the archinephros (mesonephros) and in some vertebrates (*e.g.,* the frog) where there is no development of the posterior region (metanephros), the tubules of the mesonephros serve to convey both urine and sperm. In the reptiles, birds and mammals, there is greater separation of function, the mesonephros being exclusively genital and the metanephros being exclusively urinary.

In the female, even in the lower vertebrates, the two systems are confluent only at the posterior end. It has been held that the oviduct is a derivative of the archinephric duct, but the evidence for this is not compelling.

In primitive marine animals, the blood is almost identical with sea water in composition; in typical freshwater animals the concentration of the blood is about half that of sea water. Many originally marine animals have evolved the ability to live in fresh water; relatively few animals, after having thus evolved, have returned to the sea and in none of them has the blood returned to its original 'sea water' concentration. The earliest fossil vertebrates are found in marine deposits, but the **fossil record** shows clearly that the early evolution of fishes took place in freshwater. It is assumed that the blood of early freshwater fishes, like that of other freshwater animals, was osmotically equivalent to half-strength sea water. The sharks and rays returned to the sea during the **Carboniferous period** and no doubt at that time they evolved the device of urea retention. The bony fishes returned to the sea later, in the **Mesozoic era** and solved their problem by swallowing sea water and rejecting excess salt at the gills.

Fishes

The homeostasis problem is the same for freshwater fishes as for other freshwater animals. **Water** enters the body by osmosis and salts leach out. To compensate, the kidney (which has large glomeruli) produces a relatively large amount of dilute urine (about 20 per cent of the body weight per day). This serves to remove the water but by itself is insufficient to prevent gradual loss of salts. Extremely diluted salts are taken up from the freshwater and transported directly into the blood by certain specialized cells in the gills. Nitrogenous excretion is no problem: some ammonia is carried away in the large volume of dilute urine, but most of it simply escapes to the external medium by diffusing through the gills.

By contrast, the homeostasis problem of marine fishes is unlike that of most **marine animals.** The salt content of the blood of marine fishes is less than half that of sea water (see below Evolution of the vertebrate excretory system); consequently, marine fishes tend to lose water and gain salt. This, it would seem, could be compensated most easily by the excretion of urine more concentrated than the blood, but the kidneys of fishes are not able to do this. In marine **bony fishes** the kidney has small glomeruli and produces only a small amount (about 4 per cent of the body weight per day) of urine which is of the same concentration as the blood. The fish replaces its lost water by continually swallowing sea water and the special cells of the gills, working in reverse, reject salt to the external medium. Nitrogen is excreted mostly as ammonia but also as another detoxication product, trimethylamine oxide.

In sharks and **rays** ammonia is converted to urea and urea plays an important role in homeostasis. Urea is retained in the blood to such an extent that the blood is slightly more concentrated than sea water. Thus loss of water by osmosis is prevented and these fish have no need to swallow sea water. Any excess of salt in their bodies is removed *via* the rectal gland, functionally analogous to the salt gland of birds.

Osmotic and ionic regulation in fishes is under hormonal control. This has been studied particularly in fishes such as eels and salmon, which are able to move between freshwater and sea water.

Amphibians

Direct evidence for the occurrence of filtration at the glomerulus was first provided by experiments on the amphibian kidney. Although amphibians are formally given the status of terrestrial animals, they are poorly adapted to life on land. They excrete nitrogen in the form of urea and cannot produce urine more concentrated than the blood. Their skins are permeable to **water.** On land amphibians are liable to lose water very rapidly by evaporation. In freshwater they suffer entry of water by osmosis, which is counteracted by the excretion of a large volume of dilute urine. The urine is stored in a large bladder before being voided, providing a reserve of water the animal can use when it comes on land.

When an amphibian leaves the water, a number of physiological adjustments are made that have the effect of conserving water. The rate of glomerular filtration is reduced by restriction of the blood supply and this together with an increased release of **antidiuretic hormone** results in the production of a small volume of urine of the same concentration as the blood. Antidiuretic Hormone (ADH, also known as **vasopressin,** which increases the permeability of the distal and collecting tubules to water) also increases the permeability of the bladder to water and allows the stored urine to be reabsorbed into the body.

Birds and Reptiles

The main excretory product of birds and reptiles is uric acid. Since, their glomeruli are relatively small, so also is their daily volume of urine. Not highly concentrated by mammalian standards—although it may be turbid with crystals of uric acid—the urine of birds and reptiles is conducted not to **a urinary bladder** but to the terminal portion of the alimentary canal, the cloaca; from the **cloaca** it is voided with the **faeces.** Like mammals and unlike the lower vertebrates, birds and reptiles have skins impermeable to water and thus are well adapted to terrestrial life. The relative inability of the kidney to produce concentrated urine is compensated for in birds that possess salt glands, which remove excess salt from their bodies. These organs are modified **tear glands** that discharge a concentrated solution of sodium chloride through the nostrils. Salt glands enable marine birds to drink sea water with no ill effects.

Mammals

The mammalian kidney is a compact organ with two distinct regions—cortex and medulla. The functional unit of the kidney is the **nephron.** Each nephron is a tubular structure consisting of four regions. It arises in the cortex as a small vesicle about one-fifth of a millimetre (0.008 inch) in diameter, known as **Bowman's capsule,** into which projects a tuft of capillary blood vessels, the **glomerulus.** Bowman's capsule is continuous with the **proximal convoluted tubule,** which also lies in the cortex. Following the proximal convoluted tubule is the **loop of Henle,** which descends into the medulla and then runs straight up again to the cortex, where it continues as the **distal convoluted tubule.** A **collecting tubule,** into which several nephrons open, courses through the medulla to open a wide cavity, the pelvis of the kidney. From the pelvis the ureter leads to the bladder and from the bladder **the urethra** leads out of the body.

The mechanism of urine formation involves three processes **filtration, reabsorption** and **secretion. Primary urine** is formed by filtration from the blood. From this primary urine certain substances are reabsorbed into the blood and other substances are secreted into the primary urine from the blood. The word secretion is used by renal physiologists to imply transport, other than by filtration, from the blood to urine. Filtration implies that all molecules below a certain size are allowed to pass non-selectively into the primary urine; reabsorption and secretion imply the existence of specific mechanisms for the transport of specific substances.

The membrane covering the glomerulus allows the passage of water and all the constituents of the **blood plasma** except proteins. The **glomerular capillaries** are intercalated in the course of an artery, with the consequence that the pressure of the blood in these capillaries is higher than in the capillaries in other parts of the kidney. Opposed to the blood pressure are the pressure of the fluid within Bowman's capsule and the osmotic pressure exerted by the proteins of the blood plasma; but the **blood pressure** is sufficiently in excess of the sum of these to ensure a rapid flow of fluid, the glomerular filtrate or primary urine, into Bowman's capsule. The glomerular filtrate contains the nitrogenous compounds ultimately to be excreted in the urine. As the **glomerular filtrate** passes through the proximal tubule, 80 per cent of the water and many substances of value to the body (*e.g.,* glucose), is reabsorbed into the blood capillaries surrounding the tubule. This reabsorptive process is accomplished without any change in the concentration of the tubular fluid, which remains the same as that of the blood plasma.

After traversing the loop of Henle, the remaining 20 per cent of the glomerular filtrate passes into the distal tubule, where further reabsorption, notably of salts, takes place. If this is accompanied by a proportionate reabsorption of water, the tubular fluid remains at the same concentration as the blood plasma, but if the reabsorption of water is restricted, as it may be in certain circumstances (see below), the tubular fluid becomes more dilute than the blood plasma. Under normal physiological conditions some 15 per cent of the glomerular filtrate is reabsorbed in the distal tubule. Most of the remaining 5 per cent is reabsorbed in the collecting tubule. The amount of fluid, at this point called urine, that reaches the pelvis of the kidney is only 1 per cent of the volume originally filtered at the glomerulus; but it contains nearly all the nitrogenous waste of the filtrate in concentrated solution. A few substances are also secreted from the blood through the walls of the tubule into the tubular fluid.

Kidneys

The kidneys are a pair of bean-shaped, reddish brown organs about the size of your fist. They are covered by the renal capsule, which is a tough capsule of fibrous connective tissue. Adhering to the surface of each kidney is two layers of fat to help cushion them. There is a concaved side of the kidney that has a depression where a renal artery enters and a renal vein and a ureter exit the kidney. The kidneys are located at the rear wall of the abdominal cavity just above the waistline,

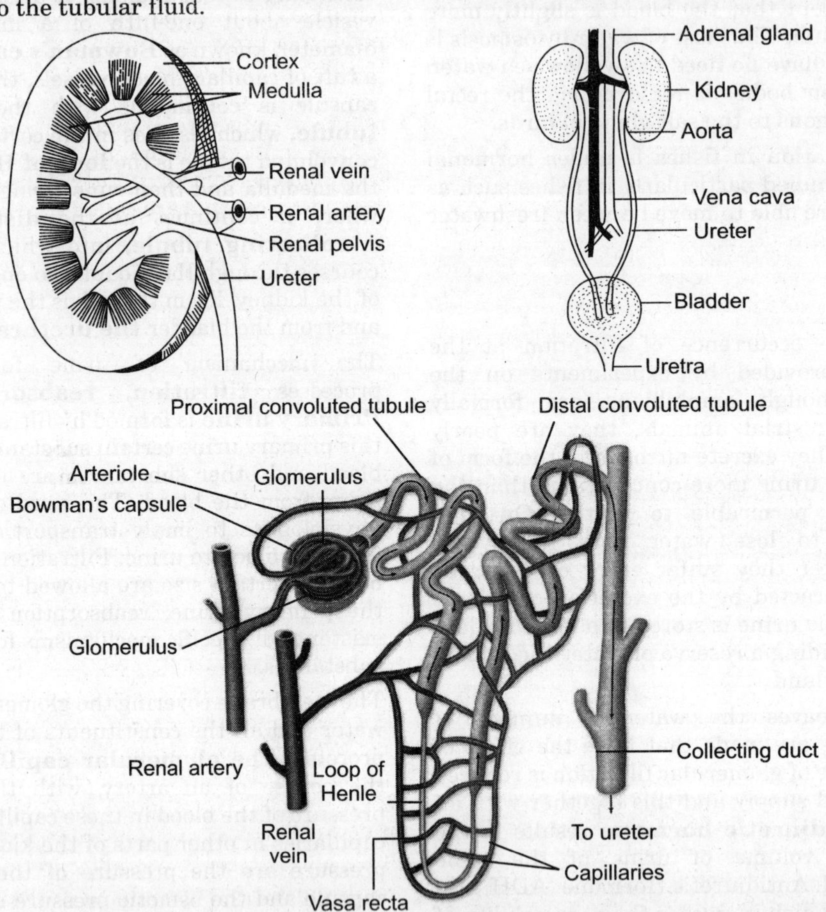

Fig. 21.1 Human excretory system

and are protected by the ribcage. They are considered retroperitoneal, which means they lie behind the peritoneum. There are three major regions of the kidney, renal cortex, renal medulla and the renal pelvis. The outer, granulated layer is the renal cortex. The cortex stretches down in between a radially striated inner layer. The inner radially striated layer is the renal medulla. This contains pyramid-shaped tissue called the renal pyramids, separated by renal columns. The ureters are continuous with the renal pelvis and are the very center of the kidney.

Nephrons

A nephron is the basic structural and functional unit of the kidney. The name nephron comes from the Greek word *nephros* meaning kidney. Its chief function is to regulate water and soluble substances by filtering the blood, reabsorbing what is needed and excreting the rest as urine. Nephrons eliminate wastes from the body, regulate blood volume and pressure, control levels of electrolytes and metabolites and regulate blood pH. Its functions are vital to life and are regulated by the endocrine system by hormones such as antidiuretic hormone, aldosterone and parathyroid hormone. Each nephron has its own supply of blood from two capillary regions from the renal artery. Each nephron is composed of an initial filtering component (the renal corpuscle) and a tubule specialized for reabsorption and secretion (the renal tubule). The renal corpuscle filters out large solutes from the blood, delivering water and small solutes to the renal tubule for modification.

Glomerulus

The glomerulus is a capillary tuft that receives its blood supply from an afferent arteriole of the renal circulation. The glomerular blood pressure provides the driving force for fluid and solutes to be filtered out of the blood and into the space made by Bowman's capsule. The remainder of the blood not filtered into the glomerulus passes into the narrower efferent arteriole. It then moves into the vasa recta, which are collecting capillaries intertwined with the convoluted tubules through the interstitial space, where the reabsorbed substances will also enter. This then combines with efferent venules from other nephrons into the renal vein and rejoins with the main bloodstream.

Afferent/Efferent Arterioles

The afferent arteriole supplies blood to the glomerulus. A group of specialized cells known as juxtaglomerular cells are located around the afferent arteriole, where it enters the renal corpuscle. The efferent arteriole drains the glomerulus. Between the two arterioles lies specialized cells called the macula densa. The juxtaglomerular cells and the macula densa collectively form the juxtaglomerular apparatus. It is in the juxtaglomerular apparatus cells that the enzyme renin is formed and stored. Renin is released in response to decreased blood pressure in the afferent arterioles, decreased sodium chloride in the distal convoluted tubule and sympathetic nerve stimulation of receptors (beta-adrenic) on the juxtaglomerular cells. Renin is needed to form angiotensin I and angiotensin II which stimulate the secretion of aldosterone by the adrenal cortex.

Glomerular Capsule or Bowman's Capsule

Bowman's capsule (also called the glomerular capsule) surrounds the glomerulus and is composed of visceral (simple squamous epithelial cells) (inner) and parietal (simple squamous epithelial cells) (outer) layers. The visceral layer lies just beneath the thickened glomerular basement membrane and is made of podocytes which send foot processes over the length of the glomerulus. Foot processes interdigitate with one another forming filtration slits that, in contrast to those in the glomeruluar endothelium, are spanned by diaphragms. The size of the filtration slits restricts the passage of large molecules (*e.g.*, albumin) and cells (*e.g.*, red blood cells and platelets). In addition, foot processes have a negatively-charged coat (glycocalyx) that limits the filtration of negatively-charged molecules, such as albumin. This action is called **electrostatic repulsion.** The parietal layer of Bowman's capsule is lined by a single layer of squamous epithelium. Between the visceral and parietal layers is Bowman's space, into which the filtrate enters after passing through the podocytes filtration slits. It is here that smooth muscle cells and macrophages lie between the capillaries and provide support for them. Unlike the visceral layer, the parietal layer does not function in filtration. Rather, the filtration barrier is formed by three components the diaphragms of the filtration slits, the thick glomerular basement membrane and the glycocalyx secreted by podocytes. 99% of glomerular filtrate will ultimately be reabsorbed. The process of filtration of the blood in the Bowman's capsule is ultrafiltration (or glomerular filtration) and the normal rate of filtration is 125 mL/min, equivalent to ten times the blood volume daily. Measuring the Glomerular Filtration Rate (GFR) is a diagnostic test of kidney function. A decreased GFR may be a sign of renal failure. Conditions that can effect GFR include arterial pressure, afferent arteriole constriction, efferent arteriole constriction, plasma protein concentration and colloid osmotic pressure. Any proteins that are roughly 30 kilodaltons or under can pass freely through the membrane. Although, there is some extra hindrance for negatively charged molecules due to the negative charge of the basement membrane and the podocytes. Any small molecules such as water, glucose, salt (NaCl), amino acids and urea pass freely into Bowman's space, but cells, platelets and large proteins do not. As a result, the filtrate leaving the Bowman's capsule is very similar to blood plasma in composition as it passes into the proximal convoluted tubule. Together, the glomerulus and Bowman's capsule are called the renal corpuscle.

Proximal Convoluted Tubule (PCT)

The proximal tubule can be anatomically divided into two segments the proximal convoluted tubule and the proximal straight tubule. The proximal convoluted tubule can be divided further into S1 and S2 segments based on the histological appearance of it's cells. Following this naming convention, the proximal straight tubule is commonly called the S3 segment. The proximal convoluted tubule has one layer of cuboidal cells in the lumen. This is the only place in the nephron that contains cuboidal cells. These cells are covered with millions of microvilli. The microvilli serve to increase surface area for reabsorption. Fluid in the filtrate entering the proximal convoluted tubule is reabsorbed into the peritubular capillaries, including approximately two-thirds of the filtered salt and water and all filtered organic solutes (primarily glucose and amino acids). This is driven by sodium transport from the lumen into the blood by the Na^+/K^+ ATPase in the basolateral membrane of the epithelial cells. Much of the mass movement of water and solutes occurs in between the cells through the tight junctions, which in this case are not selective.

The solutes are absorbed isotonically, in that the osmotic potential of the fluid leaving the proximal tubule is the same as that of the initial glomerular filtrate. However, glucose, amino acids, inorganic phosphate and some other solutes are reabsorbed *via* secondary active transport through cotransport channels driven by the sodium gradient out of the nephron.

Loop of the Nephron or Loop of Henle

The loop of Henle (sometimes known as the nephron loop) is a U-shaped tube that consists of a descending limb and ascending limb. It begins in the cortex, receiving filtrate from the proximal convoluted tubule, extends into the medulla and then returns to the cortex to empty into the distal convoluted tubule. Its primary role is to concentrate the salt in the interstitium, the tissue surrounding the loop.

Descending Limb

Its descending limb is permeable to water but completely impermeable to salt and thus only indirectly contributes to the concentration of the interstitium. As the filtrate descends deeper into the hypertonic interstitium of the renal medulla, water flows freely out of the descending limb by osmosis until the tonicity of the filtrate and interstitium equilibrate. Longer descending limbs allow more time for water to flow out of the filtrate, so longer limbs make the filtrate more hypertonic than shorter limbs. Unlike the descending limb, the ascending limb of Henle's loop is impermeable to water, a critical feature of the countercurrent exchange mechanism employed by the loop. The ascending limb actively pumps sodium out of the filtrate, generating the hypertonic interstitium that drives countercurrent exchange. In passing through the ascending limb, the filtrate grows hypotonic since, it has lost much of its sodium content. This hypotonic filtrate is passed to the distal convoluted tubule in the renal cortex.

Distal Convoluted Tubule (DCT)

The distal convoluted tubule is similar to the proximal convoluted tubule in structure and function. Cells lining the tubule have numerous mitochondria, enabling active transport to take place by the energy supplied by ATP. Much of the ion transport taking place in the distal convoluted tubule is regulated by the endocrine system. In the presence of parathyroid hormone, the distal convoluted tubule reabsorbs more calcium and excretes more phosphate. When aldosterone is present, more sodium is reabsorbed and more potassium excreted. Atrial natriuretic peptide causes the distal convoluted tubule to excrete more sodium. In addition, the tubule also secretes hydrogen and ammonium to regulate pH. After traveling the length of the distal convoluted tubule, only 3% of water remains and the remaining salt content is negligible. 97.9% of the water in the glomerular filtrate enters the convoluted tubules and collecting ducts by osmosis.

Collecting Ducts

Each distal convoluted tubule delivers its filtrate to a system of collecting ducts, the first segment of which is the connecting tubule. The collecting duct system begins in the renal cortex and extends deep into the medulla. As the urine travels down the collecting duct system, it passes by the medullary interstitium which has a high sodium concentration as a result of the loop of Henle's countercurrent multiplier system. Though the collecting duct is normally impermeable to water, it becomes permeable in the presence of Antidiuretic Hormone (ADH). As much as three-fourths of the water from urine can be reabsorbed as it leaves the collecting duct by osmosis. Thus, the levels of ADH determine whether urine will be concentrated or dilute. Dehydration results in an increase in ADH, while water sufficiency results in low ADH allowing for diluted urine. Lower portions of the collecting duct are also permeable to urea, allowing some of it to enter the medulla of the kidney, thus maintaining its high ion concentration (which is very important for the nephron).

Urine leaves the medullary collecting ducts through the renal papilla, emptying into the renal calyces, the renal pelvis and finally into the bladder *via* the ureter. Because it has a different embryonic origin than the rest of the nephron (the collecting it duct is from endoderm whereas the nephron is from mesoderm), the collecting duct is usually not considered a part of the nephron proper.

Renal Vein

The renal veins are veins that drain the kidney. They connect the kidney to the inferior vena cava. Because the inferior vena cava is on the right half of the body, the left renal vein is generally the longer of the two. Unlike the right renal vein, the left renal vein often receives the left gonadal vein (left testicular vein in males, left ovarian vein in females). It frequently receives the left suprarenal vein as well.

Renal Artery

The renal arteries normally arise off the abdominal aorta and supply the kidneys with blood. The arterial supplies of the kidneys are variable and there may be one or more renal arteries supplying each kidney. Due to the position of the aorta, the inferior vena cava and the kidneys in the body, the right renal artery is normally longer than the left renal artery. The right renal artery normally crosses posteriorly to the inferior vena cava. The renal arteries carry a large portion of the total blood flow to the kidneys. Up to a third of the total cardiac output can pass through the renal arteries to be filtered by the kidneys.

Ureters

The ureters are two tubes that drain urine from the kidneys to the bladder. Each ureter is a muscular tube about 10 inches (25 cm) long. Muscles in the walls of the ureters send the urine in small spurts into the bladder (a collapsible sac found on the forward part of the cavity of the bony pelvis that allows temporary storage of urine). After the urine enters the bladder from the ureters, small folds in the bladder mucosa act like valves peventing backward flow of the urine. The outlet of the bladder is controlled by a sphincter muscle. A full bladder stimulates sensory nerves in the bladder wall that relax the sphincter and allow release of the urine. However, relaxation of the sphincter is also in part a learned response under voluntary control. The released urine enters the urethra.

Urinary Bladder

The urinary bladder is a hollow, muscular and distendible or elastic organ that sits on the pelvic floor (superior to the prostate in males). On its anterior border lies the pubic symphysis and, on its posterior border, the vagina (in females) and rectum (in males). The urinary bladder can hold approximately 17 to 18 ounces (500 to 530 mL) of urine, however, the desire to micturate is usually experienced when it contains about 150 to 200 mL. When the bladder fills with urine (about half full), stretch receptors send nerve impulses to the spinal cord, which then sends a reflex nerve impulse back to the sphincter (muscular valve) at the neck of the bladder, causing it to relax and allow the flow of urine into the urethra. The Internal urethral sphincter is involuntary. The ureters enter the bladder diagonally from its dorsolateral floor in an area called the trigone. The trigone is a triangular shaped area on the postero-inferior wall of the bladder. The urethra exits at the lowest point of the triangle of the trigone. The urine in the bladder also helps regulate body temperature. If the bladder becomes completely void of fluid, it causes the patient to chill.

Urethra

The urethra is a muscular tube that connects the bladder with the outside of the body. The function of the urethra is to remove urine from the body. It measures about 1.5 inches (3.8 cm) in a woman but up to 8 inches (20 cm) in a man. Because the urethra is so much shorter in a woman it makes it much easier for a woman to get harmful bacteria in her bladder this is commonly called a **bladder infection** or a UTI. The most common bacteria of a UTI is *E. coli* from the large intestines that have been excreted in faecal matter.

Female Urethra

In the human female, the urethra is about 1-2 inches long and opens in the vulva between the clitoris and the vaginal opening. Men have a longer urethra than women. This means that women tend to be more susceptible to infections of the bladder (cystitis) and the urinary tract.

Male Urethra

In the human male, the urethra is about 8 inches (20 cm) long and opens at the end of the penis. The length of a male's urethra and the fact it contains a number of bends, makes catheterization more difficult. The urethral sphincter is a collective name for the muscles used to control the flow of urine from the urinary bladder. These muscles surround the urethra, so that when they contract, the urethra is closed.

There are two distinct areas of muscle the internal sphincter, at the bladder neck the external or distal, sphincter.

Human males have much stronger sphincter muscles than females, meaning that they can retain a large amount of urine for twice as long, as much as 800 mL, *i.e.*, 'hold it'.

Formation of Urine and Waste Elimination

Nitrogenous wastes are formed inside all the body cells. These wastes are transported to the kidneys by blood are changed into urine. Urine is formed in three steps—filtration, reabsorption and secretion.

Filtration

Blood enters the afferent arteriole and flows into the glomerulus. Blood in the glomerulus has both filterable blood components and non-filtrable blood components. Filtrable blood components move towards the inside of the glomerulus while non-filterable blood components bypass the filtration process by exiting through the efferent arteriole. Filtrable blood components now take on plasma like form called glomerular filtrate. A few of the filtrable blood components are water, nitrogenous waste, nutrients and salts (ions). Non-filterable blood components include formed elements such as blood cells and platelets along with plasma proteins. The glomerular filtrate is not the same consistency as urine, as much of it is reabsorbed into the blood as the filtrate passes through the tubules of the nephron.

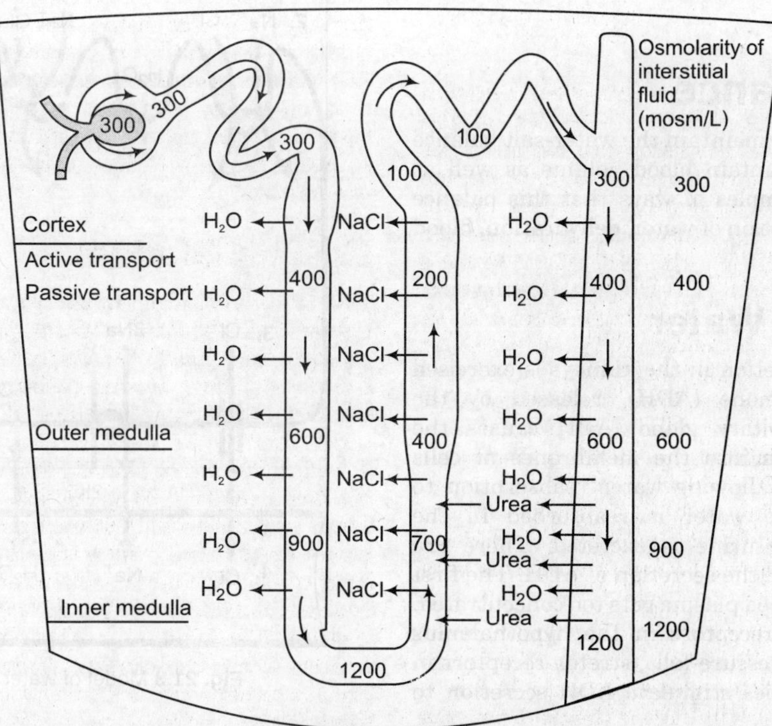

Fig. 21.2 Urine formation

Reabsorption

Within the peritubular capillary network, molecules and ions are reabsorbed back into the blood. Sodium chloride reabsorbed into the system increases the osmolarity of blood in comparison to the glomerular filtrate. This reabsorption process allows water (H_2O) to pass from the glomerular filtrate back into the circulatory system. Glucose and various amino acids also are reabsorbed into the circulatory system. These nutrients have carrier molecules that claim the glomerular molecule and release it back into the circulatory system. If all of the carrier molecules are used up, excess glucose or amino acids are set free into the urine. A complication of diabetes is the inability of the body to reabsorb glucose. If too much glucose appears in the glomerular filtrate it increases the osmolarity of the filtrate, causing water to be released into the urine rather than reabsorbed by the circulatory system. Frequent urination and unexplained thirst are warning signs of diabetes, due to water not being reabsorbed. Glomerular filtrate has now been separated into two forms reabsorbed filtrate and non-reabsorbed filtrate. Non-reabsorbed filtrate is now known as tubular fluid as it passes through the collecting duct to be processed into urine.

Secretion

Some substances are removed from blood through the peritubular capillary network into the distal convoluted tubule or collecting duct. These substances are hydrogen ions, creatinine and drugs. Urine is a collection of substances that have not been reabsorbed during glomerular filtration or tubular secretion.

Water Salt Balance

It is the job of the kidneys to maintain the water-salt balance of the blood. They also maintain blood volume as well as blood pressure. Simple examples of ways that this balance can be changed include ingestion of water, dehydration, blood loss and salt ingestion.

Reabsorption of Water

Direct control of water excretion in the kidneys is exercised by the Anti-Diuretic Hormone (ADH), released by the posterior lobe of the pituitary gland. ADH causes the insertion of water channels into the membranes of cells lining the collecting ducts, allowing water reabsorption to occur. Without ADH, little water is reabsorbed in the collecting ducts and dilute urine is excreted. There are several factors that influence the secretion of ADH. The first of these happen when the blood plasma gets too concentrated. When this occurs, special receptors in the hypothalamus release ADH. When blood pressure falls, stretch receptors in the aorta and carotid arteries stimulate ADH secretion to increase volume of the blood.

Reabsorption of Salt

The kidneys also regulate the salt balance in the blood by controlling the excretion and the reabsorption of various ions. As noted above, ADH plays a role in increasing water reabsorption in the kidneys, thus helping to dilute bodily fluids. The kidneys also have a regulated mechanism for reabsorbing sodium in the distal nephron. This mechanism is controlled by aldosterone, a steroid hormone produced by the adrenal cortex. Aldosterone promotes the excretion of potassium ions and the reabsorption of sodium ions. The release of aldosterone is initiated by the kidneys. The juxtaglomerular apparatus is a renal structure consisting of the macula densa, mesangial cells and juxtaglomerular cells. Juxtaglomerular cells (JG cells, also known as granular cells) are the site of renin secretion. Renin is an enzyme that angiotensinogen (a large plasma protein produced by the liver) into angiotensin I and eventually into angiotensin II which stimulates the adrenal cortex to produce aldosterone. The reabsorption of sodium ions is followed by the reabsorption of water. This causes blood pressure as well as blood volume to increase.

Atrial Natriuretic Hormone (ANH) is released by the atria of the heart when cardiac cells are streatched due to increased blood volume. ANH inhibits the secretion of renin by the juxtaglomerular apparatus and the secretion of the aldosterone by the adrenal cortex. This promotes the excretion of sodium. When sodium is excreted so is water. This causes blood pressure and volume to decrease.

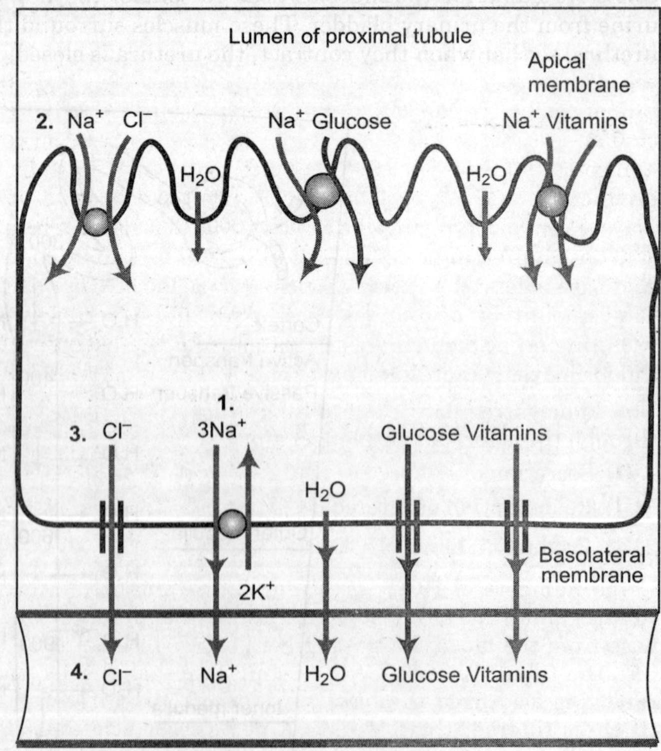

Fig. 21.3 Model of water and solute reabsorption

Micturition

Micturition is the process by which the urinary bladder empties when it becomes filled. This involves two main steps: First, the bladder filles progressively until the tension on its walls rises above a threshold level; this elicits the second step, which is a nervous reflex called the **micturition reflex** that empties the bladder or, if this fails, at least causes a conscious desire to urinate.

Although the micturition reflex is an autonomic spinal cord reflex, it can also be inhibited or facilitated by centers in the cerebral cortex or brain stem.

The micturition reflex is a single complete cycle of

(i) progressive and rapid increase of pressure.

(ii) a period of sustained pressure.

(iii) return of the pressure to the basal tone of the bladder.

Once a micturition reflex begins, it is 'self-regenerative'. That is, initial contraction of the bladder activates the stretch receptors to cause a greater increase in sensory impulses to the bladder and posterior urethra, which causes a further increase in reflex contraction of the bladder; thus, the cycle is repeated again and again until the bladder has reached a strong degree of contraction. Then after a few seconds to more than a minute, the self-regenerative reflex begins to fatigue and the regenerative cycle of the micturition reflex ceases, permitting the bladder to reflax.

Regulation of Acid Base Balance

Precise H^+ (single free proton) regulation is essential because the activities, almost all enzymes systems in the body are influenced by H^+ concentration. Regulation of H^+ balance is similar is same way to other ions in the body. To achieve homeostasis there must be a balance between the intake or production and net removal of H^+ from the body. Kidney plays a key role in regulating H^+ removal. There are multiple acid base bufferring mechanisms in body. The kidney control acid base balance by excreting either an acidic or basic urine. The amount of acid in extracellular fluid is reduced by excreting an acidic urine while bases from the extracellular fluid remove by excreting basic urine.

The kidneys regulate extracellular fluid H^+ concentration through three fundamental mechanisms:

(i) Secretion of H^+.

(ii) Reabsorption of filtered HCO_3^-.

(iii) Production of new HCO_3^-.

Large numbers of HCO_3^- are filtered continuously into the tubules and if they are excreted into the urine, this removes base from the blood. Large numbers of H^+ are also secreted into the tubular lumen by the tubular epithelial cells, thus removing acid from the blood. If more H^+ is secreted than HCO_3^- is filtered, there will be a net loss of acid from the extracellular fluid. Conversely, if more HCO_3^- is filtered than H^+ is secreted, there will be a net loss of base.

Each day the body produces about 80 milliequivalents of non-volatile acids, mainly from the metabolism of proteins. These acids are called non-volatile because they are not H_2CO_3 and therefore, cannot be excreted by the lungs. The primary mechanism for removal of these acids from the body is renal excretion. The kidneys must also prevent the loss of bicarbonate in the urine, a task that is quantitatively more important than the excretion of non-volatile acids. Each day the kidneys filter about 4320 milli equivalents of bicarbonate (180 L/day × 24 mEq/L); under normal conditions, almost all this is reabsorbed from the tubules, thereby conserving the primary buffer system of the extracellular fluid.

Both the reabsorption of bicarbonate and the excretion of H^+ are accomplished through the process of H^+ secretion by the tubules. Because the HCO^-_3 must react with a secreted H^+ to form H_2CO_3 before it can be reabsorbed, 4320 milli equivalents of H^+ must be secreted each day just to reabsorb the filtered bicarbonate. Then an additional 80 milli equivalents of H^+ must be secreted to rid the body of the non-volatile acids produced each day, for a total of 4400 milli equivalents of H^+ secreted into the tubular fluid each day.

When there is a reduction in the extracellular fluid H^+ concentration (alkalosis), the kidneys fail to reabsorb all the filtered bicarbonate, there by increasing the excretion of bicarbonate. Because HCO^-_3 normally buffers hydrogen in the extracellular fluid, this loss of bicarbonate is the same as adding an H^+ to the extracellular fluid. Therefore, in alkalosis, the removal of HCO^-_3 raises the extracellular fluid H^+ concentration back toward normal.

In acidosis, the kidneys do not excrete bicarbonate into the urine but reabsorb all the filtered bicarbonate and produce new bicarbonate, which is added back to the extracellular fluid. This reduces the extracellular fluid H^+ concentration back toward normal.

Hypernatremia

An increase in plasma sodium levels above normal is hypernatremia. Sodium is the primary solute in the extracellular fluid. Sodium levels have a major role in osmolarity regulation. For excitable cells the electrochemical gradient for sodium across the plasma membrane is critical for life. Water retention and an increased blood pressure usually are signs of hypernatremia. If the plasma sodium levels are below normal it is called hyponatremia. Signs of this are low plasma volume and hypotension.

Diuretics

A diuretic (colloquially called a water pill) is any drug that elevates the rate of bodily urine excretion (diuresis). Diuretics also decrease the Extracellular Fluid (ECF) volume and are primarily used to produce a negative extracellular fluid balance. Caffeine, cranberry juice and alcohol are all weak diuretics. In medicine, diuretics are used to treat heart failure, liver cirrhosis, hypertension and certain kidney diseases. Diuretics alleviate the symptoms of these diseases by causing sodium and water loss through the urine. As urine is produced by the kidney, sodium and water which cause edema related to the disease, move into the blood to replace the volume lost as urine, thereby reducing the pathological edema. Some diuretics, such as acetazolamide, help to make the urine more alkaline and are helpful in increasing excretion of substances such as aspirin in cases of overdose or poisoning. The antihypertensive actions of some diuretics (thiazides and loop diuretics in particular) are independent of their diuretic effect. That is, the reduction in blood pressure is not due to decreased blood volume resulting from increased urine production, but occurs through other mechanisms and at lower doses than that required to produce diuresis. Indapamide was specifically designed with this is mind and has a larger therapeutic window for hypertension (without pronounced diuresis) than most other diuretics. Chemically, diuretics are a diverse group of compounds that either stimulate or inhibit various hormones that naturally occur in the body to regulate urine production by the kidneys. Alcohol produces diuresis through modulation of the vasopressin system.

Summative Roles of the Kidneys

Regulation of plasma ionic composition Ions such as sodium, potassium, calcium, magnesium, chloride, bicarbonate and phosphates are regulated by the amount that the kidney excretes.

Regulation of plasma osmolarity The kidneys regulate osmolarity because they have direct control over how many ions and how much water a person excretes.

Regulation of plasma volume Your kidneys are so important they even have an effect on your blood pressure. The kidneys control plasma volume by controlling how much water a person excretes. The plasma volume has a direct effect on the total blood volume, which has a direct effect on your blood pressure. Salts such as NaCI can cause osmosis, the diffusion of water into the blood.

Regulation of plasma hydrogen ion concentration (pH) The kidneys partner up with the lungs and they together control the pH. The kidneys have a major role because they control the amount of bicarbonate excreted or held onto. The kidneys help maintain the blood pH mainly by excreting hydrogen ions and reabsorbing bicarbonate ions as needed.

Removal of metabolic waste products and foreign substances from the plasma One of the most important things the kidneys excrete is nitrogenous waste. As the liver breaks down amino acids it also releases ammonia. The liver then quickly combines that ammonia with carbon dioxide, creating urea which is the primary nitrogenous end product of metabolism in humans. The liver turns the ammonia into urea because it is much less toxic. We can also excrete some ammonia, creatinine and uric acid. The creatinine comes from the metabolic breakdown of creatine phospate (a high-energy phosphate in muscles). Uric acid comes from the breakdown of necloetides. Uric acid is insoluble and too much uric acid in the blood will build up and form crystals that can collect in the joints and cause gout.

Secretion of hormones The endocrine system has assistance from the kidney's when releasing hormones. Renin is released by the kidneys. Renin leads to the secretion of aldosterone which is released from the adrenal cortex. Aldosterone promotes the kidneys to reabsorb the sodium (Na^+) ions.

The kidneys also secrete erythropoietin when the blood doesn't have the capacity to carry oxygen. Erythropoietin stimulates red blood cell production. The vitamin-D from the skin is also activated with help from the kidneys. Calcium (Ca^+) absorption from the digestive tract is promoted by vitamin-D.

Renal Hormones

(a) **Vitamin-D** becomes metabolically active in the kidney. Patients with renal disease have symptoms of disturbed calcium and phosphate balance.

(b) **Erythropoietin** released by the kidneys in response to decreased tissue oxygen levels (hypoxia).

(c) **Natriuretic hormone** released from cardiocyte granules located in the right atria of the heart in response to increased atrial stretch. It inhibits ADH secretions which can contribute to the loss of sodium and water.

Thermoregulation

Thermoregulation is the maintenance of body temperature within a range that enables cells to function efficiently. Mammals, including humans, are **endotherms,** are able to maintain a constant body temperature regardless of our surroundings. The **hypothalanus** acts as your body's 'thermostat', detecting changes in body temperature and sending out messages to help restore the normal body temperature. One of the most important examples of homeostasis is the regulation of body temperature. Not all animals can do this physiologically.

Comfort Zone
(Thermal Neural Zone)

Temperature has become a strong source of selective pressure on all animals. Rate of cellular respiration increases with temperature up to a point, but above the temperature optima (temperature at which enzymes most efficiently catalyse their chemical reactions) the rates decline as the enzyme begin to denature. The chemical interactions holding the enzymes in their three dimensional shape are also disrupted.

Under constant adequate temperature conditions the retention of temperature homeostasis was shown to require a continuous functioning of the physiological thermoregulation system to prevent short term and whole day deviations of the temperature from the physiological level. Under adequate temperature conditions the thermoregulation system was shown to attain its highest sensitivity and accuracy. It is possible that this occurs owing to physiological control over the total body heat content being included into the process of thermoregulation. The body temperature falling below comfort zone will cause the animal to increase metabolism to produce heat.

Body Temperature Regulation

Animals that maintain a fairly constant body temperature (birds and mammals) are called **endotherms,** while those that have a variable body temperature (all others) are called ectotherms. Endotherms normally maintain their body temperatures at around 35-40°C, so are sometimes called warm-blooded animals, but in fact ectothermic animals can also have very warm blood during the day by basking in the sun or by extended muscle activity, *e.g.,* bumble bees, tuna). The difference between the two groups is thus that endothermic animals use internal corrective mechanisms, whilst ectotherms use behavioural mechanisms (*e.g.,* lying in the sun when cold, moving into shade when hot). Such mechanisms can be very effective, particularly when coupled with internal mechanisms to ensure that the temperature of the blood going to vital organs (brain, heart) is kept constant.

We use both in humans, body temperature is controlled by the thermoregulatory centre in the hypothalamus. It receives input from two sets of thermoreceptors receptors in the hypothalamus itself monitor the temperature of the blood as it passes through the brain (the core temperature) and receptors in the skin (especially on the trunk) monitor the external temperature. Both sets of information are needed so that the body can make appropriate adjustments. The thermoregulatory centre sends impulses to several different effectors to adjust body temperature.

Our first response to encountering hotter or colder condition is voluntary—if too hot, we may decide to take some clothes off or to move into the shade; if too cold, we put extra clothes on or turn the heating up. It is only when these responses are not enough that the thermoregulatory centre is stimulated. This is part of the autonomic nervous system, so the various responses are all involuntary.

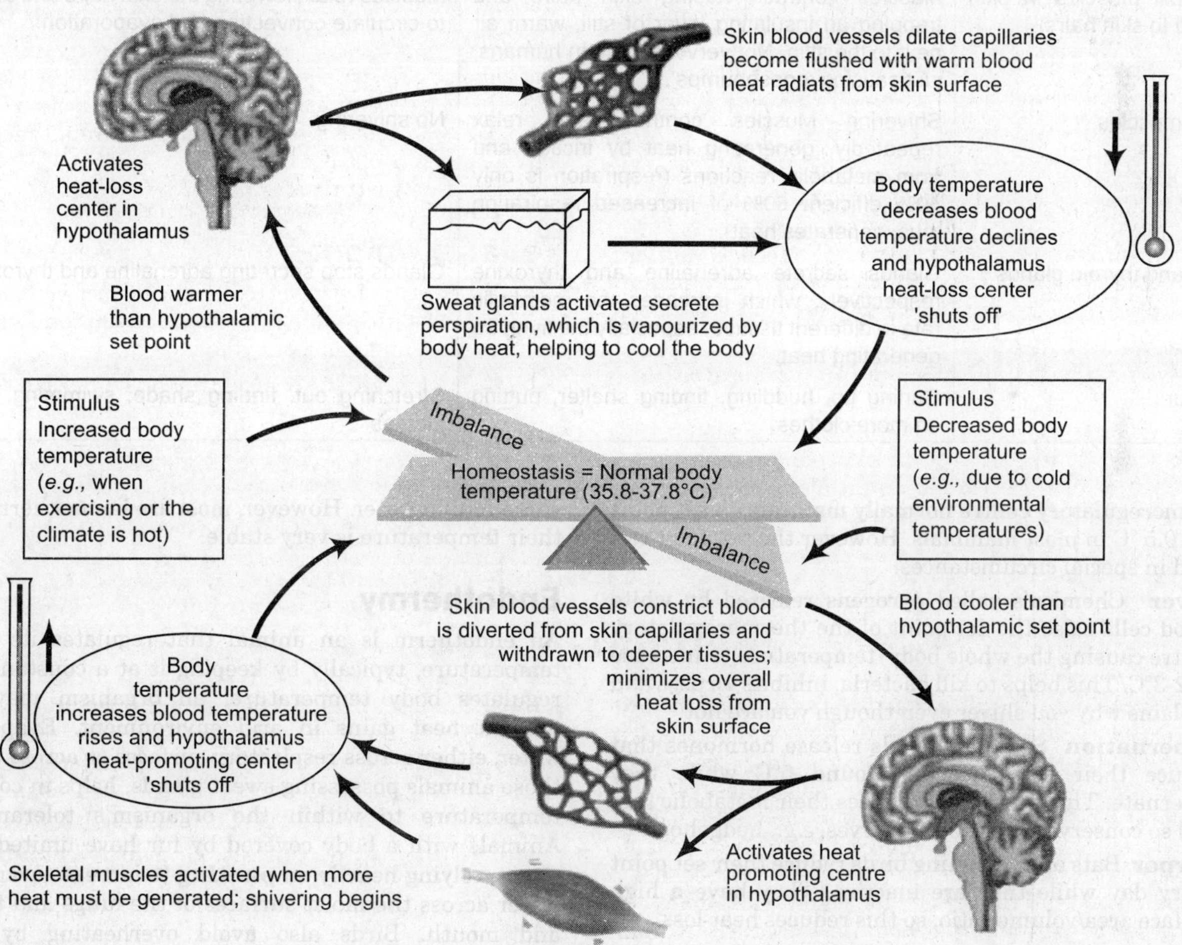

Fig. 21.4 Thermoregulation

When we get too hot, the heat loss centre in the hypothalamus is stimulated; when we get too cold, it is the heat conservation centre of the hypothalamus which is stimulated. Note that some of the responses to low temperature actually generate heat (thermogenesis), while others just conserve heat. Similarly some of the responses to cold actively cool the body down, while others just reduce heat production or transfer heat to the surface. The body thus has a range of responses available, depending on the internal and external temperatures. The exact responses to high and low temperatures are described in the table below:

Tables 21.2 **Various Responses to Temperature**

Effector	Response to Low Temperature	Response to High Temperature
Smooth muscles in arterioles in the skin.	Muscles contract causing vasoconstriction. Less heat is carried from the core to the surface of the body, maintaining core temperature. Extremities can turn blue and feel cold and can even be damaged (frostbite).	Muscles relax causing vasodilation. More heat is carried from the core to the surface, where it is lost by convection and radiation (conduction is generally low, except when in water). Skin turns red.
Sweat glands	No sweat produced.	Glands secrete sweat onto surface of skin, where it evaporates. Since, water has a high latent heat of evaporation, it takes heat from the body. High humidity and tight clothing made of man-made fibres reduce the ability of the sweat to evaporate and so make us uncomfortable in hot weather. Transpiration from trees has a dramatic cooling effect on the surrounding air temperature.
Erector pill muscles in skin (attached to skin hairs)	Muscles contract, raising skin hairs and trapping an insulating layer of still, warm air next to the skin. Not very effective in humans, just causing 'goosebumps'.	Muscles relax, lowering the skin hairs and allowing air to circulate convection and evaporation.
Skeletal muscles	Shivering Muscles contract and relax repeatedly, generating heat by friction and from metabolic reactions (respiration is only 40% efficient 60% of increased respiration thus, generates heat).	No shivering.
Adrenal and thyroid glands	Glands secrete adrenaline and thyroxine respectively, which increases the metabolic rate in different tissues, especially the liver, so generating heat.	Glands stop secreting adrenaline and thyroxine.
Behaviour	Curling up, huddling, finding shelter, putting on more clothes.	Stretching out, finding shade, swimming, removing clothes.

The thermoregulatory centre normally maintains a set point of 37.5 ± 0.5 °C in most mammals. However the set point can be altered in special circumstances:

1. **Fever** Chemicals called pyrogens released by white blood cells raise the set point of the thermoregulatory centre causing the whole body temperature to increase by 2-3°C. This helps to kill bacteria, inhibits viruses and explains why you shiver even though you are hot.
2. **Hibernation** Some mammals release hormones that reduce their set point to around 5°C while they hibernate. This drastically reduces their metabolic rate and so conserves their food reserves, *e.g.*, hedgehogs.
3. **Torpor** Bats and humming birds reduce their set point every day while they are inactive. They have a high surface area/volume ratio, so this reduces heat loss.

Homeothermy *versus* Poikilothermy

Homeothermy and **poikilothermy** refer to how stable an organism's temperature is. Most endothermic organisms are homeothermic, like **mammals.** However, animals with facultative endothermy are often poikilothermic, meaning their temperature can vary considerably. Similarly, most **fish** are ectotherms, as all of their heat comes from the surrounding water. However, most are homeotherms because their temperature is very stable.

Endothermy

An endotherm is an animal that regulates its own body temperature, typically by keeping it at a constant level. To regulates body temperature, an organism may need to prevent heat gains in arid environment. Evaporation of water, either across respiratory surfaces or across the skin in those animals possessing sweat glands, helps in cooling body temperature to within the organism's tolerance range. Animals with a body covered by fur have limited ability to sweat, relying heavily on **panting** to increase evaporation of water across the moist surfaces of the lungs and the tongue and mouth. Birds also avoid overheating by **angular fluttering,** flapping the wings near the singular (throat) skin, similar to panting in mammals, since, their thin skin has no sweat glands. Down feathers trap warm air acting as excellent insulators just as hair in mammals acts as a good insulator. Mammalian skin is much thicker than that of birds and often has a continuous layer of insulating fat beneath the dermis. In marine mammals, such as whales or animals which live in very cold regions, such as the polar bears, this is called blubber. Dense coats found in desert endotherms also aid in preventing heat gain such as in the case of the camels.

A cold weather strategy is to temporarily decrease metabolic rate, decreasing the temperature difference between the animal and the air and thereby minimizing heat loss. Furthermore, having a lower metabolic rate is less energetically expensive. Many animals survive cold frosty nights through **torpor,** a short-term temporary drop in body temperature. Organisms when presented with the problem of regulating body temperature have not only behavioural, physiological and structural adaptations, but also a feedback system to trigger these adaptations to regulate temperature accordingly. The main features of this system are stimulus, receptor, modulator, effector and then the feedback of the newly adjusted temperature to the stimulus. This cyclical process aids in homeostasis.

Thermoregulation in Vertebrates

John Hunter showed that the essential difference between the so called **warm-blooded** and **cold-blooded** animals lies in observed constancy of the temperature of the former and the observed variability of the temperature of the latter. Almost all birds and mammals have a high temperature almost constant and independent of that of the surrounding air (homeothermy). Almost all other animals display a variation of body temperature, dependent on their surroundings (poikilothermy).

Certain mammals are exceptions to this rule, being warm-blooded during the summer or daytime, but cold-blooded during the winter when they **hibernate** or at night during sleep. **JO Wakelin Barratt** has demonstrated that under certain pathological conditions, a **warm-blooded** (homeothermic) animal may become temporarily cold-blooded (poikilothermic). He has shown conclusively that this condition exists in rabbits suffering from rabies during the last period of their life, the rectal temperature being then within a few degrees of the room temperature and varying with it. He explains this condition by the assumption that the nervous mechanism of heat regulation has become paralysed. The respiration and heart-rate being also retarded during this period, the resemblance to the condition of hibernation is considerable. Again, **Sutherland Simpson** has shown that during deep **anaesthesia** a warm-blooded animal tends to take the same temperature as that of its environment. He demonstrated that when a monkey is kept deeply anaesthetized with ether and is placed in a cold chamber, its temperature gradually falls and that when it has reached a sufficiently low point (about 25°C in the monkey), the employment of an anaesthetic is no longer necessary, the animal then being insensible to pain and incapable of being roused by any form of stimulus; it is, in fact, narcotised by cold and is in a state of what may be called 'artificial hibernation.' Once again this is explained by the fact that the heat-regulating mechanism has been interfered with. Similar results have been obtained from experiments on cats.

Brain Control

Thermoregulation in both ectotherms and endotherms is controlled mainly by the **preoptic area** of the **anterior hypothalamus.** Such **homeostatic** control is separate from the sensation of temperature

Thermoregulation in Birds and Mammals

In cold environment birds and mammals employ the following adaptations and strategies to minimize heat loss:

(i) Using small smooth muscles (erector pili in mammals) which are attached to feather or hair shafts; this non-shivering thermogenesis distorts the surface of the skin as the feather/hair shaft is made more erect (called **goose bumps** or pimples).

(ii) Increasing body size to more easily maintain core body temperature (warm-blooded animals in cold climates tend to be larger than similar species in warmer climates (see Bergmann's rule).

(iii) Having the ability to store energy as fat for **metabolism.**

(iv) Have shortened extremities.

(v) Have **countercurrent blood flow** in extremities - this is where the warm arterial blood travelling to the limb passes the cooler venous blood from the limb and heat is exchanged warming the venous blood and cooling the arterial (*e.g.,* Arctic Wolf or penguins).

In warm environment, birds and mammals employ the following adaptations and strategies to maximize heat loss:

(i) Behavioural adaptations like living in burrows during the day and being nocturnal.

(ii) Evaporative cooling by perspiration and panting.

(iii) Storing fat reserves in one place (*e.g.,* camel's hump) to avoid its insulating effect.

(iv) Elongated, often vascularized extremities to conduct body heat to the air.

Thermoregulation in Humans (Acclimatization)

The skin assists in homeostasis (keeping different aspects of the body constant *e.g.,* temperature). It does this by reacting differently to hot and cold conditions so that the inner body temperature remains more or less constant.

Acclimatization is the reversible process by which an individual becomes adapted to a change in the environment. It requires adaptations to a variety of factors (like temperature, humidity and atmospheric pressure). Acclimation, by contrast, involves an adaptation to a single factor (temperature). Heat acclimatization is actually a sweat gland adaptation and a 2-week process following arrival to a hot climate such as the tropics or a desert. Gradually sweat-evaporation is increased and the NaCl loss is reduced. The sweat secretion capacity may reach up to 41 each hour with a thin sweat. The adaptation is caused by increased aldosterone secretion from the adrenal cortex. Aldosterone increases the reabsorption of NaCl and the secretion of K^+ from the sweat, during its passage of the sweat gland tubules. The larger the sweat loss the thirstier one feels because the large sweat secretion reduces the time period for NaCl reabsorption in the sweat gland tubules. The resulting high NaCl concentration in the plasma implies thirst, so heat adapted persons have to take water. Thirst is an extremely late indicator of dehydration during work in a warm climate. Tropic inhibitants are of course heat-adapted. They have an increased core temperature (set point) and their threshold for sweat and vasodilatation is typically 0.5°C higher than that of a person living in the temperature zone. An unacclimatized person who sweats profusely often losses. 15-30 g of salt each day but after 4 to 6 weeks of acclimatization the loss is usually 3-5 g/day.

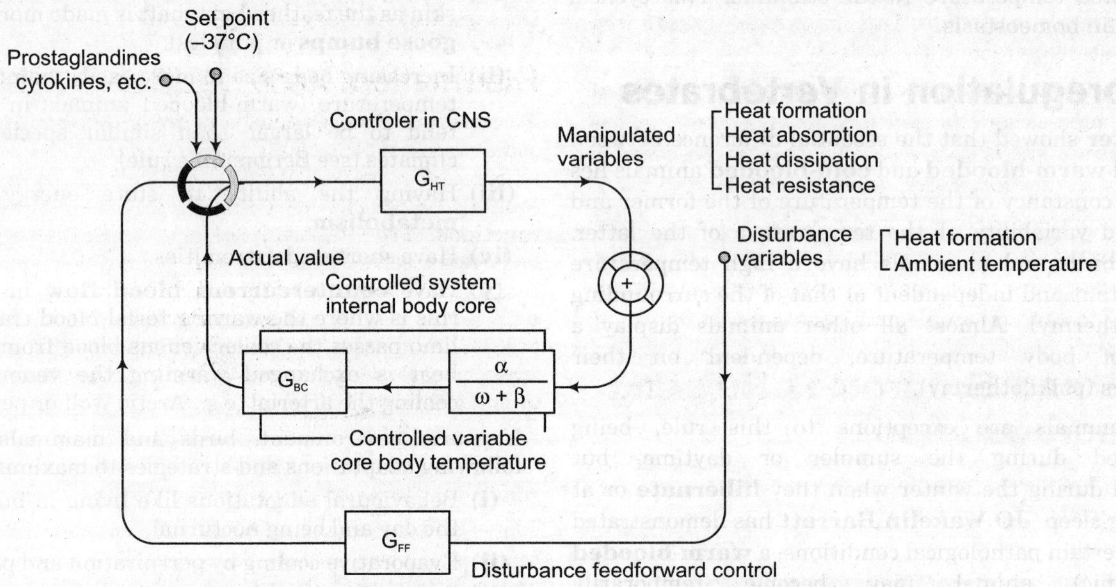

Fig. 21.5 Simplified information processing structure of human thermoregulation

(b) The hairs on the skin lie flat, preventing heat from being trapped by the layer of still air between the hairs. This is caused by tiny muscles under the surface of the skin called arrector pili muscles relaxing so that their attached hair follicles are not erect. These flat hairs increase the flow of air next to the skin increasing heat loss by convection. When environmental temperature is above core body temperature, sweating is the only physiological way for humans to lose heat.

(c) Arterioles vasodilation occurs, this is the process of relaxation of smooth muscle in **arteriole** walls allowing increased blood flow through the artery. This redirects blood into the superficial capillaries in the skin increasing heat loss by convection and conduction.

Note Most animals can't sweat efficiently. Cats and dogs have sweat glands only on the pads of their feet. Horses and humans are two of the few animals capable of sweating. Many animals pant rather than sweat because the lungs have a large surface area and are highly vascularized. Air is inhaled, cooling the surface of the lungs and is then exhaled losing heat and some water vapour.

The brain creates much heat through the countless reactions which occur. Even the process of thought creates heat. The head has a complex system of blood vessels, which keeps the brain from overheating by bringing blood to the thin skin on the head, allowing heat to escape.

In Hot Conditions

(a) Endocrine sweat glands under the skin secrete sweat (a fluid containing mostly water with some dissolved ions) which travels up the sweat duct, through the sweat pore and onto the surface of the skin. This causes heat loss *via* evaporative cooling; however, a lot of essential water is lost.

In Cold Conditions

(a) Sweat stops being produced.

(b) The minute muscles under the surface of the skin called erector pili muscles (attached to an individual hair follicle) contract (piloerection), lifting the hair follicle upright. This makes the hairs stand on end which acts as an insulating layer, trapping heat. This is what also causes **goose bumps** since humans don't have very much hair and the contracted muscles can easily be seen.

(c) **Arterioles** carrying blood to superficial capillaries under the surface of the skin can shrink (constrict), there by rerouting blood away from the skin and towards the warmer core of the body. This prevents blood from losing heat to the surroundings and also prevents the core temperature dropping further. This process is called **vasoconstriction.** It is impossible to prevent all heat loss from the blood, only to reduce it. In extremely cold conditions excessive vasoconstriction leads to numbness and pale skin. Frostbite only occurs when water within the cells begins to freeze, this destroys the cell causing damage.

(d) Muscles can also receive messages from the thermoregulatory center of the brain (the hypothalamus) to cause shivering. This increases heat production as respiration is an exothermic reaction in muscle cells. Shivering is more effective than exercise at producing heat because the animal remains still. This means that less heat is lost to the environment *via* convection. There are two types of shivering low intensity and high intensity. During low intensity shivering animals shiver constantly at a low level for months during cold conditions. During high intensity shivering animals shiver violently for a relatively short time. Both processes consume energy although high intensity shivering uses glucose as a fuel source and low intensity tends to use fats. This is a primary reason why animals store up food in the winter.

(e) **Mitochondria can convert fat directly into heat energy,** increasing the temperature of all cells in the body. **Brown fat** is specialized for this purpose and is abundant in newborns and animals that hibernate.

The process explained above, in which the skin regulates body temperature is a part of thermoregulation. This is one aspect of homeostasis, the process by which the body regulates itself to keep internal conditions constant.

Diseases and Syndromes Relating to Thermoregulation

(i) Hypothermia
(ii) Hyperthermia
(iii) Heat stroke
(iv) Raynaud's phenomenon (Raynaud's disease)
(v) Induced hypothermia
(vi) Erythromelagia (hyperthermia).

Human Heat Output Power

A human will output from around 70 W – 870 W, depending on the amount of physical activity undertaken.

Behavioural Temperature Regulation

Animals other than humans regulate and maintain their body temperature with physiological adjustments and behaviour. Desert lizards are ectotherms and so unable to metabolically control their temperature but can do this by altering their location. They may do this by in the morning only raising their head from its burrow and then exposing their entire body. By basking in the sun, the lizard absorbs solar heat. It may also absorb heat by conduction from heated rocks that have stored radiant solar energy. To lower their temperature, lizards may seek cooler objects with which to contact, find shade or return to their burrow. They also go to their burrows to avoid cooling when the sun goes down or the temperature falls.

Animals also engage in **kleptothermy** in which they share or even steal each other's body warmth. In endotherms such as bats and birds (such as the mousebird and emperor penguin) it allows the sharing of body heat (particularly amongst juveniles). This allows the individuals to increase their thermal inertia (as with gigantothermy) and so reduce heatloss. Some ectotherms share burrows of ectotherms. Other animals exploit termite mounds.

Some animals living in cold environments maintain their body temperature by preventing heat loss. Their fur grows more densely to increase the amount of **insulation.** Some animals are **regionally heterothermic** and are able to allow their less insulated extremities to cool to temperatures much lower than their core temperature nearly to 0°C. This minimizes heat loss through less insulated body parts, like the legs, feet (or hooves) and nose.

Hibernation, Aestivation and Daily Torpor

To cope with limited food resources and low temperatures, some mammals hibernate in underground burrows. In order to remain in 'stasis' for long periods, these animals must build up brown fat reserves and be capable of slowing all body functions. True hibernators (*e.g.*, groundhogs) keep their body temperature down throughout their hibernation, while the core temperature of false hibernators (*e.g.*, bears) varies with them sometimes emerging from their dens for brief periods. Some bats are true hibernators which rely upon a rapid, non-shivering thermogenesis of their brown fat deposit to bring them out of hibernation.

A estivation occurs in summer (like siestas) and allows some mammals to survive periods of high temperature and little water (*e.g.*, turtles burrow in pond mud).

Daily torpor occurs in small endotherms like bats and humming birds which temporarily reduce their high metabolic rates to conserve energy.

Normal Human Temperature

Previously, average oral temperature for healthy adults had been considered 37.0°C (98.4°F), while normal ranges are 36.1°C (97.0°F)to 37.8°C (100.0°F). In Poland and Russia, the temperature had been measured axillary. 36.6°C was considered 'ideal' temperature in these countries, while normal ranges are 36°C to 36.9°C.

Recent studies suggest that the average temperature for healthy adults is 98.2°F or 36.8°C (same result in three different studies). Variations (one standard deviation) from three other studies are

(a) 36.4-37.1°C (97.5-98.8°F)
(b) 36.3-37.1°C (97.3-98.8°F) for males, 36.5-37.3°C
(c) (97.7-99.1°F) for females
(d) 36.6-37.3°C (97.9-99.1°F).

Variations from Thermometer Placement

Temperature varies according to thermometer placement, with rectal temperature being 0.3-0.6°C (0.5-1°F) higher than oral temperature, while axillary temperature is 0.3-0.6°C (0.5-1°F) lower than oral temperature. The average difference between oral and axillary temperatures of **Indian** children aged 6-12 was found to be only 0.1°C (standard deviation 0.2°C) and the mean difference in **Maltese** children aged 4-14 between oral and axillary temperature was 0.56°C, while the mean difference between rectal and axillary temperature for children under 4 years old was 0.38°C.

Variations Associated with Development

Of the lower warm-blooded animals, there are some that appear to be cold-blooded at birth. **Kittens, rabbits** and **puppies,** if removed from their surroundings shortly after birth, lose their body heat until their temperature has fallen to within a few degrees of that of the surrounding air. But such animals are at birth blind, helpless and in some cases furless. Animals who are born when in a condition of greater development can maintain a fairly constant body temperature. In strong, healthy human infants a day or two old the temperature rises slightly when removed, but in that of weakly, ill-developed children it either remains stationary or falls. The cause of the variable temperature in infants and young immature animals is the imperfect development of the nervous regulating mechanism.

The average temperature falls slightly from **infancy** to **puberty** and again from puberty to **middle age,** but after that stage is passed the temperature begins to rise again and by about the **eightieth year** is as high as in infancy.

Variations due to Circadian Rhythms

In humans, a diurnal variation has been observed dependent on the periods of rest and activity, lowest at 11 p.m. to 3 a.m. and peaking at 10 a.m. to 6 p.m. **Monkeys** also have a well-marked and regular diurnal variation of body temperature which follows periods of rest and activity and is not dependent on the incidence of day and night; **nocturnal** monkeys reach their highest body temperature at night and lowest during the day.

The temperature curve of **diurnal** birds is essentially similar to that of man and other homoeothermal animals, except that the maximum occurs earlier in the afternoon and the minimum earlier in the morning. Also that the curves obtained from rabbits, guinea pigs and dogs were quite similar to those from man. These observations indicate that body temperature is partially regulated by circadian rhythms.

Variations due to Womens Menstrual Cycles

During the follicular phase (which lasts from the first day of menstruation until the day of ovulation), the average basal body temperature in women ranges from 36.45 to 36.7°C (97.6 to 98.1°F). Within 24 hours of ovulation, women experience an elevation of 0.15-0.45°C (0.2-0.9°F) due to the increased metabolic rate caused by sharply elevated levels of **progesterone.** The basal body temperature ranges between 36.7-37.3°C (98.1-99.2°F) throughout the **luteal phase** and drops down to pre-ovulatory levels within a few days of menstruation. Women can chart this phenomenon to determine whether and when they are ovulating, so as to aid conception or contraception.

Variations due to Fever

Fever is a regulated elevation of the set point of core temperature in the **hypothalamus,** caused by circulating pyrogens produced by the immune system. To the subject, a rise in core temperature due to fever may result in feeling cold in an environment where people without fever do not.

Variations due to Bio Feedback

A group of Monks known as the Tummo are known to practice bio feedback meditation techniques that allow them to raise their body temperatures substantially.

Variations due to Other Factors

In Simpson's and Galbraith's work, the mean temperature of the female was higher than that of the male in all the species examined whose sex had been determined.

Meals sometimes cause a slight elevation, sometimes a slight depression—alcohol seems always to produce a fall. Exercise and variations of external temperature within ordinary limits cause very slight change, as there are many compensating influences at work, which are discussed later. The core temperature of those living in the tropics is within a similar range to those dwelling in the **Arctic** regions.

Low Body Temperature

It was long theorised that low body temperature may prolong life. The transgenic mice which had body temperature 0.3-0.5 C lower than normal mice (due to overexpressing the uncoupling protein 2 in hypocretin neurons (Hcrt-UCP2), which elevated hypothalamic temperature, thus forcing the **hypothalamus** to lower body temperature) indeed lived longer than normal mice. The life span was 12% longer for males and 20% longer for females. Mice were allowed to eat as much as they wanted. The effects of such a genetic change in body temperature on longevity is harder to study in humans. The UCP2 genetic alleles seen in humans so far are associated with obesity.

Limits Compatible with Life

There are limits both of heat and cold that a warm-blooded animal can bear and other far wider limits that a cold-blooded animal may endure and yet live. The effect of too extreme a cold is to decrease metabolism and hence to lessen the production of heat. Both catabolic and anabolic pathways share in this metabolic depression and though less energy is used up, still less energy is generated. The effects of this diminished metabolism become telling on the central nervous system first, especially the brain and those parts concerning consciousness; both heart rate and respiration rate decrease; judgment becomes impaired as drowsiness supervenes, becoming steadily deeper until the individual loses consciousness; without medical intervention, death by hypothermia quickly follows. Occasionally, however, convulsions may set in towards the end and death is caused by asphyxia.

Animals cannot survive when rectal temperature fells below 16°C. At this time, temperature respiration became increasingly feeble; heart-impulse usually continued after respiration had ceased, the beats becoming very irregular, apparently ceasing, then beginning again. Death appeared to be mainly due to asphyxia and the only certain sign that it had taken place was the loss of knee jerks.

Conversely, too high a temperature speeds up the metabolism of different tissues to such a rate that their metabolic capital is soon exhausted. Blood that is too warm produces dyspnea by exhausting the metabolic capital of the respiratory centre; heart rate is increased; the beats then become arrhythmic and eventually cease. The central nervous system is also profoundly affected by hyperthermia and delirium and convulsions may set in. Consciousness may also be lost, propelling the person into a comatose condition. These changes can sometimes also be observed in patients suffering from an acute fever. The lower limit of temperature that humans can endure depends on many factors, but no one can survive a temperature of 45°C (113°F) or above for very long. Mammalian muscle becomes rigid with heat rigor at about 50°C, with the sudden rigidity of the whole body rendering life impossible.

Stress and Adaptation

Stress

Stress refers to the consequence of the failure of an **organism-human** or other **animal-to** respond adequately to mental, emotional or physical demands, whether actual or imagined. When the person perceives a threat, their nervous system responds by releasing a flood of stress hormones, including adrenaline and cortisol. These hormones rouse the body for emergency action. The stress response is the body's way of protecting the person. When working properly, it helps in staying focused, energetic and alert. Signs of stress may be cognitive, emotional, physical or behavioural.

1. **Cognitive Symptoms**
   - **(i)** Memory problems
   - **(ii)** Inability to concentrate
   - **(iii)** Poor judgment
   - **(iv)** Seeing only the negative
   - **(v)** Anxious or racing thoughts
   - **(vi)** Constant worrying
2. **Emotional Symptoms**
   - **(i)** Moodiness
   - **(ii)** Irritability or short temper
   - **(iii)** Agitation, inability to relax
   - **(iv)** Feeling overwhelmed
   - **(v)** Sense of loneliness and isolation
   - **(vi)** Depression or general unhappiness
3. **Physical Symptoms**
   - **(i)** Aches and pains
   - **(ii)** Diarrhoea or constipation
   - **(iii)** Nausea, dizziness
   - **(iv)** Chest pain, rapid heartbeat
   - **(v)** Loss of sex drive
   - **(vi)** Frequent colds
   - **(vii)** Chest pains
4. **Behavioural Symptoms**
   - **(i)** Eating more or less
   - **(ii)** Sleeping too much or too little
   - **(iii)** Isolating yourself from others
   - **(iv)** Procrastinating or neglecting responsibilities
   - **(v)** Using alcohol, cigarettes or drugs to relax
   - **(vi)** Nervous habits (*e.g.*, nail biting, pacing).

General Adaptation Syndrome

Physiologists define stress as how the body reacts to a stressor, real or imagined, a stimulus that causes stress. Acute stressors affect an organism in the short term; chronic stressors over the longer term.

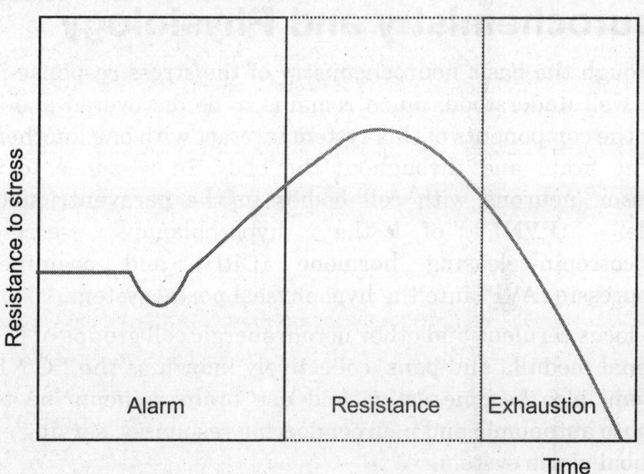

Fig. 21.6 A diagram of the general adaptation syndrome model

(i) **Alarm** is the first stage. When the threat or stressor is identified or realized, the body's stress response is a state of alarm. During this stage, adrenaline will be produced in order to bring about the fight-or-flight response. There is also some activation of the HPA axis, producing cortisol.

(ii) **Resistance** is the second stage. If the stressor persists, it becomes necessary to attempt some means of coping with the stress. Although the body begins to try to adapt to the strains or demands of the environment, the body cannot keep this up indefinitely, so its resources are gradually depleted.

(iii) **Exhaustion** is the third and final stage in the GAS model. At this point, all of the body's resources are eventually depleted and the body is unable to maintain normal function. The initial autonomic nervous system symptoms may reappear (sweating, raised heart rate, etc.). If stage three is extended, long-term damage may result, as the body's immune system becomes exhausted and bodily functions become impaired, resulting in decompensation.

The result can manifest itself in obvious illnesses such as ulcers, depression, diabetes, trouble with the digestive system or even cardiovascular problems, along with other mental illnesses.

Eustress and Distress

Where stress enhances function (physical or mental, such as through strength training or challenging work), it may be considered eustress. Persistent stress that is not resolved through coping or adaptation, deemed distress, may lead to anxiety or withdrawal (depression) behaviour.

The difference between experiences that result in eustress and those that result in distress is determined by the disparity between an experience (real or imagined) and personal expectations and resources to cope with the stress. Alarming experiences, either real or imagined, can trigger a stress response.

Neurochemistry and Physiology

Although the basic neurochemistry of the stress response is now well understood, much remains to be discovered about how the components of this system interact with one another, in the brain and throughout the body. In response to a stressor, neurons with cell bodies in the paraventricular nuclei (PVN) of the hypothalamus secrete corticotropin-releasing hormone (CRH) and arginine-vasopressin (AVP) into the hypophyseal portal system.

The locus ceruleus and other noradrenergic cell groups of the adrenal medulla and pons, collectively known as the LC/NE system, also become active and use brain epinephrine to execute autonomic and neuroendocrine responses, serving as a global alarm system.

The autonomic nervous system provides the rapid response to stress commonly known as the fight-or-flight response, engaging the sympathetic nervous system and withdrawing the parasympathetic nervous system, thereby enacting cardiovascular, respiratory, gastrointestinal, renal and endocrine changes. The HPA axis, a major part of the neuroendocrine system involving the interactions of the hypothalamus, the pituitary gland and the adrenal glands, is also activated by release of CRH and AVP.

This results in release of adrenocorticotropic hormone (ACTH) from the pituitary into the general bloodstream, which results in secretion of cortisol and other glucocorticoids from the adrenal cortex. The related compound cortisone is frequently used as a key anti-inflammatory component in drugs that treat skin rashes and in nasal sprays that treat asthma and sinusitis. Recently, scientists realized the brain also uses cortisol to suppress the immune system and reduce inflammation within the body. These corticoids involve the whole body in the organism's response to stress and ultimately contribute to the termination of the response *via* inhibitory feedback.

Impact on Disease

Chronic stress can significantly affect many of the body's immune systems, as can an individual's perceptions of and reactions to, stress. The term 'psychoneuroimmunology' is used to describe the interactions between the mental state, nervous and immune systems and research on the interconnections of these systems. Immune system changes can create more vulnerability to infection and have been observed to increase the potential for an outbreak of psoriasis for people with that skin disorder.

Chronic stress has also been shown to impair developmental growth in children by lowering the pituitary gland's production of growth hormone, as in children associated with a home environment involving serious marital discord, alcoholism or child abuse.

Chronic stress is seen to affect parts of the brain, where memories are processed through and stored. When people feel stressed, stress hormones get over-secreted, which affects the brain. This secretion is made up of glucocorticoids, including cortisol, which are steroid hormones that the adrenal gland releases.

Studies of female monkeys at **Wake Forest University** (2009) discovered that individuals suffering from higher stress have higher levels of visceral fat in their bodies. This suggests a possible cause-and-effect link between the two, wherein stress promotes the accumulation of visceral fat, which in turn causes hormonal and metabolic changes that contribute to heart disease and other health problems.

Post Traumatic Stress Disorder

Post Traumatic Stress Disorder (PTSD) is a severe anxiety disorder that can develop after exposure to any event that results in psychological trauma. This event may involve the threat of death to oneself or to someone else or to one's own or someone else's physical, sexual or psychological integrity, overwhelming the individual's ability to cope. As an effect of psychological trauma, PTSD is less frequent and more enduring than the more commonly seen acute stress response. Diagnostic symptoms for PTSD include re-experiencing the original trauma(s) through flashbacks or nightmares, avoidance of stimuli associated with the trauma and increased arousal - such as difficulty falling or staying asleep, anger and hypervigilance. Formal diagnostic criteria (both DSM-IV-TR and ICD-10) require that the symptoms last more than one month and cause significant impairment in social, occupational or other important areas of functioning.

Common Sources

Both negative and positive stressors can lead to stress. The intensity and duration of stress changes depending on the circumstances and emotional condition of the person suffering from it (Arnold; E and Boggs; K; 2007). Some common categories and examples of stressors include:

(a) Sensory input such as pain, bright light, noise, temperatures or environmental issues such as a lack of control over environmental circumstances, such as food, air and/or water quality, housing, health, freedom or mobility.

(b) Social issues can also cause stress, such as struggles with conspecific or difficult individuals and social defeat or relationship conflict, deception or break ups and major events such as birth and deaths, marriage and divorce.

(c) Life experiences such as poverty, unemployment, clinical depression, obsessive compulsive disorder, heavy drinking or insufficient sleep can also cause stress. Students and workers may face performance pressure stress from exams and project deadlines.

(d) Adverse experiences during development (*e.g.*, prenatal exposure to maternal stress, poor attachment histories, sexual abuse are thought to contribute to deficits in the maturity of an individual's stress response systems.

Adaptation

Responses to stress include adaptation, **psychological coping** such as **stress management, anxiety** and **depression.** Over the long term, distress can lead to diminished health and/or increased propensity to illness; to avoid this, stress must be managed.

Stress management encompasses techniques intended to equip a person with effective coping mechanisms for dealing with psychological stress, with stress defined as a person's physiological response to an internal or external stimulus that triggers the fight-or-flight response. Stress management is effective when a person uses strategies to cope with or alter stressful situations.

There are several ways of coping with stress, such as controlling the source of stress or learning to set limits and to say 'No' to some demands that bosses or family members may make.

A person's capacity to tolerate the source of stress may be increased by thinking about another topic such as a hobby, listening to music or **spending time in a wilderness.**

Exercise

1. .... facilitates reabsorption of water by the nephron.
(a) Loop of the nephron (b) Medulla
(c) Cortex (d) Pelvis

2. A brush border is formed in
(a) distal convoluted tubule
(b) proximal convoluted tubule
(c) Bowman's capsule
(d) loop of Henle

3. Ability of the kidneys for the production of concentrated urine is dependent on
(a) active transport
(b) passive transport
(c) countercurrent mechanism
(d) diffusion

4. Bile manufactured by liver is stored within the
(a) urinary bladder (b) gall bladder
(c) liver (d) lungs

5. Certain ions and molecules, for examples H^+ and penicillin are secreted from the peritubular capillary network into the
(a) convoluted tubules (b) peritubular capillaries
(c) loops of Henle (d) collecting ducts

6. Correct sequence of urine formation is
(a) filtration, reabsorption and secretion
(b) secretion, reabsorption and filtration
(c) reabsorption, secretion and filtration
(d) reabsorption, filtration and secretion

7. Creatinine the waste product closely regulated by the brain and kidneys is the end product of the metabolism of
(a) ammonia (b) muscle
(c) nucleotide (d) anaerobic

8. Glomerular filtrate passes from glomerular capsule into the
(a) loop of the nephron
(b) proximal convoluted tubule
(c) glomerular capsule
(d) convoluted tubule

9. If a man takes large amount of protein, he is likely to excrete more amount of
(a) glucose (b) urea and uric acid
(c) water (d) salts

10. If a person undergoes a prolonged fasting then his urine will be found to contain higher levels of
(a) ketones (b) amino acids
(c) fats (d) glucose

11. In the kidneys, osmotic pressure controls
(a) glucose absorption (b) sodium absorption
(c) water absorption (d) None of these

12. Most of the reabsorption of salts and water occurs in the
(a) distal convoluted tubule
(b) loops of Henle
(c) proximal convoluted tubule
(d) collecting tubule

13. Which one of the following statements is correct with respect to kidney function regulation?
(a) During summer when body loses lot of water by evaporation, the release of ADH is suppressed
(b) When someone drinks lot of water, ADH release is suppressed

(c) Exposure to cold temperature stimulates ADH release
(d) An increase in glomerular blood flow stimulates formation of angiotensin II

14. The basic functional unit of human kidney is
(a) Henle's loop (b) nephron
(c) nephridia (d) pyramid

15. Ornithine cycle (also known as the urea cycle) refers to the sequence of biochemical reactions taking place in the
(a) urinary bladder (b) liver
(c) pancreas (d) stomach

16. The Bowman's capsules are found in
(a) cortex (b) medulla
(c) convoluted tubule (d) loop of Henle

17. The hollow space at the centre of kidney where urine is collected after its formation is called
(a) renal pelvis (b) glomerulus
(c) distal convoluted tubule (d) urethra

18. The lungs are important organs for excretion of
(a) ammonia (b) water
(c) carbon dioxide (d) urea

19. The main nitrogen-containing waste excreted in urine is
(a) ammonia (b) creatine phosphate
(c) nucleotides (d) urea

20. The muscular tubes which take the urine from the kidneys to the bladder are
(a) urinary bladders (b) ureters
(c) urethras (d) nephrons

21. The process of dilution of urine takes place in
(a) distal tubule (b) collecting tubule
(c) loop of Henle (d) proximal tubule

22. The renal medulla consists of cone-shaped tissue masses called
(a) renal pyramid (b) adipose capsule
(c) renal cortex (d) renal pelvis

23. The size of filtration slits of glomerulus are approximately
(a) 10 nm (b) 15 nm
(c) 20 nm (d) 25 nm

24. The term 'haematuria' is used to describe
(a) blood cancer
(b) presence of red blood cells in urine
(c) internal bleeding
(d) blood poisoning

25. The yellow pigment derived from haeme breakdown and excreted by kidneys is
(a) uric acid (b) urochrome
(c) cholesterol (d) melanin

26. When the infection is localized in the urethra, it is called
(a) urethritis (b) cystitis
(c) pyelonephritis (d) haemodialysis

27. Which of the following hormones is involved in regulating the water-salt balance of the blood?
(a) Cortisone (b) Aldosterone
(c) ADH (d) ANH

28. Which of the following hormones promotes the excretion of potassium ions and the reabsorption of sodium ions?
(a) Aldosterone (b) Rennin
(c) ADH (d) None of these

29. Which of the following leads to the secretion of aldosterone from the adrenal cortex?
(a) Chymotrypsin (b) Trypsin
(c) Renin (d) None of these

30. Which of the following structures facilitates easy passage of small molecules to the glomerular capsule?
(a) Loop of the nephron (b) Peritubular capillary
(c) Convoluted tubule (d) Glomerulus

31. Which of the two waste products are removed from the blood in liver by Ornithine cycle?
(a) Urea and CO_2 (b) Uric acid and ammonia
(c) Ammonia and CO_2 (d) Urea and ammonia

32. Which of the following is incorrectly paired with its excretory system?
(a) Insect — Malpighian tubules
(b) Flatworm — flame-bulb system
(c) Earthworm — protonephridia
(d) Amphibian — kidneys

33. A freshwater fish would be expected to
(a) pump salt out through salt glands in the gills
(b) produce copious quantities of dilute urine
(c) diffuse urea out across the epithelium of the gills
(d) have scales that reduce water loss to the environment

34. Which would have the toughest time surviving over the long term in the environment given?
(a) An osmoconformer in sea water
(b) An endotherm in a warm environment
(c) An ectotherm in a cold environment
(d) An osmoregulator in seawater

35. The kidney's filtration process is non-selective, so
(a) many valuable substances are lost in the urine
(b) the proportions of substances in urine are the same as in blood
(c) it really has little control over body fluid composition
(d) useful substances must be selectively reabsorbed

36. The loops of Henle in the kidneys of a desert kangaroo rat are much longer than those in a white laboratory rat because
(a) the kangaroo rat lives in an environment where water is scarce
(b) the white rat's diet is much less varied than the kangaroo rat's
(c) the kangaroo rat cannot always find food
(d) the kangaroo rat produces more body wastes

37. Aldosterone
(a) is a hormone that stimulates thirst
(b) is secreted by the adrenal glands in response to a high osmolarity of the blood
(c) stimulates the active reabsorption of Na^+ in the distal tubules
(d) is converted from a blood protein by the action of renin

38. Which of the following statement is incorrect?
(a) Long loops of Henle are associated with steep osmotic gradients and the production of hyperosmotic urine
(b) Ammonia is a toxic nitrogenous waste molecule that passively diffuses out of the bodies of aquatic invertebrates
(c) Uric acid is the form of nitrogenous waste that requires the least amount of water to excrete
(d) Ammonia produced by a mammalian foetus is removed through the placenta and converted to urea in the mother's liver

39. The process of reabsorption in the formation of urine insures that
(a) excess hydrogen ions are removed from the blood
(b) drugs and other poisons are removed from the blood
(c) urine is always hyperosmotic to interstitial fluid
(d) glucose, salts and water are returned to the blood

40. ADH and RAAS both increase water reabsorption, but they respond to different osmoregulatory problems. Which two of the following statement are true?
I. ADH will be released in response to high alcohol consumption.
II. ADH is released when osmoregulatory cells in the hypothalamus sense an increase in blood osmolarity.
III. RAAS will increase the osmolarity of urine due to the cooperative action of renin, aldosterone and ANP.
IV. RAAS is a response to a rise in blood pressure or volume.
V. RAAS is most likely to respond following an accident or severe case of diarrhoea.
(a) I and IV (b) I and V
(c) II and III (d) II and V

41. The function of stress-induced proteins is to
(a) provide proteins that function at a lower temperature
(b) change the composition of plasma membranes to maintain fluidity
(c) regulate blood osmolarity and volume following an injury
(d) protect cellular proteins from denaturation during rapid temperature changes

42. Blood flows through the hepatic portal vessel
(a) from the aorta to the kidney
(b) from the intestine to the liver
(c) from the kidney to the inferior vena cava
(d) from the liver to the inferior vena cava

43. As your kidneys regulate your body fluid composition, which of the following is the largest?
(a) the volume of filtrate formed by the nephrons
(b) the volume of urine excreted
(c) the volume of blood flowing through the nephrons
(d) the volume of solutes added to the filtrate by secretion

44. A countercurrent heat exchanger enables an animal to
(a) produces more heat when needed
(b) reduce loss of heat to the environment
(c) slow metabolism when food is not available
(d) increase heat loss by evaporation

45. Uric acid is the nitrogenous waste excreted by birds, insects and many reptiles. An advantage of excreting uric acid is that it ...., but a disadvantage is that is ....
(a) saves water; costs energy
(b) saves energy; is highly toxic
(c) is not very toxic; wastes a lot of water
(d) is much more soluble in water than other waste; costs energy

46. Which needs to drink the smallest amount of water to maintain its water balance?
(a) A sparrow (b) A saltwater fish
(c) A freshwater fish (d) A dog

47. Most aquatic animals excrete ammonia, while land animals excrete urea or uric acid. What is the most likely explanation for this difference?
(a) They have different diets
(b) Land animals can get the energy needed to make urea or uric acid
(c) Ammonia is very toxic and it takes lots of water to dilute it
(d) Land animals cannot afford the energy needed to make ammonia

48. Which of the following sections of the mammalian nephron is incorrectly paired with its function?
(a) Bowman's capsule and glomerulus — filtration of blood
(b) Proximal tubule — secretion of ammonia and H^+ ions filtrate and transport of glucose and amino acids out of tubule
(c) Descending limp of loop of Henle — diffusion of urea out of filtrate
(d) Ascending limb of loop of Henle — diffusion and pumping of NaCl out of filtrate

49. Which of the following pairs are correctly matched?
I. Poikilo-osmotic — Animals show osmotic dependence with respect to the environment.
II. Homo-osmotic — Animals maintain body fluid concentrations constant irrespective of fluctuation in the environmental concentrations
III. Euryhaline — Animals with stand aquatic media of a wide range of concentrations.
IV. Stenohaline — Animals survive within a wide range of salinities.

Select the correct answer using the codes give below.

Codes
(a) II, III and IV (b) I, II and IV
(c) I, III and IV (d) I, II and IV

50. Match list I with list II and select the correct answer using the codes given below the lists.

List I	List II
A. Aqueous solutions of sugar, urea, NaCl, etc.	1. Lyophobic
B. Aqueous solution of proteins, starch, etc.	2. Lyophilic
C. Solutes having great affinity to solvent	3. Colloidal solution
D. Solutes having no affinity to solvent	4. Crystalline solution

Codes

	A	B	C	D
(a)	4	3	2	1
(b)	3	4	1	2
(c)	4	3	1	2
(d)	3	4	2	1

51. Match list I with list II and select the correct answer using the codes given below the lists.

List I (A Part to the Nephron)	List II (Function)
A. Ascending loop of Henle	1. Reabsorption of glucose
B. Descending loop of Henle	2. Electrolytes are actively thrown out
C. Proximal tubule	3. Passive entry of sodium
D. Collecting duct	4. Passive entry of sodim
	5. Sodium is actively thrown out

Codes

	A	B	C	D
(a)	5	4	1	3
(b)	2	4	5	1
(c)	5	3	2	4
(d)	4	5	3	1

52. Consider the following water conservation mechanisms.

I. Absence of sweat glands.
II. Dependence on metabolic water.
III. Greater ADH level in the blood.
IV. Lying more on protein-rich diet.

The kangaroo rate *(Dipodiomys)* living in deserts can survive without drinking water because of

Codes

(a) I, II and III
(b) I, II and IV
(c) II, III and IV
(d) I, III and IV

53. Consider the following statements.
For osmoregulation in aquatic medium.

I. A freshwater fish has to drink water continuously.
II. A marine bony fish has to drink water continuously.
III. A freshwater fish produces copious urine, which is hyposmotic to blood.
IV. A marine fish produces scanty urine, which is hyper osmotic to blood.

Which of the statements given above is/are correct?

Codes

(a) I only (b) IV only
(c) I and IV (d) II and III

Answers

1. (a)	**2.** (b)	**3.** (c)	**4.** (b)	**5.** (a)	**6.** (a)	**7.** (b)	**8.** (b)	**9.** (b)	**10.** (a)
11. (c)	**12.** (c)	**13.** (b)	**14.** (b)	**15.** (b)	**16.** (a)	**17.** (a)	**18.** (c)	**19.** (d)	**20.** (b)
21. (c)	**22.** (a)	**23.** (d)	**24.** (b)	**25.** (b)	**26.** (a)	**27.** (b)	**28.** (a)	**29.** (c)	**30.** (d)
31. (d)	**32.** (c)	**33.** (b)	**34.** (c)	**35.** (d)	**36.** (a)	**37.** (c)	**38.** (d)	**39.** (d)	**40.** (d)
41. (d)	**42.** (b)	**43.** (c)	**44.** (b)	**45.** (a)	**46.** (c)	**47.** (c)	**48.** (c)	**49.** (d)	**50.** (a)
51. (a)	**52.** (c)	**53.** (d)							

22

Neuroendocrine System and Reproduction

Nervous System

The **nervous system,** in association with the endocrine system, serves as the primary control center of the body working below the level of consciousness. For example, the hypothalamus of the brain is where the body's 'thermostat' is found. The hypothalamus also stimulates the pituitary gland to release various hormones that control metabolism and development of the body. The sympathetic and parasympathetic divisions of the nervous system alternatively stimulate or inhibit various bodily responses (such as heart rate, breathing rate, etc.) to help maintain proper levels. It also controls contractions like the arrector pili muscles (involved in thermoregulation) and skeletal muscles, which in addition to moving the body, also cause bone thickening and maintenance, which affects bone composition. The nervous system also regulates various systems such as respiratory (controls pace and depth of breathing), cardiovascular system (controls heart rate and blood pressure), endocrine organs (causes secretion of ADH and oxytocin), the digestive system (regulates the digestive tract movement and secretion) and the urinary system (it helps adjust renal blood pressure and also controls voiding the bladder). The nervous system is also involved in our sexual behaviours and functions.

The nervous system has three main functions, sensory input, integration of data and motor output. Sensory input is when the body gathers information or data, by way of neurons, glia and synapses. The nervous system is composed of excitable nerve cells and synapses connecting the cells to one another, to centers throughout the body or to other neurons. These neurons operate on excitation or inhibition and although nerve cells can vary in size and location their communication with one another determines their function. These nerves conduct impulses from sensory receptors to the brain and spinal

Syllabus

- Nervous system: Neurons, Central Nervous System, Brain, Spinal Cord, Peripheral Nervous System, Autonomic system, Action Potential, Neural Control of Muscle Tone and Posture.
- Sense Organs: Vision, Hearing and Tactile Response.
- Endocrinology: Mechanism of Hormone Action, Endocrine Glands, Reproduction; Male and Female Reproductive System, Types of Birth control.

cord. The data is then processed by way of integration of data, which occurs only in the brain. After the brain has processed the information, impulses are then conducted from the brain and spinal cord to muscles and glands, which is called motor output. Glia cells are found within tissues and are not excitable but help with myelination, ionic regulation and extracellular fluid.

The nervous system is comprized of two major parts or sub-divisions, the Central Nervous System (CNS) and the Peripheral Nervous System (PNS). The CNS includes the brain and spinal cord. The brain is the body's 'control center'. The CNS has various centers located within it that carry out the sensory, motor and integration of data. These centers can be sub-divided into lower centers (including the spinal cord and brain stem) and higher centers communicating with the brain *via* effectors. The PNS is a vast network of spinal and cranial nerves that are linked to the brain and the spinal cord. It contains sensory receptors which help in processing changes in the internal and external environment. This information is sent to the CNS *via* afferent sensory nerves. The PNS is then sub-divided into the autonomic nervous system and the somatic nervous system. The autonomic has involuntary control of internal organs, blood vessels, smooth and cardiac muscles. The somatic has voluntary control of skin, bones, joints and skeletal muscle. The two systems function together, by way of nerves from the PNS entering and becoming part of the CNS and *vice-versa*.

Nervous Tissue (Neuron)

All living cells have the ability to react to stimuli. Nervous tissue is specialized to react to stimuli and to conduct impulses to various organs in the body which bring about a response to the stimulus. Nerve tissue (as in the brain, spinal cord and peripheral nerves that branch throughout the body) are all made up of specialized nerve cells called neurons. Neurons are easily stimulated and transmit impulses very rapidly. A nerve is made up of many nerve cell fibres (neurons) bound together by connective tissue. A sheath of dense connective tissue, the epineurium surrounds the nerve. This sheath penetrates the nerve to form the perineurium which surrounds bundles of nerve fibres. Blood vessels of various sizes can be seen in the epineurium. The endoneurium, which consists of a thin layer of loose connective tissue, surrounds the individual nerve fibres.

Although the system forms a unit it can be divided into the following parts: the central nervous system (CNS) which consists of the brain and spinal cord, the nervous system consists of the nerves outside the CNS which connect the brain and spinal cord to the organs and muscles of the body and the automatic or involuntary nervous system consists of nerve centres and fibres inside as well as outside the central nervous system.

There are three main types of neurons, which are classified according their function: Those that conduct impulses from the sensory organs to the central nervous system (brain and spinal cord) are called sensory (or afferent) neurons, those that conduct impulses from the central nervous system to the effector organs (such as muscles and glands) are called motor (or efferent) neurons. Interneurons (also known as connector neurons or association neurons) are those that connect sensory neurons to motor neurons.

Neuroglia

Neuroglia (noo-RO¯ G-le¯ -a; -glia glue) or glia make up about half the volume of the CNS. Their name derives from the idea of early histologists that they were the 'glue' that held nervous tissue together. Neuroglia are not merely passive bystanders but rather actively participate in the activities of nervous tissue. Generally, neuroglia are smaller than neurons and they are 5 to 50 times more numerous. In contrast to neurons, glia do not generate or propagate action potentials and they can multiply and divide in the mature nervous system. In cases of injury or disease, neuroglia multiply to fill in the spaces formerly occupied by neurons. Brain tumours derived from glia, called gliomas, tend to be highly malignant and grow rapidly. Of the six types of neuroglia, four—astrocytes, oligodendrocytes, microglia and ependymal cells are found only in the CNS. The remaining two types—Schwann cells and satellite cells are present in the PNS.

Structure of a Neuron

A motor neuron has many processes (cytoplasmic extensions), called dendrites, which enter a large, grey cell body at one end. A single process, the axon, leaves at the other end, extending towards the dendrites of the next neuron or to form a motor endplate in a muscle. Dendrites are usually short and divided while the axons are very long and does not branched freely. The impulses are transmitted through the motor neuron in one direction, *i.e.*, into the cell body by the dendrites and away from the cell body by the axon. The cell body is enclosed by a cell (plasma) membrane and has a central nucleus. Granules, called Nissl, bodies are found in the cytoplasm of the cell body. Within the cell body, extremely fine neurofibrils extend from the dendrites into the axon. The axon is surrounded by the myelin sheath, which forms a whitish, non-cellular, fatty layer around the axon. Outside the myelin sheath is a cellular layer called the neurilemma or sheath of **Schwann cells.** The myelin sheath together with the neurilemma is also known as the medullary sheath. This medullary sheath is interrupted at intervals by the nodes of Ranvier. Axons and dendrites in the central nervous system are typically only about a micrometer thick, while some in the peripheral nervous system are much thicker. The soma is usually about 10-25 micrometers in diameter and often is not much larger than the cell nucleus it contains. The longest axon of a human motor neuron can be over a meter long, reaching from the base of the spine to the toes. Sensory neurons have axons that run from the toes to the dorsal columns, over 1.5 meters in adults. Giraffes have single axons several meters in length running along the entire length of their necks. Much of what is known about axonal function comes from studying the squids giant axon, an ideal experimental preparation because of its relatively immense size (0.5-1 millimeters thick, several centimeters long).

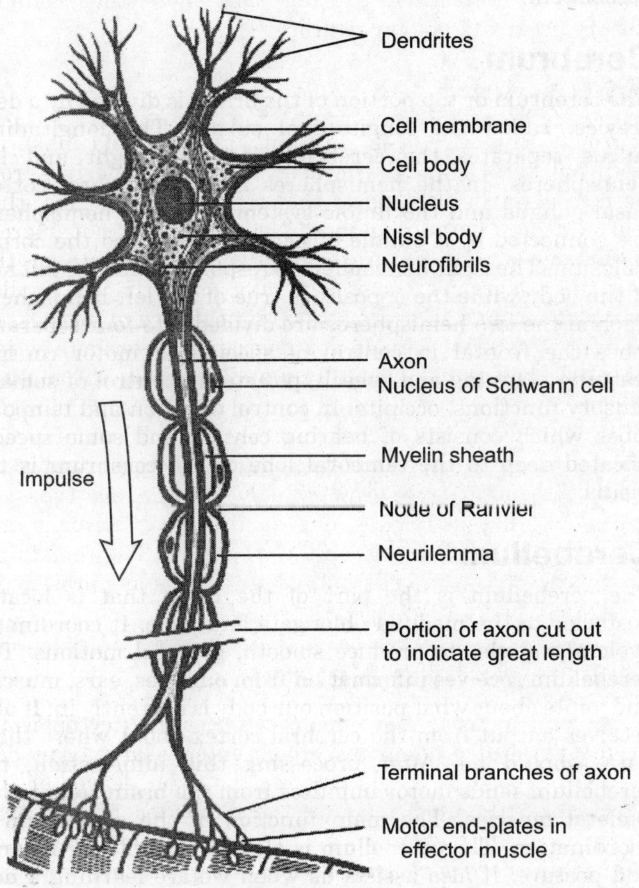

Fig. 22.1 A neuron

Nerve cells are functionally connected to each other at a junction known as a **synapse**, where the terminal branches of an axon and the dendrites of another neuron lie in close proximity to each other but never make direct contact.

Classification of Neurons

On the basis of their structure, neurons can also be classified into three main types:

Unipolar Neurons

Sensory neurons have only a single process or fibre which divides close to the cell body into two main branches (axon and dendrite). Because of their structure they are often referred to as unipolar neurons.

Multipolar Neurons

Motor neurons, which have numerous cell processes (an axon and many dendrites) are often referred to as multipolar neurons. Interneurons are also multipolar.

Bipolar Neurons

Bipolar neurons are spindle-shaped, with a dendrite at one end and an axon at the other. An example can be found in the light-sensitive retina of the eye.

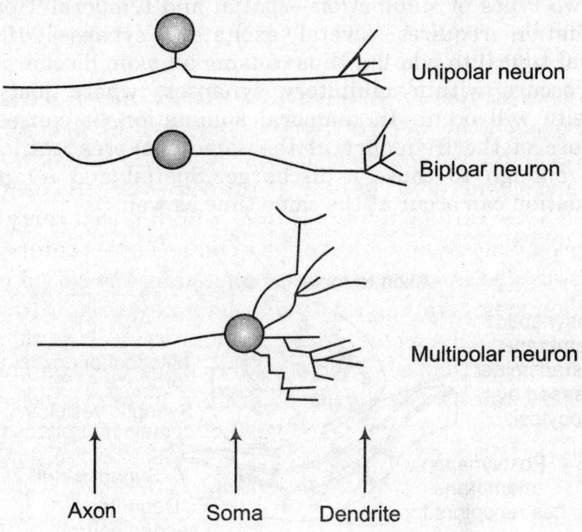

Fig. 22.2 Different types of neurons

Function

Sensory afferent neurons convey information from tissues and organs into the central nervous system. Efferent neurons transmit signals from the central nervous system to the effector cells and are sometimes called motor neurons. Inter neurons connect neurons within specific regions of the central nervous system. Afferent and efferent can also refer generally to neurons which, respectively, bring information to or send information from brain region.

Classification Based on Action

Excitatory neurons excite their target postsynaptic neurons or target cells causing it to function. Motor neurons and somatic neurons are all excitatory neurons. Excitatory neurons in the brain are often glutamatergic. Spinal motor neurons, which synapse on muscle cells, use acetylcholine as their neurotransmitter. Inhibitory neurons inhibit their target neurons. Inhibitory neurons are also known as short axon neurons, interneurons or microneurons. The output of some brain structures (neostriatum, globus pallidus, cerebellum) are inhibitory. The primary inhibitory neurotransmitters are GABA and glycine. Modulatory neurons evoke more complex effects termed neuromodulation. These neurons use such neurotransmitters as dopamine, acetylcholine, serotonin and others. Each synapses can receive both excitatory and inhibitory signals and the outcome is determined by the adding up of summation. Excitatory and inhibitory process, the release of a excitatory neurotransmitter (ACHe) at the synapses will cause an inflow of positively charged sodium ions (Na^+) making a localized depolarization of the membrane. The current then flows to the resting (polarized) segment of the axon.

Inhibitory synapse causes an inflow of Cl^- (chlorine) or K^+ (potassium) making the synaptic membrane hyperpolarized. This increase prevents depolarization, causing a decrease in the possibility of an axon discharge. If they are both equal to their charges, then the operation will cancel itself out. There are two types of summation—spatial and temporal. Spatial summation requires several excitatory synapses (firing several times) to add up, thus causing an axon discharge. It also occurs within inhibitory synapses, where just the opposite will occur. In temporal summation, it causes an increase of the frequency at the same synapses until it is large enough to cause a discharge. Spatial and temporal summation can occur at the same time as well.

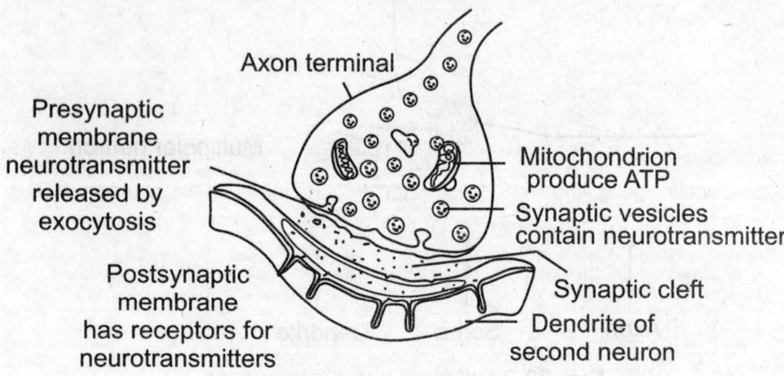

Fig. 22.3 A synapse

Central Nervous System (CNS)

The central nervous system includes the brain and spinal cord. The brain and spinal cord are protected by bony structures, membranes and fluid. The brain is held in the cranial cavity of the skull and it consists of the cerebrum, cerebellum and the brain stem. The nerves involved are cranial nerves and spinal nerves. The central nervous system (CNS) represents the largest part of the nervous system, including the brain and the spinal cord. Together, with the peripheral nervous system (PNS), it has a fundamental role in the control of behaviour.

The CNS is conceived as a system devoted to information processing, where an appropriate motor output is computed as a response to a sensory input. Many threads of research suggest that motor activity exists well before the maturation of the sensory systems and senses only influence behaviour without dictating it. This has brought the conception of the CNS as an autonomous system.

Brain

The brain is found in the cranial cavity. Within it are found the higher nerve centers responsible for coordinating the sensory and motor systems of the body (forebrain). The brain stem houses the lower nerve centers (consisting of midbrain, pons and medulla).

Medulla

The medulla is the control center for respiratory, cardiovascular and digestive functions.

Pons

The pons houses the control centers for respiration and inhibitory functions. Here, it will interact with the cerebellum.

Cerebrum

The cerebrum or top portion of the brain, is divided by a deep crevice, called the longitudinal sulcus. The longitudinal sulcus separates the cerebrum into the right and left hemispheres. In the hemispheres lies the cerebral cortex, basal ganglia and the limbic system. The two hemispheres are connected by a bundle of nerve fibres called the corpus callosum. The right hemisphere is responsible for the left side of the body while the opposite is true of the left hemisphere. Each of the two hemispheres are divided into four separated lobes the frontal in control of specialized motor control, learning planning and speech, parietal in control of somatic sensory functions, occipital in control of vision and temporal lobes which consists of hearing centers and some speech. Located deep to the temporal lobe of the cerebrum is the insula.

Cerebellum

The cerebellum is the part of the brain that is located posterior to the medulla oblongata and pons. It coordinates skeletal muscles to produce smooth, graceful motions. The cerebellum receives information from our eyes, ears, muscles and joints about what position our body is currently in. It also receives output from the cerebral cortex about where these parts should be. After processing this information, the cerebellum sends motor impulses from the brain stem to the skeletal muscles. The main function of the cerebellum is coordination. The cerebellum is also responsible for balance and posture. It also assists us when we are learning a new motor skill, such as playing a sport or musical instrument.

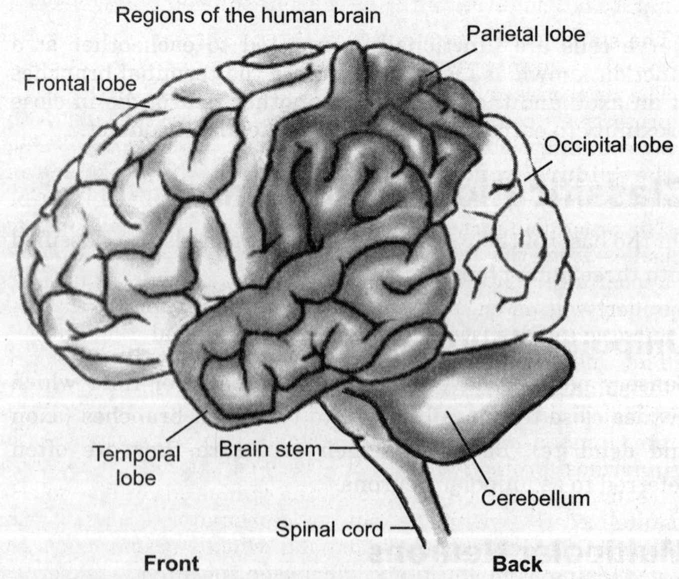

Fig. 22.4 A shaded-coated image of the brain, showing the main sections

Spinal Cord

The spinal cord is a long, thin, tubular bundle of nervous tissue and support cells that extends from the brain (The medulla oblongata specifically). The brain and spinal cord together make up the central nervous system. The spinal cord begins at the occipital bone and extends down to the space between the first and second lumbar vertebrae, it does not extend the entire length of the vertebral column. It is around 45 cm (18″) in men and around 43 cm (17″) long in women. Also, the spinal cord has a varying width, ranging from 1/2 inch thick in the cervical and lumbar regions to 1/4 inch thick in the thoracic area. The enclosing bony vertebral column protects the relatively shorter spinal cord. The spinal cord functions primarily in the transmission of neural signals between the brain and the rest of the body but also contains neural circuits that can independently control numerous reflexes and central pattern generators. The spinal cord has three major functions:

(i) Serve as a conduit for motor information, which travels down the spinal cord.

(ii) Serve as a conduit for sensory information, which travels up the spinal cord.

(iii) Serve as a center for coordinating certain reflexes.

The spinal cord is the main pathway for information connecting the brain and peripheral nervous system. The length of the spinal cord is much shorter than the length of the bony spinal column. The human spinal cord extends from the **foramen magnum** and continues through to the conus medullaris near the second **lumbar vertebra,** terminating in a fibrous extension known as the **filum terminale.**

It is about 45 cm (18″) long in men and around 43 cm (17″) in women, ovoid-shaped and is enlarged in the cervical and lumbar regions. The cervical enlargement, located from C_3 to T_2 spinal segments, is where sensory input comes from and motor output goes to the arms. The lumbar enlargement, located between L_1 and S_3 spinal segments, handles sensory input and motor output coming from and going to the legs.

The spinal cord is protected by three layers of tissue, called spinal **meninges,** that surround the canal. The **duramater** is the outermost layer and it forms a tough protective coating. Between the duramater and the surrounding bone of the vertebrae is a space called the **epidural space.** The epidural space is filled with adipose tissue and it contains a network of blood vessels. The arachnoid mater is the middle protective layer. Its name comes from the fact that the tissue has a spider web-like appearance. The space between the arachnoid and the underlying piamater is called the subarachnoid space. The subarachnoid space contains Cerebro Spinal Fluid (CSF). The medical procedure known as a lumbar puncture (or spinal tap) involves use of a needle to withdraw cerebro spinal fluid from the subarachnoid space, usually from the lumbar region of the spine. The piamater is the innermost protective layer. It is very delicate and it is tightly associated with the surface of the spinal cord. The cord is stabilized within the duramater by the connecting denticulate ligaments, which extend from the enveloping piamater laterally between the dorsal and ventral roots. The dural sac ends at the vertebral level of the second sacral vertebra.

In cross-section, the peripheral region of the cord contains neuronal white matter tracts containing sensory and motor neurons. Internal to this peripheral region is the gray, butterfly-shaped central region made up of nerve cell bodies. This central region surrounds the central canal, which is an anatomic extension of the spaces in the brain known as the ventricles and like the ventricles, contains cerebro-spinal fluid.

The spinal cord has a shape that is compressed dorso-ventrally, giving it an elliptical shape. The cord has grooves in the dorsal and ventral sides. The posterior median sulcus is the groove in the dorsal side and the anterior median fissure is the groove in the ventral side.

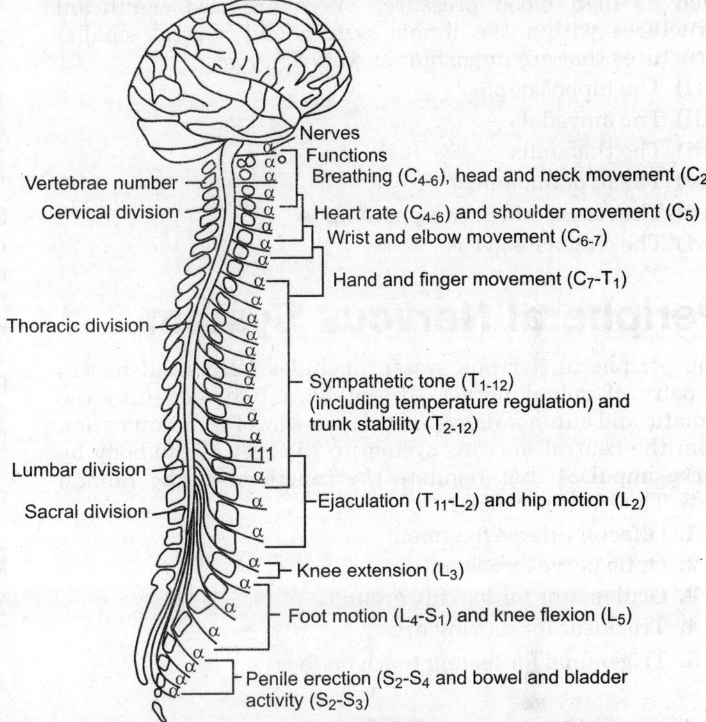

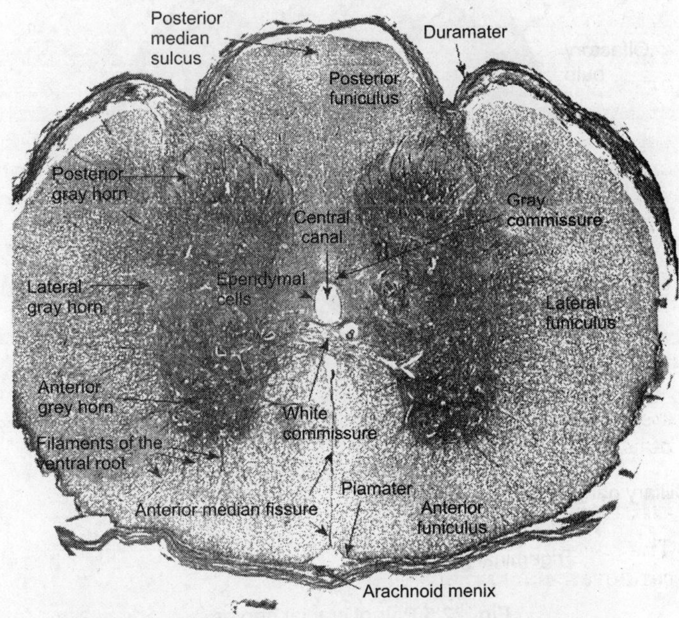

Fig. 22.5 Spinal cord: Structural and histological details

Limbic System

The limbic system is a complex set of structures found just beneath the cerebrum and on both sides of the thalamus. It combines higher mental functions and primitive emotion, into one system. It is often referred to as the emotional nervous system. It is not only responsible for our emotional lives, but also our higher mental functions, such as learning and formation of memories. The limbic system explains why some things seem so pleasurable to us, such as eating and why some medical conditions are caused by mental stress, such as high blood pressure. There are two significant structures within the limbic system and several smaller structures that are important as well. They are:

(i) The hippocampus
(ii) The amygdala
(iii) The thalamus
(iv) The hypothalamus
(v) The fornix and parahippocampus
(vi) The cingulate gyrus

Peripheral Nervous System

The peripheral nervous system includes 12 cranial nerves 31 pairs of spinal nerves. It can be sub-divided into the somatic and autonomic systems. It is a way of communication from the central nervous system to the rest of the body by nerve impulses that regulate the functions of the human body. The twelve cranial nerves are:

1. Olfactory nerve for smell
2. Optic nerve for vision
3. Oculomotor for looking around
4. Trochlear for moving eye
5. Trigeminal for feeling touch on face

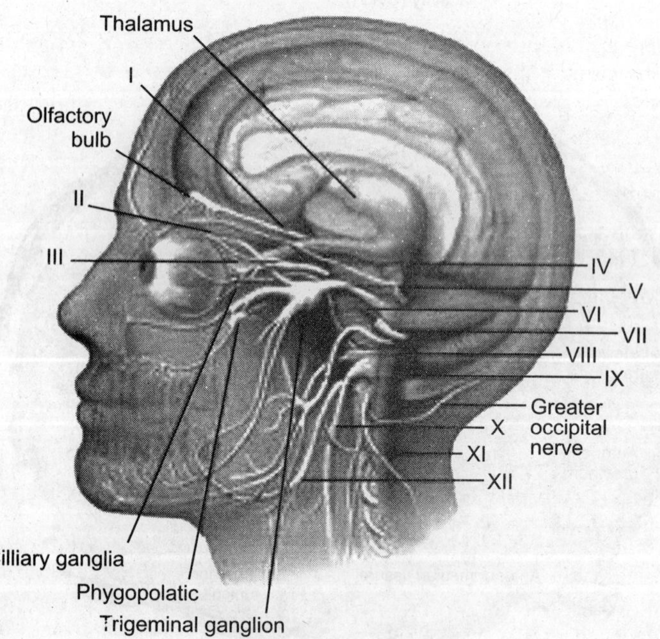

Fig. 22.6 Pair of cranial nerves

6. Abducens to move eye muscles
7. Facial to smile, wink and help us taste
8. Vestibulocochlear to help with balance, equilibrium and hearing
9. Glossopharyngeal for swallowing and gagging
10. Vagus for swallowing, talking and parasympathetic actions of digestion
11. Spinal accessory for shrugging shoulders
12. Hypoglossal for tongue more divided into different regions as muscles.

The 10 out of the 12 cranial nerves originate from the brainstem and mainly control the functions of the anatomic structures of the head with some exceptions. CN X receives visceral sensory information from the thorax and abdomen and CN XI is responsible for innervatin the sternocleidomastoid and trapezius muscles, neither of which is exclusively in the head.

Spinal nerves take their origins from the spinal cord. They control the functions of the rest of the body. In humans, there are 31 pairs of spinal nerves: 8 cervical, 12 thoracic, 5 lumbar, 5 sacral and 1 coccygeal. The naming convention for spinal nerves is to name it after the vertebra immediately above it. Thus, the fourth thoracic nerve originates just below the fourth thoracic vertebra. This convention breaks down in the cervical spine. The first spinal nerve originates above the first cervical vertebra and is called C_1. This continues down to the last cervical spinal nerve, C_8. There are only 7 cervical vertebrae and 8 cervical spinal nerves.

Lateral Cord

The lateral cord gives rise to the following nerves:

(i) The lateral pectoral nerve, C_5, C_6 and C_7 to the pectoralis major muscle or musculus pectoralis major.
(ii) The musculocutaneous nerve which innervates the biceps muscle.
(iii) The median nerve, partly. The other part comes from the medial cord.

Posterior Cord

The posterior cord gives rise to the following nerves:

(i) The upper subscapular nerve, C_7 and C_8, to the subscapularis muscle or musculus supca of the rotator cuff.
(ii) The lower subscapular nerve, C_5 and C_6, to the teres major muscle or the musculus teres major, also of the rotator cuff.
(iii) The thoracodorsal nerve, C_6, C_7 and C_8, to the latissimus dorsi muscle or musculus latissimus dorsi.
(iv) The axillary nerve, which supplies sensation to the shoulder and motor to the deltoid muscle or musculus deltoideus and the teres minor muscle or musculus teres minor.
(v) The radial nerve or nervous radialis, which innervates the triceps brachii muscle, the brachioradialis muscle or musculus brachioradialis the extensor muscles of the fingers and wrist (extensor carpi radialis muscle) and the extensor and abductor muscles of the thumb.

Medial Cord

The medial cord gives rise to the following nerves:

(i) The median pectoral nerve, C_8 and T_1, to the pectoralis muscle.

(ii) The medial brachial cutaneous nerve, T_1.

(iii) The medial antebrachial cutaneous nerve, C_8 and T_1.

(iv) The median nerve, partly. The other part comes from the lateral cord. C_7, C_8 and T_1 nerve roots. The first branch of the median nerve is to the pronator teres muscle, then the flexor carpiradialis, the palmaris longus and the flexor digitorum superficialis. The median nerve provides sensation to the anterior palm, the anterior thumb, index finger and middle finger. It is the nerve compressed in carpal tunnel syndrome.

(v) The ulnar nerve originates in nerve roots C_7, C_8 and T_1. It provides sensation to the ring and pinky fingers. It innervates the flexor carpi ulnaris muscle, the flexor digitorum profundus muscle to the ring and pinky fingers and the intrinsic muscles of the hand (the interosseous muscle, the lumbrical muscles and the flexor pollicus brevis muscle). This nerve transverses a groove on the elbow called the cubital tunnel, also known as the funny bone. Striking the nerve at this point produces an unpleasant sensation in the ring and little fingers.

Autonomic System

The autonomic system deals with the visceral organs, like the heart, stomach, gland and the intestine. It regulates systems that are unconsciously carried out to keep our body alive and well, such as breathing, digestion (peristalsis) and regulation of the heartbeat. The autonomic system consists of the sympathetic and the parasympathetic divisions. Both divisions work without conscious effort and they have similar nerve pathways, but the sympathetic and parasympathetic systems generally have opposite effects on target tissues (they are antagonistic). By controlling the relative input from each division, the autonomic system regulates many aspects of homeostasis. One of the main nerves for the parasympathetic autonomic system is cranial nerve X, the vagus nerve.

Sympathetic System

The sympathetic nervous system activates what is often termed the fight or flight response, as it is most active under sudden stressful circumstances (such as being attacked). This response is also known as sympathetico-adrenal response of the body, as the pre-ganglionic sympathetic fibres that end in the adrenal medulla (but also all other sympathetic fibres) secrete acetylcholine, which activates the secretion of adrenaline (epinephrine) and to a lesser extent noradrenaline (norepinephrine) from it. Therefore, this response that acts primarily on the cardiovascular system is mediated directly *via* impulses transmitted through the sympathetic nervous system and indirectly *via* catecholamines secreted from the adrenal medulla.

Some evolutionary theorists suggest that the sympathetic nervous system operated in early organisms to maintain survival (Origins of consciousness, Robert Ornstein, *et.al.*), as the sympathetic nervous system is responsible for priming the body for action. One example of this priming is in the moments before walking, in which sympathetic outflow spontaneously increases in preparation for action.

Organization

Sympathetic nerves originate inside the vertebral column, toward the middle of the spinal cord in the intermediolateral cell column (or lateral horn), beginning at the first thoracic segment of the spinal cord and extending into the second or third lumbar segments. Because its cells begin in the thoracic and lumbar regions of the spinal cord, the SNS is said to have a thoracolumbar outflow. Axons of these nerves leave the spinal cord in the ventral branches (rami) of the spinal nerves and then separate out as 'white rami' (so called from the shiny white sheaths of myelin around each axon) which connect to two chain ganglia extending alongside the vertebral column on the left and right. These elongated ganglia are also known as paravertebral ganglia or sympathetic trunks. In these hubs, connections (synapses) are made which then distribute the nerves to major organs, glands and other parts of the body. In order to reach the target organs and glands, the axons must travel long distances in the body and to accomplish this, many axons link up with the axon of a second cell. The ends of the axons do not make direct contact, but rather link across a space, the synapse. In the SNS and other components of the peripheral nervous system, these synapses are made at sites called **ganglia.** The cell that sends its fibre is called a preganglionic cell, while the cell whose fibre leaves the ganglion is called a postganglionic cell. As mentioned previously, the preganglionic cells of the SNS are located between the first thoracic segment and the second or third lumbar segments of the spinal cord. Postganglionic cells have their cell bodies in the ganglia and send their axons to target organs or glands.

The ganglia include not just the sympathetic trunks but also the superior cervical ganglion (which sends sympathetic nerve fibres to the head) and the celiac and mesenteric ganglia (which send sympathetic fibres to the gut).

Information Transmission

Messages travel through the SNS in a bidirectional flow. Efferent messages can trigger changes in different parts of the body simultaneously. For example, the sympathetic nervous system can accelerate heart rate, widen bronchial passages, decrease motility (movement) of the large intestine, constrict blood vessels; increase peristalsis in the oesophagus, cause pupil dilation, piloerection (goose bumps) and perspiration (sweating) and raise blood pressure. Affere messages carry sensations such as heat, cold or pain. The first synapse (in the sympathetic chain) is mediated by nicotinic receptors physiologically activated by acetylcholine and the target synapse is mediated by adrenergic receptors physiologically activated by either noradrenaline or adrenaline. An exception is with sweat glands which receive sympathetic innervation but have muscarinic acetylcholine receptors which are normally characteristic of PNS. Another exception is with certain deep muscle blood vessels, which have acetylcholine receptors and which dilate (rather than constrict) with an increase in sympathetic tone. The sympathetic system cell bodies are located on the spinal cord excluding the cranial and sacral regions. The preganglionic neurons exit from the vertebral column and synapse with the postganglionic nerons in the sympathetic trunk.

Parasympathetic Nervous System

The parasympathetic nervous system is one of three divisions of the autonomic nervous system. Sometimes called the rest and digest system, the parasympathetic system conserves energy as it slows the heart rate, increases intestinal and gland activity and relaxes sphincter muscles in the gastrointestinal tract.

Parasympathetic nervous system is composed of

(i) **Preganglionic parasympathetic fibres** These are long sized axons of neurons present in the midbrain, brainstem and lateral funiculus of sacral part of spinal cord. These come out either through some cranial nerves like oculomotor (III), facial (VII), glossopharyngeal (IX) and vagus (X) or (II), (III) and (IV) sacral spinal nerves, so these form **cranio-sacral outflow.** These form synapses with neurons of the parasympathetic ganglia.

(ii) **Postganglionic parasympathetic fibres** These are small sized axons of neurons of para sympathetic ganglia and supply smooth muscles and glands of visceral organs. These form a network in the wall of the visceral organs, called **aurebach plexus.** These have limited effect.

Postganglionic parasympathetic fibres release acetylcholine at their nerve endings, so these are called **cholinergic nerve fibres.** It involves conservation of energy and brings about relaxation, comfort, pleasure, etc., at the time of rest.

(iii) **Parasympathetic ganglia** These are present either near or inside the visceral organs. Each is a group of neurons. These are isolated ganglia and are not interlinked to form a chain.

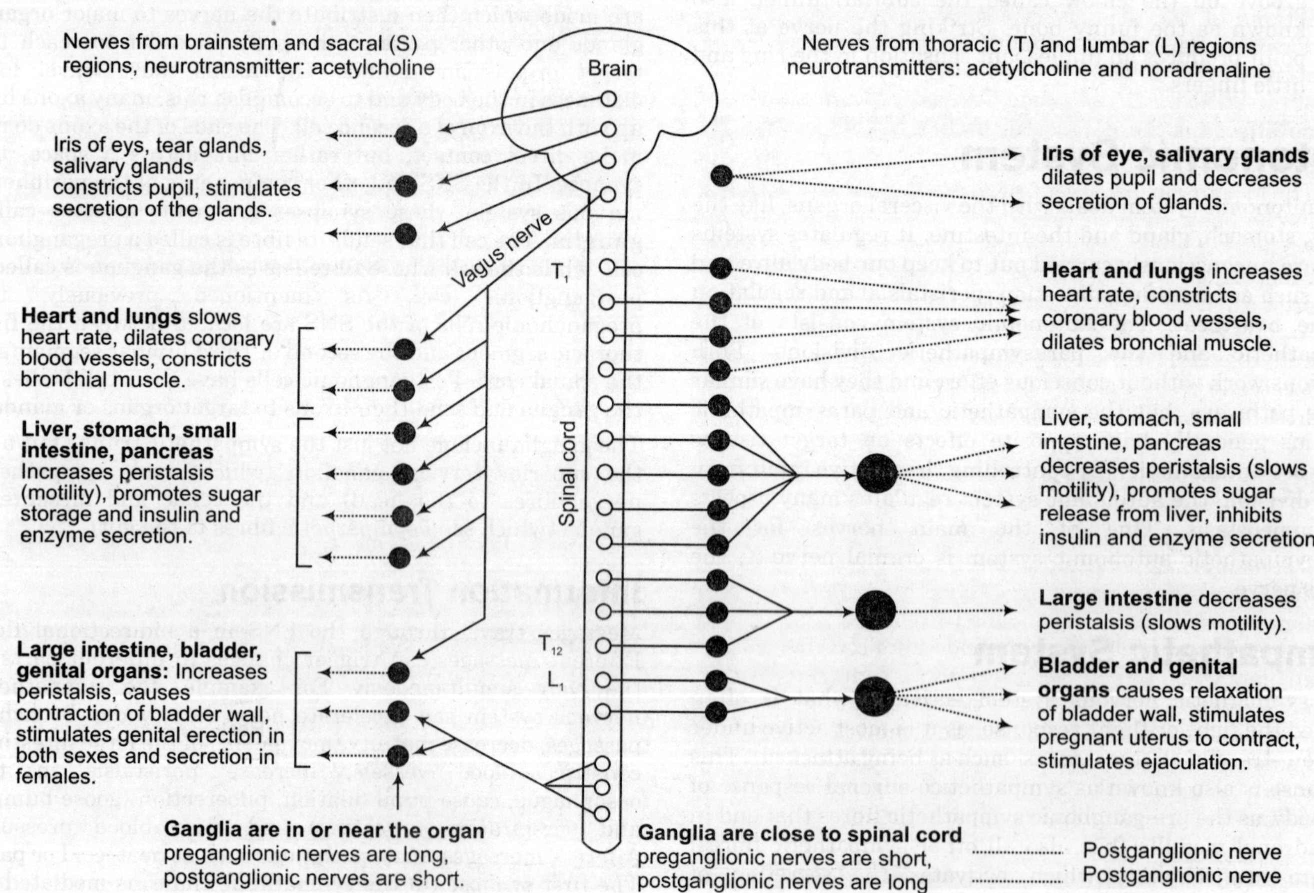

Fig. 22.7 Division of autonomic nervous system

Relationship to Sympathetic

While an oversimplification, it is said that the parasympathetic system acts in a reciprocal manner to the effects of the sympathetic nervous system; in fact, in some tissues innervated by both systems, the effects are synergistic.

Receptors

The parasympathetic nervous system uses only acetylcholine (ACh) as its neurotransmitter. The ACh acts on two types of receptors, the muscarinic and nicotinic cholinergic receptors. Most transmissions occur in two stages: When stimulated, the preganglionic nerve releases ACh at the ganglion, which acts on nicotinic receptors of the postganglionic nerve. The postganglionic nerve then releases ACh to stimulate the muscarinic receptors of the target organ. The three main types of muscarinic receptors that are well characterized are:

(a) The M_1 muscarinic receptors are located in the neural system.

(b) The M_2 muscarinic receptors are located in the heart and act to bring the heart back to normal after the actions of the sympathetic nervous system: slowing down the heart rate, reducing contractile forces of the atrial cardiac muscle and reducing conduction velocity of the atrioventricular node (AV node). Note, they have no effect on the contractile forces of the ventricular muscle.

(c) The M_3 muscarinic receptors are located at many places in the body, such as the smooth muscles of the blood vessels, as well as the lungs, which means that they cause vasoconstriction and bronchoconstriction. They are also in the smooth muscles of the Gastrointestinal Tract (GIT), which help in increasing intestinal motility and dilating sphincters. The M_3 receptors are also located in many glands that help to stimulate secretion in salivary glands and other glands of the body.

Action Potential

Action potential is a short-lasting event in which the electrical membrane potential of a cell rapidly rises and falls, following a consistent trajectory. Action potentials occur in several types of animal cells, called excitable cells, which include neurons, muscle cells and endocrine cells, as well as in some plant cells. In neurons, they play a central role in cell-to-cell communication. Action potentials in neurons are also known as 'nerve impulses' and the temporal sequence of action potentials generated by a neuron is called its 'spike train'. A neuron that emits an action potential is often said to 'fire'.

Action potentials are generated by special types of voltage-gated ion channels embedded in a **cell's plasma membrane.** These channels are shut when the membrane potential is near the resting potential of the cell, but they rapidly begin to open if the membrane potential increases to a precisely defined threshold value. When the channels open, they allow an inward flow of sodium ions, which changes the electrochemical gradient, which in turn produces a further rise in the membrane potential. This then causes more channels to open, producing a greater electric current and so on. The process proceeds explosively until all of the available ion channels are open, resulting in a large upswing in the membrane potential. The rapid influx of sodium ions causes the polarity of the plasma membrane to reverse and the ion channels then rapidly inactivate. As the sodium channels close, sodium ions can no longer enter the neuron and they are actively transported out of the plasma membrane. Potassium channels are then activated and there is an outward current of potassium ions, returning the electrochemical gradient to the resting state. After an action potential has occurred, there is a transient negative shift, called the after hyperpolarization (overshoat caused by a delay in closing the K^+ channels) or refractory period (Na^+ channels inactivated and neuron cannot respond) due to additional potassium currents. This is the mechanism which prevents an action potential traveling back the way it just came.

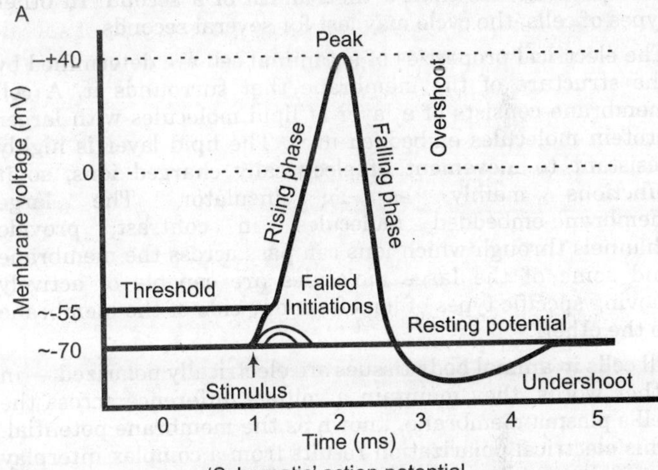

'Schematic' action potential

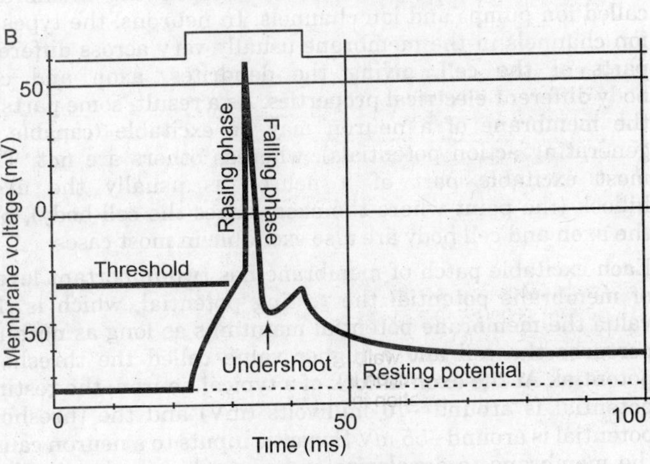

'Real' action potential

Fig. 22.8 Action potential

In animal cells, there are two primary types of action potentials, one type generated by voltage-gated sodium channels, the other by voltage-gated calcium channels. Sodium-based action potentials usually last for less than one millisecond, whereas calcium-based action potentials may last for 100 milliseconds or longer. In some types of neurons, slow calcium spikes provide the driving force for a long burst of rapidly-emitted sodium spikes. In cardiac muscle cells, on the other hand, an initial fast sodium spike provides a 'primer' to provoke the rapid onset of a calcium spike, which then produces muscle contraction.

A typical voltage for an animal cell is –70mV approximately one fifteenth of a volt. Because cells are so small voltages of this magnitude give rise to very strong electric forces within the cell membrane.

In the majority of cells, the voltage changes very little over time. There are some types of cells, however, that are electrically active in the sense that their voltages fluctuate. In some of these, the voltages sometimes show very rapid up-and-down fluctuations that have a stereo typed form: These up-and-down cycles are known as action potentials. The durations of action potentials vary across a wide range. In brain cells of animals, the entire up-and-down cycle may take place in less than a thousandth of a second. In other types of cells, the cycle may last for several seconds.

The electrical properties of an animal cell are determined by the structure of the membrane that surrounds it. A cell membrane consists of a layer of lipid molecules with larger protein molecules embedded in it. The lipid layer is highly resistant to movement of electrically charged ions, so it functions mainly as an insulator. The large membrane-embedded molecules, in contrast, provide channels through which ions can pass across the membrane and some of the large molecules are capable of actively moving specific types of ions from one side of the membrane to the other.

All cells in animal body tissues are electrically polarized — in other words, they maintain a voltage difference across the cell's plasma membrane, known as the membrane potential. This electrical polarization results from a complex interplay between protein structures embedded in the membrane called ion pumps and ion channels. In neurons, the types of ion channels in the membrane usually vary across different parts of the cell, giving the dendrites, axon and cell body different electrical properties. As a result, some parts of the membrane of a neuron may be excitable (capable of generating action potentials), whereas others are not. The most excitable part of a neuron is usually the axon hillock (the point where the axon leaves the cell body), but the axon and cell body are also excitable in most cases.

Each excitable patch of membrane has two important levels of membrane potential the resting potential, which is the value the membrane potential maintains as long as nothing perturbs the cell and a higher value called the threshold potential. At the axon hillock of a typical neuron, the resting potential is around –70 millivolts (mV) and the threshold potential is around –55 mV. Synaptic inputs to a neuron cause the membrane to depolarize or hyperpolarize, that is, they cause the membrane potential to rise or fall. Action potentials are triggered when enough depolarization accumulates to bring the membrane potential up to threshold. When an action potential is triggered, the membrane potential abruptly shoots upward, often reaching as high as +100 mV, then equally abruptly shoots back downward, often ending below the resting level, where it remains for some period of time. The shape of the action potential is stereotyped; that is, the rise and fall usually have approximately the same amplitude and time course for all action potentials in a given cell exceptions are discussed later in the article. In most neurons, the entire process takes place in less than a thousandth of a second. Many types of neurons emit action potentials constantly at rates of up to 10-100 per second; some types, however, are much quieter and may go for minutes or longer without emitting any action potentials.

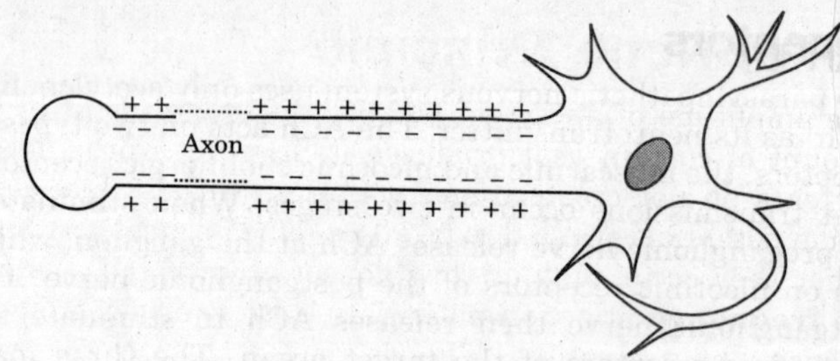

Fig. 22.9 The resting neuron

When a neuron is not transmitting an impulse, the inside of the cell is negatively charged compared with the outside of the cell. The cell is said to be electrically polarized, because the inside and the outside of the cell are oppositely charged. The potential difference (voltage) across the membrane is called the resting potential and for most nerve cells is about –70 mV. Nerve transmission is possible because this membrane potential exists.

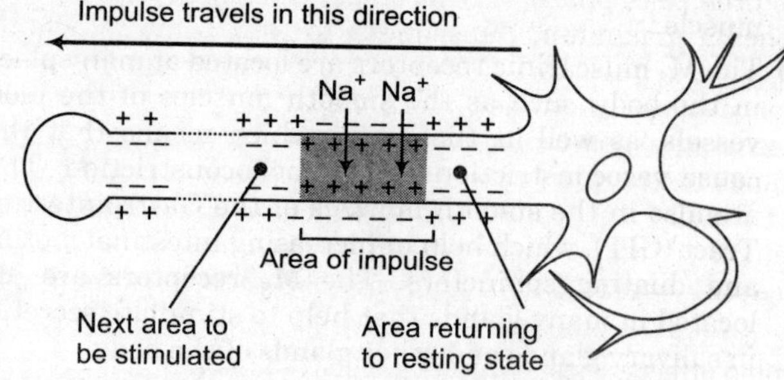

Fig. 22.10 The nerve impulse

When a neuron is stimulated, the distribution of charges on each side of the membrane changes. For a millisecond, the charges reverse. This process, called **depolarization,** causes a burst of electrical activity to pass along the axon of the neuron. As the charge reversal reaches one region, local currents depolarize the next region. In this way the impulse spreads along the axon. An impulse that spreads this way is called an **action potential.**

Although action potentials are generated locally on patches of excitable membrane, the resulting currents can trigger action potentials on neighbouring stretches of membrane, precipitating a domino-like propagation. In contrast to passive spread of electric potentials (electrotonic potential), action potentials are generated a new along excitable stretches of membrane and propagate without decay. Myelinated sections of axons are not excitable and do not produce action potentials and the signal is propagated passively as electrotonic potential. Regularly spaced unmyelinated patches, called the nodes of Ranvier, generate action potentials to boost the signal. Known as saltatory conduction, this type of signal propagation provides a favourable trade off of signal velocity and axon diameter. Depolarization of axon terminals, in general, triggers the release of neurotransmitter into the synaptic cleft. In addition, back propagating action potentials have been recorded in the dendrites of pyramidal neurons, which are ubiquitous in the neocortex. These are thought to have a role inspike-timing-dependent plasticity.

'All or None' Principle

The amplitude of an action potential is independent of the amount of current that produced it. In other words, larger currents do not create larger action potentials. Therefore, action potentials are said to be all-or-none (or boolean), since either they occur fully or they do not occur at all. Instead, the **frequency** of action potentials is what encodes for the intensity of a stimulus. This is in contrast to **receptor potentials,** whose amplitudes are dependent on the intensity of a stimulus.

Phases

The course of the action potential can be divided into five parts—the rising phase, the peak phase, the falling phase, the undershoot phase and the refractory period. During the rising phase the membrane potential depolarizes (becomes more positive). The point at which depolarization stops is called the peak phase. At this stage, the membrane potential reaches a maximum. Subsequent to this, there is a falling phase. During this stage the membrane potential hyperpolarizes (becomes more negative). The undershoot phase is the point during which the membrane potential becomes temporarily more negatively charged than when at rest. Finally, the time during which a subsequent action potential is impossible or difficult to fire is called the **refractory period,** which may overlap with the other phases.

The course of the action potential is determined by two coupled effects. First, voltage-sensitive ion channels open and close in response to changes in the membrane voltage *Vm*. This changes the membrane's permeability to those ions. Second, according to the Goldman equation, this change in permeability changes in the equilibrium potential *Em* and thus, the membrane voltage *Vm*. Thus, the membrane potential affects the permeability, which then further affects the membrane potential. This sets up the possibility for positive feedback, which is a key part of the rising phase of the action potential A complicating factor is that a single ion channel may have multiple internal 'gates' that respond to changes in *Vm* in opposite ways or at different rates. For example, although raising *Vm* opens most gates in the voltage-sensitive sodium channel, it also closes the channel's 'inactivation gate', albeit more slowly. Hence, when *Vm* is raised suddenly, the sodium channels open initially, but then close due to the slower inactivation.

Myelin and Saltatory Conduction

In order to enable fast and efficient transduction of electrical signals in the nervous system, certain neuronal axons are covered with myelin sheaths. Myelin is a multilamellar membrane that enwraps the axon in segments separated by intervals known as nodes of Ranvier, is produced by specialized cells, Schwann cells exclusively in the peripheral nervous system and by oligodendrocytes exclusively in the central nervous system. Myelin sheath reduces membrane capacitance and increases membrane resistance in the inter-node intervals, thus allowing a fast, saltatory movement of action potentials from node to node. Myelination is found mainly in vertebrates, but an analogous system has been discovered in a few invertebrates, such as some species of shrimp. Not all neurons in vertebrates are myelinated; for example, axons of the neurons comprising autonomous (vegetative) nervous system are not myelinated in general.

Myelin prevents ions from entering or leaving the axon along myelinated segments. As a general rule, myelination increases the conduction velocity of action potentials and makes them more energy-efficient. Whether saltatory or not, the mean conduction velocity of an action potential ranges from 1 m/s to over 100 m/s and in general, increases with axonal diameter.

Action potentials cannot propagate through the membrane in myelinated segments of the axon. However, the current is carried by the cytoplasm, which is sufficient to depolarize the first or second subsequent **node of Ranvier.** Instead, the ionic current from an action potential at one node of Ranvier provokes another action potential at the next node; this apparent 'hopping' of the action potential from node to node is known as **saltatory conduction.** Although the mechanism of saltatory conduction was suggested in 1925 by Ralph Lillie, the first experimental evidence for saltatory conduction came from Ichiji Tasaki and Taiji Takeuchi and from Andrew Huxley and Robert Stampfli. By contrast, in unmyelinated axons, the action potential provokes another in the membrane immediately adjacent and moves continuously down the axon like a wave.

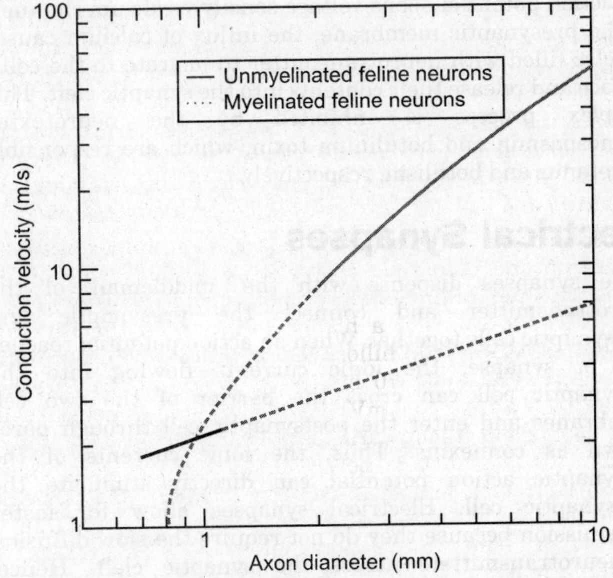

Fig. 22.11 Comparison of the conduction velocities of myelinated and unmyelinated axons in the cat

Myelin has two important advantages, fast conduction speed and energy efficiency. For axons larger than a minimum diameter (roughly 1 micrometre), myelination increases the conduction velocity of an action potential, typically tenfold. Conversely, for a given conduction velocity, myelinated fibres are smaller than their unmyelinated counterparts. For example, action potentials move at roughly the same speed (25 m/s) in a myelinated frog axon and an unmyelinated squid giant axon, but the frog axon has a roughly 30-fold smaller diameter and 1000-fold smaller cross-sectional area. Also, since the ionic currents are confined to the nodes of Ranvier, far fewer ions 'leak' across the membrane, saving metabolic energy. This saving is a significant selective advantage, since the human nervous system uses approximately 20% of the body's metabolic energy.

The length of axons myelinated segments is important to the success of saltatory conduction. They should be as long as possible to maximize the speed of conduction, but not so long that the arriving signal is too weak to provoke an action potential at the next node of Ranvier. In nature, myelinated segments are generally long enough for the passively propagated signal to travel for at least two nodes while retaining enough amplitude to fire an action potential at the second or third node. Thus, the safety factor of saltatory conduction is high, allowing transmission to bypass nodes in case of injury. However, action potentials may end prematurely in certain places where the safety factor is low, even in unmyelinated neurons; a common example is the branch point of an axon, where it divides into two axons.

Chemical Synapse

In general, action potentials that reach the synaptic knobs cause a neurotransmitter to be released into the synaptic cleft. Neurotransmitters are small molecules that may open ion channels in the postsynaptic cell; most axons have the same neurotransmitter at all of their termini. The arrival of the action potential opens voltage-sensitive calcium channels in the presynaptic membrane; the influx of calcium causes vesicles filled with neurotransmitter to migrate to the cell's surface and release their contents into the synaptic cleft. This complex process is inhibited by the neurotoxins tetanospasmin and botulinum toxin, which are responsible for tetanus and botulism, respectively.

Electrical Synapses

Some synapses dispense with the 'middleman' of the neurotransmitter and connect the presynaptic and postsynaptic cells together. When an action potential reaches such a synapse, the ionic currents flowing into the presynaptic cell can cross the barrier of the two cell membranes and enter the postsynaptic cell through pores known as connexins. Thus, the ionic currents of the presynaptic action potential can directly stimulate the postsynaptic cell. Electrical synapses allow for faster transmission because they do not require the slow diffusion of neurotransmitters across the synaptic cleft. Hence, electrical synapses are used whenever fast response and coordination of timing are crucial, as in escape reflexes, the retina of vertebrates and the heart.

Neuromuscular Junctions

A special case of a chemical synapse is the neuromuscular junction, in which the axon of a motor neuron terminates on a muscle fibre. In such cases, the released neurotransmitter is acetylcholine, which binds to the acetylcholine receptor, an integral membrane protein in the membrane (the sarcolemma) of the muscle fibre.

However, the acetylcholine does not remain bound; rather, it dissociates and is hydrolyzed by the enzyme, acetylcholinesterase, located in the synapse. This enzyme quickly reduces the stimulus to the muscle, which allows the degree and timing of muscular contraction to be regulated delicately. Some poisons inactivate acetylcholinesterase to prevent this control, such as the nerve agents sarin and tabun and the insecticides diazinon and malathion.

Neural Control of Muscle Tone

When muscles are at rest about 5% of motor units are in contraction. This partial contraction of a relaxed muscle is called **muscle tone or tonicity.** Proper control of muscle function requires not only excitation of muscle by spinal cord anterior motor neurons but also continuous feedback of sensory information from each muscle to spinal cord. The muscles and their tendons are supplied abundantly with two special type of sensory receptors. The **muscle spindles** which are distributed throughout the belly of muscles and send information to the nervous system about muscle length or rate of change of length and **Golgi tendon** organs which are located in muscle tendons and transmit information about tendon tension or rate of change of tension. The end portions of spindle fibre that do contract are excited by small gamma motor nerve fibre that originate from small type *A* gamma motor neurons in the anterior horns of spinal cord. These gamma motor nerve fibres are also called gamma efferent fibres, in contradistinction to the large α efferent fibres (type A α nerve fibres) that innervate the extrafusal skeletal muscle. The receptor portion of muscle spindle its central portion. The gamma motor nerves to the muscle spindle can be divided into two types—gamma dynamic (gamma-*d*) and gamma static (gamma-*s*). When the gamma-*d* fibres excite the nuclear bag fibres, the dynamic response of the muscle spindle becomes tremendously enhanced, whereas the static response is hardly affected conversely stimulation of gamma-*s* fibres which excite the nuclear chain fibres, enhances the static response while having little influence on the dynamic response. Whenever a muscle is stretched suddenly excitation of spindles causes reflex contraction of the large skeletal muscle fibres of the stretched muscle and also of closely allied synergistic muscles.

The Golgi tendon organ is an encapsulated sensory receptor through which muscle tendon fibres pass. About 10-15 muscle fibres are usually connected to each Golgi tendon organ and the organ is stimulated when this small bundle of muscle fibres is tensed by contracting or stretching the muscle. The major difference is excitation of Golgi tendon organ and muscle spindle is that the spindle detects muscle length and changes in muscle length while tendon organ detects muscle tension as reflected by tendon is itself. Signals from tendon organ are transmitted through large rapidly conducting type I *b* nerve fibres. These fibres transmit signals both into local areas of the cord and after synapsing in the dorsal horn of the cord, through long fibre pathways such as spinocerebellar tracts into the cerebellum and through other tracts to cerebral cortex. The local cord signal excites a single inhibitory interneuron that inhibits the anterior motor neuron. This local circuit directly inhibits the individual muscle without affecting adjacent muscles. The tendon reflex provides a negative feedback mechanisms that prevents the development of two much tension on the muscle.

Neural Control of Muscle Posture

Pressure on the footpad of a decerebrate animal causes the limb to extend against the pressure applied. This reflex is so strong that if an animal whose spinal cord has been transected for several months (*i.e.,* after the reflexes have become exaggerated) is placed on its feet, the reflex often stiffens the limbs sufficiently to support the weight of the body. This is called positive supportive reaction. When a spinal animal is laid on its side, it will make incoordinate movements trying to raise itself to the standing position called as cord righting reflex. Such a reflex demonstrates that some relatively complex reflexes associated with posture are integrated in the spinal cord. An animal with a well healed transected thoracic cord between the levels for forelimb and hind limb innervation can right itself from the lying position and even walk using its hind limbs in addition to forelimbs.

Sense Organs

Senses are the physiological methods of perception. The senses and their operation, classification and theory are overlapping topics studied by a variety of fields. Sense is a faculty by which outside stimuli are perceived.

We experience reality through our senses. A sense is a faculty by which outside stimuli are perceived. Many neurologists disagree about how many senses there actually are due to a broad interpretation of the definition of a sense. Our senses are split into two different groups. Our exteroceptors detects stimulation from the outsides of our body. For example smell, taste and equilibrium. The interoceptors receive stimulation from the inside of our bodies. For instance, blood pressure dropping, changes in the glucose and pH levels. Children are generally taught that there are five senses (sight, hearing, touch, smell and taste). However, it is generally agreed that there are atleast seven different senses in humans and a minimum of two more observed in other organisms. Sense can also differ from one person to the next.

Vision

Vision needs to have the work of both the eyes and the brain to process any information. The majority of the stimuli is done in the eyes and then the information is sent to the brain by the way of nerve impulses. Atleast one-third of the information of what the eye sees is processed in the cerebral cortex of the brain.

The human eye is a elongated ball about 1 inch (2.5 cm) in diameter and is protected by a bony socket in the skull. The eye has three layers or coats that make up the exterior wall of the eyeball, which are the sclera, choroid and retina.

Sclera

The outer layer of the eye is the sclera, which is a tough white fibrous layer that maintains, protects and supports the shape of the eye. The front of the sclera is transparent and is called the cornea. The cornea refracts light rays and acts like the outer window of the eye.

Choroid

The middle thin layer of the eye is the choroid also known as the choroidea or choroid coat, it is the vascular layer of the eye lying between the retina and the sclera. The choroid provides oxygen and nourishment to the outer layers of the retina. It also contains a non-reflective pigment that acts as a light shield and prevents light from scattering. Light enters the front of the eye through a hole in the choroid coat called the pupil. The iris contracts and dilates to compensate for the changes in light intensity. If the light is bright the iris then contracts making the pupil smaller and if the light is dim, the iris dilates making the pupil bigger. Just posterior to the iris is the lens, which is composed mainly of proteins called crystallins. The lens is attached by the zonules to the ciliary body that contains the ciliary muscles that control the shape of the lens for accommodation. Along with the ciliary body and iris, the choroid forms the uveal tract. The uvea is the middle of the three concentric layers that make up an eye. The name is possibly a reference to its almost black colour, wrinkled appearance and grape-like size and shape when stripped intact from a cadaveric eye.

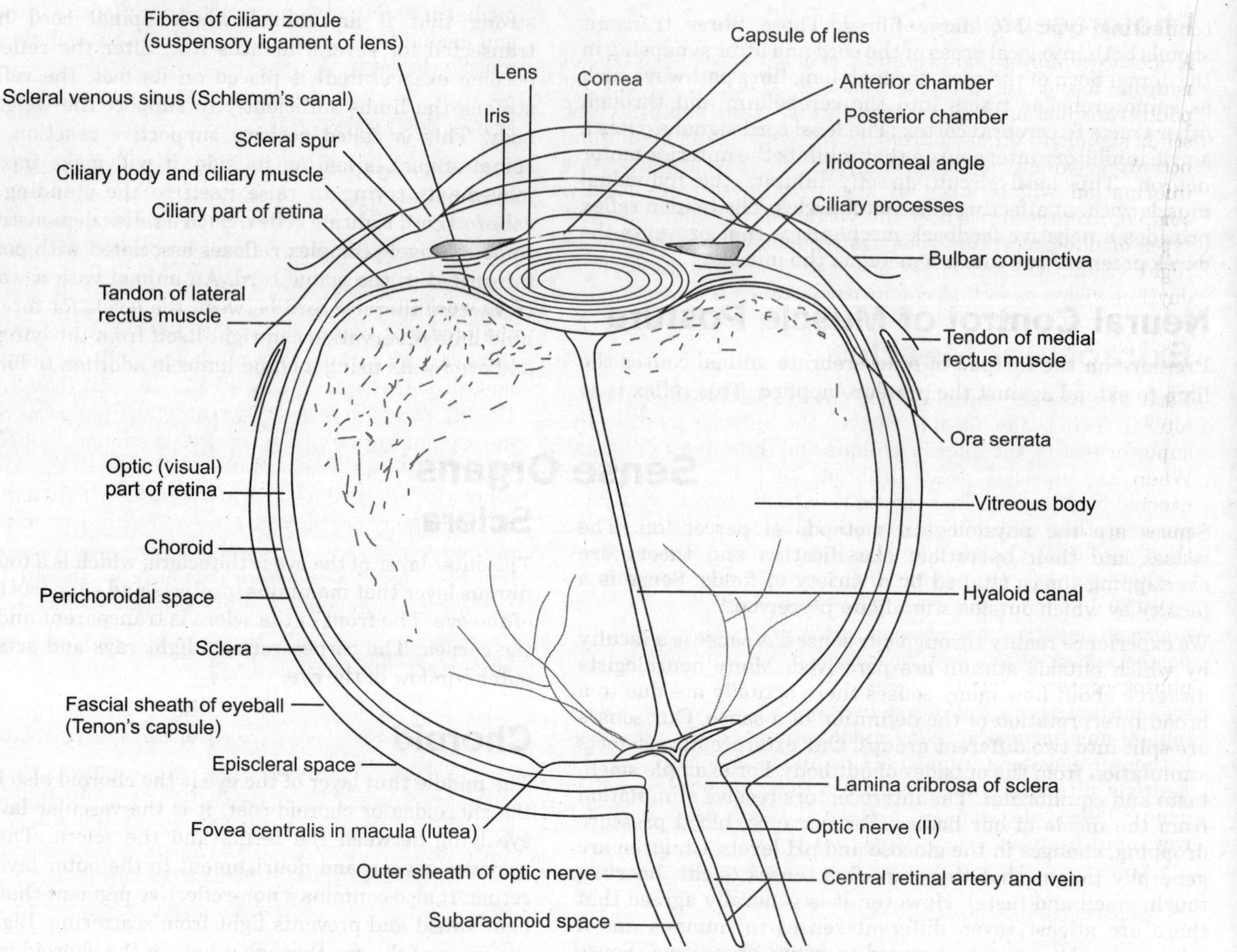

Fibres of ciliary zonule
(suspensory ligament of lens)
Capsule of lens
Lens
Cornea
Anterior chamber
Scleral venous sinus (Schlemm's canal)
Iris
Posterior chamber
Scleral spur
Iridocorneal angle
Ciliary body and ciliary muscle
Ciliary part of retina
Ciliary processes
Bulbar conjunctiva
Tandon of lateral
rectus muscle
Tendon of medial
rectus muscle
Ora serrata
Optic (visual)
part of retina
Vitreous body
Choroid
Hyaloid canal
Perichoroidal space
Sclera
Fascial sheath of eyeball
(Tenon's capsule)
Episcleral space
Lamina cribrosa of sclera
Fovea centralis in macula (lutea)
Optic nerve (II)
Outer sheath of optic nerve
Central retinal artery and vein
Subarachnoid space

Fig. 22.12 Cross section of human eye

Retina

The third or the innermost layer of the eye is call the retina. In adult humans, the entire retina is 72% of a sphere about 22 mm in diameter. The retina lays over the back two thirds of the choroid coat, which is located in the posterior compartment. The compartment is filled with vitreous humour which is a clear, gelatinous material. Within the retina there are cells called rod cells and cone cells also known as photoreceptors. The rod cells are very sensitive to light and do not see colour, that is why when we are in a darkened room we see only shades of gray. The cone cells are sensitive to different wavelengths of light and that is how we are able to tell different colours. It is a lack of cones sensitive to red, blue or green light that causes individuals to have deficiencies in colour vision or various kinds of colour blindness. At the center of the retina is the optic disc, sometimes known as 'the blind spot' because it lacks photoreceptors. It is where the optic nerve leaves the eye and takes the nerve impulses to the brain. The cornea and the lens of the eye focuses the light onto a small area of the retina called the fovea centralis where the cone cells are densely packed. The fovea is a pit that has the highest visual acuity and is responsible for our sharp central vision - there are no rods in the fovea.

Direction of light
Sclera
Choroid
Pigment layer
Rod
Cone
Horizontal cell
Bipolar cell
Amacrine cell
Ganglion cell
Optic nerve fibres

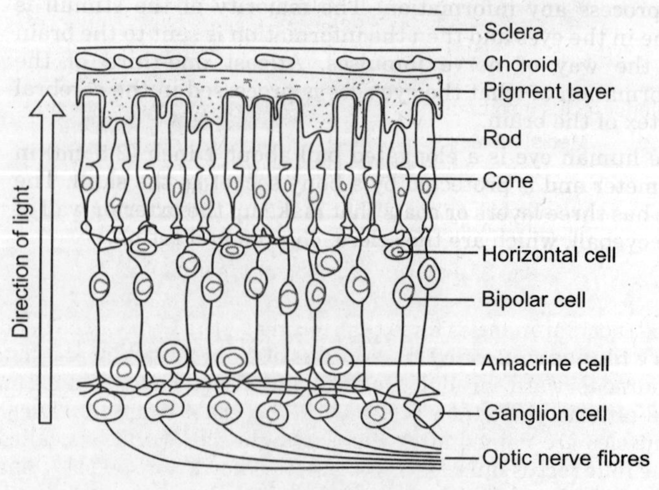

Fig. 22.13 Retina

Photoreceptors

A photoreceptor or photoreceptor, cell, is a specialized type of neuron found in the eye's retina that is capable of phototransduction. More specifically, the photoreceptor sends signals to other neurons by a change in its membrane potential when it absorbs photons. Eventually, this information will be used by the visual system to form a complete representation of the visual world. There are two types of photoreceptors rods are responsible for scotopic or night vision, whereas cones are responsible for photopic or daytime vision as well as colour perception.

Extraocular Muscles

Each eye has six muscles that control its movements the lateral rectus, the medial rectus, the inferior rectus, the superior rectus, the inferior oblique and the superior oblique. When the muscles exert different tensions, a torque is exerted on the globe that causes it to turn. This is an almost pure rotation, with only about one millimeter of translation thus, the eye can be considered as undergoing rotations about a single point in the center of the eye. Five of the retina's simplified axial organization. The retina is a stack of several neuronal layers. Light is concentrated from the eye and passes across these layers (from left to right) to hit the photoreceptors (right layer). This elicits chemical transformation mediating a propagation of signal to the bipolar and horizontal cells (middle yellow layer). The signal is then propagated to the amacrine and ganglion cells. These neurons ultimately may produce action potentials on their axons. This spatiotemporal pattern of spikes determines the raw input from the eyes to the brain.

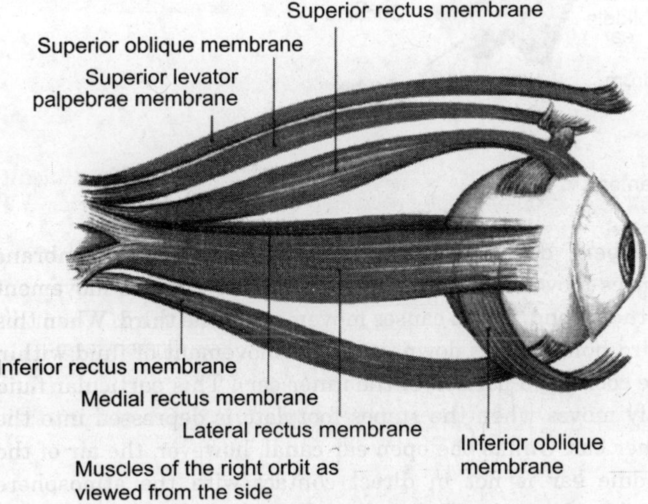

Fig. 22.14 Representation of eye muscles

Extraocular muscles have their origin in the back of the orbit in a fibrous ring called the annulus of zinn. Four of these then course forward through the orbit and insert onto the globe on its anterior half (*i.e.*, in front of the eye's equator). These muscles are named after their straight paths and are called the four rectus muscles or four recti. They insert on the globe at 12, 3, 6 and 9 o'clock and are called the superior, lateral, inferior and medial rectus muscles (note that lateral and medial are relative to the subject, with lateral toward the side and medial toward the midline, thus the medial rectus is the muscle closest to the nose).

Eye Movement

The visual system in the brain is too slow to process that information if the images are slipping across the retina at more than a few degrees per second, thus for humans to be able to see while moving, the brain must compensate for the motion of the head by turning the eyes. To get a clear view of the world, the brain must turn the eyes so that the image of the object of regard falls on the fovea. Eye movements are thus very important for visual perception and any failure to make them correctly can lead to serious visual disabilities. Having two eyes is an added complication, because the brain must point both of them accurately enough that the object of regard falls on corresponding points of the two retinas, otherwise, double vision would occur. The movements of different body parts are controlled by striated muscles acting around joints. The movements of the eye are no exception, but they have special advantages not shared by skeletal muscles and joints and so are considerably different.

Vision Process

(i) The light rays enter the eye through the cornea (transparent front portion of eye to focus the light rays).

(ii) Then, light rays move through the pupil, which is surrounded by iris to keep out extra light.

(iii) Then, light rays move through the crystalline lens (clear lens to further focus the light rays).

(iv) Then, light rays move through the vitreous humour (clear jelly like substance).

(v) Then, light rays fall on the retina, which processes and converts incident light to neuron signals using special pigments in rod and cone cells.

(vi) These neuron signals are transmitted through the optic nerve.

(vii) Then, the neuron signals move through the visual pathway-optic nerve > optic chiasm > optic tract > optic radiations > cortex.

(viii) Then, the neuron signals reach the occipital (visual) cortex and its radiations for the brain's processing.

(ix) The visual cortex interprets the signals as images and along with other parts of the brain, interprets the images to extract form, meaning, memory and context of the images.

Depth Perception

Depth perception is the visual ability to perceive the world in three dimensions. It is a trait common to many higher animals. Depth perception allows the beholder to accurately gauge the distance to an object. Depth perception is often confused with binocular vision, also known as **stereopsis.** Depth perception does rely on binocular vision, but it also uses many other monocular cues.

Hearing

The ear is the sense organ that detects sound and plays a major role in the sense of balance and body position. It is also a device used for collecting and funneling sound waves recieved by the ear. The sensory receptors for both hearing and equilibrium are found in the inner ear, consisting of hair cells that have stereocilia (long mircovilli). The stereocilia are extremely sensitive to mechanical stimulations, which are known as **mechanoreceptors.**

Anatomy of the Ear

The ear has three divisions—the outer ear, middle ear and the inner ear.

Outer Ear

(Auricle, Ear Canal, Surface of Ear Drum)

The outer ear is the most external portion of the ear. The outer ear includes the pinna (auricle), the ear canal and the very most superficial layer of the ear drum (the tympanic membrane). Although the word 'ear' may properly refer to the pinna (the flesh covered cartilage appendage on either side of the head), this portion of the ear is not vital for hearing. The complicated design of the human outer ear does help capture sound, but the most important functional aspect of the human outer ear is the ear canal itself. This outer ear canal skin is applied to cartilage, the thinner skin of the deep canal lies on the bone of the skull. If the ear canal is not open, hearing will be dampened. Ear wax (medical name - cerumen) is produced by glands in the skin of the outer portion of the ear canal. Only the thicker cerumen-producing ear canal skin has hairs. The outer ear ends at the most superficial layer of the tympanic membrane. The tympanic membrane is commonly called the **ear drum.**

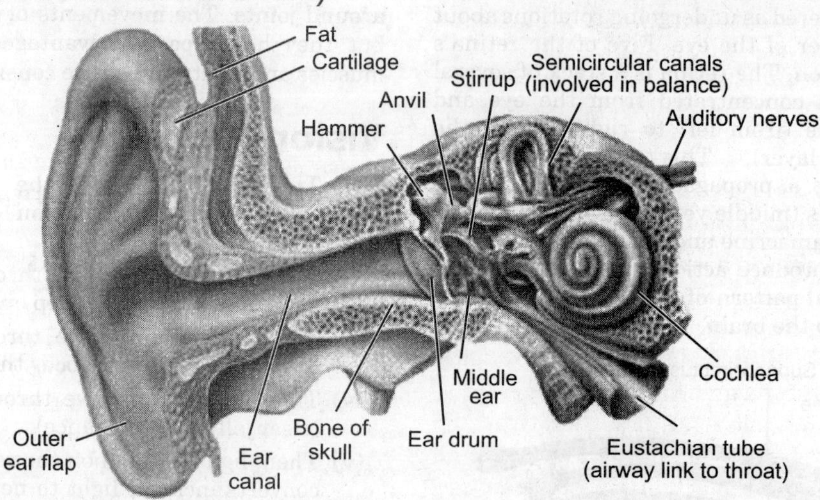

Fig. 22.15 Human ear

Middle Ear

(Air Filled Cavity Behind the Ear Drum, Includes most of the Ear Drum and Ear Bones)

The middle ear includes most of the ear drum (tympanic membrane) and the three ear bones ossicles, malleus (or hammer), incus (or anvil) and stapes (or stirrup). The opening of the Eustachian tube is also within the middle ear. The malleus has a long process (the handle) that is attached to the mobile portion of the ear drum. The incus is the bridge between the malleus and stapes. The stapes is the smallest named bone in the human body. The stapes transfers the vibrations of the incus to the oval window, a portion of the inner ear to which it is connected. It is the final bone in the chain to transfer vibrations from the ear drum to the inner ear. The arrangement of these three bones is a sort of Rube Goldberg device, movement of the tympanic membrane causes movement of the first bone, which causes movement of the second, which causes movement of the third. When this third bone pushes down, it causes movement of fluid within the cochlea (a portion of the inner ear). This particular fluid only moves when the stapes footplate is depressed into the inner ear. Unlike the open ear canal, however, the air of the middle ear is not in direct contact with the atmosphere outside the body. The Eustachian tube connects from the chamber of the middle ear to the back of the pharynx. The middle ear in humans is very much like a specialized paranasal sinus, called the tympanic cavity, it, like the paranasal sinuses, is a hollow mucosa lined cavity in the skull that is ventilated through the nose. The mastoid portion of the temporal bone, which can be felt as a bump in the skull behind the pinna, also contains air, which ventilates through the middle ear.

Inner Ear (Cochlea, Vestibule and Semi-Circular Canals)

The inner ear includes both the organ of hearing (the cochlea) and a sense organ that is attuned to the effects of both gravity and motion labyrinth or vestibular apparatus. The balance portion of the inner ear consists of three semi-circular canals and the vestibule. The inner ear is encased in the hardest bone of the body. Within this ivory hard bone, there are fluid-filled hollows. Within the cochlea are three fluid filled spaces: the tympanic canal, the vestibular canal and the middle canal. The eighth cranial nerve comes from the brain stem to enter the inner ear. When sound strikes the ear drum, the movement is transferred to the footplate of the stapes, which presses into one of the fluid-filled ducts of the cochlea. The hair cells in the organ of Corti are tuned to certain sound frequencies, being responsive to high frequencies near the oval window and to low frequencies near the apex of the cochlea.

The fluid inside this duct is moved, flowing against the receptor cells of the organ of Corti, which fire. These stimulate the spiral ganglion, which sends information through the auditory portion of the eighth cranial nerve to the brain.

Hair Cell

Hair cells are columnar cells, each with a bundle of 100-200 specialized cilia at the top, for which they are named. These cilia are the mechanosensors for hearing. Lightly resting a top the longest cilia is the tectorial membrane, which moves back and forth with each cycle of sound, tilting the cilia and allowing electric current into the hair cell. Hair cells, like the photoreceptors of the eye, show a graded response, instead of the spikes typical of other neurons. One may ask how such a wiggle of a hair bundle triggers a difference in membrane potential. Special hair cells are the actual sensory receptors which will fire off action potentials when they are disturbed. Immediately over the hair cells of the organ of Corti is an overhanging 'tectorial membrane.' When the bones of the middle ear vibrate the oval window, these vibrations are transmitted to the fluid within the cochlea and eventually cause the round window on the cochlea to bulge outward. These vibrations disturb the membrane on which the organ of Corti is located, causing the hair cells to 'rub' against the overhanging tectorial membrane. The disturbed hair cells will then fire action potentials. The current model is that cilia are attached to one another by 'tip links', structures which link the tips of one cilium to another. Stretching and compressing the tip links may open an ion channel and produce the receptor potential in the hair cell. These graded potentials are not bound by the 'all or none' properties of an action potential. There are far fewer hair cells than afferent nerve fibres in the cochlea. The nerve that innervates the cochlea is the vestibulocochlear nerve or cranial nerve number VIII. Neuronal dendrites innervate cochlear hair cells. The neurotransmitter itself is thought to be glutamate. At the presynaptic juncture, there is a distinct 'presynaptic dense body' or ribbon. This dense body is surrounded by synaptic vesicles and is thought to aid in the fast release of neurotransmitter. Efferent projections from the brain to the cochlea also play a role in the perception of sound. Efferent synapses occur on outer hair cells and on afferent dendrites under inner hair cells.

Process of Hearing

Detection of sound motion is associated with the right posterior superior temporal gyrus. The superior temporal gyrus contains several important structures of the brain, including marking the location of the primary auditory cortex, the cortical region responsible for the sensation of sound. The primary auditory area of the cerebrum and processes the basic characteristics of sound such as pitch and rhythm and is located within the temporal lobe of the brain, in an area called the Wernicke's area. This area, near the lateral cerebral sulcus, is an important region for the processing of acoustic energy so that it can be distinguished as speech, music or noise. It also interprets words that are heard into an associated thought pattern of understanding. The gnostic area of the cerebrum, helps to integrate all incoming sense patterns so that a common thought can be formed (correlated) using all arriving sensory information.

Localization of Sound by Humans

Humans are normally able to hear a variety of sound frequencies, from about 20Hz to 20kHz. Our ability to estimate just where the sound is coming from, sound localization, is dependent on both hearing ability of each of the two ears and the exact quality of the sound. Since, each ear lies on an opposite side of the head, a sound will reach the closest ear first and its amplitide will be loudest in that ear. Much of the brain's ability to localize sound depends on interaural (between ears) intensity differences and interaural temporal or phase differences. Two mechanisms are known to be used. Bushy neurons can resolve time differences as small as the time it takes sound to pass one ear and reach the other (10 milliseconds). For high frequencies, frequencies with a wavelength shorter than the listener's head, more sound reaches the nearer ear. Human echolocation is a technique involving echolocation used by some blind humans to navigate within their environment.

Process of Equilibrium

Equilibrioception or sense of balance is one of the physiological senses. It allows humans and animals to walk without falling. Some animals are better in this than humans, for example allowing a cat (as a quadruped using its inner ear and tail) to walk on a thin fence. All forms of equilibrioception can be described as the detection of acceleration.

It is determined by the level of fluid properly called endolymph in the labyrinth–a complex set of tubing in the inner ear. When the sense of balance is interrupted it causes dizziness, disorientation and nausea. You can temporarily disturb your sense of balance by closing your eyes and turning rapidly in circles five or six times. This starts the fluid swirling in circles inside your ear canal. When you stop turning it takes a few seconds for the fluid to lose momentum and until then the sense from your inner ear conflicts with the information coming from your vision, causing dizziness and disorientation. Most astronauts find that their sense of balance is impaired when in orbit, because there is not enough gravity to keep the ear's fluid in balance. This causes a form of motion sickness called space sickness.

Tactile Response

Touch is the first sense developed in the womb and the last sense used before death. With 50 touch receptors for every square centimeter and about 5 million sensory cells overall the skin is very sensitive and one of the largest and most complex organs in our bodies. These touch receptors are grouped by type and include mechanoreceptors (sensitive to pressure, vibration and slip), thermoreceptors (sensitive to changes in temperature) and nocioreceptors (responsible for pain).

Pacinian Corpuscles

Pacinian corpuscles detect gross pressure changes and vibrations. They are the largest of the receptors. Any deformation in the corpuscle causes action potentials to be generated, by opening pressure-sensitive sodium ion channels in the axon membrane. Pacinian corpuscles cause action potentials when the skin is rapidly indented but not when the pressure is steady, due to the layers of connective tissue that cover the nerve ending. It is thought that they respond to high velocity changes in joint position.

Meissner's Corpuscle

Meissner's corpuscles are distributed throughout the skin, but concentrated in areas especially sensitive to light touch, such as the fingertips, palms, soles, lips, tongue, face, nipples and the external skin of the male and female genitals. They are primarily located just beneath the epidermis within the dermal papillae. Any physical deformation in the Meissner's corpuscle will cause an action potential in the nerve. Since, they are rapidly adapting or phasic, the action potentials generated quickly decrease and eventually cease. If the stimulus is removed, the corpuscle regains its shape and while doing so (*i.e.,* while physically reforming) causes another volley of action potentials to be generated (this is the reason one stops 'feeling' one's clothes). This process is called **sensory adaption.** Because of their superficial location in the dermis, these corpuscles are particularly sensitive to touch and vibrations, but for the same reasons, they are limited in their detection because they can only signal that something is touching the skin. Meissner's corpuscles do not detect pain; this is signaled exclusively by free nerve endings.

Merkel's Discs

Merkel's discs are mechanoreceptors, making them sensitive to pressure and vibration. In humans, Merkel cells occur in the superficial skin layers and are found clustered beneath the ridges of the fingertips that make up fingerprints. They are somewhat rigid in structure and the fact that they are not encapsulated, causes them to have a sustained response (in the form of action potentials or spikes) to mechanical deflection of the tissue. Merkel nerve endings are extremely sensitive to tissue displacement and may respond to displacements of less than 1m. Several studies indicate that they mediate high-resolution tactile discrimination and are responsible for the ability of our fingertips to feel fine detailed surface patterns (*e.g.,* for reading Braille).

Ruffini Corpuscles

Ruffini corpuscles are thermoreceptors, aiding in the detection of temperature changes. Named after Angelo Ruffini, the Ruffini ending is a class of slowly adapting mechanoreceptor thought to exist only in the glabrous dermis and subcutaneous tissue of humans. This spindle-shaped receptor is sensitive to skin stretch and contributes to the kinesthetic sense of and control of finger position and movement.

Somatosensory System

The somatosensory system is spread through all major parts of a mammal's body (and other vertebrates). It consists both of sensory receptors and sensory (afferent) neurons in the periphery (skin, muscle and organs for example), to deeper neurones within the central nervous system.

General Somatosensory Pathway

A somatosensory pathway will typically have three long neurons primary, secondary and tertiary (or first, second and third).

(i) The **first** neuron always has its cell body in the dorsal root ganglion of the spinal nerve (if sensation is in head or neck, it will be the trigeminal nerve ganglia or the ganglia of other sensory cranial nerves).

(ii) The **second** neuron has its cell body either in the spinal cord or in the brainstem. This neuron's ascending axons will cross (decussate) to the opposite side either in the spinal cord or in the brainstem. The axons of many of these neurones terminate in the thalamus (for example the Ventral Posterior Nucleus, VPN), others terminate in the reticular system or the cerebellum.

(iii) In the case of touch and certain types of pain, the **third** neuron has its cell body in the VPN of the thalamus and ends in the postcentral gyrus of the parietal lobe.

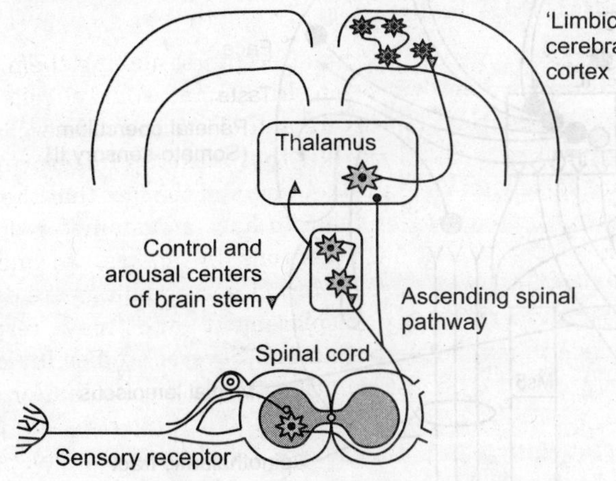

Fig. 22.16 Somatosensory pathway

Periphery

In the periphery, the somatosensory system detects various stimuli by sensory receptors, *e.g.*, by mechanoreceptors for tactile sensation and nociceptors for pain sensation. The sensory information (touch, pain, temperature, etc.) is then conveyed to the central nervous system by afferent neurones. There are a number of different types of afferent neurones which vary in their size, structure and properties. Generally, there is a correlation between the type of sensory modality detected and the type of afferent neurone involved. For example, slow, thin, unmyelinated neurones conduct pain whereas faster, thicker, myelinated neurones conduct causal touch.

Role of Spinal Cord

In the spinal cord, the somatosensory system includes ascending pathways from the body to the brain. One major target within the brain is the postcentral gyrus in the cerebral cortex. This is the target for neurons of the dorsal column medial lemniscal pathway and the ventral spinothalamic pathway. Note that many ascending somatosensory pathways include synapses in either the thalamus or the reticular formation before they reach the cortex. Other ascending pathways, particularly those involved with control of posture are projected to the cerebellum. These include the ventral and dorsal spinocerebellar tracts. Another important target for afferent somatosensory neurons which enter the spinal cord are those neurons involved with local segmental reflexes.

Role of Brain

The primary somatosensory area in the human cortex is located in the postcentral gyrus of the parietal lobe. The postcentral gyrus is the location of the primary somatosensory area, the main sensory receptive area for the sense of touch. Like other sensory areas, there is a map of sensory space called a homunculus at this location. For the primary somatosensory cortex, this is called **the sensory homunculus.** Areas of this part of the human brain map to certain areas of the body, dependent on the amount or importance of somatosensory input from that area. For example, there is a large area of cortex devoted to sensation in the hands, while the back has a much smaller area. Somatosensory information involved with proprioception and posture also targets an entirely different part of the brain the cerebellum.

Physiology

Initiation of somatosensation begins with activation of a physical 'receptor'. These somatosensory receptors tend to lie in skin organs or muscle. The structure of these receptors is broadly similar in all cases, consisting of either a 'free nerve ending' or a nerve ending embedded in a specialized capsule. They can be activated by movement (mechanoreceptor), pressure (mechanoreceptor), chemical (chemoreceptor) and/or temperature. Activation is by vibrations generated as a finger scans across a surface. This is the means by which we can sense fine textures in which the spatial scale is less than 200 μm. Such vibrations are around 250 Hz, which is the optimal frequency sensitivity of pacinian corpuscles. In each case, the general principle of activation is similar; the stimulus causes depolarization of the nerve ending and then an action potential is initiated. This action potential then (usually) travels inward towards the spinal cord.

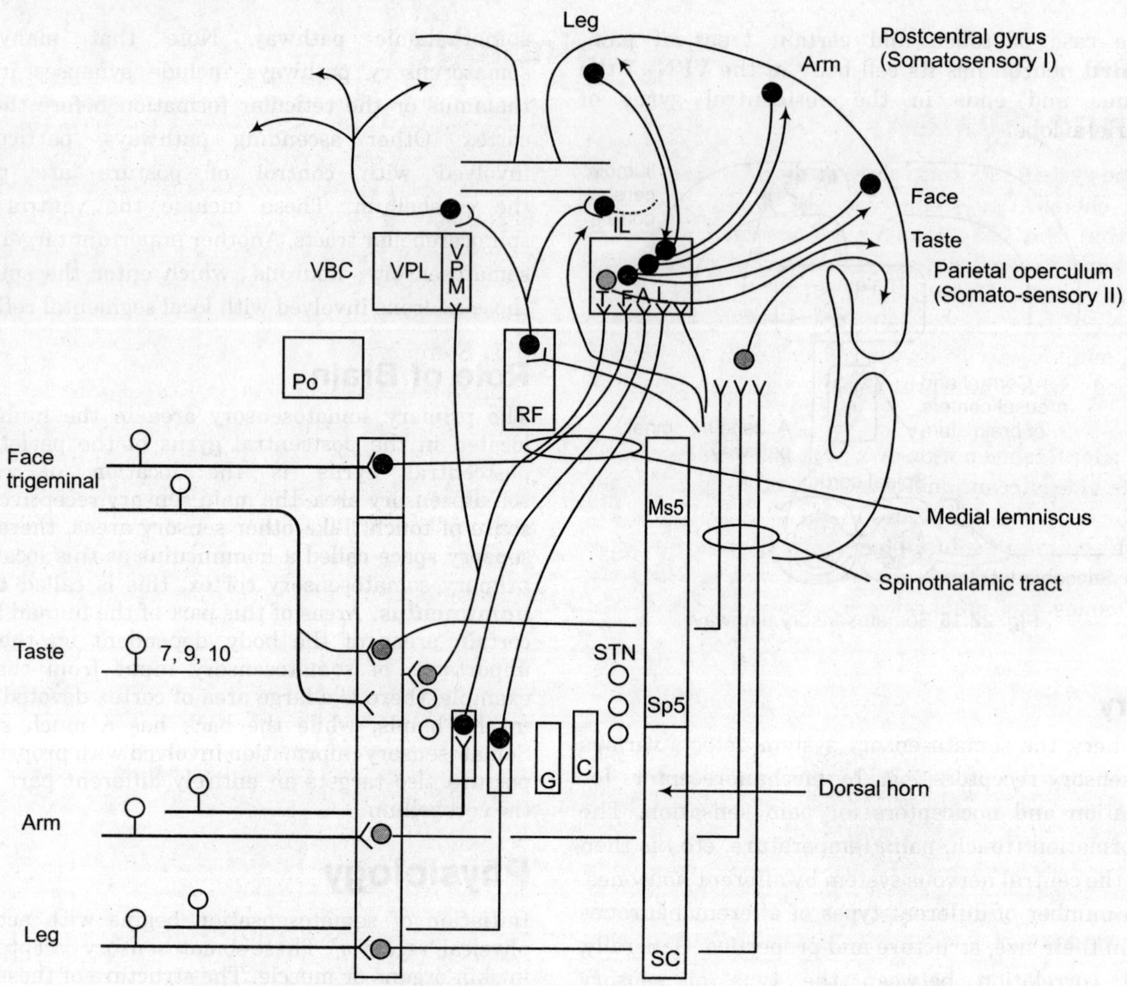

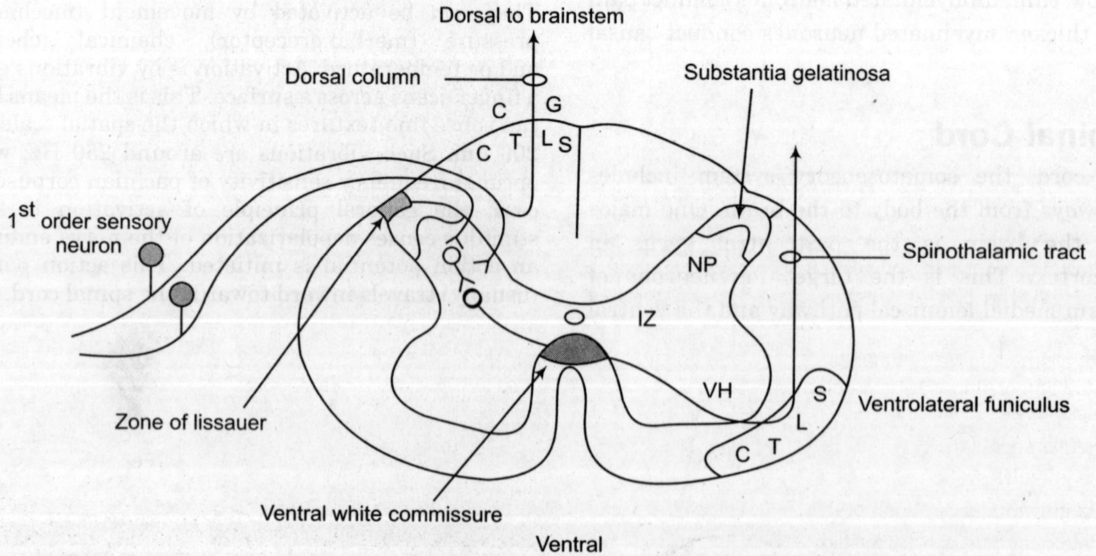

Fig. 22.17 IL-Intralaminar nucleus, VPL-Ventro-Posterior Lateral nucleus of thalamus, VPM-Ventro-Posterior Medial nucleus of thalamus, Po-Posterior nuclear group of thalamus, MRF-Medial Reticular Formation, FAL-Face/Arm/Leg, G-Gracile nucleus, C-Cuneate nucleus, Sol. n.-Solitary Tract Nucleus, Sp5-Spinal trigeminal nucleus, Ms5-Main sensory trigeminal nucleus
• NP-Nucleus Proprius, IZ-Intermediate Zone, VH-Ventral Horn

Endocrinology

Endocrine System

The endocrine system is a control system of ductless glands that secrete chemical messengers called **hormones** that circulate within the body *via* the bloodstream to affect distant cells within specific organs. Endocrine glands secrete their products immediately into the blood or interstitial fluid, without storage of the chemical. Hormones act as 'messengers' and are carried by the bloodstream to different cells in the body, which interpret these messages and act on them.

It seems like a far fetched notion or idea that a small chemical can enter the bloodstream and cause an action at a distant location in the body. Yet this occurs in our bodies everyday of our lives. The ability to maintain homeostasis and respond to stimuli is largely due to hormones secreted within the body. Without hormones, you could not grow, maintain a constant temperature, produce offspring or perform the basic actions and functions that are essential for life. The endocrine system provides an electrochemical connection from the hypothalamus of the brain to all the organs that control the body metabolism, growth and development and reproduction. There are two types of hormones secreted in the endocrine system:

1. Steroidal
2. Non-steroidal or protein based hormones.

The endocrine system regulates its hormones through negative feedback, except in very specific cases like childbirth. Increases in hormone activity decrease the production of that hormone. The immune system and other factors contribute as control factors also, altogether maintaining constant levels of hormones.

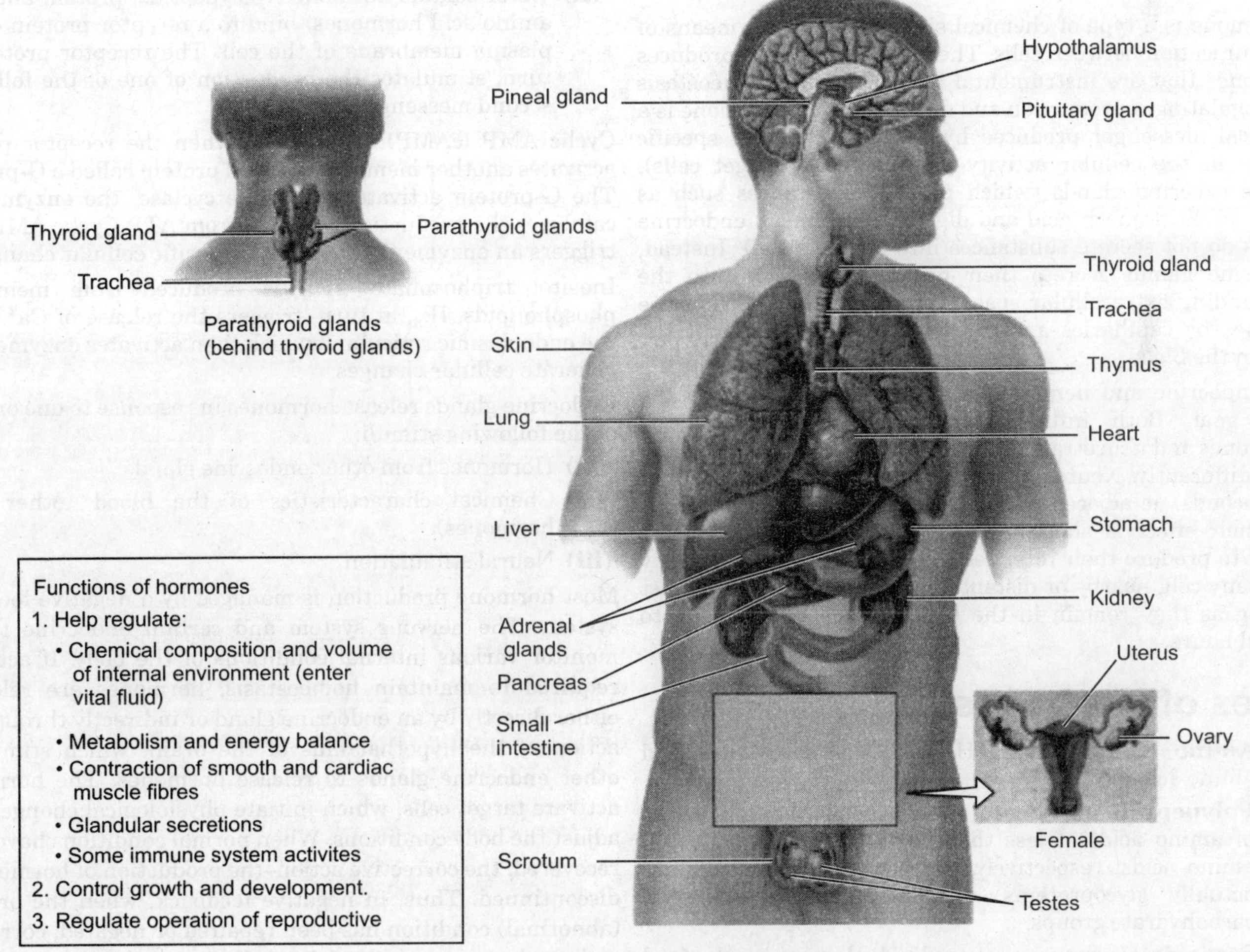

Fig. 22.18 Endocrine glands

Types of Glands

Their are mainly two types of glands–

Exocrine Glands

Exocrine glands are those which release their cellular secretions through a duct which empties to the outside or into the lumen (empty internal space) of an organ. These include certain sweat glands, salivary glands, pancreatic glands and mammary glands.

Endocrine Glands

Endocrine glands are those glands which have no duct and release their secretions directly into the intercellular fluid or into the blood. The collection of endocrine glands make up the endocrine system.

The main endocrine glands are the pituitary (anterior and posterior lobes), thyroid, parathyroids, adrenal (cortex and medulla), pancreas and gonads.

Hormones

A hormone is a type of chemical signal. They are a means of communication between cells. The endocrine system produces hormones that are instrumental in maintaining homeostasis and regulating reproduction and development. A hormone is a chemical messenger produced by a cell that effects specific change in the cellular activity of other cells (target cells). Unlike exocrine glands (which produce substances such as saliva, milk, stomach acid and digestive enzymes), endocrine glands do not secrete substances into ducts (tubes). Instead, endocrine glands secrete their hormones directly into the surrounding extracellular space. The hormones then diffuse into nearby capillaries and are transported throughout the body in the blood.

The endocrine and nervous systems often work toward the same goal. Both influence other cells with chemicals (hormones and neurotransmitters). However, they attain their goals differently. Neurotransmitters act immediately (within milliseconds) on adjacent muscle, gland or other nervous cells and their effect is short-lived. In contrast, hormones take longer to produce their intended effect (seconds to days), may affect any cell, nearby or distant and produce effects that last as long as they remain in the blood, which could be up to several hours.

Types of Hormones

(i) **Amino acid-derived** Hormones that are modified amino acids.

(ii) **Polypeptide and proteins** Hormones that are chains of amino acids of less than or more than about 100 amino acids, respectively. Some protein hormones are actually glycoproteins, containing glucose or other carbohydrate groups.

(iii) **Steroids** Hormones that are lipids that are synthesized from cholesterol. Steroids are characterized by four interlocking carbohydrate rings.

(iv) **Eicosanoids** Are lipids that are synthesized from the fatty acid chains of phospholipids found in plasma membrane.

Mechanism of Hormone Action

Hormones circulating in the blood diffuse into the interstitial fluids surrounding the cell. Cells with specific receptors for a hormone respond with an action that is appropriate for the cell. Because of the specificity of hormone and target cell, the effects produced by a single hormone may vary among different kinds of target cells. Hormones activate target cells by one of two methods, depending upon the chemical nature of the hormone.

(i) Lipid-soluble hormones (steroid hormones and hormones of the thyroid gland) diffuse through the cell membranes of target cells. The lipid-soluble hormone then binds to a receptor protein that, in turn, activates a DNA segment that turns on specific genes. The proteins produced as result of the transcription of the genes and subsequent translation of *m*RNA act as enzymes that regulate specific physiological cell activity.

(ii) Water-soluble hormones (polypeptide, protein and most amino acid hormones) bind to a receptor protein on the plasma membrane of the cell. The receptor protein, in turn, stimulates the production of one of the following second messengers:

Cyclic AMP (*c*AMP) is produced when the receptor protein activates another membrane-bound protein called a G-protein. The G-protein activates adenylate cyclase, the enzyme that catalyzes the production of *c*AMP from ATP. Cyclic AMP then triggers an enzyme that generates specific cellular changes.

Inositol triphosphate (IP_3) is produced from membrane phospholipids. IP_3, in turn, triggers the release of Ca^{2+} from the endoplasmic reticulum, which then activates enzymes that generate cellular changes.

Endocrine glands release hormones in response to one or more of the following stimuli:

(i) Hormones from other endocrine glands.

(ii) Chemical characteristics of the blood (other than hormones).

(iii) Neural stimulation.

Most hormone production is managed by a negative feedback system. The nervous system and certain endocrine tissues monitor various internal conditions of the body. If action is required to maintain homeostasis, hormones are released, either directly by an endocrine gland or indirectly through the action of the hypothalamus of the brain, which stimulates other endocrine glands to release hormones. The hormones activate target cells, which initiate physiological changes that adjust the body conditions. When normal conditions have been recovered, the corrective action–the production of hormones is discontinued. Thus, in negative feedback, when the original (abnormal) condition has been repaired or negated, corrective actions decrease or discontinue. For example, the amount of glucose in the blood controls the secretion of insulin and glucagons *via* negative feedback.

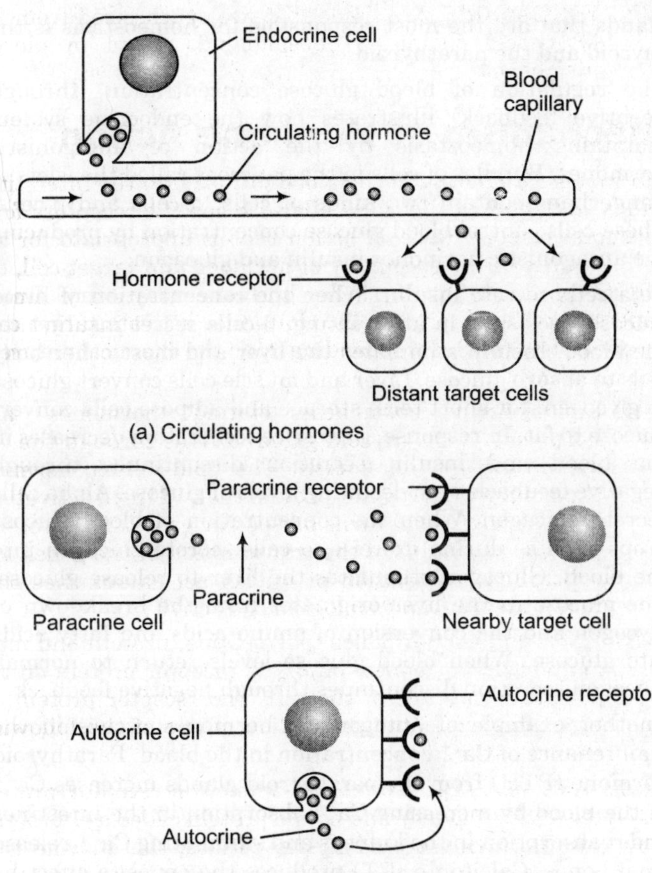

Fig. 22.19 Hormone release and site of action

The production of some hormones is controlled by positive feedback. In such a system, hormones cause a condition to intensify, rather than decrease. As the condition intensifies, hormone production increases. Such positive feedback is uncommon, but does occur during childbirth, where hormone levels build with increasingly intense labour contractions. Also in lactation, hormone levels increase in response to nursing, which causes milk production to increase. The hormone produced by the hypothalamus causing the milk let down and uterine contraction is oxytocin.

Endocrine Glands

Endocrine glands are endogeneously located and lack ducts (hence, called ductless glands). They secrete their secretion into blood for transportation to target organ. Endocrine glands of human body are –

Pituitary Gland

The hypothalamus makes up the lower region of the diencephalons and lies just above the brain stem. The pituitary gland (hypophysis) is attached to the bottom of the hypothalamus by a slender stalk called the infundibulum. The pituitary gland consists of two major regions, the anterior pituitary gland (anterior lobe or adenohypophysis) and the posterior pituitary gland (posterior lobe or neurohypophysis). The hypothalamus also controls the glandular secretion of the pituitary gland. The hypothalamus oversees many internal body conditions. It receives nervous stimuli from receptors throughout the body and monitors chemical and physical characteristics of the blood, including temperature, blood pressure and nutrient hormone and water content. When deviations from homeostasis occur or when certain developmental changes are required, the hypothalamus stimulates cellular activity in various parts of the body by directing the release of hormones from the anterior and posterior pituitary glands. The hypothalamus communicates directives to these glands by one of the following two pathways: The pituitary gland is found in the inferior part of the brain and is connected by the pituitary stalk. It can be referred to as the **master gland** because it is the main place for everything that happens within the endocrine system. It is divided into two sections—the anterior lobe (adenohypophysis) and the posterior lobe (neurohypophysis). The posterior pituitary is involved in sending hormones that control all other hormones of the body.

Posterior Pituitary

Communication between the hypothalamus and the posterior pituitary occurs through neurosecretory cells that span the short distance between the hypothalamus and the posterior pituitary. Hormones produced by the cell bodies of the neurosecretory cells are packaged in vesicles and transported through the axon and stored in the axon terminals that lie in the posterior pituitary. When the neurosecretory cells are stimulated, the action potential generated triggers the release of the stored hormones from the axon terminals to a capillary network within the posterior pituitary. Two hormones, oxytocin and antidiuretic hormone (ADH), are produced and released this way. If one's not able to produce ADH it can cause diabetes insipidus which means a person is producing large amounts of urine, resulting in loss of ions from the blood. The posterior lobe is composed of neural tissue (neural ectoderm) and is derived from hypothalamus. Its function is to store oxytocin and antidiuretic hormone. When hypothalamic neurons fire hormones release into the capillaries of the lobe.

The posterior pituitary is, in effect, a projection of the hypothalamus. It does not produce its own hormones, but only stores and releases the hormones oxytocin and antidiuretic hormone (ADH-also known as vasopressin).

Anterior Pituitary

Communication between the hypothalamus and the anterior pituitary occurs through chemicals (releasing hormones and inhibiting hormones) that are produced by the hypothalamus and delivered to the anterior pituitary through blood vessels. The releasing and inhibitating hormones are produced by specialized neurons of the hypothalamus called neurosecretory cells. The hormones are released into a capillary network or primary plexus and transported through veins or hypophyseal portal veins, to a second capillary network or secondary plexus that supplies the anterior pituitary. The hormones then diffuse from the secondary plexus into the anterior pituitary, where they initiate the production of specific hormones by the anterior pituitary.

Many of the hormones produced by the anterior pituitary are tropic hormones or tropins, which are hormones that stimulate other endocrine glands to secrete their hormones.

The anterior lobe is derived from oral ectoderm, composed of glandular epithelium it communicates with the hypothalamus *via* a network of capillaries. The anterior pituitary lobe receives releasing hormones from the hypothalamus *via* a portal vein system known as the hypothalamic-hypophyseal portal system.

Anterior pituitary secretes

(a) Growth hormone
(b) Prolactin
(c) Follicle-stimulating hormone
(d) Luteinizing hormone
(e) Thyroid-stimulating hormone
(f) Adrenocorticotropic hormone
(g) Endorphins
(h) Other hormones

It does this in response to a variety of chemical signals from the hypothalamus, which travel to the anterior lobe by way of a special capillary system from the hypothalamus, down the median eminence, to the anterior lobe. These include:

(a) TRH (Thyrotropin-Releasing Hormone)
(b) RH (Corticotropin-Releasing Hormone)
(c) DA (Dopamine, 'prolactin inhibiting factor'/PIF)
(d) GnRH (Gonadotropin-Releasing Hormone)
(e) GHRH (Growth Hormone Releasing Hormone)

These hormones from the hypothalamus cause release of the respective hormone from the pituitary. The control of release of hormones from the pituitary happens when there is negative feedback from the gland on which they act. Meaning that when the hormones increase on the effected gland the pituitary will stop sending hormones to them. Also, the heart, gastrointestinal tract, the placenta, the kidneys and the skin, whose major function is not the secretion of hormones, nonetheless, contain some specialized cells that produce hormones. In addition, all cells, except red blood cells secrete a class of hormones called eicosanoids. These hormones are paracrines or local hormones, that primarily affect neighbouring cells. Two groups of eicosanoids, the prostaglandins (PGs) and the leukotrienes (LTs), have a wide range of varying effects that depend upon the nature of the target cell. Eicosanoid activity, for example, may impact blood pressure, blood clotting, immune and inflammatory responses, reproductive processes and the contraction of smooth muscles.

Antagonistic Hormones

Maintaining homeostasis often requires conditions to be limited to a narrow range. When conditions exceed the upper limit of homeostasis, specific action, usually the production of a hormone, is triggered. When conditions return to normal, hormone production is discontinued. If conditions exceed the lower limits of homeostasis, a different action, usually the production of a second hormone, is triggered. Hormones that act to return body conditions to within acceptable limits from opposite extremes are called antagonistic hormones. The two glands that are the most responsible for homeostasis is the thyroid and the parathyroid.

The regulation of blood glucose concentration (through negative feedback) illustrates how the endocrine system maintains homeostasis by the action of antagonistic hormones. Bundles of cells in the pancreas called the islets of Langerhans contain two kinds of cells, α-cells and β-cells. These cells control blood glucose concentration by producing the antagonistic hormones insulin and glucagon.

Beta cells secrete insulin. When the concentration of blood glucose rises such in after eating, β-cells secret insulin into the blood. Insulin stimulates the liver and most other body cells to absorb glucose. Liver and muscle cells convert glucose to glycogen, for short term storage and adipose cells convert glucose to fat. In response, glucose concentration decreases in the blood and insulin secretion discontinues through negative feedback from declining levels of glucose. Alpha cells secrete glucagon. When the concentration of blood glucose drops such as during exercise, α-cells secrete glucagon into the blood. Glucagon stimulates the liver to release glucose. The glucose in the liver originates from the breakdown of glycogen and the conversion of amino acids and fatty acids into glucose. When blood glucose levels return to normal, glucagon secretion discontinues through negative feedback.

Another example of antagonistic hormones occurs in the maintenance of Ca^{2+} concentration in the blood. Parathyroid hormone (PTH) from the parathyroid glands increases Ca^{2+} in the blood by increasing Ca^{2+} absorption in the intestines and reabsorption in the kidneys and stimulating Ca^{2+} release from bones. Calcitonin (CT) produces the opposite effect by inhibiting the breakdown of bone matrix and decreasing the release of calcium in the blood.

Thyroid Gland

The thyroid gland is one of the largest endocrine glands in the body. It is positioned on the neck just below the larynx and has two lobes with one on either side of the trachea. It is involved in the production of the hormones T_3 (triiodothyronine) and T_4 (thyroxine). These hormones increase the metabolic activity of the body's cells. The thyroid also produces and releases the hormone calcitonin (thyrocalcitonin) which contributes to the regulation of blood calcium levels. Thyrocalcitonin or calcitonin decreases the concentration of calcium in the blood. Most of the calcium removed from the blood is stored in the bones. The thyroid hormone consists of two components, thyroxine and iodine. This hormone increases the metabolism of most body cells. A deficiency of iodine in the diet leads to the enlargement of the thyroid gland, known as a simple goitre. Hypothyroidism during early development leads to cretinism. In adults, it produces myxedema, characterized by obesity and lethargy. Hyperthyroidism leads to a condition known as exophthalmic goitre, characterized by weight loss as well as hyperactive and irritable behaviour. The thyroid gland is a two-lobed gland that manifests a remarkably powerful active transport mechanism for uptaking iodide ions from the blood. As blood flows through the gland, iodide is converted to an active form of iodine. This iodine combines with an amino acid called tyrosine. Two molecules of iodinated tyrosine then combine to form thyroxine. Following its formation, the thyroxine becomes bound to a polysaccharide-protein material called thyroglobulin. The normal thyroid gland may store several weeks supply of thyroxine in this bound form. An enzymatic splitting of the thyroxine from the thyroglobulin occurs when a specific hormone is releazed into the blood. This hormone, produced by the pituitary gland, is known as Thyroid Stimulating Hormone (TSH). TSH stimulates certain major rate-limiting steps in thyroxine secretion and thereby alters its rate of releaze. A variety of bodily defects, either dietary, hereditary or disease induced, may decrease the amount of thyroxine releazed into the blood. The most popular of these defects is one that results from dietary iodine deficiency. The thyroid gland enlarges, in the continued presence of TSH from the pituitary, to form a goitre. This a futile attempt to synthesize thyroid hormones, for iodine levels that are too low. Normally, thyroid hormones act *via* a negative feedback loop on the pituitary to decrease stimulation of the thyroid. In goitre, the feedback loop cannot be in operation hence, continual stimulation of the thyroid and the inevitable protuberance on the neck. Formerly, the principal source of iodine came from seafood. As a result, goitre was prevalent amongst inland areas far removed from the sea. Today, the incidence of goitre has been drastically reduced by adding iodine to table salt.

Thyroxine serves to stimulate oxidative metabolism in cells; it increases the oxygen consumption and heat production of most body tissues, a notable exception being the brain. Thyroxine is also necessary for normal growth, the most likely explanation being that thyroxine promotes the effects of growth hormone on protein synthesis. The absence of thyroxine significantly reduces the ability of growth hormone to stimulate amino acid uptake and RNA synthesis. Thyroxine also plays a crucial role in the closely related area of organ development, particularly that of the central nervous system. If there is an insufficient amount of thyroxine, a condition referred to as hypothyroidism results. Symptoms of hypothyroidism stem from the fact that there is a reduction in the rate of oxidative energy-releasing reactions within the body cells. Usually the patient shows puffy skin, sluggishness and lowered vitality. Other symptoms of hypothyroidism include weight gain, decreased libido, inability to tolerate cold, muscle pain and spasm, insomnia and brittle dry hair. Hypothyroidism in children, a condition known as cretinism, can result in mental retardation, dwarfism and permanent sexual immaturity. Sometimes the thyroid gland produces too much thyroxine, a condition known as hyperthyroidism. This condition produces symptoms such as an abnormally high body temperature, profuse sweating, high blood pressure, loss of weight, irritability and muscular pain and weakness. It also causes the characteristic symptom of the eyeballs protruding from the skull called exopthalmia. This is surprising because it is not a symptom usually related to a fast metabolism. Hyperthyroidism has been treated by partial removal or by partial radiation destruction of the gland. More recently, several drugs that inhibit thyroid activity have been discovered and their use is replacing the former surgical procedures. Unfortunately thyroid conditions require lifetime treatment and because of the body's need for a sensitive balance of thyroid hormone both supplementing and suppressing thyroid function can take months or even years to regulate.

T_3 and T_4 Function within the Body

The production of T_3 and T_4 are regulated by Thyroid Stimulating Hormone (TSH), released by the pituitary gland. TSH production is increased when T_3 and T_4 levels are too low. The thyroid hormones are released throughout the body to direct the bodies metabolism. They stimulate all cells within the body to work at a better metabolic rate. Without these hormones the bodies cells would not be able to regulate the speed at which they performed chemical actions. Their release will be increased under certain situations such as cold temperatures when a higher metabolism is needed to generate heat. When children are born with thyroid hormone deficiency they have problems with physical growth and developmental problems. Brain development can also be severely impaired.

Significance of Iodine

Thyroid hormone cannot be produced without an abundant source of iodine. The iodine concentration within the body, although significant, can be as little as $1/25^{th}$ the concentration within the thyroid itself. When the thyroid is low on iodine the body will try harder to produce T_3 and T_4 which will often result in a swelling of the thyroid gland, resulting in a goitre.

Calcitonin

Calcitonin is a 32 amino acid polypeptide hormone. It is an additional hormone produced by the thyroid and contributes to the regulation of blood calcium levels. Thyroid cells produce calcitonin in response to high calcium levels in the blood. This hormone will stimulate movement of calcium into the bone structure. It can also be used therapeutically for the treatment of hypercalcemia or osteoporosis. Without this hormone calcium will stay within the blood instead of moving into bones to keep them strong and growing. Its importance in humans has not been as well established as its importance in other animals.

Parathyroid Gland

There are four parathyroid glands. They are small, light-coloured lumps that stick out from the surface of the thyroid gland. All four glands are located on the thyroid gland. They are butterfly-shaped and located inside the neck, more specifically on both sides of the windpipe. One of the parathyroid glands most important functions is to regulate the bodies calcium and phosphorus levels. Another function of the parathyroid glands is to secrete parathyroid hormone, which causes the release of the calcium present in bone to extracellular fluid. PTH does this by activating the production of osteoblasts, special cells of the body involved in the production of bone and slowing down osteoclasts, other specialized cells involved in the removal of bone. There are two major types of cells that make up parathyroid tissue:

(i) One of the major cells is called oxyphil cells. Their function is basically unknown.

(ii) The second type are called chief cells. Chief cells produce parathyroid hormone.

The structure of a parathyroid gland is very different from that of a thyroid gland. The chief cells that produce parathyroid hormone are arranged in tightly-packed nests around small blood vessels, quite unlike the thyroid cells that produce thyroid hormones, which are arranged in spheres called the **thyroid follicles.**

PTH or parathyroid hormone is secreted from these four glands. It is released directly into the bloodstream and travels to its target cells which are often quite aways away. It then binds to a structure called a receptor, that is found either inside or on the surface of the target cells.

Receptors bind a specific hormone and the result is a specific physiologic response, meaning a normal response of the body. The activity of all the hormones or growth factors secreted by endocrine glands and circulating in blood is controlled by the exocrine system of the body. PTH finds its major target cells in bone, kidneys and the gastrointestinal system.

Calcitonin, a hormone produced by the thyroid gland that also regulates ECF calcium levels and serves to counteract the calcium-producing effects of PTH. The adult body contains as much as 1 kg of calcium. Most of this calcium is found in bone and teeth.

The four parathyroids secrete the parathyroid hormone (PTH). It opposes the effect of thyrocalcitonin. It does this by removing calcium from its storage sites in bones, releasing it into the bloodstream. It also signals the kidneys to reabsorb more of this mineral, transporting it into the blood. It also signals the small intestine to absorb more of this mineral, transporting it from the diet into the blood. Calcium is important for steps of body metabolism. Blood cannot clot without sufficient calcium.

Skeletal muscles require this mineral in order to contract. A deficiency of PTH can lead to tetany, muscle weakness due to lack of available calcium in the blood. The parathyroids were long thought to be part of the thyroid or to be functionally associated with it. We now know that their close proximity to the thyroid is misleading both developmentally and functionally, they are totally distinct from the thyroid.

The parathyroid hormone, called parathormone, regulates the calcium-phosphate balance between the blood and other tissues. Production of this hormone is directly controlled by the calcium concentration of the extracellular fluid bathing the cells of these glands. Parathormne exerts at least the following four effects:

(i) It increases gastrointestinal absorption of calcium by stimulating the active transport system and moves calcium from the gut lumen into the blood.

(ii) It increases the movement of calcium and phosphate from bone into extracellular fluid. This is accomplished by stimulating osteoclasts to break down bone structure, thus liberating calcium phosphate into the blood. In this way, the store of calcium contained in bone is tapped.

(iii) It increases reabsorption of calcium by the renal tubules, thereby decreasing urinary calcium excretion.

(iv) It reduces the reabsorption of phosphate by the renal tubules.

The first three effects result in a higher extracellular calcium concentration. The adaptive value of the fourth is to prevent the formation of kidney stones. If parathyroids are removed accidentally during surgery on the thyroid, there would be a rise in the phosphate concentration in the blood. There would also be a drop in the calcium concentration as more calcium is excreted by the kidneys and intestines and more incorporated into the bone. This can produce serious disturbances, particularly in the muscles and nerves, which use calcium ions for normal functioning. Overactivity of the parathyroids, which can result from a tumour on the glands, produces a weakening of the bones. This is a condition that makes them much more vulnerable to fracturing because of excessive withdrawal of calcium from the bones.

Adrenal Glands

Adrenal glands are a pair of ductless glands located above the kidneys. Through hormonal secretions, the adrenal glands regulate many essential functions in the body, including biochemical balances that influence athletic training and general stress response. The glucocorticoids include corticosterone, cortisone and hydrocortisone or cortisol. These hormones serve to stimulate the conversion of amino acids into carbohydrates which is a process known as gluconeogenesis and the formation of glycogen by the liver. They also stimulate the formation of reserve glycogen in the tissues, such as in the muscles. The glucocorticoids also participate in lipid and protein metabolism. The cortex of the adrenal gland is known to produce over 20 hormones, but their study can be simplified by classifying them into three categoreies glucocorticoids, mineralcorticoids and sex hormones.

They are triangular-shaped glands located on top of the kidneys. They produce hormones such as oestrogen, progesterone, steroids, cortisol and cortisone and chemicals such as adrenaline (epinephrine), norepinephrine and dopamine. When the glands produce more or less hormones than required by the body, disease conditions may occur.

The adrenal cortex secretes at least two families of hormones, the glucocorticoids and mineral corticoids. The adrenal medulla secretes the hormones epinephrine (adrenaline) and norepinephrine (noradrenaline).

Adrenal Cortex

The hormones made by the adrenal cortex supply long-term responses to stress. The two major hormones produced are the mineral corticoids and the glucocorticoids. The mineral corticoids regulate the salt and water balance, leading to the increase of blood volume and blood pressure. The glucocorticoids are monitoring the ACTH, inturn regulating carbohydrates, proteins and fat metabolism. Resulting into an increase in blood glucose. Glucocorticoids also reduce the bodys inflammatory response.

Cortisol is one of the most active glucocorticoids. It usually reduces the effects of inflammation or swelling throughout the body. It also stimulates the production of glucose from fats and proteins, which is a process referred to as gluconeogenesis.

Aldosterone is one example of a mineralocorticoid. It signals the tubules in the kidney nephrons to reabsorb sodium while secreting or eliminating potassium. If sodium levels are low in the blood, the kidney secretes more renin, which is an enzyme that stimulates the formation of angiotensin from a molecule made from the liver. Angiotensin stimulates aldosterone secretion. As a result, more sodium is reabsorbed as it enters the blood. Aldosterone, the major mineralocorticoid, stimulates the cells of the distal convoluted tubules of the kidneys to decrease reabsorption of potassium and increase reabsorption of sodium. This is turn leads to an increased reabsorption of chloride and water. These hormones, together with such hormones as insulin and glucagon, are important regulators of the ionic environment of the internal fluid. The renin-angiotensin-aldosterone mechanism can raise blood pressure if it tends to drop. It does this in two ways. Angiotensin is a vasoconstrictor, decreasing the diameter of blood vessels. As vessels constrict, blood pressure increases. In addition, as sodium is reabsorbed, the blood passing through the kidney becomes more hypertonic. Water follows the sodium into the hypertonic blood by osmosis. This increases the amount of volume in the blood and also increases the blood pressure.

Adrenal Medulla

The hypothalamus starts nerve impulses that travel the path from the bloodstream, spinal cord, sympathetic nerve fibres to the adrenal medulla, which then releases hormones. The effects of these hormones provide a short-term response to stress excessive secretion of the glucocorticoids causes Cushing's syndrome, characterized by muscle atrophy or degeneration and hypertension or high blood pressure. Under secretion of these substances produces Addison's disease, characterized by low blood pressure and stress. Epinephrine and norepinephrine produce the 'fight or flight' response, similar to the effect from the sympathetic nervous system. Therefore, they increase heart rate, breathing rate, blood flow to most skeletal muscles and the concentration of glucose in the blood. They decrease blood flow to the digestive organs and diminish most digestive processes.

The adrenal sex hormones consist mainly of male sex hormones (androgens) and lesser amounts of female sex hormones (oestrogens and progesterone). Normally, the sex hormones released from the adrenal cortex are insignificant due to the low concentration of secretion. However, in cases of excess secretion, masculinizing or feminizing effects appear. The most common syndrome of this sort is virilism of the female. Should there be an insufficient supply of cortical hormones, a condition known as Addison's disease would result. This disease is characterized by an excessive excretion of sodium ions and hence water, due to lack of mineralocorticoids. Accompanying this is a decreased blood glucose level due to a deficient supply of glucocorticoids. The effect of a decreased androgen supply cannot be observed immediately. Injections of adrenal cortical hormones promptly relieve these symptoms. Hormonal production in the adrenal cortex is directly controlled by the anterior pituitary hormone called adrenocorticotropic hormone (ACTH).

The two adrenal glands lie very close to the kidneys. Each adrenal gland is actually a double gland, composed of an inner core like medulla and an outer cortex. Each of these is functionally unrelated. The adrenal medulla secretes two hormone, adrenaline or epinephrine and noradrenaline or norepinephrine, whose functions are very similar but not identical. The adrenal medulla is derived embryogically from neural tissue. It has been likened to an overgrown sympathetic ganglion whose cell bodies do not send out nerve fibres, but release their active substances directly into the blood, thereby fulfilling the criteria for an endocrine gland. In controlling epinephrine secretion, the adrenal medulla behaves just like any sympathetic ganglion and is dependent upon stimulation by sympathetic preganglionic fibres.

Epinephrine promotes several responses, all of which are helpful in coping with emergencies the blood pressure rises, the heart rate increases, the glucose content of the blood rises because of glycogen breakdown, the spleen contracts and squeezes out a reserve supply of blood, the clotting time decreases, the pupils dilate, the blood flow to skeletal muscles increase, the blood supply to intestinal smooth muscle decreases and hairs become erect. These adrenal functions, which mobilize the resources of the body in emergencies, have been called the fight-or-flight response.

Norepinephrine stimulates reactions similar to those produced by epinephrine, but is less effective in conversion of glycogen to glucose. The significance of the adrenal medulla may seem questionable since the complete removal of the gland causes few noticeable changes; humans can still exhibit the flight-or-fight response. This occurs because the sympathetic nervous system complements the adrenal medulla in stimulating the fight-or-flight response and the absence of the hormonal control will be compensated for by the nervous system.

Pancreas

The pancreas is very important organ in the digestion system and the circulatory system because it helps to maintain our blood sugar levels. The pancreas is considered to be part of the gastrointestinal system. It produces digestive enzymes to be released into the small intestine to aid in reducing food particles to basic elements that can be absorbed by the intestine and used by the body. It has another very different function in that it forms insulin, glucagon and other hormones to be sent into the bloodstream to regulate blood sugar levels and other activities throughout the body. It has a pear-shape to it and is approximately 6 inche long. It is located in the middle and back portion of the abdomen. The pancreas is connected to the first part of the small intestine, the duodenum and lies behind the stomach. The pancreas is made up of glandular tissue: any substance secreted by the cells of the pancreas will be secreted outside of the organ. The digestive juices produced by the pancreas are secreted into the duodenum *via* a Y-shaped duct, at the point where the common bile duct from the liver and the pancreatic duct join just before entering the duodenum. The digestive enzymes carried into the duodenum are representative of the exocrine function of the pancreas, in which specific substances are made to be passed directly into another organ.

The pancreas is unusual among the body's glands in that it also has a very important endocrine function. Small groups of special cells called islet cells throughout the organ make the hormones of insulin and glucagon. These, of course, are hormones that are critical in regulating blood sugar levels. These hormones are secreted directly into the bloodstream to affect organs all over the body.

The pancreas is both an exocrine and an endocrine organ. Insulin acts to lower blood sugar levels by allowing the sugar to flow into cells. Glucagon acts to raise blood sugar levels by causing glucose to be releazed into the circulation from its storage sites. Insulin and glucagon act in an opposite but balanced fashion to keep blood sugar levels stable. A healthy working pancreas in the human body is important for maintaining good health by preventing malnutrition and maintaining normal levels of blood sugar. The digestive tract needs the help of the enzymes produced by the pancreas to reduce food particles to their simplest elements or the nutrients cannot be absorbed. Carbohydrates must be broken down into individual sugar molecules. Proteins must be reduced to simple amino acids. Fats must be broken down into fatty acids. The pancreatic enzymes are important in all these transformations. The basic particles can then easily be transported into the cells that line the intestine and from there they can be further altered and transported to different tissues in the body as fuel sources and construction materials. Similarly, the body cannot maintain normal blood sugar levels without the balanced action of insulin and glucagon. The pancreas contains exocrine and endocrine cells. Groups of endocrine cells, the islets of Langerhans, secrete two hormones. The β-cells secrete insulin, the α-cells secrete glucagon. The level of sugar in the blood depends on the opposing action of these two hormones.

Insulin decreases the concentration of glucose in the blood. Most of the glucose enters the cells of the liver and skeletal muscles. In these cells, this monosaccharide is converted to the polysaccharide glycogen. Therefore, insulin promotes glycogenesis (glycogen formation), stimulating the breakdown of glycogen into glucose for release into the blood. Insulin deficiency leads to the development of diabetes mellitus, specifically type I, juvenile diabetes. As the pancreas does not produce sufficient insulin, it is treated by insulin injections. In type II or maturity onset diabetes, the pancreas does produce enough insulin, but the target cells do not respond to it. The pancreas is a mixed gland having both endocrine and exocrine functions. The exocrine portion secretes digestive enzymes into the duodenum *via* the pancreatic duct. The endocrine portion secretes two hormones, insulin and glucagon, into the blood. Insulin is a hormone that acts directly or indirectly on most tissues of the body, with the exception of the brain. The most important action of insulin is the stimulation of the uptake of glucose by many tissues, particularly the liver, muscle and fat. The uptake of glucose by the cells decreases blood glucose and increases the availability of glucose for the cellular reactions in which glucose participates. Thus, glucose oxidation, fat synthesis and glycogen synthesis are all accentuated by an uptake of glucose. It is important to note that insulin does not alter glucose uptake by the brain, nor does it influence the active transport of glucose across the renal tubules and gastrointestinal epithelium. As stated, insulin stimulates glycogen synthesis. In addition, it also increases the activity of the enzyme that catalyzes the rate-limiting step in glycogen synthesis. Insulin also increases triglyceride levels by inhibiting triglyceride breakdown and by stimulating production of triglyceride through fatty acid and glycerophosphate synthesis. The net protein synthesis is also increased by insulin, which stimulates the active membrane transport of amino acids, particularly into muscle cells. Insulin also has effects on other liver enzymes, but the precise mechanisms by which insulin induces these changes are not well understood.

No organ except the pancreas makes significant amounts of insulin or glucagon. Insulin is secreted by β-cells, which are located in the part of the pancreas known as the islets of Langerhans. These groups of cells, which are located randomly throughout the pancreas, also consist of other secretory cells called α-cells. It is these α-cells that secrete glucagon. Glucagon is a hormone that has the following major effects it increases hepatic synthesis of glucose from pyruvate, lactate, glycerol and amino acids (a process called gluconeogenesis, which also raises the plasma glucose level); and it increases the breakdown of adipose tissue triglyceride, thereby raising the plasma levels of fatty acids and glycerol. The glucagon secreting α-cells in the pancreas, like the β-cells, respond to changes in the concentration of glucose in the blood flowing through the pancreas; no other nerves or hormones are involved.

It should be noted that glucagon has the opposite effects of insulin. Glucagon elevates the plasma glucose, whereas insulin stimulates its uptake and thereby reduces plasma glucose levels; glucagon elevates fatty acid concentrations, whereas insulin converts fatty acids and glycerol into triglycerides, thereby inhibiting triglyceride breakdown.

The α and β-cells of the pancreas make up a push-pull system for regulating the plasma glucose level.

Sex Organs

The sex organs (gonads) are the testes in the male and the ovaries in the female. Both of these organs produce and secrete hormones that are balanced by the hypothalamus and pituitary glands. The main hormones from the reproductive organs are: Testosterone is more prominent in males. It belongs to the family of androgens, which are steroid hormones producing masculinizing effects. Testosterone stimulates the development and functioning of the primary sex organs. It also stimulates the development and maintenance of secondary male characteristics, such as hair growth on the face and the deep pitch of the voice. Oestrogen in females, this hormone stimulates the development of the uterus and vagina. It is also responsible for the development and maintenance of secondary female characteristics, such as fat distribution throughout the body and the width of the pelvis.

Male

The testes produce androgens (*i.e.,* 'testosterone'). Testosterone is classified as a steroid and is responsible for many of the physical characteristics in males like.

(a) Broad shoulders

(b) Muscular body

(c) Hair

Testosterone increases protein production. Hormones that build up protein are called anabolic steroids. Anabolic steroids are available commercially and are being used by athletes because they help improve their physical ability, however, they do have major side effects such as:

(a) Liver and kidney disorders

(b) Hypertension (high blood pressure)

(c) Decreased sperm count and impotency

(d) Aggressive behaviour (roid mania)

(e) Balding

(f) Acne

Female

The ovaries produce oestrogen and progesterone. Oestrogen increases at the time of puberty and causes the growth of the uterus and vagina. Without oestrogen egg maturation would not occur. Oestrogen is also responsible for secondary sex characteristics such as female body hair and fat distribution. Estrogen and progesterone are responsible for the development of the breast and for the uterine cycle. Progesterone is a female hormone secreted by the corpus luteum after ovulation during the second half of the menstrual cycle. It prepares the lining of the uterus for implantation of a fertilized egg and allows for complete shedding of the endometrium at the time of menstruation. In the event of pregnancy, the progesterone level remains stable beginning a week or so after conception.

Table 22.1 **Endocrine Glands their Secretion and Function**

Endocrine Gland	Hormone Released	Chemical Class	Target Tissue/ Organ	Major Function of Hormone
Hypothalamus	Hypothalamic releasing and inhibiting hormones	Peptide	Anterior pituitary	Regulate anterior pituitary hormone
Posterior pituitary	Antidiuretic hormone (ADH)	Peptide	Kidneys	Stimulates water reabsorption by kidneys
Posterior pituitary	Oxytocin	Peptide	Uterus and mammary glands	Stimulates uterine muscle contractions and release of milk by mammary glands
Anterior pituitary	Thyroid stimulating hormone (TSH)	Glycoprotein	Thyroid	Stimulates thyroid
	Adrenocorticotropic hormone (ACTH)	Peptide	Adrenal cortex	Stimulates adrenal cortex
	Gonadotropic (FSH and LH)	Glycoprotein	Gonads	Egg and sperm production, sex hormone production
	Prolactin (PRL)	Protein	Mammary glands	Milk production
	Growth hormone (GH)	Protein	Soft tissue and bones	Cell division, protein synthesis and bone growth
Thyroid	Thyroxine (T_4) and Triiodothyronic (T_3)	Iodinated amino acid	All tissue	Increase metabolic rate, regulates growth and development
	Calcitonin	Peptide	Bones, kidneys and intestine	Lowers blood calcium level
Parathyroids	Parathyroid hormone (PTH)	Peptide	Bones, kidneys and intestine	Raises blood calcium level
Adrenal cortex	Glucocorticoids (cortisol)	Steroid	All tissue	Raise blood glucose level and stimulates breakdown of protein
	Mineralocarticoids (aldosterone)	Steroid	Kidneys	Reabsorb sodium and excrete potassium
	Sex hormones	Steroid	Gonads, skin, muscles and bones	Stimulates reproductive organs and brings on sex characteristics

Endocrine Gland	Hormone Released	Chemical Class	Target Tissue/ Organ	Major Function of Hormone
Adrenal medulla	Epinephrine and norepinephrine	Modified amino acid	Cardiac and other muscles	Releazed in emergency situations, raises blood glucose level, 'flight or fight' response
Pancreas	Insulin	Protein	Liver, muscles and adipose tissue	Lowers blood glucose levels, promotes formation of glycogen
	Glucagon	Protein	Liver, muscles and adipose tissue	Raises blood glucose levels
Testes	Androgens (testosterone)	Steroid	Gonads, skin, muscles and bones	Stimulates male sex characteristics
Ovaries	Oestrogen and progesterone	Steroid	Gonads, skin, muscles and bones	Stimulates female sex characteristics
Thymus	Thymosins	Peptide	T-lymphocytes	Stimulates production and maturation of T-lymphocytes
Pineal gland	Melatonin	Modified amino acid	Brain	Controls circadian and circannual rhythms, possibly involved in maturation of sexual organs

Pineal Gland

The pineal gland (also called the pineal body or epiphysis) is a small endocrine gland in the brain. It is located near the center of the brain, between the two hemispheres, tucked in a groove where the two rounded thalamic bodies join.The pineal gland is a reddish-gray body about the size of a pea (8 mm in humans) located just rostro-dorsal to the superior colliculus and behind and beneath the stria medullaris, between the laterally positioned thalamic bodies. It is part of the epithalamus. The pineal gland is a midline structure and is often seen in plain skull X-rays, as it is often calcified. The main hormone produced and secreted by the pineal gland is melatonin. Secretion is highest at night and between the ages of 0-5.

Reproduction

In simple terms, reproduction is the process by which organisms create descendants. This miracle is a characteristic that all living things have in common and sets them apart from non-living things. But even though the reproductive system is essential to keeping a species alive, it is not essential to keeping an individual alive.

In human reproduction, two kinds of sex cells or gametes are involved. Sperm, the male gamete and an egg or ovum, the gametes must meet in the female reproductive system to create a new individual. For reproduction to occur, both the female and male reproductive systems are essential. While both the female and male reproductive systems are involved with producing, nourishing and transporting either the egg or sperm, they are different in shape and structure.

The male has reproductive organs or genitals, that are both inside and outside the pelvis, while the female has reproductive organs entirely within the pelvis.

Male Reproductive System

The male reproductive system consists of the testes and a series of ducts and glands. Sperm are produced in the testes and are transported through the reproductive ducts. These ducts include the epididymis, ductus deferens, ejaculatory duct and urethra. The reproductive glands produce secretions that become part of semen, the fluid that is ejaculated from the urethra. These glands include the seminal vesicles, prostate gland and bulbourethral glands.

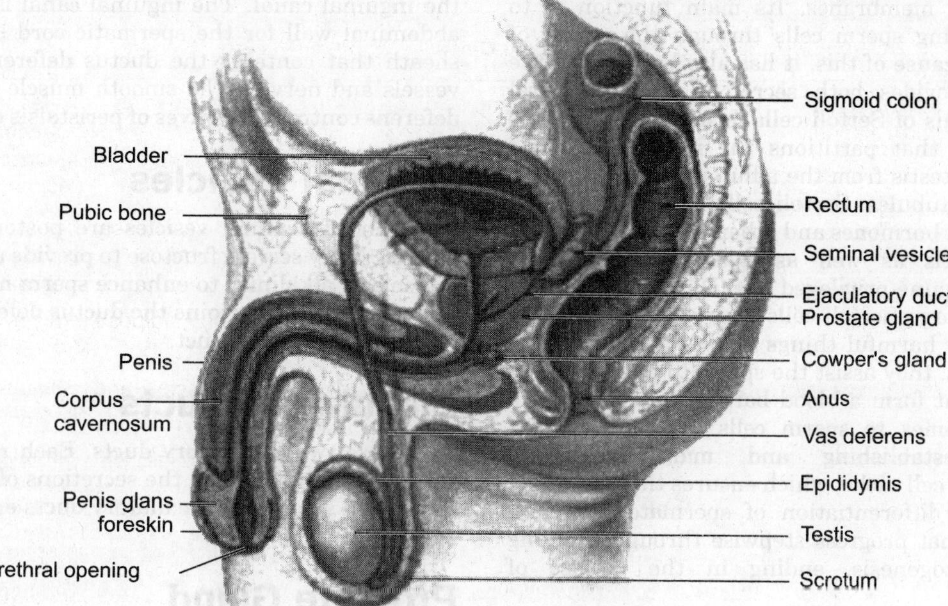

Fig. 22.20 Male reproduction system

Testes

The testes (sing. testis) are located in the scrotum (a sac of skin between the upper thighs). In the male foetus, the testes develop near the kidneys, then descend into the scrotum just before birth. Each testis is about 1½ inches long by 1 inch wide. Testosterone is produced in the testes which stimulates the production of sperm as well as give secondary sex characteristics beginning at puberty.

Scrotum

The two testicles are each held in a fleshy sac called the scrotum. The major function of the scrotal sac is to keep the testes cooler than thirty-seven degrees Celsius (ninety-eight point six degrees Fahrenheit). The external appearance of the scrotum vaires at different times in the same individual depending upon temperature and the subsequent contraction or relaxation of two muscles. These two muscles contract involuntarily when it is cold to move the testes closer to the heat of the body in the pelvic region. This causes the scrotum to appear tightly wrinkled. On the contrary, they relax in warm temperatures causing the testes to lower and the scrotum to become flaccid. The temperature of the testes is maintained at about thirty-five degrees Celsius (ninety-five degrees fahrenheit) below normal body temperature. Temperature has to be lower than normal in order for spermatogenesis (sperm production) to take place. A male can become sterile when testes have been exposed too often to high temperatures, such as when frequently in a hot tub.

The two muscles that regulate the temperature of the testes are the dartos and cremaster muscles:

Dartos Muscle

The dartos muscle is a layer of smooth muscle fibres in the subcutaneous tissue of the scrotum (surrounding the scrotum). This muscle is responsible for wrinkling up the scrotum, in conditions of cold weather, in order to maintain the correct temperature for spermatogenesis.

Cremaster Muscle

The cremaster muscle is a thin strand of skeletal muscle associated with the testes and spermatic cord. This muscle is a continuation of the internal oblique muscle of the abdominal wall, from which it is derived. It is responsible for raising or lowering the testes to keep them at the correct temperature.

Because it is skeletal muscle, it can also be contracted voluntarily. Some males, such as athletes, have the ability to consciously raise their scrotum up, to protect themselves against injury, while playing sports. However, not all males have this ability.

Seminiferous Tubules

Each testis contains over 100 yards of tightly packed seminiferous tubules. Around 90% of the weight of each testes consists of seminiferous tubules. The seminiferous tubules are the functional units of the testis, where spermatogenesis takes place. Once the sperm are produced, they moved from the seminiferous tubules into the rete testis for further maturation.

Interstitial Cells (Cells of Leydig)

In between the seminiferous tubules within the testes, are institial cells or cells of Leydig. They are responsible for secreting the male sex hormones (*i.e.*, testosterone).

Sertoli Cells

A Sertoli cell (a kind of sustentacular cell) is a 'nurse' cell of the testes which is part of a seminiferous tubule. It is activated by follicle-stimulating hormone and has

FSH-receptor on its membranes. Its main function is to nurture the developing sperm cells through the stages of spermatogenesis. Because of this, it has also been called the 'mother cell.' It provides both secretory and structural support. The junctions of Sertoli cells form the blood-testis barrier, a structure that partitions the interstitial blood compartment of the testis from the adluminal compartment of the seminiferous tubules. Sertoli cells control the entry and exit of nutrients, hormones and other chemicals into the tubules of the testis as well as make the adluminal compartment an immune-privileged site. During the time of sperm maturation, large Sertoli cells nourish the immature sperm and filter out harmful things before they reach the sperm. In these ways, they assist the sperm to mature. They are support cells that form a blood barrier with the blood. They filter what comes to sperm cells. The cell is also responsible for establishing and maintaining the spermatogonial stem cell niche, which ensures the renewal of stem cells and the differentiation of spermatogonia into mature germ cells that progress stepwise through the long process of spermatogenesis, ending in the release of spermatozoa.

Other functions during the maturation phase of spermiogenesis, the Sertoli cells consume the unneeded portions of the spermatozoa.

Efferent Ductules

The sperm are transported out of the testis and into the epididymis through a series of efferent ductules.

Blood Supply

The testes receive blood through the testicular arteries (gonadal artery). Venous blood is drained by the testicular veins. The right testicular vein drains directly into the inferior vena cava. The left testicular vein drains into the left renal vein.

Epididymis

The seminiferous tubules join together to become the epididymis. The epididymis is a tube that is about 20 feet long that is coiled on the posterior surface of each testis. Within the epididymis the sperm complete their maturation and their flagella become functional. This is also a site to store sperm until the next ejaculation. Smooth muscle in the wall of the epididymis propels the sperm into the ductus deferens.

Ductus Deferens

The ductus (vas) deferens, also called sperm duct or spermatic deferens, extends from the epididymis in the scrotum on its own side into the abdominal cavity through the inguinal canal. The inguinal canal is an opening in the abdominal wall for the spermatic cord (a connective tissue sheath that contains the ductus deferens, testicular blood vessels and nerves. The smooth muscle layer of the ductus deferens contracts in waves of peristalsis during ejaculation.

Seminal Vesicles

The pair of seminal vesicles are posterior to the urinary bladder. They secrete fructose to provide an energy source for sperm and alkalinity to enhance sperm mobility. The duct of each seminal vesicle joins the ductus deferens on that side to form the ejaculatory duct.

Ejaculatory Ducts

There are two ejaculatory ducts. Each receives sperm from the ductus deferens and the secretions of the seminal vesicle on its own side. Both ejaculatory ducts empty into the single urethra.

Prostate Gland

The prostate gland is a muscular gland that surrounds the first inch of the urethra as it emerges from the bladder. The smooth muscle of the prostate gland contracts during ejaculation to contribute to the expulsion of semen from the urethra.

Bulbourethral Glands

The bulbourethral glands also called Cowper's glands are located below the prostate gland and empty into the urethra. The alkalinity of seminal fluid helps neutralize the acidic vaginal pH and permits sperm mobility in what might otherwise be an unfavourable environment.

Penis

The penis is an external genital organ. The distal end of the penis is called the glans penis and is covered with a fold of skin called the prepuce or foreskin. Within the penis are masses of erectile tissue. Each consists of a framework of smooth muscle and connective tissue that contains blood sinuses, which are large, irregular vascular channels.

Urethra

The urethra, which is the last part of the urinary tract, traverses the corpus spongiosum and its opening, known as the meatus, lies on the tip of the glans penis. It is both a passage for urine and for the ejaculation of semen.

Table 22.2 **Structure and Function of Male Reproductive System**

Structure	Location and Description	Function
Bulbourethral glands (2)	Pea sized organs posterior to the prostate on either side of the urethra.	Secretion of gelatinous seminal fluid called pre-ejaculate. This fluid helps to lubricate the urethra for spermatozoa to pass through and to help flush out any residual urine or foreign matter (<1% of semen).
Cells of Leydig (Interstitial cells of Leydig)	Adjacent to the seminiferous tubules in the testicle.	Responsible for production of testosterone. Closely related to nerves.
Cremaster muscle	Covers the testes.	Raises and lowers scrotum to help regulate temperature and promote spermatogenesis.
Dartan's muscle	Layer of smooth muscular fibre outside the external spermatic fascia but below the skin.	Voluntary and involuntary contraction. Contraction by wrinkling to decrease surface area available for heat loss to testicles or expansion to increase surface area available to promote heat loss; also helps raise and lower scrotum to help regulate temperature.
Efferent ductules	Part of the testes and connect the rete testis with the epididymis.	Ducts for sperm to get to epididymis.
Ejaculatory ducts (2)	Begins at the vas deferens, passes through the prostate and empties into the urethra at the colliculus seminalis.	Causes reflex for ejaculation. During ejaculation, semen passes through the ducts and exits the body *via* the penis.
Epididymis	Tightly coiled duct lying just outside each testis connecting efferent ducts to vas deferens.	Storage and maturation of sperm.
Penis	Three columns of erectile tissue; two corpora cavernosa and one corpus spongiosum. Urethra passes through penis.	Male reproductive organ and also organ of urination.
Prostate gland	Surrounds the urethra just below the urinary bladder and can be felt during a rectal exam.	Stores and secretes a clear, slightly alkaline fluid constituting up to one-third of the volume of semen. Raise vaginal pH (25-30% of semen).
Scrotum	Pouch of skin and muscle that holds testicles.	Regulates temperature at slightly below body temperature.
Semen	Usually while but can be yellow, gray or pink (blood stained). After ejaculation, semen first goes through a clotting process and then becomes more liquid.	Components are sperm and 'seminal plasma'. Seminal plasma is produced by contributions from the seminal vesicle, prostate and bulbourethal glands.
Seminal vesicles (2)	Convoluted structure attached to vas deferens near the base of the urinary bladder.	About 65-75% of the seminal fluid in humans originates from the seminal vesicles. Contain proteins, enzymes, fructose, mucus, vitamin-C, flavins, phosphorylcholine and prostaglandins. High fructose concentrations provide nutrient energy for the spermatozoa as they travel through the female reproductive system.
Seminiferous tubules (2)	Long coiled structure contained in the chambers of the testis; joins with vas deferens.	Meiosis takes place here, creation of gametes (sperm).
Sertoli cells	Junctions of the Sertoli cells form the blood-testis barrier, a structure that partitions the interstitial blood compartment of the testis from the abdominal compartment of the seminiferous tubules.	Cells responsible for nurturing and development of sperm cells, provides both secretory and structural support; activated by FSH. Also called 'mother cells' or 'nurse cells'.
Testes	Inside scrotum, outside of body.	Gonads that produce sperm and male sex hormones. Production of testosterote by cells of Leydig in the testicles.
Testicular arteries (Gonadal arteries)	Branch of the abdominal aorta. It is a paired artery. Each passes obliquely downward and laterally behind the peritoneum.	Supplies blood to the testes.
Urethra	Connects bladder to outside body, about 8 inches long.	Tubular structure that receives urine from bladder and carries it to outside of the body. Also passage for sperm.
Vas deferens	Muscular tubes connecting the left and right epididymis to the ejaculatory ducts to move sperm. Each tube is about 30 cm long.	During ejaculation the smooth muscle in the vas deferens wall contracts, propelling sperm forward. Sperm are transferred from the vas deferens into the urethra, collecting fluids from accessory sex glands on route.

Composition of Human Semen

The components of semen come from two sources—sperm and 'seminal plasma'. Seminal plasma, in turn, is produced by contributions from the seminal vesicle, prostate and bulbourethral glands. Seminal plasma of humans contains a complex range of organic and inorganic constituents.

Table 22.3 **Parts of Glands in Semen**

Gland	Approximate %	Description
Testes	2-5%	Approximately 200-500 million spermatozoa sperm or spermatozoans), produced in the testes, are released per ejaculation.
Seminal vesicle	65-75%	Amino acids, citrate, enzymes, flavins, fructose (the main energy source of sperm cells, which rely entirely on sugars from the seminal plasma for energy), phosphorylcholine, prostaglandins (involved in suppressing an immune response by the female against the foreign semen), proteins, vitamin-C.
Prostate	25-30%	Acid phosphatase, citric acid, fibrinolysin, prostate specific antigen, proteolytic enzymes, zinc (serves to help to stabilize the DNA-containing chromatin in the sperm cells. A zinc deficiency may result in lowered fertility because of increased sperm fragility. Zinc deficiency can also adversely affect spermatogenesis).
Bulbourethral glands	<1%	Galactose, mucus (serve to increase the mobility of sperm cells in the vagina and cervix by creating a less viscous channel for the sperm cells to swim through and preventing their diffusion out of the semen. Contributes to the cohensive jelly-like texture of semen) pre-ejaculate, sialic acid.

Hormone Regulation

Hormones which control reproduction in males are:

Gonadotropin Releasing Hormone (GnRH):

(a) The hypothalamus secretes this hormone into the pituitary gland in the brain.

(b) There are two gonadotropic hormones, FSH and LH.

(c) Luteinizing Hormone (LH).

(d) The pituitary gland secretes this hormone after receiving a GnRH signal from the of hypothalamus.

(e) LH stimulates Leydig cells, in the testes, telling them to produce testosterone.

(f) Follicle Stimulating Hormone (FSH).

(g) The pituitary gland also secretes this hormone.

(h) Testosterone helps FSH run through the bloodstream to make Sertoli cells, located in the seminiferous tubules of the testes, to make immature sperm to mature sperm.

(i) Testosterone

(j) Also know as 'the male hormone' and 'androgen'.

(k) Testosterone is vital for the production of sperm.

Erection

The erection of the penis is its enlarged and firm state. It depends on a complex interaction of psychological, neural, vascular and endocrine factors. The term is also applied to the process that leads to this state. A penile erection occurs when two tubular structures that run the length of the penis, the corpora cavernosa, become engorged with venous blood. This is a result of parasympathetic nerve induced vasodilation. This may result from any of various physiological stimuli. The corpus spongiosum is a single tubular structure located just below the corpora cavernosa, which contains the urethra, through which urine and semen pass during urination and ejaculation, respectively. This may also become slightly engorged with blood, but less so than the corpora cavernosa.

Ejaculation

Emission is the term used when sperm moves into the urethra. Ejaculation is the term used when sperm is forced out of the urethra and penis. These are both stimulated by sympathetic nerves.

Sperm Pathway

Spermatogenesis takes place inside a male's testes, specifically in the walls of the seminiferous tubules. The epididymis is a tortuously coiled structure topping the testis, it receives immature sperm from the testis and stores it for several days. When ejaculation occurs, sperm is forcefully expelled from the tail of the epididymis into the ductus deferens. Sperm travels through the ductus deferens and up the spermatic cord into the pelvic cavity, over the ureter to the prostate behind the bladder. Here, the vas deferens joins with the seminal vesicle to form the ejaculatory duct, which passes through the prostate and empties into the urethra. Upon the sperm's exit from the testes, into the vas deferens, muscular movements take over. When ejaculation occurs, rhythmic muscle movements of peristalsis propel the sperm forward. This continues throughout the remainder of the sperm's journey through the male reproductive system.

Sperm cells become even more active when they begin to interact with the fertilizing layer of an egg cell. They swim faster and their tail movements become more forceful and erratic. This behaviour is called 'hyper activation.'

These channels are selective, allowing only calcium ion to pass. The opening of catsper channels is responsible for the influx of calcium. The sudden rise in calcium levels causes the flagellum to form deeper bends, propelling the sperm more forcefully through the viscous environment. The sperm use their tails to push themselves into the epididymis, where they complete their development. It takes sperm about 4 to 6 weeks to travel through the epididymis. The sperm then move to the vas deferens or sperm duct. The seminal vesicles and prostate gland produce a whitish fluid called seminal fluid, which mixes with sperm to form semen when a male is sexually stimulated. The penis, which usually hangs limp, becomes hard when a male is sexually excited. Tissues in the penis fill with blood and it becomes stiff and erect (an erection). The rigidity of the erect penis makes it easier to insert into the female's vagina during sexual intercourse and the extended length allows it to reach deeper into the female's oviduct, the passage from the ovaries to the outside of the body (allowing a shorter travel distance for the spermatozoa).

When the erect penis is stimulated to orgasm, muscles around the reproductive organs contract and force the semen through the duct system and urethra. Semen is pushed out of the male's body through his urethra - ejaculation. The speed of the semen is about 70 mph when ejaculation comes and it can contain 100 to 600 million sperm cells. When the male ejaculates during intercourse, semen is deposited into the fornix at the base of the female's vagina, near the cervix. From the fornix, the sperm make their way up through the cervix and move through the uterus with help from uterine contractions. Sperm hyperactivity is necessary for breaking through two physical barriers that protect the egg from fertilization. The first barrier to sperm is made up of so called cumulus cells embedded in a gel-like substance made primarily of hyaluronic acid. The cumulus cells develop in the ovary with the egg and support it as it grows.

The second barrier coating the oocyte is a thick shell formed by glycoproteins called the zona pellucida. One of the proteins that make up the zona pellucida binds to a partner molecule on the sperm. This lock-and-key type mechanism is species-specific and prevents the sperm and egg of different species from fusing. There is some evidence that this binding is what triggers the acrosome to release the enzymes that allow the sperm to fuse with the egg. When a sperm cell reaches the egg the acrosome releases its enzymes. These enzymes weaken the shell, allowing the sperm cell to penetrate it and reach the plasma membrane of the egg. Part of the sperm's cell membrane then fuses with the egg cell's membrane and the sperm cell sinks into the egg (at which point the sperm tail falls off).

Upon penetration, the egg cell membrane undergoes a change and becomes impenetrable, preventing further fertilization. The binding of the sperm to an ovum is called a zygote. A zygote is a single cell, with a complete set of chromosomes, that normally develops into an embryo.

Puberty

In addition to producing sperm, the male reproductive system also produces sex hormones, which help a boy develop into a sexually mature man during puberty. When a baby boy is born, he has all the parts of his reproductive system in place, but it isn't until puberty that his reproductive organs mature and become fully functional. As an newborn FSH and LH levels are high and after a few weeks levels drop to extremly low. When puberty begins, usually between the ages of 10 and 14, the pituitary gland, which is located in the brain secretes hormones that stimulate the testicles to produce testosterone. The production of testosterone brings about many physical changes. Although the timing of these changes is different for each individual male, the stages of puberty generally follow a set sequence.

(i) **First stage** The scrotum and testes grow larger, the apocrine glands develop.

(ii) **Second stage** The penis becomes longer and the seminal vesicles and prostate gland grow. Hair begins to grow in the pubic region. Reproductive capacity has usually developed by this stage.

(iii) **Third stage** Hair begins to appear on the face and underarms. During this time, a male's voice also deepens. Fertility continues to increase.

Ageing

For most men, testosterone secretion continues throughout life, as does sperm production, though both diminish with advancing age. Probably the most common reproductive problem for older men is prostatic hypertropy, enlargement of the prostate gland. This causes the urethra to compress and urination becomes difficult. Residual urine in the bladder increases the chance of urinary tract infections. Prostate hypertrophy is usually benign, but cancer of the prostate is one of the more common cancers in elderly men. A Turp is commonly used to correct this problem if the symptoms do not improve in response to home treatment and medication.

Erectile Dysfunction (ED) is another common problem seen in ageing males. In older men, ED usually has a physical cause, such as disease, injury or side effects of drugs. Any disorder that impairs blood flow in the penis or causes injury to the nerves has the potential to cause ED. Although it is not an inevitable part of aging, incidences increase with age about

5 percent of 40 year old men and between 15 and 25 percent of 65-year-old men experience ED. However, with proper treatment, the same can be treated effectively.

Female Reproductive System

The differences between the female and male reproductive systems are based on the functions of each individual's role in the reproduction cycle. A male who is healthy and sexually mature, continuously produces sperm. A woman's ova (eggs) are completely formed during foetal development. At about 5 months gestation, the ovaries contain approximately six to seven million oogonia, which then go through meiosis and are matured into oocytes.

The ovaries of a newborn baby girl contain about two million oocytes. This number declines to 300000 to 400000 by the time puberty is reached. On average, 400 oocytes are ovulated during a woman's reproductive lifetime. When a young woman reaches puberty around age 12 or 13, an ova (one of the matured oocytes) is discharged from alternating ovaries every 28 days. This continues until the woman reaches menopause, usually around the age of 50 years. Occytes are present at birth and ages as a woman ages. This may be one reason older women are more likely to have a hard time becoming pregnant or more likely to have children with genetic defects.

Female Reproductive System

(i) Produces eggs (ova).

(ii) Secretes sex hormones.

(iii) Receives the male spermatazoa during sexual intercourse.

(iv) Protects and nourishes the fertilized egg until it is fully developed.

(v) Delivers foetus through birth canal.

(vi) Provides nourishment to the baby through milk secreted by mammary glands in the breast.

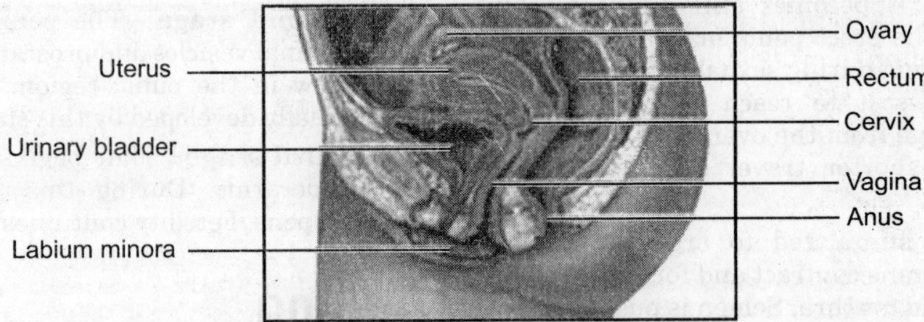

Fig. 22.21 Female reproduction system

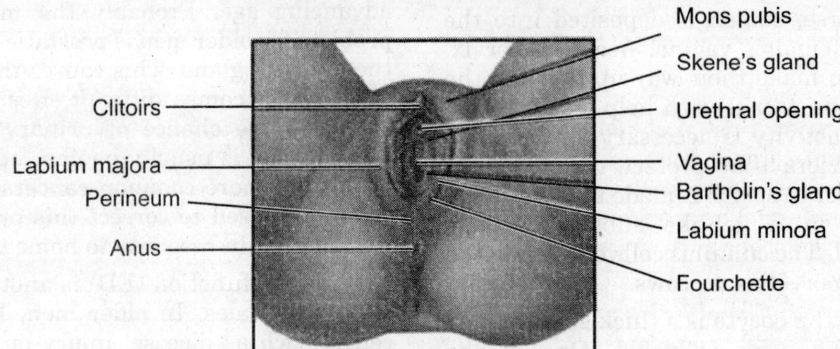

Fig. 22.22 External genitalia

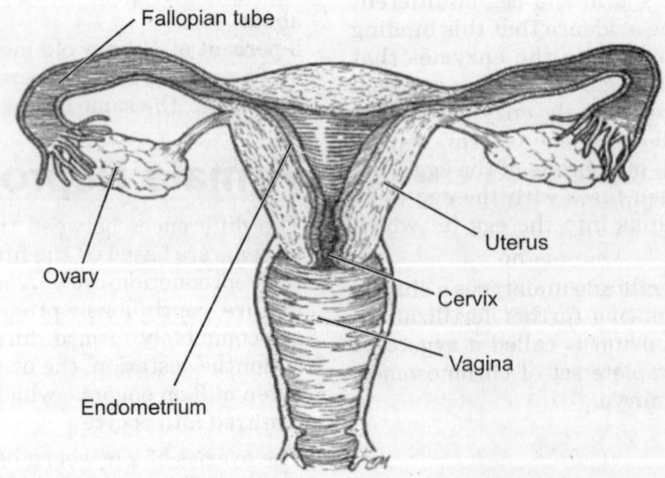

Fig. 22.23 The front view of the female reproductive organs

External Genitals

Vulva

The external female genitals are collectively referred to as the vulva. This consists of the labia majora and labia minora (while these names translate as 'large' and 'small' lips, often the 'minora' can be larger and protrude outside the 'majora'), mons pubis, clitoris, opening of the urethra (meatus), vaginal vestibule, vestibular bulbs, vestibular glands. The term 'vagina' is often improperly used as a generic term to refer to the vulva or female genitals, even though strictly speaking the vagina is a specific internal structure and the vulva is the exterior genitalia only. Calling the vulva the vagina is akin to calling the mouth the throat.

Mons Veneris

The mons veneris, Latin for 'mound of venus' (Roman goddess of love) is the soft mound at the front of the vulva (fatty tissue covering the pubic bone). It is also referred to as the mons pubis. The mons veneris is sexually sensitive in some women and protects the pubic bone and vulva from the impact of sexual intercourse. After puberty it is covered with pubic hair, usually in a triangular shape. Heredity can play a role in the amount of pubic hair an individual grows.

Labia Majora

The labia majora are the outer 'lips' of the vulva. They are pads of loose connective and adipose tissue, as well as some smooth muscle. The labia majora wrap around the vulva from the mons pubis to the perineum. The labia majora generally hides, partially or entirely, the other parts of the vulva. There is also a longitudinal separation called the pudendal cleft. These labia are usually covered with pubic hair. The colour of the outside skin of the labia majora is usually close to the overall colour of the individual, although there may be some variation. The inside skin is usually pink to light brown. They contain numerous sweat and oil glands. It has been suggested that the scent from these oils are sexually arousing.

Labia Minora

Medial to the labia majora are the labia minora. The labia minora are the inner lips of the vulva. They are thin stretches of tissue within the labia majora that fold and protect the vagina, urethra and clitoris. The appearance of labia minora can vary widely, from tiny lips that hide between the labia majora to large lips that protrude. There is no pubic hair on the labia minora, but there are sebaceous glands. The two smaller lips of the labia minora come together longitudinally to form the prepuce, a fold that covers part of the clitoris. The labia minora protect the vaginal and urethral openings. Both the inner and outer labia are quite sensitive to touch and pressure.

Clitoris

The clitoris, visible as the small white oval between the top of the labia minora and the clitoral hood, is a small body of spongy tissue that functions solely for sexual pleasure. Only the tip or glans of the clitoris shows externally, but the organ itself is elongated and branched into two forks, the crura, which extend downward along the rim of the vaginal opening toward the perineum. Thus the clitoris is much larger than most people think it is, about 4" long on average. The clitoral glans or external tip of the clitoris is protected by the prepuce or clitoral hood, a covering of tissue similar to the foreskin of the male penis. However, unlike the penis, the clitoris does not contain any part of the urethra. During sexual excitement, the clitoris erects and extends, the hood retracts, making the clitoral glans more accessible. The size of the clitoris is variable between women. On some, the clitoral glans is very small; on others, it is large and the hood does not completely cover it.

Urethra

The opening to the urethra is just below the clitoris. Although, it is not related to sex or reproduction, it is included in the vulva. The urethra is actually used for the passage of urine. The urethra is connected to the bladder. In females the urethra is 1.5 inches long, compared to males whose urethra is 8 inches long. Because the urethra is so close to the anus, women should always wipe themselves from front to back to avoid infecting the vagina and urethra with bacteria. This location tissue is the reason for bladder infections being more common among females.

Hymen

The hymen is a thin fold of mucous membrane that separates the lumen of the vagina from the urethral sinus. Sometimes it may partially cover the vaginal orifice. The hymen is usually perforated during later foetal development. Because of the belief that first vaginal penetration would usually tear this membrane and cause bleeding, its 'intactness' has been considered a guarantor of virginity. However, the hymen is a poor indicator of whether a woman has actually engaged in sexual intercourse because a normal hymen does not completely block the vaginal opening. The normal hymen is never actually 'intact' since, there is always an opening in it. Furthermore, there is not always bleeding at first vaginal penetration. The blood that is sometimes, but not always, observed after first penetration can be due to tearing of the hymen, but it can also be from injury to nearby tissues. A tear to the hymen, medically referred to as a 'transection,' can be seen in a small percentage of women or girls after first penetration. A transection is caused by penetrating trauma.

Masturbation and tampon insertion can, but generally are not forceful enough to cause penetrating trauma to the hymen.

Therefore, the appearance of the hymen is not a reliable indicator of virginity or chastity.

Perineum

The perineum is the short stretch of skin starting at the bottom of the vulva and extending to the anus. It is a diamond-shaped area between the symphysis pubis and the coccyx. This area forms the floor of the pelvis and contains the external sex organs and the anal opening. It can be further divided into the urogenital triangle in front and the anal triangle in back. The perineum in some women may tear during the birth of an infant and this is apparently natural. Some physicians however, may cut the perineum preemptively on the grounds that the 'tearing' may be more harmful than a precise cut by a scalpel. If a physician decides the cut is necessary, they will perform it. The cut is called an episiotomy.

Internal Genitals

Vagina

The vagina is a muscular, hollow tube that extends from the vaginal opening to the cervix of the uterus. It is situated between the urinary bladder and the rectum. It is about three to five inches long in a grown woman. The muscular wall allows the vagina to expand and contract. The muscular walls are lined with mucous membranes, which keep it protected and moist. A thin sheet of tissue with one or more holes in it, called the hymen, partially covers the opening of the vagina. The vagina receives sperm during sexual intercourse from the penis. The sperm that survive the acidic condition of the vagina continue on through to the Fallopian tubes where fertilization may occur. The vagina is made up of three layers, an inner mucosal layer, a middle muscularis layer and an outer fibrous layer. The inner layer is made of vaginal rugae that stretch and allow penetration to occur. These also help with stimulation of the penis. The middle layer has glands that secrete an acidic mucus (pH of around 4.0.) that keeps bacterial growth down. The outer muscular layer is especially important with delivery of a foetus and placenta.

Purposes of the vagina

(a) Receives a males erect penis and semen during sexual intercourse.

(b) Pathway through a womans body for the baby to take during childbirth.

(c) Provides the route for the menstrual blood (menses) from the uterus, to leave the body.

(d) May hold forms of birth control, such as a diaphragm, female cap, nuva ring or female condom.

Cervix

The cervix (from Latin 'neck') is the lower, narrow portion of the uterus where it joins with the top end of the vagina. Where they join together forms an almost 90 degree curve. It is cylindrical or conical in shape and protrudes through the upper anterior vaginal wall. Approximately half its length is visible with appropriate medical equipment; the remainder lies above the vagina beyond view. It is occasionally called 'cervix uteri' or 'neck of the uterus'. During menstruation, the cervix stretches open slightly to allow the endometrium to be shed. This stretching is believed to be part of the cramping pain that many women experience. Evidence for this is given by the fact that some women's cramps subside or disappear after their first vaginal birth because the cervical opening has widened. The portion projecting into the vagina is referred to as the portio vaginalis or ectocervix. On average, the ectocervix is 3 cm long and 2 and a cm wide. It has a convex, elliptical surface and is divided into anterior and posterior lips. The ectocervix's opening is called the external. The size and shape of the external and the ectocervix varies widely with age, hormonal state and whether the woman has had a vaginal birth. In women who have not had a vaginal birth the external os appears as a small, circular opening. In women who have had a vaginal birth, the ectocervix appears bulkier and the external appears wider, more slit-like and gaping. The passage way between the external and the uterine cavity is referred to as the endocervical canal. It varies widely in length and width, alongwith the cervix overall. Flattened anterior to posterior, the endocervical canal measures seven to eight mm at its widest in reproductive-aged women. The endocervical canal terminates at the internal os which is the opening of the cervix inside the uterine cavity.

During childbirth, contractions of the uterus will dilate the cervix up to 10 cm in diameter to allow the child to pass through. During orgasm, the cervix convulses and the external dilates.

Uterus

The uterus is shaped like an upside-down pear, with a thick lining and muscular walls. Located near the floor of the pelvic cavity, it is hollow to allow a blastocyte or fertilized egg, to implant and grow. It also allows for the inner lining of the uterus to build up until a fertilized egg is implanted or it is sloughed off during menses. The uterus contains some of the strongest muscles in the female body. These muscles are able to expand and contract to accommodate a growing foetus and then help push the baby out during labour. These muscles also contract rhythmically during an orgasm in a wave like action. It is thought that this is to help push or guide the sperm up the uterus to the Fallopian tubes where fertilization may be possible. The uterus is only about three inches long and two inches wide, but during pregnancy it changes rapidly and dramatically. The top rim of the uterus is called the fundus and is a landmark for many doctors to track the progress of a pregnancy. The uterine cavity refers to the fundus of the uterus and the body of the uterus. Helping support the uterus are ligaments that attach from the body of the uterus to the pelvic wall and abdominal wall. During pregnancy the ligaments prolapse due to the growing uterus, but retract after childbirth. In some cases after menopause, they may lose elasticity and uterine prolapse may occur. This can be fixed with surgery.

Some problems of the uterus include uterine fibroids, pelvic pain (including endometriosis, adenomyosis) pelvic relaxation (or prolapse) heavy or abnormal menstrual bleeding and cancer. It is only after all alternative options have been considered that surgery is recommended in these cases. This surgery is called hysterectomy. Hysterectomy is the removal of the uterus and may include the removal of one or both of the ovaries. Once performed it is irreversible. After a hysterectomy, many women begin a form of alternate hormone therapy due to the lack of ovaries and hormone production.

Fallopian Tubes

At the upper corners of the uterus are the Fallopian tubes. There are two Fallopian tubes, also called the uterine tubes or the oviducts. Each Fallopian tube attaches to a side of the uterus and connects to an ovary. They are positioned between the ligaments that support the uterus. The Fallopian tubes are about four inches long and about as wide as a piece of spaghetti. Within each tube is a tiny passageway no wider than a sewing needle. At the other end of each Fallopian tube is a fringed area that looks like a funnel. This fringed area, called the infundibulum, lies close to the ovary, but is not attached. The ovaries alternately release an egg. When an ovary does ovulate or release an egg, it is swept into the lumen of the Fallopian tube by the frimbriae. Once the egg is in the Fallopian tube, tiny hairs in the tube's lining help push it down the narrow passageway toward the uterus. The oocyte or developing egg cell, takes four to five days to travel down the length of the Fallopian tube. If enough sperm are ejaculated during sexual intercourse and there is an oocyte in the Fallopian tube, fertilization will occur. After fertilization occurs, the zygote or fertilized egg, will continue down to the uterus and implant itself in the uterine wall, where it will grow and develop.

If a zygote doesn't move down to the uterus and implants itself in the Fallopian tube, it is called a ectopic or tubal pregnancy. If this occurs, the pregnancy will need to be terminated to prevent permanent damage to the Fallopian tube, possible haemorrhage and possible death of the mother.

Ovaries

The female gonads are the paired ovaries. Ovaries are flattened and ovoid structures in resting condition located in the pelvic part of abdomen, one on each side of uterus. A layer of cells called germinal epithelium is found over the ovaries which is composed of cuboidal epithelial cells. The epithelial layer penetrates deeply as columns of cells into the underlying connective tissue. From these columns, cells multiply and grow down into the substance of ovary, some cells differentiate to become ova and become surrounded by a single layer of cells forming membrane granulosa. On acheiving puberty the granulosa proliferates to form many layers of small cells. Fluid then appears in these cells. The liquid separates the granulosa into two layers a thin layer lining the inner surface of follicle and cells which surround the ovum. These cells form a mass at one pole, thus attaching the ovum to the margin of follicle. After the accumulation of liquir the follicle is termed Graafian follicle. Each follicle contains an immature egg called primary oocyte. After the release of oocyte the lining of follicle grows inward forming the **corpus luteum** which serves as temporary endocrine tissue.

Mammary Glands

Mammary glands are the organs that produce milk for the sustenance of a baby. These exocrine glands are enlarged and modified sweat glands. Structure the basic components of the mammary gland are the alveoli (hollow cavities, a few millimetres large) lined with milk-secreting epithelial cells and surrounded by myoepithelial cells. These alveoli join up to form groups known as lobules and each lobule has a lactiferous duct that drains into openings in the nipple. The myoepithelial cells can contract, similar to muscle cells and thereby push the milk from the alveoli through the lactiferous ducts towards the nipple, where it collects in widenings (sinuses) of the ducts. A suckling baby essentially squeezes the milk out of these sinuses. The development of mammary glands is controlled by hormones. The mammary glands exist in both sexes, but they are rudimentary until puberty when in response to ovarian hormones, they begin to develop in the female. Oestrogen promotes formation, while testosterone inhibits it. At the time of birth, the baby has lactiferous ducts but no alveoli. Little branching occurs before puberty when ovarian estrogens stimulate branching differentiation of the ducts into spherical masses of cells that will become alveoli. True secretory alveoli only develop in pregnancy, where rising levels of oestrogen and progesterone cause further branching and differentiation of the duct cells, together with an increase in adipose tissue and a richer blood flow. Colostrum is secreted in late pregnancy and for the first few days after giving birth. True milk secretion (lactation) begins a few days later due to a reduction in circulating progesterone and the presence of the hormone prolactin. The suckling of the baby causes the release of the hormone oxytocin which stimulates contraction of the myoepithelial cells. The cells of mammary glands can easily be induced to grow and multiply by hormones. If this growth runs out of control, cancer results. Almost all instances of breast cancer originate in the lobules or ducts of the mammary glands.

Table 22.4 **Structure and Function of Female Reproductive System**

Structure	Location and Description	Function
Breasts	Upper chest one on each side containing alveolar cells (milk production), myoepithelial cells (contrast to expel milk) and duct walls (help with extraction of milk).	Lactation milk/nutrition for newborn.
Cervix	The lower narrower portion of the uterus.	During childbirth, contractions of the uterus will dilate the cervix up to 10 cm in diameter to allow the child to pass through. During orgasm, the cervix convulses and the external of dilates.
Clitoris	Small erectile organ directly in front of the vestibule.	Sexual excitation, engorged with blood.
Fallopian tubes	Extending upper part of the uterus on either side.	Egg transportation from ovary to uterus (fertilization usually takes place here).
Hymen	Thin membrane that partially covers the vagina in young females.	Lubrication during mating.
Labia majora	Outer skin folds that surround the entrance to the vagina.	Lubrication during mating.
Labia minora	Inner skin folds that surround the entrance to the vagina.	
Mons	Mound of skin and underlying fatty tissue, central in lower pelvic region.	
Ovaries (female gonads)	Pelvic region on either side of the uterus.	Provides an environment for maturation of oocyte.
Perineum	Short stretch of skin starting at the bottom of the vulva and extending to the anus.	Synthesizes and secretes sex hormones (oestrogen and progesterone).
Urethra	Pelvic cavity above bladder, tilted.	Passage of urine.
Uterus	Centre of pelvic cavity.	To house and nourish developing human.
Vagina	Canal about 10-8 cm long going from the cervix to the outside of the body.	Receives penis during matting, pathway through a womans body for the baby to take during childbirth. Provides the route for the menstrual blood (menses) from the uterus, to leave the body. May hold forms of birth control, such as an IUD, diaphragm, neva ring or female condom.
Vulva	Surround entrance to the reproductive tract. (encompasses all external genitalia).	
Endometrium	The innermost layer of uterine wall.	Contains glands that secrete fluids that bathe the utrine lining.
Myometrium	Smooth muscle in uterine wall.	Contracts to help expel the baby.

The Female Reproductive Cycle

Towards the end of puberty, girls begin to release eggs as part of a monthly period called the female reproductive cycle or menstrual cycle (menstrual referring to 'monthly'). Approximately every 28 days, during ovulation, an ovary sends a tiny egg into one of the Fallopian tubes. Unless the egg is fertilized by a sperm while in the Fallopian in the two to three days following ovulation, the egg dries up and leaves the body about two weeks later through the vagina. This process is called **menstruation.** Blood and tissues from the inner lining of the uterus (the endometrium) combine to form the menstrual flow, which generally lasts from four to seven days. The first period is called menarche. During menstruation arteries that supply the lining of the uterus constrict and capillaries weaken. Blood spilling from the damaged vessels detaches layers of the lining, not all at once but in random patches. Endometrium mucus and blood descending from the uterus, through the liquid creates the menstruation flow.

The reproductive cycle can be divided into an ovarian cycle and a uterine cycle (compare ovarian histology and uterine histology in the diagram on the right). During the uterine cycle, the endometrial lining of the uterus builds up under the influence of increasing levels of oestrogen (labelled as oestradiol in the image). Follicles develop and within a few days one matures into an ovum or egg. The ovary then releases this egg, at the time of ovulation. After ovulation the uterine lining enters a secretory phase or the ovarian cycle, in preparation for implantation, under the influence of progesterone. Progesterone is produced by the corpus luteum (the follicle after ovulation) and enriches the uterus with a thick lining of blood vessels and capillaries so that it can sustain the growing foetus. If fertilization and implantation occur, the embryo produces Human Chorionic Gonadotropin

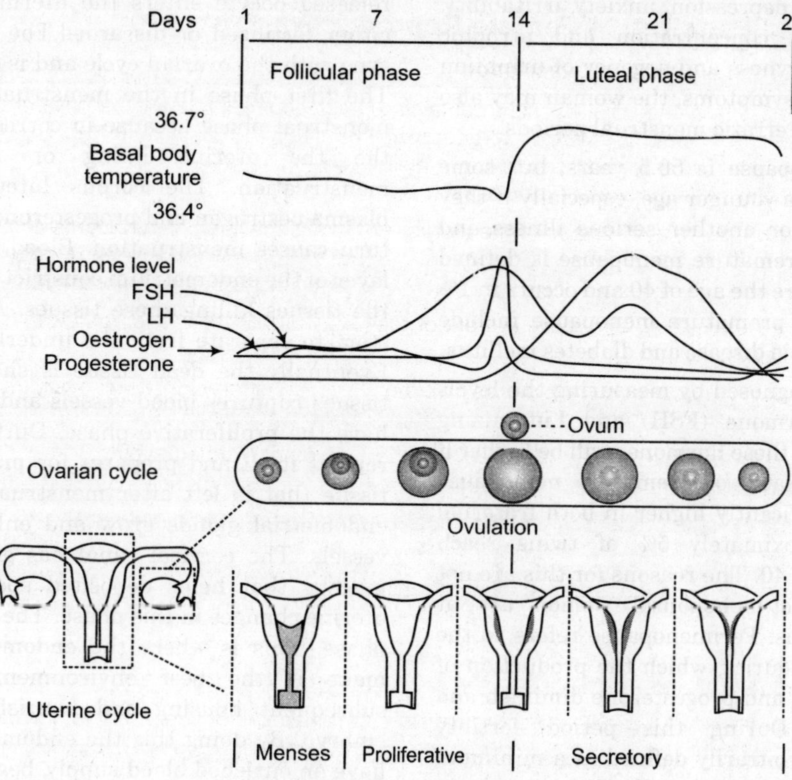

Fig. 22.24 Menstrual cycle

(HCG), which maintains the corpus luteum and causes it to continue producing progesterone until the placenta can take over production of progesterone. Hence, progesterone is 'pro gestational' and maintains the uterine lining during all of pregnancy. If fertilization and implantation do not occur the corpus luteum degenerates into a corpus albicans and progesterone levels fall. This fall in progesterone levels cause the endometrium lining to breakdown and sluff off through the vagina. This is called menstruation, which marks the low point for oestrogen activity and is the starting point of a new cycle.

Common usage refers to menstruation and menses as a period. This bleeding serves as a sign that a woman has not become pregnant. However, this cannot be taken as certainty, as sometimes there is some bleeding in early pregnancy. During the reproductive years, failure to menstruate may provide the first indication to a woman that she may have become pregnant. Menstruation forms a normal part of a natural cyclic process occurring in healthy women between puberty and the end of the reproductive years. The onset of menstruation, known as menarche, occurs at an average age of 12, but is normal anywhere between 8 and 16. Factors such as heredity, diet and overall health can accelerate or delay the onset of menarche.

Signs of Ovulation

The female body produces outward signs that can be easily recognized at the time of ovulation. The two main signs are thinning of the cervical mucus and a slight change in body temperature.

Thinning of the Cervical Mucus

After menstruation and right before ovulation, a woman will experience an increase of cervical mucus. At first, it will be thick and yellowish in colour and will not be very plentiful. Leading up to ovulation, it will become thinner and clearer. On or around the day of ovulation, the çervical mucus will be very thin, clear and stretchy. It can be compared to the consistency of egg whites.

Temperature Change

A woman can also tell the time of ovulation by taking her basal body temperature daily. This is a temperature taken with a very sensitive thermometer first thing in the morning before the woman gets out of bed. The temperature is then tracked to show changes. In the uterine cycle, a normal temperature will be around 97.0-98.0. A woman could be off by a couple of days in her calculations and still become pregnant.

Menopause

Menopause is the physiological cessation of menstrual cycles associated with advancing age. Menopause is sometimes referred to as 'the change of life' or climacteric. Menopause occurs as the ovaries stop producing oestrogen, causing the reproductive system to gradually shut down. As the body adapts to the changing levels of natural hormones, vasomotor symptoms such as hot flashes and palpitations, psychological symptoms such as increased depression, anxiety, irritability, mood swings and lack of concentration and atrophic symptoms such as vaginal dryness and urgency of urination appear. Together with these symptoms, the woman may also have increasingly scanty and erratic menstrual periods.

The average onset of menopause is 50.5 years, but some women enter menopause at a younger age, especially if they have suffered from cancer or another serious illness and undergone chemotherapy. Premature menopause is defined as menopause occurring before the age of 40 and occurs in 1% of women. Other causes of premature menopause include autoimmune disorders, thyroid disease and diabetes mellitus.

Premature menopause is diagnosed by measuring the levels of Follicle Stimulating Hormone (FSH) and Luteinizing Hormone (LH). The levels of these hormones will be higher if menopause has occurred. Rates of premature menopause have been found to be significantly higher in both fraternal and identical twins; approximately 5% of twins reach menopause before the age of 40. The reasons for this are not completely understood. Post-menopausal women are at increased risk of osteoporosis. Perimenopause refers to the time preceding menopause, during which the production of hormones such as oestrogen and progesterone diminish and become more irregular. During this period fertility diminishes. Menopause is arbitrarily defined as a minimum of twelve months without menstruation. Perimenopause can begin as early as age 35, although it usually begins much later. It can last for a few months or for several years. The duration of perimenopause cannot be predicted in advance.

Premenstrual Syndrome (PMS), it is common for women to experience some discomfort in the days leading up to their periods. PMS usually is at its worst the seven days before a period starts and can continue through the end of the period. PMS includes both physical and emotional symptoms acne, bloating, fatigue, backaches, sore breasts, headaches, constipation, diarrhoea, food cravings, depression, irritability, difficulty concentrating or handling stress.

There are two phases of the ovarian cycle the follicular phase and the luteal phase. In the follicular phase about 10-25 follicles are taken from preantral or early antral follicles to develop further. Seven days later the dominant follicle is selected to develop to full maturity. This is the pre-cursor for ovulation. Follicles themselves secrete FSH and oestrogen and these two hormones stimulate follicular growth and development. Ovulation marks the beginning of the luteal phase. This is started by the wall of the Graaffian follicle to rupture and cause a flow of antral fluid that will carry the oocyte to the ovary's surface. The ruptured follicle is then turned into a gland (corpus luteum). Which secretes oestrogens and progesterone. This is all triggered by and abrupt change in plasma LH levels. After ovulation the released oocyte enters the uterine tube, where it will be either fertilized or discarded.The uterine cycle operates in sync with the ovarian cycle and is divided into three phases. The first phase in the menstrual phase. It is named the menstrual phase because in corresponds with the shedding the the uterine lining or more commonly called menstruation. The corpus luteum degenerates causing plasma oestrogen and progesterone levels to decrease and in turn causes menstruation. Blood vessels is the outer most layer of the endometrium constrict and decrease blood flow to the tissues killing these tissues. After the tissues die they start to separate from the underlying endometrial tissues. Eventually the dead tissue is shed. This shedding of the tissues ruptures blood vessels and causes bleeding. Now we have the proliferative phase. During this phase the uterus renews itself and prepares for pregnancy. The endomitrial tissue that is left after menstruation begins to grow. The endometrial glands grow and enlarge causing more blood vessels. The cervical canal has glands that secrete a thin mucous that helps deposited sperm. Oestrogen promotes uterine changes in this phase. The last phase is the secretory phase. This is where the endometrium is transformed to make it the best environment for implantation and subsequent housing and nourishment of the developing embryo. By doing this the endometrium will do things like have an enriched blood supply, begin to secrete fluids rich in glycogen and even form a plug at the end of the cervical canal so that microorganisms can not enter. These changes in the uterus are caused by progesterone, due to the corpus luteum. At the end of the secretory phase the corpus luteum degenerates and progesterone levels fall. This will trigger menstruation.

Types of Birth Control

Birth control is a regimen of one or more actions, devices or medications followed in order to deliberately prevent or reduce the likelihood of a woman becoming pregnant. Methods and intentions typically termed birth control may be considered a pivotal ingredient to family planning. Mechanisms which are intended to reduce the likelihood of the fertilization of an ovum by a sperm may more specifically be referred to as contraception. Contraception differs from abortion in that the former prevents fertilization, while the latter terminates an already established pregnancy. Methods of birth control which may prevent the implantation of an embryo if fertilization occurs are medically considered to be contraception. It is advised to talk with a doctor before choosing a contraceptive. If you have genetics problems or blood conditions, such as factor V leiden, certain contraceptives can be deadly.

Table 22.5 **Types of Birth Control and its Methods**

Type	Procedure	Method	Effectiveness	Risks
Abstinence	Refrain from sexual intercourse.	No sperm in vagina	100%	None
Rhythm method	Intercourse is avoided for about an 8-day span every month in middle of her cycle, from about five days before ovulation to three days after ovulation.	Fertilization is only possible during 8-day span is middle of menstrual cycle.	70-80%	None
Withdrawl	The man withdraws his penis from the vagina at just the right moment before ejaculation.	Sperm are unable to enter vagina if male penis is removed at the right time.	70-80%	None
Tubal ligation (Vascetomy)	Oviducts are cut and tied.	No eggs in oviduct	Almost 90%	About 75% Irreversible
Hormonal IUD (Intrauterine Device)	Flexible, plastic coil inserted by physician.	Releases small amount of oestrogen. In most cases, stops eggs from developing and being released.	About 99%	May cause infection uterine perforation
Oral contraceptive	Hormone medication taken daily.	Stop releases of FSH and LH	More than 90%	Blood clots, especially in smokers
Contraceptive implants	Tubes of progesterone implanted under the skin.	Stops release of FSH and LH	More than 90%	Not known
Contraceptive injections	Injections of hormones	Stops release of FSH and LH	About 90%	Possible osteoporosis
Diaphragm	Latex cup inserted into vagina to cover cervix before intercourse.	Blocks entrance of sperm into uterus.	With spermicide, about 90%	Latex or spermicide allergy
Cervical cap	Latex cup held by suction over cervix.	Delivers spermicide near cervix	Almost 85%	UTI, latex or spermicide allergy
Female condom	Polyurethane liner fitted inside vagina.	Blocks entrance of sperm into uterus and prevents STD's.	Almost 85%	None
Male condom	Soft sheath, made of latex or animal membrane, encloses penis, trapping ejaculated sperm.	Blocks entrance of sperm into vagina and prevents STD's.	Almost 90%	None
Jellies, cream, foams	Spermicidal products inserted before intercourse.	Kills large number of sperm.	About 75%	UTI, allergy to spermicides
Natural family planning	Keep record of ovulation using various methods.	Avoid sexual intercourse.	About 70%	None known
Douche	Vagina cleansed after intercourse.	Washes out sperm near ovulation	Less than 70%	None known
Plan B pill	Pill taken after intercourse.	Prevents release of egg, fertilization of egg or egg contraceptive from attaching to uterus.	About 89%	Same as oral

Exercise

1. Which of the following statements is true?
(a) Peripheral nerve is similar to smooth muscle in terms of the connective tissue investment
(b) Most nerves contain afferent and efferent fibres and thus, carry both motor and sensory signals
(c) Nodes of Ranvier are most easily seen in cross-section of peripheral nerve
(d) None of the above

2. Which of the following cells is responsible for myelin formation in the peripheral nervous system?
(a) Astrocyte (b) Oligodendrocyte
(c) Schwann cell (d) Microglial cell

3. The peripheral nervous system includes the
(a) somatic nervous system (b) brain
(c) spinal cord (d) nuclei

4. The system that controls smooth muscle, cardiac muscle and gland activity is the
(a) somatic nervous system
(b) autonomic nervous system
(c) skeletal division
(d) sensory nervous system

5. A neuron with many short dendrites and a single long axon is a
(a) multipolar neuron (b) bipolar neuron
(c) unipolar neuron (d) None of these

6. Most sensory neurons are .... neurons.
(a) unipolar (b) bipolar
(c) multipolar (d) Both (a) and (b)

7. Cells found in the choroid plexus that secrete cerebrospinal fluid are
(a) astrocytes (b) microglia
(c) ependymal cells (d) oligodendrocytes

8. The most likely type of fibre that would carry the impulse for a withdrawal reflex would be a
(a) A fibre because they carry the strongest action potentials
(b) A fibre because they carry APs the fastest
(c) B fibre because they carry APs the fastest
(d) C fibre because they carry the strongest APs

9. Axons within nerves may have which of the following associated with them?
(a) Schwann cells (b) Nodes of Ranvier
(c) Oligodendrocytes (d) Both (a) and (b)

10. Action potentials are conducted more rapidly in
(a) small diameter axons than large diameter axons
(b) large diameter axons than small diameter axons
(c) unmyelinated axons than myelinated axons
(d) axons that lack a wrapping of Schwann cells

11. Clusters of nerve cell bodies within the PNS are called
(a) neuron (b) nerve
(c) ganglia (d) lymph

12. Gray matter contains primarily
(a) myelinated fibres (b) neuron cell bodies
(c) Schwann cells (d) All of these

13. Arrange the following connective tissue structures from the outermost to the innermost.
I. Endoneurium
II. Epineurium
III. Perineurium
(a) I, II, III (b) II, III, I
(c) III, II, I (d) III, I, II

14. Neurotransmitters are stored in vesicles that are located primarily in specialized portions of the
(a) soma (b) axon
(c) dendrite (d) perikaryon

15. Summation
(a) is caused by a combining of several local potentials
(b) can occur when two action potentials arrive simultaneously at two different presynaptic terminals
(c) can occur when two action potentials arrive in very close succession at a single presynaptic terminals
(d) All of the above

16. Which of the following organelles is responsible for the appearance of Nissl bodies in the cell bodies of motor neurons?
(a) Smooth endoplasmic reticulum
(b) Rough endoplasmic reticulum
(c) Golgi apparatus
(d) Mitochondria

17. Which of the following structures is a component of a reflex arc?
(a) Afferent neuron (b) Efferent neuron
(c) Sensory receptor (d) All of these

18. What is the difference between grey and white matter of the CNS?
(a) Grey matter = axons; White matter = cell bodies + oligodendrocytes
(b) Grey matter = axons + cell bodies; White matter = oligodendrocytes
(c) Grey matter = cell bodies; White matter = axons + oligodendrocytes
(d) Grey matter = axons + oligodendrocytes; White matter = cell bodies

19. What are the events whose frequency is being modulated to transmit information through the nervous system?
(a) Current potential (b) Action potential
(c) Voltage potential (d) None of these

20. Of the following processes, which occurs in dendrites?
(a) Interpretation (b) Transmission
(c) Stimulation (d) Transduction

21. Nociceptors sense
(a) pressure (b) pain
(c) heat (d) touch

22. The taste that most people sense on the back of the tongue is
(a) sweet (b) bitter
(c) salty (d) sour

23. Whether a hair cell depolarizes or hyperpolarizes depends on whether it bends toward or away from
(a) kinocilium (b) ampullae
(c) statocysts (d) otolith

24. In the cochlea, the hair cells are contained by the
(a) tectorial membrane (b) tympanic membrane
(c) basilar membrane (d) vestibular membrane

25. The amount of light entering the eye is determined by the size of the
(a) retina (b) cornea
(c) pupil (d) fovea

26. The cells responsible for colour vision in vertebrates are called
(a) rod cells (b) cone cells
(c) bipolar cells (d) cupula cells

27. Which of the following substances is involved in the electromagnetic and chemical events of vision?
(a) Rhodopsin (b) G-proteins
(c) Phosphodiesterase (d) All of these

28. Which of the following is not a mechanical stimulus?
(a) Gravity (b) Sound
(c) Touch (d) Smell

29. Nerve impulses are carried from the eye to the brain by the
(a) optic nerve (b) cornea
(c) bipolar cells (d) rod and cone cells

30. The membrane that separates the outer ear from the middle ear of mammals is called the
(a) foveal membrane
(b) basilar membrane
(c) oval window
(d) tympanic membrane

31. Which of the following is not one of the four taste classes that taste buds respond to?
(a) Bitter (b) Salty
(c) Spicy (d) Sweet

32. The endocrine system
(a) releases chemicals into the bloodstream for distribution throughout the body
(b) releases hormones that can alter the metabolic activities of many different tissues and organs
(c) produces effects that can last for hours, days or even longer
(d) All of the above

33. Each of the following is an amino acid derivative except
(a) epinephrine (b) melatonin
(c) thyroxine (d) TSH

34. When adenyl cyclase is activated
(a) *c*AMP is formed
(b) *c*AMP is degraded
(c) G-proteins are replicated in a semiconservative fashion
(d) steroid hormones enter the cell *via* receptor-mediated endocytosis

35. Which of the following hormones does not act *via* a second messenger system?
(a) Glucagon (b) Epinephrine
(c) GH (d) Testosterone

36. What hypophyseal structure receives signals from the hypothalamus *via* the hypophyseal portal system?
(a) Follicular medulla (b) Adenohypophysis
(c) Neurohypophysis (d) Pars intermedia

37. Low blood glucose typically results in the secretion of all of the following except
(a) glucagon (b) thyroxine
(c) hGH (d) PTH

38. The .... cells of the pancreas secrete insulin.
(a) F (b) chief
(c) alpha (d) beta

39. The general adaptation syndrome is activated by the
(a) hypothalamus (b) adrenal gland
(c) pituitary gland (d) thyroid gland

40. Say you ate 25 sugar cubes and then drank a litre of Mountain Dew, which hormone might be secreted in large amounts as a result?
(a) Insulin (b) Glucagon
(c) Prolactin (d) GnRH

41. Somatostatin is secreted by the
(a) pancreatic F-cells (b) pancreatic delta cells
(c) zona fasciculata (d) parafollicular cells

42. A tumour in the adrenal zona glomerulosa may cause hypersecretion of the hormones in that region. Which of the following might you expect to find in a patient with such a tumour?
(a) Increased blood sodium levels
(b) Increased blood glucose levels
(c) Decreased blood calcium levels
(d) Increased dehydration

43. Oxytocin is secreted by the
(a) adenohypophysis (b) neurohypophysis
(c) zona glomerulosa (d) pars intermedia

44. The main hormone released by the corpus luteum is
(a) LH (b) FSH
(c) testosterone (d) progesterone

45. The hormone that acts on Leydig cells is
(a) LH (b) FSH
(c) testosterone (d) progesterone

46. .... is the main hormone produced by granulosa cells.
(a) FSH (b) Testosterone
(c) Progesterone (d) Oestrogen

47. Human egg and sperm are similar in that
(a) about the same number are produced per month
(b) they have the same degree of motility
(c) they have the same number of chromosomes
(d) they are about the same size

48. The testosterone producing cells of the testes are called
(a) Sertoli cells (b) granulosa cells
(c) spermatogonia (d) Leydig cells

49. The testicular cells most involved with the construction of the blood-testes barrier are the
(a) Sertoli cells (b) granulosa cells
(c) spermatogonia (d) Leydig cells

50. The soft mucosal lining of the uterus is the
(a) ectometrium (b) mesometrium
(c) endometrium (d) ametrium

51. The anterior pituitary hormone that triggers ovulation is
(a) LH (b) TSH
(c) testosterone (d) progesterone

52. .... is the release of the secondary oocyte from the ovary.
(a) Oogenesis (b) Spermatogenesis
(c) Fertilization (d) Ovulation

53. The female homologue of the scrotum is the
(a) labia minor (b) labia antrum
(c) labia mentrum (d) labia majora

54. Ejaculation is a .... response whereas erection is a .... response.
(a) parasympathetic; sympathetic
(b) sympathetic; parasympathetic
(c) sympathetic; sympathetic
(d) parasympathetic; parasympathetic

55. An oocyte surrounded by one layer of squamous follicle-like cells is most likely a
(a) primordial follicle (b) primary follicle
(c) secondary follicle (d) Graafian follicle

56. An antrum is characteristic of .... follicles.
(a) secondary (b) Graafian
(c) primary (d) secondary and Graafian

57. The rounded region of the uterus superior to the entrance of the uterine tubes is the
(a) ampulla (b) fundus
(c) corpus (d) isthmus

58. Primary oocytes are
(a) haploid (b) diploid
(c) polyploid (d) aneuploid

59. Consider the following three tubes. Which is the correct order sperm travels through them?
I. Epididymis
II. Oviduct
III. Ejaculatory duct
(a) I, III and II (b) III, I and II
(c) II, I and I (d) II, III and I

60. The corpus luteum secretes progesterone which negatively feeds back and inhibits the release of
(a) ABP and ICSH (b) LH and ICSH
(c) LH and FSH (d) FSH and TSH

61. Which of the following is correct relative to the female anatomy?
(a) The vaginal orifice is the most dorsal of the 3 openings in the perineum
(b) The urethra is between the vaginal orifice and the anus
(c) The anus is between vaginal orifice and the urethra
(d) The urethra is the more ventral of the two openings in the vulva

62. The normal diploid number of human chromosomes is
(a) 23 (b) 22
(c) 43 (d) 46

63. Sertoli cells produce
(a) mucus (b) androgen-binding protein
(c) testosterone (d) FSH

64. Spermatogenesis begins in the
(a) epididymis (b) uterine horn
(c) seminiferous tubules (d) seminal vesicles

65. The site of oogenesis is the
(a) ovary (b) ovum
(c) oocyte (d) oviduct

66. In the 1st phase of the menstrual cycle
(a) oogonia differentiate into primary oocytes
(b) the thickness of the stratum basalis decreases dramatically
(c) the Graafian follicle ruptures
(d) the dominant follicle is opsonized

67. During ovulation, all of the following occur except
(a) rupture of the Graafian follicle
(b) oestrogen production reaches its lowest point
(c) FSH and LH plasma levels surge
(d) corpus luteum is formed

68. Which of the following would be the most likely site of fertilization?
(a) Ovary (b) Uterine tube
(c) Fundus of uterus (d) Cervix

69. Human chorionic gonadotropin
(a) begins to be produced four months after fertilization
(b) is produced by the prostate gland
(c) is produced by the corpus luteum
(d) is present only if a successful fertilization has occurred

70. In the second messenger model of hormone action
(a) a tropic hormone signals an endocrine gland to release a hormone
(b) another molecule relays the message from the membrane bound hormone to the cytoplasmic enzymes
(c) negative feedback turns off the production of the hormone
(d) genes are turned on and new proteins are synthesized

71. Ecdysone
(a) is a steroid hormone produced in insects that promotes retention of larval characteristics
(b) is responsible for the colour changes in amphibians
(c) is a peptide hormone secreted from 'bag cells' that stimulates egg laying in the mollusc *Aplysia*
(d) is secreted by prothoracic glands in insects and triggers molts and development of adult characteristics

72. The role of cAMP in hormone action is to
(a) act as the second messenger and activate other enzymes
(b) activate adenylyl cyclase
(c) bind a specific hormone to the plasma membrane
(d) release Ca^{2+} into the cell and initiate an enzyme cascade

73. When a boy goes through puberty, the steroid hormone testosterone 'puts hair on his chest' by
(a) Interacting with DNA in the nuclei of cells
(b) Causing cells to change shape
(c) Altering the permeability of plasma membranes
(d) Triggering nerve impulses in cells

74. Pro-opiomelanocortin
(a) is produced by the hypothalamus and is transported through a portal vessel
(b) is cleaved into several hormones, including ACTH, MSH and endorphins
(c) produces several releasing hormones
(d) is a precursor to the hormones of the adrenal cortex

75. Which of the following is not true of norepinephrine?
(a) It is secreted by the adrenal medulla
(b) Its action is to increase the rate and volume of heart beat and constrict selected blood vessels
(c) Its releases is stimulated by ACTH
(d) It serves as a neurotransmitter in the nervous system

76. Which of the following is not an accurate statement about hormones?
(a) Not all hormones are secreted by endocrine glands
(b) Most hormones move through the circulatory system to their destination
(c) Target cells have specific molecular receptors for hormones
(d) Hormones produce their effects through signal transduction pathways involving second messengers

77. The best description of the difference between pheromones and hormones is that
(a) pheromones are small, volatile molecules, whereas hormones are steroids
(b) pheromones are involved in reproduction, whereas hormones are not
(c) pheromones are a form of olfactory communication; hormones are a form of chemical communications
(d) pheromones are signals that function between animals, whereas hormones communicate among the parts within an animal

78. Tim once suffered a severe allergic reaction to a bee sting. The sting caused him to suffer a near-fatal drop in blood pressure called anaphylactic shock. Now he carries a kit containing a syringe of ...., which he can inject to speed up his heart if he reacts to a bee sting.
(a) insulin (b) thyroxine
(c) testosterone (d) epinephrine

79. Some glands produce hormones that stimulate other endocrine glands. Which of the following hormones specifically acts to trigger secretion of hormones by another endocrine glands?
(a) thyroxine
(b) progesterone
(c) adrenocorticotropin hormone (ACTH)
(d) antidiuretic hormone (ADH)

80. How is the level of thyroxine in the blood regulated?
(a) Thyrozine stimulates the pituitary to secrete Thyroid Stimulating Hormone (TSH)
(b) TSH inhibits secretion of thyroxine from the thyroid gland
(c) TSH-Releasing Hormone (TRH) inhibits secretion of thyroxine by the thyroid gland
(d) Thyroxine and TSH inhibit secretion of TRH

81. The function of calmodulin is to
(a) begin an enzyme cascade by phosphorylating multiple proteins
(b) bind with Ca^{2+} and regulate the activity of cellular proteins
(c) lower blood calcium levels
(d) serve as a second messenger in a signal transduction pathways

82. Which of the following hormones triggers secretion of the other two?
(a) Thyroxine
(b) Thyroid Stimulating Hormone (TSH)
(c) TSH Releasing Hormone (TRH)
(d) Any of the above can trigger secretion of the others

83. A tumour in an endocrine gland caused Jennifer to have weakened bones and unusually high levels of blood calcium. Which of the following was affected?
(a) Anterior pituitary (b) Pancreas
(c) Adrenal glands (d) Parathyroid glands

84. Researchers have found increased levels of hormones from the .... in the blood of students preparing for final exams. These hormones are produced in response to stress.
(a) thyroid gland (b) pineal gland
(c) posterior pituitary (d) adrenal glands

85. Which of the following hormones have antagonistic (opposing) effects?
(a) Thyroxine and calcitonin
(b) Insulin and glucagon
(c) Growth hormone and epinephrine
(d) ACTH and glucocorticoids

86. Every time you eat a cookie or candy bar, your blood sugar increases. This triggers an increase in the hormone
(a) thyroxine
(b) epinephrine
(c) adrenocorticotropin hormone (ACTH)
(d) insulin

87. Injections of hormone are sometimes given to strengthen contractions of the uterus during childbirth. What hormone might this be?
(a) Adrenocorticotropin hormone (ACTH)
(b) Thyroxine
(c) Oxytocin
(d) Follicle Stimulating Hormone (FSH)

88. Which of the following hormones has the broadest range of targets?
(a) ADH (b) Prolactin
(c) TSH (d) Epinephrine

89. It usually takes much longer for sex hormones and other steroids to produce their effects than it takes non-steroid hormones. Why?
(a) Steroids are bigger, slower molecules
(b) Steroids usually must be carried longer distances by the blood
(c) Steroids cause target cells to make new proteins, which takes time
(d) Steroids must relay their messenger *via* receptor

90. As a young girl, Maria suffered a head injury that damaged her pituitary. An injury to the pituitary is particularly serious because of all the functions controlled by this gland. As Maria got older, she and her doctors found that all of the following except .... were affected.

(a) metabolic rate
(b) her menstrual cycle
(c) milk production
(d) blood calcium level

91. Consider the following statements.

I. Grey matter surrounds the white matter in the brain.
II. Grey matter surrounds the white matter in the spinal cord.
III. White matter surrounds the grey matter in the spinal cord.
IV. White matter surrounds the grey matter in the brain.

Which of the statements given above is/are correct?

(a) II only
(b) I and III are correct
(c) I and IV are correct
(d) IV only

92. Match list I with list II and select the correct answer using the codes given below the lists.

List I	List II
A. Action potential	1. Myelinated nerve fibre
B. Neurosecretion	2. Donnan equilibrium
C. Resting potential	3. Hypothalamus
D. Saltatory	4. Depolarization propagation and repolarization

Codes

	A	B	C	D
(a)	1	2	3	4
(b)	4	3	2	1
(c)	2	3	4	1
(d)	4	2	3	1

93. Match list I (hormones) with list II (target) and select the correct answer using the codes given below the lists.

List I	List II
A. ACTH	1. Thyroid
B. Prolactin	2. Adrenal cortex
C. TSH	3. Mammary gland
D. Oxytocin	4. Smooth muscle of uterine wall

Codes

	A	B	C	D
(a)	1	2	3	4
(b)	2	3	1	4
(c)	2	3	4	1
(d)	3	4	1	2

94. Match list I with list II and select the correct answer using the codes given below the lists.

List I	List II
A. Sodium gate	1. Saltatory conduction of nerve impulse
B. Nodes of Ranvier	2. Synaptic transmission
C. Acetylcholine	3. Action
D. Photoreceptor	4. Transduction
	5. Dendrite

Codes

	A	B	C	D		A	B	C	D
(a)	5	3	4	2	(b)	3	5	2	1
(c)	1	4	5	2	(d)	3	1	2	4

95. Which of the following statements is/are correct?

I. Formation of rhodopsin is necessary in dark adaptation.
II. Destruction of rhodopsin is necessary in light adaptation.
III. Destruction of rhodopsin is necessary in dark adaptation.
IV. Formation of rhodopsin is necessary in light adaptation.

Codes

(a) I and II (b) II and IV
(c) I and III (d) IV only

96. Match list I with list II and select the correct answer using the codes given below the lists.

List I	List II
A. Dehydration	1. Aldosterone
B. Antidiuretic hormone	2. Osmoreceptor
C. Reabsorption of Na in the kidney	3. Blood hyperosmotic urine
D. Water diuresis	4. Vasopressin
	5. Blood hyposmotic urine

Codes

	A	B	C	D
(a)	4	1	2	3
(b)	3	4	5	1
(c)	4	1	2	5
(d)	3	4	1	5

97. Consider the following with reference to the mechanism of action of a steroidal hormone on target cell.

I. Bonding of activated complex with specific genomic site.
II. Activation of transcriptional apparatus.
III. Attachment with cytosolic receptor protein.
IV. Transportation of complex to the nucleus.
V. Formation of new proteins in the cytoplasm

What is the correct sequence of the above in said mechanism?

(a) I, II, III, IV and V (b) IV, I, III, II and V
(c) II, III, I, IV and V (d) III, IV, I, II and IV

98. Match list I with list II and select the correct answer using the codes given below the lists.

List I (Hormones)	List II (Effects)
A. Melatonin	1. Loosening of pelvic ligaments
B. Relaxin	2. Influences the activity of ovary
C. MSH	3. Pigment dispersal in melanophores
D. STH	4. Synthesis and release of glucocorticoids
	5. Metabolism of proteins and fat

Codes

	A	B	C	D
(a)	2	1	4	3
(b)	1	2	3	5
(c)	1	2	4	3
(d)	2	1	3	5

Answers

1. (b)	**2.** (c)	**3.** (a)	**4.** (b)	**5.** (a)	**6.** (d)	**7.** (c)	**8.** (b)	**9.** (d)	**10.** (b)
11. (c)	**12.** (b)	**13.** (b)	**14.** (b)	**15.** (d)	**16.** (b)	**17.** (d)	**18.** (c)	**19.** (b)	**20.** (d)
21. (b)	**22.** (b)	**23.** (a)	**24.** (c)	**25.** (c)	**26.** (b)	**27.** (d)	**28.** (d)	**29.** (a)	**30.** (d)
31. (c)	**32.** (d)	**33.** (d)	**34.** (a)	**35.** (d)	**36.** (b)	**37.** (d)	**38.** (d)	**39.** (a)	**40.** (a)
41. (b)	**42.** (a)	**43.** (b)	**44.** (d)	**45.** (a)	**46.** (d)	**47.** (c)	**48.** (d)	**49.** (a)	**50.** (c)
51. (a)	**52.** (d)	**53.** (d)	**54.** (b)	**55.** (a)	**56.** (d)	**57.** (b)	**58.** (b)	**59.** (a)	**60.** (c)
61. (d)	**62.** (d)	**63.** (b)	**64.** (c)	**65.** (a)	**66.** (d)	**67.** (b)	**68.** (b)	**69.** (d)	**70.** (b)
71. (d)	**72.** (a)	**73.** (c)	**74.** (b)	**75.** (c)	**76.** (d)	**77.** (d)	**78.** (d)	**79.** (c)	**80.** (d)
81. (b)	**82.** (c)	**83.** (d)	**84.** (d)	**85.** (b)	**86.** (d)	**87.** (c)	**88.** (d)	**89.** (c)	**90.** (d)
91. (c)	**92.** (b)	**93.** (b)	**94.** (d)	**95.** (a)	**96.** (d)	**97.** (d)	**98.** (d)		

23 Mendelism and its Extensions

Mendelian Principles

Gregor Johann Mendel (1822-1884) was an Austrian Monk out Brunn Monastery who studied at Vienna University. He worked with pea (*Pisum sativum*) due to presence of hermaphrodite flower, self-fertilization, easy hybridization, short life cycle, fertile hybrids and presence of contrasting characters on different chromosomes. Mendel presented the data and conclusion in a paper 'Experiments on plant hybridization'. His investigations were ignored but were rediscovered in 1900 and then he recognized as **Father of Genetics.** Mendel used the term **factor** for the inherited unit at that time, which are now called **genes** and the two alternative forms as **alleles.**

Syllabus

- Mendelian Principles: Dominance, Segregation, Independent Assortment.
- Concept of Gene: Allele and Multiple Alleles, Pseudoallele, Complementation Tests.
- Extensions of Mendelian Principles: Codominance, Incomplete Dominance, Gene Interactions, Pleiotropy, Genomic Imprinting, Penetrance and Expressivity, Phenocopy, Linkage and Crossing over, Sex Linkage, Sex-Limited Inheritance, Sex Influenced Inheritance.

Dominance

One of Gregor Mendel's great discoveries was the **Principle of Dominance**. He noted that when he hybridized two parents with different versions of a particular trait, one of those versions apparently disappeared in the hybrid (heterozygous) offspring. If he then mated those offspring to each other, the vanished trait reappeared in the third generation, apparently completely unchanged despite being invisible in generation two. He named the version of the trait which was visible in the hybrids the dominant and the one that was invisible in the hybrids the **recessive**.

Segregation

Mendel's Principle of Segregation, states that allele pairs separate or segregate during gamete formation and randomly unite at fertilization.

Example

The gene for seed colour in pea plants exists in two forms. There is one form or allele for yellow seed colour (Y) and another for green seed colour (y). In the figure, the allele for yellow seed colour is dominant and allele for green colour is recessive. When the alleles of a pair are different (heterozygous), the dominant allele is expressed and the recessive allele trait is masked. Seeds with the genetic make up of YY or Yy are yellow, while seeds that are yy are green. It gives 3 : 1 phenotypic ratio, while 1 : 2 : 1 genotypic ratio.

Independent Assortment

During gamete formation the segregation of the alleles of one allelic pair is independent of the segregation of the alleles of another allelic pair. This process is evident in following figure:

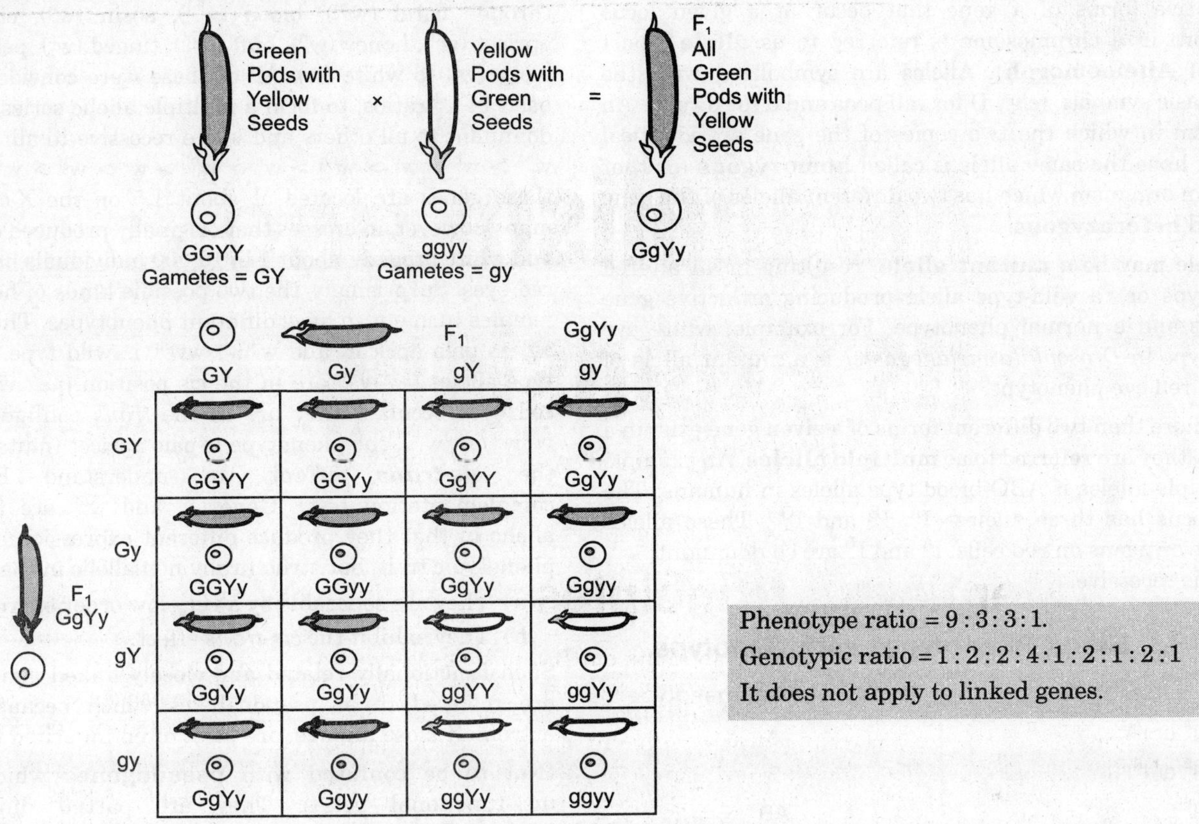

Fig. 23.1 Law of independent assortment

Phenotype ratio = 9 : 3 : 3 : 1.
Genotypic ratio = 1 : 2 : 2 : 4 : 1 : 2 : 1 : 2 : 1
It does not apply to linked genes.

- **Back cross *vs* test cross** Back cross is the cross between F_1 hybrid and one of its parent, while test cross is the cross between F_1 hybrid and its recessive parent.
- Test cross gives 1 : 1 ratio in monohybrid cross, while 1 : 1 : 1 : 1 ratio in dihybrid cross.
- CB Bridges (1921) proposed genic balance theory of inheritance in *Drosophila*.

Concept of Gene

- **Johanssen** (1909) introduced the term 'gene' and described it as 'an elementary unit of inheritance, which can be assigned to a particular trait'. Gene is a unit of inheritance composed of linear segment of DNA situated at a specific locus (gene locus), which carries coded information associated with a specific function and can undergo crossing over as well as mutation.
- **Cistron** is called functional unit of DNA.
- **Recon** is a unit of recombination.
- **Muton** is a unit of mutation.
- **Constitutive genes** or **house keeping genes** are those genes, which express themselves continuously in a cell because their products are required for the normal cellular activities, *e.g.,* genes for glycolysis, ATPase, etc. **Non-constitutive genes** (luxury genes) are not always expressing themselves in a cell. These genes are switched on or off according to the requirement of cell. These genes may be inducible or repressible, *e.g.,* nitrate reductase in plants, lactose metabolism in *E. coli*.

Alleles and Multiple Alleles

Gene can be understood as a unit of inheritance (DNA) located in a fixed place on chromosome. One of the alternative forms of a gene that occur at a given locus (position) in a chromosome is referred to as **allele** (short form of **Alleleomorph**). Alleles are symbolized with the same basic symbols (*e.g.,* D for tall peas and d for dwarf). An organism in which the two copies of the gene are identical that is, have the same allele is called **homozygous** for that gene. An organism which has two different alleles of the gene is called **heterozygous**.

An allele may be a **mutant allele**, resulting in an altered phenotype or a wild-type allele producing an active gene product and a normal phenotype. For example, white eye phenotype in *Drosophila melanogaster* is a mutant allele of normal red eye phenotype.

When more than two different forms of a given gene exist in a species, they are referred to as **multiple alleles**. An example of multiple alleles is ABO blood type alleles in humans. The ABO locus has three alleles– I^A, I^B and I^O . These alleles produce antigens on red cells. I^A and I^B are co-dominant and I^O is recessive.

Table 23.1 **Blood Phenotypes with Genotype**

Genotype	Corresponding Phenotype
I^AI^A or I^AI^O	A
I^BI^B or I^BI^O	B
I^AI^B	AB
I^OI^O	O

Pseudoalleles

Pseudoallele is one of two or more closely linked genes on a chromosome that appear to function as a single allelic pair but occupy distinct, nearly corresponding loci (plural of locus) on homologous chromosomes. Such gene pairs produce a mutant effect in the diploid state when located on homologous chromosomes but are capable of being separated by crossing over during meiosis to produce a wild-type effect when recombined on either of the homologs.

Significance of Pseudoallelism

(a) It shows the possibility of division of classical gene into a structural and a functional unit.

(b) It provides a clue for intergenic units of recombination and mutation.

The best example of pseudoallelism has been seen in the sex-linked genes for eye colour in *Drosophila*. The colour of *Drosophila* eye is determined by a series of sex-linked gene which cause the colour to vary from red or wild type (w^+ or W) through coral (w^{co}), blood (w^{bl}), eosin (w^o), cherry (w^{ch}), apricot (w^a), honey (w^h), buff (w^{bf}), tinged (w^t), pearl (w^p) and ivory (w^i) to white (w). All of these were considered, on the basis of F^2 ratios, to form a multiple allelic series, wild being dominant to all others and white recessive to all: W or $w^+ > w^{co} > w^{bl} > w^c > w^{ch} > w^a > w^{bf} > w^t > w^p > w^i >$ w. All of these genes are located at about 1.5 on the X-chromosome map. However, in crosses that originally produced only apricot and white progeny, about 1 in 10,000 individuals had wild type red eyes. Surprisingly, the two possible kinds of heterozygous females turn out to have different phenotypes. Thus, ww^+/w^+w^{ap} is pale apricot, and w^+w^+/ww^{ap} is wild type. If the wild type alleles (w^+w^+) are in the cis position (*i.e.,* w^+w^+/ww^{ap}), red eyes occur, if they are in the *trans* configuration (*i.e.,* $w^+w^+/w^{ap}w^+$), the phenotype is pale apricot (mutant). This is the ***cis-trans* effect** (to understand better see complementation test). Genes w and w^{ap} are functionally allelic in that they produce different expression of the same phenotypic trait, but structurally non allelic in that

(a) They are separable by a very low order of crossing-over.

(b) They exhibit the *cis-trans* effect.

Such functionally related and closely linked genes as these are referred to as pseudoalleles which because of their extremely close linkage, are most often inherited together.

(Not to be confused with **pseudogenes** which are the non-functional genes. They are partial duplicates of structural genes that have incorporated sufficient changes or mutations that they are not biologically active and usually are not transcribed).

Complementation Tests

Complementation testing or analysis help us know that whether the two mutations exhibiting same phenotype are the result of mutation in the same gene or different genes.

Two laboratories independently isolated and established a true-breeding strain of wingless *Drosophila* and demonstrated that each was due to recessive mutation. First assumption would be that this is because of mutation in the same gene. But since wing development in *Drosophila* involve many genes and mutation in any one of them would inhibit wing formation. To clarify this complementation analysis is done.

In complementation test, the two mutant strains are crossed and F_1 generation is analysed. There will be two cases:

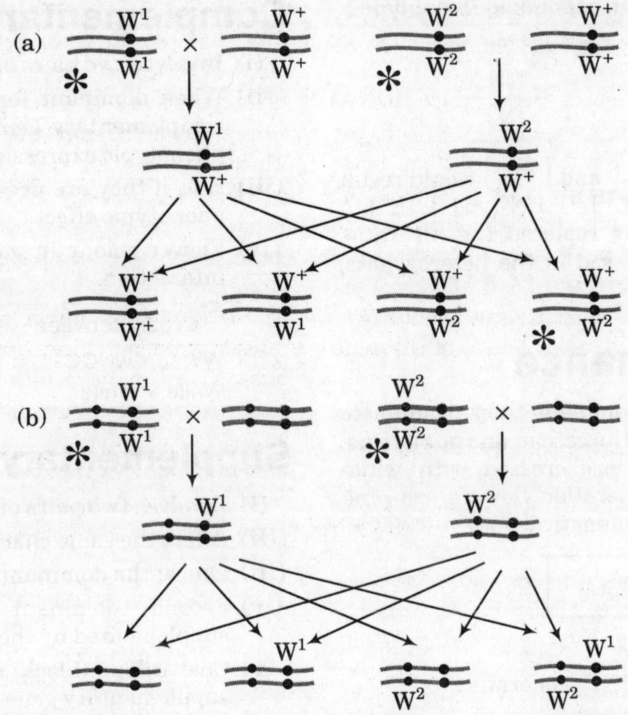

Fig. 23.2 The complementation test is used to show whether two recessive alleles that produce the same phenotype (asterisk) when homozygous are alleles of the same gene. Homozygous individuals from each mutant strain are crossed to wild type to produce heterozygotes (middle row in a and b).

(a) When heterozygotes are mated with each other, 25% of the offspring will show the recessive phenotype if the alleles are variants at the same gene.

(b) However, if the alleles are at different genes, all the offspring will be wild type. This is because individuals that carry the two recessive alleles (one at each gene) will also carry the wild-type alleles at both genes (bottom right in b).

Case 1 All offsprings develop normal wings.

Interpretation The two recessive mutations are in different genes and are not alleles of each other. This is because all the *Drosophila* flies of F_1 generation are heterozygous of two different genes and complementation has occurred.

Case 2 All offsprings fail to develop wings.

Interpretation The two mutations has occurred on the same genes and are alleles to each other. This is because the flies of F_1 generation are homozygous for the mutant alleles and complementation has not occurred here.

Complementation tests was originally developed by **Edward B Lewis** and is often called the ***cis-trans* test.** In *cis* (along side of one another), the mutations are on the same homolog, while in *trans* (opposite one another) the mutations are on separate homologs.

Extensions of Mendelian Principles

In some cases, the Mendelian principles do not found accurate as some gene interact and influenced each other. Each gene is not in a separate test tubes but they are all located in same nuclei of same cells.

Codominance

Joint expression of both alleles in a heterozygote is called **codominance.** An example is MN blood group in humans. L^M and L^N are the alleles which produce glycoproteins M and N respectively, that are present on the surface of RBCs. They act as antigens. Their expression is as given in the table.

Genotype	Corresponding Phenotype
L^ML^M	M
L^ML^N	MN
L^NL^N	N

Mating between heterozygote (L^ML^N and L^ML^N) would result into 1 M-type (L^ML^M): 2 MN-type (L^ML^N) :1 N-type (L^NL^N). A phenotypic ratio of 1:2:1 has thus replaced the 3:1 ratio, because the alleles are both expressed in the heterozygote, that is, the alleles are co-dominant.

Incomplete Dominance

When neither of the alleles are dominant then incomplete dominance is said to occur. Such is the case in **snapdragons**. When red flowered snapdragons are crossed with white flowered snapdragons, the F_1 generation flowers are pink coloured. This can be shown diagrammatically as

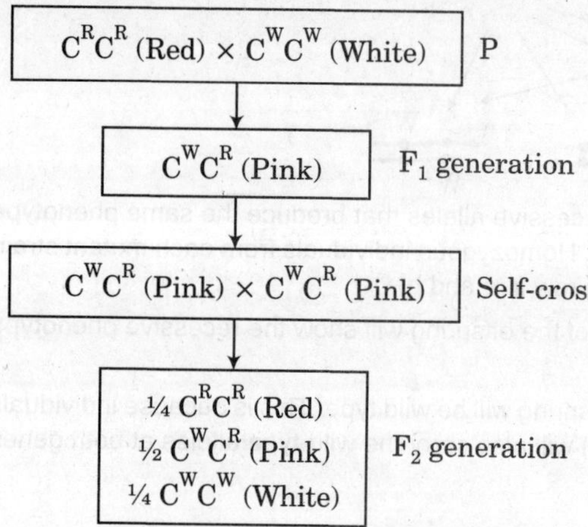

Fig. 23.3 Cross showing incomplete dominance

Another example of incomplete dominance is human biochemical disorder **Tay-Sachs disease**, in which homozygous recessive individuals are severely affected with a fatal lipid storage disorder. In afflicted individuals, there is no activity of the enzyme **hexosaminidase A.** Heterozygotes with a single copy of the mutant gene, are phenotypically normal, but with only about 50 per cent of the enzyme activity found in homozygous normal individuals.

Gene Interactions

The condition where a single character is governed by two or more genes and every gene affect the expression of other genes involved (means these genes affect each others expression) is known as gene interaction.

Gene interactions can be classified as

1. **Allelic gene interaction** As described above like co-dominance, incomplete dominance and complete dominance.
2. **Non-allelic gene interaction** Following are the different types:

Complementary Gene Interaction

(i) Involves two pairs of non-allelic genes.
(ii) When dominant forms of both the genes involved in complementary gene interaction are alone have same phenotypic expression.
(iii) But, if they are present in combination, yield different phenotypic effect.
(iv) Flower colour in garden pea follow this type of gene interaction.

Cross between	F_1	F_2
WWcc × wwCC White × White	WwCc Purple	9 purple : 7 white

Supplementary Gene Interaction

(i) Involves two pairs of non-allelic genes.
(ii) Affect the same character.
(iii) One of the dominant gene has visible effect itself.
(iv) Second dominant gene expresses itself when supplemented by the other dominant gene of a pair.
(v) Coat colour (black, albino and agouti) of mice follows supplementary gene interaction.

Cross between	F_1	F_2
CCaa × ccAA Black × Albino	CcAa Agouti	9 agouti : 3 black: 4 albino

Epistasis

(i) Involves two pairs of non-allelic genes.
(ii) Both the dominant genes affect the same character.
(iii) One of them, when present alone or along with other dominant gene expresses itself.
(iv) The other gene expresses itself only when it is alone.
(v) The recessive forms of both the genes give rise to different phenotype.
(vi) The phenomenon of masking of effect of one dominant gene by the other gene is called as 'epistasis' and hence the interaction is named as epistasis. The masking gene is epistatic gene and the masked one is hypostatic gene.
(vii) Epistasis is observed in fruit colour of summer squash (white, yellow and green).

Cross between	F_1	F_2
WWYY × wwyy White × Green	WwYy White	13 white : 3 yellow: 1 green

Polymerism or Additive Factor

(i) Involves two pairs of non-allelic genes.
(ii) Affect the same character.
(iii) When dominant forms of both the genes are present together they produce double effect.
(iv) Such genes are called as polymeric or additive genes.

(v) Polymerism or additive factor observed in case of pericarp colour of wheat (deep red, light red and colourless).

Cross between	F_1	F_2
$R_1R_1R_2R_2 \times r_1r_1r_2r_2$ Deep red × Colourless	$R_1r_1R_2r_2$ deep Red	9 deep red: 6 light Red: 1 colourless

Duplicate Factor

(i) Involves two pairs of non-allelic genes.
(ii) Affect the same character.
(iii) Dominant form of both genes, either alone or in combination produce same phenotypic expression.
(iv) Recessive forms of both the genes when together produce different phenotypic effect.
(v) Duplicate factor interaction is observed in awned and awnless condition in rice.

Cross between	F_1	F_2
$A_1A_1A_2A_2 \times a_1a_1a_2a_2$ Awned × Awnless	$A_1a_1A_2a_2$ Awned	15 awned : 1 awnless

Inhibitory Factor

(i) Involves two pairs of non-allelic genes.
(ii) Affect the same character.
(iii) One of the dominant genes inhibits or suppresses the expression of the other dominant gene.
(iv) Inhibiting gene has no visible effect.
(v) Inhibitory factor interaction is observed in plumage colour of poultry.

Cross between	F_1	F_2
CCII × ccii White leghorn × Wyandotte	CcIi White	13 white : 3 coloured

Pleiotropy

Pleiotropy (*pleio* 'many' and *tropic* 'affecting') is that phenomenon in which one gene affects multiple, apparently unrelated, phenotypes. The responsible gene is accordingly called pleiotropic gene. Pleiotropy should not be confused with polygenic traits, in which multiple genes converge to result in a single phenotype.

Suppose we take the example of an amino acid tyrosine. It is needed for general protein synthesis, and it is also a precursor for several neurotransmitters (*e.g.*, dopamine, nor-epinephrine), the hormone thyroxine, and the pigment melanin. Thus, mutation in any one of the genes that affect tyrosine synthesis or metabolism may affect multiple organ systems.

Phenylketonuria (PKU) is an example of pleiotropy in humans. Here enzyme phenylalanine hydroxylase is deficient, which is necessary to convert the essential amino acid phenylalanine to tyrosine. It results in the multiple phenotypes associated with PKU, including mental retardation, eczema, and pigment defects that make affected individuals lighter skinned.

Genomic Imprinting

Genomic imprinting is defined as the differential inheritance of genetic material from the mother versus the father. The concept of genomic imprinting suggests that in certain cases the genetic defect will produce a phenotype only when inherited from a particular parent. It is an inheritance process independent of the classical Mendelian inheritance.

The good examples of this phenomenon are **Prader-Willi Syndrome** (PWS) and **Angelman Syndrome** (AS). Both the diseases are caused by deletion of 15q11-13 (band 11 of the long arm of chromosome 15) but PWS is always paternally inherited while AS is always maternally inherited. Therefore, in case of genomic imprinting, if the gene is inherited from the father, its expression is different than if it is inherited from the mother.

1. **Prader-Willi Syndrome** (PWS)
   (i) Hypotonia in infancy
   (ii) Development delay
   (iii) Obesity
   (iv) Hypogonadism
2. **Angelman Syndrome** (AS)
   (i) Happiness disposition
   (ii) Mental retardation
   (iii) Large mouth and protruded tongue
   (iv) Seizures

In addition to these syndromes genomic imprinting has also been linked to certain cancers, *e.g.*, Wilm's tumour.

Two major mechanisms that are involved in establishing the imprint are DNA methylation and histone modification.

Penetrance and Expressivity

Penetrance and expresivity are two concepts that are different yet related. Penetrance is defined as the percentage of individuals with a given genotype who exhibit the phenotype associated with that genotype. For example, an organism may have a particular genotype but may not express the corresponding phenotype because of modifiers, epistatic genes or suppressors or because of the modifying effect of the environment.

Expressivity, on the other hand, measures the extent to which a given genotype is expressed at the phenotypic level. Different degrees of expression in different individuals may be due to variation in the allelic constitution of the rest of the genom or to environmental factors.

In simple terms, 'penetrance' refers to whether a phenotype is expressed for a particular genotype and 'expressivity' refers to the degree to which a phenotype is expressed when it is expressed. Therefore, 'penetrance' is a qualitative concept and 'expressivity' is a quantitative concept. It is clear that expressivity is dependent on penetrance.

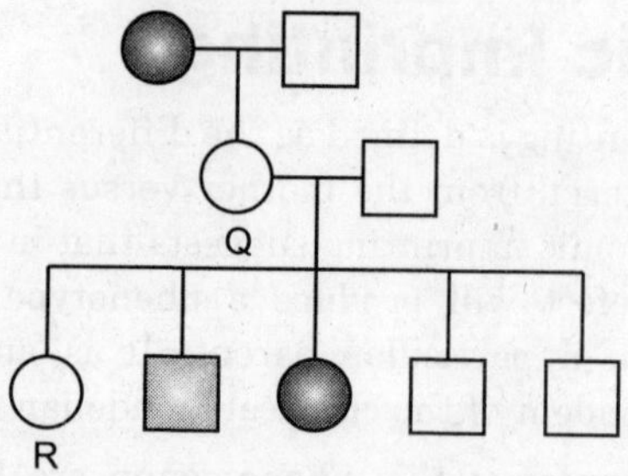

Fig. 23.4 Lack of penetrance is illustrated by a pedigree of a dominant allele. Individual Q must have the allele because it passed on to his progeny but it was not expressed in his phenotype

Phenocopy

Phenocopy is the term given to the individual whose phenotype under a particular environmental condition becomes identical or similar to the one of another individual whose phenotype is determined by the genotype. It is different from mutation and it is environmentally induced, non-hereditary phenotypic modification.

Phenocopy can be observed in the Himalayan rabbits. Himalayan rabbits are white in colour with black tail, nose, and ears. When raised in moderate temperatures they grow up to be phenotypically similar to genetically black rabbits. However, when raised in colder climates, they become phenotypically distinguishable. The Himalayan rabbits show black colouration of their coats, resembling the genetically black rabbits. Hence, this Himalayan rabbit is a phenocopy of the genetically black rabbit.

Linkage and Crossing Over

Linkage can be defined as the tendency of genes of same chromosome to remain together.

Mendel's law of independent assortment states that the segregation of alleles of one gene is independent of alleles of another gene. This law always holds true for genes that are located on different chromosomes, but for genes that are on the same chromosome, it does not always hold true.

Genes present on a single chromosome is said to be belonging to one linkage group. Therefore, there are as much linkage groups as the number of haploid chromosomes.

Linkage was discovered through a classic experiment by **William Bateson** and **Reginald Punnet.** They were studying the inheritance pattern of the gene for flower colour (P, purple, and p, red) and the gene affecting the shape of pollen grains (L, long and l, round). They crossed the pure lines PPLL and ppll and then self crossed the resulting PpLl lines. The observed frequency differed from the expected 9:3:3:1 ratio of PL: Pl: pL: pl. They observed an increased frequency of PL and pl and a decreased frequency of Pl and pL.

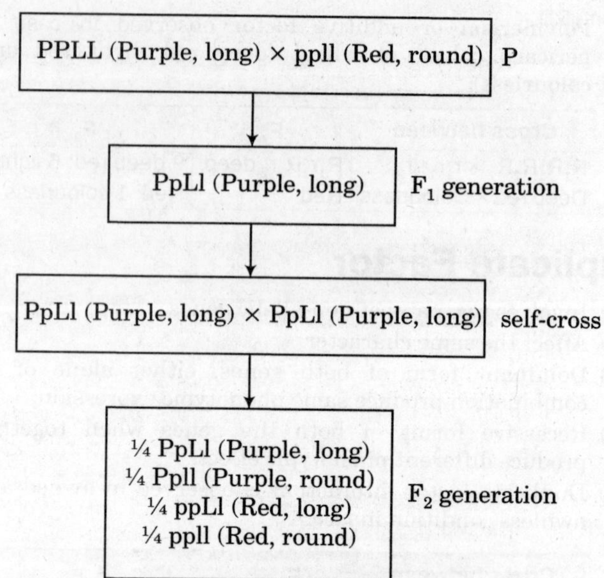

Fig. 23.5 Cross showing linkage

Phenotype and Genotype	Observed	Expected from 9:3:3:1 Ratio
Purple, long (PpLl)	284	216
Purple, round (Ppll)	21	72
Red, long (ppLl)	21	72
Red, round (ppll)	55	24

Their experiment revealed **linkage** between the P and L alleles and the p and l alleles. The frequency of P occurring together with L and with p occurring together with l is greater than that of the recombinant Pl and pL.

Genes present on the same chromosome is theoretically linked to each other, but most of the time they show independent assortment as observed by Mendel. This phenomenon is directly related to the distance between the two genes in question. The more the distance between the two gene the greater probability of their independent assortment, that is they will be separated during gamete formation. This phenomenon is facilitated by the process called **crossing-over**.

Crossing-over can be defined as the exchange of genetic material between the non-sister chromatids of a homologous chromosome. The most important features of crossing-over can be summarized as follows:

1. The genes are located on a chromosome in a linear sequence at different loci (positions).
2. The two alleles of a gene in a heterozygote occupy corresponding positions in the homologous chromosomes.
3. Crossing-over involves the breakage of each of two non-sister chromatids of the homologous chromosomes.

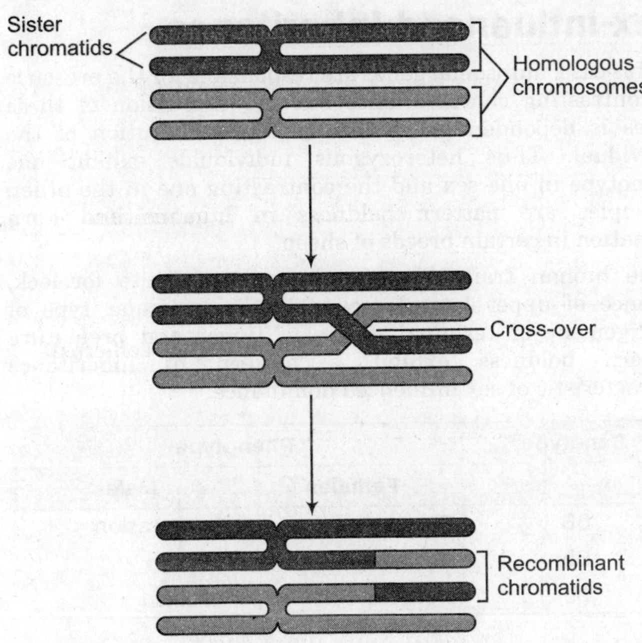

Fig. 23.6 Crossing over between homologous chromosomes

4. Crossing-over occurs at **pachytene stage** after synapsis of the homologous chromosomes has occurred in **prophase-I** of meiosis.
5. Chromosomes with recombinant combinations of linked genes are formed b the occurrence of crossing-over in the region between the two loci.

A cross-shaped structure is formed during crossing-over in which two of the four chromatids of homologous chromosome pairs appear to exchange genetic material. This structure is called chiasma (pl. chiasmata).

TH Morgan was the first to hypothesize the relation between linkage and segregation of homologous chromosomes and the occurrence of crossing-over between homologous chromosomes during meiosis.

Sex Linkage

Sex-linkage was extensively studied by TH Morgan. He discovered a white-eyed mutant in *Drosophila*. He found that when white-eyed male is mated with a red-eyed female, all the F_1 flies were red-eyed, but the F_2 flies included both red and white in the proportion of 3 red to 1 white. All white-eyed flies in F_2 generation, however were males. About half of the F_2 males were white-eyed and the rest were red-eyed, but all F_2 females had red eyes.

Interpretation Males are hemizygous for white-eye allele therefore, it was expressed. Furthermore, the mutant allele present in the X-chromosome of the original white-eyed male was passed on to his daughter therefore, all daughters become carriers (since females are heterozygote with one wild type allele present). The hemizygous males had obtained their X-chromosomes from their heterozygous mothers. Half of them received w^+ allele therefore; developed red eyes, while other half received w allele therefore; developed white eyes.

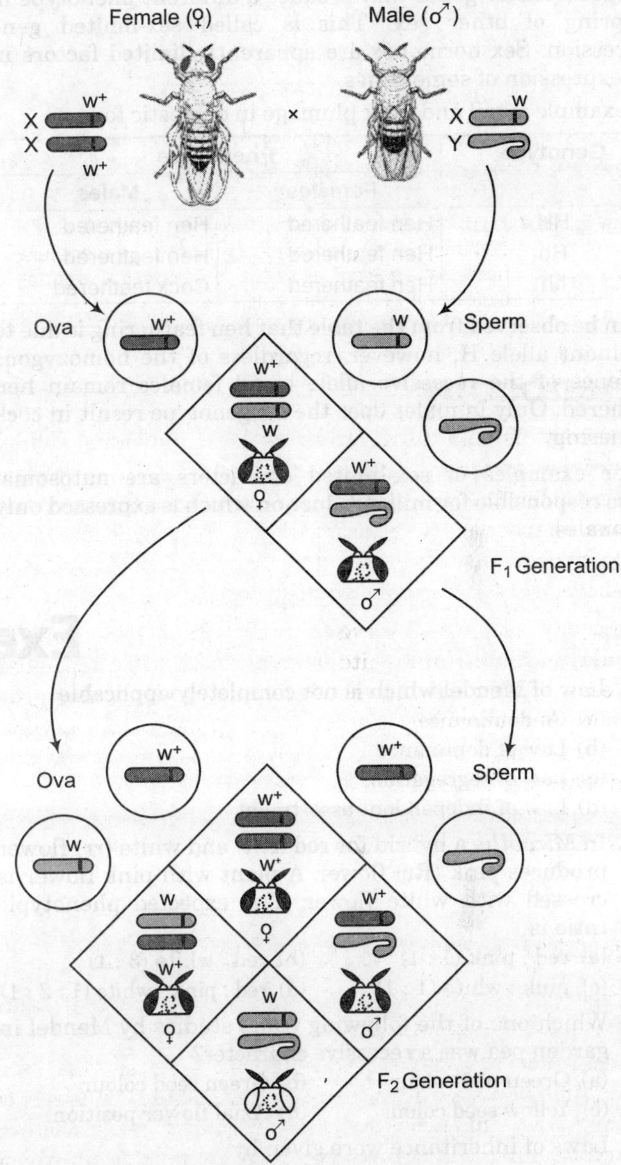

Fig. 23.7 Linkage in *Drosophila*

Pattern of Inheritance of Sex-Linked Genes

The above case was the example of X-linked sex-linkage. It follows a characteristic criss-cross pattern of inheritance in which the gene is transmitted from father to his daughter and then to his grandson. The gene is never transmitted to his sons.

However, another case is Y-linked sex-linkage in which Y-linked or holandric genes are transmitted directly from father to son and never appear in females.

Sex-limited Inheritance

One sex may be uniform in expression of a particular trait and yet transfer genes that produce a different phenotype in offspring of other sex. This is called sex-limited gene expression. Sex hormones are apparently limited factors in the expression of some genes.

An example is tail and neck plumage in domestic fowl.

Genotype	Phenotype	
	Females	Males
HH	Hen feathered	Hen feathered
Hh	Hen feathered	Hen feathered
hh	Hen feathered	Cock feathered

It can be observed from the table that hen feathering is due to dominant allele H, however, regardless of the homozygous presence of the recessive allele h, all females remain hen feathered. Only in males does the hh genotype result in cock feathering.

Other examples of sex-limited characters are autosomal genes responsible for milk production which is expressed only in females.

Sex-influenced Inheritance

In this case, autosomal genes are responsible for the presence of contrasting characteristics but the expression of these genes is dependent on the hormonal constitution of the individual. Thus heterozygous individuals exhibit one phenotype in one sex and the contrasting one in the other. Examples are pattern baldness in humans and horn formation in certain breeds of sheep.

Some human traits like certain type of white forelock, absence of upper lateral incisor teeth, particular type of enlargement of terminal gaints of finger and premature pattern boldness exhibit a pattern of inheritance characteristic of sex influenced dominance.

Genotype	Phenotype	
	Females	Males
BB	Bald	Bald
Bb	Not bald	Bald
bb	Not bald	Not bald

Exercise

1. Law of Mendel which is not completely applicable
(a) Co-dominance
(b) Law of dominance
(c) Law of segregation
(d) Law of independent assortment

2. In *Mirabilis* a hybrid for red (RR) and white (rr) flower produces pink (Rr) flower. A plant with pink flower is crossed with white flower. The expected phenotypic ratio is
(a) red : pink (1 : 1) (b) red : white (3 : 1)
(c) pink : white (1 : 1) (d) red : pink : white (1 : 2 : 1)

3. Which one of the following traits studies by Mendel in garden pea was a recessive character?
(a) Green pod colour (b) Green seed colour
(c) Yellow seed colour (d) Axial flower position

4. Laws of inheritance were given by
(a) Mendel (b) Lamarck
(c) Darwin (d) Correns

5. Mendel did his experiments on
(a) *Cajanus cajan* (b) *Pisum sativum*
(c) garden pea (d) sweet potato

6. The reason why pea plants were suitable than dogs for Mendel's experiments?
(a) Dogs have many genetic traits
(b) Pea plants can be self-fertilized
(c) There are no pedigree records of dogs
(d) The pea plants favour cross-fertilization

7. Which of the following is the monohybrid ratio?
(a) 3 : 1 (b) 9 : 7
(c) 1 : 2 (d) 9 : 3 : 3 : 1

8. If a homozygous red flowered plant is crossed with a homozygous white flowered plant, the offsprings will be
(a) all red flowered (b) half red flowered
(c) half white flowered (d) all white flowered

9. In a monohybrid cross, the genotypic ratio of F_2 is
(a) 3 : 1 (b) 1 : 2 : 1
(c) 4 : 0 (d) 1 : 1 : 1 : 1

10. A woman with straight hair mates with a man with curly hair who is known to be heterozygous for that trait. What is the chance that their child will have curly hair?
(a) No chance (b) One in two
(c) It is certain (d) One in four

11. The back cross of F_1 hybrid with the recessive parent is called
(a) test cross (b) monohybrid cross
(c) Punnett square cross (d) dominant-recessive cross

12. Which of the following cross is used to determine heterozygosite or homozygosite of parents?
(a) Test cross (b) Back cross
(c) Dihybrid cross (d) Monohybrid cross

13. Mendel's first law is called
(a) law of variation
(b) law of segregation
(c) law of inheritance
(d) law of independent assortment

14. Mendel's principle of segregation was based on the separation of alleles in the garden pea during
(a) pollination (b) flower formation
(c) seed formation (d) embryonic development

15. A cross involving F_1 hybrid and a double recessive parent is called
(a) test cross (b) dihybrid cross
(c) multiple cross (d) monohybrid cross

16. Incomplete dominance is found in
(a) *Pisum sativum* (b) *Antirrhinum majus*
(c) Both (a) and (b) (d) None of these

17. A man with blood group B marries a woman with blood group A and their child is having group B. What is the genotype of the child?
(a) I^AB^B (b) I^BI^B
(c) I^Bi (d) I^Ai

18. ABO blood group is one of the good example for which of the following?
(a) Epistasis (b) Co-dominance
(c) Pleiotropy (d) Incomplete dominance

19. Variations occur mostly due to
(a) linkage (b) segregation
(c) nutrition (d) crossing-over

20. Emasculation of flower body is achieved by removal of
(a) anthers (b) carpels
(c) flowers (d) perianth

21. Law of segregation of gametes was proposed by
(a) Mendel (b) Hugo de Vries
(c) Huxley (d) Robert Hooke

22. Phenotype ratio of dihybrid test cross is
(a) 15 : 1 (b) 3 : 1
(c) 9 : 3 : 3 : 1 (d) : 1 : 1 : 1

23. When cross is made between two species of the same genus, then the cross is known as
(a) interspecific hybridization
(b) intraspecific hybridization
(c) intergeneric hybridization
(d) intervarital hybridization

24. Which of the following statement is incorrect?
(a) ABO blood group is an example of multiple allele
(b) Sex-linked genes obey Mendelian laws
(c) Height is an example of continuous variation
(d) None of the above

25. Which of the following is not an example of incomplete dominance?
(a) Inheritance of hair phenotype
(b) Flower colour in lavendar flowers
(c) Flower colour in dog flower
(d) ABO blood group

26. If an individual with type O blood mates with an individual with type AB blood, what are the possible blood types of their offspring?
(a) A (b) B
(c) AB (d) A and B

27. If an organism is heterozygous for two traits that are linked, how many genotypes are possible in the gametes produced from a single germ-line cell? (Assume no crossing over occurs)
(a) 2 (b) 4
(c) 6 (d) 8

28. If an organism is heterozygous for two traits that are linked, how many genotypes are possible in the gametes produced from a single germ-line cell? (Assume 1 crossing over occurs)
(a) 2 (b) 4
(c) 6 (d) 8

29. Mendel's law of segregation, as applied to the behaviour of chromosomes in meiosis, means that
(a) pairing of homologs will convert one allele into the other, leading to separation of the types
(b) alleles of a gene separate from each other when homologs separate in meiosis-I
(c) genes on the same chromosome will show 50% recombination
(d) alleles of a gene will be linked and passed on together through meiosis

30. The phenomenon of independent assortment refers to
(a) expression at the same stage of development
(b) unlinked transmission of genes in crosses resulting from being located on different chromosomes
(c) association of an RNA and a protein implying related function
(d) independent location of genes from each other in an interphase cell

31. One of Mendel's pure strains of pea plants had green peas. How many different kinds of eggs could such a plant produce with regard to pea colour?
(a) One (b) Two
(c) Three (d) Four

32. If a diploid cell contains six chromosomes, how many possible random arrangements of homologous could occur during metaphase-I?
(a) 4 (b) 8
(c) 6 (d) 64

33. Determine the frequency of only one genotype, BBLl, in the offspring of dihybrid parents (BbLl).
(a) 1/4 (b) 1/8
(c) 1/16 (d) 1/2

34. An individual of genotypes, AaBbCcDd is test cross, how many different phenotypes can appear in the progeny?
(a) 16 (b) 8
(c) 32 (d) 64

35. If individuals of genotypes AaBbCc are intercrossed, how many different phenotypes can appear in their offspring?
(a) 16 (b) 8
(c) 32 (d) 64

36. If individuals of genotype AaBbCc are intercrossed, how many different genotypes can occur in their progeny?
(a) 8 (b) 64
(c) 27 (d) 9

37. In individuals of genotype AaBbCc are intercrossed. How many different F_2 phenotypes can appear assuming complete co-dominance at all loci?
(a) 8 (b) 64
(c) 27 (d) 9

38. A man is heterozygous B/b for one autosomal gene and he carries a recessive X-linked allele d. What proportion of his sperm will be bd?
(a) 1/4 (b) 1/8
(c) 1/16 (d) 1/2

39. A trihybrid cross is made between two yeast. Both with genotype A/a, B/b, C/c. What proportion of the offspring will be of genotype a/a, b/b, c/c?
(a) 1/8 (b) 1/32
(c) 1/64 (d) 1/74

40. When heterozygous black pigs are intercrossed then what is the chance of the first two offspring being black?
(a) 46 (b) 56
(c) 66 (d) 76

41. If a man blood group AB marries a woman of blood group A whose father was of blood group O, to what different blood groups can this man and woman expect their children to belong?
(a) A, AB and B (b) A and AB
(c) AB and O (d) A, O and B

42. In the human ABO blood system, the alleles A and B are dominant to O. What will be number of different possible genotypes?
(a) 4 (b) 8
(c) 6 (d) 12

43. Guinea pig, black coat colour is a dominant trait and white is recessive trait. A black female is test crossed, producing six black offspring. The probability that a heterozygous black would do this by chance alone is approximately
(a) 50%
(b) 25%
(c) 1%
(d) Cannot be determined from the above information

44. What are the minimum progeny population sizes allowing for random union of all kinds of gametes from AaBbCc parent?
(a) 64 (b) 32
(c) 16 (d) 8

45. A blue coloured flower tall parent plant (P_1) was crossed to a true breeding blue-flowered dwarf plant (P_2) and half of the progenies obtained was blue and tall and the other half blue and dwarf. In the next generation, half of all these progenies segregated only for flower colour and the other half segregate only for height. The genotype of the P_1 is
(a) heterozygous for colour and heterozygous for height
(b) homozygous for colour and heterozygous for height
(c) heterozygous for colour and homozygous for height
(d) homozygous for colour and homozygous for height

46. According to classical genetics, which of the following statements is true?
(a) Recessive alleles are detected by the phenotype of the F_1 generation
(b) The closer two genes are, the more frequently they recombine
(c) Genes on different autosomes segregate independently
(d) Gene on sex-chromosomes segregates with the same pattern as autosomal genes

47. Assuming the comparable chromosomes in different individuals is genetically dissimilar because of different alleles. How many unique zygotic combinations are possible following fertilization in an organism where $n = 3$ (assuming that no crossing over occurs)?
(a) 8 (b) 16
(c) 64 (d) 216

48. The colour of flowers of an annual species of plants is controlled by a single locus with two alleles R and r and the genotypes RR, Rr and rr and red, pink and white respectively. A large number of seeds from individuals with pink flowers were collected and planted on an island, where, because of absence of pollinators, only self-pollination is possible. What will be the most likely outcome after 25 years?
(a) About 50% plants with red flowers, 50% with white flowers
(b) Almost 100% plants with pink flowers
(c) Red, pink and white flowered plants in a ratio of 1 : 2 : 1
(d) Red, pink and white flowered plants in equal proportion

49. *Drosophila* females that have white eyes and ebony body were crossed with an inbred homozygous wild-type strain of males that have red eyes and brown body. If white colour is recessive to red and ebony is recessive to brown, what will be the phenotypic ratios for the F_2 generation (assume the genes are not linked and are all autosomal)?
(a) 9 : 3 : 3 : 1 (b) 12 : 3 : 1
(c) 9 : 6 : 1 (d) 9 : 3 : 4

50. *Drosophila* females that have white eyes and ebony body were crossed with an inbred homozygous wild-type strain of males that have red eyes and brown body. If white colour is recessive to red, and ebony is recessive to brown, what will be the phenotypic ratios for the F_1 generation (assume that eye colour gene is on the X-chromosome, the genes are not linked and body-colour gene is autosomal)?
(a) 12 : 3 : 1 (b) 3 : 5 : 7
(c) 1 : 4 : 2 (d) 1 : 1

51. In a cross between with the genotypes AaBbccDdEeFf and AaBbCCDDeeff, the probability that an offspring will be heterozygous at all these loci is
(a) 0 (b) 1/16
(c) 1/32 (d) 1/64

52. Which of the following is a mismatch?
(a) Phenotypic F_2 ratio of 1 : 4 : 6 : 4 : 1 .... polygenic inheritance
(b) Phenotypic F_2 ratio of 9 : 3 : 4 .... recessive epistasis
(c) Phenotypic F_2 ratio of 1 : 2 : 1 .... co-dominance
(d) Phenotypic F_2 ratio of 3 : 1 .... partial dominance

53. Which of the following statements is correct?
(a) Mendel had extensive training in biology and heredity prior to his groundbreaking work.
(b) Fusion of gametes is called fertilization and this creates a diploid individual.
(c) Cross-fertilization is the typical mode of reproduction for pea plants.
(d) The probability that two heterozygotes produce an affected and a heterozygous offspring is ¾. Keep in mind that each offspring is considered a separate event.

54. Which of the following statement is correct?
(a) A chi-square value lower than the critical value demonstrates that the hypothesis was correct
(b) Critical values for the chi-square test are larger when there are more degrees of freedom because each class of data is expected to show a small amount of variation
(c) A high chi-square value always means that our hypothesis is wrong
(d) A chi-square value below the critical value means that our hypothesis is correct

55. Why would you predict that half of the human babies born will be males and half will be females?
(a) Because of the segregation of the X and Y-chromosomes during male meiosis
(b) Because of the segregation of the X-chromosomes during female meiosis
(c) Because all eggs contain an X-chromosome
(d) Because, on average, one half of all eggs produce females

56. Asymmetry between reciprocal crosses is seen in
(a) pleiotropy (b) sex-linked inheritance
(c) interaction of genes (d) autosomal inheritance

57. Which of the following is not true about autosomal dominant traits?
(a) Every affected person should have at least one affected parent
(b) Males and females should be equally often affected
(c) An affected person has a 50% chance of transmitting the dominant allele to each offspring
(d) All the daughters of an affected male will be affected but none of the sons

58. Albinism is a recessive human trait. If a normal couple produces an albino child, what is the probability that their next child will be albino?
(a) 1/4 (b) 1/8
(c) 1/16 (d) 1/64

59. When a man with hypertrichosis marries a normal woman, what percentage of their sons would be expected to have hairy ears?
(a) 50% (b) 100%
(c) 0% (d) 25%

60. A man with certain disease marries a normal woman. They have 8 children (4 boys and 4 girls); all of the girls have their father's disease, but none of the boys do. What inheritance is suggested?
(a) Autosomal recessive (b) Autosomal dominant
(c) Y-linked (d) X-linked

61. Which of the following is not an example of autosomal dominant trait?
(a) Brachydactyly
(b) Marfan syndrome
(c) Familial hyper cholesterolemia
(d) Cystic fibrosis

62. A dominantly inherited trait affects a child and his grandmother, but neither parent. This best illustrates which of the following principles?
(a) Variable expressivity (b) New mutation
(c) Somatic mosaicism (d) None-penetrance

63. Cystic fibrosis is a hereditary disease that affects the respiratory and digestive systems. Cystic fibrosis occurs when two recessive genes (cc) are present. A person with one allele for cystic fibrosis is called a carrier (Cc) of the disease. If the mother is a carrier of the disease and the father is homozygous dominant, what are chances that their child will be a carrier of cystic fibrosis?
(a) 25% (b) 50%
(c) 75% (d) 100%

64. Pair of contrasting characters controlling the same trait is called
(a) factors (b) alleles
(c) alloloci (d) paramorphs

65. The term 'gene' was introduced by
(a) Mendel (b) Bateson
(c) Morgan (d) Johansen

66. Alleles of a gene are found on
(a) same chromosome
(b) any chromosome
(c) homologous chromosome
(d) non-homologous chromosome

67. An organism with two identical alleles for a given trait is
(a) one allele of a gene (b) two alleles of a gene
(c) all alleles of a gene (d) many alleles of a gene

68. The genetic, genotype and phenotype were introduced by
(a) Bateson (b) Darwin
(c) Johannsen (d) Mendel

69. Hybrids are generally superior to parents due to
(a) heterosis (b) homozygosity
(c) weak parents (d) heterozygosity

70. One gene pair hides the effect of another. The phenomenon is
(a) mutation (b) epistasis
(c) dominance (d) None of these

71. Each selection is an individual's genotype. Which are homozygous for the trait represented by H or h?
(a) HHKk (b) HhKK
(c) hhkk (d) Both (a) and (c)

72. ABO blood group is one of the good example for which of the following?
(a) Epistasis (b) Co-dominance
(c) Pleiotropy (d) Incomplete dominance

73. Some alleles of a characteristic may create multiple phenotypic effects, is an example of
(a) pleiotropy (b) anisotropy
(c) isotropy (d) karyotropy

74. When two alleles rather than one allele form a new phenotype, what is the word describing their relationship to each other?
(a) Epistatic
(b) Pleiotropic
(c) Co-dominance
(d) Incomplete dominant

75. When different genes interact with each other in a way that influences the phenotype, this phenomenon is known as
(a) epistatis
(b) pleiotropy
(c) co-dominance
(d) incomplete dominance

76. A .... is a hereditary factor and the fundamental unit of inheritance.
(a) DNA (b) gene
(c) chromosome (d) gene pool

77. In fruit flies, the allele for red eyes is dominant and the allele for purple eyes is recessive. Normal gray body is dominant, and black body is recessive. A geneticist mated a heterozygous red-gray male with a purple-black female. She predicted that there would be four phenotypes of offspring in equal numbers, but she was wrong. Instead 48% of the offspring were red-gray, 46% were purple-black, 3% were red-black, and 3% were purple-gray. She concluded that in the male, the red and gray genes were linked, and in the female the purple and black genes were linked. If this is the case, how would you account for the red-black and purple-gray offspring?
(a) This is an example of pleiotropy
(b) Body colour and eye colour are quantitative characteristics
(c) Crossing over during meiosis recombined the genes
(d) This cross shows incomplete dominance at work

78. How did Mendel's studies in genetics differ from earlier studies of breeding and inheritance?
(a) Mendel worked with plants; earlier studies used animals
(b) Mendel was able to explain the 'blending' hypothesis
(c) Mendel's work was more quantitative
(d) Mendel worked with wild species, not domesticated ones

79. Which of the following illustrates pleiotropy?
(a) In fruit flies, the genes for scarlet eyes and hairy body are located on the same chromosome
(b) Matings between earless sheep and longeared sheep always result in short eared offspring
(c) Wheat kernels can range from white to red in colour, a trait controlled by several genes
(d) The human cystic fibrosis gene causes many symptoms, from respiratory distress to digestive problems

80. Some dogs bark while trailing; others are silent. The barker gene is dominant, the silent gene recessive. The gene for normal tail is dominant over the gene for screw (curly) tail. A barker dog with a normal tail who is heterozygous for both characteristics is mated to another dog of the same genotypes. What fraction of their offspring will be barkers with screw tails?
(a) $\frac{3}{4}$ (b) $\frac{9}{16}$
(c) $\frac{3}{16}$ (d) $\frac{1}{4}$

81. Match list I with list II and select the correct answer using the codes given below the lists.

List I	List II
A. Phenotypes analysis	1. Meiotic process
B. Spermatogenesis	2. Fertilization
C. Law of segregation (Mendel)	3. Recessive type appearing in F_2
D. Chromosome mapping	4. Visible expression of the genotype
	5. Indexing gene loci

Codes

	A	B	C	D
(a)	4	2	3	1
(b)	4	1	3	5
(c)	3	2	4	5
(d)	3	2	4	1

82. Match list I with list II and select the correct answer using the codes given below the lists.

List I	List II
A. Crossing-over	1. *cis*-configuration
B. Coupling	2. *trans*-configuration
C. Coincidence	3. Recombination
D. Repulsion	4. Double cross-over

Codes

	A	B	C	D
(a)	3	1	4	2
(b)	4	3	1	2
(c)	2	1	4	3
(d)	3	4	2	1

83. Consider the following statements regarding linkage.
I. The linked genes are located on the same chromosome.
II. Crossing over between linked genes is rare.
III. Linked genes are always inherited together.
IV. Linkage affects the percentage of homozygosity following hybridization.
(a) I and III are correct
(b) I and II are correct
(c) II, III and IV are correct
(d) I, III and IV are correct

84. In *Drosophila*, black body (b) is recessive to grey body (B), vestigial (v) wing is recessive to long wing (V). The two loci are 18 map units apart on an autosome. A cross is made as indicated below

B v		b v
b V		b v
Grey long male	Bodied winged	Black-bodied vestigial-winged female

	(a)	(b)	(c)	(d)
Grey-bodied long winged	50%	—	41%	9%
Grey-bodied vestigial winged	—	50%	9%	41%
Black-bodied long winged	—	50%	9%	41%
Black-bodied vestigial winged	50%	—	41%	9%

Answers

1. (a) **2.** (c) **3.** (b) **4.** (a) **5.** (b) **6.** (b) **7.** (a) **8.** (a) **9.** (b) **10.** (a)
11. (a) **12.** (a) **13.** (c) **14.** (a) **15.** (a) **16.** (b) **17.** (c) **18.** (b) **19.** (d) **20.** (a)
21. (b) **22.** (d) **23.** (a) **24.** (b) **25.** (d) **26.** (d) **27.** (a) **28.** (b) **29.** (b) **30.** (b)
31. (a) **32.** (b) **33.** (b) **34.** (a) **35.** (b) **36.** (c) **37.** (c) **38.** (a) **39.** (c) **40.** (b)
41. (a) **42.** (c) **43.** (a) **44.** (a) **45.** (a) **46.** (c) **47.** (c) **48.** (c) **49.** (a) **50.** (d)
51. (c) **52.** (d) **53.** (b) **54.** (b) **55.** (a) **56.** (b) **57.** (d) **58.** (a) **59.** (b) **60.** (d)
61. (d) **62.** (d) **63.** (b) **64.** (b) **65.** (d) **66.** (c) **67.** (b) **68.** (c) **69.** (a) **70.** (c)
71. (d) **72.** (b) **73.** (a) **74.** (c) **75.** (a) **76.** (b) **77.** (c) **78.** (c) **79.** (d) **80.** (c)
81. (b) **82.** (a) **83.** (d) **84.** (b)

24 Gene Mapping, Extrachromosomal Inheritance and Microbial Genetics

Gene Mapping Methods

Linkage Maps Using Crossing Over

Morgan's student **Sturtevant** postulated that the greater the distance between the linked genes, the greater the chance that non-sister chromatids would crossover in the region between the genes and hence, the greater the proportion of recombinants that would be produced. Thus, by determining the frequency of recombinants, we can obtain a measure of the map distance between the genes. One **genetic map unit** (mu) is defined as that distance between genes for which 1 product of meiosis in 100 is recombinant. This is equal to the **recombinant frequency** of 1 per cent or 0.01. A map unit is sometimes referred to as a centiMorgan (cM) in honour of **TH Morgan.** The recombinant frequency can get a maximum value of 50 per cent as the rest will be parental combinations.

Linkage maps or genetic maps are constructed on the basis of recombination frequency. This method can be used to make genetic linkage maps for *Drosophila*, maize, mouse and so on in which we can observe the recombinant frequency.

Genes have been found to occur in a distinct set of **linkage groups** with each linkage group corresponding to one of the pairs of homologous chromosomes in the genome of that species. For example, mouse has 20 pairs of chromosomes therefore, 20 linkage groups. All the linked genes in a linkage group are linearly arranged.

Syllabus

- Gene Mapping Methods: Linkage Maps Using Crossing Over, Tetrad Analysis, Mapping with Molecular Markers, Mapping by Using Somatic Cell Hybrids
- Extrachromosomal Inheritance: Inheritance of Mitochondrial and Chloroplast Genes, Maternal Inheritance.
- Microbial Genetics: Transformation, Transduction : Conjugation, Sex-duction.

Two-Factor Crosses

If we take two genes at a time and observe its recombinant frequency then it is termed two-factor cross. If a cross yield a recombinant frequency of 9 per cent between gene A and gene B then the distance between the two will be 9 map units (mu). Similarly, if another cross yield recombinant frequency of 4 per cent between gene B and gene C then the distance between the two will be 4 map units (mu). One assumption here is that the distance between gene A and gene C will be addition of the above two distances.

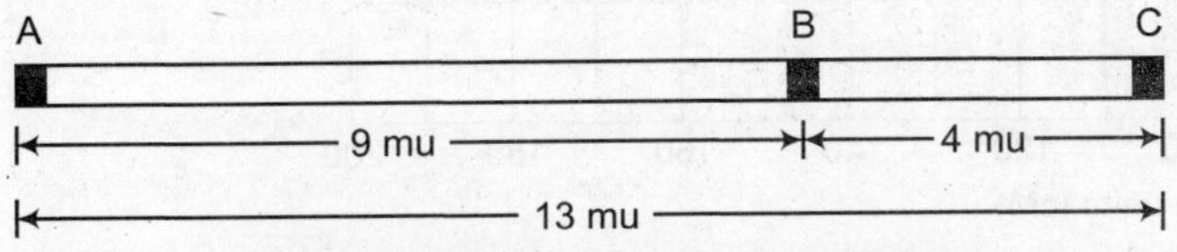

Fig. 24.1 Mapping among A, B, C genes

However, this assumption do not hold true with increased distance. It has been observed that when the distance between two genes are large, the recombinant frequency is significantly lower than what addivity principle would predict. The reason is that when two loci are far apart, double crossovers occur at significant frequencies.

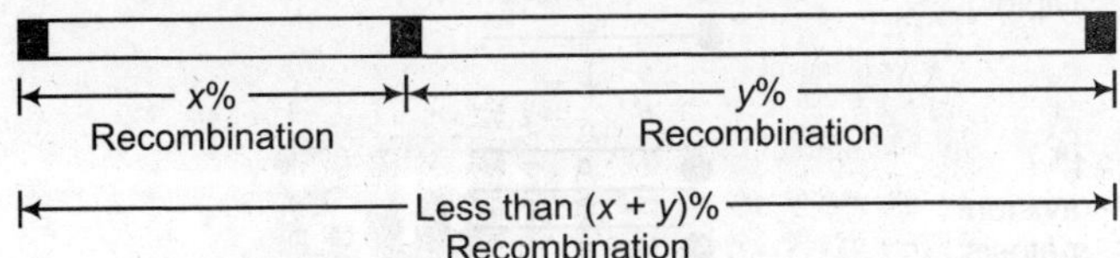

Fig. 24.2 Mapping in long distant genes

Three-Factor Crosses

These involve three pairs of alleles. They allow us to detect some of the double crossovers which were not recognizable in two-factor crosses. In addition three-factor crosses allow to order the involved pairs of alleles.

Interference

The detection of double crossing over makes it possible to determine whether exchange in two different regions of a pair of chromosomes are formed independently of each other. If recombination is independent in the two regions (which means that the formation of one crossover does not alter the probability of the second crossover), the probability of a single recombination in both regions is the product of these separate probabilities.

Such deficiencies in the observed number of double recombinants are common; they reflect a phenomenon called chromosome **interference,** in which a crossover in one region of a chromosome reduces the probability of a second crossover in a nearby region. Over short genetic distances, chromosome interference is nearly complete. The degree of interference is measured by the **coefficient of coincidence,** which is simply the ratio of the observed to the excepted frequency of double crossover gametes, that is,

$$\text{Coefficient of coincidence} = \frac{\text{observed double crossover frequency}}{\text{expected double crossover frequency}}$$

where the expected double crossover frequency is that predicted if the two crossover are independent events. In the absence of interference, the coefficient of coincidence will equal 1. Sometimes levels of interference are given as the coefficient of interference which equal 1 minus the coefficient of coincidence. The coefficient of interference will thus be 0 in the absence of interference.

Interference values between 0 and 1 indicate that positive interference has occurred. Positive interference indicates that one crossover interferes with the occurrence of a second crossover nearby.

In certain microorganism, particularly bacteriophages, coefficient of coincidence greater than 1 often occur. Coefficient of coincidence larger than 1 indicate that the occurrence of one crossover increases the likelihood of additional crossover occurring nearby (so called 'clustering' of crossovers). This second type of interference is called negative intereference.

The effect of interference on the relationship between genetic map distance and the frequency of recombination is illustrated in figure. Each curve is an example of a **mapping function,** which is the mathematical relation between the genetic distance across an interval in map units (centiMorgans) and the observed frequency of recombination across the interval. In other words, a mapping function tells one how to convert a **map distance** between genetic markers into a recombination frequency between the markers. As we have seen, when the map distance between the markers is small, the recombination frequency equals the map distance.

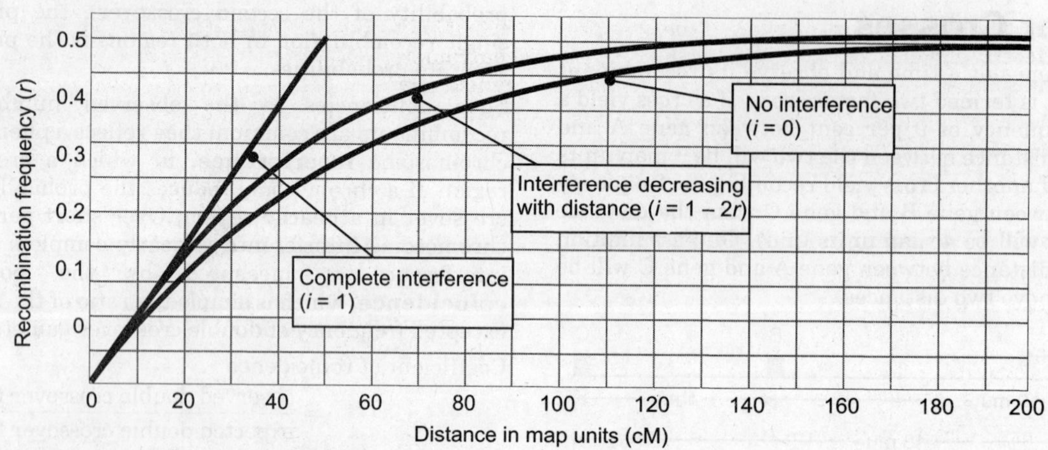

Fig. 24.3 A mapping function is the relation between genetic map distance across an interval and the observed frequency of recombination across the interval. Map distance is defined as one-half the average number of crossovers converted into a percentage. The three mapping functions correspond to different assumptions about interference, *i*.

Tetrad Analysis

In some organisms, the four haploid cells formed when a mother cell goes through meiosis are held together as a group of four cells called a **tetrad**. The knowledge that a specific group of four cells are the products of a single meiosis can be used to estimate the map distance between loci without the use of a mapping function by a procedure called **tetrad analysis**. Tetrad analysis has been extensive utilized in the fungi such as yeast and *Neurospora;* however, there are also some animals, higher plants and algae in which tetrad analysis can be performed. In some organisms such as *Neurospora,* the haploid products of meiosis are ordered such that one knows which ones separated at the first meiotic division and which ones separated at the second meiotic division. This extra information can be used to map the location of the centromeres.

When a diploid yeast (*Saccharomyces cerevisiae*) cell goes through meiosis, the four haploid spores that are formed are held together in an ascus (a tiny sac).

We characterize tetrads based upon the number of parental and recombinant spores they contain. Consider a cross between an α-mating type haploid yeast strain of genotype HIS4 trp1 with an α-mating type haploid yeast strain of the opposite genotype HIS4 trp1. These two genes are unlinked. The possible kinds of tetrads are:

Parental Ditype (PD) A tetrad containing four haploid cells of the parental class.

Non-parental Ditype (NPD) A tetrad containing four recombinant haploid cells (the two parental classes have recombined to form the reciprocal non-parental combination of alleles).

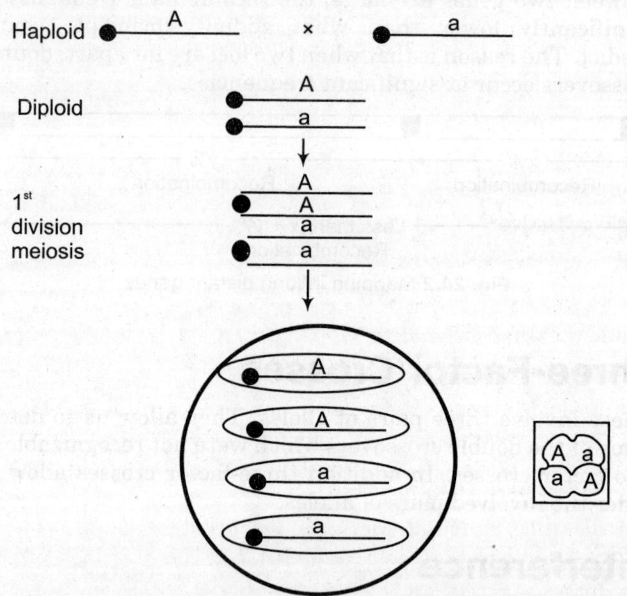

Fig. 24.4 The products of a single meiosis

Tetratype (T) A tetrad containing four kinds of haploid cells, two different parental class spores and two different recombinant class spores. In crosses involving two unlinked genes, tetratypes arise when a crossover occurs between one of the two genes and its centromere.

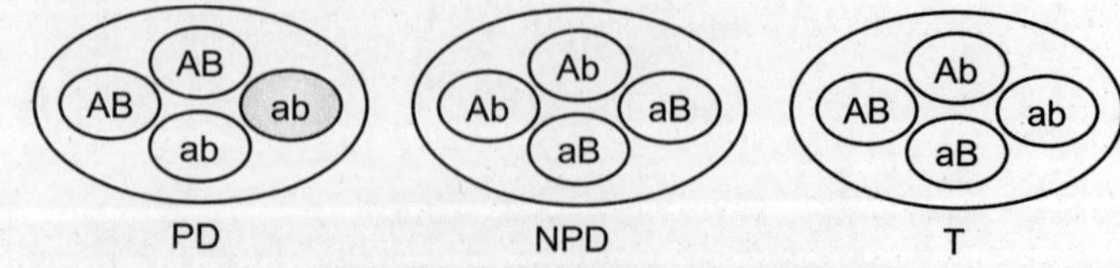

Fig. 24.5 Three forms of tetrads

If PD = NPD, then the two genes are unlinked (either they are located on different chromosomes, or they are far apart on the same chromosome).

If PD > NPD, then the two genes are linked. When PD > NPD, the haploid spores of the parental class significantly out number the haploids of the recombinant class, a sign of linkage.

Lets take an example of two linked genes, ARG3 and URA2.

Parents arg3 ura2 × ARG3 URA2

Diploid arg3 ura2 / ARG3 URA2

Meiotic Products

PD (arg3 ura2; arg3 ura2; ARG3 URA2; ARG3 URA2) = 127

NPD (arg3 URA2; arg3 URA2; ARG3 ura2; ARG3 ura2) = 3

T (arg3 ura2; arg3 URA2; ARG3 ura2; ARG3 URA2) = 70

Recombination frequency,

RF = [(NPD + 1/2T) / total number of tetrads] × 100.

In our example, this is

([3 + 1/2(70)]/200) × 100 = 19 map units.

The equation will be modified to obtain a better estimate of map distance. If we draw out the possible crossover events between two linked genes, we can see the different tetrads that result:

No crossovers ⟶ PD

Single crossover ⟶ T

Double crossover (2-strand) ⟶ PD

Double crossover (3-strand) ⟶ PD

Double crossover (3-strand) ⟶ T

Double crossover (4-strand) ⟶ NPD

Half (2/4) the strands recombine if there is a single crossover event and 4 strands recombine if there is a double crossover event (even if all of the strands don't participate, some participate more than once).

Map distance = (total rec. events/total tetrads) × 100 = [(1/2[SCO] + DCO) / total tetrads] × 100

Map distance = ([1/2 (T – 2 NPD) + 4 NPD]/ total tetrads) × 100

Map distance = (1/2 T + 3 NPD) / total tetrads × 100

For our example above, map distance = ([1/2 (70) + 3 (3)] / 200) × 100 = 22 map units.

This modified equation makes two assumptions:

1. There are no more than two crossovers in the interval.
2. There is no chromosomal interference (all types of DCOs occur with equal frequency.

Ordered Tetrads and Gene-Centromere Distance

In *Neurospora crassa*, meiosis occurs within the tight confines of a narrow ascus, resulting in the formation of ordered tetrads. Because of the precise positioning of each meiotic product within the ascus, one can infer the arrangement (and segregation) of each chromatid of homologous chromosomes during meiosis-I and II. This gives information about the distance between the gene and its centromere. (Meiosis-II is followed by mitosis; each pair of genetically identical daugthers sits adjacent to one another. Each ascus is thus made of up 8 haploid ascospores).

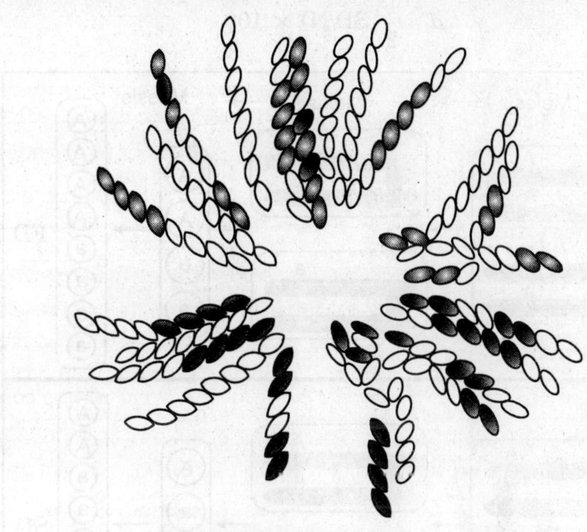

Fig. 24.6 *Neurospora crassa* colony

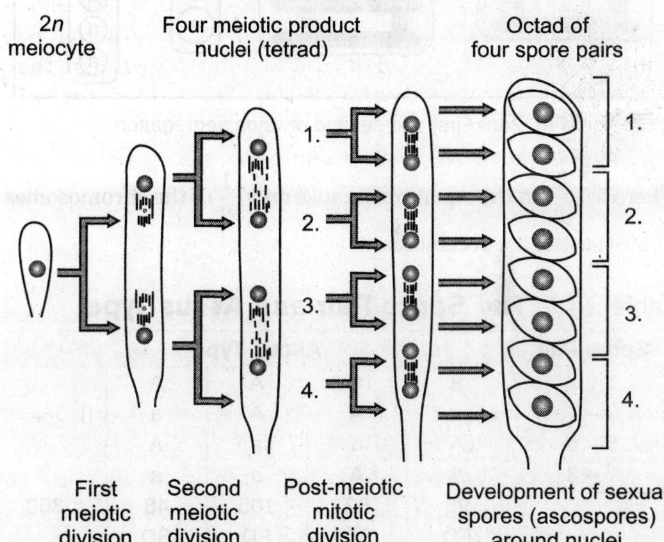

Fig. 24.7 Meiosis in *Neurospora crassa*

We will take an example in which we will look at the outcomes when there is and is not a crossover between a locus (A) and the centromere. As shown in the top panel of the figure below, when there is no crossing over, the four A spores are at one end of the ascus and the four a spores at the other end. The different alleles (A and a) segregated apart at the first meiotic division. This pattern (A:A:A:A:a:a:a:a) is called **First Division Segregation** (FD). The lower panel of the figure shows the results when there is a crossover between the locus and its centromere. Meiosis-I produces two daughter cells, each of which is Aa. The different alleles (A and a) then segregate apart at the second meiotic division. After the mitotic division, the final pattern is A:A:a:a:A:A:a:a which is called **Second Division** (SD) **Segregation**.

Since, asci showing SD have two chromosomes with recombinations between the centromere and the locus plus two non-recombinant chromosomes, we can calculate the distance between the locus and the centromere as

$$d = \frac{1}{2}\,(\text{SD/N}) \times 100$$

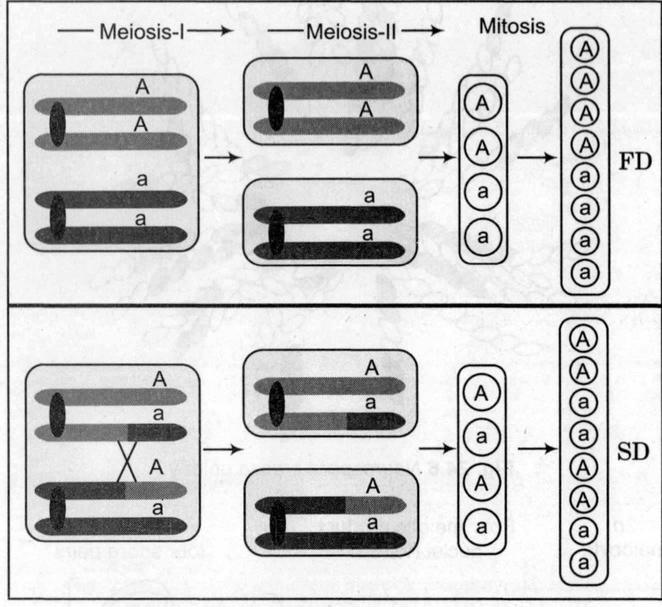

Fig. 24.8 First and second division segregation

There is a $\frac{1}{2}$ in the equation because only $\frac{1}{2}$ of the chromosomes in a SD ascus are recombinant.

Table 24.1 **The Spore Pair and Ascus Type**

Spore Pair	Ascus Type				
1 – 2	a	a	A	A	
3 – 4	a	A	A	a	
5 – 6	A	a	a	A	
7 – 8	A	A	a	a	
	95	52	105	48	= 300
	FD	SD	FD	SD	

There are a total of 300 asci of which 100 are SD, so

$$d = \frac{1}{2}\,(100/300) \times 100 = 16.6$$

or, 16.6 mu (map units)

As the distance increases up to 50 units, in theory all asci should result from second division segregation. However, numerous factors prevent this. As in diploid organisms, accuracy is greatest when the gene and the centromere are relatively close together.

Mapping with Molecular Markers

A molecular marker is a site of heterozygosity for some type of silent DNA variation not associated with any measurable phenotypic variation. Such a 'DNA locus,' when heterozygous, can be used in mapping analysis just as a conventional heterozygous alleles pair can be used.

The three most common types of markers used today are RFLP, RAPD and isozymes. Of the three marker types, RFLPs have been used the most extensively. RFLP markers have several advantages in comparison with the RAPD and isozyme markers:

(i) They are codominant and unaffected by the environment.

(ii) Any source DNA can be used for the analysis.

(iii) Many markers can be mapped in a population that is not stressed by the effects of phenotypic mutations.

The primary drawback to RAPD markers is that they are dominant and therefore, heterozygous individuals can not be distinguished. The weakness of isozyme markers is that each of the proteins that are being scored may not be expressed in the same tissue and at the same time in development. Therefore, several samplings of the genetic population need to be made.

RFLP

Restriction Fragment Length Polymorphism; a molecular marker based on the differential hybridization of cloned DNA to DNA fragments in a sample of restriction enzyme digested DNAs; the marker is specific to a single clone/restriction enzyme combination.

RAPD

Randomly Amplified Polymorphic DNA; a molecular marker based on the differential PCR amplification of a sample of DNAs from short oligonucleotide sequences.

Isozyme

A molecular marker system based on the staining of proteins with identical function, but different electrophoretic mobilities.

Mapping by Using Somatic Cell Hybrids

The linkage groups of humans can not be investigated by designed crosses used with other species. For this other methodologies like somatic cell hybridization and chromosome banding techniques are used.

Mouse-human somatic cell hybrids have been used for mapping human genes. Somatic cell hybridization was first demonstrated with mouse cells by **G Barski** and colleagues in 1960. Somatic cell hybrids are culture lines that contain the entire complement of the mouse genome and a few human chromosomes. These culture lines are developed by mixing human and mouse cells in the presence of the UV-inactivated **Sendai virus** or a chemical **Polyethylene Glycol** (PEG). Any one of them facilitates the fusing of the two cell types to form a hybrid cell. Initally, the nuclei of two cells are separate this stage is called **heterokaryon.** When both the nuclei fuse together, then it is referred as

synkaryon. For a reason that is not entirely known, most, but not all, human chromosomes are lost from the hybrid cell lines. Usually a few human chromosomes are retained. Because the human and mouse chromosomes can be distinguished by chromosome staining techniques, it can be determined which human cells are retained with a specific cell line.

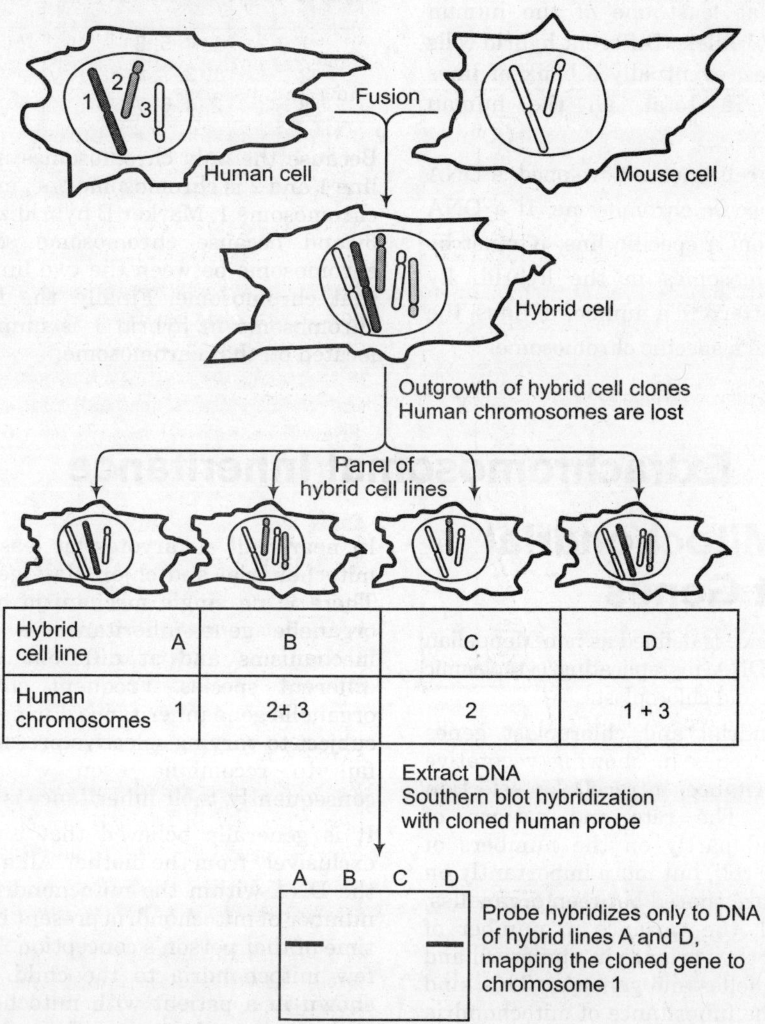

Hybrid cell line	A	B	C	D
Human chromosomes	1	2+ 3	2	1 + 3

Fig. 24.9 A diagrammatic representation of somatic cell hybridization experiment

Most somatic cell hybridization experiments are currently done using selection procedures that prevent the growth of the parental cells while allowing growth of hybrid cells produced by cell fusion. One widely used method of selection is to fuse mouse cells that can not make the enzyme Thymidine Kinase (TK) with human cells that can not make Hypoxanthine-Guanine Phosphoribosyl Transferase (HGPRT). In cells, DNA can be made either *de novo* or through a salvage pathway that uses molecular skeletons already available. The selective technique involves the application of a chemical, **aminopterin**, that blocks the *de novo* synthetic pathway, confining DNA synthesis to the salvage pathway. Two essential salvage enzymes, thymidine kinase (TK) and hypoxanthine-guanine phosphoribosyl transferase (HGPRT), are relevant to the system, as shown in the following two reactions:

$$\text{Thymine} \xrightarrow{\text{TK}} \text{Thymidilic acid (a DNA precursor)}$$

$$\text{Hypoxanthine} \xrightarrow{\text{HGPRT}} \text{Inosinic acid (a DNA precursor)}$$

The mouse cell line to be fused is genetically unable to make TK because it is homozygous for the allele tk^-, whereas the human cell line is genetically unable to make HGPRT because it is homozygous at another locus for the allele $hgprt^-$. So the genotypes of the two fusing cell lines are:

Mouse: tk^-/tk^-; $hgprt^+/hgprt^+$

Human: tk^+/tk^+; $hgprt^-/hgprt^-$

Because each is deficient for one enzyme, neither the mouse nor the human cells are able to make DNA individually. In the hybrid cells, however, the tk^+ allele complements the $hgprt^+$ allele, so the cells can make both enzymes. Therefore, DNA is synthesized and the cells can proliferate. Most human chromosomes are eliminated from the hybrid cell cultures because their loss has no effect on the cultures' ability to grow. But, to continue to grow in medium containing hypoxanthine, aminopterin and thymidine (HAT medium), a hybrid culture must retain at least one of the human chromosome that carries the tk^+ allele. Different hybrid cells are grown separately into lines; eventually a bank of lines is produced that contains, in total, all the human chromosomes.

Once, a complement of hybrid cell lines is developed, a DNA marker can be assigned to specific chromosome. If a DNA marker hybridizes to DNA from a specific line, it must be located on one of the chromosomes in the hybrid. By analyzing the hybridization pattern in a number of lines, the DNA marker can be assigend to a specific chromosome.

Table 24.2 **The DNA Markers to Specific Chromosomes**

Hybrid Line	Chromosomes	Marker		
		A	B	C
1	1, 4, 5, 8	+	–	+
2	1, 3, 7, 8	+	+	–
3	2, 4, 6, 7	–	+	–

Because the only chromosomes in common between hybrid line 1 and 2 is chromosome one, marker A must be located on chromosome 1. Marker B hybridizes to DNA from lines 2 and 3 and because chromosome seven is the only shared chromosome between the two lines, the marker must be on that chromosome. Finally, the fact that the only unique chromosome in hybrid 1 is number 5, marker C must be located on that chromosome.

Extrachromosomal Inheritance

Inheritance of Mitochondrial and Chloroplast Genes

The extrachromosomal inheritance is defined as non-Mendelian inheritance, usually involving DNA in replicating cytoplasmic organelles such as mitochondria and chloroplasts.

The inheritance of mitochondrial and chloroplast genes differs from that of nuclear genes in showing vegetative segregation, uniparental inheritance, intracellular selection and reduced recombination. The rate and pattern of vegetative segregation depend partly on the numbers of genomes and of organelles per cell, but more importantly on the extent to which genomes are shared between organelles, their distribution in the cell, the variance in number of replications per molecule, and the variance in numerical and genotypic partitioning of organelles and genomes. This kind of autonomy, as observed in the inheritance of mitochondria and chloroplast genes, has promoted many investigaters including **Margulis** to propose that mitochondria and chloroplasts were once free-living bacteria and free-living algae respectively. Over long periods of time, they established a hereditary symbiosis with their eukaryote cells and ultimately evolved into oganelles within animal and plant cells.

In humans, more than 80 proteins participate directly in oxidative phosphorylation, of which 13 are encoded by mitochondrial DNA (mtDNA). The mtDNA make up only a small portion of the total cellular DNA (less than 1 percent in somatic cell of higher animals). This mtDNA usually exists as relatively small circular molecules. The mtDNAs are usually present in multiple copies.

Similarly, chloroplasts play crucial roles in sustenance of plant cells. They contain a pigment called chlorophyll that is essential for photosynthesis. Chloroplasts contain within it the synthesizing machinery for chlorophyll production such as specific DNA, *t*RNA and ribosomes. They are capable of protein synthesis in the presence of either ATPs or light.

In nearly all eukaryotes, at least some individuals inherit mitochondrial and chloroplast genes from only one parent. There is no single mechanism of uniparental inheritance: organelle gene inheritance is blocked by a variety of mechanisms and at different stages of reproduction in different species. Frequent changes in the pattern of organelle gene inheritance during evolution suggest that it is subject to varying selective pressures. Organelle genes often fail to recombine even when inherited biparentally; consequently, their inheritance is asexual.

It is generally believed that animal mtDNA is inherited exclusively from the mother. All mitochondria, and therefore, the DNA within the mitochondria, descend from the small number of mitochondria present in the original egg cell at the time of that person's conception. The sperm contributes very few mitochondria to the child. However, it was recently shown in a patient with mitochondrial myopathy that the pathogenic mtDNA was of paternal origin. Evidence for the occasional paternal transmission of mtDNA has also been reported in sheep, mice, cattle, mussels and insects.

Carl Correns, in 1908, provided the earliest example of inheritance linked to chloroplast transmission in his studies on the four o'clock plant, *Mirabilis jalapa*. This plant has three types of branches *viz.* Green, white and variegated. He observed that the seeds derived from the branch containing **ovule** determines the colour of progeny plants regardless of the **pollen** source. Correns concluded that the inheritance was transmitted through the cytoplasm of the maternal parent because the pollen, which contributes little or no cytoplasm to the zygote, had no influence on phenotypes of the progeny. The leaf colour is dependent on the chloroplasts. Since, the chloroplasts of maternal ooplasm are the major contributers of all the future chloroplasts therefore, the colour of progeny plants appear accordingly.

However, similarly to animal mtDNA, the inheritance of chloroplast DNA has also been demonstrated to show variation from maternal inheritance.

Maternal Inheritance

Maternal inheritance is a kind of inheritance which does not follow Mendelian pattern of inheritance. Earlier the heredity pattern of mitochondria and chloroplasts were termed maternal inheritance, but now they are more appropriately called **organelle heredity**.

Many diseases in humans related to mitochondria demonstrates maternal inheritance.

1. **Myplonic Epilepsy and Ragged Red Fibre disease** (MERRF) In this, only the offsprings of affected mothers inherit the disease, while offsprings of affected father are normal. Affected individuals show epileptic seizures, dementia and deafness.
2. **Leber's Hereditary Optic Neuropathy** (LHON) This disorder is characterized by sudden bilateral blindness. Four mutations have been identified which affect the mitochondrial gene disrupting normal oxidative phosphorylation. This mutation is transmitted maternally to all offsprings.
3. **Kearns-Sayre Syndrome** (KSS) Affected individuals lose their vision, experience hearing loss and heart malfuctions occur. Mutations have been identified within mtDNA. It is also maternally inherited.

In maize, wheat, sugar-beet onion and in some other crop plants, fertility is controlled at least partially, by cytoplasmic factors. In other plants, however, male sterility is controlled entirely by nuclear genes. **Rhoades** had observed that male sterility in maize is inherited from generation after generation through the egg cytoplasm. This is also an example of maternal inheritance.

A related concept to maternal inheritance is the **maternal effect**. Maternal effect or maternal influence refers to determination of some traits in progeny according to its maternal genotype rather than its own. This effect is the result of the translation of the existing *m*RNAs or transcription and translation of the genetic information of female gamete present in the egg cytoplasm. This phenomenon contrasts the biparental inheritance.

An excellent example of maternal effect is the shell coiling in the snail *Limnaea peregra*. These snails are hermaphrodites and can undergo either cross-fertilization or self-fertilization. Some strains of this species are left-handed or sinistrally coiled shell (dd), while others have right-handed or dextrally coiled shell (DD or Dd). Maternal parents that are DD or Dd produce only dextrally coiled snails while maternal parents that are dd produce only sinistrally coiled snails.

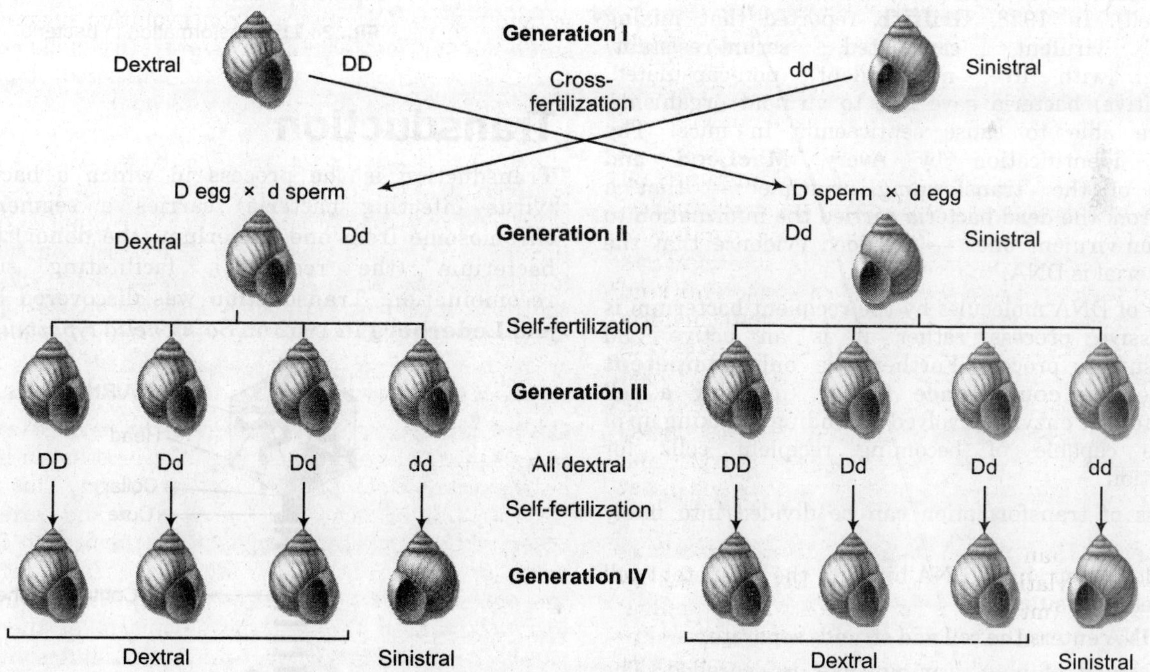

Fig. 24.10 Maternal effect on the shell coiling in *Limnaea peregra*

Microbial Genetics

The genetic material in bacteria is stored in two structures:

(i) A single main chromosome, carrying a few thousand genes.

(ii) Episomes and plasmids in which 2-3 to several hundred genes may reside.

The bacterial chromosome exists as highly condensed negatively supercoiled conformation *in vivo*. The nuclear regions of bacteria are called **nucleoids** as they are not enclosed in any nuclear membrane, as in eukaryotes.

There are three kinds of processes that mediate transfer of genetic material from one bacterium to another, making possible the recombination of genetic material. These three processes are:

1. Transformation
2. Transduction
3. Conjugation.

Of these three processes, the first two don't require cell-to-cell contact, while conjugation requires cell-to-cell contact.

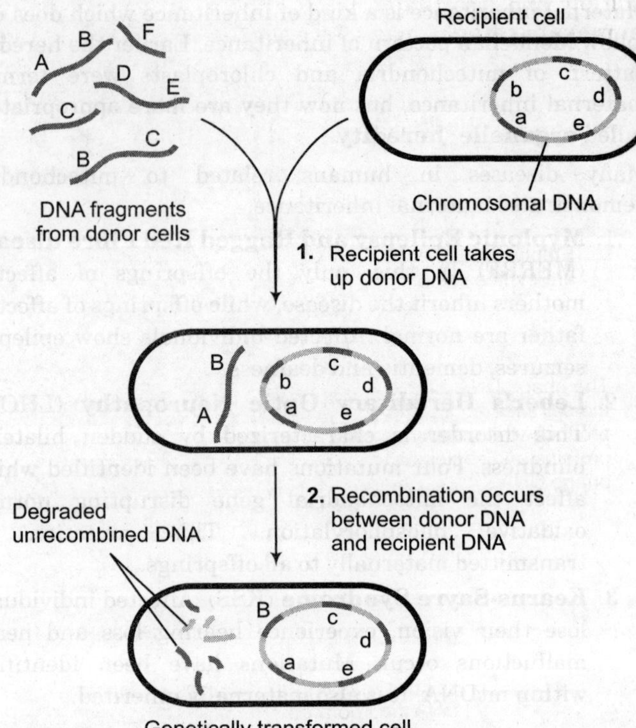

Fig. 24.11 Transformation in bacteria

Transformation

Transformation is the process of uptake of naked DNA from one bacterium (the donor cell) to another bacterium (the recipient cell). In 1928, **Griffith** reported that mixing heat-killed, virulent (capsulated, serum-resistant) pneumococci with live, non-virulent (non-capsulated, serum-sensitive) bacteria gave rise to virulent organisms, which were able to cause septicaemia in mice. The subsequent identification by Avery, **MacLeod** and **McCarthy** of the 'transforming principle' — that a substance from the dead bacteria carried the information to the live, non-virulent ones — provided evidence that the genetic material is DNA.

The uptake of DNA molecules by the recipient bacterium is not a passive process rather it is an active and energy-consuming process. Furthermore, only **competent** cells posssessing **competence factor** (probably a cell surface protein or enzyme involved in binding or taking up of DNA), are capable of becoming recipient cells for transformation.

The process of transformation can be divided into many stages:

(i) The double stranded DNA binds to the competent cell at a receptor site.

(ii) The DNA enters the cell and strands separate.

(iii) One strand of transforming DNA is degraded. The other strand pairs homologously with the host chromosome.

(iv) The transforming DNA is integrated, forming a heteroduplex.

(v) Following one round of cell division, a transformed (containing transforming DNA) and a non-transformed cell (similar to the initial recipient cell) are produced.

Transduction

Transduction is the process in which a bacteriophage (virus infecting bacteria) carries a segment of the chromosome from one bacterium (the donor) to another bacterium (the recipient), facilitating sub-sequent recombination. Transduction was discovered by **Zinder** and **Lederberg** in 1952 on *Salmonella typhimurium*.

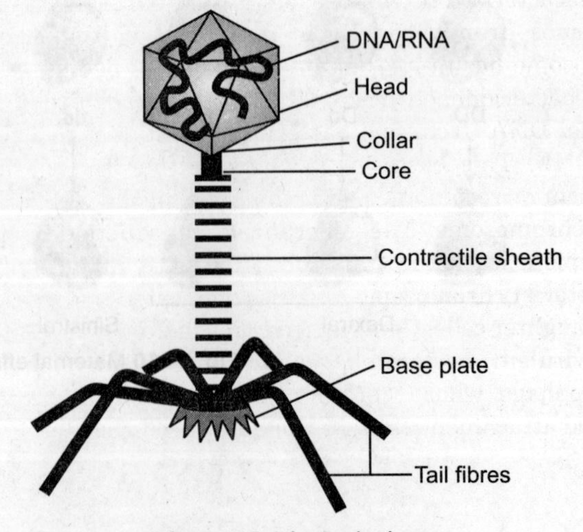

Fig. 24.12 A bacteriophage

Bacteriophages are of two types based on their interaction with the bacterial cell: **(i)** the **virulent phages** which always multiply and lyse the host cell after infection and **(ii)** the **temperate phages** may take either of two paths viz. **Lytic cycle**, during which they lyse the host cell like virulent phages or **lysogenic cycle**, during which their chromosome are integrated into the chromosomes of the host and replicate like any other segment of the host chromosomes.

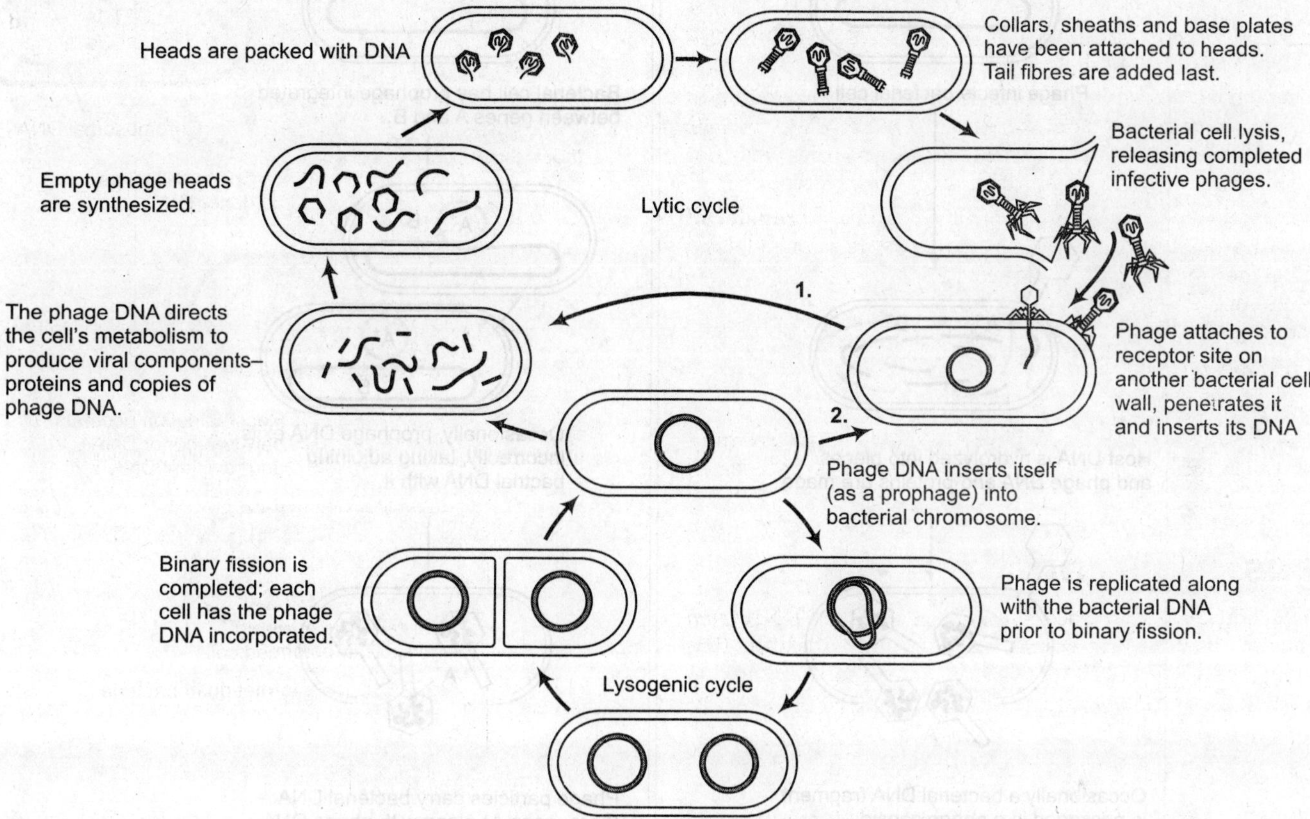

Fig. 24.13 Transduction showing both lytic and lysogenic cycles

There are two kinds of transduction:

Generalized Transduction

It is characterized by the random nature of DNA fragments and genes tranduced. Each fragment of the bacterial chromosome has finite, but small, chance of being packaged in the bacteriophage head. When this happens they inject bacterial DNA from one bacterium to another and not the viral DNA. This bacterial DNA can either remain in the cytoplasm or recombines with the homologous region of the host's chromosome. The generalized transduction is said to be complete when the transduced DNA get integrated with the bacterial chromosome and also replicated and passed on to all daughter cells. Generalized transduction is mediated by some virulent bacteriophages and by certain temperate bacteriophage whose chromosomes are not integrated at specified attachment sites on the host chromsome.

Specialized Transduction

Specialized transduction involves the transduction of both bacterial and viral DNA. It is mediated by temperate bacteriophages whose chromosomes are able to integrate at one or a few specified attachment sites on the host chromosome. They, once inside the host cell, are capable of both autonomous as well as integrated replications. As such they are the examples of **episomes,** *e.g.,* phage lambda genome. In its integrated state, the phage chromosome is called a **prophage** and the bacterium harbouring the prophage is called lysogenic bacterium.

Specialized transduction differs from generalized transduction, in the fact that here only certain genes are recombined. This is because of phage DNA always integrate into the region of bacterial chromosome between particular genes at a site called attachment site (*att*). When the phage DNA is detaching from host chromosome it sometimes carries with it genes too, but only those in between the *att* site and not others.

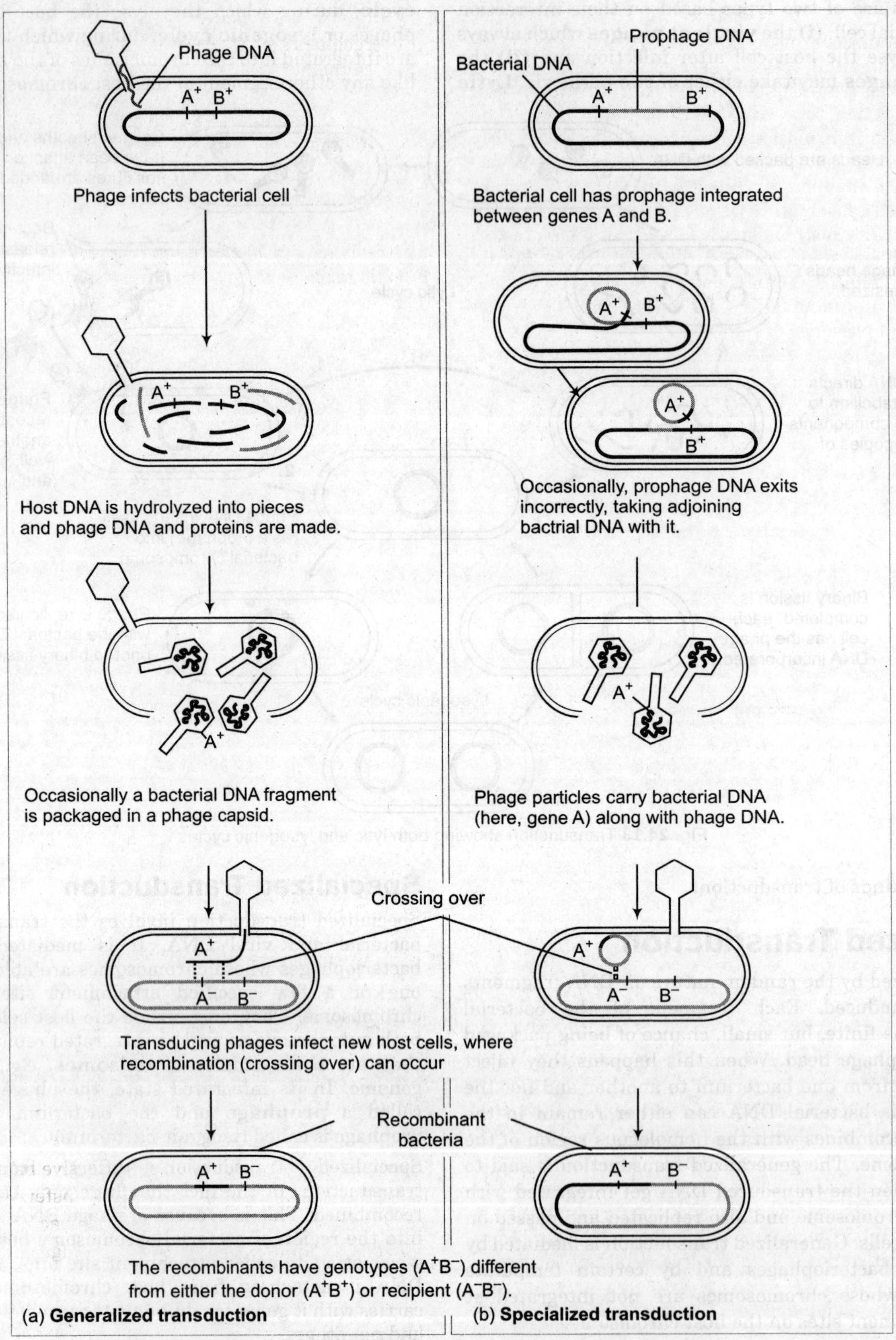

Phage DNA

A^+ B^+

Phage infects bacterial cell

A^+ B^+

Host DNA is hydrolyzed into pieces and phage DNA and proteins are made.

A^+

Occasionally a bacterial DNA fragment is packaged in a phage capsid.

A^+

A^- B^-

Transducing phages infect new host cells, where recombination (crossing over) can occur

A^+ B^-

The recombinants have genotypes (A^+B^-) different from either the donor (A^+B^+) or recipient (A^-B^-).

(a) **Generalized transduction**

Bacterial DNA

Prophage DNA

A^+ B^+

Bacterial cell has prophage integrated between genes A and B.

A^+ B^+

A^+

B^+

Occasionally, prophage DNA exits incorrectly, taking adjoining bactrial DNA with it.

A^+

Phage particles carry bacterial DNA (here, gene A) along with phage DNA.

Crossing over

A^+

A^- B^-

Recombinant bacteria

A^+ B^-

(b) **Specialized transduction**

Fig. 24.14 Figure showing generalized and specialized transduction

Conjugation

Conjugation was discovered by **Lederberg** and **Tatum** in 1946. During conjugation, cell-to-cell contact is necessary and DNA is transferred from the donor cell to the recipient cell through a conjugation tube that forms between them. The transfer of genetic information in conjugation is a one-way transfer. The donor cells have a capability to synthesize specialized surface appendages called **F pili,** the synthesis of which is controlled by a small circular molecule of DNA called an **F factor** (fertility factor). The F factor can exists in two forms, either independent of host chromosome or in the integrated state. The F factor belong to a class of genetic elements called **episomes**. There are three kinds of strains in *E. coli* based on presence of F factor:

(i) **F^- strains** which do not contain the F factor and cannot transfer DNA by conjugation. They are, however, recipients of DNA transferred from F^+ or Hfr cells by conjugation.

(ii) **F^+ cells** which contain the F factor in the cytoplasm and can therefore, transfer F in a highly efficient manner to F^- cells during conjugation.

(iii) **Hfr** (High frequency recombination) cells have F integrated into the bacterial chromosome, not in the cytoplasm.

The transfer of F factor from from an F^+ or Hfr cells to and F^- cells takes place in 90-100 minutes.

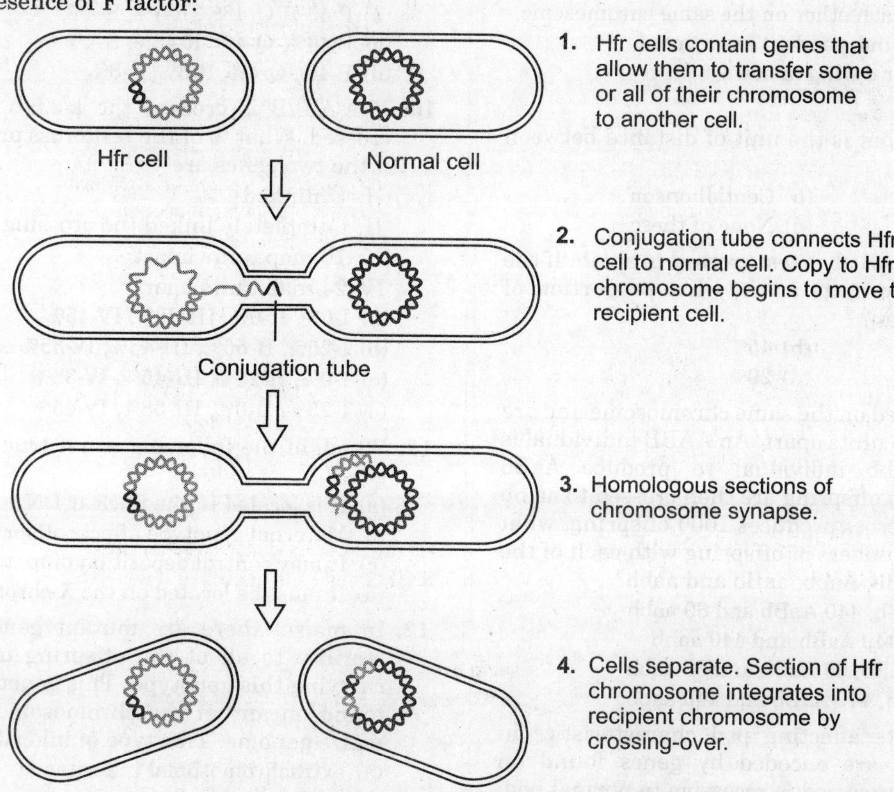

Fig. 24.15 Bacterial conjugation and recombination

Sex-duction

The integration of F factor into the chromosome in **Hfr strains** is not stable and the they are known to revert back to free state. While doing so, the F factor sometimes carry fragments of chromosomal genes alongwith it. Such an F factor that incorporates some chromosomal genes is called **F′** (F prime) **factor**. When such an F′ cell mates with F-recipient cell, it not only transfers the F factor but also the host genes that it carried with it. This process of transfer of chromosomal genes along with F factor is known as **sex-duction** or **F-duction**.

Since, F′ factors do not require packaging in a phage head as required in specialized transduction, the size of the segment of the bacterial chromosome carried by F′ is not restricted. The size of F′ factors range from carrying a single bacterial marker to those carrying up to half of the chromosomes.

Significance Among the Gram negative bacteria this is the major way that bacterial genes are transferred. Transfer can occur between different species of bacteria. Transfer of multiple antibiotic resistance by conjugation has become a major problem in the treatment of certain bacterial diseases. Since, the recipient cell becomes a donor after transfer of a plasmid, an antibiotic resistance gene carried on a plasmid can quickly convert a sensitive population of cells to a resistant one.

Exercise

1. Why didn't Mendel find linkage?
   (a) Some genes were linked, but they were too close together to cross over
   (b) All seven genes were on separate chromosomes
   (c) Mendel did detect linkage. He discovered this genetic phenomenon
   (d) Some genes were linked, but they were too far apart for crossing over to be distinguished from independent assortment, or linked genes were never tested for at the same time in the same cross
2. Linked genes
   (a) are located near each other on the same chromosome
   (b) violate the law of independent assortment
   (c) segregate together during meiosis
   (d) All of the above
3. In a genetic map, what is the unit of distance between two genes?
   (a) CentiMendel (b) CentiJhonson
   (c) CentiMorgans (d) None of these
4. A plant of genotype AB/ab is test crossed to ab/ab. If the two loci are 10 map units apart, what proportion of progeny will be AB/ab?
   (a) 5% (b) 45%
   (c) 10% (d) 20%
5. Two genes are located on the same chromosome and are known to be 12 map units apart. An AABB individual is crossed to an aabb individual to produce AaBb offspring. The AaBb offspring are then crossed to aa bb individuals. If this cross produces 1000 offspring, what are the predicted numbers of offspring with each of the four genotypes: AaBb, Aabb, aaBb and aabb?
   (a) 60 Aabb, 440 aaBb, 440 AaBb and 60 aabb
   (b) 0 Aabb, 0 aaBb, 440 AaBb and 440 aabb
   (c) 440 Aabb, 440 aaBb, 60 AaBb and 60 aabb
   (d) 60 Aabb, 60 aaBb, 440 AaBb and 440 aabb
6. Two different traits affecting pod characteristics in garden pea plants are encoded by genes found on chromosome 5. Narrow pod is recessive to normal pod; yellow pod is recessive to green pod. A true-breeding plant with narrow, green pods was crossed to a true-breeding plant with normal, yellow pods. The F_1 offspring were then test crossed to plats with narrow, yellow pods. The following results were obtained 144 narrow green pods, 150 normal yellow pods, 11 narrow yellow pods, 9 normal green pods. How far apart are these two genes?
   (a) 1 mu (b) 12 mu
   (c) 6.4 mu (d) 32.4 mu
7. A plant of genotype AaBb is test crossed to aabb. If the two loci are 10 map units apart what proportion of progeny will be AB/ab?
   (a) 50% (b) 45%
   (c) 10% (d) 5%
8. The cross between E/E.F/F and e/e.f/f is made, and the F_1 is then back crossed to the recessive parent. The progeny genotypes are inferred from the phenotypes. The progeny genotypes, written as the gametic contributions of the heterozygous parent, are in the following proportions, E.F =2/6, E.f = 1/6, e.F = 1/6, e.f = 2/6; determine the distance between e and f
   (a) 33.3% (b) 45%
   (c) 66.6% (d) 5%
9. In a haploid organism, the C and D loci are 8 map units apart. From a cross Cd x cD give the proportion of each of the following progeny classes P. CD, Q. cd, R. Cd, S. all recombinant.
   (a) P-4%, Q-4%, R-46%, S-8%
   (b) P-46%, Q-46%, R-4%, S-4%
   (c) P-46%, Q-4%, R-46%, S-4%
   (d) P-4%, Q-4%, R-8%, S-8%
10. If A/A.B/B is crossed the a/a.b/b, and the F_1 is test crossed. What % of the test cross progeny will be a/a.b/b if the two genes are
    I. Unlinked
    II. Completely linked (no crossing over at all)
    III. 10 map units apart
    IV. 24 map units apart
    (a) I-0%, II-0%, III-38%, IV-45%
    (b) I-25%, II-50%, III-45%, IV-38%
    (c) I-0%, II-25%, III-45%, IV-38%
    (d) I-25%, II-0%, III-38%, IV-45%
11. Which of the following is not true of a maternal effect gene?
    (a) It is located in the nuclear DNA
    (b) Maternal genotype affects offspring phenotype
    (c) It may control deposition of material into oocytes
    (d) It must be located on the X-chromosome
12. In maize, there are mutant genes that confer male sterility to all of the offspring of the female parent carrying this genotype. This genetic information is not found on any of the chromosomes that make up the maize genome. This type of inheritance is called
    (a) extrachromosomal inheritance
    (b) transgenic inheritance
    (c) pseudoinheritance
    (d) biparental inheritance
13. Both chloroplasts and mitochondria
    (a) are found within the nucleus
    (b) have linear DNA
    (c) carry extranuclear genes
    (d) display a Mendelian pattern of inheritance
14. Extrachromosomal inheritance is the characteristics of
    (a) virus (b) archaebacteria
    (c) prokaryotes (d) eukaryotes
15. Which of the following is not a type of extranuclear inheritance?
    (a) Sexual segregation
    (b) Vegetative segregation
    (c) Uniparental inheritance
    (d) Biparental inheritance

16. Which of the following statements is incorrect regarding mitochondrial DNA?
(a) It is double-stranded
(b) It mutates 10 times more frequently than nuclear DNA
(c) Each mitochondrion contains about 100 DNA molecules
(d) It has no introns

17. Which of the following are not true about nuclear DNAs?
(a) About 50% of the nuclear DNA codes for proteins
(b) They are tightly wrapped around histones to form nucleoprotein complex
(c) Introns interrupt the coding sequence
(d) The base pairings are bound together by hydrogen bonds

18. Which of the following statements is correct?
(a) Conjugation involves direct transfer of genetic material from one bacterium to another
(b) Gene transfer by conjugation converts a strain that cannot act as a donor to a strain that can initiate conjugation
(c) Hfr strains of bacteria contain F factors that include some genes from the bacterial chromosome
(d) Virulent phages generally follow the lysogenic cycle when infecting bacteria

19. Which of the following statements is correct?
(a) Bacteria chromosome has many origin of replication
(b) Bacterial chromosome is present mostly in positively supercoiled structure
(c) Bacterial chromosome is a circular *ss*DNA
(d) Bacterial chromosome has no centromere and telomere

20. A plasmid is
(a) a fragment of a chromosome that is transferred during bacterial conjugation
(b) a piece of DNA carrying a multiple cloning site
(c) a circular *ds*DNA which can replicate independently
(d) a piece of DNA carrying gene essential for bacteria

21. Which of the following statements regarding plasmid is incorrect?
(a) Mostly circular *ds*DNA, with multiple copies of pseudogenes
(b) A bacterial cell can harbor more than one type of plasmids
(c) Replication of plasmid may be unidirectional or bidirectional
(d) θ-replication in plasmid is more common form of replication then rolling circle replication

22. Which of the following statements is incorrect?
(a) Plasmid is present in all bacteria
(b) F factor is an example of conjugative plasmid
(c) Plasmids are also present in some eukaryotic organisms
(d) Plasmid of unknown function is known as cryptic plasmid

23. The copy number of a plasmid is the
(a) number of copies per cell immediately after cell division
(b) number of plasmids that take part in conjugation
(c) number of plasmids containing *Ori*V
(d) number of identical genes on plasmid

24. 'F' plasmids
(a) are responsible for high frequency recombination
(b) carry some chromosomal genes
(c) are those plasmids that have never been incorporated into a bacterial chromosome
(d) None of the above

25. Plasmids do which of the following?
(a) Direct synthesis of conjugation pilli
(b) Provide resistance to certain antibiotics
(c) Induce the formation of tumours in plants
(d) All of the above

26. A bacterial cell that is mostly haploid but is diploid for some regions of the genome is called
(a) heterodiploid (b) pseudodiploid
(c) half diploid (d) merodiploid

27. Which of the following processes would not contribute to genetic variation within bacterial populations?
(a) Transduction (b) Transformation
(c) Mutation (d) Meiosis

28. During conjugation
(a) cell to cell contact is required
(b) naked DNA is transferred
(c) bacteriophage mediates DNA transfer
(d) only plasmid is transferred from donor to recipient

29. *E. coli* cells containing F plasmid are capable of carrying out the following important process
(a) transduction process for transferring genes
(b) induce mutations in the chromosome
(c) conjugation, promoting horizontal gene transfer
(d) promote increased replication and cell division

30. If two populations of bacteria cultured in a U-shaped tube are separated by a membrane filter (which does not allow phage particles to pass), but recombination takes place anyway, the mechanism of genetic exchange is
(a) specialized transduction
(b) site-specific recombination
(c) conjugation
(d) transformation

31. In an $F^+ \times F^-$ cross the
(a) F^+ cell becomes an Hfr cell
(b) F^- cell becomes an Hfr cell
(c) F^+ cell becomes and F^- cell
(d) F^- cell becomes an F^+ cell

32. When cell conjugates for longer periods of time, which of the following will occur?
(a) Fewer genes will be transferred
(b) More genes will be transferred
(c) The same number of genes will be transferred
(d) It is impossible to tell because conjugation time and number of genes transferred are not related

33. High frequency recombination cells arise when
(a) they have multiple F plasmids
(b) F plasmid has been incorporated into the bacterial chromosome
(c) conjugation and transformation happen at the same time
(d) bacterial chromosomes do not break during conjugation

34. Which of the following statements is incorrect?
(a) During conjugation of an F^+ and F^- *E. coli,* a copy of the F factor is almost transferred to the recipient
(b) Conjugation between Hfr strain and F^- strain leaves the recipient strain F^-
(c) Conjugation between Hfr strain and F^- strains results in high frequency of recombination and therefore, the recipient become Hfr or F^+
(d) Conjugation between F^+ and F^- strains results in the recipient becoming F^+

35. Bacterial conjugation can be used to map genes on bacterial chromosomes. Which of the following would be the best donor strain to use if we wish to map the bio gene?
(a) Hfr: strS, bio^-, ade^-, pro^-
(b) Hfr: strS, bio^+, ade^+, pro^+
(c) Hfr: strR, bio^-, ade^-, pro^-
(d) Hfr: strR, bio^+, ade^+, pro^+

36. Generalized transduction
(a) is carried out by temperate phage only
(b) is an example of vertical gene transfer
(c) results in formation of merozygote
(d) transfers specific gene(s) from on bacteria to another

37. Gal^- mutants pof *E. coli* cannot use galactose as a carbon source. When these mutants are infected with phage λ that has been grown on wild-type *E. coli,* however, the progeny bacteria can use galactose. This genome alteration is an example of bacterial
(a) transformation (b) transduction
(c) conjugation (d) transposition

38. Presence of maltose in the medium increases transduction frequency by λ phage because maltose
(a) provides the λ phage with energy required for transduction
(b) induces the maltose receptor
(c) binds to the lambda phage surface protein, making it competent to infect
(d) keeps the bacterial cells dividing, which is required for infection by lambda phage

39. Four Hfr strains of *E. coli* were generated from the same F^+ strain. The Hfr strains donated markers in the following order
Strain 1 DQWMT
Strain 2 AXPTM
Strain 3 BNCAX
Strain 4 BDQWM
The order of the markers in the original F^+ strain is
(a) DQWMTPXACNB (b) AXPTMDQWBNC
(c) BNCAXPTMDQW (d) BDQWMNCAXPT

40. Which of the following statement is incorrect?
(a) In generalized transduction, random bits of the bacterial chromosome are packaged in a phage head
(b) Homologous recombination is a mechanism used by bacteria to incorporate new DNA into their chromosome, if it is similar to an existing sequence
(c) Horizontal gene transfer may be mediated *via* conjugation but not transduction or transformation
(d) Bacteriophage may be able to infect some strains of bacteria but not others

41. The primary difference between bacterial sex and sexual reproduction in plants and animals is that
(a) bacterial sex involves more than two individuals
(b) bacterial sex does not involve genetic recombination
(c) bacterial sex does not produce offspring
(d) eggs and sperm are different, but bacterial gametes are all alike

42. Sometimes a bacteriophages transfer a gene from one bacterium to another. This process is called
(a) transduction (b) conjugation
(c) cloning (d) DNA splicing

43. A microbiologist analyzed the DNA of *E. coli* before and after conjugation. She found that
(a) both cells lost some genes and gained others
(b) both cells gained genes but lost none of their original genes
(c) one cell most genes and the other gained genes
(d) one cell gained genes and the genes of the other were unchanged

44. Scientists wished to create an organism capable of breaking down several kinds of toxic wastes, so they combined the genes of several bacteria to create a single 'super-bacterium'. They probably did not need to use which of the following in creating the super-bacterium?
(a) nucleic-acid probes (b) F factors
(c) plasmids (d) restriction enzymes

45. A colourblind female who is a carrier for haemophilic marries a normal male. The frequency of incidence of each character among the male and female children will be such that

	Male	**Female**
(a)	50% colourblind; 50% haemophilic	50% colourblind 50% normal
(b)	50% normal; 50% colourblind and haemophilic	100% normal
(c)	100% colourblind	50% normal 50% colourblind
(d)	50% colourblind 50% colourblind and haemophilic	100% normal

46. The ability of a male *E. coli* to carry out conjugation is usually due to piece of DNA called
(a) a probe (b) an R plasmid
(c) recombinant DNA (d) an F factor

47. A genetic marker is
(a) a place where a restriction enzyme cuts DNA
(b) a chart that traces the family history of a genetic trait
(c) a nucleotide sequence near a particular gene
(d) a radioactive probe used to find a gene

48. Duchenne muscular dystrophy is caused by a sex-linked recessive allele. Its victims are almost invariably boys, who usually die before the age of 20. Why is this disorder almost never seen in girls?
(a) Sex linked traits are never seen in girls
(b) The allele is carried on the Y-chromosome
(c) Non-disjunction occurs in males but not in females
(d) Males carrying the allele don't live long enough to be fathers

49. Red-green colour blindness is a human recessive sex-linked trait. A man and a woman with normal vision have a colourblind son. What is the probability that their next child will also be a colourblind son?
(a) 0 (b)
(c) (d)

50. Most sex-linked traits in humans are carried on the .... chromosome, and the recessive phenotypes are seen most often in ....
(a) X; women (b) X; men
(c) Y; women (d) Y; men

51. Albinism and phenylketonuria are disorders due to
(a) autosomal recessive genes
(b) autosomal dominant genes
(c) recessive sex genes
(d) dominant sex genes

52. A woman carrier for haemophilia (Hh) marries a normal man (HO). Daughters of such a lady would be
(a) 75% carrier (Hh) and 25% haemophilic (hh)
(b) 50% normal (HH) and 50% carrier (Hh)
(c) 50% normal (HH) and 50% haemophilic (hh)
(d) 25% carrier (Hh) and 75% haemophilic (Hh)

53. Sex-linked traits
(a) are carried on an autosome but expressed only in males
(b) are coded for by genes located on a sex chromosome
(c) are found in only one or the other sex, depending on the sex-determination system of the species
(d) are always inherited from the mother in mammals and fruit flies

54. Linkage and cytological maps for the same chromosome
(a) are both based on mutant phenotypes and recombination data
(b) may have different sequences of genes
(c) have both the same sequence of genes and intergenic distances
(d) have the same sequence of genes but different intergenic distances

55. Which of the following is not true of linked genes?
(a) They tend to be inherited together
(b) They violate Mendel's principle of independent assortment
(c) They can form new combinations *via* crossing over
(d) They are relatively rare; most genes are unlinked

56. Morgan and his students were able to map the relative positions of genes on fruit-fly chromosomes by
(a) colouring chromosomes with dyes and observing them under a microscope
(b) scrambling the chromosomes and observing how the flies changed
(c) crossing various flies and looking at the proportions of offspring
(d) transplanting chromosomes from one fly to another

57. A cross of a wild-type red-eyed female *Drosophila* with a violet-eyed male produces all red-eyed offspring. If the gene is sex-linked, what should the reciprocal cross (violet-eyed female × red-eyed male) produce? (Assume that the red allele is dominant to the violet allele).
(a) All violet-eyed flies
(b) 3 red-eyed flies to 1 violet-eyed
(c) a 1 : 1 ratio of red and violet eyes in both males and females
(d) Red-eyed females and violet-eyed males

58. RFLP (Restriction Fragment Length Polymorphism) study is a technique for
(a) transferring genes from unrelated species
(b) isolating single genes
(c) isolating single gene products
(d) identifying genetic (DNA) homologies

59. Which of the following would never be an episome?
(a) an F plasmid (b) a prophage
(c) a provirus (d) a virulent phage

60. In his pioneering 1913 studies in *Drosophila* that resulted in the first genetic linkage map, AH Sturtevant included three genetic markers now known to cover almost the entirely of the euchromatin of the X-chromosome. The marker *w* (white eyes) is near the tip, *m* (miniature body) near the middle, and *r* (rudimentary wings) near the centromere. In two-point crosses, Sturtevant obtained recombination frequencies of 0.32 for the interval *w-m* 0.25 for the interal *m-r*, and 0.45 for the interval *w-r*. He noted that 0.45 is smaller than the sum of 0.32 + 0.25 = 0.57, which is the value expected if the frequencies of recombination over such large distances were additive. He commented that the discrepancy 'is probably due to the occurrence of two beaks in the same chromosome, on double crossing-over.' From Sturtevant's data, calculate the coincidence and the interference across the region
(a) 0.75, 0.25 (b) 0.50, 0.50
(c) 0.25, 0.75 (d) 0, 1.00

61. Genes A and B are linked 12 map units apart. A heterozygous individual, whose parents were AAbb and aaBB, would be expected to produce gametes in the following frequencies
(a) 44% AB 6% Ab 6% aB 44% ab
(b) 6% AB 44% Ab 44% aB 6% ab
(c) 12% AB 38% Ab 38% aB 12% ab
(d) 6% AB 6% Ab 44% aB 44% ab

62. Consider the following statements regarding linkage of genes.
I. Two genes are said to be linked when they independently assort
II. The strength of the linkage is determined by the distance between the two genes in question
III. The strength of the linkage is directly proportional to the distance between the two genes

Which of the above statements are correct
(a) I, II and III are correct (b) I and II are correct
(c) II and III are correct (d) I and III are correct

63. A son inherits colour blindness from his
(a) mother
(b) father
(c) mother only if she is colourblind
(d) father only if he is colourblind

64. Consider the following features.

I. Population consists of interbreeding groups of individuals.

II. Population does not form the basis unit of study in population genetics.

III. Gene frequency is the important single index characterizing the population.

Which of these are characteristic of Mendelian population?

(a) I and II (b) I and III
(c) II and III (d) I, II and III

65. Match list I with list II and select the correct answer using the codes given below the lists.

List I	List II
A. Conjugation	1. Replication
B. Nucleic acid production	2. Mutation
C. Transduction	3. Uptake of soluble DNA
D. Transformation	4. Bacteriophage transfer
	5. Cell fusion

Codes

	A	B	C	D
(a)	1	2	3	4
(b)	5	1	4	3
(c)	5	1	3	4
(d)	1	4	3	2

66. In a particular plant, genes for tall (T) plant and red (R) flowers are dominant over dwarf (*t*) plant and white (*r*) flowers. When a dihybrid of F_1 was test crossed, it produced following progenies:

Tall and Red-44
Tall and White-5
Dwarf and Red-7
Dwarf and White-44

What would be the distance between genes *t* and *r* on the basis of the data given above?

(a) 44 map units (b) 5 map units
(c) 7 map units (d) 12 map units

67. Shown below is the autoradiogram of an electrophoresis gel obtained during the sequencing a single stranded DNA by Sanger's method. The base sequence of the DNA is

A C G T

(a) 3′-AGTCGAGCT-5′ (b) 5′-TCAGCTCGA-3′
(c) 3′-TCAGCTCGA-5′ (d) 5′-AGTCGAGCT-3′

Answers

1. (d)	2. (d)	3. (c)	4. (b)	5. (d)	6. (c)	7. (b)	8. (a)	9. (a)	10. (b)
11. (d)	12. (a)	13. (c)	14. (d)	15. (a)	16. (c)	17. (a)	18. (a)	19. (d)	20. (c)
21. (a)	22. (a)	23. (a)	24. (b)	25. (d)	26. (d)	27. (d)	28. (a)	29. (c)	30. (d)
31. (d)	32. (b)	33. (b)	34. (c)	35. (b)	36. (c)	37. (b)	38. (b)	39. (a)	40. (c)
41. (c)	42. (a)	43. (d)	44. (b)	45. (d)	46. (d)	47. (c)	48. (d)	49. (c)	50. (b)
51. (a)	52. (b)	53. (b)	54. (d)	55. (d)	56. (c)	57. (d)	58. (d)	59. (d)	60. (a)
61. (b)	62. (b)	63. (a)	64. (b)	65. (b)	66. (d)	67. (c)			

25 Human and Quantitative Genetics

Syllabus

- Human Genetics: Pedigree Analysis, Lod Score for Linkage Testing, Karyotypes, Genetic Disorders.
- Quantitative Genetics: Polygenic Inheritance, Heritability and its Measurements, QTL Mapping.

Human Genetics

Pedigree Analysis

A pedigree is a family tree or chart made of symbols and lines that represent a patient's genetic family history. The pedigree is a visual tool for documenting biological relationships in families and the presence of disease. The study of inheritance pattern of a certain disease through the use of pedigree is called pedigree analysis. It is usually done by a geneticist or a genetic counsellor.

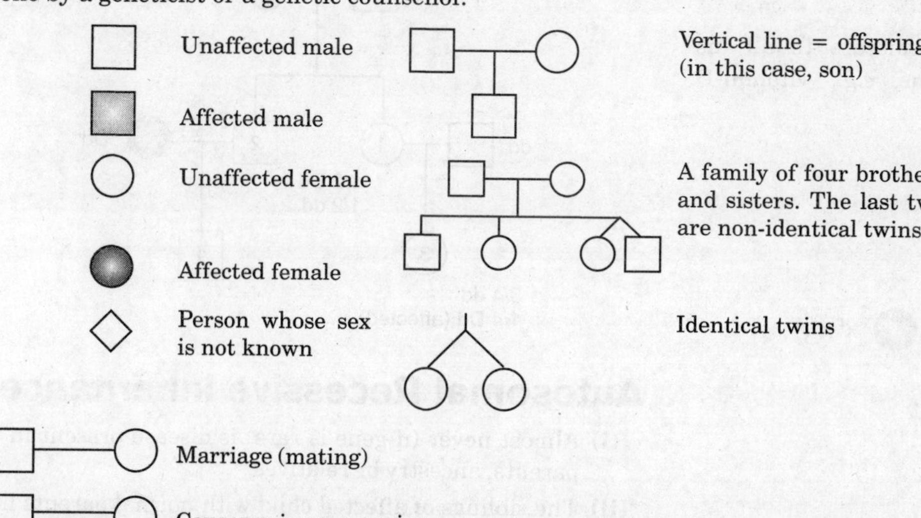

Fig. 25.1 Some basic symbols used in pedigree formation

The drawing up of a pedigree begins with the affected person first found to have the faulty trait and through whom the family came to the attention of the investigation. This person is referred as **proband.** In pedigree charts proband is indicated by an arrow below.

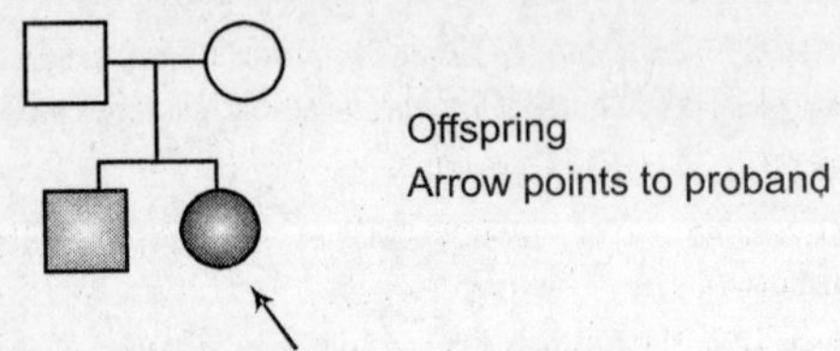

Various patterns of inheritance of a disease:

Y-Linked (Holandric) Inheritance

(i) Only males are affected.

(ii) The trait is transmitted only to sons from their fathers, *e.g.,* hairy ears, webbed toes.

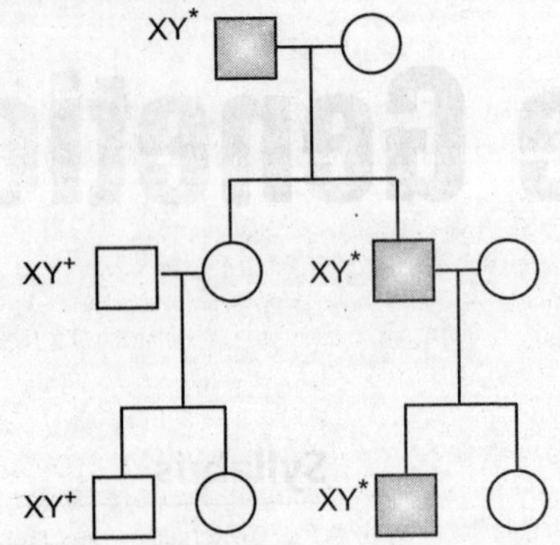

X-Linked Dominant Inheritance

(i) It manifests in heterozygote males as well as females.

(ii) An affected female transmits the disease to half her sons and half her daughters.

(iii) An affected male transmits the disease to all his daughters and none to his sons, *e.g.,* vitamin-D resistant rickets, Xg blood group.

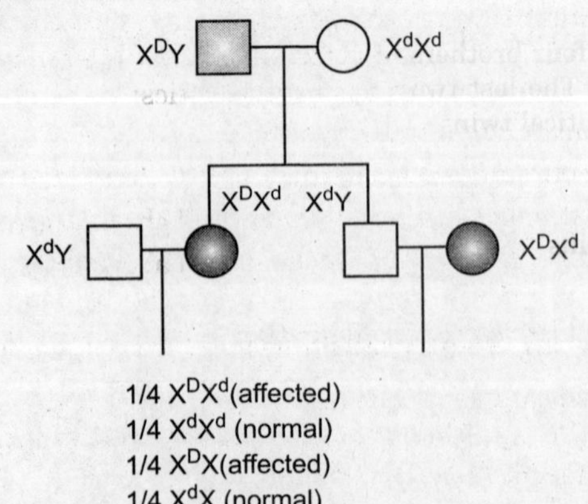

X-Linked Recessive Inheritance

(i) The disease appear almost always in males whose mothers are unaffected heterozygotes (carriers).

(ii) Each son and daughter of a carrier mother has 1:1 chance of being affected and of being a carrier respectively.

(iii) An affected male will transmit the disease to all his daughters who will become carriers. He will never transmit the disease to his sons, *e.g.,* haemophilia, duchenne muscular dystrophy, colour blindness, etc.

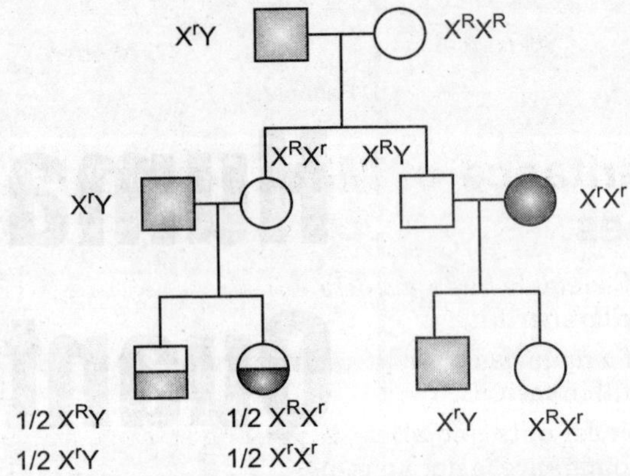

Autosomal Dominant Inheritance

(i) Each affected individual has an affected parent.

(ii) Each offspring of an affected person (with one affected and one unaffected parents) and a normal mate will have 1:1 chance of being affected.

(iii) Unaffected relatives of person will never have affected offspring, *e.g.,* cold urticaria (skin blotches, chills and weakness due to cold), polydactyly.

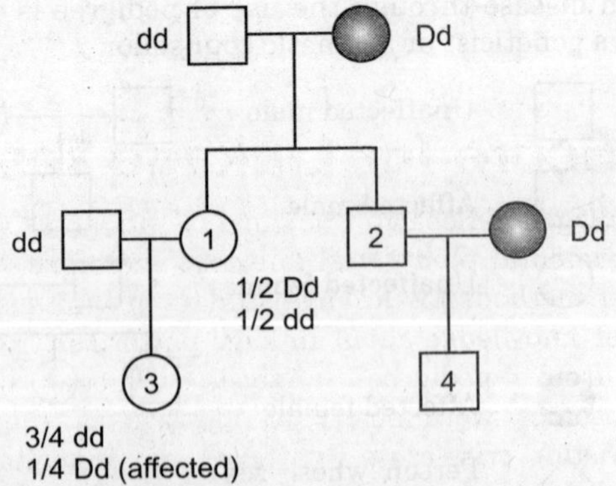

Autosomal Recessive Inheritance

(i) Almost never (if gene is rare) is disease present in the parents, ancestry or relatives.

(ii) The siblings of affected child with normal parents have a chance of 1 in 4 of being affected irrespective of sex.

(iii) The parents of an affected child are more likely to be related to each other (consanguineous), *e.g.*, cystic fibrosis, deaf-mutism, hereditary blindness.

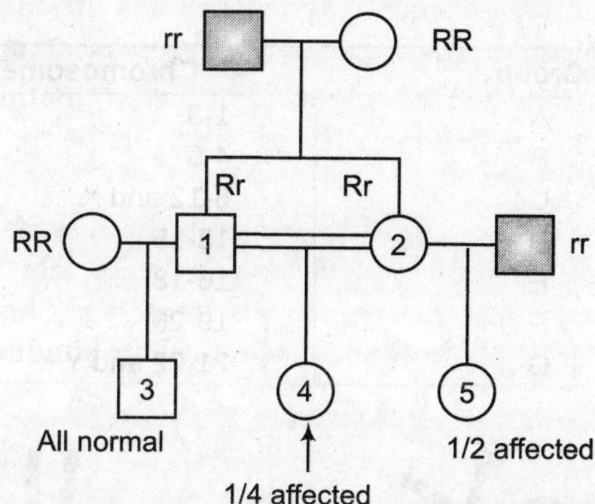

Inheritance of Mitochondrial Genes

(i) If a female has a mitochondrial trait all of her offspring will inherit it.

(ii) If a male has a mitochondrial trait none of his offspring will inherit it.

(iii) Since, only one allele is present in each individual so dominance is not an issue.

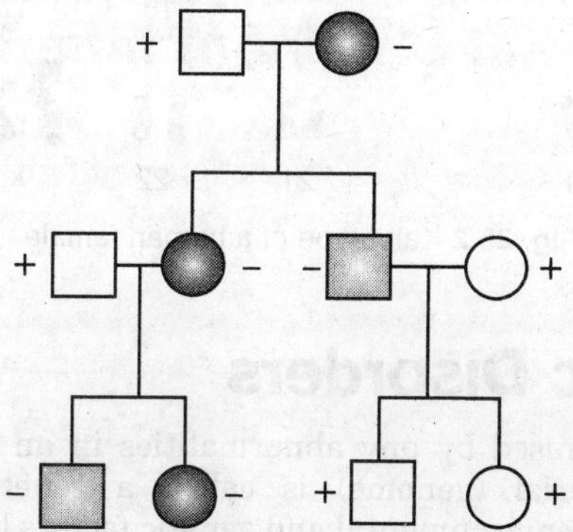

Lod Score for Linkage Testing

Since, linkage studies can't be done in human as we do with the experimental plants and animals, therefore we have to find other methods for linkage studies in humans. Much of the earlier knowledge about linkage pattern in human were gained from pedigree analysis. Those linked to X-chromosomes were easier to identify as they show a characteristic criss-cross pattern of inheritance. For autosomal traits, geneticists tried to distinguish clearly whether pairs of traits demonstrated linkage or independent assortment. Extensive data related to pedigrees were used to see if any two traits are segregating together or not. For example, through this approach it was found that the genes coding for Rh antigen and the gene responsible for elliptocytosis (oval erythrocytes) are closely linked (chromosome 1).

But this method fails, when two genes of interest are located far apart so that recombinant gametes can also form, thus linkage data are liable to be misunderstood. For this problem **Newton Morton** developed a method in 1955 called **lod score method** to assess the probability that the available data regarding linkage is truly reflective of linkage between any two genes of interest.

The word 'lod' stands for Logarithm of the odds favouring linkage. The steps followed in lod score method are:

1. A pedigree is established.
2. Recombinant frequency (θ) is calculated for various estimates.
3. Lod score is calculated for each estimate.

The formula for lod score calculation is:

$$LOD = Z = \log_{10} \frac{\text{probability of birth sequence with a given linkage value}}{\text{probability of birth sequence with no linkage}}$$

$$= \log_{10} \frac{(1-\theta)^{NR} \times \theta^{R}}{0.5^{(NR+R)}}$$

where, NR = Number of non-recombinant offsprings

R = Number of recombinant offsprings

$$\theta = \frac{R}{(R+NR)}$$

A lod score of +3 indicates the evidence for linkage between the genes in question and the being observed did not occur by chance. On the other hand, a lod score less than –2.0 is considered an evidence to exclude linkage. The lod score method represented an important advance in assigning human genes to specific chromosomes and in constructing preliminary human chromosome maps. However, with the advent of somatic-cell hybridization in 1960s and various chromosome banding techniques later, the use of lod score method for human chromosome mapping is less favoured.

Karyotypes

The word 'karyotype' means a characterization of the cell nucleus. A karyotype is the number and appearance of chromosomes in the nucleus of a eukaryotic cell. The term is also used for the complete set of chromosomes in a species or an individual organism. Karyotype analysis is a techniques where chromosomes are visualized under a microscope with emphasis on the following characteristics:

1. Number of chromosomes.
2. Sex-chromosome content.
3. Presence or absence of individual chromosome.
4. Nature or extent of chromosomal aberrations.

Steps in Karyotypes

(i) Blood sample is collected.

(ii) It is treated with phytohaemagllutin (PHA) so that WBCs got separated from RBCs.

(iii) WBCs are allowed to divide and increase their numbers in a culture medium.

(iv) After about three days, colchicine is added in the culture which prevent formation of spindle fibres.

(v) Thus we get leucocytes arrested at the metaphase stage of mitosis.

(vi) It is treated with hypotonic solution of either KCl or NaCl. The cells bursts due to osmotic swelling and metaphase chromosomes dispersed out.

(vii) Ethanol and glacial acetic acid is added in 3:1 ratio. The chromosomes got fixed.

(viii) The chromosomes are analyzed under the microscope directly or photographs are taken for later analysis.

Various banding techniques are used for better visualization of chromosomes thus obtained. The chromosomes are stained with certain dyes that show a pattern of light and dark bands (called the banding pattern). These bands reflect regional differences in the amounts of A and T versus G and C. The banding pattern for each chromosome is specific and consistent allowing identification of each of the 24 chromosomes. Some of the most used banding techniques are:

Q-banding

(a) Quinacrine mustand, a fluorescent alkylating agent used which binds to the guanine residues of DNA.

(b) With this technique polymorphic regions are distinguished such as distal long-arm of Y-chromosome, short-arm and satellites of chromosome 13-15 and 21-22.

(c) However, it is not a permanent stain and it needs a fluorescent microscope.

G-banding

(a) In this banding, the chromosome preparation is treated with trypsin (protease) and then stained with Giemsa stain.

(b) It enhances the secondary constriction regions of chromosomes 1, 9 and 16.

(c) It is a permanent stain.

R-banding

(a) Here, R stands for reverse.

(b) When heat is applied to the G-banding preparation, the staining pattern got reversed, that is, the dark bands formed in G-banding turned into lighter ones.

(c) Due to this telomere regions are better visualized.

C-banding

(a) Here, C stands for constitutive heterochromatin staining.

(b) The chromosome preparation is treated with alkali solution and then warm saline and finally stained with Giemsa stain.

(c) In this banding alongwith secondary constriction regions of chromosomes 1, 9 and 16, distal long-arm of Y-chromosome, short-arm and satellites of 13-15 and 21-22 and centromeric areas are stained.

When the chromosomes of a nucleus are depicted in a standard organized format as per their size then it is called a **karyogram** or **idiogram.** There are seven groups in humans:

Group	Chromosomes
A	1-3
B	4-5
C	6-12 and X
D	13-15
E	16-18
F	19-20
G	21-22 and Y

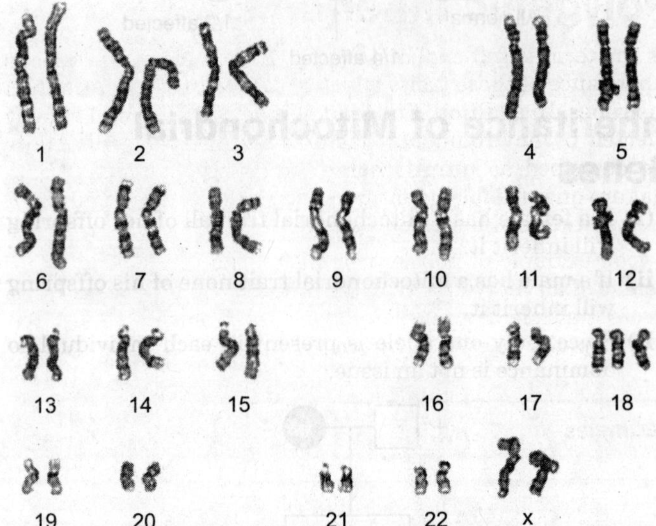

Fig. 25.2 Karyotype of a human female

Genetic Disorders

A disorder caused by any abnormalities in an individual's genetic material (genome) is called a genetic disorder. Though both environmental and genetic factors have roles in the development of any disease but when we use the term genetic disorder we mean that at least some variations in the DNA of the affected individual which either afflict or predispose that individual for developing a particular disease.

Four divisions are generally made for different types of genetic disorders:

1. **Single-gene** (also called Mendelian or monogenic) disorders: This type of inheritance is caused by changes or mutations that occur in the DNA sequence of a single gene. Some examples are cystic fibrosis, sickle cell anaemia, Marfan syndrome, Huntington's disease and hereditary haemochromatosis.
2. **Multifactorial** (also called complex or polygenic) **disorders** This type is caused by a combination of environmental factors and mutations in multiple genes. For example, different genes that influence breast cancer susceptibility have been found on chromosomes 6, 11, 13, 14, 15, 17 and 22. Its more complicated nature makes it much more difficult to analyze than

single-gene or chromosomal disorders. Some of the most common chronic disorders are multifactorial. Examples include heart disease, high blood pressure, Alzheimer's disease, arthritis, diabetes, cancer, and obesity.

3. **Chromosomal disorders** This type of genetic disorder is characterized by either abnormalities in chromosome structure or missing or extra chromosomal complement in an individual. Examples are Down's syndrome, Patau's syndrome, Edward syndrome, Turner's syndrome, Klinefelter's syndrome and cri-du-chat, etc.

4. **Mitochondrial disorders** These diseases are relatively rare. They are caused by mutations in the non-chromosomal DNA of mitochondria (mtDNA). They are always maternally inherited. The mitochondrial diseases are mentioned in the topic **inheritance of mitochondrial genes.**

Quantitative Genetics

Polygenic Inheritance

As the term is self-explanatory, polygenic inheritance means inheritance of those traits which is determined by more than one genes. In addition, this kind of inheritance is also heavily affected by environmental factors. Usually polygenic traits are described as **quantitative traits** which means traits that are quantifiable in nature and present as a continuum in a population and not as black and white categories.

A good example of polygenic trait is height in a population. Height of an individual is determined by many gene present across multiple chromosomes. And since, it can be measured and people of a population can be arranged in increasing or decreasing order this trait is quantitative trait. Other examples are skin colour in humans, yield of agricultural crops, etc.

Rh factor in humans is another polygenic trait. It needs some explanation. The Rh factor involves three different pairs of alleles located on three different loci on chromosome pair 1. The three pairs of Rh alleles (C and c, D and d, E and c) occur at three different loci on homologous chromosome pair 1. Possible genotypes will have one C or c, one D or d, and one E or e from each chromosome. For example; CDE/cde; CdE/cDe, cde/cde and CDe/CdE, etc. The different combinations that can be made are given in following chart.

Gametes→ ↓	**CDE**	**CDe**	**CdE**	**Cde**	**cDE**	**cDe**	**cdE**	**cde**
CDE	CDE/ CDE	CDE/ CDe	CDE/ CdE	CDE/ Cde	CDE/ cDE	CDE/ cDe	CDE/ cdE	CDE/ cde
CDe	CDe/ CDE	CDe/ CDe	CDe/ CdE	CDe/ Cde	CDe/ cDE	CDe/ cDe	CDe/ cdE	CDe/ cde
CdE	CdE/ CDE	CdE/ CDe	**CdE/ CdE**	**CdE/ Cde**	CdE/ cDE	CdE/ cDe	**CdE/ cdE**	**CdE/ cde**
Cde	Cde/ CDE	Cde/ CDe	**Cde/ CdE**	**Cde/ Cde**	Cde/ cDE	Cde/ cDe	**Cde/ cdE**	**Cde/ cde**
cDE	cDE/ CDE	cDE/ CDe	cDE/ CdE	cDE/ Cde	cDE/ cDE	cDE/ cDe	cDE/ cdE	cDE/ cde
cDe	cDe CDE	cDe CDe	cDe CdE	cDe Cde	cDe cDE	cDe cDe	cDe cdE	cDe cde
cdE	cdE/ CDE	cdE/ CDe	**cdE/ CdE**	**cdE/ Cde**	cdE/ cDE	cdE/ cDe	**cdE/ cdE**	**cdE/ cde**
cde	cde/ CDE	cde/ CDe	**cde/ CdE**	**cde/ Cde**	cde/ cDE	cde/ cDe	**cde/ cdE**	**cde/ cde**

Every genotypic combination with DD or Dd is classified as Rh^+. Every genotypic combination with dd is classified as Rh^-.

A related but distinct concept from polygenic inheritance is the **multifactorial inheritance.** It refers to the inheritance pattern that is affected by several factors not necessarily genetic (*i.e.*, environmental too) and may not show continuous variations as shown by other polygenic inheritance. A good example is coronary artery disease, which may be caused by a number of factors that increase the risk of disease onset. The factors include obesity, type II diabetes, high blood pressure, high levels of low-density lipoprotein cholesterol and even gum disease. Although coronary artery disease runs in families, it does not show Mendelian inheritance patterns and can occur in isolation.

Heritability and its Measurements

One important question in Biology is that whether observed variation in a particular trait is due to genetic or environmental factors, sometimes referred to as 'nature *vs* nurture' debate. Heritability is a concept that summarizes how much of the variation in a trait is due to variation in genetic factors.

The individuals of a population vary from each other because of both genes and environmental factors and also because of various interactions between genes and environmental factors. Heritability is formally defined as the proportion of phenotypic variation (V_P) that is due to variation in genetic values(V_G).

The effect of particular allele on a trait depends on the allele's frequency in the population and the effect of each genotype that includes the allele. This is sometimes termed the average effect of an allele.

There are two measures of heritability:

(i) **Broad-sense heritability** $H^2 = V_G / V_P$. This measure give the proportion of phenotypic variation due to genetic values that may include effects due to dominance and epistasis. Dominance and epistatic variation is not additive because in these cases some alleles or genes will suppress or interact with the effect of others. Broad heritability is much used when the focus is on psychological traits, as one is interested in what is the total genetic contribution to these traits. Personality traits, cognitive performance, alcoholism and mental disorders like schizoprenia are some traits that can be and have been studied using this measure of heritability.

(ii) **Narrow-sense heritability** $h^2 = V_A / V_P$. This measure give only the proportion of genetic variation due to additive genetic values (V_A). V_A can be defined as the sum of the average effects of all the alleles an individual carries. For traits other than psychological traits, mostly narrow-sense heritability is used such as in the breeding of domestic animals and plants because response to artificial selection depends on additive genetic variance.

A heritability measure close to 1.0 will mean that almost all variation in the population results from variation in genotypes and nearly nothing from environment. A heritability measure close to 0.0 for trait will mean that almost all variation is due to environmental variation.

Heritability can be estimated from simple designs such as the correlation of offspring and parental phenotypes and the difference in the correlation of monozygotic (MZ) and dizygotic (DZ) twin pairs.

In twin studies, identical (monozygotic) twins share (approximately) the same genotype while non-identical (dizygotic) twins do not. If monozygotic and dizygotic twins have equally similar environments, the differences in the correlations may be expected to be due to differences in genotype.

$$H^2 = V_G / V_P$$

or, $$H^2 = V_G / V_G + V_E$$

[as $V_P = V_G + V_E$ where, V_E is the variations due to environment]

The above equation is modified for twin studies as follows:

$$H^2 = V_{DZ} - V_{MZ} / (V_{DZ} - V_{MZ}) + V_{MZ}$$

or, $$H^2 = V_{DZ} - V_{MZ} / V_{DZ}$$

Monozygotic twins may be treated more similarly to each other than dizygotic twins. If this is the case, heritability can be overestimated (Griffiths *et.al.*, 1996, p. 833). Adoption studies may compensate for some of these difficulties, as twins that are reared apart, can be expected to live in equally similar (or different) environments. In this method those twin pairs are studied that were either reared together or reared apart. Here, the heritability equation becomes

$$H^2 = VT_{RA} - VT_{RT} / VT_{RA}$$

where, VT_{RT} = Variance in monozygotic twins reared together

VT_{RA} = Variance in monozygotic twins reared apart

One should note that heritability is not the proportion of a phenotype that is genetic rather the proportion of phenotypic variance that is due to genetic factors. Heritability is a population parameter and therefore, it depends on population specific factors such as allele frequencies, the effects of gene variations and variations due to environmental factors.

Heritability estimation is being used widely, from evolutionary biology to agriculture to human medicine. Many psychological characteristics also being investigated through heritability measurements.

QTL Mapping

Quantitative traits are those traits which are affected by multiple genes. These genes could be located on a single chromosome or at the multiple sites across many chromosomes. These genes were termed 'polygenes' by **Mather** (1949) and traits are called polygenic traits. One example is height in humans. These polygenes are now referred by a more catchy acronym 'QTL' (Quantitative Trait Loci), a term first coined by **Gelderman** (1975). A quantitative trait locus is defined as 'a region of the genome that is associated with an effect on a quantitative trait'.

QTLs identify a particular region of the genome containing a gene that is associated with the trait being studied. It make use of the molecular marker technology. In QTL mapping, it is first to find that whether there is a linkage between a molecular marker and the gene of interest or not. Where such linkage occurs, the marker locus and the QTL will co-segregate. Therefore, the basic principle of determining whether a QTL is linked to marker is to partition the mapping population into different genotypic classes based on genotypes at the marker locus, and apply correlative statistics to determine whether the individuals of one genotype differ significantly with the individuals of other genotype with respect to the trait being measured. Situations where genes fail to segregate independently are said to display 'linkage disequilibrium'. QTL mapping, thus, depends on linkage disequilibrium.

QTL mapping is the statistical study of the alleles that occur at a locus and the phenotypes that they produce. Statistical analysis is required to demonstrate that different genes interact with one another and to determine whether they produce a significant effect on the phenotype.

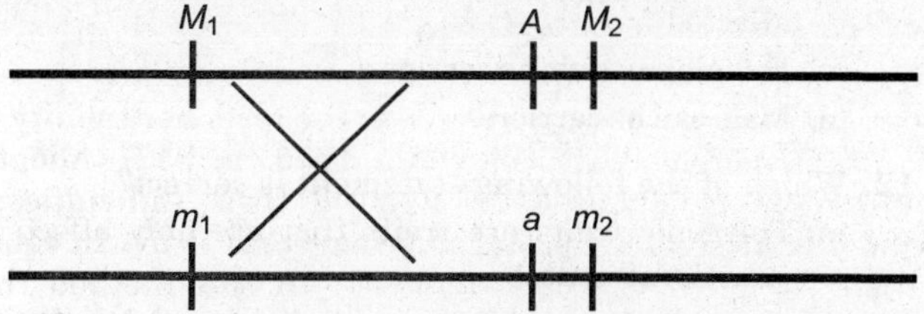

Fig. 25.3 Molecular markers used to map useful genes using recombination frequencies of linked genes

With natural populations, consistent association between QTL and marker genotype will not usually exist, except in a very rare situation, where the marker is completely linked to the QTL. Therefore, QTL mapping is usually undertaken in segregating mapping populations, such as F_2-derived populations, recombinant inbred lines (RILs), near-isogenic lines (NILs), doubled haploid lines (DHs) and backcross populations.

Objectives of QTL Mapping

(a) To identify the regions of the genome that affect the trait of interest.

(b) To analyze the effect of the QTL of the trait:

- How much of the variation for the trait is caused by a specific region?
- What is the gene action associated with the QTL (additive effect or dominant effect)?
- Which allele is associated with the favourable effect?

Salient Requirement for QTL Mapping

(a) A suitable mapping population generated from phenotypically contrasting parents.

(b) A saturated linkage map based on molecular markers.

(c) Reliable phenotypic screening of mapping population.

(d) Appropriate statistical packages to analyze the genotypic information in combination with phenotypic information for QTL detection.

Types and Size of Mapping Population

Random-mating populations are more difficult for QTL mapping, because linkage disequilibrium is a key to detecting QTLs with marker. It is essential to develop a suitable experimental mapping population using parental lines that are highly contrasting phenotypically for the target trait (for example, highly resistant and susceptible lines). Another requirement is that these parental lines should be genetically divergent. This is important to enhance the possibility of identifying a large set of polymorphic markers that are well-distributed across the genome.

Statistical Methods for QTL Mapping

(i) **Single-factor analysis of variance** (SF-ANOVA) It is extensively used, especially for isozymes. SF-ANOVA is done for each marker locus independent of information from other loci. F-tests provide evidence whether differences between marker locus genotype classes are significant or not. It is computationally simple, but suffers from major limitations:

(a) The likelihood of QTL detection significantly decreases as the distance between the marker and QTL increases.

(b) The method cannot determine whether the marker are associated with one or more QTLs.

(c) The effects of QTL are likely to be underestimated because they are confounded with recombination frequencies.

(ii) **Simple Interval Mapping** (SIM) SIM was first proposed by **Lander** and **Botstein** (1989) and it takes full advantage of a linkage map. The method evaluates the target association between the trait values and the genotype of a hypothetical QTL (target QTL) at multiple analysis points between pair of adjacent marker loci (the target interval). Presence of a putative QTL is estimated if the log of odds ratio (lod score) exceeds a critical threshold. Two more interval mapping were later developed: Composite Interval Mapping (CIM) and Multiple Interval Mapping (MIM). The interval approach is superior to the ANOVA approach in terms of both localization and estimation of the effects of QTL.

Besides the QTL mapping methods described above, several statistical packages for QTL analysis are available, some commonly used ones are Mapmaker/QTL, QTL Cartographer, QTL Mapper and Qgene.

While the methods for QTL analysis provide us with information about the putative locations and effects of QTLs influencing a quantitative trait, these do not tell us anything about molecular nature of the QTL. However, identification of putative QTL locations and DNA markers linked to QTLs have opened up opportunities for isolation and molecular characterization of QTLs *via* map based cloning.

Exercise

1. The genes in a population comprise its
   (a) gene allocation (b) gene flow
   (c) gene pool (d) genotype
2. DNA collected from a crime scene and from a suspect both have the following genotype A_1A_2 B_2B_2 C_1C_2. If the frequencies of the A_1, B_1 and C_1 alleles are 0.9, 0.99 and 0.8 respectively. Calculate the probability that another person in the suspect's group has the same pattern of these alleles.
   (a) 1.44×10^{-6} (b) 5.76×10^{-6}
   (c) 0.400 (d) 0.600
3. Who was the first person in the United States to be convicted of a crime on the basis of DNA evidence?
   (a) Nancy Hodge
   (b) Godfrey Hardy
   (c) Alec Jeffreys
   (d) Tommie Lee Andrews
4. The chromosomal theory of inheritance states that
   (a) chromosomes and their associated genes undergo segregation during meiosis
   (b) chromosomes and their associated genes undergo independent assortment in gamete formation
   (c) Mendel's law of inheritance relate to the behaviour of chromosomes in meiosis
   (d) All of the above
5. A wild type is
   (a) the phenotype found most commonly in nature
   (b) the dominant allele
   (c) designated by a small letter if it is recessive or a capital letter if it is dominant
   (d) your basic party animal
6. In a population that is in equilibrium, the proportion of individuals showing the dominant trait at a given locus having two alleles is 84%. The frequency of the recessive allele in the population is
   (a) 0.4 (b) 0.3
   (c) 0.2 (d) 0.16
7. How many A and a alleles are present in a sample of organisms consisting of 10AA, 15Aa and 4aa individuals? What are the allele frequencies in this sample?
   (a) A = 0.6; a= 0.40
   (b) A = 0.4; a = 0.60
   (c) A = 0.6; a = 0.6
   (d) A = 0.4; a = 0.4
8. In a diploid organism, what is the maximum number of alleles that can exist in a population for any given gene?
   (a) 1 (b) 2
   (c) 4 (d) Unlimited
9. Cystic fibrosis is an autosomal recessive inherited disease. Its frequency in newborns is 1 in 1700. One of the following indicated the frequency of the disease carriers
   (a) 0.024 (b) 0.047
   (c) 0.976 (d) 0.148
10. Which statement about allele frequencies is not true?
    (a) The sum of any set of allele frequency is always 1
    (b) If there are two alleles at a locus and we know the frequency of one of them, we can obtain the frequency of the other by subtraction
    (c) If an allele is missing from a population, its frequency is 0
    (d) If two populations have the same gene pool for a locus, they will have the same proportion of homozygotes at that locus
11. In human population which of statement is incorrect regarding haemophilia?
    (a) It is a sex linked recessive disease
    (b) In this disease, a single protein that is a part of the cascade of proteins involved in blood clotting is affected
    (c) Female can only be carrier
    (d) Male can be carrier
12. Which of the following statement is correct?
    (a) Polygenic traits are traits that are only affected by genetic influences
    (b) For quantitative traits, two individuals with the same genotype may have different phenotypes
    (c) Quantitative traits are probably controlled by single genes
    (d) Dominance can not be confused with overdominance if QTLs are involved
13. Which of these is an example of a quantitative trait?
    (a) A study compares rats with and without pigment in the irises of their eyes
    (b) Chinese strains of pigs have larger numbers of piglets per litter than American strains
    (c) Caterpillars exposed to juvenile hormone mimics are unable to metamorphose into adults
    (d) All of the above
14. Which of the following is/are not feature(s) of quantitative trait?
    I. Characters of degree
    II. Continuous variation
    III. Polygenic control
    IV. Discontinuous variation
    (a) I and IV (b) II and III
    (c) Only IV (d) III and IV
15. Which of the following are correct?
    I. Classical Mendelian traits are qualitative in nature.
    II. Qualitative traits show discontinuous variations.
    III. Qualitative traits are polygenic traits.
    IV. Qualitative traits are referred to as metric traits.
    (a) I and II (b) I and IV
    (c) II and III (d) III and IV

16. Wheat grain colour is controlled by four loci and following quantitative inheritance.

I. Calculate the number of different F_2 phenotypes in a certain stock of wheat.

II. Calculate the number of F_2 as extreme as one parent or the other.

(a) I-9, II-1/16 (b) I-16, II-1/256
(c) I-8, II-1/32 (d) I-9, II-1/256

17. Two pure lines of corn have mean cob lengths of 9 and 3 inches, respectively. The polygenes involved in this trait all exhibit additive gene action. Crossing these two lines is expected to produce a progeny with mean cob length (in inches) of

(a) 12.0 (b) 7.5
(c) 6.5 (d) 2.75

18. QTL analysis is used to

(a) identify RNA polymerase binding sites
(b) map genes in bacterial viruses
(c) determine which genes are expressed at a developmental stage
(d) identify chromosome regions associated with a complex trait in a genetic cross

19. There are various procedures that can be used to detect genetic disorders before birth. Among the tests discussed in this chapter, ... is the least invasive, while .... carries the highest risk.

(a) chorionic villus sampling; amniocentesis
(b) ultrasound imaging; fetoscopy
(c) fetoscopy; chorionic villus sampling
(d) fetoscopy; amniocentesis

20. The most common lethal genetic disease in the United States is

(a) sickle cell disease
(b) cystic fibrosis
(c) Huntington's disease
(d) haemophilia

21. Which of the following human genetic disorders is sex linked?

(a) Haemophilia (b) PKU
(c) Cystic fibrosis (d) Sickle cell disease

22. A multifactorial disease

(a) can usually be traced to consanguineous matings
(b) is caused by recessively inherited lethal genes
(c) has both genetic and environmental causes
(d) has a collection of symptoms traceable to an epistatic gene

23. Carriers of a genetic disorder

(a) are indicated by solid symbols on a family pedigree
(b) are involved in consanguineous matings
(c) will produce children with the disease
(d) are heterozygotes for the gene that can cause the disorder

24. If both parents are carriers of a lethal recessive gene, the probability that their child will inherit and express the disorder is

(a) 1/8 (b) 1/4
(c) 1/2 (d) 1/2 × 1/2 × 1/4 or 1/16

25. The given figure is a pedigree chart of human genetic disease. The situation responsible for the sudden reappearance of the genetic disease in generation IV is

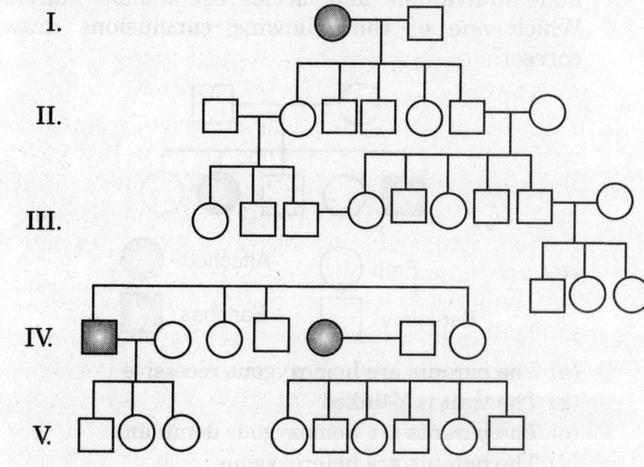

(a) congruency (b) consanguinity
(c) environmental effect (d) reverse mutation

26. Kernel colour in wheat is controlled by three genes each with two alleles and crossing extreme parents (red AA BB CC × white aa bb cc) will produce seven F_2 classes with 0.1, 2, 3, 4, 5 or 6 dominant alleles respectively in the ratio of

(a) 1 : 5 : 16 : 1 : 6 (b) 1 : 6 : 15 : 6 : 1
(c) 6 : 1 : 15 : 1 : 6 (d) 15 : 6 : 5 : 1 : 1

27. QTL stands for

(a) Quincuncial Tomography Ligation
(b) Quicker Transformation Linkage
(c) Quiescent Temperature Ligase
(d) Quantitative Trait Locus

28. Which of the following refers to inheritance of a phenotypic characteristic that is attributable to two or more genes and their interaction with the environment?

(a) Quantitative inheritance (b) Isogenic stock
(c) Heritability (d) Hybrid dysgenesis

29. Given below is a pedigree chart showing the inheritance of a certain sex-linked trait in humans. The trait traced in the above pedigree chart is

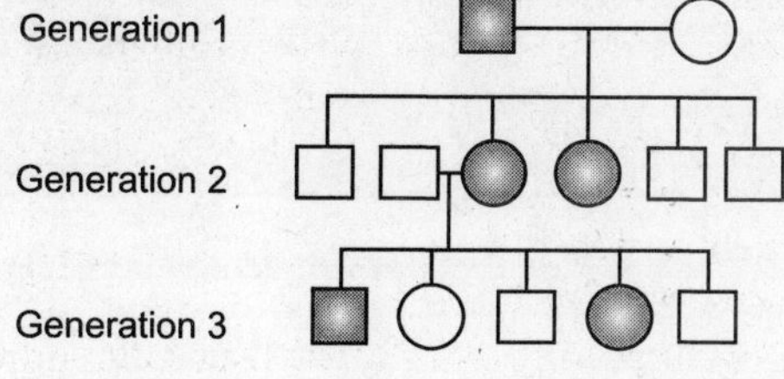

Key :
Unaffected male
Unaffected female
Affected male
Affected female

(a) dominant X-linked (b) recessive X-linked
(c) dominant Y-linked (d) recessive Y-linked

30. Given below is a pedigree chart of a family with five children. It shows the inheritance of attached earlobes as opposed to the free ones. The squares represents the male individuals and circles the female individuals. Which one of the following conclusions drawn is correct?

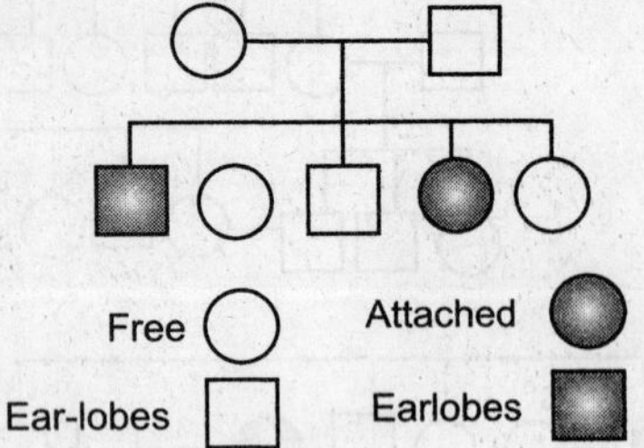

(a) The parents are homozygous recessive
(b) The trait is Y-linked
(c) The parents are homozygous dominant
(d) The parents are heterozygous

31. Consider the following diseases/syndromes
I. Huntington's chorea
II. Galactosemia
III. Duchenne muscular dystrophy
IV. Phenylketonuria

Those attribute to recessive mutations in human beings include.
(a) I, II and IV (b) II, III and IV
(c) II and IV (d) I and IV

32. Match list I (scientists) with list II (discoveries) and select the correct answer using the codes given below the lists.

List I	List II
A. Nilsson-Ehle and East H	1. DNA as transforming principle
B. Meselson M and Stahl F	2. Quantitative inheritance
C. Kornberg A	3. Semi-conservative replication of DNA
D. Avery DT MacLeod CM and McCarty M	4. Discovery of DNA polymerase enzyme

Codes

	A	B	C	D
(a)	2	3	4	1
(b)	1	3	4	2
(c)	2	4	3	1
(d)	1	4	3	2

Answers

1.	(c)	**2.**	(b)	**3.**	(d)	**4.**	(d)	**5.**	(a)	**6.**	(a)	**7.**	(a)	**8.**	(d)	**9.**	(b)	**10.**	(d)
11.	(d)	**12.**	(b)	**13.**	(b)	**14.**	(c)	**15.**	(a)	**16.**	(d)	**17.**	(c)	**18.**	(d)	**19.**	(b)	**20.**	(b)
21.	(a)	**22.**	(c)	**23.**	(d)	**24.**	(b)	**25.**	(b)	**26.**	(b)	**27.**	(d)	**28.**	(a)	**29.**	(a)	**30.**	(d)
31.	(b)	**32.**	(a)																

26 Genetic Variation

Mutation

Syllabus

- Mutation Causes of Mutant Types— Lethal, Conditional, Biochemical, Loss of Function, Gain of Function, Germinal *Verses* Somatic Mutants, Insertional Mutagenesis, Detection of Mutation.
- Structural and Numerical Alterations of Chromosomes: Deletion, Duplication, Inversion, Translocation, Ploidy and their Genetic Implications.
- Recombination

The term 'mutation' was first used by **Hugo de Vries** in 1901, for the variations he observed in the evening primrose, *Oenothera lamarckiana*. Mutation in its broad sense also include the chromosomal aberrations but in most of the modern literatures mutation refers to only **gene mutation**. Gene mutation can be defined as the change in the genetic material (generally DNA). Sometimes mutation involve change in single base-pairs, the substitution of one bp for another or the duplication or deletion of single base-pairs, such mutations are called **point mutation.**

Types of Mutation

There are various ways to classify mutations:

Spontaneous *vs* Induced Mutations

Mutations that happen naturally are called spontaneous, such as those occurring during enzymatic process of DNA replication. They are random in nature and produce genetic variations in a population, which provide the raw material for evolution. Induced mutations, on the other hand, are the result of the influence of any artificial factor like radioactive waves or UV rays of sunlight. The use of various techniques for producing mutations in experimental plants and animals by humans also fall in the category of induced mutations. **Muller** was the first to use X-rays to induce mutations in *Drosophila* in 1927.

Germinal *vs* Somatic Mutations

Mutation can occur in the DNA of either somatic cells or germinal cells (those producing gametes). Consequently, the end results are also different. Mutations arising in somatic cells are transmitted to the future generations. Only those cells will contain mutation which are derived for mutant somatic cell. If the mutation is recessive, it is of no consequence as it will not be expressed. It will have greater impact if they are dominant or if they are X-linked as they are most likely to express. But effect of such somatic mutations is generally get masked because of the presence of numerous other non-mutant cells functioning normally.

Mutations occurring either in germinal cells or gametes are of greater significance as they are transmitted to the future generations. Dominant autosomal mutations will be expressed phenotypically in the first generation. X-linked recessive mutation will be expressed only in males of the next generation and females will become carriers of the mutation. Furthermore, autosomal recessive mutation in the gametes of ether males or females may go undetected for many generations until the two copies of recessive mutations are brought together in homozygous condition.

Mutation Based on Base-pairs Alterations

Any phenotype of an organism is determined by protein which are produced by genes. The change in base sequence of gene altered the phenotype. The base sequence is changed by:

Base-substitution

This is the simplest type of gene-level mutation and involves swapping of one nucleotide for another during DNA replication. For example, in case of HbS haemoglobin type, there occur a single TA $\rightarrow$ AT base pair substitution that results into translation of valine at the 6th place of beta chain, instead of normal glutamic acid. This is the cause of sickle-cell anaemia. This type of base substitution which replaces the normal amino acid with another one in the final protein formed, is also called **mis-sense mutation**. Many base substitutions got unnoticed because the change in DNA sequence does not chance the amino acid in the final protein formed (because of the degeneracy of genetic code and wobble effect), these are called **silent mutations**. Still another kind of mutation arises when the base substitution results in the formation of termination codon that terminate the protein prematurely, thus producing faulty protein. This type of mutation is called **non-sense mutation**.

Base substitutions again can be divided into two sub-types transitions and transversions. A **transition** is the replacement of a base by the other base of the same chemical category (purine replaced by purine either A to G or G to A; pyrimidine replaced by pyrimidine either C to T or T to C).
A **transversion** is the opposite the replacement of a base of one chemical category by a base of the other (pyrimidine replaced by purine C to A, C to G, T to A, T to G; purine replaced by pyrimidine A to C, A to T, G to C, G to T).

Insertions and Deletions

An **insertion mutation** occurs when an extra nucleotide is added to the DNA strand during replication. This can happen when the replicating strand slips, or wrinkles, which allows the extra nucleotide to be incorporated. One form of beta-thalassemia is caused by insertion mutation. A **deletion mutation** occurs when a wrinkle forms on the DNA template strand and subsequently causes a nucleotide to be omitted from the replicated strand. Cystic fibrosis is an example of this form of mutation.

Frameshift Mutation

Insertion or deletion of one or more nucleotides during replication can also lead to another type of mutation known as a **frameshift mutation**. The outcome of a frameshift mutation is complete alteration of the amino acid sequence of a protein. This alteration occurs during translation because ribosomes read the *m*RNA strand in terms of codons, or groups of three nucleotides. These groups are called the **reading frame**. Thus, if the number of bases removed from or inserted into a segment of DNA is not a multiple of three, the reading frame transcribed to the *m*RNA will be completely changed. Consequently, once it encounters the mutation, the ribosome will read the *m*RNA sequence differently, which can result in the production of an entirely different sequence of amino acids in the growing polypeptide chain.

Other Categories of Mutations

There are other mutations which are not directly caused by base pair alteration. These include:

Mutations Affecting Morphological Traits

These mutations can be visualized phenotypically and important for experimental genetics. Examples include various mutant of *Drosophila*.

Mutations Exhibiting Nutritional or Biochemical Variations in Phenotype

Nutritional mutations have been studied in bacteria and fungi in which mutants fail to synthesize an amino acid or a vitamin. Biochemical mutations are those mutations which affect essential metabolic pathways resulting into disorders. Sickle-cell anaemia, haemophilia, Tay-Sachs disease, etc. are some of the biochemical disorders resulting from this type of mutation.

Behaviour Mutations

Some mutations affect the behavioural patterns of an organism, such as mating behaviour or *Circadian rhythms*. These are termed behaviour mutations. However, it is not easy to pin-point one mutation as a cause for certain behavioural pattern since multiple factors are involved in it.

Lethal Mutations

Mutations which interrupt the processes that are essential to the survival of the organism are called lethal mutations. Many biochemical disorders in humans are example of lethal mutations like **Tay-Sachs disease** and **Huntington's disease**. Lethal mutations can be further divided into recessive lethal and dominant lethal.

(a) **Recessive lethal** In case of, **Tay-Sachs disease**, the afflicted individual are homozygous recessive for the mutation. There is almost no activity of an enzyme Hexosaminidase a that is essential for lipid metabolism. The infants die during their first 3 years.

(b) **Dominant lethal** In case of **Huntington's disease** the individuals homozygous for HH die very early in life. The heterozygous Hh, display late onset about 40 years of age. The affected individuals undergo gradual nervous and motor degeneration and eventually succumb to the disease. Usually dominant lethal genes are not found in population as the individuals carrying them die before their reproduction age.

Conditional Lethal Mutations

When a mutation is lethal in one condition (restrictive conditions) and viable in another condition (permissive conditions) the mutation is called conditional mutation. There are three major classes of mutants with conditional lethal mutations are:

(a) **Auxotrophic mutants** These mutants are unable to synthesize an essential metabolite such as amino acid, vitamin, etc. that can be synthesized *de novo* by normal individuals. Such auxotrophic mutants will not be able to survive in restrictive conditions in which the particular metabolite is absent but will survive in permissive conditions in which that metabolite is supplied from outside.

(b) **Temperature-sensitive mutants** These mutants will grow at one temperature but not at another temperature. Mostly they are heat-sensitive but some cold-sensitive mutants are also available. This sensitivity is because of loss of optimal activity of some enzyme at too high or too low temperature.

(c) **Suppressor-sensitive mutants** These mutants are viable when a second genetic factor, a suppressor is present but are non-viable when the suppressor is absent. The suppressor either correct or compensate for the defect in the phenotype.

Mutation on the Basis of Function

Loss of Function

Wild type alleles typically encode a product necessary for a specific biological function. If a mutation occurs in that allele, the function for which it encodes is also lost. The general term for these mutations is loss-of-function mutations. The degree to which the function is lost can vary. If the function is entirely lost, the mutation is called a **null** or **amorphic mutation**. It is also possible that some function may remain, but not at the level of the wild type allele. These are called **leaky mutations**. Loss of function mutations are typically recessive. When a heterozygote consists of the wild-type allele and the loss-of-function allele, the level of expression of the wild type allele is often sufficient to produce the wild type phenotype. Genetically this would define the loss-of-function mutation as recessive. Alternatively, the wild type allele may not compensate for the loss-of-function allele. In those cases, the phenotype of the heterozygote will be equal to that of the loss-of-function mutant, and the mutant allele will act as a dominant.

Gain-of-function

Although it would be expected that most mutations would lead to a loss of function, it is possible that a new and important function could result from the mutation. In these cases, the mutation creates a new allele that is associated with a new function. Any heterozygote containing the new allele along with the original wild type allele will express the new allele. Genetically this will define the mutation as a dominant. This class of mutations are called **gain-of-function or neomorphic mutations**.

Causes of Mutation

Mutations occur at very low frequency in nature ranging between 10^{-7} to 10^{-4}.

There are two sources of mutations:

1. Spontaneous mutations.
2. Induced mutations through mutagens.

Spontaneous Mutations

Spontaneous mutations occur naturally without any apparent or known cause. The possible sources of spontaneous mutation are:

DNA Replication Errors and Polymerase Accuracy

Mispairing in the course of replication is a source of spontaneous base substitution. All of the bases in DNA can exist in one of several forms, called **tautomers,** which are isomers that differ in the positions of their atoms and in the bonds between the atoms. The forms are in equilibrium. The **keto** form of each base is normally found in DNA, whereas the **enol** forms of the bases are rare. The complementary base pairing of the enols is different from that of the keto forms. The figure below demonstrates the possible mispairs resulting from **tautomeric shifts.** Because of such mispairing, the enols are one source of rare spontaneous mutations.

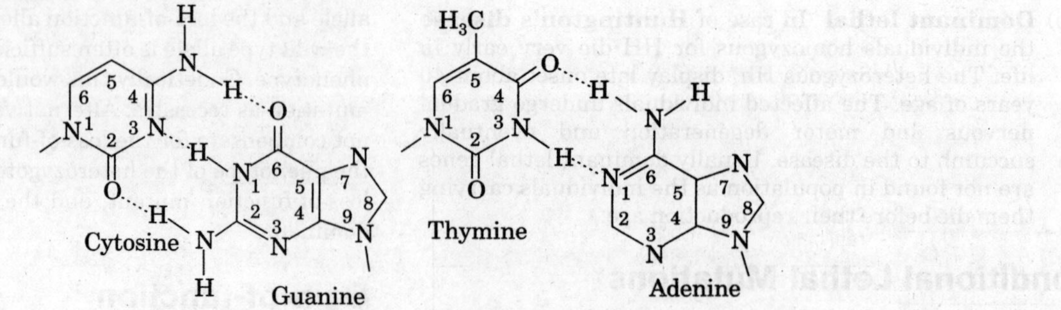

Fig. 26.1 Normal base-pairings between A-T and G-C

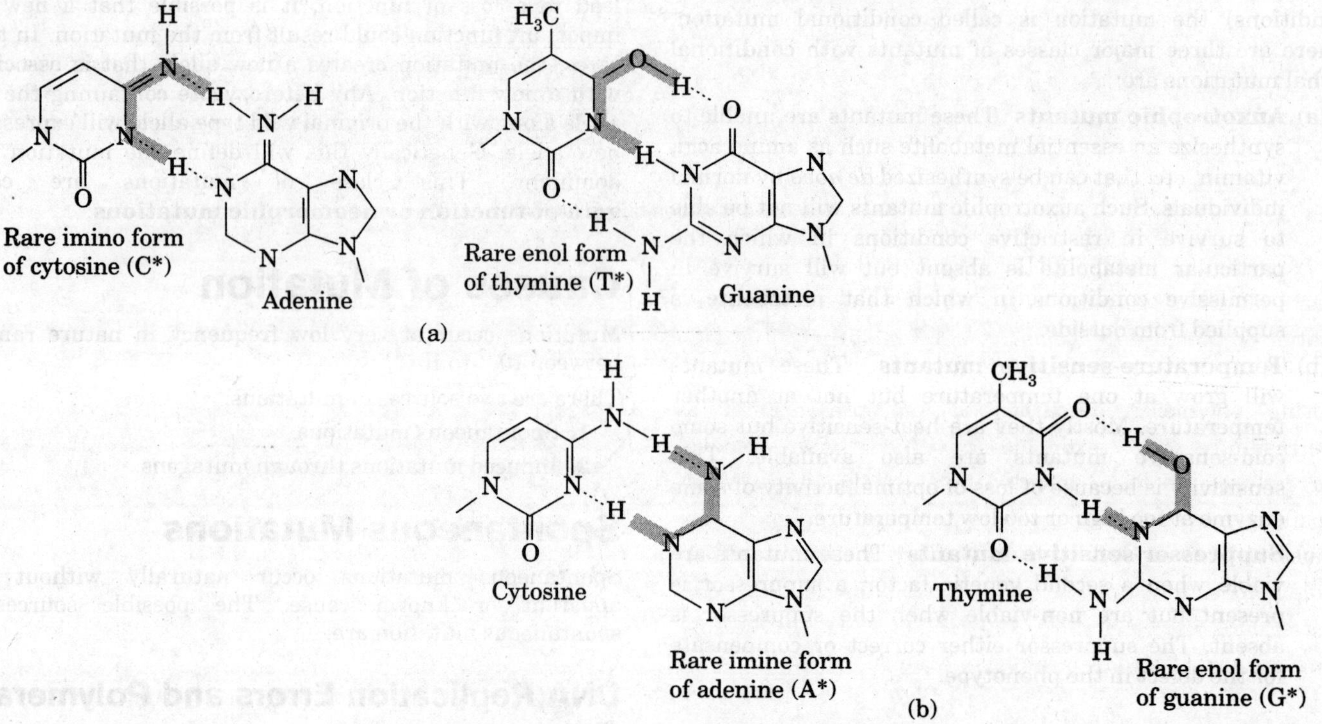

Fig. 26.2 Incorrect base-pairings because of tautomeric shifts

However, most DNA replication errors are caused by mispairings either between different but non-tautomeric chemical forms of bases (*e.g.,* bases with an extra proton, which can still bind but often with a mismatched nucleotide, such as an A with a G instead of a T), or between 'normal' bases that nonetheless bond inappropriately (*e.g.,* again, an A with a G instead of a T), because of a slight shift in position of the nucleotides in space. This type of mispairing is known as wobble. These errors in DNA replication, where an incorrect nucleotide is added will lead to a mutation in the next round of DNA replication of the strand with the incorrect nucleotide.

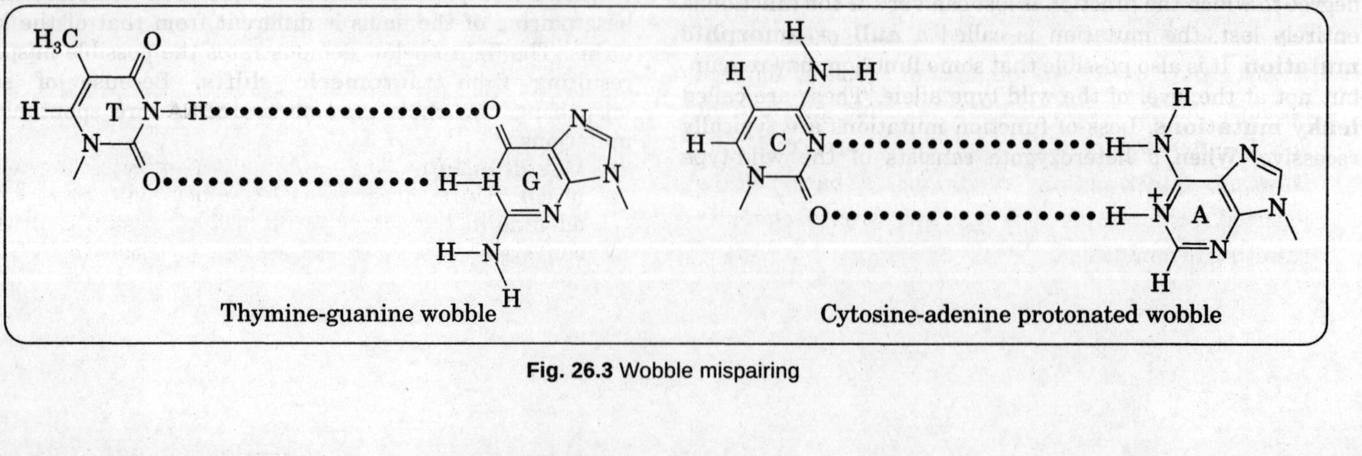

Fig. 26.3 Wobble mispairing

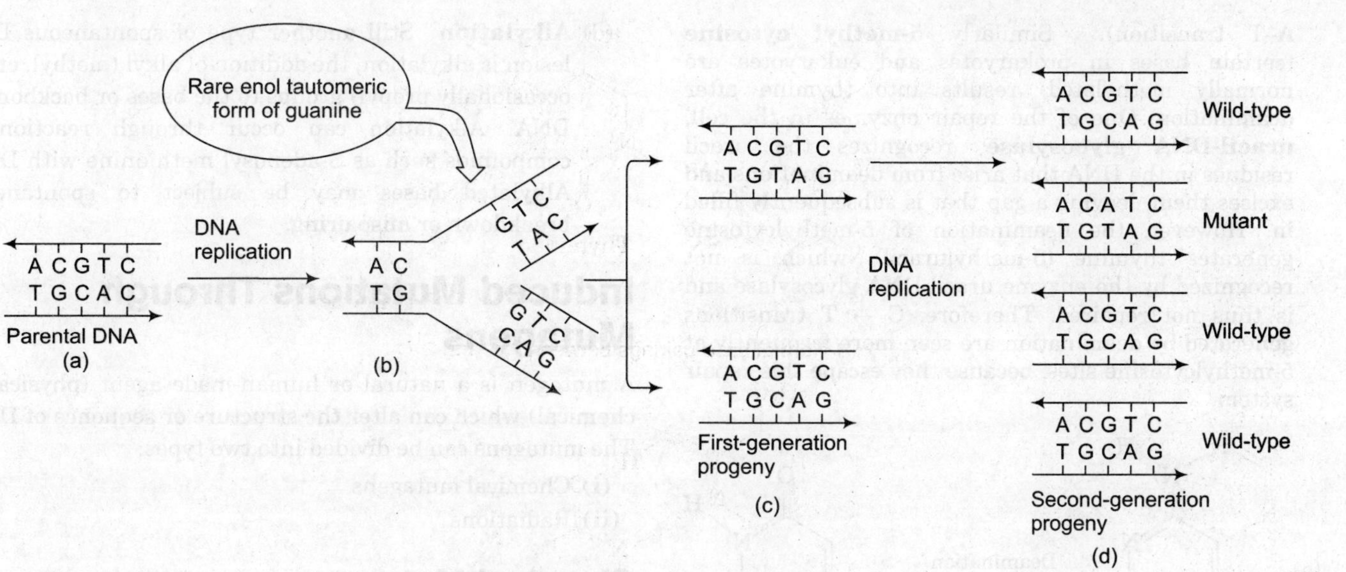

Fig. 26.4 Mutation due to tautomer

The frequency at which a DNA polymerase makes mistakes (inserts an incorrect base) will influence the spontaneous mutation frequency and it has been observed that different polymerases vary in their accuracy. One major factor affecting polymerase accuracy is the presence of a 'proofreading' 3′-5′ exonuclease which will remove incorrectly paired bases inserted by the polymerase. Most mispairing mutations are transitions. This is likely to be because an A-C or G-T mispair does not distort the DNA double helix as much as A-G or C-T base pairs do. However, transversions also can occur through mispairing. Replication errors can also lead to frameshift mutations.

Spontaneous Lesions

Naturally occurring damage to the DNA, called **spontaneous lesions,** also can generate mutations. Two of the most frequent spontaneous lesions are depurination and deamination, the former being more common.

(a) **Depurination** Depurination refers to removal of purine base from its position. The space formed after removal is called the apurinic (AP) site. If these lesions persist, they result in significant genetic damage because, during replication, the apurinic sites cannot specify any kind of base, let alone the correct one. However, under certain conditions, a base can be inserted across from an apurinic site, frequently resulting in a mutation.

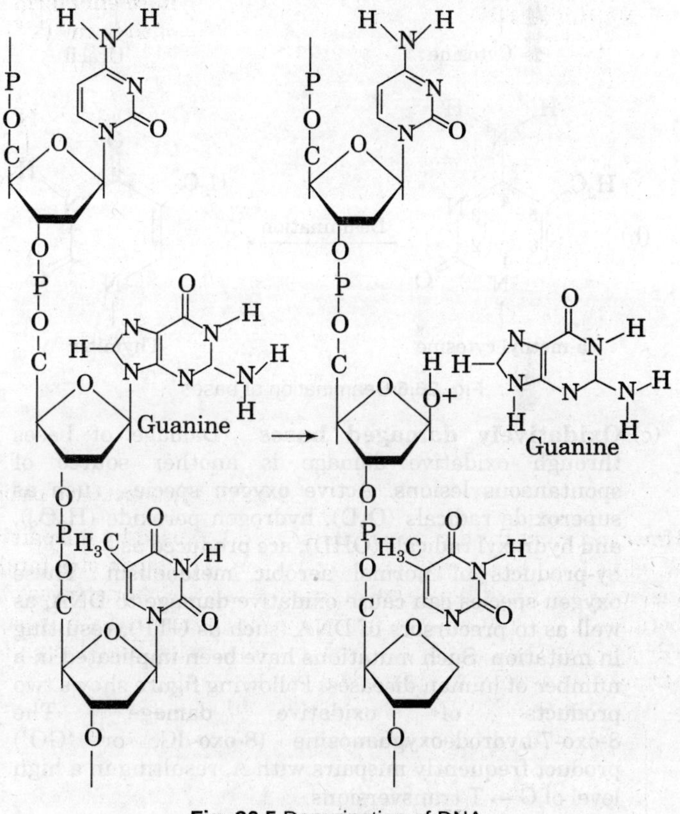

Fig. 26.5 Depurination of DNA

(b) **Deamination** The deamination of cytosine yields uracil. Unrepaired uracil residues will pair with adenine in the course of replication, resulting in the conversion of a G–C pair into an A–T pair (a G–C →

A–T transition). Similarly, **5-methyl cytosine** (certain bases in prokaryotes and eukaryotes are normally methylated) results into thymine after deamination. One of the repair enzymes in the cell, **uracil-DNA glycosylase**, recognizes the uracil residues in the DNA that arise from deaminations and excises them, leaving a gap that is subsequently filled in. However, the deamination of 5-methylcytosine generates thymine (5-methyluracil), which is not recognized by the enzyme uracil-DNA glycosylase and is thus not repaired. Therefore, C → T transitions generated by deamination are seen more frequently at 5-methylcytosine sites, because they escape this repair system.

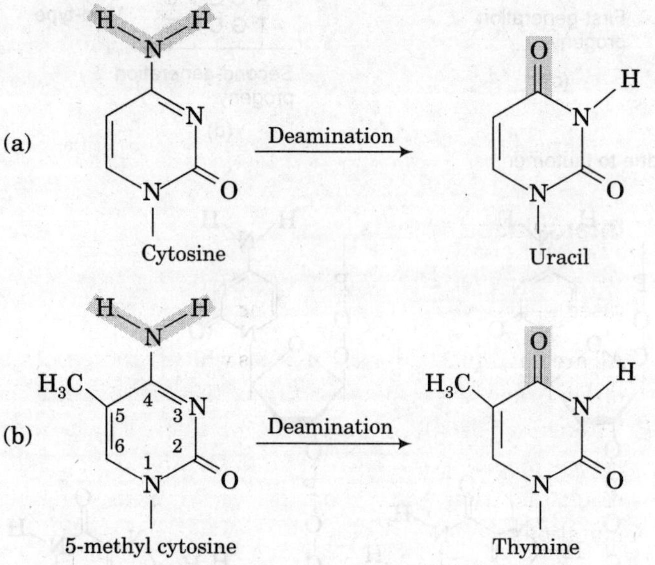

(a) Cytosine —Deamination→ Uracil

(b) 5-methyl cytosine —Deamination→ Thymine

Fig. 26.6 Deamination of bases

(c) **Oxidatively damaged bases** Damage of bases through oxidative damage is another source of spontaneous lesions. Active oxygen species, such as superoxide radicals (O_2D), hydrogen peroxide (H_2O_2), and hydroxyl radicals (ȮHD), are produced as by-products of normal aerobic metabolism. These oxygen species can cause oxidative damage to DNA, as well as to precursors of DNA (such as GTP), resulting in mutation. Such mutations have been implicated in a number of human diseases. Following figure shows two products of oxidative damage. The 8-oxo-7-hydrodeoxyguanosine (8-oxo-dG, or 'GO') product frequently mispairs with A, resulting in a high level of G → T transversions.

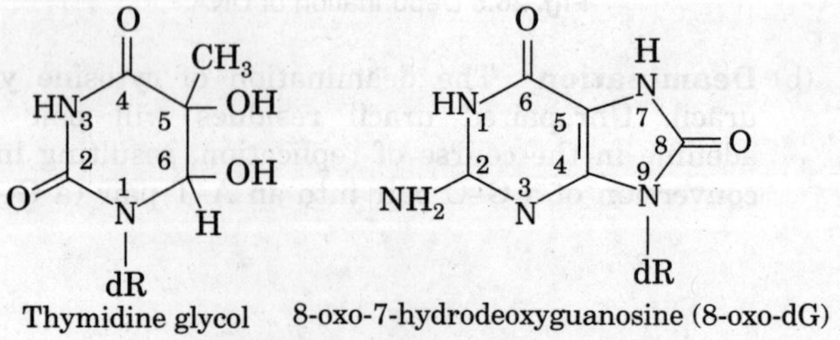

Thymidine glycol   8-oxo-7-hydrodeoxyguanosine (8-oxo-dG)

Fig. 26.7 Oxidatively damaged base

(d) **Alkylation** Still another type of spontaneous DNA lesion is alkylation, the addition of alkyl (methyl, ethyl, occasionally propyl) groups to the bases or backbone of DNA. Alkylation can occur through reaction of compounds such as S-adenosyl methionine with DNA. Alkylated bases may be subject to spontaneous breakdown or mispairing.

Induced Mutations Through Mutagens

A mutagen is a natural or human-made agent (physical or chemical) which can alter the structure or sequence of DNA. The mutagens can be divided into two types:

(i) Chemical mutagens
(ii) Radiations

Chemical Mutagens

A large number of chemicals are reported to be mutagenic. Some important one are:

Base-Analogs

These chemicals structurally resemble purines and pyrimidines and may be incorporated into DNA in place of the normal bases during DNA replication.

(a) **5-Bromouracil** (5-BU) – Resembles thymine (has Br atom instead of methyl group) and will be incorporated into DNA and pair with adenine like thymine. The presence of the bromine atom significantly alters the distribution of electrons in the base ring, so 5-BU can frequently change to either the enol form or an ionized form, the latter of which pairs with guanine. 5-BU causes G-C → A-T or A-T → G-C transitions in the course of replication.

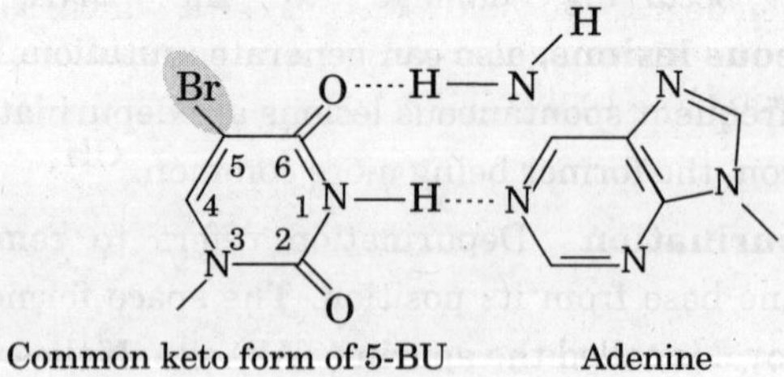

Common keto form of 5-BU   Adenine

(a)

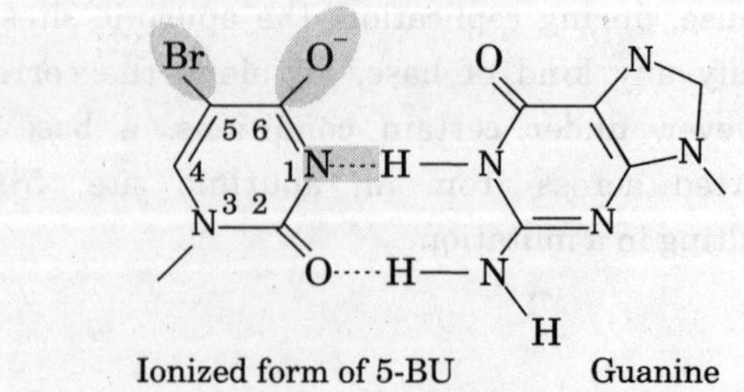

Ionized form of 5-BU   Guanine

(b)

(b) **2-Aminopurine** Adenine analog which can pair with T or in protonated form mispair with C. It causes A : T to G : C or G : C to A : T transitions. Base analogs cause transitions, as do spontaneous tautomerization events.

2-AP Thymine

(a)

Protonated 2-AP Cytosine

(b)

Guanine $\xrightarrow{\text{EMS}}$ O-6-ethylguanine Thymine GC→AT

Thymine $\xrightarrow{\text{EMS}}$ O-4-ethylthymine Guanine TA→CG

Chemicals which Alter Structure and Pairing Properties of Bases

Some of the important chemicals having such properties are:

(a) **Nitrous acid** (HNO_2) It causes conversion of C to U, G to xanthine, and A to hypoxanthine through **oxidative deaminations**. U in DNA pairs with A, xanthine in DNA pairs with C and hypoxanthine in DNA pairs with C and cause AT and GC transitions.

(b) **Nitrosoguanidine, methyl methanesulphonate, ethyl methanesulphonate** Chemical mutagens that react with bases and add methyl or ethyl groups. Depending on the affected atom, the alkylated base may then degrade to yield a baseless site, which is mutagenic and recombinogenic, or mispair to result in mutations upon DNA replication.

$C_2H_5—O—S(=O)_2—H_3C$ EMS

NG

Intercalating Agents

Ethidium Bromide, Acridine Orange, Proflavin, ICR-191, etc. (used in labs as dyes and mutagens).

All are flat, multiple ring molecules which interact with bases of DNA and insert between them. This insertion causes a 'stretching' of the DNA duplex so that DNA polymerase inserts an extra base opposite an intercalated molecule. The result is that intercalating agents cause frameshift mutations.

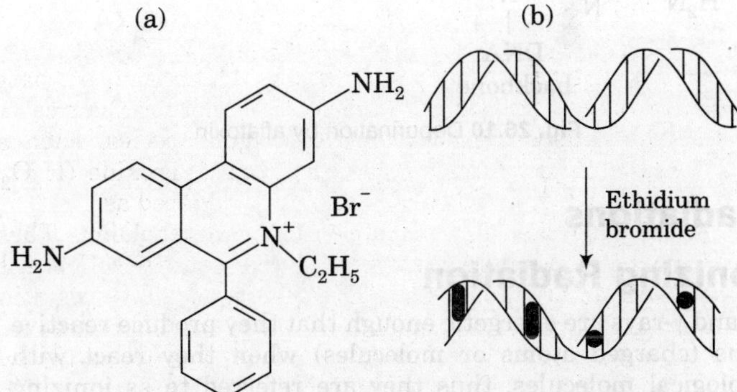

Fig. 26.8 Ethidium bromide stacked between base pairs

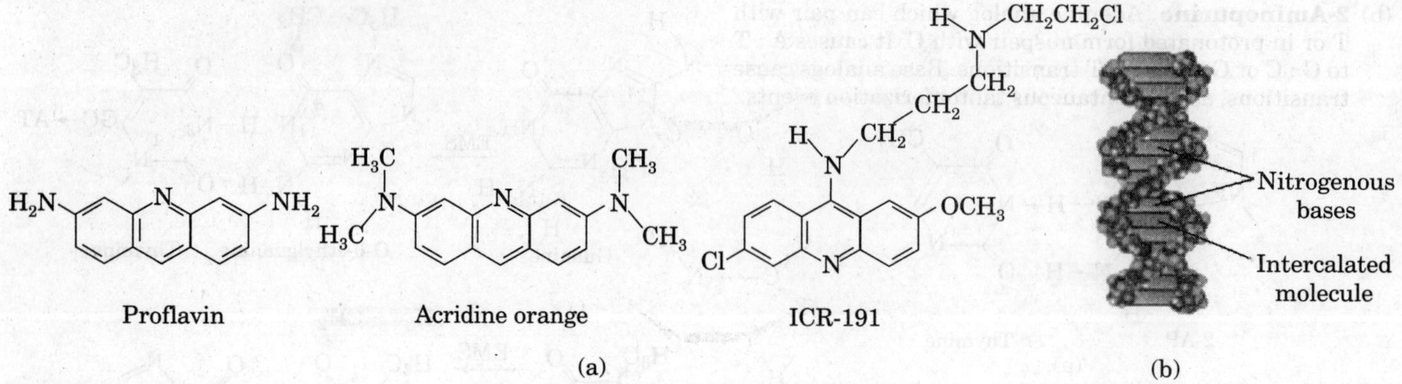

Proflavin Acridine orange ICR-191

(a)

Nitrogenous bases

Intercalated molecule

(b)

Fig. 26.9 Intercalating agents

Depurinations

Aflatoxin B_1 (AFB_1) is a powerful carcinogen originally isolated from fungal-infected peanuts. Aflatoxin forms an addition product at the N-7 position of guanine. This product leads to the breakage of the bond between the base and the sugar, thereby liberating the base and resulting in an **apurinic site.**

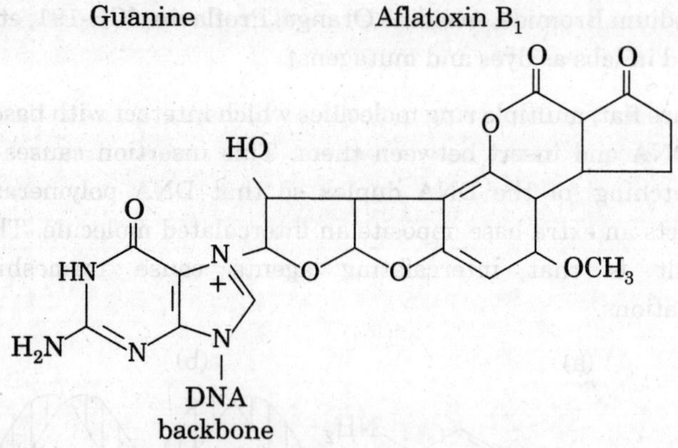

Guanine Aflatoxin B_1

DNA backbone

Fig. 26.10 Depurination by aflatoxin

Radiations

Ionizing Radiation

X-and γ-rays are energetic enough that they produce reactive ions (charged atoms or molecules) when they react with biological molecules; thus they are referred to as ionizing radiation. This term also includes corpuscular radiation – streams of atomic and subatomic particles emitted by radioactive elements these are of two types—alpha and beta-particles (alpha are helium nuclei, 2 protons and 2 neutrons; beta are electrons). Ionizing radiation produces a range of effects on DNA both through free radical effects and direct action

(a) Breaks in one or both strands.

(b) Damage to/loss of bases (mutations).

(c) Crosslinking of DNA to itself or proteins.

UV (Ultraviolet) Radiations

UV radiation is less energetic, and therefore, non-ionizing, but its wavelengths are preferentially absorbed by bases of DNA and by aromatic amino acids of proteins, so it, too, has important biological and genetic effects. UV is normally classified in terms of its wavelength **UV-C** (180-290 nm) – 'germicidal' – most energetic and lethal, it is not found in sunlight because it is absorbed by the ozone layer; **UV-B** (290-320 nm) – major lethal/mutagenic fraction of sunlight; **UV-A** (320 nm – visible) – 'near UV' – also has deleterious effects (primarily because it creates oxygen radicals) but it produces very few pyrimidine dimers. The major lethal lesions are **pyrimidine dimers** in DNA (produced by UV-B) – these are the result of a covalent attachment between adjacent pyrimidines in one strand. These dimers, like bulky lesions from chemicals, block transcription and DNA replication and are lethal if unrepaired. They can stimulate mutation and chromosome rearrangement as well. If these dimers go unrepaired then it leads to a disease called **xeroderma pigmentosum**, in which the affected individual's skin become extremely sensitive to sunlight resulting into high frequency of tumours in the epidermal cells of exposed areas.

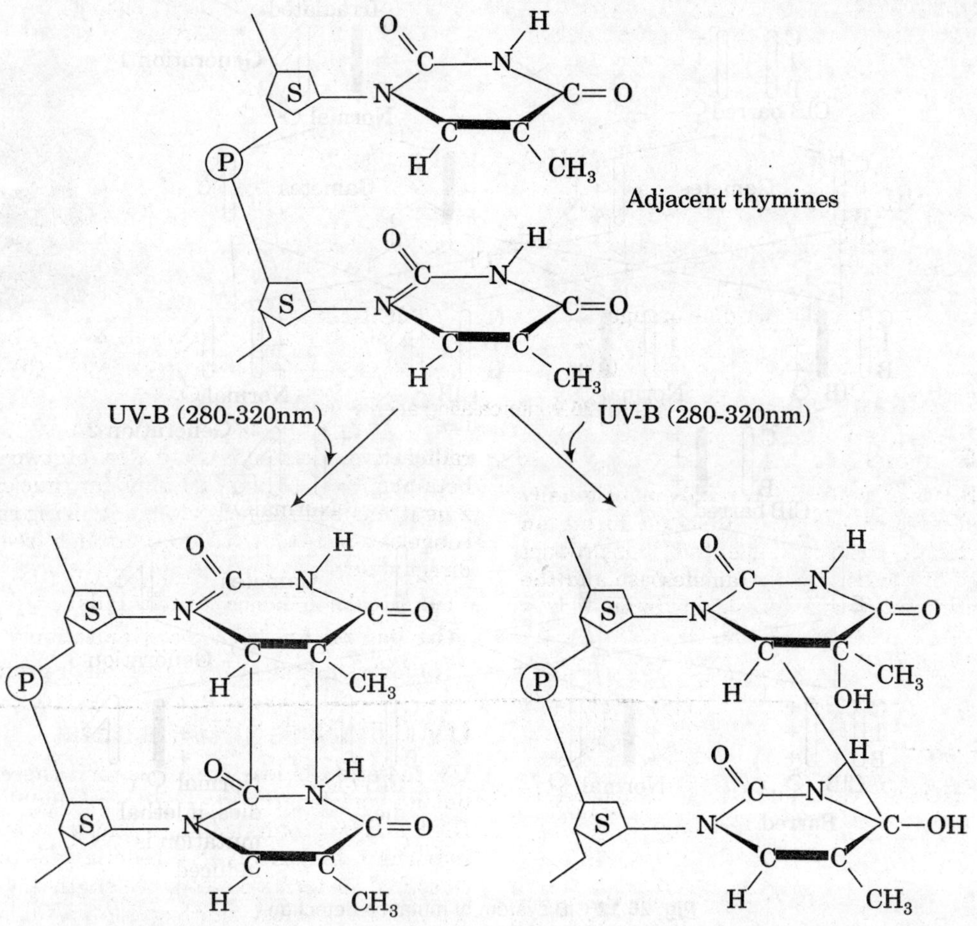

Adjacent thymines

UV-B (280-320nm) UV-B (280-320nm)

Cyclobutane thymine dimer

6-4-photoproduct

Fig. 26.11 Mutation due to UV light

Detection of Mutation

For genetic investigations detection of mutations or mutants is essential. For the ease of understanding following examples are taken as illustrations.

Detection in Bacteria and Fungi

The general principle for detection of mutation in both bacteria and fungi are same. Detection depends on a selection system by which mutant cells are isolated from non-mutant cells. As an example we take an eukaryote *Neurospora crassa*. Since, *Neurospora* is haploid in its vegetative life cycle its mutants can be easily detected as there is no need to look into heterozygosity as in diploid organisms. Wild type *Neurospora* grows on minimal culture medium of glucose, a few inorganic acids and salts, a nitrogen source and the vitamin biotin. Whereas the nutritional mutants will grow only in a supplemented or complete medium that also contains numerous amino acids, vitamins, nucleic acids, etc. Those microorganisms that are wild type and can grow in the minimal culture medium are called **prototrophs**, while those which can grow only with additional supplement are called **auxotrophs**. Thus, nutritional mutants can be identified and isolated by their failure to grow in the minimal culture medium.

Detection in *Drosophila*

Muller, in his studies of mutagenic effects of X-rays, developed many detection systems in *Drosophila*. One of them was **CB system**. The CB system is used to detect X-linked recessive lethal mutations in *Drosophila*. Here, three symbols mean

C	Inversion that suppresses the recovery of crossover products.
l	Recessive lethal allele.
B	Dominant gene duplication causing bar eye.

In this system, wild-type males are treated with X-rays and mated with heterozygous non-treated ClB females. In the F_1 generation, females expressing bar eyes are selected. They have received one X from ClB mother and one from father. Some of them have received the X-ray induced X-linked lethal mutation. When such F_1 bar females are backcrossed with wild-type males, all male progeny will die. Half of the females will be wild-type and the half will have bar eye.

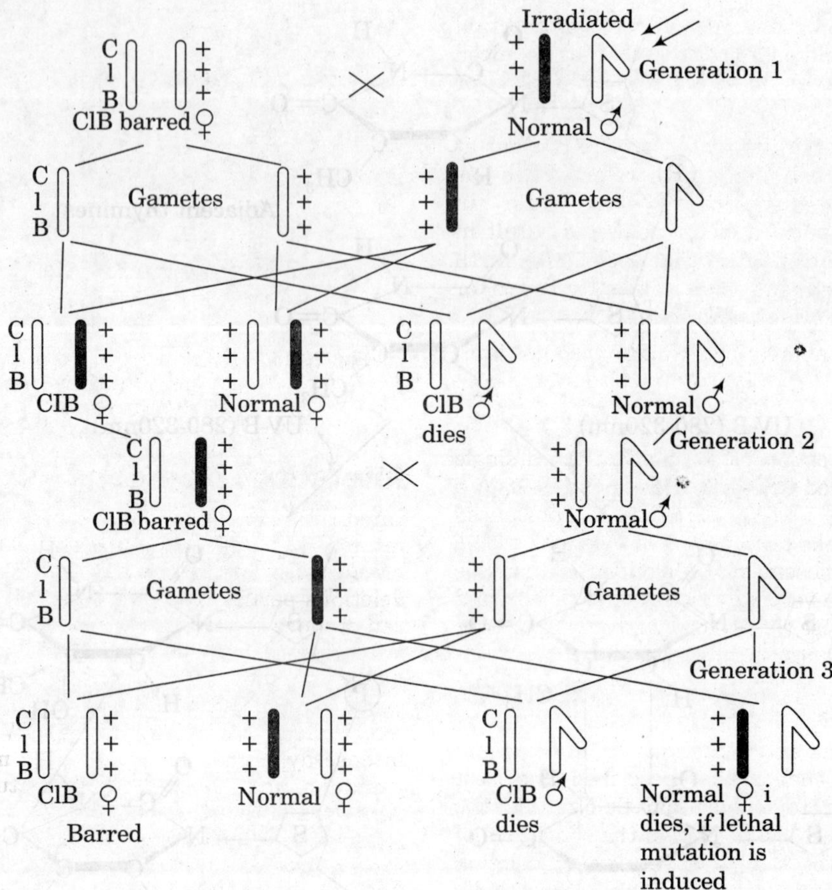

Fig. 26.12 ClB system of mutation detection

Detection in Plants

In plants, many variations are detected simply by visual observation, such as flower colour, seed-shape, etc. For biochemical mutations, plant's biochemical composition need to be analyzed. For example, isolation of proteins from maize endosperm, hydrolysis of the proteins, and determination of amino acid composition have revealed that the *opaque*-2 mutant strain contains significantly more lysine than do other non-mutant lines. Other detection techniques involve the tissue culture of plant cell lines in defined medium. The plant cells are treated like microorganisms, and their resistance to herbicides or toxins can be determined by adding these compounds to the culture medium.

Detection in Humans

For detection of mutations in humans selection techniques developed in organisms like *Drosophila* can not be used. **Pedigree analysis** is the most important source of mutation detection in humans. For details please look relevant chapter elsewhere in the book.

Structural and Numerical Alteration in Chromosomes

Due to extremely precise mitotic and meiotic cell division the somatic ($2n$) and gametic (n) chromosome number of a species ordinarily remain constant. The chromosomal aberrations may be structural or numerical.

Structural Aberrations of Chromosomes

Structural chromosome rearrangements are changes in the physical structure of chromosomes that may result in birth defects, mental retardation and increased risk for infertility or pregnancy loss. Structural chromosomal aberrations can result in genetic disease due to trisomy and/or monosomy of chromosomal segments. These aberrations may be *de novo* events or may be inherited from carrier parents. Chromosome rearrangements are considered balanced if disomy is maintained for all of the autosomes and a normal complement of sex chromatin is present, even if the positions of the homologous segments on the chromosomes have been changed. In contrast, when chromatin is lost or gained in the process the rearrangement is said to be unbalanced. Unbalanced constitutional rearrangements are generally associated with developmental delay or intellectual impairment, birth defects and poor growth, whereas balanced rearrangements often have no effect on physical or intellectual development.

Structural chromosome rearrangements that are present at conception affect every cell and are referred to as **constitutional**. Rearrangements that occur later in development affect only a portion of the cells and result in **mosaicism**. Structural abnormalities that occur after birth are referred to as acquired and may cause **tumours** or **leukaemia** by altering cell cycle regulation.

Various kinds of structural aberrations of chromosomes are:

Deletions

Abnormalities in which a portion of chromatin from a single chromosome is lost are called deletions. Deletions result in a partial monosomy and are therefore, unbalanced rearrangements. Single breaks cause terminal deletions with a subsequent loss of the chromosome end. Deletions that survive to birth are associated with a very high risk of birth defects and intellectual impairment. Those that involve tumour suppressor genes confer a high risk of cancer and/or leukaemia.

Terminal Deletions

These require a single break and capping of the broken end with a telomere. One of the earliest described and best delineated syndromes due to a terminal deletion is the **cri-du-chat syndrome** with loss of part of the short arm of chromosome 5. This may be due to a very small deletion involving a break at band 5p15.2 or one that includes virtually the entire short arm. The new-born baby has a characteristic cat-like cry. The infant has a round face with wide-set eyes, but the older child and adult develops an elongated asymmetrical face. There is severe intellectual impairment.

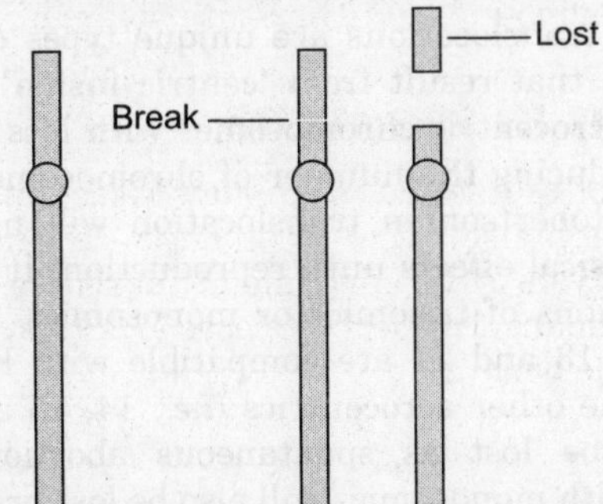

Fig. 26.13 Terminal deletion formation of a terminal deletion by a single break with loss of the terminal segment

Ring Chromosomes

A ring chromosome is formed from two terminal deletions. There is a break in both the short arm and the long arm, with fusion of the ends of the centromeric segment and loss of the two terminal segments. Ring chromosomes represent a form of terminal deletion with the added feature of being mitotically unstable due to mechanical problems during replication. Individuals with ring chromosomes have many of the features of patients with terminal deletions as well as growth retardation.

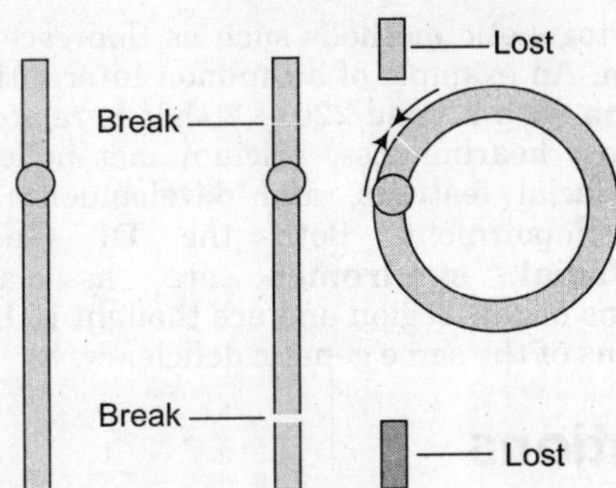

Fig. 26.14 Ring formation of a ring chromosome by a break in each arm, loss of the terminal segments and union of the centric segment

Interstitial Deletions

Interstitial deletions require two breaks with loss of the interstitial deletions. Interstitial deletions require two breaks with loss of the interstitial segment. Like terminal deletions partial monosomic caused by interstitial deletions can produce severe abnormalities and death of the embryo. It is, therefore, only embryos with small deletions that are likely to survive. Interstitial deletion of 15q 11-13 is the cause behind two syndromes that are genetically imprinted too. **Prader-Willi Syndrome** (PWS) is characterized by intense hyperphagia, obesity, poor muscle tone, hypoplastic genitalia and moderate intellectual impairment, while **Angelman Syndrome** (AS) is associated with ataxia, seizures, severe intellectual impairment, delayed or absent speech, spontaneous outbursts of laughter and characteristic facial features. Prader-Willi Syndrome (PWS) is always paternally inherited, while Angelman Syndrome (AS) is always maternally inherited (for details of genomic imprinting, please see the relevant chapter on this topic elsewhere in this unit).

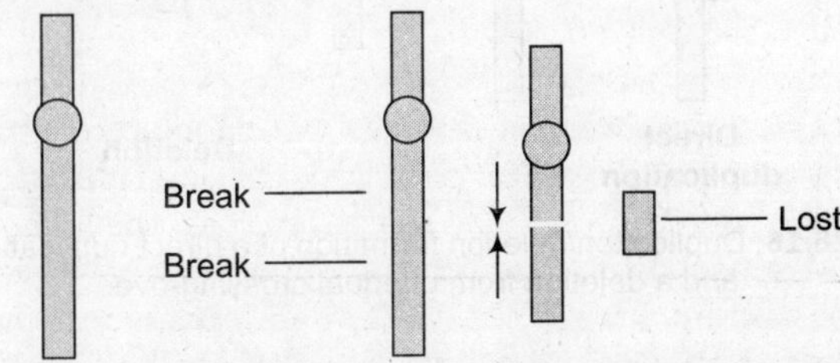

Fig. 28.15 Interstitial deletion: formation of an interstitial deletion by two breaks in the same arm, loss of the interstitial segment, and reunion of the two remaining segments

Microdeletions
(Contiguous Gene Syndromes)

A special category of interstitial deletions called microdeletions are so named because their small size often escapes detection by conventional cytogenetic methods. Microdeletions are also referred to as contiguous gene syndromes because they involve the loss of a series of closely linked genes. Contiguous gene syndromes may also be the result of small duplications. These deletions may involve only 1-2 Mb of deoxyribonucleic acid (DNA) or less, in the same chromosomal band, and are rarely visible at the microscopic level. Microdeletions must, therefore be detected using molecular cytogenetic methods such as fluorescence *in situ* hybridization. An example of a common interstitial deletion is the deletion within band 22q11.2 that is related to heart malformations, hearing loss, calcium metabolism defects, dysmorphic facial features, and developmental delay or intellectual impairment. Both the **Di George** and **Velocardiofacial syndromes** are associated with microdeletions of this region and are thought to be different manifestations of the same genetic deficiency.

Duplications

Duplications are unbalanced rearrangements that result in partial trisomy. Compared with deletions, duplications tend to be somewhat milder in effect, but they share many of the same clinical features. Duplications are believed to result primarily from unequal crossingover, especially in regions of the genome where repeat DNA sequences are found. Segmental duplications can be oriented in two ways direct or inverted. Direct duplications retain the same order of gene loci and chromosome bands in relation to the centromere as the parent chromosome, whereas inverted duplications exhibit a complete reversal of loci and bands contained in the duplication. Duplication of the proximal long arm of chromosome 22 as an extra dicentric chromosome (**cat eye syndrome**) is associated with coloboma of the eye, intellectual impairment and anal atresia. The **Bar eye** in *Drosophila* is the result of duplication of 16A region of the X-chromosome.

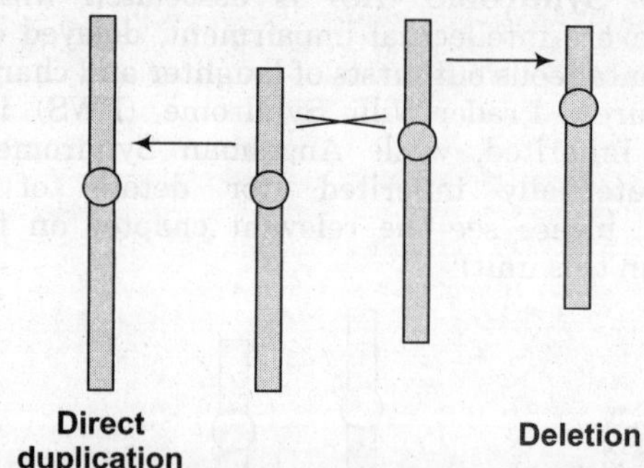

Fig. 26.16 Duplication/deletion formation of a direct duplication and a deletion from unequal crossing-over

Microduplications

Microduplications have also been reported, although they are more rare than microdeletions, and represent another type of contiguous gene syndrome. The best known of the microduplication syndromes occurs on the short arm of chromosome 11 (within band p15.5) and results in **Beckwith-Wiedemann Syndrome** with high birthweight and overgrowth of the tongue. Unlike most unbalanced autosomal chromosome rearrangements, this syndrome does not typically involve intellectual impairment or developmental delay.

Translocations

Translocations involve breaks in two different chromosomes with an exchange of segments. In humans, there are two major types of translocation reciprocal translocations in which there is no visual loss of chromatin, and Robertsonian translocations in which the long arms of two acrocentric chromosomes are joined with loss of the two short arms.

Reciprocal Translocations

A single break occurs in each chromosome, and the non-centric segments are exchanged without the visible loss of any chromatin. However, the two new derivative chromosomes may have very different morphology depending on the breakpoints. The carrier of a reciprocal translocation generally has no phenotypic effects due to the rearrangement except for possible reproductive abnormalities including infertility, spontaneous abortions and abnormal offspring. Translocations that reposition proto-oncogenes can result in dysregulation of the cell cycle and the development of tumours or leukaemia. **Chronic Myelogenous Leukaemia** (CML) is caused by the translocation of the long-arm of chromosome 22 usually on chromosome 9. (Burkitt's lymphoma) is related to translocation of chromosome 14.

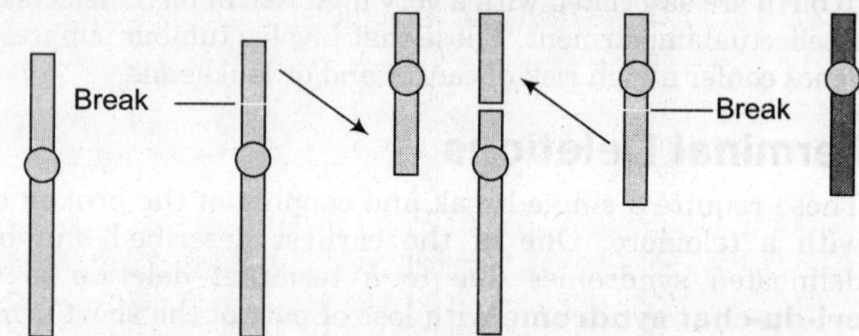

Fig. 26.17 Reciprocal translocation formation of a reciprocal translocation by a break in each chromosome and exchange of the non-centric segments

Robertsonian Translocations

Robertsonian translocations are unique types of wholearm translocations that result from 'centric fusion' of the long arms of two acrocentric chromosomes with loss of the short arms, thus reducing the number of chromosomes by one. A carrier of a Robertsonian translocation will not generally show any physical effects until reproduction. It may results in the formations of trisomics or monosomics. Trisomy for chromosomes 13 and 21 are compatible with life, whereas trisomy for the other acrocentrics (*i.e.*, 14, 15 and 22), will virtually all be lost as spontaneous abortions. All the conceptions with monosomics will also be lost prenatally.

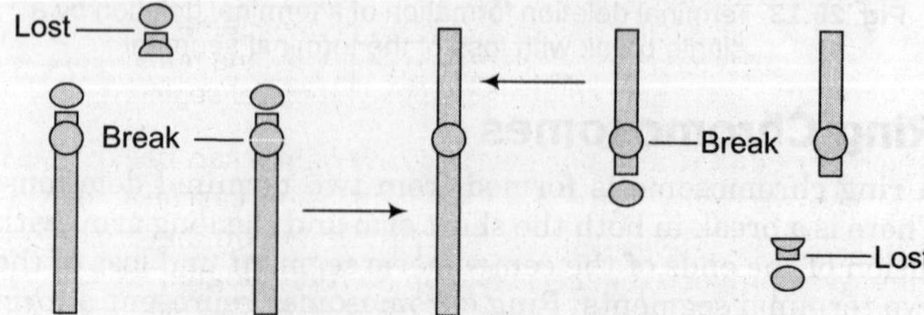

Fig. 26.18 Robertsonian translocation formation of a Robertsonian translocation by a break within the centromere of each chromosome, union of the two long arms and loss of the two short arms, reducing the chromosome number by one

Inversions

Inversions are formed by two breaks in the same chromosome with exchange of the two ends. Inversions are thus essentially formed in the same manner as translocations except that the breaks and exchange occur in the same chromosome. Two different types of inversion are found. One is a **pericentric inversion** in which one break occurs in each arm of the chromosome and, thus, the centromere is included in the inverted segment. This changes the banding patterns and may also change the shape of the chromosome due to movement of the centromere. The other is **paracentric inversion** in which both breaks occur in the same arm and, therefore, the centromere is not included in the inverted segment. This alters the banding patterns, but not the shape of the chromosome. Repositioning of protooncogenes in inverted chromosomes can activate oncogenes and disrupt normal regulation of the cell cycle causing various forms of cancer.

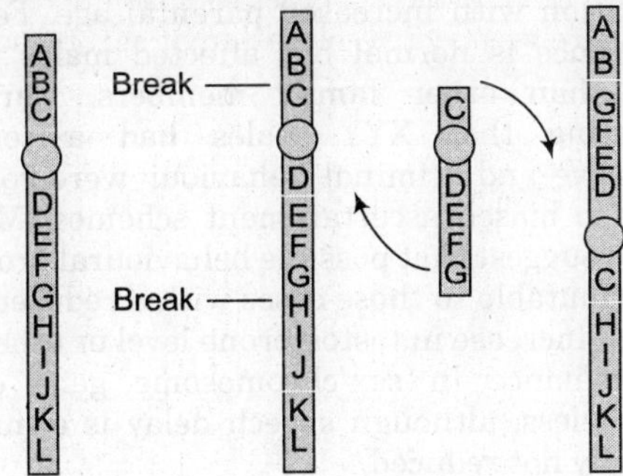

Fig. 26.19 Pericentric inversion formation of a pericentric inversion by a break in each arm, 180° rotation of the centric segment, and reunion of the terminal segments with the centric segment

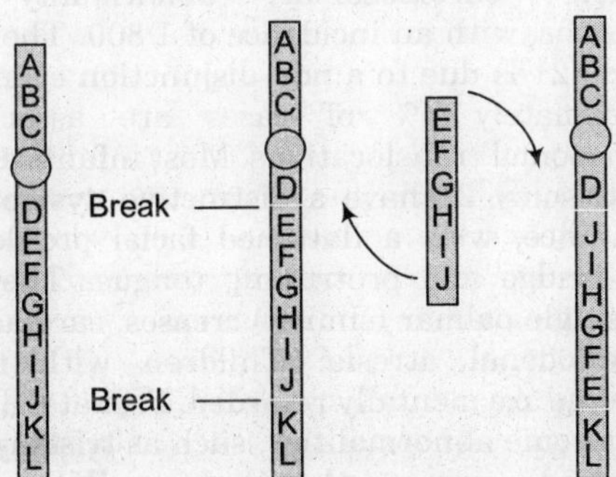

Fig. 26.20 Paracentric inversion formation of a paracentric inversion by two breaks in the same arm, 180° rotation of the interstitial segment, and reunion of the terminal segments with the interstitial segment

Both pericentric and paracentric inversions can be carried in the heterozygous state. Like translocation carriers, there is generally no phenotypic effect on inversion heterozygotes due to the inverted gene order of one homologue, except as a result of abnormalities in meiosis. Here, as in other heterozygotes for structural rearrangements, difficulties in pairing and segregation arise at the first meiotic prophase during pachytene when homologous pairing and recombination take place.

Numerical Aberrations of Chromosomes

Numerical aberrations represent a significant proportion of chromosomal changes found in humans. These errors can occur in meiosis or mitosis and therefore, be **constitutive** (present in all cells) or **mosaic** (present in some cells). They represent a significant cause of pregnancy loss as well as abnormalities found in live-births.

Meiotic Non-disjunction

The normal product of meiosis in humans is a gamete containing 23 chromosomes 22 autosomes and a sex chromosome (X or Y). Segregation of chromosomes in human meiosis is remarkably error-prone and roughly 20% of oocytes and a few percent of spermatocytes are either aneuploid, having a numerically unbalanced chromosome complement, *e.g.,* 22 or 24 chromosomes or diploid (46 chromosomes).

Chromosome non-disjunction is defined as the unbalanced segregation of chromosomes leading to aneuploidy and may occur at meiosis-I (when homologous chromosomes segregate to opposite poles) or at meiosis-II (when the two sister chromatids separate at the centromere and segregate to opposite poles). The vast majority of aneuploidy in humans is maternal in origin (*i.e.,* due to an error present in the oocyte), and its incidence increases dramatically with maternal age. The exceptions to this rule are 47, XYY (presence of an extra Y-chromosome) and 45, X (a missing sex chromosome), which are predominantly due to paternal or post-fertilization events.

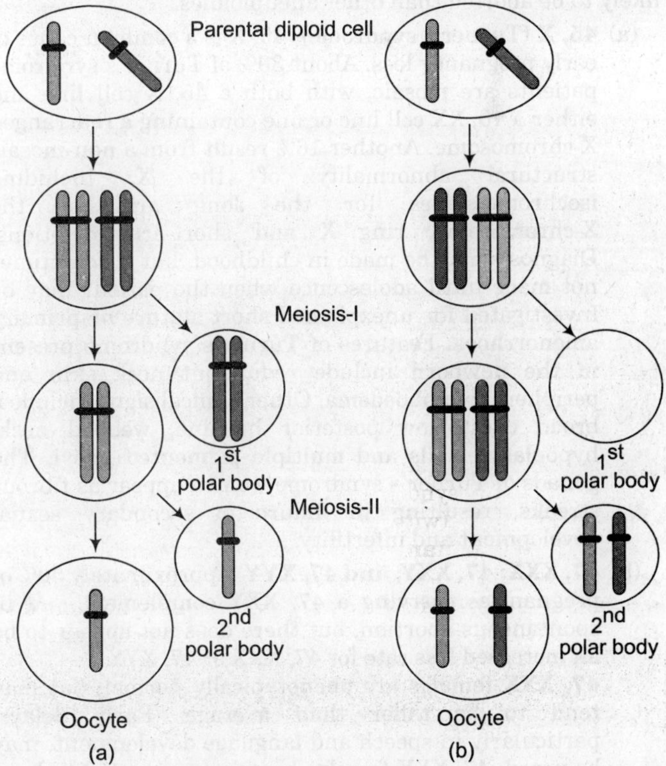

Fig. 26.21 Meiotic non-disjunction

Mitotic Non-disjunction

Chromosome segregation errors may also occur during mitotic cell divisions and thus lead to mosaicism, with the presence of both aneuploid and normal diploid cells within one individual. Mitotic non-disjunction occurring during the somatic cell divisions preceding meiosis in oogenesis or spermatogenesis may lead to germline mosaicism, and result in an increased rate of eggs or sperm with aneuploidy for a specific chromosome. Mitotic errors occurring during early development may lead to a mixture of abnormal and normal cells in the developing embryo.

Aneuploidy

Aneuploids differ from standard $2n$ chromosome complements in single chromosomes. These chromosomal errors account for about half of pregnancy losses, with most occurring in the first trimester of pregnancy. The most common abnormalities found in spontaneous abortions are trisomy for chromosome 16, triploidy (69 chromosomes in total, consisting of three complete haploid sets) and X-monosomy. Only a few abnormalities can survive to term. These include trisomy 21, trisomy 13, trisomy 18, triploidy and sex chromosome aneuploidy, with a combined incidence of 1 per 300 live-births.

Sex Chromosome Aneuploidies XXX, XYY, XXY, X

Sex-chromosome aneuploidies are relatively common, both because they occur more frequently and because they are less likely to be aborted than other aneuploidies.

(a) **45, X** (Turner's syndrome) 45, X is a common cause of early pregnancy loss. About 30% of Turner's syndrome patients are mosaic, with both a 45, X cell line and either a 46, XX cell line or one containing a rearranged X-chromosome. Another 16% result from a non-mosaic structural abnormality of the X, including isochromo-somes for the long arm of the X-chromosome, ring X and short-arm deletions. Diagnosis may be made in childhood, but is sometimes not made until adolescence when the patient may be investigated for unexplained short stature or primary amenorrhoea. Features of Turner's syndrome present in the newborn include redundant neck skin and peripheral lymphoedema. Other clinical signs include a broad chest, low posterior hairline, webbed neck, hypoplastic nails and multiple pigmented naevi. The gonads of Turner's syndrome women appear as fibrous streaks, resulting in failure of secondary sexual development and infertility.

(b) **47, XXX; 47, XXY; and 47, XYY** Approximately 50% of pregnancies carrying a 47, XXY complement end in spontaneous abortion, but there does not appear to be an increased loss rate for 47, XXX or 47, XYY.

47, XXX females are phenotypically normal, but may tend to be taller than average. Early delays, particularly in speech and language development, may be noted. 47, XXX females have been reported to have impaired scores on tests of concept formation, spatial thinking and verbal fluency. The majority of 47, XXX women can function reasonably well and become self-sufficient as adults. In addition, the majority of affected females are fertile and produce chromosomally balanced offspring.

47, XXY (Klinefelter syndrome) is the most common cause of hypogonadism and male infertility, accounting for about 10% of infertile men. The testes are small and fail to produce normal adult levels of testosterone, which consequently leads to poorly developed secondary male sexual characteristics as well as gynaecomastia (breast development). Klinefelter males have an increased incidence of learning disabilities, such as reading deficiencies, poor spelling, speech and language delays. However, overall IQ is on average only slightly decreased. Height is generally more than normal adults of their age.

47, XYY may arise from a meiosis-II error in the father or a post-fertilization mitotic event. There is no association with increased parental age. Fertility and appearance is normal but affected males tend to be taller than other family members. Early reports suggesting that XYY males had a tendency to aggressive and criminal behaviour were controversial owing to biased ascertainment schemes. More recent studies suggest that possible behavioural problems may be attributable to those cases with a reduced IQ rather than an increase in testosterone level or other effects of an imbalance in sex-chromosome gene expression. Nonetheless, although speech delay is common, IQ is generally not reduced.

Autosomal Aneuploidies

(a) **Down's Syndrome** (trisomy 21) It is the most common chromosomal abnormality amongst live-births, with an incidence of 1/800. The majority of trisomy 21 is due to a non-disjunction event; however, approximately 4% of cases are associated with chromosomal translocations. Most infants and children with trisomy 21 have a distinctive dysmorphic facial appearance, with a flattened facial profile, flattened nasal bridge and protruding tongue. They may also have single palmar (simian) creases, cardiac anomalies and duodenal atresia. Children with trisomy 21 syndrome are mentally retarded. Prenatal diagnosis for chromosome abnormalities, such as trisomy 21, can be performed using **chorionic villus sampling** (sampling from the placenta performed at 10-12 weeks gestation) or **amniocentesis** (performed at approximately 17 weeks gestation).

(b) **Trisomy 13** (Patau's syndrome) It is present in approximately 1/25000 liveborn infants. Even when liveborn, trisomy 13 is considered a lethal condition and most affected persons die in early infancy. The trisomy 13 phenotype is characterized by a range of brain abnormalities, including absence of the corpus callosum. Facial abnormalities are present. Bilateral cleft lip and palate are common. There are often extra digits on the ulnar side of the hand. Cardiac abnormalities are frequent.

(c) **Trisomy 18** (Edward's syndrome) It is more common in live-births than is trisomy 13 but is still rare, occurring in 1/8000-10000 live-births. Infants with trisomy 18 are often growth-retarded. Affected infants have a small, triangular-shaped face. Omphalocele and defects in the diaphragm are common abnormalities. Almost all hearts will have dysplastic cardiac valves, with thickened and rendundant valve leaflet tissue. Abnormalities of the genitourinary system are frequent. Survival beyond a few months after birth is rare.

Euploidy (Polyploidy)

In euploidy there is a presence of one or more extra complete haploid sets of chromosomes, that is chromosomal complement is present in multiples of n. In humans, triploidy (three haploid sets) is more common than tetraploidy (four haploid sets). Triploidy is estimated to be present in 1% of all clinically recognized pregnancies. The extra haploid set of chromosomes in triploidy may come from either the mother (digynic) or father (diandric). The digynic foetal phenotype is that of severe asymmetric growth retardation with marked wasting of the trunk and limbs and relative macrocephaly. Characteristically, there is complete soft-tissue syndactyly of the third and fourth fingers and marked adrenal hypoplasia. The phenotype of diandric triploidy differs in that the foetuses are less growth-retarded and symmetrically so, thus, the head is in proportion to the rest of the body and truncal wasting is absent. These foetuses exhibit the same congenital anomalies as the digynic triploids but do not have adrenal hypoplasia (this is another example of genomic imprinting).

In other animals too, triploids are very rare, but they have been found in *Drosophila*, salamanders, lizards, etc.

Polyploidy is an important mechanism for evolution in plants. Some plant groups have a series of chromosome numbers based on a basic number. In the genus *Chrysanthemum*, for example, the basic number is 9, and species are known that have 18, 36, 54, 72 and 90 chromosomes. Bananas, tulips, Baldwin apples, European pears, etc. are triploids that are propagated asexually.

Polyploids have been induced experimentally by several methods in various plants. Chemicals that interferes with spindle fibre formation during mitosis might result in a doubling other the chromosomes. Among the cultivated varieties of wheat, three different chromosome numbers are represented: 14, 28 and 42 ($x = 7$). The bread wheat, *Triticum aestivum* has 42 chromosomes (hexaploid).

Recombination

Recombination can be defined as the production of gene combinations not found in the parents. In nature there are varied kinds of recombinational processes, involved in different processes and playing different functions. However, during all recombinational processes some fragments of genetic material are exchanged between two distinct donor molecules, as such that genetic information from each donor is present in the offspring.

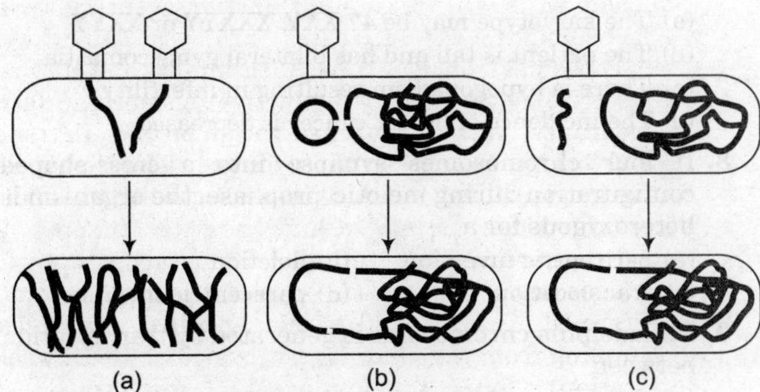

Fig. 26.22 Three recombinational processes
(a) Homologous recombination
(b) Site-specific recombination
(c) Non-homologous recombination. Note that the transforming power of site-specific recombination and non-homologous recombination is much more profound than homologous recombination

1. **Homologous recombination** When the process of recombination takes place between the regions on the chromosomes that are homologous to each other. For example, during sexual reproduction two paired homologous chromosomes exchange DNA fragments through crossing-over.

2. **Site-specific recombination** These kind of recombination takes place when the recombining DNA combines with the main chromosome at a specific site. For example, Phage integration into the bacterial chromosome. To integrate, the integrase protein (Int) catalyzes recombination between two specific sites, known as the att, or attachment sites. The attP-site is on the phage DNA and the attB-site is in the bacterial chromosome (P for phage and B for bacteria).

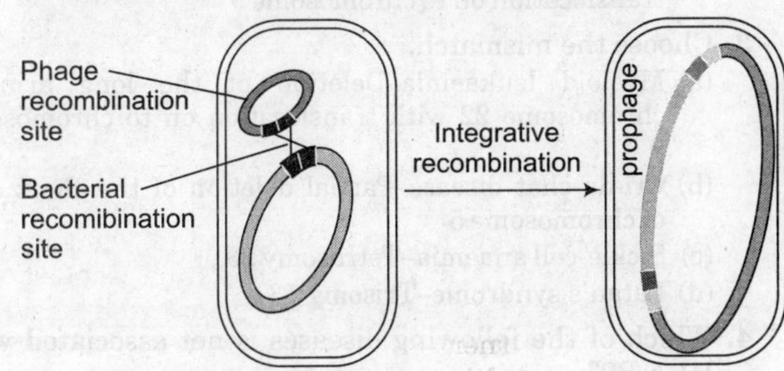

Fig. 26.23 Site specific recombination

3. **Non-homologous recombination** When the fragments of DNA are exchanged between two non-homologous chromosomes it is called non-homologous recombination. This kind of recombination takes place when translocation mutation occurs such as **Chronic Myelogenous Leukaemia** (CML) which is caused by the translocation of the long-arm of chromosome 22 usually on chromosome 9.

Another major non-homologous recombination type is **transposition**. Barbara McClintock discovered a genetic element that not only regulated the mottling but also caused chromosome breakage. She called this element **dissociation** (ds). Genetic mapping showed that the chromosome breakage always occurs at or very near the location of ds. DS does not have position this called **transposition.** Further more DS moves only if a second element called **activator** (AC) is also prevent in the same genome. Many other transposable elements have been discovered. Transposable genetic elements consist of genes that can move from place to place within the genome. There are three classes of transposable elements with different structures and mechanisms of transposition. They exist both in eukaryotes and prokaryotes and cause different effects on the chromosome they move to. For instance, they can inactivate genes by interrupting the coding sequence of a gene; they can activate an adjacent gene by providing a promoter or transcriptional activator, or they can restructure a chromosome by producing homologous sequences that might afterwards be used in homologous recombination. The existence of these 'jumping genes' which move from one chromosome to another without respect for boundaries, including species boundaries, greatly altered our views of evolution, as something smoothly driven by neutral mutations alone. Transposable elements are responsible for many mutations in most organisms in which they occur. In some genes in *Drosophila* approximately half of all spontaneous mutations that have visible phenotypic effects result from insertion of transposable element. Wrinkled seed mutation in pea also due to this. The effects of transposition are too drastic to be apparently of any use. And so are the effects of non-homologous recombination or the effects of non-sense or frameshift mutations. Nonetheless, transposition (and non-homologous recombination) is not only fairly frequent but also widely distributed throughout the living world and many are the marks it left behind in living organisms. Notwithstanding, most of the times the effect of transposition and some kinds of non-homologous recombination is deleterious. Very occasionally, though, some 'promising monsters' are formed and a completely new protein is created. In nature, in fact, very different proteins both in structure and functionality share the same construction motifs (domains) probably due to these kinds of genetic modification. (Details of transposons is given in cellular organization).

Exercise

1. Which of the following disease is not because of chromosomal abnormalities?
(a) Achondroplasia
(b) Myeloid leukaemia
(c) Cri-du-chat disease
(d) Patau's syndrome

2. Myeloid leukaemia disease is associated with the
(a) partial deletion of the short arm of chromosome 5
(b) deletion of the long arm of chromosome 22
(c) translocation of chromosome 9
(d) deletion of the long arm of chromosome 22 with translocation on to chromosome 9

3. Choose the mismatch.
(a) Myeloid leukaemia–Deletion of the long arm of chromosome 22 with translocation on to chromosome 9
(b) Cri-du-chat disease–Partial deletion of the short arm of chromosome 5
(c) Sickle-cell anaemia–Tetrasomy 23
(d) Patau's syndrome–Trisomy 13

4. Which of the following diseases is not associated with HLA-B8?
(a) Sjogren's syndrome
(b) Multiple sclerosis
(c) Myasthenia gravis
(d) Insulin-dependent diabetes mellitus

5. Which of the following trait is not a characteristic of Turner's syndrome?
(a) Premature cataract is common
(b) The cells contains 45 chromosomes
(c) The offsprings have 50% of inheriting the disease
(d) Both (a) and (c)

6. Which of the following feature is not associated with Klinefelter's syndrome?
(a) The karyotype is always 47 XXY
(b) The extrachromosome comes from the mother germ cells
(c) There is an increased incidence of lens subluxation
(d) The patient is infertile

7. Which of the following feature is not true regarding Klinefelter's syndrome?
(a) The karyotype may be 47 XXY, XXXYY or XXYY
(b) The patient is tall and has bilateral gynaecomastia
(c) There is hypogonadism resulting in infertility
(d) The incidence of breast cancer is decreased

8. If four chromosomes synapse into a cross-shaped configuration during meiotic prophase, the organism is heterozygous for a
(a) pericentric inversion (b) deletion
(c) translocation (d) paracentric inversion

9. Philadelphia chromosome is generated by translocation between
(a) chromosome 18 and chromosome 6
(b) chromosome 22 and chromosome 9
(c) chromosome 22 and chromosome 3
(d) chromosome 16 and chromosome 4

10. Retinoblastoma is cause by loss of both copies of the RB gene in the chromosome band
(a) 13p11 (b) 13q11
(c) 13q14 (d) 21q14

11. Position effect is the results of
(a) mutations (b) deletions
(c) inversions (d) transversions

12. The bridge-fragment configuration at anaphase-I is characteristic of
(a) translocation heterozygote
(b) paracentric inversion heterozygote
(c) pericentric inversion heterozygote
(d) duplication heterozygote

13. A mechanism that can cause a gene to move from one linkage group to another is
(a) translocation (b) inversion
(c) crossing-over (d) duplication

14. Pseudodominance may be observed in heterozygotes for
(a) a deletion (b) a duplication
(c) a reciprocal translocation (d) All of these

15. Which of the following chromosomal changes is usually the most damaging when in the homozygous condition?
(a) Deletion (b) Duplication
(c) Translocation (d) Inversion

16. In a trisomic individual the number of chromosomes is
(a) $2n$-1 (b) $2n+2$
(c) $2n+3$ (d) $2n+1$

17. A person with Klinefelter's syndrome is considered a
(a) monosomic (b) triploid
(c) trisomic (d) deletion heterozygote

18. If the garden pea has 14 chromosmes in its diplod complement, how many double trisomics could theoretically exist?
(a) 6 (b) 9
(c) 16 (d) 21

19. The condition in which there is one too many or one too few chromosomes is called
(a) aneuploidy (b) polytene
(c) polyploidy (d) monoploidy

20. Most cases of Down's syndrome are caused by the presence of a third copy of chromosome 21 associated with the chromosome 21 pair. This genetic condition, known as trisomy 21, is caused by
(a) a frame-shift mutation
(b) chromosome non-disjunction
(c) fragile X-syndrome
(d) chromosome translocation

21. People with Klinefelter's syndrome have 47 chromosomes, including three sex-chromosome (XXY). What is the term to describe the aberration that occurs during meiosis that results in abnormal chromosome number?
(a) Crossing-over
(b) Non-disjunction
(c) Independent assortment
(d) Pairing of homologous chromosome

22. Datura plants have been regerated from anther cultures, endosperm culture and embryo culture. Their respective ploidy levels will be
(a) n, $2n$ and $2n$ (b) n, $3n$ and $2n$
(c) n, $2n$ and $3n$ (d) $2n$, $2n$ and $2n$

23. Diagnosis of chromosome aneuploidy of unborn children is normally done by a combination of amniocentesis, cell culture, and
(a) enzyme assay (b) RFLP analysis
(c) pedigree analysis (d) karyotyping

24. The genes abcde are determined to be closely linked on the *E. coli* chromosomes. Three random short deletions are created in the region, resulting in the removal of various genes are shown below. Which of the following gene orders is possible based on the deletion analysis?
Deletion 1: Genes bde are lost
Deletion 2: Genes ac are lost
Deletion 3: Genes abd are lost
(a) abcde (b) acbed
(c) bdeac (d) cabde

25. Which statement about Down's syndrome is correct?
I. The frequency increases dramatically in mothers over the age of 40.
II. The cause is a non-disjunction when chromosomes do not separate during the first meiotic division.
III. Affected individuals have an extra autosome.
IV. The long time lag between onset of meiosis in ovarian tissue and its completion (at ovulation) is most likely the reason for increased incidence in older mothers.
(a) I and IV (b) I, II and III
(c) II, III and IV (d) I, II, III and IV

26. An individual with two normal sets of autosomes and a single X-chromosome has
(a) Down's syndrome (b) Patau's syndrome
(c) Turner's syndrome (d) Klinefelter's syndrome

27. An individual with the chromosomal description 45, X would be a
(a) normal female
(b) female with Turner's syndrome
(c) male with Klinefelter's syndrome
(d) cannot be determined

28. Which of the following statement is incorrect?
(a) The Luria-Delbruck fluctuation test was designed to differentiate between appearance of a trait due to random, spontaneous mutations *vs* appearance of the trait due to adaptation to environmental conditions
(b) A splice site mutation leading to loss of an exon can affect production of regions of the protein encoded in downstream exons even if they are spliced correctly
(c) Provided the number of base pairs is a multiple of three, insertion of additional DNA in the coding region of a protein is unlikely to have a dramatic effect on protein function
(d) DNA repair systems typically work in three major steps detection of the error, removal of the abnormality, and replacement of the removed DNA

29. Which of the following statement is correct?
(a) Chromosomal rearrangements are unlikely to produce an obvious phenotype, since they do not remove any DNA
(b) Mutational hot spots are sites in the DNA where a mutation is most likely to cause a change in protein structure
(c) Increasing environmental levels of mutagen is likely to lead to increasing frequency of deleterious alleles
(d) All of the above

30. Which statements about mutation are false?
(a) Mutations can happen at a rate of ~ 10^{-5}
(b) A change in the nucleotide sequence of a gene is a point mutation
(c) A change in the nucleotide sequence of a gene doesn't necessarily change the product of that gene
(d) Most of mutation are beneficial to the organisms that have them

31. Mutations which do not cause any functional change in the protein are known as
(a) non-sense mutations (b) mis-sense mutations
(c) backward mutations (d) silent mutations

32. A change in DNA that creates UAA codon at a site previously occupied by another codon, would result in one of the following mutations
(a) amber (b) ochre
(c) opal (d) polar

33. A single nucleotide pair is inserted near the 5′ end of a protein-coding DNA sequence. The most likely effect will be production of
(a) a protein with a single altered amino acid
(b) a protein with an almost completely altered sequence
(c) a greatly truncated protein
(d) no protein

34. A recessive mutation is one which
(a) is not expressed
(b) is expressed only when heterozygous
(c) is expressed only when homozygous or hemizygous
(d) is eliminated by natural selection

35. Thymine dimer formation during replication of DNA is caused due to
(a) gamma radiation (b) UV radiation
(c) X-rays (d) IR radiation

36. Which of the following processes would not contribute to genetic variation within a bacterial population?
(a) Transduction (b) Transformation
(c) Mutation (d) Meiosis

37. Spontaneous mutations
(a) are caused by chemicals such as acridine orange and caffeine
(b) are caused by physical agents such as UV light or X-rays
(c) are the result of errors in the base pairing of nucleotides during replication
(d) occur at a rate higher than the rate of induced mutations

38. A DNA mutation that results in no change in protein product produced is termed a
(a) mis-sense mutation (b) non-sense mutation
(c) silent mutation (d) frame-shift mutation

39. Which of the following changes to a DNA molecule is least likely to result in a deleterious mutation?
(a) Insertion of a transposable element in a coding region
(b) Deletion of a base pair in a coding region
(c) Change of a base pair in the first codon of a coding region
(d) Change of the third base pair of a codon

40. Mutations often occur as a result of base substitutions. The most common cause of base substitutions is
(a) tautomeric shifts (b) meiotic errors
(c) base insertions (d) base deletions

41. A tautomeric shift causing the substitution of one purine for a pyrimidine is called
(a) transversion (b) translocation
(c) transition (d) inversion

42. When a mutational event leads to the replacement of one codon for another coding for the same amino acid, the resulting mutation is known as
(a) frame-shift (b) neutral
(c) mis-sense (d) silent

43. When bacteria are spread on a plate containing an antibiotic, colonies of resistant bacteria appear on the plate. The Darwinian explanation for this is that
(a) the antibiotic induced the resistance
(b) resistant cells pre-existed in the population and were selected by the antibiotic
(c) no genetic change is required to exhibit antibiotic resistance
(d) the antibiotic is mutagenic

44. Using site directed mutagenesis four mutant of a protein have been generated. Which of the following missense mutations has the largest difference in terms of number of atoms between the wild type and the mutant?
(a) Ser to Cys (b) Tyr to Phe
(c) Lys to Ala (d) Arg to Lys

45. Which of the following is most likely to lead to a loss of gene function?
(a) A missense mutation in the open reading frame
(b) A change from T to C in the promoter region
(c) A frameshift mutation in the coding region
(d) A sequence change in the 3′ untranslated region

46. A bacterial protein coding gene contains a terminator codon in the middle of the coding region, yet expression of the gene in the bacterium produces a functional protein. Translation of the gene probably requires
(a) the excision of an intron
(b) a suppressor *t*RNA
(c) ribosomes that lack 5 S RNA
(d) an *m*RNA with no ribosome binding site

47. In a bacterial cell, mutation in an aminoacyl *t*RNA synthetase leads to charging of the entire *t*RNA^{ser} population with alanine. Which of the following describes the result of using these aminoacyl *t*RNAs for protein synthesis in the cell
(a) proteins synthesized using the alanyl *t*RNA^{ser} will contain neither alanine nor serine
(b) proteins synthesized using the alanyl *t*RNA^{ser} only serine where alanine would normally occur
(c) proteins synthesized using the alanyl *t*RNA^{ser} contain only alanine where serine would normally occur
(d) proteins synthesized using the alanyl *t*RNA^{ser} will randomly contain either alanine or serine where serine would normally occur

48. In genetics, suppression of a mutation refers to
(a) restoration of the original phenotype due to a second mutation
(b) restoration of the original DNA sequence by mutation
(c) prevention of expression of the mutant gene by metabolic regulation
(d) appearance of the recessive phenotype in a heterozygous diploid

49. A protein that is normally localized to the nucleus has been mutated in such a way that its localization is no longer nuclear, but cytosolic instead. The function of the protein however is 99% of the wild type protein. Which of the following could be said about the mutation?
(a) It is a frame-shift mutation
(b) It is a non-sense mutation
(c) It is a silent mutation
(d) It is a small deletion

50. Mutation is the change in
(a) gene frequency
(b) base pairs in the DNA
(c) genetic drift
(d) environmental mechanism of evolution

51. Which of the following chemical mutagen is likely to cause GC .... AT transitions?
(a) 5-bromouracil (b) 2-aminopurine
(c) acridine orange (d) hydroxylamine

52. Sites where mutations occur at rates higher than normal are known as
(a) suppressor sites (b) hotspots
(c) mutator sites (d) cistrons

53. If GUG codon is used as a starting codon then it codes for
(a) valine (b) cysteine
(c) methionine (d) leusine

54. 5-bromouracil can cause a transitional mutation in the base sequences of DNA because it
(a) bonds irreversibly with A
(b) may resemble C and bond with G
(c) is analog of T and pairs with A
(d) resembles U and would not be incorporated into DNA

55. Deamination of 5-methyl cystosine leads to the formation of
(a) thymine (b) uracil
(c) cytosine (d) hydroxymethyl cytosine

56. Mutations that are expressed only under certain environmental conditions are called
(a) transposition (b) conjugation
(c) recombination (d) conditional mutations

57. The ames test is a mass screening approach used for the detection of
(a) toxins (b) mutagenic carcinogens
(c) lactose intolerance (d) phenylketonuria

58. A chemical that resembles one of the bases and can mistakenly get incorporated into DNA/RNA is called
(a) deoxyribonucleotide (b) ribonucleotide
(c) base analog (d) nitrogen base

59. With respect to the wild type strain, a silent mutant will have
(a) same genotype and phenotype
(b) same genotype but different phenotype
(c) different genotype but same phenotype
(d) different genotype and different phenotype

60. A method to detect two mutations are located on the same gene or different genes is
(a) generalized transduction
(b) complementation analysis
(c) Hfr mapping
(d) karyotyping

61. Transposons
(a) insert into DNA by homologous recombination
(b) cannot be transferred by phage mediated transduction
(c) contain the equivalent of insertion (IS) elements
(d) can insert into plasmids but not the bacterial chromosome

62. Which one of the following statements about retrotransposons is not correct?
(a) They are mobile genetic elements residing in the genomes of all classes of organisms
(b) They are transposons that behave much like retroviruses and have a retroviruses and have a retrovirus like structure
(c) The reverse transcriptase makes a cDNA copy of the retrotransposon
(d) The retrotransposon RNA is packed into virus particles

63. L1 elements
I. are part of the viral super family of retro-transposons.
II. are found in 20000 to 50000 copies per mammalian genome.
III. are approximately 300 nucleotides in length.
IV. contain an open reading frame with homology to reverse transcriptase.
(a) I and II (b) I and IV
(c) II and IV (d) I, II and III

64. Movement of a segement of DNA from one site of the genome to another is called
(a) mutation (b) cleavage
(c) reversion (d) transposition

65. All of the following are true about transposition except
(a) transposons move from one location to a different one within a chromosome
(b) both the donor and target sites must be homologous
(c) transposon has insertion sequences that are recognized by transposases
(d) the transposon may either be excised and moved, or be replicated with the replicated piece moving

66. Which of the following are genes found in all retroviruses?
I. gag II. pol
III. env IV. onc
(a) I and II (b) I and IV
(c) III and IV (d) I, II and III

67. IS element
I. are all identical.
II. encode proteins required for transposition.
III. are flanked by direct repeats.
IV. cause a duplication of host DNA upon integration.
(a) I and II (b) I and IV
(c) I, III and IV (d) II, III and IV

68. The Alu element found in the human genome is
(a) a 7SL RNA homologue
(b) a good RNA polymerase III template
(c) about 300 bp long repeat
(d) All of the above

69. Alu elements
(a) are part of the viral family of retro-transposons
(b) are found in 20000 to 50000 copies per mammalian genome
(c) are approximately 300 nucleotides in length
(d) are transcribed

70. All of the following statements regarding genetic recombination events are correct except
(a) site specific recombination is characterized by an exchange between two identical DNA sequence
(b) the processes of transformation and transduction require extensive homology between the interacting sequences
(c) DNA replication is required for genetic recombination to occur
(d) during genetic recombination events, the DNA molecules are broken and then rejoined

71. Branch migration of a holiday junction is necessary to extend the repair/recombination segment into homoduplex regions of the interacting duplex strands. The migration is achieved by
(a) the ATP-hydrolysis-dependent activity of the RecA protein
(b) the ATP-hydrolytic action of the RuvAB helicase complex
(c) the activity of the RecBCD protein complex
(d) the tension in the DNA molecule caused by coiling

72. Gene conversion is observed when
(a) during meiosis, one molecule is placed by another allele
(b) during meiosis, the expected 2:2 ratio of alleles is replaced with a 4:0 ratio
(c) during meiosis, the expected 2:2 ratio of alleles is replaced with a 3:1 ratio
(d) All of the above

73. Which of the following describes the key difference between simple transposition and replicative transposition?
(a) In simple transposition, transposase catalyzes the removal and reintegration of the transposon, while transposase is not involved in replicative transposition
(b) In simple transposition, a double stranded piece of DNA is moved from one site to another, while in replicative transposition a single strand is moved, leaving a single strand behind
(c) Simple transposition requires DNA synthesis while replicative transposition does not
(d) Replicative transposition requires DNA synthesis while simple transposition does not

74. Which of the following chromosomal alterations does not alter genic balance but may alter phenotype because of differences in gene expression?
(a) Deletion (b) Inversion
(c) Duplication (d) Non-disjunction

75. The genetic event that results in Turner syndrome (XO) is probably
(a) non-disjunction (b) deletion
(c) parental imprinting (d) monoploidy

76. Given below is a representation of a kind of chromosomal mutation. What is the kind of mutation represented?

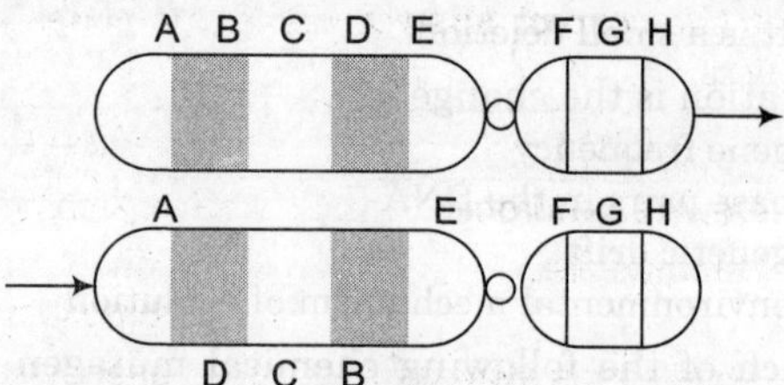

(a) Deletion (b) Duplication
(c) Inversion (d) Reciprocal translocation

77. Match list I (type of chromosomal aberration) with list II (designation) and select the correct answer using the codes given below the lists.

List I	List II
A. One chromosome pair extra to the normal complement (2n + 2)	1. Trisomic
B. One chromosome extra to the normal complement (2n + 1)	2. Monosomic
C. One chromosome less than the normal complement (2n – 1)	3. Tetrasomic
D. One chromosome pair less than the normal complement (2n – 2)	4. Nullisomic

Codes

	A	B	C	D
(a)	2	4	3	1
(b)	1	3	2	4
(c)	3	1	4	2
(d)	3	1	2	4

78. Match list I (chromosome aberrations) with list II (consequences) and select the correct answer using the codes given below the lists.

List I	List II
A. Intercalary deficiency	1. Chromosome ring formation at metaphase
B. Duplication	2. Bridge and fragment
C. Paracentric inversion	3. Change in gene order
D. Translocation	4. Two breaks followed by reunion and deletion

Codes

	A	B	C	D
(a)	4	3	2	1
(b)	4	3	1	2
(c)	3	4	1	2
(d)	3	4	2	1

79. Consider the following diseases/syndromes.

I. Huntington's chorea
II. Galactosemia
III. Duchenne muscular dystrophy
IV. Phenylketonuria

Those attribute to recessive mutations in human beings include.

(a) I, II and III (b) II, III and IV
(c) II and IV (d) I and III

80. Match list I (syndrome) with list II (chromosomes) and select the correct answer using the codes given below the lists.

List I	List II
A. Down's syndrome	1. Lack of X-chromosome (XO)
B. Haemophilia	2. Addition of X-chromosome (XXY)
C. Klinefelter's syndrome	3. Homogenestisic acid oxidase
D. Turner's syndrome	4. Trisomy of a chromosome

Codes

	A	B	C	D
(a)	4	3	2	1
(b)	4	3	1	2
(c)	2	4	1	3
(d)	2	4	3	1

81. Match list I (Human hereditary condition) with list II (Enzyme lost or dificient) and select the correct answer using the codes given below the lists.

List I	List II
A. Alkaptonuria	1. β-D-N acetyl hexasominidase A
B. Huntington's chorea	2. Glutamine acid decarboxylase
C. Cretinism	3. Homogentisic acid oxidase
D. Tay-Sachs disease	4. Iodotyrosine deiodinase

Codes

	A	B	C	D
(a)	1	4	2	3
(b)	1	2	4	3
(c)	3	4	2	1
(d)	3	2	4	1

Answers

1. (a)	**2.** (d)	**3.** (c)	**4.** (b)	**5.** (d)	**6.** (d)	**7.** (d)	**8.** (c)	**9.** (b)	**10.** (c)
11. (c)	**12.** (b)	**13.** (a)	**14.** (a)	**15.** (a)	**16.** (d)	**17.** (c)	**18.** (d)	**19.** (a)	**20.** (b)
21. (b)	**22.** (b)	**23.** (d)	**24.** (d)	**25.** (d)	**26.** (c)	**27.** (b)	**28.** (c)	**29.** (c)	**30.** (d)
31. (d)	**32.** (b)	**33.** (b)	**34.** (c)	**35.** (b)	**36.** (d)	**37.** (c)	**38.** (c)	**39.** (d)	**40.** (a)
41. (a)	**42.** (d)	**43.** (b)	**44.** (c)	**45.** (c)	**46.** (b)	**47.** (c)	**48.** (a)	**49.** (d)	**50.** (b)
51. (d)	**52.** (b)	**53.** (c)	**54.** (c)	**55.** (a)	**56.** (d)	**57.** (b)	**58.** (c)	**59.** (c)	**60.** (b)
61. (c)	**62.** (d)	**63.** (c)	**64.** (d)	**65.** (b)	**66.** (d)	**67.** (d)	**68.** (d)	**69.** (c)	**70.** (c)
71. (b)	**72.** (c)	**73.** (b)	**74.** (b)	**75.** (a)	**76.** (c)	**77.** (d)	**78.** (a)	**79.** (b)	**80.** (a)
81. (d)									

27

Classification of Livings

Principles and Methods of Taxonomy

The classification of the organism on the basis of their specialization is the conern of the biological sub-science named taxonomy or systematics. According to **G Simpson** (1961) systematics is the study of diversity of organisms and all their comparative and evolutionary relationships, are asked on comparative anatomy, comparative ecology, comparative physiology and comparative biochemistry. He regards, classification as a sub-topic of systematics that deals with ordering of organisms into groups and taxonomy as the study of principles and procedures of classification.

Histology of Classification

Classifying plants and animals into various groups is an ancient practices and can be traced back to Vedic era, in which almost 730 plants and 250 animals were subjected to various categories based on various characteristics. Greek scholors **Hippocratus** (460-377 BC) and **Aristotle** (387-322 BC) arranged animals into four major groups like insects, birds, fishes and whales. Aristotle is regarded as first taxonomist and he sub-divided plants and animals based on their habitats. **John Ray** first used Latin language for writing names of organisms. **Theophrastus** (370-285 BC), Father of Botany, classified plants on the basis of their habitats, forms and textures into four categories—tree, shrubs, undershrubs and herbs. He gives description of 480 plants in his book **Historia Generalis Plantarum.** **Carolus Linnaeus** (1707-78) a Swedish naturalist, often referred to as Father of Taxonomy developed the scientific system of naming species. It is known as binomial system of nomenclature. Linnaeus described 5900 species of plants in his book **Systema Naturae** (1735). From Aristotle to Linnaeus, every one considered only limited features in the classification. Studies of ribosomal RNA have led systematics to the conclusion that all life shares a common ancestor that these are three major evolutionary lineage called domains. As a result, diverse living organism in nature were placed into limited number of groups. This phase

Syllabus

- Principles and Methods of Taxonomy: Concepts of Species and Hierarchial Taxa, Biological Nomenclature.
- Levels of Structural Organization: Unicellular, Colonial and Multicellular Forms; Levels of Organization of Tissues, Organs and Systems; Comparative Anatomy.
- Outline Classification of Plants and Animals.

of taxonome is known as artificial system of classification. Later the organisms were classified on the basis of natural affinities. This phase represents the classical taxonomy and constitutes the natural system of classification. A modified form of natural system of classification is Phenatics (Numerical Taxonomy) emerged. Since, 1950 it employs numerical methods for the evaluation of similarities and differences between the species. All characters considered for analysis are given equal importance and weightage. This system of classification is considered better because it uses large number of comparable characters to assign a place to the species.

Simultaneoulsy another system of classification emerged in which taxonomic position of organisms were assigned on the basis of its evolutionary as well as genetic relationship. This system of classification are termed as phylogenetic classification or cladistics. This system led to the emergence of new systematics or Biosystematics. Father of new systematics is **Sir Julian Huxley** (1940). Diagram showing how organisms are related based on shared, derived characteristics such as feathers, hairs or scales are known as **cladogram.** The phylogenetic tree is also known as genealogical tree or dendrogram.

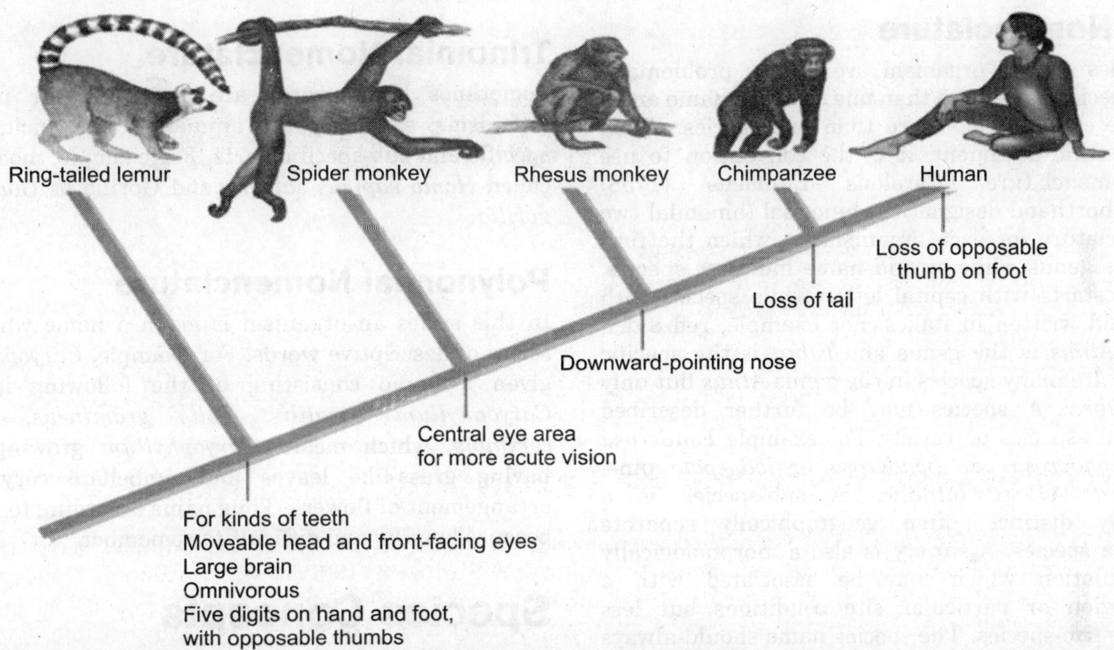

Fig. 27.1 Primate cladogram

Studies of homologous structures, comparative embryology, sequence analyses in DNA, RNA and amino acid sequences forms the basis of today's modern taxonomy. The improved tools and techniques for classification resulted in developement of new branches of systematics, such as cytotaxonomy, chemotaxonomy or biochemical taxonomy. The **cytotaxonomy** is based on the cytological information on cell, chromosomal number, and behaviour of chromosomes during meiosis. **Chemotaxonomy** or **biochemical taxonomy** is based on serology, molecular biology, comparative study of DNA sequence, chemical nature of protein, chemical constituent of plant species. **Phenetic classification** is based on overall similarities of organisms evaluated without regard to phylogeny.

Dichotomous keying used to identify organisms in which characteristics are given in pairs. Various characteristics have been read and if not matched then next key is followed.

Biological Nomenclature

Taxonomy or systematics includes following fundamental elements:

Nomenclature is assigning of name to organisms.

Classification deals with mode of arranging organisms into categories according to systematics plan such as kingdom, phylum, class, order, family, genus and species. Each category is a unit and also termed as taxon.

Identification This implies assigning taxonomic position of an organism based on similarity with already say A, B, C. All represents different species. The findings of a species D which resembles A. The identification of species D as identical to the already known species A is its identification.

Two type of name have been assigned to organism. Common and scientific.

Common or Vernacular Names

These names given to the organisms in a particular language and based on region and some pecularities of the world. These name changes with change in language and region of the world. For example the bird Indian sparrow is known as Gauraiyaa (Hindi), house sparrow (English), Pardal (Spain) and Suzune (Jaoan).

Scientific Names

This includes following practices of providing names to the organism.

Binomial Nomenclature

Common names of any organism are always problematic since, many species have more than one common name and a common name can describe more than one species. When writing a scientific document, it is the convention to use binomial nomenclature. Carolous Linnaeus (1758) introduced a shorthand designation, binomial (binomial two name) nomenclature for each organism, in which the first name indicates genus while second name indicates species. Genus always starts with capital letter while species with small letter and written in italics. For example, red alder, *Alnus rubra; Alnus* is the genus and *rubra* is the specific epithet. There are many species in the genus *Alnus* but only one *Alnus rubra.* A species may be further described according to sub-species or variety. For example *Ponderosa* pine, *Pinus ponderosa var. ponderosa* or *lodgepole* pine, *Pinus contorta* sub-sp. *latifolia.* A sub-species is a morphologically distinct, often geographically separate population of a species. A variety is also a morphologically different population which may be associated with a geographic region or particular site conditions but less distinct than a sub-species. The species name should always be used in conjunction with common names so that anyone reading the document can know exactly which species you are referencing.

Rules of Binomial Nomenclature

The rules for binomial nomenclature are framed and standardized by the following five codes of nomenclature:

International Codes of Botanical Nomenclature (ICBN)

International Codes of Zoological Nomenclature (ICZN)

International Codes of Bacteriological Nomenclature (ICBN)

International Code of Viral Nomenclature (ICVN)

International Codes of Cultivated Plants Nomenclature (ICCPN)

(a) The rules for writing scientific name are as follows:

(b) Each organisms is provided with one scientific name, consisting of two words, generic and specific.

(c) The same generic name cannot be given to different organisms domains. Three domains being, botanical, zoological and bacteriological.

(d) The same specific name can be given to organisms belonging to different genera. However, two species belonging to same genus cannot have same specific names.

(e) The genetic name is written first followed by specific name and then the name of discoverer in full or in abbreviation, *e.g., Homo sapiens* L. or *Homo sapiens* Linnaeus.

(f) The specific name starts with a small letter except when it is based after a place or person.

(g) The scientific name is printed in italics. It is underlined in hand written description, *e.g., Mangifera indica.*

(h) When a species is transferred or revised, the name of the original worker is retained but in parenthesis, *e.g., Syzygium cumini* (L.) Skeels.

Trinomial Nomenclature

Sometimes three words are also used for naming the organisms, especially the animals. These include generic, specific and sub-specific parts. For example, modern man is called *Homo sapiens sapiens* and Gorilla as *Gorilla gorilla gorilla.*

Polynomial Nomenclature

In this series an organism is given a name which include series of descriptive words. For example, *Caryophyllum* was given a name consisting of the following latin words *Caryophyllum saxatilis, Folis gramineus, Umbellatis corymbis,* which means *Caryophyllum* growing on rocks having grass-like leaves and umbellate corymb means arrangement of flowers. Thus name according to this system because lengthy and difficult to remember.

Species Concepts

Species is the fundamental or smallest unit of classification. The term species was recognized from genus by **John Ray. Ernst Mayr** defined species as. A group of potentially inter-breeding natural populations of closely resembling organisms. **Carolus Linnaeus** proposed **static concept of species** or **morphological concept** of species. He considered species as a **fixed and immutable** entity.

1. **Dynamic concept of species** was proposed by **Lamarck,** who considered species as a **mutable** and **dynamic** entity.
2. **Biological concept of species** was proposed by **Ernst Mayr.** According to this concept, a species is a group of individuals who resemble each other in morphological, physiological biochemical and behavioural characters and capable in interbreeding.
3. **Morphospecies** are the species erected on the basis of morphological characters only.
4. **Taxonomic species** are the species having a binomial name.
5. **Sibling species** are true species, which do not interbreed but are otherwise difficult to separate on the basis of morphological characters alone.

6. **Allopatric species** are species having exclusive areas of geographical distribution.
7. **Sympatric species** are species having overlapping areas of geographical distribution.
8. **Parapatric species** are species with adjacent geographic ranges meeting in a very narrow zone of overlap.
9. **Neontological species** are living species.
10. **Allochronic species** are species belonging to different time periods.
11. **Polytypic species** are species, which have more than one ideal types according to their geographical isolated areas.
12. **Linnaean species** is a taxonomic species distinguished on morphological grounds.
13. **Biospecies** is a species erected on the basis of reproductive and genetic isolation of a natural population.
14. **Macrospecies** is a large polymorphic species with several sub-divisions.
15. **Microspecies** or **Jordan's species** is a true breeding genetic unit below the rank of species.
16. **Agamospecies** is a species reproducing only asexually, *e.g., Euglena* and *Amoeba.*
17. **Gamospecies** are sexually reproducing species.
18. **Palaeospecies** are species known from fossils only.
19. **Monotypic species** are species without differentiation of sub-species or varieties.
20. **Keystone species** is a species that plays a key role or central role in the ecology of a place.
21. Mule, Hinny, Tigon and Linger are **exception to biological species concept. Mule** is the offspring of male donkey and female horse and **hinny** is the offspring of female donkey and male horse. Both Mule and Hinny are sterile. **Tigon** is the offspring of male tiger and female lion and **linger** is of female tiger and male lion. Both tigon and linger are fertile.
22. **Synchronic species** are species belonging to a same period or time.

Types of Specimen

Holotype	Nomenclature type
Isotype	Duplicate of holotype
Paratype	Any other specimen described along with holotype
Syntype	Any one of the two or more specimens cited by author, when there is no holotype
Lectotype	Specimen selected from original material to serve as nomenclature type, where there is no holotype
Neotype	New nomenclatural type, when the original material is missing.
Topotype	A specimen collected from the same locality from which the holotype was originally collected.

Taxonomic Hierarchy

It is the grouping of the species into higher categories on the basis of their similarities and dissimilarities, complexity and simplicity and hence, evolutionary relationships.

Species

It is the basic unit of classification. It is a group of individuals which are alike in morphological and reproductive characters so that they are able to interbreed freely and produce fertile offspring.

Genus

A group of species having common characteristics is called genus. It is first higher category above the species level.

Family

Family is a group of several genera which exhibit a number of characteristics among them.

Order

A group of families which share a number of common characteristics. The family–Felidae (Lion, leopard, tiger, cats) and Canidae (Dog, wolf, fox) are included in the same order Carnivora.

Class

A group of related orders is class. For example, all the insects are included in class–Insecta. They are characterized by the presence of three pairs of jointed legs and trachea. Simililarly, members of class–Aves (birds) are characterized by the presence of feathers which are modified forelimbs.

Phylum

Classes having atleast a few characters in coomoon, collectively constitute a phylum. For example, *Nereis, Pheretima* and *Hirudinaria* belong to different classes but have been grouped in a single phylum–Annelida.

Kingdom

It is the highest category in taxonomic system and includes phyla (or Divisions in plants) which are related atleast in one character. Linnaeus system of classification includes only two kingdoms–Animalia and Plantae. But Whittaker's system of classification includes five kingdoms–Monera, Protista, Fungi, Plantae and Animalia.

Taxon

Taxon is a unit of classification which may represent any level of grouping of organisms. The term was introduced by ICBN (International Code of Botanical Nomenclature) during 1956. Mayr (1964) has defined taxon to be a taxonomic group of any rank that is sufficiently distinct to be worthy of being assigned to a definite category. Simpson (1961) recognizes taxon to be a group of real organisms recognized as a formal unit at any level of hierarchical classification.

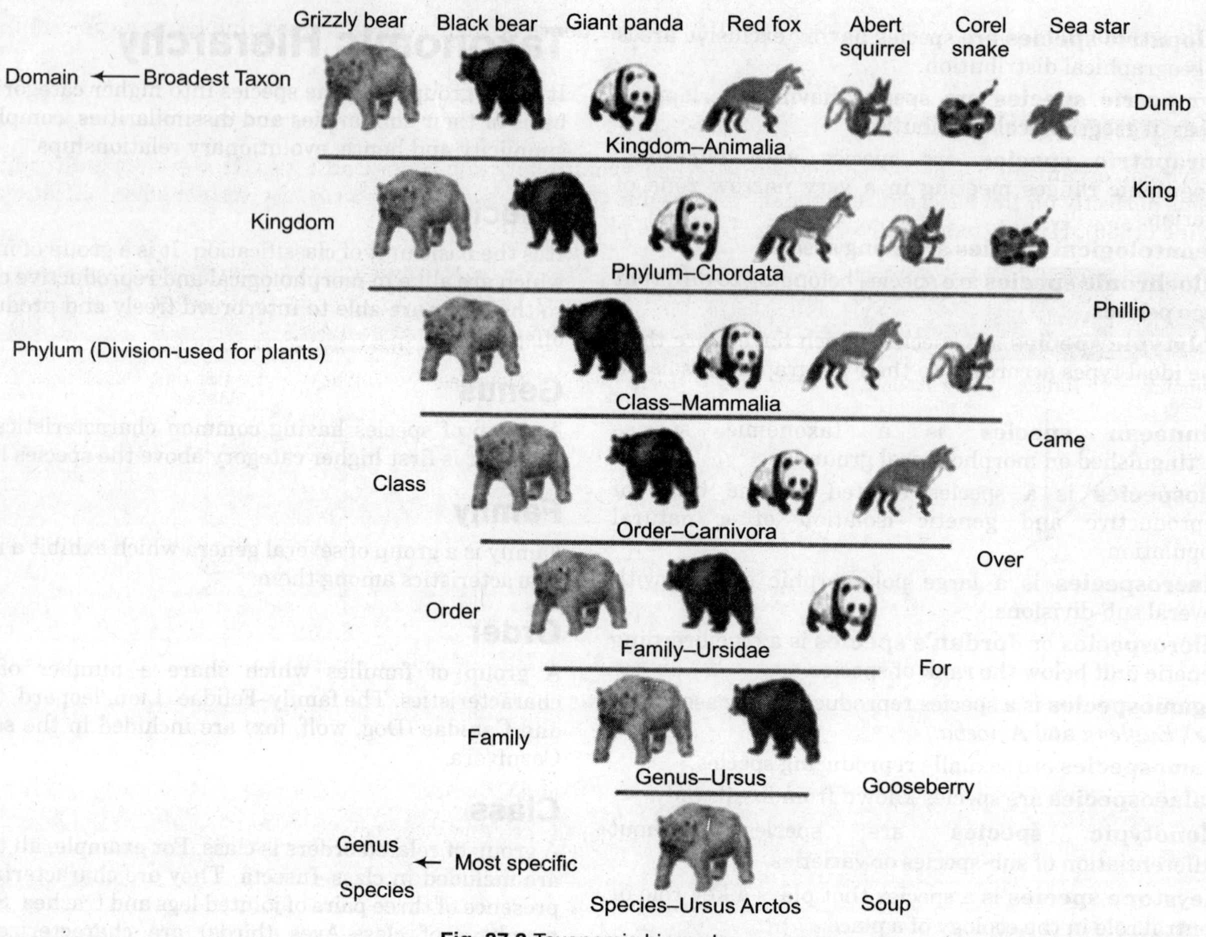

Fig. 27.2 Taxonomic hierarchy

Classification

There are three systems of classification:
1. Artificial system of classification
2. Natural system of classification
3. Phylogenetic system of classification

Artificial System

In this system of classification, only one or almost a few characters are selected arbitarily and the organisms are classified into groups on the basis of these characters.

The System of classification was first given by Pliny **the Elder (28-29AD)** in his book Historia naturalis. He divided the organisms on the basis of habit and habitat. **Linnaeus system of classification** is also an artificial system. It is commonly known as sexual system as it is based on numerical strength of sex organs. The following are the drawbacks of artificial system:

(i) The organisms which have close affinities get separated into different groups, *e.g.*, bat, whale and rat.

(ii) The organisms which have different affinities get placed together in a single group. For example, Pliny distinguished animals into flight and non-flight. So birds, bats and insects are placed under the same group though they have quite different affinities.

(iii) There is no distinct evolutionary line. In some characters they may be more advanced than their relatives while in some others they may be primitive.

(iv) The characters, which are chosen in artificial system of classification, may change with change in environmental conditions, *e.g.*, change in annual and biennial habit of radish, broad and small leaves.

Natural System

This system takes into consideration all the important characters and the organisms are classified according to their related characters. The most well known natural system of classification is **Bentham** and **Hooker's** system of classification. Natural system of classification has following advantages over artificial system:

(i) It brings about natural relationships amongst organisms.

(ii) Only closely related organisms are placed in the same group.

(iii) The organisms on the basis of their resemblances and differences are first classified into few big groups. Then these groups are further divided and subdivided into smaller groups untill the smallest division, *i.e.*, species. So, this system gives an idea about the identification of unknown organisms.

(iv) The system indicates phylogenetic relationship, *i.e.*, sequence of their evolution from simpler to more complex forms of life.

Phylogenetic System

In this system, organisms are classified according to their evolutionary and genetic affinities. However, it is difficult to classify organisms perfectly on the basis of evolutionary history due to incomplete fossil records, the system of classifications proposed by **Engler** (1886), **Hutchinson** (1926), **Tippo** (1942) are phylogenetic.

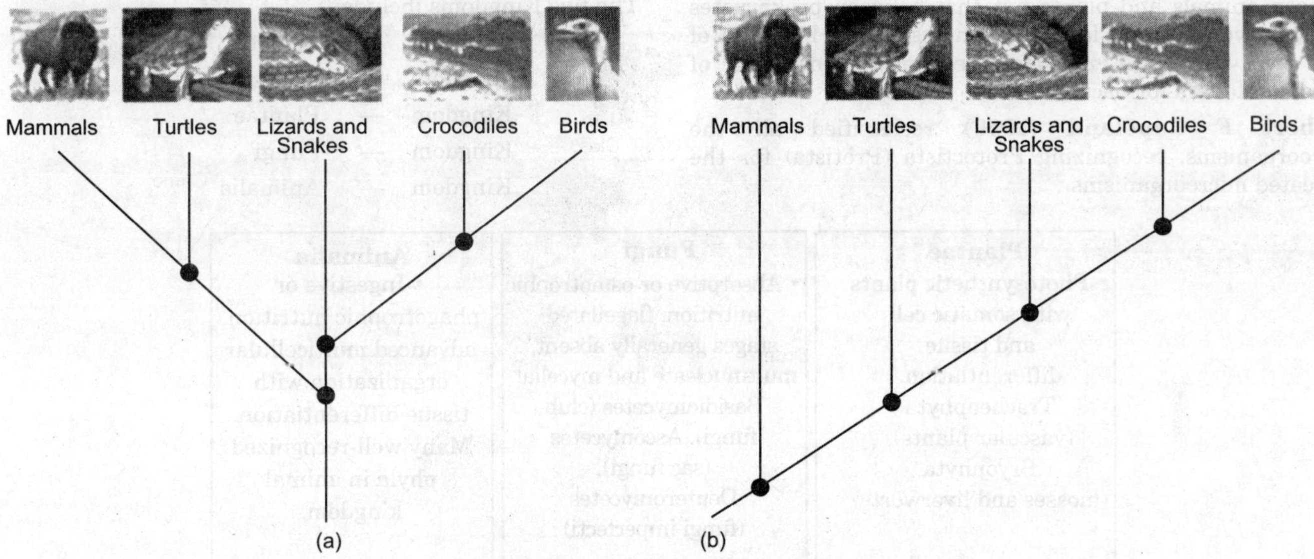

Fig. 27.3 (a) Phylogenetic tree (b) Cladogram

The Two Kingdoms Classification

Carolus Linnaeus, AL de Jussieu and **GL Cuvier** established the two kingdom classification, they named these kingdom as **Plantae** (including all plants) and **Animalia** (including all animals).

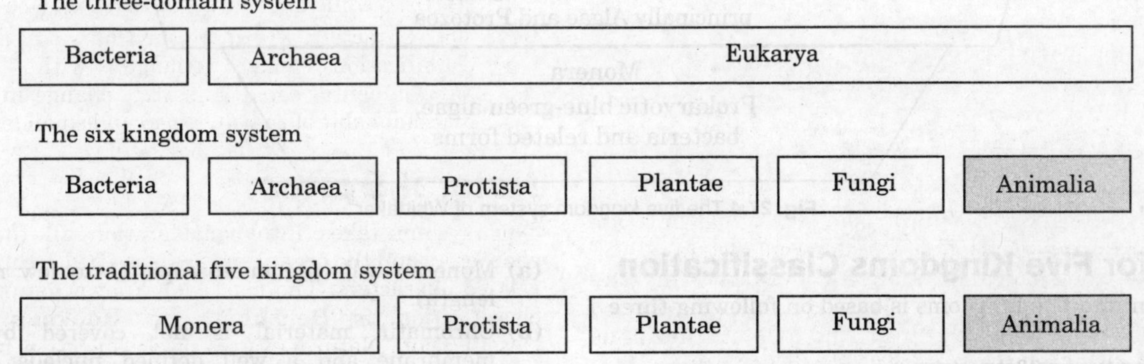

Two kingdom system of classification has been discarded due to certain limitations as given below:

(i) Fungi have certain special features of their own, they resembles plants as well as animals. They lack chlorophyll and are heterotrophic, the character which belongs to animals. But they possess cell wall and show holophytic mode of nutrition like the plants. They are immobile and have spend out appearance, the features again similar to the plants.

(ii) At the lower level of organizaion, distinction between plants and animals disappears. For example, *Euglena* has both holophytic and holozoic nutrition. Sponges are branched, fixed and irregular in outline like plants. Unicellular algae like *Chlamydomonas* are mobile possess regular shape and photosensitive organelles.

(iii) In two kingdom classification as proposed by Linnaeus, all the prokaryotes are studied under kingdom–Plantae. With the advent of electron microscopy, viruses and prokaryotes have become no relation with plants, yet they are studied under botany.

(iv) Lichens are not given an appropiate place in Linnaeus classification. Lichens represents an example of symbiotic relationship between algae and fungi. They have neither any plant character, or any animal character.

In the view of above mentioned taxonomic difficulties, during the past 50 years, biologists have recognized that most fundamental distinction among groups of organisms is not between animals and plants but that between prokaryotes and eukaryotes. Bacteria have been assigned a kingdom of their own, Monera. **Ernst Haeckel** was the innovator of kingdom Monera for bacteria.

Herbert F Copeland (1956) reclassified all the microorganisms, recognizing Protoctista (Protista) for the nucleated microorganisms.

Robert H Whittaker (1969) founded the five kingdom system recognizing kingdom–Fungi.

Five Kingdoms of Life

A new five kingdom system of classification was introduced by **Whittaker** in 1969 to replace old two kingdoms classification

The five Kingdoms include:

Kingdom — Monera
Kingdom — Protista
Kingdom — Plantae
Kingdom — Fungi
Kingdom — Animalia

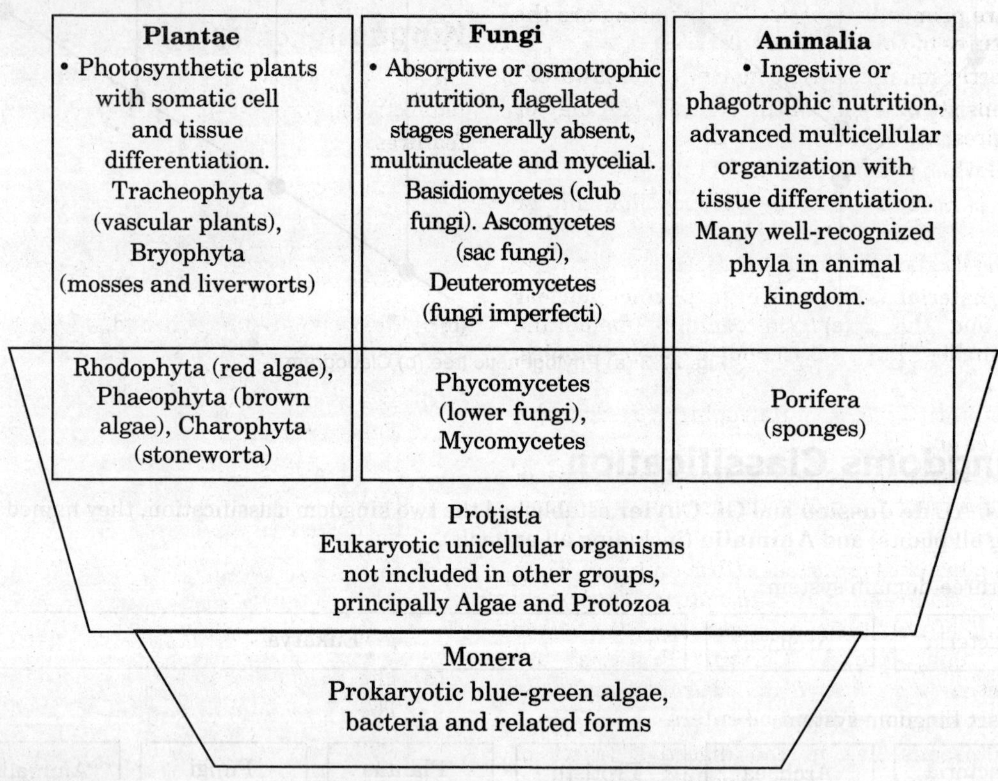

Fig. 27.4 The five kingdom system of Whittaker

Criteria for Five Kingdoms Classification

Classification into five kingdoms is based on following three criteria:

(a) Complexity of cell structure
(b) Complexity of organism's body
(c) Mode of nutrition.

Kingdom–Monera

This kingdom includes all prokaryotes, *e.g.,* bacteria, blue-green algae (cyanobacteria) and (Actinomycetes) filamentous algae. Following are the characteristics features of the kingdom–Monera

(a) Moneran cells are microscopic (1 to few microns in length).
(b) Chromatin material is not covered by nuclear membrane and a well defined nucleus is absent. Nucleus is called nucleoid or genophore.
(c) The membrane bound organelles are absent in the cell.
(d) A rigid cell wall containing mucopolysaccharides is present. Cell wall lacks cellulose.
(e) Moneran nutrition is varied, some are autotrophic, while others are heterotrophic. Heterotrophic monerans include saprobes as well as parasites. These act monerans include saprobes as well as parasites. These act as decomposers and breakdown complex organic matter into simpler ones.

(f) Some bacteria and cyanobacteria live as symbiont in higher plants. They convert free nitrogen and ammonia into nitrates and increases the soil fertility. For example, *Anabena* lives as symbiont in the leaves of a fern *Azolla*.

(g) Archaebacteria (ancient bacteria) live under drastic conditions, where no other life is possible. They are able to survive even in the absence of oxygen, high salt concentration and at high temperature (80°C) or acidic pH. **Archebacteria** are considered to be the first form of life which appeared on Earth when the conditions on Earth were not quite fit for life.

Kingdom–Protista

This kingdom includes unicellular eukaryotes. The members of this kingdom are primarily aquatic. The following are the characteristic features of this kingdom:

(a) They are mostly aquatic, may be marine or freshwater.

(b) The body consists of a single cell. The cell wall may or may not be present.

(c) The cell wall when present consists of cellulose.

(d) Locomotion is brought about by pseudopodia, cilia or flagella.

(e) Cilia and flagella show 9+2 organization.

(f) Chromatin material is covered by a distinct nuclear membrane and the cytoplasm contains membrane bound organelles like mitochondria, Golgi bodies, plastids.

(g) Some of the protistians are autotrophic, *e.g.,* diatoms, dinoflagellates and algae.

(h) Some of the protistians show heterotrophic mode of nutrition. They show ingestive (holozoic) or saprozoic mode of nutrition.

(i) This kingdom includes protozoans (first animals). They lack cell wall and are predatory in nature. They show holozoic mode of nutrition and ingest the food by the process of phagocytosis. Certain Protozoa are photosynthetic, *e.g., Euglena, Paramecium* has ingestive tract through which food enters.

(j) Certain protozoans live in the digestive tracts of cockroach and termite and helps in cellulose digestion.

Kingdom–Plantae

This kingdom includes multicellular eukaryotic plants. Their characteristic feature is the presence of photosynthetic pigments. These include chlorophyll, xanthophyll, carotene, fucoxanthin, etc., this kingdom includes:

Plants are characterized by the following features

(a) Plants are usually terrestrial, *i.e.,* fixed in the soil. However, they may grow in water as well.

(b) Immobility of plants is due to the presence of rigid cell wall which makes the cells inelastic.

(c) Most of the plants show tissue and organ level of organization.

(d) The plants do not respond sharply to the given stimulus as they lack nerve cells.

(e) Most of the plants are photosynthetic due to the presence of green pigment chlorophyll which is capable of trapping solar energy. They prepare organic food in the presence of sunlight with CO_2 and water as raw materials.

(f) Some higher plants show special mode of nutrition. Orchids are saprophytic. A few of them occur as total root parasite, *e.g., Orobanche* and total stem parasite, *e.g., Cuscuta*.

(g) Some higher plants are insectivorous, *i.e.,* they obtain their nutrients from insects. These plants generally grow in nitrogen deficit soil. In these plants, leaves are modified to various shapes so as to attract the insects. Insects are digested extracellularly by enzymes, *e.g., Drosera, Utricularia, Nepenthes* (Pitcher plant).

Kingdom–Fungi

This kingdom includes multicellular, eukaryotic, heterotrophic organisms. The following are the characteristic features:

(a) The body is composed of a large number of branched or unbranched tubular structures which are called hyphae. The hyphae form a sort of network and collectively constitute mycelium.

(b) Chlorophyll is absent and, hence they are not able to photosynthesize.

(c) The mode of nutrition is heterotrophic and absorptive. The hyphae of the fungus secretes digestive enzymes in the extracellular medium where complex organic matter is degraded into simpler ones and then absorbed in the form of solution.

(d) Fungi may obtain food from living organisms. These are called as parasite. They may also obtain food from dead organic matter and then called as saprobes.

(e) The fungal cell wall is composed of fungus cellulose. The basic unit of fungus cellulose is N-acetyl glucosamine.

(f) Hyphae of fungi (Oomycetes and Zygomycetes) are multinucleate and without any cross wall. Such a condition is called coenocytic.

(g) A large number of fungi live as parasites on plants and animals. These cause diseases like mildew, smut, rusts, leaf spots, stem rot and root rot in plants.

(h) Some fungi (generally the members of Ascomycetes) form symbiotic association with algae. Such associations are called as lichens.

(i) Mushrooms and puff balls represent the reproductive structures of some fungi. They grow on dead organic matter such as humus, logs of wood, etc.

(j) Yeasts are unicellular and casue fermentation of sugar. They are unique from other fungi which are multicellular. Because of their unicellularity, they are generally confused with protistans. They reproduce by binary fission and hence, called as fission fungi.

Kingdom–Animalia

Kingdom–Animalia includes all multicellular eukaryotic animals. This kingdom is divided into two sub-kingdoms-Chordata and Non-Chordata. Chordata is further divided into two lower chordates and vertebrate (Fishes, amphibians, reptiles, birds and mammals). Non-Chordata includes nine phylum–Porifera (Sponges), Coelentrates (cnidarians), Platyhelminthes (Flatworms), Nematodes (Round worm), Annelida (segmented worms), Arthropoda (jointed legged animals), molluscs, echinodermates (the spiny skinned animals). There are characterized by following features:

(a) The animals possess contractile muscle cell due to absence of rigid cell wall. So, they are able to move freely from one place to another. Sponges lack contractile muscle cells and, hence they are sessile.

(b) Due to the presence of nerve cells, animals show coordinated movements and quick response to given stimuli.

(c) They show organ-system level of organization. Organ systems are internal.

(d) Mode of nutrition is heterotrophic and generally holozoic (ingestive). Some parasitic forms are also present.

Table 27.1 **Characteristics of the Five Kingdoms**

Characteristic	Kingdom				
	Monera	Protista	Fungi	Plantae	Animalia
Cell type	Prokaryotic (cells lacking distinct membrane-bound nuclei)	Eukaryotic (cells containing membrane-bound nuclei)	Eukaryotic (cells containing membrane-bound nuclei)	Eukaryotic (cells containing membrane-bound nuclei)	Eukaryotic (thick cell wall)
Body form	Most unicellular; some colonial	Most unicellular; some simple multicellular	Most multicellular	Multicellular	Multicellular; organs and organ systems
Cell wall composition	Polysaccharides and amino acids	Present in some composition varies	Usually chitin	Cellulose	No cell wall
Mode of nutrition	Photosynthesis, chemosynthesis absorption	Photosynthesis, ingestion or absorption	Absorption	Photosynthesis	Ingestion
Nervous system	Absent	Absent	Absent	Absent	Present
Locomotion	Present in some	Present in some	Absent	Absent	Present

Advantages of Whittaker's Five Kingdoms Classification

(a) Separation of prokaryotes and eukaryotes is distinctly visible. Prokaryotes are grouped under kingdom–Monera whereas, eukaryotes are further sub-divided into four.

(b) The organisms which were intermediates between plants and animals, such as *Euglena*, are given proper place. They have been grouped under kingdom–Protista.

(c) Fungi are also not placed with plants. They have there own unique properties. So they are placed in a separate kingdom.

(d) The system is more natural than two kingdoms system as it shows sequential development and evolution of complex formed from simpler ones.

(e) The five kingdoms classification is based on complexity of cell structures, complexity of body organization and mode of nutrition. These factors are more fundamental than differences between plants and animals which is the basis of two kingdoms classification.

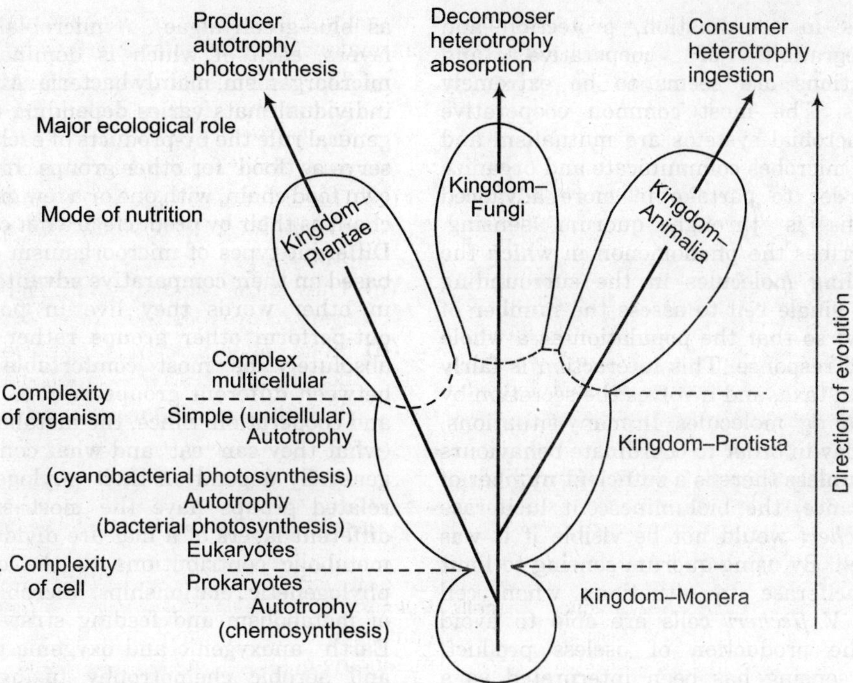

Fig. 27.5 Five kingdoms of life with divergence in modes of nutrition and morphological complexity

Drawbacks of Five Kingdom Classification

(a) A distinction between unicellular and multicellular organisms is not possible in case of algae.

(b) Each group has a large diversity. Kingdom–Monera includes both autotrophic and heterotrophic, photosynthetic and chemosynthetic, walled and wall-less organisms.

(c) Viruses have not been given proper place in this system of classification.

Six Kingdom Classification

This is the most recent classification prposed by **C Woese, O Kandler** and **ML Wheelis** in 1990. They proposed that all organisms be divided into three major groups called domains above kingdom level eukarya, bacteria and archaea. In Woese's system, the domain eukarya includes four of the six kingdoms–protists, fungi, plants and animals. After comparing the base sequences of 16 S *m*RNA from a variety of organisms, **Woese, Kandler** and **Wheelis** proposed that bacteria should be divided into two kingdoms–Eubacteria and Archaebacteria. This scheme is currently accepted by many biologists.

Virus

Viruses represent a typical group of organisms which cannot be called **prokaryotes** or **eukaryotes.** They are non-living but yet they are capable of replication. They are basically the fragments of nucleic acids enclosed in a protein envelope.

Viruses which infect the bacterial cells are known as bacteriophages. Double stranded DNA bacteriophages are very important in relation to molecular biology. Viruses are regarded as connecting link between living and non-living. Viruses have been variously defined as 'non-cellular organism' border line systems of twilight zone between living and non-living systems or matter at a level of organization at which an inert system can arouse to life and become an organisms.

Levels of Structural Organization

Unicellular Organism

A unicellular organism is a complete living entity consisting of just one cell. That cell could die in which case the organism is dead. Or it may divide into two parts, each part being a new individual and a copy of the original. Single-cell organisms, such as bacteria and Protozoa, have been so successful in adapting to a variety of different environment that they comprise more than half of the total biomass on Earth. Unlike animals, many of these unicellular organisms can synthesize all of the substances they need from a few simple nutrients, and some of them divide more than once every hour.

Colonial Organism

A colonial organism is a collection of one-celled organisms living together. Colonial behaviour is quite unique to microbes and it helps in coordination, protection and communication. Integration of cooperative and communicative interactions are seems to be extremely important to microbes. The most common cooperative interactions seen in microbial systems are mutualism and altruism. One way that microbes communicate and organize with each other in order to partake in more advanced cooperative interactions is through quorum sensing. **Quorum sensing** describes the phenomenon in which the accumulation of signaling molecules in the surrounding environment enables a single cell to assess the number of individuals (cell density) so that the population as a whole can make a coordinated response. This interaction is fairly common among bacterial taxa, and involves the secretion by individual cells of 'signaling' molecules. In many situations, the cost bacterial cells pay in order to coordinate behaviours outweighs the benefits unless there is a sufficient number of collaborators. For instance, the bioluminescent luciferase produced by *Vibrio fischeri* would not be visible if it was produced by a single cell. By using quorum sensing to limit the production of luciferase to situations when cell populations are large, *V. fischeri* cells are able to avoid wasting energy on the production of useless product. Interestingly, quorum sensing has been interpreted as a bacterial communication system to coordinate behaviours at the population level. The opportunistic bacteria *Pseudomonas aeruginosa* also uses quorum sensing to coordinate the formation of biofilms, swarming motility, exopolysaccharide production, and cell aggregation. These bacteria can grow within a host without harming it, until they reach a certain concentration. Then they become aggressive, their numbers sufficient to overcome the host's immune system, and form a biofilm, leading to disease within the host. Biofilm formation occurs when free floating microorganisms attach themselves to a surface. They secrete extracellular polymers that provide a structural matrix and facilitate adhesion. Because biofilms protect the bacteria, they are often more resistant to traditional antimicrobial treatments, making them a serious health risk. For example, there are more than one million cases of Catheter-Associated Urinary Tract Infections (CAUTI) reported each year, many of which can be attributed to biofilm-associated bacteria. Formation of a biofilm on a substratum are rather complex, but can be generalized in four basic steps deposition of the conditioning film, microbial (planktonic) attachment to the conditioning film, growth and bacterial colonization and finally biofilm formation.

A microbial mat is a multi-layered sheet of microorganisms, mainly bacteria and archaea. Microbial mats grow at interfaces between different types of material, mostly on submerged or moist surfaces but a few survive in deserts. They colonize environments ranging in temperature from 40°C to +120°C. A few are found as endosymbionts of animals. The best known physical forms are flat mats and stubby pillars called stromatolites, but there are also spherical forms. Stromatolites provide some of the most ancient records of life on Earth and are layered accretionary structures formed in shallow water by the trapping, binding and cementation of sedimentary grains by biofilms of microorganisms, especially cyanobacteria (commonly known as blue-green algae). A microbial mat consists of several layers, each of which is dominated by specific types of microorganism, mainly bacteria. Although the composition of individual mats varies depending on the environment, as a general rule the by-products of each group of microorganisms serve as 'food' for other groups. In effect each mat forms its own food chain, with one or a few groups at the top of the food chain as their by products are not consumed by other groups. Different types of microorganism dominate different layers based on their comparative advantage for living in that layer, in other words they live in positions, where they can out-perform other groups rather than where they would absolutely be most comfortable ecological relationships between different groups are a combination of competition and cooperation. Since, the metabolic capabilities of bacteria (what they can 'eat' and what conditions they can tolerate) generally depend on their phylogeny (*i.e.,* the most closely related groups have the most similar metabolisms), the different layers of a mat are divided both by their different metabolic contributions to the community and by their phylogenetic relationships. Microbial mats use all of the types of metabolism and feeding strategy that have evolved on Earth anoxygenic and oxygenic photosynthesis; anaerobic and aerobic chemotrophy (using chemicals rather than sunshine as a source of energy); organic and inorganic respiration and fermentation (*i.e.,* converting food into energy with and without using oxygen in the process); autotrophy (producing food from inorganic compounds) and heterotrophy (producing food only from organic compounds, by some combination of predation and detritivory).

There is a growing interest in the application of microbial mat and phototrophic biofilms for instance in wastewater treatment in constructed wetlands, bioremediation, aquaculture and biohydrogen production. Interestingly choanoflagellates which are the free-living unicellular eukaryotes, show colonial behaviour and considered to be the closest living relatives of the animals.

Multicellular Organism

Multicellular organisms consist of differentiated cells that perform special tasks. The entire organism requires all the different types of cells to be present, and the individual cells cannot survive without being in the organism. The Ediacara biota are the earliest widely accepted evidence of multicellular 'animals'. The difference between a multicellular organism and a colonial organism is that individual organisms from a colony can, if separated, survive on their own, while cells from a multicellular life-form (*e.g.,* cells from a brain) cannot.

The evolution of multicellularity life forms is proposed to be arisen as a result of cooperation behaviour among single cells. This idea, often referred to as the Colonial Theory, was first proposed by **Haeckel** in 1874, and claims that the symbiosis of many organisms of the same species (unlike the symbiotic theory, which suggests the symbiosis of different species) led to a multicellular organism. In a few instances, multicellularity occurs by cells separating and then rejoining (*e.g.,* cellular slime molds) whereas for the majority of multicellular types, multicellularity occurs as a consequence of cells failing to separate following division. The mechanism of this latter colony formation can be as simple as incomplete cytokinesis, though multicellularity is also typically considered to involve cellular differentiation. The advantage of the colonial Theory hypothesis is that it has been seen to occur independently numerous times. For instance, during food shortages *Dictyostelium discoideum* cells group together in a colony that moves as one to a new location. Some of these cells then slightly differentiate from each other. However, it can often be hard to separate colonial protists from true multicellular organisms, as the two concepts are not distinct. This problem plagues most hypotheses of how multicellularization could have occurred. However, most scientists accept that multicellular organisms, from all phyla, evolved by the colonial mechanism.

In the case of multicellular organisms like human body, various levels of structural organization are found, which are listed below.

(i) **Chemical** Atoms combine to form molecule.

(ii) **Organelle** All cells of humans and other complex organisms contain structures.

(iii) **Cells** The smallest units of all living things.

(iv) **Tissues** Consists of groups of similar cells that have a common function.

(v) **Organ** A structure that is composed of two or more tissue types and performs a specific function for the body.

(vi) **Organ system** A group of organs that cooperate to accomplish a common purpose.

(vii) **Organism** Represents the highest level of structural organizatin.

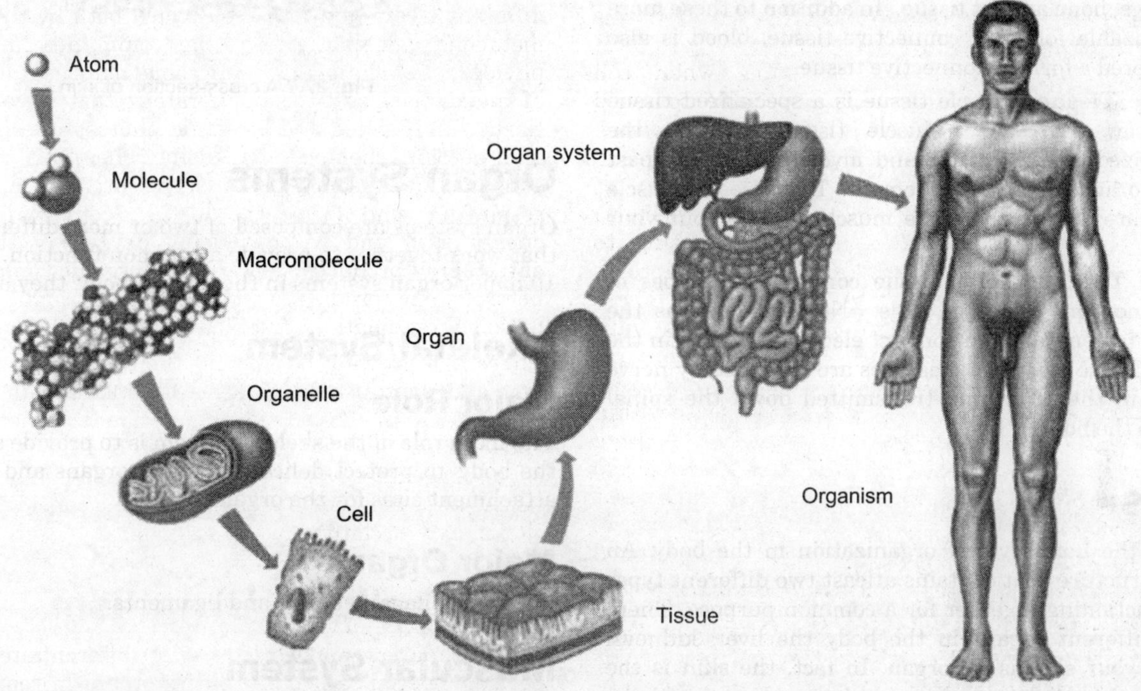

Fig. 27.6 Levels of organization

Levels of structural organization in the human body can be compared to the written language tools which we commonly used in daily life.

(a) **The chemical level and letters** Atoms and molecules can be compared to letters of the alphabet.

(b) **The cellular level and words** Cells, the smallest living units in the human body can be compared with words, the smallest elements of language.

(c) **The tissue level and sentences** Cells join together to form tissues similar to the way words are put together to form sentences.

(d) **The organ level and paragraphs** Tissues join together to form organs similar to the way sentences are put together to form paragraphs.

(e) **The system level and chapters** Organs join together to form systems similar to the way paragraphs are put together to form chapters.

(f) **The organism level and books** Systems join together to form an organism similar to the way chapters are put together to form a book.

There are many different types of cells in the human body. None of these cells function well on there own, they are part of the larger organism that is called you.

Tissues

Cells group together in the body to form tissues a collection of similar cells that group together to perform a specialized function. There are four primary tissue types in the human body epithelial tissue, connective tissue, muscle tissue and nerve tissue.

(i) **Epithelial Tissue** The cells of epithelial tissue pack tightly together and form continuous sheets that serve as linings in different parts of the body. Epithelial tissue serve as membranes lining organs and helping to keep the body's, organs separate, in place and protected. Some examples of epithelial tissue are the outer layer of the skin, the inside of the mouth and stomach and the tissue surrounding the body's organs.

(ii) **Connective Tissue** There are many types of connective tissue in the body. Generally speaking, connective tissue adds support and structure to the body. Most types of connective tissue contain fibrous strands of the protein collagen that add strength to connective tissue. Some examples of connective tissue include the inner layers of skin, tendons, ligaments, cartilage, bone and fat tissue. In addition to these more recognizable forms of connective tissue, blood is also considered a form of connective tissue.

(iii) **Muscle Tissue** Muscle tissue is a specialized tissue that can contract. Muscle tissue contains the specialized proteins actin and myosin that slide past one another and allow movement. Examples of muscle tissue are contained in the muscles throughout your body.

(iv) **Nerve Tissue** Nerve tissue contains two types of cells—neurons and glial cells. Nerve tissue has the ability to generate and conduct electrical signals in the body. These electrical messages are managed by nerve tissue in the brain and transmitted down the spinal cord to the body.

Organs

Organs are the next level of organization in the body. An organ is a structure that contains atleast two different types of tissue functioning together for a common purpose. There are many different organs in the body the liver, kidneys, heart, even your skin is an organ. In fact, the skin is the largest organ in the human body and provides us with an excellent example for explanation purposes. The skin is composed of three layers—the **epidermis, dermis** and **subcutaneous layer.** The epidermis is the outermost layer of skin. It consists of epithelial tissue in which the cells are tightly packed together providing a barrier between the inside of the body and the outside world. Below the epidermis lies a layer of connective tissue called the dermis. In addition to providing support for the skin, the dermis has many other purposes. The dermis contains blood vessels that nourish skin cells. It contains nerve tissue that provides feeling in the skin. And it contains muscle tissue that is responsible for giving you 'goosebumps' when you get cold or frightened. The subcutaneous layer is beneath the dermis and consists mainly of a type of connective tissue called adipose tissue. Adipose tissue is more commonly known as fat and it helps cushion the skin and provide protection from cold temperatures.

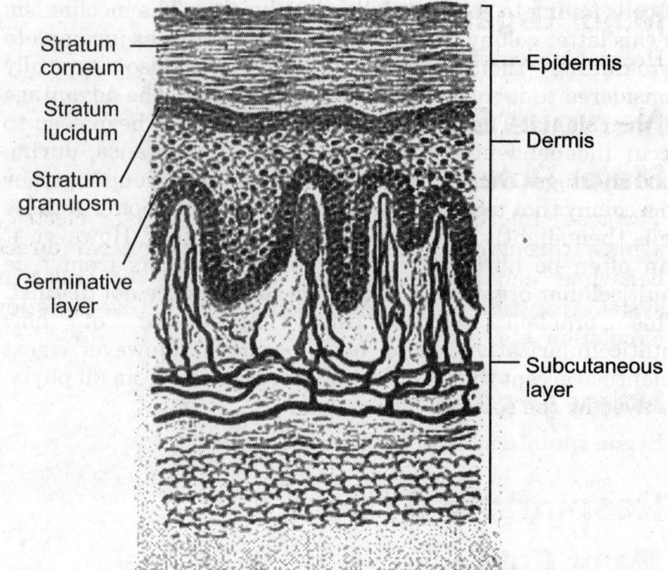

Fig. 27.7 A cross-section of skin

Organ Systems

Organ systems are composed of two or more different organs that work together to provide a common function. There are 10 major organ systems in the human body, they are the:

Skeletal System

Major Role

The main role of the skeletal system is to provide support for the body, to protect delicate internal organs and to provide attachment sites for the organs.

Major Organs

Bones, cartilage, tendons and ligaments.

Muscular System

Major Role

The main role of the muscular system is to provide movement. Muscles work in pairs to move limbs and provide the organism with mobility. Muscles also control the movement of materials through some organs, such as the stomach and intestine, and the heart and circulatory system.

Major Organs

Skeletal muscles and smooth muscles throughout the body.

Circulatory System

Major Role

The main role of the circulatory system is to transport nutrients, gases (such as O_2 and CO_2), hormones and wastes through the body.

Major Organs

Heart, blood vessels and blood.

Nervous System

Major Role

The main role of the nervous system is to relay electrical signals through the body. The nervous system directs behaviour and movement and, along with the endocrine system, controls physiological processes such as digestion, circulation, etc.

Major Organs

Brain, spinal cord and peripheral nerves.

Respiratory System

Major Role

The main role of the respiratory system is to provide gas exchange between the blood and the environment. Primarily, oxygen is absorbed from the atmosphere into the body and carbon dioxide is expelled from the body.

Major Organs

Nose, trachea and lungs.

Digestive System

Major Role

The main role of the digestive system is to breakdown and absorb nutrients that are necessary for growth and maintenance.

Major Organs

Mouth, oesophagus, stomach, small and large intestines.

Excretory System

Major Role

The main role of the excretory system is to filter out cellular wastes, toxins and excess water or nutrients from the circulatory system.

Major Organs

Kidneys, ureters, bladder and urethra.

Endocrine System

Major Role

The main role of the endocrine system is to relay chemical messages through the body. In conjunction with the nervous system, these chemical messages help control physiological processes such as nutrient absorption, growth, etc.

Major Organs

Many glands exist in the body that secrete endocrine hormones. Among these are the hypothalamus, pituitary, thyroid, pancreas and adrenal glands.

Reproductive System

Major Role

The main role of the reproductive system is to manufacture cells that allow reproduction. In the male, sperm are created to inseminate egg cells produced in the female.

Major Organs

Female (top) ovaries, oviducts, uterus, vagina and mammary glands. **Male** (bottom) testes, seminal vesicles and penis.

Lymphatic/Immune System

Major Role

The main role of the immune system is to destroy and remove invading microbes and viruses from the body. The lymphatic system also removes fat and excess fluids from the blood.

Major Organs

Lymph, lymph nodes and vessels, white blood cells, T and B-cells.

Comparative Anatomy

Comparative vertebrate anatomy is the study of structure, of the function of structure, and of the range of variation in structure and function among vertebrates. Comparative anatomy, but to be more accurately comparative morphology, deals with the study of parts and structure (forms) and the corresponding function of these forms of bodies of vertebrates. It is both descriptive and analytical and it also deals with the study of natural history. Comparative studies also deal with species of animals which no longer inhabit the Earth and are known to us by fossils records. Comparative studies are performed by comparing structures throws similarities and differences. It emphasizes the evolutionary and functional themes vertebrates possess within their innate structures. It also helps in formulating the questions we might ask in future also.

Comparative anatomy is closely related to evolutionary biology and phylogeny (the evolution of species). Comparative anatomy has long served as evidence for evolution, it indicates that various organisms share a common ancestor. Also, it assists scientists in classifying organisms based on similar characteristics of their anatomical structures. Comparative anatomy supports Darwin's theory of descent with modification, also known as evolution. A common example of comparative anatomy is the similar bone structures in forelimbs of cats, whales, bats and humans. All of these appendages consist of the same basic parts; yet, they serve completely different functions. The skeletal parts which form a structure used for swimming, such as a fin, would not be ideal to form a wing, which is better-suited for flight. One explanation for the forelimbs' similar composition is descent with modification. Through random mutations and natural selection anatomical structures gradually became better-adapted to the every organism's respective habitat.

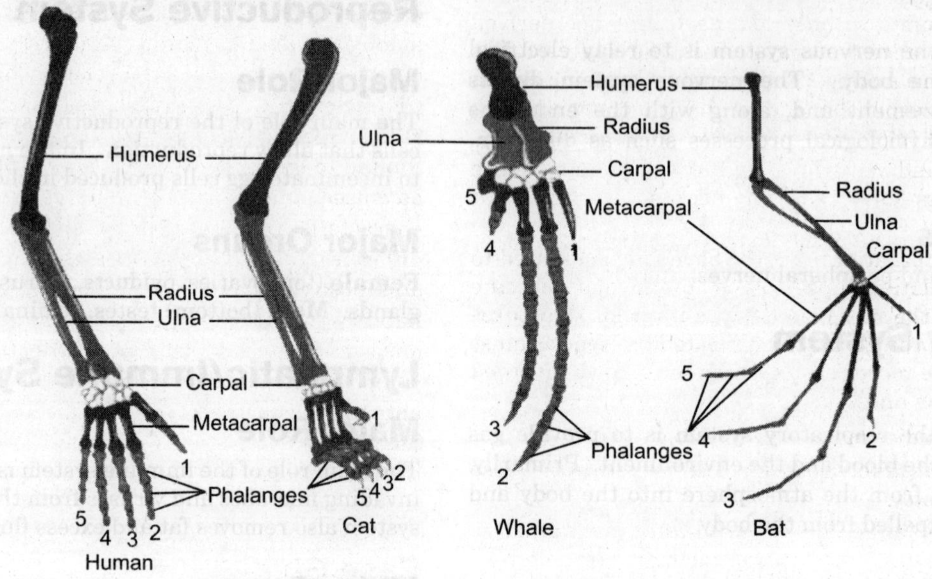

Fig. 27.8 Comparative forelimb anatomy in four mammals

The uses of comparative studies in taxonomy and allied sciences can be traced to the work associated with Linnaeus, Lamarck, cuvier, Owen (concept of homology and analogy and described the evolutionary evidence by obtaining and describing about *Archaeopteryx*), L Ag assiz (first teacher of comparative anatomy), Darwin(established the evolutionary basis, comparative, functional and adaptive morphology and anatomy), Wallace, Huxley (Published comparative anatomy of vertebrates in 1871).

Born in 1517 Pierre Belon was a French naturalist who did research and held discussions on dolphin embryos as well as the comparisons between the skeletons of birds to the skeletons of humans. His research led to what is referred to as modern comparative anatomy. **Edward Tyson** is regarded as the founder of comparative anatomy. He is credited with determining that marine mammals are, in fact, mammals. Also, he concluded that chimpanzees are more similar to humans than to monkeys because of their arms.

Marco Aurelio Severino also compared various animals, including birds, in his Zootomia democritaea, one of the first works of comparative anatomy. In the 18th and 19th century, great anatomists like George Cuvier, Richard Owen and **Thomas Henry Huxley** revolutionized our understanding of the basic build and systematics of vertebrates, laying the foundation for **Charles Darwins** work on evolution. An example of a 20th-century comparative anatomist is **Victor Negus,** who worked on the structure and evolution of the larynx. Until the advent of genetic techniques like DNA sequencing, comparative anatomy together with embryology were the primary tools for understanding phylogeny, as exemplified by the work of Alfred Romer.

Two major concepts of comparative anatomy are

1. **Homologous structures** structures (body parts/anatomy) which are similar in different species because the species have common descent. They may or may not perform the same function. An example is the forelimb structure shared by cats and whales.
2. **Analogous structures** structures similar in different organisms because they evolved in a similar environment, rather than were inherited from a recent common ancestor. They usually serve the same or similar purposes. An example is the streamlined torpedo body shape of porpoises and sharks. So, even though they evolved from different ancestors, porpoises and sharks developed analogous structures as a result of their evolution in the same aquatic environment.

The rules for development of special characteristics which differ significantly from general homology were listed by **Karl Ernst von Baer** (the Baer laws).

Uses of Comparative Studies

(i) Comparative anatomy provides structural evidence of evolution

(ii) Appearance has long been used as an indicator of the relatedness of organisms. Structure, inexorably tied to function, and also provides evidence of descent with modification. The elephant and the mammoth, for instance, clearly have similar anatomies and share a common ancestor.

(iii) Unrelated species in similar environments have evolved similar forms.

(iv) Evolution by natural selection also predicts that, given similar environmental demands, unrelated species might independently evolve superficially similar structures, a process called convergent evolution. Such outwardly similar body parts in unrelated organisms, termed analogous structures, may be very different in internal anatomy, because the parts are not derived from common ancestral structures. The wings of flies and of birds are analogous structures that have arisen by convergent evolution; the fat-insulated, streamlined shapes of seals (mammals) and of penguins (birds).

(v) Homologous and vestigial structures provide evidence of relatedness of organism adapted to different environments.

(vi) Studies of comparative anatomy have long been used to determine relationships among organisms, on the grounds that the more similar the internal structures of two species, the more closely related the species must be; that is, the more recently they must have diverged from a common ancestor.

Any comparative studies make seven basic points.

(a) If things look alike, it is because they have a close common ancestor.

(b) If things look alike, but clearly can't have a close common ancestor, the environment made different things evolve to look alike (convergent evolution).

(c) Things that look the same (for example, forelimbs) can have different functions.

(d) God would not have used the same less than optimal bone arrangement for different functions.

(e) One would expect evolution to jury-rig the same bone arrangement for different functions, and they would function less than optimally.

(f) Natural selection has the power to change the function of structures.

(g) Comparative anatomy can be used to determine how closely species are related.

Notice that if things are similar, it is evidence of evolution. It shows they have a common origin. But, if things are different, it is evidence of evolution. It shows that they have changed over time. Since, similarity is evidence of evolution, and difference is evidence of evolution, everything is evidence of evolution.

To conclude, study of comparative anatomy entails examining the morphology of various anatomical structures among species and nothing similarities and differences, in an effort to establish a relationship between species. Characteristics that are shared among a large number of similar species generally are viewed as ancestral, while those limited to one or few species are viewed as derived (or more advanced or specialized). The comparison of a variety of characteristics possessed by similar species allows us to differentiate between species that are truly closely related and those that have converged in appearance owing to similar habitats. Characteristics that show evidence of common ancestry are called homologous features. Those that have similar function but appear to be derived from differing ancestral characters are called homoplastic features. Sometimes structures that were used in an ancestor lose their use in more modern forms. We refer to these reduced structures as vestigial.

Case Studied

The typical characteristics representative of vertebrates involve notochord (atleast in the embryo); pharynx with pouches or slits in wall (atleast in the embryo); dorsal, hollow nervous system; vertebral column. Notochord is a kind of rod of living cells ventral to central nervous system and dorsal to alimentary canal. Comparative studies have revealed that in fishes and amphibians this notochord persists the length of the trunk and tail but is constricted within the centrum of each vertebra, while in reptiles, birds and mammals, notochod almost disappears duing development (*e.g.*, remains as a pulpy nucleus in the vertebrae of mammals). Interestingly in protochordates, notochord remain as the chief axial skeleton.

Outline Classification of Plants and Animals

There are more than 1.7 to 1.8 million species of living organisms described and several more to be discovered yet. All living organisms vary considerably in their form structure and mode of life. During the past 3.5 billion years on earth many living species has become extinct and still many have evolved. Linnaeus classified all the living organisms into kingdom–Plantae and Animalia but later many biologist classified living organisms by various ways. The most accepted model is five kingdom system proposed by Whittaker (1969).

Classification of Plants

Eichler (1883) classified plants (Kingdom–Plantae) into **cryptogamae** and **Phanerogamae.** Cryptogams were seedless and flowerless plants reproducing by spores, while phanerogams are flowering and seed bearing plants (also called Spermatophyta). The Cryptogamae was further divided into Thallophyta (Algae, fungi) Bryophyta and Pteridophyta while phanerogams were divided into Gymnospermae and Angiospermae.

Oswald Tippo (1942) classified plants on the basis or presence of absence of vascular tissue (Xylem and phloem) and presence or absence of embryo in life cycle. The brief outline is **(ahead):**

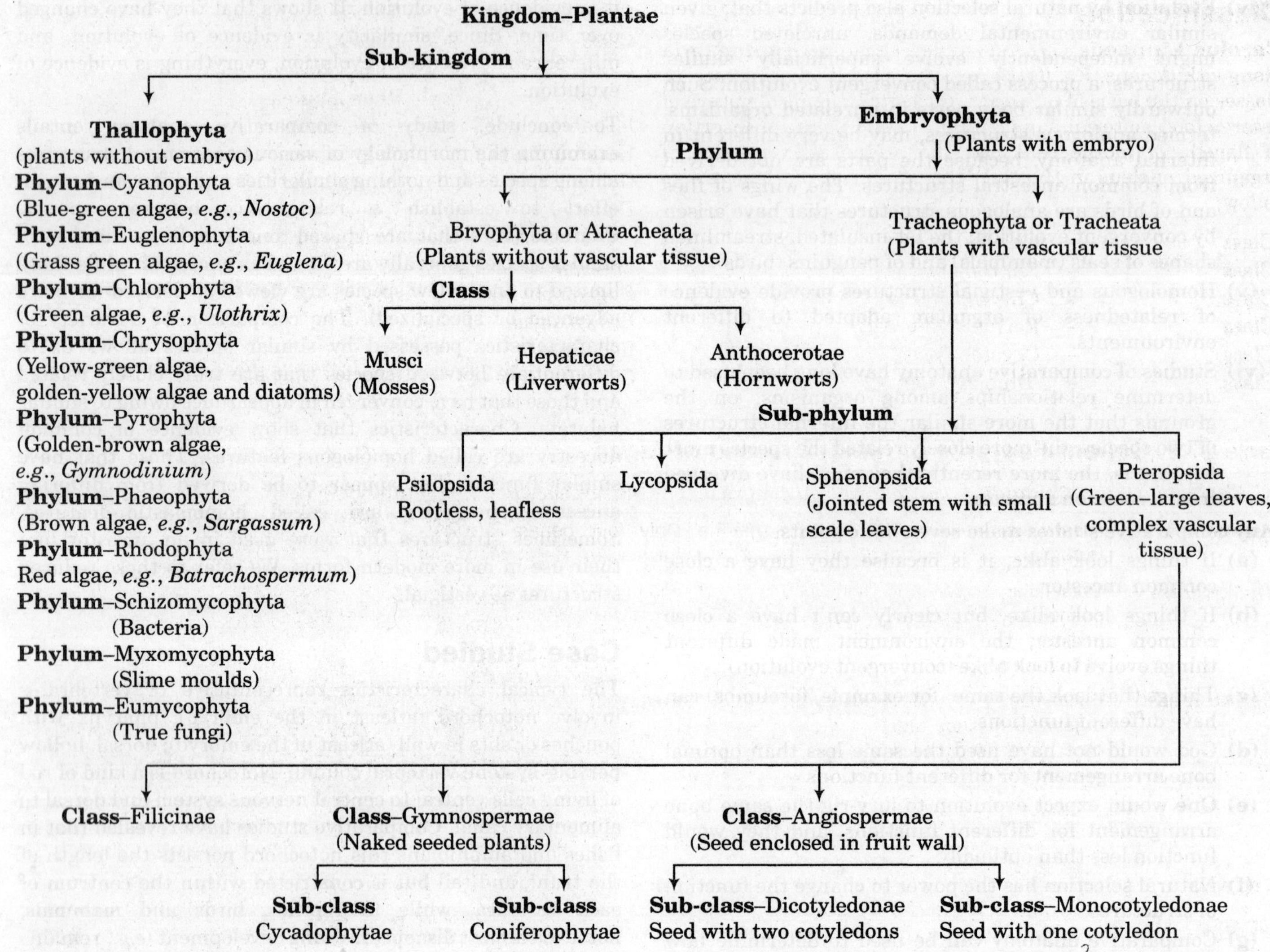

Thallophyta

Thallophytes are the plants which lack true roots, stems and leaves. Algae and fungi both have long been grouped together in **Thallophyta** because of the following features:

1. Presence of thallus-like, non-vascular plant body.
2. Presence of simple, unicellular, non-jacketed sex organs.
3. No embryo development after gametic union.

Algae

Algae are a group of chlorophyll bearing, photosynthetic, autotrophic, thalloid plants whose body is not differentiated into true roots, stems and leaves. The study of algae is called **Phycology** (*Phycos* – algae; *Logos* – study).

The term 'algae' was first used by Linnaeus (1755).

MOP Iyengar is known as **Father** of **Indian Phycology.** Some other Indian phycologists are **Y Bhardwaj, RN Singh, TV Desikachery** and **GS Venkataraman.**

(i) The algae are chlorophyll bearing organisms with a **thallus-like plant body.**

(ii) The thallus shows **little differentiation of true tissues.**

(iii) Even the complex thalli **lack vascular tissue** and epidermis with stomata.

(iv) The **sex organs are one-celled,** when multicellular, each cell is fertile and there is **no jacket of sterile cells.**

(v) There is **no embryo formation** after gametic union.

(vi) Both the generations when represented in the life cycle are independent. There are no algae with a sporophyte parasitic on the **gametophyte plant.**

(vii) Except a few, all the algae are **aquatic.**

(viii) Under favourable conditions, the gametophyte multiplies repeatedly by means of asexual spores called the **mitospores.**

Classification

Carolus Linnaeus (1754) included algae in **Cryptogamia** alongwith lichens. **FE Fritsch** (1935) classified algae into 11 classes on the basis of pigments in plastids, chemical nature of reserve food material, kinds, numbers and points of insertion of flagella of motile cells and the presence or absence of organized nucleus in the cell. The 11 classes of algae are as follow:

Class – Chlorophyceae
Class – Xanthophyceae
Class – Chrysophyceae
Class – Bacillariophyceae
Class – Cryptophyceae
Class – Dinophyceae
Class – Chlormonadineae
Class – Euglenneae
Class – Phaeophyceae
Class – Rhodophyceae
Isokontae – Green algae
Heterokontae – Yellow-green algae
Golden – Brown algae
Diatoms – Yellow or golden-brown algae
– Red, green-blue
Peridinieae
Euglenophyceae
Brown algae
Red algae
Cyanophyceae – Blue-green algae

Table 27.2 **Salient Features of Major Classes of Algae**

Character	Chlorophyceae	Bacillariophyceae	Phaeophyceae	Rhodophyceae	Cyanophyceae
Habitat	Freshwater, marine or terrestial.	Freshwater, marine or terrestrial.	Only four genera are fresh water, rest marine.	Mostly marine; a few are terrestrial.	Freshwater, marine or terrestrial.
Thallus form	Unicellular, colonial, coenobial, filamentous, thalloid or siphonaceous.	Unicellular or colonial.	Filamentous, branched usually heterotrichous.	Unicellular, filamentous, pseudoparenchymatous.	Unicellular, colonial or filamentous.
Cell structure	Eukaryotic, well organized nucleus and other cell organelles present.	Eukaryotic	Eukaryotic	Eukaryotic	Prokaryotic, membrane bound nucleus and other cell organelles like plastids, mitochondria, etc., are absent.
Cell wall	Cell wall is made up of cellulose and pectic material.	Cell wall is made up of silica and pectic material.	Outer mucilagenous layer of cell wall consists of alginic and fucinic acids and the inner layer is made up of cellulose.	Outer layer is pectic in nature, whereas inner layer is cellulosic.	Mucopeptides and muramic acid are two main constituents of the cell wall.
Flagella	Motic cells with 2, 4 or more flagella; flagella anteriorly inserted equal in length and whiplash type.	Usually 1 or sometimes 2, anteriorly inserted.	2, laterally inserted, of unequal length; one of them whiplash and another of tinsel type.	Non-flagellate, motile cells are absent.	Non flagellate, motile cells are absent.
Dominant pigments	Chlorophyll-*a*, and *b*, α and β-carotene, xanthophyll.	Chlorophyll-a, and c, β-carotene, xanthophyll (fucoxanthin).	Chlorophyll-*a* and *c*, β-carotene, xanthophyll (violaxanthin, fucoxanthin).	Chlorophyll-*a*, and *d*, β-carotene (lustein), xanthophylls,	Chlorophyll *a*, β-carotene, xanthophyll and c-phycocyanin.
Nucleus	Well organized nucleus with chromosomes and nucleolus is present.	As in Chlorophyceae.	As in Chlorophyceae.	As in Chlorophyceae.	Nuclear membrane absent, DNA not associated with histones, therefore well organized chromosomes are not found

Character	Chlorophyceae	Bacillariophyceae	Phaeophyceae	Rhodophyceae	Cyanophyceae
Eye spot	Attached with chloroplast but it has no relation with flagella.	Absent	In male gametes, eye spot is present, attached to chromatophores, it is related with flagella.	Absent	Absent
Pyrenoid	Single or compound, present either on the surface or embedded in chloroplast.	Simple or compound; one or more	Single stalked or projected.	Simple or compound; embedded, sometimes stalked.	Absent
Reserve food material	Starch and fats.	Oil volutin and chrysose.	Laminarin, mannitol, sucrose.	Foridean starch.	Special type of starch (cyanophycean starch) and protein (cyanophycin granules)
Reproduction	Reproduction by vegetative, asexual and sexual means; sexual reproduction isogamous, antsogamous or oogamous.	Reproduction by vegetative (cell division) and sexual means; sexual reproduction iso, aniso, or oogamous.	Reproduction by vege-tative (fragmentation, adventitious branches), asexual (motile and aplanospores), sexual reproduction iso-, aniso- or oogamous.	Reproduction by vegetative (cell division, fragmentation). asexual (monospores, neutral spores, tetraspores, carpospores) and sexual means; sexual reproduction complex and advanced oogamous	Multiplication only through asexual methods; sexuality completely absent.

Fungi

Fungi (*Fungour* = to flourish) are a group of **eukaryotic, achlorophyllous, non-photosynthetic, heterotrophic** organisms of diverse forms, sizes, physiology and mode of reproduction.

Mycology is the study of fungi. **PA Micheli** (1679-1737), an Italian botanist is known as **Father of Mycology,** who published *Nova Genera Plantarum.* **EM Fries** (1794-1878) is known as **Father of Systematic** Mycology, who wrote Systema Mycologium in three volumes. **HA de Barry** is known as **Father of Modern Mycology** and **Plant Pathology. EJ Butler** is known as **Father of Indian Mycology** and **Pathology.**

As per 'five kingdom system' of classification proposed by **Whittaker** in 1969; the **fungi** are a distinct kingdom of organisms. It comprises about **77000** named species and mycologists believe, that there may be as many as **1.2 million,** more species in existence.

Classification

The classification of fungi is mainly based on the following features:

(a) Nature of somatic phase whether unicellular or a mycelium, if later septate or aseptate.

(b) Kinds of asexual spores (mitospores)–sporangiospores or conidia; if former motile or non-motile; number, form and arrangement of flagella in the motile spores.

(c) Kinds of sporangia.

(d) Nature of the life cycle–whether asexual, haplontic, diplontic, haplodiplontic or haploid dikaryotic.

(e) Presence or absence or the perfect or sexual stage.

Many botanists have classified fungi in different ways. Some of which are as follows:

- In **Ostwald Tippo** (1942) classification, 8, 9 and 10 phyla of Thallophyta are that of fungi.
- **Bessey** (1950) classified the fungi in **lower fungi** and **higher fungi** on the basis of reproductive characters.

  Lower fungi Fruit bodies not formed, only one class–Phycomyceteae.

  Higher fungi Fruit bodies are formed, divided into three classes:

  Ascomyceteae Fruit body acsi; **ascospores endogenously formed.**

  Basidiomycetae Fruit body basidia; **basidiospores formed exogenously.**

  Deuteromycetae Sexual stage absent.
- **Sparrow** (1958) created nine classes emphasizing the importance of flagellation of the zoospores in the classification. He considered that flagellation should be treated as a good taxonomic and phylogenetic criterion. These nine classes

are—Chytridiomycetes, Hyphochytridiomycetes, Plasmodiophoromycetes, Oomycetes, Zygomycetes, Trichomycetes, Ascomycetes, Basidiomycetes and Deuteromycetes.

- **Martin** (1961) proposed a system of classification based on the septation of mycelium and spore characters. The outline of their classification is as follows:

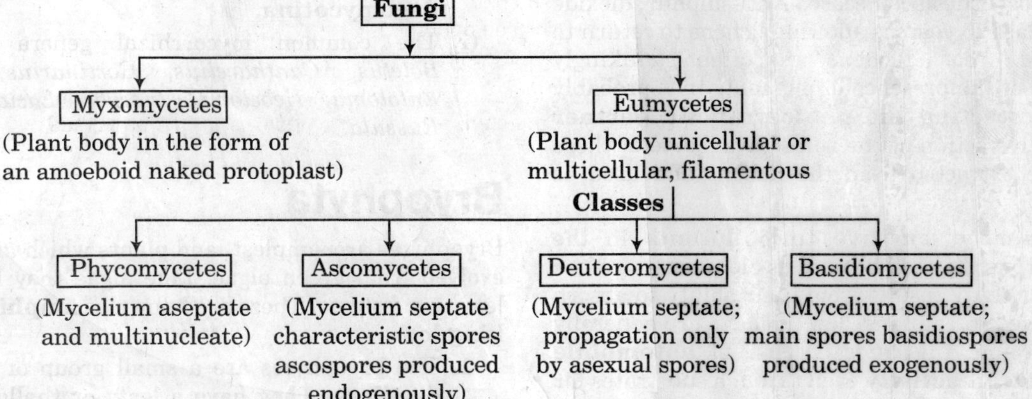

- A more natural system of classification of fungi was proposed by **Ainsworth** (1973), which has been accepted by most of the people including **Webster** (1980), **Bilgrami** (1985) and **Dube** (1987). An outline of this classification is given here.

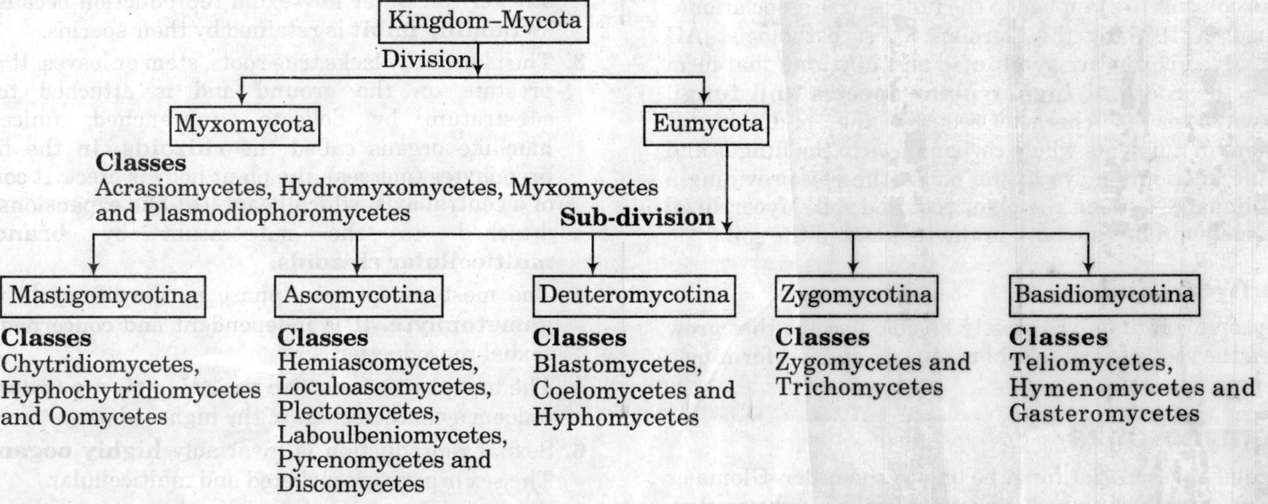

Lichens

A lichen looks like a single organisms, but it is actually a form of **symbiotic relationship** between an alga and a fungus. It is composed of a **fungal partner** (mycobiont) and one or more **photosynthetic partners** (photobiont). The photosynthetic partner is generally green algae or cyanobacteria. There are about 13500 species of lichens on the earth. In India, the lichens are much more common in Eastern Himalayas than Western Himalayas.

It is debated whether the relationship in a lichen is **mutualistic** or part of a **controlled parasitism.** On one hand, the fungus and the photobiont seem to be in a mutualistic relationship because when they are combined, they have the ability to deal with ecological conditions that neither part would be able to handle on its own. It also seems that neither partner is damaged by the other. Upon taking a closer look at a lichen, some might say that the photobiont is a captive of the mycobiont, not a partner. The fungal partner 'enslaves' the photobiont to feed from the photobionts photosynthesis.

In a lichen, the mycobiont produces a **thallus,** which houses the photobiont. There are three major morphological types of thalli, *i.e.,* foliose, crustose and fruticose.

Foliose lichens are leaf-like in appearance and structure. **Crustose lichens** are crust-like. They are tightly attached to or embedded in their substrate, and have no lower **cortex.** These consist of about 75 per cent of all lichens on earth. **Fruticose lichens** have no distinct top and bottom and are often round in cross-section.

A lichen absorbs most of its mineral nutrients from the air and rainfall. Therefore, they are a **good pollution indicators.** Lichens have been used to monitor the amount of pollutants in an environment. This is done by observing the condition of lichens as well as their chemical composition. Pollution in the atmosphere can be especially dangerous to lichens because they retain, and can accumulate, deadly amounts of heavy metals, sulphur, radioactive elements, NO_2 and ozone. Sulphur dioxide (SO_2) is especially lethal to lichens because it lowers pH and deteriorates chlorophyll, that causes photosynthesis to cease. Anti-sulphur dioxide legislation in the last 25 years is allowing lichens to return to formerly polluted areas. Lichens are often strinkingly colourful because of the presence of pigments that probably play a sole in **protecting the photosynthetic partner** from the destructive action of the sun's rays. Some of these pigments may be extracted from the lichens and used as natural dyes.

Lichens are extremely **sensitive to pollutants** in the atmosphere, and thus they can be used as bioindicators of air quality. Their sensitivity results from their ability to absorb substances dissolved in rain and dew. Lichens are generally absent in and around the cities because of **automobile traffic** and **industrial activity** even through substrates for their growth exist.

Mycorrhizae

The term mycorrhiza (sing.), which literally means fungus-root, was first applied to the fungus-tree associationss described in 1885 by the German forest pathologist **AB Frank.** Mycorrhizae are **symbiotic associations** that form between the **roots of higher plant species and fungi.** This symbiosis is characterised by the bi-directional movement of nutrients where carbon flows to the fungus and inorganic nutrients move to the plant, thereby providing a critical linkage between the plant root and soil. Mycorrhizal fungi usually proliferate both in the root and in the soil.

Ectomycorrhiza

Ectomycorrhizal fungi are mostly Basidiomycetes that grow between the root cortical cells of many tree species, forming a hartig net.

Endomycorrhiza

Arbuscular mycorrhizal fungi belong to the order–Glomales and form highly-branched structures called **arbuscules,** within the root cortical cells of many herbaceous and woody plant species.

Some Important Points about Mycorrizae

(a) Mycorrhiza sharing characteristics of both ecto and endotrophic mycorrhizae are called **ectendotrophic.**

(b) **Indian pipe** (*Monotropa indica*), a non-chlorophyllous plant, (roots parasite) belong to the family–**Ericaceae** is an example of ectendotrophic mycorrhizas.

(c) Endotrophic mycorrhiza is also called **VAM** (Vesicular Arbuscular Mycorrhiza).

(d) The fungus belongs to VAM are *Endogone, Rhizophagus, Pythium.*

(e) **Endotrophic mycorrhiza with septate fungi** are found in families of **Ericales, Orchidaceae** and **Gentianaceae.**

(f) **Orchids** are **obligately dependent** on mycorrhizal association for germination and further development.

(g) Ectotrophic mycorrhiza occurs only in about 3% of plant species.

(h) The fungi associated with ectotrophic mycorrhiza belongs to **Basidiomycotina** and some to **Ascomycotina.**

(i) The common mycorrhizal genera and *Amanita, Boletus, Cantharellus, Cortinarius, Gomphidius, Entoloma, Hebeloma, Inocybe, Lactarius, Paxillus, Russula.*

Bryophyta

Bryophytes are simplest land plants which are considered to evolved from green algae. Like algae they lack true roots, leaves and stems. These are known as **amphibians of plant kingdom.**

1. The bryophytes are a small group of primitive **land dwellers.** They have a leafy or thalloid, green plant body, which is small in structure, rarely more than 5 inches.
2. In their vegetative structure, bryophytes have become completely adapted to the land habit. However, they still rely on water for sexual reproduction because the **swimming habit** is retained by their sperms.
3. The plant body lacks true roots, stem or leaves. It grows prostate on the ground and is attached to the substratum by delicate, unbranched, unicellular hair-like organs called the **rhizoids.** In the higher bryophytes (mosses), the plant body is erect. It consists of a central axis, which bears leaf-like expansions. It is attached to the substratum by **branched, multicellular rhizoids.**
4. The most conspicuous phase in the life cycle is the **gametophyte.** It is independent and concerned with sexual reproduction.
5. The bryophytes **lack the vascular tissue** (xylem and phloem a characteristic of the higher plants).
6. Sexual reproduction is invariably **highly oogamous.** The sex organs are jacketed and multicellular.
7. Female sex organ in the form of an **archegonium** appears for the first time in the bryophytes in the plant world.
8. The sperms are **biflagellate.** Both the flagella are of **whiplash type.**
9. **Fertilization** takes place in the presence of water.
10. The fertilized egg is retained within the venter of the archegonium. It neither becomes independent of the parent gametophyte nor passes into the resting period. In both these aspects, the bryophytes differ from the algae.
11. The zygote undergoes repeated division to form an undifferentiated, multicellular structure called an **embryo.** The first division of the zygote is transverse and the apex of the embryo develops from the outer cell. Such an embryogeny is called **exoscopic.** It is the characteristic of bryophytes. No embryo stage exists in the thallophytes.

12. The venter wall enlarges with the developing embryo to form a protective, multicellular envelope, the **calyptra.**
13. The embryo by further division and differentiation produces a relatively small spore producing structure, which is not independent. It is called the **sporogonium** (sporophyte). In all bryophytes, the sporophyte is without differentiation into the stem and leaves. It is rootless and consists of a **foot, a seta** and a **capsule.** In some, the **seta** is absent (*Corsinia*) and rarely both, the foot and the seta (*Riccia*).
14. The sporophyte is simpler than the gametophyte and is originally attached to the parent gametophyte throughout its life. It is dependent upon it partially or completely for **nutrition.**
15. The sporogonium is concerned with the production of wind-disseminated, non-motile, cutinized spores, which belong to the category of **gonospores** or **meiospores.**
16. Morphologically, the **meiospores** in a given species are of one kind. Thus, the bryophytes, in general, are described as **homosporous.**
17. Each spore on falling on a suitable soil germinates to give rise to the gametophyte plant either directly or indirectly as a lateral bud from the **protonema.**
18. The occurrence of **heterologous** type of alternation of generations is a constant feature of the life cycle of bryophytes. In algae, when present, it is of **homologous** type.

Classification

Schimper (1879) gave the rank of division to the group–Bryophyta. Eichler (1883) divided Bryophyta into two classes–**Hepaticae** and **Musci. Smith, Campbell** and **Schuster** divided Bryophyta into three classes–**Hepaticae, Anthoceratae** and **Musci.**

Rothmalir named these classes–Hepaticopsida, Anthoceropsida and Bryopsida. Proskauer (1957) named Anthoceropsida to Anthocerotopsida.

Bryophyta–
- → Hepaticopsida (Liverworts)
- → Anthocerotopside (Hornworts)
- → Bryopsida (Mosses)

Pteridophyta

Pteridophytes are seedless vascular plants dominated during carboniferous period. They have vascularized root, stem and leaves.

1. **Sporophyte** represents the dominant phase and is differentiated into **roots, true stem and leaves.**
2. Vascular tissue consists of **xylem** (without true vessels) and **phloem** (without companion cells). Xylem transports water and minerals, while phloem conducts organic food.
3. Sporangia containing leaves called **sporophylls** are present. **Meiospores** are formed inside the sporangia.
4. Small, inconspicuous **gametophyte** is **independent** and **autotrophic.** Parts of gametophyte absorb water directly.
5. **Flagellate male gametes** (antherozoids) formed in male sex organs (antheridia). Water is essential for their swimming towards the female sex organs (archegonia).
6. Vegetative propagation occurs by multiplication.
7. Adventitious roots emerge from an underground, horizontally growing stem called **rhizome.** Some ferns have stem above the ground, which may attain a height of about 20 meter (*e.g.,* tree ferns-*Cyathea*).
8. Leaves are large and called **fronds.** They may be **simple** with one blade or may be **pinnately compound** (blade is sub-divided into leaflets or pinna). Pinnate leaves may be **uni, bi** or **tri-pinnate.** The growing point of leaves (apical meristem) stop growing at maturity. Young leaves show coiling like watch spring (circinate ptyxis).
9. Mature leaflets bear sporangia in clusters called **sori.** Each sorus bears a number of stalked biconvex sporangia on a placenta (cushion-shaped) covered by a membranous shealth called **indusium.** In some, **a false indusium** (turned margin or sporophyll) is present.
10. Multicellular hair or scales (ramenta) are present on the younger parts of stem, leaves and mature petiole. They have protective function.
11. Vegetative propagation takes place by **bulbils, adventitious buds** and **fragmentation.** The most unique method is seen in **walking fern**–*Adiantum caudatum,* which produce a new plant when its leaf tips come in contact with the soil.
12. Sporangium has a single-layered jacket. It has 12 spore mother cells ($2n$). Some of the marginal cells of jacket are differentiated to form a **annulus** and remaining form the **stomium. Meiosis** occurs in **spore mother cells,** which form haploid spores.
13. Haploid spore germinates to form a **prothallus** (gametophyte), which is **monoecious,** *i.e.,* has both antheridia (♂) and archegonia (♀).
14. Each male sex organ is hemispherical and has a 3-celled jacket. It contains 32-48 sperm mother cells, which produce **multiciliated sperm.** These swim in water to reach the female sex organs.
15. Archegonia is flask-shaped, embedded in prothallus. Neck opens and mucilage comes out to which the sperms are attracted. The mucilage contains **malic acid.** Sperms fuse with egg (oosphere) to form a diploid oospore.
16. **Oospore** forms the embryo stage.
17. Ferns exhibit alternation of dominant sporophyte generation with an inconspicuous gametophyte generation (heteromorphic).
18. In microphyllous leaves, the leaf trace does not disturb the vascular cylinder of the stem, *e.g.,* **lycopods** and **horsetails.** In megasporophyllous leaves, the leaf trace produces a parenchymatous leaf gap or foliar gap in the

vascular cylinder of the stem. Depending upon the development of sporangia, plants are **eusporangiate** or **leptosporangiate.**

Gymnosperms

Gymnosperms are naked seeded plants which evolved earlier then flowering plants.

1. Plant body is **sporophytic,** which is differentiated into roots, stems and leaves.
2. Root system is well-developed with **tap root system.**
3. Roots of some gymnosperms have symbiotic relations with algae such as **coralloid roots** of *Cycas*.
4. Stem in gymnosperms is usually erect, profusely branched and woody. Leaf scars are present on stem.
5. Stem of *Cycas* is **unbranched.**
6. Stem of *Zamia* is **tuberous.**
7. Leaves are **dimorphic,** *i.e.*, of two types:
   (i) **Foliage leaves** These are green, simple, needle-shaped or pinnately compound.
   (ii) **Scaly leaves** These are minute and deciduous.
8. Only scaly leaves are present in *Ephedra*.
9. In gymnosperms, xylem contains only tracheids and xylem parenchyma. Vessels remain absent.
10. Exceptionally, vessels are present in the members of Gnetales.
11. Wood is **manoxylic** (*e.g., Cycas*) or **pycnoxylic** (*e.g., Pinus*).
12. The phloem of gymnosperms lacks companion cells.
13. The leaves have thick cuticle layer and sunken stomata.
14. Usually, leaves of gymnosperms lack lateral veins. Therefore, the lateral translocation of nutrients takes place with the help of transfusion tissue.
15. Gymnosperms are **heterosporous,** which produce two types of spores, *i.e.*, **microspores** and **megaspores.**
16. **Microsporangia** occur on microsporophylls and **megasporangia** on megasporophylls, which in turn , aggregate to form compact **cones** or **strobili.**
17. The development of microsporangia is **eusporangiate** type.
18. Usually, the cones are **monosporangiate** (unisexual) but in some gymnosperms such as *Ephedra foliata, Ephedra intermedia,* bisporangiate cones are also present.
19. Male cones of gymnosperms are usually **short-lived.**
20. The **megasporangium** (*i.e.*, ovule) is usually **orthotropous** and **unitegmic,** which lies naked on the megasporophyll.
21. In Gnetales, the ovules are bitegmic.
22. Megasporophylls aggregate to form female cones, which persist for several years.
23. Male gametes are usually non-motile but male gamete of *Cycas* andf *Ginkgo* are **motile.**
24. Each archegonium contains a **single egg** and a **venter canal cell.**
25. Neck canal cells are absent in archegonium of gymnosperms.
26. Pollination in gymnosperm is **anemophillous.** It takes place by wind. The pollens are deposited in the pollen chamber where they germinate.
27. Fertilization is **siphonogamous.** It occur through pollen tube.
28. Development of embryo is **meroblastic,** which develops only from a part of the zygote.
29. The embryo is **endoscopic.**
30. There is a tendency of **polyembryony** is gymnosperms.
31. Endosperm is **haploid** (n).
32. Endosperm develops before **fertilization.**
33. *Cycas* is **dicotyledon,** *i.e.*, containing two cotyledons, while *Pinus* contains more than two cotyledons.
34. *Ginkgo biloba* is also known as **living fossil.**
35. Roots of some gymnosperms have symbiotic relations with algae such as coralloid roots of *Cycas*.

Classification

Chamberlian (1934) divided gymnosperms into two classes, *i.e.*, **class–Cycadophyta** and **Coniferophyta,** which is further divided into three and four orders respectively.

Class–Cycadophyta

It is characterized by unbranched and stumpy stems, leaves large and pinnately divided; male cones large and compact with simple sporophylls; female cones loose and consist of pinnate or simple sporophylls that bear large ovules; stems have wide cortex and manoxylic wood. It includes three orders:

(a) **Cycadofilicales** It includes all the extinct forms, *e.g., Lyginopteris.*
(b) **Cycadeoidales** It includes both living and extinct forms, *e.g., Cycadeoidea.*
(c) **Cycadales** It includes both living and extinct forms, *e.g., Cycas, Zamia.*

Class–Coniferophyta

The stems are profusely branched and the foliage gives cone-like appearance; leaves simple; male and female strobili are compact and bear complex sporophylls; wood is pycnoxylic. It includes four orders:

(a) **Cordaitales** Extinct order, *e.g., Cordaites.*
(b) **Ginkgoales** Includes extinct and one living representative, *e.g., Ginkgo biloba* (a single living species).
(c) **Coniferales** Includes both extinct and living genera, *e.g., Pinus.*
(d) **Gnetales** Includes both extinct and living genera, *e.g., Gnetum, Ephedra.*

Angiosperms

Angiosperms form a unique group of seed plants characterized by flowers, double fertilization, triploid endosperm and highly reduced male and female gametophyte.

(a) **Companion cells** are present in phloem.
(b) Vessels are found in xylem.
(c) Pollen grains germinate on the stigma.

Classification

Bentham and Hooker System

The classification of Phanerogams (seed plants) as given by **G Bentham** and **JD Hooker** (1862-1883) in *Genera Plantarum* (Three volumes in Latin) having 202 families, is as follows:

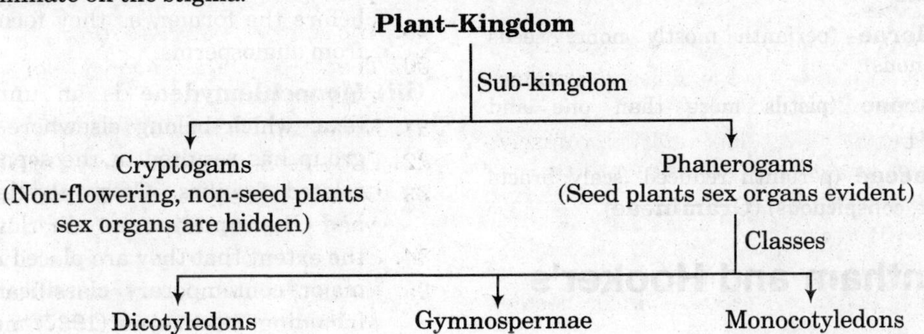

Class–Dicotyledonae

Two cotyledons in embryo, tap root present, vascular bundles with cambium arranged in a ring, secondary growth occurs in stem and roots, reticulate venation in leaves, floral organs pentamerous.

Sub-class-I – **Polypetalae** (perianth in two whorls, corolla of free petals), 3 series.

Series – **Thalamiflorae** (petals and stamens hypogynous and usually many, do disc present below the ovary, sepals free from ovary).

Orders – **Ranales** (Ranunculaceae), **Parietales** (Papaveraceae, Cruciferae), **Polygalineae, Caryophyllineae** (Caryophyllaceae), **Guttiferales, Malvales** (Malvaceae).

Series II – **Disciflorae** (sepals free or fused, stamens hypogynous, disc present below ovary).

Order – **Geraniales** (Rutaceae), **Olacales, Celastrales, Sapindales.**

Series III – **Calyciflorae** (stamens perigynous or epigynous, calyx mostly united, ovary mostly inferior).

Sub-class II – **Gamopetalae** (corolla of partially or completely connate petals, stamens mostly epipetalous, carpels apocarpous or syncarpous), 3 series.

Series I – **Inferae** (ovary inferior, stamens equal to petal length).

Orders – **Rubiales** (Rubiaceae), **Asterales** (Compositae), **Campanales.**

Series II – **Heteromerae** (ovary superior, epipetalous, androecium of 1 or 2 series, carpels mostly more than 2).

Orders – **Ericales, Primulales and Ebenales.**

Series III – **Bicarpellatae** (ovary superior, androecium of I series, carpels 2).

Orders – **Gentianales** (Apocynaceae,Asclepiadaceae), **Polemoneals** (Solanaceae), **Personales** (Scropulariaceae, Acanthaceae), **Lamiales** (Verbenaceae, Labiatae).

Order – **Rosales** (Leguminosae, Rosaceae), **Myrtales** (Myrtaceae), **Passiflorales** (Cucurbitaceae), **Ficoidales, Umbellales** (Umbelliferae).

Sub-class III – **Monochlamydeae** (flowers apetalous or perianth in one whorl), 8 series.

Series I – **Curvembryae** (Amaranthaceae).

Series II – **Multiovulate Aquaticae.**

Series III – **Multiovulate Terrestrial** (several seeded, terrestrial).

Series IV – **Microembryae** (embryo minute in endosperm).

Series V – **Daphnales** (unicarpellate, uniovulate).

Series VI – **Achlamydosporae** (ovary usually inferior, unilocular, ovules 1-3).

Series VII – **Unisexuales** (flowers unisexual), Euphorbiaceae.

Series VIII – **Ordines Anomalli** (of uncertain relationship, nearer to Unisexuales).

Class–Monocotyledonae

Embryo with one cotyledon, adventitious roots present, tap root short lived, cambium absent, vascular bundles scattered, secondary growth absent, parallel venation in leaves, floral parts trimerous, 7 series.

Series I – **Microspermae** (ovary inferior, seeds minute) (**Orchidaceae**)

Series II – **Epigynae** (ovary inferior, seeds large) (**Musaceae**)

Series III – **Coronariae** (ovary superior, perianth coloured) (**Liliaceae**)

Series IV – **Calycineae** (ovary superior, perianth green) (**Palmae**)

Series V – **Nudiflorae** (perianth mostly none, seeds albuminous)

Series VI – **Apocarpae** (pistils more than one and distinct)

Series VII **Glumaceae** (perianth reduced, scaly bracts present, conspicuous) (**Gramineae**).

Merits of Bentham and Hooker's System

(i) The system has great practical value for the identification of plants. It is very easy to follow for routine identification.

(ii) The system is widely followed for the arrangement of specimens in the herbaria of many countries including Britain and India.

(iii) The system is based on a careful comparative examination of actual specimens of all the living genera of seed plants and is not a mere compilation of known facts.

(iv) Unlike de Candolle, the **gymnosperms** are not placed among the dicots but rather in an independent group.

(v) Although the system is not a phylogenetic one, **Ranales** are placed in the beginning of dicotyledons. The group Ranales (in the broader sense including families, now separated under order–**Magnoliales**) is generally regarded as **primitive** by most of the leading authors.

(vi) Dicotyledons are placed before the monocotyledons, a position approved by all present day authors.

(vii) The description of families and genera are precise. Keys to the identification are very useful. Larger genera have been divided into **sub-genera** to facilitate identification.

(viii) The arrangement of taxa is based on overall **natural affinities** decided on the basis of morphological features, which can be easily studied with the naked eyes or with a hand lens.

Demerits of Bentham and Hooker's System

(i) The system does not incorporate phylogeny, although it was published, after **Darwin** published his evolutionary theory.

(ii) **Gymnosperms** are placed between dicotyledons and monocotyledons, whereas their proper position is before the former, as they form a group independent from angiosperms.

(iii) **Monochlamydeae** is an unnatural assemblage of taxa, which belong elsewhere. The creation of this group has resulted in the separation of many closely related families. **Caryophyllaceae, Illecebraceae** and **Chenopodiaceae** are closely related families to the extent that they are placed in the same order in all major contemporary classifications. Several authors including **Takhtajan** (1987) merge Illecebraceae with Caryophyllaceae. In Bentham and Hooker's system however, Caryophyllaceae are placed in **Polypetalae** and the other two in Monochlamydeae. Similarly, Podostemaceae, which are placed in a separate series Multiovulate Aquaticae, better belong to the order–**Rosales** (**Cronquist;** 1988). **Chloranthaceae** placed by **Bentham** and **Hooker** under Microembryeae and Lauriceae placed under Daphanales are closely allied to the order–**Magnoliales (sing. Ranales)** and are thus, placed in the same sub-class–Magnoliidae by **Cronquist** (1988).

(iv) In monocotyledons, **Liliaceae** and **Amaryllidaceae** are generally regarded as closely related and often included in the same order. In this system, they are placed under different series, Amaryllidaceae under Epigynae and Liliaceae under Coronarieae.

(v) Unisexuals is a loose assemblage of diverse families, which share only one major character, *i.e.,* unisexual flowers. **Cronquist** (1988) separates these families under two distinct sub-classes–**Hamamelidae** and **Rosidae** and **Takhtajan** (1987) under **Hamamelididae** adn **Dilleniidae.**

(vi) **Bentham** and **Hooker** did not know the affinities of the families placed under Ordines anomali and the families were tentatively grouped together. **Cronquist** (1988) and **Takhtajan** (1987) placed **Ceratophyllaceae** under sub-class–**Magnoliidae** and the other three under **Dilleniidae.**

(vii) Many large families, *e.g.,* **Urticaceae, Euphorbiaceae** and **Saxifragaceae,** are unnatural assemblages and represent polyphyletic groups. These have rightly been split by subsequent authors into smaller, natural and monophyletic families.

(viii) Orchidaceae is an advanced family with the inferior ovary and zygomorphic flowers, but the family is placed towards the beginning of monocotyledons.

(ix) In Gamopetalae; inferae with an inferior ovary is placed before the other two orders having a superior ovary. The inferior ovary is now considered to have been derived from the superior ovary.

Hutchinson System of Classification

John Hutchinson (1884-1972) gave his **phylogenetic** system of classification in **Families of flowering plants.** His classification is given on the basis of 24 principles and classified angiosperms into 411 families. He believes in monophyletic origin of angiosperms. According to him Magnoliaceae and Ranunculaceae are most primitive families while Graminal (Poaceae) most advanced.

(i) Evolution is both **upward** and **downwards.** The former leads to **preservation** and later leads to **supression.**

(ii) Evolution does not involved all the organs at the same time.

(iii) Trees and shrubs are primitive than herbs.

(iv) Tress and shrubs are primitive than climbers.

(v) Normal habit is primitive than parasitic or saprophytic habit.

(vi) Terrestrial habit is primitive than aquatic habit.

(vii) Perennials are primitive than biennials and annuals.

(viii) Dicots are primitive than monocots.

(ix) Spiral arrangement of organs is primitive than cyclic arrangement.

(x) Simple leaf is primitive than compound leaf.

(xi) Bisexual flower is primitive than unisexual flower.

(xii) Solitary flower is primitive than inflorescense.

(xiii) Monoecious condition is primitive than dioecious condition.

(xiv) **Hypogyny** is primitive than **perigyny** and **epigyny.**

(xv) Actinomorphic flowers are primitive than zygomorphic flowers.

(xvi) **Petaliferous** condition is primitive than **apetalous** (naked) condition.

(xvii) Aestivation type **imbricate** is primitive than **valvate.**

(xviii) **Polypetalous** condition is primitive than **gamopetalous** condition.

(xix) **Apocarpy** (free carpels) is primitive than **syncarpy** (fused carpels).

(xx) Free anthers are primitive than fused anthers (Syngenesious condition).

(xxi) **Polycarpy** (Many carpels) is primitive than **oligocarpy** (few carpels).

(xxii) Many stamens condition is primitive than few stamens.

(xxiii) Endospermic seeds with small embryo are primitive than one-endospermic seeds and large embryo.

(xxiv) Single fruit is primitive than aggregate fruit.

Takhtajan System of Classification

Takhtajan (1980) called angiosperms as **Magnoliophyta.** He believed that **Taxonomy without phylogeny may be likened to bones without flesh.**

He divided division Magnoliophyta into class – **Magnoliopsida** (Dicotyledones) and Liliopsida (Monocotyledones).

Classification of Animals

The goal of animal systematics is to arrange animals into groups that reflect evolutionary relationship. These groups should include a single ancestral species and all of its descendants. Such group is called a **monophyletic group.** **Polyphyletic groups** have members that can be traced to separate ancestors. A **paraphyletic group** include some but not all members of a lineage. Traditionally kingdom–Animalia has been considered monophyletic because of the impressive similarities in cellular organization. The outline classification of kingdom–Animalia is:

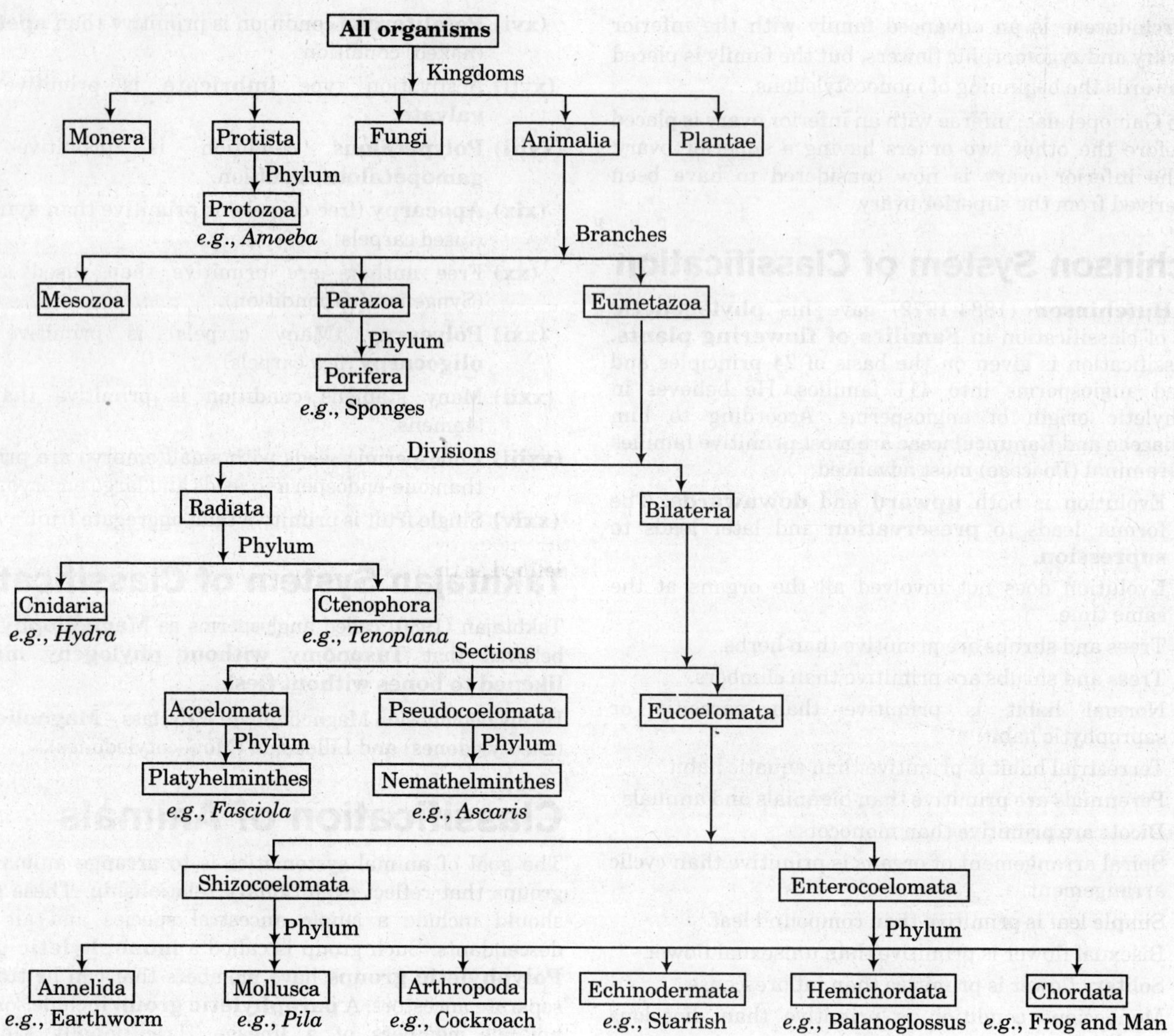

Phylum–Protozoa (Goldfuss)

(i) Protozoans are the first formed (*Gr. Protos* = first + *zoon* = animals) animals which are one-celled.

(ii) Protozoa exhibit 'Protoplasmic level of organization'.

(iii) Body symmetrical or asymmetrical, free-living or parasitic.

(iv) Locomotion is effected by **flagella, cilia** or **pseudopodia.**

(v) Excretion and respiration occurs by diffusion.

(vi) Nutrition is holophytic (*Euglena*), holozoic (*Amoeba*), saprozoic (*Mastigamoeba*).

(vii) Osmoregulation takes place in Protozoa with the help of **contractile vacuole.**

(viii) Nitrogenous waste material in Protozoa is **ammonia.**

(ix) Reproduction occurs by asexual and sexual methods.

(x) Classification of Protozoa is mainly based on **locomotory organelles.**

Classification

Phylum–Protozoa is divided into four classes:

Class – **Sarcodina,** *e.g., Amoeba, Entameoba histolytica*

Class – **Flagellata,** *e.g., Euglena, Trypanosoma*

Class – **Sporozoa,** *e.g., Plasmodium, Monocystis*

Class – **Ciliata,** *e.g., Paramecium, Opalina*

Phylum–Porifera (Robert Grant)

(i) Sponges have **no tissues.**

(ii) The cavity common to all sponges is **spongocoel** lined with flagellated choanocytes.

(iii) **Choanocytes** or collar cells are present only in sponges.

(iv) Different types of canal system in sponges are **asconoid, syconoid** and **leuconoid.**

(v) Sponges have numerous mouthlets (**ostia**) and one exit **(osculum).**

(vi) Skeleton of sponges is secreted by **Scleroblast.**

(vii) All sponges are hermaphrodites. Reproduction is asexual or sexual. Sex cells (sperms and ova) arise from undifferentiated **archaeocytes.**

(viii) Classification of sponges is primarily based on skeleton.

(ix) Excretion and respiration occur by diffusion.

(x) Development is indirect or direct. The common larval forms are **parenchymula** (*Leucosolenia* and *Clathrina*), **amphiblastula** (*Sycon*), etc.

Classification

Phylum–Porifera is divided into three classes:

Class – **Calcarea** or **Calcispongiae,** *e.g., Leucosolenia, Sycon.*

Class – **Hexactinellida** or **Hyalospongiae,** *e.g., Euplectella, Hyalonema.*

Class – **Demospongiae,** *e.g., Spongilla, Cliona, Euspongia.*

Phylum–Cnidaria (Coelenterata) (Leuckart)

(i) Cnidarians are radially symmetrical animals with **cells tissue grade of body organization.**

(ii) Body wall is **diploblastic** with two germ layers: **ectoderm** and **endoderm** (gastroderm).

(iii) The body cavity is known as **coelenteron** or **gastro-vascular cavity.**

(iv) Asexual phase is generally **polyp** and sexual phase is **medusa.**

(v) Some members like *Physalia* (Portuguese man-of-war) exhibits **polymorphism.**

(vi) The most characteristic feature of coelenterates is the presence of **nematocysts or stinging cells.**

(vii) **Nematocysts** are mainly concerned with food capture, defense and attachement.

(viii) Respiratory, circulatory and excretory systems are absent.

(ix) Reproduction is both asexual and sexual, larval stages are **Planula** (*Obelia*) and **Ephyra** (*Aurelia*).

Classification

Phylum–Cnidaria is divided into three classes:

Class – **Hydrozoa,** *e.g., Hydra, Obelia, Physalia*

Class – **Scyphozoa,** *e.g., Aurelia* (jellyfish)

Class – **Anthozoa,** *e.g., Metridium, Gorgonia.*

Phylum–Platyhelminthes (Gegenbaur)

(i) Flatworms are **triploblastic,** bilaterally symmetrical, **acoelomate.**

(ii) Flatworms have **tissue organ-system level of organization.**

(iii) **Anus is absent** like coelenterates, with **blind-sac body plan.**

(iv) Excretory organs are **protonephridia** or **solenocytes** or **flame cells.**

(v) Digestive, excretory, nervous and reproductive systems are present.

(vi) Cephalization (differentiation of head) begins in flatworms.

(vii) Monoecious or hermaphrodites with well-developed reproductive system.

(viii) Life cycle complicated with many larval stages.

Classification

Phylum–Platyhelminthes is divided into three classes:

Class – Turbellaria, *e.g., Planaria*

Class – Trematoda, *e.g., Fasciola*

Class – Cestoda, *e.g., Tapeworm* (*Taenia*)

Phylum–Nemathelminthes (Gegenbaur)

(i) **Tube within a tube** body plan and organ-system grade of body organization is present.

(ii) These are **triploblastic,** bilaterally symmetrical and **pseudocoelomate.**

(iii) A **syncytial** or cellular epidermis, is present that is generally without cilia.

(iv) Excretory system consists of **protonephridia** and canals.

(v) Skeletal, respiratory and circulatory systems are absent.

(vi) Reproductive system well-developed. Usually **unisexual** with **sexual dimorphism.**

(vii) Development may be direct or indirect. During indirect development a larva is present. **Filariform** larva is present in *Ancylostoma* (hookworm), microfilaria larva is found in *Wuchereria* (filarial worm) and rhabditiform larva is present in *Ascaris* and *Enterobius* (pinworm).

Classification

Phylum–Nemathelminthes is divided into two classes:

Class – **Rhabditea,** *e.g., Ascaris, Wuchereria*

Class – **Enoplea,** *e.g., Trichinella, Trichuris*

Phylum–Annelida (Lamarck)

(i) Annelids are bilateral, **eucoelomate** (with true coelom), **schizocoelic** segmented worms.

(ii) Annelids are characterized by **metameric segmentation.**

(iii) Presence of setae which are chitinous and unjointed.

(iv) Alimentary canal is straight, excretory organs are **nephridia.**

(v) Blood vascular system is usually closed type. Blood is red due to the presence of respiratory pigment **haemoglobin or erythrocruorin,** found dissolved in the plasma.

(vi) Development is mostly direct. If there is indirect development (*e.g., Nereis*), it includes a **trochophore** larva.

Classification

On the basis of number and presence or absence of setae phylum–Annelida is divided into three classes:

Class – Polychaeta, *e.g., Nereis, Aphrodite*
Class – Oligochaeta, *e.g.,* Earthworm (*Pheretima*)
Class – Hirudinea, *e.g., Hirudinaria.*

Phylum-Arthropoda (Vonsei Bold)

(i) Arthropods are **bilaterally symmetrical, triploblastic** and **metamerically segmented.**

(ii) Each segment basically bears a pair of lateral jointed appendages adapted for good ingestion, locomotion, respiration, copulation, etc.

(iii) Exoskeleton is light weight, tough and composed of structural polysaccharide **chitin.**

(iv) Body cavity is a fluid filled **haemocoel.**

(v) Circulatory system **open type** with dorsal heart, arteries and sinuses.

(vi) Muscular system well-developed, muscle fibres always **striated.**

(vii) Respiration by **gills** or **trachea** or **book lungs.**

(viii) Excretion by **green or coxal glands** or by **Malpighian tubules.** Excretory product is **uric acid.**

(ix) Sexes mostly separate with sexual dimorphism. Paired reproductive organs and ducts are present.

(x) Fertilization typically internal, in female's body. Eggs megalecithal. Oviparous or viviparous.

Classification

On the basis of body divisions and presence or absence of certain appendages phylum–Arthropoda is divided into four sub-phyla:

Sub-phylum – **Onychophora**, *e.g., Peripatus*
Sub-phylum – **Trilobitomorpha,** *e.g., Triarthrus*
Sub-phylum – **Chelicerata**
Class – Merostoma, *e.g., Limulus* (the king-crab)
Class – Arachnida, *e.g., Palamnaeus* (scorpion)
Sub-phylum – Mandibulata
Class – Crustacea, *e.g., Palaemon,* Cancer
Class – Myriapoda, *e.g., Scolopendra* (centipede), *Thyroglutus* (millipede)
Class 3 – Insecta, *e.g., Periplaneta, Musca*

Economic Importance of Insects

(i) The study of insects is known as **Entomology.**

(ii) Insects can be divided into two series:
  (a) Harmful insects **(b)** Beneficial insects

Harmful Insects

(a) Harmful insects can be divided into six series:

- Pests of agriculture
- Pests of store-grains
- Household pests
- Pests of domestic animals
- Disease carriers
- Poisonous insects

(b) Some important agricultural pests are: grasshoppers and locusts, cotton bollworms (pests of cotton), *Pyrilla* (sugarcane leaf-hopper), *Aphids* (pests of vegetables).

(c) Some important store–grain pests are:

Rice weevil *Sitophilus oryzae*
wheat weevil *Trogoderma granarium*
Red flour beetle *Tribolium confusum*
Pulse beetle *Callosobruchus chinensis*

(d) Some important household pests are:

Cockroaches *Periplaneta*
Houseflies *Musca*
Mosquitoes *Anopheles, Culex* and *Aedes*
Bedbugs *Cimex*
Termites *Odontotermes*

Table 27.3 **Disease Carrier Insects**

Insect	Disease
Housefly	Anthrax, diarrhoea, tuberculosis, leprosy, typhoid, cholera, etc.
Mosquitoes	Malaria, filariasis, dengue fever, yellow fever, etc.
Kissing bug	Chagas disease
Rat flea	Bubonic plague
Sand fly	Kala-azar
Tse-tse fly	African sleeping sickness
Bed bug	Typhus fever

(e) Honey bees, wasps, bedbugs and mosquitoes are poisonous insects.

Beneficial Insects

Honey Bee

- A colony of honey bee consists of three castes, *viz,* **queen, drone** and **worker.**
- Bee rearing is called **apiculture.**
- Diploid fertilized eggs give rise to queen and workers and unfertilized haploid produced males and drones.
- Natural **parthenogenesis** occurs in honey bee.

- Bee wax is a secretory product of **hypodermal glands** of the abdomen of worker bee.
- Honey is stored in the cell of comb.
- **Karl Von Frisch** decoded the language of dance by bees.
- Mouthparts of honey bee are **chewing and lapping type.**
- Different species of honey bee are: *Apis mellifera, A. dorsata, A. indica, A. florea.*
- 'Royal jelly' is secreted by worker bees.
- Honey bee is one of the most important pollinator in agriculture.

Silk Moth

- Silk is produced by an insect called silk moth.
- *Bombyx mori* is the **mulberry silkworm.**
- **Silk** is obtained from **cocoon.**
- Caterpillar feeds on mulberry leaves, its **salivary gland secretes liquid silk.**
- Silk thread is formed of two proteins namely **fibroin** and **sericin.**
- Natural silk contains nitrogen.

Lac Insects

- Lac is produced commercially by an insect *Tachardia lacca (Laccifer lacca).*
- Lac is secretion of mainly female.
- Lac is resinous substance.
- Lac is actually **secreted for its protection** and not for the food of the insect.

Red Ants

- Red ants are used for the production of **formic acid.**

Phylum–Mollusca (Johnston)

(i) Molluscs are triploblastic, bilaterally symmetrical, schizocoelic and unsegmented animals.

(ii) Most molluscs secrete a **shell** of calcium carbonate that protects and supports their soft tissues.

(iii) The body is covered by a skin fold **mantle** which secretes the shell.

(iv) Body cavity is a reduced **haemocoel.**

(v) Molluscs typically employ a feeding organ called **radula.**

(vi) Circulatory system mainly of **open type.** Blood with **amoebocytes,** respiratory pigment is copper containing **haemocyanin** dissolved in plasma.

(vii) Sense organs include eyes, statocysts and **osphradia** (chemoreceptor to test chemical nature of water).

(viii) Fertilization is generally external, development direct or through free larval forms like trochophore, veliger, glochidium, etc.

Classification

Molluscs are classified into seven classes:

Class – **Monoplachophora,** *e.g., Neopilina* (a living fossil and connecting link between annelids and molluscs)

Class – **Aplacophora,** *e.g., Chaetoderma*

Class – **Polyplacophora,** *e.g., Chiton*

Class – **Scaphopoda,** *e.g., Dentalium*

Class – **Gastropoda,** *e.g., Pila, Aplysia*

Class – **Pelecypoda,** *e.g., Unio*

- **Pearl industry** was introduced first in Japan by **Kokichi Mikimoto** in 1890.

Class – Cephalopoda, *e.g.,* Sepia, Octopus (the foot is located on the head)

Phylum–Echinodermata (Jacob Klein)

(i) Echinoderms are triploblastic, radially symmetrical often **pentamerous,** larva with bilateral symmetry.

(ii) Echinoderms are marine.

(iii) Echinoderms are uncephalized (head absent), the oral-aboral axis is perpendicular to the pentamerous plane.

(iv) A calcareous endoskeleton is present in the form of ossicles bearing protective spines.

(v) The **water vascular system** is a unique organ system that functions in locomotion, feeding, respiration and excretion.

(vi) Locomotion by external **tube feet** connected with water vascular system.

(vii) Usually dioecious, fertilization external.

(viii) Development is indirect through free swimming larval stages.

Classification

- Phylum–Echinodermata is divided into five classes:

Class – **Asteroidea,** *e.g., Asterias* (starfish)

Class – **Ophiuroidea,** *e.g., Ophiothrix* (brittle-stars)

Class – **Echinoidea,** *e.g., Echinus* (sea urchin) (commonly known as **Aristotle's lantern**)

Class – **Holothuroidea,** *e.g., Cucumaria* (sea cucumber)

Class – **Crinoidea,** *e.g., Antedon* (feather star).

Phylum–Chordata

(i) Three primary chordate characters are:

(a) Presence of notochord.

(b) Presence of single dorsal tubular nerve cord.

(c) Presence of paired pharyngeal clefts.

(ii) Presence of a post **anal tail.**

(iii) Bilateral symmetry and metameric-segmentation.

(iv) Presence of true coelom (**schizocoel** in vertebrates and **enterocoel** in protochordates).

(v) Blood vascular system closed, heart ventral with RBCs.
(vi) Sexes separate with rare exceptions.
(vii) Phylum–Chordata is divided into three sub-phylum– **Urochordata, Cephalochordata** and **Vertebrata.**

Sub-Phylum–Urochordata

(a) Notochord only in the tail region of larva.
(b) Commonly called 'tunicates'.
(c) **Retrogressive metamorphosis** results in the degeneration in adult, *e.g., Herdmania* (sea squirt).

Sub-Phylum–Cephalochordata

(a) Adult with notochord extending from head to tail, hence, the name Cephalochordata.
(b) Coelom **enterocoelous.**
(c) Circulatory system closed but without heart.
(d) Excretion by protonephridia with **solenocytes.**
(e) Nerve cord dorsal, tubuar without ganglia and brain, *e.g., Amphioxus.*

Sub-phylum–Vertebrata (Craniata)

(a) Vertebrates have well-developed **cranium** and vertebral column.
(b) Notochord is embryonic in adult replaced by vertebral column.
(c) Vertebrates are divided into two divisions:
  (i) **Agnatha** (without jaws), *e.g., Petromyzon*
  (ii) **Gnathostomata** (with jaws), *e.g.,* Pisces, Amphibia, Reptilia, Aves, Mammalia.

Class–Pisces (Fishes)

(a) Study of the fishes is **Ichthyology.**
(b) Endoskeleton is cartilaginous or bony.
(c) Heart two-chambered. It is **venous heart** pumping impure blood only.
(d) Kidneys **mesonephric.** Excretion **ammonotelic** or **ureotelic.**
(e) Lateral line receptors present.
(f) Fishes are cold blooded.
(g) Fertilization internal or external, *e.g., Scoliodon, Gambusia, Latimeria, Anguilla.*

Class–Amphibia

(a) Amphibians are cold blooded.
(b) Amphibians originated during **Devonian period** of Palaeozoic era.
(c) Endoskeleton bony, skull **dicondylic** (with two occipital condyles).
(d) Respiration by lungs, skin and buccal lining. Larvae and certain aquatic forms with external gills.
(e) Heart three-chambered with two auricles and one ventricle.
(f) Fertilization mostly external.
(g) Extraembryonic membranes are absent **(anamniota).**
(h) Larva **tadpole** which metamorphosis into adult, *e.g., Rana tigrina, Bufo melanostictus, Alytes, Salamandra.*

Class–Reptilia

(a) **Herpetology** is the study of reptiles.
(b) Mesozoic era is called **Golden Age of Reptiles.**
(c) Skin dry, cornified and devoid of glands.
(d) T-shaped **interclavicle** present.
(e) Heart is usually **three-chambered** or partially **four chambered. Crocodiles** have four-chambered heart.
(f) Kidneys are **metanephric.** Excretion uricotelic.
(g) Cranial nerves are 12 pairs but 10 pairs in snakes.
(h) Larval stage is absent.
(i) Foetal membrane is present.
(j) Fertilization is internal.
(k) **Jacobson's organ** in the roof of buccal cavity concerned with smell, well-developed in snakes and lizards.
(l) Skull is **monocondylic.**
(m) Reptiles are cold-blooded animals.
(n) **Urinary bladded** is absent in snakes and crocodiles.
(o) **Saurology** is the study of lizards.
(p) **Serpentology** is the study of snakes.

Class–Aves

(a) **Ornithology** is the study of birds.
(b) **Salim Ali** was a famous ornithologist and known as **Bird man of India.**
(c) Birds are **feathered, bipeds** and **air breathing.**
(d) Jaw bones are prolonged into toothless **beak.**
(e) Skin without glands, only cutaneous gland is **uropygial gland** or **preen gland** at tail base.
(f) The largest and most powerful flight muscle is **pectoralis major.**
(g) Bones are pneumatic or hollow and have **no bone marrow.**
(h) Skull is monocondylic.
(i) Both clavicles and a single interclavicle fused to form a V-shaped bone called **furcula** or **wishbone.**
(j) Crop secretes **pigeon milk** during breeding season.
(k) A sound box or **syrinx** producing voice.
(l) Heart is competely **four-chambered.**
(m) Females are **oviparous.**
(n) Birds are **warm-blooded** animals.

Class–Mammalia

(a) **Coenozoic era** is known as **Age of Mammals.**
(b) The study of mammals is called **Mammalogy.**
(c) Most important character of mammals is the presence of **mammary glands.**
(d) Presence of a **muscular diaphragm** separating thoracic cavity from abdominal cavity.
(e) Presence of **seven cervical vertebrae.**

(f) Teeth heterodont, thecodont and diphyodont.

(g) Respiration by lungs (pulmonary).

(h) Heart is **four-chambered.**

(i) Erythrocytes are **small, circular** and **non-nucleated**.

(j) Kidneys are **metanephric.** Excretion is **ureotelic.**

(k) Brain is highly developed with **corpus callosum** connecting cerebral hemispheres.

(l) Mammals are **viviparous,** *e.g.,* man, rabbit, duckbilled platypus, kangaroo (*Macropus*), etc.

(m) Class–Mammalia is divided into two sub-class–**Prototheria**–egg laying mammals (Oviparous), *e.g.,* Duck-billed platypus.

Theria (Viviparous), *e.g.,* Man, Rabbit, Monkey, *Macropus.*

Exercise

1. Phylogenetic system brings out
(a) reproductive similarities
(b) grouping according to morphological characters
(c) grouping on the basis of increasing complexities
(d) grouping according to evolutionary trends

2. A scientist connected with the study of variation, evolution and origin alongwith classification is known as
(a) classical taxonomist
(b) herbal taxonomist
(c) modern taxonomist
(d) new taxonomist

3. A taxon is
(a) a group of related families
(b) a group of related species
(c) a type of living organism
(d) a taxonomic group of any ranking

4. Which of the following pairs is most closely related?
(a) Dog and tapeworm
(b) Tapeworm and bacteria
(c) Mushroom and tree
(d) *Amoeba* and bacteria

5. Instead of phylum, plants use which category?
(a) Division (b) Sub-species
(c) Class (d) Sub-kingdom

6. If two organisms are in the same phylum, they must also be in the same
(a) class (b) species
(c) family (d) kingdom

7. Branches of science that deals with identification, nomenclature and classification of organisms is called as
(a) systemics
(b) taxonomy
(c) classification
(d) nomenclature

8. For revision of a group, in case of sexually reproducing organisms, basic criteria is
(a) character of delimiting a species
(b) interbreeding
(c) morphology
(d) cytotaxonomy

9. Different groups of seaweeds can generally be distinguished on the basis of
(a) colour
(b) size
(c) whether they have true leaves, stems and roots
(d) whether they are autotrophic or heterotrophic

10. Most biologists agree that seaweeds are protists, even though most other protists are microscopic unicellular creatures. Some biologists think that atleast some seaweeds should be considered plants, not protists. Which of the following would support the latter position?
(a) Certain seaweeds contain several kinds of specialized cells
(b) Certain seaweeds undergo sexual and asexual reproduction
(c) Certain seaweeds are found to be prokaryotic
(d) Certain seaweeds have very complex cells

11. Protozoans called choanoflagellates live in small clusters. They look very much like choanocytes, special feeding cells found in sponges, which are simple animals. Why might biologists find choanoflagellates of great evolutionary interest?
(a) They show how the very first organisms might have lived
(b) They might show how the first heterotrophs lived
(c) Offer hint about origin of multicellular organism
(d) They suggest what the first eukaryotes might have been like

12. Which of the following is not evidence for the role of endosymbiosis in the origin of eukaryotes?
(a) Chloroplasts have their own DNA
(b) The inner membrane of a chloroplast is similar to prokaryotic membranes
(c) Mitochondria and chloroplast both are surrounded by two membranes
(d) The DNA in the eukaryotic nucleus codes for some enzymes in mitochondria

13. Protists are a diverse group of organisms that include
(a) plants
(b) algae
(c) protozoans
(d) Both (b) and (c)

14. Among the following which statement is not a part of principles of current code adopted by XII International Botanical Congress in Leningrad (1975)?
(a) Botanical nomenclature is independent of Zoological nomenclature
(b) The application of names is determined by means of nomenclature types
(c) The nomenclature of taxonomic group is based upon priority of publication
(d) Scientific names of taxonomic group are treated as Italics regardless of their derivation

15. Different hybrid forms of the same percentage are designated as

(a) apomicts (b) nothomorphs
(c) race (d) variety

16. According to current code for botanical nomenclature, the names of class must ends with

(a) opsida (b) idae
(c) ales (d) aceae

17. A specimen or element selected by a competent worker form the original material studied by the author to serve as a substitute for the holotype if the latter was not designated in the original publication or is lost or destroyed

(a) lectotype (b) neotype
(c) isotype (d) paratype

18. Which technique is routinely used among plants for establishing genetic relationship?

(a) Amino acid sequence
(b) Serological investigation
(c) Isoenzyme profiling
(d) Chromosome morphology

19. Numerical taxonomy is also referred as

(a) statistical taxonomy
(b) phenetics
(c) computer aided taxonomy
(d) All of the above

20. Which is not a characteristic of numerical taxonomy?

(a) The greater the content of information in taxa of classification and the more character on which it is based, the better is classification
(b) Every character is of equal weight in creating natural taxa
(c) Classification is based on percentage (%) similarity coefficient for each OTU
(d) Phylogenetic inferences cannot be made form the taxonomic structure of a group and from character correlation

21. A group of plants or animals with similar traits of any rank is

(a) species (b) genus
(c) order (d) taxon

22. Basic unit or smaller taxon of taxonomy is

(a) species (b) genus
(c) family (d) variety

23. Sequence of taxonomic categories is

(a) Class-Phylum-Tribe-Order-Family-Genus-Species
(b) Division-Class-Family-Tribe-Order-Genus-Species
(c) Division-Class-Order-Family-Tribe–Genus–Species
(d) Phylum-Order-Class-Tribe-Family–Genus–Species

24. In which kingdom would you classify the archaea and nitrogen-fixing organisms, if the five-kingdom system of classification is used?

(a) Plantae (b) Fungi
(c) Protista (d) Monera

25. Put these classification terms in sequence, starting with the group with the most variation

I. Class II. Genus
III. Phylum IV. Species
V. Family VI. Order

(a) III, I, VI, V, II, IV (b) IV, II, V, VI, I, III
(c) III, I, V, VI, II, IV (d) IV, II, VI, V, I, III

26. Organisms of the same species have been classified on the basis of their

(a) structural similarities
(b) structural differences
(c) behavioural similarities
(d) behavioural differences

27. A group of freely inter-breeding organisms constitutes a

(a) species (b) genera
(c) family (d) class

28. Sub-phylum is a Linnaean classification category that is

(a) below phylum
(b) above phylum
(c) immediately below kingdom
(d) above kingdom

29. Imagine *Canus nipponicus* refers to a proposed scientific name for an imaginary organism. This proposed scientific name indicates the

(a) kingdom and phylum (b) phylum and genus
(c) genus and species (d) kingdom and species

30. Which of the following statement is correct regarding the guidelines set up for writing scientific name of any organism?

(a) Scientific names are written as the organisms genus and species
(b) The genus name is always capitalized and the species name is always lower case
(c) The scientific name should be underlined, bold or italicizes as well
(d) All of the above

31. An organelle differs from an organ in that an organelle

(a) is a substructure of a cell
(b) contains one specific type of tissue
(c) is larger than an organ
(d) cannot be stained

32. On the scale of small to large, the order of organ system is

(a) cell, organelle, organ, tissue
(b) tissue, organ, organelle, cell
(c) organelle, tissue, organ, cell
(d) organelle, cell, tissue, organ

33. Which of the connective tissue connect muscle to the skin?

(a) Fat (b) Tendon
(c) Ligament (d) None of these

34. .... supports the body and unites some of its parts.

(a) Muscle tissue (b) Connective tissue
(c) Nerve tissue (d) Epithelial tissue

35. How many levels of structural organization are present in human body?

(a) 4 (b) 5
(c) 6 (d) 7

36. Which of the following level is not involved in making human body?

(a) Molecule level (b) Cells level
(c) Organ levels (d) Organ system level

37. Prokaryotic organism includes
(a) archaebacteria, eubacteria and protists
(b) archaebacteria and protits
(c) protists and eubacteria
(d) eubacteria and archaebacteria

38. The largest unit within which gene flow can readily occur is a
(a) population (b) species
(c) genus (d) phylum

39. Unicellular eukaryotes are grouped into
(a) fungi and Plantae (b) fungi
(c) protista (d) eubacteria

40. Which of the following are protozoans?
(a) Diatoms, flagellates, amoebas and ciliates
(b) Apicomplexans, flagellates, amoebas and ciliates
(c) Amoebas, Actinomycetes, ciliates and flagellates
(d) Flagellates, ciliates, cyanobacteria and apicomplexans

41. In general, how do algae and protozoans differ?
(a) Protozoans can move and algae cannot
(b) Algae are free-living, and protozoans are parasitic
(c) Protozoans are autotrophic and algae are heterotrophic
(d) Algae are photosynthetic and almost all protozoans are heterotrophic

42. Biological kingdoms are distinguished based on whether they have species that are
(a) single or multicelled
(b) absorbers, ingesters or producers of food
(c) Both (a) and (b)
(d) None of the above

43. Cell was discovered by
(a) Leeuwenhoek (b) Robert Hooke
(c) Robert Swanson (d) Robert Brown

44. The spherical structured organelle that contains the genetic material is
(a) cell wall (b) ribosomes
(c) nucleus (d) mitochondria

45. Protoplasm found inside the nucleus is known as
(a) amyloplast (b) nucleoplasm
(c) cytoplasm (d) elaioplast

46. Which of the following statements are true about endoplasmic reticulum?
I. Smooth endoplasmic reticulum makes lipids.
II. It is also called the control centre of the cell.
III. It processes carbohydrates.
IV. It modifies chemicals that are toxic to the cell.
(a) I, II and III (b) I, III and IV
(c) I and IV (d) All of these

47. Which of the following statements are true about eukaryotes?
I. They are cells with a nucleus.
II. They are found both in humans and multicellular organisms.
III. Endoplasmic reticulum is present in eukaryotes.
IV. They have chemically complexed cell wall.
(a) I, II and III (b) I, III and IV
(c) I, II and IV (d) All of these

48. What do prokaryotic cells lack?
(a) Cell membrane (b) Cytoplasm
(c) Cell wall (d) Membrane bound nucleus

49. Which of the following is an example of cell devoid of nuclear membrane and mitochondria is?
(a) Bacterial cell (b) Sperm
(c) Protist (d) Sponge cell

50. Intracellular compartments do not occur in
(a) prokaryotes (b) lower plants
(c) eukaryotes (d) higher plants

51. Longest cells in human body are
(a) leg muscle cells (b) bone cells
(c) nerve cells (d) heart muscle cells

52. .... introduce the system for naming all the organism known as binomial clature.
(a) Carolus Linnaeus (b) R whittaker
(c) C Chamberland (d) E Haeckel

53. .... proposed a third kingdom to accommodate *Euglena* like organism and bacteria.
(a) E Haeckel (b) Carolus Linnaeus
(c) R Whittaker (d) C Chamberland

54. Artificial system of classification was first used by
(a) Linnaeus (b) de Candolle
(c) Theophrastus (d) Bentham and Hooker

55. The term 'taxon' for the first time was used by
(a) ICBN (b) ICZN
(c) de Candolle (d) Both (a) and (c)

56. Besides nomenclature of plants in wild, ICBN also gives binomial names for
(a) bacteria and fungus
(b) fungus
(c) fungus and cultivated plants
(d) cultivated plant

57. According to botanical nomenclature, which are not allowed
(a) synonyms (b) antonyms
(c) tautonyms (d) isonyms

58. The original specimen submitted by author himself is termed as
(a) holotype (b) paratype
(c) lectoype (d) isotype

59. How many codes of nomenclature are present?
(a) 1 (b) 2
(c) 3 (d) 4

60. International botanical congress are being held at four years interval since,
(a) 1867 (b) 1967
(c) 1888 (d) 1988

61. In .... E Jenner first vaccinated an 08 years old boy with pus from cowpox lesion.
(a) 1796 (b) 1797
(c) 1794 (d) 1795

62. In 1884 one of the Pasteur's associate .... that bacteria cannot pass through porcelain filters
(a) Chales Chamberland (b) R Whittaker
(c) Haeckel (d) Carolus Linnaeus

63. The .... are obligate intracellular parasite because they lack metabolic machinery.
(a) virus (b) bacteria
(c) fungi (d) plants

64. .... caspomore are present in the capsid of herpes virus.
(a) 163 (b) 161
(c) 162 (d) 160

65. Bacteriophage occur in two structural form having .... or helical symmetry.
(a) cubical (b) cylindrical
(c) rectangular (d) circular

66. The word virus is derived from Latin word
(a) bug (b) disease
(c) venome (d) germ

67. A lysogenic cycle involves
(a) early lysis of the host cell
(b) the ultimate formation of a prophage
(c) lysis by the lambda lytic protein
(d) a period of genome integration

68. The genetic alteration of a cell's genome is called
(a) transformation (b) reverse transcription
(c) genome conversion (d) invasion

69. The infectious substance of prions is
(a) protein (b) glycophosphate
(c) RNA (d) DNA

70. Viruses are considered to be
(a) non-living
(b) primitive precursors of bacteria
(c) a link between life and non-life
(d) primitive organisms

71. The first virus to be purified was the
(a) flu virus (b) tobacco mosaic virus
(c) small pox virus (d) polio virus

72. When a virus kills the infected host cell in which it is replicating, the reproductive cycle is called a .... cycle.
(a) lysogenic (b) phagocytic
(c) lytic (d) viroidal

73. Which of the following are not matched correctly?
(a) Virulent virus–lytic cycle
(b) Temperate virus–non-infecting virus
(c) Lysogenic virus–genome becomes part of host genome
(d) Lytic cycle–kills host cell

74. Which of the following statement is incorrect?
(a) Viruses are more closely related to chemical matter than to a living organism
(b) New strains of influenza continually arise because the virus mutates and recombines the gene encoding the protein that makes it resistant to antibodies
(c) The HIV virus uses the host cell's reverse transcriptase to manufacture DNA
(d) Some viruses enter the cell through endocytosis

75. Which of the following statement is true?
(a) The HIV virus uses the host cell's reverse transcriptase to manufacture DNA
(b) HIV binds to the human white blood cell receptor protein CD4
(c) HIV is a DNA virus
(d) Viruses and bacteria are the only infectious agents found in plants and animals

76. A gliding motion, the mechanism of which is not understood, is a characteristic of
(a) spirilla (b) streptococci
(c) filamentous bacteria (d) bacilli

77. Bacterial flagella
(a) undulate
(b) are of a 9+2 structure
(c) occur mostly on cocci
(d) are made of a single protein fibre

78. Bacterial ribosomes
(a) are unable to synthesize proteins in the presence of tetracycline
(b) are larger than eukaryotic ribosomes
(c) have the same RNA contents as in eukaryotic ribosomes
(d) contain the same forms of proteins as in eukaryotic ribosomes

79. Plasmids are best thought of as
(a) escaped fragments of eukaryotic DNA
(b) excised portions of bacterial chromosomes
(c) self-replicating RNA
(d) escaped pieces of mitochondrial DNA

80. Bacterial flagella are powered by
(a) the sodium-potassium pump
(b) a proton pump
(c) degradation of ATP
(d) changes in osmotic pressure

81. The first stage of .... is characterized by the appearance of a chancre.
(a) gonorrhea (b) genital herpes
(c) syphilis (d) chlamydia

82. Which of the following is a product for which bacteria are not employed?
(a) Cheese (b) Lactic acid
(c) Antibiotics (d) Turpentine

83. Chemoautotrophic bacteria include
(a) halophiles (b) myxobacteria
(c) spirochetes (d) sulphur bacteria

84. Organisms that obtain their energy by oxidizing inorganic chemical sources are called
(a) photoautotrophs (b) chemoautotrophs
(c) detritivores (d) heterotrophs

85. Which of the following statement is false?
(a) Gram positive bacteria have an outer membrane that stains purple
(b) Because the peptidoglycans wall of Gram positive bacteria is covered by an outer (lipopolysaccharide) membrane, they are more resistant to the action of most antibiotics than Gram negative bacteria
(c) Actinomycetes are flexible, helical bacteria which use axial filaments to move
(d) Both (b) and (c)

86. The mitochondria of eukaryotic cells most likely arose as a result of endosymbiosis between a eukaryotic cell and a
(a) blue-green alga
(b) non-sulphur purple bacterium
(c) red algae
(d) cyanobacterium

87. The protists are a paraphyletic group that have traditionally been grouped together because
(a) they are all genetically similar to each other
(b) they all have very similar morphological characters
(c) they are not fungi, animals or plants
(d) they all have similar nutritional modes and live in similar environments

88. Many protists are able to resist harsh environmental conditions by
(a) forming a cyst and slowing metabolism during times of stress
(b) utilizing a wide variety of nutritional modes
(c) reproducing asexually through the process of budding
(d) moving away from a harsh environment by using pseudopodia

89. The light-sensing organ in the *Euglena* is a
(a) flagellum (b) contractile vacuole
(c) pellicle (d) stigma

90. The parasitic kinetoplast that causes leishmaniasis must spend part of its life-cycle in a non-human host. What organism(s) serve(s) as the vector for this life-cycle?
(a) Small mammals (b) A sand fly
(c) A mosquito (d) A tse-tse fly

91. You are examining cells from an unknown organism under the microscope. You note that the cells have a membrane-bounded nucleus and that there are small cavities in the membranes along the internal cell surface. Based upon this information alone, you conclude that these most likely are .... cells.
(a) bacterial (b) diatom
(c) dinoflagellate (d) kinetoplastid

92. The parasitic protist that causes malaria, *Plasmodium,* must spend part of its life-cycle in a non-human host. What organism(s) serve(s) as the vector for this life-cycle?
(a) Small mammals (b) A sand fly
(c) A mosquito (d) A tse-tse fly

93. *Phytophthora infestans* is the oomycete that causes
(a) Chagas disease (b) potato blight
(c) red tides (d) African sleeping sickness

94. A biologist discovers an alga that is marine, multicellular, lacks flagella and centrioles and contains phycobilisomes. It probably belongs to which group?
(a) Rhodophyta (b) Brown algae
(c) Chlorophyta (d) Foraminifera

95. The green algae gave rise to which modern group of organisms?
(a) Photosynthetic bacteria
(b) Plants
(c) Photosynthetic euglenoids
(d) Animals

96. Protista is the connecting link between which groups?
(a) Monera and Fungi (b) Monera and Animals
(c) Monera and Plants (d) Monera and Virus

97. Which group is known as 'Jewels of plant kingdom'?
(a) Chrysophytes (b) Fungi
(c) Protists (d) Euglenoids

98. Which group has got lipids capable of storing light?
(a) Protists (b) Sporozoans
(c) Euglenoids (d) Diatoms

99. Which among the following indicates petroleum presence?
(a) Dinoflagellates (b) Chrysophytes
(c) Slime moulds (d) Protozoans

100. 'Whorling whips' are the nick name of which group?
(a) Euglenoids (b) Diatoms
(c) Red algae (d) Dinoflagellates

101. Which is the only colourless animal parasite among dinoflagellates?
(a) *Notiluca* (b) *Ceraium*
(c) *Gonyaulux* (d) *Blastodium*

102. Which is known as 'Fire algae' due to the phosphoresence activity?
(a) *Notiluca* (b) *Gonyaulux*
(c) *Plasmodium* (d) *Blastodium*

103. The only dinoflagellate which shows sexual reproduction?
(a) *Notiluca* (b) *Nematodium*
(c) *Ceraium* (d) *Blastodium*

104. Pellicle is present in .... and is made of ....
(a) diatoms; sugars (b) diatoms; proteins
(c) euglenoids; sugars (d) euglenoids; proteins

105. The red pigment that represents the eyespot in euglenoids is made of
(a) astaxanthin (b) protoxanthin
(c) xanthophyll (d) chorophyll

106. *Euglena* stores carbohydrates in the form of
(a) amylopectin (b) paramylum bodies
(c) paramylon (d) Both (b) and (c)

107. Acellular slime moulds mulitply by a method known as
(a) plasmotomy (b) binary fission
(c) spore formation (d) None of these

108. Cellular slime moulds reproduce by
(a) plasmotomy (b) binary fission
(c) spore formation (d) None of these

109. Which of the following statement is incorrect?
(a) Holozoic feeders survive, grow and reproduce using chemical energy derived from the oxidation of organic molecules
(b) The kingdom–Protista is the most diverse in the domain eukarya
(c) If an organism is capable of photosynthesis, it belongs to the plant kingdom
(d) *Trypanosoma,* the organism that causes sleeping sickness, is in the phylum of the zoomastigotes

110. Which of the following statement is correct regarding protists?
(a) One characteristic that sets the protists apart from the rest of the kingdoms is their small size
(b) Diatoms have intricate double shells made up of calcium carbonate
(c) Rusts and mildews are slime molds
(d) None of the above

111. The eukaryotic multicellular reducers are
(a) parasite (b) bacteria
(c) virus (d) fungi

112. The fungi kingdom is described as
(a) eukaryotic, multicellular
(b) eukaryotic, unicellular
(c) prokaryotic, multicellular
(d) prokaryotic, unicellular

113. Vascular invasion is characteristic of
(a) sporotrichosis (b) candidiasis
(c) mucormycosis (d) blastomycosis

114. Which of the following is not a characteristic of the fungi?
(a) They are all absorptive heterotrophs
(b) They have cell walls made of chitin
(c) Mitosis takes place within the nuclear membrane
(d) They are all motile

115. A mycelium is
(a) a specialized reproductive structure of a fungus
(b) a mass of connected fungal hyphae
(c) a mutualistic relationship between a fungus and a plant
(d) a partition between the cells of fungal hyphae

116. Which of the following statements best describes fungi?
(a) All are eukaryotic, multicellular autotrophs
(b) All are eukaryotic heterotrophs that feed by absorption
(c) All are prokaryotic, multicellular autotrophs
(d) All are eukaryotic heterotrophs that feed by ingestion

117. A wildlife pathologist is examining some skin tissue from a dead frog. She notes the presence of a fungus. She cultures some of the fungal cells and notices that some of the cells are flagellated. She concludes that the frog has a fungal disease caused by
(a) an ascomycete (b) a zygomycete
(c) a basdiomycete (d) a chytrid

118. You are walking in the woods and see a fungus that is unfamiliar to you. You remove a reproductive structure, and take it home to examine further. When you look at it under the microscope, you find a zygosporangium. Based on this information alone, this fungus is a(n)
(a) Zygomycete (b) Chytrid
(c) Basidiomycete (d) Ascomycete

119. A basidium is typically observed in the common
(a) bread mold (b) gilled mushroom
(c) lichen (d) chytrid

120. An ascomycete can be distinguished from other fungi
(a) because ascomycetes are mainly diploid
(b) because ascomycetes lack a dikaryotic phase
(c) by the presence of eight sexual spores in an ascus
(d) by the presence of gills on the mycelium

121. A lichen can be described as a mutualistic symbiosis between an ascomycete and a(n)
(a) chytrid (b) archaebacterium
(c) green alga (d) angiosperm root

122. How many species of fungi are thought to exist?
(a) 1500 (b) 100000
(c) 1.5 million (d) 1.5 billion

123. A .... is the simplest animal discussed in this chapter to have ....
(a) sponge; bilateral symmetry
(b) flatworm; a body cavity
(c) roundworm; a complete digestive tract
(d) jelly; a complete digestive tract

124. Deep in the tropical rain forest, a botanist discovered an unusual plant with vascular tissues, stomata a cuticle, flagellated sperm, cone-like reproductive structures bearing seeds, and an alternation-of-generation life cycle. He was very excited about this discovery because it would be rather unusual for a plant to have both
(a) a cuticle and flagellated sperm
(b) vascular tissues and alternation of generations
(c) seeds and flagellated sperm
(d) alternation of generations and seeds

125. The pinyon pine lives in near-desert areas in western North America. This habitat is a bit unusual for gymnosperms because they
(a) have a long life cycle for such a short growing season
(b) possess flagellated sperm that must swim to the egg
(c) produce extremely small quantities of pollen
(d) lack vascular tissues and are unable to transport much water

126. Fungal mitosis is unusual in that
(a) it occurs without spindle fibres
(b) it resembles plant meiosis, having a reduction division
(c) it results in clusters of chromosomes without a nuclear membrane
(d) it takes place within the nucleus

127. Parasexuality occurs
(a) within heterokaryotic hyphae
(b) between dikaryotic hyphae
(c) only in yeasts
(d) None of the above

128. Basidiospores are borne on the ends of
(a) basidiocarps (b) trichognes
(c) sterigmata (d) secondary mycelia

129. In the Zygomycetes, most spores are produced by
(a) somatic meiosis (b) mitosis
(c) zygotic meiosis (d) sporic meiosis

130. A small out growth which supports basidiospore?
(a) Pasmodesma (b) Ascus
(c) Sterigma (d) Oidium

131. Which of the following statement is correct?
(a) The deuteromycetes are an artificial collection of fungi that are probably not very closely related
(b) Hyphae are made up of a long string of cells, separated by septa, that prevents the mixing of cytoplasm between cells
(c) The main body of a fungus is the mushroom structure
(d) In fungi, only the reproductive cells are haploid

132. Plants are .... in nutritional mode making their own food by ....
(a) heterotrophic; respiration
(b) autotrophic; respiration
(c) autotrophic; photosynthesis
(d) heterotrophic; photosynthesis

133. A freshwater green alga, rich in protein is
(a) *Ulothrix* (b) *Chlorella*
(c) *Chlamydomonas* (d) *Spirogyra*

134. After fertilization the zygote of a seed plant becomes
(a) fruit (b) embryo
(c) seed (d) ovule

135. A pine seed has cotyledons and tissue from the ....
(a) male gametophyte (b) female gametophyte
(c) megasporangium (d) pollen grain

136. A prokaryotic autotrophic nitrogen fixing symbiont found in
(a) *Pisum* (b) *Alnus*
(c) *Cycas* (d) *Cicer*

137. Consider the following four statements whether they are correct or wrong?
I. The sporophyte in liverworts is more elaborate than that in mosses.
II. *Salvinia* is heterosporous.
III. The life-cycle in all seed bearing plants is diplontic.
IV. In *Pinus* male and female cones are borne on different trees.

The two wrong statements together are
(a) II and III (b) I and II
(c) I and III (d) Iand IV

138. In a flower, which terminal structure is part of a stamen?
(a) Anther (b) Ovary
(c) Stigma (d) Style

139. In a flowering plants megaspore undergoes mitosis and develops into a
(a) anther (b) seed
(c) ovary (d) sepal

140. Indusium is found in
(a) *Selaginella* (b) *Pinus*
(c) *Pteris* (d) *Cycas*

141. Mannitol is the stored food in
(a) *Gracillaria* (b) *Chara*
(c) *Porphyra* (d) *Fucus*

142. Meiosis occurs in the zygote of
(a) *Dryopteris* (b) *Chlamydomonas*
(c) *Funaria* (d) *Puccinia*

143. Sieve tubes and companion cells are absent in
(a) mango (b) pea
(c) angiosperms (d) pteridophyta

144. The female reproductive structure of small, non-vascular plants that produces a single egg by mitosis is
(a) archegonium (b) antheridium
(c) gemmae cup (d) sporangiophore

145. The gametophyte is not an independent, free-living generation in
(a) *Pinus* (b) *Polytrichum*
(c) *Adiantum* (d) *Marchantia*

146. The ladder-like structure found in *Spirogyra* is due to
(a) scalariform conjugation
(b) lateral conjugation
(c) direct conjugation
(d) asexual reproduction

147. The unicellular green algae that undergo both asexual and sexual reproduction are
(a) *Chlamydomonas* (b) *Selaginella*
(c) *Pinus* (d) *Dryopteris*

148. The walking fern is so named because
(a) it is dispersed through the agency of walking animals
(b) it propagates vegetatively by its shoot tips
(c) its spores are able to walk
(d) it knows how to walk by itself

149. Which of the following is a living fossil?
(a) *Spirogyra* (b) *Cycas*
(c) Moss (d) *Saccharomyces*

150. Which of the following is commonly called as 'pond scum'?
(a) *Nostoc* (b) *Ulothrix*
(c) *Spirogyra* (d) *Anabaena*

151. Which of the following plant species you would select for the production of bioethanol?
(a) *Jatropha* (b) *Brassica*
(c) *Zea mays* (d) *Pongamia*

152. The distinguishing character of imparipinnate leaf is that
(a) leaflets are large
(b) rachis is terminated by an unpaired odd leaflet
(c) rachis is strong
(d) All leaflets are borne in pairs

153. The ovary is half inferior in flowers of
(a) guava (b) peach
(c) cucumber (d) cotton

154. Which one of the following statements is correct?
(a) Flower of tulip is a modified shoot
(b) In tomato, fruit is a capsule
(c) Seeds of orchids have oil-rich endosperms
(d) Placentation in primose is basal

155. The 'Eyes' of the potato tuber are
(a) axillary buds (b) root buds
(c) flower buds (d) shoot buds

156. Green leaf-like modified aerial stems/branches with a single internode are called
(a) bulbils (b) cladodes
(c) phylloclades (d) phyllodes

157. In groundnut, the root is
(a) epiphytic (b) napiform
(c) nodulated (d) photosynthetic

158. Ginger multiplies vegetatively by
(a) bud (b) stem
(c) tuber (d) rhizome

159. Apomixis is a type of reproduction that results is the development of a/an
(a) new organism without fusion of gametes
(b) new organism from fusion products of gametes
(c) embryo from endosperm
(d) embryo from nucellus

160. Egg apparatus consists of
(a) egg (b) egg and polar nuclei
(c) egg and synergids (d) egg and antipodal cells

161. What would be the number of chromosomes of the aleurone cells of a plant with 42 chromosomes in its roots tip cells?
(a) 21 (b) 42 (c) 63 (d) 84

162. Embryo sac is also known as
(a) microgametophyte (b) megagametophyte
(c) microsporangium (d) megasporangium

163. Embryo sac is called monosporic when it develops from
(a) all the four megaspores
(b) only from two functional megaspores
(c) three megaspores
(d) one of the megaspores out of the four megaspores which are derived from division of megaspore mother cell

164. Nucellar polyembryony is reported in species of
(a) *Brassica* (b) *Citrus*
(c) *Gossypium* (d) *Triticum*

165. Endosperm of angiosperms results after fertilization from
(a) synergids (b) secondary nucleus
(c) antipodal cells (d) egg

166. Fertilization in which male gametes are carried through pollen tube is known as
(a) porogamy (b) syngamy
(c) siphonogamy (d) chalazogamy

167. Which phylum has a true coelom?
(a) Cnidaria (b) Mollusca
(c) Porifera (d) Annelida

168. Which organism possesses characteristics of plants and animals?
(a) Bacteria (b) Monera
(c) *Euglena* (d) *Mycoplasma*

169. A fat called blubber could be obtained from
(a) bats (b) porpoises
(c) dolphin (d) blue whale

170. Which one of the following phylum is characterized by absence of true coelom?
(a) Annelida (b) Mollusca
(c) Echinodermata (d) Nematoda

171. Which one of the following pairs of animals comprises 'jawless fishes'?
(a) Guppies and hag fishes
(b) Lampreys and eels
(c) Mackerels and Rohu
(d) Lampreys and hag fishes

172. Which of the following types of fish is eaten usually by humans?
(a) Jawless (b) Bony
(c) Cartilaginous (d) All of these

173. Which of the following statements is true?
(a) Invertebrates posses a tubular nerve cord
(b) Non-chordates have a vertebral column
(c) All chordates are vertebrates
(d) All vertebrates are chordates

174. Which of the following statements is true about roundworms?
(a) Roundworms may reach 5 cm in length
(b) They are non-segmented
(c) They are generally dark coloured
(d) They occur only in the soil

175. Which kind of symmetry occurs in sea anemone?
(a) Bilateral (b) Radial
(c) Asymmetry (d) None of these

176. In a sponge which of the followings are responsible for maintaining the current of water?
(a) Pinacocytes (b) Porocytes
(c) Choanocytes (d) Amoebocytes

177. Which is not an insect?
(a) Spider (b) Termite
(c) Mosquito (d) Ant

178. When tail is cylindrical and ventral scales do not extend the entire width of belly the snake is
(a) definitely poisonous
(b) can be poisonous or non-poisonous
(c) non-poisonous
(d) deadly poisonous

179. Collar cells are general characteristic of
(a) Sand worm (b) Roundworms
(c) Coelenterata (d) Sponges

180. Common character of all vertebrates without exception is
(a) body divided into head, trunk and tail
(b) two pairs of limbs
(c) exoskeleton
(d) presence of skull

181. What will you look for to identify the sex of the following?
(a) Male shark – Claspers borne on pelvic fins
(b) Female *Ascaris* – Sharply curved posterior end
(c) Male frog – A copulatory pad on the first digit of the hind limb
(d) Female cockroach – Anal cerci

182. What is common between kiwi, penguin and ostrich?
(a) They are running birds
(b) They are flightless birds
(c) They are migratory birds
(d) They have four toes

183. What colour is the blood of crayfish?
(a) Green (b) Blue
(c) Red (d) White

184. Turtles are
(a) arthropods (b) pisces
(c) reptiles (d) molluscs

185. A true coelom is lined on all sides by
(a) ectoderm (b) mesoderm
(c) endoderm (d) Both (a) and (b)

186. Which of the following possesses post anal tail?
(a) Spider (b) Scorpion
(c) Cockroach (d) Cobra

187. Tapeworm is
(a) digenetic parasite (b) nematode
(c) monogenetic parasite (d) annelid

188. Tapeworm does not possess digestive system as it
(a) doesn't require food
(b) obtain food through general surface
(c) does not require solid food
(d) lives in intestine

189. Radial symmetry is usually associated with
(a) lower grade of organization
(b) creeping mode of life
(c) aquatic life
(d) sedentary mode of life

190. Male mosquitoes usually feed on
(a) garbage (b) human blood
(c) flower sap (d) All of these

191. In which one of the following the genus name, its two characters and its class/phylum are correctly matched?

Genus	Two character	Class/ Phylum
1. *Aurelia*	(a) Cnidoblasts	Coelenterata
	(b) Organ level of organization	
2. *Ascaris*	(a) Body segmented	Annelida
	(b) Males and females distinct	
3. *Salamandra*	(a) A tympanum represents ear	Amphibia
	(b) Fertilization is external	
4. *Pteropus*	(a) Skin possesses hair	Mammalia
	(b) Oviparous	

(a) 1 (b) 2
(c) 3 (d) 4

192. Which of the following is not the main criteria for five kingdom system of classification?
(a) Cell structure and thallus organization
(b) Mode of nutrition and reproduction
(c) Phylogenetic relationship
(d) Gram staining

193. Two plants can be conclusively said to belong to the same species if they
(a) can reproduce freely with each other and form seeds
(b) have more than 90 percent similar genes
(c) look similar and possess identical secondary metaboites
(d) have same number of chromosomes

194. Reproduction is the characteristic feature of living organisms. Which of the following cannot reproduce?
(a) *Amoeba* and *Paramecium*
(b) Fungi and filamentous algae
(c) Humans and Aves
(d) Mules and worker bees

195. *Nicotiana sylvestris* flowers only during long days and *N. tobacum* flowers only during short days. If raised in the laboratory under different photoperiods, they can be induced to flower at the same time and can be cross fertilized to produce self-fertile offspring. What is the best reason for considering *N. sylvestris* and *N. tobacum* to be separate species?
(a) They are physiologically distinct
(b) They are morphologically distinct
(c) They cannot interbreed in nature
(d) They are reproductively distinct

196. What is a keystone species?
(a) A species, which makes up only a small proportion of the total biomass of a community, yet has a huge impact on the community's organization and survival
(b) A common species that has plenty of biomass, yet has a fairly low impact on the community's organization
(c) A rare species that has minimal impact on the biomass and on other species in the community
(d) A dominant species that constitutes a large proportion of the biomass and which affect many other species

197. You would expect to find the greatest number of phyla of animal .... and the greatest number of species of animals ....
(a) on land; in the sea (b) in freshwater; in the sea
(c) in the sea; on land (d) in the sea; in freshwater

198. Which of the following is not a difference between algae and plants?
(a) Plant cells have rigid cellulose walls and algae cells do not
(b) Plant zygotes and embryos are protected in moist chambers, and those of algae are not
(c) Algae lack discrete organs–leaves, stems, roots–characteristic of plants
(d) Plants have xylem and phloem and algae do not

199. 'Ordinos Anomali' of Bentham and Hooker includes
(a) seeds plants showing abnormal forms of growth and development
(b) plants represented only in fossil state
(c) plants described in the literature but which Bentham and Hooker did not see in original
(d) a few orders, which could not be placed satisfactorily in the classification

200. Which of the following is not true for a species?
(a) Members of a species can interbreed
(b) Variations occur among members of a species
(c) Each species is reproductively isolated from every other species
(d) Gene flow does not occur between the populations of a species

201. The different forms of interbreeding species that live in different geographical regions are called
(a) sibling species (b) allopatric species
(c) sympatric species (d) polytypic species

202. Phenetic classification of organisms is based on
(a) observable characteristics of existing organisms
(b) the ancestral lineage of existing organism
(c) dendrogram based on DNA characteristics
(d) sexual characteristics

203. Biological species concept emphasizes on
(a) geographical isolation
(b) reproductive isolation
(c) physiological isolation
(d) None of the above

204. Which of the following book is not associated with Carolus Linnaeus, the father of Taxonomy and Nomenclature?
(a) *Systema Naturae*
(b) *Genera Plantarum*
(c) *Species Plantarum*
(d) *Historia Generalis Plantarum*

205. Which of the following best describes how fertilization occurs in a conifer?
(a) A sperm cell swims through a film of moisture to fertilize the egg
(b) A pollen grain carried by wind fertilizes the egg
(c) A pollen grain carried by wind produces a sperm that fertilizes the egg
(d) A sperm cell carried by wind fertilizes the egg

206. During the carboniferous period, forests consisting mainly of .... produced vast quantities of organic matter, which was buried and later turned into coal.
(a) early angiosperms
(b) ferns and other seedless plants
(c) giant mosses
(d) gymnosperms

207. Which of the following is either not an excretory structure or is incorrectly matched with its class?
(a) Metanephridia — Oligochaeta
(b) Malpighian tubules — Echinoidea
(c) Flame cells — Turbellaria
(d) Thin region of cuticle — Crustacea

208. Torsion
(a) is embryonic asymmetric growth that results in a U-shaped digestive tract in gastropods
(b) is characteristic of molluscs
(c) is responsible for the spiral growth of bivalve shells
(d) describes the thrashing movement of nematodes

209. Oviparity is a reproductive strategy that
(a) allows mammals to bear well-developed young
(b) is used by both birds and reptiles
(c) is necessary for vertebrates to reproduce on land
(d) protects the embryo inside the mother and uses the food resources of the egg

210. A gastrovascular cavity
(a) functions in both digestion and circulation and has a single opening
(b) has a large incurrent siphon and smaller excurrent pores
(c) is found in the phyla–Cnidaria, Platyhelminthes and Rotifera
(d) develops from the hollow blastula stage

211. Which of the following combinations of phylum and characteristics is incorrect?
(a) Nemertea—proboscis worm, first complete digestive tract
(b) Rotifera—parthenogenesis, crown of cilia, microscopic animals
(c) Nematoda—gastrovascular cavity, tough cuticle, ubiquitous
(d) Annelida—segmentation, closed circulation, hydrostatic skeleton

212. Cephalization
(a) is the formation of a coelom by the outpocketing of the archenteron
(b) is a diagnostic characteristic of deuterostomes
(c) is common in radially symmetrical animals
(d) is associated with motile animals that concentrate sensory organs in a head region

213. Which of the following is descriptive of protostomes?
(a) Radial and determinate cleavage, blastopore becomes mouth
(b) Spiral ande indeterminate cleavage, coelom forms as split in solid mass of mesoderm
(c) Spiral and determinate cleavage, blastopore becomes mouth, schizocoelous development
(d) Spiral and indeterminate cleavage, blastopore becomes mouth, enterocoelous development

214. Phytoplankton
(a) form the basis of most marine food chains
(b) include the multicellular green, red and brown algae
(c) are mutualistic symbionts that provide food for coral reef communities
(d) are unicellular protozoans

215. The slime molds and multicellular algae are presently included in the kingdom–Protista because
(a) they appear to be more closely related to unicellular eukaryotes
(b) they lack important characteristics of the fungi and plants
(c) kingdom–Protista includes eukaryotic organisms that do not clearly belong in the other three kingdoms
(d) All of the above

216. According to the endosymbiont theory,
(a) multicellularity evolved when primitive cells incorporated prokaryotic cells that then took on specialized functions
(b) the symbiotic associations found in lichens resulted from the incorporation of algal protists into the ancestors of fungi
(c) the chloroplasts and mitochondria of eukaryotic cells began as prokaryotic endosymbionts
(d) the infoldings and specialization of the plasma membrane led to the evolution of the endomembrane system

217. There are only a few species of cartilaginous fishes, compared with the bony fishes.

Cartilaginous fishes are mostly limited to a lifestyle of swimming fast in open water. Bony fishes have adapted to many different lifestyles–clinging to seaweed, hiding

in crevices, even burrowing in the bottom. This could probably be attributed to the fact that bony fishes
(a) have more rigid skeletons
(b) are smaller than cartilaginous fishes
(c) have operculum and swim bladders
(d) have lateral line systems and paired fins

218. Imagine that you are a palontologist (a scientist who studies fossils of ancient life forms). In a recent dig, you unearthed bones of all of the following. Which could you have found in the oldest sediments?
(a) Amphibians (b) Placental mammals
(c) Dinosaurs (d) Birds

219. Which of the folowing phyla include numerous parasites and pests?
(a) Roundworms and flatworms
(b) Molluscs and roundworms
(c) Annelids and flatworms
(d) Annelids and roundworms

220. A marine biologist dredged up a small animal from the bottom of the ocean. It was uniformly segmented, with short, stiff appendages and soft, flexible skin. It had a complete digestive system and a circulatory system but no skeleton. Based on this description, this animal sounds most like
(a) a lancelet (b) a crustacean
(c) a mollusc (d) an annelid

221. 'Pil bugs' or 'sowbugs', often found under rocks and logs in moist places, are perhaps most noticed for their ability to roll up into a ball when disturbed. Sowbugs are really crustaceans, not insects. Therefore, a sowbug does not have
(a) an exoskeleton (b) gills
(c) three pairs of legs (d) antennae

222. Some recent molecular evidence indicates that cnidarians, as well as sponges, might have evolved from protists quite independently from other animals. Which of the following also suggests a separate origin?
(a) Cnidarians have no nervous tissue
(b) Cnidarians have a gastrovascular cavity
(c) Cnidarians are unsegmented
(d) Cnidarians are radially symmetrical

223. Zoologists have placed chordates and echinoderms on one major branch of the animal phylogenetic tree, and molluscs, annelids and arthropods on another major branch. Which of the following is the basis for this separation into two branches?
(a) Whether or not the animals have a skeleton
(b) Type of symmetry
(c) Whather or not the animals have a body cavity
(d) How the body cavity is formed

224. The fact that karyogamy does not immediately follow plasmogamy
(a) is necessary to create coenocytic hyphae
(b) allows for the development of more genetic variation
(c) allows fungi to reproduce asexually most of the time
(d) creates dikaryotic cells that may benefit from the presence of duplicate copies of alleles

225. An example of coevolution is
(a) wind pollination in conifers
(b) a flower with nectar guides that direct bees to its nectaries
(c) the synchronization of nutrient development and fertilization resuting from double fertilization
(d) the retention of the gametophyte generation to weed out harmful mutations
(e) the clumping of moss plants to support each other and create an absorbent mat

226. If you could take a time machine back to the Carboniferous period, which of the following scenarios would you most likely confront?
(a) Creeping mats of low-growing bryophytes
(b) Fields of tall grasses swaying in the wind
(c) Swamps dominated by large lycopods, horse-tails and ferns
(d) Huge forests of naked-seed tress filling the air with pollen

227. The name given to each of the three divisions of fungi is based on
(a) the structure in which karyogamy occurs during sexual reproduction
(b) the location of plasmogamy during sexual reproduction
(c) the location of the dikaryotic stage in the life cycle
(d) the structure that produces asexual spores

228. Match list I (animals) with list II (the group to which they belong) and select the correct answer using the codes given below the lists.

List I	List II
A. Hammerheaded shark	1. Marsupial
B. Pangolin	2. *Condrichthyes*
C. Emu	3. *Neornithes*
D. Mud puppy	4. Eutheria
	5. Urodela

Codes

	A	B	C	D		A	B	C	D
(a)	2	4	3	5	(b)	4	3	5	1
(c)	2	4	5	1	(d)	4	2	3	5

229. Consider the following statements.
I. Pisces and amphibia can be distinguished from each other on the basis of fundamental differences in the lateral line system.
II. Elasmobranchi and teleostomi can be distinguished form each other on the basis of endoskeleton.
III. *Scoliodon* and *Torpedo* are distinguished on the basis of electric organ through both belong to the class Pisces.
IV. Salamandrais distinguishable from Bufo on the basis of parotid gland.

Select the correct answer from the given option.
(a) I, II, III and IV are correct
(b) I and IV are correct
(c) II and III are correct
(d) II, III and IV are correct

230. Which of the following pairs are correctly matched?

Plant		Organ of Reproduction
I. *Oscillatoria*	—	Hormogone
II. *Nostoc*	—	Akinetes
III. *Streptomyces*	—	Conidia
IV. *Albugo*	—	Zoospore

Select the correct answer from the codes given below

(a) I, II and III (b) I, II, III and IV
(c) I, III and IV (d) II and IV

231. Match list I with list II and select the correct answer using the codes given below the lists.

List I	List II
A. Branchiopoda	1. *Daphnia*
B. Copepoda	2. *Scolopendra*
C. Chilopoda	3. *Cyclops*
D. Diplopoda	4. *Julus*

Codes

	A	B	C	D
(a)	1	3	4	2
(b)	3	1	4	2
(c)	1	3	2	4
(d)	3	1	2	4

232. Consider the following statements.

I. Claspers in sharks are posterior extensions of pelvic fin.
II. Claspers in sharks are modified pectoral fins.
III. Gonopodium in a few teleosts is specialized anal fin.
IV. Gonopodium in a few teleosts is partly modified caudal fin.

Select the correct answer from the given option.

(a) I and II are correct
(b) II and III are correct
(c) I and IV are correct
(d) II and IV are correct

233. Which of the following statements are correct?

I. Rule of Priority in plant nomenclature commenced from 1853.
II. Binomial nomenclature was introduced by Linnaeus in 1753.
III. The orchid fruit contains five distinct seeds.
IV. Gynobasic style is found in Lamiaceae.

Select the correct answer using the codes given below.

(a) I and II (b) II and IV
(c) I and III (d) II and III

234. Consider the following types of classification

I. Bentham and Hooker's system
II. Linnaeus's system
III. Cronquist's system
IV. Hutchinson's system

The correct sequence of the chronological order in which these classification systems appeared is

(a) I, II, III and IV (b) II, I, IV and III
(c) I, II, IV and III (d) II, I, III and IV

235. Consider the following statements:

In a ripe tomato, as compared to an unripe tomato, the amount of

I. vitamins is higher.
II. carbohydrates is less.
III. minerals is less.
IV. proteins is higher.

Of these statements

(a) I, III and IV are correct (b) I, II and IV are correct
(c) II, III and IV are correct (d) I, II and III are correct

236. Match list I with list II and select the correct answer using the codes given below the lists.

List I	List II
A. *Lichen*	1. *Virus*
B. *Fungi*	2. *Symbionts*
C. *Cyanobacteria*	3. *Decomposers*
D. *Bacteriophage*	4. *Flagellate*
	5. *Blue-green algae*

Codes

	A	B	C	D
(a)	2	1	4	3
(b)	1	3	5	4
(c)	5	2	3	1
(d)	2	3	5	1

Answers

1. (d) 2. (a) 3. (d) 4. (a) 5. (a) 6. (d) 7. (b) 8. (b) 9. (b) 10. (d)
11. (a) 12. (d) 13. (d) 14. (d) 15. (b) 16. (d) 17. (a) 18. (a) 19. (d) 20. (d)
21. (d) 22. (a) 23. (d) 24. (a) 25. (a) 26. (a) 27. (a) 28. (a) 29. (c) 30. (d)
31. (a) 32. (d) 33. (a) 34. (b) 35. (c) 36. (a) 37. (d) 38. (b) 39. (c) 40. (b)
41. (d) 42. (c) 43. (b) 44. (c) 45. (b) 46. (b) 47. (a) 48. (d) 49. (a) 50. (a)
51. (c) 52. (a) 53. (a) 54. (c) 55. (d) 56. (a) 57. (c) 58. (a) 59. (d) 60. (a)
61. (a) 62. (a) 63. (a) 64. (b) 65. (a) 66. (c) 67. (d) 68. (a) 69. (a) 70. (a)
71. (b) 72. (c) 73. (b) 74. (c) 75. (b) 76. (c) 77. (d) 78. (a) 79. (b) 80. (b)
81. (c) 82. (d) 83. (d) 84. (b) 85. (d) 86. (b) 87. (c) 88. (a) 89. (d) 90. (b)
91. (c) 92. (c) 93. (a) 94. (a) 95. (b) 96. (b) 97. (a) 98. (d) 99. (b) 100. (d)
101. (d) 102. (a) 103. (c) 104. (c) 105. (a) 106. (d) 107. (a) 108. (b) 109. (c) 110. (d)
111. (d) 112. (a) 113. (c) 114. (d) 115. (b) 116. (b) 117. (d) 118. (a) 119. (b) 120. (c)
121. (c) 122. (b) 123. (c) 124. (c) 125. (a) 126. (d) 127. (a) 128. (c) 129. (b) 130. (c)
131. (a) 132. (c) 133. (b) 134. (b) 135. (b) 136. (c) 137. (d) 138. (a) 139. (b) 140. (c)
141. (d) 142. (b) 143. (d) 144. (a) 145. (a) 146. (a) 147. (a) 148. (b) 149. (b) 150. (c)
151. (c) 152. (b) 153. (b) 154. (a) 155. (a) 156. (c) 157. (c) 158. (d) 159. (a) 160. (c)
161. (c) 162. (b) 163. (d) 164. (b) 165. (b) 166. (c) 167. (d) 168. (c) 169. (d) 170. (d)
171. (d) 172. (b) 173. (d) 174. (b) 175. (b) 176. (c) 177. (a) 178. (c) 179. (d) 180. (d)
181. (a) 182. (b) 183. (b) 184. (c) 185. (b) 186. (d) 187. (a) 188. (b) 189. (d) 190. (c)
191. (c) 192. (d) 193. (a) 194. (d) 195. (c) 196. (a) 197. (c) 198. (a) 199. (d) 200. (d)
201. (b) 202. (a) 203. (b) 204. (d) 205. (c) 206. (b) 207. (b) 208. (a) 209. (b) 210. (a)
211. (c) 212. (d) 213. (c) 214. (a) 215. (d) 216. (c) 217. (c) 218. (a) 219. (a) 220. (d)
221. (c) 222. (d) 223. (d) 224. (d) 225. (b) 226. (c) 227. (a) 228. (a) 229. (c) 230. (b)
231. (c) 232. (c) 233. (b) 234. (c) 235. (b) 236. (d)

28 Indian Sub-Continent and its Organisms

Natural History of Indian Sub-Continent

Syllabus

- Natural History of Indian Sub-continent: Major Habitat Types of the Sub-continent, Geographic Origins and Migrations of Species; Common Indian Mammals and Birds; Seasonality and Phenology of the Sub-Continent.
- Organisms of Health and Agricultural Importance.

Alfred Russell Wallace is popularly known as the **Father of Biogeography** and he established **biogeography** (the study of the past and present geographical distribution of organisms) by studying the distribution of animal species around the world. Some animals are found in one region and not in others. There are patterns in how species occur geographically, based on various factors such as where they evolved, how far they dispersed and how changes in the Earth affected their distribution. Biogeographic distributions demonstrate the fact that species have evolved under differing conditions in different parts of the world. Isolation of related forms over time in different environmental conditions results in the development of new specializations. Biogeography deals with the geographical distribution of both plants and animals. Communities of plants and animals in different geographical areas of the world differ widely from each other. Biogeography is divided in two branches: **1.** Phytogeography and **2.** Zoogeography. Phytogeography (plant geography) deals with origin, distribution and environmental interrelationships of plants. Zoogeography deals with the migration and distribution of animals.

Continental drift is a measurable phenomenon; it has happened in the past and continues today. Movements of up to 2-11 cm a year have been recorded between continents using laser technology. The movements of the Earth's 12 major crustal plates are driven by thermal convection currents in the mantle; a geological process known as **plate tectonics.** Some continents appear to be drifting apart while others are on a direct collision course. Various lines of evidence show that the modern continents were once joined together as 'super-continents'. One super-continent, called **Gondwana,** was made up of the Southern continents some 200 million years ago. The diagram below shows some of the data collected that are used as evidence to indicate how the modern continents once fitted together.

Sub-continent is 'a vast and more or less self-contained sub-division of continent'. The term Indian sub-continent and South Asia are used interchangeably. Due to political reasons some prefer the term South Asian sub-continent, The Indo-pak sub-continent or simply South Asia.

Indian sub-continent belongs to the Indomalaya ecozone (Oriental Realm) which extends across most of South and South-East Asia and into the Southern parts of East Asia. The Indian sub-continent bioregion covers most of India, Pakistan, Bangladesh, Nepal, Bhutan and Sri Lanka. The Hindu Kush, Karakoram, Himalaya and Patkai ranges bound the bioregion on the North-West, North and North-East; these ranges were formed by the collision of the Northward-drifting Indian sub-continent with Asia beginning 45 million years ago. The Hindu Kush, Karakoram and Himalaya are a major biogeographic boundary between the sub-tropical and tropical flora and fauna of the Indian sub-continent and the temperate-climate Palearctic ecozone.

On the basis of tectonic history, physiography and landforms, India may be divided into four regions:

(i) The Elevated Peninsular Region

(a) The North Central Highlands
(b) The South Central Highlands
(c) The Eastern Plateau
(d) The Meghalaya-Mikir Uplands
(e) The North Deccan
(f) The South Deccan
(g) The Western Ghats (Sahaydri)
(h) The Eastern Ghats

(ii) The Northern Plains of India

(a) The Plains of Rajasthan including Thar Desert
(b) The Punjab-Haryana Plains
(c) The Ganga Plains
(d) The Brahmaputra Plains

The Northern Plains of India (Punjab, Haryana, Uttar Pradesh, Uttarakhand, Bihar, West Bengal and Asom) are highly productive, intensively cultivated and densely populated.

(iii) The Himalayas and Associated Folded Mountains

(a) The Trans-Himalayas
(b) The Greater Himalayas
(c) The Lesser Himalayas and
(d) The Shiwalik of the outer Himalayas (Most of the Hill stations of India, like Gulmarg, Dalhousie, Kullu-Manali, Shimla, Mussoorie, Ranikhet, Almora, Darjeeling, etc., lie in the lesser Himalayas).

(iv) The Coastal Plains

(a) The Western Coastal Plains:
- The Konkan
- The Malabar Coast

(b) The Eastern Coastal Plains:
- The Northern Circar
- The Coromandal Coast

Major Habitat Types

Ecosystem is composed of physical environment (including its climate and altitude) and the living organisms (including plants, animals and other organisms). Habitat its the place, where a particular organism lives described in term of its climatic vegetative, topographic and other relevent factors. It may vary both in space and time. However, the conditions found in a specific habitat at a given time are unique to that habitat even though they may resemble conditions found in other similar habitats. There are four major types of habitats in the biosphere:

1. Freshwater **2.** Marine
3. Estuarine **4.** Terrestrial

Freshwater Habitat

Freshwater occupies a relatively small portion (about 3%) of aquatic area. Freshwater is of great importance to the mankind. The organisms of freshwater are autotrophs, macroconsumers and saprotrophs (the decomposers). On the basis of life form they may be categorized as benthos (bottom), plankton (floating), nekton (swimming) and neuston (resting or swimming on surface). There are generally three zones in these, *i.e.,* **littoral zone** (shallow water region), **limnetic zone** (open water zone), the **profundal zone** (bottom zone, usually absent in ponds). Freshwater habitat are generally of two types:

(a) Lentic Habitat

Such bodies has standing water like ponds, lakes, swamps, bogs, etc. The **littoral zone** has rooted or benthic plants, pytoplanktons, floating green plants rooted hydrophytes. The rooted hydrophytes may have assimilatory organs above water level (*e.g., Typha, Scirpus, Sagittaria*) or floating leaves (*e.g., Nelumbo, Nymphaea*) or completely submerged in water (*e.g., Hydrilla, Vellisneria, Nitella, Chara, Potamogeton, Ceratophyllum, Anacharis, Isoetes,* etc). The common algal species of littoral zone are *Spirogyra, Zygnema, Oedogonium, Cladophora, Chara,* etc. The consumers of littoral zone are pond snails, nymphs, rotifers, *Hydra,* flatworms and amphibians. The zooplanktons of this zone are water fleas, some Cyclopoidea, Harpacticoidea some rotifers and many ostracods. Phytoplanktonic algae are producers in **lemnetic zone** while consumers are zooplanktons (copepods, cladocerans and rotifers). The consumers commonly found in both littoral and limnetic zone are *Diaptomus sida, Bosmina, Cyclops, Diaphanosoma,* etc. The organisms of **profundal zone** are mainly depend on littoral and limnetic zone for their food as no light is penetrated this zone. Major life forms are bacteria and fungi. In lakes, the limnetic and profundal zones are relatively large as compared to littoral zone.

(b) Lotic Habitat

These habitat have running water like river, streams, spring etc. The velocity of water varies in different part of the same body. The chief producers are green algae like *Cladophora,* diatoms and aquatic mosses. The common animals found an sponges, caddisfly larvae, snails and flatworms fish and stonefly and mayfly nymphs. The zonation is longitudinal which is influenced by pH, velocity and temperature of the body.

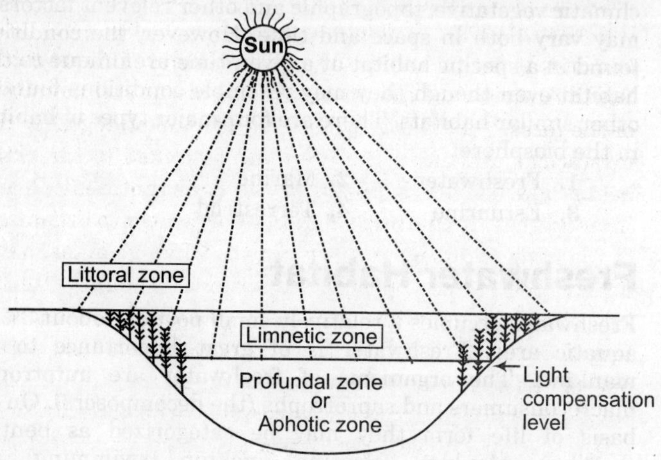

Fig. 28.1 Zonation in freshwater habitat

Marine Habitat

Marine habitat occupies about 97% of the total aquatic area. The sea is deep and continuous the all oceans are connected. As in freshwater habitat this also has zones are **neritic zone** (near shore), **intertidal zone** (zone between high and low tides, also called littoral zone). These zones are included under continental self (extending for a distance offshore). The region of open sea beyond continental self is called oceanic region. It comprises of **bathyal zone** (continental slope and rise) and **abyssal region** (ocean deeps). Depending on the light the zonation may be **euphotic** (upper oceanic zone) and **aphotic** (lower thicker zone). As in freshwater the living organisms are listed as dominated, this is not possible in marine. In this habitat the sponges, coelenterates, annelids and echinoderms are very important. Brown and red algae crustaceans, molluscs and fish are of greater importance but seed plants are of little value in sea. Insects are generally absent and the crustaceans are called **insects of the sea.** In continental shelf region the produces are phytoplanktons, diatoms and dinoflagellates. Multicellular large attached algae or seaweeds form the extensive forests or kelp beds below the tide mark near seashore. The consumers are zooplanktons (haloplankton and meroplanktons), **benthos** (sessile or relatively inactive animals), **nekton** and **neuston** (swimming animals) and bacteria.

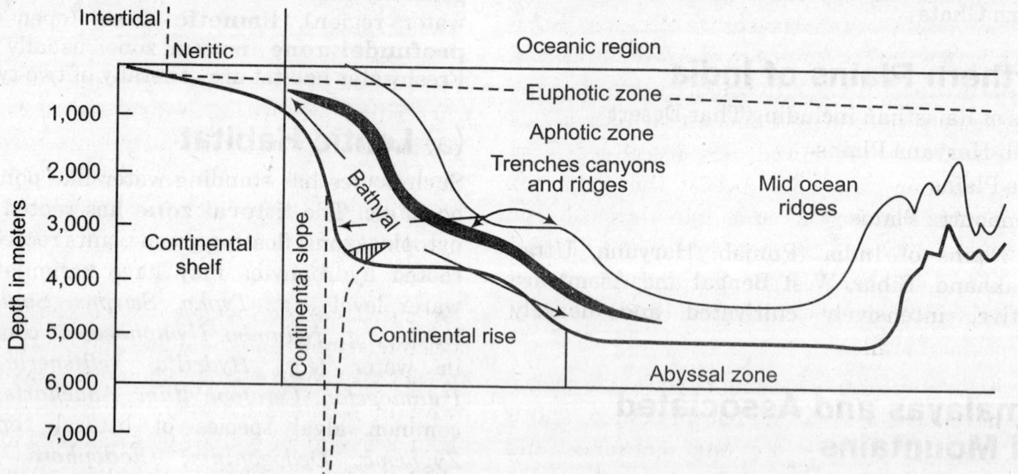

Fig. 28.2 Horizontal and vertical zonation in the marine habitat

Estuarine Habitat

A semi-enclosed coastal body of water within which seawater is mixed with freshwater from land dainage is known as **estuary.** It may be considered as a **ecotone** or transitional zone between the freshwater and marine habitat. On the basis of water circulation and stratification they are classified as **salt wedge** (highly stratified) estuary, moderately stratified vertically homogeneous and hypersaline estuary. Organisms in estuary are a mixture of endemic species and some coming from sea. The subsystems of estuary are shallow water production zones. Sedimentary subsystems, plankton and nektons. The estuaries are more productive than sea and freshwater. The producers are reefs, banks, sea grass beds or sea weed, algal mats and salt marshes. Due to their richness by producers these remain programmed for virtually year around photosynthesis. They posses distinct blooms-like red tide (due to species of *Gonyaulax* and *Gymnodinium*). These are equivalent to coral reefs and tropical rain forest as natural ecosystem and productivity. The nutrients are regenerated, recycled stored and vitamins and growth regulations are manufactured in sedimentary subsystem. Plankton and nekton move freely between shallow water production zone and sedimentary sub-system.

Terrestrial Habitat

This type of habitat is concerned with acquiring organisms on land that is much variable in time and geography. The climate (including temperature, moisture light, gases, etc.) and substrate (physiography, soil, etc.) become important in terrestrial habitat. Moisture becomes limiting factor thus, transpiration and evaporation are of chief significance in terrestrial plants life. The produces are large rooted green plants while consumers are small organisms as insects and other arthropods, herbivores, birds and mammals. The microorganisms are bacteria, fungi, Actinomycetes and protozoans. Desert is an area of terrestrial habitat having low rainfall and high temperature. The other terrestrial communities are forests grassland and cropland.

Geographic Origins and Migrations of Species

Presence of difference and diversity among the type of flora and fauna is a reflectance of the type of origins, changes, adaptations and migrations, occurred in past. Because of the type of climate changes and other stresses we often see that a species may have ranged continuously over a wide area and then have become extinct in the intermediate tracts. This kind of observation made us to believe that all the individuals of the same species, wherever found, are descended from common parents. Various naturalists across the globe has been arrived at the conclusion and hypothesized the designation of single centers of creation, by various general considerations, more especially from the importance of barriers of all kinds and from the analogical distribution of subgenera, genera and families.

With respect to distinct species belonging to the same genus, which probably have spread from one parent-source; and if we make the some allowances for our ignorance and remember that some forms of life have changed very slowly, enormous periods of time having been thus, granted for their migration, the difficulties are far from insuperable; though in this case, as in that of the individuals of the same species, they are often great. Similar to the effects of climatical changes on distribution, the last Glacial period also has played significant role and seems to have affected even the equatorial regions and which, during the alternations of the cold in the North and the South, allowed the productions of opposite hemispheres to mingle and left some of them stranded on the mountain-summits in all parts of the world.

Migration of the species also affects the ultimate fate of particular geographic regions. If the difficulties be not insuperable in admitting that in the long course of time all the individuals of the same species and likewise of the several species belonging to the same genus, have proceeded from some one source; then all the grand leading facts of geographical distribution are explicable on the theory of migration, together with subsequent modification and the multiplication of new forms. We can thus understand the high importance of barriers, whether of land or water, in not only separating but in apparently forming the several zoological and botanical provinces. We can thus understand the concentration of related species within the same areas; and how it is that under different latitudes, for instance, in South America, the inhabitants of the plains and mountains, of the forests, marshes and deserts, are linked together in so mysterious a manner and are likewise linked to the extinct beings which formerly inhabited the same continent. Bearing in mind that the mutual relation of organism to organism is of the highest importance, we can see why two areas, having nearly the same physical conditions, should often be inhabited by very different forms of life; for according to the length of time which has elapsed since the colonists entered one of the regions or both; according to the nature of the communication which allowed certain forms and not others to enter, either in greater or lesser numbers; according or not as those which entered happened to come into more or less direct competition with each other and with the aborigines; and according as the immigrants were capable of varying more or less rapidly, there would ensue in the to or more regions, independently of their physical conditions, infinitely diversified conditions of life; there would be an almost endless amount of organic action and reaction and we should find some groups of beings greatly and some only slightly modified; some developed in great force, some existing in scanty numbers—and this we do find in the several great geographical provinces of the world.

On these same principles we can also understand that why oceanic islands should have few inhabitants, but that of these, a large proportion should be endemic or peculiar and why, in relation to the means of migration, one group of beings should have all its species peculiar and another group, even within the same class, should have all its species the same with those in an adjoining quarter of the world. We can see why whole groups of organisms, as batrachians and terrestrial mammals, should be absent from oceanic islands, whilst the most isolated islands should possess their own peculiar species of aerial mammals or bats. We can see why, in islands, there should be some relation between the presence of mammals, in a more or less modified condition and the depth of the sea between such islands and the mainland. We can clearly see why all the inhabitants of an archipelago, though specifically distinct on the several islets, should be closely related to each other and should likewise be related, but less closely, to those of the nearest continent or other source whence immigrants might have been derived. We can see why, if there exist very closely allied or representative species in two areas, however distant from each other, some identical species will almost always there be found.

As the late **Edward Forbes** often insisted, there is a striking parallelism in the laws of life throughout time and space, the laws governing the succession of forms in past times being nearly the same with those governing at the present time the differences in different areas. We see this in many facts. The endurance of each species and group of species is continuous in time; for the apparent exceptions to the rule are so few that they may fairly be attributed to our not having as yet discovered in an intermediate deposit certain forms which are absent in it, but which occur above and below: so in space, it certainly is the general rule that the area inhabited by a single species, or by a group of species, is continuous and the exceptions, which are not rare, may be accounted for by former migrations under different circumstances or through occasional means of transport, or by the species having become extinct in the intermediate tracts. Both in time and space species and groups of species have their points of maximum development. Groups of species, living during the same period of time, or living within the same area, are often characterized by trifling features in common, as of sculpture or colour. In looking to the long succession of past ages, as in looking to distant provinces throughout the world, it was found that species in certain classes differ little from each other, whilst those in another class, or only in a different section of the same order, differ greatly from each other. In both time and space the lowly organized members of each class generally change less than the highly organized; but there are in both cases marked exceptions to the rule. According to one theory, these several relations throughout time and space are intelligible, for whether we look to the allied forms of life which have changed during successive ages, or to those which have changed after having migrated into distant quarters, in both cases they are connected by the same bond of ordinary generation; in both cases the laws of variation have been the same and modifications have been accumulated by the same means of natural selection.

Fortunately Indian sub-continent witness one of the vast movements of species in the form of bird migration each year. Bird migration is the regular seasonal journey undertaken by many species of birds and is marked by its annual seasonality. Bird movements include those made in response to changes in food availability, habitat or weather. Sometimes, journeys are not termed 'true migration' because they are irregular (nomadism, invasions and irruptions) or in only one direction (dispersal, movement of young away from natal area). Birds that are non-migratory are said to be resident or sedentary. Approximately 1800 of the world's 10000 bird species are long-distance migrants. Many bird populations migrate long distances along a flyway. The most common pattern involves flying North in the spring to breed in the temperate or Arctic summer and returning in the autumn to wintering grounds in warmer regions to the South. Of course, in the Southern hemisphere the directions are reversed, but there is less land area in the far South to support long-distance migration.

In the tropics there is little variation in the length of day throughout the year and it is always warm enough for a food supply (although because of competition, there may not be enough food for every bird). Migration within the tropics has been far less studied than in the temperate zones. It was once assumed that tropical birds were mostly sedentary; however, altitudinal migration and other within-tropics movements appear to be surprisingly common (citation needed). Many tropical regions have wet and dry seasons, inducing some birds to migrate or wander widely to find food. Indeed, the monsoons of India are preceded by the arrival of the Jacobin Cuckoo, the 'harbinger of the monsoon'. Indian sub-continent plays host to a number of migratory birds in summers as well as winters. It is estimated that over hundred species of migratory birds fly to India, either in search of feeding grounds or to escape the severe winter of their native habitat. The numerous wildlife sanctuaries set up in the country serve as their temporary habitat. Bird lovers from all over the country visit these sanctuaries to get a glimpse of some of the rarest species of birds in the world. Some of the most common migratory birds in India is presented here.

Fig. 28.3 Migratory birds coming to India in winter season

Common Indian Mammals and Birds

Indian sub-continent has a rich and varied biodiversity to boast of. Infact, the country is home to some of the rarest as well as magnificent wild animals and birds. Many of the species are endemic and some of them reached at the verge of extinction or endangered categories, which further necessitates the understanding and conservation strategies for the same. Common wild animals and birds of India include apes, monkeys, lemurs, bears, hyenas, sheeps, cats, civets, mongoose, dog, crocodiles, tortoise, lizards, deers, elephants, buffaloes, wild ass, rhinoceros, goats, goat antelopes, antelopes, snakes and variety of birds. Around 400 varieties of mammals, 1250 species of birds and 10000 types of insects and 2546 variety of fish, 197 species of amphibians and 408 reptile species are found in India. The common animals which represent India in various ways are as follows: Bengal Tiger (national animal); Indian peacock (national bird); King Cobra (national reptile); Gray Langur (national icon); Gangetic dolphin (national marine animal); Indian Elephant (national heritage animal). Most of the wild animals of India are being protected from poaching as well as habitat loss through the numerous national parks and wildlife sanctuaries. Indian culture preaches respect for each and every form of life, including wildlife.

Avi-Faunas in Indian Sub-Continent

Indian sub-continent is a bird watcher's paradise and is blessed with around 1301 species, of which 42 are endemic, 1 has been introduced by humans and 26 are rare or accidental. One species has been extirpated in India and 82 species are globally threatened. The Indian Peacock (*Pavo cristatus*) is the national bird of India. More recent birds discovered in India include the Bugun Liocichla which was discovered in Arunachal Pradesh in 2006. Besides this, a few birds considered to be extinct have been rediscovered an example being the Jerdon's Courser. Some others have been elevated from sub-species to full species.

Indian forests include various birds like large hornbills, serpent eagles and fishing owls, as well as the national bird of India, the beautiful peacock. Waterbirds, such as herons, ibises, storks, cranes, pelicans and others, are also found in India and are commonly seen in parks and sanctuaries. Bird life in India is rich and colourful. The birds include the beautiful peacock to the parrots and thousands of immigrant birds. Other common Indian birds are pheasants, geese ducks, mynahs, parakeets, pigeons, cranes and hornbills. In the present section, the summarized details of various Indian birds have been provided.

Black Bittern

Black bittern, of the old world origins, is a resident bird of India. The bright colour of the bird easily distinguishes it from the other bittern species. In the daytime, one can find black bitterns of India resting in trees or on the ground, amongst dense reeds. They tend to fly frequently and have a distinct booming call, mainly heard during the breeding season.

Cinnamon Bittern

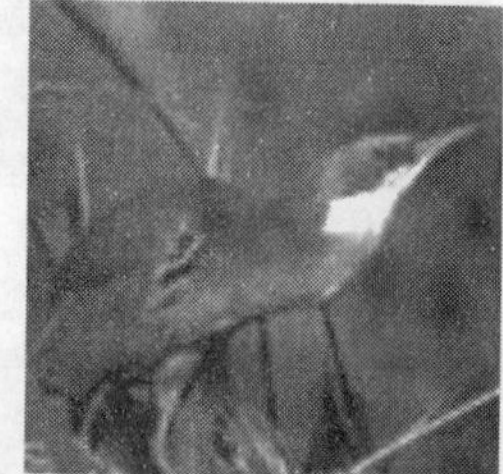

Indian **Cinnamon bittern** is a small bird, having old world origins. It is seen inhabiting the tropical parts of Asia, stretching on from India and Sri Lanka to China and Indonesia. Cinnamon bitterns of India are very shy and secretive by nature and can easily conceal themselves. One can see them only during flight, which is typically short and low.

Little Bittern

Indian Little Bittern bird is a native of the old world and is scientifically known as *Lxobrychus minutus*. The natural habitat of the bird comprises of Africa, central and Southern Europe, Western and Southern Asia and Australia. It may be quite difficult to spot a little bittern, as the bird usually spends its time hidden in dense reed beds.

Yellow Bittern

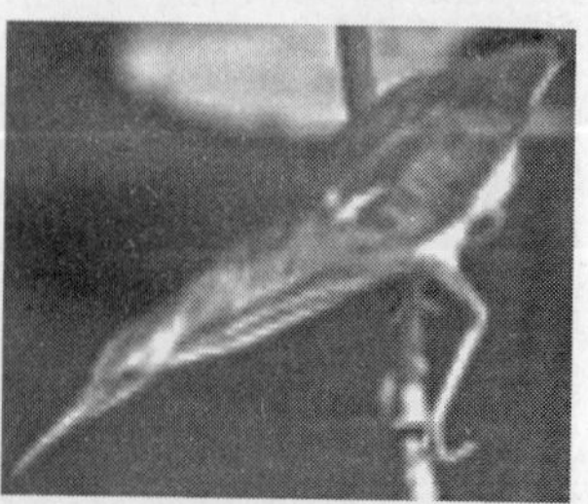

Yellow Bittern of India is one of the smallest members of the bittern species. It is found occupying the Asian countries of India, Sri Lanka, Japan and Indonesia. Yellow bitterns are scientifically known as *Lxobrychus sinensis* and are of old world origins. They are shy by nature and are brilliant in the camouflage technique.

Crested Serpent Eagle

Indian crested Serpent Eagle, a member of Accipitridae family, is scientifically known as *Spilornis cheela*. It is a specialist reptile eater, which mainly hunts snakes and lizards.

Grey Francolin

Grey Francolin, also known as grey partridge, is a resident bird of the Indian sub-continent. The species was introduced for the first time in the Andaman Islands. Since then, it has beautifully adapted itself to the country as well as its climate.

Greylag Goose

Greylag Goose, *Anser anser*, is one of the old world species of birds and was known in the pre-Linnean times as wild goose. It has ancestral relations with the domesticated geese of Europe and North America. Graylag Goose is a very frequent winter visitor to the North regions of the Indian sub-continent.

Great Indian Hornbill

Greater Indian Hornbill is considered to be the largest member of the hornbill family. Scientifically known as *Buceros bicornis,* it is usually found inhabiting the forests of Indian sub-continent, the Malay Peninsula and Sumatra, Indonesia. The average lifespan of the great pied hornbill of India exceeds 35 years and may go up to 50 years in captivity.

Grey Heron

Grey Heron, scientifically known as *Ardea cinerea*, is a bird belonging to Indian heron family. It is very strongly related to the American great blue heron as well as Australian white-faced heron. In fact, many people misunderstand the Australian white-faced Heron as the grey heron.

Night Heron

Night Heron belongs to the Nycticorax and Gorsachius genera. It is a medium sized bird, which is mainly found in the tropical regions of the Indian sub-continent. The name 'Night Heron' is derived on the basis of the fact that these birds prefer to catch their prey during night.

Pond Heron

Pond herons are one of the most commonly found species of the Indian sub-continent. Docile by nature, they can be seen in their natural habitat as well as on the outskirts of villages. The first description related to the Pond heron bird was given in the year 1832, by **Colonel WH Sykes.** The bird belongs to the old world species and is scientifically known as *Ardeola grayii*.

Peacock

Blue peacock is regarded as one of the most beautiful birds throughout the world. It is also the national bird of the Indian sub-continent. Peacock is the name given to a male peafowl, while the female is known as peahen. Scientifically known as *Pavo cristatus* (Linnaeus), the Peafowl of India is a swan-sized bird, with a long and slender neck. It is a forest bird, which usually stay on the ground. However, while roosting, it prefers to stay on trees.

Jungle Bush Quail

Jungle bush quail bird is one of the species of quails found in South Asia. The bird is usually seen in small coveys and is quite shy by nature. One can get a glimpse of the Jungle bush quails of India mainly when they burst out into flight from under the vegetation.

Painted Stork

Painted stork is a tropical species, belonging to the stork family of Ciconiidae. The bird is found in the Asian continent, covering the area from India and Sri Lanka to South-East Asia. Broad-winged soaring birds, the Painted storks of India fly with their neck outstretched. They are resident birds and are found in Indian lowland wetlands, with trees.

Black Necked Stork

Black necked stork is a large bird, known scientifically as *Ephippiorhynchus asiaticus*. It belongs to the Ciconiidae family and counts amongst the huge wading birds of the Indian sub-continent. Black necked stork is a resident bird of Southern Asia and Australia. The area inhabited by Black-necked storks stretches on from India East to New Guinea and the Northern half of Australia. Just like numerous other storks, they also fly with their neck outstretched.

There are 1228 species of birds found in India including 65 species listed in various threatened categories according to IUCN. This database provides information on the distribution of birds in various protected areas of India. Large number of information related to species distribution on various protected areas have been collected and documented in the form checklists and linking with each PAs of India is under process. The various tags have been used to highlight certain relevant categories, but not all species fall into one of these categories. Those that do not are commonly occurring, native species.

A — Accidental A species that rarely or accidentally occurs in India.

E — Endemic A species endemic to India.

I — Introduced A species introduced to India as a consequence, direct or indirect, of human actions.

Ex — Extirpated A species that no longer occurs in India although populations exist elsewhere.

Table 28.1 **IUCN Red List of Threatened Birds**

English Name	Threatened Category
Andaman Serpent Eagle	R
Asian Dowitcher	R
Baer's Pochard	V
Beautiful Nuthatch	R
Bengal Florican	E
Black Breasted Parrotbill	I
Blacknecked Crane	V
Bristled Grass Warbler	K
Brown Chested Jungle Flycatcher	V
Cinereous Vulture	V
Comb Duck	E
Dalmatian Pelican	V
Darkrumped Swift	I
Forest Owlet	I
Grass Warbler	R
Greater Adjutanat	E
Green Avadavat	R
Grey Sided Thrush	K
Himalayan Quail	Ex
Hume's Pheasant	R
Imperial Eagle	R
Indian Bustard	V
Jerdon's Babbler	V
Jerdon's/ Double Banded Courser	I
Lesser White Fronted Goose	R
Lesser Florican	E
Longbilled Bush Warbler	R
Manipur Bush Quail	R
Marbled Teal	V
Marsh Babbler	K
Masked Finfoot	V
Mishmy Wren	I
Narcondam Hornbill	R
Nicobar Scrubfowl	R
Nicobar Parakeet	I
Nicobar Pigeon	R
Pale Capped Pigeon	R
Pink Headed Duck	Ex
Plain Pouched Hornbill	I
Rufous Headed Parrotbill	R
Rufous Vented Prinia	R
Rufousnecked Hornbill	R
Rusty Throated Wren Babbler	I
Rustybellied Shortwing	I
Sclater's Monal	R
Siberian Crane	V
Snowy Throated	R
Sociable Lapwing	R
Spoonbilled Sandpiper	I
Swamp Francolin	V
Swamp Partridge/ Kyah	V
Tawny Breasted Wren-Babbler	K
Wedge Billed Wren Babbler	R
Wedgebilled Wren	R
Western Tragopan	—

Ex=Extinct, E=Endangered, V=Vulnerable, I=Indeterminate, K=Insufficiently known and T=Threatened; Source: Wildlife Institute of India

Mammalian Faunas in Indian Sub-Continent

From tropical rain forests to dry deciduous forests and mighty Himalayas, India is the home to number of wild animals. These rare and unique animals have been successfully protected in the national parks and wildlife sanctuaries of India. Eco wildlife tour in India provides you the numerous ways to come close to the mother nature. These animals have beautifully contributed in preserving the rich flora and fauna of India. More than 350 species of mammals inhabit India. Ranging from big animals like Indian Elephant, Indian Rhinoceros, Royal Bengal Tigers to small species of animals, India is teeming with variety of life force. India today has largest number of tigers, more than any other country in the world. Indian wild animals attract thousand of visitors throughout the year. Elephants are found in the sparsely populated hilly areas of Karnataka, Kerala and Odisha. A variety of deer and antelope species are also found but now-a-days these are mostly confined to the protected areas. Wild buffaloes, massive Indian bisons (gaurs), shaggy sloth bears, striped hyenas, wild pigs, jackals, Indian foxes, wolves and Indian wild dogs (dhole) are also found in forests of India. Lions are found in the rocky hills and Gir forests of Gujarat, Tigers in the Sunderbans and the Brahmaputra valley. Project Tiger was launched by the government of India in 1973-74 to protect the tiger in its natural environment. The project was initially started in nine reserves covering an area of 13,017sq.km. Wild ass is found in Rajasthan. Some of the common mammals inhabiting Indian sub-continent are presented sidewise.

Indian Asiatic Lion

Asiatic lions once used to roam around the area, stretching from Northern Greece across South-West Asia, to central India. However, today, the natural habitat of the majestic animal has been reduced to the Gir forests of India only, making the Asiatic lion almost synonymous with the Indian lion. Known scientifically as *Panthera leo persica*, the royal animal is depicted on the National Emblem of India, since, it represents power, strength and sovereignty. Gir National Park is the only remaining place in the world, where one is likely to see the Asiatic lion.

Bengal Tiger

Bengal tiger is a sub-species of tiger, which is found in the Bengal region of the Indian sub-continent. One of the most common tiger sub-species, it is also found in a number of other Asian countries, like Bangladesh, Nepal, Bhutan, Myanmar, Tibet, etc. Usually Royal Bengal Tigers of India are reddish-brown to rust-brown in colour with black stripes all over. However, a mutation may result in their colour being white also. Such a tiger is known as the White tiger. Bengal tiger is the national animal of both the Indian sub-continent as well as Bangladesh. One can visit Bengal Tiger to any Tiger Reserve in India.

Indian Clouded Leopard

The Clouded Leopard *(Neofelis nebulosa)* is a medium-sized cat found in South-East Asia. It has a tan or tawny coat and is distinctively marked with large, irregularly-shaped, dark-edged ellipses which are said to be shaped-like clouds. This unique appearance gave the mammal both its common and scientific species name (*Nebulosus* is the Latin for 'cloudy'). The Clouded Leopard was a confusion to scientists for a long time because of the appearance and skeleton. It was what seemed to be a cross in between a big cat and a small cat. The scientific name of the genus, *Neofelis*, originates from neo, which means 'new' and felis, which means 'small cat', so it literally means new kind of small cat.

Indian Leopard

Indian leopard is one of the 8-9 valid leopard sub-species found throughout the world. Known by the scientific name of *Panthera pardus*, it is the fourth largest of the four 'big cats' of the *Panthera* genus. At the same time, leopards are also the fifth largest of all cat species. The name 'Leopard' has been derived from a combination of two Greek and Latin words leo and pard, *'leo'* meaning lion and *'pard'* meaning panther. This name was given to the animal since, it was initially believed to be crossbreed of a lion and a panther.

Indian Snow Leopard

Snow leopard is a native animal of mountain ranges of central and Southern Asia, including India. It is also known as Ounce and has a scientific name of *'Panthera uncia'*. Snow leopards can live for a maximum of 18 years in then wild. In captivity, their life span increases to 20 years.

Indian Black Bear

Indian black bear is also known by the names of Asiatic Black Bear (*Ursus thibetanus*), Tibetan black bear, Himalayan black bear and Moon bear. They grow to a length of approximately 4 to 6 feet, right from the nose to the tail. The small eyes of the bear, along with its rounded ears, a long snout, a large body, a short tail and shaggy hair, differentiate it from the other types of bears. The small shoulder hump, a furry rear instep, a concave facial contour, small and curved claws and narrow ears further accentuate the difference. Last but not the least, Asiatic black bear also has a whitish V-shaped breast patch, not found in the other bear species of India.

The male black bear weighs between 220 and 480 pounds, while the females are110 to 275 pounds in weight. The senses of the Himalayan black bears of India are greatly developed and they boast of almost twice the hearing sensitivity possessed by humans. Black bears have coloured vision and their eyesight is very sharp. Even their olfactory senses (ability to smell) are highly evolved. The mating season of the Himalayan black bears is usually from late May to early July. They give birth to two cubs at a time, which stay with the mother for almost seventeen months.

Indian Black Buck

Indian black buck is also known by a number of other names like Kala Hiran, Sasin, Iralai Maan and Krishna Jinka. The scientific name of the black buck *Antelope* is *Antilope cervicapra* and it natural habitat is the Indian sub-continent. Grass forms the staple diet of the blackbucks. However, they do eat pods, flowers and fruits as supplements. The average lifespan of the Indian kala hiran is twelve years and at the maximum, they live for sixteen years. Black bucks are hunted by dogs and wolves.

Indian Deer

The name 'Deer' is given to the ruminant mammals belonging to the family–Cervidae. They are one of the most beautiful creatures on this Earth and extend to approximately 34 species. Male deer, in India as well as the world, are known as stags, harts, bucks or bulls, depending upon the species to which they belong. While, the females are known as hinds, does or cows. One can find deers widely distributed throughout the world, including the Indian sub-continent. The only continents, where deer are not found are those of Antarctica and Australia.

The 34 species of deer can be divided broadly into two categories, known as the old world group and the new world group. The former comprises of the sub-families.

Muntiacinae and Cervinae, while the latter includes the sub-families–Hydropotinae and Odocoileinae. Read on to get more information about the Indian deer.

Indian Gazelle

Indian Gazelle, also known as Chinkara, is a species of *Gazelle* found in South Asia. It belongs to the Bovidae family and is scientifically known as *Gazella bennettii*. The life expectancy of a Chinkara is between 12 to 15 years, less than that of many other deer species. Male gazelles are believed to be territorial in nature and are not prone to wandering for large distances. Gazelles come across as very nervous animals and always seem to be on alert. It is believed that the dwindling population of chinkaras is leading to a decline in the population of cheetah, their main predators, in India.

Nilgai

Nilgai, also known as Blue Bull, is one of the most commonly found wild animals of Northern India as well as Eastern Pakistan. Even though it is an antelope, it looks quite similar in appearance to an ox. Therefore, it has been given the name of Blue bull of India. The average lifespan of the Nilgai is 21 years.

Axis Deer

Axis Deer, also known as Chital Deer or Spotted Deer, is the native animal of the Indian sub-continent. It is found very commonly in India and is one of the most beautiful animals in the country. The spotted deer of India was introduced in the state of Texas in the 1930s. Since, that time, axis deer of India has become the most widespread of the entire deer species.

Brow-antlered Deer

Brow-antlered deer are known by the scientific name of *Cervus eldii*. They have a number of other names also, like Eld's Deer, Sangai Deer, Thamin Deer and even Dancing Deer. The maximum lifespan of the thamin deer of India is only ten years and the deer has three sub-species also.

Hog Deer

Hog Deer is a sub-species of deer, found in the areas stretching from Pakistan, through Northern India, to mainland South-East Asia. A population of the hog deer was introduced in a number of countries, including Australia, the United States and Sri Lanka.

Muntjac Deer

Muntjac Deer fall in the category of those deer that are shy and elusive. They are also known by the name of kakad deer or the Barking Deer in India. The reason for this name is their alarm call, which seems very much similar to the barking of a dog. Indian Muntjac Deer counts amongst the ten sub-species of the Barking Deer in the world.

Musk Deer

Musk Deer comprise of one of the most endangered deer species, not only in the Indian sub-continent, but also in the whole world. They are classified as a sub-family of the Cervidae and have four sub-species.

Sambar Deer

Sambar Deer are dark brown in colour and attain a height of 102 cm to 160 cm (40 to 63 inches). The weight of the Sambar Deer of India may touch 300 kg. There are chestnut marks on the rump as well as the underparts. Sambhur Deer of India also have beautiful manes. However, they are not spotted by birth. The spots develop gradually after birth.

Swamp Deer

Swamp Deer, also known as Barasingha, is one of the most vulnerable species of deer of the Indian sub-continent as well as the world. Presently, one can find them only in the protected sanctuaries of India. Known by the scientific name of *Cervus duvauceli*, the swamp deep of India derives its name, Barasingha, from its large antlers.

Indian Camel

The camels found in India are the single-humped camels, also known as the Dromedary camels. Long-curved neck, deep-narrow chest and a single hump characterize the Indian camel. The hump is used by the camels as reservoir of fatty tissues. In times of scarcity, the tissues are metabolized and the camel receives energy. The size of the hump is not the same in all the camels. It differs from one camel to another, depending upon its nutritional state. In times of starvation, the hump can get reduced to almost a non-existent size.

Indian dromedary camels have a heavy growth of hair on throat, shoulder and hump, which is longer than the rest of the body. On an average, the camels in India live for a period of 40 to 50 years. They are widely used by the people of Rajasthan as a means of transportation. Infact, the camels are known as the 'Ship of the Desert'. They are used for carrying goods as well as people. Indian camels also provide humans with milk, meat, wool, leather and fuel (from their dried dung).

Indian Elephant

Indian elephant, known with the scientific name of *'Elephas maximus indicus'*, is a sub-species of the Asian Elephant. It is mainly found in the Indian sub-continent, that to in the scrub forested areas. The other counties where Asian elephants are found include Bangladesh, Bhutan, Borneo, Cambodia, China, Laos, Malaysia, Myanmar, Nepal, Thailand, Sumatra and Vietnam. Since, Indian elephants are very huge and can trample all other creatures, they have no natural enemies. Even lions, hyenas and tigers attack only the very young elephants and not adults.

Golden Langur

Golden Langur or Gee's Golden Langur, is known by the scientific name of *Trachypithecus geei*. An old world monkey, it was first noticed by the scientific community in the 1950s only.

In the Indian sub-continent, Golden langurs are found mainly in the foothills of the Himalayas, along the Asom-Bhutan border. The langurs are considered to be sacred by the Himalayan people. The coat of Indian golden langur is covered with rich golden to bright creamish hair. The face is black and they have a very long tail, which may measure up to 50 cm in length.

Hanuman Langur

Hanuman Langur is believed to be one of the old world monkeys, belonging to the *Semnopithecus* Genus. They comprise of 15 sub-species and are terrestrial in nature. Earlier hanuman langurs were believed to comprise of a single species. However, now they are recognized as seven distinct species. Hanuman langur is also known by the name of Gray Langur, Entellus Langur and common Indian Langur.

Lion-tailed Macaque

Lion-tailed Macaque is one of the sub-species of macaque, found only in the Western Ghats of South India. Known by the scientific name of *Macaca silenus*, it has life expectancy of 20 years in the wild and up to 30 years in captivity. Lion-tailed macaques spend most of their time on trees and are excellent swimmers.

Long-tailed Macaque

Long-tailed Macaque is also known by some other names, like the Crab-eating Macaque or the Cynomolgus Monkey. It is an arboreal macaque, belonging to the *Macaca* genus and has the scientific name of *Macaca fascicularis*. A native of the South-East Asia, the Crab-eating Macaque of India has also been flown into outer space.

Stump-tailed Macaque

Indian Stump-tailed Macaque, also known as Bear Macaque, is known by the scientific name of *Macaca arctoides*. It can reach up to a length of 70 cm, at the maximum, excluding the tail that may grow up to 8 cm in length. Indian stump-tailed macaques weigh 6 to 13 kg and may live as long as 30 years.

Rhesus Macaque

A typical macaque, the Rhesus monkey of India is believed to be one of the best species of the old world monkeys. It is an excellent swimmer and enjoys water. Rhesus macaques are quite comfortable around humans and have the tendency to move from rural to urban areas in search of easy food. The average lifespan of rhesus macaques is approximately 15 years in the wild.

Bonnet Macaque

Bonnet Macaque, an old world monkey, is also known by the scientific name of *Macaca radiata*. Found only in India, it has been named so because of its physical appearance. Indian Bonnet macaques have a cap-like whorl of hair on their head, which radiates outward from the center. Since the coil of hair resembles a hat, they have been named as Bonnet macaques.

Assam Macaque

Assam Macaque is a diurnal primate, which inhabits the regions stretching from Nepal to Vietnam and Southern China. It is yellowish to dark brown in colour and has a hairless face. The colour of the face is red in case of adults. Assam macaques are also known by the name of Himalayan macaque and hill monkeys in India.

Arunachal Macaque

Arunachal Macaque, scientifically known as *Macaca munzala*, is a native primate of Arunachal Pradesh state of North-eastern India. It is called by the local population as munzala, meaning monkey of the deep forest. Arunachal Macaques were discovered by the Indian scientists in the year 2004 only.

Indian Red Panda

Red panda is a beautiful animal, found in only some other countries of the world, including the Indian sub-continent. Scientifically known as *Ailurus fulgens*, it is slightly bigger than the domestic cat and founds a mention in the list of endangered species. Indian red panda bear is quite apt at climbing trees and is mainly herbivorous. It is also known as the Red Fox or the common panda and is native to the Himalayan ranges of India. A one of its kind animals, red panda is believed to be a living fossil. The only other fossil close to the panda is that of *Parailurus*, which lived 3 to 4 million years ago. The lifespan of a Red Panda may range from nine years to fourteen years.

Indian Rhinoceros

Indian rhinoceros holds the distinction of being the fourth largest animal, after the three elephant species. Known by the scientific name of *Rhinoceros unicornis*, the animal is found in only two places in the world, Asom (India) and Nepal. The great Indian rhinoceros is a brilliant swimmer and has an acute sense of smell and hearing. Its maximum speed reaches 55 km/h, that to for a short period of time. The only drawback of the Indian rhino, also known as the great one-horned rhinoceros, is that its eyesight is quite poor. The sheer size of the rhinos has resulted in a few natural enemies. They may be attacked by tigers, but there are hardly any recorded incidents of a tiger killing a full-grown Indian rhino. However, they may kill unguarded calves at times.

Indian Striped Hyena

Striped hyena belongs to the Hyaenidae family and is scientifically known as *Hyaena hyaena*. Strongly related to the Brown hyena, it is basically a solitary creature. The average lifespan of striped hyenas hovers somewhere around 10 to 12 years in the wild. When kept in captivity, they can live longer also.

Indian Wild Ass

Indian wild ass, also known as khur, is one of the sub-species of wild ass belonging to Southern Asia. Its scientific name is *Equus hemionus khur*. Wild ass of India has an average age of 20-25 years.

Indian Wild Boar

Wild boar is considered to be the wild antecedent of the domestic pig of the Indian sub-continent. It belongs to the Suidae biological family, which also includes the Warthog and Bushpig of Africa, the Pygmy Hog of Northern India and the Babirusa of Indonesia. Indian wild boars are also quite closely related to peccary or javelina of North, Central and South America.

There are nearly 372 species of mammals found in India including 53 species listed in threatened categories (IUCN red list of threatened animals). This database provides information on the distribution of mammalian species in various protected areas of India.

Table 28.2 **IUCN Red List of Threatened Mammals**

Common Name	Scientific Name	Threatened Category
Asiatic Golden Cat	*Felis temmincki*	I
Asiatic Lion	*Panthera leo persica*	E
Asiatic Wild Dog/ Dhole	*Cuon alpinus*	V
Asiatic Black Bear	*Selenarctos thibetanus*	E
Banteng	*Bos javanicus*	V
Bengal Fox	*Vulpes bengalensis*	I
Brow-antlered Deer	*Cervus eldi eldi*	V
Brown Bear	*Ursus arctos*	V
Brown Palm Civet	*Paradoxurus jerdoni*	V
Clawless Otter	*Anonyx cinerea*	K
Clouded Leopard	*Neofelis nebulosa*	V
Common Otter	*Lutra lutra*	V
Desert Cat	*Felis libyca ornata*	E
Dugong/ Seacow	*Dugong dugon*	V
Ganges River Dolphin	*Platanista gangetica*	V
Gaur	*Bos gaurus*	V
Golden Langur	*Trachypithecus geei*	R
Goral	*Nemorhaedus goral*	V
Great Indian Rhinoceros	*Rhinoceros unicornis*	E
Grey/ Indian Wolf	*Canis lupus*	V
Himalayan W-toothed Shrew	*Crocidura attenuata*	V
Himalayan Marten	*Martes flavigula*	I
Himalayan Musk Deer	*Moschus chrysogaster*	V
Himalayan Shrew	*Soriculus nigrescens*	V
Hispid Hare	*Caprolagus hispidus*	E
Hoolock Gibbon	*Hylobates hoolock*	E
Indian Elephant	*Elephas maximus*	E
Indian Wild Ass	*Equus hemionus khur*	T
Jackal	*Canis aureus*	V
Kashmir Stag/ Hangul	*Cervus elaphus hanglu*	E
Leopard	*Panthera pardus*	T
Lesser Panda	*Ailurus fulgens*	V
Lion-tailed Macaque	*Macaca silenus*	E
Malabar Civet	*Viverra civettina*	E
Marbled Cat	*Felis marmorata*	I
Markhor	*Capra falconeri*	E
Nayan	*Ovis ammon hodgsoni*	E
Nilgiri Leaf Monkey	*Presbytis johni*	E
Nilgiri Marten	*Martes gwatkinsi*	I
Nilgiri Tahr	*Hemitragus hylocrius*	V
Phayre's Langur	*Trachypithecus phayrei*	I
Pygmy Hog	*Sus salvanius*	E
Red Fox	*Vulpes vulpes montana*	T
Rusty-spotted Cat	*Prionailurus rubiginosa*	K
Serow	*Nemorhaedus sumatraensis*	E
Sloth Bear	*Melursus ursinus*	V
Smooth Indian Otter	*Lutra perspicillata*	K
Snow Leopard	*Uncia uncia*	E
Stump-tailed Macaque	*Macaca arctoides*	V
Swamp Deer/ Barasingha	*Cervus duvauceli duvauceli*	E
Takin	*Budorcas taxicolour*	I
Tibetan Wild Ass	*Equus hemionus kiang*	V
Tiger	*Panthera tigris*	E

Ex=Extinct, E=Endangered, V=Vulnerable, I=Indeterminate, K=Insufficiently known and T=Threatened; Source: Wildlife Institute of India

Seasonality and Phenology of the Sub-Continent

The biodiversity of India are ancient in nature and composition and are dependent and influenced by climatic changes and anthropogenic activities. Today India's forests are protected in National Parks like Corbett and Nagarhole or in sanctuaries like Pakhui and Little Rann of Katch. The modern way of thinking has resulted in biosphere reserves and biodiversity hotspots and extensive research on them have resulted in rediscovery of new species of mammals like the Leaf Deer in Arunachal Pradesh or the Hook Nosed Frog in Western Ghats. Supporting more than 14 percent of the wild fauna and a higher percentage of the wild flora of the world the forests of India is an intricate web of life with many surprises to explore. As we proceed to an era of advanced wildlife management and as the pressure on the forests all over the world increase the need of the hour is to realize the potential resource that the forests have both economically and from the natural point of view.

Natural environment around us are changing at unprecedented rates. As wild lands shrink, human populations increase and the temperature escalates, we scramble to understand how the species around us will respond. Study of the processes governing the response of species to environmental history, climatic perturbation and human history in the context of species ecologies is the major thrust for the better understanding of their evolution. Indian sub-continent occupy a unique position because of its geographic setting, representing the intersection of three major biogeographic realms (Palearctic, Africotropical, Indomalayan); its geologically dramatic history, driven by plate tectonics, volcanism and climatic change; its ecologically diverse habitat types from the highest mountains on earth to very dry deserts and tropical forests, including biodiversity hotspots; the presence of Homonins in India for perhaps one million years and modern humans in relatively high (and ever increasing) densities for about 70,000 years impacting the Indian biota; and finally the fact that virtually nothing is known about patterns of genetic variation in native Indian species and even less is known about the impact of climate on species in this region in particular.

Variations Driving Patterns of Diversity in the Indian Sub-Continent

The geographical partitioning of genetic diversity is driven by relatively recent (~2 million years ago to the present) climatic transitions, migration events, population extinctions and ecological interactions. In the case of the Indian sub-continent, these patterns of diversity are also driven by relatively recent human impacts on wild habitats. The quatitative approach using comparative phylogeographic, demographic and population genetic approaches have been done for the diagnosis of these processes and their impact on genetic variation in Indian mammals. Phylogeography—the study of the distribution of genetic variation across the landscape- provides a framework for interpreting genetic variation within and across species. From studies around the world, we know that very different species can show congruent phylogeographic patterns driven by the biogeographic divides or climate-driven events. Unfortunately, despite its biodiversity, India lacks a phylogeographic paradigm. A priori, we might expect that phylogeographic patterns in the Indian sub-continent will be similar to Africa, with dry-zone species showing isolation-by-distance patterns and wet zone species revealing contraction-expansion dynamics. However, the Indian sub-continent is fundamentally different from Africa in three respects:

- **(i)** It is smaller and hence affords less opportunity for isolation-by-distance as well as species richness to accumulate.
- **(ii)** As far as we currently understand, few genera or families are endemic to India.
- **(iii)** The spread of elevational gradients is much greater in India than in Africa. Given the above differences, we expect phylogeographic patterns to be driven by differences/similarities in the ecologies of species.

To date, results revealed that for sympatric species of large carnivores (leopards and tigers), sub-division patterns of genetic variation across the Indian sub-continent are relatively low indicating high migration rates. Recent studies also shown that Indian tigers retain 60-70% of global genetic variability of the species, despite evidence of a relatively recent, potentially human-induced population crash 200 years ago. In the context of world wide tiger conservation, these data show that Indian populations are a critical lynchpin for the future survival and recovery of the species.

Congruent patterns of genetic variation were also predicted for two similarly sized small native cats with overlapping ranges and life histories. However, we found that jungle cats (*Felis chaus*) had high genetic variation, low population structure and evidence of population expansion, while leopard cats (*Prionailurus bengalensis*) revealed lower genetic variation and high population structure between Northern and Southern populations indicative of limited migration and lower population sizes. Niche-model analyses for leopard cats implicate a climatic barrier in central India that prevents occupancy of this region by this species today, pointing to the importance of small differences in autecology driving phylogeographic patterns. Comparisons between two macaque species, (the bonnet macaque (*Macaca radiata*) and the Arunachal macaque (*Macaca munzala*) stark differences in phylogeographic pattern. with the Arunachal macque (restricted to high elevations in the Eastern Himalaya) revealing a strong signal of population differentiation, while the peninsular bonnet macaque did not. Thus from a landscape perspective, peninsular India does not present either a historic or present boundary to gene flow and that the more isolated and restricted habitats harbor unique clades of mammals. Climate of the last 2 million years has not significantly affected the genetic diversity of the studied species and, from the perspective of the species studied, small differences in species ecology seem to significantly impact their phylogeographic patterns.

Impacts of Climate on Temporal Changes in Diversity

Understanding past changes in migration and population size in animal populations that correlate with periods of environmental change provides a framework to predict species' response to the current, accelerated rates of environmental change. Rarely, we are provided a window into the past with ancient DNA from populations. Although technical methods dealing with degraded DNA samples are well advanced, the analyses of such data are still in their infancy. Various recently developed sophisticated techniques have been applied for such stuides and results revealed that populations at the edge of the range in marginal habitats are sinks for diversity, while more central populations are larger and serve as sources of diversity. The climatic fluctuations of the Quaternary have played an important role in the organization of animal communities as we see them today. Although we know much about temperate ecosystems, we know very little about the responses of tropical species. Quaternary fossil deposit has been used in peninsular India to better understand climatic responses at low latitudes.

Cryptic Biodiversity of India and its Future

Genetic sequence data can be used as a tool to discover cryptic species and populations. It is also powerful for assigning individual specimens to specific geographic localities. Different studies reaffirm the importance of the eastern Himalaya as a biodiversity hotspot and highlight the importance of monitoring and management in this region. In many regions of peninsular India, we have a better idea of what species are present, but know very little about how populations persist in the existing, fragmented habitat matrix. For example, do tigers and leopards both depend on regions outside protected areas? If so, do these species regard similar landscape and human features as barriers? How frequently do these large felids coexist and where? Because large carnivores are elusive and rare, genetic surveys of carnivore scats can be used to answer such questions. Different non-invasive sampling and PCR-based methods to distinguish between tigers and leopards have been developed. Although India is well known for some of its large carnivores, very little is known about small carnivores. PCR-RFLP panel based method has been used for all felids and canids in the Indian sub-continent results suggested that leopard cats are more common in the Himalayas, while jungle cats are more abundant in the arid regions of central India. Finally, genetic methods can be used to quantify the most basic parameter in ecology and conservation, animal abundance. Just as the stripes on every tiger make it unique and hence identifiable, a set of microsatellite loci and their genotypes identify it as distinct from other individuals.

Phenological responses are periodic events in any plant and animal life cycle and greatly influenced by seasonal and interannual variations in climate. Because many such phenomena are very sensitive to small variations in climate, especially to temperature, phenological records can be a useful proxy for temperature in historical climatology, especially in the study of climate change and global warming. In addition to providing a longer historical baseline than instrumental measurements, phenological observations provide high temporal resolution of ongoing changes related to global warming. The concept of growing-degree/day contributes to our understanding of phenology. For, both marine and terrestrial ecosystems, the most challenging irreversible climate-related changes include altered chemical characteristics of the ambient environment, inundation of many small-islands and low-lying coastal ecosystems by sea-level rise, loss of wetland quantity and quality and increased aridity in subtropical areas. These expected irreversible changes and their cumulative effects, proceeding at unprecedented rates, will alter ecosystem characteristics resulting in potential species extinction. For documenting the effects of climate change on ecosystems at global scale different wide-ranging surveys have been conducted and analysis suggests that ecological changes in the phenology and distribution of plants and animals are occurring in all well-studied marine, freshwater and terrestrial groups. Range-restricted species, particularly polar and mountain top species, show severe range contractions and have been the first groups in which species have gone extinct due to recent climate change. Tropical coral reefs and amphibians have been most negatively affected. Predator-prey and plant-insect interactions have been disrupted when interacting species have responded differently to warming.

A comprehensive 2008 analysis of more than 29000 data series from all continents, some covering over 35 years of observations, verifies these findings and goes further by attributing such changes to anthropogenic climate change. In marine ecosystems these responses include shifts from cold-adapted to warm-adapted communities, phenological changes and alterations in species' interactions. In terrestrial ecosystems, responses include shifts to earlier onset of spring events such as leaf unfolding, blooming date, migration and reproduction timing; change in species distribution; and modification of community structure. Contributing changes in physical systems include shrinking glaciers, melting permafrost, coastal erosion, shifts in river discharge peaks and warming in lakes and rivers with effects on stratification and chemistry. For both marine and terrestrial ecosystems, the most challenging irreversible climate-related changes include altered chemical characteristics of the ambient environment, inundation of many small-islands and low-lying coastal ecosystems by sea-level rise, loss of wetland quantity and quality and increased aridity in subtropical areas. These expected irreversible changes and their cumulative effects, proceeding at unprecedented rates, will alter ecosystem characteristics resulting in potential species extinction. Various analyses world-wide explicitly considered the influence of land-use change, management practices, pollution and human demographic shifts as drivers of the observed environmental changes.

Climate Change in Relation to the Himalayas

There are evidences to indicate that Himalayas are warming at a higher rate than the global average rate. It is a matter of great concern as

(i) The region has more snow and ice than any other region in the world outside the polar caps.

(ii) Himalayas are the maker of climate of much of the South Asia.

(iii) To the Himalayas glaciers are connected nine river basins including the Gangetic basin, which alone has about 500 million population.

(iv) The Himalayas glaciers are receding faster than glaciers of the other parts of world.

Most of the research studies in recent years have clearly indicated that the planet is already under climate change and the mean temperature of the Earth is estimated to have risen by 0.75°C during last century. Some of the well known evidences for global warming are: 11 of the 12 years of the period 1995-2006 are among the 12 warmest years since 1850, retreat of glaciers, melting of the polar ice caps, increase in the area of summertime snow melt in greenland and decrease in winter hunting period of polar bears, rise of ocean level, advancement in leafing time in trees and delay in autumnal leaf dioxide (the principal green house gas) increased by 2.6PPM–the largest annual increase since, scientist began to record. The impact of global warming on coastal regions has drawn more public attention because some of the largest cities of the world are located there. However, alpine areas in mountains might see more changes and may disappear altogether from some mountain regions because they occur near mountain tops. Alpine plants and animals will have no place to march upward as temperature rises. Mountains are known to affect nearly 40% people of the world, living in mountains and connected river basins. In many regions, they represent much of the wilderness where species could migrate to escape warming. They are particularly important in tropical regions, being the only source of snow and snow-melt water. The evolution of monsoon rainfall pattern of Asia is attributed to the rise of the massive Himalayan mountain chains. The Himalayas are geoecologically important for the adjacent Gangetic Plain where, nearly 500 million people live. People have been doing agriculture in this region for several thousands years and the region is famous for the green revolution that helped India to solve its foodgrain problem. The global warming might severely affect the river connection between the Himalayas and Gangetic plains and climate regime of the entire region. Most of the talk on climate change in the Himalayas is centered on glaciers melt.

The high mountain ranges intercept cold winds from the North and trap moisture from the wind rising from oceans in the South. They have created a maritime climate in a continental location. The adjacent Gangetic plains are far more humid than their precipitation values indicate. To what extent vapours released from the forest cover occurring upto 3-4 km altitudes contribute to the high humidity in Northern India sub-continent needs to be investigated. Winters are mild allowing cultivation of crop throughout the year. The young and rising mountains have immature topography, that is why slopes particularly in the greater Himalaya are very vulnerable to erosion causing heavy silt load in the rivers originating from the Himalayas. The amount of precipitation varies widely in Himalayan ranges, some of the areas in the South of the main Himalayan ranges getting more rain than the tropical rain forest areas of Amazonia, while in the North of main Himalayan ranges there occur some of largest rain shadow areas of the planet. The Himalayas have more area under glaciers, 35100 km than any other region of the world outside polar caps. These glaciers are source of the major river systems of the Indian sub-continent. The adjacent Gangetic plain is easily one of the largest and oldest agricultural belts of the world.

Almost all kinds of forest ecosystems and extensive grasslands occur in these mountains, ranging from tropical sal (Shorea robusta, a dipterocarp) to extensive oak forest to deciduous birch forest and alpine grasslands and scrubs. Of total geographical area 593572 km^2 of Indian Himalayas, about 38% is under the cover of various forest types. These forests have 5.4 billion t C (biomass + soil) and accumulate carbon in biomass at the rate of about 65 million t yr-1. Which is about 15 % of India's emission from fossil fuel combustion? Because of high pollution and eutropification these lakes are losing their recreational values. Global warming may increase algal blooms and release of toxins from there. The data available on temperature in Himalayas indicate that warming during last 3-4 decades has been more than the global average of 0.75% over last century. Some of the values indicate that Himalayas are warming 5-6 times more than the global average. Temperature increases are more during winter and autumns than during summers and they clearly increase with altitudinal rise. In higher reaches of Himalayas (generally above 3000m) snowfall builds up year-after year to form glaciers that are long-term reservoirs of water. Many species of the alpine grasslands are able to start their growth with the supply of snow melt water, well before the commencement of monsoon in June-end. The species composition and structure and functioning of alpine meadows (buggyals) are heavily dependent on the happening in Himalayas.

How species are going to respond to warming in the Himalayan region, which is going to be more than the global mean? Warming, in general is suggested to increase the intensity of monsoon in much of the Himalayas, but a milder winter and hotter summer is likely to intensify summer-time drought, when most species produce leaves. One of the features of dominant Himalayan tree species is that in them new leaf production and leaf shedding occur simultaneously during spring, in evergreen species the former often inducing the latter. Even many deciduous species including those of adjacent low land areas drop their leaves during summer at the height of drought and then start producing new leaves after a few weeks when conditions are still dry. Normally an increase in temperature hastens the spring time leaf production. But warming may lead to extreme droughts by increasing evapotranspiration, such as the one experienced a few years ago when pre-dawn water potential in an evergreen oak dropped to –6 MPa, compared to –2.0 to –2.3 MPa during normal years. Such extreme events are expected to enable various populations that species consists of to express themselves. In a study at Nainital it is found that Banj oak (*Q. leucotrichophora*), instead of advancing leafing time, withheld leaf production (Singh SP and Tewari A, unpubl.) because of carbon drain. What seemed to have happened was that the water stress caused by a relatively warmer spring hastened the seed development. Since, trees were not left with enough carbon after investing in a rapid seed development, they withheld the spring-time leaf production. Disturbance in leaf phenology such as this can affect several other processes, such as insect herbivory, litter decomposition, predation by birds and mammals. Since, local people depend on natural forests for their day-to-day living, knowledge of these changes are important for them.

In many dominant forest species like sal, tilong anf kharsu (*Shorea robusta*, *Quercus floribunda* and *Q. semecarpifolia* respectively) seed maturation and seed germination coincide with monsoon rainfall. In a wet condition these species show varying degrees of vivipary (germination of seeds while they are still on trees). Rise in temperature or water stress may advance seed maturation, which might result in the breakdown of the synchrony between the commencement of monsoon rains and seed germination. These species would find difficult to regenerate and march upward in such a situation. Already larger oak seeds than in the past are being observed in springs, which are signs of early seed development. Regeration in Sal (*Shorea robusta*) is known to be a problem, partly becuase its seeds are ready to germinate by mid June when the commencement of monsoon is uncertain. The warming-induced early maturation of seeds can easily disrupt this delicate relationship of the events.

One of the major consequences of global warming is going to be the change in crop selection and increase in the altitudinal range of cultivated land. Tropical crops like yellow pulse (*Cajanus cajan*), corn and some millets are likely to be preferred crops in lower ranges. Among fruits, mangoes, which are already in cultivation in low valleys, may expand in area. People seasonally migrating to alpine areas along with their animals may spend several more months than in the past. In some of alpine meadows cultivation of crops like potato may become a regular feature and expand. The other major change is likely to be the enhanced decomposition of soil organic matter and the release of CO_2. Since, 1850, 160 million metric tons of CO_2 have been emitted from soils and biomass worldwide. There are indications, however, that agricultural soils can become net CO_2 accumulator by increasing productivity, improving cropping practices, erosion control measures and reduced tillage. In much of the Himalayas forest floor litter is collected and composted alongwith livestock dung. The partly decomposed organic matter is then transported to cropfields while preparing beds for seed sowing. Given that the global warming would enhance soil CO_2 emission, more forest litter would be required to maintain soil carbon level. In any case, cropfield soils in mountains would need special attention, as with better management they could become carbon sinks. Similarly, degraded hill slopes could be used to grow grasses and legumes. This in turn would promote soil carbon sequestration.

Seed predation is an important ecological and evolutionary force affecting plant community diversity, demography and phenology at individual, population and community levels. The mid-elevation non-dipterocarp wet forests in Southern Western Ghats, India are some of the largest stretches of undisturbed forest remaining in this biodiversity hotspot. Effects of the biotic and abiotic factors on phenological patterns of these tree species have been conducted and results obtained suggested that primates were responsible for some intact seed dispersal, while squirrels were obligate seed predators. For numerous tree species seed predators were the only seed dispersers. Seed predator abundance showed no significant changes across years except for the case of the lion tailed macaque, which appeared to show seasonal population movement. No community-wide mass fruiting phenomena were noticeable in the forest but there was significant variation in fruit availability between years. A few tree species appeared to show mast fruiting in certain years. A majority of the species suffered high levels of seed predation. Seed predation intensity decreased during mast fruiting events for certain species while for others it had no effect. There was no difference in predation intensity between annually and supra-annually fruiting species. Masting as a means of overcoming high seed predation at the population level in the Western Ghats was limited to only a few tree species. Seed predation also exert selective pressure to shape phonological characteristics and to favour traits such as mast fruiting that may reduce seed predation. It has been hypothesized that plants will synchronize fruiting to overwhelm seed predators. Masting phenomena have been consistently reported for temperate forests and the tropical rainforests of South-East Asia but not for the neotropics studies of phenology in Asia have focused primarily on dipterocarp forest trees which are wind-dispersed and which share similar fruit traits. Non-dipterocarp forests contain tree species with a variety of dispersal modes and phonological patterns. In the Indian sub-continent many of the studies on phenology have come from dry tropical forests. The Western Ghats region is a global biodiversity hotspot. The Southern Western Ghats are the richest in terms of flora and fauna. These forests have been subjected to clearing for plantations and reservoirs, but nevertheless there are large stretches of rain forest left intact. Different phenological studies have confirmed that fruits in the rainforests of Kakachi appear to be affected strongly by vertebrate seed predation during the pre-dispersal stage. Strong protective features of fruits and seeds appear to be a result of selection imposed by vertebrate seed predators. However, masting as a phenomenon is not only applicable for swamping seed predators but perhaps also for attracting seed dispersers.

Field ornithology has provided important data about the impacts of climate change on biodiversity. Longterm nesting record-keeping traditions in Europe have played a crucial role in advances in our understanding of these phenomena. In the context of Asia, the seasonal monsoonal rains are the primary drivers of bird nesting and some studies have sought to establish a relationship between monsoon regimes and reproduction cycles of birds across India by elucidating the manner in which the rains trigger the food cycles of birds. An important group of birds which can further enhance our understanding of the underlying causal relationships between the monsoon and bird reproduction is heronry birds. These birds depend upon wetlands for food resources and long-term heronry monitoring programmes can be useful for conservation.

Birds are excellent indicators of their environment and their study can give information about the impacts of climate change on biodiversity. The reasoning was that as sea levels rise, coastal zones across many parts of the world will be submerged, resulting in reduced foraging area for migratory waders which use these habitats as staging or overwintering sites. But, besides modelling exercises, recent empirical studies utilizing large databases have provided evidence about phonological changes in nesting and migration dates of migratory birds due to climate change. In the context of Asia, the seasonal rains (monsoon), arising due to the differential heating of the oceans and the sub-continental land mass during the summer, have a major impact on biodiversity and economy. Moisture is a crucial resource for all life processes and the monsoon brings it, albeit only in certain months of the year, by way of precipitation. Arising from the Indian ocean in May-June, moisture-laden winds move towards the sub-continental land mass. Known the summer or

'South-West' monsoon, it brings rain across large parts of Northern and NE India and also along the Western coast, but after September these winds reverse their direction and flow outwards to the sea. Known as the winter or 'withdrawal' or 'North-East' monsoon, it then brings rain across several parts, though not uniformly, of South India. Though the broad impacts of monsoon on the reproductive cycles of Indian birds have long been known, recent studies seeking to establish a relationship between monsoon regimes and nesting cycles of passerines across India have elucidated the manner in which the rains trigger the food cycles of birds. However, the influence of the monsoon can also be along non-trophic lines. For instance, nest placement in some passerines is strongly influenced by the monsoon winds. Climate change will severely impact the Indian monsoon in terms of both creating more extremes and El Nino events and also impacting phenology. Besides influencing biodiversity in general, this is bound to have an impact on birds, primarily by influencing their food cycles and indirectly their nesting times and so the question is how well prepared are we to understand these changes. Heronry birds are a good model for understanding the impacts of changing monsoon phenology, influenced by climate change, on biodiversity. While there are several detailed studies on heronry birds from India, particularly on Painted Stork at the Delhi zoo and heronries of the Keoladeo Ghana National Park at Bharatpur.

Organisms of Health and Agricultural Importance

The occurrences of diseases and searching of their causes (etiologies) goes back to antiquity. Hippocrates, a Greek physician of the 4th and 5th centuries BC, is credited with being the first to adopt the concept that disease is not a visitation of the gods but rather is caused by earthly influences. Scientists have since continually searched for the causes of disease and, indeed, have discovered the causes of many. In the development of a disease (pathogenesis) more is involved than merely exposure to its agent. Pathogenesis of disease include resistance, immunity, age and nutritional state of the person exposed, as well as virulence and level of exposure and these all play a role in determining whether the person develops a disease. There are range of organisms exist that cause infectious disease include fungi, oomycetes, bacteria, viruses,viroids, virus-like organisms, phytoplasmas, Protozoa, nematodes and parasitic plants. Not included are ectoparasites like insects, mites, vertebrate or other pests that also affect various animals, crops and humans too.

Robert Koch : Overview

In 1876-1877, the German physician Robert Koch demonstrated that a specific infectious disease (anthrax) was caused by a specific microorganism (*Bacillus anthracis*). From his work he devised what are now known as **Koch's postulates.**

Koch's Postulates

(a) The same pathogen must be present in every case of the disease.

(b) The pathogen must be isolated from the diseased host and grown in pure culture.

(c) The pathogen from the pure culture must cause the disease when it is introduced by inoculation into a healthy, but susceptible organism (usually animal).

(d) The pathogen must be isolated from the inoculated animal and be shown to be the original organism.

Exceptions to Koch's Postulates

(a) Some bacteria and viruses cannot be grown on artificial media (they multiply only within cells).

(b) Some pathogens cause several disease conditions (*e.g., Mycobacterium tuberculosis, Strepococcus pyogenes*).

Bacteria All bacteria are prokaryotes, but they are diverse in both their structure and metabolism. Bacteria are categorized according to the properties of their cell walls and characteristics such as cell shape and arrangements, oxygen requirements and motility. Many bacteria are useful, but the relatively few species that are pathogenic are responsible for enormous social and economic cost.

Eukaryotic Pathogens Eukaryotic pathogens (fungi, algae, Protozoa and parasitic worms) include the pathogens responsible for malaria and schistosomiasis. Many are highly specialized parasites with a number of hosts. Serious fungal diseases are also more prevalent now than in the past, affecting those with compromised immune systems, such as AIDS patients.

Viral Pathogens Viruses are responsible for many of the everyday diseases with which we are familiar (*e.g.,* the common cold) as well as rather more alaming and dangerous diseases, such as Ebola. Viruses were first distinguished from other pathogens because of their small size and because they are obligate intracellular parasites and need living host cells in order to multiply.

Diseases of Crops/Plants

Viruses, bacteria, fungi, nematodes, etc., cause a number of diseases in crops and natural plants.

Common Viral Diseases of Crops

Plant viruses are extremely small infectious agents that pass through fine filters and are visible only with the electron microscope. Viruses may occur naturally as complexes or strains differing in mode of transmission, virulence, host plants attacked, symptoms produced and physical and chemical characteristics (see viruses). One plant species may be susceptible to 20 to 40 different viruses. Plant viruses cause many major diseases of important food crops such as potato, tomato, wheat, oats, rice, corn, peach, orange, sugar beet, sugarcane and palms. Virus diseases are generally most serious in plants that are vegetatively propagated (*i.e.*, grown from cuttings, cut divisions, sprouts, etc., rather than from seeds; examples include potato, sweet potato, carnation, chrysanthemum, dahlia, geranium, gladiolus, lilies, orchids, tree and cane or bush fruits and strawberries).

Virus-infected plants are often more susceptible to root rots, stem or stalk rots, seedling blights and possibly other types of diseases. Among the viruses affecting plants, Tobacco Mosaic Virus (TMV) is best known and has great economic importance. Besides affecting many members of the nightshade family (Solanaceae), which includes tobacco, tomato, potato, pepper, eggplant and petunia, TMV infects more than 70 species of plants in 14 other families. Symptoms characteristically appear as dark-green leaf blotches, irregularly elevated and scattered. The remainder of the leaf becomes more and more pale green and sometimes yellow.

The virus disease curly top caused almost complete abandonment of the sugar-beet industry in parts of the world from 1916 to 1932, when it was controlled by the development of resistant varieties. Intermittently, it still causes severe damage to tomatoes, beans and other crops. The virus affects a wide range of cultivated and weeds hosts in more than 70 different plant genera. Young susceptible beet plants turn yellow and usually die quickly when infected by the virus. Spotted wilt, transmitted by onion and flower thrips, has become widespread and now is responsible for losses to tomato, potato, lettuce, pea, other vegetables and ornamentals in many parts of the world. Virus diseases of citrus are a major concern wherever these crops are grown; for example, between 1936 and 1946, tristeza (quick decline) caused the loss of 7000000 orange trees in the state of Sao Paulo, Brazil. Tristeza has attacked many millions of trees in various tropical and subtropical areas.

Common Diseases Caused by Mycoplasmas

Since, 1968, around 60 of the 'yellows' or 'witches'-broom-type" diseases previously thought to be viral in origin have been shown to be caused by tiny, unicellular organisms known as mycoplasmas. These are the simplest and smallest known organisms capable of growing on laboratory culture media. Plant mycoplasmas are characteristically delimited by a distinct double membrane that is flexible. Being soft and plastic, they assume a great variety of sizes and shapes. Aster yellows infects about 300 species of crop and weed plants in 48 families. The disease is common and destructive in most of the world where air temperatures do not persist much above 32° C (90 F). High temperatures inactivate the mycoplasma in plants and in the leafhopper vectors. Aster yellows can cause serious losses on China aster, daisies, chrysanthemum, lettuce, endive, escarole, carrot, parsnip, celery, parsley and New Zealand spinach. Diseased asters are stiff, upright and stunted with numerous yellowish secondary shoots. Flowers are green (virescent) and distorted, dwarfed or lacking.

Common Bacterial Diseases of Crops

Almost 200 species that cause plant disease infect more than 150 different genera of higher plants in more than 50 families. Bacterial diseases can be grouped into three categories: wilting, necrosis and overgrowth or hypertrophy. Wilting results from invasion of the vascular system of the plant by bacteria, examples include bacterial wilts of sweet corn, alfa-alfa, tobacco, tomato and cucurbits (squash, pumpkins, cucumbers); and black rot of crucifers. Necrosis is a condition in which plant cells are killed, forming leaf spots, stem blights or cankers and soft rots; examples are *Delphinium* black spot, fire blight of pome fruits, bacterial blights of beans and peas and soft rot of iris. Examples of overgrowth or hypertrophy, include crown gall of many plants, cane gall of brambles, hairy root of apple and olive knot.

All true bacteria (order–Eubacteriales) that cause plant disease are one-celled, rod-shaped organisms that do not form spores. Only five genera of true bacteria cause plant disease. About one half of the species are in the genus *Pseudomonas*. Another important genus, *Xanthomonas*, is characterized by the water-insoluble yellow pigment it forms when grown in the laboratory. In contrast to animal and human pathogens, those that infect plants are usually favoured by a nearly neutral (pH 6.5 to 7.5) medium and low temperatures (20 to 30°C, or 68 to 86°F). Bacterial pathogens enter plants through wounds, principally produced by adverse weather conditions, man, tools and machinery, insects and nematodes; or natural openings such as stomates (pores in leaves), lenticels (pores in bark), hydathodes (structures that discharge water from leaf interiors to the surface), nectar-producing glands and leaf scars. Most foliage invaders are spread from plant to plant by wind-blown rain or dust. Main disseminates bacteria through cultivation, grafting, pruning and transporting diseased plant material. Animals, including insects and mites, are other common transmission agents. Some bacteria, such as the causal agent of Stewart's, or bacterial, wilt of corn (*Erwinia stewarti*), are not only spread by a flea beetle but also survive over winter in this insect. When conditions are unfavourable for growth and multiplication, bacteria remain dormant on or inside plant tissue. A few, such as the crown gall bacterium, may survive for months or years in the soil.

Fire Blight

The first plant disease proved to be caused by a bacterium was fire blight of apple, pear, quince, hawthorn, Pyracantha and related plants. Fire blight, caused by Erwinia amylovora, has destroyed all high-quality pear orchards in parts of the United States. The bacteria invade flower nectaries and leaves, spread to young fruits and pass rapidly down susceptible shoots in the phloem, darkening and killing the tissue. Extensive, slightly sunken cankers, with a definite margin, form and during warm, moist weather, bacterial ooze (exudate) appears on the surface. The bacteria overwinter at the edges of cankers on the branches or the trunk. Plant parts and other trees become infected when rains splash the bacteria-laden exudate that appears at the edges of cankers.

Crown Gall

Perhaps the best known bacterial plant disease is crown gall, which derives its name from the rounded, rough growth that appears at the stem base or root crown. The disease occurs widely over the world. The causative bacterium, *Agrobacterium tumefaciens,* which is distributed with nursery stock, has a wide host range, affecting plants in more than 40 families, including peach, apple, pecan, grape, fig, raspberry, rose, willow, euonymus and sugarbeet.

Southern Bacterial Wilt

One of the most important bacterial diseases is the wilt caused by *Pseudomonas solanacearum*, which attacks tobacco, potato, tomato, eggplant, beans, bananas, peanut and numerous other vegetables and ornamentals. The disease occurs in warm temperate, subtropical and tropical areas throughout the world.

Table 28.3 **Some Important Plant Diseases Caused by Bacteria**

Disease	Causal Bacterial Species	Disease	Causal Bacterial Species
Angular leaf spot of cotton	*Xanthomonas malvacearum*	Fire blight of pear and apple	*Erwinia amylovora*
Angular leaf spot of tobacco	*Pseudomonas angulata*	Gummosis of sugarcane	*Xanthomonas vasculorum*
Black leg or soft rot of potato	*Erwinia carotovora*	Leaf spot of cucumber	*Xanthomonas cucurbitae*
Black rot of cabbage	*Xanthomonas campestris*	Leaf spot of peach	*Xanthomonas pruni*
Blight of beans	*Pseudomonas phaseolicola*	Red stripe of sugarcane	*Pseudomonas rubrilineans*
Blight of paddy	*Xanthomonas oryzae*	Scab of potato	*Streptomyces scabies*
Brown rot/wilt of potato	*Pseudomonas solanacearum*	Stalk rot of maize	*Erwinia carotovora*
Canker of citrus	*Xanthomonas citri*	Tundu of wheat	*Corynebacterium tritici*
Canker of stone fruits	*Pseudomonas syringae*	Wilt of maize	*Xanthomonas stewartii*
Crown gall of apple	*Agrobacterium tumefaciens*	Soft rot of mango	*Erwinia cartovora*
Ear rot of wheat	*Corynebacterium tritici*	Wild fire of tobacco	*Pseudomonas tobaci*

Common Fungal Diseases of Crops

Of the 100000 described species of fungi, approximately 20000 produce disease in plants. These include 4600 rusts, 700 smuts and 1000 powdery and downy mildews—a total of 6300 obligate parasites. Fungi cause the great majority of infectious plant diseases (about 75 per cent). They include all white and true rusts, smuts, needle casts, leaf curls, mildews, sooty molds and athracnoses; most leaf, fruit and flower spots; cankers; blights; scabs; root, stem, fruit and wood rots; wilts; leaf, shoot and bud galls; and many others. All economically important plants apparently are attacked by one or more fungi; often ten to 50 or more different fungi may cause disease on one plant species. Descriptions of the various fungus groups and their activity appear elsewhere. The examples below represent major types of diseases incited by fungi.

Late Blight

The causal fungus of late blight (*Phytophthora infestans*) occurs in cool, moist regions wherever potatoes are grown. A devastating epiphytotic of this disease on potatoes began in Europe in 1845 and brought about the Irish famine that caused starvation, death and mass migration of the population. In a population of 8000000, about 1000000 (about 12.5 per cent) died of starvation and 1500000 (almost 19 per cent) emigrated, mostly to the United States, as refugees from the destructive blight.

Chestnut Blight

Native American chestnuts have been practically eliminated from their natural range by a fungus (*Endothia parasitica*), accidentally imported from the orient, where blight occurs as a minor disease on native chestnuts. By 1908, chestnut blight had killed thousands of trees in areas around New York and the fungus had spread many miles in all directions. By 1925, the disease had eliminated chestnuts in Illinois; four years later, it reached the Pacific North-West. Costly efforts failed to bring the epiphytotic under control and it continued to spread, killing millions of trees and finally eliminating this valuable native hardwood species as a major forest component in Eastern North America.

Dutch Elm Disease

A serious new disease of elms was described in 1921 in The Netherlands, thus the name Dutch elm disease. The causal fungus (*Ceratocystis ulmi*) is believed to have moved to Europe from Asia during world war I. Following description of the disease, reports of its occurrence soon came from many regions in Europe and Asia. The fungus was apparently introduced into the United States in 1930 on elm burl logs imported for furniture veneer. Dutch elm disease has killed millions of elms in the Eastern two-thirds of the US and Canada and the disease has continued to spread Westward and Southward.

Black Stem Rust of Wheat

One of the oldest and still important diseases is black stem rust, which is caused by the fungus *Puccinia graminis*. All cereals and many grasses are infected by one of the six varieties of this rust. The discussion below is limited to wheat. Black stem rust occurs essentially wherever wheat is grown. In 1935 this rust destroyed almost 60 per cent of the total hard red spring-wheat crop in minnesota and the dakotas. In 1953 and 1954 outbreaks of black stem rust in the same area reduced yields as much as 80 per cent on durum wheats and 30 per cent on spring wheats.

Blister rust disease of white pines, caused by *Cronartium ribicola*, has a comparable cycle to black stem rust, but with gooseberries and currants (Ribes species) as the alternate hosts. In this case, the white pines carry the fungus spore stages equivalent to those found in the barberry of the wheat rust disease; and the stages infecting the ribes alternate host are like those found in the wheat plants.

Wood Rots

Certain higher fungi actively decompose and stain forest timber. Losses from dead trees and effects of decay on growth may approach 45 per cent of the timber losses from all causes. Such fungi may decay lumber and wood products already in use, making expensive replacements necessary.

Table 28.4 **Plant Disease Caused by Fungi**

Disease	Fungus
Black wart disease of potato	*Synchytrium endobioticum*
White rust of crucifers	*Albugo candida* or *Cystopus candidus*
Late blight of potato	*Phytophthora infestans*
Early blight of potato	*Alternaria solani*
Powdery mildews	*Erysiphe* sp.
Damping of seedlings	*Pythium* sp.
Loose smut of wheat	*Ustilago tritici*
Black rust of wheat	*Puccinia graminis-tritici*
Apple scap	*Venturia inaequalis*
Downy mildews	*Peronospore* sp.
Red rot of sugarcane	*Colletotrichum falcatum*
Tikka disease of groundnut	*Cercospora* sp.
Stem gall of coriander	*Protomyces* sp.
Wilt of arhar	*Fusarium* sp.
Leaf rust of coffee	*Haemelia vastatrix*
Blast disease of rice	*Pyricularia oryzae*
Green ear disease of bajra	*Sclerospora graminicola*
Flag smut of wheat	*Urocystis tritici*
Maize smut	*Ustilago maydis*
Loose smut of oat	*Ustilago avenae*
Covered smut of oat	*U. kolleri*
Covered smut of jowar (sorghum)	*Sphacelotheca sorghii*
Leaf spot of rice	*Helminthosporium oryzae*

Common Crop Diseases Caused by Nematodes

Nematodes parasitic on plants are active, slender, unsegmented roundworms (also called nemas or eelworms). The great majority cannot be seen with the unaided eye because they are tiny and translucent. About 1200 species cause disease in plants. Probably every form of plant and animal life is fed upon by atleast one species of nematode. They usually live in soil and attack small roots, but some species inhabit and feed in bulbs, buds, stems, leaves or flowers.

Root-knot nematodes (*Meloidogyne* species) are well known because of conspicuous 'knots' or gall-like swellings, they induce on roots. Over 2000 kinds of higher plants are subject to their attack. Losses are often heavy, especially in warm regions with long growing seasons. Certain species, however, such as the Northern root-knot nematode (*M. hapla*), are found where soil may freeze to depths of nearly a metre. Vegetables, cotton, strawberries and orchard trees are commonly attacked. Garden plants and ornamentals frequently become infested through nursery stock.

Root-lesion nematodes (*Pratylenchus* species), cosmopolitan in distribution, are endoparasites that cause severe losses to hundreds of different crop and ornamental plants by penetrating roots and making their way through the tissues, breaking down the cells as they feed. The golden nematode of potatoes (*Heterodera rostochiensis*) is a menace of the European potato industry. Great efforts have been made to control it. A related, cyst-forming species, the sugarbeet nematode (*H. schachtii*), is a pest that has restricted acreage of sugarbeets in Europe, Asia and America. The citrus nematode (*Tylenchulus semipenetrans*) occurs wherever citrus is grown, exacting a heavy toll in fruit quality and production. The burrowing nematode (*Radopholus similis*) is a serious endoparasite in tropical and subtropical areas, where it attacks citrus (causing spreading decline), banana, avocado, tomato, black pepper, abaca and over 200 important crops, trees and ornamentals, causing severe losses. Many important ectoparasites feed on plant roots—dagger nematodes (*Xiphinema*), stubby-root nematodes (*Trichodorus*), spiral nematodes (*Rotylenchus* and *Helicotylenchus*), sting nematodes (*Belonolaimus*) and pin nematodes (*Paratylenchus*). Leaf or foliar, nematodes (*Aphelenchoides* species) and bulb and stem nematodes (*Ditylenchus dipsaci*) cause severe losses in vegetable and ornamental bulb crops, clovers, alfalfa, strawberry, sweet potato, orchids, chrysanthemum, begonia and ferns.

Common Parasites of Crops

A number of flowering plants are important as parasites of other plants. Among the more important ones are mistletoe, dodder and witchweed.

Mistletoes are semiparasitic seed plants that feed on trees and obtain water and mineral salts by sending root-like structures (haustoria) into vascular tissue of the inner bark. There are three important types—American (*Phorodendron* species), European (*Viscum album*) and dwarf (*Arceuthobium* species). All produce sticky seeds spread by birds. American mistletoe, restricted to the Americas, is best known for its ornamental and sentimental uses at Christmas time.

Dwarf mistletoe is common on and very destructive to conifers in forests. Seedlings and young trees may be stunted, deformed, or killed. Conspicuous witches brooms form in the crown or spindle-shaped swellings (later cankers) in limbs and trunk. Canker and wood-rotting fungi often enter through mistletoe wounds. Dwarf mistletoes often escape detection because the scaly-leaved plants may be less than 21/2 centimetres long; they do range to 30 to 45 centimetres, however. Dwarf mistletoes occur scattered along conifer limbs and small branches.

The 170 species of dodder (*Cuscuta*) are widely distributed and called such names as strangleweed, devil's hair, pull down, hell-bind, love vine and goldthread. The leafless, yellow-orange, thread-like stems twine around a number of field and garden host plants. By extending to nearby plants, it may draw them together and downward until a tangled yellowish-orange patch is formed.

Witchweed, a small parasitic weed (*Striga asiatica*), is widely distributed in Asia and South Africa. It has been known in the coastal sandy soils of North and South Carolina since the mid-1950s but through intensive efforts is slowly being eradicated. Witchweed parasitizes the roots of many hosts, including maize (corn), sorghum, sugarcane, rice, small grains and more than 50 species in the grass and sedge families. A serious infestation may cause corn plants to be severely stunted, wilt and turn yellow or brown thus reducing the acre yield.

Diseases of Animals

Concern with diseases that afflict animals dates from the earliest human contacts with animals and is reflected in early views of religion and magic. Diseases of animals remain a concern principally because of the economic losses they cause and the possible transmission of the causative agents to humans. The branch of medicine called veterinary medicine deals with the study, prevention and treatment of diseases not only in domesticated animals but also in wild animals and in animals used in scientific research. The prevention, control and eradication of diseases of economically important animals are agricultural concerns. Programs for the control of diseases communicable from animals to man, called zoonoses, especially those in pets and in wildlife, are closely related to human health. Further, the diseases of animals are of increasing importance, for a primary public-health problem throughout the world is animal-protein deficiency in the diet of humans. Indeed, both the United Nations Food and Agricultural Organization (FAO) and the World Health Organization (WHO) have been attempting to solve the problem of protein deficits in a world whose human population is rapidly expanding.

Diseases may be either infectious or non-infectious. The term infection, as observed earlier, implies an interaction between two living organisms, called the host and the parasite. Infection is a type of parasitism, which may be defined as the state of existence of one organism (the parasite) at the expense of another (the host). Agents (*e.g.*, certain viruses, bacteria, fungi, protozoans, worms and arthropods) capable of producing disease are pathogens. The term pathogenicity refers to the ability of a parasite to enter a host and produce disease; the degree of pathogenicity—that is, the ability of an organism to cause infection—is known as virulence. The capacity of a virulent organism to cause infection is influenced both by the characteristics of the organism and by the ability of the host to repel the invasion and to prevent injury. A pathogen may be virulent for one host but not for another. Pneumococcal bacteria, for example, have a low virulence for mice and are not found in them in nature; if introduced experimentally into a mouse, however, the bacteria overwhelm its body defenses and cause death.

Many pathogens are able to live outside the animal's body until conditions occur that are favourable for entering and infecting it. Pathogens enter the body in various ways—by penetrating the skin or an eye, by being eaten with food, or by being breathed into the lungs. After their entry into a host, pathogens actively multiply and produce disease by interfering with the functions of specific organs or tissues of the host. Some common infectious and parasitic diseases of animals and the causative agents are described below:

The Black Plague

The Black Death (75 million deaths) or The Black Plague, was one of the most deadly pandemics in human history. It probably began in Central Asia and spread to Europe by the late 1340s. The total number of deaths worldwide from the pandemic is estimated at 75 million people; there were an estimated 20 to 30 million deaths in Europe alone. The Black Death is estimated to have killed between one-third and two-thirds of Europe's population.

Polio

Poliomyelitis (10000 deaths since, 1916) often called polio or infantile paralysis, is an acute viral infectious disease spread from person to person, primarily *via* the faecal-oral route. The term derives from the Greek polio, meaning 'grey', *myelon*, 'spinal cord' and -itis, which denotes inflammation. Although roughly 90% of polio infections are asymptomatic, affected individuals can exhibit a range of symptoms if the virus enters the blood stream. In less than 1% of polio cases the virus enters the central nervous system, preferentially infecting and destroying motor neurons, leading to muscle weakness and acute flaccid paralysis.

Smallpox

Smallpox (Native Americans suffer a population drop from 12 Mil. to 235,000') (also known by the Latin names *Variola* or *Variola vera*) is a contagious disease unique to humans. Smallpox is caused by either of two virus variants named *Variola major* and *Variola minor*. The deadlier form, *V. major*, has a mortality rate of 30-35%, while *V. minor* causes a milder form of disease called alastrim and kills ~1% of its victims. Long-term side-effects for survivors include the characteristic skin scars. Occasional side effects include blindness due to corneal ulcerations and infertility in male survivors. Smallpox killed an estimated 60 million Europeans, including five reigning European monarchs, in the 18th century alone. Up to 30% of those infected, including 80% of the children under 5 years of age, died from the disease and one third of the survivors became blind. To this day, smallpox is the only human infectious disease to have been completely eradicated from nature.

Cholera

Cholera (12000 deaths since, 1991) (or Asiatic cholera or epidemic cholera) is an extreme diarrheal disease caused by the bacterium *Vibrio cholerae*. Transmission to humans is by ingesting contaminated water or food. The major reservoir for cholera was long assumed to be humans, but some evidence suggests that it is the aquatic environment. In its most severe forms, cholera is one of the most rapidly fatal illnesses known—a healthy person may become hypotensive within an hour of the onset of symptoms and may die within 2-3 hours if no treatment is provided. More commonly, the disease progresses from the first liquid stool to shock in 4-12 hours, with death following in 18 hours to several days without rehydration treatment.

Ebola

The Ebola (160000 deaths since, 2000) virus first emerged in 1976 in simultaneous outbreaks in **Sudan** and **Zaire.** It is known to be a zoonotic virus as it is currently devastating the populations of lowland gorillas in Central Africa. Despite considerable effort by the World Health Organization, no animal reservoir capable of sustaining the virus between outbreaks has been identified. However, it has been hypothesized that the most likely candidate is the fruit bat. Ebola haemorrhagic fever is potentially lethal and encompasses a range of symptoms including fever, vomiting, diarrhea, generalized pain or malaise and sometimes internal and external bleeding. Mortality rates are generally very high, in the region of 80%-90%, with the cause of death usually due to hypovolemic shock or organ failure.

Malaria

Malaria (2.7 million deaths per year-2800 children per day) is a vector-borne infectious disease caused by protozoan parasites. It is widespread in tropical and subtropical regions, including parts of the Americas, Asia and Africa. Each year, it causes disease in approximately 515 million people and kills between one and three million, most of them young children in Sub-Saharan Africa. Malaria is commonly associated with poverty, but is also a cause of poverty and a major hindrance to economic development. Malaria is one of the most common infectious diseases and an enormous public-health problem. The disease is caused by protozoan parasites of the genus *Plasmodium*. The most serious forms of the disease are caused by *Plasmodium falciparum* and *Plasmodium vivax,* but other related species can also infect humans. Although some are under development, no vaccine is currently available for malaria; preventative drugs must be taken continuously to reduce the risk of infection.

Bubonic Plague

Bubonic [250 million Europeans dead (1/3 population)] plague is mainly a disease in rodents and fleas (*Xenopsylla cheopsis*). Infection in a human occurs when a person is bitten by a flea that has been infected by biting a rodent that itself has been infected by the bite of a flea carrying the disease. The bacteria multiply inside the flea, sticking together to form a plug that blocks its stomach and causes it to begin to starve. The flea then voraciously bites a host and continues to feed, even though it can not quell its hunger and consequently the flea vomits blood tainted with the bacteria back into the bite wound. The bubonic plague bacterium then infects a new victim and the flea eventually dies from starvation. Any serious outbreak of plague is usually started by other disease outbreaks in rodents, or a rise in the rodent population.

Spanish Flu

Flu (between 1918-19: 50-100 million dead), In 1918 flu pandemic (commonly referred to as the Spanish flu) was a category 5 influenza pandemic caused by an unusually severe and deadly influenza. A virus strain of subtype H1N1. Many of its victims were healthy young adults, in contrast to most influenza outbreaks which predominantly affect juvenile, elderly, or otherwise weakened patients. The Spanish flu pandemic lasted from 1918 to 1919, spreading even to the Arctic and remote Pacific islands. While older estimates put the number of killed at 40-50 million people, current estimates are that 50 million to 100 million people world wide died, possibly more than that taken by the black death. This extraordinary toll resulted from the extremely high infection rate of up to 50% and the extreme severity of the symptoms, suspected to be caused by cytokine storms. Between 2 and 20% of those infected by Spanish flu died, as opposed to the normal flu epidemic mortality rate of 0.1%. In some remote Inuit villages, mortality rates of nearly 100% were recorded.

Influenza

Influenza (36000 deaths per year), commonly known as flu, is an infectious disease of birds and mammals caused by RNA viruses of the family–Orthomyxoviridae (the influenza viruses). In humans, common symptoms of influenza infection are fever, sore throat, muscle pains, severe headache, coughing, weakness and general discomfort. In more serious cases, influenza causes pneumonia, which can be fatal, particularly in young children and the elderly.

Sometimes confused with the common cold, influenza is a much more severe disease and is caused by a different type of virus. Although nausea and vomiting can be produced, especially in children, these symptoms are more characteristic of the unrelated gastroenteritis, which is sometimes called 'stomach flu' or '24-hour flu.' Typically, influenza is transmitted from infected mammals through the air by coughs or sneezes, creating aerosols containing the virus and from infected birds through their droppings. Influenza can also be transmitted by saliva, nasal secretions, faeces and blood. Infections also occur through contact with these body fluids or with contaminated surfaces.

AIDS

Acquired Immune Deficiency Syndrome or Acquired Immuno Deficiency Syndrome (AIDS) (25 million since, 1981) is a collection of symptoms and infections resulting from the specific damage to the immune system caused by the Human Immunodeficiency Virus (HIV) in humans and similar viruses in other species (SIV, FIV, etc.). The late stage of the condition leaves individuals susceptible to opportunistic infections and tumours. Although treatments for AIDS and HIV exist to decelerate the virus' progression, there is currently no known cure. HIV, *et. al.*, are transmitted through direct contact of a mucous membrane or the bloodstream with a bodily fluid containing HIV, such as blood, semen, vaginal fluid, preseminal fluid and breast milk. This transmission can come in the form of anal, vaginal or oral sex, blood transfusion, contaminated hypodermic needles, exchange between mother and baby during pregnancy, childbirth, or breastfeeding, or other exposure to one of the above bodily fluids. Most researchers believe that HIV originated in sub-Saharan Africa during the twentieth century; it is now a pandemic, with an estimated 38.6 million people now living with the disease worldwide.

African Trypanosomiasis (Sleeping Sickness)

African trypanosomiasis is spread by the tse-tse fly, which is common to many African countries. The World Health Organization (WHO) estimates that nearly 450000 cases occur each year. Symptoms of the disease include fever, headaches, joint pains and itching in the early stage and confusion, sensory disturbances, poor coordination and disrupted sleep cycles in the second stage. If the disease goes untreated in its first stage, it causes irreparable neurological damage; if it goes untreated in its second stage, it is fatal.

Cryptosporidiosis

Cryptosporidiosis has become one of the most common causes of waterborne disease in the United States in recent years, it is also found throughout the rest of the world. It is caused by a parasite that spreads when a water source is contaminated, usually with the faeces of infected animals or humans. Symptoms include diarrhoea, stomach cramps, an upset stomach and slight fever. Some people do not exhibit any symptoms.

Dengue

World Health Organization (WHO) estimates that 50 million cases of dengue fever appear each year. It is spread through the bite of the *Aedes aegypti* mosquito. Recent years have seen dengue outbreaks all over Asia and Africa. Dengue fever can be mild to moderate and occasionally severe, though it is rarely fatal. Mild cases, which usually affect infants and young children, involve a non-specific febrile illness, while moderate cases, seen in older children and adults, display high fever, severe headaches, muscle and joint pains and rash. Severe cases develop into dengue haemorrhagic fever, which involves high fever, haemorrhaging and sometimes circulatory failure.

Hepatitis-A

Hepatitis-A is a highly contagious liver disease caused by the hepatitis-A virus. Spread primarily by the faecal-oral route or by ingestion of contaminated water or food, the number of annual infections worldwide is estimated at 1.4 million. Symptoms include fever, fatigue, jaundice, and dark urine. Although those exposed usually develop lifelong immunity, the best protection against Hepatitis-A is vaccination.

Hepatitis-B

Approximately two billion people are infected with the hepatitis-B virus (HBV), making it the most common infectious disease in the world today. Over 350 million of those infected never rid themselves of the infection. Hepatitis is an inflammation of the liver that causes symptoms such as jaundice, extreme fatigue, nausea, vomiting and stomach pain; hepatitis-B is the most serious form of the disease. Chronic infections can cause cirrhosis of the liver or liver cancer in later years.

Hepatitis-C

Hepatitis-C is a less common and less severe, form of hepatitis. An estimated 180 million people worldwide are infected with Hepatitis-C Virus (HCV); 3-4 million more are infected every year. The majority of HCV cases are asymptomatic, even in people, who develop chronic infection.

Japanese Encephalitis

Japanese encephalitis is a mosquito-borne disease endemic in Asia. Around 50000 cases occur each year; 25% to 30% of all cases are fatal.

Leishmaniasis

Leishmaniasis is a disease spread by the bite of the sandfly. It is found mostly in tropical countries. There are several types of leishmaniasis and they vary in symptoms and severity. Visceral Leishmaniasis (VL or kala azar) is the most severe; left untreated, it is always fatal. Its symptoms include fever, weight loss, anaemia and a swelling of the spleen and liver. Muco Cutaneous Leishmaniasis (MCL or espundia) produces lesions that affect the nose, mouth and throat and can destroy their mucous membranes. Cutaneous Leishmaniasis (CL) produces skin ulcers, sometimes as many as 200, that cause disability and extensive scarring. Diffuse Cutaneous Leishmaniasis (DCL) is similar to CL and infected people are prone to relapses. Approximately 12 million cases of leishmaniasis exist today.

Measles

Measles is a disease that has seen a drastic reduction in countries, where a vaccine is readily available, but it is still prevalent in developing countries, where most of the 242000 deaths (out of 30 million cases) it caused in 2006 occurred. Symptoms include high fever, coughing and a maculo-papular rash; common complications include diarrhoea, pneumonia and ear infections.

Meningitis

Meningitis, often known as spinal meningitis, is an infection of the spinal cord. It is usually the result of a viral or bacterial infection. Bacterial meningitis is more severe than viral meningitis and may cause brain damage, hearing loss and learning disabilities. An estimated 1.2 million cases of bacterial meningitis occur every year, over a tenth of which are fatal. Symptoms include severe headache, fever, nausea, vomiting, lethargy, delirium, photophobia and a stiff neck.

Onchocerciasis (River Blindness)

Onchocerciasis is caused by the larvae of *Onchocerca volvulus*, a parasitic worm that lives in the human body for years. It is endemic in Africa, where nearly all of the 18 million people infected with the disease live. Of those infected, over 6.5 million have developed dermatitis and 270000 have gone blind. Symptoms include visual impairment, rashes, lesions, intense itching, skin depigmentation and lymphadenitis.

Pneumonia

Pneumonia has many possible causes, but it is usually an infection of the *Streptococcus* or *Mycoplasma* bacteria. These bacteria can live in the human body without causing infection for years and only surface when another illness has lowered the person's immunity to disease. *Streptococcus pneumoniae* causes streptococcal pneumonia, the most common kind, which is more severe than mycoplasmal pneumonia. *S. pneumoniae* is responsible for more than 100000 hospitalizations for pneumonia annually, as well as 6 million cases of otitis media and over 60000 cases of invasive diseases such as meningitis.

Viral Gastroenteritis

Rotavirus is the most common cause of viral gastroenteritis worldwide. It kills more than 600000 children each year, mostly in developing countries. Symptoms include vomiting, watery diarrhea, fever and abdominal pain.

Schistosomiasis

Schistosomiasis is a parasitic disease that is endemic in many developing countries. Roughly 200 million people worldwide are infected with the flukeworm, whose eggs cause the symptoms of the disease. Some 120 million of those infected are symptomatic and 20 million suffer severely from the infection. Symptoms include rash and itchiness soon after becoming infected, followed by fever, chill, coughing and muscle aches.

Shigellosis

Shigella infection causes an estimated 600000 deaths worldwide every year. It is most common in developing countries with poor sanitation. *Shigella* bacteria cause bacillary dysentery or shigellosis. Symptoms include diarrhoea with bloody stool, vomiting and abdominal cramps.

Strep Throat

Strep throat is caused by the *Streptococcus* bacteria. Several million cases of strep throat occur every year. Symptoms include a sore throat, fever, headache, fatigue and nausea.

Tuberculosis

Tuberculosis causes nearly 2 million deaths every year and WHO estimates that nearly 1 billion people will be infected between 2000 and 2020 if more effective preventive procedures are not adopted. The TB bacteria are most often found in the lungs, where they can cause chest pain and a bad cough that brings up bloody phlegm. Other symptoms include fatigue, weight loss, appetite loss, chills, fever and night sweats.

Typhoid

Typhoid fever causes an estimated 600000 deaths annually, out of 12-17 million cases. It is usually spread through infected food or water. Symptoms include a sudden and sustained fever, severe headache, nausea, severe appetite loss, constipation and sometimes diarrhea.

Yellow Fever

Yellow fever causes an estimated 30000 deaths each year, out of 200000 cases. The disease has two phases. In the 'acute phase,' symptoms include fever, muscle pain, headache, shivers, appetite loss, nausea and vomiting. This lasts for 3-4 days, after which most patients recover. But 15% will enter the 'toxic phase,' in which fever reappears, along with other symptoms, including jaundice; abdominal pain, vomiting, bleeding from the mouth, nose, eyes, stomach and deterioration of kidney function (sometimes complete kidney failure). Half of all patients in the toxic phase die within two weeks; the other half recover.

Cattle and Other Domestic Animals Diseases

The world cattle population is estimated to be about 1.3 billion head, with about 30 per cent in Asia, 20 per cent in South America, 15 per cent in Africa, 14 per cent in North and Central America and 10 per cent in Europe. The 10 states in the US with the largest cattle populations are Texas, Missouri, Oklahoma, Nebraska, South Dakota, Montana, Kansas, Iowa, Kentucky and Florida. This section has a listing of the common diseases of cattles.

Anaplasmosis

Anaplasmosis is a vector-borne, infectious blood disease in cattle caused by the rickesttsial parasites *Anaplasma marginale* and *Anaplasma centrale*. It occurs primarily in warm tropical and sub-tropical areas. The disease is not contagious but is transmitted most commonly by ticks. It can also be transmitted *via* contaminated needles, dehorning equipment, castrating knives, tattoo instruments, biting flies and mosquitoes. The intracellular parasite destroys red blood cells. It causes anaemia, fever, weight loss, breathlessness, uncoordinated movements, abortion and death.

Pasture Bloat

Bloat is a form of severe indigestion marked by a collection of gas in the rumen that the animal is unable to expel. Normal digestive processes create gases consisting chiefly of carbon dioxide and methane in the rumen. Most of the gases are eliminated by belching. Gases that are trapped may form a foam or froth in the rumen which further prevents their elimination. Froth formation can be caused by many factors resulting from interactions between the animal, rumen microorganisms and differences in plant biochemistry. The main causes of bloat are an inherited tendency for bloat, certain proteins in forage (particularly in legumes), the coarseness of the roughage and the type of rumen microbial population. Pasture bloat usually occurs in animals grazing wheat pasture, lush legumes (alfalfa, ladino, red clover) or fed green-chopped legumes.

Blackleg

Blackleg is a highly fatal disease of young cattle caused by the spore forming, rod-shaped, gas producing bacteria *Clostridium chauvoei*. The spores of the organism can live in the soil for many years. The bacteria enter the calf by ingestion and then gains entrance to the body through small punctures in the mucous membrane of the digestive tract. Cattle that are on a high plane of nutrition, rapidly gaining weight and between 6 months and 2 years of age are most susceptible to the disease. The disease is not transmitted directly from sick animals to healthy animals by mere contact. Blackleg is almost entirely preventable by vaccination. The most commonly used clostridial vaccination in cattle is the 7-way type which protects against *Clostridium chauveoi* (blackleg), *Clostridium septicum* and *Clostridium sordelli* (malignant edema), *Clostridium novyi* (black disease) and three types of *Clostridium perfringens* (enterotoxemia).

Anthrax

Anthrax, a highly infectious and fatal disease of mammals and humans, is caused by a relatively large spore-forming rectangular shaped bacterium called *Bacillus anthracis*. Most outbreaks occur in areas where animals have previous died of anthrax, as the spores remain viable for decades. The predominant sign in cattle with anthrax is a progression from a normal appearance to dead in a matter of hours. Most animals are simply found dead. Once an outbreak begins in the herd animals may be observed with signs of weakness, fever, excitement followed by depression, difficulty breathing, uncoordinated movements and convulsions. Bloody discharges from the natural body openings as well as edema in different parts of the body are sometimes observed. After death, the animal's body rapidly decomposes.

Brucellosis

Brucellosis of cattle, also known as 'contagious abortion' and 'Bangs disease', is caused by infection with the bacterium *Brucella abortus*, which can also cause a disease of humans known as 'undulant fever'. Brucellosis infection of cattle causes abortion or premature calving of recently infected animals, most often between the fifth and eight month of pregancy. Although federal and state regulations have helped to control this disease, there is still a threat. Infected cows frequently suffer from retained after birth, are difficult to get rebred and sometimes become sterile.

BSE or Mad Cow Disease

Bovine Spongioform Encephalopathy (also known as BSE or 'mad cow disease') is a progressive degenerative disease that affects to central nervous system of cattle. It belongs to a group of similar but distinct neurological diseases including Creutzfeldt-Jacob Disease (CJD) in humans. The cause of BSE is unknown and there is no known treatment for this fatal disease.

BVD

BVD (Bovine Virus Diarrhea) infection can cause numerous problems, such as damage to the digestive and immune systems, pneumonia, abortions, calf deformities and others. Clinical signs in newborn calves infected with BVD include fever, nasal discharge, diarrhea and inability to move about normally.

Calf Scours

Calf scours or calf diarrhoea causes more financial loss to cow-calf producers than any other disease-related problem they encounter. But calf scours is not a disease but a symptom of a disease which can have many causes. In diarrhoea, there is a discharge of more fluid than normal from the bowel, often more frequently than normal. The discharge can be white, yellow, grey or blood-stained and is often foul-smelling. Although more common in hand-reared calves, it can also occur in calves which are being suckled by their mothers. The infectious agent that causes scours can be a virus (BVD, Rotavirus, coronavirus), bacteria (*E. coli, Salmonella, Enterotoxemia*) or Protozoa (coccidiosis, cryptosporidium).

Cancer Eye

Bovine ocular neoplasia includes a variety of benign and malignant skin tumours of the eyeball and eyelids. Benign tumours are growths that do not spread to other parts of the body and do not tend to grow into surrounding tissues. They can cause local problems with eye function, but do not affect the rest of the body. Malignant tumours are growths of cells that spread to other parts of the body and tend to invade surrounding tissues. Clearly, it is in the cattlemen's best interest from an economic, human and public perception standpoint to treat or market cattle with cancer eye as soon as practical.

Coccidiosis

Coccidiosis continues to be one of the major disease problems for cattle producers. It is caused by microscopic, one-celled parasites. Coccidiosis occurs more frequently in calves from one to six months of age, but older cattle, especially those from one to two years, are often affected. Young calves are usually infected when they are placed in pastures or lots contaminated by older cattle or other infected calves. Occasionally, mature cattle are infected when they are brought in from large pastures and crowded into small feedlots or barns.

Foot-and-Mouth

Foot-and-Mouth Disease is a severe, highly communicable disease of cattle, pigs, sheep, goats and deer. It is caused by one of the smallest disease producing viruses known. There are several different strains of the virus that cause the disease. The strain now in England and Europe is harder on pigs and cattle but milder in sheep and goats. Humans do not catch the virus. The disease is characterized by blister-like lesions on the tongue, nose and lips, in the mouth, on the teats and between the toes which then burst, leaving painful ulcers. The blisters cause a heavy flow of sticky, foamy saliva that hangs from the mouth. Infected animals sway from one foot to the other due to the tenderness of the feet. Although older cattle usually do not die from the infection, they suffer a severe illness which leaves them in a weakened state. They have high fevers, stop eating, give less milk and become lame.

Footrot

Fusobacterium necrophorum and *Bacteroides melaninogenicus* are the predominant bacteria isolated from footrot. Footrot occurs in cattle of all ages, but it is most common in adults. The disease is seen year-round, but there is increased incidence in the wet summer and fall months.

Grass Tetany

Grass tetany is a serious, often fatal metabolic disorder characterized by low levels of magnesium in the blood serum of cattle. It is also called grass staggers and wheat pasture poisoning. It primarily affects older cows nursing calves less than two months old, but it may also occur in young or dry cows and growing calves. It happens most frequently when cattle are grazing succulent, immature grass and often affects the best cows in the herd.

Infectious Bovine Rhinotracheitis (IBR)

Infectious bovine rhinotracheitis (commonly called IBR or red nose) is an acute, contagious virus disease of cattle. Often implicated as an infection which initiates the shipping fever complex. This infection usually occurs in the air passages of the head and the wind pipe. However, in females this virus also causes inflammation of the vulva and vagina and abortion. Abortion occurs about 20 to 45 days after infection.

External Parasites

Horn flies, face flies, stable flies, ticks, lice and mites are the major external parasites in beef cattle.

Johne's Disease

Johne's Disease (pronounced YO-knees) or paratuberculosis, is a chronic wasting disease that causes considerable production losses in adult cattle, sheep, goats, deer, llamas, elk and bison and other ruminants. The disease is caused by *Mycobacterium paratuberculosis*, a bacterium related to tuberculosis.

Lepto

Atleast five species of leptospira, a corkscrew-like bacteria, affect cattle in the United States. The species most commonly found are hardjo, icterohaemorrhagiae, canicola, *L. pomona* and grippotyphosa. The most common species affecting cattle is *L. pomona*. Multiple abortions in the breeding herd is often the first sign of the disease. The clinical signs in adult cattle are yellow mucous membranes and bloody appearing urine, which are seen only occasionally. The milk of lactating cows may become thick, yellow and blood-tinged. Abortion two to five weeks after infection is common, but most occur about the seventh month of gestation.

Listeriosis

Listeriosis, a disease of the central nervous system, is caused by the bacterium *Listeria moncytogenes*. This bacterium can live almost anywhere—in soil, manure piles and grass. Listeriosis is common in cattle, sheep and goats and can occur in pigs, dogs and cats, some wild animals and humans. Animals infected with *Listeria* can show signs restlessness, loss of appetite, fever and nervous system disorders. Although not seen in every case, the most notable symptom gives this disease its nickname, 'Circling Disease.' Cattle with listeriosis are often seen walking in circles.

Lumpy Jaw

Actinomycosis or lumpy jaw produces immovable hard swellings on the upper and lower jawbones of cattle, commonly at the central molar level. It is caused by an anaerobic microorganism, Actinomyces bovis. The bacterium invades tissue through breaks in the lining of the mouth caused by eating rough forage. The tumour-like swellings develop slowly and may take several months to reach a noticeable size. Lumpy jaw may be well advanced before external signs are visible. The lumps consist of honeycombed masses of thin bone filled with yellow pus. If neglected the swellings may become very large. In advanced cases openings develop and discharge small amounts of sticky pus containing gritty yellow granules.

Neosporosis

Neosporosis is found worldwide and causes to financial losses through embryonic losses, abortion, culled cattle and reduced milk production. *Neospora caninum* is a microscopic protozoan parasite that causes the disease neosporosis. Neosporosis is a major cause of abortion in cattle. Abortion can occur anytime throughout gestation.

Wooden Tongue

Wooden tongue is an infection caused the rod-shaped bacterium, *Actinobacillus lignieresii*, which lives only in the presence of oxygen. The bacteria, which live in the mouth, invade tissue through breaks in the lining of the mouth. Any rough feed can cause mouth abrasions which allow entry of infection. Wooden tongue occurs almost entirely in soft tissue with the tongue and lymph nodes of the head most often affected. The disease starts suddenly with the tongue becoming hard, swollen and painful. Affected animals drool saliva and may appear to be chewing gently. The tongue often protrudes between the lips and nodules and ulcers may be observed on the tongue. They are unable to eat or drink and rapidly lose condition. The disease is progressive and often fatal unless treated.

Ringworm

Ringworm is a transmissible infectious skin disease caused most often by *Trichophyton verrucosum*, a spore forming fungi. The spores can remain alive for years in a dry environment. It occurs in all species of mammals including cattle and man. Although unsightly, fungal infections cause little permanent damage or economic loss.

Trichomoniasis

Trichomoniasis is a venereal disease of cattle that causes infertility and occasional abortions in cows and heifers. It is caused by *Trichomonas foetus*, a small motile protozoan found only in the reproductive tract of the bull and cow. Disease organisms transferred to the cow's vagina from the bull during breeding migrate up to the uterus and cause the infection. Recently infected cows develop a mild white sticky discharge from the vulva which can last for up to two months. Large number of cows, often over 90% of the herd, will be affected in herds that have not been previously infected. Repeat breeding or infertility of individual cows can last up to five months. The reason for repeat breeding appears to be death of the embryo, often within 10 days. Eventually cows begin to cycle again and can carry a foetus to term.

Vibriosis

Vibriosis (*Campylobacter fetus*) in cattle is an infectious bacterial disease of the genital tract causing infertility and occasional abortions. It is a venereal disease spread by infected bulls when they mate susceptible cows and heifers. It is considered to be the most important cause of infertility in cattle. Good vaccines are available, but it still causes losses simply because they are not used in many herds. Infection introduced into a non-exposed or non-vaccinated herd will spread rapidly during breeding.

Warts

Warts in cattle are caused by the contagious virus papillomavirus. Four types of the virus are known to produce warts on cattle.

Pinkeye

Pinkeye (infectious bovine keratoconjunctivitis) is a common infectious disease affecting the eyes of cattle. The name describes the redness and inflammation of the lining of the eyelid and eyeball. Although pinkeye is non-fatal, it has a marked economic impact on the cattle industry. It is known to occur at all seasons of the year and in all breeds of cattle. Pinkeye and foot rot are the two most prevalent conditions affecting all breeding beef females.

Exercise

1. Which of the following is not a characteristic of a biome?
(a) It is the those ecosystem of the Earth which are facing more or less the same kind of abiotic and biotic factors spread over a large area
(b) Biomes are defined by genetic, taxonomic or historical similarities
(c) Biomes are often identified with particular patterns of ecological succession and climax vegetation
(d) Biome is a major habitat type and it is a compromise, as it has an intrinsic in homogeneity

2. Which of the following ecozones is known as oriental realm among biogeographers?
(a) Australacia ecozone (b) Afrotropic ecozone
(c) Oceania ecozone (d) Indomalaya ecozone

3. The Eastern boundary of the Indomalaya is known as
(a) Bendan line (b) Wallace line
(c) Bear line (d) None of these

4. The maximum biodiversity in India occurs at
(a) Western Himalayas
(b) North-East Himalayas
(c) Western Ghats
(d) Eastern Ghats

5. The national herbarium in our country is located in
(a) Mumbai (b) Kolkata
(c) Chennai (d) Delhi

6. Chilka lake harbours high biodiversity of
(a) pisces (b) aves
(c) reptiles (d) mammals

7. Which of the following carnivore from cat family has gone extinct in India?
(a) Tiger (b) Fishing cat
(c) Asian lion (d) Asiatic cheetah

8. Which of the following shrew is endemic to India?
(a) Mole shrew (b) Grey shrew
(c) Musk shrew (d) Kashmir shrew

9. Which of the panda is present in Indian forest?
(a) Giant panda (b) Black panda
(c) Red panda (d) White panda

10. What is the common name of *Spilornis cheela*?
(a) Indian crested serpent eagle
(b) Indian bittern
(c) Great Indian hornbill
(d) Indian peacock

11. Which of the bird species is a resident bird of the Indian sub-continent and was introduced for the first time in the Andaman Islands?
(a) Grey francolin (b) Indian bittern
(c) Great Indian hornbill (d) Indian peacock

12. The natural habitat of the Indian storks comprises of
(a) fields (b) savannahs
(c) marshes (d) All of these

13. Zoonotic diseases are the diseases which?
(a) Carried by animals but not transmitted to humans
(b) Carried by humans but not transmitted to animals
(c) Carried by animals and can be transmitted to humans
(d) Carried by humans and can be transmitted to animals

14. 'Chlamydiosis' is the zoonotic disease of
(a) cattle (b) dog
(c) pig (d) birds

15. Which one of the following diseases is a communicable?
(a) Rickets (b) Amoebiasis
(c) Diabetes (d) Cancer

16. AIDS virus spreads in the body through
(a) suppressor T-cells (b) carrier T-cells
(c) helper T-cells (d) killer T-cells

17. The cells which act as parasites in the body
(a) Schwann cells (b) Hepatocytes
(c) Kupffer's cells (d) Cancer cells

18. TAB vaccine is useful against
(a) polio (b) diphtheria
(c) pertusis (d) typhoid

19. Which of the following specimen is tested the most for the detection of carrier of typhoid?
(a) Urine (b) Blood
(c) Faeces (d) Sputum

20. Select the vital disease
(a) diabetes (b) tetanus
(c) leprosy (d) poliomyelitis

21. Kala-azar is caused by
(a) *Taenia solium* (b) *Trypanosoma gambiense*
(c) *Leishmania donovani* (d) *Wuchereria bancrofti*

22. Disease caused by *Trypanosoma gambiense* is
(a) sleeping sickness (b) kala-azar
(c) diphtheria (d) dysentery

23. In Australia, marsupials fill the niches that placental mammals fill in other parts of the world bcause
(a) they are better adapted and have outcompeted placental mammals
(b) their offspring complete their development attached to a teat in a marsupium
(c) they evolved from monotrems that migrated to Australia about 12 million years ago
(d) after Pangaea broken up they diversified in isolation from placental mammals

24. Which of the following occurs in areas a bit too warm for coniferous forest and a bit too dry for temperate forests?
(a) Desert (b) Tropical thorn forest
(c) Temperate grassland (d) Chaparral

25. Which of the following is dominated by plants that drop their leaves yearly to conserve water?
(a) Desert
(b) Coniferous forest
(c) Tropical rain forest
(d) Temperate deciduous forest

26. Winds tend to blow toward the equator because
(a) this is a very rainy area
(b) equatorial air is heated by the sun and rises
(c) air flows 'downhill' from the North pole
(d) the Earth's rotational speed is fastest at the equator

27. In order to place a newly identified species into one of the five kingdoms, the first piece of information you would need to acquire is
(a) the way in which it acquires food
(b) its life cycle
(c) the absence or presence of chloroplasts
(d) the absence or presence of a nuclear membrane

28. The primary ecological factor determining the distribution of deserts is
(a) windness (b) elevation
(c) moisture (d) temperature

29. Change of season is caused by
(a) change in the distance of the Earth from the sun
(b) the tilt of the Earth
(c) variations in output of solar energy
(d) changes in wind patterns

30. The kind of tropical forest in ia given area thorn forest, deciduous forest or rain forest depends mostly on
(a) rainfall
(b) average temperature
(c) temperature difference between day and night
(d) distance from the equator

31. The tundra biome gets little precipitation, but during the short summer season it is very wet, with many marshy areas, ponds and bogs.
(a) Water cannot soak into the frozen ground
(b) It does not rain much, but the tundra gets a lot of snow
(c) The ground is so flat that the water cannot run downhill
(d) It is flooded by melting snow from the surrounding mountains

32. If you were to compare the source (beginning) of a river to its mouth (end), you would probably find that
(a) the water is colder near the mouth
(b) there are more nutrients in the water near the source
(c) there are more phytoplankton in the water near the mouth
(d) the current is swifter near the mouth

33. In the foothills of California, between the flat valley floors and mountain forests, there is a zone of grassland with scattered oak trees. Although it is too narrow to show on out biome map, this 'oak woodland' would probably be classed as an example of
(a) coniferous forest
(b) savanna
(c) temperate deciduous forest
(d) chaparral

34. Photic or euphotic zone is how much deep from the upper surface of sea
(a) 10 m (b) 100 m
(c) 200 m (d) 500 m

35. Which of the following ecosystems have more productivity in an unit area?
(a) Grassland
(b) Marine ecosystem
(c) Pond ecosystem with algae
(d) Tree ecosystem

36. If less light falls on the pond's surface
(a) size of fishes become larger
(b) the size of fish population become smaller
(c) the size of fish population is no way connected with amount of light falling on a pond
(d) mutation will take place in fishes

37. If we completely remove the decomposers from an ecosystem, the ecosystem functioning will be adversely affected because
(a) mineral movement will be blocked
(b) herbivores will not receive solar energy
(c) energy flow will be blocked
(d) rate of decomposition of other components will be very high

38. The hypersaline waters are found in lakes located in the
(a) alpine regions (b) arid and semiarid regions
(c) tropical regions (d) All of these

39. Abyssal zone of oceans is characterized by
(a) presence of sunlight and producers
(b) absence of sunlight and all living organisms
(c) absence of sunlight but presence of producers
(d) absence of sunlight and presence of consumers and decomposers

40. In which part of the open sea producers are found?
(a) Aphotic zone (b) Abyssal zone
(c) Photic zone (d) None of these

Answers

1. (b)	**2.** (d)	**3.** (b)	**4.** (c)	**5.** (b)	**6.** (c)	**7.** (d)	**8.** (c)	**9.** (c)	**10.** (a)
11. (a)	**12.** (d)	**13.** (c)	**14.** (d)	**15.** (b)	**16.** (c)	**17.** (d)	**18.** (d)	**19.** (c)	**20.** (d)
21. (c)	**22.** (a)	**23.** (d)	**24.** (c)	**25.** (d)	**26.** (b)	**27.** (d)	**28.** (c)	**29.** (b)	**30.** (a)
31. (a)	**32.** (c)	**33.** (b)	**34.** (c)	**35.** (c)	**36.** (b)	**37.** (a)	**38.** (b)	**39.** (d)	**40.** (c)

29

The Environment and Population

The Environment

Each organism is a specialized unit which invariably depends upon the environment and other organisms for its existence. Ecology is the study of natural environment including the relations of organisms to one another and to their surroundings.

Ecological studies may focus on levels of organization that include the following:

1. **Individual organism**
2. **Population** is a group of individuals that belong to the same species and live in the same area.
3. **Community** is an assemblage of different populations that live together in a defined area.
4. **Ecosystem** is all the organisms that live in a place, together with their physical environment.
5. **Biome** is a group of ecosystems that share similar climates and typical organisms.
6. **Biosphere** is our entire planet, with all its organisms and physical environments.

The **biosphere** consists of all life on Earth and all parts of the Earth in which life exists, including land, water and the atmosphere. The biosphere extends from about 8 km above Earth's surface to as far as 11 km below the surface of the ocean.

The biological influences on organisms are called **biotic factors.** Physical components of an ecosystem are called **abiotic factors**. A biotic factor is any living part of the environment with which an organism might interact, including animals, plants, mushrooms and bacteria. An abiotic factor is any non-living part of the environment, such as sunlight, heat, precipitation, humidity, wind or water currents, soil type, etc.

Syllabus

- The Environment: Physical and Biotic Environment; Biotic and Abiotic Interactions.
- Habitat and Niche: Concept of Habitat and Niche; Niche Width and Overlap; Fundamental and Realized Niche; Resource Partitioning; Character Displacement.
- Population Ecology: Characteristics of a Population; Population Growth Curves; Population Regulation; Life History Strategies (*r* and *k* Selection); Concept of Metapopulation – Demes and Dispersal, Interdemic Extinctions, Age Structured Populations.

Physical Environment

Physical environment not only necessitates adaptations for organisms to exist in particular environments, but it also constrains the distribution of organisms, *e.g.*, vampire bat (*Desmodus rotundus*). Its Northern distribution has mean minimal temperature for January is 10°C.

Major constraints of physical environment or climate include water, air, soil, temperature and light.

1. The **Egg Rule** with special reference to birds in the Northern Hemisphere, the **egg rule** states that the average number of eggs in a set or clutch, laid by songbirds and several other kinds of birds increases as one moves North in latitude.
2. Interaction with physical environment also implies alteration of it by organism.
   (a) Life first arose in a reducing atmosphere (<1% O_2), but living things created an oxidizing atmosphere (ca. 21% O_2) within Proterozoic era.
   (b) Organisms continually create soils by weathering rocks, *e.g.*, **Negev** desert snails weather rocks at rate of 0.7-1 metric tons/ha/yr, by eating endolithic lichens (growing within rocks).
3. All organisms are constrained by physical, chemical environment (*i.e.*, according to physical laws).
   (a) **Liebig's Law of the Minimum** (1840) The distribution of a species will be controlled by that environmental factor for which the organism has the narrowest range of tolerance.
   (b) **Shelford's Law of Tolerance** Each ecological factor to which an organism responds has maximum and minimum limiting effect between which lies a range or gradient that is now known as the **limits of tolerance.**

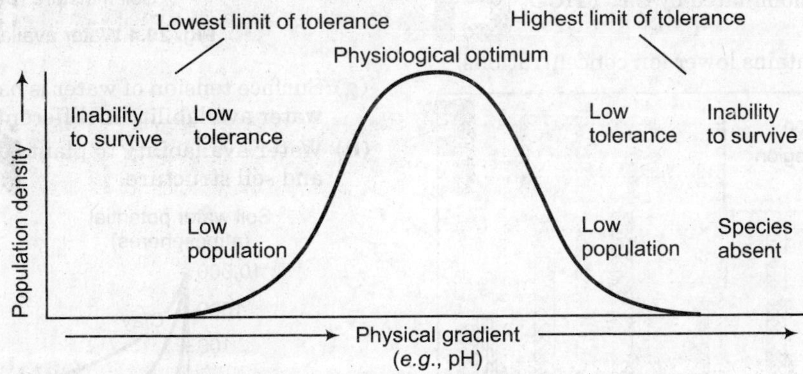

Fig. 29.1 Range of tolerance for a population of organisms of same species to an abiotic environmental factor

4. A plant or animal may have a wide range of tolerance for one factor in the environment, but a relatively narrow range of tolerance for another condition. Thus, we find that some species of freshwater fishes are eurythermal but they are stenohaline. The prefix *steno* means a narrow range of tolerance and the prefix *eury* means a wide range.
5. Abiotic factors are grouped into:
   (a) **Climatic factors** Temperature, water, light and gases.
   (b) **Edaphic factors** Soil types, pH and humus content.
   (c) **Physiographic factors** Aspect (position of the area in relation to the sunlight), slope and altitude.

All the factors are interrelated, *i.e.*, change in one factor may affect the other. The effect on the life of organism is the overall effect of all these factors at a time.

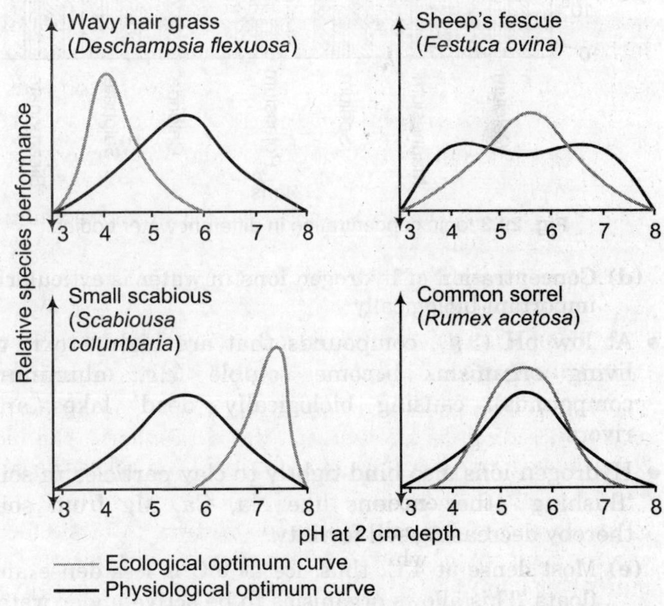

Fig. 29.2 A wide range of tolerance for one factor in the environment, but a relatively narrow range of tolerance for another condition

Water

Solvent

(a) Salts dissociate in water, some readily, —> anion availability to organisms (*e.g.*, Cl^-, SO_4^-, HCO_3^-).

(b) Transport nutrients, hormones organic substances, toxins.

(c) Leaches elements and nutrients from foliage, detritus, rocks (—> weathering) and soil.

Water Bodies Differ in Ionic Composition

(a) Seawater, accumulating ions over ions, dominated by Na^+, Cl^- and significant amounts Mg^{2+}, SO_4^{2-}.

(b) Water over limestone dominated by Ca^{2+}, HCO_3^- (hard water).

(c) Water over granite contains lower ion concentrations.

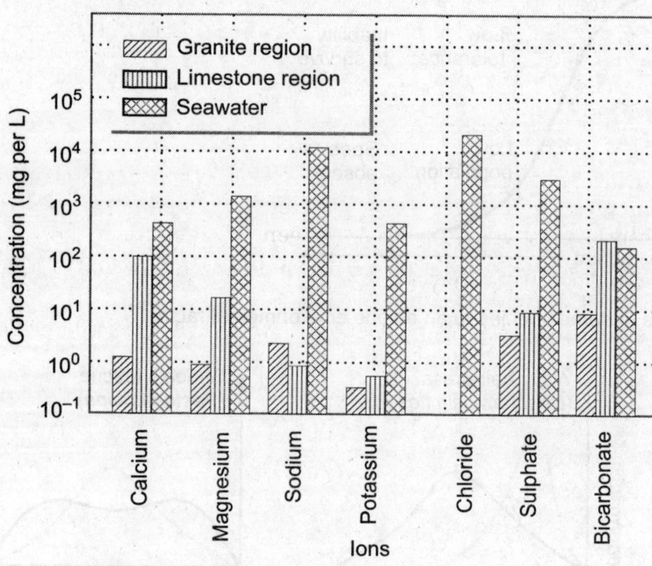

Fig. 29.3 Ionic concentration in different water bodies

(d) Concentration of hydrogen ions in water is articularly important biologically

- At low pH (3-4), compounds that are highly toxic to living organisms become soluble (*e.g.*, aluminum compounds), causing biologically 'dead' lakes and rivers.
- Hydrogen ions also bind tightly to clay particles in soil, 'flushing' other cations like Na, Ca, Mg from soil, thereby decreasing soil fertility.

(e) Most dense at 4°C; thus, ice at 0°C is less dense and floats. This allows organisms to be active under water even when surface frozen.

(f) High specific heat of water, high latent heat —> resistance to changes in state (liquid to gas, liquid to solid). Water thus tends to buffer temperature and large bodies of water tend to ameliorate climate.

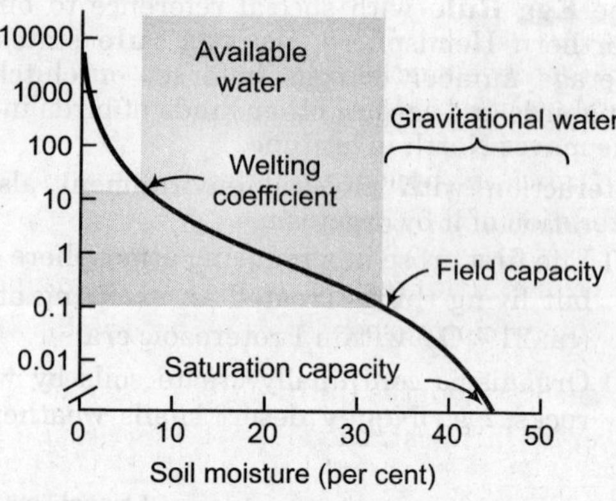

Fig. 29.4 Water availability to plant

(g) Surface tension of water is basis for **transpiration** and water availability in different soil types.

(h) Water availability to plants depends on surface tension and soil structure.

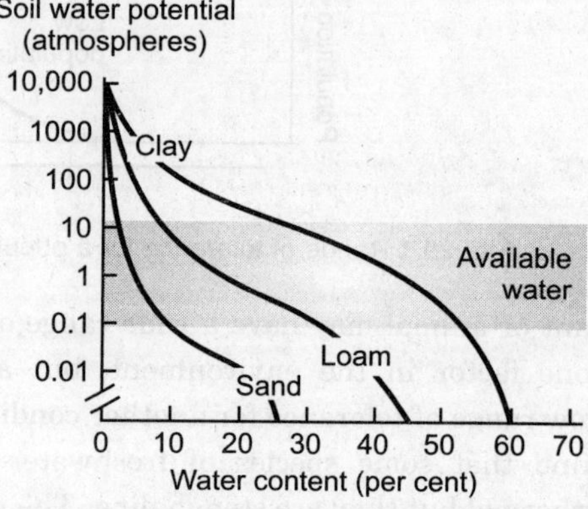

Fig. 29.5 Different soil types, with different particle sizes (and size distributions) have different soil water availability

Light

Light affects the life of plants and animals though the animal effects are far reaching. The solar energy reaching earth is transformed to other forms and great deal of solar radiation is absorbed in atmosphere. Light affect transpiration distribution of plants, overall vegetative development of plant parts community development and photoperiodism. The plants growing best in higher sunlight are called **heliophytes,** while growing in lower sunlight are called **seiophytes facultative sciophytes** are actually heliophyts which can grow under shade. While **facultative heliophytes** are actually seiophytes which can grow in full sunlight. In animals light affect the pigmentation pattern, development in some sp. (*Salmon, Mytilus*), reproduction, metabolism, vision, locomotion (phototactic) and photoperiodism. The daily response of animals to light is called **circadian rhythm** (an endogenous process).

(i) Plants absorb light only in limited range of frequencies (400-700 nm = Photosynthetically Active Region, *i.e.*, PAR).

(ii) Shorter wavelengths (ultraviolet) have higher energy, potentially damaging to organisms.

(a) Ozone in upper atmosphere absorbs ultraviolet radiation, protecting living things.

(b) Ozone hole results from loss of ozone due to chlorofluorocarbons (CFCs), produced by humans.

(iii) Longer wavelengths (infrared) have too little energy to power biochemical reactions necessary to life.

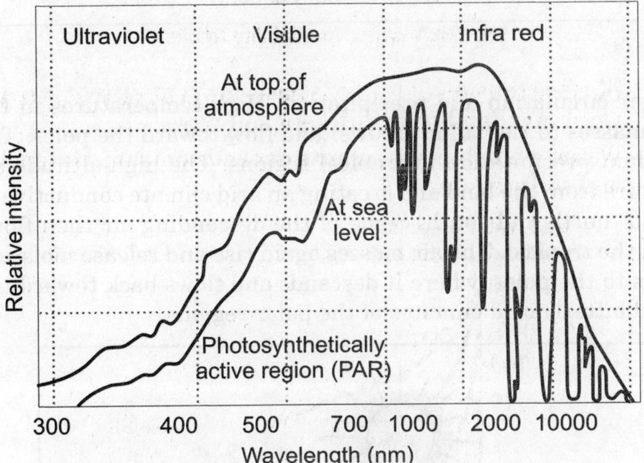

Fig. 29.6 Light wavelength and relative intensity

(iv) Different plant pigments absorb light in different parts of electromagnetic spectrum—and reflect colours that they don't absorb chlorophylls green, carotenoids yellow-red.

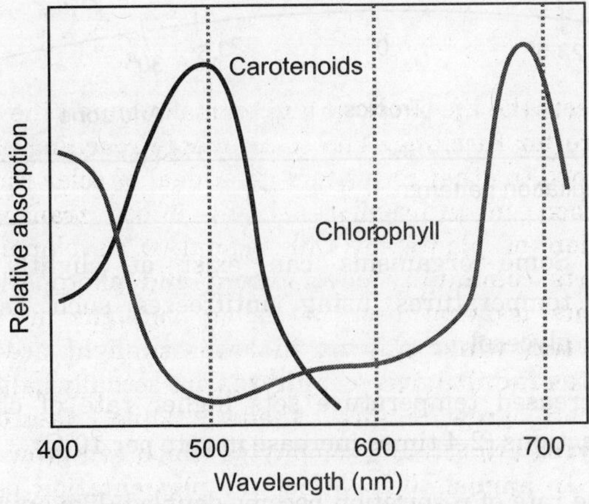

Fig. 29.7 Relative absorption of pigments

(v) Water tends to absorb longer wavelengths, scatter shorter ones thus greens penetrate deepest.

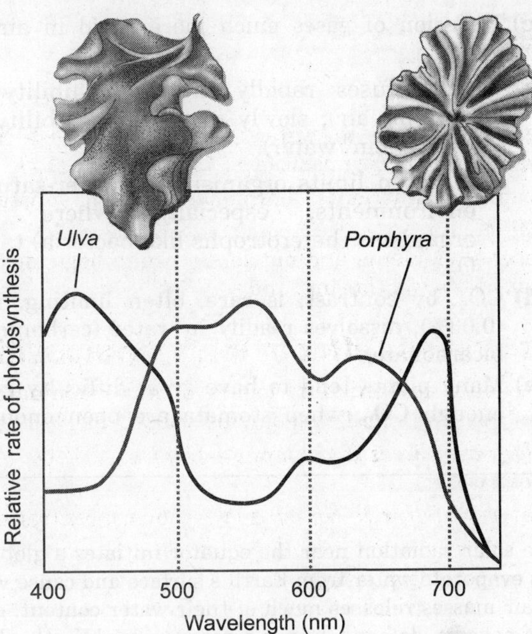

Fig. 29.8 Wavelength penetratic zone in water

Surface plant such as green alga (*Ulva*) thus has pigments like terrestrial plants; deeper water red alga (*e.g.*, *Porphyra*) absorbs most efficiently in the green wavelengths.

(a) **The activity** of an organism during the period of light in 24 hour has four categories.

(b) **Diurnal** Active in day light, *e.g.*, Butterfly, man, birds, etc.

(c) **Nocturnal** Active during night, *e.g.*, Moth, owl, bat, cockroach, etc.

(d) **Auroral** Active at dawn, *e.g.*, Bulbulcus, etc.

(e) **Vesperal** Active at dusk, *e.g.*, Rabbit.

Air

About 95% of total air is present up to height of about 20 km. The atmosphere is usually divided into four zones namely.

(i) **Troposphere** Lowest up to 20 km, having cloud formation, lightning thundering, thunderstem formation, temperature decrease at rate of 6.5 per km the upper limit called **tropopause.**

(ii) **Stratosphere** Second, of about 30 km, temperature increases due to ozone layer absorbing UV light. The upper limit called **stratopause.**

(iii) **Mesosphere** Next to stratosphere of about 40 km, temperature show down again. The upper limit called mesopause.

(iv) **Ionosphere** Above mesosphere up to 300 km. Containing gases components ionized due to radiant energy.

(a) Air composed of different substances; 78% N_2, 21% O_2, 0.03% CO_2, traces of CH_4, N_2O, etc.

(b) Air less viscous, less buoyant than water (organisms move easily phru it, but need more support).

(c) Diffusion of gases much more rapid in air than water.

- O_2 diffuses rapidly in air (solubility 0.21 cm^3/cm^3 air); slowly in water (solubility 0.01 $cm^3\ O_2/cm^3$ water).
- O_2 often limits organisms in water-saturated environments, especially, where decay organisms (heterotrophs like bacteria) take up O_2.

(d) CO_2, by contrast, is rare, often limiting, in air (0.03%); dissolves readily in water (carbonic acid, bicarbonate).

(e) Many plants tend to have great difficulty getting enough CO_2, when stomata are open enough to transpire water; this is particular problem in desert environment.

(f) Respiration is reverse of photosynthesis

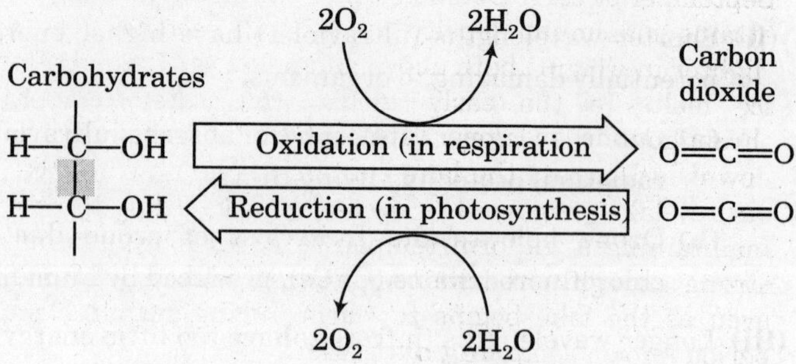

Global

Intense solar radiation near the equator initiates a global pattern of air circulation and precipitation. High temperatures in the tropics evaporate water from Earth's surface and cause warm, wet air masses to rise (blue arrows) and flow toward the poles. The rising air masses releases much of their water content, creating abundant precipitation in tropical regions. The high-altitude air masses, now dry, descend (brown arrows) toward Earth, absorbing moisture from the land and creating an arid climate conductive to the development of the deserts that are common at altitudes around 30° north and south. Some of the descending air then flows toward the poles, depositing abundant precipitation (though less than in the tropics). The air masses again rise and release moisture in the vicinity of 60° altitude. Some of the cold, dry rising air then flows to the poles, where it descends and flows back toward the equator, absorbing moisture and creating the comparatively rainless and bitterly cold climates of the polar regions.

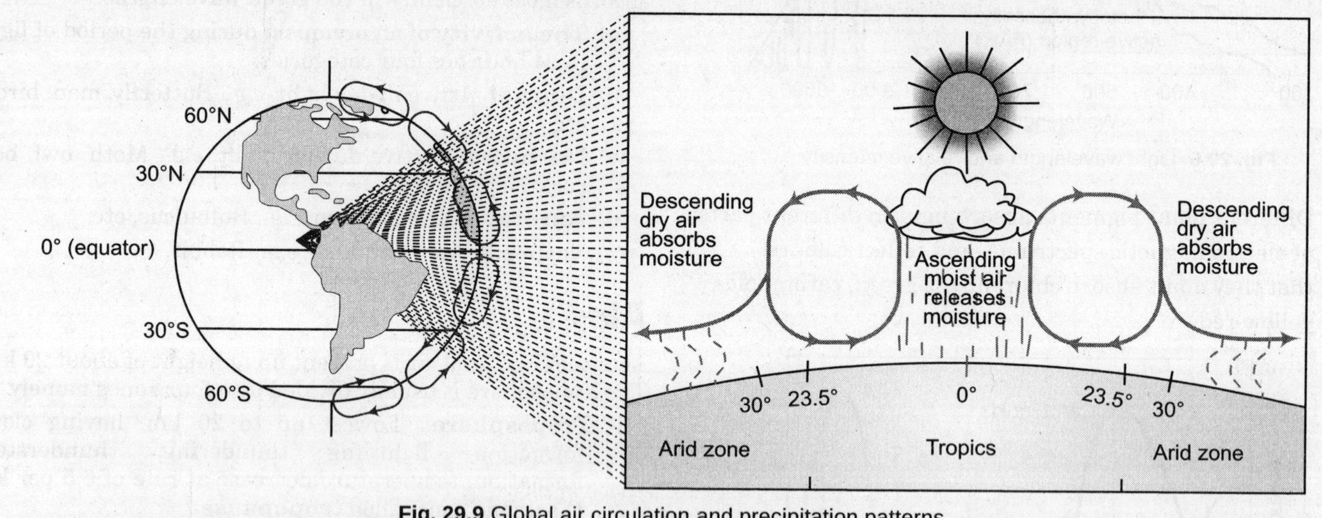

Fig. 29.9 Global air circulation and precipitation patterns

Temperature

(i) Temperatures of living things determined by range of temperatures at which water is in liquid phase. It has effects on metabolism, reproduction, growth and development crossing over and somatic expression of genes, etc.

(a) Few organisms can survive temperatures > 45°C, because of protein denaturation at high temperatures.

(b) Some organisms can exist at higher temperatures due to particularly heat-stable proteins.

(c) Most organisms cannot tolerate body (cell) temperatures below freezing, because of damage to cells from ice crystals.

(d) Some organisms can exist at slightly lower temperatures using antifreezes such as salts, glycerol.

(ii) Increased temperature sets higher rate of chemical reactions (2-4 times increase in rate per 10°C).

(iii) The rate of respiration become doubled (like animals) at the increase of 10°C above the optimum temperature, provided other factors are favourable (Vant Hoff's law). However, optimum temperature for photosynthesis is lower than that for respiration (Smith; 1974).

Thermal Stratification of Lakes

It generally begins in May or early June and ends in September or early October. Lakes can stratify because water attains maximum density at 39°F. It becomes less dense (lighter in weight) both above and below 39°F. Soon after the ice melts in the early spring, the water temperature throughout the lakes rises to 32°F. The water moves downward, across the lake bottom, to the upwind side. The entire lake begins to circulate from top to bottom, maintaining a uniform temperature. As long as winds are strong enough, the lake temperature will remain uniform, even as the lake begins to warm during spring. This is a period known as **spring overturn.**

In summer season, the temperature differential between the warm, upper layer (called the **epilimnion**) and the colder, bottom layer (the hypolimnion) increases. Between the epilimnion and hypolimnin is a relatively thin layer of water called the **thermocline.** This layer is characterized by a rapid decrease in temperature. As summer wanes and fall begins, water temperatures in the warm, upper layer begin to cool. As the upper layer cools to approximately the same temperature as the lower layer, thermal stratification disappears as wind can now mix the two layers together. This is known as **fall turnover** and is considered to have occurred when temperatures are the same from the surface down to the deepest area of the lake.

As fall progresses into winter, water cools to 39°F and below, the colder upper layer becomes less dense. This cause the lake to become stratified again. However, in winter the colder water is near the surface rather than at the bottom. Occasionally, strong winds will break up winter stratification for a few days. It will reform once calm weather returns. Often a layer of ice forms, sealing the lake surface and preserving the stratification until ice-out.

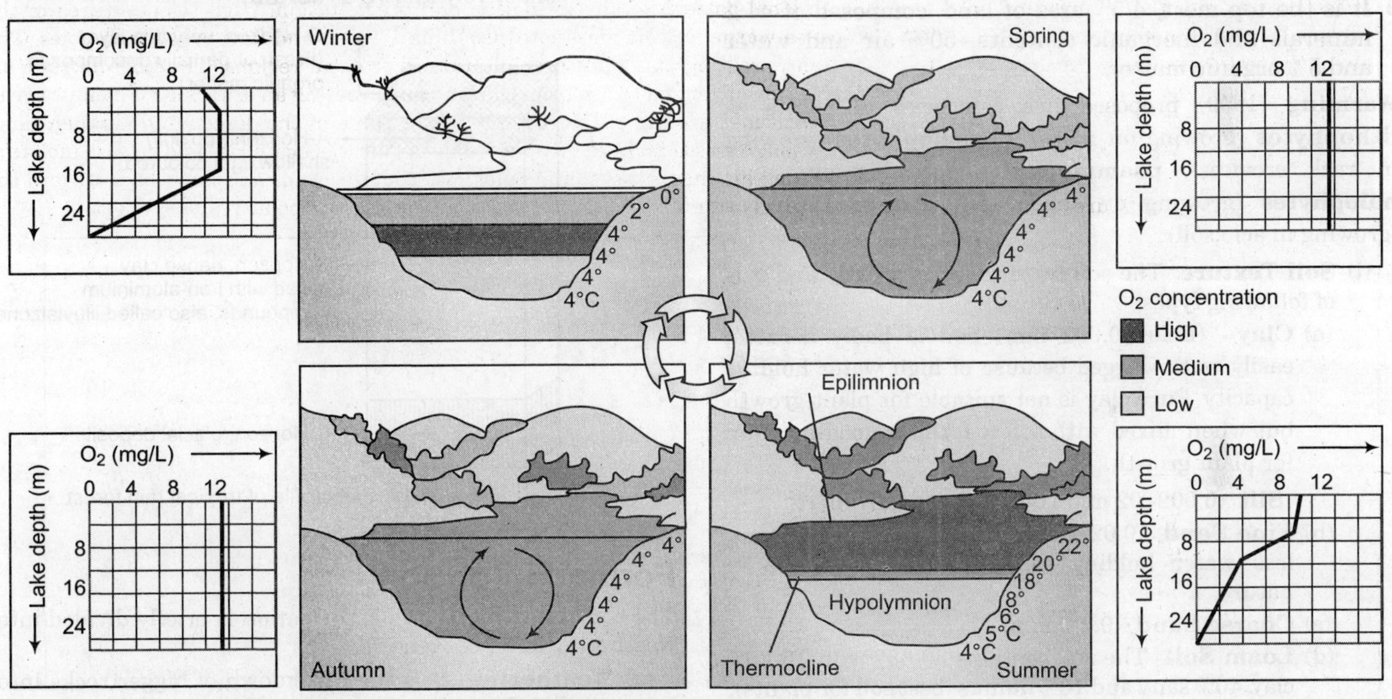

Fig. 29.10 Thermal stratification in temperate lakes

(i) In temperate lakes there is circulation of nutrients and oxygen twice a year, *i.e.,* spring and autumn. Such lakes are called **dimictic lakes.**

(ii) Temperature affects a number of morphological characters as per different rules:

(a) **Bergmann's Rule** Geographic races of a species possessing smaller body size are found in the warmer parts of the range and races of larger body size in cooler parts or warm blooded animals (birds and mammals) of cold regions are large sized than those of warmer region, *e.g.,* Polar bear is larger than black bear of temperate region. Antarctic penguin is 1m longer than that of equatorial Galapagos island.

(b) **Allen's Rule** Certain extremities of animals are relatively shorter in the cooler parts of a species' range than in the warmer parts. The tail, snout, ears and legs of mammals are relatively shorter in colder region than in the warmer regions. *e.g.,* Desert fox has the largest pinna as compared to red fox (smaller pinna) and arctic fox (smallest pinna).

(c) **Jorden's Rule** Fish found in cold water tend to have more vertebrae than those found in warm water, *e.g.,* Cod hatching at 4 - 8°C has 58 vertebrae, whereas those hatching at 10-11°C has 54 vertebrae.

(d) **Gloger's Rule** The mammals, birds and insects of warmer region (tropical) are darker and heavily pigmented than those of Arctic region (cold) except for some organisms, *Hyla* (tree frog) and *Phrynosoma* (horned toad) are dark skinned even in low temperature.

(e) **Rensch's Rule** The birds of colder regions tend to have relatively narrower wings than the birds found in warmer regions.

Temperature also affected the phenology of plants which describing periodical phenomenon of plants in relation to climate as flowering.

Soil (Pedology)

The part of earth surface which supports vegetation is called soil. The plants depends on soil for their nutrients, water supply and anchorage.

- It is the top most, 4/5th area of land, composed of 45% minerals and inorganic contents, 50% air and water and 5% organic matter.

Warming (1909) proposed five categories of plants as **lithophytes** (growing on rocks), **chasmophytes** (growing in rock crevices), **psammophytes** (growing on sand) **halophytes** (growing on saline soil) and **oxylophytes** (growing in acid soil).

(i) **Soil Texture** The soil texture varies greatly and it is of following types:

(a) **Clay** (Below-0.002 mm) Soil is badly aerated, easily water logged because of high water holding capacity. Pure clay is not suitable for plant growth but when mixed with soil it forms a good medium for plant growth.

Silt (0.002-.02 mm.) Soil is chemically inert.

(b) **Fine Sand** (0.02-.2 mm) Soil is poor in nutrient, less water holding capacity and not fertile in nature.

(c) **Coarse Sand** (0.2-2 mm)

(d) **Loam Soil** The soil contains 30-35% silt, 15-20% clay, 40% sand and 10% humus (best soil for plants).

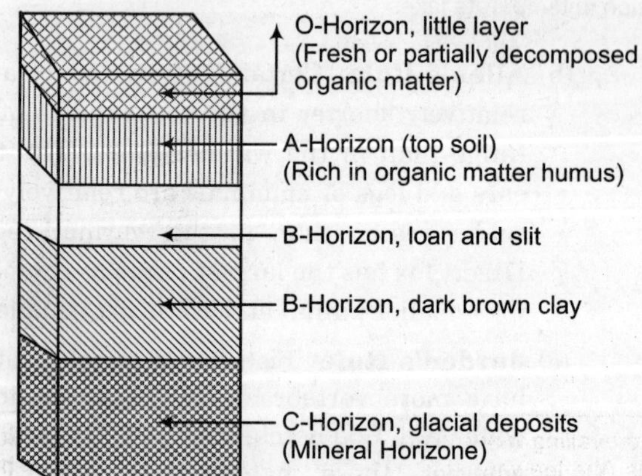

Fig. 29.11 Soil profile of temperature deciduous forest

(ii) **Organic Matter** of soil is derived from dead and living organisms. It is composed of two fractions as

(a) **Detritus/Litter** It is freshly dead and partially decomposed plant and animal residues.

(b) **Humus** It is dark coloured, amorphous, colloidal substance which determines the type of soil. It makes the soil porous and provide nutrient for plant growth. The partially decomposed litter (all dead, fresh organic matter) is called **duff.** There are two types of humus.

(c) **Morhumus and Mullhumus** Morhumus is characteristic of podsol lacking earthworm while mull humus is characteristic of brown forest soil and rich in microbs and earthworm.

(d) **Soil Profile** Soil is vertically divided into different horizons called soil profile. It develops due to withering process, accumulation of organic matter and the leaching of mineral matter. A and B are collectively known as **solum.**

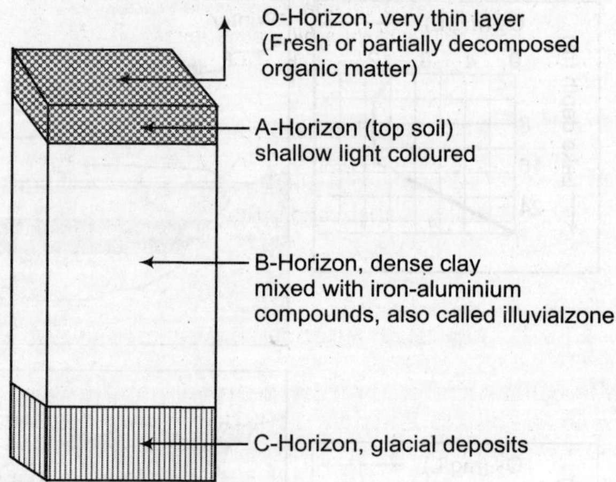

Fig. 29.12 Soil profile of tropical rain forest

Formation of Soil

The complete process of soil formation is briefly divided into weathering and pedogenesis.

(a) **Weathering** It is the breakdown of bigger rocks into smaller, fine mineral particles. The process for this may be physical and chemical. The chemical process include **hydration** (reversible change of haematite to limonite) hydrolysis, oxidation-reduction, carbonation and chelation. Chelates are metals which dissolved with organic products of microbial activity.

(b) **Pedogenesis** It is biological phenomenon during which a number of changes occur in weathered rocks material. During this process a number of organic components added due to excretion death and decay of algae, fungi, lichens, microbes, molluscs, etc. This true soil is thus, composed of organic matter and livings in addition.

Soil is generally of two types depending on place of formation and carries.

(c) **Residual soil** Soil remain at the same place where formed.

(d) **Transported soil**

Alluvial soil	–	carried by running water
Colluvial soil	–	carried by gravity
Eolian soil	–	carried by wind
Glacial soil	–	carried by glaciers

Physiographic Factors

Physiographic factors can be grouped as latitudes and altitudes, height of mountain, direction of mountains and valleys, steepness of slope, etc.

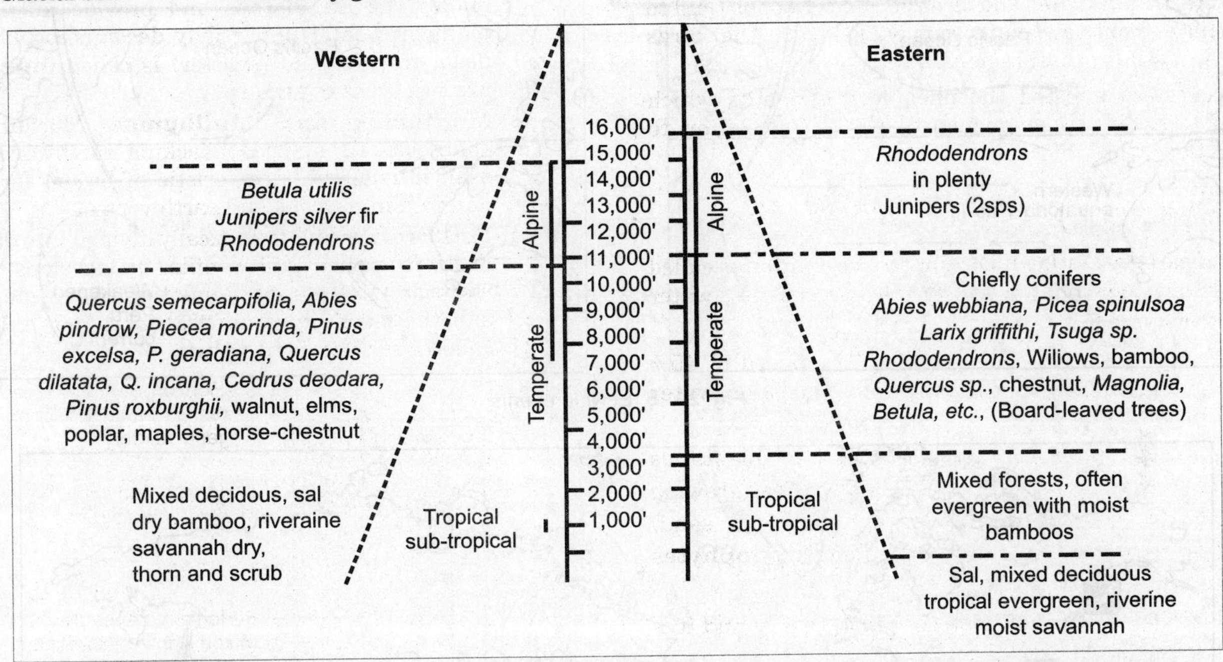

Fig. 29.13 Altitudinal zonation of Himalayas. The distribution of plants species on the Western and Eastern Himalayas

Microclimate refers to local combination of factors such as wind rate of evaporation humidity temperature, which differ from regional climate. Altitude is the height of mountain chain with increase in altitude climate changed as decrease in temperature, increase in humidity and increase in precipitation and wind velocity.

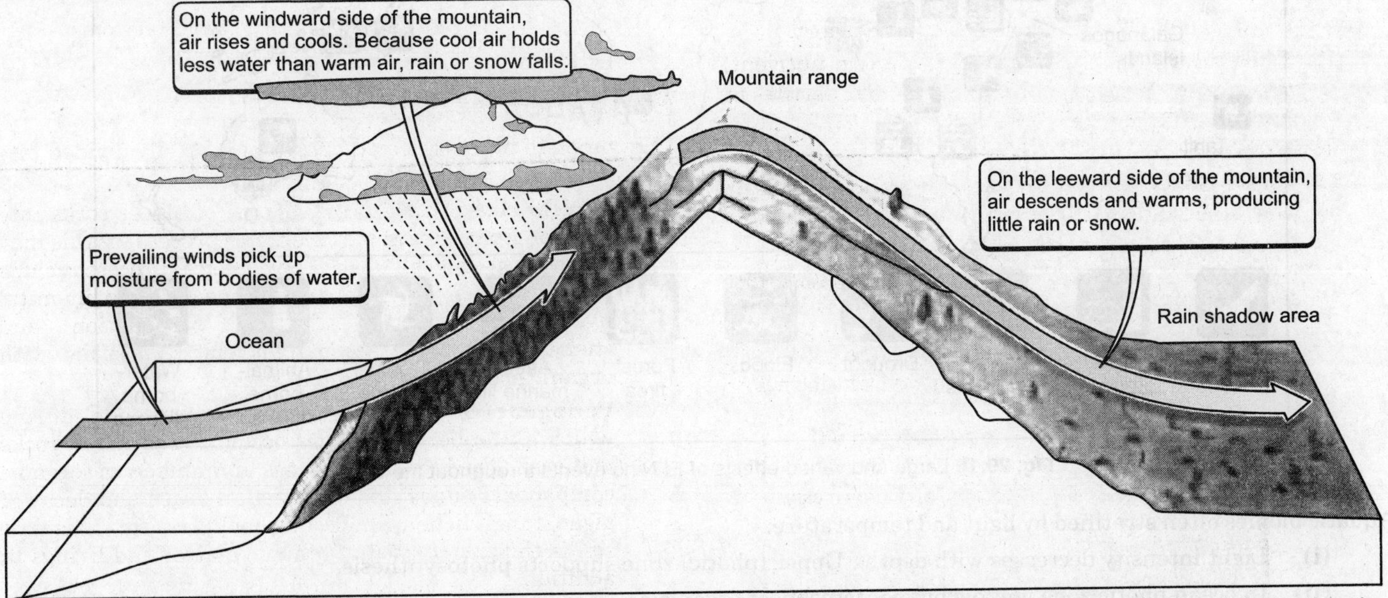

Fig. 29.14 Rain Shadow Effect. The side of a high mountain that faces the prevailing winds (the windward) receives more precipitation than the side of the mountain that faces away from the prevailing winds (the leeward side). The leeward side is thus said to be in a rain shadow. The windward side has more vegetation than the leeward side.

During an El Nino event, winds from the West push warm surface water from the Western Pacific to the Eastern Pacific. The resulting changes in sea surface temperatures cause additional changes in ocean currents, wind patterns, sea levels and patterns of precipitation throughout the world. Cold ocean currents are coloured blue; warm ocean currents are coloured red.

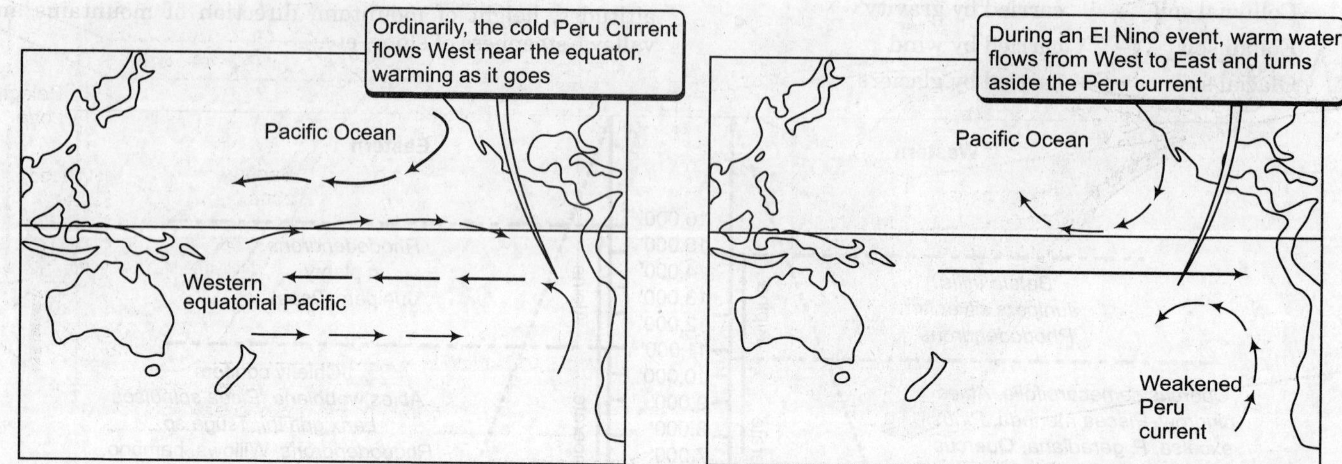

Fig. 29.15 El Nino events

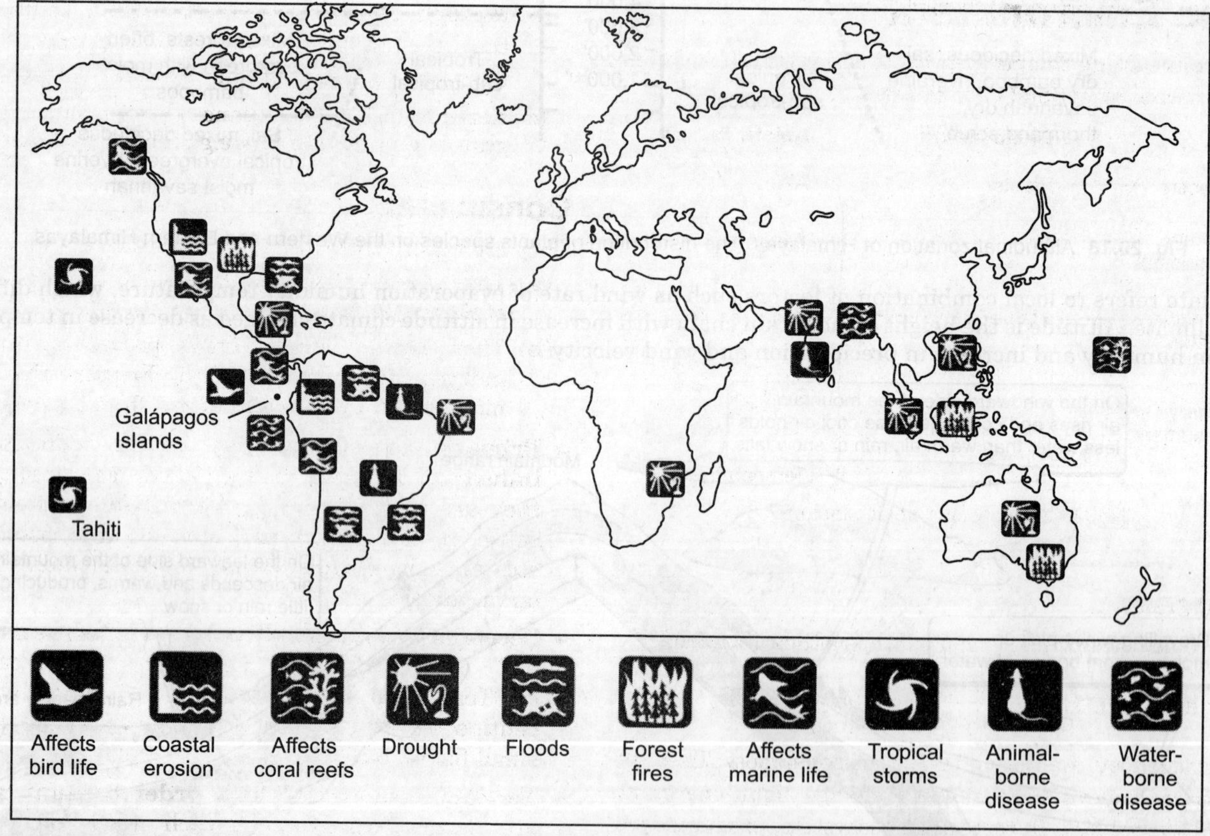

Fig. 29.16 Large and varied effects of El Nino events throughout the world

Aquatic biomes often stratified by light and temperature.

(i) Light intensity decreases with depth. Upper (photic) zone supports photosynthesis.

(ii) In ocean photic zone narrow but contains most organisms.

(iii) Aphotic zone sparsely populated.

(iv) Benthic zone (bottom) organisms often depend on rain of dead organic matter (detritus) from above.

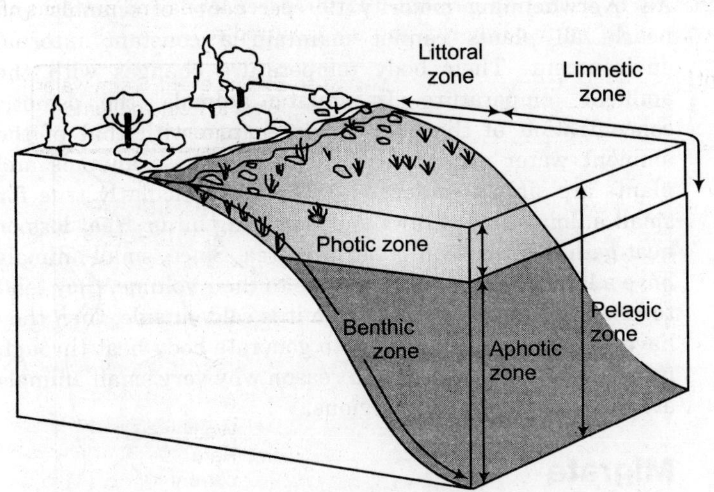

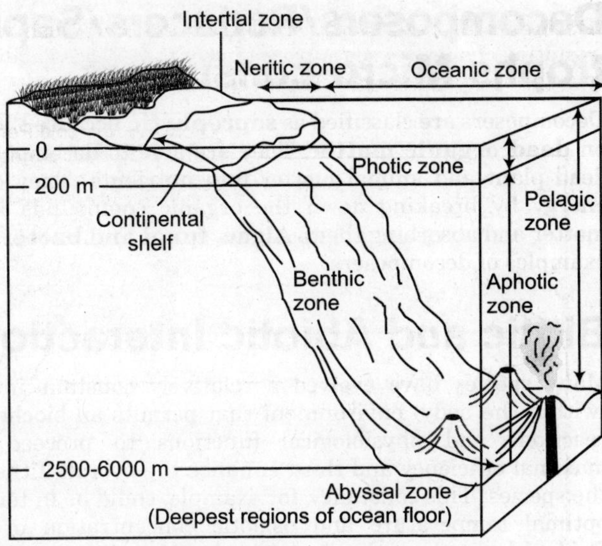

Fig. 29.17 Zonation of aquatic biomes (a) Zonation in a lake (b) Marine zonation

Biotic Environment

These are the living components of an ecosystem. It includes producers, consumers and decomposers.

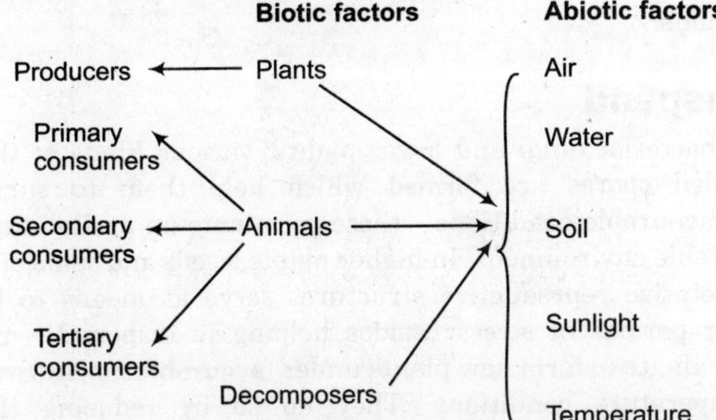

Fig. 29.18 Biotic and abiotic factors

Producers

These are **autotrophs,** *i.e.,* can synthesis their own food.

$$6CO_2 + 6H_2O \xrightarrow[\text{Chlorophyll}]{\text{Sunlight}} \underset{\text{Glucose}}{C_6H_{12}O_6} + 6O_2$$

They provide food, shelter and O_2 to the consumers. They are called **transducers** because they change light energy to chemical energy, *e.g.,* In terrestrial ecosystem, producers are green plants, phototrophic bacteria, algae, etc., and in aquatic ecosystem it is phytoplanktons (floating plants) and in shallow water it is macrophytes (rooted plants). Plants are classified according to where they grow:

(a) **Hydrophytes** Hydro means water plants that grow in water, *e.g.,* elodea, water lilies, seaweeds, algae.

(b) **Mesophytes** Meso means middle/in between plants that need moderate amounts of water, light and temperature, *e.g.,* the plants in your garden.

(c) **Xerophytes** Xero means dry/waterless plants that grow in very dry regions, *e.g.,* fynbos, cacti and aloes.

Consumers

They are **heterotrophs,** *i.e.,* feeding others.

(a) They are essential components and they occur in most of the ecosystems.

(b) They obtain energy from producers directly or indirectly. They are also called **phagotrophs** (to eat *via* mouth) which can be placed in different categories as:

- **Primary consumers/First order consumers/Key industrial animals** (Elton) They eat producers, *i.e.,* they are herbivores, *e.g.,* Terrestrial animals—Deer, cattle, rabbit, goat, horse, mouse, birds, some insects, etc. Aquatic—Zooplanktons, tadpole, snails, mosquito larva, tortoise, etc.
- **Secondary consumers/Second order consumers** They eat on herbivores, *i.e.,* they are carnivores, *e.g.* Terrestrial – fox, wolf, snake, birds, cats, frog, centipedes, etc. Aquatic—*Hydra*, water bugs, skates, small fishes, etc.
- **Tertiary consumers/Third order consumers** These are larger carnivores which feed on secondary consumers, *e.g.,* large fish, water birds (ducks, water fowls), wolves, etc.
- **Quaternary consumers/Fourth order consumers** It include carnivores which cannot be preyed upon further. They lie at the top of the food chain, *e.g.,* Lion, tiger, dolphins, whales, etc.

Decomposers/Reducers/Saprotrophs Micro-consumers

Decomposers are classified as **saprophytic** because they live on **dead organic matter**. They are able to decompose the dead plant and animal matter into nutrients. They obtain energy by breaking down the organic compounds in the matter and absorbing them. **Algae, fungi and bacteria** are examples of decomposers.

Biotic and Abiotic Interactions

Many species have evolved a relatively constant internal (within the body) environment that permits all biochemical reactions and physiological functions to proceed with maximal efficiency and thus, enhance the overall 'fitness' of the species. This constancy, for example, could be in terms of optimal temperature and osmotic concentration of body fluids. Ideally then, the organism should try to maintain the constancy of its internal environment (a process called **homeostasis**) despite varying external environmental conditions that tend to upset its homeostasis.

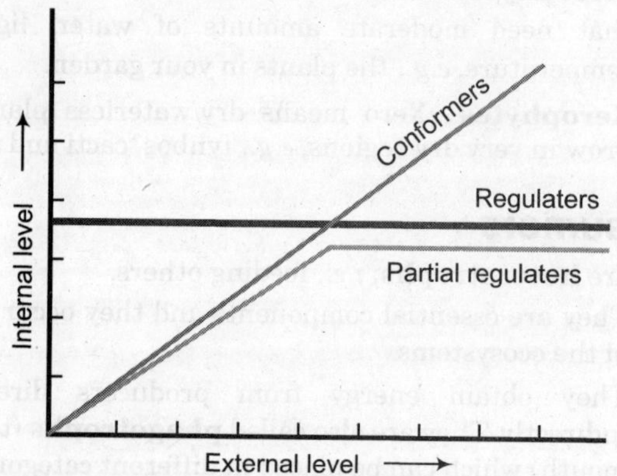

Fig. 29.19 Diagrammatic representation of organismic response

Regulate

Some organisms are able to maintain homeostasis by physiological (sometimes behavioural also) means which ensures constant body temperature, constant osmotic concentration, etc. All birds and mammals and a very few lower vertebrate and invertebrate species are indeed capable of such regulation (thermoregulation and osmoregulation). Plants, on the other hand, do not have such mechanisms to maintain internal temperatures.

Conform

An overwhelming majority (99 per cent) of animals and nearly all plants cannot maintain a constant internal environment. Their body temperature changes with the ambient temperature. In aquatic animals, the osmotic concentration of the body fluids change with that of the ambient water osmotic concentration. These animals and plants are simply conformers. This is particularly true for small animals like shrews and humming birds. Heat loss or heat gain is a function of surface area. Since, small animals have a larger surface area relative to their volume, they tend to lose body heat very fast when it is cold outside; then they have to expend much energy to generate body heat through metabolism. This is the main reason why very small animals are rarely found in polar regions.

Migrate

The organism can move away temporarily from the stressful habitat to a more hospitable area and return when stressful period is over. Many animals, particularly birds, during winter undertake long-distance migrations to more hospitable areas. Every winter the famous Keolado National Park (Bhartpur) in Rajasthan host thousands of migratory birds coming from Siberia and other extremely cold Northern regions.

Suspend

In bacteria, fungi and lower plants, various kinds of thick walled spores are formed which help them to survive unfavourable conditions – these germinate on availability of suitable environment. In higher plants, seeds and some other vegetative reproductive structures serve as means to tide over periods of stress besides helping in dispersal – they germinate to form new plants under favourable moisture and temperature conditions. They do so by reducing their metabolic activity and going into a date of 'dormancy'. In animals, the organism, if unable to migrate, might avoid the stress by escaping in time. The familiar case of bears going into hibernation during winter is an example of escape in time. Some snails and fish go into aestivation to avoid summer–related problems-heat and desiccation. Under unfavourable conditions many zooplankton species in lakes and ponds are known to enter diapause, a stage of suspended development.

Habitat and Niche

Concept of Habitat and Niche

Habitat Place or set of environmental conditions in which a particular population or species lives. Strictly, however, where an organism lives is its habitat. It is a physical and biotic environment. Habitats may be sub-divided into layers or zones.

Microhabitats

(i) **Forest canopy** Leaves, branches.

(ii) **Shrub layer** Leaves, branches, trunks.

(iii) **Herb layer** Leaves, stems, mosses, ferns.

(iv) **Litter** Dead fallen leaves, logs, (varies in depth, quality).

(v) **Soil** Topsoil, subsoil.

Ecological Niche Description of either the role played by a species in a biological community or the total set of environmental factors that determine species distribution. Every species has a range of physical and chemical conditions as well as biological interactions within which it can exist.

Dimensions of a Niche

(i) Habitat and microhabitat (Space occupied).

(ii) Food 'spectrum,' essential nutrients.

(iii) Reproductive requirements (Nutrition, nest/densites).

(iv) Seasonality When are resources required, used.

Niches identify the 'role' of an organism in its community or the way an animal makes its living.

Ecological Equivalent In ecological niche of an organism is the physical space occupied by it, its functional role in the community, *i.e.*, tropic position, its position in environment and the conditions of existence. Organisms that occupy the same or similar ecological niches in different geographical regions are known as ecological equivalents.

Niche Width and Overlap

Niche refers to the ways in which an organism interacts with its environment, so niches are closely related to environmental tolerance curves, but niches have behavioural dimensions (*e.g.*, method of locomotion running, swimming, flying) as well environmental ones (*e.g.*, temperature limits). Niches can be used to:

1. Make comparisons of the composition and organization of communities.
2. Examine shifts in the behaviour or ecology of one species in response to another species (niche shifts are commonly used to study interspecific competition).

General dimensions (components) of an animal's niche include:

1. Foraging tactics and diet
2. Reproductive tactics
3. Social organization
4. Defenses against predation
5. Environmental tolerances
6. Morphology, sensory adaptations, physiology.

Grinnell (1917) defined it as all the sites, where organisms of a species can live (where conditions are suitable for life). **Elton** (1927) described the niche as the function performed by the species in the community of which it is a member. The first definition emphasized the 'address' of the species and the second one emphasized its 'profession' (Miller 1967).

Hutchinson (1957) defined a niche as a region (n-dimensional hypervolume) in a multi-dimensional space of environmental factors that affect a species. This definition is more close to Grinnell's definition. It became popular because the range of tolerance to ecological factors can be easily measured, whereas species 'profession' is hardly measurable. It is believed that the intensity of competition is proportional to the degree of niche overlapping. However, this kind of statements should be accepted with caution because:

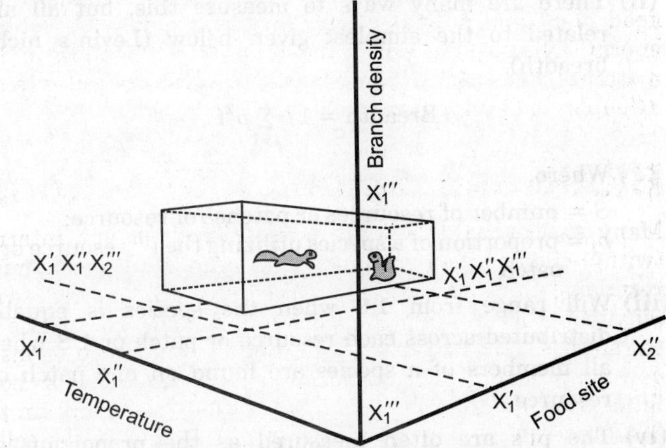

Fig. 29.20 A three-dimensional orthogonal fundamental niche x′ might define food size, in this case the mean diameter of various seeds or fruits, notably acoms; x″ might define temperature tolerance and x‴ some measure of the density of branches, between certain diameter, in unit volume of physical space (From Hutchinson 1978).

(a) Measurement of niche volume is a subjective procedure.

(b) Some important dimensions of the niche may be not known.

(c) Niches change in the life cycle.

(d) Niches change from one geographical region to another.

Measuring Niche Dimensions

(i) These ideas about competition all assume that there is a limiting resource (usually 1, but two or more have been considered).

(ii) Many have modeled resources as resource niche axes

(a) **Resource Axis** A line representing change in a resource, such as size or sugar concentration or concentration of toxins.

(b) **Species Utilization Curve** The degree to which a species can utilize a resource at some point on the resource axis.

(iii) Different species can be represented as humps along the axis.

(a) Humps (usually bell-shaped, but not necessarily so) give each species range of resources sizes utilized and its optimum resource utilization point.

(b) Ideally, if limiting similarity is correct, the overlap between species resources will not be larger than the limiting similarity ratio.

(c) Species Packing When all of the species on a resource axis are spaced so that each shows maximal overlap allowing coexistence (therefore, no additional species can be added without causing more overlap than limiting similarity would allow) the resource axis is called 'packed'.

Niche Breadth

(i) Niche breadth is the degree to which a species utilizes all available patches or resources.

(ii) There are many ways to measure this, but all are related to the simplest given below (Levin's niche breadth).

$$\text{Breadth} = 1 / \sum_{i=1}^{s} p^2 i$$

Where,

S = number of resources or patches of resource;

p_i = proportion of a species utilizing the ith resource or patch

(iii) Will range from 1.0 when the species is equally distributed across each resource or patch or 1/S when all members of a species are found on one patch or resource.

(iv) The pi's are often measured as the proportion of different food types in the guts of the species of interest.

(v) Overlap between the breadth of two species (here, designated species j and species k) may be as **proportional similarity** (between the two species).

$$PS = \sum_{i=1}^{s} (\min / p_{ij}, p_{ik})$$

Where, p_{ij} and p_{ik} are the proportions of the **least-abundant** species found on the ith patch or resource.

As a rule of thumb, a *PS* of over 70% is considered to indicate active competition between the species and lower values allow coexistence of the competitors.

This concept has been applied to comparing two different communities of species as well as two different species.

These are relative terms—specialist and generalist describe the endpoints of continuous variation in the degree of specialization in resource use, behaviour and physiology. Species that use many resources will have large value of niche breadth, reflecting a generalist pattern of resource use.

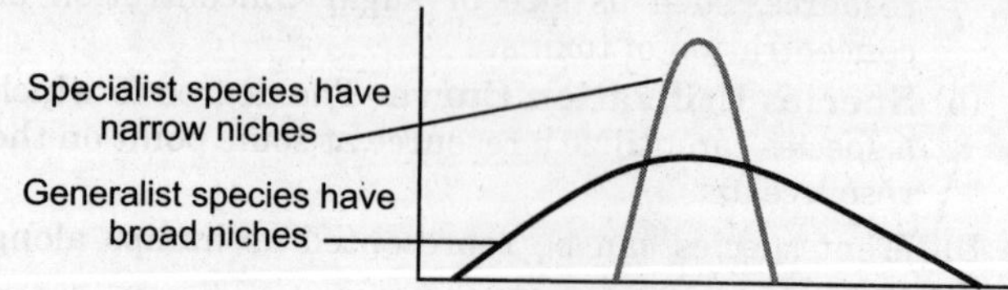

Fig. 29.21 Generalists can withstand a variety of environmental conditions and specialists can only tolerate a narrow range

Breadth can be simply represent as

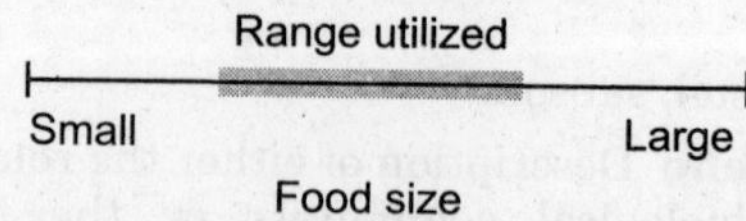

But in reality not all sizes are used equally

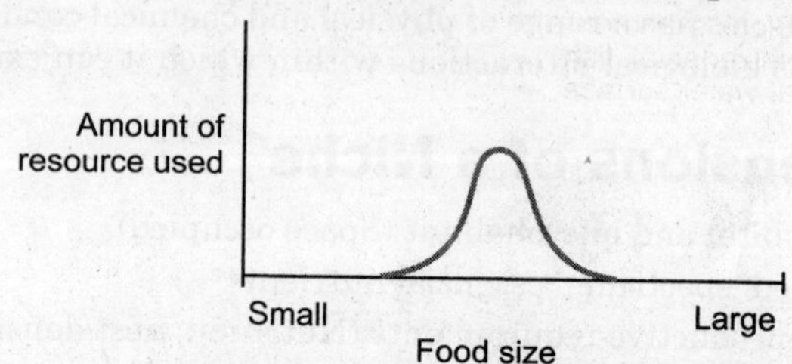

Niche breadth is variable

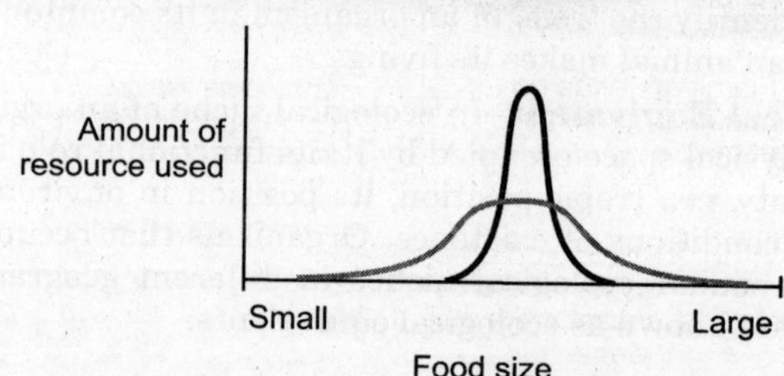

Fig. 29.22 Niche breadth is the length of resource axis that lies beneath the curve

Niche shift is change to a less used or previously unused portion of resource gradient (*e.g.*, smaller prey size) or to new resource gradient (*e.g.*, different prey species) in the presence of competitors. This may also include **niche compression** (or in the absence of competition, **competitive release** and niche expansion).

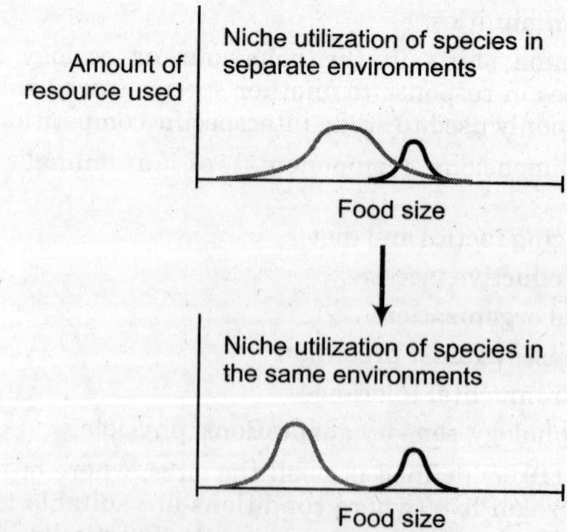

Fig. 29.23 Changes in niches

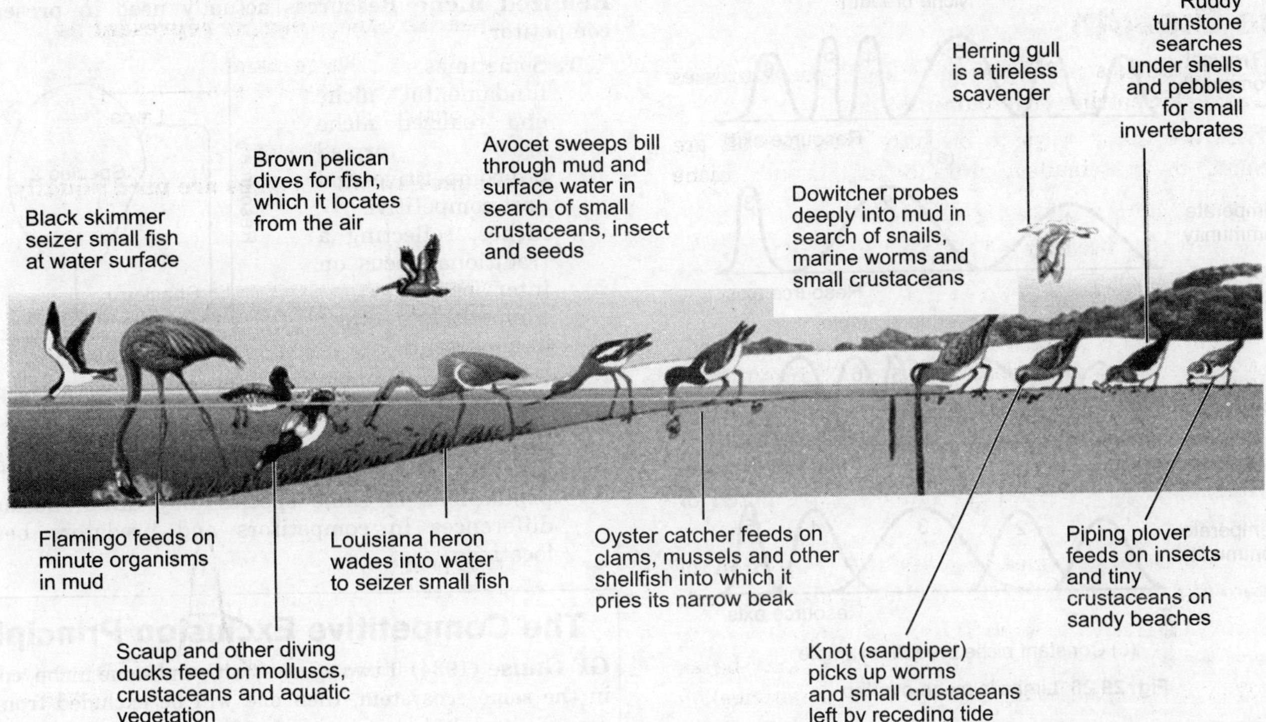

Fig. 29.24 Specialized feeding niches in birds

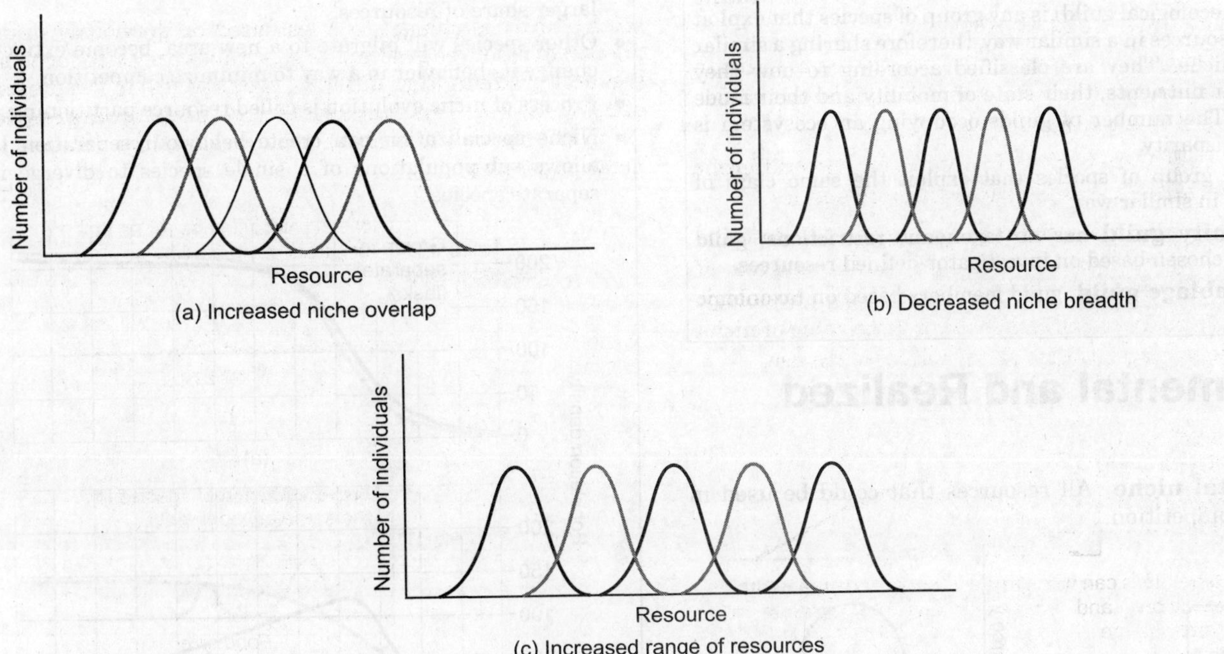

Fig. 29.25 Niche packing

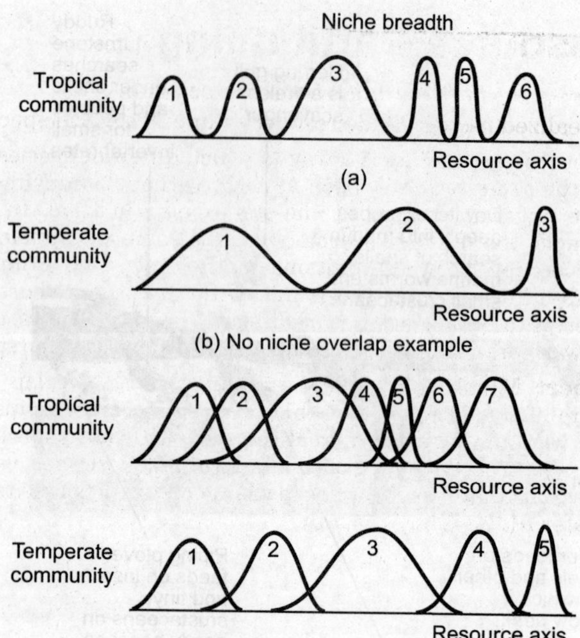

Fig. 29.26 Limits in niche overlap

Guild Concept

A **guild** (or ecological guild) is any group of species that exploit the same resources in a similar way, therefore sharing a similar ecological niche. They are classified according to how they acquire their nutrients, their state of mobility and their mode of feeding. The number of guilds occupying an ecosystem is termed its disparity.

- **Guild** is group of species that exploit the same class of resources in similar way.
- **Community guild** has no taxonomic restrictions; guild members chosen based on investigator-defined resources.
- **In assemblage guild,** guild members based on taxonomic relations.

Fundamental and Realized Niche

Fundamental niche All resources that could be used in absence of competition.

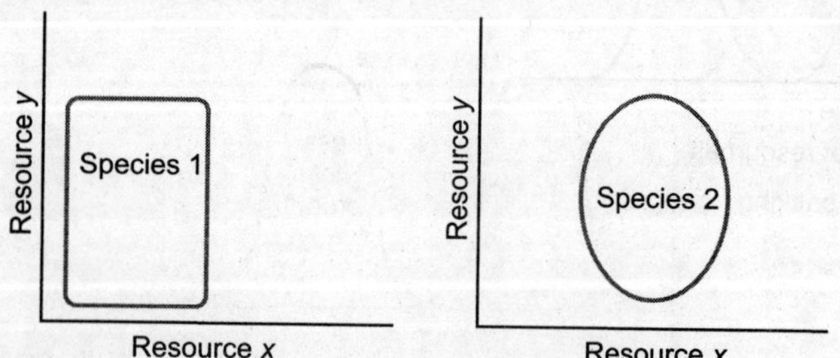

Fig. 29.27 No overlap of niches of species 1 and species 2. So coexistence is possible

Realized niche Resources actually used in presence of competitor.

1. Sometimes fundamental niche and realized niche are termed pre-competitive and post-competitive niches, reflecting a traditional focus on inter-specific competition's effect on niches.
2. Fundamental niche ≥ Realized niche.
3. Realized niche for different populations of same species may differ, because of differences in competitors and predators between locations.

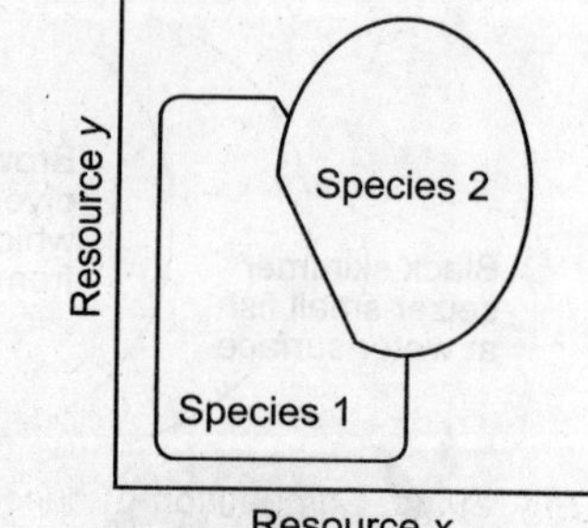

Fig. 29.28 Interspecific competition of species 1 and species 2 occurs where the niches overlaps

The Competitive Exclusion Principle

GF Gause (1934) if two species, with the same niche, coexist in the same ecosystem, then one will be excluded from the community due to intense competition **Competitive Exclusion Principle**

- One species will have a competitive edge and will gain a larger share of resources.
- Other species will migrate to a new area, become extinct or change its behavior in a way to minimize competition.
- Process of niche evolution is called resource partitioning.
- Niche specialization can create behaviour separation that allows sub-populations of a single species to diverge into separate species.

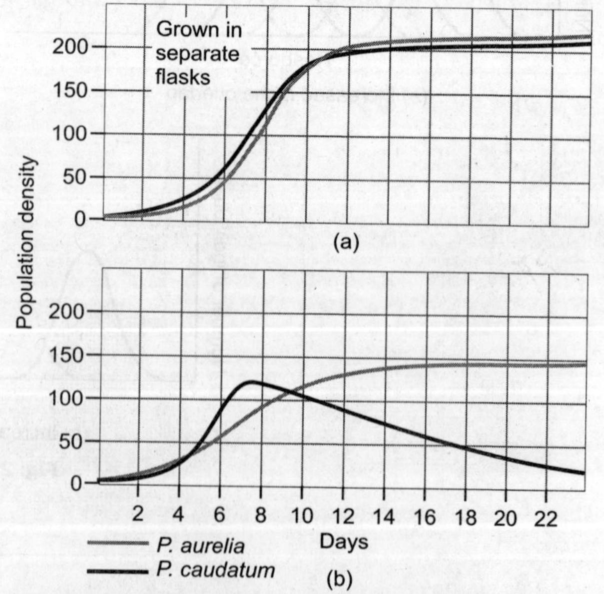

Fig. 29.29 Competitive exclusion. One species eliminates other(s)

- **Competitive exclusion of species**

Species A Species B

Fig. 29.30 Competition of species A and species B leads to competitive exclusion of one species.

- **Total exclusion of species**

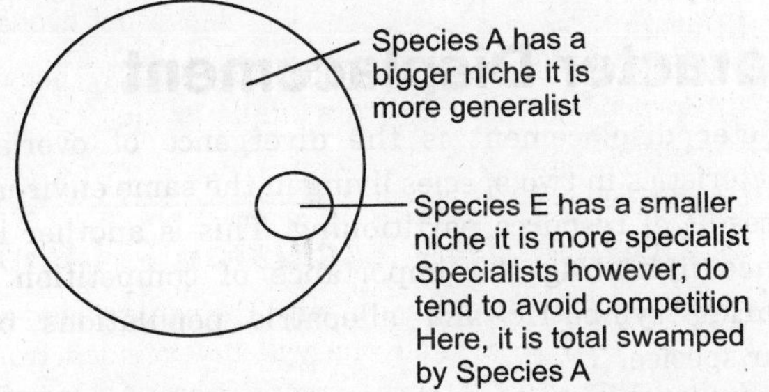

Fig. 29.31 Smaller niche of species E leads to total exclusion of species

Example Squirrels in Britain

The red squirrel (*Sciurus vulgaris*) is native to Britain. Its population has declined due to competitive exclusion, disease, disappearance of hazel coppices and mature conifer forests in lowland Britain. The grey squirrel (*Sciurus carolinensis*) is an alien species. Introduced to Britain in about 30 sites between 1876 and 1929. It has easily adapted to parks and gardens replacing the red squirrel.

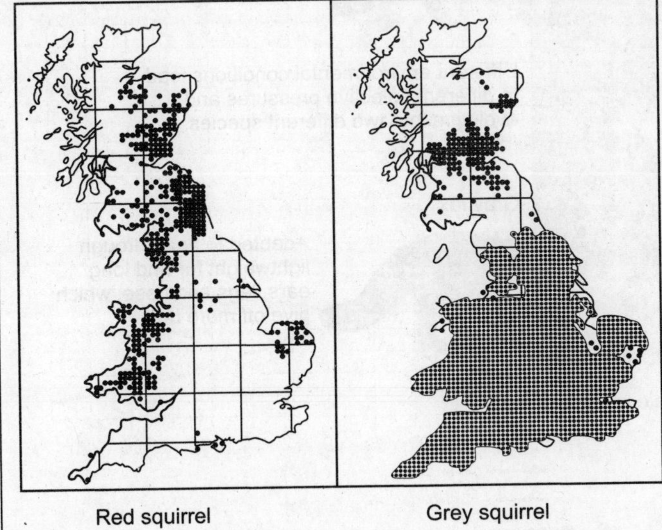

Fig. 29.32 Present distribution of the red squirrel and the Grey Squirrel

Resource Partitioning

- Resource partitioning avoids competition.
- Realized niches divide resources among several species.

Resource partitioning is a way in which different species can use the same resource, such as food, without occupying the same physical location at the same point in time. In this example, the different warblers eat the same caterpillar, but they occupy different positions in the tree. Two primarily occupy the area near the trunk, with the others share the edges of the branches, but at different heights. The result is the warblers do not overtly compete for food in the same space.

Robert MacArthur (1958) examined niche overlap in a group of five sympatric warbler species in New Hampshire that were the same size and at the same arthropod species in the same tree. With increased immigration, more species may arrive at that tree (species packing occurs), necessitating greater **niche compression.**

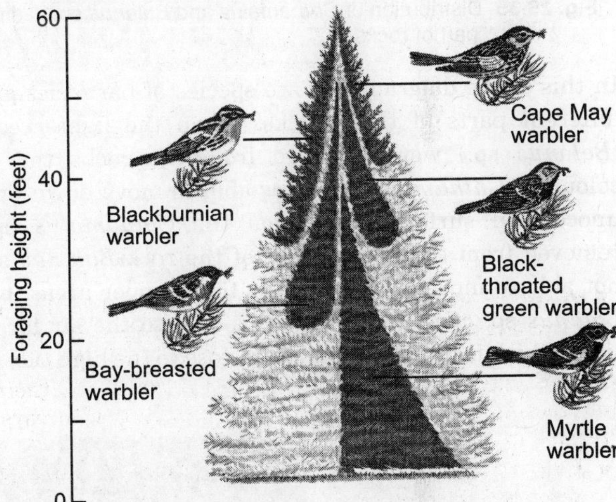

Fig. 29.33 Resource partitioning among warblers

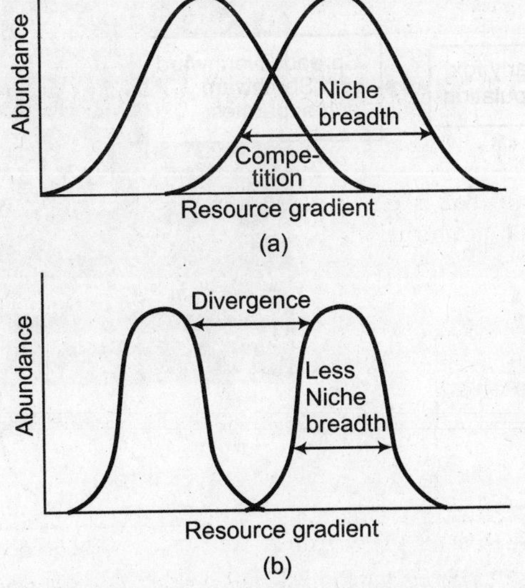

Fig. 29.34 Resource partitioning and niche specialization caused by competition

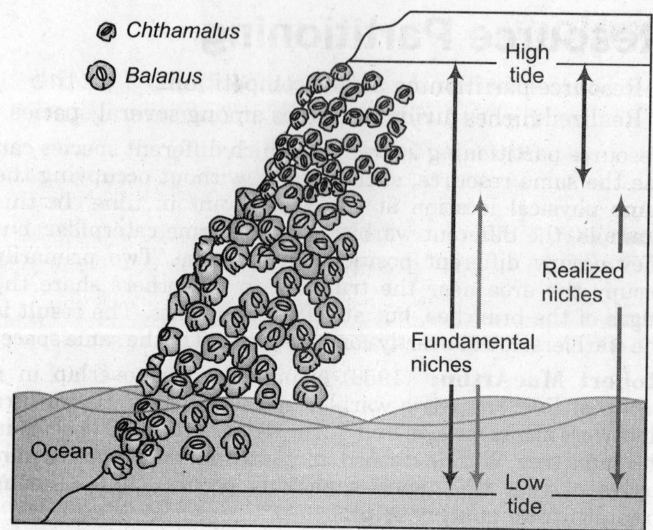

Fig. 29.35 Distribution of *Chthamalus* and *Balanus* sp. in different part of rocks

In this above diagram the two species of barnacles grow on different parts of these rocks. When the lighter coloured (*Balanus* sp.) were removed from the rocks the darker coloured (*Chthamalus* sp.) was able to move down onto the unoccupied surface. But when the *Chthamalus* sp. was removed from the upper areas of the rock *Balanus* sp. was not able to move up and occupy these upper areas, because *Balanus* sp. can't stand to be exposed to the air for a long time, which is the case with rocks close to the high tide mark.

Specialization Avoids Competition

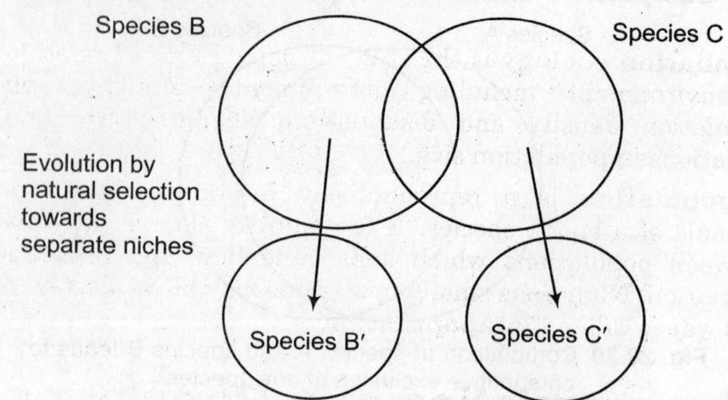

Fig. 29.36 Specialization into two separate niche

Character Displacement

Character displacement is the divergence of overlapping characteristics in two species living in the same environment as a result of resource partitioning. This is another line of evidence indicating the importance of competition when comparing sympatric and allopatric populations of the similar species.

For example two closely related species of Galapagos finches (*Geospiza fuliginosa* and *G. fortis*) have beaks of similar size when the populations are allopatric; however, on the island, where, they are sympatric, a significant difference in beak depth has occurred.

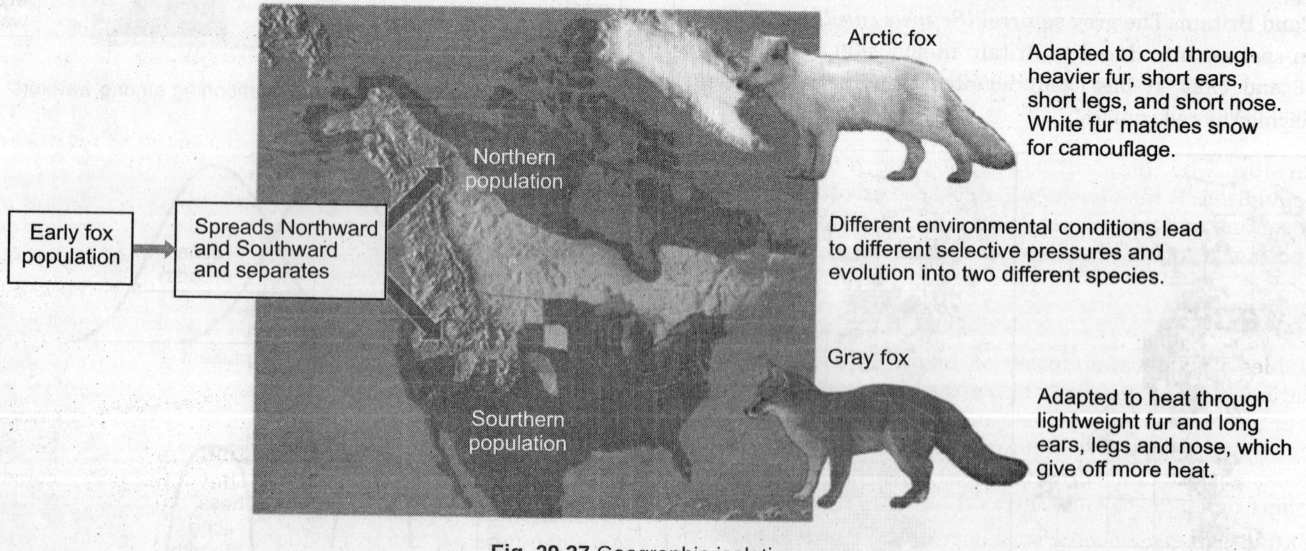

Fig. 29.37 Geographic isolation

Population Ecology

Population ecology is the study of populations in relation to environment, including environmental influences on population density and distribution, age structure and variations in population size.

A **population** is a reproductively interactive group of animals of a single species. A few individuals may migrate between populations which adds gene flow and prevents speciation. Numerous small populations may be connected in this way is called **metapopulation**.

Characteristics of a Population

Ecologists measure the rates (number per unit of time) at which births, deaths and movements take place in a population and they study how these rates are influenced by environmental factors, life histories and population densities.

The number of individuals in a population at any given time is given by the equation

$$N_1 = N_0 + B - D + I - E$$

Where, N_1 is the number of individuals at time 1; N_0 is the number of individuals at time 0; B is the number of individuals born, D the number that died, I the number that immigrated and E the number that emigrated between time 0 and time 1. If we measure these rates over many time intervals, we can determine how a population's density changes over time.

Ecads Population of individuals which although belongs to same genetic shock but differ in vegetative character, such as size, shape number of leaves, stems, etc.

Ecotype Population of individuals of a species which are genetically different. They are interfertile and come under same taxonomic species and also known as ecological or physiological races.

Dispersion The comparative spatial pattern of individuals in a population. It may be **regular** (spaced at equal distance) **random** (one individual is unrelated to other's position) and **clumed** (aggregation of individual into patches).

Life Tables

Life tables provide summaries of births and deaths in a population. A life table is constructed for determining the group of individuals born at the time (called a cohort) and the number that are still alive at later dates (survivorship). Some life tables also include the number of offspring produced by the cohort during each time interval.

A life table is an age-specific summary of the survival pattern of a population. An example of a life table based on an intensive study of the cactus finch carried out on Isla Daphne in the Galápagos archipelago.

Table 29.1 **Life Table of the 1978 Cohort of the Cactus Finch** (Geospiza scandens) **on Isla Daphne**

Age in Years (X)	Number Alive	Survivorship[a]	Survival Rate[b]	Mortality Rate[c]
0	210	1.000	0.434	0.566
1	91	0.434	0.857	0.566
2	78	0.371	0.898	0.143
3	70	0.333	0.928	0.102
4	65	0.309	0.955	0.072
5	62	0.295	0.678	0.045
6	42	0.200	0.548	0.322
7	23	0.109	0.652	0.452
8	15	0.071	0.933	0.348
9	14	0.067	0.786	0.067
10	11	0.052	0.909	0.214
11	10	0.048	0.400	0.091
12	4	0.019	0.750	0.600
13	3	0.014	0.996	0.250

Survivorship[a] = the proportion of newborns who survive to age x.

Survival rate$_b$ = the proportion of individuals of age x who survive to age $x + 1$.

Mortality rate$_c$ = the proportion of individuals of age x who die before the age of $x + 1$.

The table shows that the mortality rate. The table shows that the mortality rate for these birds was high during the first year of life. It then dropped dramatically for several years, followed by a general increase in later years. Mortality rates fluctuated among years because the survival of these birds depends on seed production, which strongly correlates with rainfall.

(i) Life tables tell why population densities change over time.

(ii) Life table data can also be used to determine how heavily a population can be harvested and which age groups should be the focus of our efforts to save rare species.

Survivorship

Graphs of **survivorship** in relation to age show when individuals survive well and when they do not. Survivorship curves in many populations fall into one of three patterns. In some populations, most individuals survive for most of their potential life span, then die at about the same age. A survivorship curve is a graphic way of representing the data in a life table.

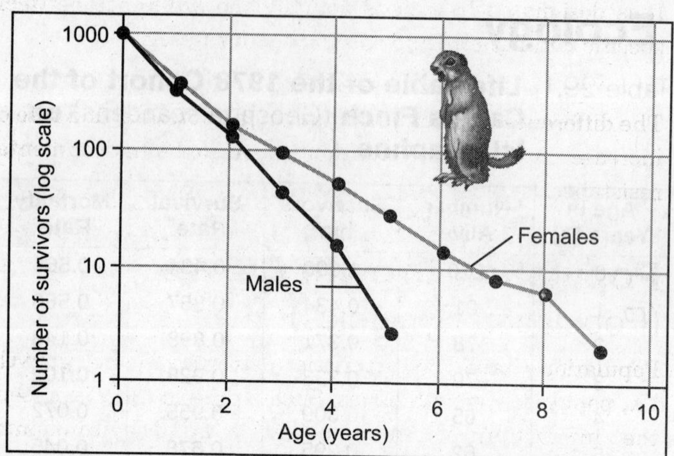

Fig. 29.38 The survivorship curve for Belding's ground squirrels shows that the death rate is relatively constant

Survivorship curves can be classified into three general types:

(i) **Type I** High survival early in life indicates parental care of fewer offspring.

(ii) **Type II** Constant death rate over life span.

(iii) **Type III** Drops sharply at start indicating high death rate for young; lots of young, no care.

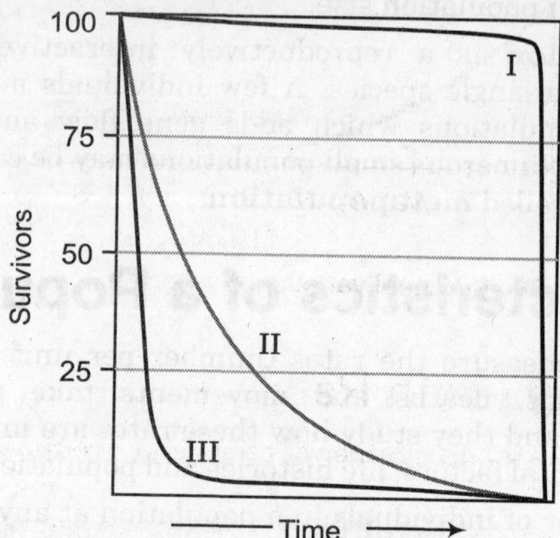

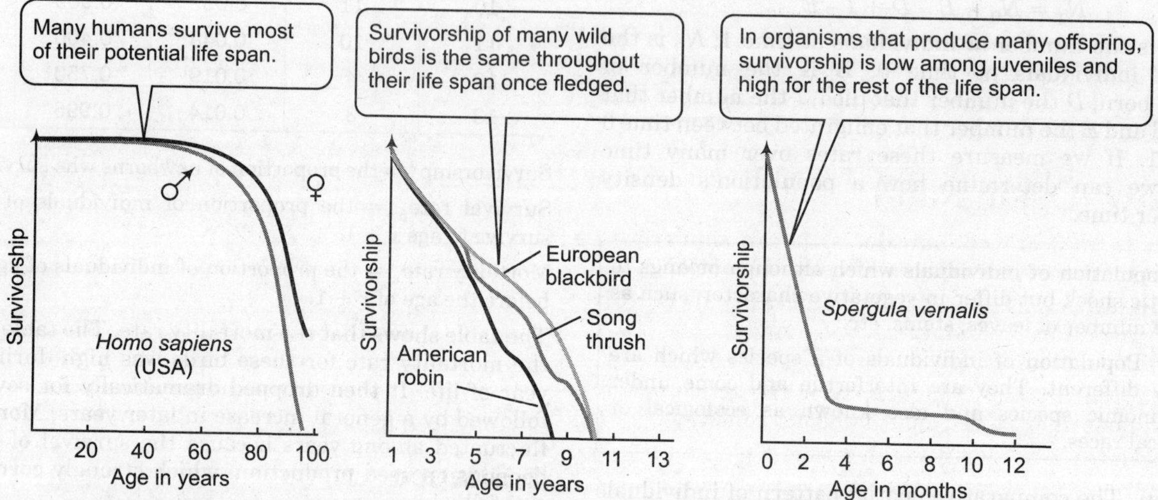

Fig. 29.39 Survivorship Curves Three common survivorship curves show the number of individuals in a cohort still alive at different times over the life span. (a) For this curve, mortality is highest at advanced ages. (b) For these species, the probability of survivorship is similar throughout much of the life span. (c) Species with this survivorship pattern have high mortality at early ages, but survive well once past a critical point

Population Density

The number of individuals of a species per unit of area (or volume) is its **population density.** Four factors—resource abundance, the size of individuals, the length of time a species has lived in an area and social organization exert strong influences on population density.

(i) Species that use abundant resources often reach higher population densities than species that use scarce resources.

(ii) Species with small individuals generally reach higher population densities than species with large individuals.

(iii) Some newly introduced species reach high population densities.

(iv) Complex social organization may facilitate high densities. some highly social species, including ants, termites and humans, can achieve remarkably high population densities.

(a) **Crude density** Diversity per unit total space.

(b) **Ecological density** Density per unit of habitat space.

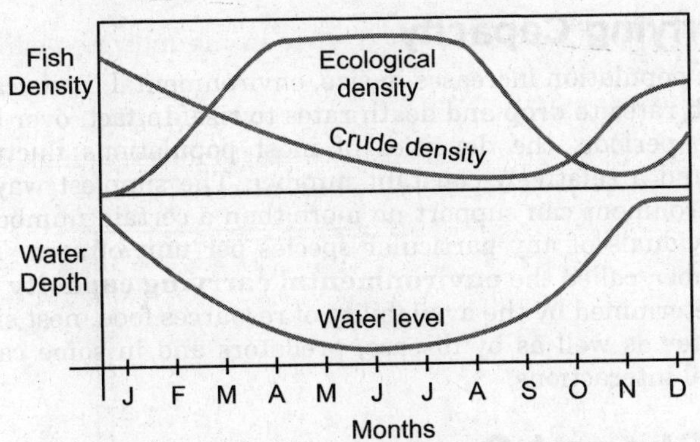

Fig. 29.40 Annual variation of fish density in a pond

Natality (Birth Rate)

Natality rate is the number of offsprings produced per female per unit time.

(i) **Maximum natality** is the maximum production of individuals, where there is no ecological limiting factors. It is limited by only physiological factors. This is also called as **fecundity rate.**

(ii) **Ecological Natality** It is the increase in population under an actual existing specific condition. It is also called as **fertility rate.**

Mortality (Death Rate)

It is refers to as death of individuals. It can similarly be classified as minimum mortality and ecological mortality.

(i) **Minimum** (specific or potential) **mortality** represents the theoretical minimum loss under ideal or non-limiting conditions.

(ii) **Ecological** (realized) **mortality** is the actual loss of individuals under given environmental condition.

(iii) **Vital index** is the birth–death ratio, *i.e.*,

$$\text{Vital index} = \frac{\text{Birth}}{\text{Death}} \times 100$$

Clutch size The number of offspring produced is related to the adult's chance of survival to the next breeding season a trade off of current fecundity *versus* adult survival and future fecundity. Clutch size usually is inversely related to the size of offspring. Organisms with a Type III survivorship curve usually produce large numbers of small eggs or offspring. Fewer larger offspring may have a better chance of surviving to adulthood, typical of Type I and II curves. Large numbers of offspring are related to the selective pressures of high mortality rates of young in uncertain environments or from intense predation. Parental investment in size of offspring, incubation and/or parental care increases survival chances of the young.

- **Biotic potential** (Chapman; 1928) It is designated as maximum reproductive power and defined as the inherent property and organism to reproduce and survive when the environment is unlimited, *i.e.*, to increase in numbers.

It is designated by r. It is actually the difference between specific natality rate and specific death rate. As

$$r = b - d$$

The difference between maximum biotic potential and rate of increase in actual condition is called environmental resistance.

Population Growth Curves (Population Dynamics)

Population have characteristic patterns of its growth, *i.e.*, population growth forms. Such a growth form represent the interaction of biotic potential and environmental resistance.

a When responses are not limiting the growth, plot is exponential.

b When responses are limiting the growth, plot is logistic.

K is carrying capacity.

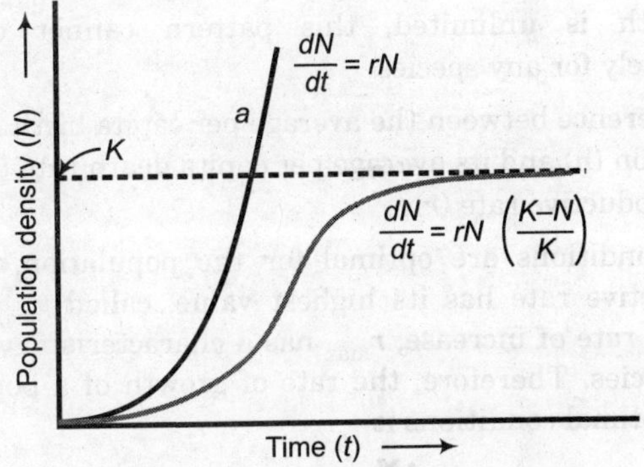

Fig. 29.41 Population growth curve

J-Shaped Curve

As the number of individuals in a population increases, the number of new individuals added per unit of time accelerates, even if the rate of increase expressed on a per individual basis called the per capita growth rate remains constant. If births and deaths occur continuously and at constant rates, a graph of the population size over time forms a continuous, **J-shaped curve**. This form of explosive increase is called **exponential growth.**

Rate of increase in number of individuals

= [Average per capita birth rate – Average per capita death rate] × Number of individuals or more concisely,

$$= \frac{\Delta N}{\Delta t} = (b - d)N$$

Where, $\Delta N/\Delta t$ is the rate of change in the size of the population (ΔN = change in number of individuals; Δt = change in time).

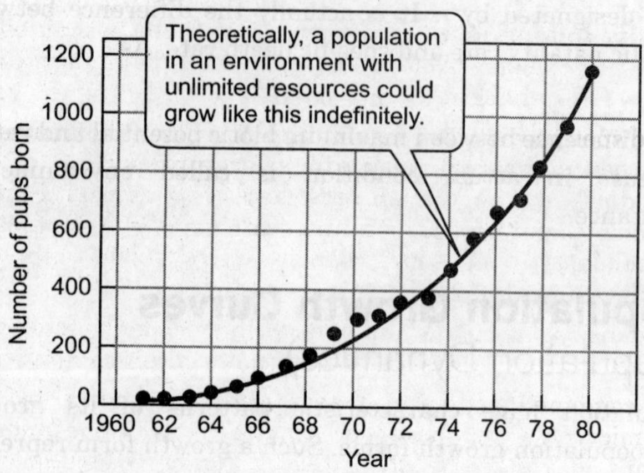

Fig. 29.42 Exponential population growth

The growth of the elephant seal population on A»o Nuevo Island, California, between 1960 and 1980 illustrates the exponential population growth curve.Theoretically, a population in a habitat with unlimited resources (including space) could continue to grow indefinitely. Since, no resource on Earth is unlimited, this pattern cannot continue indefinitely for any species

The difference between the average per capita birth rate in a population (b) and its average per capita death rate (d) is the net reproductive rate (r).

When conditions are optimal for the population, the net reproductive rate has its highest value, called r_{max} or the intrinsic rate of increase; r_{max} has a characteristic value for each species. Therefore, the rate of growth of a population under optimal conditions is

$$\frac{\Delta N}{\Delta t} = r_{max} N$$

Population Growth

The density of a population in a given habitat during a given period, fluctuates due to changes in four basic processes, two of which (natality and immigration) contribute an increase in population density and two (mortality and emigration) to a decrease.

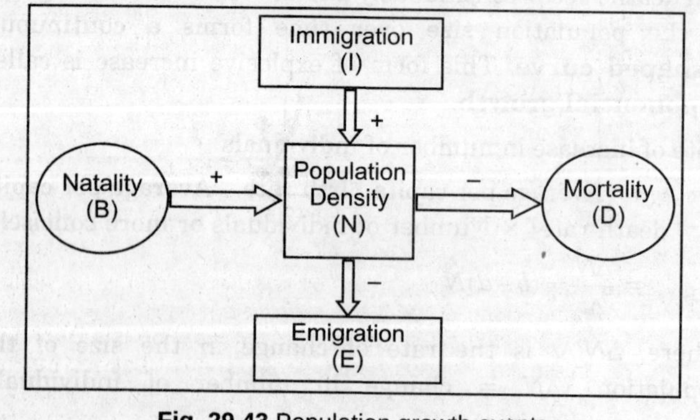

Fig. 29.43 Population growth events

Carrying Capacity

As a population increases in size, environmental limits cause birth rates to drop and death rates to rise. In fact, over long time periods, the densities of most populations fluctuate around a relatively constant number. The simplest way an environment can support no more than a certain number of individuals of any particular species per unit of area. This number, called the **environmental carrying capacity** (K), is determined by the availability of resources food, nest sites, shelter as well as by disease, predators and in some cases, social interactions.

S-Shaped Curve

The growth of a population typically slows down as its density approaches the environmental carrying capacity. A graph of the population size over time results in an **S-shaped curve**. This pattern is called **logistic growth**. The simplest way to generate an S-shaped growth curve is to add to the equation for exponential growth a term $(K - N)/K$, that slows the population's growth as it approaches the carrying capacity. Term implies that each individual added to the population depresses population growth by an equal amount

$$\frac{\Delta N}{\Delta t} = r\left(\frac{K-N}{K}\right)N$$

Population growth stops when, $N = K$ because then $(K - N) = 0$, so $(K - N)/K = 0$ and thus, $\Delta N/\Delta t = 0$.

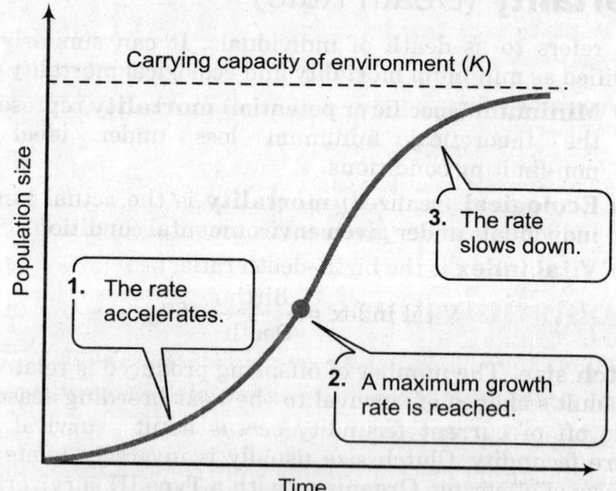

Fig. 29.44 Logistic population growth Typically, a population in an environment with limited resources stops growing exponentially long before it reaches the environmental carrying capacity

Population Regulation

Population dynamics The change in population density through time and space. The study of birth, death and movement rates that give rise to population dynamics is known as **demography**.

There is an upper limit to population density set by environment and the population is regulated at or around that level. The factors, which influences population density may be **density dependent or density independent.**

Density dependent factor increases in their proportional effect as population increases. These factors includes-competition and predation. The population in a limited environment, per capita birth and death rates usually change in response to population density; that is, they are density dependent.

Birth and death rates may be density-dependent for several reasons. **First**, as a species increases in abundance, it may deplete its food supply, reducing the amount of food available to each individual. Poorer nutrition may increase death rates and decrease birth rates. **Second**, predators may be attracted to areas with high densities of their prey. If predators capture a larger proportion of the prey than they did when the prey were scarce, the per capita death rate of the prey rises. **Third**, diseases spread more easily in dense populations than in sparse populations.

Density independent factor is not systematic in their effect as density changes. Abiotic environmental factors are often density independent.

A cold spell in winter or a hurricane that blows down most of the trees in its path may kill a large proportion of the individuals in a population regardless of its density. Factors that change per capita birth and death rates in a population independently of its density are said to be **density-independent**.

The density-dependent and density-independent factor may interact in most population to determine observed densities.

The combined action of these factors is shown by the dynamics of a population of song sparrows on Mandarte Island, off the coast of British Columbia, Canada. The number of males and females breeding each year is influenced by both density-independent and density-dependent factors.

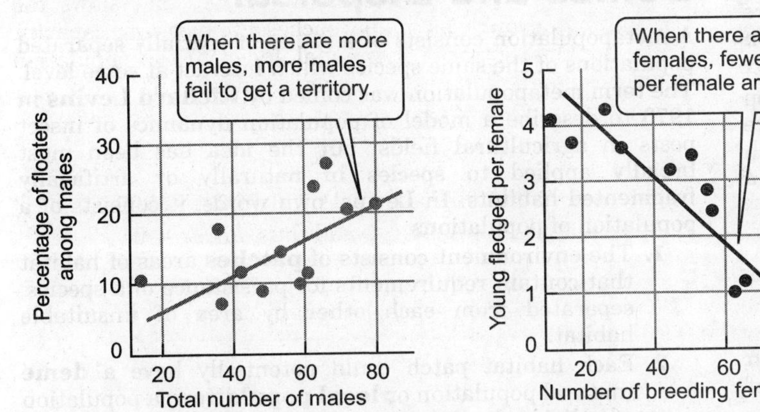

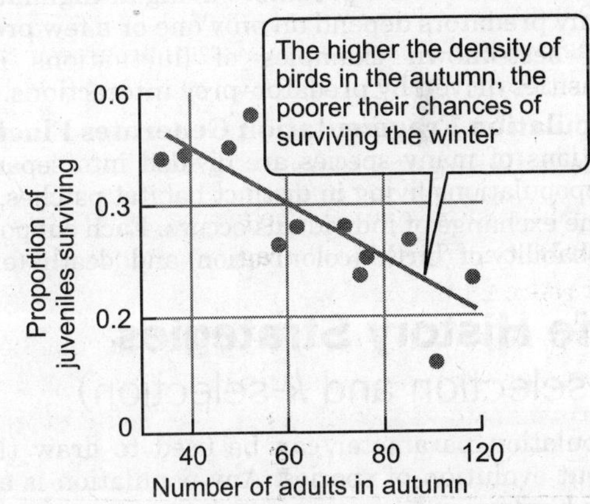

Fig. 29.45 Regulation of an island population of song sparrows. The size of the population of song sparrows (*Melospiza melodia*) on Mandarte Island, British Columbia, is determined in part by the severity of winter weather. In addition, the population is regulated by (a) The territorial behaviour of males, (b) The reproductive success of females, (c) The survival of juveniles in relation to population density

Population Fluctuations

All populations fluctuate less than the theoretical maximum, but the sizes of some populations fluctuate remarkably little. The comparison between South polar skuas and cactus finches illustrates one cause of such differences. Species with long-lived individuals that have low reproductive rates, such as South polar skuas, typically have more stable populations than species with short-lived individuals that have high reproductive rates, such as cactus finches. Small, short-lived individuals are generally more vulnerable to environmental changes than long-lived individuals. That is why insect population densities tend to fluctuate much more than those of birds and mammals and population densities of annual plants fluctuate much more than those of trees.

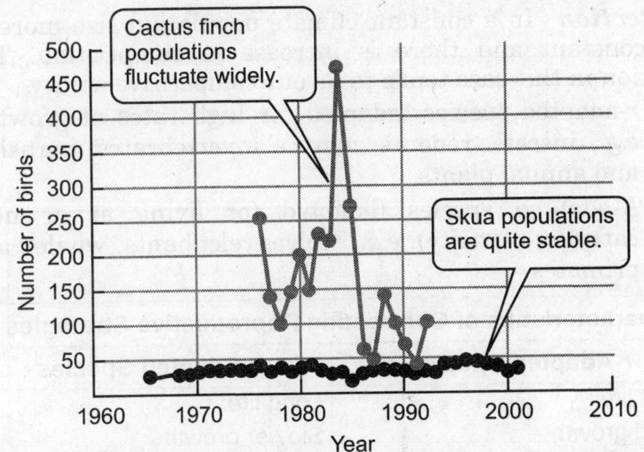

Fig. 29.46 Population sizes may be stable or highly variable populations of small, short-lived species, such as that of cactus finches (*Geospiza scandens*) on Isla Daphne in the Gal...pagos Archipelago, tend to fluctuate much more than do populations of larger, longerlived species, such as that of south polar skuas (*Catharacta maccormicki*).

Episodic Reproduction Generates Fluctuations For most species, some years are better for reproducing than other years. In Lake Erie, 1944 was such an excellent year for reproduction of whitefish that individuals born in that year dominated whitefish catches in the lake for several years.

Resource Fluctuations Generate Consumer Fluctuations Densities of populations of species that depend on a single or just a few resources are likely to fluctuate more than those of species that use a greater variety of resources. As we have seen, cactus finch populations fluctuate with the annual production of the seeds they eat, which varies greatly.

Population Interactions Generate Fluctuations Predators often cause fluctuations in the densities of their prey because predator population growth nearly always lags behind growth in populations of their prey. The predator population grows and eats most of its prey population, followed by a crash in the predator population, which no longer has enough food. Population oscillations among small mammals and their predators living at high latitudes, where many predators depend on only one or a few prey species, are the best-known examples of fluctuations in population densities driven by predator–prey interactions.

Population Fragmentation Generates Fluctuations Pop ulations of many species are divided into separated, discrete subpopulations living in distinct habitat patches, among which some exchange of individuals occurs. Each subpopulation has a probability of 'birth' (colonization) and 'death' (extinction).

Life History Strategies (*r*-selection and *k*-selection)

Population parameter can be used to draw the conclusion about evolution of species. Any population is an outcome of *r*-or *k*-selection.

***r*-Selection** Natural selection favour high reproduction rate and selection is in favour of faster development, earlier reproduction and increase fecundity. It maximizes the intrinsic rate of natural increase.

***k*-Selection** In a constant climate population size more or less constant and there is increase in competition. The selection in this case tends to favour competitive ability.

1. *r*-adapted species (adapted for high rates of growth), *e.g.*, insects, rodents, marine invertebrates, parasites and annual plants.
2. *K*-adapted species (adapted for living at or near carrying capacity), *e.g.*, wolves, elephants, whales and primates.

Characteristics of Contrasting Reproductive Strategies

r-Adapted Species	*k*-Adapted Species
Short life	Long life
Rapid growth	Slower growth
Early maturity	Late maturity
Many small offspring	Fewer large offspring
Little parental care of protection	High parental care and protection
Little investment in individual offspring	High investment in individual offspring
Adapted to unstable environment	Adapted to stable environment
Pioneers and colonizers	Later stages of succession
Niche generalists	Niche specialists
Prey	Predators
Regulated mainly by extrinsic factors	Regulated mainly by intrinsic factors
Low trophic level	High trophic level
Location temperate	Location tropical
High fecundity	Low fecundity
Density variable, well below carrying capacity	Density constant or near carrying capacity

Concept of Metapopulation—Demes and Dispersal

A metapopulation consists of a group of spatially separated populations of the same species which interact at some level. The term metapopulation was coined by **Richard Levins** in 1970 to describe a model of population dynamics of insect pests in agricultural fields, but the idea has been most broadly applied to species in naturally or artificially fragmented habitats. In Levins' own words, it consists of a population of populations:

1. The environment consists of **patches** areas of habitat that contain requirements for persistance of a species, separated from each other by area of unsuitable habitat.
2. Each habitat patch could potentially have a **deme** (natural population or **local population**) a population of individuals of the species that occur within the same patch and interact, reproduce most with each other.
3. Since, habitat patches are separated by unsuitable habitat, most likely for individuals to stay within their own patches. There is expected in most cases, however, to be some level of **dispersal**: movement of individuals from their original deme to breed in a new deme.
4. Some or all of the demes in the metapopulation are subject to **local extinction:** dying out, leaving habitat patches that do not contain the species (although habitat is suitable) for a period of time of atleast several generations.
5. The presence of suitable habitat patches that may not have the species creates the potential for **recolonization** individuals of the species dispersing into the patch and starting a new population.
6. Metapopulations may reach or approach, an equilibrium number that is a balance between local extinction and recolonization. An exception to this is a so-called 'non-equilibrium metapopulation' in which there is no ability for individuals to disperse to new patches, so no potential for colonization; such populations are expected eventually to die out.

The metapopulation approach can be applied to single species that fit the structure of demes within habitats; demes must be relatively independent from each other. This structure fits a number of species. For examples some frog species, many butterfly species, some small mammals (pikas) have also been shown to fit metapopulation expectations, Other species may appear to occur in habitat patches, but have so much movement among patches that they consist effectively of a single very large population, called a 'patchy population,' not separate demes. Example: the red-winged black bird occurs in patches of marsh habitat, but there is a lot of movement among patches.

To understand metapopulations, we need to understand what affects these two processes, recolonization and local extinction.

Factors affecting recolonization clearly, the landscape, which may have barriers to movement and the ability to disperse will affect recolonization. In addition, recolonization will be affected by

(i) Distance from currently existing demes to empty patches.
(ii) Size of currently existing demes.
(iii) Dispersal behaviour.

Thomas and **Hanski** (1997) discuss evidence on distance to existing demes and size of existing demes.

Dispersal behaviour will be affected by

(a) **Costs to dispersal** risky, may not find new habitat, increased vulnerability to predation.
(b) **Benefits to dispersal** locate mates, avoid competition, find better habitat and avoid inbreeding.

Interdemic Extinctions

Four main reasons for small local populations go extinct are:

1. **Demographic stochasticity** Random events associated with births and deaths may lead to a point at which no new individuals are born; predicted to apply only to very small populations.
2. **Environmental stochasticity** refers to random, unpredictable events in the environment that cause high mortality of individuals of the species being studied. In a small population, such events could lead to loss of the entire population.
3. **Deterministic threats** Non-random changes in the environment that create unsuitable environment. Examples human destruction of natural habitats; ecological succession (natural change in the species composition of communities over time).
4. **Loss of genetic variation** This is predicted to lead to extinction relatively slowly, so may be less important than other effects, but can impact them. Loss of genetic variation occurs through **genetic drift;** evolution that occurs because of random fluctuations in the proportions of alleles in a population. Over time, alleles become lost by chance. This decreases the potential for natural selection, so populations have less chance to adapt. Associated with genetic drift in small populations is **inbreeding depression;** decreases in production of surviving offspring because of reproduction between close relatives. In small populations, it is likely that relatives will reproduce with each other. This means that harmful recessive alleles are likely to be expressed in offspring of relatives; these individuals are unlikely to survive, so overall numbers of surviving offspring decrease. Inbreeding may have less impact on populations that have historically occurred in small patches. In such populations, past inbreeding may have rid the population of most harmful recessive alleles, so that inbreeding has ittle impact now. In contrast, populations that have historically occurred in large demes may be more subject to problems from inbreeding if demes become small since there has been no history of inbreeding so, the population is predicted to have recessive harmful alleles.

Age Structured Populations

The structure of a population changes continually because **demographic events**—births, deaths, immigration (movement of individuals into the area) and emigration (movement of individuals out of the area)—are common occurrence. The age distribution of individuals in a population reveals much about the recent history of births and deaths in the population. The timing of births and deaths can influence age distributions for many years in populations of long-lived species.

Populations that contain multiple cohorts exhibit **age structure**. More individuals in the younger cohorts indicate a growing population. It is the geometrical representation of different age group of any organisms.

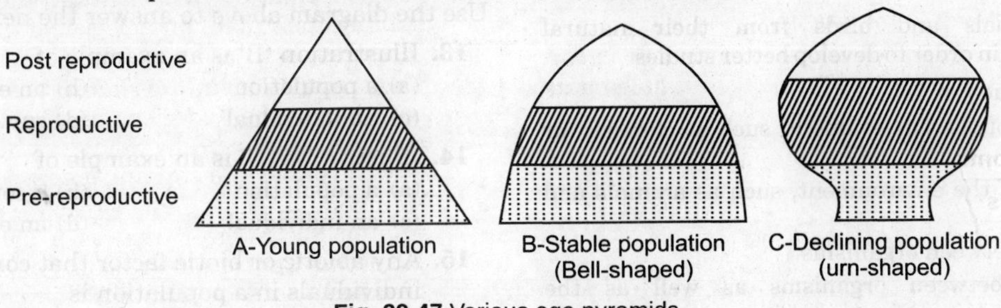

Fig. 29.47 Various age pyramids

The age pyramid represents geometrically the proportions of different age groups in the population. In young population pyramid (pyramid with broad base) the birth rate is high and population growth may be exponential while the stable population (bell-shaped pyramid) has moderate proportion of young to old, *i.e.*, rate of growth becomes show and stable. In declining population (urn-shaped pyramid) young individuals are in low percentage. The developing countries like India have a much greater proportion of young people and the side of pyramids become concave.

Exercise

1. The specific aim of ecology is to study
(a) how to best preserve diversity
(b) pollution
(c) the distribution patterns of plants and animals on Earth
(d) All of the above

2. Ecology is to environmental science as
(a) physics is to engineering
(b) environmental science is to physics
(c) engineering is to physics
(d) physics is to ecology

3. Which of the following best describes the environment?
(a) The interactions between living and non-living things
(b) The renewable and non-renewable resources that humans have developed and depend on for material well-being
(c) Our physical surroundings, including both the natural world and the structures and settlements humans have created
(d) The living and non-living things around us that humans interact with, including the structures, urban centres and living spaces people have created

4. Temperature, light, air, water, soil and climate are all .... parts of the environment.
(a) biotic (b) abiotic
(c) living (d) boreal

5. Which of the following are necessary for the survival of living things?
(a) Air, water, food and a suitable place to live
(b) Air, water and companions
(c) Temperature, light, air, water, soil and climate
(d) Oxygen, carbon dioxide, soil and energy

6. You are a wildlife biologist. Your job is to
(a) help murres find new migration patterns
(b) band all the birds in British Columbia
(c) observe animals carefully and ask questions about what you observe
(d) remove animals and birds from their natural environments in order to develop better studies

7. Ecology is the study of the
(a) abiotic parts of the environment, such as climate, air and soil
(b) biotic parts of the environment, such as animals and plants
(c) interactions between organisms
(d) interactions between organisms as well as the interactions between organisms and their environment

8. An area of soil is thoroughly wetted and allowed to drain until capillary movement of water stopped. The water contents of the soil will give an estimate of its
(a) capillary water (b) storage water
(c) field capacity (d) gravitational water

9. What is a population?
(a) A group of individuals of the same species that live in the same ecosystem
(b) All the abiotic parts of the environment
(c) The total number of different species in any one area
(d) Air, water and soil climate

10. Food, water, shelter and a space in which to live all describe an organism's
(a) biome (b) population
(c) habitat (d) community

11. When populations share their environment and interact with populations of other species, it is called a
(a) biome (b) ecoprovince
(c) community (d) species

12. If you studied ecosystems to learn about relationships between organisms and any changes in populations that take place over a long period of time, you would be
(a) an economist (b) an ecosystem
(c) an ecology (d) an ecologist

A

B

C

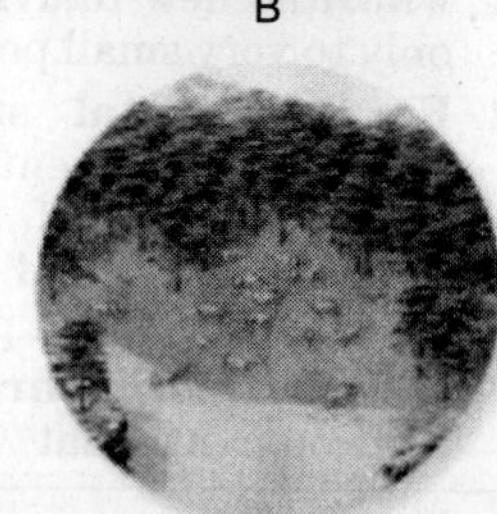
D

Use the diagram above to answer the next three questions

13. Illustration 'B' is an example of
(a) a population (b) an ecosystem
(c) an individual (d) surveying

14. Illustration 'C' is an example of
(a) a population (b) a community
(c) an individual (d) an ecosystem

15. Any abiotic or biotic factor that controls the number of individuals in a population is
(a) a pollutant
(b) chemosynthesis
(c) a bioaccumulation indicator
(d) a limiting factor

16. Which distribution pattern does territoriality produce?
(a) Random (b) Uniform
(c) Clumped (d) None of these

17. The mortality rate of organisms following a type III survivorship curve is
(a) fairly constant throughout life
(b) higher in post-reproductive years
(c) lower after the organisms become established
(d) unrelated to age

18. Which of the following is not an outcome of high population density?
(a) Toxic waste accumulation
(b) Mortality increase
(c) Predators tend to ignore prey that is overabundant
(d) Reproduction reduction

19. The statistical study of populations is called
(a) density (b) fecundity
(c) dispersion (d) demography

20. What type of survivorship curve do humans have?
(a) Type I (b) Type II
(c) Type III (d) Type IV

21. r-strategists tend to have
(a) few offspring (b) little parental care
(c) sigmoid growth curves (d) All of these

22. A community plus the non-living factors with which it interacts is called a(n)
(a) ecosystem (b) age structure
(c) biome (d) population

23. The number of individuals per unit area determines the population's
(a) survivorship (b) mortality
(c) age distribution (d) density

24. Which of the following factors will affect population growth rates?
(a) Net emigration (b) Net immigration
(c) Birth rate (d) All of these

25. What is the size of the human population today?
(a) Over 10 billion
(b) Almost 6 billion
(c) Less than 2 billion
(d) Just under 1 billion

26. Choose the factor that is unlikely to limit population growth.
(a) Predation
(b) Harsh weather
(c) Disease
(d) All are factors that could limit population growth

27. Which of these is not a density-dependent factor that could act to limit population growth as population size increases?
(a) Waste accumulation
(b) Fire
(c) Inhibitory pheromones
(d) Lowered immune function due to stress

28. An example of an organism fitting a type-I survivorship curve is
(a) an oyster (b) a human being
(c) a *Hydra* (d) lizards

29. Which of the following statement is incorrect?
(a) Clumped patterns of dispersion are indicative of an environment in which resources are unevenly distributed
(b) The sigmoid growth curve is characteristic of most survivorship curves
(c) Since humans are animals it is likely that humans will exhibit symptoms of overcrowding seen in other species
(d) The parabolic growth curve is characteristic of most survivorship curves

30. A population that has a relatively low 'R' value will most likely
(a) have large clutch sizes with relatively small offspring
(b) be found in environments that are highly variable
(c) have an early age of first reproduction and a short generation time
(d) produce fewer offspring with more competitive capabilities

31. A population carrying capacity is
(a) the number of individuals in that population
(b) reached when the number of deaths exceeds the number of births
(c) inversely related to r_{max}
(d) the population size that can be supported by available resources for that species within the habitat

32. All these terms that are characteristics of the human population in industrial countries except
(a) relatively small clutch size
(b) several potential reproductions per lifetime
(c) r-selected life history
(d) type-I survivorship curve

33. Expanding population is characterized by
I. A pyramid-shaped age structure
II. An urn-shaped age structure
III. Pre-reproductive and reproductive age groups become more or less equal in size
IV. Rapidly growing population with high birth rate
(a) I and III (b) I and IV
(c) II and III (d) III and IV

34. What is the defining feature of exponential growth?
(a) It lasts indefinitely
(b) The growth rate is constant
(c) The growth rate increases rapidly over time
(d) The growth rate is very high

35. In a life table, if nx = 800, no = 1000 and dx = 200, what is lx 200
(a) 0.8 (b) 0.25
(c) 4.0 (d) 1.2

36. Geometric growth produces what type of population growth curve?
(a) S-shaped (b) J-shaped
(c) L-shaped (d) K-shaped

37. For human populations, the highest growth rates occur in which continent?
(a) Africa (b) South America
(c) North America (d) Europe

38. Which biological factor is responsible for poor vegetation in deserts?
(a) Grazing by animals and goats
(b) Low rainfall
(c) Poor fertility of soil
(d) Native mankind

39. The logistic population growth model, $dN/dt = rN[(K - N)/K]$, describes a population's growth when an upper limit to growth is assumed. This upper limit to growth is known as the population's .... and as N gets larger, dN/dt ....
(a) biotic potential; increases
(b) biotic potential; decreases
(c) carrying capacity; increases
(d) carrying capacity; decreases

40. Bacteria and fungi act as .... within an ecosystem.
(a) primary producers (b) primary consumers
(c) secondary consumers (d) decomposers

41. A lichen is actually composed of two organisms—a fungus and an alga. They depend on each other for survival. The most specific term that describes their relationship is ....
(a) parasitism (b) mutualism
(c) commensalism (d) symbiosis

42. The theoretical growth of an organism is usually .... the actual growth.
(a) smaller than
(b) equal to
(c) greater than
(d) below the biotic potential of

43. If an organism has a population of 600 and in 30 years has a population of 1200 then what is the organism's doubling time?
(a) 15 years (b) 30 years
(c) 45 years (d) 60 years

44. If an organism began with 10 individuals and went through 25 generations, then how many individuals would be in the final generation?
(a) 3.4 × 108 (b) 3.4
(c) 6250 (d) 3.4 × 107

45. In what amount of time will enough people be born to replace everyone in New York City, Which has a population of around 8 million?
(a) One hour (b) One day
(c) One month (d) One year

46. Which of the following would be least true of a regulator?
(a) It can live in a variable climate because of its homeostatic mechanisms
(b) It may have a larger geographic range than a conformer
(c) Much of its energy budget can be allocated to reproduction
(d) It can increase its tolerance limits through acclimation

47. Ecologists use mathematical models and computer simultations because
(a) ecological experiments are too broad in scope to be performed
(b) most of them are mathematicians
(c) ecology is becoming a more descriptive science
(d) these approaches allow them to study the interactions of multiple variables and stimulate large-scale experiments

48. Which of the following changes would be likely to make terrestrial life on this planet impossible?
(a) A decrease in mean temperature by 10°C
(b) Change in atmosphere permitting all the solar radiation reaching the upper atmosphere to penetrate to the surface of the earth
(c) Change in the orbit of the earth from an ellipose to a circle
(d) Disappearance of the moon

49. The charge of the lighter coloured variety of peppered moth *Biston betularia* to its darker variety (carbonaria) is due to
(a) mutation of single Mendelian gene for survival in the smoke-laden industrial environment
(b) deletion of a segment of gene due to industrial pollution
(c) industrial carbon deposited on the wings of moth resulting in darker variety
(d) translocation of a block of genes in chromosomes in response to heavy carbons

50. Species which occupy a similar ecological niche in similar communities occupying different biogeographical regions are
(a) ecotones (b) biomes
(c) ecological equivalents (d) ecads

51. The closely related morphologically similar populations, but reproductively isolated, are designated as
(a) clines (b) demes
(c) clones (d) sibling species

52. The abundance of a species population within its habitat is called
(a) niche density (b) regional density
(c) relative density (d) absolute density

53. Human population growth was slow and gradual for a long period, but it turned sharply upward
(a) after the development of agriculture, which decreased the death rate
(b) during the last half-century, when the birth rate increased
(c) as a result of the black death, which left more food for the survivors
(d) during the industrial revolution, when the death rate dropped

54. Maximum water vapour which can be held in atmosphere is
(a) relative humidity
(b) absolute humidity
(c) saturation point
(d) absolute transpiration

55. Which of the following would generally be considered the healthiest habitat?
(a) A sink habitat populated by many endemic species
(b) A source habitat populated by many endemic species
(c) A sink habitat populated by many exotic species
(d) A source habitat populated by many exotic species

56. A population viability analysis (PVA) might take into consideration
(a) population size (b) reproductive rates
(c) availability of food (d) All of these

57. The niche of an animal is
(a) the number of individuals of the species the environment will support
(b) the same as its habitat
(c) the way the animal fits into its environment
(d) the specific place in the habitat where the animal lives

58. An oak tree produces thousands of acorns, but very few grow into mature oak trees. The oak tree exhibits a .... survivorship curve.
(a) type I (b) type II
(c) type III (d) type I or II

59. When birth rate equals death rate?
(a) A population grows rapidly
(b) The size of a population remains constant
(c) Density-dependent limiting factors do not affect the population
(d) A population goes through up-and-down cycles

60. A broad-based, pyramid shaped age structure is characteristic of a population that is
(a) growing rapidly
(b) at carrying capacity
(c) stable
(d) limited by density dependent factors

61. Plants grow sparsely in arid regions of the world
(a) only because of high temperature
(b) because no seeds fall on their soil
(c) because of several factors combining together
(d) because the soil is sandy

62. Which of the following could be a density dependent factor than might limit population growth?
(a) Fire (b) Storms
(c) Drought (d) Food supply

63. The effects of which of the following environmental factors would probably not change as a population grows?
(a) Disease
(b) Limited food supply
(c) Competition for nesting sites
(d) Weather

64. In the models that describe population, growth, *r* stands for
(a) population density
(b) a time interval
(c) total number of individuals in the population
(d) growth rate

65. A biologist wants to use the mark-recapture method to census a population of desert mice. This will not work if
(a) the mice become wary of the traps
(b) the biologist waits too long before resampling the population
(c) the mice deliberately return because the traps contain food
(d) Any of the above

66. A population grows rapidly at first and then levels off at carrying capacity if it is
(a) limited by density dependent factors
(b) limited by density independent factors
(c) an opportunistic species
(d) limited by density dependent or density independent factors

67. When needed resources are unevenly distributed, organisms often show a(n) .... dispersion pattern
(a) density dependent
(b) clumped
(c) exponential
(d) random

68. If you wanted to see what percentage of the population of Thailand is under 10 years old, you could look at
(a) a logistic curve for the population
(b) the population's age structure
(c) a life table for the population
(d) a plot of population density

69. Which of the following is the most accurate comment on the Earth's carrying capacity (*K*) for people?
(a) *K* is smaller now than it was a thousand years ago
(b) The human population is still a long way from *K*
(c) Out technology has allowed us to keep increasing *K*
(d) When it comes to humans, the concept of *K* is irrelevant

70. In wild populations, individuals most often show a .... pattern of dispersion.
(a) random (b) density dependent
(c) equilibrial (d) clumped

71. A population would grow exponentially
(a) if it were limited only by density dependent factors
(b) until it reaches carrying capacity
(c) if there were no limiting factors
(d) if it were a population with an equilibrial life history

72. To determine the density of a rabbit population, you would need to know the number of rabbits and
(a) the factors that limit population growth
(b) their birth rate
(c) the area in which they live
(d) their population growth rate

73. Which of the following shows how biotic environmental factors can affect an organisms?
(a) Mice have the highest reproductive rate of any common mammal
(b) Maple trees will not grow in waterlogged soil
(c) Some shrubs grow only where forest fires scorch their seeds
(d) Monarch butterflies live only where there are milkweed plants for food

74. An ecologist studying how cattle grazing affects population dynamics of native animals like pronghorns and prairie dogs is focusing on
(a) Populations (b) The biome
(c) The ecosystem (d) The community

75. Which of the following lists only abiotic environmental factors?
(a) Food, temperature, fire and wind
(b) Soil minerals, oxygen level and light predators
(c) Food, parasites, predators and competitors
(d) Wind, temperature, soil minerals and light

76. If you were to compare the source (beginning) of a river to its mouth (end), you would probably find that
(a) the water is colder near the mouth
(b) there are more nutrients in the water near the source
(c) there are more phytoplankton in the water near the mouth
(d) the current is swifter near the mouth

77. The tundra biome gets little precipitation, but during the short summer season it is very wet, with many marshy areas, ponds and bogs. Why?
(a) Water cannot soak into the frozen ground
(b) It does not rain much, but the tundra gets a lot of snow
(c) The ground is so flat that the water cannot run downhill
(d) It is flooded by melting snow from the surrounding mountains

78. Change of season is caused by
(a) change in the distance of the Earth from the sun
(b) the tilt of the Earth
(c) variations in output of solar energy
(d) change in wind patterns

79. The kind of tropical forest in a given area thorn forest, deciduous forest or rain forest depends mostly on
(a) rainfall
(b) average temperature
(c) temperature difference between day and night
(d) distance from the equator

80. The primary ecological factor determining the distribution of deserts is
(a) windiness (b) elevation
(c) moisture (d) temperature

81. Which of the following is not an abiotic factor that shapes ecosystems?
(a) Soil minerals (b) Predators
(c) Fire (d) Rainfall

82. Which of the following is not true? A population with a large r_{max} value
(a) probably has a short generation time
(b) probably has large clutch sizes
(c) is most likely to be regulated by density independent factors
(d) is most likely to have a large body size

83. The human population is growing at such an alarmingly fast rate because
(a) technology has increased our carrying capacity and, thus density-dependent factors have slowed reproduction
(b) the death rate has greatly decreased since the industrial Revolution
(c) the age structure of many countries is highly skewed toward younger ages
(d) All of the above

84. A type I survivorship curve is level at first, with a rapid increase in mortality in old age. This type of curve is
(a) typical of many invertebrates that produce large numbers of offspring
(b) typical of humans and other large mammals
(c) found most often in r-selected species
(d) almost never found in nature

85. The middle of the 'S' growth curve in the logistic growth model
(a) shows that at middle densities, individuals of a population do not affect each other
(b) shows that reproduction will occur only until the population size reaches K and dN/dt becomes 0.
(c) is the period when competition for resources is highest
(d) is the period when the population is increasing the fastest

86. In a range with a heterogeneous distribution of suitable habitats, the dispersion pattern of a population probably would be
(a) clumped (b) uniform
(c) random (d) unpredictable

87. The age structure of a population influences population growth because
(a) younger females have more offspring than do older females
(b) populations with shorter generation times grow more rapidly
(c) different age groups have different reproductive capabilities
(d) life tables show that mortality rates change with age

88. A type-III survivorship curve would be more likely to be found in
(a) a semelparous species
(b) a k-selected species
(c) a species that undergoes periodic molting
(d) a population that is regulated by density dependent factors

89. Density independent factors
(a) tend to maintain a population around the carrying capacity
(b) are involved in the population cycles seen in some mammals
(c) are important in the regulation of k-selected populations
(d) include climatic events and habitat disruptions

90. Which of the following is not a characteristic of a k-selected species?

(a) Usually one reproductive episode per lifetime with little parental care
(b) Extensive homeostatic capability to deal with environmental fluctuations
(c) Long maturation time
(d) Usually low mortality

91. A few members of a population have reached a favourable habitat with few predators and unlimited resources, but their population growth rate is slower than that of the parent population. What is a possible explanation for this situation?

(a) The genetic makeup of these founders may be less favourable than that of the parent population
(b) The parent population may still be in an exponential part of its growth curve and not yet limited by density dependent factors
(c) The Allee effect may be operating there are not enough population members present for successful reproduction
(d) All of the above

92. The term $(K\text{-}N)/K$

(a) is th carrying capacity for a population
(b) is greatest when K is very large
(c) is zero when population size equals carrying capacity
(d) increases in value as N approaches K

93. The ample rainfall of the tropics and the arid areas around 30° North and South latitudes are caused by

(a) ocean currents that flow clockwise in the Northern hemisphere and counter clockwise in the Southern
(b) the global circulation of air initiated by intense solar radiation near the equator producing wet and warm air
(c) the tilting of the earth on its axis and the resulting seasonal changes in climate
(d) the heavier rain on the windward side of mountain ranges and the "rainshadow" on the leeward side

94. Two communities have the same mean temperature and rainfall but very different compositions and characteristics. The best explanation for this phenomenon is that the two

(a) are found at different altitudes
(b) are composed of species that have very low dispersal rates
(c) are found on different continents
(d) have a different range of temperatures and patern of rainfall throughout the year

95. A wildlife biologist is trying to predict what will happen to a bear population if bear hunting is banned. He had the equations all worked out but then realized that he had grossly understimated the amount of food available to the bears. To make his predictions more accurate, he will have to go back to his equations and

(a) decrease N
(b) increase N
(c) decrease K
(d) increase K

96. An ecologist would suspect a population is growing rapidly if it

(a) contains many more prereproductive than reproductive individuals
(b) is near its carrying capacity
(c) is limited only by density-dependent factors
(d) shows a clumped pattern of dispersion

97. Locust populations go through periods of sudden explosive growth, followed by sudden decline in numbers. Their numbers are probably regulated by

(a) predation
(b) random dispersion
(c) logistic growth
(d) density independent factors

98. Chimpanzees have a relatively low birth rate. They take good care of their young and most chimps live a long life. The climp survivorship curve would look like

(a) a line that slopes gradually upward
(b) a relatively flat line that drops steeply at the end
(c) a line that drops steeply at first, then flattens out
(d) a line that slopes gradually downward

99. Which of the following would be true of a species with an opportunistic life history?

(a) Members of the species take a relatively long time to reach reproductive age
(b) They are regulated mostly by density dependent factors
(c) They produce large numbers of offspring
(d) The population usually stabilizes near carrying capacity

100. Match list I (plants) with list II (typical habitat) and select the correct answer using the codes given below the lists.

List I	List II
A. *Utricularia*	1. Desert
B. *Anagallis*	2. On tree branches
C. *Loranthus*	3. Water
D. *Rhizophora*	4. Wheat fields
	5. Mangroves

Codes

	A	B	C	D
(a)	3	4	5	2
(b)	4	1	2	5
(c)	5	1	2	3
(d)	3	4	2	5

101. Mark the true statement/s.

I. Unit of environment is biosphere.
II. Aquarium is artificial ecosystem.
III. Nektons are actively swimming organisms.
IV. A food chain may be parasitic or saprophytic.

Codes

(a) I and IV
(b) II and III
(c) I, III and IV
(d) III only

102. Consider the following statements.

The main objection(s) to the concept of species based upon gene flow between related populations (biological species is/are)

I. It is not applicable to many species of Protozoa and lower Metazoa and plants which reproduce asexually or parthenogenetically.

II. The occurrence of organisms in which sub-specific or specific status is disputed.

III. The occurrence of immense variety (breeds) of animals (*e.g.*, dog, horse and chicken) produced by artificial selection.

Which of these statement is/are correct?

(a) I only
(b) III only
(c) I and II
(d) III only

Answers

1. (c)	**2.** (a)	**3.** (d)	**4.** (b)	**5.** (a)	**6.** (c)	**7.** (d)	**8.** (c)	**9.** (a)	**10.** (c)
11. (c)	**12.** (d)	**13.** (a)	**14.** (b)	**15.** (d)	**16.** (d)	**17.** (c)	**18.** (c)	**19.** (d)	**20.** (a)
21. (b)	**22.** (a)	**23.** (d)	**24.** (d)	**25.** (b)	**26.** (d)	**27.** (b)	**28.** (b)	**29.** (d)	**30.** (d)
31. (d)	**32.** (c)	**33.** (b)	**34.** (b)	**35.** (a)	**36.** (b)	**37.** (a)	**38.** (b)	**39.** (d)	**40.** (d)
41. (d)	**42.** (c)	**43.** (b)	**44.** (a)	**45.** (c)	**46.** (c)	**47.** (d)	**48.** (b)	**49.** (a)	**50.** (c)
51. (d)	**52.** (a)	**53.** (d)	**54.** (c)	**55.** (b)	**56.** (d)	**57.** (c)	**58.** (c)	**59.** (b)	**60.** (a)
61. (d)	**62.** (d)	**63.** (d)	**64.** (d)	**65.** (d)	**66.** (a)	**67.** (b)	**68.** (b)	**69.** (c)	**70.** (d)
71. (c)	**72.** (c)	**73.** (d)	**74.** (d)	**75.** (d)	**76.** (c)	**77.** (a)	**78.** (b)	**79.** (a)	**80.** (c)
81. (b)	**82.** (d)	**83.** (d)	**84.** (b)	**85.** (d)	**86.** (a)	**87.** (c)	**88.** (a)	**89.** (d)	**90.** (a)
91. (d)	**92.** (c)	**93.** (b)	**94.** (d)	**95.** (d)	**96.** (a)	**97.** (d)	**98.** (b)	**99.** (c)	**100.** (d)
101. (a)	**102.** (c)								

30 Community Dynamics

Syllabus

- Species Interactions: Types of Interactions, Interspecific Competition, Herbivory, Carnivory, Pollination, Symbiosis.
- Community Ecology: Nature of Communities; Community Structure and Attributes; Levels of Species Diversity and its Measurement; Edges and Ecotones.
- Ecological Succession: Types; Mechanisms; Changes Involved in Succession; Concept of Climax.

Species Interactions

The organisms living together influence each other's life directly or indirectly. The relationship between members of different populations are based on the requirement, mode of nutrition, shelter and habits of species.

Types of Interactions

Relationship between organisms of two or more species is known as interspecific relationship. There are broadly three types of species interactions :

1. **Positive Interaction** Both the species interacting are benefited, *e.g.*, commensalism, mutualism and protocooperation.
2. **Negative Interaction** In this interaction atleast one species is harmed, *e.g.*, amensalism, competition, parasitism and predation.
3. **Passive Interaction,** *e.g.*, mimicry, camouflage and cryopsis.

Mutualism

A mutualism is an interaction in which both participants benefit (+/+ interaction). Mutualistic interactions exist between plants and microorganisms, protists and fungi, plants and insects, among animals and among plants.

(i) Most plants have beneficial associations with soil-inhabiting fungi called *Mycorrhizae,* which enhance the plant's ability to extract minerals from the soil.

(ii) Some plants have mutualistic relationships with nitrogen-fixing bacteria of the genus *Rhizobium*.

(iii) Corals and some tunicates gain most of their energy from photosynthetic protists living within their tissues. In exchange, they provide the protists with nutrients from the small animals they capture.

(iv) Termites have nitrogen-fixing protists in their guts that help them digest the cellulose in the wood they eat. The termites provide the protists with a suitable environment in which to live and an abundant supply of cellulose.

Commensalism

A commensalism is an interaction in which one participant benefits but the other is unaffected (+/0 interaction).

- An example of a commensalism is the relationship between cattle egrets and grazing mammals. Cattle egrets are found throughout the tropics and sub-tropics. They typically forage on the ground around cattle or other large mammals, concentrating their attention near the mammals' heads and feet, where they capture insects flushed by their hooves and mouths. Cattle egrets foraging close to grazing mammals capture more food for less effort than egrets foraging away from grazing mammals. The benefit to the egrets is clear; the mammals neither gain nor lose.

Amensalism

An amensalism is an interaction in which one participant is harmed but the other is unaffected (0/– interaction).

- Amensalisms are widespread and important interactions. Mammals, for example, may congregate around water holes, trampling and killing many plants. The mammals benefit by drinking water, but not by trampling and killing the plants. Leaves and branches falling from trees often damage smaller plants beneath them. The trees drop their old structures regardless of whether or not they damage other plants.

Predator-Prey/Parasite-Host Interaction

A predator-prey or parasite-host interaction is one in which one participant is harmed, but the other benefits (+/– interaction).

- Predation and competition have particularly important influences on population dynamics. If there were no competitors, predators or pathogens in its environment, a species would be able to persist under a broader array of physical conditions than it can in the presence of other species that negatively affect it. On the other hand, the presence of beneficial species may increase the range of physical conditions in which a species can persist.

Competition

If two organisms use the same resources and those resources are insufficient to supply their combined needs, the organisms are called competitors, and their interactions constitute competition (–/– interactions).

The competition may be interspecific (*i.e.,* between populations of different species) and intraspecific (*i.e.,* between member of same species). In both the types competition is at the same trophic level.

Interspecific Competition

Lotka (1925) and Volterra (1926) modified the logistic equation to include the effects of interspecific competitions and predicted that two species that relied on the same limited resource could not coexist in the same community. According to logistic model only one species survive with greater negative effect on its competitor or both species coexist indefinitely when interspecific competition is less intense. The species which begins at higher density persist while other eliminated.

The mass action approach to modeling trophic interactions was pioneered independently by the American physical chemist **Lotka** (1925) and Italian mathematician **Volterra** (1926). These authors argued that consumer and resource populations could be treated like particles interacting in a homogeneously mixed gas or liquid and under these conditions, the rate of encounter between consumers and resources (the reaction rate) would be proportional to the product of their masses (the law of mass action). The dynamics of the interaction between a resource population H and a consumer population C is then described by the differential equation

$$\frac{dH}{dt} = aH - bHC$$

$$\frac{dC}{dt} = cbHC - mC$$

where, a represents the per-capita rate of change of the herbivore in the absense of consumers, b the consumption rate of the consumer, c the constant of conversion of resources into consumer offspring, and m the per capita mortality rate of consumers in the absence of resources. The terms are described as

$cbHC$ – the rate of production of predator offspring, which is directly related to the number of prey consumed.

mC – the death rate of consumers in the absence of food. Thus, in the absence of prey, predators die according to.

aH – the growth rate of the herbivore population in the absence of predators. Thus, in the absence of predators, the herbivore population grows according to the equation $dH/dt = aH$, which intergrates to $Ht = H_0e^{at}$, the exponential growth equation.

bHC – the rate of consumption of herbivores, or their death rate due to attack by predators.

Because the exponential growth law applies to all populations all of the time it is usually more interesting and useful to study the per-capita rate of change of each population (it is also more biological meaningful because this variable describes how individual organisms respond to their environments). We do this by dividing each equation by the numbers of individuals in the population

$$R_h = \frac{dH}{Hdt} = a - bc$$

$$R_c = \frac{dc}{Cdt} = cbH - m$$

where, R_h is the per-capita rate of change of the prey and R_c is that of the predator. These equations are now known as the *R*-functions for the prey and predator populations, respectively.

Intraspecific Competition

It is density dependent factor regulating population growth. At high density female fecundity is reduced because high individual load leads to fewer successful matings due to mechanical interferance. Other point for competition cause egg mortality and larval food requirements.

Table 30.1 **Types of Ecological Interactions**

		Effect on Organism 2		
		Harm	Benefit	No Effect
Effect on Organism 1	Harm	Competition (–/–)	Predation or parasitism (–/+)	Amensalism (–/0)
	Benefit	Predation or parasitism (+/–)	Mutualism (+/+)	Commensalism (+/0)
	No effect	Amensalism (0/–)	Commensalism (0/+)	–

Mimicry

It is a type of protective resemblance in which animal mimic another animal to avoid predation. The organism which exhibit mimicry is called mimic and the organism to which it resembles is called model. Mimic is palatable to the predator and model is distasteful to the predator. There are following types of mimicry:

(i) **Batesian Mimicry** In this the two species look similar and mimic are defenseless, *e.g, Viceroy* butterfly mimics the monarch butterfly (contain toxin) which is avoided by birds for its unpleasant taste.

(ii) **Mullerian Mimicry** It is the process when the mimic shares the same defensive mechanism as the model (anti-predatory marks), *e.g.,* monarch butterfly and queen butterfly.

Camouflage/Protective Colouration

It is a type of protective resemblance with surroundings. Their body shape and colour blend with the environment, *e.g.,* birds and moths have colours matching the flowers to make their detection difficult. Stick insect resemble to dry twigs. Praying mantis resembles to green foliage and dead leaf butterfly resemble to dry leaves.

Cryopsis

It is a type of colouration which helps animals camouflage with its natural environment. It may enable animal to match/blend with its surroundings and to hide from predators, *e.g.,* stripes of zebra, tigers help to break up the outline of their bodies, which helps in protection of the animal, yellow and black striped abdomen of the wasps warns of its sting. Brightly coloured highly poisonous dart frogs are easily recognized and avoided by the predators.

Herbivory

Herbivores are organisms that eat plants. Herbivory is a form of predation in which an organism principally consumes autotrophs, such as plants, algae and photosynthesizing bacteria. More generally, organisms that feed on autotrophs in general are known as primary consumers.

Herbivores form an important link in the food chain as they consume plants in order to receive the carbohydrates produced by a plant from photosynthesis. Carnivores in turn consume herbivores for the same reason, while omnivores can obtain their nutrients from either plants or herbivores. Due to an herbivore's ability to survive solely on tough and fibrous plant matter, they are termed the primary consumers in the food cycle(chain). Herbivory, carnivory, and omnivory and call be regarded as special cases of consumer resource systems.

Carnivory

Carnivore, also called predator, animal whose diet consists of other animals. Adaptations for a carnivorous diet include a variety of hunting behaviours and the development of methods for grasping or otherwise immobilizing the prey. Wolves use their teeth for grasping, owls their claws, and bullfrogs their tongues. Some snakes (*e.g.,* rattlesnakes) use venom to immobilize their prey, and many spiders wrap their victims in thread. Most carnivores are larger than their prey species, although some of the largest carnivores prey on even larger species, for example, tigers on water buffalo and orcas on baleen whales.

Pollination

There are roughly 200000 varieties of animal pollinators in the wild, most of which are insects. Entomophily, pollination by insects, often occurs on plants that have developed coloured petals and a strong scent to attract insects such as, bees, wasps and occasionally ants (Hymenoptera), beetles (Coleoptera), moths and butterflies (Lepidoptera) and flies (Diptera). In zoophily, pollination is performed by vertebrates such as birds and bats, particularly, humming birds, sun birds, spiderhunters, honeyeaters and fruit bats. Plants adapted to using bats or moths as pollinators typically have white petals and a strong scent, while plants that use birds as pollinators tend to develop red petals and rarely develop a scent (few birds have a sense of smell). Loss of pollinators, also known as pollinator decline (of which colony collapse disorder is perhaps the most well known) has been noticed in recent years. Observed losses would have significant economic impacts. Possible explanations for pollinator decline include habitat destruction, pesticide, parasitism/diseases and others.

Pollination syndromes are flower traits that attract pollinators, and can be highly specialized. Plants and their pollinators are often in coevolutionary mutualisms.

The study of plant-pollinator interactions has proved an active and fruitful area of ecological research. Interactions between small, taxonomically constrained, groups of pollinator species such as hoverflies, solitary bees, bumble bees, birds and bats. Most pollination systems are generalized the vast majority of plant-pollinator interactions will actually be embedded in a complex, multi-order web of interactions.

Symbiosis

Symbiosis is many of the several living arrangements between members of two different species, including commensalism, mutualism and parasitism. The species involved are called symbiont's.

1. **Mutualism** In mutualism, both the interacting species are benefited, neither species can live without the other, *e.g.,* plants depend on insects for pollination; the pollinators in turn obtain nectar.
2. **Commensalism** In commensalism, one species (the commensal) obtains nutrients.shelter,support from the host species whereas the host species is substantially unaffected. *e.g.,* remoras obtain locomotion and food from sharks.
3. **Parasitism** In parasitism, one species (the parasite) depends on the other species(host) for food and shelter and in the process damages the host, *e.g., Plasmodium* (malarial parasite) used female mosquito as its vector.
4. Algae called Zooxanthellae, live inside corals. They can photosynthesize and convert sunlight into carbohydates on which the coral feeds.
5. Other microorganisms live in the guts of animals, including humans and aid in the digestion of food.
6. Many fungi are found in association with certain plants, such as fly agaric and birch trees. The hyphae penetrate the plant roots to form a partnership between plant and fungus. The fungus saps nutrients from the plant, but helps the plant in collecting water and minerals from the soils.
7. Lichens are fungi that live with algae, the fungi provides protection while the algae provides nutrients.
8. Clown fish are covered in mucus for protection against the tentacles of anemones in which they hide. The anemones in turn, are protected by the fish.
9. Cloak anemones hitch a ride on the shell of a snail occupied by a hermit crab. The anemone protects the crab in exchange for food.

The flowering plant *Myrmecodia* and *Hydnophytum* (family–Rubiaceae) from South-East Asia and North-Eastern Australia have spectacular swollen, tuber-like organs that are inhabited by ants of the genus–*Iridomyrmex*. The ants live in special chambers called **domatia.** They pack adjacent tunnels with their waste material. Nutrient ions are absorbed from the colony waste, translocated and incorporated into the plant's tissue. Bacteria and fungi in the chambers probably facilitate decomposition of the wastes. The mineral nutrients of the plant are thus augmented and the ant colony functions as a second root system.

Community Ecology

Nature of Communities

The different kinds of organisms grow in association with each other. A group of such a several species (plant/ animals) living together with mutual tolerance and beneficial interaction in a natural area is known as **community.**

1. **Bioceonosis** is coined by **Carl Mobius** (1880) for the association of organism in an oyster bed community.
2. **Synecology** is introduced by **Schroter** and **Kircher** (1902) for plant species in ocean bottom as an association or community.

A community too has its own characteristics, which are not shown by its individual component species. These characteristics which have meaning only with reference to community level of organization, are as follows species diversity, growth form and structure, dominance, succession, trophic structure, composition, structure, origin and development.

Community Structure and Attributes

The communities may be divided horizontally into sub-communities. This is called **zonation.** If communities is divided vertically it is called **stratification.** The deciduous forest community have following stratification subterranean, forest floor, herbaceous vegetation, shrubs and tree. The zonation of mountain of Western side of North America have -desert biome grassland biomass conifer forest of *Pinus junipers* zone, conifer forest of fir and pine zone and tundra biome.

The characters used to study of community structure can be grouped into two major categories—Analytical characters and synthetic characters.

Analytical Characters

These are structural characteristics which can be directly observed or measured. they may be quantitative or qualitative in native.

Quantitative Characters

(a) Frequency is the number of sampling units in which the particular species occurs. It is calculated as

$$\text{Frequency} = \frac{\text{the species occurs}}{\text{Total number of sampling unit studies}} \times 100$$

(b) Density is the numerical strength of a species in the community. It is number of individuals of a species in any unit area. It is calculated as

$$\text{Density} = \frac{\text{Total number of individual of the species in all the sampling unit}}{\text{total number of sampling unit studies}} \times 100$$

(c) Abundance is the number of individuals of any species per sampling unit of occurrence. It is calculated as

$$\text{Abundance} = \frac{\text{Number of sample unit in which the species occurs}}{\text{Total number of sampling unit studies}} \times 100$$

(d) Cover is the area generally for above ground parts which is occupied by a plant, while **basal area** refers to the ground penetrated by stem in reality.

(e) Dabenmire (1959) expressed six types of dominance. Here cover is included as important character.

Qualitative Characters

(a) **Physiognomy** General appearance of vegetation expressed by single term. Growth form of dominant species.

(b) **Phenology** Scientific study of date and time of seasonal variation in organism.

(c) **Stratification** It is the way by which plants of different species arranged in different vertical layers to fully used physical and physiological requirements.

(d) **Abundance** It has been categorized into very rare, rare, common, frequent and very much frequent.

(e) **Sociability** Degree of association between species.

(f) **Vitality** It is the capacity of growth and reproduction.

(g) **Life-form** (growth form) The sum of adaptations of plant to climate. Raunkiaer's divided it into following categories.

- **Phanerophytes** Buds naked or covered with scale, situated high on plant.
  - Megaphanerophytes (over 30 m high)
  - Mesophanerophytes (8-30 m high).
  - Micro-phanerophytes (2-8 m high).
  - Nano-phanerophytes (under 2 m).
- **Chamaephytes** Buds are close to ground surface.
- **Hemicryptophytes** Buds are hidden in soil, found in cold temperature zone.
- **Cryptophytes or Geophytes** Buds are completely hidden in soil, most of then found in arid zones.
- **Therophytes** Season plant completing its life cycle in a single favourable season.

Synthetic Characters

These are generalization or abstractions which are derived from analytical characters.

(i) **Presence and Constance** On the basis of percentage frequency it has five classes:

(a) Rare (1-20%)

(b) Seldom present (21-40%)

(c) Often present (41-60%)

(d) Mostly present (61-80%)

(e) Constantly present (81-100%)

(ii) **Fidelity** The degree with which a species is restricted in distribution to one kind of community. Such species in called indicator.

(iii) **Dominance of species** In a community only a few species determine the nature of community. Such species are called dominants. Importance Value Index (IVI) of a species in community gives the idea of its relative importance.

$$\text{Relative density} = \frac{\text{Density of species}}{\text{Total density of all species}} \times 100$$

$$\text{Relative frequency} = \frac{\text{Frequency of species}}{\text{Total frequency of all the species}} \times 100$$

$$\text{Relative dominance} = \frac{\text{Dominance of species}}{\text{Total dominance of all the species}} \times 100$$

Importance Value Index (IVI)

Importance value index is obtained by adding relative density, relative frequency and relative dominance

Methods of Community Study

There are following method used for the study of community These are:

(a) Floristic method. **(b)** Physiognomic method.

(c) Phytosociological method.

Unit of Vegetation and Classification of Community

Clemants (1916) on the basis of different unit of vegetation plant community may be classified as

1. **Plant Formation** It is major unit of vegetation and it is a climax community.
2. **Association** Each smaller communities of plant formation with two or more dominant species is called as an association. The developmental or seral communities of association is known as **associes.**
   (i) **Faciation** It is local variant of an association, this variation is due to general climate.
   (ii) **Lociation** It is a localized variant of association, it has different type of sub-dominant and secondary species.
   (iii) **Consociation** It is a local variant. In this case each community is dominated by a single species.
   (iv) **Society** It has one or more subdominant species, these species are of local importance influencing the community in local area.

Levels of Species Diversity and its Measurement

The biodiversity is a broad concept, so a variety of objective measures have been created in order to empirically measure the biodiversity. Each measure of biodiversity relates to a particular use of the data.

Whittaker described three common metrics used to measure species-level biodiversity, encompassing attention to species' richness or species evenness.

1. **Species richness** number of given species in given area.

2. **Simpson index** it is the number of species present as well as this relative abundance.
3. **Shannon index** it takes into account number of species and evenness of species.

There are three other indices which are used by ecologists:

(i) **Alpha Diversity** refers to diversity within a particular area, community or ecosystem and is measured by counting the number of taxa within the ecosystem (usually species).

(ii) **Beta Diversity** is species diversity between ecosystems; this involves comparing the number of taxa that are unique to each of the ecosystems.

(iii) **Gamma Diversity** is a measure of the overall diversity for different ecosystems within a region.

Species Richness and Productivity Influence Ecosystem Stability

Species richness might enhance ecosystem productivity because no two species in a community have the same relationship with the environment. Therefore, a richer mixture of species should result in a more complete use of the available resources. In addition, if the environment changes, a species-rich ecosystem is more likely to contain species that are already adapted to the new conditions than is a species-poor ecosystem. Therefore, ecologists hypothesized that a species-rich ecosystem should also be more stable—that is, over time it should change less in both productivity and species composition than a species poor ecosystem.

(a) Plant cover increases with species richness. (b) Variation in biomass decreases with species richness.

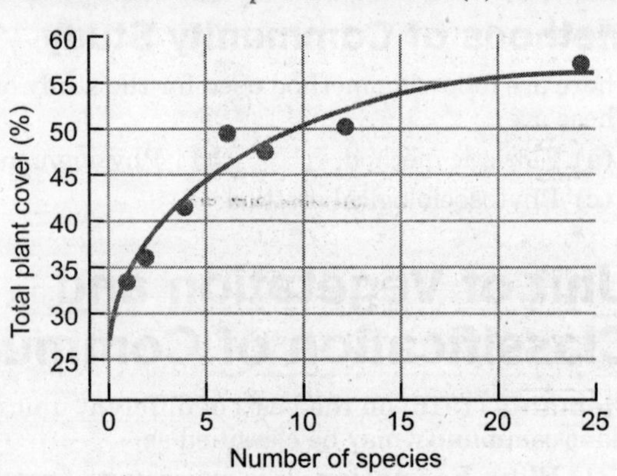

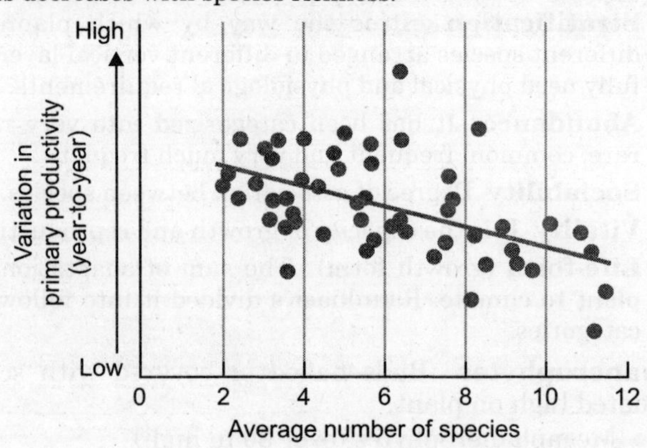

Fig. 30.1 Species richness enhances community productivity and stability net primary productivity was greater, and variation in net primary productivity from one year to the next was less, in species rich than in species poor plots of grasses.

Edges and Ecotones

Ecotone It is a transition zone between two adjacent biomes. It contains organism from adjacent biomes. The density of species is highest in this zone than neighbouring communities.

The **edge effect** is the effect of the placing side by side of contrasting environments on an ecosystem.

This term is commonly used in conjunction with the boundary between natural habitats, especially forests and disturbed or developed land. Edge effects are especially pronounced in small habitat fragments, where they may extend throughout the patch. Increasing edge effects allows more habitat structure to increase biodiversity within the area.

An ecotone is often associated with an **ecocline:** a 'physical transition zone' between two systems. The ecotone and ecocline concepts are sometimes confused: an ecocline can signal an ecotone chemically (*e.g.*, pH or salinity gradient), or microclimatically (hydrothermal gradient) between two ecosystems.

Intermediate Disturbance Hypothesis

The discovery of this general pattern generated the **intermediate disturbance hypothesis.** This hypothesis explains the low species richness in areas with high disturbance levels by suggesting that only species with great dispersal abilities and rapid reproductive rates can persist in such areas. Conversely, the hypothesis explains the decline in species richness, where disturbance levels are low by suggesting that competitively dominant species displace other species, as mussels did when sea stars were removed.

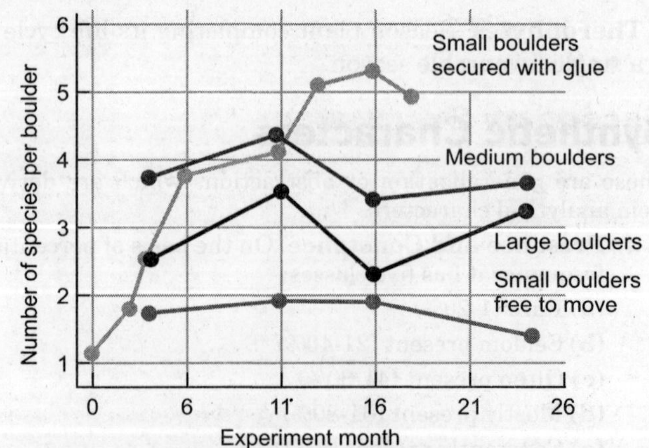

Fig. 30.2 Species richness is greatest at intermediate levels of disturbance by gluing boulders to the substratum, an ecologist showed that small boulders can support more species if they are not disturbed at high rates.

Ecological Succession

It is a natural process by which some locality become successively colonized by different group or communities. Succession can be defined in terms of following three parameters:

1. Community development involves change in species structure and community proceeds with time.
2. It results in the modification of physical environment of community.
3. It culminate in stabilized ecosystems.

Cause of Succession

(i) **Initial or Initiating Causes** Includes climatic as well as biotic factors.

(ii) **Ecesis or Continuing Causes** Includes migration ecesis, aggregation, competition, etc.

(iii) **Stabilizing Causes** These include factors such as climate of the area which result in the stabilization of the community.

Types of Succession

Based on the type of nudity of the area ecological or biotic succession is of two main types, *i.e.*, primary and secondary.

Primary Succession

It start from primitive substratum, where there was no previously any sort of living matter. First group of organism are known as pioneers.

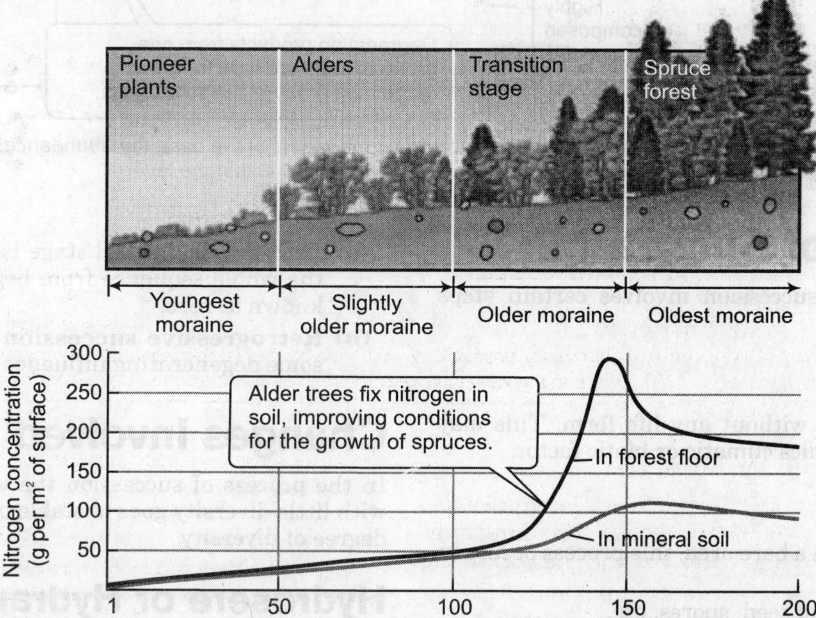

Fig. 30.3 Primary succession on a glacial moraine as the plant community occupying an alaskan glacial moraine changes from pioneer plants to a spruce forest, nitrogen accumulates in the mineral soil

Secondary Succession

It start from previously built up substrate with already existing living matter. Action of any external force such as climatic factors on biotic factors cause disappearance of community.

(a) **Autogenic succession** Plant community itself cause its own replacement of new communities.

(a) **Allogenic succession** Replacement of existing community is cause largely by external condition.

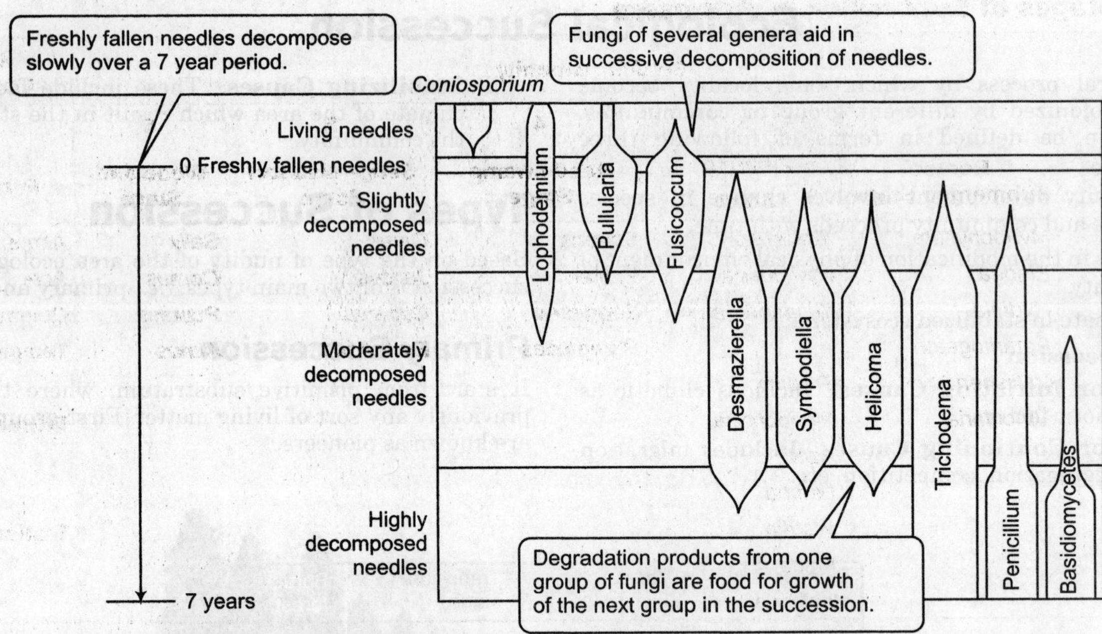

Fig. 30.4 Secondary succession on pine needles as indicated by the widths of the bars, the abundances of ten types of fungi in pine needle litter change with time, which increases with depth within the layer

Mechanisms of Succession

The complete process of succession involves certain steps namely–

Nudation

Development of bare area without any life form. This may developed due to topographics climatic or biotic factor.

Invasion

Establishment of species in a bare area, this process occurs in three successive stages:

(a) Migration spreading of seed, spores, etc.

(b) Ecesis (establishment)

(c) Aggregation.

Competition and Coaction

Interspecific or intraspecific competition for space and nutrition. Individual species affecting each other life form is called coaction.

Reaction

It is the modification of environment by organisms.

Stabilization (Climax)

Final community becomes established for longer duration of time. If it is not replaced by new community then this community is known as climax community and the stage as climax stage.

(a) Each developmental stage is known as seral stage and the whole sequence from beginning till climax state is known as sere.

(b) Retrogressive succession The biotic influence has some degenerating influence on the process.

Changes Involved in Succession

In the process of succession the unstable biotic community with little diversity goes to stable biotic community with high degree of diversity.

Hydrosere or Hydrarch

The process of succession in ponds, pools or lakes is known as hydrosere. The stages of succession can be illustrated as below

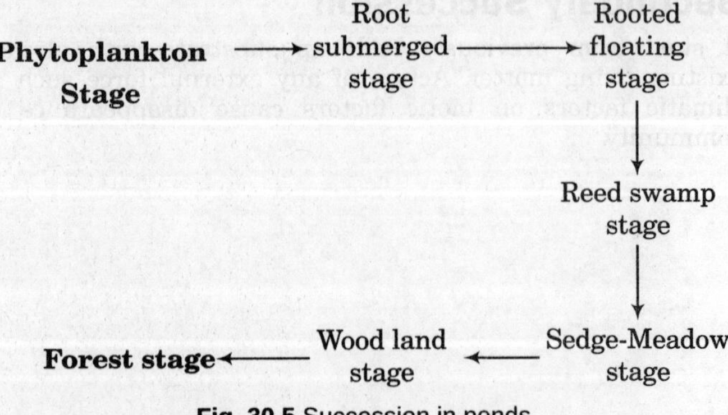

Fig. 30.5 Succession in ponds

Table 30.2 **Stages of Succession in Hydrosere**

Pioneer Community	Seral Community					Climax Community
1	2	3	4	5	6	7
Phytoplankto Stage	**Rooted Submerged Stage**	**Floating Stage**	**Reed-swamp Stage**	**Sedge-Meadow Stage**	**Woodland Stage**	**Forest Stage**
Cyanobacteria,	*Myriophyllum*	*Nelumbo*	*Scirpus*	*Carex*	*Salix*	*Almus*
Green algae,	*Elodea*	*Nymphaea*	*Typha*	*Juncus*	*Cornus*	*Acer*
Diatoms,	*Hydrilla*	*Limnanthemum*	*Saggitaria*	*Cyperus*	*Populus*	*Quercus*
Bacteria, etc.	*Potamogeton*		*Phragmites*	*Eleocharis*	*Almus*	Temperate mixed
	Vallisneria	*Trapha*				
	Utricularia	*Monochoria*				Tropical rain
		Azoll				
		Lemna				
		Wolffia				Tropical deciduous
		Pistia				
		Salvinia				

Lithosere or Xerosere

Lithosere the process of succession on the bare rock surface, various stages of succession are as follows:

Crustose lichen ⟶ Foliose lichen stage ⟶ Moss stage ⟶ Herbs stage ⟶ Shrubs stage ⟶ **Forest stage**

Fig. 30.6 Succession on rock

Table 30.3 **Stages of Succession in Lithosere**

Pioneer Community	Seral Community				Climax Community
1	2	3	4	5	6
Crustose Lichens Stage	**Foliose Lichens Stage**	**Moss Stage**	**Herbs Stage**	**Shrub Stage**	**Forest Stage**
Rhizocarpon, *Rinodina* and *Lecanora*	*Parmelia* and *Dermatocarpon*	*Polytrichum*, *Tortula* and *Griminia*	*Artistida*, *Festuca* and *Poa*	*Rhus* and *Phytocarpus*	Mesophytic trees

Species Richness and Productivity Influence Ecosystem Stability

Species whose influences on ecosystems are greater than would be expected on the basis of their abundance are called **keystone species.** Keystone species may influence both the species richness of communities and the flow of energy and materials through ecosystems.

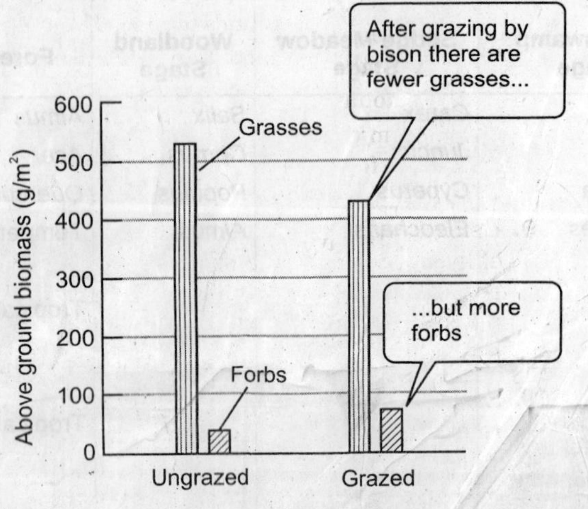

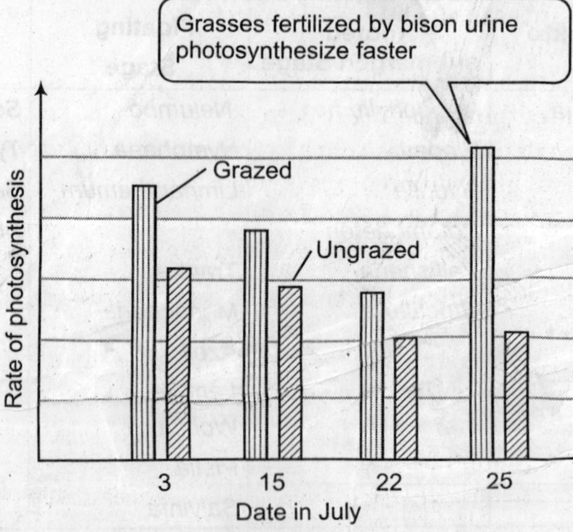

Fig. 30.7 Grazing increases plant species richness and productivity

Bison are keystone species in the tallgrass prairie ecosystem. By grazing preferentially on grasses, they increase both the density of forbs (a) and overall plant productivity (b).

Concept of Climax

When a land or water community changes over time going through a series of stages sometimes arriving at a point of stability called a **climax community.** The final, terminal and more or less stabilized community in succession is termed as **climax.** It has three principal characteristics:

1. **Unity** Climax is a unit and index of the climate of area.
2. **Stability** Climax community more on less stable with climate.
3. **Origin and phylogenetic relation** Development of organism with changing age climax communities have also simultaneously undergone changes with changing climate.

There are three popular theory of climax concept:

(i) **Monoclimax Theory** (FE Clements) Climax control by one factor.

(ii) **Polyclimax Theory** (Transley) Climax control by more than one factor.

(iii) **Climax Patterns Hypothesis** (RH Whittakar) Consider all the factor of environment.

Table 30.4 **Difference in Mature Stage** (Climax) **and Developmental Stage**

Ecological Attribute	Developmental Stage	Mature Stage
A-Community Energetics		
P/R ratio Production/Respiration	Greater or Less than 1	Approaches 1
P/B (B is standing crops)	High	Low
Food chain	Linear	Web-like
Net primary production	High	Low
B-Community Structure		
Total organic matters	small	Large
Species diversity	Low	High
C-Life History		
Niche specialization	Broad	Narrow
Life cycles	Short and simple	Long complex
D-Nutrient Cycle		
Mineral cycle	Open	Closed
Role of detritus	Not important	Important
E-Overall Homeostasis		
Production	Quantitative	Qualitative
Nutrient Conservation	Poor	Good
Stability	Poor	Good
Entropy	High	Low
Information	Low	High

Exercise

1. Which of the following statements best describes competition?
(a) Members of different species never compete for resources
(b) Competition always results in the disappearance of one of the competing species
(c) Coexisting species adapt to competition by evolving to use slightly different resources
(d) Competition always involves one species benefiting and the other being harmed by the interaction

2. Which list includes biomes in the correct order of lowest to highest rainfall?
(a) Tropical rain forest, temperate deciduous forest, grassland, desert
(b) Desert, temperate deciduous forest, grassland, tropical rain forest
(c) Grassland, desert, tropical rain forest, temperate deciduous forest
(d) Desert, grassland, temperate deciduous forest, tropical rain forest

3. In primary succession, which plants make up the early pioneer stage?
(a) Hardwood trees (b) Pine trees
(c) Grasses and weed species (d) Lichens

4. What aspect of tropical rain forests limits their use for agriculture?
(a) There are many species living there
(b) Tropical regions are hot
(c) Tropical climates have high rainfall
(d) Tropical soils are low in nutrients

5. A close physical association between organisms, such as the association of mycorrhizal fungi with the roots of plants in forests, which is beneficial to both species, is known as which of the following?
(a) Parasitism
(b) Competition
(c) Pollination
(d) Symbiosis

6. The line-intercept method of assessing plant communities measures the distance from randomly chosen points to from a .... to the nearest plant.
(a) plot (b) quadrant
(c) transect (d) allelopathy

7. Using a transect of 10 m, an ecologist found 157 individuals of a species of bluebonnet. According to her measurements, what is the density of bluebonnets?
(a) 1570 bluebonnets per metre
(b) 15.7 bluebonnets per metre
(c) 1570 bluebonnets per m^2
(d) 0.06

8. What is competition?
(a) The inhibition of a plant's germination or growth by exposure to compounds produced by another plant
(b) The interaction among individuals seeking a common resource that is scarce
(c) The amount of area a species covers in a community
(d) The sum of the relative density, relative coverage and relative frequency of a given species for a community

9. Using a transect of 100 m, an ecologist found a species of live oak to have a total intercept length of 67 m. What is the coverage of live oaks in the community?
(a) 6700 m^2 (b) 6700 m
(c) 0.67 m (d) 0.67

10. Some living things depend on each other in a very close relationship, which lasts over time. This relationship is called
(a) mutualism (b) parasitism
(c) symbiosis (d) commensalism

11. A salamander hides under the bark, fungi grows on the rotting log and other forest dwelling organisms use the hollow core as a home. This rotting decaying log is an
(a) environment (b) ecological subsystem
(c) ecotrust (d) ecosystem

12. Tapeworms live inside organisms and feed on the nutrients of the food they eat. A tapeworm is an example of
(a) mutualism (b) parasitism
(c) commensalism (d) cannibalism

13. To determine an organism's niche, all of the following must be determined, except
(a) how it is classified
(b) what it eats
(c) where it lives
(d) what relationships it has with other organisms

14. Petroleum products, which contain carbon, are burned, and the carbon escapes into the atmosphere, as carbon dioxide, but, how does it get into the petroleum in the first place?
(a) Refineries
(b) Plant respiration
(c) Decomposing plankton
(d) Photosynthesis in plants

15. Another very important cycle is the water cycle. All living things need water to live. This cycle has four main processes. The two processes that return water to the earth are
(a) evaporation and condensation
(b) condensation and precipitation
(c) transpiration and condensation
(d) evaporation and transpiration

16. Do we learn from our mistakes? Using pesticides that contained DDT was very effective in controlling insect pests on many crops. It was subsequently banned because of this harmful side effect.
(a) Birth defects in baby chicks
(b) Soft egg shells
(c) Bioaccumulation in wolves
(d) Death of small mammals

17. When each new invader to a habitat makes the habitat a little more suitable for subsequent species, succession is termed
(a) resilience (b) tolerance
(c) facilitation (d) inhibition

18. What is the relative importance of seed arrival in the colonization stage of primary succession?
(a) High (b) Medium
(c) Low (d) Static

19. What is the relative importance of facilitation in the colonization stage in favourable environment?
(a) Low (b) Medium
(c) High (d) Static

20. Not all parasitism involves feeding on the body of the host. The exception is
(a) ectoparasitism (b) endoparasitism
(c) parasitoids (d) brood parasitism

21. A lake rich in nutrients and species is classified as
(a) dystrophic (b) oligotrophic
(c) eutrophic (d) ecotrophic

22. Which of the following is an example of a plant chemical defense?
(a) Primary compound (b) Secondary compound
(c) Cactus spine (d) All of these

23. All the organisms that occur in the redwood community
(a) make up a single population
(b) use the redwoods for food
(c) have identical geographic distributions
(d) have niches that overlap

24. Which of the following is an example of a plant morphological defense?
(a) Beltian bodies (b) Mustard oils
(c) Epiphytes (d) Silica

25. Milkweeds contain
(a) cardiac glycosides (b) stipules
(c) mustard oils (d) All of these

26. Why are monarch butterflies toxic?
(a) They incorporate the toxic chemicals from the milkweed they eat
(b) They produce their own secondary compounds
(c) They breakdown the toxic chemicals from the milkweed they eat
(d) Monarch butterflies are not toxic; they only look that way

27. The evolution of two interacting species in a community is referred to as
(a) population pressure
(b) carrying capacity
(c) coevolution
(d) allopatric speciation

28. Removal of a .... from a community affects community structure significantly.
(a) keystone species (b) niche
(c) competitor (d) predator

29. Of the following types of interactions, which one is least likely to limit population size?
(a) Predation
(b) Commensalism
(c) Competition
(d) Brood parasitism

30. Which of the following statements about primary succession is false?
(a) It is initiated by pioneer species
(b) It often involves species changing the environment so that they can no longer thrive and must be replaced by other species
(c) It generally results in more complex, more self-sustaining stages than the preceding ones
(d) It is an orderly progression from pioneer species to climax species indicative of the region being studied

31. Ecologists would consider all of the following to be natural disturbances except
(a) droughts (b) floods
(c) deforestation (d) fires

32. After the eruption of Mt Saint Helens, most of the plants along the mountainside were destroyed and buried under ash. This ash provides many nutrients to plants, but only those organisms that are hearty enough to handle the extreme sunlight, high winds and shallow soil. As these first plants gain a foothold in the environment, they slowly make the environment more suitable for other, less hearty plants. Eventually, the plants that were dominant in the early stages of succession are replaced by other plants until the plant community returns to the climax community. This is a best example of
(a) pollution by volcano
(b) community succession
(c) competition between plant species
(d) None of the above

33. The red wood forests in California are the example of
(a) polluted forests
(b) stable community
(c) dynamic community
(d) community succession

34. What includes all the organisms that live and interact in the same area at the same time?
(a) Community (b) Population
(c) Genus (d) Species

35. .... is the inhibition of a plant's germination or growth by exposure to compounds produced by another plant.
(a) Alleleopathy (b) Chemopathy
(c) Phytotoxicity (d) Genopathy

36. How is milk treated in order to prevent the growth of pathogenic bacteria?
(a) Heating the milk
(b) Rapidly cooling the milk
(c) Irradiating the milk
(d) Heating the milk and then cooling it rapidly

37. What is the first step in the community succession of bacteria in milk?
(a) *Pseudomonas* and *Achrombacter* digest the butter, fat, giving the milk a putrid smell
(b) *Lactobacillus* and *Streptococcus* ferment lactose to lactic acid and acetic acid
(c) Fungi metabolize the acids into non-acidic compounds
(d) *Bacillus* metabolizes proteins into ammonia products

38. Under what conditions do fungi begin to play a role in milk succession?
(a) When the pH becomes basic
(b) When the pH becomes acidic
(c) When ammonia has been produced
(d) When the milk has been refrigerated

39. Ecological succession on sand is
(a) psammosere (b) xerosere
(c) halosere (d) hydrosere

40. Biotic succession is caused by
(a) competition amongst species
(b) occurrence of diseases
(c) changes is grazing habits
(d) adaptive ability to environmental changes

41. A community which start succession in a habitat is
(a) pioneer community (b) seral community
(c) biotic community (d) ecosere

42. Last stage of plant succession is
(a) ecotype (b) seral community
(c) climax community (d) ecotone

43. Succession in a six metre deep pond exhibits a sequence of
(a) Submerged plants → Reeds → Herbs → Floating plants → Shrubs → Trees
(b) Floatint plants → Submerged plants → Reeds → Herbs → Shrubs → Trees
(c) Shrubs → Trees → Submerged plants → Floating plants → Reeds → Herbs
(d) Submerged plants → Floating plants → Reeds → Herbs → Shrubs → Trees

44. A palatable (good-tasting) prey species may defend against predation by
(a) Mullerian mimicry (b) Batesian mimicry
(c) secondary compounds (d) aposematic colouration

45. Succession showing changes in communities at a place is called
(a) geographical succession
(b) biotic succession
(c) physiographic succession
(d) climatic succession

46. Xeric environment is characterized by
(a) precipitation
(b) low atmospheric humidity
(c) extremes of temperature
(d) high rate of vapourization

47. Last stabilized community in a plant succession is known as
(a) seral community (b) pioneer community
(c) ecosere (d) climax community

48. When goats were introduced to an island off the California coast, the goats lived in the same areas and ate the same plants as the native deer. The deer population dwindled, and the deer finally disappeared. This is an example of
(a) commensalism (b) succession
(c) a food chain (d) competitive exclusion

49. The species richness of a community refers to
(a) the relative numbers of individuals in each species
(b) the number of different species found in a community
(c) the feeding relationships or trophic structure within the community
(d) the species diversity that is characteristic of that community

50. Milkweed plants produce bad-tasting and poisonous compounds that deter most plant-eaters. But the caterpillars of monarch butterflies are able to eat milkweed leaves without being harmed. In fact, the chemicals obtained from milkweed actually protect the monarch from insect-eating birds. This example illustrates
(a) coevolution
(b) competitive exclusion
(c) mutualism
(d) the effect of a keystone predator

51. If you wanted to determine whether succession is occurring in a certain area, it might be useful to
(a) determine how many trophic levels are represented
(b) diagram its food web
(c) look at its species diversity
(d) look at old pictures of the area

52. All of the organisms in a particular area make up a
(a) food chain (b) population
(c) community (d) niche

53. When you eat an apple, you are a
(a) primary consumer
(b) secondary producer
(c) primary producer
(d) secondary consumer

54. A lichen is actually composed of two organisms, a fungus and an alga. They depend on each other for survival. The most specific term that describes their relationship is
(a) parasitism (b) predation
(c) commensalism (d) mutualism

55. Which of the following describes mimicry?
(a) An insect's bright colours warn a predator that it tastes bad
(b) The mottled pattern on a fish looks like dead leaves on the bottom of a pond
(c) Two species of mice live in the same area and eat the same kinds of seeds
(d) A harmless frog resembles a poisonous frog

56. The increasing diversity of the benthic community with depth is an example of
(a) the diversity of an area correlating with its productivity
(b) a cline that may be related to increasing environmental stability
(c) a community of intermediate disturbance reaching a higher species diversity
(d) the environmental patchiness and structural diversity of a habitat supporting diversity

57. Under which of the following circumstances would interspecific competition be most obvious?
(a) In a stable, long-established ecosystem
(b) When organisms have quite different ecological niches
(c) Among species whose trophic levels are different
(d) When a foreign organism is introduced to a community

58. The relationship between species A and species B is described as commensalism. This means that
(a) both species suffer
(b) one species benefits and the other species suffers
(c) both species benefit
(d) one species benefits and the other species is unaffected

59. Which of the following is not a property of a community?
(a) Prevalent vegetation (b) Diversity
(c) Stability (d) Density

60. According to the non-equilibrial model of succession,
(a) chance events such as dispersal and disturbance play major roles in succession and species composition remains in flux
(b) species diversity is greatest in the climax community
(c) when succession reaches a climax community, only extinctions make room for new colonists
(d) the communities with the greatest diversity have the greatest resiliency and resistance to change

61. The most important factor (s) in determining community structure
(a) may change from one community to another
(b) is predation
(c) is competition
(d) are structural diversity and environmental patchiness

62. During succession, inhibition
(a) may prevent the achievement of a climax community
(b) is evidence for the equilibrial theory of succession
(c) is one of the factors that determines the most tolerant species in an area
(d) interferes with the successful colonization of other species

63. Which of the following is not part of Gleason's individualistic concept of communities?
(a) Communities are chance collections of species that are in the same area because of similar environmental requirements
(b) There should be no distinct boundaries between communities
(c) The consistent composition of a community is based on interactions that cause it to function as an integrated unit
(d) Species are distributed independently along environmental gradients

64. Match the following lists in terms of interaction between different species.

List I	List II
A. One is benefitted other remains unaffected	1. Protocoopration
B. Both are benefitted and can live independently	2. Commensalism
C. One is benefitted and other is harmed	3. Parasitism
	4. Mutualism

Codes

	A	B	C
(a)	2	1	3
(b)	2	4	3
(c)	3	1	1
(d)	1	2	3

65. Match the following lists.

List I	List II
A. Parasitism	1. Intraspecific relationship
B. Harmful insect	2. Termite
C. Social life	3. Aphid
D. Mating competition	4. Interspecific relationship
	5. Elephant

Codes

	A	B	C	D
(a)	3	1	5	2
(b)	4	2	3	1
(c)	3	4	5	2
(d)	4	3	2	1

66. The four important steps of ecological succession consist of:

I. Invasion
II. Ecesis
III. Competition
IV. Migration

The correct sequence in which these steps appear during primary succession is:

(a) II, I, III, IV
(b) I, II, III, IV
(c) II, I, IV, III
(d) I, II, IV, III

67. Match list I and list II and select the correct answer using the codes given below the lists.

List I	List II
A. Succession on rock	1. Lithosere
B. Succession on sand	2. Psammosere
C. Succession in a salt marsh	3. Halosere
D. Succession in water	4. Hydrosere

Codes

	A	B	C	D
(a)	2	1	3	4
(b)	1	2	4	3
(c)	4	3	2	1
(d)	1	2	3	4

Answers

1. (c)	**2.** (d)	**3.** (d)	**4.** (d)	**5.** (d)	**6.** (c)	**7.** (b)	**8.** (b)	**9.** (d)	**10.** (c)
11. (d)	**12.** (b)	**13.** (a)	**14.** (c)	**15.** (b)	**16.** (b)	**17.** (c)	**18.** (a)	**19.** (a)	**20.** (d)
21. (c)	**22.** (b)	**23.** (d)	**24.** (d)	**25.** (a)	**26.** (a)	**27.** (c)	**28.** (a)	**29.** (b)	**30.** (d)
31. (c)	**32.** (b)	**33.** (b)	**34.** (a)	**35.** (a)	**36.** (d)	**37.** (a)	**38.** (b)	**39.** (a)	**40.** (d)
41. (a)	**42.** (c)	**43.** (d)	**44.** (b)	**45.** (b)	**46.** (b)	**47.** (d)	**48.** (d)	**49.** (b)	**50.** (a)
51. (d)	**52.** (c)	**53.** (a)	**54.** (d)	**55.** (d)	**56.** (b)	**57.** (d)	**58.** (d)	**59.** (d)	**60.** (a)
61. (a)	**62.** (d)	**63.** (c)	**64.** (d)	**65.** (a)	**66.** (d)	**67.** (d)			

31 Ecosystem Physiology

ECOSYSTEM

Ecology is the scientific study of interactions among and between organisms and their physical environment.

Interactions within the biosphere produce a web of interdependence between organisms and the environment in which they live.

Syllabus

- Ecosystem: Structure and Function; Energy Flow and Mineral Cycling (CNP); Primary Production and Decomposition; Structure and Function of Some Indian Ecosystems: Terrestrial Forest, Grassland and Aquatic Ecosystem Freshwater, Marine, Eustraine.
- Biogeography: Major Terrestrial Biomes; Theory of Island Biogeography; Biogeographical Zones of India.

Structure and Function

The structure of an ecosystem is basically a description of the species of organisms. An ecosystem typically has two major components–**abiotic or non-living** and **biotic** or **living components.**

Functional components of ecosystem includes :

Food Chain

A food chain is a sequence of organisms through which the food and its contained energy passes with each member becoming the food of a later member. Each level of food chain is represented as **trophic level**. A food chain may end at any trophic level but it never exceeds beyond 4 or 5 successive trophic levels. Food chain is like a series of steps of eating and being eaten up. Mainly food chains are of two types :

Grazing/Predator

Extends from producer to herbivores to carnivores, *e.g.,*

(a) Flowers → butterfly → spider → birds

(b) Grass → grasshopper → frog → snake → peacock

(c) Algae → protozoan → crustacean → small fish → large fish

(d) Phytoplankton → zooplankton → small crustacean → predator

(e) Insects → small fish → large fish

(f) Grass → deer → tiger.

Detritus Food Chain

Extends from dead organic matter to detritus feeder to the ones feeding on detritus feeders.

(a) Much larger faction of energy flow is through this chain and is a continuous process,
e.g., detritus → earthworm → frog → snake → peacock

(b) Parasites do not have any fixed trophic level since, they feed on producer, herbivores as well as carnivores, *e.g.*, aphids, ticks, mites, etc.

There are group of species, belonging to particular trophic level which exploit common resource base in a similar manner and are called **guild,** *e.g.*, grazing animals, browsing animals, etc.

Food Chains is important to maintain ecological balance, *e.g.*, if there is uncontrolled hunting of tigers it will result in increase in number of deers which will then destroy the vegetation balance and the food chain gets disturbed.

Food Web

It is the network of food chains which are interconnected at various trophic levels so as to form a number of feeding connections. In reality simple food chains are not formed in nature as every organism depends on a variety of foods available. The food web has become more complicated because of variation in taste, preference, availability and several other factors at each trophic level, *e.g.*, frogs eat insects not only of one variety but on almost every variety. Frogs are also eaten up by many carnivores as snakes, eagles, etc. Wolf not only feeds on fox but also on rabbit and deer. Man is omnivorous as it feeds on variety of plants and animals.

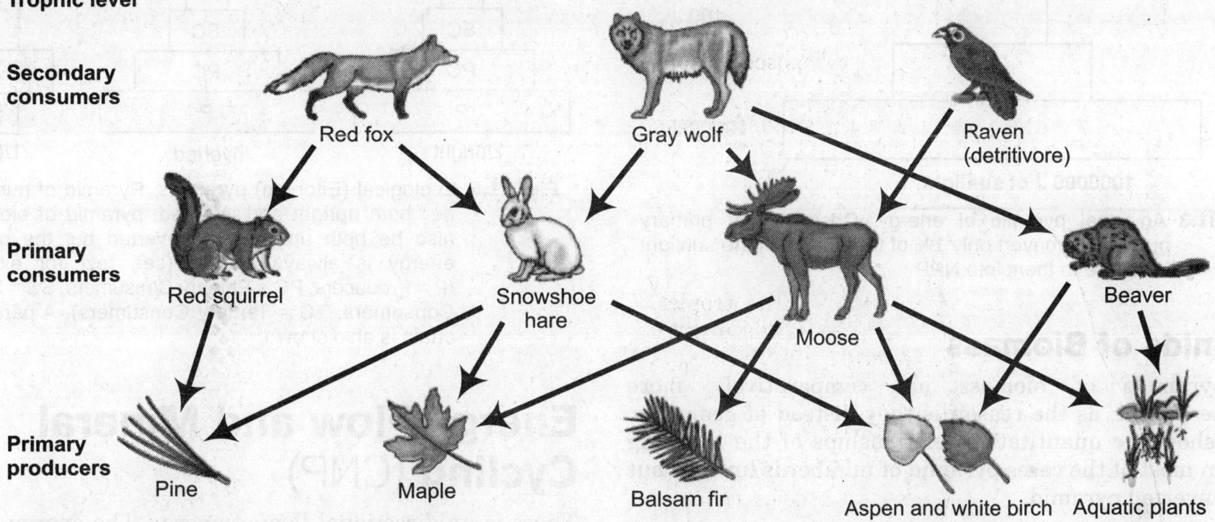

Fig. 31.1 Food Web of Isle Royale National Park. This food web includes only large vertebrates and the plants on which they depend. Even with these restrictions, the web is complex. The arrows show who eats whom

In case of food chain if one organism is removed, the organisms feeding on this would die in the absence of food but in food web many food chains overlap and if any one organism is removed, food web will tends to become stable after some time and balance is restored in the nature. Therefore, concept of food web is more real ecologically than the concept of food chain. It increases adaptability and competitiveness of the organisms.

Ecological Pyramids
(Eltonian Pyramids)

It is the graphical representation of different trophic levels. In a pyramid, base always represent first trophic level and successive levels are made towards the apex. Food pyramids are categorized as:

Pyramid of Number

It is the graphic representation of the number of individuals/unit area of various trophic levels. At each trophic level, there is increase in size and decrease in number of organisms because of their slow reproduction. In most of the cases pyramid of number is upright but can be inverted pyramid.

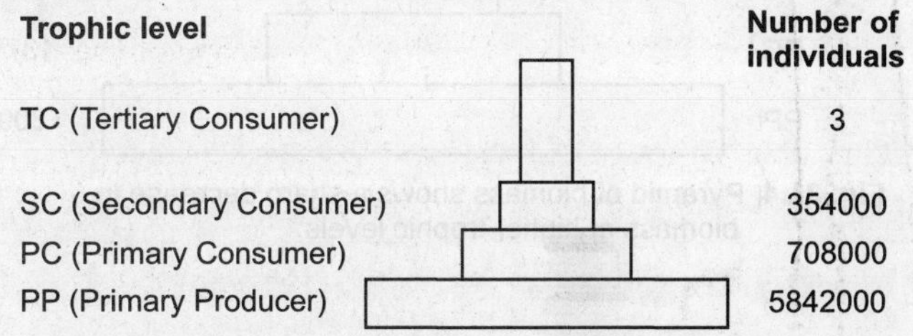

Fig. 31.2 Pyramid of numbers in a grassland ecosystem. Only three top-carnivores are supported in an ecosystem based on production of nearly 6 millions plants

Pyramid of Energy

It is a graphic representation of the amount of energy trapped per unit time and area in different trophic levels. When there is energy transfer from one trophic level to another, loss of energy is in the form of heat. According to Law of **Lindeman** (1942) only 10% of chemical energy is retained at each trophic level. The length of food chain in an ecosystem is limited to 3-4 trophic levels because there is tremendous loss of energy at successively higher trophic levels and residue energy decreases to such an extent that no further trophic level can be supported.

(a) Pyramid of energy is always upright.

(b) Such a pyramid takes into account total number, size and productivity of organisms in all trophic levels together.

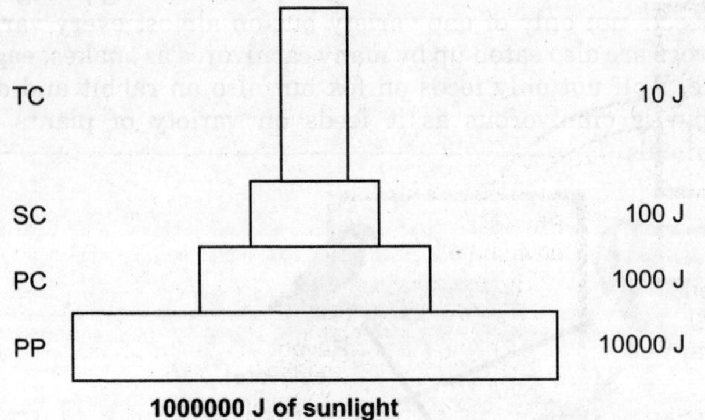

Fig. 31.3 An ideal pyramid of energy. Observe that primary producers convert only 1% of the energy in the sunlight available to them into NPP

Pyramids of Biomass

The pyramids of biomass are comparatively more fundamentalism; as the reason is they instead of geometric factor; show the quantitative relationships of the standing crops. In most of the cases pyramid of number is upright but can be inverted pyramid.

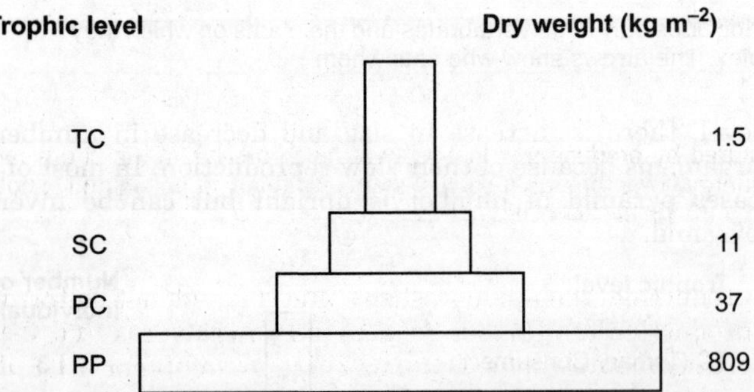

Fig. 31.4 Pyramid of biomass shows a sharp decrease in biomass at higher trophic levels

Standing Crop

The amount of living material in different trophic levels or in a component population is known as the standing crop.

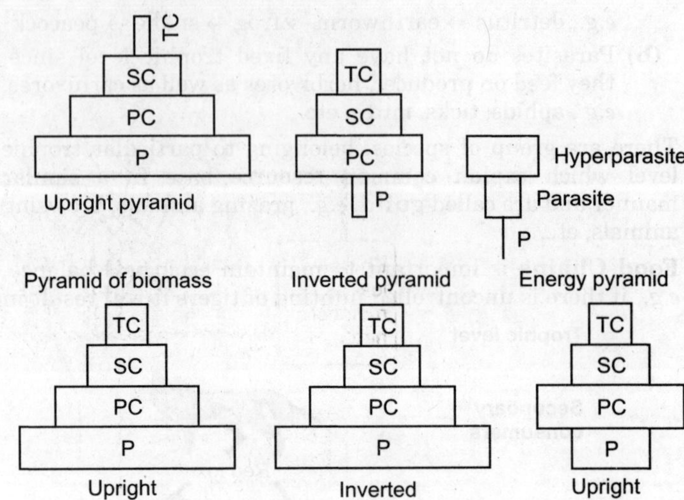

Fig. 31.5 Ecological (Eltonian) pyramids. Pyramid of numbers can be both upright and inverted, pyramid of biomass can also be both upright and inverted but the pyramid of energy is always upright (see text for explanation) (P = Producers, PC = Primary Consumers, SC = Secondary Consumers, TC = Tertiary Consumers). A parasitic food chain is also shown

Energy Flow and Mineral Cycling (CNP)

There is unidirectional flow of energy. The energy captured by autotrophs does not revert back to solar input but passes to herbivores; and that which passes to herbivores does not go back to the autotrophs but passes to consumers. Due to one way flow of energy, the system would collapse if the primary source of energy (sun) were cut off. At each trophic level, there occurs progressive decrease in energy. This is accounted largely by the energy lost as heat in metabolic reactions (respiration) coupled with unutilized energy.

Each level of an energy pyramid corresponds to a step in a food chain and is called a **trophic level. Lindemann** (1942) was the first to propose the community energetics approach or the trophic-dynamic model to ecology.

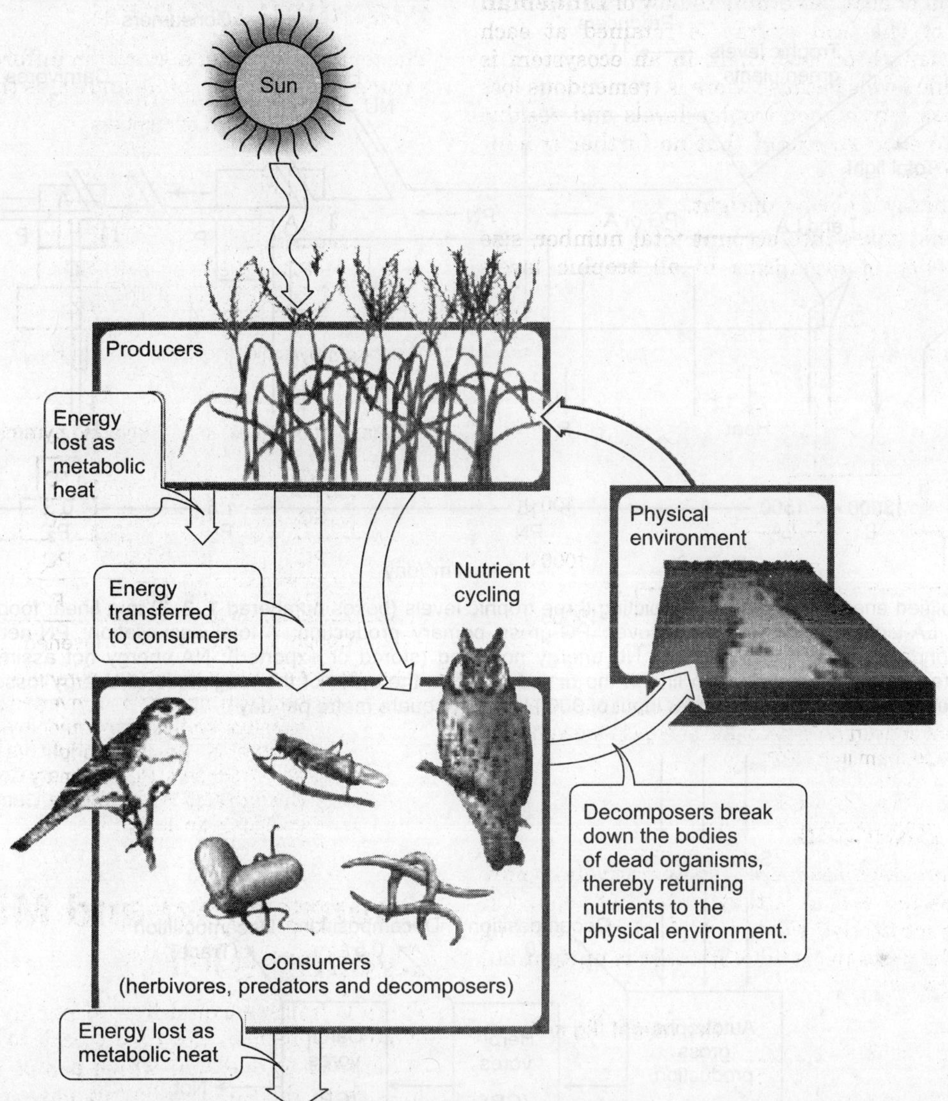

Fig. 31.6 At each step in a food chain, a portion of the energy captured by producers is lost as heat given off during the chemical breakdown of food by respiration (metabolic heat). Thus, energy flows through the ecosystem in a single direction and is not recycled. In contrast, nutrients cycle between organisms and the physical environment

Energy Flow Models

From energetic point of view it is essential to understand energy flow in an ecosystem. The main energy flow models are:

Single Channel Energy Model

Out of the total incoming solar radiations, the autotrophs (producers) only capture 0.1% of energy and rest remain unutilized. At the level of autotrophs, 21% of the converted energy is consumed in metabolic reactions of autotrophs for their growth, development and reproduction; 79.5% of net production remain unutilized and 17% of net autotrophic production are further consumed by herbivores that feed or graze on autotrophs. Decomposition accounts for 3.4% of net autotrophic production). It may be worth mentioning that collectively the three components (herbivory, not-utilized and decomposition) are equivalent to net production. These, three components when are added to consumed energy (respiration) account for gross production at autotroph level. It is also important to note that much more energy is actually available for herbivore than what is consumed by the autotrophs. However, majority of this available energy, *i.e.*, 10% remains unutilized and goes waste as heat.

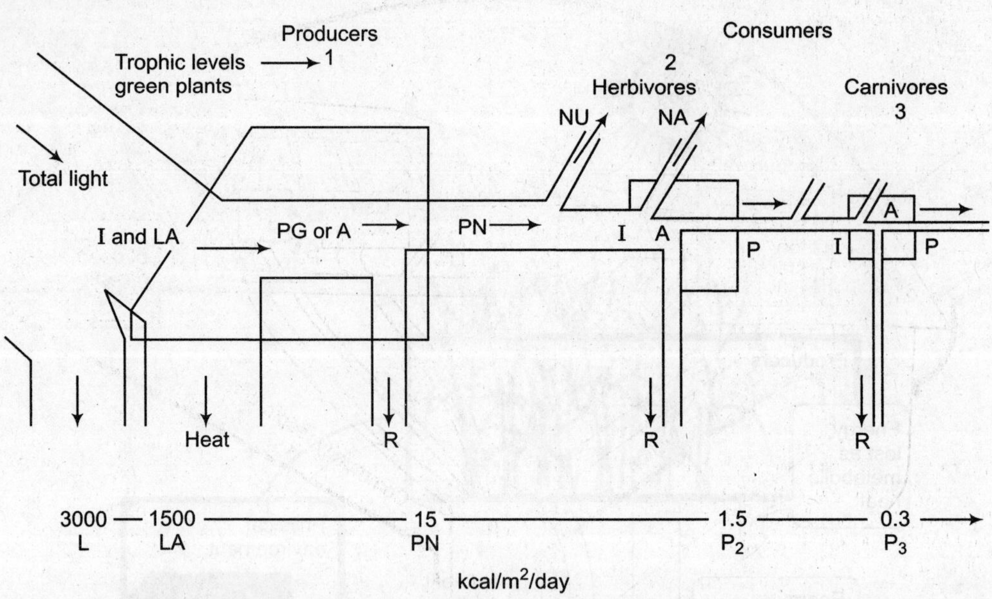

Fig. 31.7 A simplified energy flow diagram depicting three trophic levels (boxes numbered 1, 2, 3) in a linear food chain. I-total energy input; LA-Light absrbed by plant cover. PG-gross primary production; A-total assimilation; PN-net primary production; P-secondary (consumer) production NU-energy not used (stored or exported); NA-energy not assimilated by consumers (egested); R-respiration. Bottom line in the diagram shows the order of the magnitude of energy losses expected at major transfer points, starting with a solar input of 3000 kcal per square metre per day

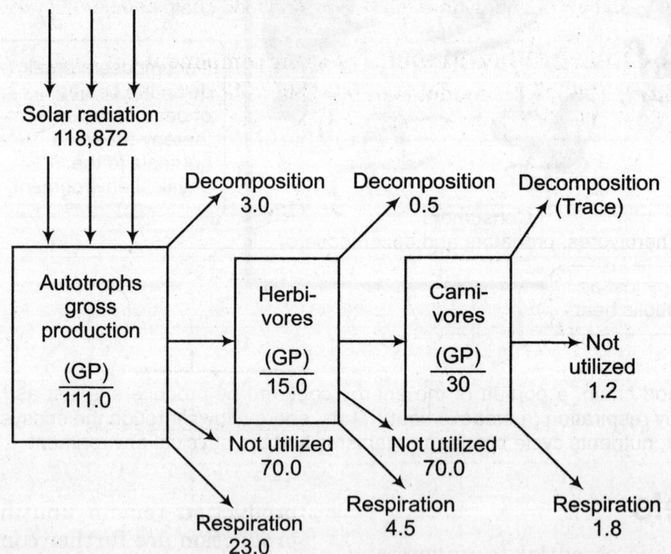

Fig. 31.8 Energy flow diagram for a lake (freshwater ecosystem) in g cal/cm²/yr (modified from Lindemann; 1942)

Y-Shaped Energy Flow Models/Diagrams

This model shows a common boundary, light and heat flows as well as the import, export and storage of organic matter. Decomposers are placed in a separate box as a means of partially separating the grazing and detritus food chains. In terms of energy levels, decomposers are, in fact, a mixed group. It separates the two chains, *i.e.*, grazing food chain and detritus food chain in both time and space.

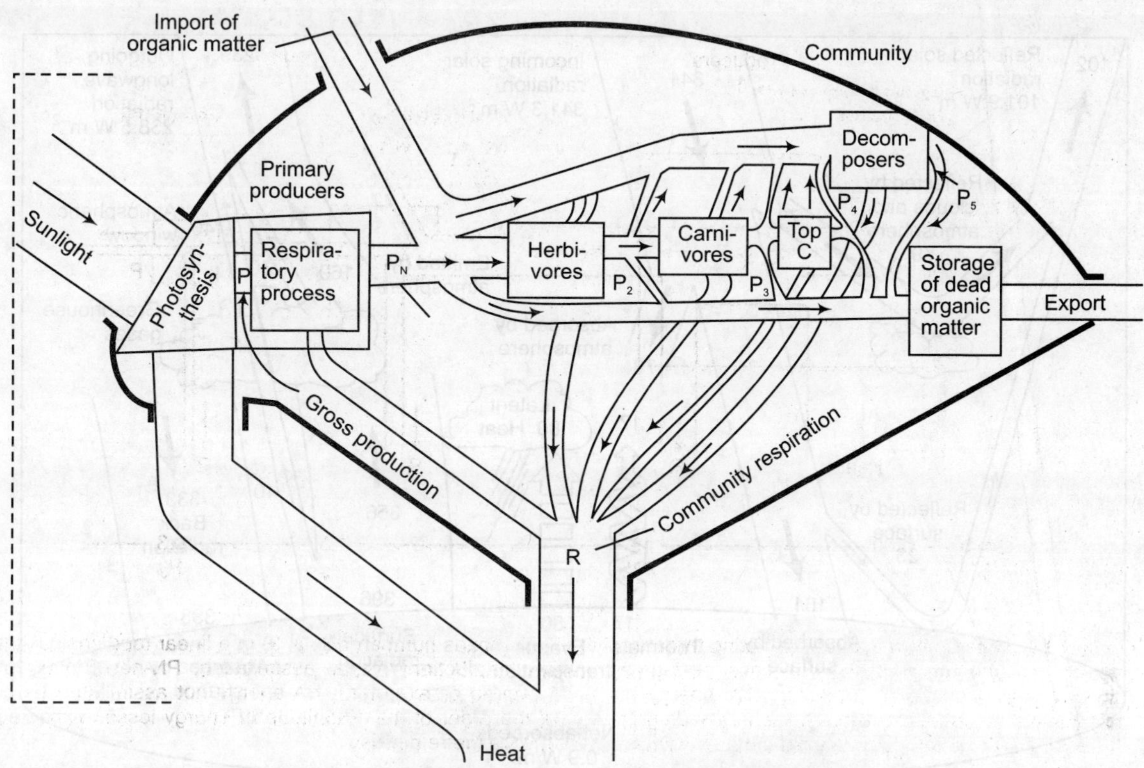

Fig. 31.9 The relationship between flow of energy through the grazing food chain and detritus pathway (After IIT Odum; 1956)

Generalized Model of Y-Shaped Energy Flow Model The basic components of an energy flow model can be examined in a universal model given by **EP Odum;** 1983. This model is applicable to both terrestrial and aquatic ecosystems.

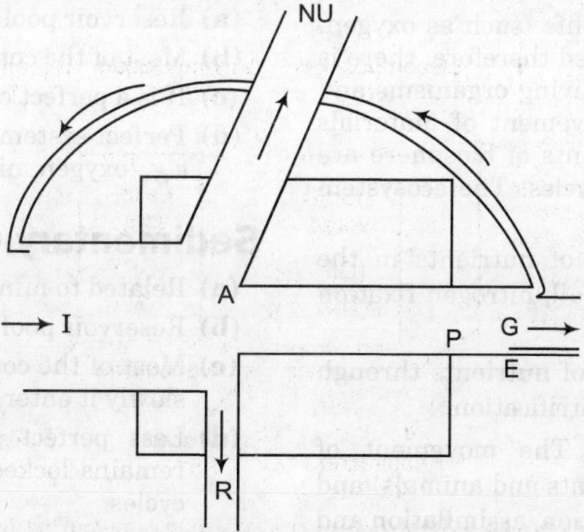

Fig. 31.10 Diagrammatic representation of a universal model of energy flow at one trophic level (After EP Odum; 1968)

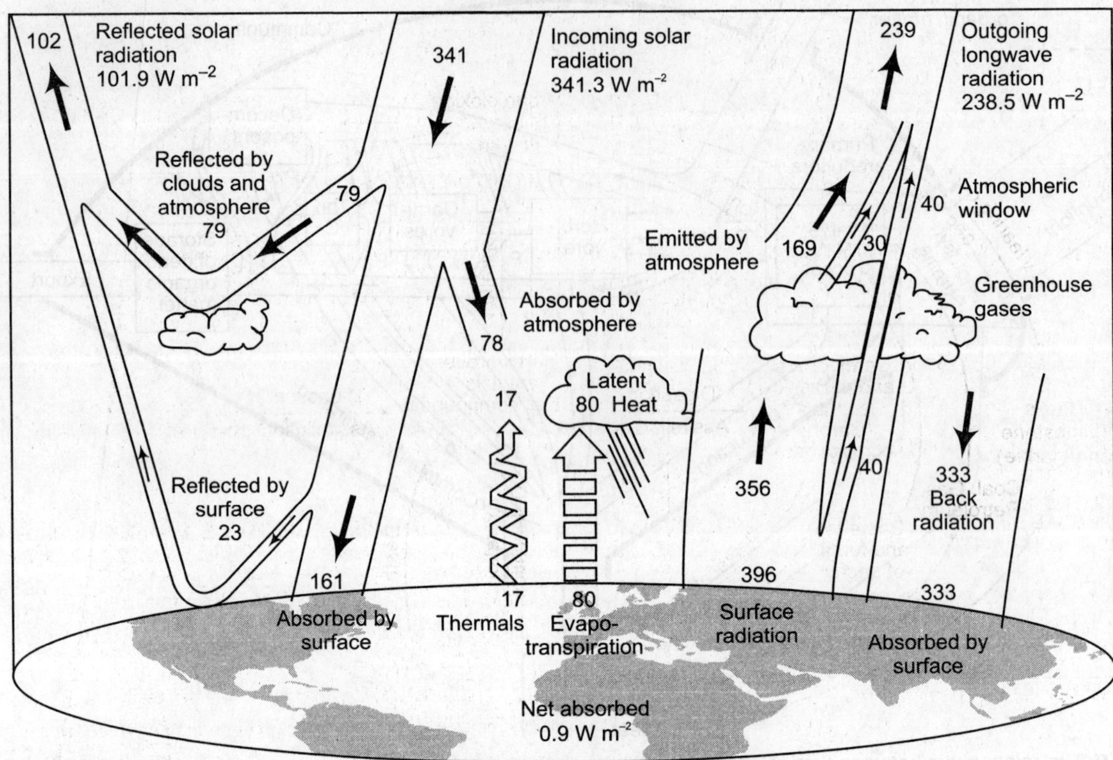

Fig. 31.11 The global energy flow

Nutrient Cycling/Biochemical Cycles

The quantity of materials required for life (such as oxygen, CO_2, N_2, minerals, water, etc.) are limited therefore, there is a cyclic exchange of material between living organisms and their non-living environment. The movement of materials through living and non-living components of biosphere are called biogeochemical cycles/nutrient cycles. The ecosystem nutrient cycles have three aspects

(i) **Input of Nutrients** The gain of nutrients in the ecosystem through rainfall, dust fall, nitrogen fixation and weathering.

(ii) **Output of Nutrients** The loss of nutrients through run off water, soil erosion and denitrification.

(iii) **Internal Nutrient Cycling** The movement of nutrients between organisms (plants and animals) and soil through the process of absorption, assimilation and decomposition.

(iv) In all biogeochemical cycles, the part of the cycle which remains out of use is called **reservoir pool** and rest is used again and again and is called **cyclic pool.** There are two types of nutrient cycles as

Gaseous Cycle

(a) Reservoir pool is atmosphere and hydrosphere.

(b) Most of the contents remain in cyclic pool.

(c) It is a perfect cycle.

(d) Perfect system as most of the time uniform circulation, *e.g.*, oxygen, nitrogen and carbon cycles.

Sedimentary Cycle

(a) Related to minerals.

(b) Reservoir pool is rocks.

(c) Most of the contents remain in reservoir pool and very slowly it enters to cyclic pool.

(d) Less perfect system as most of the time contents remains locked in reservoir pool, *e.g.*, Ca, P, S, K, Mg cycles.

Carbon Cycle

About 7×10^{13} kg of carbon is fixed by photosynthesis in a year by the producers. One hectare of a healthy forest absorbs about 30 tones of CO_2 and releases some 10 tones of oxygen annually.

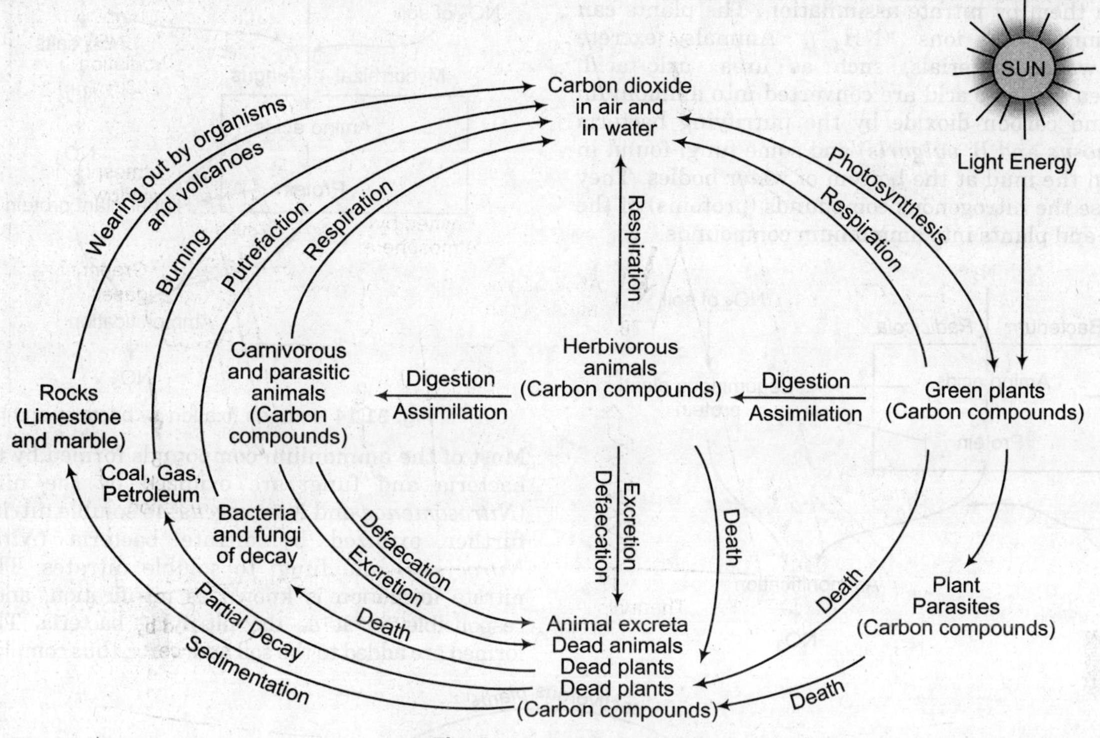

Fig. 31.12 Carbon cycle

Nitrogen Cycle

Nitrogen gas forms 78% of the air, but is not available for use as such by plants and animals. It must be 'fixed', that is, combined with other elements, such as oxygen, for use by organisms. The atmospheric nitrogen is fixed by prokaryotes, *viz.,* some soil bacteria *(Azotobacter* and *Clostridium),* by certain Cyanobacteria *(Nostoc, Anabaena, Aulosina* and *Tolypothrix)* and by the symbiotic bacteria *(Rhizobium leguminosarum)* living in the root nodules of legumes such as pea and beans.

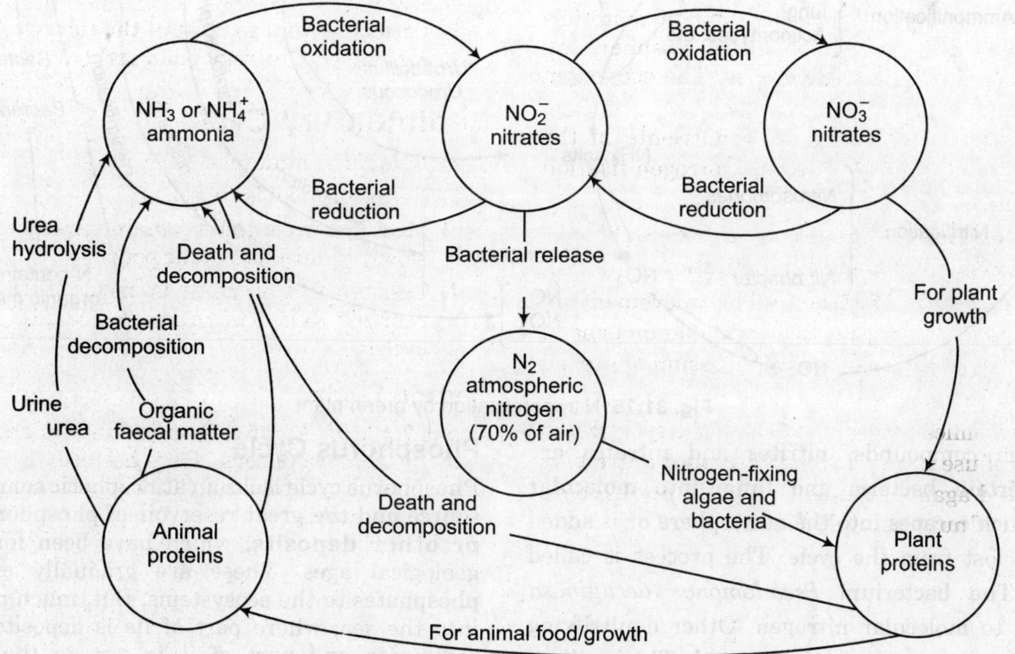

Fig. 31.13 Nitrogen cycle

The plants absorb the nitrate ions and form vegetable proteins from them by nitrate assimilation. The plants can also use ammonium ions (NH_4^+). Animals excrete nitrogenous waste materials, such as urea, uric acid, ammonia. Urea and uric acid are converted into ammonium compounds and carbon dioxide by the putrifying bacteria (*Bacillus ramosus* and *B. vulgaris*) and some fungi found in the soil and in the mud at the bottom of water bodies. They also decompose the nitrogenous compounds (proteins) of the dead animals and plants into ammonium compounds.

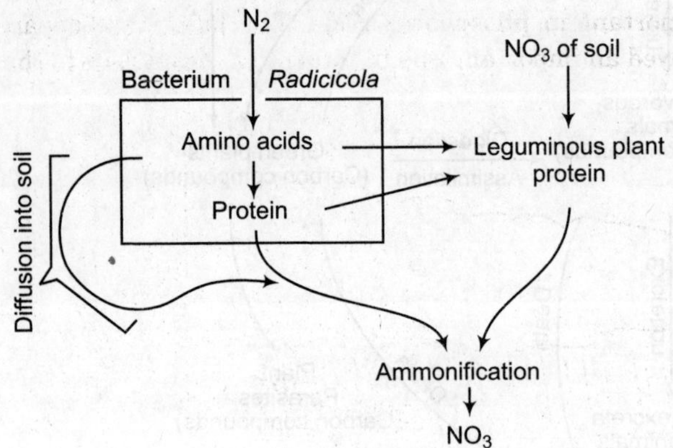

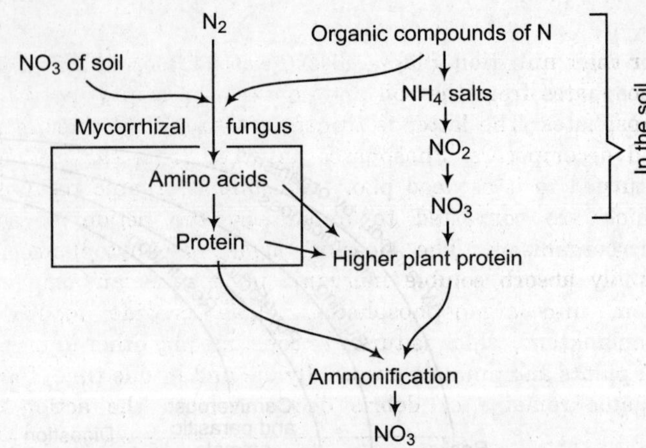

Fig. 31.14 Nitrogen fixation by bacteria and fungus

Most of the ammonium compounds formed by the putrifying bacteria and fungi are oxidized by the nitrite bacteria (*Nitrosomonas* and *Nitrococcus*) to soluble nitrites, which are further oxidized by nitrate bacteria (*Nitrobacter* and *Nitrocystis*) and fungi to soluble nitrates. The process of nitrate formation is known as nitrification, and the bacteria responsible for it as the nitrifying bacteria. The nitrates so formed are added to the soil and water, thus completing the cycle.

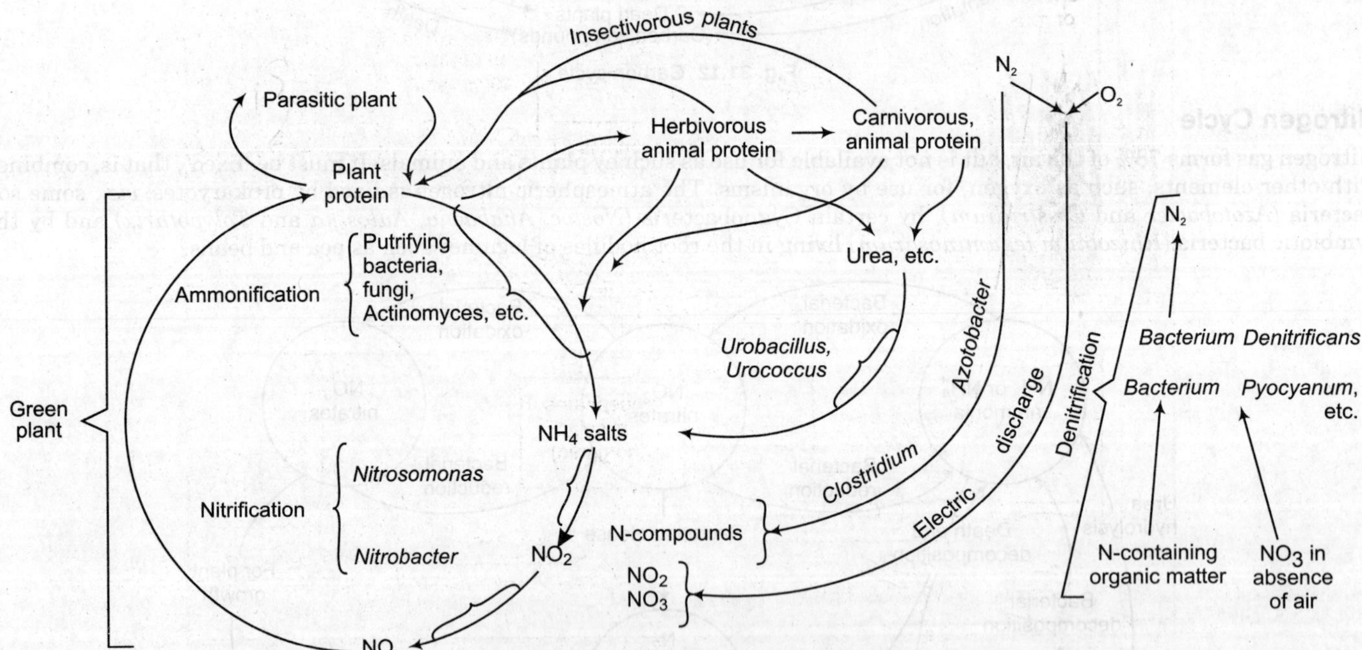

Fig. 31.15 Nitrogen fixation by green plant

Some ammonium compounds, nitrites and nitrates are converted by certain bacteria and fungi into molecular nitrogen (N_2) which escapes into the atmosphere or is added to water, and is lost from the cycle. The process is called denitrification. The bacterium *Pseudomonas aeruginosa* reduces nitrates to molecular nitrogen. Other denitrifying bacteria are *Micrococcus denitrificans* and *Thiobacillum denitrificans*.

Phosphorus Cycle

Phosphorus cycle lacks an atmospheric component. The basic source and the great reservoir of phosphorus are the **rocks or other deposits,** which have been formed in the past geological ages. These are gradually eroding, releasing phosphates to the ecosystems. But, much phosphate escapes into the sea, where part of its is deposited in the shallow sediments and part of it is lost to the deep sediments. However, the means of returning phosphorus to the cycle, are inadequate to compensate the loss.

For their nutrition, plants absorb water dissolved inorganic phosphates from the soil and convert these into inorganic phosphates. The latter is transferred to animal consumers and decomposers. Phosphates absorbed from the soil are returned to it as dead plant and animal organic residues, which are converted to humus by the action of soil microorganisms. The floating algae or phytoplanktons rapidly absorb soluble inorganic phosphates and convert them into organophosphates. Algae provide food for zooplanktons, which is turn are consumed by other animals. All plants and animals eventually die and in due time, their organic remains or debris decay through the action of microorganisms and the phosphates are released into the water for recycling.

Much phosphates get lost to this central cycle by the physical processes, such as sedimentation, which take it out of the reach of upwelling and major water circulation. Biological processes, such as the formation of teeth and bone and excretion also account for considerable losses from the major portion of the cycle. The fish and marine birds are also important in phosphorus cycle. The later have apparently played an important role in returning phosphorus to the cycle.

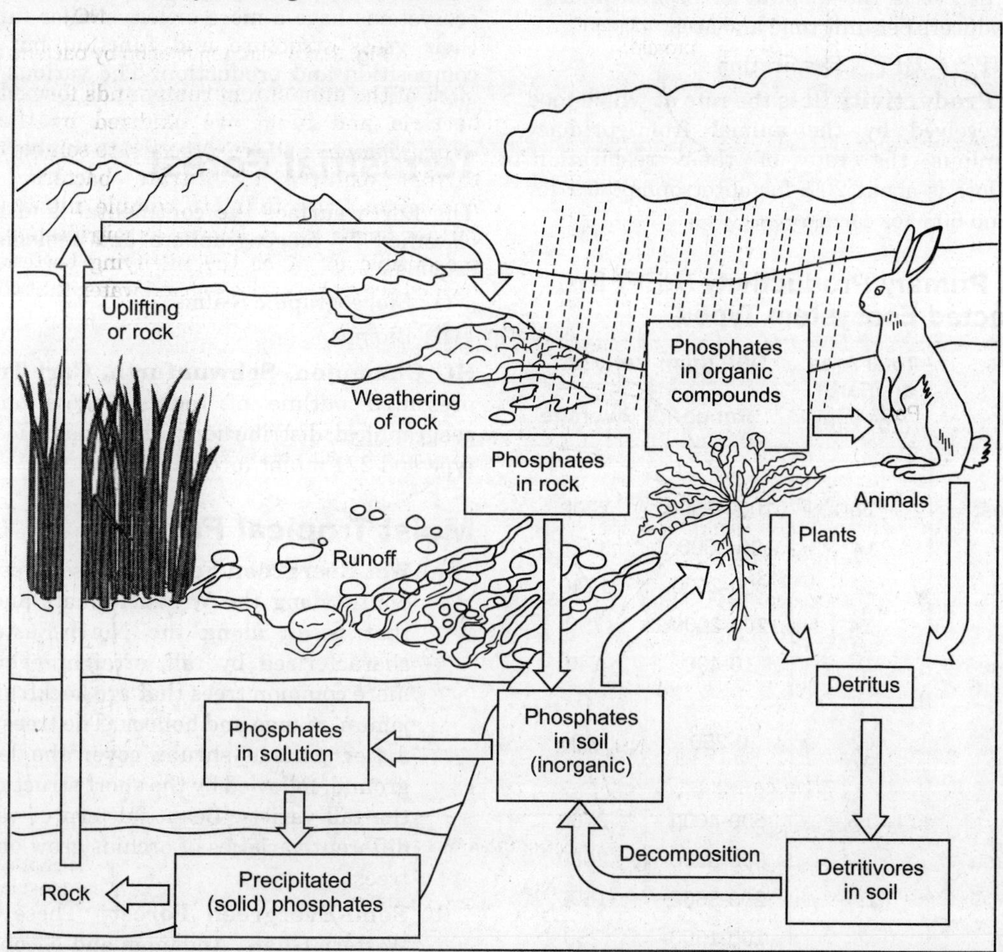

Fig. 31.16 Phosphorus cycle. The major reservoir for phosphorus is in phosphate rocks and fossil bone deposits laid down in the past geological ages. There is no atmospheric phase in the phosphorus cycle

Primary Production and Decomposition

Productivity/yield (production ecology) is the amount of organic matter produced in a single growing season/acre/hectare. It varies during different seasons in different ecosystems. The types of productivity are:

1. **Primary Productivity** It is the amount of energy accumulated in green plants through photosynthesis. It depends upon solar radiations, temperature, soil moisture, etc. It is expressed as dry matter produced or energy/unit area/time or g/m^2/yr. or kcal/m^2/year, *e.g.*, In tropical region, primary productivity may be sustained throughout year.
   (i) In temperate region, it fluctuates because of fluctuation in climate.
   (ii) In aquatic system, it decreases with the increase in depth of water.

(iii) The primary productivity is highest in tropical rain forest, coral reef, estuaries, sugarcane field (2-4 kg/m^2/yr) and is lowest in desert (less than, 200 gm/m^2/yr).

The primary productivity is of two types :

(a) **Gross Primary Productivity** (GPP) It is the organic matter produced by autotrophs of the ecosystem per unit time and area, *i.e.,* it is the rate at which solar energy is fixed.

(b) **Net Primary Productivity** (NPP) It is the part of GPP minus the energy utilized by the plants in respiration. *i.e.,* it is the amount of organic matter stored by producers per unit time and area.

$$\text{NPP} = \text{GPP} - \text{Respiration}$$

2. **Secondary Productivity** It is the rate at which food energy is received by the animal from primary producers minus the rate of their respiration. Respiration loss is about 20% for autotrophs, 30% for herbivores and 60% for carnivores.

Table 31.1 **Net Primary Productivity** (NPP) **for Selected Ecosystem Types**

Ecosystem	Total Area on Earth (10^6 km^2)	NPP (g/m^2 Per year)	
		Range	Average
Terrestrial			
Tropical rain forest	17	1000-3500	2200
Cultivated land	14	00-3500	650
Temperate forest	12	600-2500	1240
Grassland	24	200-2000	790
Tundra and alpine communities	9	10-400	140
Desert	42	0-250	40
Aquatic			
Coral reef	0.6	500-4000	2500
Swamp and marsh	2	800-3500	2000
Estuary	1.4	200-3500	1500
Lake and stream	2	100-1500	250
Ocean upwelling zone	0.4	400-1000	500
Open ocean	332	2-400	125

Ecological Efficiency

It indicates the efficiency with which organisms consume their food and convert it into biomass and make it available to the next higher trophic level. The important efficiency measures are :

$$\text{Photosynthetic Efficiency} = \frac{\text{GPP}}{\text{Incident total solar radiation}} \times 100$$

$$\text{Net Production Efficiency} = \frac{\text{NPP}}{\text{GPP}} \times 100$$

$$\text{Assimilation Efficiency} = \frac{\text{Food energy assimilation}}{\text{Food energy ingested}} \times 100$$

Ecological efficiency

$$= \frac{\text{Energy in biomass production at a trophic level}}{\text{Energy in biomass production at previos trophic level}} \times 100$$

Structure and Function of Some Indian Ecosystems

We find various types of ecosystems operating as self sufficient, interacting systems in the biosphere. About all ecosystems have a more or less similar fundamental plan of their gross structure and function but differ in species composition and production. The various Indian ecosystem are

Terrestrial Forest

The Earth surface the continental land masses have been classified by biogeographers and ecologists into following regions

(i) Biogeographic realms

(ii) Biomes

HG Champion, Schwunfurth, Carl Troll and **GS Puri** presented outline of Indian vegetation type and their geographical distribution. They identified 16 major forest type and 221 minor forest in India.

Moist Tropical Forests

(a) **Wet Evergreen Forest** These forests are found in the South along the Western Ghats and Nicobar Islands that is all along the North-Eastern region. It is characterized by tall, straight evergreen trees. The more common trees that are kackfruit, betel nut, palm, jamun, mango and hollock. The trees in this forest form a tier pattern shrubs cover the layer closer to the ground, followed by the short structured trees and then the tall variety. Beautiful fern of various colours and different varieties of orchids grow on the trunks of the trees.

(b) **Semi-Evergreen Forest** These are found in the Western Ghats, Andaman and Nicobar Islands and the Eastern Himalayas. Such forests have a mixture of the wet evergreen trees and the moist deciduous trees. The forest is dense and is filled with a large variety of trees of both types.

(c) **Moist Deciduous Forest** These are found throughout India except in the Western and the North-Western regions. The trees have broad trunks, are tall and have branching trunks and roots to hold them firmly to the ground. Some of the taller trees shed their leaves in the dry season. There is a layer of shorter trees and evergreen shrubs in the undergrowth. These forests are dominated by sal and teak, alongwith mango, bamboo and rosewood.

(d) **Littoral and Swamp Forest** These are found along the Andaman and Nicobar Islands and the delta area of the Ganga and the Brahmaputra. It consists mainly of whistling pines, mangroves, date palms and bulletwood. Their root have soft tissue, so that the plant can breathe in the water.

Dry Tropical Forests

(e) **Dry deciduous Forest** These are found throughout the Northern part of the country except in North-East. It is also found in Madhya Pradesh, Gujarat, Andhra Pradesh, Karnataka and Tamil Nadu. The canopy of the trees does not normally exceed 25 metres. The common trees are the sal, a variety of *Acacia* and bamboo.

(f) **Thorn Forest** This type is found in areas with black soil North, West, Central and South India. The trees do not grow beyond 10 metres. Spurge, Caper and Cactus are typical of this region.

(g) **Dry Evergreen Forest** These are found along the Andhra Pradesh and Karnataka coast. It has mainly hard-leaved evergreen trees with fragrant flowers, along with a few deciduous trees.

Montane Sub-Tropical Forests

(h) **Broad-leaved-Forests** These are found in the Eastern Himalayas and the Western Ghats, along the silent valley. There is a marked difference in the form of the vegetation in the two areas. In the silent valley, the *Poonspar, Cinnamon, Rhododendron* and fragrant grass are predominant. In the Eastern Himalayas, the flora has been badly affected by the shifting cultivation and forest fires. These wet forests consist mainly of evergreen trees with sparsed deciduous tree. There are oak, alder, chestnut, birch and cherry trees and a large variety of orchids, bamboo and creepers found in Eastern Himalayas.

(i) **Pine Forest** These are the found in the steep dry slopes of the Shivalik Hills, Western and Central Himalayas, Khasi, Naga and Manipur Hills. The trees predominantly found in these areas are the chir, oak, *Rhododendron* and pine. In the lower region sal, sandan, amla and *Laburnum* are found.

(j) **Dry evergreen Forest** These normally have a prolonged hot and dry season and a cold winter. It generally has evergreen trees with shining leaves that have a varnished look. Some of the more common ones are the pomegranate, olive and oleander. These forests are found in the Shivalik Hills and foothills of the Himalayas up to a height of 1000 metres.

Montane Temperate Forests

(k) **Wet Forest** Wet montane temperate forests occur in the North and the South. In the North, it is found in the region to the East of Nepal into Arunachal Pradesh, at a height of 1800-3000 metres, receiving a minimum rainfall of 2000 mm. In the South, it is found in parts of the Nilgiri Hills, the higher reaches of Kerala. The forests in the Northern region are denser than in the South. This is because over the time the original trees have been replaced by fast-growing varieties such as the Eucalyptus. Rhododendrons and a variety of ground flora can be found here. In the North, there are three layers of forests the higher layer has mainly coniferous, the middle layer has deciduous trees such as the oak and the lowest layer is covered by *Rhododendron* and champa.

(l) **Moist Forest** This type spreads from the Western Himalayas to the Eastern Himalayas. The trees found in the Western section are broad-leaved oak, brown oak, walnut, *Rhododendron*, etc. In the Eastern Himalayas, the rainfall is much heavier and therefore vegetation is also more lush and dense. There are large variety of broad-leaved trees, ferns, and bamboo. Coniferous trees are also found here, some of the varieties being different from the ones found in the South.

(m) **Dry Forest** This type is found mainly in Lahul, Kinnaur, Sikkim and other parts of the Himalayas. There are predominantly coniferous trees that are not too tall, alongwith broad-leaved trees such as the oak, maple, and ash. At higher elevation fir, juniper, deodar and chilgoza can be found.

Sub-Alpine Forest

(n) **Sub-alpine Forest** It extends from Kashmir to Arunachal Pradesh between 2900 to 3500 metres. In the Western Himalayas, the vegetation consists mainly of juniper, *Rhododendron*, willow and black currant. In the Eastern parts, red fir, black juniper, birch and larch are the common trees. Due to heavy rainfall and high humidity the timberline in this part is higher than that in the West. *Rhododendron* of many species covers the hills in these parts.

Alpine Forest

(o) **Moist** These alpines are found all along the Himalayas and on the higher hills near the Myanmar border. It has a low scrub, dense evergreen forest, consisting mainly of *Rhododendron* and birch. Mosses and ferns cover the ground in patches. This region receives heavy snowfall.

(p) **Dry** These alpines are found from the about 3000 metres to about 4900 metres. Dwarf plants predominate, mainly the black juniper, the drooping juniper, honeysuckle and willow.

Flora in India

The wide range of climatic conditions helps boasts of its rich variety of vegetation. The vegetation comprises some 15000 species of plants. According to the distribution of the flora, India can be classified into Western Himalayas, Eastern Himalayas, Asom, Indus Plain, Ganga Plain, Deccan, Malabar and the Andamans.

The **Western Himalayan region** have chir pine and other conifers deodar, blue pine, spruce, silver fir and junipers. The **Eastern Himalayan region** consists of oaks, laurels, maples, rhododendrons, alder, birch and dwarf willow. The **Asom region** is full of evergreen forests with lots of bamboo and tall grasses. The **Indus** supports very scanty vegetation and the **Ganga Plain** is under the cultivation. The **Deccan region** is full of scrubs and mixed deciduous forests. The **Malabar region** is under commercial crops like coconut, betel, pepper, coffee and tea. **Andaman region** is plentiful in evergreen and mangrove forests. Some of the dominated species in different Forests types are :

(i) **Tropical wet evergreen forest** *Dipterocarpus, Hopea, Artocerpus, Mangifera, Emblica, Michelia, Ervatamia, Lagerstroemia, Ixora.*

(ii) **Tropical semi-evergreen forest** *Artocarpus, Michelia, Eugenia, Terminalie, Terameles* and *Shorea.*

(iii) **Tropical moist deciduous forest** It is well known teak and sal forests. In South India dominated species are *Terminalia, Grewia, Gariya, Salmalia, Tectona grandis, Adina cordifolia, Melia, Albizzia, Dalbergia,* etc. In Northern India dominated species is *Shorea robusta,* other associate of sal are *Terminalia tomentosa, Dillenia* sp., *Eugenia* sp., etc.

(iv) **Dry tropical deciduous forest** In Punjab and Western UP dominated species are *Anogeissus latifolia, Acacia catechu, Terminalia tomentosa;* other associated species are *Dendrocalamus strictus, Embelical officinalis, Woodfordia floribunda.* In South mixed forest of grass, shrubs are found, species include *Terminalia Anogeissus latifolia, Tectonea grandis, Diospyros melanoxylon, Boswellia* sp; shrubs are *Dendrocalamus, Bambusa, Lantana, Helicteris,* etc. some common grasses are *Panicum Andropogon* and *Heteropogon.*

(v) **Montane subtropical forests** Some common trees are *Eugenia, Actinodaphne, Canthium, Mangifera, Ficus;* some climbers are *Piper trichostachyon, Gnetum, Scandens, Smilax macrophylla.*

(vi) **Alpine forest** Sparsely grown plants are *Sedum, Primula, Saxifraga* and lichens, etc.

Grassland Ecosystem

Halfway between the equator and the poles are temperate regions where rich **grasslands** grow. Such grasslands are often highly productive when converted to agricultural use. Many of the rich agricultural lands in the United States and Southern Canada were originally occupied by **prairies,** the another name for temperate grasslands. Grasslands occupy a relatively small area (about 19% of Earth surface). The living organisms are of three categories namely producers (mainly grasses like *Cynodon, Digitaria, Desmodium, Dichanthium, Dactyloctenium, Setaria,* etc; and few srubs). Consumers (*i.e.,* primary secondary and tertiary) and the decomposers. The primary consumers are herbivores feeding on grass like cow, deers, rabbit and some insects as *Leptocorisa, Oxyrhachis, Cincinella,* some termites and millipedes. The secondary consumers are fox, jackels, snakes, frogs, birds feeding on herbivores. The tertiary consumers are hawks. The microbes for decaying of dead organic matters are fungi and some bacteria and Actinomycetes.

Aquatic Ecosystems

(Freshwater, Marine and Eustarine)

The two main types of aquatic ecosystems are **marine ecosystems** and **freshwater ecosystems.**

(i) **Freshwater ecosystems** cover 0.80% of the Earth's surface and inhabit 0.009% of its total water. They generate nearly 3% of its net primary production. Freshwater ecosystems contain 41% of the world's known fish species. There are three basic types of freshwater ecosystems:

(a) **Lentic** slow-moving water, including pools, ponds and lakes.

(b) **Lotic** rapidly-moving water, for example streams and rivers.

(c) **Wetlands** areas where the soil is saturated or inundated for atleast part of the time.

(ii) **Marine ecosystems** can be divided into the following zones: oceanic (the relatively shallow part of the ocean that lies over the continental shelf); profundal (bottom or deep water); benthic (bottom substrates); intertidal (the area between high and low tides); estuaries; salt marshes; coral reefs and hydrothermal vents (where chemosynthetic sulphur bacteria form the food base).

Lakes and Ponds

Lake ecosystems can be divided into zones: pelagic (open offshore waters), profundal, littoral (nearshore shallow waters), and riparian (the area of land bordering a body of water).

Kinds of Lakes

(a) Hutchinson (1957) classified lakes into:

The **dimictic lakes** exhibit two overturns every year, while **monomictic lakes** may be **cold monomictic** and **warm monomictic,** the former being characterized by a circulation only during summer, while the latter has a complete circulation in winter as well. Polymictic lakes present circulations throughout the year.

(b) Based on the humic acid contents the lakes of world have been classified into **clear water lakes** and **brown water lakes,** brown water contains high humus content.

(c) Clear water lakes may be divided into two types:

- **Oligotrophic type** whose water is poor in nutritive plant material and shows nearly equal distribution of oxygen during summer and winter months and whose mud bottom contains little organic material.

- **Eutrophic type** which is rich in nutrients. At greater depth below the thermocline in summer, eutrophic lakes show a considerable reduction in oxygen content and their mud bottom is composed of typical muck. Eutrophic lakes are polluted lakes and support the growth of the microorganisms.

Table 31.2 **Classification of Wetlands or Lentic Ecosystems**

A. Inland Freshwater Area	
Seasonally flooded	Soil covered with water or waterlogged during variable periods but well-drained during much of the growing season. In upland depressions and bottomlands. Bottomland hardwoods to herbaceous growth.
Freshwater meadows	Without standing water during growing season; water logged to within few inches of surface. Grasses, rushes, sedges and broadleaf plants.
Shallow freshwater marshes	Soil waterlogged during growing season; often covered with about 15 cm or more of water. Grasses, bulrushes, spike rushes, cattails, arrowhead, smartweed and pickerelweed. A major water-fowl-production area.
Deep freshwater marshes	Soil covered with 15 cm to 91 cm of water. Cattails, reeds, bulrushes, spike rushes, wild rice. Principal duck-breeding area.
Open freshwater marshes	Water less than 3 m deep. Bordered by emergent vegetation pondweed, naiads, wild celery, water lily. Brooding, feeding, nesting areas of ducks.
Shrub swamps	Soil waterlogged; often covered with 15 cm or more water. Alder, willow, buttonbush, dogwoods. Ducks nesting and feeding to limited extent.
Wooded swamps	Soil waterlogged; often covered with 30 cm of water. Along sluggish streams, flat uplands shallowlakes, basins. North of USA: tamarack, arborvitae, spruce, red maple, silver maple. South of USA water oak, overcup oak, tupelo, swamp black gum cypress.
Bogs	Soil waterlogged; spongy covering of mosses. Health Shrubs, *Sphagnum*, sedges.
B. Coastal Freshwater Areas	
Shallow freshwater marsh	Soil waterlogged during growing season; at high tides as much as 15 cm of water on landward side, deep marshes along tidal rivers, sounds, deltas. Grasses and sedges. Important water-flow areas.
Deep freshwater	At high tide covered with 15 cm to 1.8 m of water. Along tidal rivers and bays. Cattails, wild rice and giant cutgrass.
Open freshwater	Shallow portions of open water along fresh tidal rivers and sounds. Vegetation scarce or absent. Important water-flow areas.

*(Excluding Lakes and Ponds) (Smith; 1974)

Marine Ecosystem

The marine environment can be classified into **photic** zone in which phytoplankton, zooplankton and many fishes are found and an **aphotic zone** into which light does not penetrate. The **intertidal zone** is the shallow area along the shore while neritic zone is the shallow region over the continental shelf. The oceanic zone reaches great depths. Open water of any depth is the **pelagic zone** while the bottom surface of it is the **benthic zone.** The daily cycle of tickes exposes the shoreline to variations in water nutrients and temperature and to the mechanical force of wave action. Rocky intertidal communities are vertically stratified. Adverse array of algae, sea weeds invertebrates and fishes are usually present in intertidal zones. Coral reefs are found in tropical waters in neritic zone. These are produced by the calcium carbonate skeletons of coral and serve as a substrate for other corals sponges and algae. **Benthos** are communities that occupy the sea bottom of neritic and pelagic zones. Various invertebrate and fishes inhabit the **abyssal zone.**

Estuaries

Ecosystem where a freshwater river or stream meets the ocean. These e highly productive areas often bordered by wetlands called mudflats and saltmarshes. Salinity varies both spatially and daily with the rise and fall of tides. Saltmarsh grasses, algae and phytoplanktons are the major producers. These serve as feeding and breeding areas for marine invertebrate fishes and water fowl. These are equivalent to tropical rain forest and coral reefs as natural productive ecosystem. The macrophytes are *Thalassia, Spartina, Zostora,* etc., and large blooms of *Gymnodinium* and *Gonyaulax.* Planktons and neuktons are also found.

Biogeography

Biogeography is the science that documents and attempts to explain the patterns of distribution of populations, species and ecological communities across Earth. It explaining species' distributions as why a species is or is not found in a certain location:

1. If a species occupies a particular area, either it evolved there, or it evolved elsewhere and dispersed to the area.
2. If a species is not found in a particular area, either it evolved elsewhere and never dispersed to the area, or it was once present in the area but no longer lives there.

Major Terrestrial Biomes

On land, biomes are defined by vegetation type, and in water, they are defined by the physical characteristics of the environment. The biosphere can be divided into major **terrestrial** and **aquatic** life zones called biomes. **Terrestrial biomes** cover large geographic regions and are usually named for the dominant plants that live there. The distribution of biomes is strongly influenced by patterns of temperature and rainfall.

Tropical Evergreen Forest

Tropical evergreen forests are found in equatorial regions where total rainfall exceeds 250 cm annually and the dry season lasts no longer than 2 or 3 months. They are the richest of all biomes in number of species of both plants and animals. Along with their immense species richness, tropical evergreen forests have the highest overall productivity of all ecological communities.

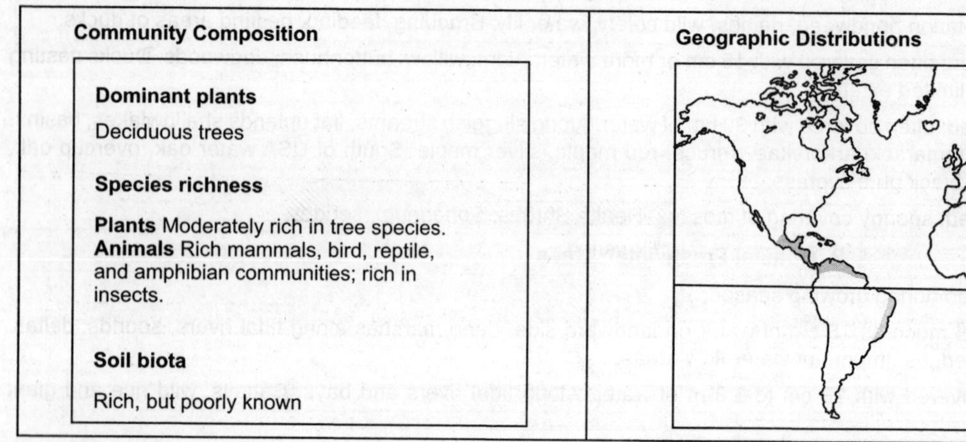

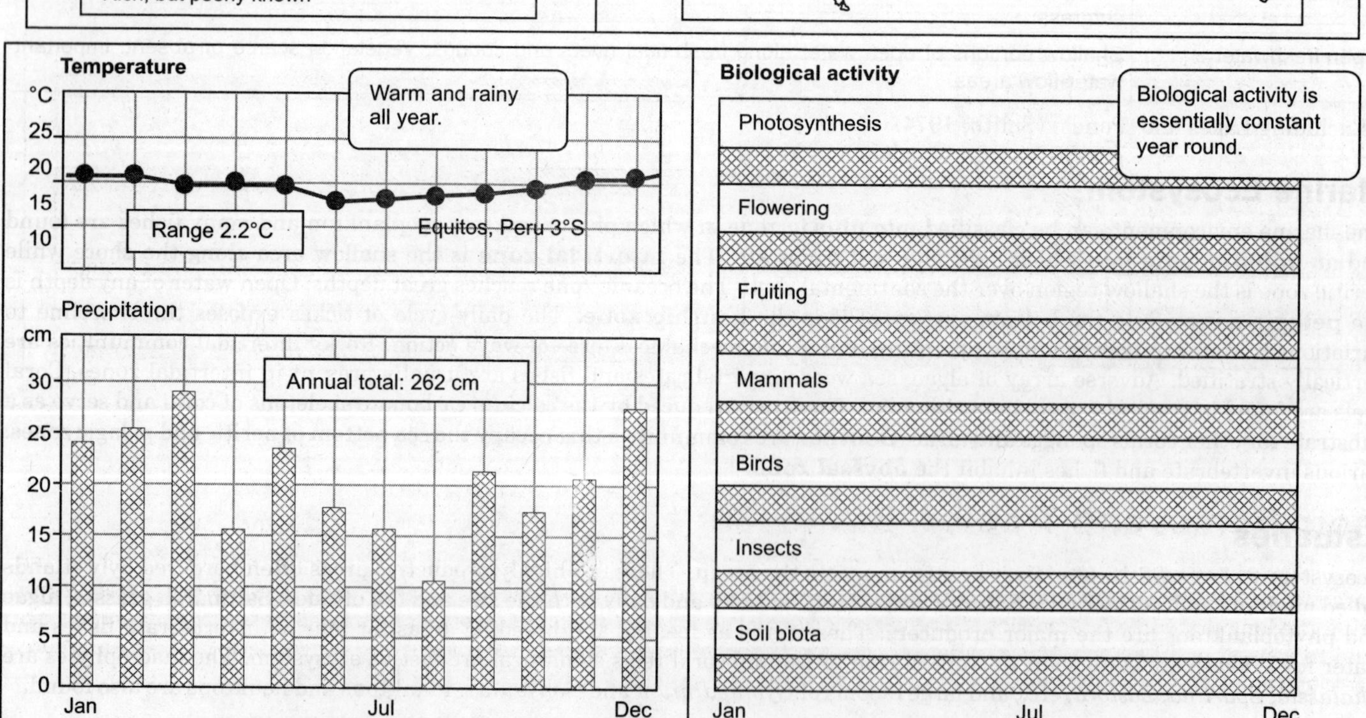

Fig. 31.17 Observation of various parameters in tropical evergreen forest

Tropical Deciduous Forest

As the length of the rainy season increases toward the equator, tropical deciduous forests replace thorn forests. Most of the trees, except for those growing along rivers, lose their leaves during the long, hot dry season. Many of them flower while they are leafless, and most species are pollinated by animals. During the hot rainy season, biological activity is intense.

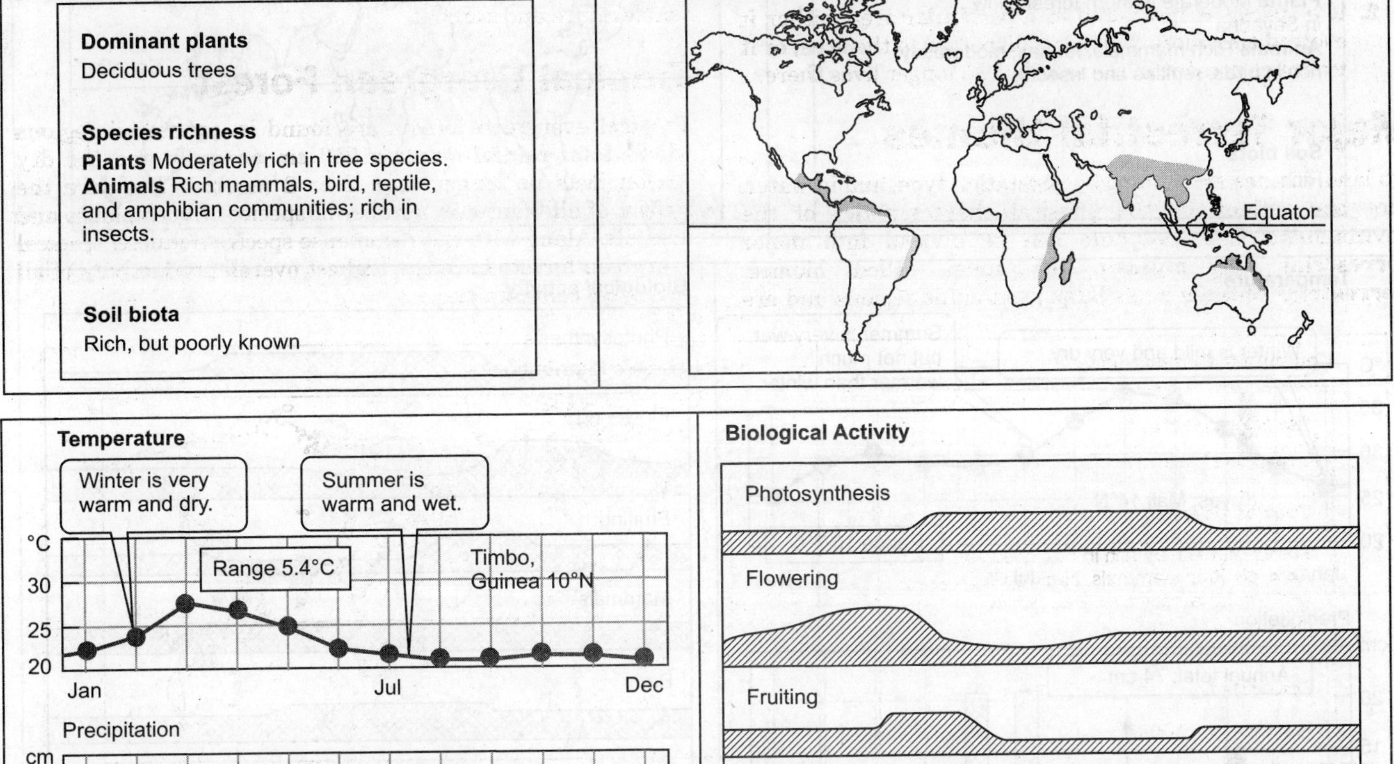

Fig. 31.18 Observation of various parameters in tropical deciduous forest

Thorn Forest and Tropical Savannah

Thorn forests are found on the equatorial sides of hot deserts. The climate is semiarid; little or no rain falls during winter, but rainfall may be heavy during summer. The dominant plants are spiny shrubs and small trees, many of which drop their leaves during the long dry winter. Members of the genus *Acacia* are common in thorn forests worldwide. The largest savannahs are found in central and Eastern Africa, where the biome supports huge numbers of grazing and browsing mammals and many large carnivores that prey on them.

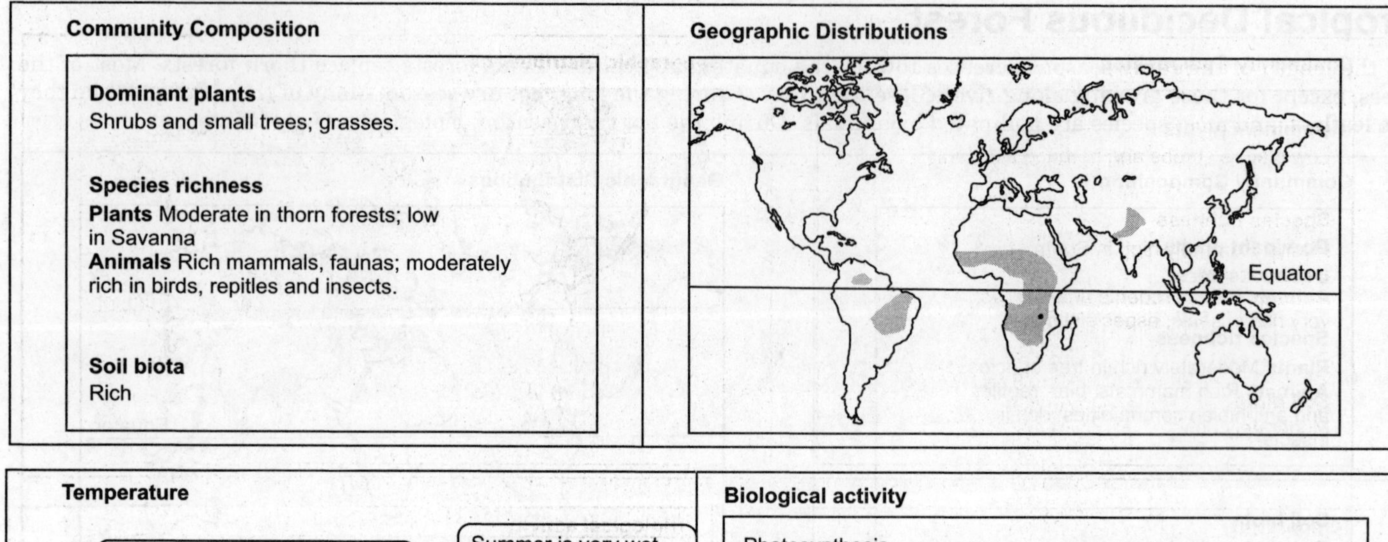

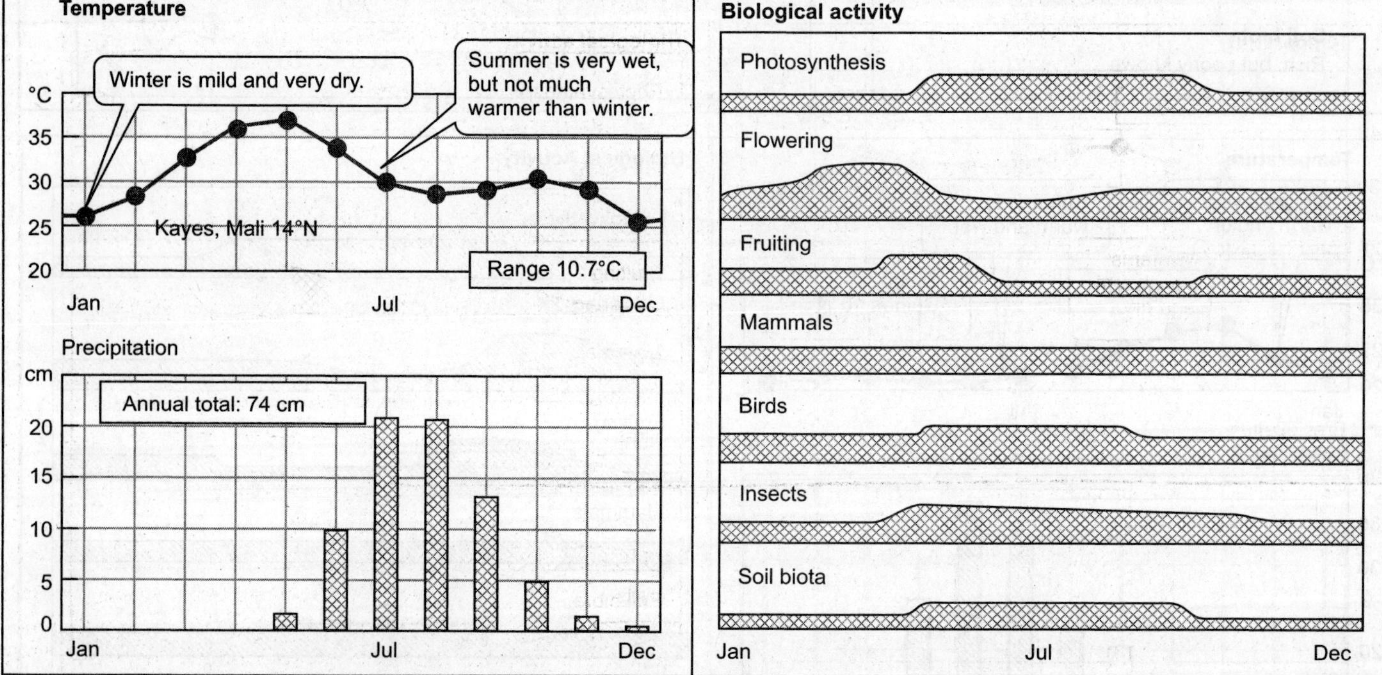

Fig. 31.19 Annual variation observation in thorn forest and tropical savannah

Hot Desert

Hot deserts receive most of their rainfall in summer, but they also receive winter rains from storms that form over the mid-latitude oceans. The driest large regions, where summer and winter rains rarely penetrate, are in the center of Australia and the middle of the Sahara Desert of Africa. Except in these driest regions, hot deserts have richer and structurally more diverse vegetation than cold deserts. Succulent plants that store large quantities of water in their expandable stems are conspicuous in some hot deserts. Pollination and dispersal of fruits by animals are common. Rodents, termites and ants are often remarkably abundant and lizards and snakes typically are rich in species and abundant.

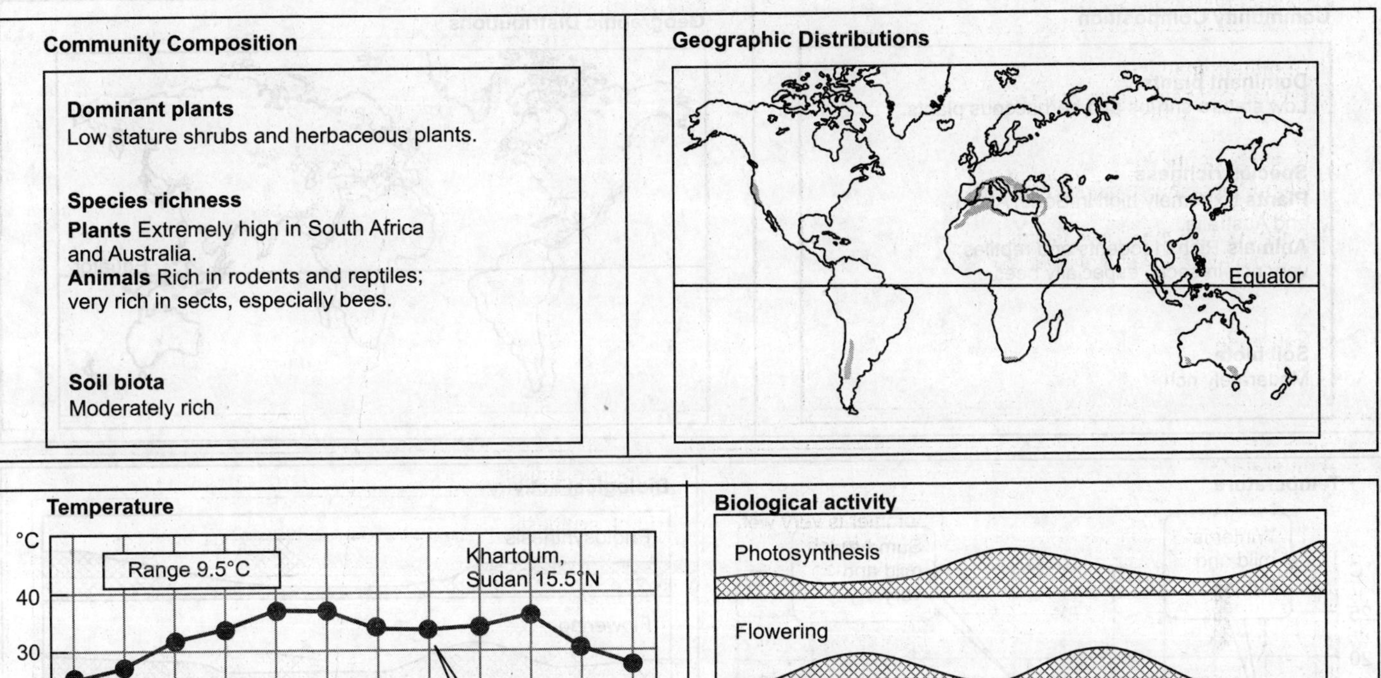

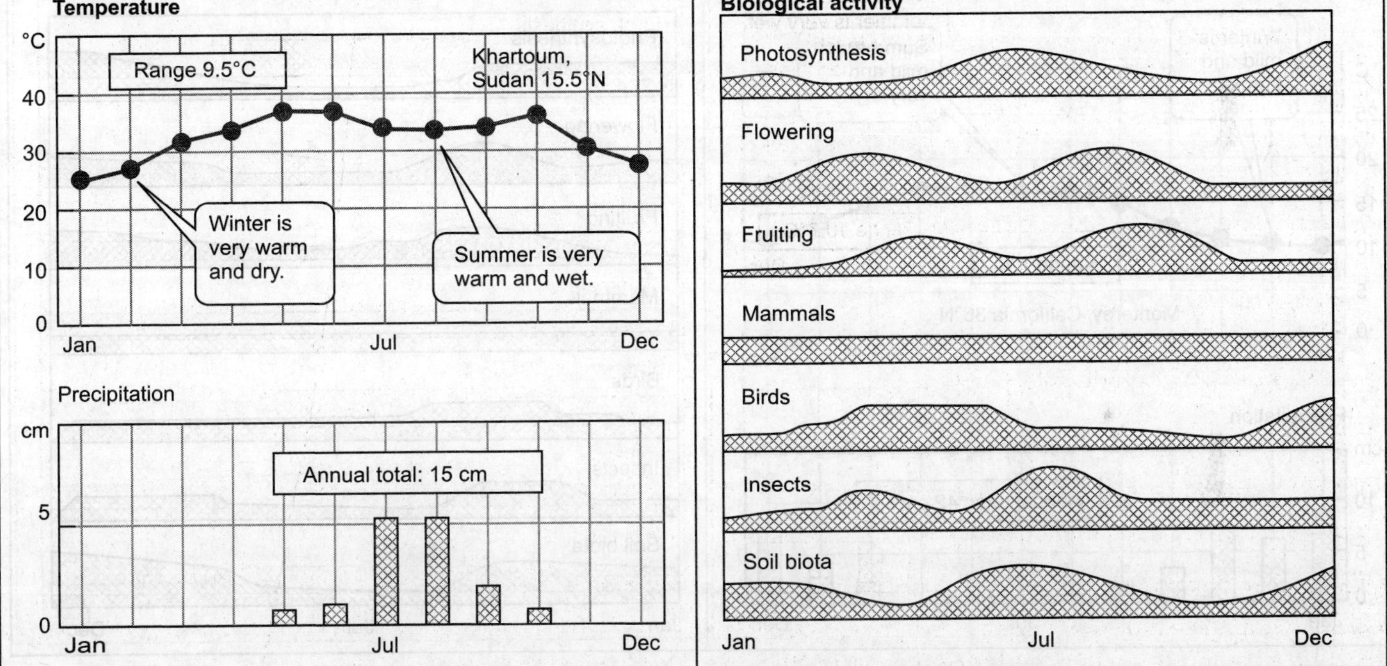

Fig. 31.20 Annual variation observation in not desert

Chaparral

The chaparral biome is found on the west sides of continents at moderate latitudes (around 30°), where cool ocean waters flow offshore. The dominant plants of chaparral vegetation are low growing shrubs and trees with tough, evergreen leaves. The shrubs carry out most of their growth and photosynthesis in early spring, when insects are active and birds breed. Annual plants are abundant and produce copious seeds that fall onto the soil. This biome thus supports large populations of small rodents, most of which store seeds in underground burrows.

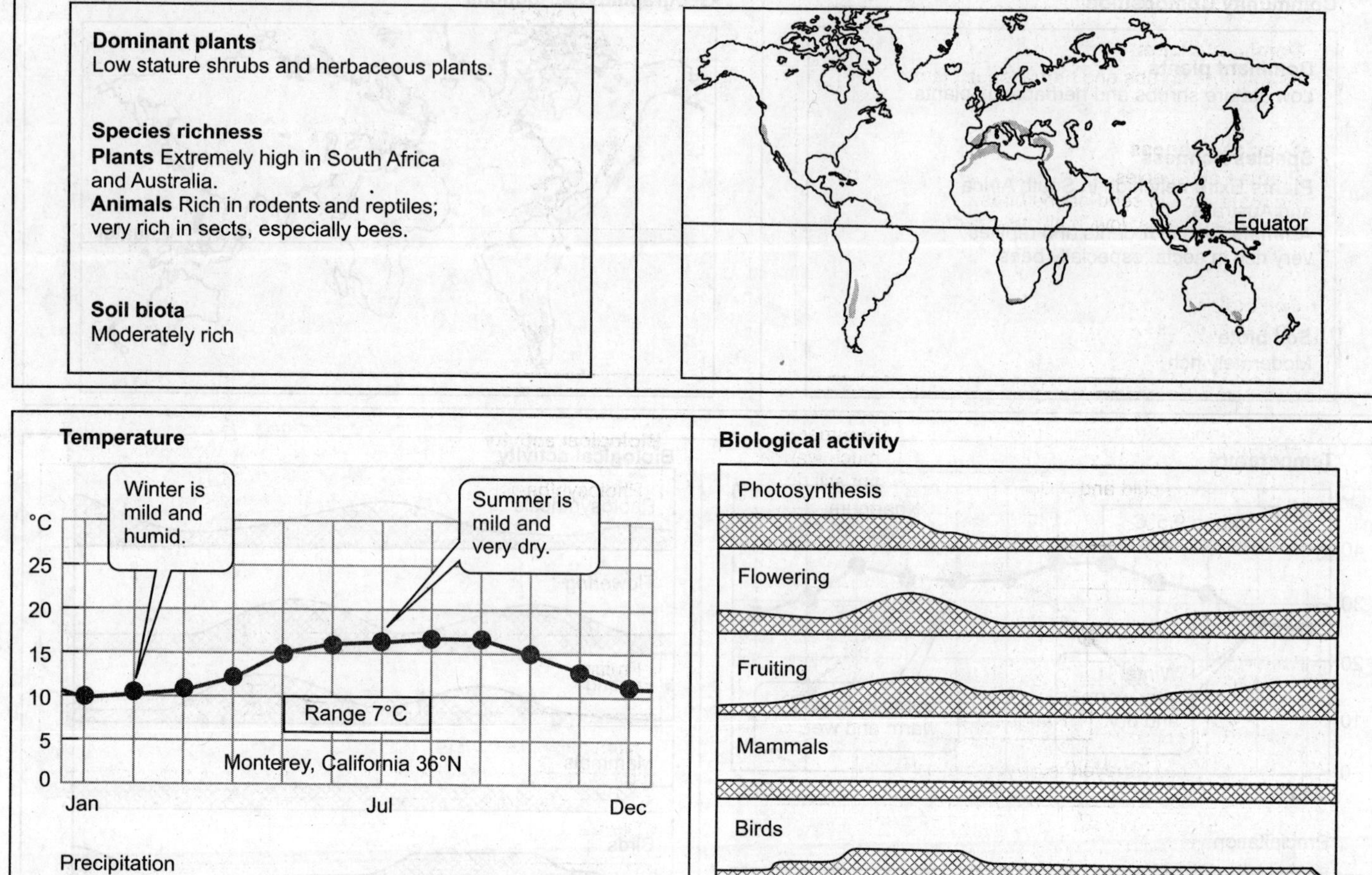

Fig. 31.21 Various parameters at Chaparral

Cold Desert

The cold desert biome is found in dry regions at middle to high latitudes, especially in the interiors of large continents in the rain shadows of mountain ranges. Seasonal changes in temperature are great. Cold deserts are dominated by a few species of low-growing shrubs. Cold deserts are relatively poor in species of most taxonomic groups, but the plants of this biome tend to produce large numbers of seeds, supporting a rich fauna of seed-eating birds, ants and rodents.

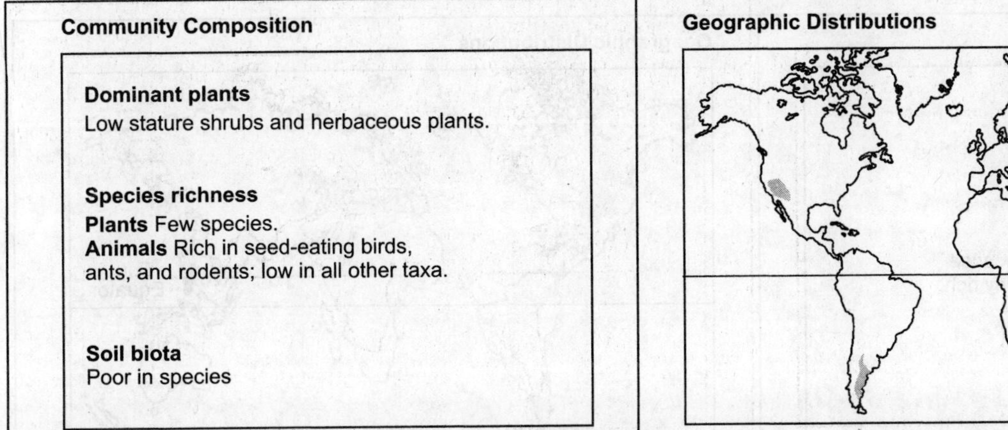

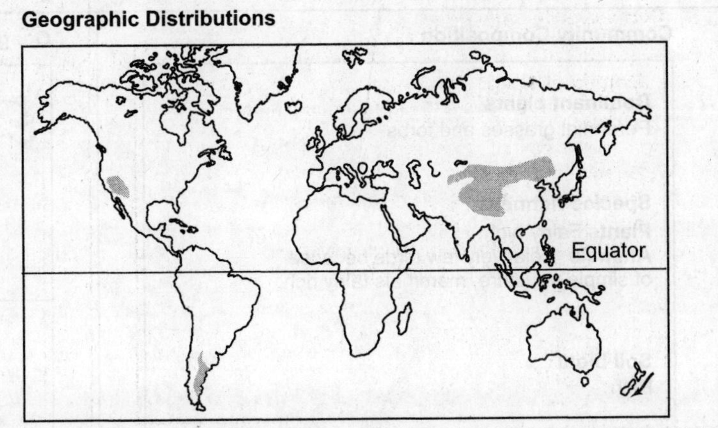

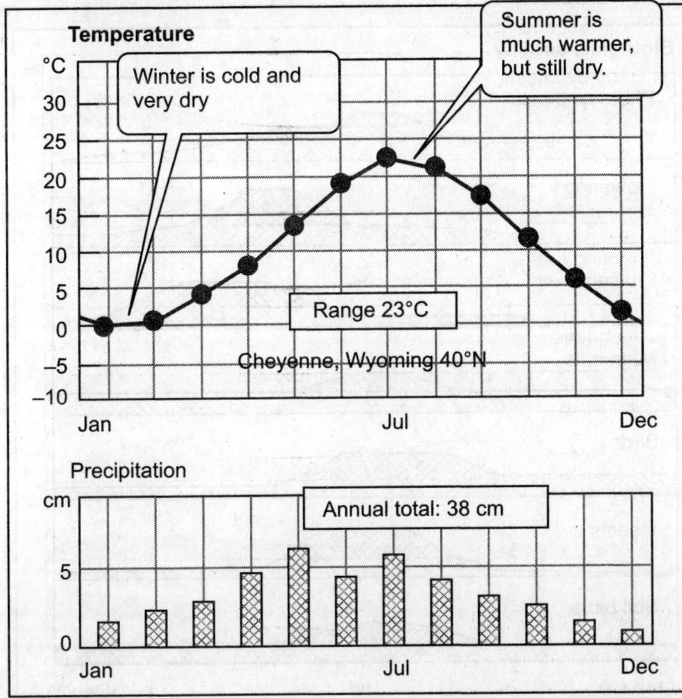

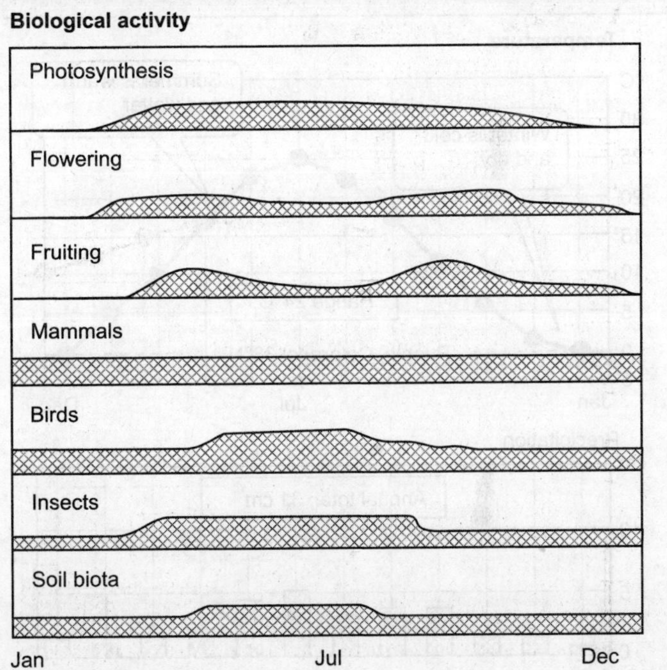

Fig. 31.22 Parameters observed annualy at cold desert

Temperate Grassland

The temperate grassland biome is found in many parts of the world, all of which are relatively dry for much of the year. Most grasslands, such as the **pampas** of Argentina, the **veldt** of South Africa, and the Great Plains of North America, have hot summers and relatively cold winters. In some grasslands, most of the precipitation falls in winter (California grasslands); in others, the majority falls in summer (Great Plains, Russian steppe).

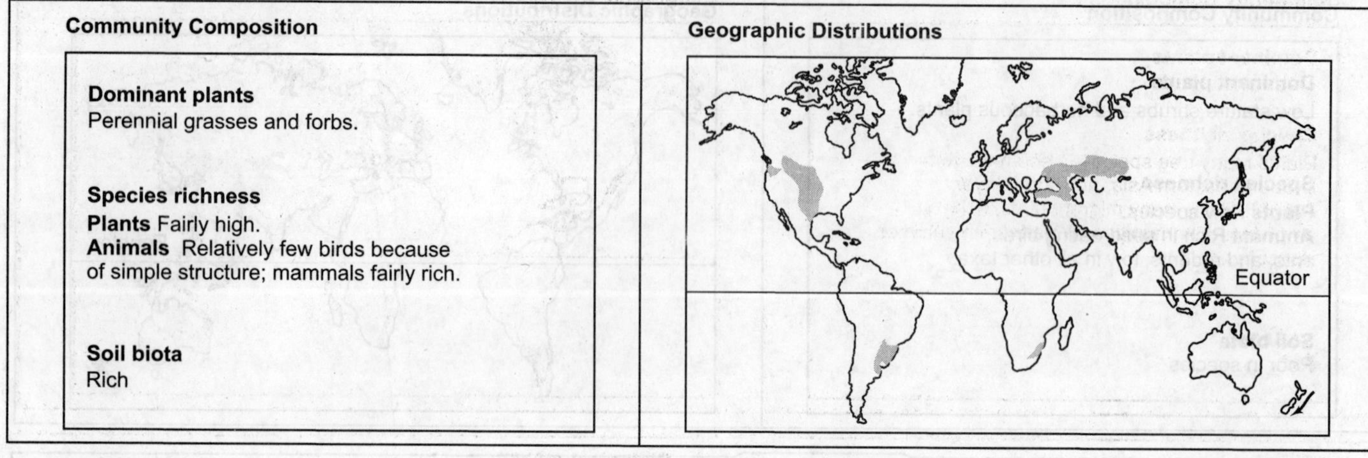

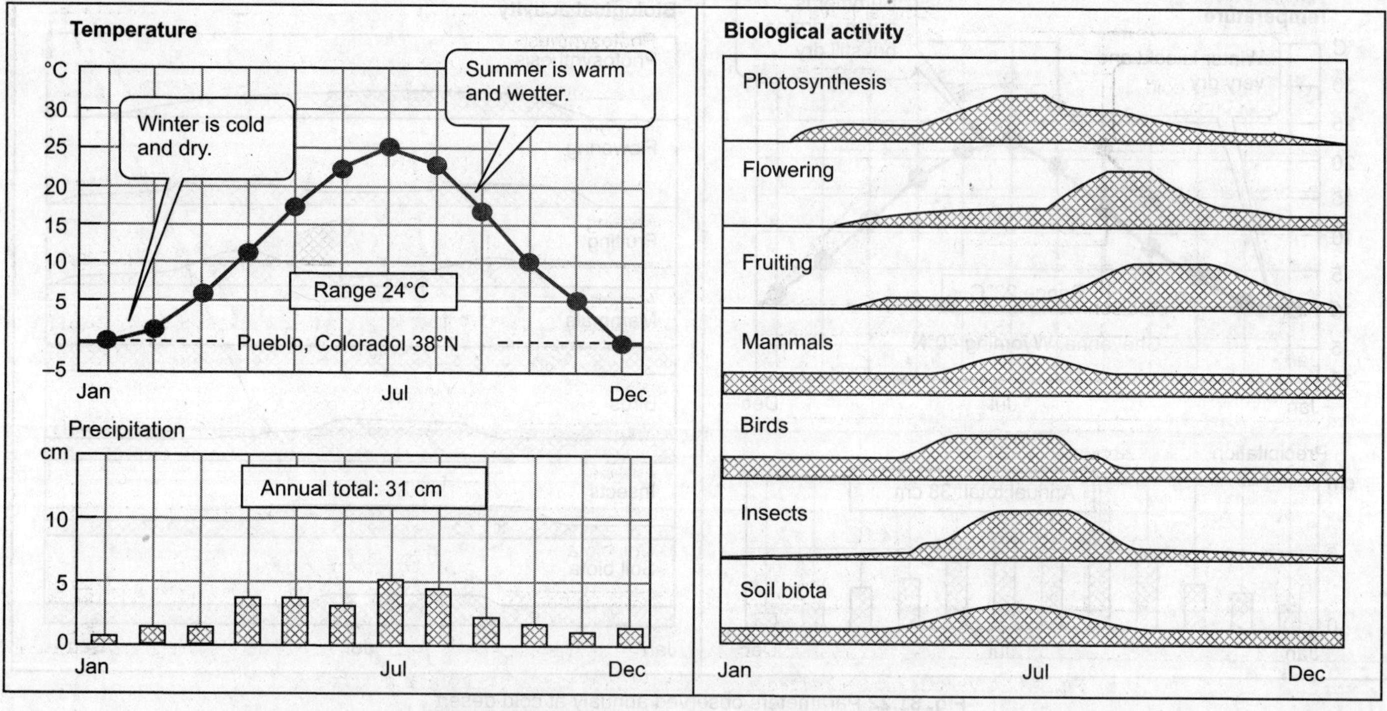

Fig. 31.23 Annual observation at temperate grassland

Temperate Deciduous Forest

The temperate deciduous forest biome is found in Eastern-North America, Eastern Asia and Europe. Deciduous trees, which dominate these forests, lose their leaves during the cold winters and produce leaves that photosynthesize rapidly during the warm, moist summers. Many more tree species live here than in boreal forests. Many genera of plants and animals are shared among the three geographically separate decidious forest biomes.

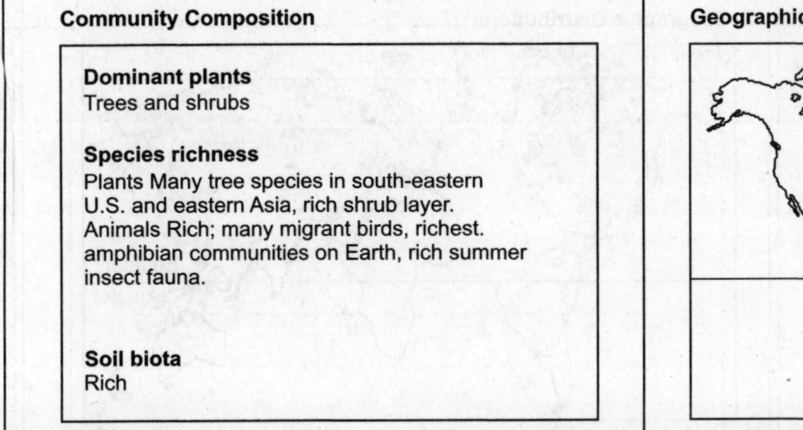

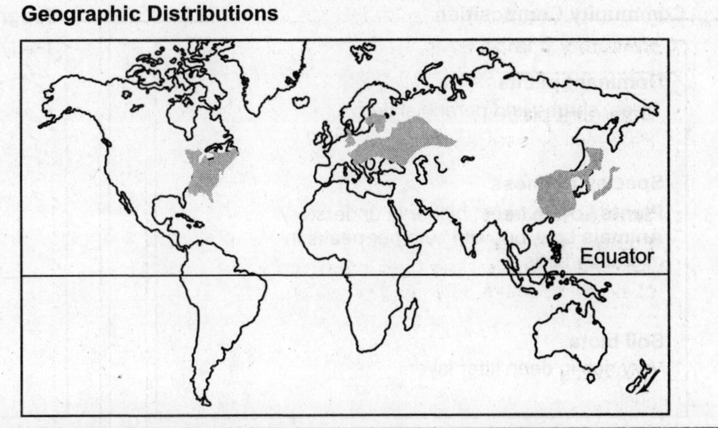

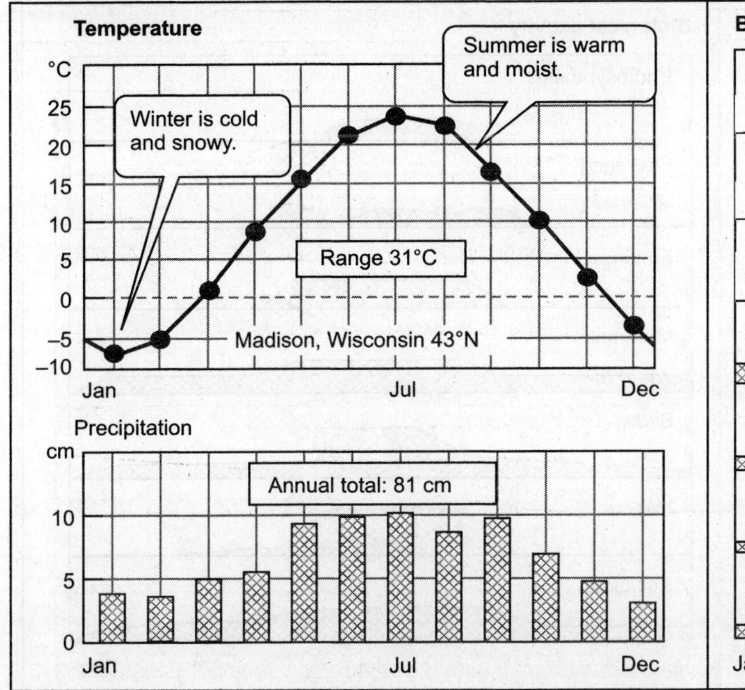

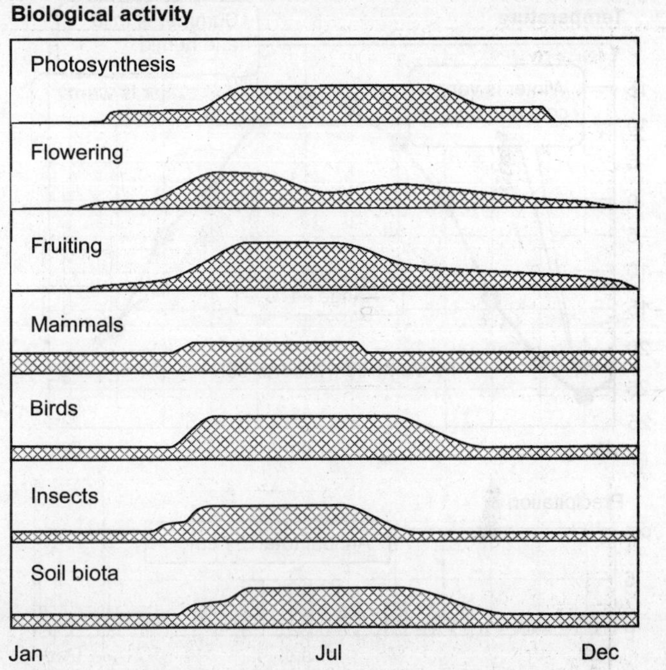

Fig. 31.24 Various annual parameters observation in temperate deciduous forest

Boreal Forest

The boreal forests of the Northern hemisphere are dominated by evergreen coniferous gymnosperms. In the Southern Hemisphere the dominant trees are Southern beeches (*Nothofagus*), some of which are evergreen. These forests are home to Earth's tallest trees. Boreal forests have only a few tree species. The dominant animals (moose and hares) eat leaves. The seeds in the cones of conifers support a fauna of rodents and birds.

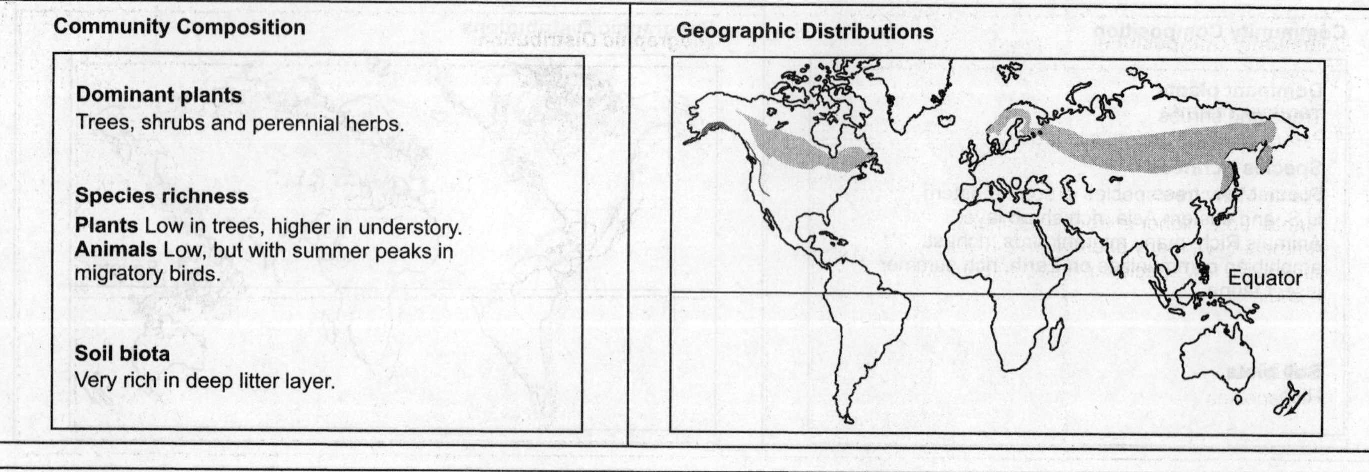

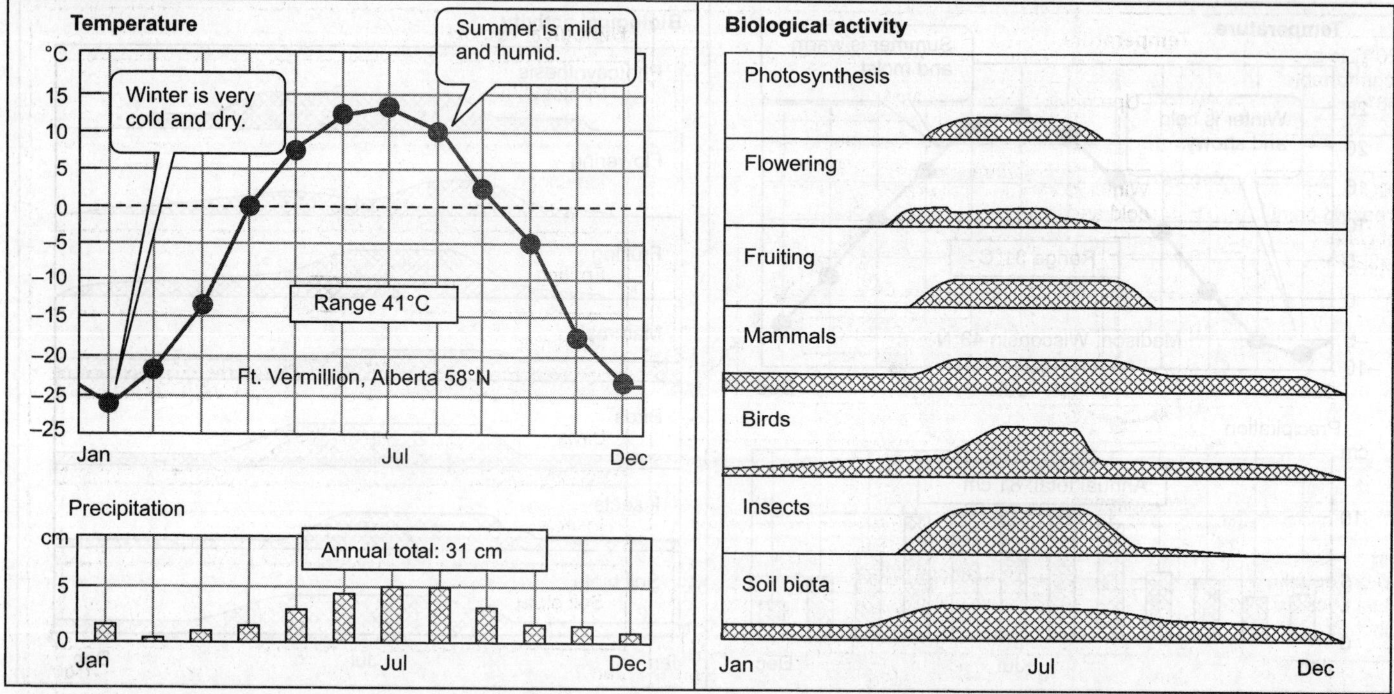

Fig. 31.25 Various annual parameter observation in boreal forest

Arctic Tundra

The **tundra** biome is found in the **Arctic** and high in mountains at all latitudes. **Arctic** tundra vegetation, which consists of short perennial plants, is underlain by permafrost soil whose water is permanently frozen.

Plants grow for only a few months each year. Most **Arctic** tundra animals either migrate into the area only for the summer or are dormant for most of the year. Photosynthesis and most other biological activities continue (albeit slowly) throughout the entire year.

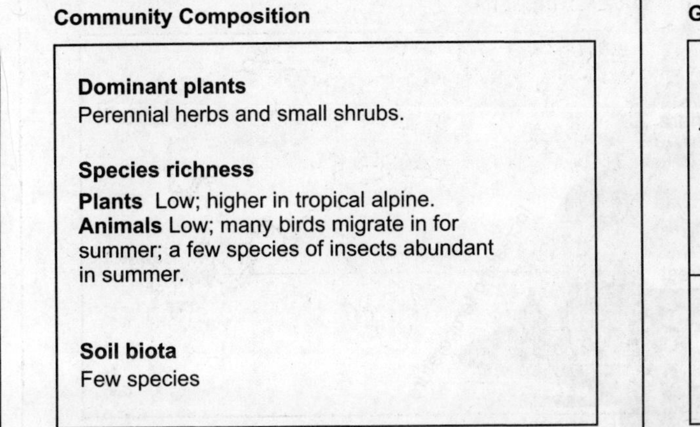

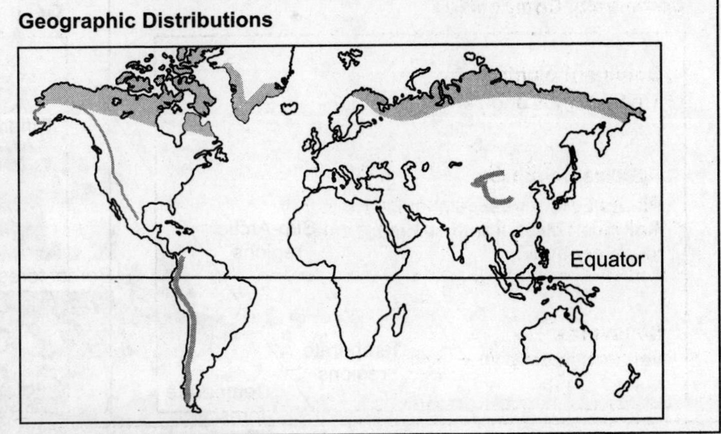

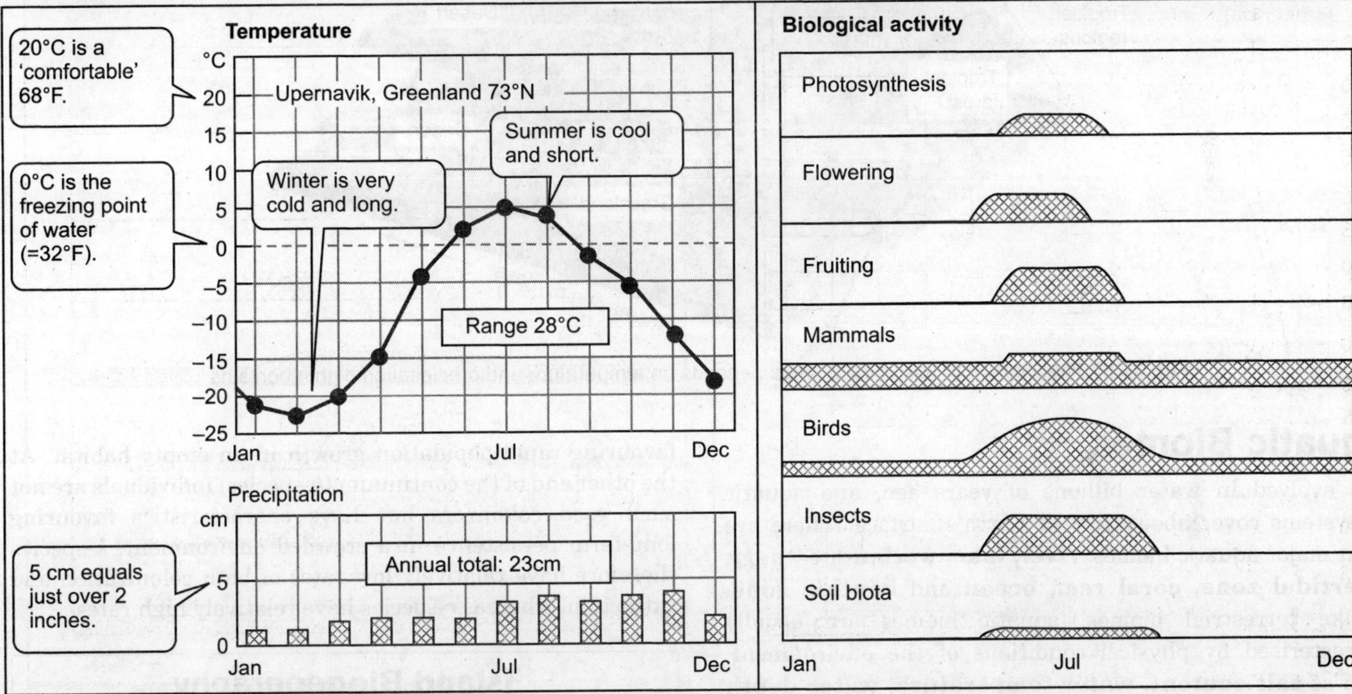

Fig. 31.26 Annual parameters observed at Arctic tundra

Climate is the single most important factor controlling the potential or natural location of terrestrial biomes. The climate of a region—most importantly, the temperature and the amount and timing of precipitation—allows some species to thrive and prevents other species from living there.

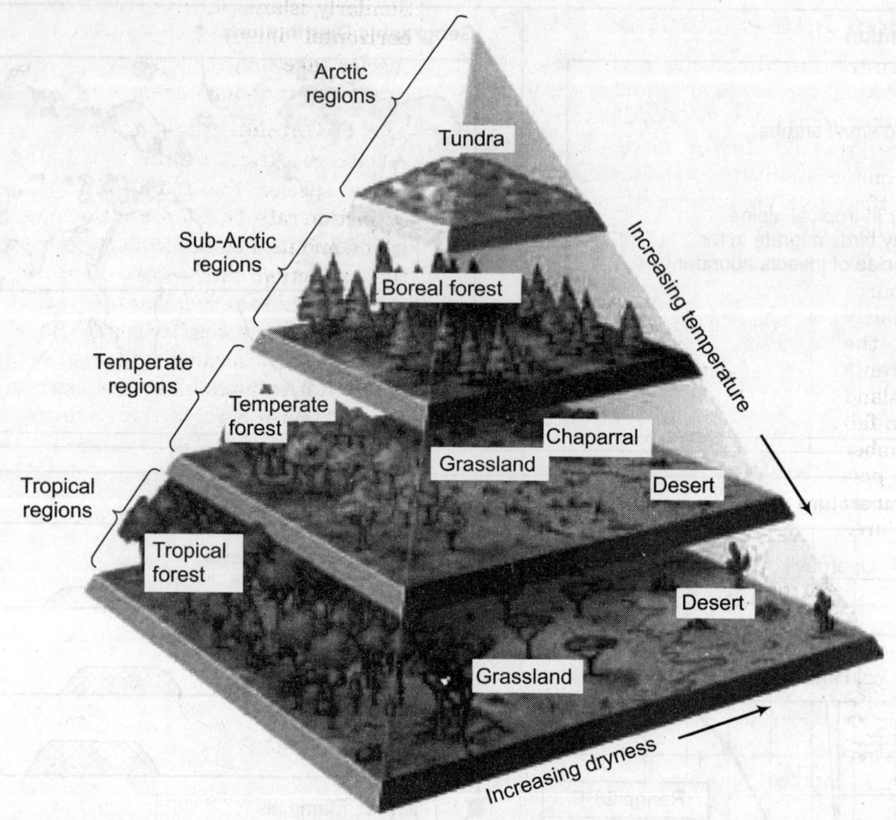

Fig. 31.27 The location of terrestrial biomes depends on temperature and precipitation high mountains

Aquatic Biomes

Life evolved in water billions of years ago, and aquatic ecosystems cover about 75% of Earth's surface. There are eight major aquatic biomes: **river, lake, wetland, estuary, intertidal zone, coral reef, ocean** and **benthic zone**. Unlike terrestrial biomes, aquatic biomes are usually characterized by physical conditions of the environment, such as **salt content, water temperature, water depth** and the **speed of water flow**.

Theory of Island Biogeography

The classic book, The Theory of Island Biogeography by **MacArthur** and **Wilson** (1967), was an important catalyst in radically changing ecological theory in general. The authors developed their ideas in the context of the dynamics of the animals and plants on real (maritime) islands, which they interpreted as reflecting a balance between the opposing forces of extinctions and colonizations. They emphasized that some species (or local populations) spend most of their time either recovering from past crashes or in phases of invasion of new territories (islands), while others spend much of their time at or around their carrying capacity. These two ends of a continuum are the *r* and *k*-species. At one extreme (*r*-species), individuals are good colonizers and have characteristics favouring rapid population growth in an empty habitat. At the other end of the continuum (*k*-species) individuals are not such good colonizers but have characteristics favouring long-term persistence in a crowded environment. *k*-species therefore have relatively low rates of both colonization and extinction, whereas *r*-species have relatively high rates.

Island Biogeography

It is a field within biogeography that attempts to establish and explain the factors that affect the species richness of natural communities. Robert MacArthur and Edward O Wilson coined the term 'Theory of Island Biogeography' as this theory attempted to predict the number of species that would exist on newly created island.Two eminent ecologist, the late Robert MacArthur of Princeton University and Edward O Wilson of Harvard developed a theory of 'Island Biogeography' to explain uneven distribution of species. **The two main predictions of Island Biogeography are:**

- Islands close to a source area should have a higher number of species than islands further from the source area for islands of equivalent areas.
- Larger islands should have more species than smaller islands for islands located at similar distances from the source area.

These two predictions have been largely supported by observational and experimental data.

The Immigration and Extinction Curve

The Immigration Curve In the theory's simplest form species from the source area disperse to an island at a rate (**the immigration curve**) depending on the distance of the island from the source area. The **fewer** species are on the island, the higher the immigration curve. The more species on the island, the lower the curve because most potential new immigrant species will have already reached the island.

The immigration curve for islands close to the source area should be fairly vertical because the potential immigrants should reach the island fairly rapidly and then fall off sharply as the number of potential new immigrant species from the source area **decreases.**

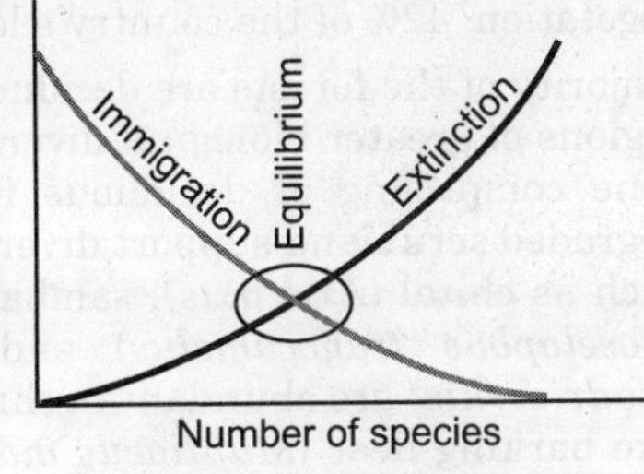

Fig. 31.28 Immigration and extinction curve

Similarly, islands far from the source area should have a more horizontal immigration curve because new immigrating species take longer to get to far away islands than to those closer into the source area.

The Extinction Curve Similarly there is a rate at which species go extinct on the island (the extinction curve). The **more** species there are on the island, the **higher** the extinction rate.The slopes of the lines depend on the size of the island and its distance from the source area. For a small island the extinction rate should increase more rapidly (the line should be more vertical) as the number of species on the island increase because smaller islands have fewer potential habitats and resources to colonize. Larger islands should have a more horizontal extinction rate (relative to the number of species already there) because there are more potential habitats and resources to use. The **slope** of the **extinction curve,** therefore, depends on the size of the island.

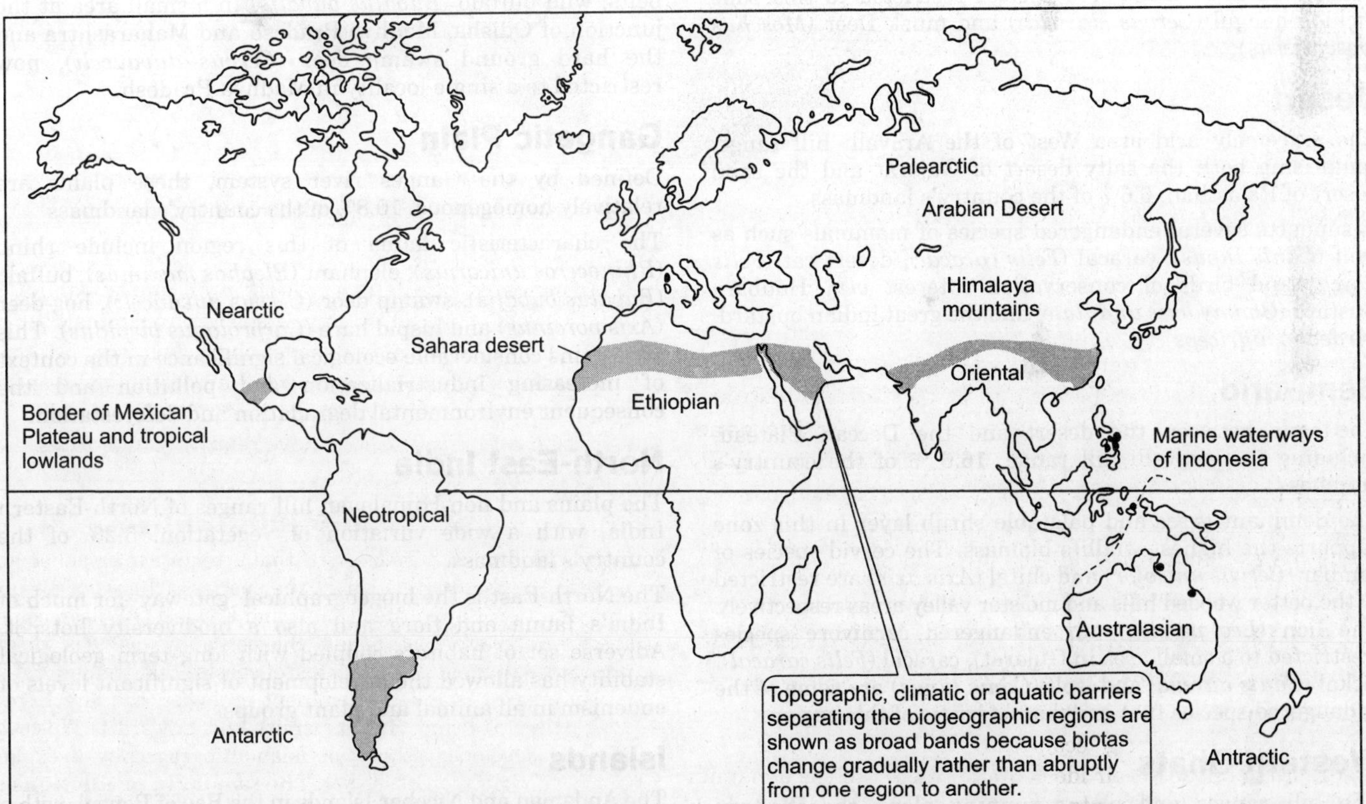

Fig. 31.29 Major Biogeographic Regions The flora and fauna of Earth's major biogeographic regions differ strikingly from one another

Biogeographical Zones of India

Biogeographically, India is situated at the tri junction of three realms namely afrotropical, Indo-Malayan and Paleo-Arctic realms and therefore, has characteristic elements from each of them. This assemblage of three distinct realms probably is a fact which is believed to partly account for its rich and unique in biological diversity. The country has 10 different biogeographic zones and 26 biotic provinces. The Biogeographic classification of India (Rodgers and Pawar 1990). They can be classified as under:

Trans-Himalayas

An extension of the Tibetan Plateau, harbouring high-altitude cold desert in Laddakh (J&K) and Lahaul Spiti (HP) comprising 5.6 % of the country's landmass.

This zone has sparse alpine steppe vegetation that harbours several endemic species and is a favourable habitat for the biggest populations of wild sheep and goat in the world and other rare fauna that includes snow leopard (*Uncia uncia*) and the migratory blacknecked crane (*Grus nigricollis*). The cold dry desert of this zone represents an extremely fragile ecosystem.

Himalayas

The entire mountain chain running from North-Western to North-Eastern India, comprising a diverse range of biotic provinces and biomes, 6.4 % of the country's landmass.

The alpine and sub-alpine forests, grassy meadows and moist mixed deciduous forests provide diverse habitat for endangered species of bovids such as bharal (*Pseudois nayaur*), ibex (*Capra ibex*), markhor (*Capra falconeri*), tahr (*Hemitragus jemlabicus*) and Takin (*Budoreas taxicolor*). Other rare and endangered species restricted to this zone include hangul (*Cervus eldi eldi*) and musk Deer (*Moschus moschiferus*).

Desert

The extremely arid area West of the Aravalli hill range, comprising both the salty desert of Gujarat and the sand desert of Rajasthan. 6.6% of the country's landmass.

It supports several endangered species of mammals such as wolf (*Canis lupus*), caracal (*Felis caracal*), desert cat (*Felis libyca*) and birds of conservation interest *viz.*, Houbara Bustard (*Chamydotis undulate*) and the great indian bustard (*Ardeotis nigriceps*).

Semi-arid

The zone between the desert and the Deccan Plateau, including the Aravalli hill range. 16.6 % of the country's landmass.

The dominant grass and palatable shrub layer in this zone supports the highest wildlife biomass. The cervid species of sambar (*Cervus unicolor*) and chital (*Axis axis*) are restricted to the better wooded hills and moister valley areas respectively. The lion (*Leo persica*), an endangered carnivore species (restricted to a small area in Gujarat), caracal (*Felis caracal*), jackal (*Canis aureus*) and wolf (*Canis lupus*) are some of the endangered species that are characteristic of this region.

Western Ghats

The hill ranges and plains running along the Western coastline, South of the Tapti river, covering an extremely diverse range of biotic provinces and biomes. 4% of the country's landmass.

This zone represents one of the biodiversity 'hot spots' with some 15000 species of higher plants, of which 4000 (27 per cent) are endemic to the region. Significant species endemic to this region include nilgiri langur (*Presbytis jobni*), lion tailed macaque (*Macaca silenus*), grizzled giant squirrel (*Ratufa macroura*), malabar civet (*Viverricula megaspila*), Nilgiri Tahr (*Hemitragus bylocrius*) and Malabar grey hornbill (*Ocycerous griseus*). The travancore tortoise (*Indotestudo forstem*) and cane turtle (*Heosemys silvatica*) are two endangered taxa restricted to a small area in central Western Ghats.

Deccan Peninsula

The largest of the zones, covering much of the Southern and South Central Plateau with a predominantly deciduous vegetation. 42% of the country's landmass.

Majority of the forests are deciduous in nature but there are regions of greater biological diversity in the hill ranges. The zone comprising of deciduous forests, thorn forests and degraded scrubland support diverse wildlife species. Species such as chital (*Axis axis*), sambar (*Cervus unicolor*), nilgai (*Boselapbus tragocamelus*) and chousingha (*Tetracerus quadricornis*) are abundant in this zone. Some other species like barking deer (*Muntiacus muntjak*) and gaur (*Antilope cervicapra*) are more frequent in, or are restricted to moister areas, but are still found in fairly large numbers. Species with small populations include the Elephant (*Elephas maximus*) in Bihar, Odisha and Karnataka, Tamil Nadu belts, wild buffalo (*Bubalus bubalis*) in a small area at the junction of Odisha, Madhya Pradesh and Maharashtra and the hard ground swamp deer (*Cervus duvauceli*), now restricted to a single locality in Madhya Pradesh.

Gangetic Plain

Defined by the Ganges river system, these plains are relatively homogenous. 10.8% of the country's landmass.

The characteristic fauna of this region include rhino (*Rhinoceros unicornis*), elephant (*Elephas maximus*), buffalo (*Bubalus bubalis*), swamp deer (*Cervus duvauceli*), hog-deer (*Axis porcinus*) and hispid hare (*Carprolagus bispidus*). This zone gains considerable ecological significance in the context of increasing industrialization and pollution and the consequent environmental degradation and deforestation.

North-East India

The plains and non-Himalayan hill ranges of North-Eastern India, with a wide variation of vegetation. 5.2% of the country's landmass.

The North-East is the biogeographical 'gateway' for much of India's fauna and flora and also a biodiversity hotspot. Adiverse set of habitats coupled with long term geological stability has allowed the development of significant levels of endenism in all animal and plant groups.

Islands

The Andaman and Nicobar Islands in the Bay of Bengal, with a highly diverse set of biomes. 0.03% of the country's landmass.

Coasts

A large coastline distributed both to the West and East, constituting 2.5 per cent of the total geographical area with sandy beaches, mangroves, mud flats, coral reefs and marine angiosperm pastures make them the wealth and health zones of India. Lakshadweep islands virtually have no natural vegetation.

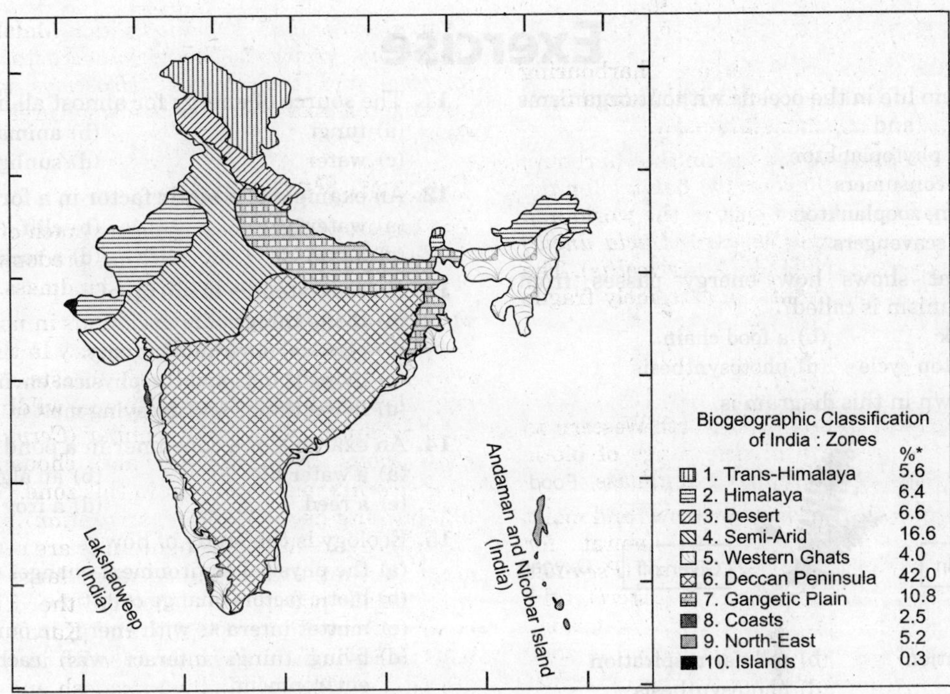

Fig. 31.30 Biogeographical zones of India

Table 31.3 **Biogeographic Zones of India**

Biogeographical Zones	Biogeographic Provinces	% of Geographical Area of India
Trans-Himalaya	Himalaya–Ladakh Mountains	3.3
	Himalaya–Tibetan Plateau	2.2
	Trans–Himalaya Sikkim	< 0.1
The Himalaya	Himalaya–North-West Himalaya	2.1
	Himalaya–West Himalaya	1.6
	Himalaya–Central Himalaya	0.2
	Himalaya–East Himalaya	2.5
The Indian Desert	Desert–Thar	5.4
	Desert–Katchchh	1.1
The Semi Arid	Semi–Arid–Punjab Plains	3.7
	Semi–Arid–Gujarat Rajputana	12.9
The Western Ghats	Western Ghats–Malabar Plains	2.0
	Western Ghats–Western Ghats Mountains	2.0
The Deccan Peninsula	Deccan Peninsular–Central Highlands	7.3
	Deccan Peninsular–Chotta Nagpur	5.4
	Deccan Peninsular–Eastern Highlands	6.3
	Deccan Peninsular–Central Plateau	12.5
	Deccan Peninsular–Deccan South	10.4
The Gangetic Plains	Gangetic Plain–Upper Gangetic Plains	6.3
	Gangetic Plain–Lower Gangetic Plains	4.5
The Coasts	Coasts–West Coast	0.6
	Coasts–East Coast	1.9
	Coasts–Lakshdweep	< 0.1
Northeast India	North-East–Brahamputra Valley	2.0
	North-East-North-East Hills	3.2
Islands	Islands-Andamans	0.2
	Islands-Nicobars	0.1

Source: Wildlife Institute of India, 2009

Exercise

1. There would be no life in the oceans without organisms called .... and ....
(a) decomposers; phytoplankton
(b) zooplankton; consumers
(c) phytoplankton; zooplankton
(d) zooplankton; scavengers

2. One model that shows how energy passes from organism to organism is called?
(a) an energy link (b) a food chain
(c) a phytoplankton cycle (d) photosynthesis

3. The process shown in this diagram is

Energy (sunlight)
Water + Carbon dioxide
Taken in
Given off
Food + Oxygen

(a) waste elimination (b) cellular respiration
(c) a food chain (d) photosynthesis

4. What do ecologists call the transfer of energy that begins with the sun and passes from one organism to the next in a food chain?
(a) A food web (b) A top consumer
(c) Energy flow (d) A pyramid of numbers

5. The amount of carbon in the environment
(a) does not change
(b) is converted to heat and lost to the abiotic environment
(c) is called the carbon cycle
(d) immediately converts to carbon dioxide

6. The way in which carbon is used and reused through the ecosystem is called
(a) energy recycling (b) the energy pyramid
(c) the carbon cycle (d) the biotic/abiotic cycle

7. When any substance is added to the environment faster than it can be broken down, stored or converted to a non-harmful form, it is called
(a) transpiration (b) concentration
(c) particle suspension (d) pollution

8. In a food chain, the organisms most affected by bioaccumulation are
(a) top consumers (b) producers
(c) phytoplankton (d) parasites

9. Which list of terms is in the correct order, from simplest to most complex?
(a) Organism, community, population, ecosystem, biome
(b) Organism, population, community, biome, ecosystem
(c) Organism, population, community, ecosystem, biome
(d) Organism, community, ecosystem, population, biome

10. The natural world that surrounds an organism is called the organism's
(a) energy (b) environment
(c) lodgings (d) nutrients

11. The source of energy for almost all life on Earth is
(a) fungi (b) animals
(c) water (d) sunlight

12. An example of a biotic factor in a forest ecosystem is
(a) waterfall (b) cliff
(c) a tree (d) a rock

13. An ecosystem is made up of
(a) living things only
(b) physical environment only
(c) living things and the physical environment
(d) living things and decaying matter

14. An example of a consumer in a pond ecosystem is
(a) a water lily (b) an algae
(c) a reed (d) a frog

15. Ecology is the study of how
(a) the physical environment changes over time
(b) biotic factors change over time
(c) matter interacts with energy in our environment
(d) living things interact with each other and their environment

16. An example of a biotic factor in a pond ecosystem is
(a) temperature (b) water
(c) fish (d) sunlight

17. An example of a producer is a
(a) fungus (b) caterpillar
(c) bird (d) moss

18. Both consumers and producers are a source of food for
(a) scavengers (b) decomposers
(c) carnivores (d) herbivores

19. In an energy pyramid, the lowest level has
(a) less energy than the top level
(b) less energy than the second level
(c) more energy than the top level
(d) the same amount of energy as the second level

20. A scientist who studies the interactions of plants and animals is called
(a) a physicist (b) a botanist
(c) a geologist (d) an ecologist

21. Two abiotic factors that affect an ecosystem are
(a) temperature and animals
(b) plants and animals
(c) water and bacteria
(d) soil and water

22. A caterpillar eats a leaf and a bird eats the caterpillar. In this interaction, the bird is a
(a) producer
(b) herbivore
(c) primary consumer
(d) secondary consumer

23. A population of rabbits is at its carrying capacity when the population
(a) reproduces (b) becomes extinct
(c) stops growing (d) can't survive

24. A crab lives on a beach where it gets food, shelter and space to live. The beach is the crab's
(a) niche (b) community
(c) habitat (d) home

25. An animal that eats only plants is a
(a) primary consumer (b) secondary consumer
(c) tertiary consumer (d) primary producer

26. An example of a biotic factor is
(a) soil (b) a rock
(c) water (d) a tree

27. An .... is made up of both living things and the physical environment.
(a) ecosystem (b) habitat
(c) niche (d) None of these

28. Living things in an ecosystem are .... factors.
(a) abiotic (b) physical
(c) limiting (d) biotic

29. Which of the statement is incorrect?
(a) The amount of light available in an ecosystem affects the types and amount of plant life that will grow there
(b) In a species, the organisms' offspring must be able to breed
(c) An ecosystem is composed of biotic factors
(d) The same niche in a habitat may be occupied by more than one species

30. Events that take place in a biome are shown in the diagram below. Which information formation is represented in the diagram?

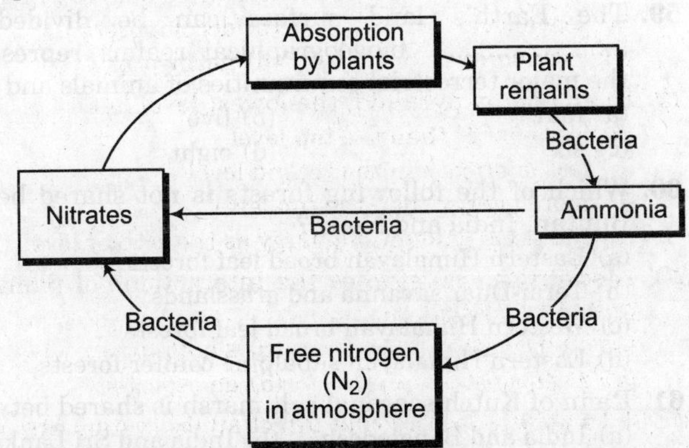

(a) Respiration and photosynthesis are interrelated
(b) Transpiration and condensation are related to the water cycle
(c) Decomposers release a material that is acted on by other organisms
(d) Predators and their prey are involved in many interactions

31. A pyramid of biomass is a representation of the
(a) amount of mass contained in biomass at different trophic levels for a particular time
(b) amount of energy contained in biomass at different trophic levels for a particular time
(c) number of individual contained in biomass at different trophic levels for a particular time
(d) type of energy contained in biomass at different trophic levels for a particular time

32. An aquatic ecosystem is an ecosystem in
(a) land (b) water bodies
(c) space (d) mountain

33. The main types of aquatic ecosystems are
(a) marine ecosystem (b) freshwater ecosystem
(c) Both (a) and (b) (d) None of these

34. Marine ecosystems cover approximately .... of the Earth's surface and contain approximately .... of the planet's water.
(a) 57%; 97% (b) 71%; 57%
(c) 97%; 57% (d) 71%; 97%

35. In the marine ecosystems the zone of bottom or deep water is known as
(a) oceanic (b) profoundal
(c) benthic (d) intertidal

36. Ecological pyramid
(a) graphically represent the trophic structure and function
(b) based on rate of energy flow is always upright
(c) producer always occupy the base of pyramid
(d) All of the above

37. The greatest amount of free energy is available at which of the following levels?
(a) Tertiary consumers (b) Secondary consumers
(c) Decomposes (d) Producers

38. Ecologists generally separate organisms in an ecosystem into three categories (producer, consumer and decomposer) based on
(a) how they obtain their energy
(b) how rapid their metabolism is
(c) the rate of succession in the ecosystem
(d) the size and complexity of the ecosystem

39. Which of the following is not recycled in an ecosystem?
(a) Water (b) Carbon
(c) Energy (d) Nitrogen

40. Which of the following is not a character of *r*-selected species?
(a) Small adult size
(b) Long generation time
(c) A high allocation to reproduction
(d) Maximum population growth

41. Parthenium is
(a) a *k*-selected species (b) an *r*-selected species
(c) None of these (d) Both (a) and (b)

42. Which of the following is not generally a feature of shifting cultivation?
(a) Relatively small field
(b) Slash and burn forest clearing
(c) Regular pesticide application
(d) Local consumption of crops

43. Biogeography deals with the
(a) geomatrical distribution of plants and animals
(b) geographical distribution of plants and animals
(c) arithmetic distribution of plants and animals
(d) None of the above

44. Phyto-geography (plant geography) deals with .... of plants.
(a) origin
(b) distribution
(c) environmental interrelationships
(d) origin, distribution and environmental interrelationships

45. Zoogeography deals with the
(a) migration of animals (b) feeding habit of animals
(c) distribution of animals (d) Both (a) and (c)

46. How many biogeographic zones can be distinguished clearly in India?
(a) 4 (b) 7
(c) 10 (d) 23

47. Which of the following biomes is correctly paired with the description of its climate?
(a) Savanna-cool temperature, precipitation, uniform during the year
(b) Tundra-long summers, mild winters
(c) Temperate deciduous forest relatively short growing season, mild winters
(d) Tropical forests nearly constant photoperiod and temperature

48. Which of the following is not a biogeographic zone?
(a) Himalayan zone (b) Gulf of Mannar
(c) Western ghat zone (d) Deccan plateau zone

49. Which of the statement does not constitute the principles of the theory of island biogeography?
(a) It proposes that the number of species found on an undisturbed island is determined by immigration and extinction
(b) The isolated populations may follow different evolutionary routes
(c) Immigration and emigration are not affected by the distance of an island from a source of colonists, *e.g.*, mainland
(d) Islands that are more isolated are less likely to receive immigrants than islands that are less isolated

50. As per the theory of island biogeography larger islands contain .... habitat areas and opportunities for more different varieties of habitat while Larger habitat ....size the probability of extinction due to chance events. In simple words habitat heterogeneity .... the number of species that will be successful after immigration.
(a) larger; reduces; increases
(b) smaller; reduces; increases
(c) larger; increases; decreases
(d) larger; increases, increases

51. The theory of Island Biogeography found its application in
(a) Conservation Biolog. (b) Comparative Anatomy
(c) Paleontology (d) Ethonology

52. Indian sub-continent is also known as
(a) East Asia (b) South Asia
(c) North Asia (d) West Asia

53. Indian sub-continent is a region on the
(a) Indian tectonic plate (b) Australian tectonic plate
(c) Japanese tectonic plate (d) Russian tectonic plate

54. According to the booklet published by the United States Department of State in 1959, which of the following country is not a part of 'Sub-continent of South Asia'?
(a) Tazikistan (b) Ceylon
(c) India (d) Pakistan

55. Which of the following ecozones is known as oriental realm among biogeographers?
(a) Australacia ecozone (b) Afrotropic ecozone
(c) Oceania ecozone (d) Indomalaya ecozone

56. Which of the fact confirm that Gondwanian elements were first introduced by India and Southern portion of India was made by the continental drift of ancient Pangea?
(a) Making of Himalayan
(b) Finding of cichlid fish and the flowering plant families like Crypteroniaceae
(c) Both of (a) and (b)
(d) None of the above

57. The WWF has identified .... terrestrial ecoregions across the Earth's land surface, as well as freshwater and marine ecoregions.
(a) 212 (b) 662
(c) 867 (d) 1023

58. Conservationists interested in preserving biodiversity have generally focused on the preservation of ....
(a) temperate rain forest
(b) tropical rain forest
(c) sub temperate rain forest
(d) mediterranean forests

59. The Earth's land surface can be divided into .... biogeographical realms representing the major terrestrial communities of animals and plants
(a) four (b) five
(c) six (d) eight

60. Which of the following forests is not shared between Bhutan, India and Nepal?
(a) Eastern Himalayan broad leaf forests
(b) Terai-Duar savanna and grasslands
(c) Western Himalayan broad leaf forests
(d) Eastern Himalayan subalpine conifer forests

61. Rann of Kutch seasonal salt marsh is shared between
(a) India and Bangladesh (b) India and Sri Lanka
(c) India and Pakistan (d) India and Bhutan

62. Which of the following is not a type of ecozone?
(a) Nearctic (b) Palearctic
(c) Neotropic (d) Endolithic

63. Which of the following is not a characteristic of a biome?
(a) It is the those ecosystem of the Earth which are facing more or less the same kind of abiotic and biotic factors spread over a large area
(b) Biomes are defined by genetic, taxonomic or historical similarities
(c) Biomes are often identified with particular patterns of ecological succession and climax vegetation
(d) Biome is a major habitat type and it is a compromise, as it has an intrinsic in homogeneity

64. The biodiversity characteristic of fauna and sub-dominant plant forms, is a function of .... factors and the biomass productivity of the vegetation.
(a) abiotic, dominant (b) biotic, dominant
(c) abiotic, inferior (d) biotic, inferior

65. In terrestrial biomes, species diversity tends to correlate positively with
(a) net primary productivity (b) moisture availability
(c) temperature (d) All of these

66. Climate is a major factor determining the distribution of terrestrial biomes. Among the following which climatic factor is important?
(a) Latitude (b) Humidity
(c) Elevation (d) All of these

67. Biodiversity generally .... away from the poles towards the equator and .... with humidity
(a) increases; increases (b) decreases; increases
(c) increases; decreases (d) decreases; decreases

68. In the terrestrial realms how many main ecoclines are possible according to Whittaker's classification?
(a) 2 (b) 4
(c) 6 (d) 8

69. Which of the following is an example of anthropogenic biome?
(a) Freshwater (b) Grasslands
(c) Rainforests (d) Croplands

70. Productivity in terrestrial ecosystems is affected by
(a) temperature (b) light intensity
(c) availability of nutrients (d) All of these

71. Secondary productivity
(a) is measured by the standing crop
(b) is the rate of biomass production in consumers
(c) is 10 percent less than primary productivity
(d) is the gross primary productivity minus the energy used for respiration

72. Which of these processes is incorrectly paired with its description?
(a) Nitrification–oxidation of ammonium in the soil to nitrate and nitrate
(b) Nitrogen fixation–reduction of atmospheric nitrogen into ammonia
(c) Denitrification–removal of nitrogen from organic compounds
(d) Ammonification–decomposition of organic compounds into ammonia

73. The ecological time scale of phosphorus cycling involves
(a) the uptake of phosphate from drinking water
(b) the weathering of rock to add PO_4^{3-} to the soil
(c) sedimentation to form rocks in the sea bed
(d) the incorporation of phosphorus into organisms that become fossils

74. Which of the following is incorrectly paired with its description?
(a) Neritic zone–shallow area over continental shelf
(b) Abyssal zone–benthic region where light does not penetrate
(c) Littoral zone–area of open water
(d) Intertidal zone–shallow area at edge of water

75. Many plant species have adaptations for dealing with the periodic fires typical of a
(a) chaparral
(b) temperate grassland
(c) temperate deciduous forest
(d) All of the above

76. Primary productivity
(a) is equal to the standing crop of an ecosystem
(b) is greatest in freshwater ecosystems
(c) is the rate of conversion of light to chemical energy in an ecosystem
(d) is inverted in some aquatic ecosystems

77. The open ocean and tropical rain forest are the two largest contributors to Earth's net primary productivity because
(a) both have high rates of net primary productivity
(b) both cover large surface areas of the Earth
(c) nutrients cycle fastest in these two ecosystems
(d) the ocean covers a large surface area and the tropical rain forest has a high rate of productivity

78. In an ecosystem,
(a) energy is recycled through the trophic structure
(b) energy is usually captured from sunlight by primary producers, passed to secondary producers in the form of organic compounds, and lost to decomposers in the form of heat
(c) chemicals are recycled between the biotic and abiotic sectors, whereas energy makes a one-way trip through the food web
(d) there is a continuous process by which energy is lost as heat, and chemical elements leave the ecosystem through runoff

79. Upwellings in the ocean
(a) are locations of reef communities
(b) occur over deep-sea hydrothermal vents
(c) are responsible for ocean currents
(d) bring nutrients rich water to the surface

80. In India, temperate evergreen vegetation occurs mostly in
(a) Rajasthan and South Punjab
(b) Eastern and Western Himalayas less than 3500 m
(c) Western Himalayas above 3500 m
(d) Western Ghats and Asom

81. The most striking difference between tropical rain forest and temperate forest is that
(a) The tropical rain forests have preponderance of angiosperms while the temperate one have preponderance of gymnosperms
(b) The trees of temperate forests are taller than those of tropical rain forests
(c) Plants of temperate forests are comparatively more mesophytic
(d) Tropical forests are comparatively more homogeneous

82. Photic or euphotic zone is how much deep from the upper surface of sea
(a) 10 m (b) 100 m
(c) 200 m (d) 500 m

83. Dense evergreen vegetation of broad sclerophyllous leaves and shrubs with fire resistant resisnous plants is known as
(a) chapparral vegetation (b) savanna vegetation
(c) steppe grassland (d) tundra vegetation

84. The number of trophic levels in a food chain is limited to 4 or 5 because
(a) the amount of food produced by producer is limited
(b) consumer's demand is high
(c) 90% of the food is lost as heat at each transfer between trophic levels
(d) activity of decomposer is poor

85. The hypersaline waters are found in
(a) lakes located in the alpine regions
(b) lakes located in the arid and semiarid regions
(c) lakes located in the tropical regions
(d) estuaries

86. Abyssal zone of oceans is characterized by
(a) presence of sunlight and producers
(b) absence of sunlight and all living organisms
(c) absence of sunlight but presence of producers
(d) absence of sunlight and presence of consumers and decomposers

87. Suppose you wanted to establish a self-sustaining ecosystem by sealing some sterlized soil, water and air in a glass container with a few organisms. You would be most likely to succeed with which of the following?
(a) Aphids, bacteria and spiders
(b) Bacteria and ants
(c) Clover, bacteria and grasshoppers
(d) Beetles, fungi and bacteria

88. Which of the following describes the climatic conditions characteristic of the coniferous forest?
(a) Mild with occasional drought and fires
(b) Cold and snowy
(c) Hot or cold but always rainy
(d) Cold and dry

89. Bacteria are especially important in
(a) the water cycle (b) the nitrogen cycle
(c) ecological succession (d) the phosphorus cycle

90. The biggest difference between the flow of energy and the flow of chemical nutrients in an ecosystem is
(a) the amount of energy is much greater than the amount of nutrients
(b) energy is recycled, but nutrients are not
(c) organisms always need nutrients, but they don't always need energy
(d) nutrients are recycled, but energy is not

91. Why is a diagram of energy flow from trophic level to trophic level shaped like a pyramid?
(a) Organisms at each level store most of the energy and pass little on
(b) There are more producers than primary consumers and so on
(c) Organisms eventually die as they get older
(d) Most energy at each level is lost, leaving litle for the next

92. Which of the following occurs in areas a bit too warm for coniferous forest and a bit too dry for temperate forest?
(a) Desert
(b) Tropical thorn forest
(c) Temperate grassland
(d) Chaparral

93. Which of the following is dominated by plants that drop their leaves yearly to conserve water?
(a) Desert
(b) Coniferous forest
(c) Tropical rain forest
(d) Temperate deciduous forest

94. Which of the following might eat phytoplankton?
(a) Great white shark (b) Beaver
(c) Seal (d) Shrimp

95. Which of the following is not true of a pyramid of productivity?
(a) Only about 10 percent of the energy in one trophic level is passed into the next level
(b) Because of the loss of energy at each trophic level, most food chains are limited to three to five steps
(c) The pyramids of productivity of some aquatic ecosystems is inverted because of the large zooplankton primary consumer level
(d) Eating grain-fed beef is an inefficient means of obtaining the energy trapped by photosynthesis

96. Which of the following statements regarding the maintenance of carbon cycle in the biosphere are correct?
I. Plants utilize solar energy to convert CO_2 and water into cellular materials and produce oxygen that animals consume.
II. Oxygen produced by the plants during carbon assimilation is not a by-product.
III. Energy used by animal comes from the oxidation of plant material releasing CO_2 and water
IV. All decaying organic matter on the Earth is ultimately degraded by moulds and bacteria to yield CO_2 that escapes into the atmosphere.

Select the correct answer using the codes given below:

Codes
(a) II, III and IV (b) I, III and IV
(c) I and II (d) I, II, III and IV

97. What is the correct sequence of the microorganisms involved in the decomposition of plant residues in the terrestrial ecosystems?
I. Actinomycetes
II. Spore producing bacteria
III. Mould fungi and non-spore producing bacteria
IV. Cellulose myxobacteria

Select the correct answer using the codes given below:

Codes
(a) III, II, IV and I
(b) III, II, I and IV
(c) II, III, I and IV
(d) II, III, IV and I

98. Match list I and list II and select the correct answer using the codes given below the lists.

List I	List II
A. The amount of energy accumulation in green plants through the process of photosynthesis	1. Gross primary productivity
B. The total organic matter synthesized by the producers in the process of photosynthesis per unit time and area	2. Primary productivity
C. Rate of storage of organic matter in plant tissues in excess of the respiratory utilization during the measurement period	3. Secondary productivity
D. Rate of energy storage at consumer level	4. Net primary productivity

Codes

	A	B	C	D
(a)	1	2	3	4
(b)	2	1	3	4
(c)	1	3	4	2
(d)	2	1	4	3

99. Match list I and list II and select the correct answer using the codes given below the lists.

List I (Type of Rain Fall)	List II (Type of Vegetation)
A. Moderate to heavy rainfall throughout the year	1. Scrub forests
B. Moderate to heavy rainfall occurring in 7 to 8 months in a year	2. Grasslands
C. Little summer precipitation but sufficient rainfall in the winter	3. Evergreen rain forests
D. Sufficient rainfall in summer and little in winter	4. Deciduous forests

Codes

	A	B	C	D
(a)	2	4	3	1
(b)	3	1	4	2
(c)	2	3	1	4
(d)	3	4	1	2

100. Barring the Himalayan region India can be divided into following four major vegetational zones:

I. Tropical deciduous forests.
II. Tropical rain forests.
III. Thorn and scrub forests.
IV. Tidal forest.

The correct sequence of the descending order in terms of the areas occupied by these zones is

(a) I, II, III and IV (b) I, II, IV and III
(c) II, I, III and IV (d) II, I, IV and III

Answers

1. (c)	**2.** (b)	**3.** (d)	**4.** (c)	**5.** (a)	**6.** (c)	**7.** (d)	**8.** (a)	**9.** (c)	**10.** (b)
11. (d)	**12.** (c)	**13.** (c)	**14.** (d)	**15.** (d)	**16.** (c)	**17.** (d)	**18.** (b)	**19.** (c)	**20.** (d)
21. (d)	**22.** (d)	**23.** (c)	**24.** (a)	**25.** (a)	**26.** (d)	**27.** (a)	**28.** (d)	**29.** (c)	**30.** (c)
31. (b)	**32.** (b)	**33.** (c)	**34.** (d)	**35.** (b)	**36.** (d)	**37.** (d)	**38.** (a)	**39.** (c)	**40.** (b)
41. (b)	**42.** (c)	**43.** (b)	**44.** (d)	**45.** (d)	**46.** (c)	**47.** (d)	**48.** (b)	**49.** (c)	**50.** (a)
51. (a)	**52.** (b)	**53.** (b)	**54.** (a)	**55.** (d)	**56.** (c)	**57.** (c)	**58.** (b)	**59.** (d)	**60.** (c)
61. (c)	**62.** (d)	**63.** (b)	**64.** (a)	**65.** (d)	**66.** (d)	**67.** (a)	**68.** (b)	**69.** (d)	**70.** (d)
71. (b)	**72.** (c)	**73.** (b)	**74.** (c)	**75.** (d)	**76.** (c)	**77.** (d)	**78.** (c)	**79.** (d)	**80.** (b)
81. (a)	**82.** (c)	**83.** (a)	**84.** (c)	**85.** (b)	**86.** (d)	**87.** (c)	**88.** (d)	**89.** (b)	**90.** (d)
91. (d)	**92.** (c)	**93.** (d)	**94.** (d)	**95.** (c)	**96.** (b)	**97.** (b)	**98.** (d)	**99.** (b)	**100.** (a)

32

Pollution and Biodiversity Conservation

Applied Ecology

Syllabus

- Applied Ecology: Environmental Pollution: Global Environmental Change; Biodiversity-Status, Monitoring and Documentation; Major Drivers of Biodiversity Change; Biodiversity Management Approaches.
- Conservation Biology

Environmental Pollution

Pollution is an undesirable change in the physical, chemical or biological characteristics of our air, land and water that may or will harmfully affect human life or that of desirable species, our industrial processes, living conditions and cultural assets (Odum; 1971). In other words, pollution is the unfavourable alteration of our environment, largely as a result of human activities (Southwick; 1976).

Air Pollution

It is the undesirable change in the physical, chemical properties of air that adversely affects the living organisms. On the basis of origin of pollutant, the pollution can be classified into

(i) **Natural Pollution** It is originated by natural processes, *e.g.*, Pollen dust, smoke (forest fire and volcanic ash), etc.

(ii) **Anthropogenic Pollution** It originates by man-made pollutions. They either have fixed source (*e.g.*, Industries, mineral smelters, power plants, etc.) or mobile source (*e.g.*, Automobiles). 80% of air pollution is due to mobile source.

On the basis of nature of pollutant, the pollution can be classified into:

Primary Air Pollutants

These exist as particulate matter or gaseous forms.

(a) **Particulate Matter** These are tiny solid particles/ liquid droplets (aerosols) that remains suspended in air, *e.g.*, soot, smoke, dust, pesticides, metal dust, mites, pollens, etc.

(b) **Gaseous Forms** It is produced by incomplete combustion of fossil fuel, automobiles and cigarette smoke. It is poisonous gas having 200 times more affinity for Hb (carboxyhaemoglobin) than oxygen. It reduces oxygen carrying capacity of Hb and also dissociation of oxyhaemoglobin. At 100 ppm concentration it causes headache and giddiness.

- **Hydrocarbon/Volatile Organic Carbon** They are produced naturally by certain types of plants (*e.g.*, pine tree), decomposition of organic matter, burning of fossil fuel and flooded rice field and swamps. Some of the hydrocarbons are carcinogenic, *e.g.*, Benzene, formaldehyde, etc.
- **Sulphur Dioxide** Burning of coal, oil refineries, smelters/putrefaction produces SO_2. It causes respiratory disorders and are harmful to plants (leaf necrosis). Epiphytes (Lichens) are the indicators of high SO_2, *e.g.*, *Paramelia, Usnea, Cladonia* and garden pea, etc.
- **Nitrogen Oxide** It is produced by combustion of fossil fuel (at high temperature) in automobiles. It contributes to acid rain that causes skin disorders, enhances heart and lung problems. It also affects the productivity of crops.
- **CFC/Freon/Aerosol** They are used as refrigerants, propellants, solid plastic foam emitted during flying jet. It react with NO_x and ozone which deplete the ozone layer which leads to the increase in UV radiations on Earth.
- **Other Pollutants** are Hg, NH_3, Pb, methyl isocyanide, phosgene (pesticide and dye manufacturing industry), etc.

Secondary Air Pollutants

These exist in the following form:

Photochemical Smog It is formed in traffic congested cities. It is mainly composed of O_3, peroxyacetyl nitrate (PAN), NO_x. It forms the brown air when solar radiations are intense, whereas it form grey air (some formation is incomplete) in lesser solar radiations. Photochemical reaction involved in formation of secondary pollutants are:

$$N_2 + O_2 \longrightarrow \text{(inside engine)}$$

$$2NO + O_2 \longrightarrow 2NO_2 \text{ (in atmosphere)}$$

$$NO_2 \xrightarrow{\text{UV ray}} NO + O$$

$$O + O_2 \longrightarrow O_3$$

$$NO + O_3 \longrightarrow NO_2 + O_2$$

$$HC + NO + O_2 \longrightarrow NO_2 + PAN$$

Ozone It is an effective oxidant that erodes building surface and causes lung cancer.

PAN It damages chloroplast so reduces photosynthetic efficiency and growth of plants. It cause irritation of eyes and inhibits ET chain.

Phenol It damages kidneys, liver, spleen and lungs.

Aldehyde It causes irritation in gastrointestinal and respiratory tract.

Acid Rain

It is the presence of acid in rain water. Normal rain water ($H_2O + CO_2$) is a weak acid of pH 6.5 but if acid rain has pH 5.6 to 4. It is formed due to nitrogen oxide (N_xO), SO_2, hydrocarbons formed during combustion of coal and petroleum. They are highly reactive in air and produces acids (H_2SO_4 or HNO_3). These acids formed in the atmosphere are deposited in tow forms:

Wet Deposition Acidic water received through rain, fog, snow, dew, mist, etc.

Dry Deposition Deposition of windblown acidic gases and particles on the ground.

- Acid rain adversely affects aquatic animals as they cannot tolerate less than pH 5, *e.g.*, mollusc, planktons, fish, etc., *Hyla vasta* (Haitian tree frog) are vanishing due to acid rain as it harms their eggs and larva.
- Low pH also damage microorganisms.
- Acids in the rain water dissolve toxic metals like Hg, Pb, Zn, Al and can also corrode marble, painted surfaces.
- It damages building materials and furnishing fabrics.
- Heritage monuments as Taj threatened by acid deposition.

Control of Air Pollution

(i) It can be controlled by selecting suitable fuel having low sulphur.

(ii) Modification of industrial processes to reduce emission.

(iii) Selection of correct manufacturing site and zone for setting up industries.

(iv) Use of efficient engines (multiple point fuel injection engine) which reduces unburnt hydrocarbons.

(v) Automobile engines operated with CNG (Compressed Natural Gas) resulting in lower toxic contamination.

(vi) Use of lead free petrol reduces toxic contamination.

The pollutants are elimination or reduction of pollutants to acceptable level is by the following methods.

Particulate Matter

(a) Use of arresters to separate particulate matter from contaminated air.

(b) Use of scrubbers is best suitable for gaseous pollutant by passing them through dry or wet packaging material.

(c) Cyclone separator and trajectory separator is used for the dust separation by centrifugal force. It is the most efficient method for course dust particle separation. It is particularly used for industrial emission with minimum moisture.

(d) Filters are used to collect extremely fine particulate matter. Different sizes of filters are available according to the size of the particles to be separated.

(e) Electrostatic Precipitators (EPs) are used for discharging of dust particle and collecting it on different charged platforms.

Gaseous Pollutants

(a) **Combustion** of gaseous pollutants at very high temperature. Petrochemical industries, paint and varnishing industries use this method.

(b) **Absorption** is especially used for toxic pollutants and vapours which are not separated by combustion or absorption. Adsorption is done on large solid surface. The periodic checking of testing of environment to check the level and source of different pollutants and to devise the strategy for their control is done by **National Environment Planning Engineering Organization** at Nagpur.

(c) **Carbon sequestration** is the process of removing carbon from the atmosphere and depositing it in a reservoir.

(d) **Biosequestration** is the capture and storage of atmospheric green house gases by biological processes *i.e.,* by increasing photosynthesis, aforestation, carbon trapping in agriculture or by use of algae.

Water Pollution

It is the undesirable change in the physical, chemical and biological properties of aquatic ecosystem and the ground water.

Types of Pollutants

On the basis of source of water pollutants, there are following types of water pollutants :

(a) **Point Pollutants** Here the effluents are discharged at specific site, *e.g.,* effluents from factories, sewage effluents (municipal waste water), etc.

(b) **Industrial Water** Contain variety of organic and inorganic pollutants which are discharged into rivers. A number of effluents are discharged into sea from costal prawn culture farms and fish processing industries. Power plants, oil refineries and many other industries use water as coolant and release hot water in the water bodies. Its temperature is 8-100 higher than the intake water, so it causes thermal pollution.

(c) **Municipal Waste** Include liquid wastes from kitchen, toilet, house hold waste water, etc., discharged into rivers and other water bodies. The domestic effluents mostly carry organic wastes, detergent etc. Dal Lake in Kashmir is highly affected by municipal waste.

(d) **Non-Point Pollutants** These pollutants enter the water bodies over a large area. It is difficult to control them. *e.g.,* City storm, water flow, agricultural runoff.

(e) **Surface Runoff** contains residues of pesticides and inorganic fertilizers (from agricultural land), biodegradable organic pollutants (from urban areas), heavy metals, acids and various inorganic compounds, etc., which contaminate water resources. On the basis of nature of pollutant the water pollution can be differentiated into:

Biological Pollutants It can be due to virus, bacteria, fungus, protozoan, helminthes, etc.

Chemical Pollutants It can be organic (*e.g.,* polychlorinated biphenyl (PCB), biocide) or inorganic (*e.g.,* PO_4, nitrates, fluorides, metals arsenic, lead, Hg, Cd.)

Physical Pollutants It is due to release of hot water from industries, oil spills (accidental discharge of petroleum in ocean or estuaries).

Effect of Water Pollution

Polluted water has a number of effects on the environment and organisms.

Effects on Aquatic Ecosystem

Higher amount of organic waste increases the rate of activity of decomposers which is collectively called **sewage fungus** and this property of becoming decomposed through microbial activity is called **putrescibility**. The higher O_2 consumption, thereby (indicator or pollution) causes a drop in Dissolved Oxygen (DO) content of water. The demand for O_2 is directly related to increasing input of organic waste and is expressed as **Biochemical Oxygen Demand** (BOD). The lower O_2 content kills many sensitive aquatic organisms like planktons molluscs, fish, etc.

(a) Biocide residues, polychlorinated bipheyls (PCB) and heavy metals, etc., can directly eliminate different species of aquatic ecosystem.

(b) High temperature of water lowers the rate of dissolved O_2 in water. It has a lower rate of putrescibility resulting in increased organic loading. Many animals as Salmon, Trout fail to reproduce under such conditions.

(c) Oil spills damage marine biodiversity and also damage coral reefs.

(d) A number of non biodegradable pollutants (DDT, radio nuclides, etc.) get accumulated in fat containing tissues in increasing concentrations along the food chain and prove hazardous to the organisms. It is called biological magnification/bioconcentration/bioamplification. In island of USA, DDT sprayed for few years resulted in sharp decline in fish eating birds because higher amount of pesticide cause cerebral haemorrhage, cirrhosis of liver, thinning of egg shell, malfunctioning of sex hormones, hypertension, etc. The decline in the population of bald eagle is attributed to this cause.

Phytoplankton ⟶ Zooplankton ⟶ Small fish ⟶ Predatory fish ⟶ Bird
0.25 ppm 0.123 ppm 1.04 ppm 4.83 ppm 124 ppm

Fig. 32.1 Process of biomagnification

Effect on Human Health

(a) Several types of pathogens in water cause diseases like jaundice, cholera, typhoid, amoebiasis, etc.

(b) Hg poisoning (by consuming fish form Hg contaminated water) causes **Minamata** disease.

(c) Cd poisoning causes **itai-itai** disease, *i.e.*, painful joints and bones.

(d) Excess of **nitrates** cause methaemoglobinea, *i.e.*, impairs O_2 transport.

(e) Excess of **fluorine** cause skeletal fluorosis, *i.e.*, deformity, of teeth, painful and stiff joints. Maize is an indicator of fluoride pollution.

(f) Excess of **arsenic** cause black foot disease. Its symptoms are peripheral neuritis, hyperkeratosis, lung and skin cancer.

Improving Water Quality

The municipal waste water and industrial effluent are treated in effluent treatment plant before they are let off in the water bodies. It involves different types of treatment as:

(a) **Primary Treatment** It is a physical process to separate large debris by sedimentation.

(b) **Secondary Treatment** It is biological process, carried out by microorganisms (oxidation of organic matter). It releases CO_2, results in formation of **sludge** or **biosolid** which is continuously aerated for further oxidation.

(c) **Tertiary Treatment** It is a physicochemical process. It removes turbidity from the waste water and involves oxidation of waste water by strong oxidizing agents like chlorine gas, perchlorate salts, O_3, UV rays, etc., to remove metals and pathogens.

Soil Pollution

Soil pollution is any undesirable change in the physical, chemical and biological properties of the soil that adversely affected their productivity. It can be:

(i) **Negative Soil Pollution** Reduction in soil productivity due to erosion and over use.

(ii) **Positive Soil Pollution** Reduction in soil productivity due to addition of undesirable substances *e.g.*, industrial waste, faulty sanitation.

(iii) **Landscape/Third Pollution** It is congregating fertile land into barren area by dumping wastes, *e.g.*, ash, garbage, rubbish, broken cans, bottles, industrial waste, etc.

Cause of Soil Pollution

Soil pollution is the results of different human activities which include:

(a) **Waste Dumps** Dumping of industrial wastes, medical or hospital wastes, radioactive wastes from nuclear testing labs, fly ash from thermal power plants and industries that settles on the ground.

(b) **Municipal Wastes** It include non biodegradable materials like polyethylene bags, plastic bottles, glass, ceramics, chemicals, needles, glass bottles, variety of pathogens, etc., from domestic and kitchen wastes, market wastes, poultry wastes and hospital wastes, etc.

(c) **Agrochemicals** Pesticides, weedicides, fertilizers and biocides residues change the properties of soil and adversely affect soil organisms.

(d) **Mining Operations** They contaminate the soil area with toxic metals and chemicals.

Control of Soil Pollution

Soil pollution can be controlled by

(i) Safer land use.

(ii) Planned urbanization.

(iii) Controlled developmental activities.

(iv) Safe disposal and management of solid wastes from industries and human habitations involve.

(a) Collection and categorizing of wastes.

(b) Recovery of solid wastes like scrap metal, plastic for recycling and reuse.

(c) Biodegradable organic waste can be transformed to organic manure.

(d) Solid waste may be disposed off by incineration (burning in the presence of O_2) and pyrolysis (combustion in the absence of O_2).

(e) Sewage sludge and solid waste may be used as land filler.

(f) Toxic chemicals, fly ash, metal containing wastes may be used as bedding material for road construction.

(g) Fly ash may be used for making bricks.

Noise Pollution

It can be defined as loud and disturbing sound that adversely affect the health of human beings. The frequency of sound is measured in **Hertz** (Hz) and unit of sound level is **decibel** (dB). Noise level of 120 dB causes discomfort in humans.

Table 32.1 **Maximum Permissible Noise Levels**

Situation	Permissible Noise, dB
Road traffic near residential areas	70
Ear protection required	85
Factory work (48 h week)	105
Prolonged noise causing permanent damage	100
Threshold of pain (30 s duration)	120
Maximum for sonic boom	150
Ear-drum rupture	180
Lungs damage	195

Source of Noise Pollution

(a) Sound amplifier
(b) Automobile and air crafts
(c) Industrial machinery
(d) Crackers bursting, etc.

Effect of Noise Pollution

(a) It affects heart beat and peripheral circulation.
(b) It causes sleeplessness and headache.
(c) It causes irritability, emotional disturbance and congential effects.
(d) It affects the concentration in work and productive performance.
(e) It causes damage to ear drum and impairment of hearing.
(f) In some birds, egg laying gets disturbed due to high noise pollution.

Control of Noise Pollution

(a) Sound proof jacket's filters must be used for machines to reduce noise from them.
(b) Industrial workers and traffic control persons may use earmuffs.
(c) There should be silent zone around 100 m area of hospitals and schools.
(d) Growing dense hedge of plants around residential area act as noise barrier (Green Muffler).
(e) Efforts must be made to increase awareness among people about the harm of noise.
(f) Noise pollution control laws should be implemented and decibel meters should be installed to monitor levels of noise pollution.

Global Environmental Change

Human activities like urbanization, industrial development, use of fossil fuel, change of land use, etc., transform the biosphere. This increases the concentration of greenhouse gases. CO_2, CH_4, N_2O and CFCs which leads to global change. These are also called **radioactive gases.**

Recognizing the problem of potential global climate change, the World Meteorological Organization (WMO) and the United Nations Environment Program (UNEP) established the **Intergovernmental Panel on Climate Change** (IPCC) in 1988. In 1988 the IPCC published an internationally coordinated assessment of the regional impacts of climate change. The IPCC found that the global mean surface temperature has increased by 0.3-0.6°C. since, the late nineteenth century. In addition, the 1990s were found to be the warmest decade of the millenium and 1998 the warmest year so far. The Panel concluded the balance of evidence suggests a discernible human influence on global climate. Computer modelling of the impact of increased greenhouse gases is extremely difficult since many factors need to be considered and little is known about how global climate functions. However, based on the best available knowledge, climate models project that the mean annual global surface temperature will increase by 1-3.5°C by 2100, that the global mean sea level will rise by 15-95 cm and that changes in the spatial and temporal patterns of precipitation will occur if the greenhouse effect increases.

Contribution in Global Warming

(i) **CO_2** (60%) It is the most abundant greenhouse gas produced by burning of fossil fuel deforestation and change of land use. Its concentration in pre industry time was 280 and in the year 2000 it was 368 ppm.

(ii) **CH_4** (20%) It is produced by freshwater wetlands, flooded rice field, biomass burning, fermentation in cattles, methanogens (bacteria). Its concentration in pre industrial time was 700 ppb and in the year 2000 it was 1750 ppb.

(iii) **CFC** (14%) It is the most stable, non flammable, non-toxic gas. Its source is leaking of air conditioners, refrigerators, evaporation of industrial solvent, aerosols and plastic foams. Its concentration in pre industrial time was zero and in the year 2000 it was 282 ppb.

(iv) **N_2O** (6%) Agriculture, biomass burning, industrial processes, burning of nitrogen rich fuel, breakdown of nitrogen rich fertilizers, nitrate contaminated ground water, etc., are the source of N_2O. In pre industrial time its concentration was 240 ppb but in year 2000 it was recorded 316 ppb.

Greenhouse Effect

Atmosphere around Earth act as window glass pane that allows solar radiations to enter the Earth surface. It does not allow long Wave Radiation (IR) emitted by Earth to escape in space. These IR radiation are absorbed by greenhouse/radioactively active gases (CO_2, CH_4, N_2O, CFC). So the atmosphere radiate part of this energy back to Earth called **Greenhouse flux**. These greenhouse gases keep the atmosphere warm and fit for living, called **Greenhouse effect**. Practically, inside a glass house, temperature is warmer than outside. It is used for growing plants that require high temperature for growth. Due to the presence of greenhouse gases, mean annual temperature of Earth is 150°C but in the absence of these gases it would drop sharply to –200°C. The excessive increase in concentration of these gases would result in retaining more and more infra red radiations. It is called **enhanced greenhouse effect.** This increase in global mean temperature is referred to as **global warming**.

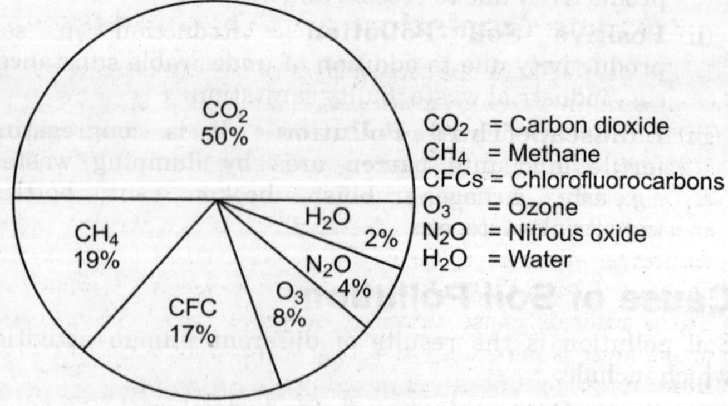

Fig. 32.2 Greenhouse gases (relative shares)

Effect of Concentration of Greenhouse Gases

- **CO_2 Fertilization Effect on Plants** The response of plants to the increase in concentration is called CO_2

fertilization effect. Due to increase in CO_2 concentration, the rate of photosynthesis will increase and the rate of transpiration may decrease due to partial closure of stomata. This will allow many species to grow in regions of water scarcity. There may be greater root production to enhance mycorrhizal development because of more photosynthetic supply to roots and more fixation of N_2 in root nodules enabling plants to grow in nutrient poor soil.

- **Weather and Climate** With the change in weather and climate, the troposphere will warm up and stratosphere will cool down which increases moisture carrying capacity of atmospheres.
  - The precipitation may decrease at lower latitudes and it is expected to increase both in summer and winter.
  - The frequency of extreme events like floods, drought, etc., may increase.
  - The climate change will pose a threat to human health.
- **Sea Level Changes** Sea level will rise due to thermal expansion of oceans (water) and melting of glaciers and greenland ice sheets. It may submerge low lying iceland that will threaten the life of one third of human population.
- **Species Distribution** Global warming shift the temperature ranges and may affect the distribution pattern of organisms. As trees are sensitive to temperature stress so a rapid rise in temperature may cause large scale death of trees and their replacement by shrub vegetation.
- **Food Production** Increase in temperature results in eruption of disease, causing plant pests, explosive growth of weeds and increase in rate of respiration. All these factors will decrease the food production.
- **Coral Reefs** Greenhouse pollutants pose a direct threat to coral reefs causing crumbling in process similar to osteoporosis in humans.

How to deal with global warming

- Reducing greenhouse gas emission by limiting the use of fossil fuels.
- Increasing the forest area for photosynthetic utilization of CO_2.
- Minimizing the use of nitrogen fertilizers to reduce N_2O.
- Developing the substitutes for CFCs.
- Making people aware of the impact of climatic change.

Ozone Depletion and Ozone Hole

In the stratosphere, the second layer of the atmosphere, ozone is present in small quantities as a protective shield for the Earth. Ozone strongly absorbs ultraviolet radiation from the sun (295-320 nm) which is injurious to life on Earth. CFCs, CH_4, N_2O (ozone destroying substances) escape into the stratosphere and causes destruction of O_3 layers. Most damaging effect of CFCs is the production of in the active chlorine (Cl and ClO radicals) in the presence of UV radiation. These radicals cause thinning of ozone layer. Thinning of ozone layer is maximum in spring season and is called **ozone hole**. It was first observed in 1985 over Antarctica.

Exhaust gases from jet aircraft and artificial satellites discharge nitric oxide (NO), nitrogen dioxide (NO_2), etc., which immediately react with ozone.

$$\underset{\text{(Ozone)}}{O_3} + \underset{\text{(Nitric oxide)}}{NO} \longrightarrow \underset{\text{(Oxygen)}}{O_2} + \underset{\text{(Nitrogen dioxide)}}{NO_2}$$

$$O_3 + NO \longrightarrow O_2 + \underset{\text{(Nitrogen trioxide)}}{NO_3}$$

Chlorofluorocarbons (CFCs) are used as coolants in refrigerators and air-conditioners. These slowly pass from troposphere to stratosphere and once there, they stay there 100 years. In the presence of ultraviolet radiation (200 nm) from the sun, CFC breaks up into chlorine-free radical (Cl) which readily consumes ozone.

$$CFCl_3 \xrightarrow{h\nu} CFCl_2 + Cl$$

$$Cl^* + O_3 \longrightarrow ClO^* + O_2$$

$$ClO^* + O \longrightarrow Cl^* + O_2$$

Effects of Ozone Depletion

- Increase in greenhouse gases, results in increase in UV radiations reaching on Earth surface (2% more in case of 1% loss of ozone).
- It inhibits photosynthesis in phytoplanktons which affects the food chains.
- It damage nucleic acids in living organisms (mutation).
- It increases the incidence of cataract and skin cancer and diminishes immunity.

Biodiversity-Status, Monitoring and Documentation

Biodiversity (Raymond F Dasmann; 1968) is the degree of variation of life forms within a given ecosystem, biome or entire planet. These variations are explained as genetic diversity (among individual of single species), species diversity (within community) and ecosystem diversity. It is measure of health of ecosystem.

1. India is known for its rich heritage of biological diversity, having already documented over 91000 species of animals and 45500 species of plants in its ten bio-geographic regions. Nearly 6500 native plants are still used prominently in indigenous healthcare systems.
2. The country is recognized as one of the eight Vavilovian Centers of Origin and Diversity of Crop Plants, having more than 300 wild ancestors and close relatives of cultivated plants.
3. India is known for its rich heritage of biodiversity. In biological diversity parlance, India is one of the **17 mega-diverse countries in the world**. With only 2.4% of the world's area, India accounts for 7-8% of the world's recorded plant (about 45000 of which approximately 15000 are of known medicinal value) and animal species (about 91000).
4. India has four out of thirty four global biodiversity hotspots, which is an indicator of high degree of endemism (of species) in India. About 5150 plant species and 1837 animal species are endemic to India. India has 16 major types and 251 sub-types of forests.
5. India has a **National Wetland Conservation Programme** covering 125 wetlands including 25

Ramsar sites under the Ramsar Convention. India accounts for about 5% of the world's mangroves (including Sunderbans delta the largest mangrove forest in the world) and partners with IUCN's Mangroves for Future programme and has established a National Institute of the Mangrove Research at Kolkata.

6. Coral reefs in India occupy an extent of 2375 sq. km. (including the Andaman Islands, which have rich coral diversity and a National Coral Reef Research Centre at Port Blair).

Centers of Origin and Diversity of Crop Plants (Vavilov Center of Diversity)

It is a region of the world first indicated by Dr. Nikolai Ivanovich Vavilov to be an original center for the domestication of plants. Vavilov developed a theory on the centers of origin of cultivated plants. He stated that plants were not domesticated somewhere in the world at random but there are regions, where the domestication started. It is believed that the center of origin is also the center of diversity.

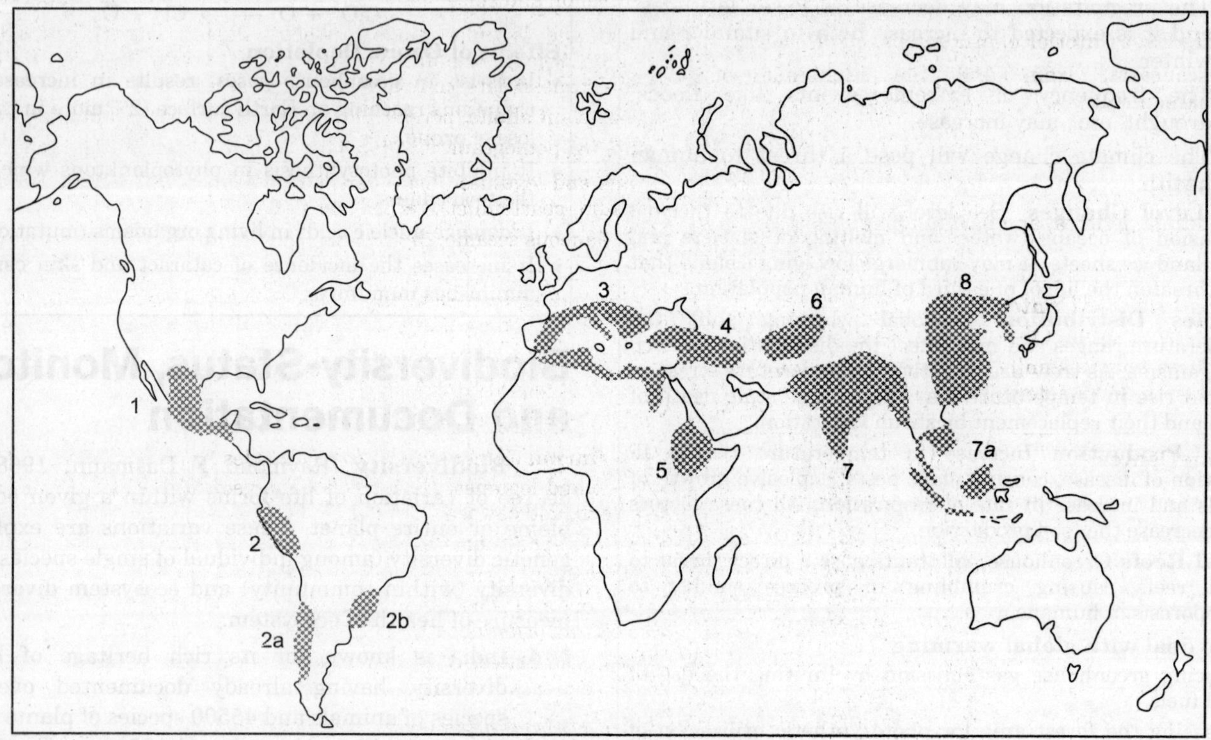

Fig. 32.3 Vavilov centers of origin

(1) Mexico-Guatemala, (2) Peru-Ecuador-Bolivia, (2a) Southern Chile, (2b) Southern Brazil, (3) Mediterranean, (4) Middle East, (5) Ethiopia, (6) Central Asia, (7) Indo-Burma, (7a) Siam-Malaya-Java, (8) China.

1. **South Mexican and Central American Center** (Southern sections of Mexico, Guatemala, Honduras and Costa Rica)	• Grains and Legumes maize, common bean, lima bean, tepary bean, jack bean, grain amarnath. • Melon Plants malabar gourd, winter pumpkin, chayote. • Fibre Plants sweet potato, arrowroot, pepper, papaya, guava, cashew, wild black cherry, chochenial, cherry tomato, cacao.
2. **South America Center**	2. **Peruvian, Ecuadorean, Bolivian Center** • Root tubers andean potato, other endemic cultivated potato species, edible nasturtium. • Grains and legumes starchy maize, lima bean and common bean. • Root tubers edible canna potato. • Vegetable crops pepino, tomato, ground cherry pumpkin and pepper. • Fibre plants Egyptian cotton. • Fruit and miscellaneous cocoa, passion flower, guava, heilborn, quinine tree and tobacco.

	3. **Chiloe Center** (Island near the coast of Southern Chile) • Common potato (48 chromosomes) and strawberry.
	4. **Brazilian-Paraguayan Center** • Manioc, peanut, rubber-tree, pineapple, cashew and purple granadilla.
3. **Mediterranean Center** (borders of the Mediterranean sea)	• Cereals and legumes Durum wheat, emmer, polish wheat, spelt, Mediterranean oats, sand oats, canarygrass, grass pea, pea and lupine. • Forage plants Egyptian clover, white clover, crimson clover and serradella. • Oil and fibre plants flax, rape, black mustard and olive. • Vegetables garden beet, cabbage, turnip, lettuce, asparagus, celery, chicory and parsnip. • Ethereal oil and spice plants caraway, anice, thyme and peppermint.
4. **Middle East** (interior of asia minor, all of) Transcaucasia, Iran, and the highlands of (Turukmenistan)	• Grains and legumes einkorn wheat, durum wheat, poulard wheat, common wheat, oriental wheat, Persian wheat, two-row barley, rye, Mediterranean oats, common oats, lentil and lupine. • Forage plant alfalfa, persian clover, fenugreek, vetch and hairy vetch. • Fruits fig, pomegranate, apple, pear, quince, cherry and hawthorn.
5. **Ethiopia** (Abyddinia, Eritrea, and part of Somaliland)	• Grains and legumes abyssinian hard wheat, polish wheat, barley, grain sorghum, pearl millet, cowpea and flex. • Miscellaneous sesame, castor bean, garden cress, coffee, okra, myrrh and indigo.
6. **Central Asiatic Center** (North-West India, Punjab, North-West Frontier Provinces and Kashmir; Afghanistan; Tadjikistan; Uzbekistan and Western Tian-Shan)	• Grains and legumes common wheat, club wheat, shot wheat, peas, lentil, horse bean, chickpea,mung bean, mustard, flax and sesame. • Fibre plants hemp and cotton. • Vegetables onion, garlic, spinach and carrot. • Fruits pistacio, pear, almond, grape and apple.
7. **Indian Center**	7. **Indo-Burma** (Hindustan Center Includes Asom and Burma) • Cereals and legumes: Rice, chickpea, pigeon pea, urd bean, mung bean, rice bean, and cowpea. • Vegetables and tubers eggplant, cucumber, radish, taro and yam. • Fruits-mango, orange, tangerine, citron and tamarid. • Sugar, oil, and fibre plants sugarcane, coconut palm, sesame, safflower, tree cotton, oriental cotton, jute, crotalaria and kenaf. • Spices, stimulates, dyes and miscellaneous: hemp, black pepper, gum arabic, dandalwood, indigo, cinnamon tree, croton and bamboo. 7a **Siam-Malaya-Java** (Indo-Malayan Center) • Cereals and legumes job's tears, velvet bean. • Fruits pummelo, banana, breadfruit and mangosteen. • Oil, sugar, spice and fibre plants candlenut, coconut palm, sugarcane, clove, nutmeg, black pepper and Manila hemp.
8. **Chinese Center** (136 endemic plants are listed in the largest independent center)	• Cereals and legumes Italian millet, Japanese barnyard millet, buckwheat, hull-less barley, soyabean and velvet bean. • Roots, tubers, and vegetables Chinese yam, radish, onion and cucumber. • Fruits and nuts pear, peach, apricot, cherry, walnut and litchi. • Sugar, drug, and fibre plants sugarcane, opium poppy, ginseng camphor and hemp.

Biodiversity Monitoring and Documentation

Monitoring biodiversity contains survey techniques and data recording sheets for remnant vegetation and wild life including mammals, birds and reptiles. Additional resources include references for identification of flora and fauna. Encompassing biodiversity and habitat monitoring as well as many other aspects of vegetation projects, this guide features seven checklists for measuring and assessing the health of forested bush. These are used to measure components including site features; plant diversity, bush health, habitat features and disturbances. The checklists promptland managers to observe three main landscape features:

(i) **Plants** types, structure and health.

(ii) **Habitats** areas where animals and plants can live and grow.

(iii) **Disturbances** processes that damage the health of plants and habitats: erosion, pest invasion, firewood collection and land clearing.

A community may be described by recording the populations that are present at a particular time measuring its **diversity.** Measurement of diversity ranges from counts of the number of species in a sample, *i.e.*, species richness to measure that incorporate the number of species and the size of individual population.

α-Diversity

Diversity within communities, α-diversity, has two components; the number of species and their relative abundances. There are many ways that α-diversity can be expressed quantitatively. One way is Simpson's Index,

$$D = 1 - \sum_{i=1}^{S}\left(\frac{n_i}{N}\right)^2$$

where, n_i is the number of individuals in species i, N is the total number of individuals in the community and S is the number of species present. This index is equivalent to calculating the probability of picking at random two individuals that are different species. It ranges from 0 in communities made up of single species to almost 1 in communities made up of many species, each present in equal numbers.

Table 32.2 **Relative Abundance of Mammal Species in Three Vegetation Type**

Mammal species	Sandstone Forest	Open Forest	Riparian Woodlan
Antechinus bilarni (sandstone antechinus)	6.3		
Dasyurus hallucatus (northern quoll)	8.6	16.7	1.2
Zyzomys woodwardi (large rock rat)	5.5		
Sminthopsis virginiae (red-cheeked dunnart)		1.1	0.4
Trichosurus arnhemensis (Northern burshtail possum)		33.3	
Pseudomys nanus (Western chestnut mouse)			3.7
Pseudomys delicatulus (delicate mouse)			0.6
Melomys burtoni (grassland melomys)			6.5
Species richness	3	3	5
Total abundance	20.4	51.1	12.4
Simpson's α-diversity	0.65	0.47	0.62

β-Diversity

β-diversity is the change in community composition we meet as we move through the landscape. If the turnover of species between sites is high, communities will be relatively different.

There are numerous indices for measuring the similarity between communities in different locations. One common coefficient of similarity is Jaccard's coefficient (S_j). It is employed when the only information available about the communities is lists of species. The coefficient is used to compare pairs of sites. Lists can be arranged in a table in which the rows (or columns) are sites and the columns (or rows) are species (Table 32.2).

Jaccard's coefficient is calculated for pairs of sites from the equation:

$$S_j = \frac{a}{t}$$

where, a is the number of species shared by the two sites and t is the total number of species, including those that are unique to either of the sites.

The coefficient may be calculated to represent the degree of similarity between any pair of sites.

Table 32.3 **List of 31 Projects for Conservation of 46 Lakes as on March 2007**

Lake	State
Banjara	Andhra Pradesh
Dal lake, Srinagar	Jammu and Kashmir
Three lakes of Bangaluru namely Vengaiahnkere, Nagavara and Jarganahalli	Karnataka
Bellandur lake, Bangaluru	Karnataka
Kotekere, Belgaum	Karnataka
Bhishma, Gadag	Karnataka
Lal Bagh, Bangaluru	Karnataka
Sharanabasveshwara	Karnataka
Akkamahadevi, Haveri	Karnataka
Chanapatna, Hasan	Karnataka
Veli Akkulum, Thiruvananthapuram	Kerala
Powai	Maharashtra
Nine lakes in Thane	Maharashtra
Mahalaxmi lake, Vadagaon	Maharashtra
Mansagar, Jaipur	Rajasthan
Ooty	Tamil Nadu
Kodaikanal	Tamil Nadu
Three lakes of Agartala	Tripura
Four lakes of Nainital District	Uttarakhand
Nainital lake	Uttarakhand
Rabindra Sarovar, Kolkata	West Bengal
Mirik	West Bengal
Bindusagar, Bhubneswar	Odisha
Kundward lake, Davengere	Karnataka
Rani Talab, Riva	Madhya Pradesh
Kotetavarekere, Chickmaglore	Karnataka
Tripuranthekeshwar, Bidar	Karnataka
Rankala, Kolhapur	Maharastra
Varhala Devi, Bhiwandi	Maharastra
Sagar, Sagar	Madhya Pradesh
Mansi Ganga	Uttar Pradesh

Biodiversity Hotspot

The concept of biodiversity hotspots was originated by Norman Myers in two articles in 'The Environmentalist' (1988 and 1990), revised after through analysis by Myers and others in 'Hotspots Earth's Biologically Richest and Most Endangered Terrestrial Ecoregions'.

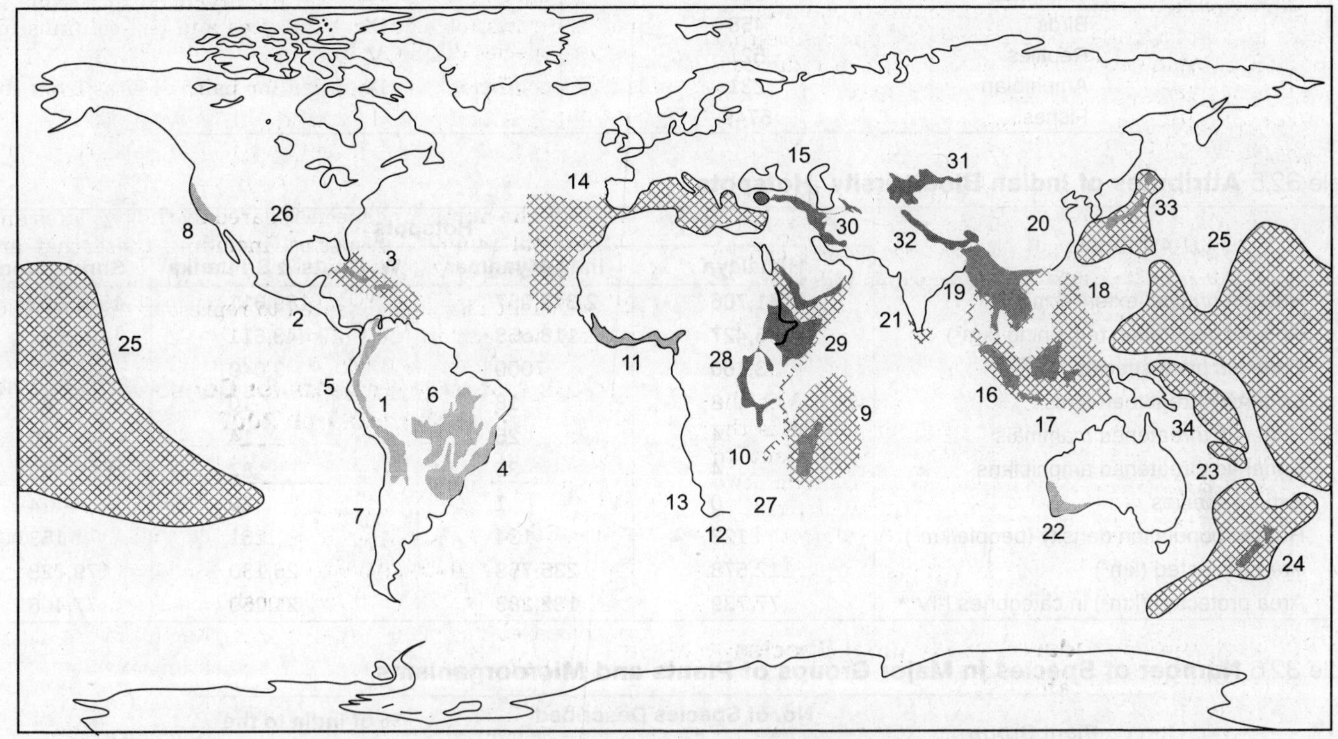

Fig. 32.4 The biodiversity hotspots of the world

The twenty five biodiversity hotspots (green) as indicated in **Myers N and *et. al.*,** (2000) Biodiversity hotspots for conservation priorities

1. The Tropical Andes
2. Mesoamerica
3. The Caribbean Islands
4. The Atlantic Forest
5. Tumbes-Choco-Magdalena
6. The Cerrado
7. Chilean Winter Rainfall-Valdivian Forests
8. The California Floristic Province
9. Madagascar and the Indian Ocean Islands
10. The Coastal Forests of Eastern Africa
11. The Guinean Forests of West Africa
12. The Cape Floristic Region
13. The Succulent Karoo
14. The Mediterranean Basin
15. The Caucasus
16. Sundarland
17. Wallacea
18. The Philippines
19. Indo-Myanmar
20. The Mountains of South-West China
21. Western Ghats and Sri Lanka
22. South-West Australia
23. New Caledonia
24. New Zealand
25. Polynesia and Micronesia

An additional nine hotspots (blue) have since been added

26. The Madrean Pine-Oak Woodlands
27. Maputaland-Pondoland-Albany
28. The Eastern Afromontane
29. The Horn of Africa
30. The Irano-Anatolian
31. The Mountains of Central Asia
32. Eastern Himalaya
33. Japan
34. East Melanesian Islands

Critiques of Hotspots

- Do not adequately represent other forms of species richness (*e.g.,* total species richness or threatened species richness).
- Do not adequately represent taxa other than vascular plants (*e.g.,* vertebrates or fungi).
- Do not protect smaller scale richness hotspots.
- Do not make allowances for changing land use patterns. Hotspots represent regions that have experienced considerable habitat loss but this does not mean they are experiencing ongoing habitat loss. On the other hand, regions that are relatively intact (*e.g.,* the Amazon Basin) have experienced relatively little land loss, but are currently losing habitat at tremendous rates.
- Do not protect ecosystem services.
- Do not consider phylogenetic diversity.

Table 32.4 **Comparative Position of Species Biodiversity in India**

Group	Estimated Number of Species	Rank Amongst Megadiverse Countries
Higher plants	18664	IX
Mammals	390	VII
Birds	458	IX
Reptiles	521	V
Amphibian	231	IX
Fishes	5749	I

Table 32.5 **Attributes of Indian Biodiversity Hotspots**

Attributes	Hotspots			
	Himalaya	Indo-Myanmar	W. Ghats & Sri Lanka	Sundarland
Hotspot original extent (km^2)	741,706	2,373,057	189,611	1501,063
Hotspot vegetation remaining (km^2)	185,427	118,653	43,611	10,0571
Endemic plant species	3,160	7000	3,049	15,000
Endemic threatened birds	8	18	10	43
Endemic threatened mammals	4	25	14	60
Endemic threatened amphibians	4	35	87	59
Extinct species	0	1	20	4
Human population density (people/km^2)	123	134	261	153
Area protected (km^2)	112,578	235,758	26,130	179,723
Area protected (km^2) in categories I-IV**	77,739	132,283	21,259	77,408

Table 32.6 **Number of Species in Major Groups of Plants and Microorganisms**

Plant Group	No. of Species Described		% of India to the World
	India	World	
Virus/Bacteria	850	8,050	10.6
Algae	7175	40,000	17.9
Fungi	14,500	72,000	20.1
Lichens	2223	13,500	16.4
Bryophytes	2500	14500	17.2
Pteridophytes	1,200	10,000	12.0
Gymnosperms	67	650	10.3
Angiosperms	17,527	2,50,000	1.0

Endemic Taxa

A species restricted to a small area and its distribution has not been found outside this area are referred to as endemic. The endemic organism are of two types :

(i) **Pleoendemics** These are the organisms whose ancestral forms were once widely distributed but at present its distribution has been restricted to a small area. These endemic species have many fossil relatives. These endemic species adopted to particular environment, can not re-established in new environment. Some example are *Ginkgo biloba* (China and Japan). *Sequoia sempervireus* (Coastal Valleys of California), *Metasequoia* sp. *Agathis australis* (China).

(ii) **Neoendemics** These are the modern species which are unable to occupy a large area, and its distribution is restricted in a confined area. Some of well known endemic flora are *Venda caerulea* (Orchidaceae), *Salmalia malabarica* (Bombacaceae), *Piper nigrum* (Piperaceae), etc. The Endemic organism is formed as a results of geographical or biological reasons. A species may become endemic due to barriers like mountains, oceans, deserts, etc. These barriers restrict its migration to new area.

- About 11058 **species are endemic to Indian region**, 6200 of which belong to flowering plants alone. Eastern Himalaya and North-Eastern region (about 2,500 species), peninsular India including Western and Eastern Ghats (about 2,600 species), North-Western Himalaya (about 800 species) and Andaman and Nicobar Islands (about 250 species) are the areas rich in endemic plants.

Table 32.7 **Endemism in Different Plant Groups of India**

Plant Group	Total Number of Species in India	Number of Endemic Species	Percentage
Angiosperms	17,527	6200	35.3
Gymnosperms	67	7	14.9
Pteridophytes	1200	193	14.0
Bryophytes	2500	629	25.1
Lichens	2223	527	23.7
Fungi	14500	3500	24.0
Algae	7175	1925	26.8

Table 32.8 **Agro-ecological Regions Harbouring Rich Crop Diversity in India**

Agro-ecological Regions	Crops
Western Himalaya	• Barley, wheat, maize, buckwheat, Amaranthus, prosomillet, finger millet. • French bean, soyabean, lentil, black gram, peas. • Pumpkin, cucumber, *Alliums* sp., ginger, Brassicaceae. • Pome, stone, soft and nut.
Eastern Himalaya	• Barlely, maize, buckwheat, Amaranthus, finger millet, foxtail millet. • French bean, soyabean, cowpea, black gram, peas, scarlet bean. • Pumpkin, cucumber, *Alliums* sp., hinger, chayote, tree tomato, Brassicaceae. • Pome and stone fruits.
North-Eastern Region	• Rice, maize, sorghum, finger millet, foxtail millet, job's tears. • French bean, soyabean, pigeonpea (perennial), black gram, rice bean, *Dolichos* bean, winged bean. • Pumpkin, chayote, cucumber, okra, eggplant, chilli/*Capsicum* sp., pointed gourd, ash gourd. • Taros, yams. • Citrus-lime/lemon/orange/grape fruit, banana. • Tea, tree cotton, juite, kenaf and mesta, large *Cardamom*, ginger, long pepper, sugarcane.
Gangetic Plains	• Rice, sorghum, barnyard millet, little millet/*Panicum*. • Chickpea, cowpea, mung bean. • Okra, eggplant, bitterground, *Cucumis* sp., *Luffa* sp. • Jackfruit, mango, lemon/lime, orange, jujube, Indian gooseberry/*Emblica*, jamun/*Syzygium*, melons. • Linseed, *Niger*, sesame, Brassicaceae. • Sugarcane, mulberry.
Indus Plains	• Durum wheat, pearl millet. • Moth bean, cluster bean, chickpea, black gram. • Okra, *Cucumis* sp. • Jujube, Khirni/Mimusops, *Phalsa*/Grewia. • Sesame, *Taramira*/Eruca, Cotton.
Eastern Peninsular Region/ Eastern Ghats/Deccan	• Rice, sorghum, finger, millet, pearl millet, foxtail millet, little millet, prosomillet, kodo millet. • Black gram, green gram, cowpea, horse gram, Mucuna, pigeonpea, *Dolichos* bean, rice bean. • Taros, yams, elephant-food yam. • Banana, mango, lemon/lime, jackfruit. • Niger, Brassicaceae, sesame. • Ginger, turmeric, chilli, kenaf, sugarcane, coconut, cotton.
Western Peninsular Region/ Western Ghats/Malabar	• Rice, sorghum, finger millet, small millet/*Panicum*. • Black gram, green gram, cowpea, pigeonpea, *Dolichos* bean, horse gram, sword bean. • Okra, eggplant, cucumber, chilli/*Capsicum*. • Taros, yams, elephant-foot yam. • Jackfruit, banana, lime/lemon, orange, juman/*Syzygium*. • Sugarcane, black pepper, turmeric, ginger, coconut, arecanut, cotton.
The Islands Regions	• Coconut, breadfruit, chilli, taros, yams, *Xanthosoma*.

Table 32.9 **Recorded Animal Species**

Taxonomic Group	Number of Species		Percentage in India
	World	India	
Protista (Protozoa)	31250	2577	8.24
Animalia			
Mesozoa	71	10	14.08
Porifera	4562	500	10.70
Cnidaria	9916	842	8.49
Ctenophora	100	12	12.00
Platyhelminthes	17500	1622	3.22
Nemertinea	600	–	–
Rotifera	2500	330	13.20
Gastrotricha	3000	100	3.33
Kinorhyncha	100	10	10.00
Nematoda	30000	2850	9.50
Nematomorpha	250	–	–
Acanthocephala	800	229	28.62
Sipuncula	145	35	24.14
Mollusca	66535	5072	7.62
Echiura	127	43	33.86
Annelida	12700	840	6.61
Onychophora	100	1	1.00
Arthropoda	970670	69903	7.20
Crustacea	35534	2934	8.26
Insecta	861696	61151	7.10
Arachnida	73440	5818	7.90
Pycnogonida	600	16	2.67
Pauropoda	360	–	
Chilopoda	3000	100	3.33
Diplopoda	7500	162	2.16
Symphyla	120	4	3.33
Merostomata	4	2	50.00
Phoronida	11	3	27.27
Bryozoa (Ectoprocta)	4000	200	5.00
Entoprocta	60	10	16.66
Brachiopoda	300	3	1.00
Pogonophora	80	–	–
Priapulida	8	–	–
Pentastomida	70	–	–
Chaetognatha	111	30	27.02
Tardigrada	514	30	5.83
Echinodermata	6223	765	12.29
Hemichordata	120	12	10.00
Chordata	48451	4994	10.40
Protochordata	2106	119	5.65
Pisces	21723	2546	11.72
Amphibia	5150	240	4.66
Reptilia	5817	460	7.91
Aves	9026	1232	13.66
Mammalia	4629	397	8.58
Total (Animalia)	1191208	88730	7.45
Grand Total (Protista+animalia)	**1222458**	**91307***	**7.45**

The **Himalayan flora** represents 71 endemic genera and 32% endemic species. Also, five families are endemic to the region (*i.e.,* Tetracentraceae, Hamamelidaceae, Circaeasteraceae, Butomaceae and Stachyuraceae), while over 90% of the species in Berberidaceae and Saxifragaceae are endemic to the Himalaya.

Table 32.10 **Richness and Uniqueness of Biodiversity in Himalayan Hotspot**

Taxonomic Group	Species	Endemic	Percentage of Endemism
Vascular plants	10,000	3160	31.60
Mammals	300	12	4.00
Birds	979	15	1.53
Reptiles	177	49	27.68
Amphibians	105	42	40.00
Freshwater fishes	269	33	12.26

Table 32.11 **Biodiversity of Western Ghats**

Group	Total Species	Endemic	Percentage of Endemism
Angiosperms	4,000	1,500	38
Butterflies	332	37	11
Fishes	288	116	53
Amphibians	156	94	78
Reptiles	225	97	62
Birds	508	19	4
Mammals	137	14	12

- The degree of endemism of plant species in Thar desert is 6.4% which is relatively higher than 3% endemism the Sahara desert. Some endemic species of Thar Desert includes *Calligonum polygonoides* (Polygonaceae), *Prosopis cineraria* (Mimosaceae), *Tecomella undulate* (Bignoniaceae), *Cenchrus biflorus* (Poaceae) and *Sueda fruticosa* (Chenopodiaceae), etc.
- Cold desert is the home of highly adaptive, rare endangered fauna, such as Asiatic Ibex, Tibetan Argali, Ladakh Uriyal, Bharal, Tibetan Antelope, Tibetan Gazelle, Wild Yak, Snow Leopard, Brown Bear, Tibetan Wolf, Wild Dog and Tibetan Wild Ass.

Table 32.12 **Ten Largest Families with Maximum Species Diversity in Indian Deserts**

Family	Species
Poaceae	111
Fabaceae	65
Asteraceae	44
Cyperaceae	36
Convolvulaceae	35
Malvaceae	28
Acanthaceae	22
Euphorbiaceae	23
Cucurbitaceae	19
Scrophulariaceae	15

Mangrove ecosystem constitutes a bridge between terrestrial and marine ecosystems and are found in the inter-tidal zones of sheltered shores, estuaries, creeks, backwaters, lagoons, marshes and mud-flats and are regarded as most productive and biologically diverse ecosystems. Mangroves are habitats, spawning grounds, nurseries and nutrients for a number of animals. They harbour several endangered species ranging from reptiles (*e.g.,* crocodiles, iguanas and snakes) and amphibians, to mammals (tigers, deer, otters and dolphins) and birds (herons, egrets, pelicans and eagles). Only a few plant families (*e.g.,* Rhizophoraceae, Avicenniaceae and Combretaceae) have developed physiological and structural adaptations to the brackish water habitat in which mangroves occur.

Table 32.13 **State/UT Wise Mangrove Cover (km^2) Assessment Since 1987**

State/UT	Assessment Year									
	1987	**1989**	**1991**	**1993**	**1995**	**1997**	**1999**	**2001**	**2003**	**2005**
Andhra Pradesh	495	405	399	378	383	383	397	333	329	329
Goa	0	3	3	3	5	5	5	5	16	16
Gujarat	427	412	397	419	689	901	1031	911	916	936
Karnataka	0	0	0	0	2	3	3	2	3	3
Maharashtra	140	114	113	155	155	124	108	118	158	158
Odisha	199	192	195	195	195	211	215	219	203	203
Tamil Nadu	23	47	47	21	21	21	21	23	35	35
West Bengal	2,076	2,109	2,119	2,119	2,119	2,123	2,125	2,081	2,120	2,118
Andman and Nicobar Islands	686	973	966	966	966	966	966	789	658	637
Puducherry	0	0	0	0	0	0	0	1	1	1
Kerala	0	0	0	0	0	0	0	0	8	8
Daman anmd Diu	0	0	0	0	0	0	0	0	1	1
Total	**4,046**	**4,255**	**4,244**	**4,256**	**4,533**	**4,737**	**4,471**	**4,482**	**4,448**	**4,445**

Major Drivers of Biodiversity Change

Biodiversity has been declining rapidly, the colonization of tropical pacific Islands by humans is said to have led to the extinction of more than 2,000 species of native birds. The factors of biodiversity change are:

Habitat Loss

Fewer natural wildlife habitat areas remain each year. Moreover, the habitat that remains has often been degraded to bear little resemblance to the natural wild areas which existed in the past.

Climate Change

Because many types of plants and animals have specific habitat requirements, climate change coud cause disastrous loss of wildlife species. A slight drop of rise in average rainfall will translate into large seasonal changes. Hibernating mammals, reptiles, amphibians and insects are harmed and disturbed. Plants and wildlife are sensitive to moisture change so, they will be harmed by any change in the moisture level.

Pesticides are deliberately spread to make the environment toxic to certain plants, insects and rodents, so it should not be surprising that other plants and wildlife are deliberately harmed at the same time. In addition, many chemical pollutants are toxic to wildlife, such as PCBs, mercury, petroleum by products, solvents, antifreeze, etc.

Hunting and Poaching

Unregulated hunting and poaching causes a major threat to wildlife. Along with this, mismanagement of forest department and forest guards triggers this problem.

Latitudinal Gradients

The diversity of plants and animals is not uniform throughout the world but shows a rather uneven distribution. In general, species diversity decreases as we move away from the equator towards the poles. With very few exceptions, tropics (latitudinal range of 23.5°N to 23.5°S) harbour more species than temperate or polar areas. Colombia located near the equator has nearly 1,400 species of birds while New York at 41°N has 105 species and Greenland at 71°N only 56 species. A forest in a tropical region like Equator has up to 10 times as many species of vascular plants as a forest of equal area in a temperate region like the Midwest of the USA. The largely tropical Amazonian rain forest in South America has the greatest biodiversity on Earth.

Grater Biological Diversity

Ecologists and evolutionary biologists have proposed various hypothesis to account for diversity:

(i) Speciation is generally a function of time had a long evolutionary time for species diversification.

(ii) Tropical environments are less seasonal, relatively more constant and predictable. Such constant environments promote niche specialization and lead to a greater species diversity.

(iii) There is more solar energy available in the tropics, which contributes to higher productivity; this in turn might contribute indirectly to greater diversity.

Species Area Relationships

German naturalist and geographer **Alexander von Humboldt** observed that within a region species richness increased with increasing explored area, but only up to a limit.

The relation between species richness and area for a wide variety of taxa (angiosperm plants, birds, bats, freshwater fishes) turns out to be a rectangular hyperbola. On a logarithmic scale, the relationship is a straight line described by the equation.

$$\log S = \log C + Z \log A$$

where, S =Species richness; A = Area; Z = slope of the line (regression coefficient); C = Y-intercept.

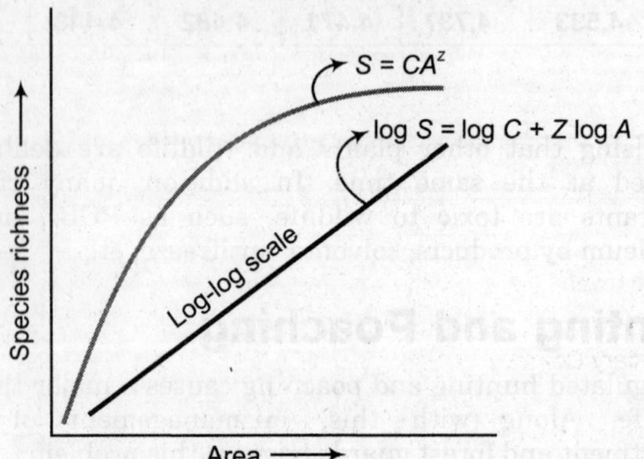

Fig. 32.5 Species area relationship. Log scale shows the linear relationship

Ecologists have discovered that the value of Z lies in the range of 0.1 to 0.2, regardless of the taxonomic group or the region. But, the species-area relationships among very large areas like the entire continents, the slope of the line to be much steeper (Z values in the range of 0.6 to 1.2). For example, for frugivorous (fruit-eating) birds and mammals in the tropical forests of different continents, the slope is found to be 1.15.

Biodiversity Management Approaches

Human applied a number of approaches for biodiversity management time to time these include:

Convention on Biological Diversity (CBD)

Biodiversity as a global issue gained importance at the 1992 Earth Summit in **Rio de Janeiro, Brazil.**

One of the key agreements adopted at Rio was the 'Convention on Biological Diversity' (CBD) which was signed by vast majority of the world's governments showing commitments for maintaining the world's ecological foundations as economic development proceeds worldwide.

The objectives of the convention are conservation of biological diversity; sustainable use of its components and fair and equitable sharing of the benefits arising from the use of genetic resources.

The CBD is the first comprehensive global agreement addressing all aspects relating to biodiversity. The institutional framework for CBD's implementation is provided by the Conference of the Parties (COP).

The COP through its decisions takes necessary steps to translate provisions of the convention into practical actions. These measures inter alia include adoption of programme of work for thematic areas (marine and coastal biodiversity, mountain biodiversity, agriculture biodiversity, dry land biodiversity, forest biodiversity, inland water biodiversity, island biodiversity) and for a number of cross cutting issues (incentive measures, alien invasive species, traditional knowledge, etc.) COP also issues specific guidance for funding through the convention's financial mechanism for implementation of programmes of convention.

Nagoya Protocol an access to genetic resources and the fair and equitable sharing of benefits arising from their utilization to the convention of biological diversity is an of genetic resources in fair and equitable way, including by appropriate access to genetic resources and by appropriate transfer of relevent technology, taking into account all rights over those resources and to technologies and by appropriate funding thereby contributing to the conservation of biological diversity. It was adopted of COP to convention on biological diversity at its tenth meeting on 29 Oct 2010 in Nagoya Japan. This Protocol will be open for signature by parties from 2 Feb 2011 to 1 Feb 2012 at United Nations headquarter.

Table 32.14 **Major Multilateral Environment Agreements (MEAs) Ratified by India**

MEAs	Year	Entry into Force	Data of Ratification by India	Issues Covered
Convention of Wetlands of International Importance	1971	21.12.1975	11.02.1982	Conservation and wise use of wetlands, primarily as habitate for the water-birds.
Convention for the Protection of World Cultural and Natural Heritage	1972	17.12.1975	04.11.1977	Protection and conservation of cultural and natural heritage.
Convention on International Trade in Endangered Species	1973	01.07.1975	20.07.1976	International trade in endangered species of wild fauna and flora.
Bonn Convention on Migratory Species of Wild Animals	1979	01.11.1983	01.11.1983	Conservation, management and wose use of migratory species of wild animals and their habitats.
Vienna Convention for Protection of the Ozone Layer	1985	22.09.1988	18.03.1991	Protection of atmospheric ozone layer above the planetary boundary layer.
Montreal Protocol on Substances that Deplete the Ozone Layer	1987	01.01.1989	19.06.1992	Protection of atmospheric ozone layer above the planetary boundary layer.
Basel Convention on Transboundary Movements of Hazardous Wastes and their Disposal	1989	05.05.1992	24.06.1992	Regulation of transboundary movements of hazardous wastes and their disposal.
United Nations Framework Convention on Climate Change (UNFCCC)	1992	21.03.1994	01.11.1993	Changes in the Earth's climate system due to anthropogenic interference.
Kyoto Protocol to the UNFCCC	1997	16.02.2005	26.08.220	Quantified emission limitation and reduction commitments for Annex I Parties.
Convention on Biological Diversity (CBD)	1992	29.12.1993	18.02.1994	Biological diversity and biological resources.
Cartagena Protocol on Biosafety to the CBD	2000	11.09.2003	11.09.2003	Regulation of transboundary movements, transit, handling and use of Living Modified Organism (LMOs).
United Nations Convention to Combat Desertification	1994	26.12.1996	17.12.1996	Combating desertification and mitigate the effects drought, particularly in Africa.
Rotterdam Convention on the Prior Informed Consent Procedure for Certain Hazardous Chemicals and Pesticides in International Trade	1998	24.02.2004	24.05.2005	Promote shared responsibility and cooperative efforts among the parties in the international trade of certain hazardous chemicals, in order to protect human health and the environment from potential harm and to contribute to their environmentally sound use.
Stockholm Convention on Persistent Organic Pollutants.	2001	17.05.2004	13.01.2006	Protect human health and the environment from persistent organic pollutants.

Conservation Biology

Principles of Conservation

The principle of this convention included in the article- 3. It defines that state have, in accordance with the charter of the United Nations and the principles of the international law, the sovereign right to exploit their own resources pursuant to their own environmental policies and the responsibilities to ensure that activities within their jurisdiction or control do not cause damage to the environment of other state or of area beyond the limits of national Jurisdication.

'Red List' of Endangered Species

The International Union of Conservation of Nature and Natural Resources an organization dedicated to accounting of ecological losses and steer the conservation efforts publishes a 'Red List' that contains the list of endangered species.

Species are classified in nine groups, set through criteria such as rate of decline population size, area of geographic distribution, and degree of population and distribution fragmentation.

Extinct (EX)	No individuals remaining.
Extinct in the Wild (EW)	Known only to survive in captivity or as a naturalized population outside its historic range.
Critically Endangered (CR)	Extremely high risk of extinction in the wild.
Endangered (EN)	High risk of extinction in the wild.
Vulnerable (VU)	High risk of endangerment in the wild.
Near Threatened (NT)	Likely to become endangered in the near future.
Least Concern (LC)	Lowest risk. Does not qualify for a more at risk category. Widespread and abundant taxa are included in this category.
Data Deficient (DD)	Not enough data to make an assessment of its risk of extinction.
Not Evaluated (NE)	Has not yet been evaluated against the criteria.

When discussing the IUCN Red List, the official term 'threatened' is a grouping of three categories: Critically Endangered, Endangered and Vulnerable.

Endangered, Threatened and Endemic Taxa

On the basis of available data any taxonomic unit at or below the species level can be categorized into extinct, endangered, vulnerable, near threatened, and this categorization process only applied to wild population inside their natural range and to populations resulting from benign introduction. It is possible to place all taxa into one of the following categories.

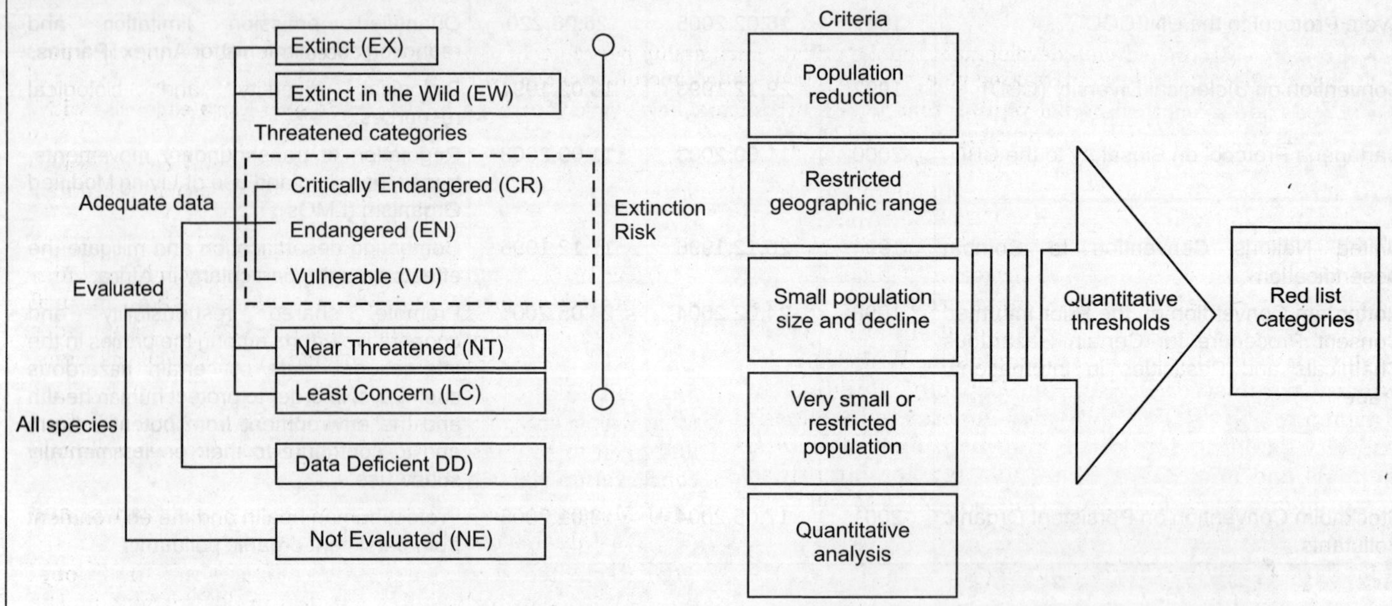

Fig. 32.6 Categorization of species

Extinct (Ex) A taxon is extinct when there is no reasonable doubt that last individual has died.

Extinct in Wild (EW) A taxon is extinct in wild when it is known only to survive in cultivation, in captivity or as a naturalized population well outside past range.

Biotechnical Approaches to Biodiversity Conservation

1. **Ecosystem conservation**
   - Restoration of degraded habitats/landscapes/ecosystems.
   - Molecular markers for assessing evolutionary potential of populations/species in ecosystems.
   - Molecular ecology of invasive species and their control through development of host specific biological methods.

- Assessment of genomic diversity and conservation of gene pools and establishment of DNA banks of grasses, legumes, orchids, etc.
- Assessment of genetic diversity of rare and endemic species and species that are critical for ecosystems functioning.
- Use of bioinformatics.
- Training and capacity building in molecular tools and techniques.

2. **Environmental biotechnology**
   - Bio and phyto remediation for restoration of environmental quality.
   - Biodegradation of xenobiotics.
   - Resources/wastes utilization/treatment through application of *r*DNA technology.
   - Augmentation of production of biodegradable plastics.
   - Use of GMOs for pollution control.
   - Biotechnological interventions for crop protection.
3. **Medicinal plants and aromatic grasses**
   - Scaling up of research leads, product development and value addition in respect of medicinal plants.
   - Development of standard and safe herbal products or isolation and characterization of therapeutically active compounds from medicinal plants.
   - Cell-culture production of therapeutic agents from plants.
   - Studies on herbal drug-modern drug interaction.
   - Network projects, mission mode programmes and creation of associated infrastructural facilities for optimal utilization of selected medicinal and aromatic plants species.
4. **Animal biotechnology**
   - Genomics, genetic characterization and development of vaccines and diagnostics for livestock.
5. **Bioresources development and utilization**
   - Biodiversity characterization through remote sensing and database development.
   - Bioprospecting of plants, microbes, marine organisms, etc., for development of novel products.
6. **Societal programme**
   - Promote entrepreneurship development, public private partnership particularly in agro food processing, self help groups and anganwadi workers for undertaking village based activities and microfinancing.
   - Create and strengthen herbal venture fund to support product development through linking traditional knowledge base with various biotechnology labs in private, public and NGO sectors.
   - Establish model bio-villages, support mobile research labs, organize training programmes, bio-melas, traditional food festivals/ shows, etc., and use other mass communication tools to create education and awareness among local people including panchayat members for judicious use of bioresources.

- Various initiatives to develop national capacities for biodiversity conservation and appropriate use of new technologies have been undertaken at different levels involving wide range of stakeholders. While an All India Coordinated Project on Capacity Building in Taxonomy (AICOPTAX) provided impetus to taxonomic capacity building for lesser known groups of plants, animals and microorganisms, India further intensified research on genetic fingerprinting of captive stock.

Major Approaches to Management

We have a moral duty to book after over planet and pass it on in a good health to our future generation. We may appreciate the fact that the most effective and efficient mechanism for conserving biodiversity is to prevent further destruction or degradation of habitat by us. There are two basic strategies to conserve biodiversity.

(i) ***In situ* conservation** This approach includes protection of a group of typical ecosystem through a network of protected areas, *i.e.*, conservation in natural habitat. It includes biosphere reserve, National Park and wildlife sanctuaries.

(ii) ***Ex situ* conservation** This approach includes protection of plants, animals outside their natural habitat for medicinal or other purposes, *i.e.*, it includes seed bank, Botanical gardens, Zoological gardens, aquarium, etc.

Most people recognize that diversity at all levels is important and need to be conserved. The points to take stress during conservation strategies are:

(a) Measures and incentives for the conservation and sustainable use of biological diversity.

(b) Regulated access to genetic resources and traditional knowledge including Prior Informed Consent of the party providing resources.

(c) Sharing in a fair and equitable way, the results of research and development and the benefits arising from the commercial and other utilization of genetic resources with the contracting party providing such resources (governments and/or local communities that provided the traditional knowledge or biodiversity resources utilized).

(d) Access to and transfer of technology, including biotechnology, to the governments and/or local communities that provided traditional knowledge and/or biodiversity resources.

(e) Technical and scientific cooperation.

(f) Impact assessment.

(g) Education and public awareness.

(h) Provision of financial resources.

(i) National reporting on efforts to implement treaty commitments.

Table 32.15 **Brief Outline of Policies, Plans and Strategies Dealing with Biodiversity**

Policies, Plans and Strategies	Brief Outline of Priorities
• National Forest Policy, 1988	Provides for national goals and guidelines relating to areas under forests, afforestation, social forestry and farm forestry, management of state forests, rights and concessions, diversion of forest lands for non-forest purposes, wildlife conservation, tribal people and forests, shifting cultivation, damage to forests from encroachments, fire and grazing, forest-based industries, etc. The policy also covers forestry education, research management, survey and database, legal support, infrastructure development and financial support.
• National Conservation Strategy and Policy Statement for Environment and Sustainable Development, 1992	Outlines the nature and dimensions of environmental problems in India as well as actions taken and constraints and agenda for action.
• National Policy and Macro-level Action Strategy on Biodiversity, 1999	Outlines a series of macro-level statements of policies, gaps and strategies needed for conservation and sustainable use of biodiversity.
• National Agricultural Policy, 2000	Seeks to actualize the vast untapped growth potential of Indian agriculture, rural infrastructure, value addition, secure a fair standard of living for the farmers and agricultural workers, discourage migration to urban areas and face the challenges arising out of economic liberalization and globalization.
• National Seeds Policy, 2002	Thrust areas include varietal development production, quality assurance, seed distribution and marketing, infrastructure facilities, etc.
• National Wildlife Action Plan (2002-2016)	Calls for adoption and implementation of strategies covering strengthening and enhancing the PA network, effective management of PAs, conservation of wild and endangered species and their habitats, restoration of degraded habitats outside PAs, control of poaching and illegal trade in wild animal and plant species, monitoring and research, HR development, ensuring peoples participation awareness and education, wildlife tourism, domestic legislation and international conventions, enhancing financial allocation and integration with other sectoral programmes.
• Comprehensive Marine Fishing Policy, 2004	Aims to maximize yield from marine fishery resources while balancing the development needs of the various categories of fishing communities.
• National Environment Policy, 2006	Stated objectives include: (i) Conservation of critical environmental resources; (ii) Intra-generational equity: livelihoods security for the poor; (iii) Inter-generational equity; (iv) Integration of environmental concerns in economic and social development; (v) Efficiency in environmental resource use; (vi) Environmental governance; (vii) Enhancement of resources for environmental conservation.
• 11th Five Year Plan (2007-2012)	Calls for a development strategy that is sensitive to growing environmental concerns and calls for careful evaluation of threats and trade-offs.
• National Forestry Action Programme (2000-2020)	Envisages developing coordinated programme for the sustainable management of forests and forest lands to meet the environmental, socio-economic and cultural needs of the present and the future generations.
• National Biotechnology Development Strategy (2007)	Prioritizes key policy recommendations and interventions relating to human resource, infrastructure development and manufacturing and regulatory mechanisms.
• National Forestry Commission Report (2006)	Contains over 350 recommendations regarding organizational structure and functions of the forestry sector.
• Final Technical Report National Biodiversity Strategy and Action Plan Project (2005)	Identified a detailed set of priority issues for the overall planning and governance as well as for the conservation of wild as well as domesticated biodiversity.
• National Action Plan on Climate Change (2008)	Eight national missions envisaged and among these four (National mission on water, sustaining himalayan ecosystems, sustainable agriculture and green India) are directly relevant to biodiversity conservation.

Biodiversity Conservation: Threats and Constraints

- **Habitat fragmentation, degradation and loss and shrinking of genetic diversity** The loss and fragmentation of natural habitats affect all animal and plant species. Various species of plants and animals are on the decline due to habitat fragmentation and over-exploitation, *e.g.,* habitats of Great Indian Bustard in Madhya Pradesh, Gujarat and Rajasthan and of the Lion-tailed Macaque in Western Ghats. Loss of habitats and over-exploitation have led to depletion of genetic diversity of several wild animals and cultivated plants.
- **Declining natural resource base and over exploitation of resources** Degradation of forests results from illicit felling, excess removal of forest products, fodder, fuel wood, forest floor litter, overgrazing and forest fires. As a result, some of the floristic and faunal components, including many keystone and endemic forest species are now left with narrow eroding populations which need to be urgently conserved.
- **Invasive alien species** The major plant invasive species include *Lantana camara, Eupatorium odoratum, E.adenophorum, Parthenium hysterophorus, Ageratum conyzoides, Mikania micrantha, Prosopis juliflora, Cytisus scoparius*, etc. Alien aquatic weeds like water hyacinth are increasingly choking waterways and degrading freshwater ecosystems. A recent intruder, the African catfish (also called Thai magur) seem to have posed even far greater threats to native fish fauna.
- **Climate change and desertification.**
- **Impact of development projects.**

National Biodiversity Authority (NBA)

- The NBA established in October 2003 pursuant to section 8 of the BDA.
- Focuses and advises GOI on conservation of biodiversity, sustainable use of its components and securing equitable sharing of benefits arising out of the utilization of biological resources.
- Regulates access to biological resources and associated traditional knowledge for research and/or commercial purposes, bio-survey and bioutilization as well as transfer of research results, seeking IPR and third party transfer of bioresources.
- Advises the State Governments in the selection of areas of importance as biodiversity heritage sites and measures for the management of such sites.
- Has constituted expert committees to perform functions such as laying down the procedure and guidelines to govern the activities such as Access and Benefit Sharing (ABS), Prior Informed Consent (PIC), Mutually Agreed Terms (MAT), Intellectual Property Rights (IPR), list of normally traded commodities, establishment of heritage sites and their management, national designated repositories and safeguarding of traditional knowledge respecting the Article 8 (j) of the CBD.
- May take measures necessary on behalf of GOI to oppose the grant of IPR which do not adhere to the PIC and MAT.
- Coordinates the activities of the State Biodiversity Boards and large number of local level Biodiversity Management Committees by providing them with technical guidance and financial assistance.
- Commissions studies and sponsor investigations and research on preparation of PBRs to document the rich valuable knowledge of local people on biodiversity and conducts capacity building programmes.

Invasive Alien Species

- 173 alien plant species recorded in India.
- India follows international quarantine regulations.
- Directorate of plant protection, quarantine and Storage, Faridabad, Ministry of Agriculture is the nodal agency to enforce the regulations; Latest regulations are 'Plant Quarantine Order 2003'.
- Environmental (Protection) Act, 1986 (Rules 1989) states 'to prohibit or restrict substances having potential to cause damage to environmental, plants and animals'.
- ICFRE has established a 'Forest Invasive Species (FIS) Cell' in Forest Research Institute (FRI) to deal with various aspects of management of FIS in the country.

Table 32.16 **Legislations Relevant to Biodiversity Conservation**

Relevant Key Legislation	Key Feature
Wildlife (Protection) Act, 1972	Deals with protection of wildlife and habitats and provides for the protection of wild animals, birds and plants and related matters, with a view to ensuring the ecological and environmental security of the country.
Indian Forest Act, 1927	Designed for forest management and protection, the transit of forest and the duty leviable on timber and other forest produce.
Forest (Conservation) Act, 1980	Designed for the conservation of forests and related matters.
Biological Diversity Act, 2002	Provides for conservation of biological diversity, sustainable use of its components and fair and equitable sharing of the benefits arising out of the use of biological resources, knowledge and related matters.
Biological Diversity Rules, 2004	Deals with operationalizing the Biological Diversity Act.
Protection of Plant Varieties and Farmer's Right Act, 2001	Provides for the establishment of an effective system for protection of plant varieties, the rights of farmers and plant breeders and to encourage the development of new varieties of plants.
The Schedules Tribes and Other Traditional Forest Dwellers (Recognition of Forest Rights) Act, 2006	Recognizes and vests the traditional rights to forest dwelling communities over access to forest goods and occupation in forest lands.

Indian Case Studies on Conservation/Management Strategy

Government of India had developed a number of strategies for conservation of biodiversity like project tiger, biosphere reserve etc.

Project Tiger

Project Tiger, launched in 1973-74, is one of our most successful conservation ventures in the recent times. The project aims at tiger conservation in specially constituted 'tiger reserves', which are representative of various bio-geographical regions falling within our country. It strives to maintain a viable tiger population in the natural environment.

The project was launched in 1973, and various tiger reserves were created in the country on a 'core-buffer' strategy. The core areas were freed from all sorts of human activities and the buffer areas were subjected to 'conservation oriented land use'. Management plans were drawn up for each tiger reserve, based on the principles outlined below.

(i) Elimination of all forms of human exploitation and biotic disturbance from the core area and rationalization of activities in the buffer zone.

(ii) Restricting the habitat management only to repair the damages done to the ecosystem by human and other interferences, so as to facilitate recovery of the ecosystem to its natural state.

(iii) Monitoring the faunal and floral changes over time and carrying out research about wildlife.

Initially, 9 tiger reserves were established in different states during the period 1973-74, by pooling the resources available with the central and state governments. These nine reserves covered an area of about 13,017sq.km *viz* Manas (Asom), Palamau (Bihar), Similipal (Odisha), Corbett (U.A.), Kanha (M.P.), Melghat (Maharashtra), Bandipur (Karnataka), Ranthambhore (Rajasthan) and Sunderbans (West Bengal).

The project started as a 'Central Sector Scheme' with the full assistance of Central Government till 1979-80: later, it become a 'centrally Sponsored Scheme' from 1980-81, with equal sharing of expenditure between the centre and the states.

Table 32.17 **The Tiger Reserve Different States**

State	Tiger Reserve	Year Estd	Total Area km^2
Uttarakhand	Corbett Tiger Reserve	1973-74	1316
Asom	Manas Tiger Reserve	1973-74	2840
Karnataka	Bandipur Tiger Reserve	1973-74	866
Madhya Pradesh	Kanha Tiger Reserve	1973-74	1945
Maharashtra	Melghat Tiger Reserve	1973-74	1677
Odisha	Simipal Tiger Reserve	1973-74	2750
Rajasthan	Ranthambhore Tiger Reserve	1973-74	1334
West Bengal	Sunderbans Tiger Reserve	1973-74	2585
Jharkhand	Palamau Tiger Reserve	1973-74	1026
Kerala	Periyar Tiger Reserve	1978-79	777
Rajasthan	Sariska Tiger Reserve	1978-79	866
Arunachal Pradesh	Namdapha Tiger Reserve	1982-83	1985
West Bengal	Buxa Tiger Reserve	1982-83	759
Chhattisgarh	Indravati Tiger Reserve	1982-83	2799
Andhra Pradesh	Nagarjunsagar-Srisailam Tiger Reserve	1982-83	3568
Uttar Pradesh	Dudhwa Tiger Reserve	1987-88	811
Tamil Nadu	Kalakad-Mundathurai Tiger Reserve	1988-89	800
Bihar	Valmiki Tiger Reserve	1989-90	840
Madhya Pradesh	Pench Tiger Reserve	1992-93	758
Maharashtra	Pench Tiger Reserve	1992-93	257
Madhya Pradesh	Bandhavgarh Tiger Reserve	1993-94	1162
Maharashtra	Tadoba-Andhari Tiger Reserve	1993-94	620

State	Tiger Reserve	Year Estd	Total Area km^2
Madhya Pradesh	Panna Tiger Reserve	1994-95	542
Mizoram	Dampa Tiger Reserve	1994-95	500
Karnataka	Bhadra Tiger Reserve	1998-99	492
Asom	Nameri Tiger Reserve	1999-2000	344
Arunachal Pradesh	Pakhui Tiger Reserve	1999-2000	862
Karnataka	Nagarhole (extension) Tiger Reserve	1999-2000	643
Madhya Pradesh	Bori-Satpura Tiger Reserve	1999-2000	1486
Asom	Kaziranga Tiger Reserve	2006	859
Chhattisgarh	Guru Ghasidas National Park	2000	1500
Odisha	Satkosia Tiger Reserve	2007	988
Karnataka	Dandeli-Anashi Tiger Reserve	2007	875
Tamil Nadu	Mudumalai National Park	2007	321
Odisha	Sunabeda Tiger Reserve	2008-09	856
Kerala/Tamil Nadu	Annamalai Tiger Reserve	2008	1019
Madhya Pradesh	Ratapani Tiger Reserve	2008-09	674
Tamil Nadu/Kerala	Parambikulam Tiger Reserve	2010	391
Uttar Pradesh	Pilibhit Tiger Reserve	2008-09	1089
Chattisgarh	Udanti and Sitanadi Tiger Reserve	2008	1580
Chattisgarh	Achanakmar Tiger Reserve	2008	963
Madhya Pradesh	Sanjay Dubri Tiger Reserve	2008	931
Maharashtra	Sahyadri Tiger Reserve	2008-09	569
Karnataka	Biligiri Rangaswamy Temple Wildlife Sanctuary	2010	–

Biosphere Reserves

Under the Man and Biosphere (MAB) Programme out of 16 biospheres in India (70,000 sq km), seven are already in UNESCO World Network of Biosphere Reserves (World total 503).

Table 32.18 **Biosphere Reserve in India**

Name of the Biosphere Reserve and Total Geographical Area (km^2)	Date of Notification	Location (State)
Nilgiri (5520)	01.08.86	Part of Wynad, Nagarhole, Bandipur and Madumalai, Nilambur, Silent Valley and Siruvani hills (Tamil Nadu, Kerala and Karnataka)
Nanda Devi (6497.03)	18.01.88	Part of Chamoli, Pithoragarh and Almora Districts and Valley of Flowers (Uttarakhand)
Nokrek (820)	01.09.88	Parts of Garo Hills (Meghalaya)
Manas (2837)	14.03.89	Parts of Kokrajhar, Bongaigaon, Barpeta, Nalbari, Kamprup and Darange Districts (Asom)
Sunderbans (9630)	29.03.89	Parts of delta of Ganges and Brahamputra river system (West Bengal)
Gulf of Mannar (10500)	18.02.89	Indian part of Gulf of Mannar between India and Sri Lanka (Tamil Nadu)
Great Nicobar (885)	06.01.89	Southern most islands of Andaman and Nicobar (A and N Islands)
Similipal (4374)	21.06.94	Parts of Mayurbhanj district (Odisha)
Dibru-Saikhowa (765)	28.07.97	Parts of Dibrugarh and Tinsukia districts (Asom)

Name of the Biosphere Reserve and Total Geographical Area (km^2)	Date of Notification	Location (State)
Dehange Debang (5111.5)	02.09.98	Parts of Siang and Debang Valley in Arunachal Pradesh
Kanchanjunga (2619.92)	07.02.2000	Parts of North and West Sikkim.
Pachmari (4926.28)	03.03.99	Parts of Betur, Hoshangabad and Chindwara districts of Madhya Pradesh.
Agasthyamalai (3500.36)	12.11.2001 (area expanded on 30.03.2005	Parts of Thirunelveli and Kanyakumari Districts in Tamil Nadu andThiruvanathapuram, Kollam and Pathanamthitta.
Achanakmar-Amarkantak (3835.51)	30.03.2005	Parts of Anuppur and Dindori districts of Madhya Pradesh and Parts of Bilaspur district of Chhattisgarh State.
Kuchch (12454)	29.01.2008	Parts of Kachch, Rajkot, Surendranagar and Patan district of Gujarat
Cold Desert (7770)	2009	Pin Valley National Park and surroundings; Chandratal and Sarchu and Kibber Wildlife Sanctuary, Himachal Pradesh.

Exercise

1. What aspect of London's 1952 smog episode prompted industrialized countries to regulate industrial air emissions?
(a) Smog is only produced by the burning of low-carbon peat
(b) It was produced by the reaction of air pollutants to sunlight
(c) It contributed to the death of thousands of people
(d) It depleted ozone

2. The Earth's ozone layer that controls the amount of solar radiation striking the planet is found in which of the following?
(a) Stratosphere (b) Tropopause
(c) Inversion layer (d) Thermosphere

3. The pattern of atmospheric conditions found across a relatively large geographic region over a long period of time is called which of the following?
(a) Climate (b) Hadley cells
(c) Seasonal cycles (d) Ferrel cells

4. Under normal atmospheric conditions, why do vertical mixing and dispersion of air pollutants occur?
(a) Warm air at the surface rises
(b) In an inversion, cool air lies below warm air
(c) Warm air is denser than cool air
(d) In an inversion, warm air lies above cool air

5. Which of the following correctly describes a secondary air pollutant?
(a) A pollutant that is less hazardous than a primary pollutant
(b) A pollutant emitted into the troposphere in a form that is directly harmful
(c) A pollutant that develops through chemical reactions with other pollutants or chemicals normally present in the atmosphere
(d) The formation of these are not as strictly controlled as primary air pollutants

6. Pollutants that produce acid rain in rural areas such as Hubbard Brook were found to come primarily from which of the following?
(a) Carbon dioxide from burning fossil fuels
(b) Pollutants from automobile exhaust
(c) Pollutants transported from urban areas
(d) The geology of the area that produces acidic soils

7. What is the principle health concern of ozone depletion in the stratosphere?
(a) Cancer and other damage to the skin
(b) Ilankovitch cycles
(c) Temperature inversions
(d) Hadley cell

8. Which of the following is not likely to happen as a result of the rising levels of CO_2 in our atmosphere?
(a) Increased incidence of skin cancer
(b) Rise in sea levels
(c) Change in climatic patterns
(d) Shifts in locations of deserts and fertile regions

9. DDT and chlordane are agricultural chemicals that were once used widely but have now been banned in the United States. They belong to a class of compounds called
(a) chlorofluorocarbons
(b) chlorinated hydrocarbons
(c) fossil fuels
(d) acid precipitation

10. Acid rain causes
(a) destruction of forests (b) gradual killing of lakes
(c) killing fish (d) All of these

11. CFCs are
(a) a cause of ozone depletion
(b) propellants in aerosol dispensers
(c) foaming agents in styrofoam
(d) All of the above

12. Which of the following statement is incorrect?
(a) We presently lack the technology to prevent acid rain
(b) Every 1% drop in atmospheric ozone content is estimated to lead to a 6% increase in the incidence of skin cancer
(c) Topsoil, groundwater and biodiversity are non-replaceable resources
(d) The first stage in addressing an environmental problem is assessing the situation

13. Information that is based upon the beliefs, cultures and values of aboriginal peoples and their thousands of years of experience in their environment is called
(a) popular ecosystem knowledge
(b) traditional ecosystem knowledge
(c) traditional ecological knowledge
(d) popular ecological knowledge

14. Scientists use .... to track changes in ecosystems by comparing the results of investigations done at different times.
(a) ecological watches
(b) organism monitoring
(c) environmental system gathering
(d) ecosystem monitoring

15. .... give scientists information about ecosystems before any events occur.
(a) A feeder watch
(b) A scattered population survey
(c) Baseline data
(d) Guideline samplings

16. A report that outlines how an activity will affect the environment is called
(a) a natural disturbance survey
(b) wetland monitoring
(c) a natural succession assessment
(d) an environmental impact assessment

17. Which of the following is not true about biodiversity?
(a) Maximum diversity occurs in tropic
(b) Introduction of exotic species may cause the loss of biodiversity
(c) Diversity of the habitats over the total landscape or geographical area is called gamma diversity
(d) Hotspot concept developed by the Norman Mayers to designate priority areas for *ex situ* conservation of biodiversity

18. Which of the following character make a species susceptible to extinction?
(a) Large population size
(b) Feeding at high trophic level in food chain
(c) Wide range of distributions
(d) Small body size

19. A species facing an extremely high risk of extinction in the immediate future is called
(a) vulnerable (b) rare
(c) endangered (d) link species

20. Choose the incorrect statement.
(a) Nilgiri biosphere reserve is the first biosphere reserve in India
(b) All land with tree cover of canopy density of between 10-40% is known as open forest
(c) Western Ghats and Eastern Himalayas are two hotspots in India
(d) The Earth summit held in 1992 at Rio de Janerio to prevent ozone depletion at stratosphere

21. Which of the following statement is false?
I. Genetic diversity helps prevent a species from becoming extinct.
II. The phenomenon in which animals with favourable adaptation reproduces more rapidly is called differential reproduction.
III. Geographic isolation is a common mechanism contributing to speciation.
IV. Biologists estimate that 99% of all species that have ever existed are now extinct.
(a) I and III (b) I and IV
(c) II and III (d) None of these

22. Which of the following best describes biodiversity?
(a) The kinds of species in a community
(b) The diversity of species in an area including their genes, populations and communities
(c) Populations of organisms that share certain characteristics and can freely breed
(d) The large numbers of species in tropical countries

23. Which of the statement below is the best description of a niche?
(a) Niche requirements include nesting sites and the location of food
(b) Habitat
(c) Niche specialists are better equipped to survive a major environmental catastrophe than generalists
(d) The occupation or activities of a species

24. Which of the following is a typical *k*-selected adaptation?
(a) Small body size
(b) Large numbers of offspring
(c) A very unstable population level
(d) Parental care of young

25. Areas set aside to protect examples of the different habitats in the province are called
(a) ecological reserves
(b) environmental preserves
(c) ecoprovinces
(d) biomes

26. Biologists might use .... to mate animals in zoos then release the young into the wild.
(a) an adaptive breeding program
(b) a symbiotic breeding program
(c) a captive breeding program
(d) an introduced species breeding program

27. .... is the careful and responsible management of something for which you are responsible.
(a) Stewardship (b) Enhancement
(c) Restoration (d) Sustainability

28. Learning about ecosystems and how to care for them will help you understand the natural world so you can
(a) take better care of all living things
(b) prevent natural disturbances
(c) prevent ecological succession
(d) increase the limiting factors in an ecosystem

29. Historically, island species have tended to become extinct faster than species living on a mainland. Which of the following reasons cannot be used to explain this phenomenon?
(a) Island species have often evolved in the absence of predators and have no natural avoidance strategies
(b) Humans have introduced diseases and competitors to islands, which negatively impacts island populations
(c) Island populations are usually smaller than mainland populations
(d) Island populations are usually less fit than mainland populations

30. An endemic species is
(a) one found in many different geographic areas
(b) one found naturally in just one geographic area
(c) one found only on islands
(d) one that has been introduced to a new geographic area

31. Which of the following does not distinguish the current mass extinction event from past events?
(a) This is the only extinction event to be triggered by a single species
(b) This is the only extinction event from which biodiversity may not recover
(c) This is the only extinction event in which the majority of losses are occurring in mainland areas
(d) This is the only extinction event in which the majority of losses are occurring on islands

32. The ability of an intact ecosystem, such as a wetland, to buffer against flooding and filter pollutants from water is a(n) .... value of biodiversity.
(a) direct economic (b) indirect economic
(c) ethical (d) aesthetic

33. Which of the following is currently considered the leading cause of extinction?
(a) Overexploitation of species
(b) Competition from introduced species
(c) Habitat loss
(d) Pollution

34. Numbers of migratory songbirds are declining in North America. Which of the following factors is important in this decline?
(a) Pollution
(b) Human disruption of breeding behaviour
(c) Habitat fragmentation in the United States
(d) Global climate change

35. All of the following are adaptations to high altitude except
(a) increased breathing rate
(b) increased erythrocyte production
(c) increased binding capacity of haemoglobin
(d) increased density of mitochondria, capillaries and muscle myoglobin

36. Comparing the mean biomass of ecosystems in kg/m^2, what type of ecosystem has the greatest biomass?
(a) Estuaries (b) Cultivated land
(c) Tropical rain forest (d) Boreal forest

37. The climate of a particular region is influenced by its
(a) solar radiation (b) latitude
(c) Both (a) and (b) (d) None of these

38. Where would you find coral reefs?
(a) In the epilimnion (b) In the abyssal zone
(c) In the profundal zone (d) In the neritic zone

39. Compared with terrestrial habitats, the oceans have .... species and .... phyla.
(a) more; more (b) fewer; fewer
(c) more; fewer (d) fewer; more

40. Which of the following statements is true?
(a) In the temperate zones of the Northern hemisphere, the Eastern edges of continents tend to be warmer than the Western edges
(b) The major circulation pattern in the atmosphere is an East-to-West one; there is very little North or South movement of air
(c) Geological features, as well as atmospheric and oceanic circulation patterns, help determine which biomes occur where
(d) Most of the great deserts lie between 40° and 60° North or South latitude

41. Approximately what percentage of the Earth's surface is covered by inland lakes?
(a) 0.3% (b) 1.8%
(c) 23% (d) 50%

42. The best predictor of future population growth rate is
(a) life expectancy (b) age structure
(c) mortality (d) undeveloped land

43. Project Tiger in India was launched in
(a) 1968 (b) 1972
(c) 1984 (d) 1993

44. Which of the following is a salient feature of Project Tiger in India?
(a) The project aims at ensuring a viable population of tigers in their natural habitats and preserving areas of biological importance as a natural heritage for the people
(b) The selection of areas for the reserves represented as close as possible the diversity of ecosystems across the tiger's distribution in the country
(c) The project's task force visualized these tiger reserves as breeding nuclei, from which surplus animals would emigrate to adjacent forests
(d) All of the above

45. The goals and objective of Project Tiger in India include
(a) identify the limiting factors and to mitigate them by suitable management
(b) the damages done to the habitat were to be rectified so as to facilitate the recovery of the ecosystem to the maximum possible extent
(c) Both (a) and (b)
(d) None of the above

46. How many biosphere reserves (categories roughly corresponding to IUCN category V protected areas) has been established by Indian Government?
(a) 10 (b) 13
(c) 17 (d) 23

47. Based on the UNESCO Man and the Biosphere (MAB) programme list .... of the seventeen biosphere reserves in India are a part of the world network of biosphere reserves.
(a) five (b) seven
(c) ten (d) thirteen

48. Which of the following biosphere is a part of the World Network of Biosphere Reserves?
(a) Sundarbans national park and Nilgiri Biosphere Reserve
(b) Nanda Devi Biosphere Reserve and Nokrek Biosphere Reserve
(c) Panchmarhi Biosphere Reserve and Simlipal Biosphere Reserve
(d) All of the above

49. One of the *ex situ* conservation methods for endangered species is
(a) wildlife sanctuaries (b) biosphere reserves
(c) cryopreservation (d) national park

50. *In situ* conservation national genetic resources can be achieved by establishing
(a) national park (b) wildlife sanctuaries
(c) biosphere reserve (d) All of these

51. Biosphere reserves are being threatened with
(a) population growth (b) rains
(c) pollution (d) All of these

52. Which one of the following is a pair of endangered species?
(a) Hornbill and Indian Aconite
(b) Indian peacock and Carrot Grass
(c) Garden lizard and Mexican poppy
(d) Rhesus monkey and Sal tree

53. Wildlife conservation means the protection and preservation of
(a) ferocious wild animals only
(b) wild plants only
(c) non-cultivated plants and non-domesticated animals
(d) All of the above living in natural habitat

54. In 1984, the Bhopal gas tragedy took place because methyl isocyanate
(a) reacted with CO_2 (b) reacted with water
(c) reacted with DDT (d) reacted with ammonia

55. In the treatment of waste water discharge, which treatment stage involves biological treatment
(a) primary treatment
(b) secondary treatment
(c) tertiary treatment
(d) reverse osmosis stage

56. Decrease in species diversity in tropical countries is mainly due to
(a) urbanization (b) pollution
(c) deforestation (d) soil erosion

57. Lichens are important in the studies on atmospheric pollution because they
(a) can grow in polluted atmosphere
(b) can readily multiply in polluted atmosphere
(c) efficiently purify the atmosphere
(d) are very sensitive to pollutants like sulphur dioxide

58. Which of the following pollutants affect more to organisms of the higher trophic level of a food chain due to biological amplification
(a) sewage and plant fertilizers
(b) detergents
(c) heavy metals mercury salts and non-biodegradable phenolic chemicals
(d) poisonous cyanides

59. How carbon monoxide, emitted by automobiles, prevents transport of oxygen in the body tissues
(a) By changing oxygen into carbon dioxide
(b) By destroying the haemoglobin
(c) By forming a stable compound with haemoglobin
(d) By obstructing the reaction of oxygen with haemoglobin

60. Photochemical smog formed in congested metropolitan cities mainly consists of
(a) ozone, peroxyacetyl nitrate and NO_x
(b) smoke, peroxyacetyl nitrate and SO_2
(c) hydrocarbons, SO_2 and CO_2
(d) hydrocarbons, ozone and SO_x

61. The phenomenon in which nutrient enrichment of a water body supports a dense growth of one or may organisms but decreases the species diversity is called
(a) biological magnification (b) species promotion
(c) eutrophication (d) None of these

62. CO is more toxic than CO_2 because
(a) it affects the nervous system
(b) it damages lungs
(c) it reduces the oxygen carrying capacity of haemoglobin
(d) it forms acid with water

63. Air pollution causing photochemical oxidants production include
(a) carbon monoxide, sulphur dioxide
(b) nitrous oxide, nitric acid fumes, nitric oxide
(c) ozone, peroxyacetyl nitrate, aldehydes
(d) oxygen, chlorine, fuming nitric acid

64. Acid rain is caused by or recent reports of acid rain in some industrial cities are due to the effect of atmospheric pollution by
(a) excessive release of CO_2 by burning of fuels like wood and charcoal, cutting of forests and increased animal population
(b) excessive release of NO_2 and SO_2 in atmosphere by burning of fossil fuel
(c) excessive release of NH_3 by industrial plants and coal gas
(d) excessive release of CO in atmosphere by incomplete combustion of coke, charcoal and other carbonaceous fuel in paucity of oxygen

65. Frequent occurrence of water blooms in a lake indicates
(a) nutrient deficiency
(b) oxygen deficiency
(c) excessive nutrient availability
(d) absence of herbivores in the lake

66. In almost of all Indian metropolitan cities like Delhi, the major atmospheric pollutant (s) is/are
(a) suspended particulate matter (SPM)
(b) oxides of sulphur
(c) carbon dioxide and carbon monoxide
(d) oxides of nitrogen

67. Cadmium pollution may cause
(a) Minamata disease
(b) Skeletal fluorosis
(c) Black foot disease
(d) Itai-itai disease

68. The greatest threat to global biodiversity is
(a) natural disasters such as storms
(b) overexploitation of natural resources
(c) competition of exotic species with native species
(d) human alteration of habitats

69. Which of the following is a greenhouse gas that may contribute to global warming?
(a) Methane
(b) Carbon dioxide
(c) CFCs
(d) Both (a) and (b)

70. A conservation group is trying to save Puerto Rico's endemic species. 'Endemic' means
(a) they live nowhere else
(b) predatory
(c) they are endangered
(d) they migrate from place to place

71. Why does the birth of a German baby have a greater impact on the environment than the birth of an Indonesian baby?
(a) The population of Germany is smaller, so one baby is a bigger increase
(b) Europe is closer to environmental disaster than Indonesia
(c) A German baby will use more resources and produce more pollution
(d) An Indonesian baby is more likely to die young

72. Exotic species
(a) are often endangered
(b) usually increase biodiversity
(c) often enhance the habitat for native species
(d) usually reduce biodiversity

73. Chemical pesticides such as DDT do the greatest harm to top predators such as ospreys and eagles because
(a) these animals are often exposed to chemical spraying
(b) their metabolism is particularly sensitive to very low concentrations of pesticides
(c) these animals are usually exposed to more than one pesticide at a time
(d) pesticide concentrations become magnified as these substances move through food chains

74. Most biodiversity hot spots are in
(a) tropical forests
(b) mountainous regions
(c) dry shrublands (chaparral)
(d) wetlands

75. Human activities such as clear cutting and road building often create edges between areas of different habitat. Edges created by human activities
(a) are usually more abrupt than natural boundaries between habitats
(b) may have their own species that are not present in adjacent habitats
(c) may be dominated by relatively few species
(d) All of the above

76. The greenhouse effect
(a) could change global weather and lead to the flooding of coastal areas
(b) could result in more C_4 plants in plant communities that were previously dominated by C_3 plants
(c) causes an increase in temperature when CO_2 absorb more sunlight entering the atmosphere
(d) could increase precipitation in central continental areas

77. An island that is small and far from the mainland, as compared to a large island close to the main land,
(a) would be expected to have a low species diversity
(b) would be expected to be in an early successional stage
(c) would have a small species diversity but a large abundance of organisms
(d) would have a high rate of colonization but a high rate of extinction

78. The island recolonization experiment of Simberloff and Wilson showed that
(a) Species diversity returns very slowly to an island after a disturbance
(b) The species diversity was highest when disturbances were intermediate in frequency and severity
(c) Whereas the same numbers of species of arthropods returned to each island, the species composition was different, indicating the importance of chance events
(d) Islands closest to the mainland had the greatest numbers of arthropods recolonize, and their community composition and diversity were the same as prior to fumigation.

79. Match the list I (National parks) with the list II (The important animals)

List I	List II
A. Kanha National Park	1. Tiger
B. Gir National Park	2. Asiatic lion
C. Bandipur National Park	3. Elephant
	4. Rhinoceros

Codes

	A	B	C
(a)	2	3	4
(b)	3	4	1
(c)	2	1	3
(d)	1	2	3

80. Match the list I (pollutant) with list II methods of control/recovery and select the correct codes.

List I	List II
A. Particulate matter from coal combustion	1. Incineration
B. Sulphur oxide fumes	2. Reverse osmosis
C. NO_2 from fumes	3. Combustion modification
D. Municipal waste water	4. Scrubber installation
	5. Electrostatic precipitators

Codes

	A	B	C	D
(a)	1	3	4	2
(b)	1	3	2	4
(c)	5	4	3	2
(d)	5	4	2	3

81. Mark the wrong statements

I. Lead is a cause of soil pollution.

II. Greenhouse effect is actually global warming.

III. Large particles are removed by cyclone reactors.

IV. CFC are used as refrigerant.

(a) I and III (b) I, III and IV

(c) IV only (d) II and III

82. Match the list I (protected areas) with list II (state) and select the correct codes.

List I	List II
A. Gulf of Mannar	1. Gujarat
B. Uttarakhand	2. Uttar Pradesh
C. Sundarban	3. West Bengal
D. Rann of Kachchh	4. Tamil Nadu

Codes

	A	B	C	D
(a)	2	4	1	3
(b)	2	4	3	1
(c)	4	2	1	3
(d)	4	2	3	1

83. Match the list I (Disease) with list II (Their cause) and select the correct codes.

List I	List II
A. Minamata disease	1. As
B. Itai-itai disease	2. Cd
C. Black foot disease	3. Hg
	4. Nitrates

Codes

	A	B	C
(a)	3	2	1
(b)	3	1	2
(c)	4	1	2
(d)	2	1	4

84. Match the list I (National parks) with list II (their location) and select the correct codes.

List I	List II
A. Keoladeo National Park	1. Gujarat
B. Gir National Park	2. Kashmir
C. Dachigam National Park	3. Bharatpur
	4. Gujarat

Codes

	A	B	C
(a)	3	1	2
(b)	3	2	1
(c)	2	3	4
(d)	3	1	4

Answers

1. (c) **2.** (a) **3.** (a) **4.** (a) **5.** (c) **6.** (c) **7.** (a) **8.** (a) **9.** (b) **10.** (d)
11. (d) **12.** (a) **13.** (c) **14.** (d) **15.** (c) **16.** (d) **17.** (d) **18.** (b) **19.** (c) **20.** (d)
21. (d) **22.** (b) **23.** (d) **24.** (d) **25.** (a) **26.** (c) **27.** (a) **28.** (a) **29.** (d) **30.** (b)
31. (d) **32.** (b) **33.** (c) **34.** (c) **35.** (c) **36.** (c) **37.** (c) **38.** (d) **39.** (d) **40.** (c)
41. (b) **42.** (b) **43.** (b) **44.** (d) **45.** (c) **46.** (c) **47.** (b) **48.** (d) **49.** (c) **50.** (d)
51. (c) **52.** (a) **53.** (d) **54.** (b) **55.** (b) **56.** (c) **57.** (d) **58.** (c) **59.** (c) **60.** (b)
61. (c) **62.** (c) **63.** (c) **64.** (b) **65.** (b) **66.** (a) **67.** (d) **68.** (d) **69.** (d) **70.** (a)
71. (c) **72.** (d) **73.** (d) **74.** (a) **75.** (d) **76.** (a) **77.** (a) **78.** (c) **79.** (d) **80.** (a)
81. (a) **82.** (b) **83.** (a) **84.** (a)

33 Origin of Life and Evolutionary Thoughts

Emergence of Evolutionary Thoughts

People thought that new living things appeared all the time through spontaneous generation from both non-living matter and other unrelated forms of life microorganisms were thought to arise spontaneously from broth, maggots from meat and mice from mixture of sweaty shirts and wheat floor. In 1668 Italian Physician **Francisco Redi** disproved the maggots from meat hypothesis simply by keeping flies (whose eggs hatch into maggots) away from uncontaminated meat. After this in mid 1800 **Louis Pasteur** in **France** and **John Tyndall** in England disproved the broth to microorganisms idea. Although their work effectively demolished the nation of spontaneous generation, it did not address the question of how life on Earth originated in the first place.

Lamarck

Jean Baptiste de Lamarck (1744-1829) proposed a mechanism that a lineage of organisms could change gradually over many generations as offspring inherited structures that had become larger and more highly developed as a result of continued use or, conversely, had become smaller and less developed as a result of lack of use. **Lamarckism** was based on the comparison between the contemporary species of his time and fossil record. He postulated:

1. **Doctrine of New Needs or Desires** The change in environmental factors like light, temperature, medium, food, air, etc., or migration, creates new needs for the organisms. To fulfil these new needs, living organisms have to put efforts which results in change in habit and habitat of the organism.

Syllabus

- Emergence of Evolutionary Thoughts: Lamarck; Darwin-Concepts of Variation, Adaptation, Struggle, Fitness and Natural Selection; Mendelism; Spontanity of Mutations; the Evolutionary Synthesis.
- Origin of Cells and Unicellular Evolution: Origin of Basic Biological Molecules; Abiotic Synthesis of Organic Monomers and Polymers; Concept of Oparin and Haldane; Experiment of Miller (1953); the First Cell; Evolution of Prokaryotes; Origin of Eukaryotic Cells; Evolution of Unicellular Eukaryotes; Anaerobic Metabolism, Photosynthesis and Aerobic Metabolism.

2. **Use and Misuse of Organs** The new habits involve greater use of certain organs and misuse use of other organs. The continuous use of certain organs makes them active and strong, while misuse makes them inactive, reduced and ultimately they disappears.
3. **Inheritance of Acquired Characters** This changes brought about by environmental factors is called acquired/adaptive characters. Lamarck believed that every generation acquire new characters and is transmitted to the new generation.

Evidences in Support of Lamarckism

(i) **Giraffe** is a mammal with very long neck and long forelimbs. They evolved from ancestors with short legs and short neck. These ancestors lived in barren land, they used to stretch their necks upward to reach the available food in the form of leaves on the tall trees, which made their neck slightly elongated that was passed to next generation.

(ii) **Snakes** are limbless snakes with long cylindrical body are produced due to continuous misuse of limbs and stretching of body to accommodate themselves in holes and protect them from powerful mammals.

(iii) **Aquatic Birds** (Ducks, Geese) have been evolved from terrestrial ancestral forms. Due to lack of food on land they had to go to water for search of food. This resulted in development of webbed toes. Their wings were not used for flying therefore, they get reduced.

(iv) **Cave Dwellers** like moles lived underground therefore, they lost eye sight due to misuse of their eyes.

Theory of Germplasm
(August Weismann; 1982)

His main contribution was the germplasm theory, according to which (in a multicellular organism) inheritance only takes place by means of the germ cells—the gametes such as egg cells and sperm cells. Other cells of the body—somatic cells—do not function as agents of heredity. The effect is one-way germ cells produce somatic cells and are not affected by anything the somatic cells learn or therefore, any ability the body acquires during its life. Genetic information cannot pass from soma to germplasm and on to the next generation. This idea, if true, rules out the inheritance of acquired characteristics as proposed by Jean-Baptiste Lamarck.

Experiment on Rats

The idea that germline cells contain information that passes to each generation unaffected by experience and independent of the somatic (body) cells, putting a final end to the theory of Lamarck and the inheritance of acquired characteristics. Weismann conducted the experiment of chopping of the tails of fifteen hundred rats, repeatedly over 20 generations, and reporting that no rat was ever born in consequence without a tail. He stated that '901 young were produced by five generations of artificially mutilated parents and yet there was not a single example of a rudimentary tail or any other abnormality of the organ'.

Criticism of Lamarckism

The two postulates, new needs and of use and misuse of organs are well accepted; but the third postulate, inheritance of acquired characters was disputed by **August Weismann** (1982) in his theory of germplasm.

Neo-Lamarckism

It is the modern synthesis of **Lamarckism.** It is based on the fact that genes are influenced by the physical and chemical factors which bring remarkable change in the offspring. The scientists who contributed to Neo-Lamarckism were : **Spencer, Brunner, Tower, TH Morgan, Mendel, Mayer, Smith,** etc., The Neo-Lamarckism states that:

(i) **Germ cells are formed from somatic cells** The regeneration in earthworm, vegetative propagation in plants and part of zygote can develop into complete body are the examples where somatic cells developed to form new species.

(ii) **Effect of environment on germ cells through somatic cells** When a pale variety of moth fed on manganese coated food, a true breeding melanic variety of moth is produced (H Harrison). Water flea in a culture of green flagellates develops some abnormalities in their structure. When their eggs are kept in ordinary water and allowed to hatch they produce individuals with same abnormality.

(iii) **Effect of environment directly on germ cells** The young potato beetles were exposed to temperature fluctuation by Tower. He found that all beetles remained unaffected but in the next generation they show marked change in body colouration.

Darwin

Darwin was influenced by Malthus essay on 'population', Wallace essay on 'The tendency of varieties to depart indefinitely form original type' and **Charles Lyell** book 'Principles of Geology.'

Darwin's theory of evolution is based on five key observations and inferences. These observations and inferences have been summarized by the great biologist Ernst Mayer as follows:

1. Species have great fertility. They make more offspring than can grow to adulthood.
2. Populations remain roughly the same size, with modest fluctuations.
3. Food resources are limited, but are relatively constant most of the time.
4. In sexually reproducing species, generally no two individuals are identical. Variation is rampant.
5. Much of this variation is heritable.

From these observations it may be inferred that in a world of stable populations where each individual must struggle to survive, those with the 'best' characteristics will be more likely to survive, and those desirable traits will be passed to their offspring. These advantageous characteristics are inherited by following generations and becoming dominant among the population through time. This is **natural selection.** If natural selection carried for enough to makes changes in a population, it will eventually leading to new species.

Darwin's theory of evolution can be summarized in following terms:

Variation

There always exists slight to great variation in form and function among the individuals of a population even within the individuals of same generation or breed. Ultimately the novalities appearance or new traits in populations originate from mutation. Mutation is a change in sequence or arrangement of DNA of an organism. The raw material for evolution is the mutation in germ line cells that passes from one generation to next. There are two types of mutations, *i.e.*, gene mutation (in the DNA) and chromosomal mutation. The frequency of mutations is relatively low. So, a significant amount of variation within sexually reproducing populations results from recombination of existing alleles.

Struggle

Since individuals multiply in geometric ratio yet the number of individuals remains roughly constant, there is struggle for existence or competition. This competition could be active or passive and take place in the food procurement, shelter selection and mate selection. This situation leads to the survival of the fittest.

Fitness

Darwin's concept of fitness is often misunderstood. By the term 'fit' Darwin meant to those individuals that are able to pass their genes to the next generation. The individual need not to be physically strong or must have plenty of resources. In the struggle of existence, individuals contributing the most offsprings to the next generation are the 'fittest' ones.

Natural Selection

New traits appear through mutations but they owe their existence to natural selection. The new traits, by themselves, are neither advantageous nor disadvantageous, it is for the natural selection to decide the importance of each mutation on merit. Selection operates in terms of fertility and fecundity, that is, the mutation that are selectively advantageous spread faster because of greater fertility and fecundity of those who possess the mutant gene. Contrarily, the genes which are considered harmful are weeded out by the opposite or negative action of selection. When it acts to remove the unwanted genes, genotypes and phenotypes, it is known as **normalizing natural selection**. Whenever, there is change in environment favouring a particular gene or genotype, the selection strategy is called **directional natural selection**.

Stabilizing Selection

Extreme variations are culled from the population (there is selection against them). Those with the established (middle range) adaptive phenotype are retained in greater numbers. This reduces the variation for the phenotypic character. In the example right, light and dark snails are eliminated, leaving medium coloured snails. Stabilizing selection can be seen in the selection pressures on human birth weights.

Directional Selection

Directional selection is associated with gradually chaning conditions, where the adaptive phenotype is shifted in one direction and one aspect of a trait becomes emphasized (*e.g.*, colouration). In the example right, light coloured snails are eliminated and the population becomes darker. Directional selection was observed in peppered moths (*Biston bitularia*) in England during the industrial revolution. They responded to the air pollution of industrialization by increasing the frequency of darker, melanic forms.

Disruptive or Diversifying Selection

Disruptive selection favours two extremes of a trait at the expense of intermediate forms. It is associated with a fluctuating environment and gives rise to **balanced polymorphism** in the population. In the example right, there is selection against medium coloured snails, which are eliminated. There is considerable evidence that predators, such as insectivorous birds, are more likely to find and eat common morphs and ignore rare morphs. This enables the rarer forms to persist in the population.

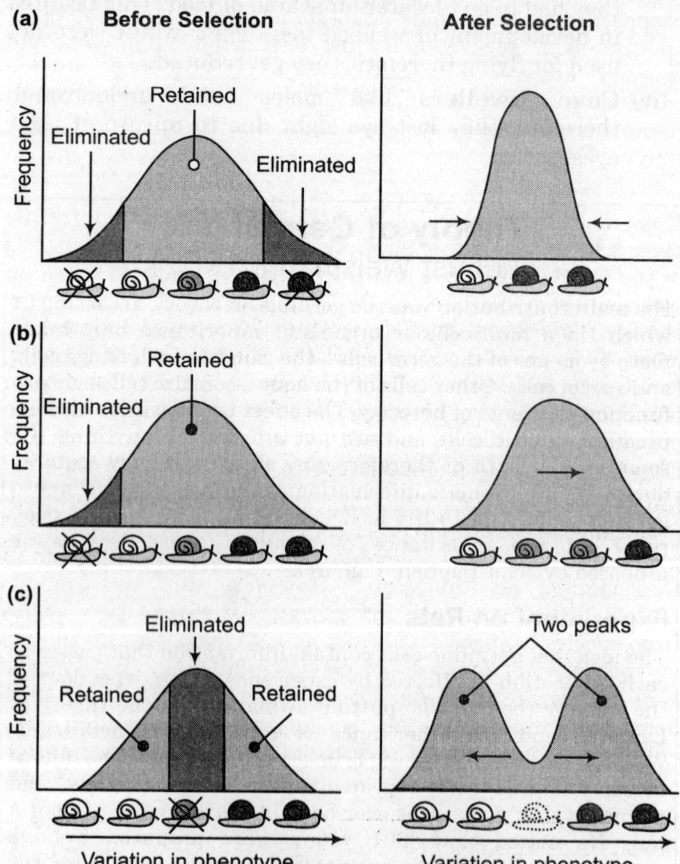

Fig. 33.1 Natural selection approaches (a) Stabilising Selection (b) Directional Selection (c) Disruptive Selection

Adaptation

This repeated and intensive selection leads to a slow but steady and certain modification through the successive generations of the form and functions of the species. This is called adaptation which is toward more fitness. The organism's body and behaviours are moulded in conformity with the external conditions.

Mendelism

The chief difficulty was that the most prominent biologists of Mendel's time were not in the habit of thinking in mathematical terms, even the simple terms used by Mendel. Even Charles Darwin, whose theory of evolution by natural selection depended on genetic variation among individuals, failed to understand the significance of Mendel's findings. In fact, Darwin performed breeding experiments on snapdragons similar to Mendel's on peas and got data similar to Mendel's, but the missed the point, still relying on the concept of blending. Mendel's pioneering paper had no discernible influence on the scientific world for more than 30 years.

Spontaneity of Mutations

Hugo de Vries, one of the rediscoverers of Mendel's work, proposed that 'mutations' (*i.e.*, changes in the phenotype of an organism, occurring in just one generation) were the primary 'engine' of evolutionary change. de Vries did his pioneering work in genetics using the evening primrose (*Oenothera lamarckiana*), which is now known for having sudden, large mutations (called 'macromutations') in its overall phenotype.

Hugo de Vries argued that these kinds of mutations were the basis for the changes in phenotype to which Darwin referred in the Origin of Species and that therefore, natural selection was neither necessary nor likely as a cause of evolutionary change. This mutational theory of evolution was accepted by most of the prominent geneticists at the turn of the century, and led to widespread public testimonials that 'Darwinism was dead.' This was, however, later accepted as false because mutations are the sources of variation in organisms and Darwin's theory of natural selection is still valid.

Mutations can occur spontaneously or they are induced. Spontaneous mutations are more important for evolutionary processes (the details of spontaneous mutations are given in the chapter on mutation). However, this spontaneous mutation, also called as 'background rate of mutation' varies from species to species and from gene to gene. Measurements of spontaneous forward mutation frequencies for various gene of phage and bacteria range from 10^{-8} to 10^{-10} detectable mutations per base-pair per generation. For eukaryotes, estimates of forward mutation rates range from about 10^{-7} to 10^{-9} detectable mutations per base-pair per generation.

Mutation is the ultimate source of all genetic variation. It provides the raw material for evolution. Without mutation, all genes would exist in only one form. Allele frequencies would not change, and thus organisms would not be able to evolve and adapt to environmental changes.

Mutation can be divided into beneficial, harmful and neutral, depending upon whether they increase, decrease or do not change the viability or fertility of their carriers. The viability and fertility in turn affect the overall fitness of the organism.

Evolutionary Synthesis

The rediscovery of Mendel's theory of non-blending inheritance paradoxically made Darwin's theory seem even less likely, as geneticists at the turn of the century believed that evolution occurred via mutation, rather than natural selection. However, the founders of theoretical population genetics eventually united Darwinian evolutionary theory and Mendelian genetics in what is now known as the **modern evolutionary synthesis.**

Ironically, one great unsolved problem in Darwin's master work, On the Origin of Species, was just that how and why do species originate? Darwin and his later followers were faced with a seeming paradox. They described evolution as a continuous, gradual change over time, but species are distinct from each other, suggesting that some process has created a discontinuity or gap, between them.

Credit for doing the most to crack this puzzle goes to **Ernst Mayer**, perhaps the greatest evolutionary scientist of the twentieth century. Along with **Fisher, Dobzhansky,** Haldane, Wright, Ford, Rensch, Chetverikov, Simpson, and **Stebbins, Mayer** achieved the 'modern synthesis' in the 1930s and 1940s that integrated Mendel's theory of heredity with Darwin's theory of evolution and natural selection. **Julian Huxley** coined the term, when he published his book, Evolution: The modern synthesis (1942). The **modern evolutionary synthesis** is now provides a widely accepted account of evolution. It is also referred to as the new synthesis, the modern synthesis, the evolutionary synthesis, millennium synthesis and the neo-Darwinian synthesis.

According to the modern synthesis, genetic variation in populations arises by chance through **mutation** (mistakes in DNA replication) and **recombination** (crossing over of homologous chromosomes during meiosis). Evolution consists primarily of changes in the **frequencies of alleles** between one generation and another as a result of **genetic drift, gene flow** and natural selection. **Speciation** occurs gradually when populations are reproductively isolated by geographic barriers.

The modern evolutionary synthesis can be summed up in the following basic tenets:

1. Mutation, genetic recombination, natural selection and isolation form the most important processes of microevolution.
2. All new traits arise due to mutations (including genetic recombination and changes in chromosome numbers), however, mutations only act as a potential source of variability.
3. Natural selection is the most vital process of microevolution and its role is more progressive and creative in bringing genetic variability.
4. Isolation, reproductive as well as geographic, form strong base for the formation of new species (that is, macroevolution). Reproductive isolation, to work effectively, requires immense contribution of mutation, natural selection and geographic isolation.

5. New species are formed by continuous action of microevolutionary processes over a long time-span cutting through geographical span.

According to evolutionary synthesis, evolution is the sum total of the five essential evolutionary processes:

(i) Gene mutation
(ii) Change in chromosome number
(iii) Genetic recombination
(iv) Natural selection
(v) Reproductive isolation

The first three processes provide the essential genetic variability without which changes can not take place. The last two processes guide populations of organisms into adaptive channels.

In addition to the above, three accessory processes affecting the working of evolution are:

(a) Migration
(b) Hybridization
(c) Genetic drift or chance factor

Origin of Cells and Unicellular Evolution

The origin of life is considered as the result of a long series of physicochemical changes, which brought about first by chemical evolution and then by biological evolution. The evloution up to formation of coacervates is termed as chemical evolution and from coacervates to simple cell structure is called biological evolution.

Origin of Basic Biological Molecules

Earth was formed about 4.5 billion years ago, and the first evidence of life was more than 3.5 billion years ago but the chemical evidence of life from as far back as 3.85 billion years ago.

The first atmosphere was made up of hot **hydrogen** gas, too light to be held by Earth's gravity. **Water vapour, carbon monoxide, carbon dioxide, nitrogen** and **methane** replaced the hydrogen atmosphere. As Earth cooled, water vapour condensed and torrential rains filled up its basins, thereby forming the seas.

In the first stage of chemical evolution, molecules in the primitive environment formed simple organic substances, such as amino acids. Ultraviolet radiation from the sun provided the energy for the transformation of these substances into organic molecules.

Further chemical evolution occurred in four stages:

1. Abiotic synthesis and accumulation of monomers, or small organic molecules, that are the building blocks for more complex molecules.

2. Joining of monomers into polymers (*e.g.,* proteins and nucleic acids).

3. Formation of protobionts, droplets which formed from aggregates of abiotically produced molecules and which differed chemically from their surroundings.

4. Origin of heredity during or before protobiont appearance.

The discovery that RNA molecules can act as catalysts in their own formation suggests that RNA or a similar molecule may have been the first gene and the first catalyst. The concentration of a self-replicating RNA molecule would increase exponentially, as one molecule formed two, two formed four, and so on. In the competition for nucleotides, the most efficient of the self-replicating sequences would win, and less efficient replicators would fade from the population.

Steps in Evolution

Free atoms
↓ Hydrogen, carbon and nitrogen
Inorganic molecules
↓ H_2, H_2O, CH_4, NH_3, CO_2 and HCN
Simple organic molecules
↓ Simple sugars, amino acids, fatty acids, glycerol, purines and pyrimidine
Complex organic molecules
↓ Polysaccharides, nucleic acid, lipids and proteins
Coacervates/microsphere
↓ Cluster of complex organic molecules bounded by fatty acid membrane and divided by budding
Pre cell/protobiont/protocell
↓ Nucleic acid controlled coacervates slow intake and outlet of components 3800 million years ago.
Free polynucleotide
↓ Self-replicating nucleoproteins
First primitive cells
↓ Anaerobic prokaryotic, chemo-heterotrophic absorbes inorganic and divide to increase their number
Chemoautotropic cells
↓ Anaerobic prokaryotic chemoautotropic, *e.g.,* Fe-bacteria, *S*-reducing bacteria, nitrifying bacteria. They used sun light for synthesis of food.
Photoautotrophic cells
↓ Anaerobic prokaryotic photoautotropic. they originated due to deficiency of inorganic compounds. They used sun light to synthesis food.
Anoxygenic
↓ They did not use water as raw material in photosynthesis. 3300-3500 million years ago.
Oxygenic cell used H_2O for photosynthesis and evolved O_2 Gas
↓ Aerobic, prokaryotic, photoautotropic cyanobacteria, procambarian, *e.g., Archaespheroides barbertonesis.*
Eukaryotes organisms
↓ Multicellular organism evolved due to endobiosis: 1600 million years ago.
Simple land plants

The division of function between DNA (genetic information storage) and protein (catalysis) was, according to the 'RNA world' hypothesis. New variants of self-replicating RNA molecules developed, with the additional ability to catalyze the condensation of amino acids into peptides. The peptide(s) thus formed would reinforce the self-replicating ability of the RNA, generating even more efficient self-replicating systems.

Sometime after the evolution of this primitive protein-synthesizing system, DNA molecules with sequences complementary to the self-replicating RNA molecules took over the function of conserving the genetic information and RNA molecules evolved to play roles in protein synthesis.

Proteins proved to be versatile catalysts and, over time, took over that function. Lipid like compounds in the primordial soup formed relatively impermeable layers around self-replicating collections of molecules. The concentration of proteins and nucleic acids within these lipid enclosures favoured the molecular interactions required in self-replication.

Abiotic Synthesis of Organic Monomers and Polymers

Various laboratory replications of the early Earth, even with the addition of low concentrations of O_2, have been able to produce all 20 amino acids, sugars, lipids, nitrogenous bases, and even ATP. The abiotic synthesis and accumulation of organic monomers could have been a natural process on primeval Earth.

The abiotic synthesis of polymers may have occurred when dissolved organic monomers splashed onto hot rocks. Fox has created polypeptides he calls proteinoids by dripping dilute solutions of organic monomers onto hot sand or rock in the laboratory.

Clay may have been an important substratum for polymerization because of its ability to concentrate organic monomers, which bind to charged particles of clay. Metal atoms, such as iron and zinc, at some of the binding sites may have functioned as catalysts, facilitating the dehydration reactions that link monomers. Iron pyrite has also been proposed as a substratum for organic synthesis.

Protobionts, aggregates of abiotically produced organic molecules, probably proceded living cells. Protobionts may have developed such capabilities as metabolism, excitability and the ability to maintain an internal chemical environment different from their surroundings.

Concept of Oparin and Haldane

In 1922, the biochemist **Alexander Oparin** proposed a theory for the origin of life early in the history of Earth, postulating that the atmosphere was very different from that of today. Rich in **methane, ammonia** and **water** and **essentially devoid of oxygen**, it was a reducing atmosphere, in contrast to the oxidizing environment of our era. In Oparin's theory, heat energy from volcanoes caused ammonia, methane, water vapour and other components of the primitive atmosphere to react, forming simple organic compounds. These compounds then dissolved in the ancient seas, which over many millennia became enriched with a large variety of simple organic substances. In this warm solution (the **primordial soup**), some organic molecules had a greater tendency than others to associate into larger complexes to form membranes and catalysts (enzymes), which came together to become precursors of the earliest cells.

Thus, Oparin postulated that 1st living cell arose spontaneously from this warm concentrated solution of organic compounds. This view was independently forwarded by **Haldane** in England. Their views were attended by much controversy and remain untested speculation for over many years—until a surprising experiment was conducted by **Stanley Miller** and **Harold Urey** using simple equipment.

Experiment of Miller (1953)

In the 1950s, Stanley Miller and Harold Urey set up an experimental 'primitive' atmosphere, containing **hydrogen gas, ammonia, methane gas** and **water vapour**. They passed a spark through these gases to simulate lightning, then cooled the system so the gases would condense and collect in a watery solution. Within days, the system contained numerous complex molecules, including amino acids, purines and pyrimidines—some of the building blocks of life. The Miller-Urey experiment simulated possible atmospheric conditions on primitive Earth to obtain some of the molecular building blocks of biological systems.

The results of the Miller-Urey experiments have undergone several such refinements:

1. In living organisms, many molecules have the L-configuration. But the amino acids formed in the Miller-Urey experiments were a mixture of the D and L-forms. Recent experiments show that natural processes could have selected the L-amino acids from the mixture.
2. There is abundant evidence of major volcanic eruptions 4 billion years ago that released carbon dioxide (CO_2), nitrogen (N_2), hydrogen sulphide (H_2S) and sulphur dioxide (SO_2). Prebiotic chemistry experiments using these molecules in addition to the ones in the original 'soup' have led to more diverse molecules.
3. Long polymers had to be formed from simpler building blocks, called monomers.
4. Miller and Urey, as well as others, suggested that life originated in hot pools at the edges of oceans.

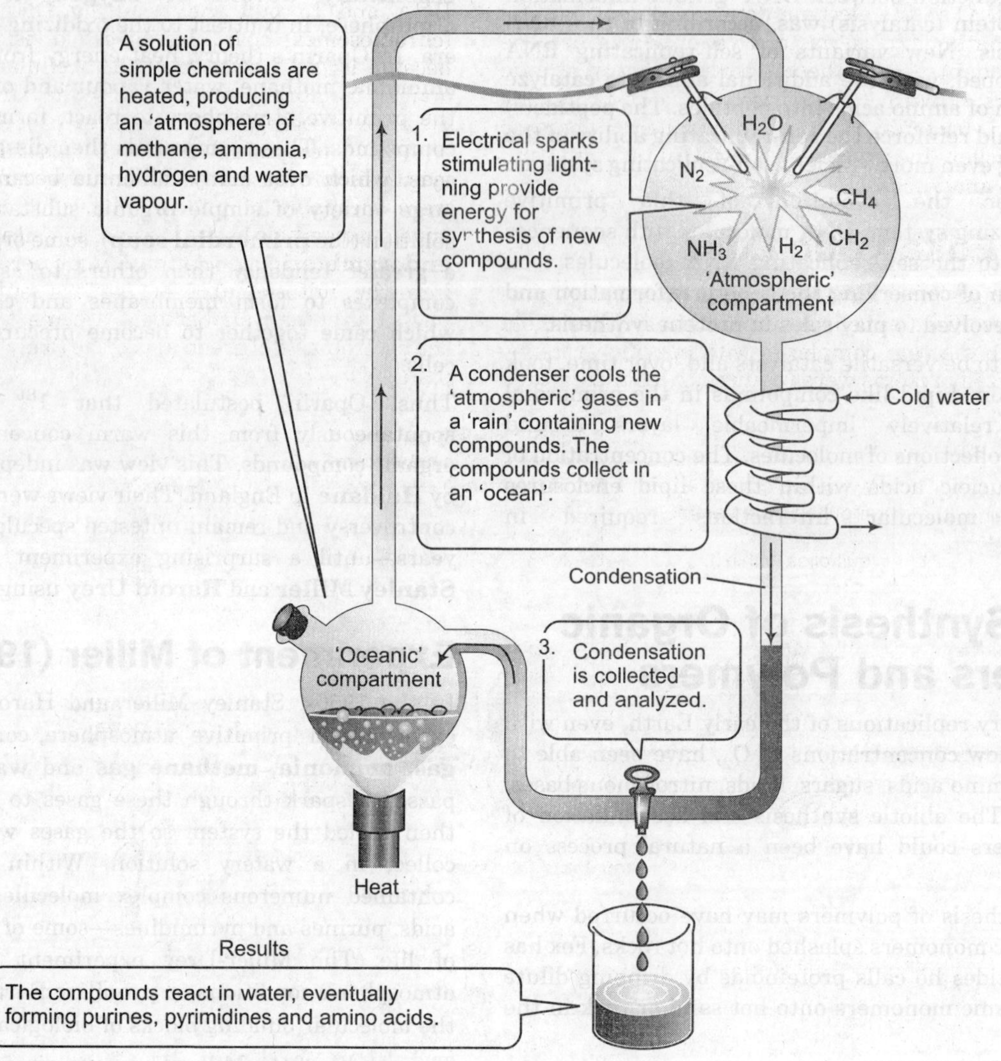

Fig. 33.2 Experiment of Stanley Miller and Harold Urey

In whatever way the earliest stages of chemical evolution occurred, they resulted in the emergence of monomers and polymers that have probably remained unchanged in their general structure and function for 3.8 billion years.

The First Cell

The earliest cells that arose in the rich mixture of organic compounds, were almost certainly chemoheterotrophs. The organic compounds they required were originally synthesized from components of the early atmosphere—CO, CO_2, N_2, CH_4, and such—by the non-biological actions of volcanic heat and lightning. Early heterotrophs gradually acquired the ability to derive energy from compounds in their environment and to use that energy to synthesize more of their own precursor molecules, thereby becoming less dependent on outside sources. The chemoheterotrophs could oxidize organic compounds to CO_2 by passing electrons not to O_2 but to acceptors such as SO_4^{2-}, yielding H_2S as the product.

Formation of Coacervates

The large organic molecules synthesized abiotically on the primitive Earth were the precursor of colloidal aggregates. These colloidal particles were called coacervates by Oparin and microsphere by Sydney Fox. When oppositely charged colloids mixed coacervates were formed. These coacervate droplets represent open systems that keep accumulating materials from their environment. In coacervates lipid molecules were joined end to end forming a layer around each aggregate which represents a simple lipid membrane. More complex microspheres and coacervates function as pre-cells or pre-bionts.

Evolution of Prokaryotes

A very significant evolutionary event in prokaryotes was the development of pigments capable of capturing the energy of light from the sun, which could be used to reduce, or 'fix,' CO_2 to form more complex, organic compounds. The original electron donor for these photosynthetic processes was probably H_2S, yielding elemental sulphur or sulphate (SO_4^{2-}) as the by product, but later cells developed the enzymatic capacity to use H_2O as the electron donor in photosynthetic reactions, eliminating O_2 as waste. Cyanobacteria are the modern descendants of these early photosynthetic oxygen-producers. With the rise of O_2-producing photosynthetic bacteria, the atmosphere became progressively richer in oxygen—a powerful oxidant and deadly poison to anaerobes.

Origin of Eukaryotic Cells

Three major changes must have occurred as prokaryotes gave rise to eukaryotes. First, as cells acquired more DNA and fold it compactly into discrete complexes with specific proteins. For this, specialized proteins were required to stabilize folded DNA and to pull the resulting DNA-protein complexes (chromosomes) apart during cell division. Second, as cells became larger, a system of intracellular membranes and a double membrane surrounding the DNA developed. This membrane segregated the nuclear process of RNA synthesis on a DNA template from the cytoplasmic process of protein synthesis on ribosomes. Finally, early eukaryotic cells, which were incapable of photosynthesis or aerobic metabolism, enveloped aerobic bacteria or photosynthetic bacteria to form **endosymbiotic** associations. Some aerobic bacteria evolved into the mitochondria of modern eukaryotes and some photosynthetic cyanobacteria became the plastids, such as the chloroplasts of green algae, the likely ancestors of modern plant cells.

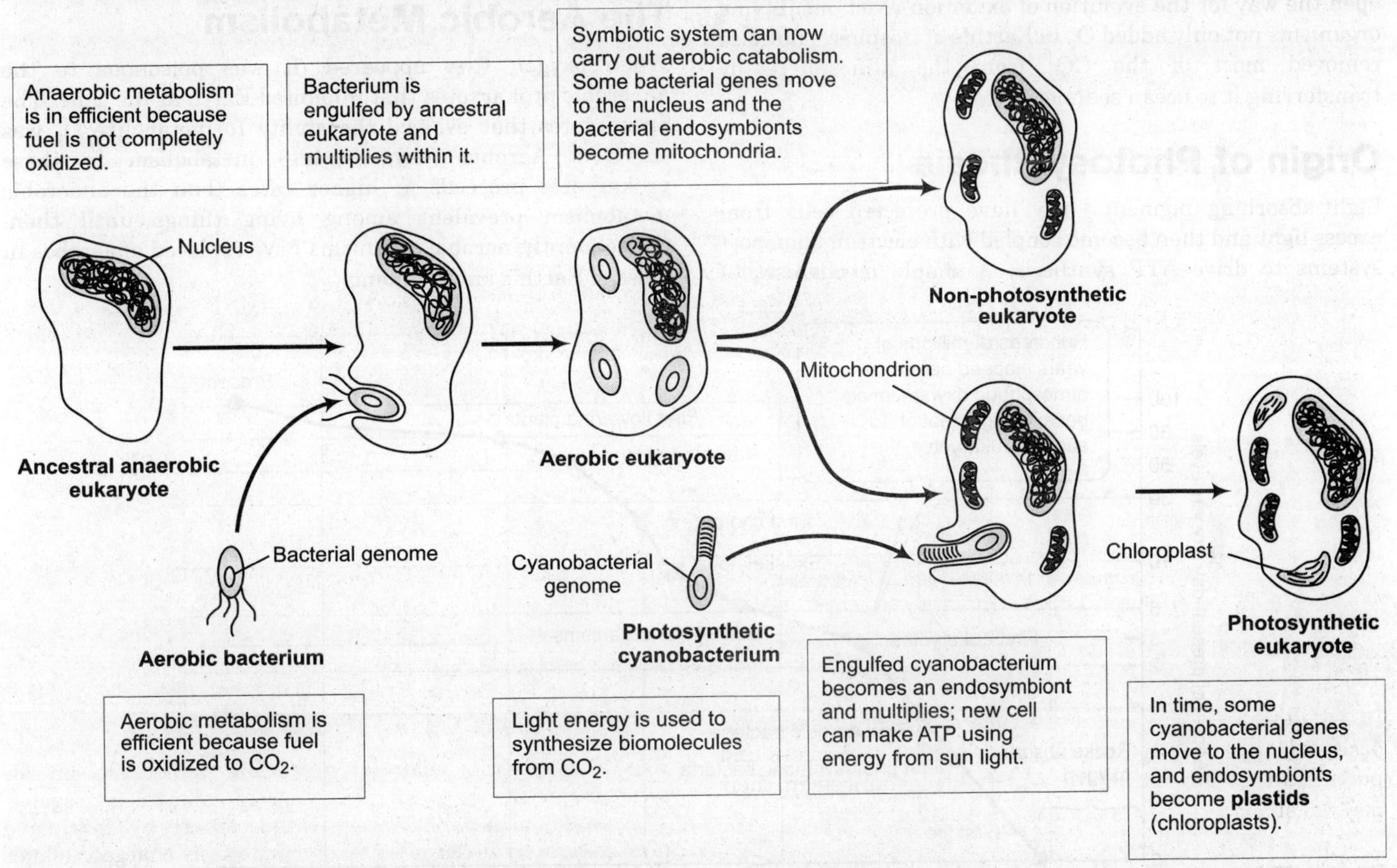

Fig. 33.3 Evolution of eukaryotes through endosymbiosis

Evolution of Unicellular Eukaryotes

Unicellular organisms, at later stage of evolution found it advantageous to cluster together and acquiring more motility, efficiency or reproductive success than their free-living single-celled competitors. Further evolution of such clustered organisms led to permanent associations among individual cells and eventually to specialization within the colony—to cellular differentiation. The advantages of cellular specialization led to the evolution of ever more complex and highly differentiated organisms. Many modern multicellular organisms contain hundreds of different cell types, each specialized for some function that supports the entire organism.

Anaerobic, Metabolism Photosynthesis and Aerobic Metabolism

All major metabolic pathways evolved in prokaryotes before these were eukaryotes probably within the first billionyears of life on Earth. Various hypothesis were based on geological, molecular and metabolic evidence.

Anaerobic Metabolism

The atmosphere of early Earth probably contained little or no free oxygen (O_2). Oxygen concentrations in the atmosphere began to increase markedly about 2.5 billion years ago, when certain bacteria evolved the ability to use water as the source of hydrogen ions for photosynthesis. By chemically splitting H_2O ($2\ H_2O \rightarrow 4\ H^+ + O_2 + 4e^-$), these bacteria generated atmospheric O_2 as a waste product; in addition, they made electrons available for reducing CO_2 to form organic compounds.

One lineage of oxygen-generating bacteria evolved was the cyanobacteria. The cyanobacteria liberated enough O_2 to open the way for the evolution of oxidation reactions. Living organisms not only added O_2 to Earth's atmosphere, but also removed most of the CO_2 from the atmosphere by transferring it to ocean sediments.

Origin of Photosynthesis

Light-absorbing pigments may have protected cells from excess light and then become coupled with electron transport systems to drive ATP synthesis. A simple mechanism of photophosphorylation has been found in some archaebacteria called extreme halophiles in which bacteriorhodopsin, a membrane bound pigment molecule, uses light energy to pump protons out of the cell. The resulting gradient is used for ATP synthesis.

The development of pigments and photosystems co-opting components of electron transport chains may have allowed some prokaryotes to use light energy to drive electrons from H_2S to $NADP^+$ and thus generate reducing power to fix CO_2 and make their own organic molecules. The nutrition of the green and purple sulphur bacteria probably is most like that of the early photosynthetic prokaryotes.

The Aerobic Metabolism

When oxygen first appeared, it was poisonous to the anaerobic prokaryotes that inhabited Earth at the time. The prokaryotes that evolved the ability to metabolize O_2 was survived. Aerobic (oxygen-using) metabolism in these prokaryotes proceeds at higher rates than the anaerobic metabolism prevalent among living things until then. Consequently, aerobic organisms have replaced anaerobes in most of Earth's environments.

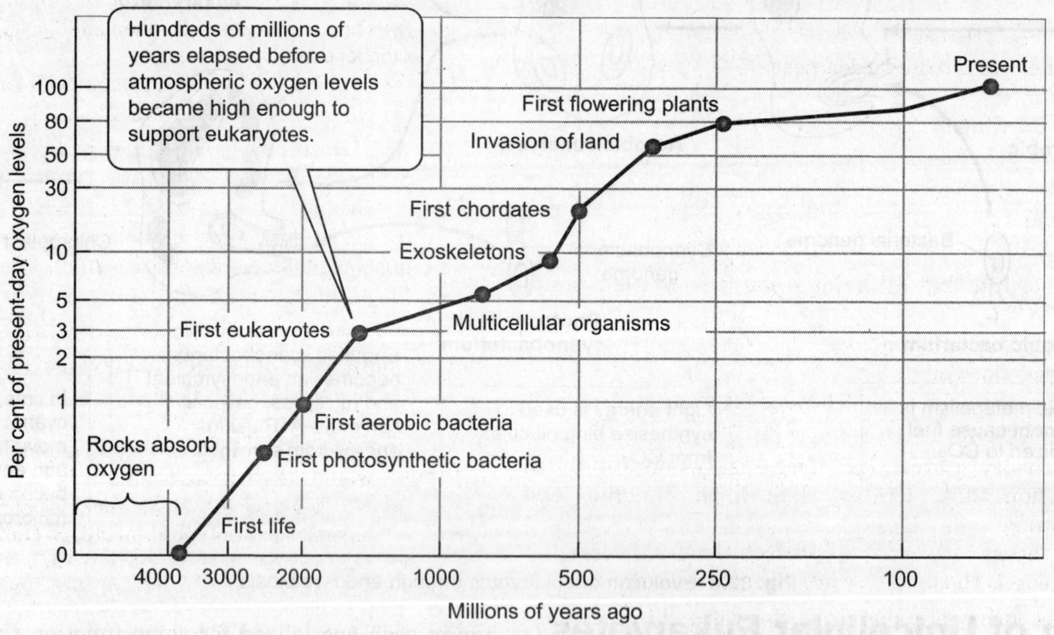

Fig. 33.4 An oxygen concentrations in the atmosphere rose, the complexity of life increased

Chemoautotrophs synthesized their own organic food from inorganic compounds in the presence of chemical energy and enzymes, *e.g.*, nitrifying bacteria, sulphur bacteria, iron bacteria, etc. Some chemoautotrophs developed porphyrins and bacteriochlorophyll and started photosynthesis. These evolved about 3500-3800 million years ago. The first photoautotrophs were anaerobic and performed anoxygenic photosynthesis, *e.g.*, *Rhodopseudomonas, Chlorobium*. Later, these developed true chlorophyll and started using the water as a reagent and O_2 was evolved during photosynthesis. Cyanobacteria were first oxygenic and aerobic photoautotrophs which were evolved about 3300-3500 million years ago. The oldest micro fossil belongs to blue-green algae, *i.e., Archaespheroids barbertonensis* about 3.3 to 3.5 billion years ago.

Exercise

1. The early Earth was a harsh environment and present day organisms that could possibly have survived that type of environment are
(a) eukaryotic organisms (b) archaebacteria
(c) protobionts (d) eubacteria

2. What was the theory put forward by Lamarck?
(a) Transformism (b) Evolution
(c) Creationism (d) All of these

3. The theory of Natural Selection was simultaneously invented by Charles Darwin and
(a) Alfred Russel Wallace (b) Jean Baptise Lamarck
(c) Thomas Henry Huxley (d) None of these

4. Who has formulated the chromosomal theory of inheritance?
(a) G Mendel (b) Morgan
(c) Sutton and Boveri (d) Darwin

5. Who is mainly credited for the Evolutionary Theory?
(a) Antony Von Leeuwenhoek
(b) Mendel
(c) Charles Darwin
(d) Mathias Schleiden and Theodor Schwann

6. Heredity or inheritance of specific traits became clearer due to
(a) Lamarck's theory
(b) Mendel worked on garden peas
(c) Darwinism
(d) Neo-Darwinism

7. .... was a predecessor of Darwin's and developed the theory of acquired characteristics.
(a) Weismann (b) Mendel
(c) Malthus (d) Lamarck

8. Who theorized that all living organisms are composed of cells?
(a) Antony von Leeuwenhoek
(b) Charles Darwin
(c) Mathias Schleiden and Theodor Schwann
(d) Robert Hooke

9. Which theory states that 'Organisms contain coded information that dictates, their form, function and behaviour'?
(a) Cell theory (b) Evolutionary theory
(c) Biogenesis theory (d) Natural Selection

10. Darwin's theory of pangenesis was refuted by
(a) recapitulation theory (b) theory of germplasm
(c) chromosome theory (d) theory of biogenesis

11. Mutation theory of Hugo de Vries was put forward while working on
(a) *Drosophila* (b) Ancon sheep
(c) *Oenothera lamarckiana* (d) *Antirrhinum*

12. In his book, 'The origin of life (1938)' Oparin submitted abiogenesis first bur biogenesis ever since, this theory is named as
(a) spontaneous generation (b) chemical origin
(c) primary abiogenesis (d) biogenesis

13. Experimental evidence for molecular evolution of life was provided by
(a) Oparin (b) Haldane
(c) Urey and Miller (d) Sydney Fox

14. By the statement 'survival of the fittest', Darwin meant that
(a) the strongest of all species survives
(b) the most intelligent of the species survives
(c) the cleverest of the species survives
(d) the most adaptable of the species to changes survives

15. In the light of modern evidences, the original theory of Darwin is now known as
(a) Re-Darwinism
(b) Neo-Darwinism
(c) Iso-Darwinism
(d) Trans-Darwinism

16. Who formulated that 'ontogeny recapitulates phylogeny'?
(a) Haeckel (b) Darwin
(c) Lamarck (d) Weismann

17. Banded iron formations in marine sediments provide evidence of
(a) the first prokaryotes around 3.5 billion years ago
(b) the evolution of chemoautotrophs that oxidized ferrous ions for energy
(c) oxidized iron layers in terrestrial rocks
(d) the release of O_2 by cyanobacteria

18. The two theories combined in the synthetic theory of evolution or Neo-Darwinism, are
(a) Evolution and Natural Selection
(b) Natural Selection and blending Inheritance
(c) Natural Selection and Mendelian Inheritance
(d) All of the above

19. Consider the first stars that formed after the big bang. Could there have been planets with life on them around those original stars?
(a) Yes
(b) Only after millions of years had passed, so that life would have time to form
(c) No, because elements such as carbon, nitrogen and oxygen were only first formed in the first stars
(d) No, because we are certain that the only life ever to exist in the universe is on Earth

20. Earth is formed about .... years ago
(a) 1.5 million (b) 1.5 billion
(c) 4.5 million (d) 4.5 billion

21. About how many years ago did life originate on Earth?
(a) 3.5 to 4 thousand (b) 3.5 to 4 million
(c) 3.5 to 4 billion (d) 3.5 to 4 trillion

22. During pre-biotic origin of life which chemical played important role in formation of nucleotide specially guanosine
(a) CH_4 (b) CO_2
(c) NH_3 (d) HCN

23. Among the following which molecule till now not synthesized by mimicking the environment of pre-biotic environment
(a) ribose (b) pyrimidines
(c) purine (d) L-amino acids

24. The difference between prokaryotes and eukaryotes is that
(a) eukaryotes do have 'true' nuclei containing their DNA
(b) eukaryotic organisms are always multi-cellular
(c) eukaryotes possess cytoskeleton
(d) eukaryotes contain large RNA/protein structures called ribosomes

25. The common feature between prokaryotes and eukaryotes is
(a) cytoskeleton structure (b) ribosomes
(c) plasmid (d) All of these

26. Prokaryotes have a .... surface area to volume ratio giving them a .... metabolic rate, a .... growth rate and, as a consequence, a .... generation time compared to eukaryotes.
(a) larger; higher; higher; larger
(b) larger; smaller; shorter; higher
(c) larger; higher; higher; shorter
(d) shorter; higher; higher; larger

27. Chemoautotrophs
(a) are photosynthetic
(b) use organic molecules for an energy and carbon surface
(c) oxidize inorganic substances for energy and use CO_2 as a carbon source
(d) use light to generate ATP but need organic molecules for a carbon source

28. Which of the following is least likely to leave a fossil?
(a) A soft-bodied land organism such as a slug
(b) A marine organism with a shell such as a mussel
(c) A vascular plant embedded in layers of mud
(d) A freshwater snake

29. Polymer formation from organic monomers may have been facilitated by
(a) the electrification of monomers by lightning
(b) proteinoid formation by pH changes
(c) amino acid concentration on clay particles
(d) sedimentary accumulation on stromatolites

30. Aggregation of prokaryotes forms stable aggregate communities. When such communities are encased in a stabilizing polymer matrix (slime), they may be called
(a) biopolymer (b) biofilm
(c) slime aggregate (d) slime polymer

31. Genetic exchange and recombination occur in bacteria and archaea in the form of
(a) horizontal gene transfer
(b) gene duplication
(c) chromosome translocation
(d) transposition

32. The primitive atmosphere of Earth may have favoured the synthesis of organic molecules because
(a) It was highly oxidative
(b) It was reducing and had energy sources in the form of lightning and UV radiation
(c) It had a great deal of methane and organic fuels
(d) It had plenty of water vapour, carbon and nitrogen, providing the C, H, O and N needed for organic molecules

33. Index fossils are fossils of
(a) unique organisms that are used to determine the relative rates fo evolution in different areas
(b) widespread organisms that allow geologists to correlate strata of rocks from different locations
(c) transitional forms that link major evolutionary groups
(d) extinct organisms that indicate the separation of different eras

34. The current model of the evolution of the first living organisms is that these were some form of prokaryotes, which may have evolved out of
(a) abiont (b) protobionts
(c) symbiont (d) neobiont

35. Which of the fact suggests that eukaryotic mitochondria and chloroplast are evolved from prokaryotes?
(a) The ribosome found in chloroplast and mitochondria are similar to in size as found in prokaryotes
(b) DNA is present in both chloroplast and mitochondria
(c) The inner membrane of chloroplast and mitochondria is similar to prokaryotes while outer membranes are similar to eukaryotes
(d) All of the above

36. Which pathway describes the invasion of eukaryote cells by two smaller prokaryote cells?
(a) Endosymbiosis (b) Parasitism
(c) Mutualism (d) Ectosymbiosis

37. The classic work 'Systematics and the Origin of Species' presented in 1942, belong to
(a) Haldane (b) Ernst Mayer
(c) Wright (d) Fisher

38. Facultative anaerobes
(a) can survive with or without oxygen
(b) are poisoned by oxygen
(c) are anaerobic chemoautotrophs
(d) are all able to fix atmospheric nitrogen to make NH_3, which is then available for plant growth

39. Which of the statement is correct?
(a) Most carbon atoms were formed during the big bang
(b) Humans are about as old as the Earth is
(c) There are ten million microns in 1 meter
(d) Carbon atoms are formed in stars

40. The order of appearance of the main groups of organisms during evolution can best be described as follows
(a) autotrophic and anaerobic heterotrophic,
(b) aerobic heterotrophic, anaerobic heterotrophic and autotrophic
(c) anaerobic heterotrophic, aerobic heterotrophic and autotrophic
(d) anaerobic heterotrophic, water oxidizing autotrophic and aerobic heterotrophic

41. Choose the most likely correct sequence for the biological evolution of life, using the codes given below

I. Aerobic prokaryotes.
II. Photosynthetic prokaryotes.
III. Anaerobic prokaryotes.
IV. Eukaryotes.

(a) I, II, III, IV (b) II, III, I, IV
(c) III, II, I, IV (d) I, IV, III, II

42. The site of life's origin is
(a) the ocean's edge (b) unknown
(c) under frozen oceans (d) near deep-sea vents

43. The earliest cellular life forms appear to have been
(a) viruses (b) one-celled plants
(c) one-celled animals (d) bacteria

44. Life on Earth is carbon based. Similar molecules could be formed with
(a) potassium (b) aluminium
(c) iron (d) silicon

45. Which of the following organisms alive today is likely to be most similar to the first life forms that evolved on the Earth?
(a) Methane-producing bacteria
(b) Cyanobacteria
(c) Algae
(d) Dinosaurs

46. Which of the following was not a source of energy on the early Earth?
(a) Lightning (b) Ozone
(c) Ultraviolet radiation (d) Volcanic eruptions

47. Within our own solar system, the most likely candidate for having life on it is
(a) Moon
(b) Jupiter
(c) Venus
(d) Europa, a Moon of Jupiter

48. Multicellular fossils appear at the beginning of the
(a) proterozoic era (b) precambrian period
(c) archean era (d) phanerozoic era

49. Miller and Urey's experiments proved that
(a) life evolved on Earth from inanimate chemicals
(b) coacervates were the first type of protocells
(c) complex organic molecules can form spontaneously under conditions that probably existed on the early Earth
(d) RNA can act as an enzyme and assemble new RNA molecules from RNA templates

50. Which of the following is not a characteristic of all living organisms?
(a) Reproduction
(b) Heredity
(c) Metabolism
(d) Movement from place to place

51. Which of the following is not found in a lipid coacervate droplet or a proteinoid microsphere?
(a) The ability to grow
(b) A nucleus
(c) A two-layer boundary
(d) Division by pinching in two

52. The Miller-Urey experiments yielded
(a) urea (b) hydrogen cyanide
(c) amino acids (d) All of these

53. What did Miller and Urey use as a source of energy in their experiments?
(a) Actual lightning (b) UV light
(c) An electrical spark (d) Radioactivity

54. A proposed hypothesis for the origin of genetic information is that
(a) Early DNA molecules coded for RNA, which then catalyzed the production of proteins
(b) Early polypeptides became associated with RNA bases, and a catalyst linked the bases into RNA molecules
(c) Short RNA strands were capable of self-replication and evolved by the natural selection of molecules that were most stable and autocatalytic
(d) As protobionts grew and split, they distributed copies of their molecules to their offspring

55. Stromatolites are
(a) synthetic molecules consisting of amino adenosine and an ester that are able to self-replicate
(b) a type of protobiont that forms when lipids assemble into a bilayer surrounding organic molecules
(c) fossils appearing to be prokaryotes that are the size of bacteria
(d) banded domes of sediment that contain the earliest fossils

56. Aerobic respiration may have originated when
(a) Some bacteria evolved antioxidant mechanisms to protect them from rising oxygen levels
(b) Photosynthetic bacteria produced an excess of organic molecules
(c) Some bacteria used modified electron transport chains from photosynthesis to pass electrons from organic molecules to O_2
(d) Some bacteria gave up photosynthesis and reverted to chemoheterotrophic nutrition

57. The hypothesis that life originated in the sea is based on
(a) that fact that most species are marine
(b) the discovery of deep-sea vents
(c) the inhospitable asteroid-crashing environment of early Earth
(d) both (b) and (c)

58. Synapomorphies are
(a) used to characterize all the species on a branch of a cladogram
(b) determined through a computer comparison of all anatomical characteristics of a group of species
(c) homologous structures that develop during adaptive radiation
(d) used to indicate the degree of morphological differences between clades

59. Consider the following geological time scales.

I. Proterozoic II. Palaeozoic
III. Mesozoic IV. Coenozoic
V. Azoic

The correct sequence of these time scales from the earliest to the most recent is
(a) V, II, I, IV and III
(b) V, I, III, II and IV
(c) V, II, III, I and IV
(d) V, I, II, III and IV

60. What is the correct chronological sequence of the following divisions of geological times?
I. Eocene II. Carboniferous
III. Devonian IV. Cretaceous
Select the correct answer using the codes given below.
(a) II, III, IV and I (b) III, IV, II and I
(c) III, IV, II and IV (d) II, III, I and IV

61. Match list I and list II and select the correct answer using the codes given below the lists.

List I	List II
A. Archeozoic	1. Soft-bodied animals
B. Proterozoic	2. Brachiopods
C. Mesozoic	3. Reptiles
D. Coenozoic	4. Mammals

Codes

	A	B	C	D
(a)	1	2	3	4
(b)	2	1	3	4
(c)	1	2	4	3
(d)	2	1	4	3

62. Match list I (Fossil) list II (Era/period) and select the correct answer sing the codes given below the list.

List I	List II
A. Trilobites	1. Mesozoic
B. Horses	2. Tertiary
C. Plesiosaurus	3. Devonian
D. Ostracoderms	4. Cambrian

Codes

	A	B	C	D
(a)	2	4	3	1
(b)	2	4	1	3
(c)	4	2	3	1
(d)	4	2	1	3

63. Match list I (theories of evolution/inheritance) with list II (proposed by) and select the correct answer using the codes given below the lists.

List I	List II
A. Catastrophism	1. Cuvier
B. Inheritance of acquired characters	2. Lamarck
C. Performation	3. Bonner
D. Pangenesis	4. Darwin

Codes

	A	B	C	D
(a)	1	2	3	4
(b)	4	3	2	1
(c)	1	3	2	4
(d)	4	2	3	1

64. Match list I (Common names of hominids) with list II (Generic names of hominids) and select the correct answer using the codes given below the Lists.

List I	List II
A. African ape man	1. *Sinanthropus*
B. Java ape man	2. *Pithecanthropus*
C. Peking man	3. *Homo*
D. Neanderthal	4. *Australopithecus*

Codes

	A	B	C	D
(a)	1	3	4	2
(b)	4	3	1	2
(c)	1	2	4	3
(d)	4	2	1	3

65. Consider the following.
I. alanine
II. glycine
III. aspartic acid
Which of the above amino acids were produced in Miller's experiment to produce organic molecules from the gaseous composition of early/primitive atmosphere of Earth?
Codes
(a) I and II only (b) II and III only
(c) I and III only (d) I, II and III

Answers

1. (b)	**2.** (a)	**3.** (a)	**4.** (c)	**5.** (c)	**6.** (b)	**7.** (d)	**8.** (d)	**9.** (d)	**10.** (b)
11. (c)	**12.** (b)	**13.** (b)	**14.** (d)	**15.** (b)	**16.** (a)	**17.** (d)	**18.** (c)	**19.** (c)	**20.** (d)
21. (c)	**22.** (d)	**23.** (a)	**24.** (a)	**25.** (d)	**26.** (c)	**27.** (c)	**28.** (a)	**29.** (c)	**30.** (b)
31. (a)	**32.** (b)	**33.** (b)	**34.** (b)	**35.** (d)	**36.** (a)	**37.** (b)	**38.** (a)	**39.** (d)	**40.** (d)
41. (c)	**42.** (b)	**43.** (d)	**44.** (d)	**45.** (a)	**46.** (b)	**47.** (d)	**48.** (d)	**49.** (c)	**50.** (d)
51. (b)	**52.** (d)	**53.** (c)	**54.** (c)	**55.** (d)	**56.** (c)	**57.** (d)	**58.** (a)	**59.** (d)	**60.** (b)
61. (b)	**62.** (d)	**63.** (a)	**64.** (d)	**65.** (d)					

34

Evolution : Methods of Studying and Mechanisms

Palaeontology and Evolutionary History

Sediments of similar composition laid down during the same geologic event are sometimes found in different geographic regions providing a time reference point. Sometimes the same stratigraphic sequence of fossils is found in different areas. With the discovery of radioactivity at the end of nineteenth century absolute measurements of geologic age became possible. Fossils are preserved remains of organisms or traces of them or even organic compounds produced by them. Hard parts of organisms are most often fossilized.

The Evolutionary Time Scale

Long before the Earth's age was known, geologists divided its history into a table of succeeding events based on ordered layers of sedimentary rock. The 'law of stratigraphy' produced a relative dating with oldest layers at the bottom and youngest at the top of a sequence. Time was divided intoeons, eras, periods and epochs.

Eon The largest time unit on the geologic time scale.

Era Sub-division of a geological eon.

Syllabus

- Palaeontology and Evolutionary History: The Evolutionary Time Scale; Eras, Periods and Epoch; Major Events in the Evolutionary Time Scale; Major Groups of Plants and Animals; Stages in Primate Evolution Including *Homo*.
- Molecular Evolution: Concepts of Neutral Evolution, Molecular Divergence and Molecular Clocks; Molecular Tools in Phylogeny, Classification and Identification; Protein and Nucleotide Sequence Analysis; Origin of New Genes and Proteins; Gene Duplication and Divergence.
- The Mechanisms: [illegible]ation Genetics–Populations, Gene Pool and Gene Frequency; Hardy-Weinberg Law; Gene Frequency Change through Natural Selection, Migration and Random Genetic Drift; Adaptive Radiation and Modifications; Isolating Mechanisms; Speciation; Allopatric Speciation Sympatric; Speciation Convergent Evolution; Sexual Selection; Co-Evolution.

Eon	Era	Period	Epoch	Myrs		Life Forms
Phanerozoic	Cenozoic	Quaternary	Holocene	0.01	Age of Mammals	Modern humans
			Pleistocene	2.6		Extinction of large mammals and birds
		Tertiary: Neogene	Pliocene	5.3		Large carnivores
			Miocene	23.0		Whales and apes
		Tertiary: Palaeogene	Oligocene	33.9		
			Eocene	55.8		
			Palaeocene	65.5		Early primates
	Mesozoic	Cretaceous		145.5	Age of Dinosaurs	**Mass extinction** Placental mammals Early flowering plants
		Jurassic		199.6		First mammals Mass extinction
		Triassic		251		Flying reptiles First dinosaurs
		Permian		299	Age of Amphibians	**Mass extinction** Coal-forming forests diminish
		Pennsylvanian		318.1		**Coal-forming swamps** Sharks abundant Variety of insects
		Mississippian		359.2		First amphibians First reptiles
		Devonian		416		**Mass extinction** First forests (evergreens)
		Silurian		443.7	Marine Invertebrates Fishes	**First land plants**
		Ordovician		488.3		**Mass extinction** First primitive fish Trilobite maximum Rise of corals
		Cambrian		542		Early shelled organisms
Proterozoic		Precambrian		2500		First multicelled organisms Jellyfish fossil (670 Myrs)
Archean				– 4000		Early bacteria and algae
				4600		Origin of life? Formation of the Earth

Fig. 34.1 Geological time scale

Major Events in the Evolutionary Time Scale

The earlist cells were primitive anaerobic bacteria. Simple molecules such as CO_2 and water were still very abundant as was energy in the dilute form of sunlight. Eventually some cells evolved the ability to use the energy of sunlight to drive the synthesis of their own complex high energy molecules from simpler molecules photosynthesis appeared. In photosynthesis of blue green algae water and CO_2 converted to organic compounds releasing oxygen as by product. Accumulation of oxygen in atmosphere provided the environmental pressure for the next great advance in age of microbes.

Table 34.1 **Major Biological Events in Geological Time Scale**

Era	Period	Age at Beginning of the Period (Million of Year)	Major Biological Event
Cenozoic	Quaternary	0.01	Sub-tropical forests gave way to cooler forests and grassland areas.
	Tertiary	65	Modern orders of mammals evolved. Humans evolved in the last 5 million years.
Mesozoic	Cretaceous	135	Continental seas and swamps spread. Extinction of ancient birds and reptiles.
	Jurassic	195	Climate warm and stable. High reptilian diversity. Birds first appeared.
	Triassic	240	Climate warm. Extensive deserts. Dinosaurs replace mammal like reptiles. First true mammals.
Palaeozoic	Permian	285	Climate cold early, but then warmed. Mammal like reptiles common. Widespread extinction of amphibians.
	Carboniferous	375	Warm and humid with extensive coal-producing swamps. Arthropods and amphibians common. First reptiles appeared.
	Devonian	420	Land high and climate cool. Freshwater basins developed. Fish diversified. Early amphibians appeared.
	Silurian	450	Extensive shallow seas. Warm climate. first terrestrial arthropods. First jawed fish.
	Ordovician	520	Shallow extensive seas. Climate warmed. Many marine inverteberates. Jawless fish widespread.
	Cambrian	570	Extensive shallow seas and warm climate. Trilobites and brachiopods common. Earliest vertebrates found late in the Cambrian.
Proterozoic		2,000	Multicellular organisms appeared and flourished. Many invertebrates. Eukaryotic organisms appeared (1,500 mya). Oxygen accumulated in the atmosphere.
Archean		4,600	Prokaryotic life appeared (3,500 mya). Origin of the Earth (4,600 mya).

Major Groups of Plants and Animals

During the Precambrian era, unicellular eukaryotic cells containing chloroplasts gave rise to first multicellular plants. The green, brown and red algae lining our shose today, some such as the brown kelp. Over 60 metres long are the discendents of these early multicellular algae. A wide variety of Precambrian invertebrate animals appear in rocks laid down between 650-544 million years ago. Like the Precambrian animals the first fossil of Cambrian animals reveal in adaptive radiation that had already yielded a diverse array of complex body plans. Coevolution of predator and prey led to increased sophistication in many kinds of animals.

The geological periods where the major groups of organisms appeared as follows:

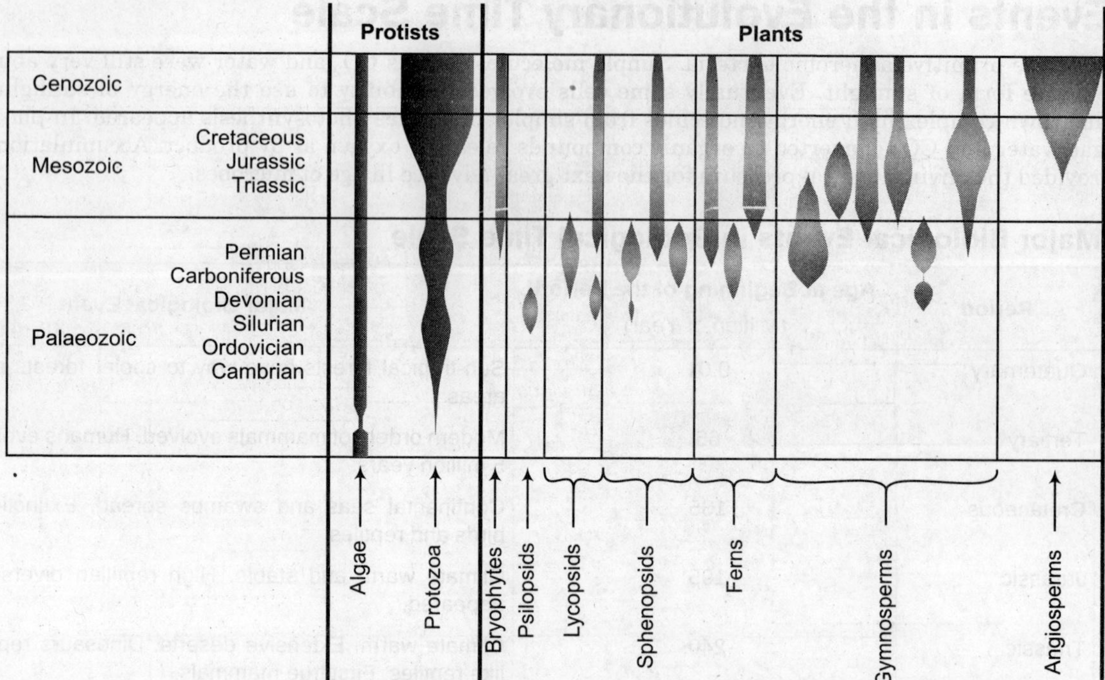

Fig. 34.2 Origin and evolution of plants

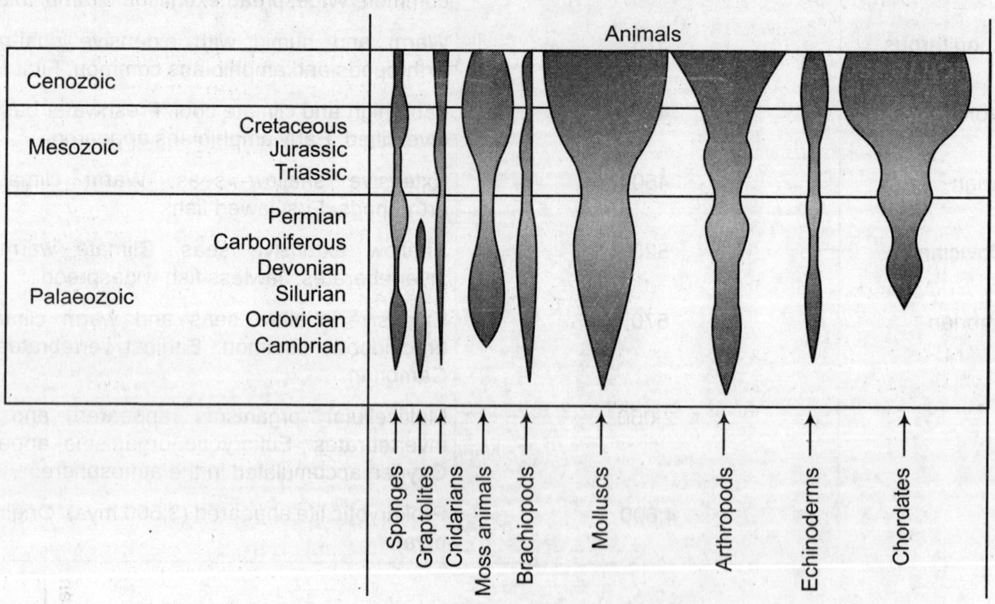

Fig. 34.3 Origin and evolution of animals

Evolution of Horse Based on Fossil Evidences

Over the past 50 million years horses evolved from small woodland browsers to large plains dwelling grazers. Three major changes include size, leg anatomy and tooth anatomy. No one is certain why horses become larger but it may have provided an advantage against predators. In any case, a large body running over hard plains favoured the evolution of large hard hooves, attached by spring like shock absorbing joints to legs with stout bones. Finally the teeth became larger with more enamel reflecting a change in diet from relatively soft leaves and buds of bushes up to abrasive blades of grasses which contain silicon (glass).

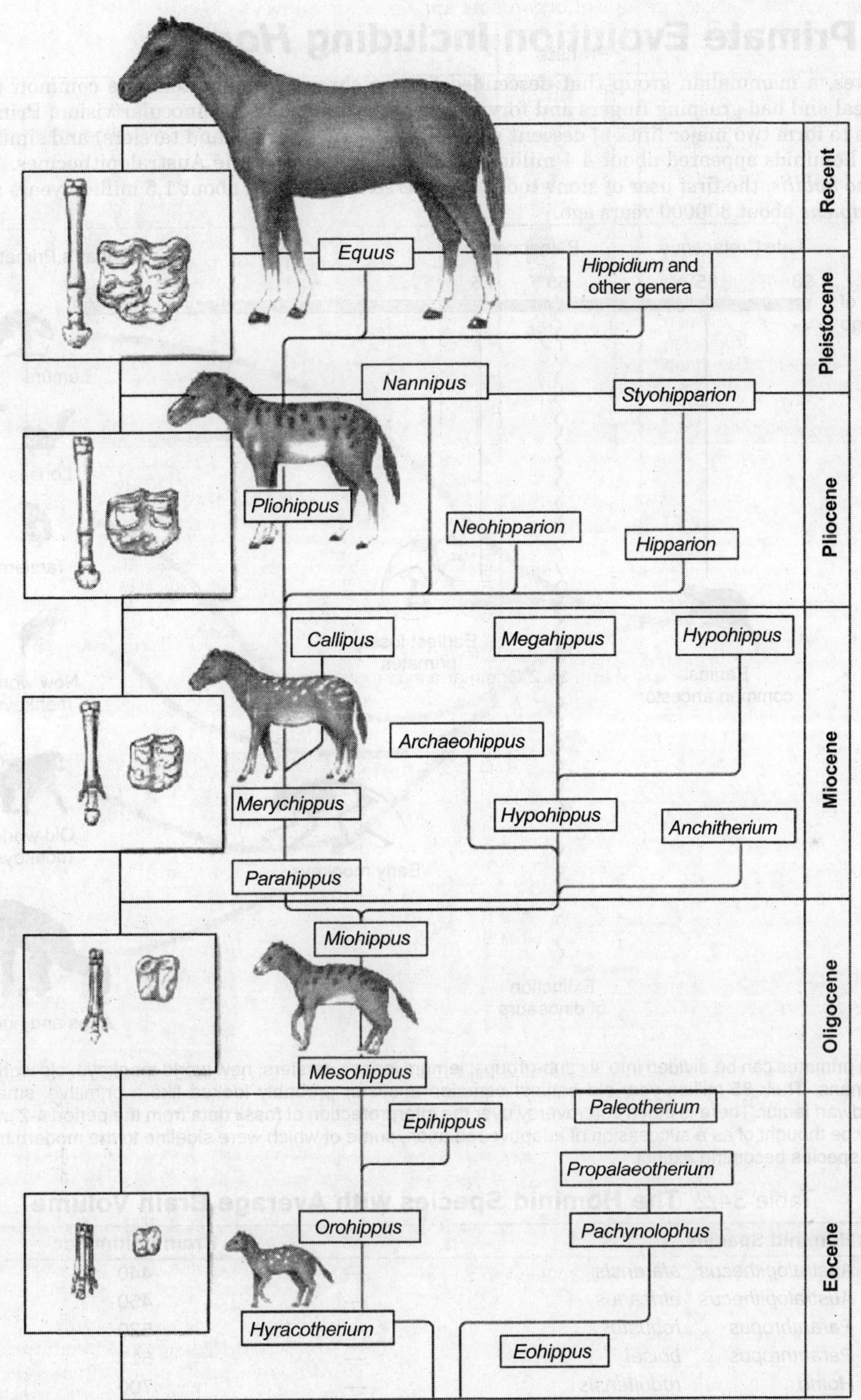

Fig. 34.4 Reconstruction of an evolutionary lineage of horse from evidence in the fossil record

The fossil record allows horse evolution to be traced back about 60 million years. *Hyracotherium (Eohippus)* was a dog-sized animal with four prominent toes on each foot. A single middle digit of the toe and vestigial digits on either side of that remain in modern horses. Evolutionary trends toward increased size, elaboration of molars and loss of toes are shown together with a hypothetical genealogy of extant and fossil genera.

Stages in Primate Evolution Including *Homo*

Humans are primates, a mammalian group that descended from a shrew-like ancestor. The common ancestor of all modern primates was arboreal and had grasping fingers and forward facing eyes capable of binocular vision. Primates radiated over the last 80 million years to form two major lines of descent prosimians (lemurs, lorises and tarsiers) and simians (monkeys apes and hominids). Earliest hominids appeared about 4.4 million years ago; these were the Australopithecines. These gave rise to and coexisted with, *Homo habilis,* the first user of stone tools. *Homo erectus* appeared about 1.5 million years ago and was eventually replaced by *Homo sapiens* about 300000 years ago.

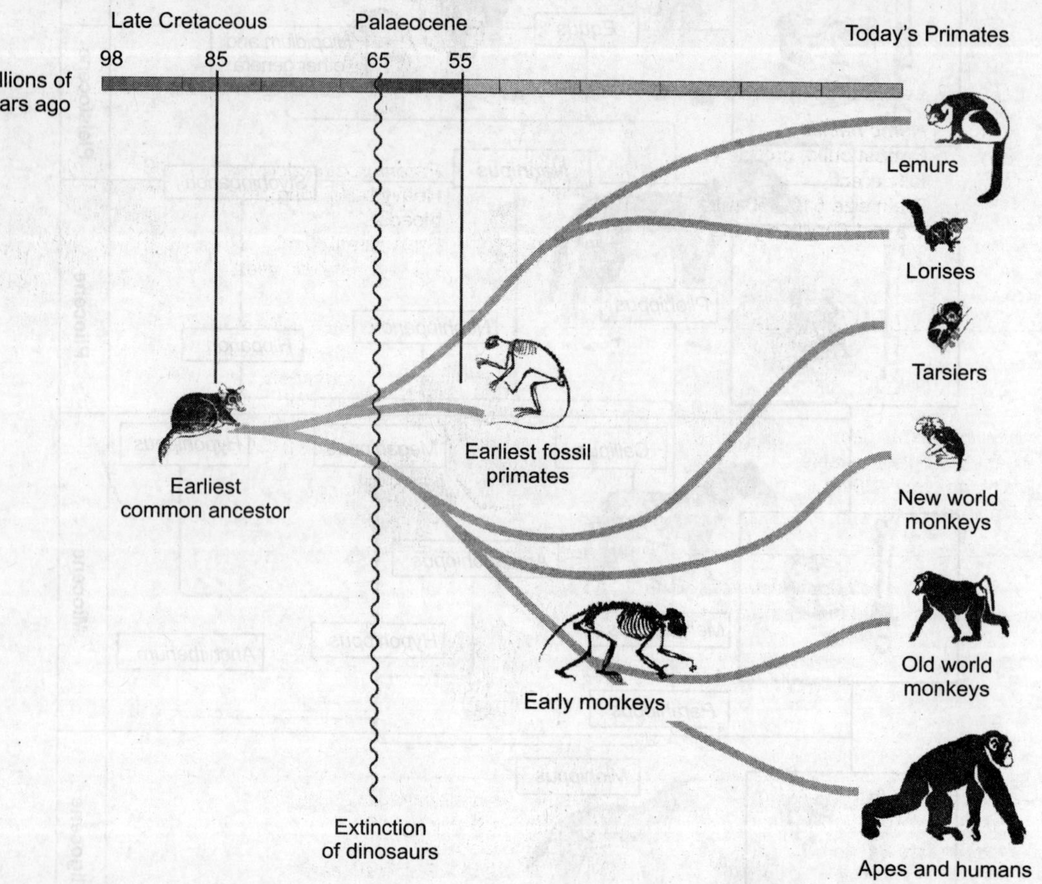

Fig. 34.5 Existing primates can be divided into six sub-groups: lemurs lorises, tarsiers, new world monkeys, old world monkeys and apes and humans. Their 85-million-year-old earliest common ancestor probably looked like a primitive, small-brained version of today's dwarf lemur. There is much controversy over the interprotection of fossil data from the period 4-2 mya. Human evolution can now be thought of as a succession of adaptive radiation, some of which were sideline to the modern human lineage and all but one species becoming extinct.

Table 34.2 **The Hominid Species with Average Brain Volume**

Hominid Species			Brain Volume cc
Australopithecus	*afarensis*	—	440
Australopithecus	*africanus*	—	450
Paranthropus	*robustus*	—	520
Paranthropus	*boisei*	—	515
Homo	*rudolfensis*	—	700
Homo	*habilis*	—	575
Homo	*ergaster*	—	800
Homo	*erectus*	—	1100
Homo	*heidelbergensis*	—	1250
Homo	*neanderthalensis*	—	1550
Homo	*sapiens*	—	1450

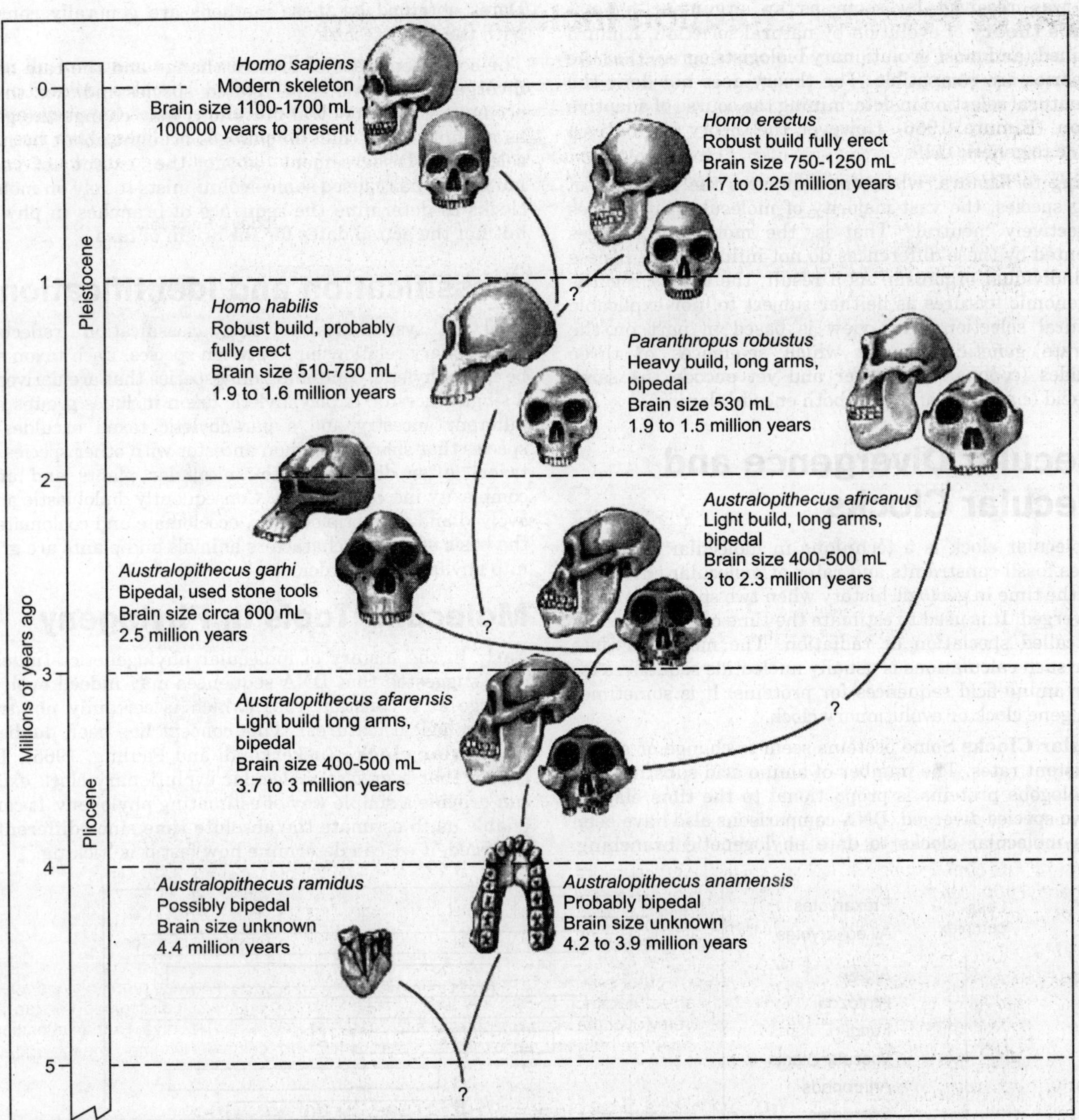

Fig. 34.6 Hominid skulls, showing several of the best-known hominid lines preceding modern humans (*Homo sapiens*)

Molecular Evolution

Concepts of Neutral Evolution

In 1968, Motoo Kimura proposed the **neutral theory of molecular evolution**. Kimura suggested that, at the molecular level, the majority of mutations are selectively neutral; that is, they confer neither an advantage nor a disadvantage on their bearers. Thus, the majority of evolutionary changes in macromolecules and much of the genetic variation within species, could result neither from directional selection of advantageous alleles nor from stabilizing selection, but rather from genetic drift.

The neutral theory of molecular evolution states that the vast majority of evolutionary change at the molecular level is caused by random drift of selectively neutral mutants. The theory was received by some as an argument against **Darwin's theory** of evolution by natural selection, Kimura maintained (and most evolutionary biologists agree) that the two theories are compatible 'The theory does not deny the role of natural selection in determining the course of adaptive evolution' (Kimura; 1986). However, the theory attributes a large role to genetic drift.

According to Kimura, when one compares the genomes of existing species, the vast majority of molecular differences are selectively 'neutral.' That is, the molecular changes represented by these differences do not influence the fitness of the individual organism. As a result, the theory regards these genomic features as neither subject to, nor explicable by, natural selection. This view is based in part on the degenerate genetic code, in which sequences of three nucleotides (codons) may differ and yet encode the same amino acid (*e.g.*, GCC and GCA both encode alanine).

Molecular Divergence and Molecular Clocks

The molecular clock is a technique in molecular evolution that uses fossil constraints and rates of molecular change to deduce the time in geologic history when two species or other taxa diverged. It is used to estimate the time of occurrence of events called speciation or radiation. The molecular data used for such calculations is usually nucleotide sequences for DNA or amino acid sequences for proteins. It is sometimes called a gene clock or evolutionary clock.

Molecular Clocks Some proteins seem to change or evolve at consistent rates. The number of amino acid substitutions in homologous proteins is proportional to the time elapsed since two species diverged. DNA comparisons also have been used as molecular clocks to date phylogenetic branching. Dates obtained by these methods are generally consistent with the fossil record.

The consistent rate of protein change and the rate of DNA divergence in groups of related species indicate that the accumulation of neutral mutations may change the genome as a whole more than do changes brought about by natural selection. Disagreement about the extent of neutral mutations has caused some evolutionists to rely on molecular clocks to determine the sequence of branches in phylogeny but not the actual dates for the origin of taxa.

Classification and Identification

Goal of systematics is that classification reflects the evolutionary relationships between species. Each taxon should be monophyletic, containing only species that are derived from a single ancestor. A polyphyletic taxon includes groups having different ancestry and a paraphyletic taxon exculdes some species that share a common ancestor with other species in the taxon. After diversion into unicellular plants and animals complexity increased slowly. Consequently diploblastic animals evolved and then triploblastic, acoelomate and coelomate. One the basis of similar characters animals and plants are grouped into phylum, class, order, etc.

Molecular Tools in Phylogeny

Early in the history of molecular phylogenetic studies, the data suggested that DNA sequences may indeed evolve and diverge at a constant rate (which is certainly not true of morphological features). This concept has been dubbed the **molecular clock** (Zuckerkandl and Pauling; 1965). To the extent that a precise molecular evolutionary clock exists, it can provide a simple way of estimating phylogeny. It can also enable us to estimate the absolute time since different taxa diverged, if we can determine how fast it is 'ticking.'

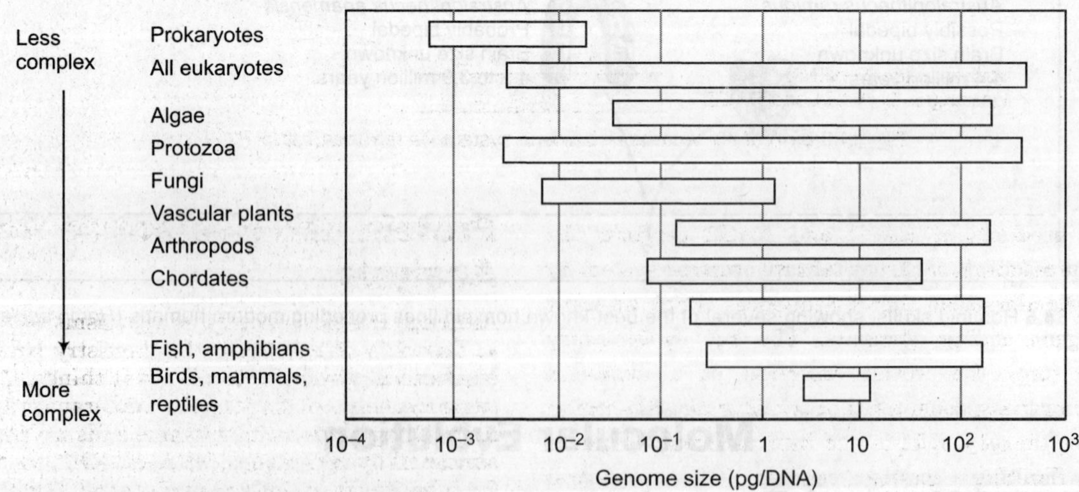

Fig. 34.7 Genome size variation. The bars indicate the range of genome size for particular clades. Taxa are arranged top to bottom in order of increasing organismal complexity

Restriction mapping of DNA compares fragments of DNA from different species cut by restriction enzymes. If two species have diverged greatly, their collections of restriction fragments will not match closely. Restriction mapping of mitochondrial DNA (mtDNA), which mutates about ten times faster than nuclear DNA, provides phylogenetic information for closely related species or populations.

DNA sequencing, determining the actual order of nucleotides in DNA, provides the most accurate information on genetic divergence between species. The sequencing or ribosomal RNA, whose genes change slowly, can be used to determine early phylogenetic relationships.

Analysis of fossilized DNA molecular systematics has now been applied to DNA extracted from fossils. Small quantities of DNA are amplified using polymerase chain reaction and tested from homology with modern species.

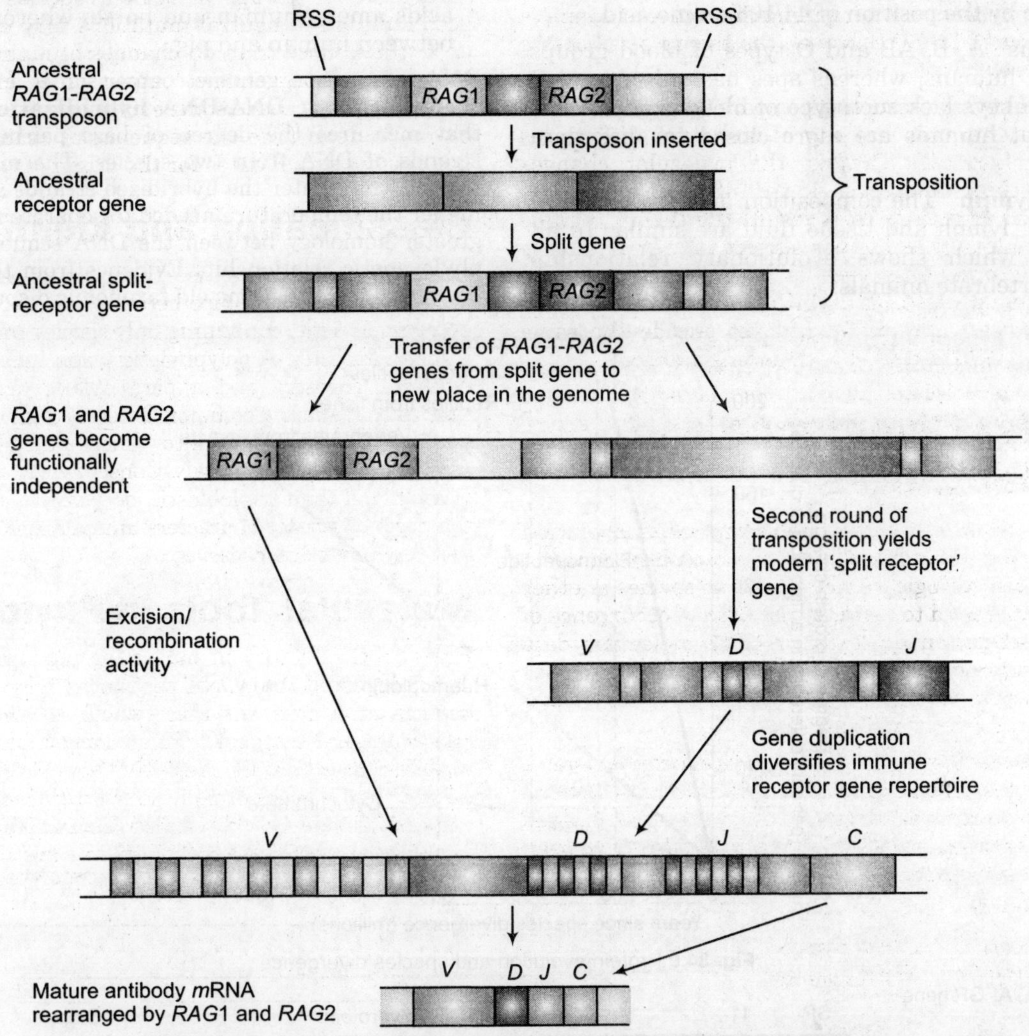

Fig. 34.8 Birth of the vertebrate immune system *via* retroposition of *RAG* genes

The protein products of *RAG*1 and *RAG*2 perform the recombination reactions of the vertebrate immune system by binding to Recombination Signal Sequences (RSS) adjacent to receptor gene coding elements. The key evolutionary events were (top) the initial insertion of a ancestral RAG-containing transposon into a progenitor variable-region receptor gene, thereby splitting it into different elements with RSS flanking coding regions (the ancestral split-receptor gene). Subsequent to this transposition, *RAG*1 and 2 genes are lost from split genes and become functionally and genomically independent.

Protein and Nucleotide Sequence Analysis

Although the biochemistry of organisms was not well known in Darwin's time, modern biochemistry indicates there is a biochemical similarity in all living things. For example, the same mechanisms for trapping and transforming energy and for building proteins from amino acids are nearly identical in almost all living systems. DNA and RNA are the mechanisms for inheritance and gene activity in all living organisms. The structure of the genetic code is almost identical in all living things. This uniformity in biochemical organization underlies the diversity of living things and points to evolutionary relationships.

- **Cytochrome-*c*** It is a respiratory pigment found in all eukaryotic cells which is a part of electron transport system. Cytochrome-*c* accepts H^+ in all eukaryotic cells. The cytochrome-*c* molecule of human and chimpanzee is identical, whereas *Neurospora* differ from human's cytochrome-*c* by the position of 44/104 amino acid.
- **Blood groups** A, B, AB and O types of blood groups are found in humans, whereas apes has only A and B type and monkeys lack such type of blood groups. This indicates that humans are more closed to apes than monkeys.
- **Blood and lymph** The composition and physiological role of blood, lymph and tissue fluid are similar in all vertebrates, which shows evolutionary relationship among all vertebrate animals.
- **Haemoglobin** Haemoglobin is a conjugated protein having two alpha chains (each with 141 amino acids in man) and two beta chains (each with 146 amino acids in man). There is single amino acid difference between human and gorilla haemoglobin chain and 26 amino acids among human and horse, whereas 10 amino acid between human and pig.

DNA comparison genome comparison is a direct measure of shared ancestry. **DNA-DNA hybridization** is a technique that measures the degree of base pairing between single strands of DNA from two species. The more extensive the pairing, the tighter the hybridized strands are bound and the higher the temperature needed to separate them, indicating a greater homology between the DNA sequences and a closer phylogenetic relationship. Evidence from this technique has been used to settle some old taxonomic disputes.

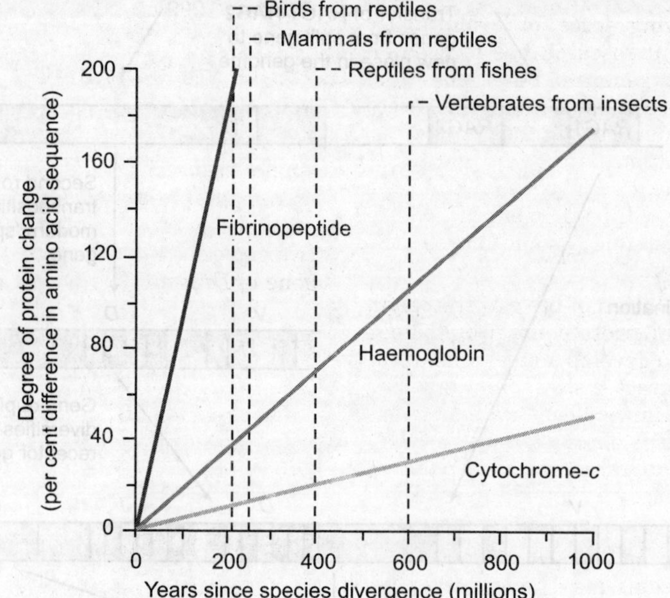

Fig. 34.9 Protein evolution and species divergence

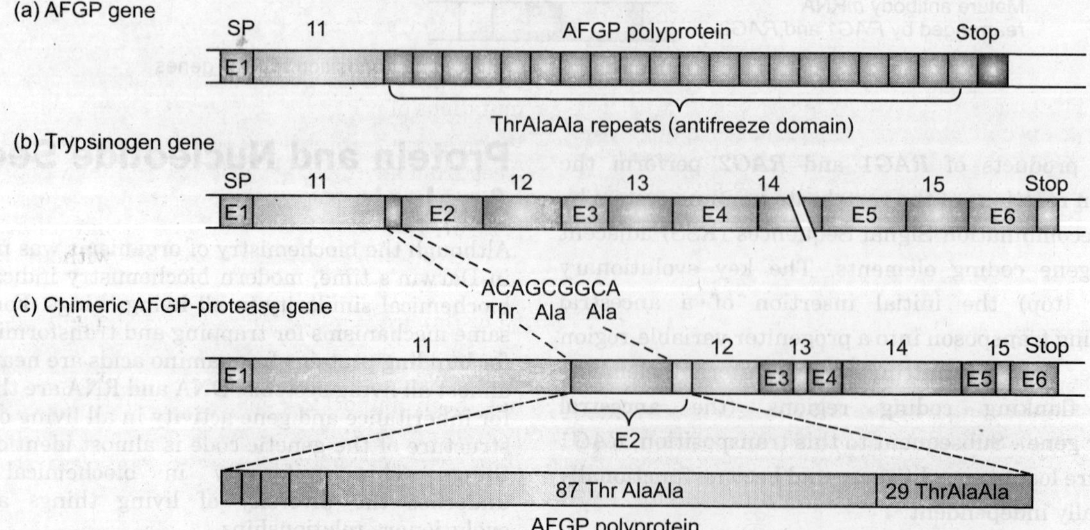

Fig. 34.10 The evolution of AFGP genes of Antarctic notothenioid fishes

(a) A typical functional AFGP gene from an Antarctic notothenioid, showing the repeated ThrAlaAla motifs encoded in exon 2 (E2) that comprise the antifreeze domain.

(b) A typical trypsinogen gene showing the single ThrAlaAla motif at the beginning of exon 2, as well as exons 1 and 6 (in red) that are also found in the AFGP gene.

(c) A chimeric AFGP gene from a giant Antarctic tooth fish (*Dissostichus mawsoni*). The exon in blue, encoding the ThrAlaAla repeats, is a many fold expansion of the single motif located just upstream of exon 2 in the trypsinogen gene.

Origin of New Genes and Proteins

New gene origination is a driving force of evolutionary innovation in all organisms. Recent research has focused on identifying the mechanisms that generate new genes and scientists have found that these mechanisms involve a variety of molecular events, all of which must occur in the germ line to be inherited by the next generation. After the germ-line mutational event, the new gene (*e.g.,* a new gene duplicate located on human chromosome 2) will be polymorphic in the population; in other words, not all second chromosomes in the population will carry the duplication.

The last step necessary for the evolution of life was the origin of genetic information. Successful protobionts would need only to grow and divide, but also to develop a mechanisms for replicating their successful characteristics, for creating instructions for making their key molecules. One hypothesis maintains that the first genes were short strands of RNA, which have been shown in the laboratory to be capable of self-replication. Cech's recent discovery of RNA catalysts called **ribozymes,** indicates that RNA molecules may have been self-replicating in the prebiotic world.

Early populations of RNA molecules may have undergone natural selection as those molecules with the most stable three-dimensional conformations and greatest autocatalytic activity within a particular environment successfully competed for monomers and generated families of similar sequences.

RNA-directed protein synthesis may have begun with the weak binding of specific amino acids to bases along RNA molecules and their linkage to form a short polypeptide. This polypeptide may have then behaved as an enzyme to help the RNA molecule replicate.

Mechanisms of New Gene Generation

These include gene duplication, transposable element protein domestication, lateral gene transfer, gene fusion, gene fission and *de novo* origination.

Gene Duplication

Gene duplication was the first mechanism of gene generation to be suggested (Ohno; 1970), and this process does indeed appear to be the most common way of creating new genes.

Transposable Element Protein Domestication

Transposable Elements (TEs) are so-called 'selfish' segments of DNA that encode proteins that allow these segments to copy or move themselves within a genome. There are two types of TEs–DNA transposons and retrotransposons.

Lateral Gene Transfer

Scientists use the term 'lateral gene transfer' to refer to the case in which a gene does not have a vertical origin (*i.e.,* direct inheritance from parent to offspring) but instead comes from an unrelated genome. It is well known that this sort of transfer occurs between bacteria and that it also has taken place between the genomes of the cellular organelles (mitochondria and chloroplasts) and the nuclear genomes (**Roger;** 1999).

Gene Fusion and Fission

Existing genes can also fuse (*i.e.,* two or more genes can become part of the same transcript) or undergo fission (*i.e.,* a single transcript can break into two or more separate transcripts), thereby forming new genes. Interestingly, it has been observed that chimeric fusion genes sometimes involve two copies of the same gene (*e.g.,* the alcohol dehydrogenase gene in *Drosophila*).

De novo Gene Origination

New genes can additionally originate *de novo* from non coding regions of DNA. Indeed, several novel genes derived from non-coding DNA have recently been described in *Drosophila* (Begun *et. al.* 2007; Levine *et. al.,* 2006).

Gene Duplication and Divergence

Gene duplication appears to be the most important process that enables proteins to acquire new functions. Gene duplication is any duplication of a region of DNA; it may occur as an error in homologous recombination, a retrotransposition event, or duplication of an entire chromosome. The second copy of the gene is often free from selective pressure — that is, mutations of it have no deleterious effects to its host organism.

When a gene is duplicated, one copy of that gene is potentially freed from having to perform its original function; the copy is redundant if the original gene is still producing the original protein. Therefore, gene duplication may allow the evolution of entirely novel protein functions without impairing cell functioning.

Gene duplication may involve part of a gene, a single gene, a portion of a chromosome, an entire chromosome, or the whole genome. Duplication of the entire genome (polyploidy) has been important in speciation, especially in plants. Autopolyploid individuals are usually viable because all of their chromosomes are duplicated. Thus, they avoid imbalances in gene expression.

Plants are the most prolific genome duplicators. For example, **wheat is hexaploid** (a kind of polyploid), meaning that it has six copies of its genome.

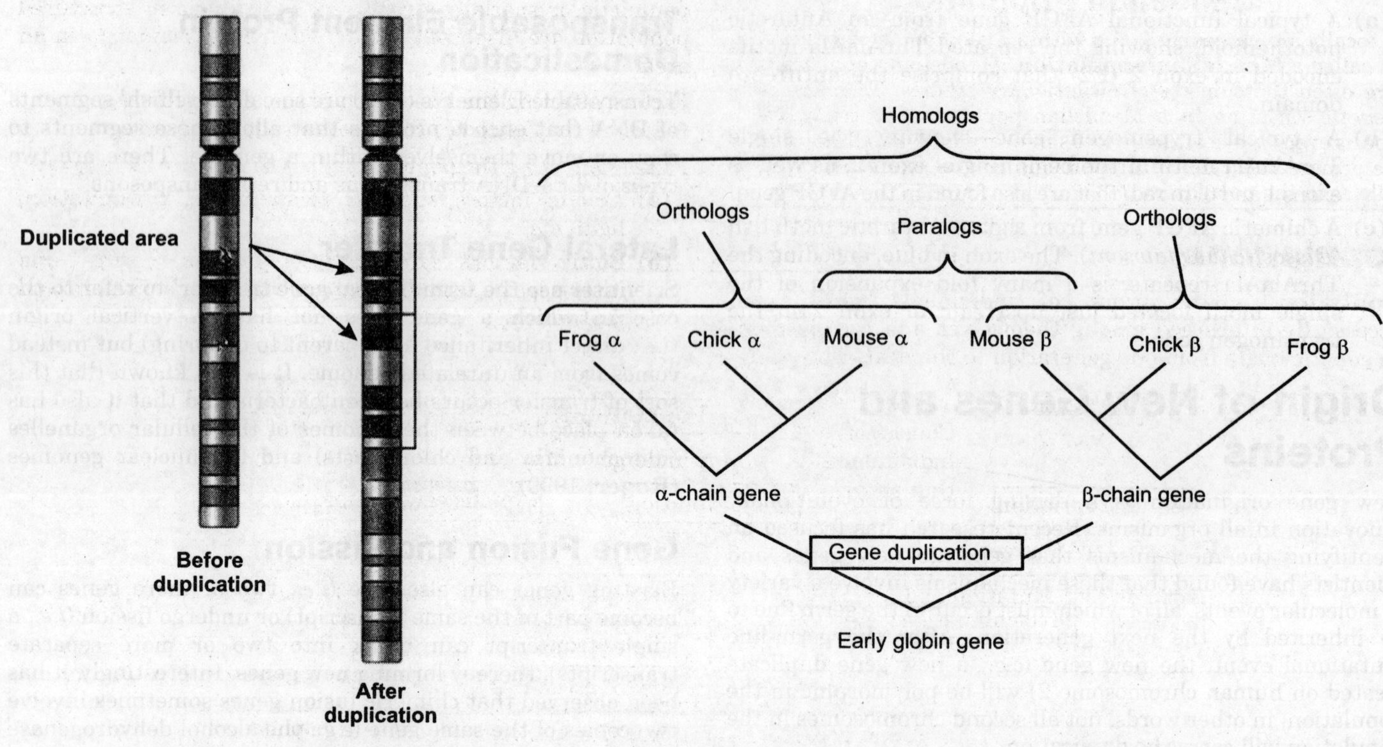

Fig. 34.11 Gene that has duplicated

Fig. 34.12 Evolution of haemoglobin through gene duplication

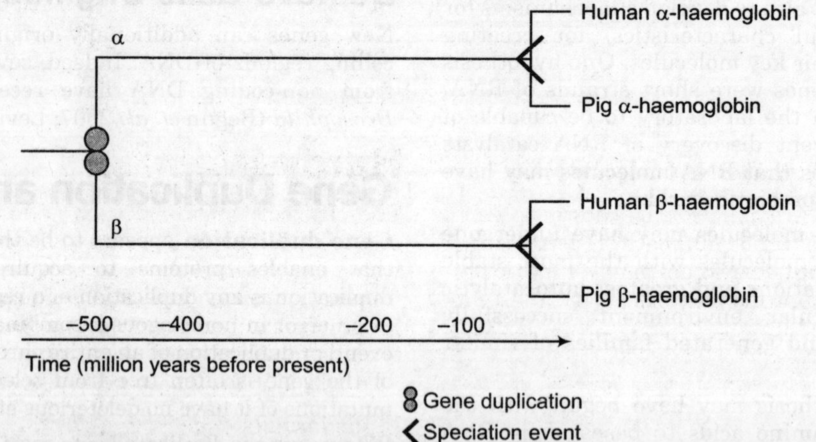

Fig. 34.13 Two genes are orthologous if they diverged after a speciation event. Two genes are paralogous if they diverged after a gene duplication event

The Mechanisms

Population Genetics

Population genetics deals with the change of a particular trait over the time leading to the process of evolution. The change of the trait is important for coping with the changing environment. The population can have low and high variation. Highly variable traits are important to cope with the changing environment compared to low variability. Variation in most traits is due the effect of many genetic differences, so called polygenic traits, which do not follow Mendelian inheritance. Variability can be studied by external appearance or by biochemical method such as RFLP.

Mendelian Population

A locally interbreeding group within a geographic population is called a **Mendelian population.** Mendelian populations are often the subjects of evolutionary studies. To measure genetic variation in a Mendelian population precisely, we count every allele at every locus in every individual in it and determine the relative proportions or **frequencies,** of all alleles in the population.

Populations

Population is the group of individuals which can successfully interbreed among themselves and can pass on the genetic traits from one generation to the next. The study of human population is called demography. Population can be panmictic or spatially structured. Individuals in structured population are dispersed evenly, clumped or randomly in an area.

Factors affecting the size of population are as follows;
(a) Birth **(b)** Death **(c)** Immigration **(d)** Emigration

Factors affecting the population growth rate are as follows;

(a) Abiotic factors such as temperature, precipitation, light, etc.

(b) Biotic factors such as competition (intra- and inter-sepcies competition), predation, parasitism and mutualism.

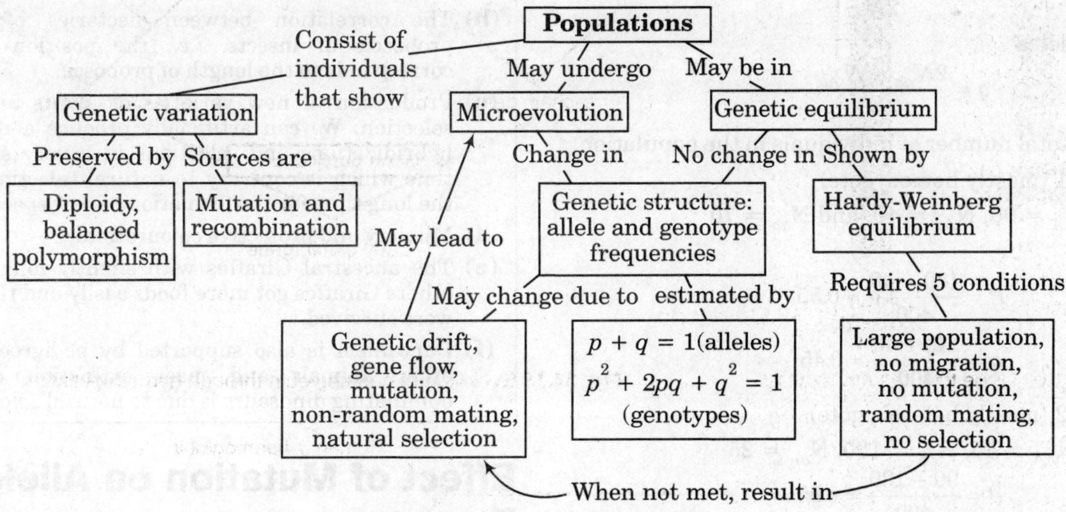

Fig. 34.14 The population framework

Gene Pool and Gene Frequency

The genetic composition of a population is known as gene pool. In simple terms, the total number of genes in a population is called **gene pool**. Gene pool is never static but changes always due to the following reasons;

(a) Gene mutation

(b) Gene flow

(c) Genetic drift

(d) Natural selection

The variation of individuals over the time in a population due to the changes in the gene pool is often regarded as microevolution. If the variations happen for a long a time so that the individuals in the population were no longer can interbreed is called macroevolution.

The occurrence of a particular gene in different individuals of a population is often measured in terms of gene frequency. **Gene frequency can have a value between 0 to 1 in proportion or 0 to 100 in percentage.** Gene frequency is often interchangeably used for allele frequency. Please note that in a single chromosome a gene at a particular locus is composed of two alleles. So, it is change of allele frequency which leads to a change in **gene frequency**.

Hardy-Weinberg Law

The British mathematician **GH Hardy** and German physician **Wilhelm Weinberg** proposed this law after their name, in which they have explained the change of gene frequency in a population, remain constant over the generations under the circumstances of random mating. The formula for Hardy-Weinberg law is

$$(p + q)^2 = p^2 + 2pq + q^2 = 1$$

In the formula, p and q denotes the proportions or frequency of alleles P and Q, respectively. p^2 is the gene frequency for PP gene, $2pq$ is the gene frequency for PQ gene and q^2 is the gene frequency for QQ gene.

The law requires following conditions to be fulfilled:

(i) Mutation is not occurring.

(ii) Natural selection is not operating.

(iii) The population is infinitely large, so that chance factor is avoided.

(iv) All members of the population breed.

(v) All mating is totally random.

(vi) Everyone produces the same number of offspring.

(vii) There is no immigration or emigration from the population.

As any population can not fulfill all these conditions, therefore every population is evolving. Within a population, random mating is occurring at certain levels but not at others. Blood type and RFLP patterns are examples for random, while intelligence and physical stature are the examples for non-random mating loci.

Calculating Allele Frequencies The gene pool and allele frequencies are the same in two different populations, but the alleles are distributed differently between heterozygous and homozygous genotypes. In all cases, $p + q$ must equal 1.

Solution

In any population

Frequency of allele A

$$P = \frac{2N_{AA} + N_{Aa}}{2N}$$

Frequency of allelea

$$q = \frac{2N_{aa} + N_{Aa}}{2N}$$

where, N is the total number of individuals in the population.

For population 1 (mostly homozygote)

$$N_{AA} = 90,\ N_{Aa} = 40, \text{ and } N_{aa} = 70$$

So,

$$P = \frac{180 + 40}{400} = 0.55$$

$$q = \frac{140 + 40}{400} = 0.45$$

For population 2 (mostly heterozygote)

$$N_{AA} = 45,\ N_{aa} = 130,\ N_{an} = 25$$

$$P = \frac{90 + 130}{400} = 0.55$$

$$q = \frac{50 + 130}{400} = 0.45$$

The concept of Hardy-Weinberg law is an ideal situation, where population are large enough with each individuals genotype in the population is reproductively fit and no mutation, selection or migration is operational. Fisher, Wright and JBS Haldane further elaborated this law under the conditions when gene frequency is changing due to the mutation, selection, genetic drift or migration.

Gene Frequency Change through Natural Selection

Natural selection is generally believed to be the prominent agent for determining the relative frequency of alleles in a population. Natural selection differentiates between phenotypes in a population with respect to their ability to produce offspring. One phenotype may better survive endemic onslaughts of parasities or predators than another, one may penetrate new habitats more effectively than another; one may mate more efficiently than other; one may even prey on the other. The important point is that some natural situation or environmental feature selectively allows one organism to develop and to propagate more efficiently and one genotype is thereby afforded greater representation in the populations gene pool. If this selective process continues over many generations, allelic frequencies will change significantly and the potential will arise for evolutionary change. Further, the natural selection process, while acting on the total phenotype, will in fact influence only the heritable portion of the phenotype. If a trait has a high heritability, selection can rapidly affect its frequency within a population, whereas selection will take a great deal longer to have any effect on a trait with a low heritability. Natural selection includes following three parameters survival rate, relative fitness and the selection coefficient.

Evidences in Support of Natural Selection

(a) Pedigree of some animals like horse, camel, elephant, etc., support Darwinism.

(b) The correlation between nectaries of flowers and proboscis of insects, *i.e.*, the position of nectarines corresponds to the length of proboscis.

(c) Production of new varieties of plants and animals by selection. We can artificially produce a new species by hybridizations and selections in a very short period of time which is contrary to natural selection which takes the long time for the formation of new species.

(d) Mimicry and protective colouration.

(e) The ancestral Giraffes with slightly longer necks than others Giraffes got more foods easily and therefore, latter were survived.

(f) Darwinism is also supported by pedigree of horse and other animals and mass extinction of giant and dominating dinosaurs is due to natural selection.

Effect of Mutation on Allele Frequency

The rate of change in gene frequency from the mutation process is very low because spontaneous mutation rates are low. The mutation rate is defined as the probability that a copy of an allele changes to some other allelic form in one generation. Thus, the increase in the frequency of a mutant allele will be the product of the mutation rate times the frequency of the non-mutant allele.

Migration and Random Genetic Drift

Genetic drift can cause evolution *via* chance fluctuation in a small population's gene pool. Chance deviations from expected results are more likely to occur in a small sample due to sampling error. **Genetic drift** is a chance change in the gene pool of a small population due to sampling error and is likely to play a role in the microevolution of populations of less than 100 individuals.

Bottleneck Effect The **bottleneck effect** occurs when some disaster or other factor reduces the population size dramatically and the few surviving individuals are unlikely to represent the genetic make up of the original population. Genetic drift will remain a factor in the population until it is large enough for chance events to be less significant. A bottleneck usually reduces variability because some alleles are lost from the gene pool.

Founder Effect Genetic drift that occurs when only a few individuals colonize a new area is known as the **founder effect.** Allele frequencies in the small sample are unlikely to be representative of the parent population and genetic drift will affect the gene pool of the new population until it is larger.

Adaptive Radiation and Modifications

Adaptive radiation is an evolutionary pattern whereby a single ancestral form (or species) diversifies (or speciates) into several or many related forms (or species). According to this concept, the different descendant taxa are similar, but each is adapted for a particular environmental niche. It is held that adaptive radiation led to the presence of over 250000 species of beetles, 14 different species of Darwin's finches on the Galápagos islands, over 25000 types of teleost fishes and different marsupials in Australia (Luria *et. al. 1981*).

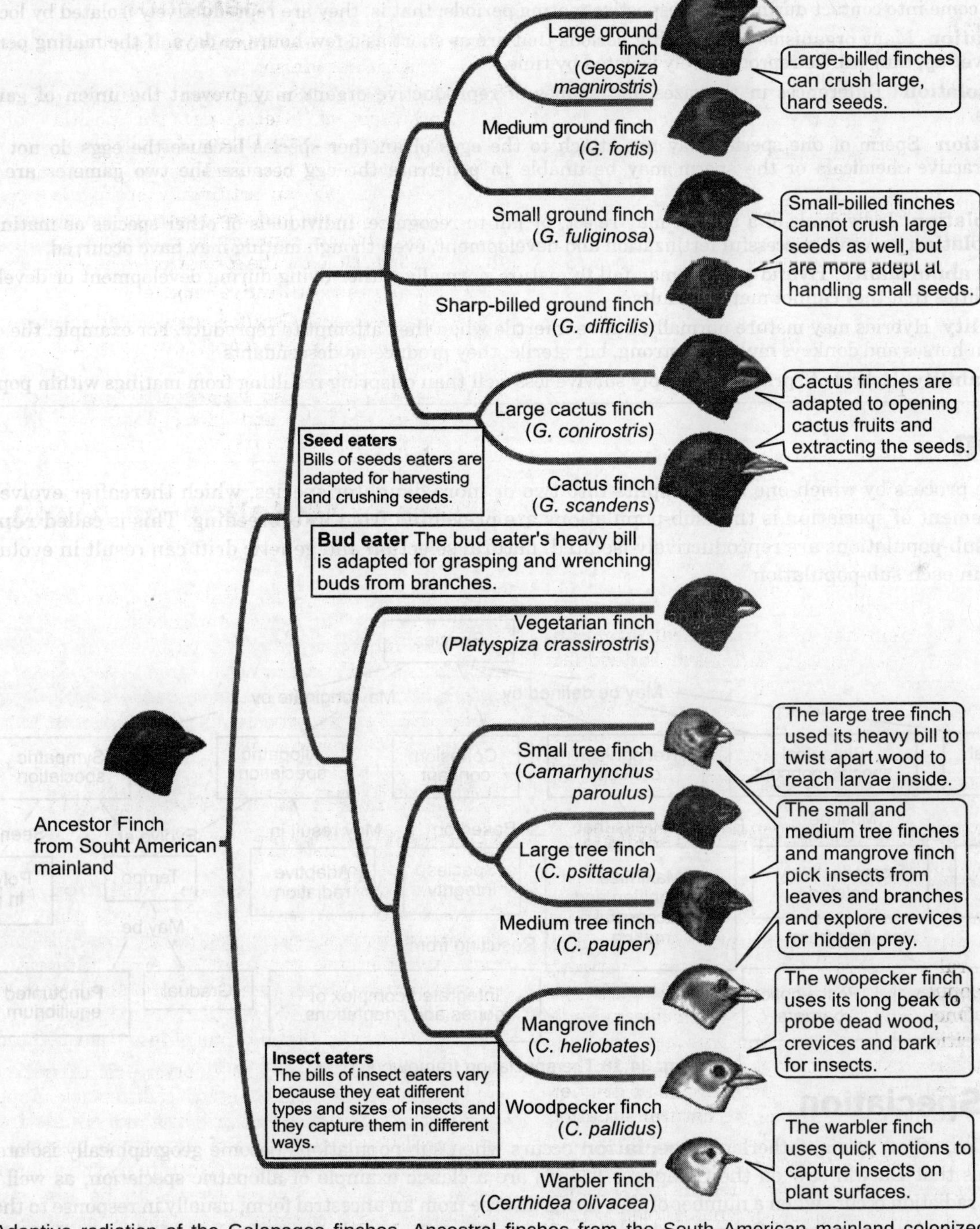

Fig. 34.15 Adaptive radiation of the Galapagos finches. Ancestral finches from the South American mainland colonized the Galapagos Islands. Open habitats and few predators promoted the radiation of finches into 14 different species

Isolating Mechanism

The reproductive characteristics which prevent species from successful breeding are called isolating mehanisms. **Isolating mechanisms are particularly important in the biological species concept, in which species of sexual organisms are defined by reproductive isolation, *i.e.,* a lack of gene mixture. Two broad kinds of isolating mechanisms between species are typically distinguished, together with a number of sub-types (modified from Mayr; 1970).**

Reproductive Isolation

Premating isolation prevents mating from taking place.

- **Spatial isolation** Individuals of different species may select different places in the environment in which to live. As a result, they may never come into contact during their respective mating periods; that is, they are reproductively isolated by location.
- **Temporal isolation** Many organisms have mating periods that are as short as a few hours or days. If the mating periods of two species do not overlap, they will be reproductively isolated by time.
- **Mechanical isolation** Differences in the sizes and shapes of reproductive organs may prevent the union of gametes from different species.
- **Gametic isolation** Sperm of one species may not attach to the eggs of another species because the eggs do not release the appropriate attractive chemicals or the sperm may be unable to penetrate the egg because the two gametes are chemically incompatible.
- **Behavioral isolation** Individuals of a species may reject, or fail to recognize, individuals of other species as mating partners.

Postmating isolation prevents successful fertilization and development, even though mating may have occurred.

- **Hybrid zygote abnormality** Hybrid zygotes may fail to mature normally, either dying during development or developing such severe abnormalities that they cannot mate as adults.
- **Hybrid infertility** Hybrids may mature normally, but be infertile when they attempt to reproduce. For example, the offspring of matings between horses and donkeys mules are strong, but sterile; they produce no descendants.
- **Low hybrid viability** Hybrid offspring may simply survive less well than offspring resulting from matings within populations.

Speciation

Speciation is the process by which one species splits into two or more daughter species, which thereafter evolve as distinct lineages. A requirement of speciation is that sub-populations are prevented from interbreeding. This is called **reproductive isolation.** When sub-populations are reproductively isolated, natural selection and genetic drift can result in evolution taking a different course in each sub-population.

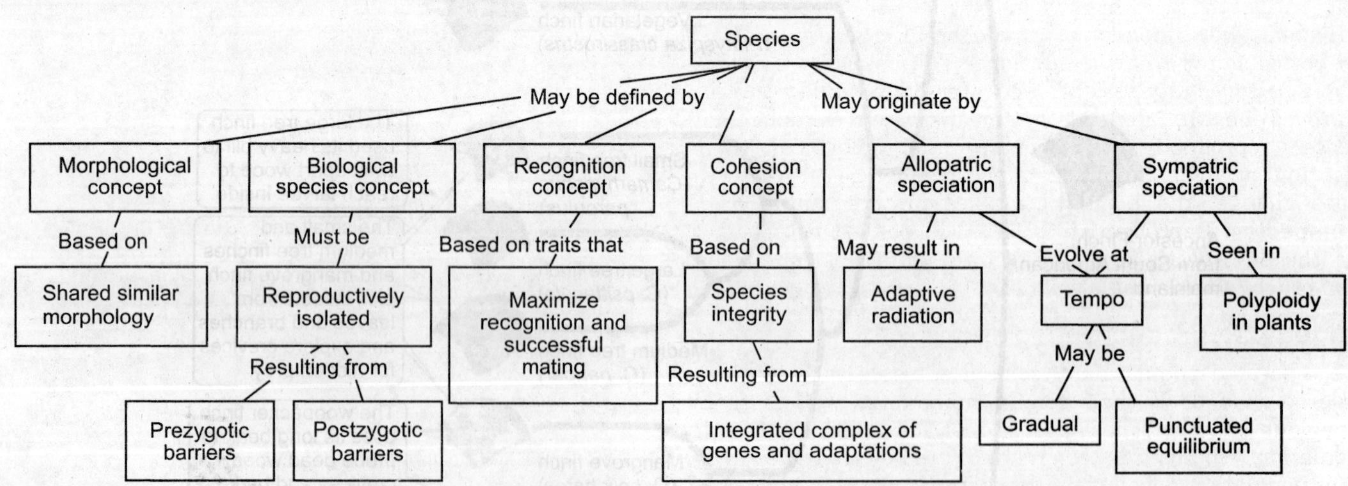

Fig. 34.16 The speciation framework

Allopatric Speciation

Allopatric (Gr. allos, other; patria, fatherland) **speciation** occurs when sub-populations become geographically isolated from one another. The finches that Darwin saw on the Galápagos Islands are a classic example of allopatric speciation, as well as adaptive radiation. Adaptive radiation occurs when a number of new forms diverge from an ancestral form, usually in response to the opening of major new habitats. Fourteen species of finches evolved from the original finches that colonized the Galápagos Islands. Ancestral finches, having emigrated from the mainland, probably were distributed among a few of the islands of the Galápagos.

Step I: Moving into New Environment

There are times when the range of a species expands for a variety of different reasons. A single population in a relatively homogeneous environment will move into new regions of their environment when they are subjected to intense competition (whether it is interspecific or intraspecific). The most severe form of competition is between members of the same species since they are competing for identical resources in the habitat. In the diagram on the right there is a 'parent population' of a single species with a common gene pool with regular 'gene flow' (theoretically and individual has access to all members of the opposite sex for mating purposes).

Step II: Geographical Isolation

Isolation of parts of the population may occur due to the formation of **physical barriers.** There barriers may cut off those parts of the population that are at the extremes of the species range and gene flow is prevented or rare. This rise and fall of the sea level has been particularly important in functioning as an isolating mechanisms. Climatic change can leave 'island' of habitat separated by large inhospitable zones that the species cannot transverse.

Example In mountainous regions, alpine species are free to range widely over extensive habitat during cool climatic periods. During warmer periods, however, they may become isolated because their habitat is reduced to islands of high ground surrounded by inhospitable lowland habitat.

Step III: Different Selection Pressures

The isolated populations (A and B) may be subjected to quite different selection pressures. These will favour individuals with traits that suit each particular environment. For example, population A will be subjected to selection pressures that relate to drier conditions. This will favour those individuals with phenotypes (and therefore genotypes) that are better suited to dry conditions. They may for instance have a better ability to conserve water. This would result in improved health, allowing better disease resistance and greater reproductive performance (i.e., more of their offspring survive). Finally, as allele frequencies for certain genes change, the population takes on the status of a **sub-species.** Reproductive isolation is not yet established but the su-bspecies are significantly different genetically from other related populations.

Stage IV: Reproductive Isolation

The separated populations (isolated sub-species) will often undergo changes in their genetic makeup as well as their behaviour patterns. These ensure that the gene pool of each population remains isolated and undiluted by the genes from other populations, even if the two populations should be able to remix (due to the removal of the geographical barrier). Gene flow does not occur. The arrows (in the diagram to the right) indicate the zone of overlap between two species after the new species B has moved back into the range inhabited by the parent population. Closely-related species whose distribution overlaps are said to be **sympatric species.** Those that remain geographically isolated are called **allopatric species.**

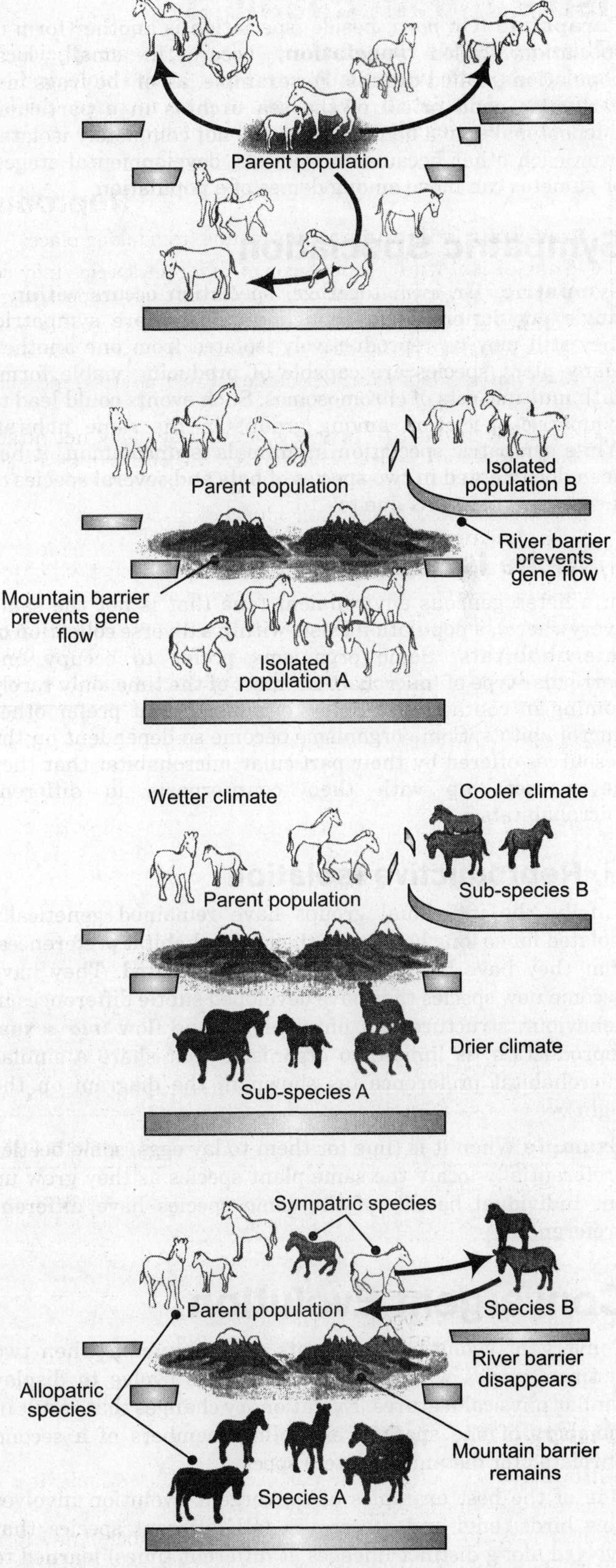

Fig. 34.17 Mechanism of allopatric speciation

Parapatric Speciation

Parapatric (Gr. *para,* beside) speciation is another form of speciation, called **speciation,** occurs in small, local populations, called **demes**. For example, all of the frogs in a particular pond or all of the sea urchins in a particular tidepool make up a deme. Demes are not completely isolated from each other because individuals, developmental stages, or gametes can move among demes of a population.

Sympatric Speciation

Sympatric (Gr. *sym,* together) speciation occurs within a single population. Even though organisms are sympatric, they still may be reproductively isolated from one another. Many plant species are capable of producing viable forms with multiple sets of chromosomes. Such events could lead to sympatric speciation among groups in the same habitat. While sympatric speciation in animals is uncommon, it has been documented in two species of bats and several species of insects and fish. It is due to

(i) Niche Isolation

In a heterogeneous environment (one that is not the same everywhere), a population exists within a diverse collection of **microhabitats.** Some organisms prefer to occupy one particular type of 'microhabitat' most of the time, only rarely coming in contact with fellow organisms that prefer other microhabitats. Some organisms become so dependent on the resources offered by their particular microhabitat that they never meet up with their counterparts in different microhabitats.

(ii) Reproductive Isolation

Finally, the individual groups have remained genetically isolated for so long because of their microhabitat preferences, that they have become reproductively isolated. They have become new species that have developed subtle differences in behaviour, structure and physiology. Gene flow (*via* sexual reproduction) is limited to organisms that share a similar microhabitat preference (as shown in the diagram on the right).

Example When it is time for them to lay eggs, some beetles preferentially locate the same plant species as they grew up on. Individual beetles of the same species have different preferences.

Convergent Evolution

Convergent evolution represents a phenomenon when two distinct species with differing ancestries evolve to display similar physical features. Evolutionary changes that result in members of one species resembling members of a second unrelated (or distantly related) species.

One of the best examples of convergent evolution involves how birds, bats and pterosaurs (all different species that evolved along distinct lineages at different times) learned to fly. Importantly, each species developed wings independently. These species did not evolve in order to prepare for future circumstances, but rather the development of flight was induced by selective pressure imposed by similar environmental conditions. Other examples are marsupial Tasmanian Wolf is similarities to placental canids, except for the narrow hips,

Parallel Evolution

Parallel evolution is the development of a similar trait in related, but distinct, species descending from the same ancestor, but from different clades. Parallel and convergent evolutionary trends can be strictly defined and clearly distinguished from one another. When both descendants are similar in a particular respect, evolution is defined as parallel if the ancestors considered were also similar, and convergent if they were not.

The patagium is a fleshy membrane that is found in gliding mammals such as: flying lemurs, flying squirrels, sugar gliders and the extinct Volaticotherium. These mammals acquired the patagium independently.

Sexual Selection

Sexual selection is the theory proposed by Charles Darwin that states that certain evolutionary traits can be explained by intraspecific competition. Darwin defined sexual selection as the effects of the 'struggle between the individuals of one sex, generally the males, for the possession of the other sex'. Sexual selection acts on an organism's ability to obtain or successfully copulate with a mate.

Selection makes many organisms go to extreme lengths for sex peacocks maintain elaborate tails, elephant seals fight over territories, fruit flies perform dances, and some species deliver persuasive gifts. The male redback spider literally flings into the jaws of death in order to mate successfully.

Co-Evolution

The term **co-evolution** is used for the cases where two (or more) **species** reciprocally affect each other's **evolution**. So for example, an evolutionary change in the **morphology** of a plant, might affect the morphology of an herbivore that eats the plant, which in turn might affect the evolution of the plant.

Co-evolution is likely to happen when different species have close ecological interactions with one another. These ecological relationships include:

1. Predator/prey and parasite/host
2. Competitive species
3. Mutualistic species

Plants and insects represent a classic case of co-evolution one that is often, but not always, mutualistic. Many plants and their pollinators are so reliant on one another and their relationships are so exclusive that biologists have good reason to think that the 'match' between the two is the result of a co-evolutionary process.

Exercise

1. The oldest known fossilized prokaryotes were laid down approximately
(a) 3.5 million years ago (b) 3.5 billion years ago
(c) 1.7 billion years ago (d) 1.7 million years ago

2. The oldest known fossil eukaryotes are about .... old.
(a) 3.5 million years ago (b) 3.5 billion years ago
(c) 1.7 million years ago (d) 1.7 billion years ago

3. Which of the era is known as age of reptiles?
(a) Azoic era (b) Palaeozic era
(c) Mesozoic era (d) Cenozoic era

4. Which of the period is also known as age of invertebrates?
(a) Ordovician period (b) Devonians period
(c) Carboniferous period (d) Jurassic period

5. First mammals appeared in .... periods.
(a) Ordovician (b) Devonians
(c) Carboniferous (d) Triassic

6. Which of the period is known as 'age of reptiles'?
(a) Ordovician period (b) Devonians period
(c) Carboniferous period (d) Jurassic period

7. Holocene epoch is known as age of
(a) Man (b) Reptile
(c) Dinosaur (d) Fish

8. Who said that origin of life followed three stages namely Chemogeny, Biogeny and Cognogeny?
(a) Lederberg (b) Cuvier
(c) Richter (d) Arrhenius

9. Which of these is not a living fossil?
(a) *Archaeopteryx* (b) Duck-billed platypus
(c) Lungfish (d) Frog

10. Human being belongs to the species of
(a) *Homo erectus* (b) *Homo habillis*
(c) *Homo sapiens* (d) Hominidae

11. Links between organisms that show branching pattern of evolutionary relationships are shown by
(a) living fossils (b) comparative embryology
(c) phylogenetic trees (d) two fossil layers

12. Evidences of evolutionary relationships is found in
(a) atmosphere (b) fossils
(c) ocean beds (d) rocks

13. The oldest microfossil so far of age 3.5 billion year ago was
(a) coacervates (b) microspheres
(c) eobionts (d) cyanobacteria

14. During fossilization, the soft parts disintegrate and the gaps created in this manner are filled by mineral deposits such as silica, calcium carbonate, etc. Such fossils are called
(a) petrifactions (b) embedding
(c) cementing (d) moulding

15. Study of fossils is called
(a) Ethology (b) Palaeontology
(c) Etiology (d) Anthropology

16. *Archaeopteryx* is the connecting link between
(a) reptile and mammals (b) reptile and amphibian
(c) reptile and fish (d) reptile and bird

17. The fossils in terms of faecal pellets that contain evidences of the food eaten, is known as
(a) coprolites (b) imprints
(c) petrifactions (d) impressions

18. How do we know how old fossils are?
(a) By digging the Earth layer for fossils and later comparing the age of the layer by the rock formation type
(b) By dating fossils is by detecting the ratios of different isotopes of the same element in the fossil
(c) Both (a) and (b)
(d) None of the above

19. Phylogenic trees are important for the understanding of
(a) evolutionary change and relationships of related organisms
(b) evolutionary stages of species and show at what stage evolutionary paths of species diverge or branch as lineages evolve and split and modifications are inherited
(c) Both of (a) and (b)
(d) None of the above

20. Evidence from fossils records are obtained by calculating age of fossil found in
(a) metamorphic rock (b) sedimentary rocks
(c) igneous rocks (d) earth crust

21. First human appeared during
(a) Oligocene (b) Miocene
(c) Pliocene (d) Pleistocene

22. Era of reptiles and gymnosperm is
(a) Precambrian (b) Palaeozoic
(c) Mesozoic (d) Cenozoic

23. The correct order of evolution of horse is
(a) *Mesohippus, Hyracotherium, Meryhippus, Pliohippus, Equus*
(b) *Mesohippus, Meryhippus, Hyracotherium, Pliohippus, Equus*
(c) *Mesohippus, Meryhippus, Pliohippus, Hyracotherium, Equus*
(d) *Hyracotherium, Mesohippus, Meryhippus, Pliohippus, Equus*

24. The oldest microfossil so far of age 3.5 billion year ago was
(a) coacervates (b) eobionts
(c) microspheres (d) cyanobacteria

25. Alternative forms of a gene are called
(a) loci (b) multiples
(c) chromosomes (d) alleles

26. Which of the following required seeing a founder effect?
(a) High rate of new mutation
(b) Population bottleneck in which the population is reduced to relatively small number of breeding individuals
(c) Lethality of homozygotes with a mutant allele
(d) Selection in favour of heterozygotes

27. Evolution only occurs when there is a change in gene frequency within a .... over time.
(a) population (b) individual
(c) organ (d) community

28. Natural selection is a .... process.
(a) random (b) not random
(c) forceful (d) waste

29. The neutral theory of molecular evolution was introduced by
(a) haldane (b) mayer
(c) kimura (d) crick

30. Number of chromosomes in a human male is
(a) 23 (b) 23 pairs
(c) 22 pairs + XY (d) 22 pairs

31. In dogs, the chromosome number is 78. How many chromosomes are present in the dog sperm?
(a) 78
(b) 39
(c) Cannot determine from this information
(d) variable

32. Homologous chromosomes which are similar in both the sexes are called
(a) sex-chromosomes (b) autosomes
(c) allosomes (d) androsomes

33. Genes are made up of
(a) nucleotide (b) nucleoside
(c) sugar (d) phosphate

34. In humans, which chromosome set is regarded as sex chromosome?
(a) XY (b) ZZ
(c) XO (d) ZW

35. Darkening of skin because of strong sunlight is an example of
(a) somatogenic (b) blastogenic
(c) Both (a) and (b) (d) None of these

36. What is the genetic material in most organisms?
(a) Chromatin (b) RNA
(c) Proteins (d) Carbohydrates

37. Which molecular structure is not a component of DNA?
(a) Nitrogenous base (b) Phosphate group
(c) Deoxyribose sugar (d) Amino acid

38. Depending on the relative importance assigned to the various forces of evolution, which of the perspectives provide evolutionary explanations for molecular evolution?
(a) Selectionists hypothesis (b) Neutralists hypothesis
(c) Mutationists hypothesis (d) All of these

39. Molecular evolution is in part a process of evolution at the scale of
(a) DNA (b) DNA and RNA
(c) RNA and proteins (d) DNA, RNA and proteins

40. Which of the fact associated with RNA made it as a strong candidate as an prevalent pioneer molecule during the initial stage of origin of life?
(a) It can store genetic information
(b) It can acts an catalyst
(c) It is a stable molecule
(d) Both (a) and (b)

41. In sexually reproducing organisms, only changes to the germ line are passed along to progeny.
(a) True (b) False
(c) Not dependent (d) Dependent

42. What is the term for a change in a single nucleotide pair?
(a) Frameshift mutation
(b) Point mutation
(c) Nonsense mutation
(d) Sense mutation

43. Very often single nucleotide mutations have no effect on the appearance or viability of an organism.
(a) True (b) False
(c) Not dependent (d) Dependent

44. It is thought that gene duplications are generated by an error in what process?
(a) DNA replication and repair
(b) Homologous recombination
(c) Transcription
(d) The replication of chromosome ends

45. Which structures in eukaryotic genes are thought to have facilitated the ability to duplicate a protein domain of a gene without damaging it in the recombination process?
(a) Introns (b) Exons
(c) Promoters (d) Regulatory regions

46. Which of the following is not true?
(a) Exon shuffling allows the generation of hybrid proteins with new functions
(b) Exon shuffling allows bacteria to become antibiotic resistant
(c) All human proteins are thought to have arisen from the duplication and shuffling of a few thousand exons
(d) Exon shuffling requires the presence of introns

47. What are homologous genes?
(a) Genes that is similar in their nucleotide sequence because of a common ancestry
(b) Genes that encode proteins that perform similar functions
(c) Genes that encode proteins that fold into the same shapes
(d) Genes that encode proteins that fold into the different shapes

48. Which of the following types of genes would be most likely to accumulate changes to its sequence?
(a) A gene that codes for a highly optimized essential protein or RNA molecule
(b) A gene that is highly conserved among a wide diversity of organisms
(c) A gene that has recently been duplicated in the genome
(d) A gene that recently deleted

49. In comparing the genomes of mammals to the relatively small genome of the puffer fish (about one-tenth the size of a mammalian genome), what tends to be missing in puffer fish?
(a) Genes
(b) Repetitive DNA in non-coding sequences
(c) Introns
(d) Exons

50. The human genome contains 3.2 ×106 nucleotide pairs divided among 22 autosomes and 2 sex-chromosomes.
(a) True (b) False
(c) Not dependent (d) Dependent

51. Which of the following is true about the human genome?
(a) About half the human genome consists of mobile genetic elements
(b) About half the human genome consists of genes coding for proteins
(c) About half the human genome consists of introns
(d) None of the above

52. Approximately how many genes are in the human genome?
(a) 13000 (b) 25000
(c) 100000 (d) 3.2 × 106

53. Evolution at genetic level is termed as
(a) microevolution (b) macroevolution
(c) gene evolution (d) point mutation

54. Which best exemplifies an active dead-end replicator?
(a) A gene in a sperm cell
(b) A gene in a body cell
(c) A meme in the mind of an active individual
(d) A computer virus on the internet

55. The hormone which is almost identical and occurs in all vertebrates is
(a) insulin (b) thyroxine
(c) glucagon (d) ACTH

56. Microevolution takes place due to
(a) somatogenic variation
(b) blastogenic variation
(c) continuous variation
(d) successive variation

57. Alternative forms of a gene are called
(a) loci (b) multiples
(c) chromosomes (d) alleles

58. Heredity or inheritance of specific traits became clearer due to
(a) Lamarck's theory
(b) Mendel worked on garden peas
(c) Darwinism
(d) Neo-Darwinism

59. On what cellular structures are genes in eukaryotes carried?
(a) Endoplasmic reticulum (b) Nuclear membrane
(c) Chromosomes (d) Mitochondria

60. Which of the following sentences is true about the evolutionary process?
(a) There is no real 'progress' in the idea of evolution
(b) Humans are unique, a totally new type of organism
(c) Progress is nature's religion
(d) Evolution of life forms was rapid in the beginning ages

61. Speciation takes place when variation occurs with
(a) mood changes
(b) death of an organism
(c) changes due to accidents
(d) geographical isolation

62. Duplications arise from an event termed that occurs during meiosis between misaligned homologous chromosomes
(a) equal crossing-over, homologous chromosomes
(b) unequal crossing-over, heterologous chromosomes
(c) unequal crossing-over, homologous chromosomes
(d) equal crossing-over, heterologous chromosomes

63. The two genes that exist after a gene duplication event are called .... and usually code for proteins with a similar function and/or structure. By contrast, ... genes are ones which code for proteins with a similar functions but exist in different species, and are created from a speciation event.
(a) homologous; paralogous (b) analogous; paralogous
(c) paralogs; orthologous (d) homologous; orthologous

64. Rett-like syndrome and Pelizaeus-Merzbacher disease are the gene dosage dependent neurological disorders which resulted because of .... in LCR.
(a) allelic homologous recombination
(b) non-allelic heterologous recombination
(c) allelic homologous recombination
(d) non-allelic homologous recombination

65. Genetic drift is caused by
(a) mutations (b) the bottle neck effect
(c) non-random mating (d) a small population size

66. Which of the following might cause the bottle neck effect?
(a) Colonization of a new island
(b) Large scale indiscriminant killing
(c) Non-random mating
(d) Random mating

67. Which of the following would decrease the number of heterozygotes in a population?
(a) Inbreeding (b) Founder's effect
(c) Mutations (d) Gene flow

68. Which of the following is an example of the founder's effect?
(a) A fertilized seed lands on a new island
(b) North American elephant hunter to almost extinction
(c) Assortive mating
(d) A bee brings pollen from a different population

69. Which of the following is an example of selective pressure?
(a) Phenylketonurics are unable to breakdown phenylalanine
(b) Fingerprints
(c) Sickle cell trait protects persons from malaria
(d) House flies are killed by DDT

70. Which of the following would cause microevolution?
(a) Mutations (b) Inbreeding
(c) Founder's effect (d) All of these

71. If 16% of deer had short legs (a recessive trait) and 50% of were eaten by lions before they could mate, how many would have short legs the next generation?
(a) 4% (b) 6.25%
(c) 8% (d) 16%

72. Among the following the evidence of evolution from biogeography is
(a) embryo development (b) plate tectonics
(c) Darwin finches (d) Darwin turtles

73. Thorns of Bougainvelia plant and tendril of cucurbits are
(a) homologous organs (b) paralogous organ
(c) analogous organ (d) orthologous organ

74. Placental mammals such as mouse, wolf, Australian marsupials such as marsupial mouse, Tasmanian wolf shows
(a) parallel evolution (b) convergent evolution
(c) divergent evolution (d) phyletic evolution

75. Which of the following is not an vestigial organ in humans?
(a) Ear muscles (b) Tail vertebra
(c) Premolar (d) Appendix

76. If a species like mice or fruit flies may get isolated if they travel on a ship to a relatively virgin island. New speciation starts because the original and new populations are not in contact anymore and do not interbreed. The original gene pool gets cut off and certain rare genes that may have surfaced in the new population may cause it manifest modified characteristics and ultimately new species. This speciation will be known as
(a) sympatric speciation (b) allopatric speciation
(c) parapatric speciation (d) None of these

77. Which speciation is thought to be the dominant mode of speciation
(a) Allopatric speciation (b) Peripatric speciation
(c) Parapatric speciation (d) Sympatric speciation

78. Mallard and Grey duck are an example of
(a) allopatric species (b) peripatric species
(c) parapatric species (d) sub-species

79. Allochrony offers some empirical evidence that .... speciation has taken place, as many examples exist of recently diverged (sister taxa) allochronic species.
(a) allopatric species (b) sympatric species
(c) parapatric species (d) sub-species

80. In the North-East Pacific Ocean Resident and transient orcas inhabit the same waters, but avoid each other and do not interbreed. The two forms hunt different prey species and have different diets, vocal behaviour and social structures. Some divergences between species could also result from contrasts in microhabitats. This is a rare example of .... speciation in animals
(a) peripatric species (b) sympatric species
(c) parapatric species (d) sub-species

81. Which variation contributes to evolution?
(a) Somatogenic (b) Blastogenic
(c) Both (a) and (b) (d) None of these

82. Which type of variations are non-inheritable from generation to generations?
(a) Somatogenic (b) Blastogenic
(c) Both (a) and (b) (d) None of these

83. Out of which of the following fields, from which field, evidences for evolution can be used?
(a) Genetics and molecular biology
(b) Palaeontology
(c) Ethology
(d) All of the above

84. Organs that have common basic form but are present in different species are known as ....
(a) homologous organ (b) analogous organ
(c) similar organ (d) different organ

85. Wings of bat and limbs of man are an example of ...., while wings of bat and wings of bird are an example of ....
(a) analogous; analogous (b) analogous; homologous
(c) homologous; analogous (d) homologous; homologous

86. Which of the statement are correct regarding the comparison of haemoglobin structure of chimpanzees, man, gorilla and gibbon?
(a) The haemoglobin of chimpanzees differs from that of man in only 8 amino acids, of gorilla in 3 amino acids and of gibbon in 1 amino acid
(b) The haemoglobin of chimpanzees differs from that of man in only 1 amino acid, of gorilla in 3 amino acids and of gibbon in 8 amino acids
(c) The haemoglobin of chimpanzees differs from that of man in only 3 amino acids, of gorilla in 1 amino acid and of gibbon in 8 amino acids
(d) The haemoglobin of chimpanzees differs from that of man in only 1 amino acid, of gorilla in 8 amino acids and of gibbon in 3 amino acids

87. Which of the biomolecules is a good and reliable indicator for pointing out the fact that chimpanzees, man, gorilla and gibbon are linked?
(a) Glucose (b) Haemoglobin
(c) Testosterone (d) Eye proteins

88. Evolutionary change and relationships of related organisms are represented in
(a) linkage trees (b) phylogenetic trees
(c) lineage trees (d) relationship trees

89. Phylogenic trees are important for the understanding of
(a) evolutionary change and relationships of related organisms
(b) evolutionary stages of species and show at what stage evolutionary paths of species diverge or branch as lineages evolve and split and modifications are inherited
(c) Both (a) and (b)
(d) None of the above

90. Leaving and going away of some members of the population to different habitats is known as
(a) genetic drift (b) gene flow
(c) migration (d) movement

91. What is the genetic material in most organisms?
(a) Chromatin (b) RNA
(c) Proteins (d) Carbohydrates

92. Which molecular structure is not a component of DNA?
(a) Nitrogenous base (b) Phosphate group
(c) Deoxyribose sugar (d) Amino acid

93. What determines the sex of a human being?
(a) The chromosome inherited from the father
(b) The chromosome inherited from the mother
(c) The chromosomes inherited both from the mother and father
(d) None of the above

94. What is common to microevolution and macroevolution?
(a) Duration of evolution (b) Type of evolution
(c) Result of evolution (d) Mechanism of evolution

95. Which of these is a living fossil?
(a) Ant (b) Crocodile
(c) Camel (d) Duck-billed platypus

96. How do we know how old fossils are?
(a) By digging the Earth layer for fossils and later comparing the age of the layer by the rock formation type
(b) By dating fossils is by detecting the ratios of different isotopes of the same element in the fossil
(c) Both (a) and (b)
(d) None of the above

97. Members of the same species which are capable of interbreeding is best described as a
(a) community (b) population
(c) ecosystem (d) biosphere

98. If 16% of the persons in a population show a recessive trait, what is the allelic frequency for the dominant allele?
(a) 4% (b) 16%
(c) 84% (d) 96%

99. For a particular human population, if the allelic frequency of the O allele for blood type was 1 and the frequency for the B allele was 5, what would be the allelic frequency for the A allele?
(a) 0.1 (b) 0.2
(c) 0.3 (d) 0.4

100. In the following population, what would be the allelic frequency for the dominant allele? 20 homozygous recessives; 320 homozyous dominants; 160 heterozygotes
(a) 10% (b) 20%
(c) 60% (d) 80%

101. If four percent of a population shows a recessive trait, what will be the frequency of carriers in the following generation?
(a) 4% (b) 8%
(c) 16% (d) 32%

102. If there is only one allele for a gene in a population, that gene is referred to as
(a) monoallelic (b) fixed
(c) common (d) monocistronic

103. Which of the following would cause deviation from the Hardy-Weinberg equilibrium?
(a) Small population (b) Isolated
(c) Random mating (d) Lack of selection pressure

104. If 36% of the population is heterozygotes for a certain gene, what percentage of the population will show the recessive phenotype in the next generation?
(a) 4%
(b) 8%
(c) 16%
(d) need more information to determine

105. Which of the following formulas lets you predict the genotypic frequency of the next generation?
(a) $p + q = 1$
(b) X^2 = sum [$(o - e)2 / e$]
(c) $p^2 + 2pq + q^2 = 1$
(d) d = 0.5 lambda / n * sin (theta)

106. The total aggregate of alleles in a population is referred to as the
(a) gene pool (b) allelic frequency
(c) genotypic frequency (d) genetic structure

107. The occurrence of large or small beak sizes among seed crackers in the absence of medium-sized beaks is an example of
(a) directional selection (b) stabilizing selection
(c) disruptive selection (d) None of these

108. Sickle-cell trait in humans is a classic example of
(a) how mutations can lead only to tragic outcomes
(b) why outbreeding is important
(c) the superior fitness seen in heterozygotes
(d) how every organism is an integrated gene complex

109. A person with sickle cell trait, having one S allele and one normal, will be resistant to malaria and eventually develop sickle cell anaemia.
(a) True (b) False
(c) No such relation exist (d) May be

110. A scientist measures the circumference of acorns in a population of oak trees and discovers that the most common circumference is 2 cm. What would you expect the most common circumference(s) to be after 10 generations of stabilizing selection?
(a) 2 cm
(b) Greater than 2 cm or less than 2 cm
(c) Greater than 2 cm and less than 2 cm
(d) Can't tell from the information given

111. In a population of wildflowers, the frequency of the allele for red flowers was 0.8. What was the frequency of the white allele, the only other allele for flower colour?
(a) 0.8 (b) 0.4
(c) 0.6 (d) 0.2

112. Using the Hardy-Weinberg Principle, which expression represents the frequency of the homozygous recessive genotype?
(a) p^2 (b) $2pq$
(c) q^2 (d) q

113. Which one of the following would cause the Hardy-Weinberg principle to be inaccurate?
(a) The size of the population is very large
(b) Individuals mate with one another at random
(c) Natural selection is present
(d) There is no source of new copies of alleles from outside the population

114. The lack of allele variation in the Nothern elephant seal population is an example of
(a) mutations (b) founder effect
(c) artificial selection (d) bottle neck effect

115. Which one of the following populations would most quickly lead to two groups with few shared traits?
(a) A population with disruptive selection
(b) A population with directional selection
(c) A population with stabilizing selection
(d) A population with no selection

116. A cross between two true breeding lines one with dark blue flowers and one with bright white flowers produces F_1 offspring that are light blue. When the F_1 progeny are selfed a 1:2:1 ratio of dark blue to light blue

to white flowers is observed. What genetic phenomenon is consistent with these results?
(a) Epistasis (b) Incomplete dominance
(c) Codominance (d) Inbreeding depression

117. What would be the frequency of AABBCC individuals from a mating of two AaBbCc individuals?
(a) 1/64 (b) 1/32
(c) 1/16 (d) 1/8

118. A gene showing codominance
(a) has both alleles independently expressed in the heterozygote
(b) has one allele dominant to the other
(c) has alleles tightly linked on the same chromosome
(d) has alleles expressed at the same time in development

119. Which component of transcribed RNA in eukaryotes is present in the initial transcript but is removed before translation occurs
(a) Intron (b) 3′ poly A tail
(c) Ribosome binding site (d) 5′ cap

120. An Hfr strain of *E. coli* contains
(a) a vector of yeast or bacterial origin which is used to make many copies of a particular DNA sequence
(b) a bacterial chromosome with a human gene inserted
(c) a bacterial chromosome with the F factor inserted
(d) a human chromosome with a transposable element inserted

121. Generation of antibody diversity in vertebrate animals takes place through
(a) the presence of as many genes in the germ line as there are types of antibodies possible
(b) infection with bacteria carrying antibody genes
(c) infection with viruses carrying antibody genes
(d) rearrangement of DNA in tissues that go on to produce antibodies

122. What is the co-transduction frequency for the A and B genes, from the following dataset?

(Assume that there has been selection for the A^+ form of the A gene).

Genotype	Number
$A^+ B^+ C^+$	10
$A^+ B^+ C^-$	30
$A^+ B^- C^+$	20
$A^+ B^- C^-$	40

(a) 10 (b) 20
(c) 30 (d) 40

123. The likelihood of an individual in a population carrying two specific alleles of a human DNA marker, each of which has a frequency of 0.2, will be
(a) 0.4 (b) 0.32
(c) 0.16 (d) 0.08

124. If the frequency of males affected with an X-linked recessive condition in a human population is .10 (one in ten), what will be the expected frequency of affected females?
(a) 0001 (b) 001
(c) 02 (d) 01

125. The following genotypes are found in a population
AA Aa aa
70 50 20
What are the allele frequencies of A and a?
(a) A = 0.86 and a = 0.14 (b) A = 0.68 and a = 0.32
(c) A = 0.63 and a = 0.36 (d) A = 0.32 and a = 0.68

126. In a random sample of a population of shorthorn cattle, 73 animals were red (C^RC^R), 63 were roan (C^RC^r–a mixture of red and white) and 13 were white (C^rC^r). Estimate the allele frequencies of C^R and C^r and determine whether the population is in Hardy-Weinberg equilibrium.
(a) C^R = 0.64, C^r = 0.36; because the population is large and a random sample was chosen, the population is in equilibrium
(b) C^R = 0.7, C^r = 0.3; the genotype ratio is not what would be predicted from these frequencies and the population is not in equilibrium
(c) C^R = 0.7, C^r = 0.3; the genotype ratio is what would be predicted from these frequencies and the population is in equilibrium
(d) C^R = 1.04, C^r = 0.44; the allele frequencies add up to greater than 1 and the population is not in equilibrium

127. Mutations are rarely the cause of microevolution because
(a) they are most often harmful and do not get passed on
(b) they may be masked in diploid individuals and are not able to be selected for
(c) they are only passed on when they occur in gametes
(d) All of the above

128. If a population has the following genotype frequencies, AA = 0.42, Aa = 0.46, aa = 0.12, what are the allele frequencies?
(a) A = 0.42 a = 0.12 (b) A = 0.6 a = 0.4
(c) A = 0.65 a = 0.35 (d) A = 0.76 a = 0.24

129. In a population with two alleles, B and b, the allele frequency of b is 0.4. What would be the frequency of heterozygotes if the population is in Hardy-Weinberg equilibrium?
(a) 0.16 (b) 0.24 (c) 0.48 (d) 0.6

130. In a population that is in Hardy-Weinberg equilibrium for two alleles, C and c, 16 per cent of the population show a recessive trait. Assuming C is dominant to c, what per cent show the dominant trait?
(a) 36 per cent (b) 48 per cent
(c) 60 per cent (d) 84 per cent

131. When human DNA is hybridized with both chimpanzee and orangutan DNA, which hybrid DNA would you expect to have the lowest melting temperature?
(a) Human-chimpanzee (b) Human-orangutan
(c) Chimpanzee-orangutan (d) Human-DNA

132. The punctuated equilibrium theory maintains that
(a) long periods of stasis are punctuated by episodes of relatively rapid speciation and change
(b) microevolution is the driving force of speciation
(c) most rapid speciation events involve polyploidy in plants
(d) evolution occurs rapidly when the adaptive landscape changes

133. Match list I with list II and select the correct answer using the codes given below the lists.

List I	List II
A. Bat, insect, bird	1. Natural selection
B. Porpois, flying lemur and man	2. Divergent evolution
C. Survival and vigorous multiplication of some bacteria when exposed to streptomycin	3. Spontaneous gene mutation
	4. Convergent evolution

Codes

	A	B	C
(a)	1	2	3
(b)	4	1	2
(c)	3	4	1
(d)	4	2	1

134. Consider the following statements.

The conditions essential for the operation of the Hardy-Weinberg law are that the

I. Mating should be at random.
II. Mutation rate should be very high.
III. Individuals should be of unequal viability and fertility.
IV. Population size should be very large.
V. Migration size should not occur.

Which of the statements given above are correct?

(a) I, II and III (b) I, III and V
(c) II, III and V (d) I, IV and V

135. Consider the following statements.

Sibling species exhibit

I. Sympatric distribution
II. Morphological similarity
III. Genetic identity
IV. Reproductive isolation of these statement

Codes

(a) III alone is correct
(b) I and II are correct
(c) II, III and IV are correct
(d) I, II and IV are correct

136. Match list I with list II and select the correct answer using the codes given below the lists.

List I	List II
A. *Latimeria*	1. Connecting link
B. Archaeopteryx	2. Mutation theory
C. HMS Beagle	3. Living fossil
D. Evening primose	4. Charles Darwin

Codes

	A	B	C	D
(a)	1	3	4	2
(b)	3	1	4	2
(c)	1	3	2	4
(d)	3	1	2	4

137. Choose the correct sequence of evolutionary events in one form of allopatric speciation, using the codes given below.

I. Geographical isolation.
II. Ecological isolation.
III. Increased pre-mating reproductive isolation.
IV. Increased genetic divergence.
V. Selection completed.

Codes

(a) III IV II V
(b) I IV III V
(c) III II IV V
(d) I II III V

138. Consider the following statements.

Instant speciation is possible due to

I. Mutation
II. Hybridization
III. Recombination
IV. Reciprocal translocation
IV. Polyploidy

Which of these statements is/are correct?

(a) I, II and III (b) III and IV
(c) V only (d) II and V

Answers

1. (b)	**2.** (d)	**3.** (c)	**4.** (a)	**5.** (d)	**6.** (d)	**7.** (a)	**8.** (a)	**9.** (a)	**10.** (c)
11. (c)	**12.** (b)	**13.** (d)	**14.** (a)	**15.** (b)	**16.** (d)	**17.** (a)	**18.** (c)	**19.** (c)	**20.** (b)
21. (d)	**22.** (b)	**23.** (d)	**24.** (d)	**25.** (d)	**26.** (b)	**27.** (a)	**28.** (b)	**29.** (c)	**30.** (c)
31. (a)	**32.** (b)	**33.** (a)	**34.** (a)	**35.** (a)	**36.** (a)	**37.** (d)	**38.** (d)	**39.** (d)	**40.** (d)
41. (a)	**42.** (b)	**43.** (a)	**44.** (b)	**45.** (a)	**46.** (b)	**47.** (a)	**48.** (a)	**49.** (b)	**50.** (b)
51. (a)	**52.** (b)	**53.** (a)	**54.** (b)	**55.** (b)	**56.** (b)	**57.** (d)	**58.** (b)	**59.** (c)	**60.** (a)
61. (d)	**62.** (c)	**63.** (c)	**64.** (c)	**65.** (d)	**66.** (b)	**67.** (a)	**68.** (a)	**69.** (c)	**70.** (d)
71. (b)	**72.** (d)	**73.** (a)	**74.** (a)	**75.** (c)	**76.** (b)	**77.** (a)	**78.** (d)	**79.** (b)	**80.** (b)
81. (b)	**82.** (a)	**83.** (d)	**84.** (a)	**85.** (c)	**86.** (b)	**87.** (b)	**88.** (b)	**89.** (c)	**90.** (c)
91. (a)	**92.** (d)	**93.** (a)	**94.** (d)	**95.** (d)	**96.** (c)	**97.** (b)	**98.** (d)	**99.** (d)	**100.** (d)
101. (d)	**102.** (b)	**103.** (a)	**104.** (d)	**105.** (c)	**106.** (a)	**107.** (c)	**108.** (c)	**109.** (b)	**110.** (a)
111. (d)	**112.** (c)	**113.** (c)	**114.** (d)	**115.** (a)	**116.** (b)	**117.** (a)	**118.** (a)	**119.** (a)	**120.** (c)
121. (d)	**122.** (d)	**123.** (d)	**124.** (d)	**125.** (b)	**126.** (c)	**127.** (d)	**128.** (c)	**129.** (c)	**130.** (d)
131. (b)	**132.** (a)	**133.** (d)	**134.** (d)	**135.** (d)	**136.** (b)	**137.** (b)	**138.** (a)		

35

Behaviour and Evolution

Behaviour is a set of activities that orient an animal to its external environment. While behaviour is most clearly apparent in terms of an observable series of movements, it may also include internal responses of an adaptive nature. The parameters of behaviours are controlled by genetics and thus are acted upon by natural selection. Thus, behavioural Biology is the study of what animals do when interacting with their environment. Behaviour can be interpreted in terms of proximate causes (immediate interaction with the environment) or ultimate causes (evolutionary differences).

Syllabus

- Approaches and Methods in Study of Behaviour; Proximate and Ultimate Causation; Altruism and Evolution-Group Selection, Kin Selection and Reciprocal Altruism; Neural Basis of Learning, Memory, Cognition, Sleep and Arousal; Biological Clocks; Development of Behaviour; Social Communication; Social Dominance; Use of Space and Territoriality; Mating Systems, Parental Investment and Reproductive Success; Parental Care; Aggressive Behaviour; Habitat Selection and Optimality in Foraging; Migration, Orientation and Navigation; Domestication and Behavioural Changes.

Concept Development of Animal Behaviour

Late 1800s

- Scientists began struggling with the neural basis of behaviour.
- Ramony Cajal Histology of the brain: neuron as the fundamental unit.

Early Mid 1900s

- **Konrad Lorenz**, **Niko Tinbergen** and **Karl von Frisch** observed animals behaviour and suggested suggest that behaviour can innate, born with rather than learned.
- Established a field of Ethology; describing animal behaviour in nature and tending to focus on behaviours that were most likely inherited rather than learned.

Mid 1900s

- Ethology combined with neurobiology: Neuroethology. Efforts to understand the neurocircuitry that was responsible for behaviour.
- Behavioural studies focused on repetitive movements: swimming, walking, flying.
- Focused on simple animals with 'simple' nervous systems; mostly a variety of invertebrates; a few vertebrate systems (lamprey swimming, tadpole swimming and bird song).

- Trying to understand learning, memory and cognition.

Late 1900.

- Neurobiological models emerged to understand how neurocircuitry can account for learning and memory: Aplysia (sea slug)-Gill withdrawal response (simple associative learning-habituation, facilitation); rat hippocampus-long term memory-synapses that show associative learning.

Present (Today)

- All of these efforts intertwine with computational (computer) and theoretical scientists seeking to understand complex brain function/cognition. Language, emotion, learning and memory.

Approaches and Methods in Study of Behaviour

Animal behaviour can be studied in lab in zoo or in wild. The complete understanding of behaviour its neural mechanism is gained through a number of methods. Psychology and ethology both relate to behaviour. The psychologists keep the animals in confinment try surgical procedures mostly in laboratories to evoke behaviour while ethologists study behaviour in wild. The study of behaviour can have two approaches:

1. **With relation to brain and physiology** Carried out in laboratories by neuroantomical neurophysiological and neurochemical methods.
2. **Study in wild or natural habitat** It uses Adlibitum, focal sampling technique, scan sampling technique all occurrence and one zero methods.

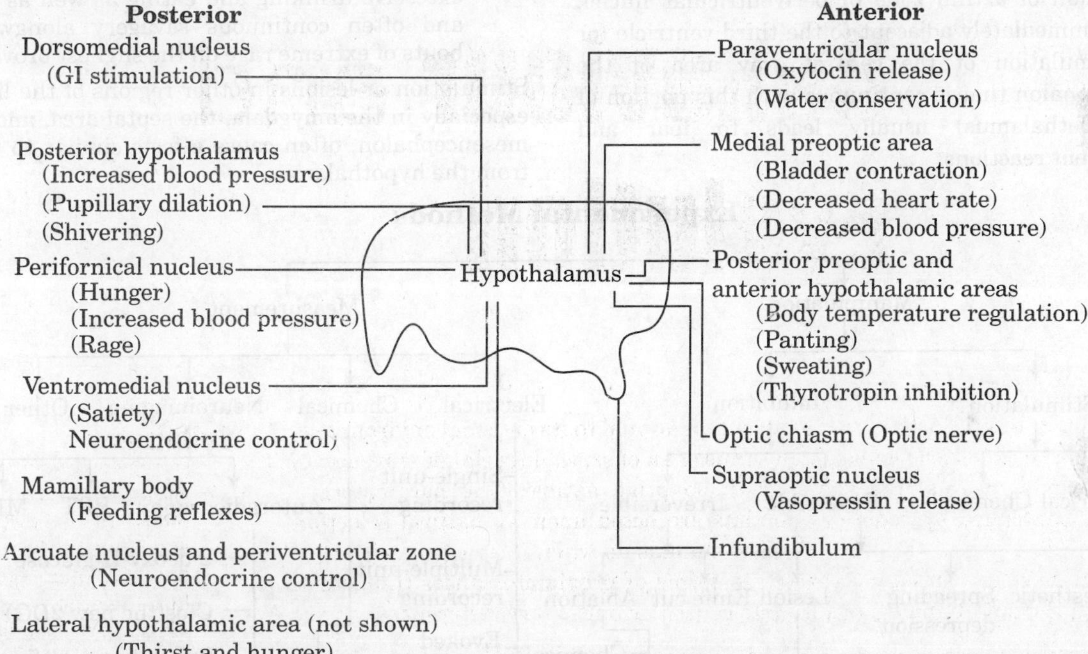

Fig. 35.1 Various control centres of hypothalamus

Neuroanatomical Method

Oldest and most crude method. Certain regions of brain are destroyed and their function is deduced from abnormal behaviour its causes in animal. The larger removal of tissue (ablation) or pathological change in tissue (lesion) may be carried out by means of cuts while the localized and small lesions are produced by passing electric current through platinum, iridium electrode to cauterize the area. The small lesions can also be created by neurotoxic kainic acid. A lesion in Broca's area of human brain causes slurring in speech and there is difficulty in understanding the words spoken by such a person though the person would talk sensibly while, if a lesion is in Wernick's area the person can talk clearly but the speech will not be articulated or coherent. The experimental finding that toad brain has zones responsible for triggerning of prey catching (optic tectum) and avoidance behaviour (TP-region) is supported by ablation experiments. The lesion experiments suggested that amygdala the medial hypothalamus and peraqueductal grey of the midbrain are responsible for control of aggression and defence **Lashly** (1938) proposed **the law of equipotentiality** to understand the neural mechanism of learning. The lesions in hypothalamus can lead to adepsia, hyperdipsia aphagia and hyperphagia. The lesion in ventromedial hypothalamus increase the hunger of animal to such a great degree that they may eat themselves which indicat that the destroyed area had **satiety centre.** While a lesion in lateral hypothalamus can cause the animal to stop eating forever because the destroyed part contained the feeding centre. This technique has also contributed in locating sensory and motor regions in the cortex.

Effect Caused by Stimulation

In addition stimulation of or lesions in the hypothalamus often have profound effects on emotional behaviour of animals and human beings. In animals some of the behavioural effects of stimulation are the following:

(i) Stimulation in the lateral hypothalamus not only causes thirst and eating, as discussed above, but also increases the general level of activity of the animal, sometimes leading to overt rage and fighting, as discussed subsequently.

(ii) Stimulation in the ventromedial nucleus and surrounding areas mainly causes effects opposite to those caused by lateral hypothalamic stimulation that is, a sense of satiety, decreased eating and transqulity.

(iii) Stimulation of a thin zone of periventricular nuclei, located immediately adjacent to the third ventricle (or also stimulation of the central gray area of the mesencephalon that is continuous with this portion of the hypothalamus) usually leads to fear and punishment reactions.

(iv) Sexual drive can be stimulated from several areas of the hypothalamus, especially the most anterior and most posterior portions of the hypothalamus.

Effects Caused by Hypothalamic Lesions

Lesions in the hypothalamus, in general, cause effects opposite to those caused by stimulation. Like

(a) Bilateral lesions in the lateral hypothalamus will decrease drinking and eating almost to zero, often leading to lethal starvation. These lesions cause extreme passivity of the animal as well, with loss of most of its overt drives.

(b) Bilateral lesions of the ventromedial areas of the hypothalamus cause effects that are mainly opposite to those caused by lesions of the lateral hypothalamus; excessive drinking and eating as well as hyperactivity and often continuous savagery alongwith frequent bouts of extreme rage on the slighest provocation.

Stimulation or lesions in other regions of the limbic system, especially in the amygdala, the septal area, and areas in the mesencephalon, often cause effects similar to those elicited from the hypothalamus.

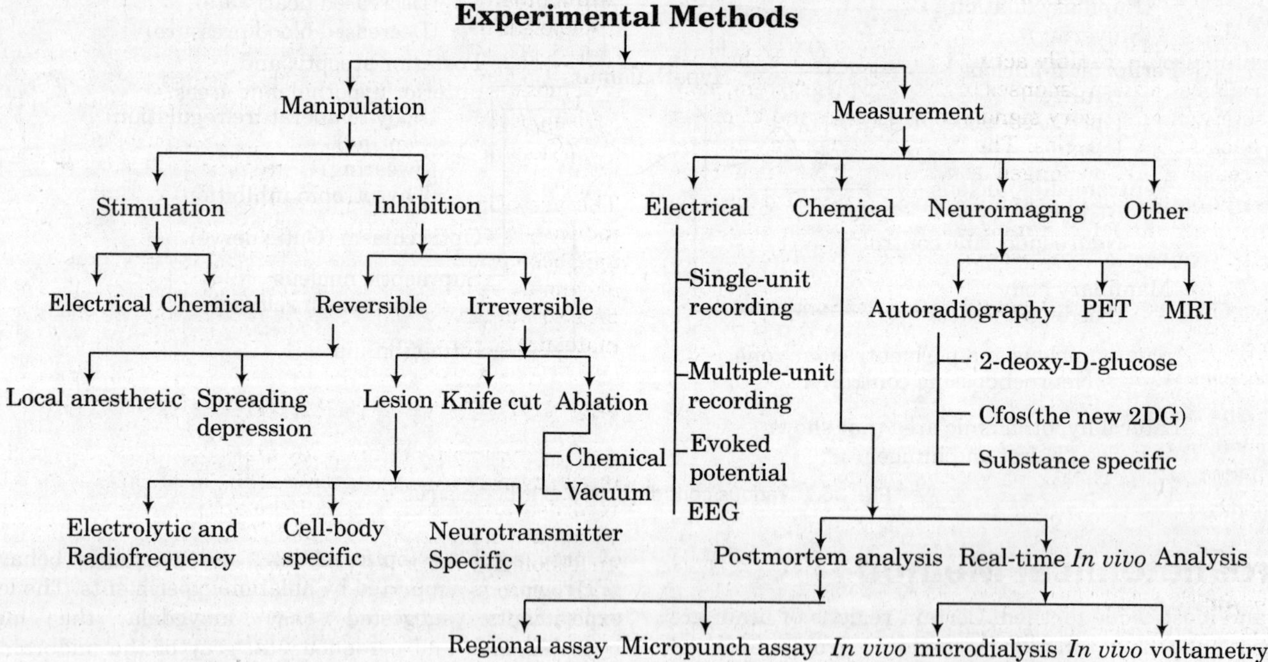

Fig. 35.2 Overview of various experimental methods used to study brain/behaviour relationships

Neurophysiological Method

Galvani (1786, 1793) discovered that twitches occurred in the nerve impulse preparations even without any metal, the nerve and muscle were producing electricity by themselves. This laid the foundation of electrophysiology. This method involves two waves.

(i) Recording the electrical activities from brain at the time of behaving.

(ii) Stimulating the brain region and eliciting behaviour.

The electrical potential of active nerve can be recorded with the aid of implanted electrods and to amplyty this activity by a sensitive instrument. The procedure of evoking behaviour artificially involves cutting the scalp in anaesthetized animals removing portion of skull by special drill exposing part of brain surface by cutting duramater. Two or more electrods lowered down in brain region. Different behaviour patterns are characterized by varying levels of response thresholds in CNS. The stereotaxic machine study the electrical activity in different parts of brain. The first successful recording of brain waves from the skull was accomplished by **Berger** (1929) who named this technique EEG (Electro Encephalogram).

In a second method, the behavioural patterns are initiated as a result of electrical stimulation to a specific brain region by electrodes implantation. As by stimulating a particular locus in the diencephalon of cat **J Flynn** (1929) elicited prey catching behaviour. By use of this technique certain brain areas are identified as **pleasure centres.** Electric stimulation frequently activates several neuronal circuits (thin lines), simultaneously releasing various behavioural responses resulting in overlapping effect while chemical stimulation activates mainly the circuits (thick line) for which the chemical stimulus is specific.

Neurochemical Method

In chemical brain stimulation technique neurons are affected more selectively in their activity by application of drugs neurotransmitters, blocking agents and hormones.

More than 50 chemical substances have been proved or postulated to function as synaptic transmitters. One group comprises small-molecule, rapidly acting transmitters. The other is made up of a large number of neuropeptides of much larger molecule size that are usually much more slowly acting.

The small-molecule, rapidly acting transmitters are the ones that cause most acute responses of the nervous system, such as transmission of sensory signals to the brain and of motor signals back to the muscles. The neuropeptides, in contrast usually cause more prolonged actions, such as long term changes in numbers of neuronal receptors long term opening or closure of certain ion channels and possibly even long term changes in numbers of synapses of sizes of synapses.

Small Molecules, as Rapidly Acting Transmitters

Class I
Acetylcholine

Class II The amines
Norepinephrine
Epinephrine
Dopamine
Serotonin
Histamine

Class III Amino acids
Gamma-AminoButyric Acid (GABA)
Glycine
Glutamate
Aspartate

Class IV
Nitric oxide (NO)

Neuropeptide, Slowly Acting Transmitters or Growth Factors

Hypothalamic-releasing hormones
Thyrotropin-releasing hormone
Luteinizing hormone-releasing hormone
Somatostatin (growth hormone inhibitory factor)

Pituitary peptides
Adrenocorticotropic hormone (ACTH)
β-endorphin
α-melanocyte-stimulating hormone
Prolactin
Luteinizing hormone
Thyrotropin
Growth hormone
Vasopressin
Oxytocin

Peptides that act on gut and brain
Leucine enkephalin
Methionine enkephalin
Substance P
Gastrin
Cholecystokinin
Vasoactive Intestinal Polypeptide (VIP)
Nerve growth factor
Brain-derived neurotrophic factor
Neurotensin
Insulin
Glucagon

From other tissues
Angiotensin II
Bradykinin
Carnosine
Sleep peptides
Calcitonin

The use of alcohol, opium, hashish to abolish pain, *i.e.,* to induce sense of well being (euphoria) relaxation and slup has long been practiced by man. If testosterone is injected in male or female rat into the central area of the proptic region located infront of the hypothalamus the both rats elicit maternal behaviour.

Ad Libitum Sampling Method

Ad libitum sampling provides ideas for future research and often reveals rare, but significant behavioural events. What is recorded are generally the behaviours of those individuals which are most easily observed. This technique is used when an ethologist is merely recording an unplanned encounter with a species, during reconnaissance observations for a later study, if the behavioural observations are being made on mother and infant relationship in deers and occasionally adult males come and interact with them, the notes could be taken on males also. In that case, we would say that interaction of adult males with mother-infant dyad were taken Ad libitum.

Focal Animal Sampling Method

In this method, a particular individual of interest receives the highest priority for recording its behaviour. To take notes using focal animal technique, the experimenter has a formulate criteria and follow them strictly. This criteria should include:

(i) Individual identification of animals of interest.

(ii) Prior decision about behavioural acts of interest.

(iii) Formation of a check sheet to be carried out in the field. Abbreviation of long descriptive words.

(iv) Each animal has to be observed at predetermind time interval, *i.e.*, (sample period).

(v) Every time the animal observation performs an act of interest its frequency and duration is noted.

Scan Sampling Method

By this method, several individuals are observed one after another and their behavioural acts are noted on a well designed check sheet. One important use of this method is to estimate the percentage of time the individuals of a group spend in various predecided activities.

Like other methods following criteria have to be decided: **(i)** Activities we are interested in **(ii)** Time duration for scan, depending upon the group size, **(iii)** Duration of interval. The scan records activities of all individuals of that group between a predetermined sample time, this task is preferably carried from drawn to dusk. If the notes are taken for a day then at the end you would know how many activities you noted (total number) and out of that percentage of other activities can be calculated.

Sampling Method

It may be desirable to focus on one or a limited number of behaviours and record all occurrences of them. In this, the notes could be more specific, *e.g.*, one can note what kind of interaction was there, agonistic or amiable? If agonistic then whether it was chase, supplant, tail pulling, threat or bite? All occurrences of selected behaviours are possible if the following factors exist:

(i) Observational conditions are adequate.

(ii) The behaviours have been carefully defined so that they all the easily recognized.

(iii) The behaviours do not occur more often (or more rapidly) than the observer can record them.

Sequence Sampling Method

In sequence sampling the focus is on a chain of behaviours. These may be performed by a single individual. The initiation of a sample period is usually determined by the beginning of a sequence and the sample period terminates when the observed sequence terminates.

One Zero Sampling Method

In this sampling method the observer scores whether behaviour occurs (one) or not (zero) during a short interval of time (sample period). It is suitable for recording states and or events, this method is also called as Hansen system (Eisenberg; 1972). It has the following features:

(i) In each sample period the occurrence or non-occurrence is scored.

(ii) Behaviour of one or two individuals is recorded in each sample period.

(iii) Occurrence refers to either an event or a state.

(iv) The sample periods are generally short.

(v) Results are presented as frequencies.

Proximate and Ultimate Causation

Sociobiology is defined as systematic study of the evolutionary basis of all forms of social behaviour in all organisms. Sociobiology provides two ways of interpreting behaviour the proximate and ultimate causation

Proximate causation Explanation of an animal's behaviour based on trigger stimuli and internal mechanisms.

Ultimate causation Explanation of an animal's behaviour based on the principles of evolution. The ultimate causation requires that the behavioural and physical traits are genetically heritable, and explains behaviour by correlating behavioural traits to mechanisms that favour evolutionary development, such as natural selection.

Altruism and Evolution-Group Selection

Edwards VC Wynne suggested that animals regulate their own population density through altruistic behaviour. For example, under crowded conditions, many birds cease reproducing. The interpretation of this phenomenon was that these birds were being altruistic: Their failure to breed was for the ultimate good of the species (**Altruism** means risking loss of fitness in an act that could improve the fitness of another individual). He suggested a mechanism called **group selection** groups that had altruistic behaviour would have a survival advantage over groups that did not.

In 1966, **G Williams**, refuted the altruistic view with the charge that individuals that performed altruistic acts would be selected. In other words, organisms not performing altruistic acts would have a higher degree of fitness. Williams held that apparent altruism had to be interpreted on the basis of benefits accruing to the individual performing the altruistic act.

Thus, biological altruism is a course of action that enhances the expected fitness of another at the expense of one's own fitness. Whether altruism occurs depends on several things on the population's initial conditions, on the definition of 'altruism' as absolute or relative fitness reduction.

Kin Selection and Reciprocal Altruism

Kin selection refers to apparent strategies in evolution that favour the reproductive success of an organism's relatives, even at a cost to their own survival and/or reproduction. The classic example is a eusocial insect colony, in which sterile females act as workers to assist their mother in the production of additional offspring. Kin selection refers to changes in gene frequency across generations that are driven atleast in part by interactions between related individuals, and this forms much of the conceptual basis of the theory of social evolution. Indeed, some cases of evolution by natural selection can only be understood by considering how biological relatives influence one another's fitness. Under natural selection, a gene encoding a trait that enhances the fitness of each individual carrying it should increase in frequency within the population; and conversely, a gene that lowers the individual fitness of its carriers should be eliminated.

Kin selection suggests that altruistic behaviour is strongest between close relatives and less common as genetic relatedness decreases. Studies show that most cases of altruistic behaviour involve close relatives and thus improve the individual's inclusive fitness.

When altruistic behaviour involves non-related animals, the explanation offered is **reciprocal altruism;** there is no immediate benefit for the altruistic individual, but some future benefit may occur when the helped animal may 'return the favour'. Reciprocal altruism often is used to explain altruism in humans.

In evolutionary biology, **reciprocal altruism** is a behaviour whereby an organism acts in a manner that temporarily reduces its fitness while increasing another organism's fitness, with the expectation that the other organism will act in a similar manner at a later time. The concept was initially developed by Robert Trivers to explain the evolution of cooperation as instances of mutually altruistic acts. The concept of 'reciprocal altruism', as introduced by Trivers, suggests that altruism, defined as an act of helping someone else although incurring some cost for this act, could have evolved since, it might be beneficial to incur, this cost if there is a chance of being in a reverse situation, where the person whom I helped before may perform an altruistic act towards me.

Neural Basis of Learning

Axons are the basic cellular units of the nervous system which transmit electrical or chemical signals from one location in an animal's body to another and in the central nervous system, interconnecting axons house memory, decision-making and other integrative functions.

Messages are usually carried between axons by neurotransmitters. The most common neurotransmitter is acetylcholine, which also often is the messenger between axons and muscles. When an action potential or nerves impulse, reaches the end of the axon, the transmitter is released and causes depolarization of the membrane of the next axon or of the muscle cells. An enzyme, acetylcholinesterase, breaks down the acetylcholine once the message is transmitted. Other commonly discussed neurotransmitters are octopamine, serotonin and dopamine, which more commonly have functions in the central nervous system.

Neural Basis of Memory

Some learning and memory can be localized to specific brain areas. Learning is the modification of behaviour by experience. Memory is the ability of the nervous system to retain what is learned and what is experienced. Even very simple animals can learn and remember, but these two abilities are most highly developed in humans.

Learning that leads to long-term memory and modification of behaviour must involve long-lasting synaptic changes.

A form of learning that is widespread among animal species is associative learning, in which two unrelated stimuli become linked to the same response. The simplest example of associative learning is the conditioned reflex, discovered by the Russian physiologist **Ivan Pavlov.**

Ivan Pavlov and Richard Thompson Experiment

Pavlov was studying the control of digestive functions in dogs and observed that a dog salivates at the sight or smell of food—a simple autonomic reflex. He discovered that if he rang a bell just before food was presented to the dog, after a few trials the dog would salivate at the sound of the bell, even if no food followed. The salivation reflex was conditioned to be associated with the sound of a bell, a stimulus that normally is unrelated to feeding and digestion. In the studies led by Richard Thompson, the eye-blink reflex of a rabbit in response to a puff of air directed at its eyes was conditioned to be associated with a tone stimulus. After conditioning, the rabbit blinked when it heard the tone.

A small and specific area of the cerebellum was discovered to be necessary for this conditioned reflex. Thus, it was possible to localize learning to an identifiable set of synapses in the mammalian brain.

Some regions of association cortex is reported to have vivid memories. Yet the destruction of a small area of the brain does not completely erase a memory, so it is postulated that memory is a function distributed over many brain regions and that a memory may be stimulated via many different routes.

There is immediate memory for events that are happening now. Immediate memory is almost perfectly photographic, but it lasts only seconds. Short-term memory contains less information, but it lasts longer—on the order of 10 to 15 minutes. Repetition, or use facilitates the transfer of short-term memory to long-term memory, which can last for days, months, or years. Neuronal mechanisms for the transfer of short-term memory to long-term memory is due to the limbic system, notably the hippocampus.

Language abilities are localized in the left cerebral hemisphere which in 97 per cent of people. This phenomenon is referred to as the lateralization of language functions. Broca's area, located in the frontal lobe just in front of the primary motor cortex, is essential for speech. In the temporal lobe, close to its border with the occipital lobe, is Wernicke's area, which is more involved with sensory than with motor aspects of language. Damage to Wernicke's area can cause a person to lose the ability to speak sensibly, while retaining the abilities to form the sounds of normal speech. Near Wernicke's area is the angular gyrus, which is believed to be essential for integrating spoken and written language.

Different regions of the left cerebral cortex participate in the processes of (a) repeating a word that is heard and (b) speaking a written word.

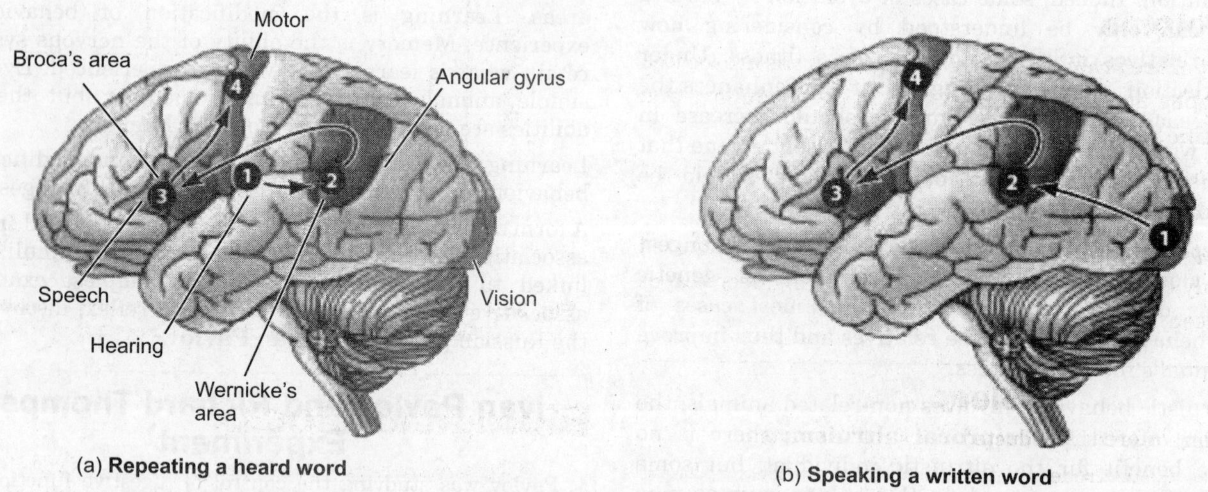

Fig. 35.3 Language areas of the cortex

Neural Basis of Cognition

Until 1993, there were a sufficient number of experimental examples of animal cognition, directed at understanding naturally occurring, complex behaviours. For example, scatter hoarding songbirds like the marsh tit (*Parus palustris*) can store many hundreds of food items, accurately retrieving a substantial proportion of this food after a few hours or days. Congeneric species, such as the great tit (*Parus major*), do not store food and therefore do not seem to require this kind of memory capacity. Comparisons of the learning and memory abilities of these and other storing and non-storing, birds revealed some evidence supporting the prediction that the storing species had the better spatial memory. Similarly, the polygynous male meadow vole (*Microtus pennsylvanicus*), which expands its range during the breeding season to search for mates, has superior spatial abilities compared with both the more sedentary female meadow vole and the male and female prairie voles (*M. ochrogaster*) – a closely related monogamous species that does not undergo range expansion.

Comparative analysis examining the relationship between specific neural substrates. For example, hippocampal volume (the hippocampus is the area of the brain playing a major role in processing spatial information) was shown to be significantly larger in food-storing songbirds than in non-storing songbirds and was also found to be larger in male polygynous voles than in conspecific females.

More recent comparative analyses have shown that hippocampal volume is enlarged concomitantly with several behaviours that apparently require an increased demand for spatial memory.

The greater size of the hippocampus in food storers appears to be caused, atleast in part, by an increase in the number of neurons, not their density and might be due to a combination of neurogenesis and inhibition of apoptosis.

Neural Basis of Sleep and Arousal

Sensory information ascending the spinal cord to final destinations in the forebrain passes through the brain stem. Many sensory fibres give off collateral branches that form synapses with a network of brain stem neurons called the **reticular system.** The reticular system is a highly complex network of axons and dendrites. Within the reticular system are many discrete groups of neurons. Such an anatomically distinct group of neurons in the CNS is called a **nucleus.** High levels of activity in the reticular system influence these nuclei to maintain the brain in a walking condition; low levels of activity enable sleep.

A dominant feature of human behaviour is the daily cycle of sleep and walking. All birds and mammals, and probably all other vertebrates, sleep. Loss of sleep impairs alertness and performance.

Since, sleep is regulated, the body must either produce a sleep-promoting substance or a wakefulness-promoting substance. It has been suggested that adenosine may play a role in the control of sleep.

(i) Acetylcholine

(a) Acetylcholine antagonists decrease EEG signs of cortical arousal while agonists increase them.

(b) Activation of cerebral cortex and increased release of acetylcholine stimulated by a group of acetylcholine neurons located in basal forebrain.

(ii) Norepinephrine

(a) Locus coeruleus is a dark-coloured group of norepinephrine cell bodies located in the pons near the rostral end of the floor of the 4th ventricle; involved in arousal and vigilance.

(b) Norepinephrine increases an animal's ability to pay attention to stimuli in the environment.

(iii) Serotonin

(a) Most of the brain's 5-hypothalamus neurons are located in raphe nuclei, which is located in the medullary and pontine region of the reticular formation.

(b) Stimulation of the neurons causes locomotion and cortical arousal.

(c) 5-hypothalamus neurons in raphe nuclei activated highly during awake states and less during deep stages of sleep.

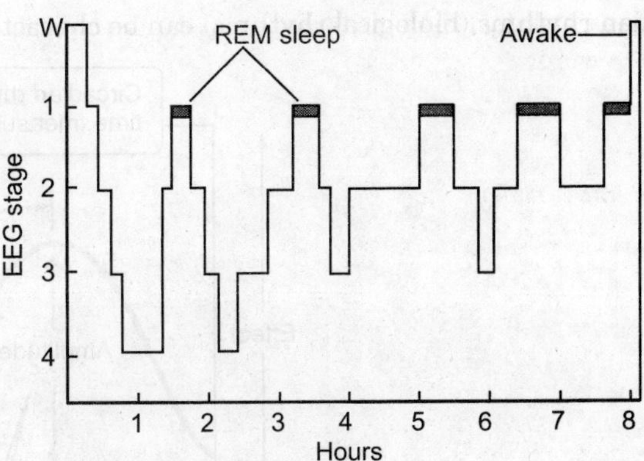

Fig. 35.4 Typical pattern of stages of sleep during a single night. During 8 h sleep, have about 4 or 5 periods of REM sleep

Sleep

- Most sleep research conducted in a sleep laboratory.
- Attaches electrodes to measure EEG, EMG (electromyogram; to measure muscle activity), and EOG (electro-oculogram; to measure eye movements).
- EEG stages
- Awake
  - **Alpha activity** Smooth electrical activity of 8-12 Hz recorded from the brain; state of relaxation.
  - **Beta activity** Irregular electrical activity of 13-30 Hz recorded from the brain; state of arousal.
- Stage 1 sleep
  - Transition between sleep and wakefulness.
  - **Theta activity** EEG activity of 3.5-7.5 Hz that occurs intermittently during early stages of slow-wave sleep and REM sleep.
- EEG stages
- Stage 2 sleep
  - EEG is generally irregular but contains periods of theta activity, sleep spindles and K-complexes.
  - Some experimenters believe that sleep spindles represent the activity of a mechanism that is involved in keeping a person asleep.
- Stage 3 and 4 sleep
  - **Delta activity** Regular, synchronous electrical activity of less than 4 Hz recorded from the brain; occurs during the deepest stages of slow-wave sleep.
- **REM sleep** A period of desynchronized EEG activity during sleep, at which time dreaming, rapid eye movements and muscular paralysis occur.
  - Dreaming during this state; tend to be narrative in form
- Stages 1-4 referred to as non-REM sleep
- Stages 3-4 referred to as slow-wave sleep
- During rest of the night subject will alternate between periods of non-REM sleep and REM sleep, each cycle about 90 min long, containing ~20-30 min of REM sleep.

Biological Clocks

Chronobiology encompasses many fields in the biological sciences which ultimately concerned with the study of biological rhythms and the biological clocks that are responsible for the generation of these rhythms.

Biological clocks exist as endogenous (internal) rhythms of fairly intense activity and usually follow a circadian (24 h) cycle. The phytochrome system functions to mark a dark or light period, but it apparently does not provide a measure of its duration. The two mechanisms may function together to enable the plant to detect the actual times spent in light and darkness.

The rhythmicity of biological clocks seems to arise from alterations of membrane permeability. Characteristics, may be due to either alterations in protein structure or alternatively, changes in the concentration or characteristics of the phospholipids of the membrane. The phytochromes, in either of their alternative structures, may alter the set point of the clock by changing the characteristics of the cell membrane. Thus, photoperiodicity may ultimately be regulated at the level of the cell membrane.

Circadian rhythms are maintained by a biological clock. A biological clock resides within the cells of all eukaryotes and some prokaryotes. The major outward manifestations of this clock are known as circadian rhythms (from the Latin circa, 'about,' and dies, 'day'). Circadian rhythms (or biological cycles) can characterize in two ways: the **period** is the length of one cycle, and the **amplitude** is the magnitude of the change over the course of a cycle. The circadian rhythms have some important characteristics:

1. The period is insensitive to temperature, although lowering the temperature may reduce the amplitude of the rhythmic effect.
2. Circadian rhythms are highly persistent; they may continue for days even in an environment in which there are no light–dark periods.
3. Circadian rhythms can be entrained, within limits, by light–dark cycles that differ from 24 h.
4. Abrief exposure to light can shift the peak of the cycle it can cause a phase shift. The resetting of the circadian rhythm by environmental cues is called **entrainment**.

Circadian rhythms (biological rhythms) can be characterized in two ways by period and by amplitude.

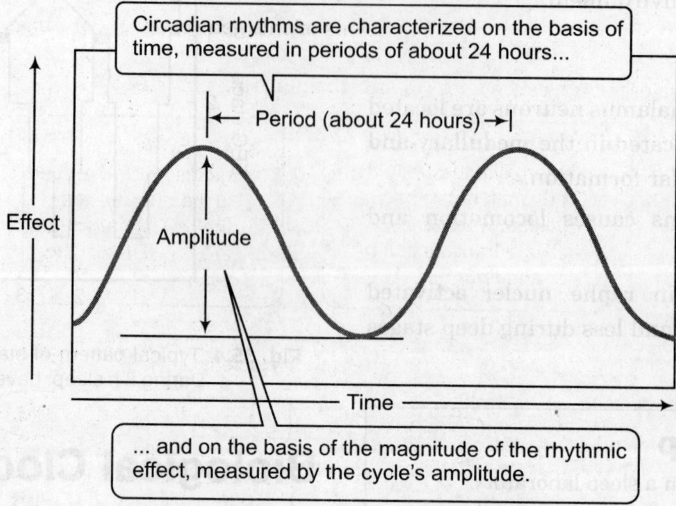

Fig. 35.5 Features of circadian rhythms

In mammals, the master circadian clock is located in two tiny groups of cells just above the optic chiasm, the place, where the two optic nerves cross. These structures are called the **Suprachiasmatic Nuclei** (SCN). If a mammal's SCN are destroyed, it loses circadian rhythmicity.

The retina of the eyes is 'classical' photoreceptors and contains photoresponsive retinal ganglion cells. These cells contain a photo pigment called melanopsin, follow a pathway called the retinohypothalamic tract, leading to the SCN. It is interesting to note that, if cells from the SCN are removed and cultured, they maintain their own rhythm in the absence of external cues.

It appears that the SCN takes the information on day length from the retina, interprets it, and passes it on to the pineal gland, which then secretes the hormone melatonin in response. **Secretion of melatonin peaks at night and ebbs during the day.**

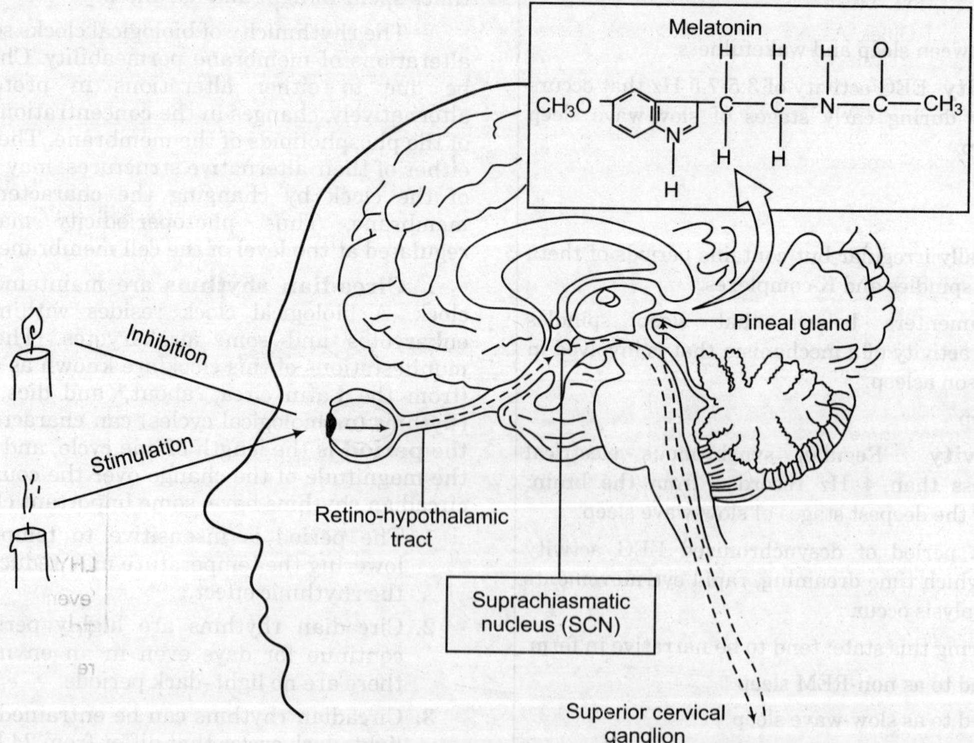

Fig. 35.6 Suprachiasmatic nucleus (SCN); the site of the circadian clock in mammals

Circadian rhythms are found in every animal group, as well as in protists, plants and fungi, but only vertebrates have SCN. In most non-mammals, the master clock contains photoreceptors that directly sense changes in light and synchronize behaviour.

Genetics of Circadian Rhythms

- A gene called period (per) was discovered in fruit flies. Mutations of this gene cause flies to have either short or long free-running circadian periods.
- Mutations of circadian gene, timeless (tim), cause a loss of circadian rhythms in fruit flies.

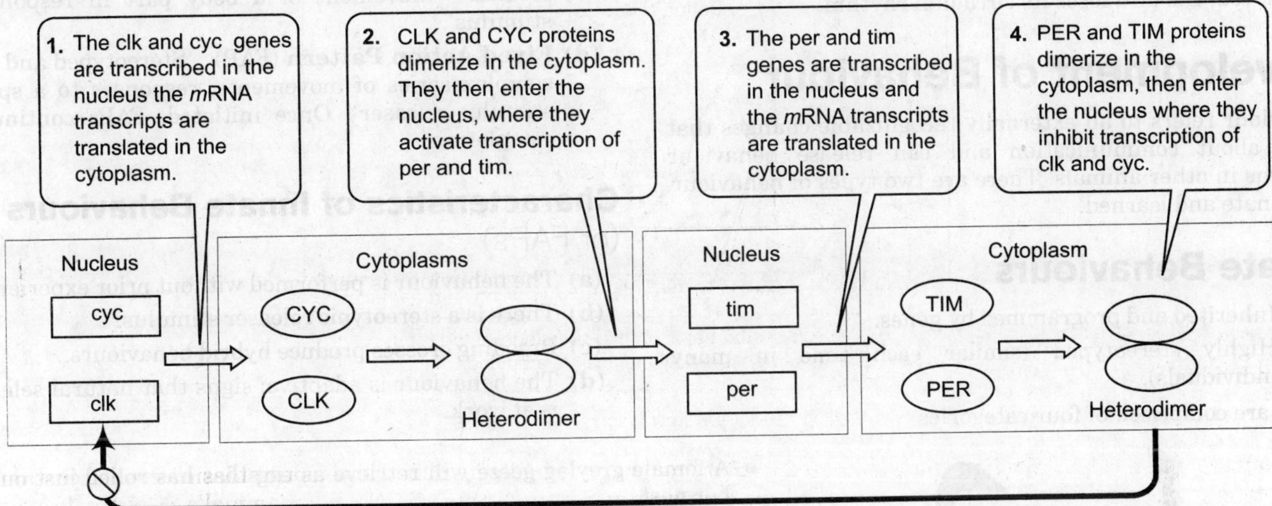

Fig. 35.7 Circadian rhythms are generated by a molecular clock. The period and timeless genes and the clock and cycle genes are homologous to 'clock genes' found in a wide range of organisms

- The PER and TIM proteins dimerize in the cytoplasm and the resulting heterodimer enters the nucleus, where it inhibits transcription of the per and tim genes.
- The PER/TIM heterodimer does this by blocking a heterodimer of two other clock genes, clock (clk) and cycle (cyc), that promotes per and tim transcription. This molecular negative feedback loop is just one of several such loops in the circadian clock of a fruit fly.
- CCA1 (Circadian and Clock Associated 1) and LHY (Late Elongated Hypocotyl) that encode closely related MYB transcription factors that regulate circadian rhythms in *Arabidopsis*. When CCA1 and LHY are overexpressed (under constant light or dark conditions) plants become arrhythimcal and *m*RNA signals reduce contributing to a negative feedback loop. CCA1 and LHY expression oscillates and peaks in early morning, while TOC1 oscillates and peaks in early evening. From past observations and studies, it is hypothesized that these three components model a negative feedback loop in which over-expressed CCA1 and LHY repress TOC1 and over-expressed TOC1 is a positive regulator CCA1 and LHY.

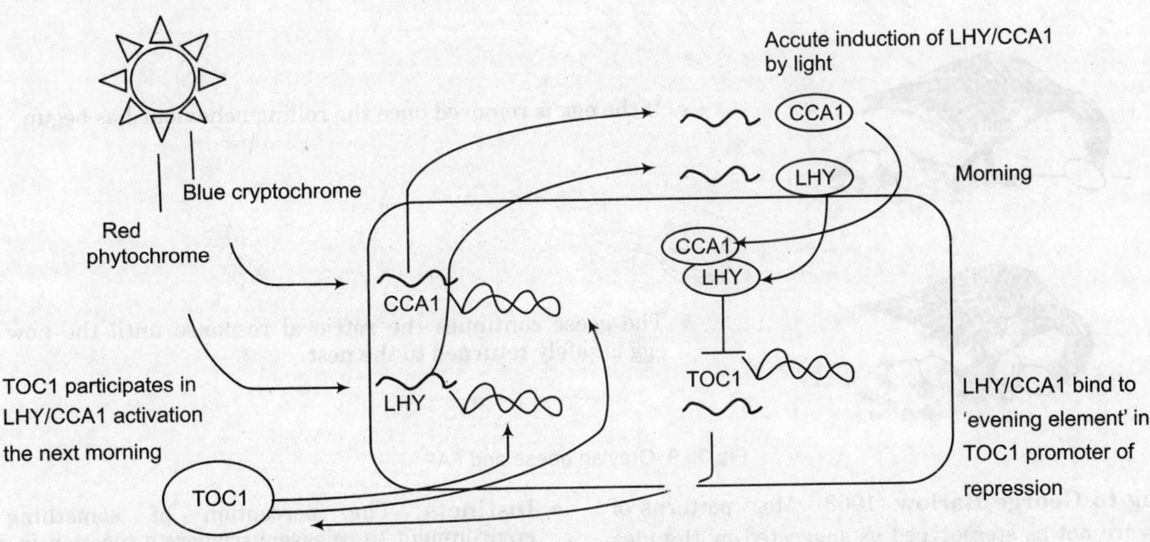

Fig. 35.8 A small portion of the transcriptional feedback loop in *Arabidopsis*.LHY and CCA1 are considered negative elements due to its repression against TOC1 in the morning while TOC1 is considered a positive element because it results in increased transcription of LHY and CCA1 during the evening because of its accumulation

In the molluscs *Bulla*, for example, the cells driving circadian rhythms are in the eyes. Birds do have SCN, but the master clock of atleast some species resides in the pineal gland, a mass of tissue between the cerebral hemispheres that produces the hormone melatonin. If the pineal gland of a bird is removed, the bird loses its circadian rhythm.

Development of Behaviour

Behaviour refers to all externally recognizable changes that bring about communication and can release behaviour patterns in other animals. There are two types of behaviour, *i.e.,* innate and learned.

Innate Behaviours

(i) Inherited and programmed by genes.

(ii) Highly stereotyped (similar each time in many individuals).

These are comprised of four categories:

(a) Kinesis 'Change the speed of random movement in response to environmental stimulus'.

(b) Taxis 'A directed movement toward or away from a stimulus; positive and negative taxes'.

(c) Reflex 'Movement of a body part in response to stimulus'.

(d) Fixed Action Pattern (FAP) 'Stereotyped and often complex series of movements, responses to a specific stimulus-releaser'. Once initiated, FAPs continue to completion.

Characteristics of Innate Behaviours (or FAPs)

(a) The behaviour is performed without prior experience.

(b) There is a stereotypic releaser stimulus.

(c) Breeding crosses produce hybrid behaviours.

(d) The behaviour is adaptive: signs that natural selection is at work.

- A female greylag geese will retrieve as egg that has rolled just outside her nest.

- She reaches beyond it with her bill and rolls it toward her with the underside of the bill.

- If the egg is removed once the rolling behaviour has begun.

- The geese continues the retrieval response until the now imaginary egg is safely returned to the nest.

Fig 35.9 Greylag geese and FAP

- **According to George Barlow** (1968) Most patterns of behaviour are not as stereotyped as suggested by the idea of the FAP. Most FAPs cannot easily be separated into fixed and orientation components. He suggested the term **Modal Action Pattern** (MAP).
- **Instincts** The perception of something in the environment (a releaser) triggers a reaction in a center in the central nervous system (the Innate Releasing Mechanism) (IRM) that then cause the performance of the instinctive act, sometimes composed of very **stereotyped movements** (Fixed Action Patterns; FAP).

Fig. 35.10 Simplified diagram of how a fixed action pattern can be triggered. The releaser is perceived by some sort of receptor, which triggers the IRM to activate certain muscles, thereby producing an instinctive movement that usually involves fixed action patterns

- A male European robin in breeding condition will attack a **tuft of red feathers** placed in his **territory.**
- The **scratching movements** of dogs, as well as many other vertebrates, are considered fixed action patterns.

Learned Behaviour

When animal modifies its behaviour in the light of experience which not passed to next generation are called learned behaviour.

It is comprised of five categories:

Imprinting

(a) Imprinting is learning that is limited to a specific time period in an animal's life and that is generally irreversible.

(b) For example, young ducks or geese following their mother have the imprint of their mother because she was the first moving organism visible to them.

(c) The outside world provides the imprinting stimulus something to which the response will be directed.

Habituation

(a) Habituation is in a sense, learning not to respond to a stimulus. The first time an animal encounters a stimulus, it may respond vigorously. But if the stimulus is presented over and over without consequence, the response to it gradually lessens and may finally disappear altogether. For example, *Hydra* contracts when disturbed by a slight touch; it stops responding.

(b) Maturation is the change in behaviour because of ongoing developmental changes in neuromuscular systems.

Conditioning (Laboratory Setting)

(a) **Classical Conditioning** The response to a normal stimulus comes to be elicited by a substitute stimulus. Classical conditioning was first described by the famed Russian biologist Ivan Pavlov.

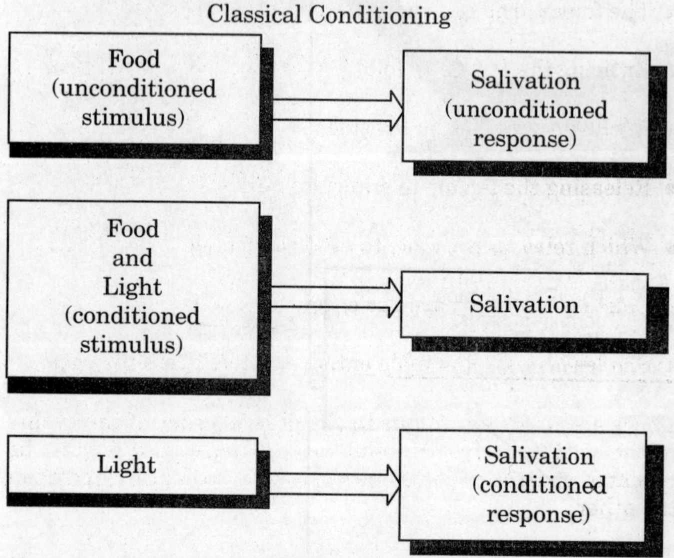

Fig. 35.11 In classical conditioning, a desirable commodity, such as food, comes to be associated with an irrelevant signal

(b) **Operant Conditioning** In operant conditioning, the reinforcement follows the behavioural response. In other words, the animal must do something. In the 1930s, psychologist BF Skinner demonstrated **operant conditioning** by employing a device now called **a Skinner box. EI Thorndike** was a pioneer in research on what was called **trial-and-error learning,** now usually called **operant conditioning.**

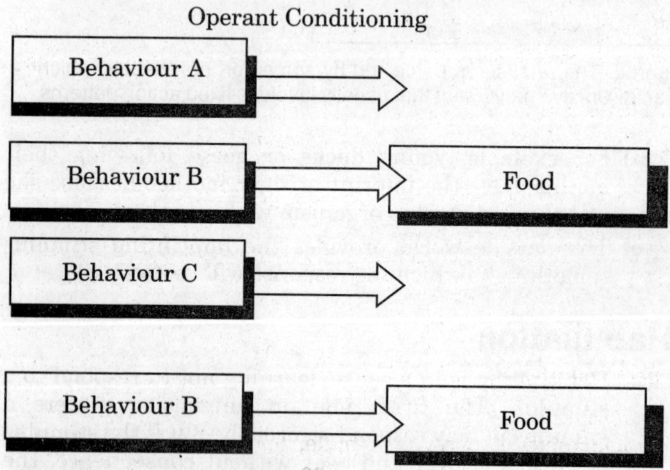

Fig. 35.12 In operant conditioning, the animal can act when given a signal, but only one action is rewarded

Observational Learning

Many vertebrates learn by observing the behaviour of other, *e.g.*, Song development in birds. Species that engage in play often have a highly social lifestyle. Play that stimulates stalking and attacking may allow animals to practice these behaviours.

Insight

Insight learning sometimes called reasoning or innovation involves the ability to perform correctly in a noval situation. It is most often observed in mammals specially primates.

Learning is a Change in Behaviour, Based on Experience

(i) Chimpanzees are highly social creatures that live in a **complex, variable** and **changing world.**

(ii) Intelligence is important under such circumstances.

Courtship

It occurs as a prelude to mating and most common in vertebrates and insects. Most animal tend to view conspecific as threatening competitors to be driven off. Complex courtship interaction unique to each species assure that individuals are not a threat and that they are of the proper species, sex and physcological mating condition. These complex rituals often consist of a series of fixed action patterns each released in sequence by the reciprocal behaviour of the other individual involved. This complex sequence is a chain of FAPs, each triggered by its own sign stimulus (releaser).

(a) A male stickleback in reproductive condition may attack a female entering his territory.

(b) After mating with a female.

- The male chases her away and defends his territory against other males.
- He entices (to attract) three to five other females with his courtship routine.
- The male guards the developing eggs from predators and fans water over them for aeration.

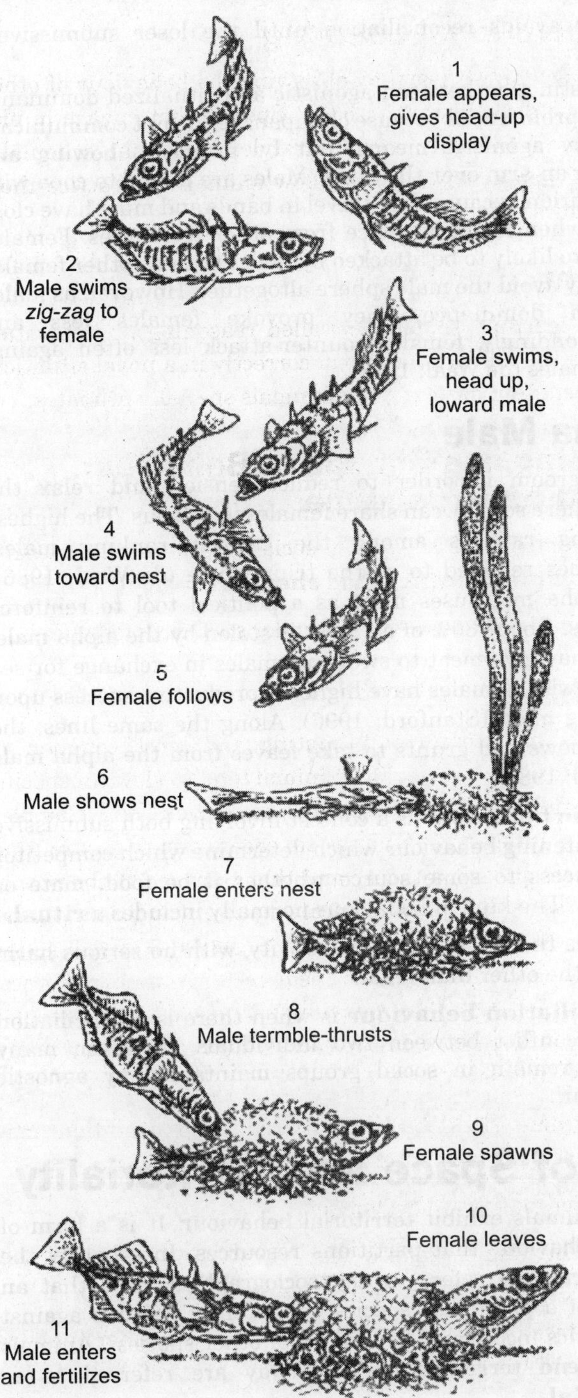

Fig. 34.13 Three stickleback courtship

- The female's head-up posture.
- Releases the male's *zig-zag* dance.
- Which releases the female's approach.
- The male turns and swims to the nest.
- Enticing the female to follow.
- At the nest, he lies on his side.
- Releasing the female to enter the nest.
- Which releases the male to prod the female.
- Causing her to release her eggs.
- She leaves nest, the male enters and fertilizers the eggs.

There are many deviations in the precise order of the events in the stickleback countership ritual. Some actions must be repeated several times if one partner is less motivated than the other.

Despite some flexibility, the component behaviour do not occur randomly. In any display, a particular behaviour is more likely to be followed bycertain actions than by others.

Social Communication

Communication is behaviour that influences the actions of other individuals. It consists of **displays** or **signals** that can be perceived by other individuals and which convey information to them. Natural selection shapes displays or signals into systems of communication if the transmission of information benefits both the sender and the receiver.

The courtship displays of a male, for example, benefit the male if they attract females. The displays also benefit the female if they allow her to assess whether the male is of the right species and whether he is strong, vigorous and has other attributes that will make him a good father.

Molecules used for chemical communication between individual animals of the same species are called pheromones. Because of the diversity of their molecular structures, pheromones can communicate very specific messages that contain a great deal of information. The mate attraction pheromone of the female silkworm moth is a good example.

Auditory (sound) **communication** is fast and effective, and can be easily modified. Non-human primates have at most forty different vocalizations, each having a different meaning. Although, chimpanzees can be taught to use an artificial language, they never progress beyond the capability level of a two-year-old child.

Visual communication involves signals used by species active during the day. For example, defense and courtship displays are exaggerated and are always performed in the same way so their meaning is clear.

Tactile communication occurs when one animal touches another. Honeybees use a combination of methods of communication, but especially tactile ones, to impart information about food distance and direction.

Social behaviour is defined as any kind of interaction between two or more animals usually of the same species. Ranges of social behaviour are: aggression, courtship, cooperation and deception. Complex behaviour increases when interactions among individuals are considered.

Social Dominance

Social organization of a group depends on the total number of individuals their age, sex, sex ratio, which in turn depend on many factors like abundance, availablity, dispersion of food, etc.

Dominance Hierarchy

de Waal (1986) contends that the male hierarchy is much more pronounced than in females and that males have coalition strategies. Female chimps are noticeably less social than males. Females are solitary and lack the social mechanisms that allow tension control and must avoid conflict with each other. Dominance is determined by conflicts, grooming and trading behaviour, involving much more than a single agonistic encounter.

Richard and **Schulman** (1982) suggest that a hierarchy minimizes the risk of fighting, allowing subordinates to avoid injury and dominant individual to avoid killing their relatives.

The competition for food and females is not affected by dominance, but the need to defend the territory favours males that attack other males. A high social rank can increase a male's fitness by allowing more access to meat and mating (Richard and Schulman; 1982).

Intragroup Aggression

de Waal (1986) explains that integration into a community consists of attraction, aggression, subordination to a senior member and finally, reconciliation and social acceptance. Males from the same community are rivals, even known to kill each other in captivity and yet also friends. Contests between males usually last two to three months and the winner avoids reconciliation until the loser submissively grunts.

The distinction between agonistic and ritualized dominance is very pronounced because chimpanzees do not communicate rank by agonistic means, but by grunting, bowing and moving an arm over the other. Males are forced to cope with competition because they travel in bands and must have close ranks when facing violence from other territories. Females are more likely to be attacked by males than by other females and may avoid the male sphere altogether. However, as males rise in dominance, they provoke females less and correspondingly, females counter-attack less often against alpha males (de Waal; 1986).

Alpha Male

Males groom in order to reduce tension and relax the atmosphere so they can share females in estrous. The highest grooming rate is among the highest ranking males, sometimes referred to as the triumvirate (de Waal; 1986). The alpha male uses meat as a political tool to reinforce alliances. About 30% of all meat is stolen by the alpha male. Males may give meat to swollen females in exchange for sex and likewise, females have higher reproductive success upon receiving meat (Stanford; 1996). Along the same lines, the female bows and grunts to take leaves from the alpha male (de Waal; 1986).

Agnostic behaviour is a contest involving both submissive an threatening behaviour which determine which competitor gains access to some source whether it be food, mate or territory. The kind of behaviour normally includes a **ritual.**

Ritual is the use of symbolic activity, with no serious harm done to the other individual.

Reconciliation behaviour is when there is reconciliation after a conflict between two individuals. However, many animals remain in social groups maintained by agnostic behaviour.

Use of Space and Territoriality

Many animals exhibit territorial behaviour. It is a form of social behaviour that partitions resources. In ethology the term **territory** refers to any sociographical area that an animal of a particular species consistently defends against conspecifics (occasionally, animals of other species). Animals that defend territories in this way are referred to as **territorial.**

The size of the territory varies with species, the function and the available resources. Territories are typically used for feeding, mating and/or rearing young.

Territoriality is often maintained by agonistic behaviour, *e.g.*, New Zealand gannets maintain their individual nesting territories by calling and pecking at each other.

Territoriality can enhance fitness if the benefits of possessing a territory outweigh the energy costs of defending one. Territorial rights are proclaimed continually in a variety of ways:

1. **Auditory** (such as bird song, or the calls of gibbons, the bellowing of sea lions and the chattering of squirrels).
2. **Scent markers**, such as urine, defecation in open areas, rubbing parts of the bodies that bear specialized scent glands against the substrate.
3. **Visual** (as in the red breast of the robin).

For example, dogs and other canids scent-mark by urination and defecation, while cats scent-mark by rubbing their faces and flanks against objects. Many prosimians use territorial marking; for example, the Red-bellied Lemur creates territories for groups of two to ten individuals in the rainforests of Eastern Madagascar by scent marking: the male Diademed Sifaka also scent marks defended territories in some of these same rainforests. The male western fence lizard defends a territory by posturing and combat, but less intensely after the mating season.

Mating Systems

Mating systems in animals inculcate different behavioural methods which depend on their natural instincts that include seeing the female genital parts, sniffing and seeing female genital part and urine.

Mating systems describe patterns of male/female pairings. Mating systems tend to be species-specific, although alternative strategies may be expressed by individuals within a species.

1. Monogamy: one male, one female, often pair bonded
   (i) Mate guarding
   (ii) Copulatory plugs
   (iii) Prolonged copulation
   (iv) Aggressive behaviour mate assistance
   (v) Serial monogamy
2. Polygyny one male, many females
   (i) Scramble competition polygyny (term coined by Thornhill and Alcock; 1983).
   (ii) Leks (A lek is a gathering of males, of certain animal species, for the purposes of competitive mating display).
   (iii) Female defense polygyny.
   (iv) Resource defense polygyny (male territoriality centered on a resource needed for breeding success).
3. Polyandry one female, many males because female choice of mates seems to drive many mating systems, polyandry, atleast superficially seems to be rare. In other words, in a population males vary in their quality and therefore in their attractiveness to females, so while all females have access to mating, only a small proportion of the males do (polygyny). There are a few cases of resource defense polyandry, in which the female is territorial and males coexist on her territory.
4. Promiscuity
5. Forced copulations as a reproductive strategy.

'In light of sexual selection, the extreme rarity of polyandry (particularly in pair bonding animals) and the moderate rarity of monogamy becomes more explicable. The relative frequency of the three basic mating systems reflects the action of sexual selection on the range of possible ecological conditions; it is usually possible for some males to monopolize several females or for females to gain by choosing those few males that will have the greatest positive effect on their fitness.

Almost all animals regardless of the kingdom for example buffaloes would lick the genital parts of the female and would smell the urine of the female frequently to detect when she is on heat. But another issue is raised whereby the male can attract the female that is on heat by vocalization of sound and bellowing.

This is a competitive feature in hoofed animals, where the vocalization sound of bulls determines and reflects on the strongest male and robust enough to mate and sire strong calves. Beside vocalization and production of sound, many animals would extend their necks and curl upper lip. This is exhibited by male animals when they feel that they would like to male and no female is ready. This is eventually done to attract any female that is willing to be mated or if any that is on heat.

Sometimes tactile stimuli are noticed in males as licking and biting of the female takes place. Bulls get the sexual desire quickly as soon as the female is on heat and arousal follows no sooner. With time the mating bull would become sexually exhausted as mating continues. When mating the bull don't concentrate on grazing and this is a factor that makes man to encourage domesticated animals to be isolated and mating would be allowed at night or early in the morning before grazing resumes.

Erection in bulls of cattle, buffaloes, wild beast, waterbucks, giraffes, rams and the goat is fast and ejaculation is fast on mounting. But elephant bulls, rhinoceros, donkey, camels, zebras and others have difficulty in mating due to the size of body mass and weight as well as the size of the male genital organ, height of female and calmness of female when mating.

One method of mating system is whereby a male has an exclusive relationship with two or more females. This is mostly exhibited by a number of primates, where the king of the jungle would mate several females, each at time when they are on estrus. The male baboon that is strong enough and can fight all other males in that group is always the king who usually would mate the females on heat during his rein and would bring forth a number of generations before it become sexually exhausted and weak to mate any more. This is a specific system in polygamous animals that is polygynic. Polygyny is the most mating system in animals that is so far well analyzed and proved and tested. It usually occurs in a number of animals for example in lions, baboon, etc.

Another mating system in animal kingdom involves polyandry, where one female has a relationship with two or more males. This is exhibited by wild dogs and hyenas.

Sometimes it is very hard to identify and to distinguish mating systems in world animals like elephants. But continuous study indicates that a polygynandry system of mating is exhibited where two or more males have almost exclusive relationship with two or more females.

Recent developments in courtship indicate that mating in animals depends on the seasons of mating that are influenced by many factors. These factors include genetic make up of animals, environment and availability of partners. Many animals depend on sensing ability of the male and from how far it can sense the pheromone hormone that is produced by females.

Copulation among wild animals usually mostly occurs when animals are safe from enemies, when environment is conducive and when females are on heat, unlike man. Mating in herbivores is highly determined by estrus cycle in females. The presence of pheromone hormone in the female's urine would make the male to be sexually active and to start mating. Usually detection of this hormone occurs during normal gracing periods whereby the males would accidentally sense the hormone or when licking the genitals of female.

In amphibians, mating highly occur when there is plenty of water, *i.e.,* during rainy season. Males' frog would fawn to attract females and communication is done through hearing of specific sounds.

Parental Investment and Reproductive Success

In evolutionary biology, Parental Investment (PI) is any parental expenditure (time, energy, etc.) that benefits one offspring at a cost to parents' ability to invest in other components of fitness (Clutton-Brock; 1991 and Trivers; 1972). Components of fitness (Beatty; 1992) include the well being of existing offspring, parents' future reproduction and inclusive fitness through aid to kin (Hamilton; 1964). Parental investment is sometimes incorrectly equated with parental care or parental effort.

Although uncommon in mammals, paternal investment is found in many species of bird, fish and in some species of insect (Perrone and Zaret; 1988, Thornhill; 1976, Wolf, Ketterson and Nolan; 1988). The study of the attendant cost-benefit trade-offs is complicated by the evolutionary history of the species, as well as by whether paternal investment is obligate or facultatively expressed (Arnold and Owens; 2002, Clutton-Brock; 1991, Fishman, Stone and Lotem; 2003). Obligate investment means that male care is necessary for the survival of his offspring. In these species, selection will favour males who invest in offspring and could eventually result in males showing high levels of paternal investment, independent of proximate conditions (Westneat and Sherman; 1993).

Male parenting in fish species is typically associated with external fertilization and male defense of nesting sites to exclude competitors (Perrone and Zaret; 1979). Under these conditions, paternal certainty is high. Males are also able to fertilize the eggs of more than one female and thus, investment does not reduce mating optunities. In contrast, paternal investment is uncommon in fish species with internal fertilization, presumably because paternity is not certain and because males can abandon females after fertilization and avoid the cost of investment.

Paternal investment does occur in some species with internal fertilization, including most species of bird and a few mammals, mostly carnivores and some primates (Dunbar; 1995, Mock and Fujioka; 1990).

Factors Associated with the Evolution and Facultative Expression of Paternal Investment

Offspring Survival

1. If paternal investment has little or no effect on offspring survival rate or quality, selection will favour male abandonment if additional mates can be found (Trivers; 1972; Westneat and Sherman; 1993, Williams; 1966).
2. If paternal investment results in relatively but not an absolute improvement in offspring survival rate or quality, selection will favour males that show a mixed reproductive strategy. Males can vary in degree of emphasis on mating and parenting, contingent on social (*e.g.,* male status, availability of mates) and ecological (*e.g.,* food availability), conditions (Westneat and Sherman; 1993, Wolf *et. al.,* 1988).

Mating Opportunities

1. If paternal investment is not obligate and mates are available, selection will favour: A. male abandonment, if paternal investment has little effect on offspring survival rate and quality (Clutton-Brock; 1991).B. A mixed male reproductive strategy, if paternal investment improves offspring survival rate and quality (Perrone and Zaret; 1979, Wolf *et. al.,* 1988).
2. Social and ecological factors that reduce the mating opportunities of males, such as dispersed females or concealed (or synchronized) ovulation, will reduce the opportunity cost of paternal investment. Under these conditions, selection will favour paternal investment, if this investment improves offspring survival rate or quality or does not otherwise induce heavy costs on the male (Clutton-Brock; 1991, Dunbar; 1995, Perrone and Zaret; 1979, Thornhill; 1976, Westneat and Sherman; 1993).

Paternity Certainty

1. If the certainty of paternity is low, selection will favour male abandonment (Clutton- Brock; 1991, Muller; 2000, Westneat and Sherman; 1993).
2. If the certainty of paternity is high, selection will favour paternal investment if: (A). Investment improves offspring survival or quality (B). The opportunity costs of investment (*i.e.,* reduced mating opportunities) are lower than the benefits associated with investment (Dunbar; 1995, Thornhill; 1976, Westneat and Sherman; 1993).
3. If the certainty of paternity is high and the opportunity costs, in terms of lost mating opportunities, are high, selection will favour males with a mixed reproductive strategy, that is, the facultative expression of paternal investment, contingent on social and ecological conditions (Dunbar; 1995, Westneat and Sherman; 1993).

Parental Care

Parental care is the attention that is taken by the parents toward rearing and protecting their offspring until they attain the age of being self reliable and independent. Some animals will extend parental care even if their progenies are able to sustain themselves. These will include man and other primates.

The most common form of parental care in amphibians is attendance of the egg clutch by either parent. Maternal care occurs in species with internal fertilization (predominantly salamanders and caecilians), and paternal care may occur in species with external fertilization (predominantly anurans). It may involve aeration of aquatic eggs, cleaning and/or moistening of terrestrial eggs, protection of eggs from predators, or removal of dead and infected eggs.

Eggs may be transported when development occurs on land. Females of the genus *Pipa* carry eggs on their backs. *Rheobatrachus* females brooded tadpoles in their stomachs, and the young emerged from the female's mouths. During brooding, the female's stomach expanded to fill most of her body cavity and the stomach stopped producing digestive secretions.

In many terrestrial and some aquatic animals the female carries the developing zygote internally prior to laying an egg or giving birth. This gives the male ample opportunity to leave the female, perhaps to search for other mates. In a sense, the female is 'stuck' with parental care after laying the eggs or giving birth, because her mate has abandoned her.

In exceptional cases, such as seahorses and midwife toads, males are the primary caregivers. These are interesting examples of how evolution can be driven to unusual solutions.

In some cases **parent-offspring** or **sib-sib** conflicts over resources are resolved by the death of juveniles. The best studied examples are egrets and prairie dogs. In other cases, males ensure their paternity by killing a female's litter and then mating with her to produce a new litter. An extreme example of this occurs in mice, in which a female aborts her litter if the male in her territory is replaced.

Paternal care rarely occurs in mammals but is found in several primate species. Male parental care includes carrying offspring, grooming them, intervening on their behalf in agonistic encounters and preventing infanticide. In order for such actions to constitute true parental care, male primates must differentiate their offspring from other members of the group and give care specifically to them and this care should increase the offspring's fitness (Buchan *et. al*; 2003). Species exhibiting paternal care of infants include cotton-top tamarins (pictured above), Coquerel's sifaka prosimians, savannah baboons, Goeldi's monkeys, titi monkeys, siamangs, Barbary macaques, and common marmosets. The actual extent of male parental care varies considerably between these species (Schradin *et. al*; 2003). Paternal care is most commonly found within monogamous mating systems but may occur in promiscuous or polyandrous groups more rarely. Obviously, male primates cannot care for infants alone due to their dependence on maternal milk (Woodroffe and Vincent; 1994).

Aggressive Behaviour

Moyer (1968) defined various categories of animal aggression:

1. **Territorial Defense** When animals attack intruders who enter their 'territory'.
2. **Predatory Aggression** When an animal attacks prey. This form of aggression is not believed to be hunger-induced, but rather involves the lateral hypothalamus and the specific 'trigger' stimuli (the animals it typically feeds on the prey).
3. **Inter-male Aggression** Occurs when another (stranger) male is present. Androgens (hormones) are believed to be important in this form of aggression.
4. **Fear-induced Aggression** Always preceded by attempts to escape. This form of aggressive behaviour is most evident when the animal is 'cornered' and is afraid. They will almost always react with aggression before they attempt to escape. The amygdala and lateral hypothalamus are believed to be important here.
5. **Irritable Aggression** This will be evoked by any attackable object or other animal. The ventromedial hypothalamus and amygdala are believed to be the crucial brain structures here.
6. **Maternal Aggression** When a female reacts with aggression in order to protect her young from harm.

Habitat Selection and Optimality in Foraging

Habitat selection refers to a hierarchical process of behavioural responses which may result in the disproportionate use of habitat to influence survival and fitness of individuals. There are several factors which are involved with an organism's choice of habitat. The important one are:

1. Habitats are heterogenous.
2. How habitat selection can relate to conservation issues.

Indeed, some ecologists employ the term 'habitat use rather than habitat selection' to avoid the connotation of birds making deliberate decisions among habitat alternatives. Birds are nearly ideal subjects for studies of habitat selection, because they are highly mobile, often migrating thousands of miles (and in the process passing over an enormous range of environments) and yet ordinarily forage, breed and winter in very specific habitats.

Foraging is the act of searching for and exploiting food resources. It affects an animal's fitness because it plays an important role in an animal's ability to survive and reproduce. Foraging theory studies the foraging behaviour of animals in response to the environment in which the animal lives. Foraging theory is discussed in terms of optimizing a payoff from a foraging decision. The payoff for many of these models is the amount of enery an animal receives per unit time, more specifically the highest ratio of energetic gain to cost while foraging. Foraging theory predicts that the decisions which maximize energy per unit time and therefore, deliver the highest payoff will be selected. Some factors affect an animal's ability to forage and acquire highly profitable resources. These are learning ability and genetic composition of animal. A central concern of ecology has traditionally been foraging behaviour. In its most basic form, **optimal foraging theory** states that 'organisms forage in such a way as to maximize their energy intake per unit time'.

In other words, they behave in such a way as to find, capture and consume food containing the most calories while expending the least amount of time possible in doing so. The understanding of many ecological concepts such as adaptation, energy flow and competition hinges on the ability to comprehend what and why animals select certain food items. Foraging can be grouped into two main categories:

1. **The solitary foraging** where animals forage by themselves.
2. **The group foraging** where animals can be seen foraging together when it is beneficial for them to do so (*i.e.,* aggregation economy) and when it is deterimental for them to do so (*i.e.,* dispersion economy).

Migration Orientation and Navigation

Migrations are long distance, regular movements, often involving a round trip each year. There mechanisms may be used in migration: Traveling from one familiar landmark to another is called piloting. Orientation occurs when an animal detects compass directions and moves in a straight line. Navigation involves the ability to detect compass direction and to determine present location relative to destination (a 'map sense').

Some species of birds and other animals orient by the heavens, using the sun or stars as directional cues. Many migrating animals are internal timing mechanisms to adjust to the changing positions of the sun and stars, both throughout the day and along the migratory route.

Many bird species are able to continue migrating under clouds or through fog, possibly because of their ability to detect and orient to Earth's magnetic field. Magnetite has been found in the heads of some birds, in the abdomens of bees and in certain bacteria, although its role in sensing the Earth's magnetic field has not been experimentally established.

Migration is a mechanism essential in studying how animal cognition functions. Migration is regular movement over relatively long distances. Migrating animals uses three mechanisms to find their way piloting, orientation and navigation.

1. **Orientation** is simply facing in the right direction.
2. **Navigation** involves finding one's way from point A to point B.

Spatial and Temporal Orientation

Behavioural information utilized by motile organisms falls into two large classes:

(i) Know how controlling instrumental behaviour (feeding, mating, etc.).

(ii) Know when/where controlling orientational behaviour.

(a) When temporal orientation.

(b) Where spatial orientation.

Animal behaviour is oriented in space and time.

Spatial Orientation

(a) Self-controlled maintenance or change of an organism's body position relative to environmental space.

(b) Occurs when certain stimuli in the environment elicit a responsive sequence of behaviour that results in a non-random pattern of locomotion, direction of body axis or both.

(c) Orientation refers to the way an organism positions itself to external cues.

Types of Orientation and Reaction Mechanisms

(a) Kinesis (kineses) type of movement that is related to the intensity of the stimulus, but not oriented with respect to the source of stimulation.

(b) Stimulus produces a change in either (a) speed of movement or (b) rate of turning.

(c) As a result, animals position is changed in relation to the source of stimulus. For example: Aggregation of woodlice.

(d) **Orthokinesis** Linear velocity influenced by stimulus.

(e) **Klinokinesis** Rate of turning affected by stimulus.

(f) **Taxis** animal's body takes up a particular direction with respect to orienting stimuli. Movements are influenced by the direction of the stimulus.

Homing and Navigation

(i) **Homing** process whereby animal returns to home.

(ii) **Navigation** process by which animal uses various cuess to determine its position in reference to a goal.

Path-Integration (Dead Reckoning)

Despite the lack of landmarks, desert ants in the genus *Cataglyphis* can quickly and directly navigate back to their colony entrance after collecting food. Ants can use information from the sun and the pattern of light reflected in the sky to orient themselves with respect to the direction of their colony.

True Navigation

(a) Ability to move to a goal in unfamiliar territory in the absence of any sensory contact with that goal.

(b) Most mechanisms for navigation involve cues that require an external frame of reference.

(c) Requires both a compass and a map.

Homing behaviour and compass orientation includes landmarks and experience, sun compass and magnetic compass.

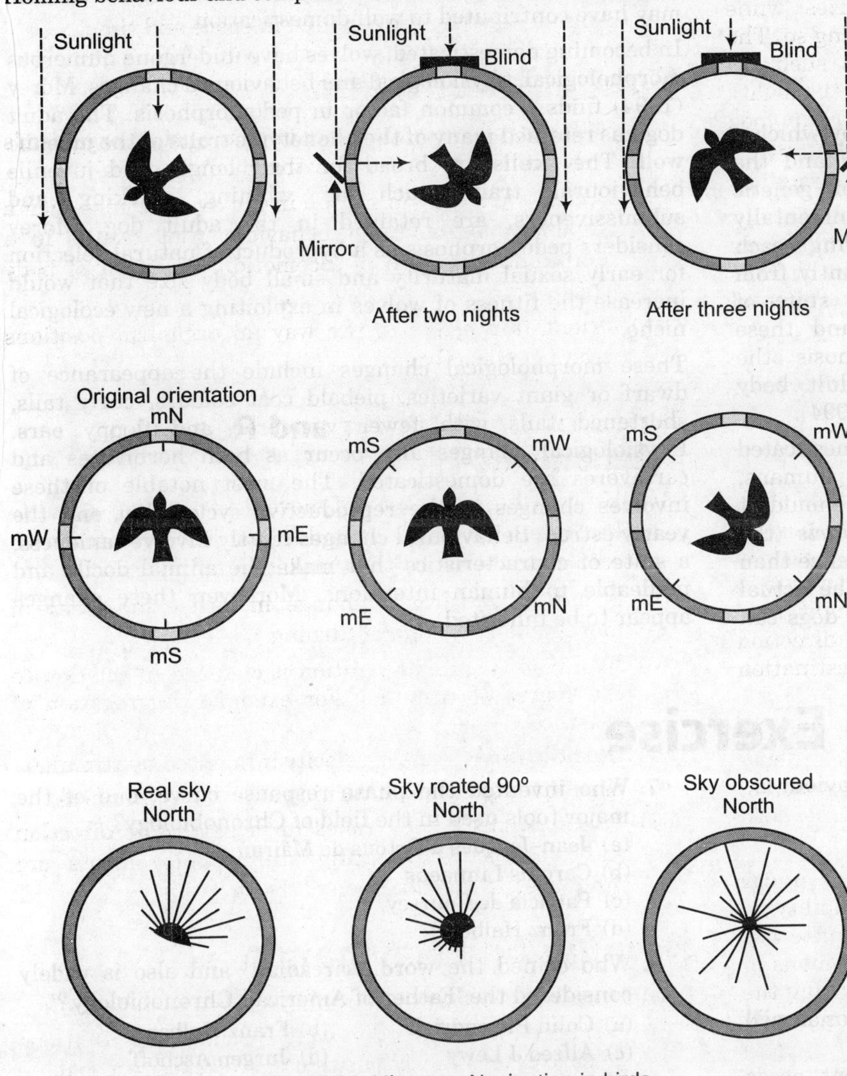

Fig. 35.14 Migratory Navigation in birds

Sun compass

Experiment have been carried out to investigate the existence of a sun compass and its importance for daytime migrations. Caged birds were placed in circular enclosures with four window. Mirrors were used to alter the angle at which light entered the enclosures. At migration time, in natural conditions, these birds clearly showed a preferred flight direction (left). When mirrors bent the suns rays through 90°, the birds turned their preferred direction (middle and right).

Magnetic Compass

An experiment that investigated the possibility of a magnetic compass being used by migratory birds used magnetic coils to mimic the Earth's magnetic field. The birds detect magnetic North, the direction of their spring migration. When the magnetic field was twisted so that North was in the East-South-East position, the birds kept their original path for the first two nights. By the third night, they had detected the change and altered their path accordingly.

Star Compass

An experiment that investigated the use of star position in the night sky used an ink pad at the base of a cone of blotting paper. Nocturnal migrants flutter in their preferred direction of travel as the amount of ink shows. In a planetarium that projected the real sky, Indigo Buntings located the Polar Star and used it to find North, the direction of their spring migration. When the sky in the planetarium was rotated 90° counter-clockwise the birds altered their direction accordingly. Simulating a cloudy night, the obscured sky confused the birds.

Domestication and Behavioural Changes

Domestic animals may be provisionally defined as those kept and bred in and around human habitation to be used constantly to human advantage.

Features favouring domestication in a wild species (Hale; 1962):

Group Structure

(a) Large social groups, hierarchical structure, males affiliated with female groups.

(b) Not territorial

Sexual Behaviour

(a) Promiscuous matings.

(b) Male does not have to establish dominance over female.

(c) Not monogamous.

(d) Sexual signals behavioural, not morphological.

Parent-Young Interaction

(a) Precocial

(b) Defined imprinting period

(c) Female accepts other infants

(d) Responses to humans

(e) Short flight distance

(f) Tolerant to environmental changes

Other

(a) Adaptable
(b) Unspecialized diet
(c) Limited agility

Price (1984) defined domestication as 'a process by which a population of animals becomes adapted to man and the captive environment, by some combination of genetic changes occurring over generations and environmentally induced developmental events recurring during each generation.' Domesticated animals differ significantly from animals in the wild. There appears to be a suite of characteristics that accompany domestication and these characteristics have be linked to pedomorphosis the retention of juvenile characteristics in the adult body (Coppinger and Smith; 1983, Price; 1984, Morey; 1994).

The dog was probably the first animal to be domesticated (although some anthropologists have said that humans, themselves, actually deserve this title). Indeed, we shouldn't even call these animals dogs, since *Canis familiaris* (the scientific name for dog) is more a name of convenience than that denoting a real species (See Isaac; 1970). The actual name might be *Canis lupus*, the wolf. Wolves and dogs can interbreed. Both natural selection and artificial selection may have contributed to wolf domestication.

In becoming domesticated, wolves have undergone numerous morphological, physiological and behavioural changes. Morey (1994) finds a common factor in pedomorphosis. The adult dog has retained many of the phenotypic traits of the juvenile wolf. The skulls are broad for their length and juvenile behavioural traits such as whining, barking and submissiveness, are retained in the adult dog. Morey considers pedomorphosis as a byproduct of natural selection for early sexual maturity and small body size that would increase the fitness of wolves in exploiting a new ecological niche.

These morphological changes include the appearance of dwarf or giant varieties, piebald coat colours, curly tails, shortened tails with fewer vertebrae and floppy ears. Physiological changes also occur as both herbivores and carnivores are domesticated. The most notable of these involves changes in the reproductive cycles that end the yearly estrus. Behavioural changes mostly involve tameness, a suite of characteristics that make the animal docile and malleable to human intentions. Moreover, these changes appear to be inherited.

Exercise

1. The study of the natural history of animal behaviour is
(a) Etiology (b) Psychology
(c) Ethology (d) Parapsychology

2. An example of associative learning would be
(a) classical conditioning
(b) operant conditioning
(c) Pavlovian conditioning
(d) All of the above

3. A song bird that hears the songs of other species as well as its own
(a) will sing the song of its own species, but needs practice
(b) will instinctively sing the song of its species perfectly
(c) will sing other songs as well as its own
(d) will be confused and not master any song

4. The most important rhythm, 'circadian rhythm' is approximately a .... cycle shown by physiological processes in all major organisms.
(a) 5 h (b) 10 h
(c) 15 h (d) 24 h

5. Which of the circadian rhythm describes animals primarily active during the dawn and dusk hours (*e.g.*, white-tailed deer, some bats)?
(a) Diurnal (b) Nocturnal
(c) Crepuscular (d) Duskurnal

6. A circadian cycle in the movement of plant leaves was first observed by
(a) Jean-Jacques d'Ortous de Mairan
(b) Carolus Linnaeus
(c) Patricia de Coursey
(d) Franz Halberg

7. Who invented the phase response curve, one of the major tools used in the field of Chronobiology?
(a) Jean-Jacques d'Ortous de Mairan
(b) Carolus Linnaeus
(c) Patricia de Coursey
(d) Franz Halberg

8. Who coined the word, 'circadian' and also is widely considered the 'Father of American Chronobiology.?'
(a) Colin Pittendrigh (b) Franz Halberg
(c) Alfred J Lewy (d) Jurgen Aschoff

9. Which of the following mating system is most common polygamous mating system in vertebrates?
(a) Polyandry (b) Polygyny
(c) Polygynandry (d) Polyandrgyny

10. In which of the mating system, a member of one sex within the social group mates with any member of the opposite sex?
(a) Monogamy (b) Polygyny
(c) Polyandry (d) Promiscuity

11. Asexual reproduction without fertilization in plants, but only when it arising by modification of sexual function is known as
(a) out crossing (b) in crossing
(c) apomixis (d) autogamy

12. Which of the species are occasionally referred to as 'opportunistic'?
(a) Allopatric species
(b) Sympatric species
(c) *r*-selected species
(d) *k*-selected species

13. Social dominance theory was first formulated by
(a) Jim Sidanius and Felicia Pratto
(b) Fischer and Fod
(c) MacArthur and Wilson
(d) Joe Felsenstein

14. Social dominance theory is influenced by
(a) Marxist
(b) Socio-biological ideas
(c) Both (a) and (b)
(d) None of the above

15. In forest, if a female songbird is attracted to male songbirds' songs. These songs warn other males to stay away from the singer's territory. Increased light during springtime triggered the male songbirds brain to produce a sex hormone. These hormones drove the birds to sing. In this songbird example, the survival aspect of the behaviour is .... and the biological aspect through which the behaviour occurs ....
(a) ultimate; proximate
(b) proximate; ultmate
(c) ultimate; ultimate
(d) proximate; proximate

16. Proximate causes are occurring during the lifetime of the individual, they involve the interactions among
(a) genotype and phenotype
(b) genotype and environment
(c) phenotype and environment
(d) genotype, phenotype and environment

17. To understand both the biological and evolutionary importance of behaviours, it's essential to determine .... causes of behaviours.
(a) ultimate
(b) proximate
(c) Both (a) and (b)
(d) None of the above

18. In its simplest version of Hamilton's rule, if C is the cost incurred by the altruist (the donor), B is the benefit received by the recipients of the altruism, and R is the co-efficient of relationship between donor and recipient. An altruistic gene will be favoured by natural selection only when
(a) $B = C/R$
(b) $B > C/R$
(c) $B < C/R$
(d) $B = C \times R$

19. Altruistic behaviour is not seen in
(a) ant (b) bee
(c) termite (d) silk worm

20. Kin selection or 'inclusive fitness' theory was originally put forward by
(a) Hamilton (b) RA Fisher
(c) JBS Haldane (d) Darwin

21. Kin selection theory contributed to the demise of the
(a) individual selection concept
(b) group selection concept
(c) population selection concept
(d) species selection concept

22. An altruistic behaviour which spreads by kin selection .... the organism's personal fitness (by definition), it increases what Hamilton called the organism's .... fitness.
(a) increases; inclusive
(b) reduces; inclusive
(c) increases; reproductive
(d) reduces; reproductive

23. Which of the correlation is the key to the evolution of altruism?
(a) Donor-recipient correlation
(b) Genetic relatedness
(c) Reproductive fitness
(d) Environmental adaptation

24. The theory of reciprocal altruism was originally developed by
(a) Hamilton (b) Trivers
(c) Cuvier (d) Darwin

25. The famous quote , 'prisoner's dilemma' is associated with
(a) weak altruism
(b) strong altruism
(c) reciprocal altruism
(d) exploit altruism

26. Hamilton equation explains any altruistic behaviour in terms of
(a) neutral genes
(b) selfish genes
(c) reproductive genes
(d) somatic genes

27. In a population of randomly interacting individuals the value of the correlation between genetic similarity and interaction strength will be
(a) 0 (b) 1/2
(c) 1 (d) 2

28. In an interesting experiment with searocket plants Susan Dudley at McMaster University in Canada compared the growth patterns of unrelated plants sharing a pot to plants from the same clone. She found that unrelated plants competed for soil nutrients by aggressive root growth. This did not occur with sibling plants. This behaviour is reflectance of the
(a) altruism in plants
(b) kinship in plants
(c) cooperation in plants
(d) aggression in plants

29. C-value paradox is often encountered mostly in
(a) prokaryotes (b) bacteria
(c) archaea (d) eukaryotes

30. Parenting is the process of promoting and supporting .... the of a child from infancy to adulthood.
(a) physical
(b) physical and emotional
(c) physical, emotional and social
(d) physical, emotional, social and intellectual development

31. Which of the following is an example of the evolution of a fixed-action pattern with finer discrimination among sign stimuli?
(a) A bluegill sunfish feeding on larger *Daphnia* when prey are abundant
(b) A chick pecking at the red spot on a parent's moving beak
(c) A bird recognizing and expelling an egg of a cuckoo from its nest
(d) A songbird learning its song after listening to a taped song of its species

32. Sociobiology
(a) explain the evolutionary basis of behavioural characteristics within animal societies
(b) applies evolutionary explanations to human social behaviours
(c) studies the roles of culture and genetics in human social behaviour
(d) All of the above

33. The ability of honeybees to fly directly to a food source, after having to wait several hours from the time of the waggle dance, indicates that
(a) the waggle dance provided directions relative only to the position of the hive
(b) bees have an internal clock that compensates for the movement of the sun during the elapsed time
(c) the bees must have been to that food source before
(d) bees are directed more by olfactory cues than by directional cues

34. In classical conditioning
(a) an animal associates a behaviour with a reward or punishment
(b) an animal learns as a result of trial and error
(c) sensitivity to unimportant or repetitive stimuli occurs
(d) an irrelevant stimulus can elicit a response because of its association with a normal stimulus

35. Circannual behaviours
(a) are often linked to changes in day length
(b) rely solely on endogenous cues
(c) involve foraging, reproduction and migration
(d) do not occur in free-running conditions

36. Supernormal stimuli
(a) may elicit stronger responses or FAPs
(b) are innate releasing mechanisms between individuals of the same species
(c) are illustrated by the removal of the cricket from near a digger wasp's nest
(d) are illustrated by the bobbing of a stick with a red spot past herring gull chicks

37. A dominance hierarchy
(a) may be established by agonistic behaviour
(b) determines which animals get first access to resources
(c) helps to avoid potential injury of competitors
(d) All of the above

38. Proximate causes
(a) explain the evolutionary significance of a behaviour
(b) are immediate causes of behaviour such as environmental stimuli
(c) indicate that much of animal behaviour is innate
(d) are endogenous, although they may be set by exogenous cues

39. Behavioural ecology is the
(a) mechanistic study of the behaviour of animals, focusing on stimulus and response
(b) application of human emotions and thoughts to other animals
(c) study of animal cognition
(d) study of animal behaviour from an evolutionary perspective of Darwinian fitness

40. The various aspects related with animal behaviour can be studied by employing following methods
(a) (i) Under natural conditions
(ii) Experimental analysis
(iii) Statistical interpretations
(b) (i) Morphological studies
(ii) Experimental analysis
(iii) Statistical interpretation
(c) (i) Under natural conditions
(ii) Statistical interpretation
(iii) Physiological studies
(d) (i) Morphological studies
(ii) Statistical interpretation
(iii) Physiological studies

41. Match list I with list II and select the correct answer using the codes given below the lists.

List I	List II
A. Oriental region	1. Gorilla, lion, giraffe and hippopotamus
B. Holarctic region	2. Tapirs, sloths, prehensile tailed monkeys and vampire bats
C. Neotropical region	3. Orangutan, tarisers, elephant and frugivorous bats
D. Ethiopian region	4. Caribou, elk, foxes of the genus Vulpes, bears and marmots

Codes

	A	B	C	D
(a)	4	2	3	1
(b)	3	4	2	1
(c)	4	3	2	1
(d)	3	4	1	2

42. Match the term in list I to this description in list II and select the correct codes.

List I	List II
A. Association	1. A dolphin learns the commands 'Throw ball' and 'Retrieve ring.' The first time the trainer says, 'Retrieve ball,' the dolphin does it correctly.
B. Imitation	2. A cat learns to come running into the kitchen when it hears the electric can opener.
C. Innovation	3. When their mother was killed, ducklings on a farm learned to follow a tractor.
D. Imprinting	4. Young monkeys see and hear their parents give a warning call when they see a snake. Next time the young monkeys give the warning call, too.

Codes

	A	B	C	D
(a)	1	2	3	4
(b)	2	1	3	4
(c)	2	4	1	3
(d)	4	2	2	1

43. Consider the following statements.

I. Reciprocal altruism help or sacrifice repaid later.
II. Kim selection present when self sacrifice relatives leads to altruism.
III. Courtship ritual minimizes agonistic behaviour before mating.
IV. Cognition is the ability to store, process and use sensory information.

Which of the above statements are correct regarding animal behaviour?

Codes

(a) I, II and III
(b) II, III and IV
(c) I, III and IV
(d) I, II, III and IV

Answers

1. (c)	**2.** (d)	**3.** (a)	**4.** (d)	**5.** (c)	**6.** (a)	**7.** (c)	**8.** (b)	**9.** (b)	**10.** (d)
11. (c)	**12.** (c)	**13.** (a)	**14.** (c)	**15.** (a)	**16.** (d)	**17.** (c)	**18.** (b)	**19.** (d)	**20.** (a)
21. (b)	**22.** (b)	**23.** (a)	**24.** (b)	**25.** (c)	**26.** (b)	**27.** (a)	**28.** (b)	**29.** (d)	**30.** (d)
31. (c)	**32.** (d)	**33.** (b)	**34.** (d)	**35.** (a)	**36.** (a)	**37.** (d)	**38.** (b)	**39.** (d)	**40.** (a)
41. (b)	**42.** (c)	**43.** (d)							

36

Applied Biology

Microbial Fermentation

The term 'fermentation' derives from the Latin word *fevere* meaning 'to ferment.' Fermentation is an ancient process dating back thousands of years. Not until the work of **Louis Pasteur** in the late 19th century was it understood how the process, which to that point was based on experience and tacit knowledge, actually worked. **Antony von Leeuwenhoek,** a **Dutch** biologist in 1680 was the first to see microorganisms in samples of fermenting beer through a microscope. Pasteur, a **French** chemist, discovered that yeasts convert sugars to alcohol and carbon dioxide during fermentation.

Fermentation is the process by which alcoholic beverages or acidic diary products (cheeses and yogurt) are manufactured. It is a way for a cell to obtain energy without using oxygen. During the process, complex organic substances are broken down into simpler ones. The cell (microbial or animal) obtain energy through glycolysis the splitting of a sugar molecule to extract its electrons. The byproduct of this process is excreted from the cell in the form of substances such as alcohol, lactic acid and acetone.

A controlled environmental for growth of **microorganism** is provided by fermentors. Fermentors (bioreactors) can be classified into two main groups based on shape, *i.e.,* tabular and stirred tanks. The main bioreactors are:

1. **Fluidized bed bioreactor** More popular in chemical industry for immobilized cells and enzyme systems.
2. **Loop or air fill bioreactor** Cooling become simpler as compare to conventional bioreactor.
3. **Membrane bioreactor** Consists of semipermiable membrane of cellulose acetate or other polymeric substance.
4. **Pulsed column bioreactor** Used as aerobic bioreactor, enzyme bioreactor or as separation unit.
5. **Bubble column bioreactor** Multistage suitable in equivalent batch process, capability to provide different environmental condition in various stages. Suitable for fungal fermentation.

Syllabus

- Microbial Fermentation and Production of Small and Macro Molecules.
- Application of Immunological Principles (Vaccines, Diagnostics). Tissue and Cell Culture Methods for Plants and Animals.
- Transgenic Animals and Plants, Molecular Approaches to Diagnosis and Strain Identification.
- Genomics and its Application to Health and Agriculture, Including gene Therapy.
- Bioresources and Uses of Biodiversity.
- Breeding in plants and Animals, Including Marker-assisted Selection
- Bioremediation and Phytoremediation.
- Biosensors.

6. **Photobioreactor** An important reactant the photon is available for photosynthetic bacteria. Used for *Spirulina* (single cell protein) and other algal protein production.
7. **Packed tower bioreactor** Consists of cylindrical column packed with inert material like wood sharing, twings, cake, polyethylene or sand. It is used for vinegar production, enzymatic conversion of penicillin to 6-amino penicillanic acid and sewage effluent treatment.

With advances in the science of **microbiology** and technologies like biotechnology, microorganisms are exploited to produce a wide variety of products using fermentation. These include :

(i) **Dairy products** Cheese and yogurt
(ii) **Beverages** Beer and wine
(iii) **Single Cell Proteins** (SCP) These are a cell monoculture of bacteria, fungi and algae. Since, the cells contain large amounts of protein. It is used as food or food supplement for human and cattle. It is regarded as a cheap source of dietary protein and is produced from methanol and byproducts of cheese production and paper making.
(iv) **Antibiotics** These are one of the most important compounds produced by fermentation. **Alexander Fleming** in 1929 was the first to discover 'penicillin', an antibiotic. Large numbers of antibiotics are being produced now by fermentation using various bacteria and fungi.
(v) **Chemicals** Citric and acetic acid, amino acids, enzymes and vitamins.
(vi) **Fuels** Ethanol, methanol and methane.

Microbial Metabolism

Microbes used in fermentation have to grow and reproduce rapidly so that they can produce metabolites. This process is related to 'metabolism'. Metabolism includes two processes—anabolism and catabolism.

Anabolism

This is the synthesis of various metabolic compounds like amino acids, proteins, nucleic acids, carbohydrates and lipids. It is an energy consuming process.

Catabolism

This is the breakdown of metabolic products to produce energy (*e.g.*, breakdown of carbohydrates to carbon dioxide, water and energy). It is an energy producing process.

Carbohydrates → Carbon Dioxide + Water + Energy

Adenosine triphosphate (ATP) is a source of energy produced through anabolism and catabolism and is broken down into **Adenosine diphosphate** (ADP).

Catabolic Pathways

Catabolic pathways are means by which organic molecules are degraded to release energy for growth or degradation. They include photosynthesis, respiration, carbohydrate catabolism, pentose phosphate pathway, Entner-Doudoroff pathway, phosphoketolase pathway, Tricarboxylic Acid Cycle (TCA) and fatty acid and hydrocarbon pathway.

There are four different phases in bacterial growth during fermentation. A good understanding of these phases is very important for effective management of the whole fermentation process.

Lag Phase

At the start of the process microorganisms are added to the nutrient medium and allowed to grow. The number of microorganisms will not increase because they try to adapt to the environment.

Log Phase

The microorganisms are adjusted to the new environment and they multiply at a very rapid pace thus, increasing the cell number exponentially.

Stationary Phase

As the microorganisms grow they produce metabolites which are toxic to microbial growth. Also, the nutrient medium is used up, slowing down or stopping cell growth.

Death Phase

Microorganisms produce toxic metabolites to the extent that they cause the death of the microorganisms.

In the first part of this chapter the industrial production of several common foods will be described. In the second section other industrial uses of microbes will be presented.

Production of Small and Macromolecules by Microbes

Microbes are commercially most important for the production of cheese, alcohol, breads and non-food industry.

Cheese Production

The discovery of the cheese-making process is very old and certainly was accidental. The process of cheese manufacturing today follows some of the primitive steps :

Milk from any mammal (*e.g.*, cow, horse, camel, whale, guinea pig, human, etc.) is mixed with renin or a similar enzyme harvested commercially from a mold today. The enzyme splits the milk protein (casein). A starter culture of a known strain of bacteria that produces desired flavours is added and the lactose is fermented to acids, which lower the pH to a point, where the cleaved casein precipitates out as a curd. The excess liquid, called whey is drained away, sometimes under pressure and the semi-dried curd collected. The curd in inoculated with special bacteria or molds or both that are known to give a particular flavour to the cheese as they grow in and on the curd. An artificial inoculums' of laboratory microbes is used for many cheeses, but many cheeses around the world are naturally inoculated by placing them in environment, where the air is known to contain microbes that produce a desired cheese. Sometimes additional ingredients like salt and herbs are added to achieve desired flavours in the product. The curd is ripened for various periods of time under specific conditions of temperature and humidity, often in caves, where these environmental factors stay constant. During ripening the final flavours and consistencies of the cheeses are produced. At the end of the incubation period the cheese is harvested packaged and sold. Each microbial strain contributes subtle different chemical flavours to its cheese.

Alcohol Fermentation

Intended alcohol production by human is known to have been around for atleast 10000 years.

Ethanol Production Process

The term 'fermentation' has numerous contextual meanings, but in relationship to ethanol production it refers to the metabolism of carbohydrates under anaerobic conditions. Any simple or complex carbohydrate can be fermented to produce ethanol. Usually this fermentation is carried out by certain ubiquitously distributed yeast, but a few bacteria are also able to produce ethanol in commercial quantities. The commercial or industrial production of ethanol is produced as follows:

A grain, usually barley, which is rich in complex glucose polymers (complex carbohydrates) is collected and wetted. As it is stored in a warm, dark place the seeds germinate (sprout) and release enzymes that breakdown or hydrolyze the polysaccharides to simple sugars which the yeast can metabolize. This process is called malting. The malt is dried and crushed to improve the extraction of the sugars. The dried material can be stored at this stage. In the next step, called mashing, the sprouted malt is suspended in water, where the enzymes continue to breakdown the polysaccharides to release simple sugars. The liquid, or malt wort or wort, containing the dissolved simple sugars is separated from the insoluble material. Hops are added to the wort, which is boiled to destroy any extraneous enzymes, to extract the hop-flavours and to precipitate the proteins which could add unwanted flavours to the final product. The hop flowers contain substances that inhibit spoilage microbes and aid in the final clarification of the product. Yeast is then added (pitched) and the mixture is placed in large closed containers, usually metal in large commercial operations so, the fermentation can proceed in the absence of air. The fermentation goes on for about 7 days at a cool temperature which is optimum for ethanol production. The brew (green beer) is usually aged (lagered) under a variety of conditions for various times as desired by individual brewers. During the ageing, chemical changes occur spontaneously that subtly alter the flavour of the product. Finally the product is usually cleared (the yeast removed), bottled and pasteurized.

The Yeasts and other Details of Fermentation

Each brewer has their own strain of yeast that is known to produce a particular flavour in their product. Companies go to great lengths to maintain the genetic purity of their yeast strain, as the wrong mutation can produce subtle changes in the product's flavour. Most ethanol for human consumption is produced by strains of two yeast species, *Saccaromyces carlsbergensis* and *Saccaromyces cerevisiae*, which are characterized as bottom and top yeast respectively, depending on where they settle in the fermenting container.

Light brews are generally made with yeast strains that convert more of the available sugars to ethanol, thus lowering the total caloric content of the beer. Wine can be made from any fruit that has sufficient carbohydrates present to be converted into enough ethanol to make it a 'wine'.

Distilled ethanol products are made from the fermentation of other grains like corn and rye. At the end of the fermentation the material is boiled and the more volatile ethanol, which evaporates first, is collected in a concentrated form. The combination of the unique starting material, the yeast strains and the ageing process all contribute to the unique flavours of distilled spirits.

Breads

The rising of bread is due to a fortuitous combination of chemical characteristics. Wheat and several related grains, makes a group of proteins called glutens. These proteins have the characteristic of forming long molecular strings when they are 'worked' or 'kneaded' that bind the bread together in the sticky mass we call dough. Gluten also contributes to the delightful flavour imparted to bread during baking. Bread rises due to the activity of contaminating yeast which metabolizes the sugar in the wheat and converts it into carbon dioxide. Because of the gluten glue, the carbon dioxide is trapped within the bread which causes the bread to rise from the pressure of the carbon dioxide buildup. This results in the formation of many small bubbles within the bread. When the bread is baked the protein is denatured and it and the starch harden into the food we know as bread. The yeast also contributes important favouring to the bread.

Non-food Industrial Microbiology

Microbes have been used for about fifty years to produce non-food chemicals for human use in industrial quantities. This section is divided into two parts, the classical industrial chemicals that can be manufactured either by microbes or organic chemical processes and the biological chemicals that can not be synthesized by organic chemical processes, but only by living cells themselves.

Industrial Organic Chemicals

Simple organic chemicals like ethanol, acetic acid (vinegar) acetone, butyric acid and lactic acid are readily made either by organic chemical synthesis or by microbial fermentation. The method of choice depends upon the price of the raw materials and on the availability of industrial facilities to carry out either process. That is, in some cases it is cheaper to manufacture ethanol by fermentation and in other cases by chemical conversion from petroleum or natural gas. Immediately preceding the first world war the process of acetone-butanol fermentation by bacteria was discovered. Today acetone and butanol are more cheaply made from petroleum, but as these natural resources run low in the next century we may have to return to the microbiological technology. The following is a partial list of organic chemicals made commercially by microbes:

(a) 2, 3-butainediol; buttery taste
(b) Enzymes
(c) Organic acids such as citric, lactic, ascorbic acid (vitamin-C). These are utilized both as foods, and in industrial chemical processes.
(d) Polysaccharides
(e) Poly-beta hydroxybutyric acid
(f) Methane
(g) Hydrogen
(h) Biological pesticides.

Pharmacological Industry

The second contribution of microbes to winning a war came through the serendipitous discovery of penicillin by the English microbiologist **A Fleming** in 1929. From this followed the antibiotic era and the huge pharmacological industry that operates world wide to day.

The following is a list of microbial produced commercial pharmacological products:

(a) Vitamins **(b)** Amino acids
(c) Nucleic acids **(d)** Antibiotics
(e) Alkaloids **(f)** Steroids

Molecular Industrial Products

The revolution in molecular Biology offers the possibility of yielding a whole new range of microbiological produces through the application of genetic engineering technology. It is now possible to move genes from one organism into a plasmid or into the genome of another organism. Under the proper conditions the cloned genes can be made to direct the synthesis of their protein product. In this way a substance that has a specific effect on another gene or gene product, but which is normally made in tiny amounts in a target organism can be made in commercially large quantities. These large quantities can then be used for therapeutic purposes. A partial list of therapeutic agents is given below :

(a) Hormones insulin, human growth hormone, somatostatin, interferons.
(b) Epidermal growth factor
(c) Insulin
(d) Platelet-derived growth factor
(e) Proinsulin
(f) Fibroblast growth factor
(g) Blood coagulating factor XIII
(h) Transgenic plants and animals.

In addition, there is a large industry in the production of genetic engineering materials which in turn are produced from genetically engineered microbes, plants or animals. These include most of the commercial restriction enzymes and plasmids as well as a number of other enzymes widely used in molecular biological research. Most of these industries, some of which are worth millions of dollars, did not exist 15 years ago. New biotech industries are appearing all the time. Biotech industries are expected to be one of the fastest growing industries in the next century, particularly as the human population ages and as the information from the human genome project comes on line. One direction that the biotech industry is going in is in the construction of transgenic plants and animals. Transgenic plants and animals are good vehicles for producing human gene products. For example, pigs and goats have had human genes incorporated in them. One interesting system involves fusing the desired gene with the milk protein (casein) of a mammal, and then when the animal lactates it produces large quantities of the human gene product which can then be cleaved from the milk protein and purified separately.

General Description of Microbial Products

All commercial fermentations utilize similar techniques. The microbes are cultivated under rigorously controlled environmental conditions conducive to optimum production of the given product in rather humongous fermentors. Fermentors are tanks that may hold 1000 of gallons of culture. They must be made of materials, usually stainless steel, that can be heat sterilized and which will not react with the microbes or with the desired products. They must be able to be tightly sealed to prevent contamination and yet must contain numerous openings for monitors, air and media. All industrial microbial processes deal with similar problems :

1. Finding the least expensive medium in which to grow the microbe so as to maximize yield and profits. Often this is a waste product from another industrial process, such as corn steep liquor, sugar processing wastes or cheese whey.
2. Maintaining strain purity and developing better strains for improving the yield. A single mutation may decrease the yield by a significant percentage or result in undesirable substances being produced. The research laboratories constantly seek better strains for the production of their product.
3. Preventing contamination by other microbes and by viruses that live on the producing microbe. The media must be sterilized prior to being inoculated with the desired organism and purity must be maintained throughout the production process. A small quantity of a contaminant may produce an enzyme that can destroy the product in 1000 of gallons of medium. For many microbes, virus present a constant danger as a single virus can infect and destroy the desired microbe in an entire tank. The sterilization of large containers and huge quantities of media represent both an engineering and microbial challenge.

4. Developing rapid and efficient methods for purification of the desired produce in a stable form that is safe to use. The product of many fermentations is unstable in the impure form or subject to unwanted modifications if it is not purified quickly. The final growth mixture may contain dangerous substances from which the desired product must be separated. As every step in the purification results in lose of the product, the search for more efficient purification procedures is never ending.
5. Always striving to improve yield by modifying the strain, nutrients or environmental conditions. As product yields are exquisitely sensitive to subtle modifications in the nutrient and the environmental conditions, these are constantly monitored For example, the pH, oxygen content, nitrogen/phosphorus ratio, etc, may be adjusted during the production process.
6. Safe and inexpensive disposal of the massive quantities of waste products remaining after the product is formed. The waste products of these large fermentations present major waste disposal problems as they are rich in organic matter that are highly polluting if released untreated into the environment. However, the cost of treatment cuts into the profit margin and increases the cost of the product.

Sterilization Methods

All the materials, *i.e.*, vessels, instruments, medium, plants, animal and microbial culture must be freed from contamination. Sterilization is the process of inactivating or removing all living organisms from a substance or surface. When a closed system is sterilized once it remains so, indefinitely since it has no opening for the entry of microbs. But in open systems continuous sterilization is required to ensure removal of all living entities at their entry points. Some physical and chemical methods of sterilization are given in tables.

Table 36.1 **Physical Methods Used to Control Microbial Growth**

Name	Mechanism of Action	Characteristic	Prefferred Use For
Heat			
1. Moist heat			
(a) Boiling or flowing	Denaturation	Kills vegetative bacterial and fungal pathogens and many viruses within 10 minutes; less effective on endospores.	Dishes, basins, pitchers, various equipment.
(b) Autoclaving	Denaturation	Very effective method of sterilization; at about 15 psi of pressure (121°C), all vegetative cells and their endospores are killed in about 15 minutes.	Microbiological media, solutions, linens, utensils, dressigns, equipment and other items that can withstand temperature and pressure.
2. Pasteurization	Denaturation	Heat treatment for milk (72°C for about 15 seconds) that kills all pathogens and some non-pathogens.	Milk, cream and certain alcoholic beverages (beer and wine).
3. Dry heat			
(a) Direct flaming	Burning contaminants to ashes	Very effective method of sterilization. to ashes.	Inoculating loops.
(b) Incineration	Burning to ashes	Very effective method of sterilization.	Paper cups, contaminated dressings, animal carcasses, bags and wipes.
(c) Hot-air sterilization	Oxidation	Very effective method of sterilization, but requires temperature of 170°C for about 2 hours.	Empty glassware, instruments, needles and glass syringes.
Filtration	Separation of bacteria from suspending liquid.	Passage of a liquid or gas through a screenlike material that traps, microbes; most filters in use consist of cellulose acetate or nitrocellulose.	Useful for sterilizing liquids (toxins, enzymes vaccines) that are destroyed by heat.
Cold			
1. Refrigeration	Decreased chemical reactions and possible changes in proteins.	Has a bacteriostatic effect.	Food, drug and culture preservation.
2. Deep-freezing	Decreased chemical reactions and possible changes in proteins.	An effective method for preserving microbial cultures, in which cultures are quick-frozen between –50° and –95°C.	Food, drug and culture preservation.

Name	Mechanism of Action	Characteristic	Prefferred Use For
3. Lyophilization	Decreased chemical reactions and possible changes in proteins.	Most effective method for long-term preservation of microbial cultures; water removed by high vacuum at low temperature.	Food, drug and culture preservation.
Desiccation	Disruption of metabolism	Invoves removing water from microbes; primary bacteriostatic.	Food preservation.
Osmotic pressure	Plasmolysis	Result in loss of water from microbial cells.	Food preservation.
Radiation			
1. Ionizing	Destruction of DNA by gamma rays and high-energy electron beams.	Not widespread in routine sterilization	Used for sterilizing pharmaceuticals and medical and dental supplies.
2. Non-ionizing	Damage to DNA by UV light.	Radiation not very penetrating.	Control of closed environment with UV (germicidal) lamp.

Table 36.2 **Chemical Agents Used to Control Microbial Growth**

Chemical Agent	Mechanism of Action	Preferred Use For	Characteristic
Phenol and Phenolics			
(i) Phenol	Disruption of plasma membrane, denaturation, inactivation of enzymes.	Rarely used	Seldom used as a disinfectant or antiseptic because of its irritating qualities and disagreeable odor.
(ii) Phenolics	Disruption of plasma membrane, denaturation, inactivation of enzymes.	Environmental surfaces, instruments, skin surface and mucous membranes.	Derivatives of phenol that are reactive even in the presence of organic material, examples include o-phenylphenol and hexachlorophene.
Chlorhexidine	Disruption of plasma membrane	Skin degerming, especially for surgical scrubs.	Bactericidal to Gram positive and Gram negative. Non-toxic, persistent.
Halogens	Iodine inhibits protein function and is a strong oxidizing agent; chlorine forms the strong oxidizing agent hypochlorous acid, which alters cellular components.	Effective antiseptic available as a tincture and an iodophor; chlorine gas is used to disinfect water; chlorine compounds are used to disinfect dairy equipments eating utensil house hold items and glassware.	Iodine and chlorine may act alone or as components of inorganic and organic compounds.
Alcohols	Denaturation and lipid dissolution.	Thermometers and other instruments; in swabbing the skin with alcohol before an injection, most of the disinfecting action probably comes from a simple wiping away (cleansing) of dirt and some microbes.	Bactericidal and fungicidal, but not effective against endospores or non-enveloped viruses; commonly used alcohols are ethanol and isopropanol.
Heavy metals and their compounds	Denaturation of enzymes and other essential proteins.	Silver nitrate may be used to prevent gonococcal eye infections; Mercurochrome disinfects skin and mucous membranes; copper sulphate is an algicide.	Heavy metals such as silver and mercury are germicidal or antiseptic.

Chemical Agent	Mechanism of Action	Preferred Use For	Characteristic
Surface active agents			
(i) Soaps and acid-anionic detergents	Mechanical removal of microbes through scrubbing.	Skin degerming and removal of debris.	Many deodorant soaps contain antimicrobials such as triclocarbon.
(ii) Acid-anionic detergents	Not certain; may invove enzyme inactivation or disruption.	Sanitizers in dairy and food-processing industries.	Wide spectrum of activity, non-toxic, non-corrosive, fast acting.
(iii) Cationic detergents (quaternary ammonium compounds)	Enzyme inhibition, protein denaturation and disruption of plasma membranes.	Antiseptic for skin, instruments utensils, rubber goods.	Bactericidal, bacteriostatic, fungicidal and virucidal against enveloped viruses; examples of quats are Zephiran^{TM} and Cepacol.
Organic acids	Metabolic inhibition, mostly affecting molds; action not related to their acidity.	Sorbic acid and benzoic acid effectiveat low pH parabens much used in cosmetics, shampoos; calcium prophonate used in bread; all are mainly antifungals.	Widely used to control molds and some bacteria in foods and cosmetics.
Aldehydes	Protein inactivation	Glutaraldehyde (Cidex^{TM}) is less irritating than formaldehyde and is used for sterilization of medical equipment.	Very effective antimicrobials; qlutaraldehyde is considered a liquid sterilant.
Gaseous sterilants	Denaturation	Excellent sterilizing agent, especially for objects that would be damaged by heat.	Ethylene oxide is most commonly used.
Oxidizing agents	Oxidation	Contaminated surfaces; some deep wounds, in which they are very effective against oxygen sensitive anaerobes.	Ozone is gaining attention as a potential replacement for chlorination; hydrogen peroxide is a poor antiseptic but a good disinfectant.

Application of Immunological Principles

Vaccines and Diagnostic Immunology

A vaccine is a preparation of microorganisms (or some part of product of them) that will induce an immune response when injected into a host. The practice of vaccination (like many medical practices) predates our understanding of the process. Many cultures afflicted with smallpox adopted the practice of intentionally exposing themselves to material from smallpox lesions, if successful, this led to a mild infection followed by immunity and if unsuccessful, it could lead to severe infection and even death. In the 18th century, **Edward Jenner** established a safer method for vaccination against smallpox. **Jenner** observed that persons that had been exposed to cowpox, which causes a mild infection in humans, exhibited immunity to **smallpox**. Jenner began deliberately exposing patients to material from (what was thought to be) cowpox lesions in the first controlled vaccination trials. Eventually, these efforts led to one of the greatest public health victories in history as there was complete elimination of smallpox from human populations.

Vaccines are critically important for control of infectious diseases for which other preventative efforts and/or antimicrobial drugs are inadequate; this is especially the case for infectious diseases caused by viruses. The goal of vaccination efforts is to provide herd immunity to a population so that, if an out break should occur, an epidemic cannot develop because there are not enough susceptible hosts. Vaccines may be of several types, depending on the targeted pathogen.

Inactivated vaccines are preparations of killed microorganisms; the original Salk polio vaccine was an inactivated vaccine.

Attenuated vaccines (of which Jenner's vaccine was an example) are viable but so weakened as to be non-pathogenic. An advantage of attenuated vaccines is that they may cause a limited infection that invokes a stronger immune response than an inactivated vaccine preparation. Attenuated vaccines are currently used for polio, measles, rubella and mumps.

Subunit (component) vaccines employ part of a virus or bacterium. The (highly recommended) vaccine for hepatitis-B virus consists of one of the capsid proteins of the virus.

Capsular polysaccharides are used as vaccines against infection with *Streptococcus pneumoniae* (agent of bacterial pneumonia) and *Haemophilus influenzae* (agent of bacterial meningitis).

Toxoids are denatured bacterial toxins; toxoids are used in vaccination against tetanus and diphtheria. Vaccine administration does carry some degree of risk. In very rare cases, an attenuated vaccine may mutate to a pathogenic form or cause a pathogenic infection in a severely immuno compromised host; this has been recorded for the Sabin polio vaccines. There may be negative reactions in some individuals; this is at the root of concerns about liability for pertussis vaccine.

Advances in molecular Biology are presently contributing to vaccine development. Attenuated vaccines can be analyzed and manipulated in efforts to avoid the possibility of 'reversion' mutants arising. Subunit vaccines can be prepared by genetic engineering; this is already the case for the hepatitis-B vaccine, which is synthesized by yeast cells DNA vaccines are currently receiving a lot of attention. The idea here is that the genes will be expressed in cells and invoke a cell-mediated immune response. Compared with whole and protein vaccines, DNA offers tremendous advantages in cost and stability.

Diagnostic immunology employs the antigen-antibody interaction to identify the presence of antigen or antibody in test materials. **Serology**, detection and measurement of specific antibodies in patient serum, is often important in identifying infectious agents, particularly (as in most viral infections) when isolation of the agent is difficult.

Precipitation reactions involve formation of large aggregates of antigen and antibody. Such aggregates form only when there is an optimal ratio of antigen:antibody. A variety of techniques, including diffusion of antigen and antibody through agar gels can be used to visualize the characteristic precipitin. Whereas precipitation reactions involve soluble antigen, agglutination reactions involve antigen bound to particles.

The precipitation reactions occur in two stages:

(i) Rapid interaction between antigen and antibody within a second and formation of complex.

(ii) Slow rate of reaction and forming lattices from antigen antibody complex within a few minute or hours.

In precipitation test, a precipitation ring appears which displays the creation of optimal ration, this zone called **zone of equivalence.**

Direct agglutination is very useful for detecting the presence of antibodies directed against antigens found on the surface of cells. ABO blood typing is a classic example of direct agglutination; in this case, it is the antigen (on erythrocytes) that is being detected. Direct agglutination is used to detect serum antibodies specific for bacterial cell surface antigens. Soluble antigens can be used in agglutination reactions if they are first bound to particles such as latex spheres or 'tanned' erythrocytes.

Indirect agglutination is particularly used for detection of streptococci. If the antigens are absorbed onto particles (*e.g.*, RBCs, latesphere, bentomile clay) soluble antigens can respond to agglutination test. When RBCs are agglutinated by certain viruses such as mumps virus, measle virus, influenza, etc., this is called viral **haemagglutination.**

Fluorescent antibody (FA) techniques use antibodies labelled with fluorescent dyes. When the labelled antibody binds to antigen, the fluorescence can be detected in a specially equipped microscope.

In direct FA tests, a specific antibody is labelled and used to identify cells exhibiting the antigen of interest.

In indirect FA tests, the fluorescent group is attached to an anti-immunoglobulin, which recognizes specific antibody bound to antigen.

Radio Immunoassay (RIA) is a highly sensitive technique which can measure 0.001 μg/mL concentration of antigen or antibody. **Barson** and **Yalow** (1960) used this technique in determining the concentration of insulin and antiinsulin in diabetics. The liquid phase RIA is based on competitive binding of radio labelled antigen and unlabelled antigen to high affinity antibody. The antigen labelled with Ist is mixed with such a concentration of antibody which saturate the antibody. By increasing amount of unlabelled antigen, the two type of antigen compete for binding to antibody site. By further increasing unlabelled antigen concentration labelled antigen could be displaced from the antibody's binding site and these become free in solution. By measuring labelled antigen amount concentration of unlabelled antigen can be determined. In solid phase RIA either antibody or antigen as immobilized on a solid phase matrix and thus comparatively simple and easy.

Fluorescence Activated Cell Sorters (FACS) are extremely valuable in counting particular classes of cells on the basis of surface antigens. In FACS, a mixture of cells (such as total mononuclear cells from blood) is labelled with one or more fluorescent antibodies. The instrument detects the fluorescence and counts different cell populations accordingly **Enzyme-Linked Immunosorbent Assays** (ELISA) have found wide applicability in diagnostic immunology. ELISAs depend on antibodies labelled with enzyme molecules that catalyze reactions which result in formation of a coloured product. The basic rule for understanding ELISAs is, 'if the labelled antibody is present at the end of the test, the colour change is seen and the test is positive.'

The double antibody sandwich method is used for detection of antigen. Specific antibody, immobilized to the bottom of a well, binds to the antigen. If the antigen is present, a second, enzyme-labelled antibody will bind to it, leading to a positive reaction.

The indirect ELISA is used to detect the presence of specific antibody in test serum. In these tests, it is antigen that is bound to the well. The presence of antibody bound to the antigen is detected with enzyme-labelled antiimmunoglobulin. An indirect ELISA is used to screen donor blood for the presence of antibodies specific for HIV.

Tissue and Cell Culture Methods for Plants and Animals

Tissue culture is the method of *in vitro* culture of plant or animal cells, tissue or organ on nutrient medium under aseptic controlled conditions.

Plant Cell Culture

Plant tissue culture is the technique used to grow an entire plant, organ, tissue or a single cell *in vitro* in the prepared nutrient medium. It can be used to study morphological, physiological or biological properties of plants and to manipulate the plant species to produce transgenic plants that yield desired biochemicals, high-yielding plants and insect/pest-resistant plants.

Plant Cell Culture Terminology

Explants

Explants are samples of parts or tissues such as roots, leaves, stem and pollen of the whole plant that are used to initiate the plant cell/tissue cultures.

Protoplasts

The naked cells whose cell walls are removed by digestion with enzymes such as cellulose and pectinase are called protoplasts. They can be prepared from explants and cells in suspensions. Protoplasts can be used to produce callus cultures. Callus is an unorganized, proliferated mass of differentiated plant cells normally formed by a wounding response.

Haploids

Haploids contain single gametophyte chromosomes (*i.e.*, *n*-chromosomes). They can be grown *in vitro* and are used in cell culture to produce whole plants.

Plasticity

The property of plants to regenerate lost or damaged parts and cell division from any existing part is called plasticity. This is very important to the survival of plants since they live over long periods of time and some parts may be damaged or lost because of various factors such as environmental conditions, predators and diseases.

Totipotency

The ability of each plant cell to express complete genetic information of the plant when provided with suitable conditions is called totipotency.

Types of Cultures

Callus Cultures

When explants are provided with favourable conditions and suitable media a mass of unorganized cells called **callus cultures** can be produced. During the callus culture cell differentiation is reversed. This is called dedifferentiation/redifferentiation.

Callus cultures require nutrient media containing plant growth hormones like auxins and cytokinins apart from the organic carbon source, vitamins and minerals. Sub-culturing (*i.e.*, providing fresh medium to the culture or transferring the culture into a fresh medium) is important because the callus cultures are slow growing and sub-culturing will provide a fresh supply of needed nutrients and hormones for effective growth.

Suspension Cultures

Callus cultures that are too soft and fragile are transferred to a liquid nutrient medium, where the cells multiply to produce a suspension in the medium; such cultures are called suspension cultures. A small sample of the callus culture is added to the liquid medium and incubated at specified temperature. The cells grow at a much faster rate than in the callus cultures hence it is important to subculture at frequent intervals. Suspension cultures are grown in conical flasks which provide a large surface area to volume ratio.

Meristem-Shoot Tip Culture

Shoot tips can be cultured in nutrient media to produce shoots which in turn can be rooted. This technique is used in micropropagation. Meristem culture (*i.e.*, culturing of extreme tip of shoot) is used for the production of virus free plants.

Microspore Cultures

Anthers containing pollens are collected and added to the nutrient medium, where the microspores (*i.e.*, pollens present inside the anthers) germinate to produce haploids. Alternatively, pollen is collected by cutting open the anthers, by homogenizing, or by centrifugation. This pollen is added to the nutrient medium and allowed to germinate to produce haploids. Embryo-like structures called embryoid were formed from another culture of *Datura innoxia* by **Guha** and **Maheshwari** (1964). Gynogenic haploids are produced by using infertilized ovules.

Embryo Cultures

Seeds and ovules are sterilized to remove microorganisms on their surfaces and the embryos are collected and then cultured to produce whole plants.

Sterile Transfer

Bio-safety cabinets are used to provide a clean environment for cell culture activities (like transfer of contents and sub-culturing) that require aseptic conditions. These cabinets are needed since microbial contamination can affect culture growth. They use HEPAA filters which can eliminate particles of sizes upto 0.3μ.

Cell/Tissue Culture Technique

Steps involved in cell/tissue culture are :

(i) The plant with desired cloning characteristics called the source plant is selected.

(ii) Explants are prepared from the source plant. The source can be any tissue such as leaf, stem and root.

(iii) Explants are surface sterilized to remove microorganisms. This can be done by using dis-infecting agents like absolute alcohol (70-80% v/v), phenol, sodium hypochlorite, or hydrogen peroxide. Initially the explants are washed with mild soap water to remove dirt then again several times with the disinfecting agent. Finally, the explants are rinsed several times with sterile water. This is done in the laminar flow cabinet or the bio-safety cabinets to ensure they are not contaminated again by the microorganisms.

(iv) The explants are transferred to vessels containing the nutrient medium and incubated to allow growth of tissue.

(v) Each new tissue gives rise to a new plant with identical genetic make up as the source plant.

Culture Medium

The culture medium should provide required nutritional supplements for the culture so that it can multiply and grow at faster rate. It should contain all elements that are required for a plant. The culture medium includes a wide range of components like a carbon source, nitrogen, iron, minerals, amino acids and vitamins. Some characteristics of the nutrients used in the culture medium are that they should be:

(i) Cheap and easily available.

(ii) Able to withstand high temperatures since, they have to be sterilized.

(iii) Able to provide the supplements to the culture, and

(iv) Be non-toxic.

The nutrients used in the culture medium can be broadly classified into the following classes.

Carbon Source

Carbohydrates are the most common source of carbon. Simple carbohydrates like sucrose, lactose and galactose are used as carbon source.

Vitamins

B-complex vitamins such as inositol, thiamine, nicotinic acid, pyridoxine, pantothenic acid, folic acid and riboflavin provide essential components like co-enzymes in various metabolic activities such as respiration, energy reactions and other metabolic pathways. B-complex vitamins also promote growth of plant tissues and organs.

Macronutrients

The components of the medium that should be provided in large amounts are called macro nutrients.

Nitrogen

It is available in different salt forms; hence, the convenient salt can be selected for the medium. Adding nitrogen-containing salts in some cases can affect the pH value. In that situation it is important to buffer the medium.

Phosphorus

This should be provided as phosphate. Salts like potassium phosphate and sodium phosphate are commonly used as phosphate sources in plant cell culture medium. Phosphates play an important role in energy transfer and enzyme regulation, and are present in vital molecules such as DNA.

Calcium

It plays roles as second messenger, enzyme co-factor, enzyme regulation, carbohydrate and amino acid mobilization, growth promoter and component of cell walls and cell membranes. Salts like calcium chloride and calcium nitrate are used as calcium source in the culture medium.

Magnesium

It acts as an enzyme co-factor, present in ribosomes and chlorophyll. Magnesium sulphate is added to culture medium as source of magnesium.

Potassium

It plays a vital role is cell homeostasis, enzyme regulation, cell division, chlorophyll synthesis and other physiological activities. Salts like potassium chloride, potassium nitrate and potassium orthophosphate can be used in culture media as potassium source.

Iron

It is essential for chlorophyll synthesis, energy production in photosynthesis and respiration. It can be provided to the culture medium by adding salts like ferrous sulphate.

Sulphur

It's functions as enzyme co-factor and is a component of amino acids and proteins. Magnesium sulphate is used as a common sulphur source in culture media.

Micronutrients

The culture medium requires some nutrients in very small amounts to help the growth and development of the cultures. These are called micro nutrients. Some of the micro nutrients added are boron, copper, cobalt, manganese, molybdenum, iodine and zinc.

Growth Regulators

Growth regulators are vital for the cell division and growth of plants. Examples are phytohormones like auxins and cytokinins.

Since, the cultures cannot produce these regulators on their own they are be added in the culture medium by dissolving first in a small amount of alcohol, acid or alkali, then, diluted with water. These hormones, both natural and synthetic, are available commercially.

Factors Affecting Cell Culture

Growth and maintenance of plant cell/tissue cultures are affected by various external factors such as those listed ahead.

Viscosity

Viscosity increases as the culture grows due to increased cell mass and accumulation of excretion products of the cells. This results in formation of foam which, in turn, affects culture growth adversely. Foaming can be prevented by adding anti-foaming agents like polyethylene glycols, polypropylene glycols and animal or plant derived fats to the medium.

Temperature

Cell culture requires temperatures between 23-29°C for optimum growth. Low temperatures cause fats to accumulate in the tissues. This is not desired. Temperatures lower or higher than the optimum range decrease the growth rate of the cells in cultures significantly.

Oxygen Supply

Oxygen is vital for culture growth, hence, a continuous supply must be provided. Stirring, aeration, and use of air-lift fermenters are some of the methods used to provide optimum oxygen to the cells in culture.

pH

Optimum pH is required for the growth of the culture. This is different for each plant specie. Most plants require pH 5-6 for optimum growth. pH in the medium may change due to production of organic acids during cell growth.

Micropropagation

This is a technique of *in vitro* propagation of plants which uses principles of conventional propagation and plant tissue culture. Micropropagation is used to produce a large number of genetically identical plants from a single parent plant under controlled conditions of temperature, nutrition and growth regulators. Further, the daughter plants can be manipulated as desired under these controlled conditions. This technique is developed from the plant tissue culture. Scientists believe that growing tissues *in vitro* under artificially controlled conditions can provide invaluable information about growth, development and other physiological functions of plants. In recent times micropropagation is the most commonly used technique for production of ornamental, flowering and other garden plants.

Stages of Micropropagation

There are five stages involved in the micropropagation technique.

Stage I Selecting and preparing the parent/donor plant.

Stage II Preparing a sterile culture.

Stage III Production of large number of daughter plantlets.

Stage IV Preparing daughter plantlets to plant in soil (also called rooting stage).

Stage V Transferring daughter plantlets to soil.

The stages are very much similar to the cell culture techniques discussed in the previous sections. The parent plant selected should be perfectly healthy so that the daughter plants can be healthy and can be produced with desired qualities. In the rooting stage the shoots with small roots are transferred to a large dish containing compost. This will help the plantlet to develop the root system and also to get used to the soil environment.

The whole process of micropropagation should be carried out in a sterile environment devoid of any microorganisms to ensure the success of the procedure. Conditions like temperature, humidity, lighting and nutrition should be controlled as specified and are vital for the success of the process. One of the disadvantages of growing the plants *in vitro* using techniques like micropropagation is that they will be sensitive to the environment and susceptible to pest and microbial attack. For example, the leaves will be sensitive to sunlight and chemicals since they lack protective wax coating.

Since, micropropagation is the most popular technique to produce plantlets on a large scale, for commercial purposes automation of the process was implemented to reduce cost of production. Cultures can be grown in bioreactors which provide more control of the conditions like temperature, nutrition and pH, thus, enhancing culture growth. Bioreactors can be modified according to the requirements to provide special features like providing nutrient medium at regular intervals, supplying nutrient medium as fine mist over the culture, removing the accumulated wastes from the bioreactor and adjusting pH. All these actions can be automated.

Protoplast Culture and Somatic Hybridization

The production of hybrid plants through the fusion of protoplasts of two different plant species/varieties is called **somatic hybridization** and such produced hybrids are known as **somatic hybrids.** The technique of somatic hybridization involves following steps:

(i) Isolation of protoplasts.
(ii) Fusion of the protoplasts of desired varieties/species.
(iii) Selection of hybrid cells.
(iv) Culture of hybrid cells and regeneration of hybrid plants from them.

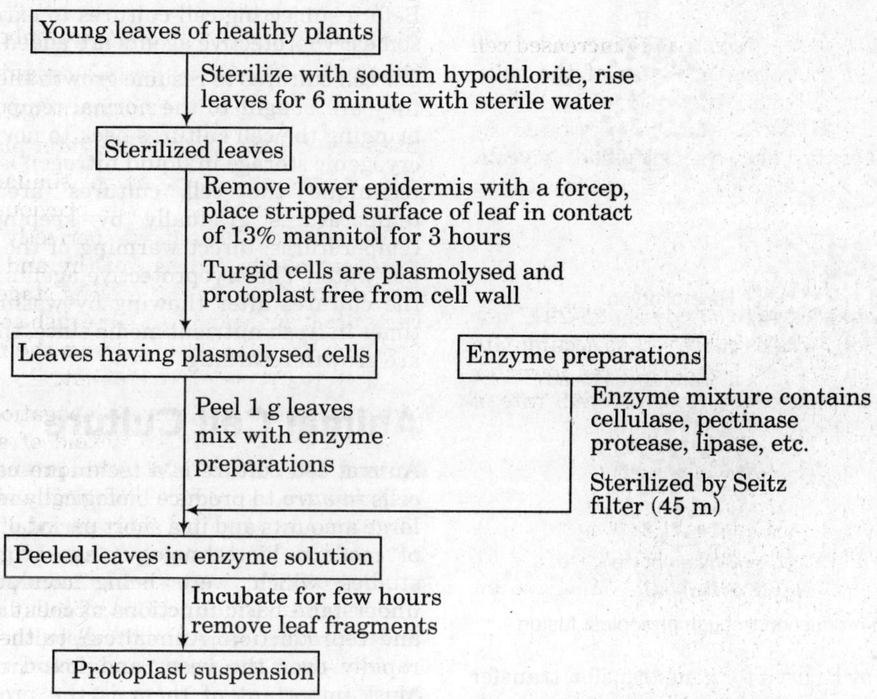

Fig. 36.1 Methods of isolation of protoplasts

Isolation of protoplasts is readily achieved by treating cells/tissues with a suitable mixture of cell wall degrading enzymes, usually pectinase and cellulase. The plant cells lacking cell wall are called **protoplasts.** Fusion between protoplasts of selected parents is induced by **Polyethylene Glycol** (PEG) solution or by a very brief high voltage electric current (electrofusion technique), when the protoplasts are cultured on a suitable medium, they regenerate cell walls and begin to divide to ultimately produce plantlets. Somatic hybrids can be identified by using several approaches.

(a) Somatic hybridization allows the production of hybrids between lines and species, that cannot be produced normally by means of sex4ual hybridization.

(b) Somatic hybridization produces asymmetric or symmetric hybrids or cybrids.

- **Asymmetric hybrids** have the full somatic complement of one fusion parent and a variable number of chromosomes from the other fusion parent.

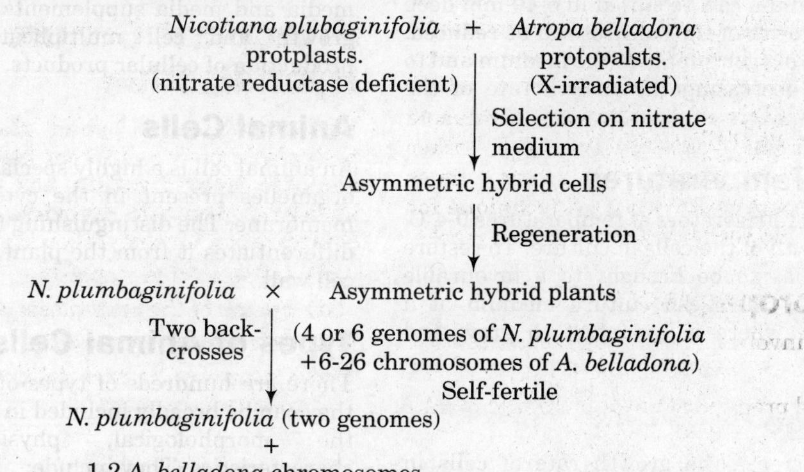

Fig. 36.2 A schematic representation of the production of asymmetric somatic hybrids between *N. plumbaginifolia* (contributes full genome) and *Atropa belladona* (contributes few chromosomes)

- **Symmetric hybrids** contain the somatic chromosome complement of both the fusion parents.
- **Cybrids** represents an extreme case in that the hybrids have the nuclear genome of only one fusion parent, but the cytoplasm of both the parents involved in fusion.

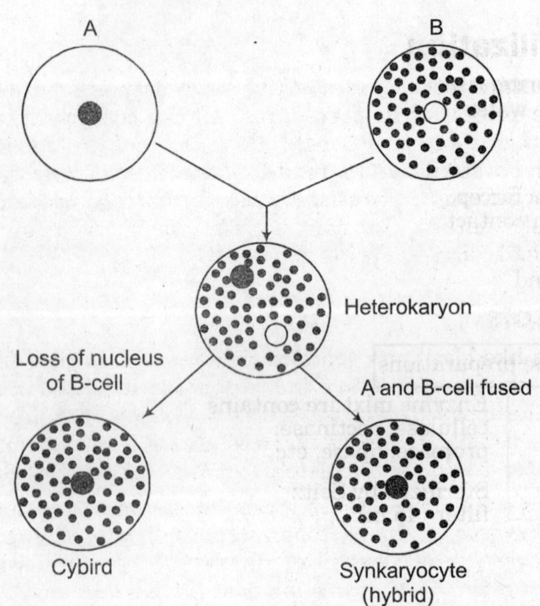

Fig. 36.3 Hybrid/cybrid production through protoplast fusion

(c) Somatic hybrids may be used for gene transfer, transfer of cytoplasm.

(d) They are used in production of useful allopolyploids.

(e) By somatic hybrids, there is a distinct possibility of development of new crop plants, *e.g.*, tomato.

Storage of Cell Cultures

Cell cultures can be stored for short periods by sub-culturing; this is also called maintenance, but to store the cultures for long periods of time other techniques are used.

Storage in Mineral Oil

The cultures on agar medium can be stored in 5-40 mm deep mineral oil so that the growth of the cultures can be reduced. Mineral oil decreases the oxygen supply to the medium and to the culture cells, thus, decreasing the growth rate of the cells/tissues.

Storage at Low Temperatures

Cultures can be stored in refrigerators at temperatures 0-4°C, which decreases the growth of the cells in culture. To restore the culture growth it has to be brought to a favourable temperature or added to the fresh culture medium at a favourable temperature, where it can start to grow and multiply.

Cryogenic Storage

Lower temperatures decrease the growth rate of cells in culture since biochemical reaction rates are lowered. Extremely low temperature like –196°C can virtually stop all the biochemical reactions in the cells thus, making it a very effective technique of storing cell cultures for a very long period of time. Such low temperatures can be achieved with liquid nitrogen. Liquid nitrogen is inert, *i.e.*, it doesn't affect or cause deterioration of the cultures, as does liquid oxygen. Before subjecting cell cultures to extreme low temperatures some cryoprotective agents are added.

For cell cultures to resume growth they should be viable once they are bought to the normal temperature. The process of bringing the cell cultures back to normal temperatures from cryogenic storage in liquid nitrogen is called thawing. In this technique the cell cultures are subjected to warm temperatures gradually by keeping the vials at room temperatures, direct warming of the vials, or immersing in hot water. The cryoprotective agents must be removed from the cultures after thawing by washing the culture several times in fresh nutrient media since, the cryoprotective agents are growth retarding.

Animal Cell Culture

Animal cell culture is a technique used for growing animal cells *in vitro* to produce biologically important compounds in large amounts and in a short period of time. It is a component of modern biotechnology that evolved from cell culture studies which were being conducted by biologists to understand basic functions of cells like growth, metabolism and reproduction. Animal cell culture technology improved rapidly over the years and found numerous applications. Most important of them is the production of biologically important compounds that have a wide range of applications in areas like pharmaceuticals, medicine, veterinary science and bio-medical science. Very large quantities of cell cultures in the range of hundreds to thousands of liters are employed to produce these compounds on a commercial scale.

Ross Harrison in 1907 was the first person to invent a technique to maintain animal cells in culture with the famous hanging drop technique; animal tissue is mounted on a glass slide sealed with cover slip where the tissue can be observed all the time. This also helped in the discovery that animal tissue can be grown from a single cell.

Later developments involved using different types of culture media and media supplements that helped to improve cell growth and cell multiplication, thus, increasing the production of cellular products.

Animal Cells

An animal cell is a highly specialized structure with different organelles present in the cytoplasm enclosed in the cell membrane. The distinguishing feature of the animal cell that differentiates it from the plant cell is the absence of a rigid cell wall.

Types of Animal Cells

There are hundreds of types of cells in an animal body but they can be broadly included in five types of tissues based on the morphological, physiological and metabolic characteristics. They include:

(a) Epithelial Tissue, *i.e.*, Squamous epithelium, cubical epithelium, columnar epithelium, ciliatory epithelium and secretory epithelium.

(b) Connective Tissue, *i.e.*, Areolar connective tissue, dense connective tissue, blood, elastic connective tissue and reticular connective tissue.

(c) Adipose Tissue.

(d) Muscle Tissue, *i.e.,* Cardiac muscle, skeletal muscle, smooth muscle.

(e) Nervous Tissue.

Cell Culture Laboratory

Design of the tissue culture laboratory is very important for the success of tissue culture since almost all the procedures dealing with cells require an aseptic environment. Cell culture laboratories should be separated from contaminating environments like microbiological laboratories or animal houses and should have restricted access so that only authorized personnel can enter and carry out procedures. These laboratories should provide clean, dust free environments by using air filters since making the whole lab sterile is practically impossible. Aseptic environments at the work place, *i.e.,* while carrying out cell culture procedures, can be provided by using laminar flow cabinets. The laboratory should have all the required equipment (refrigerator, freezer, oven, etc.), working bench to carry out the procedures, storage area, chemicals, air purifiers, air-conditioning, sinks with constant water supply, power supply and trash cans. The laboratory should be easy to clean and should have good drainage. Procedures such as sterile handling, incubation, preparation, washing and storage should be done in separate areas of the laboratory to avoid contamination.

Types of Animal Cultures

There are three types of animal cultures-tissue, cell and organ cultures.

Tissue Culture

The technique of *in vitro* cultivation of animal cells, tissues or organs in general is called tissue culture. Tissue culture can be further divided into cell culture and organ culture.

Cell Culture

These are cultures of cells obtained from some parent tissue. The cells do not have the biochemical properties of the parent tissue but they can be grown and multiplied when provided with optimum nutrition and optimum conditions.

Organ Culture

In vitro culture and growth of the whole or part of organs is called organ culture. This technique is used to maintain the organ *in vitro* allowing normal differentiation of the cells or reconstituting of the whole or part of organs while retaining all components of the tissue (anatomical, physiological and histological properties) thus resembling the organ *in vivo*. Organ culture is an extremely difficult procedure due to large experimental variation involved in the process.

Sterilization

Cell culture techniques demand strict aseptic environment for the success of its procedures. All the equipment, media and other components used in a cell culture laboratory should be sterilized to render them free of any type of microorganisms and resistant spores that can contaminate the cell culture. In this section sterilization of some individual components are discussed.

Vessels

Vessels like glassware (bottles, pipettes and culture flasks), plastic vessels, and caps of the vessels are sterilized in steps. First, the apparatus are washed several times with tap water while brushing to remove dirt and grease from the surfaces and water is drained completely to make them absolutely dry.

Pipettes are soaked in soap water overnight before cleaning with tap water to remove tough stains or traces of chemicals. Previously used glassware should be cleaned with a disinfectant immediately after use. In the next step, these apparatus are subjected to hot air sterilization at 160° C for 50-60 minutes using a hot air oven or moist heat sterilization at 121° C 15-20 minutes using an autoclave. The apparatus are then allowed to cool down to room temperature and should be used within 2-4 days.

Media

Autoclaving is the most commonly used technique for sterilization of culture media. Other liquid components such as chemicals and reagents can also be sterilized by autoclaving. The liquids are first poured in glass containers and sealed to prevent evaporation of liquids and contamination due to contact with the steam. Then, the sealed containers are placed in the autoclave for sterilization. Heat labile chemicals and culture media are sterilized by the membrane filtration technique.

Water

Water used in a cell culture laboratory has to be pure so it should be sterilized by advanced techniques such as reverse osmosis, distillation, deionization and carbon filtration. Ultra pure water can be obtained by using a combination of the above mentioned techniques. In the first stage, water is subjected to reverse osmosis or distillation, secondly, the organic and inorganic compounds are removed from the water by carbon filtration. Ionized inorganic materials are then removed from the water in the third stage by deionization and in the final stage, microorganisms are eliminated by micro pore filtration.

Requirements for Cell Growth

Culture Media

The cells in culture media require a suitable environment and optimum nutrition that are similar to *in vivo* for their survival, growth and multiplication. Culture media not only provide nutrients that are not synthesized by the cells but also optimum physical conditions like pH that are essential for the survival of cells. Factors such as temperature, oxygen and light should be controlled externally.

Based on functions the culture media can be broadly classified into four groups.

Media for immediate/short time survival of cells This media contains an instant energy source and maintains optimum osmotic pressure needed for survival of cells. The commonly used ingredients in this type of media are inorganic salts and glucose, for example, balanced salt solution.

Media for prolonged survival of cells This media should contain nutrients and supplements that cannot be produced by the cells in culture– nutrients which are essential for their long term survival such as amino acids, vitamins, growth factor and hormones. For short time survival eagle's media is commonly used.

Media for long term growth of cells This is a complex media that can provide supplements required for long term growth and multiplication of the cells. Included are enzymes, co-enzymes and serum proteins.

Media for specialized functions This is also a complex media that serves special nutrients to the cells in a culture, depending on the cell types used (*e.g.,* oestrogen for the cells of female sex organs and vitamin-A for ciliated epithelial cells). Since, the ingredients vary for each type of cell the media is prepared accordingly. Based on method of preparation culture media can be classified into two types.

Natural media This was the most commonly used culture media in the past. Natural ingredients like blood and tissues are used for the preparation of the media. There are two types of natural ingredients generally used in the preparation of natural media, namely, plasma and biological fluids.

Plasma Plasma clots were commonly used in the past for the culture of small tissues. Plasma is one of the constituents of animal blood and is prepared from the blood collected from different types of animals.

Biological fluids Serum is the clear liquid that is left out when the blood clots. It is prepared by allowing whole blood to clot and collecting the clear fluid that is separated from the clot. Serum is the most commonly used biological fluid used in the preparation of natural culture media because it contains proteins, growth factors, hormones, trace elements and fatty acids, which can enhance growth rate of the cells in culture. Culture media can also be prepared using other biological fluids like embryo extracts and amniotic fluid.

Synthetic media This type of media is prepared using different chemicals that can provide optimum nutrition and physical environment for the cells in culture, thus, promoting the cell growth. Defined media is prepared using definite amounts of chemicals in the media similar to those present in the natural ingredients. Synthetic media should also include vitamins, enzymes, amino acids, trace elements, buffers, antibiotics, indicators and antioxidants. Natural media contain all of these ingredients, so, in some cases, serum is included in the synthetic media instead of adding all the above mentioned ingredients.

Stages in Cell Culture

Cell Sources

Cells for culture can be obtained directly from organs or tissues but common sources are cell banks which are either owned by private businesses or government. The advantages of obtaining cells from cell banks are that they would have been subjected to viability and quality control tests. A protocol has to be followed when new cells are obtained by the laboratory from cell banks or any other external sources. The new cells should be quarantined and quality control tests performed before they can be added to the main cell stock of the laboratory.

Primary Culture

Primary culture is the process of establishing the culture by collecting cells directly from the animal source. Different types of cells can be collected from the animal source to establish the primary culture such as normal cells, cells from a tumour, from adults, or from embryos. Cells from different species can be used depending on the type of cell culture product. Primary cells can be obtained by one of the following processes.

Mechanical Disaggregation Mechanical disaggregation of cells from the source, involving:

- **(a)** Collecting the tissue from the animal and washing to remove blood and other unwanted tissues.
- **(b)** Mincing the tissue.
- **(c)** Rinsing the tissue with sterile BSS solution.
- **(d)** Centrifuging to collect cells.
- **(e)** Seeding the cells in large flasks with nutrient media.
- **(f)** Incubating at approximately 37°C to allow growth of primary cells.

Enzymatic Disaggregation Enzymatic treatment of the animal source is usually done with enzymes that can disaggregate the tissue into individual cells. EDTA is used since, it chelates Mg^{2+} and collagenase is often used as well. Enzymes like trypsin and pronase are used for this purpose. This process involves:

- **(a)** Collecting the tissue from the animal and washing to remove blood and other unwanted tissues.
- **(b)** Mincing the tissue.
- **(c)** Treating the tissue with 0.25% w/v trypsin for 30-40 minutes at 37°C.
- **(d)** Adding serum to neutralize trypsin.
- **(e)** Collecting the cells.
- **(f)** Seeding the cells in flasks containing nutrient media.
- **(g)** Incubating at 37°C to allow growth of primary cells.

Growing Cells

Allowing the cells to grow out of the animal tissue.

Types of Cells

There are two types of cells used in culture based on their growth characteristics. They are: adherent cells and suspension cells.

Adherent Cells

The cells are adhesive and depend on a substrate, matrix, micro-carriers, or other supporting material for their growth and development. These cells require treatment with the enzyme trypsin before they can be sub-cultured since the cells bond with the substrate.

Suspension Cells

These cells are non-adhesive or less adhesive and do not depend on the substrate or other supporting material for their growth and development. They can be maintained while held in suspension. The suspension cells can be sub-cultured easily by dilution and do not require trypsinization.

Stages of Growth

The growth of cells in culture follows a similar pattern as that of microbial growth in a fermentation tank. Cell growth can be classified into three phases or stages, *i.e.,* lag phase, log phase and stationary phase

Assessing Cell Growth

Cell growth should be assessed at regular intervals during the cell culture process so that if growth rate is low appropriate steps can be taken. Counting the number of cells in specified amount of sample is the effective way of assessing the growth rate of cells. This can be done using two types of methods.

Direct Method

The cell numbers are directly counted using a hemocytometer.

Indirect Method

The cell numbers are counted indirectly by measuring the DNA and protein in the sample to determine the number of cells present.

Secondary Culture/Subculture

This is a technique employed to maintain the cells in logarithmic phase in the culture so that they continue to grow and increase in number in a way not possible after a stage, since growth is retarded due to accumulation of wastes or to exhaustion of nutrients in the culture medium. The cells can be sub-cultured during the later stages of the lag phase. Sub-culturing is also used to obtain a culture with a homogenous population of cells from the existing primary culture. Such cultures are very useful to scale up the cell culture procedures to an industrial level and to carry out experiments on one type of cell more easily. Sub-culturing can be done either by adding fresh nutrient media to the cells in primary culture or by adding the cells from a primary culture to the fresh nutrient media.

Cell Line Preservation

Homogeneous cell lines are obtained from primary cultures and subsequent secondary cultures and the entire process is not only laborious and time consuming, but also, expensive. Cell lines are also susceptible to microbial contamination, hence, it is absolutely necessary to take appropriate steps to preserve them for later use and to prevent loss due to microbial contamination.

Cryopreservation

This is a technique of preserving the cell line at very low temperatures. At such temperatures cell metabolism is reduced significantly, but cells retain their viability when they are thawed.

Cell Banks

This is the collection and preservation of cell lines in liquid nitrogen such that their viability and other characteristics are not altered. Cell banks provide a continuous supply of cells for various procedures in the laboratory.

Cloning of a Cell Line

Cell lines are susceptible to genetic variation over the course of time. There is the possibility of growth of unwanted cells which can affect the growth and viability of the original cell lines. Cloning of cell lines is the effective way of dealing with the above mentioned situation as large number of identical cells can be produced in a short period of time. Cell lines can be cloned using three techniques.

Soft Agar Technique

This technique is used for cloning suspension cultures.

Cloning Rings Technique

This is the technique used for cloning adherent cells, where the cells are allowed to grow in conventional vessels. Small, hollow, sterile stainless steel rings called cloning rings are used to isolate each of the discrete colonies.

Limiting Dilution Technique

This is the most common technique which can be used for both suspension cells and adherent cell lines. Three dilutions of cell suspensions are prepared. Cell suspension is added to a 96 well tray followed by medium and the process is repeated for each of the three dilutions. The 96 well trays are then incubated at a suitable temperature to allow the growth of cells. The wells which show growth of colonies of single type cells are selected and further sub-cultured to produce large numbers of similar cells which can then be maintained by cryopreservation.

Organ Culture

The process of maintaining the whole organs *in vitro* without affecting its properties is called organ culture. Organ culture can be carried out by using the following methods.

Watch Glass

A clot is prepared on a watch glass using a mixture of chicken plasma and chick embryo extract. The animal tissue is placed on the clot and the watch glass is then placed in a petri dish containing moist cotton wool. The petri dish is covered and incubated at 37°C.

Single Slide

This technique is also called **Maximow single slide technique** where the organs are dissected and treated with HBSS. Chicken plasma and chicken embryo extract are added on a cover slip mixed and allowed to clot. The organ is added to the clot formed on the cover slip. The cover slip with the clot and the organ is mounted on a Maximow slide. The sides of the cover slip are sealed with wax and the slide is placed in the incubator at 37°C.

Agar Gel

The organs, after treating with HBSS, are placed in a watch glass containing agar gel along with chick embryo extract, chicken serum, **Gey solution** and **Tyrode solution.** The watch glass is then sealed with glass lid using wax and incubated at 37°C.

Cell Culture on a Large Scale

Cell culture experiments in the laboratory are useful to examine morphological, physiological and functional properties of the cells. But for bulk production of cell culture products such as vaccines, antibodies and hormones automated techniques are required. Suspension cultures are easy to scale up. Large scale cell cultures require slight modifications of the procedures used in laboratory scale.

Media

The medium should be very rich in nutrients since the cell density in large scale cell culture is very high and the nutrients are used up quickly.

Oxygen

The cells require oxygen continuously.

pH

Optimum pH for most of the cultures is 7-7.4 and this can be maintained by carbon dioxide-bicarbonate present in the medium as well as phosphates (also present in the medium). If these natural buffers fall short, pH buffers can be used.

Temperature

In large scale cell culture procedure temperatures higher than optimum range are produced that can adversely effect the growth of cells in culture, so it is very important to control the temperature. This can be done through internal heat exchangers which circulate cold water through cylinders or coiled tubes immersed in the medium.

Culture Vessels

Large volumes of cell suspensions can be handled by using large fermentation tanks and large roller bottles, depending on the type of cells being used.

Sterilization

On laboratory scales most of the equipment and vessels can be sterilized easily by autoclaving but it is difficult to autoclave large culture vessels and other equipment. *In situ* sterilization is employed for this purpose, done by pumping steam at high pressure over the surface of the vessel.

Large Scale Culture of Adherent Cells

Adherent cells are difficult to scale up since, they have to be trypsinized first. They require special vessels for culture and have special nutritional and physical requirements. The culture vessels used for large scale cell culture of adherent cells are considered below.

Roller Bottles

These are cylindrical plastic bottles of volumes in the range of 1000-1500 mL. Roller bottles provide large surface areas for the cells, as well as, good gas exchange compared to conventional culture vessels. Large numbers of bottles are stacked and placed horizontally on rollers, rotated at a specific rpm, and incubated. Roller bottles are also called Roux bottles.

The surface area of the roller bottles can be increased by filling with sterile spiral plastic film or with sterile small glass tubes.

Multi-plate Unit

This consists of flat chambers placed together and interconnected to allow transfer of culture medium between the units; the apertures in the chambers allow gas transfer. The multi-plate unit is also called cell factory.

Fermentation tanks which can support adherent dependant cells by allowing a substratum to be in suspension are generally used for adherent cell culture. Glass bead bioreactors contain small glass beads packed in the column through which the medium passes freely. The glass beads act as substratum over which the cells can grow by adhering to them.

Large Scale Culture of Suspension Cells

Suspension cultures are much easier to scale up since, what's involved is increasing the culture volume in appropriate culture vessels. Bioreactors/fermentation tanks are the most commonly used culture vessels for large scale cell culture procedures.

Stirred Tank Bioreactors

These are large steel fermentation tanks which can handle culture volumes of up to 8000 L. They are provided with either a mechanical or magnetic stirrer to ensure homogenous mixing and aeration of the contents.

Air-lift Bioreactors

These are bioreactors which do not have stirrers. The stirring action is provided by the continuous pumping of air through a sparger located at the bottom.

Membrane Bioreactors

These are generally used for treatment of waste water due to their ability to increase the rate of separation of solid wastes from the water. This property can be utilized in cell culture to improve the concentration of cells. Membrane bioreactors are also well suited to handle very large volumes of cell suspensions.

Safety in Cell Culture Laboratory

Cell culture laboratories handle harmful materials like chemicals, reagents, blood products, other animal cell products, and viruses. Some of them are carcinogenic and even classified as Biologically Hazardous Materials by the regulating authorities. Hence, it is very important that the cell culture laboratory personnel follow strict rules and protocols to ensure their personnel safety, safety of their co-workers, and thus, ensuring safety of the laboratory on the whole. Information about safety, guidelines and regulations should be made available to the personnel. **Good Laboratory Practice** (GLP) guidelines should be followed in the cell culture laboratory.

Some of the safety measures taken in the cell culture laboratory are:

Personnel Safety Measures

The personnel working in the cell culture laboratory should:

(a) Attend safety and precautions training sessions before starting the employment.

(b) Wear protective clothing like lab coat and disposable gloves to protect hands when entering the lab and should remove them before leaving the lab.

(c) Clean hands with soap or specified disinfectant before entering and leaving the lab.

(d) Wash the body parts immediately with water if contacted with harmful materials and bio-hazardous materials.

(e) Avoid eating and storing food in the laboratory.

Safe Handling of Equipment

Equipment such as glassware, autoclave, oven, centrifuge and sharp equipment like syringe and scalpels, should be handled with caution to ensure safety.

Handling Bio-hazardous Materials

Cell culture laboratories contain various bio-hazardous materials. Some steps taken to handle such materials safely are:

(a) Use of gloves while handling such materials to avoid direct contact since they are harmful.

(b) Avoidance of spilling and production of aerosols.

(c) Availability of disinfectants, decontaminants for cellular, chemical and microbial contaminants at all times in the laboratory to be used in case of spillages.

(d) Proper cleaning of work benches before and after handling of cell products.

(e) Transferring of cellular and microbial products for sub-culturing only in bio-safety hood.

Waste Disposal

Cell culture laboratory wastes should be disposed of appropriately since they contain harmful equipment like needles, broken glass, bio-hazardous materials and harmful chemicals. Other recommended practices include:

(i) Chemical wastes should be disposed in labelled containers before disposal.

(ii) Glassware should be treated with bleach solution immediately after their use.

(iii) Broken glassware, syringes, needles, other sharp objects should be treated with bleach before disposing in containers marked sharps.

(iv) Bio-hazard wastes should be disposed in special containers marked bio-hazard wastes.

(v) Disposable equipment and gloves, among others, should be sterilized prior to disposal.

(vi) Mixing of incompatible chemicals should be avoided even after disposal as this may result in dangerous reactions.

(vii) Metal cans should not be used for waste disposal; explosive resistant plastic containers should be used.

Transgenic Organisms

Extensive use of biotechnology has been made to modify both plants and animals used in **agriculture**. This frequently involves the development of transgenic plants and animals through the insertion of genes from other species into their genomes. Improvements to commercial crops include disease, drought, insect and pesticide resistance; improved nutrient content, extended fruit shelf life and pharmaceutical delivery.

Methods of Gene Transfer

Vectors containing the genes we want, must be incorporated into living cells so that they can be replicated or expressed. The cells receiving the vector are called **host cells,** and once they have successfully incorporated the vector they are said to be **transformed.** Vectors are large molecules, which do not readily cross cells membranes, so the membranes must be made permeable in some way. There are different ways of doing this.

(i) **Plant Tumours** This method has been used successfully to transform plant cells, which are perhaps the hardest to do. The gene is first inserted into the **Ti plasmid** of the soil bacterium *Agrobacterium tumefaciens,* and then plants are infected with the bacterium. The bacterium inserts the Ti plasmid into the plant cells chromosomal DNA and causes a 'crown gall' tumour. These tumour cells can be cultured in the laboratory and whole new plants grown from them by micro-propagation. Every cell of these plants contains the foreign gene.

(ii) **Gene Gun** This extraordinary technique fires microscopic gold particles coated with the foreign DNA at the cells using a compressed air gun. It is designed to overcome to problem of the strong cell wall in plant tissue, since the particles can penetrate the cell wall and the cell and nuclear membranes, and deliver the DNA to the nucleus, where it is sometimes expressed.

(iii) **Micro-injection** A cell is held on a pipette under a microscope and the foreign DNA is injected directly into the nucleus using an incredibly fine micro-pipette. This method is used where there are only a very few cells available, such as fertilized animal egg cells. In the rare successful cases, the fertilized egg is implanted into the uterus of a surrogate mother and it will develop into a normal animal, with the DNA incorporated into the chromosomes of every cell.

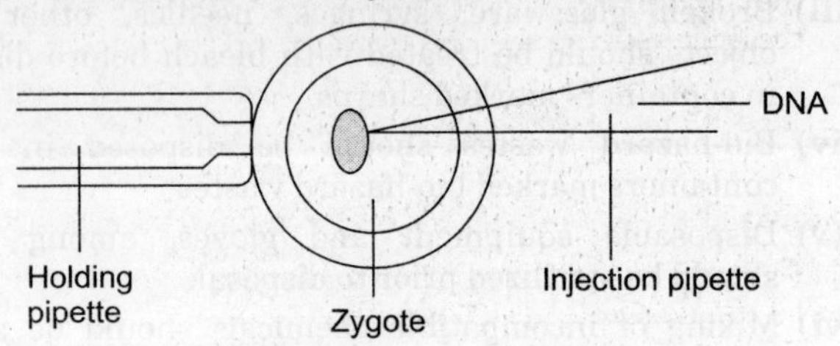

Fig. 36.4 Micro-injection

(iv) **Liposomes** Vectors can be encased in **liposomes,** which are small membrane vesicles. The liposomes fuse with the cell membrane (and sometimes and nuclear membrane too), delivering the DNA into the cell. This works for many types of cells, but is particularly useful for delivering genes to cells *in vivo* (such as in gene therapy).

Transgenic Plants

Transgenic approaches are beginning to be widely used with plants. Thus, for example, crop plants have been developed that have transgenic resistance to glycophosphate, the active herbicidal ingredient of the weed killer, roundup. Glycophosphate inhibits an enzyme needed for synthesis of amino acids, without which plants cannot grow. A bacterial gene that confers resistance to glycophosphate has been transfected into crop plants, making them resistant. A Ti plasmid vector was used for transfection of cultured tobacco cells, which were then used to regenerate plants. These plants will survive selectively, while weeds will not, in a field sprayed with glycophosphate. Similar procedures have generated 'Roundup-ready' soyabeans. Another example is the expression in corn plants of a toxin from *Bacillus thuringiensis* that kills insect pests.

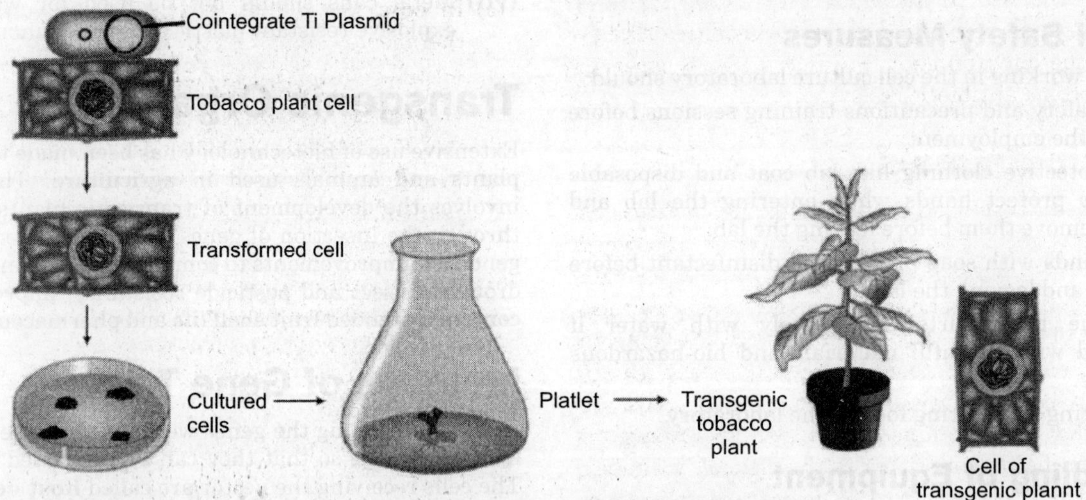

Fig. 36.5 The process of transgenic plant production

Commercial Production

A variety of transgenic plants are in varying stages of experimentation or commercial production. For example, frost-resistant and salt-tolerant plants that can be grown in otherwise hostile environments are being pursued vigorously. In some cases, unexpected new problems are encountered with genetically engineered crops. One such case is the *Flavr savr* tomato, which remains firm for a much longer time after ripening because the activity of the enzyme polygalacturonase has been greatly reduced by expression of an antisense RNA that blocks gene expression by combining with the *m*RNA. The gene encoding the antisense RNA was inserted into the plant chromosome along with a kanamycin resistance marker gene. Their approach worked the tomatoes can remain on the vines longer and are less susceptible to bruising in transit.

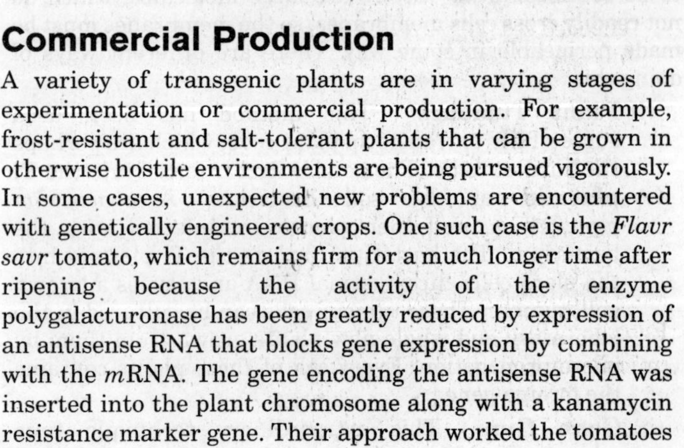

Examples of Transgenic Plants

(a) ***Bt* cotton** Pest-resistant, herbicide-tolerant and high yielding plant. It is also resistant to bollworm infestations.

(b) ***Flavr* savr tomato** With delayed ripening and better nutrient quality.

(c) **Golden rice** Vitamin-A rich rice.

(d) **Potato** With higher protein content.

(e) **Corn, brinjal** Insect resistance provided.

(f) **Soyabean, maize** Herbicide resistance provided.

Genetics

- *Flavr savr* is the result of antisense RNA technology.
- Antisense construct of the gene encoding polygal acturnase show drastically reduced expression of PG in transgenic tomato and slower fruit softening.
- The antisense **construct of ACC synthase** gene was transferrd in tomato, which reduced ethylene production to <1% of the normal.

Flavr savr

Biotechnology

- In tamato, enzyme **polygalacturonase** (PG) is responsible for softening of fruits by degrading pectin of cell wall.
- The expression of polygalacturonase has been reduced in *Flavr savr* which lead to improvement in flavour, **longer self-life** (2 weeks) and **total soluble solids.**

Physiology

- The antisense RNA technology has been used to surpress **ethylene biosynthesis.**
- The fruits remain green and hard on the plants so that they accumulate more sugar and organic acids that make the fruit sweeter and tasty.
- The new variriety called 'Endless summer' remain fresh for about four weeks.

Environmental Concerns

In many cases, there are also concerns that the transgenes could get into other types of plants. This could, for example generate herbicide resistant weeds. In addition, many of the selective procedures involved in generating recombinant vectors involve the use of antibiotic resistance. There is concern that plasmids carrying antibiotic resistance could be released into the environment causing various types of pathogens to become antibiotic resistant.

Transgenic Animals

Methods have been developed that allow cloned genes to be incorporated into germ line cells of a number of animal species. Most of the pioneering work has been done with mice, but transgenic pigs, sheep, goats and cows have also been developed. The first step is to transfect the gene in question into an embryonal stem cell (ES cell), which is then injected into an early embryo. Embryonal stem cells are cultured cells that have retained totipotent developmental potential and can become any part of the animal, including the germ cells, when injected into a sufficiently early embryo. The resulting chimeric animals are then bred with wild type mice, creating heterozygotes for the transgene. Mating of two of the heterozygotes can then generate 1/4 of the offspring that are homozygous for the transgene. In most cases, this process generates a transgenic animal that expresses the transfected foreign gene without any adverse effects on normally expressed genes from its own genome. Alternatively, it is sometimes possible to obtain random genomic incorporation of genetic material injected directly into zygotes.

Agricultural Animals

Biotechnology uses in livestock animals include: the making of transgenic animals for protein production and organ donation, *in vitro* fertilization and embryo splitting used to propagate animals with highly desirable characteristics, and the use of bovine growth hormone (BGH)(first expressed in *E. coli*) to increase milk production.

Examples of Transgenic Animals

(a) In **cow, sheep** and **goat**, transgenic varieties show therapeutic usage. Their transgenic varieties provide human proteins in their milk.

(b) In **transgenic pigs**, organ transplantation without risk of rejection is possible.

(c) **Transgenic fishes** (common carp, catfish, salmon, goldfish, etc.) contain hGH. These attain a size twice to that shown by the non-transgenic fishes.

(d) **Transgenic mouse** contains a human gene that causes breast cancer. This enables the scientists to study the very early development of cancer.

Methodology

Method for constructing transgenic animals involves two main steps:

(a) Construction of gene disruptions in a cell clone the gene on a cloning vector that contains the *tk* gene which encoded sensi-tivity to the chemical ganciclovir à insert the *neo* resistance gene into your cloned gene of interest (gene X) introduce construct into cultured cells from a mouse embryo there are three fates of the tranfected construct:

- Homologous recombination with the wild type gene on the chromosome *via* a double crossover (top in figure) cells will have a chromosomal copy of gene X which has been disrupted by the *neo* gene.
- Ectopic (Random insertion into the chromosome (middle in figure) a cells will have a chromosomal copy of gene X which has been disrupted by the *neo* gene as well as a wild type copy; also the *tk* gene and any other vector sequences will be present on the chromosome.

- **No insertion (bottom in figure) à cells will have only wild type gene X and therefore, no *neo* resistance.**

The cells in which homologous recombination with wild type gene X on the chromosome occurred will be selected for because the are resistant to *neo*. The insertion at an ectopic site will be selected against because they have the *tk* gene which renders them sensitive to the chemical ganciclovir. No insertion at all will be selected against because the cells are *neo* sensitive.

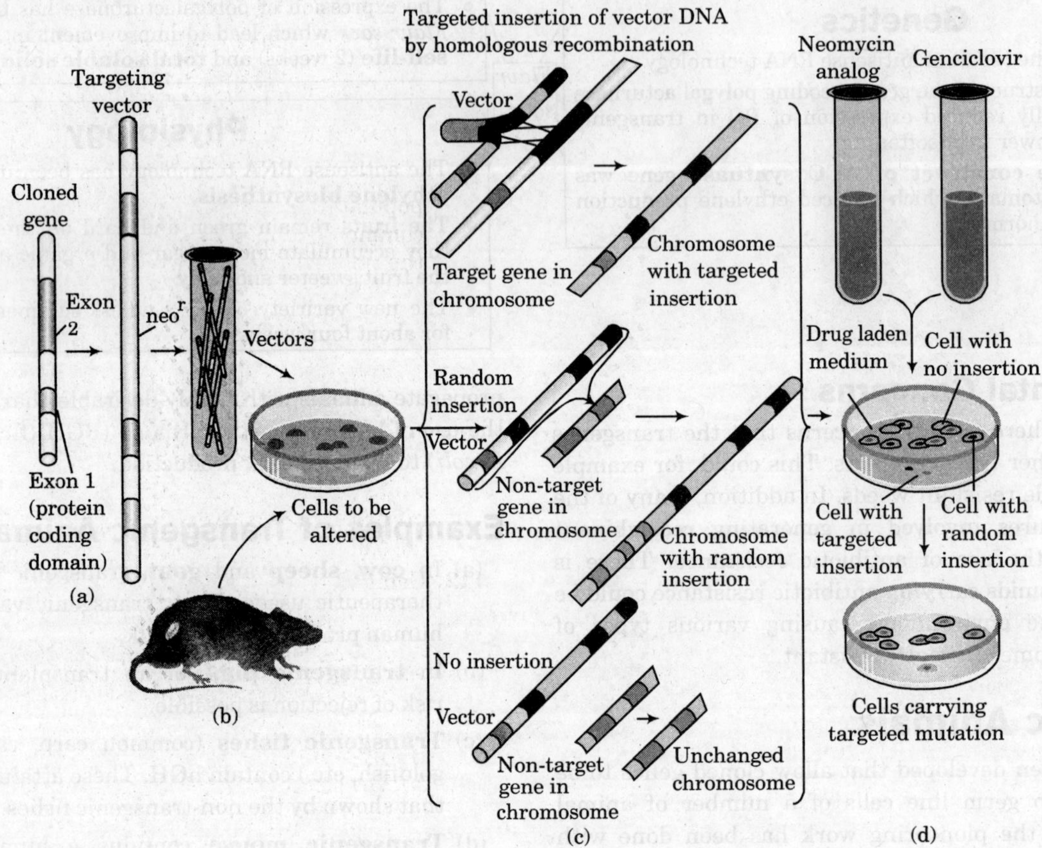

Fig. 36.6 The process of transgenic animal production

(b) **Construction of transgenic mouse carrying the mutated gene from A After disrupting a gene in the manner described in (1), the disrupted gene (m) can be put back into an animal as follows: Note that the disruption above was done in cells that came from an agouti (AA) mouse. Inject the cells (embryonic stem cells) from above into a blastocyst stage embryo from a non-agouti mouse (aa) *in vitro* (now the embryo is a mosaic of two different cell types AAMm and aaMM transplant embryo into a non-agouti pregnant mouse à examine progeny for agouti patches indicating that some of the AAMm cells survived a breed agouti mice to homozygocity for the m locus, screening for mm in candidate mice by PCR.**

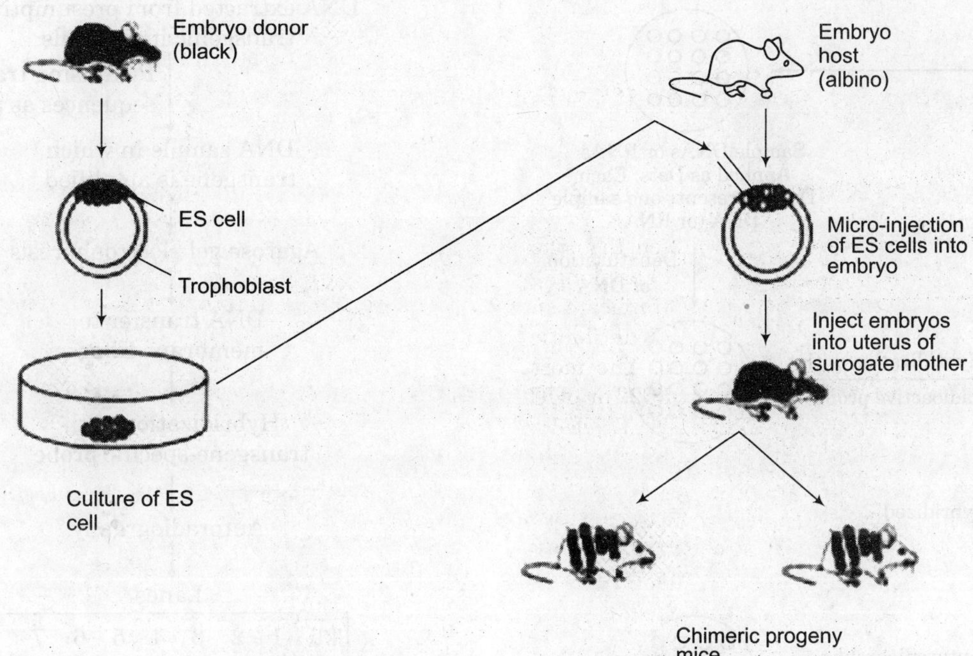

Fig. 36.7 Process of chimeric male mouse synthesis

Growth Hormone

In one the pioneering studies on transgenic animals, a mouse with multiple copies of a rat growth hormone gene was found to grow to a much larger size than a normal mouse. However, attempts to produce larger pigs with human growth hormone were less successful.

Use of Milk Gene Promoters

One very interesting application of transgenic animals has been to link genes coding for desired proteins to promoters for milk protein genes in transgenic animals. This results in the desired protein being produced in the milk of the animal, sometimes in quite large amounts. These techniques are beginning to be used, particularly in sheep and goats, to generate rather large amounts of foreign proteins in the milk. One of the advantages is that correct glycosylation of the proteins occurs in these systems.

Molecular Approaches to Diagnosis and Strain Identification

After the insertion of gene it is essential to identify the transgenic animals and plants and to confirm that they have stably integrated transgene, *i.e.*, they are transcribed and produced the protein. A number of techniques used for this purpose are:

Colony Hybridization

Used to identify bacterial colonies having specific DNA sequences. In this technique developed by **Grunstein** and **Hogness** (1975) given sequence is represented by the probe used in hybridization experiment. The colonies of master plate or replica plated into nitrocellulose filter membrane placed on agar medium. The filter is hybridized with radioactive probe and the colonies whose DNA hybridize with probe are detected by autoradiography.

Southern Hybridization

The DNA-DNA hybridization discovered by EM Southern. DNA is fragmented by mechanical shearing or restriction endonuclease and subjected to electrophoresis using polyacrylamide or agarose gel. Marker DNA fragments of known sizes are run in a separate line which permit an accurate determination of size of an unknown DNA molecule by interpolation. In many situations it is critical to detect and identify DNA fragments in a transgenics so in these animals the DNA fragment Ist denatured subjected to DNA probe. The membrane having DNA-DNA hybrid is now placed in close contact with an X-ray film.

Dot Blot Technique

Useful in detecting the presence of sequence being transferred in a number of suspected transgenic individuals and of specific transgene *m*RNA in a several such individuals or in different tissues of a single individual. Southern hybridization may be used for dot blot positive individuals to derive more precise information.

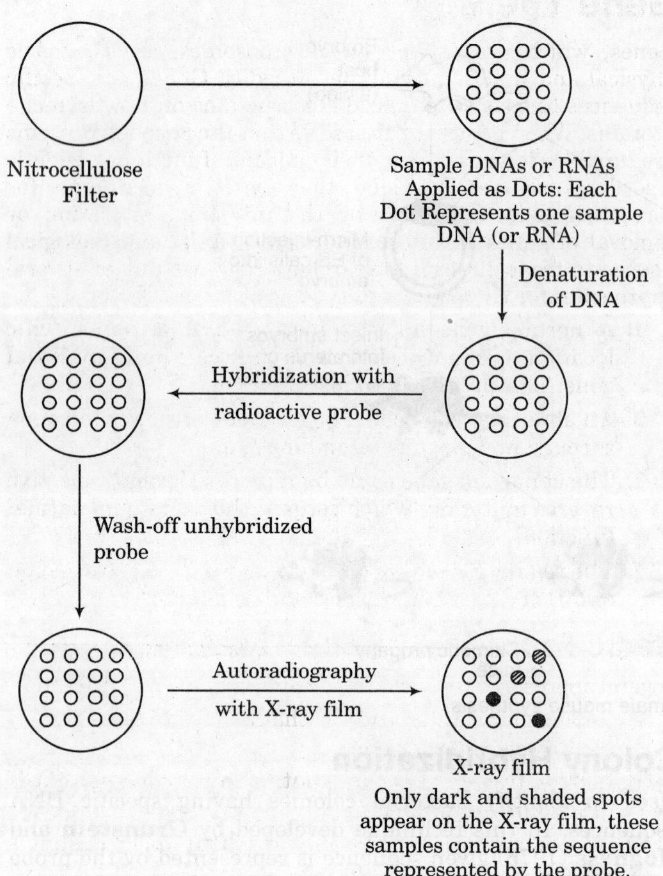

Fig. 36.8 A representation of the dot blot technique for detecting the presence of a specific sequence in transgenic organism

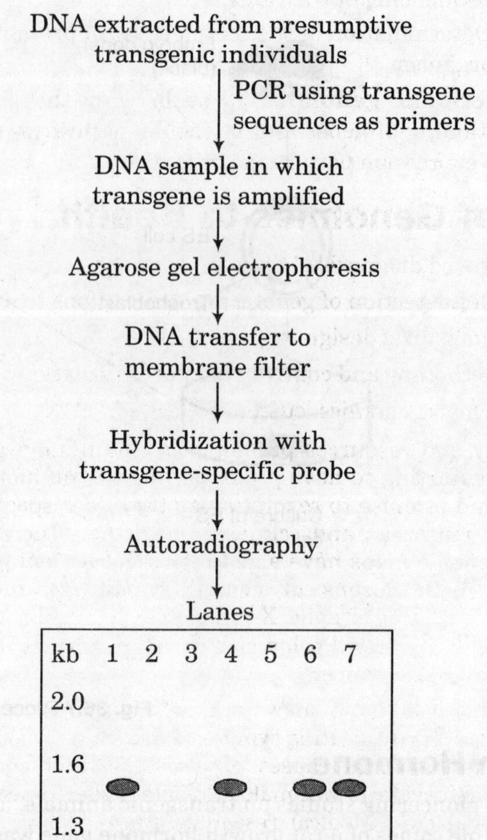

Fig. 36.9 A representation of the use of PCR for the identification of transgenic animals. Kb, kilobase; Lane 1, transgene construct used for transfection (control); Lanes 2-7, PCR amplified DNAs from presumptive transgenic animals

Transgenic organisms are easily identified when they produced a distinct phenotypic effect. A more general approach utilize either dot blot technique or polymerase chain reaction amplification. The samples which test positive for hybridization with probe are from suspected transgenic organisms. In many laboratories PCR is routinely used as first screen for transgenic organisms.

The integration of transgene into the genome of organisms is confirmed by southern hybridization. The organisms which give positive assay with southern hybridization an are confirmally transgenic organisms. The *m*RNA produced by transgenic organisms is easily detected if produces a unique sequence and subjected to RNA dot blot hybridization with a radioactive probe specific for the transgene. Detection of proteins produced by these genes are based on antibody specificity or enzymatic properties. Specific antibodies can be employed for ELISA. The expression of transgene must be allowed in two or more unrelated transgenic lines of the given animal.

Genomics

Rapid progress in genome science and a glimpse into its potential applications have spurred observers to predict that biology will be the foremost science of the 21st century. Technology and resources generated by the human genome project and other genomics research are already having a major impact on research across the life sciences.

The term 'genomics' was coined by **Thomas H Roderick** (1987) for mapping and sequencing to analyze the structure and organization of genomes. It includes sequencing of genomes, determination of the complete set of proteins encoded by an organism and the functioning of genes and metabolic pathways, in an organism. Thus, genomics not only deals with the determination of the genetic information present in an organism but also with understanding the mechanism by which this information is used by the organism.

Genomics can be divided into two domains :

1. **Structural genomics:** It includes:
   (i) Construction of high resolution genetic and physical maps.

(ii) Sequencing of the genome.

(iii) Determination of the complete set of proteins in an organism.

2. **Functional genomics** It deals with the study of functioning of genes and metabolic pathways, *i.e.*, the gene expression patterns in organism.

Role of Genomics to Health

(i) Improved diagnosis of disease.

(ii) Earlier detection of genetic pre-dispositions to disease

(iii) Rational drug design.

(iv) Gene therapy and control systems for drugs.

(v) Pharmacogenomics 'custom drugs'.

Technology and resources promoted by the human genome project are starting to have profound impacts on biomedical research and promise to revolutionize the wider spectrum of biological research and clinical medicine. Increasingly detailed genome maps have aided researchers seeking genes associated with dozens of genetic conditions, including myotonic dystrophy, fragile X-syndrome, neurofibromatosis types 1 and 2, inherited colon cancer, **Alzheimer's disease** and familial breast cancer.

On the horizon is a new era of molecular medicine characterized less by treating symptoms and more by looking to the most fundamental causes of disease. Rapid and more specific diagnostic tests will make possible earlier treatment of countless maladies. Medical researchers also will be able to devise novel therapeutic regimens based on new classes of drugs, immunotherapy techniques, avoidance of environmental conditions that may trigger disease, and possible augmentation or even replacement of defective genes through gene therapy.

Application of Genomics in Agriculture

(i) Disease, insect and drought-resistant crops.

(ii) Healthier, more productive, disease-resistant farm animals.

(iii) More nutritious produce.

(iv) Biopesticides

(v) Edible vaccines incorporated into food products.

(vi) New environmental cleanup uses for plants like tobacco.

Understanding plant and animal genomes will allow us to create stronger, more disease-resistant plants and animals reducing the costs of agriculture and providing consumers with more nutritious, pesticide-free foods. Already growers are using bioengineered seeds to grow insect and drought resistant crops that require little or no pesticide. Farmers have been able to increase outputs and reduce waste because their crops and herds are healthier.

Alternate uses for crops such as tobacco have been found. One researcher has genetically engineered tobacco plants in his laboratory to produce a bacterial enzyme that breaks down explosives such as TNT and dinitroglycerin. Waste that would take centuries to breakdown in the soil can be cleaned up by simply growing these special plants in the polluted area.

Gene Therapy

Genes, which are carried on chromosomes, are the basic physical and functional units of heredity. Genes are specific sequences of bases that encode instructions on how to make proteins. When genes are altered so that the encoded proteins are unable to carry out their normal functions, genetic disorders can result. Gene therapy is a technique for correcting defective genes by the insertion, alteration or removal of genes within an individual's cells and biological tissues to treat disease. Researchers may use one of several approaches for correcting faulty genes:

1. A normal gene may be inserted into a non-specific location within the genome to replace a non-functional gene. This approach is most common.
2. An abnormal gene could be swapped for a normal gene through homologous recombination.
3. The abnormal gene could be repaired through selective reverse mutation, which returns the gene to its normal function.
4. The regulation (the degree to which a gene is turned on or off) of a particular gene could be altered.

Basic Process of Gene Therapy

Several approaches to gene therapy are being tested, including:

(i) Replacing a mutated gene that causes disease with a healthy copy of the gene.

(ii) Inactivating, or 'knocking out,' a mutated gene that is functioning improperly.

(iii) Introducing a new gene into the body to help fight a disease.

In general, a gene cannot be directly inserted into a person's cell. A carrier molecule called a vector must be used to deliver the therapeutic gene to the patient's target cells. Vector systems can be divided into viral vectors, non-viral vectors.

Viral Vectors

Currently, the most common type of vectors is viruses that have been genetically altered to carry normal human DNA. Viruses have evolved a way of encapsulating and delivering their genes to human cells in a pathogenic manner. Scientists have tried to harness this ability by manipulating the viral genome to remove disease-causing genes and insert therapeutic ones. Target cells such as the patient's liver or lung cells are infected with the vector. The vector then unloads its genetic material containing the therapeutic human gene into the target cell. The generation of a functional protein product from the therapeutic gene restores the target cell to a normal state.

Some of the different types of viruses used as gene therapy vectors:

Retroviruses

A class of viruses that can create double-stranded DNA copies of their RNA genomes. These copies of its genome can be integrated into the chromosomes of host cells. Human Immunodeficiency Virus (HIV) is a retrovirus.

One of the problems of gene therapy using retroviruses is that the integrase enzyme can insert the genetic material of the virus in any arbitrary position in the genome of the host.

If genetic material happens to be inserted in the middle of one of the original genes of the host cell, this gene will be disrupted (insertional mutagenesis). If the gene happens to be one regulating cell division, uncontrolled cell division (*i.e.*, cancer) can occur. This problem has recently begun to be addressed by utilizing zinc finger nucleases or by including certain sequences such as the beta-globin locus control region to direct the site of integration to specific chromosomal sites.

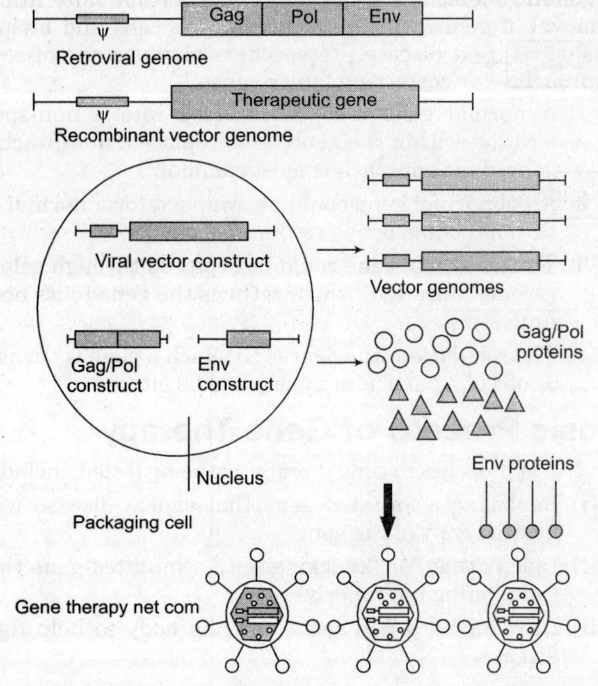

Fig. 36.10 Mechanism of producing recombinant retroviral vectors

Gene therapy trials to treat Severe Combined Immunodeficiency (SCID) were halted or restricted in the USA when leukaemia was reported in three of eleven patients treated in the French X-linked SCID (X-SCID) gene therapy trial. Ten X-SCID patients treated in England have not presented leukaemia to date and have had similar success in immune reconstitution. Gene therapy trials to treat SCID due to deficiency of the Adenosine Deaminase (ADA) enzyme continue with relative success in the **USA, Italy** and **Japan.**

Adenoviruses

A class of viruses with double-stranded DNA genomes that cause respiratory, intestinal and eye infections in humans. The virus that causes the common cold is an adenovirus.

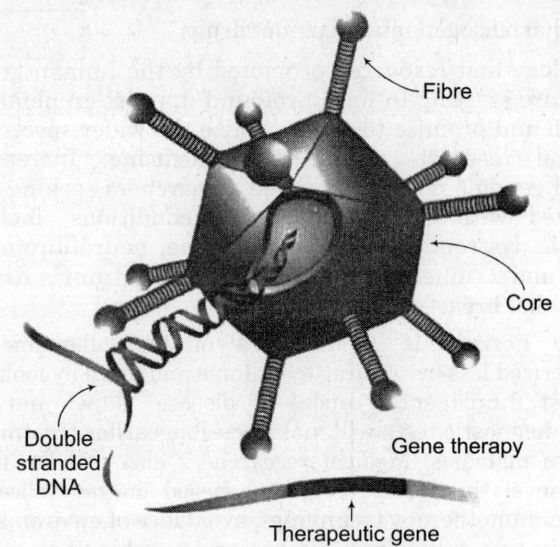

Fig. 36.11 Adenoviral particle organization

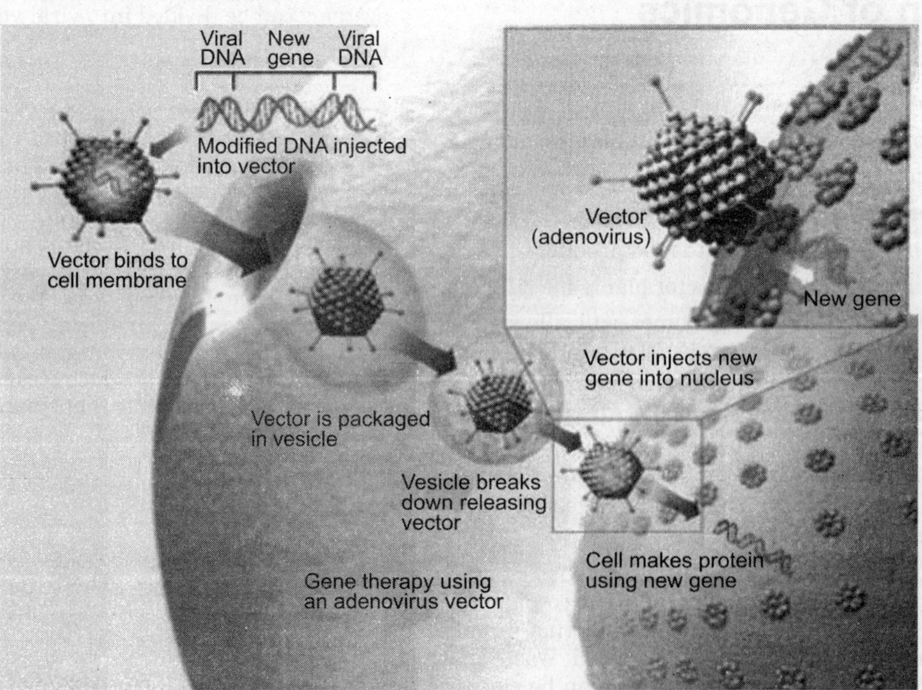

Fig. 36.12 Gene therapy using an adenovirus vector

In September, 1999, the gene therapy research community was alerted to the report of the death of a man enrolled in a gene transfer trial at the University of Pennsylvania. The Recombinant DNA Advisory Committee (RAC) has published a review which involves a discussion of the preclinical safety data, the design of the protocol, the informed consent document and any overarching scientific, safety or ethical issues relevant to the specific protocol. The review entitled **Assessment of Adenoviral Vector Safety and Toxicity** Report of the National Institutes of Health Recombinant DNA Advisory Committee was published in human gene therapy in 2002.

Adeno-Associated Viruses

A class of small, single-stranded DNA viruses that can insert their genetic material at a specific site on chromosome 19.

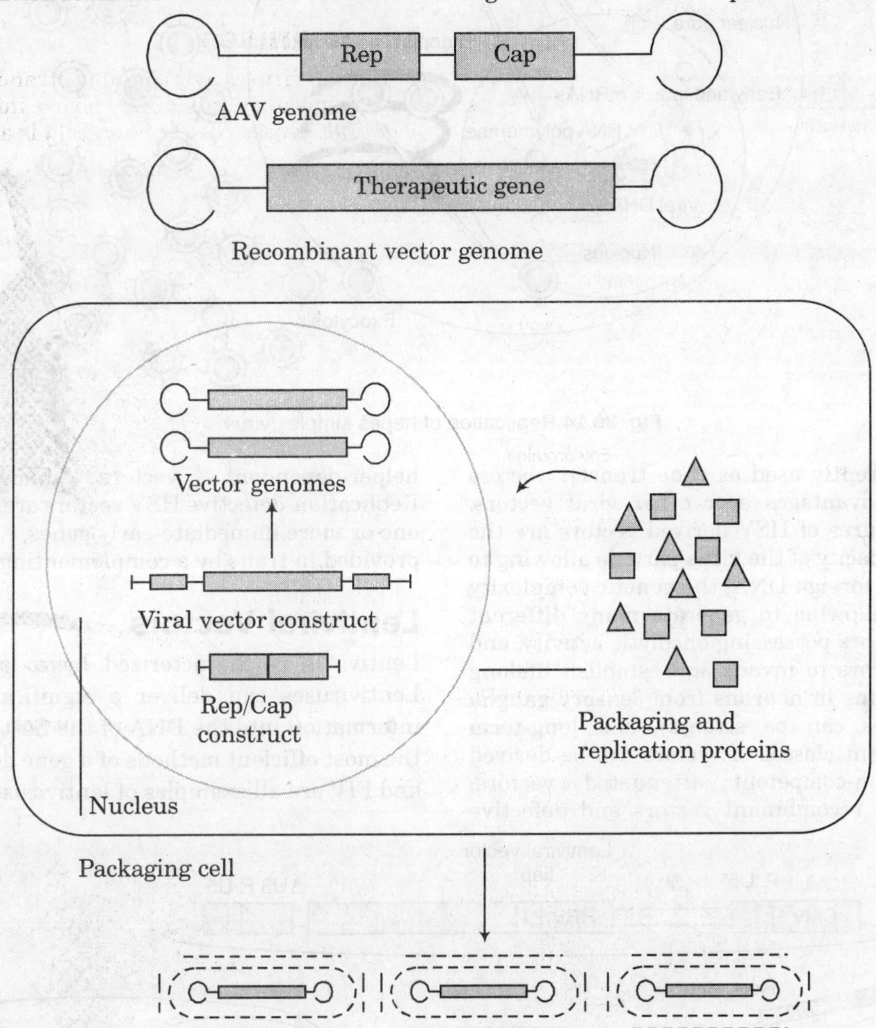

Fig. 36.13 Mechanism of producing recombinant AAV vectors

Herpes Simplex Viruses

A class of double-stranded DNA viruses that infect a particular cell type, neurons. Herpes simplex virus type 1 is a common human pathogen that causes cold sores.

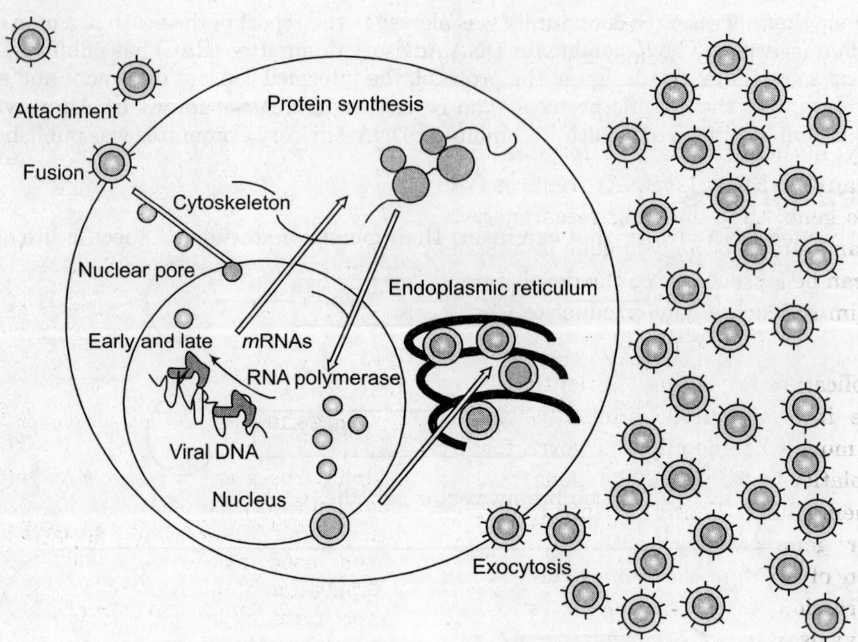

Fig. 36.14 Replication of hepes simplex virus

Herpes viruses are currently used as gene transfer vectors due to their specific advantages over other viral vectors. Among the unique features of HSV derived vectors are the very high transgenic capacity of the virus particle allowing to carry long sequences of foreign DNA, the genetic complexity of the virus genome, allowing to generate many different types of attenuated vectors possessing oncolytic activity, and the ability of HSV vectors to invade and establish lifelong non-toxic latent infections in neurons from sensory ganglia from where transgenes can be strongly and long-term expressed. Three different classes of vectors can be derived from HSV: replication-competent attenuated vectors, replication-incompetent recombinant vectors and defective helper-dependent vectors known as amplicons. Replication-defective HSV vectors are made by the deletion of one or more immediate-early genes, *e.g.,* ICP4, which is then provided in trans by a complementing cell line.

Lentiviral Vectors

Lentivirus is characterized by a long incubation period. Lentiviruses can deliver a significant amount of genetic information into the DNA of the host cell, so they are one of the most efficient methods of a gene delivery vector. HIV, SIV and FIV are all examples of lentiviruses.

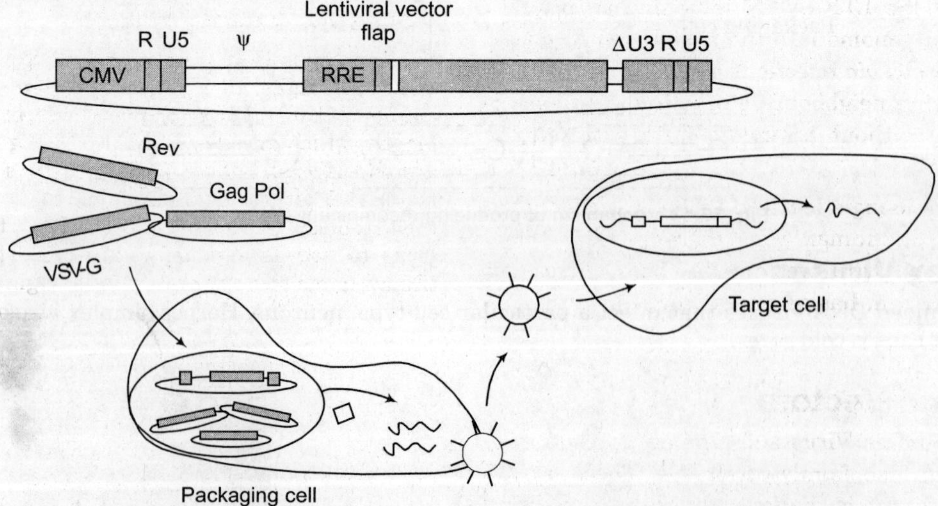

Fig. 36.15 Mechanism of producing recombinant lentiviral vectors for gene therapy

Lentivirus is primarily a research tool used to introduce a gene product into *in vitro* systems or animal models. Large scale collaborative efforts are underway to use lentiviruses to block the expression of a specific gene using RNA interference technology in high-throughput formats. The expression of short-hairpin RNA (*sh*RNA) reduces the expression of a specific gene, thus allowing researchers to examine the necessity and effects of a given gene in a model system. These studies can be a precursor to the development of novel drugs which aim to block a gene-product to treat a disease.

Another common application is to use a lentivirus to introduce a new gene into human or animal cells. For example, a model of mouse haemophilia is corrected by expressing wild-type platlet-factor VIII, the gene that is mutated in human haemophilia. Lentiviral infection have advantages over other gene therapy methods including high-efficiency infection of dividing and non-dividing cells, long-term stable expression of a transgene, and low immunogenicity. Lentiviruses have also been successfully used for transfection of diabetics mice with the gene encoding **PDGF** (Platelet-Derived Growth Factor), a therapy being considered for use in humans. These treatments, like most current gene therapy experiments, show promise but are yet to be established as safe and effective in controlled human studies.

Viral proteins involved in early stages of replication include reverse transcriptase and integrase. Reverse Transcriptase (RT) is the virally encoded RNA-dependent DNA polymerase. The enzyme uses the viral RNA genome as a template for the synthesis of a complementary DNA copy. RT also has RNaseH activity for destruction of the RNA-template. Integrase (IN) binds both the viral cDNA generated by RT and the host DNA. Processing of the LTR by IN is performed prior to insertion of the viral genome into the host DNA. Although transmission is generally *via* infectious particles, lentiviruses are capable of infecting neighbouring cells in direct contact with the host cells, without having to form extracellular particles.

The first clinical trial using a lentivial vector was conducted in 2005 (see article in human gene therapy 2005; 16(1): 17-25). The use of lentiviral vectors has been increasing because the vector system has several attractive features as outlined above.

Alphavirus Viral Vectors

Alphaviruses, like Sindbis Virus and Semliki Forest Virus, belong to the Togaviridae family of viruses. There are 27 alphaviruses, able to infect various vertebrates such as humans, rodents, birds and larger mammals such as horses as well as invertebrates. The genome of alphaviruses consists of a single stranded positive sense RNA.

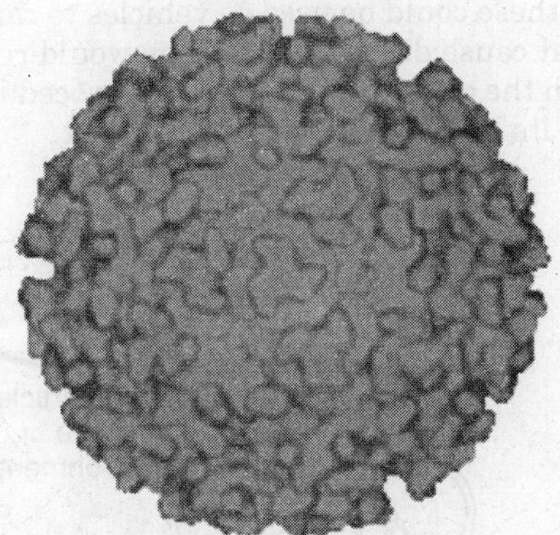

Fig. 36.16 Surface of an alphavirus (computer-generated model)

Alphaviruses are of interest to gene therapy researchers, in particular the Ross River virus, Sindbis virus, Semliki Forest virus, and Venezuelan Equine Encephalitis virus have all been used to develop viral vectors for gene delivery. Application of replication-deficient vectors leads to short-term expression, which makes these vectors highly attractive for cancer gene therapy. Alphavirus vectors carrying therapeutic or toxic genes used for intratumoral injections have demonstrated efficient tumour regression.

There are limitations to the use of alphaviruses in the field of gene therapy due to their lack of targeting, however, through the introduction of variable antibody domains in a non-conserved loop in the structure of E2, specific populations of cells have been targeted. Furthermore, the use of whole alphaviruses for gene therapy is of limited efficacy both because several internal alphaviral proteins are involved in the induction of apoptosis upon infection and also because the alphaviral capsid mediates only the transient introduction of *m*RNA into host cells. Neither of these limitations extend to alphaviral envelope pseudotypes of retroviruses or lentiviruses.

Vaccinia Viral Vectors

Vaccinia virus (VACV or VV) is a large, complex, enveloped virus belonging to the poxvirus family. It has a linear, double-stranded DNA genome of approximately 190 kb in length, which encodes for around 250 genes. The poxviruses are the largest known DNA viruses and are distinguished from other viruses by their ability to replicate entirely in the cytoplasm of the host cell, outside of the nucleus. Vaccinia virus to use as a tool for delivering genes into biological tissues (gene therapy and genetic engineering).

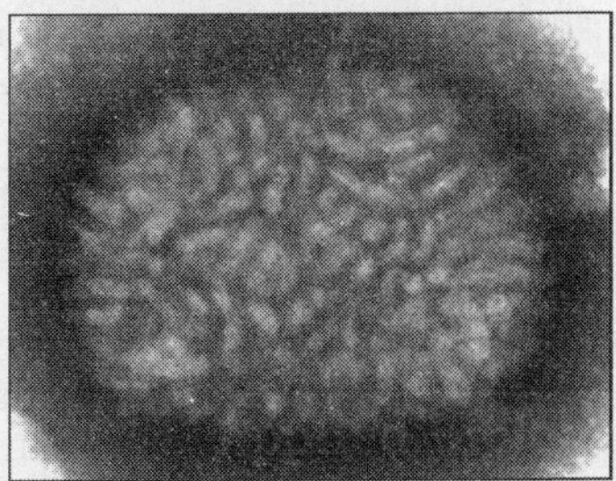

Fig. 36.17 An electron micrograph of a vaccinia virus

Viruses like these could be used as vehicles to carry 'good' genes into a human cell. First, a scientist would remove the genes in the virus that cause disease. Then they would replace those genes with genes encoding the desired effect (for instance, insulin production in the case of diabetics). This procedure must be done in such a way that the genes which allow the virus to insert its genome into its host's genome are left intact.

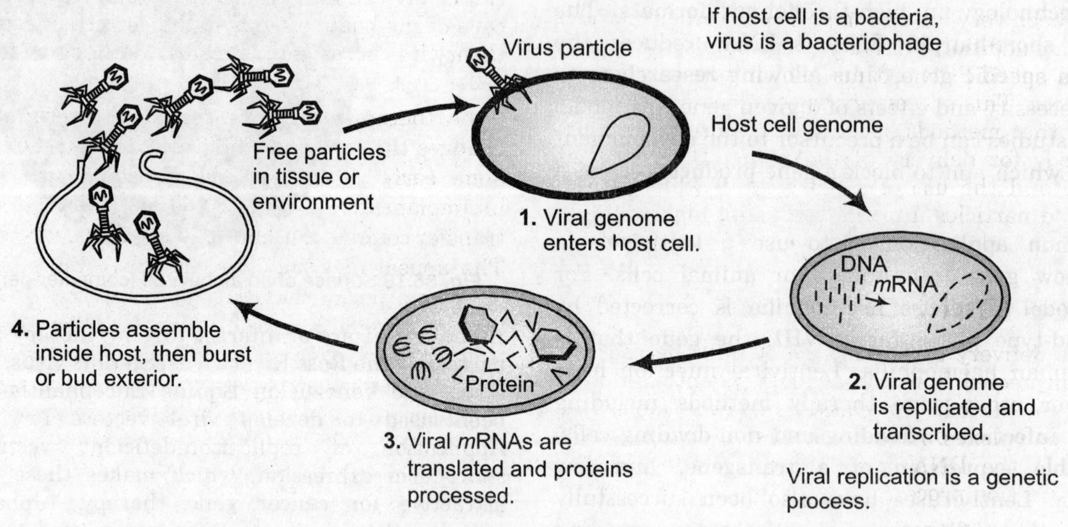

Fig. 36.18 Viruses work

Many gene therapy clinical trials rely on retroviruses or adenoviruses to deliver the desired gene. Other viruses used as vectors include adeno-associtaed viruses, lentiviruses, pox viruses, alpha viruses and herpes viruses.

Table 36.3 **A Comparison of Different Viral Vectors in Use for Gene Therapy**

	Adenovirus	Adeno-Associated Virus	Alphavirus	Herpes Virus	Retroviru/Lentivirus	Vaccinia Virus
Genome	*ds*DNA	*ss*DNA	*ss*RNA (+)	*ds*DNA	*ss*RNA (+)	dsDNA
Capsid	Icosahedral	Icosahedral	Icosahedral	Icosahedral	Icosahedral	Complex
Coat	Naked	Naked	Enveloped	Enveloped	Enveloped	Enveloped
Virion polymerase	Negative	Negative	Negative	Negative	Positive	Positive
Virion diameter	70-90 nm	18-26 nm	60-70 nm	150-200 nm	80-130 nm	170-200 X 300-450 nm
Genome size	39-38 kb	5 kb	12 kb	120-200 kb	3-9 kb	130-280 kb
Family	Adenoviridae	Parvoviridae	Togaviridae	Herpesviridae	Retroviridae	Poxviridae
Infection tropism	Dividing and non-dividing cells	Dividing and non-dividing cells	Dividing and non-dividing cells	Dividing and non-dividing cells	Dividing cells*	Dividing non-dividing cells
Host genome	Non-integrating	Non-integrating* interaction	Non-integrating	Non-integrating	Integrating	Non-integrating
Transgene expression	Transient	Potential long lasting	Transient	Potential long long lasting	Long lasting	Transient
Packaging capacity	7.5 kb	4.5 kb	7.5 kb	> 30 kb	8 kb	25 kb

Non-viral Vectors

Besides virus-mediated gene-delivery systems, there are several non-viral options for gene delivery. The simplest method is the direct introduction of therapeutic DNA into target cells. This approach is limited in its application because it can be used only with certain tissues and requires large amounts of DNA. Non-viral methods present certain advantages over viral methods, with simple large scale production and low host immunogenicity being just two. Previously, low levels of transfection and expression of the gene held non-viral methods at a disadvantage; however, recent advances in vector technology have yielded molecules and techniques with transfection efficiencies similar to those of viruses.

Naked DNA

This is the simplest method of non-viral transfection. Clinical trials carried out of intramuscular injection of a naked DNA plasmid have occurred with some success; however, the expression has been very low in comparison to other methods of transfection. In addition to trials with plasmids, there have been trials with naked PCR product, which have had similar or greater success. This success, however, does not compare to that of the other methods, leading to research into more efficient methods for delivery of the naked DNA such as electroporation and the use of a 'gene gun', which shoots DNA coated gold particles into the cell using high pressure gas.

Lipoplexes and Polyplexes

To improve the delivery of the new DNA into the cell, the DNA must be protected from damage and its entry into the cell must be facilitated. To these end new molecules, lipoplexes and polyplexes, have been created that have the ability to protect the DNA from undesirable degradation during the transfection process.

Plasmid DNA can be covered with lipids in an organized structure like a micelle or a liposome. When the organized structure is complexed with DNA it is called a lipoplex. There are three types of lipids, anionic (negatively charged), neutral, or cationic (positively charged). Initially, anionic and neutral lipids were used for the construction of lipoplexes for synthetic vectors. However, in spite of the facts that there is little toxicity associated with them, that they are compatible with body fluids and that there was a possibility of adapting them to be tissue specific; they are complicated and time consuming to produce so attention was turned to the cationic versions.

Cationic lipids, due to their positive charge, naturally complex with the negatively charged DNA. Also as a result of their charge they interact with the cell membrane, endocytosis of the lipoplex occurs and the DNA is released into the cytoplasm. The cationic lipids also protect against degradation of the DNA by the cell.

The most common use of lipoplexes has been in gene transfer into cancer cells, where the supplied genes have activated tumour suppressor control genes in the cell and decrease the activity of oncogenes. Recent studies have shown lipoplexes to be useful in transfecting respiratory epithelial cells, so they may be used for treatment of genetic respiratory diseases such as cystic fibrosis.

Complexes of polymers with DNA are called **polyplexes.** Most polyplexes consist of cationic polymers and their production is regulated by ionic interactions. One large difference between the methods of action of polyplexes and lipoplexes is that polyplexes cannot release their DNA load into the cytoplasm, so to this end, co-transfection with endosome-lytic agents (to lyse the endosome that is made during endocytosis, the process by which the polyplex enters the cell) such as inactivated adenovirus must occur. However this isn't always the case, polymers such as polyethylenimine have their own method of endosome disruption as does chitosan and trimethylchitosan.

Types of Gene Therapy

Virtually all cells in the human body contain genes, making them potential targets for gene therapy. However, these cells can be divided into two major categories: somatic cells (most cells of the body) or cells of the germline (eggs or sperm). In theory it is possible to transform either somatic cells or germ cells.

Gene therapy using germ line cells results in permanent changes that are passed down to subsequent generations. If done early in embryologic development, such as during preimplantation diagnosis and *in vitro* fertilization, the gene transfer could also occur in all cells of the developing embryo. The appeal of germ line gene therapy is its potential for offering a permanent therapeutic effect for all who inherit the target gene. Successful germ line therapies introduce the possibility of eliminating some diseases from a particular family, and ultimately from the population, forever. However, this also raises controversy. Some people view this type of therapy as unnatural, and liken it to 'playing God.' Others have concerns about the technical aspects. They worry that the genetic change propagated by germ line gene therapy may actually be deleterious and harmful, with the potential for unforeseen negative effects on future generations.

Somatic cells are non-reproductive. Somatic cell therapy is viewed as a more conservative, safer approach because it affects only the targeted cells in the patient, and is not passed on to future generations. In other words, the therapeutic effect ends with the individual who receives the therapy. However, this type of therapy presents unique problems of its own. Often the effects of somatic cell therapy are short-lived. Because the cells of most tissues ultimately die and are replaced by new cells, repeated treatments over the course of the individual's life span are required to maintain the therapeutic effect. Transporting the gene to the target cells or tissue is also problematic. Regardless of these difficulties, however, somatic cell gene therapy is appropriate and acceptable for many disorders, including cystic fibrosis, muscular dystrophy, cancer, and certain infectious diseases. Clinicians can even perform this therapy in utero, potentially correcting or treating a life-threatening disorder that may significantly impair a baby's health or development if not treated before birth.

In summary, the distinction is that the results of any somatic gene therapy are restricted to the actual patient and are not passed on to his or her children. All gene therapy to date on humans has been directed at somatic cells, whereas germline engineering in humans remains controversial and prohibited in for instance the European union.

Somatic gene therapy can be broadly split into two categories:

Ex vivo, which means exterior (where cells are modified outside the body and then transplanted back in again). In some gene therapy clinical trials, cells from the patient's blood or bone marrow are removed and grown in the laboratory. The cells are exposed to the virus that is carrying the desired gene. The virus enters the cells and inserts the desired gene into the cells' DNA. The cells grow in the laboratory and are then returned to the patient by injection into a vein. This type of gene therapy is called *ex vivo* because the cells are treated outside the body.

In vivo, which means interior (where genes are changed in cell still in the body). This form of gene therapy is called *in vivo*, because the gene is transferred to cells inside the patient's body.

Gene Doping

Gene therapy for restoring muscle lost to age or disease is poised to enter the clinic, but athletes are eyeing it to enhance performance. The non-therapeutic use of cells, genes, genetic elements or of the modulation of gene expression, having the capacity to improve athletic performance is defined as gene doping by the **World Anti-Doping Agency** (WADA).

Analogous to gene doping, non-therapeutic applications of gene therapy can be envisaged in animals for the purpose of growth stimulation and improved meat production (see also Belgian Blue Bull), for example by growth hormone, myostatin and anabolic hormones. Gene doping to improve sport performance is not limited to humans, but has also interest in for example the sport of horse racing.

Risk Factors

The concept of gene therapy seems straight forward, but this is clearly an oversimplification, and numerous problems and risks exist that prevent gene therapy using viral vectors. Viruses can usually infect more than one type of cell. Thus, when viral vectors are used to carry genes into the body, they might infect healthy cells as well as cancer cells.

Another danger is that the new gene might be inserted in the wrong location in the DNA, possibly causing harmful mutations to the DNA or even cancer. This has occurred in clinical trials for X-linked Severe Combined Immunodeficiency (X-SCID) patients, in which hematopoietic stem cells were transduced with a corrective transgene using a retrovirus, and this led to the development of T-cell leukaemia in 4 of 20 patients. See reports for first patient, second patient and third patient.

In addition, when viruses are used to deliver DNA to cells inside the patient's body, there is a slight chance that this DNA could unintentionally be introduced into the patient's reproductive cells. If this happens, it could produce changes that may be passed on if a patient has children after treatment.

Other concerns include the possibility that transferred genes could be over-expressed, producing so much of the missing protein as to be harmful; that the viral vector could cause an immune reaction; and that the virus could be transmitted from the patient to other individuals or into the environment.

However, this basic mode of gene introduction currently shows much promise and doctors and scientists are working hard to fix any potential problems that could exist. They use animal testing and other precautions to identify and avoid these risks before any clinical trials are conducted in humans.

Pseudotyping of Viral Vectors

Viral vectors have natural host cell populations that they infect most efficiently. Retroviruses have limited natural host cell ranges, and although adenovirus and adeno-associated virus are able to infect a relatively broader range of cells efficiently, some cell types are refractory to infection by these viruses as well. Attachment to and entry into a susceptible cell is mediated by the protein envelope on the surface of a virus.

Retroviruses and adeno-associated viruses have a single protein coating their membrane, while adenoviruses are coated with both an envelope protein and fibres that extend away from the surface of the virus. The envelope proteins on each of these viruses bind to cell-surface molecules such as heparin sulphate, which localizes them upon the surface of the potential host, as well as with the specific protein receptor that either induces entry-promoting structural changes in the viral protein, or localizes the virus in endosomes wherein acidification of the lumen (anatomy) induces this refolding of the viral coat. In either case, entry into potential host cells requires a favorable interaction between a protein on the surface of the virus and a protein on the surface of the cell.

For the purposes of gene therapy, one might either want to limit or expand the range of cells susceptible to transduction by a gene therapy vector. To this end, many vectors have been developed in which the endogenous viral envelope proteins have been replaced by either envelope proteins from other viruses, or by chimeric proteins. Such chimera would consist of those parts of the viral protein necessary for incorporation into the virion as well as sequences meant to interact with specific host cell proteins. Viruses in which the envelope proteins have been replaced as described are referred to as pseudotyped viruses.

For example, the most popular retroviral vector for use in gene therapy trials has been the lentivirus simian immunodeficiency virus coated with the envelope proteins, G-protein, from Vesicular Stomatitus virus. This vector is referred to as VSV G-pseudotyped lentivirus, and infects an almost universal set of cells. This tropism is characteristic of the VSV G-protein with which this vector is coated.

Many attempts have been made to limit the tropism of viral vectors to one or a few host cell populations. This advance would allow for the systemic administration of a relatively small amount of vector. The potential for off-target cell modification would be limited, as well as many concerns from the medical community. Most attempts to limit tropism have used chimeric envelope proteins bearing antibody fragments. These vectors show great promise for the development of 'magic bullet' gene therapies.

Current Status of Gene Therapy Research

The Food and Drug Administration (FDA) has not yet approved any human gene therapy product for sale. Current gene therapy is experimental and has not proven very successful in clinical trials. Little progress has been made since, the first gene therapy clinical trial began in 1990. In

1999, gene therapy suffered a major setback with the death of 18-year-old Jesse Gelsinger. Jesse was participating in a gene therapy trial for **Ornithine Transcarboxylase Deficiency** (OTCD). He died from multiple organ failures four days after starting the treatment. His death is believed to have been triggered by a severe immune response to the adenovirus carrier.

Another major blow came in January 2003, when the FDA placed a temporary halt on all gene therapy trials using retroviral vectors in blood strem cells. FDA took this action after it learned that a second child treated in a French gene therapy trial had developed a leukaemia-like condition. Both this child and another who had developed a similar condition in August 2002 had been successfully treated by gene therapy for X-linked severe combined immunodeficiency disease (X-SCID), also known as 'bubble baby syndrome.'

FDA's Biological Response Modifiers Advisory Committee (BRMAC) met at the end of February 2003 to discuss possible measures that could allow a number of retroviral gene therapy trials for treatment of life-threatening diseases to proceed with appropriate safeguards. In April of 2003 the FDA eased the ban on gene therapy trials using retroviral vectors in blood stem cells.

Gene Therapy : An Effective Treatment for Genetic Disease

(i) **Short-lived nature of gene therapy** Before gene therapy can become a permanent cure for any condition, the therapeutic DNA introduced into target cells must remain functional and the cells containing the therapeutic DNA must be long-lived and stable. Problems with integrating therapeutic DNA into the genome and the rapidly dividing nature of many cells prevent gene therapy from achieving any long-term benefits. Patients will have to undergo multiple rounds of gene therapy.

(ii) **Immune response** Anytime a foreign object is introduced into human tissues, the immune system is designed to attack the invader. The risk of stimulating the immune system in a way that reduces gene therapy effectiveness is always a potential risk. Furthermore, the immune system's enhanced response to invaders it has seen before makes it difficult for gene therapy to be repeated in patients.

(iii) **Problems with viral vectors** Viruses, while the carrier of choice in most gene therapy studies, present a variety of potential problems to the patient toxicity, immune and inflammatory responses, and gene control and targeting issues. In addition, there is always the fear that the viral vector, once inside the patient, may recover its ability to cause disease.

(iv) **Multigene disorders** Conditions or disorders that arise from mutations in a single gene are the best candidates for gene therapy. Unfortunately, some the most commonly occurring disorders, such as heart disease, high blood pressure, Alzheimer's disease, arthritis and diabetes, are caused by the combined effects of variations in many genes. Multigene or multifactorial disorders such as these would be especially difficult to treat effectively using gene therapy. For more information on different types of genetic disease, see genetic disease information.

Ethical Considerations for using Gene Therapy

(i) What is normal and what is a disability or disorder and who decides?

(ii) Are disabilities diseases? Do they need to be cured or prevented?

(iii) Does searching for a cure demean the lives of individuals presently affected by disabilities.

(iv) Is somatic gene therapy (which is done in the adult cells of persons known to have the disease) more or less ethical than germline gene therapy (which is done in egg and sperm cells and prevents the trait from being passed on to further generations)? In cases of somatic gene therapy, the procedure may have to be repeated in future generations.

(v) Preliminary attempts at gene therapy are exorbitantly expensive. Who will have access to these therapies? Who will pay for their use?

Biological Resources

Bioresources are important components for progress and economic activities of a nation. But bioresources management and utilization for human welfare is very important for the optimum utilization of the bioresources. Awareness of the importance and implications of bioresources among common people as well as elite educated citizens for safeguarding and protecting the optimum and balance way of using the bioresources needs critical studies to focus the natural bioresources wealth for the benefit of not only the present generation of our people but also to our future generations for their better, healthy and peaceful living on the Earth. The problems facing at present is the over exploitation of bioresources/natural resources which would not only have negative impact on the environment but also sometimes totally destroy and erode the important bioresources which are available at local level, regional level and national levels. Therefore, handling bioresources in a proper manner in an appropriate way is important for the optimum use without over exploitation of our bioresources wealth. Biological resources include genetic resources, organisms or parts there, populations, or any other biotic component of ecosystems with actual or potential use or value for **humanity.** Ecosystem management in a particular location is important and integral part for the conservation and protection of biological diversity of India. Ecosystem is a dynamic complex of plant, animal and microorganism communities and their non-living environment interacting as a functional unit and habitat is the place or type of site where an organism or population naturally occurs.

Conservation of Biodiversity for Sustainable Agriculture

The wide spread loss of the global biological wealth is one of the most serious crises today at International level. As many of the World's diverse life forms from microbes to higher animals and plants have a direct or indirect influence on agricultural conservation of these organisms is essential for sustainable agriculture. To feed growing population, agriculture must be intensified to provide more food. It will also be essential to increase the resilience of agriculture by maintaining a wide array of life forms with unique traits, such as trees that survive drought conditions or cattle or goat or pig that reproduce in harsh conditions. Sustainable agricultural practices can both feed people and protect oceans, forests and other ecosystems that harbor biological diversity.

It is therefore an agricultural imperative that genetic richness of the world's flora and fauna that are important in agriculture should be maintained and enhanced. The amount of diversity in these organisms is largely unknown. Unless, the nature and extent of the diversity is properly assessed and determined, its role in sustainable agriculture cannot be assessed and a critical and comprehensive strategy for its conservation cannot be formulated. It is essential to conserve species richness and genetic diversity within the species. Genetic resources means genetic material of actual or potential value and genetic material is any material of plant, animal, microbial or other origin containing functional units of heredity. For this reason, it is critical to monitor quantitative and qualitative changes in the biological diversity both in space and time. Notwithstanding the paucity of information on the nature and extent of diversity in agriculturally important species, it is clear that genetic diversity in them must be preserved for the species to continue and remain useful under changing biotic and abiotic pressures and human demands.

Value of Biodiversity

The social, ethical and economic values of bioresources have been recognized in religion, art and literature throughout humankind history. The general public often recognizes the intangible values that enrich the quality of life but the process of development tends to emphasize the more tangible economic benefits. Humanity derives all of its food and many of its medicines and industrial products from both the wild and domesticate of biodiversity. The components of biodiversity have been demonstrated to be very important to human health in both traditional and modern medical practices. Plant varieties and animal types are crucial to the healing process of traditional medicine, which forms the basis for primary health are for about 80% the people in developing countries. More than 5100 species are used in **Chinese** traditional medicines alone. It has been reported that more than 16000 antibiotics have been derived from microorganisms more particularly from streptomycetes, bacteria and fungi. The discovery of penicillin by Alexander Fleming and streptomycin by Walksman from *Penicillium chrysogenum* and S*treptomyces griseus* in 1940s respectively revolutionized in medical field and saved several millions of people in the world war. Bioactive compounds extracted from plants, microbes and animals are involved in developing all of the twenty best selling drugs in the USA. Besides economic benefits derived from medicines, there are also economic benefits from the harvesting of wild species. Wild species are also dietary mainstays providing an important source of protein in many parts of the world. Timber, ornamental plants, oils, gums and many fibres are derived from wild species. Variety in life has other benefits particularly in agriculture.

Genetic diversity provides an edge in the constant evolutionary battle between crops and livestock and pests and diseases that pray on them. Breeders and farmers also draw upon the genetic diversity of crops to increase yields per unit area and also respond to changing environmental conditions. The possibilities afforded to Biotechnology which really makes it possible to transfer gene(s) between species would further increase the opportunities for enhancing agricultural productivity by taking advantage of the genetic diversity. Overtime the greatest value of the variety of life may be found in the opportunities it provides humanity for adopting local and global climate change. The unknown potential of genes, species and ecosystems represents a never-ending biological frontier of inestimable value.

The sheer diversity of life is of inestimable value. It provides a foundation for the continued existence of a healthy planet and our own well being. Many Biologists now believe that ecosystems rich in diversity greater resilience and are therefore, able to recover more readily from stresses such as drought or human induced habitat degradation. When ecosystems are diverse, there is a range of pathways for primary production and ecological processes such as nutrient cycling, so that if one is damaged or destroyed, an alternative pathway may be used and ecosystem can continue to function at its normal level. If biological diversity is generally diminished, the functioning of ecosystems is put at risk. Possibly the greater value of the variety of life may be the opportunities it gives for adapting to change. The unknown potential of genes, species and ecosystems is of inestimable but certainly of high value.

Genetic diversity will enable breeders to tailor crops to new climatic conditions, while the Earth's biota is likely to hold still undiscovered cures for known and emerging diseases. A multiplicity of genes, species and ecosystems is a resource that can be tapped as human needs change. There is no single particular argument which on its own provides sufficient grounds for attempting to maintain all existing biological diversity. A more and pragmatic approach however recognizes that different but equally valid arguments like resource values, precautionary values, ethics and aesthetics and simple self interest apply in different cases and between them provide an overwhelmingly powerful and convincing case for the conservation of biological diversity. The many values of biological diversity and its importance for development indicate why biological diversity conservation differs from traditional nature conservations. Biological diversity conservation entails a shift from a reaction situation by protecting nature from the impacts of development to a proactive effort seeking to meet people's needs from biological resources while ensuring the long term ecological sustainability of Earth's biotic wealth. On a global level it thus involves not only the protection of wild species and their habitats but also the safe guarding of the genetic biodiversity of cultivated and domesticated species and their wild relatives. The conservation of biological diversity seeks to maintain the life support system provided by nature in all its variety and the living resources essential for ecologically sustainable development.

Animal Breeding

In animal breeding, a population is a group of interbreeding individuals, *i.e.,* a breed or strain within a breed that is different in some aspects from other breeds or strains. Typically, certain animals within a breed are designated as purebred. The essential difference between purebred and non purebred animals is that the genealogy of purebred animals has been carefully recorded, usually in a herd book or studbook, kept by some sanctioning association. Purebred associations provide other services that are useful to their members to enhance their businesses.

Selective breeding utilizes the natural variations in traits that exist among members of any population. Breeding progress requires understanding the two sources of variation genetics and environment. For some traits there is an interaction of genetics and the environment. Differences in the animals' environment, such as amount of feed, care, and even the weather, may have an impact on their growth, reproduction and productivity. Such variations in performance because of the environment are not transmitted to the next generation. For most traits measured in domestic animals, the environment has a larger impact on variation than do genetic differences. For example, only about 30 percent of the variation in milk production in dairy cattle can be attributed to genetic effects; the remainder of the variation is due to environmental effects. Thus, environmental factors must be considered and controlled in selecting breeding stock.

Genetic variation is necessary in order to make progress in breeding successive generations. Each gene, which is the basic unit of heredity, occupies a specific location, or locus, on a chromosome. Two or more genes may be associated with a specific locus and therefore with a specific trait (traits that can be observed directly, such as size, colour, shape and so forth, make up an organism's phenotype). These genes are known as alleles. If paired alleles are the same, the organism is called homozygous for that trait; if they are different, the organism is heterozygous. Typically, one of the alleles will be expressed to the exclusion of the other allele, in which case the two alleles are referred to as dominant and recessive, respectively. However, sometimes neither dominates, in which case the two alleles are called codominant.

Although no complete knowledge of the genetic makeup of any breed of livestock exists yet, genetic variations can be used for improving stock. Researchers partition total genetic variation into additive, dominance and epistatic types of gene action, which are defined in the following paragraphs. Additive variation is easiest to use in breeding because it is common and the effect of each allele at a locus just adds to the effect of other alleles at that same locus. Genetic gains made using additive genetic effects are permanent and cumulate from one generation to the next.

Additive and dominance variations are caused by genes at one locus. Epistatic variation is caused by the joint effects of genes at two or more loci. There has been little deliberate use of this type of genetic variation in breeding because of the complex nature of identifying and controlling the relevant genes.

Breeding Objectives

Breeding objectives can be discussed in terms of changing the genetic make up of a population of animals, where population is defined as a recognized breed. Choice of breeding goals and design of an effective breeding program is usually not an easy task. Complicating the implementation of a breeding program is the number of generations needed to reach the initial goals. Ultimately, breeding goals are dictated by market demand; however, it is not easy to predict what consumers will want several years in advance. Sometimes the market place demands a different product than was defined as desirable in the original breeding objective. When this happens, breeders have to adjust their program, which results in less-efficient selection than if the new breeding goal had been used from the beginning. For example, consumers want leaner beef that is tender. Thus, ranchers have changed their cattle-breeding programs to meet this new demand. These trends have gradually changed over the last few decades; for example, Angus cattle are particularly noted for the quality of beef produced. The use of ultrasound is now widespread in determining the fat and lean content of live animals, which will hasten the changing of carcass quality to meet consumer demands.

Additional complications arise from simultaneously trying to improve multiple traits and the difficulty of determining what part of the variation for each trait is under genetic control. In addition, some traits are genetically correlated, and this correlation may be positive or negative; that is, the traits may be complementary or antagonistic. Breeding methods depend on heritability and genetic correlations for desirable traits.

Heritability is the proportion of the additive genetic variation to the total variation. Heritability is important because without genetic variation there can be no genetic change in the population.

Genetic correlation occurs when a single gene affects two or more traits. The practical breeding consequence is that selection for one trait will pull along any positively correlated traits, even though there is no deliberate selection for them. For example, selecting for increased milk production also increases protein production. Another example is the selection for increased weight gain in broiler chickens, which also increases the fat content of the birds.

When traits have a negative genetic correlation, it is difficult to select simultaneously for both traits. For example, as milk production is increased in dairy cows through genetic selection, it is slightly more difficult for the high-producing cows to conceive.

Hybrid Vigour or Heterosis

Heterosis or **hybrid vigour** is the phenotypic superiority of the hybrid over either of its parents in one or more traits. Hybridization between unrelated strains generally leads to an increased vigour and fertility (hybrid vigour). The term **heterosis** was first used by **Shull** in 1914, though heterosis was first studied by **Kolreuter** (1763) followed by **Darwin** (1876). The heterosis is lost by inbreeding (self-fertilization). Heterosis is generally expressed as an increase in size and yield, but it may be expressed in several ways, such as earlier or later flowering and maturity, greater adaptability, faster growth rare, etc. Heterosis is observed both in cross and self-pollinated species.

Genetic basis of Heterosis There are two genetic hypothesis to explain heterosis–Dominance hypothesis and overdominance hypothesis. **Dominance hypothesis** states that heterosis is the result of masking of harmful effects of recessive alleles by their dominant alleles. According to **overdominance hypothesis,** heterosis is the result of superiority of the heterozygotes. There is no conclusive evidence to support or to reject either of the two hypothesis. **Heterozygotes** at certain loci are superior to homozygotes. It is generally believed that heterosis is the result of dominance and epistatic interactions; some genes may also show overdominance.

Biochemical basis of heterosis At the biochemical level, heterosis may result in one of many ways. Some of the mechanisms known so far are: reduced amount of a single gene product, separate gene products by the two alleles, combined gene product or the hybrid substance and effects in two different tissues.

Heterosis is commercially exploitted in the form of hybrid varieties or synthetic varieties. Heterosis has been extensively used in many crop species, vegetables, fruit trees and in animals.

A list of some examples of plant and animal species where heterosis is being commercially exploited.

Methods of Selection

Types of selection are individual or mass selection, within and between family selection, sibling selection and progeny testing, with many variations. Within family selection uses the best individual from each family for breeding. Between family selection uses the whole family for selection. Mass selection uses records of only the candidates for selection. Mass selection is most effective when heritability is high and the trait is expressed early in life, in which case all that is required is observation and selection based on phenotypes. When mass selection is not appropriate, other methods of selection, which make use of relatives or progeny, can be used singularly or in combination. Modern technologies allow use of all these types of selection at the same time, which results in greater accuracy.

Evaluation of Animals

Methods of ranking animals for breeding purposes have changed as statistical and genetic knowledge has increased. Alongwith increases in breeding knowledge, advancements in computing have enabled breeders to quickly and easily process routine breeding evaluations, as well as to develop research needed to rank large populations of animals. Evaluating and ranking candidates for selection depends on equating their performance record to a statistical model.

Accuracy of Selection

In some cases the accuracy of selection for a trait can be measured using a calibrated tool or a scale. Thus, measure-ments of such traits can be replicated with high reliability. Alternatively, some traits are difficult to measure on an objective scale, in which case a well-designed subjective scoring method can be effective. Because close relatives share many genes, an examination of the relatives of a candidate for breeding can improve accuracy of selection. The more complete the genealogical record, or pedigree, the more effective the selection process. A pedigree is most useful when the heritability of a trait is relatively low, especially for traits that are expressed later in life or in only one sex.

Reproductive techniques can be used to increase the rate of genetic progress. These reproductive technologies reduce the generation interval and increase selection intensity by getting more than one male calf from superior females. Both superovulation and sex-determination are now commonly used procedures. Superovulation is also used when breeders want to increase the number of female calves from a valuable cow.

Progeny Testing

Progeny testing is used extensively in the beef and dairy cattle industry to aid in evaluating and selecting stock to be bred. Progeny testing is most useful when a high level of accuracy is needed for selecting a sire to be used extensively in artificial insemination.

Breeding Systems

Crossbreeding

Crossbreeding involves the mating of animals from two breeds. Normally, breeds are chosen that have complementary traits that will enhance the offsprings' economic value. The other consideration in crossbreeding is heterosis, or hybrid vigour, which is displayed when the offspring performance exceeds the average performance of the parent breeds. This is a common phenomenon in which increased size, growth rate, and fertility are displayed by crossbred offspring, especially when the breeds are more genetically dissimilar. Such increases generally do not increase in successive generations of crossbred stock, so purebred lines must be retained for crossbreeding and for continual improvement in the parent breeds. In general, there is more heterosis for traits with low heritability. In particular, heterosis is thought to be associated with the collective action of many genes having small effects individually but large effects cumulatively.

Inbreeding

Mating animals that are related causes inbreeding. Inbreeding is often described as 'narrowing the genetic base' because the mating of related animals results in offspring that have more genes in common. Inbreeding is used to concentrate desirable traits. Inbreeding is generally detrimental in domestic animals. Increased inbreeding is accompanied by reduced fertility, slower growth rates, greater susceptibility to disease and higher mortality rates. As a result, producers try to avoid mating related animals. This is not always possible, though, when long-continued selection for the same traits is practiced within a small population, because parents of future generations are the best candidates from the last generation, and some inbreeding tends to accumulate. The rate of inbreeding can be reduced, but, if inbreeding depression becomes evident, some method of introducing more diverse genes will be needed. The most common method is some form of crossbreeding.

Inbreeding Depression

Inbreeding depression may be defined as the reduction or loss in vigour and fertility as a result of inbreeding. Inbreeding is generally accompanied with a reduction in vigour and reproductive capacity, *i.e.,* fertility. Generally, there is reduction in the size of various plant parts and in yield. In several species, harmful recessive alleles appear after selfing and the plants or lines carrying them usually do not survive. The effects of inbreeding are summarized below:

(a) Inbreeding results in the **appearance of lethal, sub-lethal** and **sub-vital** (reducing survival and reproductive rate) **characteristics (alleles)** such as, chlorophyll deficiencies-albino, chlorino, etc., rootless seedlings, defects in flower structure, etc. The plants carrying such characteristics are lost from the population.

(b) There is **reduction in the vigour** of the population. The plants become weaker and shorter due to general reduction in the size of various plants parts.

(c) The **reproductive ability** of the population decreases rapidly.

(d) The **population rapidly separates into phenotypically distinct lines,** because of an increase in homozygosity due to which there is a random fixation of various alleles in different lines. Hence, the lines differ in their genotype and consequently in phenotype. This leads to an **increase in the variance** of the population as a whole.

(e) Following inbreeding there is **increase in homozygosity** in each line, consequently the variation within a line decrease rapidly. The lines which are almost homozygous due to continued inbreeding and are maintained through close inbreeding are known as **inbred lines** or **inbreds.** Ultimately, after 7 to 8 generations of selfing, the lines become almost uniform as they approach complete homozygosity (> 99% homozygosity).

(f) Inbreeding generally leads to a **loss in yield.** The inbred lines that are able to survive and be maintained, yield much less than the open pollinated varieties from which they were derived.

The **degree of inbreeding depression** varies from one species to another. Some species, *e.g.,* onion, cucurbits, etc. exhibits little or no inbreeding depression, while in some species such as, carrot and alfa-alfa, it is very severe. On the other hand, self-pollinated species are adapted to inbreeding and do not exhibit any inbreeding depression.

Heterosis and inbreeding depression are closely related phenomena. They may be regarded as the two opposite sides of the same coin. The **genetic theories** that explain heterosis and also explain inbreeding depression. There are two main theories to explain heterosis and consequently inbreeding depression.

Line Breeding

Line breeding is a system of breeding in which the degree of relationship is less intense than in inbreeding and is usually directed towards keeping the offspring related to some highly prized ancestor. The degree of relationship is not closer than half-brother half-sister matings or cousin matings, etc. Line breeding is a mild form of inbreeding.

Plant Breeding

Plant breeding is the science of improving the heredity of plants for the benefit of human kind. The transition form wild plant to a cultivated plant started early in the history of mankind.

Some plants reproduce by (more or less strict) self-fertilization where pollen from a plant will fertilize reproductive cells or ovules of the same plant. Other plants only (mainly) allow cross-pollination where pollen from one plant can only fertilize a different plant. Asexual propagation (vegetative propagation) can also occur in plants (*e.g.,* runners from strawberry plants) which gives a new plant which is genetically identical to its parent plant. All these differences change the way plant breeders work. Apomixis is the phenomenon that seed are produced, but in an essentially asexual way, so that parent and offspring belong to one clone just as in case of 'normal' asexual propagation.

The mode of reproduction of a crop determines its genetic composition, which, in turn, is the deciding factor to develop suitable breeding and selection methods. Knowledge of mode of reproduction is also essential for its artificial manipulation to breed improved types. Only those breeding and selection methods are suitable for a crop which does not interfere with its natural state or ensure the maintenance of such a state. It is due to such reasons that imposition of self-fertilization on cross-pollinating crops leads to drastic reduction in their performance.

For teaching—purpose, plant breeding is presented as four categories—Line breeding (autogamous crops), population breeding (allogamous crops), hybrid breeding (mostly allogamous crops, some autogamous crops), clone breeding (vegetatively propagated crops).

Self-Fertilizing Crops (Autogamous Crops)

Certain restrictions caused the mechanisms for self-fertilization (partial and full self fertilization) to develop in a number of plant species. Some of the reasons why a self-fertilizing method of reproduction is so effective are the efficacy of reproduction, as well as decreasing genetic variation and thus the fixation of highly adapted genotypes. Almost no inbreeding depression occurs in self-fertilizing plants because the mode of reproduction allows natural selection to take place in wild populations of such plants.

Critical steps in the improvement of self-fertilizing crops are the choice of parents and the identification of the best plants in segregating generations. The breeder should also have definite goals with the choice of parents. Self-fertilizing are easier to maintain, but this could lead to misuse of seed.

Some of the agronomy important, self-fertilizing crops include wheat, rice, barley, dry beans, soyabeans, peanuts, tomatoes, etc.

Mass Selection

This method of selection depends mainly on selection of plants according to their phenotype and performance. The seed from selected plants are bulked for the next generation. This method is used to improve the overall population by positive or negative mass selection. Mass selection is only applied to a limited degree in self-fertilizing plants and is an effective method for the improvement of land races. This method of selection will only be effective for highly heritable traits. One shortage of mass selection are the large influence that the environment has on the development, phenotype and performance of single plants.

A developed by this method will be more uniform than those developed by mass selection because all of the plants in such a variety will have the same genotype. The seed from selected plants are not added together but are kept apart and used to perform offspring tests. This is done to study the breeding behaviour of the selected plant.

Selection of Cross-pollinated Crops

Plant species, where normal mode of seed set is through a high degree of cross-pollination have characteristic reproductive features and population structure. Existence of self-sterility, self-incompatibility, imperfect flowers and mechanical obstructions make the plant dependent upon foreign pollen for normal seed set. Each plant receives a blend of pollen from a large number of individuals each having different genotypes. Such populations are characterized by a high degree of heterozygosity with tremendous free and potential genetic variation, which is maintained in a steady state by free gene flow among individuals within the populations.

In the development of hybrid varieties, the aim is to identify the most productive heterozygote from the population, which then is produced with the exclusion of other members of the population.

Mass Selection

It is the simplest, easiest and oldest method of selection where individual plants are selected based on their phenotypic performance, and bulk seed is used to produce the next generation by mixing it. Mass selection proved to be quite effective in maize improvement at the initial stages but its efficacy especially for improvement of yield, soon came under severe criticism that culminated in the refinement of the method of mass selection. The selection after pollination does not provide any control over the pollen parent as result of which effective selection is limited only to female parents. The heritability estimates are reduced by half, since only parents are used to harvest seed whereas the pollen source is not known after the cross pollination has taken place.

Recurrent Selection

This type of selection is a refined version of the mass selection procedure and differs as follows:

(a) Visually selected individuals out of the base population undergo progeny testing.

(b) Individuals selected on basis of the progeny test data are crossed with each other in every possible way to produce seed to form the new base population.

Half-sib Selection with Progeny Testing

Selections are made based on progeny test performance instead of phenotypic appearance of the parental plants. Seed from selected half-siblings, which have been pollinated by random pollen from the population, is grown in unreplicated progeny rows for the purpose of selection. A part of the seed is planted to determine the yielding ability, or breeding value, for any character of each plant. The seed from the most productive rows or remnant seed from the outstanding half-sibs is bulked to complete one cycle of selection.

Full-sib Selection with Progeny Testing

A number of full-sib families, each produced by making crosses between the two plants from the base population are evaluated in replicated trials. A part of each full-sib family is saved for recombination. Based on evaluation the remnant seed of selected full-sib families is used to recombine the best families.

Breeding of Asexually Propagated Crops

Asexual reproduction covers all those modes of multiplication of plants, where normal gamete formation and fertilization does not take place making these distinctly different from normal seed production crops. In the absence of sexual reproduction, the genetic composition of plant material being multiplied remains essentially the same as its source plant.

Clones of mother plants can be made with the exact genetic composition of the mother plant. Superior plants are selected and propagated vegetatively; the vegetative propagated offspring are used to develop stable varieties without any deterioration due to segregation of gene combinations. This unique characteristic of asexual reproduction helped to develop a number of cultivars of fruits and vegetables including grapes, apples, pears and peaches.

Improving Asexual Plant Material through Selection

The selection in these crops is restricted to the material introduced from other sources, such as field plantations. The improvement of asexually propagated plants through induced mutations has distinct advantages and limitations. Any vegetative propagule can be treated with mutagens and even a single desirable mutant or a part of a mutated propagule (chimera) can be multiplied as an improved type of the original variety.

Selection of Asexual Plants

Selection, in the case of asexual plants, can be defined as the selection of the best performing plant and the vegetative propagation thereof. Because plants are not totally genetically stable, it can be expected that deviations would occur through the years. Selection is thus an ongoing process where deviants are selected or removed from the selection program. The main purpose of selection is to better the quality and yield of forthcoming plantations. Different approaches can be followed in the selection process of asexual plants, such as mass selection and clone selection from clone blocks.

In mass selection there are some factors that must be considered when selecting plants in a mother block, *e.g.*, vineyard. Time of selection is a big factor, because you have to select when most of the characteristics of the plant are clearly showing. With asexual perennials the best time is just before harvest. For the best results the selected plant must be evaluated during the next season, when growth-abnormalities, leave disfigurations and virus symptoms are best visualized. Mass selection is done annually on the same plant for a minimum of three years. A plant that does not conform to the requirements in any given year of the selection cycle is discarded from the program.

New Clone Development

The development and registration of new clones take place by means of local clone selection in old plantations, as well as the importation of high quality clones from abroad, for local evaluation.

A clone is the vegetative offspring of one specific mother plant; it does not show any genetic, morphologic or physiologic deviations from the mother plant. Evaluation takes place with the different selected clones after selection.

Marker Assisted Selection (MAS)

Marker Assisted Selection (MAS) is a combined product of traditional genetics and molecular Biology. MAS allows for the selection of genes that control traits of interest. Combined with traditional selection techniques, MAS has become a valuable tool in selecting organisms for traits of interest, such as colour, meat quality or disease resistance.

Molecular Markers

Until recently, researchers relied on information about how animals, plants and their relatives perform to make observations about the genes they possess. Today, researchers can use molecular markers to find genes of interest that control how plants and animals perform. Some molecular markers are pieces of DNA that have no known function or impact on animal and plant performance. Other markers may involve the gene of interest itself.

Linked Markers

One type of molecular marker is called a linked marker. Using well-designed experiments, scientists can find molecular markers that are located very close to major genes of interest. The molecular marker is said to be linked to that gene. Linked markers are only near the gene of interest on the chromosome and are not part of the DNA of the gene of interest.

Direct Markers

A second kind of molecular marker is one that is part of the gene of interest. Direct markers are easier to work with after they are found, but they often are more difficult to find than linked markers.

Three common technologies used as molecular markers are: restriction fragment length polymorphisms, simple sequence repeats and single nucleotide polymorphisms.

Restriction Fragment Length Polymorphisms (RFLPs)

Restriction fragment length polymorphisms (RFLPs) were the first molecular markers used to diagnose genetic variability in organisms. RFLP uses restriction enzymes to digest (cut) the DNA molecule and identify regions linked to a trait. The number of DNA fragments generated by one restriction enzyme digest can be in the millions, with many being several thousand nucleotides long. This makes it difficult to determine specific DNA fragments that are associated with the trait of interest on an electrophoresis gel. To help visualize specific DNA fragments, a technique called Southern blotting was developed.

Simple Sequence Repeats or Microsatellites

Simple Sequence Repeats (SSRs), also called microsatellites, are repeated units of two to six nucleotides that occur throughout an organism's genome. The sequence ATATATAT is one example of a microsatellite. The sequence GATGATGAT is another example. SSRs are useful as molecular markers because they are highly polymorphic (have many forms). SSRs have been used successfully as markers in a wide range of analysis, particularly those involving disease diagnosis and forensics.

Single Nucleotide Polymorphisms (SNPs)

On average, SNPs will occur in an organism's DNA more than 1% of the time. Because only about 3% to 5% of an organism's DNA codes for proteins, most SNPs are found outside the regions of genes of interest. SNPs found in a gene of interest are of particular interest to researchers because they are directly associated with a desired trait. Because of the recent advances in technology, SNPs are playing a greater role in selection and diagnosis of genetic traits.

Advantage of Molecular Markers

The advantage of molecular markers for researchers is that they can test for a particular trait as early as the embryo stage in animals or in the seeds of plants before they are planted. There is no longer a need for the organism to develop to a stage at which the trait can be observed, a wait that in some cases can take many years.

Bioremediation

Waste products resulting from human life have always been a serious problem. Today these waste products range from raw sewage to nuclear waste. To cope up these bioremediation seems to be a good alternative to conventional clean-up technologies research in this field which ultimately causing a rapidly growth in this field. Bioremediation is not a new technology. There has been evidence that compost piles existed as far back as 6000 BC, and in 1891 the first biological sewage treatment plant was created in Sussex, UK. However, the word 'bioremediation' did not appear in peer-reviewed scientific literature until 1987. By definition, bioremediation is the use of living organisms, primarily microorganisms, to degrade the environmental contaminants are biologically degraded under controlled conditions to an innocuous state to levels below concentration limits established by regulatory authorities.

It uses microorganisms for the degradation of hazardous chemicals in soil, sediments, water, or other contaminated materials. Often the microorganisms metabolize the chemicals to produce carbon dioxide or methane, water and biomass. Alternatively, the contaminants may be enzymatically transformed to metabolites that are less toxic or innocuous. It should be noted that in some instances, the metabolites formed are more toxic than the parent compound. For example, perchloroethylene and trichloroethylene may degrade to vinyl chloride. Apart bacteria, fungi, algae and plants have also been used for bioremediation. Biodegradation of a compound is often a result of the actions of multiple organisms. When microorganisms are imported to a contaminated site to enhance degradation we have a process known as **bioaugmentation.**

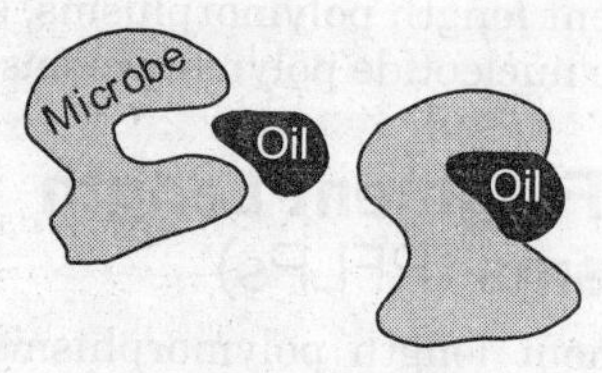

Microbe eats oil

Microbe digests oil and changes it to water and harmless gases

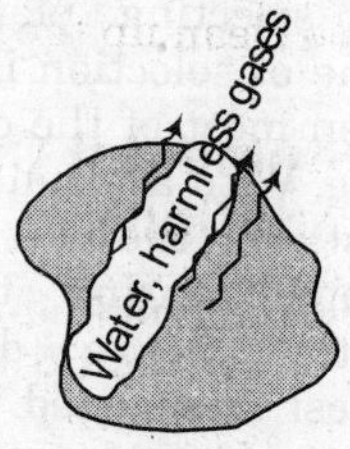

Microbe releases water and harmless gases into soil or groundwater

Fig. 36.19 Bioremediation the process

Bioremediation is very safe because it relies on microbes that naturally occur in soil. These microbes are helpful and pose no threat to people at the site or in the community. Microbes themselves won't hurt you, but never touch the polluted soil or groundwater especially before eating. No dangerous chemicals are used in bioremediation. The nutrients added to make microbes grow are fertilizers commonly used on lawns and gardens. Because bioremediation changes the harmful chemicals into water and harmless gases, the harmful chemicals are completely destroyed.

Bioremediation has been used at a number of sites worldwide, including Europe, with varying degrees of success. Techniques are improving as greater knowledge and experience are gained, and there is no doubt that bioremediation has great potential for dealing with certain types of site contamination. Like other technologies, bioremediation has its limitations. As bioremediation can be effective only where environmental conditions permit microbial growth and activity, its application often involves the manipulation of environmental parameters to allow microbial growth and degradation to proceed at a faster rate.

Microbes used for Bioremediation

Deinococcus radiodurans bacteria have been genetically modified to digest solvents and heavy metals, as well as toluene and ionic mercury from highly radioactive nuclear waste.

Geobacter sufurreducens bacteria can turn uranium dissolved in groundwater into a non-soluble, collectable form.

Dehalococcoides ethenogenes bacteria are being used in ten states to clean up chlorinated solvents that have been linked to cancer. The bacteria are naturally found in both soiland water and are able to digest the solvents much faster than using traditional clean up methods.

An enzyme from a bacterium, *Thermus brockianus*, found in Yellowstone National Park, breaks down hydrogen peroxide 80000 times faster than current chemicals in use.

The bacterium, *Alcaligenes eutrophus*, naturally degrades 2,4-D, the third most widely used herbicide in the US.

Most bioremediation systems are run under aerobic conditions, but running a system under anaerobic conditions may permit microbial organisms to degrade otherwise recalcitrant molecules. In order for microbes to clean up harmful chemicals, the right temperature, nutrients (fertilizers), and amount of oxygen must be present in the soil and groundwater. These conditions allow the microbes to grow and multiply and eat more chemicals. When conditions are not right, microbes grow too slowly or die. Or they can create more harmful chemicals. The control and optimization of bioremediation processes is a complex system of many factors. The time it takes to bioremediate a site depends on several factors:

(i) Types and amounts of harmful chemicals present.
(ii) Size and depth of the polluted area.
(iii) Type of soil and the conditions present.
(iv) Whether cleanup occurs above ground or underground.

These factors vary from site to site. It can take a few months or even several years for microbes to eat enough of the harmful chemicals to clean up the site.

Table 36.4 **Environmental Conditions Affecting Degradation**

Parameter	Condition Required for Microbial Activity	Optimum Value for an Oil Degradation
Soil moisture	25-28% of water holding capacity	30-90%
Soil pH	5.5-8.8	6.5-8.0
Oxygen content	Aerobic, minimum air-filled pore space of 10%	10-40%
Nutrient content	N and p for microbial growth	C:N:P: = 100 : 10 : 1
Temperature (°C)	15-45	20-30
Contaminants	Not too toxic	hydrocarbon 5-10% of dry weight of soil
Heavy metals	Total content 2000 ppm	700 ppm
Type of soil	Low clay or silt content	

Bioremediation is being classified in many classes based on various parameters. Based on type of degradation procedure bioremediation can be classified into three classes:

Biotransformation

The alteration of contaminant molecules into less or non-hazardous molecules.

Biodegradation

The breakdown of organic substances in smaller organic or inorganic molecules.

Mineralization

Is the complete biodegradation of organic materials into inorganic constituents such as CO_2 or H_2O_4.

These three classifications of bioremediation can occur either *in situ* (at the site of contamination) or *ex situ* (contaminant taken out of the site of contamination and treated elsewhere).

Based on the type of organism used bioremediation can also be broken down into four categories—bacterial remediation, mycoremediation, phytoremediation and compost bioremediation.

(i) Bacterial Remediation

Bacterial remediation is the process of using bacteria to break down molecular contaminants like hydrocarbons into simpler, safer components.

(ii) Mycoremediation and Phytoremediation

Mycoremediation and phytoremediation is the process of using fungi and plants respectively, to breakdown molecular contaminants like into simpler, safer components.

(iii) Compost Bioremediation

Large numbers of beneficial bacteria can be introduced into soil by brewing something called **compost tea** or through use of a product called effective microorganisms. Compost tea is a waterbased, oxygen-rich culture containing large populations of beneficial aerobic bacteria, nematodes, fungi, and Protozoa, which can be used to bioremediate toxins. It is made by adding an inoculant and a food source to non-chlorinated water and aerating it. The microorganisms present in the inoculant rapidly multiply when put in oxygen-rich water with ample food. This brew is applied to contaminated soil, where the microbial populations go to work breaking down certain types of molecular contaminants. The ease and low cost of making compost tea make it a method of bioremediation with the potential for widespread application.

Bioremediation Strategies

Different techniques are employed depending on the degree of saturation and aeration of an area.

In situ Bioremediation

In situ techniques are defined as those that are applied to soil and groundwater at the site with minimal disturbance. Bioremediation technologies that are used 'in place' without removal of the contaminated matrix. Both intrinsic and engineered bioremediation technologies can be used *in situ*.

These techniques are generally the most desirable options due to lower cost and less disturbance since, they provide the treatment in place avoiding excavation and transport of contaminants. *In situ* these techniques are generally the most desirable options due to lower cost and less disturbance since they provide the treatment in place avoiding excavation and transport of contaminants. *In situ* treatment is limited by the depth of the soil that can be effectively treated.

The most important land treatments are:

Bioventing is the most common *in situ* treatment and involves supplying air and nutrients through wells to contaminated soil to stimulate the indigenous bacteria. Bioventing employs low air flow rates and provides only the amount of oxygen necessary for the biodegradation while minimizing volatilization and release of contaminants to the atmosphere. It works for simple hydrocarbons and can be used, where the contamination is deep under the surface.

In situ biodegradation involves supplying oxygen and nutrients by circulating aqueous solutions through contaminated soils to stimulate naturally occurring bacteria to degrade organic contaminants.

It can be used for soil and groundwater. Generally, this technique includes conditions such as the infiltration of water-containing nutrients and oxygen or other electron acceptors for groundwater treatment.

Biosparging involves the injection of air under pressure below the water table to increase groundwater oxygen concentrations and enhance the rate of biological degradation of contaminants by naturally occurring bacteria. Biosparging increases the mixing in the saturated zone and thereby increases the contact between soil and groundwater. The ease and low cost of installing small-diameter air injection points allows considerable flexibility in the design and construction of the system.

Bioremediation frequently involves the addition of microorganisms indigenous or exogenous to the contaminated sites. Two factors limit the use of added microbial cultures in a land treatment unit:

1. Non-indigenous cultures rarely compete well enough with an indigenous population to develop and sustain useful population levels.
2. Most soils with long-term exposure to biodegradable waste have indigenous microorganisms that are effective degrades if the land treatment unit is well managed.

Ex situ Bioremediation

Bioremediation technologies that require removal of the contaminated matrix by excavation so it can be manipulated in some way through the use of slurry reactors, composting, biopiles, or other technologies. *Ex situ* techniques are those that are applied to soil and groundwater at the site which has been removed from the site *via* excavation (soil) or pumping (water). Bioaugmentation techniques involve the addition of microorganisms with the ability to degrade pollutants.

These techniques involve the excavation or removal of contaminated soil from ground.

Landfarming is a simple technique in which contaminated soil is excavated and spread over a prepared bed and periodically tilled until pollutants are degraded. The goal is to stimulate indigenous biodegradative microorganisms and facilitate their aerobic degradation of contaminants. In general, the practice is limited to the treatment of superficial 10-35 cm of soil. Since, landfarming has the potential to reduce monitoring and maintenance costs, as well as clean up liabilities, it has received much attention as a disposal alternative.

Composting is a technique that involves combining contaminated soil with non-hazardous organic amendants such as manure or agricultural wastes. The presence of these organic materials supports the development of a rich microbial population and elevated temperature characteristic of composting.

Biopiles are a hybrid of landfarming and composting. Essentially, engineered cells are constructed as aerated composted piles. Typically used for treatment of surface contamination with petroleum hydrocarbons they are a refined version of landfarming that tend to control physical losses of the contaminants by leaching and volatilization. Biopiles provide a favourable environment for indigenous aerobic and anaerobic microorganisms.

Bioreactors Slurry reactors or aqueous reactors are used for *ex situ* treatment of contaminated soil and water pumped up from a contaminated plume. Bioremediation in reactors involves the processing of contaminated solid material (soil, sediment and sludge) or water through an engineered containment system. A slurry bioreactor may be defined as a containment vessel and apparatus used to create a three phase (solid, liquid, and gas) mixing condition to increase the bioremediation rate of soilbound and water-soluble pollutants as a water slurry of the contaminated soil and biomass (usually indigenous microorganisms) capable of degrading target contaminants. In general, the rate and extent of biodegradation are greater in a bioreactor system than *in situ* or in solid-phase systems because the contained environment is more manageable and hence more controllable and predictable. Despite the advantages of reactor systems, there are some disadvantages. The contaminated soil requires pre treatment (*e.g.*, excavation) or alternatively the contaminant can be stripped from the soil *via* soil washing or physical extraction (*e.g.*, vacuum extraction) before being placed in a bioreactor.

Other Remediation Technologies

Intrinsic Bioremediation

Often bioremediation can be accomplished without human intervention by microorganisms that are naturally found in the contaminated matrix. For this approach to be used, it is usually necessary for the rate of contaminant degradation to exceed the rate of contaminant migration. Knowledge of the following key site characteristics are required to evaluate the likely success of intrinsic remediation; the bioavailability of contaminants, levels of nutrients, the presence of minerals to buffer the pH of the matrix, adequate levels of electron acceptors (either oxygen, nitrate, ferric iron or sulphate), and site specific contamination migration rates.

Engineered Bioremediation

In some cases, it may be desirable to construct engineered systems to supply nutrients, electron acceptors or other materials that enhance the rate or extent of contaminant degradation. This is desirable when the rate of contaminant migration, the location of environmental receptors or other liability issues dictate that steps be taken to optimize the rate of contaminant degradation in order to mitigate contaminant migration. The key site characteristics for engineered bioremediation are the same as for intrinsic remediation. However, in addition, it is important to consider factors that affect the ability to introduce chemicals to the environment such as the permeability of the soils or subsurface and the uniformity of the sub-surface.

Combination of Technologies

Non-biological treatment technologies or source removal may be used to reduce the total amount of contaminant present at the site before, or concurrent with, bioremediation. For example, excessively contaminated soils may be excavated at the source of contamination, volatile contaminants may be vacuum extracted or undissolved pools of contaminants may be pumped from aquifers.

Table 36.5 **Summary of Bioremediation Strategies**

Technology	Example	Benefit	Limitation	Factors to Consider
In situ	*In situ* bioremediation	Most cost efficient	Environmental constraints	Biodegradative abilities of indigenous microorganisms
	Biosparging	Non-invasive	Extended treatment time	Presence of metals and other inorganics
	Bioventing	Relatively passive	Monitoring difficulties	Environmental parameters
	Bioaugmentation	Natural attenuation process		Biodegradability of pollutants
		Treats soil and water		Chemical solubility
				Geological factors
				Distribution of pollutants
Ex situ	Landfarming	Cost efficient	Space requirements	See above
	Composting	Low cost	Extended treatment time	
	Biopiles	Can be done on site	Need to control abiotic loss	
			Mass transfer problem	
			Bioavailability limitation	
Bioreactors	Slurry reactors	Rapid degradation kinetic	Soil requires excavation	See above
	Aqueous reactors	Optimized environmental parameters	Relatively high cost capital	Bioaugmentation
				Toxicity of amendments
		Enhances mass transfer	Relatively high operating	Toxic concentrations of contaminants
		Effective use of inoculants	Cost	

Potential Advantages and Disadvantages of Bioremediation

The use of intrinsic or engineered bioremediation processes offers several potential advantages that are attractive to site owners, regulatory agencies and the public. These include:

Advantages of Bioremediation

Bioremediation is a natural process and is therefore perceived by the public as an acceptable waste treatment process for contaminated material such as soil. Microbes able to degrade the contaminant increase in numbers when the contaminant is present; when the contaminant is degraded, the biodegradative population declines. The residues for the treatment are usually harmless products and include carbon dioxide, water and cell biomass.

(a) Theoretically, bioremediation is useful for the complete destruction of a wide variety of contaminants. Many compounds that are legally considered to be hazardous can be transformed to harmless products. This eliminates the chance of future liability associated with treatment and disposal of contaminated material.

(b) Instead of transferring contaminants from one environmental medium to another, for example, from land to water or air, the complete destruction of target pollutants is possible.

(c) Bioremediation can often be carried out on site, often without causing a major disruption of normal activities. This also eliminates the need to transport quantities of waste off site and the potential threats to human health and the environment that can arise during transportation.

(d) Bioremediation can prove less expensive than other technologies that are used for clean-up of hazardous waste.

Disadvantages of Bioremediation

(a) Bioremediation is limited to those compounds that are biodegradable. Not all compounds are susceptible to rapid and complete degradation.

(b) There are some concerns that the products of biodegradation may be more persistent or toxic than the parent compound.

(c) Biological processes are often highly specific. Important site factors required for success include the presence of metabolically capable microbial populations, suitable environmental growth conditions, and appropriate levels of nutrients and contaminants.

(d) It is difficult to extrapolate from bench and pilot-scale studies to full-scale field operations.

(e) Research is needed to develop and engineer bioremediation technologies that are appropriate for sites with complex mixtures of contaminants that are not evenly dispersed in the environment. Contaminants may be present as solids, liquids and gases.

(f) Bioremediation often takes longer than other treatment options, such as excavation and removal of soil or incineration.

(g) Regulatory uncertainty remains regarding acceptable performance criteria for bioremediation. There is no accepted definition of 'clean', evaluating performance of bioremediation is difficult, and there are no acceptable endpoints for bioremediation treatments.

Some of the commercially available and patented bioremediation processes used worldwide, are described here

Tossom Two-step Static System

Tossom is a two-stage solid phase bioremediation technology that involves both anaerobic and aerobic treatment stages. In the first stage, explosives-contaminated soil is combined with a carbon source, an inoculum, vitamins and water to achieve anaerobic conditions. The resulting mixture is formed into a static pile or placed in a bermed construction or box to facilitate the chemical reduction of nitroaromatic and nitramine explosives.

In the second stage, the anaerobically treated soil is combined with yard waste compost and built into an aerated biopile. The biopile may be aerated by forced air conveyed through perforated piping buried within the pile or by turning the pile with a compost turner. Previous testing of TOSSSM has demonstrated TNT removal efficiencies of >99%.

Bio-In-A-BoxSM

Bio-In-A-BoxSM is a waste management process for remediating petrochemical-contaminated soils in quantities of 1000 cubic yards or less. In this process, the contaminated soil is moistened, mixed with nutrients and custom-grown microorganisms and then placed in enclosed containers called 'solid phase bioreactors' for incubation. These containers may or may not be linked to aeration and vacuum pipes, depending on the contaminants being processed. In just a few weeks, the decontaminated soil will be ready for landfill disposal or reintroduction into the environment.

The Biositesm System

The biositesm system is waste management's proprietary system for the large-scale bioremediation of soils contaminated with petrochemicals including, but not limited to:

(i) Acetone
(ii) Benzene
(iii) Toluene
(iv) Methyl ethyl ketone
(v) Methyl Isobutyl Ketone (MEK) (MIBK)
(vi) Petroleum hydrocarbons
(vii) Two and three-ring PAHs
(viii) Alcohols
(ix) Ethylbenzene
(x) Xylene

The biositesm system can also handle other contaminants, including

(a) Aliphatic chlorinated hydrocarbons (*e.g.*, Trichloroethylene).
(b) Spent molecular sieve from packing towers.
(c) Chemical manufacturing wastes.
(d) Pesticide.

DDT contaminated soils may be treated using the xenorem bioremediation process licensed from astrazeneca.

Phytoremediation

Although the application of microbe biotechnology has been successful with petroleum-based constituents, microbial digestion has met limited success for widespread residual organic and metals pollutants. Vegetation-based remediation shows potential for accumulating, immobilizing and transforming a low level of persistent contaminants. In natural ecosystems, plants act as filters and metabolize substances generated by nature. Phytoremediation is an emerging technology that uses plants to remove contaminants from soil and water. The term 'phytoremediation' is relatively new, coined in 1991. Its potential for encouraging the biodegradation of organic contaminants requires further research, although it may be a promising area for the future. Phytoremediation is well suited for use at very large field sites where other methods of remediation are not cost effective or practicable; at sites with a low concentration of contaminants where only polish treatment is required over long periods of time; and in conjunction with other technologies where vegetation is used as a final cap and closure of the site. There are some limitations to the technology that it is necessary to consider carefully before it is selected for site remediation: long duration of time for remediation, potential contamination of the vegetation and food chain, and difficulty establishing and maintaining vegetation at some sites with high toxic levels.

We can find five types of phytoremediation techniques, classified based on the contaminant fate: phytoextraction, phytotransformation, phytostabilization, phytodegradation, rhizofiltration, even if a combination of these can be found in nature.

Phytoextraction or Phytoaccumulation

Is the process used by the plants to accumulate contaminants into the roots and aboveground shoots or leaves. This technique saves tremendous remediation cost by accumulating low levels of contaminants from a widespread area. Unlike the degradation mechanisms, this process produces a mass of plants and contaminants (usually metals) that can be transported for disposal or recycling.

Phytotransformation or Phytodegradation

Refers to the uptake of organic contaminants from soil, sediments, or water and, subsequently, their transformation to more stable, less toxic or less mobile form. Metal chromium can be reduced from hexavalent to trivalent chromium, which is a less mobile and non-carcinogenic form.

Phytostabilization

Is a technique in which plants reduce the mobility and migration of contaminated soil. Leachable constituents are adsorbed and bound into the plant structure so that they form a stable mass of plant from which the contaminants will not reenter the environment.

Phytodegradation or Rhizodegradation

Is the breakdown of contaminants through the activity existing in the rhizosphere. This activity is due to the presence of proteins and enzymes produced by the plants or by soil organisms such as bacteria, yeast and fungi. Rhizodegradation is a symbiotic relationship that has evolved between plants and microbes. Plants provide nutrients necessary for the microbes to thrive, while microbes provide a healthier soil environment.

Rhizofiltration

Is a water remediation technique that involves the uptake of contaminants by plant roots. Rhizofiltration is used to reduce contamination in natural wetlands and estuary areas. In **Table 36.6**, we can see an overview of phytoremediation applications.

Table 36.6 **Overview of Phytoremediation Applications**

Technique	Plant Mechanism	Surface Medium
Phytoextraction	Uptake and concentration of metal via direct uptake into the plant tissue with subsequent removal of the plants.	Soils
Phytotransformation	Plant uptake and degradation of organic compounds.	Surface water and ground water.
Phytostabilization	Root exudates cause metal to precipitate and become less available.	Soils, groundwater and mine tailing.
Phytodegradation	Enhances microbial degradation in rhizosphere.	Soils, groundwater within rhizosphere
Rhizofiltration	Uptake of metals into plant roots.	Surface water and water pumped.
Phytovolatilization	Plants evapour transpirate selenium, mercury and volatile hydrocarbons.	Soils and groundwater.
Vegetative cap	Rainwater is evapour transpirated by plants to prevent leaching contaminants from disposal sites.	Soils

Some plants used for phytoremediation are:

(a) Alfalfa symbiotic with hydrocarbon-degrading bacteria.

(b) Transgenic *Arabidopsis* carries a bacterial gene that transforms mercury into a gaseous state.

(c) Bamboo family accumulates silica in its stalk and nitrogen as crude protein in its leaves.

(d) Indian mustard (*Brassica juncea*) accumulates selenium, sulphur, lead, chromium, cadmium, nickel, zinc and copper.

(e) Chinese ladder fern (*Pteris vittata*) accumulates arsenic.

(f) Cottonwood (with added *E.coli* gene) accumulates mercury.

(g) Tomato and alpine pennycress accumulates lead, zinc and cadmium.

(h) Poplar used in the absorption of the pesticide, atrazine.

Some of the best houseplants for filtering indoor air (and the pollutants they filter) include

(a) Green spider plant *Chlorophytum comosum* (formaldehyde).

(b) Mother-in-law's tongue or snake plant *Sansevieria trifasciata* (formaldehyde and benzene).

(c) Chrysanthemums *Chrysanthemum* sp. (benzene).

(d) Gerbera daisies *Gerbera* sp. (benzene and trichloroethylene).

(e) Varieties of *Philodendron* sp *P. scandens*, *P. domesticum* and *P. selloum* (formaldehyde).

(f) Varieties of *Dracaena* sp. *D. fragrans*, *D. deremensis*, *D. warneckii* and *D. marginata* (formaldehyde)

(g) English ivy, *Hedera helix* (benzene).

(h) Golden pothos *Epipiremnum aureum* (formaldehyde).

(i) *Peace lily Spathiphyllum* (formaldehyde, benzene and trichloroethylene).

(j) Aloe vera *Aloe vera* (formaldehyde).

Biosensor

A biosensor is an analytical device for the detection of an analyte that combines a biological component with a physicochemical detector component. According to IUPAC, a biosensor is a self-contained integrated device which is capable of providing specific quantitative or semi-quantitative analytical information using a biological recognition element which is in direct spatial contact with a transducer element.

As can be inferred from the definition a typical biosensor has two basic components:

Sensitive biological element It is typically complex chemical system usually extracted or derived directly from a biological system, *e.g.*, tissue, microorganisms, organelles, cell receptors, enzymes, antibodies, nucleic acids, etc. Bioelement interact specifically with a target compound and it generally capable of detecting the presence of a target compound in the test solution which is ultimately is the basis for biosensor.

Transducer or the detector element transforms the signal resulting from the interaction of the analyte with the biological element into another signal (*i.e.*, transducers) that can be more easily measured and quantified. Mostly transducers work in physicochemical way. Biosensor reader device along with the associated electronics or signal processors are primarily responsible for the display of the results in a user-friendly way.

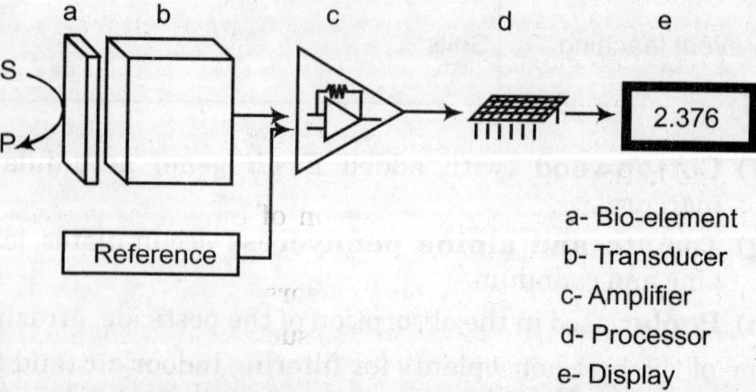

Fig. 36.20 Schematic diagram of biosensor

On the basis of signal generated and translated in some readable units, biosensors can be classified in various categories.

Optical Biosensor

Many optical biosensors based on the phenomenon of Surface Plasmon Resonance (SPR) are evanescent wave techniques. This utilizes a property of gold and other materials; specifically that a thin layer of gold on a high refractive index glass surface can absorb laser light, producing electron waves (surface plasmons) on the gold surface. This occurs only at a specific angle and wavelength of incident light and is highly dependent on the surface of the gold, such that binding of a target analyte to a receptor on the gold surface produces a measurable signal.

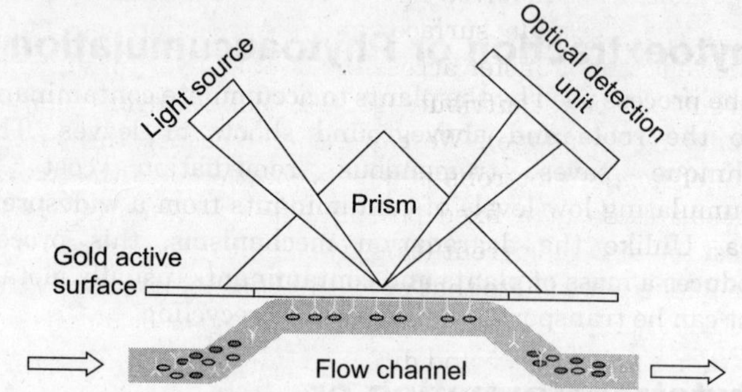

Fig. 36.21 An optical biosensor

Surface plasmon resonance sensors operate using a sensor chip consisting of a plastic cassette supporting a glass plate, one side of which is coated with a microscopic layer of gold. This side contacts the optical detection apparatus of the instrument. The opposite side is then contacted with a microfluidic flow system. The contact with the flow system creates channels across which reagents can be passed in solution. This side of the glass sensor chip can be modified in a number of ways, to allow easy attachment of molecules of interest. Normally it is coated in carboxymethyl dextran or similar compound.

Light of a fixed wavelength is reflected off the gold side of the chip at the angle of total internal reflection, and detected inside the instrument. This induces the evanescent wave to penetrate through the glass plate and some distance into the liquid flowing over the surface.

The refractive index at the flow side of the chip surface has a direct influence on the behaviour of the light reflected off the gold side. Binding to the flow side of the chip has an effect on the refractive index and in this way biological interactions can be measured to a high degree of sensitivity with some sort of energy. The refractive index of the medium near the surface changes when biomolecules attach to the surface, and the SPR angle varies as a function of this change.

Other optical biosensors are mainly based on changes in absorbance or fluorescence of an appropriate indicator compound and do not need a total internal reflection geometry. A widely used research tool, the micro-array, can also be considered a biosensor. Nanobiosensors use a immobilized bioreceptor probe that is selective for target analyte molecules. Nanomaterials are exquisitely sensitive chemical and biological sensors. Nanoscale materials demonstrate unique properties. Their large surface area to volume ratio can achieve rapid and low cost reactions, using a variety of designs.

Electrochemical Biosensor

Electrochemical biosensors are normally based on enzymatic catalysis of a reaction that produces or consumes electrons (such enzymes are rightly called redox enzymes). The sensor substrate usually contains three electrodes; a reference electrode, a working electrode and a counter electrode. The target analyte is involved in the reaction that takes place on the active electrode surface, and the reaction may cause either electron transfer across the double layer (producing a current) or can contribute to the double layer potential (producing a voltage). We can either measure the current (rate of flow of electrons is now proportional to the analyte concentration) at a fixed potential or the potential can be measured at zero current (this gives a logarithmic response). It is important to note that potential of the working or active electrode is space charge sensitive and this is often used. Further, the label-free and direct electrical detection of small peptides and proteins is possible by their intrinsic charges using biofunctionalized ion-sensitive field-effect transistors.

Another example, the potentiometric biosensor, (potential produced at zero current) gives a logarithmic response with a high dynamic range. Such biosensors are usually often made by screen printing the electrode patterns on a plastic substrate, coated with a conducting polymer and then some protein (enzyme or antibody) is attached. They have only two electrodes and are extremely sensitive and robust.

Ion-Selective Biosensor

The use of ion channels has been shown to offer highly sensitive detection of target biological molecules. By imbedding the ion channels in supported or tethered bilayer membranes (t-BLM) attached to a gold electrode, an electrical circuit is created. Capture molecules such as antibodies can be bound to the ion channel so that the binding of the target molecule controls the ion flow through the channel. This results in a measurable change in the electrical conduction which is proportional to the concentration of the target.

Resonant Biosensor

Piezoelectric sensors utilize crystals which undergo an elastic deformation when an electrical potential is applied to them. An alternating potential (AC) produce a standing wave in the crystal at a characteristic frequency. This frequency is highly dependent on the elastic properties of the crystal, such that if a crystal is coated with a biological recognition element the binding of a (large) target analyte to a receptor will produce a change in the resonance frequency, which gives a binding signal. In a mode that uses surface acoustic waves (SAW), the sensitivity is greatly increased. This is a specialized application of the quartz crystal microbalance as a biosensor.

Thermometric and magnetic based biosensors are rare.

Applications

There are many potential applications of biosensors of various types. The main requirements for a biosensor approach to be valuable in terms of research and commercial applications are the identification of a target molecule, availability of a suitable biological recognition element, and the potential for disposable portable detection systems to be preferred to sensitive laboratory-based techniques in some situations. Some examples are given below:

- Glucose monitoring in diabetes patients historical market driver.

A common example of a commercial biosensor is the blood glucose biosensor, which uses the enzyme glucose oxidase to break blood glucose down. In doing so it first oxidizes glucose and uses two electrons to reduce the FAD (a component of the enzyme) to $FADH_2$. This in turn is oxidized by the electrode (accepting two electrons from the electrode) in a number of steps. The resulting current is a measure of the concentration of glucose.

(i) Other medical health related targets.

(ii) Environmental applications, *e.g.*, the detection of pesticides and river water contaminants.

(iii) Remote sensing of airborne bacteria, *e.g.*, in counter-bioterrorist activities.

(iv) Detection of pathogens.

(v) Determining levels of toxic substances before and after bioremediation.

(vi) Detection and determining of organophosphate.

(vii) Routine analytical measurement of folic acid, biotin, vitamin-B_{12} and pantothenic acid as an alternative to microbiological assay.

(viii) Determination of drug residues in food, such as antibiotics and growth promoters, particularly meat and honey.

(ix) Drug discovery and evaluation of biological activity of new compounds.

(x) Protein engineering in biosensors.

(xi) Detection of toxic metabolites such as mycotoxins.

Exercise

1. Fermentation is the
(a) production of alcoholic beverages by microorganisms
(b) mass, controlled culture of microbes to synthesize products
(c) use of microbes in sewage and pollution control
(d) All of the above

2. Detrimental effects of microorganisms in food include
(a) flavouring (b) fermentation
(c) spoilage (d) providing protein

3. Food fermentations include
(a) leavening bread (b) pickling
(c) alcohol production (d) All of these

4. Fermentation of grains usually results in production of
(a) carbon dioxide (b) brine
(c) must (d) All of these

5. During malting, barley and other grains are broken down by
(a) heating to 95°C (b) Lagering
(c) amylases (d) yeasts

6. Milk fermentation to produce cheese is done initially by inoculating with
(a) *Saccharomyces cerevisiae*
(b) *Streptococcus lactis* and *Lactobacillus* sp.
(c) *Acetobacter* and *Gluconobacter*
(d) *Lactobacillus bulgaricus* and *Streptococcus thermophilus*

7. Pickles and sauerkraut share a common inoculum, which is
(a) *Lactobacilus plantarum*
(b) *Lactobaciluis bulgaricus*
(c) *Lactobacilus acidophilus*
(d) *Saccharomyces cerevisiae*

8. Primary methods to prevent food spoilage do not include
(a) radiation (b) heat
(c) sugar (d) exposure

9. The 'flash method' or 'high temperature short time' method exposes fluids to
(a) heat below 100 °C (b) 62.3 °C for 30 min
(c) 72 °C for 15 s (d) 134 °C for 1 s

10. Chemical preservatives do not include
(a) organic acids (b) sulphates
(c) alcohol (d) starch

11. Nitrates maintain the red colour of preserved meats and
(a) are among the most widely used preservatives
(b) inhibit germination of botulism spores
(c) maintain a high osmotic pressure to kill microorganisms
(d) prevent mold

12. Salting, as a preservative,
(a) retards growth of *Staphylococcus aureus*
(b) plasmolyzes bacteria and fungi
(c) is used to prevent growth of halophiles
(d) All of the above

13. Industrial microbiologists use 'tricks' to increase the amount of chosen end product; this may include
(a) manipulating the growth environment
(b) using small scale containers to concentrate production
(c) selecting microbial strains that lack a feedback system
(d) Both (a) and (b)

14. The production of substances in industrial microbiology occur in the sequence
(a) fermentation, downstream processing, removal of waste and inoculation
(b) inoculation, downstream processing, fermentation and removal of waste
(c) inoculation, fermentation, downstream processing and removal of waste
(d) removal of waste, inoculation, fermentation and downstream processing

15. In batch fermentation
(a) substrates are added to the system all at once and runs until product is harvested
(b) nutrients are continuously fed into the reactor and the product is siphoned off during the run
(c) new batches of microorganisms are screened for increase yield
(d) small-scale production is used to synthesize product

16. Secondary metabolites
(a) are essential to microbe function
(b) are byproducts of metabolism that are not important to microbe function
(c) are products that require additional processing before they can be packaged
(d) are harvested during the exponential phase of growth

17. Which of the following statement is true?
(a) Biotechnology, the practical application of microorganisms in making products for human use, is a relatively new science, begun since Pasteur's time
(b) Yeast cells prefer aerobic conditions to multiply in number
(c) HACCP — Hazard Analysis and Critical Control Point uses random samples for quality control of the food supply
(d) Pasteurization is used to sterilize milk

18. Which of the following statement is incorrect?
(a) Mass-produced microbial cells can be used as livestock feed
(b) Freezing at below –20°C will kill most pathogenic food bacteria and inactivate toxins
(c) Hot foods must be maintained above 60°C to inhibit microbial growth
(d) The aim of industrial microbiology is to produce chemicals that can be purified and packaged for sale or used in other commercial processes

19. When energy-depleted elements associated with a proton are accepted by an organic molecule, the process is called
(a) fermentation (b) anaerobic
(c) aerobic (d) catabolism

20. In the presence of abundant oxygen, yeast cells greatly prefer fermentation to oxidative phosphorylation, as long as sugars are readily available for consumption a phenomenon known as the
(a) hill effect (b) chloride shift
(c) crabtree effect (d) None of these

21. The pH, to be maintained for the production of penicillin is
(a) 7.5 (b) 6.5
(c) 8.0 (d) 5.0

22. Maximum application of animal cell culture technology today is in the production of
(a) interferons (b) vaccines
(c) edible proteins (d) insulin

23. The medium used in membrane filter technique was
(a) EMB agar (b) EMR-Vp medium
(c) lactose broth (d) endo agar

24. Lysol is a
(a) sterilent (b) disinfectant
(c) antiseptic (d) antifungal agent

25. Peptone water medium is an example of
(a) synthetic medium (b) semisynthetic medium
(c) differential medium (d) None of these

26. Thermal death time is
(a) time required to kill all cells at a given temperature
(b) temperature that kills all cells in a given time
(c) time and temperature needed to kill all cells
(d) All of the above

27. A culture medium the exact composition of which is not known is called as
(a) simple (b) complex
(c) defined (d) natural

28. Separation of a single bacterial colony is called
(a) isolation (b) separation
(c) pure culturing (d) All of these

29. The bacterial culture prepared by pure culture method is
(a) inoculums (b) suspension
(c) dilution (d) None of these

30. The conditions required for autoclave
(a) 121°C temperature and 15 lbs pressure for 20 min
(b) 120°C temperature and 20 lbs pressure for 30 min
(c) 150°C temperature for 1 h
(d) 130°C temperature for 2 h

31. Blood agar medium is
(a) enrichment medium (b) enriched medium
(c) selective medium (d) differential medium

32. Example of indicator medium is
(a) nutrient agar (b) nutrient broth
(c) Wilson and Blair medium (d) Czapeck-dox medium

33. Example of anaerobic medium is
(a) Robertson cocked-meat medium
(b) nutrient agar
(c) nutrient broth
(d) Mac-Conkey's agar

34. Best method for getting pure culture is
(a) streak-plate (b) agar slant
(c) Both (a) and (b) (d) None of these

35. For transfering cultures from one place to another, the device used is
(a) slant (b) needle
(c) inoculation loop (d) autoclave

36. Cultures are prepared by penetrating the inoculation loop with suspension into the medium, they are
(a) stock cultures (b) stab cultures
(c) sub cultures (d) None of these

37. Which of the following is one cardinal rule for a workable vaccine?
(a) It must last a lifetime
(b) It must contain an antigen that will provide protection but not cause the disease
(c) It must induce only the humoral immune response to be considered effective
(d) It must be administered intramuscularly to increase its effectiveness

38. How long does the protection provided by Immune Serum Globulin (ISG) last?
(a) 30 min (b) 24 h
(c) 1-2 weeks (d) 2-3 months

39. Which of the following is not a quality of an effective vaccine?
(a) It should require periodic boosters to maintains its effectiveness
(b) It should stimulate the production of memory cells
(c) it should stimulate both a humoral and cell-mediated immune response
(d) it should protect against the natural form of the pathogen

40. What is one disadvantage of using attenuated vaccines?
(a) They require fewer doses and boosters than other types of vaccines
(b) They provide long-lasting protection
(c) They produce an infection following vaccination
(d) The organisms can mutate back to a virulent form following vaccination

41. What is the agglutinogen in a viral haemagglutination test?
(a) Antibodies
(b) Antigens
(c) White blood cells
(d) Red blood cells

42. The double diffusion method allows for disease identification and diagnosis and is an application of what immunological technique?
(a) Agglutination (b) Precipitation
(c) Immunoassay (d) Antigenesis

43. Plant tissue culture is important to study the factors controlling
(a) growth and differentiation
(b) ageing and mutation
(c) pathogenecity skin grafting
(d) All of the above

44. Animal cell culture is quite popular in raising
(a) hormones (b) enzymes
(c) bacteria (d) vaccines

45. Tissue culture was developed by .... but the concept of tissue culture was conceived by ....
(a) Habertland; Haorison (b) Haorison; Habertland
(c) Haorison; C White (d) C White; Habertland

46. In plant tissue culture-callus is
(a) differentiated non-dividing mass of cells
(b) differentiated actively diving mass of cells
(c) undifferentiated non-dividing mass of cells
(d) undifferentiated actively dividing mass of cells

47. Which of the following statements regarding immunizations are true?
(a) Pneumococcal vaccines protect against infections with all types of *Streptococcus pneumoniae*
(b) MMR is the only live vaccine in the childhood immunization schedule in UK
(c) Meningococcal group C vaccine protects against all childhood meningococcal disease in the UK
(d) None of the above

48. What is an enrichment culture?
(a) Something that provides growth for all microorganisms
(b) Something that inhibits growth for all microorganisms
(c) An infectious culture
(d) Something that provides growth for a certain microorganism but not for others

49. What is an inoculating loop?
(a) A tool used to streak a microorganism in a pure culture
(b) A tool used to place agar in a pure medium
(c) A tool used to count colonies of microorganisms
(d) A tool used to view colonies of microorganisms

50. Which of the following statement is false regarding immunizations given in certain situation?
(a) A 5 year old weighing 18 kg who had prednisolone 20mg daily for 2 days for asthma attack 2 weeks ago needs MMR vaccine
(b) A 13 month old child weighing 10 kg is on Beclomethasone inhaler 100 mg twice a day needs MMR vaccine
(c) A 16 year old who has had IV immunoglobulin following severe sepsis 2 months previously due her tetanus, diphtheria and polio booster
(d) A patient with leukaemia who has completed his chemotherapy 5 months ago due his MMR vaccines before starting school

51. Which of the following statements regarding immunizations are false?
(a) MMR vaccine should not be given if a child has already had a rubella infection
(b) An adolescent who has had 5 doses of tetanus is likely to have life-long immunity
(c) Neomycin and streptomycin are both excipients of some vaccines and may cause allergic reactions
(d) Rubella vaccines may produce a very mild form of the disease

52. Which of the following was the first genetically modified animal to be sold as a pet?
(a) Glfish (b) Glofish
(c) Goldfish (d) Goldenfish

53. Genetic modification involves the insertion or deletion of genes. When genes are inserted, they usually come from a different species, which is a form of
(a) lateral gene transfer
(b) horizontal gene transfer
(c) forward gene transfer
(d) backward gene transfer

54. Which of the following method is a popular vehicle used for the transferring genetic material to animal cells?
(a) *Agrobacterium* sp. (b) HIV
(c) Lentiviruses (d) *Pseudomonas* sp.

55. The first recbacteria of *E. coli* was created in .... expressing exogenic *Salmonella* gene
(a) 1957 (b) 1973
(c) 1985 (d) 1999

56. The potential risk of using genetic engineering were first discussed in depth at the
(a) Berlin conference 1977
(b) Athens conference 1976
(c) Asilomar conference 1975
(d) New York conference 1974

57. GMOs are used in biological and medical research for
(a) production of pharmaceutical drugs
(b) experimental medicine (*e.g.,* gene therapy)
(c) agriculture (*e.g.,* golden rice)
(d) All of the above

58. To date the most widely adopted application of GMO technology is patent-protected
(a) food crops that are resistant to commercial herbicides
(b) able to produce pesticidal proteins from within the plant
(c) stacked trait seeds
(d) All of the above

59. As per, a 2007 report from the European Joint Research Commission predicts that by 2015, more than 40 per cent of new GM plants entering the global market place will have been developed in
(a) Africa (b) Asia
(c) North America (d) Latin America

60. Which of the following is famous GM crops is not developed by Monsanto?
(a) Triple-stack corn (b) *Bt* crops
(c) Bollgard (d) Golden rice

61. Transgenic animals are also becoming useful commercially. On February 6, 2009, the US FDA approved the first human biological drug produced from such an animal, a goat. The drug, ATryn, is an
(a) antidepressant (b) anticoagulant
(c) anticancer (d) antibody

62. Testing on GMOs in food and feed is routinely done by
(a) DNA microarrays (b) qPCR
(c) Both (a) and (b) (d) None of these

63. Which of the following is an example of event specific marker selected for the testing of GMO?
(a) p35S (b) tNos
(c) bar (d) *Bt*11

64. A CaMV check is important to avoid .... outcomes based on virus contamination of the sample.
(a) false negative (b) false positive
(c) true positive (d) true negative

65. Genetically modified bacteria are used to produce
(a) antidiabetic protein (b) clotting factors
(c) human growth hormone (d) All of these

66. Some chimeras, like the blotched mouse, are created through genetic modification techniques like
(a) gene inactivation (b) gene deletion
(c) gene therapy (d) gene targeting

67. Stable expressions of human proteins have not been developed in
(a) sheep (b) pigs
(c) rats (d) elephant

68. Which of the following insect has been produced as transgenic?
(a) *Drosophila melanogaster*
(b) *Pectinophora gossypiella*
(c) malaria-resistant mosquitoes
(d) All of the above

69. In 1999, scientists at the University of Guelph in Ontario, Canada, created the genetically engineered enviropig. The characteristics of this transgenic pig is
(a) it is used to produce hGH
(b) the meat obtain is of superior quality
(c) this pig is used to produce tissues for transplant purposes
(d) it excretes from 30 to 70.7% less phosphorus in manure depending upon the age and diet

70. Scientists at the University of York developed a weed *Arabidopsis thaliana* that contains genes from bacteria that can be used for
(a) killing insects
(b) increasing crop yields
(c) clean up TNT and RDX-explosive contaminants from the soil
(d) cleaning oil spillage in the field

71. .... is a product designation for a category of genetically engineered plants.
(a) Cisgenesis (b) Transgenesis
(c) Intragenesis (d) Both (a) and (c)

72. Which of the following was the first and only country to impose a ban on the 'propagation, cultivation, raising, and growing of genetically modified organisms'?
(a) Mendocino Country, California
(b) Monsanto, New York
(c) Agricultural Genetics, London
(d) None of the above

73. Which of the following is the only GMO food crop with approval for cultivation in Europe?
(a) MON810 (b) Amflora
(c) *Bt* cotton (d) Both (a) and (b)

74. Some degree of natural flow of genes, often called horizontal gene transfer or lateral gene transfer, occurs between plant species is facilitated by
(a) transposons (b) retrotransposons
(c) proviruses (d) All of these

75. The first field trials of genetically engineered plants occurred in .... in 1986, when tobacco plants were engineered to be resistant to herbicides.
(a) France and USA (b) USA and Brazil
(c) USA and Italy (d) France and Italy

76. In 1987, plant Genetic systems founded by Marc Van Montagu and Jeff Schell, was the first company to develop genetically engineered .... plants with *Bt* genes.
(a) corn (b) wheat
(c) rice (d) tobacco

77. In 1994, the European Union approved .... engineered to be resistant to the herbicide bromoxynil, making it the first commercially genetically engineered crop marketed in Europe
(a) rice (b) corn
(c) tomato (d) tobacco

78. In 1995, ... was approved safe by the Environmental Protection Agency making it the first pesticide producing crop to be approved in the USA
(a) *Bt* corn (b) *Bt* potato
(c) *Bt* brinjal (d) *Bt* tamato

79. Most genetically modified plants are generated by the
(a) biolistic method
(b) *Agrobacterium tumefaciens*
(c) lentivirus
(d) Both (a) and (b)

80. Which of the following possible avenues of hybridization leading to escape of a transgene?
(a) Hybridization with non-transgenic crop plants of the same species and variety
(b) Hybridization with wild plants of the same species
(c) Hybridization with wild plants of closely related species, usually of the same genus
(d) All of the above

81. Which of the following factors must be present for hybrids to be created?
(a) The transgenic plants must be close enough to the wild species for the pollen to reach the wild plants
(b) The wild and transgenic plants must flower at the same time
(c) The wild and transgenic plants must be genetically compatible
(d) All of the above

82. Find the unmatched.

Biomolecules Produced		Transgenic Organism
I. Human-alpha-1-antitrypsin	—	Sheep
II. Human-histo-compatibility	—	Pigs
III. Rec-lysozyme	—	chicken

(a) I only (b) III only
(c) I and III (d) II and III

83. Genetically modified plants have also been used for
(a) bioremediation (b) antigen production
(c) cry toxins (d) All of these

84. Match the gene of interest for various aspects of crop improvement.

List I (Gene insert)	List II (Aspects of crop improvement)
A. Bar	1. Tolerance to heavy metals
B. Vip3A	2. Nutritional improvement with increased vitamin-A
C. β-*lac*	3. Insect resistance
D. gshII	4. Herbicide resistance
	5. Delayed ripening
	6. Resistance to fungal infection

(a) A-4, B-3, C-5, D-6 (b) A-4, B-3, C-2, D-1
(c) A-2, B-4, C-5, D-3 (d) A-4, B-2, C-6, D-1

85. Mice which differ from a chosen strain by a single chromosomal region, containing the gene under study, is called as
(a) syngenic mice (b) perigenic mice
(c) agenic mice (d) congenic mice

86. Transgenic animals used for
(a) drug discovery (b) toxicologicals tudies
(c) pharmacokinetic studies (d) All of these

87. Which of the following is the not a example of pharmaceutical pharming?
(a) A transgenic sheep produce human factor IX
(b) Transgenic pig produce human protein C, an anticoagulant
(c) Production of hGH by yeast
(d) A transgenic sheep producing mouse Metallothionin Growth Hormone (mMThGH)

88. Which of the following sequence provide rational and well-underood marker for species or strain identification?
(a) *r*RNA (b) *m*RNA
(c) *t*RNA (d) None of these

89. Strain typing based molecular methods have been helpful for investigating outbreaks caused by
(a) *Staphylococcus aureus* (b) *Pseudomonas aeruginosa*
(c) *Klebsiella pneumoniae* (d) All of these

90. In which of the case PFGE technique failed to serve as a technique of choice for strain typing?
(a) *Staphylococcus aureus* (b) *Clostridium difficile*
(c) *Pseudomonas aeruginosa* (d) *Klebsiella pneumoniae*

91. Which of the following pair of typing system seems to be excellent in terms of strain typeable, reproducibility, discriminatory power and ease of interpretation?
(a) Biotyping and serotyping
(b) Plasmid fingerprinting and REA of chromosomal DNA by electrophoresis
(c) RFLP analysis and PFGE
(d) AP-PCR and antimicrobial susceptibility patterns

92. For which of the following bacteria, the refrence method of strain typing is serotyping rather than PFGE
(a) *Staphylococcus aureus* (b) *E. coli*
(c) *Shigella* sp. (d) *Pseudomonas aeruginosa*

93. Which of the following bacterial strain does not stand as a control strain?
(a) *P. aureus* NCTC 8325
(b) *E. coli* MG1655
(c) *Enterococcus faecalis* OG1RF
(d) *Clostridium ficicele* NIH 2332

94. Which of the following approach is used for correcting faulty genes?
(a) Normal gene insertion in a non-specific location in genome and use of homologous recombination to place a normal gene
(b) A normal gene may be inserted into a non-specific location within the genome to replace a non-functional gene, while an abnormal gene could be swapped for a normal gene through homologous recombination
(c) The abnormal gene could be repaired through selective reverse mutation, which returns the gene to its normal function and regulation (the degree to which a gene is turned on or off) of a particular gene could be altered
(d) All of the above

95. Some of the different types of viruses used as gene therapy vectors is
(a) retroviruses
(b) adeno and adeno associated viruses
(c) hepes simplex virus
(d) All of the above

96. HIV is an example of
(a) retro virus (b) adeno virus
(c) herpes simplex virus (d) a mutant bacteria

97. Find the unmatched.

	Virus Type		Genetic Material
I.	Retrovirus	—	*ds*DNA
II.	Adenovirus	—	*ds*DNA
III.	Adeno associated viruses	—	*ss*DNA
IV.	Herpes simplex viruses	—	*ss*RNA

(a) I only (b) II only
(c) I and IV (d) I, II and IV

98. Which of the following factors have kept gene therapy from becoming an effective treatment for genetic disease?
(a) Short-lived nature of gene therapy
(b) Immune response and multigene disorders
(c) Problems with viral vectors
(d) All of the above

99. Which of the following development is considered as the recent developments in gene therapy research?
(a) Nanotechnology + gene therapy yields treatment to torpedo cancer March, 2009
(b) Results of world's first gene therapy for inherited blindness show sight improvement 28 April 2008
(c) A combination of two tumour suppressing genes delivered in lipid-based nano-particles
(d) All of the above

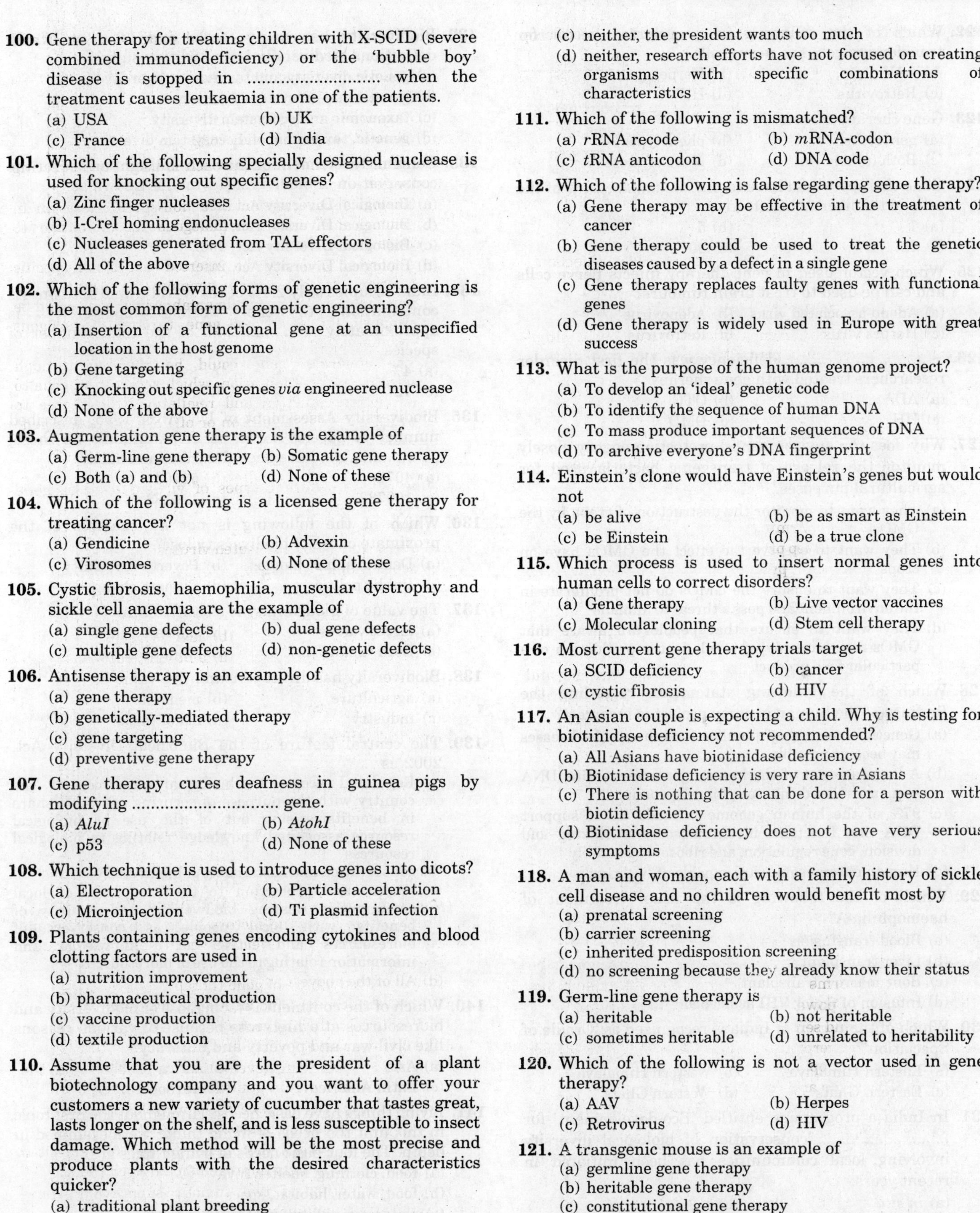

100. Gene therapy for treating children with X-SCID (severe combined immunodeficiency) or the 'bubble boy' disease is stopped in .... when the treatment causes leukaemia in one of the patients.
(a) USA (b) UK
(c) France (d) India

101. Which of the following specially designed nuclease is used for knocking out specific genes?
(a) Zinc finger nucleases
(b) I-CreI homing endonucleases
(c) Nucleases generated from TAL effectors
(d) All of the above

102. Which of the following forms of genetic engineering is the most common form of genetic engineering?
(a) Insertion of a functional gene at an unspecified location in the host genome
(b) Gene targeting
(c) Knocking out specific genes *via* engineered nuclease
(d) None of the above

103. Augmentation gene therapy is the example of
(a) Germ-line gene therapy (b) Somatic gene therapy
(c) Both (a) and (b) (d) None of these

104. Which of the following is a licensed gene therapy for treating cancer?
(a) Gendicine (b) Advexin
(c) Virosomes (d) None of these

105. Cystic fibrosis, haemophilia, muscular dystrophy and sickle cell anaemia are the example of
(a) single gene defects (b) dual gene defects
(c) multiple gene defects (d) non-genetic defects

106. Antisense therapy is an example of
(a) gene therapy
(b) genetically-mediated therapy
(c) gene targeting
(d) preventive gene therapy

107. Gene therapy cures deafness in guinea pigs by modifying .... gene.
(a) *AluI* (b) *AtohI*
(c) p53 (d) None of these

108. Which technique is used to introduce genes into dicots?
(a) Electroporation (b) Particle acceleration
(c) Microinjection (d) Ti plasmid infection

109. Plants containing genes encoding cytokines and blood clotting factors are used in
(a) nutrition improvement
(b) pharmaceutical production
(c) vaccine production
(d) textile production

110. Assume that you are the president of a plant biotechnology company and you want to offer your customers a new variety of cucumber that tastes great, lasts longer on the shelf, and is less susceptible to insect damage. Which method will be the most precise and produce plants with the desired characteristics quicker?
(a) traditional plant breeding
(b) genetic modification through genetic engineering
(c) neither, the president wants too much
(d) neither, research efforts have not focused on creating organisms with specific combinations of characteristics

111. Which of the following is mismatched?
(a) *r*RNA recode (b) *m*RNA-codon
(c) *t*RNA anticodon (d) DNA code

112. Which of the following is false regarding gene therapy?
(a) Gene therapy may be effective in the treatment of cancer
(b) Gene therapy could be used to treat the genetic diseases caused by a defect in a single gene
(c) Gene therapy replaces faulty genes with functional genes
(d) Gene therapy is widely used in Europe with great success

113. What is the purpose of the human genome project?
(a) To develop an 'ideal' genetic code
(b) To identify the sequence of human DNA
(c) To mass produce important sequences of DNA
(d) To archive everyone's DNA fingerprint

114. Einstein's clone would have Einstein's genes but would not
(a) be alive (b) be as smart as Einstein
(c) be Einstein (d) be a true clone

115. Which process is used to insert normal genes into human cells to correct disorders?
(a) Gene therapy (b) Live vector vaccines
(c) Molecular cloning (d) Stem cell therapy

116. Most current gene therapy trials target
(a) SCID deficiency (b) cancer
(c) cystic fibrosis (d) HIV

117. An Asian couple is expecting a child. Why is testing for biotinidase deficiency not recommended?
(a) All Asians have biotinidase deficiency
(b) Biotinidase deficiency is very rare in Asians
(c) There is nothing that can be done for a person with biotin deficiency
(d) Biotinidase deficiency does not have very serious symptoms

118. A man and woman, each with a family history of sickle cell disease and no children would benefit most by
(a) prenatal screening
(b) carrier screening
(c) inherited predisposition screening
(d) no screening because they already know their status

119. Germ-line gene therapy is
(a) heritable (b) not heritable
(c) sometimes heritable (d) unrelated to heritability

120. Which of the following is not a vector used in gene therapy?
(a) AAV (b) Herpes
(c) Retrovirus (d) HIV

121. A transgenic mouse is an example of
(a) germline gene therapy
(b) heritable gene therapy
(c) constitutional gene therapy
(d) somatic gene therapy

122. Which of the following is a preferred vector for transferring genes to nerve cells?
(a) AAV (b) Herpes
(c) Retrovirus (d) HIV

123. Gene therapy targets
(a) genotypes (b) phenotypes
(c) Both (a) and (b) (d) None of these

124. Gene therapy would have to 'fix' .... % of the cells in the liver to be effective.
(a) 1 (b) 5
(c) 10 (d) 50

125. Which vector used in gene therapy infects nerve cells and can be used to treat brain tumours?
(a) Adeno-associated virus (b) Adenovirus
(c) Herpes virus (d) Retrovirus

126. .... deficiency was the first disorder researchers treated with gene therapy.
(a) ADA (b) OTC
(c) HH (d) DMD

127. Why does the environmental protection agency closely monitor the release of transgenic bacteria used for agricultural purposes?
(a) They want to monitor the destruction of crops by the GMOs
(b) They want to observe the effect the GMOs have on crops
(c) They want to ensure the GMOs do not proliferate in the environment and pose a threat to humans
(d) They want to ensure that people are aware that GMOs may have played a role in the production of a particular food product

128. Which of the following statements regarding the findings of the human genome project is incorrect?
(a) Genetic screening of families for inheritable diseases may become possible
(b) A large amount of the human genome contains DNA sequences that do not code for cell protein
(c) 97% of the human genome is made up of support DNA that functions in chromosome stabilizing and division, gene regulation, and ribosome assembly
(d) Human chromosomes are capable of 'walking'

129. Which of the following is the usual treatment of haemophilia-A?
(a) Blood transfusion
(b) Liver transplant
(c) Bone marrow transplant
(d) Infusion of factor VIII as needed

130. Which of the region in India is recognized as 'Cradle of Speciation'?
(a) Eastern Himalaya (b) Western Himalaya
(c) Eastern Ghats (d) Western Ghats

131. In India a programme entitled 'Eco-development' for .... conservation of biological diversity involving local communities has been initiated in recent years.
(a) *in situ* (b) *ex situ*
(c) *ex vivo* (d) *in vivo*

132. Biodiversity has many facets and in most of the definitions biodiversity is an addition sum of
(a) genetic diversity and taxonomic diversity
(b) genetic and ecosystem diversity
(c) taxonomic and ecosystem diversity
(d) genetic, taxonomic and ecosystem diversity

133. Central Government of India has brought an act for the conservation of biodiversity, which is known as
(a) Biological Diversity Act, 1989
(b) Biological Diversity Act, 1996
(c) Biological Diversity Act, 2002
(d) Biological Diversity Act, 2009

134. India occupies only 2.4% of the world's land area but its contribution to the world's biodiversity is approximately .... of the total number of species.
(a) 4% (b) 8%
(c) 12% (d) 16%

135. Biodiversity Assessment of UNEP of 1995, described number of species so far is 1.75 million). Of these, ... have been described in India.
(a) 4076 (b) 52704
(c) 100733 (d) 126188

136. Which of the following is not an example of the proximate cause of biodiversity loss?
(a) Demographic change (b) Poverty inequality
(c) Public politics (d) Climate change

137. The value of biodiversity is classified into
(a) direct values (b) indirect values
(c) Both (a) and (b) (d) None of these

138. Biodiversity has direct consumptive value in
(a) agriculture (b) medicine
(c) industry (d) All of these

139. The central feature of the Biological Diversity Act, 2002, is
(a) Regulated access to biological resources of the country with the purpose of securing equitable share in benefits arising out of the use of biological resource associated knowledge relating to biological resources
(b) conservation and sustainable of biodiversity
(c) respect and protection to the knowledge of local communities relating biodiversity and security of benefits with local people as conservers of bioresources and holder of knowledge and information relating to the use of bioresources
(d) All of the above

140. Which of the continent is facing loss of biodiversity and bioresources at a high rate because of various reasons like civil war and poverty and illiteracy?
(a) Asia (b) Africa
(c) Latin America (d) Europe

141. Living things have basic needs. Throughout the first topic in this unit the needs of living things were examined in depth. The four basic needs of living things are
(a) food, clothing, shelter, love
(b) food, water, habitat, space
(c) water, air, habitat, protection
(d) air, water, food, habitat

142. The Nootka, an Aboriginal tribe from the West Coast of Canada, utilized the natural resources of the environment around them. They used the bark of the red cedar tree for

(a) clothing (b) canoes
(c) tipis (d) cooking utensils

143. The breadth of the concept of biodiversity reflects on the interrelationship of

(a) genes and species
(b) genes and ecosystem
(c) species and ecosystems
(d) genes, species and ecosystem

144. Which of the following statement is incorrect regarding biodiversity?

(a) Biodiversity deals with biological and geographical units such as genes, chromosomes, species, families and biogeographic regions
(b) Biodiversity is an addition sum of genetic, taxonomic and ecosystem diversity
(c) It is a measure of the amount of resources shared by the human population
(d) None of the above

145. .... diversity can be interpreted as the variation in biogeographic regions, landscapes and habitats.

(a) Genetic (b) Taxonomic
(c) Ecosystem (d) Population

146. Find the unmatched

I. Taxonomic diversity — Phyla, families, species
II. Genetic diversity — Genes and chromosomes
III. Ecological diversity — Population
IV. Biogeographic diversity — Landscape and habitats

(a) I only (b) III only
(c) I and III (d) I, II and III

147. Which of the statement is correct regarding bioresources?

(a) Bioresources are important components for progress and economic activities of a nation
(b) Biological resources include genetic resources, organisms or parts thereof, populations, or any other biotic component of ecosystems with actual or potential use or value for humanity
(c) Topsoil, groundwater, and biodiversity are non-replaceable resources
(d) All of the above

148. Which biome is characterized by heavy rainfall throughout the year, giant emergent trees, sparse ground vegetation and a great diversity of organisms?

(a) Taiga
(b) Temperate forest
(c) Tropical rain forest
(d) Tropical seasonal forest

149. The single biggest factor contributing to the increase in the human population for the last 300 years has been

(a) an increase in the global birth rate
(b) a decrease in the global birth rate
(c) an increase in the global death rate
(d) a decrease in the global death rate

150. Objects found in nature that people use to meet their basic needs are

(a) baseline resources (b) natural resources
(c) symbiotic resources (d) traditional resources

151. Which of the following is not a natural resource?

(a) Trees (b) Styrofoam
(c) Water (d) Natural gas

152. In electronic noses (e-noses) .... is placed in the soluble polymer to change the conductance.

(a) carbon black (b) polypyrrole
(c) Both (a) and (b) (d) None of these

153. The single greatest current threat to biodiversity

(a) greenhouse warming
(b) the introduction of exotics
(c) overhunting
(d) habitat destruction

154. Which of the following factors does not play a role in increased biodiversity?

(a) Complex population interactions
(b) The introduction of exotic species
(c) A higher degree of habitat heterogeneity
(d) Narrower niches

155. Choose the incorrect statement

(a) Nilgiri biosphere reserve is the first biosphere reserve in India
(b) All land with tree cover of canopy density of between 10-40% is known as open forest
(c) Western Ghats and Eastern Himalayas are two hotspots in India
(d) The Earth summit held in 1992 at Rio de Janerio to prevent ozone depletion at stratosphere

156. Which of the following statement is false?

I. Genetic diversity helps prevent a species from becoming extinct.
II. The phenomenon in which animals with favourable adaptation reproduces more rapidly is called differential reproduction.
III. Geographic isolation is a common mechanism contributing to speciation.
IV. Biologists estimate that 99% of all species that have ever existed are now extinct.

(a) I and III (b) I and IV
(c) II and III (d) None of these

157. An example of an allergenic plant created using traditional breeding is the

(a) mole (b) kiwi
(c) kangaroo (d) marsupial

158. The famous hybrid cereal created in 1875 by crossing

(a) wheat and rice (b) wheat and rye
(c) wheat and mustard (d) rice and rye

159. Cucumbers, squashes and beans are

(a) monocots (b) dicots
(c) multicots (d) ferns

160. Rice, corn and wheat are

(a) monocots (b) dicots
(c) multicots (d) ferns

161. Which of the following has no significant effect on changing gene frequency in large breeding population?
(a) Selection (b) Mutation
(c) Random genetic drift (d) Migration

162. Which of the following advancements in reproductive technologies have led to increase selection intensity *via* reduction in the number of parents needed to mate to produce the next generation of breeding animals?
(a) Artificial Insemination (AI)
(b) Embryo Transfer (ET)
(c) *In vitro* Fertilization (IVF)
(d) All of the above

163. Which of the following is false regarding various advantages of systematic breeding programs?
(a) Improvement of the efficiency in heat detection
(b) Improvement of the pregnancy rate
(c) Possibly increase involuntary culling for reproductive reasons
(d) Improve the overall reproduction performance of the species

164. Generally selective breeding is used for
(a) endangered species (b) wild species
(c) extinct species (d) domesticated species

165. Which of the following is not associated with the newly developed plant bred?
(a) Breeds (b) Varieties
(c) Cultigens (d) Cultivars

166. The cross of plants results in
(a) crossbreed (b) hybrids
(c) inbreed (d) None of these

167. The term selective breeding is synonymous of
(a) selective selection (b) discriminative selection
(c) artificial selection (d) real selection

168. The raising of the young using non-parental care givers is known as
(a) captive breeding (b) cooperative breeding
(c) confined breeding (d) company breeding

169. The cross between the Asian rice (*Oryza sativa*) and African rice (*Oryza glaberrima*) is an example of
(a) intraspecific cross (b) interspecific cross
(c) intrageneric cross (d) intergeneric cross

170. *Oryza sativa japonica* was developed in
(a) South Asia (b) Korea
(c) Japan (d) China

171. Which of the following is not a high yielding variety of wheat?
(a) Sarbati sonara (b) Sonalika
(c) Kalyan sona (d) Padma

172. Which of the following is a high yielding variety of lady's finger?
(a) Pusa purple (b) Pusa kranti
(c) Pusa savani (d) UP-301

173. Choose the high yielding variety of wheat
(a) IR-8, Jaya, Padma
(b) Ganga 101, Rankit, Deccan hybrid
(c) Sarbati sona, Sonalika, Hira moti
(d) Pusa purple, Pusa savani, Muktabeshi

174. Credit of 'Green revolution' in our country goes to
(a) Aryabhatta (b) Dr V Kurien
(c) Dr MS Swaminathan (d) Dr HG Khorana

175. Which of the following statements does not provide an explanation for hybrid vigour?
(a) Under certain circumstances, heterozygotes are superior to either possible homozygote
(b) Disease-causing, homozygous recessive phenotypes from either parent are masked in the hybrids
(c) Offspring from a hybrid cross usually possess the best of two desirable parents
(d) Inherently, hybrids have no deleterious mutations

176. Who is better known as first scientific animal breeder?
(a) Robert Bakewell (b) Robert Hook
(c) Robert White (d) Mendel

177. In animal breeding, a population is a group of
(a) interbreeding individuals
(b) intrabreeding individuals
(c) crossbreeding sub-populations
(d) None of the above

178. For what reasons additive variation is common in animal breeding programmes
(a) effects if each allele at a locus just adds to the effect of other alleles at the same locus
(b) genetic gains made using addtivte genetic effects are permanent
(c) genetic gains cumulate from one generation to the next
(d) All of the above

179. Many attempts to improve livestock in the tropics have been made, mainly by 'upgrading' with temperate breeds in crossbreeding. The major problems faced during the failed cattle breeding are
(a) the breeding programmes have been too complicated in terms of logistics, technology and requirements of resources without considering the infrastructure available
(b) indiscriminate crossbreeding of indigenous breeds with exotic breeds without enough consideration of environmental conditions for production
(c) lack of analysis of the different socio-economic and cultural roles that livestock play in each situation, usually leading to wrong breeding objectives and neglect of the potentials of various indigenous breeds of livestock
(d) All of the above

180. Mating animals of the same breed with closely related animals is known as
(a) straight breeding (b) outcrossing
(c) inbreeding (d) purebed breeding

181. Equation used to analysis of genetic progress by genetic gain per year is
(a) $\Delta A = (G\ \sigma\ gi)/I$ (b) $\Delta I = (A\ \sigma\ gi)/G$
(c) $\Delta G = (I\ \sigma\ gi)/A$ (d) $\Delta G = (A\ \sigma\ gi)/I$
Where, A is the accuracy of selection, σg is the standard deviation of the additive genetic variation in the population, i is the selection intensity (proportion selected for further breeding), and I is the generation interval (age of breeding).

182. Marker assisted selection or marker aided selection (MAS) is a process
(a) in which a marker (morphological, biochemical or one based on DNA/RNA variation) is used for indirect selection of a genetic determinant or determinants of a trait of interest
(b) which is based on the assumption that linked allele associates with the gene and/or quantitative trait locus (QTL) of interest
(c) which can be useful for plant and animal breeding especially for traits that are difficult to measure, exhibit low heritability, and/or are expressed late in development
(d) All of the above

183. Marker assisted selection (MAS) is .... selection process where a trait of interest is selected, not based on the trait itself, but on a marker linked to it.
(a) direct (b) indirect
(c) directional (d) spontaneous

184. Leaf sheath colouration, height, grain colour, aroma of rice are example of
(a) biological markers (b) morphological markers
(c) cytological markers (d) biochemical markers

185. Thymidine kinase, which makes the host sensitive to ganciclovir selection, is an example of
(a) positive selectable marker
(b) negative selectable marker
(c) beneficial marker
(d) adaptive marker

186. Generally, the markers to be used in MAS should be close to gene of interest in order to ensure that only minor fraction of the selected individuals will be recombinants. What is the probable distance is preferred?
(a) 5 cM (b) <5 cM
(c) >5 cM (d) 0.5 cM

187. In plants QTL mapping is generally achieved using bi-parental cross populations; a cross between two parents which have a contrasting phenotype for the trait of interest are developed. Commonly used populations are
(a) Recombinant Inbreed Lines (RILs)
(b) Doubled Haploids (DH)
(c) back cross and F_2
(d) All of the above

188. Which of the following technique seems to help breeders in shifting traditional breeding to marker aided selection?
(a) DNA isolation robots
(b) High throughput capillary electrophoresis
(c) Pipetting robots
(d) All of the above

189. Applied biosystems 3130 genetic analyzer used in genotyping experiments is the latest generation of
(a) NMR instrument
(b) PCR machine
(c) sequencing machine
(d) capillary electrophoresis instruments

190. The halothane gene in pigs and double muscling gene in cattle is an example of
(a) linked marker (b) direct marker
(c) morphological marker (d) positive marker

191. In general, the success of a marker-based breeding system in crops depends on a genetic map with an adequate number of uniformly-spaced polymorphic markers to accurately locate desired QTLs or major gene(s)
(a) close linkage between the QTL or a major gene of interest and adjacent markers
(b) adequate recombination between the markers and rest of the genome
(c) an ability to analyse a larger number of plants in a time- and cost- effective manner
(d) All of the above

192. Which of the following trait is not a complete quantitative trait and do not follow continuous segregation?
(a) Semidwarfism in rice
(b) Stem rot resistance in rice
(c) Submergence tolerance gene sub1 in rice
(d) None of the above

193. 'Marker-assisted background selection', a term coined by
(a) Hospital and Charcosset (b) Young and Tanksley
(c) Eisenberg and Cohney (d) Melchinger

194. Find the unmatched.

I. Rice	—	Gall midge resistance	—	Gm2		RG 329
II. Maize	—	Northern corn blight resistance	—	Hm1	—	Umc117
III. Wheat	—	Leaf rust resistance	—	Lr24	—	6 RFLP markers
IV. Chick pea	—	Cyst nematode resistance	—	rhg1	—	Sat 309 (SSR marker)
V. Pea	—	*Fusarium* wilt resistance	—	Fw	—	RFLP marker
VI. Tomato	—	Downy mildew resistance	—	P16	—	HaP1, HaP2 and HaP3
VII. Potato	—	Late Blight	—	R1 and R3	—	RFLP marker

(a) I only (b) IV and VI
(c) I, II and III (d) IV, V, VI and VII

195. Which of the following is an example of new generation marker system?
(a) Sequence Tagged Sites (STSs)
(b) Single Nucleotide Polymorphism (SNPs)
(c) Micro Satellites or Short Tandem Repeats (STRs)
(d) All of the above

196. The sequences ATATATAT and GATGATGAT are the perfect example of
(a) Single Nucleotide Polymorphisms (SNPs)
(b) Restriction Fragment Length Polymorphisms (RFLPs)
(c) Simple Sequence Repeats or Microsatellites
(d) Variable Number of Tandem Repeats (VNTRs)

197. Known for their great strength and adhesive properties, components of byssal fibres produced by .... are being studying for a variety of applications from medical sutures to adhesives.
(a) *Conus magus* (b) *Pfiesteria piscicida*
(c) *Vibrio cholera* (d) *Mytilus edulis*

198. Polyploid organisms
(a) are knockout organisms
(b) have different numbers of each chromosome
(c) are created from ES cells
(d) have extra complete sets of chromosomes

199. The gene for green fluorescent protein (GFP), a commonly used reporter gene, was cloned from
(a) *Vibrio cholerae*
(b) *SUS domesticus*
(c) *Danio rerio*
(d) *Equorea victoria*

200. Growing aquatic plants and finfish species together with shared water resources is an example of
(a) hydroponics (b) olyploidy
(c) fish farming (d) polyculture

201. Known as the 'cell from hell,' this toxin-producing dinoflagellate is responsible for significant fish kills in the mid-Atlantic region
(a) *Conus magus* (b) *Vibrio cholera*
(c) *Pfiesteria piscicida* (d) *Crassotrea virginica*

202. Which of the following is a pigment used to alter the colour of salmon?
(a) Auxin (b) AFP
(c) Hydroxyapatite (d) Astaxanthin

203. Transgenic salmon engineered to grow faster than non-transgenic strains contain extra copies of the .... gene.
(a) HA (b) AFP
(c) calcitonin (d) GH

204. Marine cone snails, *Conus magus*, are the source of
(a) hydroxyapatite used to treat arthritis
(b) prialt, a peptide used as a pain reliever
(c) calcitonin used to treat osteoporosis
(d) cells for the LAL test used to detect bacterial contamination of surgical tools

205. Limulus polyphemus are the source of
(a) calcitonin used to treat osteoporosis
(b) prialt, a peptide used as a pain reliever
(c) cells for the LAL test used to detect bacterial contamination of surgical tools
(d) hydroxyapatite used to treat arthritis

206. Marine .... is/are a primary source of agar and agarose used in laboratories for making culture medias and gels.
(a) kelp (b) molluscs
(c) fish (d) shrimp

207. Which of the following statements is incorrect about triploid species?
(a) Are an example of a polyploidy organism
(b) Are usually infertile
(c) Have an extra copy of one chromosome
(d) Have three complete sets of chromosomes

208. .... is the farming of a variety of shellfish, crustaceans, finfish and algae.
(a) Organ culture (b) Protoplast culture
(c) Tissue culture (d) Aquaculture

209. Secondary metabolites
(a) are essential to microbe function
(b) are byproducts of metabolism that are not important to microbe function
(c) are products that require additional processing before they can be packaged
(d) are harvested during the exponential phase of growth

210. Routinely used glucose biosensor estimates blood glucose level by sensing the concentration of
(a) Glucose (b) Oxygen
(c) δ-gluconolactone (d) H_2O_2

211. Which of the following enzyme pair is used in diabetes testing strips?
(a) Glucose reductase/peroxidase
(b) Glucose dehydrogenase/peroxidase
(c) Glucose oxidase/peroxidase
(d) Glucose epimerase/peroxidase

212. Which of the following hormone is measured by pregnancy kits?
(a) LH (b) Progesterone
(c) estrogen (d) hCG

213. Most of the available urea biosensor measures
(a) urea (b) ammonia
(c) carbamic acid (d) CO_2

214. Which of the following transducer type is used while constructing urease biosensors?
(a) Potentiometric (b) Amperometric
(c) Spectrophotometric (d) All of these

215. Which of the following is not a example of affinity biosensor?
(a) Antibody based sensor (b) Lectin sensor
(c) Receptor sensor (d) Enzyme sensor

216. Which of the following factor can reduce the performance of the enzymatic biosensor?
(a) Extreme pH (b) High temperature
(c) Heavy metals (d) All of these

217. The transducers included in the biosensors are
(a) magnetic (b) calorimetric
(c) Both (a) and (b) (d) All of these

218. The catalytic biosensors recognize
(a) substrates
(b) enzyme
(c) enzyme substrate complex
(d) Both (a) and (b)

219. High sample throughput using biosensors involves
(a) autosampling (b) flow systems
(c) on-line configuration (d) All of these

220. Which amongst the following is the most selling biosensor?
(a) Glucose biosensor (b) Immuno biosensor
(c) Nucleic acid biosensor (d) Urease biosensor

221. Aptasensors target .... by their ability to interact with aptamers.
(a) TAT (b) trombin
(c) Both (a) and (b) (d) None of these

222. Example of future applications of closed-loop systems with chemical biosensors
(a) regulation of anesthesia during operations
(b) control of implantable pacemakers and defibrillators
(c) control of insulin secretion from an artificial pancreas
(d) All of the above

223. The normal range of glucose in blood is .... mg/100 mL.
(a) 70-110 (b) 50-70
(c) 80-100 (d) 120-140

224. Enzyme based biosensor can measure
(a) glucose
(b) phenols in food and environment
(c) Both (a) and (b)
(d) None of the above

225. pH electrode is comprised of
(a) calomel reference electrode
(b) glass electrode
(c) Both (a) and (b)
(d) None of the above

226. The measurement of pCO_2 is based on relationship between log pCO_2 and
(a) pH (b) pO_2
(c) H_2O (d) HCO^{3-}

227. Two chambers of pCO_2 electrode are separated by a semi permeable membrane, usually made of
(a) teflon (b) silicone rubber
(c) Both (a) and (b) (d) None of these

228. Chemical fibrosensors
(a) they can be made small in size
(b) the measurements are immune to external electric interference, provided that the electronic instrumentation is properly shielded
(c) no reference electrode is necessary
(d) All of the above

229. Blood glucose can be measured using
(a) glucose oxidase method
(b) electroenzymatic approach
(c) optical method
(d) All of these

230. Lab-on-a-chip is based on
(a) photolithography (b) optical activity
(c) affinity (d) None of these

231. The biological species concept may not apply to
(a) organisms that look different but are able to interbreed
(b) organisms that do not breed in nature but may do so in captivity
(c) organisms that do not breed due to recognition adaptations
(d) populations that are geographically separated

232. According to the Hardy-Weinberg theorem,
(a) the genetic structure of a population should remain constant from one generation to the next if five conditions are met
(b) only natural selection, resulting in unequal reproductive success, will cause evolution
(c) the square root of the frequency of individuals showing the recessive trait will always equal the frequency of q
(d) genetic drift, gene flow mutations, and non-random mating are non-adaptive causes of microevolution; natural selection is the only adaptive cause

233. Introgression occurs when
(a) a hybrid successfully breeds with an individual of a parent species
(b) hybrids successfully breed with each other
(c) an allopolyploid is produced
(d) the hybrid zone remains distinct and separate

234. Allopatric speciation is most likely to occur when
(a) the splinter population is small
(b) a peripheral isolate is exposed to more severe selection pressures at the boundary of the population's range
(c) a small subset of the population becomes adapted to a new food source
(d) Both (a) and (b)

235. Genetic drift is likely to be seen in a population
(a) that has a low mutation rate
(b) in which there is assortative mating
(c) that is very small
(d) for which environmental conditions are changing

236. The Permian extinctions between the Paleozoic and Mesozoic eras
(a) resulted in mass extinction of many marine and terrestrial species
(b) coincided with the breaking apart of Pangaea
(c) made way for the adaptive radiation of mammals, birds and pollinating insects
(d) appear to have been caused by a large asteroid striking Earth

237. Gene flow often results in
(a) populations that are better adapted to the environment
(b) an increase in sampling error in the formation of the next generation
(c) adaptive microevolution
(d) a reduction of the allele frequency differences between populations

238. Which of the following is not a type of intrinsic reproductive isolation?
(a) Mechanical isolation
(b) Behavioural isolation
(c) Geographical isolation
(d) Gametic isolation

239. During cultivation of microorganisms in a fermenter, various parameters are controlled by appropriate sensor (probe). Match each probe in list 1 with the appro-ppriate response mechanism in list 2.

List I (Probe)	List II (Response)
A. Thermistor	1. Activation of acid/alkali pump
B. Oxygen electrode	2. Activation of vegetable oil pump
C. Metal rod	3. Activation of hot/cold water pump
D. pH electrode	4. Increase/decrease in stirrer motor speed

Codes

	A	B	C	D
(a)	2	3	1	4
(b)	1	2	4	3
(c)	3	2	4	1
(d)	3	4	2	1

240. Match items in list I with correct options from those given in list 2

List I	List II
A. Amperometric biosensor	1. Light beam
B. Evanescent biosensor	2. Flux of redox electrons
C. Calorimetric biosensor	3. Field effect transistors
D. Potentiometric biosensor	4. Exothermic reaction

Codes

	A	B	C	D
(a)	3	4	2	1
(b)	2	1	4	3
(c)	3	2	4	1
(d)	2	4	3	1

241. Immobilization of enzymes using entrapment method requires

I. photosensitive polyethylene glycol dimethyacrylate.
II. CNBr activation of sepharose.
III. polyfunctional reagent like hexa-methylene diisocyanate.
IV. radiation of polyvinyl alcohol.

(a) I and II
(b) III and IV
(c) I and IV
(d) II and IV

242. Two two lists given below indicate some of the fermentation products and the microbial cultures used for their production. Identify the correct set of groups from the four options.

List I (Fermentation Products)	List II (Microbial cultures)
A. Ethanol	1. *Aspergillus niger*
B. Ethanol	2. *Zymomonas mobilis*
C. Citric acid	3. *Streptomyces*
D. Cellulase	4. *Trichoderma recsei*

Codes

	A	B	C	D
(a)	1	2	3	4
(b)	2	4	1	4
(c)	2	3	4	4
(d)	1	2	2	4

Answers

1. (d) **2.** (c) **3.** (d) **4.** (a) **5.** (c) **6.** (b) **7.** (a) **8.** (d) **9.** (c) **10.** (d)
11. (b) **12.** (b) **13.** (d) **14.** (c) **15.** (a) **16.** (b) **17.** (b) **18.** (b) **19.** (a) **20.** (c)
21. (b) **22.** (b) **23.** (b) **24.** (b) **25.** (b) **26.** (b) **27.** (a) **28.** (a) **29.** (a) **30.** (c)
31. (b) **32.** (c) **33.** (a) **34.** (c) **35.** (b) **36.** (b) **37.** (b) **38.** (d) **39.** (a) **40.** (d)
41. (d) **42.** (b) **43.** (d) **44.** (d) **45.** (b) **46.** (d) **47.** (b) **48.** (d) **49.** (a) **50.** (d)
51. (a) **52.** (b) **53.** (b) **54.** (c) **55.** (b) **56.** (c) **57.** (d) **58.** (d) **59.** (b) **60.** (d)
61. (b) **62.** (c) **63.** (d) **64.** (b) **65.** (d) **66.** (d) **67.** (d) **68.** (d) **69.** (d) **70.** (c)
71. (d) **72.** (a) **73.** (d) **74.** (d) **75.** (a) **76.** (d) **77.** (d) **78.** (b) **79.** (d) **80.** (d)
81. (d) **82.** (b) **83.** (d) **84.** (b) **85.** (d) **86.** (d) **87.** (c) **88.** (a) **89.** (d) **90.** (b)
91. (c) **92.** (c) **93.** (d) **94.** (d) **95.** (d) **96.** (a) **97.** (c) **98.** (d) **99.** (d) **100.** (c)
101. (d) **102.** (a) **103.** (b) **104.** (a) **105.** (a) **106.** (b) **107.** (b) **108.** (d) **109.** (b) **110.** (b)
111. (a) **112.** (d) **113.** (b) **114.** (c) **115.** (a) **116.** (b) **117.** (b) **118.** (b) **119.** (a) **120.** (d)
121. (a) **122.** (b) **123.** (a) **124.** (b) **125.** (c) **126.** (a) **127.** (d) **128.** (d) **129.** (d) **130.** (a)
131. (a) **132.** (d) **133.** (c) **134.** (b) **135.** (d) **136.** (d) **137.** (c) **138.** (d) **139.** (d) **140.** (b)
141. (d) **142.** (a) **143.** (d) **144.** (c) **145.** (c) **146.** (b) **147.** (d) **148.** (c) **149.** (d) **150.** (b)
151. (d) **152.** (a) **153.** (d) **154.** (b) **155.** (d) **156.** (d) **157.** (b) **158.** (b) **159.** (b) **160.** (a)
161. (c) **162.** (d) **163.** (c) **164.** (d) **165.** (a) **166.** (b) **167.** (c) **168.** (b) **169.** (b) **170.** (d)
171. (d) **172.** (c) **173.** (a) **174.** (c) **175.** (d) **176.** (a) **177.** (a) **178.** (d) **179.** (d) **180.** (b)
181. (d) **182.** (d) **183.** (b) **184.** (b) **185.** (b) **186.** (b) **187.** (d) **188.** (d) **189.** (d) **190.** (b)
191. (d) **192.** (a) **193.** (a) **194.** (b) **195.** (d) **196.** (c) **197.** (d) **198.** (d) **199.** (d) **200.** (d)
201. (c) **202.** (d) **203.** (d) **204.** (b) **205.** (c) **206.** (a) **207.** (c) **208.** (d) **209.** (b) **210.** (d)
211. (c) **212.** (d) **213.** (b) **214.** (d) **215.** (d) **216.** (d) **217.** (d) **218.** (d) **219.** (d) **220.** (a)
221. (c) **222.** (d) **223.** () **224.** (c) **225.** (c) **226.** (a) **227.** (c) **228.** (d) **229.** (d) **230.** (a)
231. (d) **232.** (a) **233.** (a) **234.** (d) **235.** (c) **236.** (a) **237.** (d) **238.** (c) **239.** (b) **240.** (b)
241. (d) **242.** (b)

37 Molecular Biology and Recombinant DNA Methods

DNA technology is the chemical manipulation of the genotypes and resulting phenotypes of organisms such that living organisms are modified; alternatively, no-longer-living organisms or their no-longer-living parts may be analyzed chemically at the level of genotype. The use of DNA technology has revolutionized how scientists study the genetics, biochemistry, even the ecology and evolutionary biology of organisms, plus has allowed the development of novel biological products; indeed whole industries are now devoted to DNA-technology based on production and analysis of biological materials. Together the manipulation and analysis associated with DNA technology, genetic engineering and biotechnology are based on a number of technologies generally referred to as molecular techniques. Molecular techniques include (though are not limited to) :

- **(i)** Gene cloning (which is associated with various molecular techniques including *in vitro* restriction enzyme digests and DNA ligation plus additional, less-artificial manipulations including transformation and transduction).
- **(ii)** Creation of *c*DNA.
- **(iii)** Polymerase chain reaction.
- **(iv)** Gel electrophoresis.
- **(v)** Various blotting techniques (Southern blotting, Northern blotting, Western blotting, etc.).
- **(vi)** RFLP analysis.
- **(vii)** DNA sequencing.

Syllabus

- Isolation and Purification of Nucleic Acid (RNA and DNA)
- Analysis of RNA, DNA and Protiens, Gel Electrophoresis, Isoelectric Focusing.
- Molecular Cloning.
- Preparing cDNA Libraries, Plasmid Vectors, Phagemids, Cosmid and YACs.
- Expression of Recombinant Protiens, Isolation of Specific Nucleic Acid Sequences, Detection of Post-translation Modification of Proteins, DNA Sequencing, Site-Directed *in vitro* Mutagenesis, Gene Knock Out, Microarray.
- Isolation, Separation and Analysis of carbohydrates and lipids.

Isolation and Purification of Nucleic Acids (DNA and RNA)

Three major types of techniques or combinations of them, are employed in the isolation of nucleic acids: differential solubility, absorption methods or density gradient centrifugation. The choice of method will depend on the type of DNA being isolated and the application. A major goal of nucleic acid isolation is the removal of proteins. The separation of nucleic acids from proteins is generally easily accomplished due to their different chemical properties. In particular, the highly charged phosphate backbone makes the nucleic acids rather hydrophilic as compared to proteins which are more hydrophobic. Separating the different types of nucleic acids can be more problematic in that they all have similar chemistries. On the other hand, though, this similar chemistry results in a few basic procedures which are common to many nucleic acid isolation protocols. Most nucleic acid isolation protocols involve a cell lysis step, enzymatic treatments, differential solubility (*e.g.,* phenol extraction or absorption to a solid support) and precipitation.

Cell Lysis

Nucleic acids must be solubilized from cells or other biological material. This solubilization is usually carried out under denaturing conditions such as: SDS, alkali, boiling or chaotropic agents. These denaturing conditions efficiently solubilize the nucleic acids and generally do not adversely affect them. In addition, the denaturing conditions promote the removal of proteins during the subsequent steps and inhibit the activity of nucleases which will degrade the nucleic acids.

Enzymatic Treatment

Another approach in the isolation of nucleic acids is to degrade unwanted components. For example, inclusion of proteases (*e.g.,* proteinase K) in the lysate will promote the removal of proteins. Proteinase K is still active at 55°C in the presence of 0.5% SDS. The elevated temperature and SDS improve solubility and inhibit any DNAse activity that may be present in the lysate. Nucleases can also be used to remove unwanted nucleic acids. For example, many DNA extraction protocols include a RNAse treatment step and *vise-versa*. It is important that the RNAse be free of DNAse activity. DNAse-free RNAse is easily prepared by boiling commercial RNAse for 10 minutes. The stability of RNAse makes the preparation of RNAse-free DNAse more difficult. RNAse-free DNAse should be purchased from a reliable vendor or tested before it use.

Phenol Extraction

Phenol is an organic solvent that is used to separate proteins from nucleic acids. Proteins are hydrophobic and partition in the organic phase. Nucleic acids are highly charged and partition in the aqueous phase. The advantages are of phenol extraction are that it is easy to carry out and can be adapted to many applications. It is also easily applied over a wide range of volumes (40 μL to several mL). In particular, phenol extraction is widely used for the isolation of high molecular weight genomic DNA. Phenol extraction is accomplished by mixing the sample with an equal volume of phenol which has been previously saturated with a Tris buffer at pH 8 containing EDTA and NaCl. The phenol should be molecular biology grade phenol should and store at –20°C until preparing the saturated solution. The saturated solution is stored at 4°C. Phenol is easily oxidized, as evidenced by yellowing and the oxidation products can break DNA. Oxidized phenol should be discarded. Depending on the application, the two phases are completely mixed by vortexing or gently mixed (*e.g.,* high molecular weight DNA). The phases are separated by centrifugation and the upper aqueous phase, which contains the nucleic acids, is retained. Proteins will often be visible as flocculent material at the top of the phenol phase. The two phases need to be carefully separated in that the nucleic acids and proteins tend to be at the interface. Leaving too much of the aqueous layer behind will lead to undue loss of material and aspirating too close to the interface can include protein. The aqueous phase can be re-extracted with phenol to remove more protein. Phenol is a hazardous waste material that needs to be disposed of properly.

A common variation of phenol extraction is a mixture of phenol:chloroform: isoamyl alcohol (25:24:1). The more organic chloroform removes lipids, denatures more protein and mixes less with the aqueous phase leading to more efficient extraction.

Ethanol Precipitation

Nucleic acids can be precipitated from dilute solutions with ethanol. This precipitation can be a concentration step or a means to change buffers, especially after phenol extraction. Typically either sodium acetate or potassium acetate, pH 5.0-5.5, is added to a final concentration of approximately 0.3 M. The sodium and acidic pH will neutralize the highly charged phosphate backbone and to promote hydrophobic interactions. Two-to-two and a half volumes of ethanol are added and the sample is incubated as –20°. If the nucleic acids are small in size and/or in low concentrations an extended incubation (several hours to overnight) is needed. The precipitated DNA is collected by centrifugation. The pellet is rinsed with 70% ethanol to remove any excess salt, dried and dissolved in the appropriate buffer. A variation is to substitute ammonium acetate if the 'hard' salts are a problem. Another modification is to use an equal volume of isopropanol (instead of 2-2½ volumes of ethanol) which minimizes the increase in sample volume.

Isolation of High Molecular Weight Genomic DNA

High molecular weight chromosomal DNA is usually isolated by multiple rounds of phenol extraction and enzyme treatments as discussed above. Shear forces, which can break long DNA molecules, need to be avoided during all steps and samples should never be vortexed. Therefore, the phenol extraction is carried with gentle rocking for several hours. These precautions against shear forces are not necessary in the isolation of low molecular weight DNA. Another common modification at the ethanol precipitation step is 'spool out' the high molecular weight genomic DNA on the end of a sealed Pasteur pipet. The precipitated DNA is wrapped around the end of the pipet is then allowed to partially dry and then dissolved in the appropriate buffer. This minimizes the contamination with RNA and low molecular weight DNA fragments.

Plasmid Minipreps and Adsorption Methods

Historically, phenol extractions were used for the isolation of most forms of nucleic acids. It is now more common to use techniques based upon adsorption chromatography for the isolation of smaller DNA molecules, such as plasmids.

Various kits are available for the rapid isolation of small quantities of plasmid DNA. The procedure consists of solubilizing the bacteria in an alkali solution followed by neutralization with sodium acetate. The neutralization results in the precipitation of some of the protein and the genomic DNA which is removed by centrifugation. The soluble material is then mixed with a resin in the presence of chaotropic agents (usually guanidine hydrochloride). The resins are usually either based on silica or diatomaceous Earth. Under these conditions DNA binds to the matrix, but proteins and RNA do not. The DNA is eluted in a low salt buffer. These methods are rapid and yield a highly purified plasmid DNA which can generally be used directly in most applications without further processing.

Another common application for an adsorption method is the isolation of DNA fragments following gel electrophoresis. In this case, the agarose gel piece containing the DNA is dissolved in NaI, a chaotropic salt and the DNA adsorbed to silica. The DNA is then eluted with a low salt buffer and sometimes gentle heating.

Isolation of RNA

Most RNA isolation protocols also involve phenol extractions and are similar to DNA isolations. However, there are some differences and special considerations. In particular, precautions against RNAse activity must be taken. RNAse is an extremely stable and active enzyme. Gloves should be worn at all times and sterile plasticware should be used whenever possible to avoid introducing exogenous RNAse to the sample. Glassware needs to treated with DEPC-water and autoclaved to inactivate any RNAse. Buffers should be prepared from DEPC-water or RNAse inhibitors included. The cell lysis and solubilization of RNA will typically be carried out in guanidine salts (especially guanidine thiocyanate). Guanidine is a strong chaotropic agent and will inhibit RNAses. The strong denaturing effect of this salt will also promote better phenol extraction. The phenol extraction is the same as the DNA isolation except that the phenol is usually saturated with a buffer of pH 5-6. The lower pH will result in some DNA partitioning in the organic phase. If DNA contamination is a problem, it is possible to purchase RNAse-free DNAse. Longterm storage is best as a precipitate in 70% ethanol at –20°C.

Precipitation of RNA with LiCl

LiCl has been used to selectively precipitate RNA. Large RNAse (*r*RNA, *m*RNA) are insoluble at high ionic strength, whereas small RNAse (*t*RNA and 5 S *r*RNA) and DNA generally remain soluble. Following either phenol or guanidine extraction, an equal volume of 8 M LiCl is added. The sample is mixed vigorously and incubated at –20°. The precipitate is collected by centrifugation and reprecipitated if necessary.

Affinity Chromatography

Most eukaryotic *m*RNA contains a stretch of A residues at its 3′ end which added post-transcriptionally. It is possible to isolate *m*RNA by affinity chromatography on oligod T columns. The RNA solution is passed over an oligo-dT column under conditions which promote base pairing. Only RNA with a poly A tail binds. The poly A RNA is eluted under conditions (usually low salt and high temperature) which break the base pairing.

Density Gradient Centrifugation

Density gradient centrifugation can also be used in the analysis and isolation of nucleic acids. Double-stranded DNA, single-stranded DNA, RNA and proteins all have different densities and therefore, can be separated by isopycnic (*i.e.*, equilibrium) centrifugation. CsCl is the standard medium for the density gradient centrifugation of nucleic acids and are especially useful for the purification of large amount of highly purified DNA. The gradients are carried out in the presence of ethidium bromide which fluoresces when bound to DNA. The DNA bands are detected by illumination with ultraviolet light and easily recovered with a syringe and needle by puncturing the wall of the disposable tube and aspirating the DNA. The CsCl can be removed by dialysis or by precipitating the DNA. The %G:C content affects the density of DNA (Figure). This can result in multiple bands on CsCl gradients if DNA composed different G:C compositions are centrifuged. For example, minor bands, called satellite DNA, are often observed when total DNA from an organism is analyzed by CsCl gradients. These satellite bands are usually due to highly repetitive DNA or organellar DNA. Mitochondrial DNA is noted for its high A:T content. These satellite DNA bands can be purified from the genomic DNA by density gradient centrifugation.

Nucleic acids can also be separated according to size by rate zonal centrifugation on sucrose gradients. However, this method is not widely used since gel electrophoresis is generally a more convenient method for the size fractionation of nucleic acids.

Analysis and Quantification

The quality and quantity of isolated nucleic acids can be determined spectrophotometrically. Nucleic acids have an A_{max} of 260 nm and proteins have A_{max} of 280 nm. The A260/A280 ratio is therefore, indicative of the degree of purity of the nucleic acid. A260/A280 ratios of 1.6-1.8 or 1.8-2.0 are usually acceptable for DNA and RNA, respectively. The standard extinction coefficient used for *ss*DNA, *ds*DNA and RNA are 0.03 mL/μg, 0.02 mL/μg and 0.025 mL/μg, respectively. Formulas which take into account protein and other contaminants are also available. Indirect spectrophotometric assays for DNA quantification are also available, but rarely used. In some instances fluorometry using fluorescent dyes that bind DNA and/or RNA is used to determine nucleic acid concentrations.

Protein Isolation and Purification

(i) In order to purify a protein you need a source.

(ii) It might be blood or some other biological fluid, but most often it is a cell, usually a specific type–liver, muscle, yeast, bacteria, etc.

(iii) The cells must be broken open-homogenized—to release the protein in a soluble form.

(iv) Homogenization conditions must be worked out that release the protein from the cell without damaging the protein.

(v) Membrane-bound proteins can also be purified, but different approaches are required.

Fractional Precipitation

(a) In concentrated salt solutions, usually ammonium sulphate is used; some proteins are more soluble than others. By varying the concentration of ammonium sulphate, one can achieve some limited purification of proteins. This technique is often used in the first step of protein purification.

(b) Small proteins are more soluble than large proteins.

(c) The larger the number of charged side chains, the more soluble the protein.

Column Chromatography

(a) The invention of column chromatography was a critical event in biochemistry, because it was the basis for the development of procedures for obtaining pure proteins.

(b) Studies on pure proteins are essential for understanding the structural and functional properties of proteins.

(c) In column chromatography, an adsorbent is placed in a glass tube.

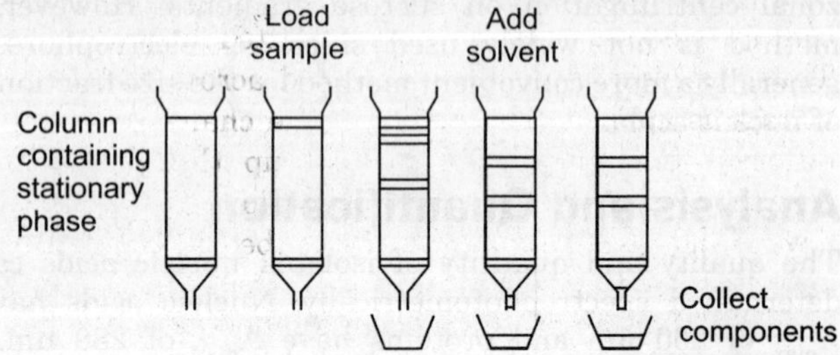

Fig. 37.1 Process of column chromatography

(d) A protein mixture is passed into the column and binds to the adsorbent.

(e) By proper choice of the eluting buffer, specific proteins can be eluted from the adsorbent and separated from other proteins in the mixture.

(f) By repeating this procedure with several different adsorbents, pure protein can be obtained.

(g) Because proteins are not very stable, low temperature (4°C) and neutral pH must often be employed.

(h) The properties of some adsorbents are described below.

Ion Exchange Chromatography

(a) Ion exchange resins have fixed charges-either positive or negative.

(b) Proteins bind to the resin *via* electrostatic interactions.

(c) The strength of these interactions depends on the net charge on the protein, which is a function of pH and the nature of the weak acid amino acid side chains and the salt concentration of the buffer-high salt concentrations reduce the interaction.

Affinity Chromatography

(a) This is a more specific interaction in which a ligand specifically recognized by the protein of interest is attached to the column material.

(b) When a mixture of proteins is passed through the column, only those few that bind strongly to the ligand will stick, while the others will pass through the column.

(c) By changing the buffer one weakens the interaction between the protein and the ligand, which causes the protein to be eluted from the column.

(d) A variation is immuno-affinity chromatography; in which an antibody specific for a protein is immobilized on the column and used to affinity purify the specific protein.

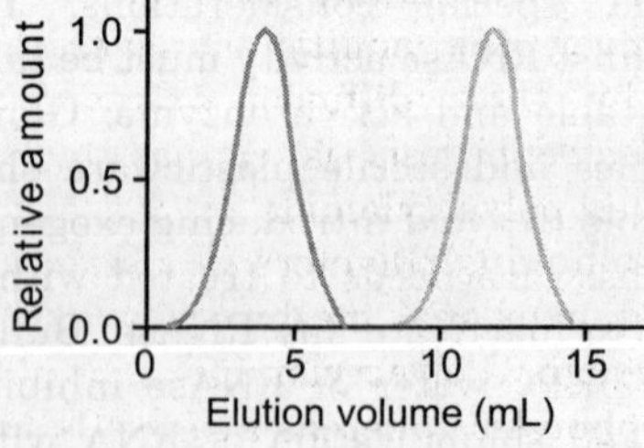

Fig. 37.2 A typical curve of protein during chromatography

Gel Filtration Chromatography (Molecular Sieve or Size Exclusion Chromatography)

(a) The column consists of material that separates proteins based on their size and shape.

(b) A wide range of molecular exclusion limits is available for separating proteins of all sizes.

(c) For any particular column dimensions and material, the volume of buffer required to elute a specific protein depends on the molecular weight of the protein. Thus, one can separate proteins by size.

(d) If one calibrates the column by determining the elution volume of proteins with known molecular weights, then a calibration curve relating elution volume and molecular weight can be constructed.

(e) Such a calibration curve can then be used to estimate the molecular weight of an unknown protein.

Dialysis/Ultrafiltration

- Semipermeable membranes are available, which allow passage of small molecules but exclude the passage of proteins. Sacs made of such material allow the salt and buffer components of a protein solution to be changed to another buffer.

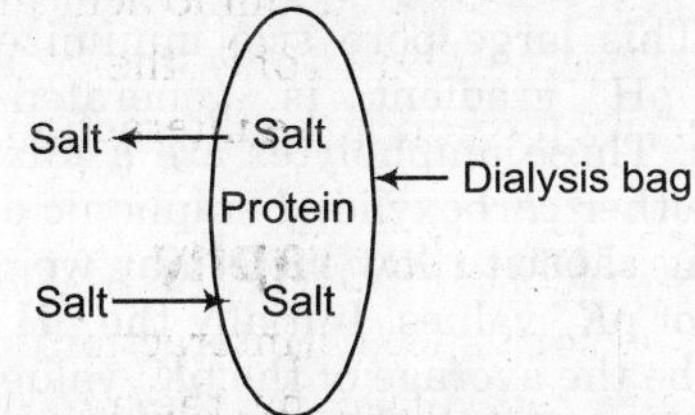

Fig. 37.3 Process of dialysis

Analysis of DNA, RNA and Protein

DNA and RNA form the nucleic acid, while protein is the structural macromolecule of the cell. These are analysed by electrophoresis centrifugation, etc.

Gel Electrophoresis

Electrophoresis of macromolecules can be carried out in solution. However, the ability to separate molecules is compromised by their diffusion. Greater resolution is achieved if electrophoresis is carried out on semi-solid supports such as polyacrylamide or agarose gels. Gels are formed by cross-linking polymers in aqueous medium. This will form a 3-dimensional meshwork which the molecules must pass through. Polyacrylamide is a common gel for protein electrophoresis, whereas agarose is more commonly used for nucleic acids. Agarose gels have a larger pore size than acrylamide gels and are better suited for larger macromolecules. However, either type of gel can be applied to either nucleic acids or proteins depending on the application. Gels are formed from long polymers in a cross-linked lattice. The spaces between the polymers are the pores. Higher concentrations of the polymer will result in smaller average pore sizes. Polyacrylamide gels are formed by covalently cross-linking acrylamide monomers with bis-acrylamide with a free radical like per sulphate (SO_4). The cross-linking of the acrylamide polymers results in 'pores' of a defined size. The total acrylamide concentration and the ratio of bis-acrylamide to acryl amide will determine the average pore size. The polyacrylamide solution is poured into a mold and polymerized. This mold can be a cylindrical tube, but is usually a 'slab' poured between two glass plates.

Since, the gel is solid with respect to the mold, all molecules are forced through the gel. Smaller molecules will be able to pass through this lattice more easily resulting in larger molecules having a lower mobility than smaller molecules. In other words, the gel acts like a molecular sieve and retains the larger molecules while letting the smaller ones pass through (this is opposite of gel filtration, where the larger molecules have a higher mobility because they to not enter the gel). Therefore, the frictional coefficient is related to how easily a protein passes through the pores of the gel and size will be the major determinant of the mobility of molecules in a gel matrix. Protein shape and other factors will still affect mobility, but to a lesser extent.

Substituting size for the frictional coefficient results in:

Mobility ≅ (voltage) (charge)/ (size)

In other words, the mobility of a protein during gel electrophoresis is primarily a function of its charge/mass ratio.

Equipment

Equipment to conduct gel electrophoresis is relatively simple. They consist of a mold to form the gels, an apparatus to hold the gel and contain buffers and a power supply capable of delivering the required voltage or current. There are many types of apparatus for carrying out electrophoresis depending on the application. Gels can be either in a vertical or horizontal configuration. Polyacrylamide gels are run in a vertical fashion and agarose gels tend to be run in a horizontal position. Gels can either be formed as cylinders by using glass tubing as a mold (often called tube gels) or formed as rectangular slabs. These slab gels are formed by polymerizing the acrylamide solution between glass plates separated by spacers. Typically the gel is 0.75-1.5 mm thick. At the top a 'comb' is used to form sample wells. Slab gels allow multiple samples to be compared on the same gel, thus eliminating gel-to-gel variations. The formed gel is placed into the apparatus to that the top and bottom of the gel are in contact with chambers containing buffer. These chambers contain electrodes which are connected to a power supply. Thus, an electric field is generated across the gel when a voltage is applied. The buffer in the chambers is generally different that the buffer making up the gel for protein electrophoresis and in some applications the buffers in the lower and upper chambers may be different. In most applications, the buffers are such that the protein has a negative charge and therefore, the anode (positve pole) will be in the lower chamber and the cathode (negative pole) will be in the upper chamber. However, there are applications in which the proteins of interest may be positively charged and therefore, the electrodes will be reversed.

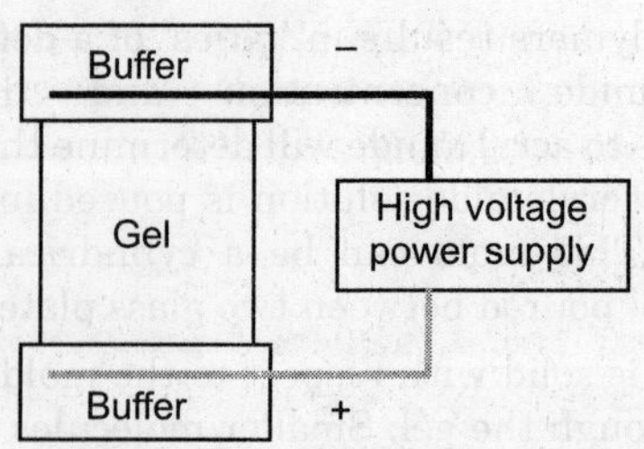

Fig. 37.4 Electrophoresis

Protein Characterization

(a) **SDS-PAGE** (sodium dodecyl sulphate-polyacrylamide gel electrophoresis) is a variant of electrophoresis in which the buffers contain SDS, a detergent that binds to proteins.

(b) Most proteins bind SDS at a constant ratio, about 1 SDS for every 2 amino acids.

(c) The large negative charge resulting from the bound SDS masks the native charge on the protein, so that all proteins have essentially the same charge to mass ratio.

(d) This means that the rate of movement in the electric field depends only on the polypeptide chain molecular weight. Mercaptoethanol is used to reduce disulphides.

(e) In addition, the SDS causes all proteins to adopt a random-coil structure, which means that shape does not affect movement through the gel.

(f) Thus, SDS-PAGE is very useful method for determining the molecular weight of the individual polypeptide chains of a protein.

(g) Western blotting is a technique for detecting a specific protein in a mixture.

(h) Gel electrophoresis and SDS-PAGE electrophoresis are primarily useful as analytical techniques, although they can be used for purification.

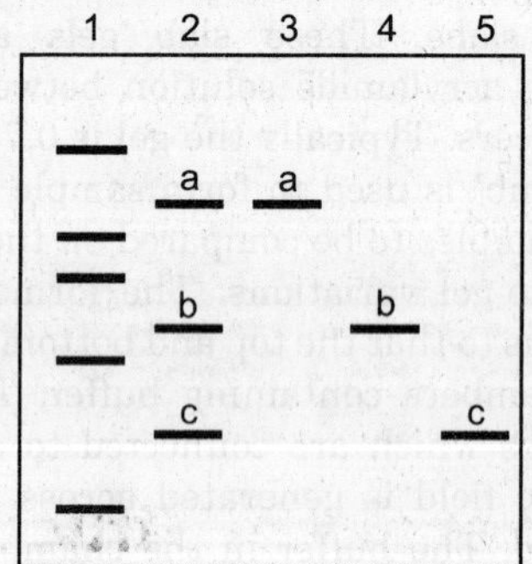

Fig. 37.5 A typical SDS-PAGE gel

(i) In this figure, lane 1 would contain standards of known molecular weight, lane 2 a mixture of three unknown proteins and lanes 3-5 the three unknown proteins.

(j) SDS-PAGE can be used to determine the molecular weight of a protein.

(k) The molecular weights of the three unknown proteins can be determined from a calibration curve constructed by plotting the log of the molecular weight of the standard proteins *vs*. the distance traveled in the gel.

(l) The distance traveled depends on the porosity of the gel. The lower the porosity the faster (further) the proteins move.

(m) Depending on the molecular of the unknown proteins, different porosity gels will need to be used.

Isoelectric Focusing

Isoelectric focusing (IEF) separates proteins based on their isoelectric points. The isoelectric point is defined as the pH at which a protein has no net charge (*i.e.*, the number of negative and positive charges are equal) and is a measure of the protein's net charge. Separating proteins according to their net charge is accomplished by generating a pH gradient in an electric field. The effect of protein size on mobility is minimized by carrying out the electrophoresis gels with large pore sizes such as low acrylamide concentrations (*e.g.*, 3.5%) or agarose. This large pore size minimizes the molecular sieving. A pH gradient is generated with **carrier ampholytes**. These ampholytes are a mixture of aliphatic amines and either carboxylic or sulphonic acid. They have a high buffering capacity, low molecular weight (300-600 Da) and a range of pK_a values. Initially the pH of an ampholyte solution will be the average of the pK_a values of the mixture. Application of an electric current will cause the ampholytes to migrate toward the electrodes according to their charges. Ampholytes that have pK_a values above the pH will be positively charged and those with pK_a values below the pH will be negatively charged. As the ampholytes migrate, this will result in changes in the local pH due to the buffering action of the ampholytes. This change in the local pH will affect the charge on the ampholytes depending upon the pK_a. The ampholytes will continue to migrate until they reach a position in which the local pH equals their pK_a (*i.e.*, no net charge). The end result is a pH gradient in which the most basic ampholytes are found at the cathode, a dilute alkali solution (*e.g.*, NaOH) and the most acidic ampholytes are at the anode, a dilute acid solution (*e.g.*, H_3PO_4). Carrier ampholytes with defined pH ranges can be purchased or prepared by isoelectric focusing. Proteins are also ampholytes and will migrate within the pH gradient until they reach a pH equal to their isoelectric point. The carrier ampholytes are needed since the protein concentration is generally not high enough to establish a stable pH gradient and the isoelectric points of the proteins may not be uniformly distributed along a pH gradient. Sample preparation is important for IEF in that many reagents can adversely affect isoelectric focusing. In particular, the ionic strength should be as low as possible. Precipitation of proteins with acetone is a method for removal of excess salts, as well as concentrating the protein. Separations can be performed under either native or denaturing conditions. Urea is the preferred denaturing agent since it is uncharged. Similarly, non-ionic detergents, such as Triton X-100 or NP-40, are less likely to interfere with the formation of pH gradients. Protein precipitation is sometimes a problem in that proteins tend to be less soluble at their isoelectric points and their local concentrations can be quite high. In addition, the high voltages and high resistance associated with IEF generates substantial heat which increases protein precipitation. Many apparatuses for IEF will have a cooling mechanism to disperse the excess heat. Inclusion of urea and NP-40 in the gels will also minimize protein precipitation. IEF is an equilibrium phenomenon since the components of the system migrate until they have no net charge. As the system approaches equilibrium the resistance approaches infinity since there are no ions to conduct the current. However, the pH gradient will start to breakdown before true equilibrium is reached and the ampholytes will migrate into the anode and cathode buffers. This gradient breakdown is accompanied by a lowering of the resistance. Therefore, the progress of IEF can be followed by performing the electrophoresis under constant voltage and monitoring the current. Initially the current will rapidly drop in concordance with the rapid migration of the ampholytes. As the ampholytes lose their net charge, the resistance increases and the current decreases (E=IR). The rate at which the current decreases levels off as the system approaches equilibrium. The current will start to rise again when the pH gradient starts to breakdown. IEF needs to be discontinued before this point. The pH gradient can be determined with marker proteins with known isoelectric points or by measuring the pH along the gel. This is accomplished by slicing the gel into pieces, eluting the ampholytes into distilled water and measuring the pH.

Two-Dimensional Gel Electrophoresis

Conventional electrophoresis separates proteins according to their charge/mass ratios. SDS-PAGE separates proteins according to subunit or polypeptide, mass. IEF separates proteins according to isoelectric point (or charge). It is possible to sequentially combine the different types of electrophoresis and run two-dimensional (2-D) gels. A common form of 2-D gel electrophoresis is to first separate proteins by IEF in 'tube' gels. These gels are then equilibrated in SDS gel electrophoresis sample buffer and subjected to SDS-PAGE in a 'slab' gel.
(It is necessary to carry out the IEF first since, SDS interfere with the isoelectric focusing.) The 2-D separation results in higher resolution since proteins are being separated according to two distinct properties (*i.e.*, charge and size).

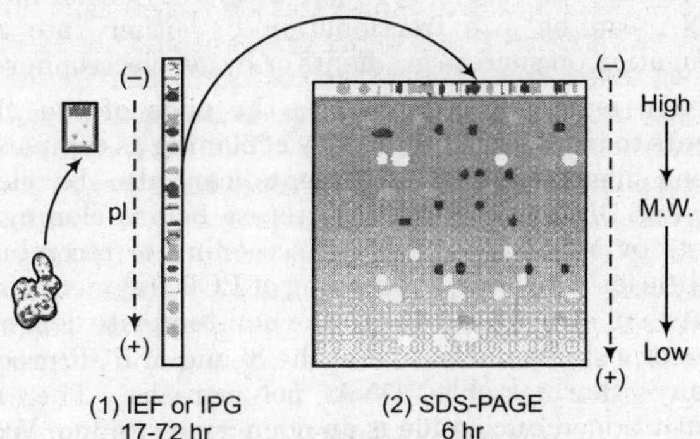

Fig. 37.6 Two-dimensional electrophoresis

Molecular weight and **shape** are fundamental physical properties of a protein. Estimates of molecular weight can be obtained using **SDS-PAGE** or **gel filtration,** as described above. One very useful technique for measuring molecular weight and shape is **centrifugation.**

Centrifugation

(i) A particle that is subjected to a centrifugal field by being spun in a centrifuge is subjected to a force, $f = m(1 - \nu\rho)\omega^2 r$, where m is the mass of the mass of the particle, r is the distance of the particle from the center of rotation and ω is the angular velocity.
(1 - nr) is the buoyancy factor which accounts for the fact that particle is buoyed up by the surrounding solvent of density r (g/mL).

(ii) ν is the specific volume of the particle (mL/g) (= 1/density of the particle).

(iii) If ν = ρ then the particle will not move.

(iv) The movement of the particle through the solvent is resisted by a frictional coefficient, *f*, that depends on the shape of the particle.

(v) The frictional coefficient is an important factor in any transport process, such as centrifugation or gel filtration.

(vi) A spherical particle has a $f = 1.0$, whereas a cigar-shaped or cylindrically shaped particle will have $f > 1.0$.

(vii) The movement of any particle under the influence of a centrifugal field is characterized by its sedimentation coefficient, *S*, which is directly proportional to its molecular mass, M and inversely proportional to *f*, $S = M\dfrac{(1 - vP)}{Nf}$ where, N is Avogadro's number.

(viii) Ultracentrifugation is used in two ways to characterize proteins.

In sedimentation equilibrium experiments, the centrifuge is operated at a relative low speed so that the forces of sedimentation and diffusion balance and the protein distributes in the centrifuge cell in a manner proportional to its molecular weight.

In sedimentation velocity experiments, the centrifuge is operated at maximal speed, which causes the protein to sediment to the bottom of the tube. The rate at which the boundary moves gives S, which when combined with M gives *f*, a measure of the shape of the protein.

Three-Dimensional Structure

(i) Whenever possible, it is highly desirable to obtain the three-dimensional structure of a protein.

(ii) Most often, this is done by X-ray crystallography, although NMR can be used, especially with small proteins (< about 25,000 daltons).

(iii) It is impressive to note that more than 10,000 structures have been determined, most in the last decade, as new, more powerful instruments have become available.

Structural Homology

(i) In addition to sequence homology for proteins with identical functions from different organisms, there are often domains in a protein that are conserved. For example, most proteins that bind nucleotides, such as ADP, have a common nucleotide-binding motif.

(ii) There are even a few cases in which proteins with entirely different functions have very similar three-dimensional structures.

Molecular Cloning

Molecular cloning or recombinant DNA, is the process by which a single gene or segment of DNA, is isolated and amplified. This is accomplished by recombining DNA fragments *in vitro* and then propagating the DNA fragments of interest. A source of nucleic acids and the ability to manipulate them are needed to carry out molecular cloning.

The source and type of nucleic acid will depend on the gene being cloned and the species of interest. The **vector,** when introduced into the appropriate host, is a replicating piece of DNA. The foreign DNA is recombined with a vector, which is then replicated by the host. Available cloning vectors include plasmids, phage/viruses or some combination of the two. Phage, short for bacteriophage, are viruses of bacteria. In order to carry out recombination between the vector and the foreign DNA, it is necessary to specifically and reproducibly cleave DNA. Restriction enzymes cleave DNA in a site specific manner and thus provide this requirement. DNA ligase is an enzyme that covalently joins two pieces of DNA. Therefore, restriction enzymes and DNA ligase allow for the recombination of foreign DNA with vector DNA. The DNA of interest is amplified by introducing the recombinant DNA (*r*DNA) into a compatible host. The vector is replicated by the host. The introduction of vector in the host depends upon the nature of the vector and host. For example, some viral vectors can be introduced by infection. Introduction of naked viral DNA or plasmid DNA is referred to as **transfection** and **transformation**, respectively. Finally, a means to detect the molecular clone of interest or a screening mechanism, is needed.

Preparation of Foreign DNA

The two major sources of foreign DNA for molecular cloning are genomic DNA (*g*DNA) and complementary (or copy) DNA (*c*DNA). Complementary DNA is prepared by making a copy of *m*RNA. One consideration in deciding whether to use *g*DNA or *c*DNA is the copy number and the level of expression of the gene of interest. Single copy genes in large genomes may require extensive screening. A gene expressed at high levels, though, will require less screening to isolate a *c*DNA clone. Conversely genes expressed at low levels will be difficult to detect in *c*DNA libraries. In addition, some genes may only be expressed at certain times or in certain tissues that are inaccessible or unavailable, thus necessitating *g*DNA libraries.

One also needs to consider how the recombinant DNA library will be screened and the questions that will be asked about the cloned gene. For example, many eukaryotic genes contain 'introns' which will result in an interruption of the open reading frame. Therefore, *c*DNA is usually a better starting material if an expression library is going to be screened or if the cloned gene is going to be used for the production of recombinant protein. Similarly, comparing *g*DNA and *c*DNA will allow for a precise mapping of the introns and splice sites.

Fragmenting *g*DNA

The extreme length of *g*DNA necessitates that it be fragmented into smaller pieces before molecular cloning. The size of the DNA fragments should take into account the vector capacity and the size of the desired clone. Restriction enzymes reproducibly cleave DNA at specific sites which are relatively easy to ligate into restriction sites of vectors. If some randomness is needed (*e.g.,* expression libraries and overlapping clones), it may be possible to carry out the digestions under 'star' conditions or to use frequently cutting enzymes under conditions where the target DNA is only partially digested.

Preliminary Southern blots are often carried out when a DNA probe is available. The *g*DNA is digested with several different enzymes and analyzed for appropriate sized fragments. The appropriateness of the size depends on the size of the genetic locus and the vector being utilized. After deciding which restriction enzyme(s) is the most appropriate, a sufficient quantity of DNA is digested and electrophoresed. The region of the gel corresponding to the desired size range is excised and the DNA isolated. This size-fractionated DNA is then used to prepare a library.

It is also possible to use a non-specific nuclease under controlled conditions to cleave *g*DNA into appropriately sized pieces. For example, DNAse I in the presence of Mn^{2+} will cleave *ds*DNA at approximately the same site on both strands. Pilot experiments are carried out to determine the optimal DNAse/DNA ratios for the production of the desired sized fragments. An application of this method is in 'shotgun' sequencing strategies which result in the production of several overlapping clones. Mung bean nuclease in the presence of formamide will also randomly cleave *ds*DNA. DNA can also be broken by mechanical shear forces. Passage of a DNA solution through a small gauge syringe needle or sonication will result in the DNA molecule being broken in random positions. Following fragmentation by either method the DNA can be size fractionation by either rate zonal centrifugation on sucrose gradients or by gel electrophoresis.

Restriction sites can be added to the ends of the *g*DNA fragments to increase the efficiency of cloning as compared to blunt-end ligations. PCR fragments can also be cloned. Amplifying DNA fragments of interest before cloning will eliminate or at least reduce, the screening of recombinant DNA libraries. However, the cloning of PCR fragments is less efficient than anticipated due to the non-template dependent addition of a single nucleotide to the 3′-end of PCR products by many thermostable DNA polymerases. The most frequently added nucleotide is an adenosine residue. Vectors containing a single 3′-T overhang (*i.e.,* TA cloning) greatly enhances the efficiency of cloning. In addition, it is possible to generate a restriction site during the amplification process (see PCR).

Preparing cDNA Libraries

The preparation of *c*DNA from *m*RNA is a multistep process. The first step in preparing *c*DNA is to isolate *m*RNA. *m*RNA tends to be less stable than DNA and requires more precautions than *g*DNA. In addition, an enrich source of *m*RNA of interest can be used. Enrichment for a particular *m*RNA could include: choice of species, tissue, developmental stage, induction of expression (*e.g.,* hormones), etc. It may also be possible to enrich for the *m*RNA of interest by size fractionation, immunological purification of polysomes or substractive libraries. The integrity of *m*RNA should be evaluated by Northern blotting and/or *in vitro* translation before proceeding with the preparation of the library. After obtaining the desired *m*RNA a DNA-RNA hybrid is synthesized with Reverse Transcriptase (RT). Reverse transcriptase is a RNA-dependent DNA polymerase isolated from retroviruses. In the presence of a *m*RNA template and primer, RT will copy the RNA template resulting in the formation of a DNA-RNA hybrid. An oligo-dT primer of 12-18 bases in length is used to initiate synthesis on poly-A messenger RNA. Sequences corresponding to restriction sites can also be included in the oligo-dT primer. For example, a common primer-linker for the synthesis of *c*DNA is 5′-(GA_{10})ACTAGTCTCGAG$(T)_{18}$-3′ which includes SpeI and XhoI sites. Random priming can also be used to increase the chances of obtaining the 5′-end of long *m*RNA or if the *m*RNA of interest lacks a poly-A tail.

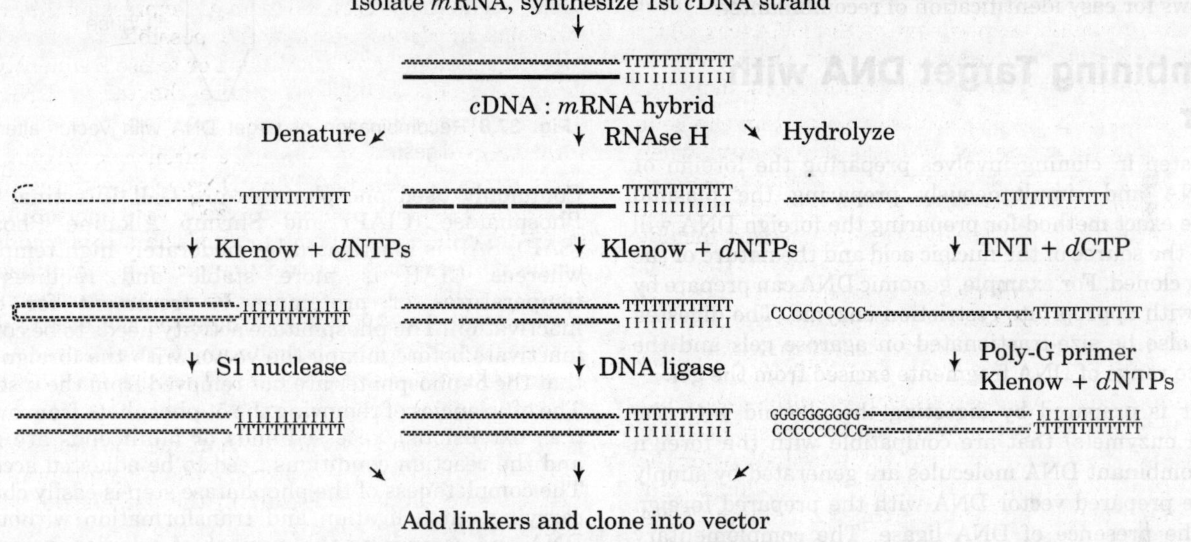

Fig. 37.7 The synthesis of cDNA

The RNA strand is replaced with a second DNA strand following the synthesis of the RNA-DNA hybrid. Three methods for synthesizing the 2nd DNA are: **1.** Self-priming, **2.** Replacement synthesis and **3.** Primed synthesis (figure). In self-priming the RNA-DNA hybrid is denatured by heating or the RNA is hydrolyzed with NaOH. The 3′-termini of single-stranded *c*DNA forms a hairpin loop that can function as a primer for DNA polymerase. Following the completion of second strand synthesis, the *ss*DNA loop is then removed with S1 nuclease. The self-priming is a poorly controlled reaction and treatment with S1 nuclease sometimes leads to loss of the 5′-end of the message.

Replacement synthesis uses the DNA-RNA hybrid as a template for a 'nick translation' reaction. The DNA-RNA hybrid is treat with RNAse H which produces nicks in the RNA strand. The nicked RNA then functions as primers for DNA polymerase. In primed synthesis, a homopolymeric tail (or other known sequence is added to the 3′-end using terminal transferase (TdT). A primer complementary to the homopolymer tail is then used to synthesize the second strand. This method may result in a higher efficiency of recombinant clones containing the complete 5′-end of the message.

The synthesis of *c*DNA results in blunt-end DNA without convenient restriction sites for cloning into vectors. Linkers are added to the termini of the *c*DNA molecules which will provide the necessary restriction sites. Restriction sites within the insert DNA are protected by methylation prior to the addition of the linkers. The overhangs are then generated by digestion with the appropriate restriction enzyme. The use of primer-linkers allow for different restriction sites on the 5′-end and the 3′-end (*i.e.,* poly-A tail) and directional cloning. Another strategy to create sticky ends is to add complementary homopolymer tails with TdT to both the insert DNA and the vector.

Plasmid Vectors

Recombinant DNA vectors function as carriers of the foreign DNA. Plasmids are extrachromosomal genetic elements found in a variety of species and are widely used in molecular cloning. They are autonomously replicating circular DNA molecules that range in size from 1-200 kb. Their replication can be under either stringent control (low copy number) or relaxed (high copy number). Stringent control means that the plasmid is only replicated when the genome is replicated, whereas relaxed plasmids are replicated continuously. Many plasmids confer antibiotic resistance and are naturally transmitted between bacteria by conjugation.

Naturally occurring plasmids have been modified to make them more useful as cloning vectors. To be useful as cloning vectors, plasmids need to be relatively small, replicate in relaxed fashion, have selectable markers (*e.g.*, antibiotic resistance) and contain unique restriction sites. The most widely used plasmids are derivatives of either pBR322 or pUC (where the lower case 'p' means plasmid). Typically modifications of plasmids include the removal of unnecessary portions or streamlining and the introduction of several useful restriction sites in one location. These restriction sites, call the Multiple Cloning Site (MCS) or polylinker, facilitate DNA cloning. This MCS is usually located within a gene which allows for easy identification of recombinants.

Recombining Target DNA with Vector

The first step in cloning involves preparing the foreign or target DNA and simultaneously preparing the plasmid vector. The exact method for preparing the foreign DNA will depend on the source of the nucleic acid and the nature of the gene being cloned. For example, genomic DNA can prepare by digesting with appropriate restriction enzyme. The digested DNA can also be size-fractionated on agarose gels and the desired size range of DNA fragments excised from the gel.

The vector is prepared by digesting the plasmid with the restriction enzyme(s) that are compatible with the foreign DNA. Recombinant DNA molecules are generated by simply mixing the prepared vector DNA with the prepared foreign DNA in the presence of DNA ligase. The complementary overhangs or 'sticky-ends', produced by the restriction enzyme(s) allow the foreign DNA and vector DNA to transiently anneal. DNA ligase catalyzes the formation of a phosphodiester bond between a 5′-phosphate and a 3′-hydroxyl (figure) and will result in the covalent joining of DNA fragments. Typically, equal molar amounts of vector and foreign DNA are mixed during the ligation reaction to minimize the formation of recombinants with tandem copies of the insert. The molar ratio of vector to foreign DNA can be increased (*e.g.*, 1.5-2) to increase the amount of target DNA incorporated into plasmids. Ligation reactions are usually carried out at lower temperatures (8-15°C) for extended time periods (2-24 hours) to promote the annealing of the short (2-4 base) overhangs.

During DNA ligations the vector can ligate with itself in cases were the vector has identical overhangs on both ends (including blunt-ends). This intramolecular formation of circles is kinetically favored and many of the vectors will not contain insert DNA (*i.e.*, be non-recombinants). The formation of non-recombinants is minimized by treating the vector with phosphatase prior to the ligation step. This pretreatment favours the formation of recombinants since, DNA ligase requires a 5′-phosphate, which can now only be supplied by the foreign DNA insert.

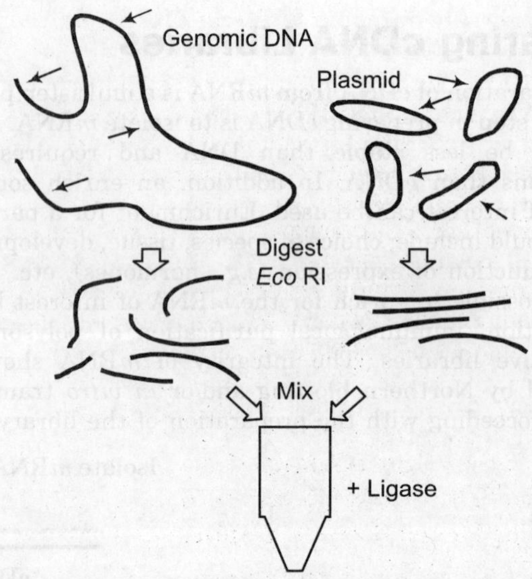

Fig. 37.8 Recombination of target DNA with vector after *Eco* RI digest

Commonly used phosphatases are Calf Intestinal Alkaline Phosphatase (CIAP) and Shrimp Alkaline Phosphatase (SAP). SAP is inactivated by moderately high temperatures whereas CIAP is more stable and requires higher temperatures or proteinase K treatment for complete inactivation. The phosphatase activity needs to be completely inactivate before mixing the vector with the foreign DNA so that the 5′-phosphates are not removed from the insert DNA. The efficiencies of removing the 5′-phosphate from overhangs (*i.e.*, extensions), recessed ends or blunt ends are different and the reaction conditions need to be adjusted accordingly. The completeness of the phophatase step is easily checked by carrying out a ligation and transformation without insert DNA and comparing the number of colonies formed to the number of colonies obtained with an equal amount of plasmid which was not treated with phosphatase.

The vector and foreign DNA can also be prepared with restriction enzymes that produce blunt ends. The advantage of blunt ends is that all blunt ends are compatible. However, the restriction sites will be lost or changed when blunt ends from different restriction enzymes are ligated together. In addition, the ligation efficiency is much lower because there are no cohesive termini to temporarily hold the two DNA fragments together. Therefore, higher DNA concentrations (both vector and foreign) and DNA ligase concentrations are needed for blunt-end ligations.

Plasmids with different protruding termini can also be prepared. Advantages of different termini are a low background of non-recombinants, tandem copies of the insert DNA are less likely and the insert DNA can only be in one orientation.

Following ligation, the *r*DNA is introduced into the host. Bacteria and in particular *E. coli*, are typically used as host cells. The two most common methods used to transform bacteria with plasmids are 'heat-shock' and 'electroporation'. In both cases, the bacteria must be made 'competent' (*i.e.*, ready to receive the DNA). In the heat shock method, the bacteria are pretreated with $CaCl_2$. The competent cells are incubated with the recombined plasmid to allow DNA to bind to the bacteria surface and then briefly incubated at 40-42°. The heating increases the fluidity of the membrane and supposedly opens up temporary 'pores' in the bacterial membrane that allows the DNA to enter.

The efficiency of heat shock is typically 105-109 colonies per µg DNA, which is relatively low. For example, a 1 µg of a 5 kb plasmid will contain approximately 2 x copies. This means that even at an efficiency of 109 colonies per µg of DNA only 0.5% of the plasmids were taken up by bacteria during transformation. Electroporation exhibits efficiencies of 109-1010 colonies per µg DNA and can be used for the transformation of prokaryotic cells. In electroporation, the competent cells are exposed to pulses of high voltage which will produce transient pores in membranes and permit DNA uptake. With both electroporation and heat shock the efficiency of transformation decreases with increasing plasmid size. After transformation with the recombinant plasmids the bacteria are plated on antibiotic containing media. The antibiotic will kill the bacteria which do not contain plasmid. Therefore, all of the colonies will represent bacteria with plasmid. However, the bacteria will have different plasmids and it will be necessary to identify the clone of interest by screening the *r*DNA library. A common method for screening *r*DNA libraries is to use a 'DNA probe' which hybridizes to the recombinant clone of interest. Sources of DNA probes include previously cloned genes or synthetic oligonucleotides that exhibit sequence homology to the gene of interest. For example, a previously cloned gene from another species that is homologous to the gene of interest can be used as a DNA probe. It is also possible to make a synthetic oligonucleotide probe from highly conserved regions of known genes. Screening expression libraries with antibodies raised against the protein of interest is also possible (see section on expression).

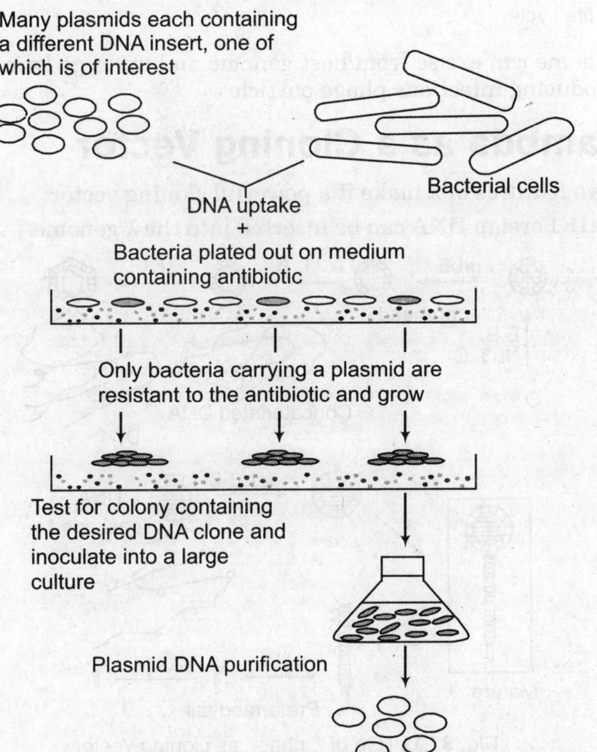

Fig. 37.9 Transformation and selection of the bacteria containing desired *c*DNA

In situations where a homologous gene has not been cloned or not much is known about the gene of interest it may be possible to develop a probe based upon a partial protein sequence (referred to as reverse genetics). A mixture of synthetic oligonucleotides, based upon all the possible codons for the polypeptide sequence, is synthesized and used to screen the recombinant DNA library. If possible, the amino acid sequence should be chosen to minimize the redundancy of the genetic code. For example, methionines and tryptophans, since they only have one possible codon and amino acids with only two possible codons are especially useful. Conversely, amino acids with six possible codons should be avoided.

It may be possible to decrease the number of degenerate oligonucleotides by adjusting for the codon usage in the species of interest. Many organisms exhibit a codon-usage bias in that not all codons are used at equal frequencies. For example, the numbers in parenheses are percentages for each the codons in *Plasmodium falciparum*. Since, *Plasmodium* species have an AT-rich genome (approximately 80%) the third codon position is very biased towards A and T and it is possible to make less degenerate probe which still may hybridize to the target sequence.

A 'colony lift' is used to detect bacteria containing plasmids of interest. In this procedure, a DNA probe is used to screen the *r*DNA library utilizing blotting techniques as discussed previously. The transformed bacteria are grown on agar plates in the presence of antibiotic. When bacterial colonies become visible a sterile nylon membrane is laid on top of the plate. Orientation marks are made on both the membrane and plate so that the pertinent colonies can be identified later. The membrane is then carefully removed and laid onto another nutrient agar plate with the colony side up. In other words, this membrane is a replica of the original master plate. Both the original plate and the membrane are returned to the incubator until the colonies are the desired size. The bacteria are lysed and the plasmid DNA is released directly onto the membrane by laying the membrane (colony side up) on filter paper saturated with buffers containing SDS. The released DNA will bind to the membrane and it is then denature by moving the membrane to a filter paper saturated with NaOH. Following neutralization, the DNA is fixed to the membrane by baking or UV cross-linking and then incubated with a radioactive DNA probe as described for Southern blotting. The probe will hybridize to plasmids containing homologous insert sequences and result in a spot on the autoradiograph corresponding to the position of the colony containing the recombinant plasmid. The positive colonies are identified on the original plate by aligning the autoradiograph with the master plate. The bacteria can be streaked on an agar plate and retested for the plasmid of interest to insure that the original bacteria colony was derived from single bacteria. Bacteria from a positive colony are expanded in liquid culture media containing antibiotic and the recombined plasmids (*i.e.,* cloned DNA) isolated for further characterized.

Bacteriophage λ

Viruses can also used as cloning vectors. The ability of a virus to replicate within a host cell is exploited as a means to amplify DNA of interest. Bacteriophages are viruses that infect bacteria and are used in various recombinant DNA methods. Phage λ has proven to be an exceptionally powerful vector for molecular cloning.

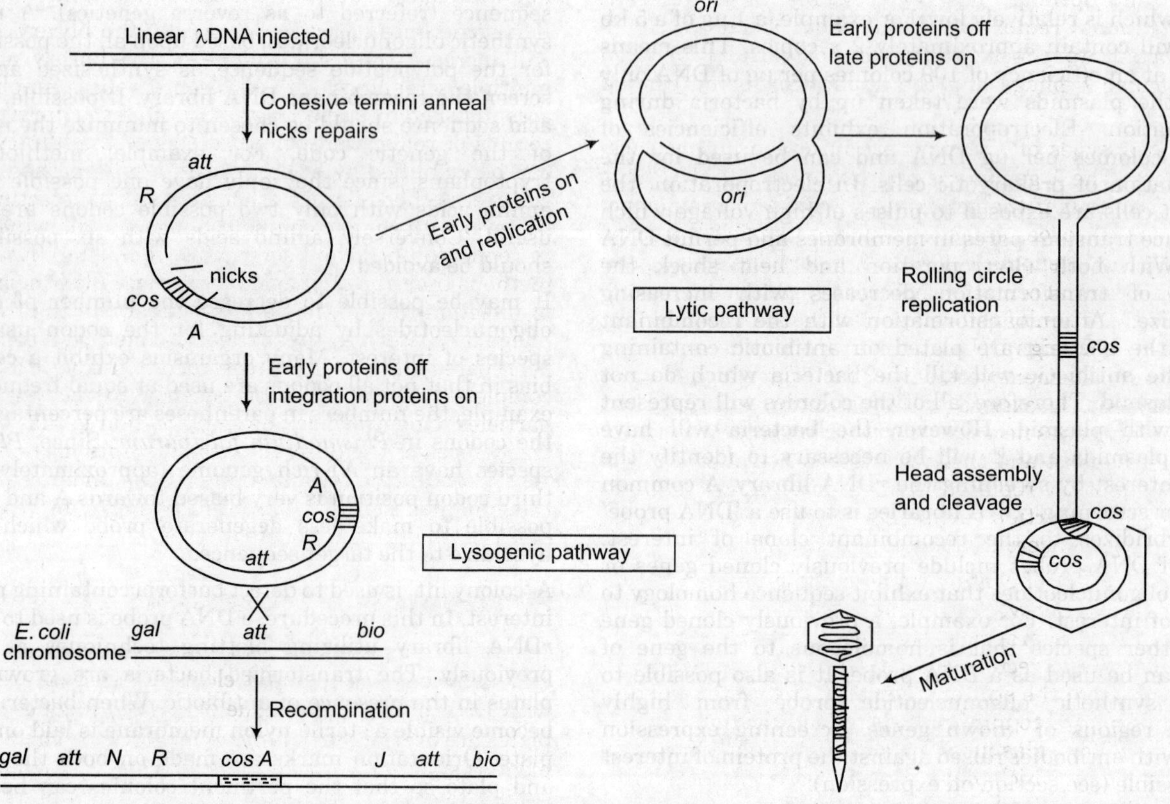

Fig. 37.10 Phage λ life cycle

(i) Phage attaches to bacteria.

(ii) DNA is injected and circularizes *vis-a-vis cos* ends.

(iii) DNA is transcribed and replicated*.

(iv) Phage assembly.

(v) Cell lysis (plaque formation).

*Alternatively can integrate into host genome and undergo a lysogeny.

Phage λ infects *E. coli* by injecting its DNA into the bacteria. The phage DNA is initially linear but forms a circle as a result of cohesive or *cos*, ends. Phage proteins are transcribed from the phage DNA and the genome is replicated. DNA replication proceeds by a 'rolling circle' mechanism that generates long linear molecules composed of consecutive λ genomes. Infectious particles are then assembled from the phage proteins and DNA. The proteins making up the phage heads self-assemble into preheads. Other phage proteins bind the linear phage DNA near the *cos* site, wind the DNA into the prehead and cleaves the DNA at the *cos* sites. A fully assembled tail structure is then attached to the prehead resulting in a mature and infectious phage particle. The phage then induces host cell lysis releasing infectious phage particles which are able to infect more *E. coli*.

The infection and multiplication of phage λ is known as the lytic cycle. Alternatively, λ can also undergo a lysogenic cycle in which λ incorporates into the host genome at a specific site and is replicated with the host. At a later time, the phage genome can excise from host genome and undergo lytic cycle producing infectious phage particles.

Lambda as a Cloning Vector

Two features of λ make it a powerful cloning vector:

(i) Foreign DNA can be inserted into the λ genome.

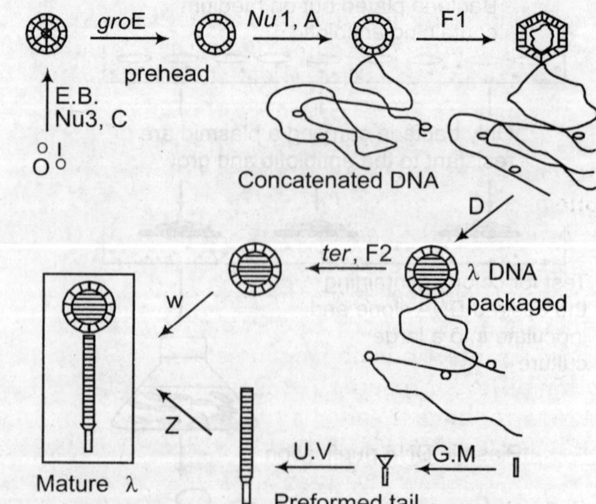

Fig. 37.11 Use of λ phase as cloning vector

(ii) Infectious phage particles can be assembled *in vitro*. Phage λ has been extensively modified to make it a more efficient cloning vector and many different λ vectors have been developed. Each particular λ vector has an optimal host and sometimes different applications require different host bacteria. It is important to choose the right host strain for each particular λ phage and the application being carried out.

The two basic types of λ vectors are insertion and replacement vectors. The λ genome is approximately 50 kb. Phage assembly can occur if the genome is 78-105% of the normal size. In other words, infectious phage particles can be assembled if the λ genome is 40-52 kb. Insertion vectors have a small non-essential central region of the λ genome removed. This removed portion of the genome allows for the insertion of up to 10 kb of foreign DNA (depending upon the particular λ vector). In replacement vectors a 13 kb fragment, called the stuffer fragment, is excised with restriction enzymes and discarded. Only genes necessary for the lysogenic cycle are on the stuffer fragment and the lytic cycle is not affected. The stuffer fragment is replaced with a foreign DNA insert of 11-21 kb. The insertion vectors are easier to work with but accommodate less insert DNA than replacement vectors.

The overall strategy of cloning into lambda is similar to that of cloning into other vectors. The λ DNA is isolated and digested with the appropriate restriction enzyme(s). In the case of replacement vectors the left and right arms will be purified away from the stuffer fragment. The vector can also be dephosphorylated to minimize vector self-ligation (as discussed for plasmids) when identical overhangs. Generally, vectors which have already been digested with restriction enzymes and dephosphorylated (*i.e.,* ready for cloning) are obtained commercially.

The vector and foreign DNA (digested with the appropriate restriction enzyme) are mixed and ligated. Generally, equal molar ratios of vector and foreign DNA work best. Ligation results in the foreign DNA being combined with the vector. In addition, the *cos* ends of phage λ are ligated together forming very long DNA molecules of sequential recombinant phage. The recombined concatenated phage DNA is then mixed with an extract containing all of the proteins needed for phage assembly. This *in vitro* packaging extract is prepared from *E. coli* which have been infected with a defective λ and usually obtained from a commercial source. One of the mutations in the defective lambda reduces the packaging of the endogenous phage DNA, but does not affect the synthesis of the phage coat proteins. Therefore, the recombined phage DNA is preferentially packaged into phage particles when mixed with extracts prepared from *E. coli* infected with this lambda mutant. Nucleases on the phage head recognize and cleave the DNA at the *cos* sites resulting in the *in vitro* assembly of an infectious phage particle. The phage particles will contain different insert DNA fragments and this mixture of recombinant phage is called a library.

The next step is to titer the recombinant library and determines the plaque forming units (pfu) per mL. Plaques are clear zones on bacteria lawn which are the result of localized bacteria lysis. The bacteria lawn is formed by mixing the phage with *E. coli* in a low concentration of agar or agarose. This mixture is then poured onto an agar nutrient plate and allowed to solidify. As the bacteria grow the plate will become opaque. Infected bacteria will result in a clear plaque due to the destruction of neighbouring bacteria following many cycles of lysis and reinfection.

It is sometimes desirable to amplify the library. Amplifying will increase the total volume of the library allowing for multiple screenings with different probes. Amplification is accomplished by subjecting a portion of the library to several rounds of replication before screening the library. Libraries can be amplified by either a plate lysate method or a liquid culture method. Both methods consist of infecting the host bacteria with the recombinant phage and allowing the phage to replicate until the bacteria are completely lysed. In both methods the ratio of phage to bacteria, called the multiplicity of infection (m.o.i.), has a large impact on the final yield of phage (*i.e.,* titer). In the plate lysate method a bacterial lawn is prepared and buffer is then added to the plate following the complete lysis of the host bacteria to recover the phage particles. One drawback of amplification is that the relative frequencies of the different recombinants may change since slowly replicating recombinants will be under represented in the amplified library. λ libraries are stable for years if stored at 4°C in the presence of chloroform.

Screening λ Libraries

The library is plated out on the appropriate strain of *E. coli* and screened. Recombinant clones of interest are identified with DNA probes in a plaque lift. When plaques appear, the plates are overlaid with a nylon membrane. The phage in the plaques stick to the membranes. In general, plaque lifts are similar to colony lifts (Figure) except that it is not necessary to continue growth after transfer to the membranes. Phage particles are lysed directly on the membrane and the recombinant phage DNA is denatured and fixed to the membrane. The membranes are then hybridized with a specific DNA probe. The recombinant phage with the insert DNA of interest is then identified by aligning the autoradiograph with the original plate.

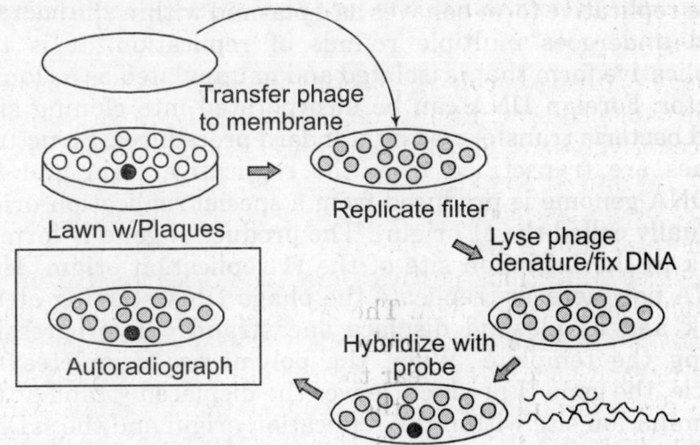

Fig. 37.12 Screening of λ phage libraries

The recombinant phage of interest are recovered by punching out the plaque of interest from the agar plate with a Pastuer pipet. The phage are eluted from the agar and can be expanded by reinfecting *E. coli*. A 'plaque purification' can be carried out by replating and rescreening the recombinant phage. It is recommended to repeat this plaque purification until all of the plaques are positive for the insert DNA of interest. The cloned phage are then expanded and the DNA isolated.

The high efficiency of λ infection and the ease at which relatively large numbers of plaques can be screened make λ a good vector for cloning genes. However, isolating DNA from λ is somewhat cumbersome compared to isolating plasmid DNA. Therefore, the recombinant DNA insert is usually subcloned into a plasmid for further characterization. This is easily accomplished by digesting the phage DNA with the appropriate restriction enzyme(s) and ligating with plasmid previously digested with the same enzyme(s). It is usually not necessary to purify the insert fragment since the phage arms are not efficiently incorporated into the plasmid or transfected into the host bacteria.

Filamentous Bacteriophage

Single-stranded DNA filamentous phage exhibit features which can be exploited for molecular biology research. For example, M13 has been widely used for the generation of *ss*DNA for DNA sequencing and site-directed mutagenesis. More recently, though, sequencing of *ds*DNA has replaced *ss*DNA and many site-directed mutagenesis applications now utilize PCR. Filamentous phage are also used for 'display' of ligands or epitopes (known as phage display).

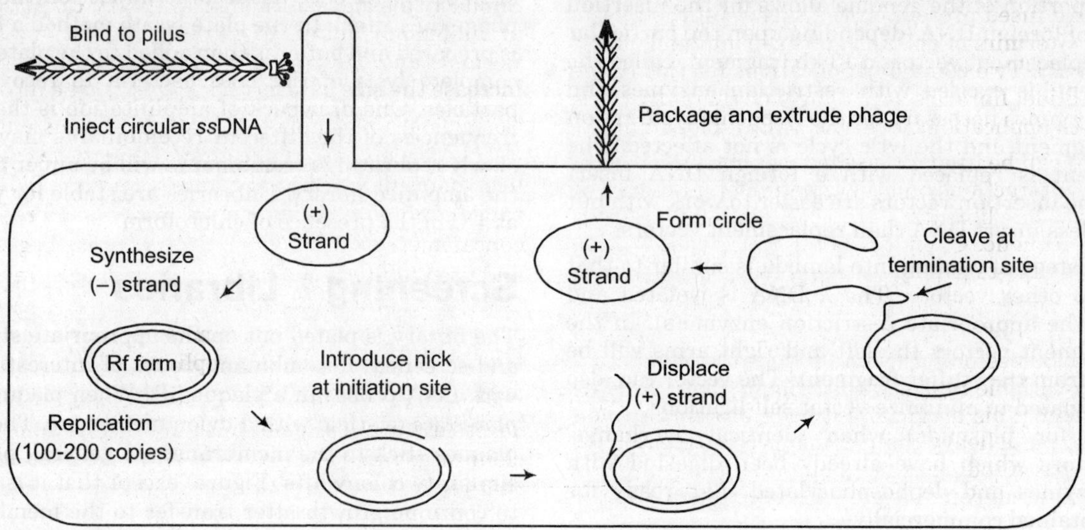

Fig. 37.13 Life cycle of filamentous phage

Life Cycle

Filamentous phage attach to the F-pili of *E. coli* and inject single-stranded circular DNA into the bacteria. The *ss*DNA is converted to a *ds*DNA form known as Replicative Form (RF). The replicative form behaves as a plasmid within the bacteria and undergoes multiple rounds of replication. It is this replicative form that is isolated and manipulated as a cloning vector. Foreign DNA can be incorporated into cloning sites and bacteria transformed by standard procedures. Structural genes are transcribed from the replicative form and the *ss*DNA genome is produced from a special replication origin (usually called the f1 origin). The product of gene II forms a nick in the initiation site of the f1 replication origin. Host DNA polymerases replicate the phage DNA starting at the nick and as plasmid displace one strand will progressing along the template. When the polymerase completes the circle, the gene II product cleaves the displaced strand at the termination site within the replication origin and the *ss*DNA is circularized.

The *ss*DNA is packaged at the membrane of the bacteria and the mature phage is extruded without lysing the cell. Phage particles containing *ss*DNA are isolated from the culture supernatant medium by differential centrifugation and the *ss*DNA is extracted from the phage particles. The phage can also be plated on a bacterial lawn to produce plaques. However, these plaques are 'fuzzy' since they are not formed as a result of cell lysis, but formed as a result of diminished host cell growth.

Phagemids

Many plasmids have been modified to include a f1 origin of replication. These 'phagemids' allow for the generation of *ss*DNA without some of the difficulties of working with M13. In particular, incorporation of foreign DNA into M13 will often severely affect phage replication. Foreign DNA is incorporated into these phagemids and propagated as conventional plasmids. Single-stranded DNA is rescued by super-infecting the transformed cells with a helper phage (*e.g.,* R408, M13KO7). The helper phage supplies enzymes (*i.e.,* gene II) that are necessary for synthesis of circular *ss*DNA molecules and the genes for the phage coat proteins. The helper phage, however, has a defect in its own f1 origin so that the f1 origin of the recombinant phagemid is the preferred substrate. The *ss*DNA is then packaged into the phage particles and secreted into the culture media with some contamination by the helper phage due to its slow replication. The exact yield of the *ss*DNA is dependent on the nature of the insert DNA.

λZAP is another example of a vector exploiting the f1 origin. In this case, a phagemid (pBluescript) is contained within the λDNA such that initiation and termination regions of the f1 origin are at opposite ends. Co-infection with a helper phage leads to the displacement of a *ss*DNA molecule from the initiation site followed by cleavage and circularization at the termination site. The *ss*DNA is then packed into phage particles and extruded from the bacteria. The plasmid containing the foreign DNA is obtained by infecting F strains of *E. coli* with these phage particles isolated from the culture supernatant. This process, called '*in vivo* excision', eliminates the subcloning step.

Phage Display

Filamentous phage have also been used for expression vectors. Peptide or protein sequences are expressed as fusion proteins with a coat protein of the bacteriophage, resulting in the display of the fused protein on the surface of the phage. Fusions to the N-termini of gp3 and gp8 have minimal effects of phage infectivity. Two common applications for this phage display are peptide libraries and single-chain antibodies. Screening in both applications is carried out by 'biopanning'.

Peptide libraries can be used for epitope mapping, analysis of protein protein interactions and the isolation of inhibitors or other ligands. The libraries are prepared by cloning oligonucleotide sequences, corresponding to random peptide sequences, into the N-terminal portion of either gp3 or gp8. The gp8 site can only accommodate peptides of approximately 6 residues.

Single chain antibodies or scFv, are produced by combining the heavy chain variable region with the light chain variable region *via* a linker. This artificial antibody protein can fold such that the light and heavy chain domains come together to form a functional binding site. Combinatorial antibody libraries are generated from naive B-cells and cloned into the gp3 site.

In both cases, the desired recombinant phage are isolated by a biopanning process. The target protein (*e.g.,* antibody for peptide libraries or antigen for scFv libraries) are absorbed to a solid support. This target is incubated with the phage display library and non-bound phage is wash away. The bound phage are eluted and amplified, thereby enriching for the phage which express peptides or proteins that bind the target. This enrichment is typically 100-1000 fold, thus 3-4 rounds of biopanning are typically carried out. (In general, the maximum complexity of the library ranges from 10^8 -10^9.) The individual phage in the final biopanning are then analyzed for the peptide sequences (*e.g.,* epitope) recognized by target protein or the scFv are isolated and used as a reagent for subsequent analyses.

Cosmids and YACS

One problem with cloning vectors is their limited size as compared to the genome size of many organisms. For example, the human genome contains more than 109 bp. Typical λ vectors will accommodate only 10-20 kb of DNA. Similarly plasmids, although in theory can accommodate an unlimited amount of DNA are rarely functional above 10 kb. Cosmids and YACS are two additional cloning vectors that increase the size of insert DNA that can be incorporated.

Cosmids are plasmids that contain the *cos* ends from λ, an *E. coli* origin of replication and a selectable marker (*e.g.,* ampicillin resistance gene). Foreign DNA with a size range of 35-45 kb is ligated with the cosmid resulting in long concatemers of DNA. The DNA is then packaged into λ heads and used to infect *E. coli*. Even in the absence of λ genes the DNA will be packaged into phage heads if the *cos* sites are appropriately spaced. Once inside of the bacteria the injected DNA will form circles and replicate as a large plasmid under antibiotic pressure.

Yeast Artificial Chromosomes (YACs) are another means to clone large fragments of DNA. YACs are linear pieces of DNA that replicate as chromosomes within yeast cells. The vector contains elements that allow for its replication in both bacteria and yeast. The centromere, Autonomously Replicating Sequences (ARS) and telomere sequences are particularly important for its function as a linear chromosome. The bacterial elements allow for the production of the plasmid in *E. coli*. Foreign DNA (100 kb-2 mb) is then incorporated so that it is a linear piece of DNA and is then introduced into yeast cells.

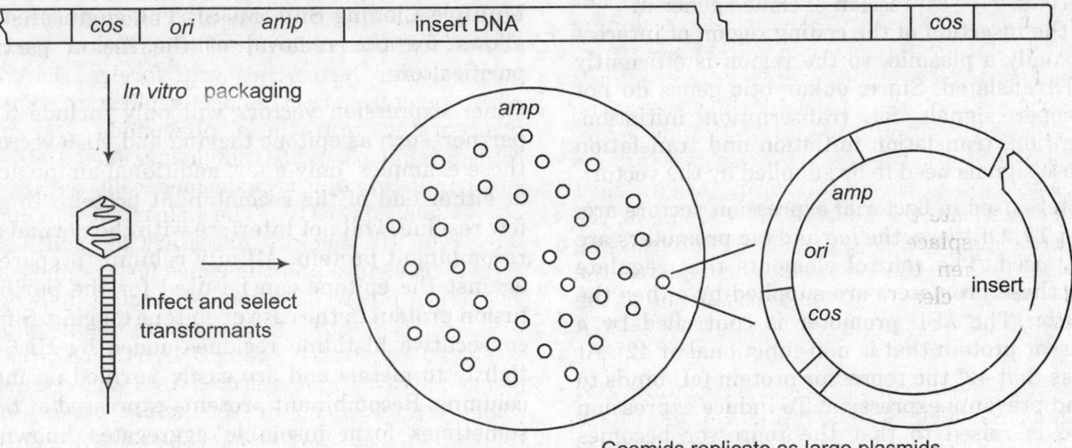

Fig. 37.14 Use of cosmid as vector

Expression of Recombinant Proteins

One potential of recombinant DNA is the production of proteins. Many systems have been designed for the expression of recombinant proteins. Although *E. coli* are easy to grow in large quantities there are some problems associated with the expression of eukaryotic proteins in prokaryotes. Therefore, expression systems in eukaryotic systems have also been devised. In addition, it is also possible to use expression vectors for the cloning of genes.

General considerations in the over production of recombinant proteins include such features as promoters and the nature of the host for expression. Ideally the recombinant protein should be cloned in conjunction with a strong promoter. Promoters are elements found on the 5′-end of genes and control their expression. A strong promoter results in a high level of gene expression. In addition to being strong, promoters should be regulatable so that transcription hosts can be turned off and on. Recombinant proteins are sometimes toxic for the host cell and this toxicity can be minimized by controlling the expression. The use of high copy number plasmids also increases the production of recombinant proteins by increasing the gene dosage.

Other features are included in many expression vectors. For example, it is often convenient to have recombinant proteins that are exported from the host cell. This can be accomplished by engineering localization signals within the recombinant protein so that they are directed to a particular cellular compartment. In addition, the recombinant protein can also be expressed as a fusion protein with another protein. This will sometimes stabilize the recombinant protein and/or assist in the purification and characterization of the recombinant protein. Proteolysis of recombinant proteins is often a major problem that is partially alleviated by cloning into protease deficient hosts.

Expression in *E. coli*

The general procedure for expression of cloned genes in *E. coli* involves the insertion of the coding region of interest into a vector, usually a plasmid, so the region is efficiently transcribed and translated. Since, eukaryotic genes do not contain the proper signals for transcription initiation, ribosome recognition, translation initiation and translation termination, these signals need to be supplied by the vector.

Common promoters used in bacterial expression vectors are: λPL, *lac*, *tac* and T7. Of these, the *lac* and *tac* promoters are the most widely used. The control elements that regulate expression from these promoters are supplied by either the host or the vector. The λPL promoter is controlled by a mutant cI repressor protein that is non-functional at 42°. At temperatures less that 42° the repressor protein (cI) binds to the promoter and prevents expression. To induce expression the temperature is raised to that the repressor becomes non-functional and expression is now permitted. One problem with this system is that heat-shock proteins may also be induced. The T7 promoter is from the T7 phage and is only transcribed by the T7 RNA polymerase (T7 gene 1). The host cell must also contain the T7 gene 1 in order to express from this promoter. To regulate expression from this promoter it is necessary to be able to regulate the expression of the T7 gene 1.

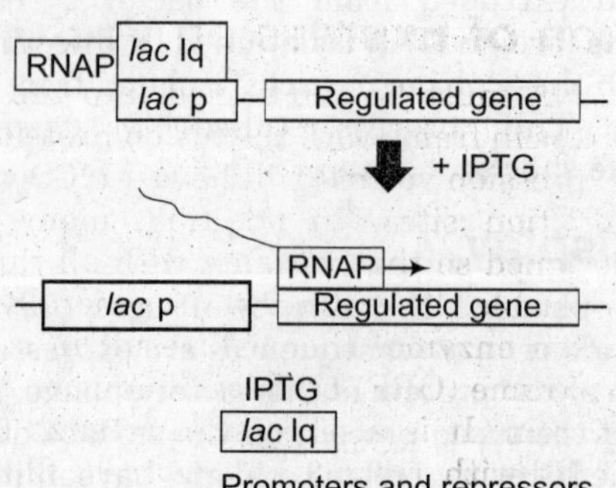

Fig. 37.15 Expression of recombinant proteins in *E. coli*

Promoters and Repressors

The *lac* and *tac* promoters are controlled by the *lac* repressor. The *lac* repressor binds to the lac promoter and prevents RNA polymerase from transcribing the gene. Host strains with *lac* Iq gene express the *lac* repressor at 10-fold higher concentrations than the normal *lac* I gene. IPTG (isopropyl-1-thio-β-D-galactopyanoside, an analog of lactose) binds to the repressor and prevents its interaction with the *lac* promoter and allowing RNA polymerase to transcribe the regulated gene. The tac promoter is a fusion of *trp* and *lac* promoters and is also regulated by IPTG. The production of recombinant fusion-proteins often stabilizes the expression of foreign proteins in *E. coli*. Several plasmids that express recombinant proteins as fusion proteins have been developed. In addition to stabilizing recombinant protein, the fusion partner is often exploited for affinity purification or for the analysis of the recombinant protein. However, for many applications the fusion partner may interfere with the activity of the recombinant protein. Some expression vectors include a protease site between the fusion partner and the Multiple Cloning Site (MCS). The engineered protease site allows for the removal of the fusion partner after its purification.

Other expression vectors will only include a small fusion partner, such as epitope tagging and His6 vectors. In both of these examples, only a few additional amino acids are added at either end of the recombinant protein. In general, these few residues will not interfere with the normal activity of the recombinant protein. Affinity columns prepared from mAbs against the epitope can be used for the purification of the fusion protein in the case of epitope tagging. Similarly, the six consecutive histidine residues added by His6 vectors bind tightly to metals and are easily purified on metal-chelating columns. Recombinant proteins expressed at high levels will sometimes form insoluble aggregates known a inclusion bodies. In some applications, it is possible to take advantage of this phenomenon. For example, the inclusion bodies can be isolated by differential centrifugation and solubilized under denaturing conditions (*e.g.*, urea). It is sometimes possible to renature the protein and regain activity. In addition, fusions with *E.coli* thioredoxin can circumvent inclusion body formation.

Preparation of Expression Vectors

The 'insert' DNA must be sub cloned into the expression vector so that it is in frame with the fusion protein (or a start ATG). Most expression vectors will have a MCS with several different restriction sites. In addition, many expression vectors are designed so that variants with all three reading frames are available. Therefore, it is generally simple to choose restriction enzymes that will result in a continuous Open Reading Frame (ORF) between the fusion protein and the foreign protein. It is also possible to shift the reading frame by cutting with restriction enzymes, filling in with Klenow and religating. Digesting with an enzyme producing a 4-base overhang will result in a -1 frameshift and digesting with an enzyme producing a 2-base overhang will produce a +1 shift. In addition, stop codons can be produced by this method with certain restriction enzymes (*e.g., Hind* III, SpeI).

Screening λ Libraries with Antibodies

It is also possible to utilize the expression vectors as a means to screen for the gene of interest. Recombinant DNA clones expressing proteins of interest can be detected with antibodies, ligands or other protein activity. λgt11 is a common vector for cloning genes using antibody probes. Foreign DNA is cloned into a *lac*-promoter controlled β-galactosidase gene resulting in the expression of fusion proteins. Recombinant phage expressing the protein of interest are detected with antibodies.

A recombinant λgt11 library is plated on a lawn of *E. coli* Y1090 and incubated at 42° until plaques are visible. An IPTG saturated nitrocellulose membrane is then laid on the plate and the incubation is continued for 1-3 h at 37°. This will induce the expression of β-galactosidase fusion proteins within infected bacteria. Upon lysis the recombinant proteins are released with other bacterial proteins into the plaque and adsorbed onto the membrane. The membrane (*i.e.,* plaque lift) is then analyzed by Western blotting using an antibody against the protein of interest. This will result in a spot on membrane which corresponds to a plaque formed by the recombinant λgt11 expressing the protein of interest. Such plaques are identified by aligning the membrane with the original plate. Rabbit antisera are often problematic due to a strong background reactivity with *E. coli* proteins. It is sometimes possible to pre-absorb the anti-sera with *E. coli* proteins to reduce the background.

It is also possible to use a cloned recombinant λgt11 phage for the production of recombinant protein. However, this is generally more difficult than subcloning the fragment into a plasmid and therefore, not widely used. The procedure involves the production of lysogens. The lysogens are induced to produce high levels of phage from which the fusion protein is expressed. The fusion protein is then isolated from the infected bacteria.

Expression in Eukaryotes

Although expression of recombinant proteins in *E. coli* is usually fairly straight forward, it is often desirable or necessary to express cloned genes in eukaryotes. Eukaryotic expression systems are often needed to insure correct folding and disulphide-bond formation, post-translational modifications and processing. Yeast, such as *Saccharomyces cerevisiae* and *Pichia* species, are useful hosts for the expression of recombinant proteins since they can be grown and manipulated like a bacteria. *Pichia* expression systems often allow for high level expression of recombinant proteins using a strong alcohol oxidase promoter which is induced by methanol. Shuttle vectors contain both a bacterial origin of replication and the origin of replication of interest. This allows for manipulations of the plasmids to be carried out in *E. coli* before transforming yeast or other eukaryotes.

The two major strategies for expression of recombinant sequences in mammalian cells are **(i)** Stable or transient expression of transfected DNA and **(ii)** The use of viral expression vectors. Mammalian and other eukaryotic cells are able to take up DNA. The introduction of DNA to cells is often cell type dependent and problematic, though. Several different methods for introducing DNA to cells are available. One of the early methods for transfecting eukaryotic cells was to incubate a calcium phosphate precipitate of the DNA with the target cells. This method is relatively inefficient. Using DEAE-dextran instead of calcium phosphate is a little more efficient. Electroporation is the application of a short pulse of high voltage. This method is effective for many cell types once the optimal conditions are determined. DNA can also be incoporated into liposomes prepared from cationic detergents. These liposomes (*i.e.,* micelles) will fuse with the plasma membrane and deliver the DNA. Similarly, protoplasts can be prepared by digesting the bacterial cell wall and fusing these protoplasts with the target cells. Finally, DNA can be directly introduced into cells by ballistics (*i.e,,* gene gun) or microinjection. The gene gun shoots small colloidal gold particles covered with DNA into cells with doing permanent membrane damage. In many cases, the foreign DNA is quickly loss from the host cell and the expression is only transient.

Several different eukaryotic viruses can also be used as cloning vectors for the expression of recombinant proteins. Lytic viruses are good for transient expression whereas episomal viruses are better for constitutive expression. Retroviruses can become incorporated into the host cell genome and possibly lead to a stable transformation.

Baculoviruses are used for the production of recombinant eukaryotic proteins. *Autographica californica* is a nuclear polyhedrosis virus (AcNPV) that infects insects. Sf9 cells, derived from *Spodoptera frugiperda,* are readily grown *in vitro* and can be infected with baculovirus. Extremely high levels of recombinant proteins can be expressed and many eukaryotic post-translational modifications are correctly made in the host insect cells. This high level of expression is driven by a strong promoter for the polyhedrin gene. The polyhedrin protein is expressed late in infection as the virus is killing the host cell and is needed for the dissemination of the virus in nature. However, the polyhedrin gene is unnecessary for viral growth in tissue culture and can be replaced with a gene of interest.

Baculovirus expression vectors consist of the viral genome (Ë130 kb) and a transfer plasmid vector which contains the regions flanking the polyhedrin gene. The target gene is inserted into the plasmid vector and host cells are co-transfected with the parental baculovirus and the engineered plasmid. Recombination between the viral genome and the plasmid results in replacement of the polyhedrin gene with the target gene. The efficiency of identifying recombinants is greatly enhance by digesting the baculovirus DNA with a restriction enzyme which, disrupts an essential gene and using a transfer vector which contains this essential gene. Recombinants between the transfer vector and the virus will have a selective advantage and produce plaques. The recombinant virus can be isolated from plaques and then amplified to produce large amounts of protein.

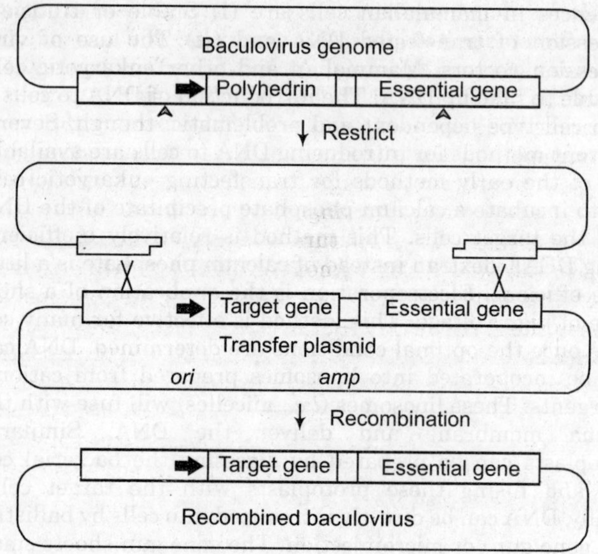

Fig. 37.16 Baculovirus as vector

Gene Identification and Large Scale Expression

Some information on proteins is already available due to previous research and protein characterization and this information is easily incorporated into the genome databases. Similarly, information on the identity and expression of proteins will be continuously generated as particular proteins are studied. However, this approach is selective in that proteins and genes which are associated with interesting phenomena will be preferentially studied and it will take substantial time to individually characterize all of the genes with unknown function. Expressed Sequence Tags (ESTS) and DNA microarrays provide a more rapid means in regards to characterizing genes and their expression. ESTs represent a collection *m*RNA sequences (*i.e.*, *c*DNA sequences) maintained in DNA sequence databases which have been cloned from a defined source and partially sequenced. The *c*DNA clones have been chosen at random from a cDNA library without selection and represent the *m*RNA profile of the source (*i.e.* organism, tissue, cell, etc.) and thus provide information about gene expression. These ESTs can also be used to assist in the identification of expression start sites and positions of introns, even in the cases of unknown genes, by aligning the genomic sequence with the EST sequence. The original clones from which the EST sequences were obtained are maintain in respositories and can be obtained and sequenced in their entirities. Microarray technology is being used to identify the expression of *m*RNA on a large scale. Protein identification. However, in many cases the genes of specific proteins have not been identified and the presence of *m*RNA does not always correlate with protein expression. The evaluation of proteins on a large scale or by high throughput methods, is not as advanced as the generation and analysis of DNA sequence. Much of protein analysis still involves the analysis of one protein at a time and requires the separation, identification and characterization of proteins resolved from complex mixtures. Gel electrophoresis of proteins is the predominant technique used in the separation and isolation of proteins. One-dimensional SDS gel electrophoresis is capable of resolving many complex mixtures of proteins into individual polypeptide chains. Two-dimensional gels (IEF + SDS-PAGE) can be used if additional resolution is needed. Proteins are then be transferred to a membrane and subjected to N-terminal microsequencing. In cases, where the N-termini are blocked it may be possible to break the protein into smaller peptides with site-specific proteases or chemicals and determine an internal sequence. However, substantially more protein is needed to determine these internal sequences. Problems with blocked N-termini and low abundance may be alleviated by a mixed peptide approach. In this method proteins are subjected to gel electrophoresis, transferred to a membrane and the band of interest excised as in a typical microsequencing protocol. The isolated protein is then cleaved into peptides with CNBr (cleaves at *Met*) or skatole (cleaves at *Trp*). On average 3-5 peptides will be generated depending on the frequency of these amino acids. The membrane is then subjected to 6-12 automated Edman cycles. Every cycle will result in several amino acid residues. This mixed sequence data are then analyzed by a computer algorithm which will sort and match the data against protein or DNA databases to identify candidate protein(s).

Isolation of Specific Nucleic Acid Sequences

Cells contain DNA in nucleus, mitochondria and chloroplast DNA isolation is a routinly procedure to collect DNA for molecular or forensic analysis. These are five steps in DNA isolation of which two optional.

1. Cell disruption or cell lysis by physical or chemical methods to expose the DNA.
2. Removing membrane lipids by adding a surfactant or detergent.
3. Removing proteins by adding proteases (optional).
4. Removing RNA by adding on RNAs.

5. Precipitating the DNA with an alcohol (ethanol or isopropanol icecold).

Presently it is possible to isolate a specific region of genome to produce unlimited copies of it and to determine sequence of nucleotide in it. Restriction endonucleases cut the DNA double helix at specific sites called recognition sites, thereby cleaving a long double stranded DNA molecule into fragments of strictly defined sizes. These enzymes are sequences specific. The recognition sequences are four to eight nucleotide long. Gel electrophoresis separates DNA molecules of different sizes. The DNA bands on agarose or polyacrylamide gels are invisible unless the DNA is labelled or stained (most commonly ethidium bromide). There are two common procedure widely used to label isolated DNA molecules.

(i) DNA polymerase copies the DNA in presence of radioactivity labelled (by p32) or chemically altered nucleotide. By this the probes having labelled nucleotides can be produced for hybridization reaction.

(ii) The polynucleotide kinase enzyme transfer a single radioactively labelled phosphate from ATP to 5′-end of each DNA chain.

Now-a-days the methods of radioactive labelling are being replaced by labelling with molecules that can be detected chemically or through fluorescence. The DNA molecule produced by this is allowed to hybridize with complementary DNA sequence and then detected with an antibody (or other ligand) that specifically recognizes its modified side chain.

Nucleic acid hybridization provides a way of detecting specific nucleotides sequences. The DNA solution is heated at 100°C or exposed to high pH (~ 13) which caused denaturation of double helix and produced single stranded DNA strands. These single stranded DNA may readily reform double helix by renaturation process. The single stranded DNA molecules used to detect complementary sequences are known as **probes** (having radioactive or chemical markers to facilitate detection). It is possible to determine the number of copies of DNA sequence present. To find a gene of interest in an organism whose genome has not yet been sequenced, a portion of known gene can be used as a probe.

Restriction Fragment Length Polymorphisms (RFLP)

Restriction fragment length polymorphisms refers to the gain of loss of restriction sites associated with a genetic locus. These polymorphisms can be used to distinguish species, strains or even individuals. Single nucleotide mutations can result in the loss or gain of restriction sites and thus generate different sized DNA fragments associated with that locus. The typical procedure is to digest the target DNA with a restriction enzyme(s), separate the fragments by gel electrophoresis and to detect the fragments of interest by Southern blotting. The changes causing the size polymorphisms do not have to be directly associated with the genetic locus being used for a probe. RFLP applications range from determining specific mutations associated with a particular gene to a genetic 'fingerprinting'. The optimal restriction enzyme(s) and probes will need to be empirically determined for a particular application. A limitation for the application of RFLP is that relatively large amounts of highly purified DNA are needed for many applications. In addition, the procedure is laborious and can take several days to carry out.

Restriction Mapping

Genetic loci can be defined by restriction maps which show the relative positions of restriction sites. The maps can be generated from sequence data or determined experimentally when sequence data is not available. Restriction maps are generated by digesting DNA with different combinations of enzymes and analyzing the digests by gel electrophoresis or Southern blotting. The sizes of the fragments will indicate the distant between restriction sites. The general procedure is to digest the sample DNA with individual restriction enzymes and combinations of the enzymes. The change in the size of the restriction fragments in double digests is used to determine the relative positions of different restriction sites. For example, in the situation on the left digestion with enzyme A produces and single 10 kb fragment and digestion with enzyme B produces a single 8 kb fragment. Carrying out a double digest with a mixture of enzymes A and B would result in the same 8 kb fragment as digesting with enzyme B alone. This indicates that both of the B restriction sites are between the A restriction sites, but no information about the distance between site A and site B is obtained. If the situation is as depicted on the right, then a fragment that is < 8 kb is produced. The size of this fragment will indicate the distance between the A and B restriction sites. A more precise map can be generated in both situations if all of the restriction fragments are detectable.

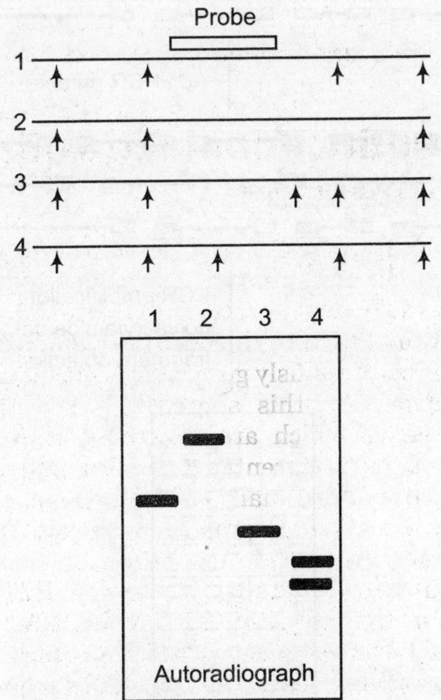

Fig. 37.17 RFLP autoradiograph

Amplified Fragment Length Polymorphism (AFLP)

It is a method based on PCR developed in 1995 by Vos *et. al.* Involves the use of RFLP and PCR techniques. Compared with the widely used RFLP, AFLP is faster, less labour intensive and provide more information. An additional advantage over RAPD is their reproducibility. The AFLP technique is based on the principle of selectively amplifying a subset of restriction fragments from a complex mixture of DNA fragments obtained after digestion of genomic DNA with restriction endonucleases. Procedures in AFLP include digestion, adaptor ligation, amplification and electrophoresis. The number of DNA bands detected by AFLP is high. It can be reduced by adding selective bases (1-3 nucleotides) at the 3′-end of the PCR primers. One additional selective base on the primer can reduced the number of DNA bands 16 folds.

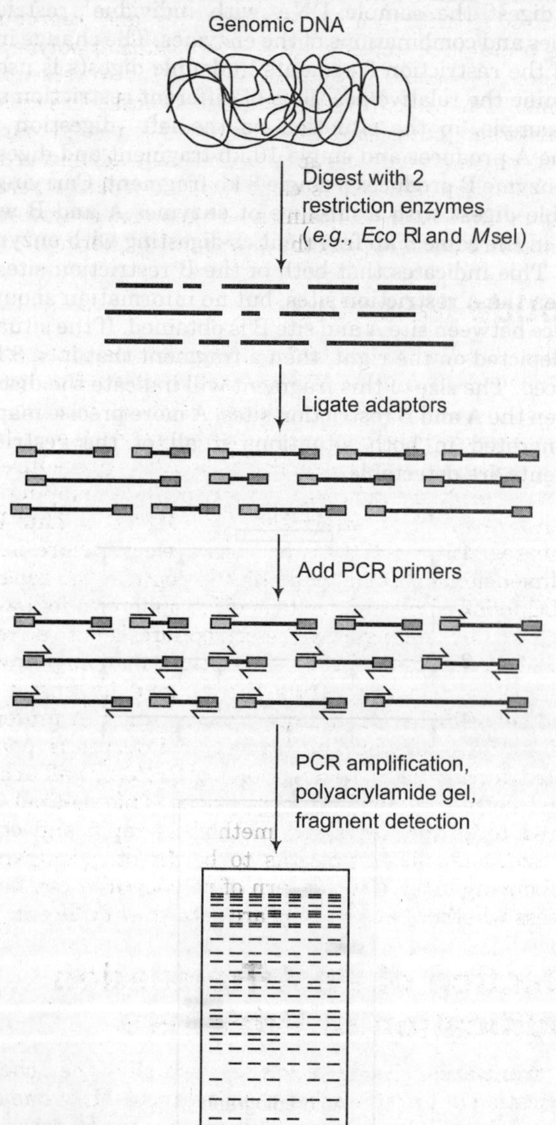

Fig. 37.18 Process of amplified fragment length polymorphism

Three additional selective bases on the primer can reduce the number of DNA bands 4,000 folds. Characteristics of AFLP include dominant marker, DNA variation is detected by presence/absence of DNA bands due to a) presence/absence of restriction sites and b) additional bases (insertion) between two restriction sites are too large. Advantages include higher reproducibility compared to RAPD and highly polymorphic.

Randomly Amplified Polymorphic DNA

It is a method based on PCR developed in 1990. RAPD is different from conventional PCR as it needs one primer for amplification. The size of primer is normally short (10 nucleotides) and therefore, less specific. The primers can be designed without the experimenter having any genetic information for the organism being tested. More than 2000 different RAPD primers can be available commercially. Genomic DNA normally has complimentary sequences to RAPD primers at many locations. If two of these locations are close to each other (<3000bp) and the sequences are in opposite orientation, the amplification will be established. This amplified region is said as a RAPD locus. Normally, a few (3-20) loci can be amplified by one single RAPD primer. Variation DNA detected by RAPD is due to the loss of RAPD loci. The loss of RAPD loci is caused by:

1. Change of sequence at primer annealing site in the genomic DNA.
2. Deletion of primer annealing site in the genomic DNA.
3. Large insertion in between two primer annealing sites.

RAPD marker is a dominant marker. Presence of a DNA band is dominant; absence of a DNA band is recessive. DNA bands of different sizes are assumed to be amplified products from different RAPD loci.

Disadvantages include: lack of reproducibility, RAPD banding patterns prone to:

(i) DNA template concentration and quality.
(ii) Different *Taq* DNA polymerases.
(iii) Different PCR machines or related equipment used in conducting PCR.

Sequencing and Mapping of Proteins

A partial amino acid sequence can provide information about a proteins identity or be used in the design of recombinant DNA probes. Through chemistry know as the Edman degradation cycle the N-terminal amino acids can be sequentially removed and then determined. Generally instruments which automate this sequential removal of amino acids and their analysis are utilized. Generally proteins or peptides to be sequence are submitted to a service provider and sequenced for a fee depending on the number of residues sequenced.

Edman Degradation Chemistry

Protein samples are usually absorbed or coupled to a membrane or glass fibre filter support which is placed in the reaction chamber of the instrument. Each cycle of the Edman degradation cycle consists of three steps: coupling, cleavage and conversion. The chemicals necessary for each of the steps are sequentially pumped into the reaction chamber. In the coupling step, the unmodified N-terminus of the peptide is reacted with phenyl isothiocyanate to form a phenylthiocarbamoyl-peptide. This is followed by addition of either liquid or gaseous trifluoroacetic acid which will cleave PTC derivatized N-terminal amino acid from the peptide resulting in the formation of an anilinothiazoline-amino acid derivitive. This unstable ATZ-amino acid is pumped from the reaction chamber into a conversion chamber, where it is converted to a more stable phenylthiohydantoin derivative. The immobilized peptide remains in the reaction chamber and the N-terminus of the next residue is available for another round of Edman degradation. The PTH-amino acid is transferred from the conversion chamber to an HPLC and the specific amino acid is determined from its elution time. Depending on the quantity and quality of the sample up to 30 cycles can be carried. Generally about one permole of amino acid can be detected although more sensitive instruments are available.

Microsequencing Following Gel Electrophoresis

The N-termini of proteins can be sequenced following separation by gel electrophoresis. This obviates the need to purify the protein to near homogeneity by more laborious conventional methods and allows one to take advantage of the high resolution of SDS gel electrophoresis. The protein of interest should not significantly co-migrate with contaminating proteins and be at least 80% pure. Generally 10-100 pmoles of the protein, which corresponds to 0.5-5 μg of a 50 kDa protein, will be needed to make carry out the analysis. If no sequence data is obtained from 100 pmoles of protein then it is generally assumed that the N-terminus is blocked (see below). Whereas if less than 10 pmoles of sample are used it may be difficult to determine if the lack of sequence data are the result of a blocked N-terminus or due to insufficient material. Following gel electrophoresis (either 1 or 2-dimensional) the proteins are electrophoretically transferred from the gels to a membrane support. The membrane of choice is a modified PVDF membrane which has good protein retention and is able to withstand the solvents, acids and bases used in the Edman degradation chemistry. The protein of interest is detected by a brief staining with coomassie blue (or other dyes) and the band excised. Components of the electrophoresis and transfer buffers, such as salts, Tris, glycine, SDS and acrylamide, interfere with the sequencing reactions and must be completely removed by extensive washing in water. The membrane piece containing the protein to be sequence is submitted to the sequencing service.

Sequencing Internal Peptides

Edman chemistry is dependent on a free amino group at the N-terminus. Apporximately half of eukaryotic cellular protein are modified (*e.g.,* acylation) at the N-terminus and do not have a free amine in this position (*i.e.,* blocked N-terminus). In addition, sometimes during the purification and preparation of proteins for N-terminal sequencing the proteins can become blocked. There are some methods (chemically and enzymatically) to remove the N-terminal blocking group of a protein or peptide. These include deformylation, deacetylation and removal of the pyroglutamate group. The choice of a particular method depends on the protein or peptide and the nature of the blocking group. However, in most cases because of the uncertain nature of the blocking group an internal peptide sequence is determined. Proteins can be treated with chemicals or site specific proteases to generate peptide fragments. For example, CNBr cleaves proteins on the C-terminal side of methionine residues. Many protease recognized specific amino acid residues and reproducibly cleave proteins at specific sites. The resulting polypeptides are then separated (typically on HPLC reverse phase columns). The peaks corresponding to peptides are collected and absorbed onto glass fibre filters as a solid support. Reverse phase chromatography is especially advantageous in this application since, it is carried out in volatile solvents. The glass fibre filters containing the peptides are submitted to the service provider and the N-termini sequenced.

Peptide Mapping

It is also possible to use site specific proteases to compare proteins and determine if they are related. The general procedure is to digest a protein with a protease and characterize the pattern of peptides formed. Each protein will exhibit a unique pattern of peptides. Such procedures are known as 'protein fingerprinting' or 'peptide mapping'. The peptides can be analyzed by HPLC, Thin-Layer Chromatography (TLC) or gel electrophoresis. In two-dimensional peptide mapping the peptides are separated by TLC followed by high voltage electrophoresis followed by separation by high-voltage electrophoresis in a second dimension. Another form of peptide mapping involves excising a protein band from the gel and loading it on a second gel of higher acrylamide concentration. A protease is added to the well and the protein of interest is partially digested during the re-electrophoresis. Proteins will exhibit a distinct pattern of smaller polypeptides. This method, often referred to as the Cleveland method, is rapid and easy to carry out and allows proteins to be directly compared in neighbouring lanes. The pattern of polypeptides can be used to assess whether two proteins are similar or different.

Detection of Post-Translation Modification of Proteins

Post translation modification is actually the chemical modification of proteins after their synthesis. It is one of the later stepsin gene expression. This process can be detected by mass spectrometry and Eastern blotting.

Analysis by Mass Spectrometry

A mass spectrometer generates gas phase ions from a sample and separates them according to their mass to charge ratio (m/z). It generates a record of their abundance, molecular weight determination of peptides and proteins, amino acid sequencing of peptides detection of post translational modification (Δm) and relative quantitation of peptides and proteins.

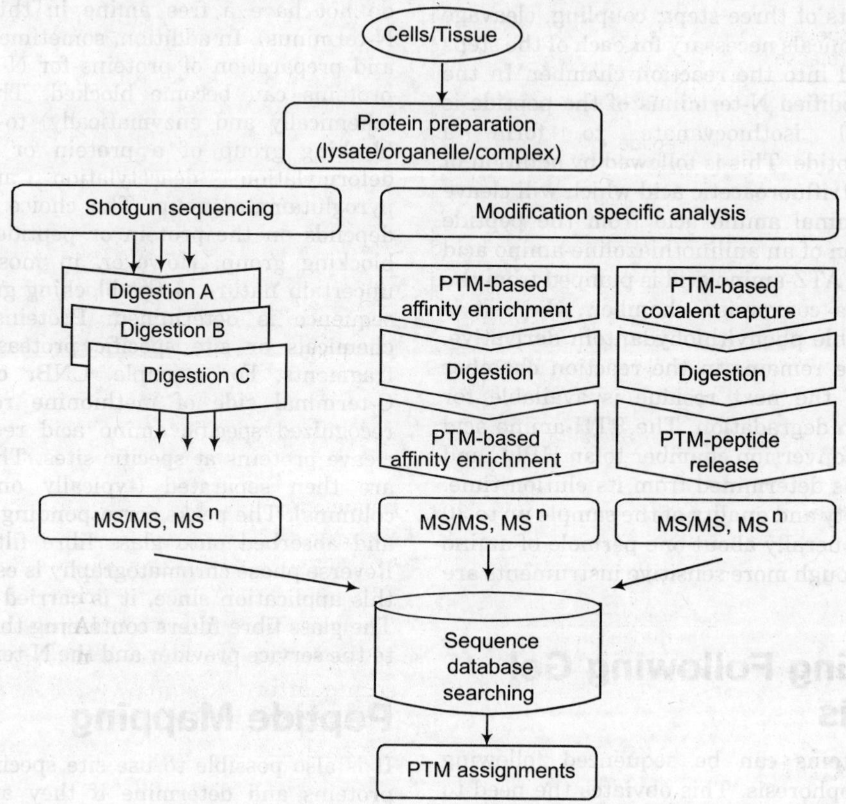

Fig. 37.19 Detection of post-translation modification

Table 37.1 **Mass Values for Some Post-translational Modifications and Frequently Observed Neutral Losses and Diagnostic Ion Signals**

PTM	Δm (MS) (DA)	Δm (MS/MS) Neutral loss (Da)	MS/MS Diagnostic ion (m/z)
Phosphotyrosine	79.966	79.966	–78.959 (neg. mode) 216.0422 (pos.mode)
Phosphothreonine	79.966	97.977	–78.959 (neg. mode)
Phosphoserine			
Acetyllysine	42.011		143.118, 126.091
Methyllysine	14.016	See. ref.	98.097
Dimethyllysine	28.031	See ref.	See ref.
Methylarginine	14.016	59.073	See ref.
Dimethylarginine	28.031		143.155
Trimethyllysine	42.047		
N-linked glycans	162.053 (hexose) 203.079 (hexosamins) 291.095 (sialic acids) 365.148 (HexHexNAc)	162.053 203.079 291.095 365.148	163.061 204.087 292.103, 274.093 366.156
Nitrotyrosine	44.985		
Palmitoyl	238.230	272.217	
Ubiquitin	114.043 (Gly-Gly tag remains after tryptic digestion)		
Methionine oxidation	15.995	63.998	
Tryptophan oxidation	3.995, 15.995, 31.990		

PTM, post-translational modifications; MS, mass spectrometry; MS/MS, tandem mass spectrometry; m/z, mass-to charge ratio.

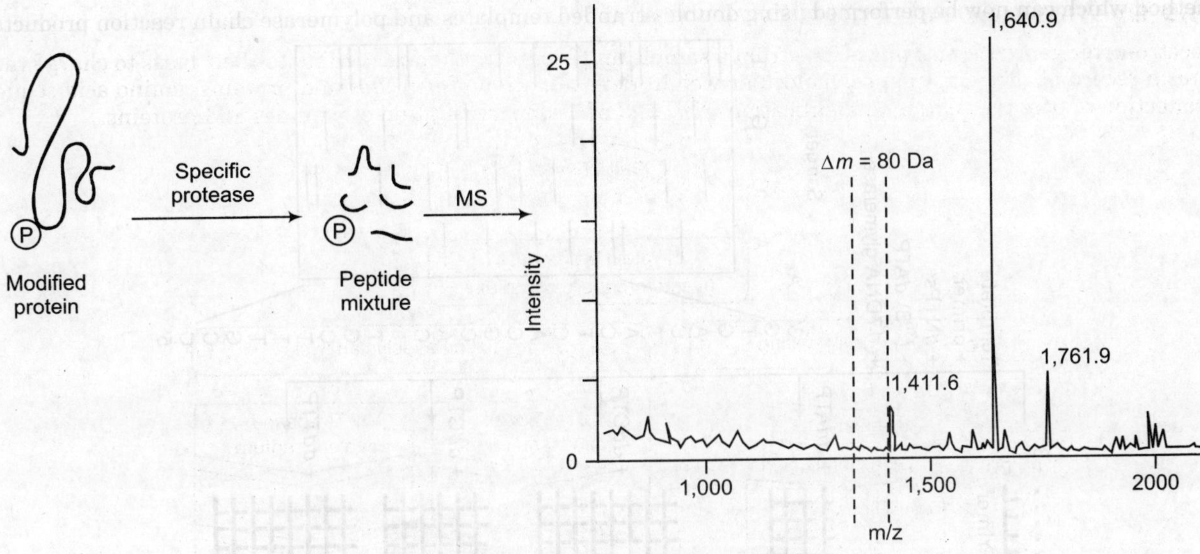

Fig. 37.20 PTM protein mass spectrometer

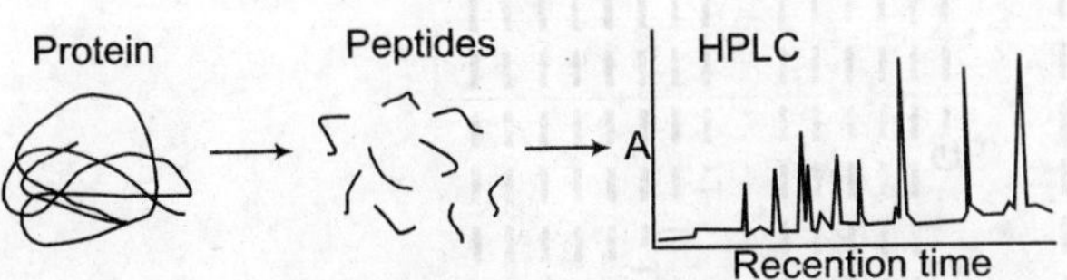

Fig. 37.21 Peptide mapping

DNA Sequencing

Each of the two main methods of sequencing long DNA molecules (chemical and enzymic) involves the production of a set of different sized molecules with one common end which are then separated by polyacrylamide gel electrophoresis (PAGE) to allow reading of the sequence. The earlier chemical method of Maxam and Gilbert requires that the DNA fragment to be sequenced is labeled at one end, usually by adding either a radioactive phosphate to the 5′- or 3′-end or a nucleotide to the 3′-end. The method works for both single and double-stranded DNA and involves base-specific cleavages which occur in two steps. The base is first modified using specific chemicals after which piperidine can cleave the sugar-phosphate backbone of the DNA at that site. Limiting incubation times or concentrations of components in the base modifying reactions ensure that a ladder of progressively longer molecules is created, rather than complete cleavage to short oligonucleotides. The specific base modification reactions use dimethyl sulphate (DMS) to methylate at G bases. Formic acid will attack the purines A and G. Hydrazine is used to hydrolyze at pyrimidines (C + T) but high salt inhibits the T reaction. Thus four lanes on the sequencing gel (G, A+G, C+T and C) allow the sequence to be determined. This method has been adapted to sequence genomic DNA without cloning. The chemical method of DNA.

Sequencing has largely been super-seded by the method of **Sanger,** which uses four specific **dideoxynucleotides** (*dd*NTPs) to terminate enzymically synthesized copies of a template. A sequencing primer is annealed to a *ss*DNA template molecule and a DNA polymerase extends the primer using *d*NTPs. The extension reaction is split into four and each quarter is terminated separately with one of the four specific *dd*NTPs, and the four samples (usually radioactive) are analyzed by PAGE. The dideoxynucleotides act as chain terminators since they have no 3′-OH group on the deoxyribose which is needed by the polymerase to extend the growing chain. The label can be incorporated during the synthesis step (*e.g.,* [α-^{35}S]*d*ATP) or the primer can first be end-labelled with either radioactivity or fluorescent dyes. The latter are used in some automatic DNA sequencers although it is more common to use fluorescent dideoxynucleotides. The original method requires a *ss*DNA template on which to synthesize the complementary copies, which means that the DNA has to be cloned into the phage vector M13 before sequencing. The *ss*DNA recovered from the phage is annealed to a primer of 15-17 nt which is complementary to the region near the vector–insert junction. All sequences cloned into this vector can be sequenced using this universal primer. A DNA polymerase enzyme (usually **Klenow** or **T7 DNA polymerase)** is added to the annealed primer plus template along with a small amount of [α-^{35}S]thiod ATP with one oxygen atom on the α phosphate replaced by sulphur (if the primer is not labelled). It is then divide into four tubes, each containing a different chain terminator mixed with normal *d*NTPs (*i.e.,* tube C would contain *dd*CTP and *d*ATP, *d*CTP, *d*GTP and *d*TTP) in specific ratios to ensure only a limited amount of chain termination. The four sets of reaction products, when analyzed by PAGE, usually result in fewer artifactual bands than with chemical sequencing. Many improvements have been made to this dideoxy method which can now be performed using double-stranded templates and polymerase chain reaction products.

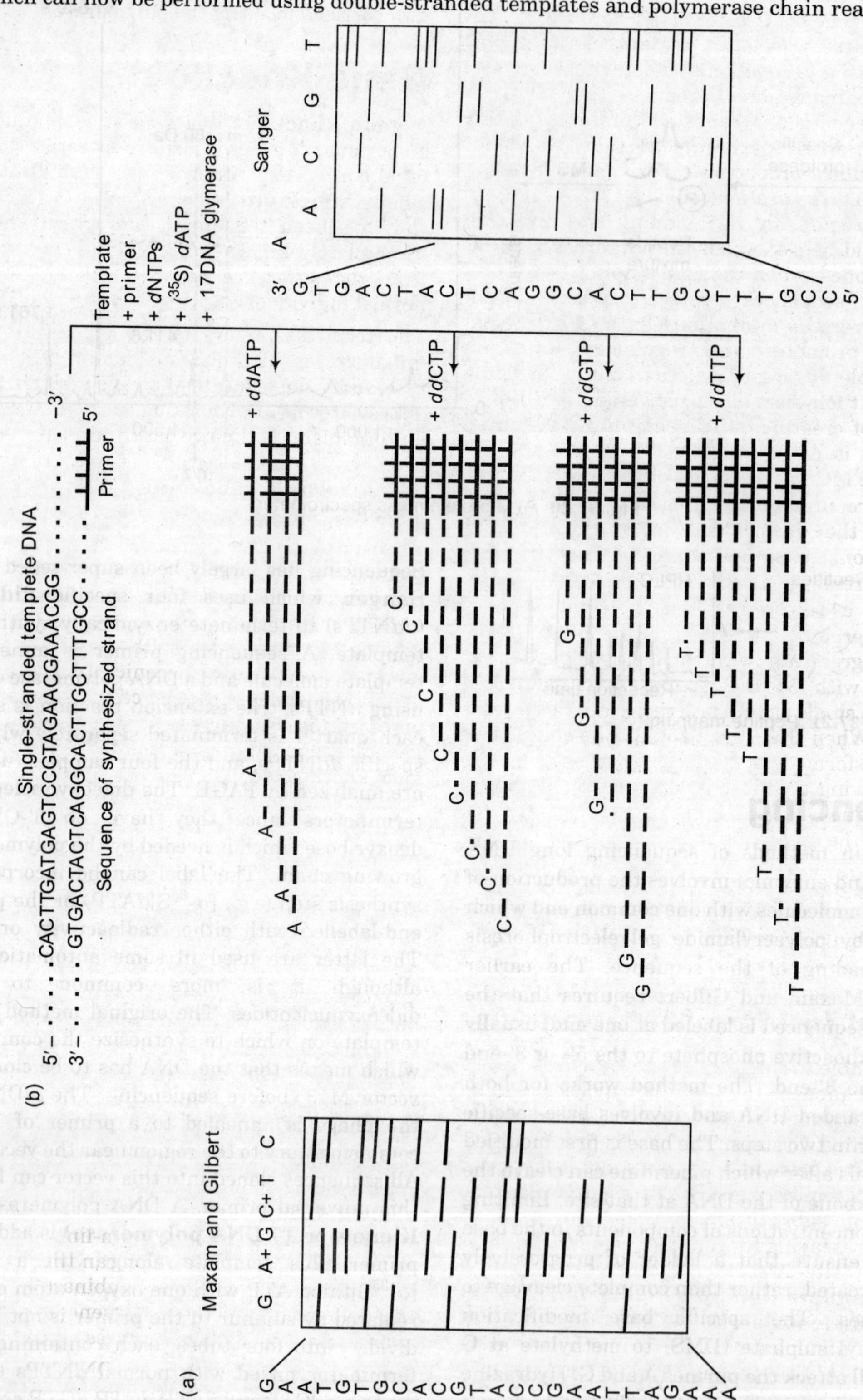

Fig. 37.22 DNA sequencing (a) An example of a Maxam and Gilberg sequencing gel; (b) Sanger sequence

Deletion Mutagenesis

In organisms with small genomes, and/or rapid generation times, it is possible to create and analyze mutants produced *in vivo*, but this is not easy or acceptable in organisms such as man. However, if cloned genes have been isolated, it is quite feasible to mutate them *in vitro* and then assay for the effects by expressing the mutant gene *in vitro* or *in vivo*. For both *c*DNA and genomic clones, creating deletion mutants is useful. In the case of *c*DNA clones, it is common to delete progressively from the ends of the coding region to produce either N-terminally or C-terminally truncated proteins (after expression) to discover which parts (domains) of the whole protein have particular properties. For example, the N-terminal domain of a given protein could be a DNA-binding domain, the central region an ATP-binding site and the C-terminal region could help the protein to interact to form dimers. In genomic clones, when the transcription start site has been identified, sequences upstream are removed progressively to discover the minimum length of upstream sequence that has promoter and regulatory function. Although it is possible to create deletion mutants using restriction enzymes if their sites fall in convenient positions, the general method of creating **unidirectional deletions** using an exonuclease is more versatile. There are several restriction sites in the MCS at each side of the insert and by choosing two that are unique and that give a 5′- and a 3′-recessed end on the vector and insert respectively, unidirectional deletions can be created. The enzyme **exonuclease III** can remove one strand of nucleotides in a 3′ to 5′-direction from a recessed 3′-end, but not from a 3′-protruding end. Therefore, it will remove the lower strand of the insert only progressively with time. At various times, aliquots are treated with **S1 or moong bean nuclease** which will remove the single strand protrusions at both ends, creating blunt ends. When these are ligated to re-circularize the plasmid, and transformed, a population of sub-clones will be produced each having a different amount of the insert removed. This technique is often used to obtain the complete sequence of clones as the one sequencing primer can be used to derive 200-300 nt of sequence from a series of clones that differ in size by about 200 bp. Approximately one in three of the deletions will be in-frame and could be used to express truncated protein. Deletion from the other end of the *c*DNA is performed in a similar way.

Site-Directed *In Vitro* Mutagenesis

It is very useful to be able to change just one, or a few specific nucleotides in a sequence to test a hypothesis. The importance of each residue in a transcription factor-binding site could be examined by changing each one in turn. Suspected critical amino acids in a protein could be changed by altering the *c*DNA sequence so that by a one nucleotide change an amino acid substitution is made, the effect of which is examined by assaying for function using the mutant protein. Originally, site-directed mutagenesis used a **single-stranded template** (created by subcloning in M13) and a **primer oligonucleotide** with the desired mutation in it. The primer was annealed to the template and then extended using a **DNA polymerase,** ligated using DNA ligase to seal the nick and the mismatched duplex transformed into bacteria. Some bacteria would remove the mismatch to give the desired point mutation, but some clones with the original sequence would be produced. Because this method was not very efficient (not all clones were mutant) and because subcloning in M13 to prepare single-stranded DNA was time consuming, much site-directed mutagenesis is now carried out using the polymerase.

Gene Knockout

A **gene knockout** is a genetic technique in which one of an organism's genes is made inoperative ('knocked out' of the organism). Also known as **knockout organisms** or simply **knockouts,** they are used in learning about a gene that has been sequenced, but which has an unknown or incompletely known function. Researchers draw inferences from the difference between the knockout organism and normal individuals.

The term also refers to the process of creating such an organism, as in 'knocking out' a gene. The technique is essentially the opposite of a gene knockin. Knockout is often abbreviated as KO. Knocking out two genes simultaneously in an organism is known as a **double knockout** (DKO). Similarly, the terms **triple knockout** (TKO) and **quadruple knockouts** (QKO) are used to describe 3 or 4 knocked out genes, respectively.

Knockout is accomplished through a combination of techniques, beginning in the test tube with a plasmid, a bacterial artificial chromosome or other DNA construct, and proceeding to cell culture. Individual cells are genetically transformed with the DNA construct. Often the goal is to create a transgenic animal that has the altered gene. If so, embryonic stem cells are genetically transformed and inserted into early embryos. Resulting animals with the genetic change in their germline cells can then often pass the gene knockout to future generations.

To create knockout moss, transfection of protoplasts is the preferred method. Such transformed *Physcomitrella* protoplasts directly regenerate into fertile moss plants. Already eight weeks after transfection the plants can be screened for gene targeting *via* PCR. The construct is engineered to recombine with the target gene, which is accomplished by incorporating sequences from the gene itself into the construct. Recombination then occurs in the region of that sequence within the gene, resulting in the insertion of a foreign sequence to disrupt the gene. With its sequence interrupted, the altered gene in most cases will be translated into a non-functional protein, if it is translated at all.

A conditional knockout allows gene deletion in a tissue or time specific manner. This is done by introducing short sequences called loxP sites around the gene. These sequences will be introduced into the germ-line *via* the same mechanism as a knock-in. This germ-line can then be crossed to another germline containing Cre-recombinase which is a viral enzyme that can recognize these sequences, recombines them and deletes the gene flanked by these sites.

Because the desired type of DNA recombination is a rare event in the case of most cells and most constructs, the foreign sequence chosen for insertion usually includes a reporter. This enables easy selection of cells or individuals in which knockout was successful. Sometimes the DNA construct inserts into a chromosome without the desired recombination with the target gene. To eliminate such cells, the DNA construct often contains a second region of DNA that allows such cells to be identified and discarded.

In diploid organisms, which contain two alleles for most genes and may as well contain several related genes that collaborate in the same role, additional rounds of transformation and selection are performed until every targeted gene is knocked out. Selective breeding may be required to produce homozygous knockout animals.

Knock-in is similar to knock-out, but instead it replaces a gene with another instead of deleting it.

Microarrays

Microarray is the exact opposite of dot blot assay (transfer of macromolecules like proteins and nucleic acids from the gel onto the surface of an immobilized membrane in the same relative position). A single probe is used in dot blot assay at a time while in microarray extremely large number of probs are spotted on to the slide. Microarrays are basically of two types:

1. **DNA microarrays** DNA sequences representing different genes of an organism are spotted onto the slide, used to determine genes being transcribed in the cells.
2. **Antibody microarrays** Consists of spots of different antibodies and used to measure abundance of proteins in samples.

Most of the hybridization methods are designed to analyze one gene at a time. The DNA microarray technology, also called gene chips, genome chips, biochips, DNA chips, provides a means to simultaneously analyzed thousands of the genes. The array is an orderly arrangement of known DNA samples. Sample spot sizes in macroarrays are generally > 300 microns in diameter and can be imaged with conventional gel and blot scanners. Microarrays contain thousands of spots that are generally less than 200 microns in diameter. Preparation of microarrays requires specialized robotic equipment and analysis of the microarrays requires special imaging equipment. The DNA microarray is fabricated by spotting known DNA samples or 'probes', on a solid support such as glass or nylon through the use of high speed robotics. The probes can either be known *c*DNA sequences (500-5000 bases) or synthetic oligonucleotides (20-80 nucleotides). The array is then exposed to flourescent-labelled *c*DNA prepared from total *m*RNA. This free 'target' DNA will bind to the spots containing homologous sequences. The identity and abundance of the complementary sequences can then be determined. It is also possible to mix DNAs prepared with different fluorescent labels. Signals are measured as absolute intensities for a given target or as ratios of two probes with different fluorescent labels representing two separate treatments to be compared or with one probe as an internal control.

Table 37.2 **A Comparison between DNA Chip and Microarray**

Characteristic	DNA Chip	Microarray
Source of DNA probe	Oligonucleotides synthesized directly onto the silicon water.	Cloned genomic DNA or *c*DNA.
Length of DNA probe	20-30 nucleotides.	Whole gene or a part of gene; much longer than that in DNA chips.
Redundancy of probes	There is no redundancy since each oligonucleotides sequence is chosen to represent a different gene.	About 30% of *c*DNA probes are redundant; redundancy can occur even with ESTs.
Cross-hybridization	Very less likely; can distinguish between sequences that are 93% identical.	May be a problem.
Prior knowledge about the genome	Sequences of the genes must be known.	Not required.
Fabrication of laboratory	Much more difficult than that of microarray.	Easier than that of DNA chip .
Cost	Much more costlier.	Relatively cheaper.
Two or more independent probes for a single gene	Can be used; each independent probe represents a different sequence of the same RNA molecule.	Usually not possible.

Analysis of Carbohydrates (CHO)

Unlike nucleic acid and proteins oligosaccharides can be branched and are joined by a number of linkages. For such analysis oligosaccharides are generally removed from their protein or lipid conjugates then subjected to stepwise degradation with specific reagents that reveal stereochemistry.

Sample Preparation for Mono, Di and Oligosaccharides

Need to isolate the CHO first before the measurement is made. Preliminary method commonly used to many isolation techniques involves food are dried under vacuum to prevent thermal degradation. They are then ground to a fine powder to enhance solvent extraction. They are then defatted by solvent extraction.

Most commonly used method for isolation is: Boil a defatted sample with an 80% alcohol solution to extract low molecular weight CHO from foods. Mono, di and oligosaccharides are soluble in alcoholic solution while the other components not.

The soluble part are separated from the insoluble part by filtration method.

- Treating the filtrate with clarifying agents or by passing it through one or more ion-exchange resins – to remove minor components such as amino acids;
  (i) **Clarifying agents** Example, heavy metal salts; Function, to form insoluble complexes with interfering substances that can be removed by filtration or centrifugation.
  (ii) **Ion-exchange** Mono, di and oligosaccharides are polar. Therefore, possible to separate by using the combination of a positively and negatively charged columns.

Methods of Analysis

CHO content can be determined by calculating the % remaining after all the other components have been measured: % CHO= 100 - % moisture - % protein - % of lipid - % mineral. This can lead to erroneous results due to experimental errors in any of the other methods.

Monosaccharides and Oligosaccharides

Chromatographic methods

HPLC

(a) **Advantages** Rapid, can tolerate a wide range of sample concentration precise and accurate and requires no prior derivatization.
(b) **Disadvantages** Require micron-filter filtration prior to injection.
(c) **Stationary phase used** Ion exhange chromatography, reverse phase chromatography and normal phase chromatography.

GC

(a) Most be converted to volatile derivatives.
(b) Involve two preparation steps.
(c) Reduction of aldehyde groups to primary alcohol groups.

Conversion of the reduced sugar into a volatile peracetate ester or pertrimethylsilyl ether derivative.

These steps must be complete 100% to ensure the measurement is accurate and precise.

Chemical Methods

Based on the fact that many of mono, di and oligosaccharides are reducing agents that can react with other components to yield precipitates or coloured complexes.

Non-reducing CHO can be determined after hydrolysis. Three categories of chemical method: titration, gravimetric and colorimetric.

Titration Methods

Example Lane-Eynon method

Use to determine the concentration of reducing sugar in a sample.

Disadvantages

The results depend on the precise reaction times, temperature and reagent concentration → must be carefully controlled. It cannot distinguish between different types of reducing sugar. It cannot directly determine non-reducing sugars. Susceptible to interference from other types of molecules that act as reducing agents.

Gravimetric Methods

CHO is heated in the presence of an excess of copper oxide and alkaline tartrate (to keep Cu^{2+} ion in solution) under controlled conditions → leads to the formation of a copper oxide precipitate: Reducing sugar + Cu^{2+} + base → oxidized sugar + CuO_2 (precipitate).

This method has similar disadvantages as **Lane-Eynon** method.

However, it is more reproducible and accurate. The concentration of precipitate present can be determined. Gravimetrically – filtration, drying and weighing.

Titrimetrically – redissolving the precipitate and titrating with a suitable indicator.

Colorimetric Methods

Can be used to determine total sugar (reducing and non-reducing sugars) due to the presence of oxidizing agent (sulphuric acid).

Example Anthrone method and phenol-sulphuric acid method.

The concentration of CHO is measured at specific absorbance using spectrophotometer.

Several methods include anthrone method, phenol-sulphuric acid method and Somogyi-Nelson Method.

Somogyi-Nelson Method is used to determine total reducing sugar and is based on the reduction of Cu^{2+} to Cu^{+} ions by reducing sugars. Cu^{+} then reduced an arsenomolybdate complex which produce blue colour that is measured spectrophotometrically.

Enzymatic Methods

It relies on enzyme ability to catalyze specific reactions. It is rapid, highly specific and sensitive to low concentrations and very little sample preparation needed. Liquid foods – directly tested while solid foods – need to be dissolved in water first.

Two most common methods are allowing complete reaction and measure the product concentration. Measuring the initial rate of enzyme catalyzed reaction.

Physical Methods

(i) **Polarimetry** A device that measures the angle that plane polarized light is rotated on passing through a solution.The concentration of CHO in an unknown sample is determined by measuring its angle of rotation and comparing it with the calibration curve.

(ii) **Refractive Index** (RI) Is velocity of light in a vacuum divided by the velocity of light in the material. RI of CHO solution increases with increasing concentration. Temperature (20°C) and w/length (589.3 nm) dependent. Used routinely in industry to determine sugar concentration of syrups, honey, molasses, tomato products and jams.

(iii) **Density** Density of an aqueous solutions increases as CHO concentration increases. Routinely used in industry for determination of CHO concentration of juices and beverages.

(iv) **Infra Red** A material absorbs infrared due to vibration or rotation of molecular groups. Measurements are normally carried out by measuring intensity of an infra red wave reflected from the surface of a sample. **Advantages** non-destructive and rapid.

Immunoassays

Low molecular weight CHO are developed by attaching the CHO of interest to a protein and then injecting it into an animal. Antibodies specific to CHO molecule is developed then and can be extracted for determining the specific CHO concentration. **Advantages** extremely sensitive, specific, easy to use and rapid.

Polysaccharides are digestible, important source of energy, *e.g.*, starch while the non-digestible types are cellulose, hemicellulose and pectins. For semi-crystalline starch, the sample can be dispersed in water and heated to a temperature where the starch gelatinizes. Addition of perchloric acid or calcium chloride to the water prior to heating facilitates to solubilization of starch.

Methods of Starch Determination

Specific enzyme is added to the starch solution to breakdown the starch to glucose. The glucose concentration is then analyzed using the methods described previously. Iodine can be added to the starch to form an insoluble starch-iodine complex that can be determined gravimetrically by collecting, drying and weighing the precipitate formed or titrimetrically by determining the amount of iodine required to precipitate the starch.

Analysis of Fibres

Fibre is also known as resistant starch. The basis of many fibre analysis techniques is, therefore to develop a procedure that mimics the processes that occur in the human digestive system. Major components of dietary fibre, cell wall polysaccharides and non cell wall polysaccharides.

Total Insoluble and Soluble Fibre Method

The basic principle: to isolate the fraction of interest by selective precipitation and then to determine its mass by weighing. A gelatinized sample of dry, defatted food is enzymatically digested with α-amylase, amyloglucosidase and protease to breakdown the starch and protein components. Total fibre content of the sample is determined by adding 95% ethanol to the solution to precipitate all the fibre. The solution is then filtered and the fibre is collected, dried and weighed. Water-soluble and water-insoluble fibres can be determined by filtering the enzymatically digested sample. Soluble fibre in the filtrate solution and the insoluble fibre trapped in the filter. The soluble component is precipitated from solution by adding 95% alcohol to the filtrate and is then collected by filtration, dried and weighed. Official method for determine fibre content and is widely used in food industry.

Disadvantages

Tends to overestimate the fibre content of foods containing high concentrations of simple sugars such as dried fruit, possibly because they get trapped in the precipitates formed when the ethanol is added. The fibre is then hydrolyzed using a concentrated sulphuric acid solution to break it down into its constituent monosaccharides. The concentration is then determined using the previous methods mentioned. Total mass of fibre in the original sample is assumed to be equal to the total mass of monosaccharides present. The concentration of insoluble and soluble dietary fibre can also be determined by this method using similar separation steps as the total, insoluble and soluble gravimetric method mentioned above. However, it does not provide information about the lignin content.

Separation and Analysis of Lipids

Lipids are insoluble in water, therefore for extraction and analysis, non-polar solvents (ethylether, petroleum ether, hexane) are used. Chloroform is used for the isolation of neutral lipids while membrane lipids are extracted with more polar solvents (ethanol or methanol). In general chloroform, methanol and water mixture (1 : 2 : 1) is used for extraction of lipids. Complex mixtures of lipids are separated by differences in polarity or solubility of the components in non-polar solvents. The lipids which contain ester or amide-linked fatty acids can be hydrolysed by treated with acid or alkali or with specific enzymes (glycosidases, phospholipases) to yield their component parts. Some methods are:

By Organic Solvents

Neutral lipids such as waxes, triacylglycerols pigments, etc., are extracted from tissues with ethyl ether, chloroform or benzene. The polar organic solvents reduce the hydrophobic interaction among lipids molecules (as in membrane lipids). The tissue is homogenized in chloroform, methanol and water mixture (1 : 2 : 1) to extract all lipids and separate it into **top phase** (methanol/water) and **bottom phase** (chloroform).

Adsorption Chromatography

Complex mixture of lipids can be separated by this method using polar material silica gel (silicic acid) packed into a glass column. The lipid mixture is loaded onto the column. The polar lipids bind tightly but the neutral lipids will not bind and will be eluted in the first chloroform wash. The polar lipids can further be eluted by increasing the polarity of the solvent. The unchanged polar lipids can be eluted with acetone, whereas very polar or charged lipids are eluted with methanol.

Thin Layer Chromatography

In this method, a thin (0.25 mm) coating of solid material (silica gel) is spread on a glass or plastic plate. The sample is applied to the plate. The spot of the sample is placed 2.0-2.5 cm from the edge. For preparative TLC the sample is applied as a band across the plate rather than as a single spot. Generally neutral lipids are separated with non-polar solvents and charged lipids with polar solvents. Lipids can be located by spraying the plate with 50% sulphuric acid followed by heating at 100°C in an even for 10 min. For further analysis the corresponding spots of the separated lipids can be scraped from the plate.

Gas Liquid Chromatography

This method is based on partitioning of compounds between a liquid and gas phase. The volatile components are separated according to their relative tendencies to dissolve in inert material packed in chromatography column and to volatilize and move carried by a current of an inert gas (as He). For analysis of fatty acids in sample of phospholipids this is first heated (in methanol/NaOH or methanol/HCl mixture) which esterified fatty acids to glycerol and into their methyl esters, the process called **transesterification**. These are loaded on

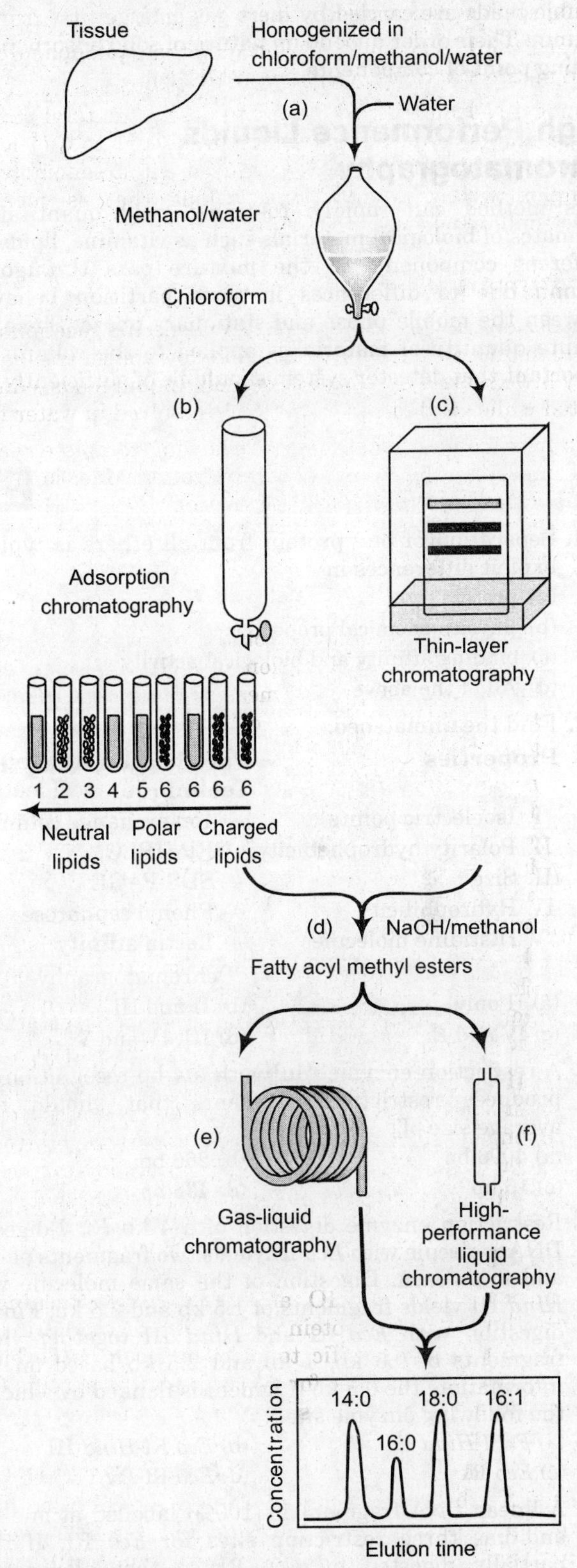

Fig. 37.23 Procedure of separation and identification of cellular lipids

the column and heated the column to volatilize the compounds. The fatty acyl esters which are most soluble in column material dissolve in that material while the less soluble lipids are carried by inert gas emerge first from the column. Their order depend on nature of solid adsorbant and boiling point of components.

High Performance Liquids Chromatography

This method can rapidly, routinely yield quantitatively estimates of biological materials such as vitamins, lipids, etc. Different components in the mixture pass through the column due to differences in their partition behaviour between the mobile phase and stationary phase. Since very minute quantity of material is applied to the column it is important that detector system should be of sufficiently high and stable sensitivity. Most commonly used detectors are refrective index, ultraviolet fluorescent, electrochemical near infrared, etc. Detector is a component that emits a response due to the eluting sample and subsequently signals a peak on the chromatogram. Quantification of compounds by HPLC involves injecting a series of known concentrations of the solution of the standard compounds on to the HPLC for detection which gives a series of peaks correlated with concentration specificity.

Mass Spectrometry

In this technique, the molecules of a compounds are ionized by ejection of an electron or by capture of proton. The resulting assortment of charged particles is then separated according to their mass. The spectrum produced is known as mass spectrum.

Exercise

1. Separation of one protein from all others is typically exploit differences in
(a) protein size
(b) physico-chemical properties
(c) binding affinity and biological activity
(d) All of the above

2. Find the unmatched.

Properties	Purification/Analytical Technique
I. Isoelectric points	— Ion exchange column
II. Polarity/hydrophobicity	— RP-HPLC
III. Size	— SDS-PAGE
IV. Hydrophilicity	— Phenyl sepharose
V. Histidine molecules	— Lectin affinity chromatography

(a) II only (b) II and III
(c) IV and E (d) III, IV and V

3. A restriction enzyme AluI with a 4-bp recognition site produces restriction fragments that should have average size of
(a) 4096 bp (b) 256 bp
(c) 16 bp (d) 436 bp

4. Restriction enzyme digestion of a 4 kb *Pst* I-digested DNA molecule with *Eco* RI yields two fragments of 1 kb and 3 kb each. Digestion of the same molecule with *Hind* III yields fragments of 1.5 kb and 2.5 kb. Finally, digestion with *Eco* RI and *Hind* III together yields fragments of 0.5 kb, 1 kb and 2.5 kb based on this information, the 0.5 kb fragment is flanked by which of the following enzyme sites
(a) *Pst I-Hind* II (b) *Eco* RI-*Hind* III
(c) *Eco* RI (d) *Eco* RI-*Pst* I

5. A linear DNA fragment is (100%) labelled at one end and has three restriction sites for *Eco* RI. If it is partially digested by *Eco* RI so that all possible fragments are produced, how many of these fragments will be labelled and how many will not be labelled
(a) 4 labelled; 6 unlabelled
(b) 4 labelled; 4 unlabelled
(c) 3 labelled; 5 unlabelled
(d) 3 labelled; 3 unlabelled

6. Bacteria protect themselves from viruses by fragmenting viral DNA upon entry with
(a) methylase (b) endonucleases
(c) ligases (d) exonucleases

7. Which of the following processes require energy?
(a) Ligation (b) Transformation
(c) Restriction digestion (d) Hybridization

8. The restriction endonuclease *Eco*521 recognizes the sequence C/GGCGG and cuts between the first C and the first G, indicated by the slash. DNA cut by which of the following enzymes (given with their recognition sequences and cut sites) could be cloned into a plasmid digested with *Eco*521?
(a) *Eco* RI (G/AATTC) (b) *XmaIII* (C/GGCGG)
(c) *SmaI* (CCC/GGG) (d) *SacII* (CCGC/GG)

9. T_4 polynucleotide kinase is used for
(a) labelling 3′-ends of DNA
(b) labelling 5′-ends of DNA
(c) creating blunt ends of DNA
(d) dephosphorylation of DNA

10. You have cut the genome of a double stranded viral genome with a restriction endonuclease and electrophoresed the products on an agarose gel. You observe only one band on the gel, equivalency to the size of the genome. This is because
(a) there are no introns in the genome
(b) the introns contain the recognition sites and have already been spliced out
(c) all of the restriction fragments are too small to detect
(d) restriction endonucleases do nor cut RNA and this virus has a *ds*RNA genome

11. A Southern transfer of *E. coli* DNA after complete digestion with *Eco* RI was probed with labelled cDNA probe of a gene which occurs only once in the *E. coli* genome. If the gene contains one *Eco* RI cleavage site near its centre, the number of radioactive bands you are most likely to find on autoradiography would be
(a) 0 (b) 1 (c) 2 (d) 3

12. The substrate for restriction enzyme is
(a) *ss*RNA (b) partially *ds*RNA
(c) cell wall proteins (d) *ds*DNA

13. If you discovered a bacterial cell that contained no restriction enzymes, which of the following would you expect to happen?
(a) The cell would be unable to replicate its DNA
(b) The cell would create incomplete plasmids
(c) The cell would be easily infected and lased by bacteriophages
(d) The cell would become an obligate parasite

14. DNA of a bacterium is not cleaved by is own restriction enzymes because the recognition DNA sequences are
(a) methylated
(b) deleted
(c) bound by inhibitory proteins
(d) not accessible to restriction enzymes

15. If the linear double stranded genomic DNA of bacteriophage T_4 is heated and cooled, one gets both linear and circular molecules because,
(a) all linear DNA on heating and cooling attain circular shape
(b) the DNA molecules are circularly permuted
(c) the DNA molecule has cohesive terminal ends
(d) the RNA component of the genomes gets hydrolyzed to result in the circularization

16. If a transcript of a given gene is degraded when mixed with DNA encoding the same gene, one could conclude that the RNA solution is contaminated with
(a) RNAse A (b) RNAse T
(c) RNAse H (d) DNAse III

17. A gene that does not contain introns has an *Eco* RI site just downstream of the translational termination codon in the 3′ untranslated region. The size of the gene is 4 Kbp. The length of 3′ UTR is 2 Kbp, the 5′ UTR is 1 Kbp and that the open reading frame is 1 kbp. Upon probing a Southern blot of an *Eco* RI digested genomic DNA with the radioactively labelled fragment containing only the open reading frame, the size of the band detected by hybridization would be
(a) 1 Kbp (b) > 2 Kbp
(c) 0.5 Kbp (d) 1.5 Kbp

18. You are attempting to clone a gene. You cut a vector with the restriction enzyme *Eco* RI. You mix your cleaved plasmid with an *Eco* RI fragment carrying the gene of interest, carry out a ligation reaction, transform the liagtion mix and plate the bacteria. When you examine plasmids from individual colonies, what do you primarily find?
(a) Plasmids that contain the *Eco* RI fragment
(b) Plasmids that contain concatamers of the *Eco* RI fragment carrying the gene (*i.e.*, multiple copies of the gene)
(c) Plasmids that do not contain the *Eco* RI fragment carrying the genes
(d) Plasmid dimers held together by the *Eco* RI fragment carrying the gene

19. To be a cloning vector, a plasmid does not require
(a) an origin of replication
(b) an antibiotic resistance marker
(c) a restriction site
(d) to have a high copy number

20. Which of the following is a desirable characteristic for a cloning plasmid?
(a) A site at which replication can be initiated
(b) One of more unique restriction endonuclease sites
(c) One or more antibiotic-resistance or drug resistance genes
(d) All of the above

21. A multiple cloning site
(a) contains many copies of a cloned gene
(b) allows flexibility in the choice of restriction enzymes for cloning
(c) allows flexibility in the coice of organism for cloning
(d) contains many copies of the same restriction enzyme site

22. Many plasmids have ampicillin marker. This implies
(a) the plasmids contain genes for ampicillin biosynthesis
(b) ampicillin is required for bacterial growth after transformation
(c) the plasmid contains the gene encoding β-lactamase
(d) ampicillin is essential for cell survival

23. BAC, which can be used to clone large DNA fragments, is derived from
(a) ColE plasmid (b) F plasmid
(c) 2μ plasmid (d) Mu phage

24. A cloning vector consisting of *cos* site inserted in a plasmid, used to clone DNA fragments of lambda phage is
(a) phagemid (b) cosmid
(c) plasmid (d) YAC

25. Which of the following is not component of YAC?
(a) Centromere (b) Telomere
(c) Origin of replication (d) *Cos* site

26. Bacterial artificial chromosomes (BACs), cosmids, phages, plasmids and Yeast artificial chromosomes (YACs) are all commonly used cloning vectors that differ in their cloning capacities, with a range from approximately 100 bp to 3000 kb. Which of the following is the proper order for these vectors in terms of increasing cloning capacity?
(a) BAC, cosmid, phage, plasmid, YAC
(b) YAC, BAC, cosmid, phage, plasmid
(c) Plasmid, phage, cosmid, BAC, YAC
(d) Plasmid, cosmid, phage, BAC, YAC

27. pBR322 which is frequently used as a vector for cloning gene in *E. coli* is
(a) an original bacterial plasmid
(b) a modified bacterial plasmid
(c) a viral genome
(d) a transposon

28. Phage T_7 promoter containing plasmids are used for over expression of cloned genes because of
(a) their convenient size
(b) their single stranded nature
(c) exquisite specificity of T_7 RNA polymerase to phage promoters
(d) T_7 infects *E. coli* and lysogenizes the cell

29. YAC is used for
(a) cloning large segments of DNA
(b) cloning only yeast genomic sequences
(c) cloning of only *c*DNA sequences
(d) all DNA except plant DNA sequences

30. For cloning a DNA fragment larger than 100 kb, which of the following vector system would be suitable?
(a) Plasmid (b) Cosmid
(c) YAC (d) Lambda bacteriophage

31. What is the difference between a PAC and BAC?
(a) One has ampicillin and another has kanamycin resistance marker
(b) One is plasmid-based vector and the other is derived from a yeast chromosome
(c) One is derived from the *E. coli* F-plasmid and other s derived from bacteriophage P_1
(d) One is derived from bacteriophage P_1 and other is derived from bacteriophage B_1

32. For a plasmid to be a cloning vector, the minimum numbers of elements required are
(a) origin of replication, multiple cloning site and selection marker
(b) origin of replication, multiple cloning site and selection marker, promoter
(c) origin of replication, multiple cloning site, selection marker and translation start site
(d) origin of replication, multiple cloning site and promoter

33. Eukaryotic genes may not function properly when cloned into bacteria because of
(a) inability to excise introns
(b) destruction by native endonucleases
(c) failure of promoter to be recognized by bacterial RNA polymerase
(d) All of the above

34. Blue-white selection is used to
(a) test the presence of a plasmid in bacteria
(b) reveal the identity of a cloned DNA fragment
(c) express the product of a cloned gene
(d) test for the presence of a cloned insert in a plasmid

35. Which of the following statements gives a correct explanation for the use of vectors containing drug resistance genes in the cloning of recombinant DNA (*c*DNA) molecules?
(a) The products of the drug resistance genes protect the *c*DNA from destruction by the host cells
(b) The drug resistance genes provide additional base sequences that enable the evctor to accommodate larger inserts of *c*DNA
(c) Entry of the vector containing the *c*DNA and the drug resistance genes into the host cell renders the later identifiable as it is now resistant to antibiotic drugs
(d) The cloned *c*DNA imparts drug resistance upon any cellular system with which it is used

36. Which statement correctly describes sequential steps in *c*DNA cloning?
(a) Reverse transcription of *m*RNA, second strand synthesis, cDNA end modification, ligation to vector
(b) *m*RNA preparation, *c*DNA synthesis using reverse transcription, second strand synthesis using terminal trasnferase, ligation to vector
(c) *m*RNA synthesis using RNA polymerase, reverse transcription of *m*RNA, second strand synthesis, ligation to vector
(d) double stranded *c*DNA synthesis, restriction enzyme digestion, addition of linkers, ligation to vector

37. The PCR is used to
(a) amplify a small amount of DNA
(b) cleavage bacteria plasmids
(c) seal sticky ends
(d) identify target plasmids

38. PCR is considered as a revolutionary technology because all of the following, except
(a) it enables as unlimited production of a DNA fragment *in vitro*
(b) it is a highly sensitive technology
(c) its experimental protocol is simple
(d) it enables the direct production of a synthetic gene that did not exist before

39. Which of the following would be eliminated by hot start PCR?
(a) Aerosol contamination from the barrel of pipetors
(b) Addition of a nucleotide to the terminal end of PCR products
(c) Infidelity of DNA copying by *Taq* DNA polymerase
(d) Formation of primer-dimers

40. The annealing temperature, at which the primers attach to the template, can be calculated by determining the melting temperature (Tm) of the primer template hybrid. What will be Tm of the primer 5′-AGACTCAGAGA- GAACCC-3′
(a) 50°C (b) 52°C
(c) 102°C (d) 43°C

41. A 200 μL of PCR mixture has 100 template DNA molecules and the reaction was performed for 10 cycles. How many molecules of amplicons will be generated?
(a) 1.024×10^4
(b) 1.024×10^5
(c) 2.048×10^4
(d) 2.048×10^4

42. Which of the following is not a potential problem associated with expressing a eukaryotic, protein coding nuclear gene in prokaryotic cells?
(a) Lack of an intron-splicing mechanism in prokaryotes
(b) Differences in the translation initiation codons used by eukaryotic cells and prokaryotic cells
(c) Stability of *m*RNA in prokaryotic cells
(d) Differences in transcriptional signals between eukaryotic cells and prokaryotic cells

43. A reporter gene
(a) acts as repressor
(b) allows gene expression to be readily measured
(c) enhances *m*RNA stability
(d) interacts with RNA polymerase

44. Most common reporter gene whose product can be directly visualized in transformed cells is
(a) NPTII (neomycin phosphotransferase)
(b) CAT (chloramphenicol acetyl transferase)
(c) β-galactosidase
(d) GFP (green fluroscent protein)

45. Shotgun approach is used for the construction of
(a) *c*DNA library (b) genomic library
(c) Both (a) and (b) (d) None of these

46. Which one of the following statements about genomic libraries are false?
(a) Genomic libraries are made from *c*DNA
(b) Genomic libraries must be representative if they are to contain all the genes in an organism
(c) Genomic libraries must contain a minimum number of recombinants if they are to contain all the genes in an organism
(d) The DNA must be fragmented to an appropriate size for the vector that is used

47. The term *c*DNA library means?
(a) Collection of *c*DNA clones by an individual researcher
(b) Compilation of *c*DNA sequences in the database
(c) Pool of *c*DNAs generated from a specific tissue inserted into an appropriate vector that can be used as a source of the *c*DNA of interest
(d) It is manual for *c*DNA research

48. What clones should a eukaryotic *c*DNA library contain?
(a) Clones that represent every fragment of DNA in approximately equal frequencies
(b) Clones that represent one copy of every coding region
(c) Clone representing transcribed DNA in approximately equal frequencies
(d) Clones representing transcribing DNA in frequencies that reflect their level of expression

49. Dideoxy DNA sequencing exclusively depends on one of the followings
(a) termination (b) ATP
(c) plasmid vector (d) vector primer

50. The genome sequencing of rice is important because
(a) the rice genome is very unique and contains genes not found in other plants
(b) the rice genome is very large compared to the DNA of other grains and so more genes will be identified
(c) it can identify genes associated with disease resistance, growth capacity, etc.
(d) it has a rapid life cycle and has many identifiable mutations

51. An analysis of chromosomal DNA, using the Southern blot technique, involves the following five major steps
I. Autoradiography
II. Blotting
III. Cleavage
IV. Electrophoresis
V. Hybridization
Which of the following sequences of steps best illustrates this technique?
(a) I, III, II, IV, V (b) III, V, II, IV, I
(c) I, II, III, IV, V (d) III, IV, II, V, I

52. Which of the following types of information cannot be determined from the traditional Northern blotting technique?
(a) The size od an *m*RNA species
(b) The half life of an *m*RNA species
(c) The strand of DNA that is transcribed into *m*RNA
(d) The amino acid sequence of the protein coded by an *m*RNA species

53. Which of the following would not be possible to address using a Northern blot?
(a) Location of restriction sites in a particular gene
(b) Spatial expression of a particular gene
(c) Temporal expression of a particular gene
(d) *m*RNA size

54. There are two different ways to determining the nucleotide sequence of a nucleic acid: the chemical sequencing (Maxam-Gilbert) method and the enzymatic sequencing (Sanger) method. The basic principle/ advantage of the Sanger method is
(a) the differential interaction of the bases with particular dyes
(b) extension of a synthetic primer and the reliable termination of DNA repair synthesis
(c) the correlation of restriction sites with end-label of the DNA
(d) the ability to 'sequence' both strands of the DNA duplex simultaneously

55. In agarose gel electrophoresis
(a) DNA migrates towards the negative electrode
(b) supercoiled plasmid migrates slower than their nicked counterparts
(c) larger molecules migrate faster than smaller molecules
(d) EtBr can be used to visualize the DNA

56. Which of the following methods would give you the most precise and accurate information about where and when a given gene is expressed?
(a) DNA microarray
(b) *In situ* hybridization
(c) Protein microarray
(d) Reporter gene fusion including introns

57. A certain purified DNA sample was cut with two restriction endonucleases E_1 and E_2. The following results were obtained from agarose gel electrophoresis

Sample cut with E_1 alone two bands of size 35 kb and 15 kb

Sample cut with E_2 alone two bands of size 40kb and 10 kb

Sample cut simultaneously with E_1 abd E_2: three bands of size 35 kb, 10 kb and 5 kb

From these data, it can be inferred that the DNA has

(a) two sites for E_1 and one site for E_2
(b) one site for E_1 and two sites for E_2
(c) one site each for E_1 and E_2
(d) three sites fior E_1 and one site for E_2

58. In order to identify the person who committed a crime. Forensic experts will need to extract DNA from the tissue sample collected at the crime scene and conduct one of the following procedures for DNA fingerprinting analysis

(a) cut the DNA and hybridize with specific micro satellite probes
(b) cut the DNA and sub-clone the fragments
(c) determine the sequence of the sub-clones
(d) (b) followed by (c)

59. The DNA fingerprinting process involves

(a) Chain terminators
(b) Degenerate oligonucleotides
(c) VNTR loci
(d) RFLPs

60. Restriction Fragment Length Polymorphism (RFLP) is

(a) the technique used to fingerprint patterns of inheritance
(b) the difference in the restriction maps between the two alleles in a diploid cell
(c) the difference in the restriction maps between two individuals of one species
(d) the difference in the restriction maps between two individuals of two species

61. Which of the following could not give rise to a restriction fragment length polymorphism?

(a) A missense mutation within the protein coding region of a gene
(b) A silent mutation within the protein coding region of a gene
(c) A single base change within the intron sequence of a gene
(d) An error in RNA splicing that mistakenly removes an exon during RNA processing

62. Positional cloning refers to

(a) using a selection procedures to clone a cDNA
(b) isolating a gene by PCR using primers from another species
(c) isolating a gene from a specific tissue in which it is being expressed
(d) mapping a gene to a chromosomal region and then identifying and cloning a genomic copy of the gene from the region

63. A mouse in which one particular gene has been replaced by its inactivated form generated *in vitro* is called

(a) transgenic mouse (b) knockout mouse
(c) nude mouse (d) mutant mouse

64. The principle of the yeast two-hybrid system is

(a) the detection of protein-protein interactions by assembling a functional transcription factor from two fusion proteins
(b) the detection of protein-protein interactions in a pair of hybrid yeast strains
(c) he detection of protein-protein interactions by studying the hybridization of two cDNA sequences
(d) the detection of protein-protein interactions between phage coat protein and target proteins

65. What sequence is a palindrome?

(a) 5′-ACGGATTCGC-3′ (b) 5′-ATG-3′
(c) 5′-CCATT-3′ (d) 5′-AGGCCT-3′

66. You want to clone a fragment of DNA into a plasmid vector such as pBR322. The plasmid is 4.36 kb long and has a single restriction site for the restriction enzyme BamHI. If you digest pBR322 with *Bam*HI, how many linear fragments will result?

(a) Three (b) Four (c) One (d) Two

67. Recombinant DNA research is dependent on

(a) cloning (b) hosts
(c) vectors (d) All of these

68. You discover a novel eukaryotic organism that glows in the dark. You believe this trait is due to a single gene, and you wish to clone the gene. Which of the following strategies is most likely to be successful?

(a) Isolate the genomic DNA from the organism, digest with a restriction endonuclease, insert into a plasmid vector and transform into bacteria. Screen colonies for the ability to glow in the dark
(b) Isolate the genomic DNA from the organism, digest with a restriction endonuclease, insert into a plasmid vector and transform into eukaryotic cells such as yeast. Screen colonies for the ability to glow in the dark
(c) Isolate *m*RNA from the organism, reverse transcribe and generate *c*DNA, insert into a plasmid vector and transform into bacteria. Screen colonies for the ability to glow in the dark
(d) Isolate *m*RNA from the organism, reverse transcribe and generate *c*DNA, insert into a plasmid vector and transform into eukaryotic cells such as yeast. Screen colonies for the ability to glow in the dark

69. You restriction map a vector using *Bam* HI, *Eco* RI and *Hae* III and obtained fragments of the following sizes. Draw a restriction map of the vector and determine which of the following statements is correct.

Results:

Bam HI alone: 4,000bp;
Eco RI alone: 4,000bp;
Hae III alone: 3,000bp and 1,000bp;
Bam HI and *Eco* RI: 3,500bp, 500bp;
Bam HI and *Hae* III: 2,300bp, 1,000bp, 700bp;
Eco RI and *Hae* III: 2,800bp, 1,000bp, 200bp;

Bam HI, *Eco* RI, and *Hae* III: 2,300bp, 1,000bp, 500bp, 200bp
(a) There are three *Hae* III sites in this vector
(b) *Bam* HI is 1,000bp away from *Eco* RI
(c) *Bam* HI cuts the smaller fragment from the *Hae* III digestion
(d) None of the above

70. A method used to prevent disulphide bond interference with protein sequencing method is
(a) cleaving proteins with proteases that specifically recognize disulfide bonds
(b) protecting the disulphide bridge against spontaneous reduction to cysteinyl sulphydral groups
(c) removing cystines from protein sequences by proteolytic cleavage
(d) reducing disulphide bridges and preventing their reformation by further modifying the –SH groups

71. In a DNA molecule cytosine is 18%. Percentage of adenine would be
(a) 32% (b) 64% (c) 36% (d) 18%

72. RAPD banding patterns prone to
(a) DNA template concentration and quality
(b) Different *Taq* DNA polymerases
(c) Different PCR machines or related equipment used in conducting PCR
(d) All of the above

73. In the creation of a microarray (biochip), fragments of DNA are placed on a
(a) microscope slide (b) circuit board
(c) silicone chip (d) membrane

74. The human genome project officially began in
(a) 1988 (b) 1990
(c) 1992 (d) 1995

75. A nucleic acid probe might be used to
(a) insert genes into a host cell
(b) make DNA for gene cloning
(c) cut pieces of DNA down to manageable size
(d) find a nucleotide sequence

76. Scientists have produced a smallpox virus that contains genes from several other disease causing microorganisms. They hope to use the virus
(a) in a vaccine against several diseases
(b) as a compact genomic library
(c) to perfect a germ-warfare weapon with no antidote
(d) as a tool for diagnosing various infectious diseases

77. It is sometimes necessary to genetically engineer mammalian cells to produce proteins because they
(a) can produce larger quantities of protein than bacteria
(b) can read eukaryotic genes and bacteria cannot
(c) can adds sugars to make glycoproteins and bacteria cannot
(d) are easier to grow than bacteria

78. A plasmid has two antibiotic-resistance, genes, one for ampicillin and one for tetracycline. It is treated with a restriction enzyme that cuts in the middle of the ampicillin gene. DNA fragments containing a human globin gene were cut with the same enzyme. The plasmids and fragments are mixed, treated with ligase, and used to transform bacterial cells. Clones that have taken up the recombinant DNA are the ones that
(a) can grow on plates with both antibiotics
(b) can grow on plates with ampicillin but not with tetracycline
(c) can grow on plates with tetracycline but not with ampicillin
(d) can grow on plates with tetracycline and are not blue

79. VNTRs are a valuable tool for
(a) forming overlapping sections in chromosome walking
(b) infecting dichotomous plant cells with recombinant DNA
(c) acting as probes in Northern blots
(d) DNA fingerprinting

80. A genomic library is
(a) where you look to find out how to make recombinant DNA
(b) a listing of the known nucleotide sequences for a particular species
(c) all the genes contained in one kind of cell
(d) a collection of cloned DNA pieces from an organism's genome

81. A genetic marker is
(a) a place where a restriction enzyme cuts DNA
(b) a chart that traces the family history of a genetic trait
(c) a nucleotide sequence near a particular gene
(d) a radioactive probe used to find a gene

82. In recombinant DNA experiments, ... is used to cut pieces of DNA and .... joins these segments to form recombinant DNA.
(a) a restriction enzyme; DNA ligase
(b) a transposon; a restriction enzyme
(c) a plasmid; DNA ligase
(d) DNA ligase; a restriction enzyme

83. Which of the following is not true of recognition sequences?
(a) Modification by methylation of bases within them prevents restriction of bacterial DNA
(b) They are usually symmetrical sequences of four to eight nucleotides
(c) They signal the attachment of RNA polymerase
(d) Cutting a recognition sequence in the middle of a functional and identifiable gene is used to screen clones that have taken up foreign DNA

84. When recombinant plasmids are added to *E. coli*, not all the bacteria take them in. This makes it difficult to spot the bacteria that actually contain the plasmids. For this reason, R plasmids are often used as gene vectors in recombinant DNA experiments. Using R plasmids would allow experimenters to find the bacteria with recombinant DNA easily by
(a) using a molecular probe
(b) killing off the bacteria without the R plasmids
(c) exposing the bacteria to restriction enzymes
(d) watching what happens when the bacteria reproduce

85. Scientists wished to create an organism capable of breaking down several kinds of toxic wastes, so they combined the genes of several bacteria to create a single 'superbacterium'. They probably did not need to use which of the following in creating the superbacterium?
(a) nucleic acid probes
(b) F factors
(c) plasmids
(d) restriction enzymes

86. Complementary DNA does not create as complete a gene library as the shotgun approach because
(a) it has eliminated introns from the genes
(b) a cell produces *m*RNA for only a small portion of its genes at any one time
(c) the shotgun approach produces more restriction fragments
(d) *c*DNA is not as easily integrated into plasmids or phage genomes

87. This segment of DNA has restriction sites I and II which create restriction fragments *a*, *b* and *c*. Which of the following gel(s) produced by electrophoresis would represent the separation and identity of these fragments?

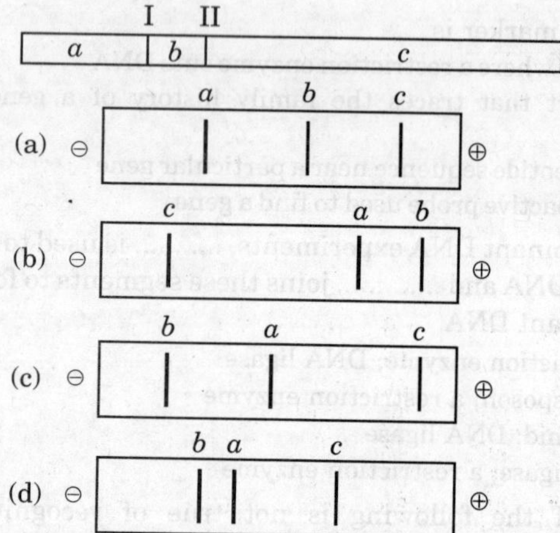

88. A crop scientist spliced genes for disease resistance into Ti plasmids and then treated tomato plants with the plasmids. Some parts of some plants resisted the disease, but most of the plants eventually died. The researcher could increase his chances for success by
(a) treating single cells and cloning whole plants from the cells
(b) using molecular probes to figure out where to put the genes
(c) using R plasmids rather than Ti plasmids to introduce the genes
(d) inserting the genes into the cells of the tomato plants with a needle

89. The role of restriction enzymes in DNA technology is to
(a) provide a vector for the transfer of recombinant DNA
(b) produce *c*DNA from *m*RNA
(c) produce a cut (usually staggered) at specific recognition sequences on DNA
(d) reseal 'sticky ends' after base-pairing of complementary bases

90. Yeast has become important in genetic engineering because it
(a) has RNA splicing machinery
(b) has plasmids that can be genetically engineered
(c) allows the study of eukaryotic gene regulation and expression
(d) All of the above

91. Consider the following steps.
I. Isolation of tissue from the plant.
II. Digestion of cell walls with cellular enzyme.
II. Preparation of culture medium.
IV. Preparation of the naked protoplasts and culturing them in the medium.

The correct sequence of the steps to be followed to culture protoplasts is
(a) I, II, III, IV
(b) I, III, II, IV
(c) IV, I, II, III
(d) IV, II, I, III

92. Consider the following statements
Tissue culture is recommended for
I. Multiplication of elite genotypes of useful trees.
II. Developing virus free plants.
III. Production of secondary metabolites.
IV. Induction of polyploidy.

Which of these statements are correct?
(a) I, II and IV are correct
(b) I, II and III are correct
(c) I, III and IV are correct
(d) II, III and IV are correct

93. Match the following lists.

List I	List II
A. Biolistic	1. Gene pulser
B. *Agrobacterium*	2. PDS 1000 He
C. Electroporation	3. Micromanipulator
D. Microinjection	4. Silicon carbide
	5. Vir operon

Codes

	A	B	C	D
(a)	2	5	1	3
(b)	2	1	3	4
(c)	5	4	3	2
(d)	1	2	3	4

94. An analysis of chromosomal DNA, using the Southern blot technique, involves the following five major steps
I. Autoradiography
II. Blotting
III. Cleavage
IV. Electrophoresis
V. Hybridization

Which of the following sequences of steps best illustrates this technique?
(a) I, II, III, IV, V
(b) I, III, II, IV, V
(c) III, V, II, IV, I
(d) III, IV, II, V, I

95. Restriction endonucleases are enzymes that

I. Cleave the 5′-terminal nucleotides from duplex DNA molecules.

II. Make sequence-specific cuts in both strands of duplex DNA molecules.

III. Promote circularization of the duplex DNA molecule by removal of the 5′-terminal nucleotides.

IV. Generate 3′-hydroxyl and 5′-phosphate ends in the cut DNA strands.

(a) I and II (b) I and II
(c) II and III (d) I, II, III and IV

96. Match list-I (enzyme) with list (characteristic/activity) and select the correct answer using the codes given below the lists.

List I (Enzymes)	List II (Characteristic/Activity)
A. Terminal transferases	1. Stable above 90ºC
B. Polynucleotide kinases	2. Cleave the ends of linear DNA
C. *Taq* DNA polymerases	3. Adds phosphate to 5′-OH end of DNA or RNA
D. Exonucleases	4. Adds a number of nucleotides to 3′-end of DNA or RNA
	5. Regulate the level of supper coiling of DNA molecule

Codes

	A	B	C	D
(a)	5	4	1	2
(b)	4	3	1	2
(c)	3	4	5	1
(d)	4	3	2	1

97. Match list I (cloning vector) with list II (character) and select the correct answer using the codes given below the lists.

List I (Cloning vector)	List II (Character)
A. Yeast episomal plasmid (YEp)	1. Integrates with host chromosome for replication
B. Yeast integrative plasmid (YIp)	2. Carries a chromosomal origin of replication
C. Yeast replicative plasmid (YRp)	3. Carries origin of replication of the 2mm plasmid

Codes

	A	B	C
(a)	3	2	1
(b)	2	1	3
(c)	3	1	2
(d)	2	3	1

Answers

1. (d)	**2.** (c)	**3.** (b)	**4.** (b)	**5.** (a)	**6.** (b)	**7.** (a)	**8.** (b)	**9** (b)	**10** (d)
11. (c)	**12.** (d)	**13.** (c)	**14.** (a)	**15.** (c)	**16.** (c)	**17.** (b)	**18.** (c)	**19** (d)	**20** (d)
21. (b)	**22.** (c)	**23.** (b)	**24.** (b)	**25.** (d)	**26.** (c)	**27.** (b)	**28.** (c)	**29** (a)	**30** (c)
31. (c)	**32.** (a)	**33.** (a)	**34.** (d)	**35.** (c)	**36.** (a)	**37.** (a)	**38.** (d)	**39** (d)	**40** (b)
41. (b)	**42.** (b)	**43.** (b)	**44.** (c)	**45.** (b)	**46.** (a)	**47.** (c)	**48.** (d)	**49** (a)	**50** (c)
51. (d)	**52.** (d)	**53.** (a)	**54.** (d)	**55.** (d)	**56.** (a)	**57.** (c)	**58.** (a)	**59** (c)	**60** (c)
61. (d)	**62.** (d)	**63.** (b)	**64.** (a)	**65.** (d)	**66.** (c)	**67.** (d)	**68.** (d)	**69** (d)	**70** (d)
71. (a)	**72.** (d)	**73.** (a)	**74.** (b)	**75.** (d)	**76.** (a)	**77.** (c)	**78.** (c)	**79** (d)	**80** (d)
81. (c)	**82.** (a)	**83.** (c)	**84.** (b)	**85.** (b)	**86.** (b)	**87.** (b)	**88.** (a)	**89** (c)	**90** (d)
91. (a)	**92.** (b)	**93.** (a)	**94.** (d)	**95.** (c)	**96.** (b)	**97.** (c)			

38

Histochemical and Immunotechniques

Antibody Generation

Antibodies are proteins that specifically recognize and bind to other molecules with a high affinity and specificity. This high degree of specificity makes antibodies powerful reagents for the characterization of proteins and other macromolecules. Antibodies are generated against specific proteins or other macromolecules by immunizing animals and collecting the sera. The immune sera contains a mixture of antibodies that recognize various epitopes on the antigen. The immune system can also respond to foreign substances *via* a cellular immune response.

Choice of Animal

A wide range of vertebrate species can be used for the production of antibodies, but the two most often used animals are mice and rabbits. Rabbits react to most immunogens and relatively large quantities of antisera are obtained. The disadvantages of rabbits are that larger quantities of antigen are needed and rabbits often exhibit a high background response to heterologous antigens. In particular, high levels of antibodies to *E. coli* antigens will complicate the analysis of antibodies against recombinant proteins. Mice are easy to handle and several different genetic strains are available. The different genetic strains provide a more uniform response to immunogens and also some control of the immune response since, the different strains may respond differently to the same antigen. In addition, mice are used models for many infectious diseases. The major disadvantage of mice is that a small amount of antisera is obtained. Adult animals should be used for immunizations (*i.e.,* rabbits 6-10 lb and mice > 7 weeks). If possible, 2-3 rabbits and 5-10 mice should be immunized with the same immunogen to control for animal-to-animal variation.

Syllabus

- Histochemical and Immunotechniqes: Antibody Generation Immunoprecipitation, Detection of Molecules Using Flowcytometry, Western Blot, Immunofluorescence, ELISA and RIA Detection of Molecules in Living Cells, *In Situ* Localization by Techniques Such as FISH and GISH.

Table 38.1 **Advantages and Disadvantages of Various Animals for Antibody Production**

Animal	Advantage	Disadvantage
Rabbit	Large amount of sera Strong antibody response Easy to maintain	Require more immunogen High background
Mice/Rat	Inbred strains Monoclonal antibodies possible Easy to maintain	Small amount of sera
Guinea pig	Generally high titer antibodies Easy to maintain	Difficult to bleed
Goat/Sheep	Very large amount of sera	Difficult to maintain
Chicken	Good for some highly conserved mammalian antigens	Difficult to maintain

Adjuvants

Adjuvants are substances that enhance the overall immune response. Most adjuvants contain two components. One component will form a deposit that prevents the rapid breakdown of the antigen and promotes a slow release of the antigen, called the depot effect. There are several different classes of adjuvants with distinct mechanisms by which the depot effect is evoked. The second component of many adjuvants non-specifically stimulates the immune system (mitogenic or polyclonal activation). For example, killed bacteria, especially mycobacteria or bacteria components are included in some adjuvants. Common bacterial components included in adjuvants are lipopolysaccharide (LPS) or muramyl dipeptide (MDP), a synthetic analogue of the adjuvant-active component from the cell walls of mycobacteria. These substances stimulate macrophages and other immune effector cells to release cytokines which then enhance the antibody response. The immuno-modulatory component may also influence the class of immunoglobin produced as well as the isotype of IgG.

Table 38.2 **Main Class of Adjuvants**

Adjuvant	Comment
Aluminium salts	The immunogen is absorbed to a gel-like precipitate of aluminium hydroxide, aluminium phosphate or alum. Action is due to efficient uptake by macrophages and slow release.
Water-in-oil emulsion	Aqueous microdroplets containing the immunogen and stabilized by a surfactant are in a continuous oil phase such as mineral oil or squalene. Immune modulators (*e.g.*, mycobacteria, MDP) are often incorporated into the emulsion. The emulsion provides a good short term depot effect and is especially useul for soluble immunogens.
Oil-in-water emulsion	The immunogen is associated with the surface of microdroplets of oil (*e.g.*, sqalane) in a continuous aqueous phase and stabilized by surfactants (*e.g.*, Tween 80). Highly suited for lipophilic or amphiphatic immunogens since, it is important for the immunogen to be incorporated into the oil phase.
Saponin	Saponins form complexes with proteins and lipids resulting in an open cage-like matrix (*i.e.*, micelles) which are sometimes referred to as immunostimulating complexes (ISCOM).
Liposomes	Immunogens can be incorporated into or absorbed to liposomes (single or multilayered bilayer vesicles) composed of phospholipids and cholestrol. Immune modulators such as LPS and MDP can also be incorporated.

Injection

It is possible to immunize by several different routes. The route of injection can also affect the antibody response, both in terms of quantity of antibody produced and in the qualitative aspects of the antibody. The volume of immunogen and how quickly the immunogen should be released into the lymphatics or circulation will influence the choice of injection method. Rabbits are generally immunized sub-cutaneously at multiple sites to stimulate regional lymph nodes. Immunization of mice with large volumes can only be accomplished intraperitoneally. Intramuscular and intradermal injections are best for slow release. However, intradermal immunizations are difficult to do correctly. Intraveneous immunization is only used for boosting and immunogens containing adjuvants should not be given intravenously. The antigen dose will depend on the animal, the purity and the immunogenicity of the antigen. In general, 0.05-1 mg and 5-50 μg of pure antigen are needed for rabbits and mice, respectively. To obtain the optimal antibody response (*i.e.*, highest titer and affinity) the animals will need to be reimmunized or boosted. Boosting promotes class switching (*e.g.*, IgM → IgG), higher levels of antibody, and an increase in the affinity of the antibody for the antigen. Typically, the boosting is carried out at intervals of 2-6 weeks and 3-4 total immunizations are given.

Initial contact with a new antigen may evoke a primary response. The primary response is characterized by a initial rise in IgM followed by IgG (Figure). Antibodies following the primary response are generally transient and will disappear from the circulation. Subsequent exposure (*e.g.*, booster injection) to the same antigen results in a much faster antibody response as well as significantly higher levels of antibodies which are predominantly IgG. Furthermore, the antibodies associated with this secondary response persist for a much longer time in the serum. This additional exposure to the antigen also results in a selection for plasma cells producing antibodies with a higher affinity for the antigen. This affinity maturation results in antibodies which react more strongly with the antigen.

Collecting and Processing Blood

Serum samples are typically collected 4-10 days after an immunization and tested for antibody titer. Clotting factors interfere with many assays, and therefore, serum is usually preferable to plasma (total non-cellular component of blood). Serum is prepared by collecting the blood without anticoagulants and allowing the blood clot for at least 30-60 min at 37°. Blood clotting can also be performed for 2-4 hours at room temperature or overnight at 4°. Incubation overnight at 4° will usually produce more haemolysis. The clot is removed and the sample centrifuged to remove any remaining blood cells. In some applications it is also beneficial to inactivate complement by heating the serum at 56° for 30 minutes.

Antibody Purification

Whole sera can be used for most immunological assays and further purification of antibodies is generally not necessary. Antibodies can be concentrated and partially purified by precipitation with 40-50% saturated $(NH_4)_2SO_4$. This will remove a substantial portion of serum albumin—the major component of serum. Higher levels of purity can be obtained after anion exchange chromatography on DEAE. The immunoglobulins elute from the column before serum albumin. Affinity chromatography using protein A or G can also be used. Protein A and G are bacterial proteins that bind IgG. The various IgG sub-classes from different animals exhibit a range of affinities for these proteins and can be differential eluted from the affinity columns at different pH values. Specific antibodies can also be purified from polyclonal sera. For example, affinity purification using the antigen as ligand can be used to isolate the antibodies specific for that protein. Monospecific antibodies can also be generated by taking advantage of the high resolution of gel electrophoresis. It is also possible to preabsorb serum to remove unwanted antibodies and to reduce background. Examples include
E. coli proteins or the fusion partner in recombinant proteins.

Immunoprecipitation

Immunoprecipitation involves the purification of antigen-antibody complexes, which are then analyzed by gel electrophoresis. This method provides a means to identify and characterize proteins in conjunction with gel electrophoresis. Initially, the technique involved the formation of large supramolecular antigen-antibody complexes due to polyclonal sera that recognized multiple epitopes on the protein. These large protein complexes are collected by centrifugation. Formation of the large complex is dependent on high concentrations of both antigen and antibody and the complexes will often contain contaminating proteins. The ability to purify the antigen-antibody complex with bacterial proteins that bind immunoglobulin has greatly increased the sensitivity and specificity of immunoprecipitation. A typical first step in immunoprecipitation is to radiolabel the protein(s). This is easily accomplished in situations where *in vitro* cell culture is possible by metabolically labeling the protein with radioactive amino acids. Proteins can also be labeled by chemical means such as iodination as long as the treatment does not adversely affect the epitopes recognized by the antibodies. It is not necessary to label the protein if it can be detected by other means such as protein staining or immunoblotting. Proteins are then solubilized under conditions which do not affect the ability of the antibody to recognize the epitope. For example, some antibodies recognize 'conformational' epitopes and denaturing agents will destroy the epitope. Generally, non-ionic detergents (*e.g.*, Triton X-100) do not adversely affect the immunoprecipitation assay. It still may be possible to use immunoprecipitation for the analysis of proteins which are only soluble under denaturing conditions if a non conformational dependent (*i.e.*, linear) epitope is recognized by the antibody. However, the denaturing agent will have to be removed before adding the antibody since, the structure of the antibody must be maintained for epitope recognition. For example, proteins can be solubilized with SDS followed by the addition of a 10-20 fold excess of Triton X-100 (or another non-ionic detergent). The excess SDS will be incorporated into mixed micelles and therefore, will have little affect on the antibody when it is added. Enough antibody should be added to precipitate all of the antigen in a sample, especially if quantitative interpretations are going to be made. In general, the formation of antigen-antibody complexes is rapid and incubations of 30-60 minutes are sufficient for maximum recovery. Longer incubations may be necessary for low concentrations of the target protein. Proteolysis can also be a problem during the incubation step. Protease inhibitors should be added and the incubations carried out on ice to minimize losses. The isolation of the antigen-antibody complex is accomplished by an affinity purification with protein A or protein G conjugated to agarose beads. Historically, fixed intact Staphylococcus areus bacteria were used to isolate Ag-Ab complexes. Protein A and protein G bind to the Fc region of IgG with an high affinity. In general, protein G binds with a higher affinity to a wider range of immunoglobulin sub-classes as well as recognizing immunoglobulins from more species than protein. These bacterial proteins have a higher affinity for antibody with bound antigen and are therefore the protein A (or G) agarose is usually added after the formation of the antigen-antibody complex. But all three components (antigen extract, antibody, and affinity matrix) can be mixed simultaneously. Generally, incubation for 30-60 minutes with continuous rocking is sufficient for complete recovery of the antigen-antibody complexes.

The antigen-antibody complexes bound to the protein A (or G) are collected by centrifugation and washed several times to remove contaminating proteins. Antigen-antibody complexes are then eluted from affinity matrix by boiling the agarose beads in electrophoresis sample buffer containing SDS and β-mercaptoethanol. Bound proteins can also be eluted with low pH and quickly neutralized if non-denatured protein is need for subsequent analyses. The sample is then subjected to SDS gel electrophoresis and immunoprecipitated proteins are detected by autoradiography or fluorography depending on the isotope. It may also be possible to detect abundant antigens by protein staining. Alternatively, it may also be possible to transfer the electrophoresed proteins to a membrane and carry out immunoblotting. IgG heavy and light chains will also be contained in the sample and can be observed as approximately 55 (IgG-H) and 25 (IgG-L) kDa bands. Most of the time this will not cause any problems unless the target protein is of a similar size and the immunoglobulin subunits interfere with the protein of interest. The immunoglobulin bands are easily control for by including an immunoprecipitation blank (B) which contains everything (*i.e.*, antibody and buffers) except the sample (S) being analyzed. Bands appearing in the sample (arrow), but not the blank will be the protein(s) recognized by the antibody. Immunoprecipitation can be used to detect a protein in a biological sample and in conjunction with SDS-PAGE to determine its molecular weight. Since, the formation of the Ag-Ab complexes can be carried out under non-denaturing conditions it is also possible to determine the quarternary structure of a protein and to analyze proteins that bind to a target protein. Other proteins binding to the protein recognized by the antibody will be co-immunoprecipitated with the target protein if the protein-protein interactions are not disrupted by antibody binding (or *visa versa*). Generally, the information obtained by immunoprecipitation is qualitative. To obtain reliable quantitative information is will be necessary to titrate the antibody and to run controls demonstrating that all of the available target protein has been immunoprecipitated.

Western Blot

Immunoblotting, also called Western blotting, is another technique used in conjunction with gel electrophoresis. In this case, proteins are first subjected to gel electrophoresis, transferred to a membrane support and the protein of interest is detected with an antibody.

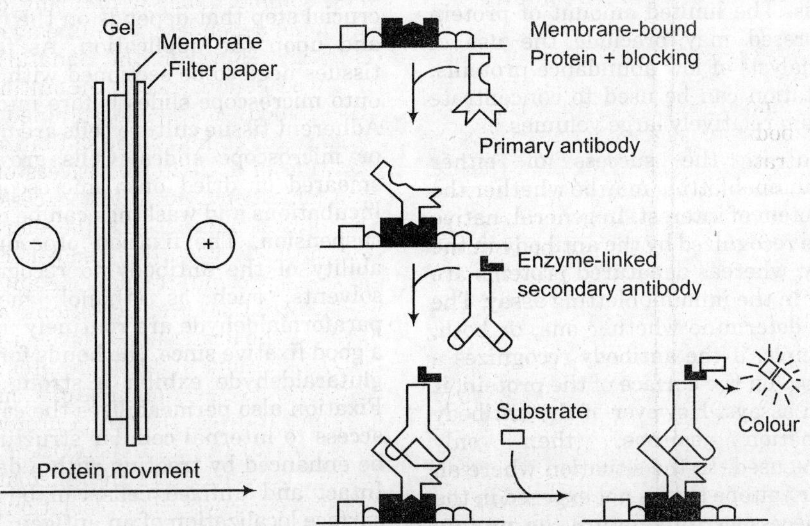

Fig. 38.1 Procedure of Western blotting

The first step in immunoblotting is antigen preparation and electrophoresis. SDS-PAGE is the most common electrophoretic system, but other gel electrophoretic systems can also be used. After electrophoresis the separated proteins are transferred to a membrane support such as nitrocellulose or PVDF (Immobilon-P). PVDF membranes bind more protein and are generally superior to nitrocellulose. Before the transfer the gel is usually equilibrated with the transfer buffer containing methanol to remove excess SDS. Excessive SDS can inhibit the binding of proteins to the membrane. The transfer of proteins from the gel to the membrane is carried out electrophoretically in a special apparatus. The gel is positioned between two electrodes that generate an uniform electric field across the thickness of the gel. A membrane is placed on the anode side of the gel. Filter papers are used to maintain buffer contact with the gel. Proteins migrate out of the gel and a replica of the gel is formed on the membrane. The completeness of the transfer can be assessed through the use of prestained proteins as size markers or by staining the gel after the transfer. Following the transfer, the membranes are washed with a buffer which removes any loosely bound proteins and which will 'block' the non-specific binding of proteins (*i.e.*, antibodies). Two common blocking agents are the detergent Tween-20 and a powdered-milk solution, called BLOTTO in lab jargon. The detergent (or milk proteins) will bind any free sites on the membrane that are not already bound with protein and prevent non-specific antibody binding. The membrane is then incubated with the primary antibody (diluted with the blocking buffer). The dilution and time of incubation will depend on antibody affinity and the amount of the target protein on the membrane. Typically incubations are carried out for one hour at room temperature. Alternatively, overnight incubations at 40 can be carried out. The membranes are then washed extensively to remove any non-specifically bound antibody followed by incubation with the secondary antibody conjugated with an enzyme. This secondary antibody recognizes immunoglobulin from the species of the primary antibody and is purchased. The secondary antibody will bind the primary antibody which is bound to the antigen. The membranes are then incubated with substrates of the enzyme which will form insoluble coloured products. This results in a coloured precipitate being formed on the membrane in the position of the target protein. Chemiluminescent substrates can also be used instead of the precipitating chromogenic substrates. Alternatively, ^{125}I-Protein A in conjunction with autoradiography can be used to detect the Ab-Ag complex.

Both immunoblotting and immunoprecipitation can identify proteins recognized by an antibody in conjunction with SDS gel electrophoresis. The choice of the assay will be affected by the experimental design, antigen concentration, antigen solubility and the ability of the antibody to recognize the antigen in the two assays. As an example of experimental design, immunoblotting will provide information about the total amount of antigen present, whereas immunoprecipitation of metabolically labelled proteins can provide information about the newly synthesized protein and/or its rate of synthesis. The limited amount of protein which can be electrophoresed may preclude the use of immunoblotting for the analysis of low abundance proteins, whereas immuno- precipitation can be used to concentrate low abundance proteins from relatively large volumes.

Another factor involved in the success of either immunoprecipitation or immunoblotting may be whether the antibody recognizes the protein of interest. In general, native non-denatured proteins are recognized by the antibody in the immunoprecipitation assay, whereas denatured proteins are recognized by the antibody in the immunoblotting assay. The nature of the epitope will determine whether one, or both, assays will work. For example, if the antibody recognizes a linear epitope that is exposed on the surface of the protein, it will likely function in both assays. However, if the antibody recognizes a conformation epitope, then only immunoprecipitation can be used. In the situation where an antibody recognizes a linear epitope that is not exposed in the native protein it will be necessary to denature the protein before carrying out the immunoprecipitation. The quarternary structure of a protein may also influence the choice of the assay. For example, an antibody that only recognizes one subunit of a multisubunit protein will only produce one band if analyzed by immunoblotting, whereas all of the protein subunits may be detected in the immunoprecipitation assay. One problem with the immunoprecipitation assay is that it is not always possible to radiolabel the antigen of interest, and therefore, detecting the target protein is difficult. Immuno- blotting provides a very sensitive method of detecting proteins after gel electrophoresis, but is limited by the amount of protein which can be electrophoresesed. Affinity purification of the target protein by immunoprecipitation and detecting the protein by immunoblotting possibly overcomes these limitations. Following immunoprecipitation and gel electrophoresis, the proteins are transferred to a membrane and analyzed by immunoblotting. This does require that the antibody works in both assays, or that distinct antibodies for each assay are available. A blank immunoprecipitation which contains the antibody, but no antigen-containing extract, should also be prepared. This blank will serve to identify the IgG heavy and light chains which may be detected with the secondary antibodies.

Immunofluorescence

Immunofluorescence is used to localize antigens to specific cell types or sub-cellular compartments. The assay can also be adapted for the detection and quantification of antibody. The general procedure is to incubate cells or tissue with the primary antibody and detect the antigen-antibody complex with a secondary antibody conjugated with a fluorochrome. Fluorescein and rhodamine, which fluoresce green and red, respectively, are two common conjugates. The location of the protein recognized by the primary antibody is determined by examining the sample under UV illumination. It is also possible to use an enzyme-conjugated secondary antibody and develop with substrates that form precipitates. The location of the precipitates is then detected by conventional microscopy. This variation is not widely used, though. The preparation of the cells or tissue for immunofluorescence is a crucial step that depends on the type of cells being analyzed and upon the application. As for microscopy in general, tissues need to be sectioned with a microtome and mounted onto microscope slides before immunofluorescence analysis. Adherent tissue culture cells are usually grown on cover slips or microscope slides. Cells grown in suspension can be smeared or dried onto microscope slides or the antibody incubations and washings can be carried out with the cells in suspension. The fixation procedure should not affect the ability of the antibody to recognize the antigen. Organic solvents, such as ethanol, methanol and acetone, or paraformaldehyde are routinely used. Glutaraldehyde is not a good fixative since, the bonds formed by the crosslinking of glutaraldehyde exhibit a strong endogenous fluorescence. Fixation also permeabilizes the cell so that the antibody has access to internal cellular structures. The permeability can be enhanced by treating with a detergent after the fixation. Intact and unfixed cells can be used to demonstrate the surface localization of an antigen. The subcellular structures recognized by the antibodies will appear as a bright image against a dark background. Comparing the epifluorescence with the bright field image is used to localize the protein of interest to a particular subcellular compartment or to a particular cell type within a tissue. Fluorescent dyes which bind to particular sub-cellular compartments can also be used to assist in the localization of the protein of interest. Dual-labelling experiments can also be used to demonstrate the extent of co-localization between two different proteins. The most convenient method is to used antibodies generated in different species (*e.g.,* mice and rabbits) as the primary antibody and then used species specific secondary antibodies conjugated with different fluorochromes. If only antibodies raised in the same species are available then it will be necessary to purify the two antibodies and conjugate them with different fluorochromes. The two different fluorochromes can be viewed separately through the use of filters specific for each fluorochrome. It is also possible to digitally merge the two images to demonstrate the extent of co-localization between the two proteins.

ELISA and RIA

The Enzyme-Linked Immuno Sorbent Assay (ELISA) involves absorbing an antigen a solid support such as a membrane (as used in immunoblotting) or a 96-well microplate. Proteins which have not been separated by electrophoresis can be bound to membranes and analyzed with primary and secondary antibodies as in the immunoblotting procedure.

Such analyses are often called dot blots. The more common format is to absorb the antigen to the wells of a 96 well microplate and to use substrates that produce a coloured soluble product. The ELISA is particularly well suited for the analysis of large numbers of samples and most of the procedure can be automated. The first step is to bind the antigen to the plate. The antigen range from a purified protein or peptide to a crude protein extract. It is also possible to use whole fixed cells. The choice of antigen will depend on the application and the nature of the antibodies being tested. Binding to 96 well microplates is accomplished by incubating the wells with a solution containing the antigen. Protein binding is due to hydrophobic interactions between the protein and the plastic. After antigen is bound to the plates, they are then blocked to eliminate nonspecific binding. Common blocking agents are bovine serum albumin (relatively cheap protein), Tween-20 (detergent) or powdered milk (very cheap protein). The function of the blocking step is to coat any protein-binding sites on the plate that could bind antibody non-specifically. The antigen-containing wells are then incubated with the primary antibody. The proper antibody dilution must be determined empirically. Serial dilutions are often carried out and the minimum titer giving a positive response will be a quantitative measure of antibody concentration. ELISAs are typically carried out in duplicate or triplicate. It is important to include negative (without antigen) controls on the same plate. Positive controls can also be included in situations where the antigen is being evaluated. After incubation with the primary antibody the wells are washed extensively to remove any unbound antibody. The wells are then incubated with a secondary antibody that is conjugated with an enzyme. Alkaline phosphatase and horse-radish peroxidase are two common enzymes. These reagents are obtained commercially and recommended dilutions will be supplied by the manufacturer. It is possible to buy secondary antibodies that are class or subclass specific (*i.e.,* made against the heavy chain). Second antibodies are made against the whole molecule will usually recognize the light chains which are shared between IgG and IgM. The plates are again washed to remove any unbound antibody. The final step is to develop the plates with a chromogenic soluble substrate.

Examples of ELISA Substrate		
Enzymes	**Substrates**	
	Soluble	Precipitating
AP	pNPP	BCIP/NBP
HRP	TMB	DAB

AP (alkaline phosphatase); HRP (horse radish peroxidase); pNPP (p-nitrophenyl phosphate); BCIP (5-bromo-4-chloro-3-indolyl phosphate); NBT (nitro blue tetrazolium); TMB (3, 3′, 5, 5′-tetramethyl-benziudine); DAB (3, 3-diaminobenzidine).

The intensity of the color will be proportional to the amount of secondary antibody which proportional to the amount of specific primary antibody in the sample. Alternatively a constant amount of a defined antibody can be used to quantify the amount of a specific protein in a sample. An ELISA reader is a spectrophotometer designed to read the individual wells in a 96-well microplate. Many ELISA readers are interfaced with a computer to assist in data management. The RIA is essentially the same as the ELISA, except 125I-protein A is used instead of enzyme-conjugate secondary antibody for the detection of the Antigen-antibody complex. The amount of radioactivity bound to the membrane filters or wells is determined instead of developing with substrates. The RIA was developed first, but the ELISA is more popular since radioactivity is not needed.

Variations to the ELISA can also be carried out. For example, the plates can be coated with the antibody instead of the antigen. The antibody will then 'capture' the antigen when extracts are added to the wells. In this case the antigen will need to be radioactive or have some type of measurable activity. If two antibodies with different specificities are available it may be possible to create a 'sandwich' type of assay. Monoclonal antibodies are especially useful for the development of antigen capture assays.

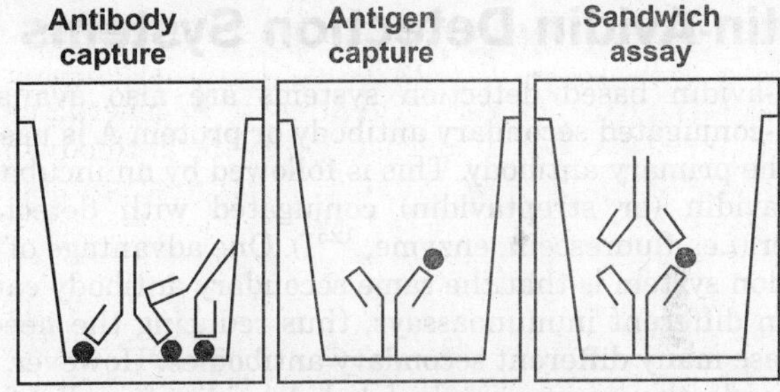

Fig. 38.2 Variations of ELISA

Direct *vs* Indirect

In summary, ELISA, immunoblotting and IFA are all techniques in which antigen is immobilized, incubated with primary antibody and the bound antibody is then detected. The bound antibody is usually detected with a second antibody, which recognizes the first antibody and is conjugated with a detectable marker (*e.g.,* radioactivity, enzyme, fluorescence). The use of a secondary antibody is referred to as indirect detection. It is also possible to label the primary antibody with the detectable marker and use the primary antibody to directly detect antigen. Direct detection methods are quicker to carry out since an antibody incubation step and the associated washing steps are eliminated. In addition, there is sometimes less background associated with direct detection methods. However, the primary antibody must be first purified and conjugated with the appropriate label. The availability of secondary antibodies from commercial sources tends to make the indirect methods easier to carry out. In addition, some signal amplification may occur during the secondary antibody step.

The most common detectable markers used to label antibodies are: radioactivity fluorochromes, biotinylation and enzyme cross-linking. In all of these labelling procedures, it is important that the modification does not affect the antibody's ability to recognize the antigen. Iodination is the preferred method for radiolabelling antibodies. Many iodination methods are gentle and do not adversely affect antibody structure. In addition, mAbs can be metabolically labelled by incubating the hybridomas with radioactive amino acids and harvesting the mAb. Arginine is a good amino acid for the labelling of mAb. Fluorescent antibodies can be made with commercially available isothiocyanate derivatives of fluorescein and rhodamine. These derivatives react with primary amines (*i.e.*, primarily lysine). The efficiency of labelling can be conveniently determined by spectrophotometry. For example, the A_{495}/A_{280} ratio should be between 0.3-1.0 following conjugation with fluorescein and the A_{575}/A_{280} ratio should be 0.3-0.7 following conjugation with rhodamine. Biotinylation with a succimide ester of biotin also labels primary amines. The labelling of free amines is usually mild and does not affect antibody function. However, the labelling should be kept to a minimum. Enzymes can also be crosslinked to antibodies. The three most common enzymes are horse radish peroxidase, alkaline phosphatase and galactosidase. Methods of cross-linking include glutaraldehyde, periodate treatment and bifunctional cross-linking agents.

Biotin-Avidin Detection Systems

Biotin-avidin based detection systems are also available. Biotin-conjugated secondary antibody or protein A is used to bind the primary antibody. This is followed by an incubation with avidin (or streptavidin) conjugated with detectable marker (*i.e.*, fluorescein, enzyme, ^{125}I). One advantage of this detection system is that the same secondary antibody can be used in different immunoassays, thus reducing the need to purchase many different secondary antibodies. However, one still needs the appropriately labeled avidin for all of the different assays. Avidin has a high affinity for biotin and several biotin molecules can be incorporated into a single antibody molecule; thus increasing the sensitivity of the assay. However, the use of the biotin-avidin systems requires an additional incubation step and the associated wash steps.

Flow Cytometry

Fluorescent microscopy provides qualitative information about individual cells. However, obtaining quantitative data is difficult and labor intensive. Fluorometry provides quantitative data, but represents the average of the population being analyzed. In other words, fluorometry does not reveal information about heterogeneity within that population. Flow cytometry can provide quantitative information on individual cells. The principal of flow cytometry is to pass cells (or particles), in single file through a laser beam and analyze the interaction of the laser with individual cells. For example, the scatter (*i.e.*, direction change) of the laser provides information about the size and shape of the cell. In addition, cells can be labelled with fluorochromes which are excited by the laser. The amount of fluorescence associated with the cells provides quantitative data on specific target molecules or their sub-cellular constituents.

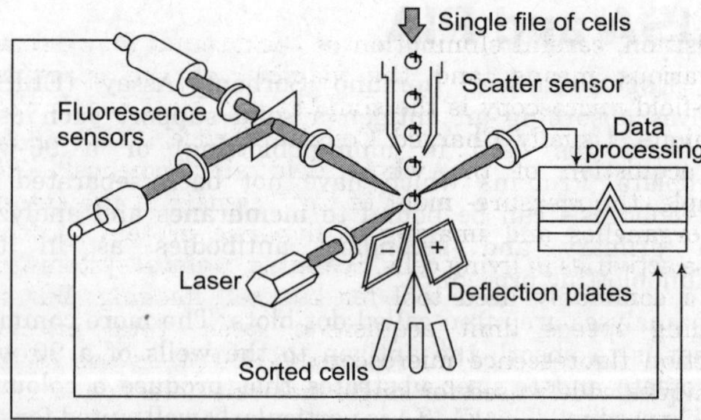

Fig. 38.3 Procedure of flow cytometry

Flow cytometry can quantify virtually any cell-associated factor or organelle for which there is a fluorescent probe (or natural fluorescence). For example, the amount of DNA per cell can be measured and provide information about the proportions of cells in various phases of the cell cycle. Through the use of multiple detectors and lasers it is also possible to analyze two or more fluorochromes with different emission spectra simultaneously. The data for the various cellular parameters being measured are accumulated for each cell and sub-populations can be identified and characterized. For example, the data can be plotted as dots defined by the fluorescence values of the two fluoro- chromes. The numbers of cells with particular characteristics are tabulated and their distributions in the cell population determined. In addition, many flow cytometers are equipped with a cell sorter, or a fluorescence activated cell sorter (FACS). Cell sorting is accomplished by passing the cells between a charged plates and applying a pulse of current to cause the cell to change directions. In this way cells with particular characteristics (*i.e.*, predetermined levels of fluorescence, scatter, etc.) can be separated from a mixture of cells. The separated cells can then be subjected to other analyses.

Detection of Molecules in Living Cells

Biochemical analysis of cell homogenates provides information about the type, amount and structure of biomolecules present inside living cells. However, an essential step is to have the knowledge of behaviour of individual cells, about molecular interactions in space and time to understand the regulatory machinery. This led to improved the novel microscopic techniques, as well as cytochemical staining methods, aiming to provide better resolution, sensitivity, specificity and versatility. Biomolecules as small as nanometer exist in the complex and well-organized microenvironment of cells. They work very efficiently and accurately in the cells. It is very important to study the molecular behaviour under physiological conditions. Single molecule visualization in living cells has been proven useful for quantitative analysis of the dynamics. Single molecule detection is a technology to study biomolecules with a high spatial and temporal resolution, such as the studies on (i) DNA transcription (ii) Enzyme reactions (iii) Molecular motors (iv) Protein dynamics and (v) Cell signaling.

For a single molecule detection there should be considered four things, *i.e.*, high-efficiency collection optics, speed of acquisition, careful elimination of background fluorescence by various means, and the viability of the specimen. Wide-field microscopy is the simplest and most widely used technique. Usually Charged Coupled Device (CCD) allows fast acquistion of the whole field simultaneously. For example, the measure- ment of Ca^{2+} signals in the cytosol and organelles and imaging of dynamic protein tyrosine kinase activities in living cells. Scanning confocal systems are now a commonly used tool for live cell imaging. But its scanning speeds limit acquisition rates. Total internal reflection fluorescence microscopy (TIR-FM) is one of the techniques widely used for single molecule detection *in vivo*. It is a technique used to observe the interfrace between two media with different diffractive indexes such as glass and water. Using the evanescent field for excitation, the excitation depth of a fluorescence microscope can be limited to a vary narrow range. This is one of the most effective ways to reduce background of fluorescence microscopy to achieve single-molecule imaging. Total internal reflection fluorescence correlation spectroscopy (FCS) is a particular example of fluctuation correlation techniques. Smaller molecules will move more quickly through the confocal volume than larger molecules. The fluorescence is measured from the volume. The number density of the fluorosphores in solution can be calculated from the magnitude of the autocorrelation. One important application of FCS in the biochemical sciences is the determination of thermodynamic and kinetic parameters. It has been shown that FCS measurements in living cells are feasible. The most recent FCS work has centered on the determination of chemical rate constants and even probing inside the cell nucleus.

Single-Quantum Dot Trackings (QDS) which are intermediary in size, are more photostable than conventional fluorophores, and have been as promising fluorescent probes. Maxime Dahan et.al. used QDs to track individual glycine receptors (GlyRs) and analyze their lateral dynamics in the neuronal membrane of living cells. The entry of GlyRs into the synapse by diffusion was observed by QD-tagged receptors and further confirmed by electron microscopy imaging. The properties of QDs make it possible to record the mobility of individual molecules at the neuronal surface, even in confined cellular compartments.

Single Molecule Detection of Signaling Molecules

Single molecule imaging is an ideal technology to study molecular mechanisms of biological reactions *in vitro*. Recently, this technology is extended to real-time observation of signal transduction. The early events in signal transduction from the epidermal growth factor (EGF) receptor (EGFR) are dimerization and autophosphorylation of the receptor, induced by binding of EGF.

Single Molecule Detection of Ion Channels

The first visualization of individual membrane proteins in living cells by fluorescence labelled ligands with 40 nm and 3D positional resolution opens new perspectives for the study of cellular organization and processes at the molecular level. The labelling of hongotoxin (HgTX1-Cy5) to the potassium channel in T-lymphocyte cell membranes and employed single dye tracing (SDT) for imaging single ion channels optically leads to resolution of channel positions to within ±40 nm in all three dimensions. The positional resolution along the optical axis (z-direction) was obtained from the accuracy of estimating the position of minimum defocusing for a single molecule. Diagnostic techniques in nuclear medicine use radioactive tracers which emit gamma rays from within the body.

In vitro methods of detection of DNA (nucleic acids) include PCR, Northern hybridization, expressed sequence tags, (EST) differential display and microarray. One class of probe called **molecular becons** are dual labelled oligonucleotide probe with a fluorophore at one end and a quencher at the other end. Hybridization with target nucleic acid opens the hairpen of this probe and physically separates the fluorochrome from quencher allowing a fluorescence signal to be emitted.

Table 38.3 **Methods for Direct Detection of *ds*DNA**

Method	Assay	Sensitivity	Sequence Restriction	Likely to be Useful in Cell
Polyamide				
Fluoresceinconjugate	FISH-like	Highly repeated sequences	None	Yes
Thiazole orange	Oligo targets	1 nM[a]	None	Yes
Triplex				
TISH	FISH-like	Highly repeated sequences	Polypurine tracts	Yes
Padlock-FITC	Spread molecules	Single molecule	Polypurine tracts	No, heat requirement
Padlock-radiolabelled	Southern	< 1 fM	Polypurine tracts	No, heat requirement
YOYO-1	Amplified DNA	4 nM[a]	None	No, intercalator
Protein				
Hin-oxazole yellow	Oligo targets	50 nM[a]	Hin sites	Delivery?
Eco RI-*nano*	Spread molecules	Single molecule	*Eco* RI sites	No, cleavage
GFP-*lac*	Live cell	256 tandern repeats	*lac* sites	Yes
SEER-GFP	Oligo targets	2.5 mM[a]	Few	Yes
SEER-LAC	Oligo targets	20 nM	Few	Yes
mCpG-SEER	Oligo targets	50 nM	Few	Yes

'Lowest concentration used in study, but lower concentrations were not examined'.

In Situ Hybridization

***In situ* hybridization** (ISH) is a type of hybridization that uses a labelled complementary DNA or RNA strand (*i.e.*, probe) to localize a specific DNA or RNA sequence in a portion or section of tissue (*in situ*), or, if the tissue is small enough (*e.g.*, plant seeds, *Drosophila's* embryos), in the entire tissue (whole mount ISH). This is distinct from immuno- histochemistry, which usually localizes proteins in tissue sections. DNA ISH can be used to determine the structure of chromosomes. Fluorescent DNA ISH (FISH) can, for example, be used in medical diagnostics to assess chromosomal integrity. RNA ISH (hybridization histochemistry) is used to measure and localize *m*RNAs and other transcripts within tissue sections or whole mounts. For hybridization histochemistry, sample cells and tissues are usually treated to fix the target transcripts in place and to increase access of the probe. As noted above, the probe is either a labelled complementary DNA or, now most commonly, a complementary RNA (rib probe). The probe hybridizes to the target sequence at elevated temperature, and then the excess probe is washed away (after prior hydrolysis using RNase in the case of unhybridized, excess RNA probe). Solution parameters such as temperature, salt and/or detergent concentration can be manipulated to remove any non-identical interactions (*i.e.*, only exact sequence matches will remain bound). Then, the probe that was labelled with either radio, fluorescent or antigen-labelled bases (*e.g.*, digoxigenin) is localized and quantified in the tissue using either autoradiography, fluorescence microscopy or immuno-histochemistry, respectively. ISH can also use two or more probes, labelled with radioactivity or the other non-radioactive labels, to simultaneously detect two or more transcripts.

FISH (Fluorescence *in situ* Hybridization)

FISH (fluorescence *in situ* hybridization) is a cytogenetic technique developed by biomedical researchers in the early 1980s that is used to detect and localize the presence or absence of specific DNA sequences on chromosomes. FISH uses fluorescent probes that bind to only those parts of the chromosome with which they show a high degree of sequence complementarity. Fluorescence microscopy can be used to find out where the fluorescent probe bound to the chromosomes. FISH is often used for finding specific features in DNA for use in genetic counselling, medicine, and species identification. FISH can also be used to detect and localize specific *m*RNAs within tissue samples. In this context, it can help define the spatial-temporal patterns of gene expression within cells and tissues.

Probes

Probes are often derived from fragments of DNA that were isolated, purified and amplified for use in the Human Genome Project. The size of the human genome is so large, compared to the length that could be sequenced directly, that it was necessary to divide the genome into fragments (in the eventual analysis, these fragments were put into order by digesting a copy of each fragment into still smaller fragments using sequence-specific endonucleases, measuring the size of each small fragment using size-exclusion chromatography, and using that information to determine where the large fragments overlapped one another). To preserve the fragments with their individual DNA sequences, the fragments were added into a system of continually replicating bacteria populations. Clonal populations of bacteria, each population maintaining a single artificial chromosome, are stored in various laboratories around the world. The artificial chromosomes (BAC) can be grown, extracted, and labeled, in any lab. These fragments are on the order of 100 thousand base-pairs, and are the basis for most FISH probes.

Preparation and Hybridization Process

First, a probe is constructed. The probe must be large enough to hybridize specifically with its target but not so large as to impede the hybridization process. The probe is tagged directly with fluorophores, with targets for antibodies or with biotin. Tagging can be done in various ways, such as nick translation, or PCR using tagged nucleotides.

Then, an interphase or metaphase chromosome pre- paration is produced. The chromosomes are firmly attached to a substrate, usually glass. Repetitive DNA sequences must be blocked by adding short fragments of DNA to the sample. The probe is then applied to the chromosome DNA and incubated for approximately 12 hours while hybridizing. Several wash steps remove all unhybridized or partially-hybridized probes. The results are then visualized and quantified using a microscope that is capable of exciting the dye and recording images.

If the fluorescent signal is weak, amplification of the signal may be necessary in order to exceed the detection threshold of the microscope. Fluorescent signal strength depends on many factors such as probe labelling efficiency, the type of probe, and the type of dye. The dye incorporation rate can be quantified photometric with specialized nano-volume photometer (starting with 0.3 μL probe volume). Fluorescently tagged antibodies or streptavidin are bound to the dye molecule. These secondary components are selected so that they have a strong signal.

FISH experiments designed to detect or localize gene expression within cells and tissues rely on the use of a reporter gene, such as one expressing green fluorescent protein, to provide the fluorescence signal.

Variations on Probes and Analysis

FISH is a very general technique. The differences between the various FISH techniques are usually due to variations in the sequence and labeling of the probes; and how they are used in combination. These few modifications make possible all FISH techniques.

Probe size is important because longer probes hybridize less specifically than shorter probes. The overlap defines the resolution of detectable features. For example, if the goal of an experiment is to detect the breakpoint of a translocation, then the overlap of the probes — the degree to which one DNA sequence is contained in the adjacent probes — defines the minimum window in which the breakpoint may be detected.

The mixture of probe sequences determines the type of feature the probe can detect. Probes that hybridize along an entire chromosome are used to count the number of a certain chromosome, show translocations, or identify extra-chromosomal fragments of chromatin. This is often called "whole-chromosome painting" or GISH. If every possible probe is used, every chromosome (the whole genome) would be marked fluorescently, which would not be particularly useful for determining features of individual sequences. However, a mixture of smaller probes can be created that is specific to a particular region (locus) of DNA; these mixtures are used to detect deletion mutations. When combined with a specific colour, a locus-specific probe mixture is used to detect very specific translocations. Special locus-specific probe mixtures are often used to count chromosomes, by binding to the centrome ricregions of chromosomes, which are unique enough to identify each chromosome (with the exception of chromosome 13, 14, 21, 22).

A variety of other techniques use mixtures of differently-coloured probes. A range of colours in mixtures of fluorescent dyes can be detected, so each human chromosome can be identified by a characteristic color using whole-chromosome probe mixtures and a variety of ratios of colors. Although there are more chromosomes than easily-distinguishable fluorescent dye colours, ratios of probe mixtures can be used to create secondary colours. Similar to comparative genomic hybridization, the probe mixture for the secondary colours is created by mixing the correct ratio of two sets of differently-coloured probes for the same chromosome. This technique is sometimes called M-FISH. The same physics that make a variety of colours possible for M-FISH can be used for the detection of translocations. That is, colours that are adjacent appear to overlap; a secondary colour is observed. Some assays are designed so that the secondary colour will be present or absent in cases of interest. An example is the detection of BCR/ABL translocations, where the secondary colour indicates disease. This variation is often called double-fusion FISH or D-FISH. In the opposite situation—where the absence of the secondary color is pathological—is illustrated by an assay used to investigate translocations where only one of the breakpoints is known or constant. Locus-specific probes are made for one side of the breakpoint and the other intact chromosome. In normal cells, the secondary colour is observed, but only the primary colour is observed when the translocation occurs. This technique is sometimes called "break-apart FISH".

Genomic *In Situ* Hybridization (GISH)

When total genomic DNA is used as a probe in hybridization experiments to chromosomal DNA in situ the process is known as GISH.Genomic *in situ* hybridization (GISH) is a molecular cytogenetic technique which now allows chromosomes from different parents or ancestors to be distinguished by means of differential hybridization of entire genomic probes. Using this technique in hybrids it is possible to determine the genome origin of paired and unpaired chromosomes in metaphase-I configurations.

Exercise

1. An amino acid contains no ionizable group in its side chain (*R*). It is titrated from pH 0 to 14. Which of the following ionizable state is not observed during the entire titration in the pH ranges 0-14?

(a) $H_2N—C(R)(H)—COOH$ (b) $H_2N—C(R)(H)—COO^-$

(c) $H_2\overset{+}{N}—C(R)(H)—COOH$ (d) $H_2\overset{+}{N}—C(R)(H)—COO^-$

2. Why is serotyping used?
(a) To identify, classify and sub-group certain bacteria into categories
(b) To determine the susceptibility of sheep red blood cells to complement
(c) To identify and diagnose a disease
(d) To verify the presence of specific antibodies that react with specific antigens

3. What is the fundamental tool in immunofluorescence testing?
(a) Specific antigen
(b) Red blood cells
(c) Fluorescent monoclonal antibody
(d) Fluorescent polyclonal antibody

4. What is injected into a patient when the tuberculin skin test is performed?
(a) Complement (b) Monoclonal antibodies
(c) Sheep red blood cells (d) Antigen

5. Which of the following counter is generally used in RIA?
(a) Alpha counter (b) Beta counter
(c) Gamma counter (d) Delta counter

6. Which of the following is a neutral stain?
(a) Picric acid (b) Gmiemsa
(c) Neutral red (d) Malachite green

7. Which of the following biomolecule show autofluorescence?
(a) Collagen fibres (b) Chlorophyll
(c) Both (a) and (b) (d) None of these

8. ELISA is used to detect viruses where the key reagent is
(a) catalase (b) DNA probe
(c) RNAse (d) alkaline phosphatase

9. Which of the following statement is incorrect?
(a) Birds, like mammals, have a 4-chambered heart, with complete separation of oxygenated and deoxygenated blood
(b) Birds tend to have larger hearts than mammals (relative to body size and mass)

(c) Avian hearts also tend to pump more blood per unit time than mammalian hearts. In other words, cardiac output (amount of blood pumped per minute) for birds is typically greater than that for mammals of the same body mass
(d) Like mammals bird's red blood cells are non-nucleated

10. The common fixative is
(a) formalin (b) glyoxal
(c) Bouin's fluid (d) All of these

11. For histological studies tissues are sectioned by using
(a) blade (b) razor
(c) knife (d) microtome

12. The application of FISH and GISH involve
(a) chromosome mapping and genome analysis
(b) phylogenetic relationship and analysis of somoclonal variations
(c) detection of alien chromatin and chromosomal aberrations
(d) All of the above

13. Which of the following statement is incorrect regarding *in situ* hybridization techniques?
(a) Application of FISH to somaclonal variants is a useful tool for identifying and understanding changes during the tissue culture process
(b) Closely related genomes in certain allopolyploid cannot be discriminated using GISH technique
(c) Multicolour or FISH can only be used successfully on polyploids with at least one known progenitor species
(d) Multicolour FISH is highly sensitive and show a higher degree of detection resolution than single colour FISH

14. Immunoprecipitation involves the purification of
(a) antigen
(b) antibody
(c) antigen and antibodies
(d) antigen-antibody complexes

15. Which of the goals is achieved by fixatives, used in electron microscopy?
(a) Stopping metabolism
(b) Fixing structures of organelles and molecules in their current position
(c) Making material accessible and stable during further processing
(d) All of the above

16. Which of the following additive is added to the fixative of EM to better preserve membranes and their contrast?
(a) Ca^{2+} and Li^{+} ions (b) Ferrocyanide
(c) Tannic and picric acid (d) All of these

17. Enzyme-linked immunosorbent assay (ELISA), is a
(a) dry assay (b) wet assay
(c) *in-silico* assay (d) *in vivo* assay

18. In ELISA which of the molecule is adsorbed on the solid stationary phase?
(a) Enzyme (b) Antigen
(c) Antibody (d) Both (b) and (c)

19. The ELISA has been used as a diagnostic tool in
(a) medicine (b) plant pathology
(c) quality control (d) All of these

20. Arrange the various steps as they are performed in sandwich ELISA
I. Antigen binding
II. Analysis
III. Polyclonal antibody binding
IV. Secondary antibody binding
V. Enzyme substrate
VI. Monoclonal antibody binding
VII. Spectro-photometric readings
(a) VI, V, I, VII, II, III, IV (b) VI, I, V, VII, II, III, IV
(c) VI, I, III, IV, V, VII, II (d) III, IV, I, V, II, VI, VII

21. Which of the ELISA contain the following steps
Antigen binding, blocking, primary antibody, secondary antibody, enzyme substrate, calorimetric reading?

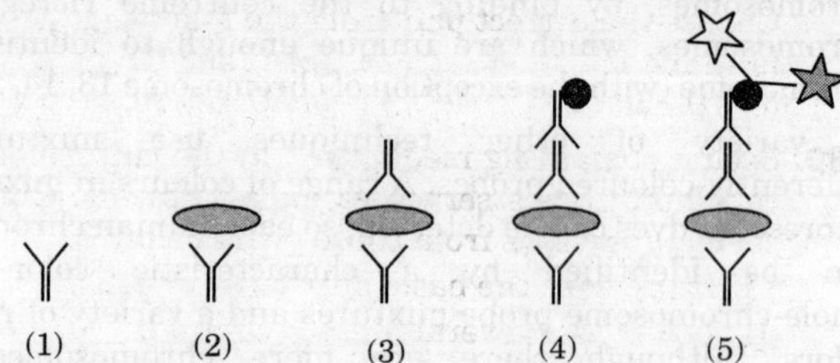

(a) Direct ELISA (b) Indirect ELISA
(c) Competitive ELISA (d) Sandwich ELISA

22. The above diagram is a representative of
(a) indirect ELISA (b) sandwich ELISA
(c) direct ELISA (d) non-competitive ELISA

23. Immuno-fluorescence is a technique used for
(a) electron microscope
(b) light microscope
(c) confocal microscope
(d) light microscopy with a fluorescence microscope

24. Which of the following membrane is used for the transfer of protein in western blot?
(a) Nitrocellulose
(b) PVDF
(c) Both (a) and (b)
(d) None of the above

25. Which of the following stain is used for checking the transfer of proteins onto the membrane after electrophoresis?
(a) Commassie Brilliant Blue G-250
(b) Commassie Brilliant Blue R-250
(c) Amido Black
(d) Ponceau S

26. Which of the following statement is incorrect regarding ELISPOT?
(a) Conceptually it is a modified version of the EIA and this assay was originally developed to enumerate B-cells secreting antigen-specific antibodies
(b) ELISPOT assay allows visualization of the secretory product of individual activated or responding cells
(c) ELISPOT assay provides both qualitative (type of immune protein) and quantitative (number of responding cells) information
(d) ELISPOT assay is comparatively less sensitive then ELISA

27. The basic difference between ELISA and RIA lies in
(a) primary antibody
(b) blocking agent
(c) type of microtitre plate
(d) label conjugated to secondary antibodies

28. The advantage of FISH over ISH is
(a) faster detection (b) higher resolution
(c) sensitivity and speed (d) All of these

29. The culture fluids of 1000 to 5000 colonies of hybridoma are screened for monoclonal antibody by
I. western blot analysis.
II. antigen capture analysis.
III. northern blot analysis.
IV. antibody capture analysis.
Choose the correct pair from the following
(a) I and II (b) II and III
(c) III and IV (d) II and IV

30. Serum containing media used in the culture of animal cells and tissues serves various functions. Choose the correct functions from those given below:
I. It provides the basic nutrients for cells.
II. It provides several binding proteins.
III. It increases the viscosity of medium and thereby, protects cells from mechanical damages.
IV. It helps in the proteolysis of trypsinised cells.
(a) I, II and III (b) I and IV
(c) I, III and IV (d) All of these

31. Match list I with list II and select the correct codes.

List I	List II
A. Western blot	1. Detect and localize specific DNA sequences
B. ELISA	2. Provide quantitative information individual cells
C. Flow cytometry	3. Detection of protein with antibody
D. Fish	4. Proteins not separated by electrophoresis are separated

Codes

	A	B	C	D
(a)	2	3	1	4
(b)	3	4	2	1
(c)	1	2	3	4
(d)	4	2	4	3

Answers

1. (a)	**2.** (a)	**3.** (c)	**4.** (d)	**5.** (c)	**6.** (c)	**7.** (c)	**8.** (d)	**9.** (d)	**10.** (d)
11. (d)	**12.** (d)	**13.** (d)	**14.** (d)	**15.** (d)	**16.** (d)	**17.** (b)	**18.** (d)	**19.** (d)	**20.** (c)
21. (b)	**22.** (b)	**23.** (d)	**24.** (c)	**25.** (d)	**26.** (d)	**27.** (d)	**28.** (d)	**29.** (c)	**30.** (a)
31. (b)									

39 Biophysical Methods

Light can be described as a wave. This wave has an electric component and a magnetic component which are perpendicular to each other. Electromagnetic radiation exhibits a direction of propagation and wave-like properties, *i.e.*, oscillations. The energy of electromagnetic radiation is defined as:

$$E = hc/\lambda = h\nu$$

where, E = Energy, h = Planck's constant, c = The speed of light, λ = The wavelength and ν = frequency. Light behaves both as a wave and as a particle.

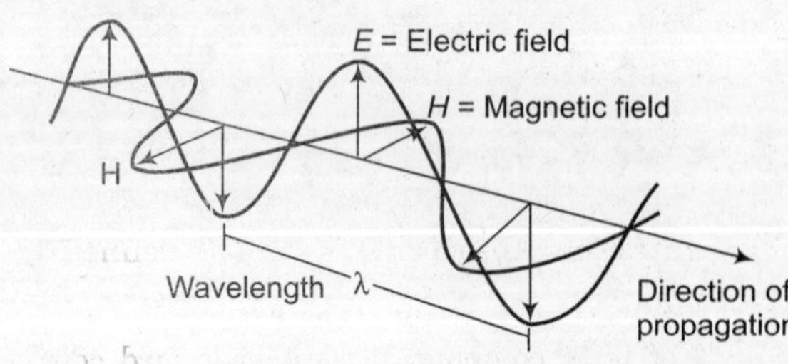

Fig. 39.1 Nature of light

Syllabus

- Analysis of Biomolecules Using UV/Visible, Spectroscopy Fluorescence, Circular Dichroism Spectroscopy, NMR Spectroscopy and ESR Spectroscopy, Structure Determination Using X-ray Diffraction and NMR; Analysis Using Light Scattering, Different Types of Mass Spectrometry and Surface Plasmon Resonance Methods.

Analysis of Biomolecules Using UV/Visible Spectroscopy

The conceptual particle of light is called a photon and is represented by $h\nu$. Electromagnetic radiation exhibits a wide spectrum and specific ranges of wavelengths have names. The energy of electromagnetic radiation is inversely proportional to its wavelength. When a light wave encounters a particle or molecule, it can be scattered (*i.e.*, direction changed), absorbed (energy transferred) or unaffected.

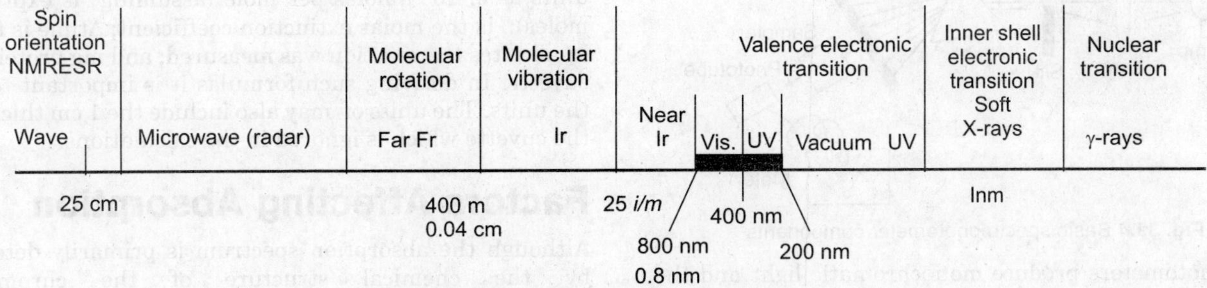

Fig. 39.2 Electromagnetic radiation spectrum

Molecules only absorb discrete packets of energy or quanta and absorption occurs when the energy of the photon corresponds to differences between energy levels in that particular molecule. These discrete energy levels, called electronic energy levels, are a property of the particular molecule and are determined by the spatial distribution of the electrons. Absorption of the energy from the photon elevates the molecule to an excited electronic state by causing an electron to move from one orbit to another. These electronic energy levels are further sub-divided into vibrational levels. The vibrational levels correspond to stretching and bending of various covalent bonds. The transitions to the excited state can occur between different vibrational levels giving a range of energy that can be absorbed by the molecule. A molecule or substance that absorbs light is called a chromophore. Chromophores exhibit unique absorption spectra and can be defined by a wavelength of maximum absorption or λ_{max}, of a broad absorption band due to the vibrational levels. The absorption spectra can consists of several absorption maxima of various amplitudes. A large number of biological molecules absorb light in the visible and ultraviolet (UV) range. The net affect of absorption is that the intensity of the light decreases as it passes through a solution containing a chromophore. The amount of light absorbed depends on the nature of the chromophore, the concentration of the chromophore, the thickness of the sample, and the conditions (*e.g.*, pH, solvent, etc.) under which absorption is measured.

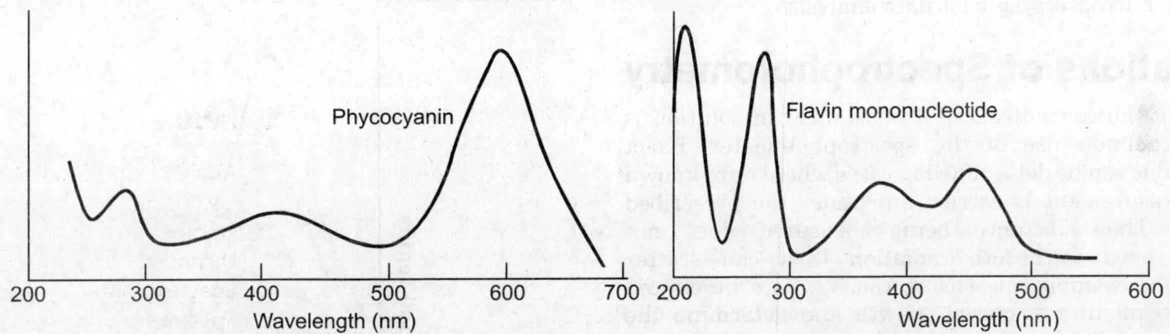

Fig. 39.3 Absorption spectrum of phycocyanin and flavin mononucleotide

Absorption is governed by the **Beer-Lambert** Law:

$$I = I_0\ 10^{-\varepsilon dc} \text{ or } \log (I/I_0) = -\varepsilon dc$$

Where, I = final light intensity, I_0 = initial light intensity,
= molar extinction coefficient, d = thickness and c = molar concentration. Absorption (A) will be defined by:

$$A = -\log(I/\ I_0) = \varepsilon dc$$

The molar extinction coefficient (ε) is defined as the A of 1 M of pure compound under standard conditions and reflects something about the nature of the chromophore. The units of ε are liter/cm·mole. However, the extinction coefficient can be expressed in other units. For example, it can be expressed in terms of mM concentration. The thickness of the sample (d) is almost always 1 cm and therefore, can be ignored in calculations. Sometimes, though, the extinction coefficient units is expressed in cm^2/mole (by converting liters to cubic centimeters) and care should be taken in making calculations. In cases where the molecular weight of the substance is not known, or varies, $\varepsilon^{1\%}$ is used as the extinction coefficient. $\varepsilon^{1\%}$ is defined as the A of a 1% (w/v) solution. It is important to precisely record the units of when looking it up or determining it experimentally since, these units will determine the concentration. It is also important to record the conditions (*e.g.*, pH, solvent, temperature, etc.) for an extinction coefficient.

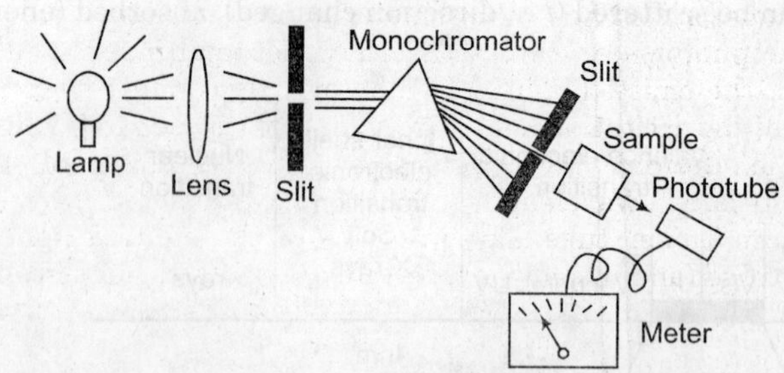

Fig. 39.4 Basic spectrophotometer components

Spectrophotometers produce monochromatic light and then accurately measure the light intensity. The major components of a spectrophotometer are the light source, a monochromator, sample holder, a light detector (phototube), and a meter. In most instruments a tungsten lamp is used for the visible range and either high pressure H2 or D2 lamps are used for UV range. Monochromatic light is generated by either 1) a movable prism, 2) a diffraction gradient or 3) filters. Monochromatic light is projected through the sample and then measured by a photomultiplier tube. A photomultiplier tube converts the energy of the light photons into electrons (see appendix). The voltage resulting from these electrons is measured by a meter and converted to an absorbance value. The Io (initial intensity) is determined by calibrating the instrument with a 'buffer blank'. The relative difference in the light intensity between the blank and the sample is then expressed as the absorbance (A). Spectrophotometers often include accessories such as chart recorders or microprocessors for data analysis.

Applications of Spectrophotometry

Determining the concentration of substances in solution is the most common use of the spectrophotometer. Exact concentrations can be determined in cases where ε are known and the measurement is carried out under the prescribed conditions. The substance being measured does not necessarily need to absorb radiation if it can scatter radiation. For example, measuring the A_{600} is a quick and easy way to monitor bacterial growth and determine the number of bacteria in cultures. In addition, since compounds exhibit unique absorption profiles, spectrophotometry can also be used to identify unknown compounds. Spectrophotometry is also a convenient method to measure enzyme activity in cases where the substrate and the product exhibit different λmax. Either the disappearance of substrate or the appearance of product over time is measured. The change in the Aλ per unit time (generally per minute) is calculated. The change in A of a blank (= identical sample without enzyme source) is subtracted from this value. The enzyme activity in terms of amount of product formed per unit time per mg protein can be calculated by factoring in the amount of enzyme, dilution factors and the extinction coefficient (see example in appendix). A typical example of a formula for the calculation of enzyme activity is:

Activity = $(\Delta A_{sample} - \Delta A_{blank})\cdot volume\cdot 10^6/\varepsilon\cdot\Delta time\cdot mg\cdot protein$ where, activity is expressed as μmoles product formed/min/mg protein; ΔA_{sample} is the change in absorbance of the sample containing enzyme; ΔA_{blank} is the change in absorbance of a sample containing everything except the enzyme; the volume in the cuvette expressed in the same units as ε; 10^6 μmoles per mole (assuming is expressed in moles); is the molar extinction coefficient; Δtime is the time in minutes the reaction was measured; and mg protein in the cuvette. In deriving such formulas it is important to match the units. The units of may also include the 1 cm thickness of the cuvette which is ignored in the calculations.

Factors Affecting Absorption

Although the absorption spectrum is primarily determined by the chemical structure of the chromophore, environmental factors can affect λ_{max} and ε. The pH determines the ionization of chromophore which in many cases will affect the absorption properties of a chromophore. Indicator dyes and pH paper are examples of this phenomenon. The polarity of the solvent or neighboring molecules can also affect absorption. Because of this effect, spectrophotometry can also be used to determine structural features of macromolecules. For example, whether particular amino acid residues are buried within the internal portion of proteins or exposed on the aqueous solvent at the protein surface can be determined by spectrophotometry. The relative orientation of neighboring chromophores also affects absorption. Hypochromism of nucleic acids is an example of orientation effects. The absorbance (*i.e.,* ε) decreases as free nucleotides (dotted line) are polymerized into single-stranded DNA (dashed line) and decreases further in double-stranded DNA (solid line).

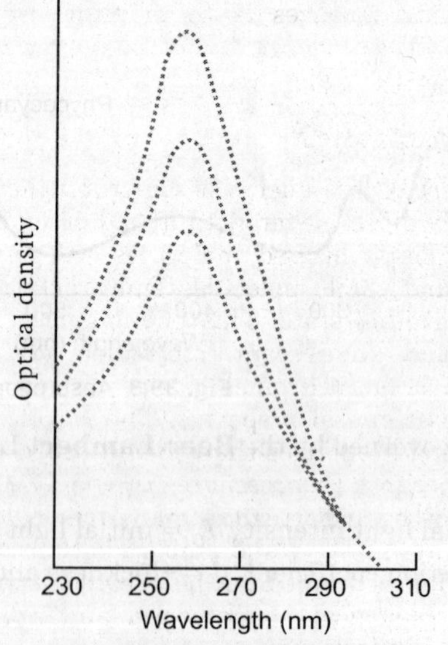

Fig. 39.5 Spectra of T_7 DNA

Variations in Spectrophotometry

It is also possible to use other spectra besides UV/visible range. For example, vibrations between the atoms of molecules can be analyzed using infrared (IR) and Raman spectrophotometries. Many molecules will exhibit characteristic 'signatures' and therefore, can be identified. Light can be polarized so that all of the waves are in the same orientation. The study of the absorption of polarized light can yield more information about the structure of molecules if the chromophores have optically active centers. Circular Dichroism (CD) measures the ability of chromophores to differentially absorb left and right circularly polarized light. Optical Rotary Dispersion (ORD) measures the ability of a optically active chromophore to rotate plane polarized light. Both CD and ORD are useful in structural studies or proteins and nucleic acids. For example, it is possible to approximate the amount of α-helix, β-sheet and random coil in proteins.

Table 39.1 **Other Forms of Spectrophotometry**

Spectrophotometry	Comment
Infrared (IR)	Vibrational
Raman	Levels
Optical Rotary Dispersion (ORD)	Polarize
Circular Dichorism (CD)	Light
Nuclear Magnetic Resonance (NMR)	Magnetic
Electron Spin Resonance (ESR)	Moments

The effects of molecules on the magnetic component of radiation can also be analyzed. Nuclear magnetic resonance (NMR) is a spectroscopic method capable of yielding information on the structure of molecules, interactions between molecules and molecular motion. This method is based upon the principle that a spinning charge (*i.e.,* the nucleus) generates a magnetic field. Similarly, an electron also possesses a spin magnetic moment which can be analyzed by electron spin resonance (ESR). A common use for ESR in biological sciences is to monitor the fluidity of membranes.

Fluorescence

Molecules absorbing the energy of electromagnetic radiation (*i.e.,* photons) will be elevated to a higher energy level or excited state. These excited molecules will return to the ground state and some molecules emit radiation on their return to the ground state. This phenomenon is known as fluorescence and fluorescent molecules are known as fluorochromes. Fluorochromes have distinct absorption spectra as well as emission spectra. The wavelengths of the emitted radiation are longer than the absorbed wavelengths (*i.e.,* lower energy). Fluorescence is widely used in the biological research. In particular, many molecules absorb in the ultraviolet range (UV) and emit radiation in the visible range. These fluorochromes can be used as sensitive probes to investigate biological phenomenon and are utilized in many different applications.

Enzyme Assays and Fluorometers

Enzyme substrates are available in which either the product or the substrate is fluorescent. As in the case of spectrophotometry, this provides a convenient method to either follow the appearance of product or the disappearance of the substrate. In general fluorescent substrates provide greater sensitivity than conventional spectrophotometric assays. The amount of fluorescence is measured using a fluorometer. The fluorometer is similar to a spectrophotometer, except that the photomultiplier tube to detect the emitted light is located at a right angle from the path of the excitation light. The sample is exposed to UV light of the desired wavelength and emitted light of the appropriate wavelength range is detected by a photomultiplier tube. The intensity of the emitted light is quantified and usually expressed as relative fluorescence units.

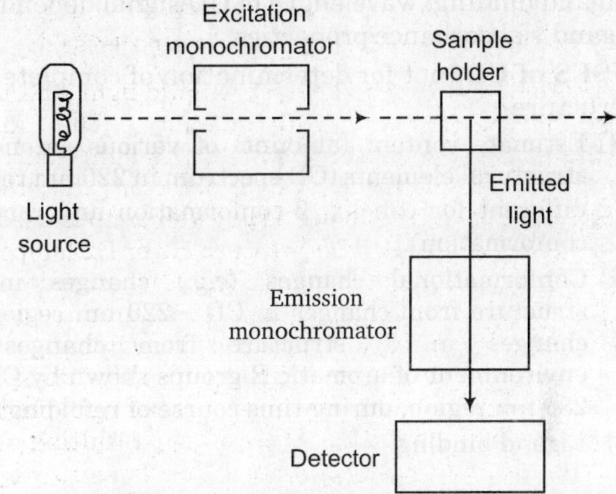

Fig. 39.6 Diagrammatic sketch of fluorometer

Circular Dichorism (CD) Spectroscopy

1. CD measures **interactions** of polarized light with **chiral protein components** that are formed into different types of 2° structure (asymmetric), and with other chromophores (ligands or prosthetic groups or aromatic *R* groups) that are asymmetrically bound.
   - **(i)** Unpolarized light consists of waves vibrating in all planes perpendicular to the direction of travel.
   - **(ii) Plane polarized light** has waves vibrating in a single plane. In plane polarized light, the varying electric field of the radiation has a fixed orientation.
   - **(iii)** In **circularly polarized light,** the direction of polarization rotates with the frequency of the radiation. If you observe a circularly polarized beam of light coming toward you, the electric field can be rotating in either a clockwise direction (right circularly polarized light) or a counter clockwise direction (left circularly polarized light).
2. Asymmetric molecules and components of molecules (*e.g.,* D and L-amino acids; right and left-handed protein helices; etc.) preferentially absorb either left or right circularly polarized light.
3. CD=different degrees of absorption of left and right circularly polarized light:

$$\Delta A = \frac{A_L - A_R}{A}$$

where, A_L is the absorbance for left circularly polarized light, A_R is the absorbance for right circularly polarized light and A

is the absorbance for unpolarized light. Since, A can be either positive or negative, a CD spectrum is unlike a normal absorption spectrum.

1. **Wavelength region for CD signal = same as absorbance for that chromophore:** ~185-240 nm (far UV) for 2° and 3° structure (**peptide bond absorbance,** aromatic *R* groups, disulphide bonds)~260-290 nm (near UV) for 3° structure (aromatic *R* groups).
2. Ligand binding: wavelength of CD signal depends on ligand's absorbance properties.
3. **USES of CD** (not for determination of complete 3-D structure).
   (i) Estimate content (amount) of various secondary structural elements (CD spectrum in 220 nm region different for α-helix, β-conformation and random conformation).
   (ii) Conformational changes (*e.g.,* changes in 2° structure from changes in CD ~220 nm region or changes in 3° structure from changes in environment of aromatic R groups shown by CD in 280 nm region, during time course of refolding).
   (iii) Ligand binding.

Electron Spin Resonance (ESR)

Electron Spin Resonance (ESR) or Electron Paramagnetic Resonance (EPR) as it is often called, is a magnetic resonance technique just like NMR. Unlike NMR, ESR is based on the spin of the electron rather than the spin of a nucleon. When placed in an external magnetic field, the spin of an unpaired electron can take on one of two orientations: aligned with, and opposed to the magnetic field. Just like in NMR, a photon with energy equal to the energy difference between the levels will cause a transition between the levels. ESR spectroscopy is a study of matter based of the energies absorbed in ESR. ESR imaging is the study of the spatial distribution of ESR signal bearing substances. Very few substances in nature have unpaired electrons. Therefore, very few substances can be studied with ESR. Nitroxide spin probes and some transition metals have an ESR signal. These substances have been studied directly by ESR, but are commonly used to probe biologic processes with ESR. Due to the much smaller mass of an electron compared to a nucleon, the electron's gyromagnetic ratio is about 658 times that of the proton's. Therefore, higher frequencies are used in ESR compared to NMR for the corresponding magnetic field strength. For a magnetic field of 1T electron spin resonance occurs approximately at 28.026 GHz, which is in the microwave region of the electromagnetic spectrum. There are four essential components in an ESR spectrometer:

1. A monochromatic microwave source.
2. A waveguide for guiding the microwave power to the sample.
3. A cavity designed to ensure a proper coupling between the sample and the incoming wave.
4. A detector for microwave power to detect the response of the sample to microwave irradiation.

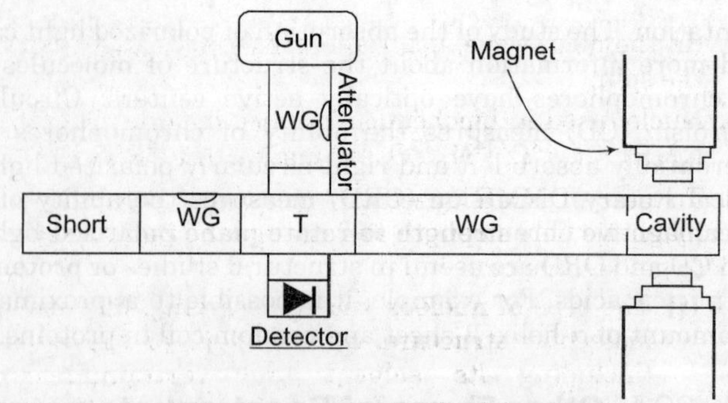

Fig. 39.7 Diagrammatic sketch of ESR

Electron spin spectroscopy is also known as Electron Paramagnetic Resonance (EPR) or Electron Magnetic Resonance (EMR) and measures the transition frequency between different electron spin states. The energy difference between an electron spin state ms = –1/2 and ms = 1/2 in a reasonably strong magnetic field of 1 Tesla is $\Delta E = 1.86.10^{-23}$ J corresponding to a frequency of 28 GHz. As opposed to the MHz frequencies encountered in NMR, the generation of such GHz frequencies is a major challenge and it is not easy to go to the highest possible magnetic fields and RF frequencies. ESR is therefore performed in a wide variety of magnetic field strength and with a correspondingly diverse set of RF radiation sources, *e.g.,* 'L-band' spectrometers in the 1 GHz range and "W-band" spectrometers in the 100 GHz range. Some spectrometers sweep the RF field frequency, others the magnetic field strength, and an increasing number of experiments is performed with pulsed fields and using Fourier transform methods as discussed for NMR spectroscopy. The excitation frequencies in ESR spectra depend on the total magnetic moment. The energy levels of a bound, unpaired electron are therefore different from that of a free electron primarily due to the electron orbital angular momentum. The orbital angular momentum is rather small for main group elements (S and P-orbitals), but can be very large for transition metals (D-orbitals). In the later case, the transition energies are strongly affected by the surrounding field of the ligands. ESR is therefore, a sensitive probe for the local environment of a transition metal and can be used to determine the oxidation state and coordination of metal centers in proteins. An example is the oxidation of poisonous compounds by the iron-porphyrin protein P-450, an enzyme found in the liver. ESR also observes the coupling of electron to nuclear spins (hyperfine coupling), carrying information about the local environment of the electronic spin probe. The information content in the hyperfine coupling is quasi identical to that in NMR spectra, but the electron acts as a local probe only for nuclear spins in close vicinity.

Nuclear Magnetic Resonance (NMR) Spectroscopy

1. **Basis** A spinning charged particle (in this case, a nucleus) behaves as a magnet, and can interact with an externally imposed magnetic field such that absorbance of electromagnetic radiation of appropriate energy

(in the microwave, *i.e.*, radio, frequency range) can flip the spin.

2. Nuclei used in biochemical studies include ^{1}H (proton NMR), ^{2}H, ^{13}C, ^{14}N, ^{17}O, ^{31}P and ^{19}F (in ^{19}F-Tyr).
3. To get an NMR spectrum (in ppm), you 'sit' on a magnetic field strength and change the radio frequency to get resonance.
   (i) The type of nucleus you're observing, but also the molecular structural environment of the nucleus (including its solvent and surroundings in 3-dimensional space) affect the width and position (position = chemical shift) of the NMR signal (peak) for that nucleus.
   (ii) Interaction with a nearby nucleus within the molecule can cause spin coupling, which is seen as splitting of the NMR signal (double peak).
   (iii) Altering the spin on one nucleus can affect the spin on a nearby nucleus (< ~5Å away), and for small proteins it is possible by NMR to do enough distance measurements between nuclei within the tertiary structure to determine the entire 3-dimensional structure.

Uses of NMR

(i) Complete 3-D structure of small proteins in solution (< 25,000 daltons).
(ii) Conformational changes (*e.g.*, during folding).
(iii) Determination of pK_a of an ionizable group, *e.g.*, His.
(iv) Follow ligand binding.
(v) Dynamics (motion in solution), *e.g.*, Tyr and Phe ring flips.

Table 39.2 **Protein Components and Uses of Various Spectroscopic Techniques**

Type	Protein Component	Use
UV-vis spectroscopy		
Absorbance	• Peptide bonds (~220 nm)	• Determine protein concentration
	• Aromatic residues [esp. W (280 nm), (Y)]	• Conformational changes
	• Some ligands and prosthetic groups	• Ligand binding
Fluorescence	• W [$1_{max, ex}$ = 280 m, $1_{max, em}$ = ~ 340 nm]	• Conformational changes
	• Some ligans and prosthetic groups	• Ligand binding
Circular Dichorism (CD)	• Secondary structure (180-240 nm) (peptide bonds)	• 2° structure (amount and type) (far UV)
	• Tertiary structure (environment of aromatic *R* groups) (260-300 nm)	• Conformational changes (2° and 3° structural changes)
	• Ligands and prosthetic groups	• Ligand binding
NMR	• Nuclei: protons (1H, esp. in aromatic residues and His) but also ^{2}H, ^{13}C, ^{14}N, ^{17}O, ^{31}P and ^{19}F (natural abundance or isotopically labelled proteins or ligands)	• Complete 3-D structure (only of small proteins) • Conformational changes • Ligand binding, including pH titrations (pK_a determination) Dynamics (motions in structure)

Structure Determination Using X-ray Diffraction

The secondary structures of proteins structure of DNA double helix and RNA, structures of lipids, membranes and polysaccharides are not simply derived. There are many techniques to study different aspects of structures of cellular molecules, but two techniques allow a resolution at the level of distinguishing individual atoms. These are X-ray crystallography (used to determine the structure of inorganic and organic crystals) and Nuclear Magnetic Resonance (used to measures the distances between atomic nuclei, rather than the electron density in a molecule) techniques.

X-Ray crystallography was first used for the elucidation of salt crystal structure, which for example gave Linus Pauling the instrumentation to study atomic distances from which he developed his theory of the chemical bond (combining structural information with quantum mechanical calculations). It makes use of the diffraction pattern of X-rays that are shot through an object X-rays have a wavelength of 0.2 Å to 2.0 Å. The wave length, as in an optical microscope, determines the resolution limit of half the applied wave length. The pattern is determined by the electron density within the crystal. The diffraction is the result of an interaction with the high energy X-rays and the electrons in the atom. The diffraction of parallel X-rays from an object containing thousands of unit molecules arranged in a regular lattice results in the enhancement and cancellation of the diffracted waves and a resulting pattern of this vectorial process can be correlated with the distribution of the electrons in the crystal.

This technique requires the growth of protein crystals up to 1 mm in size from a highly purified protein source. Crystal growth is an experimental technique and there exists no rules about the optimal conditions for a protein solution to result in a good protein crystal. Water soluble proteins are easier to crystallize than membrane proteins. The membrane proteins tend to precipitate out of solution due to unfavourable protein-protein and protein-solute interactions. The presence of detergents often interferes with regular arrangements of the protein contain large extra-membranous domains, these water soluble domains can be cleaved off from the membrane buried domain and crystallized individually. X-rays that interact with an electron cause it to oscillate. Oscillating electrons serve as a new source of X-rays that propagate away from the stimulated electron. The waves of neighboring electrons super impose and depending on their being in phase or out of phase result in a signal or in no signal at all. Diffraction by a crystal can be regarded as the reflection of the primary beam by sets of parallel planes that define the dimensions of the unit cell (the smallest repetitive pattern) of the crystal. The relationship between reflection angle, Q, the distance between the planes, d and the wavelength, λ, is given by Bragg's law:

$$\lambda = 2d \sin Q$$

By Fourier transformation the 2-dimensional distribution of the diffraction pattern can be calculated back into a 3-dimensional space of the electron distribution causing the diffraction. The distances between the spots inversely correlates with the distances of the unit cell in the crystal and the intensity of the spots with the density of electrons in the molecular structure. The exact location of the electrons, however, is lost in a single diffraction pattern that is called the phase problem. The phase problem requires at least three different protein crystals with identical unit cell geometry and the inclusion of evenly the relative phase in the individual crystal. The diffraction spots originating from the electron shell of the heavy metals can easily be identified and distinguished from other electron dens centers in the crystal. From the heavy metal location in the unit cell and the phase shift can be determined. Multiple isomorphous replacement method is used to solve the phase problem using different crystals with identical protein structures containing regularly but infrequently spaced heavy metals or protein isoforms. The amplitudes and phases of the diffraction data are used to calculate an electron density map of the repeating unit of the crystal. This is a step that involves the interpretation of the raw data. This step is sensitive to the resolution of the diffraction data, which in turn is determined by the quality of the protein crystal, *i.e.*, the regularity of the lattice of the protein in the unit cell and the regularity of the distribution of the heavy atom inclusions. The interpretation of the diffraction data needs information about the amino acid sequence of the protein because depending on the resolution of the data different amino acids can have indistinguishable electron densities (*e.g.*, Tyr and Phe or Leu and Ile). The difference in experimental structure and hypothetical structure is expressed as R-factor.

Structure Determination Using Nuclear Magnetic Resonance (NMR)

It measures the distances between atomic nuclei, rather than the electron density in a molecule. In contrast to protein crystals needed for X-ray diffraction, NMR made use of protein solutions allowing for the determination of structures at very short time ranges. With NMR, a strong, high frequency magnetic field stimulates atomic nuclei of the isotopes H-1, D-2, C-13 or N-15. The important step is to determine which resonance comes from which spin. The distance and type of neighbouring nuclei determines the resonance frequency of the stimulated atomic nuclei. This dependence on next neighbours known as chemical shift (or spin-spin coupling constant) and reflects the local electronic environment and the information contained in 1-D NMR spectra. For proteins, NMR usually measures the spin of protons. The H-1 NMR spectroscopy becomes the method of choice for biological macromolecules due to three reasons:

(i) H are present at many sites in proteins, nucleic acids, and polysaccharides.

(ii) H have a high abundance for each site.

(iii) H nuclei is the most sensitive to detect.

2-D NMR solves the problem of 1-D spectra (information about all the chemical shifts of all the H in the protein) by containing information about the relative position of H in molecular structures. 2-D NMR spectra contain information about interaction between H that are covalently linked through one or two other atoms called COSY or **correlation spectroscopy.** Alternatively, pairs of H that can be close in space, even if they are from residues that are not close in sequence (NOE spectra, or **Nuclear Overhauser Effect).** The size limit for proteins amenable to NMR solution structure analysis is about 200 amino acids. One important feature for the identification of cross peaks is that regular patterns can recognized that stem from secondary structure elements like alpha helices and parallel or anti-parallel beta sheets because they contain typical hydrogen bonding networks.

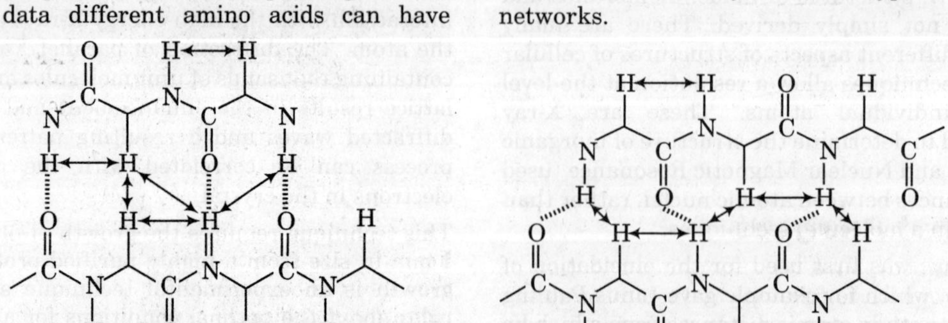

Fig. 39.8 Antiparallel (left) and parallel (right) β-sheet. Observed NOEs are shown by the arrows and the hydrogen bonds ny the dashed lines

The NMR also requires the knowledge of the **amino acid sequence,** but the protein does not have to be in ordered crystal, yet high concentrations of solubilized protein must be available. Therefore, NMR structures are called **solution structures.** In biopolymers, the primary structure logically breaks up the molecule into groups of coupled spins normally one or two groups per residue. This is true not only for proteins, but also for nucleic acid and polysaccharides.

Table 39.3 **Comparison between NMR and X-ray Crystallography**

NMR	X-ray Crystallography
Short time scale, Protein folding	Long time scale, static structure
Solution, purity	Single crystal, purity
< 20 kD, domain	Any size, domain, complex
Functional active site	Active or inactive
Domains	Domains
Atomic nuclei, chemical bonds	Electron density
Resolution limit 2-3.5Å	Resolution limit 2-3.5Å
Primary structure must be known	Primary structure must be know (except if resolution is 2Å or better for every single residue)

Mass Spectrometry

An increase in the sensitivity of protein identification can be achieved with a mass spectrometer. Mass spectrometers consist of three basic components:

(i) A small sample is ionized, usually to cations by loss of an electron (the ion source).

(ii) The ions are sorted and separated according to their mass and charge (the mass analyzer).

(iii) The separated ions are then measured, and the results displayed on a chart (the detector).

Various types of instruments utilizing different types of ionization sources and mass analyzers exist. Biological samples are ionized through the addition or loss of protons. Following ionization the masses of the components are determined. For example, in a time-of-flight mass analyzer the time it takes to traverse the length of the flight tube is a function of mass. A spectrum of the components plotted according to mass is recorded. The mass spectrometer can be used to determine accurate peptide masses or amino acid sequences of peptides. This information is then be used to identify proteins by searching databases. For example, a protein is digested with trypsin, or another site specific protease, and the resulting peptides analyzed by mass spectrometry. This acquired MS spectrum can then be compared with predicted MS spectrums of all the proteins in a database. The advantage of this method is that the analysis can be carried out quickly and can be completely automated. However, there is some ambiguity in protein identification due to peptide mass redundancy (*i.e.,* same amino acid composition but different sequence will be the same mass). In addition, factors which affect the accurate determination of peptide mass (*e.g.,* post-translational modifications) will limit the abililty to successfully identify proteins in databases. Tandem mass spectrometry (MS/MS) can be used to deduce the amino acid sequence of a peptide. In this approach ions with particular masses (*i.e.,* m/z values) are separated from the other ions and then fragmented in a collision chamber. The collision chamber is filled with an inert gas (usually argon or nitrogen) and collisions with the ions and the gas atoms result in covalent bonds being broken. The masses of the resulting fragments are then determined by a second mass analyzer. The mass spectrum of the fragments is diagnostic of the molecular structure of the parent ion. For example, peptides tend to fragment primarily along the peptide backbone at the amide bond which creates a ladder of ions that is indicative of the amino acid sequence. The sequence is used to search databases. Multiple peptides from the same protein can be analyzed in this fashion and thus, increasing the confidence of the protein identification. The disadvantage of MS/MS is that the process is not easy to completely automated. Although computer programs are available, interpretation and analysis of the mass spectrum requires some human guidance.

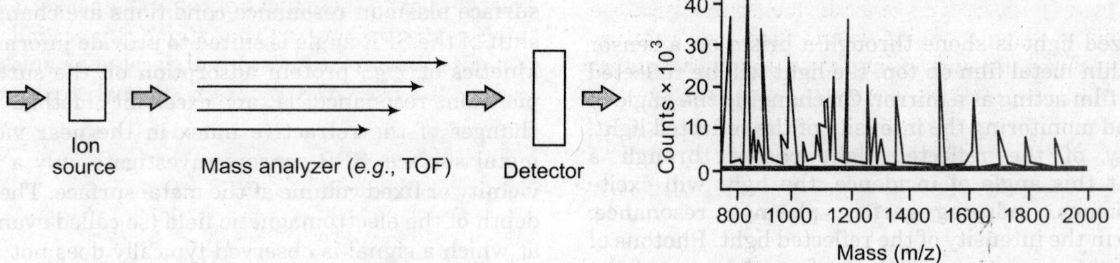

Fig. 39.9 Diagrammatic mass spectrometry

High Throughput Analyses

The procedures described above rely upon identification of proteins by gel electrophoresis followed by their subsequent identification using either one or two-dimensional gel electrophoresis. The ability of two-dimensional gels to resolve thousands of polypeptides on a single gel makes it a powerful technique in proteomics. However, 2-D gels are somewhat limited to the identification of relatively abundant proteins in the mid-to-low molecular weight ranges. Furthermore, membrane associated proteins and cytoskeletal proteins are difficult to solubilize and hydrophobic proteins do not always resolve well in the isoelectric focusing dimension. In addition, two-dimensional gel electrophoresis is a labour intensive and time consuming process and the protein 'spots' need to be further characterized by mass spectrometry or Edman degradation individually.

To overcome these limitations high through put methods to analyze complex mixtures of proteins are being developed. One approach is to combine a high throughput microcaillary liquid chromatography with Tandem mass spectrotometry. In this approach complex mixtures of proteins are treated with site-specific endoproteases. The resulting peptides are subjected to liquid chromatography (HPLC) without a prior gel electrophoresis step and then directly introduced into the Tandem MS. Elimination of the gel electrophoresis step provides provides a greater amount of flexibility in the proteolytic digestion and also increases the overall sensitivity. The first MS analysis will determine an accurate mass of the peptides which is indicative of the amino acid composition and then the fragmentation of those peptides can be used to predict the amino acid sequence. Databases are then searched for potential matches. This LC/MS/MS approach can be used to generate protein expression maps that are analogous to EST databases. Crude proteins from a particular tissue can be fractionated into cytosolic, membrane/organellar, cytoskeletal, etc., fractions and then analyzed for the expressed proteins in the mixture. This type of analysis will work best in organisms in which the genome sequence or large banks of EST sequences are available. This approach can also be used in the identification of the components of less complex protein mixtures such as large multi-protein complexes. Similarly protein-protein interactions can be discerned by affinity purifying all of the proteins that interact with the target protein and then analyzing the mixture. Methods to purify binding proteins include: coimmunoprecipitation with antibodies against the target protein, co-precipitation with an affinity tagged (*e.g.*, His6) recombinant target protein or affinity chromatography with the target protein.

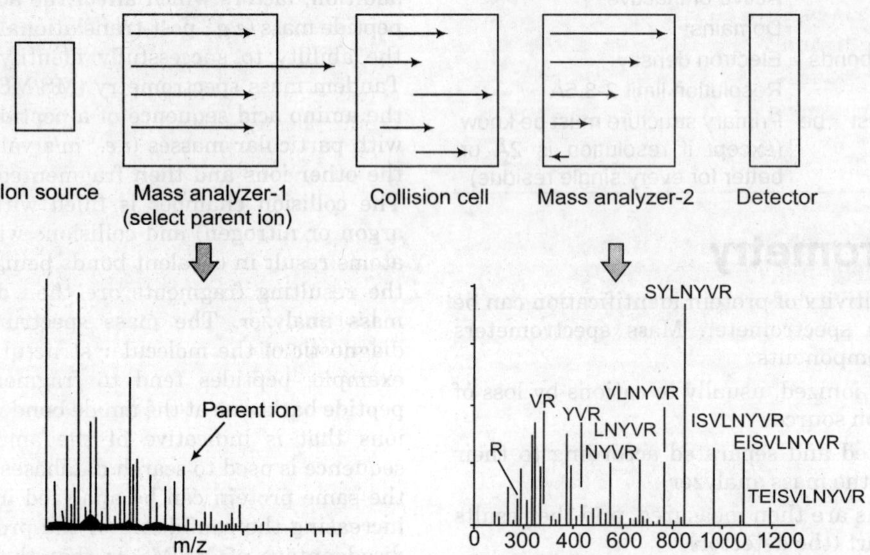

Fig. 39.10 Molecular weight determination of protein using mass spectroscopy

Surface Plasmon Resonance (SPR)

When polarized light is shone through a prism on a sensor chip with a thin metal film on top, the light will be reflected by the metal film acting as a mirror. On changing the angle of incidence, and monitoring the intensity of the reflected light, the intensity of the reflected light passes through a minimum. At this angle of incidence, the light will excite surface plasmons, inducing surface plasmon resonance, causing a dip in the intensity of the reflected light. Photons of p-polarized light can interact with the free electrons of the metal layer, inducing a wave-like oscillation of the free electrons and thereby reducing the reflected light intensity. The angle at which the maximum loss of the reflected light intensity occurs is called resonance angle or SPR angle. The SPR angle is dependent on the optical characteristics of the system, *e.g.*, on the refractive indices of the media at both sides of the metal, usually gold. While the refractive index at the prism side is not changing, the refractive index in the immediate vicinity of the metal surface will change when accumulated mass (*e.g.*, proteins) adsorb on it. Hence, the surface plasmon resonance conditions are changing and the shift of the SPR angle is suited to provide information on the kinetics of, *e.g.*, protein adsorption on the surface. Surface plasmon resonance is an excellent method to monitor changes of the refractive index in the near vicinity of the metal surface. SPR sensors investigate only a very limited vicinity or fixed volume at the metal surface. The penetration depth of the electromagnetic field (so called evanescent field) at which a signal is observed typically does not exceed a few hundred nanometers, decaying exponentially with the distance from the metal layer at the sensor surface. SPR sensors lack intrinsic selectivity: all refractive index changes in the evanescent field will be reflected in a change of the signal. These changes can be due to refractive index difference of the medium, *e.g.*, a change in the buffer composition or concentration; also, adsorption of material on the sensor surface can cause refractive index changes.

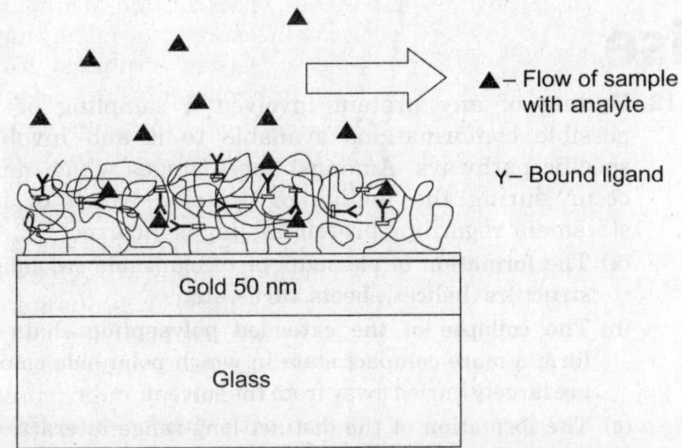

Fig. 39.11 Diagrammatic sketch of SPR

In the simplest case of an SPR measurement, a target component or analyte is captured by the capturing element or so called ligand. The ligand is permanently immobilized on the sensor surface previous to the measurement. Various sensor surfaces with immobilized ligands are commercially available, and many more can be custom-made. In the simplest case, the event of capturing the analyte by the ligand gives rise to a measurable signal, this is called direct detection. Each measurement starts with conditioning the sensor surface with a suitable buffer solution. It is of vital relevance to have a reliable baseline before the capturing event starts. At this point, the sensor surface contains the active ligands, ready to capture the target analytes. On injecting the solution containing the analytes, they are captured on the surface. Also other components of the sample might adhere to the sensor surface; without a suitable selection of the ligand, this adherence will be non-specific, and thus, easy to break. At this step, adsorption kinetics of the analyte molecule can be determined in a real-time measurement. Next, buffer is injected on to the sensor and the non-specifically bound components are flushed off. As indicated in the figure, the accumulated mass can be obtained from the SPR response (DR). Also in this step, dissociation of the analyte starts, enabling the kinetics of the dissociation process to be studied. Finally, a regeneration solution is injected, which breaks the specific binding between analyte and ligand. If properly anchored to the sensor surface, the ligands remain on the sensor, whereas the target analytes are quantitatively removed. It is vital in order to perform multiple tests with the same sensor chip to use a regeneration solution which leaves the activity of the ligands intact, as the analysis cycle is required to take place repeatedly for hundreds, sometimes even thousands of times. Again, buffer is injected to condition the surface for the next analysis cycle. If the regeneration is incomplete, remaining accumulated mass causes the baseline level to be increased. Often SPR measurements are carried out to determine the kinetics of a binding process. For realistic results it is vital to prevent immobilization from changing the ligand in a way that would influence its strength or affinity towards the target component. In addition, kinetic experiments can provide information on the thermodynamics, *e.g.*, on the binding energy of processes.

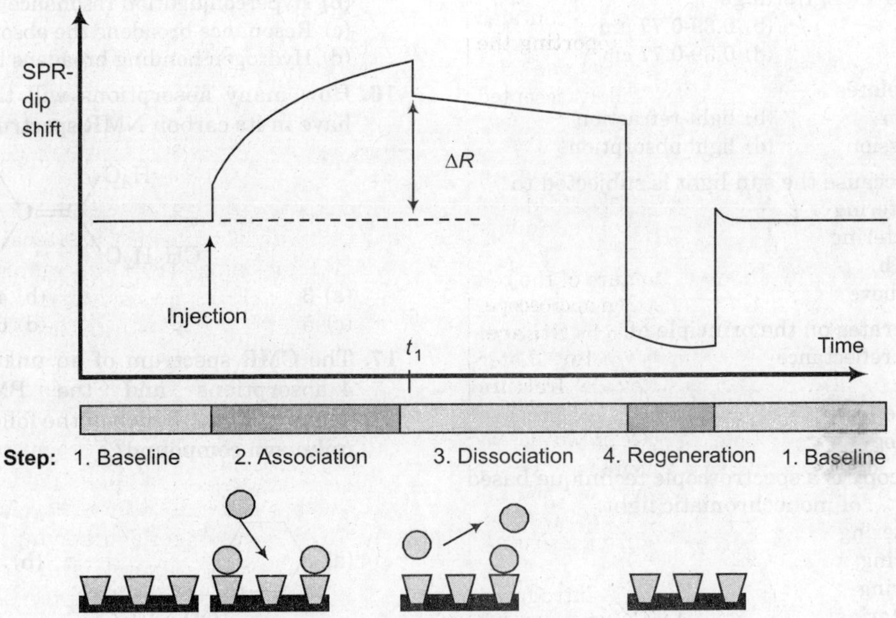

Fig. 39.12 Protein binding analysis using SPR instrument

Exercise

1. Infra red radiation spans which section of the electromagnetic spectrum?
(a) 0.25-0.78 μm λ (b) 0.78-1,000 μm λ
(c) 1,000-3,000 μm λ (d) >3,000 μm λ

2. An IR spectrum represents
(a) wavelength (μm) at *x*-axis and % transmittance at *y*-axis
(b) % transmittance at *x*-axis and at wavelength (μm) *y*-axis
(c) wave number (cm^{-1}) at *x*-axis and % transmittance at *y*-axis
(d) Both (a) and (c)

3. IR spectroscopy cannot be used for
(a) determination of functional groups in organic compound
(b) determination of molecular conformation and stereochemistry
(c) determination of molecular orientation
(d) determination of mass of the compound precisely

4. In a NMR experiment the precessional frequency for any nucleus is equal to the
(a) magnetic field strength (B_o) + magnetic ratio
(b) magnetic field strength (B_o) × magnetic ratio
(c) magnetic field strength (B_o) / magnetic ratio
(d) magnetic field strength (B_o) – magnetic ratio

5. X-ray diffraction is a analytical technique for examining
(a) crystalline solid (b) liquid
(c) powder (d) gases

6. Visible light's wavelength range
(a) 0.39-0.77 mm (b) 0.39-0.77 μm
(c) 0.39-0.77 nm (d) 0.39-0.77 cm

7. Bouguer's law relates
(a) light reflection (b) light refraction
(c) light transmission (d) light absorption

8. Sky looks blue because the sun light is subjected to
(a) Rayleigh scattering
(b) Compton scattering
(c) Both (a) and (b)
(d) None of the above

9. Optical fibre operates on the principle of
(a) total internal reflectance
(b) Tyndall effect
(c) photoelectric effect
(d) Laser technology

10. Raman spectroscopy is a spectroscopic technique based on .... of monochromatic light.
(a) inelastic scattering
(b) elastic scattering
(c) plastic scattering
(d) neolastic scattering

11. Circular Dichroism (CD) is observed only when molecule is
(a) optically active (b) planar
(c) in helix form (d) in sheet form

12. Folding of any protein involved a sampling of all possible conformations available to it and involves specific pathways. Amongst these stages which must occur during the folding of proteins which of the statement regarding protein folding is incorrect?
(a) The formation of elements of recognizable secondary structure (helices, sheets, turns, etc.)
(b) The collapse of the extended polypeptide chain to form a more compact state in which polar side chains are largely buried away from the solvent
(c) The formation of the distinct long-range interactions which characterize the native tertiary structure and are a pre-requisite for the formation of specific binding and catalytic sites
(d) The association between subunits in oligomeric proteins

13. A typical DLS instrument is based on
(a) scattering (b) interference
(c) reflection (d) diffraction

14. Which of the following bonds would show the strongest absorption in the IR?
(a) Carbon-hydrogen
(b) Oxygen-hydrogen
(c) Nitrogen-hydrogen
(d) Sulphur-hydrogen

15. Why is the oxygen-hydrogen absorption of CH_3OH such a broad band in the infrared?
(a) Rotational energy levels broaden the absorption
(b) Hyperconjugation resonance broadens the absorption
(c) Resonance broadens the absorption
(d) Hydrogen bonding broadens the absorption

16. How many absorptions will the following compound have in its carbon NMR spectrum?

H_3C CH_3
C=C
CH_3H_2C CH_3

(a) 3 (b) 4
(c) 5 (d) 6

17. The CMR spectrum of an unknown compound shows 4 absorptions and the PMR spectrum shows 4 absorptions. Which of the following compounds is the unknown compound?

(a) CH_3 (b) CH_3 CH_3

(c) 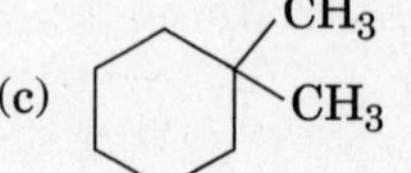

(d) CH_3– –CH_3

18. The CMR spectrum of an unknown compound shows 6 absorptions and the PMR spectrum shows 5 absorptions. Which of the following compounds is the unknown compound?

(a) $CH_3-CH(CH_3)-CH(CH_3)-CH(CH_3)-CH_3$

(b) $CH_2-CH_2-CH_2-CH_2-C(CH_3)(CH_3)-CH_2$

(c) $CH_2-C(CH_3)-CH_2-CH_2-CH_3$

(d) $CH_3-CH(CH_3)-CH_2-CH_2-CH_3$

19. What is the multiplicity expected in the hydrogen NMR spectrum for the hydrogen atoms marked by a 'star' in the following compound?

$CH_3-C(=O)-\overset{*}{C}H_2-CH_3$

(a) Singlet
(b) Triplet
(c) Quartet
(d) Heptet

20. Which of the following alkyl groups would show the multiplet pattern depicted in the diagram?

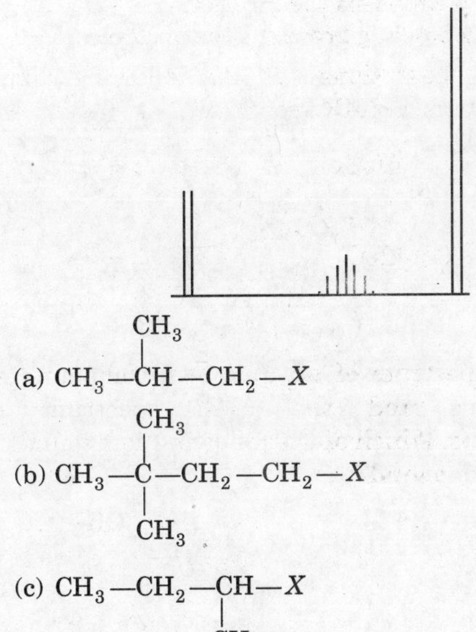

(a) $CH_3-CH(CH_3)-CH_2-X$

(b) $CH_3-C(CH_3)(CH_3)-CH_2-CH_2-X$

(c) $CH_3-CH_2-CH(CH_3)-X$

(d) $CH_3-CH_2-CH_2-X$

21. Which of the following alkenes would have the largest λ_{max}?

(a) $(H_3C)(H_3C)C=C(H)(H)$
(b) $(H_3C)(H_3C)C=C(CH_3)(H)$
(c) $(CH_3)(H)C=C(H)(CH_3)$
(d) $(H_3C)(H_3C)C=C(CH_3)(CH_3)$

22. What is the λ_{max} for the following compound? Use the provided parameters for your calculation.
Transoid base value = 214 nm
Cisoid base value = 253 nm
Alkyl groups on base = +5 m
Exocyclic C=C = + 5 nm
Extended conjugation = +30 nm

(a) 234 nm
(b) 244 nm
(c) 273 nm
(d) 283 nm

23. Which one of the following statements about ionization in a mass spectrometer is incorrect?
(a) Gaseous atoms are ionized by bombarding them with high energy electrons
(b) Atoms are ionised so they can be accelerated
(c) Atoms are ionised so they can be deflected
(d) It doesn't matter how much energy you use to ionise the atoms

24. Which compound has a molecular ion at m/z = 58, an infra red absorption at 1650 cm^{-1} and just one singlet in its nmr spectrum?
(a) Butane
(b) CH_3COCH_3
(c) CH_3CH_2CHO
(d) 2-methylpropane

25. Consider the following statements.
I. Absorption of energy from the photon elevates the molecule to an excited electronic state.
II. The disappearance of substrate or appearance of product is measured by spectrophotometry.
III. Circular dichorism measures interaction of polarized light with chiral protein components.

Which of the above statements are correct in reference to biophysical ways?
(a) I and II
(b) II and III
(c) I and III
(d) I, II and III

26. At low temperatures, peaks in the NMR spectrum of *p*-nitrophenol, $C_6H_4NO_2OH$, are observed as doublets split by ~100 Hz, because the molecule exists in equilibrium, as both protonated and deprotonated forms. At higher temperatures, the peaks coalesce to produce a single broadened peak with a line width equivalent to the separation between the individual peaks. Estimate the rate constant for proton exchange.
(a) 200 s^{-1}
(b) 5 × 10^{-3} s^{-1}
(c) 100 s^{-1}
(d) 50 s^{-1}

27. The transmittance of a 0.015 mol dm^{-3} aqueous solution of the $[Cu(NH_3)_4]^{2+}$ ion was measured to be 0.84 at 600 nm through a cuvette of optical path length 1.0 mm. Determine the molar absorption coefficient
(a) 9.0×10^{-6} dm^3 mol^{-1} cm^{-1}
(b) 6.3×10^3 dm^3 mol^{-1} cm^{-1}
(c) 5.5×10^2 dm^3 mol^{-1} cm^{-1}
(d) 50 dm^3 mol^{-1} cm^{-1}

28. The second band in the photoelectron spectrum of oxygen, O_2, at 17 eV corresponds to ionization to the excited $A^{2\pi}u$ state of the O^{2+} ion. The band consists of a long vibrational progression of peaks separated by approximately 900 cm^{-1}. The vibrational wavenumber of the ground $X_3\ \Sigma$ gelectronic state of a neutral oxygen molecule is 1580 cm^{-1}. Which of the following statements is consistent with the observed photoelectron spectrum?
(a) Ionization occurs from an antibonding orbital in O_2
(b) Ionization occurs from a bonding orbital in O_2
(c) Ionization occurs from a nonbonding orbital in O_2
(d) It is not possible to make any deductions about the nature of the ionization process

29. Chlorophyll molecules act as both donors and acceptors in fluorescence resonance energy transfer. The fluorescence lifetime of chlorophyll molecules in a dilute solution of an organic solvent was found to be 1.2 ns. When chlorophyll molecules were instead embedded in a biopolymer, the fluorescence lifetime was measured to be 820 ps. Given that R_0 = 5.6 nm for chlorophyll molecules, estimate the separation between the donor-acceptor pairs in the polymer
(a) 5.6 nm (b) 6.3 nm
(c) 8.9 nm (d) 11.9 nm

30. Surface Plasmon Resonance (SPR) detects binding of label free molecules on
(a) the surface of a chip (b) the detector
(c) on coating tube (d) None of these

Answers

1. (b)	**2.** (d)	**3.** (d)	**4.** (b)	**5.** (a)	**6.** (b)	**7.** (d)	**8.** (a)	**9.** (a)	**10.** (a)
11. (a)	**12.** (b)	**13.** (a)	**14.** (b)	**15.** (d)	**16.** (d)	**17.** (a)	**18.** (b)	**19.** (c)	**20.** (a)
21. (c)	**22.** (d)	**23.** (d)	**24.** (b)	**25.** (d)	**26.** (c)	**27.** (d)	**28.** (b)	**29.** (b)	**30.** (a)

40 Statistical Methods

Syllabus

- Measures of Central Tendency and Dispersal; Probability Distributions (Binomial Poisson and Normal); Sampling Distribution; Difference between Parametric and Non-Parametric Statistics; Confidence Interval; Errors; Regression and Correlation Levels of Significance; t-test Analysis of Variance; X2 Test; Basic Introduction to Multivariate Statistics.

Introduction

The population includes all objects of interest, whereas the sample is only a portion of the population. Parameters are associated with populations and statistics with samples. Parameters are usually denoted using Greek letter (*mu*, sigma), while statistics are usually denoted using Roman letters (x, s).There are several reasons why we don't work with populations. They are usually large, and it is often impossible to get data for every object we're studying. Sampling does not usually occur without cost, and the more items surveyed, the larger the cost. We compute statistics, and use them to estimate parameters. The computation is the first part of the statistics course (Descriptive Statistics) and the estimation is the second part (inferential Statistics).

Discrete *vs* Continuous Variables

Discrete variables are usually obtained by counting. There are a finite or countable number of choices available with discrete data. You can't have 2.63 people in the room. Continuous variables are usually obtained by measuring. Length, weight, and time are all examples of continuous variables. Since, continuous variables are real numbers, we usually round them. This implies a boundary depending on the number of decimal places. For example, 64 is really anything $63.5 <= x < 64.5$. Likewise, if there are two decimal places, then 64.03 is really anything $63.025 <= x < 63.035$. Boundaries always have one more decimal place than the data and end in a 5.

Levels of Measurement

There are four levels of measurement: Nominal, Ordinal, Interval and Ratio. These go from lowest level to highest level. Data is classified according to the highest level which it fits. Each additional level adds something the previous level didn't have. Nominal is the lowest level. Only names are meaningful here. Ordinal adds an order to the names. Interval adds meaningful differences. Ratio adds a zero so that ratios are meaningful.

Types of Sampling

There are five types of sampling: Random, Systematic, Convenience, Cluster and Stratified. Random sampling is analogous to putting everyone's name into a hat and drawing out several names. Each element in the population has an equal chance of occurring. While this is the preferred way of sampling, it is often difficult to do. It requires that a complete list of every element in the population be obtained. Computer generated lists are often used with random sampling. You can generate random numbers using the TI82 calculator. Systematic sampling is easier to do than random sampling. In systematic sampling, the list of elements is 'counted off'. That is, every kth element is taken. This is similar to lining everyone up and numbering off '1, 2, 3, 4; 1, 2, 3, 4; etc'. When done numbering, all people numbered 4 would be used. Convenience sampling is very easy to do, but it's probably the worst technique to use. In convenience sampling, readily available data is used. That is, the first person the surveyor runs into. Cluster sampling is accomplished by dividing the population into groups — usually geographically. These groups are called clusters or blocks. The clusters are randomly selected, and each element in the selected clusters is used. Stratified sampling also divides the population into groups called **strata.** However, this time it is by some characteristic, not geographically. For instance, the population might be separated into males and females. A sample is taken from each of these strata using either random, systematic or convenience sampling.

Measures of Central Tendency

There are several ways to represent frequency data for single variables. Bar charts, pie diagrams, histograms and frequency curves are commonly selected as ways to graphically represent this type of data. These tools allow us to describe or graphically represent important features of variables included in our study.

A bar chart is a series of bars where each bar represents the number or percentage of observations in that category.

A pie chart is a circular representation of a set of observed values, where the sum of all values represents the proportion of observed values in each category.

A histogram is a type of bar graphic where the height and area of the bars are proportional to the frequencies in each category of a nominal variable or intervals of a continuous variable.

A frequency curve is a graph of the frequency distribution in which the values of the variables are arrayed along the x-axis and the number of observations is depicted along the y-axis. Each data point represents the number of observations for each value of the variable and the data points are then joined together to form a line diagram.

Mean

The sum of the values of all data points, divided by the number of points; the same as the average. Gives a true center of mass for the data, but can be greatly affected by a few highly aberrant data points (outliers).

Median

The value at which 50% of the data points are higher and 50% are lower. If no data point lies at this position, then median is the average of the two nearest points. Not a true center of mass, but relatively unaffected by outliers. In a perfectly symmetrical data curve, it equals the mean.

Mode

The value with the most data points. There may be more than one (*e.g.*, a bimodal distribution).

Measures of Dispersion

Measures how closely the data cluster around the measure of central tendency.

Range

Distance from the lowest to the highest value.

Standard Deviation

A measure of how closely the values cluster around the mean. Roughly, the average distance from the mean of all data points. The more closely the values cluster around the mean the smaller the standard deviation will be. Abbreviated SD or σ.

Skewness

Refers to the symmetry of the curve. A perfectly symmetrical curve has a skewness of zero. The sign of skewness describes the direction of the long 'tail' points, not the location of the mode.

In a skewed distribution the frequency curve is not bell-shaped and value do not lie on both sides of measure of central tendency (*i.e.*, mean, mode and median) equally. The skewness may be positive or negative. A curve is said to be negatively skewed if it stopes more towards the left. In such type of distribution Mean < Median < Mode. On the other hand a curve is said to be positively skewed if it stopes more towards the right. In this situation Mean > Median > Mode.

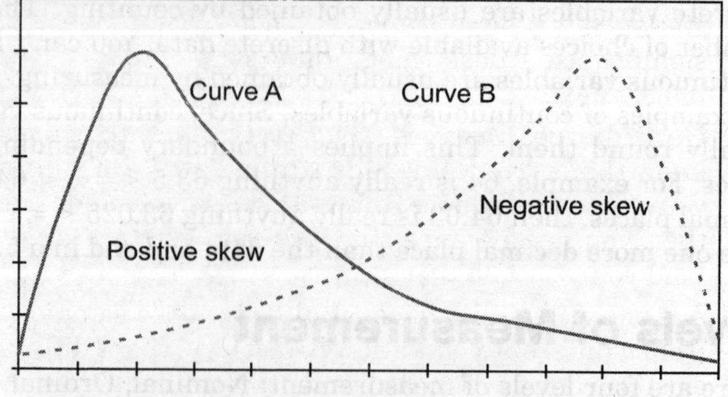

Fig. 40.1 The positive and negative skew in a curve

Relative measures of skewness also known as coefficient of skewness (Karl Pearson's coefficient of kewness) is calculated as

$$\text{Skp} = \frac{\text{Mean} - \text{Mode}}{\text{standard deviation}}$$

$$\text{or} \quad = \frac{\text{Mean} - \text{median}}{\sigma}$$

$$= \frac{\text{Median} - \text{mode}}{\sigma}$$

Measures of Dispersion

(i) **Range** (used for ordinal, interval and ratio measures), the distance between the highest and lowest values.

(ii) **Mean Deviation** (used for interval and ratio measures) Measure of dispersion that is based on the deviation of each score from the mean. The sum of these deviations is always zero.

(iii) **Standard Deviation** (used for interval and ratio measures), This is interpreted as an average of the squared deviations from the mean and is more typically used in statistics reporting than mean deviation. It is acquired by taking the square root of the sum of squared deviations for the mean divided by the number of scores minus one.

(iv) **Variance** (used for interval and ratio measures), a measure of dispersion of data points about the mean.

All of the above central tendency and dispersion statistics are real or observed. It is also useful to compare observed distributions to a theoretical (or normal) distribution. Employing the normal distribution acts are an ideal against which real distributions can be compared. The comparison provides guidelines for judging when a result can be considered unusual or unlikely to have occurred if certain conditions are present.

Inferential Statistics

It is used to determine the likelihood that a conclusion based on analysis of data from a sample is true.

(i) **p value** The probability that the observed difference could have occurred by chance (roughly, the probability that the groups really are not different after all). By convention, a *p* value less than 0.05 is considered statistically significant. Note that 'statistical significance' does not necessary imply 'clinical importance'.

(ii) **Confidence interval** The certainty with which we know that a true value falls within a range of values. If your 95% confidence interval doesn't include zero*, then you're 95% sure that the data sets are different (and your $P < .05$).

(iii) A is the probability of concluding that the sample came from a different population (*i.e.*, a significant difference exists) when in fact it didn't. By convention = 0.05. This is called a **Type I error.**

(iv) β is the probability of concluding that no difference existed when in fact it did. By convention = 0.20. This is called a **Type II error.**

Power The probability of detecting a true difference (Power = 1 – β). The larger the sample, the greater the power.

*or 1, for an odds ratio or relative risk calculation.

Probability Distribution

A **Random Variable** is a quantity resulting from a random experiment that, by chance, can assume different values. Such as, number of defective light bulbs produced during a week. Also, we said a **Discrete Random Variable** is a variable which can assume only integer values, such as, 7, 9 and so on. In other words, a discrete random variable cannot take fractions as value. Things such as people, cars or defectives are things we can count and are discrete items.

A probability distribution is similar to the frequency distribution of a quantitative population because both provide a long-run frequency for outcomes. In other words, a probability distribution is listing of all the possible values that a random variable can take along with their probabilities. For example, suppose we want to find out the probability distribution for the number of heads on three tosses of a coin:

First toss........T T T T H H H H

Second toss.....T T H H T T H H

Third toss........T H T H T H T H

The probability distribution of the above experiment is as follows (columns 1 and 2 in the following table).

(Column 1)	(Column 2)	(Column 3)
Number of heads	Probability	(1)(2)
X	*P*(*X*)	(*X*)*P*(*X*)
0	1/8	0.0
1	3/8	0.375
2	3/8	0.75
3	1/8	0.375
Total		1.5=E(X)

Mean and Variance of Discrete Random Variables

The equation for computing the **mean** or **expected value** of discrete random variables is as follows:

$$\text{Mean} = E(X) = \text{Summation } [X.P(X)]$$

where, $E(X)$ = expected value, X = an event and $P(X)$ = probability of the event.

Note that in the above equation, the probability of each event is used as the weight. For example, going back to the problem of tossing a coin three times, the expected value is:

$$E(X) = [0(1/8)+1(3/8)+2(3/8)+3(1/8)] = 1.5$$

Thus, on the average, the number of heads showing face up in a large number of tossing a coin is 1.5. The expected value has many uses in gambling, for example, it tells us what our long-run average losses per play will be.

The equations for computing the **expected value, variance and standard deviation** of discrete random variables are as follows:

Mean (Expected) Value of a Discrete Distribution

$$\mu = E(X) = \Sigma[X \cdot P(X)]$$

Variance of a Discrete Distribution

$$\sigma^2 = \Sigma[(X - \mu)^2 \cdot P(X)]$$

Standard Deviation of a Discrete Distribution

$$\sigma = \sqrt{S[(X - \mu)^2 \cdot P(X)]}$$

These are four types of discrete probability distribution *i.e.*, normal distribution, binomial distribution, poisson distribution and hypergeomatric distribution.

The Normal (Gaussian) Distribution

The normal distribution is a symmetrical (bell-shaped) curve with two intersecting properties. First, the mean, mode and median all coincide at the exact midpoint of the distribution. Second, a fixed proportion of observations or cases lies between the mean and any distance from the mean measured in terms of the standard deviation.

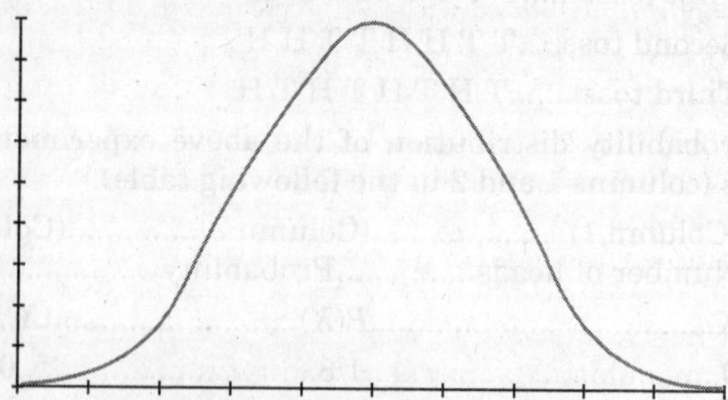

Fig. 40.2 A normal distribution curve

Under the normal distribution, 50 per cent of cases are above the mean and 50 percent are below the mean and 34.13 per cent of total area lies between the mean and one standard deviation above and below the mean (second property).This, 68.26 per cent of total cases are between one standard deviation above and below the mean. Further, 95 per cent of cases lie between two standard deviations above and below the mean of the normal distribution.

1. Mean, median and mode all have same value.
2. Curve is symmetric around the mean; skew is zero.
3. Tails of the curve get closer and closer to the x-axis as you move away from the mean.
4. 68% of values fall within 1 SD of the mean; 95% of values fall within 2 SD of the mean.
   (i) **Parametric** refers to data that approximate a normal distribution.
   (ii) **Non-parametric** refers to data that do not approximate a normal distribution.

Binomial Distribution

One of the most widely known of all discrete probability distributions is the binomial distribution. Several characteristics underlie the use of the binomial distribution.

Characteristics of the Binomial Distribution

(i) The experiment consists of n identical trials.

(ii) Each trial has only one of the two possible mutually exclusive outcomes, success or a failure.

(iii) The probability of each outcome does not change from trial to trial.

(iv) The trials are independent, thus we must sample with replacement.

Note that if the sample size, n is less than 5% of the population, the independence assumption is not of great concern. Therefore the acceptable sample size for using the binomial distribution with samples taken without replacement is [n<5% n] where, n is equal to the sample size, and N stands for the size of the population. The birth of children (male or female), true-false or multiple-choice questions (correct or incorrect answers) are some examples of the binomial distribution.

Binomial Equation

When using the binomial formula to solve problems, all that is necessary is that we be able to identify three things: the number of trials (n), the probability of a success on any one trial (p), and the number of successes desired (X). The formula used to compute the probability, the mean, and the standard deviation of a binomial distribution are as follows.

Binomial Formula

$$G_x \cdot p^x \cdot q^{u-x} = \frac{n\,!}{X\,!\,(n-X)\,!} \cdot p^x \cdot q^{n-x}$$

Mean of a Binomial Distribution

$$m = n \times p$$

Standard Deviation of a Binomial Distribution

$$\sigma = \sqrt{n \cdot p \cdot q}$$

Where, n = the sample size or the number of trials, X = the number of successes desired, p = probability of getting a success in one trial, and $q = (1 - p)$ = the probability of getting a failure in one trial.

The Binomial Table

Mathematicians constructed a set of binomial tables containing presolved probabilities. Binomial distributions are a family of distributions. In other words, every different value of n and/or every different value of p gives a different binomial distribution. Tables are available for different combinations of n and p values. For the tables, refer to the text. Each table is headed by a value of n, and values of p are presented in the top row of each table of size n. In the column below each value of p is the binomial distribution for that value of n and p. The binomial tables are easy to use. Simply look up n and p, then find X (located in the first column of each table), and read the corresponding probability. The following table is the binomial probabilities for $n = 6$. Note that the probabilities in each column of the binomial table must add up to 1.0.

Graphing the Binomial Distribution

The graph of a binomial distribution can be constructed by using all the possible X values of a distribution and their associated probabilities. The X values are graphed along the X axis, and the probabilities are graphed along the Y axis. Note that the graph of the binomial distribution has three shapes: If $p<0.5$, the graph is positively skewed, if $p>0.5$, the graph is negatively skewed, and if $p=0.5$, the graph is symmetrical. The skewness is eliminated as n gets large. In other words, if n remains constant but p becomes larger and larger up to 0.50, the shape of the binomial probability distribution becomes more symmetrical. If p remains the same but n becomes larger and larger, the shape of the binomial probability distribution becomes more symmetrical.

The Poisson Distribution

The Poisson distribution is another discrete probability distribution. It is named after **Simeon-Denis Poisson** (1781-1840), a French mathematician. The Poisson distribution depends only on the average number of occurrences per unit time of space. There is no n, and no p. The poisson probability distribution provides a close approximation to the binomial probability distribution when n is large and p is quite small or quite large. In other words, if $n>20$ and $np<=5$ [or $n(1-p)<=5$], then we may use poisson distribution as an approximation to binomial distribution.

The Hypergeometric Distribution

Another discrete probability distribution is the hypergeometric distribution. The binomial probability distribution assumes that the population from which the sample is selected is very large. For this reason, the probability of success does not change with each trial. The hypergeometric distribution is used to determine the probability of a specified number of successes and/or failures when **(i)** a sample is selected from a finite population without replacement and/or **(ii)** when the sample size, n, is greater than or equal to 5% of the population size, N, *i.e.*, ($n>=5\%$ N). Note that by finite population we mean a population which consists of a fixed number of known individuals, objects, or measurements.

Sampling Distributions

Suppose we use the sample mean, y, as our "best guess" of the population mean, μ. We assume it will be somewhat close to the target, but not exactly on every time. It is also intuitive that if we were to take another sample from the same population and calculate the sample mean for that sample, it would not only be off the target, but also be slightly different from the first sample mean.

The variability among random samples from the same population is called sampling variability.

A probability distribution that characterizes some aspect of sampling variability is called a sampling distribution. A sampling distribution tells us how close the resemblance between the sample and population is likely to be.

You can imagine describing the sampling distribution of a statistic by repeatedly taking samples from the same population over and over again, computing the statistic, and plotting all the statistics on a probability histogram. This distribution would have a shape, a mean, standard deviation, etc.

Methods of Probability Sampling

(i) **Simple Random Sample** (SRS) A sample formulated so that each item or person and each subset in the population has the same chance of being included. (*e.g.*, from N items, prob, that any one is selected $=1/N$). A simple way to implement this is to use a lottery or computer program. For example we can mark N cards and write names of items on these cards, shuffle the cards and select n cards. This will yield a simple random sample of size n.

(ii) **Systematic Random Sampling** (SysRS) The items or individuals of the population are arranged in some order. A random starting point is selected (by lottery) and then every kth member of the population is selected. If there are $N=1000$ stores along Fifth avenue and we want to select $n=100$ stores in the sample, $k=N/n$ or 10 We shuffle only the first k, and select one, say #4 Now on we systematically select stores by adding k, 2k, 3k, 4k etc to 4 So a systematic sample will have store #4, 14, 24, 34, 44, 54, etc.

(iii) **Stratified Random Sampling** (StrRS) A population is first divided into sub-groups, called **strata** and a sample is selected from each stratum, (*e.g.*, 70% males, 30% females). If a sample of 10 is selected, ($n=10$) 70% of n =7, so select 7 males and 3 females. In general, N=population size, $N1$=stratum 1(female), $N2$=stratum 2 (males), n=sample size desired. Sample should have = $(N1/N)*n$ from stratum 1 and so on. Thus,

Females in sample = $(N1/N)*n$, Males in the sample = $(N2/N)*n$.

(iv) **Cluster Sampling** A population is first divided into clusters and a sample of the clusters is selected. (Used in marketing). It works if clusters are as heterogeneous as the population.

A sampling error is the difference between a sample statistic and its corresponding parameter. We can make probabilistic statements about this sampling error only if we have a probability sample (not judgment sample).

In general, sampling distribution is for any sample statistic (mean, median, mode, standard deviation, etc) defined over a sample space consisting of all possible samples of size n from the available population of size N.

Let us first study the sampling distribution of sample mean as an example.

Sampling Distribution of the Sample Mean

(i) The sampling distribution of the sample means is a probability distribution consisting of all possible sample means based on specified sample sizes selected from the population. The sampling distribution yields the probability of occurrence associated with each sample mean over the set of all possible sample mean numbers.

Standard Error (SE) of the Sample Means (Sq. root of sampling variance or standard deviation. It is customary to distinguish between usual standard deviation (SD) and that of a sampling distribution (SE).

(ii) The standard error of the sample means is the standard deviation of the sampling distribution of the sample means.

(iii) n is the size of the sample.

(iv) s is the standard deviation of the population (assumed known).

(v) It is computed by: $\sigma_{xbar} = (\sigma/\sqrt{n})$ as a first approximation if N is not known or N is large (almost infinity).

(vi) σ_{xbar} is the symbol for the standard error of the sample means.

(vii) If σ is not known and $n \geq 30$, the standard deviation of the sample, denoted by σ is used to approximate the population standard deviation. Then the formula for the standard error becomes:

$$SE(\bar{x}) = s \text{ sub } \bar{x} = \frac{s}{\sqrt{n}}$$

Always, think of $SE(\bar{x})$ as the standard deviation of the Random Variable $\bar{x}$. What is the **shape** of the probability distribution of $\bar{x}$? The following theorem says that it is Normal and hence, the theorem enables us to solve all kinds of practical problems.

Parametric *vs* Non-Parametric Statistics

A potential source of confusion in working out what statistics to use in analysing data is whether your data allows for **parametric** or **non-parametric** statistics.

The importance of this issue cannot be underestimated.

If you get it wrong you risk using an incorrect statistical procedure or you may use a less powerful procedure.

Non-parametric statistical procedures are less powerful because they use less information in their calculation. For example, a parametric correlation uses information about the mean and deviation from the mean while a non-parametric correlation will use only the ordinal position of pairs of scores.

The basic distinction for parametric versus non-parametric is:

(i) If your measurement scale is nominal or ordinal then you use non-parametric statistics.

(ii) If you are using interval or ratio scales you use parametric statistics.

There are other considerations which have to be taken into account:

You have to look at the distribution of your data. If your data is supposed to take parametric stats you should check that the distributions are approximately normal.

The best way to do this is to check the skew and Kurtosis measures from the frequency output from SPSS. For a relatively normal distribution:

skew ~= 1.0

kurtosis~= 1.0

If a distribution deviates markedly from normality then you take the risk that the statistic will be inaccurate. The safest thing to do is to use an equivalent non-parametric statistic.

Descriptive

Name	For what	Notes
Mode	Central tendancy	Greatest frequency
Median	Central tendancy	50% split of distribution
Range	Distribution	Lowest and highest value

Association

Name	For what	Notes
Spearman's Rho	Correlation	Based on rank order of data
Kendall's Tau	Correlation	
Chi square	Tabled data	

Difference between Parametric and Non-Parametric Statistics

(i) We use non-parametric tests when we do not expect our data to conform to a parametric distribution such as the normal distribution or the t distribution.

(ii) They can also be used if other assumptions about the data needed for certain tests are violated (*e.g.*, equality of standard deviations for the two-sample t-test.

(iii) The most common non-parametric tests we shall come across are the Wilcoxon test for paired data (more properly the Wilcoxon matched pairs signed rank sum test) and the Mann-Whitney U-test (sometimes called the Mann-Whitney-Wilcoxon test, the Wilcoxon t-test, the Wilcoxon two-sample test, or the Wilcoxon W-test) for unpaired data. These tests are based on ranking the data and looking at the ranks rather than the actual values of the observations.

(iv) There is confusion over the naming of these tests in the literature. Indeed, some computer programs will do things like performing a Mann-Whitney test but express the result in terms of Wilcoxon's W.

(v) Non-parametric tests are applicable in a wider range of situations but the are, in general, less powerful: they cannot detect differences as small as the ones detectable by the equivalent parametric tests.

(vi) The phrase non-parametric does not mean we necessarily make no assumptions about the data. For example the Wilcoxon matched pairs signed rank sum test makes the assumption that the populations the samples come from are symmetric.

Correlation

The relationship between two variable is such that a change in one variable results in change in other variable and such relation is called **correlation.** The correlation may be positive, zero or negative. The correlation is positive when values of the two variables deviate together. But if one variable increase and other decrease (or *vice versa*) the correlation is called negative. There will be no relation in variable in zero correlation. There are three popular methods of studying correlation, *i.e.*, scatter diagram, rank correlation and karl Pearsons coefficient of correlation. Scatter diagram is a graphical method. The quantitative character like colour, fecundity stress, tolerance, etc., can be arranged serially and studied by rank correlation.

Sum of squares notation is the SS notation, and will make these formulas much easier to work with.

$$SS\ (x) = \Sigma x^2 - \frac{(\Sigma x)^2}{n}$$

$$SS\ (y) = \Sigma y^2 - \frac{(\Sigma y)^2}{n}$$

$$SS(xy) = \Sigma xy - \frac{(\Sigma x)(\Sigma y)}{n}$$

Notice these are all the same pattern,

SS(x) could be written as

$$SS\ (x) = \Sigma xx - (\Sigma x)\ (\Sigma x)/n$$

Also Pearson's Correlation Coefficient

$$r = \frac{n\ \Sigma xy - (\Sigma x)\ (\Sigma x)}{\sqrt{(n\Sigma x^2 - (\Sigma x)^2)\ (n\Sigma y - (\Sigma y)^2)}}$$

$$r = \frac{\dfrac{\Sigma xy - \dfrac{(\Sigma x)\ (\Sigma y)}{n}}{n}}{\dfrac{n}{\sqrt{\left(\Sigma x^2 - \dfrac{(\Sigma x)^2}{n}\right)\left(\Sigma y^2 - \dfrac{(\Sigma y)^2}{n}\right)}}}$$

$$r = \frac{SS\ (xy)}{\sqrt{SS\ (x)\ SS\ (y)}}$$

There is a measure of linear correlation. The population parameter is denoted by the Greek letter ρ and the sample statistic is denoted by the roman letter r.

Here are some properties of r

1. r only measures the strength of a linear relationship. There are other kinds of relationships besides linear.
2. r is always between – 1 and 1 inclusive. – 1 means perfect negative linear correlation and +1 means perfect positive linear correlation.
3. r has the same sign as the slope of the regression (best fit) line.
4. r does not change if the independent (x) and dependent (y) variables are interchanged.
5. r does not change if the scale on either variable is changed. You may multiply, divide, add, or subtract a value to/from all the x-values or y-values without changing the value of r.
6. r has a student's t distribution.

Hypothesis Testing

The claim we will be testing is **There is significant linear correlation.**

The Greek letter for r is rho, so the parameter used for linear correlation is rho

H_0: rho = 0

H_1: rho <> 0

r has a t distribution with n-2 degrees of freedom, and the test statistic is given by:

$$t = \sqrt{\frac{n-2}{1-r^2}}$$

Now, there are n–2 degrees of freedom this time. This is a difference from before. As an over-simplification, you subtract one degree of freedom for each variable, and since there are 2 variables, the degrees of freedom are n–2.

This doesn't look like our

$$\text{Test statistic} = \frac{\text{Observed} - \text{Expected}}{\text{Standard error}}$$

If you consider the standard error for r is

$$\text{standard error} = \sqrt{\frac{1-r^2}{n-2}}$$

$$t = \frac{r-p}{\sqrt{\dfrac{1-r^2}{n-2}}}$$

(i) The formula for the test statistic is, which does look like the pattern we're looking for.

(ii) Remember that hypothesis testing is always done under the assumption that the null hypothesis is true.

(iii) Since, H_0 is rho = 0, this formula is equivalent to the one given in the book.

Additional Note: $1 - r^2$ is later identified as the coefficient of non-determination.

There are Three Valid Conclusions

(a) There is no significant linear correlation.

(b) There is significant positive linear correlation.

(c) There is significant negative linear correlation.

(d) Use the first one if you fail to reject the null hypothesis, that is, your test statistic is not bigger than the critical value.

(e) Use the second one if you reject the null hypothesis (your test statistic is bigger than the critical value) and your test statistic is positive.

(f) Use the last one if you reject the null hypothesis (your test statistic is bigger than the critical value) and your test statistic is negative.

(g) Using the table to look up the critical values is the most common technique. However, the first technique, with the t-value must be used if it is not a two-tail test, or if a different level of significance (other than 0.01 or 0.05) is desired.

Regression

The idea behind regression is that when there is significant linear correlation, you can use a line to estimate the value of the dependent variable for certain values of the independent variable.

There are four types of regression analysis, *i.e.*, simple regression (only one independent variable) multiple regression, linear regression and non-linear regression (curvilinear regression).

The regression equation should only used

1. When there is significant linear correlation. That is, when you reject the null hypothesis that rho=0 in a correlation hypothesis test.
2. The value of the independent variable being used in the estimation is close to the original values. That is, you should not use a regression equation obtained using x's between 10 and 20 to estimate y when x is 200.
3. The regression equation should not be used with different populations. That is, if x is the height of a male, and y is the weight of a male, then you shouldn't use the regression equation to estimate the weight of a female.
4. The regression equation shouldn't be used to forecast values not from that time frame. If data is from the 1960's, it probably isn't valid in the 1990's.

Assuming that you've decided that you can have a regression equation because there is significant linear correlation between the two variables, the equation becomes: $y' = ax + b$ or $y' = a + bx$ (some books use y-hat instead of y-prime). The Triola and Bluman texts both use the second formula, however, more people are familiar with the notion of $y = mx + b$, so I will use the first.

a is the slope of the regression line:

$$a = \frac{n(\Sigma xy) - (\Sigma x)(\Sigma y)}{n(\Sigma x^2)(\Sigma x)^2}$$

$$a = \frac{SS(xy)}{SS(x)}$$

and $$b = \overline{y}\, a\, \overline{x}$$

$$b = \frac{(\Sigma y)(\Sigma x^2) - (\Sigma x)(\Sigma xy)}{n(\Sigma x^2) - (\Sigma x)^2}$$

b is the y-intercept of the regression line:

The regression line is sometimes called the 'line of best fit' or the 'best fit line'.

Since it 'best fits' the data, it makes sense that the line passes through the means. The point $(\overline{x}, \overline{y})$ is called the centroid.

The regression equation is the line with slope a passing through the point $(\overline{x}, \overline{y})$

Another way to write the equation would be

$$y' - \overline{y} = a(a, \overline{x})$$

$$y' - \overline{y} = ax - a\overline{x}$$

$$= ax + \overline{y} - a\overline{x}$$

apply just a little algebra, and we have the formulas for a and b that we would use It also turns out that the slope of the regression line can be written as $a = r \cdot \frac{S_y}{S_x}$. Since, the standard deviations can't be negative, the sign of the slope is determined by the sign of the correlation coefficient. This agrees with the statement made earlier that the slope of the regression line will have the same slope as the correlation coefficient.

Introduction to Sample from Normal Distributions

Let us take samples which are drawn from a population which has a normal distribution. The distribution of the population therefore looks like this:

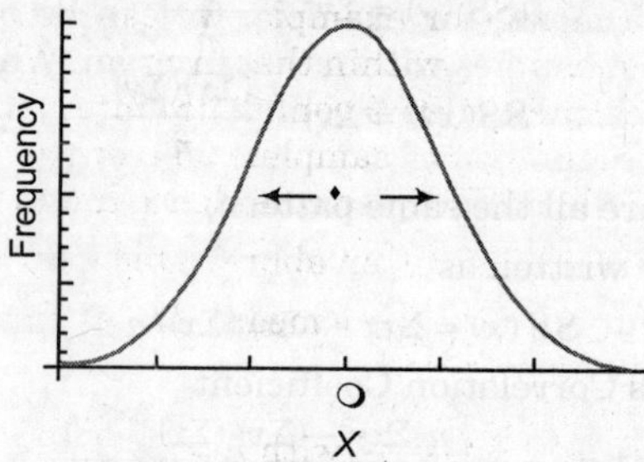

Fig. 40.3 The normal distribution of a population

The means of samples with n data points which come from this distribution will also be normally distributed. They will have a mean which is also equal to m, but the standard deviation of the sample means is equal to. Note that the larger the sample size (n), the *smaller* the variance of the distribution of sample means will be.

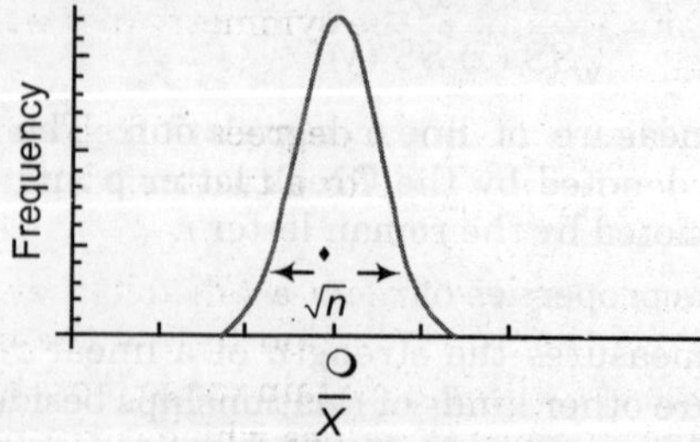

Fig. 40.4 The normal distribution with sample mean of n data points

(Again, the more data we have, the more reliable is our estimate of the mean of the distribution.)

Note that this implies:

$Z = \dfrac{\overline{X} - \mu}{\sigma / \sqrt{n}}$ has a normal distribution with mean = 0 and SD = 1.

The problem with using this fact, though, is that it implies that we know what the standard deviation of the population is. We usually only have information about the standard deviation from our sample itself, and this gives us an idea of the variance (s^2), but with sampling error. We must estimate $\sigma/\sqrt{n}$ as $s/\sqrt{n}$. Let's name a new statistic, t, which is defined as:

$$t = \frac{\overline{X} - \mu}{s/\sqrt{n}}$$

This t is distributed by a Student's t distribution with n–1 degrees of freedom.

Properties of the *t*-Distribution

Roughly shaped like the normal distribution, but with broader tails. Symmetric around zero. Converges to the normal distribution as the sample size gets large.

Confidence Intervals for the Mean

A confidence interval is a range of possible values for a parameter, which represents our best guess of what that parameter actually is. If we calculate a 95% confidence interval for a mean, for example, we can be 95% confident that the true mean lies within that interval. What this means is that if we calculated 95% confidence interval for the mean on an infinite number of samples, 95% of the time the true mean would fall within those confidence limits.

'Confidence interval' is often abbreviated CI.

The distribution of the mean is estimated by the t-distribution:

$$t = \frac{\overline{X} - \mu}{s/\sqrt{n}}, \text{ with } n = n - 1.$$

(n is the number of degrees of freedom of the distri- bution).

The t-distribution is (usually) given in tables by the probability density in the tails, called a. Some tables give both a one-tailed and a two-tailed value of $t$at the critical value; in other words, they give the value of t at the place which leaves a of the probability in either one tail or two of the distribution. (Others only give one or the other, and require the user to take account of the symmetry of the t-distribution to find the value they need).

The critical value of t, with n degrees of freedom and a given value of a is written as $t_{a(2)\cdot v}$ for a two-tailed test and as $t_{a(1)\cdot v}$ for a one-tailed test.

Since, our estimates of t follow a t-distribution, this means that we can use the t-distribution to find the probability of getting a value of t within a certain range. For the 95% CI, we want to find the range of t values which correspond to a 95% chance that our estimate falls within this range. In other words, we want to find:

$$P\left[-t_{a05(2)\cdot v} \le \frac{\overline{X} - \mu}{s/\sqrt{n}} \le t_{a05(2)\cdot v}\right] = 0.95$$

$$\left[-t_{a05(2)\cdot v} \le \frac{\overline{X} - \mu}{s/\sqrt{n}} \le t_{a05(2)\cdot v}\right]$$

Finding the confidence interval for m then becomes a matter of algebra on the inequality.

$$-t_{a05(2)\cdot v} \le (s/\sqrt{n}) \le \overline{X} - \mu\ t_{a05(2)\cdot v}\ (s/\sqrt{n})$$

$$-t_{a05(2)\cdot v} \le (s/\sqrt{n}) \le \mu - \overline{X}\ t_{a05(2)\cdot v}\ (s/\sqrt{n})$$

$$\overline{X} - t_{a05(2)\cdot v}\ (s/\sqrt{n}) \le \overline{X}\ \mu\ \overline{X} + t_{a05(2)\cdot v}\ (s/\sqrt{n})$$

So, we have

$$P[\overline{X} - t_{a05(2)\cdot v}\ (s/\sqrt{n}) \le \mu\ \overline{X} + t_{a05(2)\cdot v}\ (s/\sqrt{n})] = 0.95$$

This range in the inequality is then our 95% CI for the mean. It can also be written as $\overline{X} + t_{a05(2)\cdot v}\ (s/\sqrt{n})$

The formula for the confidence interval of the mean more generally, the $1 - a$ CI is given by $\overline{X} + t_{a5(2)\cdot v}\ (s/\sqrt{n})$

Confidence Intervals for the Variance

We can potentially calculate a CI for any estimate of any parameter. In this section will calculate the CI for the variance of a distribution.

The c^2 distribution describes the sampling properties of sample variances for normal distributions. If a variable is normally distributed, then (n-1) s^2/s^2has a c^2 distribution with n-1 degrees of freedom. Remember that the c^2 distribution starts at zero and continues to infinity. Similarly, a sample variance estimate cannot be less than zero, but can be up to indefinitely large.

This relationship between the sample variance and the c^2 distribution allows us to make inferences about the confidence we can have about our estimates of the population's variance.

We want to find the range of values which, according to our data, such that we have a 95% chance (for example) of having found the true variance within that range. Therefore, we want to allow an equal chance of having estimated too low as of having estimated too high. We therefore, want to leave 2.5% probability of guessing too high and 2.5% of having guessed too low.

The c^2 distribution is not symmetric though, which means that we have to account for each of these tails separately.

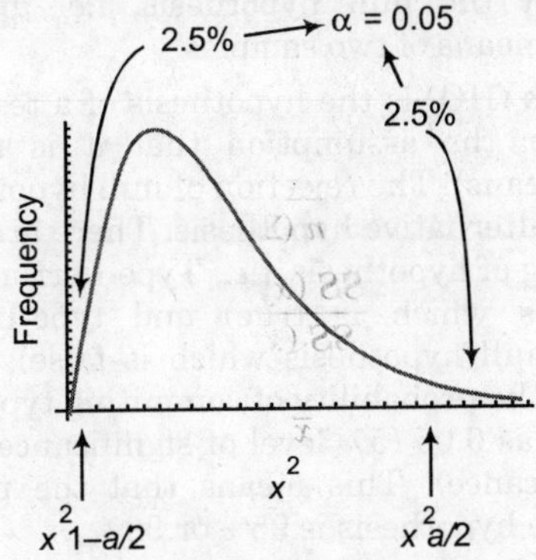

Fig. 40.5 The C² distribution

The CI for the variance of a normal distribution

The CI for variance is:

$$\frac{1\sigma^2}{X^2_{\frac{a}{2}\cdot y}} \le \sigma^2 \le \frac{1\sigma^2}{X^2_{1-\frac{a}{2}\cdot v}}$$

Derivation of CI for the Variance

The logic here is similar to the confidence interval for the mean.

$$P\left[X^2_{1-\frac{a}{2}\cdot y} \le \frac{VS^2}{\sigma^2} \le X^2_{\frac{a}{2}\cdot v}\right] = 1 - a$$

$$P\left[\frac{X^2_{1-\frac{a}{2}\cdot v}}{VS^2} \le \frac{1}{\sigma^2} \le \frac{X^2_{\frac{a}{2}\cdot v}}{VS^2}\right] = 1 - a$$

$$P\left[\frac{VS^2}{X^2_{1-\frac{a}{2}\cdot y}} \ge \sigma^2 \ge \frac{VS^2}{X^2_{\frac{a}{2}\cdot v}}\right] = 1 - a$$

$$P\left[\frac{VS^2}{X^2_{\frac{a}{2}\cdot y}} \le \sigma^2 \le \frac{VS^2}{X^2_{1-\frac{a}{2}\cdot v}}\right] = 1 - a$$

So, $$\frac{VS^2}{X^2_{\frac{a}{2}\cdot y}} \le \sigma^2 \le \frac{VS^2}{X^2_{1-\frac{a}{2}\cdot v}} = 1 - a$$

is the $1 - a$ CI for the variance of a normal distribution.

t-Test and Level of Significance

It is essential in biological experiments to compare the means of two samples to draw a conclusion. *t*-test (Student *t*-test) is applied to test the significance of difference of two means of two samples we make a choice between two alternatives.

1. To reject the null hypothesis, *i.e.*, differences between means of these two samples is significant.
2. To accept the null hypothesis, *i.e.*, no differences between means of two samples.

Null hypothesis (HO) is the hypothesis of a test for possible rejection under the assumption that it is true (*i.e.*, no difference in means). The rejection of null hypothesis leads to acceptation of alternative hypothesis. There are two types of errors in testing of hypothesis, *i.e.*, Type-I error (Rejection of null hypothesis which is true) and type-II error (*i.e.*, acceptance of null hypothesis which is false). The level of **significance** is the probability of commiting type-I error. It is usually chosen as 0.05 (5% level of significance) or 0.01 (1% level of significance). This means that the probability of accepting a true hypothesis is 95% or 99%.

One-sample *t*-Test

Often we want to do more than estimate the mean — we would like to test hypothesis about it. In this section we learn the first of many hypothesis tests about means. This is a one-sample *t*-test, which compares the mean of a single sample to some constant.

Paired *t*-Test

A very useful specialized version of the one-sample *t*-test is the paired *t*-test. The paired *t*-test asks whether pairs of data points, such as data on the same patients before and after a treatment, show any consistent differences. The data points are logically grouped into pairs, with each of the elements of the pairs having more in common with the other than with other data points.

Some other examples: same areas before and after pollution; identical twins, one treated, one not.

A paired *t*-test is just a one-sample *t*-test, where the data is the difference between the two data points in each pair.

Analysis of Variance-ANOVA

The method was developed by Fisher while studying agriculture and crop output with different fertilizer treatments, he needed test that could evaluate differences between three or more means, developed the F-distribution because problems with applying the Student's *t*-test to more than 2 sample/population means number of comparisons between all means increases with an increase in the number of samples/populations (k)

$$\frac{k\,(k-1)}{2}$$

Number of comparisons for k = 4 samples

$$\text{Number of comparisons} = \frac{4(4-1)}{2} = 6$$

Number of comparisons for k = 8 samples

$$\text{Number of comparisons } \frac{8\,(8-1)}{2} = 28$$

Alpha level becomes unstable with addition of more means, chances of making a type-I error increase with an increase in the number of means being compared

Probability – Type I Error = $1 - (0.95)^c$

c = 3 comparisons for three means

Probability – Type I = $1 - (0.95)^3$

Probability – Type I = 0.14

c = 6 comparisons for 4 means

Probability – Type I = $1 - (0.95)^6$

Probability – Type I = 0.27

Types of ANOVAs

On the basis of number of factors examine at a time ANOVA will be of following two types

One-way ANOVA

Examines one factor at a time, tests for differences among levels of the factor, focus in on analysis of variance-comparison between two types of variance among group variance (variation among the grand mean and the sample means) note that this is often referred to the group mean square (MS_g) as well as the among group variance.

$S^2{}_g = MS_g$; grand mean is the mean for all data within group variance (sum of the variation within each sample-around each sample mean).

$$S^2{}_w = MS_w = MS_e$$

note that this is often referred to the error variance or error mean square (MSe) as well as the within group variance (MSw). Evaluation uses a one-tailed F test to determine if the among group variance is greater than the within group variance.

$$F_{abs} = \frac{S_g^2}{S_w^2} = \frac{MS_g}{MS_w}$$

Two-Way ANOVA

Examines effects of two independent variables simultaneously. There are three set of hypothesis with the two way ANOVA. The null hypothesis for each of the sets are given below:

(i) The population means of the first factories equal, *i.e.,* like the one way ANOVA for the row factor.

(ii) The population mean of second factor are equal. This is like the one way ANOVA for column factor.

(iii) There is no interaction between the two factors.

Assumptions of the ANOVA

Homogeneity of variance, sample variances are equal. In Bartlett's test for homogeneity of variance the samples come from normal populations. ANOVA is robust enough to handle departures from normality and unequal variances. Problems occur when heterogeneity of variances is combined with unequal sample sizes skewness/kurtosis is combined with smaller sample sizes.

Results of ANOVA

No difference between among group variance and within group variance this tells us there is no difference among means difference between among group variance and within group variance. This tells us there is a difference among means but not which ones are different.

Multiple Comparisons Tests-only used if the results of an ANOVA yield a significant difference between among group variance and within group variance. ANOVA results only indicate that a difference exists among means, not where the difference(s) are-which means are different, have to use multiple comparisons test to detect where the differences lie. Referred to as ad hoc or a posteriori tests because they are used after you know there is a significant difference from the ANOVA. Several types of multiple comparisons tests-can be combined into three broad categories. Generic multiple comparisons tests-evaluate all possible pairs/combinations of means like Tukey's HSD test and Student-Newman-Keuls (SNK) test which are unique in that the critical value of q changes with the range of means being considered, sometimes referred to as the multiple range test. In Control group test-evaluate differences between experimental group versus the control group (not differences among experimental groups), also employs one-tailed tests which is less common practice with other multiple comparisons tests, *e.g.,* Dunnett's test.

Multiple contrasts tests - can be used like the traditional tests mentioned above to evaluate differences among pairs of mean but is better used to evaluate homogeneous groups of means against other such groups or individual means, *e.g.,* Scheffe test.

In statistics, **analysis of variance** (ANOVA) is a collection of statistical models, and their associated procedures, in which the observed variance in a particular variable is partitioned into components attributable to different sources of variation. In its simplest form ANOVA provides a statistical test of whether, or not the means of several groups are all equal, and therefore generalizes t-test to more than two groups. Doing multiple two-sample t-tests would result in an increased chance of committing a type I error. For this reason, ANOVAs are useful in comparing two, three or more means.

Models

There are three classes of models used in the analysis of variance, and these are outlined here.

Fixed-effects Models (Model 1)

The fixed-effects model of analysis of variance applies to situations in which the experimenter applies one or more treatments to the subjects of the experiment to see if the response variable values change. This allows the experimenter to estimate the ranges of response variable values that the treatment would generate in the population as a whole.

Random-effects Models (Model 2)

Random effects models are used when the treatments are not fixed. This occurs when the various factor levels are sampled from a larger population. Because the levels themselves are random variables, some assumptions and the method of contrasting the treatments differ from ANOVA model 1.

Mixed-effects Models (Model 3)

A mixed-effects model contains experimental factors of both fixed and random-effects types, with appropriately different interpretations and analysis for the two types.

A Model often Presented in Textbooks

Many textbooks present the analysis of variance in terms of a linear model, which makes the following assumptions about the probability distribution of the responses:

(a) Independence of cases–this is an assumption of the model that simplifies the statistical analysis.

(b) Normality–the distributions of the residuals are normal.

(c) Equality (or homogeneity) of variances, called **homoscedasticity** — the variance of data in groups should be the same. Model-based approaches usually assume that the variance is constant. The constant-variance property also appears in the randomization (design-based) analysis of randomized experiments, where it is a necessary consequence of the randomized design and the assumption of unit treatment additivity. If the responses of a randomized balanced experiment fail to have constant variance, then the assumption of unit treatment additivity is necessarily violated.

To test the hypothesis that all treatments have exactly the same effect, the F-test's p-values closely approximate the permutation test's p-values: The approximation is particularly close when the design is balanced. Such permutation tests characterize tests with maximum power against all alternative hypothesis, as observed by Rosenbaum. The anova F-test (of the null-hypothesis that all treatments have exactly the same effect) is recommended as a practical test, because of its robustness against many alternative distributions. The Kruskal-Wallis test is a non-parametric alternative that does not rely on an assumption of normality, and the Friedman test is the non-parametric alternative for a one-way repeated measures ANOVA.

The separate assumptions of the textbook model imply that the errors are independently, identically, and normally distributed for fixed effects models, that is, that the errors (ε's) are independent and

$$\varepsilon \sim N(0, \sigma^2)$$

Logic of ANOVA

Partitioning of the Sum of Squares

The fundamental technique is a partitioning of the total sum of squares S into components related to the effects used in the model. For example, we show the model for a simplified ANOVA with one type of treatment at different levels.

$$S_{\text{Total}} = S_{\text{Error}} + S_{\text{Treatments}}$$

So, the number of degrees of freedom f can be partitioned in a similar way and specifies the chi-squared distribution which describes the associated sums of squares.

$$f_{\text{Total}} = f_{\text{Error}} + f_{\text{Treatments}}$$

Chi-Square Analysis

Once again, we are encountering the limited ability of html to support mathematical symbols. The classical test for goodness of fit is the chi-square test, normally written as the Greek letter chi followed by the exponent 2. In these notes, chi is replaced with X and chi-squared is written as X^2. In addition, we will continue the previously introduced practice of writing 'SUM' to replace upper case sigma as the symbol for a summation.

Goodness of Fit

The chi-square test examines the extent to which observed data differ from expected values that are predicted from theory, such as a 3:1 phenotypic ratio. This relationship is sometimes referred to as 'goodness of fit'. The basic problem that must always be dealt with in statistical analysis is that data from any finite number of observations will be perturbed by random chance events. For example, tossing four heads in a row has a 1/16 probability of happening by pure chance, and does not prove that the same coin will not yield statistically equal numbers of heads and tails if tossed repeatedly.

Null Hypothesis

The starting point for chi-square analysis is the null hypothesis, which proposes that any difference between observed and expected values is due entirely to random chance events. The observed data are considered to be consistent with the expectation only if the null hypothesis is not rejected by the chi-square test. Rejection of the null hypothesis does not prove that the expectation was in error. Instead, it only says that the observed data differ from the expected sufficiently so that the probability that the deviation could have arisen by pure chance is relatively small.

Criteria for Rejecting the Null Hypothesis

The chi-square value, whose calculation will be described below, becomes larger as the probability that the observed deviation from the expected value could be due to random chance becomes smaller. After the calculations have been completed, they are converted to a probability (P value) that the observed deviation of the data from expected values could have arisen by random chance. The usual standard for rejecting the null hypothesis is a P value of less than 0.05, which means that there was less than a 5% chance (1 in 20) that the deviation of the observed data from the expectation was the result of random chance events, rather than being caused by an incorrect expectation. Thus, all that rejection of the null hypothesis actually demonstrates is that random chance events are unlikely to have caused the observed amount of deviation. In other words, a P value of 0.05 says that if the expectation is valid and the experiment were repeated over and over, 5% of the tests would yield a deviation this large or larger, whereas 95% of the tests would yield a smaller deviation.

No Proof of Validity

The chi-square test neither proves nor disproves the validity of the expectation. Statistical analysis cannot do that. A large chi-square value, which corresponds to a very low probability that the observed difference between expected and observed occurred by chance, tells us that it is highly unlikely that the expectation is valid. However, statistically unlikely events, such as winning the lottery, do occur. Thus, a rare statistical event can on rare occasions either cause the null hypothesis for a valid expectation to be rejected or cause the null hypothesis for an incorrect expectation to fail to be rejected. However, in practice, a chi-square test in which the null hypothesis is not rejected is considered to be relatively strong evidence that the expectation is probably valid. In cases where the P value comes out close to the cutoff value of 0.05, it is usually desirable to repeat the test with a larger sample size, irrespective of whether the initial test rejects the null hypothesis or not.

Calculation of Chi-square

The chi-square test begins with the difference between the observed number (O) and the expected number (E), based on the prediction being tested. Consider, for example, an F2 population of 1064 individuals that is being examined to determine whether the dominant phenotype has been expressed in the expected 3:1 ratio. In this example from Mendel's experiment with tall and dwarf peas, the expected number of dominant phenotypes is 798, whereas the observed number is only 787. The comparable values for recessive phenotypes are 266 expected and 277 observed.

Squaring the Difference

The next step is to square the $(O\text{-}E)$ value for each of the observations. This has two effects. It increases the weighting of large differences relative to that of small ones and it also makes all values positive, such that too few is no different from too many. For the dominant phenotype in our example, $(O\text{-}E) = -11$ and $(O\text{-}E)^2 = 121$.

Dividing by Expected Value and Summation

Each squared value is then divided by the expected value and the resulting fractions are added together for all observations, according to the following formula.

$$X^2 = \text{SUM } \{(O\text{-}E)^2/E\}$$

Remember that the expected values will not be the same for the dominant and recessive phenotypes. For the current example,

$$X^2 = 121/798 + 121/266 = 0.1516 + 0.4544 = 0.6065.$$

Degrees of Freedom

Because chi-square is a summed value, it increases in magnitude as the number of independent values that are examined increases. Each independent value is referred to as a degree of freedom. Tables that relate chi-square values to the probability that the observed deviation from theoretical may be significant are organized in terms of the degrees of freedom of the chi-square values.

Determining Degrees of Freedom

The number of degrees of freedom for a chi-square value is always one less than the number of observations. The reason is that the binomial expansion for n independent events yields $n + 1$ terms, as we saw earlier, with the last term being the difference between all of the rest and 1.0, and thus, not an independent observation. For example, if we look at the example presented above, the number of recessive phenotype individuals is simply the total number minus the number of dominant phenotype individuals. Therefore, these two observations provide only only one degree of freedom, since the second one is only what is left of the total after subtracting the first. Thus, in evaluating the significance of chi-square values, it is always necessary to use the line in the table for a number of degrees of freedom that is one less than the total number of observations being evaluated.

Determining the *P* value

Mathematical calculation of P values from X^2 values and degrees of freedom is sufficiently complex so that the P values are almost always obtained from a table or chart. Chi-square values corresponding to probabilities of 0.05 and 0.01 for 1 to 5 degrees of freedom.

Values that Support the Null Hypothesis

If the chi-square value is less than that for a probability of 0.05, the probability that the observed deviation could have arisen by chance is greater than 5% and the null hypothesis is not rejected. In some cases a more stringent standard may be used such that the null hypothesis is not completely rejected unless there is less than a 1% probability that the results arose by random chance. Note that for a given number of degrees of freedom, a larger chi-square value, which is indicative of greater deviation from expected values, corresponds to a smaller P value. In cases where the chi-square test indicates a P value between 0.01 and 0.05, it is often desirable to repeat the experiment with a larger population to obtain a less ambiguous result.

Rejecting the Null Hypothesis

Beyond certain values of chi-square, the probability that the deviation from expected values is caused by random chance events becomes quite small. Thus, for a chi-square value that yields a probability of less than 0.05, there is less than a 1 in 20 chance that a deviation this large could have arisen by pure chance. In other words, there is a greater than 95% chance that the expectation is invalid (or that there is some other problem with the data or its interpretation). This leads to rejection of the null hypothesis (that the observed deviation is due only to chance events). Although rejection of the null hypothesis does not prove that the expectation was wrong, it does demonstrate that the current data do not adequately support that expectation.

X^2 values that lead to rejection of null hypothesis For one degree of freedom, the X^2 value that corresponds to $P = 0.05$ is **3.84**. This is a number that you should memorize. In the example above, the X^2 value of 0.6 indicates a probability of about 80% that the observed deviation was due entirely to chance. This value does not even come close to rejecting the null hypothesis. For 2 degrees of freedom, the X^2 value corresponding to $P = 0.05$ is 5.99. For 3 degrees of freedom it is 7.82. A p value of 0.01 derived form a chi-square test is highly significant only for rejecting a null hypothesis, and not for proving an alternative hypothesis.

The need for caution in interpreting chi-square results The previous textbook for this course cautioned about reading too much into rejection of the null hypothesis. Many different aspects of the experimental design or the biology of the test organisms can cause perturbations in phenotypic ratios. One that was cited is reduced viability of certain types of homozygous recessive organisms. There can also be differences in fertilization rates. Sperm carrying certain alleles may not be as efficient. Eggs from mothers of certain genotypes may not develop as well. Even in random human births, a very careful and detailed study will reject the null hypothesis for a 1:1 sex ratio. For reasons that are still not entirely clear, slightly more boys than girls are born.

Sample Size

Another very important consideration is sample size. When sample size is small, the E values used in the calculation of X^2 may become quite small, particularly in cases where the expected numbers are a small fraction of the the total sample size, such as only 1/16 of all individuals examined expected to exhibit a double recessive phenotype in an F2 population. Because $(O\text{-}E)^2$ is divided by E for each observation prior to summation, a small E value can greatly magnify the impact of a modest amount of random chance deviation $(O\text{-}E)$ on the calculated X^2 value. Thus, in cases where the null hypothesis is rejected, it is important to examine the overall experimental design to be certain that total sample size and the numbers expected in each phenotypic class were large enough to provide reliable statistics. This is particularly important in cases where the results of a relatively small experiment look like they fit the expectation reasonably well, but fail to generate a sufficiently small X^2 value. Often in such cases, analysis of a larger experiment will yield a more acceptable X^2 value.

Multivariate Analysis

Multivariate analysis (MVA) is based on the statistical principle of multivariate statistics, which involves observation and analysis of more than one statistical variable at a time. In design and analysis, the technique is used to perform trade studies across multiple dimensions while taking into account the effects of all variables on the responses of interest.

Uses for multivariate analysis include:

1. Design for capability (also known as capability-based design).
2. Inverse design, where any variable can be treated as an independent variable.
3. Analysis of Alternatives (AoA), the selection of concepts to fulfil a customer need.
4. Analysis of concepts with respect to changing scenarios
5. Identification of critical design drivers and correlations across hierarchical levels.

Multivariate analysis can be complicated by the desire to include physics-based analysis to calculate the effects of variables for a hierarchical 'system-of-systems.' Often, studies that wish to use multivariate analysis are stalled by the dimensionality of the problem. These concerns are often eased through the use of surrogate models, highly accurate approximations of the physics-based code. Since surrogate models take the form of an equation, they can be evaluated very quickly. This becomes an enabler for large-scale MVA studies: while a Monte Carlo simulation across the design space is difficult with physics-based codes, it becomes trivial when evaluating surrogate models, which often take the form of response surface equations.

Factor analysis: Factor analysis is used to uncover the latent structure (dimensions) of a set of variables. It reduces attribute space from a larger number of variables to a smaller number of factors. Factor analysis originated a century ago with Charles Spearman's attempts to show that a wide variety of mental tests could be explained by a single underlying intelligence factor.

Applications

(i) To reduce a large number of variables to a smaller number of factors for data modeling.

(ii) To validate a scale or index by demonstrating that its constituent items load on the same factor, and to drop proposed scale items which cross-load on more than one factor.

(iii) To select a subset of variables from a larger set, based on which original variables have the highest correlations with the principal component factors.

(iv) To create a set of factors to be treated as uncorrelated variables as one approach to handling multi-collinearity in such procedures as multiple regression.

Factor analysis is part of the General Linear Model (GLM) family of procedures and makes many of the same assumptions as multiple regression.

Exercise

1. Which of the following statement is false for a 95% confidence interval?
   (a) It is a test of the null hypothesis and can only be used in parametric data
   (b) It is calculated at ± 1.96 times the standard error of the mean
   (c) Is useful when comparing data with another population
   (d) If zero difference lies within the 95% when comparing two groups to a treatment, it indicates the treatment has no effect
2. Which of the following statement is correct regarding the meta-analysis of randomized controlled trials?
   (a) Should only include peer-reviewed studies
   (b) Should include trials in which patient selection is not randomized
   (c) Provides a more stable estimate of the effect of treatment than individual trials
   (d) Gives conclusion making further controlled trials un-necessary

3. Which of the following statement is true about evidence-based medicine?

(a) Does not involve health economic assessment
(b) Is restricted to randomized placebo-controlled trials
(c) Is used to cut down waiting list
(d) Relies only on objective measurements of disease outcomes

4. Ann Landers, who wrote a daily advice column appearing in newspapers across the country, once, asked her readers, 'If you had it to do over again, would you have children?' Of the more than 10,000 readers who responded, 70% said no. What does this show?

(a) The survey is meaningless because of voluntary response bias
(b) No meaningful conclusion is possible without knowing something more about the characteristics of her readers
(c) The survey would have been more meaningful if she had picked a random sample of the 10,000 readers who responded
(d) The survey would have been more meaningful if she had used a control group

5. Which of the following are true statements?

I. If bias is present in a sampling procedure, it can be overcome by dramatically increasing the sample size.
II. There is no such thing as a 'bad sample'.
III. Sampling techniques that use probability techniques effectively eliminate bias.

(a) I only (b) II only
(c) III only (d) None of these

6. Two possible wordings for a questionnaire on gun control are as follows

I. The United States has the highest rate of murder by hand- guns among all countries.
Most of these murders are known to be crimes of passion or crimes provoked by anger among acquaintances. Are you in favor of a 7-day cooling off period between the filing of an application to purchase a handgun and the resulting sale?
II. The United States has the highest rate of murder by handguns among all countries.
Many people want to keep handguns in their homes for self-protection. Fortunately,
US citizens are guaranteed the right to bear arms by the Constitution. Are you in favour of a 7-day cooling off period between the filing of an application to purchase a needed handgun and the resulting sale?
One of these questions showed that 25% of the population favored a 7-day waiting period between application for purchase of a handgun and the resulting sale, while the other question showed that 70% of the population favored the waiting period.
Which produced which result and why?

(a) The first question probably showed 70% and the second question 25% because of the lack of randomization in the choice of pro-gun and anti-gun subjects as evidenced by the wording of the questions
(b) The first question probably showed 25% and the second question 70% because of a placebo effect due to the wording of the questions
(c) The first question probably showed 70% and the second question 25% because of the lack of a control group
(d) The first question probably showed 70% and the second question 25% because of response bias due to the wording of the question

7. Which of the following are true statements?

I. Voluntary response samples often under represent people with strong opinions.
II. Convenience samples often lead to under coverage bias.
III. Questionnaires with non neutral wording are likely to have response bias.

(a) I and II (b) I and III
(c) II and III (d) I, II and III

8. Each of the 29 NBA teams has 12 players. A sample of 58 players is to be chosen as follows. Each team will be asked to place 12 cards with their players' names into a hat and randomly draw out two names. The two names from each team will be combined to make up the sample. Will this method result in a simple random sample of the 348 basketball players?

(a) Yes, because each player has the same chance of being selected.
(b) Yes, because each team is equally represented.
(c) No, because the teams are not chosen randomly.
(d) No, because not every group of 58 players has the same chance of being selected.

9. To survey the opinions of bleacher fans at Wrigley Field, a surveyor plans to select every one hundredth fan entering the bleachers one afternoon. Will this result in a simple random sample of Cub fans who sit in the bleachers?

(a) Yes, because each bleacher fan has the same chance of being selected
(b) Yes, but only if there is a single entrance to the bleachers
(c) Yes, because this is an example of systematic sampling, which is a special case of simple random sampling
(d) No, because not every sample of the intended size has an equal chance of being selected

10. Which of the following are true statements about sampling error?

I. Sampling error can be eliminated only if a survey is both extremely well designed and extremely well conducted
II. Sampling error concerns natural variation between samples, is always present, and can be described using probability
III. Sampling error is generally smaller when the sample size is larger

(a) I and II (b) I and III
(c) II and III (d) I, II and III

11. What fault do all these sampling designs have in common?

I. The Wall Street Journal plans to make a prediction for a presidential election based on a survey of its readers.

II. A radio talk show asks people to phone in their views on whether the United States should payoff its huge debt to the United Nations.

III. A police detective, interested in determining the extent of drug use by teenagers, randomly picks a sample of high school students and interviews each one about any illegal drug use by the student during the past year.

(a) All the designs make improper use of stratification
(b) All of the designs have errors that can lead to strong bias
(c) All the designs confuse association with cause and effect
(d) None of the designs satisfactorily controls for sampling error

12. A state auditor is given an assignment to choose and audit 26 companies. She lists all companies whose name begins with A, assigns each a number and uses a random number table to pick one of these numbers and thus, one company. She proceeds to use the same procedure for each letter of the alphabet and then combines the 26 results into a group for auditing. Which of the following are true statements?

I. Her procedure makes use of chance.
II. Her procedure results in a simple random sample.
III. Each company has an equal probability of being selected.

(a) I and II (b) I and III
(c) II and III (d) None of these

13. A researcher planning a survey of heads of households in a particular state has census lists for each of the 23 counties in that state. The procedure will be to obtain a random sample of heads of households from each of the counties rather than grouping all the census lists together and obtaining a sample from the entire group. Which of the following is a true statement about the resulting stratified sample?

I. It is not a simple random sample.
II. It is easier and less costly to obtain than a simple random sample.
III. It gives comparative information that a simple random sample would not give.

(a) I only (b) I and II
(c) I and III (d) I, II and III

14. To find the average occupancy size of student-rented apartments, a researcher picks a simple random sample of 100 such apartments. Even after one follow-up visit, the interviewer is unable to make contact with anyone in 27 of these apartments. Concerned about nonresponse bias, the researcher chooses another simple random sample and instructs the interviewer to continue this procedure until contact is made with someone in a total oi 100 apartments. The average occupancy size in the final 100-apartment sample is 2.78. Is this estimate probably too high or too low?

(a) Too low, because of undercover age bias
(b) Too low, because convenience samples overestimate average results
(c) Too high, because of under coverage bias
(d) Too high, because convenience samples overestimate average results

15. To conduct a survey of long-distance calling patterns, a researcher opens a telephone book to a random page, closes his eyes, puts his finger down on the page, and then reads off the next 50 names. Which of the following are true statements?

I. The survey incorporates chance.
II. The procedure results in a simple random sample.
III. The procedure could easily result in selection bias.

(a) I and II (b) I and III
(c) II and III (d) I, II and III

16. Which of the following are true statements about sampling?

I. Careful analysis of a given sample will indicate whether or not it is random.
II. Sampling error implies an error, possibly very small but still an error, on the part of the surveyor.
III. Data obtained, while conducting a census are always more accurate than data obtained from a sample, no matter how careful the design of the sample.

(a) I only (b) II only
(c) III only (d) None of these

17. Consider the following three events.

I. Although 18% of the student body is minorities, in a random sample of 20 students, 5 are minorities.
II. In a survey about sexual habits, an embarrassed student deliberately gives the wrong answers.
III. A surveyor mistakenly records answers to one question in the wrong space.

Which of the following correctly characterizes the above?

(a) I, sampling error; II, response bias; III, human mistake
(b) I, sampling error; II, non-response bias; III, hidden error
(c) I, hidden bias; II, voluntary sample bias; III, sampling error
(d) I, undercoverage error; II, voluntary error; III, unintentional error

18. A researcher plans a study to examine the depth of belief in God among the adult population. He obtains a simple random sample of 100 adults as they leave church one Sunday morning. All but one of them agrees to participate in the survey. Which of the following are true statements?

I. Proper use of chance as evidenced by the simple random sample makes this a well designed survey.
II. The high response rate makes this a well-designed survey.
III. Selection bias makes this a poorly designed survey.

(a) I only (b) II only
(c) III only (d) I and II

19. Choose the mismatch.

I. Ordinal variable — Personality
II. Absolute measure of dispersion — Variance
III. Discrete variable — Standard error
IV. Statistic of location — Median

V. Prediction statistics	— Regression coefficient
VI. Nominal variable	— Sex
VII. Sampling statistic	— Body height
VIII. Continuous variable	— Litter size

(a) I, II and III (b) III, V and VI
(c) III, VII and VIII (d) V, VI and VIII

20. The fourth quartile of a frequency distribution is that score below which lie .... of the scores of a sample which below the fourth percentile lies .... of all the scores.
(a) All; 0.01 (b) All; 0.02
(c) All; 0.04 (d) All; 0.08

21. Mark the odd member in each of the following series.
A. (I) sum of squares (II) variance (III) quartile deviation
(IV) standard deviation
B. (I) central moment (II) range (III) standard deviation
(IV) variance
C. (I) coeffiecient of variation (II) quartile deviation (III) root-mean square (IV) mean deviation
D. (I) standard deviation (II) absolute measure of dispersion (III) range (IV) coeffiecnt of dispersion
(a) A-III, B-III, C-IV, D-I (b) A-IV, B-II, C-IV, D-III
(c) A-III, B-II, C-I, D-IV (d) A-II, B-II, C-III, D-III

22. Which of the following group better define odd items?
A. (I) standard error (II) standard deviation (III) sampling error (IV) sampling distributions
B. (I) Z score (II) T score (III) C score (IV) stanine
C. (I) statistic (II) sampling distribution (III) standard error (IV) parameter
(a) A-IV, B-I, C-IV (b) A-II, B-I, C-IV
(c) A-III, B-I, C-IV (d) A-III, B-I, C-III

23. Find out the combination of odd term in the different pairs
A. (I) student t-distribution (II) binomial distribution (III) Poisson distribution (IV) skewed distribution
B. (I) continuous distribution (II) normal distribution (III) t-distribution (IV) binomial distribution
C. (I) Poisson distribution (II) unit normal curve (III) Student's t-distribution (IV) normal distribution
D. (I) Binomial distribution (II) dichotomized variable distribution (III) Poisson distribution (IV) t-distribution
E. (I) leptokurtic distribution (II) t-distribution (II) Poisson distribution (IV) normal distribution
(a) A-I, B-IV, C-I, D-IV, E-IV
(b) A-II, B-IV, C-III, D-I, E-II
(c) A-IV, B-IV, C-III, D-II, E-III
(d) A-II, B-II, C-III, D-IV, E-III

24. Choose the mismatch.

I. Multiple regression	Partial regression coefficients
II. Phi coefficient	Genuinely dichotomous variables
III. Multiple correlation	Average ranks
IV. Slope of regression line	Regression coefficient
V. Model I regression	Treatment variable
VI. Model II regression	Classification variable

(a) II only (b) III only
(c) V only (d) VI only

25. Choose the odd item.
(a) Composite rank test (b) Chi square test
(c) Mann-Whitney test (d) Median test

26. Choose the mismatch.

I. One way ANOVA	Single independent variable
II. Interaction variance	Two way ANOVA
III. Model II ANOVA	Classification variable
IV. Model I ANOVA	Treatment variable

(a) I only (b) II only
(c) II and IV (d) None of these

27. The value of X^2 cannot be
(a) negative (b) positive
(c) zero (d) infinity

28. The value of the correlation coefficient between two variables lie between
(a) 0 and α (b) $-\alpha$ and $+\alpha$
(c) 0 and (d) -1 and 1

29. In a data $N = 11$ and calculated $r = 9$ then test of significance of 'r' by 't' test is calculated by which of the following formula?
(a) $t = r\dfrac{\sqrt{X-2}}{\sqrt{1+r^2}}$ (b) $t = \dfrac{\sqrt{N-2}}{\sqrt{1+r^2}}$
(c) $t = r\dfrac{\sqrt{N-1}}{\sqrt{1+r}}$ (d) $t = \dfrac{\sqrt{N-1}}{\sqrt{1+r}}$

30. Student's 't' test is a statistical methods to test the signi-ficance of
(a) one mean
(b) difference betwen two means
(c) find the duration
(d) establish the correlation

31. Pearson's coefficient of correlation (r) may be obtained with the help of raw scores by following one formula
(a) $r = \dfrac{\Sigma XY \dfrac{\Sigma X \cdot \Sigma Y}{N}}{N[\Sigma X^2 - (\Sigma X)^2] \times N\,[\Sigma Y^2 - (\Sigma Y)^2]}$
(b) $r = \dfrac{\Sigma XY \dfrac{\Sigma X \cdot \Sigma Y}{N}}{N[\Sigma X^2 - (\Sigma X)^2] \times N\,[Y^2 - (\Sigma Y)^2]}$
(c) $r = \dfrac{\Sigma X \cdot y}{\Sigma x^2 \cdot Y^2}$
(d) $r = \dfrac{\Sigma X \cdot y}{\sqrt{\Sigma x^2 \cdot Y^2}}$

32. The value of 'r' obtained in body wt and water % of body of 12 fishes of a species comes to 0.2515. Calculate $SE(r)$ and find correct answer

(a) 0.848 (b) 0.488
(c) 0.884 (d) 0.448

33. Which one of 't' test formula for deduction of the difference between two correlated means is

(a) $t = \dfrac{X_1 - X_2}{SE_D}$ (b) $t = \dfrac{\overline{X}_1 - \overline{X}_2}{SE\sigma}$

(c) $t = \dfrac{\overline{X}_2 - \overline{X}_1}{SE_D}$ (d) None of these

34. Which one of the following formula is correct to calculate. Standed error of the difference between means ($SE\sigma$)?

(a) $SE_D = \sqrt{SEx^2 + SEx_2^2 - 2r_{12}\ SEx_1 \cdot SEx_2}$

(b) $SE_D = \sqrt{SEx_1^2 + SEx_2^2 - 2r_{12}\ SEx_1 \cdot SEx_2}$

(c) $SE_D = \sqrt{SEx_1 + SEx_2 - r_{12}\ SEx_1 \cdot SEx_2}$

(d) $SE_D = \dfrac{\sqrt{SEx_1^2 + SEx_2 - 2r_{12}\ SEx_1 \cdot SEx_2}}{N}$

35. If the calculated value of 't' at a df on some level comes lesser than the table value then one can draw inference that

(a) the difference between two means is significant
(b) the difference between two means is insignificant
(c) not possible to draw inference
(d) the value of calculated 't' and table 't' will be same

36. The significance of difference between two means is obtained

(a) by same method in uncorrelated and correlated group
(b) by different method in uncorrelated and correlated group
(c) no set rule to obtain uncorrelated and correlated group
(d) None of the above

37. When two means are uncorrelated the following 't' formula for testing their difference is

(a) $t = \dfrac{M_1 - M_2}{\sqrt{\left(\dfrac{\Sigma x_1^2 + \Sigma x_2^2}{N_1 + N_2 - 2}\right)\left(\dfrac{N_1 + N_2}{N_1 N_2}\right)}}$

(b) $t = \dfrac{M_2 - M_1}{\sqrt{\left(\dfrac{\Sigma x_1^2 + \Sigma x_2^2}{N_1 + N_2 - 2}\right)\left(\dfrac{N_1 + N_2}{N_1 N_2}\right)}}$

(c) $t = \dfrac{M_1 - M_2}{\sqrt{\left(\dfrac{\Sigma x_1^2 + \Sigma x_2^2}{N_1 + N_2}\right)\left(\dfrac{N_1 + N_2}{N_1 N_2}\right)}}$

(d) $t = \dfrac{M_2 - M_1}{\sqrt{\left(\dfrac{\Sigma x_1^2 + \Sigma x_2^2}{N_1 + N_2 - 2}\right)\left(\dfrac{N_1 + N_2}{N_1 N_2}\right)}}$

38. In a monohybrid cross between tall and dwarf plants, 1574 tall, 554 dwarf plants were obtained in F_2 generation. By χ^2 test the result comes to 1.212. Tell;

(a) result obtained agrees with the expected ratio of 3 : 1
(b) result obtained does not agrees with the expected ratio of 3 : 1
(c) slightly in agreement with 3 : 1 ratio
(d) no result can be drawn

39. While determining degree of freedom why $df = N - 1$

(a) Because one can not change the value of one observation
(b) Because one reading is excess
(c) Because one reading is less
(d) None of the above

40. The expected frequency is calculated by one the following formula

(a) $E = \dfrac{\text{Column total} \times \text{Row total}}{\text{Grand total}}$

(b) $E = \dfrac{\text{Grand total} \times \text{Column total}}{\text{Row total}}$

(c) $E = \dfrac{\text{Column total} \times \text{Grand total}}{\text{Row total}}$

(d) $E = \dfrac{\text{Row total} \times \text{Grand total}}{\text{Column total}}$

41. Which one is not prerequisite of χ^2 test?

(a) Data should be raw
(b) Data should be qualitative
(c) Data should be random
(d) Observed frequency should be less than 5

42. One of the following formula is used to calculate χ^2 value

(a) $\chi^2 = \left\{\Sigma\dfrac{(E - O)^2}{E}\right\}$ (b) $\chi^2 = \left\{\Sigma\dfrac{(O - E)^2}{O}\right\}$

(c) $\chi^2 = \Sigma\left\{\dfrac{(O - E)^2}{E}\right\}$ (d) $\chi^2 = \left\{\Sigma\dfrac{(O\ \ E)^2}{E}\right\}$

43. While performing a Chi-square test, the data must be

(a) in raw form as scores (b) in ratio
(c) in proportion (d) in percentage

Answers

1. (a)	**2.** (c)	**3.** (d)	**4.** (a)	**5.** (d)	**6.** (d)	**7.** (c)	**8.** (d)	**9.** (d)	**10.** (c)
11. (b)	**12.** (d)	**13.** (d)	**14.** (c)	**15.** (b)	**16.** (d)	**17.** (a)	**18.** (c)	**19.** (c)	**20.** (c)
21. (c)	**22.** (b)	**23.** (a)	**24.** (b)	**25.** (b)	**26.** (d)	**27.** (a)	**28.** (d)	**29.** (b)	**30.** (b)
31. (a)	**32.** (a)	**33.** (b)	**34.** (b)	**35.** (b)	**36.** (b)	**37.** (a)	**38.** (b)	**39.** (a)	**40.** (a)
41. (d)	**42.** (c)	**43.** (a)							

41

Radiolabelling Techniques

Atomic Structure and Radioactive Decay

Atoms are composed of a nucleus, containing protons and neutrons, surrounded by electrons. Protons (p^+) have a mass of 1 atomic mass unit (amu) and a charge of +1, neutrons (n) have a mass of 1 amu and are neutral (*i.e.,* no charge) and electrons (e^-) have a charge of –1 and a negligible mass (0.0005 amu). The mass of an atom is equal to the sum of the number of protons and neutrons. An atomic mass unit is defined as the mass of a proton or neutron and approximately equals 1.66×10^{-24} grams. The number of electrons orbiting the nucleus is equal to the number of protons. The atomic number of an atom is equal to the number of protons and defines the chemical element. Isotopes are species of the same chemical element with different atomic masses (*i.e.,* a different number of neutrons). Isotopes can be either stable or unstable. Unstable isotopes will undergo nuclear rearrangements or decompose and radiation is emitted as part of this decomposition. This emitted radiation can be the ejection of subatomic particles (*i.e.,* neutrons, protons and electrons) from the nucleus or the emission of electromagnetic radiation. Alpha-radiation is not widely used in biomedical research since the relatively large α-particles are difficult to detect. Radioisotopes are found in nature and any particular chemical element is composed of a mixture of isotopes both radioactive and non-radioactive. Radioisotopes can also be synthesized. For example, bombarding nitrogen with neutrons (n) will displace a proton (p) and result in the formation of radioactive carbon (^{14}C) according to:

$$^{14}N_7 + n \rightarrow {}^{14}C_6 + p^+$$

The superscripts are the atomic masses (neutrons + protons) and the subscripts are the atomic numbers (*i.e.,* protons). The resulting ^{14}C is unstable and will decay by converting a neutron into a proton. (A neutron is composed of a proton plus an electron and this nuclear electron is ejected as a β-particle). Conversion of a neutron into a proton results in the formation of nitrogen according to:

$$^{14}C_6 \rightarrow {}^{14}N_7 + \beta \text{ (or } e^-) + \text{neutrino}$$

Syllabus

- Detection and Measurement of Radioisotopes, Incorporation of Radioisotopes in Biological Tissues and Cells.

Also emitted from the decaying nucleus is a neutrino, an entity with little mass and no charge.

Table 41.1 **Major Types of Radiation**

α-particles	2*p* 2*n* (He nucleus)
β-particles	Electron (e^-)
γ-rays	Photon ($h\nu$)

Only β and γ-radiation are widely used in biological research.

Table 41.2 **Properties of Commonly Used β-Emitters in Biological Sciences**

Isotopes	*E_{avg}	*E_{max}	Half-life
^3H	0.0055	0.015	12.3 years
^{14}C	0.05	0.15	5500 years
^{32}P	0.7	1.71	14.3 days
^{35}S	0.0492	0.167	87.1 days

*Energy expressed in MeV (mega electron volts)

Detection and Measurement of Radioisotopes

Each radioactive decay or emission, has a specific energy. These emissions have distinct energy spectrums or ranges for each particular isotope. In the case of β-radiation this energy corresponds to the velocity at which the electron is ejected from the nucleus. Each isotope is characterized by a maximal energy or E_{max}, that can be emitted and an average energy of the emissions. The average energy of the emissions is approximately one-third of the E_{max}. Radioactive decay is a random process in that the probability that a particular atom will decay is the same for each of the atoms of that particular isotope (*i.e.*, one decay does not affect another decay). However, each isotope has a distinctive rate of decay which is defined by a half life. The half-life of an isotope is the time it takes for half of the radioactivity to decay and is independent of the amount of radionuclide. Radioisotopes can be defined by the energy of their emissions and their half-life. Units of radioactivity are expressed as disintegrations (or decays) per unit time. For example, the amount of radioactivity in a sample can be expressed as disintegrations per second (dps) or disintegrations per minute (dpm). The recommended unit of radioactivity is the Becquerel (Bq) which is defined as one dps. However, the curie (Ci) is still commonly used.
The definition of one curie was originally the dps in one gram of 226Ra. This definition has been standardized to 3.7 × 1010 dps. Radioactivity is often expressed as counts (= detected disintegrations) per unit time (*i.e.*, cps or cpm). All of these units express how much radioactivity is present. Because each disintegration represents a loss of radioactivity, this value changes with time according to the half-life of that isotope. In other words, there is only half of the amount of radioactivity remaining after one half-life.

Two other terms used to describe radioactive compounds are spty refers to the disintegration rate per unit mass (*e.g.*, GBq/ecific activity and radiochemical purity. The specific activimmole) and reflects the mixture of non-radioactive and radioactive isotopes. The maximum possible specific activity is determined by the half-life. In other words, it is an inherent property of the isotope. The specific activity provides a means to convert units of radioactivity into mass units (*e.g.*, mg, moles, etc.). Radiochemical purity refers to the variety of compounds that are radiolabelled in the preparation. This is expressed as a percent and indicates the degree of purity. This can change over time due to decomposition of the compound of interest into other compounds.

Some Isotopes Used in Medicine

Bismuth-213 (46 min) for TAT.

Chromium-51 (28 d) to label red blood cells and quantify gastrointestinal protein loss.

Cobalt-60 (10.5 mth) for external beam radiotherapy.

Copper-64 (13 h) to study genetic diseases such as Wilson's and Menke's diseases.

Dysprosium-165 (2 h) for synovectomy treatment of arthritis.

Erbium-169 (9.4 d) for relieving arthritis pain in synovial joints.

Holmium-166 (26 h) for diagnosis and treatment of liver tumours.

Iron-59 (46 d) in studies of iron metabolism in the spleen.

Lutetium-177 (6.7 d) small (*e.g.*, endocrine) tumours.

Iodine-125 (60 d) in cancer brachytherapy (prostate and brain), also to evaluate the filtration rate of kidneys and to diagnose deep vein thrombosis in the leg also used in radioimmunoassays to show the presence of hormones in minute quantities.

Iodine-131 (8 d) in treating thyroid cancer and in imaging the thyroid; in diagnosis of abnormal liver function, renal (kidney) blood flow and urinary tract obstruction.

Iridium-192 (74 d) use as an internal radiotherapy source for cancer treatment.

Palladium-103 (17 d) to make brachytherapy permanent implant seeds for early stage prostate cancer.

Phosphorus-32 (14 d) In the treatment of polycythemia vera (excess red blood cells).

Potassium-42 (12 h) for the determination of exchangeable potassium in coronary blood flow.

Rhenium-186 (3.8 d) for pain relief in bone cancer.

Rhenium-188 (17 h) to beta irradiate coronary arteries from an angioplasty balloon.

Samarium-153 (47 h) in relieving the pain of secondary cancers lodged in the bone.

Selenium-75 (120 d) to study the production of digestive enzymes.

Sodium-24 (15 h) For studies of electrolytes within the body.

Strontium-89 (50 d) in reducing the pain of prostate and bone cancer.

Technetium-99 (6 h) to image the skeleton and heart muscle also for brain, thyroid.

Xenon-133 (5 d) for pulmonary (lung) ventilation studies.

Ytterbium-169 (32 d) for cerebrospinal fluid studies in the brain.

Yttrium-90 (64 h) for cancer brachytherapy and relieving the pain of arthritis in larger synovial joints.

Measurement of β-Radiation

Three methods are commonly used to measure β-radiation. None of these methods measure β-particles directly, but measure the effect of collisions between β-particles and some component of the assay system.

Geiger-Muller Counter

The G-M counter is not widely used as a quantitative instrument, but is used most often for monitoring possible radioactive contamination and estimating the amount of radioactivity. A typical G-M counter consists of a cylindrical cathode with a central anode. The tube is filled with an inert gas and sealed on one end by a mica sheet. β-particles passing through the mica sheet will dislodge electrons from the inert gas resulting in ion pairs. The ion pairs are then detected as an electrical potential between the anode and cathode. The G-M counter is unable to detect low energy isotopes since radiation needs to penetrate the mica sheet and dislodge enough electrons to create a detectable electrical potential.

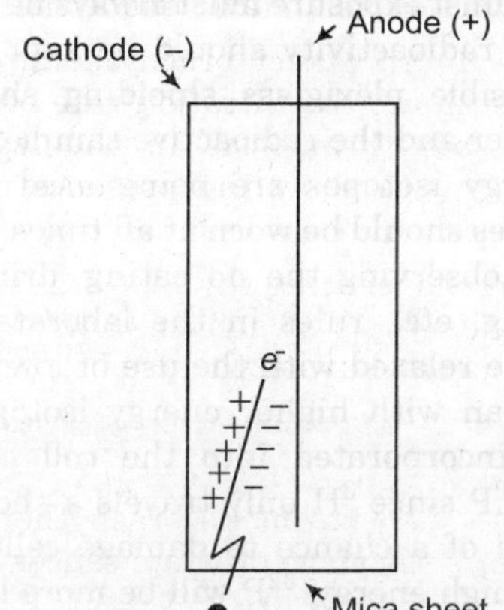

Fig. 41.1 The Geiger-Muller counter

Autoradiography

Autoradiography is the exposure of X-ray film (or a photographic emulsion) to a radioactive sample. The radioactivity behaves as light and results in the exposure of the photographic emulsion on the film. Radiation activates the silver halide in the photographic emulsion. During development the activated silver halide is converted to metallic silver. The metallic silver will appear as 'grains' on the film in positions where radioactivity is located. In other words, the exposed film will be darken in proportion to the amount of radioactivity it was exposed to. If the film is juxtaposed to the sample it is possible to precisely localize the position of the radioactivity. The two most common uses of autoradiography is in conjunction with gel electrophoresis or in conjunction with microscopy. Autoradiography of gels allows the identification and quantitation of specific proteins or nucleic. It is also possible to localize radioactive markers to particular cells in tissue sections or subcellular structures within cells by autoradiography. The typical procedure is to cover cells with a photographic emulsion and develop the emulsion after sufficient exposure. Dark grains (or spots) will appear over the cells or structures which contain the radioactive marker. It is usually desirable to use lower energy isotopes in autoradiography. High energy isotopes will travel greater distances and activate more silver halide atoms thus producing long 'tracks'.

Gamma-Ray Detection

Gamma-rays can be detected and measured by the same methods as β-particles (*e.g.,* G-M counter, autoradiography and LSC). Like β-particles, γ-rays are ionizing radiation and will be detectable with a G-M counter. Similarly, γ-rays are the same as X-rays (*i.e.,* photons) and will expose photographic emulsions. In addition, electrons (*i.e.,* β-particles) are ejected when γ-rays interact with other substances.

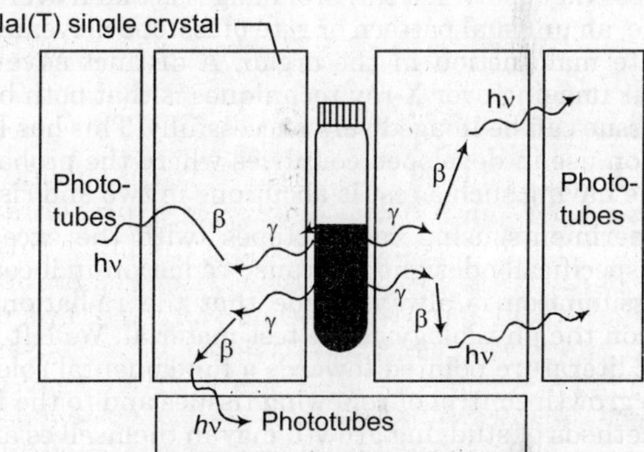

Fig. 41.2 Diagrammatic sketch for γ-ray detection

Although it is possible to measure γ-rays with a liquid scintillation counter, it is more common to use an instrument specifically designed to count γ-radiation. The counting chamber of a γ-counter is surrounded by a thallium-activated NaI crystal. When γ-rays interact with the NaI(T) secondary electrons (β-particles) are ejected. The β-particles then result in radiation in the visible range (*i.e.,* light) which is detected and quantitated by photomultiplier tubes as in scintillation spectrophotometry. The advantage of the γ-counter is that no scintillation cocktail is necessary.

Incorporation of Radioisotops in Biological Tissue and Cells

These tracers are generally short-lived isotopes linked to chemical compounds which permit specific physiological processes to be scrutinised. They can be given by injection, inhalation or orally. The first type are where single photons are detected by a gamma camera which can view organs from many different angles. The camera builds up an image from the points from which radiation is emitted; the image is enhanced by a computer and viewed by a physician on a monitor for indications of abnormal conditions. A more recent development is Positron Emission Tomography (PET) which is a more precise and sophisticated technique using isotopes produced in a cyclotron. A positron-emitting radionuclide is introduced, usually by injection and accumulates in the target tissue. As it decays it emits a positron, which promptly combines with a nearby electron resulting in the simultaneous emission of two identifiable gamma rays in opposite directions. These are detected by a PET camera and give very precise indication of their origin. PET's most important clinical role is in oncology, with fluorine-18 as the tracer, since it has proven to be the most accurate non-invansive method of detecting and evaluating most cancers. It is also well used in cardiac and brain imaging. New procedures combine PET with CT scans to give co-registration of the two images, enabling 30% better diagnosis than with traditional gamma camera alone. Positioning of the radiation source within the body makes the fundamental difference between nuclear medicine Gamma imaging by either method described provides a view of the position and concentration of the radioisotope within the body. Organ malfunction can be indicated if the isotope is either partially taken up in the organ (cold spot), or taken up in excess (hot spot). If a series of images is taken over a period of time, an unusual pattern or rate of isotope movement could indicate malfunction in the organ. A distinct advantage of nuclear imaging over X-ray techniques is that both bone and soft tissue can be imaged very successfully. This has led to its common use in developed countries where the probability of anyone having such a test is about one in two and rising.

In experiments using radioisotopes (with the exception of those specifically designed to cause radiation-induced death) the assumption is always made that the radiation has no effect on the physiology of the test material. We left that the recent literature pointed towards a fundamental role for p53 in the growth control of renewing tissues and to the fact that our methods of studying growth may in themselves affect the physiology of the cells and, in some cases, therefore invalidate the observations.

Molecular Imaging (Nuclear Medicine) of Radioactive Material

Cellular or molecular behaviour is tracked or imaged by the use of biomarkers, which are designed to attach and enhance the contrast of diseased tissue or indicate the various pathways in a physiological process. It uses very small amounts of radioactive materials to examine structure and function of organ and is often used to help diagnose and treat abnormalities developed very early in the disease. Molecular imaging is a combination of several disciplines which includes chemistry, physics, mathematics, computer technology and medicine. It differs in some ways from other forms of radiology in that these imaging studies examine organ function and structure, whereas diagnostic radiology is based primarily on anatomy. Tumours, infection and other disorders can be detected by evaluating the organ function. In a nuclear medicine imaging test, the radioisotop is injected, swallowed or inhaled. Each radiotracer is attracted to specific organs, bones, or tissues. A special camera (PET, SPECT or gamma camera) takes pictures of the distribution of the radiopharmaceutical in the body. Techniques such as PET (Positron Emission Tomography) and MRI (Molecular Resonance Imaging) are typical examples, but they require very expensive specialist equipment and also the use of radioactive materials.

Safety Guidelines

Radioisotopes are a health hazard since ionizing radiation can lead to cellular damage and DNA mutations. Radioisotopes need to be handled safely at all times and precautions against exposure must always be taken. The time of exposure to radioactivity should be kept at a minimum. Whenever possible plexiglass shielding should be placed between the user and the radioactive sample when moderate and high energy isotopes are being used. Lab coats and disposable gloves should be worn at all times. Avoid ingestion of isotopes by observing the no eating, drinking, smoking, mouth-pipetting, etc., rules in the laboratory. Some users tend to be more relaxed with the use of low energy isotopes such as 3H than with higher energy isotopes such as ^{32}P. However, ^{3}H incorporated into the cell can cause more damage than ^{32}P since ^{3}H only travels a short distance and will have more of a chance to damage cellular structures. Because of its high energy, ^{32}P will be more likely to exit the cell without doing any damage.

Exercise

1. Which of the following statement is correct regarding radioisotopes used as radiotracers?
   (a) These are the substance that reveal its presence in one way or another and thus, can be localized during an experiment
   (b) Labelled groups enable a molecule to be detected without affecting the specificity of its interactions
   (c) Radioactive molecules participate in the same reactions as non-radioactive species, but their location can be followed and the amount present can be measured
   (d) All of the above

2. Isotopes are atoms with the same number of
   (a) protons and varying number of neutrons
   (b) neutrons and varying number of protons
   (c) protons and varying number of electrons
   (d) electron and varying number of neutrons

3. Which of the following particle is the most commonly used isotopes emitted by most biologically important isotopes; easiest to detect and quantitate accurately?
   (a) Alpha (b) Beta
   (c) Gamma (d) Delta

4. What is the best sensitivity with optical fluorescence imaging?
(a) The sensitivity is about 10^{-3} – 10^{-5} mol/L
(b) The sensitivity is about 10^{-6} – 10^{-9} mol/L
(c) The sensitivity is about 10^{-9} – 10^{-12} mol/L
(d) The sensitivity is about 10^{-12} – 10^{-14} mol/L

5. Carbon dating is good for dating objects that are
(a) between 50-500 yr old
(b) between 500 and 50,000 yr old
(c) between 50,000-50,0000 yr old
(d) more than 50,0000 yr old

6. Radio isotope safety is a concern with the
(a) use of radioisotopes
(b) storage of radioisotopes
(c) sisposal of radioisotopes
(d) All of the above

7. PET scan is done using radioisotopes emitting
(a) α-rays
(b) Positrons
(c) β-particles
(d) Thermal neutrons

8. Non-stochastic effects shortly after a high dose of radiation consists of
(a) lymphopenia and haemopoietic syndrome
(b) cancer
(c) capillary occlusion and cardiac cell depletion
(d) pulmonary fibrosis and nephron loss

9. Which of the following is a preferred counter measure for the treatment of accidentally administered P^{32} isotope?
(a) ATP
(b) Potassium phosphate and dibasic
(c) Organophosphate
(d) O-phosphoric acid

10. Double chained DNA strand is made radioactive in both its chains. It is allowed to replicate twice in non-radioactive medium. The result would be
(a) all strands have radioactivity
(b) half the strands have radioactivity
(c) three strands have radioactivity
(d) radioactivity is absent in all strands

11. Match list I with list II and select the correct answer using the codes given below the lists.

List I	List II
A. Gel electrophoresis	1. Annealing
B. Serology	2. Isozymes
C. DNA-DNA hybridization	3. Southern blots
D. Restriction site analysis	4. Antiserum
	5. Sequencing

Codes

	A	B	C	D
(a)	5	2	1	4
(b)	2	1	3	4
(c)	2	4	1	3
(d)	3	4	2	5

12. A linear DNA fragment is (100%) labelled at one end and has 3 restriction sites for *Eco* RI. If it is partially digested by *Eco* RI so that all possible fragments are produced, how many of these fragments will be labelled and how many will not be labelled?
(a) 4 labelled; 6 unlabelled (b) 4 labelled; 4 unlabelled
(c) 3 labelled; 5 unlabelled (d) 3 labelled; 3 unlabelled

13. Early investigator studied various aspects (list I) of chromosomes by employing diverse techniques (list II). Match list I with list II and select the correct answer using the codes given below the lists.

List I	List II
A. The most important component of eukaryote chromosome	1. Ultraviolet absorption
B. Denaturation and renaturation kinetics	2. Density gradient equilibrium ultracentrifugation
C. Late replication of X-chromosome in mammalian females	3. Fuelgen reaction
D. Semi-conservative replication of a prokaryote genome	4. Autoradiography

Codes

	A	B	C	D
(a)	3	1	4	2
(b)	3	1	2	4
(c)	1	3	2	4
(d)	1	3	4	2

Answers

1. (d)	2. (a)	3. (b)	4. (c)	5. (b)	6. (d)	7. (b)	8. (a)	9. (b)	10. (b)
11. (b)	12. (a)	13. (b)							

42 Microscopic Techniques

Cells are small and in almost all situations a microscope is needed to observe them and their sub-cellular components. In fact the invention of the microscope led to the discovery and description of cells by **Hooke** in 1665. The microscope is still an extremely important tool in biological research. The light microscope has a limited capability in regards to the size of a particle that can be examined. The electron microscope provides additional resolution that allows for the examination of sub-cellular structures and even molecules.

Syllabus

- Light Microscopy, Resolving Powers, Aldehyde Fixation and Staining, Freeze-Etch and Freeze-Fracture Methods for EM, Image Processing Methods in Microscopy.

Light Microscopy

The principal of light microscopy (invented by Z Janssen; 1590) is to shine light through a specimen and examine it under magnification. The major optical parts of a microscope are the objective lens, the eyepiece, the condenser and the light source. The **objective lens** functions to magnify the object. The high degree of magnification of the objective lens results in a small focal length and the magnified image actually appears directly behind the objective. The **eyepiece** functions to deliver this image to the eye or camera. Eyepieces also magnify the image, but it is an empty magnification. In other words, the eyepiece enlarges the image but does not increase the ability to see fine details (*i.e.,* the resolution). The **condenser** functions to focus the **light source** on the specimen. The condensor also eliminates stray light and provides an uniform illumination. An iris diaphragm which controls the amount of light reaching the specimen is also associated with the condenser lens. In addition, the light intensity can also be controlled by adjusting the voltage applied to the lamp on some microscopes. Before using a microscope it is also important to check that all of the optical components are centered on an optical axis so that the best image and resolution are obtained. Aligning the optical components is usually simple and needs to be done periodically. The specimen is then placed on the stage and the objective lens is focused. The quality of the image produced is highly dependent on the illumination. The position of the condenser lens is adjusted so that the light is focused on the specimen and the intensity of the illumination is adjusted. On better microscopes the illumination can be controlled by both adjusting the diameter of the iris and by adjusting the voltage applied to the lamp. The amount of illumination is important for controlling resolution *vs* the contrast and the depth of field. Resolution and contrast are antagonistic in that improving one results in a loss of the other. Resolution is increased by increasing the amount of light. However, the brighter light leads to a loss in contrast. The user must decide upon the optimal mix of contrast and resolution by adjusting both the voltage (*i.e.*, intensity or brightness) of the lamp and the iris diaphragm. The iris diaphragm also has some effect on the depth of field.

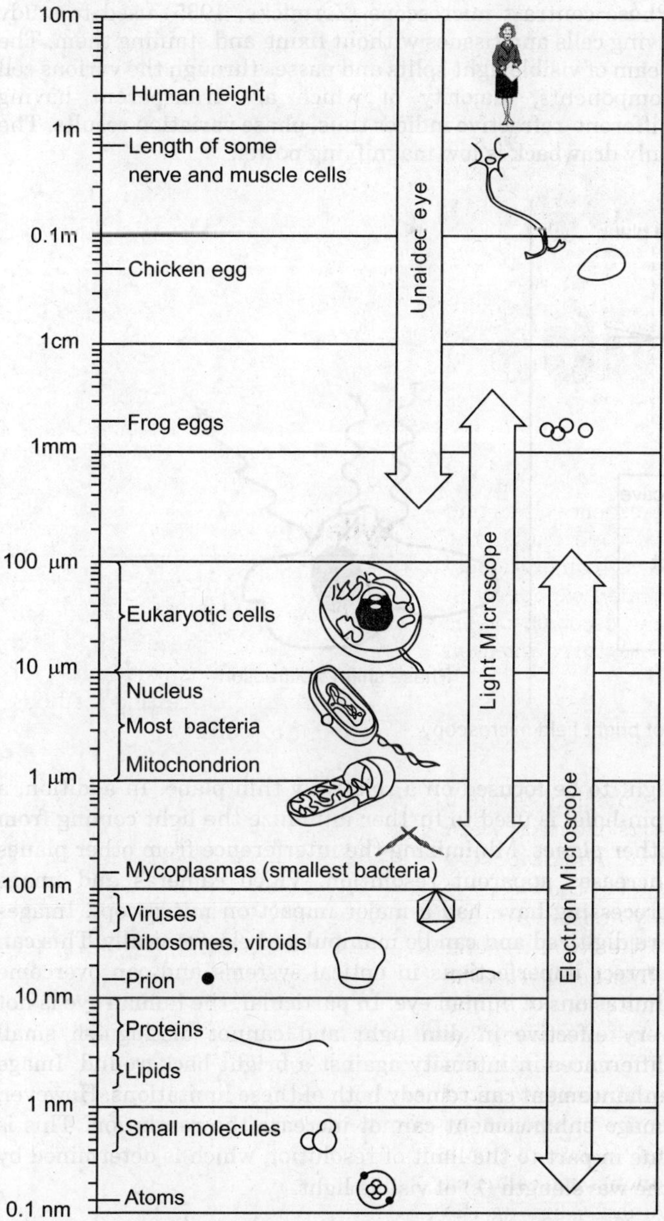

Fig. 42.1 Relationship between the sizes of various specimens and the resolution of the human eye, light microscope and electron microscope

Major Components of a Light Microscope

1. Center light source and all components on optic axis.
2. Focus objective
3. Focus condenser
4. Adjust illumination

Resolution The ability to discern fine details; typically expressed as a linear dimension describing the smallest distance needed between 2 objects so that both are seen.

Contrast Contrast refers to the number of shades in a specimen; more shades decreases the contrast, but increases the amount of information (also called dynamic range).

Depth of Field Refers to the thickness of the specimen that will be in acceptable focus.

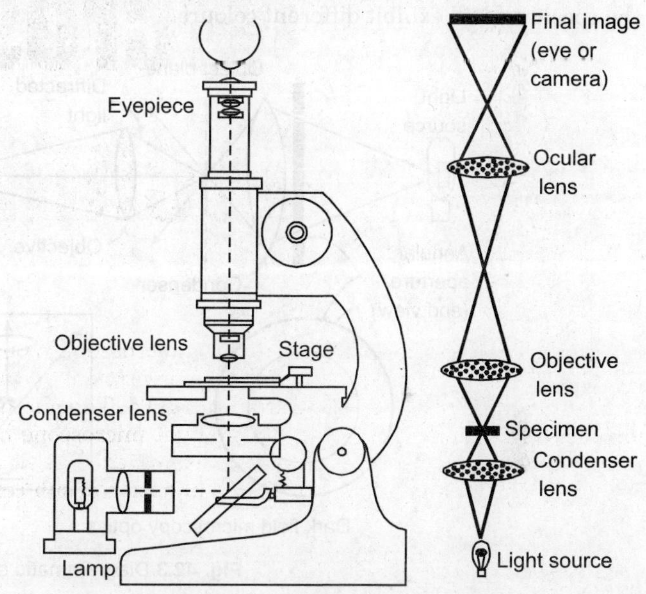

Fig. 42.2 Compound microscope

Sample Preparation

Specimens can be examined by simply placing them on a glass microscope slide under a glass cover slip. However, it is usually necessary to prepare and stain the samples before examination by microscopy. **Fixation** is a process by which cells are preserved and stabilized. Common fixatives include: acids, organic solvents, formaldehyde and glutaraldehyde. These treatments affix macromolecules in position. For example, glutaraldehyde chemically cross-links the primary amines of neighbouring proteins and organic solvents precipitate proteins and other macromolecules. Thick samples, such as tissues, will need to cut into thin sections. Following fixation the sample or cells are embedded into a supporting medium. Paraffin is a common embedding medium for light microscopy as well as various plastic resins.

- **Sectioning** is carried out with a microtome. The microtome cuts the specimen into thin slices or sections, of a specified thickness. It is also possible to collect the successive slices, called serial sections and therefore, ascertain the three dimensional aspects of the tissue or specimen being examined. The image generated by microscopy depends upon different components in the sample interacting with and impeding the light waves differentially. Biological samples are fairly homogeneous (*i.e.,* carbon-based polymers) and do not greatly impede light. Therefore, it is often necessary to **stain** cells with dyes to provide more contrast. Different dyes have different affinities for different sub-cellular components. For example, many dyes specifically interact with nucleic acids (*i.e.,* DNA and RNA) and will differentially stain the cytoplasm and nucleus. These stained sub-cellular components will differentially absorb the light waves and result in less light reaching the eyes or camera and thus appears darker. Furthermore, since the dyes only absorb certain wavelengths of light, the various structures within the specimen will exhibit different colours.

Variations of Light Microscopy

Many modifications of light microscopy that have specialized applications have been developed. In **dark-field** microscopy the specimen is illuminated from the side and only scattered light enters the objective lens which results in bright objects against dark background. This is accomplished through the use of an annular aperture that will produce a hollow cone of light that does not enter the objective lens. Some of the light hitting objects within the specimen will be diffracted into the objective lens. The images produced by dark-field microscopy are low resolution and details cannot be seen. Dark-field microscopy is especially useful for visualization of small particles such as bacteria.

Phase contrast microscope (Zermicke; 1935) used to study living cells and tissues without fixing and staining them. The beam of visible light splits and passes through the various cell components, majority of which are transparent having different refractive indices thus, phase variation results. The only drawback is low magnifying power.

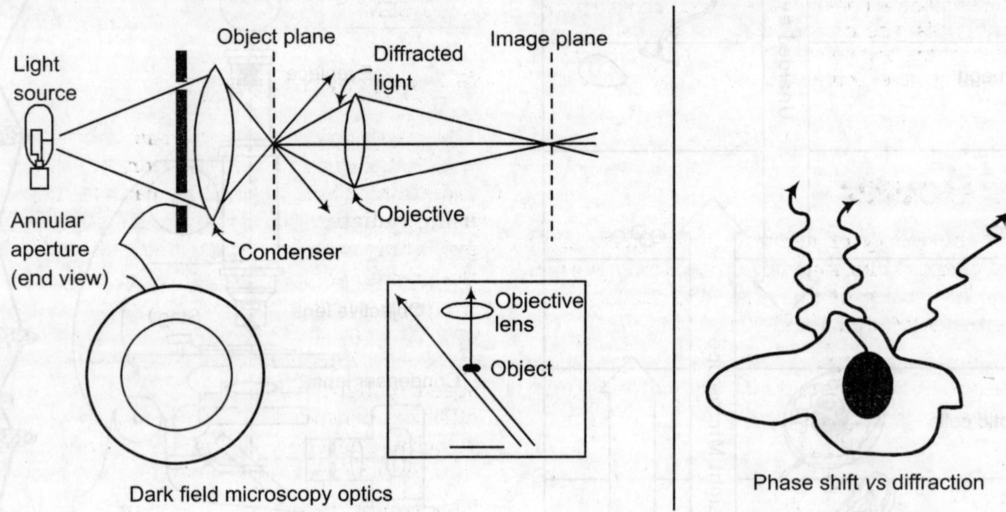

Fig. 42.3 Diagrammatic sketch of bright field microscopy

Both **phase contrast microscopy** and **differential-interference-contrast** allow objects that differ slightly in refractive index or thickness to be distinguished within unstained or living cells. Differences in the thickness or refractive index within the specimen result in a differential retardation of light which shifts the phase or deviates the direction of the light. During phase contrast microscopy the phase differences are converted to intensity differences by special objectives and condensers. Normarski optics use special condensers and objectives to recombine incident and diffracted light waves from a single source at the plane of the image. In both methods, the interference effects between the incident and diffracted light enhance small differences in the refractive index or thickness of the specimen and leads to an increased resolution without staining.

Confocal microscopy uses the objective lens as both the objective and the condenser. This allows the illuminating light to be focused on a relatively thin plane. In addition, a 'pin-hole' is used to further minimize the light coming from other planes. Minimizing the interference from other planes increases apparent resolution. Video cameras and image processing have had a major impact on microscopy. Images are digitized and can be manipulated electronically. This can correct imperfections in optical systems and can overcome limitations of human eye. In particular, the human eye is not very effective in dim light and cannot distinguish small differences in intensity against a bright background. Image enhancement can remedy both of these limitations. However, image enhancement cannot increase the resolution. This is due in part to the limit of resolution which is determined by the wavelength (λ) of visible light.

In **fluorescence microscopy**, a fluorochrome is excited with ultraviolet light and the resulting visible fluorescence is viewed. This produces a bright image in a dark background.

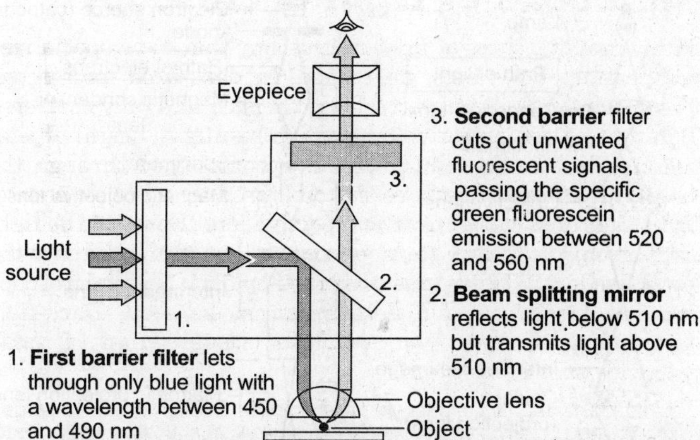

Fig 42.4 The optical system of a modern fluorescence microscope. A filter set consists of two barrier filters (1 and 3) and a dichroic (beam-splitting) mirror (2). In this example, the filter set for detection of the fluorescent molecule fluorescein is shown. High-numerical-aperture objective lenses are especially important in this type of microscopy since, for a given magnification, the brightness of the fluorescent image is proportional to the fourth power of the numerical aperture

Resolving Power

Resolution is the ability of microscope to distinguish two closely related points (also known as resolving power). Resolution gives an indication of the size of smallest object that can be distinguished by a particular lens system.

In compounds microscope, just like any other microscope, the resolving power depends upon wavelength (λ) and Numerical Aperture (*NA*) as:

$$L_m = \frac{0.61\,\lambda}{NA}$$

This equation is called **Abbe equation.**

Here, L_m = Limit of resolution, which actually is the inverse of resolving power.

NA = Numerical aperture, which is infact seen as $n \times \sin\alpha$

where, n = Refractive index of the medium

α = Half the angle width of the cone of rays collected by the objective lens from a specimen (since the maximum width is 180°, thus, $\sin\alpha$ has a maximum value of 1).

The resolution of microscope can be increased:

(i) By shortening the wavelength of visible source employed. This is the principle on which electron microscope is based. The shorter wavelength of electron beam brings about a better resolution of the object.

(ii) Another way to increase resolution is to increase the size of cone of light, *i.e.*, the numerical aperture. This can be accomplished by using oil immersion.

A microscope has magnification power also along with the resolution power. The magnifying power of a microscope can be defined as **the ratio of magnified image of a microscope to that formed in the retina of an unaided eye.** Thus,

$$\text{Magnifying power} = \frac{\text{Size of image formed with instrument}}{\text{Size of image with unaided normal eye}}$$

Table 42.1 **Resolution Power of Various Microscopes**

Microscope	Resolution Power
Compound	0.2-0.4 μm
Phase contrast	< 0.2 μm
TEM	2-10 Å
SEM	5-20 nm

Electron Microscopy

The relationship between the limit of resolution and the wavelength of the illumination holds true for any form of radiation. Thus, resolution can be increased in theory by using radiation of lower wavelengths. However, the human eye is only capable of detecting radiation with wavelengths in the range of 0.4-0.8 μm or the visible spectrum. These problems associated with the limit of resolution have been overcome by using electrons to generate an image of the specimen. Particles, such as electrons, travelling near the speed of light behave as a wave (*i.e.*, radiation) and their effective wavelength is inversely proportional to electron's velocity. Therefore, increased resolution can be achieved by examining a specimen with high velocity electrons.

The general principal of electron microscopy is analogous to light microscopy except that electrons are used to analyze the specimen instead of visible light. The illumination source is a white-hot tungsten filament, which emits high velocity electrons. The electron beam is focused by a condenser lens onto the specimen. The condenser lens, however, is an electromagnet instead of a glass. These electrons are differentially impeded by the various structures within the specimen. In other words, some of the electrons are scattered or absorbed by the atoms of the specimen. The electrons which pass through the specimen are focused with a series of magnetic objective lens onto either a photographic plate or a fluorescent screen. The electrons interact with the photographic plate or fluorescent screen as if they were photons (*i.e.*, light) and generate an image. The differential loss of electrons due to the sub-stractive action of the sample will generate an image in much the same way as the absorption of light creates an image in light microscopy.

Major Events in the Development of the Electron Microscope and its Applications to Cell Biology

1897 **JJ Thomson** announced the existence of negatively charged particles, later termed electrons.

1924 **de Broglie** proposed that a moving electron has wavelike properties.

1926 **Busch** proved that it was possible to focus a beam of electrons with a cylindrical magnetic lens, laying the foundations of electron optics.

1931 **Ruska** and colleagues built the first transmission electron microscope.

1935 **Knoll** demonstrated the feasibility of the scanning electron microscope; three years later a prototype instrument was built by **Von Ardenne.**

1939 **Siemens** produced the first commercial transmission electron microscope.

1944 **Williams** and **Wyckoff** introduced the metal shadowing techniqe.

1945 **Porter, Clade** and **Fullam** used the electron microscope to examine cells in tissue culture after fixing and staining them with OsO_4.

1948 **Pease** and **Baker** reliably prepared thin sections (0.1 to 0.2 μm thick) of biological material.

1952 **Palade, porter** and **Sjostrand** developed methods of fixation and thin sectioning that enabled many intracellular structures to be seen for the first time. In one of the first applications of these techniques, H.E. Huxley showed that skeletal muscle contains overlapping arrays or protein fila-ments, supporting the 'sliding filament' hypothesis of muscle contraction.

1953 **Porter** and **Blum** developed the first widely accepted ultramicrotome, incorporating many features introduced by **Claude** and **Sjostrand** previosly.

1956 **Glauert** and associates showed that the epoxy resin Araldite was a highly effective embedding agent for electron microscopy. **Luft** introduced another embedding resin, Epon, five years later.

1957 **Robertson** described the trilaminar structure of the cell membrane, seen for the first time in the electron microscope.

1957 Freeze-fracture tecniques, initially developed by **Steere,** were perfected by **Morr** and **Muhlethaler**. Later (1966), **Branton** demonstrated that freeze fracture allows the interior of the membrane to be visualized.

1959 **Singer** used antiboodies coupled to ferritin to detect cellular molecules in the electron microscope.

1959 **Brenner** and **Horne** develoed the negative staining technique, invented four years previously by Hall, into a generally useful technique for visualizing viruses, bacteria and protein filaments.

1963 **Sabatini, Bensch** and **Barrnett** introduced glutaraldehyde (usually followed by OsO_4) as a fixative for electron microscopy.

1965 **Cambridge instruments** produced the first commercial scanning electron microscope.

1968 **de Rosier** and **Klug** described techniques for the reconstruction of three-dimensional structures from electron micrographs.

1975 **Henderson** and **Unwin** determined the first structure of a membrane protein by computer-based reconstruction from electron micrographs of unstained samples.

1979 **Heuser, Reese** and colleagues developed a high-resolution, deep-etching technique using very rapidly frozen specimens.

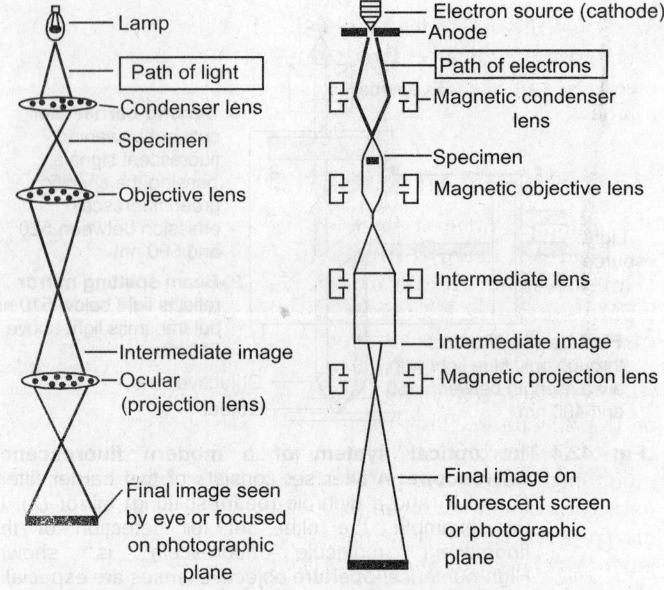

Fig. 42.5 Comparison of light and electron microscope

Sample Preparation

It is not possible to view living material with an electron microscope. Biological samples are usually fixed with glutaraldehyde, which cross-links proteins and treated with osmium tetraoxide, which stabilizes lipid bilayers and proteins. Osmium tetroxide is reduced by many organic compounds, especially lipids, which results in cross-linking. Since, electrons have very little penetrating power, samples must be embedded in special plastic resins and cut into thin sections of 0.05-0.1 μM. Removing all water from the specimen is necessary for the proper polymerization of the plastic resin. Following fixation the samples are dehydrated by exposing them to series of increasing alcohol concentrations until reaching 100%. The dehydrated sample is then put into a solution containing monomers of the embedding resin and polymerization is induced. This 'block' containing the sample is sectioned with the ultra microtome and the ultra thin sections are place onto copper or nickel grids coated with a thin carbon or plastic film for support. Contrast in electron microscopy is dependent upon atomic number of the atoms in the sample. Biological materials primarily made of carbon, exhibit low atomic number and exhibit a similar electron scattering as the carbon films on the support grid. To obtain more contrast, samples are stained with salts of heavy metals, such as osmium, uranium and lead. Staining can be carried out before the dehydration and embedding or after sectioning. Different cellular compartments and structures stain differently with the heavy metals. Electron microscopes are expensive instruments and require substantial training to operate. Electron microscopy will usually require collaboration with someone having expertise in electron microscopy. Many universities have shared instrument facilities in which users pay a fee that includes use of the instrument and technical assistance. Typically fixed samples are provided to the electron microscopy service for further processing and analysis.

Variations in Electron Microscopy

The standard form of electron microscopy involves shooting an electron beam through the sample. This is called **transmission electron microscopy**, often abbreviated TEM. **Scanning Electron Microscopy** (SEM) detects the electrons that are scattered by the specimen to form a 3-dimensional image. The sample is fixed and coated with a thin layer of a heavy metal such as platinum to form a replica of the specimen. This replica is then scanned with a thin beam of electrons and the quantity of electrons scattered along each successive point of the specimen is measured by detectors which surround the sample. Since, the amount of electron scattering depends on the angle and depth of the surface relative to the beam, the image has highlights and shadows that give it a three-dimensional appearance. The resolution of SEM is not very high (approximately 10 nm with an effective magnification of up to 20,000 times) and only surface features can be examined. Therefore, the technique is generally used to study whole cells or tissues.

Table 42.2 **Comparison Between TEM and SEM**

Transmission Electron Microscope (TEM)	**Scanning Electron Microscope** (SEM)
Resolution 2.5 nm	20 nm
Magnification 10,000-100,000 X	1000-10,000 X
Electron beam passes through the specimen and then through an electromagnetic objective lens, which magnifies the image.	Electron beam passes through the electromagnetic lenses and directed over the surface of specimen. The beam knocks out the electrons from specimen surface, which are collected, amplified and used to produce an image.
A single electron beam is used throughout for the production of a magnifying image.	Two electron beams are used, one as primary for excitation of specimen's electron and another is secondary, which is basically the collection of electrons of specimen. The secondary beam is an actual beam involved in image formation.
It has high resolutions and is extremely valuable for examining different layers of specimen.	This microscope is specially useful in studying the surface structures of intact cells and viruses.
The specimen is first killed and then used for viewing.	A living intact specimen can be used for viewing.
Provides 2-D images	Provides 3-D images.

A 3-dimensional appearance with higher resolutions than SEM can be obtained by TEM by **shadowing**. In this case, the metal coating is applied at an angle resulting in a replica reflects the height and depth of the specimen. Shadowing is often used in conjunction with other techniques. For example, in **freeze fracture** and **freeze-etching** cells are frozen in cryoprotectant and cut with a knife. Freeze-fracture will often split the lipid bilayer membranes which are then shadowed with platinum. Alternatively, in freeze-etching, the water is sublimated and replicas formed.

Negative staining can be used to visualize macromolecules and supramolecular structures such as virus particles or cytoskeletal filaments. The samples are placed on the electron transparent carbon grids and stained with heavy metals. Areas with biological structures appear more electron transparent. The fixation and manipulation of the specimen will often distort cells. Cryo-electron microscopy is used to overcome this problem. Special holders, which keep hydrated specimen at –160°C, allows viewing without fixation, staining or dehydration.

Table 42.3 **A Summary of Various Types of Microscopes**

Microscope Type	Distinguishing Feature	Principal Use
1. Light		
(i) Bright-field	Uses visible light as a source of illumination; cannot resolve structures smaller than about 0.2 μm; specimen appears against a bright background. Inexpensive and easy to use.	To observe various stained specimens and to count microbes; does not resolve very small specimens, such as viruses.
(ii) Dark-field **(Zsigmondy; 1905)**	Uses a special condenser with an opaque disc that blocks light from entering the objective lens directly; light reflected by specimen enters the objective lens and the specimen appears light against a black background.	To examine living microorganisms that are invisible in bright-field microscopy, do not stain easily or are distorted by staining; frequently used to detect *Treponema pallidum* in the diagnosis of syphilis.

Microscope Type	Distinguishing Feature	Principal Use
(iii) Phase-contrast **(Zernicke; 1935)**	Uses a special condenser containing an annular (ring-shaped) diaphragm. The diaphragm allows direct light to pass through the condenser, focusing light on the specimen and a diffraction plate in the objective lens. Direct and reflected or diffracted light rays are brought together to produce the image. No staining required.	To facilitate detailed examination of the internal structures of living specimens.
(iv) Differential Interference Contrast (DIC) **(Lebedeff; 1930)** Nomarski interference contrast microscope **(Merten, *et. al*)**	Like phase-contrast, uses differences in refractive indexes to produce images. Uses two beams of light separated by prisms; the specimen appears coloured as a result of the prism effect. No staining required.	To provide three-dimensional images.
(v) Fluorescence **(Lehmann; 1911)**	Uses an ultraviolet or near ultraviolet source of illumination that causes fluorescent microbes (green-coloured) in a specimen to emit light.	For fluorescent-antibody techniques (immno-fluorescence) to rapidly detect and identify microbes in tissues or clinical specimens.
(vi) Confocal **(Marvin Minsky; 1950)**	Uses laser light to illuminate one plane of a specimen at a time.	To obtain two and three-dimensional images of cells for biomedical applications.
2. Electron (Knoll and Ruska; 1932)		
(i) Transmission electron microscope	Uses a beam of electrons instead of light; electrons pass through the specimen; because of the shorter wavelength of electrons, structures smaller than 0.2 μm can be resolved. The image produced is two-dimensional.	To examine viruses or the internal ultra structure in thin sections of cells (usually magnified 10,000-100,000X).
(ii) Scanning electron microscope	Uses a beam of electrons instead of light; electrons are reflected from the specimen; because of the shorter wavelength of electrons, structures smaller than 0.2 μm can be resolved. The image produced appears three-dimensional.	To study the surface features of cells and viruses (usually magnified 1000-10,000X).
3. Scanned-probe		
(i) Scanning tunneling	Uses a thin metal probe that scans a specimen and produces an image revealing the bumps and depressions of the atoms of the surface of the specimen. Resolving power is much greater than that of an electron microscope. No special preparation required.	Provides very detailed views of molecules inside the cells.
(ii) Atomic force	Uses a metal and diamond probe gently forced down along the surface of the specimen. Produces a three-dimensional image. No special preparation required.	Provides images of biological molecules in nearly atomic detail and molecular processes.

Recent Developments in Optical and Electrons Microscopy

1. A fairly recent development in light microscopy is seen in the form of confocal microscope (Marvin Minsky; late 1950s). In this microscopy, the specimen is stained with fluorochromes (just like fluorescence microscope) and then one plane of small region of it is illuminated by **Laser.** Then the returned light is passed through an aperture aligned with the illuminated region. Similar planes and regions are illuminated successively until the entire specimen has been scanned. As a result, exceptionally clear two-dimensional images are obtained with improve a resolution of up to 40% over that of other microscope. **Thus, this microscope is used to obtain two and three-dimensional images of cells for biomedical applications.**
2. Since, early 1980s, several new types of electron microscopes called **Scanned Probe Microscopes** (Probe = a blunt ended instrument used for small measurement and tests) were developed. Among these, the most recent are:
   (i) Scanning Tunneling Microscope (STM)
   (ii) Atomic Force Microscope (AFM)

Scanning Tunneling Microscope uses a thin metal probe (Tungsten) that scans and produces an image revealing the bumps and depressions of the atoms on the surface of specimen. Its resolving power is much greater than that of an electron microscope (it can resolve features that are only 1/100 of the atomic size).

In **Atomic force microscope,** a metal and diamond probe is gently forced down on to a specimen. As the probe moves along the surface of specimen, a 3-D image of surface is produced.

Both STM and AFM does not require special specimen preparation, while electron microscope, on the other hand requires special preparations for visualization just like positive, negative staining, shadow casting, etc. **In electron microscope, the specimen must be first dehydrated and then placed in vacuum, while STM and AFM does require such procedure for fixation of specimen only. In these microscopes, visualization is done without modifying the specimen or damaging it with high energy radiations.** Here, mapping of the surface is done in the same manner as a blind person feels the surface of an object by its finger tips. STM was invented by **Gerd Binning** and **Heinrich Rohrer** of Switzerland in 1981 for which they got Nobel Prize in 1986.

Aldehyde Fixation and Staining

Formaldehyde and glutaraldehyde are commonly used fixatives for both light and electron microscopy. Formaldehyde is a small molecule (HCHO). The formaldehyde monomers form polymers in aqueous solutions. The liquid known as formalin is 37-40% formaldehyde by weight and most of the polymers are 2-8 units long. Higher polymers (up to 100) are insoluble in water and sold as a white powder called paraformaldehyde. To be useful as a fixative, the solution must contain monomeric formaldehyde. Dilution of formalin with a buffer at physiological pH results in an almost instantaneous formation of monomers. Conversion of paraformaldehyde to monomers requires heat (typically 60°C) and the addition of hydroxide ions. Commercial formalin contains about 10% methanol and small amount of formate ions, whereas a formaldehyde solution prepared from paraformaldehyde initially does contain any methanol or formate. Formaldehyde's mechanism of action is based on the reaction of the aldehyde group with primary amines in proteins. A cross-link between neighbouring proteins can also be formed if the primary amines are close enough together. The initial reaction of formaldehyde with protein is complete within 24 hours, but the formation of cross-links, called methylene bridges, proceeds much more slowly (several weeks). Lipids, nucleic acids and carbohydrates are trapped in a matrix of insoluble and cross-linked proteins. In practical terms, formaldehyde penetrates tissues rapidly (because of its small size), but it slowly cross-links the proteins. Glutaraldehyde contains two aldehyde groups separated by three methylene bridges (HCO—$[CH_2]_3$—CHO). These two aldehyde groups and the flexible methylene bridge greatly increase the cross-linking potential of glutaraldehyde over formaldehyde. In solution glutaraldehyde exists as polymers of various sizes which exhibit an enormous potential for cross-linking proteins. In contrast with formaldehyde, the chemical reaction of glutaraldehyde with protein is fast, but the penetration of tissue is slower, especially for the larger oligomers. Therefore, an 'EM grade' glutaraldehyde, which contains low polymers, should be used for fixation. In addition, fixation with glutaraldehyde results many leftover free aldehyde groups which cannot be washed out of the tissue. For many applications these free aldehyde groups needs need to be removed or blocked. A common blocking method is to treat with glycine or another small primary amine. The combination of formaldehyde and glutaraldehyde is also used as a fixative for electron microscopy. This takes advantage of the rapid penetration of formaldehyde molecules, which quickly stabilizes the structure of the tissue, followed by a more thorough cross-linking of proteins mediated by the more slowly penetrating glutaraldehyde.

Staining simply means colouring the specimen with a dye that emphasizes certain structures. These dyes are called **stains.**

Stains are salts composed of a positive and a negative ion (one of which is coloured called **chromatophore**).

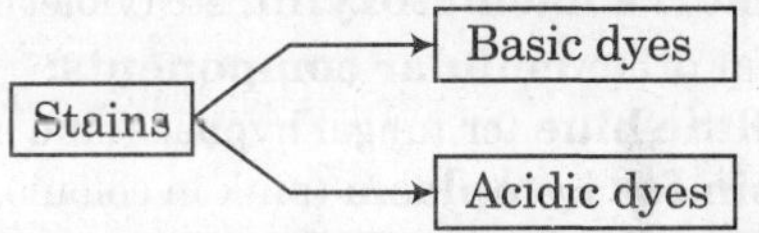

Chromatophore is positive ion basic dye, is used for staining the nucleus particularly nucleic acids, for example, **crystal violet, methyl green, basic fuchsin, safranin,** etc.

Chromatophore is negative ion.

Acidic dye is generally used for staining the cytoplasm for example, **Congo red, acid fuchsin, orange G, janus green and methyl blue.**

Staining Techniques

(i) Simple stain is an aqueous or alcoholic solution of a single basic dye. The primary purpose of a simple strain is to highlight the entire specimen so that basic structures are visible. Simple stains commonly used in laboratory are **methylene blue, carbolfuchsin, crystal violet and safranin.**

(ii) Differential stains react different with different kinds of specimen of same category (for example, **bacteria** through **Gram stain, acid fast stain,** etc).

(iii) Special stains used to colour the isolated specific parts of specimen. For example, endospore, flagella and capsule of microorganisms.

When a specimen is to be fixed, a thin film of material containing the specimen is spread over the surface of a slide. This film is called **Smear**. In the case of simple strain occasionally, a chemical is added to the solution to intensify the stain, such a solution is called a **mordant**. The other staining techniques, involve acid fast and vital staining. **Acid fast staining technique** separates species of *Mycobacterium* from other bacteria. In this procedure, all bacteria are stained with a red stain called carbolfuchsin. Afterwards, the smear is washed with acid-alcohol (decolourizer). Thus, all bacteria except *Mycobacterium* looses their colour and become transparent. The following strain (called methylene blue) strains these bacteria blue, while *Mycobacterium* species remain red thus, differentiated with others. As *Mycobacterium* causes tuberculosis and leprosy, that's why this staining technique is used as a diagnostic tool. **Vital staining** is the staining technique in which structures of living cells are stained either *in vivo* (within the body) or *in vitro* (in a preparation). Three most widely used strain for vital staining are **Janus green B** (for mitochondria, used for determination of cytochrome oxidase activity in a cell) **neutral red** (to stain plant vacuoles) and **methylene blue** (for staining the dividing cells). Generalized and most common stains for chromosomes and other cellular components are listed below:

(i) Stains for **chromosome staining:**
- (a) **Acetocarmine** (pink).
- (b) **Leucobasic fuchsin** (Warm Schiff's reagent) (pink).
- (c) **Crystal violet** (violet).
- (d) **Carbon fuchsin** (magneta).
- (e) **Gomori's haematoxylin,** etc (violet).

(ii) Stains for other **cellular components:**
- (a) **Aniline blue** for fungal hyphae (blue in colour).
- (b) **Eosin for cytoplasm** (pink in colour).
- (c) **Phloroglucinol + HCl** for lignin (red in colour).
- (d) **Ruthenium red** for pectin.
- (e) **Sudan III and IV** for suberin, cutin and oil (red in colour).
- (f) **Sudan black** for fatty substances.
- (g) **Toludine blue** for RNA.

Table 42.4 **Some Other Common Stains Used for Staining Plant and Animal Tissues**

Permanent Stains	Final Colour	Suitable For
Permanent Stains		
Aniline blue (cotton blue) in lactophenol	Blue	Fungal hyphae and spores.
Borax carmine	Pink	Nuclei; particularly for whole mounts (large pieces) of animal material, *e.g., Obelia* colony.
Eosin*	Pink	Cytoplasm (see haematoxylin also).
	Red	Cellulose, etc.
Feulgen's stain	Red/Purple	DNA; particularly useful for showing chromosomes during cell division.
Haematoxylin*	Blue	Nuclei; mainly used for sections or animal tissue with eosin as counterstain for cytoplasm; also for smears.
Leishman's stain	Red-Pink	Blood cells.
	Blue	White blood cell nuclei.
Light green or fast green	Green	Cytoplasm and cellulose (see safranin).
Methylene blue	Blue	Nuclei (0.125% methylene blue in 0.75% NaCl solution suitable as vital stain).
Safranin	Red	Nuclei; lignin and suberin of plants; mainly used for sections of plant tissue with light green as counterstain for cytoplasm.
Temporary stains		
Aniline hydrochloride or aniline sulphate	Yellow	Lignin
Iodine solution	Blue-black	Starch
Phloroglucinol + conc. HCl	Red	Lignin
Schultze's solution (chor-zinc-iodine)	Yellow	Lignin, cutin, suberin and protein
	Blue	Starch
	Blue or violet	Cellulose

*Eosin and haematoxylin are normally used to study cell for differentiation of nuclear and cytoplasmic parts.

Freeze-Etch and Freeze-Fracture Methods for Electron Microscopy

The freeze-fracturing is a method which is used to examine cellular structure under microscope when the specimen is frozen in liquid nitrogen (at –196°C) in presence of a cryoprotectant (most commonly glycerol) to prevent distortion. The frozen block is then cracked such that the fracture line passes through the hydrophobic middle of the lipid bilayers, which exposing the interior of plasma membranes. On shadowed with platinum the organic matter is dissolved away and the replica is floated of and observed under electron microscope. There are four main steps required for freeze fracture replica formation:

- **(i)** Rapid freezing of the specimen.
- **(ii)** Fracturing of the specimen.
- **(iii)** Formation of replica of the frozen fractured surface by vacuum deposition of platinum and carbon.
- **(iv)** Cleaning the replica to remove all the biological material.

When this sections of tissue are stained with osmium tetraoxide (which accentuates differences in electron density) TEM shows the trilaminar structure. This level of resolution does not reveal individual membrane protein. However, if a tissue sample is quick frozen (to avoid formation of ice crystals) and cuts with a fine knife fracture lines frequently run along the surface of a membrane splitting the bilayer into two monolayers. The surface exposed by this freeze fracture technique can be coated with a thin layer of carbon. SEM study of the resulting carbon replica shows details in bas relief of the membrane surface and the inside face of one monolayer. In many membranes, the particles are randomly positioned but in specialized regions they are clustered and ordered. As in thylakoid membranes the surface is virtually filled with particles.

Freeze-etching is sometimes used synonymously with freeze-fracture. Etching can be defined as removal of ice crystals from the surface of fractured specimen before making the replica by vacuum sublimation (*i.e.,* freeze drying). If etching step executed after fracturing standard glycerol treated specimens does not lower the ice table because glycerol can not be removed by vacuum sublimation. Etching has little effect other than cytoplasmic, nuclear and extracellular matrix give a fine granular texture. In non-glycerol treated specimens it is a valuable method for exposing natural surface of membranes or other cellular components.

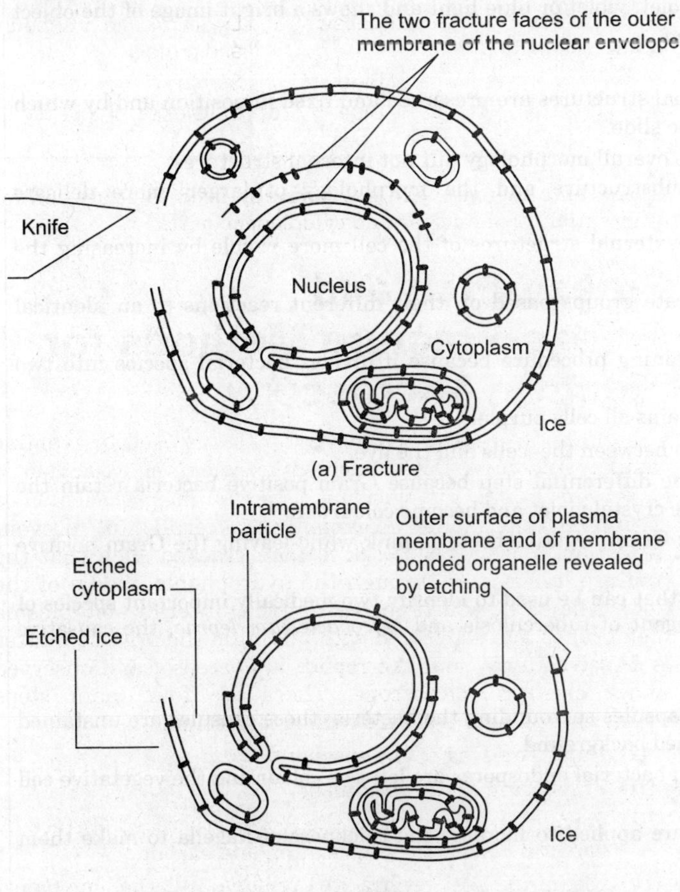

Fig 42.6 Freeze-etch electron microscopy. The specimen is rapidly frozen and the block of ice is fractured with a knife (a). The ice level is then lowered by sublimation in a vacuum, exposing structures in the cell that were near the fracture plane (b). Following these steps, a replica of the still frozen surface is prepared and this is examined in a transmission electron microscope.

The success of freeze fracture technique depends upon the tendency of the fracture plane to follow a plane through the central hydrophobic core of frozen membranes or cellular component. The resulting interior face views of the membrane give 3-D perspectives of cellular organization and structural details by macromolecular resolution. This technique has the unique ability to reveal the distribution and organization of integral membrane and proteins as intramembrane particles in the membrane plane.

Image Processing Methods in Microscopy

Image processing covers the use of techniques used to process, analyse and present image observed by a microscope. These techniques permit measurement size, shape and other features that may then be correlated with biological samples. These are of use in research, medicine, drug testing metallurgy, etc. On last decade of twenty century image acquisition was typically done with an analog video camera which was replaced by CCD camera. Which has data to a resolution of 12-16 bets. The microscopic images have an intrinsic limiting resolution. The lower resolution detector will often have a higher acquisition rate and permitting observation of faster events. In motion less object the resolution will be highest possible.

2-D Image Techniques

2-D image processing for microscopy begins with application of basic technique which most accurately reproduce the informations present in sample under microscope. These technique include arithmatic operations, image convolution, image rotation, warping, colour balancing, etc. The processing includes adjusting the brightness and contrast of image averaging images to reduce image noise and correcting for illumination informities. Image convolution is used to reduce or enhance image details by altering and pixals value. Presently a variety of algorithms have been developed for image processing some of which are of great mathematical complexity.

3-D Image Techniques

Most of the biological samples are transparent and the depth of field of the sample to focus is exceptionally narrow, therefore, it is possible to capture images through a 3-D object by using 2-dimensional equipment such as confocal microscopes. A number of software are able to reconstruct 3D model of original biological sample which may be manipulated rightly, *i.e.,* this technique turns 2-D instrument to 3-D instrument and have great application in cell biology.

Points to Remember

1. Lenses and the Bending of Light

(i) Light is refracted (bent) when passing from one medium to another.

(ii) Lenses bend light and focus the image at a specific place known as the focal point; the distance between the center of the lens and the focal point is the focal length.

2. The Light Microscope

(i) The bright-field microscope produces a dark image against a brighter background.

(ii) Resolution

(a) Microscope resolution refers to the ability of a lens to separate or distinguish small objects that are close together; magnification (total) is the product of the magnification of the objective lens and the magnification of the ocular (eyepiece) lens.

(b) The major factor determining resolution is the wavelength of light used.

(iii) The dark-field microscope produces a bright image of the object against a dark background and is used to observe living, unstained preparations.

(iv) The phase-contrast microscope enhances the contrast between intracellular structures that have slight differences in refractive index and is an excellent way to observe living cells.

(v) The differential interference contrast microscope is similar to the phase-contrast microscope except that two beams of light are used to form brightly coloured, three-dimensional images of living, unstained specimens.

(vi) The fluorescence microscope exposes a specimen to ultraviolet, violet or blue light and shows a bright image of the object resulting from the fluorescent light emitted by the specimen.

3. Preparation and Staining of Specimens

(i) Fixation refers to the process by which internal and external structures are preserved and fixed in position and by which the organism is killed and firmly attached to the microscope slide.

(a) Heat fixing is normally used for bacteria; this preserves overall morphology but not internal structures.

(b) Chemical fixing is used to protect fine cellular substructure and the morphology of larger, more delicate microorganisms.

(ii) Dyes and simple staining are used to make internal and external structures of the cell more visible by increasing the contrast with the background.

(iii) Differential staining is used to divide bacteria into separate groups based on their different reactions to an identical staining procedure.

(a) Gram staining is the most widely used differential staining procedure because it divides bacterial species into two roughly equal groups Gram positive and Gram negative.

- The smear is first stained with crystal violet, which stains all cells purple.
- Iodine is used as a mordant to increase the interaction between the cells and the dye.
- Ethanol or acetone is used to decolourize; this is the differential step because Gram positive bacteria retain the crystal violet, whereas Gram negative bacteria lose the crystal violet and become colourless.
- Safranin is then added as a counterstain to turn the Gram negative bacteria pink while leaving the Gram positive bacteria purple.
- Acid-fast staining is a differential staining procedure that can be used to identify two medically important species of bacteria-*Mycobacterium tuberculosis*, the causative agent of tuberculosis and *Mycobacterium leprae*, the causative agent of leprosy.
- Staining specific structures.
- Negative staining is widely used to visualize diffuse capsules surrounding the bacteria; those capsules are unstained by the procedure and appear colourless against a stained background.
- Spore staining is a double staining technique by which bacterial endospores are left one colour and the vegetative cell a different colour.
- Flagella staining is a procedure in which mordants are applied to increase the thickness of flagella to make them easier to see after staining.

4. Electron Microscopy

(i) The electron microscope focuses beams of electrons to produce an image.

(ii) In Transmission Electron Microscopy (TEM), electrons scatter when they pass through thin sections of a specimen; the transmitted electrons (those that do not scatter) are used to produce an image of the internal structures of the organism; TEM has a resolution about 1,000 times better.
than that of the light microscope (0.5 nm *versus* 0.2 mm).

(iii) Specimen preparation for the electron microscope involves procedures for cutting thin sections, chemical fixation and staining with electron-dense materials (analogous to the procedures used for the preparation of specimens for light microscopy); other preparation methods include shadowing or freeze-etching.

(iv) The Scanning Electron Microscope (SEM) uses electrons reflected from the surface of a specimen to produce a three-dimensional image of its surface features; many SEM have a resolution of 7 nm or less.

5. Newer Techniques in Microscopy

(i) The confocal microscope is often used to examine fluorescently stained specimens.

(a) It uses a focused laser beam to illuminate just one point on the specimen.

(b) A detector measures the amount of illumination from each point, creating a digitized signal.

(c) After examining many points (optical sections), a computer combines all the digitized signals to form a three-dimensional image with excellent contrast and resolution.

(ii) Scanning Probe Microscopy

(a) The scanning tunneling electron microscope uses a sharp probe to create an accurate three-dimensional image of the surface atoms of a specimen; the resolution is such that individual atoms can be observed.

(b) The atomic force microscope is similar to the scanning tunneling microscope in that it uses a scanning probe; however, in this microscope the probe maintains a constant distance from the specimen and is useful for surfaces that do not conduct electricity well.

Exercise

1. Which of the following statement is incorrect?
(a) In a compound microscope, the primary image is formed by an objective lens and enlarged by the optical lens to reveal a virtual image
(b) Microscope resolution increases as the wavelength of radiation used to illuminate the specimen decreases
(c) The fluorescence microscope has become an essential tool in medical microbiology to identify bacterial pathogens
(d) Fluorescence microscopy must be done on fixed and stained microorganisms

2. How does an oil immersion lens enhance the power of resolution of a microscope?
(a) Increasing the numerical aperture of the objective
(b) Reducing the spherical aberrations of lens systems
(c) Decreasing the chromatic aberrations of lens systems
(d) Preventing direct light rays from reaching the eyepiece lens systems

3. Among the following statement is incorrect?
(a) The objective lens system is solely responsible for the power of resolution of a bright-field light microscope while both the objective and the eyepiece lens systems are responsible for the magnification
(b) Polarization microscope and fluorescence microscopes use plane polarized light instead of ordinary light
(c) Mineral ions may be estimated photoelectrically in a sample from the intensities of a characteristic light wavelengths emitted by them at high temperature
(d) Fluorescence conjugated antibodies are used in direct immune-fluorescence

4. In EM, the passage of the electron beam through a very small aperture at the back focal plane of the objective .... its numerical aperture significantly, and also prevents .... electrons from forming the image.
(a) increase; scattered (b) decreases; scattered
(c) increase; reflected (d) decreases; reflected

5. Which of the following statement is false?
(a) Objective lenses with higher magnification generally have shorter working distance
(b) Even on the best light microscopes, increasing total magnification beyond 1500 cannot result in better resolution of the image
(c) Darkfield microscopy is best for visualizing live, motile microorganisms
(d) Negative stains colour the structures of interest a deep black

6. Which type of electrons is responsible in image formation in TEM?
(a) Primary electrons of the beam which transmitted through object
(b) Secondary electrons reflected from the object
(c) Secondary electrons emitted by primary electrons
(d) All of the above

7. The .... is the focal length divided by the 'effective' aperture.
(a) magnification (b) resolution
(c) numerical aperture (d) F-number

8. .... is the ability to reveal closely adjacent points as separate and distinct.
(a) Magnification (b) Resolution
(c) Numerical aperture (d) None of these

9. If green light of wavelength 500nm objective with NA 1.4 is used, then the resolution will be
(a) 178X (b) 78 nm
(c) 178m (d) None of these

10. In .... type of microscope, the field surrounding a specimen appears black, while the object itself is brightly illuminated.
(a) compound microscope
(b) phase contrast microscope
(c) dark field microscope
(d) fluorescence microscope

11. A 3-dimensional appearance with higher resolutions than SEM can be obtained by TEM by
(a) casting
(b) shadowing
(c) staining
(d) using fluorescent dyes

12. *Treponema pallidum* can be best identified using
(a) fluoresence microscope (b) bright field microscope
(c) dark field microscope (d) All of these

13. Differential staining of bacteria spore is related to
(a) Albert's staining (b) Lugol's staining
(c) Moller's staining (d) Indian ink preparation

14. Electron microscope does not help in identifying the section of bacterial spore
(a) core (b) spore cortex
(c) capsule (d) All of these

15. Which of the following statement is incorrect?
(a) Fluorescence microscopy may be used with specially stained antibodies to detect specific microorganisms
(b) Chromogenic stains which consist of a single dye rather than several dyes in combination are known as basic stains
(c) Transmission electron microscopy has a practical magnification of greater than 100,000X
(d) Acid fast stains interact with the waxy structures of the cell wall of *Mycobacterium* species

16. To improve the resolution of light microscope up to 1.5 times, we have to use
(a) red light + immersion oil between the specimen and objective
(b) blue light + immersion oil between the specimen and objective
(c) blue light + glycerine between the specimen and objective
(d) None of the above

17. In recent years, considerable attention is being given to DNA-protein interactions, because expression of genes is regulated through binding of specific proteins on regulatory DNA sequences. The pattern of protein binding of DNA can be studied by
(a) ultracentrifugation
(b) light microscope
(c) X-ray crystallography
(d) electron microscope

18. Living materials can be studied by
(a) dark field microscope
(b) interference microscope
(c) phase contrast microscope
(d) All of the above

19. The most significant drawback in electron microscope is that
(a) it is very costly
(b) it requires high technical skill
(c) it is to be lodged in vacuum
(d) living cells cannot be observed under it

20. Why can the living cells not be observed under electron microscopy?
(a) Tiemendous voltage kills the cells
(b) Cells get killed during the preparation of material to study
(c) Dehydration of cells is a must to avoid water vapours which disturb the vacuum
(d) All of the above

21. A phase contrast microscope is used to
(a) localize cell structure stained with fluorochromes
(b) to study cells and their components in a living state using a phase difference in the light rays
(c) for increasing resolving power
(d) for obtaining X-ray, diffraction pattern of DNA

22. In which of the following, UV radiation with a filter is provided in order to protect one's own eyes?
(a) Phase contrast microscopy
(b) Fluorescent microscopy
(c) Dark field microscopy
(d) Electron microscopy

23. Magnification of a compound microscope does not depend upon
(a) focal length of objective
(b) focal length of eyepiece
(c) tube length of microscope
(d) numerical aperture of objective

24. In an electron microscope higher magnification is due to the use of
(a) higher wavelengths of light
(b) high velocity electrons
(c) achromatic lenses
(d) magnetic system

25. The Feulgen nuclear reaction includes the following
(a) Removal of purines at the level of the purine deoxyribose glucosidic bond of DNA by hydrolysis
(b) Reaction of the deoxyribose with leucofuchsin to give purple colour of DNA
(c) Reaction of the free aldehyde groups with Schiff's reagent to stain DNA
(d) Both (a) and (c)

26. The resolution power of a microscope means the capacity to
(a) magnify the image
(b) distinguish between organelles
(c) distinguish between two objects
(d) distinguish between two points

27. Which of the following types of microscope uses UV-rays of higher wavelength?
(a) Ultraviolet microscope (b) Fluorescence microscope
(c) Polarizing microscope (d) Electron microscope

28. To determine the ultrastructure of a cell organelle, the most likely method to be used would be
(a) electron microscopy
(b) microdissection
(c) autoradiography
(d) phase contrast microscopy

29. DIG based technique is used for the detection of certain known DNA in an animal cell, it is preferred over radio labelling techniques because of
I. Quick result II. Safety
III. Stability IV. Easy handling
Choose the correct answer
(a) I, III and IV (b) III and II
(c) I, II, III and IV (d) I, II and III

30. Sucrose gradient centrifugation method can be used to estimate the size of

I. Proteins
II. RNA molecules
III. Ribosomes
IV. Ribosome subunits

Choose the correct answer

(a) I, II, III, and IV (b) I, II and III
(c) II, III, and IV (d) III and IV

31. Magnification of a compound microscope depends upon

I. Focal length of objective lens
II. Focal length of eye piece
III. Tube length of microscope
IV. Numerical operature of objective

Codes

(a) I, II and III (b) I, II and IV
(c) II, III and IV (d) I, III and IV

32. Match list I with list II and select the correct codes.

List I	List II
A. X-ray crystallography	1. Cell surface and larger objects
B. Phase contrast microscope	2. Examine unstained and dividing cells
C. SEM	3. Separation of subcellular components
D. Centrifugation	4. Spatial arrangement of atoms in molecules

Codes

	A	B	C	D
(a)	3	4	2	1
(b)	2	1	3	4
(c)	1	3	4	2
(d)	4	2	1	3

Answers

1. (d)	**2.** (a)	**3.** (b)	**4.** (b)	**5.** (d)	**6.** (a)	**7.** (d)	**8.** (b)	**9.** (b)	**10.** (d)
11. (b)	**12.** (b)	**13.** (c)	**14.** (c)	**15.** (b)	**16.** (b)	**17.** (c)	**18.** (d)	**19.** (d)	**20.** (d)
21. (b)	**22.** (b)	**23.** (d)	**24.** (d)	**25.** (d)	**26.** (c)	**27.** (b)	**28.** (a)	**29.** (c)	**30.** (b)
31. (a)	**32.** (d)								

43

Electrophysiological Methods

Single-Neuron Recording

It is the use of an electrode to record the electrophysiological activity (action potentials) from a single neuron.An electrode introduced into the brain of a living animal will detect electrical activity that is generated by the neurons adjacent to the electrode tip. If the electrode is a microelectrode, with a tip size of 3 to 10 micrometers, the electrode will often isolate the activity of a single neuron. The activity consists of the voltages generated in the extra cellular matrix by the current fields outside the cell when it generates an action potential. Recording in this way is generally called 'single-unit' recording. The recorded action potentials look very much like the action potentials that are recorded intracellularly, but the signals are very much smaller (typically about 0.1 mV). Recordings of single neurons in living animals have provided important insights into how the brain processes information, following the hypothesis put forth by **Edgar Adrian** that unitary action potential events are the fundamental means of communication in the brain. Microelectrodes used for extra cellular single-unit recordings are usually very fine wires made from tungsten or platinum-iridium alloys that are insulated except at their extreme tip and are less often glass micropipettes filled with a weak electrolyte solution similar in composition to extra cellular fluid. Hubel and Wiesel were awarded the Nobel Prize in Physiology or Medicine in 1981.

Syllabus

- Single-Neuron Recording, Patch-Clamp Recording, ECG, Brain Activity Recording, Lesion and Stimulation of Brain, Pharmacological Testing, PET, MRI, CAT.

The Patch Clamp Technique

It is a laboratory technique in electrophysiology that allows the **study of single or multiple ion channels in cells**.The technique can be applied to a wide variety of cells, but is especially useful in the study of excitable cells such as neurons, cardiomyocytes, muscle fibres and pancreatic beta cells. It can also be applied to the study of bacterial ion channels in specially prepared giant spheroplasts. It is a laboratory technique in electrophysiology that allows the study of single or multiple ion channels in cells. **Erwin Neher** and **Bert Sakmann** developed the patch clamp in the late 1970s and early 1980s. This discovery made it possible to record the currents of single ion channels for the first time, proving their involvement in fundamental cell processes such as action potential conduction. Neher and Sakmann received the Nobel Prize in Physiology or Medicine in 1991 for this work. Patch clamp recording uses, as an electrode, a glass micropipette that has an open tip diameter of about one micrometer, a size enclosing a membrane surface area or 'patch' that often contains just one or a few ion channel molecules. In some experiments, the micropipette tip is heated in a microforge to produce a smooth surface that assists in forming a high resistance seal with the cell membrane. The interior of the pipette is filled with a solution matching the ionic composition of the bath solution, as in the case of cell-attached recording, or the cytoplasm for whole-cell recording. Unlike traditional two-electrode voltage clamp recordings, patch clamp recording **uses a single electrode to record currents**.

Electrocardiograph (ECG)

As cardiac impulses pass through the heart, electrical currents spread into the tissues surrounding the heart, and a small portion of these currents spread throughout the surface of the body. If electrodes are placed on the skin on opposite sides of the heart, electrical potential generated by these currents can be recorded. Electrocardiograph is an instrument which records the electrical activity of the heart during a cardiac cycle. A record of the minute electrical pulses generated by the heart used to determine the condition of the patient's heart is the Electrocardiogram. Electrodes are placed on the chest and limbs, and the impulses which they detect are amplified by the electrograph to which the electrodes are connected. The ECG was developed by William Einthoven of Leiden University, England between 1903 and 1910.

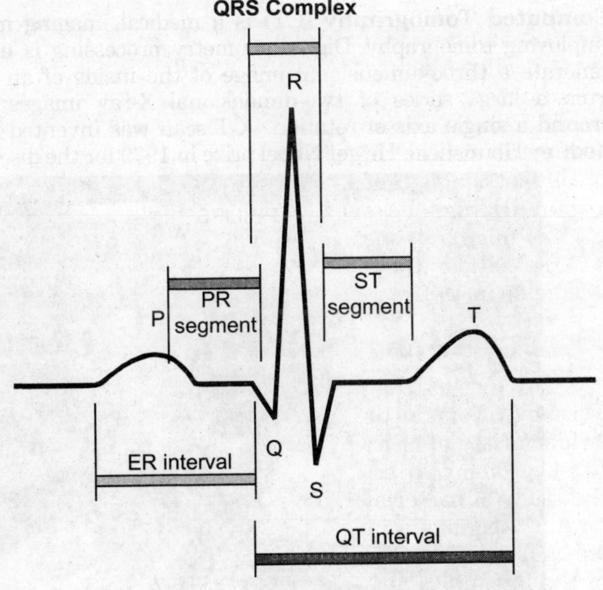

Fig. 43.1 A representative ECG signal

Electrical impulses in the heart originate in the sinoatrial node and travel through the heart muscle where they impart electrical initiation of systole or contraction of the heart. The electrical waves can be measured at selectively placed electrodes (electrical contacts) on the skin.Electrodes on different sides of the heart measure the activity of different parts of the heart muscle. An ECG displays the voltage between pairs of these electrodes, and the muscle activity that they measure, from different directions, also understood as vectors. This display indicates the overall rhythm of the heart and weaknesses in different parts of the heart muscle. It is the best way to measure and diagnose abnormal rhythms of the heart, particularly abnormal rhythms caused by damage to the conductive tissue that carries electrical signals, or abnormal rhythms caused by levels of dissolved salts (electrolytes), such as potassium, that are too high or low. In myocardial infarction (MI), the ECG can identify damaged heart muscle. The ECG cannot reliably measure the pumping ability of the heart; for which ultrasound-based (echocardiography) or nuclear medicine tests are used. A typical electrocardiograph runs at a paper speed of 25 mm/s, although faster paper speeds are occasionally used. Each small block of ECG paper is 1 mm². At a paper speed of 25 mm/s, one small block of ECG paper translates into 0.04 s (or 40 ms). Five small blocks make up 1 large block, which translates into 0.20 s (or 200 ms). Hence, there are 5 large blocks per second. A standard signal of 1 mV must move the stylus vertically 1 cm, that is two large squares on ECG paper.

Leads used in ECG

Limb Leads

Leads I, II and III are the so called limb leads. Lead I is a dipole with the negative (white) electrode on the right arm and the positive (black) electrode on the left arm.

Lead II is a dipole with the negative (white) electrode on the right arm and the positive (red) electrode on the left leg. Lead III is a dipole with the negative (black) electrode on the left arm and the positive (red) electrode on the left leg.

Augmented Limb

Leads *a*VR, *a*VL, and *a*VF are 'augmented limb leads'. They are derived from the same three electrodes as leads I, II, and III. However, they view the heart from different angles. Lead *a*VR or "augmented vector right" has the positive electrode (white) on the right arm. The negative electrode is a combination of the left arm (black) electrode and the left leg (red) electrode, which 'augments' the signal strength of the positive electrode on the right arm. Lead aVL or "augmented vector left" has the positive (black) electrode on the left arm. The negative electrode is a combination of the right arm (white) electrode and the left leg (red) electrode, which 'augments' the signal strength of the positive electrode on the left arm. Lead aVF or "augmented vector foot" has the positive (red) electrode on the left leg. The negative electrode is a combination of the right arm (white) electrode and the left arm (black) electrode, which 'augments' the signal of the positive electrode on the left leg.

Precordial

The precordial leads V1, V2, V3, V4, V5 and V6 are placed directly on the chest. Because of their close proximity to the heart, they do not require augmentation.

Waves and Intervals

A typical ECG tracing of a normal heartbeat (or cardiac cycle) consists of a P-wave, a QRS complex and a T-wave.

A small U wave is normally visible in 50 to 75% of ECGs. The baseline voltage of the electrocardiogram is known as the isoelectric line.

Typically the isoelectric line is measured as the portion of the tracing following the T-wave and preceding the next P-wave.

P-Wave

During normal **atrial depolarization**, the main electrical vector is directed from the SA node towards the AV node, and spreads from the right atrium to the left atrium.

This turns into the P-wave on the ECG, which is upright in II, III, and *a*VF and inverted in *a*VR. A P-wave must be upright in leads II and *a*VF and inverted in lead *a*VR to designate a cardiac rhythm as Sinus Rhythm. The relationship between P-waves and QRS complexes helps distinguish various cardiac arrhythmias. The shape and duration of the P waves may indicate atrial enlargement

QRS Complex

The QRS complex is a structure on the ECG that corresponds to the depolarization of the ventricles. Because the ventricles contain more muscle mass than the atria, the QRS complex is larger than the P-wave. In addition, because the His/Purkinje system coordinates the depolarization of the ventricles, the QRS complex tends to look 'spiked' rather than rounded due to the increase in conduction velocity. A normal QRS complex is 0.08 to 0.12 sec (80 to 120 ms) in duration represented by three small squares or less, but any abnormality of conduction takes longer, and causes widened QRS complexes.

PR/PQ Interval

The PR interval is measured from the beginning of the P-wave to the beginning of the QRS complex. It is usually 120 to 200 ms long. On an ECG tracing, this corresponds to 3 to 5 small boxes. In case a Q-wave was measured with a ECG the PR interval is also commonly named PQ interval instead. A PR interval of over 200 ms may indicate a first degree heart block. A short PR interval may indicate a pre-excitation syndrome *via* an accessory pathway that leads to early activation of the ventricles, such as seen in Wolff-Parkinson-White syndrome. A variable PR interval may indicate other types of heart block. The duration, amplitude, and morphology of the QRS complex is useful in diagnosing cardiac arrhythmias, conduction abnormalities, ventricular hypertrophy, myocardial infarction, electrolyte derangements, and other disease states. 'Buried' inside the QRS wave is the atrial repolarization wave, which resembles an inverse P-wave. It is far smaller in magnitude than the QRS and is therefore obscured by it.

ST Segment

The ST segment connects the QRS complex and the T-wave and has a duration of 0.08 to 0.12 sec (80 to 120 ms). It starts at the J point (junction between the QRS complex and ST segment) and ends at the beginning of the T-wave. The typical ST segment duration is usually around 0.08 sec (80 ms). The normal ST segment has a slight upward concavity.

T-Wave

The T-wave represents the repolarization (or recovery) of the ventricles. The interval from the beginning of the QRS complex to the apex of the T-wave is referred to as the absolute refractory period. The last half of the T-wave is referred to as the relative refractory period (or vulnerable period). Tall or 'tented' symmetrical T-waves may indicate hyperkalemia. Flat T-waves may indicate coronary ischemia or hypokalemia.

QT Interval

The QT interval is measured from the beginning of the QRS complex to the end of the T-wave. Normal values for the QT interval are between 0.30 and 0.44 seconds.The QT interval as well as the corrected QT interval are important in the diagnosis of long QT syndrome and short QT syndrome. The QT interval varies based on the heart rate, and various correction factors have been developed to correct the QT interval for the heart rate.The QT interval represents on an ECG the total time needed for the ventricles to depolarize and repolarize.

U-Wave

The U-wave is not always seen. It is typically small, and, by definition, follows the T-wave. U-waves are thought to represent repolarization of the papillary muscles or Purkinje fibres. It is prominent. An inverted U-wave may represent myocardial ischemia or left ventricular volume overload.

Computed Axial Tomography (CAT)

Computed Tomography (CT) is a medical imaging method employing tomography. Digital geometry processing is used to generate a three-dimensional image of the inside of an object from a large series of two-dimensional X-ray images taken around a single axis of rotation. CT scan was invented by Sir Godfrey Hounsfield. He got Nobel prize in 1979 for the discovery.

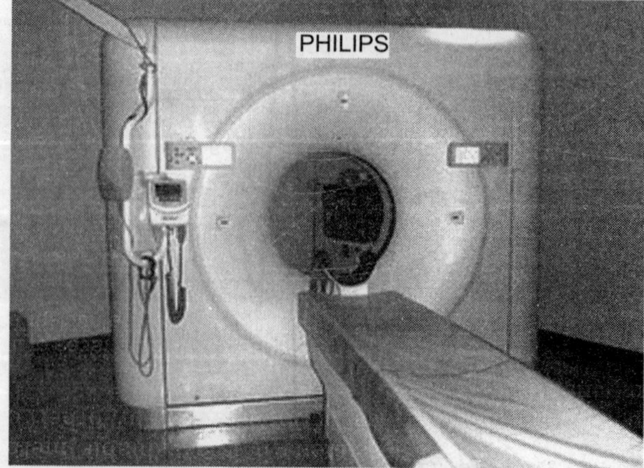

Fig. 43.2 CT scanner

The word 'tomography' is derived from the Greek tomos (slice) and graphein (to write).Computed tomography was originally known as the 'EMI scan' as it was developed at a research branch of EMI, a company best known today for its music and recording business. It was later known as computed axial tomography (CAT or CT scan) and body section rontgenography.

Positron Emission Tomography (PET)

Positron Emission Tomography (PET) is a nuclear medicine imaging technique which produces a three-dimensional image or picture of functional processes in the body. The system detects pairs of gamma rays emitted indirectly by a positron-emitting radionuclide (tracer), which is introduced into the body on a biologically active molecule. Images of tracer concentration in 3-dimensional space within the body are then reconstructed by computer analysis. In modern scanners, this reconstruction is often accomplished with the aid of a CT X-ray scan performed on the patient during the same session, in the same machine.If the biologically active molecule chosen for PET is FDG, an analogue of glucose, the concentrations of tracer imaged then give tissue metabolic activity, in terms of regional glucose uptake.To conduct the scan, a short-lived radioactive tracer isotope, is injected into the living subject (usually into blood circulation). The tracer is chemically incorporated into a biologically active molecule. The molecule most commonly used for this purpose is fluorodeoxyglucose (FDG), a sugar, for which the waiting period is typically an hour. As the radioisotope undergoes positron emission decay (also known as positive beta decay), it emits a positron, a particle with the opposite charge of an electron. After traveling up to a few millimeters the positron encounters and annihilates with an electron, producing a pair of annihilation (gamma) photons moving in opposite directions. These are detected when they reach a scintillator in the scanning device, creating a burst of light which is detected by photomultiplier tubes or silicon avalanche photodiodes.

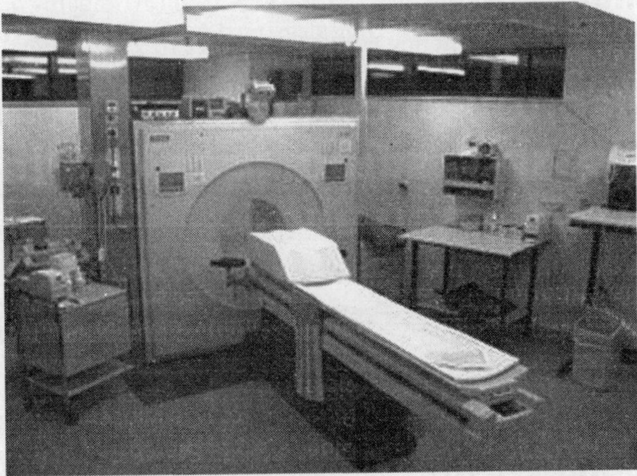

Fig. 43.3 The PET machine

Radioisotopes

Radionuclides used in PET scanning are typically isotopes with short half lives such as carbon-11 (~20 min), nitrogen-13 (~10 min), oxygen-15 (~2 min), and fluorine-18 (~110 min).These radionuclides are incorporated either into compounds normally used by the body such as glucose (or glucose analogues), water or ammonia, or into molecules that bind to receptors or other sites of drug action. Such labelled compounds are known as radiotracers.

Applications

PET is both a medical and research tool. It is used heavily in clinical oncology (medical imaging of tumours and the search for metastases), and for clinical diagnosis of certain diffuse brain diseases such as those causing various types of dementias. PET is also an important research tool to map normal human brain and heart function.

Magnetic Resonance Imaging (MRI)

Magnetic Resonance Imaging (MRI) or Nuclear Magnetic resonance imaging (NMRI), is primarily a medical imaging technique most commonly used in radiology to visualize the structure and function of the body. It provides detailed images of the body in any plane.

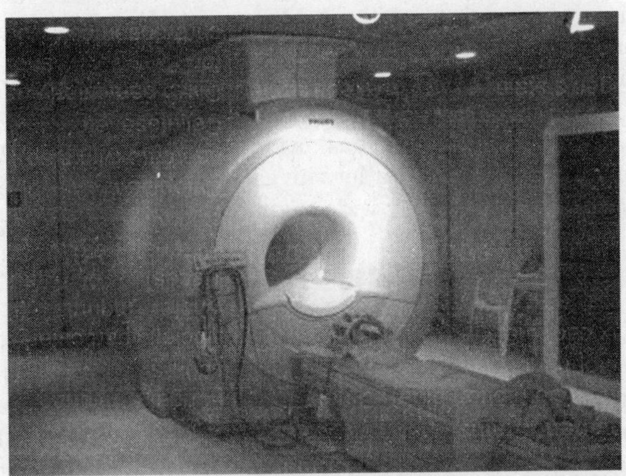

Fig. 43.4 The MRI instrument

NMR was discovered by Bloch and Purcell in 1952.MRI provides much greater contrast between the different soft tissues of the body than Computed Tomography (CT) does, making it especially useful in neurological (brain), musculoskeletal, cardiovascular, and oncological (cancer) imaging. Unlike CT, it uses no ionizing radiation, but uses a powerful magnetic field to align the nuclear magnetization of (usually) hydrogen atoms in water in the body. Radiofrequency fields are used to systematically alter the alignment of this magnetization, causing the hydrogen nuclei to produce a rotating magnetic field detectable by the scanner. This signal can be manipulated by additional magnetic fields to build up enough information to construct an image of the body.The body is mainly composed of water molecules which each contain two hydrogen nuclei or protons. When a person goes inside the powerful magnetic field of the scanner these protons align with the direction of the field. A second radiofrequency electromagnetic field is then briefly turned on causing the protons to absorb some of its energy. When this field is turned off the protons release this energy at a radiofrequency which can be detected by the scanner.The position of protons in the body can be determined by applying additional magnetic fields during the scan which allows an image of the body to be built up. These are created by turning gradients coils on and off which creates the knocking sounds heard during an MR scan.Diseased tissue, such as tumors, can be detected because the protons in different tissues return to their equilibrium state at different rates.

Applications

In clinical practice, MRI is used to distinguish pathologic tissue (such as a brain tumor) from normal tissue. One advantage of an MRI scan is that it is harmless to the patient. It uses strong magnetic fields and non-ionizing radiation in the radio frequency range compare this to CT scans and traditional X-rays which involve doses of ionizing radiation and may increase the risk of malignancy, especially in a foetus.

Functional MRI (fMRI)

It is a type of specialized MRI scan. It measures the haemodynamic response related to neural activity in the brain or spinal cord of humans or other animals. It is one of the most recently developed forms of neuroimaging. Since, the early 1990s, fMRI has come to dominate the brain mapping field due to its low invasiveness, lack of radiation exposure, and relatively wide availability.

Electroencephalography (EEG)

EEG is the recording of electrical activity along the scalp produced by the firing of neurons within the brain. In clinical contexts, EEG refers to the recording of the brain's spontaneous electrical activity over a short period of time, usually 20-40 minutes, as recorded from multiple electrodes placed on the scalp. EEG used to be a first-line method for the diagnosis of tumors, stroke and other focal brain disorders, but this use has decreased with the advent of anatomical imaging techniques such as MRI and CT. EEG was discovered in 1929 by a German psychiatrist Hans Berger . In 1932 by a British electrophysiologist, Edgar Adrian won Nobel prize for the demonstration of electrical impulses from brain.

Fig. 43.5 The EEG instrument

EEG

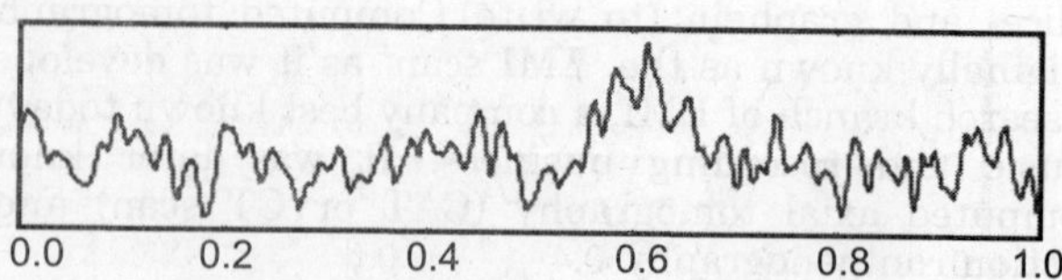

Fig. 43.6 The EEG spectrum of a patient

Second EEG

It is generally accepted that the activity measured by EEG is electrical potentials created by the post-synaptic currents, rather than by action potentials. More specifically, the scalp electrical potentials that produce EEG are due to the extra-cellular ionic currents caused by dendritic electrical activity (whereas the fields producing magnetoence-phalographic signals are associated with intracellular ionic currents).

Wave Patterns

Delta Waves

Delta is the frequency range up to 3 Hz. It tends to be the highest in amplitude and the slowest waves. It is seen normally in adults in slow wave sleep. It is also seen normally in babies.

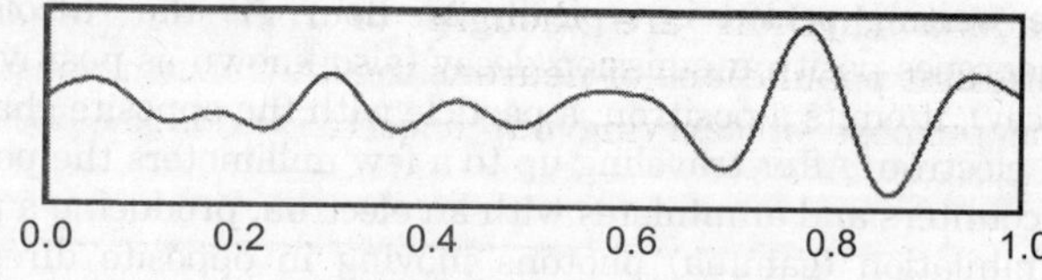

Fig. 43.7 A typical delta wave

Theta Waves

Theta is the frequency range from 4 Hz to 7 Hz. Theta is seen normally in young children. It may be seen in drowsiness or arousal in older children and adults; it can also be seen in meditation.

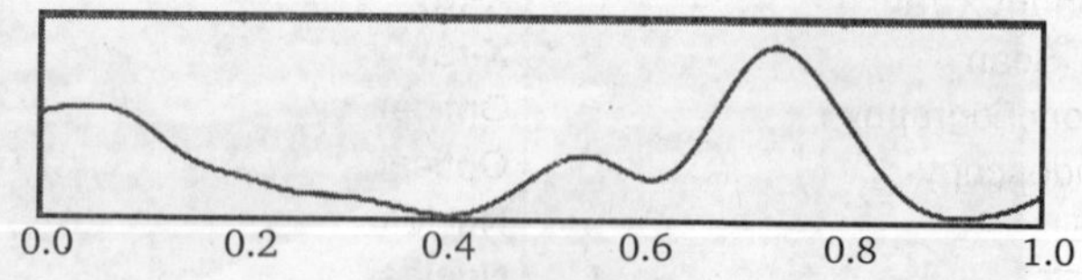

Fig. 43.8 A typical theta wave signal

Alpha Wave

Alpha is the frequency range from 8 Hz to 12 Hz. Hans Berger named the first rhythmic EEG activity he saw, the "alpha wave." This is activity in the 8-12 Hz range seen in the posterior regions of the head on both sides, being higher in amplitude on the dominant side. It is brought out by closing the eyes and by relaxation.0

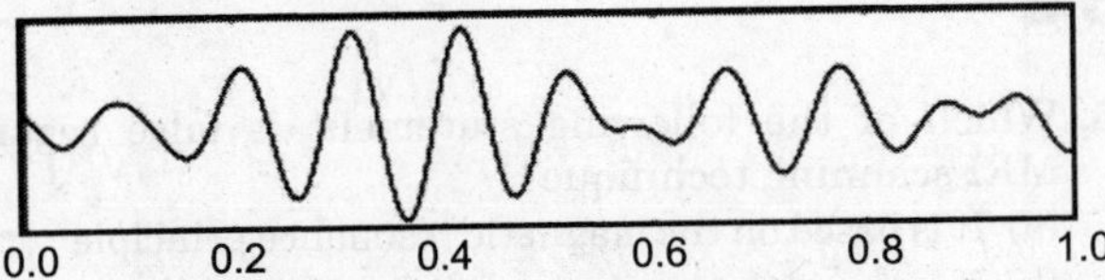

Fig. 43.9 A typical alpha wave signal

Beta Wave

Beta is the frequency range from 12 Hz to about 30 Hz. It is seen usually on both sides in symmetrical distribution and is most evident frontally. Low amplitude beta with multiple and varying frequencies is often associated with active, busy or anxious thinking and active concentration. Rhythmic beta with a dominant set of frequencies is associated with various pathologies and drug effects, especially benzodiazepines.

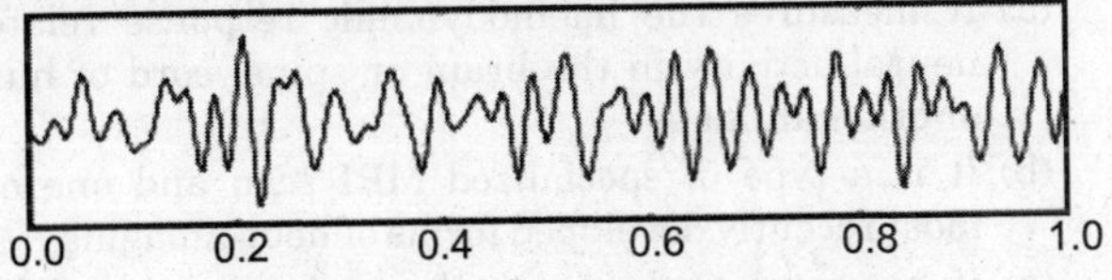

Fig. 43.10 A typical beta wave signal

Gamma Wave

Gamma is the frequency range approximately 26-100 Hz. Gamma rhythms are thought to represent binding of different populations of neurons together into a network for the purpose of carrying out a certain cognitive or motor function.

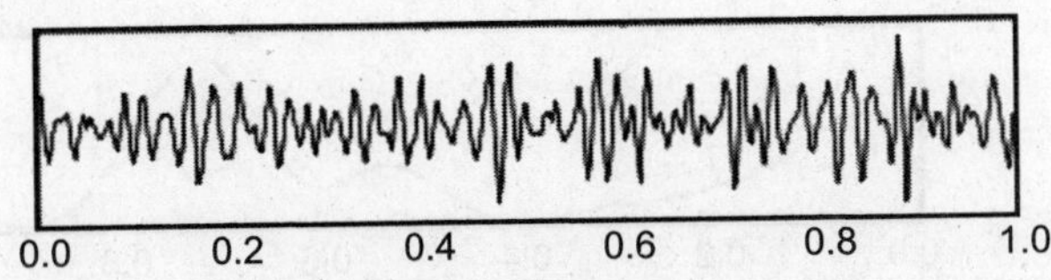

Fig. 43.11 A typical gamma wave signal

Medical Imaging Instruments

Barium X-ray	X-ray
CT Scan	X-ray
Bronchography	Optical
Endoscopy	Optical
PET	Nuclear
MET	Nuclear
Echocardiograph	Ultrasound
ECG	Bioelectricity
Electromyograph EMG	Bioelectricity
EEG	Bioelectricity

Lesion and Stimulation of Brain

A lesion is an area of tissue that has been damaged through injury or disease. So a brain lesion is an area of injury or disease within the brain. While the definition sounds simple, understanding brain lesions can be complicated. That's because there are many types of brain lesions. They can range from small to large, from few to many, from relatively harmless to life-threatening. Brain lesions can be caused by injury, infection, exposure to certain chemicals, problems with the immune system, and more. Many times and cause is not known. Some common brain lesions are:

(i) **Abscesses** Areas of infection, including pus and inflamed tissue.

(ii) **Alzheimer's disease** Nerve cells die, leaving behind damaged areas of the brain.

(iii) **Arteriovenous Malformations** (AVMs) Occurs during early development. Arteries and veins in the brain grow in a tangle and become connected by tube-like structures called fistulae. These fragile vessels may rupture, leaking blood into the brain or brain tissue may not receive enough blood.

(iv) **Cerebral Infarction** A cluster of brain cells have died this brain lesion is caused by a **stroke.**

Stimulation is the application of a stimulus to responsive structure, such as a nerve or muscle, regardless of whether the strength of the stimulus is sufficient to produce excitation. It includes:

(i) **Deep Brain Stimulation** (DBS), *i.e.*, stimulation of a specific area of the thalamus, globus pallidus or subthalamic nucleus by means of an electrode implanted in the brain.

(ii) **Functional Electrical Stimulation** (FES), *i.e.*, the application of an electric current to stimulate and restore partial function to a muscle disabled by neurologic lesions.

(iii) **Transcutaneous Electrical Nerve Stimulation** (TENS), *i.e.*, electrical stimulation of nerves for relief of pain.

(iv) **Transcutaneous Nerve Stimulation** (TNS), *i.e.*, electrical stimulation of nerves for relief of pain by delivering a current through the skin.

Deep brain stimulation is a way to inactivate parts of the brain that **cause Parkinson's disease** and associated symptoms without destroying the other parts. In this electrodes are placed in the thalamus to treat essential tremour and **multiple sclerosis** or in the globus pallidus for **Parkinson's disease.**

Exercise

1. Electrophysiological studies deal with
(a) brain (b) heart
(c) spinal cord (d) lungs

2. Which of the following statement is correct regarding 'single-unit' recording?
(a) The recorded action potentials in this study look very much like the action potentials that are recorded intracellularly, but the signals are very much smaller (typically about 0.1 mV)
(b) Recordings of single neurons in living animals have provided important insights into how the brain processes information
(c) Microelectrodes used for extra cellular single-unit recordings are usually very fine wires made from tungsten or platinum-iridium alloys that are insulated except at their extreme tip and are less often glass micropipettes filled with a weak electrolyte solution similar in composition to extra cellular fluid
(d) All of the above

3. In patch clamp setup, the word 'patch' represents
(a) the shape of glass micropipette
(b) the open tip of micropipette
(c) open tip of micropipette with a membrane surface
(d) None of the above

4. Find the unmatched regarding lead (s) type and electrodes as they placed on different body parts.

Lead Type	Body Parts
Lead I	Dipole with the negative (white) electrode on the right arm and the positive (black) electrode on the left arm.
Lead II	Dipole with the negative (white) electrode on the right arm and the positive (red) electrode on the left leg.
Lead III	Dipole with the negative (black) electrode on the left arm and the positive (red) electrode on the left leg.
Lead aVF	Positive (red) electrode on the left leg. The negative electrode is a combination of the right arm (white) electrode and the left arm (black) electrode.
Lead aVR	Positive electrode (white) on the right arm. The negative electrode is a combination of the left arm (black) electrode and the left leg (red) electrode.
Lead aVL	Positive (black) electrode on the left arm. The negative electrode is a combination of the right arm (white) electrode and the left leg (red) electrode.
Lead V1	Right hand
Lead V4	Chest

(a) Lead I only
(b) Lead aVR only
(c) Lead VI only
(d) Lead III, aVL and VI

5. Which of the following statement is false regarding MRI scanning technique?
(a) It is based on the magnetic resonance principle
(b) It provides much greater contrast between the different
soft tissues of the body than computed tomography
(c) It uses no ionizing radiation and radioactive water and uses a powerful magnetic field to align the nuclear magnetization of (usually) hydrogen atoms in water in the body
(d) It is especially useful in neurological (brain), musculo-skeletal, cardiovascular and oncological (cancer) imaging

6. Which of the following statement is correct regarding fMRI?
(a) It measures the haemodynamic response related to neural activity in the brain or spinal cord of humans or other animals
(b) It is a type of specialized MRI scan and one of the most recently developed forms of neuroimaging
(c) It has come to dominate the brain mapping field due to its low invasiveness, lack of radiation exposure, and relatively wide availability
(d) All of the above

7. Suppose you constantly faces headache problem and doctor adviced you to go for a EEG scan. When you close your eyes and relaxed a EEG signal is recorged. Which of the following wave pattern more likely you can expect?
(a) Delta wave

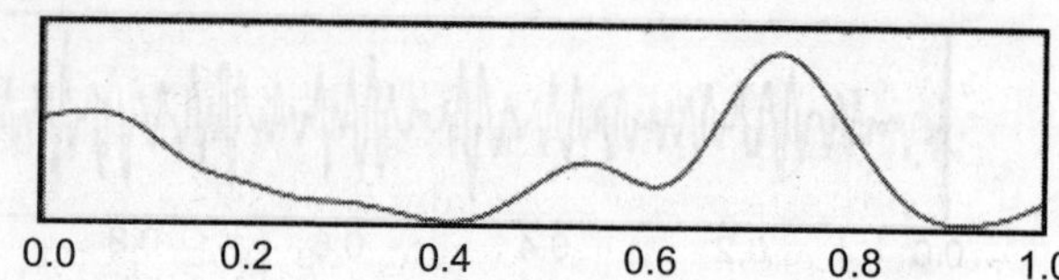

(b) Beta wave

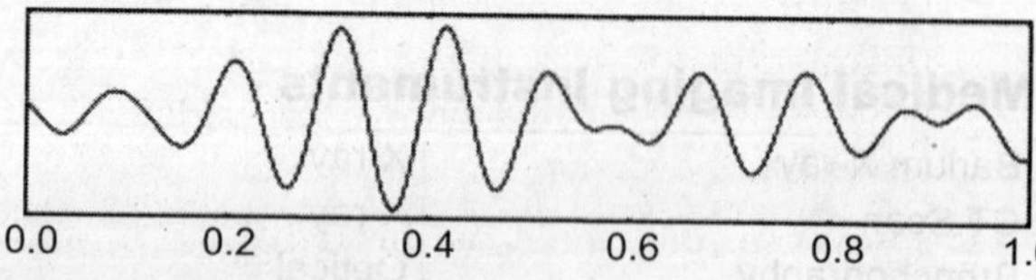

(c) Alpha wave

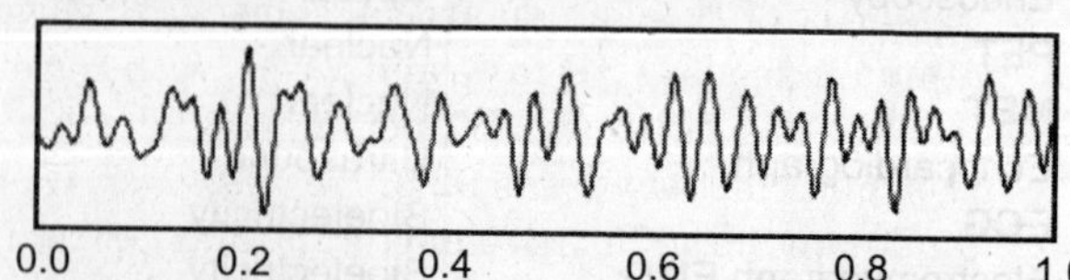

(d) Gamma wave

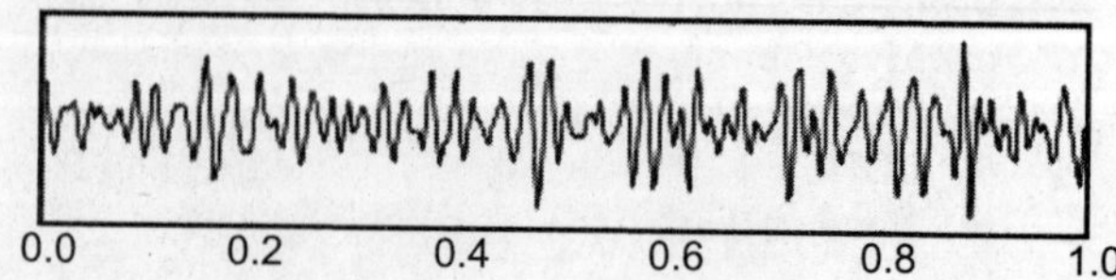

8. Which of the following statements represent the most correct interpretation of the ECG shown below?

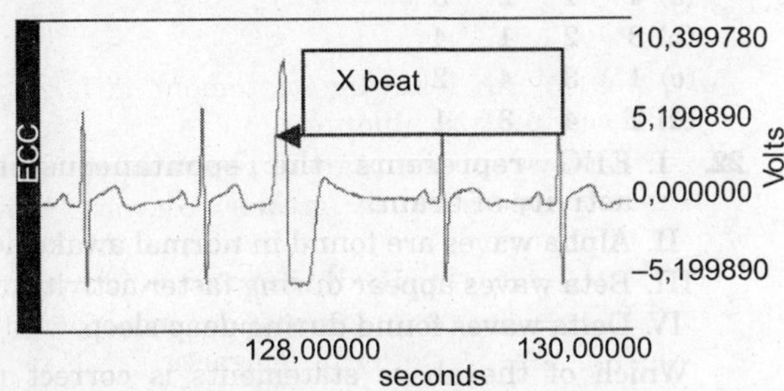

(a) X beat originated from an atrial focus
(b) X beat reset the cardiac rhythm
(c) Both heart sounds would have been present at X beat
(d) The path of spread of excitation was normal

9. A 68-year-old woman recently diagnosed with multiple myeloma presents to her GP with progressively increasing breathlessness, exercise in tolerance and ankle swelling. On examination, there is bilateral pitting leg oedema to her thighs, ascites and raised JVP. The apical impulse is impalpable. An ECG shows diffusely diminished voltage. Chest X-ray is normal and the echocardiogram shows small thick ventricles and dilated atria with a thickened interatrial septum. The ventricular myocardium has a granular sparkling texture on echo, and minimal fluid in the pericardial space is noted. What is the most likely diagnosis?
(a) Chronic pericardial effusion with tamponade
(b) Chronic pericardial effusion without tamponade
(c) Constrictive pericarditis
(d) Restrictive cardiomyopathy

10. A 32-year-old man with Wolff–Parkinson–White syn-drome presents with a 2-hour history of palpitations and breathlessness. On examination, his heart rate is 190 beats/min. ECG shows broad-complex tachycardia. What would be your first line of treatment?
(a) Intravenous amiodarone
(b) Intravenous flecainide
(c) Intravenous adenosine
(d) DC cardioversion

11. A 50-year-old male is brought to A and E with acute-onset central chest pain that started 1½ hours ago. His ECG taken on arrival showed ST elevations of 4 mm in leads II, III, aV_F and V_4–V_6 with hyperacute T waves. His pulse was 60 per minute and his BP was 146/60. The SaO^{-2} was 92%. He was given O_2 by mask and two large intravenous cannulas were inserted. Which of the following blood tests would be most useful prior to definitive treatment?
(a) Myoglobin
(b) Troponin I
(c) LDH
(d) None of these

12. The WHO criteria for the diagnosis of acute myocardial infarction (MI) requires the presence of
(a) history of ischaemic-type chest discomfort
(b) evolutionary ECG changes
(c) rise and fall in serum cardiac markers
(d) All of the above

13. A 78-year-old-man presents to Casualty with a history of syncope. An ECG shows complete heart block. Which of the following physical signs is consistent with the diagnosis?
(a) Regular cannon 'a' waves on JVP
(b) Soft first heart sound
(c) Low-volume pulse
(d) Basal systolic murmur

14. A 50-year-old-professor of economics presents with a 6-week history of progressive breathlessness and bilateral ankle swelling. The ECG shows inverted p in V_1 and partial LBBB. Echocardiography confirms dilated cardiomyo- pathy. Which of the following statements is true?
(a) There is no relevance of history of alcohol abuse
(b) A family history of similar problem is unrelated
(c) Past cytotoxic drug therapy is relevant
(d) Viral illness in the past is unrelated

15. A patient with an aortic valve replacement develops right hemiparesis. CT scan shows cerebral infarction. There is no evidence of cerebral haemorrhage. The INR is 2.0. How would you manage this case?
(a) Reverse the anticoagulation with vitamin-K
(b) Stop warfarin and start intravenous heparin
(c) Increase the dose of warfarin
(d) Continue warfarin and add intravenous heparin

16. A 58-year-old man's ECG shows a combination of a prolonged QT interval with tall T-waves. What is this suggestive of?
(a) Uraemia
(b) Hypocalcaemia
(c) Hypokalaemia
(d) Metabolic alkalosis

17. A 60-year-old man with unstable angina on long-term digoxin was being monitored on the ward with telemetry when the monitor displayed a tachycardia of 180 bpm. The printout showed discrete P waves before each QRS complex and there was an acceleration in the rate after initiation of the arrhythmia. The QRS width was 0.12 s. Which of the following is the most likely arrhythmia?
(a) Automatic supraventricular tachyarrhythmias
(b) AV nodal re-entrant tachycardia
(c) Bypass tract-mediated macroentrant tachycardia
(d) Intra-atrial re-entry

18. Levamisole used in electrophysiological experiments, is an
(a) acetylcholine antagonist (b) acetylcholine agonist
(c) acetylcholine inhibitor (d) acetylcholine blocker

19. Electropharyngeograms (EPGs) are analogous to
(a) ECG (b) EEG
(c) EMG (d) Both (a) and (b)

20. Most *C. elegans* electrophysiology so far has been done on the
(a) lungs (b) brain
(c) heat (d) pharynx

21. Match list I with list II and select the correct codes.

List I	List II
A. ECG	1. Developed by Godfrey Hounsfield
B. CAT	2. Based on detection of positrons emitted by radioisotops.
C. PET	3. Map internal tissues
D. MRI	4. Record the electric activity of heart

Codes

	A	B	C	D
(a)	4	1	2	3
(b)	3	2	1	4
(c)	1	3	4	2
(d)	2	4	3	1

22. I. EEG represents the spontaneous electrical activity of brain.
II. Alpha waves are found in normal awake adults.
III. Beta waves appear during faster activity.
IV. Delta waves found during deep sleep.

Which of the above statements is correct regarding electroencephalograph (EEG)?
(a) I, II and III (b) II, III and IV
(c) I, II, III and IV (d) I, III and IV

Answers

1. (a)	**2.** (d)	**3.** (c)	**4.** (c)	**5.** (c)	**6.** (d)	**7.** (c)	**8.** (c)	**9.** (d)	**10.** (c)
11. (d)	**12.** (d)	**13.** (d)	**14.** (c)	**15.** (b)	**16.** (a)	**17.** (a)	**18.** (b)	**19.** (d)	**20.** (d)
21. (a)	**22.** (c)								

Methods in Field Biology

Methods of Estimating Population Density

The most widely used sampling techniques for vegetation analysis involve

1. Quadrats in which individuals can be counted and measured.
2. Line transects along which the intercepted individuals are measured.
3. Points at which measurements are made of distance to and attributes of the nearest individuals.

These techniques can be adapted for almost all plant communities. Many communities of sessile or sedentary animals (*e.g.,* intertidal invertebrates) can also be sampled by these techniques.

The quadrat technique is easy to use in communities with a profile low enough that a frame can be placed over the area to be sampled, or a radius line rotated around a central point. It is also appropriate for forest communities that are open enough to allow plot boundaries to be marked easily and accurately with a tape measure. The line-transect technique is effective for low, dense communities in which quadrats are difficult to place on the surface. It is also the easiest technique to use when individual organisms are difficult to distinguish from one another, or are irregular in shape. Point-based techniques are best when individuals are widely spaced or when the dominant organisms are large and dense enough that quadrat boundaries or straight transect lines are difficult to lay out. These techniques are applied to communities of plants or animals occupying areas (stands) of two-dimensional habitat space (*e.g.,* terrestrial plant communities, sessile rocky intertidal invertebrates, and the like).

General Sampling Considerations

For any sampling procedure, it is usually most convenient to establish a baseline along one side of the stand or through the stand center. Quadrats, transects or sampling

Syllabus

- Methods of Estimating Population Density of Animals and Plants, Ranging Patterns Sampling Methods in the Study of Behaviour Habitat Characterization-Ground and Remote Sensing Methods.

points can be located randomly, in a stratified random manner or systematically with reference to this baseline. Quadrats or sampling points can be located randomly by drawing pairs of random numbers to serve as coordinates of sampling locations, one number indicating the distance along the baseline, the other the distance into the area. There is another technique for locating random points. Transects for line-intercept measurements can be initiated at randomly chosen points along the baseline. For stratified random sampling, the entire stand can be either divided into equal sub areas or transected by sampling lines at regular intervals. Equal numbers of quadrats, transects or sampling points can then located randomly within the sub areas or along the transect lines. For line-intercept sampling in a rectangular area, one randomly selected point can be used to define the locations of equally spaced transects crossing the plot. This procedure is systematic in design but unbiased in estimates of density, cover and frequency.

Quadrat Sampling

Once the quadrat sampling design has been defined, the types of quantitative data to be obtained should be determined. In sampling communities of plants or sessile animals, the species, the number of individuals, the space they cover, and the frequency with which they occur are usually the most important characteristics.

In counting the individuals of some plants and animals, such as multi-stemmed shrubs or colonial corals, an arbitrary definition of what constitutes an individual will be needed. Criteria for inclusion or exclusion of individuals occurring on the edge of a quadrat may also be necessary.

For example, plants with rooted bases lying more than halfway inside the boundary might be counted and measured as if they lay completely inside, and plants lying more than halfway outside completely excluded.

The area covered by individuals can be measured in several ways. For large woody plants, the diameter or circumference of the trunk can be measured and the basal area (cross-sectional area of the trunk) determined with a hand calculator. For smaller plants, the diameter of the crown foliage may be measured and the areal cover of the crown calculated. Often, the measurement of cover values for individual organisms is impossible or impractical. Cover can be recorded, however, as estimates of the percent of the quadrat covered by each species. Usually this is done by assigning cover class estimates. Several scales for ranking cover have been suggested, one of the most common being the following:

Considering, the difficulty of obtaining accurate measurements of the diameters of irregular canopies of many plants, cover class estimates are often as accurate as more time-consuming direct measurements.

The frequency of occurrence of a species is provided by the fraction of quadrats that contain the species. In addition to number of individuals, basal area or cover, and frequency, one may wish to record other quantitative values, such as biomass, plant height, number of tillers (grasses) or stems or numbers of flowers and fruits.

In summarizing quadrat data, density, dominance and frequency values can be determined for each species. **Density** refers to the number of individuals per unit area, dominance to the basal area or crown cover per unit area, and frequency to the fraction of sample plots containing the species. For a particular species, these values may be expressed either in an absolute form or as relative density, relative dominance and relative frequency, which show the percentage of the individual species' value with respect to the total for all species. Relative values for density, dominance, and frequency then can be combined into a single importance value, which combines these three somewhat different measures of the importance of the species in the community. These values are calculated by the following equations:

$$\text{Density} = \frac{\text{Number of individuals}}{\text{Area sampled}}$$

$$\text{Relative density} = \frac{\text{Density for a species}}{\text{Total density for all species}} \times 100$$

$$\text{Dominance} = \frac{\text{Total of basal area or areal coverage values}}{\text{Area sampled}} \times 100$$

$$\text{Relative dominance} = \frac{\text{Dominance for a species}}{\text{Total dominance for all species}} \times 100$$

$$\text{Frequency} = \frac{\text{Number of plots in which a species occurs}}{\text{Total number of plots samples}}$$

$$\text{Relative Frequency} = \frac{\text{Freqency value for a species}}{\text{Total of freqency values for all species}} \times 100$$

Importance Value = relative density + relative dominance + relative frequency

Two of the above relative values, rather than all three, may sometimes be used to obtain an importance value, so that some ecologists prefer to calculate the importance value as the average, instead of the total, of the available values.

Line-Intercept Analysis

Line-intercept analysis can yield quantitative estimates of density of individuals, areal cover, and frequency comparable to those obtained by quadrat sampling. The most satisfactory device for laying out a line transect is a measuring tape 30-50 meters in length. With the aid of the tape scale, the transect line can be subdivided into sections of any desired length, which will allow for the determination of frequency. The tape-measure scale also makes it easy to measure the length of the segments of transect line intercepted by individuals, an essential value for calculation of areal cover. In the absence of a long tape measure, a transect line of string, rope, or wire, marked off into regular intervals for the recording of frequency, can be used. Meter sticks or short tape measures are also needed for measuring other characteristics of individuals.

In recording line-intercept data, only those individuals that are touched by the transect line or that underlie or overlie the line should be recorded. For each individual encountered, three items of information should be recorded: the species, the length of the transect line intercepted (I), and the maximum width of the individual perpendicular to the transect line (M). In the case of communities with two or more quite distinct strata, such as herb, shrub, and tree strata in a forest, each stratum should be sampled separately.

In summarizing the sampling data, the following values should first be determined for each species:

(i) Total number of individuals encountered (N)

(ii) Total of intercept lengths (Σl)

(iii) Number of transect intervals in which species occurred

(iv) Total of reciprocals of maximum plant widths ($\Sigma l/M$)

With these values the standard measures of community composition can be obtained. Density and relative density are given by the equations:

$$\text{Density} = (\Sigma l / M) \times \frac{\text{Unit Area}}{\text{Total transect length}}$$

$$\text{Relative Density} = \frac{\text{Density for a species}}{\text{Total density for all species}} \times 100$$

The sum of reciprocals of individual widths is necessary for the density calculation because the chance of an individual being encountered by the transect is proportional to its width perpendicular to the transect line. The unit area in this calculation is simply the size of the area, in the same units as plant width and transects length, on the basis of which density is to be expressed.

Dominance is given by the following equations:

Dominance or cover (as % ground surface)

$$= \frac{\text{Total of intercept lengths for a species}}{\text{Total transect length}} \times 100$$

Relative Dominance

$$= \frac{\text{Total of intercep lengths for a species}}{\text{Total of intercept lengths for all species}} \times 100$$

Frequency values calculated from line-transect data can be difficult to interpret. Frequency is perhaps most simply expressed by the equation:

Frequency

$$= \frac{\text{Number of intervals in which species occur}}{\text{Total number of transect intervals}} \times 100$$

This value is somewhat misleading, however, since the chance of a species being recorded in a given transect interval is strongly related to the size of the individuals as well as to the abundance and distribution of the species. In calculating relative frequency these factors may be taken into account. A weighting factor, *F*, can be derived and used to calculate a weighted frequency, which, in turn, is used to calculate relative frequency.

$$F = (\Sigma\, l/M)/n$$

Where, n = Number of values of M

Weighted Frequency = F (number of intervals in which species occurs)

Relative frequency

$$= \frac{\text{Weighted Frequency for a species}}{\text{Total of weighted freqencies for all species}} \times 100$$

The importance value can then be calculated by summing or averaging relative density relative dominance, and relative frequency. An estimate of the total percentage of the ground surface covered by individuals can be obtained by totalling cover percentages if measurements of intercept distances were taken in a non-overlapping manner. If overlap of intercept measurements did occur, owing to the sampling of individuals belonging to different strata, total coverage must be obtained by the equation

$$\text{Total Coverage} = \frac{\text{Total transect} - \text{Total bare grond}}{\text{Total transect length}} \times 100$$

Point-quarter Technique

This technique also gives estimates of density, cover and frequency comparable to those obtained by quadrats or line-intercept measurements. In this technique (figure 1), the area around each sampling point is divided into four equal sectors or quadrants. This division can be done with a compass, or if a transect line is used, the quadrants may be formed by the line itself and a second line perpendicular to it at the sampling point. The individual nearest the point in each quadrant is then located, and the species, basal area or cover, and point-to-individual distance recorded in table 3. Basal area or cover is calculated from diameter or circumference measurements. Point-to-individual distances should be measured to the center of the organism (*e.g.*, the center of the crown or rooted base) rather than to the edge of the organism.

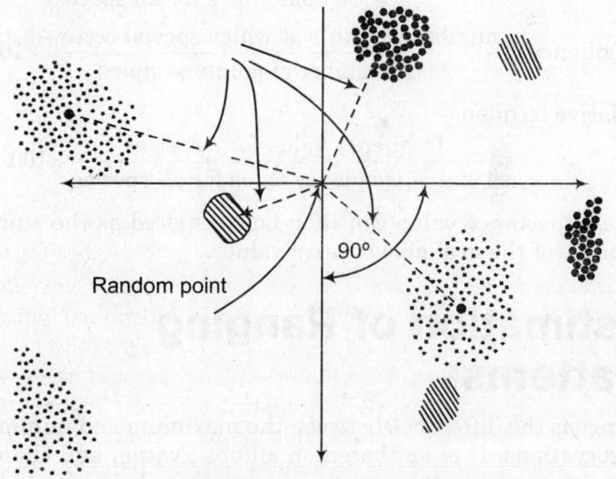

Fig. 44.1 Measured distance

To summarize sampling data, point-to-individual distances should first be totaled for all species and all points and averaged to give the mean point-to-individual distance. The square of this value is the mean area per individual or the average area of surface on which one individual occurs. Thus, the total density of individuals of all species is obtained by dividing the mean area per individual into the unit area. As an equation, this may be written:

Total density of all species

$$= \frac{\text{Unit area}}{(\text{Mean point-to-individual distance})^2}$$

In this equation, the term **Unit area** refers to the size of the area, in the same units as those for the mean area per plant, on the basis of which density is to be expressed. For example, if density is to be expressed per hectare, but the mean area per plant is in units of meters squared, the unit-area value in the calculation would be 10,000 (the number of square meters in a hectare); if density is to be expressed for a 100 m^2 area, the unit-area value equals 100.

The number of individuals of each species should next be determined. The basal area or areal cover values for individuals of each species should then be summed and divided by the number of individuals of the species, to give **average dominance values** for the various species. These average dominance values simply represent the average basal area or areal cover of one individual of each species. From these data, absolute and relative values for density, dominance, and frequency, together with the importance value for each species, can be determined by the following equations:

$$\text{Relative Density} = \frac{\text{Individuals of a species}}{\text{Total individuals of all species}} \times 100$$

Density

$$= \frac{\text{relative density of a species}}{100} \times (\text{total density of all species})$$

$$\text{Dominance} = (\text{density of species}) \times (\text{average dominance value for species})$$

$$\text{Relative Dominance} = \frac{\text{dominance for a species}}{\text{Total dominance for all species}} \times 100$$

$$\text{Frequency} = \frac{\text{number of points at which special occurs}}{\text{Total number of points sampled}} \times 100$$

Relative frequency

$$= \frac{\text{frequency value for a species}}{\text{Total of frequency vales for all species}} \times 100$$

The importance value can then be calculated as the sum or average of the available relative values.

Estimation of Ranging Patterns

Range is the difference between the maximum and minimum observations. It is not based on all observation and changes from one sample to next in a population. It is affected by sampling fluctuations. There are a number of methods used for estimation including:

Mark/Recapture Population Estimates

None of the numerous techniques available for estimating the size of animal populations is foolproof, and none can apply equally well to all populations. This is a popular method useful for estimating the population size of a single species of highly mobile animal, such as most vertebrates. It is called the capture-recapture, or mark-recapture, technique. In honor of some early contributors to its development, fishery biologists refer to the basic procedure as Peterson's method, ornithologists and mammalogists call it Lincoln's method, and diplomatic ecologists refer to it as the Lincoln-Peterson method.

Lincoln-Peterson Method

A number of individuals from a population of interest are captured, marked by some identifiable means, and released within a short period of time (*e.g.*, a day). At a later date (perhaps after a week or two), a second sample of individuals is taken from the population. Some of the individuals in this second sample may be identified as being members of the first sample because they were previously marked. Obviously, if the population is large, the marked individuals will have become 'diluted' within it, and only very few would be expected to appear in the second sample. But if the population is relatively small, then more previously marked animals would be in the second sample. Indeed, if certain assumptions about sampling and the animals' distribution are correct, then the proportion of marked individuals in the second sample is the same as that in the entire population, and the total population may be estimated as follows:

Assume the total population size to be estimated contains N individuals. From this population take a sample of M individuals, mark these animals, and return them to the population. At a later time, take a second sample of n individuals from the population; this sample contains R recaptured animals (*i.e.*, individuals captured and marked in the first sampling). Then the population size, N, may be estimated by the following considerations:

$$M/N = R/n \qquad \text{...(i)}$$

$$N/M = n/R \qquad \text{...(ii)}$$

Equation (i) says that the proportion of marked individuals in the entire population is equal to the proportion of marked animals in a random sample taken from that population. Equivalently, equation (ii) says that the ratio of the total population to the number of animals marked on the first date is equal to the ratio of the number caught on the second date to the number that were recaptured on the second date. By rearrangement of equation (ii) :

$$N = (Mn)/R \qquad \text{...(iii)}$$

So equation (iii) estimates the population size, N.

It has been shown, however, that equation (iii) over-estimates the actual population size in the long run (*i.e.*, it is biased), but this bias can be reduced by computing, a formula that assumes n/N to be a very small fraction.

$$N = \frac{M(n+1)}{R+1} \qquad \text{...(iv)}$$

The following assumptions must be met to validly use this capture-recapture procedure:

1. All individuals in the population must have an equal and independent chance of being captured. That is, the two samples taken from the population must be random samples.
2. There is no change in the ratio of marked to unmarked animals. During the time from initial capture to recapture, there must be no significant additions of unmarked animals to the population through births or immigration, and population losses from death and emigration must remove the same proportion of

marked and unmarked animals. The estimation procedure will work if mortality or emigration occurs randomly for marked and unmarked animals, for then the ratio n/R will be unaltered. If there are additions of new individuals to the population but no mortality then N will be an estimate of the population size at the time the second sample is taken. If there is both mortality and recruitment, then this method will overestimate the size of the population at the time of either of the two samples.

3. Marked individuals distribute themselves homogeneously with respect to unmarked ones so that unmarked animals have the same opportunity for capture in the second sample as do marked ones. That is, there must be a random distribution of marked individuals throughout the entire population, and marking an animal must not affect the subsequent likelihood of that animal is recaptured. One must be careful not to alter the catchability of an animal by the acts of capturing and marking it; this can happen if the catching or marking technique causes significant changes in the animal's behaviour or vigour.

These assumptions require a good deal of knowledge of the natural history of the species under study. When applying this technique, you should know the following:

1. Reproductive history of the population. Are young being added to the population? Is the catchability of animals changing during the period of measurement due to reproduction-induced changes in behaviour?
2. Mortality pattern of the species. Is the population undergoing a decline? Remember that the population may experience mortality without affecting the population estimate, as long as mortality affects the marked and unmarked alike.
3. Effects of marking on the behavior and physiology of the animal. Is the animal's movement or behaviour altered? Is the probability of mortality changed?
4. Seasonal patterns of activity and movement. Do not use this method during hibernation or migration seasons.
5. Biases in the capture of the animals. Do different individuals, sexes, or ages avoid capture or become prone to capture? Is the animal highly mobile or relatively sessile?

In addition, of course, one must use a marking technique enduring enough so the marks will last from the time of marking until the time of recapture.

As with all population estimates made from samples, there is an uncertainty caused by the error associated with examining a sample rather than the entire population. A measure of this error that expresses the uncertainty of a capture-recapture population estimate is the standard error, computed as:

$$SE = \sqrt{\frac{M^2\,(n+1)\,(n-R)}{(R+1)^2\,(R+2)}} \quad \text{...(v)}$$

The precision with which the capture-recapture technique estimates population size is inversely dependent on the number of marked animals recaptured. Thus, attempt to obtain a reasonably large R, by making n large.

Approximate confidence intervals for mark-recapture estimates may be approximated from the standard error. A 1-α confidence interval may be computed as

$$N \pm (t)\,(SE) \quad \text{...(vi)}$$

where, is student's t for $DF = \infty$ (*i.e.*, a 95% confidence interval calculation would use $t = 1.96$; and one would use $t = 2.58$ for a 99% confidence interval).

An approximate test for the difference between two population sizes estimated by capture-recapture is:

$$t = \frac{N_1 - N_2}{\sqrt{(SE)_2^1 + (SE)_2^2}} \quad \text{...(vii)}$$

where, the subscripts 1 and 2 refer to the two populations being compared (see section IB. 3.1 for principles of t-testing). For this test use $DF = \infty$.

Many modifications have been proposed to correct for some of the limitations of the **Lincoln-Peterson** technique. These newer methods often use theory and sampling procedures based on multiple markings and/or multiple recaptures. While such procedures may in some circumstances yield more accurate estimates than the Lincoln-Peterson procedure, they typically require more time and effort (and they may have more restrictive assumptions).

Some of these methods are applicable if death, migration, or emigration alters the ratio of marked to unmarked animals.

Application

Capture-recapture methods may be applied to a variety of animals. Field sampling may be done with sweep nets for larger and slower arthropods or dip nets for benthic sampling of aquatic invertebrates. Collect clams and other relatively sessile animals in a small body of water by hand, employing random plots or transects. Capture fish or crayfish with seines. Small mammals such as field mice may be live-trapped using a grid of 100 traps spaced 10 to 20 meters apart. Be sure to use the same sampling effort on all sampling days. Inanimate objects may also be subjected to experiments to test the importance of the assumptions given above and to investigate the effect of sample sizes on the standard error of the population estimate.

Identify, mark, record, and release animals as soon after capture as possible. Mark animals with an exoskeleton or shell with rapid-drying weatherproof paint; dyes or more permanent tags or bands, may be applied to vertebrates. Fish may be marked by clipping off a portion of the dorsal, caudal or anal fin. Amphibians or mammals may be toe-clipped. Consider, the permanence of the marking procedure. Markings on exoskeletons or feathers will be lost if molting occurs between samplings; also, some types of tags can physically wear off. The proper elapsed time between samplings depends largely on how long it takes for members of the first sample to distribute themselves randomly within the entire population. A week or two should suffice for most animals, but slow-moving forms may take longer.

Data in addition to numbers (*e.g.*, weight, length, age) may also be collected from these samples for use in section 4A or in other studies. To obtain an estimate of density (D), an estimate of the area (A) sampled must be had in addition to the estimate of population size (N):

$$D = N/A. \quad ...(viii)$$

The Removal Method of Population Estimation

Capture-recapture methods allow you to estimate population size with a minimum of harm to the population. However, these methods are sometimes difficult to use on natural populations because the underlying assumptions cannot be realized. If these assumptions are difficult to meet, and if the population being studied can be sampled without replacement of captured individuals, so called removal methods can be used. We shall consider only two of the simplest removal methods to convey some of the basic principles behind this approach. In practice, more elaborate sampling procedures and theory can obtain more precise and reliable results.

Removal methods of population estimation involve successive trapping of members of the population. The basis of the methods is the expectation that the number caught and removed from the population at a given time of trapping will be greater than the number caught at a later trapping. That is, as one reduces the population size, the size of the catch will decrease. Necessary assumptions of removal methods are:

(i) Each individual in the population has an equal and independent chance of being captured. That is, the sampling must be random.

(ii) Except for the effects of the trapping, the population is not increasing or decreasing in size.

(iii) The probability of capturing an individual is the same for each period of sampling.

Violation of any of these assumptions will result in inaccurate population estimates.

The first assumption relates to the collecting technique. Capture should not favor one sex, one age class, or one individual over another. Each sample taken should represent a random collection from the entire population. For example, if some members of the population consistently avoid capture, then the size of the population will be underestimated.

In capture-recapture theory, births or immigration may not occur during the study, although random mortality and emigration are acceptable. When removal methods are used, a population may have births and immigration, but (according to assumption 2 above) they must balance with normal deaths and emigration so that population size remains constant. An increase in the population size between sampling periods would give an overestimate of population size.

According to the third assumption, if the chance of capturing animals in the population changes from the first sampling period to the second sampling period, then the population estimate will be biased. Therefore, the sampling effort must be the same for each sampling period. If the probability of capture increases between sampling periods, then the population would be overestimated. In capture-recapture sampling, the probability of capture need not be constant; what is required instead is that the ratio of marked to unmarked individuals remains the same.

Trap-shyness or trap-proneness can affect the probability of capture. If trap-prone animals are more likely caught the first sampling period, the probability of their capture will be high. Therefore, during the second sampling period, the probability of capture will be lower, and fewer animals will be caught due to a higher proportion of trap-shy animals. A variety of other factors, such as bait acceptance, weather conditions, and differential activity of ages and sexes affect the probability of capture. Thus, one must assure that sampling and environmental conditions are as identical as possible during all sampling periods and that the sampling effort remains constant.

Finally, it should be realized that the error in estimating population size by these methods is smallest when large proportions of the population have been sampled. If only a very small proportion of the total population has been captured, then the confidence in the population size estimate is very low.

Regression Method

One useful method for graphical estimation of population size, N, is based on successive removals of animals from the population; one obtains a series of collections, capturing animals at different times and removing them from the population. The amount of collecting effort must be the same each time. So, for example, one may tabulate the number of fish caught in an eight-hour period, or the numbers of mammals trapped in a twenty-four-hour period, on each of several dates. The numbers of animals caught are then plotted against the total numbers previously caught.

However, one must count a very large proportion of the population and obtain enough samples to draw a reliable line through the several data points.

$$Y_i = a + b X_i \quad ...(i)$$

Where, X_i is the accumulated catch at period i, and Y_i is the number caught at period i ($Y_i = n_i$, the number caught in sample i). The slope, b, of the regression line will be a negative value, for Y_i decreases as X_i increases. Once a and b have been calculated by regression analysis, one can calculate N, which is the value of X, when $Y_i = 0$. That is, by substituting in equation 1,

$$0 = a + bN \quad ...(ii)$$

and it follows that:

$$N = -a/b \quad ...(iii)$$

To generate a confidence interval for the population you must follow the following procedure:

First calculate the sum of squares for X:

$$SS_X = SX^2 - (SX)^2/n \quad ...(iv)$$

where, n is the number of capture episodes

Then calculate the sum of squares for Y:

$$SS_Y = SY^2 - (SY)^2/n \quad ...(v)$$

where, n is the number of capture episodes

Next calculate the sum of cross products as:

$$SP = SXY - SXSY/n \quad \text{...(vi)}$$

where n is the number of capture episodes

Now calculate the variance of the slope (b) as:

$$s^2 = \frac{SS_Y - (SP)^2/SS_X}{n-2} \quad \text{...(vii)}$$

The standard error of b can now be calculated as:

$$sb = \sqrt{s^2 / SS_X} \quad \text{...(viii)}$$

Lastly, the confidence interval is calculated as:

$$\pm \frac{t}{c}\sqrt{s^2\left[\frac{(Y-\bar{Y})^2}{SS_X} + c\left(1+\frac{1}{n}\right)\right]} \quad \text{...(ix)}$$

$$\bar{X} = \frac{b\,(Y-\bar{Y})}{c}$$

Where, is the mean of the X values, Y (in this case) = 0, is the mean of the Y values, t is the tabulated value of t from the student's t-distribution at a (use a = 0.05 for 95% confidence interval) and n 2 df and,

$$c = b^2 - t^2 s_b \quad \text{...(x)}$$

The Moran-Zippin Method

This procedure for estimating population size requires fewer sampling periods than Hayne's extrapolation method, although the two population estimates should be the same or very similar. The basis of the method is as follows.

Let, N be the population size, n_1 be the number of animals caught and removed during the first sampling period, and n_2 be the number caught and removed on the second sampling period. The proportion of the original population captured in the first sampling period is then, n_1/N and after the first group of n_1 animals is removed from the population, $N - n_1$ animals remain. The proportion of this remaining number of animals captured in the second sample is $n_2/(N - n_1)$. If we can assume that the two trappings caught the same proportion, p, of animals (which is the same as saying that p is the probability of an animal being captured), then,

$$p = n_1/N \quad \text{...(xi)}$$

And $$p = n_2/(N - n_1) \quad \text{...(xii)}$$

Therefore, $$n_1/N = n_2/(N - n_1) \quad \text{...(xiii)}$$

Solving this equation for N, the population size, we find that

$$N = n_1^2/(n_1 - n_2) \quad \text{...(xiv)}$$

The standard error of this population estimate is

$$SE = \frac{(n_1)(n_2)\sqrt{n_1 + n_2}}{(n_1 - n_2)^2} \quad \text{...(xv)}$$

For the above example,

$$SE = \frac{(200)(100)\sqrt{300}}{(200-100)^2} = \frac{346410}{10000} = 34.6$$

An approximate confidence interval for our estimate of N may be calculated as:

$$N \pm (t)\ (\text{SE})$$

where, t is student's t for DF = co. (Thus, for a 95% confidence interval, use t = 1.96, and for a 99% confidence interval use; = 2.58.)

Population estimates by the Moran-Zippin method may be based on more than two samples, but the arithmetic becomes quite involved. While using data from three successive removal samples improves accuracy over estimates made using two samples, little is gained by using more than three samples.

Sampling Methods

Two possible objectives for sampling are to

1. Estimate average population density.
2. Make a map of population density.

Traditionally, random sampling plans were preferred over systematic sampling plans because random sampling helped to avoid subjective selection of sample locations. However, systematic sampling has no elements of subjectivity if sample location is selected prior to examining the area. For example, there are no subjective decisions if we sample every tenth potato plant and count Colorado potato beetles.

Moreover, systematic sampling has an advantage over random sampling if the number of samples is large because of more uniform coverage of the entire sampling area. It is especially important for making population maps. Random sampling can be used if the objective is to estimate the mean population density and the number of samples is not large (<100).

Preferential sampling of specific areas (*e.g.*, high-density areas) was always considered unacceptable. However, modern geostatistical methods and stratified sampling can take advantage of preferential sampling. This shows that the methodology of sampling evolves and old textbooks may give obsolete recipes.

Traditional statistical methods include estimation of the mean population density (M), standard deviation (SD), and standard error (SE), which is the standard deviation of the sample mean.

$$\text{SE} = \frac{SD}{\sqrt{N}}$$

or

$$S_{\bar{X}} = \frac{S_X}{\sqrt{N}}$$

The equation for standard error is derived assuming that all samples are **independent**. This is a very strong assumption which is unrealistic in many situations. Samples separated by small distance are often positively correlated. Before using standard statistics it is important to test if samples are correlated. Spatial correlations are examined using geostatistics. The simplest geostatistical test for spatial autocorrelation is the omni directional correlogram:

$$\text{p}(h) == \frac{\Sigma z_1 z_2 - N_h M_h^2}{N_h S_h^2}$$

where, z_1 and z_2 are organism numbers in two samples separated by lag distance h, summation is performed over all pairs of samples separated by distance h; N_h is the number of pairs of samples separated by distance h; M_h and s_h are the mean and the standard deviation of samples separated by distance h (each sample is weighted by the number of pairs of samples in which it is included).

Correlation decreases with distance between samples as shown below.

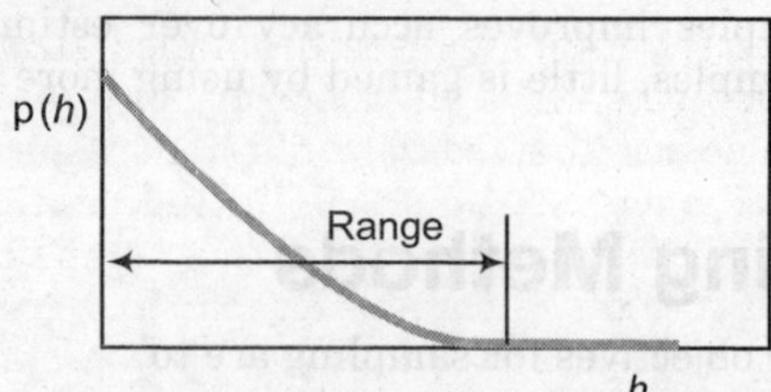

Fig. 44.2 The range of correlation

The range of correlogram is the lag distance *h* at which correlation reaches (or becomes close to) zero. Standard statistics can be applied only if inter-sample distance exceeds the range of the correlogram.

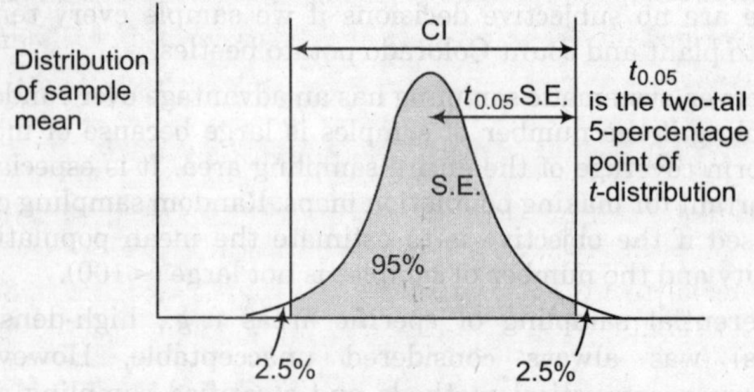

Fig. 44.3 Confidence internal of a curve

Confidence Interval (CI) is the interval where, the population mean can be found with probability of (1 – *P*), where *P* is error probability (*e.g.*, *P* = 0.05). The number of degrees of freedom d.f. = *N* – 1 (one d.f. goes for estimation of sample mean).

Precision of sample mean is

$$A = \text{SE}/M$$

There is an empirical rule that precision should be below 0.05 (or 0.1). However, this rule is not universal The only thing that matters in statistics is testing hypotheses. If null hypothesis is rejected then it does not matter whether A was above or below 0.05. However, in each specific research area, it is useful to find a precision level which is usually sufficient for rejecting null-hypotheses.

Example Insect pest population should be suppressed if its density exceeds the Economic Injury Level (EIL). A null hypothesis is tested that the average density M is equal to EIL. If EIL is within the CI for *M*, then the null hypothesis cannot be rejected and no decision can be made. In this case, more samples should be taken. If the EIL is outside of the CI, then null hypothesis is rejected, and population is suppressed if *M* > EIL, or not suppressed if *M* < EIL.

There are two major methods for planning the number of samples:

1. Two-step sampling.
2. Sequential sampling.

Two-step Sampling

The number of samples, *N*, required to achieve specific accuracy level can be estimated from equations for Standard Error (SE) and accuracy, *A*:

$$\text{SE} = \frac{SD}{\sqrt{N}}$$

$$\text{SE} = AM$$

$$N = \left(\frac{SD}{AM}\right)^2$$

where, *M* is sample mean and SD is standard deviation. Here the third equation is derived from the first two equations.

Standard Deviation (SD) is usually not known before sampling. Thus, the first step is to take N_1 samples and to estimate *N* using the equation above. Then, at the second step, take $N_1 = N - N_1$ samples.

Taking samples in two steps is possible only if population numbers don't change between two sampling dates.

Sequential Sampling

The main idea of sequential sampling is to take samples until some condition (which is easy to check) is met.

The first example is the sampling plan targeted at achieving specific accuracy. It is based on the Taylor's power law:

$$\text{In}\ (\text{SD}^2) = a + b\ \text{In}\ (M)$$

Coefficients *a* and *b* can be estimated using linear regression from several pairs of *M* and SD estimated in different areas with different average population density. Combining two previous equations we get:

$$N = \left(\frac{\exp{(a/2)}\ M^{b/2}}{AM}\right)^2$$

$$= \left(\frac{\exp{(a/2)}^2}{A}\right) M^{b-2}$$

Mean (*M*) equals to the total number of recorded individuals (*S*) in all samples divided by the number of samples (*N*). Now, we substitute *M* by *S*/*N*, and solve this equation for *S*:

$$S = \left(\frac{A}{\exp{(a/2)}} N^{(b-1)/2}\right)^{2/(b-2)}$$

Stop-lines for accuracy levels of *A* = 0.1; 0.07; and 0.05 are plotted below:

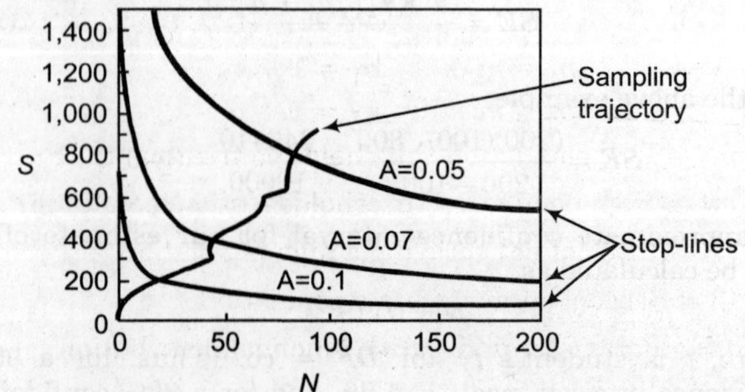

Fig. 44.4 Sequencial sampling for pest management

The blue line shows the total number of captured individuals in all samples. Sampling terminates when this line crosses the stop line for selected accuracy level.

The second example is the sequential sampling plan used for decision-making in pest management. This method was developed by waters.

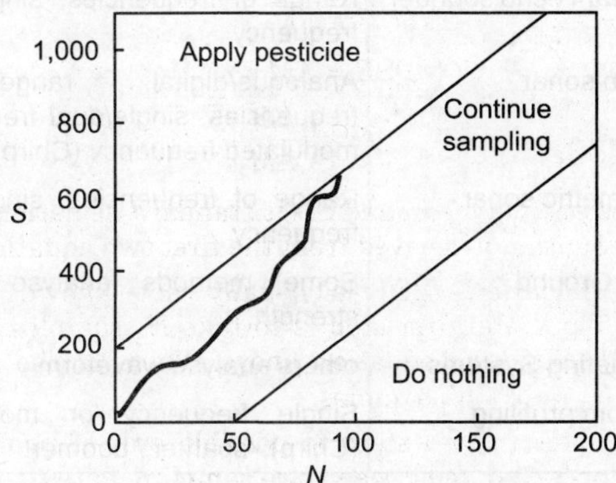

Fig. 44.5 Sequential sampling for past management

Here, the blue line again shows the total number of captured individuals in all samples. While the blue line is between magenta inclined lines, sampling continues. If the blue line crosses the upper magenta line, then sampling stops and pesticides are applied against the pest population. If the blue line crosses the lower magenta line, then sampling stops and pesticides are not applied.

Deriving the solution of this problem it is too complicated. Thus, we will consider the final result only.

If the population has a negative binomial distribution, then stop lines correspond to the linear equation:

$$S_{1,2} = bN \pm h_{1,2}$$

where,

$$b = k \cdot \frac{\log (q_2 / q_1)}{\log \left(\dfrac{p_2 \cdot q_1}{p_1 \cdot q_2}\right)}$$

$$h_1 = \frac{\log ((1-\alpha)/\beta)}{\log \left(\dfrac{p_2 \cdot q_1}{p_1 \cdot q_2}\right)}$$

$$h_2 = \frac{\log ((1-\beta)/\alpha)}{\log \left(\dfrac{p_2 \cdot q_1}{p_1 \cdot q_2}\right)}$$

$$p_1 = m_1/k \qquad q_1 = 1 + p_1$$

$$p_2 = m_2/k \qquad q_2 = 1 + p_2$$

m_1 = Low population threshold (no treatment)

m_2 = High population threshold (pesticide required)

α = Rrisk of not spraying a high population

β = Rrisk of spraying a low population

k = Parameter of negative binomial distribution

Habitat Characterization–Ground and Remote Sensing

Habitat characterization involves a detailed survey of the landscape. Surveyors have at their disposal a variety of generic technologies that sample different aspects of the environment. Remote sensing tools include optical, radar, sonar and seismic technologies, which are complemented by direct sampling tools such as grabs and corers and observational techniques like video and photography. Within each generic technology there are a variety of specific tools designed to apply that technology under different conditions or for slightly different purposes (*e.g.*, towed camera sledges, drop-frame cameras and remote operated vehicles with video). In drawing up a survey specification you should have some knowledge of the range of tools available, what data they can provide, and whether or not they are suitable for use in the conditions that might be anticipated during the survey.

Here, we look briefly at a variety of characterization tools and technologies:

Remote Sensing Techniques

The remote sensing techniques most frequently used in marine habitat mapping fall into two categories:

(i) Aerial techniques (satellite or airborne) for intertidal and shallow water work (to 20-30 m maximum in clear water).

(ii) Acoustic techniques for shallow and deeper sub-tidal work. They can be used over intertidal areas at high tide but this is unusual as there is greater risk of damage.

Aerial Techniques

For intertidal and shallow water areas, the spatial distribution of seabed facies (*i.e.*, different ground-types) can be mapped using images from satellites and aerial surveys, while topographic relief can be determined using LiDAR (a laser scanning instrument mounted on an aeroplane) or stereo aerial photography.

Acoustic Techniques

Acoustic techniques can provide information about the surface and sub-surface characteristics of the seabed. For habitat mapping it is usually the seabed surface and the top half metre of the seabed that are of greatest interest as this is where the majority of species live. Sidescan, multibeam and interferometric sonars sense swathes along the seabed that can be mosiaced to building up high-resolution images in which some sediments and bedforms can be recognised and directly mapped. Single beam echo sounders sense a series of points along the seabed and, through an Acoustic Ground Discrimination Systems (AGDS), can build coarse resolution raster images that segment the survey area into different ground types. Some techniques are better for mapping the spatial distribution of seabed facies, while others are better for mapping relief. Some can do both. Lower frequencies are used in sub-bottom profilers to penetrate the seabed to show the thickness of various sediment layers.

Seismic remote sensing techniques are considered a special case in marine habitat mapping. They are frequently used in geological surveys to show profiles through the earth's crust and can be of interest in habitat mapping when they record features at or near the seabed surface. The resolution is much lower than in acoustic surveys but the information can provide supporting evidence for interpreting the nature of the seabed, particularly over large spatial areas or in deeper waters off the continental shelf where acoustic techniques may be of limited use.

Ground-truthing Techniques

Ground-truthing techniques generally fall into two categories, observational and sampling techniques. Surveys of the shore and shallow waters tend to rely heavily on human observation, though sampling is necessary to provide quantitative data. In deeper waters, cameras can be deployed on a number of different platforms to observe the seabed but much of the ground truthing relies on the use of sampling devices to collecting samples of the sediment and the benthic infauna and epifauna that are then processed and analyzed to provide much of the physical and biological data needed to classify the habitats. Such sampling devices are normally only effective on unconsolidated sediments, so in rocky areas there is a greater reliance on video and photographic techniques.

Varieties of Tools and Techniques

Many of the different remote sensing, observational and sampling technologies can be further split into a variety of tools that have been designed and developed for specific applications or to perform optimally under specific conditions.

Table 44.1 **Varieties of Tools within Different Techniques**

Technique	Variations
Aerial Remote Sensing	
Aerial photography	Oblique or ortho-rectified photographs
Airborne digital imagery	Single, multiple or hyper spectral
Satellite imagery	Single, multiple or hyper spectral
LiDAR	Topographic, hydrographic

Table 44.2 **Acoustic Techniques**

Technique	Variations
Multibeam echo sounder	Range of frequencies, different models optimised for different depth ranges
Single beam echo sounder	Range of frequencies, single/dual frequency
Side scan sonar	Analogue/digital, range of frequencies, single/dual frequency, modulated frequency (Chirp)
Interferometric sonar	Range of frequencies, single/dual frequency
Acoustic Ground	Some methods analyse signal strength,
Discriminating Systems	others analyse waveform
Sub bottom profiling	Single frequency or modulated (Chirp), 'sparker'/'boomer'

Table 44.3 **Benthic Sampling Techniques**

Grab designs	Hamon, Day, Smith-McIntyre, Van Veen, Shipek
Core designs	Box, Nioz, Vibrocore, Mutli-corer
Trawls	Agassiz, Beam, Otter
Dredges	Oyster, Scallop, Naturalist, Rallier du Batty, Rock, Anchor
Video/photo	Towed or drop-frame cameras, ROV's

Suitability of the Techniques

The process of selecting techniques to be used in the survey must consider not only their sensing or sampling capabilities, but also whether or not they will be suitable for use under the conditions that are expected to be met during the surveys. Even the most robust sampling techniques have their technical and logistic limitations. Grab samplers are ineffective on rock substrates, optical techniques are affected by turbidity, Scubadivers would not normally work at depth >30 metres. Consequently, different combinations of sensing and sampling tools can be appropriate for different sets of circumstances.

Exercise

1. In the forest ecosystem which of the field biology tools you will prefer for species area curves?
   (a) Dominance
   (b) Basal area
   (c) Importance values of trees along a gradient of elevation
   (d) All of the above
2. Which of the following is experimental design in file biology experiments?
   (a) ANOVA designs (b) Regression designs
   (c) Mixed model designs (d) All of these
3. Footprint Identification Technique (FIT) is used for
   (a) insects (b) fishes
   (c) snakes (d) rhinos
4. Which of the following statements is true?
   (a) An equal area is covered by both vertical and oblique remote sensing imagery
   (b) A greater area can be covered in vertical rather than oblique remote sensing imagery
   (c) A greater area can be covered in oblique rather than vertical remote sensing imagery
   (d) All of the above
5. Ground based devices are categorized by the .... of the electromagnetic signal they ....
   (a) frequency; emit
   (b) wavelength; emit
   (c) frequency; absorb
   (d) wavelength; absorb
6. Bird Life International is in the process of documenting sites of global importance for conservation in its Important Bird Areas (IBA) programme. According to them which of the following bird species are categorized in Endemic Bird Area (EBA)
   (a) Globally threatened species
   (b) Restricted-range species
   (c) Biome restricted assemblages
   (d) Congregatory species
7. As per quartet method of species sampling, which of the following statement is correct for the following area?

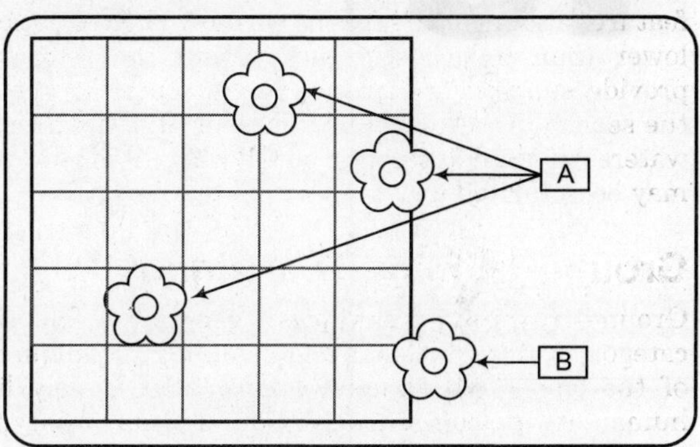

   (a) Species A will be counted while B is under revision
   (b) Species A and B both will be counted
   (c) Species A and B will not be counted
   (d) Species A will be counted while species
8. Consider the following statements.
   I. Frequency, density and dominance are summarizing in quadrate data.
   II. Line intercept analysis can yield quantitative estimates of density of individuals, cover area and frequency.
   III. Importance value index is the sum of RDom, RF and RD.

   Which of the above statements an correct.
   (a) I, II and III (b) I and II
   (c) II and III (d) I and III
9. Which of the following statements are correct in sense of Lincoln Peterson method application.
   I. Reproductive history of the population.
   II. Mortality pattern of species.
   III. Seasonal pattern of activity and movement.
   IV. Effects of marking on behaviour and physiology of animals.

   (a) I, II and III (b) II, III and IV
   (c) I, II, III and IV (d) I, III and IV

Answers

1. (d)	2. (d)	3. (d)	4. (c)	5. (b)	6. (b)	7. (d)	8. (a)	9. (c)

Computational Methods

Syllabus

- Nucleic Acid and Protein Sequence Databases, Data Mining Methods for Sequence Analysis, Web-Based Tools for Sequence Searches, Motif Analysis and Presentation.

Nucleic Acid and Protein Sequence Databases

The sequences in nucleic acid and protein contain a wealth of information of interest to molecular biologists. Bioinformatics is the application of information technology to store, organize and analyze the vast amount of biological data which is available in the form of sequences and structures of proteins (the building blocks of organisms) and nucleic acids (the information carrier). The biological information of nucleic acids is available as sequences while the data of proteins is available as sequences and structures sequence databases serve two main functions:

1. To facilitate comparisons with newly determined sequences and
2. To act as a source of data for the generation and testing of hypothesis concerning molecular sequence organization and evolution.

The large amounts of sequence data now becoming available require that algorithms for databases searching be fast and efficient and considerable progress is being made in this area. Biological databases can be broadly classified into sequence and structure databases. Sequence databases is applicable to both nucleic acid sequences and protein sequences, whereas structure database is applicable to only Proteins. DNA sequencing produces large amount of data that would be extremely tedious to analyze without computers. Several commercially available software packages will carry out routine sequence analyses. Many sequence analysis programs are also available on the internet. Some of these programs can be downloaded and used on a free standing computer. In other cases the sequence is submitted *via* the website or by email and the results of the analysis are provided. A DNA sequencing project will require the use of a computer to assist in compiling and editing the sequence data. Overlapping clones are found and assembled into contiguous sequences. Computers are also used to generate the complementary sequence, reverse the 5′→3′ orientation, or provide amino acid translations of nucleic acid sequences. It is also possible to calculate various physical, biochemical or structural properties of both nucleic acids and proteins. For example, algorithms to predict the secondary structure of either proteins or RNA are available. Specific sites or motifs within a gene, such as restriction sites, promoter elements or other DNA signals, as well as various protein motifs (*e.g.*, glycosylation sites, signal sequences, etc.) can be identified with the computer. Alignment of related sequences and homology searches are common analyses performed on both nucleic acid and protein sequences. For example, it is relatively easy to obtain sequence data, but it is quite difficult to predict protein structure and function. Protein structure and function can be approximated from similarities to known sequences. Such similarities are identified by aligning DNA or protein sequences.

Common Sequence Analyses

- Compiling and editing sequences
- Manipulating sequences
  - Complement, reverse or both
  - Translating
- Structural analysis
  - Searching for coding regions
  - Physical properties
- Comparisons and homology searches
  - Aligning sequences
  - Sites and motifs
  - Gene identification

Sequence Alignment

Alignments provide a powerful way to compare sequences for either evolutionary relatedness or structural/functional relatedness. Sequences can be compared by either global or local alignments. Global alignment forces complete alignment of the input sequences, whereas local alignments will only align their most similar segments. The choice of method will depend on whether the sequences are presumed to be related over their entire lengths or to only share isolated regions of homology.

Homologs are structures or objects that share a common evolutionary origin. Objects with similar structure or function, but no common ancestor are analogs. Homologs can be classified as orthologs or paralogs. Orthologs are homologous genes from different species that arose from a common ancestor gene. Paralogs are homologous genes that are the result of gene duplication within an evolutionary lineage (*e.g.,* species) and may have different or similar functions.

The algorithms to carry out global and local alignments are similar, but the statistics associated with the output are different. Pair-wise sequence alignments use a scoring matrix to calculate the best alignment between two sequences.

A scoring matrix contains information on how to score each match in an alignment and penalties for mismatches. For example in DNA alignments, matches are assigned a value of 0.9 and mismatch a value of −0.1. Proteins are more complicated and the scoring matrix must also take into account similarity between residues and their relative abundance. For example, tyrosine and tryptophan residues are uncommon and weighted heavier those alignments between common residues such as alanine and serine. Similarly, alignments between glutamate and aspartate are scored positively because of their chemical similarity, whereas matches between dissimilar residues are penalized. Furthermore, amino acid similarity can be defined as similar on either a chemical basis or a structural basis. No single scoring matrix can be universally used for proteins. BLOSUM and PAM are two well known scoring matrices. The gap penalty is another parameter used in sequence alignments. Mathematically, the penalty for opening a gap of length k is defined as:

$$W_k = a + bk$$

where, a is the gap opening penalty and b is the gap extension penalty. Both the opening penalty and the extension penalty can be varied and it may be useful to run alignments with different values unless it is already known the types of matches being searched for. For example, having a large open and a large extend penalty is good for analyzing closely related proteins. A large open penalty and small extend penalty may be good for situations where the distance between domains is not crucial. A small open penalty and large extend penalty (*i.e.,* many small inserts) is useful for distantly related homologous proteins. Aligning sequences involves submitting the two sequences, choosing the scoring matrix and prescribing the gap penalties. The alignment giving the best score for a particular scoring matrix and the prescribed gap penalties is returned. However, this is not necessarily the most biological significant alignment. Quite often finding the optimal alignment involves carrying out several alignments using different values for these parameters. In addition, the final alignment often involves using human insight. In contrast to pair-wise alignments, which always return the best possible mathematical match, multiple alignments are a first approximation. The human eye coupled with biological insight is much better at spotting patterns in multiple alignments that the currently available computer algorithms. Alignments are a non-trivial computational task and it is best not to treat them like a black box programs.

Databases

- Primary (original biological data) vs. secondary (value added)
- Three 1° DNA databases
  - Gen bank
  - Embl
  - Ddbj
- Sub-divisions
- Annotated.

Searching Databases

A primary database contains information of the sequence or structure alone while secondary database contains derived information from the primary database. A secondary sequence database contains information like the conserved sequence, signature sequence and active site residues of the protein families arrived by multiple sequence alignment of a set of related proteins. It is these search tools that integrate the user and the databases. One of the widely used search program is BLAST (Basic Local Alignment Search Tool).

Comparing a sequence against a database to discover similarities is one of the most frequently used and powerful tools in bioinformatics. In essence, searching a database is the same as aligning two sequences. However, to perform a pair-wise alignment of the query sequence with every sequence in the database would be too time consuming. Therefore, programs use heuristic strategies to speed up the analysis are usually used. FASTA and BLAST are the two most commonly used programs for searching databases. Both programs use rapid exact match procedures to first identify sequences which are most likely to be related. These sequences are then subjected to further analyses by alignment programs. BLAST (basic local alignment search tool) uses an approach based on matching short sequence fragments and then finds the best local alignments between the query sequence and the database sequences. Several BLAST programs are available for different types of sequence matching.

Table 45.1 **Blast Programs**

Program	Query	DB	Comments
Blastp	Protein	Protein	Compares amino acid query against protein sequences
Blastn	DNA	DNA	Compares nucleotide query against DNA sequences
Blastx	DNA	Protein	Compares 6X translations of nucleotide query against protein sequences
Tblastn	Protein	DNA	Compares protein query 6X translations of DNA sequences
Tblastx	DNA	DNA	Compares 6X translations of nucleotide query against 6X translations of DNA sequences

BLAST searches of the most current version of GenBank can be performed at the National Center for Biotechnology Information (NCBI) by cutting and pasting the query sequence onto their web page (http://www.ncbi.nlm.nih.gov/ BLAST/). The entire database or sub-divisions of the database can be searched. It is also desirable to 'filter' low complexity sequences such as long runs of repetitive sequence (*e.g.*, tracts of poly-alanine, etc.) and most BLAST programs filter by default. Such regions of sequence can give spuriously high scores against unrelated proteins. Similarly, iterative searches are prone to contamination by regions corresponding to coiled-coils or transmembrane domains. These characteristics might match the initial search and the program then emphasizes these inappropriate characteristics. The user can also choose cut-off values (*i.e.* *E*-values), the number of matches to report, and the number of alignments to show. The entire database(s) is searched and sequences with similarity to the query sequence are identified and ranked accordingly (see appendix 2 for sample output) to the alignment score derived from the pair-wise alignment. In addition to the this 'raw or bit score', the output includes a 'statistical score' and the alignments. The statistical score, or expectation value (*E*-value), provides a measure of the expected number of sequences in the database that would achieve a given alignment score by chance.

The *E*-values are more useful in terms of judging the significance of a match than the alignment score. *E*-values for proteins and DNA should be less than 0.1 and 0.0001, respectively, to be considered significant. Examining the alignments will also help in inferring whether the hit is significant. For example, protein global alignments which show 25% or greater sequence identity over a stretch of at least 80 amino acids should exhibit the same basic structure. The identified sequences can be also retrieved and subjected to further analyses. Database searches may assist in identifying an unknown gene or provide clues about its function.

Goto Swiss-Prot and search for 'human haemoglobin'

↓

Follow the links to the protein and nucleic acid Sequence entries for the alpha sub-unit of haemoglobin and download the protein and nucleic acid sequences

↓

Follow the link to the PDB entry and download the PDB file

↓

Goto BLAST and search with the human alpha haemoglobin protein sequence in the nr database

↓

Download atleast 5 sequences from different sources

↓

Do a MSA using ClustalX or ClustalW

↓

Note the conserved positions

↓

Using WebLab open the PDB file

↓

Display the same in solid ribbon by clicking the 'View-Display Style' menu

↓

Click on 'Window-New Hierarchy window' menu

↓

Click on the required residues and display them in Ball and Stick model by going to 'View-Display Style' menu

Fig. 45.1 Procedure of sequence display

Data Mining Methods for Sequence Analysis

Data Mining is an analytic process designed to explore large amount of data=typically business or market related in search of consistent patterns and then to validate the findings by applying the detected patterns to new subsets of data.

Data Mining is often considered to be 'a blena of statistics, artificial intelligence (AI), and data base research'. The process of data mining consists of three stages:

1. The initial explora- tion.

2. Model building or pattern identification with validity

3. deployment.

Concepts in Data Mining

(i) **Bagging** The concept of bagging (Voting, Averging) applies to combine the predicted classifications from multiple models or from the same type of model for different learning data. It is also used to address the inherent instability of results when applying complex models to relatively small data sets.

(ii) **Boosting** The concept of boosting applies to generate multiple models or classifiers and to derive weights to combine the predictions from those models into a single prediction or predicted classification. Boosting will generate a sequence of classifiers, where each consecutive classifier in the sequence is an 'expert' in classifying observations that were not well classified by those preceding it. It can also be applied to learning methods that do not explicitly support weights or misclassifi- cation costs.

(iii) **Data Preparation** Data preparation and cleaning is an extremely important step in the data mining process (although neglecting). The old saying 'garbage-in-garbage-out' is particularly applicable to the typical data mining projects where large data sets collected via some automatic methods (*e.g., via* the Web) serve as the input into the analysis. Analysing data which have not been carefully screened for such problems can produce highly misleading results.

(iv) **Reduction** The term is usually applied to projects where the goal is to aggregate or amalgamate the information contained in large datasets into smaller manageable information. These methods include simple tabulation, aggregation or more sophisticated techniques like clustering etc.

(v) **Drill-Down Analysis** It applies to the area of data mining, to denote the interactive exploration of large databases. The process begins by considering some simple break-downs of the data by a few variables of interest (*e.g.,* Gender, geographic region, etc). Various statistics, tables, histograms, and other graphical summaries can be computed for each group. Next, we may want to 'drill-down' to expose and further analyze the data "underneath" one of the categorizations, for example, we might want to further review the data for males from the mid-west. Again, various statistical and graphical summaries can be computed for those cases only, which might suggest further breakdowns by other variables (*e.g.,* income, age, etc.). At the lowest ('bottom') level are the raw data.

(vi) **Feature Selection** One preliminary stage is to select predictors from a large list of candidates. For example, when data are collected *via* automated (computerized) methods, it is not uncommon that measurements are recorded for thousands or hundereds of thousands (or more) of predictors. The standard analytic methods for predictive data mining become impractical when the number of predictors exceed more than a few hundered variables.

(vii) **Machine Learning** Machine learning, computational learning theory, and similar terms and often used to denote the application of generic model-fitting or classification algorithms for predictive data mining. The term Predictive Data Mining is usually applied to identify data mining projects with the goal to identify a statistical or neural network model which can be used to predict some response of interest. Unlike traditional statistical data analysis the emphasis in machine learning is usually on the accuracy of prediction regardless of whether or not the 'models' or techniques that are used to generate the prediction is interpretable or open to simple explanation.

(viii) **Meta-Learning** This applies to the area of predictive data mining to combine the predictions from multiple models. It is particularly useful when the types of models included in the project are very different. Experience has shown that combining the predictions from multiple methods often yields more accurate predictions than can be derived from any one method.

Web Based Tools for Sequence Search

Sequence homology search tools may be divided into four groups:

(i) **Pairwise searches** (*e.g.,* BLAST, Smith-Waterman): compare a single query sequence against each sequence in a large database and report significant similarities.

(ii) **Profile searches** (*e.g.,* HMMER): if supplied with several examples of a family of sequences and will attempt to construct a profile of this family, then search a database for sequences that fit the profile.

(iii) **Automated searches** (*e.g.,* PSI-BLAST): first seek out close relatives of a single query sequence, then use these close relatives to build a profile. In other words, they combine the tasks performed by pairwise and profile search tools.

(iv) **Protein family databases** (*e.g.,* PFAM, PROSITE, BLOCKS): a single query sequence is compared to entries in a database of profiles, each representing a distinct protein family. This approach shares many of the benefits of profile searches, without the duplicated effort of finding members of an already well-characterized family.

Motif Analysis and Presentation

For understanding gene regulation it is essential to identify the repertoire of Transcription Factor Binding Motifs (TFBMs) that form the building blocks of promoters and other regulatory elements. The number of TFBMs discovered remains relatively small, especially when compared with the hundered of transcription factor genes predicted in metazoan genomes. The recently developed statistical motif discovery approach, Nested MICA, is used to detect candidate TFBMs from a large set of *Drosophila melanogaster* promoter regions. Analysis of sequence conservation and motif positioning suggested that the great majority of motifs are predictive of functional elements in the genome. Many motifs showed associations with specific patterns of gene expression in the *D. melanogaster* embryo. The motifs are available through Tiffin, a new database of DNA sequence motifs. We have discovered many new motifs that are over represented in *D. melanogaster* promoter regions, and offer several independent lines of evidence that these are novel TFBMs.

Websites

List of links to molecular biology sites

http://www.expasy.ch/alinks.html

Sequence retrievial system (capable of searching numerous databases and medline simutaneously)

http://www.ncbi.nlm.nih.gov/Entrez/

Database Searches (submit a query sequence and search for homologies in the databases)

http://www.ncbi.nlm.nih.gov/BLAST/

http://www2.ebi.ac.uk/fasta3/

Translation (translate nucleotide sequence into protein sequence)

http://www.expasy.ch/tools/dna.html

Pairwise Alignments

http://genome.eerie.fr/fasta/align-query.html

Multiple Alignments

http://www.ibc.wustl.edu/service/clustal.html

http://dot.imgen.bcm.tmc.edu:9331/multi-align/Options/clustalw.html

Protein Analysis (numerous programs for analyzing proteins)

http://www.expasy.ch

http://www.ebi.ac.uk/Tools/index.html

Secondary Protein Structure

http://www.embl-heidelberg.de/predictprotein/predictprotein.html

Exercise

1. You are conducting an experiment to test the hypothesis that dairy cows will give more milk if they listen to classical music while being milk D. Your 20 experimental cows listen to classical music during milking; you collect all their milk and measure how much there is. Your 20 control cows should have all experimental conditions identical to the experimental cows except
(a) they should listen to classical music at a louder volume
(b) they should listen to classical music all the time, not just during milking
(c) they should listen to a different type of music, like heavy metal
(d) they should not listen to any music

2. A successful scientific experiment will result only in
(a) rejection of one or more hypothesis
(b) proving a hypothesis
(c) accepting many hypothesis
(d) confirming predictions

3. The application of hydropathy profile involves
(a) predicting interaction sites
(b) correlating profiles with secondary structure
(c) predicting trans-membrane regions in proteins
(d) All of the above

4. Tasks supported by data mining include
(a) prediction and segmentation
(b) dependency modeling and summarization
(c) change and deviation detection
(d) All of the above

5. According to Chou and Fasman rule, based on a database of protein structures, a set of conformational preferences parameters were calculated for each amino acid type based on
(a) relative frequency of a specific amino acid type within each protein
(b) occurrence of that amino acid in a given type of secondary structure
(c) the fraction of amino acid residues occurring in each type of secondary structure
(d) All of the above

6. Which of the following method is useful in computing the probability that an given amino acid belongs to a particular secondary structure element when there are no homologous protein sequences or structure data?
(a) PSA method (b) EMBL NN method
(c) Helical wheel method (d) None of these

7. How many types of BLAST programs have been developed to support sequence similarity searching using variety of nucleotide and protein sequence queries and databases?
(a) 2 (b) 3
(c) 5 (d) 9

8. .... program compares a protein query from a protein database.
(a) BLASTP (b) BLASTN
(c) BLASTX (d) TBLASTN

9. Which of the following BLAST program do not involve the comparing protein/nucleotide queries from a nucleotide database?
(a) BLASTN (b) BLASTX
(c) TBLASTN (d) TBLASTX

10. Find the unmatched.

	Database		Homology purpose
I.	OWL	—	Sequence
II.	GRASS	—	Structure
III.	PROSITE	—	Sequence family
IV.	CATH	—	Structure family
V.	PROCAT	—	Binding
VI.	GRID	—	Function family

(a) I and II (b) V and VI
(c) II and IV (d) II, III and IV

11. PROCAT is an example of
(a) database for sequence based protein family
(b) database for function based protein family
(c) database for structure based protein family
(d) database for energetic based protein family

12. FASTA program is more sensitive for the comparison of
(a) DNA-RNA comparison sequence
(b) DNA-protein comparison sequence
(c) DNA-DNA comparison sequence
(d) protein-protein comparison sequence

13. .... is the number of different alignment with score equal to or better than substitution score that are expected to occur by chance in a database search of this particular database.
(a) *P*-value (b) *E*-value
(c) *S*-score (d) *G*-score

14. Which of the following webserver is used to identify protein domains?
(a) BLOCKS (b) SMART
(c) DomFISH (d) All of these

15. Which of the following webserver is used to identify posttranslational modifications or cleavage?
(a) Prosite (b) NetPhos
(c) NetPico (d) All of these

16. Which of the following database is not useful for interactionstudies of protein, DNA and/or small molecules?
(a) BIND (b) LIGAND
(c) MINT (d) ECOCYC

17. BioCarta, WIT and GeneNet database is an example of protein, DNA and small molecule interaction database?
(a) Gene expression database
(b) Metabolic and signaling pathway database
(c) Operon data base
(d) None of the abave

18. Which of the following step is a part if the homology modeling?
(a) Identification of protein templates with known 3-D structures and production of an alignment between the query sequence and its templates
(b) Building a model for the query protein based on its alignment with the template structure
(c) Evaluation of the quality of the model
(d) All of the above

19. Which of the following tool is not used for homology modeling?
(a) COMPOSER (b) MODELLER
(c) CONGEN (d) PROSPECT

20. Arrange the different steps as they are followed during comparative protein structure modeling
I. Evaluate model.
II. Align target seqence with template structure.
III. Select templates.
IV. Identify related structures.
V. Target sequence.
(a) I, II, III, IV, V
(b) V, IV, III, II, I
(c) III, II, V, IV, I
(d) I, IV, II, III, IV

Answers

1. (d)	**2.** (b)	**3.** (d)	**4.** (d)	**5.** (d)	**6.** (a)	**7.** (c)	**8.** (a)	**9.** (b)	**10.** (c)
11. (b)	**12.** (c)	**13.** (b)	**14.** (d)	**15.** (d)	**16.** (d)	**17.** (b)	**18.** (d)	**19.** (d)	**20.** (b)

Solutions of Sample Questions as Provided on CSIR Website

Part 'B'

21. Which of the following bonds will be most difficult to break?

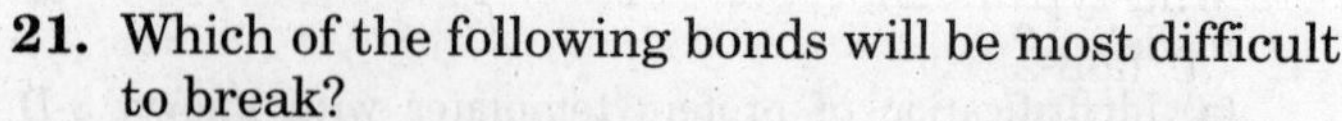

(a) C—O (b) C—C (c) C—N (d) C—S

Sol. (a) The interaction of atoms in biological molecules are primarily covalent in nature. The energy required to repture the bonds are

C—C ⟶ 82 kcal/mole
C—N ⟶ 80 kcal/mole
C—O ⟶ 84 kcal/mole
C—S ⟶ 45 kcal/mole

22. A solution of 1% (*w*/*v*) starch at pH 6.7 is digested by 15 μg of β-amylase (mol wt 152,000). The rate of maltose (mol wt = 342) had a maximal initial velocity of 8.5 mg formed per min. The turnover number is

(a) 0.25×10^{-5} min^{-1} (b) 25×10^{5} min^{-1}
(c) 2.5×10^{5} min^{-1} (d) 2.5×10^{4} min^{-1}

Sol. (c) Turnover number of an enzyme is an index of the catalytic efficiency of enzyme. It essentially represents the moles of substrate converted into product per second per mole of enzyme.

$$\text{Number of mole of } \beta\text{-amylase} = \frac{15 \times 10^{-3}}{152000}$$

$$\text{Number of moles of maltose} = \frac{8.5}{342}$$

$$\text{Turnover number} = \frac{8.5}{342} \times \frac{152000}{15 \times 10^{-3}}$$

$$= 2.5 \times 10^{5} / \text{min.}$$

23. The conformation of a nucleotide in DNA is affected by rotation about how many bonds?

(a) 4 (b) 6 (c) 7 (d) 3

Sol. (c) Nucleotide structure is more complicated than an amino acid since there are three components. But unlike amino acids, the three components are not simply different atoms or functional groups, they are three different molecules that are used to form the nucleotide: a phosphate, a sugar and a nitrogenous base. In analogy with the amino acid, the sugar and phosphate can be considered to be the 'core', with the base the '*R* group', since there is no difference in the structure of the sugar and phosphate (one for DNA and one for RNA), but there are 5 bases that compose nucleotides used in making DNA or RNA. In contrast to rotation about the two bonds hooking the alpha carbon to the amino and carboxyl groups, a nucleotide in DNA is affected by rotation about seven different bonds, six of which rotate freely. The limited rotation about bond 4 gives rise to sugar ring 'pucker', in which one of the atoms in the five-membered ring is out of the plane described by the other four.

24. Which of the following proteins acts as an energy transducer?

(a) G-protein
(b) Bacteriorhodopsin
(c) Haemoglobin
(d) Heat shock protein

Sol. (b) An energy transducer transforms one mode of energy to another. For example, for most sensory modalities sensory cells act as energy transducers, transforming the energy of the environmental stimulus into a change in the electrical potential difference across a biological membrane. Bacteriorhodopsin (bR) is an integral protein in the plasma membrane of a bacterium. Upon light absorption, bR transports protons across the membrane, converting the photon energy into the energy of a proton electrochemical gradient. bR is a single small protein and is the simplest known active ion pump and biological light energy transducer. Energy transduction is thus, the fundamental physical basis of the sensory response of most biological systems to their environment.

25. Which of the following predicted property of lipid bilayers would result if the phospholipids had only one hydrocarbon chain instead of two?

(a) The bilayers formed would be much less fluid
(b) The diameter of the head group would be much larger than the acyl chain and would tend to form micelles rather than bilayers
(c) The bilayers formed would be much more fluid
(d) The bilayers would be more permeable to small water-soluble molecules

Sol. (b) The lipid bilayer is a thin polar membrane made of two layers of lipid molecules. Lipid bilayers are large enough structures to have some mechanical properties of liquid or solids. Intrinsic curvature is defined by the ratio of diameter of head group to that of tail group. If a particular lipid has too large deviation from zero intrinsic curvature it will not form a bilayer instead form other phases such as micelles or inverted micelles.

26. **Which pump is responsible for initiating muscle contraction through depolarization of muscle cell membrane?**

(a) Na^+ pump (b) K^+ pump
(c) Ca^{2+} pump (d) Mg^{2+} pump

Sol. (a) In the sodium pump (also called sodium potassium exchange pump) ions move against the concentration gradient. This is done by active transport. When a muscle fibre is stimulated the sarcolemma becomes more permeable to sodium ions than to potassium ions so that sodium ions move along the concentration gradient. The sacrolemma positively charged inside with respect to outside. This change is called action potential and the muscle (sarcolemma) is said to be depolarized. Due to depolarization muscle fibre contracts.

27. **Which of the following statements is not true for transposable element system?**

(a) It consists of autonomous and non-autonomous elements
(b) Dissociation elements are autonomous in nature.
(c) Transposase is transcribed by the central region of autonomous elements.
(d) Certain repeats in the genome remain fixed even after the element transposes out.

Sol. (b) The maize *hAT* family members Activator/Dissociation (*Ac*/*Ds*) are composed of the autonomous *Ac* and nonautonomous *Ds* transposable elements. *Ac* is 4565 bp and encodes a 3.5 kb open reading frame (ORFa) that directs the synthesis of an 807 amino acid transposase (TPase) protein. The TPase transcript initiates at several sites within a 100-bp interval at the 5′ end of the element and spans most of *Ac*. The lack of canonical CAAT and TATA boxes in the promoter region may account for the multiple transcriptional initiation sites with *Ac* and the low levels of *Ac* transcript. *Ac* contains ~ 240 bp subterminal repeats and 11 bp terminal inverted repeats at each end. The subterminal repeat regions at both *Ac* ends contain TPase binding sites that are essential for TPase recognition and subsequent transposition of both *Ac* and *Ds*.

28. **A set of virulence genes (*vir* genes), located in the *Agrobacterium* Ti-plasmid, is activated by**

(a) octopine (b) nopaline
(c) acetosyringone (d) auxin

Sol. (c) T-DNA is ~23 kb segment of Ti-plasmid which is transferred into the plant genome during *Agrobaacterium* infection. The *vir* region contains 8 operons which together have 25 genes. This region mediates the transfer of T-DNA into plant genome hence, essential for virulence or production of crown gall therefore, called virulence region. Acetosyringone and α-hydroxyacetosyringone activate the *vir* operons whose function is essential for T-DNA transfer into plant cells.

29. **When two mutants having the same phenotype were crossed, the progeny obtained showed a wild-type phenotype. Thus, the mutations are**

(a) non-allelic
(b) allelic
(c) segregating from each other
(d) independently assorting

Sol. (b) A mutation may arise due to change in the base sequence of a gene and called gene mutation. A mutational change in phenotype is sudden heritable and is not produced due to segregation. Generally mutant alleles are recessive to their wild type or normal alleles.

30. **A conjugation experiment is carried out between F^+ *his*$^+$ *leu*$^+$ *thr*$^+$ *pro*$^+$ bacteria and F^- *his*$^-$ *leu*$^-$ *thr*$^-$ *pro*$^-$ bacteria for a period of 25 min. At this time the mating is stopped, and the genotypes of the recipient F^- bacteria are determined. The results are shown below:**

Genotype	Number of colonies
his$^+$	0
leu$^+$	13
thr$^+$	26
pro$^+$	6

What is the probable order of these genes on the bacterial chromosome?

(a) *thr, leu, pro, his*
(b) *pro, leu, pro,* and the position of *his* cannot be determined.
(c) *thr, leu, pro* and the position of *his* cannot be determined.
(d) *his, pro, leu, thr*

Sol. (c) Bacterial conjugation is a plasmid encoded mechanism of transfer of genetic material that involves cell to cell contact. The process involve a donor cell which contain a particular type of conjugative plasmid and a recipient cell which does not. Different conjugative plasmids may have slightly different *tra* regions. In the given conjugation experiment the order of genes cannot be determined.

31. **Two varieties of maize averaging 48 and 72 inches in height, respectively, are crossed. The F_1 progeny is quite uniform averaging 60 inches in height. Of the 500 F_2 plants, the shortest 2 are 48**

inches and the tallest 2 are 72 inches. What is the probable number of polygenes involoved in this trait?

(a) Four (b) Eight
(c) Sixteen (d) Thirty two

Sol. (a) In 1908 Nilsson Ehle presented the multiple factor hypothesis to explain his result on the inheritance of seed colour in wheats and maize. In crosses showing 15 : 1 ratio in F_2 seed colour is governed by two gene. 63:1 ratio is governed by 3 genes. So, the 498 : 2 or 249 : 1 ratio will probably be governed by four genes.

32. Repair of double strand breaks made during meiosis in the yeast *Saccharomyces cerevisiae*

(a) occurs mostly by non-homologous end joining
(b) occurs mostly using the sister chromatid as a template
(c) occurs mostly using the homologous chromosome as a template
(d) is associated with a high frequency of mutations

Sol. (c) An important event called crossing over takes place during pachytene stage of meiosis-I between non-sister chromatids of homologous chromosomes by exchagne and reunion. In this process one strand of double stranded DNA function as a template for the reunion of other.

33. Which of the following signaling molecules enter the cell to initiate its action?

(a) Transferrin (b) Insulin
(c) Glucagon (d) Thyroxine

Sol. (d) There are many different kind of signals including membrane anchord and secreted proteins and peptides, small lipophilic molecules (steroid hormone, thyroxine) etc. When steroid hormone and thyroxine (lipophilic molecules) enters a cell, it forms a complex with a receptor molecule. The hormone receptor complex moves to the nucleus of the cell where the receptor molecule binds to chromosome and activate the gene.

34. The mode of action of the anticancer drug methotrexate is through its strong competitive inhibition on

(a) dihydrofolate reductase (b) thymidine synthase
(c) thymidine kinase (d) adenylate cyclase

Sol. (a) Methotrexate inhibits folic acid reductase which is responsible for the conversion of folic acid to tetrahydrofolic acid. At two stages in the biosynthesis of purines (adenine and guanine) and at one stage in the synthesis of pyrimidines (thymine, cytosine and uracil), one-carbon transfer reactions occur which require specific coenzymes synthesized in the cell from tetrahydrofolic acid. Tetrahydrofolic acid itself is synthesized in the cell from folic acid with the help of an enzyme, folic acid reductase. Methotrexate looks a lot like folic acid to the enzyme, so it binds to it, thinking that it is folic acid. In fact, methotrexate looks so good to the enzyme that it binds to it quite strongly and inhibits the enzyme. Thus, DNA synthesis cannot proceed because the coenzymes needed for one-carbon transfer reactions are not produced from tetrahydrofolic acid because there is no tetrahydrofolic acid. Again, without DNA, no cell division takes place.

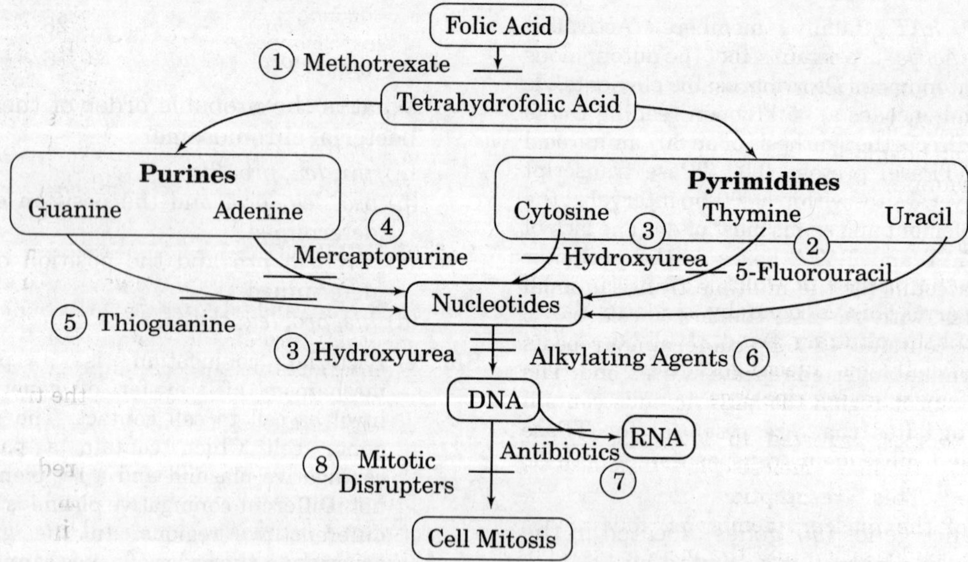

Mechanisms of Action of Anticancer Drugs

35. Which class of immunoglobulins will increase in case of a chronic infection?

(a) IgA (b) IgG
(c) IgM (d) IgE

Sol. (b) A chronic disease develops slowly and the body's reactions may be less severe but, the disease is likely to be continual or recurrent for long period. Infectious mononucleosis, syphilis, tuberculosis and leprosy falls into this category. IgG antibodies account for about 80% of all antibodies in serum. These protect against, circulating bacteria and viruses, neutralize bacterial toxins, trigger the complement system and when bound to antigens enhance the effectiveness of phagocytic cells.

36. When, prospective neuroectoderm from an early amphibian gastrula is transplanted in the prospective epidermal region of a recipient (early gastrula) embryo, the donor tissue will give rise to

(a) neural tube
(b) epidermis
(c) neural tube and notochord
(d) neural tube and epidermis

Sol. (b) Neuroectoderm gives rise to brain, spinal cord, cranial and spinal nerves, retina and posterior pituitary, while somatic ectoderm give rise to epidermis, cutaneous derivatives. Olfactory organs, anterior pituitary, etc. For inducing the neural plate to become neural tube it is necessary that chordamesoderm cells must remain in physical contact of neural plate cells. When neuroectoderm is transplanted to epidermal region, the donor tissue cannot give rise to neural tube.

37. Amphibian oocytes remain for years in the diplotene stage of meiotic prophase. Resumption of meiosis is initiated by

(a) gonadotropic hormone
(b) growth hormone
(c) oestrogen
(d) progesterone

Sol. (d) Ovulation is the process in which eggs are released from the ovary. This is done by sex stimulating hormone from the pituitary gland. Ovulation can be brought artificially by injecting crushed pituitary hormone to female having ripe eggs.

Amphibian oocytes, arrested in late prophase of meiosis (G_2), resume meiosis in response to progesterone. This resumption leads to the dissolution of the nuclear membrane, followed by chromosome condensation and the meiotic divisions up to the second metaphase. Several observations have led to the suggestion that a progesterone-induced increase in intracellular free calcium may be a necessary first step for the resumption of meiosis.

38. A group of six cells called 'equivalence group cells' divide to form the vulval structure in *Caenorhabditis elegans*. They are called so because

(a) they have similar fates during development of vulva
(b) all the six cells are competent to form vulva and can replace each other under various experimental conditions
(c) they are all under the influence of the anchor cell, signals from which initiate vulval development
(d) they interact with each other to form the vulval structure

Sol. (b) The vulva is a part of female sex apparatus, the positional information needed by the vulva progenitor cells is provided by a cell within the gonad called anchor cell. In absence of anchor cell a vulva does not develop. The signal that commits p5-p and p7p to their secondary fates might not come directly from the anchor cell but *via* p6p in the form of a different extracellular signaling compound.

39. Due to the presence of cellulose in the cell wall of plants, leaf shape is determined in the leaf primorida by

(a) rates of cell division
(b) planes of cell division
(c) cell migration
(d) cell-cell interactions

Sol. (b) A leaf initiates by periclinal divisions in a small group of cells at the side of an apical meristem. The periclinal divisions which initiate a leaf primordium are responsible for formation of lateral prominance on the side of shoot apex. Before the initiation of a new leaf primordium the apical meristem appears as a rounded mound.

40. DCMU inhibits electron transport in chloroplast by preventing the reduction of

(a) P_{680} (b) Q_A
(c) P_Q (d) Q_B

Sol. (d) DCMU (Dichloro Phenyl Dimethyl Urea) is a herbicide. Two derivative of urea (monuron and divron) and triazine herbicide bind to Q_B binding site of D_1 protein in photosystem II. The herbicide interferes with the binding of plastoquinone to the same site and thus, blocks the transfer of electron to plastoquinone.

41. In higher plant leaves, the reduction of nitrate to ammonium takes place by the combined action of nitrate reductase localized in cytosol and nitrite reductase localized in

(a) peroxisomes
(b) mitochondria
(c) chloroplasts
(d) cytosol

Sol. (c) Nitrate cannot be assimilated directly but must first be reduced to NH_4^+ by enzyme nitrate reductase and nitrite reductase. Nitrate reductase is cytosolic enzyme and the product NO_2^- then move into plastid (in roots) or chloroplasts (in leaves) where, it is quickly reduced to NH_4^+ by nitrite reductase.

42. In higher plants, the red/far-red sensory photoreceptor, phytochrome, is a light-regulated kinase. Which of the following classes of kinases does it represent?

(a) Two-component sensor regulator (histidine kinase)
(b) Two-component sensor regulator (serine/threonine kinase)
(c) Leucine rich repeat (LRR) receptor kinase
(d) Calcium-dependent protein kinase

Sol. (b) The chemical which perceives, the photoperiodic stimulus in leaves is phytochrome. Soon after perceiving the required photoperiod leaves produce a chemical which passed over to shoot apex, which undergoes differentiation to produce flowers.

Angiosperms, gymnosperms, ferns, mosses and green algae usually contain small families of three to five phytochrome (*PHY*) genes. The carboxy-terminal modules of plant phytochromes contain two predicted PAS domains followed by a sequence with apparent homology to two-component histidine kinases (TC-HKs)-the effector proteins in the 'two-component' environmental sensing systems common in bacteria, plants and fungi (Two-component systems typically comprise a receptor histidine kinase that receives the signal and relays it to a 'response regulator' protein that elicits the cellular response). However, in the plant phytochromes, amino acids critical to histidine kinase catalytic function are not conserved, and so these histidine kinase related domains (HKRDs) do not function *via* a typical Tc-HK mechanism. Bacterial and fungal phytochromes do contain functional histidine kinase domains and act *via* a two-component mechanism. Although a complete signal transduction pathway for a plant phytochrome response has not yet been described, both cytosolic and nuclear mechanisms are implicated. There is evidence that plant Phys have serine/threonine kinase activity.

43. Vesicular-arbuscular mycorrhiza (VAM) represents a beneficial association between plant roots and fungus, where fungus assists plants in obtaining ...... from the soil.

(a) iron
(b) zinc
(c) sulphate
(d) phosphate

Sol. (d) Certain fungi form association with roots of plants and the association is called mycorrhiza. These fungi convert non-available phosphorus to an available form, produce growth promoting substances and also protect against soil pathogens.

44. Unidirectional propagation of electrical signal in nervous system is

(a) proportional to the length of axon
(b) due to chemical synapse
(c) due to electrical synapse
(d) proportional to myelination

Sol. (b) A vast majority of synapses are chemical synapses. These involve the release of a chemical neurotransmitter by the presynaptic neuron, which packages into synaptic vesicle in neuron's synaptic terminal. When action potential reaches a synaptic terminal it depolarises the terminal membrane, opening voltage gated Ca^{2+} channals. The released neurotransmitter binds to specific receptors present on the post synaptic membrane.

45. A myasthenia gravis patient develops muscle paralysis because

(a) the nerve terminal at the neuromuscular junction fails to release acetylcholine
(b) although enough acetylcholine is released at the neuromuscular junction, it is destroyed by acetylcholinesterase
(c) the patient develops immunity against his own acetylcholine receptor
(d) the patient develops antibody against his own acetylcholine

Sol. (c) Myasthenia gravis, a condition in which there is extreme muscular weakness is associated with antibodies to the actylcholine receptors present on the surface of muscle membrane. It was noticed that immunization of experimental animals with purified acetylcholine receptors produced a condition of muscular weakness. This suggested a role for antibody to the acetylcholine receptor in the human disease. The antibodies reduce the availability of acetylcholine at motor end plates.

46. Inhibin from Sertoli cells of testes selectively inhibits

(a) luteinizing hormone
(b) follicle stimulating hormone
(c) thyroid stimulating hormone
(d) growth hormone

Sol. (b) When the seminiferous tubules fail to produce sperm, secretion of FSH by anterior pituitary gland increases markedly. Conversally when spermatogenesis proceeds too rapidly pituitary secretion of FSH diminishes. The cause of this negative feedback on the anterior pituitary is believed to be secretion by Sertoli cells of another hormone called **inhibin.** This hormone has strong direct effect on the anterior pituitary to inhibit secretion of salt.

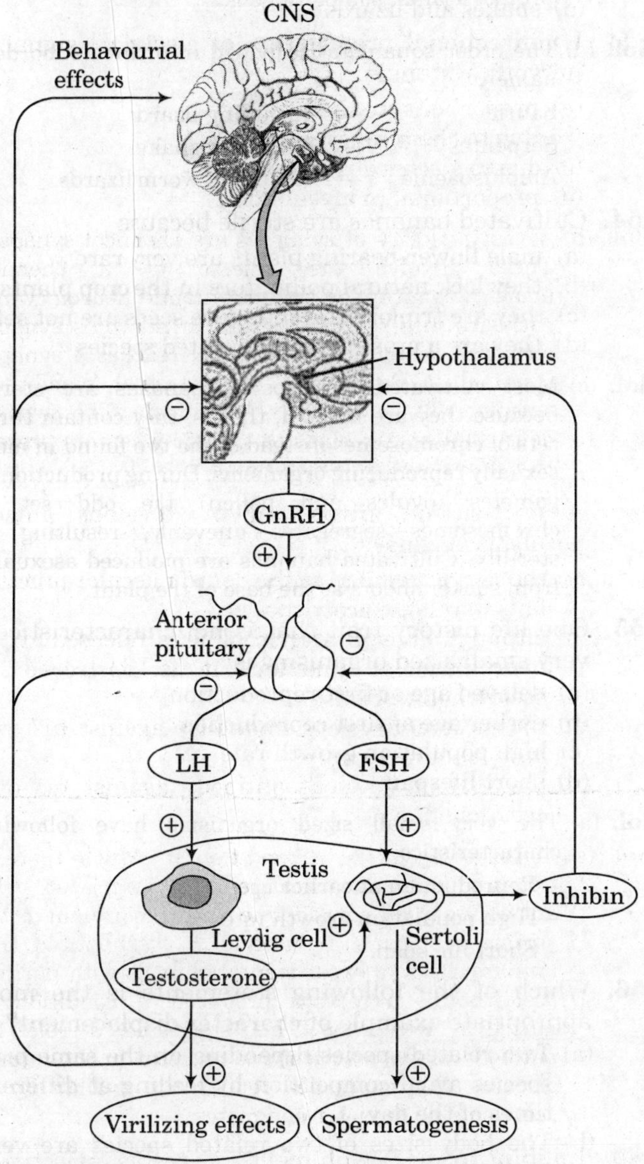

47. Hawk's retina possesses a large number of
(a) rods
(b) melanocytes
(c) cones
(d) Kuffer's cells

Sol. (c) The photoreceptor cells are of two types rods and cones. The daylight vision and colour vision is function of cones, while twilight vision is function of rods. In nocturnal animals (*e.g.*, owl) retina has mainly rods, while in diurnal animals (most birds and man) retina has mainly cones.

48. *E. coli* cells were grown in N^{15} medium for several generations and then shifted to normal medium for one generation. If the DNA isolated from the culture would be centrifuged on a CsCl equilibrium density gradient, the result will be
(a) a single band of double helix DNA consisting of one strand with N^{14} and another with N^{15} label
(b) single band of double helix DNA consisting of N^{14} and N^{15} in both the strands
(c) two bands containing double helix DNA each containing both N^{14} and N^{15} label
(d) two bands containing single stranded DNA one with N^{14} and other with N^{15} label

Sol. (d) When the *E. coli* cells were grown in N^{15} medium for several generations, all the cells except two contain the DNA with N^{15} nucleotides. When these cells shifted to normal medium two cells have purely N^{14} DNA, while other cells have one strand with N^{15} and other strand with N^{14} nucleotides in double stranded DNA.

49. Which of the following processes does not take place in the $5' \rightarrow 3'$ direction?
(a) DNA replication
(b) Transcription
(c) Nick translation
(d) RNA editing.

Sol. (d) The concept of RNA editing proposed by Benne *et al.*, in 1986 challenged the central dogma of molecular biology by demonstrating the genetic information encoded in *m*RNA can vary from that encoded in the genome. Editing occurs in a 3′ to 5′ direction and is thought to occur in four stages; *g*RNA/*m*RNA anchor duplex formation, cleavage of the *m*RNA target, the addition on delection of U residues in the *m*RNA and finally the re-ligation of the two fragments of the newly edited *m*RNA. The 5′ ends of *g*RNAs contain 10-15 nucleotides called the anchor region and it is this region that is direct complementary to a target unedited *m*RNA or pre-*m*RNA. The double stranded region formed by the binding of the *g*RNA anchor with its target pre-*m*RNA is called the anchor duplex and it forms directly 3′ to the region of the pre-*m*RNA to be edited. Anchor duplex formation brings the 3′ poly U tail of the *g*RNA into close proximity with purine rich regions of the pre-*m*RNA.

50. A deletion of three consecutive bases in the coding region of a gene cannot result in
(a) deletion of a single amino acid without any other change in the protein
(b) replacement of two adjacent amino acids by a single amino acid
(c) replacement of a single amino acid by another without any other change in sequence of the protein
(d) production of a truncated protein

Sol. (b) Coding regions of the gene have nucleotide sequences for protein synthesis. A deletion of three consecutive bases in the coding region provide two possibilities

(i) If the three bases code only a single amino acid this cause deletion of single amino acid from protein and thus functional change.

(ii) If the three bases deleted are from two nucleotide codons the whole amino acid sequence is changed in the protein molecule.

51. Deletion of the leader sequence of *trp* operon of *E. coli* would result in
(a) decreased transcription of *trp* operon
(b) increased transcription of *trp* operon
(c) no effect on transcription
(d) decreased transcription of *trp* operon in the presence of tryptophan

Sol. (b) The genes required for tryptophan biosynthesis in *Escherichia coli* are organized as a single transcriptional unit, the *trp* operon. This operon has a single major promoter at which transcription initiation is regulated by a DNA-binding protein, the L-tryptophan-activated *trp* repressor. This repressor acts by binding at one or more of three operator sites located in the *trp* operon's promoter region. One element of the *trp* operon is the leader sequence (L) that in immediately 5′ of the *trpE* gene. This sequence (about 160 bp in size) also controls the expression of the operon through a process called **attentuation.** This sequence has four domains (1-4). Domain 3 (nucleotides 108-121) of the *m*RNA can base pair with either domain 2 (nucleotides 74-94) or domain 4 (nucleotides 126-134). If domain 3 pairs with domain 4, a stem and loop structure forms on the *m*RNA and transcription stops. This structure forms when the level of tryptophan is high in the cell. If domain 3 pairs with domain 2, then the stem and loop structure does not form and transcription continues through the operon and all of the enzymes required for tryptophan biosynthesis are produce. These events occur when tryptophan is low in the cell.

52. In the endodermis of higher plants, role of Casperian strip is to control the water movement so that it flows
(a) between the cells
(b) through the plasma membrane
(c) through the cell wall
(d) through the transfusion tissue

Sol. (d) Commonly the endodermal cells are of two types primary or thin walled and secondary or thick walled. In thin walled cells certain thickening of suberin developed in the form of bands called Casparian strips. Among the thick walled cells in endodermis there occur occasionally isolated thin walled cells usually opposite the protoxylem element which are known as passage or transfusion cells. Through these cells the sap absorbed by root hairs enter the xylem elements.

53. The reptilian order squamata includes
(a) crocodiles and alligators
(b) the living fossil 'tuatara'
(c) turtles and tortoises
(d) snakes and lizards

Sol. (d) The order squamata is divided into three suborders namely

Sauria	—	Including lizards
Serpentes	—	Including snakes
Amphisbaenia	—	Including worm lizards.

54. Cultivated bananas are sterile because
(a) male flower-bearing plants are very rare
(b) they lack natural pollinators in the crop plants
(c) they are triploid and therefore seeds are not set
(d) they are a cross of two unrelated species

Sol. (c) Most cultivated varieties of bananas are sterile because they are triploid, that is, they contain three sets of chromosomes instead of the two found in most sexually reproducing organisms. During production of gametes (ovules and pollen) the odd set of chromosomes segregates unevenly, resulting in sterility. Cultivated bananas are produced asexually from sucker shoots at the base of the plant.

55. One life history trait that is not characteristic of very small sized organisms is
(a) delayed age at first reproduction
(b) earlier age at first reproduction
(c) high population growth rate
(d) short lifespan

Sol. (a) The very small sized organisms have following characteristics
- Reproduction at earlier age
- High population growth rate
- Short life span.

56. Which of the following statements is the most appropriate example of character displacement?
(a) Two related species depending on the same prey species avoid competition by feeding at different times of the day
(b) The body sizes of two related species are very similar when they are allopatric, but in geographical areas of sympatry, one species is significantly smaller than the other
(c) The food niche of a species is generally wider in the absence of competing species than in their presence
(d) Closely related species can coexist if their densities are regulated by a predator

Sol. (b) Character displacement is the divergence of overlapping characteristics in two species living in the same environmental as a result of resource partitioning. This indicating the importance of competition, when comparing sympatric and allopatric populations of similar species.

57. In a population growing logistically and approaching carrying capacity (K), the change in density (N) per unit time (dN/dt) is maximum when, N equals to

(a) K^2 (b) $\frac{K}{2}$

(c) K (d) $2K$

Sol. (b) Carrying capacity is the upper limit of a species to grow. The logistic equation assumes that the instrinsic rate of natural increase is progressively reduced as population size increases towards the carrying capacity. The logistic equation is $\frac{dN}{dt} = rN\left(\frac{K-N}{K}\right)$

When, N is more than K the $\frac{dN}{dt}$ value will be negative but when equal, the density change become zero.

58. The losses of ozone over Arctic are significantly lower than that over Antarctica because

(a) polar vortex over Arctic is not as tight as over Antarctic

(b) Arctic stratosphere warms slower in the spring

(c) concentration of chlorine in the atmosphere over Arctic is less than over Antarctic

(d) freezing of NO_2 and CH_4 are slower over Arctic than over Antarctic.

Sol. (d) Major pollutants responsible for depletion of ozone are chlorofluorocarbons, nitrogen oxides, and hydrocarbon. The threat to O_3 is mainly from CFCs which are known to deplete O_3 by 14% and NO_x would reduce O_3 by 3.5%.

59. Which of the following species replacement sequence depicts tolerance model of community succession?

(a) 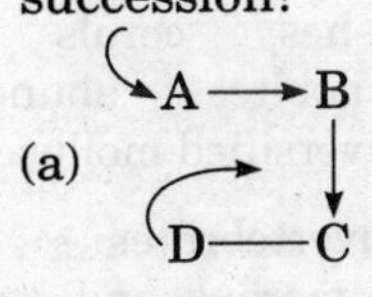

(b) 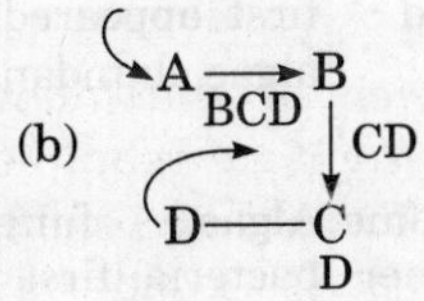

(c) 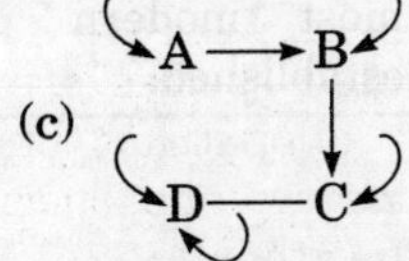

(d) A —//→ B

Sol. (b) The occurrence of relatively definite sequence of communities over a period of time in the same area is known as ecological succession. The species may increase their capacity of tolerance towards changing environment by developing ecads, ecotypes and serel community.

60. Evolutionarily, with which of the following could parental care in animals be associated?

(a) Smaller clutch size

(b) Polygamy

(c) Greater longevity

(d) Semelparity

Sol. (a) Clutch size differs greatly between species, sometimes even within the same genus. It may also differ within the same species due to many factors including habitat, health, nutrition, predation pressures and time of year. Clutch size variation can also reflect variation in optimal reproduction effort. Long-lived species tend to have smaller clutch sizes than short-lived species. The evolution of optimal clutch size is also driven by other factors, such as parent-offspring conflict. Increased parental care and smaller clutch sizes at high elevations may therefore represent a strategy to increase offspring survival in response to increased nest predation, low food availability, or changing abiotic conditions.

61. 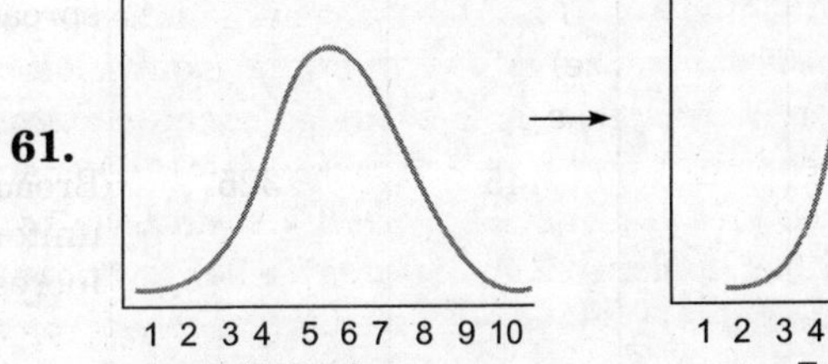

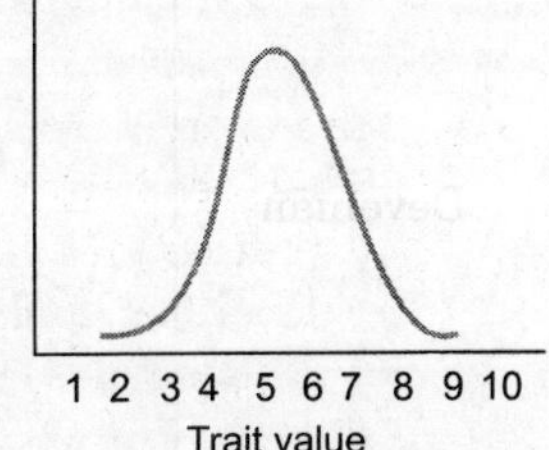

The change in a trait with time as a result of natural selection is shown above. This type of natural selection is

(a) directional

(b) disruptive

(c) stabilizing

(d) random

Sol. (c) Stabilizing selection occurs when the environment does not change. Natural selection has to produce change and if environment does not change there is no pressure for well adapted species to change.

62. During which geological period did the greatest diversification of life on Earth occur?

(a) Permian

(b) Jurassic

(c) Cambrian

(d) Ordovician

Sol. (c) **Palaeozoic Era with Notes on Events in the Evolution of Life and Environment**

Period	Epoch	Duration in Millions of Years	Time from Beginning of Period to Present in Million of Years	Geological and Climatic Conditions	Flora (plant life)	Fauna (animal life)
Permian	—	25	230	Rise of continents; climate became arid and varied, glaciation in Southern hemisphere.	Dwindling of ancient plants, decline of lycopods and horse tails.	Extinction of ammonites and trilobites, abundance of primitive reptiles; appearance of mammals like reptiles, decline of amphibians
Pennsylvanian	—	25	255	Uniform climate throughout world.	Great forests of seed-ferns and gymnosperms (great tropical coal forests)	Amphibians dominant on land, insects common, appearance of first reptiles
Mississippian (Carboniferous)	—	25	280	Climate uniform, humid at first, cooler later as land rose; spread of tropical seas	Mosses and seed ferns dominant, gymnosperms increasingly widespread (early coal forest)	Rise of insects, sea lilies at peak; spread of ancient sharks
Devonian	—	45	325	Broad distribution of uniform climates; increased temperature	First forests, first gymnosperms and first known liverworts, horsetails and ferns	Divesification in fishes sharks and lung fishes abundant, evolution of amphibians
Silurian	—	35	360	Slight climate cooling, extensive continental seas	First known land plant club mosses, algae dominant	Wide expansion of invertebrates first insects, rise of fishes
Cambrian	—	65	425	Warm climate, great submergence of land	Land plants probably first appeared, marine algae abundant	First indication of fishes, corals and trilobites abundant, diversified molluscs
Ordovician	—	75	500	Climate became progeressively warmer	Algae, fungi and bacteria: first fossils of plant life	Invertebrates numerous and varied, most modern phyla established.

63. Which of the following plant groups evolved during the Siluria period?

(a) Bryophyta (b) Psilophyta
(c) Lycophyta (d) Spherophyta

Sol. (c) Club mosses belong to Lycophyta and evolved during silurian period. (For more explanation refer solution 62).

64. Which of the following GM crops is the most widely cultivated globally?

(a) Herbicide resistant soyabean
(b) Insect resistant cotton
(c) Insect resistant brinjal
(d) Delayed ripening tomato

Sol. (a) Development of transgenic plants resistant to certain biodegradable herbicides was the first major achievement from genetic engineering in plants. Transgenic plants resistant to several herbicides, *e.g.*, glyphosate, glufosinate, sulfonylureas etc., have been successfully developed. Transgenic tobacco, soyabean, canola and tomato have been developed which are resistant to glyphosate. It inhibits the enzyme 5-enolpyruvylshikimate-3 phosphate synthase (EPSPS), which is involved in aromatic amino acid synthesis in plants.

Insect resistant cotton is also a genetically modified crop used second to soyabean.

65. PCR based DNA amplification is an essential feature of which of the following combination of molecular markers?

(a) RFLP, AFLP and SSR
(b) AFLP, SSR and RAPD
(c) RFLP, RAPD and SSR
(d) RAPD, RELP and SSR

Sol. (b) **A comparison among some of the different DNA markers used in gentic mapping**

Feature	DNA Marker			
	RFLP	**RAPD**	**AFLP**	**STS**
Efforts to generate marker	Moderate	Simple	Simpler than RFLPs	Difficult
Ease in use	Difficult	Easy	Moderate	Moderate
Number of markers scorable per cross	Unlimited	Unlimited	Unlimited	Unlimited
Plant material required	Medium	Little	Medium	Little
Reproducibi lity	High	Moderate	High	High
Use of radioactivity	Yes	NO	Yes/No	No
Use of restriction enzymes	Yes	No	Yes	No
Use of PCR	No	Yes	Yes	Yes
Dominance	Codominant	Dominant	Codominant	Codominant /Dominant
Information generated	Moderate to high	High	Very high	Very high
Time required for detection	Relatively longer	Short	Short	Short

66. The genes whose promoters are extensively used for production of pharmaceutical protein in transgenic dairy cattles are

(a) lactalbumin and ovalbumin
(b) lactoglobulin and casein
(c) lactoferrin and transferrin
(d) casein and ovalbumin

Sol. (b) The two chief objectives of transgenic cattle production are increased milk or meat production and molecular farming. The transgenic protein is secreted in milk from where it is easily harvested. Other objectives of transgenic cattle are increased properties and proportion of casein, contents of lactose and butter fat in milk and enhanced resistance to bacterial and viral pathogens.

67. A biochemist purifies a new enzyme, generating the following purification table.

	Procedure	Total protein (mg)	Activity (units)
I.	Crude extract	20000	4000000
II.	Salt precipitation	5000	3000000
III.	Ion-exchange chromatography	200	800000
IV.	Affinity chromatography	50	750000
V.	Size-exclusion chromatography	45	675000

The most effective purification step is

(a) IV
(b) III
(c) V
(d) II

Sol. (b) Chromatography is a process of separation of mixturs into components by passing the fluid mixture through a bed of adsorbant material. Enzymes possess a net charge in solution, dependent upon the pH and their structure and isoelectric point. In solutions of pH below their isoelectric point they will be positively charged and bind to cation exchangers whereas in solutions of pH above their isoelectric point they will be negaticely charged and bind to anion exchangers. The pH chosen must be sufficient to maintain a high, but opposite, charge on both protein and ion-exchanger and the ionic strength must be sufficient to maintain the solubility of the protein without the salt being able to successfully compete with the protein for ion-exchanges sites. The binding is predominaintly reversible and its strength is determined by pH and ionic strength of the solution and the structures of enzyme and ion-exchanger.

68. Similarities in sequence and function of two proteins indicate that they are members of a family that share a common ancestor. If they are from ferent species, they are called

(a) homologs
(b) orthologs
(c) paralogs
(d) proteologs

Sol. (b) The homologous genes or proteins related through the splitting of an ancestal species into two new species is said to be orthologous.

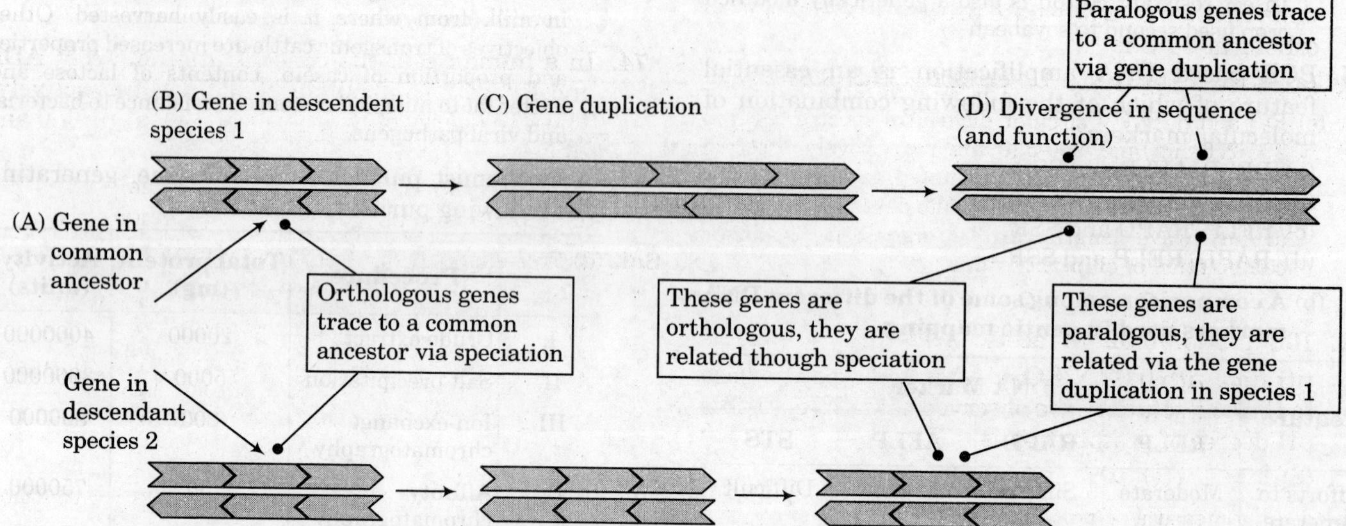

Hoemologous genes are derived from a common ancestral gene. One type of homology results when a single species splits into two new species (A and B).

69. The conformation of a 30-residue peptide is studied by NMR spectroscopy. The J_{NH} for most of the amide protons is 4Hz. The 2D NOESY spectrum shows prominent $Ni - Ni^{+1}$ connectivities. The conformation of the peptide is

(a) anti-parallel β-sheet (b) parallel β-sheet
(c) helix-like (d) unordered

Sol. (c) Using Nuclear Magnetic Resonance (NMR) spectroscopy we identify atoms in the molecules that are close together in space and from this information about the distance between atoms we derive indirectly a 3-D model of proteins. It is also possible to refine protein structures based on chemical shifts and even with insufficient information for a structrue determination. Chemical shifts can be used to distinguish between alpha helix and beta sheet *via* the chemical shift index. NOES are the by far most important source of information for the structure calculation. They are usually observed for protons separated by less than 5 Å. For most values of J more than one solution exists. Scalar couplings may be used to define dihedral angle restraint *ranges*, which sometimes help to improve convergence of the structure calculation.

Secondary structure	Theoretical 3 J_{HN}-(Hz) Value
Alpha helix	3.9
Antiparallel beta sheet	7.9
Parallel bets sheet	8.0

70. A sample of ^{32}P disintegrates at a rate of 30120 dpm. The radioactivity in microcuries (1 curie = 3.7×10^{10} dps) is

(a) 15060 (b) 1.36×10^{-2}
(c) 81.6×10^{-2} (d) 1.36×10^{-8}

Sol. (b) Rate of dissociation = 30120 dpm = $\frac{30120}{60}$ dps

$$\text{Radioactivity} = \frac{30120}{60 \times 3.7 \times 10^{10}}$$
$$= 135.67 \times 10^{-10} \text{ curie}$$
$$= 1.36 \times 10^{-2} \text{ microcurie}$$

Part 'C'

71. A protein polypeptide chain exists in α-helical conformation in a solvent and it has a value of –30,000 deg cm^2 d mol^{-1} for the mean residue ellipiticity at 222 nm ($[\theta]_{222}$) in the temperature range 20-50°C. On raising the temperature above 50°C, $[\theta]_{222}$ increases and reaches a value of –2000 deg cm^2 d mol^{-1} at 70°C and the value of $[\theta]_{222}$ remains unchanged above 70°C. The observed value of $[\theta]_{222}$ is –14000 deg cm^2 dmol^{-1} at 60°C. If one assumes that the heat-induced denaturation is a two-state process, the fraction of α-helix at 60°C is

(a) 0.40 (b) 0.43 (c) 0.50 (d) 0.57

Sol. (c) Far and near UV circular dichroism spectra covered 205-250 nm and 250-330 nm respectively. Protein secondary structure was calculated according to the method of Bohn *et. al* (1992). The observed ellipticity at any wave length can be expressed by linear combination of ellipticity value.

$$Q_{ob} = Q_\alpha + Q_\beta + Q_c$$

72. 100 mL of 0.02 M acetic acid (pK_a = 4.76) is titrated with 0.02 N KOH. After adding some base to the acid solution, the observed pH is 2.76. At this pH degree of protonation is

(a) 0% (b) 10% (c) 90% (d) 99%

Sol. (d) As a measure of proton transfer potential of an acid base pair its pK_a value is used. The stronger an acid the lower its pK_a value.

$$pH = pK_a + \log\frac{[A^-]}{[HA]}$$

$$pH - pK_a = \log R$$

$$10^{(pH - pK_a)} = R = 100$$

A_T (total concentration of acid) = $[A^-] + [HA]$

$= [HA](1 + R)$

Fraction of acid protonated

$$fHA = \frac{[HA]}{[A_T]} = \frac{1}{1+R}$$

$$\text{Degree of protonation} = \frac{R}{1+R} = \frac{100}{101} = 99\%$$

73. There are hydrogen bond donors (D), and acceptors (A). When the mixture (A + D) is transferred from water, designated as (w) to a non-polar solvent (np), the free energy change (ΔG) of transfer is 6.12 kcal mol^{-1} for the (A + D) mixture. A and D form a hydrogen bond in this non-polar solvent and ΔG for this process is –2.4 kcal mol^{-1}. When the hydrogen bonded molecule A–D is transferred from water to the non-polar solvent, ΔG for this process is 0.62 kcal mol^{-1}. The value of ΔG for the formation of hydrogen bond (A + B ↔ A – B) in water is

(a) – 0.1 kcal mol^{-1} (b) + 3.1 kcal mol^{-1}
(c) – 3.1 kcal mol^{-1} (d) – 1.78 kcal mol^{-1}

Sol. (b) Hydrogen bond is formed between a hydrogen atom involved in a polar covalent bond and another atom involved in a polar covalent bond. Free energy determines whether the reaction occurs spontaneously or not. The free energy change for the foramtion of hydrogen bond in water is equal to difference between free energy change of mixture (A + D) from water to non-polar solvent and sum of free energy change in hydrogen bond in non-polar plus free energy change in transfer of hydrogen bonded from water to non-polar solvent.

74. In a human cell, the concentration of ATP, ADP and Pi are 2.25, 0.50 and 0.825 mM respectively. The free energy of hydrolysis of ATP at pH 7.0 and 25°C is

(a) – 30.5 kJ/mol (b) – 61 kJ/mol
(c) – 15.25 kJ/mol (d) – 52 kJ/mol

Sol. (d) Free energy $\Delta G°$ = free energy at pH 7

$$\Delta G° = -RT \ln\frac{[\text{Product}]}{[\text{Substrate}]}$$

$$= -2.303 \times 298 \times L_n \frac{0.50 \times 0.825}{2.25} \times 10^{-3}$$

$$= -686.294\, L_n\, (0.1833 \times 10^3)$$

$$= -54.04 \text{ kJ/mole}$$

75. Which one of the following enzyme reaction represents non-competitive initiation?

(a) $E + S \rightleftharpoons ES + E + P$

$ES + I \underset{K_1}{\rightleftharpoons} EI$

(b) $E + S \rightleftharpoons E - S \longrightarrow E + P$

$ES + I \underset{K_1}{\rightleftharpoons} ESI$

(c) $E + S_1 \rightleftharpoons ES_1 \rightleftharpoons E'P_1 \rightleftharpoons E'$ ($\uparrow P_1$)

$\downarrow S_2$

$\rightleftharpoons E'S_2 \longrightarrow E + P_2$

(d) $E + S \rightleftharpoons ES \longrightarrow E + P$

$E + S + I \underset{K_1}{\rightleftharpoons} EI + S$

$ES + I \underset{K_1}{\rightleftharpoons} ESI$

$EI + S \rightleftharpoons ESI$

Sol. (b) Non competitive inhibitor binds at a separate site at either enzyme or E – S complex. The inhibitor binds to enzyme at a site other than active site and alters the enzyme's 3-D conformation.

76. The sequence of monosaccharides including position and configuration of glycosidic bonds in a glycoprotein is to be determined. Which one of the following methods can be employed?

(a) Glycoprotein → removal of oligosaccharides by alkaline hydrolysis → nuclear magnetic resonance analysis of cleaved mixture of oligosaccharides

(b) Two dimensional nuclear magnetic resonance spectroscopic analysis of the glycoprotein

(c) Glycoprotein → release of oligosaccharides with endoglycosidases followed by purification to separate oligosaccharides → enzymatic hydrolysis of purified oligosaccharides with specific glycosidases → mass spectroscopic analysis of smaller oligosaccharides

(d) Glycoprotein → treat with trypsin followed by MALDI analyses of tryptic peptides

Sol. (c) Goycosidic bond present between monosaccharides is broken by glycosidase. The glycoprotein is composed of carbohydrate and amino acids.

77. A bacterial culture undergoing balanced growth requires a first-order reaction. In other words, the rate of increase in bacteria at any particular time is proportional to the number or mass of bacteria present at that time. If 'N' is the number of cells at any given time 't' and 'μ' is growth rate constant this process can be expressed mathematically as

(a) $\frac{dN}{dt} = \mu N$ (b) $\frac{dt}{dN} = \mu N$

(c) $\frac{d\mu}{dt} = N$ (d) $\frac{dN}{dt} \times N = \mu$

Sol. (a) Bacteria normally reproduce by binary fission. The first step in division is cell elongation and duplication of DNA.

78. A typical animal cell (nucleated) membrane contains glycolipids and glycoproteins in the plasma membrane. To determine its topological distribution, 'lectin' is used as a probe. The following interactions may be the basis of the probing method

I. Protein-protein interaction
II. Protein-sugar interaction
III. Protein-lipid interaction
IV. Protein-sterol interaction

The appropriate answer is

(a) Only I (b) Only II
(c) I, II and III (d) Only IV

Sol. (b) Lectin is a carbohydrate binding protein. Recently plasma membrane bound lectins have been identified that recognises specific oligosaccharide on cell surface glycolipids and glycoproteins to mediate a variety of transient cell-cell adhesion processes.

79. Upon studying a considerable number of different crosses in *Drosophila*, Morgan reached the conclusion that all genes of this fly were clustered into four linked groups corresponding to the four pairs of chromosomes. Further studies revealed that linkage is not absolute and it is broken frequently. It is broken in prophase by a process called

(a) recombination (b) jumping of genes
(c) integration (d) mutation

Sol. (a) Recombination also called crossing over takes place during pachytene stage of prophase of meiosis-I. The process of crossing over involves breakage and reunion of broken ends oppositely between non-sister chromatids of homologous chromosomes.

80. A population of proliferating cells is stained with a DNA binding fluorescence dye so that the amount of fluorescence is directly proportional to the quantity of DNA. Amount of DNA in each cell is measured by flow cytometry. The number of cells with a given DNA content is plotted and following statements were made

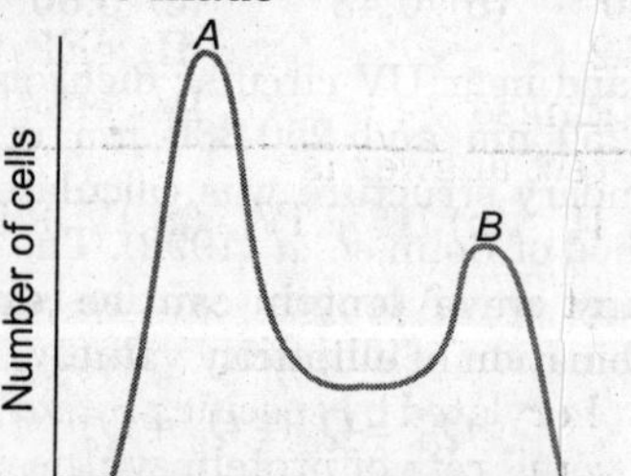

I. Peak A contains the cells of G_1-phase
II. Peak B contains the cells of G_2-phase
III. Peak A contains the cells of G_2-phase
IV. Peak B contains the cells of G_1-phase

Which of the above mentioned statement is correct?

(a) I and II (b) III and IV
(c) II and IV (d) I and III

Sol. (a) Synthesis of DNA takes place during S-phase of cell cycle thus cell in G_2 phase has double the DNA content as G_1.

81. During many important cell processes, many proteins need to undergo degradation to culminate a part of the process. For example, during cell cycle, cyclin proteins need to be degraded to allow the cells to exit mitosis. This is achieved by selective ubiquitination of cyclin followed by its degradation by proteasomes. The specific protein factor that is involved in this process is called anaphase promoting complex (APC). APC is possibly a protein which is known as

(a) E_1 enzyme (b) E_2 enzyme
(c) E_3 enzyme (d) protease

Sol. (c) **Anaphase-Promoting Complex,** also called cyclosome **(APC/C)**, is an E_3 ubiquitin ligase that marks target cell cycle proteins for degradation by the 26 S proteasome. The APC/C is a large complex of 11-13 subunit proteins, including a cullin (Apc2) and RING (Apc11) subunit much like SCF. The APC/C's main function is to trigger the transition from metaphase to anaphase by tagging specific proteins for degradation. The two proteins of most importance that get degraded in this process as substrates of the APC/C are securin and S and M cyclins.

82. During mitogenic stimulation, cells proliferate at a higher rate and it is primarily determined by an enhanced rate of protein synthesis. Among other mechanisms, MAP kinase pathway of signal transduction is involved in this. Global protein synthesis may be regulated by many mechanisms involving various steps of protein synthesis, namely, initiation, elongation and termination. Thus, many protein factors may be involved in the same. In the above process (mitogenic stimulation) the following factors are the portable targets.

I. elf-2 II. eEF-1
III. S6 kinase IV. elf-4E BP

The correct answer is

(a) I + II (b) III + IV (c) IV + I (d) II + IV

Sol. (c) Regulation of protein synthesis in eukaryotic cells involve the initiation factor eIF-2 which is phosphorylated by specific protein kinases to decrease the overall rate of protein synthesis.

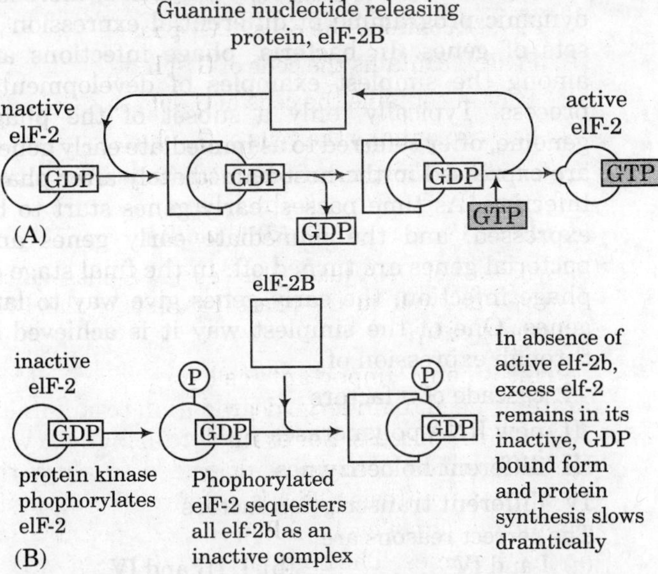

Fig. The elF-2 cycle. (A) the recycling of used elF-2 by a guanine nucleotide releasing protein (elF-2B). (B) elF-2 phosphorylation controls proteins synthesis rates by tying up elF-2B.

83. DNA repair, synthesis and recombination are intimately connected and inter dependent. An apparent commonality between processes of DNA replication and repair in the enzymatically catalyzed synthesis of DNA polynucleotide segments, which can be assembled with preexisting polynucleotides, leading to repair or replication. Synthesis of these polynucleotide segments is catalyzed by a group of enzymes DNA-dependant DNA polymerases. In the case of *E. coli*, DNA polymerase has been isolated in three distinct forms whereas five main types of polymerase have been isolated from mammalian cells. All the polymerases synthesize polynucleotides only in the $5' \rightarrow 3'$ direction. If polynucleotide chains could be elongated in $3' \rightarrow 5'$ direction, the hypothetical growing 5′ terminus, rather than the incoming nucleotide, would carry a triposphate that is unsuitable for further elongation. The $3' \rightarrow 5'$ exonuclease activity is not associated with all the polymerases and only present in

I. All *E. coli* DNA polymerases but not all mammalian polymerases.
II. Pol I, Pol II, Pol III, Pol α, Pol β
III. Pol I, Pol II, Pol δ, Pol ε, Pol γ
IV. Pol I, Pol II, Pol α, Pol ε.

The correct statements are

(a) I and II (b) I, II and III
(c) I and III (d) I, III and IV

Sol. (c) DNA poly I, II and III are found in *E. coli*.

Enzyme		Exonuclease Activity
Poly I	—	$3' \rightarrow 5', 5' \rightarrow 3'$
Pol. II	—	$3' \rightarrow 5'$
Pol. III	—	$3' \rightarrow 5'$
Pol. δ	—	$3' \rightarrow 5'$
Pol. ε	—	$3' \rightarrow 5'$

84. Bacteriophage λ genetic circuit may be represented as follows

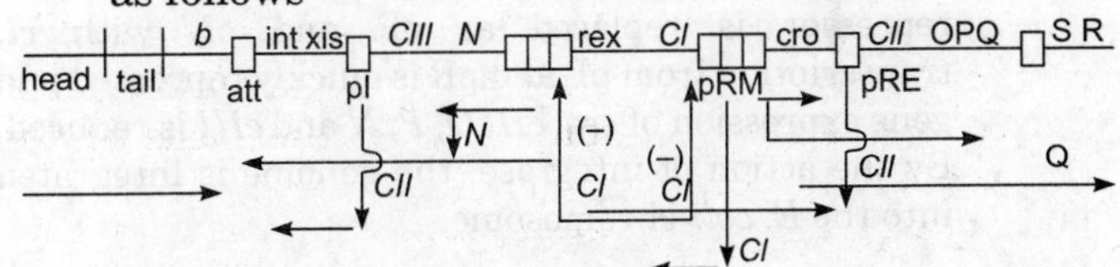

The control of gene expression occurred during the phage infection may be described as follows:

I. N and Q protein act as antiterminator
II. CI acts only as repressor
III. CII act as a retroregulator
IV. CI and CII both act as positive and negative regulator

Which one of the statements are correct?

(a) I, II and III (b) II, III and IV
(c) I and IV only (d) I, III and IV

Sol. (d) Upon injection of the λ genome into *E. coli*, it circularizes by hybridizing at the cohesive end sites (cos) and DNA ligase seals the circular chromosome. Transcription begins immediately at the promoters pL and pR. The pL transcript proceeds through gene *N* with termination of transcription about 80% efficient at *t*L1. The remainder of the transcript continues to *t*L2 transcribing the *cIII* gene where it stops. The pR transcript proceeds through the *cro* gene where termination at *t*R1 occurs 50% of the time. The remainder of the transcripts proceed through *cII*, *O*, *P* and terminate at *t*R2.

This transcription continues until sufficient *N* protein accumulates whereupon transcription at the above terminators does not occur due to antitermination. Transcription from pL then proceeds through *cIII* into *red*, *gam*, and on into the b region. Transcription from pR now proceeds through tR2 and transcription of the Q gene commences. This transcript terminates before the *S* and *R* genes.

When sufficient *cro* protein builds up it occupies the operators at oR and oL, turning off transcription from these two strong promoters. If sufficient Q proteins has accumulated, transcription starting from p'R is antiterminated and it proceeds through the S and R genes and on into the late structural genes, A through J. At this point the cell is committed to the lytic growth phase.

If sufficient *cII* and *cIII* protein accumulate, the *cII* gene product stimulates transcription from two new promoters, pINT and pRE. Transcription from pINT, proceeds through the *int* gene and from this transcript, integrase required for integration of the circular genome into the *E. coli* chromosome is made.

Transcription initiated at pRE proceeds across the antisense strand of the *cro* gene and into the *cI* gene. From this transcript, a large burst of the *cI* repressor is made.

With large amount of the *cI* reoressor formed, the *cro* repressor is replaced at oR and oL with *cl,* transcription from pL and pR is quickly repressed and gene expression of *cro, cII, O, P, N* and *cIII* is reduced. By the action of integrase, the genome is integrated into the *E. coli* chromosome.

85. *Rho* factor is involved in termination of transcription in prokaryotes. Genetic manipulations indicate that *Rho*-dependent termination requires the presence of a specific recognition sequence on the newly synthesized RNA upstream of the termination site. The recognition sequence must be on the nascent RNA rather than the DNA, as demonstrated by *Rho*'s inability to terminate transcription in the presence of pancreatic RNAse. The essential features of this termination site have not been fully elucidated. Construction of synthetic termination sites indicates that it consists of 80 to 100 nts that lack a stable secondary structure and contain multiple regions that are rich in C and poor in G.

Which of the following is/ are suggested by the above observation?

(a) *Rho* factor attaches to nascent RNA at its recognition sequence and then migrates along the RNA in the 5′ → 3′ direction until it encounters an RNAP paused at the termination site

(b) *Rho* unwinds the RNA-DNA duplex forming the transcription bubble, thereby releasing the RNA transcript

(c) *Rho* factor attaches to the RNA at its recognition sequence while RNA is in the RNA-DNA hybrid condition

(d) There may be other factors and hence *Rho* factor does not need to unwind the RNA-DNA hybrid to release the transcript

Sol. (a) The process of termination of RNA synthesis ends in two mechanisms, *i.e., rho* independent and *rho* dependent. *Rho* dependent termination requires the rho protein (a hexamer) encoded by *rho* gene. A strong pause site is present close to promotor for *rho* factor. *Rho* factor moves along RNA from its binding site to enzyme RNA polymerase. The movement is facilitated by ATP hydrolysis. Consequently the *rho* factor comes in contact of core enzyme of polymerase facilitated by Nus A and Nus G proteins.

86. During development and differentiation, there is a dynamic programme of differential expression of sets of genes. In bacteria, phage infections are among the simplest examples of developmental process. Typically, only a subset of the phage genome, offer referred to as immediate early genes, are expressed in the host immediately after phage infection. As time passes, early genes start to be expressed, and the immediate early genes and bacterial genes are turned off. In the final stage of phage infection, the early genes give way to late genes. One of the simplest way it is achieved is through expression of

I. cascade of σ factors

II. new RNA polymerases

III. different holoenzymes

IV. different transcription factors

The correct reasons are

(a) I and IV (b) I, III and IV

(c) I, II and IV (d) I, II and III

Sol. (b) The sigma (σ) subunit of *E. coli* polymerase has a specific role in initiation of transcription. It enables the enzyme to find promotor sequences to which it binds.

A number of transcription factors (initiation, elongation and termination) are required for the expression of gene. The initiation of transcription is an important control point where the cell can regulate the expression of a gene.

87. Polyclonal antibodies are raised against bovine serum albumin in rabbit. Subsequently IgG in the antiserum is purified and digested with either pepsin or papain. Out of the following possibilities, which one is correct?

(a) Pepsin-digested antibodies cannot precipitate the antigen

(b) Papain-digested antibodies cannot precipitate the antigen

(c) Pepsin digestion will produce two Fab molecules

(d) Pepsin-digested antibodies will lose all interchain disulphide bonds

Sol. (b) A single antigen would induce more than one distinct clone of plasma cells which will produce antibodies of different specificities and called as polyclonal antibodies. The structure of the IgG molecule has been determined in part by proteolytic digestions and reductive dissociation of the molecule. Digestion by papain results in the cleavage of a susceptible bond on the N-terminal side of the inter-heavy chain disulphide bridges. This yield two monovalent antigen-binding fragments (Fab) and one crystalline fragment (Fc). Pepsin cleaves the γ-chains on the C-terminal side of the inter-heavy chain disulphide bridges, resulting in one bivalent antigen-binding fragment, F(ab′)2. In this case, the Fc fragments are destroyed. Reductive dissociation of an IgG molecule splits the interchain disulphide bridges, and if the free sulphhydryl groups are blocked, results in the formation of two H chains (molecular weight 50 kDa each) and two L chains (25 kDa each).

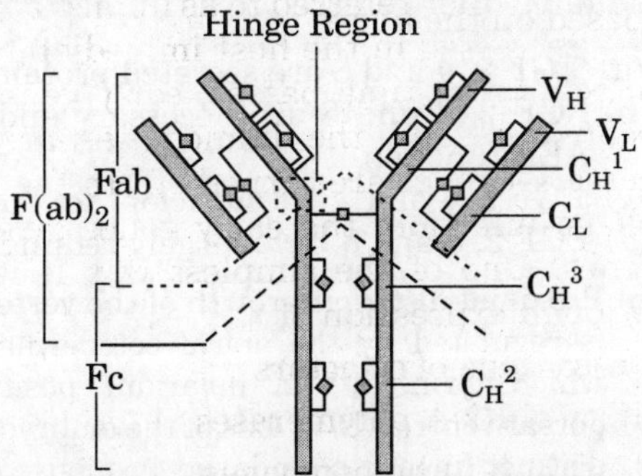

Diagram showing the structure of rabbit IgG (which exists as a single major subclass). The heavy (H) chains are composed of variable (V) and constant (C) domains and are linked by inter- and intrachain disulphide bonds(I—I). Proteolytic digestion with papain (---) yields two antigen-binding fragments (Fab) and one crystalline fragment (Fc), whereas digestion with pepsin (---) yields one $F(ab)_2$ fragment.

88. Two protein kinases, K_1 and K_2 function sequentially in regulating intracellular pathway in response to extracellular signal. The following observations are made:

I. Response is observed even in the absence of extracellular signal when a mutation permanently activates K_1

II. Response is observed even in the absence of extracellular signal when K_1 contains an activating mutation and K_2 with inactivating mutation

III. No response in the cells is detected even in the presence of extracellular signal when both kinases are inactivated by mutation

Which one of the following is correct?

(a) K_1 activates K_2 (b) K_2 activates K_1
(c) K_1 inhibits K_2 (d) K_2 inhibits K_1

Sol. (d) Since, K_1 and K_2 function sequentially, both are important for functioning but in absence of extracellular signal and a mutation permantly activating K_1 induce response but may be inhibit by K_2 if not permantly activated. Similarly, in observation (ii) response occur by inactivating K_2 and K_1 with activating mutation (not permanent).

89. Conversion of proto-oncogene to oncogene may involve the following processes

I. mutation in coding sequence
II. gene amplification
III. chromosome rearrangement
IV. mutation in non-coding sequence

Which one is appropriate?

(a) I, II and III (b) II, III and IV
(c) I, III and IV (d) I, II, III and IV

Sol. (a) The gene may be altered by a point mutation, by deletion, through chromosomal translocation, or by insertion of mobile genetic element. There are usually three way of conversion of protooncogene to oncogene.

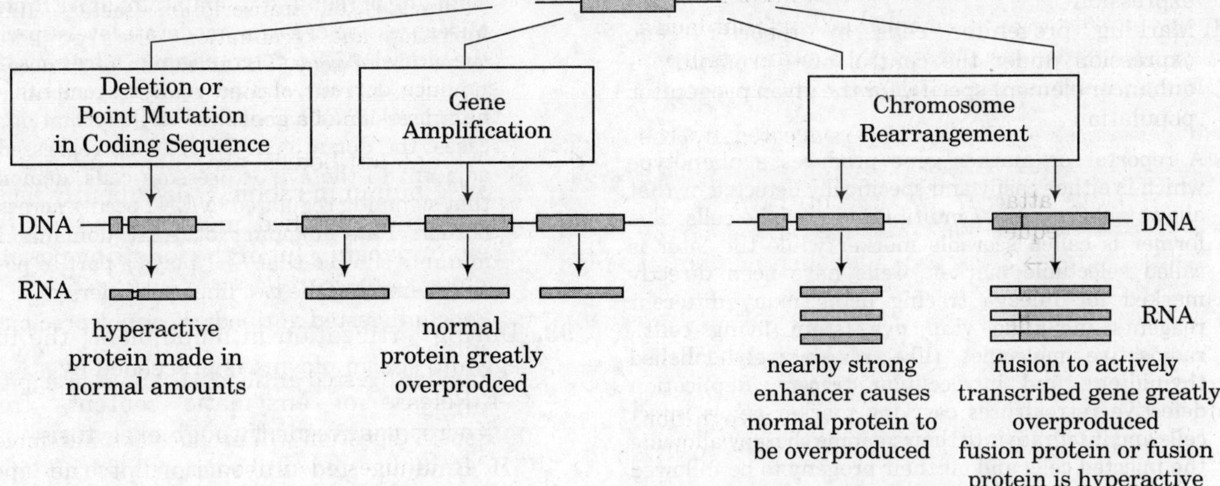

90. Opsonisation of a bacterium is a process by which specific antibody binds with the surface molecule of the bacteria. In an experimental condition, macrophage were infected with either WT: *Mycobacteria* or with opsonised: *Mycobacteria* for 2 h at 37°C. Subsequently, cells were washed and further incubated for 24 h at 37°C. Finally, bacterial load in macrophages were determined by colony forming unit (CFU). Which of the following observation is true?

(a) WT *Mycobacteria* inhibits its transport to the lysosomes and survive in macrophages
(b) Opsonised *Mycobacteria* inhibits its transport to the lysosomes and survive in macrophages
(c) WT *Mycobacteria* are targeted to the lysosomes and killed in macrophages
(d) Opsonised *Mycobateria* are targeted to the lysosomes and survive in macrophages

Sol. (a) In opsonization, complement components coat the bacterial surface allowing the phagocyte to recognise, the bacteria and engulf them. These reactions may be triggered by intrinsic ability of complement system to recognize microbial components or by antibodies bound to microorganisms. In absence of opsonins macrophages use multiple receptors to recognise and engulf a range of microorganisms. Non-opsonic uptake result in a range of survival strategies by intracellular pathogens enabling them to avoid phagosome maturation, inhibit fusion with lysosome and acidification (*Mycobacteria*).

91. Which of the following cannot be used for determination of tissue lineage of a given progenitor cell population in an animal?

(a) Marking progenitor cells with vital dye
(b) Transplanting equivalent progenitor cells from immunologically distinct but related organism
(c) Marking progenitor cells by genomic recombination coupled with reporter gene expression
(d) Marking progenitor cells by reporter gene expression under the control of a promoter — enhancer element specific for the given progenitor population

Sol. (d) A reporter or marker gene produces a phenotype which is either easily and specifically detected or that allows a differential *f* multiplication of the cells. The former is called scorable marker while the later is called selectable marker. Cells have been directly marked for lineage tracing using many different reagents including vital dye (stain living cells), radioactive molecules (like radioactively labelled thymidine), and intracellular tracers. Replication defective retroviruses carrying marker genes infect cells and integrate into their genome thereby allowing the injected cells and all their progeny to be followed overtime. Generating marked and mutant cells by recombination has been used for tissue lineage. Unlike techniques that relay on label injection or tissue transplantation cloness are produced in the natural tissue environment.

92. During vertebrate limb development, a specialised ectodermal structure, called Apical Ectodermal Ridge (AER), forms at the dorso-ventral ectodermal boundary at the distal tip of the developing limb bud. The following experimental facts about the AER is available

I. FGF 2, 4, and 8 are expressed in the AER
II. Removal of the AER causes cessation of limb growth
III. Removal of AER along with implantation of beads soaked in FGF 8 or
IV. FGF 4 or FGF 2 protein rescues the AER removal phenotype and gives rise to normal limb

Which of the following statements cannot be made based on the above facts?

(a) FGF 2, 4 and 8 are secreted proteins
(b) FGF 2, 4 and 8 are necessary and sufficient for AER function
(c) FGF 2, 4 and 8 are sufficient for AER function
(d) FGF 2, 4 and 8 have largely redundant functions

Sol. (b) Proximal-distal outgrowth of the vertebrate limb bud is regulated by the apical ectodermal ridge (AER), which forms at an invariant position along the dorsal-ventral (D/V) axis of the embryo. There are two distinct lineage boundaries in mouse ectoderm prior to limb bud outgrowth using a *Cre/loxp*-based fate-mapping approach and a novel retroviral cell-labelling technique. One border is transient and at the limit of expression of the ventral gene *En1*, which corresponds to the D/V midline of the AER, and the second border corresponds to the dorsal AER margin. Labeling of AER precursors using an inducible *Cre* showed that not all cells that initially express AER genes form the AER, indicating that signaling is required to maintain an AER phenotype. Misexpression of *En1* at moderate levels specifically in the dorsal AER of trransgenic mice was found to produce dorsally shifted AER fragements, whereas high level of *En1* abolished AER formation. In both cases, the dorsal gene *Wnt7a* was repressed in cells adjacent to the *En1*-expressing cells, demonstrating that signaling regulated by EN1 occurs across the D/V border. Fate mapping of AER domains in these mutants showed that *En1* plays a part in positioning and maintaing the two lineage borders.

93. During fertilization in amphibians, the fusion of egg and sperm plasma is preceeded by

I. Release of enzymatic contents from the acrosomal vesile through exocytosis
II. Binding and interaction of the sperm to vitelline membrane

III. Chemoattraction of the sperm to the egg by soluble factors secreted by egg

IV. Passage of sperm through extracellular envelope

Which of the following is the correct sequence?

(a) I → II → III → IV (b) II → I → III → IV
(c) III → I → II → IV (d) III → II → I → IV

Sol. (c) The fusion of haploid male gamte (sperm) to haploid female gamete (ovum) to form diploid zygote is called fertilization. The process involves following steps sequentially.

(i) Chemoattraction of sperm to the egg by chemicals secreted by egg.
(ii) Binding and interaction of sperm to vitelline membrane
(iii) Passage of sperm through extracellular envelope.

94. In many different contexts of cell differentiation, two distinct cell populations emerge from a uniform cell population. This process is referred to as lateral inhibition. Which one of the following must not be true about lateral inhibition?

I. Lateral inhibition results from morphogen action.
II. Lateral inhibition requires direct cell contacts.
III. Lateral inhibition requires reciprocal signalling between two neighbouring cells.
IV. Lateral inhibition is preceded by stochastic changes in gene expression in two neighbouring cells.

(a) IV (b) I and IV
(c) II and III (d) I

Sol. (c) Experiments with genetic mosaic show that a cell which become committed to the sensory mother cell pathway of differentiation sends a signal to its neighbours not to do the same thing, it exerts a lateral inhibition. The gene responsible for lateral inhibition are called neurogenic genes. Lateral inhibition. The gene responsible for laternal inhibiton is transmitted *via* direct cell to cell contact. If a cell that would normally become a sensory mother is genetically disabled from doing so, neighbouring proneural cell freed from lateral inhibition will become a sensory mother.

95. Which of the following statements is true about dorso-ventral patterning of *Drosophila* embryo?

I. This is dictated by the location of the nurse cells.
II. dorsal is the default fate.
III. The whole process is regulated by preventing the entry of a transcription factor to the nucleus of dorsal cells.
IV. Homeobox containing genes play a critical role in this process.

(a) I, II and III (b) I, II, III and IV
(c) I and IV (d) II and III

Sol. (d) About 20 genes are responsible for dorsal-ventral axis development in *Drosophila.* Dorsal-ventral polarization is initiated by microtubule-dependent translocation of the oocyte nucleus. Dorsal-ventral axis formation depends on

(1) Prior polarization of the anterior-posterior axis to establish the polarized microtubule cytoskeleton.
(2) Gene signaling triggering dorsalization and ventralization.
(3) Co-operation of follicle and germ line cells in receiving and processing signals.

Dorsal-ventral polarization is initiated in oogenesis, but is not irreversible as further development continues in the embryo. The path of development may be altered via injection of cytoplasmic gene products before entry into the cellular blastoderm stage.

Dorsal-ventral patterning within the ectoderm of the *Dosophila* embryo requires seven zygotic genes including *sog (short gastrulation)*. *Sog* is expressed in the ventrolateral region of the embryo that gives rise to the nerve cord. Functionally, it is homologous to the *chordin* gene of *Xenopus,* which is expressed in the dorsal lip of the blastopore and in the dorsal mesoderm, in particular the notochord. They showed by injections of messenger RNA that both *sog* and *chordin* can promote ventral development in *Drosophila,* and that *sog,* like *chordin,* can promote dosal development in *Xenopus.*

96. Which of the following is true about amphibian limb regeneration?

I. It requires a minimum number of functional nerves.
II. The blastema of an amputated limb, if transplanted in the trunk region between two existing limbs in a host, will still give rise to a limb.
III. The size of the regenerated limb is often grossly different from the original limb.

(a) I (b) II and III
(c) I and III (d) I, II and III

Sol. (a) The first stage of regeneration of limb is the epiderm from the edges of wound that starts spreading over the wound. In next few days the epidermis covering the wound begin to bulge outwards becoming more or less conical. These cells with the epidermal covering are called regeneration blastema. The mass of the cell in the interior of the limb bud becomes segregated to form the rudiments of internal parts of limb. The rudiment of the digit elongates and the whole regenerating limb continues to grow until it attains the size of normal limb.

97. In agamous mutant (flower within flower phenotype) which of the following statements is valid?

(a) Class A genes are expressed in the first two whorls, class B genes are expressed in the second and third whorls and class C genes are expressed in the third and fourth whorls.
(b) Class A genes are not expressed. class B and C genes are expressed in all the whorls
(c) Class A genes are not expressed. Class B genes are expressed in the second and the third whorls and class C genes are expressed in all the whorls
(d) Class A genes are expressed in all the whorls. Class B genes are expressed in the second and the third whorls

Sol. (a) A model was developed that attempts to explain the interactions of the different genes that control floral organ identity. All the genes are classified as expressing one of three activities, *A, B* or *C*. The A gene activities control the development of the sepal and petal, B gene activities control petal and stamen development, and C gene activities control stamen and carpel development. The two A function genes are *APETALA2* and *APETALA1*. The B gene functions are defined by the genes *APETALA3* and *PISTILLATA*.

98. Plants grown in greenhouse at 25°C when exposed first to 35°C for 6 h and subsequently to 42°C for 12 h adapt better to the high temperature (42°C) in comparison to those directly transferred to 42°C for the same duration. What is the phenomenon called and what is its main physiological basis?

(a) Acquired thermo-tolerance because of the induction of mutagens resulting into improved stability of all the proteins
(b) Induced thermo-tolerance because of the induction of heat shock proteins
(c) Induced thermo-tolerance because changes in RNA polymerase II resulting in efficient and improved transcription
(d) Acquired thermo-tolerance because of efficient post translational modification of proteins

Sol. (b) Heat shock proteins are synthesized in dramatically increased amounts following a brief exposure of cells to an elevated temperature (for example 42°C). This reflect the operation of a feedback system that responds to any increase in misfolded proteins (such as those produced by elevated temperature) by boosting the synthesis of chaperones that help the protein refold.

99. In which molecule would the radiolabel appear the earliest when wheat and sugar cane leaves are fed with $^{14}CO_2$?

(a) Wheat — malate, sugarcane —3 phosphoglycerate
(b) Wheat — aspartate, sugarcane — malate
(c) Wheat — 3 phosphoglycerate, sugarcane — 3 phosphoglycerate
(d) Wheat — 3 phosphyoglycerate, sugarcane — malate

Sol. (d) Maize, sugarcane, sorghum are C_4 plants while wheat is a C_3 plant. In C_4 plants initial CO_2 fixation takes place in mesophyll cells. The primary acceptor of CO_2 is phosphoenol pyruvate which is converted to oxoloacetate and then to malate. While in C_3 plants the CO_2 is first combined with RuBP to form 3-phosphoglyceric acid.

100. A young dicot seedling (*e.g.*, soyabean) is subjected to gravity stimulus by laying it horizontally on a surface the shoot bends upwards and root bends downward. Indicate the reason

(a) Redistribution of auxin throughout the seedlings is responsible for stimulatory unequal growth in shoots and roots
(b) Redistribution of auxin in shoots while cytokinine in roots is responsible for stimulatory unequal growth
(c) Redistribution of auxin in roots while cytokinine in shoots is responsible for stimulatory unequal growth
(d) Redistribution of cytokinine throughout the seedlings is responsible for stimulatory unequal growth in shoots and roots

Sol. (a) Auxin is synthesized in shoot apices, leaf primordia and developing seeds. Its movement is polar. It is basipetal in stem but acropetal in root. It helps in elongation of both root and shoot. Differential distribution of auxin produce plant responces like phototropism and geotropism.

101. Which of the following statements are associated with the process of photorespiration in plants?

I. Photorespiration takes place in only C_3 plants.
II. Photorespiration takes place in only C_4 plants.
III. Photorespiration takes place in both C_3 and C_4 plants.
IV. Glycolate is oxidized to glyoxylate in the peroxisome.
(E) Glycolate is oxidized to glyoxylate in the mitochondira.

(a) I and IV (b) III and IV
(c) II and V (d) III and V

Sol. (a) Photorespiration is the light dependent utilization of O_2 and release of CO_2 by photosynthetic organ of plant. It is prominant in C_3 plants and neglible in C_4 plants. It involves chloroplst, mitochondria and peroxisome. In this process the glycolate from chloroplast passes to peroxisome and in presence of oxidase enzyme forms glyoxylate

$$\text{Glycolate} + O_2 \xrightarrow{\text{Oxidase}} \text{Glyoxylate} + H_2O_2$$

102. Aspartate kinase is a key enzyme in the lysine amino acid biosynthesis in plants. With an objective of increasing the lysine content in maize seeds, maize plants were transformed with *E. coli* aspartate kinase with a strong seed specific plant promoter. Resulting transgenic plants were found to express the transgene; however, the content of lysine did not increase. Which of the following option best explain the possible reason?

(a) Bacterial proteins are not stable in plants
(b) Bacterial proteins are not properly folded in plants
(c) Proper post-translational modification did not take place in plants
(d) Lysine causes feed back inhibition of aspartate kinase

Sol. (c) In plants and bacteria lysine is synthesized from aspartic acid. L-aspartate is first converted to L-aspartyl 4-phosphate by aspartate kinase. The protein synthesis in eukaryotic and prokaryotic cells is different in processing of *m*RNA, ribosomes and post-translational modification. Therefore the eukaryotic gene can not express in prokaryotes *vice versa* (in some cases).

103. Electrical stimulation of a nerve bundle maintained at 37 ± 1° C showed *A*, *B*, *C* and *D* peaks (as shown in the diagram) when recorded at a distance of 15 cms from the stimulating site on the same bundle. The same experiment was conducted at significantly lower temperature 15 ± 1° C. Which of the following statements is correct? Lower temperature would

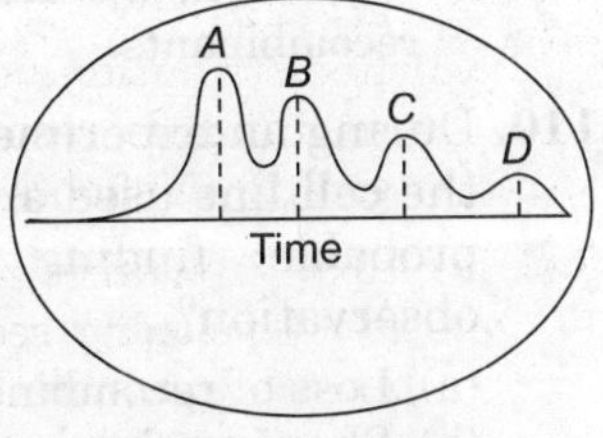

(a) not affect the record
(b) not show *A*, but would show *B*, *C* and *D* peaks
(c) not show peak *D* and may not show *C*, but would show *A* and *B*
(d) show all the peaks along with a new peak

Sol. (c) At 37°C the peak down in the sequence of $A \rightarrow B \rightarrow C \rightarrow D$. *i.e.*, *D* has lowest value. If the temperature is 15°C the peak *D* is not shown and peak *C* may not be shown.

104. A response was observed when a specific site in a rat brain was stimulated by passing electrical pulses through indwelling electrode implanted surgically. In another experiment in another rat, a cannula was surgically implanted instead of the electrode and stimulated the area by injecting excitatory neurotransmitter. However, the result of the two experiments did not match. The possibilities of variations in the results could be due to

(a) animal variations only
(b) stimulation of cell bodies or nerve fibres only
(c) difference in anatomical brain areas only
(d) variations in all the reasons mentioned in 1, 2 and 3

Sol. (d) For an impulse to be initiated the stimulus must be strong enough to depolarize the neuron. It varies among neurons and according to different conditions affecting a particular neuron. The speed of an impulse is also affected by the diameter of the axon.

105. A. In an experiment, 2 mg of a substance 'A' dissolved in 4.5 mL sterile solvent was injected as a bolus into the femoral vein of an intact frog. It was observed that the frog's heart rate increased significantly.

B. The same solution as in (a) when applied directly on the heart of the same frog after exposing the heart, the heart rate did not change.

C. The same solution as in (a) when injected to an intact cat femoral vein, the heart rate did not change significantly.

From the above observations, which one of the following statements is most likely to be correct?

(a) Substance 'A' is stimulatory on heart and the effect was inotropic.
(b) Substance 'A' acted in the brain and also might have released other hormones to increase the heart rate.
(c) Substance 'A' could not have acted on the brain but must have induced other substances in the blood to increase the heart rate.
(d) The increased heart rate was merely due to increased volume of the heart muscles.

Sol. (b) When epinephrine is infused into the femoral vein the heart will be exposed to a higher concentration as compare to when the same dose is infused into the desending thoracic aorta. Intravenous infusions of epinephrine in doses ranging from 1 to 3 μg/kg/min caused marked acceleration of the heart and a significant reduction of intraventricular conduction time.

106. In a healthy kidney given the following information:

I. Glomerular hydrostatic pressure – 75 mm Hg.
II. Glomerular capillary colloid osmotic pressure – 40 mm Hg.
III. Hydrostatic pressure in the Bowman's capsule – 20 mn Hg.

The net filtration pressure will be

(a) 55 mn Hg (b) 15 mn Hg
(c) 35 mn Hg (d) 135 mn Hg

Sol. (b) The glomerular capillaries are narrower than the afferent renal artiroles. Therefore the blood pressure in the glomerular capillaries becomes very high so that there is continuous process of ultrafiltration.

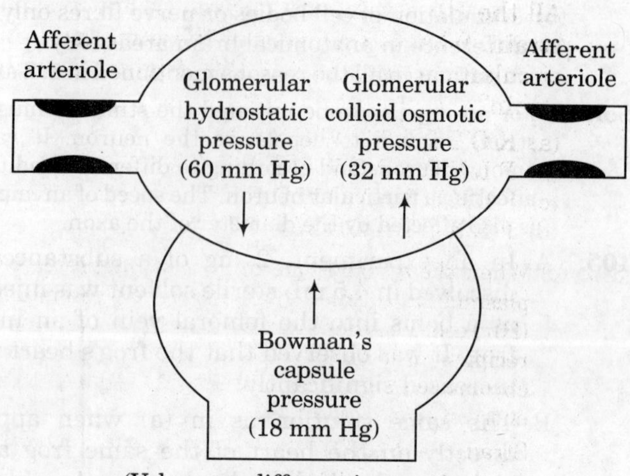

(Values are different in question)

Net filtration pressure	=	Glomerular hydrostatic pressure (75 mm Hg)	–	Bowman's capsule pressure (20 mm Hg)	–	Glomerular oncotic pressure (40 mm Hg)

= 15mmHg

107. Toll-like receptor 4 is associated with responsiveness to LPS, an endotoxin that causes lethal endotoxic shock. The mice deficient in Toll-like receptor 4 and BALB/c mice were injected with *Escherichia coli*. In addition, some BALB/b mice were also injected with the same bacteria alone or with anti-interleukin-10 (IL-10) antibody. The mice resistant to the lethal effect of the bacteria were

(a) BALB/b mice receiving the bacteria
(b) BALB/b mice receiving the bacteria and the anti-IL-10 antibody
(c) Mice deficient in Toll-like receptor
(d) BALB/c mice receiving the bacteria

Sol. (c) Many bacterial PAMPs (Pathogen Associated Molecular Patterns) activate cells *via* Toll Like Receptors (TLR). Therefore, absence of toll like receptor causes resistancy to the lethal effect of bacteria.

108. Mismatch of blood in parents may result in erythroblastosis fetalis in a new born. Match the correct cause (left column) and usual treatment (right column).

Commonest cause	Used treatment
I. Mother Rh(+) and father Rh(–)	III. replacement of neonate's blood with Rh(–) blood
II. Mother Rh (–) and father Rh (+)	IV. replacement of neonate's blood with Rh(+) blood.

(a) I and III
(b) I and IV
(c) II and III
(d) II and IV

Sol. (c) Erythroblastosis foetalis is a disease of foetus and new born child characterised by agglutination and phagocytosis of the foetus RBCs. In most instrances of erythroblastosis foetalis the mother is Rh^- and father Rh^+. The baby has inherited Rh^+ antigen from father and the mother develops anti Rh agglutinins from exposure to the foetus's Rh antigen. In turn the mother's agglutinins diffuse through the placenta into foetus and cause red blood cell agglutination. One treatment of erythroblastosis is to replace the neonate's blood with Rh^- blood.

109. In a haploid organism, the loci A/a and D/d are 8 map units apart. In a cross Ad X aD, what will be the proportion of each of the following progeny classes: (a) Ad (b) recombinants

(a) 92%, 8%
(b) 46%, 8%
(c) 92%, 4%
(d) 46%, 4%

Sol. (d) In case of linkage recombinant phenotypes ore produced by such gamets that are produced due to crossing over. The frequency of crossing over (recombination) is directly proportional to distance between genes. On test cross the value in F_2 should be in 1 : 1 ratio but due to recombination and linkage it varies, *i.e.,* 8% are recombinants (8 mapunit = 8% recombinants)

110. During an experiment, an investigator found that the cell line used are *RecA* –/–. What could be the probable finding which led him to such observation?

(a) Loss of recombination
(b) Showing aberrant all morphology
(c) Cells developed phagocytic properly
(d) Cells were aggregating

Sol. (a) Usually in case of linked gene or characters, the production of new combination of genes or characters not present in parent of a cross or generation is called recombination. It involves crossing over. Since the cell line is homozygous it means recombination is not found in these. In presence of recombination new progency cell will be formed, *i.e.,* they will be heterozygous type.

111. Find the pattern of inheritance of the trait showing incomplete penetrance from the figure shown

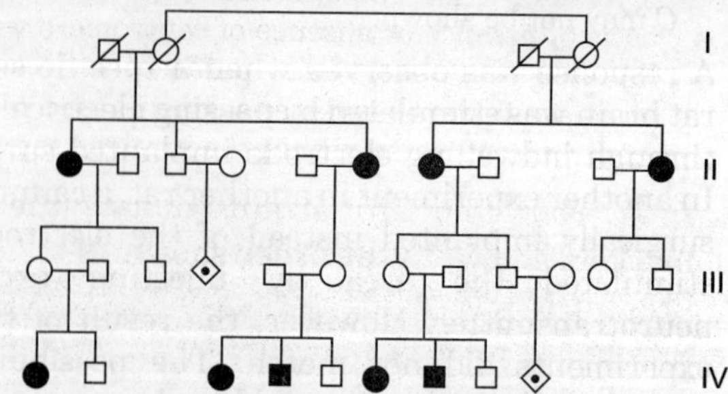

(a) autosomal dominant
(b) autosomal recessive

(c) mitochondrial inheritance
(d) X-linked recessive

Sol. (a) Many genes do not produce the concerned phenotype in all the individuals, which carry them in appropriate genotype, such a situation is called incomplete penetrance. For example a recessive gene producing partial chlorophyll deficiency in the cotyledonary leaves of lima beans shows incomplete penetrance. In the given figure if the penetrane is complete and allele is autosomal dominant it should be observed in each individual but in reality do not appear due to incomplete penetrance.

112. Which of the following assumption support the Hardy-Weinberg equilibrium?

(a) Presence of natural selection
(b) Random mating
(c) Genetic drift
(d) Assortative mating

Sol. (b) According to Hardy-Weinberg law gene and genotype frequencies in Mendelian population remain constant generation after generation if there is no migration, mutation, and random drift. The validity of Herdy-Weinberg law can be demonstrated by assuming either random union of gametes or random mating among genotypes.

113. Which of the following illustrations explain the correct pairing preceeding recombination between a chromosome (ABC•DEFG/ABC•DEFG) and its inverted homologue (ABC•DGFE/ABC•DGFE). The dot in genotype represent the centromere.

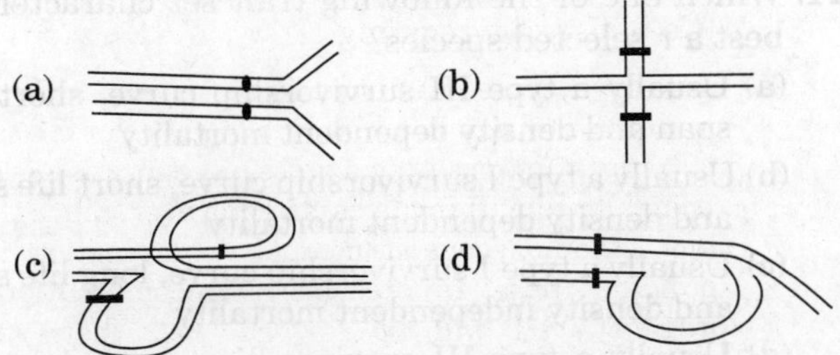

Sol. (c) When a segment of chromosome is oriented in the reverse direction; such a phenomenon is called inversion. It may be classified into two class on the basis of pesence or absence of centromere within the inverted segment, *i.e.,* paracentric (centromers located outside the inverted segments) and pericentric (centromers located within the inverted segment).

114. In *E. coli,* four *Hfr* strains donate the genetic markers shown in the order shown:

Strain 1: F L K O Z
Strain 2: C Y A Z O
Strain 3: P D W C Y
Strain 4: P F L K O

All the *Hfr* strains are derived from the same F^+ strain. What is the order of these markers on the circular chromosome of the original *E. coli* F^+ strain?

(a) K O Z P D F L W C Y A K
(b) F L K O Z P D W C Y A F
(c) F L K O Z A Y C W D P F
(d) F L K C Y A Z O W D P F

Sol. (c) When the chromosome of F^+ cell integrates with F plasmid it is called high frequency recombination (Hfr) cell. The time at which a particular gene enters a recipient is related to the portion of genes on the chromosome. A map can be obtained from the time of entry of each gene.

Strain 1 — FLKOZ
Strain 2 — OZAYC
Strain 3 — YCWDP
Strain 4 — PFLKO

115. In a family, father is homozygous dominant (AA) for a gene A and his wife is homozygous for its ressive allele (aa) showing albino phenotype. It was surprising that their child showed the albino phenotype. Which of the following phenomenon can explain the phenotype?

(a) Non-disjunction
(b) Uniparental disomy
(c) Gene conversion
(d) All of these

Sol. (d) Albinism (also called achromia, achromasia, or achromatosis) is a congental disorder characterized by the complete or partial absence of pigment in the skin, hair and eyes due to absence or defect of tyrosinase a copper-containing enzyme involved in the production of melanin. Most form of albinism are the result of the biological inheritance of genetically recessive alleles (genes) passed from both parents of an individual, through some rare forms are inherited from only one parent. There are other genetic mutations which are proven to be associated with albinism. All alterations, however, lead to changes in melanin production in the body. Segregations of chromosomes from centromere fusion heterozygotes result in non disjunction and uniparantal disomy.

116. Which of the following characteristic differentiate eubacteria from archaebacteria?

(a) Circular nature of chromosome
(b) Absence of nuclear membrane
(c) Presence of 70 S ribosomes
(d) Presence of murein in cell wall

Sol. (d) The cell wall of bacteria is composed of murein or mucopeptide while all archaebacteria lack murein. The cell wall of Archaea is composed of proteins, glycoproteins, or polysaccharides. The cell wall of Gram +ve archaebacteria consists of pseudomurein, methanochondrin or heteropolysaccharide.

117. Tropical semievergreen forests are found in the region having rainfall

(a) > 3000 mm (b) 2000-2500 mm
(c) 1200-2500 mm (d) 800-1200 mm

Sol. (b)

Forest type		Rainfall (mm)
Tropical semievergreen	—	2000-2500
Temperate broad leaved	—	1000-2500
Tropical rain	—	2000-3500
Temperate coriferous	—	500-1200

118. Presence of which of the following flora and fauna in Peninsular India is explained by the Satpura hypothesis?

(a) Chinese (b) Malayan
(c) African (d) Mediterranean

Sol. (b) Our knowledge of the biogegraphy of India, especially the Ichthyogeography was enhanced by the work, zeal and efforts of Dr. Sunder Lal Hora who propounded the Satpura Hypothesis to explain the biodiversity and Malayan affinities of the faunal and floral elements along the watersheds of the Western Ghats of South India, North East India (two of the 34 biodiveristy hot spots in the world) and the Malay Peninsula. In present day parlance, it represents 'into India' migration from the focal area of Yunnan in China passing through NE India, the Garro gap and along the Narmada-Tapti watersheds draining the Satpura mountain ranges and on to the Western Ghats. Another lineage passed thorugh the Irrawaddy System of Myanmar southwards to Malaysia, geological events and changes in watershed drainage patterns aided such migrations.

119. Complete the following sentence using options given below the sentence as a, b, c, d and e.

"Species are critically endangered when it is not endangered but is facing..........risk of extinction in the wild in the ....future".

I. high II. very high
III. extremely high IV. near
V. immediate

(a) I, I (b) II, III (c) III, V (d) III, IV

Sol. (c) Species are critically endangered when it is not endangered but facing **extremely high** risk of extinction in the wild in **immediate** future.

120. Based on Coefficient of Association table given below, which of the following taxonomic phenogram of relationship is correct?

	S	T	W	X	Y	Z
S	1.0					
T	0.8	1.0				
W	0.5	0.7	1.0			
X	0.6	0.6	0.9	1.0		
Y	0.3	0.1	0.2	0.2	1.0	
Z	0.2	0.0	0.3	0.4	0.9	1.0

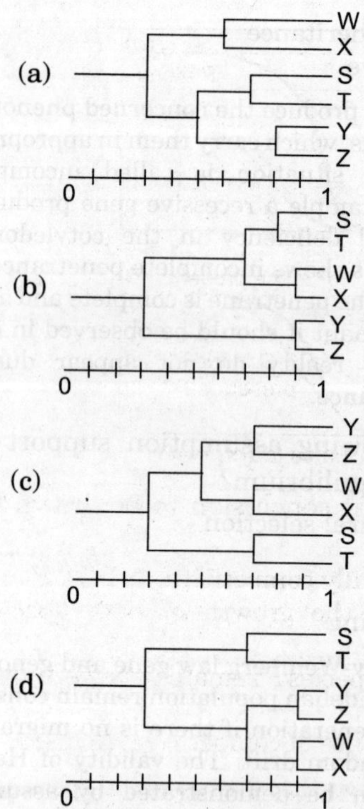

Sol. (b) Coefficient of association is an important meaasue of interrelation between two variables (attributes). In phenetic method, a phenogram is formed. Higher the coefficient of association (*i.e.*, as the value approached to 1.0) the more closely related are the species. For example the coefficient between S and T is 8 character and between T and W is 7 character.

121. Which one of the following trait set characterizes best a r selected species?

(a) Usually a type III survivorship curve, short life span and density dependent mortality
(b) Usually a type I survivorship curve, short life span and density dependent mortality
(c) Usually a type I survivorship curve, long life span and density independent mortality
(d) Usually a type III survivorship curve, short life span and density independent mortality

Sol. (d) Mac Arthur and wilson use the population parameters to draw conclusion about evolution of species. According to them *r*-selected species have small body size. concave survivorship curve, high intrinsic rate of growth, density variable below carrying capacity and good dispersal power. While, k-selected species have larger, body size, convex survivorship curve, low intrinsic rate of growth, density fairly constant at or near carring capacity and poor dispersal power.

122. The following graphs show the population growth of two species P and Q, each growing either alone (a) or in the presence of other species (b).

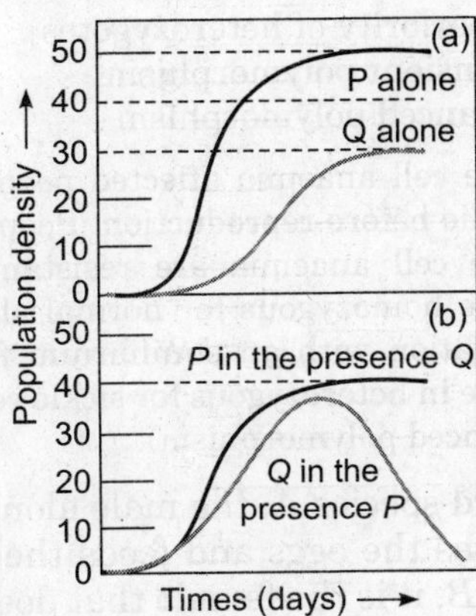

The most important conclusion to be drawn from the graph is

(a) *P* and *Q* are equally competitive.
(b) in competition, the growth of both species is adversely affected.
(c) in competition, species *P* remains unaffected while *Q* suffers.
(d) there is no evidence of competitive exclusion.

Sol. (c) In graph (b) it is clear that in presence of species *P* the growth of *Q* is adversally affected while *P* remains unaffected.

123. Three important biological parameters – generation time, population growth rate (r) and metabolic rate per gram body weight are a function of the organisms. body size. Which of the curves (a) or (b) represents the correct relation of each of the parameters to body size?

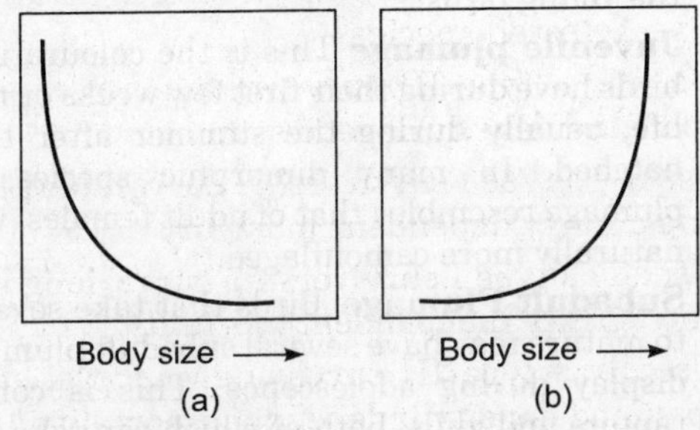

(a) Generation time – (a); population growth rate – (b); metabolic rate/g bw – (a)
(b) Generation time – (a); population growth rate – (b); metabolic rate/g bw – (b)
(c) Generation time – (b); population growth rate – (a); metabolic rate/g bw – (a)
(d) Generation time – (b); population growth rate – (b), metabolic rate rate/g bw – (a)

Sol. (c) When the body size increases the generation time increases, population growth rate decreases and metabolic rate per gram body weight decreases (although total metabolic rate increases).

124. Nearly 25% of all insect species are known to be herbivores. Yet, in spite of such heavy herbivore pressure, globally green plants tend to persist, contributing to a 'green earth'. Which of the following account for the relative success of green plants?

I. Herbivore insects are inefficient feeders.
II. Herbivore insect densities are kept low by predators.
III. Plants secrete herbivore-deterrent chemicals.

(a) II and III (b) I only
(c) II and III (d) I, II and III

Sol. (c) The transfer of food energy from producers through a series of organisms (herbivores to carnivores to decomposers) with repeated eating and being eaten is known as food chain. Various food chains are interconnected and maintain an equilibrium, thus no species become dominant. The plants also have self protecting mechanism like secreting some chemicals.

125. In the process of nitrification by organisms, the respective bacteria A and B in the following reaction are:

$$NH_4 + \frac{1}{2}O_2 \xrightarrow{A} NO_2^- + 2H^+ + H_2O$$

$$NO_2^- + \frac{1}{2}O_2 \xrightarrow{B} NO_3$$

(a) *Azotobacter* and *Nitrobacter*
(b) *Nitrobacter* and *Azotobacter*
(c) *Nitrosomonas* and *Nitrobacter*
(d) *Nitrobacter* and *Nitrosomonas*

Sol. (c) Nitrification is the phenomenon of conversion of ammonium nitrogen to nitrite and then to nitrate.

$$NH_4^+ + \frac{1}{2}O_2 \xrightarrow[Nitrosococus]{Nitrosomonas} NO_2^- + 2H^+ + H_2O$$

$$2NO_2^- + \frac{1}{2}O_2 \xrightarrow{Nitrobacter} NO_3^-$$

126. The flightless birds ostrich, rhea and emu are distributed on different continents. What is the most plausible explanation that is given by an evolutionary biologist for this discontinuous observation?

(a) The birds were able to fly earlier, but lost their flight ability later
(b) Prehistoric humans transported these birds to different continents
(c) The birds, although flightless, may have used drifting logs to cross the ocean and reach other continents
(d) All the continents used to be one single supercontinent earlier and the flightless birds were isolated after the break up of the landmass.

Sol. (d) Birds have evolved from ornithichian dinosaurs during the jurassic period. The fore limbs are modified into wings. The flightless birds like ostrich, rhea and emu were geographically separated from supercontinent and later get isolated to the area.

127. Inspite of its two-fold cost, sexual reproduction is the most dominant mode of reproduction among the living organisms. Which of the following reasons might account for this?

I. Sexual reproduction generates genetic heterogeneity through recombination

II. Sexual reproduction helps in purging deleterious mutations

III. Sexual reproduction evolved to stay evolutionarily ahead of fast evolving internal parasites.

(a) I only (b) I and II
(c) III only (d) I, II and III

Sol. (d) Sexual reproduction is usually biparental and involves fertilization, meiosis, mitosis and crrossing over. By creating variations through recombination it contributes to evolution of species.

128. A moth species occurs as two distinct morphs based on wing colour — pale and dark. In the forest there are trees with dark coloured trunks as well as those with light coloured trunks and the moths can rest on either tree. Birds capture the resting moths and eat. In a field experiment, the proportion (%) of dark and pale morphs captured from dark and light trunk trees was recorded. The most plausible conclusion to be drawn from the results is

Tree Trunk Colour	Moth morph	
	Dark	Pale
Dark	45	55
Light	48	52

(a) natural selection favours dark morphs in forests where trees with dark trunks are dominant.
(b) birds can detect dark morphs better than light morphs.
(c) pale morphs prefer to rest on light coloured trunks
(d) birds detect the moths by cues other than their wing colour.

Sol. (d) Natural selection favours dark moths in forest where trees with dark trunk are dominant, *i.e.*, the birds can not detect them. In the same way natural selection favours pale moth in forest where trees with light colour are dominant. The number of dark moth captured in dark tree trunk is lower than the dark moth in light tree trunk.

129. It is found that people with the genetic disease called sickle cell anaemia are resistant to malaria. Which of the following best describes the underlying mechanism?

(a) Frequency-dependent selection
(b) Superiority of heterozygotes
(c) Transient polymorphism
(d) Balanced polymorphism

Sol. (d) Sickle cell anaemia affected people are homozygous and die before reproduction. People heterozygous for sickle cell anaemia are resistant to malaria than people homozygous for normal allele. This produces population with an equilibrium for the numbers of people in heterozygous for sickle cell and non-carriers (balanced polymorphism).

130. In a bird species *A*, the male alone builds the nest, incubates the eggs and feeds the nestling. In bird species *B*, it is the female that does all that. In bird species *C*, both sexes contribute equally to the above activities. In species *A* and *B*, the uninvolved partner may fly away and mate again. Which sex among *A*, *B* and *C* is most likely to develop colourful plumage during breeding season?

(a) Male in species *A* and *B*, both sexes in species *C*
(b) Female in species *A*, male in species *B* and *C*
(c) Female in species *A* and *B*, neither in species *C*
(d) Female in species *A*, male in species *B*, neither in species *C*

Sol. (d) The term plumage refers to a bird's feathers, including the colour and pattern those feathers produce. There are several basic plumage that many bird species exhibit throughout the year.

- **Natal plumage** Very young birds just a few days or weeks old have natal or birth plumage. The coloration for these feathers is often plain and the feathers serve as both camouflage and insulation for the young birds.
- **Juvenile plumage** This is the colouration young birds have during their first few weeks or months of life, usually during the summer after they have hatched. In many dimorphic species, juvenile plumage resembles that of adult females, which are naturally more camouflaged.
- **Subadult Plumage** Birds that take several years to mature may have several subadult plumages they display during adolescence. This is common in raptors and gulls, both of which can take 2-3 years or longer to reach maturity. Until then, immature birds have less distinct plumage that gradually grows to resemble the adult plumage more closely each year.
- **Basic Plumage** This is a mature bird's non-breeding plumage. In dimorphic species, both genders may resemble females in basic plumage. This is also called non-breeding plumage or winter plumage, and in some species, particularly ducks, it is called eclipse plumage because of the short time males breeding plumage is 'eclipsed' by this bland coloration.
- **Breeding Plumage** This is the most brilliant, colourful plumage for many bird species. In dimorphic species it is most often the males that

develop bold breeding plumage, and it may involve extraordinary colours or unusual feather shape such as long streamers. This is also called alternate plumage, nuptial plumage or spring plumage. In some species, breeding plumage may be worn for the entire spring and summer, while for other species it may last only a few weeks.

131. If a given gene in a randomly mating population has three alleles a, b and c in the ratio of 0.5, 0.2 and 0.3 respectively, what is the expected frequency of genotypes ab and bc in the population at equilibrium?

(a) 0.1 and 0.06
(b) 0.2 and 0.15
(c) 0.2 and 0.12
(d) 0.04 and 0.09

Sol. (a) To calculate expected genotype frequencies (if the population is in Hardy-Weinberg equilibrium), use the trinomial equation (since we have three alleles)

$$(p + q + r)^2$$

which expands to ...

$$p^2 + 2pq + q^2 + 2pr + 2qr + r^2 = 1.0$$

132. The following table lists some of the enzymes of fungi and bacteria having wide variety of industrial applications, including alcoholic beverages, food, detergents and pharmaceuticals, along with their microbial original

Enzyme	Microorganism
A. Amylase	1. *Azotobacter vinelandii*
B. Asparginase	2. *Serratia marcescens*
C. Lipase	3. *Aspergillus aureus*
D. Pectinase	4. *Aspergillus oryzae*

The correct combinations are

(a) A and 4
(b) B and 3
(c) C and 1
(d) D and 2

Sol. (a)

Enzyme	Microorganism
Amylase	*Aspergillus*
Pectinase	*Aspergillus*
Lipase	Pancreas

133. Animal cell cultures are frequently used for production of therapeutic proteins. NIH3T3 (a fibroblast cell line) and CHO (Chinese hamster ovarian cell line) are some of the popular cell lines used. Choose the best combination of cell line (for transfection) and starting material for purification of human growth hormone, a secretary protein

(a) NIH3T3 cell pellet
(b) CHO and cell pellet
(c) NIH3T3 and culture medium
(d) CHO and culture medium

Sol. (d) **Chinese hamster ovary (CHO) cells** are cell line derived from the ovary of the Chinese hamster. They are often used in biological and medical research and commercially in the production of therapeutic proteins. CHO cells are used in studies of genetics, toxicity screenig, nutrition and gene expression, particularly to express recombinant proteins. Today, CHO cells are the most commonly used mammalian hosts for industrial production of recombinant protein therapeutics. The use of the Chinese hamseter in research began in 1919 where they were used in place of mice for typing pneumococci. They were subsequently found to be excellent vectors for transmission of kala-azar (also known as visceral leishmaniasis), facilitating research in epidemiology.

134. A novel vaccine (against malaria liver stage specific) has been developed by an investigator. This happened to be the parasites unique cell surface protein molecule (Mp). This Mp when injected in mice elicits humoral antibody response (IgG in nature) and can efficiently neutralize sporozoites by inhibiting their binding to the liver cells. Upon a a pre-clinical trial this vaccine failed universally despite a high titre IgG response. Which one out of the choices below is the correct answer of this failure?

(a) The liver cell surface receptor to which Mp binds is changed.
(b) The malaria parasite is successful in changing the epitope in Mp to which IgG binds
(c) IgG molecules change its binding sites for Mp.
(d) The affinity of Ig to Mp epitopes is reduced.

Sol. (b) Parasite drug resistance and difficulties in developing effective vaccines have precipitated the search for alternative therapies for malaria. The success of passive immunization suggests that immunoglobulin (Ig)-based therapies are effective. To further explore the mechanism (s) by which antibody mediates its protective effect, we generated human chimeric IgG1 and IgA1 and a single-chain diabody specific for the C-terminal 19-kDa region of *Plasmodium yoelii* merozoite surface protein 1 ($MSP1_{19}$), a major target of protective immune responses. These novel human reagents triggered *in vitro* phagocytosis of merozoites but, unlike their parental mouse IgG2b, failed to porotect against parasite challenge *in vivo*. Therefore, the Fc region appears critical for mediating protection *in vivo*, at least for this $MSP1_{19}$ epitope. Such antibodies may serve as prototype therapeutic agents, and as useful tools in the development of *in vitro* neutralization assays with *Plasmodium* parasites.

135. Following are some statements about *Agrobacterium* – plant interactions

I. *Agrobacterium* transfers a part of its chromosome into plant cell.

II. *Agrobacterium* transfers a part of one of its plasmid DNA into plant cell.

III. All the virulence genes of *Agrobacterium* are inducible.

IV. All the virulence genes of *Agrobacterium* are functional only inside the bacterial cells.

V. Some of the virulence genes of *Agrobacterium* are inducible.

VI. Some of the virulence genes of *Agrobacterium* are functional both in bacterial and plant cells.

Which of the following combination of statements is true?

(a) I, III and IV (b) II, IV and V
(c) III, IV and V (d) II, V and VI

Sol. (d) *Agrobacterium* is a gram negative soil bacterium. During infection it transfer small part pTi (tumour inducing plasmid) into the plant cell genome. All the genes present in T-DNA contain eukaryotic regulatory sequences. *Vir* region mediates the transfer of T-DNA hence is essential for virulence or production of crown gall. The operon *vir* A and *vir* G are constitutive, encode one protein each and concerned with regulation of all the *vir* operons.

136. To generate a knock-in or a knock-out mouse, it is essential to use antibiotic selection to select the stem cells that have putatively integrated the construct accurately. Each construct will have 5′ homology arm and 3′ homology arm to help in homologus recombination. A positive antibiotic selection cassette and a negative antibiotic selection cassette are also used. Negative selection cassette helps in de-selection of non-homologous recombinant stem cells.

Choose one statement indicated below that reflects the correct position of the negative selection cassette.

(a) Negative selection cassette is supplied in a separate construct.
(b) Negative selection cassette is placed between the two homology arms.
(c) Negative selection cassette is placed 3′ to the 3′-homology arm.
(d) Negative selection cassette is inserted between the promoter Exon I of positive selection cassette.

Sol. (d) The number of ways in which gene targeting constructs can be signed to produce knock-out or knock-in mice is almost limitless.

The simplest targeting construct consists of 2 long segments of genomic DNA (gDNA), called homology arms, flanking a selection cassette. The most commony used selection cassette consists of cDNA and control elements for the aminoglycoside phosphotransferase (G418 or kanamycin resistance) gene (others include resistance genes for puromycin and hygromycin).

When introduced into mouse embronic stem (ES) cells by electroporation, the gDNA homology arms can undergo a double-reciprocal recombination event with their matching sequences on one chromosome, carrying the selection cassette with them. The gDNA between the regions of homology on the chromosome is thereby replaced by the selection cassette. Where a complete knockout is desired, the sequence being replaced usually includes the TATA box, the start codon, and one or more of the initial exons. However, for various reasons it is often desirable to delete downstream exons (*e.g.*, to avoid disrupting the promoter).

One commonly used negative selection cassette contains the gene for a viral thymidine kinase (tk). The viral tk gene product allows growing cells to incorporate a toxic nucleotide analog into their DNA, thus selecting against those cells. The tk cassette is cloned into the targeting construct outside of the homology arms, so that it will not be incorporated during homologous recombination. It will be incorporated during most random integrations and help to select against those clones. Another negatively selectable marker is the gene for diphtheria toxin A (DTA). The A subunit inhibits protein synthesis but cannot be taken up by other cells.

137. Following are the different ways of obtaining human stem cells-

I. Cells from morula are dispersed and cultured to give rise pluripotent stem cells.

II. Isolated inner cell mass of a blastocyst are cultured and they become pluripotent stem cells.

III. The primordial germ cells from a foetus are collected and cultured, which grow into pluripotent stem cells.

IV. Stem cells are collected from adult tissues and grown in specific manner to develop into pluripotent stem cells.

Which of the above cell type(s) is extensively used for somatic cell gene therapy in human?

(a) I and II (b) II only (c) II and IV (d) IV only

Sol. (d) Stem cells are required whenever there is a recurring need to replace differentiated cells that cannot divide themselves. For somatic cell gene therapy the stem cell is collected from somatic adult tissue specifically growing in culture medium to develop into pluripotent stem cell.

138. RFLP and RAPD markers are commonly used in plant breeding and diversity analysis. Which of the following combination of statement about these molecular makers are correct?

I. RFLP is co dominant

II. RAPD is co dominant
III. Both the markers are ubiquitous
IV. Only RFLP can detect heterozygote
V. Only RAPD can detect heterozygote
VI. RAPD cannot detect allelic variation
(a) I, III, IV, V (b) II, III, V, VI
(c) I, III, IV, VI (d) III, IV, V, VI

Sol. (c) A **genetic marker** is a gene or DNA sequence with a known location on a chromosome that can be used to identify individuals or species. It can be described as a variation (which may arise due to mutation or alteration in the genomic loci) that can be observed. A genetic marker may be a short DNA sequence, such as a sequence surrounding a single base-pair change (single nucleotide polymorphism, SNP), or a long one, like minisatellites. They can be further categorized as dominant or co-dominant. Dominant markers allow for analyzing many loci at one time, *e.g.*, RAPD. A primer amplifying a dominant marker could amplify at many loci in one sample of DNA with one PCR reaction. Co-dominant markers analyze one locus at a time. A primer amplifying a co-dominant marker would yield one targeted product. Dominant markers, as RAPDs and high-efficiency markers (like AFLPs and SMPLs), allow the analysis of many loci per experiment without requiring previous information about their sequence.

Codominant markers (RFLPs, microsatellites, etc.) allow the analysis of only a lcous per experiment, so they are more informative because the allelic variations of that locus can be distinguished. As a consequence, you can identity linkage groups between different genetic maps but, for their development it is necessary to know the sequence.

139. Which one of the following indicate steps involved in DNA foot-printing to monitor interaction of DNA with a protein?

(a) DNA + protein → treat with restriction enzymes → run agarose gel → stain with ethidium bromide and view under UV light.
(b) Label one of the DNA strands with a radiolabel → treat one portion of labelled DNA with the protein of interest followed by reaction with DNAse → treat second portion of DNA with only DNAse. Run both the treated DNA samples on a sequencing gel.
(c) Analyze fragments obtained from the experiments described in (2) by MALDI mass spectrometry.
(d) DNA + protein → treat with DNAse followed by restriction enzymes. Run the sample on SDS page and visualize by commassie blue staining.

Sol. (b) Foot printing enables identification of the site on a DNA molecule to which a protein such as RNA polymerase, binds since binding of protein to a region of DNA protect the phosphodiester bonds of that region for cleavage by DNAse I.

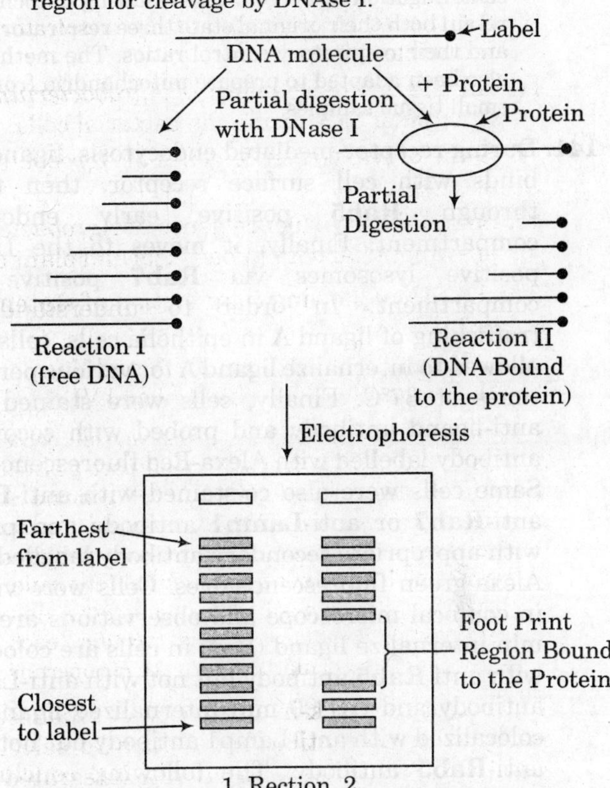

Fig. Footprinting using DNase I. In reaction I, protein-free DNA molecules are partially digested with DNase I, while in reaction II the DNA molecules are bound to the concerned protein during partial digestion with DNase I.

140. A student is asked to isolate and purify various subcellular organelles from a liver cell sample. Following sucrose density gradient centrifugation technique, and taking most care mitochondrial fraction is found to be contaminated with nuclear fraction. Which technique out of the choices given below should be appropriate to obtain a clean mitochondrial fraction?

(a) Gel filtration
(b) Percoll density gradient
(c) Immuno-magnetic separation
(d) Pulse field electrophoresis

Sol. (b) Density gradient centrifugation is concerned with actual separation, isolation and purification of subcellular organelles, plasma membrane etc. Chromatography is an important technique of cell fractionation employed for the separation of constituents of mixture, and based upon principle of portition coefficient.

Mitochondria prepared from skeletal muscle, liver are typically contaminated with sarcoplasmic reticulum fragments and salt-soulble proteins. These contaminants can be removed by density-gradient centrifugation in Percoll. The resulting mitochondria retain both their original state three respiratory rates and their respiratory control ratios. The method has also been adapted to prepare mitochondria from very small tissue samples.

141. During receptor-mediated endocytosis, ligand first binds with cell surface receptor, then traffic through **Rab5** positive early endosomal compartment. Finally, it moves to the Lamp1 positive lysosomes via **Rab7** positive late compartment. In order to understand the trafficking of ligand A in epithelia cells, cells were allowed to internalize ligand A for various period of times at 37°C. Finally, cells were stained with anti-ligand antibody and probed with secondary antibody labelled with Alexa-Red fluorescence dye. Same cells were also co-stained with anti-**Rab5,** anti-**Rab7** or anti-**Lamp1** antibody and probed with appropriate secondary antibody labelled with Alexa-green fluorescence dyes. Cells were viewed in confocal microscope and observations are (I) 5 min internalize ligand (Red) in cells are colocalize with anti **Rab5** antibody but not with anti-Lamp1 antibody and (II) 90 min internalized ligand are colocalized with anti-Lamp1 antibody but not with anti-**Rab5** antibody. The following conclusions could be arrived at from the above observations.

I. Ligand A travels to early endosomal compartment by 5 min.
II. Ligand A travels to early endosomal compartment by about 90 min.
III. Ligand A travels to lysozome by about 5 min.
IV. Ligand A travels to early endosome by about 90 min.

Identify the correct inferences.

(a) I and II (b) II and IV
(c) III and IV (d) I and III

Sol. (d) The overall rate of endocytic internalization of the plasma membrane is quite high; cultured fibroblasts regularly internalize 50 percent of their cell-surface proteins and phospholipids each hour. Most cell-surface receptors that undergo endocytosis will repeatedly deposit their ligands within the cell and then recycle to the plasma membrane, once again to mediate the internalization of ligand molecules. For instance, the LDL receptor makes one round trip into and out of the cell every 10-20 minutes, for a total of several hundred trips in its 20 h life span. In contrast, after binding its protein ligand the receptors for insulin and other growth factors generally cycle only two or three times before the complex of receptor and ligand is degraded in the lysosome—reducing the number of cell-surface receptors and thus the esnsitivty of the cells to hormone signaling. Regardless of how many times a particular receptor is recycled, internalized receptor lignad complexes commonly follow the pathway. Endocytosed cell-surface receptors dissociate from their ligands with late endosomes. Electron microscopy of liver cells pertused with asialoglycoprotein reveal that between 5 and 10 min after internalization both teh receptors and their ligands accumulate in late endosome vesicles.

142. The values of molar absorption coefficient (ε) of *Trp* and *Tyr* at 240 nm and 280 nm are the following:

Wavelenght (nm)	E_{Tyr} (M^{-1} cm^{-1})	ε_{Trp} (M^{-1} cm^{-1})
240	11,300	1,960
280	1,500	5,380

A 10-mg sample of a protein is hydrolyzed to its constituent amino acids and diluted to 100 mL. The absorption of this solution in a 1 cm path length, is 0.717 at 240 nm and 0.239 at 280 nm. The estimated content of *Trp* and *Tyr* in µmol/ g protein respectively are

(a) 586 and 28.1 (b) 58.6 and 281
(c) 586 and 281 (d) 58.6 and 28.1

Sol. (c)

143. The structure of a protein is known from X-ray diffraction studies which gave 30% α-helix, 50% β-sheet and 20% random coil. Circular dichroism (CD) measurements gave 50% α-helix, 40% β-sheet and 10% random coil. What could not be a possible explanation for these observations?

(a) Protein structure in the crystal is different from that in the solution.
(b) CD analysis for structural components is not appropriate for this protein.
(c) Contributions from other chromophores also contribute to the CD spectrum of the protein
(d) Protein contains high content of disulphide bonds.

Sol. (a) Circular dichroism spectra of proteins are extremely sensitive to secondary structure. Nevertheless, circular dichroism spectra should not be analyzed for protein secondary structure unless they are measured to at least 184 nm. Even if all the various types of β-turns are lumped together, there are at least 5 different types of secondary structure in a protein (α-helix, antiparallel β-sheet, parallel β-sheet, β-turn, and other structures not included in the first 4 categories). It is not possible to solve for these 5 parameters unless there are 5 equations. Singular value decomposition can be used to show that circular dichroism spectra of proteins measured to 200 nm contains only 2 pieces of information, while spectra measured to 190 nm contain about 4. Adding the constraint that the sum of secondary structures must equal 1 provides another piece of information, but even with this constraing, spectra measured to 190 nm simply do not analyze well for the 5 unknowns in secondary structure. Spectra measured to 184 nm do contain 5 pieces of information and we have used such spectra successfully to analyze a variety to proteins for their component secondary structures.

144. In column I are given equations and in column II what the equations represent. Column I and II are incorrectly matched.

Column I	Column I
A. $\frac{dN_1}{dt} = r_1 N_1 \left(\frac{K_1 - N_1}{K_1}\right)$	1. Polulation growth of species 1 in the presence of competing species 2
B. $\frac{dN_1}{dt} = r_1 N_1$	2. Logistic population growth of species 1
C. $\frac{dN_1}{dt} = r_1 N_1 \left(\frac{K_1 - N_1 - \alpha N_2}{K_1}\right)$	3. Population growth of prey species 1 in the presence of predator species 2.
D. $\frac{dN_1}{dt} + N_1 b_1 - d_1 N_1 N_2$	4. Exponential population growth of species 1.

The correct match in sequence of the four equations from column II is

(a) 2, 4, 1 and 3
(b) 4, 2, 3 and 4
(c) 2, 4, 3 and 1
(d) 4, 2, 1 and C

Sol. (a) The Lotka-Volterra model incorporates interspecific competition by using a parameter called alpha. Alpha is the coefficient of competition and measures the competitive effect of one species on another. Modelling the effect of one species on the population growth of another species (measured by the competition coefficients), and *vice versa*, is achieved with the following modifications to the familiar logistic growth model.

(i) Remember the logistic growth model

$$\frac{dN}{dt} = r_1 N \left(1 - \frac{N}{K}\right)$$

(ii) Population growth of species 1 in the presence of species 2

$$\frac{dN_1}{dt} = r_1 N_1 \left(1 - \frac{N_1}{K_1} - \frac{aN_2}{K_1}\right)$$

(iii) Population growth of species 2 in the presence of species 1

$$\frac{dN_2}{dt} = r_2 N_2 \left(1 - \frac{N_2}{K_2} - \frac{aN_1}{K_2}\right)$$

145. It is claimed that the mean (μ) arsenic concentration in the ground water of village is 20μg/L with σ = 3. In a random sample of 16 measurements what values of arsenic concentration should lead to rejection of the claim with 95% confidence?

(a) Values lower then 18.53 and values higher that 21.47
(b) Values higher than 21.47
(c) Values lower than 18.53
(d) Values lower than 18.07 and values higher than 21.93

Sol. (a) The 95% confidence interval, is often estimated by assuming a normal distribution of the measured parameter, in which case it can alternatively be defined as the interval limited by 1.96 (often rounded up to 2) population standard deviations from either side of the population mean (also called the expected value). The 95% confidence interval (95%) is calculated as

$$\mu = \text{mean} \pm \text{ZSE}(\bar{x})$$

$$\text{SE}(\bar{x}) = \frac{SD}{\sqrt{N}} = \frac{3}{4} = 0.75$$

$$\mu = 20 \pm 1.96 \times 0.75 = \frac{21.47}{18.53}$$

(a) 2, 4, 1 and 3 (b) 4, 2, 3 and 4

(c) 2, 4, 3 and 1 (d) 4, 2, 1 and 3

$$\frac{dN_2}{dt} = r_2 N_2 \left(\frac{K_2 - N_2 - \alpha_{21} N_1}{K_2}\right)$$

UGC CSIR
NET Life Sciences*
Solved Paper 2024

PART B

21. Following statements are made about uncompetitive inhibition of an enzyme :
A. Uncompetitive inhibitor binds to both free enzyme as well as an enzyme-substrate complex.
B. Addition of uncompetitive inhibitor lowers the v_{max} of the reaction.
C. Apparent K_M of the enzyme is lowered.
D. Apparent K_M of the enzyme remains unchanged
Which one of the following option represent the correct combination of the statement
1 B and C 2 A and C 3 A and B 4 A and D

22. Following are the pK_a's of the ionizable group in lysine.
$pK_{a_1} = 2.16$ (α-carboxylic group)
$pK_{a_2} = 9.06$ (α-amino group)
$pK_{a_3} = 10.54$ (ε = amino group)
Which one of the following option represents the *pI* of lysine
1 7.25 2 5.61 3 6.35 4 9.8

23. The enzyme alkaline phosphatase was tested for its calalytic activity using the substrate para-nitrophenylphosphate. The *kM* obtained was 10 mM and v_{max} was 100μ mol/min. Which of the following option represents the initial velocity of the reaction at a substrate concentration of 10 mM?
1 50μ mol/min 2 100μ mol/min
3 500μ mol/min 4 20μ mol/min

24. How many hydrogen bonds involving the backbone CO and NH can be observed in an α-helix consisting of 15 amino acid residues?
1 10 2 11 3 12 4 13

25. Progression across G1/S boundary followed by entry into S-phase is promoted by the activation of which one of the following protein complexes?
1 *Cdk*4/cyclin *D* 2 *Cdk*2/Cyclin *E*
3 *Cdk*4, 6/cyclin 4 *Cdk*4, 6/cyclin *D*, *E*

26. In eukaryotic cells covalently attached lipids help to anchor some water soluble proteins to the plasma membrane. One group of cytosolic proteins are anchored to the cytosolic face of membrane by a fatty actyl group (.e.g., myristate or palmitate). These groups are generally covalently attached to which amino acid present at the *N*-terminus of the polypeptide chain?
1 Glycine 2 Tyrosin 3 Serine 4 Lysine

27. To prepare individual tissue cells from a primary culture, the cell-cell and cell-matrix interaction must be broken. To achieve this, one would **NOT** use
1 EDTA 2 Trypsin 3 Collagenase 4 Separase

28. Which one of the following statements is **NOT** true about nucleosomal organisation of core particle?
1 The typical structure of DNA is altered in the middle of the core particle.
2 In core particle, DNA is organised as flat super helix with 1.65 turns around the histone octamer.
3 While forming 30 nm fibres, generally 6 nucleosomes per turn organise into a two-start helix.
4 The N-terminal histone tails in a core particle are strictly ordered and exit from the nucleosomes between turns of the DNA.

29. During replication, RNase H removes all of the RNA primer except the ribonucleotide directly linked to the DNA end. This is because
1 it can degrade RNA and DNA from their 5′ end
2 it can only cleave bonds between two ribonucleotides.
3 it can degrade RNA and DNA from their 3′ end
4 activity of RNase H is inhibited by the presence of duplex containing both strands as DNA

30. Some cells possess peptides which contains *D*-form of amino acid. How do they arise?
1 These peptides are produced by ribosome by incorporating D-amino acids at specific positions.
2 Ribosome makes peptides with L-amino acids only. However some of the amino acids in the peptides are replaced by D-amino acids by a pathways that involves excision of the L-amino acids.
3 The peptides with the D-amino acids are produced in a ribosome-independent manner.
4 Peptides with D-amino acid exist only in archeae where they are made by the presence of racemases.

31. All of the following statements about bacterial transcription termination are true EXCEPT :
1 some terminator sequences require Rho protein for terminations.
2 inverted repeat and *T*′ rich non-template strand define intrinsic terminator.
3 Rho-dependent terminators may possess inverted repeat elements.
4 Nus-A is necessary for intrinsic transcription termination.

32. Which of the following proteins is essential for both the initiation of DNA replication as well as the continued advance of the replication fork?
1 ORC 2 Geminin 3 Cdc45 4 Cdc6

* ***Based on Memory***

33. Which one of the following combinations represents the major protein or protein complex involved in chromatin condensation in yeast and human, respectively?
1 HP1 and SIR complex
2 SIR complex and HP1
3 HP1 and Su(var)
4 SIR complex and Su(var)

34. Which of the following is the causative agent of filariasis?
1 *Listeria monocytogenes*
2 *Cryptococcus neoformans*
3 *Francisella tularensis*
4 *Brugia malayi*

35. The cytoplasmic domain of the receptor of which of the following proteins does not functions as tyrosine kinase?
1 Epidermal growth factor
2 Platelet derived growth factor
3 Insulin
4 Asialoglycoprotein

36. Tumors are generally classified by
1 the virus which caused them
2 the person who discovered them
3 their metastatic ability
4 the tissue or cell of origin

37. A breakthrough in cancer therapy is expected where T-cells are taken from a patient are modified in the laboratory to attack cancer cells before re-infusion in the patient. These T-cells are called
1 cancer associated receptor T-cells
2 chimeric antigen-receptor T-cells
3 chimeric B and T-cell
4 cancer antigens recognition T-cells

38. Which one of the following statements with respect to development in amphibians is correct?
1 Gastrulation begins with the invagination of bottle cells, followed by coordinated involution of the mesodermal precursors and the epiboly of the prospective.
2 The organiser induces the Nieuwkoop center.
3 The organiser is formed by the accumulations of β-catenin.
4 In the absence of BMP inhibitors ectodermal cells from neural tube.

39. During normal development of sea urchin, β-catenin accumulates predominantly in the micromeres, which are fated to become endoderm and mesoderm. If *GSK* – 3 is blocked in the developing embryo.
1 β-catenin accumulation in the nuclei of large micromeres will be inhibited leading to the formation of ectodermal ball.
2 β-catenin will accumulate in the nuclei of all blastula cells leading to an ectodermal ball.
3 β-catenin will accumulate in the nuclei of all blastula cells leading to animal cells getting specified as endoderm and mesoderm.
4 β-catenin which accumulate in the nuclei of large micromers will be inhibited leading to animal cells getting specified as endoderm and mesoderm.

40. Which one of the following describes the function of silicon in plants?
1 Constituent of amino acids
2 Contributes to cell wall rigidity and elasticity
3 Constituent of the photosynthesis reaction centre
4 Maintenance of cell turgor and electron-neutrality

41. Most of the plant disease resistance (R) gene products contain:
1 G-Box domains
2 Transcription repression domains
3 Leucine-rich repeats
4 Enzymatic activities

42. Out of several gibberellins identified in plants, which one of the following is not bioactive?
1 GA_1
2 GA_3
3 GA_4
4 GH_5

43. Nitrogenase, a complex metal containing enzyme is involved in conversion of N_2 to NH_3. Which one of the following metals is not involved in the activity of nitrogenase?
1 Molybdenum (Mo)
2 Iron (Fe)
3 Vanadium (V)
4 Cobalt (Co)

44. Which one of the following agents cause relaxation of mesangial cells?
1 Histamine
2 Thrombaxane A_2
3 Norepinephrine
4 Dopamine

45. A patient comes to the hospital complaining of vomiting and diarrhoea. The doctor suggested that the patient take glucose and electrolyte solution orally. Which one of following membrane proteins is likely to be involved in rehydrating the patient?
1 Cystic Fibrosis Transmembrane Regulator (CFTR)
2 Sodium Glucose Transporter Protein I (SGLT I)
3 Insulin Receptor Protein (IRP)
4 Sucrase-Isomaltase Protein (SIP)

46. The dark current in retina is due to
1 Closing of Na^+ channels in the outer segment of photoreceptors.
2 Opening of K^+ channels in the inner segment of photoreceptors.
3 Opening of Na^+ channels in the outer segment of photreceptors.
4 Closing of K^+ channels in the outer segment of photorecptors.

47. Which one of the following is not present in the filtration slit diaphragm?
1 NEPH1
2 Paxillin
3 Nephrin
4 NEPH2

48. DNA was isolated from a strain of bacterium with genotype $a^+b^+c^+d^+e^+$ and transformed into bacterial strain $a^-b^-c^-d^-e^-$. The transformants were tested for the presence of the donated genes. The cotransformed genes were found as follows a^+ and b^+ : c^+ and e^+ : d^+ and c^+ : b^+ and d^+ :
What is the order of genes on the bacterial chromosomes?
1 *a b c d e*
2 *a c b e d*
3 *a b c e d*
4 *a b d c e*

49. A fly with apricot coloured eyes was crossed with a sepia eyed fly of opposite sex. In F_1 all flies were wild type. The genes responsible for the two
1 allelic
2 non-allelic
3 pseudo-allelic
4 paralogous genes

50. Human polydactyly trait having extra fingers or toes are caused by a dominant allele. In a screening it was found that out of 42 individuals having an allele for polydactyly, only 28 of them were polydactylus. Which of the following is the correct interpretation of the observation?
1 The penetrance of polydactyly is estimated to be 90%
2 The expressivity of polydactyly is 90%
3 This is an example of variable expressivity
4 The polydactyels trait is showing complete penetriance.

51. The basic difference between direct repair and base excision repair is
1 Direct repair restores original structure of altered nucleotide without replacement while in base excision repair the section of DNA containing the distortion is removed the correct base is added and resealed.
2 In direct repair, homologous recombination repairs the broken region while base excision repairs original structure of altered nucleotide by modification.
3 Direct repair restores original structure by non-homologous and joining without using homologous template while in base excision repair the section of DNA containing the distortion is repaired by using homologous recombinations.

4 in direct repair an exonuclease, a DNA polymerase and a ligase are used, while in base excision repair a tanslesion polymerase passes the bulky lesions is used by the cell.

52. Eukaryotes are classified into 5-6 super groups based on phylogenomic studies. Which one of the following statement about eukaryotic super groups is false?
1 Fungi and animals are more closely related to each other than either group is to plants.
2 Amoebozoa and opisthokonts are unikonts.
3 Land plants and green algae belong to Archaeplastida.
4 Alveolates and *Amoeba* belong to same super group.

53. What is the pattern of cleavage observed in mammals?
1 Radial 2 Spiral
3 Rotational 4 Bilateral

54. Which of the following combinations would best characterise the dominant phase of the life cycle of a pteridophyte?
1 Diploid gametophyte 2 Haploid gametophyte
3 Diploid sporophyte 4 Hapoid sporophyte

55. Which one of the following gases is present in the stratosphere at a concentration higher than its concentration in troposphere?
1 Nitrogen 2 Oxygen
3 Ozone 4 Carbon dioxide

56. The graph below shows the change in the size of four population ($A-D$) over time.

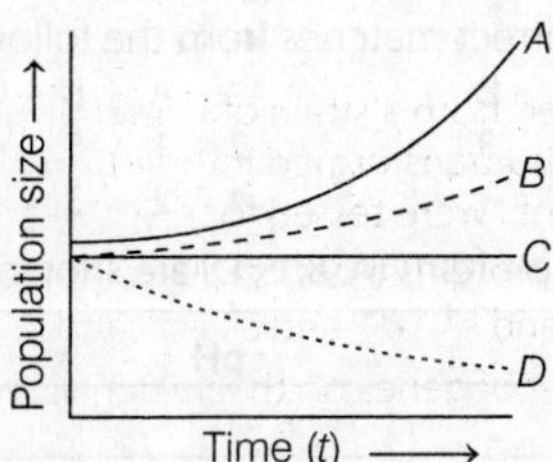

Which among the four population (A, B, C and D) would have the lowest intrinsic rate of population growth (r)?
1 A 2 B
3 C 4 D

57. Consider the following ecosystem
A. Tropical rain forest
B. Open ocean
C. Algal beds and coral reefs
D. Marshes and swamps
Which one of the following options represents these ecosystem in an increasing order of their contribution to annual world net primary production?
1 B, C, D and A 2 C, D, B and A
3 D, C, A and B 4 C, D, A and B

58. Historical frequencies of fires in an area can be determined by
1 radioactive dating of the tree remains.
2 examining the fire scars in growth rings of living trees.
3 measuring carbon content on the soil surface after fire.
4 examining records of evacuation history of the nearby villages.

59. Given below are statements on 'living fossils'. Select the correct statements.
1 Living fossils are impressions of extant organisms in old rocks.
2 Living fossils show high morphological divergence from fossil records.
3 Living fossils are always an evolutionary link between two classes of organism.
4 Living fossils are organisms that have remained unchanged for millions of year.

60. Which one of the following statements is correct for the process of speciation?
1 Allopatric speciation occurs between adjacent populations
2 Parapatric speciation may occur between geograhpically separated populations
3 Sympatric speciation occurs within one continuously distributed population
4 Sympatric speciation occurs when continuously distributed populations are fragmented

61. Which one of the following does not contribute to microevolutionary change?
1 Mutation 2 Random mating
3 Genetic drift 4 Natural selection

62. According to Hamilton's rule, altruistic behaviour can evolve when $rb>c$, where b is the extra benefit gained by the recipient as a result of the altruistic act, c is the cost to the actor arising from performing the altruistic act and r is the relatedness between the
1 individual performing the altruistic act and the offspring of the recipient
2 individual performing the altruistic act and the recipient
3 recipient and the offspring of the individual performing the altruistic act
4 individual performing the altruistic act and the members of its population

63. Analyses of nucleotide sequences of ribosomal RNA (*r*RNA) are particularly useful for evolutionary studies of living organisms because of the following reasons except
1 *r*RNA is evolutionarily ancient
2 no free-living organism lacks *r*RNA
3 *r*RNA, since critical for translation, can undergo lateral transfer amongst distant species
4 *r*RNA has evolved slowly over geological time

64. Which one of the following statements is correct?
1 If a transgenic plant heterozygous for an insert segregates into 1 : 1 ratio for the transgenic phenotype on back-crossing then it contains two unlinked copies of the insert.
2 ANOVA allows a plant breeder to test whether measurements from three or more treatments show statistically significant differences.
3 Comparative genomics allows scientists to identify regions of collinearity but not synteny between different species.
4 For genetic mapping of a quantitative trait in plants, an RIL mapping population comprising of individuals that are heterozygous at most loci is preferred.

65. Which one of the following regions of the target gene is not used for making an RNA*i* construct to knock down its expression?
1 5′ UTR of the mature transcript 2 3′ UTR of the mature transcript
3 Exonic region 4 Intronic region

66. Which one of the following options represents a combination of terms that are matched incorrectly?
1 *ddNTPs* : chain termination *ddNTPs*
2 South Western blot : Physical interaction between DNA and protein
3 5′ – 3′ exonuclease activity : Proofreading polymerase for PCR
4 Yeast two hybrid system : Interaction between proteins.

67. For a nuclear spin of spin quantum no. $\left(I=\frac{1}{2}\right)$ precessing in a magnetic field at a Larmor frequency of 300 MHz, the wavelength of incident radiation required to excite the nuclear spins must be approximately.
1 1 nm 2 1 cm
3 1 m 4 10 m

68. Widal test, a widely used serological test for enteric fever, is a type of
1 precipitation reaction
2 agglutination reaction
3 complement fixation test
4 immunofluorescence detection

69. Fluorescence microscope that requires photoactivalable probes to obtain super-resolution is
1 Structured illumination microscope (SIM)
2 *d*STORM-stochastic optical reconstruction microscopy
3 Stimulated emission depletion microscopy (STED)
4 Laser scanning confocal microscope

70. A protein solution (0.2 mL) of unknown concentration was diluted with 0.8 mL of water. To 0.5 mL of this dilute solution 4.5 mL of biuret reagent was added and the colour allowed to develop. The absorbence of this mixture taken in test tube of 1 cm diameter of 540 nm was observed to be 0.20. 0.5 mL of BSA (4 mg/mL) solution plus 4.5 mL of biuret gave an absorbance of 0.20 when measured as above. What is the protein concentration (mg/mL) in the undiluted unknown solution?
1 20
2 40
3 50
4 80

PART C

71. A schematic of a metabolic pathway is shown below.

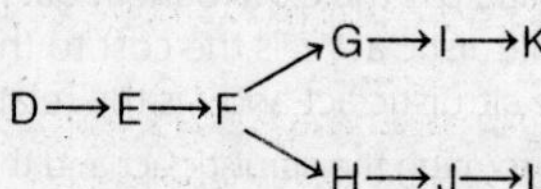

Under which of the following conditions would stoichiometric amounts of end products K and L be obtained if a concerted feedback inhibition mechanism were in operation?
1 K inhibits inhibits F→ G and L inhibits F→ H; D→ E is inhibited at equal amounts of K and L.
2 D→ E is inhibited at equal amounts of K and L; K inhibits F→ H and L inhibits F→ G
3 D→ E is inhibited at equal amount of G and H; K inhibits F→ H and L inhibits F→ G
4 K inhibits F→ H and L inhibits F→ G

72. The following statements are being made to define the Michaelis constant (K_M). It is
A. Independent of enzyme concentration (*E*) and substrate concentration (*S*).
B. Equal to the dissociation constant when the [*ES*] complex dissociates more rapidly than product formation.
C. Equal to the dissociation constant when product formation is more rapid than [*ES*] complex dissociation.
D. An intrinsic property of an enzyme and does not depend upon pH, temperature and iconic strength.
Which one of the following combination of statements is correct?
1 A and B
2 A, B and D
3 C and D
4 A and D

73. The structure of a protein with 100 residues was determined by X-ray analysis at atomic resolution and NMR spectroscopy. The following observations are possible.
A. The dihedral angles determined from the X-ray structure and NMR will be identical
B. The dihedral angles determined from the X-ray structure will be more accurate
C. β-turns can be determined only by NMR
D. β-sheets can be more accurately determined from the X-ray structure
Indicate the combination with all correct answers
1 A and C
2 B and D
3 B and C
4 A and D

74. The different arms in the *t*RNA structure are shown in column A. The specific signatures associated with the different arms are shown in Column B.

	Column A		Column B
A.	Acceptor arm	1.	Dihydrouridine
B.	Anticodon arm	2.	7 bp stem and CCA sequence
C.	TψC arm	3.	5 bp stem
D.	D-arm	4.	Pseudouridine

Choose the correct matches from the following:

	A	B	C	D
1	2	4	1	3
2	1	3	4	2
3	4	1	2	3
4	2	3	4	1

75. The ph of four proteins (A, B, C, D) are shown in the table below

Protein	pH
A	4
B	5.5
C	7
D	9

To purify 'D' from a mixture of these four proteins in a single step, using ion-exchange chromatography, what combination of buffer pH and ion-exchange resin would you select?
1 pH 11, cation exchanger resin pH 11
2 pH 2, anion exchanger resin pH 2
3 pH 6, anion exchanger resin pH 6
4 pH 8, cation exchanger resin pH 8

76. The curve *B* in the figure below shows the oxygen dissociation profile at physiological concentration of CO_2 and at pH 7. An increasing in pH would lead to oxygen dissociation profile indicated by :

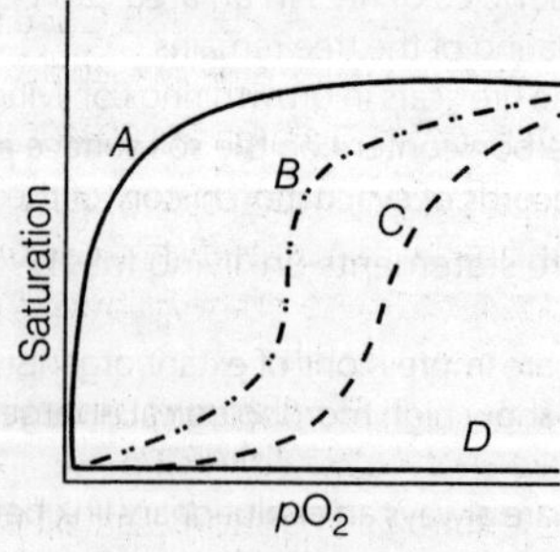

1 Curve *B* (no change in the dissociation profile).
2 Curve *A*
3 Curve *C*
4 Curve *D*

77. Following statements were made about chromosome cohesion during mitosis and meiosis.
A. Though cohesion is important for pair wise alignment of the chromosomes on the mitotic spindle, it is not important for the generation of tension across centromere.
B. Cohesion binds to the chromosome even before the initiation of *S*-phase.
C. In fission yeast, centromere specific localisation of Moa1 and Rec 8 regulates the eventuation of kinetochores at meiosis-1.
D. Cohesion exhibits uniform distribution/localisation pattern across the chromosomal length.
E. Polo/Cdc5 is a positive regulator of Separase an endopeptidase that facilitates opening of the cohesion ring.

Which one of the following combination contains all correct statements?
1 A, B and D
2 A, C and E
3 B, C and D
4 B, C and E

78. Which one of the following is valid with respect to one step growth experiment developed by Ellis and Delbruck in 1939?
1 The reproduction of large phage population is synchronised.
2 A culture is directly developed by inoculation of bacterial colony from the agar plate into the liquid medium.
3 Involves only a single step of over night culture development follow inoculation of a fresh medium with 1% inoculum.
4 Only a single carbon source such as glucose is used in the medium.

79. Given below are a few statements about nuclear transport
A. RanGTP levels are higher in the nucleus than the cytoplasm.
B. Nuclear import receptors can shuttle between the nucleus and cytoplasm.
C. NTF2 transports RanGDP into the cytosol.
D. Export of *m*RNA is not directly dependent on Ran.
E. *t*RNA and *mi*RNA export is mediated by exportins.

Which one of the following combinations contain all correct statements?
1 A, B, C and D
2 B, C and D
3 A, B, D and E
4 A, C and E

80. During cytokinesis, a small GTPase, RhoA, localizes to the equatorial membrane above the spindle midzone. The localisation/activity of RhoA is potentially modulated by
A. RhoGEF Ect2
B. Aurora B kinase
C. PLK1 kinase
D. MKLP1 kinesin
E. ATM and ATR

Which one of the following combination contains all correct statements?
1 A, B and D
2 A, B, C and D
3 B, C, D and E
4 A, C and D

81. Cellular actin levels can be as high as 100-400 μM of this, unpolymerised actin concentration can be as much as 50 – 200 μ M. However, the critical concentration for actin polymerisation *in-vitro* is about 0.2 μM. Some of the following proteins inhibit polymerization of actin in cells.
A. Thymosin-β4
B. Capping protein Cap Z
C. Tropomodulin
D. XMAP215

Which one of the following options lists all inhibitors?
1 A, B and C
2 B, C, D and A
3 C, D and A
4 D, A and B

82. To delineate the steps in endoplasmic reticulum (ER) transport, *a* PhD student homogenized pancreatic acinar cells to isolate microsomes, which retain most of the biochemical properties of the ER. For this experiment, students has planned a number of controls as mentioned below.
A. Treat one set of microsomes first with detergent and then with protease.
B. Treat one set of microsomes with protease only.
C. Treat one set of microsomes with micrococcal nuclease.
D. Treat one set of microsomes with detergent only.

Select the option that represents the best combination of the controls.
1 A, B and D
2 B, C and D
3 A and C
4 B and D

83. Following statements were made about imprinting in the human genome.
A. Imprinting control centre (IC) harbors part of the SNRPN gene.
B. Imprinting of genes in an individual cannot be tissue specific.
C. Sperms and eggs exhibit identical pattern of genome methylation, except in the sex chromosomes.
D. At imprinted loci, expression depends on the parental origin.

Select the option with all the correct statements.
1 A and D
2 B and D
3 A and C
4 B and C

84. Mitochondrial protein synthesis is of prokaryotic origin. Following statements are being made about the ribosomes from bacteria and mitochondria.
A. The bacterial ribosome consists of small and large submits of 30 S and 50 S respectively, whereas in mitochondria of mammals, these subunits are 28 S and 39 S.
B. In the bacterial ribosomes the RNA : Protein ratio is about 2 : 1 whereas in mitochondria ribosomes, this ratio is usually 1 : 2.
C. Both the bacterial and mitochondrial ribosomes consist of 30s and 50s subunits.
D. Both the bacterial and mitochondrial ribosomes consist of RNA and protein in the ratio of 1 : 1.

Choose the option that represents all the correct statements.
1 A and B
2 B and C
3 C and D
4 A and D

85. Given below are few statements about the λ infection cycle
A. Competition between C I and C II gene product determines the establishment of lysogeny *versus* lysis.
B. CI binds O_R 1first while cro binds to O_R3 first.
C. Cro binding to O_R represses CI transcription.
D. Rich medium favours lytic cycle because C II is protected from cellular protease.

Which one of the following options represents all correct statements?
1 B and C
2 A and B
3 C and D
4 A and C

86. *E. coli* mutants isolated from a genetic screen showed following classes of mutations
A. Point mutations in *lacI*.
B. Deletions immediately downstream of the transcription start site of the *lac*ZYA *m*RNA.
C. Duplications of part or whole of *lac*Y.
D. Duplications of part or whole of *lac*A.

Choose the option which is likely to result in constitutive expression of the *lac* operon?
1 Both A and B
2 Both B and C
3 Both C and D
4 Only A

87. For *Escherichia coli* chromosomal DNA replication, which one of the following statements is true?
1 DNA polymerase I is the main polymerase required for DNA replication
2 DNA polymerase I though identified originally by Kornberg as the one responsible for replication, is not important for the DNA replication process
3 Requirement of DNA polymerase I is in the context of removal of RNA primer needed for DNA synthesis, and then fill in the same with DNA equivalent.
4 DNA polymerase I is the primary enzyme for error prone DNA synthesis in response to SOS

88. Following observation were made about variations among genomes of eukaryotic organisms:
A. Single nucleotide polymorphisms are the numerically most abundant type of genetic variants.
B. Both, interspersed and tandem repeated sequences can show polymorphic variation.
C. Mitotic recombination between mispaired repeats causes change in copy number and generates minisatellite diversity in population.
D. Smaller variable segments in the genome can be identified by paired end mapping technique.
Select the option with all correct statements
1 A, B and C 2 A, C and D
3 B, C and D 4 A, B and D

89. The following statements are made with respect to DNA replication.
A. Comptothecin causes intra-strand and inter-strand cross links in DNA, loading to stalling of replication forks.
B. Prevention of reinitiation of DNA replication during the same cell cycle is mediated by regulating the loading of the interior complex ORC.
C. A glu→ ala mutation in the nucleotide building pocket of DNA polyemrase III could lead to the incorporation of ribonucleotides in the extending DNA chain.
D. A mutation in the gene encoding. Topoisomerase II could lead to entanglement of DNA daughter strands during replication.
Which one of the following options represents all correct statements?
1 A and B 2 B and C
3 C and D 4 B, C and D

90. The population that is at highest risk against influenza infection should be immunized annually. Which one of the following is the most important reason for this?
1 Influenza virus can changes its surface antigen very frequently.
2 Influenza virus has a very short incubation period.
3 Influenza virus has a resonably longer incubation period.
4 Repeated immunisation interfers with the differentiation of plasma cells from memory cells thereby decreasing levels of neutralising antibody.

91. Localised increases in the cytosolic level of free Ca^{2+} are critical to its function as second messenger. Calmodulin, a small cytosolic protein, mediates many cellular effects of Ca^{2+}. Which of the following is not correct for Ca^{2+}-calmodulin interaction?
1 Each calmodulin molecule binds six Ca^{2+} ions in a cooperative fashion
2 Binding of Ca^{2+} causes calmodulin to undergo a conformational change
3 Since binding of Ca^{2+} is cooperative, a small change in the level cytosolic Ca^{2+} leads to a large change in the level of active calmodulin.
4 One of the many enzymes activated by Ca^{2+}-calmodulin is cAMP phosphodiesterase, which degrades cAMP and links Ca^{2+} and cAMP signaling.

92. Some cellular and extracellular proteins are enlisted in List I and their typical characteristics are enlisted in List II

	List I		List II
A.	Nidogen	I.	In human genome, one gene of this protein is present but many different isoforms are there due to alternative splicing
B.	Fibronectin	II.	An intermediate filament protein that is typically expressed in epithelial and mescenchymal cells
C.	Integrin	III.	One of the principal structural proteins of basal laminae.
D.	Vimentin	IV.	Heterodimer of α and β subunit and binds to extracellular matrix proteins.

Which one of the following is the most appropriate match?
1 A-I, B-II, C-III, D-IV 2 A-II, B-III, C-IV, D-I
3 A-III, B-I, C-IV, D-II 4 A-II, B-IV, C-I, D-III

93. Following statements have been proposed for cancer cells and cancer stem cells :
A. Cancer cells mostly have mutations whereas cancer stem cells do not.
B. Cancer cells divide to form two different populations of cells whereas cancer stem cells do not divide.
C. Cancer stem cells can undergo self-renewal whereas cancer cells cannot.
D. Cancer cells are predominantly resistant to chemotherapy and radiation.
E. Cancer stem cells are found only in the bone marrow and placenta.
Which one of the following combination of statements is correct?
1 A and C 2 A and B 3 C and E 4 C and D

94. Which of the following is/are associated with the presentation of endogenous antigens by Class 1 MHC molecule by an Antigen Presenting Cell (APC), given the condition that there is no cross-presentation of antigens by the APC?
1 TAP1 and TAP2 proteins only
2 Invariant chain (Ii)
3 Proteosome-like subunits LMP2 and LMP7 only
4 TAP1, TAP2 proteins and proteosome-like subunits LMP2, LMP 7 TAP1, TAP2

95. Which one of the following statements is not correct regarding the tetrapod limb development?
1 As the limb grows outward, the stylopod forms first, then the zeugopod and the autopod is formed last. Each phase is characterised by a specific pattern of Hox gene expression.
2 The zone of polarising activity (ZPA) is maintained by the interaction of the FGFs from the AER and Shh expressed from the mesenchyme.
3 Although cell death in the limb is necessary for the formation of digits and joints, it is never mediated by the BMPs, which is only responsible for differentiating mesenchyme cells into cartilage.
4 The dorsal-ventral axis is formed in part by the expression of Wnt7a in the dorsal portion of the limb ectoderm, which maintains expression level of Shh in the ZPA and FgF4 in the posterior AER.

96. The dorsal protein involved in generating the dorsal-ventral (DV) polarity in *Drosophila*.
The following statements were made regarding the activity of the dorsal protein in establishing the DV polarity.
A. In embryos that lack Gurken protein, the Dorsal protein is not translocated to the nucleus of the follicle cells which then causes ventralisation of the embryo.

B. Though Dorsal protein acts as a morphogen, it is found throughout the syncytial blastoderm of the early *Drosophila* embryo.
C. In embryos that lack *Cactus* protein the dorsal protein can be found in the nucleus of cells with a ventral fate.
D. If the dorsal protein is blocked from entering the nucleus, the genes responsibile for specifying dorsal cell types are not transcribed.

Which of the above statements are correct?

1 A and B 2 B and C
3 C and D 4 A and C

97. Following are certain statements regarding root growth and differentiation in plants :
A. Root hair, endodermis, xylem and phloem reach maturation in elongation zone of a developing root.
B. The root epidermal cells that are incapable of forming root hairs are called atrichoblasts.
C. Quiescent center is present just above root cap.
D. In Arabidopsis, an auxin transporter (ABCB4) plays a role in root hair emergence by maintaining intracellular auxin concentration.

Which one of the following combination of statements is correct?

1 A, B and C 2 B, C and D
3 A, C and D 4 A, B and D

98. Match the terms used in vertebrates limb development in List I with their descriptions in List II.

	List I		List II
A.	EMT	I.	The cells found within the most posterior region of the limb bud.
B.	Mesenchyme	II.	The thickening of ectoderm at the apex of the developing limb.
C.	AER	III.	A loosely organised, mainly mesodermal embryonic tissue.
D.	Prgress zone	IV.	Epithelial cells making up the mesoderm of the early somatopleure undergo this transition and get included in mesenchyme cell pool.
E.	ZPA	V.	The proliferature mesenchyme that fuels limb bud growth.
F.	Autopod	VI.	The distral part of tetrapod limb.

Which one of the following combination of the statement is correct?

1 A-IV, B-III, C-II, D-V, E-I, F-VI 2 A-I, B-II, C-III, D-IV, E-V, F-VI
3 A-V, B-IV, C-II, D-VI, E-III, F-I 4 A-II, B-V, C-I, D-III, E-IV, F-VI

99. Given below are some of the statements in connection with neural tube formation in vertebrates :
A. In primary neurulation, the cells surrounding the neural plate direct the neural plate cells to proliferate, invaginate and separate from the surface ectoderm to form an underlying hollow tube.
B. In secondary neurulation the neural tube arises from the aggregation of mesenchyme cells into a solid cord that subsequently forms cavities to create a hollow tube.
C. In birds primary neurulation generates the neural tube from anterior up to the hindlimb developing region.
D. In mammals, secondary neurulation beings at the level of sacral vertebrae.
E. Anencephaly results when a failure to close the neural tube occurs resulting in the forebrain remaining in contact with amniotic fluid.

Which one of the following options gives all correct statements?

1 A, B, C, D and E 2 Only A
3 B and E 4 C, D and E

100. The following demonstrates proposed functions of different genes which determine the decision to become either trophoblast or Inner Cell Mass (ICM) blastomere during early mammalian development

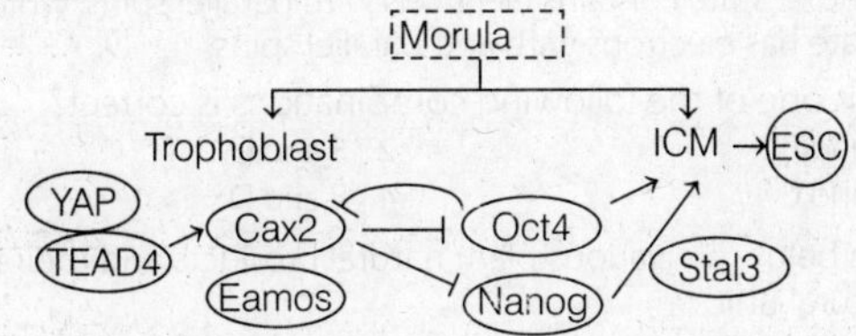

Based on the above figure, which one of the following assumptions is correct?

1 The interplay between Cdx2 and Oct4 can influence the formation of ICM
2 The ICM would form even if expression of Oct4 was inhibited.
3 YAP and TEAD4 are upstream components of Cdx2 and can be inhibited by Nanog.
4 The expression of Stat3 is optional for maintaining pluripotency of the ICM.

101. Jasmonate is known to inhibit root growth, while auxin facilitates root growth. Upon infection with pathogenic bacteria that produce coronatine, we may expect the following in plants
A. Upregulation of *COI-1* gene and inhibition of root growth.
B. Upregulation of *AuxI-1* gene and inhibition of root growth.
C. Inhibition of *AuxI-1* gene and promotion of root growth.
D. Inhibition of *COI-1* gene and promotion of root growth.

Which one of the following is correct?

1 A, B and C 2 Only A
3 Only B 4 Only C

102. Following are certain statements with regard to plant respiration
A. Metabolism of glucose into pyruvate through glycolysis generates NADH and not NADPH.
B. Metabolism of glucose through oxidative pentose phosphate cycle does not produce NADPH.
C. Cyanide forms a complex with haem iron of cytochrome oxidase leading to prevention of change in valency, which in turn stops electron transport in the respiratory chain.
D. Alternative oxidase is insensitive to cyanide and has higher K_m than that of cytochrome oxidase.

Which one of the following combinations is correct?

1 A, B and C 2 B, C and D
3 B and D 4 A, C and D

103. Blue light receptor cry 1 binds to COP1 and SPA1 complex by interacting with C-terminal region of cry1 (CCT) in a light dependent manner and regulates photomorphogenesis *via* transcription factor HY5. Read the following statements
A. cry 1 binds to COP1 and SPA1 complex leading to degradation of HY5.
B. cry 1 binds to COP1 and SPA1 complex and prevents degradation of HY5.
C. CCT is overexpressed and the plants are kept in dark.
D. CCT is overexpressed and the plants are kept in light.

Which of the following combination of above statements will result in photomorphogenesis?

1 Only A 2 Only B
3 A, B and C 4 B, C and D

104. After absorbing light, chlorophyll molecules in green plants exist in singlet and triplet states. Following are certain statements on singlet and triplet states of chlorophyll molecules

A. Singlet state is short lived compared to triplet state.
B. Singlet state is long lived compared to triplet state.
C. Singlet state contains electrons with anti-parallel spins, while triplet state has electrons with parallel spins.
D. Singlet state contains electrons with parallel spins, while triplet state has electrons with anti-parallel spins.

Which one of the following combinations is correct?

1 A and B 2 B and C
3 A and C 4 B and D

105. Given below are various plant natural products and their basic structural unit.

	List I (Natural products)		List II (Basic unit)
A.	Phenolics	I.	Five-carbon isoprene unit
B.	Alkaloids	II.	Glucose unit attached by O – β – D glycosyl linkage
C.	Terpenoids	III.	Nitrogen containing
D.	Cyanogenic glycoside	IV.	Aromatic arene ring with OH group

Which of the following options represents the correct match of natural product and the basic unit

1 A-IV, B-I, C-III, D-II 2 A-III, B-II, C-I, D-IV
3 A-III, B-I, C-IV, D-II 4 A-IV, B-III, C-I, D-II

106. The mechanism of thermogenesis in Brown Adipose Tissue (BAT) in cold are described in the following proposed statements.

A. A thermogenic uncoupling protein, UCP1 helps in the heat production in BAT.
B. Nor-epinephrine secretion from sympathetic nerve endings in BAT is decreased.
C. Lipolysis is increased by low level of nor-epinephrine in BAT.
D. A high content of mitochondria in BAT helps in oxidation of fatty acids.
E. Oxidation produces much heat as ATP synthase activity is low.

Which one of the following options represents the combination of correct statements?

1 A, B and C 2 A, D and E
3 B, C and D 4 B, D and E

107. The pressure in the 'space' between lungs and chest wall is known as intrapleural pressure. The following statements are related to the intrapleural pressure at different phases of respiration *A* . At the end of quiet expiration the tendency of the lung to recoil from chest wall is balanced by the recoil of chest wall in opposite direction and intrapleural pressure is subatmospheric.

B. At the start of inspiration the intrapleural pressure is subatmospheric.
C. The intrapleural pressure becomes more negative during inspiration.
D. The intrapleural pressure attains value above atmospheric pressure during expiration.
E. The intrapleural pressure becomes positive (relative to atmospheric pressure) during strong inspiratory efforts.

Which one of the following combinations is correct?

1 A, B and C 2 B, C and D
3 C, D and E 4 A, C and D

108. Haemoglobin (Hb) transports CO_2 in venous blood as carbamates. The following statements refer to the formation of these carbamates :

A. CO_2 interacts with amino terminal nitrogens of Hb polypeptide chains.
B. CO_2 interacts with carboxyl terminal carbons of Hb polypeptide chains.
C. Carbamates helps formation of salt bridges between α and β -chains of Hb.
D. Carbamates helps formation of disulphide bridges between α and β -chains of Hb.

Which one of the following options is a combination of correct statements?

1 A and C
2 B and D
3 B and C
4 A and D

109. Following statements are given for the ovarian hormones :

A. 17 β-estradiol, estrone and estriol are naturally occurring oestrogens.
B. They are 18 C steroids which do not have methyl group at 10th position.
C. They are 21 C steroids which have methyl group at 10th position.
D. They are primarily synthesised by granulosa cells of the ovarian follicles.
E. Their biosynthesis does not depend on the enzyme aromatase.

Which one of the following options represents the combination of correct statements?

1 A, B, and C 2 A, B and D
3 B, C and D 4 C, D and E

110. Below are given a set of statements for the glucocorticoid hormones :

A. They bind to cell surface receptors and influence stress adaptation.
B. They bind to intracellular receptors and influence stress adaptation.
C. They inhibit ACTH secretion from anterior pituitary.
D. Prolonged treatment with glucocorticoids lead to atrophic and unresponsive adrenals.
E. Their secretion does not show circadian variations.

Which one of the following combination of the statements is correct?

1 A, C and E 2 B, C and D
3 C, D and E 4 A, D and E

111. The pedigree given below represents the genotype at four different loci for the children in generation III.

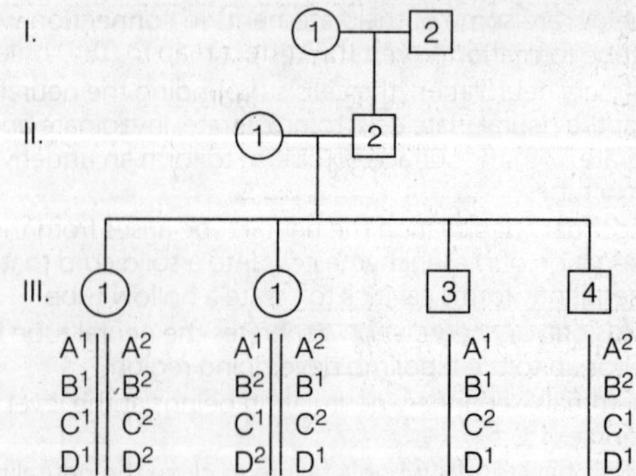

Which one of the give genotypes is likely to represent the genotype of individual II-I?

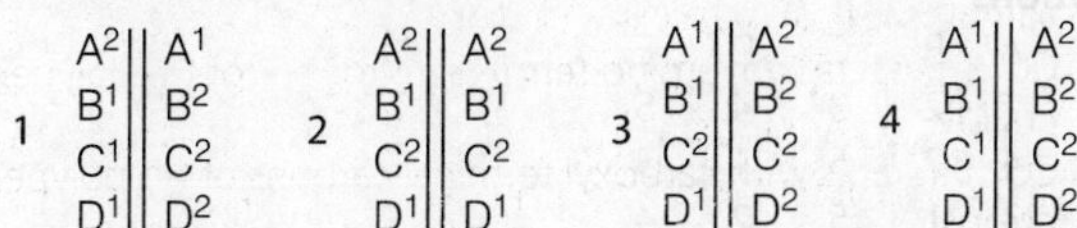

112. A *Drosophila* mutant (line A) with vestigial wings is isolated in a laboratory. The vestigial wing phenotype was observed to be recessive and mapped to gene X. Three other laboratories also isolated vestigial mutants, called line B, C and D. In order to test if the mutation in lines B-D also mapped to gene 'X', the following crosses were made and phenotype of F_1 progeny observed.

Cross	F1 progeny (wing morphology)
A × B	Vestigial
A × B	Vestigial
A × D	Normal
B × C	Vestigial
B × D	Normal
C × D	Normal

Based on the above identify the line(s) which is most likely NOT to have a mutation in gene 'X'.

1 Both lines B and C
2 Line C
3 Line D
4 Both lines B and D

113. 22 transduction was used to map the fadL gene. The result of two-factor crosses between fadL and two linked markers, purF and aroC are shown below.

Donor	Recipient	Recombinants: Selected marker	Recombinants: Second marker	Numbers obtained
fadL purF+	fadL+ purF	purF+	fadL	200
			fadL+	800
fadL aroC+	fadL+ aroC	aroc+	fadL	400
			fadL+	600
aroC+ purF	aroC purF+	aroC+	purF	500
			purF+	500

Which one of the following is the correct map for the three genes?

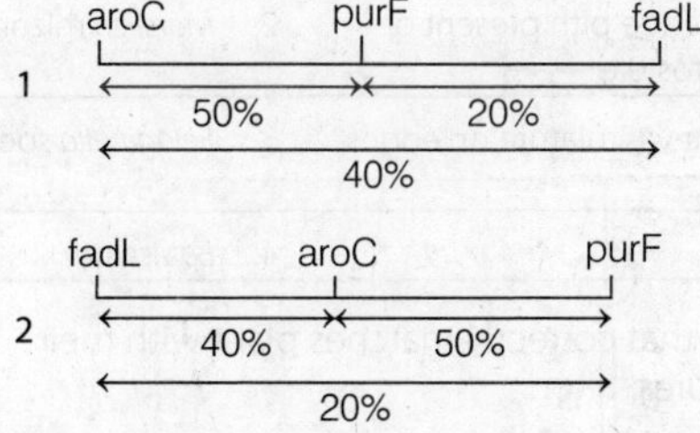

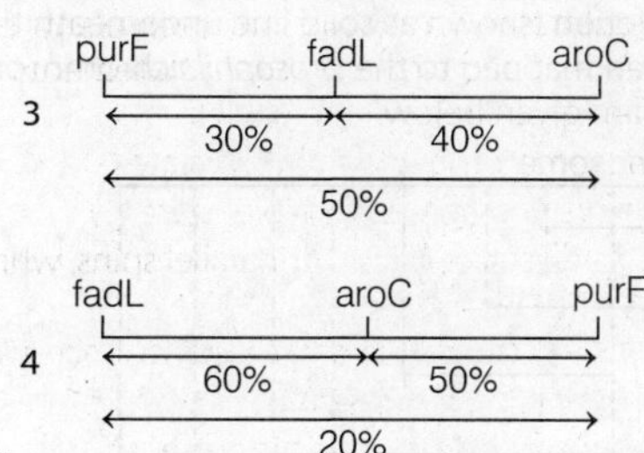

114. Two yellow mice with straight hair were crossed and the following progeny was obtained

1/2 yellow, straight hair
1/6 yellow, fuzzy hair
1/4 gray, straight hair
1/12 gray, fuzzy hair

In order to provide genetic explanation for the results and assign genotypes to the parents and progeny of this cross, the following statements were given

A. The 6 : 2 : 3 : 1ratio obtained here indicates recessive epistasis.
B. This cross concerns two independent characteristics-body colour and type of hair.
C. The deviation of dihybrid ratio from 9 : 3 : 3 : 1to 6 : 2 : 3 : 1may be due to one of the genes being a recessive lethal.
D. The lethal allele is associated with straight hair.

The most appropriate combination of statements to provide genetic explanation for this result is

1 B and C
2 Only A
3 B, C and D
4 A, C and D

115. A family was examined for a given trait which is represented in the pedigree shown below. Further, the degree of expression of the trait is highly variable among members of the family; some are only slightly affected while others developed severe symptoms at an early age.

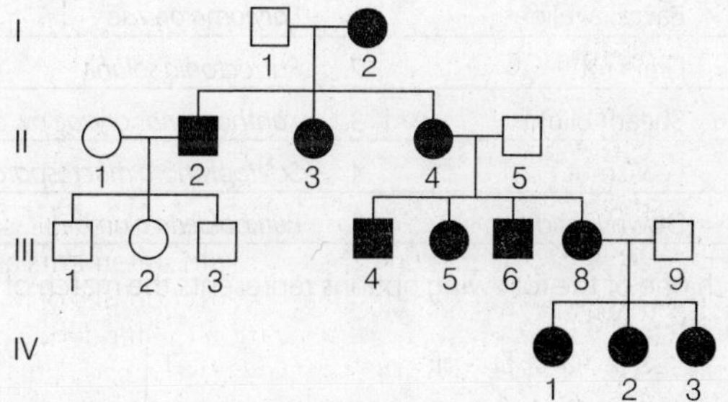

The following statements are made to explain the pattern of inheritance shown in the pedigree

A. X-linked dominant mutation.
B. X-linked recessive mutation.
C. Mitochondrial inheritance.
D. Variable expression can be due to heteroplasty.

The best possible explanation for this inheritance is

1 A and D
2 C and D
3 Only B
4 Only A

116. The location of six deletion (shown as solid line underneath the chromosome) has been mapped to the *Drosophila* chromosome as shown in the diagram given below:

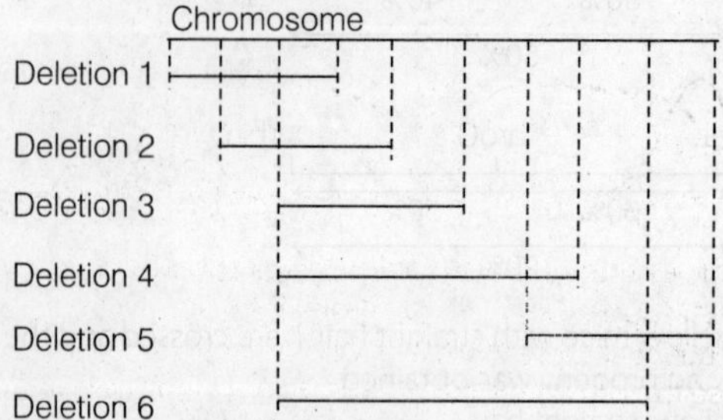

The recessive mutations a, b, c, d, e, f and g are known to be located in the region of deletions, but the order of mutations on the chromosome is not known. When flies homozygous for the recessive mutations are crossed with flies homozygous for the deletion, the following results were obtained, where the letter 'm' represents a mutant phenotype and '+' represents the wild type.

	Mutations						
Deletion	**a**	**b**	**c**	**d**	**e**	**f**	**g**
1	+	m	m	m	+	+	+
2	+	+	m	m	+	+	+
3	+	+	+	m	m	+	+
4	m	+	+	m	m	+	+
5	m	+	+	+	+	m	m
6	m	+	+	m	m	m	+e

The relative order of the seven mutant genes on chromosome is

1 bceafgd
2 bcdfgea
3 bcdeafg
4 cdeagfb

117. Given below are the names of diseases caused in rice in column X and names of the disease-causing organisms in column Y.

	Column X		Column Y
A.	Bacterial blight	1.	*Entyloma oryzae*
B.	Grain rot	2.	*Rhizoctonia solani*
C.	Sheath blight	3.	*Xanthomonas oryzae pv. oryzae*
D.	Leaf smut	4.	*Sclerophthora macrospora*
E.	Downy mildew	5.	*Burkholderia glumae*

Which one of the following options represents the match of columns X and Y.

	A	B	C	D	E
1	2	1	5	4	3
2	3	4	2	5	1
3	4	3	1	2	5
4	3	5	2	1	4

118. The table given below lists the conservation areas and the major group of organisms that they are best known for

	Column X (Conservation areas)		Column Y (Organisms)
A.	Hemis National Park	1.	Orchids
B.	National Chambal Sanctuary	2.	Gharial
C.	Nokrek National Park	3.	Nepenthes
D.	Sessa Sanctuary	4.	Snow leopard
E.	Baghmara Wildlife Sanctuary	5.	Endemic citrus species

Which on of the following options represents the correct match of column X and Y.

Options

	A	B	C	D	E
1	1	2	3	4	5
2	4	2	5	1	3
3	3	1	5	2	4
4	5	4	3	2	1

119. The table given below lists the morphological features and groups of plants.

	List-I (Plant group)		List-II (Morphological characters)
A.	Liverwort	1.	Unicellular rhizoids
		2.	Multicellular rhizoids
		3.	Presence of pyrenoids
B.	Moss	4.	Stomata on sporophyte
		5.	Dominant gametophyte

Which one of the following options represents the correct match between the two columns?

1 A-1, 3 and 5; B-2, 3 and 5
2 A-1, 3 and 4; B-2 and 4
3 A-2 and 5; B-1 and 3
4 A-1 and 5; B = 2, 4 and 5

120. The terms expressing some of the development events or specific body structures are given in Column X and the names of animals that are associated with them in Column Y

	Column X		Column Y
A.	Torsion	1.	Star fish
B.	Metagenesis	2.	*Obelia*
C.	Apolysis	3.	*Taenia*
D.	Pedicellaria	4.	Apple snail

The correct match of the following in column X with the name of animals in column Y is

	A	B	C	D
1	1	2	3	4
2	4	2	3	1
3	3	1	2	4
4	2	4	1	3

121. The table lists characteristics anatomical features and names of plants.

	Anatomical features		Plants
A.	Prostele, xylem core surrounded by phloem	1.	*Lycopodium*
B.	Siphonostele, centre pith present or medulated protostele	2.	*Marsilea* rhizome
C.	Eustele, conjoint vasculature on edges of the pith	3.	*Selaginella* species
		4.	*Equisetum*

Choose the option that correctly matches plant with their characteristics features.

	A	B	C
1	3	2	4
2	1	3	4
3	3	1	2
4	1	2	4

122. The table given below provides a list of female gametophyte features and plant genera

	Female gametophyte		Plant genera
A.	Monosporic, 8 nucleate	1.	*Allium*
B.	Monosporic, 4 nucleate	2.	*Oenothera*
C.	Bisporic, 8 nucleate	3.	*Peperomia*
D.	Tetrasporic, 16 nucleate	4.	*Polygonum*

Which one of the following options correctly matches the plant genera to female gametophyte features?

	A	B	C	D		A	B	C	D
1	4	3	1	2	2	4	2	1	3
3	1	2	4	3	4	4	2	3	1

123. The following are a few statements on shade leaves vis-a-vis, sun leaves in three species.

A. Higher amount of chlorophyll per dry weight.
B. Lower density of stomata.
C. Thicker leaves.
D. Lower rates of dark respiration per unit area.

Which one of the following combinations of above statements is correct?

1 A and D
2 B and C
3 A, B and D
4 B and D

124. The diagram below depicts energy flow within a single trophic level where 1 = amount ingested NA = amount not assimilated. *R* = respiration and P_n = Biomass production at trophic level.

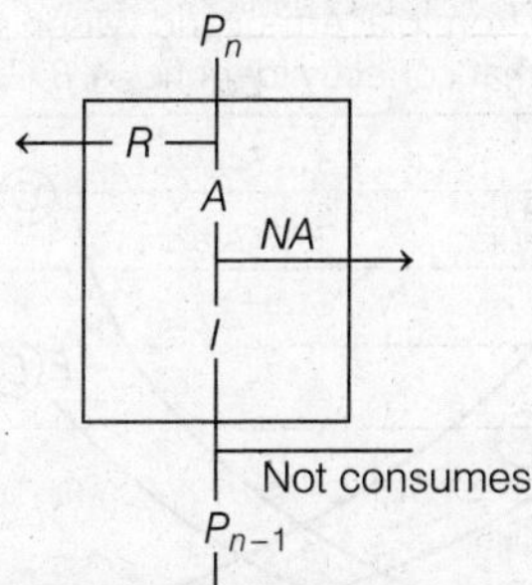

Which one of the following options represents correct values for P_n, *NA*, *R* and 1 in kcal respectively, if P_{n-1} = 1000 kCal/1/P_{n-1} = 20% *A* / 1 = 35% and P_n / *A* = 20%.

1 56 14 130 200
2 14 130 56 200
3 200 130 56 14
4 56 130 200 14

125. The following graph shows the change in proportion of biomass in foliage (leaves), branch and stemwood (bole) for a species as a function of DBH (diameter at 1.5 m above ground)

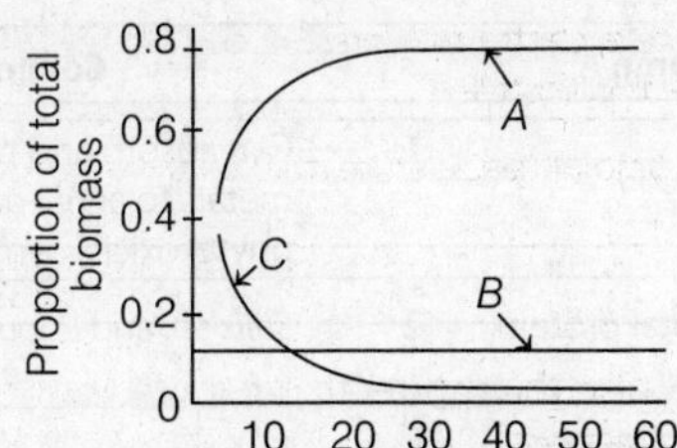

Which one of the following options correctly matches the curves (A, B and C) with stemwood, foliage and branch, respectively.

1 A, B and C
2 A, C and B
3 B, C and A
4 B, A and C

126. The graphs given below show the possible behaviour of two species over the course of succession.

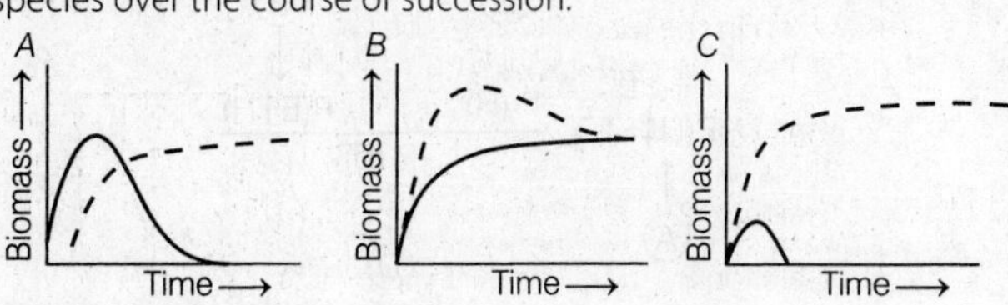

Possible effects observed during succession are

I. Total suppression
II. Convergence
III. Sequential succession

Choose the correct option matching the graphs with the possible effect.

	A	B	C		A	B	C
1	I	II	III	2	II	III	I
3	III	II	I	4	III	I	II

127. Consider the following graphs for per capita growth rate $\left(\frac{1}{N}\right)\left(\frac{dN}{dt}\right)$ as a function of population density.

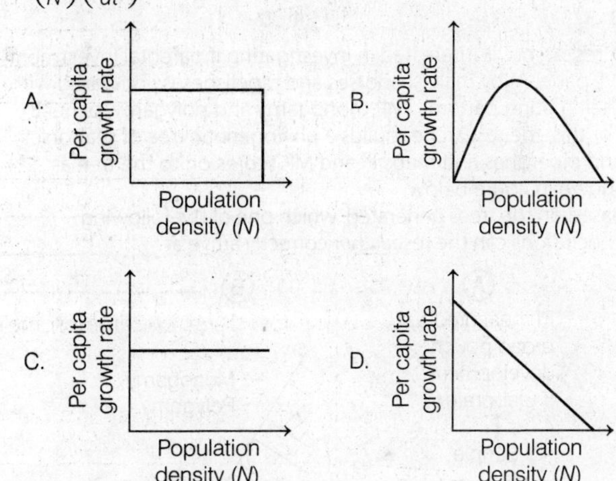

Which one of the plots correctly depicts strong Allel effect in a population?

1 A
2 B
3 C
4 D

128. In the table below, column I describes movements of organisms and column II describes the type of movement.

	Column-I		Column-II
A.	A silk moth flies at an angle perpendicular to the direction of the wind to pick up a scent trail.	1.	Mnemotaxis
B.	Bacteria burrow down into mud in the Northern hemisphere in response to the earth's magnetic field.	2.	Klinotaxis
C.	A girl reaches her school using a pharmacy and a book shop as landmarks.	3.	Magnetotaxis
D.	*Planaria* moves towards the direction of higher concentration of food by comparing the gradient of stimuli around it.	4.	Menotaxis

Which one of the following options represents the correct match of column I with column II?

	A	B	C	D		A	B	C	D
1	4	3	1	2	2	4	3	2	1
3	1	3	4	2	4	1	2	3	4

129. The following represents an equation for Bayesian statistics?

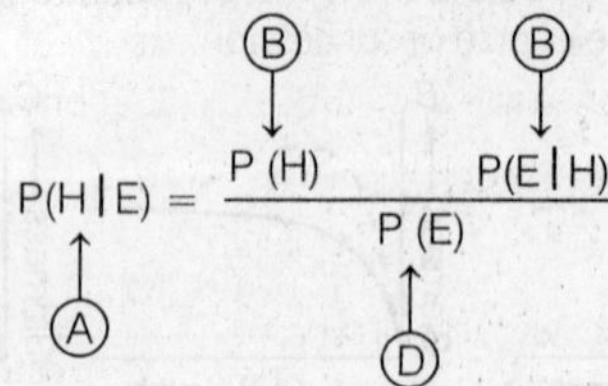

Which one of the following options correctly represents *A*, *B*, *C* and *D* in the above equation?

1 *A*-Evidence, *B*-Posterior probability, *C*-Likelihood, *D*-Prior probability
2 *A*-Likelihood, *B*-Prior probability, *C*-Posterior probability, *D*-Evidence
3 *A*-Posterior probability, *B*-Prior probability, *C*-Likelihood, *D*-Evidence
4 *A*-Prior probability, *B*-Evidence, *C*-Posterior probability, *D*-Likelihood

130. In a population, that is in Hardy Weinberg equilibrium, the frequency of the recessive homozygote genotype of trait *q* is 0.04. The percentage of individuals homozygous for the dominant allele is

1 64 2 40
3 32 4 16

131. A researcher is interested in investigating if parental investment (Pl. panel A) by male seahorses and pipefishes is correlated with their mating patterns (MP-monogamy and polygamy, panel B). For this, the researcher builds a phylogenetic tree of seahorses and pipefishes and maps PI and MP scores on to the tree as shown in figure below.
Based on the trees generated, which one of the following conclusions can the researcher correctly arrive at?

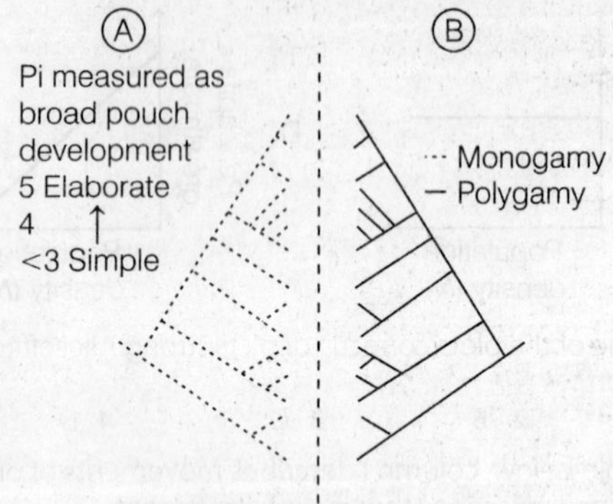

1 Polygamy is correlated with simpler brood pouches
2 Monogamy is not correlated with elaborate brood pouches
3 Monogamy is correlated with elaborate brood pouches
4 Polygamy is correlated with elaborate brood pouches

132. Given below are graphs depicting two possible dynamics of gene duplication events over a period of time during genome evolution.

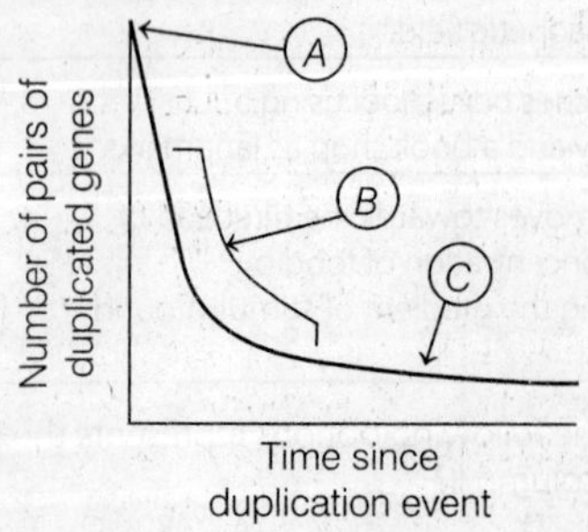

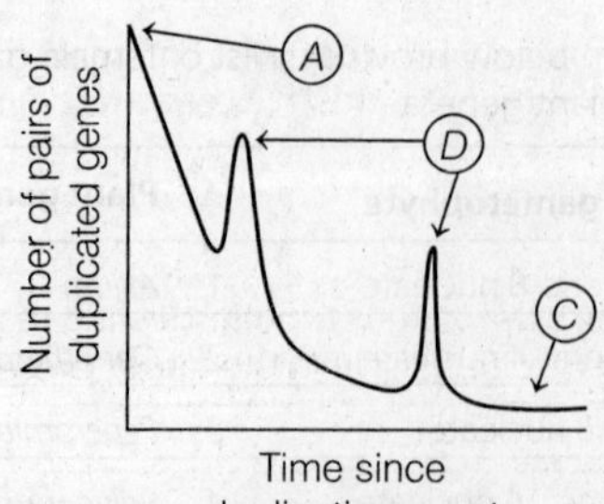

Based on the above figures, which one of the following options correctly represents the identity of *A*, *B*, *C* and *D*?

1 *A*-Gene duplication event, *B*-Random loss of duplicated genes, *C*-Remaining pairs of duplicated genes, *D*-Additional gene duplication events
2 A-remaining pairs of duplicated genes, B-gene duplication event, C-random loss of duplicate genes D-additional gene duplication events
3 A-additional gene duplication events, B-Random loss of duplicated genes, C-Remaining pairs if duplicated genes, D-Gene duplication event
4 A-Random loss of duplicated genes, B-Additional gene duplication events, C-Gene duplication event, D-Remaining pairs of duplicated genes

133. A researcher working on Island biogeography mapped how isolation controlled immigration (I), and area-controlled extinction (E), will act on number of species present on the Island. He forgot to label the size of the Islands (small or large) and the location of the Islands (near or far) on the graph.
Using information from MacArthur and Wilson's equilibrium theory, select the option that correctly identifies *A*, *B*, *C* and *D* in figure above.

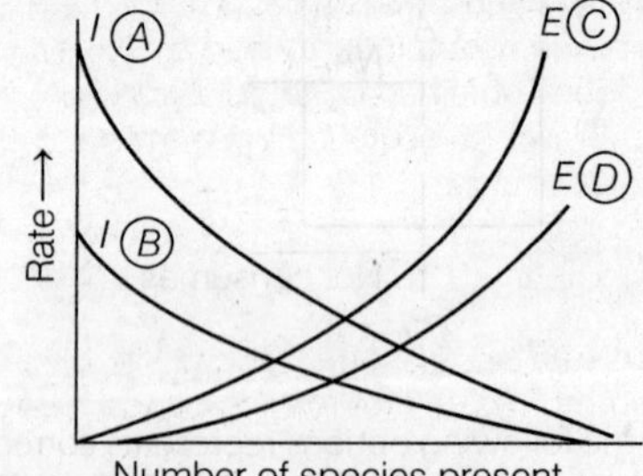

1 *A*-Large, *B*-Small, *C*-Near, *D*-Far
2 *A*-Small, *B*-Large, *C*-Far, *D*-Near
3 *A*-Near, *B*-Far, *C*-Small, *D*-Large
4 *A*-Far, *B*-Near, *C*-Large, *D*-Small

134. Given below are some terms and concepts related to phytoremediation in Column A and B.

	Column A		Column B
A.	Excluders	1.	Can absorb and transfer heavy metals to aerial parts without phytotoxicity symptoms
B.	Heavy metal protein transporter	2.	*Salix* sp. and *Populus* sp.
C.	Hyperaccumulators	3.	Transgenesis
D.	High biomass, non-accumulators	4.	Can restrict heavy metal ions to the roots and detoxify them

Which one of the following options represents the most appropriate match of all terms/concepts in columns A and B?

	A	B	C	D		A	B	C	D
1	2	4	1	3	2	3	4	2	1
3	2	3	4	1	4	4	3	1	2

135. Given below are the various protein clearing reagents (List I) and their recognition sites (List II) in the target protein.

	List-I		List-II
A.	CNBr	1.	-Asp-Ala-
B.	Trypsin	2.	-Phe-Ala-
C.	Caspase	3.	-Met-Ala-
D.	Chymotrypsin	4.	-Arg-Gly-

Which one of the following options represents the correct combination of items?

	A	B	C	D		A	B	C	D
1	3	2	1	4	2	4	2	1	3
3	4	1	2	3	4	3	4	1	2

136. Given below are few terms related to map based sequencing of genomes.

A. Partial digestion with restriction enzymes.
B. Assembly of contigs.
C. Pulsed field gel electrophoresis.
D. Cloning in cosmids/YACs/BACs.
E. Sub-cloning in sequencing.

Which one of the following options represents the correct order of steps (based on the above terms) in map based sequencing?

1 C-B-D-E-A 2 C-A-D-B-E 3 E-A-B-D-C 4 A-C-B-D-E

137. A T_0 transgenic plant contains two unlinked copies of the T-DNA of which, one is functional and the other is silenced. Segregation of the transgenic to non-transgenic phenotype would occur in a ...(i)... ratio in progeny obtained by backcrossing and in a ...(ii)... ratio in F_1 progeny obtained by self-pollination.

Fill in the blanks with the correct combination of (i) and (ii) from the options given below

1 (i)—3 : 1and (ii)—15 : 1 2 (i)—1: 1and (ii)—3 : 1
3 (i)—3 : 1and (ii)—3 : 1 4 (ii)—1: 1and (ii)—15 : 1

138 Column X lists two diseases and Column Y lists name of proteins which are commonly used for routine clinical diagnosis of these dieases.

	Column X		Column Y
A.	Myocardial Infarction	1.	Amylase
B.	Pancreatitis	2.	Creatine kinase
		3.	Lipase
		4.	Troponin

Find out the correct combination

1 A-2, B-1, A-4, B-3 2 A-3, B-4, A-2, B-1
3 A-1, B-2, A-3, B-4 4 A-4, B-3, A-1, B-2

139. A culture was started by inoculating the medium with 100 cells having a generation time of 2 hours. Assuming the culture grows in ideal synchrony for atleast 24 hours. What will be the number of cells in the culture at 2 hours and 9 hours?

1 2.0×10^2 cells, 1.6×10^3 cells, respectively
2 2.0×10^2 cells, 2.4×10^3 cells, respectively
3 2.0×10^4 cells, 3.2×10^3 cells, respectively
4 2.0×10^4 cells, 1.6×10^8 cells, respectively

140. From the steps listed below, some are used to evaluate the goodness of fit using the chi-square test.

A. The mean, variance and standard deviation are calculated
B. Variance calculated using $\dfrac{\Sigma(x_1 - \bar{x})^2}{n-1}$
C. Test statistic calculated using $\dfrac{\Sigma(\text{observed} - \text{expected})^2}{\text{expected}}$
D. The degree of freedom is calculated as $n - 1$, where n is the number of ways in which the expected classes are free to vary
E. The probability value is obtained

Which one of the following option provides the correct sequence of steps in this statistical analysis?

1 A, C, D 2 C, D, E
3 B, A, D 4 A, D, E

141. Inverse PCR is performed for site-directed mutagenesis with complementary primers (having the desired mutation) using a plasmid having the cloned gene as template. The following statements were made regarding the above experiment.

A. PCR is followed by transformation of bacterial cells directly with the reaction mixture. A large number of the transformants will have the wild type gene.
B. The PCR mixture is treated with Dpn I and then used to transform bacterial cells. Most of the transformants will have the mutant gene.
C. PCR is followed by transformation of bacterial cells directly with the reaction mixture. None of the transformants will have the mutant gene.
D. The PCR mixture is treated with Dpn I and then used to transform bacterial cells. Half of the transformants will have the mutant gene.

Which one of the following options represents a combination of all correct statements.

1 A and B 2 A and D
3 B and C 4 B only

142. The molecular ion peak $[M]^+$ of an analyte as measured by electron ionization mass spectrometry has an m/z of 149 and a relative abundance of 100%. The $[M]^+$ has a relative abundance of 6.7% and the $[M + 2]^+$ peak has a relative abundance of 5%. The abundance of the major isotope of H, C, N, O and S are ^{1}H-100%, ^{12}C-98.9%, ^{13}C-1.1%. ^{14}N-99.6%, ^{15}N-0.4% , ^{16}O - 99.8%, ^{18}O-0.2%, ^{32}S-95.0%, ^{33}S-0.75% and ^{34}S-4.2%. The most probable molecular formula of the compound is:

1 $C_7H_{21}N_2O$
2 $C_5H_{11}NO_2S$
3 $C_6H_{13}O_2S$
4 $C_6H_{15}NOS$

143. Which one of the statements given below regarding generation of monoclonal antibodies is INCORRECT?

1 Monoclonal antibodies are the product of a single stimulated B-lymphocyte
2 To generate large quantities of monoclonal antibodies, a normal stimulated antibody producing B-cell is fused with a long lived B-cell tumour
3 The hybridoma generated for antibody production is selected on HAT medium
4 For HAT selection of hybridoma, the antibody producing B-cells are pre-treated with 8-azaguanine to block salvage pathway of DNA synthesis.

144. Specimens for light microscopy are commonly fixed with a solution containing chemicals that crosslink/denature cellular constituents. Commonly used fixatives such as formaldehyde and methanol could act in various ways as described below

A. Formaldehyde crosslinks amino groups on adjacent molecules and stabilises protein-protein and protein-nucleic acid interactions.

B. Methanol acts as a denaturing fixative and acts by reducing the solubility of protein molecules by disrupting hydrophobic interactions.

C. Formaldehyde crosslinks lipids tails in biological membranes.

D. Methanol acts on nucleic acids, crosslink nucleic acids with proteins and thus stabilizes protein-nucleic acid interactions.

Which one of the following combinations represents all correct statements?

1 A and C 2 B and C
3 B and D 4 A and B

145. Run off transcription assays were performed to establish the specificity of three novel sigma factors for their promoters. Results of the experiments are shown below

	σ^A	σ^B	$\sigma^A+\sigma^B$	σ^C	
P_2		▬	▬	▬	115 bp
P_1		▬		▬	95 bp

Following inferences were made from these results

A. σ^A initiates transcription from P_2 and σ^B from P_1.

B. σ^C can initiate transcription from both promoters.

C. σ^B prevents initiation of transcription from P_2.

D. σ^A initiates transcription from P_1.

Choose the option that correctly interprets the results.

1 A, B and C 2 A and B
3 C and D 4 B, C and D

ANSWERS

PART B

21. 1	22. 4	23. 1	24. 2	25. 2	26. 1	27. 4	28. 4	29. 2	30. 3
31. 4	32. 3	33. 2	34. 4	35. 4	36. 4	37. 2	38. 1	39. 3	40. 2
41. 3	42. 4	43. 4	44. 4	45. 2	46. 3	47. 2	48. 4	49. 2	50. 1
51. 1	52. 4	53. 3	54. 3	55. 3	56. 4	57. 4	58. 2	59. 4	60. 3
61. 2	62. 2	63. 3	64. 2	65. 4	66. 3	67. 1	68. 2	69. 2	70. 1

PART C

71. 1	72. 1	73. 2	74. 4	75. 4	76. 2	77. 4	78. 1	79. 3	80. 2
81. 1	82. 1	83. 1	84. 1	85. 1	86. 1	87. 3	88. 4	89. 3	90. 2
91. 1	92. 3	93. 1	94. 4	95. 3	96. 2	97. 2	98. 1	99. 1	100. 1
101. 2	102. 4	103. 4	104. 3	105. 4	106. 2	107. 1	108. 1	109. 2	110. 2
111. 3	112. 3	113. 2	114. 1	115. 2	116. 3	117. 4	118. 2	119. 4	120. 2
121. 1	122. 2	123. 3	124. 2	125. 2	126. 3	127. 3	128. 1	129. 3	130. 1
131. 2	132. 1	133. 3	134. 4	135. 4	136. 2	137. 2	138. 1	139. 1	140. 2
141. 1	142. 2	143. 4	144. 4	145. 1					